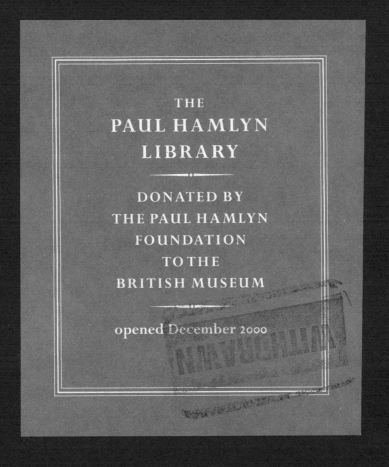

THE OXFORD
COMPANION TO
FOOD

THE OXFORD
COMPANION TO
FOOD

Alan Davidson

ILLUSTRATIONS BY
SOUN VANNITHONE

OXFORD
UNIVERSITY PRESS

OXFORD
UNIVERSITY PRESS

Great Clarendon Street, Oxford OX2 6DP

Oxford University Press is a department of the University of Oxford.
It furthers the University's objective of excellence in research, scholarship,
and education by publishing worldwide in

Oxford New York

Athens Auckland Bangkok Bogotá Buenos Aires Calcutta
Cape Town Chennai Dar es Salaam Delhi Florence Hong Kong Istanbul
Karachi Kuala Lumpur Madrid Melbourne Mexico City Mumbai
Nairobi Paris São Paulo Singapore Taipei Tokyo Toronto Warsaw
with associated companies in Berlin Ibadan

Oxford is a registered trade mark of Oxford University Press
in the UK and in certain other countries

Published in the United States
by Oxford University Press Inc., New York

© Alan Davidson 1999
Illustrations (except those indicated on page 892) © Soun Vannithone

British Library Cataloguing in Publication Data
Data available

Library of Congress Cataloguing in Publication Data
Data available

ISBN 0-19-211579-0

Typeset by Alliance Photosetters
Printed in Great Britain
on acid-free paper by
Butler & Tanner Ltd
Frome, Somerset

CONTENTS

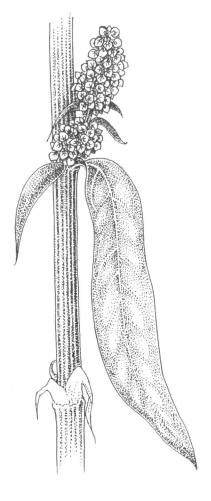

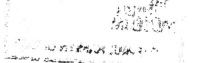

INTRODUCTION

THE book now born, in 1999, was conceived in 1976. Talking to Jill Norman, then my editor at Penguin Books, I remarked that, in writing my book on *Seafood of South-East Asia*, I had been handicapped by the lack of a good and detailed reference book on foodstuffs, of global scope. Her response was instant and simple: 'If you write such a book, we'll publish it.' Not long afterwards, my then agent, Hilary Rubinstein, suggested that this book, which I was by now planning, should appear first in a hardcover edition and in this guise would find a natural home in the Oxford Companion series. In a deal which would now be hard to imagine, let alone negotiate, Penguin, the Oxford University Press, and the separate Oxford University Press Inc. in New York all signed contracts with me for the same book, this one. My role was to produce it within about five years.

I failed on the timing; it took twenty years instead of five. Still, here it is, and the long period of gestation has carried some compensating advantages. Food history is to some extent a 'new' subject. There has been a great increase of interest in it during the last two decades, and a wealth of recently published material on which I have been able to draw; see the Bibliography.

I intended from the outset that the book should place less emphasis than people might expect on Europe and N. America, and more on other continents. I hope that I have succeeded in thus tilting the balance, but am well aware that the book proclaims its provenance (the English-speaking western world) on practically every page.

There were to be no recipes, and there are none.

I was also to avoid the risk of instant obsolescence which could have attended any attempt to be up to the minute in dealing with current topics or essaying judgements on developing situations. So there is no entry on GM (genetically modified) foods, although at the time of going to press the issues involved are prominent; and almost nothing is said (under beef) about BSE, a subject still attended by much uncertainty. Such matters are better suited to treatment elsewhere, rather than in a book whose contents may remain pertinent and valid five or ten years hence—or so I hopefully suppose.

That is by no means my only hope. Apart from our sharing the initials AD, I like to think that I have a few things in common with the great French writer Alexandre Dumas the elder. One is the hope which he expressed that, besides deserving attention from 'men of serious character', his encyclopedic *Grand Dictionnaire de Cuisine* would prove suitable to be read 'even by women of a much lighter disposition' and that the fingers of these women would not grow weary in turning his pages. I go along with that idea very strongly, all the more so because I have always assumed (quite why, I know not) that when I write it is for a female audience. Like Dumas, I cherish apposite anecdotes, and find room for them. And I echo one feature of his lifestyle, in that I do not drink wine (hence no advice in this book about wines to partner dishes). But in one respect I hope to differ from Dumas. Almost as soon as he had finished his book, and while it was 'in the press', he expired. So he heard neither praise nor criticism of the book which he regarded as the crowning achievement of his career as an author. I should like to hear both praise, for the obvious reasons, and criticisms because I am setting up machinery (notably on the Internet—at http://members.tripod.com/rdeh for collecting corrections and suggestions for any subsequent edition. All the other books I have written, even my novel, have turned out to contain errors and to be flawed by omissions. The same will certainly be true of this book, and on a larger scale. I thank here, in anticipation, all those who take the trouble to send helpful comments.

But first I must thank all those who have already helped, starting with Ralph Hancock, the encyclopedist who devoted almost a year of his time, in the early stages, to establishing the architecture of the book and making numerous contributions to its writing (especially on scientific topics). Major help was then given by Margaret Ralph, Sibella Wilbraham-Baker, and Elizabeth Gabay, in that sequence, all of them assiduous in helping with the collection of information and its orderly storage and use. Later, Andrew Dalby was brilliantly successful in tackling certain specific problems, while Candida Brazil brought her professional expertise in editing to bear on large segments of the book, pointing with perspicacity to both lacunae and superfluities.

Daniel Owen, equipped with computer know-how and ten of the fastest fingers on our successive keyboards, provided technical as well as general help. The same is true of Russell Harris, the only opera singer to be involved in the project and the only helper who combined Hebrew and Arabic with advanced computer skills.

Philip and Mary Hyman in Paris, whose unrivalled knowledge of French food history, now enshrined in the twenty-seven volumes published by the IPCF (see Bibliography), and library to match have been at my disposal for twenty years, also spared massive amounts of time to introduce me to the use of a PC.

They are among the many contributors listed on pages xi–xii, and this is the place at which I should express my gratitude to all of them, whether they contributed a whole category of entries or perhaps a single specialized one. Laura Mason worked with me for many years, being responsible for nearly 150 entries on confectionery and baked goods and for much valuable advice based on her background as a food scientist and her own remarkable survey of traditional British foods (another publication of 1999–see bibliography). Charles Perry collaborated for even more years, drawing on his rich knowledge of early Arabic cookery; Barbara Santich for equally long, the voice of Australia and my hostess when I went there; and Regina Sexton, the mellifluous voice of Ireland, throughout the 1990s. Jenny Macarthur made available the fruits of her work on food terms in other languages and wrote on African cuisines; Jennifer Brennan generously dispensed her knowledge of foods in the Orient and the Pacific islands; Doreen Fernandez lavished on me invaluable information about the Philippines, and Rachel Laudan wrote with exceptional elegance on many subjects which she had deeply explored. I thank them one and all, most heartily.

Sophie and Michael Coe were not just a help, but an inspiration. Only Michael can now be thanked, alas; I would so much have liked to place a copy of the book in Sophie's hands, with her contributions on Aztec, Inca, and Maya cuisines prominent in it. Three other contributors who have not survived to see their contributions in the book are Robert Bond, Nicholas Kurti, and Roy Shipperbottom. Each of them helped me greatly, far more than the scale of their contributions would suggest. Besides showering upon me botanical and culinary advice, especially about Asian herbs, Robert Bond, a doctor, even volunteered to fly to London from distant San Diego to minister to a faltering computer. That generous offer reminds me that my own heart faltered in 1991 and that I should repeat here my thanks to Dr Emma Vaux at the Roehampton hospital who shocked the heart out of ventricular fibrillation and started it beating correctly again with mere seconds to spare, thus enabling me to continue the writing of this book.

One of the contributors, John Ayto, and one of our most frequently quoted sources, John Mariani, must be identified as being the authors of two indispensable works of reference, dictionaries of culinary terms in Britain and the USA respectively. The other major reference book which was indispensable, and opened daily, is that of Stephen Facciola on food plants; while in the last two years, since its publication, Richard Hosking's excellent dictionary of Japanese foods has been always at my side.

Some of the sources quoted in this book, such as John Mariani, occur very often, while others may have yielded only one or two quotations, but thanks are due to all for kindly giving permission, where this was called for. The fact that there are many quotations in the book and that the bibliography is so long, reflects my wish to give readers as much information as possible about where I found the information which I am passing on to them—and where they might look for more.

For advice of great value, over and above contributions to this book or information enshrined in their own own books and essays, I thank Myrtle Allen, Samuel P. Arnold, Esther Balogh, James Beard, Ed Behr, Maggie Black, Diana Bolsmann, Lucy Brazil, Peter Brears, Lesley Chamberlain, Holly Chase, Robert Chenciner, Julia Child, Laurence Cohen (my French right hand for several years), Millard Cohen, Anna del Conte, Clive Cookson, Derek Cooper, Odile Cornuz, Ivan Day, Elizabeth Driver, Audrey Ellison, Mimi and Thomas Floegel, Gary Gillman, Peter Graham, Patience Gray, Henrietta Green, Rudolph Grewe, Jane Grigson, Anissa Helou, Bridget Ann Henisch, Karen Hess, Constance Hieatt, Geraldene Holt, Nina Horta, Richard Hosking, Philip Iddison, David Karp, Edik and David Kissin, Joy Larkcom, Gilly Lehmann, Paul Levy, Tim Low, Erich Lück, Fiona Lucraft, Cristine MacKie, Valerie Mars, Harold McGee, Joan Morgan, Henry Notaker, Elisabeth Lambert Ortiz, Sri and Roger Owen, Robert Pemberton, Eulalia Pensado, Helen Pollard, Esteban Pombo-Villar, Francesca Ratcliffe, Astri Riddervold, Dolf Riks, Gillian Riley, Alicia Rios, Claudia Roden, Françoise Sabban and Silvano Serventi, Alice Wooledge Salmon, Delwen Samuel, Elizabeth Schneider, Terence Scully, Ann Semple, Margaret Shaida, Mimi Sheraton, Birgit Siesby, Yan-Kit So, Ray Sokolov, Charmaine Solomon, Nicholas Spencer, Anne Tait, Maria José Sevilla Taylor, John Thorne and Matt Lewis, Jill Tilsley-Benham, Joyce Toomre, Arthur Tucker, Pamela Van Dyke Price, Simon Varey, Christian Volbracht, Harlan Walker, Alice Waters, William Woys Weaver, Robin Weir, Joyce Westrip, Barbara Ketcham Wheaton, Anne Willan and Mark Cherniavsky, C. Anne Wilson, Joop Witteveen, Mary Wondrausch, Barbara Yeomans, Sami Zubaida; together with John Dransfield and David Pegler at Kew; and also many members of the FAO (Food and Agriculture Organization of the United Nations) at Rome.

Realizing that no existing library had all the books, in many languages and many different fields of study, which I would need to consult, I perforce built up my own library. Doing so was in fact a pleasure, especially as I had the benefit of guidance from Elizabeth David (she who was responsible for switching the points in the late 1960s and sending me down the track which led to full-time writing). Working, at her invitation, in her own wonderful library was itself a revelation; but it was also through her that I came to know several of the specialist booksellers who helped me build up my own working library. My debt to them is considerable, not just for finding books I needed, but also in a more general way. I think especially of Ian Jackson, polymath and the most widely read man I know in nineteenth-century botanical and other literature; Janet Clarke; Mike and Tessa McKirdy; Heidi Lascelles; Jan Longone; Nahum Waxman; and, looking back a long way, that remarkable and irreplaceable figure, Eleanor Lowenstein, whose Corner Book Shop in New York City was the source of so many of my treasures.

Special responsibilities were taken on by Tom Jaine and Jane Levi, for progress-chasing on behalf of myself and the publishers, coupled with editing and writing entries (Tom) and compiling the Bibliography (Jane); the latter was a laborious task which needed much research, and in retrospect it seems almost incredible that anyone should have been so brimful of goodwill as to volunteer to do it.

Soun Vannithone, who has been doing drawings for my books ever since I first knew him when he was a student in Vientiane, Laos, applied his customary skill and sensitivity to doing drawings especially for the book. Harriet Jaine, preceded by her friend Rebecca Loncraine, took on the task of liaison with him and of organizing the several hundred drawings from which the 175 in the book were eventually chosen.

During the last seven years Helen Saberi has been working alongside me, with her characteristic diligence, wit, and good humour. I could not have wished for a better co-pilot as we neared port. Her own numerous contributions to the book are only the immediately visible signs of a lively and beneficent influence which has infused the whole. I am most deeply indebted to her.

Given the very long wait which my agents (now the resourceful team of Caradoc King and Sam Boyce at A.P. Watt) and the publishers have had to put up with, it is remarkable that there too good humour has prevailed. I thank all the successive editors who have shown patience: most recently, and over many years, Michael Cox and Pam Coote. My thanks go in particular to Pam Coote, not only for having faith in the eventual completion of the book but also for precipitating it, once delivered, into production at such high speed and with such unfailing efficiency. Under the direction of John Mackrell, the whole complex machinery of production positively purred. The copy-editors, Jackie and Edwin Pritchard, worked at amazing speed; while the multifarious aspects of design were smoothly and successfully dealt with by Nick Clarke.

Turning to home, I thank my sister Rosemary and my daughters three, Caroline, Pamela, and Jennifer, for the various forms of help and encouragement which they have willingly provided; and, above all, my wife Jane, who underpinned my work throughout the 7,250 days of gestation with unfaltering confidence in its completion and who did more, and in more ways, than anyone but myself will ever know to bring that about. Although many Oxford Companions have come into the world without any dedication, this one must certainly be so equipped, the dedication being to her with my love and gratitude.

ALAN DAVIDSON

World's End, Chelsea
March 1999

CONTRIBUTORS

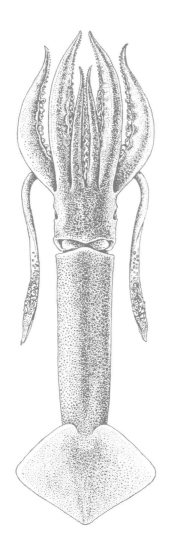

These are listed in alphabetical order of surname. Where initials appear in parenthesis at the end of an entry, this means that the person indicated wrote it originally, but that the version presented has been amplified or curtailed in more than trivial ways. Entries followed by no initials are all written by the author.

KA KATSUE AIZAWA, a Japanese scholar of food history who has lived and taught in London for many years.

AA AYLA ALGAR, who has been Mellon lecturer in Turkish at the University of California, Berkeley, is the author of two books on traditional Turkish foods.

JA JOHN AYTO, author of *The Diner's Dictionary*.

JBa JIM BAUMAN, an American resident in Paris who during his lifetime explored many aspects of food history.

CBl CAROLE BLOOM, author of *The International Dictionary of Desserts, Pastries, and Confections*.

RB ROBERT BOND of San Diego, California, wrote numerous articles for botanical and other publications on herbs and spices, especially Asian ones.

JB JENNIFER BRENNAN has written a number of major works on Asian cookery, having spent much of her life in Pakistan, India, SE Asia, Japan, and Guam.

CB CATHERINE BROWN has written several authoritative books on Scottish food and cookery with particular attention to the historical aspects.

LB LYNDA BROWN has devoted many years to writing about food, with emphasis on the growing and cooking of vegetables.

EC ELIZABETH CARTER, author of *Majorcan Food and Cookery*.

SC SOPHIE COE was the author of *America's First Cuisines* and co-author with her husband of *A True History of Chocolate*.

AD ANDREW DALBY has written essays and books about food in classical times, especially *Siren Feasts*, on food and gastronomy in classical Greece.

JD JANE DAVIDSON did the lioness's share of translating Alexandre Dumas's *Grand Dictionnaire de cuisine* for an English version entitled *Dumas on Food*.

DF DOREEN FERNANDEZ combines being a Professor of the Performing Arts with her role as one of the foremost food historians in the Philippines.

OF OVE FOSSÅ combines his career as a landscape architect in Norway with food history studies.

A and HCG ANNE and HELEN CARUANA GALIZIA are joint authors of *The Food and Cooking of Malta*.

RH RALPH HANCOCK is an encyclopedist with a special interest in food history and food science.

RuH RUSSELL HARRIS explores the byways of food history on the Internet, and does bibliographical work in this field.

AH ANISSA HELOU is author of *Lebanese Cuisine*.

RHo RICHARD HOSKING, Professor of Sociology and English at Hiroshima Shudo University in Japan for twenty years, is author of *A Dictionary of Japanese Food: Ingredients and Culture*.

CH CECIL HOURANI, an authority on many aspects of Arab culture, is preparing a book on the food and cookery of Jordan.

LH LYNETTE HUNTER, of the University of Leeds, was series editor for several important bibliographies of English cookery and household books of the eighteenth and nineteenth centuries and has written extensively on connected themes.

HY PHILIP and MARY HYMAN, Americans resident in Paris, have been deeply involved for thirty years in the study of French food and cookery and have been responsible for the historical sections of the twenty-six-volume survey thereof being published by the Conseil National des Arts Culinaires.

PI PHILIP IDDISON is a British road engineer whose hobby when he is working on projects abroad (Turkey, Thailand, the Gulf States) is to accumulate all possible data about local foods.

IJ IAN JACKSON, a polymath and antiquarian bookseller with a particular interest in nineteenth-century writing and in botany.

TJ TOM JAINE's varied career in activities connected with food, wine, and restaurants has led to his present position as publisher (at Prospect Books) of one of the leading food history lists in the world.

MK-J MARIA KANEVA-JOHNSON, author of *The Melting Pot: Balkan Food and Cookery*, is Bulgarian. Among the prizes which her book won in 1997 was the international Ceretto Prize.

NK NICHOLAS KURTI, Emeritus Professor of Physics, University of Oxford, Fellow of the Royal Society, and editor with Giana Kurti of *But the Crackling is Superb*, was author of many articles on the scientific aspects of cookery.

RL RACHEL LAUDAN's book on the foodways of Hawaii, entitled *The Food of Paradise*, won an important prize in the USA.

GL GILLY LEHMANN teaches in a French University and is a leading authority on the history of English cookery books, especially of the seventeenth and eighteenth centuries.

JEL JANE LEVI, organizer since 1997 of the annual Oxford Symposium on Food History, has reconciled her professional activities in international banking with bibliographical and other research in food history.

JL JANICE LONGONE has an unrivalled knowledge of the history of American cookbooks and is author of numerous studies thereof.

JM JENNY MACARTHUR has a long-standing hobby of collecting names in other languages for all foodstuffs, however obscure.

LoM LOURDES MARCH, one of Spain's most respected food writers, is the author of many books on subjects such as rice and olive oil.

LM LAURA MASON was responsible for the British contribution to the EU Euroterroirs project, listing and describing traditional foods of the member countries. She has also written extensively on sweets and is the author of *Sugar Plums and Sherbet* (1998).

RO ROGER OWEN has worked with his wife Sri on Indonesian food, and collaborated with her in writing *The Rice Book* (1993).

SO SRI OWEN is author of the classic *Indonesian Food* and *Cookery* (revised edition 1986) and much else on the foodways of her native country and S.E. Asia.

CP CHARLES PERRY, the leading authority on early Arabic cookery, is editing *Medieval Arab Cookery* (2000) which will on publication be the best collection of earlier and recent research in this field.

GR GILLIAN RILEY, a typographer and designer, has written on Italian food, and on food and art, notably *A Feast for the Eyes* (National Gallery, London, 1997).

AR ALICIA RIOS, a gastronomic consultant in Madrid, has written books on food history and cookery and also works in the field of aesthetics.

JR JOE ROBERTS, a travel writer, has studied and written about foodways in several continents.

FS FRANÇOISE SABBAN, of the Écoles des Hautes Études in Paris, is a leading French authority on Chinese food and cookery.

HS HELEN SABERI, author of *Noshe Djan: Afghan Food and Cookery*, has regularly contributed papers to the Oxford Symposia on Food History.

RSa RENA SALAMAN is author of *Greek Food* (rev edn 1993) and other books on food in the Mediterranean region.

BS BARBARA SANTICH, an authority on medieval cookery (*The Original Mediterranean Cuisine*) and on Australian foodways, lives in Adelaide.

RSe REGINA SEXTON, a medievalist specializing in food history, who teaches Celtic Civilization at University College, Cork, is author of the EU survey of *Ireland's Traditional Foods* (1997) and *A Little History of Irish Food* (1998).

MS MARGARET SHAIDA is the author of *The Legendary Cuisine of Persia* (1992).

RSh ROY SHIPPERBOTTOM, during his lifetime, became an expert in many disparate fields; one was traditional food and cookery in the north of England.

RSo RAYMOND SOKOLOV of the *Wall Street Journal* is the author of many books including *Fading Feast* (1981), *Why We Eat What We Eat* (1991), and *With the Grain* (1996).

JS JENNIFER STEAD, a local historian in Yorkshire, is a leading participant in the Leeds Symposia on Food History and Traditions.

LS LOUIS SZATHMARY, an authority on Hungarian cuisine, collected and published extensively in the field of food history during his lifetime.

BW BARBARA WHEATON enjoys the distinction of having her book on the history of food and cookery in France (*Savoring the Past*, 1983) translated into French and awarded a French prize.

SUBJECT INDEX

These references are to headwords. Not all headwords are included, and some may be included in more than one list.

For this purpose the whole mass of entries has been divided into four large categories. First come food plants (including fungi) and primary products derived from them. The second category is of animals, birds, and fish, etc. and products derived directly from them. Third come cooked foods and dishes of various kinds including beverages—broadly speaking, what may be put on the table for consumption other than raw foods such as fruit. The fourth category includes entries to do with culture, religion, meals, diet, and the large number of entries on national and regional cuisines.

FOOD PLANTS

AQUATIC PLANT FOODS
agar-agar; awo-nori; carrageen; dulse; funori; hairmoss; hijiki; kelp; kombu; limu; matsumo; mojaban; mozuku; nori; nostoc; ogo; sea grapes; sea lettuce; seaweeds; tengusa; wakame.

CEREALS
barley; breakfast cereals; buckwheat; cereals; corn; five grains of China; Inca wheat; maize; millet; muesli; oats; rice; rice as food; rye; sorghum; tef; triticale; wheat; wild rice.

FRUITS
akebia; akee; ambarella; apple (a feature including apple cookery and apple varieties); apricot; aquiboquil; ash-keys; azarole; babaco; bael; banana; banana flower; banana leaf; baobab; Barbados cherry; Barbados gooseberry; barberry; beach plum; bearberry; belimbing asam; berry; bignay; bilberry; biriba; blackberry; blueberry; bog myrtle; buffaloberry; bullock's heart; bush butter; calamansi; cambuca; canistel; cape gooseberry; capulin; carambola; carissa and karanda; cashew; cassabanana; ceriman; chanal; chanar; cherimoya;

cherry; cherry plum; Chinese wolfberry; chokecherry; citron; citrus fruits; cloudberry; cocona; crabapple; cranberry; cranberry tree; crowberry; currants (red, black, white); custard apple; damson; date (a feature including date varieties); date palm flower; date plum; Davidson's plum; dewberry; dogwood; doum palm; drupe; duku and langsat; durian; elderberry and elderflower; emblic; eugenia fruits; feijoa; fig; finger-lime; firethorn; genipap; gooseberry; goraka; grape; grapefruit; greengage; ground cherry; guava; hackberry; hawthorn; huckleberry; ilama; imbu; jackfruit; jambolan; jambu; jujube; juniper; kaki; kangaroo apple; ketambilla; kiwano; kiwi fruit; kokam; kumquat; lemon; lime; longan; loquat; lovi-lovi; lychee (litchi); mabolo; maidenhair berry; makrut lime; mamee; mamoncillo; mandarin; mandarin limes; mango; mangosteen; medlar; melon; mombin; mulberry; myrobalan; myrtle; namnam; naranjilla; nectarine; nightshade; nipa palm; nutmeg fruit; oleaster; orange; otaheite gooseberry; papaw; papaya; parmentiera; passion-fruit; peach; pear (including pear varieties); pejibaye; pepino; persimmon; phalsa; physalis fruits; pineapple; pitanga; pitaya; plantain; plum; plum mango; pomegranate; pomelo; pomology; pond apple; posh-té; prickly pear; prune; pulasan; quandong; quince; raisins, sultanas and currants; rambai; rambutan; ramontchi; raspberry; rhubarb; rose-apple; roselle; rowan and sorb; rukam; salak; salmonberry; santol; sapodilla; sapota; sea buckthorn; service-berries; sloe; soursop; squashberry; star apple; strawberry; 'strawberry tree'; sugar-apple; sumac; tomatillo; tree-tomato (or tamarillo); ugli; ume; wampee; watermelon; whortleberry; wood apple; yuzu.

FUNGI
agaric; amanita; beefsteak fungus; blewit; blusher; bolete (boletus); bracket fungi; cauliflower fungus; cep; chanterelle; clitocybe mushrooms; club fungus; cobweb-caps; coral fungus; cordyceps; cup fungi; enokitake; fairy ring

mushroom; false morels; field mushroom; fly agaric; fungus; grisette; guépinie; gypsy mushroom; hallucinogenic mushrooms; hen of the woods; honey fungus; horn of plenty; horse mushroom; ink cap; jelly fungus; king mushroom; matsutake; milk cap; miller; morels; mushroom (a feature including mushroom cultivation, mushroom literature, mushrooms in Russia); nameko; oronge; oyster mushroom; parasol mushroom; pholiota mushrooms; polypores; prince; puffballs; russula; St George's mushroom; shiitake; stinkhorn; stone mushroom; straw mushrooms; sulphur shelf; termite heap mushroom; toadstool; tooth fungi; truffle; wax caps; wood ear; wood mushroom.

HERBS, SPICES, CONDIMENTS

acitrón; advieh; agar wood; ajmud; ajowan; alexanders; allspice; amber; ambergris; amchur; anardana; angelica; anise (aniseed); asafoetida; ashanti pepper; balm; balsam; basil; bay leaf; bergamot; bistort; bitter berries; bitter herbs (of the Jews); black cumin; bois de Panama; borage; burnet; calamint; caper; caraway; cardamom; cassia; cayenne pepper; cherry laurel; chervil; Chinese keys; chrysanthemum; chutney; cinnamon; clary; cleavers; clove; clove gillyflowers; colombo; coltsfoot; comfrey; coriander; corkwing; costmary; costus; cowslip; cubeb; culinary ashes; cumin seed; curry leaf; curry powder; daun salam; dill; duqqa; elecampane; epazote; essence; fennel; fenugreek; five spices (Chinese); flowers; galingale; garden mace; garum; geranium; ginger; ginseng; golden needles; grains of selim; ground elder; guascas; harissa; hartshorn; hedge garlic; herb; hilbeh; hogweed; horehound; horseradish; hyssop; ketchup; khus khus; knotweed; lavender; lemon grass; lemon verbena; lime flowers; long pepper; lovage; mace; mahlab; mallow; marigold; marjoram; masala; mastic; meadowsweet; melegueta pepper; mint; mioga ginger; mitsuba; monosodium glutamate; mugwort; mustard; nam prik; nasturtium; nutmeg; orange flower water; oregano; padek; palillo; panch phoron; paprika; parsley; pennyroyal; pepper; peppermint; poppy; ras-el-hanout; rau ram; red (or pink) peppercorns; relish; rosemary; roses; rue; saffron; sage; salt; samphire; sansho; sarsaparilla; sassafras; savory (summer and winter); Screwpine; shado béni ; shichimi; shiso; sichuan pepper; silphium; smartweed; southernwood; Spanish needles; Spanish thyme; spice mixtures; spices; spice trade; spider herb; star anise; sweet cicely; tabasco; tabil; tansy; tarragon; thyme; tonka bean; turmeric; vanilla; vervain; violet; wasabi; water dropwort; wintergreen; woodruff; Worcester(shire) sauce; wormwood; ylang-ylang; zaatar; zedoary.

NUTS

acorns; almond; beech nut; Brazil nut; breadnuts; calumpang nut; candlenut; chestnut; coco de mer; coconut (a feature including coconut products); cottonseed oil; cycads; dika nut; gabon nut; ginkgo; gnetum; groundnuts; hazelnut; hickory nuts; illipe nut; Indian almond; Java olive; jojoba; karaka; kedrouvie nut; kepayang; kubili nuts; macadamia nuts; madia; manketti nut; naras; ngapi nut; niger seed; nuts; oil palms; okari nuts; olives and olive oil; oyster nut; palm; palm oil; palmyra palm; pecan; pignut; pili nut; pine nut; pistachio; safflower; sandalwood; sapucaya nut; sesame; shea butter; souari nut; sunflower; vegetable oils; walnut; water chestnut; yeheb nut.

PLANT PRODUCTS

alcohol; alginates; alkanna; ambrosia; annatto; arrowroot; arroz fermentado; balsamic vinegar; beer (in cookery); bere meal; besan flour; betel nut; birch sugar; black beans; bran; burghul; chocolate (a feature including chocolate, botany and early history, chocolate in the 19th and 20th centuries, chocolate manufacture, chocolate in cookery); chuño and tunta; coca; cochineal; cocoa; cola; cornflour; corn syrup; cudbear; dagé; dal; dibs; farina; fecula; filé; flour (a feature including milling); freekeh; glucose; golden syrup; gum; gum arabic; gum tragacanth; hemp; honey; honeydew; kecap; kermes; kimch'i; kochojang; koji; konnyaku; liquorice; madrai; malt; maple syrup and maple sugar; minchin; mirin; miso; mizuame; nata; natto; nectar; oncom; palm sugar; peasemeal; pectin; perle japon; peté; pickle; pinole; poi; ragi; raisiné; resin; rice paper; sago; salep; saps; sauerkraut; semolina; soy (soya bean) milk; soy sauce; starch; sugar (a feature including sugar beet and sugar cane); sweeteners; tapé; tapioca; tempe; tofu; treacle; tsampa; umeboshi; verjuice; vinegar; wheat products and dishes; wine (in cookery); yuba.

VEGETABLES

acacia and wattle; achocha; adlay; agave; alfalfa; amaranth; arracacha; arrowhead; artichoke; asparagus; aubergine; avocado; azuki bean; bamboo; basella; bean; bean sprouts; beetroot; bellflower root; bitter gourd; bitterleaf; bottle gourd; brassica; breadfruit; broad bean; broccoli; brussels sprouts; bulbs; burdock; butterfly pea; cabbage; cacti; calathea; callaloo; camas; capsicum; cardoon; carob; carrot; cassava; cat-tail; cauliflower; celery; chard; chaya; chayote; chia; chickpea; chickweed; chicory and endive; chilli (pepper); Chinese artichoke; Chinese cabbage; Chinese kale; Chinese spinach; Chinese water chestnut; chives; chufa; clover and melilot; cluster bean; corms; corn salad; cowpea; cress; cucumber; cucurbits; dal; dandelion; dittander; dock; elephant garlic; eringo root; fat hen; ferns; fitweed; garlic; gherkin; good king henry; goosefoot; gourd; gram; greensauce (and green sauces); haricot bean; hausa potato; hoja santa; hop shoots; horse gram; horseradish tree; iceplant; ivy gourd; jack bean; Jerusalem artichoke; jicama; junsai; kale; kapok-tree fruit; kohlrabi; kudzu; lablab bean; lath; leek; legume; lentil; lettuce; lichens; lima bean; linseed; locust tree; lotus; lupin; malabar gourd; malanga (yautia/tannia); mauka; melokhia; mesquite; moth bean; mung bean; mustard greens; nettles; New Zealand spinach; oca; okra; onion; orach; oriental onions; pacay; pacaya; parsnip; pea; pickling onions; pigeon pea; pigweed; plantain; pokeweed; potato (a feature including potatoes in cookery); pulses; pumpkin; purslane; quinoa; radish; rampion; rape; rice bean; ridged gourd; rocambole; rocket; runner bean; salsify, scolymus and scorzonera; screwbean; seakale; sea purslane; shallot; shepherd's purse; skirret; snake gourd; sorrel; soya bean; spinach; spring onions; squash; squawroot; stonecrop; summer squash; suram; susumber; swede and rutabaga; sweet potato; tamarind; taro; tepary bean; texsel greens; thistle; ti; tomato; topitambo; tree bean; tree-cotton; tree onion; turnip; udo; ulluco; urd (or urad); vegetable humming bird; vegetable lamb; vegetable marrow; vegetable spaghetti; velvet bean; vetch; vine leaves; watercress; water hawthorn; water hyacinth; waterleaf; water spinach; wax gourd; weed; wild garlic; winged bean; winged pea; winter squash; wood sorrel; yacon; yam; yam bean; ysaño; yucca; zucchini.

ANIMAL FOODS; BIRDS; FISH, ETC.

ANIMALS / MEAT / MEAT PRODUCTS

aardvark; agouti; andouille, andouillette; antelope; armadillo; bacon; badger; Bath chap; beaver; beef (a feature including beef cookery); beefeater; biltong; Bindenfleisch (or Bündnerfleisch); bison; blood; blood sausages; bone; bone marrow; brains; brawn; bresaola; buck; buffalo; bushpig; camel; cane rat; capybara; caribou; cats; cattle; caul; cervelas; cervelat; charcuterie; chateaubriand; cheeks; chipolata; chitterlings; chop; connective tissue; coppa; corned beef; crackling; crépinette; culatello; cutlet; deer; dog; dormouse; dripping; drisheen; ears; eland; elephant; elk; eyes; faggot; fat-tailed sheep; feet; foie gras; frankfurter; game; gammon; gelatin; giraffe; goat (and kid); guinea pig; haggis; ham; hare; haslet; head; heart; hedgehog; hippopotamus; horsemeat; hough; jerky; kangaroo; kidneys; kinkajou; Lachsschinken; lamb; lard; lion; liver; llama; lungs; meat; meat extracts; merguez; mince; monkey; moose; mortadella; muntjac; musk; musk ox; muskrat; mutton; muzzle; offal; opossum; oxtail; paca; palate; pancetta; pastrami; peccary; pemmican; pig; pluck; polony; porcupine; pork; prairie dog; pronghorn; puma; qawarma; rabbit; raccoon; rat; reindeer; rhinoceros; rillette; rock rabbit; saddle; salt pork; sausage (a feature including sausages of Britain, of France, of Germany, of Italy, of Spain and Portugal); sheep; skunk; spam; spiced beef; spleen; steak; stomach; sucking pigs; suet; sweetbreads; tails; tapir; tenderizers; testicles; tongue; tripe; udder; veal; venison; viscacha; warthog; water-buffalo; white pudding; wild boar; wildebeest; woodchuck; yak; zampone; zebra; zebu.

BIRDS AND EGGS
albatross; bittern; blackbird; black grouse; bobalink; bustard; buttered eggs; canvasback; capercaillie (capercailzie); capon; chicken (dishes); cock; coot, crake, moorhen, rail; crane; curassow; curlew; duck; egg; emu; figpecker; fulmar; gadwall; giblets; goose; grouse; guillemot; guinea-fowl; gull; hazel-hen; hen/chicken, breeds; heron; kiwi; knot; lark; mallard; megapode; mutton-bird; ortolan; ostrich; parrots and cockatoos; parson's nose; partridge; peacock; peacock-pheasant; peafowl; penguin; pheasant; pigeon; pintail; plover; pochard; prairie chicken; ptarmigan; puffin; quail; rook; scoter; snipe; sparrow; starling; stork; swan; teal; thrush; tinamou; trumpeter; turkey; wigeon; wild duck; woodcock.

DAIRY PRODUCTS
American cheeses; Appenzell; asiago; ayran; Beaufort; beestings; Bel paese; bleu; blue cheeses; blue vinney; bog butter; brick cheese; Brie; burrini; butter; buttermilk; caciocavallo; caciotta; Caerphilly; Camembert; Cantal; carré; cendré; Cheddar; cheese (a feature including cheese-making, cheese in cookery); Cheshire; coeur; Colwick; Cotherstone; cottage cheese; cream; cream cheese; crowdie; curd; curd cheese; Danish cheeses; Derby; Dunlop; Edam; Emmental; Explorateur; Feta; fondue; Fontina; fourme; fromage frais; Gammelost; German cheeses; ghee; Gloucester; goat's milk cheeses; Gorgonzola; Gouda; Grana; grating cheeses; green cheese; Gruyère; haloumi; hand cheeses; ice cream; ice cream sundae; Jarlsberg; kashk and kishk; kashkaval; kaymak; kefalotyri; kefir; koumiss; Lancashire; lassi; Leicester; Leiden; Liederkranz; Limburger; Liptauer; livarot; loaf cheese; maas; manchego; margarine; maroilles; mascarpone; milk; milk reduction; Mozzarella; Munster; Neufchatel; nostrale and nostrano; oka; panir; parmesan; pecorino; 'pickled' cheeses; Pont l'Evêque; Port Salut; 'pot' cheeses; potted (and processed) cheeses; Provolone; quark; queso; quroot; raclette; reblochon; rennet; resurrection cheese; ricotta; romadur; Roquefort; Russian cheeses; saanen; sage cheese; St Nectaire; Samsoe; Sbrinz; Schabziger; skyr; slipcote; sour cream; sour milk; Spanish cheeses; steppe; Stilton; Stracchino; sweet cream and curd; syr and sir; Taleggio; Tilsiter; tomme; trappist cheese; vacherin; Wensleydale; whey; whey cheeses; yarg; yoghurt; York (cheese).

EXOTIC FOODS
alligator; ant-eaters; ants; balut; bats; bear; bird's nest; caterpillar; cicadas; cockchafer; cricket; crocodile; dragonfly; frog; funistrada; geophagy; grasshopper; grubs; iguana; insects as food; larvae; lizard; locust; manna; monitor; silkworm; snails; snakes; spiders; squirrel; termites; tortoise; turtles; wasp; water bugs; witchetty grubs; worms.

FISH: FRESHWATER AND MARINE
albacore; alfonsino; amberjack; anchovy; angel shark; angler-fish; Australasian 'salmon'; barb; barbel; barracuda; barramundi; bass; big-eye; billfish; bleak; blowfish; bluefish; blue-mouth; bonefish; bonito; boutargue; bream; brill; buffalo-fish; bummalow; burbot; carp; catfish; caviar; char; cobia; cod; comber; conger eel; coral fish; crevally; crimping; croaker; cusk; cusk eel; dab; dentex; dogfish; dolphin fish; drum; eel; elvers; emperors; eulachon; fish (including fish cookery); fish pastes and fish paste products; fish sauce; fish sausages; flatfish; flathead; flounder; flying fish; frigate mackerel; fugu; fusilier; gar-fish; gefilte fish; gilt-head bream; goby; gravlaks/gravlax; grayling; grey mullet; grouper; grunt; gudgeon; guitar fish; gurnard; haddock; hake; half-beak; halibut; hammerhead shark; hapuku; hardtail; herring; hoki; horse mackerel; huss; isinglass; jack; jobfish; john dory; katsuobushi; kingfish; kingklip; kipper; ladyfish; lamprey; lemon sole; ling; lizard fish; loach; luderick; lumpfish; lutefisk; luvar; mackerel; mahseer; marlin; meagre; megrim; milk fish; minnow; moonfish; moray eel; morwong; mulloway; Murray cod; opah; parrotfish; perch; picarel; pike; pilotfish; plaice; pollack; pomfret; pompano; ponyfish; porbeagle; porgy; poutine; queenfish; rabbit fish; rainbow runner; rakefish; ray and skate; ray's bream; red cod; redfish; red mullet; rock fish; rockling; roe; roughy; sailfish; saithe; salmon; salt cod; sand-eels; sardine; saury; sawfish; scabbard fish; scad; scaldfish; scorpion fish; sea bass; sea bream; sea trout; shad; sharks; shark's fin; silverside; sinarapan; skipjack; smelt; snapper; snoek; sole; Spanish mackerel; sprat; squeteague; stockfish; striped bass; sturgeon; swordfish; tarpon; tautog; tench; threadfin bream; threadfins; tilapia; tilefish; tomcod; trevally; trigger fish; triple-tail; trout; trumpeter; tuna; turbot; wahoo; warehou; weever; wels; whitebait; whitefish; whiting; wolf-fish; wrasse; wreckfish; zander.

SEAFOOD OTHER THAN FISH
abalone; ark-shell; bailer shell; bivalves; blacang; blue crab; carpet-shell; cephalopods; chiton; clam; cockle; conch; crab; crab, common/European; crayfish; crustaceans; cuttlefish; date-shell; dog cockle; dolphin; dugong and manatee; Dungeness crab; fan shells; fiddler crab; flat lobster; flying squid; gaper; geoduck; giant clam; goose-necked barnacle; hamaguri; heart shell; hermit crab; horn-shell; horseshoe crabs; jellyfish; kona crab; krill; lagoon crab; land crabs; lavignon; limpet; lobster; mangrove crab; mantis shrimp; marron; molluscs; murex; mussel; nautilus; Norway lobster; ocean quahog; octopus; otter shells; oyster; oyster crab; palolo; pearl oyster; pelican's foot; periwinkle; piddock; pipi; pismo clam; prawn; quahog; razor clam; red crab; rock crab; sand-bug; sand crab; scallop; sea anemone; sea cucumber; sea turtles; sea urchin; seals; shellfish;

caramel; crumble; custard (with custard sauce, custard powder); dariole; desserts, general; eve's pudding; figgy pudding; firni; floating island(s); flummery; fool; fruit jellies; fruit salad; fruit soups; frumenty; halo-halo; hasty pudding; junket; keshkul-e-fuqara; kheer; khoshab; kisel; meringue; milk puddings; mince pie; muhallabia; nesselrode pudding; paloodeh (paluda); pandowdy; panna cotta; pavlova; payasam; pudding (general); quaking pudding; queen's pudding; rice puddings; roly poly pudding; saxon pudding; shoofly pie; shrikhand; snow; sponge puddings; spotted dick; suet puddings; summer pudding; Sussex pond pudding; syllabub; thunder and lightning; trifle; upside down cake; vareno zhito; water ices; zabaglione.

EVERYTHING ELSE

COOKERY BOOKS: THEIR AUTHORS AND OTHER PEOPLE

Accum, Frederick; Acton, Eliza; American cookbooks; Apicius; Appert; Archestratus; Athenaeus; Avicenna; Beeton, Mrs Isabella; Brillat-Savarin, Jean Anthelme; Carême, Antonin; Cavalcanti, Ippolito; Cervio, Vincenzo; Cole, Mrs Mary; Cooper, Joseph; David, Elizabeth; Digby, Sir Kenelm; Dumas, Alexandre, Père; English cookery books and books on food; Escoffier; Farmer, Fannie; Fisher, M. F. K.; Forme of Cury(e); French cookbooks; Galen; German cookery books; Glasse, Hannah; Gouffé, Jules; Grigson, Jane; Grimod de la Reynière; Hartley, Dorothy; Heinz, Henry J; Hippocrates; Italian cookery books; La Varenne; Leslie, Eliza; Lincoln, Mary; Linnaeus; May, Robert; Menagier de Paris; Petronius; Platina; Pliny; Raffald, Elizabeth; Rombauer, Irma; Rorer, Sarah Tyson; Rumford, Count; Rumohr; Simmonds, Peter Lund; Simmons, Amelia; Smith, E.; Spanish cookery books; Taillevent; Theophrastus; Verral, William; Ward, Artemas; Woolley, Hannah.

CULINARY TERMS AND TECHNIQUES

à la; alla; antipasto; au bleu; baking; ballottine; balti; barbecue; bard; basting; bento; bisque; blanch; blanquette; boil; bombe; bouquet garni; braise; brandade; cacciatora; carbonade, carbonado; cardinal; casserole; caudle; chafing dish cookery; chartreuse; chaud-froid; civet; clarification; coffin, coffyn; colbert; collar;

collop; condiment; confit; conjurer; coulis; court bouillon; crème; croquette; crouton; culinary terminology; daube; deglazing; devil; dough; duff; duxelles; échaudé; entrée and entremets; fines herbes; fisnogge; flame; florentine; fraise; fricandeau; fricassée; frying; fumet; galantine; galette; gallimaufrey, gallimaufry; glaze; gratin, gratiner; griddle; grill (broil); gyuvech; hors d'oeuvres; Japanese culinary terms; jug; kickshaw; kitchen; larding; macedoine; macerate; marinade, marinate; matelote; mezze; mirepoix; mocha; mousse; mousseline; nouvelle cuisine; panada, panade; parboil; parfait; pâté; pil-pil; plank; poach; posset; ragout; ramekin; red-cook; rissole; roast; roux; salamander; şalş; sashimi; sauté; scald; score; searing; shortening; simmer; soffritto/sofrito; souffle; spatchcock; spitchcock; staple foods, staples; steam; stew; stir-fry; stock; stufato; stuff, stuffing; supreme; surtout; sushi; sweet-and-sour; tandoor; tapas; tartare; tempura; terrine; timbale; tinola; tzimmes; vandyking; vindaloo; wok cookery; zakuski.

CULTURE; DIET; FOODWAYS; RELIGION

afternoon tea; ambigu; banquet; bistro; brasserie; breakfast; Buddhism and food; buffet; cannibalism; carnival foods; chef; Christianity and food; Christmas foods; chuck, chuck wagon; clambake; cockaigne (land of); Columbian exchange; cook; cordon bleu; culinary mythology; dietary laws; diner; dinner; Easter foods; eat; elevenses; epicure; fairy food; fast foods; fasting; feasts; food history; four humours; funeral food; futurist meals; gender/sex and food; gourmand; gourmet; high tea; Hinduism and food; Hogmanay; hospitality; Jains and food; Japanese tea ceremony; Jewish dietary laws; Lent; lunch; markets; meals; merenda, merienda; Muslims and food; Noah's ark (the food problem); organic food; Passover (and food); picnic; politics and food; Ramadan; restaurant; sardi/garmi; service à la française; service à la russe; sin eating; smörgåsbord; soul food; stage meals; street food; subtleties; taboo; tasting (against poison); tex-mex; Thanksgiving; tiffin; vegetarianism; washing up; wedding meals and cakes; white trash cooking; yin-yang.

NATIONAL AND REGIONAL CUISINES

Afghanistan; Albania; Algeria; Anglo-Indian cookery; Anglo-Saxon food; Angola and Mozambique; Antarctica;

Arab cuisine; Arabian food; Argentina; Armenia; Australia; Austria; Azerbaijan; Aztec food; Babylonian cookery; Balearic islands; Balkan food and cookery; Bangladesh; Basque food and cookery; Bedouin food; Belgium; Belorussia; Bolivia; Bosnia-Herzegovina; Brazil; Bulgaria; Burma; Byzantine cookery; Cajun food; Cambodia; Canada; Canary islands; Catalan cookery; Celtic feasting; Central America; Central Asian Republics; Chile; China; Classical Greece; Classical Rome; Colombia; Creole cookery; Croatia; Cyprus; Czech and Slovak Republics; Dagestan and Chechnya; Denmark; Dutch cookery; East Africa; Ecuador; Egypt; England; Estonia; Ethiopia; Faeroe Islands; Finland; France; Fulachta fiadh; Georgia; Germany; Goa; Greece; Guyana (with Surinam and French Guiana); Hawaii; Hokkaido; Horn of Africa; Hungary; Iceland; Inca food; India; Indonesia; Inuit cookery; Iran; Iraq; Ireland; Ireland and the potato; Israel; Italy; Japan; Jewish cookery; Jordan; Korea; Laos; Latvia; Lebanon and Syria; Libya; Lithuania; Luxembourg; Macedonia; Madagascar (Malagasy Republic); Madeira; Malaysia, Singapore & Brunei; Maldives; Malta; Mauritius; Maya food; medieval cuisine (general); medieval cuisine (the sources); Mexico; Moghul cuisine; Moldova (Moldavia); Mongolia; Morocco; Nepal; New Zealand; Norway; Okinawa; Orkney and Shetland; Pacific Islands; Pakistan; Papua New Guinea; Paraguay; Parsi food; Pennsylvania Dutch; Peru; Philippines; Poland; Portugal; Romania; Russia; Scotland; Seychelles; Slovenia; Southern Africa; Spain; Sri Lanka; Sub-Saharan Africa; Sudan; Sweden; Switzerland; Taiwan; Tatar cuisine; Thailand; Tibet; Tunisia; Turkey; Ukraine; Uruguay; USA; Venezuela; Vietnam; Wales; West and Central Africa; West Indies; Yemen; Yugoslavia.

SCIENTIFIC TOPICS

acids; additives; adulteration; alkali; altitude and cookery; amino acids; aphrodisiacs; appetite; autoclave; autolysis; bacteria; baking powder; bicarbonate of soda; botulism; browning; calcium; calories; canning; carbohydrates; cellulose; chelation; cholesterol; climate; coagulation; collagen; colloid; colour and cooking; colour, colouring of food; composition of foods; cookery—skill, art or science?; cooking; cream of tartar; curdling; denaturation; diet; digestion; distillation; drying; emulsion; enzymes; fats and oils; fermentation; fibre; flavour;

NOTES ON USING THIS BOOK

The book has been written with the intention that browsing through it should be a pleasure. However, most readers are likely to use it in the first instance for looking up a particular topic.

To look up something, the first step, obviously, is to see whether it is a headword. The 2,650 headwords, printed so that they stand out clearly on the page, are in alphabetical sequence. (Note that, for this purpose, spaces between words are ignored, so that AARDVARK comes before À LA.) The 41 feature articles on staple foods and the like sometimes combine entries on different aspects of the subject (e.g. the bread feature article includes a general entry on bread, followed by entries on bread varieties, bread chemistry, and bread in cooking). In these instances, all the relevant headwords can be found across the top of the page at the start of the feature article.

If the topic sought is not a headword, the next step would be to look for it in the selective index at the back of the book. The entries there lead, in every instance, from a word which is not a headword to the headword/s of the entry or entries where it will be found.

The index caters for synonyms (e.g. Dublin Bay prawn and NORWAY LOBSTER). It provides help in a situation where there is an English name for something but a name in another language has wide currency (e.g. a reader looking for langouste is directed to SPINY LOBSTER). Finally, and perhaps most important, it provides signposts for readers who are looking for topics which are actually presented as sub-topics within entries of larger scope (e.g. a reader looking for vermicelli will be directed to PASTA SHAPES).

Another way of using the book would be to start with the subject index (pp. xiii–xviii), a thematic listing of headwords which shows at a glance the whole range of entries in a particular field of interest such as fruits, fish, baked goods, national and regional cuisines.

Cross-references are indicated by small capitals. They appear only where they are likely to be helpful to the reader; and normally only once within any given entry. Thus, an entry about a country whose inhabitants are addicted to garlic might contain the word 'garlic' 20 or 30 times, but only the first occurrence in that entry would be in small capitals.

Bibliographical references in the standard form 'Mariani (1993)' direct the reader to an item in the Bibliography (pp.867–884). If a book is referred to in a less precise way, it will probably not be in the Bibliography.

The little heading 'READING' which occurs at the end of some entries directs attention to useful works which have not already been the subject of bibliographical references within the entry. In fact, 'READING' usually means 'further reading'.

The list of contributors (pp. xi–xii) is prefaced by an explanation of the system used in identifying contributors at the end of entries by their initials.

CAUTIONS

Within the book there are occasional specific warnings, for example about the overriding need to have reliable expert identification of fungi before eating them and about measures of legal protection from interference which apply to certain species of plants or animals. But the book would have made tedious reading if warnings of this sort had been included wherever and whenever they might conceivably be appropriate. Hence the need for the following two general cautions which apply to the entire content of the book.

1. The fact that something is mentioned in the book as being eaten or having been eaten by humans does not in itself imply that to eat it now or in the future would be appropriate, legally permissible, or safe.

2 The same applies to methods of preserving or cooking foods or dealing with them in any other way. Mentions of such methods do not in themselves imply that they accord with current international or national regulations or may safely be adopted.

It might be added out of earshot of legal advisers that common sense will normally tell readers in what contexts they should heed these cautions.

AARDVARK *Orycteropus afer*, an animal of southern Africa which is truly 'one of a kind'; it has no relations, although it can be counted as a member of the category of ANTEATERS.

Dutch colonists gave it its name, which means 'earth pig', because it resembles in some respects the pig and because of the amazing efficiency with which it can burrow into the ground, notably to create the system of tunnels in which it lives. These tunnels have many entrances (or exits) and by retreating into them during daytime the aardvark achieves a fair degree of security against large predators. Its own food consists largely of termites, plus various insects, all of which it catches on its sticky tongue. It may cover a considerable distance during the night, guided by its excellent sense of smell, in search of such sustenance. Although it attains a large size (maximum length 1.8 m/6' maximum weight 100 kg/220 lb), it is rarely seen, due to its timorous and nocturnal habits.

The reputation of the aardvark as food for humans is good. It is commonly described as tasting like pork.

ABALONE the common name used since the mid-19th century in N. America, and now generally adopted, for large single-shell molluscs of the genus *Haliotis*. Ormer and ear-shell are other English names.

An abalone can be regarded as a large and highly evolved kind of LIMPET, using the term in its general sense. It possesses seven holes in its shell through which water is drawn to be filtered through a pair of gills, and a very large oval 'foot' or adductor muscle by which it adheres firmly to its rock. It is this foot which is the edible part. Obtaining it is not easy, since the creature normally lives at a depth which makes it necessary to dive and then prise the shells away from the rock. However, the rewards are commensurate with the task, since abalone fetches a good price and its beautiful shell also has some commercial value.

The Chinese and the Japanese are the greatest enthusiasts for this delicacy, and it is noticeable that the finest and largest abalones, such as *H. asinina*, are found in the Pacific, off the coasts of Japan, Australia, New Zealand, and California. Dried or canned abalone is widely used in the Orient, and everywhere expensive, although fresh abalone costs even more.

The species familiar in the Mediterranean and on the European Atlantic coast as far north as the Channel Islands is *H. tuberculata*, which may measure as much as 12 cm (5"). This has been esteemed since classical times, when Aristotle described it, but the abalone is not a noticeable feature of Mediterranean cuisines, perhaps because it has never been abundant there. It is more common on the Atlantic coast of France, and there are interesting Breton recipes for preparing it. Its reputation in the Channel Islands is high.

In California the various species include black, red, green, white, and pinto abalones. The red abalone, *H. rufescens*, is the premier species, and was formerly the only one for which there was a commercial fishery. It could grow up to a size over 25 cm (10–11"), but large specimens are now rare.

Commercial fishing for any species of abalone is prohibited in the states of Washington and Oregon. A Californian project for the establishment of a new country, Abalonia, consisting of artificial reefs for the cultivation of the red abalone, outside the (then) territorial limits, came to grief when the first hulk being towed out for this purpose sank in the wrong place.

For the Japanese, abalone has been an important shellfish since antiquity. Whereas HAMAGURI, the Japanese clam, with its matching pair of shells, has been a symbol of marital harmony, abalone, because of its single shell, has long been used by poets as a symbol of unrequited love.

Japanese fishing for abalone is often done by husband-and-wife teams—the wife diving into the sea, and the husband taking charge of the boat and lifeline. (This is said to be because women can hold their breath longer than men.) The diving women, called 'ama' (sea-women), now go about their task with the aid of neoprene suits which enable them to stay under water longer in pursuit of the shrinking population.

The flesh of all abalones is tough, and must be tenderized by beating with a mallet, to break up the muscle fibres, before cooking. Processing, which is a skilled business, usually ends with the cutting of the trimmed meat into steaks.

The Japanese consider that an abalone whose flesh has a bluish tint will be tougher in texture, and best eaten raw as *mizugai*, i.e. the flesh is diced and floated in iced water or buried in crushed ice, to be eaten with a dipping sauce. Abalones with yellowish flesh, on the other hand, are thought to be more tender and suitable for grilling, or steaming.

In New Zealand the Maori name paua has been generally adopted for the species found there, especially the large and black-footed abalone *H. iris*, which enjoys some protection, so that the New Zealand liking for paua fritters and chips will not lead to the exhaustion of stocks.

ACACIA AND WATTLE *Acacia* spp. There are over 600 species, most of them native to Australia but others distributed throughout Africa, S. Asia, and the warmer parts of the Americas. They belong to the family Fabaceae (Leguminosae) whose members, including the familiar beans and peas, characteristically produce seeds in pods.

Many varieties are edible in part (for example, seeds, roots, gummy exudations) and have been exploited for this purpose by Australian Aborigines. Low (1989) explains that some acacias have several times the protein content of wheat; that the dried seeds were ground and baked as a form of damper (see BREAD VARIETIES); and that the species called mulga (*A. aneura*) is so abundant in the Northern Territory that its seeds could feed a quarter of a million people in an average year. However, virtually all edible wattles were eaten only in desert regions; the exception being the coast wattle,

A. sophorae, whose pods and peas were eaten in S. Australia and Tasmania.

It is a far cry from Aborigines in the Australian desert to the renowned chef ESCOFFIER in the capitals of Europe. However, acacia/wattle bridges the gap. Escoffier adopted the European practice of stripping off the flowers of acacia, which have a light but definite perfume, and making fritters of them. He did this with cultivated acacia flowers, first steeped in liqueur brandy and sugar.

Many acacias exude gums, of which the best known is GUM ARABIC, extracted from incisions in the bark of *A. senegal*.

ACCUM FRIEDRICH CHRISTIAN (1769–1838), chemist and food investigator, was born in Buckebourg, Westphalia. After training as a chemist, he went to London in 1793 and worked for the apothecaries to King George III.

He lectured on science at the Surrey Institute, opened a laboratory, and began to publish work on mineralogy. He then became an engineer with the London Gaslight and Coke Company and published, in 1815, his *Practical Treatise on Gas Light*. Turning to the investigation of food, he published *Adulterations of Food and Culinary Poisons* (1820). He was appalled by the adulteration of food carried on by men who, 'from the magnitude and apparent respectability of their concerns would be the least obnoxious to public suspicion'. He asserted that 'spurious articles are everywhere to be found, made up so skilfully as to baffle the discrimination of the most experienced judges'. Accum was not fooled; and he gave his scientific attention to a number of 'substances used in domestic economy which are now very generally found sophisticated [adulterated]—tea, coffee, bread, beer, wine, spiritous liquors, salad oil, pepper, vinegar, mustard, cream, confitures, catsup and other articles of subsistence'. His book gave methods of detecting adulterations and culinary poisons and listed brewers and grocers who had been prosecuted for adulterating beer and tea.

The powerful revelations in *Culinary Poisons* of the unscrupulous and dangerous techniques used to defraud the public were introduced by a title-page decorated with a dramatic image: a pot inscribed with a quotation from the Second Book of Kings. The chilling announcement that 'There is Death in the Pot' is entwined by snakes and topped by a draped skull.

His book *Culinary Chemistry* (1821) gave 'Concise Instructions for Preparing Good and Wholesome Pickles, Vinegars, Conserves, Fruits, Jellies, Marmalades and Various other Alimentary Substances

employed in Domestic Economy, with Observations on The Chemical Constitution and Nutritive Qualities of Different Kinds of Food'.

Accum became librarian of the Royal Institution, but he was charged with embezzlement and dismissed. He was reputed to have used the free endpapers of books as notepaper. When tried, he was acquitted, but left England to avoid a continuation of the proceedings against him, which were said to have been inspired by those whose swindles he had exposed. Back in Germany, he became a professor at the Berlin Technical Institute and continued to teach until his death in 1838.   RSh

ACHAR (also acar, achard), an Indian name for PICKLE. As Achaya (1994) notes, a Persian or Arabic derivation is commonly given for the name, but Rumphius in the mid-18th century noted that the name *axi* or *achi* was among those used in America for the CHILLI pepper and he (Rumphius) thought that this was the origin of the Indian word achar (no doubt because chilli pepper is an important ingredient for pickles).

There are other theories about the origin of the word. *Hobson-Jobson* (1903; see Yule and Burnell, 1979) has the following interesting entry:

[The word is] adopted in nearly all the vernaculars of India for acid and salt relishes. By Europeans it is used as the equivalent of 'pickles' and is applied to all the stores of Crosse and Blackwell in that kind. We have adopted the word through the Portuguese; but it is not impossible that Western Asiatics got it originally from the Latin *acetaria*.

Among the interesting early citations which *Hobson-Jobson* gives is one from the 16th century which identifies cashews conserved in salt as achar, and another from the 17th century which gives mango as the prime example (conserved with mustard, garlic, salt, and vinegar).

However this may be, the term has achieved wide currency. It is well known in Malaysia, for example, whither S. Indians had no doubt taken it when they arrived in force in the 19th century; and it is familiar also in S. Africa, having been brought perhaps by the 'Cape Malay' immigrants whose influence on the cuisine there is considerable. Indians may also have taken the term to the W. Indies, where it is used in many of the islands. What seems to be an echo of the term occurred in N. America in a Boston publication of 1837 which referred to 'Yellow Pickle, or Axejar'; see also CHOW-CHOW.

Although the term penetrated to the far north of the Indian subcontinent (notably in Nepal), it failed to reach Afghanistan and does not seem to have crossed the mountain barriers into C. Asia, nor to have travelled westwards to the Levant.

ACHOCHA the fruit of a tropical American tree, *Cyclanthera pedata*, widespread in Mexico and S. America, of the CUCURBIT group. The gourds or fruits, which are about 5 cm (2") long, yellowish-white, and prickled on the upper part, are cooked as a vegetable, notably in Peru. The name achocha (or achuccha) is a native one, used in that country.

The fruits are sometimes stuffed before being cooked. Young ones, which taste something like cucumber, may be eaten raw.

Herklots (1972) records that, mysteriously, this plant has come to be cultivated and eaten in parts of Nepal, where it is called *korila*. He describes the tiny black seeds, vividly, as being like 'diminutive mud turtles with head and neck outstretched and projections at the corners where the feet would emerge beneath the carapace'.

ACIDS a large group of substances essential to the working of the body and widespread in food. The scientific definition of an acid is a substance that dissolves in water to release hydrogen ions, dissolves metals releasing hydrogen gas, and reacts with a base to form a salt. All these properties are relevant to food.

First, the release of hydrogen ions—that is, hydrogen atoms with a positive electrical charge—means that acids tend to remove oxygen from other substances, and combine it with the hydrogen to form water. Oxygen tends to spoil foods (see, for example, FATS AND OILS), so acids act as preservatives, as in PICKLES and some fermented foods such as SAUERKRAUT and YOGHURT.

Second, many compounds formed by acids and metals are important in foodstuffs. These include ordinary SALT, sodium chloride, which can be made from sodium and hydrochloric acid. Other examples are BICARBONATE OF SODA, CREAM OF TARTAR, calcium oxalate (see OXALIC ACID), and saltpetre (see NITRATES AND NITRITES).

Third, the reaction of an acid with a 'base' (roughly the same as an ALKALI) is the means by which BAKING POWDER evolves gas and thus raises cakes.

Acids may be classed as strong or weak, according to the quantity of hydrogen ions they can release. One of the strongest, hydrochloric acid, is found in the stomachs of animals, where it helps to break down food. Strong acids are corrosive and this one is no exception; the stomach lining must be constantly renewed as it is eaten away. Many complex organic acids are so weak that their effect is negligible, for example the AMINO ACIDS of which protein is composed. Some organic acids, however, are quite strong, such as citric acid in citrus fruit, malic acid in apples, and acetic acid in VINEGAR. The strength of acids (and of alkalis) is measured on the pH scale (see PH FACTOR).

The old belief that certain foods are 'acid forming' and thus in some way bad for the body is no more than a myth.   RH

ACITRÓN the candied 'flesh' (stem) of the large cushion-like *biznaga* cactus, *Echinocactus grandis*. This confection is sometimes called just *biznaga* in Mexico, where it is made, usually shaped into bars of about 2 cm (1") square. It is used for desserts, for sweet TAMALES, and sometimes in less expected ways, e.g. in the beef hash called *picadillo*.

Acitrón can be found at most Mexican markets or bakeries, in the SW of the USA (as 'cactus candy') as well as in Mexico. It does not have a pronounced flavour of its own, but provides an interesting texture. Candied citron may be substituted; indeed, this has always been what the term *acitrón* has meant in Spain.

ACORNS the nuts borne by oak trees, *Quercus* spp. Of the hundreds of species around the world, many yield acorns suitable for animal fodder, but only a few bear acorns acceptable as human food. These have been eaten since prehistoric times, and still are, but their use has greatly diminished.

The best and sweetest acorns are from the ilex (or holm, or holly) oak, *Quercus ilex* var *rotundifolia* (formerly *ballota*), which grows all round the Mediterranean and in W. Asia. It is common in Spain and Portugal, and varieties of it are cultivated there for their acorns, the best of which are comparable to and eaten like chestnuts. The Duchess who, in *Don Quijote*, asked Sancho Panza's wife to send acorns from her village would have been seeking especially fine specimens of this kind. Such acorns are longer than most, and cylindrical in shape. The Spanish name *bellota* is derived from the Arabic *ballūṭ*, from which comes the former variety name *ballota*. This name is also used by Mexicans, but in reference to the acorns of *Q. emoryi*.

The common oak of Britain and NW Europe, *Q. robur*, is one of the many unpalatable species with nuts having a high content of tannin; these have only been used as human food in times of famine.

In N. America, however, there are several native species whose acorns are palatable and constituted a food of some importance for Indians and early white settlers. The Cahuilla Indians were not numerous, but the detailed account of their treatment of acorns by Bean and Saubel (1972) illuminates vividly the whole question of acorn-eating in the past. For the Cahuilla, these nuts were a food resource of great value, providing less protein and carbohydrate than barley or wheat, but much more fat. Of the four *Quercus* spp which they used, the California black oak, *Q. kellogii*, was rated top, since its acorns had 'outstanding flavor and the most gelatin-like consistency when cooked, a prerequisite for good acorn mush'. However, a really skilled acorn mush-maker would mix acorns of different species; and the whole complex of activities involved in harvesting, preparing, and cooking acorns called for great expertise, much equipment, and due ceremonial.

Acorns themselves and cakes made from acorn meal have remarkable keeping properties. Acorn meal can be used in much the same ways as cornmeal.

ACTON ELIZA (1799–1859), regarded by some as the most accomplished cookery writer in the English language, spent her early life in Suffolk, the county where her father's family belonged, and also spent some time in France. As an adult she lived in Tonbridge (in Kent) and Hampstead (in London). She never married and for much of her life her household consisted of her mother and herself.

Her book *Modern Cookery for Private Families* was published in 1845, revised by her in 1855, and stayed in print until almost the end of the century. It then had to wait almost 100 years before being reprinted in full (1994), although a generous selection of her recipes had been republished in 1986, accompanied by admirable essays from Elizabeth Ray and Elizabeth David. A separate book, *The English Bread Book*, appeared in 1857.

The high praise which her work has attracted has been due to a combination of elegant, precise, and lucid writing on the one hand with meticulous and observant activity in the kitchen on the other. The 'Obs.' appended to many of her recipes constitute exactly the kind of comment which is invaluable to the cook.

Elizabeth Ray (Acton, 1986) points out that 'although she is basically a very English cook, many of her receipts are labelled "French", and appear as a matter of course in the main body of [her] book'. Other foreign recipes, in contrast, appear in a separate chapter on 'foreign and Jewish cookery' (Eliza Acton mentions more than once 'a certain Jewish lady' who gave her recipes; and it is interesting that these are Ashkenazi rather than Sephardic). Among Elizabeth Ray's further comments are the following:

Eliza Acton's muse had once flown further than the kitchen: the story has often been written of how the maiden lady of the eighteen-thirties, already a poet with a modest reputation, took 'further fugitive verses' to her publishers—to be told that they would rather have a cookery book instead. *Modern Cookery for Private Families* was the result, and posterity has agreed with her publishers: the cookery book survives, but not the verses.

Nevertheless, an unmistakable literary talent appears even in her receipts, in the style itself, and in the engaging titles she bestows on some of her dishes. 'The Elegant Economist's Pudding' for example, is an appetising name indeed for what is, in fact, a way of using up left-over Christmas pudding. 'Poor Author's Pudding' is contrasted with 'The Publisher's Pudding', which 'can scarcely be made *too rich*'. The italics are her own, the poor author's.

It is tempting to compare Eliza Acton to Jane Austen, at least for elegance of style and quiet wit. However, although Eliza Acton was the product of that period of English history which Jane Austen so charmingly described in her novels, she was writing at a time when the nature of English society was undergoing radical changes, largely because of the Industrial Revolution; and the beneficial innovations which she introduced into the art of recipe-writing were especially appropriate in that they heralded many new developments in food distribution (the railways) and kitchen technology as well as in other aspects of Victorian life.

Elizabeth David (1984) drew attention to Miss Acton's 'singleness of purpose . . . and meticulous honesty'; and (Acton, 1986) described her book as 'the greatest cookery book in our language'.

ADDITIVES substances added to food to make it more appetizing or to preserve it. The term tends to be used in a pejorative sense for unwanted chemicals introduced by the food industry for purely commercial reasons; but even salt and pepper are additives in the strict sense.

The laws of many countries require all the ingredients of processed foods, including additives, to be listed on the package. In the USA additives are listed by name, but in the EC they are classified by a three-figure number. These 'E numbers' are a useful guide to the purpose of additives—though not infallible, because many have more than one function. The numbers are assigned to both natural and synthetic additives, as well as 'nature identical' ones—that is, exact synthetic copies of natural substances such as the green colour chlorophyll (E140). Some numbers are not preceded by E, which often means that their status is under consideration; as with Brown FK (154), a dye used only in Britain to make pale, lightly smoked kippers look more attractive. A very

few were assigned numbers but have since been banned, such as the 'azo' (nitrogen-based) dye Allura red AC (E129).

Substances used as COLOURINGS have E numbers beginning with 1. They include natural caramel (E150), and synthetic azo dyes such as Green S (E142), used in canned peas, and the notorious yellow tartrazine (E102), which some people believe causes hyperactivity in children.

General preservatives have numbers beginning with 2. They include sorbic acid (E200), extracted from fruits or made synthetically, and very widely employed. Saltpetre or sodium nitrate (E250) is used in cured meats. Acetic acid (E260) is the active principle of vinegar.

Antioxidants which, among other things, prevent FATS AND OILS from going rancid, have numbers from E300 to E322. These include some vitamins used as preservatives as well as dietary supplements, such as vitamin C or ascorbic acid (E300) and various forms of vitamin E, the tocopherols (E306–9).

The remainder of the numbers beginning with 3 go to substances which are both antioxidants and general stabilizers. One of the commonest is butylated hydroxyanisole or BHA (E320), added to potato snacks, biscuits, pastry, sauces, and fried foods. Citric acid (E330) is used to prolong the keeping time of pickles, bottled sauces, dairy products, and baked goods.

Emulsifiers (see EMULSION) and other stabilizers have numbers beginning with 4. These include natural GUMS such as gum arabic (E414), PECTIN (E440a), and the dauntingly named polyglycerol esters of polycondensed fatty acids of castor oil (476), used to make chocolate coatings flow smoothly.

Anti-caking agents, which prevent powdered ingredients from going lumpy, have numbers beginning with 5. Surprisingly, many of these are inorganic minerals; for example talc (553b) and kaolin or china clay (559).

Flavour enhancers have numbers beginning with 6. The best known is the controversial MONOSODIUM GLUTAMATE (621). Another is maltol (636), extracted from malt but also, improbably, from larch bark and pine needles, and used to brighten the taste of synthetic coffee, maple syrup, and vanilla flavourings.

Numbers beginning with 7 and 8 are not used. Those from 901 to 907 are given to glazing agents, some of which are surprising: for instance beeswax (901) and shellac (904). 'Improving agents', used mainly to soften the texture of mass-produced baked goods, have numbers from 920 to 927. One of these, the amino acid L-cysteine (920), is also used as a synthetic chicken flavour. It is extracted from feathers and hair.

A few substances, mostly common ones, have no number; for example GELATIN, STARCH, and the artificial flavour vanillin.

Many large supermarkets offer free booklets listing additives, which are useful to people worried about food allergies.   RH

ADLAY *Coix lachryma-jobi*, a cereal plant with large, starchy, tear-shaped grains. It is native to SE Asia, where it has long been used for food, though generally only as second best when there is a shortage of a main staple crop. It is most widely grown in the Philippines.

The plant travelled westwards long ago, through India. It is now found wild in Spain and Portugal, and there is a dwarf form, probably introduced by the Portuguese, in Brazil.

Varieties may have hard or soft seed coats. The hard-shelled kinds are very hard, and the grains have an attractively lustrous appearance. They have been used in many regions as beads, sometimes for rosaries, which is why 'Job's tears' figure in their botanical name. (Naturally occurring round lumps of the shiny mineral chrysolite, similarly used, have the same name.)

Soft-shelled varieties, especially that called 'Ma-Yuen', are preferred for eating, for example in macrobiotic diets. After being husked and roasted they may be ground to a coarse flour, which can be used for making bread if mixed with flour from a conventional cereal.

ADOBO a culinary term of the Philippines which usually refers to pork, or chicken and pork, stewed with vinegar, bay leaf, peppercorns, garlic, and soy sauce until brown and aromatic. It may be served with its sauce, or fried crisp. The sauce may also be thickened with mashed chicken liver.

The word comes from the Spanish *adobo*, referring to a pickling sauce of olive oil, vinegar, and spices (or to the Mexican paste of ground chillies, spices, herbs, and vinegar); and from *adobado*, pork pickled with the above or with wine and onions.

Adobo has long been called the quintessential Philippine stew, served with rice both at daily meals and for feasts, and also taken on journeys, since the stewing in vinegar ensures that it keeps well without refrigeration. It is palatable hot or cold. Although chicken and/or pork are the basic adobos, there are many others, for example with squid, various shellfish, catfish, and *kangkong* (WATER SPINACH, swamp cabbage). More exotic examples are *agachonas adobadas* (with snipe), *adobong bayawak* (with MONITOR lizard), and *adobong kamaru*, in which the mole CRICKET is featured.

The Philippine adobo is thus vinegar-stewed food of almost any kind, not a dish of Spanish or Mexican derivation but a native dish which was given a Spanish name by the Spaniards who came and saw something similar to their own *adobado*. Raymond Sokolov (1991) is correct to emphasize that 'Filipino *adobo* stands by itself, fully formed and always distinct from the "adobo" dishes of Mexico and Spain'.　　　　　　　DF

ADULTERATION the mixing of foodstuffs with inferior or spurious substances, has been going on for as long as food has been sold. Roman bakers were accused of adding chalk to bread. More usually it is goods of high value that are adulterated, for example spices. In England in 1316 the Guild of Pepperers issued a decree banning the moistening of saffron, ginger, and cloves to make them heavier, as they were sold by weight. Often highly noxious adulterants were used: cayenne pepper, which easily loses its red colour, was tinted with cinnabar, an extremely poisonous mercury compound.

The increase in trade brought about by the Industrial Revolution turned adulteration from minor fraud to big business. According to Shipperbottom (1993), mustard in the 1850s rarely contained more than 20% real mustard seed, the rest being wheat or pea flour, linseed meal, and plaster of Paris, coloured with turmeric and spiced with cayenne pepper. Ground pepper was adulterated with powdered bones. A common ploy was to sell real spices which had already been used; for example, ground ginger was made from ginger root that had already been used to flavour ginger beer, so that it was more or less tasteless.

Until the advances in chemistry at the end of the 18th century it was hard to prove that foods had been adulterated. The first systematic analysis was undertaken in Britain by the German chemist Friedrich Christian ACCUM, who published *A Treatise on Adulterations of Food and Culinary Poisons* in 1820. This was prefaced by the famous dictum: 'There is death in the pot.' It surveyed not only foods and spices, but also wine, spirits, tea, and coffee, all expensive and therefore much adulterated; and it described analytical methods that could be used to detect substitutes.

Laws were passed to outlaw such frauds, without much success; an anonymous book published in London in 1859, *Tricks of the Trade*, told many horror stories, and an intrepid analyst of the early 1870s disclosed that mushroom ketchup was being simulated with a liquid made from rotting horse livers. From the 1850s to the 1870s the British doctor Arthur Hill Hassall published articles exposing frauds of all kinds, leading

to the passing of Acts of Parliament in 1860, 1872, and 1875, the last of which required that processed foods should be labelled with a full list of their constituents.

Hassall's work was brought together in a book of nearly 900 pages (1876) which contained remarkable illustrations of adulterations revealed under the microscope, and which is still a sort of 'bible' on the subject. The same applies to the magnificent American book by Wiley (1911), who was the principal architect of the world-renowned FDA (Food and Drug Administration) of the USA.

Fraudulent practices, including adulteration as well as substitution (of inferior products) continue, more actively in some parts of the world than in others. The worst of them have been eliminated or subdued in countries which have established adequate systems of control, but the plugging of loopholes is a perennial task.

One widespread modern (but not new) form of adulteration is the addition of water to increase the weight of (especially) processed meats—these can be treated with polyphosphates, chemicals which allow the meat to absorb large amounts of water. Obnoxious though this sort of thing is, it is less iniquitous than some of the old forms of adulteration by actively toxic substances.
　　　　　　　　　　　　　　　　　　(RH)

ADVIEH the Persian name for a SPICE MIXTURE, includes a wide range of such products, indeed an almost infinite range, given that even in modern times the mixtures are normally prepared in the home, according to the preferences and practices of the cook and the particular purpose of a given mixture. Not every Persian housewife uses it every time. Some cooks only sprinkle a little turmeric or cinnamon, or perhaps a little powdered coriander seed for fragrance or a bayleaf to 'cut' the muttony flavour of the meat, while others will make up a blend or even several different blends: one for delicate and fragrant dishes, another for hearty day-to-day meals, and a third for an aromatic sprinkling when serving festive dishes. The individual sprinklings or the blends are all known collectively as *advieh*.

A popular *advieh* blend from the south of Iran includes coriander seed, turmeric, cinnamon, cumin, cardamom, and black pepper and is reminiscent of a CURRY POWDER (although more delicate since not including hot chillies, red peppers, ginger, and garlic, none of which would ever appear in any Persian *advieh* recipe). Some mixtures also include nutmeg or cloves.

Advieh from the sunny upland of the Persian plateau and from the north-western region contains dried rose petals which give

a rare and heady fragrance when sprinkled over delicate rice dishes during the steaming process.　　　　　　　　　　　　　　MS

AFGHANISTAN a landlocked country at the heart of Asia, is the crossroads for four major cultural areas: Persia and the Middle East; C. Asia; the Indian subcontinent; and the Far East. It is a land of contrasts and extremes—scorching deserts; high, inaccessible snow-capped mountains; and green, fertile plains and valleys, some of which are subtropical.

Afghanistan was a crossroads on the ancient Silk Road which linked East and West and which played a vital role in the exchange of foods, plants, skills, and knowledge. Other influences came with invading armies: Alexander the Great; Genghis Khan; the Moghul Babur and the Persian Nader Shah; and then the British with their Indian troops in the 19th century and the Russians in the 20th century (although the latter left a negligible cultural influence behind them).

The names Afghan and Afghanistan mask the diversity of ethnic groups in the country: Pushtun, Tajik, Turkmen, Hazara, Uzbek, etc. This was another factor which made the country a melting pot for different cultures and traditions. Its cuisine reflects internal diversity, besides mirroring the tastes and flavours of its neighbours.

Bread is the staple food, usually made with wheat flour in the form of either NAN, which is leavened and baked in a TANDOOR, or CHAPATI. Bread is very often eaten on its own with tea (*chai*) but it is also used as a scoop for food or as an accompaniment to dishes such as soup.

Although bread is the staple, rice is of great importance. Long-grain rice is used for the many sorts of PILAF; also for *chalau*, the basic white rice which is accompanied by meat or vegetable stews (KORMA) or *burani* (vegetables with yoghurt, see BURAN). Short-grain rice is used for the basic sticky rice called *bata* which is served with a stew or vegetables, both savoury and sweet SHOLA, and other rice desserts.

Pasta and noodle dishes (on which generally see NOODLES OF ASIA) also play an important part in the Afghan cuisine, as do savoury fried pastries such as BOULANEE (pastry stuffed with Chinese chives or mashed potato), *sambosa* (see SAMOSA), and PAKORA. These are often served for lunch or as one of the numerous snack foods available from street vendors (*tabang wala*).

Lamb is the favourite meat although goat, beef, water-buffalo, camel are also eaten, as are poultry and game. Since Afghanistan is a Muslim country, pork is not eaten. Lamb is often made into KEBABS. These include the fiery hot speciality of Jalalabad, *chappli kebab* (which means sandal kebab, named after its sandal-like shape); rib or *shinwari* kebab, named after one of the large Pashtun tribes; *shami* or *lola* kebabs which are made with ground meat, potatoes, split peas, and fried in oil. *Dumba*, the fat from the FAT-TAILED SHEEP, is grilled with kebabs to provide more succulence or boiled with lamb to make *dopyasa*.

Fish does not play an important part in the Afghan diet. In the winter some sea fish (but not shellfish) are imported from Pakistan and river fish such as trout or *sheer mahi* can be found. JALEBI are traditionally served with fish during the winter months.

Dairy products loom large in the Afghan diet. Yoghurt (*mast*) is used extensively in cooking. It is often strained to make a creamy substance called *chaka*, which in turn is sometimes dried and formed into balls which harden and resemble grey pebbles. This is called QUROOT. Cheese (PANIR) is also made. In the springtime a snack called *kishmish panir* is a dish of white cheese served with red raisins. *Qymaq*, another milk product, is similar to the Middle Eastern KAYMAK. It is sometimes eaten with nan for breakfast, but is better known for its use in the Afghan tea called *qymaq chai* (see below), which is made for special occasions.

Desserts, sweets, cakes, biscuits, and pastries are considered to be luxuries. Many resemble those of Iran, the Middle East, and India. Milk-based puddings include FIRNI and sweet rice dishes. HALVA is popular as are pastries such as BAKLAVA and the pastry shaped like elephant ears called *goash-e-feel*.

Abrayshum kebab (*abrayshum* meaning silk) is an unusual Afghan sweet which is made with egg in such a way that the egg forms threads which are then rolled up like a kebab and sprinkled with syrup and ground pistachio. The egg threads are supposed to resemble silken threads, hence the name; see Saberi (1993).

For the Afghan New Year, a pre-Islamic festival marking the first day of spring, a traditional dried fruit and nut compote called *haft mewa* is prepared.

At the end of every meal fresh fruits in season are served. In summer this would include melons and grapes of which there are numerous varieties and for which Afghanistan is famous. Grapes are made into both red and green raisins. Nuts (pistachios, almonds, walnuts, pine nuts) are used extensively in cooking, mainly as garnishes, but are also eaten as snacks.

Tea, both black and green, is consumed copiously all over Afghanistan. *Chaikhana* (tea houses) are an important institution. They not only furnish tea from a constantly boiling samovar, but very often provide meals and accommodation for travellers.

Tea is seldom drunk with milk, but often flavoured with cardamom. Sugared almonds called *noql* are a common accompaniment. *Qymaq chai* is served for special occasions. This special tea (see, again, Saberi, 1993) is made from green tea in such a way that, with the addition of bicarbonate of soda and the process of aeration, the tea becomes red. Milk is added, producing a purply pink tea which is then topped with *qymaq*.   HS

AFTERNOON TEA one of a pair of tea meals (the other being HIGH TEA), both of which are essentially British and which, although alike in having tea as the beverage served, stand in high contrast to each other in other respects.

Mrs Beeton (1861) expressed succinctly the material difference when she remarked that 'There is Tea and Tea' and went on to say that 'A "High Tea" is where meat takes a more prominent part and signifies really, what is a tea-dinner . . . The afternoon tea signifies little more than tea and bread-and-butter, and a few elegant trifles in the way of cake and fruit.'

Although the custom of taking a cup of tea, at least occasionally, at a suitable time in the afternoon may have been adopted by some ladies in the late 17th century, it seems clear that neither afternoon tea nor high tea, the meals, started to become established until late in the 18th or early in the 19th centuries. Since almost all authors rely on the indefatigable Ukers (1935), who had scoured available literary and artistic sources for indications on this point, he must be allowed here to speak for himself:

Dr Alexander Carlyle wrote in his autobiography of the fashionable mode of living at Harrowgate in 1763 that, 'The ladies gave afternoon tea and coffee in their turn.' For the custom of afternoon tea as a distinct and definite function, however, the world is indebted to Anna, wife of the seventh Duke of Bedford, 1788–1861. In her day, people ate prodigious breakfasts. Luncheon was a sort of picnic, with no servants in attendance. There was no other meal until eight-o'clock dinner, after which tea was served in the drawing-room. The Duchess of Bedford struck out a new line; she had tea and cakes served at five o'clock, because, to quote herself, she had 'a sinking feeling'.

Fanny Kemble, the actress, in her *Later Life*, records that she first became acquainted with afternoon tea in 1842 at Belvoir Castle, seat of the Dukes of Rutland. She added that she did not believe the now universally-honored custom dated back any further than this.

In the 20th century afternoon tea has kept to a formula: tea (in a pot, with milk and sugar, or perhaps lemon if China tea is served); dainty small sandwiches (cucumber, very thinly sliced, is a favoured filling); scones with butter and jam (optional); some form of little cakes or slices of a large cake; biscuits (optional); and a serviette or napkin to complete the generally dainty picture. The effect is charming and may be achieved by a hostess (or host) with far less expenditure of effort and money than a full meal, or even a high tea, would require.

A variant of afternoon tea is the Devon cream tea, which towards the end of the 20th century was advancing relentlessly across all the other counties of England, and indeed appearing in Scotland, Wales, and Ireland, sometimes described as just 'cream tea'. This calls for scones, clotted cream, and jam.

For afternoon tea in Australia see Barbara Santich (1988).

AGAR-AGAR the Malay name for a GUM which was discovered in Japan. The name originally applied to a mucilage extracted from a red SEAWEED of the genus *Eucheuma*. This was in use only locally. The type of Japanese agar-agar which is important both in Japanese cooking and worldwide comes from red algae of the genus *Gelidium*. This gum, known in Japan itself as *kanten*, is referred to by many names, including grass jelly and seaweed jelly, also Japanese or vegetable gelatin (although true GELATIN is an animal product).

Agar-agar is the most powerful gel-former of all gums, owing to the unusual length of its carbohydrate molecules. Agar-agar gels are unique in withstanding temperatures near boiling point. They are thus ideal for making jellied sweet dishes in tropical climates, without any risk of their melting or sagging, and for ASPIC coatings.

The marine plants from which agar-agar is made are gathered and left on the beach to dry and bleach before being sold to a factory. There they are beaten and washed in fresh water to clean them, then boiled to extract the gum. This is frozen, then thawed. As the water runs out of it, the impurities are carried away. The purified gum is finally dried.

The method of purifying *kanten* by freezing and thawing is said to have been discovered accidentally by a Japanese innkeeper during frosty weather in 1658. Since then the product has gained widespread popularity in Japanese cuisine not only for making jellies but also as a general thickener for soups and sauces. It is also used in China (as *dai choy goh*), in the Philippines (*gulaman*), and elsewhere in SE Asia.

During the 19th century agar-agar was imported by western countries for making desserts. When it was discovered that agar-agar jelly was an ideal medium for the experimental growing of bacteria, this trade expanded. Agar-agar also began to be more widely used in the food industry.

The Second World War stopped trade with Japan, and western countries looked at their own native seaweeds. They found some which yielded what were often inferior substitutes for agar-agar, but also discovered or reappraised others which gave useful gums such as ALGINATES, carrageenan (see CARRAGEEN), and furcellaran (see GUM). Since then agar-agar has been less dominant in the market, although some continues to be imported from Japan, to be used as a thickener, emulsifier, and stabilizer in numerous products.

The seaweed called OGO in Japan is the source of a similar product.

AGARIC an old term for any mushroom, is derived from the classical Greek name for mushroom, *agarikon*, which in turn comes from the town of Agara, once famous for its mushrooms. The name has survived in both popular and scientific nomenclature, but with meanings which differ somewhat from each other (and, incidentally, from the meaning in classical times).

The scientific classification Agaricales comprises all the families of 'mushroom-shaped' fungi, i.e. those which have caps with radiating gills underneath and which grow on stems. All these might therefore be correctly called agarics. But in ordinary speech they are not.

Nor is the name agaric restricted, as would have been convenient, to the 'true' mushrooms, of the genus *Agaricus*, such as the common FIELD MUSHROOM, the cultivated mushroom, and their numerous close relations. The trouble is that this genus was known as *Psalliota* until the end of the 19th century, by which time a wider and looser application of the name agaric was too well established to be narrowed in conformity with the change. Thus we still have 'orange agaric' as a common name for both the oronge, *Amanita caesarea*, and the saffron milk cap, *Lactarius deliciosus*; and 'fly agaric' as the name for *Amanita muscaria*, a harmful species. In contrast, in the genus *Agaricus* only one species, the wood agaric, has a common name which includes the word agaric.

Because of the possible confusion, the term agaric is not used in this book in a general sense, but only when it is part of an established common name.

AGAR WOOD *Aquillaria agallocha*, a fragrant wood commonly used in oriental incense, has occasional culinary uses. Paula Wolfert (1973), calling it aga wood, identifies it as one of numerous possible ingredients in the Moroccan spice mixture known as RAS-EL-HANOUT. In Morocco it goes under the Arabic name of *oud kameira*.

AGAVE a tall perennial plant, of which there are many species in the genus *Agave*, almost all originating in Mexico or nearby

regions. Some, notably *A. americana* and *A. deserti*, yield food. They are often called **maguey**.

Four major parts of the agave are edible: the flowers, the leaves, the stalks or basal rosettes, and the sap.

Each agave plant will produce several pounds of edible flowers during the summer. The starch in the buds is converted into sugar, and the sweet nectar exudes from the flowers.

Agave leaves are best in winter and spring when the plants are rich in sap. (They often have on them larvae of the agave skipper butterfly, *Megathymus stephousi*; these were roasted on the leaves by the Indians and then picked off and eaten as a delicacy.)

The stalks, which are ready during the summer, before the blossom, weigh several pounds each. Roasted, they are sweet and taste like molasses.

When mature (six to eight years old) the agave provides a fourth food, its sap, which may be tapped at the rate of half a gallon a week for two months or more. In its fresh state this is transparent with a greenish tinge, sweet but with a bitter taste; it makes a pleasant refreshing drink, called *agua miel* (honey water), or can be boiled down to make a syrup or sugar. However, fermentation sets in quickly; within a few hours, if left to itself, the sugar of the sap will be converted into carbonic acid and alcohol, and on the way to becoming vinegar or the alcoholic drink pulque.

Agave is and was cultivated extensively in the highlands of Mexico, especially as the source of pulque. There is, in effect, a whole cuisine in this region based on these plants.
READING: Sophie Coe (1985, for use by Aztecs); Bean and Saubel (1972, for use by Cahuilla Indians).

AGOUTI (sometimes spelt aguti), any of a number of *Dasyprocta* spp. C. and S. American rodents of the family Dasyproctidae. The common (or golden) agouti is found most abundantly in the forests of Guiana, Brazil, and N. Peru but the range of the genus extends northwards through C. America to Mexico; one species, *D. cristata*, is found in the W. Indies. The name agouti comes from the Tupi-Guaraní name, *aquti*.

Agoutis are only about 50 cm (20") long overall but do not have much of a tail, so there is quite a bit of body, weighing around 3.5 kg (nearly 8 lb) and giving plenty to eat. They are nocturnal. Burton (1962) reports that: 'A hunter's trick is to toss stones into [the] air; these falling to [the] ground sound like falling fruit to agutis, which come out to feed.' Fruit is the animal's favourite food but it also eats vegetable matter, leaves, roots of ferns, etc.

Charles Darwin and his shipmates, in S. America in the course of their voyage round the world aboard the *Beagle*, ate agouti, which Darwin described in his journal as 'the very best meat I ever tasted'. (However, he thought agouti and cavy were interchangeable names, so he may have meant a GUINEA PIG.)

Simmonds (1859), who managed to produce relevant comments on the edibility of virtually every four-footed creature, has this to say:

The white tender flesh of the agouti . . . when fat and well dressed, is by no means unpalatable food, but very delicate and digestible. It is met with in Brazil, Guiana, and in Trinidad. The manner of dressing them in the West Indies used to be to roast them with a pudding in their bellies. Their skin is white, as well as the flesh.

The US National Academy of Sciences, reviewing in 1991 the potential for raising agoutis commercially, commented that its meat is leaner and gamier than that of the PACA, which is generally preferred, but that it is nonetheless a promising resource.

AÏOLI described by Blancard (1927) as the 'triumph of the Provençal kitchen', is in effect a garlic MAYONNAISE. But it is not just a sauce; it can take the form of *Aïoli garni* which is a whole dish in itself, traditionally served on Christmas Eve and incorporating beef or a boiled chicken.

Among the items which aïoli accompanies are potatoes, beetroot, fish and other seafood, and boiled salt cod. It may also be amalgamated with fish stock to make a thinner and pale yellow sauce to be poured over the fish in the famous Provençal dish called *Bourride*.

Aïoli does have a reputation for being indigestible, if eaten in quantity. Olney (1974) comments: 'A more easily digestible but less silken aïoli may be prepared by substituting boiled potato . . . for the egg yolks.' The same author observes that the quality of the olive oil is important; and that an aïoli 'is traditionally prepared in a marble mortar with a wooden pestle; the weight of the mortar prevents it from slip-sliding around as one turns the pestle with one hand while dribbling the oil with the other.'

See also CATALAN CUISINE, for the Catalan *allioli*.

AJMUD *Trachyspermum roxburghianum*, a plant of the umbelliferous family (to which celery, for example, and a number of important flavouring herbs belong). The seeds are used in India and SE Asia for flavouring pickles, chutneys, and preserves, as well as 'curry' dishes. The leaves, which smell of carrots, are also used to some extent as a substitute for PARSLEY. The seeds are an important minor spice in many parts of India. The name ajmud is also used of CELERY seed.

It is cultivated in SE Asia, often in kitchen gardens, and also in India.

AJOWAN *Trachyspermum ammi*, an umbelliferous plant of India and the Near East, related to CARAWAY and AJMUD. Its seeds constitute a spice which is used as a flavouring (e.g. sprinkled on biscuits and bread in Afghanistan), and also possesses useful antioxidant and preservative qualities. The flavour of the spice has been described as 'a combination of anise and oregano with a hint of black pepper'.

The seeds, sometimes referred to as carom seeds, yield an essential oil, thymol; this is mainly used in toothpaste and for medical purposes, but also for flavouring purposes.

Some authors have said that an English name for ajowan is LOVAGE, but this is a mistake, although both plants belong to the same family.

A related spice, used in Ethiopian cookery, consists of the seeds of bishop's weed, *Ammi majus*.

AKEBIA the fruit of either of two oriental climbing shrubs in the genus *Akebia* of the family Lardizabalaceae.

Although appreciated in their native region (China, Korea, and Japan), the fruits are rarely cultivated there and have not been introduced elsewhere on a significant scale. Each plant produces up to three pendent fruits, purplish in colour. Those of *A. trifoliata* may reach a length of 12 cm (5"). They burst open when ripe to reveal thick, semi-transparent flesh and numerous black

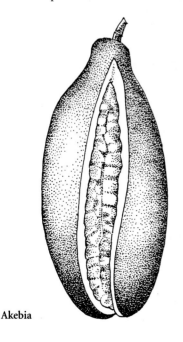

Akebia

seeds. This flesh, which has only a faint flavour, is edible, and so is the skin.

Akebia is often mentioned in Japanese literature where it is evocative of pastoral settings. Spring is when the young leaves and buds are eaten. The fruit, a delicacy of autumn, is sometimes eaten as is, but may also be stuffed with MISO (bean paste) and chicken mixture. For this dish the seeds are removed, the stuffing put in, and the whole then tied up with a thread and lightly fried. As is often the case, it is the stuffing rather than what is stuffed that is tasty.

The dried leaves are made into a tea in Japan.

AKEE (or ackee), the curious fruit of a W. African tree, *Blighia sapida*, introduced to the W. Indies by Captain Bligh of HMS *Bounty* (whence the generic name *Blighia*). It is a member of the same family as the LYCHEE of SE Asia.

The name 'akee' may be a corruption of the Mayan *achee*, which was a name applied to several plants whose flowers attract honey bees.

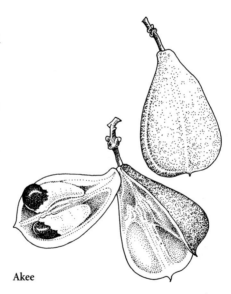

Akee

The fruit is comparable in appearance to a peach, but in structure to an orange, as it has segments. It measures 7–10 cm (2–4") long, is usually red when ripe, but sometimes yellow. When fully ripe, it splits open spontaneously, exposing three shiny, black seeds partly surrounded by a fleshy, cream-coloured aril (seed coat).

This aril is the only edible part; the rest of the fruit is not safe to eat. Morton (1987) states that the toxin (hypoglycin, a propionic acid) has been shown to reside in the seeds and in unripe arils. What is in the unripe arils is largely dispelled by light when the fruit splits, but what is in the seeds remains; squirrels never eat the seeds.

The akee is to be eaten at the peak of ripeness, just after the capsule splits, an occurrence which is often followed by a race between man and bird to reach the succulent fruit first. The aril is oily and does not keep for long.

Akee can be eaten raw but are usually cooked. Since their texture resembles that of brains (or, say some, scrambled eggs), they are sometimes known as 'vegetable brains'. The flavour is mildly sweet and delicate. In the W. Indies they are cooked as a vegetable, for example in the national dish of Jamaica, salt fish (usually cod) and ackee (the alternative spelling being preferred). They are canned and exported to Britain for the W. Indian community.

In Africa, the fruits are eaten raw, or cooked in a soup, or fried in oil.

W. Indians sometimes apply the name akee to a related fruit, *Melicoccus bijugatus*: see MAMONCILLO.

À LA a French phrase which introduces a name indicating how a dish has been prepared: thus, *Sole à la normande, Potage à la Rothschild*. In the whole phrase the words *façon de* or *mode de* are usually understood: thus, *Sole à la [façon] normande; Potage à la [mode de] Rothschild*. Sometimes the missing words are included in the phrase: thus, *Tripes à la mode de Caen*. Sometimes the words *à la* are omitted: thus, *Sole normande* may appear all by itself.

It is rare for these phrases to be self-explanatory. The great majority are in code, and in the 19th century and the first half of the 20th century, when the coded terms were most freely used, even chefs and restaurateurs and the most sophisticated diners needed a lexicon devoted to their interpretation, such as (to cite the title of the English version) *Hering's Dictionary of Classical and Modern Cookery* (Bickel, 1977), a book commonly used by chefs in the past and one which still has some currency as the 20th century draws to a close.

Alexandre DUMAS the elder (1873) poked fun at the system, building a whole edifice of witty comment on the basis of a turnip recipe which he came across, *Navets à la d'Esclignac*:

What can possibly have earned M. d'Esclignac the honour of giving his name to a dish of turnips? In this field, there is no odder subject of study than the books written by cooks and the strange way in which they suddenly make up their minds to make a sauce of, to put on the grill, or to roast our famous men.

This is what we find in one single book, in the section on soups:

Potage à la Demidoff
 à la John Russell
 à l'Abd-el-Kader
 à la ville de Berlin

à la Cialdini
au 15 Septembre 1864
au héros de Palestro
à la Lucullus
à la Guillaume Tell . . .

Dumas gives scores of other examples, many drawn from other categories of dishes.

If the system had not got out of hand, in the way mocked by Dumas, it could have been more useful. The coded terms were capable of conveying a lot of information with great brevity. Thus a restaurateur composing his menu in the year 2000 might have to write: 'Poached eggs, Abyssinian style—dressed on flat croquettes of sweet potatoes, hollowed out and stuffed with chestnut, coated with white butter sauce mixed with shredded white Italian truffles', whereas his predecessors in 1900 could just have put down *Œufs pochés à l'abyssinienne* in the expectation that at least some customers (even if they could not interpret all the 312 other terms for serving poached eggs in Hering's manual) would know what to expect from this one.

To continue the case for the defence, it is of some interest (if true) that a dish has a national, regional, or ethnic connection (*à la polonaise, à la niçoise, à la juive*). It is normally of less interest, as Dumas noticed, to have a personal connection indicated, although there are some worthy examples: it may be thought that Parmentier deserves to have his name perpetuated by the names of potato dishes. In this connection there is an interesting point to which the famous chef ESCOFFIER, a great one for dedicating dishes to persons he admired (or wished to gratify), paid attention. In the case of a dedication the words *à la* are inappropriate; the dish is not in the style of Dame Nellie Melba but named in her honour—so *pêches Melba*, not *pêches à la Melba*.

Any attempt to create a little all-purpose lexicon of *à la* phrases comes up against the difficulty that many of them change in meaning according to what it is that is being cooked or garnished. Thus *à l'anglaise* applied to potatoes is one thing, whereas it has different messages if it refers to fish or to a custard. The difficulty is well understood and circumvented by clever organization in various recently published pocket guides to French culinary terms. There is a corresponding, albeit different, problem with the Italian ALLA.

Despite this problem, it is worth mentioning that the *à la* phrases include a pleasant group which indicate that down-to-earth and practical, non-aristocratic, ladies are the inspiration for certain dishes: *à la bonne femme, bourgeoise, fermière, ménagère*. And it is fairly safe to assume that *à la provençale* portends the presence of tomato and garlic, *soubise* the use of onion, and so on.

ALBACORE *Thunnus alalunga*, one of the most prized members of the TUNA family. Its long pectoral fins distinguish it from its relations and account for its alternative common name, longfin tuna, and the specific name *alalunga*. Maximum length: 125 cm (nearly 4'). Colour: dark blue on the back, lighter below, like other tuna.

The albacore is a fish of the seven seas, but is most abundant in the open waters of the Indo-Pacific, and in the Atlantic. The world catch fluctuates around 200 MT, roughly twice as great as that of the bluefin tuna, but far less than that of the yellowfin tuna. Its relative importance is greater in the Atlantic area, but it is not a common fish in the Mediterranean.

The meat of the albacore is noticeably lighter than that of other tuna, and is the only tuna meat which can be labelled 'white meat tuna' in the USA. For the same reason it has common names meaning 'white tuna' in some languages. It is widely regarded as one of the best tuna for eating, but the Japanese, who can be regarded as the chief connoisseurs, dissent; they do not normally use it for SASHIMI (raw fish) or SUSHI, the two preparations calling for fish of top quality. It is canned in Japan as 'chicken of the sea'.

The French name is *germon* or *thon blanc*, in francophone countries *albacore* means the yellowfin tuna, *T. albacares*.

ALBANIA the smallest and least known of the Balkan countries, is known to Albanians as *Shqipëria*, meaning 'Land of Eagles'—an appropriate name since two-thirds of the country is mountainous. Its language, the sole survivor derived from ancient Illyrian, is like no other, although now it contains a considerable number of words of Turkish, Slavonic, and Italian origin, especially noticeable in a culinary context.

The decades after the Second World War, when Albania was the sole European client state of communist China, have left little or no trace in Albanian kitchens.

Until the Turkish occupation of the country in the first year of the 16th century, the Albanians were Christians—Eastern Orthodox in the south, Roman Catholic in the north. The following centuries, however, saw a gradual Islamization of the population until, by the 19th century, Islam had become the predominant religion. Except in the traditionally Orthodox south, where food remained Graeco-Mediterranean in essence, and the coastal zone, where Italy exerted a considerable influence, Albanian cookery evolved as a result of this Islamization and under the influence of Turkish food and culinary practices.

On a national scale, bread, cheese, yoghurt, and pasta are valuable staples in the diet. The standard Albanian loaf is dark beige in colour, on the heavy side, with a slightly sour flavour. Cheeses follow the general pattern of the Balkan region and include a white brine cheese similar to the Greek FETA.

Sheep's, cow's, and occasionally water-buffalo's milk is used to make yoghurt (*kos*), which in taste and consistency is identical to Bulgarian yoghurt, although the list of micro-organisms involved is not quite the same.

Pasta, *makaronash*, is very popular. Scores of pasta products, commercial as well as home made, are served in dozens of different ways—as a main dish for lunch or supper, or, if the meal is to be without pasta, as a starter which, in Albanian, is called *antipaste* (from the Italian ANTIPASTO). A regular restaurant *antipaste* is *Kanelloni alla toskana* (from Italian cannelloni) which consists of a couple of pancakes stuffed with minced 'veal' (immature beef) and given a gratin finish. Another national *antipaste* is *Byrek me djathë* (from Turkish BÖREK), a small triangular pastry which accommodates a filling of white cheese and eggs.

The MEZZE ritual and various other features of Turkish cookery, including some use of rice and PILAF dishes, Turkish coffee, and some Turkish sweets, have been preserved. Food traditions generally are still strong among the older generation, as well as in the villages populated by Albanians in Yugoslavia (in Kosovo, Montenegro, and the town of Tetovo in Macedonia) whose isolation from the mother country has strengthened traditions. But even in those parts, women's emancipation and the slow dismantling of the social system of the extended family and the clan are eroding ancient food habits.   MK-J

ALBATROSS Joseph Banks, recording in his journal many details of Captain Cook's famous voyage in *Endeavour*, states that albatross was eaten aboard as the ship approached Tahiti. His entry for 5 February 1769 enthuses that the birds were 'so good that everybody commended them and eat heartily of them tho there was fresh pork upon the table'.

ALCOHOL colloquially refers to potable liquids containing quantities of ethyl alcohol (C_2H_5O), and is the sense used here. Technically, alcohol denotes a class of organic compounds distinguished by the presence of a hydroxyl group (an oxygen atom combined with a hydrogen atom, linked to a carbon atom). Minute quantities of some of these are responsible for complex flavours in items as diverse as fruit and Scotch whisky.

Apart from its use as a drink, to which many volumes have been devoted, alcohol has a role as an ingredient in cookery. Many examples of the use of locally popular alcoholic drinks in the foods of different areas exist, from beer in Belgium to saké in the Orient. Grape-based alcohols—wine, champagne, port, sherry, Marsala, brandy, and other spirits distilled from grapes—have a global importance. The wide distribution of viticulture, the extensive trade in wines, their distinctive flavours, and the influence of French kitchen practice have all contributed to this. However, dietary laws forbid Muslims to use alcohol in any form, including as an ingredient.

Use of alcohol in food can be divided very roughly into two categories: cooked or uncooked. Lower-proof alcohols such as wines, ciders, and beers are almost always cooked; those of higher alcohol content (such as sweetened, flavoured liqueurs) are more likely to be used with no further cooking. There are exceptions, such as champagne (with a relatively low alcohol content) which is poured over peaches or berries; and the vermouths and anise-flavoured spirits of Mediterranean countries (high proof), used principally as flavourings in fish cookery.

In cooked dishes, the addition of wine, beer, cider, or other alcohol is usually made before cooking (even some time before, as in a MARINADE). It has a noticeable effect on taste, even if used in relatively small quantities. The drinks themselves have distinctive flavours, which become more concentrated during cooking, as a proportion of the liquid in a dish inevitably evaporates. Alcohol also combines with acids and oxygen to give (respectively) esters and aldehydes, groups of aromatic compounds, which no doubt contribute to the result.

It is sometimes debated whether any alcohol will remain in a STEW after cooking. The answer is 'almost certainly not'. The theory of stews demands that they should be cooked at temperatures high enough to coagulate the proteins in the meat (over 60 °C), but not as high as the boiling point of water (100 °C). The practice of most cooks is to let a stew perceptibly 'simmer', at a temperature somewhere around 95 °C (203 °F). Ethyl alcohol vaporizes at 78 °C (172 °F). So any alcohol in the cooking liquid of a conventionally prepared stew will be evaporated ('boiled off'). An alcoholic drink used to FLAME food will inevitably lose its alcohol in the heat of the process. Likewise, when rice wine is added to stir-fried dishes in Chinese cuisine, the fierce heat of the wok will be enough to evaporate the alcohol content.

Fortified wines and spirits have several uses in cookery. The high alcohol content is often exploited by flaming, or they can be used in sauces, as drinks of lower proof are.

They are also used as ingredients in sweet dishes, an extensive and important role shared with liqueurs, cordials, and eaux-de-vie. Uncooked, they add potent flavours. Thus a little Madeira may be added to consommé immediately before serving. Sherry, brandy, and Marsala add flavour and an alcoholic kick to creamy puddings such as trifle, syllabub, cranachan, brose, tiramisu, zabaglione, and egg nog. These dishes, many deriving from recipes such as the possets of 16th-century England, have a long history as restoratives. Some are served warm, perhaps speeding absorption of alcohol and enhancing the 'pick-me-up' effect (alcohol provides a source of quickly available energy because it is absorbed into the blood stream without prior digestion). Higher-proof alcohols are extensively used in confectionery, combined with chocolate in puddings and sweets, in icings, cakes, sweet sauces, and used to enhance raw or cooked fruit-based desserts.

Finally, alcohol contributes to the preservation of food. Wine marinades help meat, fish, and game keep a short time in hot weather. In combination with sugar syrup, wine makes elegant and attractive fruit conserves.

See also BEER; WINE.   (LM)

ALEXANDERS *Smyrnium olusatrum*, a large umbelliferous plant with yellow flowers, native to the Mediterranean region but able to thrive further north. It resembles

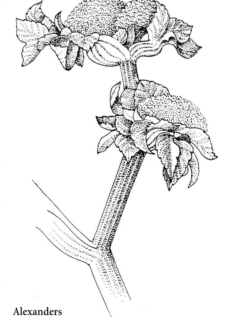

Alexanders

CELERY and was for a long time widely grown for use as a vegetable or herb.

Alexanders is intermediate in flavour between celery and parsley, but with a bitter aftertaste which may have been diminished by the practice of earthing up and blanching the young shoots. It was used in medieval times as an alternative to, and in the same way as, the bitter sorts of celery then current. Evelyn (1699) commended the use of young shoots in salads or 'in a vernal pottage', while Caleb Threlkeld (1727) gave a recipe for an Irish 'Lenten Potage', a soup based on alexanders, watercress, and nettles; see Grigson (1955).

Alexanders was supplanted in the 18th century by the improved kinds of celery which were then developed. It is now almost forgotten as a foodstuff, although it still grows wild in much of Europe, including Britain. It is common around the sites of medieval monastery gardens, where it had been cultivated as *petroselinum Alexandrinum* (Alexandrian parsley—hence the common name).

Alexanders is sometimes called 'black lovage' or 'wild celery'; although both LOVAGE and celery belong to different genera. In Newfoundland the name is applied to another umbelliferous plant, a type of wild angelica.

ALFALFA is the American and more usual name of a leguminous plant, *Medicago sativa*, which is often called lucerne in Britain. Apparently a native of Media (Iran), from which comes its generic scientific name, it was said by Pliny to have been introduced to Europe in the course of the invasion of Greece by the Persian Emperor Darius in 491 BC. Laufer (1919) states that it was introduced to China as early as the 2nd century BC.

Alfalfa is now grown worldwide in warm temperate (and cool subtropical) regions, especially in the USA, the Russian Federation, and Argentina. Its main uses are as a forage crop for feeding cattle and as a green manure.

Alfalfa has been used for human consumption in Europe in times of shortage, e.g. in Spain during the Civil War, when it was the basis of dishes such as alfalfa soup. The mature plant is coarse and has a grassy flavour. The young leaves, which are better, have been eaten as a vegetable, e.g. in China. The seeds can be ground into a meal, but it is now more common to use them for producing alfalfa sprouts, widely eaten as a salad vegetable.

ALFONSINO *Beryx splendens*, a fish of temperate waters, especially the N. Atlantic between Madeira and the Portuguese coast, but also parts of the Pacific, e.g. in the vicinity of Japan, Hawaii, and New Zealand. Both it and the nannygai (see below) belong to the family Berycidae. Both are in turn related to other fish of the families Holocentridae and Apogonidae, and share with them a tendency to be called, vaguely, 'redfish' (see REDFISH).

Maximum length: 60 cm (25"). The colour is rose red, and orange below, with all fins and the inside of the mouth bright red. The flesh is palatable. In Japan it is thought to be at its best during the winter months.

Centroberyx affinis is a related but slightly smaller fish of southern Australian and New Zealand waters which has an attractive coloration—'a beautiful glowing golden orange on the head and body and fins, with darker red-orange longitudinal bands along each row of scales' (Ayling and Cox, 1982). It is called golden snapper or koarea in New Zealand; nannygai in New Zealand and Australia; and, officially, redfish in Australia, the Aboriginal name nannygai having been deemed less attractive for commercial purposes. It makes reasonably good eating, although somewhat bony.

ALGERIA in terms of area, is the second largest political unit in Africa and the Middle East, but by far the greater part of its area consists of Sahara desert. There are small numbers of nomads (see BEDOUIN FOOD) and settlements at some oases, but most of the 25 million inhabitants of the country live on the fertile coastal strip, called the Tell, which is bounded to the north by the Mediterranean and to the south by the Plateau which marks the beginning of the Atlas Mountains; and most of the rest to the Plateau, whose different climate makes it suitable for sheep farming and the cultivation of cereals.

As elsewhere in N. Africa, meat dishes are usually of lamb, mainly grilled or spit roasted or stewed (see TAGINE); and cereals are principally represented in COUSCOUS and various breads. The round Arab bread baked in clay ovens in the countryside is standard fare but French bread became established in the big cities (Algiers, Oran, Bône) during the long period, lasting 130 years, when Algeria was a French colony (counted by the French as part of Metropolitan France and only achieving liberation after a long and bitter war).

MOROCCO, Algeria, and TUNISIA together constitute what is called the Maghreb (or, if LIBYA is included, the greater Maghreb). Ingredients and cooking styles vary to some extent from one country to another, but it would be fair to say that there is at least as much culinary coherence as political solidarity between the three. All three have exerted an influence on France through their cuisines, exporting such items as couscous, MERGUEZ sausages, Arab-style pastries, etc. Returning French colonists, including the so-called *pieds-noirs*, have in turn contributed dishes to the French repertoire, as have Algerian immigrants (if only by bringing into being shops and market stalls which carry Algerian ingredients, which thus become more accessible to the French).

ALGINATES a general name for various gums extracted from SEAWEEDS in the category of brown algae. These include Californian kelp, *Macrocystis pyrifera*; several wracks of the genus *Ascophyllum*; and oarweeds of the genus *Laminaria*, which grow around the coast of Britain. The USA and Britain are the chief producers.

Alginates have become increasingly important recently, in line with the growth of the processed food industry, and are now among the most widely used gums. They have excellent thickening, suspending, emulsifying, stabilizing, gel- and film-forming properties, and can be dispersed in both hot and cold water. They are used in ice cream, where they prevent ice crystals from forming, and in other desserts and syrups, bottled salad dressings, and many dairy products including processed cheese; but they are not used in domestic cookery.

ALIGOTE an unusual dish of mashed potato in which very fresh CANTAL cheese is melted, the whole then being vigorously beaten to produce a smooth elastic texture. The elasticity of this dish, which is a speciality of Auvergne, is such that a pair of scissors has to be provided when it is served.

The success of the dish depends on choosing suitable potatoes; on using butter and cream when mashing them, to produce a very rich and smooth texture; and on the rapidity as well as the vigour of the beating.

Aligote is often served with a coarse sausage of the region. See Graham (1988).

ALKALI an odd-looking word which comes more or less straight from the Arabic *al-kali*, meaning the calcined ashes of plants such as saltwort. In food science it means 'any substance which neutralizes or effervesces with acids and forms a caustic or corrosive solution in water' (*NSOED*). It can also mean a soluble salt (or mixture of such salts) of an alkaline nature. See ACIDS, and also pH for an explanation of the scale by which the acidity or alkalinity of a substance is measured.

Very few foodstuffs are alkaline. Indeed, McGee (1984) remarks that 'egg albumen and baking soda are the only alkaline ingredients to be found in the kitchen'. However, a number are almost neutral, e.g. milk. So adding milk (or yoghurt) to a mixture will normally reduce the acidity of the mixture.

ALKANNA a red or brown dye extracted from the roots of plants of the BORAGE family, *Alkanna tinctoria* and *A. officinalis*, which has been used both for fabrics and as a food colouring since the time of the early Arab civilizations. Its name comes from the Arabic *al hinnā*, meaning 'the dye' (not to be confused with the red dye commonly called henna, which comes from plants of the genus *Lawsonia*).

The original alkanna plant is a native of the Levant. Both this and other kinds of borage which yield dye are now found, both wild and cultivated, in much of Europe and around the Mediterranean. Old English names are (dyer's) alkanet and orcanet.

The dye gives a red colour when dissolved in oil or alcohol, but only a dull brown in water. Medieval recipes call for its use in meat dishes. Nowadays, despite competition from artificial colourings, it is used in sausage skins, ice cream, and drinks and to deepen the artificial colour of margarine.

ALLA the Italian equivalent of the French *À LA* as an indicator of the style in which a dish has been prepared, has been used with relative restraint. Most *alla* phrases are topographical; those referring to a person, or to an ingredient or utensil or general concept (*alla casalinga*, in the style of home cookery), are rare.

This is a difference between Italian practice and that of France. Another difference, although only of degree, is that in Italy the meaning of phrases such as *alla romana/milanese/fiorentina/napoletana* will almost certainly vary according to what it is that is being cooked, whereas in France such variations, although they occur, are somewhat less common.

As with the French term, *alla* is really an abbreviation, for *all'usanza di*, meaning 'in the manner or style of'.

ALLIGATOR an animal now better known as food than its slightly larger relations, the various species of CROCODILE. A tradition of eating alligator in the south of the USA, especially Louisiana, seemed likely to die out when fears that the alligator would become extinct caused it to be given protected status; but the tradition was strong enough to prompt the creation of alligator farms, where they are now bred for the table (besides furnishing valuable leather).

Of the various species which are found in tropical swamps around the world, *Alligator mississippiensis* is the most notable. Although its heartland is the Mississippi delta, its range extends from Texas to the Carolinas. It is usually eaten when young and about half its maximum length of about 3 m (10'). The meat is white and flaky, resembling chicken or (as one authority described it) flounder; it is thus suitable for many methods of preparation and cooking. It would still be premature, in the closing years of the 20th century, to predict how widespread its consumption in the western world will eventually be; but the signs are that the practice of farming alligators will spread and grow to the point at which their meat is generally available.

ALLSPICE the dried, unripe berry of *Pimenta dioica*, a tree of tropical America which is mainly cultivated in Jamaica and is the only spice whose production is confined to the New World. Efforts to introduce it to other parts of the world have been largely unsuccessful.

The English name allspice was given to the spice because its flavour resembles a mixture of other spices, especially CLOVES and black PEPPER; some people also detect hints of NUTMEG and CINNAMON. But allspice is not the only name current in English; 'pimento' is much used in commerce, as a result of confusion long ago.

The allspice tree belongs to the myrtle family, and is not related to the pepper or to capsicum plants. However, when Spanish explorers encountered the plant in Jamaica at the beginning of the 16th century, they thought that the berries resembled those of the pepper and gave them names such as 'Jamaica pepper' and 'pimento' (from *pimienta*, the Spanish word for peppercorn).

The green berries, when dried, become reddish-brown. Their aroma and flavour come mainly from their volatile oil of which the major constituent is eugenol, the principal flavouring element in cloves. The source of their pungency has not been finally identified, but a tannin, quercitannic acid, is present, producing some astringency (again, as in cloves).

Allspice may be used whole, in pickles and marinades; or ground, in cakes and puddings and with cooked fruits. Its essential oil, pimento berry oil, can be used instead of the ground spice for flavouring purposes, but lacks some of the characteristics of the spice. Distillation of this oil takes place mainly in Europe and N. America. A less expensive oil is made from the leaves, in Jamaica, and exported as pimento leaf oil.

The popularity of allspice varies considerably by region. It is used extensively in N. America; and much more in N. than S. Europe. During the latter part of the 20th century, a general order of importance among importing countries was this: USA; Germany; the former Soviet Union (imports fluctuated considerably according to price); Sweden; Finland; UK; Canada.

ALMOND the nut borne by the beautiful almond tree, *Prunus amygdalus*, is delicately flavoured and highly versatile, has been cultivated since prehistoric times, and is the most important nut in commerce. The USA (California) is the main producer, supplying over half the world's crop, followed by Spain and Italy. Almonds are also grown in most other Mediterranean countries, and in Portugal, Iran, Afghanistan, and Australia.

The almond belongs to the same genus as the apricot, cherry, etc., but it differs from them in having a leathery fruit, which can only be eaten when immature, and a comparatively large stone and kernel. Its ancestors are thought to be several wild trees of W. and C. Asia, whose small, dry fruits produce bitter kernels. The tree fruits only in warm temperate climates, tolerating neither spring frosts nor tropical humidity. Thus, when it spread from its region of origin, this was along a restricted band of W. Asia to the W. Mediterranean.

The oldest mention of almond cultivation is in the Bible. Aaron's rod, which miraculously bore flowers and fruit, was of almond wood (Numbers 17: 8). The ancient Greeks cultivated almonds, and their name for the nut, *amygdalon*, has become, via Latin, the botanical name of the species and, in corrupted form, its name in modern European languages. The Romans regarded the almond as a Greek nut, calling it *nux Graeca*. In classical times Phoenician traders introduced its cultivation into Spain; and it was being grown in the south of France (Provence is just within the northern limit of its cultivation) as early as the 8th century BC.

Turkestan, Afghanistan, and Kashmir mark the almond's eastern limit. The Chinese, although they have tried at various times to cultivate the true almond, have generally used instead the indigenous 'Chinese almond' (see below).

Majorca, where large-scale planting began in the latter half of the 18th century, is an important place for almonds. Read and Manjon (1978) remark that 'in the early spring Majorca is a sea of white blossom', and describe the harvest which starts towards the end of August thus:

The fruit is first shaken down on to large canvas sheets, the tough green skin is then cut off and the nuts are left to dry in the sun and then despatched in sacks for cracking, roasting or milling. The female kernels, which occur in pairs, are usually ground for confectionery, while the larger male nuts are roasted or salted.

Both **bitter and sweet almonds** are cultivated. Those with bitter kernels contain prussic acid and are poisonous; but their taste is so disagreeable that no one is likely to eat enough of them to be made seriously ill. The poison and much of the bitterness can be driven off by heat, so that bitter almonds can be used in various ways, e.g. the extraction of a wholesome oil for flavouring purposes. Varieties used for dessert are sweet. These have the characteristic 'almond' flavour, but only mildly and some varieties not at all.

The main commercial distinction is between hard (or thick) shell varieties; softshells; and the extra thin papershells. The last two kinds are generally preferred both for dessert and for processing.

Well-known **varieties** include Jordan (nothing to do with the country of that name, but a corruption of the Spanish *jardín*, meaning garden) and Valencia, both semihard-shelled Spanish types, and the Californian papershell Nonpareil and softshell Ne Plus Ultra. The numerous Italian varieties of almond are almost all hard shelled. Their names are subordinate to commercial quality classifications such as 'Avola scelta' (choice Avola).

Uses of almonds are in many instances of great antiquity. They were of great importance in early Arabic and medieval European cookery, partly as a source of the 'almond milk' which was used in early versions of BLANCMANGE (and which is still current in refreshing drinks such as ORGEAT and *horchata*—see CHUFA). Since then, although 'green' (immature, soft) almonds are eaten in some places as titbits and many almonds are roasted and salted for consumption as snacks or with drinks, the main importance of the nut has been to the confectionery industry. Such products as MARZIPAN and NOUGAT (and its many relations) and MACAROON all depend on it. The Spanish range of almond-flavoured cakes, biscuits, etc. is probably the most extensive in the world.

Products of the almond are numerous. Almond paste, much used in confectionery and baking, is the basis of marzipan, as mentioned above. To produce the paste, blanched kernels of sweet almonds are ground, mixed with water and sugar, and cooked to a smooth consistency. Ground or powdered almonds, both sugared, are available. See also SUGAR ALMONDS.

The terminology of oils, essences, and extracts of almond is confusing, and, as remarked in *Law's Grocer's Manual* (c.1895), 'it is highly important to be certain as to which is intended'.

Almond oil, a delicate and expensive product, formerly in high repute as a superfine culinary oil, is made from bitter almonds; it is still used in some superior confectionery.

Oil of bitter almonds, or almond essence, is not the same. It is made from the presscake left after the extraction of almond oil. This residue retains poisonous substances, and has to be steeped in water for half a day, then distilled. The result is a highly concentrated almond flavouring.

Other 'almonds'. Because the almond is so well known and so highly esteemed, the name has been borrowed for application to other nuts. The 'Chinese almond' is a near relation; it is a special kind of APRICOT grown in China for its kernels alone. But some other 'almonds' are of unrelated species. The INDIAN ALMOND is described separately; the 'Java almond' under PILI NUT. The name 'almondette' is used for the CALUMPANG NUT, and 'almendrón' (Spanish for 'big almond') for a relative of the SOUARI NUT.

ALTITUDE affects cooking because at high altitudes atmospheric pressure is lower, so that water boils at a lower temperature. As a rule of thumb, boiling point falls one-third of a degree C for every 100 m above sea level (0.18 °F per 100').

A lowered boiling point does not prevent food from cooking, since most of the changes that occur in food when it is cooked take place well below 100 °C (212 °F); for example, fish cooks at a mere 63 °C (145 °F), egg yolk at 70 °C (158 °F), and starch at 60–85 °C (140–185 °F). In the world's highest capital city, La Paz in Bolivia at 3,800 m (12,400') above sea level, water boils around 87 °C, so these temperatures are easily attainable. However, water at a lower temperature contains less heat, and the time it takes to boil food is therefore much increased; it can take several hours to boil a potato. Roasting and baking are less affected, since in these processes most of the heat is transferred into the food directly by conduction.   RH

AMANITA is a genus of fungi which has to be treated with special attention, since it includes several edible species but also the notorious death cap and destroying angel, besides several species which are poisonous to a lesser extent. McIlvaine (1902) gives an eloquent description of the *Amanita* species.

They are the aristocrats of fungi. Their noble bearing, their beauty, their power for good and evil, and above all their perfect structure, have placed them first in their realm; and they proudly bear the three badges of their clan and rank—the volva or sheath from which they spring, the kid-like apron encircling their waists, and patch marks of their high birth upon their caps. In their

youth, when in or just appearing above the ground, they are completely invested with a membrane or universal veil, which is distinct and free from the skin of the cap. As the plant grows the membrane stretches and finally bursts. It sometimes ruptures in one place only and remains about the base of the stem as the volva. When such a rupture occurs the caps are smooth. In most species portions of the volva remain upon the cap as scruff or warts—or as feathery adornment; any or all of which may in part or whole vanish with age or be washed away by rain. Extending from the stem to the margin of the cap, and covering the gills, is the partial veil—a membranaceous, white texture of varying thickness. As the cap expands this veil tears from it. Portions frequently remain pendant from the edges, the rest contracts to the stem as a ring, or droops from it as a surrounding ruffle, or, if of slight consistency, may be fugacious and disappear, but marks remain, or the veil itself will always be traceable upon the stem.

The main edible species of the genus are the BLUSHER, GRISETTE, and ORONGE (or Caesar's mushroom). These are described in separate entries, as is one harmful species, the FLY AGARIC. In Europe the most dangerous species are *Amanita phalloides* (death cap), *A. virosa* (destroying angel), and *A. verna*, described respectively as occasional, uncommon, and rare. Eating as little as 20 g (less than 1 oz) of one of these was likely in former times to prove fatal, but medical treatments have now been devised which can save victims from death. Symptoms usually appear after a delay, so anyone who may have eaten one should seek medical advice at once. See the warning below.

The same species occur in N. America, along with a few other dangerous relations. *A. phalloides* is known in S. Africa; both it and *A. verna* occur in China; *A. verna* and *A. virosa* are present in Japan. These are all woodland fungi which appear in the late summer or autumn, except for *A. verna* which, as its specific name indicates, comes up in the spring.

Warning See the general warning under MUSHROOMS, ad fin. So far as the *Amanita* mushrooms are concerned, the most important precaution is to avoid any mushroom in which the following three features are present: a volva or the remnants thereof at the base of the stem (often out of sight near the surface of the soil); a ring or traces thereof near the summit of the stem; and white or yellowish-white gills under the cap.

AMARANTH *Amaranthus* spp, a large group of plants of which many provide edible green leaves and some provide, or formerly provided, grain. They occur all round the world, mostly in the tropics. Many of the species are primarily used as

ornamental plants in gardens, but the edible ones alone are a bewildering array, especially in Latin America, SE Asia, and W. Africa; and classification of the genus has been frequently revised.

One of the most prominent of the amaranths whose leaves are eaten, *A. tricolor*, is described under BASELLA (and is also known as Chinese or vine spinach).

The best-known species which has provided a grain food is *A. caudatus*; for this, and general remarks on the use of amaranths as a cereal crop, see INCA WHEAT.

Other species which are eaten on more than a minor and local scale include:

• *A. cruentus*, a plant of temperate zones, cultivated in India and elsewhere, often called 'bush greens' in Africa;
• *A. spinosus*, one of the several species treated under CALLALOO;

besides three which have the discouraging names *A. dubius*, *A. hypochondriacus*, *A. lividus*.

But there are many others, including at least two which are used for food colouring. These are *A. hybridus*, known as *sangorache*, the source of a dye for colouring *chicha* and ceremonial maize dishes; and a hybrid form called *komo* which produces the pink colour in Hopi wafer bread (*piki*).

Amid all the confusion of botanical and common names, the name 'amaranth' itself is confused. It is derived from the Greek *amarantos* (unfading), because of an ancient belief that it was immortal. However, a false idea arose that the name meant 'love flower' (Latin *amor*, love, and Greek *anthos*, flower) and its name thus acquired a final 'h'. Vernacular names such as love-lies-bleeding and florimer (*flor-amor*) reflect this misunderstanding.

AMBARELLA *Spondias dulcis* (formerly *S. cytherea*), a tree native to the Society Islands, but now widely distributed in tropical and subtropical regions of both hemispheres, especially in SE Asia and the Pacific islands. It is cultivated, but not on a large scale.

The greyish-orange plumlike fruits are produced in pendent clusters of two to ten. Each fruit is about the size of an egg, and contains several seeds surrounded by a yellowish pulp. The taste of the pulp is pleasantly sour; the flavour midway between apple and pineapple; and the aroma sometimes resinous and pungent. The unripe fruits are made into relishes, pickles, and also soups. The ripe fruits are used for sauces and preserves.

Ambarella (the Sinhalese name) is widely known as Otaheite (Tahiti) apple in former British colonies, and as Jew plum in Jamaica. The fruit is much in evidence in Trinidad,

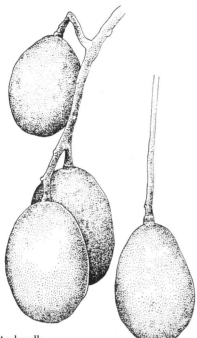

Ambarella

where it is known either by the French name *pomme cythère* or as golden apple. Other names include Brazil plum (or hog plum), and Tahitian quince (although in Tahiti itself the name *vi* is used, and this name is occasionally used elsewhere too).

Related species include the MOMBIN (yellow and red) and IMBU.

AMBER a fossilized resin familiar in jewellery, used to have a role in food and drink. The Arabs regarded it as an APHRODISIAC, and used it for this purpose; and under the influence of this tradition it was sometimes added, in powdered form, to both sweet dishes and beverages in Europe. But see also AMBERGRIS, with which amber has sometimes been confused.

AMBERGRIS an intestinal secretion of the cachalot or sperm whale, sometimes found in the animal itself but more often floating on the sea or washed up on the beach, used to have a minor culinary role. It is a waxy solid, occurring in lumps which weigh anything from a few ounces to 90 kg (200 lb). The French saw a resemblance between it and true AMBER and, since its normal colour is ashy grey, called it *ambre gris*. From this name are derived the English ambergris and variants thereof such as ambergrease. Like MUSK, it was used in conjunction with other aromatics, such as CARDAMOM, to perfume foods, mostly confectionery. The practice, not uncommon in the 17th century, seems to have died out in Britain in the 18th century. Hannah Glasse

(1747) used it in only one of her 900 recipes, and that (for Icing a Great Cake Another Way) came from an earlier book.

However, the use of ambergris apparently continued in France in the 19th century. The reliable encyclopedist Trousset (1879) states that it was sometimes used as an aromatic flavouring, but in very discreet quantity. According to Favre (*c*.1883–92), the 'ambre' used by Brillat-Savarin in his *chocolat des affligés*, recommended by Dumas (1873), was ambergris (not amber).

Lane (1860) describes the use of ambergris by wealthy people in Egypt to flavour their coffee. The usual method was to melt a little ambergris in one pot and pour hot coffee from another pot over it. But some preferred to place a small piece of ambergris (about two carats) in the bottom of a cup and add coffee; the small piece lasted two or three weeks.

Landry (1978) states that the Chinese were the first to appreciate the flavour of ambergris, which they imaginatively referred to as the 'flavour of dragon's saliva', and sprinkled in powdered form on boiling tea.

AMBERJACK a common name for fish of the genus *Seriola*. The Mediterranean species, *S. dumerili*, one of the largest (up to 125 cm/50") and best known, also occurs in the Caribbean region, on the eastern seaboards of S. and N. America, and in the warmer parts of the Indo-Pacific. Its name was bestowed because it has yellow (amber) streaks running along its sides and belongs to the family of fish (Carangidae) loosely referred to as JACKS.

Just how many other species there are in the genus seems to be uncertain, but there is no doubt about *S. lalandi*, which is well known in Australia as yellowtail kingfish and in California as Californian yellowtail, and occurs elsewhere too (e.g. S. Africa, Argentina).

Although the amberjacks are pelagic fish, rarely caught in quantity and not well known in the markets, they are familiar to sport fishermen in many parts of the world; and the smaller specimens make good eating.

AMBIGU a distinctive sort of evening meal, or supper, which enjoyed some popularity among the upper classes of England from roughly the middle of the 17th century until the middle of the 18th. It was less formal than a dinner, but was nonetheless carefully planned and provided substantial fare. The meaning of the French word which was appropriated to use in England in this way can be 'a mixture of different things', and this meaning was reflected in the wide variety of dishes laid

out on the 'sideboard' for an ambigu. The dishes were mainly cold, as for a supper.

Charles Carter, author of the last of the great English 'court cookery books' (1730), provided table layouts for no fewer than ten ambigus (or ambogues, as he called them). One example incorporates the explanation that it was for a masquerade and shows empty plates set on the table 'to eat on, for none Sat Down'.

AMBROSIA the food of the gods in classical mythology. The term may mean food in the narrow sense of eatables, in which case it is the counterpart of NECTAR, the drink of the gods; or it may mean food in the wider sense of sustenance, when it embraces drink also.

What the gods were actually supposed to eat is a matter of conjecture.

In the English language any especially delicious food may be called ambrosia; but this usage has become uncommon.

AMCHUR a dried product prepared in the northern states of India from unripe MANGO flesh. Immature fruits which have become windfalls are peeled and then marketed in the form of slices or powder.

Amchur is used as a souring agent for curries, including certain vegetable curries, just as tamarind pulp is; and it is also used in chutneys and soups. Pruthi (1976) observes that the main purpose of its addition is to lower the pH of the gravy so that the dish will keep longer.

AMERICAN CHEESES are mostly versions of European ones, especially CHEDDAR. Two which can claim to be American originals are described under BRICK and LIEDERKRANZ.

The American cheese industry is centred on Wisconsin, where a state law has obliged restaurateurs to serve two-thirds of an ounce each of Wisconsin butter and Wisconsin cheese with every meal. New York State ranks second in production of cheese. Other states known for their cheeses are California, Colorado, Illinois, Kentucky, Ohio, and Vermont.

American Cheddar was first made in New England early in the 17th century, and was being exported to Britain by the end of the 18th century. The Cheddar technique, adapted to a greater or lesser extent, now produces numerous varieties of which the following are noteworthy.

Club cheese, see POTTED CHEESE.

Colby, a highly popular American cheese named for the town of Colby in Wisconsin, resembles Cheddar but has a softer and more open texture, and is moister. Two steps in the regular Cheddar manufacturing process, that known as 'cheddaring' (slicing up the curd) and the subsequent milling, are omitted when Colby is made. Several American cheeses with other names are really varieties of Colby.

Colorado Blackie has a black rind.

Coon is a premium variety of American Cheddar which has a dark rind due to the conditions in which it is aged.

Cornhusker, developed in Nebraska, is like Colby but contains less fat.

Herkimer County cheese, the pride of New York State cheese-makers, is aged for a year or more. It has a crumbly texture, a sharp and nutty flavour, and an attractive pale orange colour.

Longhorn does not refer to a kind of cow but to a particular size of Cheddar.

Monterey (or Jack, an alternative name now little used) is named for Monterey County in California, where it originated in the 1890s. It comes in two main varieties; a whole-milk semi-soft cheese, and a cheese for grating which is made with skimmed or semi-skimmed milk. Both are made by a process resembling that used for Colby, but more rapid.

Sage, or Vermont sage, see SAGE CHEESE.

Store cheese is a name for plain Cheddar of the kind which was a stock item in village stores.

Tillamook, see below.

Vermont (State) cheese is a Cheddar with a tangy flavour.

Besides the above, there are of course the cheeses just called Cheddar or American Cheddar.

The Cheddar made in Tillamook, Oregon, prompted the publication in 1933 of a book in two volumes, the first of which is scarce and the second unobtainable. The title is *The Cheddar Box*. Volume I is a normal book, describing in picturesque language the history of the cheese made at Tillamook. Volume II looked like a book but was really a box containing a 2 lb (1 kg) cheese. Brown (1955) recalls borrowing a first volume whose flyleaf was thus inscribed:

This is an excellent cheese, full cream and medium sharp, and a unique set of books in which Volume II suggests Bacon's: 'Some books are to be tasted, others to be swallowed, and some few to be chewed and digested.'

Another American cheese which deserves mention is Philadelphia cream cheese (see CREAM CHEESE). And numerous artisanal cheeses, including many of goat's milk, are now being made.

AMERICAN COOKBOOKS The history of cookbook publishing in the United States exemplifies the abundance and diversity that characterize American society. In recent years a flow of cookbooks numbering in the thousands has steadily issued from American publishing houses. This is in stark contrast to the record of the early years; America came late to cookbook publishing. Although the settlers carried cookbooks with them to the New World and imported cookbooks, especially from England, and kept manuscript receipt books, cooks in the original colonies had been preparing food for more than 100 years before the first cookbook was published in America.

Then in 1742 William Parks, the printer at Williamsburg, Virginia, published E. SMITH's the *Compleat Housewife*, first issued in London in 1727. During the following half-century, this book and several other English works were reprinted in Boston, New York, and Philadelphia, most notably Susannah Carter's *The Frugal Housewife* (1772) and Richard Briggs's *The New Art of Cookery* (1792). When Parks printed *The Compleat Housewife*, he claimed to have made some attempt at adapting it to American tastes and practices. However, no cookbook seriously attempted to reach an American audience for more than another 50 years.

The year 1796 marked the first appearance of a cookbook written for Americans and adapted to the American way of life: Amelia SIMMONS's *American Cookery . . . Adapted to This Country, and All Grades of Life.* Although *American Cookery* borrowed heavily from English cookbooks, its genius was its recognition and use of American products and practice. So many firsts and milestones of American cooking appear in this small volume that it has justly been hailed, in its specialized sphere, as another declaration of American independence.

Two conflicting trends were evident during the 60 years following the publication of *American Cookery*. English works, including the major contemporary classics by RAFFALD, Rundell (see ENGLISH COOKERY BOOKS), GLASSE, Henderson, Nutt, Kitchiner, Soyer, and ACTON, were being reprinted regularly, often with special adaptations for the American audience. But, increasingly, cookbooks written by Americans for Americans were capturing the market.

Although reprints and pirated editions of Amelia Simmons's book continued to appear (a dozen by 1830), no important new cookbook was published until 1824 when Mary Randolph's *The Virginia Housewife* was issued. This was the first regional American cookbook and set a pattern for the many to follow, including such early classics as Mrs Lettice Bryan's *The Kentucky Housewife* (1839); Thornton's *The Southern Gardener and Receipt Book* (1840); Philomelia Hardin's *Every Body's Cook and Receipt Book . . . Designed for Buckeyes,* Hoosiers, Wolverines, Corncrackers, Suckers (1842); Mrs Howland's *The New England Economical Housekeeper* (1844); the *Carolina Housewife* (1847); and *Mrs Collins' Table Receipts: Adapted to Western Housewifery* (1851).

The 1820s also brought the first printings of works by two of America's most influential cookery authors, Eliza LESLIE and Lydia Maria Child. Miss Leslie's various works were to dominate American cookbook publishing for the next 30 years. Mrs Child's only book on cookery, *The Frugal Housewife*, went through at least 35 printings between its first appearance in 1829 and 1850 when it was allowed to go out of print, arguably because of her increasingly public work in the cause of anti-slavery as well as the publication of more modern cookbooks.

In 1827 the first book on household management written by a black American appeared, *The House Servant's Directory* by Robert Roberts. Additional black-authored works on cookery and household management published in the 19th century include Tunis Campbell's *Hotel Keepers', Head Waiters', and Housekeepers' Guide* (1848) and the first southern-black cookbook, *What Mrs. Fisher Knows about Old Southern Cooking* (1881). From this meagre beginning and by the end of the 20th century, interest in and generation of black culinary literature had grown to become a significant specialized area of publication.

During the 1830s cookbooks by the American and English authors previously mentioned were printed and reprinted in New England, New York, Pennsylvania, Maryland, and Ohio. The works of Mrs Child, Miss Leslie, and Mrs Randolph clearly dominated this decade, although other authors appeared, including 'A Boston Housekeeper', whose *The Cook's Own Book* (1832) was the first alphabetically arranged culinary encyclopedia to appear in the United States.

The last year of the decade brought the publication of the first of many cookbooks of another major figure in American culinary history, *The Good Housekeeper* (1839) by Sarah Josepha Hale. As editor for 40 years of *Godey's Lady's Book*, the most influential American magazine of the 19th century, Mrs Hale was the arbiter of national taste for much of that period.

By the 1840s new authors appeared on the culinary scene: Catherine Beecher, Mrs Cornelius, Mrs Crowen, Mrs A. L. Webster, and Mrs Howland, although earlier writers continued to be influential, especially Miss Leslie, Mrs Hale, and Mrs Child. Cookbooks began to be published in new cities, including some in the Midwest and the south.

By this time, certain trends had appeared that are still a part of the American cooking scene: economy and frugality; management and organization; and a preoccupation with baking, sweets, and desserts. Several other themes of American cookery appeared in the 1830s and 1840s: vegetarianism, diet and health, and temperance; representative were Sylvester Graham's *A Treatise on Bread and Bread-Making* (1837), William Alcott's *Vegetable Diet* (1838), and Miss C. A. Neal's *Temperance Cook Book* (1841).

Many of these same themes continued in the cookbooks of the 1850s, as did the domination of writers already mentioned. In addition, several new authors emerged, all of them American women, such as Mrs Abell, Mrs Bliss, and Mrs Chadwick.

By the mid-19th century, women were writing the majority of American cookbooks; works by male professional chefs and male medical doctors were the exception. This trend has more or less continued to the present time, although the last few decades have seen increasing numbers of male cookbook authors.

By 1860 more and more cookbooks were being published, and they had become an integral part of the publishing industry. The upheaval of the Civil War (1861–5) caused a decline in the publication of all books, including cookbooks. Following the Civil War, cookbooks were written to help southern women adapt to their changed circumstances. Of these, Mrs Hill's *New Cook Book* (1870) and *Mrs Porter's New Southern Cookery Book* (1871) were among the most influential.

Then, in the 1870s, three major cookbook explosions occurred, the effects of which are still with us.

The first was a Civil War legacy: cookbooks compiled by women's charitable organizations to raise funds to aid victims of the War and their families. When the War ended, these groups turned their attentions to other charitable causes. The trickle of these early books published in the 1860s and 1870s has now become a flood, as hundreds of such books are issued in the United States each year. In the earlier years when women were without full political rights, the fund-raising cookbook proved to be one very effective way for them to participate in and influence the public life of the nation.

Several cookbooks which began life as fund-raisers were reissued, under varying titles, for many decades and became American classics; notably, *Buckeye Cookery* (1876) and Mrs Kander's *Settlement Cook Book* (1901).

The second major development was promotional literature, the advertising pamphlets issued by the growing number of national food and kitchen equipment companies. Tens of millions of such pamphlets have flooded the American market in the last 150 years; every household probably has a few in a kitchen drawer. These bits of culinary ephemera were often extremely handsome; they merit further investigation as they document trends in American foodways.

The third important force was the growth of the cooking school and home economics movements. These began with the influential cooking schools founded in New York by Professor Pierre Blot and Juliet Corson, and intensified with the great cooking schools and their teachers—Sarah RORER in Philadelphia and Mary LINCOLN and Fannie FARMER in Boston. These schools dominated American cookbook publishing for the remainder of the 19th century and early into the 20th. Mrs Rorer authored more than 60 books and pamphlets as well as serving as editor for major food and household magazines. Fannie Farmer's *Boston Cooking-School Cook Book* (1896) went on (with many revisions and new editions) to become one of the best-selling and most influential cookbooks in America.

It is useful to place in more general historical context the facts outlined in the 19th-century chronology presented above. That period, the first post-colonial century, saw profound changes in the land and peoples of America, and all of this ferment was reflected in the cookbooks of the time. The talented women authors cited above were influential beyond their cookbooks. Not only were they recognized culinary authorities, but they were also reformers active in all the major social and cultural events of their day from consumer issues to women's rights. Their books went through numerous editions. They reached millions of households with their classes, journal articles, and cookbooks, and in all they did, their social consciousness was manifest.

As America moved westward a cookery literature useful to the pioneers appeared. Among the most popular were works authored by Dr A. W. Chase. His books, in endless variations, were written to enable the frontiersmen and women to do for themselves, out in the wilderness, everything that was necessary to survive, from cooking to shoeing horses.

With the settlement of the continent and the rise of cities, massive tomes addressed to the urban housewife appeared, complete with information on how to deal with servants and how to entertain properly.

In addition to cookbooks and advertising pamphlets, national magazines and almanacs offering household advice and recipes became ever more popular in the latter half of the 19th century. Long a part of American life, these publications, general in nature at first, turned increasingly to specialized subjects that included women's topics and cookery. Cooking magazines continue to play a very influential role in American cookery.

The large waves of immigration that began late in the 19th century produced a special cookery literature. Books in almost every European language, sometimes bilingual, were available through the country. Some contained American recipes to teach the new immigrant, in his native language, how to cook American food; others had recipes from the old country, with or without altered ingredients to suit the new homeland. In addition to the foreign-language cookbooks published to fill the needs of immigrants, foreign and international cookbooks began to be written for the American housewife. By 1920, an American cook could find books on the cuisines of most cultures.

In general, the ethnic works mirrored the successive waves of immigrants: German, still prominent in the Midwest; and French, with historic roots in St Louis, Detroit, and northern Maine, but especially in New Orleans and Louisiana. There (mixed with Spanish, Caribbean, African, Southern, and Italian) it was the basis of CREOLE and CAJUN cookery, both of which endure in the kitchen and on the printed page. Other major ethnic influences came to include the Hispanic, Mexican, African, Chinese, Italian, Jewish, Scandinavian, Middle European, and Shaker—all overlaid on the English and native American base. The large new waves of immigration in the last quarter of the 20th century introduced still more cuisines to America, mainly Asian and Latin American, and the cookbooks followed.

The First and Second World Wars, the Depression, and Prohibition (1920–33) all influenced the cookbooks of the first half of the 20th century. The period is best noted, however, for the appearance of the American classic *The Joy of Cooking* (1931) by Irma ROMBAUER.

In the last half of the 20th century, radio, television, magazines, newspapers, and food industry publications created the culinary stars and authors: real, such as Julia Child, James Beard, and Craig Claiborne, and imaginary, such as Betty Crocker. That era also saw the rise of cookbooks by celebrity chefs and restaurateurs, such as Alice Waters of Chez Panisse. In addition to recipe books, America has had its complement of gastronomic literature, best exemplified by the works of M. F. K. FISHER.

The social ferment of the 1960s reinvigorated a culinary literature popular in the 19th century; books on vegetarianism and healthful eating became very popular. In addition, numerous books emphasizing sustainable agriculture and ecological concerns began to appear. These works continue to capture a large share of the cookbook market.

The commemoration of America's bicentennial in 1976 generated much interest in America's culinary past. From that time to the present, books on regional American cuisine, facsimiles and first-time printing of manuscripts, culinary bibliographies, food newsletters, and scholarly food history works have been issued with increasing regularity. Cookbook collecting, both private and institutional, has become a vigorous national pastime. The year 1996, the bicentennial year of the first American cookbook (Amelia Simmons's *American Cookery*), was commemorated nationwide by a cornucopia of lectures, symposia, and media coverage. An exhibition at the University of Michigan displayed one cookbook published in America in each of the 200 years since 1796, giving vivid testimony to the richness and diversity of this body of literature; see Jan Longone (1996*a*), also Janice B. and Daniel T. Longone (1984).   JL

AMINO ACIDS the substances of which PROTEIN is made. Twenty-four of them are known to be involved in the synthesis of protein, of which 20 are important. These are glycine, alanine, proline, *valine, leucine, isoleucine, methionine, phenylalanine, tryptophan*, aspartic acid, glutamic acid, tyrosine, cysteine, serine, *threonine*, asparagine, glutamine, *histidine, lysine*, and *arginine*. The names in italics are those of the 10 'essential' amino acids for humans. These cannot be made in the body, and have to form part of the diet. The others can be made by altering other amino acids. Other animals have different sets of essential acids.

Amino acids have part of their chemical structure in common. Their general structure is R-CH-NH$_2$-COOH, where R is a group of atoms which varies from one acid to another; in the simplest, valine, this is simply one hydrogen atom. The -NH$_2$ group is known as an amino group, the -COOH group as a carboxyl group; the latter is a characteristic part of organic acids.

Proteins consist of chains of linked amino acids. When one acid is joined to another the amino group of one acid loses one hydrogen atom, and the carboxyl group of the other acid loses one hydrogen and one oxygen atom. The two groups then link thus: -NH-CO-. This is known as a 'peptide bond'. The two hydrogen and one oxygen atoms join to form a molecule of water, H$_2$O.

The peptide bond can be broken by putting the two parts of the water molecule back in, so that the amino and carboxyl groups resume their original form. This is known as HYDROLYSIS, and is

fundamental to the cooking and digestion of protein.

The molecules of living things are 'chiral'—they can exist in either of two forms which are mirror images of each other, known as 'laevo-' (left-handed, L for short) and 'dextro-' (right-handed, D) forms. As a rule only L forms are found in nature, and this applies to all amino acids except glycine, which is too simple to have more than one form.

The food industry uses some amino acids on their own. L-glutamic acid and its salt MONOSODIUM GLUTAMATE are both used as flavour enhancers. The SWEETENER aspartame is made from aspartic acid.   RH

ANARDANA a spice consisting of the dried seeds of the POMEGRANATE, is used in India, especially in the north, for acidifying chutneys and some curries. The seeds and pulp are separated from the rind of the fruit and dried in the sun for 10–15 days, turning a reddish-brown. The spice is marketed in this form and ground before use. The seeds of the wild pomegranate called *daru* which grows on the lower Himalayas reputedly yield the finest anardana.

Julie Sahni (1980) remarks: 'Many chefs prefer pomegranate over mango powder, as pomegranate seeds impart a distinct sweetish-sour taste to a dish instead of just a sour taste.'

This spice is also sometimes used to flavour dishes in Iran and the Middle East, although the syrup made from fresh pomegranate seeds is in more common use in that region.

ANCHOVY a fish of the family *Engraulidae*. Species are found in all the warm oceans, and it is interesting to observe the varying uses made of them in different regions of the world.

The anchovy of culinary renown is *Engraulis encrasicolus* of the Mediterranean, the Black Sea, and the warmer waters of the E. Atlantic coasts. In earlier centuries it was mainly consumed as salted anchovies, which were sold from barrels. It is now more familiar in the form of canned anchovy fillets, which are used to impart a distinctive and salty flavour to many dishes. The preserved anchovies of Collioure, in the south of France, are reputedly among the best.

However, the practice of eating fresh (unsalted, and not canned, but often frozen) anchovies is spreading to other European countries from those where the abundance of the catch had already made it a familiar delicacy, for example Portugal, Spain, and above all Turkey. The Turks are beyond doubt the greatest enthusiasts in the world

for anchovies, which they call *hamsi*. The intense and proprietorial feelings inspired by *hamsi* in Turkish hearts have found expression in some remarkable poems recited by itinerant troubadours on the Black Sea coast, one of which is cited by Davidson (1981) along with an impressive list of the culinary uses to which *hamsi* are put in Turkey, including their incorporation in a kind of bread.

On the western side of the N. Atlantic, the striped anchovy, *Anchoa hepsetus*, arouses little interest.

In the Indo-Pacific region anchovies present a different picture. *E. ringens* occurs off the coast of Peru and adjacent countries in shoals so enormous that the catch of the *anchoveta* (its Peruvian name) has often been the biggest by weight in the whole world. The cold Humboldt current, which flows northwards in those parts and is very rich in zooplankton, accounts for its abundance. This species is made into fish meal.

In Asian waters there are anchovies of the genera *Stolephorus* (long-jawed anchovy); *Coilia* and *Setipinna* (hairfin anchovies, with sharply tapering rear ends); and *Thryssa* (the moustached anchovy, which has rearward extensions to its upper jaw which are thought to resemble a moustache or the whiskers of a cat, and whose Thai name means 'cat fish'). These are all good food fish, but do not have the special importance in Asian cuisines which the European anchovy has in Europe. The explanation may be that in SE Asia a special taste which corresponds in gustatory effect to that of the European anchovy is already provided in the daily diet by the FISH SAUCES of the region. These may, incidentally, be made from anchovies.

ANDOUILLE and *andouillette* are tripe-based sausages, but otherwise they have little in common. The former is generally a large sausage, frequently smoked and eaten cold in slices as a starter; the latter is a small sausage that is never smoked and is generally grilled and served hot as a main dish. There are numerous versions of each. The words may derive from the Latin *inductile*, meaning something drawn out.

Andouilles were served on the best French tables in the Middle Ages, but in the centuries since then they have mutated into a more rustic sort of speciality. The use of the term *andouille* as a slang word meaning 'imbecile' might seem to fit with this new role, but it is hard to explain and appears to be incompatible with the existence of lively associations of *andouille*-lovers.

Andouilles or aunduyle, stuffed with chopped TRIPE and other entrails, were known in Britain in the 13th century and were still being mentioned in the 17th and 18th centuries, but both the word and the recipe passed out of use.

The most famous *andouilles* are from Normandy (*andouille de Vire*) and Brittany (*andouille de Guéméné*). Both are smoked, and both are eaten cold. Thin slices have an interesting appearance on the plate, with little white squiggles of tripe and CHITTERLING or (in the case of Guéméné, which is made with larger pieces of chitterling rolled up) white spirals. However, in some parts of France an *andouille* is simply a large sausage which is poached with beans or cabbage and eaten either hot or cold.

The best-known *andouillettes* are those of Troyes (by far the most widely imitated), which are made exclusively of pure pork 'innards'; and those from the Beaujolais region, made with calf's mesentery. All are cooked before eating; grilled *andouillettes* with mustard and puréed potatoes are a popular dish of French bistro cookery.

HY

ANGEL FOOD CAKE

sometimes called angel cake, a light, pale, and puffy American sponge cake. It is made with egg whites to which cream of tartar is added to prevent darkening. Mariani (1994) writes: 'The egg whites give it a texture so airy that the confection supposedly has the sublimity of angels.' The cake is often baked in a ring-shaped ('tubular') mould.

This is a plain cake, but may be flavoured with nuts and/or spices, or enriched with fillings or frostings.

Angel food cake was known in the USA in the 1870s, according to Mariani (and the name appeared in print in the 1880s). Some perceive it as a good way of using up surplus egg whites.

ANGEL'S HAIR

cabello de ángel, a speciality of Majorca but familiar in other parts of Spain, has been well described by Janet Mendel (1996) as 'fine golden strands of candied fruit . . . made from the flesh of the *sidra*, a type of large squash, striated in green and yellow, which seems to be used for nothing else but this'. The pulp is cooked, then cooked again with sugar to produce a stringy jam which is used for various sweet purposes, e.g. as a filling for ENSAIMADAS. It is widely obtainable in canned form. References to it in culinary literature often say that it comes from a 'pumpkin'.

ANGEL SHARK

Squatina squatina, which occurs in the Mediterranean and E. Atlantic, with close relations in warm temperate oceans all round the world, is a fish with unusual features and interesting names. It is correctly termed a shark, having cartilaginous rather than true bones and possessing most of the other characteristics of sharks; but is regarded by scientists as representing an evolutionary stage between sharks and rays.

Certainly it does not look like a conventional shark. On the contrary, it is generally agreed to present an ecclesiastical appearance. Medieval sages saw its large pectoral fins as wings and its tapering body and tail as angelic robes. From being an Angel, it was later demoted to the rank of Monk by Norwegians, who according to the ichthyologist Rondelet, writing in the 16th century, were impressed by a specimen washed up on the shore and noted that 'it had a man's face, rude and ungracious, the head smooth and shorn. On the shoulders, like the cloak of a monk, were two long fins.' It is still often called monkfish, although promoted to Bishop by some authorities; and an Australian species has even attained the rank of Archbishop, no doubt because of its ornate dappling of denticles (McCormick, Allen, and Young, 1963). A well-known medieval woodcut shows the fish in episcopal guise.

The W. Atlantic species is *S. dumerili*. Both it and *S. californica* of the E. Pacific are comparable in size (maximum length about 1.5 m: 5') and eating quality (better than most people realize, and better than the common run of edible sharks) to *S. squatina*.

Generally, the angel shark can be treated like a RAY. It is always safe to bake a sizeable chunk of 'wing' with added flavours, whether these are Mediterranean or Asian.

Although the angel shark is sometimes called angel fish, it has nothing in common with the small reef fish of the Indo-Pacific to which that name properly belongs.

ANGELICA

the name for a group of tall umbelliferous plants with thick stems, in the genus *Angelica*. Of the many species, growing in most temperate regions of the world, the most famous and useful, growing in Europe, is *Angelica archangelica*.

Parkinson (1629) observed that all Christian nations call this plant by names

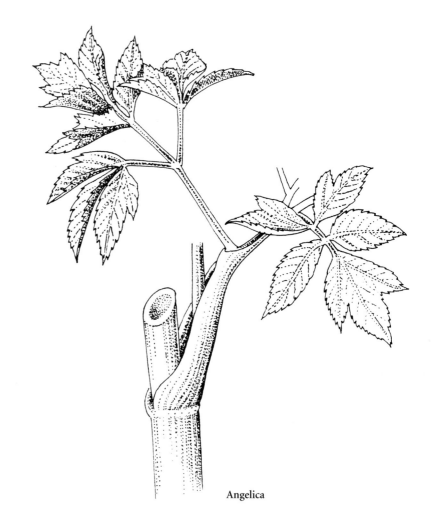

Angelica

signifying its angelic associations, and 'likewise in their appellations hereof follow the Latine name as near as their Dialect will permit'. The basis for the angelic associations is not clear, although it may be connected with the plant's reputation as an antidote to poisons; and the archangelic ones might be due to the fact that the flower would be in bloom on 8 May (old calendar), the day of St Michael the Archangel.

A. archangelica grows well in Scotland, Germany, Scandinavia, and Russia. It is among the few tall plants which can withstand the weather in Iceland and the Faeroes. It will also thrive further south, and is grown in both France and Italy; and likewise in many parts of N. America, where it has been introduced as a cultivated herb. It differs from most members of the genus in having smooth stalks and leaves in all its parts, and has a distinctive scent, often described as musky.

Formerly the leaf stalks were blanched and eaten like celery, and the leaves were candied. The roots were made into preserves, and angelica water was a well-known cordial. Its use as a vegetable survives in some countries, e.g. Greenland and the Faeroes, where it is eaten cooked. Nowadays, however, much the most common use is to candy the stalks, cut into short pieces, for use in cakes and CONFECTIONERY. In England it is frequently used to decorate a TRIFLE. Most of the angelica grown commercially for candying comes from France and Germany.

The candied stalks have been sold as 'French rhubarb' in the USA. Elsewhere, the addition of a little angelica to stewed rhubarb is thought to be a good way of reducing the acidity.

Growing and candying angelica have been a speciality of Niort in France since the latter part of the 18th century, and the Niortais now have a monopoly in France. (Tales about the origin of their specialization are of doubtful validity, and it was not an invention of Niort—the art of candying angelica was already being practised in the south of France around 1600; but claims have been made that the angelica grown at Niort is superior to any other.) The process of candying angelica as practised at Niort is elaborate, involving many stages and takes up to a year or more. Angelica jam is made and so are chocolate-coated pieces of candied angelica.

ANGLER-FISH *Lophius piscatorius*, a fish of bizarre appearance and considerable size (maximum length 2 m: 6.5'), which is also called monkfish (a confusing name, also applied to ANGEL SHARK). It has an extensive range from the Black Sea through the Mediterranean and up to Iceland. On the American side of the N. Atlantic its close relation *L. americanus* is known as goosefish.

The angler-fish is a master of camouflage, concealing itself on the seabed in a manner well described by the Duke of Argyll (quoted by Goode and associates, 1884, who omit to say which duke):

The whole upper surface is tinted and mottled in such close resemblance to stones and gravel and seaweeds that it becomes quite indistinguishable among them. In order to complete the method of concealment, the whole margins of the fish, and the very edge of the lips and jaws, have loose tags and fringes which wave and sway about amid the currents of water so as to look exactly like the smaller algae which move around them and along with them. Even the very ventral fins of this devouring deception, which are thick, strong and fleshy, almost like hands, and which evidently help in a sudden leap, are made like two great clam-shells, while the iris of the eyes is so coloured in lines radiating from the pupil as to look precisely like some species of *Patella* or limpet.

Thus disguised, the angler-fish agitates the 'fishing-rod' above its head and prepares to engulf in its vast mouth the smaller fish which come to investigate. It even has a spare fishing-rod. The main one projects forward and has a piece of tissue on it which serves as 'bait'. But in case this is bitten off, there is another behind which can be brought forward. It bears no bait normally, but apparently grows a piece of bait if it is brought into use.

The ability of the fish to swallow large prey is astonishing. Bigelow and Schroeder (1953) report that an angler 1 m (3.3') long has a mouth which gapes 23 cm (9") horizontally and 20 cm (8") vertically; and that an angler 65 cm (26") long was found to contain a codling 57 cm (23") long.

Naturally, such a remarkable creature has attracted many interesting vernacular names. The American name goosefish (bestowed because it stuffs itself) is matched by bellyfish, allmouth (N. Carolina), and the cognate 'lawyer' in parts of New England. The Scots name Molly Gowan has no obvious explanation, but the Irish 'frogfish' is understandable and is echoed by many names in other languages.

The tail of the angler-fish, or rather the tail-end of its body, is the part which is skinned and marketed. In the Netherlands it is sold as *ham* or *hozemondham*. The merits of the angler-fish became widely acknowledged in Europe during the 1960s to the 1980s, but its acceptance as human food in N. America has advanced rather more slowly.

The flesh is so firm and white that it invites comparison with that of the lobster; indeed, there have been instances of a lot of angler-fish being used to supplement a little lobster. It may be poached or steamed, or opened out butterfly-fashion and grilled. Slices can be fried. The head, when obtainable, makes a good soup.

Angler-fish

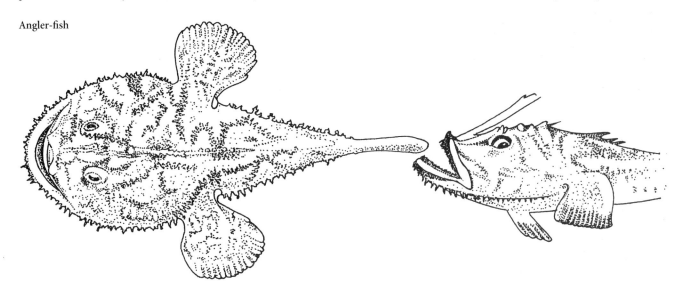

ANGLO-INDIAN COOKERY a product of British rule in India or, more precisely, a result of the interface between Indian cooks and British wives of British officers and officials stationed in India, could be viewed as an example, on a grand scale, of CREOLE FOOD; or, more simply, as the most interesting 'colonial kitchen' which resulted from the imperial era of British history.

There is a rich literature. One outstanding item is the wonderful dictionary known as *Hobson-Jobson* ('A Glossary of Colloquial Anglo-Indian Words and Phrases, and of Kindred Terms, Etymological, Historical, Geographical and Discursive'). Others are provided by those 19th-century English authors (notably Colonel Kenney-Herbert, on whom see ENGLISH COOKERY BOOKS OF THE 19TH AND 20TH CENTURIES) who produced manuals intended for use by the English memsahibs in dealing with their cooks. Recently, serious contributions of a historical and gastronomic nature have been made by Jennifer Brennan (1990) and Burton (1993).

The scope and scholarship of these books can hardly be reflected in a short article, but it will be appropriate to mention a few of the dishes or foodstuffs regarded as typical of Anglo-Indian cookery.

Mulligatawny soup is an ingenious adaptation necessitated by the British requirement for soup as a separate course, a concept unknown in India. As Burton explains:

Such soups as there were had been used as thin sauces, poured over plain rice and mixed with dry curries, but never drunk by themselves, due to the Indian custom of serving all the dishes of a meal at the outset rather than course by course.

The simplest of these 'rice-mixers' consisted merely of spices boiled in water, perhaps with the addition of fried onions. In the north of India the recipe was enriched by yoghurt and known as *shorwa*; in the south, where lentils were often added, the dish was called *saar*. In the Tamil version tamarind was included and the soup called *rasam*. When used metaphorically the *ras* part of *rasam*, like *saar*, means 'essence'—and essences are what they were.

Hobson-Jobson explains the etymology: 'The name of this well-known soup is simply a corruption of the Tamil milagu-tannir, "pepper-water"; showing the correctness of the popular belief which ascribes the origin of this excellent article to Madras.' From the same source we learn that British officials in the Madras Presidency were known as 'mulls' (after mulligatawny) whereas those at Bombay were 'ducks'.

The simple concept of pepper water was greatly elaborated in some recipes for mulligatawny (which might call for a score of ingredients) but the basic prescription was always for some chicken or mutton, fried onion, curry powder, and stock or water.

Kedgeree, originally khichri, is a common Indian dish which was already being described by visitors hundreds of years ago. *Hobson-Jobson* quotes from the Arab traveller Ibn Batuta (1340): 'The munj (Moong) is boiled with rice, and then buttered and eaten. This is what they call Kishri, and on this dish they breakfast every day.'

By 'moong' is meant mung bean. The description remains correct, although other 'lentils' (the term is used in various ways—see LENTIL) can be used and it is usual to add flavourings (onions, spices). It seems to have been under British influence and for British tables that flaked fish or smoked fish was built into the dish, replacing the 'moong' or 'lentils'; and again due to the British that chopped hard-boiled eggs came into the picture (plus, in de luxe versions, ingredients such as cream). It was this transformed dish which became famous as kedgeree, a British breakfast speciality.

CURRY is an Indian category of spicy sauces or dishes transformed for Anglo-Indian purposes. CURRY POWDER, pre-mixed and packaged, was a major result of this development.

Country captain is a chicken dish of mysterious origin. Burton (1993) explains that:

The term 'country' used to refer to anything of Indian, as opposed to British, origin, and hence the country captain after whom this dish is named may have been in charge of sepoys. It seems more likely, however, that he was the captain of a country boat, since the recipe turned up midway through the nineteenth-century at ports as far apart as Liverpool and the American South (where many Americans mistakenly think the dish originated).

Hobson-Jobson had reached much the same conclusion; and thought that the origin of the dish was to be found in a SPATCHCOCK with onion and curry stuff, of Madras.

WORCESTERSHIRE SAUCE is a sort of transplant from India to England.

The long-term effects of Anglo-Indian cookery on English cookery are perceptible in the popularity of curry dishes and of CHUTNEYS, but not much else. A separate matter is the arrival of Indian restaurants in Britain, mainly in the second half of the 20th century, and the introduction of their kitchen terms, e.g. VINDALOO, into the British culinary vocabulary (although not into British kitchens).

See also TIFFIN.

READING: Kenney-Herbert (1885).

ANGLO-SAXON FOOD a subject which has generally been neglected, is now illuminated by the two volumes (1992, 1995) from Ann Hagen on *Anglo-Saxon Food and Drink*. The first covered 'Processing and Consumption', the second 'Production and Distribution'. The author approached the subject from a background of archaeology but harnessed to her purposes a wealth of literary evidence. Since, for many readers, the interest of her study, which she defines as extending from the beginning of the 5th century to about 1100, lies as much in her diligent and ingenious use of source material as in the substance of the information she gathered (which is in any case so extensive and disparate that it would be difficult to summarize), it seems best here to cite her own account of the sources.

The area covered is Anglo-Saxon England and the Celtic west of Britain, with occasional reference to continental sites.

Primary material is of two kinds: documentary and archaeological. Material in the vernacular was supplemented from Latin manuscripts. Writings on all kinds of subjects were used, from laws, chronicles and sermons, to poems and medical recipes. Surviving manuscripts have been preserved by chance, so there will always be lacunae in the documentary record. Moreover, this is very heavily weighted towards the end of the Anglo-Saxon period, with few Old English manuscripts surviving from before the tenth century. While place-names are often recorded for the first time after the Conquest, where Old English elements are involved it is reasonable to assume they were in use in the Anglo-Saxon period. . . .

Archaeological evidence is available for the whole period and is the main source of data for early Anglo-Saxon England, but, as with manuscripts, the recovery of evidence is a matter of chance.

Soils preserve material differentially, and recovery techniques themselves will bias a sample of animal or plant material. Different methods of quantifying the numbers of animals from an animal bone sample produce different results. Problems of interpretation (that the absence of fish bones may indicate not that few fish were eaten, but that many fish were eaten, bones and all, or that animal bones in graves may not represent foodstuffs) are dealt with in the text.

Chemical analysis and electron spin resonance techniques can add to our picture of what the Anglo-Saxons ate and how they cooked it. Human skeletal material provides information about diet not available from other sources. Excavated structures relate to the processing (mills, kitchens) and consumption (halls) of food.

People who have never had occasion to study this subject are likely to be aware of only one incident in Anglo-Saxon cookery, to wit King Alfred and his burnt cakes. It is interesting to see how this is handled by a culinary historian. Ann Hagen has compared three versions of the story, finding that in one the loaves are burning at the fire; in a second they are on a pan with the fire underneath; while in the third the bread is being baked under the ashes of the fire. So we learn that 'cakes' seems to be a misunderstanding for loaves of bread, and are led by an analysis of the source material into a survey of baking equipment and techniques used in Anglo-Saxon times, plus the interesting point that Old English has both masculine and feminine forms for bakers; and a quotation which shows that barley bread and pure new butter were considered a good food for Anglo-Saxon invalids. On top of all this, we discover that although Alfred's cakes were loaves, the Anglo-Saxons did also have cakes, described as well spiced, and possibly enriched with cream, eggs, butter, honey, and preserved fruits. Whether the Anglo-Saxons had crumpets or only pancakes seems, however, to be an open question.

ANGOLA AND MOZAMBIQUE

though not adjacent and geographically very different, were both once Portuguese colonies and their cooking was influenced thereby and also by the trade between them. Laurens van der Post (1977), describing the 'two wings' of cooking in Africa which the Portuguese created and which were held together by their presence, puts it well:

Roughly, one is South American, or more specifically Brazilian, and is most evident in Angola. The other is a compound effect, in Mozambique, of the Portuguese experiences of the East from its Arabian outposts in Zanzibar to the coast of Malabar in India and Malacca on to the Celestial Empire. Since there was a constant coming and going between Angola and Mozambique from the earliest days, these two schools naturally borrowed freely from one another. Yet it is surprising that they retain nuances of their own. Rice, spice and the fruits of the Orient feature more prominently in Mozambique than they do in Angola.

He goes on to describe how life in Saint Paul de Luanda (founded in 1575, the oldest city established by Europeans south of the Sahara, and now simply Luanda) was for centuries like that of a Brazilian city, including many aspects of food, such as the seasoning. Indeed, he says that 'Muamba chicken', a strong claimant for the title of national dish of Angola, is 'purely Brazilian' in origin.

The enormous influence which the Portuguese had on the diet of Africans was perhaps based not so much on their cooking styles but on their talents as gardeners and importers of many plants now thought of as basic foods in Africa. From the Americas via Angola they introduced maize, tomatoes, potatoes and sweet potatoes, chillies, sweet peppers, and cassava/manioc. From the east via Mozambique came oranges, lemons, dozens of spices, new kinds of rice and beans, and probably bananas and sugar as well as many tropical fruits. The Portuguese introduced the domestic pig, chickens, olives, and salt cod as well as coffee and tea. Through the interchange between these two former colonies these foods spread to most of Africa and made a huge difference to the basic diet of the continent.

Angola was the country most ravaged by the slave trade (the depopulation is estimated at some three million people), and the most heavily settled by the Portuguese themselves. It is Africa's largest state, but even since independence in 1975 has remained one of the most sparsely populated, with a population not much over 10 million. It is mostly high plateau, with a coastal strip cooled by the Benguela Current. The area was settled about 2,000 years ago by Bantu herders from the north who subsisted mainly on dairy products from their cattle, grain pastes called *funge* (which has become the *funchi* of Barbados), and wild green vegetables. Thus it remained until the Portuguese, looking in the early 16th century for routes to the Spice Islands, established bases for re-victualling.

The Portuguese passion for fish and salt cod, in particular, has remained. One dish, *Esparregados de bacalhao*, reflects the combination of cuisines, being salt cod with cassava leaves, sweet peppers, guinea pepper, and palm or sesame oil. Another seafood dish of Portuguese origin is a soupy dish of cuttlefish with limes, powdered sesame, olive oil, and TABIL.

These are by no means the only links with Portuguese cuisine. European-style bread is still liked in the towns. Goat meat is popular as it is in Portugal; in Angola it is usually cooked in a pot with garlic, chillies, and cloves. Another common dish is *Assola de mais*, cooked dried beans mixed with fresh maize fried in pork fat. Also, van der Post observed that in both Angola and Mozambique great care is taken to use the blood of a slaughtered animal—whether as an ingredient or in a sauce or dressing, even for yellow rice—and it has been suggested that this may reflect medieval Portuguese practice.

In **Mozambique,** most of which is lower lying than Angola, and thus more tropical, besides facing across the Indian Ocean to India and SE Asia, a large Goanese settlement made curry and coconut preparations popular. But Mozambique is known above all for the dishes called piri-piri (see PIL-PIL), which may have originated there. Piri-piri in Mozambique means basically a small hot chilli, but any dish flavoured with chillies is now known as a piri-piri, a usage which has become international. The sauce by this name differs from most chilli sauces in that it is made with oil, lemon juice, and garlic.

Dishes flavoured or thickened with cashew nuts are also common. A notable coastal dish is *Matata*, made with clams, nuts, and green leaves, traditionally pumpkin.

Another Portuguese legacy is a liking for sweet dishes, especially those made with eggs. Coconut puddings and candies are common in Mozambique. JM

ANISE or aniseed, the plant *Pimpinella anisum* and especially its seed. A native of the Levant, it was known to the Greeks by the 4th century BC. Culinary use extends at least as far back as classical Rome, for Pliny wrote of the seed: 'Be it green or dried it is wanted for all conserves and flavourings.' It is now grown in warm climates all over the world but especially in SE Europe, N. Africa, and India.

The plant, especially the seeds, has a sweet and unmistakable taste. Anethole, the principal essential oil in the seeds, is what gives the flavour to drinks such as the French pastis, ouzo in Greece, and arak in Turkey; and this use has been dominant in modern times. 'On the Aegean coast [of Turkey] a familar winter sight, in February, is the loading of bags of anise on board Turkish ships bound for overseas ports, a particularly aromatic undertaking' (Kalças, 1974).

However, anise is also employed as a flavouring for breads in some European countries, e.g. northern Spain, and in the Middle East; and likewise for cakes and in sweets, among which anise comfits used to be popular, and creams. Indians use the seeds in some curry-type dishes; and anise turns up, in discreet quantity, in various recipes for seafood.

The seeds are sometimes chewed after meals, e.g. in Afghanistan and India, as a means of sweetening the breath and as an aid to digestion. They are slightly roasted first for this purpose.

Aniseed balls, a popular English sweet, are mentioned under DRAGÉES.

STAR ANISE is different but also contains anethol.

ANNATTO *Bixa orellana*, a small to medium-sized tree, native to tropical America. This is often grown for purely ornamental purposes because of its red-veined leaves, clusters of pink flowers, and thick, spiny pods which open to reveal scarlet seeds. But it is also useful in other, including food, contexts.

In the Caribbean the seeds were used extensively in the past by the Caribs as body paint (hence 'redskins' as a name for American Indians) and for medicinal purposes (they are a rich source of vitamin A). They were also and still are used for food colouring. Annatto oil or lard is made from the hard orange-red pulp surrounding the seeds. The coloured and flavoured lard (*manteca de achiote*) is used in a number of

Caribbean islands, e.g. to colour codfish cakes in Jamaica.

Annatto was being imported into Europe by the 17th century (when many European chocolate recipes called for it). In the 18th century it was being used by cheese-makers in England to give an orange or red colour to Cheshire cheese and red Leicester. The colour is derived from bixin, which is a carotene pigment. So is the pigment which produces the natural yellow colour of butter and cheese, which comes from the fresh grass eaten by the cattle in summer. In winter, cattle eat fodder which lacks the pigment and dairy products are naturally paler. They also tend to be paler than average at any time of year in certain regions; CHESHIRE cheese, for example, is a pale ivory unless something is done to brighten it. MARIGOLD petals have been used in the past, but the colour which they provide is relatively weak and may be accompanied by an unwanted flavour. Annatto imparts practically no flavour, even when added in amounts sufficient to make cheese bright orange. So annatto was preferred for this purpose. In recent times, however, it has been partly replaced by beta carotene, which is obtained by an industrial process from other sources.

The whole seed is ground and used as a spice in some regions. Mexican *achiote*, ground to a paste ready for use, is imported to the USA.

ANTARCTICA a continent about which very little has been written from a gastronomic point of view. However, as Kurti (1997) points out, there is some material available. Laws (in Kurti and Kurti, 1988) provides 'A Perspective of Antarctic Cookery', in which he writes:

Delicacies included young crabeater seals, especially filet or liver, leopard seal brains, seal chitterlings (the small intestine of one species can be several hundred feet long), fish and shag. The eggs of several sea birds were appreciated though the whites of penguin eggs are an off-putting translucent bluish-grey and are better in cakes and omelettes than fried or boiled. Particularly to be avoided were giant petrels (flesh or eggs), and elephant seals which, although the subject of my PhD thesis, are repulsive, however cooked.

Laws also cites a publication *Polar Record 9*, evidently from the late 1950s or 1960s, which carried an essay by a cook (Gerald T. Cutland), recording dishes which he had prepared using Antarctic raw materials (e.g. Braised Seal Heart and Escalopes of Penguin).

It can be expected that in the course of the 21st century there will be some developments in Antarctic cuisine, although the commendable international agreements which limit human intrusions into the continent will ensure that undesirable radical changes do not occur. On the other hand, it can be expected that controlled exploitation of Antarctic seafood will increase. The FAO had already published in the 1980s two excellent volumes of Species Identification Sheets for the Edible Marine Fauna of the Continent.

ANTEATERS the name given, for the obvious reason, to various wild animals found in S. America, Africa, and SE Asia, of which the AARDVARK is perhaps the best known. Anteaters have long snouts which they thrust into ant-heaps in order to devour the ants or termites. Alternatively they may climb trees in search of tree ants, as do the pangolins or scaly anteaters of the genus *Manis*. The nature of their diet, which they catch with a sticky tongue, has resulted in their having no or merely vestigial teeth.

The name pangolin is sometimes used for these animals. In S. Africa there is the Cape pangolin, *Manis temminckii*. The Indian pangolin, *M. crassicaudata* is sometimes eaten by hill tribes, and is also found in SE Asia (Malaysia). The Chinese pangolin is *M. pentadactyla*.

Anteaters generally have tough flesh, but are edible. In S. America they are often stewed, which helps to tenderize the meat.

ANTELOPE any of a group of ruminant mammals of Africa and Asia. They are typically graceful, having long legs and horns, and include the ELAND, WILDEBEEST, gazelle, springbok, hartebeest, impala, etc.

The name antelope is a general one which may be derived from a Coptic term which according to Burton (1962) applied originally to the mythical unicorn but now covers the wide range indicated in the preceding paragraph. Most antelopes are good runners (the S. African sassaby, for example, is said to be faster than any horse) and many of them graze in herds on plains. Some are of graceful appearance, while others such as the wildebeest (gnu) are ungainly. Almost all antelopes are African species.

There is one animal which is sometimes called an antelope which differs from true antelopes in two respects: it belongs to the New World, and it has branched horns. This is the PRONGHORN.

Brief notes follow on a number of the species or groups of species which count as antelopes.

- Dik dik, *Madoqua saltiana*, a diminutive and attractive animal of Somalia and Ethiopia.
- Gazelle, a name used of many species of small fawn-coloured antelopes found in Asia and the drier parts of Africa. They are speedy creatures and have conspicuous black and white face markings. The Dorcas gazelle, *Gazella dorcas*, one of the smallest, measures less than 60 cm (2') high at the shoulder; found in N. Africa from Algeria to Egypt and Sudan.
- Hartebeest, *Alcelaphus* spp, one of the largest African antelopes. Its meat is far inferior to that of the slightly larger eland.
- Impala, *Aepyceros melampus*, a favourite prey of lions. 'A herd of impala in full flight leaping in a giant follow-my-leader across roads is one of the most striking sights of Africa' (Burton, 1962). The meat is usually tender, faintly aromatic, and good to eat if it has been larded before cooking.
- Kudu, *Strepsiceros strepsiceros*, another of the largest African antelopes, but with inferior meat.
- Saiga or steppes antelope, *Saiga tartarica*, of the steppes from C. Asia to NW China, which figures in Kazakh cuisine (see CENTRAL ASIAN REPUBLICS).
- Springbok, *Antidorcus marsupialis*, which has qualities similar to those of the impala.
- Blackbuck or Indian antelope, *Antilope cervicapra*, an animal of the plains of India and Pakistan.

ANTIPASTO an Italian term which literally means 'before the meal' and refers to foods served as appetizers before the meal proper begins. Typical items are olives, pieces of raw or cured ham, marinated mushrooms or other vegetables, and items of seafood.

As the popularity of Italian food increased in the second half of the 20th century this term acquired wide currency in English. However, Ayto (1993) points out that the English language first took the word over at the end of the 16th century, naturalizing it to 'antepast'.

For corresponding terms in other languages, each with its own slightly different meaning, see HORS D'ŒUVRES, MEZZE, TAPAS, and ZAKUSKI.

ANTS insects of the order Hymenoptera, living in large social groups with a complex organization and hierarchy. Their colonies typically comprise winged males, wingless sterile females (workers), and fertile females (queens).

Ants have been a food resource for Aborigines in Australia, who relished especially the honey ants, *Melophorus* spp, which they call yarumpa. Bodenheimer (1951) furnishes a good description:

The 'honey ant' itself is a modified worker of the colony, which is so overfed by the ordinary workers that its abdomen swells to the size of a marble, about 1 cm. in diameter, in consequence of the liquid honey stored within. With the exception of a few transverse plates (tergites and sternites), the abdominal walls are reduced to an extremely fine membrane, through which the honey can be clearly seen. The insect's viscera are compressed into a small space near the vent. The ant in this condition is naturally unable to move from the spot. It appears that the inflated ants in this extraordinary way provide for the needs of the colony during the barren season of the year, acting as living barrels, which can be tapped as required. . . . When a native wishes to partake of the honey, he grips one of the ants by the head, and placing the swollen abdomen between his lips he squeezes the contents into his mouth and swallows them. As regards the taste, the first reaction the palate receives is a distinct prick of formic acid, which is no doubt due to a secretion produced by the ant in self-defence. But this is both slight and momentary; and the instant the membrane bursts, it is followed by a delicious and rich flavour of pure honey.

So-called 'white ants' are TERMITES and belong to another order.

APHRODISIACS in the usual sense of foods or drinks which stimulate the sexual appetite and improve performance, are prominent on the list of human 'wannahaves', but virtually non-existent. Alcoholic drinks may affect appetite and (sometimes detrimentally) performance, but are outside the scope of this book. So are drugs. That leaves, for consideration here, substances which can be classified as food.

A study of the literature on the subject shows that most foods have, in one culture or another, been perceived as aphrodisiacs. No doubt foods which contain nutrients and therefore help to maintain human bodies in working order can be said to be aphrodisiacs in the very weak sense that they help to maintain the sexual function as well as the numerous others which our bodies are expected to perform. But this sense is so attenuated as to be without significance.

There are a very few substances which improve blood circulation in the genital areas. The most notorious is 'Spanish fly', also known as cantharides. It consists of the powdered bodies of a bright green beetle of N. Africa, which in the past was sometimes an ingredient in the Moroccan spice mixture RAS-EL-HANOUT. It can be very harmful indeed, and its sale in the spice markets of Morocco was finally banned in the early 1990s. However, it continues to be the subject of tall tales and anecdotes. One Moroccan, asked by a researcher whether he had any personal experience of the effects of Spanish fly, dissolved into laughter and, between laughs, related how his wife had once added some to a pan of spaghetti which she was boiling. When she came to serve this, she found that every single strand of spaghetti was standing bolt upright in the pan.

Johimbine, a substance derived from a S. American tree, improves blood circulation and is considered by some medical authorities as being useful for some people in facilitating the erection of erectile tissue; but it is a drug, not a food. The same applies to the male hormone, testosterone; it is not present in any foodstuffs.

Otherwise, one is left with the psychological effects of certain foods. It may be that sexual appetite is increased for some people if they eat something which they know has an aphrodisiac reputation (oysters); or which is thought to bear some resemblance to sexual organs (carrots, figs); or which is so rare and expensive that it creates an atmosphere of luxury or thoughts of wealth and power (such thoughts being sometimes linked to sex). What this comes down to is that a person's mind may be turned to thoughts of sex by eating something which is in some way a symbol thereof. But this is not a very compelling idea. A remark attributed to a Roman prostitute, that kissing and embracing are the most effective aphrodisiacs, rings true and makes the nibbling of carrots or sucking of figs seem, by comparison, pathetically feeble.

The same verdict, 'pathetically feeble', could be applied to a book by one master of English prose (Norman Douglas) and furnished with an approving preface by another (Graham Greene). It is called *Venus in the Kitchen* (1952) and, whether regarded as a joke or as a source of information, is an embarrassing failure.

There are other books which attempt to deal with the subject seriously, but they—while not irritating their readers by misplaced levity—provide no real food for either sex or thought. Typically, they list foods which have been deemed to be aphrodisiacs in various cultures around the world, to about 1% of which they are able to attach an unconvincing testimonial, such as that a medieval herbalist stated that he had a colleague whose nephew believed that he had been excited after eating the food in question, but which are otherwise unsupported by anything more substantial than superstition and legend.

The negative nature of this survey may prompt the question: why have so many people looked for something that is not there? The answer must surely spring from two sources. First, human beings are subject throughout their adult lives, to a greater or lesser degree, to sexual urges (these being necessary to ensure propagation of the species). Secondly, it is not always easy to satisfy these urges, and an obstacle frequently encountered is outright unwillingness, or at least lack of a matching simultaneous desire, on the part of the prospective partner. If, therefore, a human

being of either gender knew of a seemingly innocuous food which, when ingested by the prospective partner would immediately produce a flood of sexual desire, how happy that human being would be and how often would this knowledge be utilized! In short, the concept of a truly aphrodisiac food is on a par with that of finding a crock of gold at the end of a rainbow.

APICIUS is unique among surviving texts from the Roman Empire: it is the only classical cookery book. It is a businesslike collection of recipes, apparently for banquets at which no expense was to be spared, for many costly spices are called for. There are about 470 recipes in total, over 200 of which are for sauces alone. Most of the remainder are for meat, fish, and vegetable dishes, these too typically including strongly flavoured sauces. There are a few recipes for sweet dishes and one or two for flavoured wines.

The great number of spices in many *Apicius* recipes implies a fashion of cuisine in which the flavour of the main ingredient would often be unrecognizable, and there is independent evidence that this approach to cookery—the 'disguised' dish—was at times in fashion at Rome. The recipes probably come from many different sources, some no doubt inserted by cooks and copyists who worked with earlier versions of the text. It has been suggested that several recipes which give exact quantities for ingredients may come from a dietary guide for invalids and may be Greek in origin.

A few recipes are named after individuals; one or two very elaborate ones are named after a certain Apicius (see below). *Patina Apiciana*, one of these, happens to be mentioned by another source of about AD 200. But *Apicius* as a whole is impossible to date precisely. Some work under this name existed by the time the 'Lives of the Later Caesars' (*Historia Augusta*) was compiled in the late 4th century AD. Because of an anecdote in this (highly unreliable) source, it has been suggested that *Apicius* was intended for reading rather than for practical use. Against that, the language of the text as we know it is the Vulgar Latin of the Roman lower classes: *Apicius* is indeed a very important example of this variant of Latin, the direct ancestor of the modern Romance languages such as French, Spanish, and Italian. However, educated people, those with leisure for reading, demanded classical grammar, a cultured style, and a careful choice of words, none of which is offered by *Apicius*. It is best to conclude that it was used as an aide-mémoire for those who worked in the kitchens of the wealthy.

Apicius survived the Middle Ages in two 9th-century manuscripts, one now in the Vatican, the other in the library of the New

York Academy of Medicine. Numerous copies were made from these in the 15th century as humanist scholars became interested in the work. The first printed edition appeared at Milan in 1498. No earlier English translation exists than the interesting but unreliable version by J. D. Vehling (Chicago, 1936).

Apicius is in origin a Roman personal name: the first known Apicius was a legendary gourmet of about 100 BC. Apicius became a kind of nickname, given to various cooks and gourmets. Stories tell of another, M. Gavius Apicius, of the time of Tiberius (AD 14–37) and yet another under Trajan (98–117). It was said, for example, that M. Gavius Apicius chose to live in Minturnae, Campania, because prawns grew bigger there than anywhere else. Then he heard that bigger prawns were to be found in Libya, and set out immediately. As his ship approached land it was met by a fishing-boat offering fresh prawns for sale. On learning that they were not, after all, any bigger than those of Minturnae, Apicius ordered his ship to turn and make straight for home.

The recipe text bears this same name *Apicius*, meaning 'The Gourmet', but there is no need to suppose that any of it was written by any of these individuals.

Other texts are known to have carried this same name *Apicius*. One that survives is the *Excerpta Apicii* ('Outline Apicius') occupying a few pages of an 8th-century manuscript in the Bibliothèque Nationale in Paris. The compiler was 'the Illustrious Vinidarius', illustrious once but unknown now. It contains 31 brief recipes preceded by an interesting list of spices and flavourings said to be required in every kitchen.

The most convenient edition of *Apicius*, with parallel English translation, is *The Roman Cookery Book: A Critical Translation of The Art of Cooking by Apicius* by Barbara Flower and Elisabeth Rosenbaum (London, 1958). See also Carol Déry, 'The Art of Apicius', in *Cooks and Others* (Oxford Symposium Papers, 1995); Jon Solomon, 'The Apician Sauce', in *Food in Antiquity* (Exeter, 1995). (Note: John Edwards's *The Roman Cookery of Apicius* (London, 1984) includes the first English translation of the *Excerpta Apicii* of Vinidarius.)   AD

APPENZELL or Appenzeller, a Swiss cheese which takes its name from the Canton of Appenzell and has an exceptionally long history. Some authorities believe that it can be traced back to the 8th century AD.

Appenzell is made from whole unpasteurized milk by a process similar to that used for Gruyère and Emmental. But before being left to mature the rind is washed with spiced white wine or cider. It comes in a small wheel shape, weighing about 6 to 10 kg (15 to 22 lb); has a brownish rind and a golden-yellow interior with some small holes or 'eyes'; is firm but elastic in texture; and has a flavour which develops from mildly fragrant to moderately strong as the cheese ages.

Appenzell rass (*rass* meaning sharp) is a version made from skimmed milk, marinated for much longer, and consequently more tangy in flavour.

APPERT NICOLAS (1749–1841), a Frenchman of great importance in the history of food conservation, came to public notice when the well-known gastronomic writer GRIMOD DE LA REYNIÈRE, in the third year of his *Almanach des Gourmands* (1806), wrote about him admiringly as one who had found a method of bottling a large number of fruits and vegetables. Food treated in this manner had the advantage of keeping for a long time and thus allowed the gourmand to sample dishes which recalled 'the month of May in the heart of winter'. According to Grimod, 'the petits pois above all else were as green, as tender and as delicious as those eaten in season'.

Appert was a maker of *confitures* (in his time, conserves of fruit) and it was natural that it should have been a member of this profession who brought about a new technique to guarantee the conservation of foodstuffs. However, Appert's work had a much wider scope than just fruits, for he discovered that any food which had been hermetically sealed in bottles and sterilized by boiling (in an autoclave) would keep for months, even years. Moreover, it would still taste almost identical to freshly cooked products, a taste which would not survive salting, drying, smoking, or any of the other conserving procedures which were known of at that time.

When Appert published in 1810 his *Art de conserver* he introduced housekeepers to the principle of conserving meats and vegetables and, at the same time, won a prize of 12,000 francs which the French government had offered for an invention which would ease the problem of feeding the army and navy.

Although in his early experiments and in the world's first canning factory, which he opened in 1812, he had worked with jars and bottles, he switched from these to tin-plated cans in 1822.

Appert's successes are all the more striking when one considers that several more decades were to elapse before Pasteur made the bacteriological discoveries which permitted a full understanding of why Appert's techniques worked.   (HY)

APPETITE the desire to eat, is regulated by both physical and mental factors. It might be said that the physical feeling of wanting food is hunger, and the mental one is appetite; but the two sensations are so interlinked that the distinction is not useful.

Most obviously, we feel hungry because our stomach is empty. The time the stomach takes to empty after a meal depends on the nature of the food and how long it takes to digest; sugary foods take the least time, followed by other carbohydrates, proteins, and finally fats. Fats also inhibit the movements of the stomach wall, further slowing digestion.

Several hours after a meal the stomach signals its emptiness with the familiar 'hunger contractions'. These stimulate nerves in the stomach wall which send messages to the appetite regulating mechanism of the brain. By this time the level of glucose in the bloodstream, high immediately after a meal, has fallen considerably, and this is detected by the liver which in turn sends a warning to the brain.

Two parts of the brain directly control appetite: the 'appetite centre' and the 'satiety centre'. Both are in the hypothalamus, a primitive part of the brain not under conscious control. It is the appetite centre that responds to nerve impulses from the stomach and liver and relays them to the conscious mind, creating a desire to eat.

The amount we eat is controlled by the satiety centre, in a way which is not well understood. Clearly the stomach sends messages to the brain reporting how full it is, but the exact degree of fullness that gives a feeling of satiety varies not only from person to person, but from day to day in the same person. There must be some way in which the mechanism detects the amount of energy a person is using, and thus how much food is required; but the details are still mysterious.

The entire regulatory apparatus is sometimes called the 'appestat' on the analogy of a thermostat, which regulates temperature. In most people it is remarkably accurate, so that they stay the same weight for years at a time. But some people eat more than they need, and gain weight; less often, others eat too little and lose weight.

The appestat tends to be most accurate when a fair amount of energy is being used and plenty of food is being eaten to fuel it. At low levels, when a person is inactive, control slips a little. The person will feel less hungry and eat less, but perhaps not little enough. So sedentary people often gain weight gradually. People may also be in the habit of eating a certain amount of food, whether they need it or not. This can lead to 'middle-age spread': someone becomes less active over the years but continues to eat as much as before.

Although the regulatory mechanism is not under direct conscious control, it is strongly influenced by mental events. We see some foods as appetizing, owing mainly to a memory of what these or similar foods taste like. This recognition prompts the appetite centre to prepare for eating and digestion. The salivary glands begin to function—that is, the mouth waters—and the stomach signals its readiness by hunger contractions. Likewise, the smell of food being cooked, although sometimes unattractive, is often enough to arouse appetite, for example when one has just got up in the morning and smells toast or bacon or coffee aroma from the kitchen. Another stimulus to eating is simply the time of day: we expect to eat at lunchtime, so we feel hungry. Yet another is the actual consumption of some preliminary titbit, such as the *amuse-gueules* which are offered in some restaurants, or, on a larger scale, the numerous small items which are found in HORS D'ŒUVRES, MEZZE, ZAKUSKI, etc.

The satiety centre's reminder that we have eaten enough may be overridden if the food being eaten is especially tasty, or merely because we have a certain amount on our plate and expect to (or are expected to) finish it.

Appetite may also be repressed. Foods of repellent aspect or smell, seeing or remembering unpleasant events, and psychological depression can all have this effect—though some people eat more when unhappy, finding food comforting. In western societies where there is social pressure to be slim, people may feel guilty about eating. In severe cases this, or other malign factors, can lead to eating disorders such as anorexia nervosa and bulimia.   RH

APPLE (*see page 26*)

APRICOT *Prunus armeniaca*, a fruit belonging to the rose family and closely related to the plum, peach, cherry, and almond. The apricot's original wild ancestor has long since vanished, but it is generally accepted that its home was in, or mainly in, China, and that it was the Chinese who first cultivated the fruit, before 2000 BC. Laufer (1919) gave a plausible account of its spread westwards by silk dealers, which resulted in its reaching Iran (where, significantly, it had only a descriptive name, *zard-alu*, meaning 'yellow plum') in the 2nd or 1st centuries BC, and Greece and Rome in the 1st century AD.

The Greeks, wrongly thinking that the fruit originated in Armenia, called it 'Armenian plum'; hence *armeniaca* in the botanical name. The Romans, impressed by its early ripening, named it *praecocium*, meaning precocious. From this derives the name 'apricot'.

The fruit is now widely grown in the warmer temperate parts of the world. The main regions of cultivation are: a band stretching from Turkey through Iran and the Himalayas to China and Japan; S. Europe and N. Africa; S. Africa; Australia; and California. There are many varieties differing in size, colour, and flavour. The diversity found in the great apricot belt from Turkey to Turkestan is astounding: white, black, grey, and pink apricots, from pea to peach sized, with flavours equally varied. In the Near East white apricots are common, with pale skin and pink blush. Their translucent flesh resembles that of a white peach, and is of surpassing delicacy and sweetness.

A fresh apricot is ranked high among fruits, as is evident from the praise of the connoisseur Leclerc (1925), who wrote of 'Le parfum très pénétrant de l'abricot, sa saveur balsamique et douce dont on ne retrouve l'équivalent dans aucun autre fruit.' He thought the flesh of the apricot combined in a unique way the subtle and disturbing fragrances of the Orient with the robust and straightforward smells of the French countryside.

The apricot certainly possesses a potent sensory appeal. In one of his books, John Ruskin described it as 'shining in a sweet brightness of golden velvet'. But appearances can be deceptive. Apricots can acquire their orange colour before they are fully ripe and before their superb flavour has developed. Fruits picked in this state, for commercial purposes, will never taste as they should.

Hence the efforts made in Britain, from the 16th century onwards—King Henry VIII's gardener brought the apricot to England from Italy in 1542—to grow the fruit there, in spite of the unpropitious climate.

However, it was only in the 18th century, that real success was achieved, notably by Lord Anson at Moor Park in Hertfordshire; the variety called Moor Park (or Moorpark) became famous in other European countries and is still grown. But the vast majority of apricots sold in the UK are imported, and despite the rapidity of modern transport these cannot match in flavour a fully ripe fruit picked from the tree in, say, N. Africa or California.

The apricot reached Virginia in N. America early in the 18th century, but the climate of the eastern states is not fully suitable. The Spaniards had earlier taken the fruit to Mexico. It was from there that its cultivation spread to California during the 18th century; and that is the state where it has since been principally grown. California's classic variety, the Blenheim, is lusciously sweet and perfumed. In California's golden age of the apricot, between the wars, flourishing groves of

Blenheim made the Santa Clara Valley (surrounding San Jose, south of San Francisco) the world's leading area of production. Unhappily, the development of 'Silicon Valley' caused most of the growers to move to the east, on less suitable land, where inferior varieties have come to be dominant.

The consumption of freshly picked apricots out of hand is a well-known pleasure, but most apricots are fated to be dried or otherwise processed. Dried apricots are one of the best of dried fruits and at their best if they have been sun dried. Fully ripe fruits are used, so they have the real apricot flavour.

The dried apricots from Hunza are small and unprepossessing, but have a notable reputation, since the inhabitants of Hunza enjoy remarkable health and longevity, both attributed in part to this fruit. (Apricots are among the more nutritious fruits, and are particularly rich in carotene.)

Apricots are usually treated with sulphur dioxide, a preservative, before being sun dried. Apricots which have not been so treated are darker in colour, with a caramelized, almost figlike, flavour.

Turkey produces the so-called 'apricot leather', dried apricot flesh in the form of thin sheets, which the cook melts down for use; these have a highly concentrated flavour. Meebos is an unusual S. African conserve. Ripe but firm apricots are brined, then stoned and pressed flat, salted, and part dried in the sun over several days. The resultant sheets are stored in jars with layers of sugar between them and on top, and will keep for months.

In China, from at least the 7th century AD onwards, apricots were preserved not only by drying, but also by salting and even smoking. The black smoked apricots of Hupei were famous, and apricots in general were greatly esteemed as a food, being considered good for the heart.

Apricot jam, made from fresh or dried fruit, is not only a good spread but also an important ingredient for the confectioner. It is used as a sweet adhesive in cakes such as SACHERTORTE; and in diluted form as the apricot glaze which 'finishes' many confections.

In Middle Eastern cookery apricots are also used in sweetmeats, for example stoned and stuffed with almonds or almond paste, the two flavours of the related fruits complementing each other to perfection. But apricots are used in savoury dishes too, to give a 'sweet-and-sour' effect. The fruit blends particularly well with lamb, as in the Arab *mishmishiya* (which might be translated as 'apricotery' and goes back to the 13th century). It is also met in PILAF dishes of C. Asia and Iran.

(*cont. on page 31*)

The apple, *Malus pumila*, one of the first fruits to have been cultivated, is now the most important fruit in Europe, N. America, and temperate regions in both northern and southern hemispheres.

There are about 7,000–8,000 named varieties, although only a small proportion of these are of commercial or historical importance. An alphabetical list of some interesting ones is given under APPLE VARIETIES below.

ORIGINS

The large, sweet apple familiar in modern times is essentially a cultivated product, much changed from the tiny, sour fruits, such as those of the CRABAPPLE, which were its wild ancestors. The natural strategy for an apple tree, in order to propagate itself most effectively, was to produce hundreds of tiny fruits instead of a small number of large ones. The apple's wild relatives in the rose family, e.g. the ROWAN and HAWTHORN, all do this. It was no easy task to persuade apple trees, by selection, to evolve against their natural bent to give larger apples, some of which may now weigh over 500 g (1.25 lb).

The original wild crabapple of Europe, *Malus sylvestris*, is not the direct ancestor of the cultivated apple, although it and other small wild apples contributed to the apple's development through interbreeding. The main ancestor of the modern apple was *M. pumila* var *mitis*, a native of the Caucasus where it still grows wild. Early, small, apples were pale green, yellow, or red and consisted principally of core, the part of the apple which is useful for the tree's reproduction; it is the seed box, consisting of five compartments, each usually holding two seeds. The edible fleshy part surrounding the seed box is called the torus. Selective breeding enlarged the torus whilst leaving the core little larger than it had been originally.

The production of reliable, consistent apple trees is not easy. Apple seeds grow into trees resembling their parents no more than human daughters resemble their mothers. The flowers of most varieties can be fertilized only by the pollen of other varieties. And there is a natural tendency for offspring to revert to the wild state. As Behr (1992) puts it: 'Without the techniques of grafting (or of rooting a branch), each tree in the world would constitute its own variety, distinct from every other.' These techniques are a legacy to the modern world from classical times.

APPLES IN CLASSICAL TIMES

The first written mention of apples, in Homer's *Odyssey*, is not specific, since the Greek word *melon* is used for almost any kind of round fruit which grows on a tree. Thus the legendary 'apples' of Greek myth—given by Paris to Aphrodite, or thrown down by Hippomenes to distract Atalanta, or growing in the Hesperides—may have been other kinds of fruit, or no particular kind at all.

In later Greek writings a distinction was made between the apple and the related QUINCE, which had been growing in the E. Mediterranean region before the arrival of the apple. The 'apples' with which the Shulamite in the Song of Solomon asked to be comforted would probably have been quinces. The Hebrew word used, *tappuach*, meant 'apple' later, but not necessarily then.

The Bible is not specific about the nature of the tree of the knowledge of good and evil. The notion that it was an apple came much later, possibly because of the high opinion of the apple which was general in Roman times, or perhaps later still when the apple had become the standard fruit of W. Europe, the one which would come to mind first whenever fruit was mentioned. Paintings of the temptation of Eve always show an apple; but these are all European, the Jews being forbidden to make religious pictures.

At some time in the classical period it was discovered how to produce apples of a consistent variety: by taking cuttings ('scions') of a good tree and grafting them onto a suitable rootstock, where they grow into branches producing the desired fruits. The process is first described in *De Agricultura*, written in the 2nd century BC by Cato the Elder.

The Romans considered the apple a luxury fruit, better than the fig. It seems at least probable that two or three varieties known to them are identical with kinds grown today. See Api and Court pendu plat under apple varieties below.

LATER HISTORY OF APPLES IN EUROPE

After the fall of the Roman Empire the cultivation of apples lapsed into disarray. Although the Arabs preserved many classical techniques, including that of grafting trees of all kinds, they were not in a position to reorganize European apple-growing, since they invaded Europe from the south, through hot regions unsuitable for apples.

However, apples continued to be grown, and certain distinct types were recognized. In England the two leading kinds were the Costard, a large variety, and the Pearmain. These were both known in the 13th century. There are recipes for apple dishes in 14th-century works such as the MENAGIER DE PARIS and the FORME OF CURY(E), which also includes one for a CAUDLE made with apple blossom.

Grafting was reintroduced and became systematic by the 16th century. Good new varieties of apples were developed, mostly in France, and soon spread to England where their superiority over native apples was acknowledged, although the conservative English would not allow the newcomers to supplant entirely the older kinds. The new apples included the first Pippins, from which many good eating varieties were developed.

From the same ancestors came the Reinettes, mostly small, dull coloured, and very late to ripen. The Reinettes were most important in France, and are still widely grown there. Apples of this type also spread to other countries, e.g.

Boskoop (or Belle de Boskoop), a late variety popular in the Netherlands.

Apples of other types known in Britain before 1600 were the Nonpareil; the White Joaneting; and the Royal Russet, ancestor of a long succession of russet apples with a matt brown skin and a pearlike flavour.

In N. Europe, especially in Scandinavia and Russia, the climate required apples which would ripen quickly in the short summer. The most satisfactory were of a type whose best-known example now is White Transparent. All are light coloured, sometimes with a crimson flash or stripes, and with soft, juicy flesh.

APPLES IN OTHER CONTINENTS

Emigrants to America at first took apple pips rather than scions, which would have died on the voyage, in order to establish the domestic apple in the New World. This procedure gave rise to entirely new varieties, which were further diversified by interbreeding with native American crab-apples. As a result American apples became and remain a distinct group. Some have European characteristics, such as Boston Russet, a variety raised in the mid-17th century. Others are unlike their ancestors. For example, the famous Newtown Pippin is quite different from any European pippin.

A two-way trade in varieties arose. Gravenstein, the best of the N. German and Danish apples, became popular in the USA. American Mother, a red, juicy, mid-autumn apple, enjoyed a vogue in Britain in the 19th century.

The spread of apple cultivation in America was encouraged by a notable eccentric, Johnny Appleseed, born John Chapman in Leominster, Massachusetts, in 1775. He collected large amounts of apple seeds from cider mills and journeyed up and down the country planting them wherever he went.

Apples could also be grown successfully in some parts of the southern hemisphere, and new varieties were developed there too, e.g. Bismarck, a brilliant crimson cooking apple, in Tasmania. S. Africa, Australia, New Zealand, and Chile are now all major exporters of apples to the northern hemisphere, taking advantage of the reversed seasons to sell when local apples are scarce.

In the Middle East and most of Asia the climate does not suit apples except in some cooler, hilly areas. Thus they are grown in the upland, but not the lowland, parts of Lebanon. India produces apples in the northern hills and some are grown in Nepal and on the mountain slopes of E. Java. China has grown apples since well before AD 1000, but they are not a major crop, and are far less esteemed than pears. Japan produces apples more extensively, and has contributed the variety Mutsu to the international repertoire.

In the latter part of the 20th century, production of apples was highest in Italy and France. In N. America, the leading states were Washington, Michigan, and New York.

PREFERENCES IN APPLES

National tastes affect not only the choice of varieties but also the categorization of apples.

In Britain apples are divided clearly into eating and cooking varieties, a distinction which is much less rigid in other countries. (An English cooking apple disintegrates to a purée when cooked. This effect is brought about by a high content of malic acid, which is characteristic of early, soft, green-skinned apples of the Codlin type, such as Grenadier; and of the late, long-keeping, red-striped Lane's Prince Albert family which includes the familiar Bramleys.)

As for eating apples, the British are catholic in their taste. It may still be possible to discern some traces of the effects produced by the Victorian and Edwardian custom of taking DESSERT with port; this prompted enthusiasm for apples with a 'nutty' flavour which would complement the port. It was also partly responsible for a small tide of gastronomic prose about apples which washed over England in the late 19th and early 20th centuries (see POMOLOGY), and which embodied language which resembled writing about fine wines. But none of this had much effect on the vast majority of British people. They accept with docile pleasure the imported Golden and Red Delicious, but their greatest favourite is still the Cox. They are not deterred by the curious appearance of the Russets, which has caused these to be neglected in other countries.

In the USA apples are judged more by their appearance, and red varieties are preferred. While some deep red apples are good, there are also insipid varieties such as Rome Beauty which sell on their looks alone; and there are popular varieties of other colours: Golden Delicious is of American origin. Few kinds are sold purely as eating or cooking apples, and most are used for both purposes.

STORAGE AND PRESERVATION, AND APPLE PRODUCTS

Storing apples is simple in principle, but exacting in practice. The requirements are that the apples should be of a well-keeping—which means late—variety; that they should be absolutely sound, for even a small bruise or a break in the skin releases enzymes which hasten decay; that the place should be dry and cool; and that the apples should not touch each other, lest infection be spread by contagion.

The practical details were understood early. Pliny the Elder (1st century AD) warned against trying to store windfalls or apples picked on wet days. He recommended a cool, dry room with windows on the side away from the sun which could be opened on warm days. The apples were to be stored in a way that would permit free circulation of air around them.

From early times apples were preserved by drying. The usual method in medieval Europe was to peel and core the apples and dry them whole, threaded on strings: this required a warm and airy drying room. The later method of cutting apples across into rings is more reliable, since these dry faster.

An unusual old drying method was the preparation of Norfolk 'biffins'. These were apples which were dried, whole and unpeeled, in warm bread ovens so that they shrivelled into a form like roundish, red prunes. The partial cooking helped to preserve them. They were close packed in layers as they dried. The *pommes tapées* of the Loire Valley in France are somewhat similar, but are peeled first; then dried in special ovens for about five days, during which they are occasionally 'tapped' with a mallet to encourage them to subside into a flattish shape, for ease of storage. It is usual to soak them in red wine before eating them. Similar treatment produced *poires tapées* in the past but, although they were famous in the 19th century, these have virtually disappeared.

Apple butter, which is apple sauce concentrated by boiling it down with cider, was a traditional European product associated especially with the Dutch. It was they who introduced it to America, now its principal stronghold.

All these old preservation methods were made less necessary at the beginning of the 20th century by the introduction of chilled storage, and more recently by inert nitrogen storage. (Nitrogen, which makes up three-quarters of the atmosphere, is harmless to fruit. It is only the oxygen in the air which contributes to spoilage; so, if this is removed, keeping time is much prolonged.)

The main commercial apple product is cider (the alcoholic kind—see CIDER for the American meaning of the term). This is a major industry in parts of France, especially Normandy, and the west of England; and the traditional cider-making in the Basque region of Spain is being revived. Although overshadowed in terms of quantity by alcoholic drinks (including calvados and applejack), fresh apple juice is an important product. The best is bottled under varietal names.

VERJUICE, formerly used as souring agent in the same way as vinegar, was sometimes made from apples, though more usually from crabapples. Cider vinegar is mentioned under VINEGAR. Apple PECTIN is extracted from apple pomace (pulp, including rejects and trimmings).

OTHER USES OF NAME 'APPLE'

Since apples were the fruits best known to the Europeans who colonized the other continents, they naturally used the name as a point of reference in describing strange fruits which they met. Thus misuse of the name 'apple' for unrelated fruits is more prevalent than with any other fruit name. A few examples are CUSTARD APPLE, ROSE-APPLE, SUGAR-APPLE, WOOD APPLE; and, of course, PINEAPPLE—the most famous example of all.

READING: Joan Morgan and Alison Richards (1993), Rosanne Sanders (1988).

Apple varieties

The general section on apple above explains what a large number of varieties there are, some of great antiquity. This alphabetical list gives brief details of just a few, not including the most recent arrivals whose staying power is not yet fully established.

Allington Pippin is one of the sweet/sharp varieties which exemplifies the manner in which an apple's taste can change with age. As Joan Morgan (1985) points out, it 'can be almost bitter sweet in early November but mellows to a definite pineapple flavour by Christmas'. It also exemplifies complexity of flavour; one enthusiast claimed that he had found 'pine and grape, the scent of quince and pear . . . the breath of honey from the hive in its gelid pores'.

Api (Pomme d'Api) or Lady apple, a small, hard, winter apple which may have originated in Roman times. Lister (1698), describing his visit to Paris in that year, wrote that it was served there for show more than use, 'being a small flat apple, very beautiful red on one side, and pale or white on the other, and may serve the ladies at their Toilets a Pattern to Paint by'. The flavour, residing chiefly in the perfumed skin, is good.

Bismarck, unusual among British-type cooking apples in having a bright red skin, was introduced from Tasmania, its place of origin, in 1890.

Blenheim Orange, one of the best apples of the Pippin family, was popular in England for a century after its introduction around 1818. It is large, dull yellow and red, and has crisp flesh and a flavour of unusually acid quality. Season: midwinter, so traditionally a Christmas apple.

Bramley's Seedling or Bramley, the most widely sold cooking apple in Britain, has a very long keeping season, from early autumn right through to next summer. It is usually very large and often irregular in shape. It is harvested commercially as a green apple, or green with faint red stripes, but will turn yellow if left on the tree; and there are also crimson varieties.

Calville blanche d'hiver, an old French variety, is a connoisseur's apple. It is large, ribbed, golden, juicy, and scented. Season: January and February.

Cider apples are of varieties quite distinct from eating or cooking apples, and are indeed almost inedible. Their chief characteristics are sourness, astringency, and bitterness. (In N. America 'cider' usually refers to unfermented apple juice, to which the above does not apply: see CIDER.)

Cortland, a modern American variety bred from Ben Davis and McIntosh, is useful for fruit salads because its flesh hardly browns when cut. Largish, yellow and red, with a sweet, moderately acid flavour. Season: late autumn.

Costard, an extinct family of British apples, was one of the first types to have a distinct name, which was already in use in the 13th century. The first important kitchen apple, large and flavourful, much used in pies until it began to disappear towards the end of the 17th century. 'Costard' was medieval slang for 'head'. The name survives in the word 'costermonger', although such a person may now sell any kind of fruit or vegetable.

Court pendu plat, an old French variety dating from

before 1600, may well be a survival from Roman times. It is small, flattened in shape, green with faint red stripes, and richly flavoured.

Cox's Orange Pippin, one of the best of the large family of Pippins (see Pippins, below). Since its introduction in the first half of the 19th century it has become the most popular British apple. It is a medium-sized, round apple, dull brownish-green with faint red stripes and a red flush on one side. It usually has a matt brown russeted area around the stem. The texture is crisp, the flavour solidly acid but balanced by sweetness. The skin is strongly scented and should be eaten. Season: late autumn to spring, but the best is midwinter.

Delicious, a red apple, whose name is often applied by an inept abbreviation to the unrelated Golden Delicious. Delicious began as a chance seedling on the farm of Jess Hiatt of Peru, Iowa, in 1872. He marketed it as Hiatt's Hawkeye. Stark Brothers, a large fruit-growing concern, bought out Hiatt and renamed the variety Delicious. Since the 1940s it has been the leading American apple, is also widely grown elsewhere and has given rise to new varieties such as Starking (sometimes Star King). The fruit is large, red, and elongated, with five projections at the bottom end. The flavour is sweet but insipid, lacking in acid. Season: autumn to early winter.

Discovery, so named because it was a chance discovery by an amateur grower, was first marketed on a large scale in the 1970s. A bright green and crimson apple, like a brighter version of a Worcester Pearmain, the flesh often has a pink tinge on the sunny side. The flavour is unusual, with a hint of raspberries.

Ellison's Orange is highly flavoured, tasting of aniseed and pear drops.

Faro, a French apple, red, large, juicy, sweet with a little acidity. Grown in Brie, a region renowned for apple cultivation, and known as long ago as the 14th century. For table use during winter and for making a TARTE TATIN.

Flower of Kent, a large, green variety now almost forgotten, but said to be the apple whose fall inspired Sir Isaac Newton to formulate his law of universal gravitation.

Gillyflower, a variety mentioned by many early authors such as Evelyn (1699) and praised for its rich and aromatic flavour.

Gladstone, a large early summer apple of pleasing flavour and aroma.

Golden Delicious, an American apple which appeared as a chance seedling on a W. Virginia farm in about 1900, is now the most widely grown apple in many countries. It is not related to Delicious: the name is due to the fact that the same nursery firm bought the rights to both varieties. The apple is elongated, tapering to five points, pale green becoming yellow and sometimes aquiring a faint flush. The texture, at first light and crisp, later becomes flabby. The flavour varies. When the apple is grown in a cool climate, so that enough acid is formed, it can be good; but when grown in a warmer region it is insipid. Popular with growers because the tree

crops heavily and the apples keep from early autumn to spring, albeit becoming more limp as time passes. Golden Delicious retains its shape when cooked, so it is a good choice for dishes containing sliced apples which are exposed to view, such as the French *Tarte aux pommes.*

Granny Smith is unusual, perhaps unique, in being a brilliant, almost emerald, green even when fully ripe. Much grown in warm climates, notably in S. Africa, Australia, Chile, and France. The texture is crisp and juicy, the flavour distinctive, with a hint of almond.

Gravenstein originated in N. Germany or Denmark before 1800. Scions were taken to California around 1820 and it soon became a popular American variety, especially for cooking; but it is also eaten by those who like rather acid apples. It is large, roundish and slightly lopsided, yellow with bright red and orange stripes. The texture is reasonably crisp, the flavour sharp and aromatic.

Greening or Rhode Island Greening is a pale green apple first grown from seed in 1748 by a Mr Green at Green's End, Rhode Island. Crisp and sharp in flavour, it is usually sold as a cooking apple, but is a good dessert apple too. It has a long season from late autumn to spring.

Idared (sometimes Ida Red), an American apple bred in the 1940s from the better-known Jonathan and Wagener, has become popular with British growers too because of its long keeping qualities. A medium-sized, round, red and yellow apple with a sweet, moderately acid flavour which makes it a satisfactory dessert variety; it also cooks well.

James Grieve, an English apple classified as 'early dessert', has a pleasantly balanced flavour and yields plenty of delicious juice.

Laxton apples, a large and important group, owe their name to the horticulturist Thomas Laxton (1830–90), whose sons produced thousands of cross-bred apples, from which many of the best British dessert apples are derived. A high proportion of them retain the family name Laxton. They bear a general resemblance to Coxes, but are usually brighter green, with less striping and russeting. The texture is crisp and the flavour light. The best-known late Laxtons include Laxton's Pearmain and Laxton's Superb. Laxton's Fortune is a yellow and red striped mid-season variety.

McIntosh, a popular Canadian variety which has been designated Canada's national apple. It was named for John McIntosh of Ontario, who discovered it in E. Ontario as a chance seedling in (probably) 1811. The apple is medium-sized, green or yellow overlaid with red stripes. The area where it grows is near the northern limits of apple country. Its texture is soft and juicy, the flavour a pleasing combination of tart and sweet; and it is aromatic. Good to eat out of hand, also a good cooking apple.

Macoun, a large, red American apple bred from McIntosh, which it surpasses in flavour. It also keeps better.

Mutsu, of Japanese origin, is grown in Britain under the name Crispin. A very late, long-keeping variety, developed from Golden Delicious but generally larger, of a duller green hue, with a more acid and more interesting flavour. For both cooking and eating.

Newtown Pippin, a fine, old established American variety, is little grown today because the tree is awkward to manage. Newtown was on Long Island, where Flushing now is. The original tree was found growing there soon after 1700. It produced a heavy crop of yellowish-green apples which were crisp but juicy, acid but sweet, and had exceptional keeping qualities.

Northern Spy, a large, yellow and red striped American apple resembling Baldwin but far better; indeed, it was for long the ne plus ultra of the cracker-barrel connoisseur and something of a legend for country people as well as urban gastronomes.

Pearmain, the oldest English apple name, was recorded in a Norfolk document of 1204. It is derived from the old French apple name 'parmain' or 'permain', referring perhaps to a group of apples rather than a single variety. All that modern Pearmains have in common is the green and red colouring typical of many British apples. The best known is Worcester Pearmain, an early autumn apple which has a good, sharp flavour, with a hint of strawberry, and a crisp texture when fresh, but does not keep. Its red parts are distinctively dark. Most other Pearmains ripen later.

Pippin, originally meaning any apple grown from a pip, is a name derived from the French 'pépin', meaning both 'pip' and the apple. By the 16th century the term had come to denote a hard, late-ripening, long-keeping apple of acid flavour. The first pippins brought over from France to England were cider apples, but eating varieties were soon developed. In relatively recent times Ribston Pippin became popular, and from it Cox's Orange Pippin (see above) was bred. Sturmer Pippin does well in the southern hemisphere, notably S. Africa and Australia.

In America the name 'Pippin' was used for different kinds of apple, the most famous being a purely American variety, Newtown Pippin (see above).

Reinette, an old French apple name, originally meant an apple propagated by grafting (Latin *renatus*, meaning 'reborn'). The name soon came to denote instead a type of apple which was late ripening and long keeping, with a dull green skin, sometimes flushed and often 'russeted'. It had firm, slightly dry flesh, and a good, sharp flavour. Golden Reinette has been popular in France since before 1650. Orléans Reinette, an 18th-century variety which is unusually sweet, is generally regarded as better.

Rome Beauty, an American apple, is named for Rome, Ohio, near where it was discovered around 1820 by the farmer Joel Gillett. One of his grafted trees had shot from below the graft. The stray branch began to produce large, red striped apples of handsome appearance and rock-like solidity. These keep crisp for a long time, but the flavour is insipid. Used for cooking, especially baking, because it keeps its shape well.

Russet is the name of a group of apples with distinctive matt brown skin, often spotted or with a faint red flush, and of a flattened lopsided shape. The flesh is crisp and the apples keep well. The flavour is unusual and pearlike.

Russets are used both for eating and for cooking. Their size varies from tiny to very large. Royal Russet, a variety known in England before the 17th century, remains popular on the mainland of Europe as a cooking apple. In Britain Egremont Russet and Golden Russet are the most popular kinds. An American variety, Roxbury Russet, is claimed to have originated in Roxbury, Massachusetts, in the early 17th century. If true, this would make it America's oldest named variety.

Wealthy, a large, bright red American apple, grows well in northern climates. It was developed for that purpose in the 1860s by Peter Gideon, the first American to breed apples scientifically. The name was not bestowed to suggest opulence, but was Mrs Gideon's (Puritan) Christian name. Has a good, sharp flavour suitable for table or kitchen use. Season: mid-autumn.

White Joaneting, an English apple known before 1600 (the Jenneting of Elizabethan writers), is still sometimes grown because it ripens before any other apple, in July. Its shiny skin is yellow, sometimes with a red flush. It has a good flavour and is juicy, but does not keep.

White Transparent, an apple of Scandinavian or Russian origin introduced to Britain and the USA in the mid-19th century. Very pale with a transparent skin and a mild flavour. The taste is mild but agreeable. Season: late summer. To be used as soon as ripe, while still crisp, and for cooking rather than dessert. Yellow Transparent is similar.

Winesap, an American apple, of medium size, elongated, bright red with a little yellow on the shaded side, and with firm, aromatic flesh.

Worcester apples form a group of which the Worcester Pearmain (see Pearmain) is the best known. Firm, sweet flesh with a strawberry flavour is characteristic of them.

York Imperial, a large American apple with good keeping qualities, much grown for use in the food-processing industry. It has crisp flesh with an attractively aromatic flavour, but its lopsided shape and patchy colour are unprepossessing, so it is seldom sold retail.

READING: Bultitude (1983); Joan Morgan and Alison Richards (1993); Muriel Smith (1971).

Apples in cookery

Most of the dishes made with apples that we know today are of early origin. For example, to cook apples with fatty meats, so that their sharpness offsets the fat, is a practice which dates back at least as far as classical times when APICIUS gave a recipe for a dish of diced pork with apples. Likewise the combination of fatty fish such as herring with apple, still popular in the Netherlands and N. Europe, is of ancient origin. The versatility of apples was already being exploited in medieval times; the *FORME OF CURY* and the *MENAGIER DE PARIS* (14th century) give a range of recipes for apple sauce, FRITTERS, rissoles, and drinks.

Before the introduction of the domestic oven apples were roasted whole in front of an open fire. Practical difficulties in cooking them evenly led to the development of more complicated 'apple roasters'. These were metal racks incorporating curved tinplate reflectors to heat the far side of the apples.

Apple pie is perhaps the most famous apple dish, and exhibits interesting variations. The American apple pie, with pastry underneath and on top, is derived from the medieval raised pies (of which the British pork pie and French *pâté en croute* are surviving examples) and various sweet and savoury dishes completely enclosed in 'coffyns' (see COFFIN) or pastry cases. In contrast, the modern British apple pie is normally baked in a deep pie dish with a crust on top only. This form too has a long history, since pies with an upper crust only had emerged as early as the 17th century. It was common in Britain to add verjuice for extra sharpness; and old recipes often included quinces which not only sharpened the flavour but gave an attractive pink colour.

In France the classic dish is *Tarte aux pommes*, which is topless. This is made on a round or square base of puff pastry (or simply short pastry), spread with raw apple slices arranged in elegant rows, baked, then often glazed with apple jelly. The choice of apple is important; the typical low-acid apples of the southerly growing areas, which retain their shape when cooked, are best. See also TARTE TATIN—cooked with apples underneath pastry and served 'upside down'.

Further east the *Apfeltorte* (covered apple tart) and the well-known *Apfelstrudel* of German-speaking regions return to the completely enclosed form, which is also found in the apple dumplings which are traditional all over N. Europe as well as in Britain.

Apple dumpling (*Rabot de pommes* in French) used to be a conventional boiled dumpling: in 1849 Eliza Acton recommended wrapping it in a knitted cloth to make a decorative pattern on the surface. Soon after, it became usual to bake it, the method now preferred. A whole apple is peeled, cored, and filled with a sweet mixture (e.g. brown sugar, butter, and cinnamon plus a little grated lemon rind). The apple is then wrapped in shortcrust or puff pastry and baked. Why it should retain the name 'dumpling', when it is made in this way, is not clear; but it does.

The standard accompaniment for apple pie is cream. A recipe of 1708, written in heroic couplets by the English satirist William King (one of the minor Augustans but possessed of a sometimes pleasing wit), cautions against tasting the pie until the cream has had an opportunity to 'give a softness to the tarter juice'. (The recipe sounds good. It includes quinces, brown sugar, cloves, and a little orange flower water.) It is a modern American practice to serve the pie with ice cream, giving an attractive contrast of heat and cold. In Britain it was often eaten with cheese, especially Derby.

Apple cakes are made by several different methods. In England they are plain cakes based on creamed or rubbed-in mixtures with chopped or grated raw apples, and are a speciality of the south-west. Swedish applecakes, on the other hand, are puddings made from layers of apple purée with fried and spiced bread crumbs, reminiscent of Apple BROWN BETTY or Apple CHARLOTTE.

The preceding paragraph shows how indistinct are the boundaries between CAKE and CRUMBLE and PUDDING.

There are many other sweet or dessert confections which can feature apple. See, for examples, COBBLER; PANDOWDY.

Apricot kernels are similar to almonds and, like almonds, contain small amounts of prussic acid which is destroyed by roasting them. They are used in making apricot brandies and liqueurs; and the Italian *amaretti di Saronno* (see MACAROONS) owe some of their flavour and texture to them.

Other species and hybrids are noteworthy. The Chinese, and later the Japanese, have cultivated an apricot of a different species, *P. mume* (now *Armeniaca mume*), commonly known in the West as 'Japanese flowering apricot', although it is of Chinese origin, and often misdescribed as a type of plum. See UMEBOSHI.

Some apricots are dark in colour, for example, the 'black apricot' of N. India, *Armeniaca × dasycarpa*, which looks like a purplish-black plum but has a true apricot flavour.

A few plum-apricot hybrids with velvety purple skin, scarlet flesh, and an apricot aroma have been developed recently in California, bearing names like plumcot and aprium.

'San Domingo apricot' and 'South American apricot' are not apricots but other names for the MAMMEE.

AQUIBOQUIL the purple fruit of a woody plant, *Lardizabala biternata*, which grows in Chile and Peru and belongs to the family Lardizabalaceae. This family also includes the AKEBIA fruit, and seems to specialize in fruits of a sausage-like shape and a blue or purple colour. Akebia fruits are purplish, aquiboquil are deep purple, and the species *Holboellia fargesii* has fruits (also edible) which are metallic blue in colour.

Aquiboquil fruits are esteemed in Chile, partly perhaps for their shape and colour but also for their agreeably sweet taste. The name is sometimes spelled 'aquibuquil'.

ARAB CUISINE The vast majority of Arabs live in the Fertile Crescent, the Nile Valley, or the northern parts of Tunisia, Algeria, and Morocco. There is a 1,000-mile gap between the Egyptian and Tunisian population centres, and from the later 8th to the early 16th centuries, the sparsely inhabited southern shore of the Gulf of Sirte was nearly always a no man's land between rival states. As a result, a line can be drawn through the middle of Libya dividing Arabs into easterners and westerners, who differ in language, customs, and cuisine.

Although the first impression of Arab food that results is one of bewildering variety, there are common culinary features throughout the Arab world. The everyday protein sources are usually dairy products and pulses (above all LENTILS, CHICKPEAS, and BROAD BEANS). Pulses are often made into pastes, called *baisar* in the west; in the east, the pastes are turned into little fried cakes (*ta'miyya*, FALAFEL). Milk is scarcely ever consumed fresh but made immediately into YOGHURT (*laban*), clotted cream (*qishta*, KAYMAK), clarified butter (*samn*, see GHEE), or cheese (*jibn*). A common breakfast is cheese or yoghurt with olives or dates.

Beef is eaten in Iraq and water-buffalo in Egypt, but the preferred meat nearly everywhere is LAMB. The most tender cuts go for KEBABS, the others for stews and ground meat. Markets often have butchers or cooked meat shops that specialize in the head and trotters, that is, the non-organ meats that are not suitable for stews and kebabs. Among fowl, chicken is popular but squab (see PIGEON) runs a close second in Egypt and N. Africa.

Because of Islamic dietary law, pork is rarely eaten in the Arab world, even by Christians. Islam also prohibits wine. Perhaps as a result of this, meat dishes are often given a sweet flavouring, or even more often a sour flavouring (with lemons—fresh, pickled, or dried—or yoghurt, vinegar, POMEGRANATE juice, SUMAC, or TAMARIND), which would not occur to cooks in parts of the Mediterranean where wine is a regular part of the meal.

The preferred grain has always been wheat, though rice is the staple of S. Iraq and has prestige value elsewhere in the eastern Arab world. Most breads, whether cooked in the TANDOOR or the European-style brick oven, are flat. Paper-thin breads (*raqîq*, *marqûq*, *khubz sâj*) command special admiration. Throughout the area, bakers also make ring-shaped breads (*samîd*) and biscuits (*ka'k*).

Vegetables are stewed with meat when possible, but cold stewed vegetables dressed with oil (much like *légumes à la grecque*) are virtually universal. They may descend from Christian Lenten dishes. When vegetables are stuffed with rice and dressed with oil, they are called *yalanji* to distinguish them from meat-stuffed vegetables, just as in the Middle Ages vegetarian Christian dishes, often oil dressed, were called *muzawwarât* (the Arab word meaning, like the Turkish *yalanji*, 'counterfeit'). Vegetables made into vinegar pickles include some rarely preserved this way in Europe, such as turnips.

Sweets and pastries are commonly flavoured with nuts but scarcely ever with fruits (with the exception of dates), which are usually eaten out of hand, either fresh or dried. In cookery, fruits are treated much like vegetables. Mixed dried fruits are often poached together and served cold, like the cold vegetable dishes. Fruits are frequently stewed with meat in the same way that vegetables are, though in Egypt, Syria, and Lebanon this is now rare, probably because of the influence of Turkish cuisine, which avoids this combination.

A particular characteristic of the Arab world is the mixing of flatbread—fresh, stale, or toasted—with other ingredients. Stewed meat mixed with bread, a dish known as THARÎD, was the favourite of the Prophet Muhammad, and it is no accident that Muslims make *tharîd* as far away as Xinjiang. But the Arab countries make many other such dishes as well, such as the *tashrîb* of Iraq, the *fatta* of Egypt and Syria, and *fatût* of Yemen (which is anything you wish—meat, scrambled eggs, a mixture of honey and melted butter—mixed with toasted flatbread). In a sense, these dishes are the equivalent of the complex PILAFS that developed in Iran. During the Middle Ages, the Moors of Spain and N. Africa were obsessed with creating an ultra-thin bread for particularly elegant *tharîds* and this was one theatre for the development of both puff pastry and the strudel-like pastry sheets known as WARQA in Morocco today.

The cuisine of the nomads and oasis-dwellers of Arabia, monotonously based on DATES and BARLEY, had little to offer the outside world apart from *tharîd* and the barley and date dish *'asîda*, which subsequently developed into a more refined sort of sweet in many Arab countries. The distinctive cuisine of the Arab empire that began to develop during the days of the caliphs adopted much from the conquered peoples. From Egypt, it took *ka'k* (the Coptic *k'aak'e*) and *mulûkhiyya*, a stew based on the leafy vegetable MELOKHIA. (Its gluey consistency is an acquired taste. Curiously, in Morocco, the name *mulûkhiyya* is applied not to this mallow but to another gluey vegetable, OKRA.) From the Aramaic-speaking people of the Fertile Crescent, it took a number of grain dishes: the sweet *khabîsa*, the hearty porridge-like dish *harîsa* (made with meat and whole wheat, the latter beaten to a purée at the end—see HALEEM) and a sweetened dish of whole wheat served on religious occasions, called *'ashûre* (see AŞURE) by Muslims and *kilbeh* by Christians.

But the overwhelming influence, which affected cookery not only throughout the Arab world but much of the non-Arab Muslim world as well, came from Iran. There had been a cult of gastronomy at the court of the Sasanian Empire and the caliphs of Baghdad gratefully adopted it. As a result, the Arabic food vocabulary is as saturated with Persian words as English is with French. Among them are *turshi* (vinegar pickles), *sanbûsak* (the small triangular meat pie known as SAMOSA in India), *shurbâ* (soup, often with a grain thickening, see SHORBA), *yakhni* (meat stewed with a vegetable), *kufta* (ground meat, nearly always formed into balls, whether to be grilled, fried, or stewed—see KOFTA), *zulâbiyâ* (lattice-shaped fritters, known as JALEBI in

India), and *fâlûda* (see PALOODEH, also known, depending on when and how borrowed from Persian, as *bâlûza* and *balta*), even the ubiquitous term MEZZE.

The relative sophistication of the various influences is symbolized by three basically similar sweets of a puddingy or porridgy consistency. At least in its original form, the Arabian *'asîd* is the peasant's basic meal of whole grain, the Aramaean *khabîsa* is based on flour, and the Iranian *fâlûda* is thickened with cornstarch (cornflour).

The new cultural constellation of the court of Baghdad also called into being new dishes. Several that are named after famous personages have survived to the present, the most widespread being *muhallabiyya* (see MUHALLABIA), a smooth pudding made from rice flour, and *bûrâniyya* (see BURAN). In the later Middle Ages, the crêpe called QATÂ'IF developed in an unexpected direction and gave rise to the very delicate and sophisticated sweet also known as *kunâfa*.

Other dishes universal in the Arab world have less clear-cut antecedents, such as the date-stuffed pastry called MA'AMOUL in the east and *maqrûd* in the west; the delicate butter cookie *ghuraiba* (see GHORAYEBAH); and the dish of fish and rice found in all coastal areas, *sayyâdiyya*.

Around the 12th century, parallel innovation in grain cookery took place in Iran and the western Arab world which largely superseded the traditional mushy grain preparations of the earlier Middle Ages. In N. Africa and Spain, COUSCOUS was invented. The Iranian innovation was pilaf (a method of cooking rice partly by steaming, designed to keep each grain separate), known in Arabic as *rizz mufalfal*. At a later but unknown time, *bulghur* (see BURGHUL—boiled crushed wheat dried in the sun) was invented somewhere in the east, probably in N. Iraq or what is now SE Turkey. Couscous spread to Syria in the Middle Ages and bulghur is known as far west as Tunisia today (but KIBBEH, a purée of meat and *bulghur* used in countless Syrian and Iraqi dishes, has spread no further west than Egypt).

The culinary differences that we see among the Arab countries today are due to the existence of three great areas of culinary innovation: Iran (a continuing influence upon Iraq); Moorish Spain, where there was a great cross-fertilization of Muslim, Christian, and Jew, of Arab, Berber, and Spaniard; and the Ottoman Empire, where, by Sultan Mehmet II's design, there was an even greater cultural fusion in the metropolis of Istanbul (see TURKEY). But these are at bottom local colourings of a cuisine that had taken its basic shape in the 9th century.   CP

READING: Perry (1998*b*), Zubaida and Tapper (1994).

ARABIAN FOOD a term used to indicate the food of Saudi Arabia, Kuwait, Bahrain, Qatar, the United Arab Emirates, and the Sultanate of Oman, which constitute the Gulf Co-operation Council countries of Arabia. They cover some 2.5 million square km (965,000 square miles) and have a population of about 25 million, of whom a substantial proportion are expatriates. This results in the availability of a very wide range of foods. (There is a separate entry for YEMEN.)

The terrain is varied with extensive desert areas, a long coastline, and mountains in the eastern and western fringes. The monsoon reaches the southern coast but the majority of the land receives only occasional rainfall. The agriculture does, however, achieve a wide range of produce although it is only well developed over limited areas of the peninsula.

The indigenous Bedouin tribes have a strong but basic food culture (see BEDOUIN FOOD). Historically the region's food has been influenced by the surrounding cultures, Ottoman to the north, the HORN OF AFRICA to the west, and IRAN and INDIA to the east. This has resulted in a diverse and well-developed cuisine in the main population centres.

The presentation of food and the format of meals is similar to what one finds to the north, in LEBANON AND SYRIA.

LAMB is the most popular meat and *Khouzi*, baked whole lamb, could be considered to be the national dish of several of these countries. The lamb is stuffed with a chicken, eggs and rice spiced with the *baharat* spice mixture (see below), saffron, and onions. The baked lamb is served on the bed of rice liberally garnished with almonds and GHEE. Lamb is also frequently cooked on skewers either as pieces or as ground meat, *Kebab mashwi*. Chicken is the second favourite and is also available freshly roasted from *shawarma* stalls. These stalls sell the Gulf version of doner kebab (see KEBAB); vertical spit-roasted lamb pieces are sliced and served in some form of flatbread such as *mafrooda* or hollowed-out roll with tomato, parsley, and TAHINI dressing.

The *baharat* spice mix is prepared from black pepper, coriander, CASSIA, cloves, cumin, CARDAMOM, nutmeg, and paprika. Another important flavouring ingredient specific to this region (and for which there is no real substitute) is *loomi*, dried Omani limes. They are used in meat dishes and also for a refreshing sweet tea.

Fish and prawns feature significantly in the region's food as all the countries are coastal. *Hammour* (grouper) and *zubaidi* (silver pomfret) are particularly esteemed. *Machbous* is a dish of prawns cooked with rice, fresh herbs, and vegetables.

Savoury dishes are eaten with rice or flat-bread. Yoghurt, *laban*, and strained yoghurt, *labneh*, are the most important milk products and are used in a number of dishes. Fresh salt pickles are prepared as an accompaniment to snacks and meat.

Vegetables and pulses are available in wide variety as accompaniments for the meat and fish. Large quantities of fresh herbs are sold in the markets in bunches, mainly parsley, spinach, mint, and coriander but including Ceylon spinach (see BASELLA), basil, dill, PURSLANE, rocket, spinach beet, MELOKHIA, radish tops, spring onions, FENUGREEK, MALLOW, and DANDELION.

Dates were the most important fruit and continue to be consumed in large quantities, particularly during the fresh date season and Ramadan, the month of fasting. Other fruits which are now available and popular include mango, melon, watermelon, orange, and banana.

Sweet dishes are often based on dates. BAKLAVA is a popular import from Turkish cuisine and the small stuffed pancakes called '*ataif* (see QATA'IF) are a RAMADAN speciality adopted from northern neighbours.

Dibis, date molasses (see DIBS), is extracted from dates as they dry and is used in many sweet dishes. There is also a large consumption of honey which particularly appeals to the sweet tooth of the populace.

Coffee, the main drink, has strong associations with the renowned hospitality of the people. It is prepared from finely ground, well-roasted beans and is usually flavoured with cardamom. Tea, the second drink of the region, is usually taken black and very sweet.   PI

READING: Lamees Abdullah Al Taie (1995).

ARCHESTRATUS was a Sicilian Greek of the 4th century BC who 'circumnavigated the world to satisfy his hunger' (Athenaeus), or, more accurately, who travelled widely and gathered his knowledge of the middle Mediterranean into a poem, *Hedypatheia*, thus becoming the world's first known food writer. For a while his work was well known: in the century after it first appeared Archestratus, unfairly, was a byword among moralists for having encouraged gluttony. The complete poem is now lost, and it would be quite unknown today had not Athenaeus in the *Deipnosophists* cited it extensively. These surviving extracts have recently been collected in English (translated by J. Wilkins and S. Hill, 1994).

From what remains of his work we can learn much of Archestratus' gastronomic opinions and even something about himself. His views were set down as practical instructions to one or two named friends, in rough but lively and highly quotable

hexameter verse. His chief concern, repeated over and over again in different words, was that the true flavour of fresh produce, chosen in the right place at the right time of year, should be allowed to come through and not be covered up with layers of spices and strong seasonings. 'Let no Syracusan and no Greek of Italy come near you when you make this dish,' he says of SEA BASS. 'They do not know how to prepare good fish, but wickedly spoil it by cheesing everything and dousing it with watery vinegar and pickled SILPHIUM.' He deals mainly with the seafood of Greek coastal cities, from Sicily in the west to Byzantium (Istanbul) in the east. Over fifty place names occur, and a similar number of fish species. These local specialities, as named by Archestratus, often agree with what other ancient sources have to say: this applies, for example, to the fine bread, the anchovies, and the Hymettan honey to be looked for on the Athenian market. Of the produce of many smaller cities, however, we would know little or nothing if it were not for a mention by Archestratus.

He had strong views on the food that should accompany wine at a supper. 'As you imbibe, have served some such relish as this: tripe or boiled sow's womb marinated in cumin and sharp vinegar and silphium, and the tender tribe of birds, such as are in season. Have nothing to do with those Syracusans who simply drink, like frogs, without eating anything.' In another fragment he recommends hare, cooked rare, for a similar occasion. But Archestratus had no time for fancy dinner parties or complicated menus. 'All to dine at one hospitable table,' he wrote; 'there shall be three or four friends altogether or at most five, or you would have a tentful of plundering mercenaries.' Sicilian cities were prey to bands of mercenary soldiers in Archestratus' time: this is the one sly political reference in his poem. Its publication can be dated fairly closely, between about 360 and 348 BC, because it is only during this short period that a reader could have been recommended to visit all the cities named.   AD

READING: Dalby (1996).

ARGENTINA The rolling grassland each side of the River Plata which includes URUGUAY and central Argentina is the world's richest agricultural terrain. The home of nomadic Indians before the arrival of the Spanish, no people had exploited it, nor tilled its soil. It was to prove ideal for imported cattle and sheep, as well as for any temperate crops the new colonists might wish to introduce.

The second largest republic in Latin America is more than just pampas:

landscapes vary from the Andes in the north and west, whose foothills support vineyards of high quality, to the rugged terrain of Patagonia in the far south, home of myriad sheep. Nonetheless, it is the superficially romantic life of the gaucho, on the move over immeasurable grasslands, that has marked the character of Argentine, and Uruguayan, cooking.

Before meat processing had made the twin jumps to canning, then refrigeration, cattle were exploited for by-products such as hides, or for JERKY. (Buccaneers were so called because they ate *boucan*, a French word for jerky, and the griddle it was dried upon, derived in turn from the Tupi-Guaraní language of Paraguay.) Locals, therefore, could eat as much meat as they wanted, so long as the hide was retained. W. H. Hudson comments on the gauchos' terrific waste of meat, excess being fed to the dogs by the barrowload. Since refrigeration allowed export of raw meat, the character of Argentine beef has been improved by Scottish and English breeding stock.

Most commonly, meat is grilled or roasted on the open fire. This may be a *parrilla* (large, movable barbecue), or the meat can be roasted (*asado*), with carcasses and joints set on iron rods planted round the perimeter of the fire. Cooked *con cuero*, with the hide on, it is said to be juicier. Butchered in this fashion, it is sometimes baked in a pit. Although able to pick only the tenderest meat, the Argentinians have proved to be both omnivorous and careful of resources. Offal is popular: tongues cooked with almond sauce, tripe and sausages, sweetbreads grilled on the barbecue, and, most famously of all, the PUCHERO or boiled dinner of calf's head, chicken, sausage, and beef with green corn. Economical cuts like the rib or flank are also essential for *Matambre* (literally, hunger-killer) which is a roll of flank steak filled with vegetables and hard-boiled egg eaten cold, in thin slices, or hot.

Offcuts and trimmings from the meat could be served as cold cuts (*fiambres*), or were used in an EMPANADA, a crescent-shaped pastry turnover with a distinctively rolled edge filled with spiced chopped meat, vegetables, or cheese, common as a street food and for snacks. *Fiambres* may come with olives and butter, or with a relish or sauce like *chimichurri*, some versions of which are almost a hamburger relish of corn oil, onions, and pimentos, while others are more like a spicy vinaigrette. Peppery relishes also claim a place at the barbecue.

Stews that include the tougher cuts combined with indigenous vegetables such as pumpkin and corn (MAIZE) are exemplified in the *Carbonada criolla*, cooked in the shell of the pumpkin itself, or in the

adaptable LOCRO which is a soup-stew with wheat or corn as a base, enriched with SQUASH. The lack of good green vegetables in Argentina, also noted by British visitors to Uruguay, meant that *chichoca de zapallo* (squash cut into strips and dried) was a winter staple. Although most Indians living on the pampas were wiped out in the campaigns of General Rosa of 1879–83, leaving a population that is 97% European, their staples have persisted, for instance *humitas*, a rough purée of corn with milk, eggs, pimentos, and cheese. Wrapped in corn husks and steamed like *tamales*, it is known as *humitas en chala*. Other corn dishes, porridges of grits like *mazamorra*, or savoury hominies served with cabbage and sausages, are also common.

Argentina does not only eat beef, though no other country in the world consumes more per capita. Mutton is the meat of Patagonia, once supplemented by the guanaco (see LLAMA) like that shot by Darwin on Christmas Eve in 1833 to feed the crews of the *Beagle* and *Adventure*. Chicken and turkeys are esteemed. Seafood is rich on the Atlantic shore, but Argentine fish cookery has not the reputation of Chile's.

Spanish origins are most easily marked by an affection for sweet milk confections like the *dulce de leche* which is a soft fudge for spreading on bread, or use as a sauce for puddings. In *The Honorary Consul* (1973) Graham Greene wrote: 'Every three months Doctor Plarr flew down to Buenos Aires and spent a weekend with his mother who was growing more and more stout on her daily diet of cream-cakes and *alfajores* stuffed with *dulce de leche*.'

Spanish influence, however, is not universal. Italian settlers, especially around the city of Mendoza, have made their own contribution to national preferences (noodles and sun-dried tomatoes, to name two), just as German-speaking migrants have guided the charcuterie industry of Buenos Aires, while in Patagonia there are the Welsh.   TJ

ARK-SHELL the name given to BIVALVES of the family *Arcidae*. The double shell, when viewed from the end, looks something like a decked ship (or Noah's ark). Some ark-shells are attached by a byssus, like that of the mussel, to a substrate, but others are unattached burrowers. *Arca noae* is a Mediterranean species which is sometimes eaten raw, but is better in the Ligurian dish *Pasta con le zampe* (*zampe* being the Ligurian name for ark-shells).

Ark-shells of tropical waters, in the genus *Anadara*, include a very large one, *A. senilis*, a W. African species which is almost globular in shape and may measure 14 cm (6.5") in diameter. *A. granosa*, the principal

species of SE Asia, is only half that size. *A. inaequivalis*, another species of the Indo-Pacific region, is markedly asymmetrical. All these species are known as 'bloody cockles' or 'bloody clams' because their flesh is red and they exude a red liquid, being possessed of the red blood pigment haemoglobin. This deters some people from eating them, although they should be valued as a good source of iron.

A. granosa is of commercial importance in Malaysia and Indonesia. After being parboiled to open them, and removed from their shells, the creatures may be eaten with a sweet-and-sour sauce; or fried; or used in curry dishes.

The species appreciated in Japan, *A. broughtonii*, is called *akagai* and is eaten raw when absolutely fresh, otherwise prepared in any of several ways.

ARMADILLO any of a number of American mammals in the family Dasypodidae, related to the sloths and the anteaters. *Tolypeutes tricinctus*, the three-banded armadillo or *apara*, and *Dasypus novemcinctus*, the nine-banded or Texas armadillo also called *peba*, are among the better known. The former has a range from the south-west of the USA to Argentina, the latter belongs to Argentina and Brazil. Armadillos are mostly of moderate size, up to about 60 cm (2') in body length, and are covered with bony scales. Their food consists mostly of insects.

An armadillo is edible, indeed good to eat, provided that seven glands have first been removed from legs and back. The animal may then be cleaned and baked in its own scaly covering. In Brazil it is usual to add a lot of parsley with the seasoning. One authority recommends armadillo sausages, well flavoured with coriander seed, basil and bay leaves, garlic, and nutmeg.

The Browns in their *South American Cook Book* (1939) have the following to say about armadillos:

In Brazil the armadillo (*tatú*) has as many quaint legends and fancies woven around it as has the possum in our own South, for this curiously armored animal, with its comical head and rattling, plated tail, has the ability to roll into an impenetrable ball, dig itself into the earth so rapidly that no man with a shovel can keep up with it, and do other quaint tricks that no other animal is equipped to perform. The resemblance does not end here, for the armadillo when cooked tastes rich and porky, more like the possum than any other game. It is so easily captured and so universally liked that almost everybody from Mexico to the Argentine eats armadillo, and down in Texas during the Depression it was popularized under the apt name of 'Hoover Hog'.

The same authors explain that there are three sorts of armadillo in Brazil, and that it is only the sweet, white-fleshed little *tatú mirim* which is fit for the table. When this has been dressed and the glands removed, the meat is usually baked in the armoured shell with seasonings and a little minced parsley.

ARMENIA one of the three countries of the Caucasus and, like the other two (GEORGIA and AZERBAIJAN), formerly a republic in the Soviet Union, has a culinary importance which transcends its present boundaries. Armenians are to be found not only in neighbouring Russia, Turkey, and Iran but also in many other places. They have been among the great emigrants of history and their communities in the USA (where they first arrived in the 17th century) are prominent. Many such Armenians have been successful in the food industry. They have speciality foodshops, delicatessens, restaurants, and bakeries.

Tradition has it that the original kingdom of Armenia was founded by a descendant of Noah in the region of Lake Van (believed to be the area where Noah's ark landed after the deluge). In the 2nd century BC Armenia lost its independence to Rome, and thereafter was taken over by the standard roll-call of successive conquerors: Persia, Byzantium, Islam, Mongols, Turks, Persians (again), and Russia. In addition, the Armenians took to Christianity at a very early date (around the beginning of the 4th century) and have maintained their own Church ever since, with consequent attention to Lenten foods etc. Thus a wealth of cultural and culinary influences have been brought to bear on the Armenians. However, they may have influenced others more than others influenced them, as Jean Redwood (1989) suggests:

A long unbroken religious cohesion and a strong national consciousness over the centuries, despite decimation and dispersion of their numbers over the globe, has kept their culture intact. Because of this they have tended to influence rather than be influenced in their manner of cooking. They travelled around the Caucasus more than the other nationalities and were the main commercial traders.

As in the other Caucasian countries, lamb, aubergines, yoghurt, and bread are basic features of the diet. However, there are important differences between the countries in several respects, including the use of cereals. Whereas Georgians particularly like maize and Azerbaijanis favour rice, Armenians use a lot of BURGHUL (cracked wheat), notably in their *plov* dishes (see PILAF). Also, their practice of combining wheat processed in one way with wheat processed in another, and their liking for mixed flours (wheat, potato, maize), produce flavours which are hard to replicate where these ingredients are not readily available.

MEZZE are important to Armenians and include the standard items of the region such as those made with aubergines, lentils, beans, and chickpeas which are also renowned in Armenia; *boeregs* (see BÖREK), toasted pumpkin seeds, roasted and salted pistachios, DOLMA (which according to some originated in Armenia and went from there to Turkey), *basturma/pastourma*, a pungent, spiced meat similar to the Romanian PASTRAMI (but with fenugreek), and various sausages. LAVASH is the bread commonly served with mezze.

Salads too, often including slices of fresh or pickled cucumbers, tomatoes, and lemons, are served at most meals either as a first course or as a side dish, e.g. with the spitted chicken which is a popular dish throughout the Caucasus but takes on its Armenian character from this accompaniment.

Lake Sevan is famous for its trout, called *ishkhan*, which are prepared and cooked in several ways: by stuffing it with fruits such as prunes, damsons, or apricots before baking; by poaching; by first marinating the trout with red peppers; or serving with a walnut sauce.

Typical Armenian soups are prepared with a tomato, egg-and-lemon, or yoghurt sauce flavoured with onion or garlic and herbs. A cucumber and yoghurt soup called *Jajik* is common. Fruits, which are abundant in Armenia, are often added to soups and stews (in line with the general Caucasian liking for sweet and sour). Apricots, for which Armenia is noted, feature in many Armenian soups. The most favoured and best-known type of soup is *bozbash*, basically made with fatty breast of lamb plus selected fruit and vegetables. One kind, *Shoushin bozbash*, practically unknown outside the Caucasus, is a fragrant combination of meat, quince, apple, and mint.

Meat cookery provides few surprises. The ubiquitous KOFTA are *kiufta* here. *Kyurdyuk*, lamb fat from the FAT-TAILED SHEEP, is used in cooking instead of butter, although for certain purposes sheep's milk butter, with its characteristic and different flavour, may be used.

Cheese is a basic Armenian food, served at almost every meal, besides being used in cooking. One of the numerous types is a 'green' cheese, described as similar to ROQUEFORT. Others match the generality of cheeses in the Near East and the Balkans (for which see FETA, HALOUMI, KASHKAVAL).

Armenians incorporate herbs in their cheeses (and also on their salads) in an imaginative way. One Russian author has said that they use no fewer than 300 herbs in their kitchens. Use of spices is moderate.

Rosewater, orange flower water, and honey are used to flavour many desserts and pastries, mostly similar to those made all over the region such as *paklava* (see BAKLAVA). Armenians also use a lot of pine nuts and pistachios.

ARRACACHA *Arracacia xanthorrhiza*, a plant which belongs to the same family as CELERY, PARSNIP, and CARROT (and is sometimes called Peruvian or white carrot), is unique among the cultivated members of this family in being native to the New World. It is a popular vegetable in the northern part of S. America and parts of the Caribbean; but attempts to grow it elsewhere have failed.

The roots, which resemble those of a large carrot or a small, blunt parsnip, grow in clusters. The colour of the flesh ranges from white to pale yellow or purple, and the texture is like that of a potato. The flavour has been described as a mixture of parsnip, celery, and carrot; or of parsnip and roasted chestnut.

ARROWHEAD (or arrowleaf), *Sagittaria sagittifolia*, a perennial water or marsh plant of Europe, Asia, and America, is named for the shape of its leaves, but it is the starchy, tuberous roots which are usually eaten and for which the plant is cultivated in Asia.

A distinction was formerly made between *S. sagittifolia* and what were regarded as two other species: *S. sinensis* of China and Japan, and *S. latifolia* of N. America. However, all are now classified as a single species.

In N. America arrowhead has long been gathered from the wild by Indians (for whom it was probably the most valuable of the available root crops) and sometimes by white inhabitants. This has the Chinook name 'wappatoo', now rendered as 'wapato', meaning potato; and is also called 'duck potato' because water birds are fond of the leaves.

Quinn (1938) states that arrowhead was the most valuable of American Indian root crops, and describes the procedure thus:

The Indian women gathered them by wading into the water, pushing a light canoe ahead of them, locating the tubers with their toes and tossing them into the handy canoe. They boiled them in wooden kettles with hot stones, or roasted them on sticks stuck in the ground near the fire, or in stone-lined kilns.

The tubers are more or less round and enclosed in a sheath. Once this is removed they may be cooked like new potatoes, without prior peeling. But the flavour is more pronounced than that of potatoes and at its best when the tubers are roasted to a

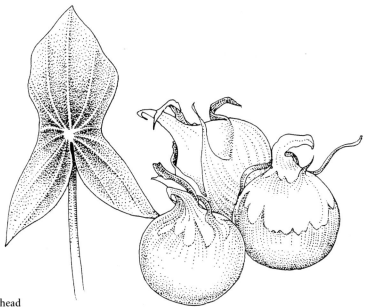

Arrowhead

mealy consistency. Cooking destroys bitter and possibly toxic substances in the tubers, and takes away the acrid taste which they have in the raw state.

ARROWROOT the common western name for a starch which is usually made from the swollen roots of *Maranta arundinacea*. This plant, originally native to the W. Indies and S. America, is now widely grown in Asia, Africa, and the Pacific islands. The name is also loosely applied to miscellaneous starchy roots grown in many other parts of the world.

. True W. Indian arrowroot can be eaten whole, boiled or roasted; but it is fibrous, and better when reduced to a starch by pulverizing and washing the roots. There are two varieties, red and white, of which the first is considered superior.

Arrowroot starch is a delicate product, with remarkably fine grains, and is therefore a traditional invalid food. It makes a light-textured, translucent paste without any flavour of its own, and will set to an almost clear gel. The Chinese use it as a thickener for soups and sauces which cornflour would make undesirably opaque. It is also lighter than cornflour and less obviously starchy.

A root native to tropical America but now grown in Africa, Australia, Hawaii, and the W. Indies is *Canna edulis*. It and close relations are known in French as *tous les mois* (meaning every month, because it is always available), which name has been corrupted into 'toleman' or 'tulema'. It is also called **Queensland**, African, Sierra Leone, or purple **arrowroot**. All the species are used for starch.

East Indian arrowroot is widely used in SE Asia, especially Burma, Malaysia, and

Indonesia. It comes from plants of the genus *Curcuma*, which also includes the spice turmeric and belongs to the same family as ginger. The principal species used for starch is *C. angustifolia*.

Indian/South Sea/Polynesian/Tahiti/Hawaii arrowroots are from *Tacca leontopetaloides* (or, possibly, close relations). One Hawaiian name is *pi* (not the same as the better-known POI, which is a starch made from TARO).

Brazilian arrowroot is CASSAVA, in the form of coarse flour.

Wild or Florida **arrowroot**, also called wild sago and 'coontie', comes mainly from *Zamia floridana*, which grows in the south of the USA. Like many of the other roots or tubers which yield edible starches, this must be carefully processed to ensure that the result is safe to eat.

Oswega arrowroot is an old name for CORNFLOUR.

ARROZ FERMENTADO (fermented rice), also called *arroz amarillo*, an unusual food made in the Andes regions of Ecuador. Unpolished rice is moistened, spread on a floor, and covered. Moulds including *Aspergillus* spp (related to those which ferment SOY SAUCE etc), and bacteria including *Bacillus subtilis* (which ferments NATTO) soon grow in it. Full fermentation takes a fortnight and generates considerable heat. The rice is turned over with a shovel at the halfway stage. The final product is golden brown with a sharp, pungent flavour.

ARTICHOKE *Cynara scolymus*, a member of the THISTLE family. The

cultivated globe artichoke is an improved form of the wild CARDOON, *C. cardunculus*, which is a native of the Mediterranean region with a flower head intermediate in size and appearance between artichoke and common thistle.

The true artichoke may have evolved originally in N. Africa, although some have suggested Sicily as its birthplace. It is first mentioned as being brought from Naples to Florence in 1466.

The artichoke differs from the cardoon chiefly in the size of its flower head, which is greatly enlarged and fleshy. When this is an immature, small bud, the whole head is edible. Later, but while it is still a bud and before it opens, it assumes the form in which artichokes are generally consumed. At this stage the bracts (leaves resembling petals) have become tougher and only their fleshy bases are edible. The eater must be equipped with front teeth and patience. The bracts are picked off the cooked head one by one, a procedure which has given rise to the Italian phrase *la politica del carciofo*, meaning a policy of dealing with opponents one at a time. Then they are dipped in melted butter or vinaigrette dressing, and their bases are nibbled off. When they are all gone, a bristly structure, the inedible 'choke', is revealed. This is carefully cut off to reveal the 'heart' or 'bottom', the best part.

In Italy, the very young, wholly edible buds have long been eaten just as those of the cardoon were in classical times. They may be deep fried (*Carciofini alla Giudea*) or pickled. At a slightly later stage, but before the bracts become really tough, the heads may be stuffed; this is a popular dish in Arabic cuisine, which strongly favours the stuffing of vegetables. Sometimes the young stems and leaf midribs are cooked and served like any other stem vegetable.

After the artichoke became established, it enjoyed a vogue in European courts, and had a reputation as an aphrodisiac. In modern times it has become more commonplace, and is relatively cheap in S. Europe, where it thrives. It is, however, sensitive to frost, so in N. Europe, including Britain, has to be imported and costs more. The British do not eat artichokes much. Nor are they generally popular in the USA, although they are grown in California and commonly eaten wherever French influence persists, as in Louisiana.

In France itself, the *artichaut de Paris* (also known by its varietal name Gros Vert de Laon) enjoyed a high reputation until the latter part of the 20th century when competition from growers in S. Europe more or less stifled the cultivation which had been flourishing in the environs of Paris since the 16th century.

Names meaning 'wild artichoke' are

applied to various other members of the thistle family, notably *C. humilis* in N. Africa.

ASAFOETIDA a dried gum resin which is obtained from the rhizome or taproots of some of the species of the giant fennels, plants of the genus *Ferula*, particularly *Ferula assafoetida*. These are perennial, umbelliferous plants which grow in a wide arc from the Mediterranean to C. Asia.

The three species which are used to produce the spice asafoetida are *Ferula assafoetida*, *F. foetida*, and *F. narthex*, of which the first two at least are native to both Iran and Afghanistan, while the third is known in Afghanistan and is sometimes called Chinese hing.

The name asafoetida comes from the Persian word *aza* which means mastic resin and the Latin word *foetida* meaning stinking. This name was no doubt given because of the spice's pungent and strong odour. It is interesting to note here that the Indian word hing was used in English from the 16th century; but in England it is now only recognized by oriental and Asian grocers. The apothecaries' Latin name *asa foetida*, used in Latin, French, English, and other European languages since the 14th century, has become the most familiar name.

The plants, by the time they are four or five years old, have massive, thick, fleshy, and woody carrot-shaped taproots, and it is at this stage that the resin is collected. The collection is done before the plant has flowered in spring/early summer. The soil is scraped away from the roots to expose the upper part and a deep incision is made. A milky resinous juice exudes, which starts to coagulate upon exposure to air. This juice has a very strong fetid odour, somewhat similar to that of garlic, mainly due to the presence of sulphur compounds. The freshly exuded resin has a pearly appearance, although the colour darkens during drying in the air. When the product sets to a solid resinous mass, the colour can vary from a greyish or dull yellow colour to black (which should be rejected) but it is usually reddish-brown.

The spice is commercially available in several different forms: 'tears', 'mass', 'paste', and 'powdered'. The tears are the purest form and are rounded or flattened, 5–30 mm ($\frac{1}{5}$–$1\frac{1}{6}$") in diameter.

Lump asafoetida, sometimes called mass, is the most common commercial form, consisting of tears agglutinated into a more or less uniform mass or lump. Powdered asafoetida often contains additions, notably gum arabic, turmeric, and flour (which may be added to diminish the fetid odour, to prevent lumping, or to add colour).

Although it seems that most of the 500 or so tons of ferula gum resins produced annually come from Iran and Afghanistan, asafoetida is now mainly used in India, where it is used as a flavouring for various dishes, and valued for its supposed antiseptic qualities. It is said to counteract flatulence and is often used in the cooking of pulses and other 'windy' vegetables such as cauliflower. It is also a popular flavouring for curries, PAKORA, KOFTA, fish, KACHORI (a kind of POORI stuffed with dal), and in pickles.

Asafoetida is used as a substitute for onions and garlic by the Kashmiri and Hindu Brahmans and by Jains, whose strict vegetarian diets forbid them to use onions.

In Afghanistan it is still used in the preparation of dried meat, on which it is sprinkled with salt. It is thought to have preservative qualities and to be a tenderizer. Strabo, in his *Geography*, records that Alexander the Great's soldiers used it for this last purpose on their march through Afghanistan.

Asafoetida is not well known in the West although it is said to be one of the supposedly secret ingredients of WORCESTERSHIRE SAUCE.

Only small amounts of asafoetida are needed for flavouring food. A pinch of the powder will do. When this is added to hot oil and fried, it changes character and the powerful smell becomes an oniony aroma. Chandra Dissanayake (1976) describes how in some cases when people dislike the flavour and smell of asafoetida, a small piece the size of a small marble is stuck to the inner side of the lid so that the steam melts a very small portion into the dish. This piece of asafoetida can be used over and over again.

Just how far back the use of asafoetida goes is an open question, but cuneiform tablets show that it was cultivated for medicinal purposes as long ago as 750 BC in Babylon and the Greeks and Romans certainly knew it. The Greeks called it *silphion medikon*, meaning silphium from Media (Iran), and the Romans used asafoetida as a substitute for SILPHIUM which was a highly prized spice. (Asafoetida, like silphium, was expensive and APICIUS describes how to make it last longer by keeping a small piece in a jar of pine nuts which then become impregnated with the strong flavour. When required for cooking, a few of the nuts were crushed and added to the dish. Fresh nuts were then placed in the jar to replace those removed.)   (HS)

READING: Helen Saberi (1993).

ASHANTI PEPPER *Piper guineense*, a kind of PEPPER grown and used in W. Africa, especially Guinea, is also known under the name Benin pepper (and, sometimes, Guinea pepper). It is milder than regular black pepper.

ASH-KEYS the fruits of the European ash, *Fraxinus excelsior*. The name is given to them because they hang in pendent clusters, like a bunch of keys. Each fruit has a 'wing' attached to help dispersal.

Ash-keys in the green state are sometimes pickled. The practice used to be more widespread, and there are many recipes in 17th- and 18th-century cookery books. That by Evelyn (1699) is precise:

Ashen Keys. Gather them young, and boil them in three or four Waters to extract the bitterness; and when they feel tender, prepare a Syrup of sharp White-wine Vinegar, Sugar, and a little Water. Then boil them on a very quick Fire, and they will become a green colour, fit to be potted so soon as cold.

The keys have a slightly aromatic and bitter taste. Hulme (1902) justly observed: 'After one's first taste one is not conscious of any special hankering for them.'

Other species of ash in various parts of the world yield edible exudations (see MANNA) or have bark and roots from which a tonic substance is extracted; but the main value of all species is in the wood.

ASIAGO an Italian cheese named for the commune of Asiago in the province of Vicenza, had only local importance until the 20th century, but is now better known and has become a protected name. It is made from cow's milk, in the form of wheels weighing from 9 to 14 kg (20 to 30 lb). It is called *mezzanello* and used as a table cheese when six months old. *Asiago vecchio* and *stravecchio* have been aged for 12 and 18 months respectively, and are used for grating, especially over MINESTRONE. It is not unlike the GRANA cheeses.

ASPARAGUS is the young shoot of a curious, almost leafless plant, *Asparagus officinalis*, of the lily family. There are several other *Asparagus* spp, native to various parts of the Old World.

The wild form of *A. officinalis* grows in marshy places in Europe, e.g. in Poland and Russia. In the cultivated form, selective breeding and special growing techniques have combined to give a greatly thickened, fleshy shoot which has been prized as a delicacy since ancient times. However, the much thinner shoots of wild asparagus are often edible and are still eaten.

The name 'asparagus' was used in classical Greece and Rome. Bitting (1937) traces it back to the Persian word *asparag*, meaning a sprout, and recounts the subsequent development of the name in English. 'Sperage' was current in the 16th and 17th centuries, but was displaced by 'sparagus' and by the appealing term 'sparrow grass'. During the 19th century 'asparagus' took over, and 'sparrow grass' came to be thought of as a term used by the illiterate. However, 'grass' has remained in use among those who grow or process asparagus.

The early Greeks are not known to have cultivated the plant, but the Romans grew asparagus in their gardens from quite early times, as Cato and Columella attest. By the 1st century AD Pliny the Elder could describe asparagus spears grown at Ravenna, in heavily manured soil, as being 'three to the pound' (larger than modern kinds). Pliny's ascription of medicinal virtues to asparagus was echoed and amplified in later centuries; its medical reputation may have been helped by the noticeable although harmless odour which it imparts to the urine of those who eat it. The specific name *officinalis* means 'of the dispensary'.

After the fall of the Roman Empire, asparagus cultivation continued in Syria, Egypt, and Spain, with help from the Arabs who occupied all these countries. Eventually it arrived in the main part of Europe: France before 1469 and England by 1538. Cultivation was well below the standard reached by the Romans; Gerard's *Herbal* of 1597 describes the shoots as being only the size of a large swan's quill, thinner than a pencil.

Asparagus was not grown on a large scale in N. America until the latter half of the 19th century. During the same period it was spread to China and the Malay peninsula by European influence. The Malay name, *saparu keras*, is evidently a corruption of 'sparrow grass'.

The peculiar way in which asparagus has to be grown explains its high price. For the first two years after sowing, a bed of asparagus is unproductive. In the third year the shoots are thick enough to be marketed, and the bed continues to yield good asparagus for another couple of seasons, but quality then declines. So at any given time a grower has half his land in an unproductive state. Furthermore, careful tending and hand harvesting are essential.

The careful tending used to include some strange practices, including the burial of horns, especially those of sheep, in the beds. Remarking on this, Bitting (1937), whose essay on all aspects of asparagus and its production and conservation is unrivalled, observes that the detailed description of asparagus husbandry given in *Adam's Luxury and Eve's Cookery* (1744) can serve to represent standard European practice of that time, which is in turn the foundation of modern practice.

Sometimes the asparagus bed is earthed up to keep the shoots white, and they are excavated and cut when they appear at the surface. In Belgium, Germany, and most of France white is preferred. In Britain, most of Italy, and much of the USA (but with local differences) coloured asparagus is usual; but asparagus which is grown for canning is almost always blanched.

Asparagus is normally cooked, preferably by steaming in the special tall utensil designed for the purpose. Conventionally it is served lukewarm, not hot, with melted butter or HOLLANDAISE or some such rich, mild-flavoured sauce. However, eating asparagus raw is not unknown. John Evelyn (1699) wrote that 'sperage' was 'sometimes, but very seldom, eaten raw with *Oyl*, and *Vinegar*', and the most tender spears are occasionally still eaten raw, especially in the USA.

The asparagus of Argenteuil, near Paris, enjoyed great fame from around 1830, when a certain M. Lhérault-Salbœuf began to introduce improvements in asparagus-growing. These led to giant blanched stalks which, according to one critic, had no flavour and would only be eaten for the sauce. The quest for ever larger stalks resulted, by the 1930s, in some which measured up to 18 cm (7") in circumference and over half a kilo (1.25 lb) in weight. However, Parisians preferred the asparagus of Argenteuil to any other kind. At least two important cultivars are named for Argenteuil. Cultivation there ceased in 1990, but the methods used live on elsewhere.

Jersey Giant, with purple tips, is one of several varieties which compete in terms of heavy production and size of shoots; it has the advantage of being a purely male type (the male being, in this particular arena, more vigorous than the female). Some varieties are naturally dark green, some light green, and some violet.

Because cultivated asparagus is expensive, substitutes have been used. Some are wild species, e.g. *A. acutifolius*, of the Mediterranean region, which has a particularly strong flavour. Others include the shoots of both wild and cultivated HOPS, *Humulus lupulus*, known as 'hop tops'.

So-called 'Bath asparagus' in England is *Ornithogalum pyrenaicum*, a beautiful wild lily which was formerly sufficiently abundant to be gathered before flowering and sold in the markets at Bath and Bristol, for eating like asparagus.

ASPIC the name for a clear savoury JELLY used for holding together or garnishing cold meat or fish dishes, has an uncertain derivation and dates back only to the late 18th century, when it meant the whole dish not just the jelly element.

Aspic is properly made, as its great proponent CARÊME would have insisted, from knuckle of veal or calf's foot, but ready-to-use powdered aspic is widely used.

AŞURE (Noah's pudding), made in Turkey and other countries of the Middle East and Balkans, can correctly be described as a 'legendary' pudding. The word *aşure* comes from the Arabic *ashura* which means the tenth day of the holy month of Muharram, the first month of the Muslim calendar. According to tradition a number of significant events happened on this day: Adam met Eve; Abraham was delivered from the fire; and Jacob was reunited with Joseph. It was also on this day, according to legend, that a special pudding was made by Noah and his family when the waters of the great flood subsided and they were able to leave the ark. The pudding was made with all the foodstuffs remaining on board; wheat, rice, beans, chick peas, dried fruits, and nuts. Nowadays the ingredients vary according to the harvest of the country, availability, and preference.

In modern times a pudding of this name has been made in memory of Noah's survival and as a token of thanksgiving, to be offered to relatives, friends, and neighbours, and a symbol of generosity.　　HS

ATHENAEUS author of *The Deipnosophists* ('professors of dining' or perhaps 'professors at dinner'). This is a compilation of Greek wisdom and anecdote on food, dining, and entertainment, threaded together in the form of a series of dinner conversations, by a Greek scholar who probably lived and worked in Rome about AD 200, when (as Gibbon said) 'the Empire of Rome comprehended the fairest part of the earth, and the most civilised portion of mankind'.

Athenaeus (Athenaios) was born in the old Greek trading post of Naucratis in Egypt. Nothing is known of his life, but *The Deipnosophists* was not his only work: he had written something on the rulers of Syria, and had compiled a commentary on *The Fishes* by Archippus, a 5th-century BC comedy (now lost) which had no doubt been full of obscure names of fishes. The conversations in the *Deipnosophists*, though evidently fictional, involve some real people, including the famous physician GALEN (died AD 199) and the great jurist Ulpian (died *c*. AD 223), who comes across here as a pedant. It is possible that Athenaeus knew these people, but it is unwise to imagine (as some have done) a real literary circle somehow matching the one in the *Deipnosophists*. These conversations are a way of recording the researches of Athenaeus himself.

There is a sequence of topics, at times almost lost in continual digressions. Book 1 dealt with the literature of food, food and drink in Homer, and wine; books 2–3 hors d'œuvres, bread; book 4 the organization of meals, music; book 5 lavish display and luxury; book 6 parasites, flattery; books 7–8 fish; book 9 meat, poultry; book 10 gluttony and more wine; book 11 cups and dishes; book 12 social behaviour; book 13 love, women; book 14 more music, desserts; book 15 wreaths and perfumes.

The speakers are ready with quotations from a dizzying range of earlier Greek literature: literary (comedies, memoirs, epics), historical, medical, scientific, lexicographical. Several hundred authors are cited, many of whom are otherwise quite unknown: usually full references are given including author, title, and book number. Some of these quotations are extracted from dictionaries and other secondary sources but even so Athenaeus must have read widely in the older literature of Greece. Possibly the most recent author cited in the *Deipnosophists* is mentioned at the end of a survey of names for loaves.

'Allow me not to list—since, sadly, memory fails me—all the cakes and sweets given by Aristomenes of Athens in *Religious Requisites* III,' [said Pontianus.] 'I myself, when young, knew this author as an old man, an actor in classical comedy and a freedman of that very cultured monarch Hadrian, who used to call him "Athenian Partridge".'

'Freedman!' said Ulpian. 'Now which early author used that word?'

Someone said that Freedmen, is the title of one of Phrynichus's plays . . . We were at last about to get to grips with the bread when Galen said: 'We shan't start dinner before we have told you what the medical fraternity have to say about bread.'

The dialogue format gave Athenaeus the excuse to incorporate masses of fascinating material which any other structure would have excluded. The great advantage of it to any historian using the book is that it allowed the bringing together of verbatim quotations from many genres, bearing on the topic in different ways, contributing to a more rounded picture of Greek social life. The format also allowed Athenaeus to lay down quick, trenchant, even scurrilous opinions which would have had to be toned down if he had been writing plain history. Admittedly it brought artistic problems. Real conversation is desultory and repetitive: so is Athenaeus. However, he was an assiduous student of Greek social history, and his work is a treasury for modern readers interested in ancient food—as well as for literary scholars who burrow in it for fragments of lost works, from Sappho to Archestratus.

The *Deipnosophists* survived the medieval period in one 10th-century manuscript now in Venice—but the whole of books 1–2 and a few other pages were long ago lost. Although an abridgement known as the Epitome helps

to fill the gaps, the abridged books 1 and 2 which it offers are unattractive to read.   AD

ATOLE (or atolli), a beverage made from ground maize, of Maya origin. Diana Kennedy (1986) uses a quotation from *Travels in the New World* by the 18th-century writer Thomas Gage to show how it appeared to the incoming Europeans:

Here are also two cloisters of nuns [in the Dominican convent in Oaxaca], which are talked of far and near, not for their religious practices, but for their skill in making two drinks, the one called chocolate and the other atole, which is like unto our almond milk, but much thicker, and is made of the juices of the young maize or Indian wheat, which they so confection with spices, musk and sugar that it is not only admirable in the sweetness of the smell, but much more nourishing and comforting to the stomach. This is not a commodity which can be transported from thence, but is to be drunk there where it is made.

The last comment no doubt reflects the fact that, unlike the other important maize drink of the Maya, POSOLE, atole calls for a cooking vessel, which would have been a heavy clay pot. So, while soldiers or messengers on the road could mix their *posole* with water in the lightweight and almost unbreakable calabash cups which they carried with them everywhere, they would not normally be carrying the wherewithal for preparing atole. Sophie Coe (1994) compares the two beverages in other respects, and describes some of the more complex forms of atole and some of the myths about it.

AUBERGINE (or eggplant, the name used in N. America), *Solanum melongena*, botanically a fruit but usually counted as a vegetable. It originated in India, and is now grown in suitable climates worldwide.

Both its names are of interest. 'Aubergine' has a complicated derivation, which prompted Leclerc (1927) to write:

The word aubergine is amongst those which must fill with joy the souls of those philologists whose innocent mania is to claim that every term in the language derives from Sanskrit; without in the least being forced into the tortuous acrobatics which such exercises usually entail, they may elegantly and painlessly prove that *vatin gana*, the name of the aubergine in Sanskrit, gave birth to the Persian *badingen*, from which the Arabs derived *albadingen*, which via the Spanish *albadingena* became the aubergine.

The Arabic name produced the usual modern Indian name *brinjal*. Meanwhile, through the Provençal corruption *meringeane*, another French name, *melongene*, became the species name of the fruit.

'Eggplant' is not an appropriate name for the varieties sold in western countries, most of which look like purple truncheons. However, small round white eggplants are still popular in Spain in pickled form (*en escabeche*). And in Asia there is a wide range of varieties with smaller fruits, including pale green and white ones which may be spherical or egg shaped. In Australia it may be eggfruit, and in W. Africa it is often called garden egg.

A third group of names, surviving in the modern Italian *melanzana* and Greek *melitzana*, comes from the Latin *mala insana*, meaning 'apple of madness'.

Although the aubergine is believed to be of Indian origin, the first surviving mention of it is in a Chinese work on agriculture of the 5th century AD, the *Ts'i Min Yao Shu*.

Aubergines soon became popular throughout Asia and the Near East, since their mild flavour and spongy texture suited them for many combinations with other vegetables and meat. They arrived in Europe both through the invasion of Spain by the Moors and by means of Italian trade with the Arabs, which became important in the 13th century. A writer of this time, Albertus Magnus, mentions them. The first types to reach Europe were egg shaped, which explains the name 'eggplant'; they included purple and whitish or yellow ones.

For a long time Europeans considered the aubergine inedible, gave it insulting names, and grew it only as an ornamental plant. But during the 15th century it gradually gained acceptance. By 1500 it was well enough known for the early Spanish and Portuguese colonists to take it to America, where it grew well and became a popular vegetable, which it still is. In the W. Indies it bears the name 'brown jolly', presumably a corruption of *brinjal*, due to Indian immigrants.

Back in Europe, the aubergine has for some time been firmly established in regional cuisines: in Greek MOUSSAKA; in the Levantine *baba ghanoush*—grilled, puréed aubergines with garlic, lemon juice, and parsley ('poor man's caviar'); in the Italian *melanzane parmigiana* (topped with melted GRANA cheese); and in the Provençal mixed vegetable stew RATATOUILLE *niçoise*, where it blends harmoniously with tomatoes, onions, and sweet capsicums. A frequent use in the Near East is to stuff aubergines; the shape of the larger varieties is highly suitable for this purpose.

The most famous aubergine dish, eaten all over the Arab world, is called *Imam bayildi*—'the priest fainted'. This consists of aubergines stuffed with onions (also, in some recent recipes, with tomatoes) and cooked with olive oil. There are two stories about the origin of the name. One is that the priest fainted because of the deliciousness of the dish; the other is that he fainted when he heard how much oil his wife had used in making the recipe. The ability of aubergines to soak up vast amounts of oil is legendary. One way to avoid it is to cover slices with salt and leave them for a while so that the salt collapses the cells. This technique was devised to draw out the bitter juice which primitive varieties contained; but with modern aubergines bitterness is not a problem.

In India, Iran, and Afghanistan, aubergines are made into a hot pickle. There and in China and SE Asia the small, round varieties, including some no bigger than grapes, are the ones most often seen in the markets. Aubergines are nearly always eaten cooked, but the small fruits of a related wild species, *S. torvum*, are sometimes eaten raw (and also cooked) in Indonesia.

Facciola (1990), writing of the related *S. aethiopicum*, the African scarlet eggplant or garden egg, states that the orange-red fruits, which are cooked and eaten like aubergines, are sometimes known as 'tomatoes of the Jews of Constantinople', the reference being to the Ladinos, Jews expelled from Spain to Constantinople at the end of the 15th century. He speculates that their ancestors may have carried this crop with them when they were expelled from Timbuktu a century earlier.

AU BLEU a method of cooking certain freshwater fish, especially TROUT. The fish should be still alive when the procedure starts. It is then killed by banging its head on something solid, gutted through the gills, sprinkled with vinegar, and put at once into a boiling COURT BOUILLON. The effect of the vinegar on the mucus which covers the body of the fish is to turn it blue; and the sudden immersion in boiling liquid, given the totally fresh state of the fish, is to cause the body to arch into a crescent shape, a characteristic of this technique.

AUSTRALASIAN 'SALMON' is now the official marketing name in Australia for two species of fish which are not even distantly related to the salmon of the northern hemisphere, but belong to the family Arripididae. They are two species: *Arripis trutta* (also known as 'salmon trout') and *A. truttaceus*. In the same genus there is another species which makes better eating. This is *A. georgianus*, popularly known as the ruff or tommy ruff (again, nothing to do with anything bearing that name in the Old World), but now officially called 'Australian herring' (one more aberration).

A. trutta is abundant in the waters of southern Australia, and in New Zealand, where it is known by the Maori name

kahawai. It may reach a length of 90 cm (3'). The flesh is not highly esteemed, although Roughley (1966) pointed out that its texture and flavour improve when it is canned.

The ruff, on the other hand, although a smaller fish, makes good eating; its flesh is tender and tasty.

AUSTRALIA It is something of a paradox that the world's geologically oldest continent should be developing one of the world's newest cuisines.

Australia is a large island of some 7.7 million square km (2.9 million square miles) (including the smaller island of Tasmania, to the south), surrounded by nearly 37,000 km (23,000 miles) of coastline. While nearly two-thirds of the continent is classified as having a temperate climate, there are many different climatic zones, including palm-fringed coasts and tropical rainforests as well as arid deserts. Much of southern Australia experiences a typical Mediterranean climate with hot dry summers and predominantly winter rainfall.

Australia was physically isolated from the rest of the world for over 40 million years and has enormous biological diversity. It is rich in flora (for example, its 25,000 plant species are more than Europe has) but relatively poor in fauna with just over 2% of the world's freshwater fish species.

When the first Aborigines arrived in Australia, at least 60,000 years ago, primitive humans all lived as hunter-gatherers; the beginnings of agriculture in the northern hemisphere were not yet apparent. In Australia they remained hunter-gatherers, in some areas developing a rudimentary agriculture but typically practising 'firestick farming' (deliberate burning of small patches of land to encourage plant growth and make hunting easier) as a way of curating resources and ensuring continuity of food supply, particularly of medium-size mammals. While they tended to live in harmony with the environment, they also had an impact on it; Aboriginal hunting may have been responsible for extinction of some of the giant marsupials which existed some 30,000 years ago.

As in all hunter-gatherer societies, the Aborigines ate a very wide variety of plants (fruits, roots, tubers, leaves, flowers), insects (WITCHETTY GRUBS, Bogong moths), small reptiles (SNAKES, lizards, goannas), and larger game (KANGAROO, EMU, wallaby). They developed techniques of dealing with potentially harmful foods such as CYCAD seeds (*Macrozamia* spp) which, when eaten untreated by some of the early explorers and settlers, caused violent vomiting and diarrhoea. Their harvesting was not indiscriminate; they knew the right time of the year for maximum flavour and

nutritional value, how to identify ideal conditions of ripeness and palatability, how to dig roots so as not to disadvantage the harvest in following seasons. They also developed a kind of gastronomic code such that certain animals or certain parts of animals had greater prestige—for example, the liver of BARRAMUNDI.

Much of this local knowledge was ignored by the first white settlers who arrived (the majority as convicts) in 1788, and who sustained themselves with predominantly imported rations until about the turn of the century. From the 1830s, however, there were many who emigrated voluntarily, attracted by the potential of a new land. These colonists were more enthusiastic about the local resources and were happy enough to accept and incorporate indigenous foods, especially those having some resemblance to familiar ones, as this account by Mundy (1862) of a dinner in Sydney in 1851 demonstrates:

The family likeness between an Australian and an Old Country dinner-party became, however, less striking when I found myself sipping doubtfully, but soon swallowing with relish, a plate of wallabi-tail soup, followed by a slice of boiled schnapper, with oyster sauce. A haunch of kangaroo venison helped to convince me that I was not in Belgravia. A delicate wing of the wonga-wonga pigeon and bread sauce, with a dessert of plantains and loquots, guavas and mandarine oranges, pomegranates and cherimoyas, landed my imagination at length fairly at the Antipodes.

Virtually all species of wildlife were considered edible game—emu, possum, bandicoot, wombat, flying fox, echidna (described as excellent eating, with a flesh resembling pork). Kangaroo, in particular, was much esteemed, and was even sold on a commercial basis in the main towns. The tail was made into soup, and the meat generally roasted, stewed, or 'steamed'. The 'kangaroo steamer', nominated as the national dish of Tasmania during the 19th century, was made of finely chopped or minced kangaroo plus salt pork or bacon, similarly prepared, a little seasoning and a very small amount of liquid, cooked slowly in a tightly closed pot beside the fire.

Ingredients from the plant world were also eaten or used in cooking but, being more peripheral to sustenance, were less often written about. The Tasmanian pepper leaf (*Tasmannia* spp) was used as a spice, and fruits such as lillypillies (*Eugenia* spp), rosella (*Hibiscus sabdariffa*, see ROSELLE), and local 'currants' (*Leptomeria* spp) were made into jams and jellies; in a letter to Eliza ACTON in 1853 William Howitt describes using a preserve of native currants in fruit puddings. Such indigenous fruits seem, however, to have been an acquired taste, and neither as desirable nor as sweetly satisfying as fruit from imported species which had been cultivated and selected over many centuries and which thrived in the temperate climate. (A recipe for native currant jam calls for almost twice as much sugar as fruit.) Among other wild plants, pigweed (PURSLANE, *Portulaca oleracea*) and FAT HEN (*Chenopodium* spp) were cooked as a kind of substitute for spinach; pigweed was also eaten raw in salads.

In the early days of the colony cooking was often a matter of improvisation. Pieces of meat were jammed on sticks and cooked over an open fire (the 'sticker-up'). Damper cooked in the ashes (see BREAD VARIETIES) became the ubiquitous substitute for oven-baked bread; because of the difficulty of obtaining yeast, carbonate of soda and tartaric acid were used as rising agents. The same dough, cooked as small flat cakes in a frying pan, produced 'leather-jackets'; fried in fat, they were known as 'fat-cakes'.

Damper and meat were inevitable partners in the monotonous bush diet, washed down by plenty of tea (up to three pints per day, according to one contemporary account)—a consequence in part of the cheapness and abundance of meat and of the primitive living conditions, but also a reflection of the basic rations decreed since convict days: flour, meat, tea, and sugar. Australian annual meat consumption in the 19th century was amongst the highest in the world, averaging around 125 kg (nearly 300 lb) per person. Meat was eaten three times a day, but little attempt was made to develop imaginatively complex dishes around this ingredient; rather, people continued what Muskett (1893) called 'the conventional chain of joints, roasted or boiled, and the inevitable grill or fry'. Colonial Goose and Carpet Bag Steak (a thick slab of rump, slit through the centre and filled with fresh oysters, then grilled over the coals and sauced with anchovy butter), which first appeared in cookery books at the end of the 19th century, may have been exceptions. (Colonial Goose, also known as Barrier Goose and Oxford Duck, was simply a boned leg of mutton with a sage-and-onion stuffing.) Vegetable cookery was also unimaginative (protracted boiling in plenty of water), and the range of vegetables typically eaten was rather limited, though home gardens produced a great diversity of vegetables, including a variety of salad greens. Tomatoes flourished, and were far more commonly eaten than in England, for example; a series of correspondence in the *Melbourne Argus* in 1856 shows that they were eaten in salads, stewed, roast, fried, baked with breadcrumbs, made into sauces for immediate use or for keeping, pickled, and made into jam.

One reason for this dullness of the daily fare was the lack of culinary skills amongst colonial cooks, amply testified by visitors to Australia; another was the stoic resistance to 'dressed up' dishes, a carryover of the English heritage. Further, at a time when physical labour demanded substantial meals for men, men's tastes demanded plain, wholesome food and plenty of it. Thus there was little incentive to develop 'dainty dishes' for main courses, and even less when thrift and economy were considered more important than flavour. Stews were basically meat, water, salt and pepper, and a little flour. As in England, however, there were pretensions to a French-style cuisine amongst an educated minority; a menu from a Sydney restaurant, Paris House, in 1910 listed 'Filets de Soles, Marguery', 'Artichaut vinaigrette', 'Bouchées Luculus', and 'Petit Poussin en Casserole et Salade'.

One area in which Australian women excelled, and where their creativity was indulged and expressed, was baking. Novelist Hal Porter (1963) fondly recalled his mother's ritualistic weekend baking in the 1920s:

Saturday afternoon is for baking. This is a labour of double nature: to provide a week's supply of those more solid delicacies Australian mothers of those days regard as being as nutritionally necessary as meat twice daily, four vegetables at dinner, porridge and eggs and toast for breakfast, and constant cups of tea. . . . Mother, therefore, constructs a great fruit cake, and a score or more each of rock cakes, Banburies, queen cakes, date rolls and ginger nuts. . . . three-storeyed sponge cakes mortared together with scented cream . . . cream puffs and éclairs.

Turn-of-the-century recipe books usually devote considerably more pages to pies, puddings, cakes, scones and biscuits, etc. than to savoury dishes of meat, fish, poultry, and vegetables. While most of these sweet recipes were direct imports from Britain, a number of Australian specialities were developed, including anzacs (see BISCUIT VARIETIES), butterfly cakes (small cup cakes with a circular wedge cut from the top, the hollow filled with whipped cream, and the two halves of the wedge placed on the cream so as to look like butterfly wings), melting moments, LAMINGTONS, the SPONGE CAKE, the Australian BROWNIE, a simplified version of BARM BRACK, and PAVLOVA.

It would be easy to describe Australian cuisine as static during the first half of the 20th century, though tastes subtly shifted from mutton to lamb. Suggested family menus show little change, with dishes such as roast mutton, braised steak, steak and kidney pudding, and SHEPHERD'S PIE, typically followed by stewed fruit and baked and steamed PUDDINGS. Nevertheless, some subtle changes are evident. First, a more urbanized population was less reliant on

native foods and ingredients, and both local game and fruits faded from use. Second, changes in technology ushered in new dishes. With the introduction and acceptance of refrigerators came ice creams and ice blocks and an increased variety of chilled desserts (especially dishes using commercial gelatin and jelly crystals); with electric and gas stoves, and the new oven-to-table cooking and serving dishes, came casseroles (cooked in the oven) and 'mornays', a mainstay of mid-century entertaining.

On the other hand, the post-war period introduced enormous changes in what was produced, cooked, and eaten in Australia. Increased affluence coincided with a growing interest in wine, food, and eating out, and with increased numbers of restaurants. Travel brought contact with other cultures and cuisines, both Asian and European, and familiarity with new ingredients and foods; and at the same time waves of immigrants from Europe, particularly Mediterranean Europe, and then Asia, made these ingredients and foods available in Australia. The once traditional Sunday family dinner of roast leg of lamb with mint sauce has been replaced by the casual BARBECUE where kangaroo sausages may cook alongside bratwurst or MERGUEZ, chicken SATAYS next to oregano-marinated lamb KEBABS. The net effect has been the virtual extinction of the British-inherited diet and cuisine and the encouragement of distinctly and characteristically Australian culinary expressions. This has involved a reappraisal of indigenous resources, including kangaroo, emu, and other game as well as native fruits, seeds, and herbs, such as the QUANDONG, MACADAMIA NUT, bush tomato (*Solanum* spp), wattle seed (see ACACIA AND WATTLE), and wild lime (*Microcitrus* spp). Other additions to the larder are the wide variety of Asian vegetables, fruits, and herbs which can be grown in Australian climates. There is increasing recognition of regional diversity, such as the particular qualities of oysters from different sources, and of the gastronomic identity of different regions. The potential of long-established and climatically sympathetic species such as OLIVES (first introduced to Australia in 1800) is being realized. Specialized, small-scale agriculture and food initiatives—growing PISTACHIOS or producing goat- and sheep-milk cheeses analogous to traditional Mediterranean varieties—are being encouraged.

Australian kitchens have embraced Asian culinary techniques and flavour combinations; stir-frying is probably as common as were grilling and frying in Muskett's day (most gas cooker tops are now specifically designed to accommodate a wok) and GINGER, GARLIC, and SOY SAUCE are as much staple ingredients as TOMATO sauce. In restaurants, 'Australian' cuisine acknowledges influences from both Asia and Europe, especially the Mediterranean regions, adapted to accommodate Australian ingredients. BS

READING: Symons (1982), Beckett (1984), Isaacs (1987), Low (1989), Cherry Ripe (1993).

AUSTRIA one of the two most direct heirs of the former Austro-Hungarian Empire, might be expected to have interesting culinary traditions, and does not disappoint. Special features of the Austrian cuisine include the layer cakes such as SACHERTORTE for which Vienna is famous. HUNGARY, as the other direct heir of the former empire, enjoys similar fame for cakes; and it is hard to know whether Vienna or Budapest is the richer in Konditorei, establishments where coffee and cakes can be enjoyed.

Although the neighbouring CZECH AND SLOVAK REPUBLICS may geographically lie at the centre of Europe, Austria is perhaps the archetypal C. European country and, having a common frontier with Italy, has played an important role in the transmission of foods and dishes from the Mediterranean region to countries further north. In this respect the S. Tyrol is of particular interest. It is there that one sees most clearly the interplay of Italian and Austrian dishes, symbolized (as Wechsberg, 1969, points out) by the title of a S. Tyrolean cookbook, *Spaghetti and Speckknödel*. The latter are dumplings made with *Bauernspeck*, carefully cured and smoked bacon, a prominent speciality of the whole of the Tyrol.

Nockerln, the Austrian (and Hungarian) version of Italian GNOCCHI, are small DUMPLINGS which accompany many main dishes; not to be confused with *Salzburger Nockerln*, a sweet soufflé-like confection.

However, it is not only from Italy that southern influences have played on the Austrian kitchen. The Turkish influence is also apparent, e.g. in the pastry for STRUDEL (see also FILO), although not for some other things, such as the CROISSANT, for which it is sometimes given credit (see CULINARY MYTHOLOGY).

Austria is the country to which the institution of MEHLSPEISEN belongs. Austrians would also like to think that the KUGELHOPF, which they certainly prepare very well, had its origin in their country; but the matter is dubious and likely to remain so, given the difficulty of pinpointing the origin of something which has such a long history and is found in such a wide span of European countries. However, there can

be no such doubt about their beloved *Linzertorte*, from Linz, a jam tart decorated with a lattice work of its nut pastry—see TORTE AND KUCHEN.

Writers who have commented on the general characteristics of Austrian cuisine, not least the illustrious and above-mentioned Wechsberg, remark on the tendency of Austrians to have more than three meals a day (they add in a second breakfast, *Gabelfrühstück*, and a tea meal, *Jause*) and their liking for substantial dishes, including many with meat. Along with Wienerschnitzel (see VEAL), which is better known internationally, the Austrian boiled beef dishes, of which *Tafelspitz* is probably the most popular, and Viennese steaks, *Wiener Rostbraten*, and various other beef, pork, and lamb dishes often feature in Austrian menus. *Bauernschmaus* is something like the Alsatian *choucroute garnie* (see SAUERKRAUT). Potatoes also lend weight to Austrian menus. The yellowish and waxy 'Kipfler' potatoes (of the variety whose English name is Austrian Crescent—*Kipfel* meaning croissant) are especially good for the potato salad (with finely chopped onion and condiments) to which Austrians are exceedingly partial. Austrians also attach importance to what they call their 'winter vegetables', which help to keep them going in cold weather, especially if prepared with butter or cream.

There are, naturally, regional differences between the nine provinces in Austria, some reflecting differences in recent history (e.g. the occupation of Lower Austria and Burgenland by the Soviet army after the Second World War, which delayed post-war economic recovery) as well as in geographical features and neighbouring influences. Carinthia in the south has the highest mountain, numerous lakes to provide freshwater fish, and is also the home of *Nudeln*—small, folded noodle squares with many different fillings, *Kasnudeln* (with cheese) being the best known. Styria, bordering on former Yugoslavia, has a reputation for hearty eating (shared, admittedly, with the rest of Austria) and can boast a number of interesting soups, e.g. *Stoss-Suppe* (sour cream and milk, potato, and caraway).

READING: MacDonogh (1992b).

AUTOCLAVE the industrial counterpart of the domestic pressure cooker (see PRESSURE COOKING), a vessel in which temperatures considerably higher than the normal boiling point of water can be reached by increasing the pressure. At atmospheric pressure water boils at 100 °C (212 °F); at 20 lb pressure at 126 °C (259 °F).

An autoclave, like a domestic pressure

cooker, makes it possible to cook in a shorter time. It is also important in sterilization, since the higher temperatures which it attains are effective in killing bacteria which can withstand normal boiling.

See also CANNING.

AUTOLYSIS a process of self-digestion, when the enzymes naturally present in what had been a living organism proceed, after the death of the organism, to break down its cells or tissues. For example, when game birds are hung to tenderize them, autolysis of the connective tissues occurs.

This process is used in the making of yeast extract, where the yeast is broken down by its own enzymes.

AVGOLÉMONO literally 'egg-lemon', the Greek name of a characteristic E. Mediterranean sauce. The name in Arabic (*tarbiya*) and Turkish (*terbiye*) literally means 'treatment; improvement'. Avgolémono may be used either as a sauce for fish, lamb, or vegetables (particularly artichoke) or as a flavouring in various casserole dishes and soups (which it also thickens).

The recipe is simple. Lemon juice is whisked into beaten egg and then hot cooking liquid (e.g. fish broth) is whisked into the mixture. The temperature of the added liquid must be well below boiling point, so that the egg will not coagulate. In some versions of the sauce cornflour is added. Sometimes the sauce is made with only yolks of eggs.

AVICENNA the name by which a famous Persian physician and writer of the 11th century is generally known, although his Arabic name was Ibn Sina. He was born near Bokhara, where his father was a Persian official, and lived his life in various Persian cities, including Ispahan. He is often referred to as an Arabic philosopher; this is perhaps because he did his studying of philosophy, medicine, astronomy, and mathematics in Arabic, the medium through which he knew the writers of classical Greece such as Aristotle.

His own medical work, the *Canon*, was for many centuries the basis of much of medical teaching in the Arabic and western worlds. His principal writings were published in Latin towards the end of the 15th century, and reprinted many times.

The chief importance of Avicenna lay in his preservation and wide dissemination of medical lore from the classical world. In the context of food, he had much responsibility for the transmission of the ideas usually referred to as the FOUR HUMOURS, which deeply influenced medieval cookery in Europe and remained influential until at least the 18th century.

AVOCADO (or avocado pear), *Persea americana*, a fruit unlike any other, with its buttery flesh and single large stone. Of all fruits the avocado is highest in protein and oil content. The latter may reach 30%; and the avocado is therefore a powerful source of energy.

The avocado tree, a member of the laurel family, is native to subtropical America, where it has been cultivated for over 7,000 years, as archaeological remains demonstrate.

There are three original races of the species. The Mexican type, which was called by the Aztecs *ahuacatl* (which meant 'testicle' and is the source of 'avocado'), has a plum-sized, smooth-skinned, purple or black fruit, and foliage with an anise scent. It matures in the autumn and is hardier than other kinds. The Guatemalan type bears larger fruits with a rough skin which is green, purple, or black in colour; these fruits mature in spring or early summer and store well. The W. Indian type has the largest fruits, up to more than 1 kg (2 lb 3 oz) in weight with a smooth skin, usually light green and of medium thickness.

All cultivated avocados are descended from these three types. Many of them are hybrids; for example Fuerte, a prominent Californian variety, and Hass, now the leading cultivar in California, are both Guatemalan/Mexican hybrids. In all there are now at least 500 varieties, of various shapes, sizes, and colours, grown in many countries around the world.

One of the first Europeans to taste the avocado was Fernández de Oviedo, who noticed its external resemblance to a dessert pear, so ate it with cheese; but other Spaniards preferred to add sugar, or salt and pepper. They all praised it. The same applies to the first mention in English, in 1672, by W. Hughes, the royal physician, after a visit to Jamaica. He said that it was 'one of the most rare and pleasant fruits of the island. It nourisheth and strengtheneth the body.'

However, despite such favourable comments, the avocado was slow to spread from its native region. For Europeans, it remained for a long time no more than a tropical curiosity; and commercial cultivation in N. America only began in California in the 1870s and in Florida from about 1900.

Avocados are now grown in Africa, Israel, Australia, Madeira, and the Canaries, as well as in many parts of their native continent.

The avocado ripens off the tree. If picked when fully grown and firm, it will ripen in one to two weeks in a warm room but much more slowly in a refrigerator. The fruit is ripe when it is faintly but perceptibly squashy, especially at the stem end.

The flavour of the avocado is subtle, but so mild as to be easily overwhelmed. It is often served in halves, with a vinaigrette dressing (or a stuffing of, for example, shrimp) in the hole left by taking out the stone.

Perhaps the best-known avocado dish is **guacamole**. So far as pre-Columbian use of the avocado is concerned, Sophie Coe (1994) comments:

The one recipe that we may be sure of is the Aztec ahuaca-mulli, or avocado sauce, familiar to all of us today as guacamole. This combination of mashed avocados, with or without a few chopped tomatoes and onions, because the Aztecs used New World onions, and with perhaps some coriander leaves to replace New World coriander, *Eryngium foetidum*, is the pre-Columbian dish most easily accessible to us. Wrapped in a maize tortilla, preferably freshly made, or even on a tortilla chip, it might ever so distantly evoke the taste of Tenochtitlan.

Avocado leaves, toasted and ground, are occasionally used as a mild spice; those of one variety have an anise-like flavour.

AWO-NORI sometimes spelled *aonori*, the Japanese name of a green seaweed, *Monostroma latissima*, and also of a seasoning prepared from it. The name means 'green nori', NORI being the Japanese name for the most important of the red seaweeds, but used also of certain green and brown ones.

This green seaweed grows in tissue-thin broad 'leaves', perforated by numerous holes. It is sold as dried sheets as well as in powdered form for use as a condiment.

Other kinds of *aonori* include *suji-aonori* (*Enteromorpha prolifera*, called *limu ele'ele* in Hawaii) and *usuba-aonori* (*E. linza*, a worldwide species), both of which have a spicy aroma.

AYRAN (also eyran, airan), the Turkish and Arabic name for a refreshing YOGHURT drink prepared in the Middle East, especially during hot, dry summer months. Yoghurt is mixed with water and thoroughly blended, then seasoned with salt and either freshly chopped mint or dried crushed mint. Finely chopped cucumber is sometimes added. In Iran and Afghanistan a similar drink is made, called *abdugh* and *dogh* respectively.

Other yoghurt drinks made in India include LASSI and *mattha* (literally, BUTTERMILK); *chaach* is yet another, sweetened and flavoured with lemon, mint, and ginger.   HS

AZAROLE (or azerole), *C. azarolus* (sometimes called Naples medlar but no relation to the ordinary MEDLAR), a native of the E. Mediterranean area and Iran. The fruit is cherry sized, red, yellow, or white, or a mixture of colours. Its flesh is crisp and slightly granular, with a strong aroma and a sharp but agreeable flavour. There are three or four hard pips. The fruits have a pit at the end away from the stem, resembling that of the medlar, which partly explains the name 'Naples medlar'.

Azarole has been grown since classical times all over its native region and as far west as Majorca and Spain. It has been introduced to N. America, where there are now named cultivars.

Azeroles are made into jam, eaten as a fresh fruit, and used to flavour a liqueur. READING: Iddison (1994).

AZERBAIJAN is the largest and most populous of the countries of the Caucasus. Of the other two, GEORGIA is to the north and ARMENIA to the south. The other southern neighbour is IRAN, which now includes much of the larger Azerbaijan of former times.

Like Armenia, Azerbaijan underwent— and still bears the marks of—a succession of invasions, including Romans, Persians, Arabs, Mongols, and Turks, the last of whom dominated the country from the 11th century. In recent times, Azerbaijan was a republic in the Soviet Union. Around 70% of the present population are of Tatar stock, speak a language related to Turkish, and are Muslims.

The range of scenery, which is generally beautiful, includes semi-desert, alpine meadows and the coastline on the Caspian Sea. Not much land is devoted to agriculture, but crops are highly diversified, including citrus fruits, vegetables, nuts, and rice. Azerbaijan's rice and fruit, including their grapes, have been prized since ancient times and play an important part in the cuisine.

Naturally enough, there are many points of resemblance between Azerbaijan and Georgia and Armenia. For example, all the Caucasian countries show a liking for sweet and sour. *Kavourma* (see KORMA) in Azerbaijan is often made with sweet and sour flavours, the latter coming from the juice of unripe grapes or lemon juice.

However, there are also noticeable differences. The MEZZE typical of Armenia and Georgia are largely absent. The traditional start to an Azerbaijani meal is simplicity itself: fresh vegetables and herbs— radishes, spring onions, tomatoes, cucumbers, watercress, coriander, and so on. In a full-scale meal, this could be followed by a further introductory course of fresh fruits such as damsons or peaches, lightly fried and maybe sprinkled with lemon juice.

Soups such as the dumpling soup called *Dyushbara* (see JOSHPARA) are popular, as are soups with pasta, rice, yoghurt. CHICKPEAS and PRUNES or damsons may feature in these, as may chestnuts (an Azerbaijani speciality, roasted, blanched, shelled, and cooked in milk). Soups are often flavoured with herbs such as dill or crushed dried mint; and SAFFRON from Iran, which has been described as the national spice of Azerbaijan, can be used here as well in other dishes. Meatballs can be incorporated in the famous soup/stew called *Bozbash* (see also ARMENIA), which exemplifies the tendency in the whole region to create dishes which are on the frontier between soups and stews.

The Caspian coastline, despite pollution, has continued to yield some valuable STURGEON (and caviar), and also other fish, which Azerbaijanis prepare with an enterprising variety of ingredients, including coriander, tarragon, WALNUTS, and fresh and dried fruit such as prunes. POMEGRANATE seeds and pomegranate syrup are favourite accompaniments, as are walnuts. These stock Caucasian items also appear with poultry and game (e.g. in the dish FESENJAN, shared with Iran); and the syrup (or alternatively sour plum sauce) accompanies the ubiquitous kebabs (*shashlik*), which may also be flavoured with SUMAC. Stuffed meatballs may turn out to have sour plums, chestnuts, quince, or prunes inside.

But the pride of Azerbaijani cuisine probably lies with its magnificent *plovs*, related to the *polo* of Iran (usually PILAF in English). A *plov*, served after the fresh vegetables, soup, and a main dish of meat such as kebabs, is considered the centrepiece of the meal. One special *plov* is that made with *kazmag*, a thin round layer of dough made with egg which lines the bottom of the casserole before the rice is put in. The rice, when served, is garnished with wedges of the by now golden brown and crisp *kazmag* crust. The numerous toppings for *plovs* include orange peel and nuts, dried BARBERRIES or other dried fruits, chestnuts, beans, lentils, and so on. Demonstrating further versatility, a *plov* may also be made with fish and even eggs.

According to Pokhlebkin (1984), describing a full Azerbaijani meal: 'The plov is followed by a thick sauce made of grape juice, raisins, almonds and dried apricots. This is the preliminary to the dessert course, which is generally extremely varied, including jams, halvah, sherbets and cakes, served with strong black tea.'

AZTEC FOOD unlike MAYA FOOD and INCA FOOD, is a subject for which relatively rich written source material exists.

Admittedly, all of it has to be read with an eye open for prejudices of one kind or another on the part of the authors, faults of memory, flights of imagination, and vagueness or error in nomenclature. However, the chronicle of Bernal Díaz del Castillo, who accompanied Cortés (the Spanish invader) but wrote his account much later in Guatemala, and the illustrated work in Spanish and Nahuatl (the language of the Aztecs) of Father Sahagún, written in the 1530s, are full of fascinating detail for food historians.

The Aztecs, coming south from the deserts of N. Mexico, had in the 14th century occupied sites in the valley of Mexico, an area rich in lakes, whose produce (fowl of many kinds, fish, frogs, water insects, algae) the newcomers adopted with enthusiasm. They flourished and established their dominion over a wide area. The power wielded by their emperor Motecuhzoma (Montezuma is a Spanish mangling of his name, which means 'angry like a lord') was such that one might have expected them to withstand a relatively small force of Spaniards under Cortés. However, the New World had never seen anything remotely like these strangers with their ships, horses, and cannons. The impact was something like the effect which would be produced on the western world today by a combination of the Second Coming with an invasion by beings from outer space. The question was: were the newcomers gods or mortals? And Motecuhzoma tested the matter with gifts of food. His first offerings made the Spaniards feel ill because he had caused them to be splattered with blood, thinking that this would be suitable for gods. Later, Sahagún tells us, they feasted agreeably on 'white tortillas, grains of maize, turkey eggs, turkeys, and all kinds of fruit'. He gives a list of 25 'fruits', including four varieties of SWEET POTATO, sweet manioc (see CASSAVA), AVOCADOS, and some CACTI. It is said that they flinched from CHOCOLATE at first, but when the Indians set the example they drank and found it good.

When Cortés and his men, including Bernal Díaz, who was later to record the events, reached the capital of Motecuhzoma, they were entertained at what seemed to them to be a most sumptuous banquet, although it was a standard palace meal. The description by Bernal Díaz of how Motecuhzoma was served and ate, and of the thousands of jars of foaming chocolate, is famous. It contrasts strongly with the general impression of the Aztecs as an abstemious and frugal people, who subsisted on meagre fare and for whom fasts (of which the simplest form was abstaining from salt and chilli) were part of the way of life. Indeed, this contrast illustrates a fundamental dualism in Aztec thought. In

food matters they sought to maintain an equilibrium between abstinence and indulgence.

MAIZE was the staple food of the Aztecs and the focus of a large part of their religion; the cult of the rain god Tlaloc was celebrated so that the rain would fall on the maize, and there was a maize god, Cinteotl, and a maize goddess, Chicomecoatl, as well. Maize was especially revered in the blue-husked form, but Sahagún devotes a highly poetic passage to the white:

The white maize ear—that of the irrigated lands, that of the fields, that of the chinampas . . . is small; it is hard, like a copper bell—hard, like fruit pits; it is clear; it is like a seashell, very white; it is like a crystal. It is an ear of metal, a green stone, a bracelet—precious, our flesh, our bones.

The food value of the maize was greatly enhanced by the process called NIXTAMALIZATION.

Beans and CHIA were important enough to figure as items of tribute paid to the Aztec state, as were AMARANTH and squash seeds. CHILLI was available in many guises. To quote Sahagún again:

The chilli seller . . . sells mild red chillies, broad chillies, hot green chillies, yellow chillies, *cuitlachilli*, *tenpilchilli*, *chichioachilli*. He sells water chillies, *conchilli*; he sells smoked chillies, small chillies, tree chillies, thin chillies, those like beetles. He sells hot chillies, the early variety, the hollow-based kind. He sells green chillies, sharp-pointed red chillies, a late variety, those from Atzitziuacan, Tochmilco, Huaxtepec, Michoacán, Anauac, the Huaxteca, the Chichimeca. Separately he sells strings of chillies, chillies cooked in an *olla*, fish chillies, white fish chillies.

The short list of domesticated creatures was headed by TURKEY and included dog (carefully bred and raised to make succulent eating) as well as, on a much smaller scale, the bees.

The culinary sophistication of the Aztecs is apparent from the extraordinarily long list of spices and flavourings which they would use with chocolate. For this and also for information about the Aztec kitchen, the cooks who worked in them, and Aztec table manners, as well as numerous other connected matters (including the extent and nature of the cannibalism practised), see Sophie Coe (1994). (SC)

AZUKI BEANS (also transliterated, less correctly, as adzuki) are the small, red beans of the annual plant *Vigna angularis* which has for long been cultivated in the Orient. China is probably its original home; and it was introduced into Japan some time between the 3rd and 8th centuries.

After the soya bean, this is the legume most widely used in Japanese cookery. It is tender in texture and has a mild, sweet taste.

It may be used like any other pulse, and the beans may be 'popped' like corn, or dried and ground to produce azuki bean meal. But its main use in Japan is to produce the fresh, sweet bean paste called *an* which is the basis of many Japanese sweet confections. It is made by boiling and pounding the beans and adding sugar syrup, and comes in two varieties: *koshi-an*, a smooth purée, and *tsubushi-an*, in which there are still chunks of bean. The corresponding dried product is *sarashi-an*.

Azuki beans are steamed with sticky rice to make the festive dish 'red rice' (*sekihan*), which is made to celebrate happy family events and for numerous special festivities such as eating *Azuki-gayu* (rice porridge with azuki) on 15 January.

Azuki bean paste is used in China as a filling for MOONCAKES and for Chinese New Year dumplings.

The azuki bean, which has been introduced to Hawaii, the southern USA, S. America, New Zealand, certain African countries, and India, is now widely available. So are cans of azuki bean paste, usually Japanese or Chinese.

BABA a sweetened bread or cake made from rich dough, baked in tall, cylindrical moulds. The shape is Slavic in origin, and of great antiquity. The 12th-century Danish chronicler Saxo Grammaticus describes a Baltic pagan harvest-festival bread as a 'cake, prepared with mead, round in form and standing nearly as high as a person'. The word means 'old woman' or 'grandmother' and refers to the vertical form, an anthropomorphic usage similar to the derivation of PRETZEL from *bracelli*, because the twist of dough resembles folded arms. Conversely, the cylindrical shape also recalls ancient Slavic phallic idols. Imperial Russian copper baba moulds as high as 40 cm (16") are recorded, and it was evident that a true cylinder was the ideal shape, for the dough was not allowed to rise over the top of the mould. In the less well-endowed 20th century, empty cans are often dragooned into service as moulds, and the dough may balloon over the top.

If the shape is Slavic in origin, the same may not be true of the actual recipe—it has been suggested by Lesley Chamberlain (1989) that this came from Italy:

The recipe for it probably came to Poland from Italy in the sixteenth century via Queen Bona, as a transplant of the Milanese panettone. Since then much ritual has surrounded the baking of this fragile masterpiece. Precious pastrycooks declared it needed to rest on an eiderdown before it went in the oven, after which baking took place in an atmosphere of maternity. Men were forbidden to enter the kitchen and no one was allowed to speak above a whisper.

On the other hand, there are rival claims from the Ukraine. Savella Stechishin (1979), writing in an attractive and undogmatic manner, says that baba or babka is one of the most distinctive of all Ukrainian breads, traditionally served at Easter. The name 'baba' is the colloquial Ukrainian word for woman or grandma, while 'babka' is a diminutive of the same word. (The name 'babka' is more commonly used, as the modern loaves are smaller and the name sounds daintier.) She confirms the theory that the shape of the loaf, suggesting a statuesque matron, gave the bread its name and that the fluted tube pan used resembles the skirt of a peasant woman.

Stechishin speculates that the baba-bread may have originated in prehistoric times when a matriarchal system existed in the Ukraine. Apparently priestesses performed various religious rituals some of which may have been connected with fertility (of the soil); hence a special type of ritual bread, the baba-bread, may have been a feature of the ritual. She goes on to say that this event was probably held in the spring, which eventually blended with Easter festivity.

Be all this as it may, the baba's homeland is generally regarded as being W. Russia and Poland. It is related to other Russian festive breads or cakes, such as the Easter *kulich* (see EASTER FOODS), or the *krendel* which is baked in a figure-of-eight shape to celebrate name days. They, however, are fortified with dried fruits and nuts, while the baba was originally plain. Polish and Ukrainian recipes commonly include other flavours (from ingredients such as saffron, almond, cheese, raisins).

Other additions, noticeable in the *Baba au rhum* and other versions which are now part of the international repertoire, consist in adding dried fruits and, more important, soaking the cake in an alcoholic syrup (often rum-based) after it has been made. These changes seem to have been made in France after the baba emigrated westwards to Alsace and Lorraine. This had happened by 1767 (when the term first appears as a French word) and the baba eventually became a well-known French confection. (The last king of Poland, who abdicated in 1736 and was an exile in France, supposedly had a hand in this, but the stories which are recounted in French and other reference works are not convincing.)

To make a baba, yeast is mixed to a liquid batter with flour, eggs, and milk; this is allowed to rise, and then melted butter is beaten in. As for other yeast-risen cakes, much beating is necessary to impart air to the mixture. More eggs are used than in a BRIOCHE dough, for example, and the recipe delays the addition of butter until after the first rise to enable the yeast to work to its full effect. Hence a baba is lighter and spongier than a brioche, with an open texture that makes it ideal for soaking up the syrup or liquor added after cooking (to many its chief attraction).

See also KUGELHOPF, whose history may have been intertwined with that of the baba and SAVARIN, a derivative of baba.

BABACO *Carica pentagona*, a large fruit of Ecuador (where it may also be called *chamburo*), has now been introduced for cultivation elsewhere, e.g. in New Zealand and Europe as far north as the Channel Islands, and is also available in N. America. The plant is not known in the wild, and botanists suggest that it may be a hybrid, perhaps of the mountain pawpaw, *C. candamarcensis*, and another fruit of Ecuador.

The plant is relatively small, given the number and size of fruits which it bears. The fruit may reach a length of 30 cm (1'), is star-shaped in section, and has tender juicy flesh of a pale apricot colour with a mild and faintly acid taste and a delicate fragrance. Since it is normally seedless and the skin (green, turning to yellow when ripe) is soft, the entire fruit can be eaten; or it can be liquidized to make a refreshing drink or be used in ice creams. A little sugar or honey is often added.

BABYLONIAN COOKERY by which is meant that of the Mesopotamians in what is called the Old Babylonian period, has been the subject of recent research, based on a study of three tablets of ancient cuneiform text. These, which are dated to around 1700 BC and were probably found in the south of Mesopotamia, constitute between them a collection of recipes, perhaps the oldest surviving one.

Eveline van der Steen (1995) gives reasons for thinking that these recipes were intended for use in a religious context; and that what would otherwise be puzzling features of them can be explained on the assumption that they are all for versions of a meat-in-sauce dish which would be served to a god in his temple, accompanied by bread (probably mixed barley and wheat) and date cakes, etc. The god (probably Marduk in this instance, as he was the city god of Babylon) would eat behind closed curtains. Leftovers would go to the king.

It was only in 1995 that Bottéro published a full translation and commentary; and discussion will no doubt continue. It does seem clear, however, that these fragments of evidence should not be interpreted as reflecting the food of the common people of the time.

BACON the side of a PIG cured with salt in a single piece. The word originally meant pork of any type, fresh or cured, but this older usage had died out by the 17th century.

Bacon, in the modern sense, is peculiarly a product of the British Isles, or is produced abroad to British methods, specifically for the British market. Denmark is the leader in this field. In Britain itself, many regional variations on cuts and cures for bacon exist. It was formerly sold by cheesemongers, rather than butchers, and the association is still maintained in some shops.

Preserved pork, including sides salted to make bacon, held a place of primary importance in the British diet in past centuries. Pigs were kept by everyone, fed economically on scraps, waste, and wild food. Their salted and smoked meat was useful to give savour to otherwise stodgy dishes, and was especially important for the poor. Cobbett, in *Cottage Economy* (1823), considered the possession of a couple of flitches of bacon did more for domestic harmony than 'fifty thousand Methodist sermons and religious tracts. The sight of them upon the rack tends more to keep a man from stealing than whole volumes of penal statutes.' Victorian and early 20th-century investigations into the conditions of the poor discovered that bacon was a staple of all households except for the most poverty stricken. At this time, it was thought desirable that bacon should be very fat; bacon fat and lard were then much more important sources of fat in the British diet than they now are.

British pigs for both fresh and salted meat had been much improved in the 18th century. During the 19th, Yorkshire Large Whites, Middle Whites, Tamworths, and Lincolnshire curly-coated pigs were the breeds favoured for bacon. However, in mid-century the Danes, seeking a new market for their pigs, bred a very productive bacon pig, the Landrace, and began to export large amounts of bacon to Britain. Nowadays many bacon pigs are hybrids, with Yorkshire Large White and Landrace prominent in their make-up.

The first large-scale bacon curing business was set up in the 1770s by John Harris in Wiltshire. (The Harris firm still exists, though it was taken over by a larger corporation in 1962.) Until this time pigs for London's bacon had been driven long distances on foot before being killed there, which exhausted them and spoiled the meat. Harris realized that it would be more practical to make the bacon where the pigs were and send that to London.

Wiltshire remains the main bacon-producing area of Britain, and the standard commercial method of curing bacon is known as the 'Wiltshire cure'. This was originally a dry cure. The prepared sides of the pig (legs still on, for this method) were strewn with salt and stacked skin side down. (It is during this process that a chemical change, aided by salt-tolerant bacteria and the presence of small amounts of nitrate in the 'pickle', produces the characteristic pink colour of the lean.) After 10 to 14 days, the salt was brushed off and the sides matured for a week before packing. Since the First World War, however, brine has been used, both injected into the sides, and for soaking, in place of dry salt. After maturing, the sides may be smoked.

A Wiltshire side is a large piece of meat, and is divided up for various purposes. The shoulder yields the cheapest bacon; the most valued is back and streaky bacon (from the loin region and the belly respectively); while the legs, removed after curing, provide what is called GAMMON; and other parts of the side may become 'boiling bacon'.

The Wiltshire cure is but one of a number of techniques, reflecting regional preferences for bacon types; while people in the south of England favoured Wiltshire bacon smoked over oak or pine sawdust, people in the north liked 'green bacon' (unsmoked and often cured separately from the legs). Ayrshire bacon, a supremely good Scottish version, is made from skinned and boned meat, rolled and lightly cured. The dry method of curing bacon is still used on some farms; bacon so made is distinguished by its dryness and firmness.

The main British use of bacon is in the thin slices called rashers (formerly, COLLOPS), often fried and served with eggs. Although associated with the 'traditional' English breakfast, this combination is a favourite meal at more or less any time of day. Larger pieces of bacon, or bacon hocks, boiled and served hot or cold with mustard, were much used as standby dishes in poorer households. There are, or were, all kinds of economical dishes, intended to make a little bacon go a long way: cereal and pulse

POTTAGES were early items in this group. Somewhat later, bacon pudding was a common dish in many parts of Britain, in times when every cottager kept a pig. Most regional varieties are suet rolls, or sometimes round puddings, containing bacon, onion, and often sage.

Similar economical practices exist also in many European countries where smoked pork belly is used more as a flavouring than as a meat in its own right.

Preserved pork products which share some of the qualities of bacon are made in other countries. The French use the word *lard* to mean any kind of bacon, but also either fresh or cured (e.g. smoked) pork fat, which they use to add fat to other lean meat when this is roasted, or in other composite dishes. Streaky bacon is termed *lard de poitrine* (*fumé* if smoked, or just *poitrine fumée*). This is added to such dishes as *Choucroute garni* (see SAUERKRAUT). *Lard salé* or *petit salé* is any salt pork, cut into small pieces.

The general German word for bacon is *Speck*, but the Germans tend to use streaky bacon or pure fat only, reserving the rest of the side for other products, for example, LACHSSCHINKEN from the loin. *Speck* is typically cut up small and used to add flavour and fat to boiled dishes.

Italian and Spanish cooks use fatty streaky bacon as an ingredient in made dishes. The Italian PANCETTA and the Spanish tocino are both usually unsmoked; when smoked, the name 'bacon' is often used in either language.

Naturally, there is no bacon in the Middle East, where Islam forbids the eating of pork, or in Jewish cookery; but the strong attraction of bacon is implicit in some ingenious bacon substitutes.

There is no Chinese equivalent to bacon. The closest product is finely sliced streaky pork, sometimes cured, used in many Chinese dishes.   (LM)

BACTERIA minute single-celled organisms which are present more or less everywhere. They resemble plants more than animals, but are usually considered as belonging to a third kingdom, Protista, in which they constitute the group *Schizomycophyta*. With a few exceptions, they do not feed by the ordinary plant process of photosynthesis but live, according to type, on an enormous range of substances including practically everything found in food, as well as in live animals or plants. They reproduce by splitting in half and some, in ideal conditions, can do this every 20 minutes, so they can spread very fast.

The effect of bacteria in foods ranges from highly desirable to harmful. The great majority are neither, though if they are allowed to grow unchecked in food they may spoil it with off flavours from their waste products, or by producing enzymes which cause softening or gases which cause bloating.

Of the really useful species the most familiar are the lactic acid-producing bacteria which cause fermentation in milk products of all kinds, in PICKLES and SAUERKRAUT, in *salami* (see SAUSAGES OF ITALY), and in many of the SOYA BEAN products of the Orient. There are many varieties, each producing characteristic flavours and other effects. It is quite usual for types to work in sequence, one kind replacing another as the acidity increases and often living off the waste products of its predecessor. Typically, *Leuconostoc* spp in plants and *Streptococcus* spp in milk start a fermentation and are succeeded by *Lactobacillus* spp which produce and can tolerate high levels of lactic acid.

Other useful bacteria include acetic acid-producing types such as *Acetobacter aceti*, which turns alcoholic liquids to vinegar; propionic acid producers such as *Propionibacterium shermanii*, which creates the special flavour of Swiss cheese and also forms its 'eyes' by giving off carbon dioxide; *Bacillus subtilis*, which ferments certain vegetable products such as NATTO and ARROZ FERMENTADO; and a motley crew of bacteria which co-operate with MOULDS and YEASTS to develop the flavour of surface-ripened cheese: the most assertive of these is *Bacterium linens*, which gives LIMBURGER cheese its pungent aroma.

It seems safe to assume that all useful bacterial fermentations were discovered by accident, the species involved being endemic in the relevant food or in the environment. It is, however, impossible to be sure that the right organisms are naturally present. Conditions can be adjusted in their favour, as when, in making YOGHURT, the milk is kept above 32 °C (90 °F) so that *Streptoccocus thermophilus* and *Lactobacillus bulgaricus*, which thrive in such warmth, can outgrow and dominate rivals. In commercial food production it is usual to ensure the growth of the right bacteria by first killing off all those present, often by pasteurization, and then adding a pure culture of the desired type. After fermentation the food may be pasteurized again to stop further bacterial action.

Bacteria also have useful effects in living creatures. Nitrogen-fixing bacteria in the root nodules of leguminous plants (such as peas and clover) take in nitrogen direct from the air and pass it on to the plant, both feeding the plant and enriching the soil. Herbivorous animals could not, unaided, digest the cellulose in the plants which they eat. It is bacteria in their digestive tracts which break down the cellulose and change it to digestible sugars. Humans have gut bacteria as well, but these do not supply nourishment from cellulose. They do, however, break down certain plant substances: scientific opinion is still divided on how far, if at all, the process aids the nutrition of the host. One unwelcome by-product is wind.

Some cause disease. For example bacteria in unpasteurized milk have been known to infect those who drink it with polio, tuberculosis, typhoid, diphtheria, undulant fever, and foot and mouth disease. They also cause food poisoning. Fatal BOTULISM is due to toxins created by *Clostridium botulinum*. *Staphylococcus aureus*, a species common on human skin, produces toxins which cause what used to be called 'ptomaine' poisoning; and *Salmonella* spp, abundant in many kinds of raw meat, especially chicken, are a common cause of less serious poisoning (see SALMONELLA). *Campylobacter jejuni*, widespread in animals, causes diarrhoea and a typhoid-like illness.

Harmful bacteria in food can be difficult to suppress. Many species can grow in a wide range of conditions and can survive, to resume growth when they have a chance, in a much wider one.

Aerobic bacteria are those which breathe air and stop breeding (but do not die) when air is excluded. Other, anaerobic, types breed only in airless conditions and stop (but again survive) when air is admitted. Certain types prefer particular temperatures. Thermophilic bacteria breed fastest between 42 °C (104 °F) and 75 °C (160 °F); mesophilic bacteria between 10 °C (50 °F) and 40 °C (104 °F); while psychrophilic bacteria, although they breed fastest between 150 °C (590 °F) and 20 °C (68 °F), can continue to breed right down to −5 °C (23 °F). One example of the way temperature favours different types of bacteria is the spoilage of unpasteurized milk. At room temperature, mesophilic bacteria turn milk sugar to lactic acid so that the milk goes sour. In a refrigerator these organisms are repressed; instead, psychrophilic bacteria attack the milk protein and turn the milk alkaline and smelly.

Only heating well above their preferred temperature, or antiseptic chemicals, can kill bacteria. Chilling, even freezing, or drying causes them to stop growing; but when warmth or moisture return they at once start again. Some bacteria which themselves are killed by heating form spores from which fresh bacteria can later develop; and these spores can survive very high temperatures. The most dangerous of these is *Clostridium botulinum*.

Another problem is that of bacterial toxins. Both *C. botulinum* and harmful *Staphyloccocus* spp poison not by their presence but by the toxins they produce. If they have been allowed to grow for long enough to produce an appreciable amount of toxin, the food is poisonous and remains so no matter how much it is heated.

All these harmful bacteria are common and we are constantly exposed to them; yet they seldom cause illness except in people with weak immune systems—the very young, the very old, and those who are already ill. A healthy person's immune system can kill any bacteria as long as these do not arrive in overwhelming numbers.

BADGER any of a group of stocky omnivorous mammals, of which the European representative is *Meles meles*. Various other species inhabit Asia, Africa, and N. America. They are large, burrowing, nocturnal animals, with strong claws and a thick coat. The European badger has a distinctive striped black and white head and an average weight of around 10 kg (22 lb).

In Ireland, badgers have been eaten and cured in much the same way as we now cure bacon. In England badger fat has been used for cooking, and badgers eaten. Jaine (1986*a*) consulted some of the few written sources before cooking and eating part of a badger which had been mistakenly caught in a fox trap:

The badger is one of the cleanest creatures, in its food, of any in the world and one may suppose that the flesh of this creature is not unwholesome. It eats like the finest pork, and is much sweeter than pork.' So writes Richard Bradley in the early eighteenth century while including a recipe from one R.T. in Leicestershire for brining the gammons before spit-roasting them. Waverley Root calls badger the food of eighteenth-century English peasants seeking more succulent fare. He is accurate in this, for it was by no means dry, and had a pronounced layer of fat over the ham. Where we differ from all those people whose written coments we could find is in comparing it to pork or sucking pig. . . . We found that the most useful comparison was to mutton. The meat was dark, succulent and strong-tasting, but in no way like pork, having a particular smell to it.

Badgers now enjoy a considerable measure of protection in Britain.

BAEL *Aegle marmelos*, a tree which grows wild in much of N. India and SE Asia, belongs to the same family, Rutaceae, as the citrus fruits. It is not related to the quince, although sometimes called Bengal or Indian quince. The fruits, which look something like greyish-yellow oranges, may have a thin hard shell or a less hard but thick rind, depending on the variety.

The ripe pulp is yellow, gummy, and full of seeds. However, it has an aromatic, refreshing flavour. It can be eaten as is or made into a jelly, marmalade, nectar, squash, or sherbet.

Morton (1987) observes that the bael tree was grown by the famous botanist David Fairchild, at his home in Coconut Grove, Miami; this was after he had acquired a taste for the fruit, served with jaggery (see PALM SUGAR) in Sri Lanka. The fruit is similarly served in Indonesia.

Hindus hold the tree sacred to Shiva and use its leaves in his worship. It is sacrilegious to cut down a bael tree, but to die under one assures immediate salvation.

BAGEL a dense round yeast bun with a hole in the middle. A slightly enriched dough is shaped into rings, given a short rise, then thrown into violently boiling water for a matter of seconds before baking. The brief boil makes the crust chewy rather than crisp, a texture reinforced by the short rising time. The crust may be brushed with egg to give gloss (an effect also achieved by putting sugar into the poaching water), and it may be coated with onion flakes, poppyseeds, or sesame. Sweet versions are also made, a common kind containing raisins and cinnamon.

The bagel is a Jewish bread, apparently originating in S. Germany, migrating to Poland and thence to N. America, where it has become the most famous and archetypal Jewish food. Its name derives from the Yiddish *beygel* from the German dialect word *beugel*, meaning 'ring' or 'bracelet'. Its history means, of course, that it is an Ashkenazi rather than a Sephardi food (see JEWISH COOKERY). As Claudia Roden (1996) points out: 'Because of their shape—with no beginning and no end—bagels symbolize the eternal cycle of life.'

The bagel has become generally popular throughout N. America, filled sometimes with cream cheese and lox (smoked salmon from Nova Scotia) or cream cheese and jelly/jam. Some Canadians say that the bagels of Montreal, imprisoned in time in the east-end bakeries of the city, with their wood-fired ovens, and given their preliminary boiling in honey-flavoured water, are best of all: especially the sesame or poppyseed versions. New Yorkers, however, claim that the special quality of New York water makes theirs the best. Wherever they are made, bagels are best eaten very fresh; otherwise they become leathery and have to be split and toasted. (Jewish joke: 'A bagel is a doughnut with rigor mortis.')

In the Rhône Valley, there is a ring-shaped, anis-flavoured roll, called *rioute* and eaten as a snack with wine, which is also briefly boiled before baking. Otherwise the technique applies only to the bagel.

BAILER SHELL *Cymbium melo*, one of the largest edible gastropods (creatures living in single shells). The shell, which may measure 25 cm (10") across, is yellow and red with purplish or black spots. The inhabitant of the shell is itself black with yellow lines, like a huge and exotic snail. This Indo-Pacific species is rarely seen in the markets, but makes good eating and is prized by fishermen in SE Asia, where it is usual to boil the creatures, or fry them with vegetables, or roast them and dip them in a chilli sauce.

The shell itself is of value. 'The flaring apertures of bailer shells make them especially useful, as their name suggests, for the quick bailing of small boats and canoes caught in tropical squalls. They are also used in native markets as scoops for sugar, flour and salt' (Mary Saul, 1974).

BAKED ALASKA a dessert which combines hot MERINGUE and cold ICE CREAM. It is made by placing a well-chilled block of ice cream on a base of SPONGE CAKE, masking it with uncooked meringue, and then baking it in a hot oven for just long enough to brown and set the outside. The recipe exploits the insulating properties of air, trapped in the sponge and meringue, to keep the ice cream solid whilst heating the outside.

Mariani (1994) remarks, in an interesting note, that Thomas Jefferson seems to have devised a dish of this type, but gives main credit for the scientific thinking which led to the dish in its present form to Count RUMFORD. He also observes that the famous chef Charles Ranhofer, to whom some give credit for creating the dish, called it 'Alaska, Florida' in his own mammoth cook book (1893), and that its modern name seems only to have appeared in print in the first decade of the 20th century, e.g. in the 1909 edition of Fannie FARMER's *Boston Cookery Book*.

A French name for a somewhat similar confection is *Omelette* (*à la*) *norvégienne*. This has been current since 1891 and the alternative name *Soufflé surprise* began to be used shortly afterwards. Claudine Brécourt-Villars (1996) mentions also the name *Omelette suédoise*. She concurs in seeing Count Rumford as responsible for the whole idea, but joins Mariani in making a reference to a culinary surprise of this genre which was prepared by a French chef called Balzac for the astonishment of a Chinese delegation visiting Paris in 1867.

BAKED BEANS familiar as a canned product, are derived from a traditional New England dish, Boston baked beans, for which navy beans (see HARICOT BEAN) are baked with spices and molasses (see TREACLE) in a dish in the oven. The Boston connection seems to have arisen because Puritan families in or around Boston used baked beans as a sabbath dish. Use in print of the term 'Boston baked beans' dates back to the 1850s.

BAKEWELL TART (or BAKEWELL PUDDING) is more of a TART than a PUDDING, but was always known as a pudding until the 20th century. It is still so called in the Derbyshire town of Bakewell, but the name 'tart' is now generally prevalent.

Medieval precursors date back to the 15th century and were called 'flathons' (see FLAN). There were two main kinds. One was filled with a sweet, rich egg custard over a layer of chopped candied fruit on the pastry shell. A second version was originally made without eggs, butter, or milk, and was a Lenten flathon; the filling was of ground almonds and sugar made into a liquid paste and flavoured with spices. In the succeeding centuries names such as 'egg tart' and 'almond tart' came into use.

The name 'Bakewell pudding' first occurs in Meg Dods (1826), referring to the custard version; but thereafter the name was used for both.

The recipe for Bakewell Pudding given by Eliza Acton (1845) was essentially a rich custard of egg yolks, butter, sugar, and flavouring—ratafia (almond) is suggested—poured over a layer of mixed jams an inch (2 cm) thick and baked. Miss Acton noted that 'This pudding is famous not only in Derbyshire, but in several of our northern counties, where it is usually served on all holiday occasions', which suggests that it had been known for some time. In this form, it bears some resemblance to various 'cheesecake' recipes of the preceding century.

During the latter part of the 19th century the custard version fell into disuse, and the recipe evolved towards its modern forms. Mrs Beeton (1861) gave a recipe for a pudding much closer to the one now known, in which ground almonds were used instead of the candied peel, with a layer of strawberry jam only half as thick under the custard mixture, and the whole contained in a puff pastry case. Since then, Bakewell Pudding has shown a tendency to a thinner jam layer and higher proportion of almonds in the filling.

There are now two principal versions. One is the 'pudding' recognized by the inhabitants of Bakewell; this is thus described by Laura Mason (1999):

Bakewell pudding as understood in the late 20th century consists of a puff pastry case with a layer of jam (strawberry or raspberry) covered by a filling of egg, sugar, butter and almonds, which is baked.

A legend current in Bakewell, especially in the 'Old Original Bakewell Pudding Shop', is that the pudding was accidentally invented in the 1860s, when a cook in a local inn made a mistake. This appears to be without foundation, since the pudding was already well known.

The other current version is a shortcrust case with a filling of something like almond sponge cake over a layer of jam.

BAKING in English, refers primarily to the action of making up all sorts of flour-based goods such as breads and cakes, and cooking them, usually in an oven, although some are 'baked' on a GRIDDLE. A group of items produced at one time may be referred to collectively as 'a baking', and the day on which they are produced as a 'baking day'. Some N. European languages have similar words (such as German *backen*, from the same root as the English word) but S. Europeans have no equivalent to this general concept.

Baking also has a more general meaning, denoting the cooking of food, uncovered, in an enclosed oven: many Sunday 'roasts' are actually baked, as are foods cooked in a TANDOOR. It is also used of food wrapped in a protective cover (for instance, aluminium foil) and placed in the ashes of a fire (e.g. 'baked potatoes'). A CLAMBAKE is a primitive, and now rather special, variant on the idea of baking.

In English, 'baking' in the primary sense has been used with reference to bread and other flour-based items since the Middle Ages. The recipes and methods were transmitted from royal and noble households to country houses. In the 16th and 17th centuries the skills of the pastry-cook were added to those of the worker with yeast dough, so that in modern Britain domestic and commercial bakers take in skills from both fields of expertise, in contrast to France, for example, where the *boulanger* and the *pâtissier* remain clearly separated.

Home baking has long been an important activity in England, but the skills required and the emphasis have changed over the centuries. Until the 19th century it was only in southern England that wheat flour was predominant; before this time, only relatively wealthy households had enclosed ovens. These were wood fired, providing falling heat until cold again, a process which took roughly 24 hours, necessitating a concentrated one-day baking session. Heated infrequently, they were used whilst very hot to bake coarse and fine breads, followed by cakes and biscuits as the heat declined. Poorer households, with no oven of their own, used dutch ovens, or griddles, or sent their dough to public bakehouses. The coal-fired range, developed in the 19th century, and 20th-century gas and electric ovens made the home baker's life easier.

In the southern part of England, baker's bread was commonly being bought, even by poor people, well before the 19th century. The habit of home baking has lasted much longer in N. England and in Scotland. Peter Brears (1987) comments that in Yorkshire:

The period from around 1850 up to the Second World War can now be seen as a 'golden age' of home baking, when almost every housewife took a great pride in baking all the bread, cakes and puddings eaten by her family, instead of relying on mass-produced convenience foods.

A similar practice of home baking prevails in some other European countries, especially in the north and especially at Christmas and the New Year. (LM)

BAKING POWDER a raising agent used in breads, cakes, and biscuits. It consists of a mild acid and a mild alkali which react together when wetted, generating carbon dioxide which forms bubbles in the dough. The reaction begins at once, so there is no need to leave the dough to 'ripen' as when using yeast.

The alkaline component of baking powder is usually BICARBONATE OF SODA, also known as baking soda. The first type, invented in the USA in 1790, was 'pearl ash', potassium carbonate prepared from wood ash. This provided only the alkali; the acid had to come from some other ingredient, for example sour milk. Pearl ash reacted with fats in the food, forming soap which gave an unpleasant taste. Soon it was replaced by bicarbonate of soda, which still reacts in this way but to a much smaller extent. An American name used for either of these alkali-only agents was saleratus.

True baking powder, containing both bicarbonate of soda and an acid, was introduced around 1850. The acid was CREAM OF TARTAR or tartaric acid, both of which conveniently form crystals. This was mixed with a little starch to take up moisture and so keep the other components dry, so that they did not react prematurely. A disadvantage of this mixture was that it sprang into rapid action as soon as it was wetted, so that the dough had to be mixed quickly and put straight into the oven before the reaction stopped.

Modern baking powder still uses these substances, but some of the cream of tartar (or tartaric acid) is replaced with a slower acting substance such as acid sodium pyrophosphate. This hardly reacts at all at room temperature, but speeds up when heated, so that bread and cakes rise well in the oven.

The starch in baking powder is not fully effective in keeping it dry, so that the components react together slowly in storage and the powder gradually loses its effect. Any that has not been used within a few months should be discarded.

BAKLAVA a popular Middle Eastern pastry much imitated elsewhere. It is made of many sheets of FILO pastry laid flat in a pan, brushed with melted butter and given one or sometimes more layers of a sweetened filling of minced nuts (PISTACHIOS, ALMONDS, or WALNUTS). The whole is soaked in a honey or sugar SYRUP, often with a little lemon juice. Before baking, the sheet is cut into diamond-shaped fingers. After baking, these are separated into individual pastries.

The origins and earliest history of baklava are discussed under FILO.   CP
READING: Perry (1983*b*, 1987*a*, 1989).

BALEARIC ISLANDS namely Majorca, Minorca (Anglicized versions of Mallorca and Menorca), plus Ibiza and Formentera, are, with Catalonia on the mainland, the surviving territory of CATALAN COOKERY. However, they call for separate consideration because there is a high degree of contrast between the relatively sophisticated cuisine of Catalonia, especially Barcelona, and the more down-to-earth peasant-style cookery of the islands.

The Balearics are of course not only part of the Catalan region but also part of Spain, and it is noticeable that many of the foods and dishes popular in the islands echo, albeit under somewhat different names, those of Spain. Thus, to take a few examples, *bunyols* (Mallorquin) are *buñuelos* (Castilian Spanish), doughnuts; *arros brut* (a winter dish of rice with rabbit and other game, snails, and vegetables, well spiced) is the Spanish *arroz brut*; *pan-cuit* is the bread and garlic 'soup' known as *sopa de ajo* in Castilian and familiar in the south of France and elsewhere in the Mediterranean.

Mention of 'soup' prompts a quotation from Elizabeth Carter (1989), author of a fine book on *Majorcan Food and Cookery*. She remarks that:

The Mallorcan word *sopes* has misled many foreigners into thinking that they were ordering a soup. Actually, *sopes* are thin slices of Majorcan country bread, *pan payes*, a circular, beige-coloured bread made from wheat; this bread is left unsalted, a tradition said to date from the Moorish occupation.

Thus *Sopes mallorquinas* is a Majorcan bread and cabbage dish, almost all bread and sliceable rather than suppable. The same bread is used for *pamboli*, bread with salt and olive oil—and perhaps tomato, in which case it matches the famous *pa amb tomàquet* of mainland Catalonia.

A typical cooking dish is the *greixonera*, a shallow earthenware vessel with four small handles and a rounded bottom. It has no lid (although a small one upside down or large cabbage leaves can be used) and features in a very large number of recipes. *Pastanagues morades ofegades* ('black', i.e. purple, carrot hotpot) is an example of a dish in Majorca which does require a cover while it is being cooked. It also, helpfully, contains a lot of typical Mallorquin ingredients: currants and pine nuts (Moorish influence); *sobrassada* (the most famous of the Majorcan sausages, spicy and reddish-orange); *butifarró* (a blood sausage spiced with cinnamon, fennel seeds, and black pepper); *todas especias* (a home-made spice mixture of cinnamon, peppercorns, and cloves); and lard (amply used in the islands, where the pig is enormously important).

The prominence of the pig in Majorca inspired George Sand, one of the most famous (and critical) of the residents (but not for very long), to write that she would never have got to the island in the first place had it not been that

[the pig] came to enjoy in Majorca rights and privileges which nobody had so far dreamed of offering to humans. Houses have been enlarged and ventilated; the fruit which used to rot on the ground has been gathered, sorted and stored; and steamships, previously considered needless and unreasonable, now run between Majorca and the mainland.

Majorca is famous for its apricots and almonds. The trees enhance the beauty of the island and its fruits the dessert table. The same applies to figs and plums; in their dried form these are among the specialities of Minorca and Ibiza, where one delightful way of packing dried figs involves thyme, sprigs of fennel, and pretty baskets.

The dessert table is also embellished by sweet dishes which betray the culinary influence of the Moors, notably baked items with almond, and the wonderful almond ice cream called *gelat d'ametilla*. *Orxata d'ametilla*, a sweet iced drink which is 'almond milk' in English, is another example and is not found elsewhere in Spain except for Valencia.

BALKAN FOOD AND COOKERY is a subject which implicitly poses the question: what are the Balkans? They take their name from the Turkish *balkan*, referring to the chain of mountains in central Bulgaria, and then by extension to the entire peninsula which stretches south from the rivers Danube and Sava to the southern tip of Greece. Thus 'the Balkan peninsula' embraces the whole of former Yugoslavia, Romania, Bulgaria, Albania, Greece, and European Turkey. It divides the Ionian Sea from the Aegean Sea; and it links W. and C. Europe with the Middle East.

Working out what peoples were in a particular territory 10,000 years ago in any part of Europe is no easy matter, and it is perhaps especially difficult in the Balkan peninsula. Waves of people from C. Asia swept down into, or through, the area in the past, long before it became part of the Roman Empire, and among them were certainly some Celts (still represented by the Albanians). More floods of people poured in during the centuries following the fall of the Western Roman Empire: Ostrogoths, Huns, Alans, Slavs, etc.

Cookery is thought to have begun in the 7th/6th millennia BC by the Balkan autochtonous population. This view is based on archaeological studies of oven floors and of items like a clay model of a loaf, from near Stara Zagora, dated to *c*.5100 BC; and evidence indicating that it may well have been in the same region, earlier still, that milking of domestic animals first took place.

Be that as it may, the waves of nomadic invaders and settlers abated during the period of the Roman Empire, but resumed after its fall, thus ensuring a further enrichment of the already complex cultural patterns in the Balkans. The next period of stability was that of Turkish domination, from roughly the 14th to the beginning of the 20th century. These centuries of integrated life under Turkish political control have led to the creation of a common Balkan culture, a sameness in demeanour, in outlook, in eating attitudes and habits.

The similarity of dishes quickly becomes apparent to the traveller; MOUSSAKA, KOFTA (*köfte* in Turkish), BAKLAVA, sour soups—all these and many others are part of an older shared heritage. There are, understandably, numerous variations reflecting the differences in climate, religious beliefs, and economic conditions.

Bread and other flour-based products are the bedrock of the Balkan diet, supplemented by milk, cheeses (especially of the FETA and KASHKAVAL types), YOGHURT, and large quantities of fruit and vegetables. Like most E. Europeans, the Balkan peoples could be defined as grain-eaters, in contrast to westerners who are predominantly meat-eaters.

The southern part of the peninsula, in the olive-growing Mediterranean region, is different. Setting it aside, one can say that, in essence, Balkan cooking is an amalgam of indigenous gastronomic heritage enriched by Greek, Turkish, and C. European adoptions, bridging the span between E. Mediterranean and W. European cookery traditions.

For the countries which count as being in the Balkans or have been strongly influenced by Balkan culture, see ALBANIA, BULGARIA, ROMANIA, YUGOSLAVIA,

BOSNIA-HERZEGOVINA, CROATIA, MACEDONIA, SLOVENIA; plus of course GREECE and TURKEY (because part of it is in the Balkan peninsula, and the entire Balkans have been so strongly influenced by it).

MK-J

READING: Maria Kaneva-Johnson (1995), Mirodan (1987).

BALLOTTINE a French term which refers to a hot or cold dish consisting of meat or poultry that has been boned, stuffed, rolled, tied up (often inside a cloth), and braised or poached. Its name is a diminutive form of French *ballotte*, which in turn is derived from *balle*, meaning 'bale', to which a ballottine has an obvious resemblance in form, although very much smaller.

BALM also known as lemon/common/sweet/bee balm, or melissa, *Melissa officinalis*, a perennial plant of the Mediterranean region and W. Europe, belonging to the MINT family. It has pale green, deeply veined and downy leaves.

The name balm is a shortened form of BALSAM, which is something different, a resinous preparation often but not necessarily derived from plants called balm.

Lemon balm is used as a flavouring herb. Its lemony aroma, more pronounced in fresh than in dried leaves, enables it to substitute in some contexts for lemon juice and makes it a refreshing addition to salads. It is used for soups, with fish, and in sauces; as a flavouring for milk and yoghurt and for certain drinks; and also, especially, to make balm tea. In the English countryside this balm tea was traditionally sweetened with honey; a nice touch, since *Melissa* is the Greek for honey bee and was given to the plant as its generic name because bees like it (as Virgil tells us—he grew thyme, lavender, and balm for the benefit of his bees).

Since classical times, balm has been considered to be a cure for melancholy and associated ailments.

BALSAM sometimes called BALM but not to be confused with the plants bearing that name, is a compound of plant resins mixed with volatile oils, insoluble in water, used in the past for medicinal purposes but also sometimes as a flavouring.

These substances were originally obtained from the Near and Middle East, as balsam of Gilead or Mecca, and their use for medicinal purposes was in line with the Arabic tradition. Pomet (1712) devoted a lengthy passage in his history of drugs to describing these and other sorts and explaining their various remarkable features, such as how the Sultan of Turkey caused each of the small trees which yielded the true balsam of Gilead to be guarded by soldiers. The discovery of the New World added balsam of Peru and of Tolu (now Santiago de Tolu, in Colombia) to the list; and these too were described by Pomet.

Balsam of Tolu is produced by collecting the resin from incisions in the bark of the plant *Myroxylon balsamum* and letting it harden into cakes in the sun. It can then be used as an alcoholic tincture or dissolved in water with the aid of mucilage or egg yolk. It occurs in some early English recipes, e.g. Artificial Asses' Milk (Hannah Glasse, 1747), but has declined from having little culinary significance to having none.

See also BALSAMIC VINEGAR.

BALSAMIC VINEGAR which takes its name from 'balsamic', meaning health giving, is a traditional product of the province of Modena in Italy, produced on an artisanal scale and greatly superior to any 'balsamic vinegar' which comes from factories.

Making the real thing takes a long time; see box.

Before any of the balsamic vinegar can be sold under the traditional label of authenticity, it is sampled blind by members of the guild of balsamic vinegar-makers, and has to be approved. The merits of the 'real thing' are undisputed, but may have been exaggerated towards the end of the 20th century by its becoming a fashionable ingredient in sophisticated restaurants in western countries; and the production of inferior kinds in factories has been encouraged by the glint of the gold which is attracted by the name.

The book by Professor Benedetto Benedetti (1986), who acknowledges no fewer than 19 other professors and experts as involved in its composition, covers the technical and legal aspects as well as history, traditions, etymology, and medical properties; a thorough work.

READING: Anderson (1994).

BALTI the name of both a cuisine, that of Baltistan in the far north-east of PAKISTAN, and of the wok-like utensil (*karahi*) which is the main piece of equipment used by Balti cooks.

Until the last quarter of the 20th century Balti food was virtually unknown outside Baltistan. However, the chance which led one emigrant to settle in Birmingham, the second city of England, and to open a modest eating place there for the benefit of other emigrants led to surprising results. The 'Baltis', as the eating places also came to be called, multiplied at phenomenal speed, breaking through the 100 barrier in Birmingham within a dozen years or so and also establishing outposts in other English towns and cities. The extent of the 'invasion' may not be quite as great as it seems, since a number of existing restaurants from the Asian subcontinent have changed their names or menus so as to embrace Balti dishes and profit from their popularity. However, even with allowance made for this the spread of the Balti houses has been remarkable.

The distinguishing features of Balti food have been well defined by Chapman (1993), who opens the introduction to his excellent,

---

MAKING AND USING THE TRUE TRADITIONAL BALSAMIC VINEGAR

THE must from specially cultivated varieties of grape is reduced by slow simmering to a half or a third of its volume and after a year's fermentation and acidification sets off on its long slow journey from youthful zest to sumptuous maturity, siphoned from one container to another in a *batteria* of barrels of decreasing size, each made from a different wood which adds its own aromas to the slowly concentrating liquid. This traditionally takes place under the rooftops of homes in the region, from the Este palace in the centre of Modena, where the ducal *acetaia* flourished in the 18th century, to the attics of ordinary families. Here the extremes of temperatures and climate contribute to the maturing process as the aceto balsamico concentrates by evaporation during the stifling summer heat and rests and matures during the cold, clammy winters.

This densely perfumed brew needs to be used with respect for its qualities, a few drops in a salad of fresh garden herbs and leaves, or crisp white chicory; a dribble across a simple home-made vanilla ice cream; a scant teaspoon swirled into the cooking juices of some simply grilled or fried meat or chicken; a last-minute addition to a savoury strawberry salad with spring onions and cucumber. A small dose in a liqueur glass makes a fine after-dinner digestive, reminding us of its medicinal use in the past and hence its name, a balsamic cure-all.

GR

and amusing, book on the subject by dispelling any possible misapprehension that the whole Balti phenomenon belongs to the realm of fantasy: 'There really are Balti people who live in Baltistan. Once it was a kingdom complete with its own royals. Now it is the northernmost part of Pakistan.' He explains that the term 'Balti' refers both to the area of origin of this cuisine and also to the utensil used for cooking and serving:

Known also as the karahi, the Balti pan is a round-bottomed, wok-like, heavy cast-iron dish with two handles. The foods served in the Balti pan are freshly cooked aromatically spiced curries. Balti food at its best is very aromatic but not excessively spiked with chillies. Traditionally it is eaten without rice or cutlery. Balti bread is used to scoop up the food using the right hand only.

Chapman's analysis of the origins of Balti cooking includes a bow to CHINA (notably Szechuan); to TIBET; to MOGHUL CUISINE; and to the 'aromatic spices of Kashmir' (see KASHMIR). He gives clear notice to his readers that other sources have been tapped to produce many of the dishes served in Balti restaurants in Britain, and points out that many of the people operating or working in these restaurants may never have been anywhere near Baltistan.

BALUT an oriental delicacy particularly associated with the Philippines, is a boiled fertilized duck's egg, and is savoured for the variety of textures within: the broth, the very young chick, the yolk. It is eaten by cracking the top of the shell, sprinkling a little salt within, and sipping the broth, then opening the whole egg and eating the rest with rock salt.

The Chinese are said to have brought to the Philippines the idea of eating duck eggs at this stage of maturity. The process has, however, been indigenized, and is now done (in towns like Pateros, in Rizal) in very native ways. Eggs delivered to the balut-maker (*mangbabalut*) are laid under the sun briefly to remove excess moisture and to bring them to the ideal warmth for keeping alive the zygote within. The eggs are then taken to a *garong*, a deep wooden trough lined with rice husks, in which are set bamboo-skin baskets (*tuong*) lined with paper and husk and wrapped in cowhide. Into these baskets are placed the eggs, separated in 100-egg sacks of netting (*tikbo*). The eggs are kept warm in these sacks by a system of transferring each *tikbo* from one *tuong* to another twice a day, thus keeping the warmth even. Eggs at the bottom of the basket are warmest, those on top the coolest, and the transferring evens this out.

On the 9th day the eggs are held up against an electric bulb; opacity shows that the zygote has developed. A clear, transparent egg has not developed one, and

is set aside to be boiled as *penoy*. A failed balut (e.g. when water seeps in through the permeable membrane and contaminates the fluid inside) is called *abnoy*, and has a sulphurous smell. It is, however, beaten and fried, and/or made into *bibingkang itlog*, which is eaten with a vinegar dip.

The perfect balut, to the Filipino, is 17 days old, and called *balut sa puti*; the word 'balut' also means 'wrapped in', and *put* means 'white', i.e. the chick is 'wrapped in white', not mature enough to show feathers, claws, or beak. Filipinos in the USA make 16-day-old balut, with the chick hardly visible at all, to serve to non-Filipinos. Beyond 17 days, the chicks develop, and vendors are said to sell this at bus and train stations, where they do not expect to see their customers again (but they would not worry about their Vietnamese customers, who are said to prefer 19-day-old balut).

Most balut are sold by vendors (*magbabalut*), who carry them in lined baskets that keep the eggs warm, and offer a tiny spill of paper containing salt with each egg. The most omnipresent of food vendors, they ply the streets in early dawn (to sell to those coming from nightclubs or night work), throughout the day and into the night, with a distinctive cry: 'Balu-u-ut!' that has inspired a popular song.

Balut, popularly believed to be an aphrodisiac, is now also served in restaurants as an appetizer (rolled in flour, fried, and with a vinegar-chilli dip), *adobado* (cooked in vinegar with garlic), or baked in a crust with olive oil or butter and spices as a 'surprise' (*Sorpresa de balut*).   DF

BAMBOO plants of the grass family, belonging to the genera *Bambusa*, *Dendrocalamus*, *Giganthocloa*, *Phyllostachys*, and others. Some of the several hundred species grow to 30 m (100') tall. The stems of all kinds are hard and tough: indeed, bamboo scaffolding is stronger, weight for weight, than steel. However, the very young shoots, harvested just as they appear above ground, are tender enough to be edible, and are a popular vegetable in China, Japan, Korea, and SE Asia.

Many, but not all, species of bamboo have edible shoots. Most contain prussic acid, but in edible kinds there is none or only a little, which can be destroyed by cooking. The species most commonly used in China and Japan are *Phyllostachys pubescens* and half a dozen other members of that genus, plus *Sinocalamus* spp. *Bambusa* spp are also eaten. Herklots (1972) quotes an authority on Chinese bamboos as declaring that the shoots of *Phyllostachys dulcis* (pah ko poo chi, sweetshoot bamboo) have the best flavour.

Cultivated bamboo shoots are grown by earthing up the base of the plant with pig manure, which promotes rapid growth and blanches the shoots, making them less bitter. As soon as the tips appear, the shoots are dug up, severed at the base, and prepared for consumption, usually by trimming and boiling. Subsequently they need only a brief heating through if added to a mixture of stir-fried vegetables.

Fresh bamboo shoots can be kept in a refrigerator, and slices taken off as needed. Canned bamboo shoots are almost indistinguishable from the fresh article. Since they come already prepared and cooked, they can be used straight from the can. The species *Thyrsostachys siamensis* is an important species in Thailand for bottling and canning.

Dried shoots are also available; and pickled shoots are considered a delicacy in several Asian countries, e.g. Burma.

Although people in western countries tend to think of bamboo shoots as typically Chinese, and they are indeed prominent in Chinese cookery and horticulture (there being numerous cultivated species, becoming ready at different seasons), it is arguable that the Japanese interest in bamboo shoots is even more intense. Indeed, the use of bamboo in Japanese kitchens is a whole subject in itself, diverging somewhat from the general practices already described. Katsue Aizawa (private communication, 1991) writes:

The young shoots of bamboo, which normally come out in April and May, are a typical spring vegetable in Japan. The shoots of mosochiku (*Phyllostachys pubescens*) are thought to be the best, and Kyoto is famous for them.

The harvester of bamboo shoots looks for cracks on the surface of the earth and digs up the emerging shoots almost before they come out. For only very young shoots are edible, and they are known to make amazingly rapid growth (more than a metre, which is over 3', in 24 hours).

After initial preparation, shoots are cooked with dashi and soy sauce, boiled with rice, put in soup, etc. They are thought to have a special affinity with WAKAME (a seaweed commonly eaten in Japan), and these are often cooked together, the dish being called *wakatakeni*.

Tender parts of the skins that tightly envelope bamboo shoots (called *kinukawa*) are also edible. They are often used as a garnish for clear soup.

The leaves of mature bamboo are sometimes used as food wrappings, e.g. for glutinous rice (steamed in large bamboo leaves, for the Boys' Festival in May) and for the candy called *sasaame*, a speciality of Niigata.

Bamboos and other canes often have edible seeds. The seeds of some *Bambusa* spp resemble rice and are often called bamboo rice. They are as palatable and rich in protein as any cereal grain, but each plant produces only a few seeds.

A unique and highly prized substance derived from bamboos of the genus

Bambusa is *tabashir*. This is a concretion intermediate in nature between sugar and a stony mineral which occasionally forms from the liquid inside the joints of bamboo stems. *Tabashir* is as rare as a pearl in an oyster and nearly as expensive. It has a long history of use for medicinal purposes.

BANANA a fruit which belongs to the tropics and has its origin in SE Asia, has achieved a remarkably high level of consumption in temperate countries. For consumers there, bananas are almost uniform in appearance, being varieties which ship well and look good. But in the tropical regions where bananas grow there are countless varieties, varying widely in appearance and eating qualities. There are, moreover, both eating bananas and cooking bananas, usually called PLANTAINS. The latter have an entry of their own, dealing with their varieties and culinary uses, but they are not a separate species and therefore figure in this entry in their botanical aspect.

The banana plant is a strange growth, which looks like a palm tree, but is not a tree. It is a perennial herb which grows a complete new 'trunk' every year, and dies back to its roots after it has flowered and fruited. This is all the more remarkable in that some kinds grow to a height of 12 m (40'). The 'trunk' is in fact composed of overlapping bases of leaves wrapped tightly to make a fairly rigid column. New leaves constantly emerge at the top, forming a crown of leaves which are blown into tattered strips by the wind (a neat evolutionary adaptation to lower their wind resistance, for the 'trunk' is not as strong as a real tree trunk and risks being blown down).

Eventually the flowering stem emerges at the top, bearing a large flower surrounded by red bracts, the whole growth having a strikingly phallic appearance. The bananas develop some way back from the flowering tip of the stem. The increasing weight causes the stem to bend over, so that the fruits point upwards. They are arranged in 'hands' of 10 to 20 bananas set in a double row in a half spiral around the stem. There may be up to 15 hands in a complete bunch, which can weigh 45 kg (100 lb) or more.

The history and botanical classification of bananas are subjects best left to experts, e.g. Purseglove (1985), for they are of extreme complexity. A starting point is the wild banana of the Malaysian/Indonesian region, *Musa acuminata*, sometimes known as the 'monkey banana', whose fruits were no doubt used for food from very early times. This species and a hybrid between it and an inedible wild species, *M. balbisiana*, are the ancestors of most modern cultivated bananas. They are often described as being

in the series of *Eumusa* (good banana) cultivars, and may be distinguished from each other by what is called their 'ploidy'. For most purposes it is enough to know the names and characteristics of the cultivars.

It seems likely that edible bananas date back several thousand years in India. They were certainly known by repute to the Greeks in the 4th century BC, when the army of Alexander the Great encountered them on trees in India. Pliny the Elder, writing several centuries later, recorded the incident and cited the Indian name *pala* for the fruit. This name passed into classical Greek and is reflected in some modern Indian names. The classical writer Theophrastus repeated a legend that wise men sat in the shade of the banana tree and ate its fruit, whence the pleasing but now obsolete botanical name *M. sapientium*, meaning 'banana of the sages'.

The banana reached China about AD 200, when it is mentioned in the works of Yang Fu. However, it was grown only in the south, and was considered a rare, exotic fruit in the north, an attitude which lasted well into the 20th century.

During the 1st millennium AD the banana also arrived in Africa, probably taken directly from the Malay region to Madagascar. By the end of the 14th century the fruit was being cultivated right across the continent to the west coast.

During the same period it was taken eastward through the Pacific islands. The Arabs had spread cultivation through their lands south of the Mediterranean before AD 650, but no further north than Egypt, the climate in S. Europe being too cool for the plant. Consequently, the banana remained unknown to most Europeans until much later.

The first serious European contact with the fruit came not long after 1402, when Portuguese sailors found it in W. Africa and took it to the Canary Islands. That is why the

European name 'banana' comes from a W. African word, the Guinean *banema* or *banana* (also *bana*, *gbana*, etc. in neighbouring regions). The Canaries have remained an important banana-growing area ever since, and it was from there that a Spanish missionary, later Bishop of Panama, took banana roots to America in 1516, after which the new plant spread quickly through C. America and the northern parts of S. America. For some reason the Spaniards saw a likeness between the banana tree and the totally different plane tree (*plateno*), which is how the plantain got its confusing name.

Another myth now appears. The spread of the banana in S. America was so rapid, often anticipating the progress of the colonists, that some early writers were convinced that it had existed in S. America, among the Inca, before the Spanish Conquest.

During the 19th century occasional small consignments of bananas were sent by fast ships from the Canaries to Europe and from Cuba to the USA. Early varieties had not been bred for keeping qualities, so the fruit had to arrive in little more than a fortnight and was an expensive luxury. But all this began to change in the 1870s, when two American entrepreneurs began to ship bananas from the Caribbean to New Orleans, Boston, and New York. They also set up plantations on virgin soil in producing areas. In 1899 they merged their interests to form the United Fruit Company, which had and still has great influence in C. America and the islands, for most of the trade of these lands depended on it; hence the derogatory name 'banana republics'.

However, whatever view is taken of this influence, the company must be given credit for making the banana a familiar and reasonably priced fruit in temperate lands. Other companies followed its lead, and handsome, big, yellow, Caribbean bananas began to appear in Europe as well, ousting the small brown Canary ones.

BOTANICAL NAMES FOR BANANA

THE story of the botanical names for the banana is interesting. *Musa* goes back to the Sanskrit 'moca', but does not seem to have attained its Latinized form until the Middle Ages, via the Arabic 'mauz', first used in the 13th century. (Theories that the name came from that of the doctor of the Emperor Augustus, Antonius Musa, or from the south Arabian trading city of Moka seem to be without foundation.) The old specific name *sapientium*, whose origin is explained elsewhere in this entry, was reserved for sweet, eating bananas. Plantains or cooking bananas were assigned to *M. paradisiaca*, another name with a story behind it. In an Islamic myth, probably of Indian origin, the banana was the fruit of the tree of knowledge of good and evil, in the Garden of Eden (which was fittingly situated in Sri Lanka). Furthermore, after the Fall, Adam and Eve covered their nakedness with banana leaves rather than those of the fig. This may account for the common W. Indian practice of calling a banana a fig. It is certainly true that large pieces of banana leaf would have been much more effective for Adam and Eve than small fig leaves.

COMMERCIAL VARIETIES

The main commercial varieties of the banana are **Gros Michel** and **Cavendish Gros Michel**. Gros Michel is the familiar, big, yellow eating banana which has for decades been the main export variety. It is thick skinned, robust in shipment, reliable in quality, and of adequate flavour. It has long been grown in SE Asia and Sri Lanka. In Malaysia and Indonesia it is called 'pisang Ambon' (Amboyna banana). Introduced to the W. Indies in 1835, it soon became the dominant variety, and is often called the Jamaican banana.

Cavendish bananas are a group of southern Chinese origin. The most popular cultivar is **Dwarf Cavendish**, so named because the plant has a short stem. This variety can stand a cooler climate than most bananas. The Canary banana is a subvariety of Dwarf Cavendish.

Cavendish bananas are shorter, blunter, duller coloured, and thinner skinned than Gros Michel. The flavour of most kinds is better, and they are preferred in Asia, where they are the leading variety. They are now replacing Gros Michel in the W. Indies and parts of S. America.

Lacatan is another export variety very similar to export types of Dwarf Cavendish. It is the lakatan of the Philippines, where it is regarded as the best banana in the world. It is highly aromatic and its pulp is sweet, firm, and light orange-yellow when ripe.

Other varieties, including some particularly good ones, are usually eaten only in the regions where they are grown, because their skins are too thin or their lives too short to permit export except by air, as a luxury item.

The **silk banana** is grown in tropical regions worldwide. In the French W. Indies alternative names are used, meaning 'plum, apple, or pineapple fig'. It has very white flesh and a sweet but sharp taste. A similar variety, also widely grown but less important, is the **lady's finger** or **apple banana**.

A small, thin-skinned, deep yellow banana of bulbous shape is called **sucrier** or **bird's fig** in the W Indies and **pisang mas** (golden banana) in Malaya and Indonesia. It is a major variety in New Guinea, with a flavour which is sweet and pleasing.

The **Mysore** banana grows well in poor soil and is often cultivated in the more barren parts of Asia. It is quite a good eating variety and is of great importance in India. In Thailand it has a name meaning 'milk of heaven'.

Both in Asia and the W. Indies there are several kinds of **red banana**, sometimes green striped, with pink flesh. They are delicious, but frail and short-lived. Nevertheless a few are exported to the USA.

The bananas grown for export are suitable for being picked when only two-thirds ripe, and continue to ripen during shipment. The ripening process involves a chemical change in which starch is converted to sugars (made up of sucrose 66%, fructose 14%, and glucose 20%). Protopectin is also converted to soluble pectin. As bananas ripen they give off ethylene gas. Most fruits do this during ripening, but bananas produce an exceptionally large amount. (Ethylene causes ripening and development of colour, as well as being produced by it, so one fruit can help another to ripen. A ripening banana put in a lidded box with green tomatoes turns them red. It also helps a hard avocado to ripen overnight.)

Apart from being eaten fresh, bananas may be made into interesting desserts, e.g. banana fritters and Caribbean sweet dishes in which bananas are flavoured with rum. In India, bananas are made into various confections, such as *panchamrutham*, spiced and sweetened with honey.

Other parts of the banana plant are also used as food or in connection with food. See BANANA FLOWER and BANANA LEAF.

BANANA FLOWER also called banana heart, the inflorescence of the BANANA, is used in many Asian cuisines. The 'flower' (technically, the male part of the flower) is sheathed in outer reddish petals. When these are removed, the paler inside, which is what is eaten, is first debittered by boiling in a change of water, and then used or further cooked in various ways. The flowers may be sliced and used in salads. Or they may be cooked in curry-type dishes with the immature green fruits (i.e. half-formed bananas), as in Malaysia. In Indonesia they are often served as a hot vegetable, e.g. sliced and simmered in coconut milk.

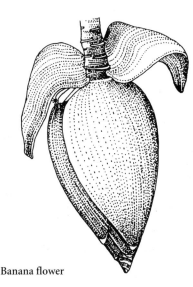

Banana flower

BANANA LEAF a material of great use to cooks in the tropics, is used to wrap up many foodstuffs in the markets, and again in the kitchen, in almost all the regions where the BANANA grows.

These uses, although familiar, have not often been described in detail. However, Monina Mercado (in Cordero-Fernando, 1976) devotes an entire essay to its virtues in the Philippines for these purposes. She points out that most rural cooking in her country is done over a wood fire, and that this usually results in what is in the bottom of the pot being burned. But if a piece of banana leaf is in this vulnerable position, all will be well.

Lining a pot of rice, a piece of banana leaf at the bottom will not burn before the top is done to fluffy whiteness. And even if the bottom should burn to a brown crisp—the cook has gone away to chat over the fence—the crust, stuck to the banana leaf . . . would be a delicacy: golden brown and toasty crisp, subtly flavored with burnt banana leaf.

This flavour is a perfect partner for rice. Monina Mercado describes the flavour as 'cool but not mint cool; faintly smoky and lightly fragrant, but far from aromatic'.

Banana leaf is selected with care for use in cookery. Very young leaf, thin and yellow, is strong and makes the ideal wrapping for something which needs to be cooked for some time. If mature, dark green leaf is used, it is first made pliant by softening it over a flame. This process enhances its flavour.

Foods are often wrapped in banana leaf to be steamed. In Java this mode of cooking is called *pepesan* and may include salt fish, spices, and young coconut, or meat and spices, or simply vegetable and spices. Banana leaves also provide impromptu plates and tablecloths and containers for rice and other foods, as Monina Mercado explains:

Simply as a container, banana leaf is as versatile as the imagination. Twisted into a small cone pinned together with a sliver, it holds peanuts, boiled corn or betel. Twisted into a large fat cone tied with twine, it holds take-home *pancit* from the Chinese restaurant. The same large fat banana leaf cone holds the farmer's lunch for the day; hot newly-cooked rice with a bit of fish on top.

A mature banana leaf is very large. When a cookery book says 'Take a banana leaf' it usually means 'Take a piece of banana leaf'. In western countries it is sometimes possible to obtain banana leaf for free from shops which import tropical produce wrapped in it. This will always be the dark green, mature leaf.

BANBURY CAKES are named after the town in Oxfordshire with which they have been associated since at least the 17th century. The cakes were sold from a shop there in 1638, by one Betty White according to some local records. (This shop, in Parsons Street, was certainly known as 'The Original Banbury Cake Shop' in 1833 and its history is documented since then, including the export in the 19th century of considerable numbers of the cakes to India.)

The first known recipe, by Gervase Markham (1615), required a rich, sweet, spiced, yeast-leavened dough to be divided into two portions. One was left plain, and the other was mixed with currants. The portion with the currants in was then sandwiched between thin layers of plain paste. If the quantities given in the recipe were used to make just one cake, the final product would have been very large, weighing about 4 kg (8 lb). Similar cakes were known elsewhere, one example being the Shrewsbury SIMNEL CAKE; in Scotland, one has survived down to the present day in the form of BLACK BUN, made at New Year.

By the first part of the 19th century, recipes show that Banbury cakes could be made either as large flat pastries, scored and broken into oblong pieces after baking, or as individual confections enclosed in puff pastry, similar to those still known.

Dorothy Hartley (1954) says that the cakes 'used to be carried around, all hot and crisp and fresh, in specially made chip baskets, wrapped in white cloths'. She adds that they were always eaten fresh and hot.

Modern Banbury cakes are small and oval, made of light flaky pastry with a crisp top achieved by a powdering of sugar before baking. The filling is of butter, chopped peel, dried fruit, sugar, and mixed spice.

ECCLES CAKES are similar to Banbury cakes.

BANGLADESH formerly E. Pakistan, is a largely Muslim country which corresponds roughly to E. Bengal (W. Bengal being largely Hindu and part of India). The geography of Bangladesh is therefore dominated by the great rivers which flow into the Bay of Bengal (and are apt to create floods during the monsoon season) and by the enormous alluvial delta which they have created. The climate is subtropical. Population density is remarkably high.

Fish and rice are the staples. Well-known fish include the hilsa, *Hilsa ilisha*, a SHAD and therefore full of small bones; and the bekti/bhekti/begti (etc.), which is *Lates calcarifer*, the giant sea perch which is one of the best fishes in the Indo-Pacific and well known in Australia as BARRAMUNDI. Rice is considered to be a food of higher status than bread, so when rice is served there will not be bread. However, many breads, mostly corresponding to the range available in India, are made. An example is provided by

LUCHI, a kind of fried bread like the northern Indian POORIS. Stuffed, e.g. with green peas, these become KACHORI.

As Bangladesh is so heavily populated, the proportion of poorer people existing on a basic diet and vulnerable to the famine conditions which occur from time to time is relatively high. The diet for such people would indeed be basic. As Chitrita Banerji (1997) writes:

Many poor peasants in Bangladesh remain content daily with just rice, an onion or two, some chillies and the handful of *shak* [any kind of leafy green eaten as a vegetable] or boiled potato. Urban workers living in slums often feel lucky if they can manage a regular supply of rice and *dal*.

However, for the better off there are sophisticated dishes and confections, reflecting the prowess of Bengali cooks and demonstrated particularly in the amazing range of confectionery for which they are world famous. A professional sweet-maker, called *moira*, is a figure of importance, who, according to the author quoted above is traditionally pictured as 'a huge, immobile mountain of flesh, sitting in front of his stove or in front of a huge platter of white *chhana* which he manipulates with the ease of long practice'. For one extraordinary British legacy which survives in the hands of these sweet-makers, see LADIKANEE.

BANKETBAKKERIJ a Dutch baker's shop specializing in pastries, cakes, and Dutch *koekjes* (see COOKIE). In some shops it is possible to drink a cup of coffee and enjoy a cake on the premises.

It is traditional in Holland for a person having a birthday to buy cakes for his friends or colleagues, and these cakes would normally be obtained from the banketbakkerij.

Varieties made and sold at the banketbakkerij include the following. They are seldom made at home.

Speculaas (*speculoos* in Belgium and *Spekulatius* in Germany), Christmas biscuits made of wheat flour, butter, sugar, and a mixture of spices in which cinnamon is predominant. The dough is baked in decorative moulds. The biscuits are crisp and flattish and may have cut almonds pressed into the underside. For special occasions, a very large *speculaas* may be made in a special mould. The Abraham, as Ileen Montijn (1991) explains, is baked for a man's 50th birthday:

a large, flat, edible doll, once made of bread dough, nowadays more cake-like and elaborately decorated, or even mistakenly taken to be a kind of gingerbread man. . . . The basis for this is in the Bible, John, 9: 57: 'Then said the Jews unto him, Thou art not yet fifty years old, and hast thou seen Abraham?' The giving of Abraham dolls to people

on their fiftieth birthday (and Sarah dolls to women, as a kind of consolation prize) has . . . become more rather than less popular.

One variety of *speculaas* has a rich filling of almond paste sandwiched between two biscuit layers.

Taai-taai, chewy Christmas biscuits made in the same way as GINGER BISCUITS from rye flour and molasses, honey or syrup, and no fat. They are flavoured with aniseed rather than ginger. Like *speculaas*, they were traditionally baked in carved wooden moulds in various shapes, mostly human, but also representing biblical scenes, ships, and so on. The industrial production of both *speculaas* and *taai-taai* began around 1880 and one result was a great loss of variety in the moulds. Today, however, all *speculaas* and *taai-taai* are still sold in traditional moulded shapes, however rudimentary. Two exceptions are *Pepernoten* (see below) and filled *speculaas*.

Pepernoten, like German *Pfeffernüsse* (see GINGER BISCUITS), often made with rye flour. Traditionally these are strewn around by Black Peter, St Nicholas's assistant, on the saint's day of 6 December.

Banketletters, flaky pastry with an almond paste filling, cut out in letter shapes for St Nicholas's Day. The commonest letters are S for *Sinterklaas* (Santa Claus) and M for *Moeder* (Mother). (These pastry letters have now been largely replaced by chocolate letters, production of which began around 1905.)

Sprits, a very old variety, round, made from a liquid dough, piped from a forcing bag.

Beschuit met muisjes (rusk with little mice), offered to family, friends, and colleagues when a baby is born. The mice are white and pink sugar-coated aniseeds. They are a very ancient food, having been used to decorate dishes in the Middle Ages. They were called *trigy* then. Aniseed, like fennel, is a traditional cure for stomach disorders and colic in babies.

Wellington, a long almond biscuit, rounded at each end with a narrower waist.

BANNOCK a griddle-baked flatbread from the highland zones of Britain, made from barley, oats, or even PEASEMEAL, water or buttermilk. One made from a mixture of flours was called a meslin bannock (see maslin in BREAD VARIETIES).

The derivation of the word may be from the Gaelic *bannach*, itself stemming from the Latin *panicium*. Bannock is hence a generic term for bread in those non-wheat-growing regions, and Wright's *Dialect Dictionary* has found it current throughout N. and W. Britain. In Scotland, the bannock was pre-eminently made with barley (or BERE MEAL, bere being a primitive form of barley that does better in acid soils); in England, more often of oats. It is thicker than the OATCAKE, and larger than a SCONE, 'about the size of a meat-plate'. Like scones, the bannock was unleavened until the introduction of bicarbonate of soda.

Originally, bannocks were baked in the embers, then toasted on the GRIDDLE before eating, though the more usual method now is to bake entirely on the griddle. An English–Latin wordbook of c.1483 translates bannock as *focacius* (hearth bread), or *panis subcinericius* (bread baked in the ashes). The dough was moister than an oatcake. Dr Johnson encountered bannocks on his trip to the Highlands in 1773 and noted that 'I learnt to eat them without unwillingness; the blackness of their colour raises some dislike, but the taste is not disagreeable.'

The jannock, though it may seem phonetically related, is principally a Lancastrian and north country word, not seen before the 16th century, for unleavened oaten bread.

Not every bannock is a simple hearth bread. Those of Selkirk are festive breads similar to lardy cakes; Pitcaithly bannocks are a rich shortbread; Gayle bannocks, in Wensleydale, were griddle cakes made with much lard, flour, and currants, and the staple diet of local quarrymen.

BANQUET the English word, and its close relations in other languages (French *banquet*, Italian *banchetto*, etc.) have had different meanings at different times. Today, the meaning of banquet in English is: a formal and sumptuous meal, usually of a ceremonial nature and for a large number of people. The word embraces the meal in its entirety.

However, in the 16th and 17th centuries this was not so. The whole of a formal and sumptuous meal would then have been called a FEAST; and the word 'banquet', at that time, referred to the final, sweet, course or episode of the feast. This often took place in a separate room, not the one in which the main part of the feast had been consumed; and its character was different.

In medieval times, it had been common for wine and spices to be served as the finale to any important meal, after the tables had been cleared. The purpose of this ceremony, called the 'voidée' in accordance with its French origin, was originally medicinal. The spices and the spiced wine were selected and prepared in a manner thought to aid digestion.

However, the serving of these items sometimes became merged with the serving of the last course of the feast, which consisted in various sweetmeats and which was also modelled on a French practice. And as time passed, the two things were separated

again, but now in reverse sequence; the spiced wine was served first, and this was followed by the service of sweetmeats.

Hence the interesting and pleasant characteristics of the English banquet of those times. Some nobles began to design and build special rooms, or even special buildings, for their banquets. These were often secluded; not necessarily by being built some way from the main house—there was a fashion for building them on the roof. One can imagine the merriment with which the important guests would file along a corridor and then mount perhaps several staircases, finally emerging from a small circular staircase onto the roof, enjoying a panorama of the surrounding countryside, and passing into a small private room in which the sweetmeats would be laid out ready, with exquisite artistry.

Often, there would be no servants; or, if there was one, he would be gone once he had seen to it that the guests were all present and comfortable. Part of the pleasure lay in the 'withdrawn' and private atmosphere of the banquet, when people could relax completely, indulge in indiscreet talk, and so forth.

The scent of flowers and the sound of music, being played by musicians who were nearby but out of sight, could complete the charming environment.

Examples of banqueting rooms given by Jennifer Stead (1991*a*) include the earliest known banqueting room on a roof, that of Sir William Sharington, who, in the middle of the 16th century, had an octagonal lookout tower incorporating two banqueting rooms, which still survive.

A banqueting room could also be set in a garden; in the Renaissance period the garden itself was seen as a source of inspiration and refreshment for intellect and spirit and senses alike, one might say a banquet for the mind as well as a feast for the eyes. Indeed, the room might itself be made of garden materials. Queen Elizabeth caused a temporary banqueting house to be erected in Greenwich Park for the entertainment of the French Ambassador and his staff. This was made entirely of boughs and blossoms. And at Cobham Hall in Kent a living lime tree was converted into a banqueting house comprising three rooms at different levels, with stairs between them, and accommodating fifty people in all.

The theme of water was generally popular, and the sound of water splashing in a fountain was considered to be a highly appropriate background noise for banquets. It was not uncommon to combine the function of 'water house' (a building which housed the pumps and pipes which supplied water to the house and to the gardens) with that of banqueting room. And some banqueting rooms took the form of grottoes,

where elaborate decorations of sea shells and a damp atmosphere conducive to the growth of ferns and suchlike plants created a wettish environment which was thought to have particular charm.

All this has long been lost. Few are the instances in modern times of a 'banquet' which offers true pleasure to the participants.

BAOBAB *Adansonia digitata*, a broad, spreading tree with a thick, spongy trunk. It belongs to tropical Africa and bears fruits whose pulp is a popular food and seasoning. This is often called 'monkey bread'. Another name, 'cream of tartar tree', refers to the whitish-yellow pulp of the fruit, which contains tartaric acid. Pastoral tribes use the pulp to sour milk. The fruit pulp is also remarkably rich in ascorbic acid.

Various kinds of porridge and gruel are also made, either from the seeds or the flesh of the fruit. The young shoots and leaves of the tree are eaten in soup or as a pot-herb.

BAOZI steamed buns which are found, with various fillings and in slightly different forms, all over China.

Unlike JIAOZI, baozi are leavened. When they are made in western countries, commercial yeast is used and the resulting buns are softer than they would be in China, where it is still usual to keep some uncooked dough from the last batch to leaven the next one.

Fillings may be savoury, for example the Cantonese roast meat called *chahsiu*; or sweet with fillings such as mixed sugared nuts, sweet red bean paste, dried JUJUBES boiled and mashed, or simply sugar.

BAP 'the traditional morning roll of Scotland' (Marian McNeill, 1929), which is also made in Ireland, is a soft roll. The term, which has been in use since the late 16th century, is of unknown derivation.

Dough for baps is lively, sometimes including butter or lard to ensure tenderness; the crust is well dusted with flour before baking in a hot oven. Shapes vary, from triangular to square to torpedo (Dublin), though round is now most common. It is customary to press a floured finger into the centre of each bap before baking to prevent blistering of the crust. In Scotland, baps are never sweetened, but currant baps are made in Ireland.   LM

BARA BRITH a moist Welsh bread containing currants, raisins, or sultanas, candied peel, and sweet spice. The name literally means 'speckled bread', referring to the fruit. Bara brith is often served sliced and buttered for AFTERNOON TEA or HIGH TEA. Originally a yeast cake, but recent recipes sometimes use raising agents such as bicarbonate of soda.

See also BARM BRACK and TEA BREADS AND TEA CAKES.

BARB a name commonly but loosely applied to most of the numerous species of fish in the genus *Barbus*. This consists of freshwater fish only, and falls in the CARP family.

The principal European species is called BARBEL. The various fish called MAHSEER in the Indian subcontinent (assigned to the genus *Barbus* by some authorities, but to the genus *Tor* by others) belong to the same group.

Generally, however, *Barbus* spp are small and more valued as aquarium fish than for eating.

BARBADOS CHERRY *Malpighia punicifolia*, is the most important member of a group of small fruiting trees and shrubs of which most are native to tropical and subtropical America. It is also known as acerola, and as the W. Indian/Puerto Rican/native/garden cherry. It is much cultivated in the W. Indies, where the fruit is eaten fresh or made into pies and preserves; and has been introduced to other areas with suitable climates, such as Brazil and Hawaii.

The fruit is bright red and the size of a cherry (up to 3 cm/1" in diameter). The shallow furrows running down the outside betray the position of the three stones which are to be found inside. The flesh is juicy and subacid, more like a raspberry than a cherry in flavour. When cooked it tastes like a tart apple. It is remarkably rich in vitamin C, outdoing even rose hips in this respect and having a twentyfold advantage over oranges, weight for weight.

BARBADOS GOOSEBERRY the edible fruit of a vigorous, climbing, leafy cactus, *Pereskia aculeata*, grown mainly in the W. Indies and C. America. Its numerous common names include lemon vine, blade apple, and gooseberry shrub.

The small, often pear-shaped, fruits have a thin skin which is yellow or reddish in colour, and contain small soft seeds. When ripe, they are juicy and somewhat tart. They can be eaten raw, but are usually stewed or preserved with sugar, or made into jam.

BARBECUE meat (or other food) cooked in the open air on a framework over an open fire; or an event incorporating such cooking; or the framework and accompanying apparatus required for this.

The word comes from the Spanish *barbacoa*, which in turn had probably come from a similar word in the Arawak language, denoting a structure on which meat could be dried or roasted. When the word first entered the English language, in the 17th century, it meant a wooden framework such as could be used for storage or sleeping on, without a culinary context. However, by the 18th century it took on the first of its present meanings, and—at least in the USA—the second one too. The third meaning, like the apparatus itself, became commonplace in the latter part of the 20th century.

Barbecues, naturally, occur most often in countries where the climate is right for outdoor cooking. Texas (and N. America generally) and Australia are examples of regions where the cult of the barbecue is most noticeable. In the southern states of the USA the traditional barbecue was of pork. Traditions everywhere have been expanded in recent times to accommodate other meats (emphasis on spare ribs and sausages, steaks and chops), poultry (especially chicken), fish, and various vegetables (usually as an accompaniment). Rivalry between different kinds of barbecue sauce is intense. The whole barbecue scene and the atmospherics surrounding it are considerably affected by a cultural circumstance, to wit the general practice of having men rather than women do the barbecuing.

BARBEL a name usually applied only to *Barbus barbus*, a C. European species of freshwater fish in the CARP family. Other *Barbus* spp are called BARB.

The flesh of the barbel is bony; so it is not greatly esteemed or used as food. The roe is said to be toxic, and may sometimes be so, but Blanchard (1866) recalls that the naturalist Bloch ate barbel eggs, as did other members of his family, without ill effect.

BARBERRY a shrub of the genus *Berberis*, of which many species grow wild throughout the temperate regions of Europe, Asia, and America. A closely related genus, *Mahonia*, familiar in western countries as an ornamental garden shrub, also has a wide distribution. Some shrubs which were formerly thought of as true barberries have now been reassigned to *Mahonia*.

All these species bear berries which are edible but sour. *Berberis* berries are generally red, varying from coral to deep crimson, almost black. *B. vulgaris*, the common barberry of Europe and Asia, has elongated, bright red berries which hang in clusters. *Mahonia* berries are usually blue or bluish. Several *Mahonia* species bear the name Oregon grape (or hollygrape), and others are associated with Mexico or the south-west of the USA. Among the latter, for which *agrito* is a common name, *M. swaseyi* is a promising candidate for improvement by selection.

Traditional uses of barberries, called 'poor man's red currant' by early settlers in N. America, include preserving them in syrup or vinegar to provide a sharp flavouring; and making them into a jelly or jam, e.g. the French *confiture d'épine-vinette*, a speciality of Rouen and Dijon which is made from a seedless variety of *B. vulgaris*.

Most European barberries are too sour to eat fresh, but several species found in the south of the USA and Mexico are sweet enough to have been eaten thus by American Indians. Their tart flavour is popular in Iran where they are used in PILAF dishes and in stews. In India some species, e.g. *B. vulgaris* and *B. aristata*, are sun dried to make 'sour currants' and used like raisins in desserts.

BARD a culinary operation described with his usual lucidity by Stobart (1980):

A bard was an armoured breastplate for a horse. In cooking, it is a breastplate of fat, salted fat or bacon, a thin slice of which is tied around meat or fowl to protect and moisten it during roasting. This is particularly necessary when the meat lacks its own fat; the bard also helps to keep rolled meat neatly in place.

BARFI an Indian sweetmeat made principally of dried milk (*khoya*, see MILK REDUCTION and INDIAN SWEETS) with various additions. The name comes from the Persian word for snow, presumably because plain barfi is white and might be thought to resemble snow. In this plain form, barfi is among the simplest of all Indian sweets. It is common, however, for its already pleasant taste to be improved by adding ingredients such as coconut, carrots, pistachios, or white pumpkin, and by spicing with cardamom.

The prepared mixture is simmered until thick, left to cool, and cut into small cubes. The same mixture formed into flat round tablets may be called *pera* in Bengal and Nepal (echoing the Afghan term *sheer pera*).

Some barfi mixtures are precisely the same as those for SANDESH and the usage of the names overlaps; as does the habit of colouring the confection in several different colours, layered so that cut pieces are striped.

BARLEY *Hordeum vulgare*, the oldest cultivated cereal in the Near East and Europe (and possibly anywhere, for it may have come before cultivation of rice in the Far East). In the ancient world it was for long the most important food grain; but it is now used primarily for animal fodder, secondly for making MALT for beer and other products, and only thirdly as a food grain.

The name barley derives from the Old English *bære*, which survives in Scotland as bere (see BERE MEAL) without the suffix 'ly' which was originally given to turn it into an adjective (meaning 'of barley').

ORIGIN, TYPES, AND EARLY HISTORY

Barley originated as a wild grass of the Near East, often called *H. spontaneum*, but now classed in the same species as cultivated barley, *H. vulgare*. Wild barley, or remains of it, have been found in N. Africa, Asia Minor, and temperate Asia as far east as Afghanistan. It has fragile ears, from which the seeds fall when mature: a feature necessary to a wild plant which has to propagate itself, but unsuitable for a cultivated crop. Domestication led to the emergence, as early as the 6th millennium BC, of cultivated barley with firmly attached grains, which then became dependent on cultivation for its survival.

Types of barley are described as '2-rowed', '4-rowed', and '6-rowed'. These terms are explained in technical books about cereals, but are hard for lay people to understand, at least without diagrammatic pictures. It is perhaps enough to know that the earliest cultivated forms of barley, and most modern varieties are 2-rowed, whereas 6-rowed barley, which in antiquity seemed to give a better yield, was the chief barley of the ancient world. This is why the barley ears depicted on ancient Greek coins, for example, do not look like modern barley, being shorter and fatter.

Most barleys of whichever row number have seed husks terminating in stiff bristles (awns). It is awnless types, with reduced husks, which are known as 'naked' barleys. These are most common in the east.

The oldest known remains of barley are at Tell Mureybat, Syria, a site dating from about 8000 BC. A considerable store of grains was found but they are of the wild type and evidently gathered rather than cultivated. (It is also at this site that the earliest wild WHEAT was discovered. Many of the oldest sites in Syria, Palestine, Mesopotamia, and Asia Minor have both barley and wheat; but barley is more abundant and found in more places, and it seems almost certain that it was cultivated earlier.)

During the whole of the ancient period up to classical times barley was the chief staple grain of the whole Near East, including Egypt and Greece. It reached Spain in the 5th millennium BC and spread north from there to what is now France and Germany, although it probably did not reach Britain until the Iron Age, around 500 BC. In its

eastward movement it reached India in the 3rd millennium BC and China in the 2nd.

At the beginning of the **classical era** in Greece, barley was still the leading staple food all around the eastern end of the Mediterranean. It was eaten as porridge and made into unleavened bread and malted for beer.

During the last centuries BC in Rome barley gradually became less esteemed. This must have been partly due to improvements in bread-making. Barley contains much less GLUTEN than wheat, this being the substance which gives wheat bread its firm, elastic texture and ability to rise. Leavened bread can be made from barley, but it is always dense, coarse in texture, and dark, although the flavour may be mild and pleasant. Also, BARLEY BREADS stale quickly, because they lack the water-retaining powers of the gluten network in wheat or the natural gums in RYE. Thus increasing skill in making well-risen bread, and the universal preference for light-coloured bread, led to a demand for wheat from those who could afford it.

However, the ancient Egyptians, who made good bread themselves, did not abandon barley; and it did not fall into general disuse. It remained cheaper than wheat and was much eaten by the poor. It was considered a strengthening food (wrongly, for it contains less protein than wheat). At the Eleusinian games winners were awarded sacks of barley. Roman gladiators were fed on it, and were known as *hordearii*, 'barley men'.

MORE RECENT HISTORY

In **Europe,** after the fall of the Roman Empire, barley bread was considered inferior to rye bread and greatly inferior to wheat; but barley bread was used even by the rich, as trenchers, which served instead of plates. Barley remained the chief bread grain of Europe as regards quantity rather than quality until the 16th century, and lingered in remote areas, for example, in the north and west of Britain, for some time longer. In the 19th century in the form of bonnag, it was still the main kind in the Isle of Man.

Barley had other uses in Europe apart from bread, being added to soups and stews or made into porridge, gruel, and beverages such as barley water (see below). Barley also continued to be grown for use in making alcoholic drinks.

As for the **Orient,** barley had arrived in China before wheat, and evidence of its cultivation is very ancient. It was quite widely eaten in the north; though as a cheap alternative to wheat, MILLET was preferred. It was cooked in broth, or used like rice, or made into flat cakes; and it was malted to make malt extract, which was used as a sweetener. This product was made in China

from early times, and was later to become the principal sweetener of Japan, where barley is still an important food, chiefly in pearl form (see below).

In TIBET, and in the adjacent western parts of China, barley is a more important crop. Its resistance to the severe mountain climate gives it a major role through the whole Himalayan area to northern India. The staple food of Tibet, TSAMPA, is toasted barley (or other grain) ground to a flour.

Barley went to the **New World** with early European settlers. Columbus could not make it grow on Haiti, but the Spanish did better in Mexico and in 1602 it was grown in Massachusetts. In the USA it was seldom used for bread, since there was maize as a second-class alternative to wheat, but it was made into beer. As in Europe, barley was and remains a major fodder crop.

BARLEY PRODUCTS AND DISHES

As well as being ground into barley meal (for a particular kind of which, see BERE MEAL), barley is sold in various forms. Whole barley grain for use in soups and stews may have some or all of the bran ground off. Unground grain, with the bran intact, used to be called Scotch barley and was the cheapest kind. Pot barley has some of the bran removed, and pearl barley is ground to complete whiteness. The bran has a distinct but pleasant flavour, whereas pearl barley has almost none. 'Patent barley' is meal made from pearl barley, which is used as a thickener and to make babies' cereal feeds.

Barley water used to be made at home by boiling pearl barley in water. The infusion was cooled, sweetened, and sometimes flavoured with orange or lemon. Ready-made and bottled barley water is now more usual. It is a traditional drink of infants, invalids, and tennis players at Wimbledon. See also ORGEAT.

BARLEY SUGAR is a sweet which was originally prepared from flavoured barley water made into a syrup with sugar and boiled to the verge of caramelization. Nowadays there is no longer any barley in it, but the name persists.

Among the **dishes** made from barley, barley PORRIDGE is more delicate than oatmeal porridge, to the point of being rather insipid. It was usually made with milk rather than water. A sweet version with nuts, *Belila*, is traditionally made by Sephardic Jews to celebrate a baby cutting its first tooth. Another porridge-like dish in Britain was barley berry, or aleberry, made by boiling stale barley bread in mild ale until thick. This was served with honey and cream. Lothian barley pudding, still made, is a plain boiled pudding made from pot barley, currants, water, and a pinch of salt, and served with sugar and thin cream or milk. Dorothy Hartley (1954) cites an old

English dish, Barley bake with celery; barley, chopped celery, and mutton broth are the main ingredients. However, the barley dishes which survive most strongly in Britain are probably soups with pearl barley, exemplified by Scotch barley broth; see SCOTCH BROTH. A larger range of barley dishes is to be found further north, e.g. in RUSSIA and the Baltic countries.

In conclusion, it is noteworthy that Sokolov (1996), in a masterly survey of cereal grains, declared barley to be his favourite and furnished an anthology of recipes which should go a long way to convince any sceptics.

BARLEY BREADS Since BARLEY suffers from a lack of GLUTEN, though high in other proteins and starch, these breads have commonly been unleavened, GRIDDLE breads, such as BANNOCKS. If a leavened barley bread is wanted, it is best to mix barley with wheat; such mixtures have been usual in parts of Europe where wheat cultivation was marginal, or in times of dearth. If a light crumb structure is desired, the fibrous and indigestible outer bran of the barley is best discarded. The flavour of barley bread is sweet and nutty.

Barley's tolerance of many soils and climates has given it wide geographical spread; hence it was a breadcorn of ancient Egypt and Greece, as well as of the lake-dwellers of Glastonbury in Iron Age Britain. That said, its earliest and most enduring use has been as the starchy base to POTTAGES and GRUELS, or as raw material for beer.

The Greek author Archestratus (5th century BC) is cited by Athenaeus as claiming that the best barley comes from Lesbos, closely followed by Thebes and Thasos: 'get hold of a Thessalian roll, rounded into a circle and well pounded by hand. They call this *krimnitas*, others call it *chondrinos* [these names come from terms describing coarsely milled barley].' However, a century on, Aristotle thought barley less health giving than wheat, and it is evident that richer, more cosmopolitan communities such as Athens, where there existed a body of professional bakers able to manipulate leavenings, favoured wheaten bread as lighter and more digestible. The same was true of classical Rome; *panis hordeacius* was by and large for slaves and the poor.

The way in which barley has declined as a breadcorn consequent on increasing wealth and sophistication is illustrated in medieval Provence and Languedoc where its use, which had been considerable, almost vanished in the 14th century as wheaten bread, or a mixture of wheat and rye, became universal. It continued far longer in northern and western regions where climate favoured its cultivation. In Tudor Britain, the north-country traveller Fynes Morison observed: 'the English husbandmen eat barley and rye brown bread', but, 'citizens and gentlemen eat most pure white bread'. Come the *Corn Tracts* of 1764, it was estimated that barley contributed less than 2% of the raw material for bread in south-eastern counties, as opposed to nearly 48% in Wales and over 24% in the south-west. In northern districts, it was by then displaced by oats. In those areas where it was still popular, the commonest mode of cooking was as an unleavened hearth bread, under an inverted cauldron with hot coals heaped above.

An interesting barley bread survives, although tenuously, in the mountainous Jura region of France. This is *bolon* (or *boulon*), which has a history stretching back to medieval times, but was made with oats until late in the 19th century, after which a mixture of barley and other cereals began to be used and then just barley. This bread, which comes in small loaves weighing about 60 g (2 oz) each, is remarkably hard, too hard to be eaten in the normal way, but suited to its particular purpose which is to be eaten in a sort of PANADA (*bolons* broken into a casserole, warm water plus milk, garlic or onion). As explained in IPCF (1993), it will keep for a year.

Barley was widely cultivated in Scandinavia, and is an important element in flatbreads in Norway, Sweden, and northern Finland, also Orkney and Shetland (see BERE MEAL). Bonnag is a barley bread which has survived in the 20th century in the Isle of Man.

In Iraq, the distinction between wheaten and barley bread is identical to that in Europe: it is synonymous with poverty or meanness. 'I remember the gibe shouted from one shopkeeper to another across the market: "What do they have for supper?" Answer, "Barley bread and water melon"' (Zubaida, 1990).

A curious sidelight on the history of barley doughs is their use to make condiments in the medieval Arab world, described by Perry (1998). Unleavened, unseasoned barley doughs were rotted in closed containers for 40 days, to make *budhaj* (literally 'rotten'), then dried and ground into flour which was further rotted as a wetted mixture with salt, spices, and wheat flour to make a liquid condiment called *murri*; or with milk to make *kamakh*.

See also PAXIMADIA, a kind of barley 'biscuit' made from a barley bread in Greece and elsewhere.

BARLEY SUGAR a simple, old type of English boiled syrup sweet, with a distinctive twisted shape. Originally, in the 17th century, the sugar syrup was made with barley water, an infusion of boiled barley which gave it an agreeable, mild flavour. Now the most usual flavouring is lemon juice, whose acidity favours the making of a clear, uncrystallized sweet. The syrup is cooked to the hard crack stage (see SUGAR BOILING), poured out onto a slab in a sheet, and quickly cut into strips which are twisted before they harden.

In France a special *sucre d'orge* was being made by the Benedictine nuns of Moret-sur-Loing in the 17th century. After enjoying great popularity in the 18th century it underwent various vicissitudes, (including a move to another town, Provins, and a commission given by Napoleon to a former nun, Félicité, to keep him supplied with the product) before finishing up in modern times back in Moret, but with its manufacture in secular hands. There is reputed to be a secret ingredient, known to only one person and tantalizingly called *poudre de perlimpinpin*; it has proved to be imperceptible to chemical analysis. This barley sugar is not twisted, as in England, but comes in triangular pieces (*berlingots*) or 'rods'.

BARM BRACK or BARN BRACK, an Irish fruit bread containing dried fruit, peel, and something in the way of spice (one tradition being the use of caraway seeds). The name is generally spelled with an 'm', suggesting the original use of barm (the yeast drawn off fermenting malt) as the raising agent. However, as long ago as 1904 one authority was upholding the spelling with an 'n' on the ground that this was an Anglicized version of the Irish *bairgain breac*, two words meaning respectively 'bread' and 'speckled'. This view was endorsed by Florence Irwin (1949), a sparkling, very Irish and authoritative writer, and indeed by the less sparkling but also authoritative OED. Whichever view should prevail, it seems clear that 'brack' represents an adjective, not a noun.

Cathal Cowan and Regina Sexton (1997) provide the fullest description and history of barn brack, and indicate its symbolic roles at Hallowe'en and the New Year.

See TEA BREADS AND TEA CAKES; and BARA BRITH, for a similar Welsh product.

BARRACUDA fierce fish with large jaws and a devastating array of teeth, belong to the genus *Sphyraena*. The great barracuda, *S. barracuda*, is found in tropical waters all round the world, but especially in the Caribbean and adjacent waters. A solitary fish (unlike some small relations, which swim in shoals), it is potentially dangerous. So far as direct attacks on human beings are concerned, it is reputedly (but the matter is doubtful) a greater peril than any shark; and it is also one of those fish which in certain conditions can cause in humans who eat it what is called cigatuera poisoning. Its maximum length is not far short of 2 m (6'). The same applies to *S. jello*, a species found only in the Indo-Pacific. A smaller species of the Caribbean region, *S. guachancho*, known as the guachancho, seems to be free of the cigatuera danger.

The Mediterranean species, *S. sphyraena*, may be up to 120 cm (4') in length but is usually much smaller. A resemblance to the freshwater PIKE is acknowledged in names such as the French *brochet de mer* and the Italian *luccio marino*.

Barracuda steaks are good when fried, and may also be prepared in other ways.

BARRAMUNDI a name of Australian Aboriginal origin used both for a fine sea fish, *Lates calcarifer* (also known as giant sea perch), and for fish of the family Osteoglossidae (bony-tongued fish).

The former is considered to be less deserving of the name barramundi, but this is so familiar in northern Queensland that it seems likely to stay. It is a prized game fish, attaining a very large size (maximum length 1.5 m/5'), golden-brown or greenish above and silvery below, with small red eyes. Throughout its range, from the Persian Gulf to the Philippines, it is prized for its excellent flesh, and it is of major commercial importance in India. Although a marine species, it does enter fresh waters. How it came by its Anglo-Indian name 'cock-up' seems to be a mystery.

The latter are freshwater fish, living in slow-flowing rivers. The two Australian species are *Scleropages leichardti*, the spotted barramundi, and *S. jardini*, the northern barramundi. They have a maximum length of 90 cm (35"), the same as that of their Asian relation *S. formosus*. The flesh of all three is good.

BASELLA (or Ceylon spinach, also called vine spinach or Malabar nightshade), *Basella rubra*, a climbing plant whose succulent red or green leaves are eaten like SPINACH. Widely cultivated in tropical Asia and China, and now also in Africa and the New World. It is probably a native of India, where the variety previously distinguished as *B. alba*, with green leaves, is the one most commonly eaten (and is what is usually meant by the name Indian spinach).

The plant, which is prolific, is commonly grown as an annual or biennial. The bright red juice from the fruits is used, especially by the Chinese, for colouring foods such as pastries and agar-agar; and is sold in powdered form for these purposes in various countries including Indonesia. The leaves are mucilaginous, and are often used in Asia as an ingredient for soup, including a Chinese 'slippery soup', or as a pot-herb, in stews or with other vegetables. Young leaves may be eaten as salad greens, but are preferred as cooked greens, like spinach; the green form retains its fresh green colour, whereas the red form loses much pigment to the water, and is less attractive. The leaves have a very mild flavour; while the stems, which also become mucilaginous when cooked, tend to be somewhat bitter. In general, basella leaves can be prepared in any of the ways suitable for spinach.

CHINESE SPINACH is something quite different.

READING: Martin and Ruberté (1975).

BASIL an aromatic herb in the genus *Ocimum* of which there are several species and numerous horticultural varieties.

The best known to cooks is *Ocimum basilicum*, native to India, SE Asia, and NE Africa, and very commonly used in the Mediterranean countries. This is an annual plant, typically reaching a height of 60 cm (2'). *O. basilicum* var *minimum* is a small-leafed species, the most perfumed of all, called Nano verde (green dwarf) by seedsmen in Italy. *O. basilicum* var *citriodorum* is a lemon-scented basil; and *O. basilicum* var *purpurascens* is purple leaved. These varieties are sometimes listed as cultivars.

Other species are as follows:

- *O. sanctum*, tulsi or holy basil, regarded by Hindus as a holy plant, and much used in SE Asia. It has a clove-like fragrance.
- *O. gratissimum*, a shrubby species known as tree basil or East Indian basil and now found in many parts of the world, used for both culinary and other (e.g. mosquito-repellent) purposes. It occurs in various forms, one of which is clove-scented; but this is not the form favoured for culinary purpose. *O. gratissimum* var *viride*, known as tea-bush or green basil, is used in W. Africa as a herb for flavouring savoury dishes, or in salads.
- *O. canum*, known generally as hairy or hoary basil, but also called 'partminger' and (in Nigeria) curry leaf; its leaves are used similarly.

The early reputation of basil in Europe was characterized by a remarkable capacity to inspire approval or denigration. Referring to the polemic it aroused in classical writings, Culpeper (1653) records it as 'the herb which all authors are together by the ears about'. The potency of its associations goes some way towards explaining the suspicion with which it was sometimes regarded. These tend to be erotic or funerary and often are both: the fusion of meanings can be seen in the story by Boccaccio which later inspired Keats's poem *Isabella*. In addition to this, a widespread belief that basil bred scorpions is reiterated in the old herbals.

Basil reached England from S. Europe in the 16th and N. America, up to parts of New England, in the 17th century. Since all basils, to a greater or lesser degree, are plants of warm climates, none grows freely in more northerly regions.

In the cuisines of S. and W. Europe, and their descendants in the New World, especially in the W. Indies, basil is known particularly for its affinity with the tomato, but goes well with many other partners. It is an essential ingredient of the Italian PESTO, but has many other uses.

Dried basil loses its fragrance. The herb can be preserved for a while in olive oil or honey. However, Alicia Rios (personal communication) keeps basil by layering in salt in a sealed jar, the purpose being to get a basil-perfumed salt as a base for flavouring soups and sauces rather than as a means of preserving the basil.

In Asia, the use of basil is uneven. It is imported in Iran. In contrast, Julie Sahni (1980) writes:

Because of the sacred association of basil with the Hindu God Vishnu, the use of this herb in Indian cooking has been severely limited. However, in many Indian homes a delicious brew of basil leaves, shredded ginger, and honey, known as 'Tulsi ki Chah', is served during the winter.

Among Buddhist and Muslim peoples this special consideration does not apply, and basil of various species is freely used in most countries of SE Asia. In Thailand, a minor use is in a delicious dessert, *Mang nak lam ka-ti*, best described as giving the effect of tiny black jelly-baby fish afloat in a caviar-studded sea of milk, what looks like caviar being sweet basil seeds. The seeds are also used in Iran and Afghanistan in a special kind of SHERBET drink.

BASQUE FOOD AND COOKERY distinguishes that area in the south-east corner of the Bay of Biscay, comprising a little of France and a larger part of Spain, where the Basque people have lived since prehistoric times. María José Sevilla (1989), whose survey of *Life and Food in the Basque Country* treats the subject comprehensibly and with due attention to historical and sociological factors, quotes an expert opinion that the Basque culture goes back 50,000 years. What is clear is that from as far back as records stretch the Basques have been great seafarers. Indeed, everything about them depends on the sea and the mountains (the Pyrenees, at whose western end their territory lies).

Basque fishermen are prominent in TUNA fishing, and used to be responsible for much of the COD fishery in the N. Atlantic; the Basque people are still devoted to SALT COD.

Other items which the Basques particularly relish include fungi, among which the MOREL and CHANTERELLE feature as *karraspina* and *saltxaperretxiku* (this opportunity being taken to display the unusual appearance of Basque words). They also love dried beans. The catalogue of what they enjoy, and of things like the roast lamb which is prepared for feast days, could be continued at great length. It is perhaps more important to mention here an institution which appears to be almost unique to the Basques: the existence of numerous gastronomic societies, of a highly democratic nature but for men only. These seem to have their origin in the 19th century and to have served originally as lunch clubs for men (but not snooty, like London clubs—they were catering for all social strata), and perhaps as a way of getting round the restricted opening hours of the cider houses (the Basque country is famed for its cider). Seafaring traditions (men being away on their own for long periods) and politics and perhaps to some extent a male desire for peace and quiet (Basque women being not only beautiful but also formidable)—all these and other factors may have blended to produce the idiosyncratic results which may still be observed, especially in San Sebastian. They are to be visited in mid-January, when the societies open their doors to all visitors and women for the Tamborrada, probably the most important festival of the year, marked by the marathon drumming sessions of which Luis Buñuel gave such a dramatic description in his book *My Last Breath*.

BASS a fish name long used in Europe for the excellent fish described under SEA BASS, and widely adopted in N. America and elsewhere for naming fish related to or deemed to bear some resemblance to the European species.

One of the finest American bass is *Morone saxatilis*, the STRIPED BASS, or striper, which is treated separately, together with the black sea bass, *Centropristes striatus*, and the white perch, *Morone americanus*, which might just as well have been called a bass but was not. See SQUETEAGUE for a species which has been called white sea bass.

Two freshwater game fish of N. America bear the name bass. These are *Micropterus dolomieui*, the smallmouth bass; and *M. salmoides*, the largemouth bass, fish of moderate size (the latter and larger has a maximum length of 80 cm/32").

Channel bass is an alternative name for the red drum (see DRUM). Stone bass is an alternative name for the WRECKFISH.

In SE Asia, 'bass' occurs in the names of some members of the grouper family. Thus 'hump-backed sea bass' is an alternative to polka-dot grouper (see GROUPER), and 'giant sea bass' is the usual English name for both the huge *Promicrops lanceolatus* and the even huger *Stereolepis gigas* (for both, again, see GROUPER).

BASTING an operation familiar to all cooks, may have one or both of two purposes: to keep moist, and therefore tender, the surface of something being cooked; or to add more flavour, as when a piece of fish or meat has been in a marinade before being cooked, and is then basted with the marinade during the cooking process.

Where flavour is the aim, the use of herbs, e.g. a sprig of rosemary, to apply the liquid to the surface may be helpful. However, the best tool is a sort of syringe; but this seems to have been unavailable to cooks until the 20th century, spoons having been used previously.

BATALIA PIE a dish with a puzzling name which was current in the 17th and early 18th centuries in England. The name, which is often spelled 'battalia', is derived by the *NSOED* via French *béatilles* from the Latin *beatillae*, meaning small blessed objects. Thus this pie would be one containing especially fine titbits such as cockscombs and sweetbreads. John Nott (1726) gives two recipes, one for Battalia Pye and the other for Battalia Pye of Fish. The latter incorporates battlements and towers in the pie-case, which would suggest an alternative origin for the name if the correct one had not already been established. Nott's first pie had sweetbreads, but the other lacked the sort of titbit called for by the *NSOED*. It seems likely that any precise meaning which the term originally possessed had been eroded in the course of time.

BATH CHAP the lower (or sometimes the upper) jaw bone of a pig, with attached cheek, brined (and in the past also dried), cooked, and often pressed in a mould. In appearance a Bath chap is like a cone cut in half vertically; the curved upper surface being covered with light brown or orange breadcrumbs and the interior being streaky with pink lean and white fat in layers. Bath chaps are often eaten cold, making a tasty dish.

The word 'chap' is simply a variant on 'chop', which in the 16th century meant the jaws and cheeks of an animal. These are probably what Mrs Raffald (1782) intended when she gave a recipe 'To salt chops' with salt, saltpetre, bay salt, and brown sugar.

This called for the meat to be dried afterwards; it would probably be expected to keep for several months. *Law's Grocer's Manual* (*c*.1895) notes that both the upper and lower jaws were used, the lower one which was meatier and contained the tongue selling at about twice the price of the upper.

Why this English speciality has been associated with Bath is not clear, except that Bath is situated in an important bacon-curing part of England.

For a similar Italian product, see *guanciale* under PANCETTA.　　　　　　LM

BATS flying mammals of the order of Chiroptera, are mentioned in the Bible among the unclean animals which the children of Israel were not supposed to eat, and this fact alone suggests that they must be edible and tempting. In fact the fruit-eating bats of India and SE Asia, and other places such as Mauritius, although taboo to the Hindus as well as the Jews, are widely eaten. They are clean animals living exclusively on fruit, and have a taste which has been compared (like so much other exotic animal fare) to that of chicken.

Newly arrived passengers at Vientiane airport in Laos are surprised to see youths waving very long poles high in the air on the short stretch of four-lane highway to the city centre. They are trying to knock down bats, to be eaten. Eaten they are, and protein they provide, but (like insects) they are often absent from official statistics about food consumption.

R. J. May (1984) gives a description of how 'flying fox nets' are hung across cleared flight paths by roadsides in Papua New Guinea, and explains that the flying fox is a large species of fruit-eating bat, *Dobsonia moluccensis*. In his view the flesh is richer than chicken and more like that of a game bird. These flying foxes are usually cooked over an open fire, so that the fur is singed off, and the skin is removed before eating.

Flying foxes are also very commonly eaten by Sulawesan Christians (but forbidden to Muslims). They tend to be curried in a rich brown RENDANG style sauce. Restaurants which serve dog often serve flying fox also.

BATTENBERG CAKE a commercially produced cake popular in Britain. It consists of four square lengths of SPONGE CAKE, two coloured pink and two left yellow, stuck together with apricot jam. When cut this gives a chequered cross-section. A sheet of almond paste is wrapped round the outside.

The cake appears to be of late 19th-century origin. The first record in print is 1903. Ayto (1993) states that the cake was 'named in honour of the marriage of Princess Victoria of Hesse-Darmstadt, granddaughter of Queen Victoria to Prince Louis of Battenberg in 1884'. Prince Louis later took British nationality and Anglicized his name to Mountbatten. Ayto also observes that the two-tone Battenberg cake 'was probably designed to mimic the marbled effect of many German breads and cakes'.

BATTER is a semi-liquid preparation consisting of eggs, milk, and flour in varying proportions. Lighter batters can be made by replacing some of the milk with water or beer.

One of the main uses of batter is to coat foods which are to be deep fried, either little pieces of vegetable, fish, meat, fruit to make FRITTERS; or larger items, such as fish fillets. The texture and viscosity of the mixture is important, for it must be thick enough to adhere to the food, but not so thick that the coating becomes excessive and heavy. The batter cooks very quickly in the hot fat and forms a crisp shell around the food, preventing scorching, whilst retaining flavour and juices.

Wherever deep-frying is an important cooking method, something similar to batter will have evolved to fulfil this role, although the ingredients may differ substantially from those used in Europe. Japanese TEMPURA recipes call for various combinations of flour, egg (or egg yolk alone), and water; Chinese deep-fried recipes for wheat flour, cornflour, and water; and the Indian PAKORA, a type of vegetable fritter, uses a batter of chickpea flour and water.

In the USA, the meaning of 'batter' extends to some thicker mixtures such as those for cake and for spoon bread (sometimes called 'batter bread', see CORN BREAD).

More generally, cooked in a thin layer in the bottom of a frying pan, a batter makes PANCAKES or crêpes (see also FRAISE). Poured in a thicker layer in a large tin, and baked in the oven, it becomes YORKSHIRE PUDDING.

However, despite the fame of this last item in its savoury version, most **batter puddings** are sweet. One example is the French CLAFOUTIS, which contains fruit. Fruit is also an ingredient in many of the English batter puddings, of which Dorothy Hartley (1954) gives an impressive range, from medieval to modern times. Some are boiled or steamed, for example the Gotham pudding from the little town of that name in Nottingham, which incorporates slices of candied peel and, after being steamed, is to be served 'with cowslip wine and sugar'. Another steamed batter pudding belongs to Tiverton in Devon, incorporates ginger and other spices as well as candied lemon rind, is

served with butter and sugar, and 'should be eaten at once while light and spongy'. However, many, e.g. Kentish cherry batter pudding, are baked.

Tewkesbury (or Welsh) saucer batters are small baked puddings made by quickly baking two saucerfuls of batter, putting fruit on one and inverting the other on top of it to make a lid. These ingenious snack meals, 'ready by the time the kettle boils' for tea, may be unique to the Tewkesbury area and other fruit-picking districts. However, their small size is echoed in small baked batter puddings made elsewhere: for example the American POPOVER, and the Austrian *Pfitzkauf* ('puff up') which is eaten as a dessert with fruit.

See also HASTY PUDDING.

BAVAROIS *bavaroise*, terms which can confuse because they look alike and also because the second sometimes equals the first but can also refer to something quite different.

The dessert called bavarois (originally *fromage bavarois*) usually consists in an egg CUSTARD (*crème anglaise* in France) mixed with whipped CREAM and set with GELATIN in a mould. It first appeared in print early in the 19th century, when CARÊME gave a recipe. Although its English name is sometimes 'Bavarian cream' and some French authorities believe that it was brought to France by a French chef who had been working in Bavaria, the connection is not clearly established. However, the great chef ESCOFFIER, when he declared the title 'Bavarois' to be illogical and suggested that 'Moscovite' would be more appropriate, may be taken to endorse by implication the topographical derivation.

A bavarois may vary in flavouring, shape, and accompaniments. It can also vary in name, for the form *bavaroise* (the feminine noun *crème* being understood, or in some instances present) occurs; see Höfler (1996).

However, the long established and correct meaning of *bavaroise* is a beverage, something like a CAUDLE, which is described in detail by Favre (*c*.1905). It has hot tea with milk as an essential ingredient, into which is whisked a mixture of sugar and egg yolks, to be followed by some kirsch. Escoffier explains that it is to be drunk from special glasses while still frothy, and that it can be flavoured in various ways.

Favre also admits the existence of a bavaroise sauce, involving horseradish, vinegar, and crayfish butter, said to be suitable for tasteless fish. In case anyone should still think his treatment of the subject incomplete, he takes pains to demolish the erroneous idea that something called *Colbert* is at all like a *bavarois* or *bavaroise*. It has neither the same constituents, the same

taste, nor the same qualities, he thunders. See, however, COLBERT.

BAY LEAF from the tree *Laurus nobilis*, is one of the most widely used herbs in European and N. American cooking. The tree is indigenous to the Mediterranean region, but will grow much further north. It belongs to the family Lauraceae, which also includes cassia, cinnamon, sassafras, and the avocado.

The bay was the laurel with which poets and victorious warriors and athletes were crowned in classical times. In French it has kept the name *laurier*, and a notorious trap for translators of French recipes is to render this as 'laurel leaves', which in English may be taken to mean the larger leaves of *Laurocerasus officinalis*, the cherry laurel; these can be used in minuscule quantity for flavouring custards and the like, but are harmful in larger amounts.

Bay leaves appear as a constituent of a BOUQUET GARNI, in a COURT-BOUILLON, and in many forms of marinade. In N. Europe they are regularly used in fish dishes and in fish pickles or marinades. In many countries a bay leaf is added to potatoes which are to be boiled. However, their use is not confined to savoury dishes. In Britain they have often been used for flavouring custards and milk puddings.

In the north-west of the USA, the leaves of *Umbellularia californica*, the California bay (or California laurel, or Oregon myrtle), are used in similar ways for savoury dishes. They have a stronger flavour than European bay leaves.

'Bay leaves' in the Indian subcontinent are likely to be leaves of the CASSIA tree, *Cinnamomum aromaticum*.

In the W. Indies, the name bay leaf is used for the leaf of the 'bay-rum tree', *Pimenta racemosa* (in the family Myricaceae), whose bark and fruits are used for flavouring by cooks and whose leaf oil is an industrial food flavouring.

BEACH PLUM *Prunus maritima*, the best-known wild plum in America, is found along the eastern seaboard from New England to Virginia. The cherry-sized, crimson or purple fruits were among the first foods that the early colonists learnt to adopt. They make an excellent jelly; this is sometimes served with soft-shelled crabs, since the two products share the same season. They can also be used in many candies, desserts, and beverages, and to flavour meat and fish dishes.

An impressive conspectus of this fruit's role in the kitchen is given by Elizabeth Post Mirel (1973). In what could serve as a model work on a minor fruit, she includes historical matter, observing that the first

European sighting of a beach plum was by Giovanni da Verruzano in 1524, when he was exploring the coast of New York. But it was not until Humphrey Marshall (1785) wrote his scientific description of *Prunus maritima* that its botanical identity was established. Efforts have been made since then to cultivate the beach plum. Although cultivation remains rare, there are named cultivars in existence. This helps to preserve the identity of the beach plum, which is not always easy. The plant is highly variable in form, so much so that at one time botanists proposed two species, the high and the dwarf. Also, there are many other wild fruits which have similar characteristics; Mirel, citing Canada plums to the north, wild goose plums to the south, and Allegheny plums to the west, states helpfully that any of her recipes for beach plum can be used for 'any wild plums you can find'.

BEAN a term loosely applied to any legume whose seeds or pods are eaten, and which is not classed separately as a PEA or LENTIL.

The nutritional and agricultural advantages of beans and other legumes are discussed under LEGUMES. See also: DAL; GRAM; PULSE; and (for what is perhaps the single most famous bean dish) FUL MEDAMES.

Beans have a good reputation. The English expression 'full of beans' means 'in an energetic, cheerful mood'. There is a corresponding Portuguese phrase: *cheio de feijão*.

Most beans familiar in the West were formerly classified in the genus *Phaseolus*, which is named on account of the shape of the pods it bears, to suggest a swift sailing boat; but many of these species have now been assigned to the genus *Vigna*.

Since the common names of beans are often confusing, the following table is provided to show what botanical species there are and what common names are usually applied to them (with headwords of other entries in small capitals as usual).

- *Phaseolus acutifolius*. TEPARY BEAN, dinawa.
- *P. aconitifolius*. MOTH BEAN.
- *P. coccineus*. RUNNER BEAN, scarlet bean.
- *P. lunatus*. LIMA BEAN, sieva bean, Madagascar bean, butter bean.
- *P. vulgaris*. HARICOT BEAN, kidney bean, cannellini, French bean, navy bean, black bean, pinto bean, snap bean, common bean, frijol, chumbinho, opoca.
- *Vigna angularis*. AZUKI BEAN, feijao, adsuki.
- *V. mungo*. URD, black gram.
- *V. radiata*. MUNG BEAN, green gram, golden gram.
- *V. umbellata* var *umbellata*. RICE BEAN, frijol arroz.

- *V. unguiculata* (formerly *sinensis*), COWPEA, black-eyed pea (or, sometimes, black-eyed bean).
- *V. unguiculata* ssp *sesquipedalis*, asparagus bean, yard-long bean, dow gauk.

Bean species in other genera are:

- *Bauhinia* spp. TREE BEAN.
- *Canavalia ensiformis*. JACK BEAN, sword bean, chickasaw lima, feijão de porco, haba de burro.
- *Cyamopsis tetragonoloba*. CLUSTER BEAN, guar.
- *Vicia faba*. BROAD BEAN, fava bean, haba, fève.
- *Glycine max*. SOYA BEAN.
- *Lablab purpureus* ssp *purpureus*. LABLAB BEAN, hyacinth bean, bonavist bean, field bean, Indian butter bean, Egyptian kidney bean, seme, louvia, frijoles caballeros.
- *Macrotyloma uniflorum*. HORSE GRAM, Madras gram.
- *Mucuna* spp. VELVET BEAN.
- *Pachyrrhizus tuberosus*. YAM BEAN, jicama, potato bean, Mexican water chestnut, saa got.
- *Psophocarpus tetragonolobus*. WINGED BEAN, Goa bean, asparagus pea.

For bean products see: BLACK BEANS, GUM, KECAP, MISO (bean paste or sauce), NATTO, SOY SAUCE, TEMPE, TOFU (bean curd).

Coffee 'beans' are not beans: they are the twin stones of a fruit. Vanilla 'beans' or pods are the fruit of an orchid rather than a legume. Locust 'bean' refers to CAROB.

BEAN SPROUTS are produced by allowing seeds to germinate and grow for a short time to form shoots. The Chinese have been sprouting MUNG and SOYA BEANS for 3,000 years, and bean shoots, always popular in E. Asia, are now widely available elsewhere.

Sprouts of all kinds are highly nutritious. Germination breaks down some of the starch and protein in the seeds and makes them more digestible; and the green shoots contain vitamin C which was not present in the seeds. Raw sprouts contain substances which inhibit the action of the digestive enzyme trypsin and must be cooked to make their protein available. Only a little cooking is necessary, such as the Chinese method of quick stir-frying, which preserves the crunchy texture of the sprouts.

BEAR of various species, has sometimes been used for meat, the paws being particularly valued. Bear's grease, the fat, was esteemed for cookery by the French settlers in the Mississippi Valley, and is said to have been preferred in New Orleans, at some time in the 19th century, to butter or hog's lard.

Generally, this all belongs to history, although local consumption may continue in some remote places.

BEARBERRY *Arctostaphylos uva ursi* and other species of the same genus. This is a low scrubby plant which grows wild in northern and Arctic regions of Europe, Asia, and America. It provides dry, unappetizing fruits which are eaten only in times of famine, or by bears, as its botanical name doubly indicates (*Arctostaphylos* and *uva ursi* mean 'bear's grapes' in Greek and Latin respectively). However, the berries of *A. alpina*, the alpine bearberry, which are less dry and reasonably pleasant to eat, are consumed in Lapland and parts of Russia.

BÉARNAISE SAUCE is made by beating butter into a reduction of something acid (vinegar or lemon juice) with shallots and flavouring herbs (tarragon, chervil), and egg yolk, then heating the result until it begins to thicken. It is a robust sauce, often served with grilled steak or grilled fish of a substantial sort, like salmon.

McGee (1990) gives an illuminating account of the scientific aspects of preparing this sauce, and emphasizes that the ratio between egg yolks and butter, accounted sacrosanct by many authorities, can safely be varied within widely spaced limits. Flexibility, within rather narrower limits, can also be shown in the exact choice of ingredients and in the sequence of operations.

Béarnaise is a 'mother sauce' from which by slight modifications some other minor sauces may be devised.

BEATEN BISCUITS are small and round in shape, about 1 cm (0.5") thick, with a crisp, short texture, and slightly cracked sides. A speciality of the southern states of the USA, they are an exception to the general N. American habit of using the word 'biscuit' to indicate a soft product similar to a British scone.

To make beaten biscuits, flour, salt, and a little lard are mixed to a stiff dough with milk and water (or whole milk, for a richer result). Then the dough is beaten with a rolling pin for half an hour or more, until it blisters. It is then rolled, cut into rounds or squares (traditionally by a cutter which presses six prongs into the centre of the biscuit as it cuts). They are baked until pale brown on the outside, but should remain white within. Bernard Clayton Jr. (1973) commented that: 'The true mark of the beaten biscuit buff is splitting the biscuit with the tines of a fork. Never the knife or fingers.'

The first references to these southern beaten biscuits appear in the mid-19th century (Karen Hess, 1981). The method of repeatedly hitting a stiff plain dough with a wooden pin is related to the traditional bakers' method of kneading with a brake, a wooden lever attached at one end to the wall above the kneading table. This was worked up and down by hand, or, with a larger version, by 'riding the brake', i.e. by sitting on it as on a see-saw whilst an assistant moved the dough back and forth beneath it. As an alternative to hand beating, a special 'beaten biscuit machine', consisting of two wooden or metal rollers (like a miniature clothes mangle) was devised; these are now prized antiques. The recipe and kneading show some similarity to SHIP'S BISCUITS which were intensively worked, with a brake, by trampling, or by putting the dough through rollers.   (LM)

BEAUFORT

a cheese from the French Jura and Savoie regions, is the best of the French cheeses of the GRUYÈRE type. Like real Swiss Gruyère (as opposed to EMMENTAL) it has few and small holes, and a nutty flavour. Other French cheeses of this type include Comté (or Gruyère de Comté) from the Franche-Comté district, which has larger holes and a coarser, distinctive flavour. All are made in the characteristic large wheel shape, usually weighing up to 60 kg (140 lb), and occasionally as much as 130 kg (290 lb, the greatest weight of any cheese in normal production).

From Françoise Botkine (1993) we learn that:

The whey left over from Beaufort proper is used to make Sérac (from the Latin, *serum*, meaning whey). Sérac is a white cheese, lean and compact like Italian Ricotta. Together with Tomme, Sérac used to constitute the staple diet of the mountain people, who kept their Beaufort to sell at market, since it was their sole means of earning money.

BEAVER

Castor canadensis, a member of the family Castoridae. These animals have stout bodies about 1 m (40") in length with a tail of about 30 cm (12") characteristically broad and flat which serves variously as a rudder, propeller, and signal gun when the animal is in the water. Mature animals reach weights up to 30 kg (over 60 lb).

Beavers live in 'colonies', each 'colony' consisting of a family unit of up to 12. They are well known for their building of elaborate dams and 'houses' or lodges. The dams cause an overflow of river banks, forming a beaver-pond in which they construct their lodge.

A beaver's diet is strictly vegetarian; they feed throughout the year on bark, twigs, tree buds, grass, berries, lily roots, and other aquatic plants.

Although the beaver's industrious habits, wholesome diet, and generally meritorious lifestyle have endeared it to many human beings, the fact remains that beavers are also prized for their flesh, and are eaten.

According to Ashbrook and Sater (1945) 'beaver meat is dark in colour, fine in texture and tender'. They go on to say that:

A beaver skinned and dressed will weigh a little more than half as much as before, that is, a fair-sized animal will dress 25–30 lbs. This should include the tail and liver, which are especial delicacies. The tail is fatty tissue, rich and palatable when cooked, and was greatly relished by early trappers and explorers. The liver is large and almost as tender and sweet as that of a chicken or goose. The body meat has rather a gamy flavor, but if properly cared for and cooked is excellent and was generally preferred by trappers to any other game, even in the early days when buffalo, elk, and deer were abundant.

The beaver is a versatile animal in the kitchen. The range of recipes for cooking it includes a pot roast, barbecued beaver, baked, fried, stewed, fricasseed, or in a meat loaf or pie. Ashbrook and Sater, on whom this list is based, also observe that many Indians smoke their meats before cooking to eliminate the gamy flavour.

BÉCHAMEL

the name of a sauce which plays a large part in European cuisines; not only in France, although that is where the name originated.

The question of its origins has been discussed by Sokolov (1976):

Gastronomic literature is filled with tedious pages and trifling disputes. Béchamel has inspired more than its fair share of this piffle. People *will* argue about whether the correct spelling should not be béchamelle; whether the Italian version, balsamella from the Romagna district, is the original of the best-known and easiest mother sauce.

In such matters prejudice will always rule, for there is no evidence one way or the other. We can only point to the appearance of sauce called béchamel during the reign of Louis XIV. And, as so often, this original sauce bore only a slight resemblance to the modern sauce. While we think of béchamel as an all-purpose white sauce made of scalded milk, roux, and flavorings, Carême made it by enriching velouté with cream.

Sokolov also dismisses as intrinsically unimportant the debates which have taken place in modern times about whether a béchamel must be made with veal or need not be.

What is common to almost all accounts of béchamel in modern times is that it is prepared with a ROUX and scalded milk, usually flavoured, and that once assembled it is cooked gently for quite some time.

See also VELOUTÉ (similar, but stock-based rather than milk-based) and WHITE SAUCE.

BEDFORDSHIRE CLANGER

a tube-shaped PASTY with a SUET crust and an interior division, one end containing a savoury filling, the other a sweet filling. The clanger was thus a meal in itself, which could be taken to work and constituted a counterpart to the dual-function version of the Cornish pasty.

BEDOUIN FOOD

The Bedouin (or Beduin) were nomadic herdsmen who lived in the deserts of Arabia and N. Africa. The number of true nomads is now in decline but their food culture has survived to influence the more sedentary populations which have developed in these regions.

Bedouin existence depended on their herds and flocks. The CAMEL was the supreme possession providing transport, milk for food and drink, meat, hair, hides, and dung for fuel. Camels were, however, a Bedouin's wealth and would rarely be slaughtered for meat. Any camel meat usually came from the slaughter of surplus bull calves or injured or sick beasts. The camel enabled man's penetration of the extensive desert areas, as they are capable of sustained travel in search of pasture with only intermittent water supplies. Where daily access to water could be assured, herds of GOATS and SHEEP were kept by the Bedouin, primarily for milk and meat but also for their skins which were used as water and food containers.

Bedouin hospitality rules varied but the common version required that a host was duty bound to provide at least a minimum of board and lodging for three and one-third days. After that time the guest was required to leave but was still under the host's guardianship for a further three days. Frequently a beast would be slaughtered for the first meal to demonstrate the host's wealth, social standing, and to uphold tribal honour. Whilst this meal was being prepared, COFFEE or some other light refreshment such as DATES and BUTTERMILK would be served and the guest would be politely questioned to extract useful information. These gatherings were strictly male affairs. If women were in the encampment they would be segregated and would prepare the meal, although slaughter and butchery were men's work.

The main dish of boiled MUTTON or camel calf served to an honoured guest was called *mansaf*. It would be presented on a bed of rice or wheat and would normally be a festival dish for the Bedouin. These meals were served to the guests first. Food was generally eaten speedily. Once the guest had taken his fill he would leave the food to allow someone of lower standing to have his turn. After rinsing his hands he would retire to wait for everyone to finish, after which more coffee would be served. After all the men had eaten, any remaining food would be taken to the women and young children. A host would often abstain from eating, taking a supervisory role to ensure that the hospitality was worthy.

Routine Bedouin fare was a basic and monotonous diet of milk, bread, and DATES. Bedouin culinary requirements ranged from the need to sustain a small group travelling independently, probably with grazing flocks, to the provision for large tribal groups who might be settled in one area for several weeks. Thus bread, which was a staple, could be simply cooked in the embers of the fire by wandering herdsmen. In a tribal encampment large quantities of *shirak* or *rukak* (thin unleavened breads) would be required and would be prepared and cooked on a metal sheet over the fire. Access to fresh provisions might be close at hand in a nearby oasis or could be several days' march away.

Small game was simply thrown on the fire to cook in its fur and was eaten in its entirety. On the other hand, a butchered beast for a feast in a large camp would be cooked in a *jidda*, a large stewpot, and served on rice, liberally drenched with rendered animal fat or *samn* (clarified butter—see GHEE). Wheat was grown in Arabia whilst rice was imported from Iraq or India.

Cooking utensils were simple and robust, appropriate to the nomadic lifestyle. The *jidda*, made of tinned copper, came in a variety of sizes, large sizes being required for festival meals. It was accompanied by a shallow dish, *sahen*, for serving food. Wooden bowls and serving dishes were also used. Much cooking was an improvised affair—three stones to make a tripod support and a search for dried plant roots in the desert sand or some dried camel dung for fuel.

Bedouin food was dominated by a number of staple items. Apart from their animal stock and milk products the staple items were dates, wheat and rice, flour, and *samn*.

Dates were of prime importance to survival in the desert. They were an ideal food, readily obtainable as they grew in all the oases; non-perishable, easy to consume, economical to transport, and providing excellent nutrition as a balance to the other main dietary constituents.

Milk, *haleeb*, from camel, goat, and sheep was consumed, although the preference was for camel's milk. Of the three, it was drunk whole and the other two usually after the butter had been made as they were

considered to be too rich. During the spring grazing, herdsmen would subsist solely on their camel's milk.

Samn was a major product of the Bedouin herds for consumption and also as an item of commerce. The *samn* was prepared by churning either fresh milk or yoghurt in a skin which was inflated by blowing into it at regular intervals. The fresh butter was heated with a little flour and occasionally coriander and cumin. Once the *samn* had been poured off into the storage skin, the curds and flour were eaten and not wasted.

Yoghurt was drained and salted to make a sun-dried food for storage, *jamid*. Initially like a cheese, the drained yoghurt eventually became rock hard (see KASHK AND KISHK). It was reconstituted by pounding in a mortar and mixing with water or sieving into hot water. As a traveller's food it could be gnawed in its natural state.

Water was a precious commodity. Throughout the deserts it was only dependably found at some waterholes and at various springs associated with oases. It was transported in a waterskin made from goat hide.

Coffee, *kahwa*, was the prime social drink and a marker of hospitality. The ring of coffee pestle on the mortar as the freshly roasted beans were crushed was the signal for men to gather at the coffee tent for the exchange of news and retelling of stories. Guests were received by the host who would frequently prepare the coffee himself.

Coffee was always freshly roasted in a roasting spoon, then cooled in a wooden tray before being pounded and subsequently brewed in a pot made of clay or tinned brass. It was served in small ceramic cups and was often flavoured with cardamom.

Game formed an important element of Bedouin food though it was not available on any regular basis and would at times be an item of last resort, e.g. the eating of carrion and the prohibited foods (*harram*, as opposed to *halal*, permitted foods). Small game such as jerboa and lizards could be dug out of burrows with a camel stick. Locusts were consumed, generally roasted or parched over the fire. If not consumed immediately the dried flesh could be ground up into meal and stored in a skin to be added to stews at a later date.

With food resources at a premium there was little prospect of regular meals for the Bedouin. One meal a day would be adequate and it could easily happen that there would be no real meal, a few dry dates and some camel milk sufficing.   PI

BEECH NUT a small nut of fine flavour, which has been gathered from beech trees, *Fagus* spp, and used for human food since prehistoric times. However, its main use has

been for feeding animals, especially pigs. The nuts are often called beechmast, or simply 'mast' (a term applied also to ACORNS).

The generic name for beeches comes from a Greek word meaning 'to eat', indicating the importance which the nuts have had as food. However, the names in Germanic languages, *Buche, Buke*, etc., are all related to 'book'. Loewenfeld (1957) speculates that this may be because runic tablets and early 'books' were made of beech; she notes also that the same is true of the first letters cut by Gutenberg for printing purposes.

Beech trees are large and beautiful, and belong to temperate climates. The main European species, *F. sylvatica*, is found throughout Europe and temperate W. Asia to the northern edge of India. *F. grandifolia*, the principal N. American species, is common in most of the USA and southern parts of Canada.

The small triangular nuts are borne in pairs inside a cup with four prickly brown sides. The nuts change from green to brown as they ripen; the husks open out; and the pairs of nuts are then 'blown on windy days in thousands from their coverings to the ground, where they lie hidden among the carpet of rustling golden leaves' (Claire Loewenfeld, 1957).

There is no doubt about the attraction of this 'mast' for animals. Squirrels, badgers, dormice, and larger animals such as deer are greedy for it. The value of beech woods for the purpose of feeding domesticated animals and poultry used to be very great. Howes (1948) says: 'it is no exaggeration to state that in times gone by the value of many an old estate in Britain was estimated more by the amount of mast the woods on it produced, which of course included acorns as well as beech nuts, than on its actual area.'

In general, beech nuts have been regarded as food for humans in times of famine or scarcity. Roasting makes it possible to peel them without difficulty, and they are then rubbed and sieved to rid them of small hairs, after which they can be dried and salted and eaten whole; or ground into meal for making bread. The meal can also be used in cakes and biscuits. In N. America, Indians and white settlers alike made use of beech nuts in times past.

The oil which can be obtained from the kernels is above average in keeping quality and flavour, and has been used by rural populations in Europe both for cooking and as a salad oil.

BEEF (*see opposite page*)

BEEFEATER the popular name in England for Yeomen of the Guard, dates

(cont. on page 69)

Beef

The meat of domestic CATTLE, *Bos taurus*, eaten mainly in N. Europe, the Americas, and Australia. The word derives from Anglo-Norman *bœuf*; less desirable parts of the animal are referred to in English with the Saxon prefix 'ox' (OXTAIL, ox cheek, etc.), reflecting the social divide which existed in England after the Norman Conquest.

Beef usually comes from castrated males (steers, or bullocks), which are killed at about 18 months to 2 years, providing tender meat. Heifers not required for breeding are also used. Up to the age of 6 months, the meat of young cattle is regarded as VEAL.

The quality of beef from a particular animal is partly dictated by its breed, a subject discussed under CATTLE. Fodder is also important. Grass-fed beef is considered to have the best flavour, although many cattle are intensively reared on grain. To rear cattle using grain, or pasturing them on land suitable for growing grain, is an inefficient use of food resources; see MEAT, where many other matters relevant to beef are also discussed.

Medieval contributions to the art of **beef cookery**—beyond simple roasting and boiling—were the development of the PIE, and BRAISING. BEEF OLIVES also originated during this time: slices of meat spread with a stuffing of, say, breadcrumbs, onion, herbs, rolled up, and braised.

Broiled or grilled steaks were also popular. During the 16th century these were made into 'carbonadoes', a name which referred to a method of scotching the meat with shallow criss-cross cuts to help make it tender. See CARBONADE, CARBONADO.

As the thick POTTAGES of medieval cookery went gradually out of fashion, they were partly replaced with 'made dishes' of meat in sauce: for example braises, RAGOUTS, DAUBES, and HASHES (from the French *hachir*, to chop).

Beef was also treated by SALTING. Some was cured with spices and molasses, and simmered for immediate consumption; a great deal more was barrelled in brine or smoked for long keeping. Another way of dealing with beef was to souse and collar it; the piece was rolled and tied and cooked in salted liquor. Cheaper cuts were used for POTTING; Scottish potted HOUGH is made from shin of beef.

During the 19th century, beef acquired a position of primary importance in European haute cuisine. The coarser cuts went into the pot to provide a foundation for stock-enriched sauces, or to be cooked and boiled down for CONSOMMÉ. The OFFAL was used up in economical dishes. (In England beef suet went into the crust for English SUET PUDDINGS.) Even the bones were roasted and the BONE MARROW extracted to spread on toast. Whenever possible, a piece of beef was added to the composite boiled meat dishes of peasant and bourgeois cookery, such as the New England boiled dinner, French POT-AU-FEU, Italian BOLLITO MISTO, Spanish COCIDO (*cozido* in Portugal), and Romanian *ciorbă* (see SHORBA), which provide broth or soup for a first course, and a plain meat course to follow.

One side effect of this, especially in Britain, was that large amounts of cold beef had to be 'used up' in other dishes. Mrs Beeton devoted much space to 'cold meat cookery' including baked beef, a precursor to SHEPHERD'S PIE; a beef RAGOUT; broiled beef and oyster sauce (slices of cold meat broiled, served with mashed potatoes and covered in oyster sauce); and bubble and squeak (see COLCANNON). RISSOLES, HASHES, and CURRIES were other methods for using leftovers. Thus evolved the English habit of serving a large roast of beef on a Sunday, and making the remains into a series of dishes for the other days of the week.

The study of food science advanced during the 19th century with the discovery of proteins, then known as albumen, in fluid extracted from meat. It was erroneously thought that meat could be 'sealed', allowing a crust to form on the

---

BEEF CUTS

BEEF carcasses are large and, except on the rare occasion of an ox-roast (when the entire carcass is roasted whole over an open fire), are always divided into smaller cuts or joints. This is a more complex task than dividing pigs and sheep, and the pattern of division varies between and within countries.

In Britain, the main cutting lines run at right angles to major muscle groups, cutting through fat deposits and bone. The most expensive and tender cuts, used primarily for roasting, or for cutting into STEAKS, come from the ribs and sirloin. An exceptionally tender piece of meat is located underneath the backbone in the region of the sirloin; if removed in one piece it is known as the 'fillet', and used as a superior roast or for steaks. Both sides of the rump together, with the back part of the sirloin attached, constitute a 'baron' of beef.

Most other cuts of beef are traditionally cooked by moist methods. Silverside, topside (the 'round', frequently called for in old cookery books), and brisket are left as joints; neck, chuck, shin, and flank are cut up for pies and stews.

A simplified version of the British pattern is followed in the USA, but with more emphasis on making pieces suitable for grilling (broiling). Much of the less tender meat is minced (ground) and used for dishes such as HAMBURGERS.

The French cut their beef in a different pattern, dissecting muscles to provide a higher proportion of meat for grilling and frying. For instance, a cut from the fore rib which in Britain would be used exclusively for roasting is divided by the French into the tougher muscles, which are sold for stew, and tender ones, sold as best-quality steak.

Whether the bone is left in the joint or not is a matter of taste; it conducts heat, helping the joint to cook, and contributes to flavour. On the other hand, a boned and rolled joint is easier to carve.

BSE

(Bovine Spongiform Encephalitis)

Bovine Spongiform Encephalitis, colloquially known as 'mad cow disease', came to light in Britain in the mid 1980s and was subsequently identified in some other European countries. Exactly how it started is a much debated question, but the former practice (discontinued in Britain in 1988) of recycling dead sheep and cattle meat as animal feed (and changes in the 1970s in the regulations governing this practice) are widely viewed as a prime factor.

Efforts to eradicate BSE had a particularly severe effect on cattle farming (millions of animals destroyed) and the meat trade in Britain. Extensive enquiries are still continuing in 1999 into it and into 'new variant CJD', the form it has apparently taken when transmitted, with fatal results, to humans.

It remains to be seen how many people will come down with new variant CJD (whose incubation period is very long but still undetermined) over the next few decades. Estimates range from under 100 to many thousands. It is likely that existing bans on eating certain parts of the animal will gradually be lifted, with the ban on eating brains lasting longest.

outside early in cooking, thus preserving these precious fluids. This belief is not entirely extinct, and is sometimes quoted as the reason for browning beef or other meat in hot fat before stewing it. It belongs, however, to the realm of CULINARY MYTHOLOGY. McGee (1990) writes well and in detail on this, and on 19th-century preoccupations with MEAT EXTRACTS, which affected attitudes to beef and provoked much activity in Britain in making 'beef tea', and in the production of items such as Oxo.

Some of the above might suggest that the British have been especially prone to entertaining mistaken ideas about beef cookery. However, they have earned for themselves an enviable reputation for roasting beef:

> The English men understand almost better than any other people the art of properly roasting a joint, which is also not to be wondered at; because the art of cooking as practised by most Englishmen does not extend much beyond roast beef and plum pudding.

Thus wrote the Swede Per Kalm after his visit to England in 1748. Like many other clichés, that of the *rosbif*, the beef-fed Englishman with a fleshy face and high colour, contains more than a grain of truth. For centuries visitors have commented upon the excellence and quantity of beef eaten in England. They also noted the English liking for rare beef, a taste which according to Rumohr (1822) led many continental visitors to believe that it was actually raw meat which was being eaten. With the disappearance of open fires from most kitchens, what is known as 'roast' meat today is actually oven baked; but the principle is still based on the use of dry heat. YORKSHIRE PUDDING, gravy, roast potatoes, boiled greens, and horseradish sauce are the usual accompaniments to roast beef.

British cooks perform adequately in other areas of beef cookery, offering such specialities as Boiled beef with carrots (for which a cut such as round, slightly salted, is used) and various pastry-based items, including STEAK AND KIDNEY PUDDINGS or pies, and several items which belong to the PASTY category: Cornish pasties and the Forfar Bridie. A much grander pastry dish is Beef Wellington, an English equivalent to the French *Bœuf en croûte*; a fillet of beef, perhaps embellished first with other expensive ingredients such as truffles, is baked in a pastry case.

French cookery is famous for slow-cooked rich stews, in which the beef may be left in one piece, or cut up. *Bœuf à la bourguignonne*, cooked with wine, salt pork, and garnished with mushrooms and small onions, is probably the best known. A rich beef stew is also characteristic of Flemish cooking, where it is known as *carbonnade* (see CARBONADE), and contains onions and beer, and is topped with a crust of mustard-flavoured bread. Italians, too, make hearty meat stews; those from the north are more likely to contain beef, such as a Lombardy *stufato*, a stew of beef with tomato. Further south, the *Stufato alla romana* is based on shin of beef.

Braised beef is popular in C. and E. Europe. For German *Sauerbraten* (see GERMANY), a cut suitable for pot-roasting is marinated in a mixture of wine vinegar, water, and spices for two days or so, then cooked in the marinade, and served with potato dumplings.

A famous beef dish of Russian cookery is Beef Stroganov. It consists of strips of fillet steak browned swiftly in butter, served in a sauce of shallots, wine, and soured cream. There is some disagreement over which Stroganov, Alexander Grigorievich Stroganov, who lived in the Black Sea port of Odessa, and did much entertaining, or a 19th-century diplomat, one Count Paul Stroganov, is the person honoured. Another beef dish which has become internationally popular is the Hungarian GOULASH.

Cured beef remains important. See PRESERVATION, SALTING, DRYING, and also CORNED BEEF, PASTRAMI, and BINDENFLEISCH.

Towards the end of the 20th century, trends in beef consumption, in those countries where it has been high, reflect various factors. A tendency to eat less red meat is one. Disquiet over BSE (a topic where the available information and current attitudes are liable to relatively rapid change—see box) is another. In those parts of the world where for various reasons there is no strong tradition of eating beef, there may be a slight tendency towards increased consumption, caused by the general 'internationalization' of foods or, as in Japan, by the development of a new connoisseurship. In the area around Kobe, Japanese *shimofuri* beef is raised on a diet including rice, rice bran, beans, beer, enhanced by regular massage. This is very fine and some distinctive methods for cooking it have evolved.

back to the 17th century. It was wrongly supposed during much of the 19th century to be derived from the French word *buffetier*, meaning someone who attends at the sideboard. Weekley (1958) exposes the fallacy, declares that the word simply means 'eater of beef', and continues: 'In the 16th century the compound had two special meanings: (1) a burly Englishman, as compared with less favoured races, (2) a pampered menial. The Yeoman of the Guard was both.'

Beef olives familiar in England, originated in medieval times, when cooks would take slices of beef or veal (or mutton), spread them with a stuffing of, say, breadcrumbs, onion, and herbs, and braise them. When they call the result 'olives', this was a mistake; a corruption of the name of the dish, 'aloes' or 'allowes'. This came from the Old French *alou*, meaning lark; the idea was that the small stuffed rolls looked something like small birds, especially ones which had lost their heads in being prepared for the table. In this connection it is interesting that, although the standard French word for these rolls is *paupiettes*, there is an alternative name, *alouettes sans tête*, literally 'larks without heads'. Also, in English they are still often called 'veal birds'. Corresponding terms in other countries are: Italy, *involtini*; Poland, *zrazy*; Czechoslovakia, *ptachky*; and Germany *Rouladen*.

Beefsteak fungus (also called ox-tongue fungus), *Fistulina hepatica*, a large bracket fungus which grows like a shelf from the trunks of oak and chestnut trees. It is found in Europe and parts of the USA, e.g. New Jersey and Pennsylvania, and some regions of southern Africa including Swaziland. It has pores, not gills, and belongs to the group of Polypores. The pores, however, are formed by small tubes which remain distinct and independent from each other, a feature which distinguishes this species from other polypores.

The common names are explained by Badham (1863):

This fungus, which, in the earlier stages of its development, frequently resembles very closely a tongue in shape, structure, and general appearance, presents later a dark, amorphous, grumous-looking mass, bearing a still more striking likeness to liver.

The upper surface is usually sticky, or gelatinous when wet, and of a blood-red colour which darkens with age. Underneath, the flesh is mottled and veined, resembling raw meat, and exudes a juice like blood when cut.

A beefsteak fungus can grow to an enormous size. Badham remarked that he had himself picked one which measured nearly 150 cm (5') round and weighed over 4 kg (8 lb), and that he had heard on good authority of a specimen weighing 14 kg (30 lb).

The fungus has an acid flavour, betraying the presence of tannins. This is more apparent when it is eaten raw, for example sliced into a salad, than when it is cooked. For either purpose it should first be peeled and have its pores removed, and then be sliced. The slices should be salted and put aside for a while to remove excess water and acidity. They may be fried or stewed or grilled. Badham comments on this too:

No fungus yields a richer gravy, and though rather tough, when grilled it is scarcely to be distinguished from broiled meat. . . . its succulency is such that it furnishes its own sauce, which a friend of ours, well versed in the science of the table, declares each time he eats it to be 'undeniably good'.

Beer as an alcoholic beverage has no place in this book, but it does have two claims for inclusion. One is that the early history of brewing is closely bound up with that of bread-making, as both were early and obvious ways of using cereals. The other is that beer is an ingredient in certain dishes.

It was in ancient Egypt and the Near East that the beer and bread connection was apparent from early times. But the same connection is found at later times elsewhere, for example in N. Europe. Studies such as some of those edited by Astri Riddervold (1988) provide details.

As for beer as an ingredient, this is prominent in the north of France and Belgium, especially for various versions of carbonade, for each of which a specific beer may be required. In Britain, beer is used in curing or cooking ham and it does occur occasionally in other culinary contexts, of which Elizabeth Craig (1955) has provided details. Its uses in Germany, for example in meat cookery and certain sweet soups, are more noticeable.

Beestings for which the correct technical name is colostrum, is the milk produced by a cow, or any other mammal, immediately after giving birth: it is markedly different from normal milk and contains various substances which favour and protect the newborn animal. For cooks the important point is that it contains much more of the lactalbumin proteins than usual, so that it is thick when raw and sets to a custard when cooked.

Tradition attributes mystical curative powers to beestings, and it has often been used to make special curds and other dishes for invalids.

Beeton ISABELLA (1836–65), author of the most famous cookery book in the English language, does not correspond at all to the general impression which people have of her. The sheer size and scope and authoritative air of this book, *Beeton's Book of Household Management*, have caused people to imagine a matronly figure, in middle age, if not older, perhaps looking somewhat like the standard image of Queen Victoria, during whose reign Mrs Beeton lived.

In fact, she was a beautiful young woman, married to a bright and enterprising young publisher, who started at the age of 21 to produce material for her husband's *English Woman's Domestic Magazine*, including the collection of vast numbers of recipes and information about how to run a household. She was only 25 years old when her work appeared in book form, and only 28 when she died (of puerperal fever, contracted after giving birth to her fourth child—and having lost the first two in infancy).

Her book, in its first edition, was a triumph of organization, common sense, and kitchen skills. Mrs Beeton had borrowed from her great predecessor, Eliza ACTON, the innovative method of setting out recipes in a standard way, with appropriate brevity but also with the requisite details. And she was well served by her friends and by contributors to the magazine for which she worked. Yet, whatever benefits of this nature she enjoyed, the compilation and editing of what was the greatest work on cookery and household management in the 19th century called for an extraordinary talent. This she displayed, with occasional flashes of a pretty wit, to lighten what might otherwise have seemed too didactic an approach to her readers. Didactic, of course, she had to be because the task she had set herself was to instruct both mistress and housekeeper in all aspects of housekeeping, while supplying background information on the natural history of foodstuffs (a feature in which she anticipated developments which in the main did not take place until a hundred years later) and explaining points of etiquette and wrapping up the whole package with advice on lifestyles and morals which was intended to ensure that her readers approached their tasks in the appropriate frame of mind. To do all this required an almost military approach ('As with the commander of an army . . . so is it with the mistress of a house,' she wrote) and a decisiveness which would ensure that readers were not left bemused by too many alternatives or vague instructions. After all, their days would hardly be long enough to cope with their manifold tasks, even if they completely eschewed the 'faffing around' which messes up the day for so many people. Mrs Beeton recommended early rising ('one of the most essential qualities'). She noted with approval that Lord Chatham gave this advice: 'I would have inscribed on the curtains of your bed, and the walls of your chamber, "If you do not rise early, you can make progress in nothing."'

However, a great book such as hers could not be based solely on such exhortations to readers, comprehensive scope, good organization, and a clear style. The something more which was necessary to make it great was that intangible quality which is hard to pin down but which radiates almost palpably from the finest cookery books, an emanation which tells the readers that the author really knows what she is about.

Given that her book merits such high praise it is all the more unfortunate that its later history was on the whole a sad one. Sam Beeton ran into financial difficulties in 1867, while seriously ill and still suffering from the shock of bereavement. He relinquished all his copyrights, including his late wife's book, to the publishing firm Ward, Lock & Tyler. Elizabeth David (1984) has chronicled what happened thereafter. To begin with, the new publishers were content to reprint and to produce abridged volumes. However, a new and considerably changed edition came out in 1888, containing much which Mrs Beeton had not written and would not have written. In 1906 there followed a completely revised edition, with the cookery sections re-edited by a well-known chef and author, C. Herman Senn. Elizabeth David comments that, although this carried the book considerably further away from the down-to-earth approach of the original author, grafting on to it 'refined little things in dariole moulds' etc., such as Edwardian professional chefs delighted to produce, and adding 'other laughable little items' which left Mrs Beeton's reputation vulnerable to critical scorn, the Senn edition was 'a wonderful and beautiful book' and was still a coherent whole.

It was at this point that references by Sam Beeton to his 'late wife' dropped out of the book, leaving the unwary to suppose that she might still be alive and tendering her advice; and from then on it was downhill all the way until eventually, by the 1960s, the revised book did not contain a single recipe as written by the author. Fortunately, two other publishers subsequently produced facsimile reprints of the first (1861) edition, so that those who would like to savour Isabella Beeton's recipes and homilies directly from the original source may easily do so.

BEETROOT one of four useful forms of the versatile plant *Beta vulgaris*. The two which provide vegetables for human consumption are the red, globular roots of beetroot itself, and its leaves; and the stalks and leaves of CHARD. Mangelwurzel, treated with beetroot in this entry, is also cultivated for its edible root, but used for animal fodder. The fourth form is SUGAR BEET, whose roots are an important source of sugar.

All these cultivated forms are descended from the sea beet, *B. maritima*, a wild seashore plant growing around the Mediterranean and Atlantic coasts of Europe and N. Africa. This has only a small root, but its leaves and stems are sometimes eaten. Early Greek writers such as Theophrastus referred to the cultivation of this plant. By about 300 BC there were varieties with edible roots.

Red beet, known as Roman beet, and yellow-rooted varieties spread through Europe and Asia in succeeding centuries.

In Europe a yellow kind developed into fodder beet. In Germany it was known as Mangoldwurzel (beet root), which was corrupted to Mangelwurzel (root for time of need) because it would only be eaten when nothing else was available.

However, until well after medieval times, beet roots remained long and relatively thin. The first mention of a swollen root seems to have been in a botanical work of the 1550s and what is recognized as the prototype of the modern beetroot, the 'Beta Roman' of Daleschamp, dates back only to 1587.

In Britain the common beets were originally all light in colour. The red beet, when introduced in the 17th century, was described by Gerard (1633) with some enthusiasm ('a most excellent and delicate sallad'). It soon found its way into the recipe books. Evelyn (1699) declared that cold slices of boiled red beetroot (such as are still familiar to everyone in Britain) made 'a grateful winter Sallet', while adding that it was 'by the French and Italians contriv'd into curious figures to adorn their Sallets'. The anonymous but authoritative authors of *Adam's Luxury and Eve's Cookery* (1744) gave two recipes, one for frying red beets as a garnish for carp and other fish, and the other 'To make the Crimson Biscuit of red Beet-roots'.

The scarlet colour of beetroot is due to the combination of a purple pigment, betacyanin, and a yellow one, betaxanthin. Yellow roots have little of the former. The pigments are much more stable than most red plant colours, and are sometimes extracted and used as edible food colourings.

A cultivated beetroot may be as small as an orange or as large as a grapefruit. Although red, globular varieties are dominant, there are some with flattened tops, some with golden or even white flesh, and some which are shaped like thick carrots. Prolonged cooking makes the colour fade. When whole beetroot is boiled, the skin is left on to avoid damage to the cells and letting the colour leak out.

See BORSHCH, for what is probably the best-known beetroot dish.

BEIGNET the French term denoting a general class of small, light, batter-coated, deep-fried items equivalent to the English FRITTER. This meaning has been kept in the state of Louisiana, where French influence is strong, and beignets are a speciality of New Orleans.

'Beignet' also has a specific gastronomical meaning of deep-fried choux pastry, sometimes distinguished with the name *beignet soufflé* (because the paste puffs up considerably when cooked). These may be served sprinkled with icing sugar, or filled with jam, or with a savoury filling such as chopped ham or grated cheese. A small, round, plain one is known as a *pet de nonne* ('nun's fart').

Choux paste is popular in many countries for making fritters. The Italians use it to make *bigné*, simple lemon-flavoured puffs sprinkled with sugar made for St Joseph's Day. Spanish *buñelos de viento* ('puffs of wind') are made for various feast days, such as All Saints; they become *buñelos de San Isidro* when filled with custard and served during the May festival of that saint. *Sonhos* ('dreams', a Portuguese and Brazilian name) are lemon-flavoured choux beignets soaked in cinnamon-flavoured syrup. LM

BELGIUM a country fashioned in its present form in 1839, is made up of a Flemish part in the north and a Walloon (French-speaking) part in the south, plus the bilingual capital Brussels in the centre. The division is not just between languages. The scenery differs (flat in the north, mountainous in the south) and so do the pattern of employment, indices of wealth, birth rates, and—perhaps most important—personality profiles. The Walloons are generally held to be softer in outlook, more pleasure-loving, and more gastronomically inclined; whereas the much more numerous, and richer, Flemish are seen as diligent and determined go-getters. Any such generalizations are liable to many exceptions, but few would deny them a certain validity.

Given this split, is it reasonable to speak of a Belgian cuisine? In fact, the singular word does fit, if one takes into account certain national dishes, the dissemination of regional specialities from both parts across the whole country, the liking shared by both the Flemish and Walloons for certain ingredients—e.g. EEL, SHRIMP, MUSSELS, GAME, CHARCUTERIE (e.g. *boudin blanc*, see WHITE PUDDING), and HAM, CHICORY and the fine varieties of PEAR which Belgian growers in the 18th and 19th centuries did so much to develop; plus the important unifying role of the capital. In terms of culinary sophistication Brussels ranks above, say, Amsterdam and Strasbourg, Milan and Geneva. The very names of streets in the capital excite the appetite. *Belgian Cuisine* (Belgian Tourist Office, 1981) cites among others impasse du Potage (Soup Dead-end), rue des Harengs (Herring Street), rue des Faisans (Pheasant Street), and impasse des Groseilles (Gooseberry Dead-end).

The national dishes certainly include *Moules et frites* (mussels with chips), skilfully cooked at hundreds of restaurants and roadside stalls and especially at places like Ostend on the North Sea coast. Another would be CARBONADE, which belongs to the south but not exclusively, witness the version cooked in beer and called *Carbonnade à la flamande*. Another candidate would be the famous dish of eel cooked with herbs, which has different names in north and south (*Paling in't groen* and *Anguilles au vert* respectively). Yet another would be WATERZOOI.

Specialities of the Flemish-speaking north include *Asperges op zijn Vlaams*. This is ASPARAGUS the Flemish way (the cooked asparagus is accompanied by potatoes, boiled or braised cooked ham, hard-boiled egg, melted butter, and grated nutmeg), and Malines is its capital city. HOP SHOOTS (in their short season in early spring), are a speciality of Poperinge in Flanders but popular throughout Belgium.

For the historically minded, it is interesting to note certain traces of Spanish rule, such as what Belgians call *escavèche* (see ESCABECHE). Going even further back, one may savour what is supposed to be Charlemagne's grandmother's soup. Now known as *Potage liégeois*, this is a pea and bean soup, one example of the numerous and particularly good soups which Belgians enjoy. Another one associated with Liège is *Soupe Tchantches*, named after a mythical comic figure of Liège, who has been made into a marionette. It is a vegetable soup with the addition of fine vermicelli and milk. *Truleye* (from *truler*, to crumble) is a cold soup into which gingerbread is crumbled, but there is also a hot version made with beer, sugar, butter, and nutmeg.

Southern Belgium is a land of châteaux and fortresses, among the pastures of Hainaut in the west and the rugged hills of the Ardennes in the east. The Ardennes is noted for its famous smoked raw ham and for charcuterie and PÂTÉS in general, but

perhaps even more so for its game, wild boar (*sanglier*, here at its very best), deer, and rabbit. It is in this region and elsewhere that one also finds one of the many excellent Belgian TARTS, such as *tarte au sucre* or *tarte au riz*. Not far away is Spa, known for the Spa biscuits which are probably the best-known product of a well-established biscuit industry (one cannot say long established, since it was only around 1900 that it began to achieve its present prominence; but of course many of its products such as *speculoos*—see *speculaas* under BANKETBAKKERIJ—are of great antiquity).

Passing from the dessert course to FRIANDISES, one has to note that the chocolatiers of Belgium, mostly of Greek origin (Daskalides, Léonidas, etc.) are acclaimed internationally for the unsurpassed quality of their products. These, with coffee, follow nicely after what many visitors to Belgium would consider to be one of the national desserts, namely the *Dame blanche* (meringue, ice cream, and chocolate sauce). HS

READING: Belgian Tourist Office (1981, an unpretentious but invaluable reference work for regional specialities); Rosine de Dijn (1992).

BELIMBING ASAM *Averrhoa bilimbi*, a fruit-bearing tree, native to Malaysia, which has no English name. 'Asam' refers to the sourness of the fruit, which is related to the sweeter CARAMBOLA. The fruit is also distinguishable by its smooth, unridged, yellowish-green skin, looking a little like a gherkin.

Juicy and acid, the fruit is used in Malaysia, Indonesia, and the Philippines for making pickles, e.g. the Malay *sunti*; in curries; and for stewing as a vegetable. In Indonesia it is caramelized with sugar to make a sweetmeat known as *manisan* (something sweet). The sour flavour which it imparts to a dish is well liked in the region. Dried slices of the fruit are available in the markets, and the fruit can be bought in candied form in the Philippines.

Julia Morton (1987) observes that in Costa Rica the uncooked fruits are made into a relish and served with rice and beans.

Towards the end of the 18th century the bilimbi was carried from Timor to Jamaica, and was planted throughout mainland C. America, as well as in Cuba and Trinidad. It is also grown extensively in Zanzibar.

BELLFLOWER ROOT *Platycodon grandiflorus*, a foodstuff used extensively in Korea, where it is known as *toraji* and is one of the vegetables associated with the first full moon of the year. It makes a delicious vegetable side dish, prepared with spices, vinegar, and SOY SAUCE. The roots have to

be carefully prepared to rid them of their bitter taste. Fresh root must be parboiled and repeatedly rinsed. Dried root must be soaked and washed several times. Either way, the root is usually cut into strips, which will have a distinctive, but mild flavour. Pickled *toraji* is also available.

In Japan, the dried root is included in the medical herb mixture used to flavour *o-toso*, the MIRIN-based liqueur drunk at New Year.

BELORUSSIA once known as White Russia, is a vast flat country with many large rivers, lying between RUSSIA, LATVIA, LITHUANIA, POLAND, and the UKRAINE. A Russian author, Pokhlebkin (1984), comments:

There is some difficulty in establishing exactly what constitutes traditional Byelorussian cooking, because of the continuous social and religious upheavals the region has undergone.

The peasants of Byelorussia belonged to the Russian Orthodox Church; the petty gentry were mainly Unitarian; the nobility, chiefly Polish or Lithuanian in origin, were exclusively Roman Catholic. The cooking traditions of the ruling classes resembled the Polish and German cuisines, while the small-town artisans and merchants were influenced by Jewish cooking, after the seventeenth century when the Jews began to settle there *en masse*. Only the peasants maintained the real traditions of the Slavic tribes from which they descended.

Given the geographical position of the country and the habits of its neighbours, it is no surprise to find that potatoes loom large in the diet (mealy ones are preferred) and that there are lots of DUMPLINGS (*kletski*), both savoury and sweet; that there are RYE BREADS; that BARLEY and OATS are used; and that there is much emphasis on dairy foods.

Unusual items typical of Belorussia include:

- *Zhur*, a type of oat KISEL which can be sweet (often made with honey and fruit) or savoury. The latter is a kind of soup which is served hot and has a slightly acid or sour taste, produced by soaking the oatmeal overnight; it is served with potatoes.
- *Mokanka*, a dish which succeeds in combining four milk products (curd cheese, sour cream, milk, and buttermilk) to which, when they have been blended, chopped spring onion and dill are usually added. This can be eaten as a thick and creamy hors d'œuvre or as a cold main dish with potato and perhaps cucumber and pancakes.
- *Drachona/drachena*, a pancake-type cake/scone made with rye flour and buckwheat and served with sour cream and jam.

READING: Bolotnikova *et al.* (1979).

BEL PAESE one of the best-known Italian cheeses, was not made until the 20th century. In his survey of 451 Italian cheeses, Di Corato (1977) dates it precisely to 1906, at Melzo in the north of Italy, and gives credit for its invention to Egidio Galbani. The name was not bestowed in allusion to the beauty of the northern Italian landscape, as some authors have it, but was taken from the title of a book, well known at the time, by the Abbot Stoppani.

The inspiration for Bel Paese was French. The process by which it is made closely resembles that used to produce PORT SALUT and Saint-Paulin: whole milk, and surface-ripening for a relatively short time. Like the French cheeses, Bel Paese has a semi-soft but elastic texture, with a flavour which is mild when the cheese is young and more pronounced after it has been kept for a while. It is sold in small wheel shapes, weighing about 2 kg (4.5 lb) and with a characteristic wrapping which features the head of the Abbot Stoppini and a map of Italy. (The Bel Paese made in the USA has what seems to be the same wrapping, but inspection reveals that the map on it is of the Americas.)

This is a fairly rich cheese, with a fat content of 45–50%. Italians find that it goes particularly well with pears.

BENTO a Japanese term applied to the small items of food which go into packed lunch or picnic boxes, and to the box itself. The box can vary from utterly simple to very grand, and the contents likewise—but they are always elegantly arranged and they always include rice. This is almost always non-glutinous rice (*uruchi mai*). For special occasions, glutinous rice (*mochigome*) is used and always steamed. With the addition of little red azuki beans it is called *seki-han* (red rice) and could appear as bento.

Of course there is more to a bento than the rice, and the accompaniments (called *o-kazu* in Japanese) are many and various. Pickles are a must and so is fish, usually grilled, but there may be some small pieces of meat and certainly a salad of cooked vegetables such as spinach, BURDOCK, or COLTSFOOT. Shredded raw cabbage and a twist of cold spaghetti are quite common, as is mashed potato and hard-boiled egg. Slices of rolled omelette, *kamaboko* (see FISH PASTES), and boiled pumpkin are also popular.

Expensive bentos will have plenty of prawns and expensive fish, salmon, for example, or fried oysters. Cheap bentos will have mackerel and lots of fried foods— potato croquettes, slices of pork fried in a coating of egg and breadcrumbs, or squid done the same way.

Finally, there is usually a small piece of fruit—a wedge of apple, a small piece of watermelon, or a few grapes.

Perhaps the best-known kind of bento is the *ekiben* sold at all major railway stations, each station having its own distinct bento featuring local specialities. The station bento for Hiroshima is shaped like a wooden rice paddle (a famous local product) and contains oysters (also a famous local product) set on top of *Chirashi sushi*, a kind of seasoned rice decorated with a variety of colourful things such as green peas, shredded pink ginger, shredded omelette, slices of SHIITAKE mushrooms (cooked), a sprinkling of powdered green seaweed, with a slice of lemon for the oysters. The pickles are wedged into the handle of the rice-paddle box and are also a local speciality (Hiroshima *nazuke*).   RHo

BERE MEAL a speciality of ORKNEY AND SHETLAND, is made from a special variety of BARLEY which thrives in those northern islands and has been used for many centuries as the basis for local BANNOCKS and PORRIDGE and similar preparations.

Catherine Brown (1996) explains that this special northern variety of barley is known as 'bigg' or 'bere' (pronounced 'bare' in the north) and has four ear rows rather than the usual six, 'yielding a lower amount per acre but producing a grain of remarkable flavour. Between 12 and 15 tons are grown in Orkney each year, and every Orkney baker makes a daily supply of the bere bannock—a 15 cm (6") round, 1–2.5 cm (0.5–1") thick, flat, girdle-baked, soft scone.' Characteristic of these bere bannocks are the grey-brown colour and robust earthy tang. They were originally made, before raising agents were developed in the 19th century, in the form of 'a very thin soft chapati-type pancake, like a modern potato scone'.

The crofters for whom bere bannocks were taken for granted as daily fare in the past would have been surprised to learn that at the end of the millennium bere meal would be classified as one of the cherished traditional foods of the European Community, thus part of the European culinary heritage.

BERGAMOT the name for herbs of the genus *Monarda*, especially *M. fistulosa*, in the MINT family. These are indigenous to Mexico and N. America. Some are used as flavouring herbs, additions for salads, or pot-herbs.

M. fistulosa var *menthifolia*, known as oregano de la sierra, provides in the south-west of the USA a flavour akin to that of true OREGANO.

M. didyma is also known as Oswego tea, indicating its former use in making a

beverage, or as bee-balm (but see also BALM).

There is no connection with the bergamot orange (*Citrus bergamia*), except for the coincidence that *M. citriodora*, lemon bergamot, has a citrus aroma. Bergamot oil (used to flavour what is known as Earl Grey tea) comes from the orange, not the herbs. The bergamot orange is not edible and is grown only for its fragrant oil, although its peel is sometimes candied. It is grown (almost exclusively) in the Italian province of Calabria.

BERLINGOT a French sweet made from boiled sugar, striped with pulled sugar. These sweets are made all over France, but the best known are from Carpentras, where berlingots in their current form (shaped like HUMBUGS, although an official definition describes them as being 'of indefinable shape') have been manufactured since the mid-19th century. Flavourings include mint (most commonly), coffee, aniseed, and many sorts of fruit essence. It is the stripes of pulled sugar which seem to distinguish the *berlingots de Carpentras* from those made elsewhere, for example at Nantes (which city may have a better claim to be the place of origin of the berlingot, which was already known in the Nantais version in the 18th century).

BERRY is a name commonly applied to various small fruits. There is a difference between everyday usage and the botanical definition. A typical version of the latter is: 'a many-seeded inferior pulp fruit, the seeds of which are, when mature, scattered through the pulp.' This definition includes the BILBERRY, CRANBERRY, CURRANT, GOOSEBERRY, and GRAPE. But it also includes unexpected items: CUCUMBER, BANANA, DATE, PAPAYA; APPLE, PEAR (both pomes); and the citrus fruits ORANGE and LEMON, and it excludes a number of fruits commonly referred to as berries. Thus the HUCKLEBERRY is not a berry but a drupe (a fruit with a stone or stones, hard casings around the seeds). The BLACKBERRY and RASPBERRY are strictly 'etaerios of druplets', clusters of little fruits with stones. MULBERRY is a composite fruit called 'sorosis', as is the PINEAPPLE. The STRAWBERRY is a 'false' fruit, being the swollen receptacle which bears an 'etaerio of achenes', i.e. the pips which are the true fruits of the plant.

Fortunately, the *NSOED* also allows a commonsense definition: 'Any small globular or ovate juicy fruit not having a stone.' In Old English, berrie used to refer chiefly to the grape. Etymologically it is difficult to unravel the word and the limits of its application. Various derivations have been proposed, some leading back to Sanskrit words. One possibility, not the one most favoured by lexicographers, is that the word is of Celtic origin, and means 'red', comparing it with Middle Irish 'basc', which also means red.

The notion of a classification based on colour, 'red' being wide enough to include the orange-through-to-black colour range found in berries, tallies with a recurrent theme in Graeco-Romano mythology, where the colour of the berry in question is explained as being the result of blood spillage: the blackberry is from the blood of the Titans; the raspberry is stained red with the blood of the nymph Ida. (And the mulberry is black from the blood of Pyramus and Thisbe, the ill-fated lovers in the ill-fated play acted by Bottom and his cronies in *A Midsummer Night's Dream*.)

BESAN FLOUR a principal product of the CHICKPEA. Because the chickpea is known in S. India as Bengal GRAM, besan flour is also known as gram flour or Bengal gram flour. Whichever name is used, it is a basic ingredient in Indian cookery. It is made by milling very finely what is called *channa* (or *channa dal*), the small Indian chickpea, husked and split. Its protein content is very high, its texture fine, and its colour pale yellow.

Besan flour mixed with water provides batter coatings for FRITTERS such as PAKORA. It is used for various savoury noodles, and plays a part in certain sweetmeats. Among these are *bundia* (or *boondi, bonde*), tiny confections made from a sweetened batter incorporating besan flour (or other pulse meal) dribbled through a perforated ladle into hot oil. The mixture forms pea-sized balls which are coated in syrup.

Besan flour is also an ingredient of dumplings and for thickening and emulsifying curries. Stobart (1980) points out that cooks in western countries, where besan flour is virtually unknown, will find it a highly effective thickener.

BESTILLA a Moroccan pigeon pie made on special occasions and often very large. The name is generally derived from the Spanish *pastel*, 'pie'. It is the Moors' adaptation of the large medieval European pie, using their own variety of layered pastry.

This pie is made in a large dish lined with half a dozen thicknesses of a pastry similar to FILO, called WARQA. Above this comes a layer of sugar, cinnamon, and browned almonds; then a creamy mixture of eggs and stock; more sheets of pastry; small pieces of meat from as many pigeons as required, previously cooked; more of the egg and

stock mixture; and a crust of several more sheets of pastry, the top one cut in a decorative pattern, glazed with egg, and sprinkled with sugar and cinnamon.   CP

BETEL NUT a popular stimulant in the Indian subcontinent and SE Asia, is the fruit of the areca palm, *Areca catechu*, which grows wild in Sumatra and the Philippines and is cultivated in other regions. The nut, which may also be called areca nut, contains a stimulating alkaloid (arecoline) and tannins which give it a pleasantly astringent taste.

The usual way of consuming betel nut is in the form of 'pan'. The nuts are gathered either green or ripe, according to taste. Green nuts are shelled, boiled to mellow the flavour, and sun dried. Ripe nuts are simply dried. The nuts are then crushed with lime and catechu, a scarlet and astringent extract made by boiling chips of wood from the areca palm. The mixture is wrapped in a betel leaf, which comes from a different tree, *Piper betle*, to make small packages. Elaborate equipment may be used for the various stages of preparation, and the provision of betel nut for guests used to be an important element in hospitality. All this is now on the decline.

Packages of pan are chewed, not swallowed. The effect is mildly stimulating. Pan sweetens the breath but stains the saliva bright red and eventually blackens the teeth. It is thus easy to see who has been using it. Indians believe that pan aids the digestion. No claim has been made for it as a source of nutrients.

The so-called betel leaf, mentioned above, is used as an edible wrapping for morsels of food in SE Asian countries, e.g. Thailand.

BETTY or **BROWN BETTY**, a N. American baked pudding, consisting of alternating layers of sugared and spiced fruit and buttered breadcrumbs. A little fruit juice is used to moisten the whole, and it is baked until browned and crisp on top. Although various other fruits can be used, Apple brown Betty is the favourite. The name seems to have first appeared in print in 1864, when an article in the *Yale Literary Magazine* listed it (in quotation marks, implying that it was not then a fully established term) with tea, coffee, and pies as things to be given up during 'training'. That author gave brown in lower case and Betty in upper case; and, in default of evidence to the contrary, it seems best to go along with the view that Betty is here a proper name.

BICARBONATE OF SODA NaHCO$_3$, has been used in cookery for so long that,

despite its chemical label, it has largely escaped the growing opposition to 'chemical' additives. It is an alkali which reacts with acid by effervescing—producing carbon dioxide. It is therefore a leavening agent in baking, if used in conjunction with, say, tartaric acid (see CREAM OF TARTAR) or lemon juice. See BAKING POWDER and LEAVEN.

The alkaline properties of bicarbonate of soda can also be used to soften the skins of beans and other pulses. And a pinch added to the cooking water makes cabbage and other green vegetables greener, by its effect on the pigment chlorophyll. However, it also induces limpness (by breaking down hemicelluloses) and the loss of vitamins B$_1$ and C; and the practice, which dates back to classical Rome and used to be recommended in Britain and N. America, has largely died out. McGee (1984) provides a detailed explanation and cites a forthright injunction from Tabitha Tickletooth (1860):

Never, under any circumstances, unless you wish entirely to destroy all flavour, and reduce your peas to pulp, boil them with soda. This favourite atrocity of the English kitchen cannot be too strongly condemned.

See also COLOUR AND COOKING.

BIG-EYE the name given, for the obvious reason, to fish of the genus *Priacanthus*. Of the several species found in SE Asian waters, *P. tayenus* may be taken as typical: up to 30 cm (12") long, abundant (at Hong Kong, for example), but not highly esteemed. Chan (1968) writes:

The rather unpleasant brilliant crimson-red colour, the tough skin with firm and rough scales, and the unusually large eyes are probably the cause of its unpopularity. However, it is of excellent edible quality. It can be roasted, baked or steamed. When it is ready for the table, the skin is very easily peeled off, and the flesh is extremely palatable.

The name 'big-eye' is sometimes applied to other sorts of large-eyed fish, usually in adjectival form, as in 'big-eyed scad'.

BIGNAY *Antidesma bunius*, a tree native to SE Asia, where it is occasionally cultivated, and N. Australia, is also known as 'Chinese laurel', 'salamander tree', or 'currant tree'.

The tree bears long clusters containing as many as 30 or 40 berries, each of which is up to 2 cm (0.75") in diameter. These clusters are very colourful, because the berries ripen unevenly; white, yellowish-green, and red ones are to be seen in the same cluster as ripe purple ones. Even ripe fruits are rather too acid for eating raw, but their high pectin content makes them excellent for making jam and so forth. The whole cluster may be

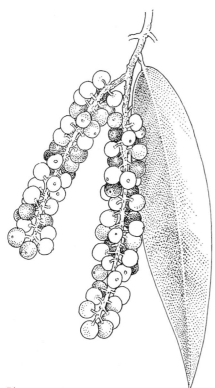

Bignay

picked, even when all the berries are not yet ripe, for this purpose. The berries may also be used in a sauce suitable for fish.

The genus includes numerous other species which are put to similar uses. *A. ghaesenbilla*, the blackcurrant tree, is a species with a wider distribution, including tropical Africa.

BILBERRY the fruit of a group of low scrubby plants in the genus *Vaccinium*, especially *V. myrtillus*, which typically bear dark bluish-purple berries with a characteristic bloom on their smooth skins. They are distinct from the CRANBERRY and BLUEBERRY, although they belong to the same genus and the name WHORTLEBERRY is sometimes applied to both.

Other names in use in Britain are whinberry, because the plant grows among whins (a Scots term for gorse); and blaeberry, 'blae' being a north country and Scots word for blue.

Bilberries are sparsely distributed on the plants, and picking a large quantity is tiring work. They are good to eat raw, being less acid than cranberries, but are also often made into pies, tarts, jams, preserves, and sauces.

In Ireland, Lammas Sunday (the last of July) is also known as Garland, Height, or Bilberry Sunday. Marking the beginning of the harvest, this was an occasion when bilberries were gathered and festivities took

place. In County Down there has been since prehistoric times a cairn where, on the first Sunday of August, the 'blaeberries' were picked and put into little rush baskets made there and then; a procedure which accompanied courting, as suggested by the saying that 'many a lad met his wife on Blaeberry Sunday'.

In N. America bilberries may also be called whortleberries, as noted above, and less aptly 'huckleberries', a name better reserved for the true HUCKLEBERRY, whose structure is different. The bilberries of N. America are plants of the far north, characteristic of Labrador, the mountainous parts of New England and the Lake Superior region. They are generally less good than the BLUEBERRY.

The term 'bog bilberry' is applied to more than one species, but especially to *V. uliginosum*, whose berries are of inferior quality.

BILLFISH a name given to the various species of large fish which have their upper jaws prolonged into a pointed rostrum, snout, or 'bill', which may be either round in section or, in the case of the 'sword' of the swordfish, flat. The purpose of the bill seems to be to stun the smaller fish on which billfish prey.

Billfish, in general, provide excellent flesh, usually paler than that of tuna and with good keeping quality. In many regions they constitute a major resource for so-called 'big game fishing'. Commercially, they are of greatest importance to the Japanese, whose share of the world catch, in terms of both fishing and consumption, is over two-thirds.

Billfish fall into four groups, treated under MARLIN, SAILFISH, spearfish (see MARLIN), and SWORDFISH. For a catalogue of all the species see Nakamura (1985).

BILTONG a dried, or dried and smoked, meat of southern Africa which exists in two principal forms.

Biltong made from beef is formed by taking a good piece of muscle 45–60 cm (18–24") long and 15 cm (6") in diameter, with no tendon and just a little fat, and trimming it into an elongated oval shape. It is then rubbed with salt, pepper, coriander seed, and fennel seed, moistened with vinegar; left to marinate for a few days, then hung up to be wind dried, and finally hung in the chimney to be smoked. Leipoldt (1976) writes: 'the result should be a dark-coloured, firm, elongated piece of dried meat, which cuts easily and when sliced is a tender garnet-red segment, surrounded by a thin, more darkly covered integument that need never be pared off before eating. Its taste is deliciously spicy.'

The same author explains that game biltong 'as made in the field' is markedly different. It is game meat cut into thin strips, rubbed with salt and perhaps crushed coriander seed, and sun dried until very hard. Bits are cut off and chewed by those with strong teeth; or it is pounded or grated to provide something which even the dentally disadvantaged can manage. Powdered game biltong spread on bread and butter is recommended. ZEBRA is said to make the finest biltong of all, but almost any game animal can be used.

BINDENFLEISCH also called **Bündnerfleisch**, a Swiss air-dried meat, traditionally made in the Grisons during the winter. It is treated before drying by being dipped in white wine and rubbed with a pickle of salt, herbs, and onion. It is served in very thin slices with a dressing of oil and vinegar. See also BRESAOLA.

Brési, a dried meat speciality of Franche-Comté in France, is clearly a close relation of Bindenfleisch and Bresaola.

BIRCH SUGAR a sugar obtained by boiling down the sap of the sweet/black birch tree, *Betula lenta*, and other species in the genus.

Birch sugar is considerably less sweet than maple sugar (see MAPLE SYRUP) and the sap from which it comes is not available until about a month after the maple sap is running. Medsger (1972) notes that the inner bark of the black birch has a sweet, spicy WINTERGREEN flavour and was generally eaten by boys. He further notes:

It is claimed that in 1861, after the Battle of Carricks Ford, the edible bark of Black Birch probably saved the lives of hundreds of Garnett's Confederate soldiers during their retreat over the mountains to Monterey, Virginia. For a number of years after that, the route the soldiers took could be traced by the peeled birch trees.

BIRD'S NEST the eponymous ingredient of Chinese bird's nest soup is an expensive delicacy. The nests belong to a species of swiftlet, *Collocalia whiteheadi*, which is found in the Philippines and New Guinea. Patricia Arroyo Staub (1982) has explained that

The gathering of these nests is a formidable task of the intrepid souls who scale cliffs and mountains. Contrary to popular belief, the bird's nests are not found in the faces of cliffs but in caves. Hence the gathering involves work in the nooks and crannies of caves which are dark and slippery. This makes it a rare and highly prized delicacy which is most precious to a Chinese food gourmet and which has become popular among Filipinos. . . .

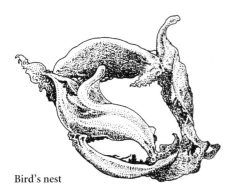

Bird's nest

However, due to its ability to swell in boiling water, very small amounts are needed to make soup.

In making their nests, the birds cement a scaffolding of tiny twigs together with a sticky substance which has been variously identified as coming from regurgitated seaweed, such as AGAR-AGAR, or as being simply the birds' own saliva. Since it is the sticky substance which is finally absorbed by the persons eating the bird's nest soup, it seems to be an open question whether they are consuming a plant food or an animal food. Several authorities have referred apologetically to this area of doubt, but have pointed out that the high cost of a bird's nest of the right sort has tended to rule out any analytical research.

BIRIANI a term of Persian origin meaning 'fried', refers to a spicy dish of layered meat and rice. In a relatively elaborate form with garnish which could include silver leaf (see GOLD AND SILVER LEAF), this is a feature of MOGHUL CUISINE. It is essential to use basmati rice and to flavour the dish with SAFFRON.

BIRIBA the fruit of the tree *Rollinia mucosa* (probably=*R. deliciosa*, although some botanists distinguish two species), which has an extensive natural range in Latin America, from N. Argentina to S. Mexico and including the Caribbean islands. It is cultivated in some places, e.g. in the vicinity of Iquito (Peru). In Brazil it is often grown in domestic yards or gardens, but plays little part in commerce. It is better known in the north and north-east, notably Belém dó Pará, than elsewhere.

The fruit is 7–10 cm (3–5") long and has a creamy-yellow skin. The white or cream-coloured flesh is sweet, juicy, and of a good flavour, making the biriba one of the finest of the annonaceous fruits of tropical America.

BISCUIT is a word which covers a vast range of flour-based items, generally small in

size, thin, and short or crisp in texture. A more precise definition is difficult, as Garrett (*c*.1898) discovered; he concluded that a crisp or brittle texture was the only shared characteristic and that 'Pastrycooks and confectioners, both British and foreign, appear to have mutually agreed to retain this feature as the only one necessary to distinguish a tribe of kinds which differ from each other in almost every other particular'. However, he had reckoned without N. America, where 'biscuit' means a soft, thick SCONE-type product, and the words COOKIE and CRACKER are used for items similar to English biscuits. (In modern Britain the application of the word 'biscuit' to breads which are soft and fresh has survived on Guernsey, and in the north-east of Scotland, where 'soft biscuits' are flat buns made from bread dough kneaded with butter and sugar. This is possibly the origin of the N. American habit of referring to scones as biscuits.)

Apart from considerations of size and texture, a biscuit is also defined to a certain extent by usage. Biscuits rarely form part of a formal meal except when cheese is served. They are mostly eaten as snacks and served as offerings of hospitality, together with drinks. They may be sweet or savoury, are simple to make in quantity and keep well when stored.

The name 'biscuit' is derived from the Latin *panis biscoctus*, 'bread twice cooked'. This name was applied to such products as RUSKS, made from plain dough baked in a loaf, cooled, sliced, and then dried in gentle heat to give a crisp, dry product which kept well. Double cooking was also used for SHIP'S BISCUIT, a durable staple food made from stiff flour and water dough for sailors on long voyages and armies on campaign. The Italians produced this type of *panis biscoctus* commercially in the Middle Ages. The English equivalent was a hard and unattractive food. Froissart in his *Chronicles* (about 1400) writes enviously of Scottish soldiers who carried bags of oatmeal and made themselves delicious fresh OATCAKES instead wherever they camped.

Other methods not requiring an oven were devised for producing crisp products from flour and water; one was to cook the mixture in a thin layer on a heated plate to make a WAFER. These were popular in the Middle Ages and, in various forms, still are. The method of deep frying is even more ancient. The Romans made thin sweet biscuits in this way; one of the few recipes of APICIUS to deal with this branch of cookery describes how a thick paste of fine wheat flour was boiled and spread out on a plate. When cooled and hardened it was cut up and fried until crisp, then served with honey and pepper. This biscuit is made of a mixture similar to the Roman pasta known as *lagani* (see LASAGNE), whose name may

have passed down (possibly via the Arabic *lauzinaj*) to the medieval LOZENGE, for which a thin sheet of dough made from flour, water, sugar, and spices was cut into pieces and fried.

The boiling and frying technique remained in use in the Middle Ages for making cracknels, which were small, crisp, sweet biscuits. They continued to be made well into the 19th century (and bequeathed their name to a sort of brittle toffee filling for chocolates). The simnel was another medieval product, which was boiled first and then baked. It was thicker than a cracknel, and resembled a sweet bread. In the 17th century the original simnel died out and the name was transferred to SIMNEL CAKE.

Sweetened, spiced mixtures of the GINGERBREAD and HONEY CAKE type have been popular in Europe for centuries. Over the years, thinner versions such as British ginger biscuits and German LEBKUCHEN developed.

Another special category of rich sweet biscuit popular since the late Middle Ages is that of confections aerated with foamed egg whites, in which the flour is partly or wholly replaced with ground nuts (see NUT BISCUITS, MACAROON, etc.).

The discovery that beaten egg was an effective aerating agent gave rise to several types of biscuit (usually spelt 'bisket') popular in the 17th and 18th centuries. Foamed egg white, or whole egg, and sugar were mixed with fine flour and baked in small thin rounds or fingers, or baked in a roll, sliced, sugared, and dried like a rusk. These progenitors of modern MERINGUES and of sponge biscuits (see BOUDOIR BISCUITS) passed under many names, but towards the end of the 17th century the recipes had become codified. 'Italian' biscuit, based on egg whites alone, was an early form of meringue. SAVOY biscuit, which originated in France sometime early in the 17th century, appeared in English recipe collections in the late 17th and early 18th centuries. It was made from whisked eggs and sugar, mixed with flour. A number of other 'biscuits' based on similar ingredients but mixed in a slightly different order also appeared: Lisbon biscuits, Naples biscuits, and Spanish biscuits, given in 18th-century cookery books, were all of this type. 'Common biscuit' was an egg, sugar, and flour biscuit flavoured with a spice such as coriander, rosewater, or sack.

Another popular 17th- and 18th-century biscuit was the JUMBLE, or knot, made from a light mixture of eggs, sugar, and flour and rosewater or aniseed.

A new French *croquant* (crunchy) biscuit reached Britain around 1600. It was based on flour, sugar, and egg whites. Several kinds of very light egg white biscuits made of a mixture similar to that of croquant are of long standing in Europe. These include the various thin biscuits such as the French TUILE, curved into a tile shape while still soft after cooking.

Flat, pastry-type products, baked only once, were known in the 16th century as 'short cakes'. They were made of rich shortcrust pastry with added eggs, leavened with a little yeast but kept thin. (Yeast always presented a problem in biscuit-making, since it was likely to give an uneven rise. 'Docking'—pricking holes in the rounds— was one method of dealing with this. Many modern biscuit varieties still have these holes.) In the north of England short cake mixtures were pressed into moulds to make funeral biscuits (see FUNERAL FOOD) which were given to the mourners at a burial. Both short and croquant mixtures—as well as puff pastry—were used for making flat biscuits to be eaten by themselves, and as a base for mixtures of dried fruit and other sweet things. Biscuits based on mixtures in which butter and sugar were creamed together probably developed during the 18th century.

In Britain the relative importance of the basic biscuit mixtures changed greatly during the following two centuries. That of RUSKS diminished, and fried biscuits died out (although in parts of Europe, the Middle East, and India frying continues to be an important method for cooking biscuit batters). Spiced biscuits remained popular and were influenced by shortened mixtures. NUT BISCUITS, always a select delicacy, became a specialized branch of biscuit-making, verging on sugar confectionery. Sponge finger biscuits continued to be made after the larger sponge cake became a separate variety in the 18th century.

Enriched 'short cakes' became much more important, developing into many regional English biscuit specialities such as Derbyshire wakes cakes (flavoured with currants, caraway seeds, and lemon zest), Goosnargh cakes (from Lancashire, flavoured with coriander), SHREWSBURY CAKES (flavoured with cinnamon), and all biscuits based on a short pastry mixture such as modern SHORTBREAD and digestive biscuits. Rich short butter-based doughs are also specialities of C. and N. Europe.

Cheese-flavoured biscuits have their origins in medieval cheese tarts and pastries; but the totally plain, unsweetened biscuit for eating with cheese did not come into use until the 18th century. An early British plain biscuit was the Bath Oliver (see BISCUIT VARIETIES). Plain biscuits also developed into fancy salted crackers, 'cocktail biscuits' for nibbling at drinks parties.

In France, because sailors used so many biscuits, the great seaport of Nantes became associated with biscuit production, especially in the 19th century. Famous biscuits made here include *petit beurré; paille d'or*, a very fragile biscuit, enclosing raspberry jelly between two wafers; and the round *beurré nantais*.

During the 19th century supplies of cheap sugar and flour, plus chemical raising agents such as BICARBONATE OF SODA, led to the development of many sweet biscuit recipes. In Britain several entrepreneurs laid the foundations of the modern biscuit industry. The firms of Carrs, Huntley & Palmer, and Crawfords were all established by 1850. Since the mid-19th century the range of commercially baked biscuits based on creamed and pastry type mixtures has expanded to meet demand, and accounts for the majority of biscuits sold under brand names in Britain today. Chocolate-coated biscuits, however, only became a lucrative business after the Second World War.

See also BISCUIT VARIETIES, and in addition: BANKETBAKKERIJ; BEATEN BISCUITS; BOUDOIR BISCUITS; BRANDY SNAPS; COOKIE; CRACKER; GINGER BISCUITS; GINGERBREAD; HONEY CAKE; JUMBLES; LEBKUCHEN; MACAROON; NUT BISCUITS; OATCAKE; PAXIMADIA; RUSK; SAVOY; SHIP'S BISCUIT; SHORTBREAD; SPONGE CAKE; SPRINGERLE; TUILE; WAFER; WATER BISCUITS; some of which have already been signposted above in particular contexts.

LM

BISCUIT VARIETIES both home baked and factory made, are so numerous that no one has ever catalogued them all, worldwide. The entry for BISCUIT provides signposts to entries for many kinds. The present entry provides a further selection.

Abernethy biscuit, a plain, semi-sweet Scottish biscuit, sometimes flavoured with caraway seed. Named after Dr John Abernethy (1764–1831), a Scot who became chief surgeon to St Bartholomew's Hospital. He used to take lunch at a baker's shop, where he ate ordinary 'captain's biscuits'. After he suggested the addition of sugar and caraway, the baker gave the new biscuit his patron's name; see Marian McNeill (1929).

Afghan, a New Zealand biscuit made from a creamed mixture with the addition of cornflakes, and flavoured with cocoa. These biscuits have no obvious connection with Afghanistan, but serve to illustrate the fact that wherever British colonists plant their feet, as in New Zealand, biscuits spring up around them and may be given whimsical names.

Anzac a New Zealand biscuit made with butter, golden syrup, rolled oats, and coconut, named after the Australian and New Zealand Army Corps Anzac which fought at Gallipoli in 1915.

Bath Oliver, a flat biscuit with a hard, crisp texture, made from flour, butter, yeast, and milk. The biscuits are 'docked'—pricked all over before cooking—which prevents them from rising and blistering too much. The original biscuits were created by Dr W. Oliver of Bath around 1750. The town was a fashionable health resort and this biscuit was introduced as a diet item. It is now popular with cheese. True Bath Olivers have an imprint of Dr Oliver in the middle of the biscuit.

Bourbon, a British commercially made sweet biscuit which has no known connection with the French royal family. It is a crisp sandwich biscuit of rectangular finger shape, composed of two chocolate-flavoured biscuits with a stiff chocolate paste filling.

Captain's biscuit, an old-fashioned British biscuit, commercially made and once popular as a plain biscuit for eating with cheese, but now rare. 'Thin captains' and 'thick captains' were made from flour and water, with a small quantity of butter and eggs, and the mixture kneaded together very thoroughly. After baking the captains were set in a dry warm place to dry out.

Charcoal biscuit, eaten in the 19th and early 20th centuries as an antidote to flatulence and other stomach troubles. It was based on ordinary flour mixed with powdered willow charcoal, made into plain dough with a little butter, sugar, and eggs.

Cigarette russe, a thin sweet biscuit popular in France. It is made from a soft, creamed dough, which spreads out very thin in the oven. While still soft after baking, the biscuits are rolled into cylinders. See also TUILE and BRANDYSNAPS.

Digestive, the British name for a popular commercial biscuit. It is of the pastry dough type, made from coarse brown flour. It is thick, fairly crisp, but also crumbly and, being only moderately sweet, goes well with hard English cheese. The biscuit has no particularly digestive properties and is banned from sale under that name in the USA. Alternative names are 'wheatmeal' and 'sweetmeal'. Recipes for home-made digestives generally include oatmeal to give the required texture.

Doigt de Zénobie (Zénobie's finger), the common French name for a sweet, crumbly, finger-shaped Middle Eastern biscuit made from semolina and butter, raised with yeast, sprinkled with cinnamon, and saturated with warmed honey.

Garibaldi, a popular British biscuit named for the famous Italian patriot, but almost certainly unknown to him. It is a sweet, rather chewy biscuit containing currants, and is known colloquially as 'squashed-fly biscuit', from the appearance of the currants.

Langue de chat (cat's tongue), a thin, flat, French biscuit, named for its elongated oval shape. It is made from a beaten mixture of sugar, cream, flour, and egg white.

Maria, the most popular of Spanish biscuits, accounting for nearly half the biscuits eaten in Spain. It was invented in England by the firm of Peek Frean in 1875, to mark the wedding of the Grand Duchess Maria of Austria to the Duke of Edinburgh. The crisp, thin round, stamped 'Maria', was an immediate success, but, although Marias were first produced in large quantities in Spain around the turn of the century, it was not until after the Civil War that they became an integral part of Spanish culture. They are dunked in milk, coffee, or tea. There are now numerous versions, all with a delicate design and 'Maria' stamped on top.

Miroir, a French product composed of an outer ring of almond paste with a mixture of sugar, butter, and eggs in the middle. When baked the biscuit has a flat centre and a raised lumpy outer edge, reminiscent of a mirror in a frame.

Oreillette (little ear), a French carnival biscuit, sweet and deep fried. Several other types of fried biscuit are called 'ears', from the way they curve and fold during cooking, for example the Middle Eastern *hojuelos de Haman* (Haman's ears) and Afghan *goash-e-feel* (elephant's ears).

Petit beurré, a famous French biscuit which has been made at Nantes since the 1880s. It was invented by Louis Lefèvre-Utile, so is known by the initials LU and may be called *p'tit lu*. Tradition requires that one eats the four projecting corners first; these are darker than the main body of the biscuit.

Polvorone, a Spanish and Mexican biscuit made from a simple pastry dough based on lard and mixed without liquid. They are flavoured with nuts or spiced with cinnamon, and rolled in icing sugar after baking. The biscuits are small, thick, dry, and apt to crumble; they come individually wrapped in fringed tissue paper.

Sablé (sandy), a French sweet biscuit made from a rich pastry mixture bound with egg, variously flavoured. The name refers to the texture; there is a place called Sablé, where production of *sablés de Sablé* has taken place since the 1920s, but the sablés of Normandy, which date back to the 19th century, came first.

Snickerdoodle, a biscuit made from a creamed mixture enlivened with nutmeg, nuts, and raisins. It is a speciality of the Pennsylvanian Dutch, a community with many sweet biscuit and cookie recipes.

Tostada, the second most popular biscuit in Spain, is a close rival to the Maria (see above) and not unlike it, but rectangular in shape.

Vanillekipferl (vanilla crescent), popular in Germany and C. Europe, especially as a Christmas speciality. It is made from a rich pastry-type dough containing almonds and flavoured with vanilla or lemon peel.   LM

BISON the name applied to two species of large animal in the family Bovidae, whose fate, broadly speaking, has been to be eaten up already and thus no longer available:

- *Bison bison*, the American bison (or N. American buffalo, or just buffalo), dark brown and bearded, once existing in enormous populations, reduced by 1890 to near-extinction, now surviving in a population of viable size under rigorous protection measures. During the relatively brief period that it provided game meat, the bison was liked particularly for its tongue, hump, and marrow. Hooker (1981) cites Susan Magoffin, who travelled the Santa Fe Trail in 1846–7 and kept a diary of what she ate, as saying that buffalo hump soup was 'superior to any soup served in the "best" hotels of New York and Philadelphia and the buffalo marrow superior to the best butter or most delicate oil'.
- *B. bonasus*, the European bison (sometimes called aurochs, but see CATTLE) survives only in zoos and parks, and forest reserves in Poland.

The name 'Indian bison' is sometimes applied to the gaur, *Bos gaurus*, a huge and vigorous wild animal whose range extended from the Indian subcontinent to Malaysia but which is now far less common than it used to be. It is essentially a hill animal and is said to thrive best in the hills of Assam. The seladang of Malaysia is a race of gaur.

See also BUFFALO; WATER-BUFFALO.

BISQUE a rich soup of creamy consistency, especially of crayfish or lobster. An earlier use, for soups of game birds, has fallen into desuetude. Wine and/or cognac often enter into the recipes.

When the word was first adopted from the French language, it came over as 'bisk', and it thus appears in *The Accomplisht Cook* of Robert May (1685). His recipes, incidentally, illustrate the wider use of the term in his time. He gives two recipes for Bisk of Carp, both involving many ingredients and having plenty of solid matter in them. And his Bisk of Eggs sounds even more surprising to modern ears.

BISTORT *Polygonum bistorta*, is a KNOTWEED. A knotweed is so called because its roots are knotted or twisted; bistort means twice twisted.

Bistort, the best-known European member of a populous genus, is found from Britain to Siberia and bears attractive pink flower spikes in the summer. It is sometimes called patience-dock or passion-dock, the former name by confusion with the latter

and the latter because associated by Christians with the Passion and eaten at Passiontide.

In the same family, Polygonaceae, there is another plant, *Rumex patientia*, which is the plant with the strongest claim to the name patience-dock; see DOCK. It too is associated with Easter, perhaps because of an understandable confusion between patience and Passion.

Under yet another name, Easter mangiant, bistort leaves are an important ingredient in a traditional Easter dish of Cumbria, Herb pudding. Geoffrey Grigson (1955) explains 'Easter mangiant' as a corruption of Easter-mangeant, *mangeant* being French for 'eating' or 'fare', and he unravels the origins of the even more puzzling name 'Easter ledger', found in the Lake District. Here he realized that an old name for bistort (cf William Turner's *Herbal* of 1548) was astrologia—hence Easter ledger. Astrologia comes from *aristolochia clematis*, a plant which was an ancient antidote to demons and poisons, and a charm plant for successful conception and birth. The *Grete Herball* of 1526 says that bistort 'hath vertue . . . to cause to retayne and conceyve'.

As further evidence of the superstition that bistort enhanced fertility, Grigson points to the unicorn tapestry in the Cloisters in New York, probably woven for the marriage of Francis I of France in 1514. The wounded unicorn recovers from its wounds amid obvious symbols of fertility:

Symbol in part of the consummation of the marriage, the unicorn is tethered by a gold chain to the pomegranate tree of fertility. Against its flank, and below its hind legs are depicted two of the plants of desire, the Early Purple Orchis and the aptly named Lords-and-Ladies (*Arum maculatum*); and touching a white foreleg is— *Polygonum bistorta*, the plant of virtue in retaining and conceiving.

The Herb pudding referred to above is made from bistort and other herbs, barley, and hard-boiled egg, to be eaten with veal and bacon. In the 1930s this pudding was still being boiled in a cloth, with the added barley, then turned out and served with butter and raw egg. Another version of the same thing, now perhaps the better known, is DOCK PUDDING, a springtime hasty green pudding whose principal ingredient is bistort.

Jennifer Stead (1995a) has fully explored this complex of topics, and the history and distribution of these puddings in various parts of England. One conclusion of her essay is that the puddings probably had a pre-Christian origin.

BISTRO a term which dates back only to the late 19th century in French and to the early 20th century in English, is elastic in its meaning but always refers to an establishment where one can have something to eat, as well as drinks. Such an establishment would normally be small, and its menu would be likely to include simple dishes, perhaps of rustic character and not expensive.

If it is correct that the word comes from a Russian one meaning 'quick!', this would fit in with the general idea that one can eat quickly at a bistro. However, the concept of simple inexpensive food served in a French atmosphere has wide appeal, and as a result the use of the term, whether as a description of eating places or of food, had, towards the end of the 20th century, begun to be annexed by more pretentious premises.

HY

BITTER BERRIES *Solanum aethiopicum*, also spelled bitterberry (one word), are a small orange/red pea-sized relation of the AUBERGINE which are eaten in Africa as a vegetable by the wealthy but more often used to season steamed PLANTAIN or beans, sometimes mixed with sesame seeds or peanuts. They are very bitter and not the same thing as the Asian pea-sized aubergine, *Solanum torvum*, less bitter and often eaten raw.

Bitter berries are sometimes known as the 'tomato of the Jews of Constantinople', the Ladinos, expelled to Constantinople from Spain about 1500, whose ancestors had been expelled from Timbuktu in about AD 1400. These 'berries' are initially green, turning orange or red as they ripen, seldom more than 2 cm (1") in diameter. They are widely cultivated throughout most of tropical Africa. The Buganda people of Uganda celebrate the birth of twins by serving plantain and bitterberry sauce to the parents. It is thought to help milk production. JM

BITTER GOURD (or bitter cucumber), *Momordica charantia*, neither a true gourd nor a cucumber, although a member of the same CUCURBIT family as both. Another English name, balsam pear, is even less fitting. Names in India and the Philippines are, respectively, karela and ampalaya.

The plant is thought to be a native of India, but has been grown elsewhere for a long time and its use in SE Asia goes back a considerable way.

The knobbly fruit has a bitter taste, akin to that of a fresh, i.e. unpickled, GHERKIN. It is used as a vegetable in various tropical regions, including most SE Asian countries. It varies considerably in size (from 2.5 to 25 cm/1 to 10") and also in colour. Indonesians cultivate it as a garden vegetable and recognize numerous forms,

including a large whitish one and smaller green ones.

In India the fruits are cooked in curry dishes; or sliced and fried; or stuffed with GRAM and onion and fried; or, notably in Kerala, sliced, salted, and dried for use in the rainy season.

When bitter gourds are fried and curried in Sri Lanka, the curry may incorporate coconut milk, Maldive fish, and GORAKA.

In the Philippines the vegetable is well known; ampalaya leaves are consumed almost as much as ampalaya fruits.

A close relation, *M. balsamina*, sometimes referred to as the balsam apple, is pickled in India when young and green, and cooked in curry dishes and stews when ripe and red. The fruit is smaller than that of *M. charantia*.

BITTER HERBS (OF THE JEWS) are the bitter plants which form part of the food at the Feast of the PASSOVER, symbolizing the bitter times which the Jews endured in Egypt. The festive Seder (Passover) table includes a plate of at least one of these bitter herbs, known collectively as *maror*. Those commonly used (the choice varies) are LETTUCE (often romaine lettuce, although some Jews think that endive is meant), CELERY, CHICORY, cress, and grated HORSERADISH.

BITTERLEAF a name given to *Vernonia amygdalina*, an African shrub, and some other plants of the same genus. The leaves are used in W. and S. Africa as a pot-herb or for seasoning. Cultivation, practised on a small scale, had produced plants whose leaves are less bitter than those gathered from the wild.

These leaves are readily available in Nigerian markets, either fresh or dried.

BITTERN *Botaurus stellaris*, a marsh bird of Europe and Asia, which belongs to the same family as the HERON. The bittern is a large bird (average total length 75 cm/30") and was prized as food in Britain in the 16th century. The flavour has been compared to that of hare.

The bittern makes migratory journeys from the temperate regions of Europe and Asia to India and Africa. It has close relations in N. America, S. Africa, and Australasia.

BIVALVES a category of marine MOLLUSCS distinguished by having two hinged shells. These can be tightly closed in most species, which can therefore survive for an appreciable time after being removed

from the water: examples are the OYSTER and the MUSSEL.

Bivalves which lack this ability, and cannot therefore be kept alive for long after being taken, include the RAZOR CLAM and SOFT-SHELLED CLAM. These should not really be called clams at all, since they cannot 'clam up'; see CLAMS.

Of the bivalves which are cultured, the oyster and mussel are by far the most important. Culture of the latter has been so far developed that it is now, in terms of consumption, the most popular bivalve. Bivalves collectively constitute a major food resource and have the advantage over their companion categories in the mollusc world, the gastropods (single shells) and the CEPHALOPODS, that they are less apt to arouse feelings of distaste or revulsion. They also benefit from having in their ranks such undisputed delicacies as the oyster and SCALLOP.

BLAA (originally blaad, also spelled blah and bla), a special bread of Waterford in Ireland. It is a type of ordinary batch bread dough made into small round pieces, bigger and lighter than a bap, very soft, about 3.5 cm (1.5") high and 10 cm (4") in diameter, the top dusted with flour and therefore white.

Waterford bakers believe that the blaa was introduced by Huguenots who came to Waterford from France in the late 17th or early 18th century and set up an industrial area called New Geneva. It is thought locally that the blaa derived from the CROISSANT they brought with them (although this cannot have been a croissant like those now sold in France). An eccentric poem on the subject includes the following:

But the real delicacy are Blaas, fresh from the
    oven,
Smothered in butter, you'd ate half a dozen . . .
You can fill them with ham or a slice of red lead,
In the summer you could try some dillisk instead.

In present practice at Waterford they are eaten with butter for breakfast, a mid-morning snack, or lunch. A filling of dillisk (DULSE) may still be used; also popular are blaa butties—blaa with chips or a filling of luncheon sausage. RSe

BLACANG (also spelled blachan), the Malay and most common name for a SE Asian fermented shrimp paste, which is called *terasi* or *trasi* in Indonesia, *kapi* in Thailand, and *bagoong* in the Philippines. What is called *balichão* in Macao is more or less the same thing. A form of blacang is also found in Burma and Sri Lanka.

This has a somewhat different flavour from the fish pastes of the region but plays the same sort of role in cookery. Blacang is always cooked. It may be crushed or ground and mixed with other spices and flavourings into a paste which is then fried; or it may be fried or grilled by itself before being combined with other spices.

BLACK BEANS a term which may refer either (*a*) to a kind of HARICOT BEAN, namely the Mexican black beans which are widely eaten in Latin America and give their name to black bean soup, or (*b*) in the sense treated here, to black SOYA BEANS, fermented and preserved by salting.

The latter, known as *chi* to the Chinese, have been an important relish in their cuisine since the Han dynasty (beginning in the 2nd century BC). Yan-Kit So (1992) remarks on this, noting that the evidence is supplied by inscriptions discovered in 1972 on bamboo slips in a Han tomb in Hunan province. She also explains that:

Black beans are also made from cooked soy beans which, halfway through their hydrolytic decomposition, are dried at a very high temperature and become darkened as a result of oxidation.

The agricultural writer Jia Sixie (*c.* AD 540) was the first author to explain how these black beans are prepared, in a work which had the engaging title 'Essential Skills for the Daily Life of the People' (*Qimin Yaoshu*).

Since the soya bean commonly occurs in a black form, as well as in other colours such as light brown, it is natural to think that it is this black form which is fermented. However, it is not necessarily so. Beans lighter in colour may be used and will darken as a result of the fermentation.

Fermented black beans are prepared in many regional varieties. In most processes the raw beans are salted and allowed to soften under the influence of their own enzymes at a high temperature; enzyme action also darkens the colour. Some varieties are made by a wet pickling process using brine, vinegar, or wine. The end product, which is always salted, may be had in cans or dry packs and keeps well.

Fermented black beans have a strong flavour, but the black bean sauce prepared from them is delicate.

BLACKBERRY is a name which usually refers to the common European blackberry, *Rubus fruticosus*, also known as bramble; but it is also a collective name for a large group of fruits in the same genus which grow throughout the cooler parts of the world, particularly in upland and northern regions.

There are said to be over 2,000 varieties of blackberry, counting both the frequent and naturally occurring hybrids and the cultivars.

The genus *Rubus* also includes RASPBERRIES. The untrained eye cannot always distinguish between a blackberry and a raspberry, since the shapes and sizes of the fruit, leaves, and thorns vary, and there are both red blackberries and black raspberries. However, when a blackberry is picked, it comes off the plant with its receptacle, the solid centre to which the druplets (the round, juicy parts) are attached. When a raspberry is picked, the cluster of druplets comes away from the receptacle, which remains as a hard, white cone on the stem. A good blackberry has druplets which are large in relation to the hard part.

Blackberries are more highly esteemed in Britain and N. Europe than in other European countries. During their season they are commonly gathered and eaten fresh, as they keep for only a short time; or they may be used in desserts such as the British blackberry and apple pie. They are sometimes preserved by bottling but lose much of their evanescent flavour. They make an excellent jelly but a somewhat pippy jam. Tea made from blackberry leaves is a traditional cure for indigestion and is believed to purify the blood.

In Britain it used to be considered unlucky to pick blackberries after a certain date, sometimes Michaelmas (29 September) but with regional variants, as in Warwickshire, 12 October, the day of the traditional 'Mop' or hiring fair. Later than this, the devil was believed to have stamped or spat on the berries.

In Scandinavia, elsewhere in N. Europe, and Asia blackberries and DEWBERRIES are common but there are also species peculiar to the far north. These include the juicy, flavourful, red Arctic bramble, *R. arcticus*; but the most famous is the golden CLOUDBERRY, *R. chamaemorus*.

In W. and C. Asia blackberries grow as far south as Iran and are also common in the Himalayas. One Himalayan species, *R. procerus*, bears large thimble-shaped berries and is sometimes called Himalayan Giant; it is now found growing wild in the USA. The wild black berries of the Far East are more usually black raspberries than blackberries. In New Zealand, European blackberries introduced by white settlers are common.

Blackberries in the USA are highly diverse. The indigenous species vary across regions, and have also been interbred with imported varieties. They include the Oregon evergreen or cutleaf blackberry, *R. laciniatus*, originally from Europe (thought to have arrived in Oregon via the South Sea islands, whither someone from England had taken it), whose leaves are separated into 'fingers'. American Indians used both berries and leaves in the same way as Europeans, but also preserved them for the winter by drying them. Dried berries of all kinds were often pounded with dried meat and fat to make PEMMICAN.

There is much cultivation of blackberries (and of the related dewberry) in the USA. Native species developed for cultivation are erect woody plants rather than trailing brambles; they include *R. alleghaniensis* and *R. argutus* (tall or highbush blackberry), often interbred with imported strains.

Blackberries and raspberries are often crossed to give varieties such as the loganberry and tayberry (see RASPBERRY).

BLACKBIRD *Turdus merula*, a familiar European songbird, which ranges from the southern parts of Norway and Sweden down to the Mediterranean.

The English nursery rhyme about four-and-twenty blackbirds baked in a pie might suggest that large blackbird pies were once common fare; but since 'when the pie was open'd, the birds began to sing,' the allusion must be to the medieval conceits known as SUBTLETIES, which often featured such surprises. However, blackbirds were eaten in the Middle Ages and the 17th century and even later (see, for example, a recipe for Blackbird pie given by Mrs Beeton, 1861). In a few regions of continental Europe blackbirds are still used in pies or to make terrines.

BLACK BUN as its alternative name Scotch bun indicates, is a Scottish institution, a festive cake eaten at Hogmanay. Originally this cake belonged to Twelfth Night but moved to the secular festival of New Year when religious reformers banned Christmas as a festival.

Although the 'bun' has a long and puzzling history, the name 'black bun' only came into use in the early part of the 20th century. The recipe for it which was given by Meg Dods (1826) was entitled Scotch Christmas Bun. This was originally made with bread dough enriched with spices, dried fruit, eggs, and brandy and then wrapped in a plain casing of bread dough. Meg Dods said that it was made by all the leading bakers in Edinburgh in the weeks before Christmas and exported in sizes up to 16 lb (8 kg) to other parts of the United Kingdom.

Back in the 18th century the same thing or something very like it appeared as 'plum cake'. The 'bun' term may have been introduced to avoid confusion with the meaning which the Scots had for 'cake' as a hard biscuit, as in oat 'cakes'.

By the late 19th and early 20th centuries it had become so intensely spicy and fruity that the bread dough was abandoned, very little flour was added to the spice and fruit mixture, and the whole mixture was wrapped in short pastry crust. At this stage the bun could almost be described as an English CHRISTMAS PUDDING in a crust. The filling had become so dark as to deserve the epithet 'black'. It seems to have been after the author R. L. Stevenson described it as 'a black substance inimical to life' that the name 'black bun' came into use.

The composition of the filling has varied over the centuries. All Scottish bakers who make the bun have their own spice mix, and flavours range from strong peppery versions to milder cinnamon-flavoured ones. Black treacle is a modern addition which did not appear in early recipes, and this of course enhances the blackness.

Size and shape also vary. A black bun may be circular or loaf shaped. In many households there is a strong tradition of serving the bun with Scotch whisky; but the bun may of course be found in households where Scotch whisky is never consumed.

(CB)

BLACK CUMIN is a name which can either indicate a rare, dark, variety of true CUMIN or (more commonly) a spice consisting of the seeds of *Nigella sativa*, native to the Levant.

In spite of being called black cumin, the latter does not resemble cumin in taste; nor is it botanically related. (It is, however, closely related to love-in-the-mist, *N. damascena*, whose seeds are also used as a condiment.)

Nigella sativa is sometimes cultivated on a small scale in N. India, but is mainly collected from wild plants in forests. The seeds are small, dull black, roughly wedge shaped, and pungent. They are used in India, and also in the Middle East for sprinkling on bread, flavouring vinegar and pickles, etc. much as true cumin is.

The name most used in India seems to be *kalonji/kalaunji*. The Arabic name *habba sauda* means 'black seed', but the alternative name *habbat al-baraka* means 'seed of grace', which suggests that at one time it had religious significance.

It is not unusual to find nigella seeds labelled 'onion seeds', reflecting a common misconception. A further source of confusion is that they are sometimes called 'black caraway' rather than 'black cumin'.

BLACK FOREST GATEAU

Schwarzwälder Kirschtorte in German, a baroque confection of layers of chocolate cake, interspersed with whipped cream and stoned, cooked, sweetened sour cherries. The cake layers are often sprinkled with kirsch, and the whole is covered with whipped cream and decorated with chocolate curls.

This confection is not one which has a long history. It has been suggested that it was created in the 1930s in Berlin, but firm evidence is elusive. What is certain is that in the last decades of the 20th century it made a triumphant entry into the dessert course of restaurants in Britain (and no doubt elsewhere) and reigned for a time as 'top favourite'. This is no doubt due to the fact that, properly made, it is delicious.

BLACK GROUSE *Tetrao tetrix*, also known as black game or blackcock (the male, the female being grey hen), a European game bird, male specimens of which have an average total length of about 50 cm (21"). Its range extends from N. Europe to NE Asia. Males are blue-black in colour, females brown.

The reputation of the black grouse as a table bird is good. It can be roasted, perhaps with thin rashers of bacon and vine leaves clothing it, or fillets can be taken and cooked in a suitable sauce.

BLANCH a verb which for the gardener means to earth up (e.g. stalks of celery) and thus keep white, and which for the cook means to immerse briefly in boiling water.

The blanching carried out in the kitchen may whiten, as when pieces of rabbit are blanched prior to being cooked, but it more commonly serves other purposes. Fruits and nuts may be blanched to permit peeling them. If vegetables or herbs are blanched before they are frozen, this deactivates enzymes and 'sets' their colour. And vegetables to be cooked in the French manner are first blanched, so that their colour will be preserved (after which they are 'refreshed' in cold water and subsequently heated in butter). Blanching lasts for a shorter or longer time according to what is being blanched and for what purpose; but it never lasts long.

BLANCMANGE an Anglicization of the French *blanc manger* (white food), now means a sweet, jellied dessert made from milk and cornflour, to which flavour and colour are often added. The addition of colour to something whose name indicates that it is white is not and never has been perceived as a problem or paradox in Britain. Until recently, an observer at any children's party was likely to hear requests such as: 'May I have some more of the pink blancmange please?' In France, however, *blancmanger* is typically white and is made with gelatin and almond milk.

The ancestor of the homely modern dish was honoured on medieval and Renaissance menus all over W. Europe. The 14th- and 15th-century English *blancmangers* were made of shredded chicken breast, sugar, rice, and either ground almonds or almond milk, but there were many variations on the idea on the Continent; furthermore, there was a whole family of related dishes. Professor Constance Hieatt (1995) has described the fundamental difficulties, perplexities, and traps strewn in the way of any culinary detective attempting to clarify the history of so widespread and popular a dish.

It has long been speculated that it derives from the Middle East, whence both rice and almonds were imported. One of the most widespread dishes in medieval Arab cuisine was *isfidhabâj* (a Persian name which also means 'white food'), and the recipe translated by Arberry (1939) is lamb stewed with almond milk. However, Perry (1989) points out that this happens to be the only *isfidhabâj* recipe in Arab culinary literature containing almond milk; the others show little or no resemblance to the European dish. It seems likely that *blancmanger* does reflect eastern influence, but the exact source and path are obscure.

Ayto (1993) draws attention to the two recipes given by PLATINA (1475), one of which he, Platina, says plainly comes from APICIUS. The surviving manuscripts of *Apicius* do not include this recipe, however, and Maestro Martino, from whom Platina avowedly took the recipe, does not mention the connection himself. So, while it is possible that the Romans made a dish called *cibaria alba* (although the name would imply coarse food such as that supplied for slaves) the question remains uncertain.

Although modern people are always surprised to learn of a sweet made from chicken breast, this was common in medieval Arab cuisine, where chicken was sometimes literally candied. The concept survives in the contemporary Turkish rice and chicken dessert *Tavuk gögsü kazandibi*, whether this is an idea picked up from the Arab sources or conceivably a version of *blancmanger*. CP

READING: C. Anne Wilson (1973); Scully (1995).

BLANQUETTE a French and to some extent international culinary term indicating a dish of white meat (veal, poultry, also lamb) served in a WHITE SAUCE which masks it. The meat is usually cooked in a *fond blanc* ('white', i.e. uncoloured, stock) which is then used as the basis of the sauce.

Blanquette is the equivalent of the English 'blanket', which originally meant white woollen cloth, but the English word has not been put to the same use (although it is occasionally used in the kitchen, e.g. for 'pig in a blanket', where the blanket is of batter).

BLEAK *Alburnus alburnus*, a small European freshwater fish which is not widely eaten but is used in one famous speciality of Burgundy, *friture de Saône*. Its French name is *ablette*.

Fritures, mixed fried dishes, date back to the Middle Ages, and the emphasis was always on fish. Medieval household accounts in Burgundy contain mentions of *petits poissons*, a term which evidently included not only bleak but also small LOACH and BARBS.

Eating a dish of these fish, fried, was formerly associated with the end of the harvest. In modern times the tradition is maintained in small restaurants on the banks of the Saône. The small bleak (about 9 cm/3.5" long and weighing 5–10 g/about 0.25 oz) are preferred because when fried their skins are agreeably crisp and crunchy, while the inside remains succulent.

BLEU meaning blue, an element in the name of many of the various French blue cheeses. One of the best known is *bleu d'Auvergne*, a rich, sharp cheese made from whole milk, but there are numerous others; Rance (1989) describes 46 *bleus*. *Bleu de Bresse* and *bleu des causses* (mentioned under ROQUEFORT) are two of them. *Bleu du Haut-Jura* comprises *bleu de Gex* and *bleu de Septmoncel*, names which seem to have become largely interchangeable; but see Rance on the interesting history and special qualities of *bleu de Gex*.

There is no connection between these cheeses and the fish cookery technique called AU BLEU.

BLEWIT a corruption of 'blue hat', which is a good name for a bluish-lilac edible mushroom which is common in Europe and the USA. There are two main species, the wood blewit, *Lepista nuda*, and the field blewit, *L. saeva*.

The wood blewit has a cap measuring up to 12 cm (4") across, growing on a relatively short stem. Cap, gills, and stem are all likely to be bluish-lilac. The field blewit is almost as large, but its cap tends to be pale grey or brown, the gills pale grey, and the stem greyish with just a blue or lilac tinge.

Blewits are found in the autumn, one kind in woods and the other in fields, often growing in large 'fairy rings'. They will also thrive on lawn mowings or discarded straw. The flavour is fresh, rather like that of new potatoes, and the texture delicate. The wood blewit is generally preferred to the field blewit, but both are highly esteemed.

In Britain the blewits are more familiar in the Midlands than elsewhere. Dorothy Hartley (1954), who says that they have remained popular wherever French people settled, believed that they are best stewed. Having given a recipe for cooking them in milk with onion and a sage leaf, as one would cook reed tripe, and serving the result with its sauce in a well of mashed potato, she remarks that: 'The likeness to a very delicate dish of tripe and onions is curious, both in texture and flavour. . .' Roux-Saget and Delplanque (1985) comment that appreciation of the blewit in France varies from region to region, that specimens growing at high altitudes are peppery, and that those growing under oak trees are best.

BLINI in Russian, is the plural of the word *blin*, which denotes a small PANCAKE. The same is correct in English, but in colloquial English, as in this entry, blini can serve as both singular and plural.

A blini is about 10 cm (4") in diameter, and rather under a centimetre thick. Blini, to be authentic, should be made from a batter of BUCKWHEAT flour leavened with yeast, and further lightened with beaten egg white and whipped cream. Special little cast-iron pans, each one the right size and shape to cook a single blini, are made in sets of six. These fit into a holder and can be used in the oven or on top of the stove. The finished pancakes are eaten hot with butter, herring, smoked fish, chopped egg, or—best known in the West—caviar and sour cream.

Many observers remark that the traditional blini recipes make crumbly, strongly flavoured pancakes. Lighter blini have evolved using mixtures of wheat and buckwheat flour, with or without the yeast. French influence, important in Russian cuisine during the 19th century, may have encouraged these developments.

Blini are important to Russian eating habits, and have a history which stretches back to the Middle Ages. Lesley Chamberlain (1983) says that the name is derived from *mlin*, meaning something ground (i.e. flour or meal generally). She gives their place in the sequence of foods at a main meal:

In a full Russian *obed*, *blini* are served after the cold *zakuski*. They may be followed by consommé, then pies and then the main meat course. For all this you would need a gargantuan appetite. . .

Blini were especially important during the *Maslenitsa* (or 'butter festival'), the week leading up to Lent, as a treat eaten twice a day by everyone; street vendors did a roaring trade, and cooks who could make good blini were in heavy demand. The old Russians had other occasions for eating blini. Three times a year the middle and lower classes held

prayers for the dead, after which they had a ceremonial meal of blini. At funerals blini, boiled wheat (cf VARENO ZHITO), and vodka were consumed beside the grave, and a small offering of each poured into the grave in a completely pre-Christian manner.

Pancakes similar to blini, *nalesniki* and *rakuszki*, are known in Poland; and buckwheat is used in pancake batters in SE Europe. Since the late 19th century, blini and buckwheat pancakes generally have become popular in NW Europe and the USA.

Blintz (blintze), a name derived from the Russian *blin*, is an egg batter pancake of JEWISH COOKERY. A blintz may be either sweet or savoury: with cinnamon sugar and sour cream; or filled with lox (smoked salmon), cottage cheese, chives, etc.   (LM)

BLOOD of all the component parts of an animal the one which is most apt to engender the kinds of emotion which underlie, or accompany, food taboos. Yet in many cultures it is highly esteemed as food and free of inhibitions.

In the past, and even to some extent in present times, blood has been a staple food of nomadic tribes (Berbers, Mongols, etc.), for whom it is a renewable resource; they draw it from living animals (horses, cattle, camels), then staunch the wound. In some instances the blood was drunk just as it came from the animals. In others it was mixed with milk before being drunk. In yet others, it was cooked before consumption. Reference is often made to the Masai of E. Africa, who obtain blood from their cattle by firing an arrow, at close range, into a vein in the neck of the live animal. The wound is plugged after the desired amount has been extracted. The bleeding of horses was also a common practice of early trappers and explorers in the days of the settlement of America. If the blood was not consumed in liquid form, it was preserved with salt, cut into squares and reserved for eating during times of scarcity.

In a wide-ranging essay, Birgit Siesby (1980) draws attention to a striking contrast between attitudes which have their origin in the Middle East and those of the Nordic peoples. All concerned seem to have started from the premiss that blood is the very soul of the animal, but opposite conclusions were drawn. In the Middle East, Jews banned the eating of blood and so did early Christians and Islam. The Nordic peoples on the other hand did not find it proper to waste the souls of animals, but thought on the contrary that by drinking the blood they might partake of the strength and qualities of the slain beasts. The introduction of Christianity did not make the Nordic peoples give up their traditional blood dishes (black soup, black pudding, paltbread—a kind of black rye bread made with blood, dark beer, and spices).

It should not be thought, however, that Nordic attitudes to blood were free of superstition. Bringéus (in Arnott 1975) describes a strange and ritual dialogue which took place between people involved in boiling blood sausages; ritual smackings of the sausages (with sexual incantations); special blessings; and the practice of placing the spleen of the slaughtered pig in the kettle with the sausages as 'sausage saviour'.

Siesby also goes into the nutritional aspects, demolishing (in part by citing interesting experiments with Swedish policemen) the myth which gained currency in the 1920s that the iron in animal blood could not be absorbed by the human body. On the contrary, it is the best available source of iron.

Blood is used as a thickener in stews such as a CIVET. For other current main uses of blood, see BLOOD SAUSAGES; also DRISHEEN (Ireland) and DINUAGAN (the Philippines).

BLOOD SAUSAGES sausages filled with blood, with cereal or other vegetable matter to absorb this, and fat. The most familiar type is the black pudding or *boudin noir*, English and French terms for much the same thing. It is a pudding in the old sense of something enclosed in a sausage skin.

The black pudding is probably the most ancient of sausages or puddings. Some would claim this distinction for the HAGGIS, but the earliest mention in literature is of something tending more towards black pudding, at least in its filling. Book 18 of Homer's *Odyssey*, around 1000 BC, refers to a stomach filled with blood and fat and roasted over a fire.

The reason for the great antiquity of such dishes is clear enough. When a pig is killed it is bled, and a large amount of blood becomes available. This has a very short keeping time if not preserved. Putting it into one of the vessels which the entrails of animals conveniently furnish, along with other OFFAL with a limited keeping time, is an obvious solution.

The oldest detailed recipe for black pudding, in the compilation attributed to APICIUS (material of the first few centuries AD), calls for lengths of intestine, rather than a stomach, as the container. It is a rich recipe with no cereal, but chopped hard-boiled egg yolks, pine kernels, onions, and leeks. Common black puddings of the time were probably made with cereal.

In medieval Europe it was not unusual for even relatively poor families to own a pig, which was slaughtered in the autumn. Black puddings were therefore made everywhere. They always included fat and onions, but not invariably cereal. An English recipe of the

15th century is for a black pudding made with the blood and fat of a porpoise with oatmeal, spiced with pepper and ginger. It was boiled, then lightly grilled. This was a dish for nobles.

Black puddings have remained popular in many European countries and regions. In Britain they are now eaten mainly in the Midlands and the north, often flavoured with PENNYROYAL as well as other herbs and spices. The cereal filling is generally oatmeal (see OATS). Continental European versions contain little or no cereal, and rely mainly on chopped onion to absorb the blood.

The blood used is generally, but not always, pig's blood; see DRISHEEN for an exception. The taste of blood is unassertive, like that of liver, so all blood puddings depend on additional flavourings for their particular character.

The French *boudin noir* is made from pig's blood and fat, chopped onion, and cream, and is seasoned with salt, pepper, and mixed spices. There are many local variations, containing herbs and brandy (*boudin de Lyon*), apples (*boudin noir alsacien*), spinach (*boudin de Poitou aux épinards*), etc. In Auvergne milk is used; in Brittany calf's blood is added to the pig's blood. In the north of France and Belgium, very rich *boudins* containing large amounts of cream, lard or butter, and sometimes eggs, are made. *Boudin noir de Paris*, also called *boudin à l'oignon*, is one of the only two *boudins* on the list of 14 in the official French Code de la Charcuterie to contain cooked onion. *Boudin à la flamande* has currants and raisins. The term *boudin noir à l'anglaise* is used for a black pudding with cereal, which is made in France as well as England.

The principal French *boudin* competition is held every year at Mortagne-au-Perche in Normandy, attracting hundreds of entries from all over Europe. The category for *boudins* made with cereal has several times been won by British entries.

Allied to the *boudin* but of a different composition is a product of the Pays de la Loire, named *gogue* or *cogne*. This is a sort of

sausage in which green vegetables (chard, spinach, parsley) are dominant, with some meat and also, in a relatively small quantity and in order to bind the mixture, some pork blood. The mixture is encased in a pig bladder or a large intestine.

There are several kinds of Spanish black pudding, or *morcilla*. The most renowned comes from Asturia, where it is made from the local black pig, and forms part of the regional speciality *Fabada*, a bean stew with mixed meats. An Andalusian *morcilla* includes almonds, pimentos, and parsley. The Italian black pudding, *sanguinaccio*, is a large type of blood sausage bound in a net.

Germany has some unusual types of *Blutwurst* verging on a conventional SAUSAGE. The normal, plain type is often smoked. Swedish blood sausage is made with rye meal and raisins. Hungarian *kishka*, ring-shaped and dark in colour, are also made elsewhere in E. Europe and in the USA. They use ground rice to absorb the blood, contain some meat, and are highly seasoned.

In the USA black puddings are not generally popular, but are eaten by some ethnic groups. There is a W. Indian black pudding made with sweet potato or rice and with pumpkin, and spiced with chilli peppers.

All blood puddings are cooked as soon as they are made, and either eaten at once or allowed to dry. They have a limited keeping time of a few weeks. When required, they may be heated through in boiling water, or slashed and grilled, fried in slices, simply sliced and eaten cold, or used in various made dishes.

WHITE PUDDING (*boudin blanc*) is a different product: no blood.

BLOWFISH or pufferfish, the English names for numerous species of fish in the families *Lagocephalidae* and *Tetraodontidae* (but for the latter see also TRIGGERFISH). All have hugely inflatable stomachs, and powerful beaks which can bite through a crab shell or a fishing line. Many are edible, subject to the stringent precautions which apply to some of them, especially the

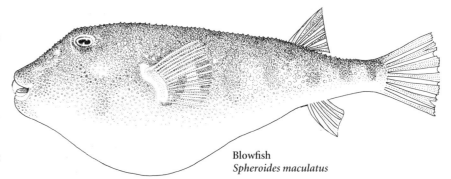

Blowfish
Spheroides maculatus

Japanese FUGU, which is the best known. Others which are eaten include *Spheroides maculatus*, found in W. Atlantic waters as far north as Long Island, also known as northern swellfish and marketed as 'sea squab'. Zachary (1969) provides fuller advice than other authors on how to prepare and cook this delicacy.

BLUEBERRY the small bluish fruits of various scrubby ('low-bush') and bushy ('high-bush') plants of the genus *Vaccinium*. The most important N. American species are named below. In C. and N. Europe, the corresponding species is *V. myrtillus*, but this is preferably called BILBERRY.

Wild blueberries are found wherever suitable conditions (acid soil and enough moisture at all seasons) exist, as far north as the limits of human habitation. Most commercially cultivated blueberries are grown in N. America, especially New Jersey, Michigan, Indiana, N. Carolina, Washington, Oregon, and British Columbia; but cultivation also takes place in parts of W. Europe and has been started in New Zealand.

The blueberry is the most recent example of a fruit plant taken from the wild and brought into commercial cultivation, a development which began in New Jersey in 1920. The cultivars then introduced served as the basis of a new agricultural industry which put to good use acid, boggy soils which had previously been thought worthless for cultivation. The cultivated varieties of blueberry are mostly hybrids of three native American species, the high-bush *V. corymbosum*, the 'rabbit-eye' *V. ashei*, and the low-bush *V. angustifolium*. The fruits of cultivated varieties are far removed from wild blueberries and may be four times as big. The selection and breeding of commercial varieties has been aimed not only at size but also at a pleasing combination of acidity and sweetness.

Although the name blueberry is now standard for the commercially produced fruit, there has been much confusion in popular nomenclature in the past. New England colonists called the berries hurtleberries (=whortleberries), and later huckleberries and no doubt bilberries too. For the approved use of other common names applying to fruits of the genus *Vaccinium*, the whole of which is pervaded by confusion, see BILBERRY, CRANBERRY, HUCKLEBERRY, WHORTLEBERRY.

Facciola (1990) provides an excellent conspectus of all these species. He observes that *V. corymbosum* var *pallidum*, the Blue Ridge blueberry, has the reputation of being superior to all other blueberries. He also lists *V. floribundum*, the Colombian blueberry, known locally as *mortiño*; this is an example of a good blueberry from somewhere other than N. America and Europe.

Wild blueberries were used extensively by the Indians of N. America. Besides eating them fresh, they dried them in the sun, to be used later like currants in puddings, cakes, and PEMMICAN; a practice 'decidedly worth imitating, the berries drying readily in a week or ten days and being immune to decay' (Fernald and Kinsey, 1943). They pounded the dried berries with parched meal or used them as a flavouring for meat and in soups.

The use of blueberries as fresh or stewed fruit, and in such American dishes as blueberry pie and blueberry muffins, or with ice cream, is well known. They make an excellent jelly and are prized for this purpose in France (and also for jams, tarts, and cakes).

BLUE CHEESES owe their flavour and appearance to a blue mould, usually *Penicillium roqueforti* or *P. glaucum*. Some of the finest blue cheeses, such as Roquefort, continued until recent times to be of 'natural' formation in the sense that they picked up their special moulds from their surroundings; but virtually all blue cheeses are now deliberately inoculated with the chosen mould, so that their development is fully under control. In the larger and harder blue cheeses, the mould is encouraged to penetrate throughout by stabbing the cheese with copper needles which carry mould spores to the interior. Even the hardest blue cheeses have a fairly open-textured curd which allows mould to grow between the granules, giving a marbled appearance to a slice of the cheese.

The characteristic flavour of blue cheese is largely due to the action of the lipase enzymes produced by the mould. These break down fats in the cheese to yield fatty acids, especially butyric acid; methyl ketones; alcohols; esters; and other compounds.

See also BLEU; BLUE VINNEY; GORGONZOLA; ROQUEFORT; STILTON.

BLUE CRAB *Callinectes sapidus*, the most famous American crab, has a natural range which extends down the eastern seaboard from Delaware Bay to Florida and beyond, but is mainly caught in the Chesapeake Bay area. It has been introduced into the E. Mediterranean and is now part of the marine fauna there.

Adults are large, up to more than 12 cm (5") in width. However, at the annual National Hard Crab Derby, held at Crisfield in Maryland, the champion crab-pickers manage to 'pick' (remove all the meat from) a whole crab in about 40 seconds.

These are handsome crabs, and their scientific name is suitably honorific. *Callinectes* means 'beautiful swimmer' and *sapidus* means 'tasty'. Warner (1976), whose admirable book has all the information one could desire about the blue crab and ways of catching it and the people who live by catching or dressing it, remarks that it was Dr Mary J. Rathbun who gave it its specific name and that, although in her long career at the Smithsonian Institution she identified and described 998 new species of crab, this was the only instance in which she alluded to culinary quality.

The marketing of soft-shell crabs is a major part of the industry in Chesapeake Bay. (The other place where it is practised extensively is Venice, the species used there being the common European crab.) For a general account of the periodic shedding of their 'shells' by crustaceans, see CRUSTACEANS.

The blue crab is very soft indeed when it has shed, and will normally take refuge in some relatively safe nook for a day or so while its new shell becomes reasonably hard. It is not feasible to catch the crabs while they are soft. They have to be caught in advance and kept in special floats until they shed. These floats are patrolled frequently so that crabs which have shed can be culled at once.

A crab which is just about ready to shed is called a 'comer' or 'peeler'. The condition can be recognized by the appearance of a red line along the edge of the 'paddlers' at the rear of the crab. During the actual process of shedding, the crab is a 'buster', 'peeler' (again), or 'shedder'. At the moment of emergence from the old shell, it is a 'soft crab' in the full sense of the term. Soon afterwards, as a slight hardening becomes apparent, it is termed a 'paper shell'. Further hardening turns it into a 'buckram' or 'buckler'. At this stage the new shell is still flexible, but the crab is no longer soft enough to be treated as a soft-shell crab, and its muscles are thin and watery. Within 24 hours or so of shedding, the new shell will be hard and the crab can resume a normal life.

There is a further complication in all this. The female must mate with a male immediately after her own shedding. When she is almost ready, a male will pick her up, clasping her beneath him, and carry her to a suitable spot. She then sheds and mating takes place. Crabbers are pleased if they catch a couple on this amorous journey, since they gain simultaneously a hard male and a female shedder.

Soft-shell crabs have to be conveyed to market with extreme rapidity if they are to be sold fresh. Many are frozen in the soft state, which permits marketing them in distant places. They are suitable for frying, preferably in clarified butter, or grilling.

The genus *Callinectes* is represented in other parts of the world. For example, there is *C. latimanus*, the blue-legged swimming crab of W. Africa, which is a large species (carapace up to 30 cm/12" across) living in the muddy bottoms of lagoons. Its meat is of fine quality and the Ewe people regard it as the king of crabs.

BLUEFISH *Pomatomus saltatrix*, a prime example of a fish which has a very wide distribution, yet is thought of in certain places as being purely local. For anglers on the eastern seaboard of the USA, the 'blues' are 'theirs'. In Turkey, one will meet people who suppose that the beloved *lüfer*, as they call it, is not to be found except in the region of the Bosporus. Yet this species is found in many parts of the world, in temperate and semi-tropical seas. It is the 'elft' of SE Africa and is well known in Australian waters as 'tailor'.

Bluefish, which may reach a length of 1.2 m/4', are among the most voracious of fish. Swimming in groups, they ruthlessly attack shoals of smaller fish, often killing far more than they can eat. Jordan and Evermann (1902) describe this vividly:

they move along like a pack of hungry wolves, destroying everything before them. Their trail is marked by fragments of fish and by the stain of blood in the sea, as, when the fish is too large to be swallowed entire, the hinder portion will be bitten off and the anterior part allowed to float or sink. It has even been maintained that such is the gluttony of this fish, that when the stomach becomes full the contents are disgorged and then again filled!

Bluefish are, moreover, said to be cannibals, which may help to explain why the fish in a shoal are all of the same size; if some were larger they would eat the smaller ones.

The shoals move in accordance with changes in water temperature. Fishing progresses up the eastern seaboard of the USA from spring to summer to autumn. The annual migrations of bluefish through the Bosporus gives rise to corresponding seasonal fisheries there.
READING: Hersey (1987).

BLUE-MOUTH *Helicolenus dactylopterus*, a fish of the family Scorpaenidae (see SCORPION FISH) and thus related to, but inferior to, the rascasse and the REDFISH. Maximum length 45 cm (18"); red above and rosy below; the mouth and pharynx blue. A fish of moderately deep waters, known on both sides of the N. Atlantic and in the W. Mediterranean.

BLUE VINNEY (or vinny) is or was a highly esteemed blue cheese made by an accidental mould infection of Dorset cheese (a notably hard skimmed-milk cheese).

The name 'vinney' comes from an Old English word meaning 'mould'. There are various picturesque tales about how the mould in question came from old boots or saddles etc. and it may well be true that maturing was sometimes done in harness rooms. However, it seems to have been a chancy business; and without the mould Dorset cheese has little attraction. These factors and difficulties arising from controls on milk marketing and cheese-making in the mid-20th century were enough to account for blue vinney's virtual disappearance in the latter part of the century. However, some is still made.
READING: Rance (1982); Laura Mason (1999).

BLUSHER the common English name for an edible mushroom, *Amanita rubescens*, abundant in woods throughout the temperate regions of Europe and N. America in late summer and autumn. Those who gather and cook it are rewarded by a good flavour and pleasant texture. But it should not be eaten raw; and it must be positively identified, since it could be confused with other, harmful members of the genus AMANITA, namely the panther cap (sometimes called 'false blusher') and the FLY AGARIC, both of which may be found growing with it in woodlands.

The true blusher is up to 13 cm (5") tall and 10 cm (4") across the cap. This is brown, speckled with fragments of the typical *Amanita* veil unless these have been washed off by rain. The stem is strong, up to 2.5 cm (1") thick, and bears the usual *Amanita* volva (basal sheath) and ring. The latter is clearly marked with close-spaced lines where it has pressed against the gills of the immature cap. The rings of the panther cap and fly agaric lack these lines. The other feature which distinguishes the blusher from either of its dangerous relatives is its 'blush'. If any part of it is bruised or cut it stains red.

Blushers are not to be eaten raw. It is best to simmer them in water, then discard the water and continue the cooking by pan-frying or grilling. Blushers will add a touch of piquancy to a dish of milder mushrooms.

BOBALINK (sometimes spelled bobolink), *Dolichonyx oryzivorus*, a small N. American bird which migrates southwards and fattens on wild rice, after which it becomes a prized table delicacy. They are commonly offered in the markets, in this condition, as reed or rice birds, being called bobalinks only when alive and further north, in the summer. All this is explained by de Voe (1866), who said that in his time they had many admirers among epicures when they were at their best, in the autumn.

BOBOTIE a dish which has been popular in SOUTHERN AFRICA for centuries. Typically, it is a CURRY-type dish baked in the oven, containing finely minced meat with a blend of sweet/sour ingredients and topped with an egg and milk sauce. It reflects the influence of spices from the Dutch East Indies, used by the Cape Malays, but often incorporates local ingredients such as apricots, almonds, etc. A version with yellow rice and raisins is well known, but there are innumerable variations, including fish boboties.   HS

BOG-BUTTER the product of a discontinued custom, practised since medieval times, of preserving fresh butter in bogs. It is associated with Iceland, India, Ireland, Morocco, and Scandinavia (Evans, 1957).

In Ireland many examples have been found in bogs whilst turf-cutting. These finds, of various weights, had been wrapped in cloth and packed into wooden boxes or baskets. In some cases the butter was flavoured with wild garlic. It is believed that the butter was placed in bogs not only for preservation purposes but possibly also to develop a desired rancid flavour. It has also been suggested that the butter was a votive offering to the fairies (see FAIRY FOOD). Evans believes that the custom continued in Ireland until at least the 19th century.   RSe

BOG MYRTLE (or sweet gale), *Myrica gale*, a shrub which grows in boggy places in most of the cooler parts of the northern hemisphere. It is smaller than and unrelated to the true MYRTLE.

The leaves and small, winged fruits yield an agreeably aromatic wax, which smells rather like bay. The leaves were used to make a tea in both China and Wales; but a more general use in Europe was to make gale beer, to which they were added in place of hops. The fruits have also been used in France, Sweden, and N. England to flavour soups and meat dishes. Fernald and Kinsey (1943) say: 'The nutlets of Sweet Gale have been used in France . . . as an aromatic spice, having a delicious fragrance suggestive of sage.' But it was more usual to soak them in hot water to release the wax, which was made into scented candles. So another name for these plants is candleberry.

BOIL a verb which indicates one of the fundamental cooking operations, familiar in every kitchen. Water, at sea level, boils at 100 °C (212 °F). That is not a coincidence. The centigrade scale was established by defining the freezing point of water as 0° and its boiling point, when it turns to steam, as 100°.

Nor is it a coincidence that the point at which water boils is easily recognized. When water turns to steam, the process is heralded by some bubbles coming to the surface and is accompanied, when in full swing, by rapid bubbling. So, cooks have no problem with an instruction such as 'bring to the boil'. Even from the far side of the kitchen one can tell when this has been achieved.

This ease of recognition is a considerable convenience, and, taken in conjunction with the ready availability of water as a cooking medium, would go a long way towards explaining the popularity of boiling as a cookery technique. But there is still a fundamental question to be answered: what is it about this precise temperature which makes it suitable for cooking a wide range of comestibles? Might not 5° less or more, or even greater variations, be better?

On one level, the last question can be answered in the affirmative. It is frequently better to poach something, at a temperature just below boiling point; or to cook at a higher temperature. Since water turns to steam at 100 °C, the latter option requires using a different cooking medium (e.g. oil) or changing the water to a solution (e.g. of sugar in water, which will reach a far higher temperature) or altering the boiling point of the water by resorting to PRESSURE COOKING.

On another level, one could answer the question differently, pointing out that most foods consist mainly of water (the proportion is often more than 90%), and that it is therefore unsurprising that 'bringing to the boil' is an efficient way of cooking; it takes the main constituent of the foodstuff to as high a temperature as it can normally reach.

Vigorous, rapid boiling of water (or other liquid with the same characteristics) does not produce a higher temperature, but simply causes more commotion in the pot (normally pointless) and increases the rate at which water evaporates (useful if one is reducing the liquid). The point is brought out in this quotation from ACCUM (drawing on Count RUMFORD and thus uniting in one passage two of the greatest writers on the science of cookery):

Count Rumford has taken much pains to impress on the minds of those who exercise the culinary art, the following simple but practical, important fact, namely; that when water begins only to be agitated by the heat of the fire, it is incapable of being made hotter, and that the violent ebullition is nothing more than an unprofitable dissipation of the water, in the form of steam . . . it is not by

the bubbling up, or *violent boiling*, as it is called, that culinary operations are expedited.

When the cooking medium is something other than water, the situation is different; then there may well be situations in which vigorous boiling is required. See BOUILLABAISSE for one, the point there being to create an emulsion of the water and oil. JAM recipes often call for rapid boiling at the end of the process, this being designed to promote evaporation and, by increasing the proportion of sugar in the sugar solution, to allow the jam to reach the relatively high temperature which will ensure a good set. Other examples could be given.

Finally, an interesting point from Tabitha Tickletooth in a book called *The Dinner Question* (1860). This extraordinary author, whose massive and matriarchal image on the cover of the book is generally supposed to represent the real male author in drag, holds forth on many topics, including potato cookery. Having established the need to choose the appropriate variety of potato for the dish being prepared, Tabitha goes on to give a cooking tip of importance. It is reproduced here with its explanatory footnote.

When [the potatoes] have boiled five minutes, pour off the hot water and replace it with cold* and half a tablespoonful of salt.

*The reason for this innovation on the general practice is, that the heart of the potato being peculiarly hard, the outside, in the ordinary course, is done long before it is softened. By chilling its exterior with cold water, the heat of the first boiling strikes to the centre of the vegetable, and as its force gradually increases when the water boils again, by the time the outside has recovered from its chilling, the equilibrium is restored, and the whole potato is evenly done.

BOILED SWEETS a general term indicating CONFECTIONERY made by the process of SUGAR BOILING. The name is used especially with reference to hard, glassy 'high boiled' sweets such as DROPS, which are actually highly concentrated sugar solutions.

TOFFEE, FUDGE, HUMBUGS, BULLSEYES, and various items of PULLED CANDY, such as ROCK, also count as boiled sweets. Small drops in different colours, plus striped balls and lengths of cut rock, are often sold as a mixture. Sweets made by sugar boiling are especially popular in W. Europe and N. America.   LM

BOIS DE PANAMA a name applied to two plant products which some would classify as spices but which are valued for their foam-making ability rather than for any aromatic quality.

The first of these, and the one which has prior claim to the name bois de Panama, is the dried inner bark of *Quillaja saponaria*, an

American tree. It is clear from Seigneurie (1898) that this dried bark was an article of commerce at the end of the 19th century, and that it had a food use. If it is brought to the boil in plenty of water and then left to simmer for a couple of hours, or until the volume of water has been greatly reduced; and if the result is strained and left to cool, and then whisked, it becomes foamy and brilliant white. A warm sugar syrup can then be incorporated in this foam, producing a white elastic mousse with excellent keeping qualities. This mousse is called *naatiffe* (spelled in various ways, e.g. *natef*) and is used in the Middle East—especially Egypt and the Lebanon—to accompany sweetmeats such as KARABIJ (finger-shaped pistachio nut pastries). The *naatiffe* has a faintly bitter-sweet (almondy, say some) taste and plays a role more or less comparable with that of whipped cream in western countries.

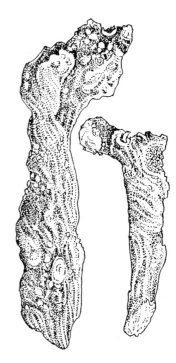

Pieces of **Bois de Panama** bought in a Lebanese market

The second product is the dried root of *Saponaria officinalis*, the herb known as soapwort. This grows in the Middle East as well as in many other places. It is quite unrelated to the tree described in the preceding paragraph but happens to share with it the ability to create foam. This is because of the presence of certain saponins, which also make it possible to manufacture shampoos from either the bark of the tree or the root of the herb.

A further coincidence is that the dried bark and dried root are similar in appearance. It seems clear (see Helen J. Saberi *et al.*, 1994) that confectioners in the Middle East see little difference, for their practical purposes, between the two; and that the name bois de Panama, sounding more exotic and attractive than soapwort, came to be the preferred name for both. The fact that usage of *naatiffe* was particularly strong in the Lebanon and Syria, where French was spoken, no doubt had an influence.

Helen J. Saberi *et al.* (1994) and other correspondents of the journal *PPC*, in which they were recording their research, drew attention to further ramifications, notably that plants of the genus *Gypsophila* can also be used to produce a white foam, used e.g. in Turkey in the confection of one type of HALVA.

BOLETE (or boletus), a general name for a large group of edible fungi which includes the genus *Boletus*. The most highly esteemed members of this genus are described under CEP, a name properly applied to them alone, although often used more loosely (but not current in the USA, where every species in the group is a 'boletus' or 'bolete').

As explained under MUSHROOM, there is a fundamental difference between an AGARIC and a bolete, immediately apparent to anyone looking under their caps. An agaric, such as the common field mushroom, has gills in the form of fine, radiating 'plates'. A bolete has instead a mass of tubes, looking rather like foam rubber. The tubes terminate in pores, which may be very fine or quite coarse. (The group of POLYPORES also has these tubes, but is distinguished from the boletus group by other features.)

Boletes (boletus mushrooms) were all grouped by early mycologists in the single genus *Boletus*. Now, although this genus remains the chief one in the group, a number of others are recognized, including *Boletinus*, *Leccinum*, *Suillus*, and *Gyroporus*. The common name bolete (or boletus, as some have it, despite the difficulty of then providing a plural form) is, however, normally applied to all of them. Boletes are found in most parts of the world, including China, Japan, SE Asia, Australia, and Africa, as well as Europe and N. America.

Many boletes besides the ceps are worth eating, but their stems tend to become infested with insects or maggots and often have to be discarded. The same applies to older specimens whose tubes have become soggy. Some *Boletus* spp are harmful: see the warning at the end of this entry. Others are excessively bitter or peppery, or edible but of no gastronomic interest.

Good species include the following. (E indicates European, NA North American, AS Asian, and AU Australian):

- *Boletus appendiculatus*, which has a reddish-brown cap and pale yellow or creamy flesh which stains blue if cut. (E)
- *B. regius*, with a red or purplish cap and yellow tubes and stem. French, *bolet royal*; German, *Königsröhrling*. (E, NA)
- *B. badius*, with a brick-red or ochre-brown cap and white flesh, usually free of maggots. French, *bolet bai*; German, *Maronenröhrling*. (E, NA)
- *B. erythropus*, which, as the specific name indicates, has a red foot (more precisely, a yellow or orange one, densely covered with tiny red dots) and is therefore *bolet pied rouge* in France. The flesh turns blue when cut, which puts many people off; but it is good to eat. (E, NA)
- *B. mirabilis*, which has a maroon cap, white to yellow flesh, and bright yellow spores. It is found mainly in the Pacific north-west and the Rocky Mountain region, and is unusual in that it grows on rotting coniferous logs or stumps as well as on the ground. Excellent. (NA)
- *B. zelleri*, with a very dark cap and yellow flesh, highly esteemed in the Puget Sound region, where amateur mycologists abound. (NA)

Of the several edible species in the genus *Leccinum*, the best known is perhaps *L. aurantiacum*, sometimes called orange-cap boletus. It grows near aspen trees or pines, has a large, rusty red cap, and a stout, white stem covered with what look like particles of soot but are really tiny tufts of dark hair. German, *Rotkappe* or *Kapuziner*. Recommended (E, NA).

The genus *Suillus* includes *S. luteus*, known as *numeiguchi* in Japan, *bolet jaune* or *nonette* in France, *Butterpilz* in Germany, and *smörsopp* in Sweden, where it is highly esteemed. Its chestnut or sepia cap has a glutinous surface, earning it the English name 'slippery Jack', and it is found in coniferous woods (E, NA, AU). The same applies to *S. granulatus*, the granulated boletus, a species whose flesh is pale yellow (E, NA, AU).

There are other edible species in this genus, all with glutinous caps and all growing in association with conifers. *S. grevillei* (formerly *Boletus elegans*) is always found with larch trees; so it is the *bolet du mélèze* in France and the larch bolete in England and N. America. *S. pictus*, known as painted bolete, is common wherever the white pine grows in the USA.

In the genus *Gyroporus* there is one exceptionally fine mushroom: *G. cyanescens* (E, NA), *indigotier* in France, because its pores stain blue readily; indeed their surface can be 'written on' with any sharp instrument. The French mycogastronomist Ramain (1979) counted it the best of all the boletus family, including the ceps.

Any edible boletus can be prepared like a cep. Peeling is necessary for the slippery Jack tribe, whose viscous caps do need it, but not otherwise. The spongy texture of the cap makes these mushrooms less suitable than others for use in salads, and it is better to cook them, taking full advantage of their juiciness.

Some French authorities, mindful that the flesh of *Leccinum aurantiacum* turns black if cooked in the ordinary way, recommend coating thick slices with beaten egg and breadcrumbs and pan-frying them in this protective cover; a technique which can be applied to other species.

WARNING. It is advisable to be very sure of the identification of any species which has red pores under the cap. It could be one of several, such as *Boletus luridus*, which are poisonous when raw and can cause gastric upsets even when cooked. Or it could be a species which is poisonous in any circumstances, e.g. *B. satanas*, the devil's boletus, happily rare. On the other hand, the delicious *B. erythropus* has red pores.

BOLIVIA This inland country was once part of the Inca Empire; see INCA FOOD. It was then called Alto Peru and, true to that name, is high in the Altiplano that stretches east from the border lake Titicaca, and even higher in the true Andes beyond, before swooping down to a moist and barely explored jungle in the Oriente region. If the staple crop of the Altiplano is the POTATO, then the COCA bush might seem the most important in the high mountains, for the leaves counteract altitude sickness, and the jungle will supply the full gamut of tropical produce, from CASSAVA, to SWEET POTATO and COCONUT.

The Indian culture that resulted in the ruined city of Tiahuanaco was overlaid by the Inca, in turn giving way to the Spanish. Two Indian languages, Aymará and Quechua (the Inca tongue), are still current, Europeans accounting for only 17% of the population, and mestizos for another 30%. The cooking of Bolivia reflects this strong Indian element, and the relative barrenness of the country. Once local circumstances have been taken into account, however, there is much in common between the high regions of Bolivia and the cooking found in other Andean countries such as PERU and ECUADOR. All love the spice of CHILLI peppers, rely on stews and substantial vegetable dishes rather than roasts, and often colour their foods with ANNATTO.

The potato is in its heartland here. Western visitors have written of potato shows at La Paz where up to 89 separate named varieties have been displayed (though there may be as many as 300 in existence), but most particular are the frost-resistant white and purple varieties which are used for the manufacture of CHUÑO, the freeze-dried potato that provides food for the whole year, whether as a simply sauced day-to-day staple, for example with accompaniment of hot peppers or cheese, or as an ingredient of a more complex *chupe* (stew). Other potatoes, such as the yellow-fleshed *S. andigenum* so popular in Peru, are also grown in milder ground.

MAIZE does not grow well at Bolivian altitudes, but around Lake Titicaca, QUINOA provides a cereal staple, though maize has by now entered the national repertoire in such dishes as *Pastel del choclo*. These three staples, potato, quinoa, and maize, have all been used to make alcoholic drinks of varying potency.

Bolivians share with Peruvians an affection for *cuy* (GUINEA PIG), especially useful as they are unable to rely on a coastal region for fish, or a pampa that would support large meat animals. They have used the llama for transport, but not for milk or meat. RABBIT is another small meat animal that has found favour—the dish *Conejo estirado* is so called because the animal is stretched to make it more tender. The freshwater fish of the two great lakes Titicaca and Poopù are certainly eaten, travellers reporting them excellent fried.   TJ

BOLLITO MISTO
a N. Italian dish of various boiled meats; the name means literally 'boiled mixed'. The mixture of meats varies according to the region but, as Anna del Conte (1987) explains, 'should include beef, veal, chicken, tongue, *cotechino* (sausage) and half a calf's head'. The meats are cooked in boiling water at different times according to how long they take to cook.

A Bollito misto is accompanied by various sauces, the most common one being *salsa verde* (a piquant parsley sauce), although *salsa rossa* (a tomato sauce) is also popular. The dish is usually made for a large number of people, at least 12, and in restaurants it is often wheeled around on a special trolley with separate compartments keeping the meat hot in its stock and carved specially for each person; this prevents the meats from drying out. Del Conte asserts that the best Bollito misto is to be had in Piedmont, but people in Lombardy and Emilia-Romagna might well disagree.   HS

BOMBE
the French word for bomb, refers also to a kind of rich, frozen dessert. It is properly *bombe glacée* as a culinary term but commonly occurs as just plain bombe (now accepted as an English word), with or without an epithet to indicate the flavouring

or other aspect of it. The principal constituent is a bombe mixture, which is typically made with egg yolks, sugar, whipped cream, and water. ICE CREAM of various kinds is used in addition, being placed in the mould so as to surround the bombe mixture or be interleaved with it, always with the aim of producing an attractive pattern when the finished dish is served and cut open.

The name bombe reflects the fact that the moulds originally used for this confection were more or less spherical, as were bombs such as assassins would hurl in past times. The shape of the moulds subsequently evolved into forms such as those advertised by Mrs Marshall (1894), notably a section of a cone.

For another frozen dessert of the same family, see PARFAIT.

BONBON
a French term often used for any small SWEET or CANDY. It has entered many other languages, becoming *bombon* in Spanish, and *bombom* in Portuguese. It was adopted into English around the end of the 18th century and, according to Ayto (1993) 'probably reached its heyday as a more delicate alternative to the foursquare *sweet* [see also SWEETIES] in the late Victorian and Edwardian eras, when bonbonnières (small decorated boxes for holding sweets) graced fashionable sideboards and tables'.

The general use of the word *bonbon* in French to refer to a sweetmeat or 'goody' is recorded as early as the beginning of the 17th century. Originally a child's term for a FRIANDISE, or sweet delicacy, it now refers, 'broadly speaking, to a multitude of sugar based products flavoured with fruits and essences, in a variety of shapes, made by confectioners; and the term *bonbon de chocolat* is also in use for items with chocolate centres'. The explanation is from the fine encyclopedia of *épicerie* by Seigneurie (1898).

In France, as elsewhere, bonbons and sweets have been given as gifts at festivals. In 18th-century France, this custom became a fine art, with small highly decorated boxes called *bonbonnières* or *drageoirs*, which were made of precious materials and given as presents and tokens of regard.

Jarrin (1827), a confectioner working in London, observes of bonbons that:

There is great demand for these articles in France, particularly on New Year's day; and the various envelopes in which they are put up, display the usual ingenuity of this gay and versatile people: fables, historical subjects, songs, enigmas, jeux des mots, and various little gallantries, are all inscribed upon the papers in which the bon-bons are inclosed, and which the gentlemen present to the females of their acquaintance.

According to Gunter (1830), eponymous founder of the famous London confectioners, bonbons were composed 'of syrup boiled to a blow, essenced, and formed in moulds of lead. They may be tinted with liquid colouring.' Flavourings such as rose, cinnamon, orange flower, lemon, vanilla, bergamot, or vanilla are quoted; alternatively, liqueurs could be used.

Twentieth-century bonbons and sweets made in France include numerous skilfully marketed regional specialities, traditional or modern, unobtainable anywhere else. These are often based on local produce, and divide roughly into four categories: sweetmeats made from fruits; nut-based confectionery; chocolates; and traditional boiled sugar items.

Fruit confections include *pâtes de fruits* (FRUIT PASTES) made in many parts of France, particularly the Auvergne; and *fruits confits*, whole CANDIED FRUITS such as apricots or pears. These are a speciality of the city of Apt, but are also manufactured throughout Provence and in the Auvergne. Other fruit-based confections may depend upon the cultivation of a particular fruit in a small area. In this category are *pruneaux d'Agen* (see PRUNE), and *cotignac d'Orléans*, a clear paste made from quinces (see QUINCE PRESERVES).

Nut-based confectionery includes the famous NOUGAT de Montelimar, and other Provençal *nougats*, *turrons*, and nut BRITTLES; and MARRONS GLACÉS. PRALINES are another nut-based speciality, referring in this sense to confections made from nuts covered in an irregular sugar coating.

The manufacture of CHOCOLATE in France was, historically, associated with the port of Bayonne in the south-west, although other towns now practise this. Confectioners throughout France offer their own chocolates, the shapes and fillings of which are limited only by their imagination.

A number of boiled sugar specialities have evolved in France. DRAGÉES or SUGAR ALMONDS have been made in Verdun for at least seven centuries. Centres for dragées are also made from many regional specialities such as liqueurs or fruit pastes; spices are sometimes used, for example in *anis de Flavigny*.

BARLEY SUGAR, *sucre d'orge*, is made in various localities, particularly spa towns such as Vichy. Other boiled sugar sweets which are well known are: *bergamottes de Nancy* (flavoured with bergamot oil); *bêtises de Cambrai* (flavoured with mint and caramelized sugar); and BERLINGOTS. Boiled sugar is also used to make outer casings for sweets filled with pastes made from local fruits or nuts.

French boiled sugar specialities of the toffee type are called, collectively, CARAMELS. Caramels are specialities of N. and

W. France; as in Britain, many different flavourings are used with them. Well-known varieties are *niniche de Bordeaux* and *negus de Nevers*.

PASTILLES, which in France means little sweets of hard, perfumed sugar, are made in many areas. They are scented with different essences, and may be shaped as fruits or flowers, or simply made in little drop shapes. These were the 19th-century bonbons which filled the New Year's gifts mentioned by Jarrin. Some have therapeutic value, such as the 'digestive' pastilles of Vichy, or the 'throat' pastilles, made with honey, at Saint-Benoît-sur-Loire.

Other traditional bonbons are *violettes de Toulouse* (CANDIED VIOLETS); and candied ANGELICA, a speciality of Niort and the Poitou. *Reglisse*, LIQUORICE, is made in the south-east, particularly in the Marseilles area; and CACHOUS, also based on liquorice, are made in Toulouse.   LM

READING: Combet and Lefrèvre (1995); Lallemand (1990); Annie Perrier-Robert (1986).

BONE except insofar as it contains BONE MARROW, is of little use to the cook save for making stock for soups. It may, however, be of indirect use; it is often said that meat cooked on the bone has more flavour than meat without the bone.

Experiments carried out by Papin (1681) with his 'New Digester or Engine for Softning Bones' (see PRESSURE COOKING), and repeated by Davidson (1988*a*), show that bones cooked under pressure for sufficiently long will disintegrate, yielding both marrowfat and a pulp which can be used for thickening sauces and kindred purposes. In this way bones can be eaten. They are rich in calcium.

This applies to bones of animals and birds. Those of fish, although they too can be used to produce stock for soups, are different in that they have no marrow. Indeed, in many languages there is a different word for fish bones, no doubt because the small ones are perceived as a nuisance; those who have not taken the trouble to learn how to separate the flesh of a fish from all its bones, large or small, often find themselves greatly inconvenienced by the latter.

BONEFISH the unpromising name of *Albula vulpes*, a fish of the HERRING family, related to the TARPON and the LADYFISH; it is itself sometimes called ladyfish. The French name *banane* and Portuguese and Malay names with the same meaning, allude to its 'underslung' shape.

The bonefish, which is found worldwide in tropical waters, has a maximum length of 90 cm (35"). It has elusive habits (whence the

scientific name, which means 'white fox') and is highly regarded as a game fish but not often seen in the markets. It has too many bones for convenience at table, but is otherwise good to eat.

Anglers esteem the fish because of the desperate and vigorous way in which it fights for its life when hooked. Fishing for it is a favourite sport in Hawaii, where many are killed, compared with what seems to be a zero rate of fatalities among the much bigger human gladiators who pit themselves against it.

BONE MARROW the soft, nutritious substance found in the internal cavities of animal bones, especially the shin bones of oxen and calves. The French term is *moelle*.

The spinal marrow of oxen and calves is sometimes known as 'ox pith'. Pieces of it, or of the same thing from sheep, are commonly called *amourettes* in French.

Marrow was formerly a prized delicacy, to be cooked and served in its bone from which it would be removed with a special silver marrow scoop.

Dorothy Hartley (1954) provides charming drawings which show how marrow bones were baked in Georgian times, with a small paste crust sealing the cut end, and how they were boiled if the marrow was to be served on hot buttered toast. She says that in the Middle Ages marrow was a well-loved food, mainly used for sweet dishes. Later, in the time of Queen Victoria, marrow was considered to be a man's food and 'unladylike', although Queen Victoria herself apparently ate marrow toast for tea every day. Dorothy Hartley comments that this 'was certainly not correct diet for her plump Majesty'. She does, however, further comment that: 'Marrow is the most liked and digestible fat, and should be given to children and invalids who require building up.'

Sheila Hutchins, writing in 1971, mentioned that baked marrow bones were 'still served hot in a napkin at City dinners and a few old-fashioned public houses' in London. More remarkably, she gave two recipes for marrow pudding, one of which was the family pudding of Sir Watkin Williams-Wynn. According to Sir Watkin, the recipe dated from the mid-18th century and the pudding was still, when Sheila Hutchins interviewed him, being 'served regularly with hot jam sauce at his table and at that of the dowager Lady Watkin Williams-Wynn' (at the age of 95). The preferred jam was raspberry jam.

BONITO *Sarda sarda*, a fish of the scombrid (MACKEREL and TUNA) family which occurs on both sides of the S. and N.

Atlantic, as far north as Cape Cod in the west and the south coast of Britain in the east; throughout the Mediterranean; and in the Black Sea, whence it migrates south at the end of the year, returning in the spring. The name is also used in connection with other species, e.g. the striped or oceanic bonito (see SKIPJACK).

The back of the bonito is steel blue with dark blue slanting stripes; its sides and belly silvery. Its maximum length is 90 cm (3'), although it is never as big as this in European waters.

These are shoaling fish and vigorous predators, with the habit of leaping out of the water when in pursuit of prey such as herring and squid.

There are similar species, mostly slightly bigger, in the Indo-Pacific region. *S. orientalis*, the oriental bonito, has a range right across the Indo-Pacific. *S. chiliensis* is present on much of the western coasts of both N. and S. America. Both these are of commercial importance.

The compact and light-coloured flesh of the bonito, which is excellent, is often canned. Spaniards (and Turks) are among the greatest connoisseurs of and enthusiasts for this fish. Note, however, that *bonito* on a menu in the north of Spain could well be *bonito del norte*, the ALBACORE.

BORAGE *Borago officinalis*, an annual or biennial plant common in the Mediterranean region and as far north as C. Europe and Britain, has pretty blue flowers, hairy leaves with a mild cucumber flavour, stalks which may be cooked as a vegetable, and a reputation for enlivening those who eat it.

Borage leaves, and often the flowers too, are added to various drinks, but for the sake of the flavour rather than in response to testimonials such as the following. Burton, the famous 17th-century authority on the *Anatomy of Melancholy* (1st edn 1621) named borage as a good plant 'to purge the veins of melancholy'. Gerard (1633) wrote: 'Those of our time use the leaves in sallads, to exhilarate and make the minde glad.' Evelyn (1699) declared that borage would 'revive the Hypochondriac and chear the hard Student'.

Whatever it does for human beings, the plant certainly has a strong attraction for bees; hence another English name, bee-bread.

When they are small and young, the leaves are a good addition to salads. Larger leaves, whose prickly hairs are a nuisance, can be cooked as a vegetable, as they are, for example, in parts of Catalonia and in Liguria. Borage abounds in Liguria and is put to other uses there, such as stuffing for pasta. Stalks cooked as a vegetable are popular in some of these Mediterranean regions, but perhaps even more so in Galicia.

BORDELAISE SAUCE one of the important sauces incorporating sauce ESPAGNOLE. There are three stages in making it. First, thin slices of streaky salt pork with diced carrot and chopped onion are sweated in a pan. Then red or white Bordeaux wine (if white is used the sauce is called Bonnefoy), shallots, peppercorns, and other ingredients are added and the whole greatly reduced. The sauce ESPAGNOLE and stock are then added, brought to the boil, strained, returned to the pan, and slowly reduced again. This sauce goes well with roast meat and in *Cèpes à la bordelaise* (see CEP).

BÖREK a distinctive family of Near Eastern pastries, eaten both during meals and as snacks. The wrapper may be plain bread dough but rich layered pastry is more characteristic, either FILO or rough puff paste, made by the familiar sequence of buttering, folding, and rolling. The filling is usually savoury, of meat or cheese, but sweet versions have been made throughout the pastry's recorded history. Originally, börek was cooked on the *saj*, the flat sheet of iron used by the nomadic Turks; now the cooking method may be frying or baking (although the Kalmuk Mongols boil their deviant *büreg*).

One form of börek, the Tunisian *brik*, has evolved into what might be regarded as a separate species, such is the importance of *Brik à l'œuf* (described under TUNISIA).

Börek came to occupy such a high place in the Turco-Iranian cuisine of W. Asia that it was even considered a rival to PILAF. The rise of börek is reflected in a curious poem by the 14th-century Persian poet Bushaq-i At'ima, describing an imaginary battle between börek and pilaf, which are personified as two rival monarchs.

Bushaq's mention is one of the earliest, two others occurring in 14th-century Turco-Arabic glossaries. Among the Turkish languages, the word börek is found only in those of Turkey and its immediate neighbours in the Crimea, the Caucasus, and Turkmenistan, and this fact suggests that börek was indigenous to that area.

Not only the point of origin of börek within its present range but also the question of its relationship with similar items elsewhere (Indian SAMOSA, Afghan *sambosa* and BOULANEE, Iraqi *sambusak*, etc.) has been the subject of debate. Ayla Algar (1991) treats the matter at length. She also observes that in later centuries popular consumption of börek in Turkey soared to such great heights that at one time there were 4,000

börek shops in Istanbul, compared to just 1,000 bakeries.

Natural historians who are looking for the point of origin for a species of plant often look for the region of greatest diversity, and there are good grounds for maintaining that this is likely to be where the plant originated. Adapting this approach to the history of börek, Ayla Algar has this interesting passage, quoted because of its value as an example of how this natural history approach can be used in the culinary matters:

Börek remains central to the popular cuisine of Anatolia, and it would hardly be an exaggeration to say that Anatolia feeds itself primarily on different varieties of dough! . . .

The broad and lasting popularity of börek would be impossible without the great diversity that is concealed by the uniform name of this food. There is great variety in the techniques of preparing and layering the doughs, in the fillings that are used, in the shapes that are given to the final product, and in the methods of cooking that are used; some of these variations are regional in nature.

No doubt other cuisines have had roughly comparable dishes—the spring rolls of the Chinese, the *lumpia* of the Malays and Indonesians, the *sanbusa* of the Iranians (now surviving only in India in the form of *samosa*). But no other cuisine can boast of a whole family of dishes akin to *börek*, an Ottoman legacy found not only in Turkey but also in the Balkans and North Africa. Even the Russian *pirog* (more familiar in its diminutive form, *pirozhki*) may be derived from *börek*, according to the Finnish scholar Georg Ramstedt.

BORSHCH a BEETROOT soup which can be served either hot or cold. It is essentially a dish of E. Europe, this region being taken to include RUSSIA, LITHUANIA, POLAND (where the name is *barszcz*) and, most important, the UKRAINE. Ukrainians count it as their national soup and firmly believe that it originated there. They are almost certainly right, especially if (as suggested under BURAN) one can properly apply to such questions the principle followed by botanists: that the place where the largest number of natural variations is recorded is probably the place of origin of a species. There are more kinds of borshch in the Ukraine than anywhere else; these include the versions of Kiev, Poltava, Odessa, and L'vov.

Borshch, which is also counted as a speciality of Ashkenazi JEWISH COOKERY, can be made with a wide range of vegetables. However, the essential ingredient is beetroot, giving the soup its characteristic red colour. Sour cream is usually added on top, just before serving.

The stock used can be beef (meat or bones or both), pork, chicken, goose or, in a vegetarian version, mushroom. *Rassol*, the

liquid in which beetroot is preserved, adds more flavour to the soup, as does KVASS, if used. Spicy sausages or chopped ham are optional additions, as are dumplings. A common and important accompaniment consists of *pirozhki* (see PIROG).

The traditional fast-day variant was based on mushroom stock and included in its range of vegetables the young green leaves from spring beetroot (the actual beets being omitted).

See also CHŁODNIK.   (HS)

BOSNIA-HERZEGOVINA independent since 1992, is a well-wooded, predominantly mountainous country with many fertile plains and a small outlet on the Adriatic.

During the four centuries of Turkish occupation most of the Slavs in what is now Bosnia-Herzegovina embraced the Muslim faith. Their descendants account for about a third of the present population, the remainder being mainly Serbs and Croats.

The republic boasts modern, large-scale agriculture with maize as the chief cereal, and intensive rearing of cattle, pigs, and sheep. Orchards are numerous with plums as the major fruit crop.

Bosnian Muslims have never been enthusiastic observers of the law of Islam which prohibits the drinking of alcohol, and practically never gave up drinking wine and their beloved *šljivovica* (plum brandy). Indeed, the favourite pastime, even now, is the evening gathering called *akšamluk* (from Turkish *akşamlatmak*, to entertain for the night), where men would engage in friendly conversation, enlivened with many glasses of the native brandy and sustained by multifarious MEZZE dishes.

The tradition of good restaurant food in Bosnia dates back to the second half of the 15th century (*c*.1462) when the first inn with a cook was recorded. A list of nearly 200 dishes which were served at the end of the 19th century in the eating houses in Sarajevo was given by the Bosnian Ali efendi Numanagić in a newspaper published in 1939. However, by the beginning of the 20th century many of these dishes had disappeared from Bosnian restaurant menus.

Bosnians and Herzegovinians like to taste their way through a menu, and it is an old restaurant practice to serve small amounts of six or more different, but complementary, dishes arranged side by side on a plate. For example, *Baščaršikski sahan* (high-street platter) could consist of one skewer of *šiš ćevap*, a stuffed onion, green pepper, and tomato, a few fried tiny meatballs, and stuffed vine or cabbage leaves which are called *sarma* in Bosnia, or *japrak* in Herzegovina; the juices from the various saucepans are then mixed together, poured over the food, and the whole dish garnished with a few tablespoons of YOGHURT.   MK-J

BOTTLE GOURD *Lagenaria siceraria*, is also called calabash or white-flowered gourd, by way of distinguishing it from the yellow-flowered *Cucurbita* spp. It is generally regarded as a native of Africa, but has been cultivated in Asia and America since prehistoric times.

Archaeological evidence from the Peruvian highlands shows that the bottle gourd was there in the period 13000–11000 BC. There are numerous other reports from the Peruvian coast and Mexico of its presence somewhat later, 7000–4000 BC.

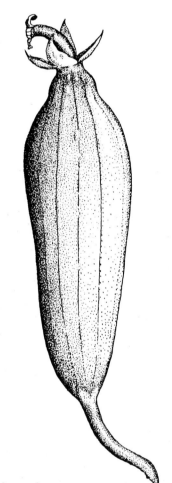

Bottle gourd

That it reached America in this very distant past is certain; but how it did is a question which has prompted lively debates. It has been shown that the gourd's hard shell is sufficiently water resistant to float across the ocean from Africa, and that the seeds inside will remain viable longer than such a crossing requires. But gourd seeds would not germinate if cast up on a beach; human intervention would be required.

Heiser (1979) has summed up well the alternative sets of difficulties. On the one hand, is it to be supposed that when a bottle gourd floated across the Atlantic, probably to Brazil, nearly 15 millennia ago, there was an agriculturist waiting who realized its worth and knew what to do? Or, on the other, is it plausible to suppose that pre-Columbian contacts across the S. Atlantic (generally conceded to have taken place, but without agreement on how and when) happened quite so long ago and provided for the carriage of these gourds or at least the transmission of knowledge about them? Other gourds present like problems, but the bottle gourd is the archetypal enigma of its kind.

In its wild form the bottle gourd is bitter and more or less inedible, and even recent works sometimes refer to it as of negligible use in the kitchen. However, selection and cultivation have transformed it into a sweet and valued foodstuff. One could even say 'a range of foodstuffs', for the bottle gourd now takes many forms. Besides the dozen or more important cultivars of *L. siceraria* itself, there are two separate varieties: *L. siceraria* 'Clavata' and *L. siceraria* 'Longissima', of which the former is used especially for *kampyo* (see below), while the latter is exceptionally thin and long (120 cm/48" or more) and has alternative common names such as *cucuzzi* and New Guinea bean.

Collectively, this group of vegetables offers wide scope in cookery. As Facciola (1990) points out, the young vegetables may be eaten boiled, steamed, fried, pickled, added to soups and curries, or made into fritters.

The same author and others describe a product which the Japanese make. This is *kampyo*, ribbon-like strips of the dried peeled pulp of the fruit. When seasoned with SOY SAUCE, these form a common ingredient of rolled SUSHI, and of certain Buddhist ceremonial dishes. The strips, which are sometimes called 'dried gourd shavings', are reconstituted in lightly salted water before use, e.g. in tying foods into little packages, rolls, or bundles. If such packages are simmered, these ties become soft and transparent and can be eaten with the food they enclose.

In China the bottle gourd is stir-fried and eaten with chicken or shredded pork, sliced onion, and 'cloud ear' black fungus (see WOOD EAR). In India it is enjoyed with curries but is also steamed and given for medicinal purposes.

When fully mature the bottle gourd ceases to be suitable for eating. Like its wild predecessor it is hard and woody and its greatest use reverts to being a bottle or container for both liquid and dry materials—or being made into other objects such as a musical instrument or a ladle. In

Afghanistan, for example, the larger fruits are made into water-holders for hookahs (Aitchison, 1890); and Heiser (1979) gives a memorable account of the range of penis sheaths made from these gourds in (especially) New Guinea.

BOTULISM a rare but very dangerous form of food poisoning caused by a toxin produced by the bacterium *Clostridium botulinum*. This organism is widespread in the environment, for example in river mud. It is anaerobic—that is, it functions only in the absence of oxygen—and will not grow in an acid medium; but it can survive unfavourable conditions by forming spores. These withstand high temperatures and can persist in cooked meat (the name botulism is derived from the Latin *botulus*, a sausage, because of incidents involving such foods) and non-acid canned vegetables, if these have not been prepared properly. To kill all spores food must be heated to 121 °C (250 °F) for three minutes, which is possible only in a pressure cooker or a commercial AUTOCLAVE.

Even this may not be sufficient if the organism has had time to produce its toxin, which has been described as the most poisonous substance known; 1 gram (0.035 oz) could kill between 100,000 and 10 million people, depending on how it is administered. Albert (1987) states:

Botulism is not a common disease. Outbreaks mostly follow consumption of a consignment of canned seafood, such as tuna, where every can in a faulty batch is likely to be infected. The second commonest source of infection seems to be home-preserved peas and beans, insufficiently heat-processed.

BOUCHÉE the French word for mouthful, refers to a small VOL-AU-VENT. A *petite bouchée* (a very small shell for cocktail snacks) is smaller still.

BOUDOIR BISCUITS are in effect the same as sponge biscuits or sponge fingers, ladyfingers (N. America) and SAVOY biscuits (an older term). They are long, finger-shaped, crisp sponge biscuits based on whisked egg and sugar mixtures with a crystallized sugar topping. In France they are also called *biscuits à la cuiller*.

Helen J. Saberi (1995a) has investigated the history and significance of the unusual name 'boudoir biscuits'. Although boudoir entered the English language from French long ago and its application to these biscuits could therefore have arisen in England, it seems clear that the French were the first to use the name. Boudoir comes from the French verb *bouder*, to pout, and normally refers to a woman's private room where she would receive only her intimate friends—who could pout and nibble sponge fingers as much as they wished in this cloistered environment.

What is surprising about the adoption of the name in England is that the English had previously been eating these biscuits in a completely different environment, at funerals. Thus at one bound, early in the 20th century, the biscuits leaped from the funeral parlour to the boudoir. The new name stuck, presumably because it excited the imagination of Englishwomen, and remained prevalent for most of the 20th century. It is often embossed on the bottom of the biscuits.

BOUILLABAISSE the best known of a large number of Mediterranean fish soup/stew dishes, which include the Greek *Kakavía* and the Catalan *Suquet*, is associated particularly with Marseilles. An essay by Davidson (1988*b*) deals with its history and the technique for making it, prefaced by this account of its distinguishing characteristics:

- the dish requires a wide variety of fish, including *rascasse* (see SCORPION FISH), some fish with firm flesh (to be eaten) and some little ones (to disintegrate into the broth), and maybe some inexpensive crustaceans (small crabs, *cigales de mer*, etc.);
- onions, garlic, tomatoes, parsley are always used—and saffron too (though this item is costly);
- the liquid used consists of water (some white wine is optional) and olive oil, a mixture which must be boiled rapidly;
- the fish (i.e. the ones to be eaten, not the ones which disintegrate) are served separately from the broth, which is poured over pieces of toasted bread (of which there is a special sort at Marseilles for the purpose).

On the history, it is widely supposed that the dish had a primitive origin: fishermen sitting on the beach after the day's fishing and preparing for themselves, with a few staples which they had brought along, a one-pot supper which would use up the least saleable items in their catch. There is no reason to doubt this, but a study of written sources shows that when the dish was brought into the world of restaurants and cookery books it was rather different.

The earliest recipe which is clearly relevant was given by Jourdain Le Cointe in his *La Cuisine de Santé* (1790). It was not headed Bouillabaisse but *Matellotte du Poisson*. It portrayed fishermen disembarking on a river bank where their wives would light a clear fire and bring to the boil in a small cauldron a mixture of many of the ingredients of a 20th-century bouillabaisse (but with the olive oil as an optional item), into which little fish from the nets would go. The first recipe to appear under the name Bouillabaisse (precisely, *Bouillabaisse à la Marseillaise*) was given in *Le Cuisinier Durand* (1830) and advised using expensive SEA BASS and SPINY LOBSTER; it had thus moved away from the primitive scene on the shore or the river bank. Soon afterwards, in 1839, *Le Cuisinier méridionale* had a recipe with a similar title, advocating a mixture of sea fish and freshwater fish; indeed, the anonymous author of the book listed eight of each category, again including sea bass and spiny lobster.

The work already cited considers four principal explanations of the origin of the word 'bouillabaisse' and opts for that favoured by Littré in his great dictionary of 1883: that the expression should be interpreted as *bouillon abaissé*, literally 'broth lowered', i.e. the level of the broth is lowered by evaporation during cooking—or, as we would say, it is 'reduced'. On the question whether and why rapid boiling is necessary, and what various authors mean when they say that this achieves 'amalgamation of the oil, water and wine', clues provided by Harold McGee (1984) and conclusive experiments in the kitchen of Philip and Mary Hyman, recorded by Davidson, led to the explanation that an EMULSION is being formed.

Incidentally, Davidson had criticized two American ladies whose cookery book included a recipe for a bouillabaisse which was based on two cans of soup (one of tomato and one of pea) and included no fish, no herbs, and no olive oil. It has emerged, however, that a partial exoneration of these supposed miscreants is in order. In two of the best-known traditional Provençal cookery books there are recipes for 'bouillabaisse' which contain no fish. The term must be allowed to have more elasticity than might be supposed.

BOULANEE are savoury pastries made in Afghanistan, to be served either crisp and hot, straight from the frying pan, or cold. The dough (plain, unleavened, made with just flour, salt, and water) is rolled out thinly like FILO pastry into rounds which are folded over into half-moon shapes after the stuffing has been put in. The typical stuffing is of *gandana* (Chinese CHIVES), but mashed potato can be used. The pastries are shallow fried and seem to have no exact equivalent outside Afghanistan; they differ from the families of BÖREK, SAMOSA, etc. in not using layered pastry and by virtue of their special filling.   HS

BOUQUET GARNI a French term which came into the English language in the mid-19th century, means the little bundle of herbs which is cooked with various dishes to impart flavour to them. This little bundle began to figure in French cookery in the 17th century, as part of the move away from highly spiced medieval dishes to the more subtle (and less expensive) flavours which herbs could provide. However, even in 1656 the writer Pierre de Lune thought it necessary to explain to his readers what a bouquet garni was (according to him, a strip of bacon, chives, thyme, cloves, chervil, parsley).

The popularity of the bouquet garni increased during the 18th century and ever since then it has been an important item in the French kitchen. The standard bouquet garni is now a bundle of thyme, bay leaf, and parsley; but the composition of the bundle is variable and cooks have their own preferences.

In England and in other countries too, bunches of herbs have been used since medieval times, but the convenience of a single phrase to indicate them was missing until the French one spread abroad.

BOUTARGUE the French, and most widely used, name for a product consisting of the eggs of GREY MULLET, removed in their intact membrane, salted, pressed, dried in the sun, and covered with a protective coat of wax. The name is thought to come from the Arabic *bitârikh*, via the Provençal *boutargo*. This would suggest that Arabs first devised the delicacy, a hypothesis supported by its popularity in Tunisia, when they were en route from the Arab heartlands to Spain.

Boutargue, now an expensive delicacy (which is often described as a speciality of Martigues in Provence and spelled *poutargue*), is thinly sliced for consumption. It can then be served as is or on toast, in any case with a simple dressing of olive oil, lemon juice, and pepper.

BOXTY an Irish variation of potato bread made of grated raw potato, mashed potato, and flour. The name is probably an Anglicization of the Gaelic *bacús*, a term used to describe an oven or baking implement such as a GRIDDLE or pan.

Boxty bread has a particular association with a number of midland and northern counties, especially Cavan, Tyrone, Fermanagh, and Derry.

Boxty PANCAKES and boxty DUMPLINGS are also prepared and the consumption of such was held to augment a girl's marriage prospects:

Boxty on the griddle,
Boxty on the pan,

If you don't eat your boxty,
You'll never get a man!

Traditionally boxty was prepared as part of the Hallowe'en (31 October) and New Year's Day festive fare. It was also eaten throughout the year and often replaced bread at the midday meal or evening supper. A more substantial form of boxty consisting of milk, salt, and potatoes was known as 'dippity'. Another variant dish called 'stampy' was made in the same fashion as boxty bread but prepared with the new season potatoes and often enlivened with cream, sugar, and caraway seeds. In the south-west regions the end of the potato harvest was marked with a 'Stampy Party' when the harvest workers and helpers were treated with copious amounts of stampy bread. RSe

BRACKET FUNGI a term which applies to various fungi which grow directly out of, for example, tree trunks, rather than on stems, which they lack completely or have only in a rudimentary form. Typically they form dense ranks of shelflike (bracket-like) protuberances. See SULPHUR SHELF and BEEFSTEAK FUNGUS for the best-known edible examples; and POLYPORES for some others.

Almost all the fungi in this group live by eating wood. On the debit side they are the principal source of damage to timber; but on the credit side they can claim to be vital to the well-being of forests and woods—which would clog up completely if these fungi were not present to devour fallen logs and branches etc. The very few which are counted as edible provide a means for human beings to eat wood at one remove.

BRAINS especially those of calf and lamb, have been accounted a delicacy, valued mainly for their creamy texture. They can be poached in a COURT BOUILLON, or braised, or made into FRITTERS. Poached brains in brown butter with CAPERS are a popular dish in France, and something similar is well liked in Italy.

In the 1990s marketing and consumption of calf's (or cow's) brains, together with some other organs, ceased in W. Europe because of fear that human beings might be affected by BSE (bovine spongiform encephalitis—see BEEF).

Generally, brains are a very rich food, of which a little goes a long way. In regions like N. America, where attitudes to OFFAL (variety meats) tend to be negative, the brains of slaughtered animals would be likely to finish up with members of immigrant ethnic groups. However, in most countries they are marketed and eaten without any special inhibitions, although

(one might add) without overpowering enthusiasm.

BRAISE a verb and also, less often, a noun, indicating a method of cooking with a small amount of liquid in a closed vessel. Some vegetables are braised, but the technique is used mainly for meat dishes. Braised oxtail is a well-known example in England.

The term, derived from the French *braiser*, first came into use in English in the mid-18th century. Few other languages have a term with the same meaning; for example, there is no Italian or Spanish equivalent. See, however, KORMA for a Middle Eastern and W. Asian equivalent. And French, the richest language in this respect, has two other terms, *à l'étouffée* and *à l'étuvée*, which are virtual equivalents for 'braised'.

The term **pot-roast** has almost the same meaning as braise, although the technique has a different origin, best explained by quoting the Irish author Florence Irwin (1949), who deserved, if anyone did, the title of her own book *The Cookin' Woman*:

Even 30 years ago there were a few ranges in farmhouses. These and also the cottages had hearth fires or open grates in their kitchens. All roasting was done in a pot-oven. These ovens were pots with flat bottoms standing on three legs. The lids were depressed. Sometimes they were suspended over the peat fire on the crook and on the lid red turn (peat) embers were placed. When there was a hearth fire, some embers were taken to the side of the main fire, the pot placed over these on the hearth, and embers placed on top, thus having both upper and under heat.

In this pot the fowls were roasted, also joints of beef. When basting had to be done the lid and embers were removed and replaced when the meat had had due attention.

Although pot roasting has gone on for a long time, Mariani (1994) observes that the term first appeared in print in 1881.

BRAN the husks which are removed when grain is milled to produce flour. The husks usually have a part of the endosperm adhering to them; the more the better in terms of the value of the bran. Because it contains a significant amount of FIBRE, bran is considered to be a useful dietary supplement for people who would otherwise not be ingesting enough fibre.

Bran is used in preparing certain kinds of pickle.

BRANDADE a French culinary term which occurs almost exclusively in the name of one SALT COD dish: *Brandade de morue*, made by vigorously beating milk and olive oil into the previously poached fish to make a thick white purée. The dish is a speciality

of the land-locked city of Nîmes in the Languedoc province of France and the first published recipe is to be found in a cookbook published by a chef from Nîmes, the *Cuisinier Durand*, in 1830. It had begun to be prominent in Paris at the beginning of the 19th century. According to GRIMOD DE LA REYNIÈRE (1805) a Parisian restaurateur made his fortune from serving *Brandade de merluche* (salted and dried hake). Although Grimod describes this dish as being laced with garlic, and many modern recipes still consider garlic to be characteristic of brandade, Durand's recipe notes: 'one may add a little garlic to this preparation, if one is not afraid of it, but it is not essential.' Similarly, people who labour under the misapprehension that potato should be included can be referred to a late 19th-century author who explained that this was not used in the south of France, although further north, where olive oil was less popular, potato was used in order to prevent the flavour of the dish being too strong, and to make it more digestible. Recent authorities have speculated that changes such as these, which have been made outside the south of France in order to make the famous dish more accessible, are now being reflected, if only to a slight extent, in the procedures followed in the south of France itself. If so, this would be an interesting example of how an 'internationalized' version of a dish may eventually begin to compete with (and potentially oust) the authentic version in the region of origin. HY

BRANDY SNAPS crisp, lacy baked items which stand on the frontier between BISCUITS, WAFERS, and sugar CONFECTIONERY. They are made from butter, sugar, and GOLDEN SYRUP, mixed with flour, and flavoured with ginger, brandy (sometimes), and lemon juice. Teaspoonfuls of the mixture are dropped on to trays and baked gently. During baking the mixture spreads into a thin sheet; this is lifted off the tray with a spatula while warm, and rolled round a wooden spoon handle to give a hollow cylinder. When cold, it may be filled with whipped cream.

On the question whether brandy is or is not used (which seems to make no difference to the flavour) the delightfully ponderous comments by Garrett (*c.*1898) are relevant:

These delights of our youth were probably originally made with a Brandy flavouring as one of their ingredients; but with that lack of discriminative taste peculiar to uneducated palates, the presence of the Brandy flavour was not sufficiently appreciated to render its presence essential to the success of the manufacture; hence, as the 'snaps' could be made cheaper without Brandy, and yielded more sweets for the same money, the spiritous prefix became but a name.

Brandy snaps are traditional English 'fairings', treats to buy at the fair, and are sometimes sold flat rather than rolled. Black treacle was used in earlier versions.   LM

BRASSERIE a word which dates back to early medieval times, originally referred to premises where beer was made, but acquired by extension in the mid-19th century the meaning of a place where beer was served, and then, more recently, of a 'cafe-restaurant' where beer would certainly be available but in which the serving of meals might be the dominant activity. A *brasserie alsacienne* is a common feature of French cities, Alsace being the home of famous beers.

A brasserie can be and often is quite modest, although large and relatively pretentious examples can be found. Drawing a line between a brasserie and a BISTRO is no easy matter.   HY

BRASSICA the generic name of the highly diverse and complex group of vegetables typified by the CABBAGE. The genus also includes KALE; BRUSSELS SPROUTS; CAULIFLOWER; BROCCOLI and calabrese; KOHLRABI; CHINESE CABBAGE; CHINESE KALE; numerous types of MUSTARD and MUSTARD GREENS; RAPE; SWEDE AND RUTABAGA; and TURNIP.

The name of the genus is derived from a Celtic word for cabbage, *bresic*, which corresponds to the Latinized *brassica* and has since, by frequent usage, become an English word too.

BRAWN a moulded, jellied cold meat preparation, usually made from a pig's head, but also sometimes from a sheep or ox head or, in some parts of Britain, rabbit. The meat is lightly cured in brine, then boiled until it can be trimmed and boned. The essential feature of brawn is that it is made of gelatinous meat, such as is furnished by a head, so that when the meat is cooked the rich broth extracted from it can be boiled down to make the jelly in which the coarsely chopped meat is set. Brawn is usually moulded in a cylindrical shape, like a cheese; hence the American name 'head cheese' and the French *fromage de tête*.

In medieval Britain brawn was made from wild boar, then abundant. Indeed, the term had originally meant the flesh of wild boar. Brawn, in the narrower sense which the word acquired, was valued for its fatty rich quality, and was eaten at Christmas, a tradition which persisted to modern times.

In those days it was not made into a moulded jelly, but was kept in a pot, covered with a pickling liquor of ale, VERJUICE, and salt, from which it was taken out to serve. It was often made into a rich POTTAGE or sliced and served in a thick, sweet wine sauce. By the 14th century it had acquired its traditional accompaniment of a mild mustard sauce.

By the 16th century the British wild boar had become rare, and pigs, specially fattened on whey, were used instead. In the 17th century, when the POTTING of meats was newly fashionable, brawn became a potted preparation, baked in wine in its pot, then drained and filled up with butter. From the 18th century on it assumed its modern form of a jellied product.

Early brawns were heavily spiced, but the plainer tastes of the 18th century reduced the amount of flavouring, and nowadays only a small amount of sage or other herbs, and perhaps a little lemon juice, are usual.

French *fromage de tête* often has its surface decorated by applying vegetables cut into shapes to the mould before the meat is put in.

In Italy the term *coppa cotta* is applied to brawn; this is not the same as *coppa crudo* (see COPPA).

BRAZIL is the largest and most populous Portuguese-speaking country in the world; indeed in all Latin America more people speak Portuguese than Spanish. Unlike the conquistadores further north, colonists did not have to cope with an advanced Amerindian culture, but the impact of the climate and existing foodways and food resources was still profound. Hence CASSAVA was of fundamental importance, as were native varieties of BEANS, PINEAPPLE and other tropical fruits, and the use of spices like the MELEGUETA PEPPER (malagueta in Brazil), not to mention cooking methods like foods wrapped in leaves once exemplified in the dish *Muqueca*, though this is now more often a stew.

The Portuguese first settled the north-east of the country, with their capital Salvador in Bahia province. Along this coast they established sugar cane plantations, and brought African slaves, principally from W. Africa (notably Guinea) and Sudan, to work them. More than 3,500,000 negroes were settled in Brazil before the slave trade ceased in 1853. Their food preferences changed the accent of **Bahian cuisine.** Dendê oil (giving its characteristic orange colour, see PALM OIL), the extensive use of COCONUT, and vegetables such as OKRA and PLANTAINS are all African imports, which extended to whole recipes, such as *Vatapá*, the fish or chicken stew with dried shrimp, peanuts, palm oil, and coconut milk which is said to have

originated with the Yoruba of W. Nigeria. *Caruru*, a fish dish which uses okra, onion, dried shrimp, melegueta pepper, dendê oil, and green vegetables, does not have coconut milk but does call for cashew nuts. *Molho de Nagô* (Nagô sauce), made from dried shrimp, lemon juice, okra, and melegueta peppers, is named after a part of Brazil but specifically recalls the Yoruba tribe which was said to have brought it with them.

African influence was reinforced by most cooks in the province being drawn from the slave population. There has been an interesting example of syncretism between the Roman Catholic religion and the traditional beliefs and customs of the black slaves and their descendants, especially apparent in Bahia. The Yoruba tribe in Africa, who are said to have the highest rate of twin births in the world, celebrate twins in music, sculpture, and also food. In Brazil they are honoured with a feast of *Caruru* (see above) which takes place on the feast day of the twin Roman Catholic saints Cosmas and Damian. And offerings are also made to a female figure who seems to be a hybrid between the Virgin Mary and an African female 'goddess'.

The complex lines that go towards Bahian cookery are completed by the Portuguese contribution of materials such as SALT COD, dried shrimp, olives, wine, almonds, garlic, and onions as well as basic cookery processes—for example the *refogado* (the Portuguese equivalent of a SOFFRITTO).

Other notable dishes from the **northern region,** substantial ones which are suitable for special occasions, are *Xinxim de galinha* where chicken is cooked with dried shrimp, peanuts, and palm oil; and *Efó*, fresh and dried shrimp with greens (for instance mustard leaves). Cassava meal (*farinha*) is ever present on the table in the form of lightly toasted meal, in a gourd or wooden bowl, to be sprinkled over most dishes. *Farinha* is often eaten as an accompaniment in the form of *farofa*, with the meal toasted in butter to produce the consistency of loose toasted breadcrumbs, or it may be mixed with boiling water.

Beans and legumes are equally important as a bulk food, and as accompaniments to meat or fish. *Acarajé* are FRITTERS, a popular street food, made from dried beans that have been skinned and ground, then mixed with dried shrimp and fried in dendê oil. They are served with a sauce of shrimp, melegueta pepper, and ginger. And beans are central to *Feijoada*, the national dish, sharing the support of a bewildering array of mixed fresh and preserved meats with rice.

The **south of the country** was developed later than Bahia and the northerly coast. COFFEE was the cash crop, starting round São Paulo in the 1830s, and it was European immigration rather than the slave trade that marked the character of the country. The cuisine of SE Brazil (São Paulo, Rio de Janeiro, Minas Gerais) is at once more cosmopolitan and has more direct links with its Portuguese original—though that itself was already a multifaceted cuisine, drawing on Arab inspiration, exemplified in a dish like *Cuzcuz paulista*, where COUSCOUS is replaced by cornmeal, and layers of chicken and vegetables are packed with the meal into a hemispherical steamer and turned out moulded for presentation at table. Several nationalities, not least Germans and Italians, flocked to the industrial region that grew around São Paulo, and the mines in the backcountry, and contributed their own skills in cheese-making and preserved meats.

Beef is reared in the region nearest Uruguay and on the central plateau of Mato Grosso. Here, the grill is called the *churrasco*, restaurants *churrascarias*, and the cowboys *gauchos* as in Argentina. Their diet of grilled meats, cassava, and mate (as they spell MATÉ) is much like that of W. H. Hudson's Uruguayans (see URUGUAY).

Fresh meat has always been important to the Brazilian diet, but preserved meat has relatively more importance in the dry north-east region. Beef is eaten. Sun-dried beef is called *carne sêca* or *charque* (see JERKY). Pork fat is in very general use.

Minas Gerais, the region between Rio de Janeiro, São Paulo, and Bahia, is famous as the source of the best cooks in Brazil, and of some of the best Brazilian food. The *Feijão* of the region is among the best of the numerous Brazilian dishes based on beans (and originally reflecting the W. African love of beans) and is eaten all over the country.

Sweet dishes are plentiful, and many of them remind the consumer of Portugal— just as do the *fios de ovos* (egg threads, now used also as a garnish for turkey etc.) that delight the most skilled Brazilian cooks. Egg-based custards (among which *Quindim*, which incorporates coconut, is the most popular) and confections of Brazilian fruits and BRAZIL NUTS are prominent. However, the best-known dessert, found in popular restaurants and middle-class households, is *Romeu e Julieta*, a piece of GUAVA paste with fresh cheese, echoing the combination of quince paste and cheese in Spain and Portugal. (TJ)

BRAZIL NUTS borne by the tree *Bertholettia excelsa*, are among the finest of all nuts, and commercially the most important of the many kinds which grow in S. America. Yet they are hardly cultivated at all. No one has managed to grow the tree on a commercial scale outside Brazil; while in Brazil, although there are a few plantations, the bulk of the crop comes from wild

trees, harvested by local people using unsophisticated methods.

The tree is enormous, up to 50 m (150') tall and with a crown as much as 30 m (100') in diameter. It grows in the dense jungle of the Amazon basin and, like most tall jungle trees, has branches only near the top. For practical purposes it is unclimbable, and the nuts are harvested by waiting for the fruit which contains them to ripen and fall to the ground. The fruit is round and large, about the size of a coconut. It weighs up to 2 kg (4.5 lb) and has a thick, woody shell. Inside are the nuts, arranged like the segments of an orange, and each having its own woody covering. There are one or two dozen in each fruit. When the fruit is ripe they come loose from their fibrous attachments and rattle about inside. Brazilians call the nuts *castanhas* (chestnuts) and the gatherers *castanheiros*. Other names are 'Para nuts', because much of the crop comes to market through the state of Para, and 'cream nuts' because of the flavour.

The outer shell of the fruit is called *ourico*, and can be used to make cups or ornaments or as fuel. Despite its hardness, it can be gnawed through, after it has fallen to the ground, by rodents such as the AGOUTI. Howes (1948) tells us that:

It is now known that these animals, after eating a few nuts, are prone to bury the remainder in selected spots in much the same way as squirrels do in other countries. No doubt some of these nuts are later missed or forgotten by their 'owners' and so germinate and grow into trees. It is thus that these small animals are of service in propagating and disseminating one of the largest and most useful trees of the forest.

The fall of an *ourico* is a dangerous event, since it is large, heavy, and hard and drops from a great height. When one hits damp ground it embeds itself to some depth. A *castanheiro* who is hit on the head by one may well be killed. So no one goes near the trees on windy or rainy days, and when the *castanheiros* do go they often wear broad wooden hats as protection. Their time is divided between finding and gathering *ouricos* on safe days, and preparing them on dangerous ones. The *ouricos* are opened with a few heavy blows of a machete and the nuts tipped into running water. This not only washes them, but also separates bad nuts, which usually float while the sound ones sink.

Brazil nuts are sold both shelled and unshelled. Shelling is often done at primitive factories, sometimes using nothing more complicated than a hand-operated lever and piston arrangement resembling a gigantic garlic press. Larger works have roller crackers. The nuts are expensive to transport in the shell, and are among the most difficult of nuts to crack with domestic nutcrackers, so the trend is towards marketing them

ready shelled. However, shelled nuts quickly become rancid, so they must be dispatched and sold quickly.

Brazil nuts have a high oil content, up to 65% (as well as up to 20% protein). This oiliness is shown in their unusually tender texture and rich, mild flavour. Medium-sized and large nuts are sold for eating fresh. Small ones are in strong demand by the confectionery industry.

A small amount of oil is made from the nuts for local use as a high-quality salad oil. This resembles almond oil in composition, and has a pleasant, nutty flavour.

The related SAPUCAYA NUT is considered by some to be even better than the Brazil.

BREAD (*see opposite page*)

BREADFRUIT the large, starchy fruit of a tall tree, *Artocarpus altilis*, native to the Pacific islands. When Europeans began to explore the Pacific the breadfruit was already being grown throughout the region, although still a newcomer in some islands. It belongs to the same genus, in the mulberry family Moraceae, as the JACKFRUIT.

The fruit is round and grows up to the size of a man's head. It is a composite fruit with a structure like that of the PINEAPPLE, and its skin is similarly marked with a hexagonal pattern of fissures. The fruits are divided into two broad categories: seedless and seeded. Most of the numerous cultivated varieties (there are over 200 named cultivars) are seedless; the others have large, edible seeds. The name 'breadnut' is sometimes, unsuitably, used for the latter kind.

French and British explorers who encountered the fruit included Captain William Dampier, at Guam, in 1686, and Captain Cook when he was voyaging in the 1770s. Such explorers were so enthusiastic in their praise of the fruit that thought was given to the potential benefits of introducing it to the W. Indies. The French seem to have effected small-scale introductions in the 1770s and 1780s; but it was left to the British government, responding to appeals from their W. Indian colonies, where it was expected that this large and abundant fruit would be useful as a cheap food for the slaves, to consider a more ambitious scheme. As Popenoe (1932) tells the tale:

The outcome was that notorious voyage under William Bligh, in the *Bounty*, which forms certainly the most dramatic incident in the history of plant introduction. The expedition sailed from England in 1787, and reached Tahiti, after a cruise of ten months, in 1788. A thousand breadfruit plants were obtained and placed on board ship in pots and tubs which had been provided for the

(*cont. on page 103*)

Bread

The fundamental food in many parts of the world, so much so that the word 'bread' is often equivalent to 'food', and by extension, in 20th-century English vernacular, to 'money'. Christians who recite the Lord's Prayer ask for their 'daily bread', and Anglo-Saxons called their lords *hlafward* (loaf guardian) and their ladies *hlaefdige* (loaf kneader). But bread is by no means the universal staple; in parts of Asia there is a corresponding equivalence between 'rice' and 'food'.

Bread's place in the scheme of human survival has ensured its role in religion, magic, and custom. Hence the breaking and blessing of bread that is central to meal-taking in Orthodox Jewish custom; the extension of this rite to the Christian Eucharist; the loading onto bread of countless superstitions and customary rituals, from the hanging of a loaf in the house on Good Friday to ward off evil spirits, the cutting of a cross on loaves 'to let the Devil out', to eating buns marked with a cross at Easter (but the cross has symbolism older than Christianity, and cutting a loaf this way may reflect other customs, such as sun or fire worship, fertility rites, or the ritual division of a loaf into portions).

Bread is a deceptively simple foodstuff that required technological progress in various fields: an agriculture capable of raising gluten-rich cereals; a technique for converting grain into flour, i.e. milling; a method of imparting lightness to a dough by way of leavening; a means of cooking more complex than a flat stone on a fire. Until these were in place, societies had to be satisfied with GRUELS and POTTAGES, or at best some form of PANCAKE or WAFER.

AGRICULTURE

It is no chance that bread is the staple of Europe, W. Asia, and the Near East. The cereals which grow naturally in these regions include those whose composition—including especially GLUTEN—is such that they can form a cohesive loaf. The best in this respect is WHEAT and its predecessors emmer, spelt, and einkorn, which contain the most gluten, followed by RYE and BARLEY. (Others such as MILLET and OATS, though lacking GLUTEN, can still be pushed together into dense cakes. In contrast, RICE, the staple of E. Asia, is unsuited to bread-making.)

It is commonly believed that the domestication of the predecessors of wheat began in the region of Anatolia, Iran, and Syria before 7000 BC, and that this represented the start of settled agriculture and the development of cereal crops and, in consequence, bread.

MILLING

The flour which is needed for bread-making has to be produced by some sort of grinding. Use of a pestle and mortar is the most primitive means, but normally produces a coarse grind which is more suited to porridges and gruels than bread. The next step up is to organize two stones to grind against each other. The saddle quern, beloved of archaeologists, provides the first example.

As explained in the entry on FLOUR, this domestic device led to others, the harnessing of water power in classical Rome, and the adoption of wind power from about AD 1000. However, the principle remained the same and the grinding had to be followed by sieving or bolting, until the 19th century when something quite new emerged: the efficient, fast roller mill, first tried in Hungary in the 1820s, perfected in Switzerland in 1834, and then quickly adopted all over Europe and America. Its multiple steel rollers not only ground the grain, but also separated the various fractions (bran, germ, endosperm) without the need for bolting. For the first time, truly white flour was available at a low price.

LEAVENING

The third essential for a risen loaf was a gas-forming agent or LEAVEN. The discovery of this has been credited to the Egyptians. It was probably by accident when a batch of dough became infected by the wild yeast spores which float in the air everywhere. If, for reasons of economy, the apparently spoilt, rotten dough was baked anyway, it would have been realized that the bread was lighter and had a special, good flavour. Later came the discovery that a piece of leavened dough could be kept to spread the infection to the next batch. Egyptian leavened and unleavened bread of various shapes and sizes has been found, preserved by the dry desert sand. An inscription of the 20th dynasty lists 30 different kinds of bread. From 2000 BC or earlier there were professional bakers.

When the Israelites fled from Egypt in the Exodus they left their leaven behind. (In contrast, the more provident prospectors of the American west carried their cultures with them; hence San Francisco sourdoughs.) The Israelites thereafter had to exist on unleavened bread (Exodus 12: 34–9). This was the origin of the Passover bread MATZO. But unleavened bread continued in use in many societies. The Romans, especially old-fashioned ones in the early days of the Empire, felt that it was traditional, correct, and healthy, the newfangled leavened doughs being an import from luxurious Greece.

Ultimately, the Romans did borrow the use of ale-barm or brewers' YEAST (*Saccharomyces cerevisiae*, used to make beer and wine, now replaced by varieties of distillers' yeast), from subjected Germanic tribes. This was a means of leavening also known to Celts in Spain. If the original Egyptian leaven was a combination of spontaneous lactic fermentation of flour and water with assistance perhaps from soured milk and further reinforcement from the spores of wild, airborne yeast, brewers' yeast induced an alcoholic fermentation, and was more predictable. The breads of some societies have relied mainly on lactic fermentation—which is the base of the whole family of sourdoughs—while others, especially the British Isles, have long depended on straight alcoholic fermentations using brewers' yeast. An inhibiting factor in the adoption of brewers' yeast was its availability: it could not survive extremes of heat, and not all communities had alcohol on the bubble week in, week out. There are countless recipes in English recipe books for making a barm, indication that it was not always to be found.

BREAD OVENS

The first breads would have been cooked on flat stones heated directly in the fire. The bakestone remained the preferred method of cooking flat or unleavened breads in many cultures, from Mexico to Scotland, and is still in use. However, a natural step to take was to cover the bakestone with an inverted pot to contain the heat, and then to turn this makeshift arrangement into a domed, igloo-shaped or beehive, oven. A free-standing structure of this sort, with its own source of heat, merely replicates on a larger scale the principle of the stone and pot. Early examples have been found in Mesopotamia, Egypt, and the Balkans.

The conventional account of the development of these ovens has them first appearing in Egypt. However, archaeologists working in the Balkans have unearthed models of near-conical (igloo-shaped) clay bread ovens dating from the middle of the 5th millennium BC, and a site in Bulgaria has yielded a clay model of a loaf carbon-dated to c.5100 BC. The pattern of finds would indicate that these ovens were not known south of Macedonia—in Crete, for instance, there are none dating from before c.1500 BC—and the loaf model is of leavened bread, not an unleavened disc. These facts hint at the possibility that bread was first developed in C. Asia and came to the Mediterranean by both a southern (Mesopotamian and Egyptian) and a northern (Balkan) route.

The beehive oven is heated by burning a fire on its floor. When the fire has heated the structure, it is raked out and the risen dough put in its place. The doorway is sealed, and the bread cooks in a falling heat radiating from every surface, the oven space capturing and recycling any moisture that evaporates from the loaves. (See also TANDOOR for a somewhat similar oven of the Near East and Asia.)

The technical development of ovens did not quicken pace until the 18th century when improvements in design allowed the more efficient retention, or even introduction, of moisture—hence the crackling thin crusts of Viennese and, eventually, Parisian loaves—and led to methods of remote heating rather than burning fuel on the oven sole. This facilitated more continuous production, as the oven did not have to be prepared and cleaned between each firing, and permitted ovens of greater size: more usually with a flat arched roof than a dome.

During the 19th century, there were many experiments in conveying heat, just as other materials than brick, clay, or stone, particularly steel, were tried for the oven's construction. Superheated steam, pipes filled with oil, oil burners, gas jets, and, latterly, electricity replaced wood and coal. Equally, there have been many improvements in the delivery of bread to the oven itself over the deft manipulation of a loaf on a baker's peel. The fullest expression of this is the travelling oven, where the goods to be baked moved through a heated space, going in cold and emerging fully baked.

HISTORY OF BREAD PRODUCTION

Although ovens can be built any size, there are advantages of time and function in having them fairly large. The same may be said of mills. Hence bread-baking has often been a communal activity to avoid duplication of expensive resources. Grain is ground at the village mill, often in Europe in the hands of the political master; dough is baked in a communal oven, owned either by the lord or the community, or in the hands of a tradesman who gains his living therefrom. In feudal Europe, bread seemed a gastronomic expression of the social order. In modern France and Switzerland, there are still examples of communal ovens, though few now work. In Greece and the Near East, the village baker cooked bread fashioned in the homes of his customers, as well as baking joints of meat after the first heat had gone off, just as did his professional equivalents in societies where ovens were at a premium. In Quebec, too, the oven was a community venture.

Small hand mills have always been used among pioneer societies, or in scattered settlements, and small ovens were built, for instance in the fireplaces of farmhouses, especially where they were isolated from near neighbours. There was a trade in the construction of small earthenware 'cloam' ovens from 17th-century N. Devon potteries, exported to colonists in N. America as well as remote farms of SW England. Otherwise, the mass of people had to wait for the development of the cast iron kitchen range to have an oven on site and ready.

The nature of bread production—that it should usually be on a larger scale than that of other foods—also gave rise to its early organization into a professional trade. Full-time bakers are identifiable from the records of ancient Egypt; the 5th-century BC Greek author Archestratus refers to Lydian, Phoenician, and Cappadocian bakers; in Rome there was a bakers' guild from approximately 150 BC; in 12th-century London and Paris bakers' guilds were among the earliest craft brotherhoods. The complexity of production also led to sectional groupings: millers were, of course, distinct, but bakers in 14th-century London were divided between those who made white bread and brown, and the town governments of Provence at the same period distinguished between bakers and oven-keepers.

Professional organization, as well as the importance of the food itself, determined the nature of government controls over bread—an early candidate for every form of interference in most western societies, whether to ensure honest retailing, satisfactory ingredients, or acceptable prices.

Langland's 'Bakers and brewers, bouchers and cokes—For thees men doth most harme to the mene puple' only needs to add millers to the list to complete the gallery of poor men's rogues.

It could be said that the early history of bread was dominated by efforts to ensure its distribution to as many people as necessary to avoid civil unrest, or to control its distribution to the advantage of the rulers over the ruled. In contrast, the history of bread since the Industrial Revolution has been driven by technological change and its consequences. This shift was mirrored by the change in the nature of government controls. At first, as indicated above, they were preoccupied with price, fair dealing, and the nature of trade. Latterly they have centred on improvements either to replace constituents removed by the technical processes of milling and baking, or actually adding nutrients to the benefit of the consumer, or controlling the manipulation of the raw material first suggested by technical imperatives—for example which chemicals should be allowed to accelerate the ageing of flour.

Technical changes have come about through greater understanding of how bread is made, and through the replacement of human effort by machines. The effect of roller milling (already mentioned), was matched by the mechanization of kneading, which took hold in most of Europe and America in the last quarter of the 19th century (though there had been simple mechanical aids even in ancient Rome, and 17th-century man was familiar with the dough-breaker) and improved the baker's lot immeasurably. Taken together, these permitted large-scale production of white bread from the newly developed cornlands of N. America (which offered harder wheat than before experienced) and the creation of veritable bread factories. Subsequent change has been to improve industrial efficiency, to reduce the amount of time taken in production, and to exercise control over raw materials to obtain consistency. The outcome has been the plant bakery operating some form of accelerated dough development through high-speed mixing, dependent on chemical treatments to flours to maximize performance, and normally adding a cocktail of chemicals called 'improvers' (not in themselves harmful) to the dough. The result has been less individualistic and less characterful, less tasty in short, and so successful that the same measures have been adopted even by small-scale producers.

KINDS OF BREAD AND HEALTH ASPECTS

The history of bread in particular countries is touched on in the section on bread varieties below, or specific entries (BARLEY BREADS, ROLLS, MUFFINS, etc.), but the general tendencies are clear.

Although many grains have contributed to a variety of breads, depending on geography, climate, and agricultural development, wheat has been pre-eminent. Its gluten content ensures a lighter, more appetizing texture. With few exceptions, a light and refined loaf has been viewed as a better loaf. Wherever a distinction has been drawn between bread for the rich and bread for the poor, the poor get the heavier, browner loaf.

Some countries have retained a taste for RYE, especially in N. and E. Europe, and for the lactic fermentation or sourdough that gives rye bread more even texture and better balance of flavours. Few countries where wheat is readily or cheaply obtainable, however, have continued to depend on the lesser bread grains such as barley, oats, or millet, and even less on bean or chestnut flour, which once were staples in times of dearth or areas of poverty.

Exceptions to this rule have arisen when bread is the subject of considerations other than appetite or preference. No foodstuff bears greater moral and philosophical burden. Since ancient Greece, certain types have been seen as health-giving, and by extension, bestowing some sort of moral worth on the consumer. Dr Thomas Muffat advocated eating brown bread in *Health's Improvement* (1595) and such arguments reached their most extreme with the views of the American Dr Sylvester Graham, whose name was adopted by the French to signify wholemeal bread. In the 20th century, further work emphasized the importance of bran to human digestion, adding a new element to the debate already raging about the respective advantages and disadvantages of white and wholemeal bread (the former had no nutritional capacity, said some, while others accused the latter of inhibiting calcium take-up).

Part of the background to this bubbling pot of controversy was undoubtedly the aftermath of exposures of ADULTERATION of white flour with substances such as chalk dust and alum in 18th- and 19th-century England. Was the whitest of breads the purest or was it the most suspect? This sort of problem, plus the developments just mentioned, resulted in temporary reversals, especially among the better off, of the general trend towards light, white breads made with harder flours.

BREAD BEYOND EUROPEAN CULTURES

In countries where wheat or grains suitable for breadmaking were not grown, other crops formed the dietary staple. In Japan, it was rice, though much barley was grown, and bread was only familiar in treaty ports where western trading ships were allowed. However, a series of rice famines in the 19th century led the Japanese to take bread more seriously. By the early 20th century it was common, and made by professional bakers. The usual product was dryish, sweetened, and cakelike. Nowadays, mass-produced western bread has made inroads on the original kinds.

Indian bread varieties are influenced by the availability and cost of the various cereals, wheat being common in the north but expensive, and by the fact that only the more prosperous households have had ovens. The medium-sized clay TANDOOR oven produces NAN, a crisper and bubblier relative of PITTA BREAD, but most Indian breads are cooked on bakestones and are more in the nature of pancakes.

Leavening is often provided by palm yeast, obtained by the spontaneous fermentation of palm sap as it turns into toddy.

In China wheat has long been grown in the north, though always a comparative luxury, the poor having to make do with millet and other grains. Barley is also grown. The Chinese adopted the rotary mill driven by animals after it had reached them from the Persians. Watermills and windmills were known by the Chinese but not harnessed to grinding corn. The Chinese were also ignorant of the bread oven; so their bread, like that of the Newari people of Nepal, was made by steaming, or the flour was converted to some form of flat pasta.

See also TORTILLA; TAMALES; and some items in CORN BREADS and BARLEY BREAD. (TJ)

Bread varieties

The archetypal bread is made of wheat flour, water, and yeast, which are allowed to ferment together, shaped, and then baked in an oven. However, as bread is such a widespread and ancient food innumerable variations have developed.

Some interesting and important breads or near-breads are treated separately: BABA; BAGEL; BANNOCK; BARLEY BREADS; BRIOCHE; BRUSCHETTA; CHOEREK; CORN BREADS; CROISSANT; DANISH PASTRY; DOUGHNUT; FARL; FRENCH BREAD; GINGERBREAD; GRIDDLE BREADS; KUGELHOPF; MUFFIN; OATCAKE; PANETTONE; PITTA; PRETZEL; PUMPERNICKEL; RYE BREAD; SODA BREAD; SOURDOUGH; STOLLEN; TEA BREADS.

Other breads or groups of breads include the following:

Ashcake, any kind of bread cooked in the ashes of a fire, particularly an American CORN BREAD.

Biscuit, historically this word was applied to soft enriched breads baked in Guernsey and NE Scotland.

Bloomer, English name for a long loaf with rounded ends, slashed diagonally in evenly spaced deepish cuts just before baking. The shape is common to most European countries (it is known in France as *bâtard*). Now made from an ordinary white bread dough, bloomer loaves were formerly made from a high-grade flour, enriched with milk, butter, or lard. The origin of the name is obscure. One possible explanation is that the loaf 'blooms' or rises in the oven, rather than being confined in a mould; another that the shape resembles a thick bar or 'bloom' of iron as made in medieval iron foundries or 'bloomeries'.

Boston brown bread, a traditional American bread made from mixed grains, usually a blend of rye and wheat flour with cornmeal, buttermilk, and molasses. Raised with bicarbonate of soda, the mixture is placed in a tall cylindrical mould and steamed, not dry baked in the normal way. The Puritan community in New England served this bread on the sabbath with Boston baked beans.

Brown bread, a general term still used in England, denoting anything from a loaf made from wholemeal flour to one made from white flour with a little fibre and possibly some caramel colouring added.

Ciabatta. This Italian word means 'old slipper/shoe', an apt description for the baggy, rough oval shape of these loaves. They are characterized by large holes in the crumb, and a distinctive, slightly sour flavour. The irregular shape comes from the use of a very wet dough, which, in turn allows large bubbles to form in the loaf. The flavour is derived partly from olive oil and malt, and hints at the use of a sourdough starter.

Coburg/cob, a popular English crusty loaf, made from plain white dough. Round in shape, the crust may be cut in a number of ways. A cross gives the loaf four distinct corners, which, on a pan-baked loaf, rise into a spectacular top or 'cauliflower'. With one spreading cut, it is called 'Danish' by some bakers, and with a chequerboard pattern of little cuts, exposing more surface to brown, it becomes a crusty loaf, a porcupine, or, according to Eliza Acton, a college loaf. Or it may be 'docked', punctured with small holes by a special utensil consisting of formidable spikes set in a rounded piece of wood.

The docked loaf, and a round loaf with a plain, uncut crust, may be known as a cob, which is not an abbreviation of Coburg, but an old word for head. Cob loaves were formerly small, round, and baked from coarse flour. The name 'Coburg' only came into use in the 19th century, possibly introduced by German bakers who settled in London.

Cornish splits, small round cakes made of plain white dough, split and eaten hot with butter, or cream and jam or treacle.

Cottage loaf. This is actually two round loaves of ordinary bread dough baked one on top of the other, the top one always being smaller than the bottom one. Assembling the two to give the correct shape requires practice and fine judgement of the texture of the dough. It is now rare, although it was formerly very common in England. The shape is also known in France, where the BRIOCHE is a richer and more elegant version of the same idea; and *pain chapeau* of Finisterre looks like an English cottage loaf. Elizabeth David (1977) suggests that the shape may have evolved from joining two loaves together to economize on floor space in old-fashioned brick ovens.

Crackling bread, see CRACKLING.

Crispbread, flat, unleavened bread from Scandinavia, commonly made from rye flour and distinctly crisp after it has been dried out. It can be stored for a long time. In the Scandinavian countries it bears names such as *knäckerbröd*.

Damper, Australian term for unleavened bread which is cooked in ashes or a Dutch oven.

Farmhouse, an English loaf shape, a short, thick, rounded oblong, often with the word 'farmhouse' impressed on the sides. Now made of ordinary white dough, it meant a loaf baked from brown wheatmeal (wholewheat) dough in the 19th century. The name is a conscious appeal to the supposed 'goodness' of the rustic loaf as baked in the country.

Flatbreads, any bread made into a thin cake before baking, or, more usually, cooking on a GRIDDLE. Different grains are responsible for the wide variety. Many are unleavened, such as Scandinavian crisp bread, Mexican TORTILLA, Jewish MATZO, and British OATCAKE; others, such as Indian NAN, are raised with yeast.

Granary, a British type of bread, which takes its name from a specific type of flour composed of mixed brown wheat and rye with malted, cracked wheat grains. The resulting loaves, usually in a round or oval shape, have a soft, sweetish, slightly sticky crumb.

Grissini, Italian crisp bread sticks made from plain dough, placed on the table as a 'nibble' in restaurants. German *Salzstange* (see below) are a more elaborate version of the same idea.

Graham bread, originally the very coarse wholemeal bread advocated by the early 19th-century American food reformer and self-styled physician the Reverend Sylvester Graham. Now widely applied to any wholemeal product.

Harvest loaf, a special loaf made for harvest thanksgiving, in which the dough has been modelled into a wheatsheaf shape. Ordinary white bread dough can be used if the loaf is intended to be eaten. If it is purely decorative, recipes call for large amounts of salt which control the amount by which the bread rises, giving a sharper sculpture and acting as a preservative.

Hovis, loaves baked from a proprietary flour to which concentrated wheatgerm has been added.

Manchet, a soft, fine white bread, often enriched, made for the noble and wealthy people in England during the medieval period and beyond (see Elizabeth David, 1977, for interesting historical details).

Maslin bread, of historic interest, was made from maslin, a mixture of rye and wheat, from medieval times until (in some places) the 18th century. The rye made it fairly dense, but it had a good flavour.

Milk bread. As the name suggests, the dough for this is mixed with milk instead of water (a little butter can be added too). It makes a loaf with a closer texture and softer crust than water.

Plaits, bread is often made more special by dividing up the dough, making each piece into a rope, and plaiting the pieces together. This is the standard shape for some loaves, notably the CHALLAH. Intricately plaited loaves of up to eight strands (in German, *Zopf*) or plaits shaped into hearts, stars, clover leaves, and butterflies are made for special occasions, especially in C. Europe.

Potato bread. Mashed potato was sometimes used to replace some flour when grain was scarce, or as an economy measure in poor households. Carefully handled, in a proportion of about four parts flour to one of potato, it can give a very good result, which keeps and toasts well and is now liked for its own sake. Mashed potato, added to leaven, encourages fermentation.

Pugliese, a soft Italian white bread, enriched with olive oil.

Pulled bread, the crumb of a white loaf, 'pulled' apart into chunks and dried in the oven.

Salt stick (German: *Salzstange*), thin, crisp, usually leavened bread stick covered in salt, used as a snack. They are made in several countries, especially in C. Europe, where they are often sold with beer in beer halls, since they stimulate thirst.

Stotty cake, not a cake but a flat round loaf which is a speciality of NE England (e.g. Durham and Newcastle upon Tyne).

Vienna, British term for a glazed, bright golden, crusty white loaf cooked with the aid of steam in the oven to give a very light texture. It is usually baked in a pointed oval shape, which is slashed the entire length. A similar method is used for making FRENCH BREAD such as baguettes.

Wholemeal (French, *pain intégrale* or *pain complet*; German, *Schrotbrot*), bread made from flour which has been ground from the entire grain, including all the bran and germ, with no additives. The dough does not rise as high as white bread dough, because the bran particles in the flour cut the gluten strands. Wholemeal bread has become increasingly fashionable in many western countries since the 1960s. Claims for the health-giving properties of wheatgerm and bran have had a lot to do with this.

Bread chemistry

This section seeks to explain how 'bread represents the *culinary* domestication of grain, an achievement that made it possible to extract pleasure as well as nourishment from the hard, bland seeds' (McGee, 1984).

Any cereal flour consists mainly of STARCH and PROTEINS. WHEAT flour contains five groups of proteins, classed as albumin, globulin, proteoses, glutenin, and gliadin. When flour is wetted, the first three, being soluble, disperse, leaving glutenin and gliadin. It is these, which wheat has in greater quantity than any other cereal, which form GLUTEN. Kneading the dough draws out the glutenin, whose long, thin, chainlike molecules form strands, while the shorter molecules of gliadin create bridges between them. As the network of strands develops, it absorbs water, resulting in that familiar change in the texture of dough from a shaggy mass of short chains and imperfectly absorbed liquid, through a certain stickiness, to a smooth, plastic, and elastic substance. RYE flour, which contains little gluten and some natural gums, remains sticky and makes a denser loaf. BARLEY has very little gluten indeed.

The amount of gluten-forming protein in wheat varies according to breed and circumstances of growth. The greatest, contributing to the lightest breads with the greatest volume, is found in wheats grown in a single short summer season, particularly from the prairies of N. America. They are known as 'hard' wheats and may contain 13–14% protein. Before there was large-scale export of N. American grain, hard wheats were obtained especially from Hungary and the plains of C. Europe. Other European wheats tended to be 'softer', running from 7 to 11% protein, and best suited for 'shorter' products such as cake and pastry, though they lent character, even greater flavour, to traditional breads. As Europe has tended to greater agricultural self-sufficiency, so has there been much effort directed towards increasing the protein content of indigenous, winter-sown wheats.

The performance of gluten is affected by the age of flour: maturity causes beneficial chemical changes to the glutenin. The effect of time can be replicated by oxidants introduced after milling, though some have been banned from commercial use. Vitamin C or ascorbic acid, one of the permitted ADDITIVES, has the same effect.

Other substances have important consequences on the performance of gluten in a bread dough. SALT may inhibit yeast activity, just as it makes gluten less extensible, but it also reduces the action of protein-digesting ENZYMES in flour which, if left unchecked, could damage the gluten far more than a little salt. This is why an orthodox bread dough, if unsalted, is often denser than a properly seasoned mixture.

FATS, for instance butter, lard, oil, or liquids such as milk, also have a contradictory effect. Too much, the gluten will be broken up and will not form the long strands necessary for maximum expansion; just enough, approximately 3% of the total weight of a dough, and they appear to reinforce the contribution of natural lipids in wheat to make gluten more stretchy. Fats also have a tenderizing effect. In part this is due to their assault on long strands of gluten—the longer and more elastic they are, the 'tougher' will be the bread; and by coating the starch granules, fats delay the release of moisture, keeping bread apparently fresher. Finally, when much butter or lard is added to enriched doughs, by coating the flour particles, it protects them from the action of the yeast. This is a reason many recipes call for a delay in adding fats until fermentation has begun.

The major component of flour, more than 70% of total weight, is STARCH, from the endosperm of the wheat grain. This affords the bulk of the loaf which is structured and supported by the framework of gluten. Starch also provides yeast with the SUGARS necessary for life and fast breeding. These come from granules damaged in the milling process which are vulnerable to the enzyme amylase, which is present in the flour and will eventually break down the starch into its constituent sugars. (The amylase is usually sufficient to invigorate modern yeasts, although in the past extra help was often needed; this was one reason for sugar or honey being a usual part of domestic bread recipes.) The sugars in starch, having fed the yeast, also contribute to the final tex-

ture and appearance of a loaf. Their caramelization (see CARAMEL) gives colour to the crust.

The grain of wheat also consists of BRAN and germ. For white bread these are largely excluded from the flour, by sifting if it is stoneground, or by the very process itself if roller-ground. The wheatgerm is high in natural fats and nutrients, as well as imparting flavour. When it is left in flours, for instance wholemeals, they tend to keep less well as the fats run the risk of going rancid. Hovis bread, a British brand, adds the wheatgerm back into the flour after its first exclusion in the milling process.

Bran also has its own flavour, and is enjoyed for its mechanical effect on the human body, which has some parallels with its performance in a bread dough. Bran particles are sharp and rough, though fine milling may reduce their effect—hence the greatest volume in a wholemeal loaf will usually be obtained from a fine flour. These cutting edges, which irritate the bowel, tend also to disturb the cell structure that builds up in a maturing dough as the carbon dioxide expands. The bran interrupts and punctures the thin cell walls.

Not all leavened breads use brewer's or distiller's YEAST and the consequent alcoholic fermentation to obtain volume. Some depend on LEAVEN, which is a lactic fermentation provoked by bacteria joined with a mild alcoholic fermentation from less vigorous strains of wild yeasts, though both methods have a single end: to introduce carbon dioxide into a dough which is capable of expansion yet resilient thanks to the gluten, and bulk and nutrition thanks to the starch. Other leavenings, for instance soda activated by soured milk, BAKING POWDER, or the simple introduction of carbonic gas (as once practised by the Aerated Bread Company), are often used for short doughs that do not develop gluten to the same extent.

Yeasts, but not baking powder, contribute flavour as well as the impetus to rise. This flavour is developed by the amount of fermentation rather than the absolute amount of yeast added at the beginning. Hence, a dough which is made over a number of hours, or even days, will start with a very small quantity of yeast, but will develop a stronger flavour than a short-time dough made with an initially large amount of yeast. In the case of a lactic fermentation that taste is more or less sour; hence the term SOURDOUGH. Dried yeast contains a higher level of waste products, which give it stronger flavour.

Yeasts need nutrients in order to multiply up to a number sufficient to do the work of fermentation. These are contained within the flour itself, though modern bakery techniques accelerate development by adding various improvers, often malt based. Fermentation occurs when the sucrose and maltose in the flour are acted upon by enzymes in the yeast to produce glucose and fructose, which are then converted to alcohol and carbon dioxide.

Yeast activity is also influenced by temperature. It cannot function at all over 56 °C (130 °F), when the cells die. It is perceptibly slowed if the figure drops below 21 °C (70 °F). It is moribund when frozen. Cold fermentations are feasible, even advantageous, for instance with Vienna bread (see BREAD VARIETIES above). Dough can be developed in the refrigerator, but warmth is sensible for even and convenient fermentation. The optimum is between 24 °C (75 °F) and 27 °C (80 °F). The fermentation of natural leaven bread is more temperature sensitive than that raised with brewer's yeast. If it is too cold, the lactic fermentation will develop too much sourness, will be swamped by cold-tolerant bacteria that taste 'off', and the wild yeasts will not perform well.

It is not merely the ambient temperature that is important, for the baker is more interested in the heat of the dough itself. This is why he will adjust the temperature of the water or liquor at the outset of making a dough with a view to accelerating fermentation, slowing it down, or in reaction to the air temperature depending on the season of the year. His ideal is consistency, which is why draughts are to be avoided: so that one part of the dough (out of the draught) does not ferment more quickly than the part being chilled.

The first mixing of the dough is important to later stages because the baker must ensure even distribution of ingredients and even wetting of the flour. Hence yeast is often mixed in the water, and the first mixing is a comparatively rapid process. Pockets of flour that are not properly wetted will prove very difficult to eradicate at the later stage of kneading. Before the advent of mechanical mixers, the creation of a dough was nearly always in two stages. First a wet sponge was made with most of the liquor, the yeast and a portion of the flour. This was allowed to ferment, then the rest of the flour would be added. This alleviated the work of mixing great weights of flour at once, as well as economizing on yeast (by allowing it more time) and developing more flavour. In France this method is called *sur poolish*; it was also much favoured in Scotland.

After mixing, the dough is kneaded in order to develop the gluten to its maximum. The harder the wheat the more kneading is required. The dough is then left to rise until approximately doubled in size. It is covered so that a skin will not form where it comes into contact with the air. The rising further conditions the gluten as well as allowing the yeast to ferment. This stage has been accelerated in modern commercial baking by high-speed mechanical mixing: the Chorleywood Process. The gluten is conditioned by the mixer and large quantities of high-active yeast are used to obtain rapid fermentation.

Once risen, the dough is knocked back to its original size, thus evening out the distribution of yeast and gas bubbles, then moulded into loaves. The ensuing second rise or 'proof', also under cover or in humidified and heated proving cabinets, doubles the bulk once more. It is never the intention that the loaves should rise to their maximum during proof. A final expansion is reserved for the oven. If they do rise as far as they can before exposure to heat, they will probably collapse in the oven.

Baking is the final process in making bread. It needs a very hot oven to give it an initial fierce heat, after which the temperature can be allowed to fall gradually. This was the principle of a wood-fired brick or stone oven heated with a fire which was raked out just before the bread was put in. The intention of all bread-baking is to strike heat into the centre of the bread as quickly as possible, from as many angles as possible. A brick oven, which radiates from the floor, sides, and roof (and which retains heat far better than the thin metal walls of modern domestic ovens), is ideal. The heat needs rapid conveyance so that the yeast can be killed before it causes too much expansion and so that the outside of the loaf can be set so as to avoid any semblance of collapse or sagging. A 1 kg (2 lb) loaf will need 20 minutes at 500 °F (260 °C) before its centre reaches 130 °F (54 °C). Chinese steamed rolls, which are cooked on a quite different principle, gain their heat shock from the great latent heat in steam, many times that of boiling water, which is released when it condenses on a cold surface like dough.

When the raw bread is first exposed to the heat, the yeast is goaded into a last furious burst of activity. When the water in the dough boils (at a temperature slightly above normal boiling point, because of the presence of salts, sugars, and other dissolved materials in the dough), steam continues to expand the loaf. The direction of the 'spring' is usually influenced by the baker slashing the top of the loaf in a particular way before he sets it in the oven.

Expansion is stopped by the formation of a rigid crust. This can be delayed by making steam in the oven, keeping the outside soft for longer. Traditional bread ovens are hermetically sealed, thus allowing recirculation of steam during the baking process, and ovens developed by Viennese bakers in the 18th century, later adopted by the French, were designed to optimize the benefits of steam to loaf expansion and crispness of the crust. Most commercial ovens now have means of introducing steam, which helps to gelatinize the surface starch and give a high-gloss finish. Domestic bakers can either put a tray of water in the bottom of the oven, or spray their loaves with water during the first minutes of baking.

From the outside in, first the crust then the crumb solidifies. From 140 °F (60 °C) the starch partly sets to a gel and the proteins coagulate at 160 °F (71 °C). When all expansion has stopped, the loaf continues to cook at a lower temperature. Coagulation becomes complete and water evaporates from inside the loaf (a cooked loaf will weigh 12% less than raw). The crust loses most water and turns brown as a result of reactions between proteins and sugars. The colour of the crust is important in determining the final taste of the loaf. Crust coatings such as egg wash or milk give good colour, but cause softness.

As soon as bread is cooked and has cooled (paradoxically, an important part of the cooking process), it begins to stale. This is caused by a breakdown in the gel structure called 'retrogradation', in which the network of starch molecules subsides and shrivels. It is not so much a simple loss of water, but 'a change in the location and distribution of the water molecules' (McGee, 1984). Much of the water migrates to the crust, which gets leathery. Slight retrogradation is desirable: it improves the cutting texture of the loaf, especially in rye breads. Staling is accelerated by refrigeration, stopped by freezing, and slowed by keeping at room temperature. It can be temporarily reversed by reheating. Emulsifiers are added by commercial bakers to delay staling.

Bread in cooking

This is an extensive subject that E. S. Dallas (1877) thought the English well equipped to address: 'the best bread for cooking purposes is known in the French kitchen as *pain Anglais*—it is the English pan loaf.'

Bread may be used as crumbs, dried or soft; entire, as either a loaf or a slice; or as small pieces cut off a larger slice.

When breadcrumbs are dried, they may consist of the raspings of a crust. When bread was baked in ovens with only approximate temperature controls, or was cooked over very long periods of time, it often had crusts that were too hard, or too thick and tough. A bread rasp, therefore, to thin or remove the crust, was essential kitchen equipment. 'French' breads in English 18th-century recipes were invariably rasped. More refined dried crumbs are made with crustless slices dried out in the oven before pounding. Hard crumbs obtained in these ways could be used to coat foods for frying, as in 'egged and crumbed', or spread on a dish before browning under a grill or in a hot oven. The GRATIN crust benefits from absorption of the juices from below and fats such as butter or cheese placed on top by the cook.

Soft breadcrumbs are the crumb of the bread, slightly staled, then grated or processed into small particles. They may also be used to coat foods before frying (lighter and less fat-absorbing than dried crumbs) or to form a crust to gratins, but most important has been their function as thickening agent to many sauces and soups, and to give bulk to a PANADA or a STUFFING. Bread, either cut into small pieces or made into crumbs, was the most common thickening agent in medieval European cookery, ground almonds running second, as a flour-based ROUX is a comparatively complex development. Bread sauce is a modern descendant in Britain, but there are more survivors in countries like Spain where medieval cookery has been less overlaid by classical French inventions; hence the dish of liver called *chainfaïna* which is finished with a handful of crumbs to bind the juice, and many other examples. There is a group of Mediterranean cold sauces—sauce ROUILLE, some versions of AïOLI, SKORTHALIA, and the Genoese sauce for *Cappon magro*—where the bread helps the emulsification of the oil,

while the Levantine TARATOR is a combination of nuts and breadcrumbs moistened with lemon juice or broth and TARAMOSALATA gains softness and lightness from crumbs.

Crumbs are also used to thicken soups—both red and white GAZPACHOS in Spain, for example, or the simple bread soups of the Italian countryside, with the *Panada di Milano*, an egg and Parmesan enriched soup like *stracciatella*, at the pinnacle of elaboration. *Panzanella* is a Tuscan salad of bread soaked in water, tomato and salad vegetables, basil, and olive oil. The likely derivation of the name, from *pan* (bread) and *zanella* (little soup tureen), seems to imply that it, too, began life as a bread-thickened soup. An alternative method of combination is to place slices in a bowl and pour the soup on to them. Equally, the bread may be floated on top of the soup, laden with cheese, and browned under a grill, as in French onion soup.

In German lands, particularly Bavaria where bakers even sell Knödel-loaves, bread is used to make DUMPLINGS (*Knödel*). Stale crusty breakfast rolls are sliced and soaked in milk, mixed with eggs and flavourings, moulded without kneading, then poached. Dumplings can be sliced and fried afterwards, and may themselves be served with fried breadcrumbs as a garnish.

Crumbs are added to recipes to give them body. Hence the whole family of meat and poultry stuffings, and the incorporation of crumbs into many steamed pudding mixtures. Crumbs are also added to SAUSAGE, HAMBURGER, and MEAT LOAF mixtures, often to extend the meat content, but also to absorb fat and lighten the whole.

Slices of bread may be cut into smaller shapes and fried or toasted to produce CROUTONS ('little crusts'). Cubes of bread thus treated are added to soups at the table; larger shapes are served with stews or sauced meats. In England they were called sippets. Croutons are added to salads to give body, taste, and texture. Caesar SALAD is one instance, but in the Middle East, *fattoush* is also a mixed salad with toasted PITTA BREAD broken into it.

If bread is hollowed out, it can be used as a container as well as absorbing the juices from whatever is placed within, be it oysters or some more elaborate stew, but a more common method is to use a whole slice of bread, or a pair of them, for supper dishes, often involving cheese, like CROQUE-MONSIEUR, *Mozzarella in carossa*, or WELSH RABBIT. The oldest was a popular titbit called PAIN PERDU (lost bread) in the Middle Ages, where a slice of bread was soaked in cream and eggs, honey and spices, then fried. Elaborations of the theme are practised in Italy on toasts called BRUSCHETTA, and the Catalan *Pa amb tomaquèt* is toast rubbed with ripe tomato and drizzled with olive oil, so popular that a book, *Teoria i práctica del pa am tomaquèt*, was written on the subject.

See also BREAD PUDDINGS.

purpose. Before the ship was out of the South Seas the crew, who had become enchanted with Tahitian life, mutinied and took charge of the ship, putting their commander and the eighteen men who remained loyal to him in a launch and setting them adrift. The mutinous crew sailed back to Tahiti, whence some of the members, accompanied by a number of Tahitians, migrated to Pitcairn's Island and established there an Utopian colony.

Bligh and his companions managed to reach the E. Indies, more than 3,000 miles away, in their open boat, and Bligh later returned to Tahiti to collect, this time, over 2,100 plants which he landed in Jamaica in 1793. Their fruits were not a great success with the slaves, but the seedless breadfruit flourished so well in the island that Jamaica became and remains the principal producer of that kind. In some other parts of the Caribbean and C. America the seeded kind is preferred or grows better. Usage also follows an irregular pattern. In some areas the fruits are used to feed livestock, whereas in others (e.g. Trinidad, with its large Asian population) they are highly esteemed as human food.

The breadfruit is also grown in tropical Africa, Mauritius, and Réunion (where Valentin, 1982, lists ten ways of eating it).

Breadfruit is nearly always picked before it is fully ripe. It is seldom eaten raw, but is usually boiled, roasted, or fried, or cooked in an underground pit with hot stones. The naturalist Alfred Wallace encountered breadfruit in Ambon (the Moluccas), and expressed his enthusiasm as follows:

It is baked entire in the hot embers, and the inside scooped out with a spoon. I compared it to Yorkshire pudding; Charles Allen [Wallace's collecting assistant] said it was like mashed potatoes and milk. It is generally about the size of a melon, a little fibrous towards the centre, but everywhere else quite smooth and puddingy, something in consistence between yeast-dumplings and batter-pudding. It may be eaten sweet or savoury. With meat and gravy it is a vegetable superior to any I know, either in temperate or tropical countries. With sugar, milk, butter or treacle, it is a delicious pudding, having a very slight and delicate but characteristic flavour, which, like that of good bread and potatoes, one never gets tired of.

Other ways of using the fruit include drying slices and grinding them into flour for bread. Or the fruit may be buried in a pit and allowed to ferment into a strong-smelling green pulp which is made into cakes. Local names for this product include 'MADRAI', 'mahe', and 'mandraiuta'. In Hawaii breadfruit is sometimes allowed to ripen until it is beginning to soften and turn brown, then baked. It is also used as a substitute for TARO in making a starchy porridge, POI.

The seeds in the seeded varieties are numerous, large, chestnut-like, and rich in protein. These are eaten fried or boiled. The surrounding flesh is edible but inferior, and is usually discarded.

In her excellent description of the breadfruit and its uses, Elizabeth Schneider (1986) remarks that the fully ripe flesh 'may be as soft and creamy as an avocado, or runny as ripe Camembert, or tender as rising yeast batter, with an aroma that matches'. She adds that in the countries where it is cultivated, breadfruit is given much the same culinary treatment as potatoes and sweet potatoes.

The breadfruit is not entirely suitable for use as a staple food. It contains a lot of starch, but is low in protein, fat, and e.g. vitamin A. But in the islands where it is used as a staple these deficiencies are balanced by plentiful seafood and other resources.

BREADNUTS a name loosely applied to the starchy seeds of the fruits of certain trees of the family Moraceae. The most important of these fruits are described under BREADFRUIT and JACKFRUIT.

Some other trees of this family, growing in C. and S. America, bear fruits containing edible 'breadnuts'. The best known is the snakewood tree, *Brosimum alicastrum*, whose relatively small fruits usually contain one seed each. These have been consumed in various ways, whole or dried and ground, sometimes in savoury dishes and sometimes with sugar, honey, or cornmeal; but they are not much eaten nowadays.

BREAD PUDDINGS an important category. Many desserts include bread whether in the form of breadcrumbs or pieces or slices of bread. There is also a whole class of desserts; see, to take only a few examples, QUEEN'S PUDDING, POOR KNIGHTS OF WINDSOR, or SUMMER PUDDING and certain types of CHARLOTTE and the like, where the role of bread is simply to line the recipient.

It is safe to assume that from the very distant past cooks have sometimes turned stale bread into a sweet pudding, if only by soaking it in milk, sweetening it by one means or another, and baking the result. The addition of some fat, preferably in the form of butter, and something like currants is all that is needed to move this frugal dish into the category of treats, and this is what has ensured its survival in the repertoire, even of cooks who never have stale bread on their hands.

This enhanced product is known as **bread and butter pudding** and this same dish can also be made with something more exotic than plain bread, for example, BRIOCHE, PANETTONE, slices of plain cake, etc., and can be enlivened by judicious spicing or by reinforcing the currants with plumper sultanas and mixed peel. But such elaborations must be kept under strict control, so that what is essentially a simple pudding does not lose its character under the weight of sophisticated additions.

The likely history of the pudding can be illuminated by looking back at medieval 'sops' and at the medieval practice of using a hollowed-out loaf as the container for a sweet dish. More immediately recognizable antecedents began to emerge in traditional regional British cookery of more recent times. One such, Wet Nellie, is described by Helen Pollard (1991) as follows:

Wet Nellie, a Liverpudlian dish, was originally a cheap way of using stale bread and crusts. These were crumbled and mixed with suet, sugar or syrup and a little spice before baking and cutting into pieces. The bottom piece of a pile was considered the best value for money as, hopefully, the syrup would have soaked through the other layers. 'Wet' probably refers to the sticky syrup, 'Nellie' being derived from Nelson. A similar dish is known as Nelson's cake or Nelson's slice in Plymouth, and in Norfolk where Nelson was born.

Helen Pollard comments that all these variants of bread pudding could be eaten hot as a pudding or cold as a cake.

Bread jelly, made from soaked bread in the same way as FLUMMERY from oatmeal, then flavoured with cinnamon and lemon, was popular in the 19th century.

Eliza Acton's several recipes are, as usual, elegantly worded and completely precise. The range she offers illustrates clearly how the transition from a 'common' version to a 'rich' version can be effected without compromising the essential simplicity of the dish. It is in her recipe for the common version that she introduces the charming word 'lemon-grate', this being an alternative flavouring to nutmeg.

This is the place to mention an Egyptian dessert which bears a marked similarity to bread and butter pudding, and which was originally a simple dish of rural areas, although it has recently become popular in Cairo, where it can take more sophisticated forms. It is called *Om Ali* (mother of Ali), and is made with bread (but in Cairo, the bread is often replaced by FILO pastry), milk or cream, raisins, and almonds. Claudia Roden (1985) mentions the intriguing theory that *Om Ali* was introduced to Egypt 'by a Miss O'Malley, an Irish mistress of the Khedive Ismail'.

Another Middle Eastern bread sweet, *Eish es serny* (palace bread), is made by drying large round slices cut horizontally through a big loaf to make enormous rusks, which are then simmered in a sugar and honey syrup flavoured with rosewater and coloured with caramel.

Travelling further east, an Indian dessert in the Moghul style, *Shahi tukra*, is made with bread fried in ghee, dipped in a syrup flavoured with saffron and rosewater, and covered with a creamy sauce in which decorative slices of almond are embedded.

These are but a few examples of bread and butter puddings which occur outside the context of western cookery. Other examples could be furnished from Turkey, Sri Lanka, and Malaysia.   HS

BREAKFAST the first meal of the day; literally the meal with which one breaks one's fast. Opinions have varied over the years and around the world as to what foods are suitable for this. Individual tastes play a part, and are perhaps at their strongest early in the day: *chacun à son goût*, as Major L. (author of *Breakfasts, Luncheons and Ball Suppers*, 1887) said when noting a baronet's alleged preference for apple tart and home-brewed ale first thing in the morning. The type and quantity of food depends on the daily schedule; those who labour hard may break their fast with a drink and a little bread, followed by a larger second breakfast two or three hours later, and guests at a 'wedding breakfast' will almost certainly have eaten an ordinary breakfast earlier in the day.

The most flexible versions of breakfast are probably the C. and N. European buffets of breads, pastries, cheeses, and cold meats, or their Middle Eastern equivalents of bread, yoghurt, fruit, and preserves. Really substantial breakfasts include the modern British fry-up, and the N. American subspecies of this, with numerous variations on the theme of eggs, plus options of WAFFLES with MAPLE SYRUP. India provided Victorian British cooks with inspiration for kedgeree (see ANGLO-INDIAN COOKERY); traditional Indian breakfasts include DAL, rice, breads, SAMOSAS, and fruit. Comforting bowls of hot cereal mixtures are popular, from Scottish oatmeal PORRIDGE to the rice porridges eaten across much of Asia, of which CONGEE is the best known. Minimal approaches to breakfast include CROISSANTS and *café au lait* in France, chocolate and churros (see FRITTER) in Spain, and many variations on the bowl of MUESLI theme for those who think that cereal, nuts, and dried fruit are a key to good health.

The British feel that breakfast is one area in which they are experts. In fact, few British people eat a traditional English (or Scottish, Irish, or Welsh) cooked breakfast at home; but they do expect a 'full English breakfast' of fried bacon, eggs, sausages and tomatoes, plus toast, butter, marmalade, and tea or coffee to be available in any hotel or café. Fried bread, potatoes, mushrooms, fancy jams, and regional frills such as porridge, black pudding (see BLOOD SAUSAGES), laverbread (see NORI), or GAMMON are

provided at the discretion of the proprietor. A KIPPER is often an alternative to the fried breakfast. This sort of breakfast is commonly believed to reflect some golden era of the more leisured past—usually, the world of the late 19th-century country house.
READING: Eileen White (1994); Read and Manjon (1981).

BREAKFAST CEREALS which need no cooking or preparation but can be used straight from the packet, were among the earliest convenience foods. Their history is enmeshed with that of the American vegetarian, health food, and water cure movement, and also that of the Seventh Day Adventist Church, which enjoined a meatless diet.

In the early days of the 19th century the Revd Sylvester Graham, a man of strong views on diet despite his lack of medical qualifications, had advocated the use of wholemeal flour. Graham bread, CRACKERS, and flour were already in common use in 1858 when Dr James C. Jackson took over an unsuccessful water-cure resort in Dansville, New York, and renamed it 'Our Home Hygienic Institute'. Patients were subjected to a rigorous routine of baths and less pleasant treatments, and fed a very restricted diet including various grain products. The stodgy monotony of the fare palled with all but the most enthusiastic. Graham experimented with new ways of presenting the same ingredients, and in 1863 perfected a product which he called Granula. It was made from Graham flour and water baked in a very slow oven until it dried into a brittle mass, which was roughly broken up, baked for some time longer, and ground into smaller pieces. The result was rather like the cereal Grape Nuts, with a pleasantly 'toasted' flavour. However, it had to be soaked overnight in milk before the stone-hard crumbs softened enough to eat. Jackson not only served his patients Granula but put it on the market, together with Somo, a 'health coffee' also made from grain. Granula was a modest success but highly profitable, for it was sold at ten times the cost of its ingredients.

In 1866, a group of Seventh Day Adventists at their central colony in Battle Creek, Michigan, set up their own water-cure establishment, the Western Health Reform Institute. There were the same problems with monotonous diet. One Adventist, John Harvey (J. H.) Kellogg, was sent as a young man to New York to study medicine. Here, living in a boarding house where cooking was impossible, and restricted to the vegetarian diet required by his religion, he realized the need for a ready cooked cereal that needed no preparation. In

1875 he graduated, and next year returned to Battle Creek, where he reorganized the Institute into the Battle Creek Sanitarium. Here, he experimented with his idea for a cereal, and achieved success with a mixture of wheat, oat, and maize meal, formed into biscuits, baked, and ground. He put it on the market, also under the name 'Granula' (an obvious choice, being Latin for 'little grain'), but was forced by legal action by the makers of the original Granula to change the name. So it became Granola. It enjoyed considerable commercial success, along with a whole range of vegetarian products and coffee substitutes manufactured by Kellogg's Sanitarium (later Sanitas) Health Food Company. As with Granula, ingredients were cheap and the 'mark-up' high. Mrs Kellogg did much of the development work for new lines while her husband administered the sanitarium and the business.

Then, in 1893, a Denver lawyer, H. D. Perky, who suffered from indigestion and had become converted to health foods, invented a completely different product: Shredded Wheat. The grain was steamed until thoroughly softened, then rolled between one grooved and one plain roller to form strands which were chopped into biscuits. The early versions were soft and moist, and kept poorly, so sales were limited. But Perky had patented all the important parts of the process.

In 1894 Kellogg, who had heard of Perky's product from a patient, went to visit him in Denver. Perky was discouraged and thinking of giving up. Kellogg at first offered Perky $100,000 for his patents, and the deal was nearly concluded. However, Kellogg, seized by timidity when it came to actually parting with money, withdrew the offer. He was later to regret this, particularly since in his conversation with Perky he had described the way in which Kellogg products were dried by slow heating, so that they kept in perfect condition for a long time. Perky began to dry Shredded Wheat and sales took off. He built a huge factory, the 'Conservatory of Food', at Niagara Falls.

The envious Kellogg and his wife experimented furiously to create a rival. Batch after batch failed; but finally they developed a process in which whole wheat was cooked, allowed to stand for several hours and passed through plain rollers, which flattened each grain into a flake. The flakes were then dried. J. H. Kellogg wanted to break the flakes up into granules, but W. K. Kellogg, who helped him to scale the process up for mass production, dissuaded him. In 1895 the new flakes went on sale under the name 'Granose', and were an instant success. There were soon many imitations: it was easy to circumvent Kellogg's patents by varying the process slightly. Most of the new firms set up their factories at Battle Creek itself to capitalize on the now famous name. One early rival which has survived, Force, was based elsewhere in Buffalo.

During the 1890s the Kelloggs had experimented with maize as a grain for making flakes: in fact corn flakes. The early types all went rancid. It was not until 1902 that they managed to make a corn flake of reasonable quality, and even then it did not sell well.

Charles W. Post had been a patient at the sanitarium in 1891. He was an inventive man: his creations included a fireless cooker; a water-powered electric generator; and the Post Currency Check, a kind of postal order. In 1892 he set up his own medical boarding house, La Vita Inn, at Battle Creek. Here he invented and marketed Postum, a most successful (commercially speaking) cereal coffee substitute. In 1898 he made another financial killing with his granular wheat cereal Grape Nuts, which he ingeniously sold in very small packets, 'because it was concentrated'. However, it was of quite orthodox composition. It got its name because Post erroneously supposed the maltose sugar in the product to be 'grape sugar' (an old name for dextrose; see SUGAR), and because it had a nutty flavour as a result of toasting. By 1903 Post was making over a million dollars a year: no mean sum in those years.

In 1906 Post launched a new product, a corn flake considerably better than Kellogg's 1902 version. The flakes were thick with an attractively bubbly texture. The 'health and godliness' image of Battle Creek was still strong and Post had the unfortunate idea of calling his product 'Elijah's Manna'. There was widespread protest, and he had to withdraw it. In the same year the Kelloggs struck back with their own Toasted Corn Flakes. However, it was not old J. H. Kellogg who was selling it: it was his younger brother, W. K., whose signature still appears on the packet and has been turned into the Kellogg trade mark. J. H. had had a characteristic attack of cold feet over the investment required to launch a new product—in fairness, he himself had considerable trouble with corn flakes. The brothers quarrelled and W. K. founded his own Kellogg Toasted Corn Flake Company, independent of J. H.'s firm.

In 1908, Post relaunched his product as Post Toasties. Both the Kellogg and the Post products were enormously successful: there was plenty of room for them and others in an expanding breakfast cereal market. By 1911, 108 different brands were being manufactured in Battle Creek alone. W. K. Kellogg in particular became enormously rich and contributed large sums to charity, setting up the Kellogg Foundation in 1930.

But J. H.'s sanitarium went bankrupt in 1933. Both brothers lived to the age of 91.

The name 'corn flake' was freed for use by rival firms through legal action by the Quaker Oats Company, who were seeking to diversify into cold cereals—they had been making their rolled porridge since the early days of the grain food boom.

Most modern cereals are no more than mere modifications of the original types with added sugar or flavourings, or in new shapes. All Bran was invented in the 1920s by W. K.'s son John L. Kellogg; it was a convenient way of using up bran left over from other products, and its laxative properties, discreetly promoted by euphemistic advertising, were in a way a return to the original health food image. The only really different cereals are the puffed wheat and rice types. These are made by heating the grain inside a sealed cylinder in which pressure builds up considerably. After an hour at 285 °C (550 °F) the grain is softened and all the water inside has turned to steam, superheated by the pressure. Then the cylinder is suddenly unsealed. The high steam pressure inside each grain causes it to expand enormously. The puffed grains are then dried off before they can collapse.

Despite their origins in the health food movement, cereals have no special nutritional value. A cereal made of any grain, whole or husked, has only the food value of that grain, with slight losses of proteins and carbohydrates destroyed during cooking, and substantial losses of the rather frail B vitamins. In fact, in most countries, cereals are artificially 'fortified' with extra vitamins, as revealed in the small print on the packet. Cereals are usually eaten with milk, which provides nutrients which they lack (and with sugar, which provides nothing but calories).

Bruce and Crawford have provided an entertaining and detailed chronicle of the whole process of *Cerealizing America* (1995), the homeland of breakfast cereals, with much on advertising the various products.

RH

BREAM *Abramis brama*, a fish of the carp family which has a wide distribution in C. and N. Europe. This is the freshwater bream, not closely related to the numerous species of SEA BREAM.

The bream has a maximum length of 80 cm (32"), but is generally a little under half that size. It favours stagnant or slow-flowing waters and muddy bottoms. It is counted a good food fish in many European countries.

The silver or white bream, *Blicca bjoerkna*, has an almost similar range but is of much less interest as a food fish. Other freshwater breams are of even less interest, but there are

some close relations, which hybridize with the bream and amongst each other, which count as edible. One, the ide, *Leuciscus idus*, is the object of a fishery in Russia.

BRÈDES a name used in Réunion and Mauritius (and in francophone islands of the Antilles) for various dishes made with the leaves and stems of many different cultivated and wild plants, or for the plants themselves. The dishes may be of a bouillon-like character (cooked with plenty of water) or thick (cooked with their own juices). In the latter case they are called *étouffée* (see BRAISE).

Among the vegetables used for this category of dish are WATERCRESS, MUSTARD GREENS, christophine (see CHAYOTE) and PUMPKIN shoots, and (under the local name *songe*) various sorts of CALLALOO.

The name *brèdes* has an interesting derivation. In classical Greek and Latin *bliton* and *blitum* meant green leaves that are eaten boiled (like spinach), and the same meaning was preserved in French *blette*, Spanish *bledo*, and Portuguese *bredo*. Portuguese sailors, who were the first to establish settlements around Africa and in the Indian Ocean, naturally applied their name to any greens which they came across which were eaten boiled, and the word then migrated in slightly altered form into regional French and French creoles. See Chauvet (1998).

See also SOUTHERN AFRICA for the Cape Malay dish *Bredie*, which normally includes greens along with meat, and which acquired its name by the same route.

BRESAOLA dried beef, from a choice lean cut, as prepared in the Alpine region of Italy. It undergoes a maturing stage which leaves it dark red in colour; and is served in very thin slices with a dressing of olive oil and lemon juice and pepper.

This product is akin to BINDENFLEISCH.

BREWIS an ancient term of which BROSE is a variant, originally meant bread soaked in fat or DRIPPING and then came to mean a BROTH, often thickened with bread or oatmeal or the like. In this connection Theodora FitzGibbon (1976) has an interesting description of brewis as a 'tea-kettle broth' which was made in Wales 'from oat husks, soaked in water and then boiled with fat bacon, salt and pepper'. She also recorded that in modern times the dish was being made 'with finely cut bread crumbs and a lump of butter'.

In recent times the term is most commonly met in Newfoundland, where it refers to a hard bread, also called 'hard tack' (see SHIP'S BISCUIT). Len Margaret (1980), who has the combination of fish and brewis as part of the title of his survey of old recipes of Newfoundland, explains that the dish involves SALT COD, SALT PORK, brewis, and salt, the role of the salt pork being to provide 'scruncheons' (small cubes fried until golden brown) to be sprinkled over the fish and brewis.

BRICK CHEESE is one of the main kinds made in the USA and one of the few which can claim an American origin (although possibly modelled on a German cheese called *Box*). First made in Wisconsin, around the 1870s, it is now manufactured in other states and Canada also.

The name may refer to the brick-like shape and size bestowed on it by the forms in which it is made, or to the actual bricks traditionally used in pressing it.

Brick is a whole-milk cheese with an elastic texture, less firm than CHEDDAR, with irregular holes or 'eyes', and easy to slice.

BRIE one of the most famous soft cheeses in the world, has been made in much its present form since early medieval times; or, if the account of the Emperor Charlemagne sampling and praising a wonderful local cheese near Meaux is reliable, since the 8th century or even earlier. Because of its renown it has been much imitated; and its name, unfortunately, is not protected. Genuine Brie, from around the city of Meaux (to the east of Paris), is rich, mild, and creamy. It is a mould-ripened cheese, made from whole milk. When fully ripe it is runny, and a slice will not hold its shape. It is to be eaten entire, rind and all, as Charlemagne was reputedly taught to do.

During the first half of the 19th century connoisseurs of cheese esteemed very highly the *Brie de Meaux en pot*, although this seems originally to have been a way of selling cheeses which were not suitable, because 'too far gone' towards the liquid state, for normal presentation. In the course of time what had been an expedient developed into a new field for displaying expertise, and the *Brie en pot* continued to be a delicacy in strong demand from its devotees until late in the 19th century.

The Brie de Meaux is accorded the title of *Roi des Fromages et Fromage des Rois* (King of Cheeses and Cheese of Kings) by Androuet and Chabot (1985), partly because of this cheese's long association with the French royal court. It is of interest that this Brie was originally consumed fresh, not ripened, as an 18th-century painting in the Musée des Beaux Arts at Chartres demonstrates.

There are other notable varieties, e.g. Brie de Melun, which in its traditional form underwent a long ripening to give a darker colour and stronger flavour. The Brie of Montereau and that of Nangis are both renowned.

The continuing replacement of the traditional breeds of cow in the region by the Frisonne-Holstein breed is thought to have caused some deterioration in flavour of most Brie cheeses. And the large quantities of industrially produced Brie are not nearly as good as the traditional product.

The milk from which Brie is made is never heated above lukewarm. After it is curdled, the curd is ladled into circular hoops standing on straw mats, through which it drains gently without pressing.

The cheese is salted, dried, and ripened in a complicated process involving several stages. A white MOULD, *Penicillium camemberti* or *P. candidum* (two strains of what is essentially the same organism), is either endemic in the first drying room or deliberately innoculated, and soon covers the surface. In later stages it is joined by YEASTS and bacteria, and the surface becomes streaked with reddish brown. During this time the cheese is kept in a fairly damp, cool cellar. Enzymes produced by the organisms break down proteins in the cheese, softening it and developing the flavour. The unripe cheese has a chalky centre which gradually disappears as the enzymes spread from the outside inwards. Time, temperature, and humidity are all critical. Refrigeration, which would disrupt the desired sequence, is to be avoided.

Brie is made in three sizes, from 18 cm (7") to 40 cm (16") in diameter. It is seldom more than 3 cm (1") thick. The smallest size or Petit Brie, sometimes known as Coulommiers (although what is properly called a Coulommiers cheese is a vexed and vexing question), is ripened for a shorter time than the others and is milder, with a pure white crust.

READING: Île-de-France in the IPCF Series (1993, includes bibliography); Rance (1989).

BRILL *Scophthalmus rhombus*, a FLATFISH of European waters which is closely related to the TURBOT; indeed, it could be described as a slightly smaller (maximum length 60 cm/24"), shallow-water version of the other. It differs slightly in shape, and also in having scales but not having tubercles. It is not as fine to eat, but good nonetheless.

BRILLAT-SAVARIN JEAN ANTHELME (1755–1826), the best known of three pioneering writers on gastronomy at the beginning of the 19th century (the other two being his fellow Frenchman GRIMOD DE LA REYNIÈRE and the German RUMOHR). McGee (1990) notes succinctly that he became a lawyer, fled the French Revolution, spent two years in New York teaching languages and playing the violin in a theatre orchestra, returned to France, and eventually became a judge on the Court of Appeals in Paris. He had a lifelong fascination with science and medicine, which accounts for much of the content of his gastronomic work. He published this privately and anonymously in 1826 under the title *La Physiologie du goût: ou, méditations sur la gastronomie transcendante*. The book has since gone through many editions in many languages, of which the English translation with commentary by M. F. K. FISHER (1972) is an outstanding example.

McGee points out that Brillat-Savarin and his book are remembered today mainly for a handful of epigrams which appear in the first two pages of the book, and that the physiological content is now mostly forgotten and was largely ignored even by the many writers who imitated its title and eclectic mixture of aphorism, anecdote, and exposition. Balzac, who wrote an admiring biographical essay on Brillat-Savarin, published the *Physiology of Marriage* in 1829, and less notable scholars dilated in succeeding decades on the physiology of the opera, the cafe, the umbrella, billiards, and 'the ridiculous,' among other things. In this short-lived genre, *physiology* was reduced to a synonym for character or portrait. These books aspired only to the form and fame, not the substance, of *The Physiology of Taste*.

Brillat-Savarin may have been responsible for a temporary change in the word's meaning, but he himself used *physiology* literally, to mean a scientific analysis of the workings of living beings. Roughly a third of his book is devoted to the chemistry and physiology of food and eating. Delightful as the aphorisms and anecdotes are, *The Physiology of Taste* would be a lesser book without its attention to science. Like the astringent tannins in a red wine, this element lends the whole a certain solidity and dimension, and has helped it age well.

Pointing out that Brillat-Savarin had been delighted, on one academic occasion, to be mistaken for 'a distinguished foreign professor', and that he presented his book as the work of an anonymous 'Professor, member of many learned societies', McGee notes that:

He gives a medical cast to much of his material; his anecdotes are often case histories, his recipes prescriptions. The Professor delivers a formal lecture to his cook on the theory of frying, since 'the phenomena which take place in your laboratory are nothing other than the execution of eternal laws of nature.'

McGee also observes that Brillat-Savarin's closest friend Anthelme Richerand, another native of the town of Belley but a good deal younger than Brillat-Savarin, had published a book whose title translates as *New Elements of Physiology* and that:

It was at Richerand's country house that Brillat-Savarin began writing his book and that the anecdote of the huge turbot is set; in the dialogue that follows the opening aphorisms, it is Richerand who convinces him to publish.

This connection and knowledge of some other authors and books whose influence on Brillat-Savarin can be traced helps modern readers to understand the nature and original purpose of *La Physiologie du goût*. Some such readers may value it by these criteria, but it has to be admitted that the book is more honoured by the quotation of the aphorisms and the perusal of the most entertaining anecdotes than by the serious study which Brillat-Savarin and his friend Richerand would have thought appropriate. The whole episode provides a good example of how a book, once it leaves its launching pad, may rocket away on an unexpected path.

It is noteworthy that serious appreciation of Brillat-Savarin was particularly noticeable, towards the end of the 20th century, in Australia.

READING: MacDonogh (1992*a*).

BRIOCHE a light but rich French bread/cake, made with flour, butter, and eggs, and raised with yeast.

The word, which has been in use since at least the 15th century, is derived from the verb *broyer*, meaning to break up, and refers to the prolonged kneading of the dough.

The brioche may have originated in Normandy. In support of this theory is the fact that the quality of the butter is what determines the quality of a brioche and that Normandy has been famed for its butter since the Middle Ages. Whatever the truth, the brioche arrived in Paris in the 17th century. Cotgrave translated the term, in his *Dictionarie of the French and English Tongues* (1611) as 'a rowle or bunne, of spiced bread'. The earliest surviving recipe is in *Suite des dons de Comus* (1742) and prescribes brewer's yeast (whereas baker's yeast is now used) and a relatively small amount of butter. In modern times, brioches can be made with little or much butter, the standard having become 500–750 g (1–1.5 lb) butter to 1 kg (2 lb) flour. Lacam (1890) gave an amusing table of five grades, all the way up from 125 g butter/500 g flour (*brioche très commune*) to 625 g butter/500 g flour (*brioche princière*).

Since some time in the 19th century it has been customary to bake a brioche in a deep, round, fluted tin, narrow at the base and flaring widely at the top. The traditional Paris brioche is made by placing a small ball of dough on top of a larger one, thus producing the shape known as *brioche à tête* (brioche with a head). In this form brioches range from individual size to large ones which yield a dozen servings. The brioche of Nanterre (close to Paris, on the west) is made by placing several small balls of dough around the sides of a rectangular mould. These balls coalesce and the resulting shape is officially known as parallelepipedic. Both these forms of brioche are given a shiny glaze of egg.

Brioche dough takes some time to prepare, as it usually has three, rather than two, rising periods. In France brioches are mostly bought from specialist shops, e.g. *viennoiseries*, rather than being made at home.

The dough also lends itself to the addition of ingredients such as cheese or raisins, for variations of flavour. A plainer brioche dough, with fewer eggs and less butter, may be used for a savoury brioche, for example one which encases sausage. A filled sweet brioche may contain fruit, confectioner's custard, whipped cream, etc.

The *brioche Vendéenne*, whose fame and consumption has now spread from the woodlands of the Vendée throughout France, is a plaited brioche usually flavoured with brandy/rum/orange flower water; it used to have a special association with Easter but is now generally popular for any festive occasions.

One form of brioche is a highly localized speciality of the Savoie village of Saint-Pierre-d'Albigny. It is called *Main de Saint-Agathe* because it is made in the form of a hand, with allusion to the severed hand (severed when she unsuccessfully tried to save her breasts from being cut off) of that saint, the patron saint of young mothers and wet-nurses, who is venerated in this village. The dough is flavoured with saffron or anise.

Brioche is usually eaten at breakfast or teatime, with coffee or hot chocolate; and in its modern form it constitutes a delicacy, slightly closer in British eyes to cake than to bread. However, 'Qu'ils mangent de la brioche' (usually translated into English as 'let them eat cake'), the statement attributed to Marie Antoinette on being told that the people of Paris were rioting because they had no bread, has achieved more notoriety than it deserves. Eighteenth-century brioche was only lightly enriched (by modest quantities of butter and eggs) and not very far removed from a good white loaf of bread.

Interesting comparisons may be made between brioche and BABA, SAVARIN, and KUGELHOPF (all based on similar ingredients, but mixed in a different order, and with different results).

READING: Île-de-France in the IPCF Series (1993, includes bibliography).

BRITTLE a very hard confection usually made from plain sugar syrup cooked almost or actually to the CARAMEL stage and poured over nuts. Brittle is a simple and ancient sweet, and has been made for centuries in many countries. It is very similar to some dark types of NOUGAT made with honey and nuts only (no egg white). Two examples are the Provençal *croquant* made with sugar, honey, and almonds; and Italian *croccante* with sugar, sometimes a little butter (which makes it less hard), and almonds.

Similar confections of nuts, especially pistachios, almonds, and cashews, or sesame seeds, are popular in parts of the Arabic-speaking world. Versions of nut and sesame seed brittle are to be found in many parts of Asia; from the Afghan *hasta shireen* and the Iranian *sohan asali* (best from the holy city of Qum, according to Nesta Ramazani, 1974) to regions further east, where some are based on jaggery (see PALM SUGAR). Peanut brittle is a popular sweet in N. America.   (LM)

BROAD BEAN *Vicia faba* (or *Faba vulgaris*), the original bean of Europe, W. Asia, and N. Africa, has been an important staple food for millennia (long before the HARICOT BEAN was imported from America), and is also known as fava bean (from the Latin name). Remains of broad beans have been found in many of the earliest inhabited sites investigated by archaeologists throughout this region.

After 3000 BC their cultivation spread to China, where in some southern provinces they now rank second to SOYA BEANS in importance. They are also cultivated in the temperate regions of N. America; in some dry, mountainous parts of S. America where the native haricot bean does not grow well; and in the Sudan and Uganda.

The primitive type of broad bean was small and not unlike the horse bean which is now grown as a fodder crop. Improved garden varieties fall into two main classes: Windsor beans with short pods containing four large beans, and longpod beans, which have about eight smaller ones. There are at least three dozen popular cultivars available, and their beans vary considerably in size and colour; they may be white, pale green, green, buff, brown, chestnut, etc. The useful notes given by Facciola (1990) include the information that Green Windsor was formerly used for Brown Windsor soup (see SOUP), and that Red Epicure beans are like chestnuts in flavour as well as in colour.

'Field beans', grown mainly for animal fodder, are similar to garden broad beans, but are allowed to grow larger before they are picked.

When the beans within the pods are only fingernail size and still green they are often eaten raw, especially in Italy. As they mature, most varieties become grey tinged with pink, although some of the better kinds remain green. Up to medium size, they are eaten boiled, sometimes with an added flavouring such as SAVORY (in France and Germany). When large and old the beans develop tough skins which have to be removed. At this stage they are best dried. The dried *Ful medames* which are the Egyptian national dish are a local, brown variety of broad bean.

There is a mysterious shadow over the history of broad beans, and an actual problem which may be linked with it. From the beginnings of recorded history, these beans have aroused superstitious dread. The ancient Egyptians, although they cultivated them, regarded them as unclean, and the Greek writer Herodotus claims that their priests would not even look at one, let alone eat it. In Greece in the 6th century BC, the followers of Pythagoras were forbidden to eat beans, but no satisfactory reason was given. There seems to have been a general belief that the souls of the dead might migrate into beans. This was later rationalized by the Roman writer Diogenes Laertius: 'Beans are the substance which contains the largest portion of that animated matter of which our souls are particles.' One crude origin of the idea could have been the tendency of beans to cause wind. The Greek word *anemos* means both 'wind' and 'soul'. Whatever the cause, beans were associated with the dead and were eaten at funeral feasts. This was not only a Roman practice. The word 'beano' was originally applied by the ancient Celts to a funeral 'beanfeast'.

The actual and enduring problem is that of favism, a form of poisoning which afflicts certain susceptible people when they eat broad beans, and sometimes even when they breathe the pollen of bean flowers. The result is severe anaemia and jaundice. Only a tiny proportion of the population suffers from this trouble, which is hereditary and seems to affect peoples native to the European and Mediterranean lands where the bean originated. It has been suggested that Pythagoras himself was a sufferer and that this was the reason for his ban. However, such an explanation would have to be stretched considerably to account for all the other derogatory and mystical beliefs about the bean which were entertained in the past.

BROCCOLI *Brassica oleracea*, Cymosa group, is one of the most puzzling members of the cabbage family. The trouble is that, although shopkeepers and shoppers can usually distinguish it easily from the CAULIFLOWER, botanists cannot.

Like the cauliflower, broccoli is a sort of cabbage in which flowers have begun to form but have stopped growing while still in bud. In the cauliflower the buds are clustered tightly together to form the familiar white head. In broccoli, or at least

what is called 'sprouting broccoli', they are in separate groups, each group on its own thick, fleshy stalk. Besides **sprouting broccoli** (which is ready for consumption in the spring, after overwintering, and may have purple, green, or white flower heads), the main category of this vegetable is **calabrese,** an annual broccoli which is harvested in summer; it is green or purple. A third category, **romanesco,** matures later in the year, displaying yellowish-green multiple heads, grouped together. However, the development of numerous cultivars has resulted in a highly complex situation.

One plausible theory about its origin is that broccoli developed before the cauliflower. Vilmorin (1883), drawing on his great experience as the premier seedsman of France, thought that when gardeners first tried growing cabbages for their shoots (as opposed to compact heads) they began to develop prototypes of broccoli, and that it was from these that cauliflowers, which were regarded as superior because of their white and compact form, evolved.

The first clear description of broccoli occurs in the 1724 edition of *Miller's Gardener's Dictionary*, where it was described as a stranger in England 'until within these five years' and was called 'sprout colli-flower' or 'Italian asparagus'. It seems to be generally accepted that the broccoli thus introduced to England, and no doubt to other European countries at about the same time, came from Italy. Broccoli is an Italian word meaning 'little arms' or 'little shoots'. The Italian connection is maintained in the name calabrese, which refers to the Italian province of Calabria.

Broccoli reached N. America later in the 18th century, but did not become popular there until the 20th century. In the latter part of the century its consumption has increased dramatically. About 90% of the crop in the USA comes from California.

Broccoli is less demanding than cauliflower in respect of climate, and thrives in many parts of the world. For what is often called Chinese broccoli, the sort preferred in China, see CHINESE KALE.

Broccoli is rich in nutrients, best preserved by cooking briefly, with little water, or stir-frying. A dressing of lemon butter or HOLLANDAISE sauce suits it.

BROSE one of the most basic words in the vocabulary of Scottish cooks, was used originally to refer to one of the simplest Scottish dishes, to wit a dish of oatmeal (see OATS) mixed with boiling water or milk, with salt and butter etc. added. It differs from PORRIDGE in that the oatmeal is not cooked.

Depending on what was locally available, a brose could be made with BARLEY meal or

(for pease brose) PEASEMEAL. Indeed, Marian McNeill (1929) relates that mixtures of several meals (for example, oatmeal, BERE MEAL—made from certain kinds of barley—and peasemeal) could be used, and that beggars, who might be given small quantities of different meals, were apt to use this technique.

Other ingredients are also added to the basic brose. Green brose is often made in the spring with young NETTLE tops, SPRING ONIONS, or whatever is available. Kail brose is made with KALE/kail, meat stock being poured over the oatmeal. Neep brose is made with SWEDE.

Atholl brose is an alcoholic version which combines oatmeal, water, honey, and whisky (cream is an optional addition, especially for festive occasions). There is a legend which suggests an early origin and explains how the name Atholl came to be used. The Duke of Atholl is said to have foiled his enemies during a Highland rebellion in 1475 by filling the well from which they normally drank with this ambrosial mixture, and so intoxicated them that they were easily taken.

BROTH a term which usually means the liquid in which meat has been cooked or a simple soup based thereon. It is a close equivalent to the French *bouillon* and the Italian *brodo*, but differences between the evolution of cookery in English-speaking countries and those of the cuisines which use other languages have given it, so to speak, a flavour of its own.

The word comes from a root which means simply to brew, without specifying the presence of meat, and there are early examples of broths made with just vegetables; indeed, the term 'vegetable broth' (and to a lesser extent 'fish broth') would not seem surprising. However, for several centuries, broth has usually implied meat. It has also been prominent in invalid cookery. Thus Garrett (*c*.1895) gives recipes for pectoral broth and nutritive broth as well as for quick broths and cheap broths and (less usually) a rich broth. The same thoughtful author points to a paradox of terminology: if one does something interesting to a broth, then it will probably change its name and become a soup or consommé or whatever. The one broth which stands out as an exception to this paradoxical rule, because so good and so famous and yet remaining a broth, is SCOTCH BROTH, also known as Scotch barley broth. Sheep's head broth (see HEADS), another Scottish speciality, enjoys equal prestige but less currency.

It could be said that broth occupies an intermediate position between STOCK and SOUP. A broth (e.g. chicken broth) can be eaten as is, whereas a stock (e.g. chicken stock) would normally be consumed only as an ingredient in something more complex. A soup, on the other hand, would usually be less simple, more 'finished', than a broth.

BROWNIES rich American chocolate-flavoured squares baked as a single cake, then cut up and eaten as a dessert or snack. The name comes from the deep brown colour.

Although the origin of brownies is not clear, they have been eaten in the USA since the 19th century, first appearing in print in the 1897 *Sears, Roebuck Catalog*.

Some brownies have an almost fudgelike consistency, while others are more like biscuits. They are generally made of flour, sugar, and cocoa, or unsweetened cooking chocolate, with melted butter, eggs, a little vanilla flavouring, and chopped pecans or walnuts.   LM

BROWNING of foods is a familiar occurrence in the kitchen, and often a welcome one. People prefer loaves to be brown outside, and like a slice of bread to be browned when toasted. Grilled or roasted meat should have a brown exterior. On the other hand, no one likes to see cut fruits or vegetables turning brown, as many will if remedial action is not taken.

Some compounds formed during browning have distinctive flavours, often ones which are liked, such as that of CARAMEL, but sometimes stale and even repulsive. An understanding of the different ways in which browning occurs will help to illuminate these contrasts.

There are four main causes of browning, which may act separately or in combination at various temperatures.

The simplest is caramelization, which happens only at high temperatures. It is caused by the breakdown of SUGARS or, indirectly, of starches which first decompose into sugars.

Another kind of browning directly affects STARCH when it is heated in dry conditions; this is known as dextrinization.

A very common cause of browning is a more complicated reaction known as sugar-amine browning. Sugars and AMINO ACIDS (or proteins, which are composed of amino acids) react together, usually at cooking temperatures but sometimes at room temperature or below.

ENZYME browning is also widespread. It occurs at low or moderate temperatures only, since the enzymes which cause it are quickly destroyed by heat.

CARAMELIZATION

Sugar molecules begin to disintegrate at temperatures above 170 °C (340 °F). They break up in various ways, and the number of different compounds which can thus be yielded is over a hundred. Some of them are brown in colour and bitter in taste, producing the characteristic colour and flavour of caramelization. If heating is continued, caramelized sugars break down further into pure black carbon.

The various types of sugar differ noticeably in the extent to which they caramelize. Fructose and sucrose caramelize readily, but dextrose (glucose) hardly does so at all. The pentose sugars, whose molecules contain only five carbon atoms instead of six, caramelize very well. Since small amounts of these are present in wheat bran and in rye, wholemeal and rye breads tend to colour quickly when toasted.

Caramelization can take place both in air and away from it, as at the bottom of a saucepan. The sticky black coating on the bottom of an overheated pan is mostly caramel and carbon.

Caramelized sugar can be used as a brown colouring and is the basis of 'gravy browning', which is made from glucose. Such products are popular in Britain and northern countries, though little seen elsewhere.

An example of pure caramelization is the well-known dessert CRÈME CARAMEL. Sugar and water are boiled until the sugar is caramelized, and this is then used to line a small mould. A vanilla-flavoured custard is poured in, and the mould is paced in a bain-marie in the oven. See also CRÈME BRÛLÉE.

Curiously, the sweets called 'caramels' have not undergone caramelization. They acquire their flavour and pale brown colour largely from sugar-amine reactions caused by heating the milk with which they are made.

DEXTRINIZATION

Dextrins are the remains of starch molecules which have been broken down by heating, or by enzymes in the course of digestion. When starch is heated in dry conditions these products include pyrodextrins, which are brown in colour and have a characteristic flavour recognizable in bread crust and toast.

Again, excessive heating can yield black carbon.

SUGAR-AMINE BROWNING

This occurs in a wide variety of foods which contain both sugars and proteins. It is also called the 'Maillard effect', after the Frenchman who first identified it. It is strange that there is no more common term for it, since such reactions are a fundamental part of cooking. The products are not only coloured but also have flavours which give much of the taste of roasted and grilled foods.

The chemistry is complex and many different compounds are formed at various stages. The reactions can take place both in air and without it. The coloured end products are known as melanoidins. Proteins, whether whole or in the form of isolated amino acids, are not all equally prone to engage in these reactions. Sugars, too, vary in their behaviour. Ordinary sugar (sucrose) does not react at all. But in most foods there are other sugars which do; and some sucrose will anyway be split into simple sugars during cooking, or by the action of yeast in bread dough.

Sugar-amine reactions are usually desirable, as in cooked meat, roasted coffee beans, dried prunes, and maple syrup; but they may also be unwelcome, as in fruit juices. It is therefore useful to know both how to encourage and how to inhibit them.

Among the encouraging factors are a high temperature and alkalinity. Thus, in making maple syrup, the desired colour and flavour are deliberately developed by concentrating the syrup at a high temperature and taking advantage of its slight natural alkalinity. BICARBONATE OF SODA, the mild alkali which is added to some cakes and biscuits and peanut BRITTLE, promotes browning. Certain organic acids, such as fruit acids, also help, as do phosphates, iron, and copper. The provision of additional sugar and protein, as when milk is brushed on to bread to help the crust turn brown, is an obvious technique.

Inhibiting factors are fewer. Moderate, but not extreme, drying of a product slows down browning. Sulphur dioxide blocks it effectively, in a manner not yet fully understood. This chemical is therefore added to various food products some of which, including fruit squashes, would otherwise discolour quickly even at room temperature.

ENZYME BROWNING

This typically occurs in fruits and vegetables that have been cut or bruised, breaking open their cells and allowing the natural enzymes in them to decompose other substances into compounds with a dark colour and, often, an 'off' flavour. This is seldom desirable; an exception is the preparation of 'black' tea, where the leaves are deliberately bruised to allow enzymes to work.

We normally try to frustrate the enzymes responsible for this kind of browning. The simplest way is to cook the food, which destroys the enzymes. Freezing, on the other hand, does not, so vegetables to be frozen must be thoroughly blanched beforehand to prevent them from slowly browning after they are frozen. Salt blocks the action of the enzymes, but such large quantities are needed that it is not generally used for the purpose, although sliced apples may be left in brine for a short time before they are used. Acids have the same effect and are

more practical. Lemon juice, vinegar, and
ascorbic acid (vitamin C) are all used.
Sulphur dioxide (which forms sulphurous
acid in water) is used for commercial dried
fruit. Finally, enzyme browning can be
prevented by the exclusion of air, since,
unlike the other kinds of browning, it needs
oxygen to work. Putting foods in water is
not effective by itself, because of the air
dissolved in the water. Syrups afford better
protection. Vacuum packing, although the
vacuum is never total, is quite effective. The
use of an inert gas, as when apples are stored
in nitrogen, is best of all.

COMPLEX BROWNINGS

The browning of bread crust and of toast
involves the first three mechanisms acting
simultaneously. Sugars released into the
dough by the action of yeast, or painted onto
the loaf, undergo caramelization. On the dry
outside of the loaf starch breaks down into
pyrodextrins. In the moister conditions just
below the surface, sugar-amine browning
also takes place. The same three, and
especially the last two, occur when
breadcrumbs are sprinkled on top of a
dish and heated to produce a brown crust
over it.

There is an element of caramelization in
the browning of foods which are deep fried;
but this is subordinate to the more
important sugar-amine browning.   (RH)

BROWN SAUCE (BOTTLED) of one
kind or another is seen on the tables of most
British cafés and has a certain popularity in
other countries. It is a commercial
descendant of the home-made KETCHUP of
earlier times, and also related to WORCESTER
SAUCE which is, however, much more
concentrated, and a condiment rather than a
relish.

Brown sauces come in bottles of various
shapes, and bear labels which make
interesting reading for connoisseurs of food
additives. They combine sweet, vinegary,
and spicy elements, and often have a gummy
texture.

The best-known variety is HP sauce. HP
stands for the Houses of Parliament, in
whose members' restaurant it is in fact
available. Its history is the subject of an
interesting book by Landen and Daniel
(1985). As this book explains, many other
memorably named brands have come and
gone, or survive.

The BROWN SAUCES (*sauces brunes*) of
French cuisine are an entirely different
matter; see the next entry.

BROWN SAUCES *sauces brunes*, a group
of sauces in French cuisine which are based
on what the French call GLACE DE VIANDE or

ESPAGNOLE. A general characteristic of these
sauces is that they are rich in flavour and
colour. However, depending on what
ingredients are used to enhance the basic
sauce, they present considerable diversity in
appearance and flavour.

The most famous of them is perhaps
BORDELAISE. Some others are *bigarade* (with
the juice of bitter orange); *chasseur*,
supposed to be like what hunters would put
on their meat after the hunt; *Madère*, with
Madeira; *piquante*, which is piquant;
poivrade, peppery; and *Robert*, dating back to
the 14th century and mentioned in the 16th
by Rabelais, who attributed it to a certain
'Robert', whose identity is still a mystery.

See also BROWN SAUCE (BOTTLED) above,
which is English and a quite different affair.

BRUSCHETTA a Tuscan dish designed to
show off the new season's oil at the time of
the olive harvest. To make it, RUSKS or
TOAST of household bread are rubbed with
garlic and drenched with oil. Coarse salt is
added to taste.   LM
READING: Taruschio and Taruschio (1995).

BRUSSELS SPROUTS *Brassica oleracea*,
Gemmifera group, a many-headed
subspecies of the common cabbage. The
main head never achieves more than a
straggly growth while many miniature head
buds grow around the stem. (The
phenomenon may sometimes be induced in
a normal cabbage by cutting off the top
before the head has formed.)

Some authors have referred to the
possibility that they were known in classical
times, and cite stray references from Brussels
in the 13th century and documents about
wedding feasts of the Burgundian court at
Lille in the 15th century. However, sprouts
only became known in French and English
gardens at the end of the 18th century and a
little later in N. America, where Thomas
Jefferson planted some in 1812. Jane Grigson
(1978) comments that in modern times
Brussels sprouts have become quite
prominent in Britain as accompaniments to
the Christmas turkey, game, etc. Having
done some sleuthing in 19th-century cookery
books, she records that:

As far as I have been able to find out, Eliza Acton
was the first in England to give a recipe in her
Modern Cookery of 1845. In fact she gives several
suggestions in one recipe, including the Belgian
style of pouring buttery sauce over them, or
tossing them in butter and a spoonful or two of
veal gravy; she says that this is the Belgian mode as
served in France, which makes one conclude that
she had eaten them when she had spent a year
there as a young girl round about 1820.

The flavour of young sprouts, properly
cooked, is delicate and pleasing. At least one

variety, Rubine Red, has purple leaves and
sprouts, a sweet taste and pleasing flavour.
In Belgium sprouts are traditionally cooked
with peeled chestnuts.

Sprout tops are sold as greens. The flavour
is intermediate between those of cabbage
and of sprouts.

BUCK a term which has some potential
for causing confusion. In Britain it is used to
refer to the male of the fallow DEER and the
roe deer (as distinct from the male of the red
deer, which is called stag). However, the
term is also much used, both in its English
form and in its Dutch spelling *bok*, as a suffix
to the name of various deer and ANTELOPES:
for example roebuck and springbok. When
so used, the name applies equally to the male
and the female of the species. Terms such as
'wild buck', or 'buck' by itself, used in
southern Africa, are to be interpreted in this
last sense.

BUCKWHEAT *Fagopyrum esculentum*, a
plant of the same family as rhubarb, sorrel,
and dock, is grown for its seeds; these
resemble those of cereals. Being hardy,
growing quickly even in unfavourable
conditions and capable of producing two or
even three crops a year, it is most used in
regions with cold climates or poor soils
where true cereals do not grow well. For
many centuries it was a vital food source for
the inhabitants of mountainous regions of
Japan where the climate is too cold, the soil
too poor, and the land too limited for
growing rice. The main producer and
consumer is now the Soviet Union.

The plant bears small clusters of seeds of
a curious shape, triangular in cross-section
with pointed ends. They are named from a
supposed resemblance to beech nuts, which
are also roughly triangular but much larger.
(The name is derived from the Dutch
bockweit, and its literal translation,
'beechwheat', has been used in English.)

There are several species of buckwheat, all
native to temperate E. Asia. The wild
ancestor of the cultivated type is thought to
be perennial buckwheat, *Fagopyrum dibotrys*,
which grows in the Himalayas and China.
From this came the main cultivated species,
brank buckwheat, *F. esculentum*, which may
have originated from Yunnan province, in
S. China. Tartary buckwheat and, to a lesser
extent, notch-seeded buckwheat are
cultivated in mountainous and northern
regions, where they resist the harsh climate
better.

Although buckwheat has certainly been
gathered from the wild for a long time in its
native region, deliberate cultivation may not
be very ancient. The first written records of
the plant are in Chinese documents of the

5th and 6th centuries AD. It appears to have reached Japan from Korea in antiquity and an official chronicle (*Shoku-Nihongi*), completed in 722, contains the earliest known mention of buckwheat in Japanese literature.

Buckwheat reached E. Europe from Russia in the Middle Ages, entering Germany in the 15th century. Later it came to France and Italy where it was known as 'Saracen corn', a name which survives in both languages; and Spain, where a name derived from Arabic was used. For several centuries it was grown as a crop of minor importance in most of Europe, including Britain, but it has now lost popularity in W. Europe. Buckwheat was grown by early European settlers in N. America, and figures in traditional dishes there. Some is also grown in parts of Africa and Brazil.

Buckwheat is similar to a typical cereal in nutritional value. It contains a substance, rutin, which is supposed to be beneficial in cases of high blood pressure.

The **uses** of buckwheat both in the form of husked whole grains and as flour are manifold. The flour, however, is not suitable for making ordinary bread, except when mixed with other cereal flour. It has an unusual flavour which is not universally liked.

The most renowned of all buckwheat dishes is KASHA, a speciality of **Russia and E. Europe.** Whole buckwheat grain may be cooked in the same way as rice, and is also made into sweet, baked puddings. Buckwheat flour is most often made into pancakes, notably the Russian BLINI. Lesley Chamberlain (1989) says that 'Buckwheat flour is widely used in traditional bread and cakes in Slovenia.' In the German-speaking countries of C. Europe *Schmarren*, thick pancakes which are torn up when partly cooked and the shreds browned, are sometimes made from buckwheat, although stale bread is a more usual base (see PANCAKE). Buckwheat pancakes are a traditional N. American breakfast dish. They also appear in the cuisine of N. China.

Buckwheat noodles have been made in China and Russia, but are a particular speciality of **Japan**. There they are called SOBA, which is also the name for buckwheat in its original state. It was only from the 17th century that the Japanese began to use buckwheat for noodles. Previously, it was commonly eaten in other, simpler, forms, such as GRUELS, PORRIDGES, PANCAKES, and DUMPLINGS. The simplest way of eating it had been *sobagaki*, something like Italian POLENTA. Boiling water was poured over the flour, the whole stirred vigorously, and the result eaten at once with SOY SAUCE. *Sobagaki* is still made, always with buckwheat; and some Japanese prefer it to

noodles as being the purest way of eating buckwheat.

The **leaves** of species grown for grain are customarily used for animal fodder, but those of wild perennial buckwheat are cooked as a vegetable in the Himalayas and N. China. In Tibet, and probably elsewhere, they are eaten as a salad green, resembling coarse sorrel.

Buckwheat **flowers** yield an interesting, strongly flavoured, dark HONEY.

BUDDHISM AND FOOD a topic of interest in connection with the cuisines of countries where Buddhism is the or a main religion: Sri Lanka, Burma, Thailand, Laos, Cambodia, and Japan. Although Buddhism began in India, in the 6th century BC, and was at one time the state religion of India, its importance there has greatly diminished.

In common with Hindus, Buddhists believe in reincarnation and that the soul of the human being may have inhabited, or may inhabit in the future, an animal. In principle, therefore, Buddhists abstain from killing or injuring any living creatures, from which it would logically follow that they should all be vegetarians. In practice, abstention from eating meat is strictly observed by monks and devout laymen, but many Buddhists do eat meat.

Buddhist monks, in many Buddhist countries, go out in procession each morning so that people in the neighbourhood can offer them food; and they may not eat any solid food after midday. The goal of Buddhists is the state of perfection called nirvana, and lay people win merit and aid their own progress towards nirvana by feeding the monks. This helps to offset any negative marks acquired from eating flesh. In any case, Buddhists believe that the real wrong consists in killing an animal, not in eating it, so that many Buddhists will eat with a clear conscience meat from an animal which has had a fatal accident, or just died, or been killed by a non-Buddhist. According to Fieldhouse (1986), Buddhists in Thailand—and no doubt elsewhere—see no problem in fishing and eating their catch since the fish are not perceived as being killed, but merely removed from the water.

See also TIBET for further evidence of the flexible and practical ways in which Buddhists interpret for food purposes the requirements of their religion.

BUFFALO an ambiguous term which has been well described/clarified by an FAO book (1977) with a foreword by W. Ross Cockrill, who is an expert on the water-buffalo.

When reference is made to buffaloes, it may be to several different animal species, all of which are called buffaloes. The big-game hunter, for example, may be describing experiences with the ferocious African buffalo; or a North American may be talking of the days of Buffalo Bill and of the vast herds of American bison; but a traveller from the Far East would, undoubtedly, be praising the virtues of the Asian water buffaloes.

The same book explains that within the order of ruminant animals the family Bovidae comprises, besides the tribes of sheep, goats, and antelopes, that of the Bovini. This tribe, in its turn, is divided into three groups: Bovina, (domestic) cattle; Syncerina, the African buffaloes; and Bubalina, the Asian water-buffaloes.

The Bovina group embraces *Bos*, domestic cattle; *Poëphagus*, the YAK; *Bibox*, the banteng, the gaur, and the kouprey; *Bison*, the American bison, *Bison bison*; and the European bison, *Bison bonasus*. The Syncerina group comprises the African buffaloes, of which the Cape buffalo, *Syncerus caffer caffer*, requires mention here, since it constituted a large piece of game, much of which would be turned into BILTONG.

See also BISON and WATER-BUFFALO, which two entries deal with the animals which may be called buffalo and retain interest as food.

READING: Roe (1972, on the N. American buffalo).

BUFFALOBERRY the fruit of the thorny N. American shrub *Shepherdia argentea*, which grows in the dry north-western Great Plains region. The small scarlet berries were a staple food of the region; they become sweet and ready for eating, raw or cooked, after frost. They are also known as silver buffaloberry, rabbit-berry, and Nebraska currant.

These berries are considered to be a fine accompaniment for buffalo steaks or tongue, an affinity which accounts for their common name. They are also used to make drinks and jellies.

The closely related soapberry, sometimes also called russet buffaloberry, is *S. canadensis*. Fernald and Kinsey (1943) observed that these berries were a popular food for Indians, especially in the form of a cream-like foam tinged with red, which could be produced from them and then sweetened. The foam is due to the presence of 'a bitter principle saponin', an interesting echo of what happens with BOIS DE PANAMA. White settlers in Canada, perhaps inspired by the foam, managed to make a beer of these berries.

BUFFALO-FISH *Ictiobus cyprinellus*, the largest member of the sucker family

Catostomidae in N. America, is abundant in shallow waters of lakes in the region of the Great Plains and has some commercial importance. A toothless creature, it feeds on plankton and is usually caught at a weight of 3–5 kg/5–10 lb.

This fish may also be called lake buffalo or blue buffalo, but is correctly termed 'bigmouth buffalo'.

BUFFET a term which may either indicate a sort of sideboard (usually for the display of silver or other tableware or for the setting out of prepared foods); or tables of food set out for guests to help themselves; or a meal for which such an arrangement has been made; or a refreshment room in a railway station (*buffet de la gare* in France); or a railway carriage serving refreshments (buffet car).

In France, a *buffet garni* is a buffet laid out with consideration for artistic as well as gastronomic considerations. Favre (*c.*1905) supposed that the poet Désaugiers was thinking of one such when he penned the lines:

> Aussitôt que la lumière
> Vient éclairer mon chevet,
> Je commence ma carrière
> Par visiter mon buffet.
> A chaque mets que je touche
> Je me crois l'égal des dieux,
> Et ceux qu'épargne ma bouche
> Sont dévorés par mes yeux.

The contrast is extreme between such a scene and what one might witness if present at dawn in the 'buffy-car' of a British railway train. Yet the sharpness of this contrast itself bears witness to the utility of a word which, after an obscure debut in the English language, has elbowed its way firmly into common parlance and now seems irreplaceable.

BULBS of plants are used for food, the obvious example being those of the ONION family. Plants of related families also often have bulbs (or corms: a distinction unimportant to cooks) which are or used to be eaten, especially by N. American Indians and in Asia.

The common lily (*Lilium* spp) exists in many wild forms and cultivated varieties, nearly all of which have edible bulbs, though not all are palatable. Apart from the American Indians, the Japanese make some use of lily bulbs in traditional dishes. They are known as *yurine. Yamayuri* and *oniyuri* are cultivated for the purpose. But there are more important edible plants in the lily family. These include CAMAS, formerly a staple food of the north-west of the USA. Emerson (1908) records that the Tatars of C. Asia took advantage of a mouse, *Mus*

socialis, which had the habit of collecting lily and other bulbs in a cache for its own use. The Tatars would rob the cache.

Asphodel bulbs (*Asphodelus* spp) were eaten in the classical era by Greeks and Romans. They were mainly a food of the poor, but Pliny mentions that when the bulbs were roasted and pounded with oil, salt, and figs they were considered a delicacy. The Bedu still eat these bulbs.

Tulip bulbs, of *Tulipa* spp, have been widely eaten by nomadic tribes in C. Asia, where these plants are native. They are also sometimes used in Italy. During the Second World War the Dutch ate the bulbs of their flowering varieties; see Salzman (1983) and Holthuis (1984) for reports on their palatability. The film star Audrey Hepburn, then a teenager in Utrecht, has recorded how turnips and tulip bulbs helped her to survive in 1945. In this connection it is interesting that Dutch settlers in S. Africa had earlier made a practice of eating various 'bulbs' (mainly corms, as explained below, which they knew by names such as *sanduintjies* and *geeluintjies*). Leipoldt (1976) comments that all the edible *uintjies* are cherry sized, almond white inside, and easily removed from their fibrous husk. 'They taste somewhat like chestnuts and, when boiled have the same crisp consistency, can be mashed easily and blend perfectly with many flavourings.'

A special type, the edible tulip (*Amana edulis*, syn *Tulipa edulis*), is grown in Japan to make starch. *Erythronium japonicum*, a plant of the lily family found in Hokkaido and Honshu and known as *katakuri*, is similarly used; a starch known as *katakuri-ko* is extracted from the bulb. It is of high quality and used for confectionery. Since it is expensive and only a small amount is produced, cheaper and inferior potato flour is used as a substitute and often goes by the same name.

The iris family includes a number of species with edible 'bulbs' (actually, corms). Those of the tiger iris, *Tigridia pavonia*, of C. and S. America have an agreeable chestnut flavour, and are eaten by Indians.

A crocus, *Crocus sativus*, is most notable as the source of SAFFRON, but its corms are often eaten in the poorer parts of Greece and the Levant, where they grow wild; again, they have a nutty flavour.

The corms of many aroids (the arum lily family) are important tropical root crops: see TARO, SURAM, and for tannia, MALANGA.

BULGARIA which might claim to be the heartland of the Balkans, has a capital city, Sofia, which is approximately equidistant from the Adriatic and Black seas, and Istanbul, Athens, and Tirana. At an altitude of 550 m (1,800') and surrounded by

mountains, it is the second highest capital in Europe after Madrid. Three-quarters of the land of Bulgaria lies below 600 m (2,000') and much of it is arable, the remainder consisting of high mountains. Most of the highlands are forested, and above the forests are summer pastures with a large number of sheep.

The Danubian plain, north of the Balkan range, is devoted to the cultivation of cereals, mainly wheat and maize, the rearing of cattle, pigs, and, to a lesser extent, water-buffaloes. Temperate fruits such as apples, pears, cherries, and quinces flourish in most parts of the country, with a predominance of apricots on the banks of the Danube. Along the Black Sea coast and in the lowlands there are almonds, walnuts, chestnuts, figs, and peanuts, whereas cultivation of rice and lentils is confined to the warmest regions of the south. There are no olives or citrus fruits, so they have to be imported. Except for them and some spices, very few foodstuffs are brought into the country, mainly because of the Bulgarian preference for home produce as against imported less-known items, which are often alien to the national taste.

A peculiarity in the general eating pattern is that, historically, Bulgarian consumption of FISH has been one of the lowest in Europe, despite the fact that the country has an outlet on the Black Sea and has rivers and streams which are rich in fish (some of which are luxuries in other parts of Europe). Consumption towards the end of the 20th century increased, but is still low by European standards. Many Bulgarians eat fish, *riba*, only in the months with an 'r' in them, and most are biased against eating fish with milk or yoghurt at the same meal.

Whatever the reason for fish's relatively low priority in the diet, there is no doubt about the Bulgarian enthusiasm for YOGHURT. Two-thirds of the milk output, mostly cow's milk, is sold as plain yoghurt though there are also other sorts. Thick sheep's yoghurt, which can claim a very ancient ancestry, is preferred to any other. Whether or not the ancient Thracians made yoghurt is open to question; but it is certainly true that in the 7th century AD— that is, seven centuries before the incursion of the Ottoman Turks into the Balkan peninsula—a form of yoghurt was already being prepared by the Bulgar-Turks, who used as a starter culture either spontaneously fermented sheep's milk, or sheep's cheese which was creamed with water and mixed with the warm milk. This form of yoghurt, called *katuk*, is still made in highland dairies and many rural areas towards the end of the ewes' lactation period. When ready, the yoghurt is stored for the winter sealed with a protective layer of sheep's butter.

It is interesting that the Bulgar-Turks' cultured milk has survived in an almost unchanged form to the present day. Even more interesting is the fact that although its contemporary Bulgarian name is obviously derived from the Turkish *katik*, meaning 'anything eaten with bread, as a relish', the same term, applied to the same or similar product, was used in the Bashkir, Uzbek, and Tatar republics of the former USSR—a fact which suggests an all-Turkic origin somewhere in the steppes of C. Asia.

A main characteristic of present-day Bulgarian cooking is the widespread use of SUNFLOWER oil rather than animal fats. Sunflower oil has also almost entirely replaced the walnut and sesame cooking oils of the past, as well as the imported olive oil. Lard or butter are sometimes used in stews and pastries, but beef fat is avoided to such an extent that in many households minced beef is first thoroughly defatted and then cooked with sunflower oil.

Another national feature is the delight in red-coloured food and drinks—a trait probably inherited from the so-called Proto-Bulgars (4th century onwards) who used crushed red rock or red clay mixed with red wine as a curative. Red foodstuffs are considered healthy and invigorating; red apples are preferred to green or yellow, and there are many folksongs which eulogize red wine—but never white. When peppers were introduced in the 16th century (the hot chilli type) and the cottage production of ground chilli pepper began, stews took on a crimson glow. A Bulgarian stew, *yahniya* (from Turkish *yahni*), can be meatless, or with meat and vegetables, but it is always red, and always cooked with lots of onion. Long, slow cooking allows the onion to melt and thicken the meat or vegetable juices, giving the stew its quite distinct taste and flavour. Meat stews are often cooked with fruits such as quince. See also GYUVECH.

Minimum frying is an attribute of the old Bulgarian cuisine. The frying technique was almost unknown in the villages before the Turkish conquest, probably because the traditional clay baking dishes could not withstand the high temperature necessary for frying, and copper pans were few and quite expensive. The use of *zapruzhka*, a small stew-enrichment sauce based on fried onion and flour, is a late occurrence of the last hundred years or so. Nearly all fried dishes of modern Bulgarian cookery are adoptions from GREECE, TURKEY, and C. Europe.

As for bread, the *pitka* is noteworthy; this is a large roll or bap-shaped loaf sometimes offered with a saucer of *choubritsa* or *sharena sol. Choubritsa* is a powdered mixture of dried winter SAVORY (*Satureja montana*), cumin, fenugreek, salt, pepper, and occasionally chilli powder. One tears off a piece of *pitka* and dunks the torn surface into the *choubritsa* before eating it. This goes well with fish dishes and also with the *shopska salata*, a salad incorporating mild red peppers, which one should have first.

Turning to another aspect of Bulgarian cooking, it is noticeable that food preparation runs in close harmony with the seasonal cycle which determines the ingredients that enter the pot. Meat of older animals or poultry is cooked with pulses, cabbage, SAUERKRAUT, potatoes, or almost any winter fruit: prunes, dried apricots, and chestnuts. Young animal flesh is combined with spring onion and green garlic, spinach, young broad-bean pods, or tiny peas. The cooking together, for example, of lamb with haricot beans or dried okra is considered an inadmissible culinary blunder.

Traditionally, the lamb-cooking season started in April, on St George's Day. The young chickens of the season were roasted for the first time on St Peter's Day in June. Baked carp stuffed with walnuts was served in December on St Nicholas's Day, roast pork at Christmas, and goose or cock on the first day of January. The practice was based on the ancient Bulgarian solar calendar in which the new year started after day zero (22 December, day one being the shortest day of the year).

Summer is the time for vegetables served in their own right, and also for salads and for uncooked tomato or yoghurt soups. Ice-cold yoghurt drinks, unsweetened compotes, and fresh fruit are then welcome. Cherries, strawberries, grapes, and peaches are brought home from the market in their wooden crates; melons and watermelons, by the cartload, are piled up in the cellar, later to be joined by a couple of barrels of sauerkraut—one of whole cabbages for salad and to provide leaves for stuffing, the other with shredded cabbage for cooking.

Bulgaria is famed for its attar of roses, the liquid gold (see ROSES), as is ROMANIA. For other neighbours see YUGOSLAVIA; MACEDONIA; GREECE; TURKEY.   MK-J

BULLOCK'S HEART the common W. Indian name for the fruit of *Annona reticulata*, a tree native to that region, which thrives in coastal and lowland regions and spread to C. America and S. Mexico in early times. Later, the Portuguese were largely responsible for disseminating it, via Africa, to other tropical areas, and it is now found in such areas all round the world.

The coloration of the fruit (reddish or brownish on the sunny side, dull yellow on the other) and its shape show enough resemblance to the heart of a bullock or other large mammal to justify the W. Indian name; but other names are often used. The fruit is generally regarded as having the best claim to the name CUSTARD APPLE, and this name would have priority if it were not applied in a confusing way to several other species. Other names in use are sweet sop (in contrast to the SOURSOP), and even CHERIMOYA (a misleading error, since the bullock's heart has less flavour than that excellent fruit, and is also inferior to the SUGAR-APPLE).

The size of the fruit varies from 8 to 16 cm (3–6") in diameter, and it may weigh up to 1 kg (over 2 lb). The skin, thin but tough, may be faintly or distinctly 'netted' (hence the term 'netted custard apple' sometimes used). The flesh, which is yellowish-white,

Bullock's heart

has a custard-like and somewhat granular texture. It can be sieved and used in ice cream and milk shakes. If eaten as a dessert fruit, it may need a sprinkling of sugar.

BULLSEYE a traditional British hard boiled sweet, round and with a swirly pattern of brown or black and white. The syrup may be made with brown sugar, cooked to the soft crack stage and divided into unequal parts. The smaller part is pulled to make it white and opaque. The larger is flavoured with an acid mixture, such as lemon juice and tartaric acid, so that it remains a clear brown. The two syrups are recombined briefly, pulled into a strip, cut up, and rolled. Alternatively, separate batches of syrup, one of which is coloured, can be made.   LM

BUMMALOW *Harpadon nehereus*, a fish of the family Harpadontidae and related to LIZARD FISH, belongs to Asian coastal waters and estuaries and especially the west coast of India. It is of considerable commercial importance in India, where it has accounted for as much as 10% of the catch of marine fish. In dried form, when it makes a popular accompaniment for curry-type dishes, it acquired the English name 'Bombay duck', and this has been adopted so widely (even as *bombeidakku* in Japan) that it is now often used as the name of the fish, whether dried or not.

It is a small fish (maximum length about 40 cm/16" but usually caught at about half this size) and pale in colour, almost translucent when alive. The flesh is soft and flaccid, but the fish does not have a soft disposition; on the contrary, it is an active predator, hunting in shoals and using its needle-like teeth to devour small crustaceans.

Although some bummalow are eaten fresh, more than three-quarters of the catch is sun dried, and it is this version which is generally consumed.

BUN a term which has a more restricted meaning in Britain than in the USA, where it simply means a bread roll of some kind, sweet or savoury. British buns are sweeter and richer than plain breads, or than MUFFINS or CRUMPETS. The term has been used in English since the 15th century. It is derived from the old French *bugne*, 'swelling', referring to the bulging shape. The word survives in French for a puffy FRITTER.

The following are a few of the many sorts of bun.

Bath bun. In the 18th century, the original Bath buns were made from a rich, BRIOCHE-like dough, strewn with caraway COMFITS. A similar bun is still made in the Bath area, from a rich yeast dough containing flour, butter, sugar, and eggs shaped into rounds with a lump of sugar under each. After baking, they are sprinkled with crushed lump sugar. Some recipes require candied peel, currants, or sultanas. Eighteenth-century 'Bath cakes' may have been the ancestors of both these and SALLY LUNNS. The popularity of such confections led to Bath buns being much copied, not always with the original delicacy.

Black bun is not a bun; see separate entry.

Chelsea bun, a square bun made from a spiral of yeast dough containing eggs and flavoured with grated lemon peel, ground cinnamon or sweet mixed spice. When the dough has risen for the first time, it is rolled out into a rectangle and a mixture of equal quantities of currants, brown sugar, and butter is spread over it. Folding, rolling, and re-rolling follow and the buns are glazed after being baked. These buns originated in the Bun House of Chelsea, which was built around the beginning of the 18th century. It enjoyed the patronage of the Hanoverian royal family and flourished until its demolition in 1839.

Colston buns, a speciality of Bristol in England, still made in that city, take their name from Sir Edward Colston (1636–1721), a Merchant Venturer. They are based on a lightly enriched yeast dough, flavoured with sweet spices, and contain a little dried fruit and candied peel. The 'dinner-plate size' is marked out into eight wedges; in the 'ha'penny starver' size they are small individual buns.

Hot cross bun, a round bun made from a rich yeast dough containing flour, milk, sugar, butter, eggs, currants, and spices, such as cinnamon, nutmeg, allspice, and cloves. In England, hot cross buns are traditionally eaten on Good Friday; they are marked on top with a cross, either cut in the dough or composed of strips of pastry. The mark is of ancient origin, connected with religious offerings of bread, which replaced earlier, less civilized offerings of blood. The Egyptians offered small round cakes, marked with a representation of the horns of an ox, to the goddess of the moon. The Greeks and Romans had similar practices, and the Saxons ate buns marked with a cross in honour of the goddess of light, Eostre, whose name was transferred to Easter. According to superstition, hot cross buns and loaves baked on Good Friday never went mouldy, and were sometimes kept as charms from one year to the next. Like Chelsea buns, hot cross buns were sold in great quantities by the Chelsea Bun House; in the 18th century large numbers of people flocked to Chelsea during the Easter period expressly to visit this establishment.

London bun, a finger-shaped bun made from a rich yeast dough which may include currants, and sometimes caraway seeds. The bun is topped with white sugar icing after baking. The way in which the icing spreads out prompted an alternative name, 'candlegrease buns'.

Saffron bun, made from the same dough as is used to make the bread called 'saffron cake'. Saffron was also an ingredient in Devonshire revel buns, an old variety served on special occasions such as revels. They were made from a rich yeast dough, contained currants, were additionally flavoured with cinnamon or nutmeg, and were sprinkled with powdered sugar after baking. Florence White (1932) explains that a revel was 'an anniversary feast to celebrate the dedication of a church', and says that the buns were traditionally baked on sycamore leaves.   (LM)

BURAN the nickname of the wife of a 9th-century caliph of Baghdad, has evolved from a special dish served at her wedding into a whole family of dishes which have found their way to many parts of the world. Thus the memory of the Princess, who died in 884, is honoured every day on many thousands of tables. Her name and the vegetable here called eggplant (but described under AUBERGINE) have become inextricably linked.

The story is of exceptional interest. First, her wedding celebrations were of fabulous magnificence. Secondly, the dish named for her and its descendants are a virtually unique case of a dish whose history can be traced from the date of its introduction over a period of 1,000 years. We can watch with unusual clarity the evolutionary processes that affect a dish over the centuries as it spreads thousands of miles into new physical and social settings.

To return to the wedding, the Caliph al-Mamun (son of Harun al-Rashid) was the bridegroom, and he had a remarkable surprise when he arrived at the wedding palace which had been specially erected for the occasion. He was led to a tray of woven gold, and as he stood on it, all unsuspecting, a thousand pearls were poured over his head. And this was merely for the sake of a literary reference: the court poet had once compared the bubbly surface of a glass of white wine to 'pearls scattered like pebbles on a field of gold'. That set the tone and scale of the celebrations. The party began during RAMADAN, the month when Muslims fast during the daylight hours and celebrate with all-night feasts, and lasted the better part of a month.

The wedding food must have been supremely lavish but no record of it survives. However, by the middle of the 10th century the poet Kushajam refers to a dish named for Buran, *badhinjan buran*. This means 'Buran's eggplant', and *The Book of Dishes*, written in the 10th century by a friend of the poet, gives two recipes for it. The recipes look rather pedestrian to us: eggplant slices salted and then fried with flavourings. However, it is reasonable to suppose that the dishes had been served at the wedding feast or were otherwise intimately associated with the Princess. At that point in history, eggplants were exotic newcomers from India, known under a name of Indian origin, *badhinjan*, that was to give rise to the name of the vegetable in most European languages: Spanish *berenjena*, Italian *melanzane*, French aubergine. In the 10th century its place in the kitchen and on the table was still precarious. Indeed, in some quarters it met scorn and hostility. In one 11th-century anecdote a Bedouin was asked, 'What do you say of eggplant cooked by Buran?' He replied, 'Even if Mary the mother of Jesus split it and Sarah the wife of Abraham cooked it and Fatimah the daughter of the Prophet served it, I would have no taste for it.' Perhaps the bitter taste accounted for this in part. The plain-looking 10th-century recipes contain an innovation after all—the salting, which leaches out some of the eggplant's bitterness. Whatever the reason, this eggplant dish spread to all the medieval Islamic lands and Buran's name has been applied to a vast range of dishes descended from it, in Spain and the Balkans as well as the Islamic heartland that extends from Morocco to India.

By the 13th century, the dish had become *buraniyyah* ('Buran stew'), in conformity with the usual way of naming dishes and perhaps because meat had now been added. Arabic cookery manuscripts from Spain show several variations on the theme of fried eggplant with stewed meat. This theme is still familiar in Morocco and Algeria, where *braniya* remains a popular dish; and it was alive in Syria as recently as the 15th century. However, as early as the 13th century, *buranniyah* had begun the process of differentiation that commonly happens to popular dishes; it had started to become a category of dishes.

The first recorded example of this differentiation is a recipe, probably from Iraq, for 'buranniyah of gourd' (in a compilation whose title translates as *The Book of Familiar Foods*, 17th century). The other elements of the dish had already changed. Now the 'lead ingredient' itself was removed; eggplant was changed to gourd. The door was open for the invention of new *buraniyyahs* made with other vegetables. The result can be seen in modern Egypt and Syria, where a dish called burani is made with zucchini, spinach, mallow, or other vegetables (but not with eggplant, which had meanwhile become the main ingredient in a whole array of new recipes which caused the old eggplant *burani* to be forgotten).

Differentiation proceeded elsewhere, on radical lines, and in a manner reminiscent of the adaptive radiation by which one species of bird (such as Darwin's finches in the Galapagos) may spread into and adapt itself to new environments, being transformed after a score of generations into birds so different that they are classified as new species. *Buraniyyah*, as it spread, met and reacted to various cultures and different religious needs, including the preoccupation in Christian areas with meatless dishes for fast days. It is tempting to suppose that Christianity brought about the vegetarian *boronía* of Spain and the vegetarian but otherwise entirely different *buranija/borani* of the Balkans.

Be that as it may, we can reconstruct the family tree of this dish as follows. A fried eggplant dish is introduced to the Islamic world and is soon enriched with meat. A meatless form survives in Spain; the version with meat survives unchanged in N. Africa and as a category of meat and vegetable dishes (but not using eggplant) in Egypt and Syria. The Balkans follow a recipe probably developed in Turkey from eggplantless dishes of the Syrian type by the addition of wheat or rice, which can be replaced in Bulgaria and (former) Yugoslavia by green beans.

This 'tree' has to be completed by a description of what is perhaps the most distinctive new 'species' in the family, an Iranian dish with yoghurt. We find it mentioned in the writings of a 14th-century Persian food poet named Abu Ishaq of Shiraz: a dish of fried eggplant dressed with sour milk products. This is the ubiquitous *Borani-ye-bademjan* of Iran, also found in Iraq, Georgia, Armenia, Afghanistan, Pakistan, and India. Against the background described above, it will be no surprise to hear that this in turn has differentiated into a broad category of (usually cold) vegetable dishes dressed with yoghurt. These may be made with chard, squash, spinach, beets, lentils, cardoon, or beans, and occur in Iran, Armenia, and Turkey.   CP

READING: Perry (1984).

BURBOT *Lota lota*, the only freshwater species of the COD family, has a range which extends right round the northern regions of the northern hemisphere. It can tolerate brackish waters, and is thus found in the Finnish archipelagos of the E. Baltic. Maximum length (reported from Siberia) 125 cm (50"), but specimens in the markets are unlikely to exceed a third of this length and will weigh 500 g (18 oz) or less. Coloration is drab, except for the so-called 'golden burbot', which are reddish yellow.

Burbot have firm tasty flesh, so make good eating. The liver is reputedly a delicacy and the eggs are sold as a form of 'caviar' in some places.

BURDOCK *Arctium lappa*, a plant of the daisy family, Compositae, which, with its smaller relation *A. minus*, is common all over the northern temperate zone, and which furnishes edible roots. These are long (up to 120 cm/4' in length) and usually slender (around 4 cm/1.5" in width).

A. lappa is the popular vegetable *gobo* of Japan, the only country where it is eaten on a large scale, although it enjoys some popularity in Hawaii, where the Japanese introduced it. In Japan, a distinction is made between two forms, one with green and one with purplish stalks. The varieties most esteemed are Ouragobo, from Oura near Tokyo, and Horikawagobo, an old favourite from Horikawa near Kyoto. The root of the former is unusual in being thick, short, and hollow inside.

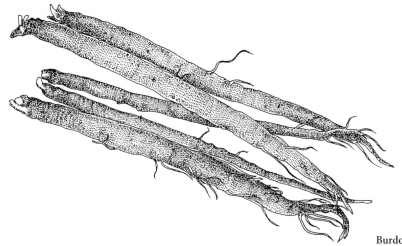

Burdock

The Japanese do not often cook *gobo* as a vegetable in its own right, preferring to combine it with other vegetables. However, *Kinpira* is a well-known dish in which slices of burdock and carrot are lightly fried, then cooked with sugar and soy sauce and sprinkled with sesame seeds: a New Year dish and a popular item for lunch boxes.

Not only the root but also the inside part of the young shoot is edible. Gerard's *Herbal* (1633), referring to the plant as 'clot-burre', said of the young shoot: 'The rind peelld off, [it] being eaten with salt and pepper, or boyled in the broth of fat meate, is pleasant to be eaten.' The instruction to peel off the rind is important, since it is bitter. Burdock is still used on a small scale in Britain: the root is used to flavour 'dandelion and burdock', a soft drink akin to the better known American ROOT BEER. American Indians also ate burdock roots and shoots. Wild burdock root resembles salsify but is slightly bitter, so has to be boiled in two changes of water. The shoot is not unlike asparagus, and can be successfully candied.

BURGHUL also known as bulgur/bulgar and as cracked wheat, is a product made by parboiling WHEAT, parching it to dry it, and coarsely grinding it. The outer layers of bran are then removed (by sprinkling the dried wheat with water and rubbing by hand) and the grains cracked. The result, burghul, is prepared for eating by steaming or boiling, and has a distinctively nutty taste, due to the inner layers of bran. It may be served like rice, for example in making a PILAF; or combined with minced meat in the various kinds of MEATBALL or CROQUETTE popular in the Near East (see KOFTA); or used as the basis of TABBOULEH, in which it is mixed with parsley, onion, garlic, mint, oil, lemon juice; or used in KIBBEH, another important dish of the Near East.

Aykroyd and Doughty (1970) state that the above method of preparing wheat 'is an old one, followed mainly in the areas of W. Asia and N. Africa, where wheat has long been cultivated'. Burghul (from the Turkish *bulgur*, from Persian) has also been a staple food in the Balkans since the 14th century, when it was introduced by the Ottoman Turks.

Abdalla (1990) has given a full account of burghul from the point of view of Assyrians, including what may be the most detailed published account of its production, the songs sung while this is going on, etc.

BURMA which achieved independence in 1948 with the end of British rule, includes many different ethnic and cultural groups, in particular the Burmans, the Shans, the Chins, and the Mons. It has five terrestrial neighbours (INDIA, BANGLADESH, CHINA, LAOS, THAILAND) as well as a long sea coast. Important food crops include RICE and SUGAR CANE.

The similarity between the cuisines of Burma and Thailand is noticeable. However, it is Burma's two big neighbours, India and China, which have probably exerted the greatest influence on Burmese cooking. This dual effect is symbolized by the choice which Burmese cooks frequently exercise between 'Indian curry power' (*garam masala*) and 'Chinese curry powder'. Indeed, the Indian influence is perhaps most apparent in the form of aromatic seasonings and CURRY dishes. From China have come many rice and NOODLE dishes, SOY SAUCE, and dried mushrooms; pungent fermented fish seasonings, described below, may well derive from the Vietnamese tradition of FISH SAUCE, although fish sauces are omnipresent in the region and probably had no single point of origin.

Rice is the staple food of the Burmese and is served piping hot at every meal even though the other dishes such as curries may be served at room temperature. The rice is preferred cooked moist, fluffy, and just sticky enough to hold together when eating as the traditional method of eating is with the fingers. A Burmese dish called *Htamin lethoke* literally means rice mixed with the fingers. And rice noodles are one of the fundamental ingredients in the national dish, MOHINGA.

Other ways of cooking rice again illustrate the dual influences of India and China. *Danbauk* or PILAF rice cooked with GHEE, instead of the peanut (see GROUNDNUT or SESAME oil which are Burmese staples (peanut for frying, sesame for other purposes), is of Indian and Muslim origin; while fried rice, as a one-dish meal, more or less as found throughout SE Asia, is of Chinese origin.

Other noodles are also popular and are available dried or fresh and are generally used as a base for curries. A festive Burmese dish called *Oh-no kauk-swe* is made with chicken and noodles and richly flavoured with coconut milk curry.

LEMON GRASS is one of the most popular flavourings, and GINGER is another. There are also a number of prepared condiments, of which several are essential to the Burmese table. *Ngapi* is the basic fish paste of the country and comes in forms which vary according to the fish (or other seafood) used and the techniques of fermentation. *Ngan-pya-ye* is a fermented liquid FISH SAUCE, and is a staple ingredient. So is *balachaung*, a powerful home-made condiment with an intense flavour; this is a paste of very finely shredded dried SHRIMP, garlic, ginger, turmeric, a little added shrimp paste, onion, and sesame oil (see BLACANG).

Although these staple condiments are firmly based on seafood, the general Burmese attitude to sea FISH is surprisingly unenthusiastic. Freshwater fish are greatly preferred. When marine fish are eaten, their smell of the sea is masked by the use of turmeric and ginger.

Davidson (1977), after discussing the matter with senior fishery officials in Rangoon, offered the following analysis of the Burmese mistrust of seafood:

Sea fish, some believe, have a soporific effect on people who eat them; a belief which I have not met elsewhere, but which is entitled to sympathetic examination by any research worker who can devise methods of testing the hypothesis. A more widespread belief is that eating sea fish upsets people, making them nervous and agitated. For that reason invalids and pregnant women are expected to eat freshwater fish only.

Among the interesting dishes which the Burmese make with freshwater fish is one described by Mi Mi Khaing (1978) for stuffed fish from Inle Lake. The author explains that this lake is

one of Burma's scenic attractions. Across its wide expanse are semi-aquatic villages where floating island gardens are built by towing bits of vegetative land and staking them in place. The rowing of people here is renowned. Men, women, and children use a leg to row with when their arms get tired. They stand straight at the prow, wrap one leg around the oar, and row. They catch delicious carp called *ngapein* for this recipe.

The stuffing for the fish includes the roe and typical Burmese spices and condiments, plus marigold leaves—an unusual touch. Another recipe for carp, or in this instance catfish, is for what the author translates as Kneaded fish rice.

A one-dish meal, this is sold at five-day bazaar meets in the Shan uplands. A strong-fingered man sits cross-legged: around him basins of cooked fish, rice, and flavoring ingredients. He debones, kneads hard, mixes rapidly, dresses, and serves each portion on a counter at which the queue sits on haunches. As in all Shan areas, hot tea and chillies are on the house, with buffalo skin crisps and garlicky shoots as extras.

In the realm of sweet dishes the Burmese have much to offer. Mi Mi Khaing explains that the categorization to which western cooks are accustomed is different from the Burmese one. There, a super-category of tongue-twisting complexity exists; in English it comes out as 'Confections-Desserts-Salivators-Tongue Titillators'. The point is that it groups along with desserts and confectionery those other items which the Burmese call *thayesa*, 'foods for salivary juices', nibbles which are eaten at any time, to relieve hunger or boredom.

Although the dish of pickled tea leaf, *lepet* (or *lephet*), is often called a salad it is really a dessert and is always eaten after a meal. It is very important in the Burmese cultural structure. Aung Aung Taik (1993) describes how *lepet* is made:

by lightly steaming young tea leaves and then pressing them tightly into clay vessels or large bamboo stems and storing the containers in the ground, preferably close to a river bed to ensure a steady temperature.

Lepet is usually served with tea, from a special lacquer box. Inside the box are different compartments filled with *lepet*, fried garlic, toasted sesame seeds, fried broad beans, and salt. Very beautiful *lepet* salvers were formerly made for court use. At the other end of the scale, an ordinary tin plate may be used for the *lepet* served at village meetings, for which it acts as a stimulant as well as a mark of occasion. For those who have had a rich meal and take *lepet* afterwards, it serves to clear the palate into sweetness and, again, to stimulate.

The Burmese resemble other Asians in being enthusiastic snackers, with ample provision of snack stalls. There are also plenty of tea houses; the Burmese like their tea strong, sweet, and served with milk.

(HS)

BURNET the name for two common European herbs which bear dark crimson or deep brown flowers; hence the name, which is derived from the French *brunette*.

Salad burnet, *Sanguisorba minor* (syn *Poterium sanguisorba*), is the species usually cultivated in gardens. Its leaves, which have a pleasant cucumber flavour, have been eaten since classical Greek times and were commonly used in salads from the 15th to 19th centuries. In recent times they have still been used, as *ensalada italiana* in Spain, especially Catalonia. They are also added to drinks in the same way as the better-known BORAGE.

Great burnet, *Sanguisorba officinalis*, is a larger plant of similar uses.

BURRINI also called manteche, are pear-shaped Italian cheeses, each of which encloses a centre of fresh butter (*burro* or *manteca* being the Italian for butter). This, being sealed from the air, does not go rancid, but does acquire a cheesy flavour.

Burrini, with bread, make a popular snack. They are found throughout the south of Italy, but especially in Calabria and Puglia, in the regions where CACIOCAVALLO and PROVOLONE are produced. They may be regarded as an offshoot of the latter cheese, since their cheese coats are made by the same process.

These are small cheeses, typically weighing from 100 to 300 g (3.5 to 11 oz). They are made in pairs tied together with string, so that they can be hung over rods to dry. This

has led to their being given the nickname *testicoli du mulo* (mule's testicles).

BUSH BUTTER (tree), *Dacryodes edulis*, which grows in tropical Africa and is occasionally cultivated, is also known as African or native pear, *safu*, and *eben*. Facciola (1990) observes that the purple plum-sized fruit

is eaten raw, roasted, boiled, or with curries. When placed in hot water it softens and swells, and all the flesh then slides easily off the seed. It is usually salted and tastes like a warmed ripe avocado, with a slight sour flavour. Has a 7% protein content, which is high for a fruit.

BUSHPIG *Potamochoerus porcus*, an African animal which belongs to the pig family, Suidae, and is related to the larger WARTHOG. The bushpig is also known as Red River hog in W. Africa and sometimes as *bosvark* in S. Africa.

The meat of this animal, like that of the warthog, can be cooked like pork but does not taste like pork.

BUSTARD the name for birds of the genus *Otis*, which come in two sizes, large and little. Even the little bustard, *O. tetrax*, is a large bird, but the great bustard, *O. tarda*, is very large indeed—measuring 1 m (40") from tip of beak to end of tail, and having a wing span of around 150 cm (60").

Bustards frequent steppes and open plains, and spend more time walking than flying. Both species have wandered north to Britain and Scandinavia, but belong more to S. Europe, N. Africa, and the Near East. They have anyway become rare. Brand (1859) recalled that earlier in the 19th century these birds 'were bred in the open parts of Norfolk and Suffolk, and were domesticated at Norwich. Their flesh was delicious, and it was thought that good feeding and domestication might stimulate them to lay more eggs; but this was not the case.'

BUTTER is made from cream which is further concentrated so that the final product is more than 80% fat. In this form it keeps for longer than fresh milk or cream, and has therefore been used since antiquity (although not everywhere—the ancient Greeks, whose usual cooking medium was olive oil, seem not to have used butter except as an ointment).

Butter is made not only from cow's milk but from WATER-BUFFALO's milk in India, and sheep's milk in various parts of Asia. It is only exceptionally made from CAMEL's milk. Milk from the dri (female YAK) is rich

in butterfat; and that from a *dzomo* (yak/cow hybrid) can also be used.

Structurally, butter is a water-in-oil EMULSION. It is made from CREAM, which is an oil-in-water emulsion containing, in the richest grades, over 40% fat (the words 'fat' and 'oil' are interchangeable in this context). When cream is churned, by some kind of revolving paddle, this disturbs the emulsion, forcing the fat globules together until they join up into a continuous mass with water droplets trapped in it. Much of the water, with milk sugar dissolved and proteins dispersed in it, is forced out in the form of BUTTERMILK.

Most butter is made from cream which has 'ripened' by the action of lactic acid-producing BACTERIA, which are present naturally in unpasteurized milk and cream. Since one can never be certain that the right bacteria are there in adequate strength, it is usual to add starter cultures of bacteria chosen to produce substances which give desirable flavours. *Streptococcus* spp, in addition to fermenting the lactose (milk sugar) to lactic acid, convert the citrates in milk to diacetyl and acetyl methyl carbinol, of which the first is a major and the second a minor contributor to butter flavour. *Leuconostoc* spp also produce acid and other flavouring substances such as alcohols and esters. Some of the latter, the delta lactones, are the chief factors in the flavour of foods cooked in butter. Butter made from unripened cream is called 'sweet cream butter' and has less flavour.

Naturally, butter from different species of animal differs in flavour, but another effect comes from the diet of the animal, in particular from aromatic herbs. This is why butter from certain areas, for example Normandy, has such a high reputation.

After churning, the butter is further worked, and also washed in plain water, to remove as much of the buttermilk as possible and improve the texture and flavour. (Most of the lactic acid is in the buttermilk and if it were all retained the butter would taste too sour.) This also improves keeping quality, as does the addition of salt, which discourages the growth of bacteria.

Butter, whether salted or not, is not a fully preserved food; indeed, it begins to deteriorate (albeit slowly) at once. The fat is broken down by oxidation (the effect of the oxygen in the air) and hydrolysis (the effect of the water) so that it becomes rancid. One way of making butter keep longer is to clarify it: that is, to remove all the water. This is done by heating it gently so that the emulsion breaks down and the fat rises to the top of the water. The fat may then be left to solidify and be lifted off the water, or, more usually, the water evaporated by continued heating. The latter method is the one used to make GHEE. The prolonged heating develops a slightly burnt taste, caused by reactions between the small amounts of proteins and sugar remaining in butter from the original milk; but the taste is quite pleasant. The heat also completely eliminates bacteria, further improving keeping quality.

Butter is a fine cooking medium; the excellent flavour which it imparts to food is matched by no oil or other fat. This is due partly to lactones, as mentioned, and partly to protein-sugar reactions brought about by heating. These reactions also give an attractive brown colour to food cooked in butter. However, butter stands up to heat less well than oils; if it is overheated, protein breakdown goes too far, resulting in a strong burnt taste and too dark a colour. (This problem is lessened by mixing butter half and half with oil, or by using ghee.)

Butter has a lower melting point than hard white fats such as lard and hardened vegetable cooking fat. It is therefore more difficult to make good PASTRY with butter than with these fats. Moreover, the latter also have larger fat crystals, better able to hold the flour grains well apart and prevent them from coalescing into a dense mass. Despite this, butter's superior flavour balances its disadvantages in other ways and it is often used for rich shortcrust, and almost always for the flaky and puff varieties.

BUTTERED EGGS a method of preserving freshly laid eggs by rolling them in fresh butter in the palms of the hands. The process is associated especially with the Cork region in S. Ireland. The butter is absorbed quickly into the hot porous egg shell. When the egg cools, the hardened, buttered shell acts as a barrier against the absorption of air into the egg cavity. The sealed shell will keep the egg fresh for up to six months. Eggs preserved in this way have a shiny and polished appearance, whilst the cooked egg has a buttery flavour.

This preservation technique was devised to ensure a winter supply of eggs, when the hen's laying potential was at its lowest. In Ireland the religious custom of abstaining from egg-eating during Lent and the associated ritual of saving them for the Easter Sunday egg feast may also encourage this process of preservation. During the two World Wars the demand for buttered eggs in Ireland was particularly high because fresh eggs were rationed and the only ones available in abundance were of the buttered variety.

In other contexts, and especially in older books, 'buttered eggs' may refer to scrambled eggs.   RSe

BUTTERFLY PEA also called *anjan* or *anchan*, is *Clitoria ternatea*, a leguminous plant described by Charmaine Solomon (1996) as:

A vivid cobalt-blue pea flower native to tropical regions, which yields a blue dye when crushed in water. Used to colour sweets and cakes in Malaysia, Singapore and Thailand. Particularly spectacular are the blue tapioca and rice flour, pork-filled dumplings from Thailand called *chor lada*, sometimes shaped like flowers.

The Malay name is *bunga biru*, meaning 'blue flower'.

BUTTERMILK was originally the liquid squeezed out when cream was churned to make BUTTER. In composition it resembled a light, skimmed milk; but it was also mildly sour as a result of the 'ripening' of the CREAM to make butter.

Buttermilk was drunk in N. Europe throughout the Middle Ages; and in Britain it was for many centuries a 'perk' of shepherds and dairymaids. In the 17th century, and on into the 18th, both buttermilk and WHEY became fashionable city drinks (being drunk by the diarist Pepys, for instance, in 1664).

In recent times, after a long period when buttermilk was in low esteem, more people have come to regard it as a healthful alternative to ordinary milk, having much less fat. Its slightly sour taste is seen as an attraction: less cloying than whole milk and more interesting than plain skimmed milk.

If buttermilk is strained, it yields some CURDS which are put to various uses in e.g. C. Asia, the Middle East, and Scandinavia. See KASHK. In the Netherlands buttermilk is hung up in a cloth until all the whey has drained, and then eaten on a rusk with sugar and cinnamon. This is called *hangop*.

Meanwhile, however, much of the available buttermilk had come to be used for making into other food products and was no longer available for sale as buttermilk. What is now sold as 'cultured buttermilk' is actually ordinary skimmed milk which has been slightly fermented with cultures of the same organisms as those which 'ripen' the cream for butter. Subsequently, it is heat treated to kill the bacteria and stop fermentation, so it cannot be used for any purposes which require 'live' buttermilk, although it is perfectly effective in many recipes, e.g. for making scones.

BUTTERSCOTCH a very crisp form of TOFFEE containing butter, and sometimes also milk or cream. The quantity of butter in formulae used by various manufacturers differs, but, by law, any product made in the UK which includes the word 'butter' in the name must contain at least 4% butterfat in

the finished item. Salted butter is usually stipulated, and oil of lemon added as a flavouring.

The origin of the name is unknown, but it does not appear to have any direct link with Scotland.   LM

.

BYZANTINE COOKERY Constantine I, the first Christian emperor of Rome (306–37), established his new eastern capital at a site that was unrivalled for its beauty and unmatched as a centre for administration and commerce. The Greek colony of Byzantion had prospered on its exports of tuna, mackerel, and other Black Sea produce. Now renamed Constantinopolis, it was destined to rule the later Roman ('Byzantine') Empire for 1,100 years. After the Turkish conquest in 1453 Constantinople (Istanbul) would be the Ottoman capital for nearly 500 years more.

The civilization of Constantinople is now sometimes seen as a poor imitation of that of CLASSICAL GREECE, and of CLASSICAL ROME. Its life and culture, like those of most other societies, did indeed arise from a synthesis of what had gone before: a synthesis that continued to develop and did not cease to innovate.

This is certainly true of Byzantine cuisine. Dried meat, a forerunner of the *pastirma* of modern Turkey, became a delicacy. Among favoured game were gazelles of inland Anatolia, '*dorkádes* commonly called *gazélia*'; wild asses, of which herds were maintained in imperial parks; and sparrows. Turning to seafood, the Byzantines appreciated salt roe, *oiotárikhon* (literally 'egg pickle'; hence the modern term *botargo*, see BOUTARGUE); by the 12th century they had tasted CAVIAR, *kabiári*, the new fish delicacy of the Black Sea. Still later they imported kippered herrings, *réngai*, from distant Britain. Fruits unknown to the classical menu included the aubergine and the orange.

New dishes multiplied; old recipes were adapted to new tastes. Where ancient cooks had wrapped food in pickled fig leaves, *thrîa*, it was in Byzantine times that stuffed vine leaves were used in these recipes, which thus become the parents of modern *dolmádhes* (see DOLMA). Vinegar flavoured with squill (also known as 'sea onion', *Urginea maritima*) was a favourite condiment. It was probably the Byzantines who first tried ROSEMARY as a flavouring for roast lamb, and who first used SAFFRON in cookery: both these aromatics, well known in the ancient world, had not previously been thought of as food ingredients. NUTMEG was sprinkled on the PEASE PUDDING that was a fast-day staple.

Cheeses included *mízithra* (produced by the pastoralist Vlachs of Thessaly and Macedonia) and *prósphatos* (FETA, the marketing of which in Crete in late Byzantine times is described by an Italian pilgrim, Pietro Casola). As for bread, the bakers of Constantinople were in the most favoured of trades, according to a 9th-century code: 'bakers are never liable to be called for any public service, neither themselves nor their animals, to prevent any interruption of the baking of bread.'

It is among sweets and sweet drinks that we can best sense the distinctive flavour of Byzantine cookery. There are dishes that we would recognize as puddings; *groûta*, a sort of FRUMENTY, sweetened with honey and studded with CAROB seeds or raisins; rice pudding served with honey. QUINCE marmalade had already entered the repertoire, but other jams or conserves now made their appearance, including pear and citron or lemon. The increasing availability of SUGAR (*sákhar*) assisted the confectioner's inventiveness. Rose sugar, a popular medieval confection, may well have originated in Byzantium.

Flavoured soft drinks (required on fast days) and flavoured wines became popular: the ones flavoured with mastic, aniseed, rose, and absinthe were especially well known, alongside the spiced wine known by its Latin name *konditon*. They are distant ancestors of the *mastikha*, vermouth, absinthe, and pastis of the modern Mediterranean. A remarkable range of aromatics, unknown to earlier inhabitants of the region except as perfumes or in medicines, belonged to the liquid diet of Byzantium: spikenard, gentian, *tejpat*, gum benzoin, camomile, and violet were among the ingredients in these concoctions.

Two influences combined to produce the great range of powerful flavours that we can sense at the heart of Byzantine cuisine. One was the Church calendar, with its numerous fast days (see FASTING) on which both meat and fish were ruled out: the rich (including rich abbots and ecclesiastics) gave their cooks full rein to produce fast-day dishes as piquant and varied as could be conceived. The second influence was that of dietitians. By contrast with earlier dietary manuals, the Byzantine ones were written for non-specialists. The effect of each ingredient on the FOUR HUMOURS had been codified; the desired balance must be maintained by a correct choice of dish and by a correct adjustment of ingredients, varying for the seasons, the weather, the time of day, and each individual's constitution and state of health. Dietitians sometimes recommended vegetarian meals, eaten with vinegar or other dressing. Spices and seasonings became ubiquitous, used both during the cooking process and at table to amend the qualities of each dish. Fresh figs, if eaten in July, must be taken with salt. A daily glass of *konditon*, strong in spikenard, was recommended in March: anise wine was appropriate for April. The dietary manuals are important sources of culinary history: *botargo* is first mentioned in the 11th century by Simeon Seth, who said that it 'should be avoided totally'!

Annual fairs were a focus for the food trade: important fairs were held at Thessalonica and Constantinople around St Demetrius' Day. Constantinople was a place for specialized food markets. Sheep and cattle were driven to market here from pastures far away in the Balkans, and eastern spices followed long-established trade routes through Trebizond, Mosul, and Alexandria. The populist emperor Manuel (1143–80) liked to sample the hot street food of the capital, paying the proper price and waiting for the change like any other citizen.

Medieval travellers to Byzantium did not always like the strange flavours they encountered. *Gáros*, the venerable FISH SAUCE, was still much used and was an acquired taste. Most foreigners and even some Byzantines disapproved of retsina: 'undrinkable', said Liutprand of Cremona, snootily, in the 10th century. If we had had to rely solely on this supercilious commentator, we would never have known of the range of Byzantine meat and fish dishes—roast pork basted with honey wine, skate spiced with caraway, wild duck with its sauce of wine, *gáros*, mustard, and cumin-salt; and we would never have heard of calavance (certain kinds of PULSE) cooked in honey vinegar. But even strangers were seduced by the confectionery, the candied fruits, and the sweet wines. William of Rubruck, a 13th-century diplomatic traveller, looking for worthwhile presents to take from Constantinople to wild Khazaria, chose fruit, muscat wine, and fine biscuits.

The food of the poor of Constantinople was no doubt limited, though a poetic catalogue of a poor family's larder (*Prodromic Poems* 2. 38–45) includes numerous vegetables and locally grown fruits along with a considerable list of flavourings: vinegar, honey, pepper, cinnamon, cumin, caraway, salt, and others. Cheese, olives, and onions made up for any scarcity of meat. *Timarion*, another satirical poem of the 12th century, offers a salt pork and cabbage stew as a typical poor man's meal, eaten from the bowl with the fingers just as in contemporary W. Europe. The basic food of the Byzantine army was cereal, whether as loaves, biscuits, or porridge. The future emperor Justin II (518–27) had nothing but army biscuits to keep him alive on his long walk from Illyria to Constantinople in 470. This barley biscuit, *paximádion*—still known in the Greek countryside today under that name (see PAXIMADIA and Aglaia Kremezi, 1997)—has many descendants: it is Arabic *bashmat*, *baqsimat*, Turkish *beksemad*, Serbo-Croat *peksimet*, Romanian *pesmet*, and Venetian *pasimata*.

Inns and wine shops generally provided only basic fare: though it is in a 6th-century Byzantine source, the Life of St Theodore of Syceon, that we hear for the first time anywhere in the world of an inn that attracted customers by the quality of its food.

The cuisine of the Byzantine Empire had a unique character of its own, though it is difficult now to reconstruct. It forms a bridge between the ancient world and the food of modern Greece and Turkey.   AD
READING: Dalby (1996).

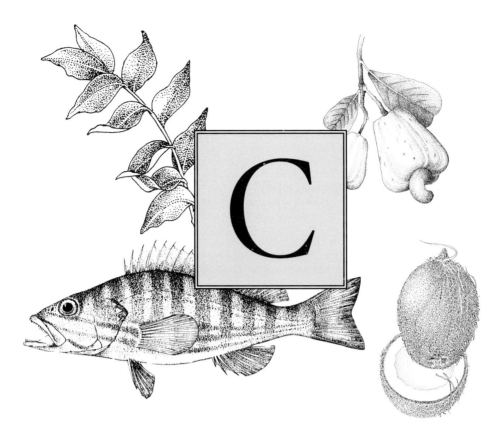

CABBAGE *Brassica oleracea*, var *capitata*, the first cultivated vegetable in the diverse genus *Brassica*, is the ancestor of most of its numerous relations such as CAULIFLOWER and BRUSSELS SPROUTS.

The original wild plant, known as wild or sea cabbage, still grows in some coastal areas of Europe, is occasionally gathered and eaten, and has a cabbagy flavour. However, it is a spindly plant with few leaves and no 'head'. Indeed, it is more like KALE, another of its descendants. Other wild brassicas grow around the eastern end of the Mediterranean and in the Balearic Isles. These and the wild ancestors of our mustard plants were no doubt interbred with wild cabbage during the early stages of its cultivation.

Cabbage has been highly valued as a food since the time of the ancient Egyptians. From surviving pictures and reliefs it is clear that Egyptian cabbage was headless. The Greeks, too, cultivated headless cabbages and invested them with a religious significance. They ascribed the origin of cabbage to the chief of the gods, Zeus, believing that when he was earnestly trying to explain two conflicting prophecies, he worked himself into a sweat and that from

this sweat sprang cabbage. There may be some connection here with the strong smell of cooking cabbage.

Both the Greeks and the Romans thought cabbage a very healthy food, which it is; and a protection against drunkenness, which it is not. A Greek proverb states roundly: 'Cabbage served twice is death.' This sounds sinister but seems to have reflected no more than a dislike of leftovers on the part of people who knew nothing of Bubble and squeak. The saying was used to disparage anything stale or secondhand.

At some time in the 1st century BC the first headed cabbages appeared. The head, an enlarged terminal bud, was at first a small one at the top of a long stem, but Pliny the Elder in the 1st century AD was already writing of a head 30 cm (12") in diameter. He probably knew of this only by hearsay, since the new, headed cabbage is now thought to have evolved in N. Europe, where it later developed into the hard, white 'Dutch' or 'drumhead' varieties. But it was not until well into the Middle Ages that headed cabbages spread throughout Europe to supplement the staple 'colewort' or KALE.

Cabbage arrived in N. America in 1541, on the occasion of the third voyage of Jacques Cartier, but the first written record of its being planted in what is now the USA is dated 1669. The immigrant cabbages came mainly from Germany and the Low Countries, no doubt because German settlers were anxious to make sauerkraut. However, boiled cabbage was established at an early date as a traditional dish in New England, where British connections were dominant.

VARIETIES AND GROUPS
The categorization and nomenclature of brassicas have beeen difficult, and rival systems have found favour at different times. Attempts in the 20th century to introduce order into what is essentially an unruly scene have involved the creation of what are called Groups. By this device, reflected in some of the names below, a main variety of a species can be subdivided at a level higher than that of commercial cultivars.

When new varieties began to be developed, one of the earliest, in the 16th century, was the red cabbage, now classified as *B. oleracea* var *capitata*, Rubra group. It was followed by many types of loose-leafed cabbage, light or dark green and sometimes tinged with red or purple. The increasing number of varieties made it possible to extend the growing season from the first spring greens, picked before a head has formed, to winter's end.

The cabbage which is generally rated the best as a cooked vegetable, the Savoy cabbage, has wrinkled leaves and a loose head. It was a variety separately developed in Italy and probably descended from the old Roman types. It is now classified as var *capitata*, Subanda group.

The most suitable cabbage for SAUERKRAUT is a hard white cabbage, var *capitata*, Capitata group. The same cabbage is also used for COLESLAW. See also KIMCH'I.

One curious survivor from the early days of headed cabbages is the enormously tall Jersey or walking stick cabbage, whose stem is as high as a man and has been recorded as reaching 5 m (16').

Two other types of cabbage stand outside the main line. One is Portugal or Braganza (or Galician) cabbage, also called by its Portuguese name, *couve tronchuda*. This variety, developed well before the 17th century, has no proper head but instead wide, spreading leaves with very thick midribs. It looks rather like seakale, and its ribs may be cooked in the same way. The other outsider is the Kerguelen cabbage, a botanical oddity. It grows only on the Antarctic islands of Kerguelen and Heard, and could not possibly be related to any European cabbage. Yet it closely resembles an ordinary leafy cabbage. It is classified in a separate genus as *Pringlea antiscorbutica*.

CHINESE CABBAGES do not belong to the same species as European brassicas and are treated separately.

The name 'cabbage' is applied to a few other plants of quite different kinds, such as the 'palm cabbage' (see PALM).

COOKING CABBAGE

The smell of cooking cabbage, which few people like, comes from various sulphur compounds. All vegetables contain and give off substances of this type, but those in cabbage (and some related brassicas) are usually copious and pungent. In particular, cabbage contains a moderate quantity of 'mustard oils' (isothiocyanates), the substances which give mustard, horseradish, and onions their characteristic 'bite'. The taste is quite noticeable in the raw leaves.

One way of reducing the sulphurous smell is to stir-fry cabbage sliced into thin strips in the Chinese manner. The coating of hot oil seals the surface and reduces the emanation. For the same reason more flavour is re-tained, while the texture is appetizinglycrisp.

Red cabbage presents a special problem. If exposed to even slightly alkaline conditions it loses its red colour, going progressively mauve and slate blue or, when cooked, dirty green. Hard water is often alkaline enough to discolour its sensitive anthocyanin pigments. All traditional recipes for red cabbage therefore include acid fruit, vinegar, or wine, additions which not only preserve the colour, but also improve the flavour. Red cabbage pickles well, and is popular in this form in Britain.

CABINET PUDDING There are many variants of cabinet pudding, hot, cold, and even made with ice cream. The political link, though unexplained, is constant. Ude (1828) gives, as an alternative name, *poudin à la chancelière*. Another name is Diplomat pudding, which may just be a translation of the French *Pouding à la diplomate*. Only the names differ; the puddings are all alike.

The general method is to grease a pudding basin; stick currants or glacé fruit to the grease; line it with sponge fingers or soaked MACAROONS; and then fill this lining with layers of dried fruit, sponge fingers, and CUSTARD (in cold versions including GELATIN). Most versions include some spirit or liqueur as a flavouring. Hot ones are boiled; cold ones are made with a custard or cream that needs no further cooking.

CACCIATORA *alla cacciatoria*, the Italian version of a culinary phrase which occurs in many languages, meaning 'huntsmen-style' and usually indicating the presence of forest mushrooms. The Poles say *bigos* and the French *chasseur*.

CACHOU a French term, possibly connected with the CASHEW nut, for a small, scented, hard sugar sweet sucked by tobacco smokers to freshen the breath. It is often perfumed with violets or other flowers. A popular French variety is *cachou Lajaunie*, invented by the pharmacist Leon Lajaunie in Toulouse in 1890. These, based on LIQUORICE, scented with mint, and mixed with various secret ingredients, are a relatively modern example of a confection with a history that extends back at least to the 17th century, when 'kissing COMFITS', flavoured with musk, were served as part of the BANQUET course in England.   LM

CACIOCAVALLO one of the principal and oldest cheeses of the south of Italy, is usually made from cow's milk, although a mixture of cow's and ewe's milk is sometimes used. The compressed curd is fermented in hot whey and then sliced and covered with hot water to give it further elasticity and to permit shaping it into the typical caciocavallo forms, which are gourd- or spindle-like. A finished cheese has a pointed bottom and a neck and head at the top and weighs about 200 g (7 oz).

The cheeses are hung in pairs joined by a cord to drip-dry. One explanation (among several) of their name is that they then look like saddle bags: thus 'cheese on horseback' (*cacio a cavallo*, *cacio* being an old word for cheese).

Caciocavalli vary in the time they take to mature; but young ones are always mild (*dolce*) and suitable for eating at table, while older ones develop a sharp taste (*piccante*) and may be used for grating. They are good quick-melting cooking cheeses at any age.

Scamorza is another Italian cheese, belonging to the region of buffalo milk (although now made from cow's milk), of the same group; but the name can also be applied to a type of MOZZARELLA.

The Balkan cheeses described under KASHKAVAL are all related to caciocavallo, but made from ewe's milk. Which came first is a question which is unlikely ever to be resolved; so far as etymology is concerned, some believe that the Balkan name derives from the Italian one, others the contrary.

CACIOTTA an Italian word meaning 'little cheese', is used as a general name for a wide variety of cheeses, which have nothing in common except their small size (up to about 1 kg or 2 lb), a tendency to be round and flattish in shape, and the fact that they are mostly made on farms or by small-scale producers. They are not confined to, but are most common in, C. Italy. They may be made with cow's, sheep's, or goat's milk, or a mixture; may be young and moist or aged and sharp; and vary greatly in flavour.

The general name caciotta often embraces a cheese properly called caciofiore, so named because it is made with the creamy top (*fiore*) of the milk; or, say some, because it is usually prepared with a vegetable RENNET extracted from the flower (*fiore*) of the CARDOON.

This is a yellow, buttery cheese, coloured with SAFFRON, now hard to find outside the areas of production in Umbria although it used to be on sale elsewhere. Caciofiore Aquilano is the most renowned; according to di Corato (1977) its flavour is so delicate that it was formerly regarded as one of the finest presents which anyone could give or receive.

CACTI a large group of plants of which some are edible. The best known are AGAVE, BARBADOS GOOSEBERRY, PITAYA (strawberry pear), PRICKLY PEAR, and YUCCA.

There is also *Peniocereus greggii*, a night-blooming cactus (hence the name *reina de la noche* in Mexico), which is sometimes eaten in e.g. Louisiana; it bears tubers which can be made into fritters or French fries, or roasted.

CAERPHILLY a pale, almost white cheese called after the Welsh town of that name, otherwise famous for its ruined castle. The Welsh justly claim the cheese by origin, for Caerphilly became a centre of cheese production in the first half of the 19th century; but most Caerphilly cheese is now made in the English counties of Somerset and Wiltshire.

There were two reasons for the move to England. The growth of the Welsh population around the beginning of the 20th century increased the demand for milk in Wales, so less was available for cheese-making; but the demand for cheese had also risen. Across the border the makers of CHEDDAR, who had ample supplies of milk, saw an opportunity to expand their activities and speed up their financial return by starting to make Caerphilly too. Cheddar has to be kept for a long time before it matures, whereas Caerphilly ripens in 10 days.

Nonetheless, a revival of the Welsh farmhouse version of this cheese in the 1980s has ensured that its Welshness (as *caws Caerffili*, *caws* meaning cheese) continues to be recognized.

Caerphilly is a moist, whole-milk cheese with a crumbly, softish texture and a mild, acid tang, which was a favourite of Welsh miners. Some attribute this preference to the saltiness of the cheese; additional salt is supposed to be needed by persons doing heavy manual work. Others point to the fact that it does not dry out; and that it can be cut into wedges which fit in the flattish miner's wallet and are convenient to eat in the cramped conditions underground. A third explanation is that it is more digestible than most cheeses, which matters to men working (and digesting) in cramped positions. All three explanations probably have some truth in them.

CAJUN FOOD Acadians ('Cajuns') are descended from the French settlers of 17th century Nova Scotia, a colony they named Acadia, from *akade*, the Miçmac Indian word for 'plenty'. When they were driven off their land and into exile in what was called the *Grand Dérangement* of 1755, some went back to France and some to the French Caribbean islands, but others arrived in the French colony of Louisiana just as it was being handed over to Spain in 1766.

The Spanish government granted the Acadians the uninhabited land around the Atchafalaya where, in time, they learnt to harvest the natural bounty of the swamps and marshes growing rice and raising cattle on the prairies.

Interestingly, Cajun food has retained very little of its Canadian ancestry and although many of the dishes have French names, only a few have recognizable Gallic origins. The predominant influence is African, as are many of the staples: okra, aubergine, field peas, peanuts, even rice. This is due to the geographic proximity of another francophone minority—the Creoles, sometimes incorrectly called 'black Cajuns'. See CREOLE FOOD for the various meanings of this term. The point here is that the Creoles of Louisiana, many of African or part-African descent, were better equipped by their previous history than were the Cajuns to deal with the crops which were suited to the hot climate; and this applied in the kitchen as well as in the fields.

TABASCO sauce is the standard condiment of the Cajun table. When a dish is described as 'sauce piquant' (Crawfish sauce piquant, Chicken sauce piquant, Alligator sauce piquant, etc.) it means that it is served in a fiery hot reddish gravy, the fiery heat being supplied by Tabasco.

Gumbo (see OKRA) is the most celebrated Cajun/Creole dish. It is a spicy, soupy stew that can feature a variety of ingredients—chunks of ANDOUILLE sausage, pieces of chicken or game, crab claws, or shucked oysters. The common basis of all gumbos is the ROUX, a roughly equal combination of flour and fat cooked until very nearly burnt; it is the dark smoky roux that gives the gumbo its colour and flavour. After the roux, vegetables are added, then the main ingredients that will give the gumbo its specific identity. A traditional Lenten version is meatless; it is called Gumbo zerbes (*gumbo aux herbes*) and sometimes Gumbo Zaire. The word 'gumbo' comes from *kingombo*, a W. African name for okra. (There is a legend that one particularly enterprising slave brought okra seeds to the New World hidden in her hair.) However, okra is no longer considered crucial to a gumbo; it used to be added to give a mucilaginous texture to the dish, but this is less appreciated now than it was by previous generations. Likewise FILÉ powder made from the dried leaves of the SASSAFRAS tree would be added during the final stages of cooking to give the gumbo a 'stringy' texture. One used either okra or *filé* to achieve the desired texture, never both.

Jambalaya is a New Orleans dish that has been adopted by the Cajuns. It probably came from the period of Spanish rule in Louisiana, and represents a slurring together of *jamón* and PAELLA. In a traditional jambalaya, chicken, sausage, ham, and chopped vegetables are cooked and added with seasonings and liquid to an iron pot full of rice.

'Dirty rice' is rice cooked in chicken stock with chopped chicken giblets and sometimes bits of pork. *Maque choux* is a corn dish that varies in consistency from a stew to a chowder or soup. It always contains corn and frequently features tomato, onion, and cayenne pepper.

The most emblematic of all Cajun ingredients is the crawfish (see CRAYFISH). It is honoured with its own festival in Breaux Bridge. The simplest way to prepare crawfish is to boil them in water that has been seasoned with a ground mixture of mustard, coriander, and dill seeds, cloves, allspice, bay leaves, and, most important, dried chillies.

Crawfish bisque is a rich, roux-based crawfish soup filled with sweet crawfish tail meat, often served with a bowl of rice on the side which is added to taste. At the bottom of the bowl rests a crawfish shell stuffed with chopped crawfish meat, herbs, and breadcrumbs to soak up the flavour of the soup. Sometimes a *boulette* (a round cornmeal fritter usually seasoned with onion, pepper, and tender crawfish tails) is substituted for the stuffed shell.

The French influence is most evident in the traditional preparation of pork products. A *boucherie* is the slaughtering and preparing of a hog, originally both a social event and a means of distribution and now (despite refrigeration and modern slaughter methods) continued for social reasons. *Boudin* (see BLOOD SAUSAGES) is a well-seasoned sausage of rice and pork as well as varying amounts of giblets, while the traditional *boudin rouge* is a blood sausage or black pudding. *Chaudin* is a type of HAGGIS, made with a pig's stomach, while *paunce* is a stuffed calf stomach. *Gratons* are pork scratchings (see CRACKLING). *Tasso*, a lean, smoked seasoning meat quite similar to beef JERKY but moister and more highly spiced, may be made from either pork or beef, and is typically used to flavour stews and soups.   JR

READING: Mitcham (1978); Schweid (1980).

CAKE is a term with a long history (the word is of Viking origin, coming from the Old Norse *kaka*) and a subject which has many aspects. This entry is concerned with definitions and history; there is another on CAKE-MAKING, while categories of cake and individual cakes which have their own entries are ANGEL FOOD CAKE, BANBURY CAKES, BATTENBERG CAKE, BLACK BUN, BLACK FOREST GATEAU, CHIFFON CAKE, CHRISTMAS FOODS, COVENTRY GODCAKES, CUP CAKE, DEVIL'S FOOD CAKE, EASTER FOODS, ECCLES CAKES, FRUIT CAKES, GACHE, GALETTE, GATEAU, GÉNOISE, GINGERBREAD, HONEY CAKE, LAMINGTON, LARDY CAKE,

MADEIRA CAKE, MADELEINE, MARBLE CAKE, MOONCAKES, PANCAKE, POUND CAKE, QUEEN CAKE, ROCK CAKES, SACHERTORTE, SAFFRON CAKE, SAVOY, SEED CAKE, SIMNEL CAKE, SPONGE CAKE, STOLLEN, SWISS ROLL, TEA BREADS AND TEA CAKES, TENNIS CAKE, TIPSY CAKE, TORTE AND KUCHEN, TWELFTH NIGHT CAKE, UPSIDE DOWN CAKE, VICTORIA SANDWICH CAKE, WEDDING MEALS AND CAKES.

Definition is not easy, but the following corresponds to English usage. Cake denotes a baked flour confection sweetened with sugar or honey; it is mixed with eggs and often, but not invariably, with milk and fat; and it has a porous texture created by the mixture rising during cooking.

It is not surprising that the frontiers between cake and BREAD, BISCUIT, BUN are indistinct. The progenitor of all is bread in its simplest form. As techniques for baking and leavening developed, and eating patterns changed, what were originally regarded as forms of bread came to be seen as categories of their own, and named accordingly. The point is well brought out by Ayto (1993) who observes that certain Roman breads, enriched with eggs and butter, must have achieved a cakelike consistency and thus approached one of these indistinct frontiers. He continues:

Terminologically, too, the earliest English cakes were virtually bread, their main distinguishing characteristics being their shape—round and flat—and the fact that they were hard on both sides from being turned over during baking. John de Trevisa (1398) gives an early definition: 'Some brede is bake and tornyd and wende [turned] at fyre and is called . . . a cake.' It is this basic shape that lies behind the transference of the name to other, completely different foods, such as fishcakes, pancakes, and potato cakes.

The process whereby cakes evolved from breads was such that some items were inevitably left perched on the frontier—they could be one thing or the other, as in the case of tea breads and tea cakes.

Europe and parts of the world such as N. America where European influence is strong have always been the stronghold of cakes. One might even draw a line more tightly, round English-speaking areas. No other language has a word which means exactly the same as the English 'cake' (although some echo it with strange-looking forms such as 'kek', when meaning to refer to English-type cakes). The continental European GATEAU and TORTE often contain higher proportions of butter, eggs, and enriching ingredients such as chocolate, and often lean towards PASTRY rather than cake. Central and E. European items such as BABA and kulich (see EASTER FOODS) are likewise different.

The occidental tradition of cakes has little application in Asia. In some countries western-style cakes have been adopted on a small scale, for example the small sponge cakes called KASUTERA in Japan. But the 'cakes' which are important in Asia are quite different from anything occidental; for examples, see MOONCAKES and RICE CAKES OF THE PHILIPPINES.

The **history of cakes,** in the broadest sense of the term, goes a long way back. Among the remains found in Swiss lake villages were crude cakes made from roughly crushed grains, moistened, compacted, and cooked on a hot stone. Such cakes can be regarded as a form of unleavened bread, as the precursor of all modern European baked products. Some modern survivors of these mixtures still go by the name 'cake', for instance OATCAKES, although these are now considered to be more closely related to biscuits by virtue of their flat, thin shape and brittle texture. Over many centuries, by trial and error and influence from other cultures, baking techniques improved. From the basic method for making what was essentially desiccated porridge, leavened and unleavened cereal mixtures evolved into breads, cakes, and pastries.

Ancient Egypt was the first culture to show evidence of true skill in baking, making many kinds of bread including some sweetened with honey. Later the products of the island of Rhodes achieved a reputation in the classical world. Although they were probably rather breadlike, they were eaten as desserts, not staples, thus occupying a similar niche to modern cakes.

The ancient Greek word for cake was *plakous*, which comes from the same root as the word for 'flat'. From this was derived the Latin word *placenta* (and the modern anatomical use of 'placenta', the unborn baby's food supply). In the 2nd century BC Cato described a type of *placenta* resembling a modern cheesecake. A Roman cake known as a *satura* was flat and heavy, made from barley with raisins, pine nuts, pomegranate seeds, and sweet wine. (The name of this cake, full of added ingredients, is linked to the word 'saturate'; and to 'satire', which at first meant a literary hotchpotch.)

By the early centuries AD the Romans had acquired considerable skill in the control of YEAST, the only leavening known at the time; and barbarian peoples to the north and west of the Empire were adept at using barm, foaming yeast drawn from the top of beer, as a raising agent. During the medieval period there was no clear distinction between bread and cake in terms of richness and sweetness. Both words passed from Anglo-Saxon into English. Possibly 'cake' meant something small at the beginning of the period, since it was generally translated into Latin as *pastillus*, a little cake or pie. However, by the time Chaucer was writing in the late 14th century, immense cakes were being made for special occasions. Chaucer himself mentions one made with half a bushel (13 kg/28 lb) of flour. Sweet cakes containing currants, butter, cream, eggs, spices, and honey or sugar were often made. Raised with yeast, these would now be regarded as enriched fruit breads.

Cakelike survivors of this enriched bread type are still found today in the form of Alsatian KUGELHOPF and Welsh BARA BRITH. And from these enriched yeast-leavened mixtures developed a number of modern creamed cakes, particularly FRUIT CAKES. (Quite how the creaming method evolved is uncertain. It is initiated with sugar and fat and ended by adding flour, and thus is a reversal of bread-making, which begins with flour. See CAKE-MAKING.)

Italian pastry-cooks worked in both France and England during the 16th century and introduced many new baked goods. Some items, such as Genoese and Naples 'biscuits', had Italian names which they were to keep for centuries. Recipes such as these, which did not include yeast, were the precursors of whisked sponges (see CAKE-MAKING). The earliest surviving British recipe to use a real SPONGE CAKE mixture was given by Gervase Markham (1615). All such recipes were probably used to make small, thin, crisp cakes which their makers called 'biscuit'.

Recipes for 'biscuit'-type cakes are found in many 17th-century cookery books, along with yeast-leavened plum (fruit) cakes, GINGERBREAD, and small items of the MACAROON type. Spiced buns and cakes such as WIGS became common breakfast foods.

During the 18th century yeast was finally abandoned as a leavening for fruit cakes in favour of the raising power of beaten egg. Cake recipes of this period call for the mixture to be beaten for a very long time, to incorporate as much air as possible.

By the 17th century most of the ingredients important to modern cake-making had become known in Europe. Spices and dried fruits had been imported since the Middle Ages; citrus fruits were arriving in increasing quantities from the Mediterranean. The COLUMBIAN EXCHANGE with the New World brought chocolate and vanilla to the attention of Europeans. Colonization of the W. Indies and the development of sugar plantations meant that sugar was cheaper and easier to obtain; and treacle, available in Britain from 1660 onwards, replaced honey in many products such as gingerbread.

Moulds, in the form of cake hoops or pans, have been used for forming cakes since at least the mid-17th century. Paper hoops could be improvised to contain the mixture; Sir Kenelm Digby (1669) favoured wood over metal hoops, as he found the latter were liable to rust. Metal cake hoops were similar to modern flan rings, open at the bottom, and placed on a baking sheet as a base. Elizabeth David (1977) conjectures that expanding cake hoops were known, and could be adjusted according to the amount of mixture to be baked. Cake hoops were prepared by buttering them, and floured paper was placed underneath them. Cake 'pans' (now known as tins in England, but still called pans in the USA) were also used.

Most cakes were eaten as incidental items to accompany a glass of sweet wine (the origin of the MADEIRA CAKE) or a dish of tea. They had not found a real place in a set meal, except among the miscellaneous sweetmeats offered as dainties at the end. At large banquets, elaborately decorated cakes might form part of the display, but would probably not be eaten. In the mid-19th century when France, under Russian influence and followed by other western European countries, began to adopt the sequence of courses known as SERVICE À LA RUSSE, it became possible to have a purely sweet course. Cakes adopted a new form to fill this role. The medium-sized rich cake, iced, filled, and decorated, appeared. See GATEAU, a term used both in France and in Britain.

During the 19th century, technology made the cake-baker's life much easier. The chemical raising agent BICARBONATE OF SODA, introduced in the 1840s, followed by BAKING POWDER (a dry mixture of bicarbonate of soda with a mild acid), replaced yeast, providing greater leavening power with less effort. Supplies of white flour, granulated sugar, and cheap shortening such as margarine all helped to make cake baking popular. Another important contribution made by technology was the development of ovens with reliable temperature control.

In most of NW Europe and N. America a well-developed tradition of home baking survives, with a huge repertoire of cake recipes developed from the basic methods. Most of these rely on additions such as chocolate or glacé cherries for their effect. Many probably owe their inspiration to recipe leaflets handed out by the manufacturers of baking powders and shortenings from the late 19th century onwards. The ability to bake a good cake was a prized skill among housewives in the early to mid-20th century, when many households could produce a simple robust, filling 'cut and come again' cake, implying abundance and hospitality. Although the popularity of home baking and the role of cakes in the diet have both changed during the 20th century, cakes remain almost ubiquitous in the western world and have kept their image as 'treats'. (LM)

CAKE-MAKING lays much emphasis on texture. Indeed, for the consumer, texture is the most obvious feature which distinguishes cakes from other cereal products. A high proportion of enriching ingredients inhibits the formation of gluten, giving a more tender product than BREAD; and a soft, spongy 'risen' crumb sets cakes apart from BISCUITS and PASTRY.

Nowadays **four basic methods** are used in Britain and countries with similar baking traditions. All involve producing a BATTER which entraps tiny air bubbles. This is poured into a mould and baked. Heat causes the air to expand and make the cake rise; eventually PROTEIN and STARCH in the liquid phase of the cake coagulate and gelatinize, giving what in scientific terms is a stable foam and in common parlance a cake.

Many of the properties of cake batters are derived from the careful use of beaten egg to trap air. This is best seen in the **'whisking' method,** used to make the original forms of SPONGE CAKE, known as SAVOY and GÉNOISE. This starts with prolonged whisking of eggs and sugar which incorporates air, distributing it through the mixture as tiny bubbles. Immediately before baking, flour is folded into the batter. During baking the air expands, leavening the mixture with a network of little holes surrounded by walls of coagulated egg proteins; hence the name 'sponge cake'.

The **'creaming' method** is the other main way of making cakes; it always incorporates fat, and the results are known as 'shortened' cakes. To make these sugar is mixed or 'creamed' with fat to a soft, fluffy mass, incorporating air; eggs are beaten in, one by one; and finally flour is folded in, usually with the addition of baking powder. During baking the air bubbles in this heavier mixture are augmented by tiny pockets of carbon dioxide gas generated by the BAKING POWDER when moisture and heat are applied. An example of the creaming method is the VICTORIA SANDWICH CAKE.

Shortened cakes requiring low proportions of fat may be made by the **'rubbing in' method,** the fat and flour being worked together before the other ingredients are added. ROCK CAKES are made this way.

The **'melting' method** ('muffin method' in the USA), is used for making some types of heavy cakes such as PARKIN and some sorts of GINGERBREAD; the fat, sugar, and any liquid required are heated gently, before beating in eggs, flour, and baking powder.

There are **several variants** on the basic recipe for shortened (creamed method) cakes.

- Sometimes the baking powder is replaced by bicarbonate of soda plus an acid ingredient such as vinegar or cider or buttermilk. The two react together to give

carbon dioxide; the finished cake may be called a soda cake or a cider cake or a vinegar cake.
- Soft fats developed specifically for baking allow a 'dump' or 'all in one' method to be used, in which all ingredients are placed in the bowl of an electric mixer and intensively worked.

That the order in which ingredients are added affects the result is plain from a comparison between creaming and rubbing in. In creamed cakes an airy batter of fat, sugar, and egg is mixed with flour at the last minute, allowing minimal time for protein and starch in the flour to cross-link. For rubbed cakes, cold fat is combined with dry flour before any liquid is added, and this separates the particles and prevents the flour proteins from linking to form gluten when liquid is added to the mixture. It also inhibits starch gelatinization during cooking, and the result is a yielding texture.

Cakes baked in industrial bakeries use the same basic principles as home-baked cakes. Special fats which incorporate an emulsifier, usually glyceryl monostearate, are available to the commercial baker. These 'superglycerinated' fats cream, emulsify, and shorten the mixture more efficiently than ordinary baking fats, allowing use of a higher proportion of sugar and moisture per unit of fat than the domestic cook. Such cakes are sometimes called 'high ratio cakes' in the trade. However, industrially produced cakes are poor things by comparison with those which are hand made.

Two major reservoirs of skill in cake baking exist: the (usually male) *pâtissier* who has learnt the classical tradition as a trade; and the housewife, whose skills are based on informal traditions derived from friends and family, but whose cakes may be just as accomplished as those made by professional bakers.

Within Europe, the Scandinavians and the British make a speciality of home baking. The Swiss, Germans, and Austrians (particularly the Viennese) are accomplished bakers, both at home and professionally. In France and S. Europe *pâtissiers* are more important than home bakers. (LM)
READING: Olney *et al.* (1980); Barbara Maher (1982).

CALAMANSI (or kalamansi or calamondin/kalamondin), formerly known as *Citrus mitis*, is now classified as × *Citrofortunella mitis* (*Citrus reticulata* × *Fortunella* sp), i.e. a hybrid of the MANDARIN orange and the KUMQUAT. It is a small citrus fruit of the Philippines which plays an important role in Filipino cookery.

The fruits, which look like small mandarins, are very acid. The juice can be used like lemon juice to season dishes, or made into a refreshing drink. Other uses of the juice include acting as a marinade or a dip. It will also arrest browning in bananas, as lemon juice does; and is good to squeeze over papaya for breakfast, or over *pansit* (see NOODLES OF ASIA). In addition, the fruits can be pickled. The preserved peel is often used as a flavouring.

CALAMINT a name used of various species of herb in the genus *Calamintha* (or, possibly, close relations in other genera). *C. sylvatica* (formerly *officinalis*) is cited by Morton (1976), alongside summer and winter SAVORY, as having been used in Roman kitchens for its strong aroma and pleasantly pungent flavour, reminiscent of MINT. It is sometimes, reputedly, called by names such as 'mint savory'.

Modern Italian authorities record only very occasional culinary uses and point to a frequent confusion with another herb which is a kind of marjoram and bears Italian common names such as *nepitella*.

CALATHEA the common and generic name for certain plants of the W. Indies and S. America which have small, round tubers resembling new potatoes. These were cultivated in the Caribbean islands and Peru before the arrival of Europeans. *Calathea allouia* is still cultivated on a small scale, mainly in Puerto Rico. Two other species, *C. macrosepala* and *C. violacea*, have flowers which are cooked and eaten by some C. American Indians. The former may be called *chufl*.

Calathea roots, sometimes called 'sweet corn roots', have an agreeable flavour, free of the bitterness and toxins which afflict many tropical roots. A starch extracted from them is used to produce 'Guinea arrowroot'.

The names for this plant in Trinidad and Dominica, *topi tambo* and *topitambour* respectively, are corruptions of the French name for the Jerusalem artichoke, *topinambour*.

CALCIUM a chemical element vital to living things. In its pure form it is a light, whitish metal; but it is seldom thus seen because it reacts violently with water to form lime (calcium hydroxide).

The bones and teeth of animals, including people, are largely composed of calcium sulphate. Calcium also plays an important role in the working of the nerves and muscles, and in the clotting of blood. Quite a lot is required in the diet. An adult needs about 500 mg a day; growing children need slightly more, and pregnant and lactating women about 1,200 mg.

The main dietary sources of calcium are grains, dairy products, fish (especially small ones of which the bones are eaten) and green vegetables, especially watercress. To absorb calcium, the body needs adequate vitamin D. Lack of either can cause bone diseases such as rickets in children and osteoporosis in older people.

The outer coats of cereal grains contain phytin, a chemical which opposes the uptake of calcium. Strict vegetarians who eat wholemeal bread and coarse porridge are therefore at risk of calcium deficiency. In many countries including Britain extra calcium is added to bread in the form of chalk (calcium carbonate) which, surprisingly, can be digested to release the calcium.   RH

CALLALOO (or *calalú, calulu, caruru*, etc.) is the name given to various green leaves which form the chief ingredient of the soup called callaloo, popular in the W. Indies and Brazil. Some of the plants yielding leaves for this purpose are listed below. The first three are the most used.

- TARO, *Colocasia esculenta*, usually called 'dasheen' in the W. Indies, a root crop with edible leaves—this is the plant used in Trinidadian callaloo soup.
- Tannia (see MALANGA), another root crop which has edible leaves. The species *Xanthosoma brasiliense* is called *calalu* in Puerto Rico.
- Several sorts of AMARANTH, including the species known as CHINESE SPINACH; prickly callaloo, *Amaranthus spinosus*, in the W. Indies; and yellow amaranth or *caruru* (*A. flavus*), in Brazil.
- Spanish callaloo or W. Indian foxglove, *Phytolacca octandra*, a species of POKEWEED.
- Branched callaloo, *Solanum nodiflorum*, a type of NIGHTSHADE.

The soup in its simplest form will have flavourings such as garlic and other herbs, probably some other vegetables, and (often) coconut milk, plus perhaps a little salt pork. Sometimes salt beef or salt cod are used, or corned beef or crab. Elisabeth Lambert Ortiz (1973) observes that in Martinique and Guadeloupe there is a more elaborate form, with creole rice and a salt cod salad as accompaniments.

CALORIES units for the measurement of energy, including energy obtained from food. In the eyes of scientists the unit is now obsolete, but the word is part of everyday language, at least in English, and shows no sign of falling into disuse.

Strictly, a calorie is the amount of heat required to raise the temperature of 1 gram

of water by 1 °C. This is a very small amount, and dietitians found it more convenient to use the kilocalorie (kcal), 1,000 calories, in their calculations. Unfortunately they called this a 'Calorie' with a capital C. The use of the capital was often misunderstood or omitted, causing much confusion. In popular usage 1 kcal is 'a calorie'.

In the modern system of measurement the unit of energy is the joule (J), defined as the work done when a force of 1 newton is exerted over a distance of 1 metre (a newton is roughly the force of a mass of 100 grams resting on the earth's surface). This is also inconveniently small, so dietitians use kilojoules (kJ), 1,000 joules. One kilocalorie is equal to 4.18 kJ. Dietary information on food packaging normally gives energy values in both units.

All the following figures are approximate. A very active man uses 3,600 kcal (15,100 kJ) a day, a very active woman 2,500 kcal (10,500 kJ). A sedentary man needs 2,600 kcal (10,900 kJ), a sedentary woman 2,100 kcal (8,780 kJ). Most people's needs lie between these extremes. The amount of energy used by an adult per hour is: asleep, 70 kcal (295 kJ); sitting, 85 kcal (360 kJ); standing, 90 kcal (380 kJ); walking slowly, 185 kcal (780 kJ); running at a gentle sustainable pace, 500 kcal (2,100 kJ); and walking briskly upstairs, 1,000 kcal (4,200 kJ).

The 19th-century chemist who deserves credit for being behind the whole apparatus of 'recommended daily intakes' and 'energy values' for foods, Jacob Moleschott, is the subject of an interesting essay by Jane O'Hara-May (1984).   RH

CALSONES ('breeches'), a Sephardic Jewish stuffed pasta which is widely consumed in the Middle East. They may be square in shape like RAVIOLI or in half-moon or oblong shapes. Calsones are mostly home made, using egg in the dough, and usually filled with a cheese and egg mixture.

Calsones with RESHTEH (tagliatelli) were a famous Jewish dish in Aleppo, Syria. The calsones and reshteh were mixed together, dressed with melting butter, and served with yoghurt.

As for the origin of calsones, Claudia Roden (1996) suggests that they came to the Aleppo community with the Italian Jews who left Italy at various times, beginning in the 16th century, when there was a mass emigration eastwards following the expulsion of Jews from Italy.

READING: Claudia Roden (1996).

CALUMPANG NUT from the tree *Buchanania lanzan*. This member of the CASHEW family is native to India and Burma and is cultivated there and in SE Asia. Other members of the genus are found throughout SE Asia and in N. Australia.

The acid fruits are edible, but of less importance than the kernels. These are irregularly round or pear-shaped and about 6 mm (0.25") long. They resemble almonds and pistachio nuts in flavour, and are popular in sweetmeats such as SHRIKHAND in India, and elsewhere. Some are exported to western countries as 'almondettes'.

CAMAS *Camassia quamash*, a member of the lily family belonging to the western USA, whose edible bulbs were a staple food for the natives of the Pacific north-west. Camas was observed by early explorers to grow in great abundance, and still does, although

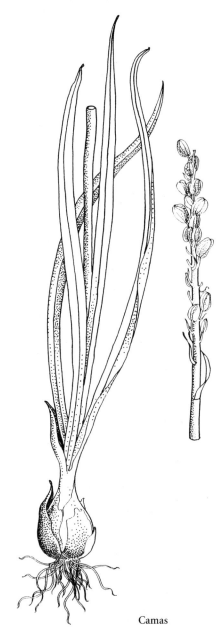

Camas

European settlers ploughed many camas fields up in favour of more familiar crops.

The camas plant takes several years to bloom, but its bulb was not harvested until the blue flowers appeared. This was partly because there are other types of camas belonging to the genus *Zigadenius*, which are highly poisonous. Their flowers are cream (or occasionally green), in contrast to the blue (or occasionally white or pink) ones of the edible kind.

There were three camas harvests, of which the first was in the spring. The bulbs then gathered were thought to be best boiled or raw, while those from the main (summer) and autumn harvests were baked, traditionally in a fire pit. The brown meal which resulted from the baking would be formed into cakes and stored in maple-leaf-lined baskets in trees to provide food for the coming months. The flavour of camas bulbs has inspired many comparisons, not all compatible with each other. It has been likened to that of mealy potatoes, gingerbread, baked pears, maple sugar, quince, dates, and figs. It provides carbohydrates and some protein, with minerals and fibre.

Few recipes for camas have been published. Hope (1983) states that 'the Nez Perce of today eat baked camas with sugar and cream. It is known that most new potato recipes adapt to camas. If overcooked, camas turns dark and soggy. If the taste is bland, the texture and nutrition of camas can still be used to advantage in a meat or vegetable pie.' Early settlers in Oregon and California had made camas pie or venison-camas stew.

CAMBODIA a country better known since the 1970s for bloodshed and turmoil than for its cookery, has nonetheless an interesting culinary history. It has been said that the work done by the cooks of the royal palace and of the aristocracy at Phnom Penh during the first half of the 20th century reflected the same capacity for taking pains and using highly developed techniques which had been displayed by the builders of Angkor Wat, Cambodia's most famous monument, in the distant past. By all accounts, such cooks produced dishes of a visual appeal equal to or surpassing those of any other cuisine. This is now no more than a piece of history, and a piece which has been insufficiently recorded.

However, the popular traditions of the people of Cambodia, like those of other countries which have been subjected to oppression or warfare, live on. Two 'snapshots' of Cambodian food which were taken in the third quarter of the 20th century retain their interest and much of their validity. The first of these was by Ung Teng (1967) and took the form of his doctoral

thesis, on traditional Cambodian foods and their nutritional value.

Rice comes first, with rice products and ways of cooking. Ung Teng explains that both regular and glutinous rice are used, and that consumption is not confined to the two meals of the day but extends to snacks at various times and to festive occasions, when special rice confections may be made. Rice vermicelli is a main product, and is the basis of many simple dishes, including *Kutiev*, also known as *Soupe chinoise*.

Kralan is an unusual speciality, glutinous rice which needs no kitchen recipient, since it is cooked in hollow sections of bamboo, after being mixed with coconut cream and shredded coconut and given additional flavourings. The stuffed sections of bamboo are set in a fire for an hour, after which the contents are well cooked and the outside can be peeled like a banana. A rice dish which takes more time and trouble and is reserved for festive occasions is *Ansam chrouk*, a kind of stuffed rice cake; the stuffing is of haricot beans and pork meat or fat, and an outer covering of banana leaf, tightly secured, is provided. This preparation has numerous variations. TAPÉ is an example of a fermented glutinous rice preparation.

Rice is not the only important cereal. MAIZE plays more of a part than one might think. This is not 'red' maize, produced for animal fodder and mainly exported, but white maize, cultivated in smaller quantities for human consumption. Like rice, it has its retinue of derivative products and special dishes.

Besides *tuk trey*, their version of the FISH SAUCE which is used throughout SE Asia, Cambodians have two special fermented fish products, which help to add protein to rice-based dishes: these are *prahoc* and *pha-âk*. The preparation of both starts with cleaned, not whole, fish and takes many weeks. *Prahoc* finishes up as a sort of dry paste, still incorporating chunks of fish. *Pha-âk*, on the other hand, is preserved in brine and incorporates rice, perhaps including the special red or black form of glutinous rice.

The second snapshot is by Professor Andras Hellei (1973), who surveyed on behalf of the FAO (Food and Agriculture Organization of the United Nations) the eating patterns of the Khmer people. So far as the ordinary people were concerned, he wrote, the pattern was to have two meals a day, one at about 1 a.m. and one at dusk. The basis of each meal was rice, and the invariable accompaniment soup (*samla*). Whenever possible, Cambodians would add further accompaniments, taking one from each of three broad categories known as:

- *chhâ*, a sauté of meat or poultry, with vegetables or poultry, or vermicelli, or perhaps condiments only;

- *aing*, a dish of grilled meat, poultry, or fish;
- *chion*, a dish of fried meat, poultry, or fish.

Fish would be dominant in the grilled and fried dishes, and these would be freshwater fish. Cambodia has a relatively short coastline, but vast resources of lakes and rivers, abounding in fish.

As in neighbouring LAOS and THAILAND, foods wrapped in edible leaves are common. Sour and acid tastes are liked, and are manifest in the use of lime juice, tamarind, etc. Lemon grass is among the favourite flavouring herbs.

A characteristic sweet rice dish is made with black glutinous rice.

CAMBUCA *Marlierea edulis*, a tree of the MYRTLE and eucalyptus family, grows wild in Brazil, especially in the region of São Paulo. Its yellowy-green fruits, which look rather like 'flying saucers' some 6 cm (just over 2") in diameter, are appreciated locally, but have become difficult to obtain. The juicy pulp has a sweet-sour flavour.

The name is from the native Indian word *cambuci*, meaning a jar, and was given because the shape of the fruit resembles that of a certain type of water container.

CAMEL either of two large ruminant mammals of the genus *Camelus*. The one-humped Arabian camel, *C. dromedarius*, is also known as the dromedary. *C. bactrianus* is the two-humped Bactrian or Asian camel. Both provide milk. Camel's milk, a staple food for desert nomads, contains more fat and slightly more protein than cow's milk. Stobart (1980) remarks that it 'has very small fat globules and cannot readily be churned to make butter'. It can be made into a kind of yoghurt.

However, the principal use of camels is for carrying goods and people in desert regions of Africa and Asia. As the chief beasts of burden in these areas, they are too valuable to be slaughtered for food, but in the past, when there were probably many more camels than there are now, they were valued for their meat. This is still eaten in some regions. When camels were domesticated it seems that the development of their 'local fat accumulations', i.e. their humps, increased; and it is generally considered that the best part of the camel for eating is the hump.

As for the distant past, ancient Greek writers spoke of whole roast camels at Persian banquets; and the Roman emperor Heliogabalus is said to have relished camel's heel (among many other outlandish delicacies)

CAMEMBERT one of the most famous of the French soft cheeses, belongs to the Vallée d'Auge in the department of Orne, where the village Camembert gave it its name. That is still the home of true Camembert, although 'Camembert' is now manufactured worldwide.

The making of good cheeses at Camembert was mentioned as early as 1708, but Rance (1989) believes that the cheeses made there then were not closely similar to the Camembert of modern times; they were smaller, brownish, and undistinguished.

Although some of the details are obscure, it seems clear that a certain Marie Harel was responsible for creating Camembert as we know it, at the end of the 18th century. She introduced changes in the method of making the cheeses and also began to use larger moulds, the size still familiar. It may be that the new cheeses were not known as Camembert until Napoleon III was presented with one of them in the middle of the 19th century, asked where it came from, and ruled that it should be known by that name.

However, Camembert remained a cheese of only local importance until in 1880 the chipboard cheese-box, in which it is still housed, was patented and permitted dispatching the cheeses over considerable distances. The introduction of *Penicillium candidum* in 1910 (*P. glaucum*, the local natural blue mould, was formerly used) finally set Camembert on the road to world renown.

The true Camembert is made from untreated cow's milk (*lait cru*), is not less than 10 cm (4") across, and contains at least 45% fat. The cheese is cut by hand, drained and salted, then sprinkled with the mould, poured into tall perforated forms, and left to settle and drain until it takes the characteristic round shape. The cheeses are then cured until the characteristic white surface mould appears, and are ripe when the inside has become soft and smooth, turning from white to creamy yellow.

There is some debate about the ideal time to eat a Camembert. Rance says:

To my mind, the most delicious stage of the cheese is when there is still a trace of that white at its heart in a moist but not melted state. This is called l'âme, the spirit or soul of the cheese in Brie. The combination of the two consistencies and flavours is as delightful to the palate as the aroma is to the nose. For me this is the smell of heaven.

READING: Lanarès (1982).

CANADA a huge country whose area exceeds that of the USA, although its population is not much more than a tenth as large, includes vast areas which are too chilly for all but trappers and other rugged people whose professions take them there. It is also remarkable that Canada is much wider, west to east, than the USA, thus giving scope for a wonderful six-day coast-to-coast train ride (still available in the late 1990s).

In fact the railways used to provide some of the best dining in Canada. It used to be said, with some justification, that the dining cars of the CPR and CNR (the two major railroads) and their hotels in the principal cities were the best places to eat. P. and J. Berton (1974), while emphasizing that this was all in the past, provide a charming description of the good fare to be had:

As the decades rolled on Canadian railway dining became known the world over, for it was without doubt superior to any other. The mounds of crackling crisp Canadian bacon, the evenly grilled Calgary sirloins, the plump, pink spring lamb chops, the succulent goldeyes with their melting pat of parsley butter, the juicy lake fish, slightly charred, the Oka and cheddar cheese and the hot seasonal blueberry pies—all these came to be associated almost exclusively with our transcontinental train service. It is perhaps not too much to say that, if there is a distinctly Canadian style of cuisine, it is this; and not too surprising that, in an artificial nation bound together by bands of steel, it should spring directly from our dining cars.

Old railway hands also fondly recall the rich, steaming coffee of the old CPR, served from silver tureens.

Following an imaginary route from the extreme east over to the Pacific, a touring epicure would first encounter the conservative cuisine of Newfoundland where, despite modern intrusions, traditional seafood dishes such as fish and BREWIS (straight out of medieval England), and home baking continue to thrive—indeed, the epicure will find that home baking thrives more or less all along his route, whether derived from Scotland or the Ukraine or France or elsewhere. The seafood traditions, of both French and British origin, are equally noticeable in the Maritimes (Nova Scotia, New Brunswick, and Prince Edward Island), and among the Scottish traditions there are various oatmeal delicacies including oatmeal bread sweetened with molasses.

Given the excellence of the seafood in Atlantic Canada, it is unfortunate that Canada has had its name usurped by the so-called 'Canadian method' of determining cooking times for fish. The method is deeply flawed, for it flies in the face of one of the laws of physics, as explained under FISH COOKERY, and should be disowned.

Quebec, the French-speaking province, vast and including much of the St Lawrence River, up which the Frenchman Jacques Cartier sailed in 1535, marvelling at the fertility of the region, is the home of many French dishes which have evolved in interesting ways in their new environment, and indeed of new dishes created by the application of French cooking techniques to New World ingredients. *Cretons* (originally pork scratchings, now a pâté-like spread of spiced cooked pork), *Tourtière* (a hot spiced pork pie), *Tarte au sucre*, *Pouding du chômeur* (an economy pudding for the unemployed)—these are but a few notable examples. Best known of all is probably the Québécois pea soup, made with dried yellow split peas, smoked pork hock or ham bone, and seasonings.

Further west lies Ottawa, the capital, in Ontario, a province of lakes, berries, cornmeal-coated juicy back bacon, maple syrup, and other good things. The province also harbours the great multicultural city of Toronto; and Ingersoll, birthplace of the Canadian Cheddar cheese industry. Recently, some of these cheeses have recovered the old, true taste, following a return to the use of raw milk by some cheese-makers. The Ontario cuisines include a strong German element, with Mennonite and Amish communities adding their distinctive notes, e.g. in home-smoked sausages in the Kitchener-Waterloo district, and other Old Order dishes such as the (dried fruit-cum-meat) Schnitz pie, or the charmingly named molasses dessert SHOOFLY PIE.

Next come the Prairie provinces: Manitoba, Saskatchewan, and Alberta. There are Arctic CHAR, WHITEFISH, PICKEREL, etc., in the rivers and lakes of this region, but the fame of these provinces rests mainly on their contribution to world stocks of wheat and other grains. The influence of Scandinavians, including a tiny group of Icelanders, is noticeable in the region, as are the food traditions which immigrant Jews brought with them from Europe. However, the influence from the UKRAINE is perhaps the strongest; there are about half a million Canadians of Ukrainian origin, and the best book on Ukrainian cookery was published in Manitoba, where pierogi (see PIROG) are practically a 'national dish'.

Over on the Pacific rim, in the far west, British Columbia provides its own matchless sockeye and coho SALMON in numerous incarnations (including the Indian method of wind-drying it as a fish JERKY). Here too are echoes of Victorian England, surviving harmoniously with modern and ethnic manifestations to rival those of Perth in Western Australia (just a hemisphere away); there is much evidence of Chinese and other Asian cuisines in the exciting city of Vancouver. Indeed, such evidence is visible elsewhere, for the pattern of immigration to Canada changed radically in the latter part of the 20th century, with major inflows from Asia (especially Hong Kong, China, and Taiwan), Africa, and the Caribbean, all adding new dimensions to Canadian foodways.

This survey has left out the north, for which (to some extent) see INUIT COOKERY, but otherwise gives a panoramic view of the variegated belt of regions, circling a sixth of the northern hemisphere, to which the transcontinental railroad used to give a special sense of identity which is not in the gift of air transport.

READING: Ladies of Toronto and Chief Cities and Towns in Canada (1877); Edna Staebler (1968, for Mennonite cuisine); Julian Armstrong (1990, for Quebec); Marie Nightingale (1971, for Nova Scotia).

CANAPÉ a French word which basically means sofa or couch, has become a culinary term in France since the late 18th century, when it was applied by analogy to the thin pieces of fried or toasted bread which served as supports for various savoury toppings. A century later, in the 1890s, it became an English word referring to a titbit of this kind. Now that yet another hundred years have passed, the usage continues, although it sounds old-fashioned and is most likely to be found in contexts such as catered receptions or 'cocktail parties'. The modern practice of offering guests in western restaurants a titbit before the meal proper begins, calling it an *amuse-gueule*, may go someway towards extending the lifespan of canapés, although often departing from the 'something sitting on a square of toast or a cracker' formula.

Canapés may be hot or cold. If hot, they come close to what are called SAVOURIES in British English. In either case they are capable of being classified as HORS D'OEUVRES in some culinary contexts. Large canapés trespass on the territory of the open SANDWICH.

CANARY ISLANDS called by the Romans 'the fortunate isles', have had human beings in residence and enjoying their remarkably agreeable subtropical climate since the time of the Cro-Magnon culture in the south-west of France. Indeed, the first inhabitants, known as Guanche, arriving about 2000 BC, probably came from that culture and thus shared a common ancestry with the Spanish conquistadores who took the islanders under Spanish rule at the end of the 15th century. So the cuisine which had existed in the islands and that which was brought in by the Spaniards already had some features in common. Both alike were influenced by the arrival of new foods from the Americas (see COLUMBIAN EXCHANGE), for example the MAIZE which has become an important crop in Gomera.

The first major crop-plant introduction after the conquest was SUGAR CANE, brought

in by Portuguese experts from Madeira. This was the main crop for a century but succumbed to competition from the New World. Meanwhile vines had been imported and produced wines which are often named in 18th-century English recipes (sack, malvasia). However, the most important successor crop was the BANANA, which has continued to be the major export of the islands with growing support from potatoes, tomatoes, citrus fruits, etc.

The effect of mass tourism has been to submerge to a large extent the indigenous dishes of the islands, including items such as *gofio*, formerly the staple food and still eaten by the islanders but probably invisible to visitors. This was made from wheat, maize, or barley, roasted and ground, then mixed with water to make a kind of bread. However, many good things can be had, including a large range of seafood (simply grilled or in a fish soup), and items such as the local version of jacket potatoes, *Papas arrugadas*. These are boiled in heavily salted water and eaten with their jackets which have a white deposit of salt on them. For local flavours, the piquant sauce called *mojo* is important. It goes with most things, including fish, and exists in various forms, but always based on oil, vinegar, garlic, and herbs. The red form includes red peppers and saffron; the green form has parsley and coriander.

Sweetmeats and desserts include many items based on almonds (and usually reflecting Spanish mainland inspiration) but also some maize sweets such as *frangollo*.

CANDIED FRUIT whole fruits preserved by soaking in syrup for several days until the sugar replaces the moisture in the fruit. The result is very sweet and firm textured, retaining the shape, and usually the colour, of the original.

The lengthy process is not difficult, but requires patience and attention to detail. Fruit is prepared by cooking briefly in water to soften it, before immersion in syrup. The syrup is drained every day and the concentration increased by dissolving more sugar in it, before it is poured over the fruit again. (If the fruit was added to a highly concentrated syrup from the beginning, the result would be shrivelled and tough. When the concentration increases gradually, shape and tenderness are retained.) Finally, the fruit is drained and allowed to dry in very gentle heat for several days. If desired it can be coated in caster sugar to become 'crystallized fruit' or dipped in concentrated sugar syrup to give the smooth coating called *glacé* in French.

Candied fruits keep well. Citrus and stone fruits, pears, figs, and pineapple all respond to preservation by this method. Large items, such as whole pineapples or grapefruit, are usually cut into pieces before preservation, but may be treated whole for a particularly magnificent display. Soft fruits are little used, as they disintegrate before soaking is completed.

The long process and the high-quality fruit required means that, like MARRONS GLACÉS, candied fruit is now an expensive luxury. In Britain such sweetmeats are associated with Christmas. The one exception is glacé cherries, which are relatively cheap. These are important ingredients in home baking, and, along with candied ANGELICA, are frequently used for decorating desserts. Other candied fruits are rarely used as ingredients, except in a few luxurious sweet dishes such as *Riz à l'impératrice.*

The French regions of the Auvergne and Provence (particularly the city of Apt) are well known for candied fruit of all types; also the north-eastern city of Strasbourg, where candied mirabelle plums, flavoured with kirsch and stuffed with fruit paste, are made. Elizabeth David (1965) observed that:

Italian preserved and candied fruit is spectacular. Whole pineapples, melons, citrons, oranges, figs, apricots, red and green plums, pears, even bananas in their skins, are sugared in the most skilful way, and make marvellous displays in the shops of Genoa and Milan.

The Spanish and Portuguese also enjoy candied fruit. Candied plums are a speciality of the town of Elvas, in Portugal. These two nations also left a legacy of confectionery recipes in their former colonies, with the consequence that candied fruit, and fruits in syrup, are now popular in Mexico, S. America, and the Philippines.

On the other side of the world, in China, preserved fruits are made by salting, sugaring, and drying, particularly citrus fruit, plums, and kumquats.

The preservative qualities of syrups in relation to fruit were known to the Romans; instructions for the preservation of whole quinces in concentrated grape juice are given in the cookery book ascribed to APICIUS. An alternative method was recommended by the physician Dioscorides, in which pieces of peeled quince were wedged together in a vessel full of honey and stored for a year.

The date at which sugar was substituted for honey, and the evolution of the sophisticated method of gradually increasing syrup concentration, are unknown. A French agricultural writer, Olivier de Serres, gave some details of the method in 1600, so it was known in France by then; and versions of such recipes had already appeared in English cookery books in the late 16th century. However, instructions were sometimes sketchy, and the process of slowly increasing concentration poorly understood.

Sometimes the cook was required to cut the fruit into *chips*—thin slivers—which would produce an acceptable result after only one or two boilings in syrup.

At this time, such confections were known in England as SUCKETS. Dry and wet suckets (a 'wet' sucket was fruit stored in syrup) were popular from at least the mid-16th century onwards. All kinds of fruit were used, as well as items which would now be classed as vegetables, or are no longer eaten, including lettuce stems and mallow stalks from the MARSHMALLOW plant; and stalks of ANGELICA, then as now a favourite non-fruit item for candying.

Roots, such as those of ELECAMPANE, were used too. Those of sea-holly (ERINGO ROOT) were favourites for candying and had a powerful reputation as aphrodisiacs. Eringo was invoked in this role by Falstaff in *The Merry Wives of Windsor* (1598): 'Let the skie rain potatoes, . . . haile kissing comfits, and snow eringoes.' Day (1996a) has more to say on this and on the orchid tuber called satyricon which was another top-rated aphrodisiac.

Most things, it seems, could be made into suckets. Nuts were also preserved; a recipe for sucket of green walnuts was given by Sir Hugh Platt (1609).

Although the word 'sucket' went out of use, sugar-preserved fruits, both dry and wet, continued to be made. Eighteenth-century recipe books contain numerous recipes for them under the title of 'preserves', or 'conserves', plus other related confections of fruit and sugar.

By the mid-19th century, dry candied fruits seem to have moved out of the realm of the domestic cook. Imported varieties continued to appear on the tables of those who could afford them, but home preservation of fruit in syrup, a less exacting process, became a popular substitute. Fruits were now also being preserved in syrup by CANNING, the descendant of all the 16th- and 17th-century suckets.

One preserve which does carry on the tradition of wet suckets as the Elizabethans would have understood them is preserved GINGER root in syrup. Imported from China, the traditional round porcelain jars in which it is stored make charming Christmas displays in British shop windows.   LM

CANDIED VIOLETS violet flowers preserved by a coating of sugar syrup. Hot syrup is poured over the fresh flowers, and stirred until the sugar 'grains' or recrystallizes. This method is still used occasionally for rose petals, and was applied to orange flowers in the past. Almonds and orange peel were also treated this way, and the results of such recipes were referred to as PRALINES. Candied violets are still made

commercially at Toulouse in France, where they are known *as violettes de Toulouse.*

A simpler technique, used by home cooks, is to brush flower petals with egg white or gum arabic solution, and then dredge them with caster sugar. The principal use of candied flowers in modern times is as decoration for chocolates or cakes.   LM

CANDLENUT an edible nut borne by the large tree *Aleurites moluccana*. This is native to the region of E. Malaysia but is now cultivated from India to the Philippines and in the Pacific islands. It bears a round, hard fruit up to 10 cm (2") in diameter with a wrinkled papery outer wrapping and tough inner coat enclosing either one or two waxy white kernels. These bear some resemblance to WALNUTS and are therefore sometimes called Indian or Tahiti walnuts. The Malay name is *buah keras* (hard nut) and the Indonesian is *kemiri*.

The nuts contain a toxin which makes them unsuitable for consumption raw, but they are widely consumed as a flavouring ingredient, after suitable preparation, in SE Asia and especially in Java. The usual practice there is to roast the nuts until they can be cracked open and then to sauté the kernels, crushed with other ingredients such as shallots, garlic and chilli peppers, shrimp paste, to produce an aromatic mixture which is fried before being used in savoury dishes. A mixture of this sort is a standard ingredient in Indonesian cookery.

The candlenut is very oily, and was used in the past for making primitive candles, as its name indicates.

The strength and weight of the shells is such that whole nuts cannot economically be exported. But kernels are available in western countries, not always whole since the process of extracting them is difficult.

CANDY a term derived from the Arabic *qandi*, meaning a sugar confection. In the USA it is a general term for SWEETS of all kinds; in Britain it is used in a more restricted range of meanings, notably to indicate sweetmeats coated or glazed with sugar. For candied fruit, peel, and vegetables, see under CANDIED FRUIT etc. There is a separate entry for SUGAR CANDY.

CANDYFLOSS a confection made by spinning granulated sugar, which can be coloured and flavoured as desired, in a special machine. The sugar is melted in the machine and forced through small holes by centrifugal force. This produces threads which are collected on a stick, to give something which looks like a huge lollipop made from cotton wool. It becomes sticky if stored, and therefore is made freshly for each customer.

Candyfloss is a popular item at fairs and festivals in many countries. Another sweet which has a thread-like texture is *saray helvasi*, made in Turkey and Iran, from flour, oil, and sugar. The mixture is worked to give numerous fine, parallel threads, rather like a skein of silk. LM

CANE RAT *Thryonomys swinderianus*, a large African rodent which also goes by the name grasscutter (especially in W. Africa) and ground-pig (a misnomer which has been current in S. Africa, perhaps because of its bristly hairs). It can live in various environments, mostly but not always in damp areas; enjoys an excellent vegetarian diet (roots, young shoots, bark, etc.); and is capable of causing havoc in some crops such as sugar cane.

The cane rat may reach a length, not including the tail, of nearly 60 cm (24") and provides a substantial amount of good meat. It is eaten on a large scale in sub-Saharan Africa.

CANISTEL *Pouteria campechiana*, an interesting tropical fruit which is sometimes called egg-fruit (or the equivalent in other languages), or yellow sapote (see also SAPOTA), because of its orange flesh; or by names meaning 'drunk' since it ferments after falling to the ground. It occurs wild in S. Mexico and a few C. American countries, and is cultivated in them and neighbouring countries and also in Puerto Rico, Jamaica, and (especially) Cuba.

The fruit can measure up to 12 cm (5") long; and contains from one to four hard brown seeds. The skin of the ripe fruit is yellow and shiny. Inside, the flesh is relatively firm but becomes softer towards the centre. 'It has been often likened in texture to the yolk of a hard-boiled egg. The flavor is sweet, more or less musky, and somewhat like that of a baked sweet potato' (Morton, 1987).

CANNELLONI a large and eminently stuffable form of PASTA, formed by wrapping a sheet round itself in the shape of a tube. Cannellini are similar but smaller.

Fillings may include meat, sometimes seafood, often cheese or vegetables, usually incorporating a sauce or with a sauce poured over, or both.

CANNIBALISM formerly practised in many parts of the world (see the excellent surveys by Tannahill and Harris listed below), is now extremely rare.

When cannibals ate human flesh, it was often for ritual reasons, e.g. in connection with human sacrifices which were enjoined by some form of religion; or because it was thought that the virtues of dead relations or the martial abilities of dead enemies, or whatever, would be absorbed by the act. There have, however, been cultures in which human flesh was consumed, straightforwardly, as food, and evidence is available for the curious about which parts of the body were preferred, how the flesh was cooked, with what accompaniments it was eaten and so forth.

READING: Reay Tannahill (1975); Harris (1978).

CANNING is an example of preserving food by SEALING. Its history is inseparable from that of bottling; so the two are treated together here. Each involves heating food to sterilize it and sealing it in an airtight container. However, the use of metal containers (cans) soon became dominant in the canning industry, while bottling in glass containers was the usual practice in domestic kitchens (although it has continued to be used in the food industry for specialized or expensive or visually attractive items (e.g. fruit in syrup)).

The theoretical basis of canning was not established until 1861, when the French scientist Louis Pasteur showed that MICRO-ORGANISMS were the principal causes of food spoilage. But empirical knowledge had pointed the way from early times. As explained under SEALING, the medieval raised pie was a confection which could serve as a preserving container; and the old practice of POTTING certain foods must have produced at least a vague realization that cooking plus excluding air made food keep. In 1680 such notions were given concrete form by the anonymous author of *A Book of Receipts According to the Newest Method*, who wrote:

To keep Gooseberries, Damsons, or Bullies [bullaces]. Gather Gooseberries at their full Growth, but not ripe, Top and Tail them, and put them into Glass Bottles, put Corks on them but not too close, then set them on a gentle Fire, in a Kettle of cold Water up to the Neck, but wet not the Cork, let them stand till they turn White, or begin to Crack, and set them till cold, then beat in the Corks hard, and Pitch them over. You may also do them in an Oven if you please, or cork them down hard, and pitch them over, and they will keep without scalding.

This recipe seems to have had no influence, perhaps because of the misguided advice at the end, which may have tempted people to try the invalid alternative technique 'without scalding'. Otherwise, subject to some minor problems, the recipe should have worked.

The decisive step forward into the era of successful bottling and canning of foods was not taken until the beginning of the 19th century, when the Frenchman Nicolas APPERT perfected a method of bottling which won the approval of the French government and was described in his book *L'Art de conserver* (1810). An English translation appeared in 1811, and an American edition in 1812.

Appert's technique was as follows. Food of any type—meats, soups, fruits, and vegetables—was placed in a stout wide-mouthed jar, and this was closed with a stopper composed of several layers of cork with the grain running crossways to reduce porosity. The stopper was sealed with an odd but effective mixture of cheese and lime, and wired down as for champagne. The jars, enclosed in sacking in anticipation of some bursts, were then heated in a water bath. Appert worked out cooking times for each type of food. All his mixtures were either liquid themselves or packed in liquid. Tests carried out from 1806, including the shipment of jars across the equator, vindicated the technique.

Parallel work was taking place in England. In 1808 Bryan Donkin was awarded five guineas for a method of bottling fruit, which

Canistel

he had borrowed without acknowledgement from Appert. His corks were kept moist, and thus airtight, by storing the jars on their sides in the manner of wine. Not long afterwards he introduced the use of tinned iron containers in place of glass jars—hardly surprising, as he was a partner in an ironworks. This idea had already been patented twice in Britain, in 1810; it is not clear whether Donkin was aware of this. In any event there was no legal challenge when he began to manufacture canned foods in 1812. He offered samples to the Royal Navy and to several explorers, and the firm of Donkin, Hall & Gamble became an established naval supplier from 1818.

Two cans made for an Arctic expedition of 1824, one of veal and one of carrots, survived unopened and were investigated 114 years later. The contents were in sound condition, only slightly spoiled by the slow chemical attack of the tin coating; they could have been eaten safely, but the investigators did not dare try.

These early cans were bulk containers, holding 1 or 2 kg (2–4 lb). The metal was thick and the seams were hand soldered; the cans had to be opened with a hammer and chisel. They were not completely closed before heating, as Appert's jars had been; a small hole was left for the escape of steam. This was quickly soldered when the contents boiled, and heating was continued for the full processing time. To verify that all cans had been properly sealed, and that no air had been drawn in when the can cooled and pressure inside fell, the cans were left in a warm place for a month. Any faulty can would bulge, as a result of gas being formed inside from the spoilage of the food.

In the late 1840s, when still larger cans were being made—net weight over 6 kg (14 lb)—a scandal was caused by the discovery that many such cans of meat went bad. It can now be seen that this was because the distance from the outside of the can to the middle was so great that heat did not have time to diffuse right through the solid block of meat, and the centre did not reach boiling point. Cans with liquid or partly liquid contents did not suffer from the problem, however large they were, because convection currents could carry heat around inside them. Admiralty investigators, although not understanding this, wisely recommended that no cans should have a capacity of more than 2.7 kg (6 lb), and that the navy should have its own cannery, which was established in 1856 at Deptford.

This was still several years before Pasteur's discovery, and long before the great resistance to heat of certain spore-forming bacteria had been discovered. Nevertheless, there was a feeling that greater heat was desirable, and experiments were made to raise the boiling point of the water bath (with salt, which unfortunately corroded the outside of the cans) and by PRESSURE COOKING. AUTOCLAVES (large pressure cookers) were, however, feared because they sometimes exploded, and it was not until the end of the century that they came into general use.

The earliest canned foods had been expensive items, whose use was only warranted for special situations—ships at sea for long periods, Arctic explorations. But meat was scarce and dearer than usual in Britain in the 1860s, and it became economically feasible to import canned mutton and beef from Australia. In the 1870s the USA entered the British market, followed later by S. American countries. The canned meat thus imported was cheap food for the poor. It was widely disliked for its coarse, fatty nature, as shown by some of the nicknames it acquired. The Royal Navy called theirs 'Sweet Fanny Adams', after the victim of a notorious murder in 1867, whose victim was hacked into small pieces. This tradition proved to be durable. During the Second World War the cans of meat supplied to Axis troops were labelled 'AM'. The Germans called it 'Alter Mann' (old man), and the Italians 'Asino morte' (dead donkey).

Canned fruits and vegetables were at first only prepared for the luxury trade or special purposes, but evolved into an inexpensive item for the mass market. Canning of tomatoes on a large scale began in Pennsylvania in 1847–9, at a time when this fruit had not yet won acceptance in the English-speaking world. A lively marketing campaign by the canner, who sent samples to President Polk and Queen Victoria, overcame doubts, and it was largely due to this campaign for the canned product that tomatoes came to be a common and popular food. By the 1880s large quantities of canned tomatoes were being sent to Britain from the USA. Peas, first canned on a large scale in Baltimore in the 1850s, had also progressed down market from luxury to staple. Californian peaches were widely sold in cans from the 1860s, but canned pineapple, from Hawaii, did not appear until 1892.

Cans of pork and beans were made for the fishing fleet, in Portland, Maine, in 1875; and these may be regarded as the parents of the cans of 'baked beans'.

The first canned fish were sardines, which were commercially canned at Nantes as early as the 1820s. Sardines spoil quickly and, unless they are to be eaten on the spot, always need preserving in some way. Traditionally they had been salted and sometimes smoked. Canning in oil gave a product more like the fresh fish, and which was esteemed as a delicacy.

Another familiar canned product is condensed milk. Appert himself had bottled condensed milk for the French government trials, and others continued to make it thereafter, sometimes sweetening it. The object was not only to preserve milk ('fresh' milk sold in towns in the early 19th century was often sour and contaminated) but also to reduce its inconvenient bulk. The breakthrough that made condensed milk popular was achieved by Gail Borden of Brooklyn, New York, who in 1856 patented a vacuum evaporation process which worked at temperatures below boiling point and resulted in a less obviously 'cooked' taste. Borden's condensed milk was sweetened, but unsweetened evaporated milk followed. (The sugar has a preservative function, and unsweetened milk has to be treated at a higher temperature.)

By the 1880s canned foods had an important place in popular diet. Cans looked much like those of the 20th century, and the metal was thin enough to permit opening with a can opener. Sealing, however, was still done by a cumbersome soldering process.

Modern methods require, for most foods, an initial blanching at a temperature slightly below boiling point. This destroys enzymes that might discolour the food or give it an off flavour, and also removes air, which helps when filling the can.

Filling is done on a continuous production line. The can is packed with food and topped up with brine, sauce, or syrup as appropriate, leaving a head space of 6 mm (0.25 ") to allow for expansion. Then the lid is clamped on by a machine which produces a double seam. It is important that the contents are hot when this is done, so that when the can is heated later it will not burst. If necessary the can may be warmed with hot water or steam.

The can is then heated in an autoclave, which allows the contents to be heated well above boiling point. The high pressure outside the can also keeps it from bursting. The cooking temperature varies with the acidity of the food. The bacteria which cause BOTULISM cannot grow in acid conditions, so acid foods such as canned fruit and tomatoes need be heated only just enough to bring the centre of the can to boiling point. Other foods have to be heated to 121 °C (250 °F) or more for at least three minutes to destroy the spores of this dangerous organism—which is why canned vegetables often seem 'overcooked'.   (RH)

CANNOLO (or cannoli, the plural form more familiar in N. America), a Sicilian sweetmeat made from flour, mixed with Marsala, cinnamon, cocoa, egg, and a mixture of water and vinegar (which is said to keep it crisp). The thinly rolled dough, cut in circles, is wrapped around metal tubes and deep fried. When cool, the cannolo is filled with sweetened RICOTTA, chocolate chips, and candied orange peel, or liqueur-flavoured ricotta in which case the ends are dipped in chopped nuts. These cakes are made for carnival, in February.

CANTAL is a French, semi-hard, cow's milk cheese from Auvergne in the Massif Central. Its history is ancient; indeed, Pliny seems to have mentioned a cheese very similar to Cantal, although the Salers cattle now used to make the cheese were probably not in existence then.

The cheese is characterized by its tall drumlike shape, and can weigh up to 45 kg (99 lb). The flavour, which should be nutty in a mature cheese, is often compared to that of CHEDDAR. Rance (1989) points out that Cantal, coming from a region of volcanic rock, tends to have a metallic flavour, whereas Cheddar, coming from limestone, does not. The rind of Cantal changes colour as it matures, from yellowish up to three months (*Cantal jeune*) to russet and then to grey streaked with gold after six months (*Cantal vieux*). The inside is smooth, ivory coloured, and firm.

READING: Graham (1988).

CANVASBACK *Aythya valisineria*, a wild duck of N. America, known especially from the saltwater marshes and bays of the eastern seaboard, but also present on the Pacific coast, is the largest of what Americans refer to as 'bay ducks'. De Voe (1866) observes that up to the early part of the 19th century there was little or no distinction made in the markets between this duck and relations such as red-heads and broad-bills; but that from the 1820s onwards the superiority of this species (if taken from suitable feeding grounds) was widely recognized. In the two paragraphs quoted below de Voe explains how the canvasback received its common name and dilates upon its merits.

Canvas-back duck received its name from the fact that a portion of the back of the drake resembles a piece of canvas. The bill of this duck is black, and higher at the base than the red-heads, and nearly in a straight line with the head, about 3" long.

This, no doubt, is the finest and choicest wild-duck known for the table, when in season, which generally appears to be in the latter part of November and through December; and then, provided they have been killed in the Susquehanna, Chesapeake, Potomac, and Delaware Rivers, feeding on what is commonly called wild celery, they are very fat, fine, tender, and with that delicious flavours much admired. If taken at any other season and place they are but little better than some of the common sea-ducks.

CAPE GOOSEBERRY *Physalis peruviana*, is thought to be a native of Peru and Chile, but the cape in its name is the Cape of Good Hope; the fruit enjoyed an early vogue in S. Africa, whither it was taken before 1807 and whence it travelled on to Australia and New Zealand. It thrives particularly in New South Wales and New Zealand.

It has been introduced to many other countries, including India, Sri Lanka, and Malaysia. It is now widely known by the Hawaiian name poha, since it is cultivated and consumed with especial enthusiasm by the Hawaiians. It is also among the fruits which are sometimes called GROUND CHERRY.

The plants bear throughout the year in Hawaii. They are annuals in temperate regions, but perennial in the tropics.

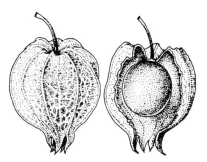

Cape gooseberry

The Cape gooseberry has not become popular in N. America, despite 'its having been reported on with enthusiasm by the late Dr David Fairchild in his well-loved book, *The World was My Garden* (1938). He there tells of its fruiting "enormously" in the garden of his home in Maryland, and of the cook's putting up over a hundred jars of what he called "Inca Conserve" which "met with universal favor". It is also remarkable that it is so little known in the Caribbean islands' (Morton, 1987).

The fruit, as usual with PHYSALIS FRUITS, is enclosed in a papery thin calyx or husk, which is cream in colour. It is this feature which accounts for the attractive Chilean name *amor en bolsa*. The fruit itself is about the size of a cherry, yellow-green or orange, with a thin, waxy skin; and the juicy pulp within contains many small seeds. The flavour is distinctive and pleasant, and the fruits may be eaten raw, alone or in composite desserts. They make a good jam, but their relatively low pectin content makes them unsuitable for jelly.

CAPER the pickled olive green flower bud of *Capparis spinosa*, a Mediterranean shrub. This is cultivated for the buds in France, where Roquevaire in Provence is the 'caper capital', and also in Spain and Italy. The plant, which is sprawling and has tenacious spines (hence one Turkish vernacular name meaning 'cat's claw'), bears small fruits which may also be pickled.

Fresh capers are not used. The characteristic and slightly bitter flavour which is the virtue of capers, and which is mainly due to the formation of capric acid, is only developed by pickling.

The buds are picked before they start to open, and pickled in vinegar. The most prized ones are called *non pareilles* in France, followed in increasing order of size and diminishing value by *surfines*, *capucines*, *fines*, and *capotes*. Because the buds develop fast, plants have to be picked over more or less daily, a procedure which affects their cost.

Pickled caper fruits are popular in Spain. They are somewhat larger than a grape—in fact, they somewhat resemble a coarse green grape with faint white stripes, or perhaps a lilliputian watermelon—and they have a seedy, slightly starchy texture like okra, but the flavour is that of the caper bud, though less intense. They are eaten like olives.

Capers are used in a number of sauces, for example TARTARE, RÉMOULADE, and RAVIGOTE. They are suited to seafood. In the Mediterranean region they are particularly used with salt cod, and go well with mutton. Capers are also used to flavour the Austrian cheese LIPTAUER, and in various Provençal dishes, including *tapenado*; and, sparingly, to decorate or flavour salad dishes.

C. decidua, which yields pink fruits and flower buds, usually pickled or used as a pot-herb, is the caper of N. India.

CAPERCAILLIE (sometimes given as capercailzie), *Tetrao urogallus*, a bird which belongs to the same family (Tetraonidae) as the GROUSE; and has been described as 'a very large grouse'. The average total length of an adult male is 85 cm (34"). As a result of forest clearance and other unfavourable factors, this magnificent game bird became extinct in Britain around the end of the 18th century, but successful introductions have since then taken place in parts of Scotland.

Various subspecies are recognized, but there is also another species, *T. parvirostris*, the Siberian capercaillie.

The reputation of the capercaillie as a table bird is less high than its splendid appearance and size might suggest. This is largely because the male birds in particular are likely to eat fir cones which give them a flavour of turpentine.

CAPIROTADA (also capirottata and other variant spellings), a Spanish term whose ancestry and original meaning are not entirely clear (see Barbara Santich, 1982, and Perry, 1983*a*), but which generally indicated a thick sauce served with meat or the whole dish of meat plus sauce, or sometimes a 'medley'.

In recent times something of the same name has appeared in New Mexico as a pudding. Davidson (1984) described some he ate as 'a bread pudding, flavoured with cinnamon, dotted with raisins, laced with rum, and topped (like so many New Mexican dishes) with melted cheese, forming an orange "skin" with raisins peeking through it. Indeed there was a thin layer of melted cheese over every layer of bread.'

Villa and Barrios (1978) give a recipe for Capirotada, which they describe as a Mexican bread pudding, 'one of Mexico's most popular Lenten dishes and one of the most exciting and tempting desserts of the world'. Bread is the most important ingredient but nuts and cheese also loom large. These authors, like Davidson, point to the puzzling gap between the Spanish savoury sauce or dish and the New World pudding. The question poses itself: by what process of evolution (or misunderstanding?) did the one turn into or give rise to the other? The answer may lie in the use of bread. The earliest appearance in print of a recipe using the name capirotada is in the Spanish version of the book published earlier by Ruperto de Nola in Catalan in 1520 (see CATALAN COOKERY), and this recipe, which is a meat (partridge) plus sauce recipe entitled *Almodrote que es capirotada*, calls for slices of bread (such as were called 'sops' in medieval England). This basic ingredient could have provided the bridge to the later pudding version.

Farga (1963), in his pleasantly discursive survey on food and gastronomy in Mexico (which includes a valuable short section on previous books and periodicals on the subject, comprehensive lists of game and fish, and other such items), gives capirotada in his glossary, describing it as being in Mexico 'a dessert made of white bread fried in lard, with sugar, cheese, cinnamon, raisins and pine nuts'. This is in line with other information, but Farga adds the following, potentially useful for further research:

Elsewhere in the hemisphere, it is a Creole dish made of meat, toasted corn, cheese, lard and spices. This name is also given to a combination of fragrant herbs, eggs, garlic and other products used as a batter for other dishes, or as a sauce.

CAPON a castrated young domestic COCK, castrated in order to become fatter and tastier for table use. It is no longer legal to produce capons in Britain, where they had sometimes been used as a Christmas bird instead of turkey; but the practice no doubt continues in some parts of the world.

CAPSICUM the botanical and also to some extent the common name for a genus of plants which includes a wide range of species: those referred to as peppers, sweet (or bell, or green) peppers, pimento, pimiento, chilli (and in other spellings).

Some of these common names, notably PEPPER and pimento (see ALLSPICE), are also used for fruits of other genera. Hence the need to use the name capsicum here for the *Capsicum* genus as a whole.

The CHILLI peppers, the hot ones, are described under their own heading.

The capsicums are a genus of the family Solanaceae, and are therefore related to the New World tomato and potato, and, in the Old World, to the aubergine and deadly nightshade. All capsicums are native to the Americas. The first two of the three species listed below are the most important.

- *Capsicum annuum*, to which species all modern cultivated sweet capsicums and most of the hot ones belong. This originated in Mexico, where remains dating back to around 7000 BC have been found. Despite its botanical name, which means 'annual capsicum', it is perennial in its native habitat.
- *C. frutescens*, a close relation (but not recognized by all botanists as a separate species), may have evolved more recently than *C. annuum*. It is a perennial. It produces mainly very hot fruits; among its cultivars is the well-known TABASCO.
- Bonnet pepper (with bulging fruits shaped like a Scotch bonnet, popular in the W. Indies) belongs to the species *C. chinense*, which despite its name is not Chinese; it is widespread in the north-east of S. America.

Besides this closely related group *annuum/frutescens/chinense*, there are two other S. American cultivated species of peppers. *C. baccatum* is native to the west coast of S. America, and *C. pubescens* to the Andes. *C. baccatum* varieties are usually called *aji* and *C. pubescens* is known as *rocoto* (or *locoto*) from the name of the pepper in the Quechua language of the Inca.

One of Columbus' reasons for trying to take a short cut to the E. Indies, which resulted in his accidentally 'discovering' America, was to obtain spices, which were in great demand and very expensive. So, when he found the Caribbean islanders using hot capsicums in their food, he was gratified and brought quantities back from, probably, his very first voyage.

Hopefully likening them to black pepper (*pimienta*), he called the capsicums 'pimiento'. He also recorded that they were called *axi* by the Taino people of Santo Domingo. The word was pronounced 'ashi' by the Taino and by Columbus, but the sound changes of 16th-century Spanish led

to the modern spelling and pronunciation, *aji*. Europeans learned the word chilli after the conquest of Mexico, but *aji* had become the standard word in colonial Spanish; hence its continuing use in Spanish America outside Mexico and C. America (where 'chilli' is the name for all capsicums). In Brazil, the word *pimenta* has remained the name for capsicums in general.

The naming of new foods often involves conflicts of interests among market-makers. The Spanish wanted hot capsicums to be classified as peppers, and most European consumers were happy to fall in line. Within a year of Columbus' return, Peter Martyr described them as 'pepper more pungent than that from the Caucasus'. Dutch traders, however, who were importing 'ordinary' (*Piper* spp) PEPPER from the E. Indies feared that this cheap new spice would outsell their expensive one. They therefore tried to enforce the use of the Nahuatl (Mexican) Indian name chilli, and were partially successful.

The sweet peppers became popular in most countries only at the beginning of the 20th century, as demand grew for a greater variety of vegetables. But spices were what the market had wanted, and the hot peppers had been a success in that role from the start, spreading eastward with extraordinary speed (see CHILLI), in striking contrast to the slow and hesitant manner in which the potato and tomato were accepted in Europe and Asia.

In English-speaking countries, pimiento (adopted into English from Spanish in the 19th century) usually refers to sweet (bell) peppers, the large red or green fruits which can be eaten raw in salads, cut into slivers for stuffing olives, or cooked as a vegetable; they are conveniently designed for stuffing. Piedmont is famous for the exceptionally large and handsome specimens grown there. Ivory or yellow varieties are known as wax peppers. There are also small, mild red cherry peppers.

Intermediate between sweet and hot types, but often mild enough to use whole in cooking, are the Ancho peppers of Mexican cuisine. Slightly hot peppers such as these often have a flavour of superior richness and interest. Another group in this category, classed by growers as Anaheim peppers, provide the Hungarian PAPRIKA.

Capsicums are rich in vitamins A and C and in carotenoids, which provide flavour and in some cases colour, the most important red colouring agent being capsanthin. (There are green varieties which lack capsanthin, though they may develop orange patches when ripe; other 'green' capsicums are simply unripe.)   (RO)

CAPULIN *Prunus salicifolia*, a true cherry (so called also by names such as *cereza* or *cerezo*, meaning cherry), has been cultivated since early times in the cooler mountainous regions of C. and northern S. America, where it grows abundantly.

The dark red fruits contain a pale green, sweet, and juicy pulp. They can be eaten either raw or stewed, and made into jam. They have been and remain an important food in the region.

The unrelated 'Jamaican cherry', *Muntingia calabura*, in the family Elaeocarpaceae, is also often known as capulin or capuli in Latin America. It is indigenous to C. and tropical S. America, but is now widely grown elsewhere, e.g. India, Malaysia (where it is known as 'Japanese' or 'Chinese cherry'), and the Philippines. Its small red or yellow fruits have a light brown, soft, juicy pulp, filled with minute yellowish seeds, too small to notice when eating. It has a sweet, figlike flavour.

CAPYBARA *Hydrochoerus hydrochoeris*, also known as water pig/hog or water cavy, belongs with the GUINEA PIG to the family Caviidae. This is the largest living rodent, indeed the size of a pig, 120 cm (48") long (not counting the tail which is either missing or of negligible size). The range of the capybara is from Panama to Paraguay; it is usually found living in troops or family groups, in the vicinity of rivers, lakes, or marshes. It can swim considerable distances under water. It is hunted both on land and water, and can be tamed, but has not yet been domesticated except on an experimental basis.

The capybara lives on vegetable matter, and the flesh is 'remarkably good eating' (Simmonds, 1859). Others have noted a resemblance to pork, but have commented that careful preparation is needed, especially trimming off the fat, to avoid a fishy taste. Dried and salted meat, which is commonly available, is free of this problem.

The US National Research Council (1991) draws attention to one special feature about the capybara as food.

Centuries ago, Venezuelans and Colombians petitioned the Pope for special dispensation to eat this semiaquatic animal on traditional 'meatless' days; approval was granted, and since that time the capybara has been an important food during Holy Week.

CARAMBOLA *Averrhoa carambola*, a small tree or shrub thought to be native to Java or other parts of Indonesia, and perhaps also Sri Lanka. It is cultivated in SE Asia, India, and Sri Lanka; and to a lesser extent in other tropical countries. It bears an elongated yellow-green fruit up to 13 cm (5") long which has five prominent ridges

running down it so that a cross-section is star shaped. Hence the alternative name starfruit.

The fruit has a waxy, orange-yellow skin, with a crisp, yellow, juicy flesh when ripe. There are two distinct sorts of carambola, one small and very sour, the other larger, with a bland but sweeter flavour.

The Javanese propagate the trees vegetatively by 'air layering', a technique which involves making a parcel of soil around a branch so that it strikes root and can be cut off and planted. Growing fruit from seed may produce a sour-fruited tree, which would not suit the Javanese, who eat the fruit as dessert and like it to be as sweet as possible.

The ridges are removed before the fruit is eaten fresh. The carambola is also cooked. The Chinese and Indians both use the unripe fruit as a vegetable as well as the ripe fruit for dessert.

CARAMEL a food product used both as a brown colouring and for its bitter-sweet flavour, is produced in the final stage of sugar boiling when sugar is heated above 170 °C (340 °F). The exact temperature at which caramel begins to form depends on the composition of the sugar; the figure given applies to sucrose, common white sugar. The fructose present in honey caramelizes more quickly; but the dextrose (glucose) which is also present in honey is slower. The pentose sugars found in small amounts in various vegetables caramelize particularly well, and toast made from wholemeal bread owes its dark colour to the caramelization of pentoses in the wheat bran.

The formation of caramel is, as a matter of chemistry, very complex. Some of the reactions take in oxygen, but others release it; so the process can go on in a closed container, which ordinary burning cannot. As the sugars are degraded they are changed into over a hundred different compounds, some of which are brown and bitter. If the temperature rises much above caramelization point, or is maintained at it for too long, the taste becomes too bitter and the colour very dark. At a very high temperature the sugar burns to black carbon.

The caramel topping in desserts such as CRÈME BRÛLÉE is made by exposing a layer of sugar on the surface to direct heat, e.g. under a grill.

Caramel colouring has several uses. An old-fashioned product still sometimes met is gravy browning, a concentrated caramel syrup which can be made at home from sugar and water. (It serves only to add colour, whereas stock cubes or 'gravy mixes', which also often contain caramel, provide

both colour and flavour.) Caramel colouring made from corn syrup is used to tint many brown foods, including bottled brown sauces and some drinks.

Caramel is used extensively in **confectionery.** BARLEY SUGAR (which formerly contained barley, but now does not) is simply sugar which has been slightly caramelized and then abruptly cooled to solidify it to a glassy state. See also PRALINE, SPUN SUGAR, and TOFFEE APPLE.

However, the word is more familiar in a confectionery context as meaning a kind of TOFFEE. Caramels and toffee are based on similar recipes, using sugar syrup enriched with milk, butter, or cream, and the choice of name for a particular confection in this category may appear arbitrary. This is recognized by confectioners, and stated in *Skuse's Complete Confectioner* (13th edn, 1957):

The difference between toffee and caramel is essentially one of texture and the two types of confection merge into one another without any clear dividing line. Toffee should be hard, 'chewy', unlike butterscotch which is hard and brittle; caramel is soft-eating with a clean fracture.

'Caramel' sweets made with milk owe their flavour and colour to a different effect which has been named 'Strecker degradation'. This occurs in heated milk when the sugar and protein in it react together. The effect is also noticeable in condensed and evaporated milk, and in the aroma of various roasted products including cocoa.

CARAWAY *Carum carvi*, a plant cultivated for its 'seeds' (the split halves of the dried fruits), which are an important spice, used mainly to flavour breads, especially rye bread, and other bakery goods (see COMFITS; CAKE; BISCUIT; WIGS; MERINGUE) but also cheeses (see LIPTAUER; TILSITER; LEIDEN) and PICKLES. It is an ingredient in the Arabic spice mixture TABIL and the N. African paste HARISSA. The seeds have a warm, sweet, biting taste.

The plant, which is indigenous to W. Asia and the Mediterranean region, may be the oldest cultivated spice plant of Europe. It is now mainly grown in E. and SE Europe, Germany, the Netherlands, N. Africa, and the USA. It is Germans who use it most freely, not only in cakes and breads but also in certain cheeses and pickles and in some meat dishes.

The main constituent of its essential oil is carvone, which can now be produced synthetically.

Redgrove (1933) comments: 'Mixed with a trace of sugar, and lightly sprinkled on bread and butter, powdered caraway seed forms an admirable accompaniment to gorgonzola cheese, a combination which has only once to be tasted to be highly appreciated.'

Munster cheese is traditionally served with caraway seeds.

CARBOHYDRATES an important category of substances in food, include all SUGARS, STARCH, CELLULOSE, HEMICELLULOSES, PECTIN, and the various sorts of GUM. They make up most of the solid matter in plants. Animals, however, whose solid matter consists mostly of proteins, contain only a little carbohydrate (apart from any undigested food they may have on board).

Plants store energy in the form of carbohydrates. When people and animals eat the plants they release this energy and can use it for their own purposes. Carbohydrates are the main source of energy for most peoples of the world. In an average western diet, for example, 55 to 65% of the energy comes from carbohydrates, the rest from fats and proteins. In a typical Japanese diet the figure for carbohydrates is about 80%.

Carbohydrates are not a requirement for survival as are proteins, essential fatty acids, vitamins, or minerals. The Inuit (better known as Eskimos) live largely on meat and fish and get their food energy from protein and fats. However, in most parts of the world this would be a wasteful way to live, since foods rich in protein and fat are relatively expensive, and their vital nutrients are lost if they are simply 'burnt as fuel'. A diet with plenty of carbohydrates and a smaller, but sufficient, quantity of protein and fat allows the body to 'burn' the carbohydrates and exploit the vital nutrients in the other substances to its best advantage. A further consideration is that a diet with virtually no carbohydrates throws the body into an abnormal metabolic condition known as ketosis, characterized by foul-smelling breath.

In chemical terms, carbohydrates consist of carbon, hydrogen, and oxygen. (The term carbohydrate means 'carbon with water' and water consists of hydrogen and oxygen.) Plants make them by taking in carbon dioxide from the atmosphere and water from the soil; energy from sunlight falling on the leaves powers a series of chemical reactions which convert these substances to carbohydrates, which the plants retain and use, and to oxygen. This process is known as photosynthesis. The oxygen replenishes the supply in the atmosphere which is steadily used up by animals breathing and by the burning of fuels.

The molecules of carbohydrates may be relatively simple, or may consist of thousands of atoms. But they are all based on molecules of simple or 'single' sugars, which can be joined together in long, often branched, chains to make the more complex carbohydrates. These simple or 'single' sugars, called monosaccharides, are described in the entry for SUGAR, where it is also explained that all digestion of carbohydrates is a process of breaking down large molecules to monosaccharides and changing them to dextrose. Slightly more complex carbohydrates are the disaccharides or 'double' sugars which include sucrose (ordinary white sugar), maltose (malt sugar), and lactose (milk sugar). Oligosaccharides ('few' sugars) include raffinose (three units) and stachyose (five units), both found in legumes.

Carbohydrates with a large number of sugar units are called polysaccharides ('many' sugars). They include starch, cellulose, hermicelluloses, pectin, and gums, all of which occur naturally in plants. In starch all the units are of the sugar dextrose, but this is not true of all carbohydrates. Inulin, a substance found in Jerusalem artichokes and asparagus, is made of fructose units.

The links between the units in these substances cannot all be undone by the human digestive system, so undigested portions of molecules pass through the gut. Here there are BACTERIA which can break the links. The chemical reactions by which they do this evolve gas, which is why peas and beans cause wind.

Carbohydrates present in animals include some dextrose (glucose) in the blood. The amount is small, only about 5 g (0.2 oz) in an adult man, but it is important because of its role as a reserve of short-term energy. When the level falls low it is topped up from a 250 g (11 oz) store of glycogen, another carbohydrate, in the liver, the conversion being regulated by a hormone, insulin. Faulty control results in the disease diabetes.

There are a few other animal carbohydrates, notably chitin, the substance which constitutes the hard outer casing of insects and crustaceans.

The main mechanism by which carbohydrates are broken into their constituent sugars is HYDROLYSIS, in which the links between the monosaccharide molecules are undone by the insertion of a molecule of water. This is assisted by heat; by acid conditions, as in the stomachs of most animals; and by digestive enzymes.

The exact way in which carbohydrate bonds are made differs from substance to substance. Particular enzymes undo particular types of bond. The human digestive system has enzymes which can hydrolyse starch, but only to a certain degree. One type of starch molecule has a branched, treelike structure. An enzyme begins at the tip of a branch and dismantles the bonds all down it until it reaches a fork, where there is a differently shaped bond which it cannot break. The result is that the branched molecule is reduced to a form like a lopped tree. The indigestible remainder is called a limit dextrin.

There are other kinds of dextrin. Starch hydrolysed by heating it in acid breaks more indiscriminately to form a type of dextrin found, for example, in corn syrup. It is slightly sweet, and sticky enough to be used as a gum ('British gum'). Starch heated dry forms pyrodextrins, some of which are compounds with a brown colour and a distinctive flavour (see BROWNING).

The human digestive system has no enzyme which can break down cellulose. But cows and other herbivorous animals have bacteria in special auxiliary stomachs 'upstream' of their true stomach which can and do break the bonds. Thus cows can gain nourishment from grass, which is practically non-nutritious to humans. However, indigestible carbohydrates do play a role in the diet. Dieticians refer to them as 'crude fibre' or 'roughage'. They act as a bulky medium to help food travel through the intestines (see CELLULOSE).

Digestion of carbohydrates is given a head start by cooking food, which, since the process involves heat and water, performs some preliminary hydrolysis. This, and the swelling and disruption of the cellulose and hemicelluloses and dispersion of the pectin which together form the cell walls of plants, cause vegetables and fruits to soften when cooked. The cellulose is not actually dissolved or much dispersed in normal cooking conditions, though hemicelluloses are dispersed to some extent even by the fairly weak acids and very weak alkalis used in cooking.

One further class of carbohydrates occasionally encountered is the dextrans: slimy, gummy, or rubbery substances, complex in composition. These are formed by bacteria, including those active in pickles. Usually they are no more than a nuisance, something to be skimmed off; but some are now grown deliberately and used as gums by the food industry (see also NATA). (RH)

CARBONADE AND CARBONADO two terms which are easily confused and which may indeed have been interchangeable, in the English language, for part of the 17th century. Both are derived from the Latin *carbo*, meaning charcoal (as is the Italian *carbonara*, which occurs in the phrase *alla carbonara*, meaning 'in the style of charcoal-burners').

Carbonade, also spelled carbonnade, now means, for English-speaking readers, a beef dish made with onions and braised in beer. This corresponds to *Carbonnade à la flamande*, not simply a Flemish speciality but also one of the national dishes in BELGIUM and well known in the NE corner of France.

Historically, *carbon(n)ade* has another meaning in French: a piece of meat fiercely grilled (broiled) on the outside but with the inside still rare. The appearance of the word in the French language goes back to the 16th century (even earlier in the form *charbonnade*), but it has been replaced in recent times by the English word 'steak' (in various spellings, as in *bifteck* (beefsteak) or *steak frites* (steak with French fries).

Carbonado, on the other hand, is a purely English term, and obsolete (at least in England); it was formerly used to mean a piece of meat or fish which had been scored and then grilled (broiled).

Dallas (1877) in *Kettner's Book of the Table* commences his entry on carbonade by saying: 'If cookery is ever to be a science it must be exact in its nomenclature, and cooks must not be allowed to confuse common-sense with their ignorant use of terms.' Unfortunately, he seems himself to have made this confusion, believing that the appearance of the French word 'carbonade' in England, with the meaning of a stew, represented a corruption of the word 'carbonado', which had been used by no less an authority than Shakespeare in the sense indicated above ('He scotcht him and notcht him like a carbonado'). Although Dallas's indignation was apparently misdirected, it did have the advantage that it prompted him to some fine polemical writing (in which, for carbonade understand carbonado):

The shoulder of mutton is usually roasted, but being flat and comparatively thin, is easily grilled; and a carbonade of it, or to speak more strictly, of its blade, has for centuries been a celebrated dish. But let no one be deceived by French receipts. Let the reader go back to the word carbonade, and understand what it really means. It is a broil which has been first slashed and scored, as in devilled meats, in order to be penetrated by pepper, salt, and other condiments—but above all by the taste of fire. This we can understand. In this sense the bladebone of mutton makes an admirable carbonade. But the French cooks have determined, for the glory of the Prince of Soubise, that in their sense a carbonade of mutton shall mean a bladebone planted or larded all over with fat bacon and then stewed or brazed with a goodly faggot of vegetables. Let Mossoo have this if he likes; but John Bull, having easy access to the Southdowns, where the wethers grow fragrant on banks of thyme and trefoil, is apt to turn almost an Israelite when he hears of a proposal to dibble his shoulders of mutton with splinters of bacon.

In conclusion, and in an attempt to prove everyone right, it is to be remarked that, since the charcoal of classical Rome is accepted as the point of origin for both carbonade and carbonado, a reconciliation of contending points of view can be achieved by supposing that in one region one of the resulting medieval and post-medieval terms first meant charcoal grilled; then charcoal

grilled and subsequently braised; and, finally, browned in the pan and then braised. This sequence may not yet have been fully established, but it is plausible and could have coexisted with the continuation of other and more conservative meanings of the terms in other places or subcultures.

CARDAMOM the dried fruit of a perennial herb, *Elettaria cardamomum*, is the third most expensive spice, after saffron and vanilla. The plant, indigenous to S. India and Sri Lanka, belongs to the GINGER family.

As far back as the 4th century BC the Greeks were buying spices called *amomon* and *kardamomon*, and later Greek and Roman writers distinguish varieties of both; but from the descriptions by Dioscorides and Pliny it is not clear which of them, if any, was what we would now call true cardamom.

It is certain, however, that cardamoms of the true kind have been an article of trade with India and Sri Lanka for about a thousand years. India is at present the largest producer; Guatemala comes second, Sri Lanka and Tanzania rank third, while other countries, including Papua New Guinea, produce on a smaller scale.

The fruits, which are three angled and ovoid or oblong, are picked before they are fully ripe (when they would be apt to split) and cured by drying, after which they should be hard and of a good green colour. Some are bleached before sale, a practice which perhaps began as a means of disguising poor coloration but which now seems to be responsive to the demand of certain markets. Each fruit contains three cells in which there are numerous small seeds. These seeds, which turn from white to brown to black as the fruit ripens, provide the pleasing aroma of cardamom, and its warm, slightly pungent flavour. The essential oil which can be distilled from them contains cineole, which is responsible for a eucalyptus-like note in the flavour.

The emphasis placed above on 'true' cardamom suggests that there are other kinds, i.e. 'false' cardamoms. As explained below, there are lots of these. However, from the point of view of the cook, the important distinction is between the green (or white, if they have been bleached) cardamom fruits (the true ones) and the larger brown or black fruits which come from some of the other species.

Green cardamoms are normally used for flavouring sweetmeats, desserts, and tea, notably in India and W. Asia, or in certain delicate savoury dishes. In addition, a popular and traditional use is to chew them as a breath-cleanser; and they are also regarded as a good digestive (when taken, for example, in sweet green tea after a meal).

The brown or black cardamoms, which are coarser in taste and aroma and tend to smell of camphor, are used more in meat and vegetable dishes, pickles, and as a flavouring for a PILAF (e.g. in Afghanistan).

Both black and green cardamoms are among the spices used in Asian spice mixtures such as *garam masala*.

In Arab countries cardamom is mainly employed as a flavouring for coffee. Its use in Europe has been most noticeable in Scandinavia and Germany, where it is added as a flavouring to various baked goods, and also to some pickles.

When whole cardamoms are used to flavour dishes, they are not meant to be eaten; but when the seeds, or ground seeds, are used, they are of course consumed.

VARIETIES, AND 'FALSE CARDAMOMS'
What are sold as cardamoms in western countries are normally true cardamoms, but distinguishing between the commercial categories of these, and the various 'cardamoms' of commerce in other parts of the world, is complicated by three factors.

First, the species which provides the true cardamom, *E. cardamomum*, comprises two botanically recognized varieties, *E. cardamomum* var *cardamomum* and *E. cardamomum* var *major*. The former is, strictly speaking, the only true one. The latter is the wild cardamom of Sri Lanka, has larger fruits, and is less highly esteemed.

Secondly, distinctions are made by region of origin. The Malabar and Mysore types of true cardamom differ in the composition of their volatile oils and therefore in their organoleptic qualities, which are also affected by the presence of sugar in the mucilage surrounding the seeds of Mysore cardamoms and its absence in those from Malabar.

Thirdly, there are the 'false cardamoms', some closely related to the true cardamom and sharing to some extent its desirable characteristics, others further removed and less satisfactory as substitutes. Burkill (1965–6) commented that if the word 'cardamom' is used in its widest sense it refers to various species of no fewer than six genera of plants. It is in this large category that the big brown cardamom fruits, referred to above, are found. Among those listed by Purseglove *et al.* (1981) are:

- The Nepal or large cardamom; a native of the E. Himalayas, markedly inferior, with a 'harsh' rather than subtle aroma.
- The Java (or Siam or round) cardamom, *Amomum compactum*; has a strong smell of camphor.
- The large round Chinese cardamom, *Alpinia globosa*; also smells of camphor.
- Thai or 'bastard' cardamom, *Amomum xanthioides*.

- The Ethiopian or Korarima cardamom, *Aframomum korarima*, smelling of camphor, 'harsh', dark brown in colour.
- Madagascar cardamom, *Aframomum angustifolium*, used as a substitute for pepper in the areas where it is grown.

The confusion sometimes extends to MELEGUETA PEPPER, a quite different spice.

CARDINAL at one time the name for a drink based on rum, has become a French culinary term indicating the colour scarlet, the colour of a cardinal's headgear. It may turn up in connection with a SAUCE, a garnish, or a CONSOMMÉ. It is usually obtained from the coral of a LOBSTER.

CARDOON *Cynara cardunculus*, a member of the THISTLE family, a native of the Mediterranean region with a flower head intermediate in size and appearance between ARTICHOKE and common thistle.

Long before the artichoke was developed, the ancient Greeks and Romans regarded the cardoon as a great delicacy. It was first described in the 4th century BC by the Greek writer Theophrastus, who stated that it was a native of Sicily. (Probably it was originally introduced from N. Africa.) Not only the flowering heads but also the stems and the midribs of the main leaves were eaten. Young buds were pickled in vinegar or brine with SILPHIUM and CUMIN.

The cardoon remained popular through the Middle Ages and continued to appear in English cookery books through the 18th and into the 19th century, but in recent times cultivation and consumption have been greater in N. Africa and S. Europe than in W. Europe. The blanched stalks or ribs of the inner leaves are favoured in Spain for the Madrid version of the nationally renowned COCIDO and in other dishes too.

In addition, wild cardoon heads are gathered in Italy and Spain and used as a vegetable RENNET for making certain kinds of cheese. As a wild plant, the cardoon is notably persistent and fast-spreading. Accidentally introduced to S. America, California, and Australia, it has now become a troublesome weed.

Schneider (1986), as so often, has an evocative and precise description of:

the fleshy, silver-gray stalks. They grow in bunches, like celery, but are flattened, longer, and wider, with slightly notched sides and a brushed-suède finish. Cooked, the cardoon is soft and meaty. The flavor is complex, bitter and sweet, with hints of artichoke heart, celery, and oyster plant.

CARÊME ANTONIN (1783–1833). Here is the man who became and remains the most famous of 19th-century French chefs. His students and their successors studied his books, or at least paid lip-service to him, well into the 20th century. Gastronomes and food writers have praised him as a great genius of haute cuisine, and have held him up as an outstanding example of how a lowly apprentice, of a humble background, could rise to the topmost pinnacle of his profession. His grandiloquent claim that there are five branches of the fine arts, and that the greatest of these is confectionery, is famous.

That is one way of looking at him, and it corresponds to the image which he sought to create in his writings. Like Soyer in England, he was a great self-promoter. Yet to study his books and work with his recipes produces a different impression: of a man who was conceited, whose recipes were written in a tangled prose, whose menus were pretentious and heavy, and whose *pièces montées* are to modern eyes an extravagant waste of ingredients.

The truth lies somewhere in between. It is certainly true that he rose from the bottom to the top. Born into a poor family as one of either 15 or 25 children (depending on which account is accepted), he was apparently told at the age of 10 by his father to go forth and support himself, whereupon he was taken in by the proprietor of a cheap tavern, where he learned the first elements of his métier. Eight years later—having presumably learned to read and write by now—he began to work for Bailly, one of the best pastry-cooks in Paris, who had the statesman Talleyrand among his distinguished clients. There Carême rose to a position of responsibility. Bailly allowed him to take two afternoons each week to visit the nearby old royal library (which was later to become the Bibliothèque Nationale), where he studied architectural prints in the Cabinet des Estampes and read cookbooks from other countries and from past times.

At the end of three years he was ready to move on, first to another pastry-cook, whom he describes only as the successor to M. Gendron, and then opening his own shop on the rue de la Paix in 1803, which continued to operate for a decade. All through the 19th century one can see the luxury trades in France being democratized. Luxury goods and activities which had been almost exclusively the prerogatives of the court and the very rich became available to anyone who could pay for them. Excellent ingredients could be bought in the markets and shops; beautifully prepared food could be bought in restaurants. As the century went on the same thing happened with travel, clothing, and reading matter. But with the single exception of this shop, about which he has little to say, Carême held aloof from this more commercial sphere, restricting his services to the more exclusive world of power and great wealth. After his youthful work in the tavern, he never cooked in a restaurant: and in this respect his great students, Jules GOUFFÉ and Félix Urbain Dubois, resembled him.

It is not surprising, then, that at the same time as he opened his shop he set out on what was to become an intermittent but spectacular career as a specialist pastry-cook at the great imperial, social, and governmental banquets.

For the rest of his life his activities cycled between working on these events, writing and working for longer periods of time with a single employer, and trips abroad to serve monarchs and diplomats.

From 1804 to 1814 he was directing the kitchens of Talleyrand. During the same period he organized special events such as the festivities for the marriage of Napoleon to Marie-Louise of Austria (1810).

Carême never let patriotism interfere with his own career interests. For example, after the defeat of Napoleon, the English and Russians occupied Paris. Alexander I, the Tsar of Russia, accompanying his army, engaged Carême's services during his stay at the Élysée-Napoleon palace (1814), and again for several weeks the following year. The great public eating event of 1815 was the banquet Carême organized for the Allies near Châlons in Champagne. It presented immense logistical problems, most of which were overcome.

In the same year he published his first two books: *Le Pâtissier royal parisien*, an illustrated two-volume compendium of recipes for all the preparations that an accomplished pastry-cook would need to know, with extensive general observations about the composition and execution of the most elaborate menus, and *Le Pâtissier pittoresque*, which contains more than a hundred engravings of designs for *pièces montées*, with more or less sketchy instructions for executing them.

There followed a period of brief, high-profile engagements and frenetic travel. July of 1816 saw him in England, directing the kitchens of the Prince Regent, first at Carlton House in London, and subsequently at the Royal Pavilion in Brighton. He directed the Tsar's kitchens at the Congress of Aix-la-Chapelle in 1818, and later, after more work in Vienna and London, agreed to go to St Petersburg. To his annoyance, the Tsar was making a 40-day visit to Archangel, and Carême found Russian kitchen politics and cost-controls not to his liking, so he returned to Paris again; but, although the Russian visit was a fiasco, it made a deep impression on him.

While his career continued to develop on these lines, he continued to produce books. In 1821 he produced his *Projets d'architecture dédiés à Alexandre 1er* and *Projets d'architecture pour l'embellissement de Paris*, both of which attempted to use the insights gained from making *pièces montées* to advance the cause of planning the monumental city, based on his studies in the Cabinet des Estampes. This is perhaps the place at which to mention that, although his designs for *pièces montées* were meticulously drawn, they display disconcerting discrepancies. Elevations do not always match their accompanying floor plans. When one compares the plates in the works on architecture and travel to which he refers with his own designs, one finds that he has played some very strange games indeed with proportion and scale. Typically, he appropriates from monumental structures one or more ornamental features, cramming them together without any intervening plain areas. The designs he produced for the embellishment of St Petersburg reveal a similar lack of proportion, bordering on the grotesque. The eclecticism that was to characterize 19th-century art and architecture was exactly to his taste. It seems not to have mattered to him at all if one used a 'Turkish cabana' or a 'Babylonian ruin', a 'Chinese temple' or an 'English belvedere'. It must be said, however, that there is a playfulness to them which can be quite charming.

His next publication was the *Maître d'hôtel* (1822). Later, while working for James de Rothschild, the head of the French branch of the great banking house, he published *Le Cuisinier parisien* (1828). He had a further and more ambitious plan, which he did not live to execute in its entirety. No doubt he was worn out by a life that began in deprivation and continued with the stress of organizing so many high-visibility meals and with his decades of hard work in carbon-monoxide-laden kitchens; there is a moving passage in his last book in which he displays great sympathy for those working in kitchens, and describes vividly the terrible conditions with which they (and he) had to contend. Anyway, he retired from Baron de Rothschild's service to work on his last project. Unfortunately he died with only three volumes of this work, the extensively illustrated *L'Art de la cuisine française au XIXe siècle*, completed. His student, Pluméry, added the remaining two volumes which Carême had planned to write.

Carême's own perception of his place in the history of France and that of cuisine was exaggerated. He was a creature of the troubled times in which he lived. His attitude towards his employers and other gastronomes was one of enthusiastic servility, more deeply tinged with self-interest than he would have acknowledged. He was well repaid. He became a society pet. The Tsar gave him a diamond ring,

Metternich a gold snuffbox. It was probably a real advantage to him that he lacked a sense of proportion, because his exaggerated self-importance carried him further than modesty would have done, and because it helped to fuel the ambitions of generations of chefs, in France and abroad.   BW

CARIBOU *Rangifer arcticus*, a large member of the DEER family, Cervidae, and a close relation of the REINDEER. The caribou has importance as food for the indigenous inhabitants of Alaska, and other parts of the far north of the American continent, although its meat is thought to be not quite as good as that of the reindeer. However, the difference between the two animals is small and some authorities have been tempted to classify them as a single species.

The name itself is said to be derived from a Micmac Indian name meaning 'snow-shoveller'.

Gillian Riley (1990), describing the experiences of Vilhjalmur Stefansson, who from 1906 onwards spent over two decades living as an Inuit on a diet of nothing but meat and water, quotes this intrepid experimenter at length on how caribou meat was divided between a family and its dogs:

The children get the kidneys and the leg marrows nearest the hoof. All Eskimos known to me think the sweetest meat is nearest the bone; they boil the hams and round shoulder bones and the children pick from these the cooked lean that goes so pleasantly with the uncooked fat of the raw lower marrows. Perhaps the whole family and my visitors will share the boiled caribou head. The Eskimo likes the tongue well enough, and the brains; but what he prefers from the head is the jowl, and after that, the pads of fat behind the eyes. His next preference is brisket, then ribs, then pelvis. From the hams and shoulders he will peel off the outside meat as dog food, but will keep some of the inside meat for his family. The neck of the caribou is considered halfway between human food and dog food. Dog food, especially if the team is big, would consist first of the lungs, but not the windpipe or the bronchial tubes, for the Eskimo likes cartilage. The liver goes to the dogs and everything else from the body cavity except the kidneys. The heart is considered intermediate, not especially bad but not especially good. The dogs get the stomach and the entrails, but not the fat from the entrails. They also get the tenderloin and much of the meat from the backbone; but the Stone Age Eskimo likes to leave some meat on the vertebrae; he enjoys picking them when boiled.

CARISSA AND KARANDA, two closely related fruits of which the former is indigenous to S. Africa and the latter to S. Asia. *Carissa* is a botanical as well as a common name, referring to the genus of thorny, fruiting shrubs to which both fruits belong.

Carissa, the more popular of the two species, *Carissa macrocarpa*, is also known as

Natal plum and amantungula. In its native S. Africa the fruit is gathered from wild trees but also cultivated on a small scale; and it has now been introduced elsewhere, e.g. Florida and Hawaii. Its fruits look like small scarlet plums, with dark red streaks on the skin, and red flesh inside, flecked with white. The whole fruit can be eaten out of hand, without peeling or deseeding. The texture is slightly granular, the flavour mildly sharp. In the semi-ripe stage the fruits are used for making jellies and jams. Ripe fruits are said to make a good filling for pies.

The karanda, *C. carandas*, is cultivated in India (where it was popular with British residents because it reminded them of the GOOSEBERRY) and some parts of SE Asia and E. Africa. Its fruits resemble the carissa and are used in similar ways, and also for pickling when unripe. The tree grows wild in Malaysia and Indonesia, where its fruits have an additional use in curry dishes.

CARLING from Carling/Carlin/Care Sunday, the fifth Sunday of LENT, when it is a tradition in the north of England to serve a dish made of dried peas, known as carlings. Constance Cruickshank (1959), author of an exceptionally charming book on Lenten food, cites a couple of old recipes. In the less common of the two, the carlings (like brown split peas) were soaked for 24 hours, then tied in a cloth and boiled as a pudding for three hours, after which they were rubbed through a sieve, beaten with salt, butter, and cream—finishing up like PEASE PUDDING but brown instead of green—and served with any kind of meat. The more usual recipe also starts with soaking and boiling, but then requires the carlings to be drained, fried briefly in butter, then: 'mix with more butter and lots of sugar and add a small glass of rum. Eat while hot.' It was the latter recipe which prompted someone to say that he didn't care for the greyish-brown peas but that the gravy was wonderful.

This author's account of the etymology and history is so good and interesting that it deserved to be quoted at length:

Originally peas and beans were fasting fare, and Brand presumed that their connection with this day goes back to the Roman association of beans with funerals. I quote his deductions though they are open to doubt. 'In the old Roman Calendar so often cited, I find it observed on this day, that "a dole is made of *soft Beans*". I can hardly entertain a doubt but that our custom is derived from hence. It was usual amongst the Romanists to give beans in the doles at funerals: it was also a rite in the funeral ceremonies of heathen Rome. Why we have substituted peas I know not, unless it was because they are a pulse somewhat fitter to be eaten at this season of the year. They are given away in a kind of dole at this day. Our Popish ancestors celebrated (as it were by anticipation) the funeral of Our Lord on this Care Sunday.'

However this may be, by the eighteenth century carlings came to be regarded as matters of jollity. A passage from 1724 says, 'There lads and lassies will feast . . . on sybows [onions], and riforts [radishes] and carlings', a reference which occurs also in an old Scots song. And we cannot imagine that those parties at the inns were occasions of great sobriety. It appears that the carlings which survived were a festive form of the original plain parched peas.

There are a number of theories about the origin of this name, in one or other of its forms. The Yorkshire people who observed their Carlin Sunday on Mothering Sunday, are said to have got the name from the word for old woman. A more usual derivation, from the other spelling, is that it comes from Care or Carle Sunday, in the way, suggests Brand, that presents from fairs are called fairlings, or as we should say, fairings.

Quite another explanation, again of this spelling, is that a ship was wrecked with a cargo of peas and the starving peasants seized the food and have ever after commemorated the event. According to this picturesque legend, the name carling comes from part of the boat's structure, which no doubt was also washed up. Some say it was an Australian boat, others put it back to Commonwealth days; but in sober fact the name was known well before that date. The first appearance noted in the *Oxford English Dictionary* is in Turner's Herbal of 1562, 'the perched or burstled peasen which are called in Northumbria Carlines'.

Perhaps it is no wonder that such an old and persistent custom should have such a varied appearance today. It must at one time have been very widespread. Scotland knew it and most of the north of England. I am told by a firm which supplies the peas, that the custom is still observed to a certain extent in Northumberland, Durham and parts of Cumberland and Yorkshire; though they say that the tradition has been much weakened since the break in the war years.

CARNIVAL FOODS
could be regarded as a worldwide phenomenon, if the word 'carnival' is taken in its wide sense, meaning any occasion of riotous revelry. However, in the narrower and more commonly used sense it refers to the day or week before LENT and especially Shrove Tuesday (Mardi Gras), when Christians bid farewell to meat for 40 days.

Carnival (a term derived from two Latin words meaning 'meat, goodbye') is celebrated most noticeably in Roman Catholic countries such as Italy, Spain, France, where various cities hold traditional processions with dancing, mummers, masks, lights, special street foods, etc. The custom travelled to the New World and is conspicuous in New Orleans and Rio de Janeiro, for example. However, some would say that the calypso and carnival tradition in Trinidad (and Tobago) eclipses by its size and exuberance anything else in the world. DeWitt and Wilan (1993) provide a vivid description of carnival time in Trinidad and of the street foods consumed by the revellers.

On the origin of carnivals in Europe, Constance Cruickshank (1959) has written:

Many of these rites undoubtedly stem from pre-Christian times. It is well known that the great Pope Gregory deliberately charged his missionaries to graft the new on to the old by purifying pagan rites and the sanctification of existing customs. In particular ancient rituals of the death of winter and the rebirth of spring can still be traced in the rites and customs of the Christian year.

Which of the carnival foods enjoyed in modern times can be traced back to pagan times is an interesting question. One obvious candidate is the PANCAKE, the entry for which includes much relevant material. Another is the FRITTER. An 18th-century poem entitled 'The Oxford Sausage' neatly pairs these items:

Let glad Shrove Tuesday bring the pancake thin Or fritter rich, with apples stored within.

CAROB
Ceratonia siliqua, a long-lived evergreen tree bearing large, brown, leathery pods and seeds, rich in sugar. These, often referred to as locust beans, have been used for food in the E. Mediterranean region since ancient times.

Cultivation of the carob was practised by the ancient Greeks, who valued it highly as a sweetmeat. When the pods ripen they become full of a sweet gum with a distinctive taste and smell. Locust gum is produced by grinding the endosperm.

The Bible relates that when John the Baptist was in the desert he lived on locusts and wild honey. Opinion is divided about whether the insect or the plant is meant. Both are nutritious and locally available, and the original Greek has the same ambiguity as the English. The gum is still sometimes made into a sweetmeat called St John's bread.

Carob pods are used for animal fodder in tropical Africa and parts of Asia, but are also used as human food and have acquired, during the latter half of the 20th century, the status of a 'health food' in western countries.

Broken carob pods, called kibble, are roasted and ground to produce a brown powder which has a flavour similar to CHOCOLATE or MOCHA, and is used as a substitute for chocolate. Its fat content is only 0.7%, whereas that of chocolate ranges from about 25% to 50%, depending on the form in which it is offered.

Anissa Helou (1994) reports that in the Lebanon a thick dark syrup called *dibess kharroob* is extracted from carob pods. 'The long pods are picked when dark and ripe and taken to a special press to extract their juice. *Dibess kharroob* is served with pita bread as a sweet dip and is eaten alone or mixed with tahini. The ripe pods can also be chewed on as a sweet snack.'

In classical times carob seeds were used as weights by goldsmiths. The Greek word for the seed, *keration*, meaning 'little horn', gives us the modern term for a jeweller's carat weight.

The carob has been introduced to California, Mexico, S. Africa, Australia, and India.

CARP
the common name applied to a limited number of species in several genera of the very extensive family Cyprinidae; especially *Cyprinus carpio*, the best known and the one which is usually meant when a recipe refers to 'carp'. This is a large fish, deep-bodied and reaching a length of up to 1 m (40"). It is native to the Danube River and others which flow into the Black Sea and the Aegean, but has been very widely introduced elsewhere, indeed one might almost say everywhere, mainly because of its value as a food fish. It grows quickly and is well suited to fish-farming operations.

This carp has firm flesh and has a high reputation as food in some countries, notably in C. Europe, besides being esteemed by Jewish communities, for whom it is a traditional holiday dish. However, carp which have been living in stagnant ponds are liable to acquire a muddy taste; and the flesh of larger specimens, wherever they have been living, tends to be coarse. So their gastronomic reputation, averaged around the world, is no more than moderate.

The three other best-known carp, at least for food purposes, are as follows (but note that they may all be referred to as 'Chinese carp'):

- The grass carp (properly grass-eating carp—it grows rapidly when fed on grass cuttings), *Ctenopharyngodon idellus*, a larger fish (maximum length 125 cm/50").
- The big-head carp, *Aristichthys nobilis*, is relatively dark in colour and has a larger head than the others. It is a popular choice for fish farming in SE Asia.
- The silver carp, *Hypophthalmichthys molitrix*, is less esteemed as a food fish, but can be a useful addition to fish farms because it feeds on nanoplankton and does not therefore compete with other fish for the higher forms of plankton. It has a greenish-brown back.

CARPET-SHELL
Ruditapes decussatus (formerly *Venerupis decussata*, or *Tapes decussatus*), an edible BIVALVE which is better known to connoisseurs of seafood under its French and Italian names: *palourde* and *vongola* respectively. Although the range of the species extends as far north as Britain, it is little known there. The erudite Lovell (1884) recorded that people in Hampshire

knew it as butter-fish, and preferred it to the cockle, but any such enthusiasm had waned a 100 years later. The name carpet-shell is given because the pattern on the shell was thought to resemble those of certain carpets. The more general name VENUS SHELL may also be used, since the carpet-shell belongs to the family Veneridae.

The carpet-shell has a maximum width of 8 cm (3"), but usually measures much less. Its twin shells, or valves, are usually of a light colour (whitish, yellow, pale brown) with darker brown streaks or rays. It is highly esteemed as food, and may be prepared according to any of the standard recipes for small clams, or eaten raw as oysters are.

Besides French and Italian recipes, there are numerous Spanish and Portuguese ones. In Portugal there is an ingenious device called cataplana, like an aluminium or copper globe but in two parts which are hinged together. When this is closed, with carpet-shells inside and olive oil and other ingredients of an aromatic nature, it can be set to steam. The results are excellent, especially if a little bacon or chopped Portuguese sausage has been included.

The golden carpet-shell, *Venerupis aurea*, is the French *clovisse jaune*. It is only half the size of *Ruditapes decussatus*. The golden colour which gives it its name is on the inner side of the valves, not the outside. This species has other small relations, which share the name *clovisse* with it. Its range extends from the Mediterranean to Norway.

Mention should be made here of two other species. *Venerupis pullastra* is a close relation of the carpet-shells, although lacking their carpet-like pattern and thus more apt to be called venus shell than carpet-shell in English. It is the *almeja babosa* of Spain, *poulette* or *coque bleue* in French. Some think it superior to the carpet-shells, but it lives less long out of water and is therefore less common in the markets. The other is *Ruditapes philippinarum*, an oriental species which has been introduced to Spain, where it is being 'farmed' under the name *almeja japonesa*.

CARRAGEEN *Chondrus crispus*, one of the red SEAWEEDS. It is found on both sides of the N. Atlantic but associated especially with Ireland, where the Gaelic *carrigín*, meaning a little rock, provided its most common name and whence comes 'Irish moss', one of the numerous alternative names. The beautiful fan-shaped fronds, which are purplish or reddish-green, are important as the source of carrageenan, a substance which has gelling properties similar to those of AGAR-AGAR, an Asiatic product of related red seaweeds in the family Gigartinaceae.

Carrageen may be made into a delicious jelly dessert, as explained by Myrtle Allen (1987), who points out that only enough to produce a gel should be used and that a flavouring of vanilla or cocoa enhances the result. It is also used widely in Irish folk medicine as a trusted cure for coughs and colds. A curative draught is prepared by simmering some fronds in milk or water, after which the liquid is strained and sometimes flavoured with honey and lemon juice.

Carrageen

The same name is often used for *Gigartina stellata*, a related plant; and has been used in New Zealand for other relations which grow in the southern hemisphere.

Carrageen is an important ingredient for the food industry, because of its capabilities to produce and stabilize consistencies, and most of what is harvested is used in this way.

CARRÉ the French word for 'square', is used as a generic term for cheeses that are square in shape and flat. Examples are *carré de l'Est*, made in Lorraine, and the cheese of the same name which is made in the Franche-Comté.

CARROT *Daucus carota*, an important root vegetable which had an unpromising origin. The wild carrot, which grows in much of W. Asia and Europe, has a tiny and acrid-tasting root. However, when it is cultivated in favourable conditions the roots of successive generations enlarge quickly. So the evolution of cultivars with enlarged roots is easily explained; indeed, what is puzzling is that it seems to have taken a very long time for *D. carota* var *sativa*, as the modern cultivated carrot is known, to appear.

The puzzle is all the greater because archaeologists have found traces of carrot seed at prehistoric lake dwellings in Switzerland. Also, the plant is included in a list of vegetables grown in the royal garden of Babylon in the 8th century BC. Here there is a clue: the plant is not in the list of ordinary vegetables but in that of aromatic herbs. It was probably being grown for its leaves or seeds, both of which have a pleasant carrot fragrance. It seems likely that this had also been the purpose of carrot cultivation in classical times, for there is little or no evidence to suggest that the Greeks and Romans enjoyed eating the roots.

Many writers state that the carrot in something like its modern form was brought westwards, at least as far as the Arab countries of the E. Mediterranean, from Afghanistan, where the very dark red, even purple, carrots of antiquity are still grown. The introduction is variously dated at the 8th or 10th century AD, i.e. the period of Arab expansion into the Middle East and C. Asia. This fits well enough with the fact that the earliest surviving clear description of the carrot dates from the first half of the 12th century, and was by an Arab writer, Ibn al-Awam. He described two kinds. One, which was juicy and tasty, was 'red'; probably the purplish-red carrot referred to above and seldom seen now. The other, coarser and of inferior flavour, was yellow and green: this sounds like a predecessor of the typical hot-climate variety still grown in the Middle East and India. Ibn al-Awam said that carrots were eaten dressed with oil and vinegar or in mixtures with vegetables or cereals.

Ibn al-Awam was writing in Andalusia, whither the Arabs had brought the carrot by his time, and whence it reached other parts of Europe. For example, it came into use in France, the Netherlands, and Germany in the 14th century, and in Britain in the 15th. The Dutch were foremost in the cultivation of carrots, and improved Dutch varieties were brought to England in the reign of Queen Elizabeth I. From contemporary botanists' descriptions, and in particular from a painting (*Christ and the Adulterers* by Pieter Aertsen, Amsterdam, 1559) it is clear that all these carrots were pale yellow or purple, the purple kinds gradually falling from favour. In the mid-16th century a white type was described in Germany. (White carrots still occasionally appear as freaks in normal-coloured crops.)

The first sign of truly orange carrots is in Dutch paintings of the 17th century, and they were first described, also in the

Netherlands, in the 18th. They soon assumed the dominance which they have had ever since. The orange colour is due to the presence of carotene, in its beta form; this is converted in the body to vitamin A. (The earlier purplish colour was provided by an anthocyanin pigment.)

Cultivated carrots of the European type were brought to the New World before 1565, when Hawkins mentions that they were grown on Margarita Island, off the coast of what is now Venezuela. These carrots were enthusiastically received by the American Indians, who had few good sweet roots to compare with them. In Oregon the Flathead Indians, though otherwise scrupulously honest, were said by a surveyor for the Pacific Railroad to be unable to resist digging up the white settlers' carrots.

Modern carrot varieties are specialized into different shapes. The conventional, and oldest, fairly long and tapered shape is that of 'main crop' carrots, which grow slowly and are ready from the middle to the end of the season. They keep well both in the ground and in storage, and generally have the best flavour for use as cooked vegetables. 'Early' carrots, the second principal category, are often narrow and cylindrical, for example Amsterdam.

Carrots contain quite large amounts of sugar, and have occasionally been used as a source of refined sugar; but in this role they cannot compare with the sweeter but otherwise useless sugar beet.

Despite this sweetness, carrots are most commonly met, in western kitchens, as an ingredient for savoury soups (*Potage Crécy* is the famous French carrot soup) and stews, or as a cooked vegetable in their own right, or grated to be eaten raw as a salad item.

Carrots being cooked by themselves are often slightly sweetened to bring out their natural sweetness, either with sugar or by browning to caramelize their natural sugar and convert some of their starch to sweetish dextrin. Another way of accentuating the flavour is by adding a little of one of their umbelliferous relatives: celery leaves, fennel seeds, chervil, or parsley.

In the Middle Ages in Europe, when sweeteners were scarce and expensive, carrots were used in sweet cakes and desserts. In Britain, for example, carrot puddings (and puddings made from other sweet root vegetables, such as parsnips) often appeared in recipe books in the 18th and 19th centuries. Such uses were revived in Britain during the Second World War, when the Ministry of Food disseminated recipes for carrot Christmas pudding, carrot cake, and so on and survive in a small way to the present day. Indeed, carrot cakes have enjoyed a revival in Britain in the last quarter of the 20th century. They are perceived as 'healthy' cakes, a perception

fortified by the use of brown sugar and wholemeal flour and the inclusion of chopped nuts, and only slightly compromised by the cream cheese and sugar icing which appears on some versions.

The role of carrots has a different emphasis in Asia. They are often conserved and preserved in jams and syrups. Shredded carrots are used as a colourful garnish for PILAF, notably in Iran and C. Asia. In Afghanistan and the Indian subcontinent, they are also the basis of some types of HALVA and KHEER.

CASHEW *Anacardium occidentale*, a small tree which bears a strange fruit. As the drawing shows, it has two parts: at the stem end a cashew 'apple', and projecting from the other end of the apple a smaller cashew 'nut'. In fact the 'nut' is the true fruit, and it is only after the 'nut' has reached its full size that the 'apple' develops, as a fleshy expansion of what is called the receptacle of the nut. The degree of expansion is considerable; the apple may be over 10 cm (4") long.

Cashew

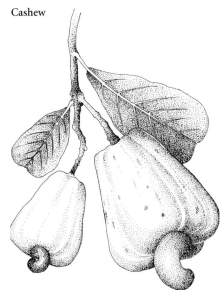

When the apple is ripe, it and the nut fall to the ground together. Each then poses a problem. The apple keeps only for a very short time; it will spoil within a day at ordinary room temperature. The nut is in a hard double shell, between the two parts of which there is a caustic substance, as explained below, so the kernel is difficult to extract. In some countries the fruit is prized, for immediate consumption, or to be preserved in syrup or dried and candied; and the nuts are discarded. In other countries, the emphasis is on the nuts, and the fruits are left on the ground for animals to eat. Monkeys like them.

The native region of the cashew is thought to be NE Brazil. As long ago as the 16th century it was taken from there by the Portuguese to the E. Indies, whence cultivation spread to India. The Portuguese turned the Brazilian Tupi name *acaju* into *caju*, and names in most languages come from this. (In French *acajou* means 'mahogany', which has caused confusion. The two trees are unrelated.)

The cashew 'apple' is generally pear shaped; yellow or red; quite sour; and tending to be astringent and fibrous. However, a good fruit can be eaten raw, if sweetened. In Indonesia it is an ingredient in *Rujak*, a spicy fruit salad. However, it is usual to boil the fruit in slightly salted water for a few minutes to reduce the astringency, and it still needs sugar.

The nut is not easy to extract. The tissue between its two layers of hard shell contains strongly irritant substances, cardol and anacardic acid. This tissue has medical uses, including burning off warts, an indication of its great corrosive power. The usual way of treating the nut is to roast it whole, driving off the irritants and making the shell brittle enough to crack without crushing the contents.

The nuts, which have a delicate texture and a mild almond flavour, are highly esteemed. They are widely eaten as a snack or appetizer. The USA imports large quantities annually. In S. India and China they are often added, whole or ground, to savoury dishes.

The species *Semecarpus anacardium*, known as marking nut (because its outer shell yields a black, resinous liquid which can be mixed with lime to produce an indelible ink), is related to the cashew, and may be called oriental cashew. Both fruit (when cooked) and nut (once freed of toxins, e.g. by roasting) are edible, but neither is important as food.

Because its fruits resemble cashew 'fruits', the Malay rose apple (see ROSE-APPLE) is sometimes called French cashew or Otaheite cashew, but it is not related to the true cashew.

CASSABANANA *Sicana odorifera*, also known as *sikana* or musk cucumber, is found throughout tropical America, sometimes being grown as an ornamental vine. It is popular for its fruit in some places, notably Cuba, Puerto Rico, and Mexico. *Melocotón* is one name often used.

The fruit resembles a large, wide-bodied CUCUMBER (measuring up to 60 × 12 cm/24" × 5") in shape, and has a hard, shiny shell, which can be red, purple, or black in colour. The orangey-yellow, juicy flesh is melon-like in texture and smell, and the central cavity contains a soft pulp surrounding massive rows of tightly packed, flat, oval seeds.

Although refreshing when eaten raw, the cassabanana is more popularly used for making jams. Unripe fruit is good for soups and as an addition to stews. It keeps well in a cool, dry place, and according to Morton (1987) some people like to store it in the linen cupboard, where its pleasant melon-like fragrance is thought to repel moths.

CASSATA a speciality of Sicily, where it is a traditional Easter food, was originally a sort of cake, filled with RICOTTA beaten up with sugar, chocolate, vanilla, candied fruit (especially small cubes of pumpkin), and a liqueur. This filling, according to a description quoted by Carol Field (1990), is enclosed 'in alternating squares of sponge cake and almond paste coloured green to look like the pistachio paste with which cassate were originally made. The cake is iced and decorated in a flourish of baroque extravagance with ribbons of candied pumpkin sweeping around a candied half orange set in the center, and it is dotted with glacéed cherries and sprinkled with silver sugar balls.'

There is an echo here of some of the 16th-century recipes of Scappi (see ITALIAN COOKERY BOOKS), for mixtures of ricotta or the like with egg white, nuts, and spices, enclosed in pastry or set on a pastry base.

Nowadays, however, the name cassata is better known, internationally and in Italy, as a kind of ICE CREAM exhibiting three colours—typically chocolate, white (for vanilla), and green (pistachio or candied angelica).

CASSAVA *Manihot esculenta*, a tropical root crop which is outranked, in volume consumed, only by the SWEET POTATO. The plant is native to C. or S. America, where it has been in use since prehistoric times, and is the only member of the spurge family, Euphorbiaceae, which provides food. Brazil and Indonesia are the principal producing countries, but cassava has become important in the economies of many tropical countries worldwide. It is marketed mainly in the form of cassava flour, but can be eaten as a vegetable (as can the young leaves) or processed into a wide range of other products.

Cassava tubers are cigar shaped, with a brown, often pinkish, rind which is usually hairy, and ivory white flesh. They vary considerably in size, but are typically 25 cm (10") long and 5 cm (2") thick. They are borne in clusters of up to ten, and may spread out widely and deeply from the stem of the plant.

Varieties fall into two main groups: bitter and sweet, of which the first is the more cultivated, although cultivars of the latter are chosen when the plants are being grown for their leaves. The only cassava product with which most people outside the tropics are familiar is TAPIOCA, a refined starch. The cassava plant itself is sometimes known by this name, though the word in its original American Indian usage always meant the prepared product. Other names for cassava often used are **manioc** and **yuca,** also of American Indian origin.

The original wild species from which the cultivated one evolved is, or are, lost or unrecognized. Selection of plants for cultivation would have been directed at reducing a serious disadvantage of the plant; that it contains two substances, a glucoside and an enzyme, which react together to produce poisonous prussic acid. The reaction begins, slowly, when the tubers are uprooted and speeds up when they are cut or peeled and exposed to the air. At worst, the amount of poison can be fatal. However, prussic acid is freely soluble in water and driven off by heat, so the American Indians were able to evolve various soaking and heating processes to remove it. It was also the American Indians who bred the two main races of cassava.

Bitter cassava has a high yield of large, starchy tubers but contains an appreciable amount of poison, so that it can be consumed only after thorough treatment. Sweet cassava is of lower yield and its tubers are comparatively watery; but they contain less poison and that mainly in the skin, so that after peeling the tubers may be safely eaten as a cooked vegetable or, less often, raw, and the leaves are safe to use as a vegetable. Nearly all tapioca and other cassava products are made from bitter cassava.

As a staple food, cassava provides much carbohydrate, but very little protein; so in regions where people depend almost exclusively on cassava, malnutrition is common. Nevertheless cassava, properly supplemented with a source of protein, has a unique advantage over other roots. After the roots have grown, which they do quickly, typically in six months, they can be left in the ground for as long as three years without deteriorating. Thus cassava can be a reserve food against shortage.

The first European explorers in the **W. Indies** found cassava in use everywhere, in the form of meal and of dried, flat cakes. They made use of it themselves on their voyages. Cassava meal, now usually known by the Portuguese name *farinha* (flour) or the Creole name *couac*, was made by a sequence of processes which began with grating the peeled tubers and squeezing the moisture from them, and which ended with

heating, either briefly to make a porridge or for longer to make a dry meal which would keep for some time.

Cassava continues to be an important food in the Caribbean region. Hawkes (1968), who writes at length on this topic, comments that: 'Boiled, hot cassava is most often served as a vegetable in the American tropics dressed simply with butter, additional salt if needed, a couple of good grinds from the pepper mill, and a few drops of lime or sour-orange juice.' His highest praise is reserved for a soup/stew dish of tripe (*mondongo*) and cassava and 15 other ingredients.

A special cassava product made only in the Caribbean is cassareep. This is a thick syrup prepared by boiling down juice from the tubers with sugar, cloves, and cinnamon. Its unique flavour is essential to the W. Indian stew PEPPER POT. A corresponding product/sauce, *tucupi*, plays a similarly important role in Brazil.

In **Brazil** a superior variety of cassava, mandiba, was ground extra fine, then pressed. Some of the fine starch escaped with the juice; but this was extracted from the liquid (*tipioca*) and heated to make pellets (*tipioceto*). That was the origin of the modern tapioca process. However, farinha was the normal everyday product, and still is in regions where cassava is the staple food.

The Indians also made a cassava beer; and they boiled the young leaves as a vegetable, a practice which continues. Like the tubers, the leaves must be cooked to remove poison. The early European explorers brought back only meal, not cuttings from which the plant could be grown, but slave traders later took cuttings to Africa, where the plant was in use by the end of the 16th century. By the late 18th century it had spread to E. Africa and was already a major food in a region beyond the southern limit of yam cultivation.

The usual **African practice** is to cook the tubers, then pound them to make a type of porridge called FOO-FOO in W. Africa. Sometimes this is given a short fermentation to improve the flavour. The pulp can be dried to make a dry meal called *gari*. Cassava also provides beverages, both non-alcoholic ones and beer.

Cassava arrived in the Malay peninsula and Indonesia during the 18th century, and in India by 1800. Neither in India nor in SE Asia did it become as important in diet as in parts of Africa. Much is grown, but most of it is made into tapioca for export. However, in Indonesia, the Javanese, with their customary skill in fermentation processes, have developed a fermented cassava delicacy, TAPÉ, as well as using fermented tuber peelings as a seasoning for rice.

During the 19th century cassava was introduced to the Pacific islands and became an important food in Polynesia. In Hawaii it is often used as an alternative to TARO in making the fermented porridge POI.

CASSEROLE 'a covered heat proof vessel in which food is cooked and served' (*NSOED*) or, by extension, the food cooked in such a vessel. The word has a complicated history, starting with a classical Greek term for a cup (*kuáthos*), progressing to a Latin word (*cattia*), which could mean both ladle and pan, then becoming an Old French word (*casse*, via the Provençal *casa*), which then became *cassole* (diminutive *cassolette*) and casserole. Besides explaining this, Ayto (1993) draws attention to the remarkable fact that there has been a complete and sudden change in the meaning of casserole in English in the last 100 years:

When English took it over from French at the beginning of the eighteenth century it meant a dish of cooked rice moulded into the shape of a casserole cooking pot and then filled with a savoury mixture, say of chicken or sweetbreads. It was also applied by extension to a border of rice, or even of mashed potato, round some such dish as fricassee or curry: Mrs Beeton's recipe for a 'savoury casserole of rice' describes such a rice border. Then some time around the 1870s this sense of *casserole* seems to have slipped imperceptibly but swiftly into a 'dish of meat, vegetable, and stock or other liquid, cooked slowly in the oven in a closed pot', its current sense.

On the French side, it is of interest that when Favre (1883–92) wrote his huge culinary encyclopedia a casserole was defined as a tinned copper cooking pot, well suited to being displayed on the wall in order to impress visitors with the wealth and highly civilized lifestyle of the owners 'who live on food prepared in these gleaming vessels'.

There are many situations in which the use of a casserole, as the term is now understood, is helpful to the cook. It is economical in the use of fuel; beneficial where long, slow cooking is desired to achieve a mingling of flavours, or tenderness; convenient when something has to be left cooking unattended; and appropriate for any household which likes to have food brought hot to the table in the vessel in which it was cooked (a point which is also of interest to whoever in the household attends to the washing up). Historically, casserole cookery has been especially popular in rural homes, where a fire is in any case burning all day and every day, and for special situations such as the requirement in JEWISH COOKERY for one-pot dishes for the sabbath.

Although casserole is a western term, the use of cooking pots which would be called casseroles in Europe or the Americas is almost universal in Asia. In China, for example, as Gerald and Anne Nicholls (1989) explain:

Sandpots are the casseroles of Chinese cooking. They are used for 'clear simmering' which involves the long, slow cooking of meat or fish with vegetables in water or fragrant sauces. They are also used for making soups and for cooking rice. They are thus an important part of the Chinese kitchen.

They are made of a mixture of sand and clay, and come in a variety of shapes and sizes. They are called sandpots because their rough unglazed exteriors have a sandy texture. There are wide pots, shallow pots, large pots and small, pots with two handles and pots with one handle. Some have rounded sides and others are straight or bowed. Some are designed to rest on a charcoal burner; a sort of chafing dish. Many come with matching lids.

See also pot-roasting, under ROAST.

CASSIA a spice resembling and related but inferior to CINNAMON (hence often known as 'false' or 'bastard' cinnamon), is the product of numerous plants, notably: Chinese cassia, *Cinnamonum cassia*; Indonesian cassia, *C. burmannii*; and Saigon cassia, *C. loureirii*. Each has a number of alternative names. Thus Chinese cassia may also be Kwangtun, Yunnan, Honan, or Chinese-junk cassia. Distinguishing between the various kinds is not easy. Rosengarten (1969) remarks that in the period when imports from China to the USA were banned, US chemists had to devise a system of testing cassia bark by gas chromatography in order to identify and exclude any of the Chinese kind.

Cassia is marketed and used like cinnamon, in the form of cured and curled 'quills' of bark, or powdered. But cassia 'buds', the dried, unripe fruits, are also used in China and elsewhere, much in the manner of cloves, to lend their powerful aroma to confections and other items such as pickles.

The distinction between true cinnamon and cassia was recognized from early times. Indeed, way back in the 5th century BC, the Greek historian Herodotus was in no doubt about their being different. Cinnamon sticks were used by huge birds in Arabia for the construction of their cliff-top nests, and the way of gathering the spice was to tempt the birds into flying back to their nests with pieces of meat so heavy that the nest would then collapse and its constituent parts flutter down to the Arabs waiting far below. Cassia was quite a different matter. It grew in shallow lakes, protected by batlike creatures which squeaked alarmingly and tried to ward off the Arab cassia-pickers; but the latter were clothed in leather gear from head to foot, and, provided that they could shield their eyes from the squeaking assailants, could gather the crop.

Such pleasing fantasies were no longer current in the Middle Ages, when the two spices were distinguished more by status. John Russell, in his *Boke of Nurture* (15th century), said that cinnamon was for lords, but canelle (cassia) was for common people.

Good cassia is, however, a respectable spice, and Chinese cassia in particular has been cultivated for a long time in S. China and is of commercial importance. Although the flavour is less delicate than that of cinnamon, the quills are more robust. The colour is reddish-brown, compared with the tan of true cinnamon.

CASSOULET a renowned composite meat dish which appears, with many variations, throughout the Languedoc. The consistent elements are haricot (white) beans and some forms of pork and sausage. Goosefat is frequently the cooking medium.

Anatole France claimed in his *Histoire comique* that the cassoulet he used to eat in a favourite establishment in Paris had been cooking for 20 years, thus placing cassoulet squarely within the POT-AU-FEU category of dishes, which traditionally live on the stove through decades while subjected to daily subtractions and replenishments. It is true that long slow cooking is essential but it need not be carried to such extreme lengths.

The name cassoulet comes from that of the glazed earthenware vessel in which the dish is cooked. Although it is generally agreed that the haricot beans are the most important ingredient, others being subject to variation, the earliest versions of cassoulet must have had Old World beans since the haricot beans did not arrive in France via Spain from the New World until the 16th century. The variations exhibited by the best-known recipes concern the meat. The cassoulet of Castelnaudary has ingredients on the lines noted above, with pork and pork products supplying all the meat. That of Carcassonne may include leg of mutton and partridge in season. In Toulouse there will be Toulouse sausage and the possibility of mutton and duck or goose. The *Larousse gastronomique* (1997) cites other versions from Montauban and Comminges and quotes a gastronomic 'decree' of the 1960s, stating that a true cassoulet must contain at least 30% pork (which can include sausage), mutton, or *confit d'oie* (goose). However, the same work acknowledges the existence of a fish cassoulet made with salt cod.

CATALAN COOKERY is a more important subject, especially in a historical context, than most people realize; but it requires definition, lucidly provided by Grewe (1981) in a pioneering paper:

I understand by the word Catalan primarily a language evolved from Latin, that is more akin to Provençal and the Langue d'Oc than it is to Castilian or Spanish.

By the Catalan Region I mean the region where Catalan is spoken, that is Catalonia, Valencia, the Balearic Islands and Roussillon. This region is called in Catalan 'els paisos Catalans' or 'las terras catalanas'. . . . The continental section is a triangular strip of land that extends along the western Mediterranean, from the Roussillon in the North, now part of France, to Alicante in the South. Its coastline is approximately 700 km long.

During the late medieval period the Catalan area was considerably but temporarily enlarged, by the incorporation of Sicily in the 13th, Sardinia in the 14th, and Naples in the 15th century. The resulting influence of Catalan cuisine on Italian cuisines can be clearly traced by comparing the important Catalan text known as the *Sent Sovi* (Grewe, 1979) with Italian 15th-century works such as those of Martino and Platina.

The *Sent Sovi* was one of two great Catalan culinary texts of the medieval period. The other is the *Libre del coch* (Book of the Cook), ascribed to Mestre Robert (also known as Robert/Ruperto de Nola). Colman Andrews (1988), who provides, in what is the first and best book in English on Catalan cuisine, a good survey of Catalan writing on the subject, believes that the *Libre del coch* dates back to the 15th century, although the first known edition was published in Barcelona in 1520.

The BALEARIC ISLANDS, which are treated separately, were also an acquisition of the medieval period, but a permanent one.

The term Catalonia, which refers to the mainland only, means the north-eastern region of mainland Spain, comprising the four provinces of Barcelona, Girona (Gerona), Lleida (Lérida), and Tarragona. This region is unique in Spain for its pervasive Roman heritage. Latin is the foundation of Catalan; there are almost no traces of pre-Roman words. After all, the Romans conquered the Catalan region in the 3rd century BC and retained it until AD 476, a period of over 600 years. In Grewe's view, Rome laid the foundation for what was to become the Catalan cuisine, just as Latin was the foundation of Catalan.

However, other influences have been at work. That of the Arabs, coming after the Romans, was important. It was the Arabs who improved the rich soil of the region by irrigation; and it was the Arabs who were responsible for introducing new plants, e.g. aubergine, spinach, sugar, bitter orange, saffron, which have been prominent in Catalan cookery ever since.

The question arises: what, now, are the distinguishing characteristics of Catalan cuisine? Andrews suggests that the cuisine is built on four basic preparations: *allioli*, *sofregit*, *picada*, and *samfaina*. These can be described as follows:

- *Allioli*, an emulsion of garlic and olive oil, which is closely similar to the Provençal aïoli, is the ubiquitous condiment at Catalan tables—often made with egg, although purists denounce this version.
- *Sofregit*, onion (plus, often, tomato) lightly fried with garlic and herbs, is the starting point for many Catalan dishes (as are the related SOFFRITTO/SOFRITO for Italian and Castilian dishes).
- *Picada*, described by Andrews as 'a thickening and flavoring agent made up of such ingredients as garlic, fried bread, olive oil (or some other liquid), and various nuts, herbs and/or spices, all pounded together with a mortar and pestle', is added to a dish at the moment of its completion, as a liaison to thicken the sauce and heighten flavour. Andrews suggests that there is no real parallel to the *picada* in other cuisines, although the Italian PESTO has some points of similarity.
- *Samfaina* is difficult to distinguish from the French RATATOUILLE (a speciality of Nice), although in the opinion of Andrews possibly antedating the latter and in any case having a more fundamental role in Catalan cookery than ratatouille has ever enjoyed in the south of France.

Pork is another cornerstone of Catalan cooking, often in the form of *butifarra*, a white sausage spiced with cinnamon, nutmeg, and cloves, and lard is as commonly used as olive oil. The inventive spirit of the cuisine is seen in its flair for unusual combinations of ingredients, one example being lobster and chicken. The region is unique in Spain for its dishes of meat and poultry cooked with fruits, the most celebrated example being *Oca con peras*, baby goose with pears. Nuts embellish and enrich a range of savoury foods and bitter chocolate is used as a flavouring for meat, and sometimes for seafoods such as spiny lobster.

Sweet dishes and confectionery are well liked by the Catalan people. Back in the 15th century the famous Italian writer PLATINA was already praising Catalan skill in making Lenten confectionery.

See also ROMESCO.
READING: Patience Gray (1986).

CATERPILLAR a stage through which butterflies and moths pass in the process of metamorphosis. In the whole category of INSECTS AS FOOD, caterpillars are moderately prominent, partly because they are easy to catch and partly because the larger caterpillars at least are nutritious and contain enough fat to make them tasty morsels. Examples of the consumption of caterpillars could be quoted from many parts of the world. One which is well known because it has achieved a certain totemic significance for modern Australians (and was always important in this respect for the Aboriginals) is the WITCHETTY GRUB (grub being a term which is often synonymous with caterpillar).

Another well-known caterpillar is that of the Emperor moth, *Imbrasia belina*, of southern Africa. This is a large, colourful, and spiny caterpillar which is associated with the mopane tree and is commonly called the 'mopane worm'. Where available, they are a local delicacy; and have also been made available elsewhere in dried form or canned in a peri-peri (PIL-PIL) or tomato sauce.

CATFISH the name given to a large number of fish in more than two dozen different families, both freshwater and marine, which share the characteristic of having barbels like cats' whiskers. They typically have a somewhat flattened head and a scaleless skin. This last point means that they cannot be eaten by observant Jews (not a serious deprivation in biblical times, since the ones which are best as food are mostly found at distances of 5,000 to 10,000 miles from the Holy Land).

Perhaps the most renowned catfish, from the cook's point of view, are the group in the family Ictaluridae of N. America, especially *Ictalurus furcatus*, the blue catfish (or Mississippi cat, as it is sometimes called) of the southern USA and the channel catfish, which ranges from way up north down to Florida and the north of Mexico. Their maximum lengths are respectively 1.5 m (5') and 1.2 m (4'), so both are large fishes and of great commercial value. In the southern states catfish fillets are usually dredged in cornmeal and fried, to be served with HUSH PUPPY and COLESLAW.

The longest (although not the heaviest) catfish is the WELS, but it is an unprepossessing fish of no great merit. In contrast, the largest catfish (by weight), is the best, indeed is one of the finest fish in the world for eating. This is *Pangasianodon gigas*, the giant catfish of the Mekong, which may weigh over 300 kg (nearly 700 lb) and measure 3 m (10') in length. Until recently, it was something of a mystery, indeed a great mystery; no one had ever seen a young specimen, less than a metre in length, and only myths were available to satisfy curiosity about its spawning habits. Everything to do with it was surrounded by legends and extraordinary rites took place near Vientiane (capital of Laos, on the Mekong River) when the season for fishing it opened. See Davidson (1975) for detailed information about all this, about ways of cooking parts of the fish, and about the excellence of its eggs—referred to as 'Laotian caviar', reddish in colour and eaten on rice cakes. It had been thought that the species inhabited only the Mekong River and that it faced extinction. However, in the last decades of the 20th century Thai fishery experts established that it was present in some major tributaries and also managed to breed the fish in captivity. Thus the future of this majestic creature seems to be assured.

Marine catfish include species in the family Ariidae, which have some commercial value in SE Asia, being eaten for example in Thailand and the Philippines. Elsewhere in the world there are other edible catfish, but none of great gastronomic value.

CATS especially domesticated cats, are rarely eaten, for reasons discussed under DOG. Stray pieces of evidence are occasionally cited to demonstrate that people in some parts of Asia do sometimes eat them, and Schwabe (1979) was able to find some recipes, but the practice seems to be very limited and is probably on the decline. Simoons (1994), in his comprehensive work on food avoidances from prehistory to the present time, barely mentions the subject.

CAT-TAIL the most usual common name for bulrushes of the genus *Typha*, which occur in temperate regions round the world and provide a surprisingly large variety of foodstuffs. *Typha* comes from the Greek word for a cat's tail, referring to the seed stalk, not the long tapering leaves.

In N. America *T. latifolia* is the main species. Fernald and Kinsey (1943) cite impressive testimonials from early writers to the food value of the rootstocks, when well filled with starch in the autumn and winter, and refer also to notable experiments carried out at Yale. These showed that mice throve on 'cat-tail flour'; and it seems that similar results were obtained when, 'as a check, Yale students substituted for the mice'. However, other parts of the plant also provide food. In the south-western states, Indians regarded the young flowering spikes, excepting the tough core, as a delicacy, whether raw or cooked. Fernald and Kinsey, full of enthusiasm, say that the flavour and consistency are somewhat suggestive of both olives and French artichokes.

It is often remarked that the inner part of the stem of this cat-tail is or has been eaten, raw or cooked, as 'Cossack asparagus'; but those who pass on this titbit of information fail to say who used this seemingly improbable name. A clue to the small mystery is provided by a passage in *Sturtevant's Notes on Edible Plants* (1919), where Lindley (1846) is said to have recorded

use of the name. In the same work, reference is made to 'Clarke's *Travels in Russia*'; this traveller found the people of the Don devouring young cat-tail stems 'with a degree of avidity as though it had been a religious observance. It was to be seen in all the streets and in every house, bound into faggots.' After the outer rind had been peeled off, the tender white parts inside offered, for the length of about 45 cm (18"), 'a crisp, cooling, and very pleasant article of food'. To round out the picture, a distinctive category of persons, namely 'Cossack officers who have travelled extensively', are cited by Fernald and Kinsey (1943) as stating that the cat-tail 'is only fit for food when it grows in the marshes of the Don'.

The same species (but sometimes referred to as *T. orientalis*) occurs in marshy places throughout New Zealand, where it is known as *raupo*. The Maori made full use of this plant. The rootstock were used, much as in N. America, and the young shoots were also eaten. But the greatest delicacy was a part not eaten in N. America. As Crowe (1981) puts it:

The yellow pollen, pungapunga or pua, was the most important food of the raupo; it was collected at the height of the summer, from the very top of the seed stalk—above the brown seed head. A party of fifty to sixty men, women and children would take part in the harvesting, which was done in the early morning and late evening, to avoid the pollen being blown away. The flower-stalks would be collected and then left in the sun for several days to dry, being brought in each night to avoid the dew. The pollen was then stripped from the stem and sifted to separate out the down. Colenso says that it looks exactly like 'the ground yellow mustard of commerce, and when put up into bottles would be mistaken for it'. The Northern Waori Maori mixed the pollen with water to form a porridge which they called rerepe . . . I have made pollen gruel along these lines with a taste and smell reminiscent of sweet corn. The more common preparation, however, was to form this pollen into cakes with a little water, place the cakes in leaf lined baskets, and then cook them in the earth saying that they remind one strongly of 'London gingerbread'.

The versatility of the product was further demonstrated by the Tuhoe tribe, who mixed it with crushed green manka beetles and steamed the mixture in an earth oven.

In the Indian subcontinent *T. latifolia* (greater cat-tail) and *T. angustifolia* (lesser cat-tail) are both found. The roots, shoots, and pollen of the latter have all been used for food, the pollen being treated as a flour and bread made from it.

CATTLE a collective term which covers animals in the genus *Bos* of the family Bovidae, including *Bos taurus*, the domesticated European animal which is the source of BEEF; but also *B. indicus*, the

humped ZEBU cattle of Africa and India, *B. javanicus*, the banteng of Indonesia, *B. frontalis*, the mithan or gayal of Assam and Nepal (a domesticated descendant of the wild gaur). These are all domesticated animals, as is the WATER-BUFFALO, *Bubalus bubalis*, for which the term cattle is also applicable. See also BISON; BUFFALO; YAK.

It is less usual to use the term cattle for species which exist only in the wild, and an expression such as 'wild cattle' would usually refer to the wild ancestors of modern domesticated species.

The history of cattle shows their immense economic and social significance, reflecting their value as draught animals in many parts of the world; that of their MILK and MEAT, plus their dung (used as fuel); and their importance as sacred animals in India, and even, in Africa, as currency.

European domestic cattle and the Indian zebu are thought to share an ancestor in the shape of *Bos primigenius*, the wild cattle or aurochs common in Eurasia between about 30 degrees and 60 degrees N. at the end of the last ice age. Shown in cave paintings in France and Spain, these were a favourite quarry of palaeolithic hunters, and were eventually hunted to extinction. The last one was killed during the early 17th century AD in the forests of central Poland. Domestication of cattle probably started because wild cattle were attracted to the fields of grain grown by early farmers and robbed these abundant supplies of food. Cross-breeding with wild stock no doubt continued for some time. Exactly where domestication took place is uncertain, but by 3000 BC there is evidence for several well-defined breeds in representations of cattle from both Mesopotamia and Egypt.

The early importance of cattle as meat animals is unclear. Egyptian tomb paintings show cattle drawing ploughs (motive power may have been the original purpose of domestication), and trampling corn to thresh it. Scenes of milking, slaughtering and butchering cattle, and hunting wild cattle in swamps are also shown.

Cattle have had great religious significance in many cultures. Bulls, especially, were held in awe for fertility, strength, and vigour, and were thought to be associated with the power of natural phenomena such as thunder and earthquakes. Numerous examples of cattle deities are to be found in early Eurasian civilizations, from the Assyrian statues of winged bulls with human heads, to Hathor, the cow goddess of Egypt. The development of these cults, west and east, has led to important differences in the use of cattle as providers of food in European and Indian culture.

In Europe, the bull cult was important in several early civilizations. A famous example was that of Minoan Crete, where wall-paintings at Knossos depict acrobats vaulting over the backs of bulls, a practice which contributed to the Greek myth of the Minotaur. Cattle cults also existed from early times in the Iberian peninsula, where the bullfight has survived into the 20th century.

In Asia, the picture is different. Although the Hindu attitude to the cow does not stretch back into remote antiquity—the ancient Indus Valley civilization used beef for food, and appears to have had a bull cult—it has for long been firmly established that no Hindu would ever contemplate killing a cow and eating its flesh. Here all the products of the live cow (including dung and urine) are regarded as purifying, and have their place in ritual. See HINDUISM AND FOOD; and, for other religious factors which influence the attitudes of many Asians, BUDDHISM AND FOOD and JAINS AND FOOD.

CATTLE IN BRITAIN IN HISTORICAL TIMES
From prehistoric times domesticated cattle have been important in the British Isles. In Ireland they represented a form of wealth, and the title of one of the earliest surviving pieces of epic literature, 'The Cattle Raid of Cooley' (*Táin Bó Cuailnge*), speaks for itself.

The native domestic cattle were based on the gene pools of those brought by neolithic farmers and their successors, the Beaker people, with some aurochs blood. Some of the small, sturdy black breeds of British cattle may descend from this ancient stock. British cattle were exported to the Continent both before and after the arrival of the Romans. According to Julius Caesar, the Britons lived on milk and flesh.

Cattle were raised mainly as draught and plough beasts by the Saxons. Beef became increasingly important, and the custom of cattle droving, walking cattle to market in lowland England from Wales and the north of England, was established by the 13th century. (Cattle droving from Scotland came later and lasted until the coming of the railways.) Feral cattle roamed in the forests and were hunted until the reign of Elizabeth I, their range gradually receding northwards as the forests of lowland Britain were cut down. Such were the 'wild white' cattle enclosed in parks such as Chillingham in the Middle Ages.

The quality of beef available to the consumer increased greatly between the 17th and 19th centuries. This was due to the development of fodder crops such as turnips and clover, and to selective breeding. In the 18th century, gentlemen farmers such as Robert Bakewell of Dishley in Leicestershire took an active interest in improving livestock. Cattle purchased from Holland were used to improve English cattle in the eastern counties, and the recording of pedigrees began.

CATTLE BREEDS

THE concept of breeds is a relatively recent one. A breed is not the same as what is called a landrace. The latter is a genetic stock in a particular area which has adapted over the centuries to the local conditions. A breed has been bred in controlled conditions, with documentation in the form of a herd book. One can become the other; for example, Highland cattle prior to the mid-19th century were a landrace, but more recently have become a breed (herd book established 1885).

Some breeds have been enormously influential because used for the establishment or improvement of herds far from their native lands. British breeders have been to the fore in all this, and British bulls have been among Britain's most important exports. The breeds whose genes are most widely distributed include:

- *dairy breeds*: Dairy Shorthorn, Jersey, Swiss Brown, Friesian/Holstein.
- *beef breeds*: Beef Shorthorn, Hereford, Aberdeen Angus, Devon.

These four breeds are all British and have been genetically influential since the 19th century.

In contrast, the following six continental breeds have only become fashionable since the Second World War, mainly because they are former 'traction breeds' and lean:

Charolais	Blonde d'Aquitaine
Limousin	Chianina
Simmental	Belgian Blue

Many 19th-century breeds of beef cattle are now rare and confined to a few specialist farms. Most calves in Britain are cross-breds with blood from both native and continental breeds.

By the end of the 18th century the improved Shorthorn breed had become the most important. This breed produced several animals of great size, which have left their names, and portraits of curious rectangular looking beasts with disproportionately tiny heads and legs, on pub signs all over the country. One of the best known was the Durham Ox, bred in 1796, which had a successful career as an exhibition animal. Such animals commanded huge prices (1,000 guineas was paid for a Beef Shorthorn bull at a time when a labourer's wage was less than £1 a week) and specimens were exported all over the world.

By now many different breeds of *B. taurus* were emerging, to fulfil the three basic purposes—dairy, draught, and beef—of cattle in agriculture.

The physiology of dairy cattle, directed at converting food into rich supplies of milk, means that they are lean, and a result of their value as milk producers is that they are several years old at slaughter. Their meat is never first-class beef. Some types of dairy cattle are bred to be 'dual purpose', that is to be efficient milk producers which also yield good beef. The black and white Friesian/Holstein is an example.

Breeds intended as draught cattle are generally very large and carry a high proportion of lean meat. Their importance as a means of traction has waned in Europe, but during the late 20th century several 'traction breeds' have become important as suppliers of beef in their native countries, and as sires for cross-bred beef animals in Britain. Examples are the French Charolais, Limousin, Simmental, and Blonde d'Aquitaine, the Italian Chianina, and the Belgian Blue. The Charolais and the Belgian Blue are especially popular because of a phenomenon known as 'double muscling', which means that the muscles are much bulkier in relation to the amount of bone in the animal.

Finally, there are the traditional beef breeds, bred to produce the best-flavoured and tenderest meat. Several of these are of British origin, such as the Shorthorn and the Hereford, instantly recognizable for its red body and white head. Both are also popular in the USA. The classic Scottish beef animals are the Highland, the Galloway, and the Aberdeen Angus.

The concept of breeds and associated matters are explained in the box, with a list of the most influential breeds.

For preparation and consumption of beef, see BEEF. (LM)

READING: Juliet Clutton-Brock (1981); Valerie Porter (1991, a magnificently illustrated global survey).

CAUDLE The original, basic caudle was a hot drink made from ale, or occasionally wine, thickened with strained egg yolks, sweetened with honey or sugar, spiced, and gently heated until the eggs thickened. From the start there were thicker versions containing breadcrumbs. Caudel ferry, coloured with saffron, might be solid enough to slice, and was sometimes served in a dish in alternate quarters with BLANCMANGE to make a yellow and white pattern. Caudles thickened with breadcrumbs or cereals were considered suitable for those with delicate digestions; by the 18th century both thick caudles and POSSETS were commonly recommended as foods for invalids.

From the 16th century on, 'caudle' came also to mean a mixture used like a CUSTARD or sauce to fill up a pie or tart. This might be as simple as plain butter and verjuice (acid fruit juice, used as vinegar), or a thicker mixture of wine, egg yolks, butter, sugar, and flavourings. One peculiar type of drinking caudle which enjoyed a vogue around the beginning of the 18th century was tea caudle. It arrived in the following way, according to Sir Kenelm Digby (1669):

The Jesuit that came from China, Ann[o] 1664, told Mr Walker, that they used tea sometimes in this manner. To near a pint of the infusion, take two yolks of new laid eggs, and beat them very well with as much fine sugar as is sufficient for the quantity of liquor; when they are very well incorporated, pour your Tea upon the Eggs and Sugar, and stir them well together. So drink it hot.

This odd concoction may be a confused version of a Chinese dish, 'tea eggs', in which hard-boiled eggs are cooked for hours in salted tea until they soften again. However, this is never a sweet dish. The English version sometimes included alcohol.

Dorothy Hartley (1954) recalls an oatmeal caudle which was just what labourers needed to sustain them on a long drive home from a winter market. Moira Buxton (1993) also remarks on this beneficial aspect of caudles, while indicating the 'diversity of kind and usage' which this drink/sauce displayed over the centuries. She states that the degree of comfort which could be given by means of a caudle eventually gave rise to the verb 'coddle', which was later applied to eggs as well as people and produced the derivative verb 'mollycoddle', meaning to pamper unduly.

The most luxurious of all dishes of the caudle type is ZABAGLIONE, which is generally supposed to have been invented in the early 16th century at the Florentine court of the Medici.

CAUL an edible membrane surrounding the intestines of animals, is defined in the dictionaries in a manner which leaves one wondering what it looks like and which does not hint at culinary uses. In contrast, Jane Grigson (1987b) gave this illuminating description to the members of the Oxford

Symposium on Food History, holding up a sheet of caul fat as she spoke:

The caul is a large web of fat which encloses the intestines. It is not the fatty frill called mudgeon or mesentery that actually holds the intestines together—what the French call *fraise*—but a cloth-like semi-transparent sheet about a metre square, or a little less. If you see it at all in a butcher's shop, it will most likely be hanging in a greyish-yellowy-white droop, looking like a worn-out dishcloth. Unappetising. Something you would never think of asking for unless you knew its value and usefulness. . . .

Supposing you run a bit of caul fat to ground, you should soak it in warm water (with a splash of vinegar if it looks particularly unappetising or smells slightly odd). Then you will be able to stretch it out slowly, slowly, and its beauty will be revealed.

Now you can appreciate the names it has been given. Caul used to apply mainly to the little netted caps that people wore. *Crépine*, which is the French word, is related to *crêpe* meaning both pancake and those kinds of crinkled cloth known as *crêpes* and *crêpe de chine*.

Grigson goes on to explain that the caul, with its fine fat, is a wonderful basting medium when wrapped round pheasant, partridge, a calf's liver, or other meats which benefit from being basted. The method was called *en crépine* in France, where it 'was so much a matter of everyday kitchen knowledge' that one does not find specific references to it. CARÊME used it for the sides and base of a dish called *Fromage d'Italie*; he used pork fat for the top of this, whereas in bourgeois kitchens the caul, trimmed to fit, would completely envelope this and other sorts of pâté, cooking on top to 'a rich brown webbing' with perhaps a bay leaf or two showing through.

Caul fat is used to enclose English and Welsh FAGGOTS. See also CRÉPINETTE and HASLET (harslet).

CAULIFLOWER *Brassica oleracea*, Botrytis group, a variety of the common CABBAGE in which flowers have begun to form but have stopped growing at the bud stage. The same applies to BROCCOLI. The thick stems under the buds act as storage organs for nutrients which would have gone into the flowers and eventual fruits had their development not been aborted. All these varieties are therefore richer in vitamins and minerals than other brassicas.

The tendency to produce a 'sport' or freak growth of this kind has been noticed in wild cabbages, so prototypes of the cauliflower may have originated spontaneously in different places. Selective breeding would then have produced the present forms. Be that as it may, the origin of the cauliflower and its relatives is obscure. It is thought that they were first grown in the Near East, but no one is sure when. The belief of Cypriots

that the cauliflower originated in Cyprus derives tenuous support from the old French name for it, *chou de Chypre* (Cyprus cabbage). Jane Grigson (1978), in a charming passage, evokes the idea:

The largest cauliflower I have ever seen, a great curdled depth of white cupped in green leaves, was about 45 cm across. It was so large that the elderly Turk who was carrying it, in the outskirts of Nicosia, could not get his arm right round. Only enough to clamp it to his side, as he shuffled along in his droopy black clothes.

However, she then dismisses the Cypriot claim in favour of the Arabs; and it is generally believed that it was the Arabs who introduced (or reintroduced) the cauliflower to Europe after the fall of the Roman Empire.

Young white cauliflower florets are eaten raw in salads. Cooking a cauliflower whole may require making incisions at the base of the sturdy stem, lest it remain tough while the delicate florets become overcooked. English cooks have often liked to cover a whole cooked cauliflower with a cheese sauce.

The Chinese, for whom the cauliflower is a relatively recent introduction, dismantle the vegetable completely, separate the florets and finely slice the stem, then stir-fry it.

CAULIFLOWER FUNGUS (or cauliflower mushroom), *Sparassis crispa*, which bears some resemblance to the white part of a cauliflower, or to a large sponge, measures up to 60 cm (2') across, and grows on rotting conifer stumps in the autumn, mainly in Europe and N. America. It should be picked and cooked young, while still pale cream in colour, or dried and used for its attractive, faintly nutty flavour.

The French reserve the name *clavaire chou-fleur* (cauliflower) for *Ramaria botrytis*: see CORAL FUNGUS.

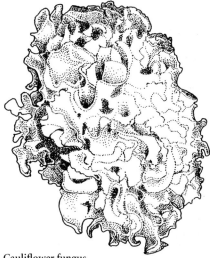

Cauliflower fungus

Jordan (1975) observes that large specimens can be kept fresh by putting the base in a bowl of cold water in a cool, dark place, and that portions may then be cut off for use as required. Slices can be sautéed until tender, or stewed gently in butter and milk, with the addition of herbs and seasoning.

CAVALCANTI IPPOLITO, Duke of Buonvicino (1787–1859), author of one of the most popular ITALIAN COOKERY BOOKS of the 19th century. It is not known whether he had another occupation. The book was first published at Naples in 1837, under the title *La cucina teorico-pratica*. No copy of this edition is recorded as surviving. The second edition was in 1839 and there were six further editions, all at Naples, by the time of his death. The title was modified and the contents revised in successive editions, one of the important changes being the introduction in the second edition of a section in Neapolitan dialect on the authentic domestic cookery of Naples. Editions continued to appear up to 1904.

Cavalcanti's work was original in that it was not based on the French recipes which were characteristic of other Italian cookery books of the period. He laid emphasis on the use of local ingredients, and can justly be regarded as one of the earliest regional cookery writers. His recipes were notable for their precision, both in measurements and in the description of how to carry out certain culinary operations.

CAVIAR in English and *caviare* in French, terms derived from the Turkish *khavyar* (from which come also many names in other European languages, but not the Russian term, which is *ikra*), mean the salted eggs (roe) of various species of STURGEON; and by extension (improperly, some would say) edible eggs of other fish, especially if they bear or can be made to bear some resemblance to sturgeon eggs.

As long ago as the mid-15th century caviar was mentioned by Rabelais as the finest item for what would now be called HORS D'ŒUVRES. It has always enjoyed a reputation as a luxury food (witness Shakespeare's 'caviar for the general'), but it was only in the 19th century that its adoption by the most prominent restaurants and hotels of W. Europe sealed this reputation.

Production of caviar has for long been centred on the Caspian Sea, where Russians and Iranians between them account for much of the world output, and the Black Sea. The main distinctions are between the species of sturgeon from which the caviar comes, as set out below, but there is one term which refers to technique rather than species: *malossol*, meaning lightly salted and indicating caviar of particular excellence, from fish caught at the beginning of the season.

Distinctions by species yield the following terms:

- *sevruga*, from *Acipenser stellatus*, the main source of Caspian caviar;
- *beluga*, from *Huso huso*, the great (because largest) sturgeon;
- *osciotr*, from *Acipenser guldenstaedti*.

Some would say that the best of these three is beluga, and its eggs are certainly the largest, but it does not travel as well as sevruga, which may therefore be a better choice for anyone not in the vicinity of the Caspian. It is osciotr which provides the very rare 'golden' caviar, which is the subject of many legends and anecdotes but is not special in any respect except its colour (it comes from albino fish).

The ripest eggs, taken towards the end of the season, are processed to make 'pressed caviar', which has a stronger flavour.

Sturgeon are confined to the northern hemisphere, but not to the Caspian and Black Seas. There are sturgeon in N. America, for example, which are the source of some caviar; and within living memory there was a population of *A. sturio* in the Gironde estuary in SW France sufficient to produce most of the caviar consumed in France.

Those with professional knowledge and experience of caviar are virtually unanimous in recommending against providing garnishes such as chopped onion to go with it. Their recommendation would be to open the (chilled) tin only a few minutes before serving the contents, preferably from the tin itself but otherwise from a porcelain saucer and in any case with a non-metallic implement, and accompanied only by very thin toast (or BLINIS) and a delicate unsalted butter (or sour cream), with the use of lemon discouraged.

The finest salmon eggs are considered by many to be comparable with caviar and do not need to be labelled 'caviar' to make them attractive. However, the name is sometimes used and has recently been applied to the reddish eggs of the chum (or dog) SALMON, *Oncorhynchus keta*, of the N. Pacific and Arctic. Otherwise, 'caviar' may refer to substitutes such as LUMPFISH roe, skilfully processed in Denmark to present an attractive appearance and to be palatable.

CAWL a Welsh term thoroughly explained by Bobby Freeman (1996). She begins by saying roundly:

There is no translation for *cawl*. In its literal sense it means soup or broth. But as it is used here it conveys a dish which is a whole meal in itself, whether the broth is taken first, then the meat and vegetables, or all together in a bowl, eaten with a special wooden *cawl*-spoon (to avoid burning the mouth on the hot broth). It is pronounced 'cowl'.

She proceeds to explain that the basic ingredients are a piece of bacon, with cabbage and potatoes and leeks, but that there are many local and regional variations. Meat, beef or lamb, can be featured with the bacon or instead of it. If parsley sauce is featured, this will not be the sort made with milk, but one which is based on the potato-cooking water. Oatmeal dumplings and 'trollies' (again, untranslatable, the name is connected with the troll of folklore and means little curranty dumplings or puddings) may go in. So may carrot and parsnip, and swedes or broad beans, and savory. Freeman cites a poem by the Welsh poet Dewi Emrys, translated by the Herald Bard of Wales, which contains the following evocative lines about a cawl:

with leeks and potatoes and stars on its face.
You'll see the cauldron on the tripod there
and the gorse blazing gaily beneath it.
You shall have the ladle full, and filled again,
and that lovelier than any mixture;
you shall have a wooden spoon in the bowl as well
and a great hunk of a fine old cheese.

There are other broth-and-meat-and-vegetable dishes, but nothing quite the same as this Welsh one.

CAYENNE PEPPER a highly pungent spice made from the ground seeds of *Capsicum frutescens*, chilli pepper (see CHILLI). The name 'cayenne' itself probably came from the Tupi language (of the Amazon basin in S. America). Since it sounded like Cayenne, the name of a place in what was formerly French Guiana, it was commonly supposed to be that name, and it was further supposed that the name was given because the spice came principally or originally from Cayenne. What is now marketed as cayenne pepper may come from Asia or Africa.

Explaining the term 'Nepaul (or Nepal) pepper' which bobs up in some older recipe books, Law (*c*.1895), in his comprehensive 'grocer's manual', states that it was a superior kind of cayenne pepper produced in Nepal and exported from there in tins.

Cayenne is added to some dishes made with cheese and to some crab and lobster dishes, and in very small quantities to much besides.

CELERY *Apium graveolens*, exists in three forms. The original wild plant has thin, hollow green stalks and an abundantly leafy top. It looks much like any other small umbelliferous hedgerow plant, and is sometimes called 'smallage' (from 'small ache', *ache* being an old French name for celery). From this two main cultivated types have been bred. The ordinary stem kind (var *dulce*) has greatly thickened, solid, pale green or white stems. In **celeriac** (var *rapaceum*) the base of the stem is enlarged to the size of a medium turnip, while the stem itself is no larger than in the wild form.

Wild celery has always been a common plant in Europe and the temperate parts of Asia, especially near the sea, and has been used since ancient times. It is mentioned in Homer's *Odyssey* as *selinon*, from which modern names are derived. Since it has a very strong flavour and is bitter, it was used more as a flavouring than as a vegetable. It also had medical and religious uses: to both the Egyptians and the Greeks it was associated with funerals, where it was made into garlands. (There is some ambiguity in classical literature between celery and its relative parsley, the Greek name *selinon* and the Latin *apium* often being used for both.) The seeds were used as a condiment.

Celeriac

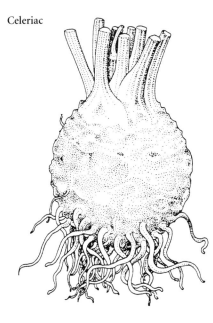

During the Middle Ages celery continued to be used as a medicine and flavouring. Milder varieties, probably originating in Italy, appeared in the 16th century. The practice of earthing up the growing plant dates from these times. This encourages the growth of the stems, blanches them from green to white, and improves the flavour.

The first mention of **cultivated celery** is by the French horticulturalist Olivier de Serres in 1623. The new plant soon came into its own as a salad vegetable. Ray (1686–1704) says: 'Smallage transferred to culture becomes milder and less ungrateful, whence in Italy and France the leaves and stalks are esteemed as delicacies, eaten with oil and

pepper.' (Nevertheless, wild celery remained in use, and can still be bought in France, as *céleri à couper*. Cut up and added to soups and stews, it gives a better flavour than does cultivated celery. It is also better for use in sauces such as Italian RAGÙ.)

Later breeding has produced 'self-blanching' varieties of cultivated celery which do not need to be earthed up, thus saving considerable labour. Some of these are distinctly green, but none is more than slightly bitter.

The Chinese, who had been using wild celery as early as the 5th century AD, developed cultivated varieties of celery independently. Their celery is thinner, juicier, and more strongly flavoured than the European kind. They do not blanch it, since they value the strong flavour. They always eat it cooked, usually in mixtures of vegetables.

Both wild and cultivated celery were taken to America at a date which is not known, but certainly well before the first mention of four types of cultivated celery in a catalogue of 1806. The wild plant is now common throughout the USA; and cultivated celery is highly popular as a salad vegetable; indeed, the English-speaking nations are now the main consumers of stem celery.

Celeriac has quite a long history. Wild celery has a small but edible root which, like any part of the plant excluded from light, is of comparatively mild flavour. In 1536 the botanical writer Ruellius mentioned that the root of smallage was eaten, both cooked and raw; and in 1575 another writer, Rauwolf, said that it was considered a delicacy in the Arab world. Thus the idea of developing a variety with really large roots arose naturally enough, and such a variety was mentioned in J. Bauhin's posthumous *Historia Plantarum* (1613). Celeriac became popular on the mainland of Europe, but for some reason has never made much headway in English-speaking countries.

Uses of the two varieties are quite different. Cultivated celery is often eaten raw as a salad vegetable. It keeps very well if stood upright in a jug containing a little water, and refrigerated. It also makes a fine cooked vegetable.

Celeriac has a milder, sweeter taste than celery and is equally good cooked or grated raw in salads or cut *en julienne* and served as *céleri en rémoulade*. It can be served as a purée.

Celery seed, often used as a flavouring, has a strong celery fragrance (due to the essential oil of celery, apiol) but is bitter, so must be used with discretion. A hint of celery flavour may be imparted to meat dishes by using ready-made celery salt.

Substitutes for celery which have been used in the past are ALEXANDERS (often wrongly called 'wild celery') and LOVAGE.

CELLULOSE is the main structural material of plants. It is tough, insoluble in water, little affected by ordinary cooking, and wholly indigestible by humans and most animals. Nevertheless, it is still an essential part of human diet.

Herbivorous animals such as cows can digest and be nourished by cellulose. Cellulose is a CARBOHYDRATE of the polysaccharide type; its molecules consist of long chains of simple sugar molecules. To digest cellulose, a digestive system must produce enzymes which can split the big molecule into individual sugar units. Herbivorous animals act as host to bacteria which produce such enzymes. In the ruminants (cows, deer, and others) these bacteria live in a series of auxiliary stomachs 'upstream' of the true stomach. Other herbivorous animals have different arrangements, but digestion is always a slow, multi-stage process aided by bacteria.

Cellulose is necessary in the human diet precisely because it is not digested. It acts as 'crude FIBRE' or 'roughage', an inert, bulky medium which helps to carry digestible food through the system. Its bulk is increased by the considerable quantity of water it absorbs. Deprived of roughage, the system works too slowly and the result is constipation and other bowel disorders. These are typical troubles of people in the West whose food is over-refined and low in cellulose.

There is another benefit from roughage. The bran around cereal grains, which is mostly cellulose and otherwise useful only as fibre, contains useful amounts of B-group vitamins which can be dissolved out of it.

CELTIC FEASTING an integral part of aristocratic Celtic society. The Celts were the Iron Age inhabitants of Europe in the pre-Roman period. By the 3rd century BC aspects of a common La Tène Celtic culture were established throughout Europe, stretching from Ireland to Romania and Hungary. The eating and feasting habits of the Celts were recorded by a number of classical writers, the most important of these being Posidonius, a Syrian Greek philosopher who in his *Histories* provides eyewitness accounts of the Gauls in the 1st century BC. Although his work does not survive intact, it was an important source of information for a number of later Greek writers, notably Diodorus Siculus (1st century BC) and ATHENAEUS (fl. *c.* AD 200). Detailed accounts are also found throughout the corpus of early medieval Irish saga literature, much of which is believed to reflect Iron Age Celtic society.

Athenaeus, quoting Posidonius, describes the informal feasting arrangements of the Celts as follows: 'the Celts place dried grass on the floor when they eat their meals, using tables which are raised slightly off the ground.' This practice is confirmed by Diodorus Siculus, who states: 'they do sit not on chairs when they dine, but sit on the ground using the skins of wolves and dogs.' The classical material indicates that the feast was centred around the cauldron and roasting spits and was characterized by an abundance of roasted and boiled meats, which were eaten with bare hands. Athenaeus, again citing Posidonius, describes various regional foods as follows:

They eat only small amounts of bread, but large quantities of meat, either boiled, roasted, or cooked on spits. They dine on this meat in a clean but lion-like manner, holding up whole joints in both hands and biting the meat off the bone. If a piece of meat is too difficult to tear off, they cut it with a small knife which is conveniently at hand in its own sheath. Those who live near rivers, the Mediterranean, or Atlantic also eat fish baked with salt, vinegar and cumin. They also use cumin in their wine. They do not use olive oil because of its scarcity, and because, due to its unfamiliarity, it has an unpleasant taste to them.

Two important Irish sagas, the c.8th-century *Fled Bricrend* (Bricriu's Feast) and the c.9th-century *Scéla Mucce Meic Dathó* (The Tale of Mac Dathó's Pig), supply complementary descriptions of the feasting fare. In the first, Bricriu entices the warriors to attend the feast with a promise of:

a fine beeve that since it was a little calf neither heather nor furze entered its mouth, but full new milk and green grass and corn—and a boar of seven years, that since it was a piglet nothing has entered its mouth but porridge made on fresh milk and gruel in the spring; full milk curds and full new milk in summer; nut kernels and wheat in autumn; and meat and broth in winter. One hundred wheat cakes cooked in honey; twenty-five bushels of wheat were brought for these cakes, so that each bushel made just four cakes.

Mac Dathó's feast consisted mostly of meats boiled in the cauldron, and each warrior had only one chance of taking a portion of meat from the pot, for, as Gantz (1981) explains: 'each cauldron contained beef and salted pork, and as each man passed by he thrust the flesh-fork into the cauldron, and what he brought up is what he ate; if he brought up nothing on the first try, he got no second chance.'

Diodorus Siculus notes that the nobles grew long moustaches that covered the mouth and these became 'entangled in the food' when they were eating and acted as 'a sort of strainer' while they were drinking.

Celtic society was extremely hierarchical. That seating at feasts was graded in accordance with social rank is clear from Athenaeus, citing Posidonius, and from the Irish sagas. Moreover, the sagas show that the distribution of meat cuts was dictated by social class. In the early medieval text *Suidigud Tellaig Temra* (The Settling of the

Manor of Tara—see Best, 1910) which describes the great feast at the banqueting hall of Tara in County Meath, 'choice fruit and oxen and boars and flitches' are given to the kings and nobles, 'red meat from spit of iron, and bragget and new ale' to the warriors, 'veal and lamb and pork' to the young men and maidens, and 'heads and feet' to the jugglers, rabble, and common people.

More importantly, the feast was a ceremonial manifestation of the warfaring nature of society. The lord's economic and territorial interests depended on the loyalty of his warriors, and one means of ensuring such support was in hosting great feasts. Athenaeus recalls Posidonius' description of Lovernius, a chieftain of the Gauls, who in a bid to win support for his opposition to the Romans 'made a square enclosure one and a half miles each way, within which he filled vats with expensive liquor and prepared so great a quantity of food that for many days all who visited could enter and enjoy the feast prepared, being served without a break by the attendants'.

In a heroic society, the communal aspect of the feasting was an appropriate means of rewarding the prowess of the individual warriors. Diodorus Siculus states that the bravest warriors were honoured with the finest portions of meat, referred to as 'the champion's portion' in the Irish sagas. However, Athenaeus tells us that according to Posidonius the allocation of the 'champion's portion' might provoke fights, even to the death. The contentious distribution of the choice cuts of meat is the theme of the two Irish sagas already mentioned, *Fled Bricrend* and *Scéla Mucce Meic Dathó*. In the latter tale, as the following excerpt from Gantz (1981) vividly shows, the feasting ends in a bloody brawl:

Blows fell upon ears until the heap on the floor reached the centre of the house and the streams of gore reached the entrances. The hosts broke through the doors, then, and a good drinking bout broke out in the courtyard, with everyone striking his neighbour.

Overall the Celtic feast seems to have been a riotous affair, dominated as much by alcohol and violence as by food.

Many features of the Celtic feast seem to have been retained by the Irish Gaelic nobility until well into the early modern period. They were still sitting on straw as they feasted in the 16th century. For a contemporary illustration, see John Derricke's woodcut of MacSweeney, an Ulster chief, dining with his colleagues, in *The Image of Irelande with A Discovery of Woodkarne* (1581).   RSe

CENDRÉ a French term used to describe cheese coated with ashes, ideally of vine

roots (*sarments*), but now more usually with industrially powdered charcoal mixed with salt. It gives the surface of the cheese a bluish or greyish hue, with a speckled effect.

CENTRAL AMERICA consists in the string of states extending down the land bridge connecting N. to S. America, from the southern provinces of MEXICO to Panama itself. From north to south, after Mexico, these are: Belize, Guatemala, Honduras, El Salvador, Nicaragua, Costa Rica, Panama. Except for Belize (which has only a Caribbean coastline) and El Salvador (facing only the Pacific), all these republics have ocean views on both sides.

Although this looks like a 'region' on the map, the term is not entirely appropriate, since the area includes a bewildering variety of habitats and climates. There are high mountains and tropical coastal plains, temperate pine forests and deep jungle, pasture land and orchard zones—providing homes for a rich palette of foods and fruits, and foster homes for many imports by colonists, not least the cash crops SUGAR CANE, BANANAS, and COFFEE.

In terms of history and culture as well as geography, the area falls into two parts. The upper part is known as **Mesoamerica** and it was that part which was under the sway of the powerful Aztecs in the north and the Maya further south when the Spanish Conquest took place. For Mesoamerica, evidently, the foodways described under AZTEC FOOD and MAYA FOOD have constituted important culinary traditions whose influence can still be detected. Maya influence has endured particularly in Guatemala and Honduras, and especially in the highland zones away from CREOLE or Ladino influence. (Many people in C. America are mestizos, which means of mixed Indian and Spanish descent. Those of them who speak Spanish are Ladinos, while the term 'creole' is used of English-speakers.) The continuity from ancient Maya times to modern Guatemala is well brought out by Copeland Marks (1985).

The Maya staple was MAIZE and so it remains, consumed as solid food or in drinks or gruels. TAMALES and TORTILLAS are perhaps the most prominent reminders of the ancient past, but there are others, for example the product now called POSOLE, a semi-fermented maize dough, which can be diluted to make a beverage, or used in other ways; and ATOLE, a thickened maize gruel which can be eaten with simple additions of chilli, squash seeds, beans, etc., or as an ingredient in more complex dishes with turkey, vegetables, or fruit.

Apart from the Maya heritage and other native Indian traditions, the factor which has done most to mould present-day foodways, both in Mesoamerica and in the more southerly republics of C. America, has been the influence of the Spanish, as the original colonists. Names of dishes and menu language are much as in SPAIN. New foods brought by the Spanish from Africa and Asia, for instance COCONUT, BREADFRUIT, RICE, have had a great impact on the cuisines, especially those of the more southerly republics, where the Mayan inheritance was unimportant, and on the Caribbean coast.

The Caribbean coast also served as a place of entry for Caribbean foodways. Since these came from islands where the sea is always near at hand, they took root most easily in the coastal strips. The Carib-speaking Miskito Indians of Nicaragua, and indentured African and (Asian) labour imported to work the plantations and forests in British Honduras (now Belize), also brought their own influences to bear. At one remove, Andean food customs that had passed into general currency in Colombia were also common usage in Panama (which was indeed part of Colombia until the beginning of this century).

Combinations of rice and bean are common in the region; *Frijoles con arroz*, *Gallo pinto*, and *Casado* are just a few examples. In Costa Rica the second of these items is a traditional breakfast, sometimes with sour cream or fried eggs enhancing the mixture of rice and black beans. Also in Costa Rica, the third item makes an economical meal, with meat, fried plantain, beef, and perhaps avocado providing the extra ingredients. Some dishes are specialities of one country. Belize has a SPINY LOBSTER soup and Honduras a TRIPE soup (*Mondongo*); Guatemala makes liberal use of a tomato sauce, often with chilli, called *chirmol*; El Salvador uses pineapple in some unexpected ways, for example in stews as well as more conventionally in what has been called the Salvadorian national dish *La semita*, a pineapple tart.

Belize provides CONCH soup or fritters, echoing practice in the Caribbean islands. It also offers an exotic meat from the forests, locally called gibnut, a small deerlike rodent which provides excellent meat; see PACA, the alternative name for it, which has wider currency.

Salvador is thickly strewn with *pupuserías*, selling *pupusas*, which are small thick tortillas variously filled (beans, sausage, cheese). Panama, whose cuisine is the main subject of an excellent book by Gladys Graham (1947), who extends her cook's-eye view to take in neighbouring countries and Caribbean islands. Her book and others provide useful reminders that certain ingredients, for example the orange-red colouring *achiote*/ANNATTO, the ROSELLE fruit, CHAYOTE, and some others little known elsewhere, are constant elements in the cuisines of the area.

CENTRAL ASIAN REPUBLICS a convenient grouping which includes one trio of cuisines, Uzbekistan, Tajikistan, and Turkmenistan, plus one pair, Kazakhstan and Kyrgyzstan. (Tatarstan is another republic to the north in the Volga region of Russia, but TATAR CUISINE has its own entry.)

The Russian author Pokhlebkin (1978 in Russian, 1984 in English) has given a conspectus of the foods and foodways of all the constituent parts of the Soviet Union as it was when he wrote, including these five republics. This is a valuable reference (and almost the only one for some areas), but things have changed since then; and, as Pokhlebkin was intent on displaying diversity rather than uniformity, his account does not always give sufficient prominence to the strong Soviet/Russian influence on other republics.

He explains that both geographical and historical factors have brought about a convergence between the cuisines of the Uzbeks (originally nomadic shepherds) and the Tajiks (who occupy more mountainous territory). They are the most subtle and sophisticated cuisines of C. Asia. Both use a lot of lamb (often made into KEBABS such as *shashlyk*), virtually no fish, and few eggs. Their dishes include many thick soups and semi-liquid main courses. Flatbread is usual, often made in a *tandyra* (see TANDOOR). That of the Uzbeks is renowned for its quality and decoration (see NAN).

Some Uzbek soups are euphoniously called *shurpa* (cf SHORBA), and a prominent range of main dishes there go under the name *plov* (see PILAF). Noodle dishes include *mantu* (see MANTOU) and a range of popular items which are of Chinese origin. These were brought to Kazakhstan, Uzbekistan, Kyrgyzstan, and Tajikistan in the 1880s by Muslim Chinese and Uighurs fleeing the collapse of their revolt against the Manchus. The noodles are recognizably of the Chinese type (they include the showy 'stretched noodle' made by repeatedly folding and stretching dough until it separates into strands), except that they are seasoned with mutton, rather than pork. The best known are *laghman* (from the Chinese *liang mian*, cold noodle), noodles served with a sauce on top; *manpar* (*mian piar*, sliced noodle), round or square slices of dough in soup or stew; and *shima* (*zi mian*, fine noodles), vermicelli in soup.

Turkmenians were mostly nomadic shepherds. Their cuisine has some distinctive characteristics. Unlike some other C. Asians, they eat fish (in dishes incorporating fruit or fruit juices or a sweet-and-sour sauce), especially in the area close to the Caspian Sea. On the other hand, dishes composed entirely of meat (mainly lamb) are popular. Some tribes eat young camel (and brew their black tea with hot camel's milk).

Kazakhstan (covering a vast area of steppe) and Kyrgyzstan (next door but small and mountainous) are, from the point of view of outside observers of their cuisines, remarkably similar. Pokhlebkin remarks that the Kazakhs never drink milk as such, either hot or cold, but do enjoy numerous milk products, of which the best known is KOUMISS (fermented mare's milk—there is also *shubat*, fermented camel's milk, thicker and with a higher fat content). Most of their dishes, some of which are borrowings from RUSSIA, are eaten cold. Many feature one or other kind of OFFAL. The same author remarks that the Kyrgyz use more cereals in their cooking, going for porridge-like sour soups, and have a distinctive taste in tea which they prepare 'with twice as much milk as water and with salt, pepper and a fried flour-butter mixture added'.

CEP a Gascon (and now English) term which is *cèpe* in French, refers to some of the finest edible fungi. The Gascon word meant tree trunk; and it and 'cèpe' have sometimes been used as a synonym for the general term BOLETUS, which covers a larger group of fungi, but is more properly restricted to the four species which most French authorities agree to be true *cèpes*.

Lemoine and Claustres (1977) define true ceps as follows. They have flesh which is white and stays white; a broad foot, sometimes as broad as the cap is wide and giving the whole cep a shape like that of a champagne cork; a handsome, hemispherical cap; and tubes which are first white, then yellow, and finally green. (These tubes, which form a spongy mass under the cap, are the most notable characteristic of the boletus group. They are quite unlike the radiating ribs of ordinary mushrooms, but serve the same function, i.e. they constitute the gills on which the spores are carried. Species other than ceps may have tubes of different coloration.)

Ceps, like certain other edible fungi (e.g. CHANTERELLES and TRUFFLES), have a mycorrhizal relationship with trees; i.e. they exchange nutrients, through their mycorrhizae or filamentous root systems, with tree roots. Some show a marked preference for trees of a particular species. Like other boletus mushrooms, ceps are liable to infestation by larval insects. Young specimens are most likely to be free of this nuisance. The four ceps, with the French names which are most often used for them, are as follows:

- *Boletus edulis, cèpe de Bordeaux;*
- *B. aestivalis* (or *reticulatus*), *cèpe d'été* (or *réticulé*);
- *B. aereus, tête de nègre* (or *cèpe bronzé*);
- *B. pinicola, cèpe des pins* (or *cèpe acajou*).

The *cèpe de Bordeaux* is the best known of these, and is distributed all over Europe although the inhabitants of Bordeaux have succeeded in asserting a proprietary claim to it. It is found from August to November, often in the vicinity of oak or chestnut trees, less often beech trees. The species occurs in southern Africa (e.g. in pine plantations in what used to be the E. Transvaal); and it is well known in N. America, where it is called the king boletus and has a fruiting season from late August into the late autumn. There are American records of king boletes weighing over 2 kg (5 lb) and measuring 30 cm (1') across the cap.

This, anyway, is the principal cep. It has a glossy brown cap which looks like a glazed bun (whence the English common name 'penny bun') or a shiny stone (the German name *Steinpilz* means 'stone mushroom'). The Italian name, which usually appears in the plural as *funghi porcini*, means 'piglet mushrooms' and presumably refers to the fat stem. Generally, the favourite.

Some, however, find the *cèpe d'été* even better. It is the first of the four to appear, having a season from May to September but a noticeable preference for dry weather. The cap is velvety, and pale brown; the foot covered with a distinctive network of white lines.

The *tête de nègre* has a darker cap, occasionally even black, which is sometimes distinctively 'crackled'. It thrives in airy oak forests and the maquis, and prefers warm climates such as those of S. Europe, although found as far north as the south of Sweden, and in Russia.

The *cèpe des pins* does not choose only pines as its arboreal partner, but grows also beside chestnuts, oaks, and even beech trees. Its cap is first plum-coloured, then dark reddish-brown. In France it is most common in the west, the centre, and the south. Its distribution includes all Europe, as far north as Murmansk; N. Africa; and parts of Asia, including China.

All these ceps are excellent. The most famous recipe for them, *Cèpes à la bordelaise*, seems to have undergone changes when it was adopted outside its region. Bontou (1898), describing how he introduced the dish to Paris in the 1880s, says that the oil and garlic used in the *bordelaise* had to be changed to butter for Parisian tastes.

Ceps, especially *B. edulis*, are often dried and keep their flavour well. The addition of a few dried ceps to a stew or to a dish of bland cultivated mushrooms improves these greatly.

CEPHALOPODS a category of marine MOLLUSCS, many of which are important as food: notably SQUID, CUTTLEFISH, and OCTOPUS. All these lack allure; they look like bags with heads on top and eight or ten arms or tentacles sprouting therefrom; and the name cephalopod, which is of Greek derivation, itself means 'head-footed'. This construction, which is entirely logical for the kind of life they lead, appears strange, even repugnant, to most human eyes, and accounts for the widespread but diminishing reluctance to eat them.

Such reluctance may have been caused in part by tales of huge cephalopods—'krakens', giant squid—overwhelming sailing ships; and by the common notion that a large octopus can catch a diver under water and hold him until he drowns. There are various species of giant squid. The largest are indeed of terrifying size, reaching about 25 metres (60') in total length, but these are feeble creatures. The stronger and fiercer ones which are found in the waters of the Humboldt Current are not large enough to menace anything bigger than a rowing boat. An octopus of unusually large size could drown a man, but there is no recorded instance of this happening. An entertaining investigation into all these matters is provided by Lane (1957).

The Japanese, incidentally, are an important exception to what was said above about human attitudes to cephalopods such as the octopus. They consider the octopus a cheerful, good-natured, and somewhat comical creature. It is often personified, especially in its boiled state, when it has turned red and its 'feet' curled up, and figures in fairy tales, and as toys, mascots, etc. The other cephalopods do not receive this affectionate treatment, but there is no negative feeling about them.

The pearly NAUTILUS is an exception to most generalizations about cephalopods. Setting it aside, it can be said of cephalopods that they have only internal 'shells'; that they have three hearts and blue blood; and that they can move very rapidly by a kind of jet-propulsion. The ink which they secrete, and can eject to baffle predators, is an important element in the preparation of certain dishes, but more usually removed, still in its sac.

Generally, the flesh of cephalopods is of an interesting consistency, with no layers of fat, no gristle, no bones, indeed nothing to inconvenience the cook. That of the octopus must normally be tenderized by one means or another; but suitable cooking methods are enough to turn squid and cuttlefish into agreeable fare. All can be dried. Squid are particularly suitable for being stuffed.

The supply and consumption of octopus is unlikely to increase much, and the same applies to cuttlefish; but squid still constitute an underexploited marine resource.

For a catalogue of *Cephalopods of the World*, see Roper and Sweeney (1984).

CEREALS are plants of the grass family whose seeds are used as food grains; they are named from the Roman corn goddess Ceres. Cereals include WHEAT, RICE, BARLEY, OATS, RYE, MAIZE, MILLET, and SORGHUM, all of which have been used as food since prehistoric times, and cultivated since antiquity.

Mangelsdorf (1953) has given an eloquent description of their importance:

When he domesticated wheat, man laid the foundations of western civilization. No civilization worthy of the name has ever been founded on any agricultural basis other than the cereals. The ancient cultures of Babylonia and Egypt, of Rome and Greece, and later those of northern and western Europe, were all based upon the growing of wheat, barley, rye and oats. Those of India, China and Japan had rice for their basic crop. The pre-Columbian peoples of America—Inca, Maya and Aztec—looked to corn [maize] for their daily bread.

Although the cereal grains constitute the world's most important single class of food, and provide protein of good quality, this protein is 'incomplete'; it generally lacks just one essential amino acid, lysine, which is easily supplied by small amounts of pulses or animal foods. Thus in regions where cereals make up a very large part of diet—and in much of the Orient 90% of food energy comes from cereals such as rice—nutrition is reasonably balanced, a result which could hardly be achieved with any other single kind of food, except perhaps potatoes. Even in western countries, where a more varied diet including far more animal food is eaten, cereals play an important part. In a typical British diet one-third of the energy and one-third of the protein come from cereals.

Many cereals are eaten as cooked grains, often in the form of PORRIDGE. Virtually all are made into FLOURS which can be used to bake bread etc.

A few plants of other families provide seeds resembling those of cereals and used in the same way, and are sometimes included informally in that category. These include AMARANTH, CHIA, BUCKWHEAT, and QUINOA.

See also FIVE GRAINS OF CHINA. BREAKFAST CEREALS are also described separately.
READING: Kahn (1985), Sokolov (1996).

CERIMAN the fruit of the familiar 'Swiss cheese plant', *Monstera deliciosa* (sometimes known as monstera), grown as a houseplant for the sake of its unusual leaves, which have holes in them. The plant, a creeper of the arum lily family, is a native of Mexico and

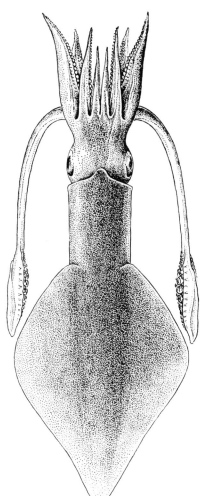

Among cephalopods
the OCTOPUS,
with its eight tentacles
is easily recognized,
so not illustrated.
Those shown here
are less familiar,
except in regions
(the Mediterranean,
the Orient,
and SE Asia),
where they have
been eaten
and enjoyed
since antiquity

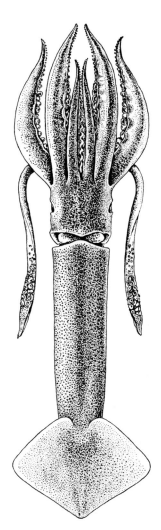

Top left, a SQUID
Loligo forbesi
of the NE Atlantic
Top right, a
flying squid
Illex illecebrosus.
To the right,
the CUTTLEFISH of
the Mediterranean,
Sepia officinalis
(Three drawings
from Muus, 1959.)
On the far right
the mini-cuttlefish
Rossia macrosoma

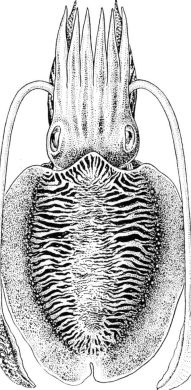

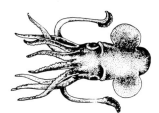

Guatemala. In its natural habitat it grows to a great size and bears fruit which somewhat resemble green corn cobs and which take just over a year to ripen on the plant.

The fruit, like that of any arum lily, for example the poisonous 'lords and ladies' common in the English countryside, is composed of a mass of berries on a spadix, the fleshy central spike first seen in the flower. In the case of the ceriman the spadix itself is eaten. Provided that the fruit is fully ripe, and carefully peeled, the flavour and texture are delicious; somewhere between banana and pineapple and mango, with a special aromatic quality. But it is rarely encountered outside its native region, although an English trade publication of about 1935 recorded that even then it was imported in limited quantities from Madeira during the winter; and recently some cultivation has taken place in Queensland, California, and Florida.

Professor Julia Morton (1987) explains that oxalic acid present in the unripe fruit, or even the ripe fruit, can cause irritation for some people, so that it is best to eat sparingly on the first occasion. If cut at the right moment (when the tile-like sections of rind separate slightly at the base), the fruit will ripen progressively towards the apex over a period of almost a week. The rind will then be loose for the whole length of the fruit, and the flesh will come away from the core.

The ripe flesh can be served in a fruit salad, or with ice cream; or sections of it can be stewed with sugar and lime juice and conserved.

CERVELAS and CERVELAT are names given to SAUSAGES made in France and Germany respectively. The latter has its own entry. Both names and the Italian must have had a past connection with similar terms meaning 'brain' but the connection has been lost; for no recent or modern recipes for cervelas call for brains as an ingredient.

The typical French *cervelas* is a short, stumpy fresh sausage, made from pure pork or pork and beef flavoured with garlic, and spiced with coriander, allspice, and nutmeg. It is matured for a few days, and may be smoked lightly. Popular in much of E. France, these sausages are cooked by poaching in water or red wine before being served with a sauce, or a potato salad, or cold, sliced and seasoned with a mustardy vinaigrette and sliced onion. The name is also used in Lyons for a *saucisson à cuire* (see SAUSAGES OF FRANCE) frequently laced with pistachio or truffles.

The name *cervelas* is the origin of the word *saveloy*, a word used to denote a degraded product, including cereal, often sold by British street vendors in the 19th century from a large pot of hot water. Of the various recipes used in Britain none seems to be closely related to those used in France. A 1930s recipe for 'London Saveloys' from *Dalton's Meat Recipes* (a book written by a Yorkshire butcher to encourage the use of proprietary rusk and spice mixtures which he had developed) calls for 'Lean beef . . . with pork fat, hearts, melts, bacon ends, cooked meat trimmings', plus rusk and gives the impression that the product acted as a means of using up leftovers. Saveloys were encased in weasands, giving them a wider diameter than normal, and smoked and coloured. The size and colour appear to have been the identifying characteristics.

CERVELAT a German sausage which takes several forms—it may be spreadable but is usually intended for slicing—and is usually mild in flavour. The several types include *Braunschweiger* (Brunswick) Cervelat, of beef, lean pork, fat bacon, and seasoning. This fairly large sausage is cured for three weeks and then cool smoked.

See also CERVELAS, a French sausage which has an etymological connection with the German product. (This adds to the confusion already pervading foreigners' perceptions of Cervelat, a confusion caused by the fact that one observer will have encountered the spreadable sort and another the sliceable kind and each may be convinced that what he or she ate or bought is the one and only authentic sort.)

CERVIO VINCENZO (*c*.1510–*c*.1580), for most of his life an officer of the household of Cardinal Alessandro Farnese, was famous as a carver and is now remembered for his posthumous book on the subject, *Il trinciante di Vincenzo Cervio*. This was first published at Venice in 1581, 'edited by Cavalier Reale', and including a separate section by Reale. The extent of Cervio's own contribution to the book remains uncertain.

Cervio believed that the only true method of carving was the Italian one: to hold the meat or other food up in the air, on a fork, and apply the knife to it in this posture. This technique transformed a practical operation into a spectacular exercise of virtuosity. In contrast, the German practice was to carve foods anchored on a plate or table.

Il trinciante was the most complete, but not the first, treatise on carving in the Renaissance period. The earlier works by Romoli (*Singolare dottrina*, 1560) and Scappi (1570; see ITALIAN COOKERY BOOKS) would have been familiar to Cervio, but were no doubt considered by him to be insufficiently comprehensive. Such a criticism could not be made of his own book, which devotes 10 chapters to the status and duties of a carver, and no fewer than 76 chapters to the carving of particular foodstuffs. It contains, however, only two illustrations. Cervio's book provides, incidentally, much information about the foods eaten at an Italian court of that period.

CEVICHE (the spelling preferred to seviche, which is, however, often used), a speciality of C. and S. America, particularly in Spanish-speaking countries (Ecuador, Peru, Mexico are noted for it): raw fish (usually fillets) marinated in lime or lemon juice with olive oil and spices and often served as an appetizer. The name is said to come from the Latin *cibus* (food) via Spanish *cebo* (fodder, food, bait) and *cebiche* (fish stew).

When fish is cooked by heat, the main effect in terms of food chemistry is that its protein is 'denatured'. The citric acid in lemons or limes has a similar effect, although this is not called 'cooking'.

The same technique is used in some places in the Mediterranean region, e.g. in making *Acciughe al limone* at Boccadasse near Genoa, but not with the same name (and probably without a long history, since if it dated back a long way it would presumably have spread as widely in the Mediterranean region as ceviche has in America).

For a corresponding practice, of wider scope, in the Philippines, see KINILAW. See also ESCABECHE; this is something different but comparable, and it has been suggested that it could be a European ancestor, etymological as well as culinary, of American ceviche. See Barbara Santich (1985).

CHAFING DISH COOKERY as practised in modern times, depends on a piece of kitchen equipment which changed its form twice; once between classical and medieval times, and then again when open-hearth cookery gave way to the use of ovens in the 19th century. Chafing is derived from the French *chauffer*, to heat.

The prototype in classical times was described by Cicero as 'a kind of saucepan of Corinthian brass, made with such art that its contents cook instantly and almost without fire. This simple and ingenious vessel possesses a double bottom; the uppermost one holds the light delicacies destined for dessert and the fire is underneath.'

In medieval times a chafing dish was a portable brazier to hold burning coals or charcoal, designed to be set on a metal stand and to have a dish of food on top. This was a piece of equipment to be found in the stillroom, up to the 17th century, and often used in preparing medical prescriptions. But it was also, and increasingly, used for cookery, since it made possible the cooking or heating of dishes away from the fierce heat of the hearth where the main cooking activity took place. See Karen Hess (1981). The name chafing dish could be applied to either the brazier or the dish on top of it, but it is clear from references by Hannah Glasse (1747) to a chafing dish of coals that the former meaning was common.

As Elizabeth David (1980) has explained, this device 'ultimately became the elegant silver-plated chafing dish set over a spirit lamp and used for the table cookery of Edwardian dishes'. By then the 'dish' had become the dish containing food to be cooked or heated. Chafing dish cookery enjoyed a considerable vogue in the period from about 1890 to the First World War. READING: Schloesser (1905).

CHALLAH (or challa or chollah), pronounced 'hallah', a Jewish sabbath bread which is made with eggs and white flour, and sometimes coloured light gold with saffron.

The bread is braided or twisted and glazed with beaten egg and sprinkled with sesame or poppy seeds. Two loaves are served at each of the three sabbath meals, as a remembrance of the double portion of manna which fell for the Israelites in the wilderness to provide food both for the sixth day and for the succeeding sabbath day.

For certain festivals, e.g. Rosh Hashana and Yom Kippur, the challah may be rounded rather than braided. It might then be decorated with a dove wing or ladder made from surplus dough.

When the challah is prepared, a small piece of the dough is pinched off to be put in the oven and burned while the challah bakes, as a symbolic offering for the priesthood. Indeed, the meaning of the word *challa* in biblical Hebrew is this bit of dough, 'the priest's share'.   (HS)

CHAMP a simple yet hearty Irish dish of mashed potatoes moistened with milk and butter and flavoured with chopped onions or scallions or nettle tops. The popularity of the dish is reflected in the diversity of regional names, which include bruisy, cally, goody, pandy, panada, and poundies. (Lots of butter was used for pandy, and 'a sup of cream and salt' added, the intention being to make it attractive to children—but adults also yearn for it.)

Champ was prepared especially for the festival of Hallowe'en (31 October) when large quantities of potatoes were pounded with a cylindrical wooden implement called a beetle. Florence Irwin (1937) gives an evocative description of the procedure as follows:

The man of the house was summoned when all was ready, and while he pounded this enormous potful of potatoes with a sturdy wooden beetle, his wife added the potful of milk and nettles, or scallions, or chives, or parsley, and he beetled till it was as smooth as butter, not a lump anywhere. Everyone got a large plateful, made a hole in the centre, and into this put a large lump of butter. Then the champ was eaten from the outside with a spoon or fork, dipping it into the melting butter in the centre. All was washed down with new milk or freshly churned buttermilk

It was customary to offer champ to the fairies at Hallowe'en or All Soul's Night (1 November). A bowlful was left on field posts or under hawthorn and whitethorn bushes.   RSe

CHANAL the fruit of *Gourliea decorticans*, a small tree native to Chile. It resembles the JUJUBE, being fleshy and subacid, and is a food of some importance in the Chaco region.

CHANAR a fruit of the Argentine which according to Emerson (1908) possesses such remarkable qualities that, even though it has not proved possible to establish its botanical identity, it must have a place in the present book, and be described in Emerson's own words:

The Indians are extremely fond of fruit and of all which appeal to them most that called *chanar* is the chosen; but one must know how and when to eat it, for if even bitten into before it is fully ripe it will pucker the mouth to such an extent that speech becomes an impossible task. When the *chanar* is ripe and fully grown it is about the size of an egg and is also shaped very much like one. Its flavour is beyond description, and the way the Indians eat this fruit best shows in what estimation it is held. Early in the morning all hands repair to the *chanares*—chanar orchard (for, though wild, the trees grow in immense tracts) and proceed to eat of the fruit until locomotion, except in a crawling way, becomes almost impossible, and as soon as they have arrived at this state they crawl to the river, drink as much water as they can possibly hold, and then crawl back to the trees, where they stretch themselves out at full length and sleep until night, when they repeat the operation.

CHANTERELLE a French name adopted as the English one for an excellent edible mushroom, *Cantharellus cibarius*, which the French themselves as often call *girolle*. It grows all over Europe and in many parts of the USA, particularly W. Virginia, appearing in late summer and autumns in woods of all kinds. It also occurs in parts of Africa, for example Zambia, and in China. It is a small fungus, never more than 8 cm (3") high or wide, and usually much less. It has a distinctive shape aptly described by Jane

Grigson (1975) as 'a curving trumpet, with delicate ribs running from the stalk through to the under edge of the cap like fine vaulting'. Its colour is a bright apricot-orange; and the smell sometimes resembles that of apricots, especially in European specimens.

There are three related species in Europe:

- *C. cinereus* is grey (*chanterelle cendrée* in France).
- *C. tubaeformis* has a brown, sometimes very dark, cap and a yellow stalk, and is more funnel shaped than the other two. It is called *chanterelle en entonnoir/en tube/en trompette* in France. It occurs also in the USA.
- *C. lutescens*, a mountain species known as the *chanterelle jaunâtre/jaunissante* in France, is similar, but yellow or orange all over. It appears on the markets as late as January or February, and has an aroma like that of the mirabelle plum. (Note: there is doubt about its status as a species in Europe, and about its relationship with what has been called *C. lutescens* in N. America and China.)

The flesh of these species is thin, and they dry well, whereas *C. cibarius* does not.

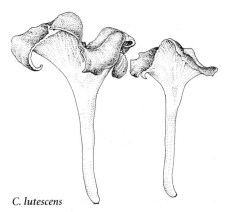

C. lutescens

N. America has a broader range of chanterelles than Europe, but among the seven or eight edible species which occur there only a few are of high merit. *C. subalbidus*, the white chanterelle, which is meaty and has a fine flavour, is possibly the best of these; but it is only found in the north-west, in coastal areas. *C. fallax*, in contrast, is found throughout the continent. It is known as the black trumpet, being grey-brown or darker in colour, and has a fine fragrance. The name 'fragrant chanterelle' is, however, reserved for *C. odoratus*, which is only rated 'edible' when young. *C. minor* (the small chanterelle, an eastern species) and *C. lateritius* (the smooth chanterelle, of the north-east) are both superior to it.

In Zambia, besides *C. cibarius*, at least three other species are found. *C. miniatescens*, called *chitondo*, is the most widely eaten mushroom in Zambia and 'is even eaten by individuals who will not consider other species' (Pegler and Piearce, 1980).

Chanterelles keep and travel well, so are often in the markets fresh. They are also sold dried and in cans. The flavour is strong and good, and is held to go well with eggs, perhaps partly because the colours make an attractive combination. The texture is relatively tough, so chanterelles should be cooked gently and for longer than ordinary mushrooms. Soaking them in milk overnight before cooking them is said to help. As for many kinds of mushroom, it is a good idea to start the cooking over a low heat, so that the chanterelles exude their own juices and are cooked in these.

CHAPATI a basic unleavened flat circular bread which is served throughout India, Pakistan, and elsewhere in this region.

Chapatis are made from finely milled wholewheat flour, called chapati flour or *atta*, and water. The dough is rolled into thin rounds which vary in size from region to region and then cooked without fat or oil on a slightly curved GRIDDLE called a *tava*. Chapati breads are made every day in N. Indian homes as a staple for scooping up food or dipping in soups.

Alternative names for chapati are ROTI and *phulka*. The latter, however, which literally means 'puffed', refers to a somewhat thicker product, which is baked for a second time over a flame after it has been griddle baked, and which then puffs up.   HS

CHAR (also known as Arctic char, and sometimes spelled charr, which purists prefer as the original version), *Salvelinus alpinus*, a fish of the SALMON family which occurs in both sea-run and freshwater forms. The former are larger (up to 1 m/40"), and have metallic blue or green backs, and yellowish sides marked with small spots. The coloration of the freshwater races is highly variable, and some of them attain only a small size.

The distribution of the Arctic char at sea is circumpolar. In the N. Atlantic area it descends as far as northern Labrador, Iceland, and N. Norway; but landlocked freshwater populations are found further south (for example, Lake Windermere in England, and Lac Léman in France/Switzerland, where it is the *omble chevalier*).

The Arctic char has several close relations, listed below. The first two of these are known in common parlance as 'trout', although, if common names matched biological distinctions, they would be called char. (The chief differences between true

trout, of the genus *Salmo*, and char is that char have noticeably smaller scales and brighter colouring—pinkish spots on back and sides.)

- *S. fontinalis*, generally known as the brook trout or speckled trout, but sometimes called brook char. See under TROUT.
- *S. namaycush*, the lake trout. See under TROUT.
- *S. malma*, the Dolly Varden, adorned with particularly numerous and bright little spots, pink, yellow, orange, and named after a female character, who liked brightly coloured clothes, in Dickens's *Barnaby Rudge*.

Potted char from Lake Windermere in England was counted as a great delicacy in the 18th and 19th centuries, and examples of the special dishes used for this are not uncommon in antique shops.

CHARCUTERIE literally means cooked meat, from the French *chair cuit*. It now refers almost solely to PORK products, which are sold by a specialist *charcutier* and include HAMS, SAUSAGES, sausage meat and forcemeats (see STUFF), TERRINES, PÂTÉS and *pâtés en croûte*, GALANTINES, CRÉPINETTES, *gayettes*, *boulettes*, ANDOUILLES, ANDOUILLETTES, *boudins noirs* (see BLOOD SAUSAGES) and *boudin blancs* (see WHITE PUDDING), PIES, and some ready-cooked dishes, including TRIPE. Some *charcuteries* also sell veal sausages and terrines of game.

The history of the *charcutiers* in France, as an organized body, goes back to the 15th century, when they were allowed to sell only cooked pork and raw pork fat. During Lent, when meat was not eaten, they sold salt herrings and saltwater fish. In later centuries they progressively increased the range of products, acquiring cooked tripe after the Revolution.

Charcuterie was considered an affair of regional or bourgeois cookery rather than of haute cuisine until, at the end of the 19th century, a pork butcher named Louis-François Drone published *Traité de la charcuterie ancienne et moderne*, which for the first time took the subject seriously.

The leading regions of France for charcuterie are the Auvergne and Alsace, where there is a long tradition of pig rearing. Italy, Germany, and other countries including Britain have many specialities which could be classed as charcuterie; but they do not have shops which sell the same range of products as a French *charcutier*. This range has not been immutable, but has remained remarkably constant. Zola (1873, here in an English translation), describing in a few deft paragraphs Lisa, the beautiful *charcutière*, and the display over which she

presided in the Paris market, selected some typical items for the verbal picture which he painted:

In front of her, displayed on white porcelain plates, were sausages from Arles and Lyon from which slices had been cut, tongues and chunks of boiled ham, a pig's head drowned in jelly, an open jar of rillettes and a tin of sardines whose punctured metal revealed a lake of oil. To the left and right, on the floor, were cheeses from Italy, brawn, a local pale pink ham, a red-fleshed York ham, covered in a thick layer of fat. There were more round and oval plates, plates of stuffed tongue, truffled galantine, brawn with pistachio nuts, while next to her, within reach, were larded veal, liver and hare pâté in yellow terrines.

READING: Jane Grigson (1967).

CHARD *Beta vulgaris* ssp *cicla*. Also called Swiss chard, leaf beet, seakale beet, white beet, and spinach beet. It is related to SUGAR BEET, but it produces large leaves and fleshy stalks, rather than a bulbous root. Its leaves taste something like SPINACH, but are coarser. The stalks may be a pale celadon colour or vivid scarlet (rhubarb or ruby chard). The stalks and leaves are generally cooked separately in different ways.

The history of chard has been traced back to the famous hanging gardens of ancient Babylonia, and the vegetable evidently has a long history in the Arab world. From the Arabic name *silq* came the Spanish *acelga*. However, the word 'chard' derives from the Latin and French words for thistle, although chard is not related to the thistle, and eventually came to mean the stalk or ribs of some vegetables such as chard or CARDOON which is related to the thistle. By the 19th century seed catalogues were adding 'Swiss' to the name. This was presumably to distinguish it from cardoon, but it is not clear why the term 'Swiss' was chosen, although Jane Grigson (1978) evidently believed that the epithet originated in Dutch. Evelyn (1699) had not used it; he referred to the 'Rib of the *White Beet* (by the *French* call'd the *Chard*)' with approval and made the interesting comment that it 'melts, and eats like Marrow'.

The *cicla* in the vegetable's scientific name derives from *sicula*, which refers to Sicily, one of the places where chard first grew. Chard is popular around the Mediterranean especially in Provence and Nice, and in Catalonia, including the Balearic Islands, where the leaves are often prepared with pine nuts and raisins, a dish with Arabic origins. A Moroccan TAGINE of chard, *Marak silk*, has chard leaves and stalks, onion and coriander, all chopped, and rice cooked together. Paula Wolfert (1973) observes that 'in Tetuán this dish is often accompanied by a dish of boiled lentils'.

CHARLOTTE a PUDDING made in a mould lined with sponge fingers or bread slices. There are two principal kinds: baked and unbaked.

The best-known baked charlotte is Apple charlotte. The mould is lined with buttered bread, sometimes previously fried; filled with stewed apples; topped with more bread or breadcrumbs; baked until the crust is brown above and below; and turned out. It seems clear that this charlotte began life in Britain. The *OED* gives the earliest relevant appearance of 'charlotte' in print as 1796, and at least one recipe for Apple charlotte was published within ten years or so. The name may have been bestowed in honour of Queen Charlotte (1744–1818), wife of George III, said to be a patron of apple growers.

The principal unbaked charlotte is *Charlotte (à la) russe*. Here the mould is lined with sponge fingers. In some fancy versions, these are omitted from the bottom, which is covered with a decorative arrangement of glacé fruit with a layer of JELLY (US jello) cementing it into a mosaic. The mould is filled up with a rich cream filling containing GELATIN, so that it sets and can be turned out (in one piece, one hopes). The history of this item seems to have begun with the famous French chef CARÊME, at the beginning of the 19th century, probably when he was working for the Prince Regent in England, and perhaps after he had come across the British baked charlotte. In fact he called his invention *Charlotte à la parisienne*; it is said to have acquired the name *russe* at a banquet in honour of Tsar Alexander I, or because of the switch in France to SERVICE À LA RUSSE. Claudine Brécourt-Villars (1996) dates the appearance of the term *charlotte* in a French recipe book to 1806 (virtual simultaneity with England).

The Russians, for their part, adopted and adapted the Apple charlotte as *Sharlotka*, made in a mould lined with brown or white breadcrumbs and filled with alternate layers of apples and raisins, and of sweetened, spiced, fried dark breadcrumbs soaked in white wine.   (RH)

CHARTREUSE a French word which (besides meaning the famous French liqueur flavoured with ANGELICA and HYSSOP) refers to a dish of PARTRIDGE cooked with cabbage.

CHATEAUBRIAND is the name given to a large piece of fillet STEAK, either much thicker than usual or big enough to serve at least two people, or both. There is some disagreement, e.g. between French and American butchers, over the exact size and nature of the cut.

A tedious accretion of tales about the origin of the name was robustly hacked out of the way by Dallas (1877) in *Kettner's Book of the Table*; indeed, the author of this would have gone further and banished the term altogether, as had the members of a certain London club (so he tells us) when a fancy chef sought to install it in their menu.

CHAUD-FROID a French term, literally meaning 'hot-cold'. This seemingly contradictory term designates dishes covered with a thick sauce while hot, then chilled and served cold. Those who prefer to believe that one individual is always responsible for every great dish will like the story which attributes this creation to a certain chef named Chaufoix who is said to have worked in the kitchens of Louis XV. Classicists, on the other hand, will be pleased to know that, according to Favre, an earthenware vessel was uncovered at Pompeii bearing the inscription *Calidus-frigidus* and containing 'remains of cooked meat in jelly'; hence, according to this author, the Romans invented not only the dish but its name as well.

Historical polemic aside, this dish does not come into its own until the 19th century in France and, ever since, chauds-froids have been indispensable elements in well-dressed French buffets. Their popularity stems not only from their often spectacular presentation but from the fact that they offer guests a rare opportunity to sample dishes without the usual dipping and dripping associated with nibbling hot or cold foods with accompanying sauces.

Giving instances of the lavish hand with which ESCOFFIER dedicated dishes to people, Shaw (1994) remarks that 'The aptly named *Chaud-froid Félix Faure* commemorates the French President who in 1899 died suddenly at the Elysée while making love to his mistress, Madame Steinheil.'   HY

CHAYA *Cnidoscolus chayamansa*, also known as tree spinach, is a shrub indigenous to C. America, belonging to the family Euphorbiaceae. It may have future potential as a food resource, given the impressive content of nutrients in its abundant green leaves. These are covered with stinging hairs, and are not eaten raw; but, when young and tender, they can be cooked and eaten like SPINACH.

A regional speciality of Yucatan is *Tzotobilchay*, a TAMALE made of MAIZE dough, ground SQUASH seeds, and chaya leaves.

CHAYOTE *Sechium edule*, also called custard marrow, vegetable pear, mirliton (Louisiana), christophine (Trinidad), choko, and many other names, is a fruit of the GOURD family which is peculiar in having one large seed.

There are pear shaped and round; light and dark green; smooth and hairy, and knobbly varieties. A common one is pear shaped but larger than a pear, pale green, and longitudinally ridged with 'knuckles' at the base so that it looks something like a clenched fist. Its name in the south of China means 'Buddha's hand gourd'.

The chayote originated in Mesoamerica, and was cultivated by the Aztecs. Its name comes from the Nahuatl word *chayotl*. Unlike other gourd vines, it is perennial, and develops large, starchy tubers which are also eaten. The young leaves and shoots may be used as a green vegetable, and the large seed (protruding when mature) is edible; Elizabeth Schneider (1986) bids one 'cook it along with the squash for a delicious nibble that tastes somewhere between a lima bean and an almond'.

After the conquest of Mexico the chayote was taken into cultivation elsewhere and has become popular in Spain, N. America, SE Asia, China, and Australasia.

David Fairchild, meeting the chayote for the first time in Jamaica in the last years of the 19th century, was enthusiastic:

The chayote has a firmer, more agreeable texture than squash and an equally delicate flavor. Upon entering a chayote arbor, one sees hundreds of fruits hanging from the thick canopy of leaves like large green or white pears. When the small yellow flowers are fertilized, the fruits grow with outstanding rapidity, maturing in only a few days.

Fairchild sought to popularize the fruit in the USA, but he was a prophet ahead of his time; it did not catch on then. And opinions still vary: insipid and watery, say some, delicate and sweetly fresh say others.

Chayote is usually cooked. It is suitable for any standard method and well fitted for being stuffed, in halves. In parts of Latin America it is sometimes used in sweet dishes, on the lines of pumpkin pie. In other continents it has been adapted to local preferences. Thus the Cantonese like to have it boiled in soup with pork meat.

CHEDDAR the most famous and widespread hard cheese in the world, takes its name from the village of Cheddar, by Cheddar Gorge in the English county of Somerset. However, the name has now come to indicate a technique of cheese-making rather than a place of origin, for Cheddar cheese is now made not only in other parts of the British Isles but also in other continents.

'Cheddaring', which is just one step in the many which lead to the final product, refers to the cutting of the curd into slabs which are piled upon each other to produce a smooth mass; it is not a term which would be used by any but cheese-makers.

Cheddar cheese is made from whole cow's milk and, in its traditional form, matured for a considerable time—a year to eighteen months if it is to be savoured at its best. To produce such cheeses obviously requires a considerable investment of time and effort, all the more so since the Cheddar normally is and always has been a big cheese. Cheddars used to be called corporation cheeses in Somerset, because they were made by all the dairies of a parish putting their milk together. The results were impressive. One of the most weighty contributions to Queen Victoria's wedding celebrations was a Cheddar cheese over 9' (2.7 m) in diameter and registering 1,250 lb (567 kg) on the scales. Two villages had combined to make the monster.

However, small quantities of milk left over from making the big Cheddars were used to make small ones, in the form of a little round loaf called a truckle; and it is still possible in the west of England to buy farmhouse truckles which have an excellent flavour, full and 'nutty' as a Cheddar should be, and with the firm but creamy texture and the pale glow which are the marks of real quality.

Such cheeses, made by small producers in limited quantities, have qualities far surpassing mass-produced versions. Nonetheless, many of the latter represent excellent value for those who seek an unpretentious cheese which goes well with bread and ale, keeps well, and melts satisfactorily when heated.

CHEEKS of animals, for example of the pig, because they usually yield rich, savoury juices, are a good choice to include in stews, pies, and sausages. However, because cheek muscles are exercised constantly, the meat tends to be tough and may need long cooking. COD cheeks, on the other hand, are tender morsels, perhaps because cod are not eating all the time and do not exercise their cheeks in making noises.

See also BATH CHAP; PANCETTA (for *guanciale*).

CHEESE (*see opposite page*)

CHEESECAKE not a CAKE in the ordinary sense, is really a kind of TART. Most cheesecakes have a pastry shell or a biscuit base (made of crushed biscuits mixed with melted butter) topped with sweetened cheese, often CURD CHEESE, stabilized to avoid curdling during baking by combining it with egg, or flour or some other cereal, or both. A range of flavourings may be added

to this mixture, and the cheesecake may be garnished with fresh fruit or with a sweetened fruit 'topping'.

Nowadays the USA has more cheesecake recipes than anywhere else. The best known is perhaps Lindy's cheesecake, named after the famous but now defunct New York restaurant. A biscuit dough base supports a filling of cream cheese, eggs, sugar, and flour, flavoured with orange and lemon rind.

The concept of cheesecake is both ancient and widespread. There is a vague description of what appears to be a Roman cheesecake in Cato's *De Re Rustica* of the 2nd century BC. An entry in the account books of the Countess of Leicester in 1265 is for 'cheese for tarts', but the earliest actual recipe for a cheesecake is found in the FORME OF CURY (14th century). Hannah Wolley's *Queen-Like Closet* (1664) gives a cheesecake recipe which sounds quite modern. It includes currants and is flavoured with sack, rosewater, and spices. Various continental European recipes use local curd cheeses. QUARK is widely used in sweet tarts in C. Europe.

In France the term *talmouse*, of medieval origin, originally denoted something close to what would now be called a cheesecake. It now describes a small savoury triangular cheese tart served as an HORS D'ŒUVRE.

Some unusual Italian recipes include a combination of RICOTTA with POLENTA; or even ricotta with almonds, rum, and beetroot leaves—comparable to the medieval use of spinach in sweet flans. A special Easter cheesecake, *pastiera napoletana*, is made in Naples. It is rich but not unusual, except that the ricotta filling is stiffened with pearl TAPIOCA. It includes candied peel, lemon rind, and cinnamon.

In Russia PASKHA, an enriched mixture of curd cheese, spices, nuts, dried fruit, and sugar, is traditionally eaten in Russia at Easter.

There are several Indian recipes of the same general character, for example *karrah panir*, made with a shell of coarsely chopped almonds; and a sort of coconut cheesecake.

CHEF is a French word, which has entered other languages, denoting a professional cook. It is a contraction of the phrase *chef de cuisine* hence originally a description of rank as much as, if not more than, occupation. There are chefs in many other fields, not least *chef de bureau* (administration), *chef d'équipe* (fire-fighting, industry, or sport), *chef de patrouille* (scouting), or *chef d'état* (politics). Even within the sphere of professional catering there is the *chef de rang*: the waiter in charge of a group of tables in a grand restaurant.

Although there had obviously always been cooks in charge of other cooks—there is the 15th-century description of the chief cook

whose job was tasting and testing, not cooking—the phrase itself did not appear before the beginning of the 19th century, passing quickly from France to England and other countries which had adopted the lingua franca of haute cuisine. Before that chefs were called cooks, sometimes qualified as man-cooks, master-cooks, cook-maids, professed cooks, principal cooks, or even (in the case of La Chapelle on the title-page of *The Modern Cook*, 1733) 'chief cook'. In particularly grand and conservative establishments in France before the Revolution, the head cook might be called *écuyer de cuisine*, supported by ranks of specialists such as *rôtisseurs*, *pâtissiers*, and so forth, as well as a body of *cuisiniers*.

The adoption of a new professional description must surely reflect a change in cooks' circumstances. The necessary preconditions of change and adjustment, both of material facts, and of more delicate matters of professional identity and self-esteem, were found in post-Revolutionary France. The households of the old nobility were disbanded, their masters either dead or in exile, and many of those employed in the kitchens, or in more senior positions such as maîtres d'hôtel, turned restaurateur (another new professional group that arose at this time) to provide food to all-comers, so long as they could pay. Others entered service with new families whose establishments were less elaborate. The settled hierarchies of the *ancien régime* were in disarray.

Into this vacuum floated the possibility of a new breed of cook: the artist-cook, described with eloquence and conviction by the most influential practitioner and writer of these decades, Antonin CARÊME (1783–1833), who both orchestrated developments in contemporary haute cuisine and acted as role model to many aspiring cooks. His meteoric passage through the kitchens of all Europe gave cooks the necessary impetus to reappraise and improve their standing. In his view, the cook should create the menu, order supplies, provide the artistic inspiration necessary for the great set-pieces of ceremonious dinners, and oversee the cooking. He sought to combine the two roles of maître d'hôtel and artist-cook, hence his praise of a former employer, the Princess Bagration, for allowing him both to cook and to supervise the serving of his dinners.

Carême offered an intellectual platform for cooks to redefine their professional status, while the way in which high cookery was developing towards stratified working methods to achieve complex culinary ends gave practical reasons for at least some cooks to rise to the top of the heap. Carême himself had made visible his own self-esteem (*cont. on page 161*)

Always made from MILK, is in other respects of great variety. Its taste may be almost imperceptible, as in some fresh cream cheese, or very strong, as in the most aged blue cheeses. The texture, which depends largely on water content, can be virtually liquid, as in a ripe BRIE, or dry and friable, as in many kinds of GRATING CHEESES. The fat content ranges from 1% (SCHABZIGER) to 75% (the richest CREAM CHEESES such as *Brillat-Savarin*).

Size also varies greatly. Some tiny goat's milk cheeses weigh less than 25 gm (1 oz), a mere five-thousandth of the 130 kg (290 lb) of certain cheeses of the GRUYÈRE family; and this is without counting freaks such as the 1,250 lb (567 kg) CHEDDAR cheese made in 1840 by a group of Somerset farmers as a wedding present for Queen Victoria. In 1964 the weight record was taken by an American Cheddar over 28 times as large made in Wisconsin, America's chief milk-producing area. It weighed 15,190 kg (34,591 lb) and took 43 hours to make, even with the benefit of modern machinery.

Some cheeses are made fresh daily and used at once: for example fromage blanc and fresh RICOTTA (see also WHEY CHEESES). PARMESAN and other types of GRANA may be aged for four years; the record age for an individual cheese, 200 years, goes to the hard Swiss cheese SAANEN. In France alone there are 324 (General de Gaulle speaking to Winston Churchill) or 450 (conventional reckonings by French experts) or 750 (Rance, 1989) named varieties of cheese; and the total worldwide must be over 1,500—without counting many nameless types made by small farmers and herdsmen.

Cheese is also one of the oldest of made foods, dating back to the prehistoric beginnings of herding. As with all fermented products, it seems likely that the discovery of cheese was accidental. It could be that the curdling action of RENNET was noticed when a herdsman poured milk into a pouch made of an animal's stomach. The numerous kinds of bacteria which invade milk products are common in all parts of the world. Once any kind of cheese had been formed by chance, its owner would have observed not only that the taste was pleasant but that it kept well—always a problem with milk products—and even kept hard and dry.

The earliest records of milking, some cave paintings in the Libyan Sahara dating from 5000 BC or before, show what might be cheese-making; and the ancient Sumerians and Egyptians certainly made cheese. Traces of actual cheese have been found in an Egyptian tomb of about 3000 BC. And there is no doubt that cheese was familiar in pre-classical Greece, as we know from Homer's description of Circe serving cheese to Odysseus, and was a staple food of classical Greece and Rome.

The history of cheese-making after the fall of the Roman Empire is more obscure, but it clearly continued and re-emerged in the Middle Ages as a familiar and important food. The first printed cookery book appeared in 1475. The first printed book on the subject of cheese, the famous *Summa Lacticiniorum* (see Irma Naso, 1990) was published only two years later and was the earliest of what would now be called single-subject food books. It was the first of many (for a very few of which see Reading, below, and entries for individual cheeses).

Cheese is commonly made from cow's, sheep's, goat's, and water-buffalo's milk. The more exotic kinds of milk, such as mare's and camel's, are largely reserved for other kinds of milk product, although it is possible to make cheese from the latter and cheese is certainly made from reindeer's milk.

From a nutritional point of view, cheese is a most valuable food, concentrating as it does most of the nourishment of the milk. The solids extracted from milk to make cheese contain virtually all the fat and fat-soluble vitamins, most of the proteins, and a fair amount of the minerals. Left behind in the whey are almost all of the sugar, some protein, and the water-soluble vitamins and minerals. (Whey itself may be concentrated to make WHEY CHEESES.)

The virtues of cheese are not, however, limited to being wholesome and nutritious; the sensory experiences which it offers provide an important field in which food connoisseurs can show their paces.

READING: Nantet, Rance, *et al.* (1993); Evan Jones (1976); Rance (1982, 1989); Maggie Black (1989).

Cheese-making, principles and techniques

Since there are so many types of cheese it is impossible to give an account of how a 'typical cheese' is made; the following descriptions simply set out some of the commoner processes. Some cheeses which are made in exceptional ways are described under their individual names.

'RIPENING' THE MILK

In most cheeses the first stage is to 'ripen' the milk by letting lactic acid-producing BACTERIA sour it; this develops flavour which will be apparent in the finished product. In primitive cheese-making the bacteria were left to chance. Most modern cheese is made from pasteurized milk, virtually free of bacteria, to which selected cultures are added. For example, Swiss cheeses such as GRUYÈRE and EMMENTAL, whose manufacture is rigidly controlled, depend on a culture of *Streptococcus thermophilus*, *Lactobacillus bulgaricus*, and *Propionibacterium shermani*. The most significant flavourings produced by these three are respectively (and to simplify greatly) diacetyl for a 'buttery' taste, lactic acid for sharpness, and propionic acid for the characteristic 'Swiss' flavour. The propionic bacteria also give off carbon dioxide gas which forms the bubbles that appear as 'eyes' in the cheese. Milk is kept fairly warm during ripening to encourage the bacteria to grow.

SETTING THE CURD

The next step, almost invariably, is to set the curd; i.e. to extract the solid component of the milk. Usually RENNET is used; vegetarian cheeses and some minor varieties (see CACIOTTA; PECORINO) may be curdled with vegetable extracts. For a general description of this process, see CURDLING. The casein fraction of the proteins coagulates and shrinks, trapping the fat globules and forcing out the WHEY. The milk is kept at a temperature near blood heat while it separates.

WORKING THE CURD

Once the curd has formed it is worked in one way or another to produce the characteristic texture of the particular type of cheese. For the very softest types of French cheese it is simply lifted from the whey with a perforated ladle and set in perforated tin hoops or other forms and allowed to drain by the force of gravity. But for most cheeses, which are harder, the curd is cut up or even passed through a mill or shredded with a wire 'harp' to break it down into grains. This both helps the drainage of whey and determines the size of the grains or flakes which are discernible in many hard cheeses, especially English ones. In 'cheddaring', the method by which CHEDDAR and many related hard cheeses are made, the cut curd is stacked in a tall pile to force out whey, and then milled to break the grains down to a small size. Some AMERICAN CHEESES such as 'washed curd', 'stirred curd', and 'granular' types, as well as other kinds of softer than normal Cheddar, are given less drastic treatments so that more moisture is left in the curd. Salt may be added now or later.

HEATING THE CURD

For some cheeses, including EMMENTAL, GRUYÈRE, GRANA, and other compact, even-textured types, the curd is heated well above boiling point, sometimes as high as 57 °C (134 °F)—not quite hot enough to coagulate the protein. (For different reasons, much higher temperatures are used in whey cheeses and SCHABZIGER, where coagulation is necessary.) These cheeses are called 'cooked' or 'semi-cooked', depending on the degree of heating. The effect is to shrink the grains and consolidate the texture. Despite the heat, at least some of the bacteria survive to develop flavour in the finished cheese.

One important variant of the cooking process is the *pasta filata* or 'plastic curd' process, used for Italian cheeses such as MOZZARELLA, PROVOLONE, CACIOCAVALLO and its relations such as KASHKAVAL. Here the curd is immersed in very hot water at about 60 °C (140 °F), which causes it to soften and become pliable. It is then repeatedly pulled out into long, thick strands, by hand or machine. The curd achieves a putty-like consistency which allows it to be moulded to any shape.

FORMING THE CHEESE

Next, the curd is formed into cheeses. Forms vary greatly in size and shape. Sometimes they are lined with cloth bandages to help the cheese retain its shape when it is removed. There is still some whey in the curd: the form is perforated to allow drainage. Some primitive forms are or were made of coiled straw—though the basketwork pattern on the PECORINO or MANCHEGO cheese is today more likely to be the result of a stamped metal form. The pressure on the cheese in its form may be as great as a ton and a half for a full-size Cheddar.

Some blue cheeses including ROQUEFORT are inoculated with a culture of blue mould at the forming stage. STILTON is inoculated after forming; other English blue types such as CHESHIRE and WENSLEYDALE are allowed to become infected by their surroundings.

TREATMENT OF THE FORMED CHEESE

A formed cheese, once it is stiff enough to remove, is now usually salted if salt has not been added already. Salt may be rubbed on the outside, or the cheese may be soaked in brine for hours or days. 'PICKLED' CHEESES such as FETA are kept in a mixture of brine and whey for long periods. The salty exterior of the cheese represses the growth of unwanted micro-organisms. Some cheeses such as APPENZELL are marinated in alcohol, giving special flavours.

MATURING THE CHEESE

The final step is to mature the cheese. Times and conditions for this process vary greatly. Dry surroundings are necessary for cheeses which are to be hardened; a moist environment suits soft cheeses and promotes the growth of surface organisms (see below). Warmth speeds ripening. The longer-matured cheeses are generally kept cool. There may be successive stages of maturing in different conditions.

Two important classes of cheese are ripened largely by MOULDS, YEASTS, and BACTERIA which invade them from the surface, and attention must be paid to the surface of each cheese to ensure that the desired species of micro-organisms grow on the surface and to the right extent. The curing rooms, called 'cellars', for traditionally made cheeses are, usually, naturally infected with the required organisms.

BRIE, CAMEMBERT, and similar cheeses are ripened mainly by a white mould, *Penicillium candidum*, or a relative. This is inhibited by salting, but otherwise allowed to grow unchecked. The cheese, at first acid, dry, and hard, is softened by proteolytic (protein-breaking) enzymes released by the mould, which spread from the outside inward. That is why these cheeses are always made rather flat and thin.

The other class of surface-ripened cheeses receive a more catholic mixture of bacteria, yeasts, and to a small extent moulds. For example, LIMBURGER is ripened largely by the bacterium *Brevibacterium linens*, which gives it its famous smell. The strong smell of many bacterial surface-ripened or 'surface smear' cheeses is in fact more or less confined to the surface; the inside is usually quite mild in aroma and flavour. Surface bacteria tend to grow too fast, and are kept in check by frequently washing or brushing.

Some cheeses show features of both the above classes, i.e. of the cheeses ripened by surface moulds and of the bacterial surface-ripened cheeses. They include quite large, hard and semi-hard cheeses such as the French *tomme de Savoie* (see TOMME) which develops red, grey, and yellow patches of surface mould.

Other surface treatments include coating with soot or ash (said to slow maturation) or with leaves, or 'marc' residues (grape pips and skins left over from wine-making) to impregnate the cheese with their flavour.

However, many cheeses are matured without any surface treatment: Emmental, EDAM, and SAMSOE are examples. The surface is cleaned during maturing, and may be oiled, waxed, or varnished partly to keep it clean and partly to stop drying and shrinkage.

All through the maturing period and, ideally, during shipping and up to the moment of retail sale, a cheese is kept in an environment whose temperature and humidity favour its proper maturation.

Cheese in cookery

A subject which has attracted relatively little attention from cookery writers, perhaps because dishes in which cheese is a principal ingredient (e.g. FONDUE, CHEESECAKE, WELSH RABBIT) are not numerous and cheese is more often eaten as a separate item or treated as a condiment or garnish (as in the use of PARMESAN on PASTA, or melting cheese on top of something as a finish).

However, so far as France is concerned (and with a look over the frontier to Switzerland, and some glances at other culinary cultures), there is the strikingly rich study by Peter Graham (1988), which shows that there are more examples of cheese cookery in the regions of France than one would suppose. To take one example, the *Tourteau fromagé* of Charente-Maritime, made in the traditional way, is an interesting dish made with (usually) goat cheese; it is cooked in two *moules*, one fitting tightly inside the other, and its pastry crust is burnt looking on the outside as a result of the very high heat employed.

Elsewhere the choice of a particular cheese for cooking depends largely on national or regional tastes and on what people think appropriate for their own cuisines: thus FETA for Greek and HALOUMI for Lebanese dishes, and so on. But choice is also determined by questions of texture and of behaviour when heated.

A good melting cheese is high in fat and not too hard or dry. Thus low-fat, skimmed-milk cheeses do not melt well because they are relatively high in proteins which it is easy to coagulate (coagulation starts at about 60 °C/140 °F), causing stringiness or leatheriness. When melted cheese is required, the cheese should be heated only as much as is necessary to melt it. Some coagulation may be inevitable because of the nature of the cooking process; but use of a soft, moist cheese will postpone or avert the onset of stringiness.

One cheese which behaves well in many cooked dishes is GRUYÈRE, the cheese of choice for a *Gratin savoyard*, the principal cheese for a classic *fondue suisse* (which will include two other cheeses, ideally Bagnes and *vacherin fribourgeois*), and for certain cheese soups in the Savoie, Jura, and Switzerland.

Soft cheeses with a very high water content, for example cream and curd cheeses, give a very tender texture, as required in CHEESECAKE and DANISH PASTRIES.

Graham makes the interesting general point that the whole genre ('evolved by generations of peasant cooks') of starchy envelopes or bases (RAVIOLI, PIES, TARTS) holding a cheese-flavoured filling or topping had the original function of eking out the cheese but has the bonus of providing new textural and aromatic combinations.

---

while cooking for Lord Stewart, the British envoy in Vienna, in 1821 by putting a tube of card into the floppy bonnet customarily worn by cooks to make the 'high bonnet' that is now the chef's hat or *toque*.

In his own writings, Carême refers to the rank of *chef de cuisine*. He describes how 20 cooks turn a convoluted tarantelle 'in a chasm of heat' during the preparation of a meal, where not a sound is heard save from *le chef*, who alone has the right to speak. In *L'Art de la cuisine française au XIXe siècle* he describes how the *chef des cuisines* became maître d'hôtel, and the title-page of his *Pâtissier royal parisien* (1815) describes him as *chef pâtissier*. The English translation of Carême by William Hall, 'cook to T. P. Williams, Esq.', published in 1836 under the title *French Cookery*, describes the author as 'some time chef of the kitchen of His Majesty George IV'.

The combination of practical and intellectual ambition that is evident from Carême's writings—a man with a mission for his craft—is wittily underscored some years later by W. M. Thackeray in his novel *Pendennis* (1848–50). He describes the arrival at Sir Francis Clavering's opulent country seat of

Monsieur Alcide Mirobolant, formerly Chef of his Highness the Duc de Borodino, of his Eminence Cardinal Beccafico, and at present Chef of the bouche of Sir Clavering, Baronet:— Monsieur Mirobolant's library, pictures, and piano had arrived previously. He was aided by a professional female cook who had inferior females under her orders. It was a grand sight to behold him in his dressing-gown composing a menu. He always sate down and played the piano for some time before. Every artist, he said, had need of solitude to perfectionate his works.

This is the artist-cook with a vengeance, modelled, it is thought, on Alexis Soyer (1809–58), chef of the Reform Club. Mirobolant's emotional scrapes notwithstanding, his tender sense of personal dignity was most deeply affronted by the hero of the novel calling him 'cook'.

The concept of the artist-cook had also been encouraged by middle-class enthusiasts for fine cooking in post-Revolutionary France such as GRIMOD DE LA REYNIÈRE who invested much intellectual effort in the creation of a menu (a joint activity of the cook and the employer). In his *Manuel des Amphitryons* (1808) is an early use of the term 'chef', introduced when discussing the various functions in the kitchen. He recommends specialization; life is too short to learn more than one trade to perfection. In a large kitchen, he observes, 'the chef and his aide are employed exclusively on the range', the *rôtisseur* and *pâtissier* on the spit and the oven respectively.

It was the invasion of territory hitherto occupied by the steward of the household (in England) or the maître d'hôtel (in France) that gave the cook new status. Maîtres d'hôtel had often themselves trained as cooks—the great Monsieur de Saint-Clouet, cook to the Duke of Newcastle, eulogized by William VERRAL in *A Complete System of Cookery* (1759) went on to become maître d'hôtel to the Duc de Richelieu. They wrote cookery books, for example Beauvilliers, *L'Art du cuisinier* (1814), and they had books written for them such as Massialot's *Cuisinier roïal* (1691), 'necessaire à tous Maîtres d'Hôtels, & Ecuïers de Cuisine'. But when the cook began to compose his own menus as well as design his own *pièces montées* and supervise the order of service, it was a definite extension of his duties into the realm of the steward, and would be utter conquest when the clerk of the kitchen and provision of all supplies became subject to the chef as well. The job definitions of the British cook and author Charles Elmé Francatelli (1805–76), a student of Carême's, indicate the shifts in function. At the outset of his career he was *chef de cuisine* (so called) to the Earl of Chesterfield and several other noble households where presumably he had independence within his own sphere. In 1841 he became 'maître d'hôtel and chief cook in ordinary' to Queen Victoria. The royal household was conservative enough to retain the old offices and their titles, but the chef has now combined the two most relevant to his calling.

In its passage into other languages, particularly English, the word *chef* has come to stand alone, and describe function more than status. As with other words that were once all to do with rank, it has been universalized and democratized. Every cook is a chef, though a short-order chef in a hamburger restaurant occupies a position light years from the original connotation of overall command. For many years, however, the usage was quite precise. A *chef de cuisine* is still by profession a cook, who happens to control the work of other cooks. Victor Hugo, discussing Carême's patronage of the arts during his time with James de Rothschild (*Choses vues*, 1847–8), calls him *cuisinier* never *chef*; the French trade association was one of *cuisiniers*, not *chefs*; the French chef and writer Pierre Hamp in his autobiography *Kitchen Prelude* (1932) was careful to restrict the name to those who were properly so called, remembering from his time under Escoffier at the Savoy that 'Another cook, head of department, who also left was Bozzone, the sauce man, the next in rank after M. Charles, an Alsatian who was called "chef", for

Escoffier went by the name of "Kitchen Director".'

It was in fact the organizational reforms by Escoffier's generation that caused the extension of the term 'chef' to a wider body of workers. The functions of large commercial kitchens were rearranged. Hitherto, independent sections had each produced a certain type of finished dish, but under the new regime the departments, called *parties*, were split along operational lines according to the components of a dish: one making sauces, another supplying raw ingredients, a third doing the grilling, and so on. A single dish would call for contributions from several *parties*, thus would take less time to go to table than when in the hands of a single cook. It is a process of industrialization (see Mennell, 1985). Pierre Hamp may not have used the terms, but eventually the men in charge of these new departments were called *chefs de partie*. Their assistants were sous-chefs, and apprentices and learners began to be called commis-chefs. Soon everybody, except the washers and cleaners, was some sort of chef.

It was a small jump to the complete confusion of chef with the word 'cook', at least within the sphere of hotels and restaurants—and at least to outsiders, for if you were working inside the kitchen, there was never more than one man who demanded to be called 'Chef'. 'Cook' remained the usual description of one who worked in an institution, no matter whether man or woman, and of women who were employed as cooks in domestic service. Men-cooks in private households in the 20th century were often given the courtesy title of chef, although Anatole, Aunt Dahlia's matchless Frenchman in P. G. Wodehouse's *The Code of the Woosters* (1938), remained simply a cook.

Chefs were invariably male, largely because a large restaurant kitchen was a man's world. Women who worked commercially remained cooks, *cuisinières*, or

'mères' such as Mère Poulard of omelette fame. Since technology and social progress have allowed the entry of more women into once all-male brigades, so they have also been given the same titles. The professional cook is hard to find outside domestic service and the school kitchen. Memories of the original meaning of the word 'chef' as a description of rank not function persist however. Chefs still cook, there is no verb 'to chef'.   TJ

CHELATION the phenomenon which occurs when a metal atom is trapped inside a molecule of an organic substance, whose numerous and smaller atoms form a 'cage' round it. Globin in meat chelates iron. Chlorophyll in plants chelates magnesium. In both instances chelation is responsible for colour changes (the red colour of meat and the green colour in plants). See COLOUR AND COOKING.

CHERIMOYA the fruit of *Annona cherimola*, a tree native to the mountains of Peru, where prehistoric terracotta vases modelled from it have been dug up, and Ecuador. It has since been introduced to subtropical regions around the world and is cultivated in many of them. Its name comes from the Peruvian *chirimuya*, meaning cold seeds; presumably an allusion to the wet freshness of the fruit and the large number of seeds which it contains.

'Deliciousness itself,' declared Mark Twain on sampling it. Its particular excellence is often obscured by the undiscriminating application of the name 'custard apple' to both it and some of its close relations (see CUSTARD APPLE, SUGAR-APPLE, and BULLOCK'S HEART). The development of hybrids has added to the confusion. But the cherimoya is distinct from and superior to its congeners, and the tree may be distinguished from the others by the velvety underside of its leaves.

Cherimoya

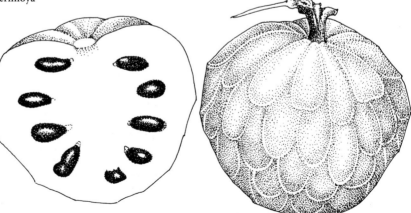

The fruit has been likened in appearance to a globe artichoke, although a glance will show that the 'scales' on its surface are not separate like the leaves of an artichoke but mere protuberances (and are anyway not present in all varieties). The skin is light green and thin. 'The flesh is white, melting in texture, and moderately juicy. Numerous brown seeds . . . are embedded in it. The flavor is subacid, delicate, suggestive of the pineapple and banana.' Thus wrote Popenoe (1932). Other commentators have found hints of papaya and vanilla in addition to pineapple and banana and have noted that the custard-like flesh is made more interesting by a touch of the granular texture of pears.

A fruit may weigh anything from about 100 g (3.5 oz) to 2–3 kg (5 lb) or even more. Shape too varies greatly. One expert on the genus gave a list of the principal forms: Smooth, Tuberculate, Mammillate, Umbonate, and Finger-printed (*anona de dedos pintados* in Costa Rica, its surface covered with what look like fingerprints in wax).

However, the development of new varieties and of hybrids such as the **atemoya** (a cross between the cherimoya and the sugar-apple, now a fruit in its own right, with its own named varieties), is obscuring the traditional classification of forms.

CHERRY a favoured fruit of painters and poets. True cherries, of which there are several species, belong to the genus *Prunus*, which also includes PLUMS, PEACHES, APRICOTS, and ALMONDS, all in the ROSE family. Cultivated cherries are descended from two wild species: *Prunus avium*, ancestor of the sweet varieties; and *P. cerasus*, from which sour cherries come. Both are native to W. Asia.

The sweet cherry was described in about 300 BC by the Greek writer Theophrastus. It and the sour cherry were probably both being cultivated in the Mediterranean area before this time. The ancient Greek name *kerasos*, from which 'cherry' is derived, has been said to come from the city of that name in Asia Minor (now Giresun in Turkey); but it is more probable, as Casaubon first pointed out in his great edition (1597–1600) of Athenaeus, that the city took its name from the fruit.

The wild sweet cherry is also called 'gean' (from the old French *guine*), and 'mazzard' (a name especially applied to small black fruits). The fruits are small, usually dark red, and either sweet or bitter, but never sour. The wild sour cherry, *P. cerasus*, is borne by a smaller and hardier tree which has spread further north, for example in Scandinavia.

By the 1st century AD, when Pliny the Elder was writing, at least eight varieties of cherry were under cultivation in Italy and were highly prized. The Romans certainly played a part in spreading interest in the cherry, and Pliny mentions cultivation as far away as Britain.

There is plenty of evidence that cherries were still being cultivated, e.g. in monastery gardens, and appreciated during the medieval period. In medieval art cherries represented a sweet, pleasing character, and the delights of the blessed.

In England, the emergence of Kent as the principal cherry county was already clear in the 16th century. By the 17th century, around the time when colonists were taking the cherry to New England, two dozen or more named varieties were being grown in England, and the number has increased ever since. Parallel developments have taken place in continental Europe, where Germany is by far the largest producer (worldwide) of both sweet cherries and sour cherries; and in the USA, the second largest producer in the world for both kinds. American production is concentrated in three states: California, Oregon, and Washington.

The number of cultivated cherry varieties, worldwide, is now estimated to be about 900 sweet and 300 sour. There is therefore scope for confusion over the names of varieties, and of groups of varieties. The main groups are explained in the box.

Sweet cherries are usually eaten raw as dessert fruit. Sour cherries have a good flavour when cooked and adequately sweetened, and are preferred for making cherry pies and other dishes. The variety Montmorency, for long considered to be the finest cherry on the Paris markets, is now a rarity in France, sought after by connoisseurs for making conserves or bottling in brandy, but is still a popular variety in the USA.

Meat dishes with sour cherries exist in many cuisines from England to Persia. In many parts of N. Europe cherry soup is popular. Sour cherries are dried and used to give a sourish flavour to many dishes in the Caucasus and in Iran.

The black Morello cherry is essential for black cherry jam, *Schwarzwälder Kirschtorte* (BLACK FOREST GATEAU), *Kirschstrudel* (cherry STRUDEL), and the white spirit kirsch.

The griotte cherry is used in the confectionery items called *griottes* which are a speciality of the Franche-Comté. Long-stalked griotte cherries, such as are plentiful in the vicinity of Besançon, are enclosed with kirsch in a chocolate covering.

The small, very sour marasca or maraschino cherry was originally grown near Zara, the capital of Dalmatia (now in Croatia), where it was made into maraschino liqueur, now also made in Italy. The special flavour of this drink is due to the stones being crushed to release the almond taste of the kernels, in contrast to kirsch, where the stones are left whole.

Maraschino cherries in syrup are prepared by stoning and bleaching the cherries, then adding syrup, bitter almond oil, and red or green colouring. Glacé cherries are made by the more ordinary method of candying.

The MAHLAB or St Lucy's cherry (so named because it was planted at a convent dedicated to that saint) is native to Asia Minor and continues to have uses in e.g. Turkey and Cyprus. It belongs to the same genus as the mainstream cherries. So does the CHOKECHERRY, which is more interesting than it sounds.

Other 'cherries' belonging to unrelated genera may or may not have hard stones. They include the BARBADOS CHERRY, cornelian cherry (a DOGWOOD), ground or winter cherry (PHYSALIS FRUITS), and Surinam cherry (PITANGA).

GROUPS OF CHERRY VARIETIES

Sweet cherries have often been classed into two main groups: bigarreau with firm, dry flesh; and guigne (the French equivalent of 'gean') with soft, juicy flesh. However, hybridization has blurred this old distinction. Sweet cherries of the firmer (bigarreau) sort include the justly popular 'white' (in reality light red and yellow) Napoleon, Bing (a fine red cherry, named after his Chinese workman by an American grower, now dominating US fresh sweet cherry production), and Rainier (a cross of Bing and Van, delicate and exquisitely sweet). Softer (guigne) varieties include Black Tartarian and Coe's Transparent (with a clear skin, but too delicate to be shipped).

Sour cherries are classified into two groups: amarelle or relatively light coloured, with clear juice; and griotte, dark or black, with coloured juice. Montmorency (which originated in the valley of that name in the Île-de-France, where a Fête de la Cerise is still held annually) is a famous variety of amarelle; and Morello the best-known griotte.

Sweet-and-sour cherries are intermediate between the above categories. They often go under the name Duke (Royale in France). This kind of cherry came to England from Médoc, which name was adapted to May Duke, later abbreviated to Duke.

CHERRY LAUREL a shrub of the E. Mediterranean region, *Laurocerasus officinalis*. It is sometimes confused with the unrelated bay tree (see BAY LEAF) which it rather resembles, although it is larger, with larger and glossier leaves. Since the French for bay leaf is *laurier*, unwary translators of French recipes sometimes advise cooks to use 'laurel leaves', which could lead to serious consequences since these leaves contain prussic acid, and have been known to cause poisoning.

However, cherry laurel leaves, with their bitter almond flavour, do have a limited use in flavouring rice puddings and custards, although they must always be used with caution because of their toxicity. A liquid distilled from the leaves and available commercially is used in the food industry.

CHERRY PLUM *Prunus cerasifera*, a plum which is also known by the old name myrobalan plum. It is round, with a tiny point at the end away from the stalk, and larger than a cherry but smaller than most plums: typically about 3 cm (just over 1") in diameter. The usual colour is red, but some cultivars have amber or yellow fruits. It is thought to have originated in W. Asia and the Caucasus and is used in cooking in SE Europe and the Near East.

CHERVIL a name derived from the Greek *chaerophyllon*, meaning herb of rejoicing, is applied to two quite different cultivated plants, and to one wild one. The most familiar chervil is an umbelliferous plant, *Anthriscus cerefolium*, which looks rather like curly-leafed parsley but is sparer, more feathery, and more upright. Originally a wild plant native to W. Asia, it was first cultivated in Syria, according to Pliny the Elder (1st century AD). The Syrians ate chervil as a raw or cooked leaf vegetable; but in Roman cuisine it was used as a flavouring herb, as it is now. It has consistently enjoyed a reputation for restorative powers. As Gerard (1633) said: 'It is good for old people: it rejoiceth and comforteth the heart and increaseth their strength.'

Chervil leaf has a light, mild flavour between those of parsley and of anise or liquorice, but more delicate than any of these. Its flavour is spoiled by heat, so it has to be added towards the end of cooking. It does not dry successfully, and must be used fresh.

Chervil is given most prominence in French cuisine. It is a constituent of FINES HERBES, and is often used with tarragon, in BÉARNAISE SAUCE, for instance. Elsewhere, its use is of less importance.

Wild chervil is another name for the common wild plant cow parsley, *A. sylvestris*,

which has also been used as a flavouring herb in England and the Netherlands. Although it belongs to the same genus as cultivated chervil it is a bigger plant with a stronger, coarser flavour. In Japan its young shoots and leaves are used in Sansai cooking (a vegetarian cuisine associated with Buddhist temples, using ferns, roots, wild herbs, young shoots, etc.). *Cryptotaenia japonica*, Japanese MITSUBA, may also be referred to as 'wild chervil'.

Turnip-rooted chervil, *Chaerophyllum bulbosum*, an umbelliferous plant native to S. Europe and the Caucasian region, is quite different from cultivated or wild chervil. The root is the part eaten, while the leaves are slightly poisonous. It is mainly eaten in E. Europe, Germany, and Holland, and is nowadays almost unknown in other countries.

The root is round, seldom larger and often smaller than a small carrot, grey outside and yellowish white within, with a mealy texture like a floury potato. It is usually boiled.

Typically, Vilmorin-Andrieux (1883) not only described this plant, but had something to add:

the Prescott Chervil, a native of Siberia, which produces large edible roots like those of the variety just described, is grown much in the same way. Its roots are longer and larger than those of the Common Tuberous-rooted Chervil, but their flavour is coarser and more like that of the Parsnip.

CHESHIRE is thought to be Britain's oldest named cheese. It is mentioned in the Domesday Book at the end of the 11th century, but was probably made long before then.

Good Cheshire must (unlike Cheddar) be made in its region of origin; this is around Chester, the county town of Cheshire. The flavour of the cheese depends on the salty, marl and sandstone, grazing land along the River Dee and its tributaries; also no doubt on the cattle, those same cattle which, in Charles Kingsley's sad poem, Mary was invited to call home across the sands of Dee.

Cheshire is a large, hard-pressed, drum-shaped, whole-milk cheese typically weighing 30 kg (70 lb). The texture is crumbly but not moist, and the flavour mild and slightly acid. It was formerly made in early-, medium-, and late-ripening varieties, of which the last, aged for as long as 10 months, was considered best. Now, however, it has been standardized at a medium, six-month, ripening time.

In its natural state Cheshire is a pale cream colour. However, it is often coloured orange with ANNATTO (since the end of the 18th century, before which carrot juice was used), a practice which probably originated

as a means of giving the cheese a rich look, in rivalry with other, deeper-coloured cheeses. There is also a highly regarded blue Cheshire, locally known as 'green fade' cheese.

Gerard (1633) records the preference for rennet made from lady's bedstraw in making Cheshire cheese, 'especially about Namptwich [Nantwich] where the best Cheese is made'. This practice seems to have died out by the end of the 18th century.

Giant Cheshire cheeses have been recorded. In 1909 an order for 20, each to weigh 300 lb (136 kg), was executed with success. But this exploit seems to have been surpassed by cheese-makers in the town of Cheshire, Massachusetts, who established a tradition of giving mammoth cheeses to an incoming president of the United States, and whose cheese for President Jackson, after it had stood in state for weeks at the White House while Democrats ate their fill from it, still left the floor a foot deep in fragments; see Brown (1955).

The French and Germans make a cooking cheese called 'Chester', originally intended to resemble Cheshire (which enjoyed an international reputation long before Cheddar did, and was mentioned in the first printed cheese book, of 1477—see Naso, 1990). But, nowadays at least, 'Chester' bears only a slight resemblance to its original.

CHESTNUT a name given to many nuts, originally and primarily to those of the European 'sweet' or 'Spanish' chestnut tree, *Castanea sativa*, and later to various Asian and American relatives. These trees belong to regions with a temperate climate.

Chestnuts contain more starch and less oil than most other nuts and have had a special role as food for this reason. The European chestnut was formerly a staple food of great importance, but has now become more of a luxury.

HISTORY
The European chestnut, despite its name, is of W. Asian origin. Around 300 BC the Greek writer Xenophon described how the children of Persian nobles were fed on chestnuts to fatten them; and it was the Greeks who brought the tree to Europe, from Sardis in Asia Minor. But it flourished more in S. Europe than in its region of origin and deserved the name European long before this came into common use. The more specific name Spanish chestnut probably arose because the best chestnuts imported into Britain came from Spain.

The Romans had the tree in regular cultivation by 37 BC, when Virgil described it in his *Eclogues*. The Latin name, from which came the botanical name and modern European names, was bestowed on it for the town Castanea in Magnesia, where the tree was especially common. The Romans made chestnuts into flour, which was used to extend wheat flour, a practice which survives in S. Europe. APICIUS gave a recipe for chestnuts cooked with lentils. The Romans also took the tree north, to Gaul and then to Britain.

Wild chestnuts are common all over S. Europe, especially in Italy, Corsica, S. France, and Spain. The trees, of medium size, are hardy and long-lived. One at the foot of Mount Etna was thought to be 2,000 years old when it was killed by the volcano erupting.

USES

Nuts of wild varieties are relatively small but of good flavour. They have been an adequate staple food for peasants in poorer regions, and remain a useful foodstuff in the country-side. Rural uses of wild chestnuts include the original Italian POLENTA, a porridge which was made with chestnut meal before the introduction of maize from the New World; and bread and biscuits made of chestnut meal mixed with cereal flour.

Chestnut bread is characterized by large, irregular holes. Although the European chestnut has almost the same proportions of protein, starch, and fat as wheat, it lacks gluten to bind the bread together, and can only be used in moderate amounts. A higher proportion of chestnut meal is used in Italian *necci*, flat cakes baked on hot stones and resembling Indian CHAPATI. Chestnut meal, called *farina dolce* (sweet flour) in Italian, is often used as a thickener in Italian dishes. In Italy chestnuts which have been dried to keep through the winter are called *secchielli*; in Spain *pilongas*. They need to be soaked or steamed before they can be used.

Howes (1948) remarks on the importance of chestnuts in Corsica.

A generation ago, there were old inhabitants in the more remote parts of the island who admitted they had never eaten ordinary or wheat bread, so dependent were they on chestnuts and chestnut flour.

In Britain the chestnut grows as far north as the Caledonian Canal. Evelyn (1644) gave the tree a warm recommendation.

Tis likewise observed, that this tree is so prevalent against cold, that where they stand, they defend other plantations from the injuries of the severest frosts: I am sure being planted in hedgerows, etc. or for avenues to our country-houses, they are a magnificent and royal ornament.

This prompted the planting of many more chestnut trees in England. However, again according to Evelyn, the nuts were not used for human food as much as they deserved to be.

But we give that fruit to our swine in England, which is amongst the delicacies of princes in other countries; . . . The best tables in France and Italy

make them a service, eating them with salt, in wine or juice or lemmon and sugar; being first roasted in embers on the chaplet; and doubtless we might propagate their use amongst our common people, being a food so cheap, and so lasting.

Whereas wild chestnuts are a food of the poor, the large cultivated chestnuts are a luxury. Trees of these varieties produce only a single, large nut in each burr (nut-case) instead of several small ones. Many European languages have a different name for the finest cultivated nuts, e.g. *marrons* in French, as opposed to *châtaignes* for the wild chestnut or the ordinary cultivated kind. (However, there is no clear dividing line. Some *châtaigniers* are hard to distinguish from *marronniers*.)

The biggest and best *marrons* are grown in the region of Lyons, where they are candied to make the famous MARRONS GLACÉS.

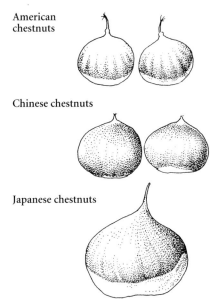

American chestnuts

Chinese chestnuts

Japanese chestnuts

However, French production of the cultivated chestnut has declined so much that most of their *marrons glacés* are now made with imported chestnuts.

Chestnuts are often employed in stuffings for poultry, e.g. turkey. Other chestnut preparations include purées for serving with meat and game; chestnuts cooked with Brussels sprouts; French chestnut soups and soufflés; the Italian *castagnaccio*, a semi-sweet baked dish incorporating other nuts and sultanas; numerous puddings (of which the Austrian NESSELRODE PUDDING is the best known); many gateaux and cakes, in which chocolate is often combined with the chestnut; and chestnut ice creams.

Special perforated pans for roasting chestnuts over a fire used to be common items of equipment in Britain and elsewhere in Europe. In some European cities it is still possible in winter, especially just before

Christmas, to buy freshly roasted chestnuts from stalls or barrows.

OTHER SPECIES

Outside Europe there are chestnuts of several other *Castanea* species. The Chinese chestnut, *C. mollissima*, has been cultivated in China for at least as long as its European counterpart, and used in much the same way: dried, roasted, or made into meal. It has nuts of good flavour, whose relatively thin skin can be peeled off easily. The Japanese chestnut, *C. crenata*, has large, starchy nuts which are usually eaten boiled, when they have some resemblance to potato. The American chestnut, *C. dentata*, once a common tree, especially in the Appalachians, bore excellent nuts, richer in oil than European chestnuts. The tree was widely cultivated until the the 20th century, when chestnut blight almost wiped it out. (European chestnut trees, which were also cultivated, were affected by the blight, but less so. The Chinese chestnut, which is resistant to it, is now the main species cultivated in the USA.)

Another American species, the dwarf chestnut, *C. pumila*, has small nuts of no commercial value, but of good flavour. It is sometimes called chinquapin, a name of American Indian origin, which is better reserved for trees of the genera *Castanopsis* and *Chrysolepis*, related to the chestnut but smaller and of a bushy character. American chinquapins include the golden chinquapin of the north-west of the USA, *Chrysolepis chrysophylla*. In E. India and SE Asia various species are cultivated to a limited extent. The nuts of all these are used in the familiar ways; boiled, roasted, or dried and ground to meal.

HORSE CHESTNUTS

The horse chestnuts, *Aesculus* spp, are not closely related to true chestnuts or chinquapins, and the resemblance of their fruits is coincidental. The species common in Europe, *A. hippocastanum*, known as *marron d'Inde* in France, originally grew in Asia Minor and Greece. In 1557 a Flemish doctor resident in Constantinople sent some nuts to the great botanist Matthiolus in Vienna, remarking that in Turkish they were called *kastane* and used in a horse medicine. The large, handsome tree, which thus came to be called 'horse chestnut', then became popular as a shade tree. Its nuts, however, are bitter and inedible because of the presence of large amounts of tannins. These are soluble in water, so the nuts can be processed to produce an edible starch which, ground to meal, makes a famine food.

OTHER 'CHESTNUTS'

Other plants bearing nuts termed 'chestnuts' are less similar to the true kind. These include some leguminous plants such as the Tahiti (or Polynesian or Fiji) chestnut, *Inocarpus edulis*, a tree of the tropical Pacific islands. The large, single, seeds, locally called *mape* and other names (*ivi* in Fiji), may be boiled or roasted, or grated to become an ingredient of breads or puddings. They are almost a staple food on some of the more remote islands. However, most authors follow Burkill (1965–6) in describing them as indigestible. They are sometimes fermented like BREADFRUIT seeds, and it may be that this process, which makes it possible to store them underground for long periods, also reduces the indigestibility.

See also WATER CHESTNUT and CHINESE WATER CHESTNUT.

READING: Ariane Bruneton-Governatori (1984), a truly remarkable work covering the 'ethnohistory' of the European chestnut and its manifold uses.

CHEWING GUM a confection of SUGAR, flavouring, and an insoluble base which is eventually spat out and discarded by the user. Originally it was made from chicle, the latex of the tree *Manilkara zapota* (see SAPODILLA), which is native to C. and S. America. A sweet based on a mixture of chicle, sugar, and a flavouring (LIQUORICE or SASSAFRAS) was patented in 1871. By the end of the 19th century, several entrepreneurs were making handsome profits from the manufacture of such items as Chiclets, Gumballs, and Spearmint Gum. The foremost of these, William Wrigley, made clever use of marketing techniques and expanded the market considerably.

The sweet became popular in Europe after soldiers from the USA brought it in their ration packs during the First World War. In the late 20th century, chewing gum seems to be a global phenomenon.

The demand for chicle has long outstripped supply, and a number of patented substitutes based on blends of resins, oils, and rubbers are now used instead.

Bubble gum is a similar product, based on a highly elastic latex mixture, usually coloured pink. Children enjoy seeing who can blow the largest bubble with it.   (LM)

CHIA an American plant of the same genus as the common European herb sage, was grown for its seeds by the Aztecs in ancient Mexico, who used them as a cereal. The main species grown was *Salvia columbariae*, golden chia, the seeds of which were roasted and ground, to form a meal called PINOLE, then mixed with water so that the meal swelled into a glutinous mushy mess. This was eaten as a porridge or made into cakes.

The name 'chia' is also applied to *S. hispanica*, Mexican chia, the uses of which are admirably summarized by Facciola (1990).

When soaked in water, the seeds form a gelatinous mass which is flavored with fruit juices and consumed as a cooling drink. The gelled seeds can also be prepared as a gruel or pudding. Sprouted seeds are eaten in salads, sandwiches, soups, stews etc. Due to their mucilaginous properties, they are sprouted on clay or other porous materials, and clay animals or 'chia pets' are sold commercially for this purpose. The seeds are ground into meal and made into breads, biscuits, muffins and cakes.

CHICKEN dishes are possibly the most nearly ubiquitous menu items of a non-vegetarian kind. They may be taboo in certain circumstances in some cultures, but are generally available to all irrespective of religion and with fewer financial constraints than other flesh.

The history of the species is discussed under HEN/CHICKEN BREEDS. It has also been the subject of a fine book by Page Smith and Charles Daniel (1975), which carries the story from antiquity through publication of the famous book on chickens by Aldrovandi (1600) up to the late 20th century and does not shrink from describing the horrors of some intensive rearing practices. It is these practices which have tended to turn chicken—once something of a luxury for most people—into an inexpensive meat, lacking flavour and provoking uneasy qualms of conscience. This consideration applies in many parts of the world. The 'free-range chickens' of, for example, Britain have equivalents in distant places. Thus *gai ban* (yard chicken) in Thailand is superior to *gai yang*, a cooped chicken.

The lack of flavour has meant that chickens are particularly suited to dishes which involve distinctive added flavours. Many ethnic cuisines are rich in such dishes, and many of them have become popular in the western world on tables where they would formerly have been seen as almost unimaginably exotic. The simple roast chicken, with a simple flavouring of herbs,

which was a Sunday treat in England in the first half of the 20th century may still be a treat, but only for people who are prepared to make the effort and meet the expense of procuring a chicken which has been properly reared in a good environment (e.g. certain French chickens whose origin, as explained under HEN/CHICKEN BREEDS, is officially established by metal tags).

Among well known or particularly interesting dishes are the following.

Hindle wakes, a strange name for a dish, comes from 'hen de la wake', meaning hen to be eaten at the wake (fair). A medieval festive dish, to be eaten cold, it presents a fine appearance with white meat, black stuffing, and yellow and green trimmings. See Elizabeth Ayrton (1975).

Coronation chicken, devised for the coronation of Queen Elizabeth II in 1953, has proved remarkably persistent as a menu item, never in sophisticated restaurants, but otherwise popping up all over the place. It is cooked pieces of cold chicken served with a curried mayonnaise sauce, often accompanied by apricots.

Chicken à la Kiev is a chicken breast coated with breadcrumbs and stuffed with flavoured butter which spurts forth when punctured by the diner's fork. It has been described by Lesley Chamberlain (1983) as a 'Soviet hotel and restaurant classic', which so far as she could discover had no pre-revolutionary history.

Chicken Marengo is the name of a dish supposedly cooked for Napoleon's supper immediately after the battle of Marengo in 1800. The chicken is fried, then cooked in a sauce of white wine, garlic, tomatoes, and perhaps mushrooms, which were supposedly the ingredients which the chef had to hand on the original occasion; but he would not have had tomatoes at that early time and the first printed recipe for the dish makes no mention of them.

Southern fried chicken is a dish which arouses strong emotions whenever there is discussion among Americans about techniques, ingredients, or accompaniments. Mariani (1994) does a masterful job in setting out the various points which may be

TERMINOLOGY OF CHICKENS

This is a complex area. Apart from anything else, there is an awkward overlap in Britain between 'chicken' and 'boiling fowl' (a mature hen, called *poule* in French, now less often marketed, but formerly a great standby). A poussin is a baby chicken weighing around 450–500 g (about 1 lb), best suited to being grilled. Spring chicken (a term falling into disuse, since chicken alone now has this meaning), French *poulet*, will weigh about 1–2 kg (2 to 4.5 lb). A French *poularde*, e.g. from Brittany, may be a chicken which has been reared and fed in an exemplary manner for most of its life, but then confined and fattened for the table.

Chicken breasts are referred to as *suprêmes* in menu French, see SUPREME.

disputed. He also identifies antecedents in the 19th century ('Maryland fried chicken' crops up in the 1870s), but remarks that the dish did not acquire fame as a southern speciality under its modern name until the early decades of the 20th century. The only conclusions one can reach after reading Mariani are that there are lots of ways of making southern fried chicken but that there is only one appropriate way of eating it—with the fingers.

Tampumpie, a dish from the Solomon Islands (not otherwise represented in this book), is recorded by Emerson (1908), who explains that it is made in a stone oven. Sliced taro or yam is placed in this, with a prepared fowl in the centre and a mass of grated coconut over all. Water is added and the dish cooked. 'While the oven is a primitive affair it is most effective, and in the hands of a native woman who is at all desirous of pleasing her lord and master it can be made to do wonders.'

See also SPATCHCOCK, TINOLA, SATAY, TIKKA.

CHICKPEA *Cicer arietinum*, a small LEGUME which was first grown in the Levant and ancient Egypt, but is now an important food in many parts of the world, especially the broad band of countries extending from India through the Middle East to N. Africa, with offshoots of importance in places to which the Arabs took it, e.g. Sicily and Spain.

The seeds of larger varieties are curled at the sides and have been likened to a ram's skull. This accounts for the botanical name, *arietinum* (aries being ram). As for the generic name, *Cicer*, this was Latin for chickpea, and it is said that the family of the famous Roman orator Cicero had an ancestor who had a wart on his face shaped like a chickpea and that this is how they got their name.

The chickpea was certainly used by the Romans, but regarded as a food for peasants and poor people. Its rustic image is shown by the longing of the poet Horace, when sickened by city life, for a dish of chickpeas and pasta.

Much earlier, in the 2nd millennium BC according to Achaya (1994), the chickpea was one of the pulses eaten in India, where it is a major foodstuff, known as *channa*. It makes a popular form of DAL (split pulse). Whole chickpeas are known as Bengal gram. Finely milled chickpea flour, known as BESAN FLOUR, is used to make batter for PAKORA/FRITTERS etc.; and there are similar uses in Afghanistan and Iran, including biscuits.

Despite its reputation, the chickpea is the basis of some of the most popular Middle Eastern dishes, notably *hum(m)us*, which is the Arabic word for chickpea but also

signifies a ubiquitous paste of chickpea and TAHINI (sesame paste) with garlic and lemon; and FALAFEL. Still in the Arab sphere, it is an ingredient in N. African COUSCOUS; and continues to betray Arab influence in many Spanish soups and stews.

Spanish migrants took chickpeas to Latin America, but they have never been as important there as the native haricot beans. Nor are they much eaten in regions east of India, except by peoples of Indian origin in and around the Malay peninsula.

Chickpeas are almost always sold in dried form, whether split or not, and are of an ochre or pale brown colour in this form. However, they may be eaten fresh, as Patience Gray (1986) explains:

Gathered fresh in May, though no one will believe it, they are a short-lived delicacy, brilliant green, growing two to a pod; eaten raw they have a refreshing taste of lemon. Cooked in a dish of rice they delight the eye. But, as the May sun in southern latitudes quickly dries them, they are imagined, even by Italians, to be born brown and born dry.

The same author relates how:

In northern Italy, chickpea flour is used to make appetizing pizze, thin as flannel, in Carrara called Calda! Calda! The name arose from boys carrying them in covered baskets, shouting their piping hot wares, along the rocky torrent of the carrione, down which the famished quarrymen returned at evening on foot from the marble mountains.

Alluding to the notorious toughness of chickpeas (even when soaked, and cooked for a long time), Théophile Gautier is said to have written that 'garbanzos . . . sounded in our bellies like pieces of lead in a Basque drum'. Fortunately, modern varieties are less intractable, although a preliminary soaking and relatively long cooking are still normal. *Channa dal*, being split and skinned, cooks much faster than whole chickpeas.

CHICKWEED *Stellaria media*, is the best known of a group of related small plants which have played a minor role in the diet of various peoples.

Chickweed is so called because poultry like it. A pleasant old English name for it is 'hen's inheritance'. It grows wild in temperate regions all over the world, and resists the cold, so that it is a useful source of greenstuff in winter. The classical Greeks and Romans liked chickweed and sometimes even cultivated it, although supplies from the wild are abundant. It was also popular in ancient Japan. The young green leaves may be raw or cooked. The flavour is between that of spinach and cabbage. The plant is best eaten in the spring.

A related plant, sea chickweed (or sea purslane), *Arenaria peploides*, is eaten

pickled by the Inuit (Eskimos) of Alaska, whose diet is otherwise almost exclusively animal.

CHICORY AND ENDIVE, *Cichorium intybus* and *C. endivia*, two closely related plants whose common names are beset by much confusion, in French as well as English. It is convenient to treat them together, and to exhibit the common names in tabular form.

Scientific name	English	American	French
C. intybus (green)	chicory	chicory, sugarloaf	*chicorée endive*
C. intybus (blanched)	witloof, French endive	witloof chicory, Belgian endive, French endive	*chicorée à grosses racines*
C. intybus (red-leaved)	radicchio	radicchio red chicory	*chicorée sauvage à rouge feuille*
C. endivia (broad-leaved or batavian)	endive	endive, escarole, batavia, chicory	*chicorée scarole*
C. endivia (curly-leaved)	curly endive		*chicorée frisée*

Chicory and endive both belong to the genus *Cichorium*, which in turn belongs to the large family Compositae which also includes lettuce, and many other edible plants, and also dandelion (whose leaves resemble those of wild chicory).

CHICORY

Chicory, *Cichorium intybus*, describes a group of perennial cultivated plants developed from wild chicory, a common plant of Europe, W. Asia, and Africa. The wild plant was also called succory (or 'blue succory' because it has blue flowers) in England in the past. The French and Italian names *barbe de capucin* and *barbe di capuccino* mean 'Capuchin monk's beard'.

Chicory was used as a vegetable and for salad in classical Greece and Rome, but was not apparently cultivated. The leaves of the wild plant are not too bitter if gathered young.

From the 16th century onwards modern cultivated forms, with larger and less bitter leaves, were developed. The wild plant had anticipated many characteristics of these in its polymorphic natural state, including a tendency to produce leaves tinged with red.

Cultivated chicory varieties include:

- green, leafy types of which **Sugarloaf** is a well-known 'heading' example, while

Grumolo and Spadona are semi-heading or loose leaved;

- **Catalogna** (sometimes known as asparagus chicory), a loose-leaved variety of Italian origin, distinguished by long and relatively thick white stalks, and with narrow leaves rather like those of a dandelion (and whose young, slightly asparagus-flavoured flower shoots are also eaten). Some types have curly leaves, though not as frizzy as those of the curly endive;
- the red-leafed types popular in Italy, all of which have now become popular in other countries also, especially in the last two decades of the 20th century and usually under the name **radicchio**. Among these are radicchio di Treviso (probably the oldest), radicchio (variegato) di Castelfranco (Veneto), and rosso di Verona. Colours are in the range of bronze/red/pink/variegated. If grown in normal light these chicories tend to be brown because of the presence of green chlorophyll, so they are often covered up;
- the **Witloof** types, white, blanched varieties forced in dark cellars, originating in France and Belgium in the late 19th century and now very widely adopted—see below;
- large-rooted varieties whose roots provide the coffee substitute (again, see below), and whose leaves may also be edible.

Within these categories further distinctions can be made between broad- and narrow-leaved varieties, curly and non-curly leaves, heading and semi-heading and non-heading (heading can be encouraged by tying the leaves together), and so on.

The practice of taking up chicory plants in the autumn, cutting off their leaves, and replanting the roots in a dark cellar so that they regrow small, white leaves originated in France. The original French variety called, like the wild plant, Barbe de Capucin is unusual in that the roots are replanted on their sides in angled banks and the shoots grow horizontally. Around 1850 a Belgian grower, experimenting with uses for old mushroom compost, discovered the superior cigar-shaped form Witloof (meaning white leaf). This is grown vertically from roots buried under a deep covering of soil, sand, or sawdust so that the developing shoot is forced together into a compact shape. It is harvested as soon as it shows above ground, part of the root being taken with the shoot.

The large-rooted variety of chicory which is used as a coffee substitute was developed in Holland during the second half of the 18th century, when coffee was newly fashionable and very expensive. All over Europe people experimented with substitutes: grains, figs, acorns, and all kinds of root, especially dandelion and chicory. Chicory was judged most acceptable and special, large-rooted kinds were bred to meet the demand. Although the roasted root does not taste like coffee and contains no caffeine, this chicory became popular in Europe during the 19th century, and fields of blue-flowered plants were a common sight. Chicory was used both by itself and as an adulterant of real coffee. Even now, coffee mixed with up to 20% of chicory is available, especially in France and Spain.

ENDIVE

Endive, *C. endivia*, is a close relative of chicory, but is a hardy annual or biennial, not a perennial. Wild forms grow in the same area as chicory, but also extend further to the east, to India and beyond. The wild plant is particularly abundant in Italy. It is thought to have originated in the remote past as a hybrid between chicory and another member of the genus *C. pumilum* (one of the wild *lakhanika* or *radicchie* gathered in Greece and Italy); but it has been a distinct species since prehistoric times. Cultivated types are curly endive (confusingly called in French *chicorée frisée*, meaning 'frizzy chicory') which resembles a huge, untidy green wig; and broad-leafed varieties commonly termed 'batavia' and 'escarole'.

The ancient Egyptians ate and probably cultivated endive. The Greeks and Romans certainly cultivated it, preferring it to chicory, since in its natural state endive is slightly less bitter. The Romans may well have blanched it, for they were acquainted with the procedure, and Pliny distinguishes chicory from endive by saying that chicory is darker as well as more bitter. Only the broad-leafed types were known to the Romans and for some time afterwards. The first curly, but still broad-leafed, endive is described in 1586. The curly, narrow-leafed type which is now the most popular one emerged much later.

Broad-leafed endive, which is often blanched by putting a box over the plant, is called 'escarole' in the USA. Indeed, the names endive, escarole, and chicory are used interchangeably for *C. endivia*. Another name, originally that of a cultivar, is **batavia**. (The Batavi are an ancient tribe who in classical times inhabited what is now Holland, and their name has often been applied to things Dutch, including this vegetable.)

Curly endive may be plain green, as in the cultivar Ruffec, or green with red midribs, as in Pancalière. It sometimes grows to a formidable size, well over 30 cm (1') in diameter. A common way of partly blanching it is to put a tile on top of the plant, which flattens its growth and produces a green outside and a white heart.

USES

Both chicory and endive are most commonly used as salad vegetables. It is usual to balance their bitterness by including something slightly sweet such as red capsicum; or emollient, such as chopped hard-boiled egg, in the salad. A dressing of hot diced bacon with the melted fat is another successful expedient.

When the vegetables are cooked, as they sometimes are, they can be first blanched (in the cooking sense, after which (to take one possible example) they can be dressed with olive oil and garlic and heated through again. A well-known cooked chicory dish is *Endive au jambon sauce mornay* (parboiled Witloof wrapped in ham, covered in cheese sauce, and baked).

CHIFFON CAKE a very light American cake, unusual because it uses oil instead of a solid fat. Flour, sugar, and baking powder are mixed together, and then oil, egg yolks, and water, with a flavouring (vanilla, lemon peel, spice), are beaten in. Finally, very stiffly whisked egg whites are folded into the mixture. The cake is baked in an oblong or ring tin.

Mariani (1994) explains that 'chiffon pie' first appeared in print in N. America in 1929, to be followed soon afterwards by 'lemon chiffon', but that chiffon cake came later and, according to one source which he cites, 'was invented by a professional baker and introduced in May, 1948': the first basically new cake for 100 years.

CHILE This long, thin country, more than 2,600 miles from tip to toe, is sandwiched between the Andes and the Pacific Ocean. 'The soil is so fertile, that the husbandmen have very little trouble; for they do but in a manner scratch up the ground and without any kind of manure it yields an hundred fold,' wrote a visiting British admiral in the 18th century. True of the temperate to subtropical central zone of wide fertile valleys, where table grapes and stone fruits are grown and vineyards planted, it can hardly be said of the high desert of the northern third, nor of the rain-washed forests of the south, as far as Tierra del Fuego, where neither climate nor terrain is suitable for settled agriculture.

The lie of the land protected Chile from invasion, though the Inca occupied its northern part, and the Spanish succeeded them; not without a fight, so that full occupation was not achieved until 1800, less than 20 years before Independence. The stubborn resistance of the Araucanians, who lent their name to the monkey puzzle tree (*Araucaria araucana*) and delighted in its piñons, left a strong Indian influence. *Porotos granados* combines three of the staples of Indian diet—beans (most authentically 'cranberry beans', the preferred variety of *Phaseolus vulgaris*), squash, and green or immature corn. Corn also figures in a second, *Pastel del choclo* (the Spanish for ear of corn), where beef is given a topping of ground fresh corn sprinkled with sugar. *Humitas*, a purée of green corn with onions, peppers, and tomatoes, popular too in Argentina, is a third Indian dish of wide acceptance.

Lack of plains on an Argentine scale left cattle rearing as second string to growing fruit and edible crops. Argentine beef is imported, and its cuisine has come too, but sheep are reared in the south, and, in the province of Chiloé, pigs have long been farmed, which may account for certain pork recipes like *Chancho a la chilena*, a casserole of pork and vegetables given spice by *Salsa de ají colorado* (chilli is *ají*, here and in Peru). The sauce called *pebre*, made with onions, vinegar, olives, garlic, chilli, and coriander, is another seasoning of cold meat; and an infusion of garlic and paprika with either oil or lard called *color* is a cooking medium (made hot or not with chilli) that finds favour.

Although meat, apart from beasts such as the GUINEA PIG, derives mainly from imported species, some important plants had an early home in Chile: the POTATO, the bean, and the ancestor of the European cultivated STRAWBERRY, *Fragaria chiloensis*, which was brought to France from Chile in 1714 by Amédée Frézier. So many grew round Concepciùn, he wrote, that 'people sell them at the market like other fruits' (Darrow, 1966).

The long, deeply indented coastline, particularly to the south, combined with the cool Humboldt Current, cause a wealth of seafood. Giant sea urchins called *erizos* are often served raw with a parsley sauce; species such as mussels, scallops, abalone, and oysters were a staple of Indian diet, gathered freely on the foreshore, and latterly have been cooked in stews such as *Chupe de mariscos*, with breadcrumbs and cheese, or steamed in stone-lined pits in the same way as a CLAMBAKE, called here *curanto*—often a cook-all method where several items are placed in and around each other, the top layer being ears of corn and potatoes. The giant GOOSE-NECKED BARNACLE, *Megabalanus psittacus*, called *pico, picorico*, or *picoroccos*, is a delicacy only found on this coast, as is the *congrio*. This is not a conger, but a CUSK EEL, *Genypterus chilensis*, other species of which, various in coloration, are also caught. Slices may be broiled, or it is stewed with tomatoes and potatoes.   TJ

CHILI CON CARNE known in Texas, its home territory, as just 'chili', is a Spanish-American term which means CHILLI with meat. It first appeared, with a slightly different spelling, in a book by S. Compton Smith entitled *Chile con Carne*, or *The Camp and the Field* (1857). Mariani (1994), in explaining this, comments that the term came into more common usage only at the end of the century, and has now come to be applied to a wide spectrum of recipes. Thus, he writes: 'In New Mexico one may find lamb or mutton used instead of beef, while Cincinnati chili and many other northern versions contain red kidney beans, a variant that Texas purists would consider tantamount to a criminal act.'

Hooker (1981) has a charming passage on the early history:

Chili con carne may have already existed among poor Mexicans of San Antonio in the Mexican province of Texas during the 1820s. It was not until about 1880, however, that writers first mentioned the Mexican-American 'chili queens' of San Antonio who came about dusk each evening to the downtown plazas with carts in which were crude tables and stools and cauldrons of cooked chili con carne. Each chili queen had a large, ornate lamp with a brightly coloured globe, and the women themselves dressed gaily.

Chili's realm expanded slowly. By 1890 a chili parlour existed in McKinney, a large town north of Dallas, and in 1893 a 'San Antonio Chilley Stand' was set up on the grounds of the Columbian Exposition in Chicago. Soon the dish, made with or without beans, won followers in New Orleans, St Louis, Cincinnati, and Chicago among other places. In Cincinnati, due to some E. Europeans, chili served on spaghetti became the accepted form. In 1908 a San Antonio company canned chili and other canners followed.

Chili has since spread not only all over the USA but also all over the world. Chili contests ('cook-offs') held annually in Texas have international participation. However, Texas, while taking pride in the world-conquering aspect of chili, manages to keep its own to itself, e.g. by having it as the Texas State Dish since 1977. And it seems to be only or mainly in Texas that the affectionate alternative term 'a bowl of red' is commonly used. Indeed, that is the title of the book by Tolbert (1972) which, with others such as *The Great American Chili Book* by Bridges (1981, complete with chili-bibliography), provides chiliheads with plenty of witty chili-literature.

CHILLI a general term, derived from the Nahuatl language, for a wide range of fruits of the genus *Capsicum* (but not including the larger, mild-tasting pimiento or sweet pepper, for which see CAPSICUM).

Five species of capsicum are cultivated, but most modern cultivars are bred from either *C. annuum* or *C. frutescens* (with *C. chinense* well behind in third place). The second of these may have evolved later; by and large, its fruits are hotter. This hotness could be the result of natural selection, in the wild plant, as a defence against the seeds being eaten, or of selection by growers over the very long period of cultivation.

Chillies (also called chilli peppers) vary in size, shape, and colour, and most of all in taste, ranging from relatively mild to very pungent and extremely hot. Most are long, thin, and pointed, but there are many other shapes, and sizes vary over a wide range. In Laos, the smallest kind are known as 'mouse droppings'; whereas some Cayenne chillies are 30 cm/12" long.

Wild chillies were being gathered and eaten in Mexico *c.*7000 BC, and were cultivated there before 3500 BC. Columbus probably came across them on his first voyage, and may have brought plants back to Europe. At any rate, the Spaniards and Portuguese took them to India and SE Asia within a few years, and they spread quickly to the Middle East, the Balkans, and Europe—to Italy by 1526, Germany by 1543, and Hungary (see PAPRIKA) by 1569. In short, they were welcomed in every region where people were already accustomed to eating food with hot spices. It is now hard to imagine what (for example) INDONESIA or INDIA (at present the world's largest producer of chillies) was like without them.

Chillies are 'hot' because they contain capsaicin, an irritant alkaloid which is found mainly in the interior tissue to which the seeds adhere. Capsaicin has at least five separate chemical components; three give an immediate sensation in the throat and at the back of the palate, the other two a slower, longer-lasting, and less fierce hotness on the tongue and mid-palate. Each type of chilli can be rated for average hotness, but individual fruits from the same bush can vary greatly in their capsaicin content. Capsaicin is odourless and, paradoxically, flavourless; it irritates the skin and any delicate area. It is barely soluble in water, so cold drinks are little help if one has taken a mouthful of chilli. One ancient codex shows an Aztec parent propelling a (presumably naughty) daughter, arms bound and huge tears already starting from her eyes, towards the clouds of smoke rising from burning chillies. Synthetic capsaicin is used in anti-mugger sprays.

Cooks use chilli for flavour, not merely for hotness. However, people accustomed to chilli do like the heat, and as they become inured to it (usually early in life) they need more and more to generate the same sensation in the mouth. Therefore, when cooking Mexican or S. Indian dishes for people whose mouths are not so hardened, it is important to use much less than the 'authentic' amount of chilli in order to produce an 'authentic' effect.

Even people who have never tasted chilli will usually agree, when they encounter it for the first time in a mild form, that its flavour is subtle and attractive, and its gentle warmth stimulates not only the taste buds but appetite and digestion also. In larger amounts, they find that it burns the mouth and inflames the stomach. Why should a food that causes pain be so widely popular? One theory is that the discomfort in the mouth causes the brain to produce endorphins, natural opiates that give pleasure. If this is true, however, then inflaming one's skin or eyes by touching chillies should have the same effect, and no one pretends that smarting eyes are pleasant. A likelier explanation is that people whose diet is rather bland and unvarying crave something to pep it up, and chillies provide flavour and excitement at low cost. It may also be true that chillies, or chemicals within them, are mildly addictive. In chilli-eating areas, children usually start to eat this adult food from the age of 10 or 11, and rapidly become so used to it that they miss it quite badly if they are deprived of it.

In the USA, the heat of a chilli is expressed in Scoville Heat Units. This scale, derived from a test devised in 1912, refers to the number of times that extracts of chillies dissolved in alcohol can be diluted with sugar water before the capsaicin can no longer be tasted. Where bell peppers would score 0, Anaheim score 1,000, and Jalapeño and Cayenne are rated at 2,500–4,000. Higher up the scale, Tabasco peppers rate 60,000–80,000. DeWitt and Gerlach state that Habaneros range from 100,000 to 300,000 Scoville units. In SE Asia there are no recognized scientific units, but the general rule is 'the smaller, the hotter'; the strongest chillies being the little green ones often called bird peppers, a variety of *C. frutescens*. However, in C. America the name bird pepper, first used by an English writer in Panama in the 1680s, is applied to varieties of *C. annuum* and *C. baccatum*.

Chillies, even the hottest, are eaten fresh and whole in many countries, or are chopped up and used as a garnish, or ground up and mixed with other ingredients in a cooked dish. They may also be dried or roasted before being used in cooking; these processes affect the flavour.

When handling chillies, disposable plastic gloves should be worn or the fingers rubbed with salt. To calm a mouth which has been set on fire by hot chillies, some recommend slices of cucumber (perhaps in yoghurt, as in the Indian preparation *raita*), while others suggest plain boiled rice, and there are also advocates for something sweet (logical,

CULTIVARS OF CHILLI

Anaheim, *C. annuum*, was developed in California *c.*1900 for the new cannery at Anaheim. Long, blunt-nosed green/red pods, ranging from mild to hot.

Ancho, *C. annuum*, is called poblano when green, from the valley of Puebla, south of Mexico City. Broad, somewhat heart-shaped fruit; used green, or dried and used in sauces or for grinding to powder. Fairly mild to hot.

Cascabel, *C. annuum*, is called Cascabel ('jingle bells') because the seeds rattle in the pod. The shape may be like a button mushroom. Very pungent. Not to be confused with Cascabella.

Cayenne, *C. annuum*, has thin, pointed pods, 10–30 cm (4–12") in length. Named for Cayenne in French Guiana, where it probably originated, though it is not cultivated in Latin America today. Used mostly in hot sauces, also for grinding as CAYENNE PEPPER. Pungent and hot.

Chiltecpin, *C. annuum*; the Nahuatl name means flea-chilli, because this one is very small and bites sharply. It is also one of the many so-called bird peppers. Used fresh and dried.

Fresno, *C. annuum*, was developed by Clarence Brown in the early 1950s and named for Fresno, California. Wide, stubby pods, used mostly when still green for seasoning, sauces, and pickling.

Guajillo, *C. annuum*, is so called ('little gourd') because the seeds, in a dried pod, rattle. This is the red, dried form of Mirasol.

Habanero, *C. chinense*, has short, wide, lantern-shaped, orange-coloured pods, with an aroma of tropical fruit. Very, very hot. It may have originated in Cuba, as the name (meaning 'from Havana') suggests. A closely related variety, **Scotch Bonnet**, belongs to the Caribbean, and can be light green, yellow, or red.

Jalapeño, *C. annuum*, has blunt, almost oval pods. Named for the town of Jalapa in Veracruz state, Mexico. Hot. Much hyped in the USA, where it is the most popular hot chilli and enters into many commercial products. Large dried and smoked Jalapeños, called chipotles, are wrinkled and warm brown in colour.

Mirasol, the fresh, yellow form of Guajillo, is called Mirasol because the fruits grow pointing up at the sun; dried ones are also called Cascabel. It imparts a yellow colour and a distinctive flavour to dishes cooked with it. Very popular in Mexico for stews and sauces.

Pasilla, *C. annuum*, has long, narrow pods of a unique dark brown colour, which dry raisin black and wrinkled, hence the name, the diminutive form of *pasa*, a raisin. (Fresh pods, which reach the market only in small numbers, are called *chilacas*.) Relatively mild.

Peperoncini, *C. annuum*, has, small, curved pods. A sweet red chilli, used while still green to make a pickle to accompany Italian salads.

Serrano, *C. annuum*, has small, tubular pods like little torpedoes. Named for the mountain ridges (*serranías*) in Mexico where it probably originated. Mainly eaten while still green, either fresh or made into sauce, e.g. guacamole (see AVOCADO). Hot, with a sharp acidic taste which makes it good for a fresh salsa.

Tabasco, *C. frutescens*, is the only chilli of this species commercially grown in the USA. Tabasco pods are red or yellow. Virtually all available production is used for TABASCO pepper sauce.

given the criterion used for the Scoville scale).

For many dishes it is important to use the appropriate variety of chilli. Some of the commonest, most useful, or most interesting are briefly described in the box. It is chiefly in the Americas that one finds a wide range of strikingly different types and cultivars. Note that attractive names like Cascabel are often applied to different varieties, seemingly almost at random.

In India, the most important distinction is between green and red chillies, though Camellia Panjabi (1994) points out that local varieties often give quite different flavours to regional dishes—for example, in Goa. She mentions Kashmiri chillies, which are grown all over the place and are highly valued because they give a bright red colour to food as well as a moderate hotness. 'The gourmets of northern India use a bright yellow dried chilli grown around the Sonepat area in Punjab for their white or yellow curry dishes.'

In Indonesia and Malaysia, practically all chillies are either large (*C. annuum*) or small (*C. frutescens*); the former are *cabai* (or *lombok*), the latter *cabai rawit* or *lombok rawit.* All are hot, but the smaller *rawit* types are especially so. Bird chillies (*cabai burung* in Malaysia) are also called bird's-eye chillies because they are as small, vivid, and sharp as the eye of a bird. Colour is important (*merah* is red, *hijau* is green): *cabai merah* are dried and powdered, or are fresh ones crushed and used to give body to a hot sauce.

Chilli products include chilli powder, which is made in many countries from any type of chilli which is locally available. It varies considerably in hotness and flavour. (In N. America, 'chile powder'—also known as 'Mexican' or 'creole' chile powder—is a spice mixture for making CHILI CON CARNE, containing cumin, clove, and garlic powder as well as hot pepper.)

The whole subject of chilli is adorned by legends, mostly to do with the heat. Jean Andrews quotes one charming legend from Bancroft (1882), as follows:

This pungent condiment is at present day as omnipresent in Spanish American dishes as it was at the time of the conquest; and I am seriously informed by a Spanish gentleman who resided for many years in Mexico and was an officer in Maximillian's army, that while the wolves would feed upon the dead bodies of the French that lay all night upon the battlefield, they never touched the bodies of the Mexicans, because the flesh was completely impregnated with chile. Which, if true, may be thought to show that wolves do not object to a diet seasoned with garlic.

See also CAYENNE PEPPER and PAPRIKA and TABASCO. Important commercial sauces based on chilli include *salsa picante*, ubiquitous in Mexico.
READING: Jean Andrews (1984); DeWitt and
   Gerlach (1990); Miller (1992); Naj (1992).   (RO)

CHINA: EATING AND COOKING. In the mythology of ancient China, Han, the Chinese man, is distinguished from savages and barbarians by two features of his eating habits: he eats cereals and uses fire to process his food.

In China, dietary practice involves two extremes; 'eating to live' and 'eating for pleasure'. The former in effect meant the ingestion of cereals, the foodstuff capable of sustaining life, whereas the latter was achieved by cooking animal or vegetable matter, perceived as being of secondary importance, and destined to be an accompaniment to the cereals.

The make-up of the Chinese menu reflects this opposition/correlation between what is necessary and what is superfluous. A Chinese meal is usually made up of a starchy food (the essential dish called *zhushi*, 'principal food'), and of one or several accompanying dishes based on animal or vegetable products (called *fushi* or 'secondary food'). This model, which holds true throughout all Chinese territories, is

executed differently in different regions and in different social classes. A contrast is drawn, in general, between N. China, a WHEAT area, and S. China, where RICE predominates, with a line between the two drawn by the Blue River (Yangtze); but the situation is made more complex because there are other starches besides wheat and rice.

Starches, which include cereals and tubers, are classified according to a scale of values. Cereals are always preferred to tubers, which are eaten only in case of dire necessity; but some cereals such as rice and wheat are much more highly prized than others, and ultimately their consumption can depend just as much on local habits as on economic factors. Specific regional preferences are nowadays completely blurred in certain areas by the rising standard of living. In Beijing, rice is eaten as much as wheaten products, whether of the NOODLE family or steamed breads (MANTOU). On the other hand, the inhabitants of the poor rural areas in the north and centre eat dishes based on MAIZE and MILLET more often than noodles or *mantou*, which are considered to be luxury items. South of the Yangtze, where rice is primarily cultivated (with wheat, as a secondary or fall-back crop), rice is usually eaten, and at feasts flour made from glutinous ('sticky') rice appears in the guise of cakes. It is in areas lacking in natural resources, or in periods of scarcity, that cereals are supplemented or even replaced by tubers: taro in the subtropics, sweet potatoes or potatoes in temperate and cold areas.

Similar variations are to be found in the attendant dishes, which can be anything from vinegar or a simple puréed pepper sauce to prepared and elegant meat dishes.

The relationship between the essential and the superfluous manifests itself also in relation to taste. Cereals, simply cooked in water or steam, without salt, marry well with flavourful side dishes which are seasoned to perfection and cooked by the most sophisticated methods. The neutral taste of the cereal symbolizes the consumption of the 'essential', while the palatability of the accompanying dishes produces the 'pleasure' derived from the combining of different flavours. And, although the cereal is indeed cooked, the simplicity of its transformation, which is achieved without the use of any aromatics, suffices to place it outside the category of the art of cookery.

Indeed, the art of cookery in China is concerned only with dishes prepared to accompany a cereal in daily life or, on the other hand, to be eaten by themselves on feast days. In fact, the ordinary menu, centred on cereals, loses its relevance as soon as one celebrates. No longer is it a question of subsistence but, on the contrary, of

feasting by ingesting dishes which despite their richness and variety will satisfy the appetite in the same ways that cereals do on ordinary days. These last, moreover, disappear from the meal, or play only a minor role at the end of a banquet, appearing furtively and usually not actually eaten. In this case, 'eating for pleasure' supersedes 'eating to live' and the banishment of cereals symbolizes the triumph of gourmandise over physiological necessity.

The contrast of 'eating to live' and 'eating for pleasure' is to be seen in daily life also. Although cereal-based meals are eaten at regular times and are consumed in order to maintain the 'vital principle', between-meal snacks give the leisure to eat items destined to give pleasure to the palate. Thus were conceived the street foods called *xiaochi* ('small foods'), titbits which can be eaten at any time of day or night in the towns. Extremely varied, they consist of savoury or sweet dishes, thick soups, bouillons, custards, jellies, doughnuts, omelettes, cakes of all description which are eaten without ceremony, simply to please the taste buds or to fill a small hole in the stomach.

These minor dishes are the most obvious and immediate markers of regional specialization. They often figure as famous gastronomic items, not to be missed if the opportunity arises to taste the local food when visiting this or that place. Thus in Beijing, for example, it would be mungbean milk (*douzhi*); in Shanghai, little vegetarian buns (*sucai bao*); in Jiaxing, glutinous rice cakes wrapped in lotus leaves (*zongzi*); in Jinhua, crispy cakes (*subing*); in Canton, rice porridge (*zhou*); in Fuzhou, fishballs; and in Xiamen, oyster omelette (*haozijian*).

The existence of local specialities is in keeping with the very ancient concept in China that each region can be represented by its natural products, and notably its edible foodstuffs. The system of tributes, sent annually to the emperor from the provinces, has probably contributed to the recognition of certain products as indigenous to the various Chinese regions. Nevertheless, the identification of regional cuisine is not just related to climate or ingredients; it also comes from a history in which politics, economy, and culture intermingle.

The division of China by regional styles of cooking is based on a historical evolution dating from the 12th century. At that time the little town of Hangzhou, situated at the south of the mouth of the Yangtze, was transformed into the capital after the court took refuge there as the result of pressure from the Mongols. It became a place for exchanges and intense mixing among populations which had emigrated from the north, tradespeople from the west, and the local inhabitants. Restaurants representing the tastes of the four horizons prospered, and thus was born the concept of 'regional culinary style'.

Nowadays, the culinary division of China most often recognized distinguishes four great cooking styles. These correspond in general to the four cardinal coordinates: northern style, centred on Beijing and the Yellow River valley stretching to the east up to the Shandong; central and western style, concentrated around Sichuan but also including Ghuizou, Yunnan, Hunan, and Hubei; the south-eastern style which includes Shanghai, Zhejiang, and Anhui; and finally the southern style, from Canton, Guangdong, and Fujian to the east. This classification, which is somewhat artificial, does not take into account certain important differences—thus it does not seem appropriate to associate Fujian with Guangdong. However, the scheme fits in with a desire to classify the world according to the ancient correlation between the macrocosm and the microcosm which linked the cardinal points to flavours, colours, climates, animals, cereals, etc. The identification of tastes plays a particularly important role in the appreciation of Chinese cuisine, and it is quite often one or several dominant flavours which give a regional cuisine its character

The inhabitants of the Yellow River basin to the north are reputed to like strong smells, such as those of garlic, vinegar, and soy sauce. PEKING DUCK with its fat, crackling skin would be virtually inedible without its accompaniment of raw spring onions and a sweet and sour sauce. The same applies to mutton, which is normally eaten in winter in these regions and is associated with garlic and a 'balsamic' vinegar whose mild acidity goes marvellously well with its musky taste.

In Sichuan, considered to be the land of aromatics, spices are liked, particularly the hotter and more pungent ones, such as hot chilli peppers and SICHUAN PEPPER. All the dishes are flavoured with fermented bean paste (*dou ban jiang*), or sesame oil and sesame purée, which produce harmonious flavours with some highly evocative names: 'strange taste' (*guai wei*), 'familiar taste' (*jiachanh wei*), 'peppery-scented' (*xiangla wei*), etc.

In the lower plains of the Yangtze, 'the kingdom of fish and rice', it is tender vegetables which are appreciated, accompanied by freshwater fish and crustaceans. Here dishes with a delicate and subtle flavour are prepared, enhanced by the refreshing presence of ginger and the kick of Shaoxing wine. It is the only region where sweet and sweet-and-sour flavours are really appreciated and admirably used in cooking.

The complexity and richness of Cantonese cuisine do not permit reducing it to a few dominant flavours, the art of the Cantonese cook being to excel in marrying all the flavours, or on the contrary to privilege each one individually. Seafood has pride of place. Freshness is exalted, for example, by steaming fish in the simplest possible fashion; oyster sauce enhances poached poultry, or green vegetables barely blanched. But Canton is also famous for its whole-roasted milk-fed pigs and its gleaming lacquered meats hung temptingly in the front windows of restaurants.

These different regional cuisines, originating in geographical areas equal to or larger than a European country, might have had little or nothing in common. However, they have a common base of flavourings, procedures, and techniques which by general consensus are perceived as being Chinese. Although it is difficult to speak of one single Chinese cuisine, and one can even doubt its very existence, it is true that three aromatic ingredients are indispensable to the Chinese culinary scene, and are used throughout the entire territory: fresh ginger, soy sauce, and spring onions. Without these it would seem impossible to prepare Chinese food. Their inclusion in a dish gives a touch and smell which one can define as typically 'Chinese'.

As to culinary procedures and techniques they are also common to all the regions, allowing for the fact that certain dressings and ways of making things are more sophisticated here or there. The order of execution of culinary work is in part influenced by the way the food is consumed. In China, kitchen space is clearly separated from the dining area. This means that once dishes leave the kitchen, they require no further attention prior to being eaten with chopsticks or a spoon, the only utensils admissible at table.

Carving and seasoning therefore constitute the two key stages of the preparation of a dish before its final transformation by cooking. Thus meats and vegetables are first cut up, shaped, sculpted, and cooked in such a way as to make it possible for them to be picked up, separated, or torn apart with recourse only to the consumer's two available implements. In the exceptional instance of a piece of meat being cooked whole, either the flesh is prepared in such a way that it can be detached without special effort by the use of chopsticks; or, in the case of PEKING DUCK for example, the meat is cut up in the kitchen after cooking, as soon as it is taken out of the oven. The current practice of cutting up the duck in front of the assembled company, in restaurants generally open to foreigners, is a recent concession, encouraged by the growth of tourism, to display the virtuosity of the great chefs.

Once the ingredients are properly cut up into cubes or strips, sliced, shredded, chopped, etc., they are placed on a plate with the flavourful ingredients needed for the recipe: soy sauce, vinegar, ginger, pepper, sesame oil, whatever, depending on the final preparation.

The method chosen for cutting up this or that ingredient must facilitate both the use of chopsticks and the seasoning. The flavours are thus enhanced by the chosen shapes. One of the most striking examples of this relationship between shape and taste is that of cuttlefish, whose flesh is slashed with regular cross-hatched lines which cause the flesh to retract in such a way during cooking as to give the impression of little flowers, each of whose petals is thus impregnated to perfection with sauce.

All cooking methods are used in China, but the oven does not exist at the domestic level. Roasting is therefore elevated to the level of professional cooking, and is done in big drum-shaped vertical ovens. One could say that in China steaming takes the place held by roasting in the West. Yet the cooking method considered as most emblematic of Chinese cooking by the Chinese themselves is STIR-FRYING (*chao*). It consists in frying the various ingredients of a dish very rapidly over an extremely intense heat, most often separately one after the other, then reassembling them with their seasoning before serving them. This cooking method allows small pieces of food to be seared and cooked very superficially, thus retaining their texture and flavour. Vegetables thus prepared are crisp and have beautiful colour, two qualities considered to be essential by Chinese gourmets. Chinese cooking is also remarkably economical when it comes to utensils; only one sort of knife is used for cutting up food, and stir-frying—in common with other cooking methods— needs but one cooking pot, the distinctive kind of iron frying pan known in the western world under the Cantonese name WOK.

What we might call 'passing over a flame' rather than 'cooking' plays a major role in Chinese cookery. In fact, what counts for more than the idea of 'cooking' is that of 'preparation to the correct and desired point', which means that a foodstuff can, depending on its nature or on the recipe, need either very light cooking or, on the other hand, several cooking procedures destined to contribute varied flavours and consistencies to the dish. Raw things do not belong to any Chinese category. Every food must have been subject to some form of preparation leading to its 'preparation to the correct and desired point' in order to appear on the table; transformation by heat for a dish which is included in the menu, or transformation by steeping, pickling, or preserving if it is a question of a condiment or something to act as a standby.

One finds again in this exigency the figure of the Chinese myth which defined the Chinese man as a cook who is able to 'transform' foodstuffs by cooking and who eats cereals. This picture of the cook whose activities served even in antiquity as a point of reference for the art of government is without a doubt intimately connected with the great fame of Chinese cooking. Thus, because from early days it was a skilled profession, passed down from generation to generation with its laws and techniques, this activity has become the 'haute cuisine' recognized today with its schools and styles. It includes not only four great regional styles of cooking, but also a Muslim 'haute cuisine', in which pork and its by-products are excluded, and a great vegetarian cuisine, aimed at those who, Buddhist or not, wish to enjoy their food without attacking the lives of living creatures.   FS

CHINESE ARTICHOKE *Stachys affinis*, an oriental root vegetable which is related neither to the globe artichoke (see ARTICHOKE) nor to the JERUSALEM ARTICHOKE. Of these three confusingly named plants it was the last to arrive in Europe.

The plant reached France in 1882, when the doctor of the Russian Legation in Beijing sent it to M. Pailleux, a prominent *acclimatiseur*, and it began to appear as a market vegetable five years later. Pailleux saw to it that it was called Crosne du Japon, from Crosnes the village where he lived. The root achieved, and retains, some popularity in France (it was an ingredient in the so-called *salade japonaise* for which Dumas (1873) helped to create a vogue), but it is not much in evidence elsewhere in Europe or America.

Chinese artichokes

The Chinese artichoke tuber is small, typically 5 cm (2") long. It is whitish and composed of up to a dozen bulging segments. Jane Grigson (1978) comments that 'if you rubbed one or two clean in your hand, you would soon notice the beauty of form and pearly translucency that have made Chinese poets compare them to jade beads'.

It is likely that the English name was bestowed because of a vague resemblance to the Jerusalem artichoke, but it could have been prompted by a comparison of its flavour with that of the globe artichoke. In 1927 two eminent authorities, the discriminating Dr Leclerc and the cookery writer Mme Saint-Ange, both declared independently that its flavour lay between those of salsify and artichoke; and Dr Leclerc also praised the digestibility of the tuber.

The tuber must be used quickly after it is pulled up, for it discolours and deteriorates quickly. However, it can remain in the ground for quite a long season from autumn to the end of winter, and is a useful winter vegetable for those who can obtain it. There is no need to peel a Chinese artichoke provided that it is well cleaned. It can be eaten raw and grated in salads; plain boiled; fried (usually after a short parboiling); or as a pickle.

CHINESE CABBAGE a name with a bewildering number of applications. Confusion is compounded by the fact that many Chinese names for species or varieties are taking their place in the English language, in parallel with the increased cultivation of these plants in western countries; and by the lack of agreement among botanists on their botanical classification. What is said about classification and nomenclature below is offered 'under every reserve', as the French say; and there is much to be said for the advice offered by one expert author, which is to forget the names and shop by picking up or pointing.

There is, however, one thing which it is helpful to know, as a clue: the Chinese word for vegetable is *cai* (*choy* or *choi* in Cantonese). There is no single word for cabbage, but the names for cabbages reflect their appearance. Thus *bai cai* (*pak choi* in Cantonese) is literally 'white vegetable', i.e. white cabbage; while *da bai cai* is 'big white vegetable [cabbage]'.

The development of cabbage plants in China parallels that of the European CABBAGE in Europe. Both evolved by cultivation from wild ancestors; both have been important foods since the remote past; and both now exist in numerous varieties which can be bought almost all the year round. Chinese cabbages belong to the same genus, *Brassica*, as European ones. For other Chinese brassica vegetables see MUSTARD GREENS and CHINESE KALE.

With the sweeping reservations mentioned above, here is a list of Chinese cabbages, to which might be added a little group of polymorphic and variously coloured 'loose-leafed' varieties).

Brassica rapa ssp *chinensis* is sometimes known in the west as **bok choy,** pak choi, and kindred names), also sometimes as Chinese chard cabbage, or Chinese white cabbage. There are many varieties, including those called 'spoon', taking their name from the resemblance of the leaf stalk base to a Chinese soup spoon or ladle. Pak chois of one variety or another are available for all seasons.

All are open in form rather than hearted, generally with fairly smooth, oval green leaves on thick stalks which are pearly white (except for some, e.g. the variety Shanghai, which have pale green stalks). Both stalks and leaves shrink greatly when cooked. The flavour is mild but cabbagy. The Chinese harvest some as young plants, 'chicken feathers' for use in soups and salads; some when they are still small but already clumping; and others when they are mature.

B. rapa ssp *chinensis* var *parachinensis*, whose Mandarin name is *cai xin*, is sometimes called by its Cantonese name choi sam (or choy sum) in western countries, but is also referred to as Chinese flowering cabbage, since it is grown for its flowering shoots (as is another flowering brassica, CHINESE KALE). A popular vegetable in Hong Kong and S. China, it is sold as bunches of leaves rather than as whole plants, and is distinguished by its small yellow flowers and delicate green stems, which are slightly grooved.

B. rapa ssp *chinensis* var *rosularis* is the Chinese **flat-headed** or 'rosette' cabbage (*wu ta cai* in Mandarin and *taai gwoo choi* in Cantonese), a variety which grows in the shape of a plate, spreading over an area up to 30 cm (1') or more in diameter although only 5 cm (2") high. It withstands some frost, and is much grown in the region of Shanghai. It has rounded leaves and green leaf stalks. Young plants, with small leaves surrounding the central rosette, are best. This cabbage is widely considered to have an exceptionally good flavour.

B. rapa var *pekinensis*. This is possibly the vegetable with the best claim (in a chaotically uncertain world) to the name 'Chinese cabbage', although like the other brassicas of China it goes under many names, including **Chinese leaves**, napa, Peking or Tientsin cabbage, *bai cai* or *chih-li* (versions of the Mandarin names of two principal cultivars); and sometimes an approximation to the Cantonese *wong nga baak*. These cabbages have more than one shape, for example long and narrow like a cos lettuce, or less long and barrel shaped in profile. The long narrow form has almost no flavour of its own, which makes it useful as a vehicle for other flavours; the Chinese frequently use it in this way, e.g. with a highly flavoured meat sauce. It can also be eaten raw, in salads.

In Japan, the Chinese cabbages most commonly met are those of the last variety listed, which have been widely cultivated since the end of the 19th century. The Japanese name is *hakusai*, and uses are in dishes such as *nabemono* and *tsukemono* (see JAPANESE CULINARY TERMS).
READING: Joy Larkcom (1991); Elizabeth Schneider (1986).

CHINESE KALE (or Chinese broccoli), *Brassica oleracea* var *alboglabra*, a species distinct from both European kale and other Chinese brassicas, distinguished by its white flowers and a white bloom on the leaves, which are borne on thick, smooth stems.

Chinese kale

The leaves have a stronger flavour than Chinese flowering cabbage (see CHINESE CABBAGE), but the peeled stalks are a delicacy. When young and tender (in bud but not in flower), Chinese kale may be cooked whole by boiling or steaming, like broccoli. Slightly older shoots have a better flavour, but their stems may need peeling and chopping. The latter is anyway necessary before stir-frying, the usual Chinese method of cooking this vegetable.

CHINESE KEYS one of several unsatisfactory names for the rhizomes of *Boesenbergia pandurata*, a plant of SE Asia which belongs to the GINGER family. Light brown multiple roots (7–12 cm/3–5" long, 1 cm/0.5" in diameter) hang down from a central corm, like a bunch of keys. The flesh is bright yellow with a creamy core and has a distinctive lemony-ginger aroma.

Chinese keys are available fresh, dried, or powdered. Their sweet, aromatic flavour is an important ingredient in the green curry paste used in Thai curries of chicken, duck, and fish as well as in soups and sauces. They can also be steamed and eaten as a vegetable; pickled; or eaten raw when young.

Despite the name 'Chinese keys', they are not found in Chinese cookery, and they

seem to be unknown in the Indian subcontinent.

CHINESE SPINACH *Amaranthus tricolor*, an annual plant, probably indigenous to India, whose leaves are grown and sold there and in SE Asia as well as China, for use like SPINACH. It is one of the numerous plants in the AMARANTH group, and not botanically related to spinach.

The leaves exhibit striking variations in colour, especially in Bengal, where cultivation is intense. Those of one variety familiar in China have red centres. It is usual to cut Chinese spinach into 5 cm (2") lengths and stir-fry it. Leaves and stalks alike become limp when cooked, and have a mild flavour.

CHINESE WATER CHESTNUT *Eleocharis dulcis*, is not a nut and is a completely different plant from the WATER CHESTNUTS of the genus *Trapa*. It is related to the European and African CHUFA. The 'nut' is really the corm of a kind of sedge. It resembles a gladiolus corm, round, flattened, usually between 2.5 and 5 cm (1–2") in diameter, and mahogany brown. As sold in the markets, it has rings of leaf scars on it.

This water chestnut is generally considered superior to *Trapa* nuts. It is peeled before use. The white interior can be eaten raw, out of hand as a snack or sliced into a salad, and is crisp with a pleasantly sweet and nutty taste. If cooked quickly it retains its crisp texture, which is the main quality for which the Chinese prize it.

In Cantonese cuisine it is used in various sweet dishes; also grated, combined into shapes with minced meat and other

ingredients, and steamed. It is especially associated with the Chinese New Year; but in Cantonese restaurants it is served as a DIM SUM all the year round.

It is this water chestnut which is the source of the water chestnut flour, *man tai fan*, which is an important Chinese ingredient.

The Chinese cultivate this water chestnut in tanks, and export it both fresh (e.g. to SE Asian countries) and canned.

CHINESE WOLFBERRY *Lycium chinense*, a small shrub of E. Asia whose small red berries have had a reputation as a medicine and tonic in China since ancient times. A Chinese name for them means 'drive-away-old-age berries'. They have little use in the kitchens of either China or Japan (where the name is *kuko*). However, since they impart a sweetish taste, they have a limited use as a flavouring ingredient in some dishes, for example the oxtail soup of Sichuan.

The plant, which occurs wild in most of Asia and has become naturalized in Europe, may also be referred to as Chinese boxthorn. Its thin, bright green leaves can be used to flavour rice or consumed as a vegetable; they play a leading role in a Cantonese soup which usually also contains pork liver. They wilt quickly and need only be cooked very briefly.

CHIPOLATA a small SAUSAGE filled with lean pork, pork fat, and cooked rice, and using a sheep's intestine as the casing. Chipolatas are popular in France, where they are finger width, relatively long, and usually pan fried. They are sometimes used as a garnish for other dishes.

Chinese water chestnuts

The name is derived from the Italian *cipollata*, meaning something containing onion as an ingredient or flavouring (*cipolla* = onion), and this is the meaning which is still valid in Italy; but the sausages called chipolatas outside Italy contain no onions and the origin of this usage is a mystery.

The explanation may be that the dish with onions which was correctly called *Cipollata* often or at least sometimes contained sausages of a distinctive kind, and that non-Italians, especially the French, began to think that it was these sausages which deserved the name. Thus the first recorded mention of the word in France, in *Les Dons de Comus* (1742), is in a recipe for chicken wings *en chipoulate*, beginning 'Take the wings, bacon and small sausages about the size of your little finger.' Courchamps, in his *Dictionnaire général de la cuisine française* (1853 edn), is even more illuminating; he defines 'chipolata' as 'a kind of stew of Italian origin', and then gives a recipe which calls for 'twelve little sausages called *chipolates*'.

Thus the notion of small size as a distinguishing feature of chipolata sausages goes back a long way; and this is the notion which has become prevalent in Britain, where the term 'chipolata', in popular usage, indicates any small sausages, such as the so-called 'cocktail sausages' and other miniature versions of ordinary sausages.

CHITON an unusual marine MOLLUSC, whose 'shell' is a flexible girdle surrounding eight overlapping plates. Various species occur on shores round the world, typically living under rocks, and feeding on vegetation. They are not normally considered as food, but the fleshy foot muscle is eaten in some countries, e.g. in New Zealand, parts of S. America, and the Caribbean region.

Gibbons (1964) is alone in devoting a whole chapter to chitons as food. Emphasizing the extent to which American Indians of the north-west ate them in the past, he draws particular attention to:

the Giant Sea Cradle, or Gum Boot, *Amicula stelleri*, the largest chiton in the world, attaining a length of 13 inches. These and several other large species were eagerly sought by the West Coast Indians, and they became favorite seafoods of the Russians who first settled southeastern Alaska.

The 'gum boot' is unique in having a foot large enough to yield what can be called a 'steak' (as with ABALONE steak—and methods of preparation, including pounding, are similar). Smaller chitons have scant amounts of edible meat, but this is enough to warrant local exploitation of some, such as *Acanthopleura echinata* of Chile and Peru.

Chitons are used in the island of Tobago to make pak roo tea, a soup which has a distinctive flavour and a reputation for health-giving properties.

CHITTERLING(S) the small intestine, or part thereof, of a pig (or, less often, another animal—Hannah Glasse (1747) refers to calf's chitterling), especially when prepared for use as food. Jane Grigson (1967) remarks that 'The unforgettable name is of unknown derivation, but appears in the 13th century in dog-latin form in a description of women washing "chitterlingis" down by the waterside.' The form 'chitlings' is also in use.

Chitterlings have a twofold use in the making of SAUSAGES such as ANDOUILLES and ANDOUILLETTES; chopped up, they provide an ingredient for the filling, while they are also used to furnish casings.

Apart from sausages, there are only a few dishes in which chitterlings are a main ingredient. In England, chopped chitterlings were used in the 16th century in a kind of WHITE PUDDING; and a chitterling pie was known in England in the 18th century. Indeed, C. Anne Wilson (1973) quotes a passage from Ellis (1750) which emphasizes the need to wash them and scour them with salt very thoroughly, and continues thus: 'Others boil sage in their water to take off their hogoo [*haut goût*, i.e. strong flavour], for the preparation of chitterlings will prove the cleanliness or sluttishness of a housewife as much as any meat whatsoever will.' If dealing with chitterlings was a kind of hallmark for hygiene in the kitchen, their use must have been common.

Although chitterlings have largely dropped from view in Britain, their use continues in those countries where all forms of OFFAL are eaten, even though cooks there may have no precisely equivalent term. (There are many recipes which call for intestines, a more general term which would often include chitterlings.)

CHIVES *Allium schoenoprasum*, the smallest and the most delicate member of the ONION family, are the cultivated descendant of a wild plant of C. Europe, which is still found, mostly in rocky and mountainous regions. Wild chives and closely related species are found throughout the northern temperate zone of the Old and New World.

The leaves of chives, which are thin, hollow, and round in cross-section, are the part used. When cut they re-grow, so that a clump of chives can provide leaves from spring to autumn. It dies down in winter but reappears next spring. During its dormant period the clump can be spread by division of the small bulbs.

Chives must have been used in the wild form since early times but the first mention of them seems to be by Gerard (1633), by which time they were being cultivated.

The name 'chive' comes from the Latin *cepa* (onion). The German name, meaning 'cut leek', probably reflects their early use as a treatment for wounds. They have antiseptic qualities.

Chopped chive leaves make a pretty green garnish, and provide a discreet onion-like flavour. They are used mainly in the cooking of C. and N. Europe, and are at their best in mild, creamy sauces and egg dishes, or as a garnish for soups and salads.

Chives of the European type have long been known and cultivated in China, but more use is made there, and in Japan and E. Asia generally, of the so-called **Chinese chives**, *A. tuberosum* (syn. *A. odorum*). This is also available in the West, sometimes called 'kuchai'; this name, spelled in various ways, is a corruption via Malay of its Cantonese name, *gau choi*.

The leaves of Chinese chives are bigger, flat and solid in cross-section, with a stronger and more garlic-like flavour than European chives. Indeed, the plant is more closely related to GARLIC, but the name 'chives' has stuck because they are often used like European chives. Two main kinds are grown: a large one which is used as cooked vegetable (in mixtures and with discretion); and a small one which is grown for its flowering stems, used as a seasoning and garnish. (The white flowers of the latter, *gau choi fa*, have a delicate flavour. In contrast the flowers of European chives, which are purple, are never used, and the buds are picked off to stop the plant from going to seed.)

Gau wong are blanched Chinese chives, lacking colour and limp, but appreciated for certain purposes because they are tender. They are frequently added to noodles or noodle soups.

CHŁODNIK a cold soup of Poland, usually made when CRAYFISH are in season. It is based on a stock of grated BEETROOT, water, vinegar, and a little sugar which is then chilled before adding the crayfish and other vegetables such as spring onion, radishes, cucumbers, and DILL. Thick soured cream is stirred into the soup, and this, with the beetroot, gives it its characteristic pink colour. It is garnished with slices of lemon and chopped hard-boiled (US hard-cooked) eggs.   HS

CHOCOLATE (*see page 176*)

Chocolate BOTANY AND EARLY HISTORY, CHOCOLATE IN THE 19TH AND 20TH CENTURIES, CHOCOLATE MANUFACTURE, CHOCOLATE IN COOKERY

Botany and early history

The cacao tree provides, with its seeds, the raw material for chocolate. Linnaeus, a chocolate-lover, assigned the species to a botanical genus which he named *Theobroma*, 'food of the gods'. In this genus 22 species are now recognized, all native to C. and S. America, and two are cultivated. *Theobroma bicolor* is grown from Mexico to Brazil and produces *pataxte*, which can be drunk on its own or mixed with chocolate drinks. But vastly greater is the importance of *T. cacao*, the source of chocolate.

Cacao is the usual term for the tree and for its seeds (misleadingly, 'cocoa' has sometimes been used in English). A complex process of roasting, fermenting, and grinding turns these seeds into chocolate. Efficient extraction of cacao butter (a valuable and nutritious substance) leaves a residue which is marketed as 'cocoa powder' (see COCOA), or, mixed with sugar, as 'drinking chocolate'.

Where cacao grows, the sweet pulp that surrounds the fresh seeds in their pod is a prized delicacy, whether eaten raw or fermented into an alcoholic drink. Green cacao pods used to be brought, as an expensive luxury, to the Aztec emperor at Tenochtitlan, far to the north-west of the cacao country.

THE CACAO TREE AND ITS PRODUCT

The tree is indigenous to the region of Latin America that lies between S. Mexico and the northern Amazon basin. The cacao tree is an evergreen, achieving a height of 6–12 m (20–40'), depending on growing conditions. It is a prima donna, requiring shade when young, and susceptible to fungi and pests. Diseases are controlled by breeding resistant varieties; the one commonly used is the Forastero. The Criollo, grown by the Aztecs at the time of the Conquest, is delicate and little used today, although it produces finer beans. Hybrid varieties are also grown. Cacao is cultivated under banana or rubber trees which provide shade, and alternative sources of income if the cacao crop fails.

Cacao flowers, which are pollinated by a species of midge, grow directly on the trunk of the tree. Only a few flowers develop into fruit, or *pods*, an average annual yield being about 30 per tree. These are shaped like large, oval melons, saffron yellow or red depending on variety, and spring straight from the tree trunk. The tree produces pods and flowers simultaneously throughout the year, but commercial harvesting only takes place twice a year.

Ripe pods are collected, split, and the contents scraped out. The seeds, or *beans*, and their surrounding pulp are exposed to the sun making the pulp ferment. This step is essential for good flavour when the beans are used in chocolate manufacture (see below). Fermentation develops 'flavour precursors', breaking down sugar to glucose and fructose, and turning some protein into free amino acids and smaller peptides.

After fermentation the beans are dried and exported to manufacturers. They lose 50% of their weight during drying, the average annual yield of a single tree being no more than 0.5–1 kg (1–2 lb) of dried beans.

CHOCOLATE IN PRE-COLUMBIAN AMERICA

Cacao was well known to the classic Maya, whose remarkable civilization flourished and died in Yucatan and Guatemala in the 1st millennium AD. Alongside deceased Maya dignitaries were buried implements for use in the afterlife, including jars and bowls for chocolate. The identification of the word *ka-ka-w* in the inscriptions on these pots was a breakthrough in the decipherment of Maya phonetic writing. Moreover, traces of theobromine and caffeine, two active constituents of chocolate, have been found in some of them. An 8th-century painted vase shows chocolate being poured from a cylindrical jar, held high, into a bowl, thus demonstrating how the Maya raised froth in their chocolate: the froth was the most desirable part of the drink. They sometimes flavoured chocolate with chilli, with vanilla, and with other ingredients less easy to identify. They probably liked to drink their chocolate hot, as did the Maya of Spanish colonial times.

Linguists believe that cacao is in origin not a Maya but a Mixe-Zoquean word (perhaps *kakawa*), suggesting that the Maya learnt to use the product from the earlier Olmec culture, which flourished in the Veracruz and Tabasco provinces of Mexico between 1500 and 400 BC. Olmec hieroglyphs have not been deciphered, so we cannot read what they themselves said of cacao. No linguistic or archaeological evidence allows us to trace cacao or chocolate further back than this. The successor Izapan civilization spread Olmec culture, and perhaps cacao cultivation, to the Pacific littoral of Mexico and Guatemala: it was perhaps from the Izapans that the Maya would have learnt of chocolate.

Cacao will not grow everywhere where C. American civilizations flourished. Thus the beans became a commodity of trade, an object of warfare, and also a currency. By later Maya times long-distance traders had brought knowledge of chocolate to distant parts of Yucatan and also to the valley of Mexico, far to the west, where the Nahuatl-speaking Aztec were to establish their power. In due course cacao became a major source of the wealth of the Aztec merchants.

Aztec 'puritanism', however, linked with their reputed origins as poverty-stricken migrants from the north, led to an ambivalent attitude towards chocolate. One legend told of an expedition to retrace their steps, at the end of which the powerful emissaries of the Aztecs were told by the aged goddess of their ancestral home: 'You have become old, you have become tired because of the chocolate you drink and because of the foods you eat. They have harmed and weakened you.' But they did not stop drinking it, and huge quantities of cacao beans arrived as tribute in the valley of Mexico each year, both for use and for storage.

Like the Maya, the Aztecs frothed their chocolate by pouring it from vessel to vessel. They drank it from calabash gourds, or from cheaper earthenware; they liked it cold rather than hot, and invented new ways of flavouring it. By adding honey to their cacao they were apparently the inventors of sweetened chocolate, which almost the whole world now prefers. To the Aztecs, chocolate was a drink for warriors and the élite. The drinking of chocolate, like the smoking of tobacco, did not take place during a meal but immediately after it. Aztec soldiers on campaign were supplied with tablets of ground cacao, to be stirred into water as 'instant chocolate'.

Chocolate lent itself to flavour mixtures. Both Maya and Aztecs mixed ground cacao with maize to make *pinole*, and made a different drink by mixing cacao butter with maize. Modern Mexicans still flavour chocolate, as the Aztecs did, with the petals of the 'ear flower', *Cymbopetalum penduliflorum*. The Aztecs liked to add the leaves or seeds of *acuyo* (*Piper sanctum*), petals of *Magnolia mexicana*, and several other herbs and flowers. Modern Mesoamerican peoples sometimes add black pepper, allspice, or annatto: the latter not only contributes flavour but colours the drinker's mouth red, a reminder of the link sometimes made in Mesoamerican thought between chocolate and blood.

To the Maya and the Aztecs the ceremonial importance of chocolate was profound. It was provided generously at the banquets at which noblemen and merchants displayed their wealth. It was offered to the gods, and was used to anoint newborn children on the forehead, face, fingers, and toes in a rite resembling baptism.

CHOCOLATE REACHES EUROPE

On his third voyage to the New World, on 15 August 1502, Columbus captured a Maya trading canoe laden with cacao beans and other produce. He may have learnt that the beans were money but he never found out that a drink was made from them.

However, when the Spaniards under Cortés invaded Yucatan and then the valley of Mexico itself, between 1517 and 1526, they soon realized the full value of the black 'almonds' (as they at first called them) of which so many millions were stored at Tenochtitlan. At first disgusted by the frothy, dark beverage that was present at every Aztec banquet and festival, the conquistadores soon learned to appreciate it. Rumour credited it with aphrodisiac properties (perhaps simply because it was taken in late evening, when the meal was over), and long argument would centre on the question whether chocolate was a food sufficiently nourishing to be ruled out during Lent. In contrast to the Aztec view of it as a drink for warriors, chocolate has sometimes been seen by Europeans as a woman's drink. This may have something to do with the fact that the conquistadores were taught to like it by their Mexican wives, concubines, and domestic servants. By 1590, 'the Spanish men—and even more the Spanish women—are addicted to it', wrote José de Acosta of his Mexican observations.

It was from an innovation of this period that the name chocolate originally comes. Hot water with a mixture of ground cacao and ground sapote kernels, maize, and other flavourings made a refreshing drink first described by the Spanish scientist Francisco Hernandez in the late 16th century. Its new name, *chocolatl*, appears to be a Spanish-inspired blend of Maya *chocol* 'hot' and Nahuatl *atl* 'water'—an appropriate formation for the melting pot of cultures that was colonial Mexico. The word was soon applied to all the products of cacao.

The Spaniards in Mexico also appear to have invented a new means of producing the much-loved froth of drinking chocolate. Where Maya and Aztecs had achieved the effect by pouring, colonial Mexico developed the *molinillo* or swizzle stick, which required a chocolate pot with a well-fitting, pierced lid. Meanwhile cane sugar, introduced to America in early colonial times, became an ever more popular flavouring in chocolate drinks. Other flavourings, including cinnamon and anise, were also tried.

The reputation of chocolate travelled faster than the substance itself. It is mentioned in many early European works on botany, but this does not mean that it was actually available in Europe. Hence the dates that follow are later than those that will be found in some other reference books.

Chocolate is known to have reached the Old World by 1544, when a party of Kekchi Maya from Guatemala, led by Dominican friars, paid a visit to the future Philip II of Spain. They brought him chocolate, maize, and other New World products. As a commodity of trade, cacao beans began to reach Spain in 1585. In the 17th century the Spanish court was well known throughout Europe for its prowess in preparing chocolate drinks. Spain soon adopted the chocolate cup and saucer, *mancerina*, which had been invented in S. America—by the Marques de Mancera (Viceroy of Peru from 1639 to 1648) after he had seen a guest at a reception accidentally spill her clumsy traditional chocolate pot.

As an expensive, exotic spice, chocolate was gradually introduced to the rest of Europe with emphasis on its medicinal virtues. By 1644 chocolate was known at first hand to a Roman physician, Paolo Zacchia, who describes it as 'a medicine brought here from Portugal not many years ago, to which it was sent from the Indies, called *chacolata*'. According to a Florentine chronicler, 'a drink used in Spain called *ciocolatto*' was first sold in Florence in 1668 'in little earthenware beakers, hot as well as cold according to taste', and by then it was already known at the court of Cosimo III de' Medici. The Grand Duke's physician had written in 1666 of experiments with new flavourings for chocolate, including ambergris, musk, jasmine, citron peel, and lemon peel.

By the later 17th century Italian cooks had experience in the addition of chocolate as a flavouring to savoury and sweet dishes, including sorbets and ice creams. The poet Francisco Arisi, in 'Il cioccolato' (1736), detailed the over-use of chocolate in cookery:

One cook, running short of cheese in his kitchen, sprinkled two *bolli* of chocolate, well grated, on a fine polenta. The novelty was well received: the Apicii [gourmets] demanded the recipe. At a dinner I attended I found it made into a sauce, though, to tell the truth, it did not whet my appetite. It has been put into nougat; it has a place of honour in cakes; one day, no doubt, a cook will serve it with roast quail.

It was also in Italy that chocolate would reach its highest fame as a vehicle of poison (a reputation it already held in early colonial Mexico). Pope Clement XIV, who suppressed the chocolate-loving Jesuits in 1773, was widely believed to have been poisoned by way of a bowl of chocolate in the following year.

The first recorded chocolate-drinker in France, in the early 17th century, was Alphonse de Richelieu, elder brother of the more famous Cardinal. He used it 'to moderate the vapours of his spleen'. In 1659 David Chaliou was granted a monopoly for selling chocolate throughout France. By 1671, according to the letters of Mme de Sévigné, chocolate was much in vogue at the court of Versailles, alternately praised for its medicinal virtues and blamed for unexpected side effects: 'The Marquise de Coetlogon took so much chocolate during her pregnancy last year that she produced a baby as black as the Devil. It died.'

In the late 18th century the French still sometimes flavoured their chocolate with chilli, in the old Mexican and Spanish style, but they always added sugar and cinnamon and often vanilla. Martin Lister, a traveller of 1698, had already blamed the obesity of Parisian women on their habit of drinking sweetened chocolate. In the course of the 18th century French confectioners tried flavouring biscuits and sweetmeats with chocolate. The marquis de Sade was said to have given a ball at which were served chocolate pastilles laced with cantharides. He himself loved chocolate, and frequently wrote to his wife from prison demanding supplies of chocolate pastilles, biscuits, and cakes.

Chocolate was first sold in London about 1657 by a Frenchman with a shop in Gracechurch Street: he advertised it as 'an excellent West India drink [which] cures and preserves the body of many diseases'. An enlightened entrepreneur, he not only sold chocolate ready to drink but offered to teach his customers how to make it themselves, with the help of a recipe book which they were encouraged to buy. The diarist Samuel Pepys, in the 1660s, several times recorded a morning drink of 'Chocolatte'. It may have been in England that the use of milk in a chocolate drink first became popular. England's supply of chocolate came from the plantations of Jamaica, captured from the Spanish in 1655. By the end of the 17th century, chocolate was available in New England too.

The chocolate houses which sprang up in London at this period became fashionable meeting places, precursors of men's clubs: they had been briefly banned by Charles II in 1675 as hotbeds of radical politics. The Garrick Club began life as 'The Cocoa-Tree Chocolate-House' and was an early headquarters of the Jacobite party. White's originated in 1693 as 'White's Chocolate House', originally Whig, later Tory.

At the end of the 18th century chocolate remained a drink for the rich, and particularly for rich ladies. As such it figures in Mozart's *Cosi fan tutte*. A maid enters carrying a chocolate pot and cups:

What an abominable life a lady's maid leads! Sweating, toiling, labouring from morning till night . . . and we get nothing out of it ourselves. I've been beating the chocolate for half an hour: now it's ready. Am I just to stand and smell it, my mouth dry? Isn't my mouth just as good as yours? O gracious mistresses, why should you get the real thing and I only the smell of it? By Bacchus, I'm going to taste it—Oh! It's good!

Through all this period, the preparation of chocolate for drinking remained very close to pre-Columbian practice. Toasting, winnowing, breaking, and grinding of the beans was highly labour intensive. In the 18th century there were 150 chocolate-grinders in Madrid. They plied their skilled trade from house to house, many drinkers preferring to keep a close eye on the quality and purity of their favourite drink by having it ground at home. The *metate*, the sloping stone on which chocolate beans were ground by hand, would still be familiar in 19th-century France and in 20th-century Spain and Italy.

CHOCOLATE CULTIVATION SPREADS

As demand grew and the population of Mexico and Guatemala declined through disease and serfdom, other tropical countries began to be exploited as cacao producers. The Mesoamerican variety of cacao, originally the only one known in the Caribbean and the one that provided all the cacao of Europe up to the end of the 18th century, is called Criollo. It was this which now began to be cultivated in Venezuela, and in Jamaica, Trinidad, and several of the smaller W. Indian islands. In the 17th and 18th centuries Europe's supply came mainly from these Caribbean plantations and, in declining quantity, from America itself.

In Ecuador and in parts of the Amazon basin in the 17th century Spanish and Portuguese prospectors found a distinct variety of cacao—that now known as Forastero—growing wild, and succeeded in establishing plantations of it. From Brazil (where the Jesuits had controlled the trade) the Portuguese took seedlings of Forastero cacao to Sao Tomé and Fernando Po, off the coast of W. Africa. By the end of the 19th century cacao was being cultivated in several W. African countries, and by the early 20th century it had been planted in Sri Lanka, Malaya, Java, Sumatra, New Guinea, the New Hebrides, and Samoa. W. Africa is now the world's main source of chocolate, and the bitter Forastero variety accounts for 80% of world production.

When the cacao of Trinidad was almost wiped out by a blight, it was supplemented with Forastero plantings. Soon afterwards the hybrid Trinitario variety emerged there, combining some of the flavour of Criollo with the hardiness of Forastero.

READING: Coe and Coe (1996).   SC/AD

Chocolate in the 19th and 20th centuries

Already by the end of the 18th century there had been a perceptible increase in the amount of chocolate being eaten, in slabs and pastilles, in ices and sorbets, as an ingredient in desserts and main dishes, in pastas and soups. This was all full fat chocolate; the raw cacao bean is about 50% fat by weight. Attempts to reduce the fat content of chocolate during processing had been made in the late 17th century; but it was not until the Dutchman van Houten developed a screw press, patented in 1828, that real success was achieved. It removed about two-thirds of the cocoa butter from the chocolate paste, leaving a residue which became known as COCOA. This dispersed easily in water and was considered more digestible than full-fat chocolate. Alkalizing, or 'Dutching', was a process which also originated with van Houten, who found that treating cacao during processing with potassium carbonate led to a milder flavour and darker colour.

A use was soon found for the excess cocoa butter. Added to the ground beans it created a smooth paste which could be moulded, and was solid when cold, but melted easily in the mouth. By 1842 Cadbury Brothers were selling a block chocolate, described on their price list as 'French'; and by 1847 Fry's were marketing 'Chocolat Délicieux à Manger'. Prices remained high, due to import duty levied on cacao beans. This was reduced in 1853, and imports of cheap sugar also helped lower the price but chocolate was still a luxury. Mrs Beeton (1861) instructed that chocolate, served in an ornamental box, should be placed on a glass plate as part of the dessert. Cocoa, now a cheap by-product, became the less desirable version of chocolate.

Major contributions made by the Swiss to the art of chocolate manufacture included that of Rodolphe Lindt, who in 1880 increased the amount of cocoa butter in his formula and developed the process of conching. In 1876 Swiss confectioner Daniel Peter produced the first milk chocolate, using dried milk, a new product manufactured by Henri Nestlé. It developed as a means of using milk in areas where it was cheap and plentiful. Milk and chocolate liquor were mixed, dried, and cocoa butter added. This is very similar to the modern 'milk crumb' process described in the section on chocolate manufacture below. The Swiss dominated the market for milk chocolate until the early 20th century.

Chocolate reached a wider audience when it was included amongst rations for troops during the First World War. Between the wars, the price of chocolate continued to fall as prices of materials fell, technological advances reduced manufacturing costs, and concentration in the industry brought economies of scale. By the dawn of the Second World War, **chocolate confectionery** was outselling sugar confectionery in England, and has continued to do so ever since.

Chocolate confectionery is a mixture of chocolate mass (processed cacao), cocoa butter, and sugar (see CHOCOLATE MANUFACTURE), often with additions of dairy produce and other confectionery.

Block chocolate, for eating or incorporation into other foods or drinks, is the primary manifestation of chocolate confectionery. That sold in Britain comes in three basic types: plain, or dark, which is a mixture of chocolate mass, cocoa butter, and sugar; milk chocolate, which includes milk solids and has a lower proportion of chocolate mass; and white, which is not really chocolate as it contains no mass, but is a mixture of cocoa butter, milk solids, sugar, and flavourings. In continental Europe and N. America, 'plain' chocolate is subdivided into categories of sweet, semi-sweet, and bitter-sweet. Unsweetened chocolate, which is hardened chocolate mass, is used by confectioners and bakers.

Nuts, dried fruit, biscuits, wafers, and sugar confectionery are often added to chocolate.

Chocolates, or *pralines* as they are called in parts of continental Europe, are sweetmeats made by coating small pieces of sugar confectionery or nuts with melted chocolate. Popular fillings include FONDANT flavoured with fruit, coffee, or mint; MARZIPAN; TOFFEES or CARAMEL; and PRALINE, mixed with chocolate to give a nut-flavoured paste.

Chocolates can be made by hand dipping. In theory this is simple, the centres being lowered on a special 'dipping fork' into molten chocolate, covered, and then deposited on paper to set. In fact, this skill takes years to learn properly. This method is mostly used by craft confectioners, for whom investment in production line methods would be expensive, but who wish to produce high-quality, individual chocolate selections. There are two automated methods for making chocolates: **enrobing,** in which the centres are transported under a curtain of molten chocolate, and **shell moulding,** which is time consuming and therefore more expensive. For this, molten chocolate is deposited in moulds to form the shell, which is then filled; a lid of chocolate seals the filling in before the chocolate is unmoulded. This method gives a better finish and allows for more elaborate shapes than enrobing. It is used for shapes such as Easter eggs and other novelties.

Liqueur chocolates, which magically enclose liquids, can be made by shell moulding, or by depositing the syrup into impressions made in trays of starch. Left undisturbed for some time, the syrup 'crusts' (by forming sugar crystals on all surfaces) and can be lifted out and enrobed. Another method for making chocolates with semi-liquid syrup fillings relies on the use of an enzyme to act on solid sugar centres after they have been coated with chocolate.

Other confections include TRUFFLES: these are based on *ganache*, a paste of chocolate and cream or butter with flavourings of spirits, nuts, or essences. Chocolate is used for panned sweets or dragées, either as centres which are coated with thin, crunchy sugar shells, or to cover dried fruits and nuts. For the latter, chocolate is sprayed onto centres rotating in revolving pans; cool air is blown over them to harden them.

Chocolate is popularly perceived as comforting, and perhaps 'addictive'; and maintains a reputation as an aphrodisiac. How much of this image is due to intrinsic properties, and how much to clever marketing and associations with luxury and pleasure is debatable. The basic combination, in chocolate, of fat and sugar is well calculated to give pleasure. And chocolate does contain phenylethylamine, a naturally occurring chemical in the human brain, responsible for the euphoric feelings associated with being in love. However, experiments to discover if eating chocolate has a measurable effect on this aspect of body chemistry have proved inconclusive.

Chocolate also contains theobromine, a stimulant which acts on the muscles; and caffeine (but in much smaller quantities than tea or coffee). This stimulant effect was noticed by early European consumers such as Thomas Gage (1648), who drank chocolate when he wished to work late at night.

Finally, chocolate is nutritious: depending on the formula (milk or plain) it yields up to 600 calories of energy per 100 g (3.5 oz), mostly in the form of fat and sugar, useful amounts of protein, and iron. Because it is such a concentrated food source, it features in the survival kits of soldiers and mountaineers.

Perhaps for these reasons the term 'chocolate' has acquired in some parts of the world a much more general meaning: something sweet which is easy to eat from the hand. This is true in Kazakhstan, where 'Kazakh chocolate' (*zhent*) turns out to be a block of sweet matter made from millet, curd cheese, sugar, raisins, and butter (with not a whiff of even a chocolate substitute). And in Afghanistan children who are offered toffees will exclaim delightedly: 'chocolates!'

Chocolate manufacture

has been an important industry in W. Europe since the late 18th century. Some great names in chocolate manufacture— Dröste, van Houten (Holland); Lindt, Suchard (Switzerland); Menier (France); and Fry, Cadbury, Rowntree (England) can trace their history back to the mid-19th century and often earlier. Chocolate is manufactured in the USA by Walter Baker and Co. (founded 1779) and by Hershey. A curious aspect of chocolate manufacture, at least in England, is the link with nonconformist religions, the three principal companies all being founded by Quaker families.

Chocolate manufacture is a complex process, requiring substantial investment in machinery. The raw material is cacao (see the section on chocolate: Botany and Early History above) which is imported from the country of origin as fermented, dried beans. Over 30 varieties are available, and the manufacturer's first concern may be **blending,** using several varieties of bean to produce the desired flavour.

After cleaning, the first process in manufacture is **roasting.** This is important for developing flavour, and reduces moisture content to a level appropriate during later processing. It also facilitates removal of the shells from the beans during the next process, winnowing, when they are cracked between rollers, and the husks removed, leaving only the kernels or nibs. The nib (the cotyledon of the seed) is the part of the bean used for chocolate and cocoa manufacture. It may be further treated by alkalizing, altering flavour and colour.

Then the nib is reduced to a paste by **grinding.** Originally stone mills, echoing the Aztec use of stone implements for chocolate preparation, were employed, but now metal mills with sophisticated temperature controls are used. Temperature is important because the heat produced by friction during grinding releases the fat, or cocoa butter, from the nib. The mass emerges from the grinder in a liquid state known as chocolate liquor, chocolate mass, or pâte.

This liquor is the essential ingredient for chocolate manufacture. It is often made by individual manufacturers.

Cooled and hardened, the liquor becomes basic **unsweetened chocolate.** Some liquor is used to make COCOA; this is done by pressing it to release more cocoa butter, and grinding the residue to powder. (The extra cocoa butter is used to enrich liquor during chocolate production.)

For **plain chocolate,** liquor is mixed with powdered sugar. Cocoa butter is added to adjust the consistency. A stiff paste emerges and goes for **refining,** which reduces the size of the particles in the mixture, so that they are imperceptible to the palate. The mass is passed through a series of steel rollers, each of which rotates faster than the one before. These have a shearing action and the mass emerges almost as powder.

The next process is **conching.** This is said to have gained its name from the shell-like shape of the 'conche', a long heated stone trough, curved at each end. It was fitted with a roller to work the chocolate mass back and forth at a temperature of 55–85 °C (131–85 °F), constantly turning the chocolate and exposing fresh surfaces to the air. During conching flavour develops, moisture content is lowered further, and more fat is squeezed out of the cocoa particles. Stone conches are still used, as well as modern rotary conches which knead the mass intensively. Conching may take from several hours to a week, depending on the quality required. Towards the end of conching and desired flavourings are added. Vanilla is the most common in European and N. American chocolate. Others often used are mint, orange, and coffee.

Chocolate couverture is chocolate with a very high cocoa butter content, intended as a long shelf-life product for bakers and craft confectioners. Milk solids may also be added. It is specially prepared for coating, and manufactured so that at a given temperature it will cover evenly, but not flow off centre. (The term 'couverture' can cause confusion, since it was used in England to describe a cheap product from which most of the cocoa butter has been removed and replaced by hydrogenated fat and a stabilizer. This is now called chocolate-flavoured covering.)

Milk chocolate is usually made by the 'milk crumb' process. Fresh milk, concentrated to a solids content of 30–40% is used; sugar is added and the mixture further condensed, under vacuum, to a dry-matter content of about 90%. This is mixed with chocolate liquor, giving a stiff mixture which is dried and broken up. Processing then follows the same steps (adding cocoa butter, mixing, and refining, and conching) as for plain chocolate. Conching for milk chocolate takes place at a lower temperature (45–60 °C/113–40 °F) for a longer time; this prevents the lactose (milk sugar) from aggregating and giving a lumpy consistency.

After conching, the chocolate mass, plain or milk, is used for chocolate confectionery (see the section on chocolate in the 19th and 20th centuries above). However, before being moulded, the chocolate has to be stabilized, or **tempered,** by heating to a temperature of 49–50 °C (120–2 °F), and then cooling it, whilst stirring, to about 29 °C (84 °F) for plain, or 28 °C (82 °F) for milk. The object of this process is to 'seed' the mixture with cocoa butter crystals of a uniform and stable type, which will keep well during storage. If nuts, dried fruit, biscuit, etc. are to be added, they go in at this stage. The mixture, warmed slightly, is then deposited in moulds, shaken to remove air bubbles, and chilled, before unmoulding and wrapping.

Chocolate is best stored at temperatures below 18 °C (64 °F), to prevent undesirable changes (such as the formation of a harmless but unsightly whitish 'bloom') in the cocoa butter crystals.   LM

Chocolate in cookery

In Europe and N. America chocolate is an important flavouring for puddings, desserts, baked goods, and ice creams. It combines well with nuts, fruits, orange, mint, coffee, and spirits.

In the form of COCOA, it provides a concentrated chocolate flavour for cakes, biscuits, and icings, and is sometimes added to pastry. Block chocolate is used for richer cakes, and to flavour creams, mousses, soufflés, sauces, and ice cream.

Some famous confections include chocolate by definition. Examples are SACHERTORTE, BLACK FOREST GATEAU, devil's food cake, Poires belle Hélène, ÉCLAIRS, FLORENTINES, BROWNIES, and chocolate chip cookies.

The foregoing are all sweet items. N. Europeans, who think of chocolate exclusively in terms of sweetness, are often surprised to discover that it can be used to flavour savoury dishes, especially sauces for game. The pre-Columbian Americans who were the first to use chocolate would have been equally surprised, for they would have regarded a use of this sort as sacrilege (see MOLE on this point, and also for an example of later Mexican use of chocolate as an ingredient in a savoury sauce).

In Europe it seems to have been the Italians who first explored such possibilities. There are firmly dated Italian recipes of the 1680s which reflect such novel experimentation. This became so widespread that an Italian poet cited by Coe and Coe (1996) in a poem listed among those who misused the beverage *cacao* not only those who misguidedly blow the froth off their cups, or take snuff with it, or mix it with coffee, but also those who put it into meat pasties and kindred dishes.

It may have been from Italy that the idea passed to France. It made an early appearance there in Massialot (1691) as 'Wigeon in a ragout with chocolate', but this recipe seems to have been swiftly forgotten.

The Spanish have been more consistent in taking up the idea. They continue to make 'Catalan-style' dishes which are sometimes seasoned with chocolate. Chocolate is also still used, in small amounts, in Italy in *salsa agrodolce* (sweet-sour sauce), which is served with boar and hare. In Latin America, it is used more widely, perhaps reflecting Spanish influence as much as or more than any post-Columbian indigenous tradition.

Chocolate must be melted gently, using a bain-marie, a slow oven, or a microwave on a low setting. If it gets too hot (over 44 °C, 111 °F), the flavour is impaired and it 'seizes'—goes hard and grainy.

CHOCOLATE SAUCE is best made with semi-sweet or bitter chocolate, often with a little butter and vanilla. It goes particularly well with vanilla ICE CREAM, and cools so rapidly on contact with the ice cream that it solidifies almost at once, providing a contrast in texture as well as in flavour. This combination is called a *Dame blanche*, especially in Belgium. Chocolate sauce with PEAR, as in *Poires belle Hélène*, is another good combination.

Certain sauces with other names incorporate chocolate as an ingredient. In Spain, for example, it is used in a sauce for spiny lobster. In Mexico it is used in some versions of MOLE.

CHOEREK (or choereg, choereq, churekg etc.) (the name has seemingly innumerable transcriptions) means 'holiday bread'. This is an enriched bread (using e.g. sour cream, butter, egg), oven baked, made in a variety of shapes and sizes and flavours in the Caucasus. The most common shape is 'knotted' or braided bread, but it also occurs in snail shapes in Georgia. Flavourings include aniseed, MAHLAB (a spice derived from black cherry kernels), vanilla, cinnamon, and grated lemon or orange rind.

In Turkey a similar bread is called *paskalya coregi*, meaning Easter bread, a role which is also played by the Greek version, *tsoureki*; see EASTER FOODS. Etymological considerations suggest that the Greek name comes via Turkey from the Caucasus, rather than the other way round.

CHOKECHERRY *Prunus virginiana*, which grows widely in the USA, is so named because of the fierce sourness and astringency of the fruit when unripe. As William Wood (quoted from Fernald and Kinsey, 1943) wrote in 1634, 'they so furre the mouth that the tongue will cleave to the roofe, and the throate wax horse with swallowing those red Bullies. English ordering may bring them to be an English Cherrie, but yet they are as wilde as the Indians.' However, when the fruit was fully ripe, it was used by whites and Indians alike. The latter had many traditional uses and used the fruits in PEMMICAN, their preserved dried meat.

Gibbons (1971) points out that there is a considerable difference between eastern and western chokecherries. The latter, *P. virginiana* var *Melanocarpa*, he assures his readers, can be eaten fresh from the tree, make a wonderful jelly but are even better if turned into juice and made into a soup with lemon rind, cinnamon, and a little cornflour.

CHOLESTEROL a complex fatty alcohol, is essential for the proper working of the digestive and nervous sytems. It is present in foods of animal origin, large amounts being found in egg yolk. There are many kinds of cholesterol, of which two are of interest to human health; these are known as 'low density lipoprotein' (LDL) and 'high density lipoprotein' (HDL). LDL is notorious as a contributory cause of atherosclerosis—clogging of the arteries with fatty deposits—as well as gallstones. HDL, in contrast, is wholly beneficial and helps to keep the arteries clear. But it should be noted that some LDL is necessary; it is only harmful in excess.

In Harvard during the 1950s, Konrad Bloch and Feodor Lynen worked out the role of cholesterol in the body and its link with atherosclerosis, for which they won a Nobel prize in 1964. It became clear that many people in western countries had dangerously high levels of LDL and that this was caused, at least partly, by eating fatty foods. In particular, there were worries about foods which were themselves high in cholesterol, and some people stopped eating eggs altogether.

It is now thought that the main cause of high LDL levels is not eating cholesterol itself, but a combination of too much saturated fat (see FATS AND OILS) in the diet, and lack of exercise.   RH

CHOP as a concept noun in the context of meat cookery, emerged in the 17th century. Slices of meat the size of individual portions, they were in their way forerunners of hamburgers, served up to busy city dwellers in the London chophouses that proliferated from the 1690s onwards. Right from the start chop seems usually to have been applied to cuts containing a bone and chopped from the loin, shoulder, or particularly ribs. It did, though, take a little time to bed down as a solo term: at first people spoke of 'a chop of mutton', for instance, rather than simply 'a chop' (on 9 July 1663 Samuel Pepys recorded 'Had a chop of veal'). In modern usage, chop is applied to cuts of lamb or pork, but not beef (a corresponding section of which would be too big to form a single portion that could fit onto the average plate).   JA

CHOP SUEY a dish whose ingredients can vary—indeed, its very nature is that this should be so—but which usually includes things like bits of pork or chicken, beansprouts, water chestnuts, bamboo shoots, and other vegetables such as celery, all chopped, plus soy sauce and perhaps some stock; the whole to be stir-fried or simmered and served with rice or noodles.

Chop suey may be a prime example of CULINARY MYTHOLOGY. The general perception of this dish in the western world is that it is a sort of parody of Chinese food, invented in San Francisco towards the end of the 19th century and spreading out from there to become a standard item in the American repertoire, and indeed known all over the world. Various accounts have been given of its birth. They all agree in supposing that a Chinese cook, confronted by a demand for food at an hour when none of his proper dishes was still available, improvised a mixture from leftovers and then, in response to questions from the people who had demanded food, said that the dish was called 'odds and ends' in Chinese. However, there are numerous candidates for the role of the demanding diners: drunken miners, a San Francisco political boss, railroad workers, a visiting Chinese dignitary who was suffering from indigestion, etc. etc. This variation in the supposed identity of principal characters is typical of mythology.

It has been left to Anderson (1988) to show what seems more likely to have been the true origin of the dish.

chop suey is not—as many would-be connoisseurs believe—an American invention. As Li Shu-fan points out in his delightful autobiography, *Hong Kong Surgeon* (1964), it is a local Toisanese dish. Toisan is a rural district south of Canton, the home for most of the early immigrants from Kwangtung to California. The name is Cantonese *tsap seui* (Mandarin *tsa sui*), 'miscellaneous

scraps.' Basically, it is leftover or odd-lot vegetables stir-fried together. Noodles are often included. Bean sprouts are almost invariably present, but the rest of the dish varies according to whatever is around.

CHOUQUETTES or petits choux, a small item of PÂTISSERIE in France which resembles soft PETITS FOURS secs (dry as opposed to the other category of petits fours which are moist, e.g. miniature SAVARINS) and whose name (in either version) has been adopted as a term of endearment. It has nothing to do with a cabbage, as the present author mistakenly supposed; he wondered in his youth why he should be addressed as a small cabbage and only discovered in the eighth decade of his life that this had not been the intention of female friends who in the distant past had applied the phrase to him.

The term is of long standing. A street cry in the 16th century was 'Choux, petits choux, tout chauds.' Cotgrave (1611) in his French–English dictionary gave the term as 'tichous' and translated this as 'Little cakes made of eggs and flower [*sic*], with a little butter (and sometimes cheese among) eaten ordinarily with sugar and Rosewater'. The author of the *Thrésor de santé* (1607) regarded cheese, and cheese of a certain kind not just any cheese, as obligatory rather than optional. However, towards the end of the century, the great dictionary of Furetière (1690) described something closer to the modern petits choux, without cheese.

Chouquettes are among the most popular Parisian FRIANDISES, eaten at tea when warm and soft, semi-dry at other times. Wedding cakes can be constructed from them, with confectioner's cream inside.

CHOW-CHOW an American term which came into use in the mid-19th century and was defined by the grocer Artemas Ward (1923) as: 'a mixture of pickles of various sorts, especially mixed vegetables, in mustard. Also, and originally, a Chinese sweetmeat consisting of pieces of orange-peel, ginger and numerous other articles put up in sirup.' Weaver (1993) suggests that chow-chow was derived from a 'root recipe' for 'Yellow Pickle, or Axe-jar', for which he cites a publication of 1837. See also ACHAR.

CHOWDER a term first used in N. America in the 1730s, may well be derived from the French word *chaudière* meaning the sort of iron cooking pot which early French settlers took to what are now the Maritime Provinces of Canada. When they encountered the Canadian Micmac Indians they found that the latter had a great appetite for their native clams but were having to cook them with hot stones placed in water in a hollowed-out piece of tree trunk. It has been suggested that a natural marriage took place between the clams which the Indians had and the pots which the settlers brought. Indeed, it seems likely that this combination of European technology with American foodstuffs was happening at many places more or less simultaneously, so that there could be no way of telling where the first real 'clam chowder' was made.

Chowder always means a hearty soup, usually but not invariably of seafood; and clam chowder is its best-known form. Indeed, one should say forms in the plural, for in New England, which along with the Maritime Provinces of Canada has for long been the main home territory of chowders, there are lively arguments about what is an authentic clam chowder. Mariani (1994) describes this thus in his excellent long essay about chowder:

By the end of the century certain New England regions became known for their various interpretations of chowder—one might find cream in one spot, lobsters in others, no potatoes elsewhere—but most were by then a creamy white soup brimming with chopped fish or clams, crackers, and butter. In Rhode Island, however, cooks often added tomatoes to their chowder, a practice that brought down unremitting scorn from chowder fanciers in Massachusetts and Maine, who associated such a concoction with New York because the dish came to be called, for no discernible reason, 'Manhattan clam chowder' sometime in the 1930s. By 1940 Eleanor Early in her *New England Sampler* decried this 'terrible pink mixture (with tomatoes in it, and herbs) called Manhattan Clam Chowder, that is only a vegetable soup, and not to be confused with New England Clam Chowder, nor spoken of in the same breath'.

READING: Thorne (1978).

CHOW MEIN one of a pair of prominent Chinese-American dishes, the other being the somewhat similar CHOP SUEY. Mariani (1994) notes that the term first appeared in print in 1903.

Chow mein is related to and takes its name from *chao mian*, a Chinese dish consisting of previously boiled noodles stir-fried with meat and vegetables. There is, however, an important difference. In chow mein the noodles are deep fried in bundles, which are crisp and brittle when they emerge; whereas in the Chinese dish the noodles are soft.

CHRISTIANITY AND FOOD a subject with surprisingly few negative aspects. Alone among the major religions of the world, mainstream Christianity has no general

taboos which would forbid Christians ever to eat a whole category or categories of foods, such as the prohibitions described under MUSLIMS AND FOOD, HINDUISM AND FOOD, and JEWISH DIETARY LAWS. It is true that in the early centuries AD Christians continued to follow many of the Jewish laws which are stated in the Old Testament, but these were gradually jettisoned and in effect replaced by the Christian system of abstinence and FASTING (which see for the distinction between the two terms).

However, there are many feast days and fast days for Christians, in proportions which vary from church to church. See CHRISTMAS FOODS and EASTER FOODS for outstanding examples of feast days, to which can be added several forms of harvest festival and thanksgiving days.

Feasts, generally speaking, are not a problem. However, it is true that within Christianity a broad distinction can be drawn between those denominations which look with favour on the pleasures of food and drink, albeit perhaps urging moderation, and those which place emphasis on the dangers of all fleshly pleasures and which seem to be saying, in effect, that one must eat but that one should not do so for, or even with, enjoyment. The name of Calvin is prominent in the latter group, although Janny de Moor (1995) has shown that his own attitude was more ambivalent than has been generally supposed.

The main food issue which has confronted Christian ecclesiastical authorities, especially those of the Roman Catholic Church, has been that of FASTING (taking this term to include abstinence); not the principle, but the extent. It seems unlikely that the evolution of ideas on the modalities will ever reach a terminal point. See also LENT.

Of the symbolic foods which play a role in Christianity, the most important by far (and the most puzzling for non-Christians) are those which feature in the mystery of 'Holy Communion' where consumption of wafers and wine is held by some believers not merely to represent but to be consumption of the flesh and blood of Jesus Christ. Obviously, no allusion to CANNIBALISM is intended; in many parts of the world Christian missionaries have been foremost in trying to eradicate that abhorrent practice. But when it comes to explaining just what is supposed to be going on, there are problems (of which Caroline Walker Bynum, 1987, gives a sympathetic description with well-researched history).

CHRISTMAS FOODS include in virtually all Christian countries or communities provision for a main meal on Christmas Day, or Christmas Eve, which in

turn incorporates a main dish which is symbolic of Christmas. This main dish is liable to change, the only constant factor being that it is perceived as 'special'. Thus the TURKEY which has during the 20th century provided the main dish for most families in England does not represent an antique tradition, for it was only in the 19th century that it began to replace the GOOSE; and there are signs that the reverse process may now be under way. There is a similar question mark over the traditional CHRISTMAS PUDDING, whose ancestry (as plum POTTAGE or plum PUDDING) can be traced back for many centuries but which in its present configuration and status can also be counted as mainly a product of the 19th century, and which may also yield ground in the coming millennium to lighter alternatives. In other countries it is possible to observe similar gradual evolutions, although what is subject to change may be quite different: a carp, for example, rather than a bird.

What is, however, relatively common ground and relatively unchanging is the seasonal frenzy of baking in most European countries, as households (one used to say housewives, but patterns of activity change) make a stock of special foods for the Christmas period.

Mention of the Christmas period is highly relevant because, although Christmas is often taken to mean Christmas Day plus perhaps Christmas Eve and what is called Boxing Day in England, its more extensive meaning covers a long period, beginning with Advent in early December and continuing to Twelfth Night on 6 January. It is this longer timespan for which the baking frenzy caters.

Many of the bakery products, such as English MINCE PIES, Scandinavian GINGER BISCUITS, and German LEBKUCHEN, are indeed consumed throughout the season. Others are kept for specific days, which vary from country to country. In the Netherlands, Germany, and C. Europe 6 December (St Nicholas's Day) is important; as is 13 December (St Lucy) in Sweden; Christmas Eve and Christmas Day in Britain, the USA, France, and S. Europe; New Year's Eve and New Year's Day in Scotland; and 6 January (Epiphany) in France, Spain, and Portugal.

Although Christmas is supposed to commemorate the birth of Christ, a number of important pagan festivals which took place at midwinter have been incorporated. Their echoes still persist in the feasting, especially in the shapes of foods baked for this time of year.

All special breads made for Christmas involve doughs mixed with quantities of butter, eggs, and sugar. Many are spiced, or flavoured with lemon zest, and further embellished with nuts and dried or candied fruit.

In Switzerland and Germany on St Nicholas's Day the saint is thought to reward good children with sweets but punish bad ones with a switch. In the Netherlands his role is to deliver presents to children. For this day Swiss bakers make *Weihnachtsmänner*, Father Christmases, and *Grittibanzen*, dough men. Shaped from lightly enriched dough, they range from simple figures with currant eyes to ones carefully dressed in fringed scarves and jackets, carrying walking sticks. Gingerbread and honey cake mixtures are also made into men for autumn and midwinter festivals over most of N. Europe, including Britain. There are no records of these having been made in the Middle Ages, but Bachmann (1955) conjectures that they represent a winter god, and refers to gods modelled in dough, mentioned in the Norse sagas.

On the day of the Immaculate Conception (8 December) the inhabitants of Madeira bake their *bolo de mel* for the coming Christmas. This honey cake (now sweetened with molasses), heavy with walnuts, almonds, and candied peel, is leavened by a piece of dough from bread-baking. Any honey cakes left from the previous year are eaten up on this day.

In Sweden St Lucy's Day is celebrated with rich saffron-flavoured buns. The dough is mixed with fruit, candied peel, and almonds, and shaped into plaits, crosses, and buns called *Lussekatter*, St Lucy's cats. Traditionally, one of the daughters of the house gets up to prepare a breakfast of these buns, and dresses in a long white robe with a crown of lingonberry twigs and lighted candles on her head to serve them.

As the season progresses other breads make their appearance especially on Christmas Day. In England, the 'traditional' Christmas cake, a rich FRUIT CAKE, has largely usurped the place of sweet spiced and decorated fruit breads. These cakes, round and covered in marzipan and a thick layer of royal icing, are made well in advance.

Breads have also been replaced by rich cakes in France, where the *bûche de Nöel*, a roll of light SPONGE CAKE, is covered in chocolate or coffee buttercream textured to resemble bark. The conceit is carried further by mounding the cream over small pieces of cake stuck to the main roll, to represent trimmed branches. The ends of the roll and the cut faces of the 'branches' are finished with a vanilla cream, imitating pale newly cut wood, and the whole is decorated with leaves made from icing, or meringue mushrooms.

Christmas breads are part of the celebrations in Scandinavia. The Danish *julekage* is a Christmas fruit loaf, lightly enriched, kneaded with candied fruit, and flavoured with lemon peel and cardamom, and candied fruit; *julbröd* is the Swedish name for a similar loaf. Various kinds of coffee bread and *Wienerbrød* DANISH PASTRIES) are baked in special Christmas shapes such as stars. These share the table with a plethora of Christmas biscuits such as *pepperkaker* (ginger snaps) and *peppernotter* (ginger nuts). The Norwegian *kransekake* (garland cake) is made from a marzipan-like mixture of ground almonds, icing sugar, and egg white, gently heated, and made into rings in graduated sizes; up to 14 rings may be made, for which special tins are available.

C. Europe provides a wealth of breads. Some, such as KUGELHOPF (an Austrian favourite), are made throughout the year. *Hutzelbrot*, a heavily fruited and spiced bread, is sold at all the Advent markets which are a popular feature of Christmas in Germany. Swiss Christmas *Birnbrot* includes kirsch in its spiced pear filling, which is encased in a lightly sweetened and enriched dough. *Tannenzapfen*, 'pine cone cake', a Swiss Christmas speciality, is made from thin layers of sponge built up into the shape of a pine cone lying on its side, covered in coffee-flavoured buttercream, and stuck all over with split toasted almonds to resemble the scales on the cone. Dresden STOLLEN is one of the most famous German Christmas breads; plainer Stollen are also made, some aniseed flavoured, as are SPRINGERLE biscuits. German and Swiss bakers make lightly enriched doughs into intricate plaited shapes such as the *Weinachtszopf*, a straight plait with dried fruit; or crowns, wreaths, and stars for Christmas and New Year displays. The plaits are said originally to represent women's hair cut off in sacrifice as part of mourning ritual (a custom observed through much of ancient Europe by the inhabitants of Greece and Rome, as well as the Germanic tribes). They are also very decorative shapes which show off a baker's skill.

Baking is somewhat less important in Mediterranean countries, where nut and sugar confections such as nougat sustain the sweet toothed. However, the principal Italian festive bread, PANETTONE, is on sale everywhere at Christmas. *Christopsomo*, Greek Christmas bread, is rich, sweet, aniseed flavoured, and marked with a Greek (equal-armed) cross.

The Church celebrates 6 January as Epiphany, the day on which the Christ child was shown to the three Kings. This date is also Twelfth Night, the last of the twelve days of Christmas. It has inherited some of the pagan customs associated with Roman Saturnalia, and its cakes are of such interest that they have separate entries; see TWELFTH NIGHT CAKE and (for France and other Latin countries) *galette des rois*, see GALETTE.

(LM)

CHRISTMAS PUDDING the rich culmination of a long process of development of 'plum puddings' which can be traced back to the early 15th century. The first types were not specifically associated with Christmas. Like early MINCE PIES, they contained meat, of which a token remains in the use of suet. The original form, plum POTTAGE, was made from chopped beef or mutton, onions and perhaps other root vegetables, and dried fruit, thickened with breadcrumbs, and flavoured with wine, herbs, and spices. As the name suggests, it was a fairly liquid preparation: this was before the invention of the pudding cloth made large puddings feasible. As was usual with such dishes, it was served at the beginning of a meal. When new kinds of dried fruit became available in Britain, first raisins, then prunes in the 16th century, they were added. The name 'plum' refers to a prune; but it soon came to mean any dried fruit.

In the 16th century variants were made with white meat such as chicken or veal; and gradually the meat came to be omitted, to be replaced by suet. The root vegetables also disappeared, although even now Christmas pudding often still includes a token carrot. The rich dish was served on feast days such as All Saints' Day, Christmas, and New Year's Day. By the 1670s, it was particularly associated with Christmas and called 'Christmas pottage'. The old plum pottage continued to be made into the 18th century, and both versions were still served as a filling first course rather than as a dessert.

Not all plum puddings were rich, festive, or ceremonial. Plum DUFF, essentially a suet pudding with less fruit and other enrichment, remained popular for centuries.

Even before Christmas pudding had attained its modern form, its consumption on Christmas Day had been banned by Oliver Cromwell. This was not simply a sign of his Puritan attitudes. The Christian Church everywhere was conscious that Christmas was merely a veneer of the old Celtic winter solstice fire festival celebrating the 'rebirth' of the sun after the shortest day, 21 or 22 December. This is still frankly celebrated in the Orkneys with the rite of Up Helly A, when a ship is burnt. Signs of paganism keep emerging: for example the Yule log, a huge log which is kept burning for all twelve days of the festival, and is still commemorated in the traditional French log-shaped Christmas cake. Other relics are the candles on the Christmas tree (imported from Germany in the time of Prince Albert), and the flaming pudding itself. There had been a similar official attitude in Scotland towards the consumption of the BLACK BUN on Twelfth Night.

What currently counts as the traditional Christmas pudding recipe has been more or less established since the 19th century. Usual ingredients are: suet; brown sugar (not always); raisins; sultanas; currants; candied peel; breadcrumbs; eggs; spices such as cinammon, nutmeg, and cloves, or allspice or mixed spice; and alcohol (e.g. stout, rum, brandy). Optional ingredients include flour, fresh orange or lemon peel, grated carrot or apple, almonds. The result is a remarkably solid pudding which has to be boiled for many hours then preferably left to mature for up to a year and reboiled on the day. A large pudding resists this treatment better than small ones—though few are as large as the one made in Devon in 1819, which weighed over 400 kg (900 lb).

The pudding is traditionally served with rum or brandy butter (US hard sauce) made from butter, sugar, and spirit. It is topped with a sprig of holly and set alight with rum or another spirit. This part of the tradition is still widely observed, but recipes for the pudding itself have been evolving in the direction of something lighter and more digestible.

The shape of the pudding is traditionally spherical, from being tied up in a floured pudding cloth. Most modern puddings are made in a basin covered with layers of foil and greaseproof paper.   RH

CHRYSANTHEMUM the name applied to most of the numerous species of plants of the genus *Chrysanthemum* in the daisy family. In the western world these plants are well known as a source of garden flowers and florists' blooms. There is, however, one species which is important in the Orient for its edible leaves and flowers. This is the garland chrysanthemum, *Chrysanthemum coronarium*. It is mainly in Japan, China, and Korea that its leaves and young shoots are cooked as a green vegetable.

This species, grown extensively in the northern regions of Japan, is known to the Japanese as *shungiku* or *kikuna*, meaning 'spring' or 'leaf' chrysanthemum. The leaves, if sufficiently young and tender, may be eaten raw; but it is usual to parboil them, refresh them in cold water, and serve them as *sunomono* (see JAPANESE CULINARY TERMS). They may also be added to 'one-pot' dishes such as *sukiyaki*, or be fried as TEMPURA.

Kikunori, boiled and dried chrysanthemum petals which come in sheet form, are a product of Ainai in the Aomori Prefecture of Japan. They can be used as a garnish, like fresh petals.

Another traditional preparation in N. Japan is called *kikumi*. Hamada (in Yashiroda *et al.* 1968) gives an evocative description:

In late autumn, the cooking chrysanthemum opens its medium-sized, double yellow flowers.

We used to help my grandmother gather the flowers, remove the green involucre from beneath the flowerhead and separate the rays, or florets. These are then washed and drained. After they are momentarily boiled, they are marinated in a bottle of Japanese rice wine and blended with soy sauce and pickled apricots. This completes the process, and the flowers are then ready for use in making kikumi. Kikumi is served in a deep bowl from which everyone helps himself. Such a bowl lasts two or three days even if served at every meal. The fragrance of the cooked chrysanthemum florets, blended with the sharp wine, pungent soy sauce and sour apricots, makes a very agreeable combination of flavors. It tastes of deepening autumn and makes me long for one or two haiku [seventeen-syllable Japanese poems] to capture the feeling.

CHUCK CHUCK WAGON, terms which belong to the era of the cowboy in the west of the USA. Chuck was what they ate, and the chuck wagon was where the cook prepared it. 'Come an' Get It' was the cry with which the cook announced that food was ready. It is also the title of the admirable book by Adams (1952) which records with picturesque details the equipment and supplies of the chuck wagon, the idiosyncrasies of the cooks and their helpers (called wranglers), and the nature of the food (in which loomed large meat stews, such as SONOFABITCH STEW, SOURDOUGH bread, dry biscuits, 'frijoles and fluff-duffs', and strong coffee often without sugar but with insects and Carnation milk).

CHUFA *Cyperus esculentus*, a sedge common in S. Europe and Africa, has small, edible tubers a little less than 20 mm (just over 0.8") in diameter. These are black, with a nutlike texture and a sweetness which increases when the tubers have been stored for a few weeks and become slightly wrinkled. Their resemblance to nuts accounts for many of their common names including nut grass, tiger nut, earth almond, and earth nut. Chufa itself is a Spanish dialect name.

The same genus, *Cyperus*, embraces many common plants of boggy places all over the world, including several others with edible tubers; and also the Egyptian papyrus rush (nut), *C. papyrus*, from which the ancient Egyptians made their writing paper. A near relative is the larger and better-known Chinese WATER CHESTNUT.

Chufa, which grows freely, has been used as food since early times, e.g. in ancient Egypt. The plant is sometimes cultivated, e.g. in the coastal regions of Ghana. The tubers may be eaten raw or roasted. In Spain they are made into a refreshing milky drink, *horchata*.

The plant was introduced into the USA in 1854; an act now regretted, for it has become a troublesome weed. It is grown in the southern states, mainly for feeding pigs, but people also occasionally eat it.

CHUÑO AND TUNTA two dried potato products developed in the foothills of the Andes in S. America over 2,000 years ago. Dawn and Douglas Nelson (1983) believe that the process must have been discovered accidentally and that it was only in the Andes that the necessary climatic conditions existed; these were that every autumn should have long periods of sub-zero temperatures at night followed by bright sunshine and drying winds during the day. The Nelsons point out that the varieties of potato used are almost tasteless and are reserved for this purpose. They continue:

The freshly lifted potatoes are washed clean without damaging the skins and laid out on soft turf or straw padding to be exposed to severe night frost. As soon as they have thawed in the morning they are trodden with bare feet so that the skin remains intact but the fluid resulting from cell rupture is extruded. On the first pressing over 30% of the fluid may be lost. They are left in position and dried by the sun and wind. The process is repeated for five successive days. From the sixth day onwards no further pressing takes place and they are straw-covered to a sufficient depth to prevent further freezing at night. Once dried they are as hard as stone and can be stored indefinitely, and even a minor degree of damp does not seem to damage them unduly. This product is called chuño.

The preparation of tunta begins in similar fashion but includes a soaking in a pond for two months, followed by a final sun-drying. Tunta, which is also called 'white chuño', is pure white inside and readily disintegrates into a fine white flour.

Potatoes treated thus are frost-proof, capable of almost indefinite storage, light in weight, and highly portable (especially tunta). For use, chuño are simply reconstituted with water and may be added to the native stew called *chupa*, or used otherwise in savoury dishes. The uses of tunta are similar to those of wheat flour in Europe and N. America.

No doubt these products helped to make the Inca migrations possible; and they have always been regarded by Peruvian Indians as essential for journeys. Travellers who are carrying *charqui* (dried LLAMA meat, see JERKY) and chuño need only add water to have the makings of a nutritious stew. The Nelsons calculate that a month's ration of this food would weigh only 9 kg (20 lb).

CHUTNEY the ordinary English spelling of the Indian word which used to be spelled *chutni* and is now *chatni*.

In Indian cuisine a *chatni* is a spicy relish eaten as a side dish to add interest to less piquant food, such as rice or DAL. It is freshly prepared for each meal by grinding spices and herbs (e.g. ginger, chilli pepper, mint, coriander leaves) and mixing them to a paste with (e.g.) garlic, or tamarind, or limes, or coconut. Whole pieces of fruit or vegetable (especially mango) may be in the relish. An Indian *chatni* is always vegetarian and has a sour tang.

Generally, ingredients vary according to region and tastes. Thus coconut chutney is the most popular relish in S. India, while herb and coconut chutney is typical of W. India; purely herb chutneys are eaten in W. and N. India. A chutney made with unripe mangoes—the one which has become most popular in the western world—is also a favourite in N. India; while walnut chutney (also chutneys with sour cherries or pumpkin or radish) is popular in Kashmir. Tomato (green or ripe) chutney is the one which knows no frontiers; it is eaten all over India.

The British encountered *chatni* early in their colonial days and adopted it with enthusiasm, tending perhaps to emphasize the sweet aspect of what is essentially sour or sweet and sour. British chutneys are usually spiced, sweet, fruit pickles, having something of the consistency of jam. Highest esteem is accorded to mango chutney, imported from India, but the sorts of chutney have been legion; *Law's Grocer's Manual* (1895), listed, among others, chutneys called Bengal, Cashmere, Colonel Skinner's, Lucknow, Calcutta Howrah, and Major Grey's. The last named is famed in India as well as Britain.

CICADAS insects of the family Cicadidae, the males of which make shrill chirping noises, are in some regions of N. America referred to as 'locusts'. Those who have explored the history and scope of insect-eating mention them in various contexts as providing food for human beings. Thus the indefatigable Bodenheimer (1951), ever scrupulous in fully citing his sources, tells us that a Mr W. S. Robertson informed Asa Fitch, who used the statement to support a report by the Revd A. Sandel of Philadelphia (1715), that 'the Indians use the different species of cicadas as an article of diet, every year gathering quantities of them. They are prepared as food by roasting in a hot oven and are stirred until they are well browned.'

Other authorities from the past are summoned up to confirm that the diet which cicadas themselves eat is thoroughly wholesome and that, at least after the wings have been removed, they may be eaten with enjoyment and nutritional benefit.

CIDER a term with two meanings. In N. America it usually refers to unfermented APPLE juice. In Britain, cider is an alcoholic drink, for which special cider apples are used; this has some limited uses in cookery and in making cider VINEGAR. This kind of cider is also made elsewhere in Europe, notably in parts of France and Spain.

CINNAMON the dried bark of *Cinnamomum verum*, a tree indigenous to Sri Lanka, has been an important spice since antiquity; but there was then, and indeed still is, confusion between cinnamon and CASSIA bark. In French, for example, the single word *cannelle* applies to both. And in the USA the term cinnamon can legally be applied to *C. cassia*, whereas the British Pharmacopoeia requires cinnamon to be the product of *C. verum*.

Purseglove *et al.* (1981) have surveyed the historical problems of identification and the opinions expressed on the possible use of cinnamon in very early times. They draw attention to the likelihood, explained by Burkill (1965–6), that the barks entering into the cinnamon trade have changed in the course of time and continue:

It seems probable that the ancient Greeks and Romans had both cinnamon and cassia, but the Arab traders who supplied them protected their business interests by deliberately shrouding the sources of their products in mystery. Both Herodotus (5th century BC) and Theophrastus (4th century BC), who believed that cinnamon and cassia came from the region of Arabia, offered fantastic stories. Thus Theophrastus:

they say it grows in valleys where there are snakes with a deadly bite, so they protect their hands and feet when they go down to collect it. When they have brought it out they divide it into three portions and draw lots for them with the sun, and whichever portion the sun wins they leave behind. As soon as they leave it, they say, they see it burst into flame. This is of course fantasy.

During the 12th to 14th centuries Arabic writers alluded to true cinnamon from Ceylon, and recognized its superiority. Finding it was one of the goals of 15th- and 16th-century explorers. Columbus thought that he had found it in Cuba in 1492, but the bark brought to him probably came from a tree of the genus *Canella*, the W. Indian 'wild cinnamon'. It was the Portuguese who eventually found cinnamon in its wild state in Ceylon, in 1505, and it was mainly for the cinnamon that they proceeded to occupy the island. When the Dutch took over the island in 1636, they inherited the monopoly in cinnamon, and began its cultivation. After the British conquest in 1796, the East India Company acquired the monopoly and kept it until 1833, when trade in cinnamon was freed.

The second most important source of true cinnamon is the Seychelles Islands, where it was introduced in the late 18th century by the French. In 1815 this source also passed into British hands. Some true cinnamon is also produced in the Malagasy Republic.

Cultivators of cinnamon manage their rootstocks in such a way as to encourage the formation of numerous straight shoots, in bush form. When these growing stems are about as high as a human being, they are harvested and taken away in bundles for peeling and processing.

Peeling involves first the stripping off of the outer bark. The inner bark is then rubbed with a heavy brass rod to loosen it, incisions are made round it and down each side, and it is prised off in half sections. The curled strips thus obtained are subsequently scraped clean and formed into compound quills, about 1 m (40") long; each quill consists of many strips rolled together into a cylindrical shape, and trimmed and dried. For retail sale, they are cut into shorter lengths. Cinnamon is also commonly sold in powdered form, often (whether this is stated or not) in a mixture with powdered cassia bark.

Although it is always cinnamaldehyde and eugenol, with other minor components, which impart the characteristic odour and flavour of *C. verum*, the chemical composition of cinnamon products varies considerably. It and other factors affecting quality are influenced by the soil on which the shoots are grown, the cultivar used, the techniques of processing, etc.; so appraisal is a matter for experts.

The quills themselves are the subject of a complicated system of grading, in which the main groupings are Fine, Mexican, and Hamburg.

Cinnamon bark oil is the source of the cinnamon essence which is used for culinary purposes. Cinnamon leaf oil is a different product, whose very high eugenol content gives it a clovelike aroma.

In European cookery, cinnamon is mainly used for flavouring baked goods and confectionery. CHOCOLATE with cinnamon was a combination favoured by the Spanish in the 16th century, when supplies of the new commodity were shipped back to the homeland from S. America. Cinnamon is also a favourite spice for fruit COMPOTES and kindred sweet dishes. Outside Europe, it is used as often in savoury dishes. Meat stews of the Middle East such as Moroccan TAGINE and Iranian *khoresht* are often spiced with cinnamon; indeed, in Lebanon and most of Syria the only spices used on meat are cinnamon and ALLSPICE. As part of the traditional *garam masala* (see MASALA), it is used extensively for the aromatic dishes, for example PILAF.

It is sometimes served at table as a condiment, for example to sprinkle over melon. Cinnamon toast is especially popular in N. America. Elizabeth David (1970) points out that in England silver casters were often intended to be filled with cinnamon (not sugar) to be sprinkled on TOAST and MUFFINS.

CITRON *Citrus medica*, a citrus fruit resembling a huge, rough LEMON. Some varieties may be as much as 30 cm (1') long. Most of the bulk is thick, dense rind; inside this the flesh is dryish and may be either sour or sweet, with a weak lemon flavour. The rind, which has a unique, resinous fragrance, is the most useful part.

The citron, like the lemon and LIME, is native to NE India, where it was used from early times as a perfume and in medicine. The earliest reference to it is in the *Vajasaneyi Samhita*, a collection of religious texts dating from before 800 BC, in which it is called *jambila*. The fruit seems always to have had a curious connection with religion and magic, and a high reputation as medicine, being regarded as an antidote to almost any poison and indeed almost a panacea.

Before 600 BC the citron had spread to Persia, then ruled by the Medes. From there it reached Babylonia, where it came to the notice of the exiled Jews, who later brought it back to Palestine. In 325 BC the army of Alexander the Great, returning from India to Macedonia, brought word of the citron to Europe; and soon afterwards the Greek writer Theophrastus described it, using the term 'apple' in its very general sense (usual in classical times), and under the heading 'the trees and herbs special to Asia':

The Median or Persian apple is not eaten, but is very fragrant, as also is the leaf of the tree. And if the 'apple' is placed among clothes, it keeps them from being motheaten. It is also useful when one has drunk deadly poisons, for being given in wine it upsets the stomach and brings up the poison: also for producing sweetness of breath.

Early attempts to grow the citron in Greece and Italy failed. However, the fruits, which keep very well, were imported as an exotic delicacy. Eventually, around the 1st century AD, perhaps because of a slight warming in the Mediterranean climate, it became possible to grow the fruit in parts of S. Europe (or further north in hothouses).

Later the citron gave its name to the whole group of citrus fruits as they became known in Europe, simply because it had been the first of them to arrive. There was also a confusion with its smaller and juicier relative the lemon (French *citron*, German *Zitrone*).

The citron did not reach China until the 4th century AD. When it did, a freak form

(sometimes classified as var *sarcodactyla*) developed in which the fruit was separated into five (or more) lobes looking like the fingers of a hand. This variety, called *fo shu kan* (Buddha's hand), was considered a symbol of happiness. For this reason and because of its especially fine scent, it was placed on household altars. Later it also became popular in Japan.

The ordinary citron also had religious symbolism from an early date. Perhaps because of its splendid size it came to represent wealth. In India the god of wealth, Kuvera, is always represented as holding a citron in one hand and a mongoose spewing jewels in the other.

In Orthodox Jewish practice a particular variety of citron, Etrog (which is also the Hebrew word for citron), is used during the joyous Feast of the Tabernacles, following the biblical commandment (Leviticus 23): 'And ye shall take you on the first day the fruit of a beautiful tree . . . and ye shall rejoice before the Lord your God seven days.' The Hebrew phrase *pri etz hadar*, literally 'the fruit of a beautiful tree', has always been identified with the *etrog*.

What is clear is that early uses of the citron were purely religious or medical. Even as late as the times of Pliny the Elder (about AD 75) it did not figure as an ordinary food. Soon afterwards, however, the practice of cutting the rind into strips for culinary use began. The Romans soaked it in vinegar or GARUM (fish sauce) and other liquids. APICIUS gives several recipes.

After the fall of the Roman Empire the citron remained important in Arab cuisine. The Baghdad physician Muwaffaq Ed-Din Abd el-Latif bin Yusuf mentions an Egyptian citron containing 'another citron complete with its yellow peel'—in other words, a navel. There were other varieties, 'some of them as big as a watermelon'. The gradual introduction of sugar to the Arab world and later to Asia allowed citron rind to be candied.

Citrons are now used almost exclusively for the manufacture of candied peel; the Buddha's hand variety is candied in China. Etrog citrons are in heavy demand in Jewish communities throughout the world for the

Feast of the Tabernacles. The main producers are Italy, Greece, Corsica, Morocco, and Israel. Some are grown in the USA.

Although the citron is not particularly juicy, juice can be got from it. This was used for making a refreshing soft drink which was the precursor of lemonade. In Italy it was called *acquacedrata*, and in the 17th and 18th centuries the vendor of this, with a tank on his back, was a familiar sight in Italian cities. The term *acquacedrata* for lemonade is still occasionally heard.

World production of citrons is small. Apart from the two varieties already mentioned, Corsican (described as a 'sweet' citron because of its lack of acidity) and Diamante (acid flavoured) are of some importance. The cultivar Earle, which resembles Diamonte, originated in Cuba.

CITRUS FRUITS There are separate entries for CALAMANSI, CITRON, GRAPEFRUIT, LEMON, LIME, MANDARIN, MANDARIN LIMES, ORANGE, POMELO, UGLI, YUZU. Here, these fruits are considered as a family.

All citrus fruits are native to a region stretching from E. Asia southwards to Australia. Collectively they now constitute the third most important group of fruits; only the apples and pears, and the banana and plantain, surpass them in quantity produced and consumed.

Botanists have calculated that the history of the citrus trees goes back 20 million years, to a time when Australia was joined to Asia. Given this span of time, and the ease with which hybridization takes place, it is remarkable that so much of the development of the fruits has taken place in historical times, even in the last few centuries—the grapefruit dates back only to the 18th century.

One feature which gives citrus fruits a special quality is their unique internal structure. Inside the rind, the fruit is filled with small vessels called pulp vesicles, which contain juice. The vesicles are grouped in larger containers termed locules, one locule being one segment of e.g. an orange. The

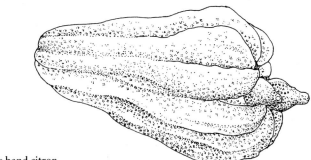

Buddha's hand citron

botanical name for this type of fruit is 'hesperidium'.

Citrus fruits all have a more or less acid taste, due mainly to the presence of citric acid. This is widely used as a flavouring. In powder form, it is sometimes known as 'sour salt'; and in the Near East it is known under the Turkish name *limon tuzu*, meaning lemon salt.

They also contain varying amounts of sugar and of bitter substances. The proportions of these constituents and the juiciness of the pulp determine whether they are edible or not. Most of the edible kinds have a strong orange or yellow colour, caused by various carotene pigments. (The colour of pink grapefruit is caused by a red carotene pigment, lycopene, but the deep red of blood oranges comes from an anthocyanin, the usual pigment of red fruits.) Tropical species tend to contain the green pigment chlorophyll which may mask the yellow colour, so that the fruits, e.g. limes, are green. If some species from cooler climates are grown in the tropics they too bear green fruits.

Why and where citrus fruits were first cultivated is not clear. However, the *Monograph of Citrus*, a Chinese document which was written in AD 1178, provides a detailed discussion of the growing of 27 varieties of sweet, sour, and mandarin oranges, as well as citrons, kumquats, and the trifoliate orange. The text indicates that, in China at least, cultivation had been practised for a long time.

Meanwhile citrus fruits had been spreading westwards. In India the *Vajasaneyi Samhita*, a collection of religious texts dating from before 800 BC, mentions the lemon and citron. The orange does not appear until about AD 100, in a medical treatise, the *Charaka Samhita*.

The citron was the first citrus fruit to reach Europe, which is why the whole group of fruits is called after one of its less important members. Its spread was helped more by its significance in religion and magic than by its culinary quality.

The orange and lemon seem to have arrived in Europe during the 1st century AD. A mosaic from Tusculum (now Frascati) of about AD 100 shows a basket containing lemon, citron, what are probably two oranges and another, smaller fruit which might be a lime.

After the fall of the Roman Empire the Arabs cultivated and disseminated the bitter orange, pomelo, lime, and sweet orange, between the 12th and 15th centuries. (The mandarin did not reach the western world until the beginning of the 19th century.)

The introduction of citrus fruits to the New World began directly after Columbus' first voyage. From the 16th century onwards their spread in the Americas was rapid,

culminating in the large industries which now exist in Florida and California. Orange and lemon trees were first planted in S. Africa by Dutch settlers in the mid-17th century. Orange, lime, and lemon arrived in Australia by the end of the 18th century.

Saunt (1990) provides an interesting table giving figures for world citrus production by main type and by hemisphere (northern/southern) and country. He points out that until recently the USA had led world production, but that Brazil is now in the lead. These two countries produce over 40% of the world citrus crop, but most of what they produce is processed rather than eaten fresh. Indeed, a third of the world's citrus output is processed, mostly into frozen concentrated juice. The figures cited by Saunt show that, as one would expect, 'Oranges are by far the most extensively produced citrus fruit.'

CIVET a French term which is usually met nowadays in the phrase *civet de lièvre*, which is a kind of HARE stew whose sauce has been thickened with the animal's blood. However, in the early Middle Ages civets were made with eggs, veal, oysters, and much besides. As the author of the MENAGIER DE PARIS (14th century) explained to his young bride, the essential features of the civet were simply some fried onions and the use of breadcrumbs to bind the sauce of whatever dish was being made. Etymologists would say that if one were to go even further back one would find that a civet was simply a dish containing *cives*, i.e. onions or spring onions (the word *cives* varied in meaning in medieval times).

By the 17th century most of the aforementioned civets had disappeared and the *civet de lièvre* was by far the most important civet. In modern times the name of the dish does not evoke *cives* or thickening with breadcrumbs but simply a dish of blackish colour, bound with blood and usually made with game. Another interesting change is in the status of the dish; it belonged originally to 'grande cuisine' but is now thought of rather as a rustic dish.

HY

CLAFOUTIS a speciality associated with the Limousin region of C. France. In its original form it is a CUSTARD or FLAN with numerous cherries (traditionally, the first red ones of the summer) embedded in it, the whole being baked in a large earthenware dish and served either hot or cold.

There have been debates about the type of cherry to be used and whether or not the fruits should be left with their stones in, as traditionalists recommend. Modern recipes often call for lining the dish with pastry, so

that the end result looks more like a cherry tart than a true clafoutis.

In the course of this century the clafoutis has gone from being a local preparation to national status as a popular dessert, and this has exposed it to experimental variations by innovative chefs. Although other fruits which are related to cherries, such as small plums and greengages, can legitimately be used in a clafoutis, the use of mangoes, for example, may be thought to be straying too far from the original.

CLAM a general name variously applied to a few, some, or many (but never all) edible BIVALVES. Clam is a shortened form of clamshell.

Strictly, the name should refer only to those bivalves which can close their hinged shells completely, since it is derived from the verb clam, meaning shut. On this basis, almost all bivalves would qualify as clams; although, paradoxically, the SOFT-SHELLED CLAM and the RAZOR CLAM would not, since their shells always gape open slightly. In practice, however, those bivalves which are very well known and have their own names, for example the OYSTER and the MUSSEL, are rarely referred to as clams. And the name is used so much more in N. America than in Britain that some British people have the impression that clams are an American phenomenon. In fact, the clams which are eaten with such gusto in N. America exist also on the European side of the Atlantic; but they are rarely consumed in Britain or other countries to the north of France, although a start has been made in cultivating some species on the south coast of England and it is reasonable to suppose that the American pattern of consumption will eventually be replicated in NW Europe. Meanwhile it is of interest that the French reserve their word 'clam' for the species called QUAHOG in N. America.

The American interest in clams, especially the above-mentioned quahog (or littleneck or hardshell clam), the SOFT-SHELLED CLAM, and the SURF CLAM, no doubt derives from the experience of early settlers in adopting some of the eating habits of the American Indians, who had not failed to take advantage of the rich harvest on their shores. See also CLAMBAKE and CHOWDER.

For important clams of the Pacific coast of N. America see WASHINGTON CLAMS; PISMO CLAM.

In Australasia the name 'clam' is not in common use, although many bivalves which could well be called clams (see e.g. TOHEROA; TUATUA; PIPI) are prized. In SE Asia the name occurs in a somewhat haphazard fashion wherever English-language terms are in use, but most notably for the GIANT CLAM.

Particulars are given under HAMAGURI of the species most favoured in Japan and a few others.

European bivalves which might well be called clams are described under CARPET-SHELL, VENUS SHELLS, and VERNI. Some of these are found in other parts of the world too.

Minor uses of the name 'clam' include 'sand clams', for some of the very numerous clams which live in the sand. It is not a current term in English-speaking countries, except for some supposedly common names which are used only by conchologists, but has been applied to some SE Asian clams, as mentioned under VENUS SHELLS.

CLAMBAKE an American institution which can be approached in various ways: as a matter for anthropological or sociological study (see the essay by Kathy Neustadt in Humphrey and Humphrey 1988); or as a rite whose differing details in the various states where it happens should be ritually compared; or in a sit-back-and-let's-just-enjoy-it mode. The last is chosen here. The enjoyable prose which constitutes the rest of this article is from the great Mrs Lincoln (1891).

An impromptu clam bake may be had at any time at low tide along the coast where clams are found. If you wish to have genuine fun, and to know what an appetite one can have for the bivalves, make up a pleasant party and dig for the clams yourselves. A short thick dress, a shade hat, rubber boots,—or, better still, no boots at all, if you can bring your mind to the comfort of bare feet,—a small garden trowel, a fork, and a basket, and you are ready. Let those who are not digging gather a large pile of driftwood and seaweed, always to be found along the shore. Select a dozen or more large stones, and of them make a level floor; pile the driftwood upon them, and make a good brisk fire to heat the stones thoroughly. When hot enough to crackle as you sprinkle water upon them, brush off the embers, letting them fall between the stones. Put a thin layer of seaweed on the hot stones, to keep the lower clams from burning. Rinse the clams in salt water by plunging the basket which contains them in the briny pools near by. Pile them over the hot stones, heaping them high in the centre. Cover with a thick layer of seaweed, and a piece of old canvas, blanket, carpet, or dry leaves, to keep in the steam. The time for baking will depend on the size and quantity of the clams. Peep in occasionally at those around the edge. When the shells are open, the clams are done. They are delicious eaten from the shell, with no other sauce than their own briny sweetness. Melted butter, pepper, and vinegar should be ready for those who wish them; then all may 'fall to'. Fingers must be used. A Rhode Islander would laugh at any one trying to use a knife and fork. Pull off the thin skin, take them by the black end, dip them in the prepared butter, and bite off close to the end. If you swallow them whole, they will not hurt you. At a genuine Rhode Island clam bake, blue-fish, lobsters, crabs, sweet

potatoes, and ears of sweet corn in the gauzy husks are baked with the clams. The clam steam gives them a delicious flavour. Brown bread is served with the clams, and watermelon for dessert completes the feast.

CLAPSHOT a Scottish potato and turnip dish which is a recommended accompaniment for HAGGIS. The traditional recipe, according to Marian McNeill (1929), calls for potatoes and turnip to be cooked separately then mashed together with the addition of butter and chives.

CLARIFICATION is the process of clearing a liquid of suspended particles. True, butter is not thought of as a liquid, and butter is clarified (see BUTTER and GHEE), as are other fats; but otherwise the definition holds.

In the kitchen, things which may need clarification are STOCK, clear SOUP, ASPIC, JELLY, etc. The agents of clarification are various. Filtration is simplest but will not catch the smallest particles. A change in temperature may suffice, if followed by drawing off the liquid from above or from below. Or 'hunter-catchers' may be let loose in pursuit of the particles, as when egg white and eggshell are employed or a few slices of potato are heated in used cooking oil. Even more drastic are the 'hunter-killers', in the shape of proteolytic or pectolytic enzymes which do not merely trap the offending material but destroy it.

CLARY also known as clary sage, *Salvia sclarea*, is a herb of S. and C. Europe whose aromatic leaves were more used in the past than now. The German name, *Muskateller-salbei*, indicates their past use to give a flavour to Muscatel wine (also to vermouths and some liqueurs). Clary is said to have been introduced to England in the 16th century. Evelyn (1699) commented: 'when tender not to be rejected, and in *Omlets*, made up with *Cream*, fried in sweet *Butter*, and eaten with *Sugar*, Juice of *Orange*, or *Limon*.' However, culinary use is now rare.

CLASSICAL GREECE Our knowledge of ancient Greek cuisine is tantalizingly incomplete, although (as explained by Dalby, 1996) there is a larger corpus of evidence than has been generally realized. This reflects the fact the subjects other than food have tended to preoccupy classical scholars.

HISTORICAL SURVEY

In the civilization depicted in the Homeric epics, the *Iliad* and *Odyssey* (8th century BC),

there is little evidence of any elaborate methods of cookery. Meals as described in these poems consisted of bread with unspecified relishes, spit-roasted meat, and red wine; but there are references also to fish, cheese, honey, and orchard fruit (apples, pears, figs, pomegranates). There is no sign of any long-distance trade in foodstuffs, whether luxuries or necessities. Named wines and aged wines were appreciated.

But there is room for endless debate on how closely the 'Homeric' world resembled any real time and place.

By the 5th and 4th centuries BC a highly developed cuisine was practised in many Greek towns. Greeks of the mainland knew that this had come about under overseas influence. Some recipes were said to be Lydian (from the rich and civilized kingdom in W. Asia Minor) or Ionian (from the Greek settlements in and near Lydia). Others had come from the prosperous Greek colonies in Sicily; Sicilian cooks were famous. There was widespread trade in wine, oil, and luxury foodstuffs and an awareness that quality could be linked with geographical origin. Athens, which had during the 5th century rapidly become a large city, depended on imports even for staple foods. Growers of fruit and vegetables developed varieties that varied in quality, time of ripening, and soil and water requirements.

After Alexander's conquests a material civilization with many Greek features, now known as 'Hellenistic', spread through the E. Mediterranean and Near East. The local food habits of towns in Greece were attracting antiquarian interest, but the wealthy demonstrated their wealth by lavish entertaining in a new style influenced by Macedonian, Persian, and other cuisines and customs. No sudden change occurred when most of the region became part of the Roman Empire. The cookery of Rome (see CLASSICAL ROME) itself came under strong Hellenistic influence. Meanwhile trade within the Mediterranean area continued to grow; crop varieties were exchanged and tested in new environments; new fruits (peaches, cherries, lemons) were introduced from the East; spices began to be imported from Persia, India, and beyond.

STAPLE FOODS

The staple foods of Greeks when leading a settled life were WHEAT and BARLEY. At home these were baked into loaves in clay ovens or under ashes; travellers and soldiers probably more often boiled them as gruel or porridge. Poor people supplemented this diet with little more than fruit, mushrooms, and vegetables gathered from the wild. Many could afford to add olive oil and flavourings such as cheese, onion, garlic, and salt fish (e.g. anchovy, goby). On the tables of the wealthy, the variety of fish and meat dishes and the many savoury and sweet confections were still typically preceded by wheat and barley loaves.

THE MENU

An elaborate dinner in 4th-century BC Athens began with the serving of loaves in baskets.

A relatively light first course consisted of a variety of appetizing relishes, *paropsides*, to eat with the bread; quantities served were small. A single large platter might be offered in turn to each guest, containing a selection of perhaps half a dozen of the following: oysters, SEA-URCHINS, shrimps fried in honey, *aphye* 'small fry', fried or stewed sliced squid, pieces of *galeos* (smooth hound, see DOGFISH) baked or boiled and served with MULBERRY sauce, pieces of STURGEON, pieces of EEL, slices of salt TUNA; little FIGPECKERS in sweet pastry, *thria* (minced salt fish or other ingredients baked in a pickled fig leaf), cheese; *bolboi* (grape hyacinth BULBS) baked in ashes and served with a cheese and SILPHIUM sauce; asparagus, cauliflower, cabbage, lettuce, and other vegetables, olives of different types, garlic. Sliced egg is mentioned as a garnish. At a very large gathering whole fish dishes might also be served as entrées. At more everyday dinners *etnos* (pea or bean soup), *phake* (lentil soup), or *bolbophake* (bulb-and-lentil soup) took the place of daintier delicacies here.

The first course might be divided from the second by the serving of some small CAKES. Some descriptions, however, imply that the two courses were scarcely distinct. The baskets of BREAD would be replenished to accompany the main dishes next described.

The main course consisted of a selection of more generous fish, poultry, and meat dishes. Most frequently listed are eel, conger eel, tuna, sea bass, skate, ray, red mullet, grey mullet, *glaukos* (an unidentified fish), hake, sole, sea perch; chicken, duck, goose; beef, pork, WILD BOAR, mutton, goat, HARE (the only game commonly available in Athens). Meat was spit roasted or grilled, not oven roasted. Whole animals required to be slaughtered and prepared by a professional *mageiros* ('butcher-cook') with appropriate religious ritual: if this became too expensive the main course might be limited to fish. Meat could, however, be included more cheaply in the form of ham, tripe (served in silphium sauce), pigs' trotters (see FEET), UDDER, womb, intestines, liver, snout, ears, and cheeks, lamb's and kid's HEAD and feet, ox tongue, intestines, and feet, pork and beef sausages, and blood puddings; generally, see OFFAL, BLOOD SAUSAGES, etc.

Between main course and dessert wine was first served. It continued to circulate

during dessert and the conversation and entertainment that followed. It was normally drunk much diluted with water. Wines of Chios, Lesbos, Thasos, and the coast of Macedonia had lasting popularity.

Dessert, called *deuterai trapezai* (literally, 'second tables'), consisted of cakes and sweetmeats (mostly very sweet, with an emphasis on HONEY and SESAME), cheese (served with honey), eggs (presumably hard boiled), CHICKPEAS, nuts such as walnuts and almonds, fresh fruit such as quinces, pears, grapes, and figs, and dried fruit, especially figs and raisins.

The invariable constituent of the first two courses was bread, and of the third, wine.

Meals in Ionia and the Aegean islands were apparently not very different from those in Athens. Elsewhere in Greece barley was commoner than wheat, which Athens could afford to import from the Black Sea. In S. Greece and Crete our limited information suggests that more game was available, that meat broth and cheese (both served early in the meal) were important, and that fish was not much eaten.

The Hellenistic menu differed from the classical Athenian in several ways. New kinds of bread became popular, some apparently native to Cappadocia and Syria. Oven-roasting of meat was introduced from the East, allowing the development of large and elaborate stuffed meat dishes, which afterwards became typical of Roman cuisine. Following Macedonian preference, wine was served earlier in the meal and with less admixture of water. Fresh fruit and salad vegetables might be offered among the hors d'œuvres. Meat might appear in the first course and in the dessert (as roast THRUSHES, for example).

CHOICE OF COOKING METHODS AND OF FLAVOURINGS

Much cooking was probably done out of doors, and took the form of grilling, roasting, frying, or boiling over a fire, or baking in hot ashes; the clay oven was perhaps reserved for bread. Cooks depicted in Athenian comedy of the 4th century BC happily list the methods they preferred for preparing various dishes (and, in particular, various kinds of fish). Although all too brief for the non-initiate, these laconic instructions are consistent enough with one another to carry some conviction: there clearly was a body of knowledge that professionals and household cooks learnt and transmitted by word of mouth and by example. At least one cookery book, by Mithaecus, had been written (there were others later) but only a few scraps survive. Also in the 4th century Archestratus of Syracuse had written a humorous gastronomic poem, evidence that the expertise of cooks could be acquired by

interested laymen and that travel and trade was encouraging the appreciation of local produce and regional cuisine.

Comedy cooks sometimes list the range of ingredients they would expect to have at hand. These lists include thyme, oregano, fennel, dill, sage, rue, parsley, fig leaf, coriander leaf, and other herbs; raisins, olives, capers; onions, garlic, and leek; cumin and sesame seed; almonds; olive oil, vinegar, grape juice; eggs; pickled fish, salt. This list contains no eastern spices (pepper was just beginning to be known) and indeed nothing not found close to Athens. In classical Athenian cuisine the only commonly used ingredients that had to come from far away were *silphion* (dried silphium sap) and *kaulos* (silphium stem) from Cyrenaica; *horaion* and other forms of salted tuna, of which Byzantium was a major exporter; *garos* (see GARUM) manufactured at several Black Sea ports; and sumach. The trade in these products, like that in fish generally, in wine, and in wheat, was in Greek hands.

WHEN AND HOW TO EAT

Greeks commonly ate two meals a day, a lighter *ariston* at the end of the morning and a heavier *deipnon* in the early evening; among the leisured classes the latter might lead into a *potos* or *symposion* (a drinking-party, often with things to eat as well) which could go on all night.

In some areas of S. Greece the typical meal in classical times appears to have been a communal one, served in a public hall. In 'Homeric' houses, large or small, meals took place in the one main room, *megaron*; diners sat on chairs and stools. In Athens and other cities, by the 4th century, houses of the middle and upper classes had more rooms than this, and ordinary meals would take place in a less public location. One room, *andron*, was however reserved for men's entertaining and was furnished with couches on which guests reclined (one or two per couch), a fashion imported from eastern civilizations. At the beginning of the meal a small table, freshly scrubbed, was placed in front of each diner or of each couch. Food from the serving dishes might be taken directly onto the table, or onto bread, and eaten with the fingers; for soups and stews a bowl might be supplied. Bread served for spoons. When dessert was about to be brought the tables were changed.

THE SOCIAL CONTEXT OF FOOD

In classical Athens, and in much of the rest of Greece in the 5th and 4th centuries BC, women who were present at men's dinners and symposia were in the categories of *hetairai* ('girl friends' and prostitutes) and hired entertainers. Celebrations and family parties might be held at home or might take place at a temple, either out of doors or in purpose-built dining rooms. When not entertaining, a man might be served with food by his wife or household women. Slaves and children of both sexes ate with the women. In all these cases it was the rule that free men ate apart from the rest of the household, whether at a different time, in a different place, or from different dishes.

Throughout the ancient period food was a medium of patronage and dependence. In the more public circumstances of Homeric households women, children, servants, beggars, and animals are described as present at the fringes of men's meals, sometimes favoured with gifts of food and drink; in an age that knew nothing of money, entertainment was a good way to request and repay services. Later, the dependants (*episitioi*, *parasitoi*) of powerful Athenians, the serf caste (*helotai*) of Sparta, and the courtiers (*kolakes*, flatterers) of monarchs were fed by their masters, and similarly paid for their food with more or less tangible services. Cities offered dinner in the *prytaneion*, a public building containing dining rooms, as a welcome to ambassadors and as a reward to benefactors. Democracies provided food, or a subsistence allowance, in return for jury service and attendance at public functions. Food or the means to buy it was also, naturally, provided in return for military service, at least where the fruits of victory were to go to the state: on freebooting expeditions, from which the participants benefited, they had to feed themselves.

In classical Athens professional (male) COOKS, whose work was linked to religious observances, possessed relatively high status. They hired out the services of themselves and their slaves; in each household help would be available to them from those who did the everyday cooking.

Literature depicts men, not women, preparing meat. Women, however, typically carried out most other culinary tasks, particularly grinding flour and baking bread. At men's entertainments service was provided by the host's male slaves or by servants hired for the occasion. His household women would not be seen. Entertainment during a *symposion* might be got up by the participants (in the form of songs, riddles, and competitive games) or arranged by the host, who could hire slave acrobats and musicians.   AD

READING: Dalby (1996); Athenaeus (1927–41); Vickery (1936); Brothwell and Brothwell (1969); Lissarrague (1987); Berthiaume (1982).

CLASSICAL ROME Roman gastronomy, or gluttony, impresses all who read the literature of the great Mediterranean empire of the past. Feasting was a central feature of its society. The cuisine of Rome, much influenced by that of CLASSICAL GREECE and the Near East, is the direct ancestor of the national cuisines of most of W. Europe. It can be reconstructed through descriptions in Latin literature, through ancient scientific and technical writings—including the recipe book known as *Apicius*—and through archaeology. Notable here are the finds at Pompeii, the city buried in AD 79 by the disastrous eruption of Mount Vesuvius.

HISTORICAL OUTLINE
Founded, it was said, by Romulus and Remus in 753 BC, on the banks of the Tiber in C. Italy, Rome was a country town whose power grew and grew until it was the centre of what may fairly be called a world empire. In the 3rd and 2nd centuries BC Rome fought and defeated the Carthaginians of N. Africa, opening the way to domination of the whole W. Mediterranean. In the 2nd and 1st centuries BC successive victories in Greece and the East ensured that a single political entity was governing the entire Mediterranean and its hinterland by the time of Christ—the time at which the first two emperors, Augustus (ruled 27 BC–AD 14) and Tiberius (14–37), were establishing their power. Later conquests included Britain (from AD 43) and Dacia (modern Romania, AD 106). Crises in the 3rd and 4th centuries led to the division of the Empire into two parts, which had quite different fates. In the East, the Byzantine Empire (see BYZANTINE COOKERY) was the direct continuation of the Roman. The Western Empire crumbled, disappearing in AD 476, but the 'barbarian' kingdoms that succeeded it inherited Roman dietary ideas and developed a way of life which had many Roman features.

Even before the eastern conquests, Rome had become rich enough to spend enthusiastically on imported luxury foods and wines, and the fashion for lavish banquets grew. The price of slave cooks rose steeply. Moralists inveighed against these developments, but in vain. Meanwhile, other changes affected the Roman diet. Successively, new territories were providing the opportunity for experimentation in agriculture and food production. Romanization in the provinces encouraged the demand that what was available in the capital should also be available more widely. The effect on Britain, for example, was that vines, peaches, walnuts, celery, coriander, and carrots were first planted here in Roman times, and wine, olive oil, olives, figs, lentils, chickpeas, rice were among commodities now first imported.

Many special features of Roman administrative and economic life have left their marks on the food and cuisine of the vast region that was once the Empire. Great frontier armies, whose zones of recruitment ensured movement and mixture of populations, required reliable, standardized supplies on well-built roads. Inscriptions show that periodic markets existed (every eight days in Italian towns; twice a month in N. Africa; monthly or three times a month in Asia Minor) encouraging local and regional trade. Annual fairs, often religious in spirit, attracted wide interest; tax concessions, and special local coin issues, are evidence of the importance of these fairs in fostering travel and trade.

THE LITERATURE OF FOOD
For modern readers Roman prose literature begins, about 175 BC, with the *Farming Manual* of the statesman Cato, which includes recipes for cakes, for preserves, and for flavoured wines suitable for farmhouse production. Later the personal, sometimes satirical poetry of the Augustan period is full of information on food and dining among the élite. The largest surviving fragment of the *Satyricon* by Petronius (probably Nero's courtier, died AD 66) is the famous 'Dinner of Trimalchio', a vigorous satire on the luxurious lifestyle of the newly rich. The series of biographies of emperors by the imperial archivist Suetonius (*The Twelve Caesars*, written about 115) opens a window into palace lifestyles, in which feasts might indeed turn into Roman orgies. Lives of poorer people are depicted in the fictional *Metamorphoses* (*The Golden Ass*) of Apuleius (born 125), and in some saints' lives. The encyclopedic work by PLINY (died 79 AD), *Natural History*, devotes books 12–19 to a survey of plants and their products, with close attention to fruits, vegetables, and wines, and is in Latin. Meanwhile medical, scientific, and scholarly texts were usually written in Greek, the second language of the Empire: examples are a dietary manual, *On the Properties of Foods*, by the famous physician GALEN (129–99), and the *Deipnosophists* of ATHENAEUS (c. AD 200), a miscellany of literary research on food, wine, and entertainment. The only recipe book that survives from the ancient world is, however, in Latin. This is APICIUS, compiled perhaps in the 4th century AD.

It was a commonplace of Roman food writing to despise complicated dishes designed for show rather than for taste. Yet, in practice, Rome bought the luxury foods and spices of the whole Mediterranean and beyond: the pepper of S. India and even the cloves and ginger of the Spice Islands made their way to Rome. The recipes of *Apicius* are so lavish in spices that the flavour of the main ingredients must often have been swamped. Whatever poets said, rich households must have spent much money and slave labour on the finding of rare ingredients and the elaboration of showpiece dishes. The parrot WRASSE and the DORMOUSE fetched high prices not because of their flavour but because of the way they looked on the table. PEACOCKS, and peahen's eggs, were likewise in demand for their rarity more than their quality. Fashion ruled.

It was also a commonplace to boast of the freshness and simplicity of the farm produce that one was offering to one's guests. The moral of these literary menus was that the host was at heart an old-fashioned Roman who, like Cato, kept a close eye on his farm and his farm manager. Cato's own fulsome praise for CABBAGE goes together with stories later told of some emperors' food preferences. Augustus 'preferred the food of the common people, especially the coarser sort of bread, little fish, new hand-pressed cheese, and green figs from a twice-bearing tree' (Suetonius).

STAPLE FOODS AND MAJOR FLAVOURINGS

Rome's status as an overgrown city-state is signalled by one of the special privileges enjoyed by inhabitants of the city: the free BREAD ration. Interruptions in this led to riots: its continuity was eventually assured by Rome's annexation of Egypt at the suicide of Cleopatra in 30 BC. Thereafter, huge grain ships left Alexandria regularly through the sailing season, bringing wheat to Ostia at the mouth of the Tiber. It was on such a ship that St Paul reached Italy after having been shipwrecked on Malta. Roman bakers baked leavened bread, both white and wholemeal. Small-scale baking required a dome-shaped baking-crock, *testum clibanus*: fragments of these are often found by archaeologists. A commercial bakery, complete with fossilized loaves, has been excavated at Pompeii.

The traditional staple food of early Italy had been not wheat bread but *puls*, emmer (see WHEAT) PORRIDGE. To early writers this was so well known that no recipes were needed, so none survive. The staple diet of the Roman provinces varied considerably, depending on climate and local custom. Although BARLEY had been considered a respectable, even a desirable, food in parts of Greece and Italy, Roman soldiers came to look on barley as 'punishment rations'. This served to increase the demand for wheat wherever Roman armies were stationed. In Britain and Gaul, however, malted barley was indeed required for the manufacture of beer, a local speciality for which there was a steady demand in legionary camps.

Always in use in the Roman kitchen were OLIVE OIL, FISH SAUCE, and wine. All three were manufactured and distributed on a large scale. Fish sauce was the major source of dietary salt: scarcely any *Apicius* recipes call for pure salt. Must and wine concentrated by boiling were also much used in flavouring, as were honey and dates. Many recipes begin with the instruction 'Pound pepper and lovage', a reminder that both local LOVAGE and exotic PEPPER and aromatics were appreciated. Other commonly used flavourings were ONION, MUSTARD, DILL, FENNEL, RUE, SAVORY, THYME, MINT, PINE NUTS, CARAWAY, CUMIN, GINGER, and ASAFOETIDA, the C. Asian substitute for the SILPHIUM (*laserpicium*) that had been so much appreciated by the Greeks.

Pliny and Galen—both connoisseurs, to judge from their writings—provide full information on the wines that Romans drank with their meals. Italy had many fine wines to boast of. Falernian wine, from hillsides in N. Campania, was one which kept its reputation throughout the Empire. Italian vintages were known by the name of one of the consuls elected for the year: the Opimian vintage, of 121 BC, was legendary, its wines still valued (though not truly drinkable) 200 years later. It was in Roman times that the wine-growing regions of Spain, Gaul (France), and Germany came to real economic importance. Long-distance transport of wines was less risky if they were 'cooked' and sweetened with honey: it was in this form that Greek wines were enjoyed in Rome.

FOOD IN ROMAN SOCIETY

Romans tended to eat little during the first part of the day: a breakfast, *ientaculum*, was a snack that many did not trouble to take at all, and only the greedy wanted a big lunch, *prandium*. There was no better preparation for a big evening meal, *cena*, the one big meal of the day, than a couple of hours at the baths. These were fashionable meeting places, ideal locations for informal business discussions. One could easily spend a whole evening at the baths, for food and wine were available: as Jérôme Carcopino said rather censoriously in *Daily Life in Ancient Rome* (1940), 'many congregated there to overeat and drink and indulge other disreputable tastes'.

City dwellers in imperial Rome, many of whom lived in tenement flats, had little opportunity to cook anything but the simplest of food for themselves unless they wished to risk setting fire to the whole building: these *insulae* did sometimes burn down because an occupant had tried to cook without safety precautions. Street food was, however, always available to the city dweller. Cakes and sweets, mulled wine, hot sausages, and porridge were on sale from street stalls and at cookshops. 'In the tavern all are equally free,' wrote Juvenal (born 67 AD) with an undertone of disapproval: 'all drink from a common cup, the couch is barred to no man, the table is no closer to one than it is to another.' The philosopher Seneca (died 65 AD) gives us the sounds of the busy street just outside his apartment window: 'pancake-sellers and a sausage-vendor and a confectioner and all the proprietors of cookshops, selling their wares with miscellaneous shouts, each in his distinctive accent.'

For the peasant population of the ancient countryside, cooking was a shared task, but more often performed by the wife. Large households had kitchens staffed with slaves, the skilled cook himself often being an expensive and carefully chosen acquisition.

Typical larger Roman houses had a special dining room, the *triclinium*. Three couches arranged in a U, each large enough for three diners, surrounded a central table. A house with a big enough garden might well have a garden dining area, too, shaded by vines and creepers, with three stone couches sloping gently upwards to the middle—to be made comfortable with cushions and pillows. The open side of the square was for waiters to come and go.

Servants took off guests' sandals as they reclined, and brought water to wash their hands. A sequence of dishes began with the *gustatio*, appetizers, followed by a sweet aperitif, *mulsum* or *conditum*. The appetizers might be more varied and more costly than the main course, though not so bulky. We know of a religious dinner, attended by Julius Caesar, at which sixteen appetizers awaited the priestly celebrants. They ranged from SEA-URCHIN and CLAMS to slices of VENISON and WILD BOAR.

The main courses were accompanied by bread and wine. Waiters must have been forever coming and going, bringing new courses, clearing away, supplying perfumed water for finger-rinsing: for diners ate with their hands, with the occasional help of a knife. Music and dance, performed by slaves, might well accompany the drinking, which tended to continue long after the meal itself was over.

A napkin, which lay in front of the diners as they reclined, might serve as a knapsack to take home the little gifts of food or wine with which a host would regale his friends as they departed. Similar gifts were made to dependants not lucky enough to be invited to a real dinner. Martial (1st century AD) wrote a collection of short poems intended to accompany such gifts. They are the most obvious sign that hospitality helped to articulate the patron/client relations that permeated Roman society. Latin poems often seem to beg for dinner invitations— and poets were only the most vocal among the crowd of hangers-on of the rich and powerful. The Greek satirist Lucian (2nd century AD) wrote a convincing sketch of daily life in a rich Roman household, addressed to a friend who had been offered a post as private tutor: placed at the lowest table, Lucian warned, he would be sneered at by slaves and would taste little of the fine cuisine except the mallow leaves which garnished the serving dishes.

Upper-class Romans, like Etruscans but unlike Greeks, did not segregate the sexes at meals. Roman women, it was said, once sat demurely at the foot of their husbands' dining couches: but by imperial times they too reclined. It was also said that in the old days women did not drink wine, and that the kiss a Roman husband gave his wife when returning home was a way of assuring himself that this rule had been kept.   AD

READING: J. André (1981); White (1970); Gowers (1993); Andrew Dalby and Sally Grainger (1996).

CLEAVERS *Galium aparine*, a herb also known as goosegrass, which has a wide distribution in Europe, Asia to Siberia, and N. and S. America. Its common names are justified by the way in which the narrow pointed leaves stick or 'cleave' to persons or animals, and the practice of feeding it to goslings and geese.

The plant was formerly used as an ingredient in soups which would otherwise have been too greasy.

Parkinson (1629) had remarked that 'Clevers . . . is of subtill parts: it is familiarly taken in broth to keepe them lean and lanke, that are apt to grow fat.' The same author noted that 'the herb serveth well the Country people in stead of a strainer, to cleare their milke from strawes, haires, or any other thing that falleth into it.' The Greek author Dioscorides had recorded this practice in classical times and such sieves were still in use in Sweden in the 20th century.

Of the scores of supposed 'coffee substitutes', the seeds of cleavers are among the least implausible. The plant is related to the coffee plant, and its roasted seeds do have a similar aroma.

Cleavers is also called bedstraw, a name which it shares with its close relation *G. verum*. This plant, often called lady's bedstraw, is native to temperate Europe but has become naturalized in N. America. It is not normally eaten, but its flowers contain substances which can curdle milk and they have sometimes been used instead of RENNET in cheese-making. The French name *caille-lait* means 'curdle-milk'.

G. odoratum is WOODRUFF.

CLIMATE a factor which varies considerably (from Greenland's icy mountains to India's coral strands, as the hymn puts it), and which largely determines what foods can be grown where.

A change in climate may have consequences so severe as to destroy entire communities. A classic example is the Viking colony in Greenland, set up in the 11th century when the average temperature there was high enough for the growing of BARLEY and the grazing of CATTLE. In the 1370s the temperature fell steeply and the colony, unable to adapt to the changed conditions, collapsed. The original inhabitants, the Inuit, who lived by hunting and fishing, were much less affected by the cooling climate and have continued to live in Greenland.

The decline of the early Maya civilization in the Yucatan peninsula of Mexico can also be attributed to climate change. In this case the weather became drier, a gradual shift which had been going on since 1600 BC. By 150 BC the land could no longer feed the people, who were obliged to abandon their cities and migrate inland. Lack of rain also caused the collapse of the Bronze Age Canaanite civilization in Palestine around 2000 BC.

It should be realized that climate change was not the only factor in these cases. The Viking colonists had allowed cattle to overgraze their pastures, and their arable land was badly affected by soil erosion. The Maya had become city dwellers, with more and more people making ever greater demands on a limited area of agricultural land. The Canaanites seem to have blamed the wrath of the gods for their troubles, and failed to adapt their agriculture to the drier conditions.

There is also a vicious circle at work. Lower rainfall reduces the amount of vegetation covering the ground, which reduces the amount of moisture that evaporates into the air. This depresses the formation of clouds, so that rainfall decreases further.

All these failures occurred because people failed to adapt to changing conditions. However, failure is not inevitable. In Palestine around the 2nd century AD, by now even drier than when the Canaanites had abandoned it, the Nabateans successfully irrigated crops by a complex system of rainwater channels and underground reservoirs. The Ethiopians adapted to changes in their climate (which was becoming drier) by growing TEF, a drought-resistant cereal.

Less dramatic examples concern crops grown at the limit of their climatic range. In the early Middle Ages there were vineyards in S. England and wine was made. The fall in temperature that forced the Vikings out of Greenland also affected Europe. From 1400 it was simply too cold for GRAPES to ripen. Europe continued to get colder; at the low point, in the 17th century, the Thames often froze so hard in winter that fairs were held on the ice. During the 19th century the climate slowly became milder, and by the middle of the 20th century it was once again warm enough to grow grapes in the south of England. Other crops have also been introduced; for instance, it is now possible to grow the hardier varieties of MAIZE.   RH

CLITOCYBE MUSHROOMS i.e. those of the genus *Clitocybe*, lack genuine, popular English names (though funnel-cap and funnel agaric are cited by some authors), and are not commonly eaten. However, a few of the numerous species, whose particular merits are described by Jordan (1975) and others, deserve mention.

C. flaccida, sometimes referred to as the tawny funnel-cap, has an orange or reddish brown cap, typically about 6 cm (2") across. It is common in the autumn in coniferous woods. The acid taste can be turned to advantage if the fungus is pickled, or made into ketchup, or used in a piquant dressing for roast beef.

C. geotropa is often called *tête de moine* (monk's head) in France, and likewise *Mönchskopf* in Germany, since its buff cap, which may measure up to 20 cm (8") across, recalls a 'shaven crown'. It appears in the autumn, often forming circles or lines, in clearings or grassy parts of woods, and makes good eating if picked young.

C. infundibuliformis is funnel-shaped, as the specific name indicates, and has a cap of variable colour: buff, ochre, brown, or reddish. A common species, whose season is summer and autumn. The aroma recalls anise and lavender.

C. odora, the anise clitocybe (similarly, *clitocybe anise* in France and *seta anisada* in Spain), has a more powerful aniseed smell, and is too strong to use by itself, but makes a good condiment, chopped or dried and ground, for addition to stews. Widely distributed in Europe and N. America, and known in Japan.

CLOOTIE DUMPLING a Scottish speciality which is a sweet PUDDING steamed in a 'cloot' (cloth). A whole clootie dumpling—the best known of these sweet dumplings but not the only one—is of a round, flattened, ball-like shape, weighing anything from 115 to 900 g (4 oz to 2 lb), but the product is often sold in cut slices. Standard ingredients are flour, breadcrumbs, suet, dried fruit, eggs, treacle, spices, sugar, and milk, with a raising agent and often with some apple or carrot.

The clootie dumpling can be regarded as the sweet version of HAGGIS, the savoury pudding boiled in a sheep or pig's stomach bag. Using a cloth or linen cloth instead, the sweet pudding mixture was made originally as the Scottish alternative to a celebration fruit cake for holidays, birthdays, and during winter solstice celebrations, known in Scotland as the Daft Days.

Easily made in the common domestic setting where there was no oven and the cooking was done solely over a fire in a large pot, these special-occasion dumplings usually contained a selection of 'surprises':

a ring signifying marriage; a coin—wealth; a button—bachelordom; a thimble—spinsterhood; a wishbone—the heart's desire; a horseshoe—good luck. Compared with rich celebration fruit cakes, or an English CHRISTMAS PUDDING, the dumpling mixture is much plainer. Clootie dumplings are sometimes served with cream. When cold they are often fried with bacon and eggs for breakfast. CB

CLOUDBERRY *Rubus chamaemorus*, one of the most delicious of all berries and one of the most costly, since it is confined to the northern regions of Europe and N. America and can be gathered in limited quantities only. In N. Scandinavia, where Finland, Sweden, and Norway meet, and the cloudberry thrives, the inhabitants of these peace-loving countries have been known to engage in 'cloudberry wars'; and the Swedish Ministry for Foreign Affairs maintains, or used to have, a special section for cloudberry diplomacy. In northern N. America, where the fruit may also be called the baked-apple berry or just 'bakeapple', it is not so highly esteemed, but is nonetheless a prized item. The berries are red when nearly ripe, and golden with a tinge of orange when ripe, and soft and juicy. They keep very well because of their high content of benzoic acid.

Bears are partial to cloudberries. News that cloudberries are plentiful in a given region is often followed by news that bears have been sighted there. But the reports of bears being sighted may be fabricated by local people to discourage others from coming to pick the berries.

Two varieties are recognized in Norway; *molte* and *bekkemolte* (brook cloudberry) which is a little bigger and with a stronger colour.

Most people encounter cloudberries in the form of preserves of one kind or another. Cloudberry jam is outstanding, and a fine accompaniment to ice cream or filling for pancakes. Cloudberries freeze successfully and can be kept thus for years.

CLOVE the dried, unopened flower bud of an evergreen tree, *Syzygium aromaticum*, which belongs to the myrtle family and is native to the Moluccas (in E. Indonesia). Cloves are an important culinary spice, mainly cultivated in Zanzibar (Tanzania), the Malagasy Republic, and Indonesia. Indonesians use over 30,000 tonnes a year in the manufacture of their 'kretek' cigarettes, the largest single use of cloves.

The English name is short for CLOVE GILLIFLOWERS, from the French *clou de girofle*: literally, 'nail of clove', referring to the shape of the dried bud. The similarity to a nail is also noted in the Spanish,

Portuguese, Italian, and Persian names. In Arabic individual cloves are called *masamir qaranful*, 'nails of clove', just as in French.

Cloves were in use in China as early as the 3rd century BC, and have also been used in India since ancient times. They spread from Egypt throughout the Mediterranean region and then further north in Europe between the 2nd and 8th centuries AD.

Marco Polo, in the 13th century, mentioned seeing clove plantations in the E. Indies. The Portuguese, after taking possession of the Moluccas in 1514, controlled the clove trade for a century. The Dutch wrested the islands and the monopoly from them early in the 17th century, and used draconian measures to restrict the growing of cloves to the single island of Amboina; the penalty for cultivating or selling them elsewhere was death. French efforts to break the monopoly by securing plants and growing them in Mauritius began to succeed towards the end of the 18th century; and subsequently led to the important plantations of Madagascar and Zanzibar.

Varieties of clove are defined by their place of origin. In the trade, Penang cloves are considered best, those of Zanzibar second, and Madagascar cloves third.

Some authorities do not accept the separation of the genus *Syzygium* from *Eugenia*. Be that as it may, the clove is closely related to the ROSE-APPLE, JAMBOLAN, and PITANGA. The tree is small and evergreen, and may live for a century or more. It flowers twice in the year, and it is the fully grown but still closed buds which are harvested to be dried and marketed. The four petals, with the stamens inside, form the quadrangular nail-like head of the clove.

Eugenol, which is also present in CINNAMON, is the substance which gives cloves their distinctive aroma.

There are two picking seasons in the year. The clusters of cloves have to be picked by hand, at just the right moment, when most of them will have developed a pink flush. Clove-picking, except for the young, small trees, or the lowest branches of big ones, is difficult. After picking, the stems are removed and the cloves carefully dried, when they assume their familiar brown colour. They keep well if stored in dry conditions, but some of the volatile oil will evaporate if storage is prolonged.

In India and some other Asian countries cloves are much used in connection with BETEL NUT chewing, but also have a role as a conventional spice in cookery. In western countries, they are a common pickling spice, e.g. in soused herring; they are also often stuck into onions and hams, and for various festive foods such as CHRISTMAS PUDDING, or drinks such as mulled wine. However, their main destination in the English

kitchen, according to Elizabeth David (1970), is apple pie, whose taste, in her opinion, they spoil. She thought that the best use of whole cloves was in the 'extraordinary candied walnuts of Turin', black and soft after being cooked and half-crystallized, each with a clove stuck into the stalk end.

The addition of a single clove, or a fragment of one, is recommended in a wide variety of dishes, both sweet and savoury. Stobart (1980) comments that the addition of a clove to beef stock or to a stew gives it a richness whose source will be unidentified, and opines: 'As a flavouring, cloves are best when kept below the level of recognition.' READING: Tidbury (1949).

CLOVE GILLIFLOWERS an ingredient specified in early English recipes, especially of the 17th and early 18th centuries. What are meant are pinks, *Dianthus caryophyllus*, whose flowers were considered to have an attractive aroma like that of cloves. The spelling of 'gilliflowers' was highly erratic; 'jelly-flowers' occurs in Robert May (1685) as a garnish for a salad, and 'gilliflewers' in Hannah Glasse (1747), to make a syrup, and there are numerous other variations.

CLOVER AND MELILOT leguminous plants which have leaves growing in groups of three, go together. Their main use is in feeding animals and providing nectar for bees; but although their importance for human food is thus at one remove it is considerable.

The common clovers, especially *Trifolium repens*, are among the most widely distributed and nutritious forage legumes of the world. The 'sweetclovers', of the genus *Melilotus* are among those favoured by honey bees. They also serve other purposes, for example as flavourings for certain soups, breads, and cheeses. The Swiss green cheese SCHABZIGER is usually flavoured and coloured by several herbs; exactly which is hard to determine, but *M. officinalis* and blue melilot, *Trigonella caerulea*, a species said to have been brought to Switzerland from Asia Minor by returning Crusaders (Montandon, 1980), are often cited.

CLUB FUNGUS a curious growth of which the various species include a few which are edible. A typical club fungus resembles a small white or yellow baseball bat standing on end, and may be as much as 30 cm (1') tall. *Clavariadelpha pistillaris* has a more swollen top than most, and is almost the shape of a light bulb. Either can be cooked in any way suitable for an ordinary mushroom. Neither is especially good.

Although club fungus may be found in groups, each club is separate. It thus differs from the related CORAL FUNGUS.

CLUSTER BEAN *Cyamopsis tetragonoloba*, a leguminous plant known also as guar, whose pods grow in groups looking something like small bunches of bananas. It may be native to the Indian subcontinent, where it has been grown for centuries, mainly as a forage crop or for green manure. The young pods may be cooked in curry-type dishes, or fried. Sometimes the fully developed seeds are eaten as a vegetable.

In the 1950s it was discovered that the bean yields a gum which is of value in the food industry as an emulsifier, thickener, and stabilizer for salad dressings, ice cream, and other products. The plant is now cultivated in the south-west of the USA, and elsewhere, as a source of guar gum.

COAGULATION a technical term more familiar to cooks than is the companion term 'flocculation'. The two are often confused, but have different meanings, and the distinction between them is worth knowing.

Flocculation and connected words such as flocculent (and the charming but neglected word 'floccose') are all derived from the Latin *floccus*, meaning a tuft or a lock of wool. Cirrus clouds may be described as having a flocculent appearance; and it is easy to see the resemblance between them and the loose, ragged patches of solid matter in a sauce which has separated.

Coagulation, on the other hand, refers to what is for the cook a much more serious state of affairs. Protein coagulates, i.e. hardens into a 'cooked' state, if subjected to a temperature of 74 °C (165 °F). This process is irreversible, as is readily understood if one imagines, for example, trying to unscramble scrambled eggs. Flocculation, in contrast, can be remedied. The two terms, with their different meanings, are subsumed in the vaguer term, CURDLING. This may suffice to indicate what is meant, but it is often better to use whichever of the two more precise terms is applicable.

COBBLER an American term for a deep-dish PIE of cooked fruit (often apple or peach) with a thick crust on top. This usage seems to date back to the 1850s. Mariani (1994), comments:

This dish is called Bird's nest pudding or 'crow's nest pudding' in New England; it is served with a custard but no topping in Connecticut, with maple sugar in Massachusetts, and with a sour sauce in Vermont.

Cobbler dough can also be used as a topping for stewed meat dishes.

Cobbler can also refer to a kind of mixed alcoholic drink, and that meaning was recorded earlier than the above one.

See also PANDOWDY.

COBIA *Rachycentron canadum*, a fish of the open seas found in tropical waters all round the world except for the E. Pacific. Exceptionally, it may reach a length approaching 2 m (6') and a weight of 40 kg (100 lb). The back and sides of adults are brown, with silvery stripes running along them. These stripes are presumably responsible for the common name 'sergeant-fish'. Another common name is 'crab-eater'; bestowed because this voracious fish does eat crustaceans, including crabs, with enthusiasm, although its diet includes other fish. In Australia it is officially known as 'black kingfish'.

The cobia is a fine game fish, and good to eat. Its flesh has been compared to that of SPANISH MACKEREL, but is slightly coarser in texture.

COBWEB-CAPS a family of fungi of which there are 230 species in Britain alone. The English name refers to the gossamer veil which protects the gills when the cap is in its unexpanded state, and which bears some resemblance to a spider's web. This feature is the most noticeable characteristic of these mushrooms, which in other respects such as size and coloration vary to a bewildering extent. They occur in China and Australia as well as in Europe and N. America.

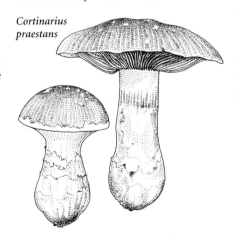

Cortinarius praestans

Although a German author lists 40 cobweb-caps as edible (plus five toxic ones), only a few of these fungi are eaten by any save dedicated enthusiasts. For example, Phillips (1981) gives a straightforward 'edible' rating to only one European species, *Cortinarius violaceus*. However, French and Italian sources also recommend the

brown-capped *C. praestans*, while Scandinavian authorities give a high rating to *C. crocolitus*, which has a yellowish cap with a tawny centre. Serzhanina and Zmitrovich (1978) list no cobweb-caps as 'officially edible' in Russia but point to literary evidence of some being eaten.

In the USA several of the species have been praised and McIlvaine (1902) reported that the number eaten had doubled in his time from less than a dozen to about a score. This notable increase may, however, have been largely attributable to his own experiments. He found *C. violaceus* (the American variety, which differs from the European, although both have a violet tinge) the best of the family; *C. turmalis* (yellow tan, plentiful in pinewoods, e.g. Maryland) of great value; *C. cinnabarinus* (red-flesh) radish flavoured; and the rare *C. intrusus*, which flourishes in cultivated mushroom beds, conservatories, etc. in the vicinity of Boston, 'delicate, savoury, and a most accommodating renegade from its kind', offering the additional convenience that it is available in February, generally a poor month for edible fungi.

There are several toxic species, so positive identification of any cobweb-caps to be eaten is essential. Young specimens should be chosen. There is no need to scrape off the scaly excrescences from the cap. All parts are fleshy and edible, and the flavour is mild.

COCA a stimulant traditionally used in the Peruvian Andes and surrounding regions. It is the leaf of a small shrub, *Exythroxylon coca*, which grows at fairly high altitudes and of a less important species, *E. novogranatense*, grown lower down. Its use was originally a royal privilege among the Inca, but it is now widespread.

Coca leaves are chewed. They contain small amounts of the alkaloid cocaine. The effect is to increase endurance and suppress hunger, valuable among poor mountain folk who work hard and long on little sustenance. However, prolonged use causes addiction and lack of interest in food.

The traditional way of taking the drug is to chew the fresh leaves with lime and the ash of plants such as QUINOA. The leaves must be used soon, as they do not keep. For use in western countries, the cocaine is extracted by a straightforward chemical process which was discovered in 1860. At first cocaine was used only as a stimulant, but it soon became, and still is, widely abused. It may be sniffed in powder form or dissolved and injected. In 1884 it was discovered that cocaine was a local anaesthetic.

At this time the drink Coca-Cola was first being produced and marketed. Coca and cocaine did not then have their present evil reputation, so the name was given to the drink to encourage the idea that it was stimulating. Coca-Cola have always sought to keep their formula (in its successive versions, ably chronicled by Pendergrast, 1994) secret, but it is generally assumed that for a long time now it has contained no coca. It does probably contain COLA, a harmless stimulant.

READING: Mortimer (1974).

COCHINEAL a crimson dye used as a food colouring, is made from the dried, pulverized bodies of an insect, *Dactylopius coccus*, which is a parasite on cactus plants in America. When the female insect has mated, it settles on the cactus and becomes permanently fixed there, sheds all its limbs and swells into a round lump which looks more like an excrescence on the cactus than an insect. (The Latin word *coccus* means berry.) Several other kinds of insect behave thus, one of them being the KERMES bug which is native to the Old World and is also used to made a red dye.

The dye-making properties of the cochineal bug, already well known to American Indians, were soon recognized by the early European settlers in America. The kermes with which they were familiar in the Old World was expensive and the abundant cochineal insect could be used to make a cheap substitute. After exports to Europe began in 1518, the new product was first used to adulterate kermes but soon supplanted it; it gives a better colour. (It is said that in the 18th century the coats of the highest ranks in the British army were dyed red with cochineal, those of the middling grades with kermes, and those of the 'redcoats' of lower rank with a mere vegetable dye.)

Cochineal is now 'cultivated' in special plantations of cactus in several parts of tropical America. The dye is still popular despite competition from artificial colourings.

COCIDO a Spanish meat and vegetable stew with a long history and a number of variations both within SPAIN and outside. It is the subject of a remarkable essay by Alicia Rios (1984), who explains that in all its numerous versions it is based on

slow and prolonged cooking that unites water, meat and horticultural products in a single pot. A single dish while it is cooking, it is tripled upon serving, for it provides three different courses (*vuelcos*, meaning overturns). The first course, or *vuelco*, is the soup; the second *vuelco* consists of a platter presenting the chickpeas with the beef, chicken and pork on top of them; and in the third vuelco the vegetables and sausages are served.

The Madrid version, *cocido madrileno*, is described as the central dish of that city's gastronomy. There, the water is almost as important as the meat and vegetables. The purity of the water from the local sierras is seen as the secret of the success of this cocido. 'It is still actually possible to see some purist people go with their water jug to the fountain of Plaza de Alcala to gather the water that will produce the miracle in the kitchen.'

The pot traditionally used (and now often replaced by a pressure cooker) is of earthenware, pot-bellied, glazed inside, and furnished with a tightly fitting lid. This is the famous *olla*, to which reference is made under OLIO.

So far as vegetables are concerned, the CHICKPEA is almost everywhere a 'must'. As Alicia Rios puts it:

The chickpea presides over all cocidos and is the ancestral, unifying element of this family of dishes. Although all cocidos demand the presence of this golden leguminious pod, shaped, as the saying goes, like 'an old woman's head and a dressmaker's backside'—it can be substituted by the white and red bean, as in the 'Euskaldun' cocido from Euskadi, the Basque country.

The orthodox Madrid cocido is otherwise characterized by potatoes and cabbage almost exclusively. However, the further one draws away towards the coast from the central plateau where Madrid is located, the more numerous the vegetables which are used. The variations are extensive:

Some cocidos will be salty, as in Castilla and the north: Leon, Santander, Galicia, Euskadi. In Andalucia and in the east (the Mediterranean basin), we find, perhaps because of the Moorish influence, a sweeter range of cocidos—containing onion, carrot, pumpkin or squash, sweet potato and even pears and quince; a wide range of nuances that includes the salty-salt, and the salt-sweet, and the sweet-sour (which can be achieved by a tomato sauce with a hint of vinegar in it). The presence in these regions of some meat balls called 'pilotas' . . . are symbolic traces of the hard-boiled eggs in the Sephardi *adafina*.

The cocido has emigrated with Spaniards to other Spanish-speaking countries, and has been modified in its new environments. In the Philippines, for example, it is a festive dish which may have a luxurious combination of beef, pork, salt pork, ham, chicken, and sausages, and may incorporate among the vegetables *pechay* (*petsai*, a kind of CHINESE CABBAGE) and *saba* bananas.

See also PUCHERO, another basic Spanish dish which has undergone modifications abroad.

COCK a male bird (as opposed to hen, a female bird), both terms being most usually applied to domestic fowl. Breeds of domestic fowl are described under HEN/CHICKEN BREEDS. The majority of dishes based on domestic fowl find their place under CHICKEN DISHES. There are, however, some recipes which specifically call for a cock (or cockerel, a young cock); and of these the best known are the Scottish COCK-A-LEEKIE and the French Coq au vin.

Although **Coq au vin** is well known and was featured in numerous menus in the third quarter of the 20th century, it does not have a long history. The flesh of a cock has always been regarded as somewhat tough and indigestible, and with few exceptions cooks of earlier centuries saw no merit in cocks except as a source of cockscombs (much in demand as a garnish) and sometimes for making a *bouillon* (see BROTH). One of the very first recipes for Coq au vin, that of Brisson published in Richardin's *L'Art du bien manger* (1913), was presented as a real 'discovery', the author having been surprised to find the dish in Puy-de-Dôme, and surprised by how good it was. The ingredients in this case were the cock, good wine of Auvergne, bacon, onion, garlic, and mushrooms. Wine from Burgundy has since become the one commonly used, and indeed many recipes just say 'red wine'.

The upsurge of interest in regional cuisines has recently brought to light other similar traditions for preparing Coq au vin. In Franche-Comté the bird is simmered in *vin jaune*; and in Alsace in Riesling. In both these regions morels and cream are gladly added if available. Indeed, knowledgeable food experts no longer speak of Coq au vin in the singular but of coqs au vin in the plural, while acknowledging that these dishes were doubtless simmering away for long years before the first recipes were published and before the gastronomes 'discovered' the virtues of simple country fare.   HY

COCKAIGNE (or Cockayne), LAND OF, an imaginary land of idleness and plenty (especially of food and drink) whose name is derived from a Middle Low German word meaning small cake.

The rivers in Cockaigne are of wine, the pavements of pastry, and the houses of cake, and visitors from the real world are bemused to find roast geese and fowls wandering around requesting that they be eaten, while buttered larks fall from the sky: etc. etc. These and other gastronomic features of the imaginary land vary from culture to culture. Thus in Italy there are mountains of Parmesan, while in Ireland, according to 'the Vision of MacConglinne' (thought to date back to the end of the 12th century) there are such strange visions as 'A loch of pottage fat Under a cream of oozy lard', and 'A forest tall of real leeks, Of onions and of carrots', besides 'Hedges of butter'. However, despite the numerous variations, the core idea is remarkably consistent in early European literature.

A painting by Bruegel of this fantasy land has provided its best-known image in art. This hangs in Munich.

COCK-A-LEEKIE a Scottish soup/stew of chicken and leeks. The name came into use in the 18th century, but the dish itself is commonly said to date back to medieval times, when it contained onions and prunes (and/or raisins), and was probably served as two dishes—the chicken and the broth.

Modern recipes are generally for just one dish, not two; they provide for cutting up the chicken meat before the soup is served; and they are virtually unanimous in insisting that chicken and leeks between them provide plenty of solid matter.

Onions have retained their place in the recipes, but raisins have largely disappeared and there has been controversy over the prunes. Marian McNeill (1929) lent the full weight of her authority to including them, one on each plate. However, she cited opposing views and referred also to a compromise solution which, according to Meg Dods (1826), was favoured by the French statesman Talleyrand, famous for his diplomacy; he came to the conclusion that prunes should be boiled in the soup but removed before serving.

COCKCHAFER also called may-bug, *Melolontha melolontha*, one of a group of insects known as chafers because of the way they attack plants. They are vegetarians and have been recommended as wholesome and delicious fare for human beings. Holt (1885) portrayed a world in which 'insects eat up every blessed green thing that do grow and us starve. Well, eat them and grow fat!' He particularly recommended 'a good dish of fried cockchafers'. Bodenheimer (1951) was able to marshal similar testimonials from French authorities, including the writer Catulle Mendés, who 'tore off the head and wings, and crunched the remainder, the taste of which he compared to a dish of chopped chicken in butter taken with salt.'

However, Bodenheimer devotes more space to the consumption of the white grubs of cockchafers and cites Simmonds (1885) as the narrator of an 'amusing story, how a few years ago at the Café Custoza in Paris a great banquet was given for the special purpose of tasting the white grubs or cockchafer worms. This insect, it appears, was first steeped in vinegar, which had the effect of making it disgorge the earth, etc., it had swallowed while still free; then it was carefully rolled up in a paste composed of flour, milk and eggs, placed in a pan, and fried to a bright golden colour. The guests were able to take this crisp and dry worm in their fingers. It cracked between their teeth. There were

some fifty persons present, and the majority had a second helping.'

Similar evidence may be available from 20th-century sources, but it is elusive.

COCKLE a confusing name which is applied to many edible BIVALVES in different parts of the world. It would be convenient if it were reserved for members of the families Cardiidae (true cockles) and Glossidae (heart-cockles, see HEART SHELL). As the information supplied below shows, there seems to be little hope of tidying up the nomenclature to this extent; but some encouragement may be derived from reflecting that the word 'cockle' is derived from classical Greek and Latin words meaning simply 'shell', and that its meaning has at least become narrower than that.

The archetypal cockle, known as the edible or **common cockle**, is *Cerastoderma edule*, which has an extensive distribution from the Barents Sea and the Baltic to the Mediterranean and Senegal. As is true of most bivalves bearing the name cockle, it looks something like a human heart when viewed from the side. In Scandinavian languages and German it is therefore called 'heart mussel' (mussel being a term of much wider application in those languages than in English).

The common cockle, which is what Molly Malone was selling when she called 'Cockles and mussels, alive alive-oh' in the streets of Dublin, has a maximum measurement of about 6 cm (2.5"). The colour of the shells is brown, pale yellow, or grubby white. Like its close relations, the cockle can be eaten raw, or cooked, and is a valuable and delicious food. It benefits from the opportunity to purge itself by being left in a pail of clean sea water for a few hours before consumption.

The **spiny cockle**, *Acanthocardia aculeata*, occurs in the Mediterranean and the E. Atlantic coast as far north as the Channel Islands and Devon. It may reach a size of 10 cm (4"). The creature inside the shell is red; hence the alternative name bloody cockle. The **prickly cockle**, *A. echinata*, has a range extending further north, to Norway and the Baltic. *A. tuberculata* is a Mediterranean species, whose shell is covered with tubercles rather than spines or prickles, and which is another kind with a red inhabitant, well known at Naples as *fasolare*.

On the American side of the Atlantic there are two important cockles. The so-called **Iceland cockle**, *Clinocardium ciliatum*, ranges from Greenland down to Massachusetts. The much larger giant **Atlantic cockle**, *Dinocardium robustum*, is a southerly species, rare north of Florida.

It is on the Pacific coast of N. America that confusion becomes rampant. There the name cockle, often prefixed by such terms as

'sea', 'sand', 'mud', or 'bay', is among those given to a whole range of CLAMS and VENUS SHELLS. However, there are also some true cockles present. The outstanding one is the **basket cockle**, *Clinocardium nuttalli*, which can measure 110 mm (4"). It is fished extensively in Puget Sound and British Columbia. But the largest by far is the rarer *Laevicardium elatum*, the smooth giant cockle, measuring up to 15 cm (8") and distinguished also by having a bright yellow shell. (There is an E. African giant cockle which is even larger, as big as a coconut.)

In Britain cockles, which abound on sandy shores and in estuaries all round the coast, provide the most valuable mollusc fishery. The cocklers of the Gower peninsula in Wales are the most picturesque of the people engaged in the fishery; and the Welsh seem to have a wider range of cockle recipes than the English (see, for example, Tibbott, 1976, for *Cocos ac wyau*—cockles and eggs— and also for a description of itinerant Welsh cockle-sellers). But the best British cockles are generally held to be the Stiffkey (pronounced stookey) blues from Norfolk; these owe their blueness to the anaerobic mud which they inhabit.

In New Zealand a common venus shell, *Chione stuchburyi*, is called a cockle.

See also DOG COCKLE.

COCOA can be a confusing term because until about the end of the 19th century it was often used in English to mean what is properly called cacao. See CHOCOLATE: BOTANY AND EARLY HISTORY; and also CHOCOLATE MANUFACTURE.

As the term is now understood, cocoa is the substance left after the cocoa butter (needed for enriching chocolate confectionery, see CHOCOLATE IN THE 19TH AND 20TH CENTURIES) has been extracted from the chocolate mass and powdered. It can be used to provide a chocolate flavour in baked goods, icings, and puddings. It is also mixed with sugar and vegetable fat to make 'chocolate-flavoured coating', used for covering cakes and biscuits.

However, its most important use is to provide the drink called cocoa, for which purpose it is mixed with sugar and boiling milk or water. And the most important aspect of this use is undoubtedly the brewing of 'kye' (as it is known) for those who are keeping a watch at night on the bridge of any ship in the (British) Royal Navy. The art of making the 'kye' really strong, so that a spoon stands up in it, requires an apprenticeship of many years.

Not even this naval 'kye' can quite match the punch which was delivered by an ancestral 'cocoa' prepared by the indigenous Indians of C. America, according to Emerson (1908), in the 16th century. This beverage still had all the cocoa butter in it, but there were other reasons to beware of it:

for, besides being at boiling heat, the beverage also contains a very liberal supply of native peppers, noted the world over for their extreme heat, and one small sip of this chocolate is generally enough to make a man think that he has awakened in another world, and all doubt about which one it is is removed at once. The outside world has very little interest for him at this time. It is the inside one that calls for immediate attention.

COCO DE MER or sea-coconut, *Lodoicea maldiviana*, a palm which grows only on certain of the Seychelles Islands and which bears huge (up to 20 kg/45 lb) fruits which take many years to ripen fully. These are sometimes called 'double coconut', because they usually comprise two lobes (sometimes more); but it is a misnomer because they do not closely resemble the true COCONUT.

The nut within the fruit is a rare delicacy, if eaten when the fruit is about 10 to 12 months old. At this stage it yields a translucent, jelly-like substance which has a melting consistency and a pleasant sweet taste. (If the fruit is left to ripen fully it will eventually, years later, have an interior as hard as ivory.)

The terminal buds are also eaten. However, the coco de mer is perhaps best known in the Near East as the source of dervish begging bowl—see KESHKUL-E-FUQARA, describing the milk pudding which was a typical offering. In a remarkable paper about this whole complex of subjects, Jill Tilsley-Benham (1986a) recalled early ideas about the origin of the strange fruits of *L. maldiviana*:

Borne by the Indian Ocean, sometimes for a thousand miles, the huge seeds are washed up on the shores of Zanzibar, the Maldives, Ceylon, Sumatra and south India. Until its home was discovered in 1743, legend declared that it grew beneath the sea and ancient sailors spun their yarns of palm trees, swaying underneath the waves, which vanished magically when they dived to cull its fruit. Other stories gave its provenance as the lagoons of Java where the griffin, lazily digesting its meal of elephants and tigers, would rest among its shady fronds. Naturally, a fruit of such rarity was precious, and this combined (no doubt) with its suggestive shape, made of it an aphrodisiac for kings. When split apart and polished the shells were used (again only by the aristocracy) as vessels which were reputed to keep food and liquid free from taint of poison. In the 18th century, when the double coconut's home was traced, matters took a different turn, and even a beggar afterwards could boast his *vaisselle de l'Isle Praslin*, as the bowls were sometimes known.

COCONA *Solanum sessiliflorum*, a fruit related to the NARANJILLA, but with different characteristics and much less known outside its native region in Latin America (especially Ecuador, Colombia, and Brazil). When ripe, the smooth skin often has the colour of a TOMATO; and the aroma of a fruit freshly cut open is also reminiscent of the tomato. The pulp in the centre is yellow and pleasantly acid, while the flesh surrounding it has a milder taste and is cream in colour. As with the tomato, the seeds in the pulp are not noticed when the fruit is eaten. The shape may be round or conical; a fruit of conical shape may be 10 cm (4") long.

The cocona is cultivated in its native region. It is used like tomatoes in connection with savoury dishes, also made into jams etc. The juice, sweetened, is a popular drink.

The variety *alibile* has been developed as a dessert fruit.

COCONUT (*see opposite page*)

COCONUT ICE a traditional home-made English confection made from grated coconut mixed with sugar syrup cooked to the thread stage (see SUGAR BOILING). The mixture is stirred, giving a slightly grainy texture. Often half the mixture is coloured pink, the rest being left white. One batch is poured on top of the other to set, giving a striped confection when cut. Fresh coconut is said to give the best flavour, but desiccated coconut is frequently used.

This confection is not frozen. How it came to be referred to as 'ice' is unknown; possibly natural colour and the slightly crystalline, smooth yet tender texture had something to do with this. In most countries, including the rest of the English-speaking world, similar confections are referred to simply as coconut candies or coconut creams.

The pink or white 'pralines' of New Orleans are a fresh coconut confection of this type.

For no very clear reason, a number of sugar and coconut confections, popular in Britain in the early 20th century, carried the prefix 'Jap' or 'Japanese'. Jap nuggets (small fruit-flavoured sweets) and Japanese dessert (something like coconut ice but harder and more caramel-like) are two examples. In Scotland, a coconut-covered cake is still known as a 'Jap cake'. (LM)

COD which has by any criteria been one of the most important fish in the history of mankind, as Kurlansky (1997) has eloquently explained, continues to be one of the foremost marine food resources, both as fresh or frozen fish and in the form of bacalao (dried and salted cod, see SALT COD) and STOCKFISH (dried cod). The American (New England) term 'scrod', the origin of which has been the subject of various explanations, is applied to small specimens (under 50 cm/20") of cod or haddock. Although an (unconvincing) explanation of the origin of this term is cited by Davidson (1979) and a more plausible one by Mariani (1994) it is best left as '[origin obscure]' which is how Craigie and Hulbert (1938) put it.

The N. Atlantic cod, *Gadus morhua*, is the better-known one, but the smaller N. Pacific species, *G. macrocephalus*, is also important. Some authorities count the Greenland cod as a separate species, *Gadus ogac*, but others do not, although it is recognizably different (no white lateral line); its range centres on Greenland, where it is *ugaq*.

There was a time, before all the fishing grounds had been exploited, when one Atlantic cod was recorded as reaching a weight of over 90 kg (200 lb) and a length of nearly 2 m (6'). This seems almost incredible nowadays when the maximum weight is in the region of 10–11 kg (25 lb) and an average market specimen weighs only 4–5 kg (10 lb).

Exploitation of the fishing grounds then known was already heavy in medieval times, largely because of the demand for salted and dried cod for LENT, but this was nothing remotely like the present scouring of the sea with sophisticated equipment (on which see Warner, 1977, whose description can instructively be compared with that of Rudyard Kipling in his novel *Captains Courageous*).

The range of the Atlantic cod is from the Bay of Biscay up to Arctic waters and down to Cape Hatteras on the other side, but the best fishing grounds are in the northern part of the range, e.g. round Iceland and on the famous Grand Bank off Newfoundland. The appearance of cod at the southern limit of its range is due to seasonal migrations.

Coloration of cod varies. The lateral line is pale and the body colour greenish or grey, or even of a reddish hue, depending on habitat, all dappled with lighter spots or patches.

Cod feed mainly on other fish, but also eat crustaceans and have been known to devour inanimate objects, such as a 'book in three treatises' which was taken from one captured in 1626 and presented, fittingly, to the Chancellor of Cambridge University (Day, 1880–4).

Trawls, seine nets, and lines can all be used for catching cod. As it has become scarcer and more expensive, its culinary merits have been more widely recognized. Its reputation suffered in the past from its being, in salted and dried form, of unattractive appearance; it was perceived as a prime example of 'penitential' food. In more recent times, it was disdained by some because available in much larger quantity

(*cont. on page 201*)

Coconut

The fruit of *Cocos nucifera*, the most useful tree in the world. It provides not only food and drink, but also vessels to serve them in and fuel to cook them, as well as textile fibre, thatching and basket materials, timber, medicines, chemicals, and many other valuable or useful products.

The coconut tree is a palm, usually tall, which flourishes on seashores in the moister parts of the tropics. It tolerates salty conditions and actually prefers light, sandy soil, since it needs a supply of air to its roots. This is provided by the ebb and flow of the tide lowering and raising the water table under it, so drawing air into the ground round the roots and then expelling it again. The roots are shallow, though widely spread; so the effect of strong winds is to give the palms their characteristic list. The huge leaves are often 6 m (20') long, with a massive midrib and drooping leaflets.

The 'nut' is technically a drupe, i.e. a fruit with a hard stone. A whole coconut, as usually sold, is only the stone of the fruit, the husk having been removed before shipping, to lessen the weight and to be used for other purposes.

The outside husk or exocarp is smooth and very tough, green to reddish brown becoming grey as the fruit matures. In a few varieties it is ivory-coloured. Between this outer husk and the nut is a thick, loose layer of coarse brown fibres, the mesocarp. The shell of the nut itself, which constitutes the endocarp, is hard, woody and brown, with three 'eyes' in one end. It is through one of these eyes that the shoot emerges when the seed germinates.

Inside the shell is a thin brown coat, the testa, which adheres firmly to the kernel, which is hollow and contains liquid. In the young nut the kernel is soft and the liquid copious, but unpleasant and purgative. As the fruit ripens, the kernel gradually hardens to a creamy gelatinous texture and the liquid becomes a sweet and refreshing drink. This liquid can conveniently be called 'coconut juice' or 'coconut water'. (What is usually called 'coconut milk' is different—see under coconut products, below.) In the mature fruit the amount of liquid is less, but still pleasant to drink; while the kernel is quite solid and slightly fibrous. The kernel, when removed and dried, becomes the product known as copra in commerce.

When they are mature, the fruits of many kinds of coconut palm fall off the tree, and it is better not to be standing underneath when this happens. The fruits of others do not fall and have to be gathered. It is possible to train monkeys to do this.

ORIGIN AND NOMENCLATURE

Botanists disagree about whether the species originated in the region of the E. Indies and Melanesia, as most think, or in tropical America, as a minority have vigorously argued.

The minority view is supported by the fact that almost all the coconut palm's relations are American, the one important exception being the oil palm, which is African. Yet the coconut has, at most, an exiguous history in C. America in pre-Columbian times; the evidence that the earliest Spanish invaders found it growing on the west coast of the Isthmus of Panama is uncertain; and if it was growing there it is odd that its cultivation was not widespread, since it is so useful. In contrast, the coconut has been been known in E. Asia and the islands for a very long time indeed; it exists in greatest variety in that region; and there is other evidence (including the number of species of insects associated with it in the various regions) that it did originate there, probably in Melanesia.

There is also an interesting diversity of views about the origin of the name 'coconut'. Child (1974) gives a good account of these and comes down in favour of the etymology which commands most acceptance, that 'coco' was first used towards the end of the 15th century by Portuguese seamen, who applied to the nut, with its three 'eyes', the Spanish word *coco*, referring to a monkey's or other grotesque face.

When Linnaeus gave a scientific name to the tree in the 18th century, he toyed with *Coccus* (*coccus*, berry in Latin) but settled on *Cocos*.

It was also in the 18th century that the notorious confusion between coconut and cocoanut began. The blame for this seems to rest with Dr Johnson, who confused the two in a single entry in his dictionary (1755); and one still occasionally comes across 'cocoanut' when 'coconut' is meant. The term 'coker-nut', an old variant of coconut, was at one time in commercial use in the Port of London, to avoid the confusion, and remains in popular use.

EARLY HISTORY AND DISSEMINATION

The coconut is mentioned in Indian documents BC (see Achaya, 1994), but remained unknown in the western world for a long time.

No part of Asia west of India is suitable for it, and climate also barred it from China, although it was known in the south, and was taken north as an exotic delicacy.

Marco Polo encountered coconuts in Java and Nicobar in the 13th century; and Vasco da Gama found the palms growing on an island off Mozambique in 1497/8. It seems likely that Arab traders had been responsible, much earlier, for introducing it to E. Africa.

As for the New World—whether or not the coconut had already existed on the west coast of Panama—what really mattered were the introductions of it by the Spanish (to Puerto Rico in the first instance) and by the Portuguese (to Brazil, in the 16th century). Cultivation soon spread to all suitable regions; and began in Florida much later, towards the end of the 19th century.

The main growing and exporting countries are now the Philippines, Indonesia, India, Sri Lanka, Mexico, Malaysia, and Papua New Guinea. Substantial crops are also grown in W. and E. Africa; around the Caribbean; and in Brazil.

VARIETIES/CULTIVARS

There are countless kinds of coconut palm which can be

distinguished by visible characteristics, including size, colour, shape, etc. of nut, but all belonging to the single species *Cocos nucifera*. In the past, botanists attempted to classify these kinds, giving them varietal names such as *Cocos nucifera* var *typica*. (These attempts corresponded, by and large, to the distinctions made by growers and consumers; but they, naturally, used vernacular names in their own languages for the various kinds which, to their mind, were significantly different. The Malay and Indonesian languages are particularly rich in vernacular names.)

If, however, it is accepted that there are no truly wild coconut palms in existence, and that all the different kinds are, ultimately, based on cultivated palms, it is not appropriate to speak of 'varieties'; the term used should be 'cultivars'. This principle holds good even for the particular kinds which have evolved on isolated islands or atolls.

One thing which can safely be said is that coconuts differ considerably in what they offer to the consumer. Some are rich in oil; some are outstandingly good to eat; some bear small, indeed dwarf, fruits; and so on. The best-known groups or kinds may be listed thus.

- The common, tall, coconut palms, those usually selected for commercial plantations, provide the typical coconuts of commerce; they fall into subgroups according to location, so that there is Jamaica Tall, West African Tall, Panama Tall (Choco), and so on.
- Dwarf palms start bearing fruits sooner than the tall ones, but have a shorter economic life and their copra is of less good quality. Their fruits vary in size; one of the smallest-fruited kinds is the Cocos Niño of the Philippines. Dwarf Malay Golden and Dwarf Malay Green have been introduced to the Caribbean region.
- The Macapuno coconut of the Philippines has no cavity occupied by liquid but is full of a gelatinous flesh which can be eaten with a spoon. Any given tree will only bear some such nuts, the others being normal.
- The San Ramon, also from the Philippines, bears the largest known nuts.
- The King coconut from Sri Lanka is known for the high sugar content of its liquid.
- The Maldivian coconut, which has evolved in an isolated mid-ocean position, has the smallest fruit of all: no bigger than an egg.

The so-called COCO DE MER, or 'double coconut', is not a true coconut, and is described separately.

HARVESTING AND PROCESSING
Except where a harvest of ripe nuts (as opposed to 'green' or not fully ripe ones) was required, and these were of kinds which drop off the tree when ready, harvesting was a dangerous business. A man would have to climb the straight, unbranched, tall palm, using a rope or leather loop as a safety device while ascending and to steady himself while gathering at the top of the palm. Accidents were frequent.

The employment of trained monkeys to do the job, referred to earlier, was only possible in a few places and on a small scale.

In modern commercial plantations, especially those using new dwarf cultivars, the nuts may be harvested from the ground, using hooked knives mounted on long bamboo poles.

The husk is removed by striking the end of the fruit against a spike. The husk, which contains useful fibre, known as coir, is not discarded but is set aside to produce, for example, coconut matting.

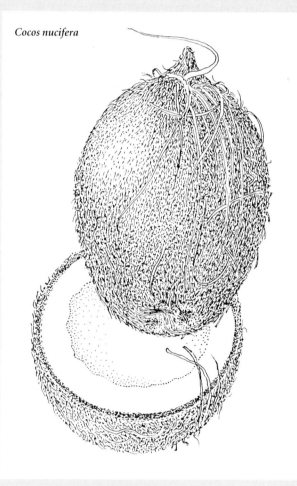

Cocos nucifera

The nut is removed and may be used in various ways. 'Green' coconuts, which are harvested for their refreshing juice, have their tops sliced off with a machete, the remainder being used as a cup from which to drink the juice. Mature coconuts, harvested for their copra, also yield some juice. If two of the three 'eyes' are pierced with a spike, it can be poured off into a glass and drunk. The nut is then struck hard against, for example, a concrete floor, so that one of the three ridges at the 'eye' end takes the force of the blow; whereupon it should split open.

COCONUT PRODUCTS

Copra is the name for dried coconut meat. The water content of copra should be 5% or less, compared with close to 50% before drying. The oil content is high, around 70%, and coconut oil (see below) is produced from copra.

Coconut milk or cream is a thick sweet liquid produced by pouring boiling water over grated coconut, leaving it to cool, and squeezing the liquid from the pulp through a straining cloth. Twice as much water by volume as there is grated coconut produces 'milk' of normal thickness; half that amount of water will yield the thicker 'cream'. The same pulp can be used several times to produce a decreasingly rich milk.

Coconut milk is a standard ingredient in the cookery of the southern part of the Indian subcontinent and SE Asia. It is an emulsion, as is cow's milk, but contains less protein and more fat. If it is made to separate, the fat rises to the top and can be removed as coconut oil, which is obtained for domestic use in this way.

Coconut milk can be made from desiccated coconut.

Coconut 'cream', in the sense of rich and thick coconut milk, is not the same as the commercial product called 'coconut cream', which is a solid white preparation furnished with instructions on how to reconstitute it with hot water.

Desiccated coconut is made from the white part of the kernel only, after the brown skin has been removed. It is sterilized, frayed out with water into a wet pulp, dried and sieved into grades (of which the finest is called 'macaroon').

Coconut oil can be made from fresh coconuts, a procedure still used locally in coconut-growing areas, but is normally extracted from copra (see above) by pressing.

The oil has a high proportion of saturated fatty acids, and is therefore resistant to rancidity. It is liquid in the temperatures which prevail in its countries of origin, but solidifies at temperatures below 85 °F/30 °C. Almost tasteless after processing, it is extensively used in making margarine, confectionery, and bakery goods, and for frying. It is especially important in the south of India as a cooking oil.

Among the sweet products of the coconut is **coconut syrup,** which is made by heating coconut milk and invert sugar together. The result is similar to 'golden syrup', which is pure invert sugar. **Coconut honey** is a darker product made in the same way but with a little of the brown rind included and longer cooking. **Cocolait** is a commercially made coconut milk with its composition adjusted to resemble that of cow's milk.

Toddy, an alcoholic liquor, is made by tapping the tree, which is done by cutting off the tip of a flower stem. The sap released ferments quickly and spontaneously. The resulting toddy can be drunk raw; or distilled to make arak; or used as a source of YEAST for bread; or allowed to turn into VINEGAR. Alternatively, unfermented sap can be boiled down to make jaggery or gur, types of PALM SUGAR. However, tapping damages the tree, so it is preferable to use other, less useful, palms for these various purposes.

See PALM for palm heart, an extravagant product, procured only at the expense of killing the palm.

Finally, there is also one rare and valuable product: the coconut 'pearl' which occasionally forms inside a nut, in a manner which is not fully understood but which may be the result of germination being arrested by a defective eye. In structure, composition (calcium carbonate) and appearance it is remarkably like a pearl from an oyster, although often larger, up to the size of a cherry. It has a white or bluish lustre, and various kinds of medical and magical powers are traditionally attributed to it.

---

and much more cheaply than nowadays. In fact, its flesh, which separates into large flakes, is excellent, especially if really fresh. This was recognized in the 19th century, when floating cod chests were used to keep cod alive for the market at English ports such as Harwich; and even in the 1980s it is customary to buy cod alive from big tanks in the fish market at Bergen, Norway.

Cod is susceptible to all standard methods of FISH COOKERY. Cod roe is a delicacy. So are the cheeks and 'tongues' (more properly, throat muscles), which by themselves constitute the Belgian dish called *Kaaksjes en keeltjes* (Ostend dialect). Finally, the head of a cod, in places where people are knowledgeable about these things, is greatly prized; and one of the most fascinating and scholarly food controversies ever to be debated had to do with the traditional consumption of dried cod's heads in ICELAND.

See also RED COD and MURRAY COD (neither of them a true cod). For a catalogue of all the numerous species in the order Gadiformes, see Cohen *et al.* (1990). READING: Jensen (1972).

CŒUR is a term used to describe cheeses in the form of a heart, usually after being placed in a mould or when drained in a heart-shaped basket such as *Cœur à la crème*—cheese curds which are then covered with cream and sugar and served as a dessert. Another example of a cheese taking this shape is the cœur d'Arras.

COFFEE a beverage, and at one remove an important food flavouring, made from roasted beans of the coffee plant, mainly *Coffea arabica*. Other species are *C. robusta* (now reclassified as *C. canephora*), and a couple of minor ones suited to the climate of W. Africa.

The earliest written mention of the drink is in the work of Rhazes, an Arabian physician active in the 10th century, but cultivation may have begun several centuries earlier. A rich mythology, full of dancing goats and sleepy monks, was woven around the discovery of the plant in Arabia.

Legend and history seem to agree that the berries were eaten whole at first, or mixed with fat. Later, the fermented pulp was used for a kind of wine, and in about AD 1000 a decoction was made of the dried fruit, beans, hull, and all. The practice of roasting the beans was started around the 13th century. In YEMEN, by the end of the century, the beverage had acquired its name, *Qahwah*, originally a poetic name for wine. This may reflect the excitement felt in Sufi circles at the discovery of a drink to replace wine in religious ceremonies. Whether or not this is true, it seems likely that its stimulant properties were welcomed as a means of prolonging hours of prayer. These stimulant properties are due to caffeine; see the box.

Dervishes and Muslim pilgrims were largely responsible for spreading the use of coffee throughout the Middle and Near East and N. Africa, by the end of the 15th century. Intensive cultivation had by now begun in the Yemen, using plants from Ethiopia, where they originated.

The arrival of coffee in W. Europe and the question often posed, where were the first European coffee houses, has set many pens in motion. It does seem that Venice, or anyway Italy, had the honour of being the pioneer. However, France (to whom the honour was accorded by Emerson, 1908) was certainly among the pioneers, apparently antedating Britain by several years.

Its popularity in France appears to have been given a boost, a little later, by the exotic parties given by the Turkish Ambassador there in 1688–9. The heady atmosphere of these occasions is captured by Isaac d'Israeli in his *Curiosities of Literature* (1817):

On bended knee, the black slaves of the Ambassador, arrayed in the most gorgeous Oriental costumes served the choicest Mocha coffee in tiny cups of egg-shell porcelain, hot, strong and fragrant, poured out in saucers of gold and silver, placed on embroidered silk doylies fringed with gold bullion, to the grand dames, who fluttered their fans with many grimaces, bending their piquant faces—be-rouged, be-powdered and be-patched—over the new and steaming beverage.

References to coffee in the writings of various English travellers to the East had occurred as early as 1599 (Anthony Sherley's description of 'damned infidells drinking a certaine liquor, which they do call Coffe'). The first British coffee house was opened in Oxford in 1650 by Jacob, a Turkish Jew. Two years later, Pasqua Rosee, who was either Armenian or Greek, opened one in London.

Coffee has been seen as a subversive substance at various points in its history. At one time, Islam perceived the conviviality it fostered as a threat to religious life; the mosques were empty, the coffee houses full. At another time, as Kolpas (1979) explains, authorities in the Vatican saw coffee as a threat to Christianity, 'Satan's latest trap to catch Christian souls'. Fortunately the then Pope, Clement VIII, did not fall for this line of thought. The story goes that he demanded to taste coffee and then announced that this was something which Christianity must make its own.

During the first half of the 18th century coffee plants reached the New World and their cultivation on a much larger scale began, leading to the present situation when many countries are competing. Brazil is the largest producer in quantity. Jamaica (the Blue Mountain estates) is widely thought of as producing the very finest coffee. Mexico produces much and so does Indonesia (where the coffee of Sumatra is most highly esteemed). S. India is another important

CAFFEINE AND COFFEE

Caffeine (which is present also in tea and chocolate, although in smaller proportions) is the constituent of coffee which give it its 'kick'. By itself, it is without aroma and has just a faint bitter taste.

For those who wish to enjoy the characteristic aroma and flavour of coffee without the kick, there are decaffeinated coffees available.

The caffeine is removed from the green berries, preferably by the method which involves soaking them for hours in hot water; drawing off the water, which will contain virtually all the caffeine; removing by means of a solvent the caffeine from the water; removing the solvent from the water (from which it is easily separable); restoring the water to the berries; drying them and dispatching them for further processing in just the same ways as apply to non-decaffeinated beans. This method should result in ridding the coffee of 97% of its caffeine, in no appreciable loss of desirable aromas and flavours, and in retention of virtually none of the solvent used.

It was, of course, the kick provided by the caffeine which prompted the religious, political, social, and medical arguments about coffee drinking which have resounded down the centuries from medieval times to the present. Such arguments have rarely, if ever, applied to the use of coffee as a food flavouring.

region of production; and, in Africa, Kenya and Tanzania have joined Ethiopia in that role. The coffees of all these places have their special characteristics; indeed, qualities vary from estate to estate, since the nature of the soil, the altitude, and many other factors all make significant differences—as in wine-making. And, again as with wine, a whole complex system of nomenclature and description has grown up. However, as Davids (1976), the best guide to this and several other aspects of the subject, points out, the labelling of coffee constitutes a much less satisfactory source of information than what one finds on wine labels.

However, coffee is not a food, and coffee terminology and nomenclature hardly enter at all into the food uses of coffee, for example as a flavouring, especially for ICE CREAM, in various desserts, and in CONFECTIONERY. In recipes involving those functions, it is usually prescribed as just 'coffee', or 'strong coffee'.

Coffee flavouring combines well with CHOCOLATE. See also MOCHA.

For the imposing battery of equipment (especially the world-conquering Italian espresso machine) with which it is processed and brewed, see the great work of Ukers mentioned below (for the historical side) and Bersten (1993) for a more recent and highly illustrated survey.
READING: Ukers (1922); Claudia Roden (1977); Stella (1996).

COFFIN or coffyn, a term meaning a thick pastry case for a PIE, was in use from the late Middle English period to the 16th century. It thus antedated the use of the same term (from the early 16th century) in what is now the familiar sense of a receptacle for a corpse, and should therefore not be

regarded as having lugubrious or sinister connotations.

Coffins could be open or have a lid. They might be eaten or they might not; and, although we do not really know how the pastry was made, it seems likely that it would have been too coarse and heavy to appeal to the better off and more fastidious diners, albeit welcome to the poor and hungry.

C. Anne Wilson (1973) makes this comment:

To make a bakemeat for a special occasion two or more coffins could be united, as in the handsome 'chastletes' or little castles. For this, four coffins were made of 'good paste' and arranged on four sides to form a fifth one at the centre. The tops were carved to look like battlements. They were baked blind and then filled with separately coloured mixtures, yellow for the middle, and white, red, brown and green for the four sides. The edifice was baked again and served forth.

COLA or kola, a popular stimulant which comes from, and has traditionally been used in, W. Africa. Cola 'nuts', not real nuts but the interior part of the fleshy seeds of plants of the genus *Cola* (especially *C. nitida* and *C. acuminata*), are chewed fresh, or dried and ground to powder for making into a drink. They have a similar effect to TEA or COFFEE, since they contain the same alkaloid, caffeine. They also contain smaller amounts of theobromine, as does the related COCOA 'bean', and of kolanin, a heart stimulant.

Cola trees are large and grow best in tropical rain forests. Of the two main species, *C. nitida* is cultivated over most of tropical W. Africa, and *C. acuminata* is grown as far south as Angola. The seeds may be pink, white, or purple, white being preferred. The taste is slightly bitter, but it is claimed that food eaten afterwards tastes sweet. Indeed, Smith (1886) stated that these seeds have the effect of causing water drunk afterwards to taste 'like white wine and sugar'. A cola nut is often eaten before a meal for this sort of reason, and because it is said to have digestive properties.

Although the formulae of Coca-Cola and similar drinks are supposed to be secret, it seems safe to assume that they contain cola; see Pendergrast (1994).

COLBERT a French culinary term. One can hardly repress a yawn on learning that the name was that of a French statesman of the 17th century, whose chef gave his name to a sauce, a manner of preparing sole, and a soup. When one reflects that Claudette Colbert, the most beautiful and perhaps the best loved of Hollywood film stars of the 1930s–1940s, was of French origin, but that it is not she who is meant here, one can only lament that the French system of honouring people by naming dishes for them (see À LA) petered out in the early part of the 20th century. On the other hand, one would not wish Claudette to have been associated with an anachronism; and the presence (according to Favre, c.1905) of BRUSSELS SPROUTS in the supposedly 17th-century *Soupe à la Colbert* seems to be one (see Meiller and Vannier, 1991). All the same, she could have had her name on the mysterious iced *crème*, which Favre (again) believed to have been called Colbert (although his only mention of it is not under Colbert, but under BAVAROIS, where he merely said that it should not be confused with a bavarois).

COLCANNON originally an Irish dish of boiled potatoes and cabbage or KALE mashed together and flavoured with onions, shallots, or leeks and cream or butter. It is similar to CHAMP. The word 'colcannon' is from the Gaelic *cál ceannann* which literally means white-headed cabbage. However, the 'cannon' part of the name might be a derivative of the old Irish *cainnenn*, translated variously as garlic, onion, or leek. Therefore it can be suggested that in its earliest form colcannon may have been a simple mixture of some brassica and allium.

One of the earliest Irish references to the dish as a mash of potatoes and cabbage is found in the Diary of William Bulkely, of Bryndda, near Amlwch in Anglesey, who made two journeys to Dublin in 1735. In his diary entry for 31 October 1735 he describes the dish as follows:

Dined at Cos. Wn. Parry, and also supped there upon a shoulder of mutton roasted and what they call there Coel Callan, which is cabbage boiled, potatoes and parsnips, all this mixed together. They eat well enough, and this is a Dish always had in this kingdom on this night.

The dish was introduced into England in the 18th century, where it became a favourite of the upper classes. Here according to Salaman (1949) a more elaborate mash was prepared of potatoes and Brussels sprouts, highly flavoured with ginger, and moistened with generous amounts of milk and butter. There existed, however, towards the end of the 18th century, the ancestor of what would eventually become the native English counterpart of colcannon. This was the dish called **bubble and squeak,** at first made of beef and cabbage fried, but subsequently and nowadays usually made of potato and cabbage (or another member of the cabbage family). Jane Grigson (1978) comments wittily on an early version of bubble and squeak (from the eccentric Dr Kitchiner, who prescribed Wow Wow sauce to go with it); and makes the connection with colcannon, which she evidently and rightly prefers to its later English rival.

In Ireland colcannon was associated traditionally with Hallowe'en (31 October) festivities, when it was used for the purposes of marriage divination. Charms hidden in bowls of colcannon were portents of a marriage proposal should unmarried girls be lucky enough to find them, whilst others filled their socks with spoonfuls of colcannon and hung them from the handle of the front door in the belief that the first man through the door would become their future husband.

Colcannon is served in individual serving bowls and topped off with a decent knob of butter.   (RSe)

COLE MRS MARY (fl 1788–91), author of *The Lady's Complete Guide; or Cookery in All its Branches* (1st edn 1788, 3rd edn 1791), chiefly remarkable for the stand she took on plagiarism. She was the first cookery writer to cite in a systematic way the other books from which most of her recipes were drawn. Even in those numerous instances where she had collated into a single version, which she could have called her own, the recipes of several earlier writers, she took pains to acknowledge them. In her preface she claimed credit for this innovation and castigated earlier writers, among whom she names HANNAH GLASSE, for dishonesty. 'If all the writers upon Cookery had acknowledged from whence they took their Receipts, as I do, they would have acted with more candour by the public. Their vanity to pass for Authors, instead of Compilers, has not added to their reputation.'

A curious feature of Mrs Cole's book is that its subtitle contains references to a number of 'Cooks of Eminence who have published in France' and says that some of Mrs Cole's recipes are translated from them. These French authors include the 'Duke de Nivernois', Commo (*Histoire de cuisine*), and Disang (*Le Maître d'hôtel*). None of them, however, is known to the standard bibliographers of French writings on cookery. Indeed, research suggests that, except for the possibility that the first of these was the French Ambassador in London at about that time (see Noble, 1992), all are imaginary persons, whose names were printed in jest, by way of mocking those English authors who made a great to-do about following French authors. There is, however, no other trace in the book of a jesting spirit at work. Nor is other information about Mrs Cole, such as would fortify a judgement on the matter, available.

COLESLAW a term derived from the Dutch *koolsla*, formed by combining two Dutch words, *kool* meaning cabbage, and *sla*, an abbreviated word meaning salad. The salad in question is normally shredded cabbage mixed with MAYONNAISE and nowadays often with additions such as a little shredded carrot.

The form 'cold slaw' is also commonly met, and it is customary to say that this is simply the result of a misunderstanding on the part of people who do not know how the term originated. However, it is to be remarked that the earliest uses in America recorded by Craigie and Hulbert (1938) are in this form; they have citations for it from 1794 ('a piece of sliced cabbage, by Dutchmen ycleped cold slaw') and 1821, whereas the earliest for cole-slaw is from 1842.

Ayto (1993) remarks that the confusion here between cole and cold has led to 'slaw' being regarded, particularly in America, as an independent term for a cabbage dish—he even cites a reference in a Baltimore newspaper to 'hot slaw'.

It seems clear that coleslaw reached England from the USA, and that acceptance of the term in the correct form 'coleslaw' was probably facilitated by the fact that there was an English word 'cole' meaning cabbage.

COLLAGEN a tough PROTEIN which is one of the main structural materials of the bodies of animals. Tendons and cartilage are mostly collagen; it provides most of the strength of skin; bone is a composite of collagen and the hard mineral calcium phosphate. Collagen is also found in many other tissues, including muscle.

The 'gristle' in meat is collagen. It is not only hard to chew but impossible for a human to digest. However, it may be boiled down to make GELATIN, which is digestible although of low nutritional quality.

See also CONNECTIVE TISSUE.   RH

COLLAR a verb which has been used in a culinary sense since the 17th century, but rarely in modern times. It means to roll up and tie with string.

COLLEGE PUDDING Almost every Oxford and Cambridge college has a pudding named after it. Generally they are fairly plain boiled SUET, breadcrumb, and dried fruit puddings, sometimes with eggs and milk. The oldest recipe, from Cambridge, is dated 1617. Trinity College, Oxford, has a rich version with egg yolks, eggs, brandy, and spices.

At New College, Oxford, a similar mixture is made into small DUMPLINGS the size of eggs, and deep fried, then served rolled in sugar. This technique recalls medieval recipes antedating the invention of the pudding cloth. New College pudding became well known outside Oxford.

Other examples from Cambridge are Peterhouse pudding, in which a SUET PUDDING mixture lightened with eggs is baked in a pastry tart case; and Magdalene pudding, a rich baked sponge pudding made lighter by beating the egg whites separately, flavoured with brandy, nutmeg, and lemon rind.

See also CRÈME BRÛLÉE.

COLLOID a mixture of substances in which one is in the form of very small particles dispersed through the other. Examples are smoke (solid specks in air), foams (gas in a liquid), sols (solids in liquid, as in a mixture of starch and water), gels (sols that have 'set' by the solid particles linking into a network), and EMULSIONS (one liquid dispersed in another). The substance which is split into particles is known as the disperse(d) phase; the other substance in which the first is dispersed is called the dispersion medium.

COLLOP (a word of obscure derivation, says the *OED*, perhaps connected with coal) had from early times the primary meaning of a rasher of salt BACON, to be fried, often with eggs; 'a peculiarly British fashion of eating bacon, not known elsewhere in Europe'. The comment is from C. Anne Wilson (1973).

Later, the term came to have the more general meaning of a slice of meat. Hannah Glasse's recipe for Collup and Eggs, and her recipes for Scotch Collop, illustrate this development in the meaning of the word. Scotch collops were a well-known dish from the 17th to the 19th centuries, although the manner of preparing them changed with the passage of time.

It is still usual to speak of venison collops; and by extension the word seems to have acquired in some places the general meaning of thick slice (Mary Hanson Moore, 1980, records that her mother, in Yorkshire, served as 'collops' thick slices of potato which had been fried in DRIPPING until golden brown).

There was some confusion between the nouns collup (or collop) and scollop (or scallop). Indeed, there still is. It is compounded by the circumstance that the French word for a slice of meat is escalope (see VEAL); and by the formation of a verb 'to scallop' which sometimes is and sometimes is not connected with scallop shells. Hannah Glasse's recipe for making Collups of Oysters is a fine example of such confusion. It has nothing to do with collops, but requires the oysters to be put into scallop shells.

COLOMBIA a country with two coasts, Caribbean and Pacific, and three mountain ranges, the East, West, and Central Cordilleras at the tip of the Andes, which cut off the coastal plains from the vast expanse of jungle stretching towards BRAZIL. The deep valleys between the Cordilleras, and the separation of each of the lower-lying areas from each other by these ranges, are reasons for distinctive regional characteristics being commonplace in Colombian cuisine, whether it be the coconuts, tropical fruits, and fish of the Caribbean coast so well described by the novelist Gabriel García Márquez, with affinity to the cookery of VENEZUELA, or highland dishes of the capital Bogotá, showing some of the Indian influences shared with PERU, ECUADOR, and BOLIVIA.

Different altitudes ensure varied growing conditions and underpin the country's agricultural wealth: an enormous variety of fruits (often consumed as fresh juices); CASSAVA on the coasts; coffee, maize, beans, and potatoes in the highlands. Firm yellow-fleshed potatoes (*papas criollas*) are marks of a common Andean culture, which are eaten fried or boiled or in casseroles typical of highland cooking. *Papas chorreadas* (literally 'poured-upon potatoes') are dishes in which boiled potatoes are smothered by a sauce, e.g. tomato, cheese, and coriander or spring onion and curd cheese.

Ajiaco de pollo is a chicken stew with potatoes and corn, derived from *ajiaco Santafereño* (named after the first name of the capital city), which was originally a stew of an Andean bird now extinct, plus three sorts of potatoes (some to keep firm and whole, the others to thicken) and corn. In its present form it includes cream and capers. These last items, imported from Spain by early settlers, are typical of the 'new' ingredients which have transformed

old Indian dishes both here and in Venezuela.

Staples such as RICE, BEANS, and POTATOES are universal; Colombia is the only Latin American country where rice is more important than MAIZE. However, as in Venezuela, the small patties of cornbread called *arepas* accompany meals in some areas, e.g. Antioquia; and green corn is made into fritters, or used to make the dough for EMPANADAS, or for thickening.

Cassava (yuca in Colombia) finds its way into many soups and stews, e.g. *sancochos*, stews comparable to *olla podrida* (see OLIO) or BOLLITO MISTO, commonly made with chicken, sweet potatoes, cassava, and plantain, and flavoured with fresh coriander. Cassava is used as a thickener in the lowlands; and cassava flour is the basis of *pan de yuca*, an outstandingly light bread of the highlands which incorporates also curd cheese.

Cassava may also be sliced and fried as one of many ingredients for a *picada* (hors d'œuvre). Similar chips are made with PLANTAINS, another staple of the coasts, and their leaves are used as wrappings for steamed foods such as TAMALES.

Tropical fruits have spread from the lowlands to the fertile valleys of the higher ground, be they guava, papaya, or the universal avocado which may be mixed into a soup like *ajiaco Santafereño*; served as a salad accompaniment; or used in a sauce such as *ají de huevo*, which combines avocado, hard-boiled egg, and chilli. Colombians like their food piquant (*picante*), and enjoy the flavour of coriander leaf.

The coasts provide much seafood, and freshwater fish are plentiful in the wide rivers flowing into the Caribbean. These are usually fried or stewed, e.g. in a *sancocho de pescado*.

The COCONUT is yet another important ingredient in the coastal regions. It shares with rice the star role in *Arroz con coco*, a PILAF with RAISINS (another common element in Colombian recipes). It also occurs in soups and stews, e.g. of rabbit or rodents such as PACA.

Though the jungle may yield some picturesque sources of protein, be they ANTS or wild PECCARY, beef is perhaps the most important meat, raised either here or on the eastern plains, bordering Venezuela. Its eating quality is not as fine as Argentine or pampas-reared cattle, so Colombians have been wont to treat it with tenderizing methods, either chopping it into small dice, or subjecting it to two cooking processes—notably applied to 'difficult' cuts like skirt (*sobrebarriga*), which is braised in beer and spices and then roasted.

The Spanish influence is still felt, not least in some sweet dishes such as *Arroz de leche* (a rice pudding with raisins and cinnamon). Other dessert dishes, e.g. the almost ubiquitous fruits boiled in light syrup, are a hybrid: Spanish methods and local fruits.

TJ

COLOMBO a spice mixture used in the French Antilles, especially Guadeloupe. The name comes from the city in Sri Lanka, and the mixture itself seems to derive from 'curry powders' of Sri Lanka, but with differences. According to Landry (1978), it consists of allspice, garlic, coriander, saffron, cinnamon, and perhaps tiny fragments of dried mango (see AMCHUR) or TAMARIND pulp. It is said to be a very good flavouring for fish dishes, and for plantains, sweet potatoes, etc.

The name colombo may be applied to a dish prepared with it.

See also WEST INDIES.

COLOUR AND COOKING See also the following entry, on COLOUR, COLOURING OF FOOD.

The particular substances in foodstuffs which are responsible for their colour are known as pigments. Most of them belong to closely related groups of chemicals, the special spacing of whose atoms brings about different light-trapping effects. Minor chemical differences between the members of the group give different colours. All this applies to natural and artificial colours alike. Examples of the former are the green chlorophyll pigment in plant leaves and the orange pigment present in carrots, carotene. The latter include many pigments derived from coal tar (all 12 of the artificial colours permitted by EEC regulations are coal tar derivatives).

Most plants contain several pigments, whose relative proportions may vary considerably, producing colours which differ noticeably from each other. This is not only true of broad categories such as, say, apples, but applies to apples of one particular variety or strain. Hereditary variations produce differences in chemical composition, and even minute differences of this kind affect colour. Sometimes the results are quite dramatic, even freakish.

CHELATION is another phenomenon which affects colour, among other things.

The groups of pigments discussed below are chlorophyll; carotenoids; flavonoids including anthocyanins, betazyanin, and betaxanthin; and the various kinds of globin. All but the last are plant pigments.

CHLOROPHYLL

People like green vegetables to stay green when cooked, not to turn olive. Chlorophyll is not soluble in water, so the green which is to be preserved will not leach out into the cooking water, which is one blessing. However, there are lots of other things which can affect it. Chlorophyll is a complex substance. It is quickly affected by an alkali or an acid, and by the application of heat.

The effect of an ALKALI, whether already present in the cooking water or added in the form of BICARBONATE OF SODA, is to prevent the replacement of the central magnesium atom in chlorophyll with hydrogen. The vegetable then acquires an unnaturally bright green colour. Some might find this attractive, but the penalties to be paid are formidable. Not only is there a heavy loss of vitamin C, but the cell walls of the vegetable are disrupted and it becomes mushy, even slimy. So it is best to avoid alkaline water and not to add bicarbonate of soda.

ACID has a different effect. Chlorophyll reacts with acid to give an olive-coloured product called pheophytin. This is clearly not wanted, except in artichokes! But acids are naturally present in vegetables. A possible solution is to cook the vegetables in plenty of water, so as to dilute their natural acids, and to leave the pan uncovered to allow volatile acids to escape. But this increases the loss of vitamin C. The dilemma must be resolved according to the individual cook's priorities, or by resorting to a different method of cooking, described below.

The effect of HEAT, in brief, is to decompose the chlorophyll, producing once more the unattractive olive colour. The effect is not immediate. If a green leaf or pea is dropped into boiling water its colour at first intensifies, for reasons which experts still debate but which are probably due to physical action, e.g. the removal of the layer of air between the outer skin of a pea and the inside; and it is only a little later that the green changes to olive. The extent of the change will depend on the temperature and time of cooking. Less of the chlorophyll will be decomposed, and more of the green colour retained, if the vegetable is cooked briefly. Cutting up such vegetables as cabbage makes it possible to shorten the cooking time.

However, there is still one more hazard to consider: the action of the ENZYMES present in vegetables, which tend to cause fading of the chlorophyll in green vegetables which are being stored for a time. The enzyme which affects chlorophyll is called chlorophyllase. When blanching green vegetables before freezing them, it is a good plan to bring them to the boil as quickly as possible, thus hustling this enzyme through its temperature of maximum activity (70 °C, 160 °F) and then quickly destroying it.

The above comments apply particularly to cooking green vegetables by boiling. It will have become clear that there are inescapable disadvantages in this. An alternative is to stir-fry the vegetables quickly, after cutting them up small. This will reduce the loss of vitamin C and of colour.

CAROTENOIDS

These constitute a large group of yellow, orange, and red pigments found in both plants and animals. The most common carotenoid is B (beta) carotene, which has already been mentioned as the pigment responsible for the colour of normal carrots. It is, incidentally, the constituent of CARROTS which our bodies break up to produce vitamin A, an aid to night vision.

The carotenoids, like chlorophyll, are insoluble in water. Unlike chlorophyll, they are not affected to any great extent by the presence of an alkali or an acid. The application of heat may speed up the gradual fading which will anyway be induced by exposure to air and by prolonged storage. But it does not produce very noticeable changes. One particular change which occurs is something of an oddity. The carotenoid pigments in SWEDES turn to a deeper yellow when these vegetables are cooked.

One example of a carotenoid pigment in an animal is the red colour of cooked LOBSTERS and certain other crustaceans. A live lobster is purple or slate-coloured. So is a dead, uncooked lobster. In these situations the red pigment is chemically bonded to a protein and does not appear as red. Cooking breaks the bond and 'releases' the red colour.

The yellow colour of EGG yolks is due to the pigment zeaxanthin (which may be enhanced by including factory-made beta carotene in the hens' diet). Zeaxanthin occurs naturally in MAIZE too. Chickens fed on maize absorb it and acquire a yellow tint to their flesh. Zeaxanthin is not affected significantly by cooking.

FLAVONOIDS

This general term embraces some groups of pigments whose names invite confusion: flavones, flavanols, etc.

Flavones occur in what are thought of as 'white' vegetables—white ONIONS, POTATOES, CAULIFLOWER, and white CABBAGE are all examples—and may in certain circumstances produce a yellowish or brown colour. If this occurs because of cooking the vegetables in 'hard' (in slightly alkaline water), a little lemon juice will deal with the problem.

Tea contains a common flavone, quercetin, and this is why it becomes slightly paler when a slice of lemon is put into it.

Flavones can also produce trouble when vegetables containing them are cooked in aluminium vessels, which may produce yellow or brown chelates; or from contact with iron pans, steel utensils, and cans, which may cause green, blue, red, or brown chelates. See CHELATION. Again adding lemon juice will forestall this kind of change.

THE ANTHOCYANIN GROUP

The pigments in this group are related to the flavones etc., but give red, purple, and blue colours. They are present, for example, in STRAWBERRIES and other berries, CHERRIES, red APPLES, and POMEGRANATES; and also in red CABBAGE, AUBERGINES, and RADISHES. They are soluble in water, and all show a marked sensitivity to the pH factor. In an acid solution they are usually red, whereas in an alkaline one they are violet or blue. If flavones or flavanols are also present, a green colour will be produced by the mixture of yellow and blue.

Since these pigments occur in so many fruits, their behaviour is of interest to those making fruit punches. To achieve a pleasing red colour, for example use red or blue fruit juices and ensure acidity by adding lemon juice.

The most mutable of this group of pigments is that found in red cabbage. In definitely acid conditions it is red. When the pH factor is around neutral it is violet. And once the balance has swung over to the alkaline side it becomes blue-grey. When cooked in alkaline conditions (over pH 8) it turns green. So, to keep it red, it has to be cooked in acid conditions, with the addition of a little lemon juice if necessary.

Related pigments known as proanthocyanins are responsible for the pink colour of cooked PEARS and QUINCES. However, they will only turn pink in acid conditions. Cooks tend to like the colour; but food processors, in curious contrast, take pains to avoid it when canning pears, by ensuring non-acid conditions. (Perhaps they are concerned to give the impression that canned pears are not 'cooked'.)

BETACYANIN AND BETAXANTHIN

These two pigments, present in BEETROOT, fall outside the main groups. Betacyanin is red-violet, betaxanthin yellow. When a beetroot is cooked, its cell walls are made porous and these colours leak out, creating the familiar deep red effect. Betacyanin is an unusually stable red pigment. However, if a highly alkaline cooking medium is used, it may turn yellow. Acid conditions, on the contrary, will make the red colour more purple; and the addition of an acid to beetroots which have turned out yellow will make them red again.

TANNINS

Tannin is usually thought of as something present in TEA, which is quite correct. However, the term has a more general application, referring to a whole group of substances which are related to the flavonoids but distinguished by the fact that they combine an astringent quality with a tendency to produce dark hues such as blackish-blue and blackish-green. They are generally what give unripe fruits an astringent taste. As the fruits ripen, they cease to have this effect. Green PERSIMMONS contain an especially large amount of tannin, which is why they have a markedly astringent, puckery taste. When the persimmons ripen, the membranes enveloping the cells in which the tannin lurks become hard and insoluble and this taste ceases to be evident.

Other examples of tannin at work include one of the few instances of their activity being welcome. The leaves of the tea plant, when intended to produce a black tea, are bruised in the course of processing in order to release the tannins and let them darken the leaves. But most other examples are of undesirable changes.

GLOBINS: COLOUR IN MEAT

Globins, which provide the red colour in meat, are examples of CHELATION. They are numerous, and each has a name which consists of -globin with a prefix attached. Some explanation of how one globin changes into another, and so on, promotes understanding of the colour changes in meat, whether fresh, cured, or cooked.

In the meat of a dead animal, some of the colour comes from the red haemoglobin in the blood, but most comes from the myoglobin in the muscle tissue. Fresh myoglobin combines with oxygen from the air to give bright red oxymyoglobin, which is what the surface of recently killed meat exhibits. Inside such meat the unoxygenated myoglobin remains purple.

Prolonged exposure to the air, as when meat is hung, causes a further oxidization of the myoglobin, which now becomes metmyoglobin. This, left to its own devices, would be brown. But there are BACTERIA at work on the surface of the meat and these appropriate some of the available oxygen, with the result that a purplish shade is produced. So the surface of properly hung beef should be a depressing purple-brown, not an attractive deep red.

Two qualifications must be added. First, animals which are thoroughly bled after being killed lose their haemoglobin. Also, they are not usually hung. So they have a flesh of a light, clear pink colour. Secondly, meat sold in shrink-wrapped trays is to some extent protected from oxidation, so its surface remains purplish red, with less of a brown tinge.

When raw meat is cooked, the outside turns brown and the brown colour gradually spreads inwards. The interior lightens from purple to pink. Both these changes occur because heat denatures the myoglobin.

Outside, where oxygen is present, brown haemichrome is formed. Inside, where it is not present, pink haemochrome is the result.
READING: McGee (1984).

COLOUR COLOURING OF FOOD The use of added colour in food, to make it look more appetizing, or for purely aesthetic reasons, or to give it a symbolic character, has been a feature of many cuisines since classical times and probably even earlier.

Red, yellow, and green have been the most usual additions. GOLD AND SILVER LEAF are used in the Indian subcontinent.

Vivid, even lurid, added colours have for long been employed in SE Asia, especially the region which was Indo-China, and the Philippines. The Chinese themselves are fairly exuberant in this respect, for example in some of their coloured bean curd (see TOFU) concoctions. The Japanese are more restrained, tending to rely in their delicate arrangements on the natural colours of the foods themselves, placed in subtle contrast with each other; but they are not averse to giving pink preserved ginger (*beni shoga*) a redder tone, or to colouring their *kamaboko* (see FISH PASTES).

Most traditional colourings are vegetable substances, and many of them provide flavour as well as colour.

Plants which yield stable yellow colours include SAFFRON; MARIGOLD petals, once used for colouring cheese; and ANNATTO, which is extracted from a S. American tree, *Bixa orellana*, and is still used for colouring dairy products. There is also TURMERIC yellow (curcumin), which is different in not being a carotenoid colour, but it does give a yellow.

Red is not so easy. Traditional red colouring include KERMES and COCHINEAL, both of which are pigments made by crushing masses of tiny insects. The kermes bug was known in Europe from ancient times. Cochineal comes from another insect, *Coccus cacti*, which is a parasite on cactus plants in C. America. It was first exported to Europe in 1518, as a cheap means of 'stretching' the expensive kermes. But since it actually gives a better colour, it soon supplanted the older dye.

The red available from plants is usually an unstable anthocyanin pigment, which will turn blue or grey in certain circumstances. Sanders, from SANDALWOOD, was formerly used and figures in English recipes up to the 17th century.

Another red dye, CUDBEAR, comes from a lichen. ALKANNA, made from borage roots, gives a good red when dissolved in an oil or alcohol but turns brown in water. Red PAPRIKA contains a good carotene pigment which has long been used in situations where the potential added flavour of paprika is acceptable. BEETROOT juice gives a reliable red, and is sometimes used by jam manufacturers. And some red fruits, such as the ELDERBERRY, have been used for particular purposes, such as making red wine redder.

Green has never been a problem. The juice expressed from SPINACH contains abundant natural chlorophyll. In SE Asia pandanus leaf (see SCREWPINE) is widely used. PISTACHIO nuts, although expensive, are used in ice cream.

Brown, when wanted, is also easy. CARAMEL has been used for many centuries, and the term has come to indicate a particular golden shade of brown. COFFEE and CHOCOLATE have been used more recently. See, however, BROWNING.

Blue has not been favoured, although there is a recipe in the 15th century MENAGIER DE PARIS for a blue aspic for fish, achieved by the use of heliotrope, and this is not the only example; see Barbara Wheaton (1983, chapter 11 for an 18th-century sky blue sauce; and 1984, rebutting the charge that this was a hoax). Indigo, a plant dye, has had some insignificant uses in the kitchen. Much more important, in SE Asia, is *anjan* (see BUTTERFLY PEA).

Black can come from charcoal, which is tasteless and harmless. LIQUORICE is an alternative, but it does have a flavour of its own.

In short, most desired colours can be added to foods by using natural products. Sometimes this can be done cheaply. But often the expense is such that the food industry has looked for substitutes which can be manufactured at low cost; what are usually called artificial added colours, hence the next topic.

ARTIFICIAL ADDED COLOURS

Passing over horror stories of toxic mineral compounds used in the distant past, we find that since the discovery of coal tar dyes in the 19th century most of the artificial colours used by food processors, and to some extent by caterers, fall into this category. These dyes are stable, and minute quantities of them suffice. Some of them, however, are deemed to be dangerous or potentially so, and the varying opinions held by the authorities in particular countries are reflected in a bewildering range of different regulations about what is and what is not permitted. The EEC has managed to produce a unified list for its member countries. But the United States authorities ban some EEC colours and permit some which are not on the EEC list.

See also ADDITIVES.

COLTSFOOT a name given to various plants of the daisy family for the shape of their leaves. *Tussilago farfara*, the common coltsfoot of Europe, Asia, and N. America, is little used, although a wine and a herbal tea are made from its yellow petals.

In contrast, *Petasites japonicus*, the sweet coltsfoot of Japan, is an important herb which is cultivated for the market. Both the leaf stalks and the unopened flower buds are used in Japanese cooking. The combined flavour of leaf stalks and buds is considered to be appropriate for spring dishes.

The buds, *fuki-no-to* in Japanese, appear in the early spring, before the leaves. Buds of both yellow (staminate) and white (pistillate) flowers serve equally well, furnishing a bitter flavour which is greatly appreciated. They are chopped and used as a garnish for clear soup, or used for *nimono* (see JAPANESE CULINARY TERMS) after being parboiled and soaked in water.

The leaf stalks are blanched in boiling water and peeled before use; they often figure in such dishes as *nimono*, TEMPURA, *aemono* (see JAPANESE CULINARY TERMS).

The Japanese also have a giant sweet coltsfoot, *P. japonicus* var *giganteus*. This tall plant, which may be almost 2 m (around 6') high, is called *Akita-buki* after the city of Akita in N. Japan. There is a story that, in the 18th century, a lord of the Akita clan boasted to a group of lords assembled further south in Edo (now Tokyo) that in his province there grew a sweet coltsfoot 'which attained a leaf the size of an umbrella and a leaf-stalk as thick as a bamboo cane. The other lords laughed away his words as a fanciful tale; the *fuki* they knew was a common herb with a hat-sized leaf and a pencil-thin stalk only two feet high.' But the lord from Akita sent his fastest messengers north to fetch some plants, which they managed to keep fresh on the return journey and by which the Edo lords were confounded.

The leaf stalks of this larger species may be treated like the smaller ones, or pickled for use in winter as a green vegetable; and the flower buds are also used.

COLUMBIAN EXCHANGE the name given to the massive exchange of plants, animals, people, knowledge, etc. (not forgetting diseases) which took place between the Old World and the New World in the period following Columbus' voyages.

To say that Columbus 'discovered' the New World is both true and untrue. Others from Europe (and probably Africa) had crossed the Atlantic before him. Vikings had even set up settlements, later abandoned, in N. America. But none of this earlier activity left easily observable marks on the historical record, whereas the sequence of events that followed Columbus' exploits altered the face of our globe so manifestly and strikingly that even an observer from outer space would have remarked the changes.

Like certain other subjects which would seem at first sight to be so ramified that no one book could handle the task of description and assessment, this subject attracted an author equal to the task. Crosby (1972) produced an elegant and succinct survey of what he termed 'the biological and cultural consequences of 1492'. This work remains of unmatched brilliance.

In the way of food and drink, what passed from New World to Old makes an impressive list: CHOCOLATE, MAIZE, POTATO, TOMATO, CAPSICUM peppers, CASSAVA, SQUASHES and PUMPKIN, GROUNDNUT (peanut), and many BEANS. In addition there were important fruits; PINEAPPLE, AVOCADO, GUAVA, PAPAYA. And there was one important bird, the TURKEY.

Traffic in the other direction included some highly important plant foods (WHEAT, OLIVES, GRAPES, and CITRUS FRUITS and many others, the BANANA, SUGAR CANE, many garden vegetables such as CABBAGE and LETTUCE, and lots besides. But it may be that the animals brought from the Old World were even more important in their long-term effects, whether directly as food (CATTLE, PIGS, SHEEP) or in promoting food production by providing new sources of power (the first horses to exist in America since the Pleistocene were those brought by Columbus in 1493).

Crosby draws attention to the statistics on population growth in the world as a whole in the post-Columbian era. He suggests that rapid worldwide human population growth had probably 'occurred only twice before in all history; once when man, or protoman, first developed tools and again when man invented agriculture. And then it happened again, after the century in which Europeans made highways of the oceans. Is there a connection between Christopher Columbus and the population explosion?' His answer is yes, the transfer of Old World plants and (especially) Old World animals greatly enhanced the capacity of the Americas to feed a growing population; and the arrival in the Old World of a whole new set of food plants paved the way for a rapid increase in the population there.

Most recent authorities would acknowledge (as Crosby did, although less evidence had accumulated when he wrote than is now available) that some things were 'exchanged' before Columbus; for example, MAIZE had reached some parts of the Old World before Columbus set sail. However, this did not change the broad picture. As Crosby puts it: 'There is no doubt whatsoever that no crop of one hemisphere was a significant source of food for large numbers of people of the other hemisphere before 1492.'

COLWICK one of the best known of the old English soft cheeses, is named after the village of Colwick, near Nottingham, and has traditionally been made in the counties of Nottingham and Leicester. Special tin moulds, circular in shape and perforated to allow drainage of whey, are used. A whole Colwick cheese weighs about 700 g (1.5 lb) and has a 'dished' top, which means that its upper surface has sagged into a concave shape. This effect is produced by lining the mould with cheesecloth and pulling this up and inwards from time to time as the cheese drains. As a result, a Colwick cheese is an ideal recipient for fresh raspberries or grapes or other small fruit. This is one of the cheeses which may be called SLIPCOTE, from having a loose skin.

COMBER the name for at least four species of fish, found in the Mediterranean and E. Atlantic, which are smaller relations of the GROUPERS in the family Serranidae.

Serranus cabrilla may be taken as typical. It has a market length of around 30 cm (12"), and is reddish marked with vertical bands and some horizontal stripes below. The comber is appreciated in Spain, especially Galicia, whereas in some other countries it is thought to be fit only for fish soups, or at best fried.

S. scriba is called the 'lettered perch' because of the marks like scribbling on its body.

COMFIT an archaic English word for an item of CONFECTIONERY consisting of a seed, or nut coated in several layers of sugar, equivalent to the French DRAGÉE. In England these small, hard sugar sweets were often made with CARAWAY seeds, known for sweetening the breath (hence 'kissing comfits'). Up to a dozen coats of syrup were needed before the seeds were satisfactorily encrusted. Comfits were eaten as sweets, and also used in other sweet dishes: for example SEED CAKE was made with caraway comfits rather than loose caraway seeds as in the 19th century.

Confectioners as early as the 17th century recognized that by varying the proportions of sugar in the syrup they could change the final texture, making 'pearled' comfits or 'crisp and ragged' comfits.

The word 'comfit' remained in use in English up until the 20th century: Alice, of *Alice in Wonderland*, has a box of comfits in her pocket. During the 20th century, however, it has become obsolete, and the confectionery produced by this method is now known under individual names—SUGAR ALMONDS, HUNDREDS AND THOUSANDS, GOBSTOPPERS are a few examples.   LM

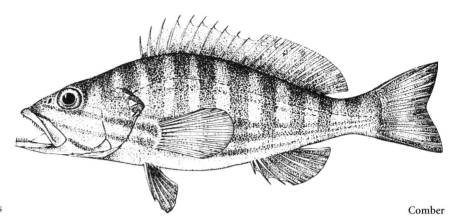

Comber

COMFREY *Symphytum officinale*, a fast-growing European plant, and its several relations (including Russian comfrey) belong to the same family, Boraginaceae, as the herb BORAGE. Early uses were mainly medicinal; an old name is 'boneset'. Pamela Michael (1980) draws attention to a remarkable belief first recorded by William Coles in the 17th century. She writes:

He described the roots as 'so glutinative, that they will fasten together pieces of meat that have been cut asunder, making them all into one lump, if they be boyled in a pot therewith', which seems to be rather a pointless exercise, but Culpeper, too, while extolling the healing properties of comfrey, repeated the strange formula 'so powerful to consolidate and knit together that if they (the roots) be boiled with dissevered pieces of flesh in a pot, it will join them together again'.

Comfrey has been used sporadically as a flavouring herb for homemade wine and, in Bavaria, for butter. Also both the leaves and the stems of comfrey have been eaten, usually boiled. In Bavaria the leaves are dipped in batter and fried. The stems can be blanched by earthing them up, which makes the astringent flavour milder. However, although some have advocated comfrey has a 'health food' for humans, cultivation has been mainly for animal fodder.

COMPOSITION OF FOODS a subject that has engaged scientists for thousands of years. The first serious attempt to classify nutrients was as part of the medical doctrine of the FOUR HUMOURS, itself based on the theory that all matter was made of four elements, air, fire, earth, and water. This theory was developed by the Greek philosophers Pythagoras and Empedocles in the 6th and 5th centuries BC and elaborated by GALEN (2nd century AD). The doctrine had great influence until quite recent times, but was essentially philosophical rather than empirical and did not illuminate the question: of what are foods composed?

The first attempt to discover the composition of foods by experiment dates from 1667, when the newly founded French

Académie des Sciences began to analyse plant substances by distillation, classifying the products into categories such as 'subtle oils' and 'urinous spirits'. By 1721 they had examined over 1,400 plants without useful results.

Further progress had to wait for the discovery of the true nature of chemical elements in the second half of the 18th century—especially the discovery of oxygen, made independently in 1772 by the German Carl Wilhelm Scheele and 1774 by the Englishman Joseph Priestley. Scheele also discovered many of what we now call organic acids, for example lactic acid in sour milk and citric, malic, and tartaric acids in fruits. In 1807 in France, Théodore de Saussure correctly stated that alcohol consists of carbon, hydrogen, and oxygen. Between 1809 and 1814 Joseph-Louis Gay-Lussac and Louis-Jacques Thénard began to work out the characteristic composition of acids, oils, and carbohydrates. Most importantly, in 1846 the German Baron Justus von Liebig classified foodstuffs by their content of carbohydrates, fats, and oils, and what were then called 'albuminoids' or 'nitrogenous matter', now known as proteins.

It was also realized that small amounts of some substances—their nature still unknown—were essential to health. The work of James Lind during the 1750s on the prevention of SCURVY was to lead to the discovery of vitamins at the beginning of the 20th century. The role of minerals—inorganic substances necessary in small amounts—was also gradually elucidated. The last major discovery was that of the role of fibre in digestion, which was not fully established until 1978, by Alison Paul and D. A. T. Southgate.

We now know that food consists of the following substances:

• PROTEIN, the chief structural material of animals, provided in the diet by both animal and plant foods. It allows the body to rebuild and maintain itself; any excess is used as a source of energy. An important subclass of proteins is the ENZYMES, which regulate chemical reactions in the body.

- CARBOHYDRATES, including fibre, provided by plant foods. These are the main source of energy in most diets. Fibre (see CELLULOSE) is not digested, but its bulk carries waste matter through the gut.
- FATS AND OILS, which are essentially the same thing. Solid fats are found mostly in meats; liquid oils in fish and plant foods. They provide essential fatty acid, and carry fat-soluble vitamins.
- MINERALS, inorganic substances required in small amounts. Daily needs range from about half a gram of calcium to one ten-thousandth of a gram of iodine.
- VITAMINS, organic substances which take part in vital chemical reactions, but which the body cannot make itself. Requirements per day range from about a gram for choline (a B-group vitamin) to a couple of micrograms of cobalamin (vitamin B12).
- Last but not least, WATER. All the processes of life take place in a watery environment.

These are the substances necessary to life and health. In addition, food contains a huge diversity of substances which provide FLAVOUR, texture, and COLOUR and make eating a pleasure rather than a duty. ALCOHOL, though not usually considered a foodstuff, does provide energy. Equally, food may well contain harmful substances which can cause FOOD POISONING and other troubles. The chemistry of living things is immensely complex; the more that is discovered, the more it becomes apparent how little we know.   RH

COMPOTE a dish of fruit cooked in a light sugar syrup. The fruit may be fresh or dried (in which case it is soaked before use, possibly with a liqueur or in tea) and may have added flavouring such as cinnamon or lemon zest. It may be served warm or cold, as a dessert. It is often offered in its poaching liquid, which may be such a light syrup as to resemble water in its liquidity, but the more luxurious form (recommended, for example, by Molokhoviets in her classic Russian cookery book of the late 19th century; see Joyce Toomre, 1992) the liquid is considerably reduced before being poured over the fruit in the serving dish.

Compote has been something of a speciality of Russia and E. Europe, down to the Balkans. In those parts, its name appears in forms such as *kompot*. In regions where good desserts are rare, compote is distinguished by being almost invariably wholesome and palatable.

The derivation of the word is interesting. Ayto (1993) remarks that both compote and compost are derived from the past participle of the verb *componere* (to bring together). In

Old French *composte* was used for a dish of fruit stewed in syrup; and this usage was followed for a time in England, e.g. in a 15th-century recipe for 'pears in compost'. C. Anne Wilson (1973) observes that this is one dish where the transition from honey to sugar as the sweetener can be traced, honey and spices having been used in the original compost, 'which was kept and eaten cold as a sort of winter salad', but replaced by a sugar and wine syrup in the 15th century. In the course of the 16th century the modern meaning of compost (a heap of decaying leaves in the garden) was becoming established and the term therefore became increasingly unsuitable for a dish of fruit to be eaten. For the latter purpose the variant compote, borrowed from the French, where it was a later version of composte, came into use.

As with so many culinary items, the frontiers of compote are not always easy to define. Jars of compote can be bought which are bottled; and something very similar to compote appears under other names (see, for example, KHOSHAB) in countries of the Near East and C. and W. Asia.

CONCH a common name used loosely in some parts of the world for a wide range of large, single-shell MOLLUSCS; and more precisely in the Caribbean region, for example, to denote members of the genus *Strombus*, some of which are important as food. True conchs are all inhabitants of tropical waters, and all are herbivorous; whereas WHELKS, which superficially resemble them, are often found in colder waters and are carnivorous.

Strombus gigas, the Queen conch, is known in Bermuda and parts of Florida as well as throughout the W. Indies. Its shell is highly decorative, rosy on the inside, and may be 30 cm (1') long. The creature within is like a huge snail with horns tipped by bright golden eyes. Its white flesh is compact and will be rubbery unless carefully prepared.

A conch will have been extracted from its shell and cleaned before sale, but it may still have to be tenderized in one way or another before it is ready for use. The first step is often to marinate it in lime juice. Beating is usual, as for ABALONE or OCTOPUS. Typical W. Indian conch dishes are *Daube de lambis aux haricots rouges* (conch stew with red kidney beans) and *Matété de lambis* (rice and conch stew). Prepared conch flesh may also be eaten raw in seafood salads.

CONDIMENT a word derived from the Latin *condire*, meaning to preserve or pickle, is defined by the *NSOED* as: 'Anything of pronounced flavour used to season or give

relish to food, or to stimulate the appetite.' In practice, it is used more of items employed at table than of the same or similar items in the kitchen; but both usage and scope are flexible. Thudichum (1895) devoted an interesting essay to categorizing condiments, taking the term in its broadest sense.

CONFECTIONERY (*see page 210*)

CONFIT a term which comes from the French verb *confire*, 'preserve'. Meat, typically goose, duck, pork, or turkey, is cooked in its own fat, covered in its own fat, and then preserved in a pot. Confit keeps well and this improves the tenderness of the meat and the flavours. Confit can be eaten hot or cold and is sometimes added to dishes to add extra flavour.

See also RILLETTE and QAWARMA (the Middle Eastern equivalent preserve of lamb in fat). Another example of the confit technique is given under MUTTON-BIRD. READING: Renée Valéri (1977).

CONGEE a watery 'porridge' (of the category often called GRUEL) made with RICE, preferably glutinous, in S. China, where it is known as *zhou*. Plain congee is usually eaten as the first meal of the day. It is a bland dish and may be accompanied by salted fish or other strongly flavoured food to provide contrast.

Chicken congee, *ji zhou*, is a more nourishing and flavourful version. A MILLET congee is also made. Florence Lin (1986) mentions both these and also provides an illuminating tip for anyone who has to take in a bowl of hot congee at high speed:

First you fill the rice bowl to the brim with congee. Then, holding the bowl with the palm of your hand, you put your mouth against the rim and suck the congee while your palm turns the bowl. With one breath of sucking along the rim of the bowl, you can swallow a quarter of a bowl of congee. This is because the congee is cooler at the rim. If you needed three bowls to quell your hunger, it didn't take long to get them with this method.

Congee is a prominent street food. It is easily digested and perhaps for this reason is regarded as a good pick-me-up after exercise or illness.   HS

CONGER EEL *Conger conger*, a voracious fish of the Mediterranean and E. Atlantic with a close relation in the W. Atlantic, *C. oceanicus*. It may be up to 2 m (80") in length and is of variable colour, mostly grey or brownish.

(*cont. on page 211*)

Confectionery

A term with blurred edges but generally indicating a delicacy which is sweet, is usually eaten with the fingers, and keeps for some time. The word 'confection' is related to medieval Latin *confecta* and the English word COMFIT, with meanings associated with the preparation of a mixture, and preservation in sugar.

Some but not all confectionery items are associated with particular festivals, for example Easter eggs (see EASTER FOODS); or locations, as in seaside ROCK; or rewards and luxury, for instance hand-made CHOCOLATES.

Some are small pastries. Most, however, at least in W. Europe and N. America are sweets (American candy), made with a lot of sugar and additional ingredients to give flavour and texture. SUGAR BOILING is one method used to produce many favourites in this category.

Middle Eastern confectionery is rather different, using cereal ingredients. TURKISH DELIGHT is thickened with CORNFLOUR, and many forms of HALVA have a basis of SEMOLINA. Here and in Asia proper, although sugar-based sweets are made, there is no division between sugar confectionery and pastry or other sweet dishes.

Milk products are important ingredients in Indian confectionery. (See INDIAN SWEETS; MILK REDUCTION.) The textures of many Indian confections are produced by varying this and the proportions of cereals and pulses, from curd alone to cereal or pulse alone. The sugar content of an Indian sweet may be quite high, but with a few exceptions, sugar is not used to govern the texture.

Preferences as to the flavour of sweets differ between West and East. In a typical western sweet, with its high concentration of sugar, the intense sweetness may be offset by a contrasting flavour such as the sharpness of acid fruit or the bitterness of CARAMEL, CHOCOLATE, COFFEE, or black TREACLE. Asian sweets, with a lower proportion of sugar, especially those of India, generally rely on spices and perfumes as flavouring agents. Westerners often find them stodgy in texture and insipid in flavour. As an example of an extreme and illiberal view, one may take that of J. W. L. Thudichum (1895), who wrote:

The so-called confectioneries made by native Hindoos, in the Indian and colonial Exhibition in London, were, either indifferent to flatness, or simply repulsive.

The stalactite-like pipes made of syrup and starch, resembling bullose macaroni, baked in foetid oil, no amount of enthusiasm could find attractive, or even, consumable.

Indians may find western confections equally deplorable, but have been more tactful in their criticisms.

Further east, in China and Japan, the sweet tooth is less evident. That is not to say that sweets do not exist: sugar sticks and candied fruits, as well as sweet pastries and raw sugar cane for chewing, are mentioned in ancient Chinese writings. Both the Chinese and the Japanese have long made malt extract for use as a sweetener. But sweets have been an occasional luxury, to be eaten at festivals, for example.

When sugar first became known in Europe it was a rare and costly commodity, valued mainly for its supposed medicinal qualities and finding its place in the pharmacopoeia of the medieval apothecary. This history no doubt accounts in part for the way in which sugar-based sweets have been treated as a category apart from other sweetmeats.

Sugar gradually became more widely available in Europe during the Middle Ages. In Britain, it was considered to be an excellent remedy for winter colds. It might be eaten in the form of candy crystals, scented and coloured with roses or violets. Or it might be made into little twisted sticks which were called in Latin *penida*, later Anglicized to 'pennets'. The tradition of *penida* survives most clearly in American stick CANDY which is similarly twisted and flavoured with essences supposed to be effective against colds, such as oil of WINTERGREEN. The British BARLEY SUGAR which was first made in the 17th century was for a long time sold in twisted sticks, which have only recently begun to disappear. A vast range of 'cough sweets' also carries on the apothecaries' tradition, as do other confections: MARSHMALLOW and LIQUORICE have both been used as medicine.

While sugar was still an expensive luxury, HONEY, though not cheap either, was widely available. There is a widespread and longstanding tradition of simple home-made sweets based on honey (even if sugar is used in modern versions because it is now cheaper), from Ukrainian forms of NOUGAT to the old-fashioned TOFFEES of Wales and Ireland.

Confections made either in the home or by tradesmen known as comfitmakers in the 16th and 17th centuries in England included many fruit-based items such as SUCKETS, FRUIT PASTES, PRESERVES, conserves, MARMALADES, JELLIES, and CANDIED FRUITS. CANDIED VIOLETS were also fashionable. Many of these confections have some basis in the desire to preserve fruit for winter use; some were regarded as medicinal or aphrodisiac. MARZIPAN was also popular; and COMFITS, or sugar-plums, gave their name to the trade. These sweets were important components of the final course or BANQUET in the meals of wealthy households. This involved all kinds of sweetmeats, tarts, spiced cakes, and GINGERBREAD, consumed with sweet wines. Even the crockery might be edible, when made from a confection called sugar plate, a mixture of powdered sugar, rosewater, and GUM TRAGACANTH.

Sweets were served at other times: served with wine for visitors, given as presents, and copiously fed to expectant and nursing mothers to build up their strength. It was an era of a prodigiously sweet tooth, and nowhere more so than in Britain. Foreign visitors commented on the sugar-rotted, blackened teeth of the English aristocracy, including those of Queen Elizabeth herself, mentioned by a German observer at the end of the 16th century as an affliction from which the English suffered, as a result of consuming too much sugar.

Throughout the 17th and early 18th centuries, making confections at home was regarded as a suitable pastime for elegant and wealthy ladies. Their realm often also included beauty preparations, perfumes, and medicines. Sir Hugh Platt's *Delightes for Ladies* (1609) is an example of a work focused on such interests. The survival of such books has resulted in our knowing more about home-made sweets of that period than about professionally made ones; yet there were numerous professional confectioners, some making their products for sale and some in the employment of rich households. It would have been a hardy lady who dared to try to make a banquet centrepiece herself.

During the 17th and 18th centuries the skills of sugar boiling diffused from Italy and France. Some confections, such as suckets of lettuce stalks or ERINGO, disappeared. New flavourings, in the form of COFFEE and CHOCOLATE, were tentatively used (their main use at this time was for drinks). An innovation confined mainly to Britain was TREACLE or molasses from SUGAR CANE. This was first used in the 1660s for GINGERBREAD, but soon found its way into confectionery. Black treacle TOFFEE is an old-established sweet, still highly popular in Britain. By the mid-18th century, the banquet course of a large dinner, with its abundant sweets had gone out of fashion. Sweets and sweet dishes still appeared as part of the second course, but they were less important than before. Plenty of sweets were still eaten at other times. This shift in practice coincided with a change in the nature of the

dense, sugary fruit pastes and conserves which had been a feature of the banquet. A rough notion of the importance of hygiene in the sealing of jars of preserves was developing, and there was no need to reduce preserves to such a dry consistency. Thus the old suckets and marmalades began to yield to jams of the modern type.

Chocolate became important in confectionery in the 19th century, when the Dutchman Conrad van Houten invented a process for removing much of the naturally occurring fat associated with cocoa. This allowed the use of chocolate for bars and for coating purposes. See CHOCOLATE IN THE 19TH AND 20TH CENTURIES. During the same period advances in science led to understanding of the principles behind sugar boiling, and the application of technology allowed the production of cheap sweets on a large scale. Throughout the early part of the century, these were frequently coloured with derivatives of mercury, arsenic, and lead and were the cause of illness and sometimes death. Concern on this score was partly responsible for the legislation which now controls food standards in Britain.

By the end of the 19th century, many of the confections familiar today were in production. The companies producing them had become household names through vigorous advertising campaigns. Whatever else western adults may have forgotten about their childhood, the likelihood is that they recall effortlessly the names—and texture and flavour—of the confectionery they enjoyed as children.

For a French term which corresponds in important respects to confectionery, see FRIANDISE.   (LM)
READING: Laura Mason (1998).

The conger comes out to feed at night, hiding by day in rocky crevices, often close to the shore. It is the biggest and most terrifying fish which bathers may disturb if probing among inshore rocks; and is fierce enough to do battle with the redoubtable OCTOPUS, whose chief enemy it is. Since a large, old conger retains all these ferocious characteristics, it is curious that for Alice (in Wonderland) an old conger was the 'drawling master, who came once a week to teach drawling, stretching, and fainting in coils'.

The flesh of the conger seems to be more esteemed in Spain and on the Atlantic coast of France (it is even complimented by the name *bœuf bellilois* in Belle-Île), and in SW England and Wales, than in other regions. The bony tail-end is best reserved for soup, but a middle cut can be poached or braised, or even roasted like meat, with good results.

The range of *C. conger* in the E. Atlantic extends down to S. Africa; but in other parts of the southern hemisphere, notably Australasian waters, it is replaced by various other congers. In Indo-Pacific waters the principal conger is *Muraenosox cinereus*, a species which sometimes enters fresh waters.

CONJUROR a 19th-century device for cooking meat rapidly with burning paper as the fuel. It seems to have been descended from the 'necromancer' to which Hannah Glasse (1747) referred, ascribing its invention to an actor, Mr John Rich, and declaring it to be much admired by the nobility (in 1735). However, the necromancer can be traced further back, to Bradley (1736), who gave a recipe for 'Thin Beef-Collops Stew'd. From Oxford' which uses the same technique. Stead (1983) surmises from this that the method and the equipment might have been previously practised by students at Oxford University ('student bed-sitter makeshift cookery'), but also utilized by the theatrical profession when in need of a hot meal and away from normal cooking facilities.

The best description of the conjuror is that of Eliza Acton (1845), which was accompanied by a good illustration:

Steaks or cutlets may be quickly cooked with a sheet or two of lighted paper only, in the apparatus called a conjuror. Lift off the cover and lay in the meat properly seasoned, with a small slice of butter under it, and insert the lighted paper in the aperture shown; in from eight to ten minutes the meat will be done, and found to be

remarkably tender, and very palatable: it must be turned and moved occasionally during the process. This is an especially convenient mode of cooking for persons whose hours of dining are rendered uncertain by their avocations. The part in which the meat is placed is of block tin, and fits closely into the stand, which is of sheet iron.

CONNECTIVE TISSUE is the name given to the various structures which support muscles in meat. On eating, it is usually referred to as gristle and considered undesirable. It contributes to the toughness of meat. Before cooking, connective tissue is visible as semi-transparent membranes between muscles; it is also there invisibly as very thin fine layers supporting bundles of muscle fibres and individual fibres.

The protein COLLAGEN is responsible for the tough qualities of connective tissue. It is composed of coiled fibrous molecules, each one a sequence of AMINO ACIDS held in a helix by hydrogen bonds and cross-links between the acids. The number of links increases as the animal ages; it is this, not an increase in the proportion of connective tissue generally, that makes the meat of older animals tougher than that of youngsters. The proportion of connective tissue varies according to the position of the meat in the animal's body. The more there is present, the tougher the meat will be, and the cheaper the cut.

Heat alters the fibres of connective tissue, initially by making them shorter and thicker, and then by altering the structure. Long cooking breaks down the bonds and cross-links of the collagen, and eventually some of it becomes soluble, leaching out of the meat to form GELATIN (this is the reason why cold gravy often forms a gel). The change occurs whether water is added or not. Whilst heat softens collagen, it hardens the muscle fibres in meat, to the extent that they become dry and mealy by the time the collagen has broken down. Cooking methods for meat therefore involve a compromise which aims to minimize the hardening of the muscle and maximize the softening of connective tissue. Moist methods are successful for tough cuts of meat, partly because water is a more efficient medium for heat transfer than air, but also because the sauces produced (e.g. when using traditional casserole recipes) enhance flavour and provide the moisture which the meat needs.

Connective tissue in fish is much more fragile and less noticeable.   LM

CONSOMMÉ meaning a clear SOUP, has been used in English since the early part of the 19th century, but has been a French culinary term since the 16th century. It is the past participle of the verb *consommer*, meaning to consume or accomplish or finish, and indicating in this context a 'finished' soup as opposed to a simple stock or broth. *Double consommé* is a clarified consommé.

Little fragments of this or that may be introduced into a consommé at some stage in its production, or just when serving, and the nature of these is, in classical French cookery, reflected in the name given to the consommé. Garrett (*c*.1895) gives nearly three dozen different recipes, but sensibly distances himself from any taxonomical discussion:

Several futile attempts have been made by gastronomers to classify Consommés, as they have also tried in vain to draw distinctions between broths, soups, Consommés, potages and bouillons; but as the receipts for what would be intermediaries of these classifications outnumber the classified soups themselves, it will not be advisable in this work to introduce such a useless arrangement.

A consommé may be served hot or cold, usually at the beginning of a meal. The simplest consommé of all, in France, is the BROTH (*bouillon*) from POT-AU-FEU.

COOK (*see opposite page*)

COOKERY SKILL, ART, OR SCIENCE? This question is sometimes posed. The answer must be that cookery can be any or all of these; it depends on who is cooking, in what context, and for what purpose.

The language used in medieval cookery texts (mostly manuscripts) is consonant with **the skill view.** Yet there is also a touch of what would now be called 'science' in some of them, because they assume that the choice of foods and combinations of foods is a branch of medicine, or at least a close ally thereof; see GALEN and FOUR HUMOURS.

Next, **the art view.** This, necessarily has to be combined with the skill view. If cookery is an art, then according to the normal usage of the terms 'art' and 'artist', it is only done well and properly by a limited number of people—corresponding in practice to the great chefs of the time. They are the artists, who stand out like mountaintops among the foothills. Lower down come the vast majority of practitioners, who go through similar but less complicated and subtle motions in their kitchens, and who are no more than artisans.

The art view becomes noticeable in the 16th century, at least in the English language. The work of Jos. Cooper (1654) bore the title *The Art of Cookery*; and the phrase 'the whole Art of Cookery' appeared two years later in the subtitle of M. Marnette's *The Perfect Cook*. But it was in the 18th century that the titles chosen for cookery books laid most emphasis on its being an art. The most famous of the 18th-century cookery books, that of Hannah Glasse, is called *The Whole Art of Cookery Made Plain and Easy*; but she also wrote *The Complete Confectioner or The Whole Art of Confectionery Made Plain and Easy*. In this latter book she unveiled yet another connected art, that of making artificial fruits.

Finally, **the science view.** This seems to have found its first clear expression, in English, in a not very good book by Francis Collingwood and John Woollams: *The Universal Cook . . .*, first published in 1792. Their preface begins by disavowing any intent 'to discover what was the food of our first parents in the garden of Eden, or in what manner they performed their culinary operations: it is sufficient for us to know at present that Cookery is become a science.' (It is true that they almost immediately refer to it as an art, in traditional style, but they then repeat the term 'science' with emphasis.)

In the course of the 19th century the aspects of science (even if it was pseudo-science) which underlie cookery came increasingly to notice. The activities and writings of Count Rumford are highly

relevant here. McGee (1990) has brought out not only the connection between the work of the best-known French gastronomic writer, BRILLAT-SAVARIN, and the science of his day, but also the importance of Liebig and of concepts such as osmazome in culinary thinking of that era. Among the relevant books of the period one of the best was called *The Chemistry of Cookery* (by Mattieu Williams, 1st edn 1885).

Another was *Science in the Kitchen* by the American Mrs Kellogg (1904), who had charge of the experimental kitchen at the famous sanitarium at Battle Creek (see BREAKFAST CEREALS). She stated optimistically:

Cookery, when based upon scientific principles, ceases to be the difficult problem it so often appears. Cause and effect follow each other as certainly in the preparation of food as in other things; and with a knowledge of the underlying principles, and faithfulness in carrying out the necessary details, failure becomes almost an impossibility.

The 20th century has seen, on the whole, an increasing tendency to treat the most prominent chefs as artists. At the same time, however, the works of McGee and others (e.g. the French author Hervé This) have reminded readers that much of the art displayed has to rest on a scientific basis. And, of course, the vast majority of people have continued their lives on the tacit assumption that cookery is a skill, which some people have more than others.

COOKIE the name used in N. America for a small, flat, sweet confection, which approximates to a sweet BISCUIT as eaten in England, although cookies tend to be richer and have a softer, chewy texture. The name first appeared in print as long ago as 1703.

Generations of immigrants from all over Europe have contributed to the American tradition of cookies. Early Dutch settlers introduced their recipes for various types of *koekje*, Dutch for 'little cake' (see BANKETBAKKERIJ), the name which needed only slight adaptation to become cookie. English, Scandinavian, German, and E. European settlers introduced numerous types of biscuit, including many which could be classed as cookies, and maintained their connection with feast days. Cookies were originally associated, in the USA, with New Year's Day; references cited by Craigie and Hulbert (1938) from the early part of the 19th century show that cookies and cherry bounce (a cherry cordial) were the correct fare with which to greet visitors on that occasion, although already threatened 'by plum-cake and outlandish liqueurs', as one author put it.

(*cont. on page 214*)

Cook

A noun which is sometimes difficult to disentangle from CHEF; the two terms can certainly overlap in meaning, although chef normally indicates a professional cook in an establishment of some standing while plain 'cook' can mean someone who cooks for a living, but also an amateur domestic cook, usually a woman.

Cooks figure often in literature. An anthology of references to them could be a large book in itself. To give only the barest taste of the subject, three very different passages from three different authors are offered here—a mere twitching back of the curtain, for no more than seconds, on this richly variegated population (which must surely number hundreds of millions of mainly women).

For the medieval period, Bridget Ann Henisch (1976):

As one peers down the tunnel of time, trying to catch glimpses of the medieval cook at work, there is at first disappointingly little to be seen. Neither he nor his equipment were considered worthy of a center-stage position, and so they must be hunted down patiently in the nooks and crannies of art and literature. Kitchen scenes are hard to find, but many a cauldron bubbles in exotic settings: devils tend their pots over the fires of hell in a Last Judgement, cooks stir their dinner on the back of a whale at the bottom of a page. A stewpot perched on the head of a rakish monster in a manuscript border, a stumpy little man carved on a bench end, clutching a ladle as long as himself, these are the scraps which make up the patchwork quilt of first impressions.

Such random clues suggest that cooks were exceedingly cross and their kitchens in perpetual uproar. Dogs were everywhere, looking for dinner. According to a proverb recorded in the sixteenth century, 'The cook is not so sone gone as the doges hed is in the porigpot.' Medieval dogs never deigned to wait for a back to be turned. A misericord in St George's Chapel, Windsor, shows four enormous hounds piling into a cauldron, indifferent to the cook just poised to hurl his ladle. . . .

Animals may have been incidental irritations in the kitchen, but the cook's principal distractions were his fellow humans. The scene which appears most frequently in art shows the cook repelling boarders, beating off the tasters and nibblers who hover hopefully round his precious stewpot. A polished flirt knew exactly how to make defenses crumble. In a border of the fourteenth-century *Smithfield Decretals*, he has one arm round the cook, while deftly fishing a joint out of her cauldron with the other.

Only lovers can get away with such shameless depredations; husbands are clouted as soon as they creep within range. On a misericord in Bristol Cathedral, the husband has actually managed to get as far as lifting the lid of the stewpan, but his wife has him firmly by the beard, while a pot, shown by the artist in mid-flight past the poor man's ear, testifies to female bad temper and worse aim. . . . The kitchen was a classic battleground for the sexes, although which was regarded as the aggressor depended naturally on the point of view. A sequence of border scenes in the *Smithfield Decretals* shows a husband toiling to please, fetching water, washing dishes, grinding corn, baking bread, but beaten up after every task by an implacable wife. In the fifteenth-century poem *A Young Husband's Complaint*, the henpecked victim is barked out of the kitchen in every verse, and hit on the head whenever he asks for dinner. . . .

. . . In popular belief, cooks were expected to be drunk: the medieval phrase 'a temperance of cooks' is heavy with sarcasm, and Chaucer's cook runs true to type by being so full of liquor that he falls off his horse.

When not actually quarreling, cooks seem to have had an alarming sense of humor and plenty of time in which to indulge it. Among the stories written down in the twelfth century about the Saxon outlaw Hereward and his guerrilla warfare against the Norman conquerors, one tells how he slipped into the King's camp disguised as a potter. His first stop was at the kitchen, to show his wares. There the cooks, inevitably, were drinking on the job while they prepared the King's meal. As spirits rose, one of them had the brilliant idea of shaving off the potter's beard with his chopping knife. Hereward had to fight his way through a suddenly menacing circle of kitchen staff, armed to the teeth with razor-sharp equipment. Being no mere peddler but a hero in disguise, he not only escaped but left behind him several concussed cooks and, doubtless, one King crossly roaring for his ruined dinner.

In the 18th century, there is a vivid description of the interface in a kitchen between a chef and a cook, from the racy pen of William VERRAL. The chef has just prepared a menu for a dinner that he is to give in a private home.

My next step was to go and offer a great many compliments to Mrs. Cook about getting the dinner; and as it was her master's order I should assist her, I hoped we should agree; and the girl, I'll say that for her, returned the compliment very prettily, by saying, Sir, whatever my master or you shall order me to do, shall be done as far and as well as I am able. But Nanny (for that I found to be her name) soon got into such an air as often happens upon such occasions. Pray, Nanny, says I, where do you place your stewpans, and the other things you make use of in the cooking way? La, Sir, says she, that is all we have (pointing to one poor solitary stewpan, as one might call it,) but no more fit for the use than a wooden hand-dish. Ump, says I to myself, how's this to be? A surgeon may as well attempt to make an incision with a pair of sheers, or open a vein with an oyster-knife, as for me to pretend to get this dinner without proper tools to do it; here's neither stewpan, soup-pot, or any one thing else that is useful; there's what they call a frying-pan indeed, but black as my hat, and a handle long enough to obstruct half the passage of the kitchen. However, upon a little pause I sent away post haste for my own kitchen furniture. In the meantime Nanny and I kept on in preparing what we could, that no time might be lost. When the things came we at it again, and all was in a tolerable way, and forward enough for the time of day; but at length wanting a sieve I begg'd of Nanny to give me one, and so she did in a moment; but such a one!—I put my fingers to it and found it gravelly. Nanny, says I, this won't do, it is sandy: she look'd at it, and angry enough she was: rot our Sue, says she, she's always taking my sieve to sand her nasty dirty stairs. But, however, to be a little cleanly Nanny gave it a good thump upon the table, much about the part of it where the meat is generally laid, and whips it into the boiler where I suppose the pork and cabbage was boiling for the family, gives it a sort of rinse, and gave it me again, with as much of the pork fat about it as would poison the whole dinner; so I said no more, but could not use it, and make use of a napkin that I slily made friends with her fellow-servant for; at which she leer'd round and set off; but I heard her say as she flirted her tail into the scullery, hang these men cooks, they are so confounded nice.—I'll be whipt, says she, if there was more sand in the sieve than would lay upon a sixpence. However, she came again presently, and I soon coax'd her into good humour again; come, says I, Nanny, I'm going to make fricasee of chicken, observe how I cut'em (for I'll show ye how to do any part of the dinner), and she seemed very attentive. When I had cut mine, there, says I, do you take that, and cut it in the same manner; and indeed the girl handled her knife well, and did it very prettily: then I gave her directions how to proceed; and it was done neatly, notwithstanding the story of the sandy sieve. I then took in hand to show her in what manner it was to be finished for the table. And now, dinner being dish'd up, Nanny was vastly pleased, and said, that in her judgment it was the prettiest and best she had ever seen.

M. F. K. FISHER (1984) next. She provides a searching and indeed disquieting examination of those people (mainly women) who 'love to cook'.

There is another category of people who 'must live to cook,' and I belong to it . . . It is the cooks of this third gastronomical world, who must be most careful about confusing the love to cook with the love to control and dominate. They/we can be a rapacious and ruthless lot, in the need to keep families undoubting and devoted. We must watch ourselves and our own skills and trickeries like wary buzzards, so that we stay honest . . . or at least overt.

It is probably fortunate that most of us practitioners of the art of making our loved ones believe that we love to cook, because we love *them*, can often watch our own kind at work.

We have all had the chance, for instance, to recognize how fallible people can be. Say that an Italian friend invites us to a 'strictly family' meal. 'If you haven't tasted my mother's spaghetti,' and he rolls his eyes ecstatically and spreads his hands outwards in a slightly helpless gesture straight from either Milan or Genoa, 'Ah, *mama mia*, you have never tasted true spaghetti!'

So you go, as if to a Special Mass, to an intimate kichen-table meal, which means that Papa is in his shirtsleeves and a sulky daughter-in-law has consented to drop in with a couple of howling babies, who are mercifully invisible in Grandma's bedroom. And Mama, in very high heels because this afternoon was her Society of the Daughters of the Circle of Holy St. Genevieve, teeters dutifully between stove and the big table where we all sit, tumblers of cheap rot-gut red on the ready, waiting for the platter of lukewarm overcooked packaged pasta that one of

her boys carried dramatically ahead of her as she sinks, exhausted but beatific, into her chair. Somebody tosses the puddle of bottled tomato-mushroom sauce into the limp pasta; we all sprinkle it with imitation Parmesan cheese and moan and grunt in voracious bliss. 'Mama Mia!' the men mutter, rolling their eyes. . . .

Of course it is not always mothers who command this blind if occasional devotion, but they seem dominant, at least in our Western society, and I can think of many I have known, here and in Europe and Mexico. In the Mid-West, for instance, I know a woman who honestly believes that The Kitchen is holy. It is the fountain-head of our whole society, and something never to be touched by doubting foreigners or the subversive anti-Christian elements that are trying to eat away our good American trust in Mom-the-Flat-and-Apple Pie. . . .

When she is not filling her temple, her shrine, with the heady incense of fried chicken, and Aunt Jennie's recipe for corn-bread and Gramma Jenkin's mince-meat pudding, with a kettle of plum butter chucklin' on the back burner, she is energetically making plaques, dozens of them.

She sells them at the County Fair, to benefit her Church missionary activities. They are of varnished pine, and after many years of turning them out between stirring her peach conserve and making the best canned corn this side of Sioux City, she is whiz at using the electric script-burner Paw gave her on their twenty-fifth anniversary.

Sometimes she puts a design of entwined hearts at the top, for newly married couples, but usually the plain ones are the best-sellers. They say

WELCOME TO MY KITCHEN
AROUND THIS TABLE
FAMILY AND FRIENDS SHARE
THE WARMTH
OF LOVE AND TOGETHERNESS

Sometimes she changes the words a little, but the message is always the same, that we are invited to worship at her kitchen and its stove. It is there that we will find real love, because *she* loves to cook.

At the risk of sounding sacrilegious, but always with the courtesy due any fellow-culprit, I think that people who have so candidly, even voluptuously, designated themselves as high priests at their own altars, are potential egomaniacs.

The American habit of making up rolls of cookie dough and keeping them in the refrigerator or freezer may have come from Germany; the doughs for some German biscuits such as *Heidesand* are made into rolls and chilled before slicing. Pieces are sliced off and baked as required. These are often known as 'icebox' cookies, and usually made from a rich creamed mixture. A type of icebox cookie has spread to the Chinese community; made from an almond-flavoured creamed mixture, it is known as *hsing jen ping*. Fortune cookies, twists of plain dough which enclose slips of paper carrying prophecies, are a commercial invention

of the Chinese community in N. America.

An alternative to recipes based on creamed doughs is provided by soft mixtures of a dropping consistency, used to make 'drop cookies'.

Of the numerous recipes which have evolved in America, one of the best known is that for the chocolate chip, or Toll House cookie, which according to Mariani (1994) did not appear in recipe books until the 1930s; it was created by Mrs Ruth Wakefield who owned the Toll House Inn in Whitman, Massachusetts.

In Scotland the term 'cookie' has been in use since around 1700, but the original

meaning is uncertain. It now refers to a lightly enriched bread bun, which may be split and filled with cream, or ornamented with icing.

COOKING a subject which can be approached as a matter of definition (answer: cooking food is preparing it, by the application of heat, for being eaten) or through many different questions, e.g. how? (see the numerous articles on cookery techniques, such as FRYING), by whom? (see COOK, CHEF).

In this article the question is why? And this is one question to which the Latin epigram *Tot homines [et feminae] quot sententie* does not apply, since most *homines* and *feminae* have not had occasion to think about it at all. Those who have, and who have expressed their thoughts, usually produce several answers, including the promotion of digestibility and an increase in enjoyment; and the order in which such factors are listed provides interesting evidence of the authors' attitudes to eating.

Here are some quotations, which seem to advance, respectively, one, two, three, and five reasons for cooking.

[In more primitive times] *only to live* has been the greatest object of mankind; but, by-and-by, comforts are multiplied and accumulating riches create new wants. The object, then, is not only to *live*, but to live economically, agreeably, tastefully and well. Accordingly, the art of cookery commences; and although the fruits of the earth, the fowls of the air, the beasts of the field, and the fish of the sea, are still the only food of mankind, yet these are so prepared, improved, and dressed by skill and ingenuity, that they are the means of immeasurably extending the boundaries of human enjoyments. Everything that is edible, and passes under the hands of the cook, is more or less changed, and assumes new forms. Hence the influence of that functionary is immense upon the happiness of the household. (Mrs Isabella Beeton, *The Book of Household Management*, 1st edn, 1861)

It is to be noted that the object aimed at in cooking food is twofold: First, from an aesthetic point of view, to improve its appearance when it comes to table, and to develop in it new flavours; second, with a hygienic purpose, to partially sterilise the food, thereby enabling it to remain longer sweet, and good. (W. T. Fernie, *Meals Medicinal*, 1905))

The purposes of cooking are threefold—(1) to assist digestion by preparing the food for the action of the digestive juices, (2) to quicken the flow of saliva and other digestive secretions by making it pleasing to the palate and other senses, and (3) to destroy by heat any disease germs or parasites that it may contain. (Artemas Ward, *The Encyclopaedia of Food*, New York, edn of 1923)

[Reasons for Cooking]
(1) to render mastication easy; (2) to facilitate digestion; (3) to increase the food value; (4) to eliminate any risk of infection from harmful bacteria; (5) to make the food agreeable to the palate and pleasing to the eye. (Editors of *Mrs Beeton's Book of Household Management*, Ward, Lock, London, 1948 edn.)

Thus we pass from the cheerful hedonism of Mrs Beeton herself, undiluted by any other thoughts (and anticipating by two years the publication of John Stuart Mills's *Utilitarianism*, which would establish the maximization of happiness as a guiding principle), to mixed formulae in which the aesthetic or enjoyment factor is successively first, second, and a feeble fifth. However, it does not follow that there is a widening gulf between cookery and pleasure; but rather that there has been progressively more understanding in the last 150 years of the variety of reasons which exist for cooking food (coupled perhaps with a decreasing ability to write on the subject in an attractive manner).

The reasons for cooking can perhaps be represented thus:

to increase our enjoyment of it	to make it more digestible
	and often
to enhance its nutritional value	to prevent it spoiling and help it to keep

And in many instances only one or two of these reasons may apply, or may be dominant.

For consideration of how we would get on if we adopted the recommendations of those who completely oppose any cooking, see RAW FOOD.

COOPER JOSEPH, known only from his book *The Art of Cookery Refin'd and Augmented*, whose title-page declares him to have been 'chiefe cook' to King Charles I. This was published in 1654, five years after the execution of the King. It is curious that no trace of Cooper survives in records of the royal household, although the names of other 'master cooks' are there. It seems clear that he did not rise from the ranks in the King's kitchen; and probable that he only cooked for the King during the confused period of the Civil War, in the 1640s (Richardson and Isabell, 1984).

Perhaps for this reason, and because only one copy of the book is known to survive (in the British Library), his work has been neglected. Yet the book is attractive; is written in a personal, even conversational style; and includes some distinctive features, such as a short 'discourse' on the various kinds of pastry. Of small format and only a little over 200 pages in length, it is comparable to *The Compleat Cook* by 'W.M.' (a compilation of recipes belonging to the exiled Queen Henrietta Maria, published in 1655), but much slighter than *The Accomplish't Cook*, the comprehensive work by Robert MAY first published in 1660.

COOT (*Fulica* spp), **crake** (mainly *Porzana* spp), **moorhen** (*Gallinula* spp), **rail** (many genera, notably *Rallus*) are all marsh birds of the family Rallidae, represented around the world. Few of them make good eating. None is sufficiently appreciated in Europe, although there have been times when moorhens were plentiful in London markets and coots have been counted as good fare in N. America. The exception is the corncrake (also called landrail), *Crex crex*, which is less marsh-loving in its haunts and is highly regarded in the autumn, after the harvest, when it is well fed and ready to make its annual migration south to Africa.

This family includes the swamp-hen, *Porphyrio melanotus*, which has a wide distribution in Australasia and feeds on swamp-reeds. It has been praised as good table fare by at least one writer on the birds of New Zealand.

COPPA (cup), an Italian product made from cured, raw pork collar compressed inside a large sausage skin. It is unsmoked and very dry and hard. Widely made in C. Italy and Corsica, coppa is a rough-looking product, but is highly esteemed and quite expensive. It is always eaten raw and is sometimes called *coppa cruda* (raw) to distinguish it from a completely different product called *coppa cotta* (cooked), which resembles BRAWN.

CORAL FISH a name sometimes used in English for certain of the numerous species of small fish which have their habitat in the coral reefs of tropical waters. These include species in the family Pomacanthidae (otherwise known as angel fish) and Chaetodontidae (butterfly fish). It is characteristic of fish of the coral reefs to be deep bodied and prettily coloured rather than good to eat, although most are edible.

Other fish to which the name 'coral fish' is not specifically applied but which can conveniently be grouped under the name include some more angel fish (family Chelmonidae), batfish (Drepanidae), and leaf-fish (Platacidae).

CORAL FUNGUS of which the most common edible varieties are *Ramaria botrytis*, *R. aurea*, and *R. flava*, is abundant in woods throughout Europe and N. America in the autumn and Australia in the spring, having a global distribution. It is a conspicuous growth, measuring up to 15 cm (6") wide and high, but is often ignored by mushroom gatherers since it looks like coral rather than a mushroom. *R. botrytis* is usually off-white with pink tips, and *R. aurea* golden.

Both species are good to eat when young and sound. They may be cut up and cooked like any mushrooms, and are also good pickled in vinegar. The bitter-tasting tips of the former should be cut off. Identification of the latter should be positive, since some other coral fungi of similar coloration are unsafe to eat.

Some common names for coral fungi incorporate a reference to cauliflower. However, what is properly called CAULIFLOWER FUNGUS in English belongs to another family.

CORDIAL whether adjective or noun, is derived from the Latin word for the heart, *cor*. As a noun, it may mean a medicine, or medicinal food or drink, with the property of stimulating the heart and therefore the circulation. The term came also to mean a fruit SYRUP or concentrated and sweetened fruit-based beverage, presumably because it was believed that a preparation of this sort would have this effect. This sense of the word dates back to medieval times.

A well-known French cordial is *cassis*, made with blackcurrant juice. Another, this time one of those strong alcoholic drinks which are generally referred to as liqueurs, is RATAFIA.

References to cordials were far more frequent 100 years ago than now, and the sense of the term far wider. Fernie (1905), for example, devotes a dozen pages to 'Cordials and Restoratives', and his lists of the former include:

Alcohol, Beer Soup, Coffee, Egg Cordial, Liebig's Meat Extract, the Mints, Quinces, Ratafia, Rum Punch, Tea Caudle, and Wine Whey. Others may usefully be added, to wit, Allspice, Caraway, Cinnamon, Cloves, Grapes, Honey in Mead, Raisins, Rosemary Wine, Saffron, and the Garden Thyme. The four Cordial flowers of the English simplers were the Rose, the Violet, the Alkanet, and the Borage.

These are by no means all. Fernie quotes a 17th-century author as declaring that 'Marmalade of Quinces is known to be a good Cordial'; and he refers to GINSENG as a marvellous cordial root, and gives even higher praise to pure brandy.

CORDON BLEU was originally a title reserved for the Chevaliers of the Order of Saint Esprit (the highest order of chivalry under the Bourbon kings), to whom it belonged because of the blue sash which they wore. Towards the end of the 18th century, in England as well as in France, the term was being applied to anyone who excelled in a particular field of activity, one example of which was cookery.

In the course of the 19th century its scope was gradually focused onto cooks alone, and for the French it was now denoting precisely a very skilful female cook (*une cuisinière très-habile*). At that time only professional female cooks could be cordons bleus, but in the 20th century, in France, the term has been used rather of gifted amateur cooks, and a professional woman cook would prefer to be CHEF (a title for long withheld from women) or just *cuisinière*. Outside France, in contrast, anyone, whether man or woman, who shows a special aptitude for cooking is likely to be pleased at being called cordon bleu, although chefs already well known would probably feel that it was a distinction more appropriate for lesser beings than for themselves. (HY)

CORDYCEPS the only English name available for fungi of the genus *Cordyceps*. These grow, oddly, as parasites on live insects or worms. One of them, *C. robertii*, is eaten in China and Tibet, where it has mysterious names such as the Chinese *tung chong ha cho*, meaning 'winter worm summer grass' (sometimes shortened to *tung chong cho*, which translates even more puzzlingly as 'winter worm grass').

The explanation of these names is that during the winter the fungus grows only inside its host. In the summer, however, it produces an exterior growth. So what appeared to be, and was, a live worm or larval insect can change into something which looks like and is a kind of plant. Tibetans believe that this is a real metamorphosis, and that the 'insect-plant' can move around as they hunt for it; but what has happened is that the fungus first consumes the nutrients provided by its host and only then, having thus killed it, sends up the brown stalk which is what can be seen above ground. The top of this stalk is thickened by spore-bearing globules and resembles a very small bulrush.

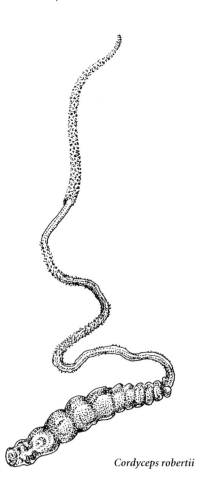

Cordyceps robertii

C. robertii occurs not only in the southwestern provinces of China and Tibet, but also elsewhere, for example in New Zealand. However, it is only used as a food by Chinese and Tibetans. The dried stalks, because they are hard to find, are expensive. In China they have a reputation as a restorative and APHRODISIAC, and it is therefore customary to eat them in a rich chicken broth in the late evening.

CORIANDER also known as cilantro, *Coriandrum sativum*, a plant of the family Umbelliferae, is related to PARSLEY, for which reason it is sometimes known in the Orient as Chinese parsley. This is a misnomer, in that the strong flavour of its leaves is quite different from that of parsley; but not entirely misleading, since its leaves are used in many tropical and subtropical parts of the world in the same way as parsley leaves are in temperate climates.

The plant reaches a height of 60–90 cm (2–3'), and has a much branched stem and finely divided leaves. The small flowers are white or pinkish.

Coriander, which is indigenous to S. Europe and the Mediterranean region, was already being cultivated in ancient Egypt for medicinal and culinary purposes. Its dried seeds have been used there and in S. Europe since classical times as a spice. The Roman statesman Cato recommended chopped fresh coriander as a garnish to encourage an invalid's appetite.

Use of the seeds has continued to be widespread in Europe. In contrast, the leaves, which are so widely used in Latin America and SE Asia (with fish and seafood, meat and poultry, in salads and soups as a garnish, often lavishly), are little used in Europe, with the notable exception of PORTUGAL; Portuguese use of the leaves derives from Africa, where Portuguese settlers took it over from the native Africans in, for example, Angola.

The seeds are used as an aromatic spice in a great many foods from stews to cakes and breads. In the Middle East fresh coriander is so widely used that it is sometimes called 'Arab parsley'. Both seeds and leaves are used extensively in India. The seeds are a standard item in *garam masala* and occur in numerous curry-type dishes, as do the leaves.

Both uses of the plant are linked by its characteristic and strong smell. The very name coriander is said to be derived from the Greek word *koris*, meaning bed-bug. The foliage of the plant, and its seeds in the unripe stage, have an odour which has been compared with the smell of bug-infested bedclothes. However, this smell disappears from the seeds when they ripen and is replaced by a pleasant, spicy aroma. The leaves, on the other hand, retain it. Europeans often have difficulty in overcoming their initial aversion to this smell.

Coriander has now become popular in all of Asia other than Japan, where it is unknown. In Thailand even the roots are used; they are ground and added to stews and curry-type dishes, as in India. It is usual in Asia and Latin America to find fresh coriander for sale with its roots still in place, so the Thai example can be followed without difficulty elsewhere.

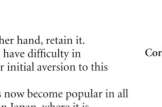

Coriander

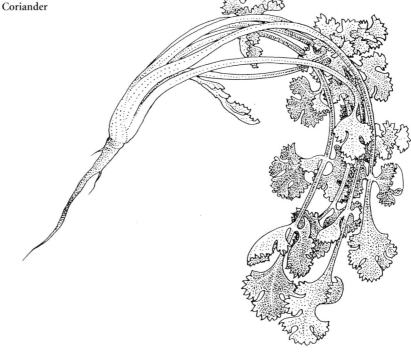

CORKWING *Glehnia littoralis*, a plant of the west and east coasts of the N. Pacific, is used mainly in Japan, where it is known as *hama-bofu* and is a valued flavouring herb.

It commonly grows by the shore, with glossy green leaves fanning out over the sand from its reddish stalks. The young leaves and leaf stalks are marketed in Japan and used as an accompaniment for fish dishes and *sunomo* (vinegared salads, see JAPANESE CULINARY TERMS), or pickled. They have a pleasing aroma and flavour, said to taste like a cross between ANGELICA and TARRAGON.

CORMS the thickened underground stems of certain plants, resembling BULBS. They are sometimes referred to as 'solid bulbs'.

CORN a general name for cereal crops, is also commonly used in the USA and elsewhere as a name for MAIZE. The latter usage is especially prevalent with regard to the kinds of maize eaten as vegetables; the terms 'sweet corn' and 'corn on the cob' are examples. But maize is a single species, and is considered in all its forms in the entry for it. That entry includes, at the end, references to various products and preparations whose names incorporate the word 'corn'.

Corn in the wide sense crops up in the Bible and in expressions such as corn-fed, corn exchange, cornfield.

CORN BREADS a term which refers to breads based on MAIZE. There are two traditions: the first is that of the Americas, where maize originated, while the second is that of Europe and Europeanized societies for whom maize was an ancillary rather than a staple, and where corn breads were usually variations on wheaten breads rather than forms in their own right.

The corn breads of the AZTEC and MAYA, TORTILLAS and TAMALES, remain highly visible in MEXICO and the rest of what was Mesoamerica, and have become prominent in N. America too, and indeed

internationally. Coe (1994) cites amazingly long lists compiled by a Spanish observer of the various kinds of tortilla and tamale which were on sale when the Spaniards arrived in America. Although tamales, in particular, were and are usually stuffed, it remains correct to refer to them, as well as to tortillas, as breadstuff.

Arepa is an alternative corn bread, of equally long ancestry, current in VENEZUELA and, to a lesser extent, COLOMBIA. In this case a larger-grained maize, with higher starch content, was formed into rolls or small cakes and cooked first on a GRIDDLE, then baked.

All these pre-Columbian breads were made with nixtamalized maize flour (see NIXTAMALIZATION), a technique which was not known to the Inca, further south in the Andes area, who seem to have hardly eaten any bread at all.

N. American Indians also depended on maize as a staple, and made various kinds of bread with it, often using wood ash to improve it. The Navajo, for example, mixed a small amount of cedar ashes with cornmeal for their bread. These native breads were often adopted by the settlers; Robert Beverley (1705) noticed that bread in 'Gentlemen's Houses' was usually of wheat, 'but some rather choose the Pone, which is the bread made of Indian Meal'. The reference is to the celebrated **corn pone;** the binomial form is to be preferred, since pone by itself could sometimes refer to a bread made of something other than corn.

These early American corn breads, including the **hoe cakes** and **johnny cake**

which attracted praise from Benjamin Franklin (in a widely quoted letter to the *London Gazette*), were griddle or hearth baked. Hoe cakes were cooked on a greased iron blade; johnny cakes were also thin and griddled. However, the whole complex of terms for such corn breads presents as unpromising an aspect to the lexicographer as the proverbial brown paper bag full of snakes. It is best just to accept that usage varied with place and with time, and that the origin of terms is often uncertain. As Karen Hess (see Mary Randolph, 1984) puts it:

It must be understood that among the scores of johnny cakes, pones, ash cakes, hoe cakes, bannocks, and even various fried cakes, differentiation was not rigorous. Each colony, each community had its own versions and names, a tradition that faded as the iron kitchen range made all hearth cakes virtually obsolete, except perhaps in Rhode Island where questions of choice of cornmeal, additions or no, and texture of their fried *jonny cakes* still stir lively interest.

Hess comments that the diversity and far-flung distribution of the breads argues for the derivation of johnny cake from journey cake, a term which had been in use in England, rather than the various other hypotheses which have been advanced.

Later recipes are more elaborate, mixing cornmeal with wheaten flour and sometimes raising agents to make a lighter bread, more orthodox in European eyes. Thus the steamed Boston brown bread (see BREAD VARIETIES) to eat with baked beans includes cornmeal, while anadama bread, also of New England, mixes corn and wheat flours with molasses.

Spoon breads were soft, rich corn breads made with milk, butter, and beaten egg. Cf the old English term 'spoon-meates', referring to breadlike foods which were best eaten with a spoon.

The cornmeal favoured in southern states is whiter than that used in the north, just as southern corn breads are normally thinner (not more than 2.5 cm/1") than northern.

Maize bread became popular in IRELAND in the mid- to late 19th century following the distribution of maize as a famine relief food. Commonly called 'yellameal' or 'Indian meal' bread, it was baked over the open fire in a pot oven. Usually a quantity of wheat flour was used in its preparation and the bread was leavened with bicarbonate of soda.

Elsewhere in Europe maize was a virtual staple in north-east ITALY and in ROMANIA, but not elsewhere. It is rare in Europe to find true corn breads, or even breads using a proportion of cornmeal.

CORNED BEEF so called because the beef is preserved with 'corns' (grains) of salt. In the form known in modern times it is then chopped and pressed and packed in characteristic rectangular cans. Much of it comes from Uruguay.

Ayto (1993) says that the name dates from the 17th century and gives a citation: 'Beef . . . corned, young, of an Ox,' Robert Burton, *Anatomy of Melancholy*, 1621. He adds that until the 19th century the adjective 'corned' was applied to pork as well as beef; and that usage in N. America is different (corned beef there means salt beef, especially from the brisket, while what is called corned beef in Britain becomes 'canned pressed beef').

Appreciation of corned beef in Britain is largely a matter of generations. People whose gastronomic experiences go back to the Second World War or the decades immediately following it are largely to view corned beef with some affection. A classic English salad dish consists of slices of corned beef served with lettuce leaves, tomato quarters, slices of beetroot, and 'salad cream' (NB, not mayonnaise). This is delicious. Corned beef hash is another favourite.

It may be, however, that enthusiasm for corned beef has been even higher in Ireland, where it has been a traditional dish for Christmas, Easter, and on St Patrick's Day, and where the combination of corned beef and cabbage provides one of the country's best-known dishes.

Emphasizing its long history in the Irish diet, Regina Sexton (personal communication, 1996) points out that a similar product is mentioned (as *bóshaille*) in the 11th-century Irish text *Aislinge meic Con Glinne*: 'many wonderful provisions,

pieces of every palatable food . . . full without fault, perpetual joints of corned beef.' She adds that corned beef has a particular regional association with Cork City. From the late 17th century until 1825, the beef-curing industry was the biggest and most important asset to the city. In this period Cork exported vast quantities of cured beef to Britain, Europe, America, Newfoundland, and the W. Indies. During the Napoleonic wars the British army was supplied principally with corned beef which was cured in and exported from the port of Cork.

Some of the exports from Cork may have gone to the Pacific islands in many of which corned beef is a long-established popular food, almost a staple. In some of the islands it goes under the name of keg.

CORNFLOUR is the British, and cornstarch the American, name for a fine starch prepared from MAIZE. It is not the same as cornmeal or maize meal, which are relatively whole flours containing most of the maize grain. Cornflour is made by softening maize in weak acid, grinding it, separating the bran, and washing all non-starchy substances out of the ground meal.

Because cornflour has a very fine texture and contains no gluten it has less tendency to form lumps than ordinary flour. Another advantage is that it has virtually no flavour, whereas the grainy flavour of wheat flour requires some cooking before it goes away. For these reasons cornflour is popular as a thickener in western cooking.

Cornflour is also used as a thickener in oriental dishes, but not nearly as much as western books about, for example, Chinese cooking suggest. The texture imparted by cornflour is unsuitable for many oriental dishes, and the fact that it makes liquids cloudy excludes its use for others. For a survey of the thickeners most used in Chinese cookery, see TAPIOCA; ARROWROOT.

CORNISH SPLIT a small round BUN (about 6–7 cm/2.5" in diameter) of lightly enriched, yeast-raised dough, made in Cornwall in the West Country of England. They can be eaten hot with butter, or cooled, split, and filled with clotted cream (see CREAM) and strawberry jam, or a combination known as THUNDER AND LIGHTNING, which is clotted cream and GOLDEN SYRUP.

Similar buns are made in Devon, where they are called Devonshire splits (the old Devon dialect names of 'chudleighs' or 'tuffs' for these seem to be dying out); and E. Scotland, where they are called cookies.

LM

CORN SALAD *Valerianella locusta*, also known as lamb's lettuce, a common and hardy wild plant of Europe, W. Asia, and N. Africa, has been cultivated in Europe since at least the 16th century and is naturalized in N. America.

The leaves form pretty rosettes, and can either be harvested at seedling stage on a cut-and-come-again basis or used at maturity. They have a tender texture and a pleasant mild taste, which make them a good ingredient for salads. Evelyn (1699) commended 'corn-sallet' for use in salads during the winter and spring. Different varieties for summer and later sowings are now available, and the appearance of the early spring crop continues to give particular pleasure.

Corn salad is most popular in France, where it is *mâche*, and in Germany. In Britain its use has declined since the 18th century; whereas in N. America its popularity has been increasing.

V. eriocarpa, Italian corn salad, belongs to the Mediterranean region and has longer, paler leaves than the main species.

CORN SYRUP a heavy, watery-white SYRUP made from MAIZE starch, is also known as 'liquid glucose' or 'glucose syrup'. (This is not quite correct, since it does not consist entirely of GLUCOSE, otherwise known as dextrose, but includes a substantial amount of dextrin. However, it gives the right impression.)

Corn syrup is used in the food industry as a sweetening agent in place of sugar, especially for the manufacturing of soft CONFECTIONERY, ICE CREAM, and similar foods. It is useful because glucose, although less sweet than ordinary sugar (sucrose), crystallizes much less readily. Also, corn syrup has no flavour of its own, and in some parts of the world it is less expensive than ordinary sugar.

In human digestion, glucose is formed by the hydrolysis (breaking down) of starch and other carbohydrates. Until recently, all corn syrup made industrially was produced by a method which mirrored on a large scale what happens inside humans: the heating of maize starch with an acid broke down the large molecules of starch into their component parts, mostly molecules of dextrose (glucose).

Recently, a new method has been adopted: hydrolysis carried out by enzymes, which can work at a moderate temperature. Nor is this all. Certain bacteria (*Streptomyces* spp), with which the syrup can be inoculated, will produce other enzymes which convert some of the dextrose to fructose, which is considerably sweeter than either glucose or ordinary sugar (sucrose). If this procedure is followed, the result is a 'light fructose' syrup which is much sweeter than ordinary corn syrup, although its energy value is no greater than that of any other common sugar.

Ordinary corn syrup can be refined further into what is called 'corn sugar' or 'solid glucose'. This has a lower content of dextrin, but it is still not pure glucose.

COSTMARY *Tanacetum balsamita*, a perennial plant which originated in W. Asia but achieved a wide distribution in Europe and was taken to N. America by early settlers. It has a distinctive fragrance with hints of BALSAM or MINT, and is sometimes called mint geranium; or alecost, because it was used in flavouring ale; or Bible leaf, because its large leaves were used as markers in church.

Its use in ale is of historical interest only, and the other roles of its pretty leaves, as in making a tea or being added to salads, have largely disappeared. Although Joy Larkcom (1984) lists it as a salad plant, she advises that the leaves should be used sparingly since their flavour is strong. Di Corato (1978), writing about the use of flavourings in Italy, echoes this advice but mentions too that the leaves are added to some rustic soups and that in Piedmont they are used as an ingredient of stuffings, e.g. for courgettes. He also records a use of the seeds for flavouring meats and sweets.

COSTUS *Saussurea lappa*, a plant of the Himalayan region whose root is sometimes used as a spice. It has been identified as one of the spices used in classical Rome, where its name was *costum*. Dalby (1996) records its use (along with a wide range of other aromatics) in Byzantine drinks, which featured numerous flavoured wines.

Costus turns up as an ingredient in the GREENSAUCE for which a recipe is given by Alexander Neckham (12th century AD) and occasionally in later medieval recipes. Generally, however, its profile in European kitchens has been a low one.

The plant has an interesting aroma, among whose components a smell like that of violets has been distinguished.

COTHERSTONE a cheese from the north-east of England, was introduced as a farmer's version of the old monastic WENSLEYDALE cheese. It was originally made from sheep's milk, but from the 17th century cow's milk has been used. It is looser in texture than Wensleydale. Although popular locally, it was not widely known south of Yorkshire, and is now rare.

COTTAGE CHEESE is now in every supermarket and it is obvious that any connection between it and cottages can only be historical. Its ancestors, which were as commonly called 'cottagers' cheeses', were indeed home-made and constituted an important category in the group of simple so-called 'bag cheeses' (drained in a cloth bag), all of which were suitable for making in cottages.

Mention of cottages brings to mind the English countryside, but the name 'cottage cheese' originated in N. America in the 19th century and was little used anywhere else until the 20th century. Bartlett (1848), whose reference is said to be the earliest in print, had the following entry in his dictionary: '*Smear-Case*, a preparation of milk made to be spread on bread, whence its name, otherwise called "cottage-cheese".'

By 'smear-case' he meant *Smierkase*, a Pennsylvania Dutch term. It is interesting that in this early definition the spreadability on bread is given as the chief characteristic. Bartlett was on the right track here. A very wide range of simple, fresh cheeses have been made in both N. America and Britain under the umbrella term 'cottage cheese'; but the vast majority, if not all, have been spreadable. It would also be fair to say that skimmed cow's milk is the standard basis for such cheeses, although some recipes call for adding a proportion of whole milk, and some of the cheeses are even enriched by a little cream.

Commercial manufacture started around 1915 in the USA. Factory-made cottage cheese is made from powdered skimmed milk by a scaled-up version of the same simple process. Production and consumption are greatest in the USA, where a number of different kinds are available. Sweet-curd cottage cheese is a variety made with RENNET, and of low acidity. In this the particles of CURD are large and resemble kernels of popped corn; so it is sometimes called popcorn cheese. Small-grained varieties are apt to be called 'country-style' or 'farm-style'.

Cottage cheese is usually sold in tubs, often with flavouring agents such as CHIVES added. These are desirable since, unlike the tangy cottagers' cheese of the past, which was naturally soured, it has little flavour of its own. Its growth in popularity has evidently been due to its combining a good supply of protein with a low calorie count and relatively low cost.

COTTONSEED OIL a product of the cotton plant, which is not normally thought of as a source of food. Up to 1880 the seeds were usually discarded after the surrounding fibres, for which the plant was grown, had been removed. Then it was discovered that an edible oil could be pressed from the seeds, and cottonseed oil became an important by-product of the large cotton industry. The chief producers include the USA, India, Sudan, Egypt, and also Brazil.

The oil emerges from the mill in a dark and impure state, and must be thoroughly refined before it is fit for use. The refined product is light, flavourless when fresh, and high in polyunsaturates. It goes rancid quickly on exposure to air. For this reason it is mostly used in the manufacture of vegetable margarine and cooking fats; but it can also be bought as a salad or cooking oil and, if used promptly, is suitable for these purposes.

COULIBIAC the western form of the Russian name for a PIE in which the filling, often but not always fish (and likely to include also chopped hard-boiled eggs, dill or parsley, and KASHA), is cooked inside an envelope (shaped like a shallow loaf) of yeast dough. (A flaky pastry dough may be used, but is less good.)

Pamela Davidson (1979) gave a detailed recipe for it, including a description of the *vyaziga* (dried spinal cord of cartilaginous fish such as STURGEON) which adds a distinctive element to taste and texture if incorporated in the filling; and quoted the following passage from Gogol's *Dead Souls*. Chichikov has just retired to bed after another gorging session with his host Petukh, but unfortunately his bedroom is next to Petukh's study, and through the wall he can hear Petukh ordering the following day's culinary delights:

'Make a four-cornered fish pie,' he was saying, smacking his lips and sucking in his breath. 'In one corner put a sturgeon's cheeks and dried spinal cord, in other put buckwheat porridge, little mushrooms, onions, soft roes, and brains and something else—well—you know, something nice . . . And see that the crust on one side is well browned and a little less done on the other. And make sure the underpart is baked to a turn, so that it's all soaked in juice, so well done that the whole of it, you see, is—I mean, I don't want it to crumble, but melt in the mouth like snow, so that one shouldn't even feel it—feel it melting.' As he said this Petukh smacked and sucked his lips.

COULIS a French culinary term which came originally from the Latin *colare* (to strain) and which has achieved wide currency in English-speaking countries, has been well described by Ayto (1993):

A coulis is a thin purée or sieved sauce made typically of vegetables or fruit (tomato coulis is a common manifestation of it). Nouvelle cuisiniers' penchant for using fruit coulis, especially made from raspberries, at every opportunity has recently made the term familiar to English-speakers, but in fact it had first crossed the Channel nearly 600 years ago, in the form 'cullis'. This was a sort of strained broth or gravy made originally probably from chicken, but subsequently from any meat or even fish, and used as a basis for sauces or simply poured over meat dishes.

COURT BOUILLON a flavoured liquid intended for the cooking of eggs, vegetables, or seafood, and in use in France and elsewhere for many centuries. In modern times its use is reserved almost exclusively for seafood, especially fish. The ingredients include salt; an acid element (lemon juice, white wine, vinegar); spices (notably peppercorns); and aromatics such as onion, shallots, garlic, celery, a BOUQUET GARNI). Court bouillons prepared with wine are the most common. In early English cookery books the term is often spelled in strange ways, e.g. corbolion (May, 1685). However, there was little difference between early English recipes for the preparation and early French ones. La Varenne (*Le Cuisinier françois*, English translation 1653) gave several recipes for fish cooked in a court bouillon. That recommended for a perch consisted of 'wine seasoned with all sorts of spices, such as salt, pepper, clove, peel of orange or lemon, "chibbolds", and onions'.

Stobart (1980) points out that:

Meats and vegetables are less often cooked in *court-bouillon* for an obvious reason. A *court-bouillon* is prepared in advance by boiling the flavouring ingredients *before* the food is put in to cook. This is necessary with fish, and shell fish, as they spend only a short time in the cooking liquid. But with meats and vegetables, which take longer to cook, the flavouring materials can usually be boiled while the food is cooking.

COUSCOUS a grain product consisting of tiny balls of dough which are steamed and served like rice, mixed with a stew or sauce. It is a staple food throughout N. Africa; in Morocco and Algeria, some of the local names for it are identical to the word for 'food' in general. It has become part of the cuisine in neighbouring African countries from Chad to Senegal, in the eastern Arab countries (where it has been known since the 13th century as *moghrabiyyeh*, 'the North African dish'), and elsewhere.

In dried form couscous might be mistaken for an exceptionally small soup noodle, but it is made by a wholly different technique that does not involve kneading. Instead, a bowl of flour is sprinkled intermittently with salted water while the fingers of the right hand rake through it in sweeping, circular movements, causing the dough to coagulate in tiny balls. They are also shaped by rubbing with the palm of the hand against the side of the bowl. From time to time the granules are sieved to ensure uniform size.

When the process is complete, they are dried.

The usual sort, called *seksu* in Berber or *kuskusu* in Arabic, are about 2 mm in diameter. *Berkukes* or *mhammsa* has larger granules, 3 mm or larger. An ultrafine couscous called *seffa* or *mesfuf*, 1 mm in diameter, is made in Morocco and Algeria.

The granules are steamed in a device which the French call *couscoussier*. It resembles a double boiler of which the upper part (the *keskas* or *couscoussier* proper) has a perforated bottom. This is set over a pot of boiling water, or more often the stew with which the couscous will be served. The swelling granules are removed and worked with the hands one or more times during steaming to ensure that they remain separate.

Berkukes, however, because of the difficulty of steaming the large granules thoroughly, is usually thrown into the stew for a while after steaming. Both *berkukes* and *kuskusu* may be steamed over water rather than stew, in which case they are usually sauced with milk or yoghurt. *Mesfuf* is always steamed over water and served with butter and sugar or raisins.

The stirring and rolling process by which the couscous granules are formed amounts, it has been suggested, to a way of preserving grain. Couscous is traditionally made from freshly ground whole grain, which is much better suited to the purpose than bolted flour, because starch readily accumulates around the larger and harder particles of BRAN and germ, much as a pearl forms around a grain of sand. The resulting granule is in effect a grain turned inside out, with the part of the flour that can deteriorate protected from the air by an envelope of starch. It can thus be kept without spoiling for months or years. This would explain why *Berkukes* is the couscous traditionally carried by travellers on long journeys—it has the thickest starch casing.

The wide spread of couscous has been influenced also by economic and aesthetic reasons. One of the attractions of couscous is that, unlike pasta or leavened bread, it is a light and elegant grain food that is held together not by gluten but by the weaker proteins found in all grains, and therefore need not be made with expensive wheat flour.

In many parts of Morocco and N. Algeria, BARLEY couscous (often called *abelbul*) or maize couscous (*abaddaz*) is commoner than the wheaten sort. A speciality of the Kabyle Berbers of Algeria is *ahethut*, made from barley, bran, and ground ACORN meal. Particularly in W. Africa couscous is also made from MILLETS (*Sorghum bicolor*, *Pennisetum americanum*), the local grain *fonio* (*Digitaria exilis*), and minor grains such as *Diplotaxis ecris*; some of them wild.

The Tubu, who inhabit the Sahara east of the Tuareg lands, sometimes harvest a variety of GOOSEFOOT, *Chenopodium murale et vulvaria*, which makes a black couscous. In season, heads of unripe wheat or barley (in Berber, *azenbo*; in Arabic, *frik*, see FREEKEH) may be gathered and dried over the fire so that they can be ground and made into a highly esteemed green couscous.

Other grain products are sometimes steamed like couscous, such as whole or cracked grains, grain-shaped noodles similar to European soup pastas, and even vermicelli. There is a medieval recipe for steaming breadcrumbs like couscous.

Algerian folklore has it that couscous was invented by the Jinn. Whoever the inventor was, there is no evidence for its existence before the 13th century, and the invention probably took place in N. Algeria and Morocco following the 11th-century collapse of the Zirid kingdom. In 13th-century books written in Spain and Syria, both *kuskusu* and *muhammas* can mean either couscous or a small soup noodle, and the recipes suggest that the stirring process originated as a hasty noodle method that saved kneading.

Couscous has continued to spread beyond the S. and E. Mediterranean. At some point it entered Sicilian cuisine (*cúscusu trapanese*). In S. Brazil *cuscuz paulista* is a steamed mixture of maize meal and vegetables (the *cuscuz* of N. Brazil, however, is a totally different product, not steamed at all, made by mixing TAPIOCA, COCONUT meat, milk, and sugar with boiling water). Couscous is now a common dish in France and increasingly elsewhere in Europe and N. America.   CP

READING: Magali Morsy (1996).

COVENTRY GODCAKES have now, according to Laura Mason (1999), become extinct. They were small, triangular sweet pastries filled with mixed dried fruit. Flaky or puff pastry could be used.

Coventry children formerly gave these to their godparents at Easter. The triangular shape may be a reference to the Trinity.

COWPEA *Vigna unguiculata*, an annual LEGUME which exists in many forms. It originated in Africa but soon spread to Europe, where it was known during the classical era, and to Asia, where it became very popular. In the 16th century it was taken to America by the Spanish. It is one of the main food crops in Haiti. The plant needs a hot climate and in the USA it will only grow in the south.

Cowpeas can be divided into those grown for their seeds (beans or peas), which are usually dried, and those grown for their immature pods. The former, short plants with short pods, are those most often grown in Africa, India, and the USA. The latter, tall climbers with exceptionally long pods (the name 'yard-long bean' is not always an exaggeration) are favoured in SE Asia. But in some regions, such as the W. Indies, both sorts are cultivated. All are now assigned to *V. unguiculata* and the subspecies listed below, although some used to be classified as separate species.

Yard-long bean

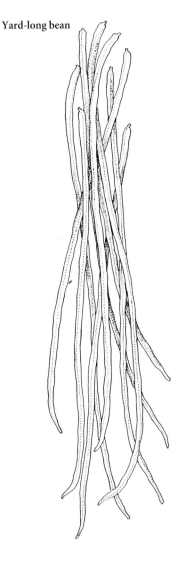

V. unguiculata is the **black-eyed pea** or bean, or southern pea, of the USA, the cavalance of the W. Indies, and the type most widely cultivated in India and Africa. The pods are up to 30 cm (1') long and hang straight down. (It was this bean which originally bore the French name *mogette*, a diminutive of *monge*, meaning a nun. The effect of the black eye in the centre was thought to be reminiscent of a nun's head attire. But the name was transferred, after discovery of the New World, to certain beans of *Phaseolus* spp and now applies, for

example, to the *haricots blancs* grown in the NW Vendée in France. The areas of production are all marshy.)

V. unguiculata var *cylindrica* has short pods which point upwards. It is cultivated in various parts of the tropics. In the USA it is known as the field pea, and is grown for animal fodder.

V. unguiculata var *sesquipedalis* is the **yard-long bean,** with very long, thin, curved pods, which can be a metre (over 3') long. Unlike the two preceding plants it is grown purely for its immature pods, not for its seeds. Other names include Bodi bean, Chinese bean, snake bean, asparagus bean (a puzzle, since it neither looks nor tastes like asparagus), and in the Netherlands Antilles *boonchi*. 'The beans are flexible enough to wrap around the skewered meat and vegetables in the Aruba dish Lambchi and Boonchi' (Ortiz, 1975).

The **uses** to which cowpeas are put vary by region and by type.

In the USA, the seeds of *V. unguiculata* are used as a dried pulse. The 'black eye' of the common variety is the hilum, or attachment point of the pea to the pod. The most famous American dish using cowpea is HOPPIN' JOHN.

In India the dried seeds are eaten whole or made into a DAL (split pulse) of inferior quality.

In Nigeria the dried seeds are second only to the peanut (GROUNDNUT) as a staple legume. Some tribes in W. Africa eat the young shoots and leaves as a vegetable, like spinach, and the young green pods may be eaten like French beans; but it is the seeds which are used as food and seen in the markets all over W. Africa. These may be white, yellow, brown, or mottled, the white being regarded by some authorities as the best. Irvine (1934), writing of the Hausa, explains that:

The seeds are generally boiled and eaten or put in soup or made into special pea soup. Sometimes they are pounded when dry and made into a kind of pea meal which is cooked in various ways, generally in the form of balls or doughnuts, which are eaten in or with soup or fried in oil. The pea meal is sometimes made into a form of porridge.

In China and SE Asia both *unguiculata* var *sesquipedalis* and *unguiculata* var *cylindrica* are grown for their pods alone. Indonesians often eat yard-long bean pods raw.

The **maloga bean,** a native Australian cowpea, *V. lanceolata*, also has edible pods. It is of special interest, partly because it has both ordinary pods and underground ones (like the groundnut) and partly because its long parsnip-like root is not merely edible when roasted but has been declared 'one of the best vegetables available to the Aborigines'.

Wild mung is the name sometimes given to a related plant, *V. vexillata*, which grows

in Ethiopia and the Sudan. It has edible tubers, which, once peeled, yield flesh which can be eaten raw or cooked and is outstandingly rich in protein.

COWSLIP *Primula veris*, a perennial plant of Europe and the temperate zone of Asia, which bears yellow flowers and is closely related to the primrose.

'Cowslip is not the most elegant of names. It is a polite form of Cowslop . . . "cow dung", "cow pat", obviously from a conception that the cowslip sprang up in the meadow wherever a cow had lifted its tail. . . . Cowslop or no, the deliciously coloured and deliciously scented flowers make the best and most delicate of country wines' (Grigson, 1955).

Cowslips are usually gathered from the wild. However, at least one English author was recommending them for cultivation in the herb garden in the early part of the 17th century. Evelyn (1699) recommended the juice of cowslip leaves as suitable for 'qualifying' TANSY leaves which were to be fried and then eaten with bitter orange juice and sugar. Evelyn also listed cowslip among eight flowers which were to be infused in vinegar and eaten in composed salads or alone. There is still a traditional use of the leaves as a salad green in Spain.

The cowslip and its relation the primrose, *P. vulgaris*, were not always clearly distinguished. Parkinson (1629) felt it necessary to state: 'I doe therefore . . . call those onely Primroses that carry but one flower upon a stalke, and those Cowslips, that beare many flowers upon a stalk together constantly.' Primrose leaves are occasionally eaten, and the flowers can be used in salads or for colouring sweet puddings. The flowers may also be crystallized (even while they are still growing on the plant, according to Sir Hugh Platt, quoted in Phillips, 1983). The same applies to cowslip flowers.

In the USA the name 'cowslip' is used for the marsh marigold.

CRAB an outstandingly successful form of CRUSTACEAN, so much so that since the first crabs evolved in the Jurassic the number of species has multiplied to such an extent that within the order Decapoda (which includes LOBSTER, PRAWN, SHRIMP) some 4,500 of the 8,500 species are crabs.

The typical crab is thought of as a creature which scuttles sideways across the sea bottom or beach; and many crabs answer to this description. However, there are also swimming crabs and land crabs, and the range of sizes and configurations is huge. The tiny oyster (pea) crab is the size of a pea, whereas the giant Japanese spider crab may measure 3.6 m (12') from claw tip to claw tip. The constant feature is possession of two claws and eight walking or swimming legs or 'feet', and that the whole creature is, like other crustaceans, contained within a hard exoskeleton which serves as protective armour except at those times when it has to be shed, as its occupant grows, and replaced by a new and larger one.

The most important crab fisheries take place in the N. Pacific, especially the Bering Sea, where king crabs of the genus *Paralithodes* and snow crabs of the genus *Chionoecetes* are taken in larger quantities than any other groups. These are processed in one way or another before reaching the consumer.

The W. Atlantic, including the Gulf of Mexico and the S. American coast down to Brazil, is another important region for crab fisheries, especially that for the blue crab, centred in Chesapeake Bay. The blue crab is third in catch by volume, worldwide.

The Pacific coastal waters of N. America yield the Dungeness crab, which, with its E. Atlantic opposite number, the feebly named but delicious 'edible crab', constitutes the fourth largest group.

It may be that a lack of full statistics for crab catches in SE Asia has prevented the regional group consisting of the mangrove crab (*Scylla serrata*) and swimming crabs (*Portunus* spp) from attaining their proper place in the league table. Thailand is, however, recognized as the third largest producer (after the USA and Japan), with the former Soviet Union and Brazil competing for fourth place.

Some crabs, such as the Dungeness and the European edible crab, yield meat from both claws/legs and body. The blue crab provides mainly body meat. Others, notably the king and snow crabs, furnish leg meat.

There is a similarity of flavour and texture between the white (claw/leg) meat of a crab and lobster meat. The latter is held in higher esteem, at least among those who can afford to buy it; but partisans of the more plebeian crabmeat challenge this, declaring that it can be just as good, or even better.

For particular species or groups, see BLUE CRAB; CRAB, COMMON; DUNGENESS CRAB; FIDDLER CRAB; HERMIT CRAB; HORSESHOE CRAB; KONA CRAB; LAGOON CRAB; LAND CRABS; MANGROVE CRAB; OYSTER CRAB; RED CRAB; ROCK CRAB; SAND CRAB; SHORE CRAB; SNOW CRAB; SPIDER CRAB; STONE CRAB; SWIMMING CRABS.

CRAB COMMON, or European crab, *Cancer pagurus*, the familiar large edible crab of W. and N. Europe. It may occasionally be found in the W. Mediterranean, but this is doubtful. The maximum width of the carapace is over 25 cm (10") and the weight

of the largest specimens can be as much as 5 kg (11 lb). The usual colour is pinkish or reddish-brown, with black tips to the claws.

There are some places where these crabs seem to grow larger than elsewhere. Street (1966) mentions the rocks round Cadgwith on the Lizard Peninsula in Cornwall as one, and comments that the explanation is not known.

These edible crabs are of great importance in commerce, being more abundant than LOBSTERS and yet, in the opinion of many, producing meat of comparable quality. White meat comes from the claws only. The body produces brown meat, including the exceptionally large liver, which is a delicacy. On average the yield of meat from a crab will be one-third of its whole weight; and about two-thirds of this yield will be brown meat.

The meat varies in quality according to a number of factors. That of the male, which has larger claws than the female, is generally preferred. The sex of a crab can be easily determined by looking at the tail, which is curled up under the body; that of the female is broad and round, while that of the male is narrower and pointed.

It is usual to sell these crabs cooked; to which end they are steamed in huge containers, which used to present a dramatic sight at the old Billingsgate fish market in London.

CRABAPPLE sometimes shortened to 'crab', is the name given to any very small and sour apple, wild or cultivated, from any of numerous species in the genus *Malus*. The modern cultivated apple is classified as *M. pumila*, which is one of these species. Its ancestry probably includes also *M. silvestris*, the common crabapple found in the British Isles; and *M. baccata*, the Siberian crab, also plays a role here. Other species grow in the Orient and N. America, and many of them have a history of local use in early times.

Generally, crabapples are edible and nutritious, but most of them are extremely sour and astringent. The main use for the fruit now is to make crabapple jelly which, with sufficient sugar added, has a tart astringency superior to that of plain apple jelly.

CRACKER a name first used in N. America, from the mid-18th century onwards, for a plain, unsweetened, dry, hard, bread product; thus corresponding to part of the domain covered by the wider English term BISCUIT (of which another major part belongs to the American term COOKIE). When crackers are broken into pieces they make a cracking noise, which accounts for the name.

Crackers may be leavened or unleavened. Those of the former sort were formerly

baked by a particular method which called for a dough leavened with bicarbonate of soda (hence the term 'soda cracker') and left to stand until pockets of carbon dioxide formed in the mixture. When biscuits of this dough were placed in a very hot oven they rose quickly, giving the characteristic texture.

Unleavened crackers may be made from flour and water only (as are MATZOS) or with the addition of a little salt. Some examples of this sort are the small oyster cracker, used on top of seafood CHOWDERS, and the crackers known as SHIP's BISCUIT (or pilot biscuit or sea biscuit).

The Graham cracker, which is sweet, is made from Graham (wholemeal) flour.

The cracker barrel was an institution in American general stores and groceries which sold crackers loose in bulk. The term was first used in print in the 1870s.

In Britain crackers are generally thought of as a specific commercially made biscuit, the 'cream cracker', invented and first marketed by W. and R. Jacob of Dublin in 1885. Jacobs were also the first people to pack them in airtight cartons, so that crackers were soon exported all over the world. Cream crackers are made from flour, salt, and a very little fat, moistened with milk, or milk and water. The mixture is rolled very thin, 'docked' (punched with holes), cut into squares, and baked until pale brown. These crackers are now usually eaten with cheese.

Cream crackers, as Rachel Laudan (1996) informs us, achieved fame in Hawaii's Chinatown as Krim Krakers, from Singapore. Hawaii is quite a wonderful place for biscuit historians. The lore associated with 'saloon pilots', Hawaii's own name for crackers (or hard tack or sea biscuits), has much fascination. Laudan writes that:

Sea biscuits were known as pilot bread from New England through the West Indies. New England seamen must have brought the use of the work 'pilot' for a sea biscuit with them to Hawaii. My suspicion is that 'saloon' was added as the crackers became richer and finer than the original hardtack, because the saloon on a ship was usually reserved for the better-off passengers. Along with salted meat and fish and pickled meats, saloon pilots are one of many symptoms of the atavism of Hawaii's food. Neither crisp and tender like soda crackers, nor elegantly spotted with brown like water biscuits, their thickness, their chewiness, and their relative lack of salt make saloon pilots closer to what I imagine hardtack must originally have tasted like.

For a completely different sort of cracker, from SE Asia but increasingly familiar in the western world, see PRAWN CRACKERS.
READING: Layinka Swinburne (1997).

CRACKLING in England, is the skin on roast PORK. Correctly cooked, it becomes very crisp and brittle. To produce good crackling, the raw skin is scored in close parallel lines right through the fat and down to the flesh. The meat is roasted without basting; any contact with liquid or fat makes the crackling tough and leathery. The skin can be removed and roasted separately if desired. To the English, crackling is a standard part of a meal involving roast pork. Many countries follow this pattern, but some remove the skin and fat for use in other dishes. This is particularly true in France.

Most countries make use of pork skin cooked until crisp. Sometimes this is a by-product of rendering LARD. Such items are the equivalent of English pork scratchings, and are known as *cracklings* in the USA, *grillons* or *grattons* in regional French, *cretons* in Quebec, and *chicharrones* in C. American and Spanish Caribbean cookery. Usually eaten as snacks, or with bread or mashed potatoes.

In N. America the cracklings are mixed with cornmeal to make crackling bread, a term which came into use in the 1840s and which has a pleasing alternative name, 'goody-bread'. There are many variations on this theme. German *Speckkuchen* is relatively rich, made from a flat sheet of bread dough studded with pieces of fat bacon. Spanish *torta de chicharrones* is sweetened and flavoured with lemon zest.

In some parts of the world, especially where pork is not eaten, cracklings are made from lamb fat. Thus the version of crackling bread eaten in Afghanistan uses lamb crackling. See also FAT-TAILED SHEEP for a reference to lamb crackling sandwiches in Iran.   (LM)

CRACK SEED important in Hawaii, is a wider category of confectionery items than the name might suggest. The category also goes by the Chinese name of *see mui* (pronounced see moy), and it was Chinese immigrants from Canton who brought crack seed to Hawaii in the 19th century. It is, essentially, preserved fruit, often with the stones ('seed') left in and frequently cracked ('crack') to expose the kernels and enhance flavour.

Rachel Laudan (1996) explains that everyone in Hawaii, not just the Chinese, snacks on crack seed and that what had been in its home country (China) a recognized but minor kind of food has here 'exploded into a cacophony of variants and a much greater importance'. Describing a crack seed store, she writes:

The jars are full of preserved fruits, red and brown and green and black, some of them gleaming with syrup, some frosted with sugar, and yet others wrinked and dusted with salt, as many as forty or fifty different varieties. Their names are poetry: li hing mui, Maui-style sweet plum, . . . apricot poo ton lee, . . . Hilo slice ginger, . . . guava peel, . . . licorice peach, . . . wet lemon peel, . . . honey mango, . . . rock salt plum, etc etc.

Some of the innovative expansions of the genre are due to the Yick Lung Company (the name means 'profitable enterprise'), and the range of tastes and flavours has become remarkably wide including the very salty as well as the sweet. Anise is one flavour which is common. The products seem to be quite addictive in a harmless way. Children pick up crack seed to chew on as they make their way home from school. 'Homesick students away on mainland call and beg "Send seed".'
READING: Rachel Laudan (1996).

CRANACHAN a Scottish dessert which became prominent in that role in the latter part of the 20th century, was originally a harvest festival version of the simple oatmeal GRUEL which was known as CROWDIE. For the festive version a coarser cut of oatmeal was used and cream was substituted for the water or BUTTERMILK which provided the liquid element.

The basic modern version of 'cream crowdie' or cranachan is based on lightly toasted coarse-cut oatmeal and whipped cream, with honey or sugar as a sweetening agent. Other flavourings may be added. Fresh soft fruits such as raspberries may be incorporated in the mixture or served with it. In restaurant versions there may be a whole panoply of ingredients, including even Scotch whisky.

The entry for CROWDIE explains that that term has two senses. Oddly, the other sense, a kind of soft cheese, may also be involved in cranachan; recipes may call for a mixture of such cheese and whipped cream, rather than just the whipped cream.

CRANBERRY the most important of the berries borne by a group of low, scrubby, woody plants of the genus *Vaccinium*. These grow on moors and mountainsides, in bogs, and other places with poor and acid soil in most parts of the world, but are best known in N. Europe and N. America. All yield edible berries. The genus also includes the BILBERRY (see also BLUEBERRY).

The generic name *Vaccinium* is the old Latin name for the cranberry, derived from *vacca* (cow) and given because cows like the plant. This accounts also for the common name 'cowberry', which is *lingon* in Swedish, giving rise in the middle of the 20th century to the English term 'lingonberry'. The origin of the name cranberry is obscure, apart from the dubious suggestion that cranes eat the berries. The common names of these berries are confusing and sometimes overlap with those of berries in other genera or families. See CRANBERRY TREE; HUCKLEBERRY; WHORTLEBERRY.

The plants to which the name cranberry was originally given are two species which occur in Europe as well as in other temperate parts of the world: *Vaccinium oxycoccus* and *V. vitis idaea*. The former is sometimes called the small cranberry. The latter, which replaces it in the more northerly regions and at higher altitudes, can be termed mountain cranberry, or foxberry. Either can be cowberry, or lingonberry (as mentioned above). Both plants bear reddish oval berries about 8 mm (0.3") across with a piquant flavour. This fits them for making sharp sauces to go with game; and they also provide excellent jellies or preserves.

When the Pilgrim Fathers arrived in N. America they found a local cranberry, *V. macrocarpon*, which had berries twice the size of those familiar to Europeans, and an equally good flavour. American Indians were accustomed to eating these fresh or dried, and to adding the dried fruits as an ingredient in PEMMICAN (a dried, preserved meat product). Cranberries contain large amounts of benzoic acid, which is a natural preservative and accounts for this practice; the berries will keep for months without treatment of any kind. It was no doubt these large American cranberries which, at an early stage in the evolution of THANKSGIVING Day dinner, were made into sauce to accompany the turkey, which became established as its centrepiece.

For a long time now the American cranberry has been both cultivated and exported. Even in former times its remarkable keeping properties enabled it to withstand long sea voyages stored in barrels full of plain water. Cranberries for storage were selected, by tipping them down a flight of stairs. The sound berries bounced and fell to the bottom, while damaged ones stayed on the steps. This principle is still used in modern sorting machines.

Most cranberries on sale in Europe are imported from the USA, but there is some European cultivation of *V. macrocarpon*, and as a result of escapes the plant is sometimes found growing wild on European moors. Cranberry juice, with its high vitamin C content, is a popular product.

Various *Vaccinium* spp in other parts of the world produce fruits comparable to the cranberry but of less importance. One such is *V. reticulata* of Hawaii, which bears the ohelo berry, red or yellow in colour, sweet enough to eat raw, and suitable for jam if its low pectin content is strengthened.

CRANBERRY TREE (also called high-bush cranberry), *Viburnum trilobum*, a shrub or small tree of Canada and the northern states of the USA, which bears berries similar in appearance and quality to the CRANBERRY, but with large stones inside (and belonging to a different family). A few cultivars have been developed. A similar species in Europe, *V. opulus*, has also been cultivated in some places.

The berries of the American cranberry tree produce an excellent jelly, and can be used for most purposes in the same way as cranberries proper. They have the same tart but pleasant flavour.

CRANE *Megalornis grus*, a stately long-legged bird which generally resembles the STORK and the HERON. It is a migrant, breeding in NE Europe and flying south for the winter. Its distribution may have extended as far west as Britain in the Middle Ages and earlier, since there is a record of King Ethelbert II of Kent asking a missionary in Germany in AD 748 to send him a couple of goshawks for hunting cranes. Cranes were certainly among the birds hunted by falconry in various parts of Europe.

Witteveen (1986–7), in the only survey of the subject available in English, remarks that cranes were cooked in CLASSICAL ROME, usually by braising them in a sauce; that roasting them was the preferred method in Italy from the 14th century; and that the same was true of England, where the roasted bird might be served with the sauce called cameline (later galandine—see GALANTINE).

Up to the 16th century, cranes were likely to appear on the menus of banquets, but this practice petered out in the 17th century, although cranes, especially young ones, continued to be eaten.

Sir Thomas Browne (1902) had remarked in the 17th century that cranes were often seen in Norfolk in hard winters and must have been more plentiful in earlier times, when they figured in bills of fare for banquets. It may be that increasing scarcity in W. Europe, perhaps reflecting changes of climate and of the migratory patterns of the bird, was largely responsible for the disappearance of the crane from banquet tables. However, this disappearance coincided, generally speaking, with the similar disappearance of other 'great birds' such as the PEACOCK, for which the arrival of the TURKEY from the New World is thought to have been partly responsible.

CRAYFISH CRUSTACEANS which can be regarded as the freshwater counterparts of the marine LOBSTER. Those in the northern hemisphere belong to the family Astacidae, those in the southern hemisphere to the family Parastacidae.

The name 'crayfish' prompted remarks by the English zoologist T. H. Huxley (1880):

It might be readily supposed that the word 'cray' had a meaning of its own and qualified the substantive 'fish'—as 'jelly' and 'cod' in 'jellyfish' and 'codfish'. But this certainly is not the case. The old English method of writing the word was 'crevis' or 'crevice', and the 'cray' is simply a phonetic spelling of the syllable 'cre' in which the 'e' was formerly pronounced as all the world, except ourselves, now pronounce that vowel. While 'fish' is the 'vis' insensibly modified to suit our knowledge of the thing as an aquatic animal.

In fact, *crevis* and *crevice* were Old French terms, which survive in the modern *écrevisse*. The term 'crawfish', allowed by some as an alternative to crayfish, was coined in the USA in the 19th century and is still used in Louisiana.

The distribution of crayfish is surprisingly patchy. There are none in the tropics except for those in Papua New Guinea. There is a species in Madagascar, but none is indigenous to the African mainland. Crayfish are absent from most of Asia and have only found two habitats in S. America. It also seems odd that there should be over 250 species in N. America, but only 7 in Europe and 4 in E. Asia; and that the 110 species in Australasia should only be matched by 10 in the whole of the rest of the southern hemisphere.

The demand for crayfish is also erratic. It is most intense in Scandinavia and France; growing in the USA, where it was for long confined to the region around Louisiana, and in Australia; but non-existent in many countries.

Crayfish vary greatly in size. Many species are too small to be worth eating. The smallest is a mere 2 cm (0.75") long from head to tail (the claws being excluded in measuring the creatures), whereas the largest, the giant Tasmanian crayfish, may be 30 times as long and can weigh as much as 4.5 kg (10 lb).

They also vary in habits. Aquatic crayfish live in permanent bodies of water: rivers or streams, and sometimes lakes. Semi-aquatic crayfish can survive out of water for a long time and normally live in burrows connected with water by 'shafts' of their own construction. Land crayfish are seemingly independent of water, although they can only live on land which has water below it. But they are small creatures, with tiny tails, and are used only as bait. Some species are large enough to be potentially interesting as food, but still inedible. Those which are regularly eaten, apart from the famous YABBY and MARRON of Australia, include the following:

- *Astacus fluviatilis*, the European crayfish, wiped out in many European countries by a plague which began in the 19th century but became most disastrous in the 20th.

- *Pacifastacus leniusculus*, the signal crayfish of the north-western USA, introduced to crayfish farms in Sweden because immune to the plague which destroyed most European crayfish.
- *Euastacus armatus*, the Murray (River) cray of Australia, the second largest freshwater crayfish in the world.

READING: Lesley Morrissy (1978).

CREAM ranges in richness from British 'top of bottle', which contains barely more fat than MILK itself, to double cream, which is almost half fat. Examples of the fat contents of different grades in Britain and the USA are: 'half and half' cream 10–12%; British single cream 20%; US medium cream 25%; whipping cream 35%; and British double cream 48%.

In France the term CRÈME has a wider meaning. However, so far as the narrower sense is concerned, French official regulations define only two kinds of *crème*, *crème fraîche* (often referred to as just *crème*, but it is not 'just cream' in the English sense, being lightly fermented) and *crème légère*. The former must contain at least 30 grams of fat per 100 grams: the latter need only have 12. However, although these are the only categories with legal standing, other terms are used. *Crème épaisse* (or *crème double*) will have a fat content higher than the minimum prescribed for *crème fraîche*, but its thicker consistency may also be due to loss of water content, and it is usually more acid, having been allowed to ripen. *Crème fluide* has a fat content of around 35% and has not ripened; it is used for whipping (see below). *Crème à café*, a light cream with a 15% fat content, is what the Swiss use for the purpose indicated by its name.

Cream separates naturally from unhomogenized milk, in which the fat globules are just too large to remain suspended in the emulsion. Being lighter than water, they slowly collect at the top. The old method of collecting cream was to leave milk, unrefrigerated, in a broad earthenware pan until the cream had separated to the required extent: up to 12 hours for single cream and 24 for double. It was then skimmed off. During this time, lactic acid-producing bacteria were active in the milk and the cream, 'ripening' them and developing a creamy taste by converting lactose (milk sugar) to lactic acid and citrates to diacetyl. The cream, any butter made from it, and the remaining skimmed milk all have this pleasant, slightly sour flavour.

Nowadays cream is separated mechanically in a centrifuge, a revolving circular vessel in which the cream migrates to the centre, from which it is drawn off. Any degree of extraction, even separating

CREME

double cream from the thinnest milk, can be obtained in a few minutes. Consequently the cream has no chance to ripen; and since what is sold as 'fresh' cream must be promptly pasteurized to kill almost all the bacteria in it, modern cream does not have much flavour. (Batches of cream to be made into BUTTER and SOUR CREAM are treated differently. They are inoculated with starter cultures of chosen bacteria.)

Bottled, canned, and UHT ('ultra high temperature') cream are subjected to treatment similar to that for sterilized or UHT milk. A slightly 'cooked' flavour results.

Whipped cream adds a touch of luxury to almost any dessert and is essential for certain sweet confections such as ICE CREAM SUNDAES. When cream is whipped, the mechanical action introduces air bubbles into it. These are stabilized by the fat globules in the cream clumping at the air–liquid interface all around each bubble. The clumps of globules are stabilized by a coating of protein molecules (see EMULSIONS). To whip properly, cream has to have a reasonably high fat content: at least 30%, and 40% gives a lighter foam. Whipping cream is intermediate in fat content between British single and double cream. The clumping of the fat globules, and thus the successful whipping of the cream, is aided if the viscosity of the fat is increased by chilling the cream (to below 10 °C/50 °F—and chill the bowl and whipping implement too).

Whipped cream will not retain its airy bulk for long without assistance. When used as a topping for a TRIFLE, for example, it can be stabilized by adding egg whites, one to every 125 ml or 5 fl oz. of cream. MOUSSES and cold SOUFFLÉS using cream include either egg whites or GELATIN to hold up the fragile foam.

In cooking with cream, the main problem is that it curdles (see CURDLING) far more easily than milk. Even the freshest cream will separate at boiling point. So a soup or dish to which cream is added before serving must not be allowed to reach boiling point thereafter.

Clotted cream, regarded by the inhabitants of Devon and Cornwall, where it is chiefly made, as an exclusively English product, is in fact a close relation of the Near Eastern KAYMAK etc.; and it has been suggested that Phoenician traders, who came to Cornwall more than 2,000 years ago in search of tin, may have introduced there the Near Eastern technique for making it. The traditional West Country method is to put milk in shallow pans until the cream has risen (12 hours in summer, 24 in winter), then heat the whole to about 82 °C (180 °F), keep it there for half an hour, and allow it to cool overnight. Clotted cream made in

factories is produced more quickly by what is called 'direct scalding'. Clotted cream has a distinctive 'cooked' taste, keeps for much longer than ordinary cream, and is too thick (at about 60% fat content) to pour.

In Devon and Cornwall there was a traditional practice, barely surviving at the end of the 20th century, of making butter from clotted cream. The dairymaid would stir the cream with her forearm until the butter was formed.

The south-west of England is also the home territory of cream teas (see AFTERNOON TEA).

CREAM CHEESE 'although so called, is not properly cheese, but is nothing more than cream dried sufficiently to be cut with a knife.' Thus Mrs Beeton in 1861. Her comment was pertinent in that the simplest form of cream cheese is made by draining CREAM through a muslin and leaving it for a few days until it becomes as firm as BUTTER. But what is normally offered as cream cheese is produced in a more sophisticated manner, and is rarely made from cream alone.

Most kinds of cream cheese are made from a mixture of cream and MILK, inoculated with lactic acid-producing BACTERIA chosen to produce the desired degree of acidity. The mixture may or may not need RENNET to precipitate the CURD. Although the bacteria are allowed some time in which to do their work, a cream cheese is not matured. Most commercial varieties are pasteurized, to kill the bacteria once their work is done.

The most important cream cheese, in terms of quantity, must be Philadelphia cream cheese; it has for long been the principal American variety, and cream cheeses are said to account for a quarter of all the cheese eaten in the USA.

Well-known French cream cheeses include examples of both *double crème* and *triple crème*, which have a minimum fat content of 60% and 75% respectively. *Caprice des dieux* is in the former class. Fontainebleau, which has whipped cream blended into it, is *triple crème*, as is Boursin (plain or with a range of added flavourings). Two *triple crème* cheeses from the Île de France are EXPLORATEUR, much of which is exported to Belgium, and *délice de Saint-Cyr*, whose white rind is marked with reddish spots. *Brillat-Savarin* is a *triple crème* cheese from Normandy.

A cream cheese such as Fontainebleau is often eaten for dessert, with sugar.

The Scottish caboc, known since the 15th century, was Sir Walter Scott's favourite kind of cheese. It became extinct but has been revived as a rich cream cheese, made from double cream and given a crust of

toasted pinhead oatmeal. It comes in 'logs' of 120 g (4 oz).

CREAM OF TARTAR a mildly acidic substance used as an ingredient of BAKING POWDER, and occasionally to give a sour taste to soft drinks. In the food industry it is also used to help SUGAR to 'invert' in the making of syrup.

Scientific names for cream of tartar are acid potassium tartrate and *di*potassium L-(+)-tartrate. It is an 'acid salt'; that is, a SALT formed by the partial neutralization of an acid so that the product remains slightly acidic.

It is usually made by purifying tartar, the whitish crystals which precipitate out of wine. This is also a source of tartaric acid, which is an alternative constituent of baking powder. RH

CREAM PUFF a delicate confection consisting of a round choux PASTRY shell filled with whipped CREAM (or, sometimes, *crème pâtissière*). These puffs have an obvious relationship with PROFITEROLES (which are smaller) and ÉCLAIRS (which are a different shape).

Cream puffs may be dusted with icing sugar. This certainly applied to the cream puffs in a famous story, 'The Garden Party' by Katherine Mansfield, referred to by Barbara Maher (1982); they were 'beautifully light and feathery', and Cook shook off the extra icing sugar as she arranged them. However, the puffs are sometimes iced, e.g. with a chocolate icing.

Cream 'buns' in English bakeries may be the same thing but are sometimes ordinary sweet buns with a cream filling.

CRÈME a French word which not only means CREAM, the dairy product, but is also a culinary term.

In the French kitchen, there is no word to match the English term 'custard', and *crème* has to fill the gap. The thin pouring-sauce type of CUSTARD is *crème anglaise*.

Crème pâtissière is the equivalent of confectioner's custard, though the English term tends to denote a less rich kind than the French mixture. *Crème pâtissière* is made from egg yolks, milk, sugar, and a little flour, with vanilla or some other flavouring; the light version used in ÉCLAIR fillings and Saint-Honoré (see GATEAU) also contains beaten egg whites.

Crème au beurre (buttercream) is a richer variant made with butter instead of milk, and omitting the flour. It is much used for filling cakes.

Crème frite (fried cream), an ingenious French invention, might be described as a

FRITTER containing ice cream. A very thick, sweet custard strengthened with flour is frozen, cut up, egged and breadcrumbed, and quickly deep fried. The centre remains at least partly solid.

Petits pots de crème are little boiled custards in individual cups. (The correct term for the correct vessel is a RAMEKIN, French *ramequin* from a Flemish or German word meaning 'little cream'; the term also embraces dishes made in such a container.) A custard turned out to serve is a *crème renversée*. Both the 'right way up' and the reversed type have numerous flavours and names, and exist in large and small sizes.

See also the following two entries, CRÈME BRÛLÉE and CRÈME CARAMEL.

CRÈME BRÛLÉE is a French term for a rich baked CUSTARD made with CREAM, rather than with milk. The custard is topped with a layer of sugar (usually brown) which is then caramelized by use of a SALAMANDER or under a grill. CRÈME, meaning 'cream', is derived from the Latin *chrisma* through the old French *cresme*. The term *brulé* is applied to dishes such as cream custards which are finished off with a caramelized sugar glaze.

In English, the dish is Burnt cream. This term was in use as long ago as the beginning of the 18th century, but the French term had already been used by Massialot in 1691 and has priority, although it fell into disuse in France for a while in the 19th century (oddly, at just about the time when English people were adopting it in place of their own English term).

Crème brûlée is also sometimes known as Trinity cream because of its association with Trinity College, Cambridge, where the college crest was impressed on top of the cream with a branding iron. Florence White (1932) says of Caramel Cream.

This recipe is given by Miss Eleanor L Jenkinson, sister of the late Cambridge University Librarian in the Ocklye Cookery Book (1909). Miss Jenkinson says: 'It is amusing to remember that this recipe, which came from a country house in Aberdeenshire in the 'sixties, was offered to the kitchens of Trinity College, Cambridge, by an undergraduate, and rejected with contempt. When the undergraduate became a Fellow, just thirty years ago (in 1879), he presented it again; this time it was accepted as a matter of course. It speedily became one of the favourite dishes of May week.'   HS

CRÈME CARAMEL a sweet dish which is essentially a CUSTARD but, because there is no French term corresponding to custard and because it is seen as something originally French, is known as a CRÈME. The entry for that term explains that a boiled custard is often served in France in little individual containers. If some caramel syrup is poured into the container before the custard is put in, and the custard is subsequently turned out when served, it will have a more interesting appearance and flavour; and will qualify as a crème caramel.

In the latter part of the 20th century crème caramel occupied an excessively large amount of territory in European restaurant dessert menus. This was probably due to the convenience, for restaurateurs, of being able to prepare a lot in advance and keep them until needed. Latterly, however, it seems to have been losing ground.

A kindred dish is described above under CRÈME BRÛLÉE.

CREOLE FOOD The first thing that comes to mind on hearing the term is the food of the Mississippi Delta, a blend of French and American Indian cooking. But it is worth considering also the example of linguists who use 'creole' to refer to the language spoken by the children of individuals who by reason of migration, trade, or conquest had developed a rudimentary pidgin to deal with foreign-language speakers. Unlike pidgins, creoles develop complex grammars and extensive new vocabularies and have proved a rich resource for investigating the origin and growth of languages. In a parallel manner, creole foods—foods eaten by the descendants of parents from very different culinary traditions—offer the promise of throwing light on the çauses of culinary change.

Creole foods probably go back many centuries, perhaps even millennia. The conversion of China and Japan to Buddhism, for example, or the conquest of much of the Mediterranean by the Arabs led to the conjunction of radically different food traditions. But the best-documented creole foods follow the European expansion beginning in the 16th and 17th centuries. The Portuguese encouraged marriage with local women leading to creole foods in Brazil, Goa, Malacca, and Macao. Spanish imperialism resulted in two of the richest and most complex creole foods, the Mexican and the Filipino. Creole foods with a strong British strain were to be found in the eastern part of the USA and in India, and with a marked Dutch emphasis in what used to be the Dutch E. Indies and in South Africa. The French, in turn, contributed to contemporary Vietnamese cuisine. This simple picture of European colonists coming up against indigenous food traditions is complicated by the massive migrations, forced or voluntary, of other peoples. As a result of the need for labour on the great plantations of the tropical world—sugar, cotton, and rubber, for example—creole foods of two non-European groups and creole foods with three or more roots are common: Nonya (Chinese-Malaysian) in the Malaysian Peninsula, Chinese-Indian-European in Mauritius, black-American Indian-English in the south of the United States, Indian-Pacific island in Fiji, American-Japanese-Chinese-Hawaiian in Hawaii.

To clarify what is meant by creole foods, it is worth excluding two other kinds of foods: variant foods within a given tradition (food dialects, to continue the linguistic metaphor) and diaspora foods. An example of variant foods within the same tradition would be the French and the English. Viewed on the grand scale, the philosophies of food in England and France, however strikingly different they may appear to inhabitants of the two countries, are essentially the same. So too are the methods of preparing foods, the times and natures of the meals, and the range of ingredients, particularly the staples. The exchanges that have occurred regularly between English and French food do not add up to a new creole tradition. Neither do diaspora foods where a given group disperses to new lands retaining their philosophy of food, either by virtue of its strength (Jewish or Chinese) or by virtue of near-disappearance of the indigenous population and its foods (Europeans in Australasia and much of Latin America). In these cases, the group may absorb new ingredients and even parts of menus (chilli, salt beef) while retaining a recognizable culinary tradition.

It might seem that—except for their mere existence—nothing general could be said about creole foods. But in fact they share certain general characteristics at the level of philosophy, at the level of menu and methods of preparation, and at the level of ingredients. The philosophy of a creole food—theories about how food contributes to physical and spiritual health, about when a people should feast and when they should fast, and about what counts as a meal—differs from the parent traditions. In Hawaii, for example, all ethnic groups now feast on a baby's first birthday (a baby luau) and a meal now consists of Asian rice with American quantities of meat. Second, the menu changes, foods are prepared in new ways, and foods expand into different slots. An instance would be Mexico where leavened wheat bread and distilled liquor (tequila) joined unleavened corn tortillas and naturally fermented beverages (pulque) in the diet. Third, the ingredients themselves change. Typical of a creole cuisine is the reliance on two or more staples from the different contributing cuisines (maize, wheat, and sweet potatoes in the American south or wheat, maize, and rice in Mexico). Also typical, given the displacement of peoples concerned, is the heavy use of preserved foods, often the traditional European sailor's diet or the tinned goods developed in the last century (the condensed milk belt across S. and SE Asia, salted and preserved meats and fish, hard tack or crackers).

Thus true creole foods develop their own dynamic, something more than the sum of the parts of the contributing traditions. In the past, most were created by default, by peoples who were forced by circumstance to change their habits. Even so, among them are some of the world's great cuisines, the Mexican, for example. The scale of migration in the late 20th century, the increased knowledge of methods and ingredients of different food traditions, and the willingness to experiment with new foods that follows on abundance suggests that creole foods are likely to become a yet more important part of the world culinary scene.   RL
READING: Mitcham (1978).

CRÉPINETTE a small flat French SAUSAGE encased in CAUL (French *crépine*). A crépinette is usually made with minced pork, but lamb, veal, or chicken can be used.

These sausages are highly seasoned and sometimes include chopped TRUFFLE. They are usually buttered before being grilled and served with a purée of potatoes.

CRESS a name derived from a Greek word meaning to creep, and loosely used for a large number of low-growing plants with small leaves, whose common use is in salads, although they may also be cooked. Most of them belong to the same family as the MUSTARDS and they are usually more or less pungent in taste; leaves or seeds of some have been used as a peppery condiment.

Some cresses grow in water. The only one of these to be cultivated is described under WATERCRESS.

The other main cultivated cress is **garden cress**, *Lepidium sativum*, and it is this, with its tiny leaves, which ought to be present in boxes labelled 'mustard and cress'. It is a native of W. Asia, but its main use is in Europe and N. America.

The 'wild cress' called DITTANDER or poor man's pepper and 'Virginian cress' (pepperwort, peppergrass) are both peppery. So is winter cress, *Barbarea vulgaris*, also called yellow rocket, and its close relation *B. verna* (American or land cress). The latter can be used in place of watercress, if necessary. Both are candidates for winter salads.

Pará (or Brazil) cress, *Spilanthes acmella* 'Oleracea', can be used to give some pungency to salads, but is distinctly milder

than the parent *S. acmella*, known as the toothache plant or Australian cress. However, we are here moving away from plants of the mustard family and into the realm of pot-herbs which belong to the family Compositae and just happen to have 'cress' as part of one of their common names.

CREVALLY or crevalle, a name loosely applied to various fish in the family Carangidae, sometimes with an epithet attached, as in 'jack crevalle'. The name is derived from the Latin *caballa* (meaning mare) via the Spanish *caballa* (a name for certain carangid fish). However, it is hard to disentangle the relationship between 'crevalle/crevally' and TREVALLY. If, for example, one considers the list of species which are highly prized in Hawaii as 'crevalle' (or *ulua*, the local name) one finds that a couple of large ones, *Caranx melampygus*, the blue crevalle, which may attain a length of over 90 cm (35"), and *C. ignobilis*, which can be half as long again, feature in Australia as blue-finned trevally and giant trevally respectively.

See also JACK.

CRICKET the name used for various jumping, chirping INSECTS of the family Gryllidae, especially *Gryllus campestris*, the field-cricket, and *Acheta domestica*, the house-cricket of 'cricket on the hearth' fame. Bush-crickets are mainly tree-dwelling grasshoppers. These insects, generally speaking, are edible and there is evidence from many parts of the world of certain species being eaten, often after being roasted.

The mole-cricket, *Gryllotalpa africana*, according to Bodenheimer (1951) is dug up from its deep burrows in Thailand and eaten with enthusiasm, especially by ethnic Lao. In the Philippines little mole-crickets called *kamaru* are first boiled in vinegar (see ADOBO), then fried in butter. They are crunchy on the outside, soft in the inside.

See also GRASSHOPPER and LOCUST.

CRIMPING the process of gashing the flesh of fish soon after it has been caught and before rigor mortis sets in, in order to make it contract and become firmer. The basic meaning of the verb to crimp is to contract, and gashing is merely the means to this end; but in the course of time means and end became confused and people thought that crimp meant gash.

The term dates back to the end of the 17th century and the process was widely used in the 19th century but has largely fallen into disuse.

CROAKER a general name applied to a large number of species of fish in the family Sciaenidae. This family includes 200 or more species, some of whose members will be found under DRUM (another general name), KINGFISH, and MEAGRE. The name croaker, although imprecise, is used with reason, since it is normally applied only to those sciaenid fish which can make a croaking (or drumming) noise. Scott (1959) explains that the croaking

comes from their ability to produce a loud, croaking sound, similar to that of a frog. The large swim-bladder is used as a sounding box. The noise is not only heard when the fish has been pulled out of the water but is clearly audible by underwater listening devices and to the Malay 'Jeru selam' who lowers himself under the water and listens for the noises made by shoals of fish from which he can deduce the size of the shoal, species of fish and their approximate position, after which he directs his fishermen to set the net to capture the fish. Even persons drifting in a small boat while fishing have been mystified by the loud 'frogs' chorus' suddenly starting up all round them, the source of which remained unseen until they started to catch the still-croaking vocalists.

According to Read, who quotes ancient Chinese authors to this effect, the listening devices used by Chinese fishermen were long bamboo tubes lowered to the sea bottom, and it is in the fourth moon of every year that the croakers 'come in from the ocean in file several miles long, making a thundering noise'.

In general, the croakers of S. and SE Asia enjoy only moderate esteem, and some are downright insipid. The best is probably *Protonibea diacanthus*, the spotted croaker, which is also the largest (maximum length 120 cm/48"); besides lots of small spots it has dark blotches along its brown or greyish back. The runner-up may be *Nibea soldado* (or *Pseudosciaena soldada*) which reaches a length of 70 cm (28") and, although essentially a marine fish, enters fresh waters in Cambodia and even ascends the River Mekong as far as the north of landlocked Laos, 2,000 km (1,250 miles) from the sea. It can be recognized by its high-arching greenish back, which was responsible for the name 'greenback jewfish'. (Jewfish is or was a common alternative name for croakers and drums, but the reason for this is obscure.)

CROATIA an almost exclusively Roman Catholic country, includes the old district of Slavonia and the ancient littoral province of Dalmatia. Until 1992 it was part of Yugoslavia.

The revival of national awareness, which took place in the 19th century, included also a lively interest in Croatia's own gastronomic past, reflected in publications such as *Croatian Cookbook* (1976) which includes recipes from the 1876 original bearing the same title.

There is a marked distinction between inland and coastal cookery, due not only to contrasting climatic conditions, but also to differences in history. The connection of Croatia proper with Austria and the Austro-Hungarian Empire has strongly influenced its cuisine, which is C. European in character. The people of Dalmatia, on the other hand, were ruled for nearly four centuries by Venice before coming under Austrian rule, and it was not until the beginning of this century that they were united with Croatia. Not surprisingly, Dalmatian cookery is similar, after a fashion, to that of S. Italy and other parts of the Mediterranean, though the Dalmatians use more meat, especially smoked meat, and much less garlic and olive oil than is common in the rest of the Mediterranean.

MK-J

CROCODILE an animal which needs no description, exists in various species of which the most notable are *Crocodylus niloticus*, the Nile crocodile, and *C. acutus*, the American crocodile. The former, which is the larger (maximum length 5 m/16'), had an extensive range in the past (as far north as Palestine for example) but is now found only in the northern part of the Nile and its delta. The latter is found in swamps in Florida.

Asia also has a freshwater crocodile, *C. palustris*, considered to be sacred in many of the regions where it is found. There is also a marine species *C. porosus*, perhaps the largest of all crocodiles and the only one with a reputation for attacking human beings. A large specimen killed in 1970 in Irian Java, New Guinea was thought to have taken 55 human victims while it was alive. This crocodile often swims many miles out to sea, will travel up rivers so far as the water remains salty, and is able to run swiftly on land. This species is now being 'farmed' in some places within its range, e.g. Papua New Guinea. Its range extends from the north of Australia to the south of India and across to the Philippines.

All crocodiles are surprisingly agile, both in and out of the water, and have a carnivorous diet. Considered as food themselves, they are far less prominent than the related ALLIGATOR, but have been eaten locally and have attracted various comments, such as a recommendation to prefer the legs. In those Pacific Islands where *C. porosus* is found, the meat of young specimens is preferred by the islanders and is thought to have a flavour and texture somewhere between fish and chicken.

In the Northern Territory of Australia the farming of both freshwater and marine crocodiles has become established; and it is illegal to sell crocodile meat other than the farmed products.

CROISSANT a French word meaning crescent or crescent shaped, is the name traditionally given to a buttery breakfast roll or bread popular in France. Croissants are made with a yeast-based dough, rolled to incorporate the butter exactly as is done when making puff pastry.

The bending of a little roll into a crescent shape, as probably happened in various parts of the world at various times, does not constitute the invention of the familiar, puffy, buttery croissant. There is more to the croissant than shape.

In fact, the croissant in its present form does not have a long history. See CULINARY MYTHOLOGY for the erroneous idea that it came into being in Vienna in the 17th century. The earliest French reference to the croissant seems to be in Payen's book *Des substances alimentaires* published in 1853. He cites, among the *Pains dits de fantasie ou de luxe*, not only English 'muffins' but 'les croissants'. The term appears again, ten years later, in the great Littré dictionary (1863) where it is defined as 'a little crescent-shaped bread or cake'. Thirteen years later, Husson in *Les Consommations de Paris* (1875) includes 'croissants for coffee' in a list of 'ordinary' (as opposed to 'fine') pastry goods. Yet no trace of a recipe for croissants can be found earlier than that given by Favre in his *Dictionnaire universel de cuisine* (*c.*1905), and his recipe bears no resemblance to the modern puff pastry concoction; it is rather an oriental pastry made of pounded almonds and sugar. Only in 1906, in Colombié's *Nouvelle Encyclopédie culinaire*, did a true croissant recipe appear. The history of the croissant, and its development into a national symbol of France, is a 20th-century history.

For many years, croissants in France were served only at breakfast with a large cup of coffee but, with the advent of what the French call 'Le Fast Food' in the late 1970s, a massive attempt was made to counteract the spread of the American hamburger through the creation of numerous French eateries called 'Croissanteries'. In these establishments the previously plain, buttery roll was split open lengthwise and garnished, sandwich fashion, with every imaginable filling from ham to chestnut cream. The spread of these establishments, in which plain croissants were sold as well, strengthened the French attachment to what is considered a national food. Croissants are, indeed, to be found throughout France and, despite the infringements on their traditional form of consumption by the developments described above, they

continue to be the French breakfast food par excellence.

Croissants can vary dramatically in taste because, as with many butter-based doughs, bakers find butter too expensive a commodity and prefer to substitute cheaper products or simply use less butter than is required for the very best results. Consequently, almost every bakery in France offers up two kinds of croissants to the customer: one labelled simply 'croissant' and the second 'croissant au beurre'. Although the second must be made with butter, the first can be made with almost anything the baker wishes to substitute for it (generally margarine). Strangely enough, a growing number of French people have come to prefer the substitute to the real thing, since the breadier butterless version lends itself better to dunking into the breakfast coffee— a habit much indulged in by many croissant-eaters. The rise of the butterless croissant has been accompanied by a progressive straightening of the butter croissant and a pronounced curving of its rival, making them easily distinguishable from each other. Be they 'au beurre' or not, croissants are a French speciality to be found on breakfast trays around the world.

HY

CROQUEMBOUCHE a French term which means 'crunch in the mouth' is the name for a whole range of elaborate French pastries which traditionally play an important role at weddings, baptisms, christenings, etc. The crunchiness is the result of glazing the component parts with sugar cooked to the stage before caramel.

The typical shape of a modern croquembouche is an inverted cone, formed by piling small choux pastries (see PROFITEROLE) on top of each other. However, when Alice Wooledge-Salmon (1981) investigated the history of these confections she found herself in a whole new world of architectural structures which had their origin in the SUBTLETIES displayed in medieval tables and evolved, under the influence of CARÊME in particular, into the category of *grosses pièces de fonds*, where they kept company with Turkish mosques, Persian pavilions, Gothic towers, and other *pièces montées*. The shape in those days was that of a Turkish fez, something like that of the confections later known as *sultanes*. The same author goes on to explain, vividly and in detail, how the whole genre spiralled upwards out of control towards the end of the 19th century, but then subsided to manageable dimensions—permitting the survival of a relatively plain range of croquembouches through the 20th century, the basic form being simply a conical pile of choux balls on a NOUGAT base with a spun sugar *aigrette* (plume) or other decoration at the top.

CROQUE-MONSIEUR a popular French snack, consists of a thick slice of GRUYÈRE cheese and a thin slice of HAM sandwiched between layers of buttered bread and then toasted on both sides until the cheese has completely melted. Croque-monsieur can also be prepared by frying the sandwich on both sides in butter until crisp. Sometimes the sandwich is dipped in egg and breadcrumbed before frying.

Croque-monsieur literally means 'crunch-sir' or 'munch-sir' (*croquer* being the French verb 'to crunch' or 'to munch'), but where the term originally comes from is not clear. It first appeared on French menus early in the 20th century.

A croque-madame is a more recent invention, with the addition of chicken, or a fried egg on top.

CROQUETTE a French culinary term which was adopted into English too, as long ago as the beginning of the 18th century. Ayto (1993) points out that Phillipps (1706) gave the following meaning: 'In Cookery, Croquets are a certain Compound made of delicious Stuff'd Meat, some of the bigness of an Egg, and others of a Walnut.'

As Phillipps thus indicated, a croquette is always quite small, but highly variable in shape (a ball, a cylinder, an egg shape, a rectangle, etc.); the basic ingredient is either vegetable or meat or fish (although occasionally something sweet); cooking is achieved by coating the croquette with breadcrumbs and deep-frying it, so that the exterior becomes golden and 'crunchy' (*croquant*).

Potato croquettes are frequently met. Croquettes of SALT COD are especially good.

HY

CROUTON derived from the French *croûton*, has been an English word since early in the 19th century, whereas two other connected French culinary terms, *croûte* and *croustade*, have remained French—the former, no doubt, because the English word crust already had a somewhat similar meaning, and the latter because it is a more specialized term which the chefs and menu-writers who use it are happy to leave in its French form.

All these terms derive from the Latin word *crusta*, meaning 'shell'. Thus the outside of a loaf of bread is the crust or *croûte*.

Croûton, the diminutive form, usually refers to the familiar little cubes of toasted or fried bread which might originally have been cut from a crust. (By extension, croutons/

croûtons can refer to similar little cubes of some other substance such as aspic.) It first appears in French in the 17th century when it is described as 'a little piece of bread crust served with drinks'. In recent times, croutons are often added to fish soups and occasionally to certain SALADS, e.g. Caesar salad.

A dish served *en croûte*, e.g. *Bœuf en croûte*, is more likely to be in a pastry case than enclosed by pieces of bread. This is another example of a natural extension of meaning. A *pâté en croûte*, therefore, is a pâté baked inside a pastry casing (indeed, all *pâtés* used to be *en croûte* since *pâté* like *pâte* is derived from the Latin *pasta* meaning 'paste' or 'dough', hence pastry).

Croustade, the third member of the trio, may refer either to a pastry case or to the pastry case and its filling. In classical French cooking these were elaborately sculpted and were likely to have not only a rich filling but also fancy garnishes. Nowadays *croustades* are considered old-fashioned in France; they may still be encountered on buffet tables at grand receptions, or as an accompaniment to drinks.

HY

CROWBERRY the fruit of *Empetrum nigrum*, a plant which grows in the far north of Europe, Asia, and America. It is a low creeping bush with needle-like leaves, somewhat like a prostrate yew. Its berries lack flavour, but are edible. They are small, round, shiny, and black, with half a dozen pips or so, and a firm pulp.

The crowberry grows as far south as Scotland, where it has occasionally been used for food, but prefers the regions above 60 degrees N. In most languages there is a separate name for the variety which is found in the more northerly parts of its range and at higher altitudes. Crowberries are abundant in Greenland.

American Indians of the north-west and Alaska used to gather crowberries for winter food, preserving them by drying or, in Alaska, by placing them with other berries in seal oil. The Inuit still gather and freeze them for the winter.

CROWDIE a fresh cheese made in Scotland from tepid milk to which RENNET has been added to form CURDS; a little salt and sometimes cream is added after the WHEY has drained away. Much crowdie used to be made by crofters in the Highlands. Production diminished after the Second World War, when crofters were leaving the land, and few of those remaining had cows; but since the 1970s it has increased again.

Marian McNeill (1929) gives a Highland recipe recorded earlier by Sir Walter Scott for crowdie to be served at breakfast. This called for two parts of sweet-milk curd and

one part of fresh butter, worked together and pressed in a mould until firm enough to slice. In areas where whey was a popular drink, this was a useful way to use up the curd, especially as a stiff, finely blended curd would keep for months. Lowlanders, in contrast, only made and used what they called 'one day's cheese'. It is, however, from the Lowland Scots word 'cruds' (meaning curds) that the name crowdie comes.

Crowdie was also, in former times, the name for a mixture of finely ground oatmeal (see OATS) and water, stirred to a batter-like consistency but uncooked. Marian McNeill explains that Crowdie in this sense 'was at one time a universal breakfast dish in Scotland', and that it could be made with fresh BUTTERMILK instead of water. Indeed, to celebrate harvest home a festive crowdie could be made with cream and sugar. This 'cream crowdie' may still be met under that name, but is now better known as CRANACHAN.

CRULLER an American FRITTER made of a dough similar to that for a DOUGHNUT but with more eggs, or sometimes with choux PASTRY. The first dough is made stiff enough to roll, and is cut into strips which are usually plaited together; the choux pastry is piped on to a piece of paper in a ring or figure of eight, and tipped off into the hot oil. After frying, crullers are sprinkled with icing sugar. Chinese deep-fried egg twists, made from a dough of flour, oil, sugar, and eggs, are made in a similar shape.

The distinguishing feature of a cruller is not its composition but its shape, which is always doubled or interlaced in some way.

Similar shaped items are made in Scandinavia, for example the Swedish *klenäter* (little things, trifles) and Norwegian *fattigmenn* (beggarmen) based on foamed eggs and sugar mixed with flour and butter, flavoured with lemon or cardamom. These are sometimes actually known as crullers.

LM

CRUMBLE is the name of a simple topping spread instead of pastry on fruit pies of the dish type with no bottom crust, such as are popular in Britain. Recipes for crumble do not appear in old books of English recipes, nor is it recorded until the 20th century. Crumble is much quicker and easier to make than pastry and it seems probable that it developed during the Second World War. It is like a sweet pastry made without water. The ingredients of a modern crumble are flour, butter, and sugar; a little spice is sometimes added. (The original wartime type used some other fat—whatever was available.) The butter is cut into the dry ingredients, and the mixture spooned onto the pie filling without further preparation, after which the pie is baked. The butter melts and binds the solid ingredients into large grains, but they do not form a solid layer like a true pastry. The texture can only be described as crumbly. Apple crumble is probably the best-known form. But other fruits are often used. Numerous variations are permissible, for example the addition of coconut to the crumble mixture in Australia.

Crumble may have been inspired by a similar cinnamon-flavoured topping traditional in Austria and C. Europe for a rich tea bread or cake. The topping is called Streusel, and the cake *Streuselkuchen* (German *streusen*, to scatter). Streusel contains much less flour in proportion to sugar than British crumble, so that when baked it has a crisp and granular rather than crumbly texture, and remains firmly attached to the top of the cake. It is spread over a coating of melted butter on the raw cake, which helps it to adhere.

CRUMPET a type of thick, perforated PANCAKE made from a yeast-leavened BATTER containing milk. Crumpets are cooked on a lightly greased GRIDDLE, confined in ring moulds. Since the 19th century, the leaven in the batter has been boosted by a little BICARBONATE OF SODA just before cooking. Batter consistency is important: the characteristic mass of tiny holes will not develop if it is too thick.

Crumpets are only turned briefly on the griddle, the underside taking on a pale gold colour and smooth surface, while the top remains pallid. This is intentional as they undergo a second cooking by toasting after which they are spread lavishly with butter on the holey side. Dorothy Hartley (1954) says that crumpets may 'vary locally from large brownish dinner-plate size made with an admixture of brown flour in some mountain districts, to small, rather thick, very holey crumpets made in the Midlands'.

The earliest published recipe for crumpets of the kind known now is from Elizabeth Raffald (1769). Ayto (1993), in an entertaining essay, discusses a possible 14th-century ancestor, the crompid cake, and the buckwheat griddle cakes (called crumpit) which appeared from the late 17th century onwards. He also illuminates the sexual connotation of crumpet, pointing out that it is now used of sexually attractive men as well as women, and that there was an analogous use of muffin (for women) in 19th-century Canadian English.

It seems clear enough that there is a connection with Welsh *crempog* (pancake) and Breton *krampoch* (buckwheat pancake).

Reading the collection of crumpet, MUFFIN, and PIKELET recipes made by Elizabeth David (1977) underlines the confusion of method and terminology between these three forms of yeasted pancake cooked on a griddle. A consensus might be that crumpets are made with a thinner batter than muffins, hence the need to confine them in rings (though this was not invariable), and hence too the holes in the top. Muffins are baked thicker, thick enough to be pulled asunder after toasting which crumpets would never be. Pikelets seems a northern usage—though perhaps originally Welsh if the proposed derivation from *bara pyglyd* ('pitchy bread') is accepted. Again the consensus is that the pikelet is near identical to a crumpet, though the batter is thinner still and baked without a ring on the griddle, thus much more like a yeasted pancake.

CRUSTACEANS a mainly aquatic class of creatures, sharing with other arthropods such as insects and arachnids the characteristics of being invertebrates, with jointed limbs, segmented bodies, and an exoskeleton (exterior skeleton) of chitin.

Most crustaceans are edible, although some are not worth eating and some are so small that they have been disregarded as human food; but interest has been growing in KRILL, the collective term for the minuscule amphipods which abound in polar waters, and very small crustaceans of this sort already enter into the composition of certain SE Asian shrimp pastes. On a larger scale, the best-known examples are the various sorts of LOBSTER, SHRIMP, PRAWNS, and CRABS; but there are others, including the GOOSE-NECKED BARNACLE.

Like other arthropods, crustaceans can only grow if they are able to cast off periodically their rigid exoskeleton or shell, and grow a new and larger one in its stead. For a lobster or crab to ease itself out of its existing shell, at the very time when this is becoming too tight a fit, is an extraordinary feat. The emerging 'soft-shelled' creature is highly vulnerable for a short time, until the new shell is hard, and in the case of certain crabs (see, for the main example, BLUE CRAB) may find that its condition is exploited by human beings.

The meat of crustaceans is of fine quality. The fact that many crustaceans, being omnivorous, may act as scavengers and eat the corpses of fellow aquatic creatures need not be a deterrent. Carrion (other than what human beings themselves lay out as bait!) is only a very small proportion of the diet of any of them, and many crabs, for example, feed on algae or even on land plants.

CRYSTALLIZE to cover with a coating of SUGAR crystals. There are two methods of doing this. The simplest is to roll a slightly sticky food, such as a CANDIED FRUIT, in caster or granulated sugar. The second, more complicated, but technically more correct definition, is a process used during the manufacture of sugar CONFECTIONERY. Sweets such as FONDANTS are arranged in a layer on a grid, which is lowered into a sugar solution. This is left undisturbed for some time in a warm place. During this time, a layer of sugar crystals is deposited over the surface of the sweets, giving a sparkling appearance when they are drained.

'Crystallized fruit' is also a term used loosely to indicate candied fruits in general.

LM

CUBEB a largely obsolete spice, is a kind of PEPPER from a climbing plant, *Piper cubeba*, which is native to Indonesia (hence sometimes called Java pepper) and has been cultivated there in the past. It is occasionally called for in medieval Arabic cookery books, nearly always as one component of a mixture of hot spices. In Europe the cubeb was a minor spice of late medieval times and the 17th century and was still being mentioned (sometimes as Benin pepper) in some recipes in 18th-century European cookery books.

Like true black pepper, it consists of the dried berries, and these are about the same size, but longer and grey (almost black) in colour and with stalks attached (hence yet another name, tailed pepper). They have a pleasing fragrance and a hot, camphorous, pepperminty taste. They are now little used except for medicinal purposes, although the oleo-resin from them is sometimes an ingredient in commercial pickles, sauces, etc.

CUCUMBER *Cucumis sativus*, one of the oldest cultivated vegetables, grown for some 4,000 years, may have originated in S. India. Cucumbers were known in Europe in classical and medieval times, and were introduced by Columbus to Haiti in 1494, after which they soon spread all over N. America

Like other CUCURBITS, cucumbers have a very high water content (96%). Of the large number (around 100) of varieties now cultivated, about two-thirds are for eating, and one-third for pickling; the longer fruits of the former are sold fresh, whereas the pickled cucumbers are relatively short and come packed in their pickle in jars.

A high proportion of the cucumbers sold for eating are now grown in greenhouses. They are seedless and self-pollinating, of uniform shape and length, and free of the bitterness which used to be a feature of cucumbers and accounts for the instruction in older recipes to debitter them. They are also said to be more easily digestible than their predecessors.

Besides its use in salads, and as a conventional garnish for cold salmon, sliced, chopped, or grated cucumber is often dressed with yoghurt and a little vinegar; in Indian *raita*, Turkish *cacik*, and Greek *tsatsíki*, etc.

Cucumber can also be made into a fine soup. In England, thin and delicate cucumber sandwiches are a requirement for certain functions in the AFTERNOON TEA category.

The term GHERKIN, which applies to the cucumber varieties grown for pickling, includes not only the small fruits of dwarf varieties of *C. sativus*, but also the fruits of *C. anguria*, sometimes called West Indian gherkin or (because of its spiny exterior) bur(r) cucumber. This latter species is well known from Brazil through the W. Indies to Texas and Florida. In Jamaica it is called maroon cucumber, 'maroon' meaning 'run wild'; and in Trinidad cackrey.

DILL is often used in pickling cucumbers; hence the use of the term 'dill pickles'. In France it is usual to sell especially small gherkins, which are fruits of varieties selected or developed for the purpose and go under the name *cornichons*.

CUCURBITS an extensive family of plants with a vinelike habit of growth. Many bear edible fruits which, whether they are eaten as fruits or as vegetables, have well-established common names: the various kinds of sweet and 'pickling' MELON, the WATERMELON, the CUCUMBER, GHERKIN, the CHAYOTE, the CASSABANANA, and the KIWANO, all treated in their respective entries, are examples of these.

However, within the family Cucurbitaceae there is one genus, *Cucurbita*, which poses intractable problems of nomenclature, because the common names in use tend to be loosely applied, vary from one part of the world to another, and overlap with each other. The names in question are pumpkin, gourd, summer squash (including marrow/zucchini/courgette), and winter squash; and there is no fully effective way of sorting out the confusion.

The various botanical species can be distinguished under their scientific names, as is done below, but this is of less help than one would expect, since a single species may contain numerous varieties, of which one may usually be called a squash while another is termed pumpkin. The solution adopted, as the capitalized English names indicate, has been to provide separate entries for all the recognized common names, thus allowing familiar usage to prevail, at the cost of having some entries overlap with each other as the names do.

All members of the genus *Cucurbita* are of American origin.

C. pepo embraces many sorts of PUMPKIN, SUMMER SQUASH (including the British VEGETABLE MARROW, Italian ZUCCHINI/French courgette, besides the American Pattypan, Yellow Custard, Sunburst and Crookneck squashes), and the curious VEGETABLE SPAGHETTI. *C. pepo* is the most important species in the group and the one which can be traced furthest back. Remains of its rind and seeds dating back at least to 7000 BC have been found by archaeologists in Mexico.

C. maxima, which originated in the region of Bolivia, includes the larger kinds of WINTER SQUASH, e.g. the cultivars Hubbard and Buttercup. This species is little known in Europe.

C. moschata, a species which grows only in warm regions, includes some sorts of PUMPKIN, such as the large cream-coloured Cheese; some of the smaller sorts of winter squash, including the Winter crookneck and the Cushaw (see WINTER SQUASH); and no summer squashes.

C. ficifolia is the MALABAR (or ivy-leaved) GOURD of S. and C. America.

The name 'cucurbit' is not a properly botanical term, although derived from the name of the family, Cucurbitaceae, and that of the genus *Cucurbita* within it. Botanists call the fruits 'pepos' and count them, weird though this seems, as 'berries'. They answer to the definition of a berry as a simple, fleshy fruit, without internal divisions, enclosing seeds (or, exceptionally, a single seed), and not having a separate, peelable skin.

Cucurbits have abundant, watery, and sometimes fibrous flesh. Their nutritional value is generally low, although some of them such as the watermelon and the pumpkin have edible seeds which are highly nutritious.

Norrman and Haarberg (1980) have contributed a semiotic study in which a very wide range of references, and not only in English, to cucurbits is exposed. There is a considerable emphasis on the ridiculous connotations of some of them and on their association with sex, but the very wide reading and open-minded approach of the authors ensures that the study is balanced.

CUDBEAR also called archil or orchil, a dye extracted from various lichens, notably *Rocella tinctoria*, which grow around the Mediterranean. It has for long been used as a food colouring, and gives a purple red or clear red in most foods.

The lichen is first soaked in water and treated with ammonia to give a blue liquid. This is heated to make the ammonia evaporate, leaving a strong, concentrated red colour.

Cudbear was used illicitly, in former times, to deepen the colour of red wine. It is still used in bottled sauces and bitters.

CULATELLO ('little backside'), an Italian product made from pieces of PORK hindquarter pressed together in the manner of a HAM. It comes from the neighbourhood of Parma and is almost as expensive as the better known *prosciutto di Parma*. The meat, which is all lean, is salted, soaked in wine, and packed in a bladder. It is moist, delicate, and pink, and always eaten raw.

CULINARY ASHES put to good use in various regions and cultures of the world, are made by burning certain bushes or trees until they crumble into ash. Among N. American Indians, Creeks and Seminoles use hickory, and Navajos use primarily juniper branches. Hopis may use various materials, such as spent bean vines and pods or corn cobs, but Hopi women prefer ashes made from green plants, since they are more alkaline. They especially prize the ash from the four-winged saltbush *Atriplex canescens*, also called *chamisa*. When burned, green chamisa bushes yield culinary ashes high in mineral content. In explaining all this, Juanita Tiger Kavena (1980) adds:

The Hopi practice of adding culinary ashes to corn dishes therefore raises the already substantial mineral content of these foods. In addition to increasing nutritional value, chamisa ashes enhance the color in blue corn products. When one is using blue cornmeal for any dish, the meal will turn pink when hot water is added, so Hopi women mix chamisa ashes with water to make an 'ash broth' which is then strained and added to cornmeal mixtures. The high alkaline content of the chamisa ashes create a distinctly blue-green color, which holds a religious significance for the Hopis.

CULINARY MYTHOLOGY potentially a subject for a whole book, is here confined to a small number of notorious examples.

CATHERINE DE' MEDICI TRANSFORMED FRENCH COOKERY

Catherine de' Medici arrived in France from Italy in 1533, as the 14-year-old fiancée of the future Henri II of France. She was accompanied by a train of servants including cooks. The myth consists in the idea that she and her retinue between them transformed what had been a rather primitive cuisine at the French court into something much more elegant and sophisticated, on Italian lines.

Barbara Ketcham Wheaton (1983) is not alone in demolishing this myth—far from it, since it has become an almost routine activity for food historians. However, she has mustered more evidence and more detail on this matter than most of her colleagues. She shows that French court cuisine was not transformed (in any direction) in the 1530s and 1540s, and that in any case the interchange of ideas of people between France and Italy had begun before Catherine was born and continued after her death. Italian culinary practice could exert such influence as it may have had on the French by means of the steady traffic and also through books (e.g. PLATINA); but the French in the 16th century had a conservative outlook which in any case immunized them against sudden and foreign influences. Where Catherine did eventually have an effect, it was less on the cooking and more on the attitudes and expectations of the diners, for the wonderful festivals or masquerades which she planned and executed (this was after the death of her husband Henri II) developed into an institution of great visual and dramatic significance.

MARCO POLO'S SUPPOSED INTRODUCTION OF PASTA FROM CHINA TO THE WESTERN WORLD

This durable myth, which requires that nothing should have been known of PASTA in Italy until 1295, when Marco Polo returned from the Far East, can easily be shown to be wrong by citing references in Italy to pasta of an earlier date. What is interesting about the myth is the question of how it arose. An explanation was offered to a distinguished audience at Oxford University by the famous Italian authority Massimo Alberini:

As far as I can make out, the 'Chinese' story originates from an article entitled 'A Saga of Catai' that appeared in the American magazine *Macaroni Journal* in 1929. There it was written that a sailor in Marco Polo's expedition had seen a Chinese girl preparing long strands of pasta, and that the sailor's name was Spaghetti. Obviously an unlikely tale.

It is tempting to add that the *Macaroni Journal* explanation may itself be a myth; but no better explanation has been offered. The question of interaction between oriental and occidental forms of pasta and the extent to which particular forms may have travelled either eastwards or westwards, through C. Asia, is a different one, of a subtlety and complexity sufficient to deter myth-makers from trying to intervene in it. (To be effective, a myth must be comprehensible at the lowest level of intelligence.)

PURPOSE OF SPICING IN MEDIEVAL TIMES

As Gillian Riley (1993) has written: 'The idea that spices were used in the Middle Ages to mask the flavour of tainted meat has been expressed with considerable conviction by many writers about food and cookery.'

The same author demonstrates that:

(*a*) no convincing evidence has been produced to support this idea;
(*b*) in particular, the alleged recommendations in medieval texts to use spices for this purpose cannot be found;
(*c*) the supposition that the 'tainted meat' theory is the only way of accounting for heavy consumption of spices in the Middle Ages is based simply on a misconception, since consumption of spices in that period was not unduly heavy—and indeed could not have been, given their cost;
(*d*) detailed evidence about how cattle were slaughtered, how meat was sold, how cooks kept it and cooked it in particular places at particular times—all this can now be studied in detail and produces no evidence in support of the myth.

Riley believes that the frequent use of the words 'tainted meat' is significant in implying a derogatory and backward glance at cultures less fortunate than our own; and that the 'disguising' role allocated to spices betrays a killjoy attitude which could not acknowledge the simple fact that they add to the pleasure of eating and were so perceived by people in the Middle Ages.

ORIGIN OF THE CROISSANT

According to one of a group of similar legends, which vary only in detail, a baker of the 17th century, working through the night at a time when his city (either Vienna in 1683 or Budapest in 1686) was under siege by the Turks, heard faint underground rumbling sounds which, on investigation, proved to be caused by a Turkish attempt to invade the city by tunnelling under the walls. The tunnel was blown up. The baker asked no reward other than the exclusive right to bake crescent-shaped pastries commemorating the incident, the crescent being the symbol of Islam. He was duly rewarded in this way, and the croissant was born.

This story seems to owe its origin, or at least its wide diffusion, to Alfred Gottschalk, who wrote about the croissant for the first edition of the *Larousse gastronomique* (1938) and there gave the legend in the 'Turkish attack on Budapest in 1686' version; but who subsequently, in his own book (1948) on the history of food, opted for the 'siege of Vienna in 1683' version.

In fact, the world-famous CROISSANT of Paris (and France) cannot be traced back beyond the latter half of the 19th century, at the very earliest. The first relevant mention in any dictionary definition of the word was in 1863, the first recipe under the name 'croissant' (but describing an oriental pastry) in 1891, and the earliest recipe which

corresponds to the modern croissant in 1905.

EFFECT OF SEARING MEAT

Harold McGee (1990) introduces and deals with this myth succinctly:

It's in the best of cookbooks and the worst of cookbooks, the simple and the sophisticated. 'Sear the meat to seal in the juices,' they say. This catchy phrase is probably the best-known explanation of a cooking method. It originated with an eminent scientist. And it's pure fiction.

A nineteenth century German chemist, Justus von Liebig, conceived the idea that high temperatures quickly coagulate proteins at the surface of a piece of meat, and that this coagulum forms a juice-trapping shell that keeps the interior moist. The cooking technique that Liebig accordingly recommended—start the meat at a high temperature to seal it, then reduce the heat to cook it through—ran counter to the traditional ways of roasting and boiling. Despite this, or perhaps exactly because it offered a modern 'scientific' alternative to tradition, the technique caught on immediately in England and America, and eventually in France. Unfortunately, Liebig never bothered to test his theory by experiment. When home economists did so in the 1930s, they found that seared beef roasts lose somewhat more moisture than roasts cooked throughout at a moderate temperature. But Liebig's brainchild continues to turn up in many recipes for roasting, frying, and grilling. It refuses to die.

McGee also explores the question of why it refuses to die; and explains how easily, by simple visual observation, even the most stubborn adherent may be convinced that the myth is indeed a myth.

THE ORIGIN OF CHOP SUEY

Various legends have been current. They agree in supposing that a Chinese cook (usually in California), confronted by a demand from exigent diners for food at an hour when everything on the menu was 'off', improvised a mixture from leftovers and said that the dish was called CHOP SUEY, meaning 'odds and ends' in Chinese. The identity of the demanding diners varies (in a manner typical of mythology): drunken miners, a San Francisco political boss, railroad workers, a visiting Chinese dignitary, etc.

Anderson (1988) gives the true explanation. Chop suey is a local Toisanese dish. Toisan is a rural district south of Canton, the home for most of the early immigrants from Guangdong to California. The name is Cantonese *tsap seui* (Mandarin *tsa sui*), meaning 'miscellaneous scraps'.

CULINARY TERMINOLOGY has been discussed to such good effect in *Kettner's Book of the Table* by Dallas (1877) that it is his words which are here offered.

In one point, however, accuracy is well within our reach, and nearly all the cookery books—even those produced under the eyes of great artists—make a mock of it: we can be accurate in language. In the whole range of literature and science, there is nothing to be found comparable to the inaccuracy and corruption of culinary language. It is something astounding. It seems as if all the ignorances in the world had conspired together to darken speech and to stupefy cooks. There is no science of cookery possible without a correct phraseology. Science is but another name for clear and classified knowledge; and the first step to it is precision of speech. It is for this reason that in the following pages the reader will find more than usual attention paid to the naming of dishes and to their history. At the present moment the vocabulary of dinner is a mass of confusion and ridiculous mistakes, which is every day becoming worse and worse through the ignorant importation of French names (originally themselves bad enough) into English bills of fare. It comes of abominable pretension. A leg of good English mutton—the best in the world—will be entered as a Gigot of Pré Salé. What on earth has become of the English Southdowns that they should be described as a French Salt Marsh? I have seen a fillet-steak served with tomatos entered as 'Filet de Boeuf à l'Orientale,' under a notion that tomatos came originally from the East and not from the West, and that the people of the East are given to beef. This is not merely pretension: it is perfidy. You order the Oriental fillet expecting one thing, and you get something quite different.

Some people may innocently argue—'What harm is there in a wrong word so long as the dish is good? We eat the food and not the name.' But this is to mistake human nature. A hungry taste is apt to be querulous, and resents disappointment. Also there is a peculiar fastidiousness in what has never yet been thoroughly analyzed—that peculiar condition known as Acquired taste. Perhaps there is no such thing in persons who are grown up as a perfectly pure and natural taste. The taste may be sound and even fine, but it is always more or less influenced by custom and by association, until it breeds an Acquired taste which is not to be reasoned with and which will not be denied. The Greenlander takes to tallow; the southern Frenchman glories in garlic; the East Indian is mighty in pepper. No force of reasoning can prove to them that other tastes are better; they have an Acquired taste which insists on being pampered. And precisely the same phenomenon occurs, though in a less marked way, when we get a dish which we know, which we expect, and which does not correspond to its name. A very pleasant Julienne soup can be made without sorrel; but those who look for the sorrel always feel that without it the Julienne is a failure. An acquired taste has been created, which suffers under disappointment as cruelly as when the Greenlander is deprived of his whale-blubber, the Gascon of his garlic, and the East Indian of his curry.

Bad as it is, however, it is not on the perfidy or the pretension of wrong names that it is most necessary to insist. The great wrong about them is that they are a bar to all chance of science and of progress in cookery. An idea has got abroad and has been much fostered by French authorities, that cookery as practised by the great artists is perfect, and that there is nothing more to be done except to ring the changes on what these artists have achieved. It is probable enough that we shall

not get many more new foods or combinations of savour; but it is quite certain that with the progress of science we ought to attain our results by simpler and shorter processes, with aim more precise and with success more assured. But nothing at all is possible until we first of all understand each other by agreeing upon terms about which there shall be no mistake. It is for this reason that . . . [I dwell] so much upon the mere grammar and vocabulary of the kitchen. Till we have settled our definitions there is no use in talking. And therefore, while in . . . composing receipts . . . I have done my utmost to simplify processes, to discard mere subtleties and variations, and to cut down useless expenses and tedious labour, I have gone first and foremost on the principle that the greatest waste of all in the kitchen is the waste of words. It is a simple fact . . . that the language of the kitchen is a language 'not understood of the people.' There are scores upon scores of its terms in daily use which are little understood and not at all fixed; and there is not upon the face of this earth an occupation which is carried on with so much of unintelligible jargon and chattering of apes as that of preparing food. . . . We sorely want Cadmus among the cooks. All the world remembers that he taught the Greeks their alphabet. It is well-nigh forgotten that he was cook to the king of Sidon. I cannot help thinking that cooks would do well to combine with their cookery, like Cadmus, a little attention to the alphabet.

CULLEN SKINK a fish soup associated with the fishing village of Cullen in NE Scotland, happened to be singled out for mention by Marian McNeill (1929) in her pioneering survey of traditional Scottish cookery. However, it is but one of a number of such soup/stews, based on smoked haddock and incorporating milk, with potato as a thickener. Catherine Brown (1996) affirms that these were made by fishwives all along the coast.

In fact the word 'skink' comes from the German word *Schinke* (ham) and has the same meaning in Scotland as HOUGH, i.e. the part of an animal corresponding to the human ankle or shin; so the archetypal skink is a soup made from shin of beef. Presumably the people in places such as Cullen adapted this to the fishy version.

CUMBERLAND SAUCE served cold with cold meat, is made with redcurrant jelly, mustard, pepper and salt, blanched 'matchsticks' of orange peel, and port wine. Elizabeth David (1970), having conducted characteristically thorough research into its origins, observes that: (*a*) there is a legend that it was named for the Duke of Cumberland who was brother of George IV; (*b*) the first reference to it by name was in a French book, Alfred Suzanne's *La Cuisine Anglaise*, of 1904; (*c*) what was essentially the same recipe had been published by Soyer in 1853, but without the name; and (*d*) the

famous chef ESCOFFIER, who flourished in the Edwardian era, popularized the recipe given by Suzanne and was responsible for the commercial success of the sauce.

If there were any need to confirm these findings, one could add that the sauce had not appeared in any of the late 19th-century compilations, such as *Law's Grocer's Manual* (*c*.1895), in which, had it become known and commercially available by then, it would certainly have figured; and that the Duke of Cumberland of the legend, who had become King of Hanover, died in 1851, more than 50 years before Suzanne made his reference to Cumberland sauce.

CUMIN SEED or cumin (sometimes cummin) for short, a spice consisting of the dried, seedlike, fruits of *Cuminum cyminum*, a pretty little annual herb of the parsley family, Umbelliferae. It probably originated in the E. Mediterranean region, but is now grown also in India, China, Japan, and Indonesia.

Cumin was well known in antiquity. There are biblical references to threshing the harvested plants with rods to collect the 'seeds', a procedure still followed in some places in the E. Mediterranean.

Pliny (1st century AD) paid cumin a high compliment ('when one is tired of all seasonings, cumin remains welcome'); and to judge by the collection of recipes attributed to Apicius the Romans used it frequently.

It was popular in England in medieval times, but later was largely eclipsed by CARAWAY. Cumin is still much used elsewhere, e.g. in pickling mixtures. In the Netherlands and Switzerland it spices certain cheeses; and in France and Germany it flavours some cakes and breads.

Cumin is an ingredient of the Iranian spice mixture ADVIEH; the Afghan *char masala*, the Indian *garam masala* (see MASALA) and other CURRY POWDERS.

In N. Africa cumin seeds are used in meat and vegetable dishes. Their use in Spain for stews and for breads continues, but on a diminishing scale; as is perhaps implied by a curious Spanish saying, 'me importa un cumino', meaning 'I couldn't care less'. The popularity of cumin in Latin America, originally due to Spanish influence, and the popularity of Mexican food such as CHILI CON CARNE (in which the cumin which is always present in chilli powder is a prominent flavouring) in the USA have combined to make cumin an important spice for N. Americans.

There is an uncommon variety of true cumin whose seeds are black or near-black. Names for this include *siyah zira* in Iran and Afghanistan, and *kala jeera* or *kala zira* in

India (or, a corruption of the name in Iran, *shia zira*). See also BLACK CUMIN.

CUP CAKE the name given in Britain and generally in the USA to any small cake baked in a cup-shaped mould or in a paper baking cup. In the USA the term may originally have been related to the American measuring system, based upon the cup. Elizabeth Ellicott Lea's *Domestic Cookery* (1845) gives a recipe for cup cake which is a large cake, baked 'as pound cake'. The cake is made from four cups of flour, three of sugar, one of melted butter, and one of sour cream with a teaspoonful of saleratus (BAKING POWDER) dissolved in it. Three eggs are added and the cake is flavoured with brandy and nutmeg.

CUP FUNGI a large group of fungi, some edible. They all belong to the order Pezizales in the class Ascomycetes, the fungi which form their spores in small sack-shaped cells.

The scarlet elf cup, *Sarcoscypha coccinea*, is one of the most eye-catching edible fungi. It grows on fallen branches from winter to spring and looks just like a scarlet cup of a size which would suit an elf. It is common in N. America as well as Europe. Children in the Jura are said to eat it raw on bread and butter; and one French author suggests adding the cups, with a little kirsch, to a fresh fruit salad.

The orange peel fungus, *Aleuria aurantia*, is not dissimilar, but its cup has a surface which is less smooth and resembles an orange skin turned inside out, being whitish outside and orange within. It too is a European and N. American species. In Italy it is considered edible, even raw in salads, but lacking in flavour.

Otidea onotica, the hare's ear fungus, is of the shape indicated by its name and creamy yellow in colour. It needs to be well cooked; and can then be used in salads, but has little flavour.

CURASSOW the name for a bird in one group of the family Cracidae. The other two main groups have the names *chachalaca* and *guan*. All these birds bear a general resemblance to the HEN, PHEASANT, or TURKEY. The *chachalacas*, relatively small, can look like scrawny hens as they scratch around in barnyards. Curassows, on the other hand, are large and may be compared to turkeys. Their size gives them more importance as table birds. The great curassow, *Crax rubra*, may weigh as much as 4.5 kg (10 lb).

Some authorities believe that the relationship between these birds and the families of turkey, GROUSE, GUINEA-FOWL,

etc. is so close that they should all be grouped in one large family.

The name curassow comes from the Caribbean island of Curaçao, whence the first specimens to be seen in Europe. Whether or not this family of birds originated in S. America, that is certainly the region where they evolved most rapidly and are best known. The northerly limit of their range is the frontier between Mexico and Texas; the southern limits are N. Argentina and Uruguay.

These birds may be prepared and cooked like their counterparts among domestic fowl such as CHICKEN and turkey.

CURD or curds is the solid part of MILK which has been separated by CURDLING with RENNET or an ACID. Separating the curd in this way is the first step in making almost all kinds of cheese.

The curd contains the main milk PROTEIN, casein, and the milk fat. The liquid fraction, whey, contains the milk sugar and the remains of the protein. Curds and WHEY are eaten together as JUNKET, a bland 'nursery' dessert. Also, of course, curds and whey were providing sustenance for Little Miss Muffet until the spider frightened her away.

Curd can be eaten as it is, with sugar or salt, cream or whey. 'Cruddes' as they were once called, have been a poor man's staple and middle-class 'milk-meat' for centuries. Samuel Pepys, the diarist, recorded having curds and cream or whey as a snack on several occasions. In modern times, curds have more often been used to make curd cakes or tart fillings (as in Yorkshire curd tarts), and similar dishes.

The word 'curd' is also used in other contexts, notably in the name of bean curd (see TOFU), a comparable substance made from SOYA BEANS; and for a kind of fruit preserve of which lemon curd is the archetype (and which may also be described as a 'cheese', especially when made with damsons).

CURD CHEESE a term which at first sight is puzzling since virtually all cheeses are made from CURD. It is generally taken to mean any soft cheese made from unfermented curds, and as corresponding to the Russian *tvorog* and the German QUARK. In contrast, COTTAGE CHEESE is defined as being made from unpressed curds, and therefore having a different texture.

The fat content of curd cheeses is typically higher than that of low-fat cottage cheeses but lower than the CREAM CHEESES.

CURDLING the separation of an EMULSION such as MILK or MAYONNAISE.

Cooks normally use the word when something has gone wrong, but the deliberate curdling of milk is part of the normal process of making CHEESE and other milk products. The term is also used vaguely for various misfortunes that produce a lumpy texture. Other words used in this context are flocculation, which means the formation of any kind of lumpy or fluffy masses and is understood here to mean a lumpiness that can be reversed; and COAGULATION, which means an irreversible hardening—if a sauce coagulates, the only thing to do is to throw it away and start again. The term coagulation is normally used only of PROTEIN.

Foods that curdle in the true sense include all the emulsified sauces made with egg and oil; some cake batters; and milk, cream, and yoghurt, as well as any sauces, soups, or stews to which these are added—although in these cases separation may occur for more than one reason.

An **emulsion** is a mixture of two liquids in which one liquid forms tiny droplets suspended in the other. In cookery one liquid is generally an oil of some kind, the other water or some watery liquid such as vinegar. When the mixture curdles, the droplets run together into larger drops. If the mixture is left to stand, the two liquids may separate completely so that one floats as a layer on the other. This is a familiar event in vinaigrette dressing, which is an unstable, temporary emulsion. When separated it can be remixed simply by shaking hard in a jar with a lid.

Milk and mayonnaise are stable emulsions—at least over a time scale of hours or days. The droplets are maintained by an emulsifier, a substance which forms a protective boundary layer around them. Emulsifiers are sensitive to changes in their environment, and if the temperature or acidity of the mixture changes they may stop working. In this case more than shaking or stirring is required to reform the emulsion.

Mayonnaise may curdle if the oil is added to the egg yolk faster than the two can be beaten together, so that there is no time for the physical work of beating to break the oil into small enough droplets. It may also separate if the ingredients are not all at the same temperature, or if an ingredient such as vinegar is added without adequate stirring, so that it forms regions of excessive acidity. Even when mayonnaise has been successfully made it may separate if put in the refrigerator, which makes the oil begin to solidify.

In all these cases the emulsion may be repaired by stirring it into another egg yolk. This must be done as gradually as when making the original mixture. If no more eggs are available, sometimes the mayonnaise can be reunited by stirring it into a spoonful of water, but, since there is much less emulsifier around when this method is used, it does not always work.

Milk does not consist only of fat and water; it also contains protein molecules suspended in the water. It can separate in two ways. In fresh, unhomogenized milk the droplets of fat float to the surface, forming a layer of 'top of milk'. The milk can be remixed by shaking it. But when milk separates into semi-solid curds floating in clear whey it cannot be remixed. In this case not only the fat but some of the protein has separated, and the protein has begun to coagulate into a solid that cannot be liquefied again. Similarly, when milk is boiled the heat makes protein coagulate into a skin on the surface, which cannot be stirred back into the milk. The technical term for an irreversible change in protein is 'denaturing'. This change can also be brought about by adding acid or alkali to milk.

Many hot dishes call for CREAM or YOGHURT to be stirred in just before serving. It is important that the liquid should not then be allowed to return to the boil. If it does, the milk protein will coagulate, producing a granular texture which cannot be rectified. (If cream is added to an acid sauce, for example one containing tomatoes, it may separate even if it does not boil.)

Yoghurt and SOUR CREAM are even less stable than fresh cream because of their acidity. However, yoghurt that is to be used in cooking can be prevented from curdling by first stirring in cornflour or egg white while it is slowly brought to the boil. These act as physical binders to thicken the mixture.

In this context, lumpiness in a WHITE SAUCE needs a word of explanation. White sauce is partly an emulsion, because it is made with milk, so it can curdle like any other mixture made with milk. But it is also a 'sol', a dispersion of starch such as FLOUR or CORNFLOUR in liquid, and it is this other aspect of the sauce which usually causes trouble. The major cause of lumpiness here and precautions to be taken are explained under STARCH.   (RH)

CURLEW *Numenius arquata*, a drab-coloured bird of about 60 cm (24") in average total length, of migrant habits, with breeding grounds in the north of Asia and Europe.

The curlew is not a common article of food, although it used to enjoy some popularity. Birds which have been feeding at sea or on the coast tend to have a fishy taste. Those taken from inland moors, where they eat berries and insects, are greatly preferable.

The Scots name for curlew is whaup.

The godwits mentioned in early English cookery books are marsh birds of the genus *Limosa*, not unlike the curlew, but smaller. They had a high reputation as table fare. Sir Thomas Browne (1902), writing in the 17th century about the natural history of Norfolk, observed that they 'were accounted the daintiest dish in England and I think, for the bignesse, of the biggest price'.

CURRANTS the fresh fruits which may be red, white, or black, have nothing to do with currants in the other sense (see RAISINS, SULTANAS, AND CURRANTS), but belong to a separate genus of plants, *Ribes*, which also includes GOOSEBERRIES. They are small, round berries which often retain, at the end opposite the stem, withered remnants of the flower from which they grew.

Wild currants, both red and black, grow worldwide in northern temperate regions. Cultivated species are virtually all derived from European and Asian types. Native American currants were used by Indian tribes, especially for making PEMMICAN (preserved dried meat, fat, and fruit), but one of them, *R. aureum*, the golden currant, is so good that cultivars of it have been developed by a process of selection.

The redcurrant was first mentioned in European literature in a German manuscript of the early 15th century. A drawing appears in the Mainz *Herbarius* of 1484. It was domesticated in Europe in the 16th century, mainly in the Netherlands and Denmark. The first species used was *Ribes sativum*, but the more prolific *R. rubrum* was later adopted, and there are many hybrids between these and other species. Wild redcurrants taste much the same as cultivated ones.

The **whitecurrant,** now relatively uncommon, is a variant which arises spontaneously in several redcurrant species.

In Britain **redcurrants** are essential for the making of at least one delicacy, SUMMER PUDDING; and redcurrant jelly is a fine accompaniment for lamb and other meats. Redcurrant juice is a popular drink in and around Germany. Generally, the popularity of redcurrants is most noticeable in the northern parts of Europe, including Scandinavia.

In other parts of Europe, especially the far south, currants of whatever colour have never caught on. The most common Latin languages use the same name for 'currant' and 'gooseberry'. Even when, in Paris in the 18th century, redcurrant juice became a fashionable drink, the fruit was known as *groseille d'outre mer* (overseas gooseberry). However, there is at least one exception to this general statement. Bar-le-Duc, a town in NE France, is known for its exquisite preserve made from redcurrants. The process for making this is exacting; it requires that the currants should be individually pierced with a quill to remove the seeds, before being boiled with sugar syrup and some redcurrant juice. (Similar preserves are made with whitecurrants or tiny strawberries. All may be served with cream cheese for dessert.)

The **blackcurrant**, *R. nigrum*, was first cultivated a century later than the red, and for a long time was considered to be distinctly inferior. Its flavour, though pleasant, lacks the brilliance of that of the redcurrant, especially when the fruit is raw. The original blackcurrants grew in N. Europe and in Asia as far east as the Himalayas. They have been crossed with other Asian species to produce the plants now cultivated.

Early uses in Britain were partly medicinal, as a cure for sore throats. The leaves were made into a tea said to have strengthening properties. Blackcurrants also became popular for jam. In France the alcoholic cordial *crème de cassis*, made in the vicinity of Dijon in Burgundy from locally grown blackcurrants, won worldwide fame.

The discovery of vitamins at the beginning of the 20th century gave a boost to consumption of the blackcurrant, since it is outstandingly rich in vitamin C. Half a dozen blackcurrants have more of this than a large lemon. Blackcurrant juice is now widely used as a healthful drink.

CURRY a term adopted into the English language from India, has changed its meaning in migrating and has become ubiquitous as a menu word. It now denotes various kinds of dish in numerous different parts of the world; but all are savoury, and all spiced.

The Tamil word *kari* is the starting point. It means a spiced sauce, one of the sorts of dressing taken in S. India with rice, and soupy in consistency. Different words in Tamil refer to stewlike dressings (meat, fish, poultry, vegetables, in small quantities) and to 'dry' dressings. Europeans, however, fastened on the word *kari* and took it to mean any of these dressings. *Hobson-Jobson* (1903; Yule and Burnell, 1979), who gives the fullest (and most entertaining, but in some respects confused) account of the term's history up to the beginning of the 20th century, observes that the Portuguese took over the word in this manner, and cites evidence that a recipe for *karil* appeared in a 17th-century Portguese cookery book, probably reflecting a practice which had begun in the 16th century.

The earliest apparent mention in print in the English language occurs in a translation (1598) of a Dutch traveller's account of voyages in the E. and W. Indies. Referring to Indians, this text states that: 'Most of their fish is eaten with rice, which they seeth in broth, which they put upon the rice, and is somewhat sour but it tasteth well and is called Carriel, which is their daily meat.'

This account was reasonably correct. However, the first curry recipe in English, 'To Make a Currey the India Way', was provided by Hannah Glasse (1747), and her instructions plainly lead to the making of a stew of fowls or rabbits, with but a spoonful of rice and several spices. This recipe, echoed by many later ones, exemplifies the transposition which had taken place. What had been an Indian sauce to go with rice has become an English stew with a little rice in it. Meanwhile, however, *kari* itself had been changed by the introduction to Asia from the New World of capsicum plants, and the hot red pepper made from them. From that time on *kari* included this pepper, whereas previously it had contained nothing more pungent than black pepper.

The traditional S. Indian *kari* does not have a fixed set of ingredients, but a typical mixture was and remains the following, all roasted and ground to a powder: *kari patta* (CURRY LEAF); CORIANDER, CUMIN, and MUSTARD seeds; red and black PEPPER; FENUGREEK; TURMERIC; and less certainly CINNAMON, CLOVES, CARDAMOM.

Such a mixture is always freshly prepared in India. The British, becoming accustomed to it and wishing to have it available in Britain, created commercial ready-mixed CURRY POWDER, which reflects the above mixture with more or less accuracy (often less—some terrible tales are told of what has been found in them, and they were often made with spices of inferior quality and stretched with sago flour).

Use of the word 'curry' in English spread to Malaysia, and was matched in the Dutch E. Indies by the Dutch word *karie*. Many Indians were in SE Asia, and dishes based on either their practice or European transmogrifications of it exist throughout the region, and also in E. Africa. Indeed, they are now a worldwide phenomenon.

CURRY LEAF the shiny green aromatic leaf of the small tree *Murraya koenigii*, a member of the family Rutaceae to which the citrus fruits belong. The tree grows wild in much of S. and SE Asia, and is cultivated in some countries. The leaves, disposed in a feather-like arrangement, have a pleasing fragrance and are widely used as a flavouring in cookery, including CURRY dishes and in many kinds of CHUTNEY, in S. India, Sri Lanka, and some parts of SE Asia, e.g. the north of Thailand. Names for the leaf in India vary, but *kari patta* (plural) is widely used.

The function of curry leaves, like that of MAKRUT LIME leaves, corresponds to some extent to that of the BAY LEAF in western

Curry leaf

countries (and to that of coriander leaves in N. India). If used fresh, either whole or broken up (to intensify their aroma), they are fried before being incorporated in the dish; this makes them brown and crisp. Whole leaves are usually removed from a cooked dish before it is served.

The leaves retain their aroma when dried, and in places where there is not an abundant fresh supply they can be bought in semi-dried, dried, or powdered form. (Powdered leaves might be expected to be an ingredient of curry powder, but they are not.)

The leaves of the related *M. paniculata*, sometimes referred to as jasmine orange, are likewise used to flavour curry dishes.

In Nigeria, curry leaf is a common name for partminger (see BASIL).

CURRY POWDER of the kind sold commercially, represents an attempt by British (originally and still primarily) manufacturers to provide in ready-made form a spice mixture corresponding to those used in S. India. The latter are called *kari podi*; *kari* because they incorporate *kari* leaves (see CURRY LEAF).

A mixture in S. India, as noted already under CURRY, is likely to include also CORIANDER, CUMIN, and MUSTARD seeds; red and black PEPPER; FENUGREEK; and TURMERIC—with the possible additions of CINNAMON and CLOVES and CARDAMOM, and *channa dal* (split CHICKPEAS). All these are roasted and ground to a powder. The powder is freshly prepared when needed.

Since it was this sort of mixture which the British in India sought to replicate in

standard forms, it is to the most notable writer on ANGLO-INDIAN COOKERY that we turn for information. Colonel Kenney-Herbert (1885) gave as ingredients in his 'stock receipt for curry powder' 'turmeric, coriander-seed, cumin-seed, fenugreek, mustard-seed, dried chillies, black pepper corns, poppy-seed, dry-ginger'. The first seven items correspond to the first seven in the preceding paragraph, and only the last two are different; thus the resemblance is close.

Commercial mixtures had been available to cooks in Britain from late in the 18th century (at least one recipe (H. Glasse, 1796) of the 1790s calls for 'curry powder'), but seem not to have been a common article of commerce until later. Such mixtures, then and subsequently, have varied considerably but have usually contained many or most of the ingredients mentioned above (except cardamom, which has hardly ever been used).

At the close of the 19th century, *Law's Grocer's Manual* listed 12 recipes for curry powder, drawing on 19 ingredients. These included rice flour; and an excess of this or an addition of sago flour were mentioned as two of several possible adulterants.

In recent times, increased awareness of what Indian cooking in its authentic form is like has created a demand in Britain for curry powders which bear a closer relationship to it. However, the uses to which the powders are put in western countries—uses which stem back to Anglo-Indian cookery—do not, generally speaking, correspond to Indian practices. The whole curry powder scene is always going to be irreconcilable with its origins.

It is, incidentally, not only the British who use curry powder. In France *poudre de curry* is obtainable, and in Denmark, with its long tradition of trade with the Orient, there has for long been a 'karry' powder available (but a relatively mild version.

See also CURRY and MASALA.

CUSK also known as torsk or tusk, a fish of the cod family which has a range stretching right across the northerly waters of the N. Atlantic. Its habits are unlike those of its brethren; it does not mass in shoals but tends to a solitary and sedentary existence, growing slowly in the cold Arctic waters (maximum length 110 cm/44"). It has only one dorsal fin, and just one barbel.

There is some commercial fishing for the cusk, which may be marketed either fresh or salted. Its flesh contains a moderate amount of oil and is well suited to grilling or baking.

CUSK EEL the general name for two fine edible sea fish of the southern hemisphere,

Genypterus capensis and *G. blacodes*. They belong to the family Ophidiidae, and are not true eels although somewhat eel-like in shape. They also bear a resemblance to the CUSK (hence cusk eel) and the LING.

G. capensis may reach a length of 1.5 m (5'), and is generally pinkish with brown blotches. It belongs to the Cape of Good Hope region and is known there as *kingklip*, a name which according to van der Elst (1988) is a contraction of the old Dutch word *koningklipvisch*, meaning king of the rockfish. It counts as one of the finest table fishes of S. Africa.

The liver of the *kingklip* is greatly appreciated, a point which also applies to *G. blacodes*, a smaller species of Australasian waters which is of less commercial interest and which locally bears the misnomer ling.

CUSTARD a mixture of milk and eggs thickened by gentle heating, is a basic item of western cooking and occurs in many dishes in either a dominant or subsidiary role.

In the vocabulary of the French kitchen, there is no word for 'custard', and thus it is easy to forget the role that custard mixtures play in things as diverse as QUICHE Lorraine and ÉCLAIRS. The word used is CRÈME, which see for this and its other meanings; but see also CRÈME CARAMEL and CRÈME BRÛLÉE for connected subjects.

Custard was much used in the Middle Ages as a filling and binder for other fillings in the FLANS and TARTS which were highly popular at the time and for long afterwards. That is how it got its name; 'custard' is derived from 'crustade', a tart with a crust.

The use of custard-filled 'pies' or tarts was memorably extended in the 1920s, when the throwing of custard pies into the faces of characters in silent films became a standard Hollywood procedure. Lorna Woodsum Riley (1987) devoted a chapter of her appropriately titled *Reel Meals* to the subject, recalling that the comedienne Mabel Normand, around 1913, launched the first such missile, probably at Fatty Arbuckle; that Arbuckle himself developed into a champion pie-thrower (able to toss two at once in opposite directions); that the *pâtisserie* which supplied the pies to Keystone Studios soon developed a special ballistic version of the pie, with heavy-duty pastry and especially slurpy 'custard', demand for which from film-makers—who might stage scenes in which a thousand or more pies would be thrown—grew to such an extent that the *pâtisserie* was eventually making nothing else.

Two other medieval preparations, CAUDLE and POSSET, have a history linked with that of custard, and in some instances have virtually been custards. Although in their plainest form they were drinks, they were often thickened to a fair degree of solidity.

One way of cooking custards was to bake them in a bread oven after the bread was taken out and when the oven was fairly cool, or in one of the small side ovens which became increasingly usual at the end of the Middle Ages. Another device used at this time, the chafing dish gently heated with a layer of hot coals under it, provided an ideal way of making custards. Sometimes the thick kind of medieval custard was further stiffened by adding breadcrumbs. This was done with both tart fillings and free-standing custards. Other 'enforcements', as the term was, were flour and finely pounded meat, for example pork flavoured with sage. There was at this time no clear distinction between savoury and sweet, and meat might coexist with quantities of sweet ingredients such as sugar and fruit, as well as almonds, herbs, and spices.

A gelling agent was sometimes added to custards for serving cold. Some old local British recipes make use of CARRAGEEN moss. Custards liquid enough to pour were also made, variously flavoured. These might be poured onto bread to make a 'sop', or onto poached eggs.

In the 16th century 'fruit creams' became popular. These were sweet made with eggs, cream, and puréed fruit. Early types of FOOL were similar. During this time it became usual to make custards in dishes or individual cups rather than in a pastry case, though many types of custard tart continued to be popular.

Much later, when ICE CREAM arrived in Britain, custard mixtures were used for it as well as straight cream ones, one reason being that a rich emulsion was less prone to form unwanted ice crystals during freezing.

Custard sauce is made from the same ingredients as custard, but is runnier. It is now very much more common than a true custard, at least in Britain. Indeed, the term 'custard' by itself usually refers to the sauce, as in 'Prunes and Custard' (to select a menu item which many people, although unjustly, regard as offputting—what could be better than *prunes d'Agen* with a well-made custard sauce?).

What is unclear is just when the transfer of custard to the sauceboat began to happen. There are various mid-19th-century recipes for rich custards including flavourings such as bitter almonds, chocolate, various liqueurs, and lemon zest, but they were served cold, probably alone. Mrs Beeton (1861) does, however, give a recipe for a 'custard sauce for tarts or puddings' of eggs and milk, so the transition had begun by the time she was writing.

What is abundantly clear is the importance in all this of the invention of **custard powder.** This product is not a dried form of real custard. It consists mainly of cornflour and sugar, coloured and flavoured, to which hot milk is added to make a sauce. It was invented by Alfred Bird, who opened a shop in Birmingham in 1837 under the sign 'Alfred Bird F.C.S., Experimental Chemist'. Johnston (1977) says that:

it was not the pursuit of scientific knowledge which prompted him to devise a new custard based on cornflour rather than eggs, but rather his concern to find a compromise between his wife's partiality to custard and her allergy to eggs.

Demand for Bird's product increased steadily during the second half of the 19th century. Competitors, using formulae whose ingredients included arrowroot, sago flour, or potato starch, coloured with turmeric or chrome yellow, and flavoured with cassia or bitter almonds, also entered the market. Bird's, however, promoted their product with skilful salesmanship, and became so closely identified with custard powder that few competitors survived.

A principal factor in the success of custard powder was that, as it did not contain eggs,

'CUSTARDS' IN ASIA

Chinese cooking does not normally use dairy products, but contains several dishes in which eggs are combined with water and sometimes oil or fat to give the effect of a custard. One such, 'steamed eggs', is made with mixed meats or seafoods covered with an egg mixture lightly seasoned with soy sauce and wine and steamed over water.

A Japanese savoury baked custard, *Chawan mushi*, is made by pouring a mixture of eggs and DASHI (stock) over a mixture of cooked chicken, seafood, and vegetables in individual lidded china cups. These dishes are the only Japanese ones normally eaten with a spoon.

Steamed egg 'custards' are known in Korea, and a few, savoury or sweet, turn up in the cuisines of the Indian subcontinent. As for SE Asia, there is a Thai and Lao sweet custard, *sankhaya* or *Sankhagnaa mak phao,* which uses COCONUT milk. This is mixed with eggs and sugar and poured into containers made from young coconuts still soft enough to carve with a knife, formed into elegantly shaped pots with a lid and a foot. These pots are steamed until the custard inside sets.

there was no longer any risk of the sauce curdling in unskilled hands. During the late 20th century, the old egg-based custard sauce has become a rarity.

CUSTARD APPLE a name widely applied to various annonaceous fruits, and referring to their creamy pulp, which does taste something like custard. Nothing called custard apple is related to the true APPLE. The fruits most likely to be intended by the term are CHERIMOYA, SUGAR-APPLE (alias sweetsop), BULLOCK'S HEART, and (in the USA) POND APPLE. Of these, bullock's heart is the fruit with the best claim to the name.

There is, however, an African fruit to which the name **wild custard apple** is properly given. This belongs to *A. senegalensis*, which grows throughout tropical Africa. The fruit is oval/round and 2.5–10 cm (1–4") in length. The fleshy pulp is orange or yellow, with a scent of pineapple, and full of seeds. It is considered by some to be the finest of the fruits indigenous to Africa.

CUTLET a term used in butchery and meat cookery which has more than one meaning. The first is a neck CHOP of MUTTON or LAMB. The second is one which applies to VEAL; a veal cutlet is a flat piece of veal (on or off the bone, depending on whether it incorporates a small piece of bone). Thirdly, a cutlet may be a round patty formed of minced meat (or a substitute, as in 'nut cutlet'), like a RISSOLE or CROQUETTE.

The word is derived from the Latin *costa* (rib) through the French *côte* (rib) and *côtelette* (chop). This derivation suits the first meaning. In the other two meanings cutlet is treated as though it were a diminutive of cut (the noun), so meaning a small piece (of meat).

See also the discussion under *Costoletta alla milanese* in the article on VEAL, where the Italian terms *costoletta* and *cotoletta* are explained.

CUTTLEFISH an edible CEPHALOPOD (the group of molluscs which also includes SQUID and OCTOPUS). The species familiar in the Mediterranean and E. Atlantic is *Sepia officinalis*, which has a maximum body length of about 25 cm (10") and is usually dark in colour with markings as shown in the drawing. Like other cephalopods, it has ink sacs which secrete a dark ink, intended for ejection when a predator threatens it. That of the cuttlefish was formerly used to produce the colour sepia. Both cuttlefish and squid may be called inkfish.

In the Indo-Pacific area there are a number of species of cuttlefish, of which those most commonly consumed are:

- *Sepia pharaonis*, slightly larger than *S. officinalis*, and most abundant off the Arabian Peninsula, although its distribution extends across to Japan and Australia;
- *S. esculenta*, a smaller species of Korean and Japanese waters and the E. China Sea; and,
- *S. latimanus*, the largest cuttlefish (up to 50 cm/20"), found in SE Asian and N. Australian waters.

Japan is by far the most important market in the world for cephalopods, and the Japanese generally pay more for cuttlefish than for squid or octopus; but this may be partly because supplies are smaller.

The Chinese, remarking that 'the cuttle has ink in its bosom', have called it 'the clerk of the god of the sea'. Other Chinese names in use at Hong Kong include *mak mo* (nanny inkfish) and *foo ban woo chak* (tiger-blotched black thief).

There are also some very small cuttlefish, such as *Sepiola rondeleti* and *Rossia macrosoma* in the Mediterranean. They are only 3 to 6 cm (about 1" to 2") long, and are often offered for sale ready cleaned and fried, when they make delicious morsels. It is these which the French call *suppions* and the Spaniards *globitos* or *chipirones*. They can be distinguished from baby specimens of *Sepia* spp by the prominent 'ears' which project from their tiny bodies.

Cuttlefish can be cooked like squid or octopus, but need no special treatment to make them tender.

CYCADS are exceptionally primitive plants; they were familiar to the dinosaurs, 100 million years or more ago. They and the GINKGO, the sole surviving species of an equally ancient group, are among the oldest of seed-bearing plants.

A cycad looks like a palm tree with fernlike leaves, but proves that it is not a palm by producing cones, often resembling those of a pine but sometimes far larger. The biggest ever found, from a S. African cycad, *Encephalartos caffer* (source of the so-called 'Kaffir bread'), weighed 42 kg (92 lb).

The plants are long-lived—some are more than 1,000 years old—and highly resistant to drought and harsh treatment. Cycads of several genera are found throughout tropical and subtropical regions worldwide.

The large, nutlike seeds found between the scales of the cones are no delicacy, being starchy and bland, but provide a useful food to many peoples. However, they are toxic in their natural state, and have to be processed quite elaborately before they are safe to eat.

In Malaysia and Indonesia the young leaves are cooked and eaten. They are tender and mucilaginous, and reputedly have a flavour between that of cabbage and of asparagus.

The main African genus is *Encephalartos*. Besides *E. caffer*, mentioned above, there is *E. hildebrandtii* (source of the so-called 'Hottentot bread'). These species variously yield stem sago and seeds, yielding a flour which, after being sun dried and soaked to make it safe, is used for porridge or bread.

There are also cycads in the warmer parts of the Americas. In the W. Indies and Florida, *Zamia floridana* is cultivated on a small scale for the production of starch from the roots. This is known in Jamaica as 'wild sago' or 'arrowroot' and in Florida as 'Florida arrowroot'. Other names for the plant are 'coontie', a Seminole word, or 'seminole bread'. During the American Civil War a number of Federal soldiers died after eating the roots without giving them the careful washing treatment used by the Seminoles. Likewise, as Low (1989) explains, cycads in Australia, used by Aborigines after detoxifying them, caused fearful agonies among early European arrivals, e.g. Captain Cook's crew. The latter did not know what precautions had to be taken.

CYPRUS an island in the E. Mediterranean which has two mountain ranges, an extensive coastline, and a population of under a million, has had a turbulent history, which is reflected in its food.

A Greek colony 4,000 years ago, it has since been conquered by Egypt in the 6th century BC, later by Persians, Macedonians, Romans, Byzantines, Arabs, Venetians, and in 1571 by Turks until 1878 when it came under the British. Subsequently it became a British crown colony in 1925. In 1960 it became an independent state but there was continuing strife between its Greek and Turkish populations until in 1974 a full-scale war broke out. Turkey invaded the island and brought about its present division into two parts.

Cyprus is a fertile island with a clement climate. Its gastronomy reflects the surrounding Mediterranean foodways (especially those of GREECE, TURKEY, and LEBANON AND SYRIA), and the fact that it is geographically closer to the Arab East rather than the European West.

There is a strong link with BYZANTINE COOKERY. Spices are used in a generous way, especially coriander. This was also a favourite feature in Byzantine cooking when cumin and coriander were added to several dishes and in particular to plainly boiled Lenten pulses such as chickpeas and lentils. A number of labour-intensive and intricate dishes such as *koubes* or *koupes*, *koupepia* (the local name for DOLMA), and the sweet-and-savoury Easter cheese pies called FLAOUNES still have their place in the island's gastronomic pantheon. This feature of intricacy could betray either Byzantine or Arab influence.

Vegetables are the protagonists on the daily table and there is a universal love for pulses. A bewildering array of greens, some wild and others cultivated, which are used, after being boiled, for salad, e.g. MALLOW shoots, Swiss CHARD (with black-eyed beans), RAPE before it flowers, and so on. Greens are often sautéed and made into omelettes such as *Strouthia omeletta*—an omelette with young pea shoots.

Similarity between Greek Cypriot cuisine and that of Greece is shown by landmark items such as egg-and-lemon sauces added to chicken and fish soups and casseroles; grilled and fried fish; various pies; and breads such as the delicious *elioti* (made with olives and olive oil). There are also two dishes which may have come straight from ancient Greece. One is *louvana* (*fava* in Greece), a purée of yellow split peas similar to the ancient *etnos*. The other is *tra(c)hanas* (see TARHANA), which is cracked wheat boiled with milk and then rolled into thick breadcrumbs, sun dried and stored for the winter, to be made into a porridge-like soup with a lightly fermented taste.

However, many Cyprus favourites are quite unknown in Greece, e.g. the Arab dip hummus made with CHICKPEAS, and the Arab KIBBEH which are rissoles made with a layer of cracked wheat (see BURGHUL) on the outside and stuffed with a fried mixture of spicy minced meat, onions, and parsley, appropriately Hellenized under the name *koupes* which means cups.

TARO (*kolokassi*) a vegetable which was known in Byzantium but is not known in Greece, is often included in Cypriot casserole dishes, for which the general name is *kapamas*. These casseroles can be made with lamb or pork. Taro has other uses; it is often cooked with dolmas or boiled with celery and lemon and served as a salad.

Other prominent dishes are *Tavas* (a Persian word, meaning frying pan), which is cubed beef or lamb, potatoes, tomatoes, and cinnamon, covered and roasted slowly in a low oven; and *Afelia*—a casserole of pork, red wine, crushed coriander seeds, and cinnamon. Of the numerous grilled meats the star is *sheftalia*, a spicy sausage made with pork or lamb and wrapped in CAUL.

Cypriots are no exception to the general rule that people like sweet things. Their favourites include *loukoumades* (see JALEBI), and GLIKO. RSa

CZECH AND SLOVAK REPUBLICS

for most of the 20th century perceived as a single country, may conveniently be considered together even after separation, since so much of their culinary histories is shared.

The western part of the Czech Republic, adjoining Poland, Germany, and Austria, corresponds to the former kingdom of Bohemia, whose territory represented quite precisely the centre of Europe and which was poised on the frontier between the German and Slavonic parts of that continent. The territory was also a rich one for agriculture.

Bohemia had a high reputation for cookery skills and is said to have provided many cooks for Vienna, the capital of the Austro-Hungarian Empire, to which Bohemia belonged. There was no doubt an influence in both directions, with results still visible. Generally, however, Czech fare tends to be more robust than that of neighbouring Austria, with considerable emphasis on root vegetables and DUMPLINGS as well as on the meat which they accompany and the soups which they fortify.

Czech dumplings (*knedliky*) are unforgettable. The huge loaf-sized ones, which are served in slices with stews, are one of the first things which a visitor notices. They are the leviathans of a massive range which extends all the way down to the tiny liver dumplings which are traditionally served in soup by the bride to her new husband, and which includes ham dumplings, cheese/curd dumplings, sweet fruit dumplings, and many others.

On the sweet side, Bohemian traditions have left a legacy of tearooms and coffee houses and sweet things to eat in them, including various sorts of STRUDEL, biscuits, and yeast buns, as well as numerous large cakes such as *makovy kolac* (poppyseed cake with sultanas), *bublanina* (bubble cake, a sponge with cherries, or other fruit, baked into it), and *streuselkuchen* (crumble-topped cakes). See also MEHLSPEISEN, since this food category of the Austrian Empire remains valid and important in both the Czech and Slovak Republics.

Lesley Chamberlain (1989) records that the foremost Czech cookery writer was Magdalena Dobromila Retigova, a literary figure of the early part of the 19th century who was prominent in the Czech National Revival movement; and that much may also be learned about food in daily life in Bohemia from the work of another pioneering woman writer, Bozena Nemcova (1820–62), whose semi-autobiographical 'novel' featured a grandmother who was a repository of knowledge about the good old foodways which were threatened by newfangled sophistication from alien sources.

What is now the Slovak Republic, adjoining Hungary, was in the past exposed to culinary influences from that country and, at one remove, from Turkey. Some of the ingredients and dishes which arrived from the south became, naturally enough, part of the culinary heritage of the Czech people also; examples are dishes of the GOULASH family.

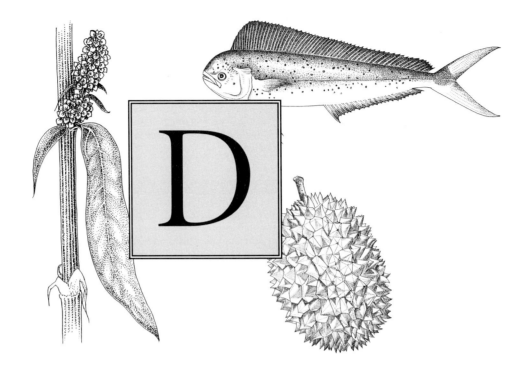

DAB *Limanda limanda*, a FLATFISH of the NE Atlantic, with a range from the White Sea down to France. It has a brown back, often freckled, and may reach a length of almost 40 cm (16"), although commonly little more than half of that. A good fish, with a pleasing flavour, well suited to being fried either whole or in fillets, depending on size; but less esteemed in Britain than in continental Europe. In Jutland dabs are salted and dried and sold under a name which means 'dried Jutlanders'.

In other parts of the world, where English-speaking colonists arrived and found species of fish which they thought similar to the dab which they had known in Britain, the name is often used for other members of the family Pleuronectidae. Thus *Hypoglossoides platessoides* is properly called the American plaice, but is also known as sand-dab or long rough dab. (This particular fish is the very embodiment of confusion in nomenclature since it has also been called a flounder and a sole, while its scientific name suggests an association with the halibut!)

DAGÉ an Indonesian food produced by bacterial fermentation in the same way as the Japanese NATTO. Dagé may be prepared from leftover TEMPE or ONCOM; from various kinds of seeds; from the presscake left after oil extraction from groundnuts or other nuts; or from other vegetable waste. Rice straw is often used to start the fermentation, though the usual wrapping is banana leaf. Dagé is most often used as a condiment for rice, and may also be deep fried or mixed with vegetables.

DAGESTAN AND CHECHNYA adjoin each other in the region lying just north of the Caucasus (see AZERBAIJAN and GEORGIA), one mountainous and the other on the edge of the steppe. Both border on the Caspian Sea.

Very little has been published about their cuisines, but a series of pioneer papers by Magomedkhanov (1991 and 1993; Magomedkhanov and Luguev 1990) has given quite a bit of detail about the food habits and customs of Dagestan, which may be supplemented by the relevant chapter in

Chenciner (1997). The diet is a simple one, built on enduring traditions. A roll-call of the daily fare would include mutton (KEBABS, especially *shashlik*), dried meat, pasta DUMPLINGS, stuffed PANCAKES, flatbreads such as LAVASH, cheese and the other dairy products of the region, HONEY. Tea is the beverage.

Fish does figure in the diet, including STURGEON, but CAVIAR is not eaten by the local people, being reserved for export. Special patrol boats operate in the Caspian to control poaching.

Magomedkhanov and Luguev (1990) have given a detailed description of the feast which follows the end of RAMADAN and is given by a recently bereaved family. It seems that the symbolism of some of the items or procedures is no longer fully understood, but that what is in effect a remarkably elaborate ritual is carried out with great fidelity. There are seven 'breads' (some being pancakes, always garnished with melted fat from a FAT-TAILED SHEEP's tail on top and clarified butter underneath; and one being a glazed and baked sandwich with a complex filling), and seven sweets, including a sort of 'sherbet' in toffee-like slabs, *kompot* (blackcurrants, apricots, rowanberries), and *chelob* rice (cf the *chelow* rice of Iran) variously flavoured (ground apricot kernels, cannabis seeds, honey). Main dishes number three, and are items which also appear in daily fare: cold boiled meats; *plov* (PILAF); and *pilmeni* (PEL'MENI), filled with e.g. *tvorok* (curd cheese).

The above account omits one highly important item: the mountain ram, which is the symbol of Dagestan, symbolizing independence and virility. The role which it plays in the cuisines of the region is described by Chenciner and Salmonov (1988) in a paper delivered at Oxford University which bore the memorable title of 'Little Known Aspects of North East Caucasian Mountain Ram and Other Dishes'. This recorded the culinary aspects of a journey through Dagestan and Chechnya. In a passage which vividly illustrates the continuity of foodways in the region, he describes eating *khingali* (large diamond-shaped PASTA) boiled in ram's broth and served with pure GARLIC juice and pure WALNUT juice, to be eaten with large chunks of boiled ram on the bone. He explains that a 10th-century Arabic text describes similar NOODLES, also served with garlic and walnut flavourings, boiled meat (probably onager—see HORSEMEAT), and broth.

Still on the topic of sheep, Chenciner observes that both main types of sheep are eaten: the plains sheep with fat tails, and the mountain sheep without. He quotes from Thomas Love Peacock (1823):

> The mountain sheep are sweeter,
> But the valley sheep are fatter,
> We therefore deemed it meeter
> To carry off the latter.

DAL (or dhal), whether the word is used to denote an ingredient or a dish prepared from it, is one of the principal foods of the Indian subcontinent. In the first sense it is a split PULSE (as opposed to GRAM, which is whole; but the distinction is not always observed, even by Indians). In the second sense it refers to a dish, of which there are at least 60 kinds, made from BEANS, PEAS, or LENTILS. A combination of LEGUME, such as dal, with cereal is especially nutritious.

One of the most common dals is made from *channa*, the Indian CHICKPEA. The split chickpeas are larger than the grains of other types. The colour is a medium yellow.

Several types of lentil, known as *masur*, are the usual source of dal consumed in Bengal and by Muslims. One common kind is *malika masur*, which is pinkish. The term 'Mysore dal' is sometimes used for lentils.

MOTH BEAN dal is brown, like Middle Eastern lentils. Both this and *malika masur* are often cooked to a purée or porridge.

The most popular dal in the south of India is made from the PIGEON PEA, *Cajanus cajan*, known as *tur* or *arhar*. It has a fine texture and is usually orange, with a few flecks of other colours.

URD (or urad) is a kind of bean, *Vigna mungo*, which yields an expensive and highly regarded dal; this is pale yellow in colour and is special to S. India, where it is used in savoury pancakes etc. Other names for this are *mash, maan*, and *ulutham*. Although the bean has a black coat, the very best dal, made from it, *dhuli urd*, is washed to pure white. Lower grades have black and green flecks. The grain size is very small.

The MUNG BEAN, similar in size to urd but with a green coat, gives a light, delicate dal of a cream or yellow colour with green flecks.

There are other dals made from ordinary peas, similar to European split peas but of various colours. HORSE GRAM, LATH, and COWPEA provide inferior dals.

Dals differ in flavour and texture, as well as in the cooking time required. An Indian recipe will say which type of dal should be used.

Methods of cooking dal also vary. In S. Indian recipes the aim is generally to produce a liquid, souplike consistency, while in northern dishes a thicker texture is usually preferred. Some recommend cooking dal without preliminary soaking and without adding salt until the end, because of its toughening effect. The dissolved salts in hard water have a similar effect, so soft water is advised. Others recommend soaking the dal for as long as overnight, but allow the addition of salt at the beginning of cooking. Whatever the advantages of either method for taste and texture, the second requires less cooking time and saves expensive fuel.

DAMSON a small oval PLUM which, together with the somewhat rounder bullace plum, is classified as *Prunus institia* (a botanical name whose spelling is much disputed—*insititia* is preferred by many authorities). The species, native to E. Europe and W. Asia, is considered to be older than *P. domestica*, the plum proper. Growing wild in hedgerows it is small and sour, suited only to making jam, but cultivated varieties have a fuller range of uses.

The damson had been known in W. Europe since prehistoric times (remains have been found, for example, in excavations of prehistoric Swiss lake dwellings), but was also growing in the Near East. It received its name because it was from Damascus, in Syria, that this damson reached Italy in times BC. When in about 1200 the Duke of Anjou brought the fruit back to France from a Crusade, a further baptism took place; the fruit was now called Damascene, while the shorter form 'damson' was still applied to

fruits of the same species which had been known earlier in Europe. (There is evidence that in medieval times and indeed right up to the 19th century a distinction was preserved, at least in some quarters, between W. European damsons and Near Eastern Damascene plums.)

Britain took a more prominent role than other European countries in developing the cultivation of improved kinds of damson. Examples include Farleigh and Bradley's King, two 19th-century varieties. Shropshire is a PRUNE variety, selected for drying. Varieties of bullace include Black (purplish with greenish yellow flesh) and White (amber with yellow flesh).

The astringency of the fruit generally requires that it be cooked with plentiful sugar, as in damson jam or damson cheese. The description by Dorothy Hartley (1954) of such a cheese, 'crimson in a pool of port wine on a gold-washed dish', is a vivid celebration of the place of honour once held by this delicacy at British tables.

DANDELION *Taraxacum officinale*, one of the most widespread wild plants of temperate regions worldwide. Leaves, root, and flowers are all edible. Dandelions belong to the large family Compositae, in which their nearest edible relative is wild CHICORY; they resemble this in the variable form of their leaves and the slight bitterness of leaves and root. *T. officinale* is a native of Europe and Asia. There are also native American species, but there, too, *T. officinale* has spread everywhere thanks to its airborne seeds.

During the Middle Ages in Europe dandelion acquired its two common names which are shared by several languages. 'Dandelion' comes from the French *dent de lion* (lion's tooth), which refers to the (usually) serrated leaves. The other name, the common French *pissenlit* and its English local equivalent 'pissabed' refer to the diuretic properties attributed to dandelion root. These are not recognized by conventional medicine; however, dandelion leaves are allowed to be an excellent source of vitamin C, and all parts of the plant are rich in vitamin A and iron.

When the European dandelion became common in N. America with the arrival of white settlers, the Indians also began using it as a food and for its medicinal qualities.

Cultivation of the dandelion began around the middle of the 19th century in France and Britain. Roots were taken up and planted in dark cellars to produce blanched shoots similar to the French cultivated *barbe de capucin* (see CHICORY AND ENDIVE). These are still well known in France, but largely forgotten in Britain.

In the USA there is a small market for cultivated dandelion greens. These are of selected varieties with large, fleshy leaves. Selection and blanching through darkness combine to give larger leaves which are not bitter, in contrast to wild dandelions, which have to be picked when very young and small if the flavour is to be acceptable.

Dandelion leaves are usually made into a salad. A traditional dressing, known in France as *aux lardons*, is hot BACON fat with small pieces of chopped bacon. This allays the slight bitterness and gives an agreeable blend of flavours. The leaves may also be cooked, which allows slightly older wild plants to be used, but the leaves must always be picked before the plant flowers.

The root can be chopped in salads or cooked. Dandelion root is one of the innumerable things which were tried in the 19th century as a coffee substitute. Unusually, it is still available for this purpose. The root is roasted until brown all through, then ground; but the flavour does not resemble that of real coffee, and the drink contains no caffeine.

An unusual French product is *cramaillotte*, a brownish-orange jelly made from dandelion flowers, with orange, lemon, and sugar. To judge by early references to the medicinal properties of dandelion flowers, this jelly may originally have been appreciated for this reason, but it is nowadays esteemed mainly for its fine taste. It is made by a specialist at Quarré-les-Tombes (Yonne), a village in whose neighbourhood there are fields of wild dandelion.

DANISH CHEESES The names of Danish cheeses, of which there are 11 officially sanctioned by the government, would seem to suggest that there are 11 distinct cheeses belonging to Denmark; but this is not so. One Danish cheese, SAMSOE, is a cheese in its own right, since it has characteristics which distinguish it clearly from the Swiss cheese on which it was originally modelled: but other kinds, although some of them also have names derived from places in Denmark where they are made, are more or less copies of cheeses of other nationalities.

Rather than irritate the consumer with names of the 'German Brie' or 'Finnish Emmental' type, it was agreed at the Stresa Convention of 1951 that Danish cheeses should have their own names which, with indications where appropriate of what they imitate, are as follows:

- Samsoe resembles the Swiss cheese Emmental;
- Elbo is a loaf-shaped version of Samsoe;
- Esrom resembles Port Salut;
- Havarti resembles Tilsiter;
- Danbo resembles the E. European Steppe;
- Fynbo resembles Gouda (with eyes);
- Maribo resembles Gouda (without eyes);
- Molbo resembles Edam;
- Tybo is a square version of Molbo;
- Danablu (Danish blue) resembles Roquefort (a rather distant copy);
- Mycella resembles Gorgonzola.

DANISH PASTRIES are rich confections based on a yeast dough with milk and egg, into which butter (essential for the flavour of the pastry) has been folded by a method similar to that employed for making CROISSANTS. Before baking, the pastry is cut into small sheets and filled. Of the various fillings, the most 'correct' must be the traditional Danish one, *remonce*; this is a Danish (not French, and of unknown etymology) term which means butter creamed with sugar and often ALMONDS or MARZIPAN too. But confections called Danish pastries are made in vast numbers outside Denmark, and common alternative fillings include differently flavoured sugar and butter mixtures, almond or hazelnut mixtures, jam, *crème pâtissière*—alone or in any combination, often with dried fruit or candied peel.

The individual pastries are shaped by folding them in various ways, each of which has its own name. *Spandauers* are squares, with the corners folded to the middle, and *kammar* (combs) are narrow folded pastry strips filled with *remonce*, and nicked with short cuts to make 'teeth'. Crescents, pinwheels, and whorls are all made, as are large marzipan-filled plaits, custard-filled strips which are cut into slices after baking, and unfilled *kringler* (the pretzel shape, which is the sign of the baker's trade in Denmark). Most types are glazed with syrup or iced after baking, and decorated with nuts.

The Danish name for Danish pastries is *Wienerbrød*, 'Vienna bread' (the name by which these recipes are known throughout Scandinavia and N. Germany, where they are also popular). The reverse also applies; in Vienna a similar thing is known as *ein Kopenhagener*. However, as Birgit Siesby (1988) has pointed out, the Danish *Wienerbrød*, which must be counted as the 'true' Danish pastry, is very different from the sticky pastry *Kopenhagener* sold in Vienna and from British and American 'Danish pastries'. They are expected to be very light and crisp, so Danish bakers make them fresh two or even three times a day. They are eaten at any time of day, often with tea or coffee.

DARIOLE a French term which migrated into English long ago but is now little used in either language. In modern usage, and in either language, it means a cooking utensil shaped like a very small flowerpot, in which flavoured custards or small savoury confections can be prepared, as well as the preparation itself.

Originally it meant a small cup-shaped flan baked in a thin pastry case. This was a popular dish in France for many centuries. In the 16th century Rabelais praised the darioles baked by a certain Guillot in Amiens, which led some later authorities to state that the dariole was invented at Amiens at that time. In fact, however, references to *darioles de cresme* (cream darioles) are found as early as the 14th century in Paris.

DASHI the basic Japanese soup stock, is made by simmering flakes of dried bonito (KATSUOBUSHI) and pieces of giant kelp (KOMBU). It has a delicate flavour and is well suited to making clear soups; but it has many other culinary uses, and has been described as the primary constituent of Japanese cooking. Instant dashi in the form of a powder in packets or in liquid form in bottles is available, as *Dashi-no-moto*.

DATE (*see opposite page*)

DATE PALM FLOWER 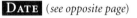 an interesting food item which is found in the markets of date-producing countries and has been described as follows by Iddison (personal communication, 1996), writing in the United Arab Emirates:

The flowers of a date palm appear in the January–February period. The flowers of the male palms are a minor commercial commodity, appearing in the markets for pollination purposes. The enclosing sheath or *spadix* should be intact or only just splitting for this purpose. Fortunately this is also the condition in which the flower is edible and it is common for farmers to reduce the number of flowers on a female palm to improve date size and quality. In the Al Ain market the female flowers were on sale for consumption and were more common than the male flowers. They weighed 300–400 grammes and the tough sheath enclosed a cramped mass of flower buds. These could be rubbed off the spikelets and were tried as a salad with a little lemon dressing as recommended by Popenoe (1913). There was no distinctive flavour apart from a slight astringency. Local people eat the flowers pounded together with small dried fish, *gashr*, as a dip for bread.

DATE PLUM *Diospyros lotus*, a fruit which is related to neither the date nor the plum, but is closely akin to the American PERSIMMON, *D. virginiana*. It grows from the Mediterranean as far east as Japan and Korea. It is not eaten in Japan and is grown there only for its ornamental value.

Date DATE VARIETIES

The fruit of a palm tree, *Phoenix dactylifera*, is a staple food in the desert regions of N. Africa and the Middle East; indeed, in such regions the tree is often the essential plant on which life depends, a universal provider which is said to have 800 distinct uses.

The tree, like all palms, has a single growth point at the tip, so the removal of this terminal bud kills the tree. Starting at ground level, the plant grows a new section every year, with fresh leaves on top of the previous year's section. The leaves live for an average of five years. Thus the tree consists of about five leafy sections on top of a stack of sections whose leaves have died, and this stack rises higher and higher away from the ground. The date palm is a long-lived tree and may eventually exceed 30 m (100') in height. However, commercial growers usually cut down their trees when they are 15 m (50') tall because of the difficulty in managing them, since they flower and fruit only at the top.

Trees may be male or female, and only the latter produce fruit. Although natural pollination may occur by wind, cultivated trees are (and have been since time immemorial) artificially pollinated. One male provides enough pollen for 100 or more females.

The fruits are produced in large bunches of over 10 kg (20 lb) in weight and containing as many as 1,000 dates. An average yield is about 50 kg (100 lb) of fruit from each tree every year, but good trees may produce two or three times as much. A single date fruit is up to 5 cm (2") long, depending on the variety.

The area of **origin** cannot be pinpointed, but must have been somewhere in the hot, dry region stretching from N. Africa through the Middle East to India—quite probably oases in the region of the Persian Gulf. Cultivation is of prehistoric origin. The palm is often shown in carvings from the earliest period of the Egyptian and Mesopotamian civilizations, and it is clear that dates were then already a staple food.

The classical Romans were fond of dates, which they had to import from their Eastern Empire. The best ones came from Jericho in Palestine. Since sugar was then almost unknown, the fruit was used as a sweetener, or else stuffed to make a sweetmeat. The recipes of APICIUS include several dishes in which dates are used in sauces for meat or fish.

The Chinese came to know the date in early times but, since they could not grow date palms in their climate, even in the southern provinces, they imported dates from Persia from the time of the T'ang dynasty (AD 618–907) onwards.

Most dates are still grown in their Old World region of origin, the biggest **producers** being Egypt, Iraq, Iran, and Saudi Arabia. Large quantities are also grown in N. African countries, Pakistan, and the Gulf countries. Some are grown in the Canary Islands, and even in S. Spain, which is at the extreme northern limit of cultivation. Beyond this the tree may grow, but it will not bear fruit.

The production of dates in the drier parts of the American tropics and in the hotter parts of the USA, especially California, expanded considerably after the US industry was established at the beginning of the 20th century, but levelled out in the 1960s and is a small percentage of world production.

USES AND TYPES

The chief food value of the date lies in its very high sugar content, which can be 70% by weight in a dried date, although the semi-dried dates sold in western countries only contain about 50%. The fruit contains a fair amount of protein, plus vitamins A and some of the B group. It is not a perfectly balanced staple food; but desert Arabs nonetheless exist in good health for long periods on almost nothing but dried dates and milk, which makes up most of the deficiencies.

Three main types of date are grown. **Soft** dates have a high moisture content, relatively little sugar in the fresh fruit stage, and a mild flavour. They are grown in the Middle East mainly for eating fresh, though they are also matured, dried, and compressed into blocks. Because of the naturally mild flavour and the concentration of sugar caused by the drying, these compressed dates are very sweet. Soft dates are not often seen in the West, although there is an international export trade within the Middle East. There is also a sporadic trade reaching further afield, as for example, during the fasting month of RAMADAN in Indonesia where dates are suddenly to be seen on every street corner, being considered a suitable way to 'break' the fast, whereas at other times they are unobtainable.

Hard dates, also called 'bread' or 'camel' dates, are dry and fibrous even when fresh, and when further dried become extremely hard, friable, and again intensely sweet, though with a good flavour. They may be left whole or ground into flour. Either way, they remain in good condition for years. These were the staple food dates of the Arab world, particularly for nomads. However, with the arrival of modern packaging and marketing, these dates are probably passing into history.

The dates most popular in the West are of the **semi-dry** type. It is these which are sold packed in the familiar long boxes with a stem, or plastic imitation thereof, between the rows. The dates grown in the USA are nearly all of this type. The flavour is less sweet than that of the other types, and more aromatic and distinctive.

When dates are classified by their degree of ripeness and the extent to which they have been dried, it is the Arabic terms which are used internationally. These start with khalal, which refers to fruits which have reached full size but are still green and not really edible; progress through bisr (marked by colour change and the commencement of conversion to sugars) and rutab (softening and darkening); and end with tamr, the stage when the dates are ready for packing.

For details of some of the numerous named varieties of date, see the section on DATE VARIETIES which follows.

For other products of the date palm, see PALM SUGAR, SAGO, and DATE PALM FLOWER. See also PALM, for the delicacy known as 'palm cabbage' or 'palm heart' (the terminal bud at the top of the tree which can only be obtained at the cost of killing the tree, so normally taken from a less valuable species of palm).

Date varieties

The date is a fruit whose qualities and uses vary considerably according to the variety being grown. And there are very many varieties, as an interesting book by Popenoe (1913) attests in a readable manner.

The reproductive characteristics of the date palm ensure that growing plants from seed is a lottery with regard to the eating qualities and productivity of the palm. The only way to ensure particular characteristics is to propagate vegetatively. In practice date orchards are developed in this way as particular palms are selected for desirable aspects such as fruiting season, bearing capacity, keeping and transport characteristics, and above all flavour. Various numbers are quoted for the named varieties in any one of the main producing countries, with 600 being a common figure. Certain varieties have come to dominate the market and it is these dates which have entered world commerce.

When first studied in detail in the early part of the 20th century many of these varieties had a localized distribution in one country or even in one cultivated area. Improved transport and communications have enabled the spread of particularly fine examples to challenge the past domination of Deglet Noor in world commerce. In the main producing countries 30 to 40 named varieties will be found in the markets during the season and represent the diversity which is still available to local consumers.

A selection of the main world varieties with the characteristics which have ensured their popularity follows:

- **Asharasi,** an excellent dry date of Iraq with a rich nutty flavour; the flesh at the tip is translucent amber shading to creamy-white at the stalk.
- **Barhi** (Barhee), a prime date of Arabia, valued for its delicate and rich flavour. The ripening date develops its sweetness at an early stage making it a popular fresh date, and it also cures well.
- **Deglet Noor,** an attractive date originating in Tunisia which has become important in the USA and dominates the European trade. It is very sweet and mild in flavour and has translucent flesh. The principal sugar present at commercial maturity is sucrose, unlike most other varieties whose sucrose has inverted to glucose and fructose at maturity.
- **Fardh,** one of the staple dates of Oman which keeps well. The fruit is red-brown at the fresh stage with moderate sweetness but rather insubstantial flavour.
- **Gundila,** one of the dominant and premium varieties in Sudan. It is large; seven dates were a breakfast ration for a schoolchild in the 1960s.
- **Halawi** (Halawy). The name means sweet and aptly describes this pale-coloured soft date from Mesopotamia; it is a major commercial date for export although not particularly favoured on its home territory.
- **Hilali,** an Arabian date which is available as a fresh date at the very end of the season. It has excellent flavour but does not cure well and so must be eaten fresh.
- **Khadrawi** (Khadrawy), a heavy cropping, soft, premium date from southern Iraq, popular because it has a rich flavour but is not cloying.
- **Khalas,** the most famous date of Arabia, originating in the Hofuf oasis and now widely planted. The fruit has a caramel flavour when cured and is also excellent fresh. Its name means quintessence, an apt description.
- **Khustawi,** one of the premier dates of Iraq with a sweet and rich flavour which makes it a favourite dessert date. The yield is quite low but it has excellent keeping qualities.
- **Khidri,** a large maroon red date which originates from Egypt and has a firm chewy texture. It is medium sweet and has a mild flavour with a hint of raisin.
- **Medjool** (Medjul), a substantial deep red date with thick flesh, little fibre, and a rich flavour. It is widespread in commerce, for instance reaching Singapore from the USA during Ramadan.
- **Mactoum,** a finely flavoured small date which has spread from its origins in Iraq down the Gulf. It has a good balance of sweetness and astringency in the semi-ripe state.
- **Naghal,** the earliest ripening date of Oman and UAE, available fresh from May and cropping heavily, has average flavour and is mostly eaten fresh.
- **Yatimeh,** a popular N. African date eaten fresh and cured, soft and syrupy, drying to firm but tender with a pronounced flavour, the syrup sometimes dripping from the ripe bunches.
- **Zahidi,** the principal commercial date of Iraq, is sold in three stages of maturity from soft to dry. The palm is prolific and easy to maintain and the fruit has a high sugar content, leading to its use as an industrial source of sugar.

PI

Besides growing wild, it has served as an introduced and cultivated plant since ancient times, and it is no longer possible to establish its original distribution. It has been present in the Mediterranean region for a long time, and is one of the several fruits reputed to have been the 'lotus' of the so-called lotus-eaters of Homer; but see JUJUBE.

The fruit is cherry-sized and yellowish-brown to blue-black in colour. It is simultaneously sweet and astringent, and of a pleasant flavour bearing some resemblance to that of DATES. A seedless variety has been reported from China, but most date plums contain numerous brown, flattened seeds.

Asians appreciate the fruit, often drying it for winter use.

DATE-SHELL *Lithophaga lithophaga*, a member of the MUSSEL family, but slimmer than common mussels. It embeds itself in rocks, which makes it difficult to gather, but has a very good flavour and is worth the effort.

Distribution is throughout the Mediterranean. The coast near La Spezia in Italy, and parts of the Adriatic coast of Yugoslavia, are places where it is abundant.

The date-shell is not a mechanical borer. It makes its hole in the rock by applying to it an acid secretion whose exact composition is unknown, which softens the rock. Then it scrapes the debris away and repeats the process, until it is completely, or almost completely, encased in the hole. The purpose of this manœuvre is to gain protection against predators. The water lapping into the hole provides nutrients.

L. subula, the rock-boring mussel of California, is a Pacific counterpart of the date-shell, but is not often eaten. It is, however, to Californian authors (Ricketts and Calvin, 1978) that we owe the Syllogism of the Date-mussel.

Major premise: the date mussel's acid secretion attacks calcareous matter. Minor premise: the date mussel's own shell is calcareous. Conclusion: the date mussel's acid secretion attacks its own shell.

The authors also give the explanation. The date mussel's shell is covered with a thick brown layer of horny material, which protects it against the acid. And it is the colour of this material which, besides the shape of the mussel, is likened to a date in popular nomenclature.

DAUBE a French culinary term indicating both a method of cooking and a type of dish. In both respects the meaning of the term has evolved noticeably since it was first used.

In the 18th century, when the French town of Saint-Malo made a speciality of *daubes*, and sent them all over France, these preparations were diverse: artichokes *en daube*, celery, pork cutlets, goose—all these and many other foodstuffs besides were prepared *en daube*. *Daube* in fact referred to the method of preparation, which was to cook meat or other foodstuffs in a TERRINE or pot with aromatics and wine or vinegar to point up the flavour. The cooked foodstuff was then removed to be eaten 'dry' (without the sauce) and often cold (with jelly formed during the cooking clinging to it). If the food was eaten in its sauce, it ceased to be *en daube* and became *en compote*. Thus what is now called *Bœuf en daube*, the one dish in which the term remains common currency, would then have been presented as *Bœuf en compote*.

Daubes remained popular in the 19th century, but changed character and status; they now tended always to be meat dishes, usually of beef, and they began to be regarded as belonging to *l'ancienne cuisine*, a kind of relegation carried further in the 20th century when they have come to be thought of as rustic preparations and are met but rarely. The copper *daubière* used to prepare them has become a curiosity in antique markets.   HY

DAUN SALAM meaning 'salam leaf', the dried leaf of the tree *Syzygium polyanthum*, which plays an important part in Indonesian cookery.

If a single leaf is placed in the pan during cooking it gives a subtle aromatic flavour to the dish. It is used in e.g. *Nasi goreng*; and its role is generally comparable to that of the BAY LEAF in western, and the CURRY LEAF in Indian, cuisines. When cooking has been completed, the leaf is normally discarded. Powdered *daun salam* is available.

DAVID ELIZABETH (1913–92), the food writer to whom is given by common consent most credit for leading British tastes, from the 1950s onwards, in a new direction. Her keynote was struck, clear and melodious as a church bell in the Greek island where she had lived for a while, by *A Book of Mediterranean Food* (1950). Like the book which she acknowledged as a principal trigger for her own writing (*The Gentle Art of Cookery* by Mrs Leyel and Olga Hartley, 1925), it was inspirational rather than didactic. Although it impinged on a relatively small number of people (until the late 1950s and 1960s, when it and her other early books were published by Penguin in paperback for a wider audience) its influence began to show at once, for its content and style, echoed in the brilliant jacket by John Minton, matched a mood which was there in the post-war years but had not previously found expression.

French Country Cooking (1951) and *Summer Cooking* (1955) were charming, unpretentious books which echoed her keynote in size and style. *Italian Food* (1954) was more substantial: the first of the author's books to qualify as a reference work in addition to having literary and inspirational merits. Indeed, after successive revisions, it remains one of the best surveys of its subject. The same is true of the even larger *French Provincial Cooking* (1960), in which some aspects of her food writing which had been nascent in the Italian book (a section on cookery equipment, a short bibliography) came into full blossom. With its really extensive bibliography it marked the author's steady movement towards research in books as well as in markets and kitchens; and its illustrated section on French kitchen equipment brought this aspect into prominence and foreshadowed the beautiful kitchen shop which Elizabeth David subsequently planned, opened, and personally ran in Pimlico (not far from where she lived in Chelsea, London). It was unfortunate that a disagreement with her partners brought her own participation in the shop enterprise to an end.

During the 1960s she was busy with journalism (especially a series of articles in the *Spectator*, where she was given a free hand to write as she pleased, with results evident in *An Omelette and a Glass of Wine*, 1984, the volume in which these and other essays were collected). The shop also took up much of her time and energy. It was not until 1970 that the next book, *Spices, Salt and Aromatics in the English Kitchen*, came out. This had several remarkable features. One was that it included a charming tribute to Mrs Leyel, co-author of the *Gentle Art of Cookery*, for the inspiration and stimulus which she had supplied and an affectionate analysis of the merits of Mrs Leyel's writing. Another was that she included in it material about Anglo-Indian cookery, perhaps reflecting in part the short period after the war when she lived in India (accompanying the military husband she had married in Cairo).

English Bread and Yeast Cookery (1977) represented the zenith of her scholarly writing. It at once became a sort of bible for home bakers and people interested in the very strong baking tradition of the British Isles, but its relatively narrow focus and its length and weight were in contrast to the earlier, lighter books. *Harvest of the Cold Months* (1994), on which she had begun work, was prepared for its posthumous publication by her long-time editor and close friend Jill Norman.

Elizabeth David valued her privacy and was highly selective in offering glimpses, in her writings, of personal feelings. Her strong negative feelings against food snobbery, pretentiousness of all kinds, and careless writing were never concealed, but a natural kindliness prompted her to express these, for the most part, in general terms rather than personal attacks. And she allowed her admiration for a chosen few (e.g. Norman Douglas, the famous travel writer with whom, when she was in her twenties and he in his seventies, she formed a close friendship in the south of France and, later, Capri) to be fully apparent. Her writings did reflect, but not as much as they could have done, the breadth of her interests and knowledge in the arts (especially painting), history, and literature.

READING: Lisa Chaney (1998); Artemis Cooper (1999).

DAVIDSON'S PLUM *Davidsonia pruriens*, otherwise known as ooray, the fruit of a small tree found in the rainforests of Queensland and northern New South Wales in Australia. As one would expect from its generic name, it is excellent. Cribb and Cribb (1975) state:

We regard the ooray as one of the best native fruits we know. Its blue-black, plum-like fruits with a few loose hairs on the surface have a soft, juicy purple flesh with relatively small flattened seeds with fibrous coats. The fruit is very acid, but stewed with sugar or made into jam or jelly, it provides a distinctive and most enjoyable food for anyone who likes a sharp taste in preserves.

DEER properly any animal of the family Cervidae, although the word is sometimes used to include other animals with generally similar characteristics. The family includes CARIBOU and REINDEER, which are both large animals, as well as the MOOSE, which is the largest living deer with a shoulder height up to 2.25 m (7' 6"). There are also numerous much smaller deer, such as the engaging MUNTJAC or barking deer of SE Asia, which stands little more than 50 cm (20") at the shoulder, and a number which are smaller still, including the tiny *chevrotain* or mouse-deer.

The deer which are the main sources of meat for human consumption, whether they are truly wild deer or 'farmed' animals from a protected environment, belong to just four species, all of an intermediate size. Their use in cookery is described under VENISON (the name usually applied to the meat of deer, with certain exceptions such as reindeer meat). The four species are:

- The **roe deer**, *Capreolus capreolus*, of N. Europe (French, *chevreuil*). This was almost extinct in the Scottish Highlands in the 18th and 19th centuries but has now been re-established there.
- The **fallow deer**, *Dama dama* (French, *daim*), is a Mediterranean and European species.
- The **red deer**, *Cervus elaphus* (French, *cerf*), of Europe is the largest of the four. It has close relations in N. Africa and Asia.
- The **white-tailed** (or Virginian) **deer**, *Odocoileus virginianus*, is the most abundant and typical deer of N. America, hunted in the eastern part of the continent.

As common and widely distributed animals, deer have been important in the human diet since prehistoric times. Archaeological evidence from various sites around the world, and from as far back as half a million years ago, can be mustered to demonstrate this.

Although deer have never been fully domesticated, some human control has been exerted in their management, in Europe and perhaps in ancient Egypt also, from very early times. A simple form of management was to fence in a relatively small area and keep enough captured deer inside the fence to ensure an adequate supply of venison when needed. On a larger scale, there were extensive deer parks, a common phenomenon in medieval Europe. Generally speaking, these parks had a dual function. They provided sport for the aristocracy and big landowners; and they were a source of valuable meat. A feature of European history for many centuries (and even in the 20th century) has been a ding-dong struggle between those who would enclose for such purposes as much land as possible, denying access to the general population, and those who sought to minimize the enclosures. Hence many a battle of wits, or armed struggles, between poachers and gamekeepers.

One circumstance which affected the position in Britain during the 19th century was the Victorian fashion for all things Scottish, encouraged by Queen Victoria's enthusiasm for spending long periods at Balmoral. The fashion led to management of red deer herds, on a large scale, for sport in the Scottish Highlands. The enthusiasm for deer stalking had as its main objective the larger and older animals, the ones looking like Landseer's famous 'Monarch of the Glen'; whereas the younger deer were the best to eat. Thus a certain dichotomy arose, in this context, between sport and gastronomy, which had so often been partners in the past.

These were not the only results. Nichola Fletcher (1987) writes that:

Strangely, though, the passion for deer stalking was indirectly responsible for the emergence of modern deer farming. In the late 1870s a shipment of deer from Invermark in Angus was imported into New Zealand. Several others followed suit and were released for sporting purposes. The deer thrived and multiplied in the lush forests, eventually causing serious destruction, and ultimately were classed as vermin to be slaughtered by any means possible. However, the price paid for the by-products of the extermination campaign (tails, pelts, velvet antlers) by Oriental medicine-makers was such that one or two entrepreneurs decided to farm these pests, much to the derision of their neighbours.

The same author, herself a deer farmer and an authority on venison, points out that deer farming in New Zealand began only in the late 1960s, and in Britain (Scotland) just a year or two later. Venison may now be either wild, park, or farmed, and it is important to know the origin and age of the deer when deciding how to cook it.

DEGLAZING a simple process by which liquid—stock, wine, water, or cream—is added to a container after browning meat or other food, to dissolve the residue. The bits adhering to the base and sides of the pan are scraped off and incorporated into the liquid. The residue includes soluble proteins and other substances which have leached from the food onto the surface of the pan; heating induces appetizing colour and flavour changes (the Maillard reaction) in these. Deglazing is a thrifty process, ensuring that the concentrated flavours are retained and become part of the sauce served with the food.   LM

DENATURATION in a food context, describes what happens to PROTEINS as a first result of being heated (or as a result of acidification, or of violent agitation, or of being cooled below a critical temperature). Their structure is shaken loose, and an 'unfolding of molecules' takes place. This unfolding exposes the protein chains to each other to a greater extent, opening the way to cross-bonding between them, which will result eventually in first flocculation and then COAGULATION.

When denaturation takes place, some of the physical and biological properties (but not the nutritional qualities) of the proteins are affected. These changes are usually, but not invariably, irreversible. In contrast, the further changes which typically occur when proteins are subjected to higher heat and which bring about coagulation, are always irreversible.

It is natural to think of denaturation as happening to the protein in something visible and solid, such as a piece of fish or meat. However, it applies just as well to protein in a liquid (milk or blood) or in a gel (egg white).

From the point of view of the cook, it is sufficient to know the above, and to remember that denaturation is not an 'all or nothing' occurrence, but a matter of degree; slight denaturation may well be imperceptible.

DENMARK and SWEDEN are the two Nordic countries which, for historical and geographical reasons, have been most influenced in culinary matters by GERMANY. Denmark shares with the neighbouring parts of the Netherlands (see DUTCH COOKERY), especially Friesland, traditions of dairy farming and of a certain simplicity of food. The picture is completed by allowing for a more sophisticated and long-range influence, that of FRANCE, which had some effect on the eating habits of the wealthier classes.

With coastlines on both the North Sea and the Baltic, Danes have always had a fine supply of seafood. They are well known for their EELS and SHRIMP (often called Tivoli prawns, after the pleasure gardens), and their green-salted HADDOCK (*grønsaltet kuller*), among other delicacies, and for being devotees of PLAICE, which Danish housewives like to buy alive. The old fish market in Copenhagen was on the Gammelstrand, where a stocky statue of a lady fishmonger stands on the canal bank, impassively eyeing a pair of famous fish restaurants.

Like the Dutch, the Danes had an important trade with the Orient in past centuries. This accounts for their use of curry powder (of a mild sort), but they also have their own condiments. In any Danish fish shop there will be a bucket of *fiskesennep*, fish MUSTARD, a mixture of coarsely ground yellow and brown mustard seeds with mild Danish VINEGAR (made from molasses) and salt.

Frikadeller, meat patties, are everywhere. Pork is popular and the art of raising pigs, in particular those which produce a high proportion of the large amount of BACON eaten annually in Britain, is highly developed.

Classical Danish cookery books, from Fru Mangor (1837) onwards, tended to give more attention to French models than to the authentic traditions of Danish regional cookery; but a good survey of the latter by Westergaard (1974) showed how rich these traditions are. They include some unusual sweet soups, based on fruit and thickened with barley or sago.

Denmark's international fame rests mainly, to judge by frequency of mention, on a single item, DANISH PASTRIES, although these are not Danish in origin and the Danes themselves refer to them as *Wienerbrød*. However, the runner-up in the international renown stakes would be a truly Danish item, *smørrebrød*, literally 'bread and butter'; i.e. open sandwiches, made with RYE BREAD and having any of scores of special toppings.

White bread is used if the topping is of shrimp or something similar.

DENTEX *Dentex dentex*, a sizeable (maximum length 1 m/40") and important fish of the Mediterranean and E. Atlantic from NW Africa to the Bay of Biscay. The colour of this fish changes as it grows older, from grey to a faintly rosy hue and then to a bluish-grey; and the number and disposition of the dark spots vary. The quality of the dentex is almost as good as that of the GILT-HEAD BREAM and it is in keen demand. Few individuals survive long enough to reach the maximum size, and those in the markets are usually in the range 20–50 cm (8–20").

There are several close relations. *D. maroccanus* is smaller, crimson in colour, and present in the W. Mediterranean and warm waters of the E. Atlantic. *D. gibbosus* is rosy in colour and if it survives into old age develops a noticeable forehead, giving it an intellectual appearance. It is found chiefly in the W. Mediterranean whereas *D. macrophthalmus*, crimson and large eyed, is more common in the eastern basin of that sea. All make good eating.

A large dentex may be stuffed and baked, using white wine and Mediterranean aromatics. Smaller specimens can be grilled whole.

DERBY an English cheese made by a process similar to that of CHEDDAR. It is pressed less hard and therefore retains a higher moisture content; it is also more definitely primrose yellow in colour, with a closer and more flaky texture, and a milder and more acid flavour.

Derby is of a thick disc shape and weighs 4 to 14 kg (9 to 31 lb). A smaller version flavoured with sage and coloured green with spinach juice was traditionally made at harvest time and Christmas; this survives as sage Derby in British cheese shops and delicatessens. See also SAGE CHEESE.

DESSERTS a collective name for sweet dishes considered suitable for the last course of a meal, including CAKES, ICE CREAMS, CREAMS, raw and cooked fruit, PUDDINGS, PASTRIES, and PIES. Cheese may also be included amongst desserts. In Britain, 'dessert' is sometimes regarded as an elegant synonym for the words 'pudding', or 'sweet', which are used in the same collective sense.

The word derives from French *desservir*, meaning to remove the dishes, or clear the table. Originally 'the dessert', singular, denoted a course of fruit and sweetmeats, either placed on the table after the meal, or served at a separate table; in English, it

replaced the word BANQUET, an older name for a similar course, during the 18th century. The change in emphasis from the 18th-century French 'dessert' to the 20th-century miscellany of sweet 'desserts' appears to have taken place in N. America. The word had a wider meaning for Americans as early as the end of the 18th century, whereas this usage was not common in England until the 20th century.

Originally, dessert, apart from providing something sweet to nibble, was designed to impress. Mrs Beeton (1861) lists numerous fresh fruits considered suitable, and refers to 'choice and delicately-flavoured cakes and biscuits' served with 'most costly and recherché wines'; plus candied fruits and other morsels such as chocolate (following French fashion). She devoted many words to presenting and garnishing the dessert in china, silver, and glass, and commented that 'as late as the reigns of our two last Georges fabulous sums were often expended upon fanciful desserts'.

The latter probably owed much to French inspiration, where, during the early to mid-18th century, the dessert comprised impressive pyramids of fruit and sweetmeats, displayed in rococo style on tables decorated with flowers and tall candelabra. Finishing touches were provided by setpieces resembling anything from a Greek temple to a Chinese pavilion, modelled out of more or less edible ingredients.

A formal dessert in the old sense is now a rarity. One interesting survival is the Provençal *gros souper* on Christmas Eve, which finishes with a ritual presentation of *les treize desserts*, the 13 desserts, based on local fruits, nuts, baking, and confectionery. Elisabeth Luard (1990) quotes a Provençal woman talking about these:

We dried our own apricots, made quince paste, and we always had les mendiants, the four begging orders of friars: almonds for the Dominicans, figs for the Franciscans, hazelnuts for the Carmelites, dried currants for the Augustines. We made the dark nougat at home with hazelnuts and honey, and it was so hard you needed a hammer to break it. But we always bought the white nougat, which is a factory-made speciality of Montélimar.

Other possibilities include local orchard fruit; enriched breads such as *pompe à l'huile* (a BRIOCHE-type bread enriched with oil); imported oranges; and sweet or savoury *panade* (TARTS). Traditions vary between areas and families, but there are always 13 items, and they are said to represent Christ and the twelve apostles.

LM

DEVIL a culinary term which according to the *NSOED* first appeared as a noun in the 18th century, and then in the early 19th century as a verb meaning to cook something with fiery hot spices or condiments. Theodora FitzGibbon (1976) remarks, however, that 'Boswell, Dr Johnson's biographer, frequently refers to partaking of a dish of "devilled bones" for supper', which suggests an earlier use. The term was presumably adopted because of the connection between the devil and the excessive heat in Hell.

Devilled bones and devilled kidneys are just two examples of the dishes in this category, which could be referred to as 'devils'. Writing about this noun, FitzGibbon distinguishes between brown devils, wet devils, and white devils, explaining the differences between these. An earlier authority, Dallas (1877) in *Kettner's Book of the Table*, had stated that devils were of two kinds, the dry and the wet, but had also commented:

It is the great fault of all devilry that it knows no bounds. A moderate devil is almost a contradiction in terms; and yet it is quite certain that if a devil is not moderate he destroys the palate, and ought to have no place in cookery, the business of which is to tickle, not to annihilate, the sense of taste.

The dilemma thus stated may have proved insoluble, for devilling has fallen out of fashion.

A certain parallel exists in France in the form of dishes 'à la diable'.

One of the British SAVOURIES which was popular for a time bore the name Devils on horseback and consisted of prunes stuffed with chutney, rolled up in rashers of bacon, placed on buttered bread and sprinkled with grated cheese, and cooked under the grill. The absence of cayenne pepper or other hot condiments suggests that in this instance the word 'devil' was introduced as a counterpart to 'angel' in Angels on horseback rather than in the sense described above.

DEVIL'S FOOD CAKE is an American dark chocolate cake. Noting that the first recipe appeared in 1905, Mariani (1994) suggests that the cake received its name 'because it is supposedly so rich and delicious that it must, to a moralist, be somewhat sinful, although the association is clearly made with humour'. Its dark colour, achieved by chocolate frosting which covers the entire cake, contrasted with the snowy white of the earlier ANGEL FOOD CAKE.

DEWBERRY *Rubus caesius*, is closely related to and resembles the BLACKBERRY, and has a similar distribution; but it bears smaller fruits with fewer and larger druplets, which are covered by a purple bloom. Hulme (1902) declared the dewberry to be more succulent than the blackberry; but

Grigson (1955) points out that it varies from season to season in abundance and quality, and that in a poor season it deserves the local Wiltshire name 'token blackberry'.

Other dewberries include *R. canadensis*, with juicy fruits, and *R. ursinus*, the Pacific or California dewberry, whose large berries have many uses and are sometimes dried. There is some cultivation of these berries.

DHANSAK a well-known example of PARSI FOOD in Gujarat, India; *dhaan* meaning rice and *sak* meaning vegetables. Dhansak is a meat, vegetable, and lentil CURRY served with brown PILAF rice. The Parsis use a mix of DALS but always include *moong dal* (see MUNG BEAN) in this dish. A specific spice mixture, *dhansak masala*, is prepared just for this dish.

When the Parsis settled on the western coast of India, they adopted Gujarati as their language and absorbed local influences into their cuisine, but maintained many of their own culinary traditions, including the use of mung beans, of which this dish is the most famous example.   HS

DIBS an Arabic word which refers to a thick sweet syrup made by boiling down grape juice. It is made in various Middle Eastern countries, and is closely related to the Turkish PEKMEZ and kindred products described under that head.

A similar product is prepared from dates; this is *dibis* (the same word, with a different regional pronunciation) in the Gulf States, where it is used in many sweet dishes.

DIET what a person or a group of people habitually eat. The diet of most people reflects a combination of availability and inclination, both of which factors depend to some extent on the prevailing culture as well as on economic influences.

Special diets are followed by persons suffering from various disabilities or illnesses; diabetics are a well-known example. They are also followed, in the western world, by people who are 'slimming', and expressions such as 'I'm on a diet' commonly relate to that situation.

Dietary supplements, especially vitamins, may be necessary in certain situations. There is much debate over the extent of this need, which must anyway vary according to what a person's basic diet provides. When foodstuffs (such as flour for making bread) are 'fortified' with such supplements (e.g. calcium, iron, B vitamins), it is sometimes a case of putting back what was originally there before the foodstuff was processed (e.g. to produce white flour).

National or ethnic diets vary considerably according to what are the STAPLE FOODS in a given area or group. Personal diets vary to an infinite extent. The literature and the popular press often draw attention to examples which will appear freakish to most people (e.g. an English child who for several years would eat nothing except jam sandwiches) and which may, on analysis, prove to be adequate, or nearly so, or dangerously deficient.

READING. The literature is vast. For Britain, Drummond and Wilbraham (1939); Burnett (1966); Oddy and Miller (1976); McLaughlin (1978); Maisie Steven (1985). For Australia, Santich (1995b). For the USA and more generally, Levenstein (1988). For slimming diets, Schwartz (1986).

DIETARY LAWS in the widest sense of the term, would embrace secular legislation such as the sumptuary laws which various governments from classical times up to the present have passed in an effort to stem excesses of gluttony, flagrantly unfair distribution of foodstuffs, and other practices perceived as harmful to the state. However, the term would not normally be applied to legislation, for example during the Second World War, to provide for rationing of essential foods. Indeed, the phrase is commonly used with almost exclusive reference to 'laws' associated with religious beliefs. In this connection, see BUDDHISM AND FOOD, CHRISTIANITY AND FOOD, HINDUISM AND FOOD, JAINS AND FOOD, JEWISH DIETARY LAWS, MUSLIMS AND FOOD. It will be apparent from these other entries that dietary laws of this type vary considerably, in scope, content, and severity, from one religion to another. Some attempts have been made to find a pattern underlying these phenomena, or a rationale explaining what human needs they satisfy; but the results are not impressive. Like the religions which have given rise to them, the religious dietary laws resist 'explanation'. And it must be taken into account that there are very large numbers of people whose choices of what to eat are not influenced by any such laws.

See also TABOO, VEGETARIANISM, and, on a different but not wholly unrelated plane, ORGANIC FOOD.

DIGBY SIR KENELM (1603–65), an adventurous and romantic figure of 17th-century England whose eccentric and posthumously published recipe book has earned him the interest and esteem of food historians.

His father, a convert to the Roman Catholic Church, died when he was still a boy; and it was a Protestant uncle who took him, at age 14 and for two years, to Spain, where he began his lifelong habit of collecting medical and culinary recipes. Later, at Oxford, he studied under a famous mathematician and astrologer, and also fell in love, with a notorious beauty, Venetia Stanley. Opposing the match, his mother packed him off on on a three-year Grand Tour of France and Italy, but he married Venetia when he returned and the marriage lasted happily for eight years, until Venetia's sudden death in 1633.

After Venetia's death, Digby had a spell as an Anglican, but then reverted to being a Catholic and spent some time, after the execution of King Charles, as a spokesman seeking toleration for the Catholics in England. This and other politico-religious activities were accompanied by activity in the newly formed Royal Society and by much writing. He wrote prolifically, including works of literary criticism and philosophy. However, his most lasting work has proved to be one which he never saw in print. This was his collection of recipes, assembled after his death and published by his laboratory assistant Hartman for his own profit under the title *The Closet of the Eminently Learned Sir Kenelme Digbie Kt. Opened: Whereby is Discovered Several ways for making of Metheglin, Sider, Cherry-Wine, &c. Together with Excellent Directions for Cookery: As also for Preserving, Conserving, Candying, &c.*

This book begins with 106 recipes for mead, metheglyn, and other drinks mostly based on fermented honey and herbs. Some had been contributed by sundry friends and professional cooks, others were the fruits of Digby's own research. They are followed by POSSETS, SYLLABUBS, and CREAMS, and by soups and gruels for health and nourishment. There follows a somewhat jumbled collection of savoury dishes. Recipes for fruit preserves, tonic sweetmeats (including the remarkable 'Cordial Tablets', whose worth has been proved in the late 20th century), cosmetic cures, and a perfume for tobacco round off the collection. Because it has an engagingly amateur, yet learned, air about it and reflects the attractive enthusiasm of the author, the book, which has been twice reprinted in the 20th century, seems sure to continue finding appreciative readers.

DIGESTION the process by which the body breaks down food and extracts nutrients from it. The word was first used by medieval alchemists to describe a chemical reaction which dissolved materials. When the French scientist Denis Papin invented the first pressure cooker (see PRESSURE COOKING) in 1679, he called it a *digesteur*.

The digestion of food takes place in stages.

It begins in the mouth where the ENZYME ptyalin, present in saliva, begins to break down starch in food to sugars. Chewing food, by breaking it into small pieces, exposes a large surface area for digestive enzymes to work on.

The chewed food passes down the oesophagus into the stomach. The gastric juice in the stomach contains hydrochloric acid, which helps to break down proteins and starch by the process of HYDROLYSIS, assisted by movements of the stomach wall. At the same time the enzyme pepsin begins to dismantle the PROTEINS into smaller pieces known as polypeptides, each consisting of a few AMINO ACIDS. Food remains in the stomach for several hours. The time is influenced by the amount of fat in the food, which relaxes the stomach wall and slows down the whole process. Fatty foods seem more 'filling' because they remain in the stomach for longer.

Some of the nutrients liberated in the stomach are absorbed through the stomach wall into the bloodstream. These include any available glucose (other sugars are dealt with later), and water-soluble MINERAL salts and vitamins of the B group and C. Any alcohol is also absorbed here; it circulates in the bloodstream, thus producing the well-known effects on the brain, and is eventually broken down to sugar by the liver.

The partly digested food moves out of the stomach to the duodenum, which is the first section of the small intestine—its name is derived from the Latin *duodeni* ('twelve each') because it is about 12 finger widths long. It contains pancreatic juice, provided by the pancreas; and bile from the gall bladder, which emulsifies fats (breaks them into small droplets—see EMULSION). Three types of enzyme are at work here. Amylases continue to break down starches to sugars (ptyalin, already mentioned, is also an amylase). Trypsin carries on with the breakdown of proteins. Lipases start work on the fats, separating them into the fatty acids and glycerol of which they are composed. By the time the food leaves the duodenum, the stomach acid has been neutralized and the rest of digestion takes place in slightly alkaline conditions.

The food now continues along the small intestine, which is 6 m (20') long in a human adult. It is moved by peristalsis, rhythmical contractions of the intestinal wall. Here more enzymes work on sugars. Invertase splits sucrose into glucose and fructose (see SUGAR). Maltase breaks maltose down to glucose. Lactase turns lactose to glucose and galactose (but see LACTOSE INTOLERANCE). At the same time erepsin separates the protein fragments into single amino acids. More lipases complete the breakdown of fats. The liberated nutrients, including those vitamins and minerals that were not

absorbed by the stomach, filter through the intestinal wall into the bloodstream.

Next, the remains of the food move into the large intestine, a wider tube which runs up from the bottom of the abdomen, across under the stomach, and down again to the anus. The main function of this stage is to absorb more water from these food remains so that they become a compact mass of faeces, ready to be eliminated. Here dietary fibre (see CELLULOSE) is important. It retains water, so that the faeces remain fairly fluid, and its bulk also helps to keep them moving.

The intestine contains bacteria which help to break down undigested solids, and also make some vitamins of the B group which can be absorbed and used by the body. These bacteria can digest some carbohydrates that the body cannot deal with. As far as is known, the body gets no useful sugars from the process. One by-product is the gas methane, which causes flatulence.

The whole process takes from several hours to several days. It does not always go smoothly, especially if one overloads the system by consuming a lot of rich, fatty food. Stress such as anxiety can increase the rate of secretion of stomach acid and irritate the stomach lining; or, conversely, it may reduce secretion so that digestion is slow and difficult. The resulting symptoms are loosely described as indigestion, dyspepsia, acidity, or heartburn—which is nothing to do with the heart, and is felt some way above the place where the trouble actually occurs. It used to be thought that peptic ulcers were caused by excessive stomach acid burning a hole in the lining of the stomach or duodenum. In the 1990s the cause was identified as a bacterium, *Helicobacter pylori*, which thrives in the harsh conditions of the stomach. It can be killed with antibiotics.

Advice on how to promote good digestion takes many forms, often recommending particular diets or foodstuffs. Indeed, some foodstuffs recommend themselves by their names, e.g. the famous digestive biscuits of Britain which, however, have no effect one way or the other. On the other hand, the *promenade digestive* recommended by some French (and other) authors does seem likely to be beneficial.   RH

DIKA NUT the seed of the small, mango-like fruit (sometimes called wild mango) of a W. African tree, *Irvingia gabonensis*, associated particularly with Gabon.

The seeds or kernels, called *agbono* or *apon*, which are oily, are sometimes eaten as nuts, or used in cooking like nuts, e.g. in Nigeria as an ingredient in soups or as a seasoning element. But they are more commonly processed into a stiff paste known as dika bread or Gabon chocolate. This is done by grinding the kernels, then heating them to melt the fat, and sometimes adding pepper or other spices. The result may also be smoked. The product is used as seasoning for meat, fish, plantain dishes, etc.

Crude dika paste as described above can be heated to yield a product called dika butter, which is comparable to cocoa butter.

DILL *Anethum graveolens*, a herb indigenous to W. Asia, known in the Mediterranean region and S. Russia since long ago, has become naturalized in most of Europe and N. America and is now cultivated in many parts of the world.

However, although popular in W. Europe, dill has special associations with the Nordic countries, Poland, and Russia, where the leaves and seeds are used most abundantly, e.g. with fish—fried, boiled, and in particular GRAVLAKS; on potatoes; for flavouring pickled cucumbers, gherkins, etc. ('dill pickle' is well known); with yoghurt and sour cream. The Nordic connection is apparent in the name dill itself, which derives from the Old Norse *dilla* meaning to lull (dill water is used for soothing babies in England; and dill is a main ingredient in the gripe water used for the same purpose).

Dill is also often teamed up with broad beans in a PILAF and in KOFTA in Iran.

Dill belongs to the PARSLEY family and is closely related to FENNEL; the two plants are hard to tell apart. However, dill is an annual whereas fennel is perennial; and fennel has an anise flavour which dill lacks.

What is called Indian dill was formerly recognized as a separate species, but is now regarded as a subspecies or variety, *Anethum graveolens* 'Sowa'. The plants are taller than European dill and the seeds have a more pungent and bitter flavour which is preferred for use in curries.

DIM SUM an important institution of Cantonese cuisine which has become increasingly visible in 'Chinatowns' outside China, has been described by Yan-Kit So (1992) in terms which cannot be bettered, as follows:

Literally translated as 'so close to the heart', they are, in reality, a large range of hors d'œuvres Cantonese people traditionally enjoy in restaurants (previously teahouses) for breakfast and for lunch, but never for dinner, washed down with tea. 'Let's go yumcha (to drink tea)', is understood among the Cantonese to mean going to a restaurant for dimsum; such is the twin linkage between the food and the beverage. The familiar yumcha scene at a Cantonese restaurant, which is often on several floors, is one of young girls pushing trolleys replete with goodies in bamboo baskets piled high or small dishes set next to each other. As they mill around the dining

tables, they call out the names of their wares and place the baskets or dishes on to the tables when diners signal their wishes.

The range of dimsum in a restaurant easily numbers several dozen and they come under these main varieties: the steamed, the fried and the deep-fried. Among the steamed variety, which are served in small bamboo baskets, 'char siu bao'—buns made with flour stuffed with 'charsiu' or roast pork—are the most basic. Next come 'hargow'—crescent-shaped transparent skin dumplings made with glutenless flour stuffed with shrimp; 'siumai'—open-top minced pork dumplings wrapped with wonton skin made with wheat flour; and 'fanguo'—flat dumplings made with glutenless flour stuffed with chopped mushrooms, bamboo shoots and pork. Three kinds of 'tsuenfun'—steamed rice flour dough sheets stuffed with either charsiu, shrimp or minced beef—are sought after for their silken, slippery texture. Among the deep-fried variety the favourites are spring rolls, 'wugok' or taro croquettes, which have an almost honeycomb appearance, and 'harmshuigok'—round dumplings made with glutinous rice flour tasting slightly sweet-savoury. 'Law Baak Go' and 'Wu Tow Go'—savoury puddings made with white radish and taro—are often served shallow-fried.

Besides dumplings, a range of steamed dishes served in bamboo baskets is also popular. Pork spareribs chopped into small cubes and seasoned with black beans or a plum sauce, duck's webs deep-fried then steamed in a spicy sauce, and steamed beef balls seasoned with tangerine peel are but the obvious examples. Beef tripe or 'gnauchaap' and chicken feet, the latter enjoyed perhaps more for their texture than flavour, are, for many Europeans, an acquired taste. But most people adore the dishes of suckling pig, roast pork and cold chicken found on the trolleys of those restaurants which have kitchens specialising in them.

DINER an important American institution which originally, in the middle of the 19th century, was a railway dining car. However, by extension it came to mean a cheap roadside restaurant which could be either a disused railway dining car, or something built to resemble this, or something else giving the impression of mobility. Although diners, almost by definition, offer modestly priced food of an unsophisticated nature, they offer scope for connoisseurship and even minor cults, and various publications had been devoted to them in the latter part of the 20th century.

DINNER the main meal of the day, whether eaten at mid-day or in the evening. In Britain, the timing and composition of dinner has varied considerably over the centuries, and also regionally, by social class, and according to occasion. The same would be true, although sometimes with less striking differences, of other western countries, and the same principle of variation can be observed elsewhere—

although the concept of 'dinner' begins to fray at the edges once one tries to transfer it to peoples whose languages and historical roots are quite different from those of Europe.

A modest dinner may be referred to as 'supper'; but that term also signifies a meal eaten some time after dinner, e.g. at the end of a ball or after the theatre.

A survey of the successive changes in the hour of dinner in England was conducted with notable thoroughness and wit, drawing largely on literary sources, by Palmer (1952). READING: Tabitha Tickletooth (1860).

DINUGUAN a culinary term of the Philippines, comes from the word *dugo* (blood), and is a stew of meats—variety and/or otherwise—cooked in blood, vinegar, garlic, and hot peppers.

Most dinuguan are made from pork internal organs (heart, liver, intestines, pancreas) and meat and/or fat. They are usually by-products of the butchering of a pig, using up the blood and the organs that do not go into other dishes, or of the making of *lechon* (whole, spit-roasted pig).

Although dinuguan is found throughout the Philippines, there are regional variations. There is *dinuguan manok* made with chicken meat, internal organs, and blood. Beef dinuguan from Nueva Ecija is called *cerkely*. The Pampanga variant is light coloured, filled with soft internal organs, headmeat, and fat, and is called *tid-tad*. There is dinuguan with coconut milk. Most versions have whole chillies for fragrance.

Dinuguan is often served with rice at lunch, dinner, and feasts, but a bowl of it is also popular for the mid-afternoon *merienda* (snack) or breakfast, when it is accompanied by *puto* (see RICE CAKES OF THE PHILIPPINES) or in some places, bread.   DF

DISTILLATION separating a liquid from a mixture by boiling it off and condensing the vapour. The best-known use of the technique is to make alcoholic drinks such as brandy; but there are other, food-related, uses; flavourings such as rosewater (see ROSES) and ORANGE FLOWER WATER are prepared by a type of distillation.

Distillation can also be used to produce drinking water from sea water, a process described by Aristotle in the 4th century BC. At that time the Egyptians were already distilling turpentine from pine resin, and probably also making small amounts of alcohol for medicinal use. It was only with the rise of Arab science that the distillation of alcohol was carried out on an appreciable scale. Islam prohibits the consumption of alcoholic drinks, but certainly by the time the technique reached European countries in the 14th and 15th centuries it was being used for that purpose.

The principle of distillation is that different liquids boil at different temperatures. Ethanol, the type of alcohol found in drinks, boils at 78 °C (173 °F), considerably lower than the boiling point of water at 100 °C (212 °F). Brandy is made by heating wine to a temperature between these figures in a closed vessel—a still. The alcohol boils but the water does not. The alcohol vapour passes out through a tube at the top of the still. This tube continues as a long downward spiral in which the vapour gradually cools and condenses back to a liquid. The whole process is accompanied by complications which often make it necessary to repeat the distillation at least once to achieve the required strength and purity.

Drinking water is distilled from sea water in a vacuum still, in which pressure is reduced to lower the boiling point so that less heat is required. Even so, it is an expensive process and largely restricted to rich countries such as the Gulf States.

Distilled, and thus very strong, VINEGAR is used for making pickles. The boiling point of acetic acid, at 118 °C (244 °F), is higher than that of water so the distillation of vinegar is a process of boiling away unwanted water.

Steam distillation is used to extract essential oils from flower petals, herbs, and spices. The materials to be distilled are mashed in water. Steam is bubbled through them to heat and evaporate the oils, which are carried away by the steam. Since the oils do not mix with water, they are easy to recover from the condensed liquid.

Destructive distillation is the heating of a solid in a closed vessel until it decomposes into other substances. Artificial 'smoke' flavouring is made by the destructive distillation of wood.   (RH)

DITTANDER one of the more puzzling herb names. Geoffrey Grigson (1955) quotes Turner (1548) as saying that the name properly belonged to *Dictamnus albus*, pepperwort in English and *Pfefferkraut* in German; and added that the old form 'dittany', which it should have replaced, remained obstinately in currency. Other authors link either or both names with CRESS and other herb families. Thus Karen Hess (1981), Facciola (1990), and Tucker (1994) all identify 'dittany of Crete' with *Oreganum dictamnus*.

It is thus no easy matter, when considering recipes for preparations like GREENSAUCE, to determine what a reference to either dittander or dittany really signifies.

DIVINITY an American confection related to NOUGAT and MARSHMALLOW. It is

made by cooking a sugar syrup to the firm- or hard-ball stage (120 °C or 124 °C (255 °F), see SUGAR BOILING), and then beating it into whisked egg whites. Occasionally egg yolks are used instead of the whites, to give a yellow result. Vanilla is often used as a flavouring, and nuts, glacé cherries, or candied angelica added. 'Sea foam' is a name sometimes given to divinity made with soft light-brown sugar, rather than ordinary granulated sugar.   LM

DOCK a name applied to several plants which belong, like the SORRELS which they resemble, to the genus *Rumex*. Some are edible, notably patience dock, *R. patientia*, which is thought to have originated in S. Europe and W. Asia and was known as a food plant in classical times. It has been cultivated in some parts of Europe. The name 'patience dock' is also applied, in parts of England, to BISTORT; and it is this other plant which is almost invariably meant when reference is made to the English tradition of eating 'patience dock' at Easter. See DOCK PUDDING.

R. crispus, curled dock, and *R. obtusifolius*, broad-leaved or bitter dock, have also been eaten as green vegetables. The latter, which is

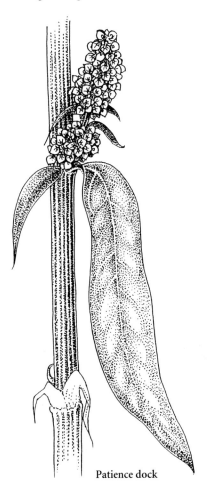

Patience dock

the well-known remedy for nettle stings, was formerly used for wrapping butter, so may be called butter dock. It has been introduced to N. America and Australasia and is sometimes grown as a garden vegetable.

R. alpinus, mountain dock (or monk's rhubarb), belongs to the mountain regions of C. Europe and the Balkans. It is eaten in salads and also cooked as a spinach substitute. It too was formerly employed to preserve butter.

Other docks are used as food in various parts of the world. *R. abyssinicus*, Abyssinian spinach or Spanish rhubarb dock, also has a connection with butter; it was used in the Congo for dyeing it a brick red colour. *R. crispus*, referred to above, is a tall herb which has succulent leaves and stems which can be stewed like rhubarb; indeed, Low (1989) asserts that in Australia some people prefer it to rhubarb.

DOCK PUDDING a mixture of 'dock' (i.e. BISTORT, *Polygonum bistorta*), oatmeal, onions, and nettles, thickened with oatmeal and boiled together. There are those who profess to love it, and those who loathe it. It tastes something like a cross between spinach and asparagus. Once cooked, it is fried by the dollop or slice in plenty of old-fashioned, real, bacon fat to counteract the strong taste and green slimy consistency. When it has a crisp, fatty, salty outside, it is more palatable.

Dock pudding has become synonymous with Calderdale (in W. Yorkshire), especially Mytholmroyd, Hebden Bridge, and Todmorden, ever since 1971. It was in that year that the first competition to find the World's Champion Dock Pudding Makers was held there. However, dock pudding is by no means unique to Calderdale. The truth is that bistort has been used in many similar pottages and puddings for centuries, in many areas of England and S. Scotland.

Up to the 17th century, oatmeal POTTAGE (poddige, porridge) was a universal food in Britain, eaten by rich and poor alike. It was often enlivened, both for flavour and food value, with green herbs such as daisy, tansy, dandelion, nettles, kale, etc. But at Easter time, it was invested with a special significance, partly as a seasonal ritual, partly as a vital spring blood cleanser and anti-scorbutic. (Up to the 19th century, many people had scurvy by February because of a lack of green stuff in winter.) The Easter connection of bistort pudding is reflected in various local names for bistort: passion dock or patience dock (from Passiontide), pash-docken (Littondale), Easter mangiant, Easter giant, Easter ledger, etc. It is called passion or patience dock in Yorkshire, Derbyshire, and N. England, and known mainly as patience dock in Cheshire and Lancashire.

Dog the supreme example of animals which are regarded in the western world not just as pets but as true companions, in activity and thought, for human beings, and consequently not to be even imagined as potential food. So strong are the feelings of revulsion which the mere mention of such an idea can provoke that some writers have excused themselves from even mentioning the subject. This taboo is almost as strong as that governing CANNIBALISM and, generally speaking, very much stronger than that affecting the HORSE (another animal 'companion'). Feelings of hesitation or sadness over eating a lamb or a young pig, even though these other animals may be treated as pets and show signs of intelligence, are on a different plane. Although they may occasionally be overwhelming for individuals, they lack the strength and near universality in the western world of the feelings about dogs (and CATS).

However, the situation has been quite different in some other parts of the world, and even in Europe in past times. Dalby (1996) has summed up the situation in classical Greece:

Aristotle in the *Study of Animals* . . . brackets pig and dog together as *synanthropeuómena*, 'animals symbiotic with man'. Both were eaten in classical Greece, but dog, *kyon*, was not a food of which one boasted. It is never listed in the comedy menus or in the gastronomic poetry of the fourth century. Roast dog was, however, recommended for certain diets by the author of the Hippocratic dietary text *Regimen*, puppy meat for others.

Simmonds (1859) who shrank from nothing in *The Curiosities of Food*, a book devoted to 'dainties and delicacies of different nations obtained from the animal kingdom', mentions consumption of dogs in various parts of the world, including Africa, but lays emphasis on China and the Pacific islands. He explains that in China special breeds of dog are fattened for the table, 'and the flesh of dogs is as much liked by them as mutton is by us'. The practice has been widely attested.

Turning to the Pacific islands, he refers to a traveller who had the experience of eating young dog in the Sandwich Islands. This person had to admit that everyone found it to be excellent, and that to his own palate 'its taste was what I can imagine would result from mingling the flavour of pig and lamb'. However, he had qualms and indeed, on reflection, 'felt as if dog-eating were only a low grade of cannibalism'.

One interesting point which is brought out in the anecdote from the Sandwich Islands is that the dogs eaten there were 'fed exclusively on vegetables, chiefly taro'. This is seen as a mitigating circumstance, which fits in with the widespread disinclination of human beings to eat the flesh of other carnivores (whether they are pets or companions or not).

The situation in the Philippines has been described in various books about food by Filipino authors, including Gilda Cordero-Fernando (1976) and Alegre (in the book of essays by Doreen Fernandez and himself, 1988). The latter explains the interplay between the legal situation, the variable manner in which legal prohibitions are implemented, the way in which dog meat in Pampanga, for example, is part of the culinary tradition along with other exotic items, and what goes on in dog meat restaurants.

Generally, Simoons (1994) provides the best survey of this troubling subject, drawing on information about many cultures in various parts of the world and exemplifying by well-chosen incidents the strong emotions which it continues to arouse.

Dog cockle the inappropriate English name given to a BIVALVE, *Glycymeris glycymeris*, which has a distribution from Norway and the Baltic down to the Mediterranean and the Canaries, and which is eaten in France, Spain and Portugal, and Italy. It may measure just over 6 cm (2.5"), and the shells are usually white or cream, with irregular zigzag markings. Well worth eating, but not outstandingly good.

Dogfish a name given in a loose way to many of the smaller species of shark in many different languages. Why? The question is perplexing, all the more so since the doggy theme not only crosses species and genus boundaries (thus *Squalus acanthias* is 'spur dog' and *Mustelus asterias* is 'smooth hound') but also extends into terms descriptive of lifestyle (newly born spur dogs are called a 'litter' of 'pups'). Another puzzle, dealt with separately, is the English vernacular name HUSS.

This system of names does not extend to larger sharks, except for the PORBEAGLE (*Lamna nasus*). The species to which it applies are those which have a maximum length of anything from 60 cm (2') to twice that. Most of them have tough, rough, sandpapery skins (which in some instances are used in place of sandpaper for smoothing). They are regarded as a nuisance by fishermen in N. America, and sometimes so in Europe; but on the whole they are seen by Europeans—and indeed everywhere except N. America—as a marketable commodity. Whereas special techniques are needed for catching large sharks such as the porbeagle, dogfish come up frequently in trawls along with other fish.

There are so many dogfish around the world that only a small proportion of them can be mentioned. They all have a maximum length of about 1.5 m (60"), but a normal adult length of half or two-thirds as much.

- *Squalus acanthias*, the **spur dog**, found all round the world in temperate waters; officially, along with some other *Squalus* spp, 'greeneye dogfish' in Australia.
- *Mustelus canis*, the **sand shark**, common in warm and temperate waters of the W. Atlantic.
- *M. asterias*, the principal Mediterranean and NE Atlantic member of the genus; known as **smooth hound**.
- *Scyliorhinus stellaris*, the **nursehound** or **huss**, also of the Mediterranean and NE Atlantic.
- *Centrophorus moluccensis*, which with other members of the same genus is marketed as **Endeavour dogfish** (the name is that of the research vessel *Endeavour*) in Australia.

Whatever the true explanation of the name 'dogfish', it was not bestowed in order to make these fish seem attractive to consumers. Indeed, fishmongers have consistently rechristened them by more flattering names, some of which, like the British 'rock salmon' or the Venetian *vitello di mare* (veal of the sea), are outrageously misleading, although others such as the Australian 'flake' seem venial. Anyway, insofar as these euphemisms work, they must be applauded, since there are two reasons for encouraging consumption of dogfish. One is that they breed fast and are voracious predators, feeding often on small specimens of more valuable species. The other is that they are good to eat, if properly prepared. Even in N. America, they have been marketed and eaten with appreciation in times of need, such as the First World War. The most serious fish cookery book ever published in the USA, that by Spencer and Cobb (1922), devotes earnest attention to them.

Like all sharks, dogfish have no true bones but make do with a cartilaginous skeleton. This is good from the cook's point of view, since there are no tiresome small bones to contend with and it is easy to lift off fillets of whatever size seems suitable. The corresponding disadvantages are more apparent than real. Dogfish do not have a delicate flavour; but this simply means that they do not need to be cooked in a delicate way. They are fine in fish and chips, or covered with a robust sauce.

Dogwood a small tree or shrub of which varieties grow in Europe, N. Asia, and N. America, bearing small, round, cherry-like fruits which are eaten in some countries.

The best fruit of any Old World species is that of *Cornus mas*, commonly called cornel or **cornelian cherry.** It is bright red and may be as large as a small plum. The flavour is acid and slightly bitter. The fruit was formerly used in W. Europe to make pies, sauces, and confectionery, or pickled as a substitute for olives.

It is perhaps in Turkey that the fruits are most prominent. Evelyn Kalças (1974) writes:

It is to be found in late summer piled on huge trays in Turkish markets and fruit shops. Though not considered very tasty by most westerners, I have found the tartness quite tasty, and the jelly or jam made from it is flavorsome. A number of the whole fruit taken from the jam can be added to any fruit salad as an attractive and tasty contrast. There is a fascinating Turkish legend about this fruit. It seems that when Seytan—the Devil—first saw the Kizilcik tree covered with blossoms when no other fruit showed even a bud, he said to himself: 'Aha! This tree will produce fruit first of all. I must be first there to secure it.' So he gathered up his scales and basket and took up his position under the tree. He waited and waited, but all other fruit trees came into bloom and fruit formed on them. Still the Kizilcik fruit was not ready and ripe for eating. Seytan was patient, but he wondered what had happened. Then to his great surprise he discovered that this was one of the very last fruits to ripen at the end of summer, so his chagrin was great. Ever since then the Turks have called the tree:—'Seytan alditan agaci'—the tree that deceived Satan.

The same author relates, as evidence of the use of the tree in antiquity, that the famous and un-untieable Gordian knot was formed from a thong of its leathery bark. (Alexander the Great, acquainted with the problem, drew his sword and severed the knot, then went on to fulfil the prophecy that whoever could undo it would conquer the world.)

Fernald and Kinsey (1943) cite a report by the great Swedish botanist Linnaeus that the Lapps used to make a 'dainty' using the berry of *C. suecica* mixed with whey, then boiled until the mass was as thick as flummery. After the stones had been strained out, this pudding would be eaten served with cream.

American dogwoods include the miner's dogwood, *C. sessilis*, whose fruits are sweet when fully ripe, and the less flavourful bunchberry, *C. canadensis.* Both these and others were widely used by Indians.

DOLMA vegetables stuffed in the E. Mediterranean style. There are two main categories: those with meat stuffings (usually extended with grain), which are served hot, often with a sauce such as broth thickened with lemon juice and eggs; and those with rice stuffings (often enriched with nuts, raisins, or pulses), which are served cold, dressed with oil. The latter are also known as

yalanji dolma (Turkish *yalanci*, 'counterfeit'; namely meatless).

In Turkey, a distinction may also be made between dolma ('stuffed thing'), made from a hollowed-out vegetable (aubergine, courgette, sweet pepper, or tomato; less often potato, artichoke, cucumber, carrot, or celery), and *sarma* ('rolled thing'), where the filling is rolled in an edible leaf, such as vine leaf or cabbage. A sort of *sarma* may also be made from separated layers of boiled leek or onion rolled around a stuffing.

Dolmas are vernacular food in Turkey, the Balkans, the southern Caucasus, Iran, C. Asia (where the word differs in form according to the local Turkish language: *dolâma* in Turkmen, *tulma* in Tatar), and in Egypt, the Fertile Crescent, and Arabia. *Kaldolmar* ('cabbage dolmas') have long been part of Swedish cuisine also, as an unplanned consequence of Charles XII's sojourn in Turkey after his defeat by the Russians at the battle of Poltava. When he returned to Sweden in 1715, he was followed by his Turkish creditors—and their cooks—who remained until 1732.

This distribution, as well as the name dolma itself, indicates that this dish belongs to the court cuisine of the Ottoman Empire. Vegetables had been stuffed before Ottoman times, but only sporadically. For instance, the ancient Greek *thrion* was a fig leaf stuffed with sweetened cheese, and some medieval Arabic cookbooks give recipes for aubergine stuffed with meat (and also, curiously, for the reverse: chunks of cooked aubergine coated with meat like a SCOTCH EGG). However, it was in Istanbul that stuffed vegetables were first treated as a regular culinary genre.

The Ottoman origin is somewhat obscured by the fact that in some countries stuffed vegetables may be referred to by a native name meaning 'stuffed', such as *yemistos* (Greek) or *mahshi* (Arabic). Indeed, some Arabic dialects rarely if ever use the word 'dolma'. Nevertheless, the signs of Turkish origin are clear. In places as remote as Kuwait and Damascus, instead of *mahshi waraq 'inab* (stuffed vine leaf) one may say *mahshi yabraq* (in Kuwait, *mahshi brag*),

which comes from the Turkish *yaprak* (leaf).   CP

DOLPHIN the name properly given to various large marine mammals of the family Delphinidae, the name porpoise being reserved for some of their smaller relations; but porpoise is used instead of dolphin in some parts of the world.

From classical antiquity, and perhaps even earlier times, the dolphin has been regarded as a friend of man, to be respected rather than caught and eaten. General concern for the preservation and well-being of marine mammals (see also DUGONG and WHALE) has reinforced this attitude in the 20th century, and dolphins only appear in the present book because they have been eaten in the past in Europe and may still be in some other parts of the world.

The two best-known species are *Delphinus delphis*, the common dolphin, and *Tursiops truncatus*, the bottlenose dolphin. Delightful legends and tales from classical Greece and Rome have been recounted by Alpers (1960) in a work which deals also with the remarkable swimming speed of these creatures, their playful disposition, and a pleasing vindication of the description of them given by Aristotle.

It was at Genoa that the general rule of abstaining from eating dolphins was breached. There the dried flesh of dolphins, known as musciame, has regularly been for sale.

The DOLPHIN FISH is something quite different, a true fish not a mammal.

DOLPHIN FISH *Coryphaena hippurus*, is not to be confused with the DOLPHIN, which is a marine mammal. The dolphin fish is found all round the world in tropical and semi-tropical seas, but nowhere, with the possible exception of the waters round MALTA, in the quantities desired. It may attain a length of 1.5 m (5') and is a remarkably handsome fish, but its iridescent colours of blue-green, silver, and gold fade rapidly once it is taken from the water.

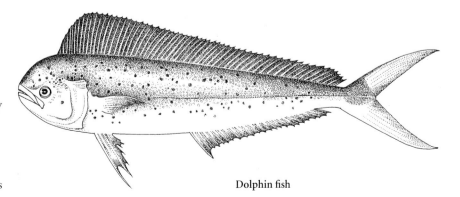

Dolphin fish

It has the habit of swimming in small shoals around patches of flotsam, or floating logs, and is attracted by rafts or drifting boats. It eats other fish.

A smaller species, *C. equisetis*, the pompano dolphin fish, also has a circumglobal distribution and is not easily distinguished.

The dolphin fish has excellent flesh. Slices or steaks may be grilled, fried, or steamed. In Malta they are made into a pie with vegetables.

DORMOUSE *Myoxus glis*, distinguished from other dormice by being called the fat or edible dormouse. It inhabits much of S., C., and E. Europe and was appreciated by the Romans in classical times as food. They fattened dormice on special diets, then stuffed and baked them. An adult dormouse may measure 18 cm (7"), head and body, and has a tail of about equal length.

DOSA a S. Indian PANCAKE, crispy on the surface but slightly spongy inside with a faintly sour taste. Dosas may be eaten as an accompaniment, to scoop up other food, but are most often eaten for breakfast, together with a SAMBAR (S. Indian DAL, hot and soupy) and coconut CHUTNEY.

Dosas can be made with a variety of batters, each giving a slightly different texture or colour, but the traditional dosas are made with rice and lentils (*urd dal*) mixed with water, a little butter and sometimes flavoured with fenugreek, then left to ferment overnight. The mixture is then ground to a batter the next day before being fried on a griddle or on a traditional dosa *kalu* ('dosai stone'). The dosa *kalu* is in fact made of cast iron. Other types of dosa include:

- *Rava dosa*, sometimes called *sooji dosa*, made with semolina and rice and flavoured with cumin, ginger, asafoetida, and nuts.
- *Narial dosa*, which includes coconut.
- Jaggery dosa, made with flour, rice flour, coconut, and flavoured with jaggery and cardamom.

Dosas are often filled (or rolled up) with a variety of vegetables and spices, when they are called *masala dosa*.   HS

DOUGH a malleable, uniform mixture of FLOUR (or meal, which is coarser) and water. Other liquids, leavening, eggs, sweetening, flavouring, and shortening ingredients are added as recipes dictate. Doughs are common in cuisines which exploit the properties of wheat (those rooted in Europe and SW and C. Asia), where their most significant use is in making wheat BREAD. A BATTER is made from similar ingredients to a dough, but is thin, and mixed by beating, not kneading.

Methods and relative proportions of ingredients used for making wheat-based doughs vary according to the desired product, encouraging or discouraging the development of GLUTEN to give varied textures. See also BREAD CHEMISTRY. Bread dough is made with high-protein flour, leavened with yeast or sourdough, and kneaded with water to develop the gluten, yielding a characteristic spongy appearance and chewy texture. Gluten development is also encouraged in pasta and noodle dough, which is heavily kneaded but unleavened; these have a relatively low moisture content when fresh and are often dried to give compact, long-keeping foods. Pastry doughs, and those for shortbread-type biscuits and cakes, use soft flour, with a high proportion of shortening (fat), and are usually unleavened, giving a crisp, friable result.

These are generalizations, and there are numerous exceptions, including doughs for unleavened breads (e.g. CHAPATI); pastry doughs in which gluten development is encouraged, such as FILO; and doughs for unleavened biscuits or CRACKERS, such as water biscuits. Manipulation, cooking, and special operations for particular products are all used to give individual character to dough-based items as disparate as a PRETZEL or PANETTONE.

Rye is also used to make bread doughs, but is less versatile; oats and barley have limited, regional applications. Doughs based on rice, maize, and other grains are made in non-wheat cuisines, but generally lack the primary importance of wheat doughs.

Staple grains other than wheat have different protein contents, and do not develop gluten as wheat-based doughs do. They include those used for unleavened breads, such as maize-flour TORTILLAS; and those which are steamed, including maize-flour TAMALES and the numerous glutinous rice cakes made in E. and SE Asia, for instance *puto* (see RICE CAKES OF THE PHILIPPINES) and the Japanese MOCHI.

(LM)

DOUGHNUT (also donut), a term which originally had and in some places retains a more general meaning, but now indicates particularly the ring-shaped snack food which has become one of the culinary emblems of the USA. This is made from a soft dough, leavened with yeast or baking powder, shaped into a ring, and deep fried, and often sprinkled with fine sugar afterwards. It is commonly dunked in coffee.

The history of the doughnut in America had begun by the first decade of the 19th century, when Washington Irving wrote in a comical description of Dutch settlers in New Amsterdam (later New York) that 'The table . . . was always sure to boast an enormous dish of balls of sweetened dough, fried in hog's fat, and called dough nuts, or oly koeks.' The 'oly koeks' were Dutch in name and possibly German in origin. They were, as Irving said, just balls of dough; there was no hole. The same was true of the many other doughnut-like confections which could be found all over C. Europe, where they had a long-standing association with carnival, saint's days, and festivals. It must have been around the middle of the 19th century or soon afterwards that they acquired the characteristic hole. Mariani (1994) draws attention to a catalogue of 1870 which offered equipment for cutting out the holes.

Not all American doughnuts have the hole. They may be filled, e.g. with a blob of jam; this produces the 'jelly donut', similar to the *Berliner Pfannkuchen* of Germany. Fillings have been quite common in parts of Europe, e.g. an apple filling in Denmark.

The usual mixture for an American doughnut is a combination of flour, eggs, and milk, raised by baking powder or by bicarbonate of soda activated by sour milk. The formula echoes many used in Europe in a broad region stretching from the Ukraine (*pampushky*, Christmas doughnuts filled with jam or poppy seeds), through Germany (all sorts of *Krapfen*), and into the Netherlands (*oliebollen*) and Denmark.

The water content of doughnut mixtures is important; the dough must be stiff enough to be shaped, but still contain plenty of moisture to give the light spongy texture of the cooked product. When small pieces of the dough are dropped into boiling fat, they quickly heat through to well above normal boiling point, so that superheated steam puffs them up to lightness before the outside hardens. The presence of air or gas bubbles formed by beaten egg or yeast also helps the process. Since the speed with which heat penetrates a doughnut (or anything else) varies in proportion to the square of half the maximum thickness, and since the thickness of a doughnut is greatly reduced by making it in a ring shape, the doughnut with a hole cooks far faster than those without.

The frontier between doughnut and fritter is often indistinct, so it is difficult to give any list of doughnuts without wandering into disputed territory. With this proviso, a very few interesting kinds of doughnut are described below, moving in a grand sweep from the Old World through the New World and the Pacific and leapfrogging most of Asia back to the Near East.

- **Rosquilla,** a Spanish doughnut made from a sweet dough with wine and anise-

flavoured oil, shaped into a ring and dusted with icing sugar and cinnamon.
- **Cala,** a New Orleans doughnut, familiar also in Trinidad and elsewhere, made from a yeasted dough of cooked rice, eggs, flour, and sugar, flavoured with nutmeg.
- **Andagi,** the doughnuts of Okinawa, admired and eaten in Hawaii, are not yeast doughnuts but cake-type doughnuts leavened with baking powder. The dough is soft and is formed with great dexterity into small balls which quickly turn from pale gold to a rich brown in the boiling oil.
- **Malasadas,** other doughnuts introduced to Hawaii, where they are enormously popular, by Portuguese immigrants from the Azores in the late 19th century. Made with an eggy dough and milk or cream (or evaporated milk). Sometimes rolled in honey as well as in sugar, and with a touch of vanilla or nutmeg.
- **Sufganiyah,** made in Israel for Hanukkah, using a yeast-leavened dough enriched with milk, eggs, and sugar. After deep-frying it is filled with jam, often apricot, and rolled in caster sugar.   (LM)

DOUM PALM *Hyphaena thebaica,* a native of Egypt. The Revd John Montgomery (1872), viewing it from a British standpoint, said that it 'produces a fruit, the thick, brown, mealy rind of which has a remarkable resemblance to gingerbread'. This is confirmed by Corner (1966), who also remarks that elephants enjoy the fruits.

DRAGÉE the French name for a sweetmeat composed of a nut or some other centre coated with layers of hard sugar. Almonds are the nuts usually chosen; alternative centres are seeds, fruit pastes, or chocolate, and occasionally liqueurs.

The manufacture of dragées is carried out using heated rotating pans, shaped a little like concrete mixers, in which a batch of almonds (for example) is tumbled. A 'charge' of sugar solution, mixed with gum arabic, is added. The rotating action of the pan causes the sugar to coat the centres, and the heat dries them; when the 'charge' is used up, another is added and the process is repeated until the sweets have reached the desired size. The sugar solution can be coloured and flavoured as the confectioner wishes; and the dragées may be polished after the final coat of sugar. The appearance and texture of the finished product is influenced by the proportion of sugar in the syrup.

Sweets made by this process, known as 'panning', include SUGAR ALMONDS, and other nut-based dragées; jelly beans; nonpareils, or HUNDREDS AND THOUSANDS; and chocolate-centred dragées such as

'Smarties'. GOBSTOPPERS are also made by panning, as are the French sweets called *anis de Flavigny.* Silver dragées, often used for cake decorations, are dragées given a final tumbling with a little gum solution and sheets of fine silver leaf in a glass pan.

Dragées have long been a great speciality of French confectionery. These sweets may have their origin in sugar-coated pills made by apothecaries. However, the original word 'dragée' is obscure although it occurs as early as the 13th century in the archives of Verdun in the north-east of France.

The word does not appear to have entered English until the middle of the 19th century, when the older terms sugar-plums or COMFITS began to be displaced. These usually employed whole spices, such as coriander and aniseed, for the centres. Aniseed balls, which are simply flavoured with aniseed, are descendants of these.

Manufacturing dragées, or comfits, by hand was a skilled task, which has long been the preserve of professional confectioners. Details of their trade secrets rarely survive, but in this case we are fortunate as instructions were published by Sir Hugh Platt (1609) in 'The arte of comfetmaking, teaching how to couer all kinds of seeds, fruits or spices with sugar' including details of equipment, materials, and quantities. 'A quarter of a pound of Coriander seeds, and three pounds of sugar will make great, huge and big comfets.' Comfits were used for decorating other sweet dishes, such as MARZIPAN, and, until the 19th century, caraway comfits (as opposed to loose caraway seeds) were used in SEED CAKES.

Jarrin (1827) observed that 'The best comfits are made at Verdun' and gave instructions after the method of confectioners of that town. He also noted that large hollow egg shapes were made in sugar paste: 'They are usually filled with imitations of all sorts of fruits. In Paris they put in a number of nick-nacks, little almanacks, smelling bottles with essences, and even things of value for presents.' These were then coated with sugar in the same manner as other comfits. Gunter (1830) disagreed with Jarrin: 'I have been exceedingly surprised to hear it asserted, that the French make *better* comfits than the English; they decidedly fail in this compound and would appear . . . to know as little of *Comfit* as *comfort.*'

The manufacture of dragées was successfully mechanized in the mid-19th century and few would now attempt to make them by hand except out of curiosity. More recently, the range has narrowed.

Varieties listed in *Skuse's Complete Confectioner* (1957) under colourful names such as green peas and coral beads, rifle balls, red and white currants, vanilla and chocolate beans, and pearls seem to have

vanished; but many sweets made by panning, e.g. sugar almonds and jelly beans, are still enduring favourites.   (LM)

DRAGONFLY a kind of insect which is eaten in many Asian countries. Pemberton (1995) collected data about their capture and ways of eating them from a number of countries and by personal investigation in Bali (Indonesia). He noted that the Balinese often use the sticky latex of the jackfruit tree as a means of capture. He recalls the report by Covarrubias (1937)

that children caught dragonflies by holding latex tipped poles higher than the places where dragonflies were perched. This induced the 'rank conscious' dragonflies to fly up and land on the tip of the poles, where they became stuck.

Thus among dragonflies, as among other and larger species, excessive consideration for rank may spell doom.

Pemberton found that several cooking methods were employed in Bali, including some which involved coconut milk and other ingredients such as ginger, garlic, and shallots. The simplest method was to place the dragonflies directly on a grill. Cooked in this way they 'had a carbonized crispy quality with a subtle, fat flavor'.

In Laos the preferred species for eating is *Anax guttatus,* which can be caught by placing a lighted candle in a large bowl of water; the unfortunate insects are attracted by the flame, singe their wings, and fall helpless into the water. Other information comes from Japan and Korea. The general impression given is that dragonflies are widely eaten, but are not an important foodstuff anywhere; catching them is a sort of 'sport', and this aspect is as important as anything to do with nutrition or flavour.

DRIPPING (drippings in USA), the fat that drips from joints of meat, especially BEEF, when they are roasted. Stobart (1980), harking back to the days 'when meat really had fat on it', says:

When cold and solidified, some brown meat jelly was usually trapped and preserved under the fat. When the fat (especially of beef dripping) was mixed with the jelly, salted, and spread on toast, it used to be a standard—and delicious—appetite stopper for farm workers and children at tea time on raw evenings in winter or after skating. Dripping was also commonly clarified and used as a cooking fat. In that case, the distinction between dripping and rendered fat is mainly one of usage. Chicken fat, so much a part of Jewish cooking, is not called 'chicken dripping'.

DRISHEEN a type of blood pudding made only in Cork city in S. Ireland and prepared with a mixture of sheep and beef bloods. The exact quantity of each blood used is critical; the product is too light and fragile if too much sheep blood is used and it is too dark and heavy if too much beef blood is used. The bloods are blended and a little salt is added. The mixture is left to solidify and once coagulated is scored with a knife and left overnight. By morning the blood has separated into serum and coagulated blood residue. The serum is drawn off and poured into prepared beef casings. The puddings are boiled for about five minutes. Its shape resembles an inflated bicycle tube, the colour is a brownish-grey, and it has a distinctive blancmange-like texture.

The origins of the pudding can be traced to the commercial developments of the city between 1685 and 1825. In this period Cork became the largest and most important port in the British Isles for the exportation of salted beef. The beef cuts were exported to England, Europe, and America and the blood by-product of the city's slaughter houses was used in the manufacture of the pure blood pudding of Cork.

The pudding is simply prepared by boiling lightly in milk and is served with a rich buttery white sauce, which is seasoned with plenty of pepper. It is also sliced and fried in butter. A mixture of tripe and drisheen is another common dish. RSe

DROPS small round confections originally made by 'dropping' a mixture in rounds to set. In common with words such as KISSES and LADDU (Hindi) the word describes a shape rather than a recipe. Acid, fruit, and GUM drops are all still produced. Chocolate is also made into drops, as are cake and biscuit mixtures, e.g. SPONGE drops.

Acid drops (a contraction of acidulated drops) are small clear sweets made from sugar boiled to the hard crack stage (see SUGAR BOILING), with the addition of tartaric acid to give a sour flavour. *Fruit drops* are similar confections, highly coloured, flavoured with natural or synthetic essences. *Pear drops* are a popular British sweet, coloured half-red, half-yellow, roughly pear shaped and flavoured with jargonelle pear essence, or synthetic pentyl acetate.

All these are descended from earlier fruit confections. Recipes which would have produced something close to a modern conception of fruit drops were given by La Varenne in *Le Parfait Confiturier* (1667). Acid juices such as lemon or pomegranate were added to boiled sugar. The acid had the desirable effect of keeping the sugar mixture clear and hard when it cooled, instead of 'graining', i.e. recrystallizing to granulated sugar. Other drop recipes called for

powdered sugar mixed with fruit juices, giving a result similar to ICING. In the late 18th and early 19th centuries, extra acid in the form of vinegar or tartaric acid (or in one recipe oil of vitriol, sulphuric acid), were added to boiled sugar, and modern drops evolved.

Other flavourings included coffee, and perfumes such as rose, violet, and bergamot. The latter survives as a French regional speciality, *bergamottes de Nancy*. PEPPERMINT is still used as a flavouring in Britain. Overtly medicinal ingredients, such as horehound, wintergreen, and liquorice, turned the confections into cough drops. *Paregoric*, added to some cough drops, originally referred to a camphorated opium compound, now reduced to a harmless flavouring.

Boiled sugar drops are usually made into attractive and varied shapes by putting the mixture, whilst still warm, through 'drop rollers' which both shape and cut the mixture.

'Gum' drops and 'jelly' drops rely on gelling agents for their textures and are shaped by starch moulding. LM

DROP SCONE or dropped scone, a term used to cover a group of baked goods which are equally well known under names such as Scots pancake.

Catherine Brown (1990) remarks that

The term dropped scone seems to have been adopted to distinguish between the thick Scots pancake and the thin French crêpe also known as a pancake. In England the term dropped scone seems to have been universally adopted, while in Scotland it is possible to come across both terms.

In any event, this excellent PANCAKE is made from a thick creamy batter of flour, milk or BUTTERMILK, a sparing amount of egg and sugar (or GOLDEN SYRUP), with BICARBONATE OF SODA and CREAM OF TARTAR. The pancakes are cooked on a greased girdle (see GRIDDLE). They are best eaten warm with butter or jam, or both.

The Welsh name for the same thing, in parts of Glamorganshire, is *froes*, or Welsh dropped scone. Bobby Freeman (1996), in the course of a disquisition on the importance to Welsh people of pancakes in general, speculates that Scottish miners coming south to Glamorganshire may have brought their recipe with them.

DRUM the name given to certain fish of the family Sciaenidae which are notable for the noise they can make; cf the similar name CROAKER, applied in the same family. The noise is produced by a snapping of the muscles attached to the air bladder, which acts as a resonance chamber. A curious fact is that certain other fish in the family (e.g. of

the genus *Menticirrhus*, see KINGFISH) which lack an air bladder and cannot therefore 'drum', are still subject to the family impulse to make a noise, which they do by grinding their teeth.

Of the species which bear the name drum, which is mostly used on the eastern seaboard of the USA, the following are the best known:

- **sea drum** or **black drum,** *Pogonias cromis*, a large fish (maximum length 140 cm/56", although a length of 100 cm/40" is more common), silvery with a brassy lustre fading to grey on death. It is abundant from the Carolinas southwards. Young specimens make good pan fish.
- **red drum,** or channel bass, *Sciaenops ocellata*, slightly larger than the sea drum. It is not really red, but one ichthyologist declared that he could detect 'a tint, an evanescent, metallic, reflection of claret from the scales'. Again, the smaller specimens make the best eating.

See also SQUETEAGUE, another N. American species of the sciaenid family.

In the southern hemisphere other species of the same family occur, indeed scores of them, and some of these are referred to as drums, although mostly having a more specific common name which is used more often, e.g. *Argyrosomus hololepidotus* in S. African waters, better known as the kob.

DRUPE the technical term for the category of fruits which have a layer of flesh surrounding a single 'stone', which is called a nut if edible. Examples are PEACH and ALMOND.

DRYING the simplest and oldest method of food PRESERVATION, is used in almost every part of the world, and for foods of all kinds. Drying a food reduces its water content to a level so low that the micro-organisms and enzymes which cause spoilage cannot function.

When carried out by traditional methods, drying is a gradual process. Food, however, begins to decay immediately, so drying is a race against spoilage. Various factors influence the rate at which food dries. The larger its surface area in relation to its volume, the more quickly it loses liquid. In practice this means that it has to be in small pieces or cut into flat sheets, as when fish to be dried is split and opened out, or figs are squashed. The air has to be dry. It is helpful if there is a wind. Heat speeds drying, since hot air can hold, and thus carry away, more moisture than cold air; but it also speeds up decomposition. A problem which affects all dried foods containing fat is rancidity caused by the oxygen in the air. This is most severe in oily fish, whose oil is highly unsaturated and goes rancid easily. These cannot be successfully dried.

Drying is often combined with SALTING, which arrests spoilage at once. The SMOKING of food also helps to dry it, as well as depositing a layer on the surface which is antiseptic and excludes oxygen to avoid rancidity.

Chemical agents may be used to arrest spoilage while drying takes place. The chief of these (apart from salt) is sulphur dioxide, which creates acid conditions and is effective against both enzymes and micro-organisms. It is widely used on dried fruit. Pepper and spices, which are mildly antiseptic, aid the preservation of some dried foods.

MEAT

Meat can be dried without salt if it is cut into thin strips. However, many dried meats include salt, often added mainly for flavour. The 'dry-salting' of large pieces of meat, such as some kinds of bacon or ham, is not really a drying procedure, since it relies almost entirely on the action of the salt.

Genuinely dried meats include the Latin American *charqui* (or *tassajo*), made with beef, and its mutton equivalent *chalona*. The name *charqui* has been Anglicized to JERKY (or jerked beef). Such foods were, and to some extent still are, used by travellers, cowboys, and other people who had to carry their food with them. See also BILTONG. Typically, these products consist of thin strips, air dried, usually salted, sometimes lightly smoked, often peppered or spiced.

Dried meats are often made in mountainous areas where windy conditions (and at great altitudes, low air pressure) favour drying: for example, conditions are good for drying pork in Nepal.

Thicker pieces of dried meat in which drying plays a significant part in the preservation process include some beef products such as the northern Italian BRESAOLA and the Swiss BINDENFLEISCH, two products made in adjoining border regions. See also PEMMICAN.

FISH AND OTHER SEAFOODS

Plain dried fish, prepared without salt, has been superseded by salted, dried fish, or fish preserved in other ways, in many parts of the world where it was formerly usual. In N. Europe, where the climate allows simple air-drying, it continues in use alongside combined salting and drying. Only white fish, whose flesh is not oily, are suitable for either process and, for drying without salt, they have to be fairly small.

In ancient Egypt, classical Greece, and the Near East salt was readily obtainable, and fish was salted to dry it from early times, as well as being preserved in brine. In medieval Europe STOCKFISH was a major food, and

was the subject of considerable trade. The name, originally a German word, was a general one for any dried white fish, most often cod, but also pollack, whiting, hake, and others. These might be dried with or without salt, although the modern usage of the term 'stockfish' is for an unsalted kind only. SALT COD is the prime example of the salted kind.

EGGS

Eggs are difficult to dry, and it was not until the early 20th century that a workable process was developed, by German engineers in China. From the 1930s onwards other countries, including the USA and Britain, began to dry eggs, for baking and other processed foods. During the Second World War dried egg was used in Britain and elsewhere, for different and obvious reasons, but domestic use of the product has since almost ceased, although its quality has improved. Eggs may be dried whole, or separated into yolks and whites.

MILK

Dried milk is another modern product, foreshadowed by the Indian condensed milk *khoya* (see MILK REDUCTION). This is evaporated and coagulated by slow heating, often carried to the point at which the product is quite dry and crumbly. It is not intended to keep, but is used as an ingredient in confectionery. Dried milk is now made either by drum or spray drying.

FRUITS AND VEGETABLES

Sun-drying of most fruits is easy in warm, dry climates if there is no objection to the fruit becoming brown or black, as is considered normal in RAISINS, PRUNES, and FIGS. Dried figs were a main article of the diet of ordinary people in classical Greece and Rome. In Arabia and N. Africa dried or partly dried DATES are still a staple food.

Sun-dried tomatoes, formerly best known in the Mediterranean region (see Patience Gray, 1986, for an account of their preparation in Apulia and of how they can be stuffed), became fashionable as a speciality food in N. America and W. Europe in the closing decades of the 20th century.

In medieval Europe dried fruits were much in demand. Currants, prunes, figs, and dates were all imported from Mediterranean countries on the same ships that brought spices. Rich people used them liberally in pies, tarts, and pottages. The medieval mistrust of raw fresh fruit did not extend to exotic dried kinds. APPLES were also dried. Rather than being sliced into rings as in more recent practice, they were peeled and cored but left whole. Threaded on strings and hung across an airy room they became brown, leathery, and sweet through concentration of their sugar as they shrank.

Vegetables are in general less suitable for drying by simple processes than are fruits. They are watery and lack sufficient protective sugar or acid to resist decay. If air-drying were attempted many vegetables would simply go bad, or leaves would wither and brown. (There are exceptions. The leaves of MELOKHIA, which is made into a soup loved by Egyptians, are sometimes air dried.)

Attempts were made long ago to dry some vegetables for use as military rations to ward off SCURVY, but it was not understood until the 20th century that the procedure would make them almost useless for that purpose. The first process was patented in 1780, but was unsuccessful, as were other early attempts, e.g. to produce by drying an instant mashed potato. Indeed, some would say that full success has still not been achieved. Modern dried vegetables (other than freeze dried, for which see FREEZING) are prepared in an air draught whose temperature is a compromise between the conflicting needs of fast drying and flavour preservation. The vacuum method, which satisfies both requirements, is sometimes used for better-quality products.

Among dried vegetable products, much the most important are grains. Generally, whole grains harvested in favourable conditions need only a little air-drying to make them keep, although in wet climates, such as that of Britain, fuel-burning grain dryers often have to be used.

PULSES—peas, beans, lentils, chickpeas, and the like—are typically staple foods of dry areas, such as India and Mexico, where they can be spread out in the sun and left to dry naturally inside their protective seed coats.

SPICES AND HERBS

Hard spices such as cinnamon and nutmeg are little altered by the small amount of drying necessary to preserve them. Drying may bring about a desirable change in flavour, as in pepper where the pungency increases.

Among herbs, woody types such as rosemary and thyme stand up to drying well; slightly more fleshy plants such as marjoram and sage reasonably well; and fleshy moist ones like mint not very well. Worst is probably basil which, however carefully dried, loses the 'top notes' of its fragrance and has little virtue left.

FUNGI

Fungi have been dried with great success since early times. In a dry climate they can be air dried without any special preparation other than cutting the larger ones into slices. All kinds shrink considerably, concentrating the flavour. The best known of the dried mushrooms on sale in Europe is the CEP; the

Italian *funghi porcini* are of this kind. The British mushroom which was most dried in former times was the champignon or FAIRY RING MUSHROOM. The Chinese dry many fungi, especially the WOOD EAR.

BEVERAGES AND SOUP

Various beverages are prepared from dried ingredients. TEA leaves and COFFEE beans are obvious examples. Instant coffee and tea are made by brewing the drink and drying the liquid in a spray dryer (see below) or, in the case of high-quality instant coffee, by freeze-drying. Other dried plant substances used to make infused drinks are CHICORY (dried root), COCOA (dried powdered seeds), GUARANA (dried powdered seeds, made into smoked cakes), COLA 'nut' (dried powdered seeds), and MATÉ (dried leaves).

For an interesting form of dried soup, see PORTABLE SOUP.

DRYING TECHNIQUES

Of modern mechanized drying techniques, the most commonly used is continuous tunnel drying. The food is loaded onto wire mesh trays which are drawn slowly through a long tunnel through which heated air is blown. By the time the food emerges from the far end of the tunnel it is fully dried.

A refinement of the tunnel dryer is the fluidized bed drier, used for small items such as peas. The food travels along perforated plates through which warm air is blown from below. The air lifts and transports the food while it is drying. The further it goes the hotter the air gets. In the case of peas, moisture content falls from 80% to 50%. The food is then transferred to a stationary drying bin where it is finished off slowly with warm air. Finally, after a total of, say, 16 hours, the moisture content is down to 5%.

Stationary bin or cabinet driers are used throughout for less robust foods. In a closed cabinet a partial vacuum can be applied to the food, which allows the use of lower temperatures and so avoids damage to delicate fruits and vegetables.

Liquids such as milk, fruit or vegetable juices, and pastes such as those for breakfast cereals, may be dried in drum driers. Two heated stainless steel drums revolve slowly, almost touching. The liquid is poured into the gap between the drums and trickles down slowly. It dries on the lower surfaces of the drums and is scraped off by a blade. Usually drying is assisted by a partial vacuum.

Another drying method for liquids or semi-liquids, including milk, eggs, and instant coffee, is spray drying. A large, funnel-shaped chamber, typically 3 m (10') high, has a whirling nozzle at the top through which the liquid is misted into the chamber. Hot air is also blown in at the top.

The mist dries to a powder and collects at the bottom. The product is less damaged by heat than in drum drying. The fine powder has to be slightly moistened and formed into granules to make a product which will dissolve without bedding down into a lumpy mass.

DUCK a bird which exists in many wild species right round the world (see WILD DUCK), but of which the domesticated kinds are those commonly eaten. Domestication began over 2,000 years ago in China, and was being practised in classical Rome (witness Columella, 1st century AD) and has been pursued with enthusiasm in many parts of the world. In Europe and N. America almost all domesticated breeds stem from the MALLARD duck, but they exhibit considerable differences in size, appearance, etc.

A duck (of either gender—the term drake is not used in a culinary context) is usually six months old or more, while a duckling is younger. The French terms are canard and caneton.

Some breeds of duck, e.g. Indian Runner, are reared for laying purposes, and may produce as many as 200 eggs (larger than hen's eggs) a year. But the demand for duck eggs has never been overwhelming (except perhaps in the Philippines—see BALUT) and most ducks are bred for table use. The principal such breeds are:

- Aylesbury, named after an English town, in the county of Buckinghamshire, which offered propitious surroundings for duck-rearing. These are white ducks. The meat is pale and tender. Laura Mason (1996) quotes a charming passage from Mrs Beeton (1861) about what was once a cottage industry. Mrs Beeton said that in parts of Buckinghamshire:

  [the birds were raised] in the abodes of the cottagers. Round the walls of the living-rooms, and of the bedroom even, are fixed rows of wooden boxes, lined with hay; and it is the business of the wife and children to nurse and comfort the feathered lodgers, to feed the little ducklings, and to take the old ones out for an airing.

  However, enquiries in the 1990s showed that there was only one producer left.
- Norfolk. Most English duck and ducklings are labelled 'Norfolk', that county being the most important British centre of production of birds which match the needs of restaurants and conform to the latest hygiene requirements.
- Peking. A fine breed. When first imported to Britain in the 19th century it was used to give new vigour to the Aylesbury breed, but was later bred for its own sake. In the USA it gave rise to what has become the

most successful breed ever in the western world (see next item).
- Long Island. Best, best known, and most widely sold of American ducks, this breed is descended from white Peking birds imported from China in 1873. These were introduced first to Connecticut and then to Long Island, where they flourished well. They grow fast to a good weight.
- Nantes. From early in the 19th century the small Nantais ducks (strictly speaking, from Challans, Nantes being the point from which they were dispatched to Paris) enjoyed a good reputation, and this eventually came to rival that of the larger Rouen breed. Nantais ducks are beheaded and bled before sale.
- Rouen. A famous French breed, traditionally smothered to death so as to preserve all the blood inside. The famous dish *Caneton à la rouennaise* calls for the carcass of the cooked bird to be squeezed in a special press, to extract all the juices, and in a brilliant marketing operation which began in 1890 has every instance of the dish numbered (in a sequence which is poised to reach one million early in the 3rd millennium—Charlie Chaplin was 253,652, way back).

Muscovy ducks are of a different species: *Cairina moschata*, of C. and S. America. They make good eating, especially when crossed with other ducks to diminish their tendency to muskiness. (Their name has nothing to do with muskiness or with Muscovy, nor do they merit the name 'Barbary duck' sometimes given to them.)

One of the most interesting treatments given to duck in the kitchen belongs to Wales. This is Welsh salt duck, the recipe for which first appeared in print in the charmingly eccentric book by Lady Llanover (1867). This was described and praised by Elizabeth David (1970), who drew attention to the resemblance between it and 'Nanking fresh salted duck', while remarking that the latter is eaten cold while the Welsh dish was originally intended to be eaten hot with an onion sauce.

In England the most familiar and excellent combination is roast duckling with apple sauce and peas, a dish of the late spring. In France (and, alas, in debased international cuisine) there is the well-known *Canard à l'orange* (or *à la bigarade*, using the recommended Seville oranges); and a good dish of duck with turnip. In other countries there are combinations which reflect the characteristics of their cuisines, for example duck and red cabbage in Poland; the use of sour cream, apple, etc. in E. Europe; the Iranian braised duck with walnut and pomegranate sauce (see FESENJAN).

PEKING DUCK is, however, probably the most famous of all duck dishes.
READING: Stobart (1980); Judy Urquhart (1983).

DUFF A steamed PUDDING containing fruit, especially raisins as in 'plum duff'.

It is hard to know how to pronounce the word dough, since it might be thought to rhyme with enough or rough. It seems to have been for this reason that the pronunciation 'duff' emerged in the north of England, and then became a term in its own right, having the basic meaning of dough but usually with reference to a steamed pudding made with dough.

On both sides of the Atlantic plum duff began as something very plain and unpretentious. For example in a chapter devoted partly to 'fluff-duffs' Adams (1952) records complaints by cowboys that the cook 'jes' bogged down a few raisins in dough an' called 'er puddin'. And in England a duff was for long counted as a cheap and filling item which would appear frequently in school or other institutional menus, especially for sailors. However, plum duff can claim one illustrious relation, namely CHRISTMAS PUDDING, of which the ancestral manifestation was little more than dough and dried fruits.

DUGONG AND MANATEE, the names used in SE Asia (and other Indo-Pacific regions, including N. Australia and E. Africa) and the W. Indies respectively for certain marine mammals in the order Sirenia, also commonly referred to as sea cows. The former is *Halicore dugong*, while the latter name corresponds to three species: *Trichechus manatus*, the W. Indian manatee (with two subspecies, the Florida manatee and the Antillean manatee); *T. inunguis*, the Amazonian manatee (*inunguis* because its flippers do not have the fingernails possessed by other manatees); and *T. senegalensis*, the W. African manatee.

The name dugong is probably a corruption of the Malay name duyong. These creatures were in the past quite common in Malayan waters, especially in estuaries and other coastal areas but also some way upstream in major rivers such as the Mekong. Now, however, they are rare and protected.

The dugong was formerly eaten in Malaya, and its cousin the manatee, according to Simmonds (1859), was eaten in the W. Indies with appreciation, having delicious white flesh like pork. The same author expressed qualms which must have affected many people:

It appears horrible to chew and swallow the flesh of an animal which holds its young (it has never more than one at a litter) to its breast, which is

formed exactly like that of a woman, with paws resembling human hands.

This description helps to explain why both the dugong and the manatee have given rise to tales about mermaids, marine creatures with breasts and a forked tail. The semi-human characteristics of mermaids may in turn explain why some people in SE Asia believe that the dugong engages in philanthropic activities. Thus there are tales about how, if a pirogue sinks in the River Mekong, 'a score or more of dugongs will appear and form a circle round the crew as they flounder in the water. The dugongs utter wheezing sighs of concern and are evidently bent on protecting the men from possible attacks by large and predatory fish.'

The manatees, like the dugong, have been hunted and eaten locally in the regions where they occur and are now also threatened by pollution and accidents with motor boats and fishing gear.

DUKU AND LANGSAT, two SE Asian fruits, are both classified as *Lansium domesticum*, although one can readily be distinguished from the other and the two of them recognized as separate botanical varieties. *L. domesticum* var *domesticum* corresponds to the name duku and is the more widely cultivated. *L. domesticum* var *pubescens*, which is the langsat, is often called 'wild langsat' but it too is cultivated. Each variety has some desirable characteristics.

Cultivation takes place mainly in Indonesia (especially Java), Malaysia, and Thailand.

The tree, of medium size, takes about 15 years to reach maturity, but then bears tight clusters of fruit twice a year.

Langsat has about 20 fruits in a cluster, each oval and just under 4 cm (1.75") long, with thin, pale fawn skin. Duku has only about 10 fruits to a cluster. They are round and larger, about 5 cm (2") in diameter, with thicker skins. The flesh of both fruits is usually white, but in some cultivated varieties of duku it is pink. It is juicy and refreshing, with a taste ranging from sour to sweet. Each fruit is composed of five segments, some of which may contain bitter, inedible seeds. The fruits may be eaten raw or preserved with sugar.

According to folklore in the Philippines, where the fruits are known as *lanzones*, they used to be so sour as to be quite inedible, and indeed toxic. But it happened one day that a beautiful woman with a child, travelling through the countryside, could find nothing else to eat but *lanzones*. She accordingly picked one and gave it to the child. From then on the fruit acquired its present desirable characteristics; for the woman was none other than the Virgin Mary. However, the transformation which

she wrought was not complete, since some *lanzones* still turn out to be very sour.

DULSE *Palmaria palmata*, probably the most widely distributed of the edible red seaweeds; it occurs in both northern and southern hemispheres, in the Indo-Pacific as well as the Atlantic, in temperate and cold waters. The rose-red or purplish plants have an average height of 30 cm (12"). Nutritious, slightly salty to taste, they are accounted among the most delicious seaweeds, although there are many countries in which they occur but are not normally eaten.

Ireland is where dulse has been consumed with the greatest enthusiasm since ancient times. It is mentioned as an item of hospitality (together with onions and salt) in the 7th-century Irish secular laws *Corpus Iuris Hibernici*. In modern Ireland dried dulse is chewed as a snack particularly in coastal regions and it is often used as a relish with potatoes or boiled milk. Because of this association with Ireland, the English common name 'dulse', which is essentially the Irish name, has come to be in widespread use, even in countries where English is not spoken.

DUMAS ALEXANDRE, PÈRE (1802–70), even by 19th-century standards an astonishingly prolific writer. The collected edition of his works comprises 303 volumes. Ironically, it does not include *Le Grand Dictionnaire de cuisine*, which was his last work and the one on which, to judge by statements which he made in his last years, he expected his reputation to rest most firmly. In fact, he is far better known as the author of such books as *The Three Musketeers* and *The Count of Monte Cristo*. But he has also retained a reputation as an authority on food and cookery; a reputation which is not entirely deserved, unless one takes the view that his quixotic personality and abundant enthusiasm entitle him to a greater meed of praise than what he actually wrote would warrant.

The dictionary was published posthumously and bore the date 1873, although copies were already being distributed in 1872. It remained in print until the 1950s, in the original edition. The surviving copies were then destroyed, which paved the way for a number of coffee-table editions. Some of these were provided with illustrations, of which the first edition had only two.

The book, which contains about 750,000 words, is poorly organized and heavily weighted down with recipes from other sources and quotations, not always acknowledged, from other writers such as Brillat-Savarin. The information which it offers is frequently inaccurate, and it is plain that when Dumas made his compilation he was unaware of or chose to ignore a number of important reference books which were available in France in the 1860s. He says himself that when he withdrew to Normandy to write the book he took only a small collection of notes and books and relied rather on his memory. This may have been a good thing, for the result was that the book was studded with personal reminiscences which were written with verve and are entertaining. The merit of the book lies in this aspect of it. It therefore cries out to be abridged. But the only abridgement published in France (*Le Petit Dictionnaire de cuisine*, 1882) discarded much of the good material instead of focusing attention on it. No critical study of the book has ever been made in France. Authoritative writers such as André Maurois have, however, praised it in general terms and have thus provided some cement for Dumas's gastronomic reputation.

For examples of Dumas' entertaining style, see GOOSE and HERMIT CRAB. See also the next page, under England.
READING: Alan and Jane Davidson (1978, especially introductory matter).

DUMPLING (*see opposite page*)

DUNDEE CAKE a rich, buttery Scottish FRUIT CAKE containing sultanas, ground almonds, and candied peel. Before baking, the top is covered with whole blanched almonds.

The name appears to have been first recorded in the late 19th century. According to sources in the city of Dundee, the cake originated as a by-product of the orange marmalade made by Keiller's, the famous and long-established marmalade-makers of that city, who found it convenient to make the cakes during the part of the year when they were not making marmalade (and may well have had citrus peel to spare).

Laura Mason (1999) further observes that the bakers in the city had a gentleman's agreement that only Keiller's should make Dundee cake, a situation which lasted until the company became part of a multinational in the 1970s. The agreement had not, however, extended to other parts of Britain, and the cake was widely copied in the 20th century. Bakers further south also confused it with rich fruit cakes as known in England, and tended to think that it was merely the topping of almonds which distinguished it from the latter.   LM

DUNGENESS CRAB *Cancer magister*, the most important commercial crab of the

Pacific north-west coast of the USA. Carapace width may be as much as 20 cm (8"). The back is reddish-brown or purplish in life, turning to red or orange when the crab is cooked. This crab and *C. pagurus* (see CRAB, COMMON) are closely related and match each other in quality.

Ricketts and Calvin (1978) remark in connection with this species:

The exoskeleton of a crab presents a formidable barrier to love-making; and although it seems to be the general rule that mating of crabs requiring internal fertilization can take place only when the female is still soft from molting, the process has not often been observed.

They proceed to describe what two members of the Oregon Fish Commission saw when watching two Dungeness crabs mate in an aquarium. They watched for 192 hours, perhaps a record in the field of voyeurism.

A smaller relation, *C. productus*, called the red crab (but to be distinguished from the species described under RED CRAB), is not exploited commercially; although it is quite large enough to eat, the ratio in weight of meat to shell is unfavourable.

DUNLOP a hard, cow's milk cheese, took its name from the native dairying cattle of Ayrshire, whose lowlands constitute the finest dairying region of Scotland. This all happened centuries ago, long before anyone had thought of manufacturing rubber tyres, still less of using Dunlop as a brand name for them. The coincidence almost spelled doom for the cheese, since the Milk Marketing Board, fearing that customers would suppose, even if only subconsciously, that Dunlop cheese would be rubbery, tried to drop the name in favour of the far less precise 'Cheddar'.

It is said that Dunlop cheese came into being in 1690 or just afterwards, when an Ayrshire farmer's daughter, Barbara Gilmour, who had been living in Ulster, in exile from religious persecution, returned with a recipe for making cheese which, at the time, was quite revolutionary. It involved using full cream cow's milk instead of skimmed milk, and pressing it until it was quite hard and had acquired a superior keeping quality and flavour. While the old cheese was described as 'common cheese', the new cheese became known as 'sweet-milk cheese' or 'new milk cheese'. By the 1790s, when parish accounts were compiled, it had become established as 'Dunlop cheese', made in five parishes of Ayrshire and two of neighbouring Lanarkshire.

The growth of the urban and industrial markets of C. Scotland, especially Glasgow and Paisley, encouraged production during the latter part of the 19th century. As late as 1930, at least 300 farms were still making Dunlop cheeses. 'Each farm had a fully

matured cheese open for cooking, and a softer one for eating. At breakfast, porridge was followed on alternate days by bacon and eggs or toasted cheese on a scone made from home-ground flour, eaten in front of the fire' (Rance, 1982).

Although the shadow of Dunlop tyres and Milk Marketing Boards, as mentioned above, fell over the cheeses in the period of and after the Second World War, some cheese-makers, especially on the Isle of Arran, maintained the Dunlop name and tradition; and these now seem assured of survival. By comparison with Scottish Cheddar cheeses, Dunlop has a more mellow, 'nutty' flavour and a softer, creamier texture.   CB

DUQQA a spice mixture used in the Near East. The word is derived from the Arabic verb meaning 'to pound'. Claudia Roden (1985) explains that the ingredients in the mixture vary from one family to another, although typically including SESAME and CORIANDER seeds, CUMIN, salt and pepper, and perhaps hazelnut. She also quotes a 19th-century source which lists ZAATAR or wild MARJORAM or MINT, with sesame and coriander seeds and CINNAMON, plus CHICKPEAS. Roden emphasizes the texture:

It is a loose mixture of nuts and spices in a dry, crushed but not powdered form, usually eaten with bread dipped in olive oil. In Egypt it is served at breakfast time, as an appetizer, or as a snack in the evening. . . . Roast or grill the ingredients separately. Pound them together until they are finely crushed but not pulverized. . . . *Dukkah* should always be a crushed dry mixture, and definitely not a paste.

Landry (1978), bringing a French perspective to the subject, lists among possible ingredients nigella (BLACK CUMIN), millet flour, and even dry cheese, and paints an evocative picture of the Egyptian fellaheen sprinkling the mixture on bread such as *pain baladi*, which they eat in the fields.

Duqqa is commonly sold on the streets of Cairo in little cones of twisted paper; the simplest version being just a mixture of dried crushed mint, salt, and pepper. In Near Eastern markets in the USA, a brand of 'dokka' is sold consisting of parched wheat flour flavoured with cumin and caraway, to be mixed with oil and used as a dip.   HS

DURIAN *Durio zibethinus*, a tropical fruit notorious for its taste and smell, either or both of which may provoke reactions ranging from revulsion to adulation.

The large oval fruit grows on a tall tree native to W. Malaysia and cultivated elsewhere in SE Asia. 'Duri' is the Malay word for spike, and the tree takes its name

(*cont. on page 263*)

A term of uncertain origin which first appeared in print at the beginning of the 17th century, although the object it denotes—a small and usually globular mass of boiled or steamed dough—no doubt existed long before that. A dumpling is a food with few, indeed no, social pretensions, and of such simplicity that it may plausibly be supposed to have evolved independently in the peasant cuisines of various parts of Europe and probably in other parts of the world too. Such cuisines feature soups and stews, in which vegetables may be enhanced by a little meat. Dumplings, added to the soup or stew, are still, as they were centuries ago, a simple and economical way of extending such dishes.

The dough for most dumplings has always been based either on a cereal, whichever was the staple in a given region (oats, wheat, maize, etc.), or on one of the vegetables from which a bread dough can be made or partly made (potato, pulses, etc.). Other ingredients for the basic and original dumpling were few: salt, water, and perhaps leaven. If herbs were added, for flavour or colour, this did not compromise their simplicity. Green dumplings, dumplings with herbs, were quite common. In Scotland a green suet dumpling used to be made in spring with dandelion and nettle leaves, hawthorn buds, and anything else that came to hand. Spinach was often used in a similar way, e.g. in Germany and Austria.

However, despite its simplicity, the humble dumpling, or anyway the range of foods to which the name is applied, has evolved in the course of time from the prototypes into something more complex. A first step was provided by the filled dumpling, in which the dough encloses something else, for example apple in an apple dumpling, and a sour Zwetschke cooking plum (its stone replaced by a lump of sugar) in the Austrian and Czech *Zwetschkenknödel*. The legitimacy of fruit-filled dumplings is rarely challenged; but it must be acknowledged that their existence takes the dumpling, at a single step, out of the role of supplement to a main dish and into the role of dish-in-itself.

Similar considerations apply to dumplings into which richer ingredients (such as finely minced liver in *Leberknödel*, the liver dumplings of S. Germany and Austria) have been incorporated. Yet it is no long step from them to the kind of product which reverses the proportions, being essentially a MEATBALL. In this connection see also KIBBEH and KOFTA, noting that a kibbeh from Iraq may be a meatball inside a semolina covering (which gives it some claim to be called a dumpling), whereas others have no such covering and at the most incorporate a little cereal as binder or extender. An object of the latter sort is not a true dumpling; it is but one of the numerous tribe of dumpling lookalikes, things which are neither dumplings nor English but have been called dumplings, when an English name for them has been required, on the basis of form and cooking method without regard to the third criterion, composition.

However, these excursions beyond the original meaning of the term are as nothing by comparison with what has happened in the Orient, where English-speakers, seeking a term which could be applied to various kinds of oriental filled pasta (see MANTOU; JIAOZI; etc.), unhappily chose 'dumpling'. This heinous excursion is explained at more length under DUMPLINGS OF ASIA.

Returning to Europe, it would be fair to say that dumplings are almost ubiquitous in that continent, but by no means of equal importance in the various countries. They are more popular in colder climates, for the obvious reason. But even there they vary considerably in popularity. It might be generally agreed that there are three regions in which they have flourished most: England, which English people like to think of as the home of the archetypal and most authentic dumpling; the much larger area of C. Europe (including Bavaria, Austria, Bohemia), which is one vast hotbed of Germanic dumplings; and the specialized habitat provided by Italy for GNOCCHI, so intimately linked with pasta and outside the common run of dumplings that they are treated separately. Each of the first two regions will be considered in turn.

ENGLAND

Early dumplings were probably balls of bread dough taken from the batch used to make bread. However, people soon began to make dumplings from other ingredients, e.g. suet or white bread. By 1747 Hannah Glasse could give no fewer than eight recipes for dumplings, of which two were for 'hard' dumplings made from plain flour and water, 'best boiled with a good piece of beef'; two were for apple dumplings; and others were for Norfolk dumplings, yeast dumplings, white bread dumplings, and suet dumplings. When she indicated size, she usually said 'as big as a turkey's egg'.

Norfolk is the chief dumpling county of Britain, but the history of its honourable (and plain) dumplings has been obscured by French intervention. The story told by DUMAS in his *Grand Dictionnaire de cuisine* (1873) that the Duke of Norfolk was fond of dumplings, and that they are named after him, is wrong, as is the recipe Dumas gives. Indeed, the recipe is so wildly wrong that it looks as though Dumas was the victim of a practical joker when he visited England, possibly the same person who told him that Yermouth [*sic*], home of bloaters, was in Ireland.

A good description of how Norfolk dumplings were and are made is given by Mrs Arthur Webb (*c*.1935):

The farmer's wife very skilfully divided a pound of dough (remember, just ordinary bread dough) into four pieces. These she weighed, and so cleverly had she gauged the size that they weighed approximately 4 oz each. She kneaded, and rolled them in a very little flour until they were quite round, then put them on a plate and slipped them into a large saucepan containing fast-boiling water. The saucepan lid was put back immediately, and then, when the water came to the boil once more, 15 minutes' rapid boiling was allowed for the dumplings.

Dumplings in Norfolk are not a sweet. They are a very substantial part of what might be the meat course, or they might serve as a meat substitute. In the villages I found that they were sometimes put into a very large pot and boiled on top of the greens; then they are called 'swimmer'.

Eliza Acton (1845), apparently referring to Norfolk dumplings, specified several accompaniments: wine sauce, raspberry vinegar, or sweetened melted butter with a little vinegar.

Suffolk dumplings, unlike those of Norfolk, are made of flour and water, without yeast. (Eliza Acton recommended adding milk to make a thick batter.) They are steamed or rapidly boiled, so that they rise well. They may be eaten with meat gravy, or with butter or syrup. They often include currants if intended as a sweet dish.

Oatmeal dumplings are common in N. Britain, where oats are widely grown. Derbyshire dumplings, relatively small, are made from equal amounts of wheat flour and oatmeal, with beef DRIPPING and onion; to be added to a beef stew half an hour before serving.

CENTRAL EUROPE

In the region of Bavaria (see GERMANY), AUSTRIA, and Bohemia (see CZECH AND SLOVAK REPUBLICS), the common material of dumplings is stale bread. This is broken into small pieces and soaked in water or milk, and combined with any available enriching ingredients: bacon, eggs, cheese, chopped liver, or herbs. There are sweet types stuffed with fruit. In some of the more refined kinds flour or semolina or (since the 19th century) potatoes are used in the basic mixture.

Another kind is the *Nockerl*, made from a softer dough of flour with butter, milk, and egg (or leftover noodle dough may be used). Because the dough is soft, it is not rolled into balls to make the dumplings; small pieces are picked off with the fingers and thrown into the boiling water (or the dough is spread on a *Nockerlbrett*, a thin wooden board from which little bits can be flipped into the water, using a knife). Small ones are sometimes formed by pressing the dough through a coarse wicker sieve, and used as garnishes in soup. This technique, the dough itself, and the name *Nockerl*, are clearly influenced by the Italian GNOCCHI. (*Salzburger Nockerln* are something different; not dumplings but sweet egg confections which defy any conventional classification.)

The *Dampfnudel* ('steam noodle') is interesting. This is a medium-sized German dumpling made of yeast dough, cooked in a shallow bath of milk in a tightly lidded pan. The heat transmitted through the bottom of the pan browns the underside of the dumpling, which rests on its bottom. The steam above the milk, slightly superheated by pressure due to the close-fitting lid, hardens and browns the top. The middle, surrounded by boiling milk, which transmits less heat to it than does steam, remains soft and extensible so that the dumpling rises and, when cooked, has a brown top and

bottom and a soft, white central zone. It is served with meat, or as a dessert with jam and butter or a sweet sauce.

Potato dumpling types are exemplified by *Kartoffelkloss*, small, light German dumplings of potato, flour, breadcrumbs, and egg. Another name for this dumpling is *Glitscher* ('slider') because it goes down easily. Other potato dumplings include the Russian *pampushka*, a dumpling made from a mixture of raw grated and cooked mashed potato enclosing a filling of cooked minced beef and onion or curd cheese, egg, and herbs. It is boiled in salted water and served with sour cream and onions.

See also CLOOTIE DUMPLING.

Dumplings of Asia

These are different from European ones. Indeed, what English-speakers in the Orient call dumplings are more like what would be called filled pasta in Europe. The Chinese type of dumpling, in particular, with its thin wrapper of wheat flour and water paste folded over the filling and pressed shut, bears a close resemblance to RAVIOLI.

Chinese records of dumplings go back at least as far as the Sung dynasty (AD 960–1279), when they were described as being sold (with other foods) from stalls much in the way that snacks are in modern China. MANTOU are among the best-known Chinese manifestations of the genre, but probably originated in C. Asia rather than in China itself.

Whatever the truth may be about their ultimate origin, this type of oriental filled 'dumpling' has spread westwards; it is met in Tibet as *momo*, in Russia as PEL'MENI (usually with a meat filling), and in Jewish cuisine as the similar KREPLACH.

In their home country, these Chinese dumplings take various forms. WONTON (a pun on the Chinese for 'chaos') are dumplings made from a wheat dough which is usually bought in prepared sheets, folded over a filling, most often of minced pork and onion, with the edges left untidy and wavy (hence the name).

JIAOZI (the word means 'corners') are small semicircular dumplings made by folding a circle of plain flour and water dough over a filling, usually savoury such as chopped pork and cabbage. The joint is pressed to seal each tightly before they are boiled. All the dumplings are put simultaneously into boiling water, which at once goes off the boil. It is brought back to the boil and cooked three times: this is said to make the dough firm.

In many parts of Asia the dumplings commonly met are **rice dumplings**.

T'ang t'uan (boiled ball) is a small Chinese dumpling made of a kneaded dough of glutinous rice. It has a filling, usually a savoury one such as pork and onion, and is cooked by the same method as jiaozi.

Another small Chinese dumpling made of glutinous rice flour, but this time with a sweet filling, is *yüan hsiao*. The filling, which must be of a fairly solid consistency (e.g. a mixture of crushed nuts and sesame seed, sugar, and fat), is damped and rolled in a tray of dry flour, and picks up a coating. Then it is boiled by the same method as for jiaozi. This sweet dumpling is traditionally eaten on the 'Festive Night' of the 15th day of the New Year, and that is what its name means.

Japan also has glutinous rice dumplings, MOCHI. For these, the dough is wrapped round fillings of, for example, red bean paste; or the dough itself can be made into little shapes and wrapped in cherry or oak leaves. In either case the dumplings are steamed. They are featured at the Japanese New Year; and it has been known for sumo wrestlers to be mustered to achieve a sufficiently strong initial pounding of the cooked rice.

Ondé ondé is the name of a small Indonesian sweet dumpling, also made of glutinous rice flour, which contains a knob of brown sugar; it is rolled in grated coconut after boiling.

One more example, this time using sago, comes from Thailand. This is *saku sai mooh*: small **sago dumplings** enclosing a filling of pork, onion, and groundnuts; cooked by steaming; served hot or cold.

---

from the hard, spiky shell which the fruit develops. A full-grown fruit may weigh 2 kg (5 lb) or more. Since the tree may be as high as 30 m (300') and the fruit drops off when ripe, it is wise to take care when walking near such trees in the durian season. Death by durian is not uncommon. (Another hazard at this time is the appeal the fallen, split fruit has for tigers and other wild animals.)

A durian in the **ripening stage** changes rapidly. While still on the tree it develops its famous odour, which has prompted many people to search for an accurate description. Comparisons have been made with the civet cat, sewage, stale vomit, onions, and cheese; while one disaffected visitor to Indonesia declared that the eating of the flesh was not much different from having to consume used surgical swabs.

However, others have expressed enthusiasm with equal vigour. Alfred Russel Wallace in his *Malay Archipelago* (1869) declared himself 'a confirmed durion eater', and went so far as to announce that 'If I had to fix on two (fruits) only as representing the perfection of the two classes, I should certainly chose the durion and the orange as the king and queen of fruits.' In what did this perfection consist? Here is Wallace's own description of the edible part of the fruit:

A rich butter-like custard highly flavoured with almonds gives the best general idea of it, but intermingled with it come wafts of flavor that call to mind cream-cheese, onion-sauce, brown-sherry, and other incongruities. Then there is a rich glutinous smoothness in the pulp which nothing else possesses, but which adds to its delicacy. It is neither acid, nor sweet, nor juicy, yet one feels the want of none of these qualities, for it is perfect as it is. It produces no nausea or other bad affect, and the more you eat of it the less you feel inclined to stop. In fact, to eat durions, is a new sensation worth a voyage to the East to experience.

Some have found that while the smell repels them, the flavour attracts. A strange synergistic effect causes the components of the smell to combine with the unsmelled but tasted substances to produce the characteristic rich, aromatic flavour. This increases until it becomes overpowering to all but the staunchest devotees of the fruit. Even Indonesians acknowledge that prolonged exposure to the smell may have negative effects, and as a result, the carriage of durians on public transport is forbidden. Even during its two days normal ripening time a durian becomes slightly alcoholic. The Javanese believe it to have APHRODISIAC qualities, and also impose a strict set of rules on what may or may not be consumed with the durian or shortly after. As with several other very strong fruits, it is considered particularly unwise to take sweet drinks such as coffee, as the effects could supposedly be fatal. In some parts of the region people bury durian deliberately in order to ferment them prior to consumption; this because they prefer their durians slightly on the high side, much as someone in the West might have a penchant for very aged blue cheese.

Patterns of **consumption** have changed. As it deteriorates swiftly, durian used to be eaten only in the region where it was grown. Now, with export by air possible, it is widely available. The procedure is to split open the shell, revealing the large seeds, each with a generous coating of sticky pulp surrounding it. This is gnawed or sucked off. Some people advise drinking water out of a segment of the shell afterwards, to counter the heating effect of the durian. In the Philippines too the fruits are used for many confectionery items (fruit bars, jams, various candies, types of nougat). A specialized and delicious product of Davao is magnolia durian ice cream.

Unripe durians may be cooked as a vegetable (but not in the Philippines, where all uses are sweet rather than savoury). Also durian is sometimes cooked and made into a sausage-shaped cake which retains some of its proper flavour and very little smell. Malaysians make both sugared and salted preserves from it. The large seeds are often boiled or roasted and eaten as nuts.

Among the uses of durian Wallace cites the following: as a fermented side dish called *tempoya*; mixed with rice and sugar as *lempog*; minced with salt and onions and vinegar as *boder*; made into a sauce or prepared with ice and syrup; and the seeds roasted, cut in slices, fried in coconut oil, and eaten with rice or coated in sugar for use as a sweetmeat. However, his enthusiasm and list of uses provoked an attack in a quasi-limerick which was printed in *Horticulture*, 9 (1973).

The durian—neither Wallace nor Darwin agreed on it.
Darwin said: 'may your worst enemies be forced to feed on it.'
Wallace cried 'It's delicious'.
Darwin replied 'I'm suspicious,
For the flavour is scented
Like papaya fermented,
After a fruit-eating bat has pee'd on it.'

DUTCH COOKERY i.e. that practised in the Netherlands (and closely connected with the Flemish-speaking part of BELGIUM), has shown great continuity since medieval times to the present, as befits people who can count conservatism among their numerous

Durian

virtues and who have not only conserved (against the encroaching sea) their precious agricultural land but have even enlarged it by creating new polders in the Zuyder Zee.

Although this is not the place to discuss the complex political history of the Low Countries in general or of the Netherlands in particular, mention must be made of one great event, the Reformation, because, when this put an end to religious paintings (of the Madonna and saints and so forth) in N. Europe, the great school of Dutch painters turned perforce to secular themes; and it is to this change that we owe the abundance of still lifes of food, paintings of market scenes, etc., which do so much to bring alive for us the foodways of the 16th and 17th centuries.

Nor is the influence of Dutch explorers and traders and the colonial period to be overlooked. The fact that INDONESIA was for so long a Dutch possession (until 1951) has left its mark on recent food history. The study by Eloise Smith van Niel (1997) of the Dutch colonial kitchen in Indonesia deals mainly with the other side of the coin, but touches on changes in the home country. These consist mainly in the presence of Indonesian restaurants, some few offering truly Indonesian fare but mostly providing a Dutch-style 'rijsttafel'.

There has not been much Indonesian influence on domestic cooking. However, on the takeaway front, Indonesian prepared foods—SAMBALS, SATAY, *loempia* (see LUMPIA) etc.—have become part of standard Dutch fare; and most butchers and poulterers sell strips of beef or chicken ready prepared and spiced for *Bami goreng* or *Nasi goreng*.

The conservatism of the Dutch in their kitchens was instilled in the female population by means of the popular cooking schools which were prominent in the first half of the 20th century, catering for the rapidly growing middle classes in cities throughout the country. The teachers developed a scientific approach in their courses, in which nutritional values were dominant and questions of palatability and pleasure were considered to be of secondary importance. The best known of all cookery-school cookbooks is *Eenvoudige berekende recepten* (Simple Calculated Recipes) by Martine Wittop Koning, first published in 1901 and going through 62 editions until 1952.

There are other classic Dutch cookery school manuals which were characteristic of the first half of the 20th century. These are very substantial and thorough cookery books, and a roll-call of them evokes in majestic fashion the principal cities of the kingdom: Amsterdam (which had two), Rotterdam, The Hague, etc. They have an honoured place in the long history of cookery books published in the Netherlands, a history which began (if one excludes books

published in what is now Belgium) in the 17th century and has now been comprehensively chronicled by Witteveen and Cuperus (1998).

As a group, these cookery school manuals appear to have no parallel in other countries, and they do serve to exemplify those qualities of solidity, patience, discrimination, and adherence to tradition which have helped to ensure that many kinds of Dutch produce are of the highest quality.

Until sometime after the Second World War most families in the Netherlands were large, and the country was not rich. Thus, most Dutch cooking was subsistence cookery, making the best use of the cheapest available local products. It was also customary to supplement the family's diet by fishing in the nearby canals, rivers, and lakes, and even the fishmongers generally supplied freshwater fish, including EEL (which, in smoked form, is one of the greatest Dutch delicacies). In recent years, however, there has been a noticeable change to seafood, due to pollution in the inland waterways.

Dutch eating habits generally followed the seasons, and there were specific winter dishes: *Boerekool met worst* (cabbage with sausage); *Stamppot* (mashed potatoes mixed with various vegetables especially brassica varieties); and also specific dishes for feast days, such as hot chocolate with *speculaasbrood*—spicy biscuits—on Sinterklaas Day, or *Olliebollen* (fried raisin yeast bread) and *Appelflappen* (apple turnovers) on New Year's Eve. The appearance of certain foods in the market, such as MUSSELS, the new HERRING, and game, would add their nuances to home cookery at their respective seasons.

Traditionally, the Dutch diet centred around potatoes, vegetables, and meat. In wintertime a meal could consist of one of the famous Dutch soups (*Erwtensoep*, a split pea soup; *Bruinebonensoep*, a brown bean soup) eaten with rye bread and bacon. Desserts were generally varieties of *pap* (gruel) made from oatmeal, semolina, tapioca, or pudding rice cooked in either milk or buttermilk. On Sundays, the *pap* would be thicker (*pudding*), with the addition of some luxury item such as vanilla and eaten with boudoir biscuits and perhaps a fruit sauce. A famous Sunday dessert was *Watergruwel* (pear tapioca cooked in the juice of berries with lemon peel, cinnamon, currants, and raisins, sweetened with sugar).

Dutch diet changed drastically during the years of the Second World War, when there was a great scarcity of foodstuffs and rationing was introduced. Winter 1944 is considered to be the low point of this century, when the Dutch people were reduced to eating, among other famine foods, BULBS (experienced by the young

Audrey Hepburn, as noted in that entry, in the form of bulb flour).

With the improving economic situation after the War, and the influx of people from the former colonies (e.g. about 35,000 Moluccans in 1947) and also guest workers from Italy and Spain, followed by others from Turkey, Morocco, and Cape Verde, new and exotic products appeared in the markets and shops, and food customs underwent some radical changes. If it would be true to say that the hallmarks of Dutch cooks are simplicity, quality, and a sort of conservatism which fends off gimmicks yet gives a slow and cautious welcome to beneficial innovations, then the passage of time will show which of these changes have come to stay and which have only enjoyed a temporary and superficial favour.

See also BANKETBAKKERIJ; EDAM; GOUDA; SPICE TRADE.

DUXELLES is cuisine French (not in standard French dictionaries) designating a mixture of chopped mushrooms sautéed in butter with onions and/or shallots and used as a garnish with many dishes.

Why this mixture is called a *duxelles* (or Duxelles) is the subject of much conjecture. One school argues that it was named after the Marquis d'Uxelles whose cook, La Varenne, wrote a popular cookery book in the 17th century (La Varenne himself, however, does not include a recipe for *duxelles* nor does he use this term).

A second school associates it with the town of Uxel in Brittany. These authors write *duxel* rather than *duxelle* but, unfortunately research looking into early atlases shows no reference to a town of this name in NW France (there is a town named 'Uxelles' in E. France and a hamlet of the same name in Burgundy).

To complicate matters, in the 18th century, dishes said to be *à la Duxelle* seem to characteristically contain crayfish (*écrevisses*) rather than mushrooms and, in what may be the earliest use of the term in a mushroom sense, Beauvilliers (1814) calls the preparation *La Ducelle* and describes not a mushroom garnish but a mushroom-based SAUCE. Around 1820 a revised edition of Viard's *Cuisinier impérial* contains a similar mushroom sauce called *La Durcelle* but it was not until the 1830s that Carême used the modern spelling in a mushroom preparation labelled *Sauce à la duxelle*.

The sauce becomes a 'dry' garnish (*Duxelles sèche*) in Escoffier's day (around 1900), and in the course of this century both its spelling and preparation have been standardized by chefs who consider it an indispensable component of classic French cuisine.

HY

EARS of some animals are good to eat, notably those of calf and PIG. The cartilaginous meat has to be softened by lengthy cooking, after which a crisp finish can be given to the ears by breadcrumbing and baking or grilling.

A German dish, *Erbensuppe mit Schweinsohren*, is a split pea soup with pig's ear. Some recipes for MOCK TURTLE SOUP use ears simmered and cut into strips.

EAST AFRICA is here taken to extend from Uganda, Kenya through Tanzania to Malawi and Zimbabwe, taking in also Zambia, Burundi, and Rwanda. For the Somali Republic, see HORN OF AFRICA. ANGOLA AND MOZAMBIQUE have their own entry, as does MADAGASCAR (MALAGASY REPUBLIC).

Apart from the coastal plains, most of the terrain of these countries is highland plateau, enjoying some of the best climates in Africa, free of the humidity of W. Africa and the aridity of the desert regions.

One of the most remarkable things about the food of the highland Africans of E. Africa is the almost total lack of meat in the diet, in spite of the abundant game and long tradition of breeding CATTLE. These were regarded as wealth, not food, and the famous Masai and related peoples lived almost entirely on milk products and the BLOOD of the animals. Others, before the introduction of MAIZE, lived mostly on MILLET, SORGHUM, and BANANAS with such greenstuffs as could be gathered.

The earliest foreign settlers were the Arabs who established colonies along the coast from about AD 700. They traded in slaves and ivory and introduced spices, ONIONS, AUBERGINES, and possibly even COCONUT. Arabic roots are evident in the widely used Kiswahili language but the Arabs seem to have made little impact on the cooking of the Africans, except that CAMEL hump is still eaten in Zanzibar, the island off the coast of Tanzania. The same applies to the Germans, who were the first European colonists in this part of Africa. The British scarcely had any more impact though they trained large numbers of African men, never women, in European cooking. There were complex traditions where women cooked only indoors within their own homes, while the men were responsible for open-air cooking such as grilling and barbecueing. But it was the British encouragement to Asians to settle in E. Africa which affected local cooking most. Few households now do not possess a large tin of curry powder, *mchuzi*.

The most common staple food is a thick porridge known variously as *ugali, sadza, nsima,* or *posho* made from maize or finger millet. *Sukuma wiki*, which means 'leftovers', is a Kenyan dish made from cooked meat, tomatoes, capsicums, and green leaves, usually served with *ugali*. A Kikuyu dish, *Irio*, often served with curried chicken, is made from beans, maize, and potatoes or CASSAVA mashed to a thick pulp. The local green bananas, green when ripe, are also a popular starch when boiled in banana leaves and mashed. They feature in the Ugandan dish of *Matoke n'yama*, literally bananas and meat, which is flavoured with tomatoes.

Cassava and YAMS are also grown, though not as widely as in W. Africa. As elsewhere in Africa, the starch is regarded as 'real food' and the relishes as accompaniments. The COWPEA is also an important source of protein among those who do not eat much meat or fish. BEANS feature as part of most daily diets and in such dishes as *Janjalo muchuzi* of Uganda which has red kidney beans with fish, onions, and tomato. E. Africans also eat a large amount of green leaves, especially those of AMARANTH, SESAME, OKRA, cowpea, and PUMPKIN; these are often cooked with peanut (see GROUNDNUT) paste. As in most of Africa, BAOBAB leaves are used as a vegetable and dried as a flavouring.

Much of the excellent seafood taken from coastal waters is salted and dried and sent inland. One of the biggest catches on the coast is the SHARK known as *papa*, which is mostly dried. TURTLE meat and soup were once very popular. The Asian influence means that many fish dishes are cooked with coconut milk, which is a more commonly used ingredient in E. Africa than in the central and western countries.

The many lakes supply numerous species of fish; both TILAPIA and CATFISH (*chambo* and *mlamba* respectively in Malawi) are farmed in many areas and now exported.

European hunters found a paradise in the mountains of E. Africa. Although many of the animals are now protected there is plenty of game and ANTELOPE farming programmes have been started.

Insects such as the red LOCUST, CRICKETS, GRASSHOPPERS, and flying ANTS are collected in season and either fried with salt to make popular snacks or dried for later use. *Imbrasia epimethea*, cousin to the mopane worm (see WORMS) of southern Africa, known here as *madora*, and the CATERPILLARS known as *harati* are also popular snacks.

Milk products and honey are an important part of the diet and many cheeses are now made, including adaptations of European cheeses.

STREET FOOD, the cheapest form of eating in most of Africa, is likely to include the Indian fried pastries called *sambusas* (see SAMOSA); *mandazi* (a sort of DOUGHNUT or FRITTER); grilled corn cobs, rice and coconut pancakes; and *mkate mayai*, a fried pancake filled with minced meat and egg. *N'yama choma*, almost a national dish in Kenya, are kebabs of goat usually served with a mash of green banana, washed down with the local beer.   JM

EASTER FOODS are primarily those of Easter Sunday, the day on which Jesus rose from the dead, a day of special rejoicing for Christians, who rejoice too at reaching the end of the long Lenten fast. This time also marks the beginning of spring, the season of renewal, and a cause for general rejoicing. The concept of renewal/rebirth is responsible for the important role played by the EGG in Easter celebrations, a role which no doubt antedates Christianity.

There are also special foods associated with other days in the Easter calendar (see LENT; PANCAKE; FRITTER; CARLING), but these are mostly connected with fast day fare rather than with feasting.

In Europe, there is a general tradition, not confined to Christians, that Easter is the time to start eating the season's new LAMB, which is just coming onto the market then. For Christians there is the added symbolic significance that Jesus is regarded as the lamb of God. In Britain, a leg, shoulder, or saddle is roasted at this time and served with new potatoes and mint sauce. For the French, a roast leg of lamb, the *gigot pascal* (*pascal* and the English paschal refer equally to the Jewish PASSOVER and Christian Easter), is the traditional Easter Sunday lunch. In Italy, too, and Greece baby lamb or kid (see GOAT), plainly roasted, is a favourite Easter dish.

Easter breads, cakes, and biscuits are a major category of Easter foods, perhaps especially noticeable in the predominantly Roman Catholic countries of S. and C. Europe (and in E. Europe where the influence of the Greek and Russian Orthodox churches hold sway), but prominent too in N. Europe and in Christian countries or communities outside Europe. Traditional breads are laden with symbolism in their shapes, which may make reference to Christian faith—crosses, fish, and lambs—or be relics from pagan practices—hares, eggs, and the cylinder shapes of E. European breads. In general, they are not as rich as the Christmas breads (see CHRISTMAS FOODS), using less butter, sugar, and fruit, although eggs are freely used.

In England breads or cakes flavoured with bitter TANSY juice used to be popular Easter foods, but are no longer made. SIMNEL CAKE has come to be regarded as an Easter speciality, although it was not always so. The most popular English Easter bread is the hot cross bun (see BUN), the small spiced breads traditionally baked on Good Friday, and the only English breads to retain the cross, traditionally cut in rising dough 'to let the devil fly out', after the Reformation.

In Scandinavia coffee breads and cakes are baked in special Easter shapes. The Finns make an interesting Easter bread which they call *Pääsiäisleipä*. Based on a mixture of wheat and rye flour, enriched with cream, butter, eggs, raisins and almonds, flavoured with cardamom and lemon zest, it is traditionally baked in a milking pail, giving a cylindrical loaf.

The most famous Russian Easter bread, *kulich*, also has a tall narrow shape. This shape is Slavic and of great antiquity; see BABA and SAVARIN. The *kulich* is based on a baba dough, with more sugar, plus additions of candied peel, almonds, raisins, and

saffron. The bulging top is iced and decorated, usually with Cyrillic letters standing for 'Christ is risen'. Traditionally the *kulich* is taken to be blessed at midnight mass on the eve of Easter Sunday. In some families it replaces bread for the entire Holy Week. It is served with PASKHA, a sweetened confection based on curd cheese.

In Georgia there is CHOEREK, enriched with sour cream, butter, and egg, flavoured with aniseed (often also with vanilla and MAHLAB, from black cherry kernels) and made into snail shapes or braided wreaths.

In Germany and Switzerland, Easter gives the bakers an opportunity to show off their skills in baking rich breads in elaborate plaits and other shapes. Some towns have specialities, such as the *Bremener Osterklaben*, a loaf similar to the Dresden STOLLEN. Other specifically Easter breads are *Osterkarpfen* (a dough fish with halved almonds representing scales); *Eier im Nest* (a yeast dough nest with coloured eggs in it); and *Osterhase*, the Easter hare, who is said to hide coloured eggs in the garden on the morning of Easter Sunday. Sarah Kelly (1985) suggests that many or all of these items may have migrated north from Greece or Italy. Italian influence also gives the *Taube* (dove—see below).

The Greek *lambrópsomo*, an almond-topped Greek Easter bread that breaks the Lenten fast, is rich in eggs and butter, two foods forbidden during Lent. They are shiny loaves with decorations of spring flowers, leaves, or buds shaped in dough. Red eggs, signifying both rebirth and the blood of Christ, are an important part of the decoration. Another festive bread, made at Easter and also for the New Year, braided and variously flavoured according to regional preferences, is *tsoureki* (see CHOEREK); it too is topped with one or more red eggs. Other loaves are made in a cloverleaf shape said to symbolize the Trinity.

Symbolic eggs also occur in Italian, Corsican, and Portuguese Easter breads, indeed all over the place.

The Italian *colomba* (dove) is made of PANETTONE dough baked in a vaguely dove-shaped tin and topped with candy sugar. Italian *pignola* bread, an enriched bread including pine nuts, sultanas, lemon zest, and candied orange peel, is made into rolls, coated with ground hazelnuts, and sprinkled with more pine nuts.

In contrast, the Castilian Spanish Easter bread, *hornazo*, is a large savoury loaf based on plain household bread dough, enriched with olive oil and bacon fat, and containing pieces of *chorizo* (see SAUSAGES OF SPAIN AND PORTUGAL), other pork products, and hard-boiled eggs.

In France there is a special biscuit, called *agneau pascal* (Easter lamb), which is made in the shape of a recumbent lamb, with a meringue topping to represent the wool.

(LM)

READING: Constance Cruickshank (1959).

EAT an apparently simple verb which one would suppose to have simple equivalents in all languages. However, one example will suffice to show that this is not so.

The Maya languages (see MAYA FOOD) divide up the world of edibles in quite a different fashion from English categories (flesh food, fruits and vegetables, breadstuff, etc.). Thus in the Tzeltal language the verb 'to eat' is used only when asking the question: 'What are you eating?' Otherwise the verb differs according to the substance being eaten. One verb is used for things that are chewed and the pulp spat out, as is done with sugar cane and maize stalks. Another verb is used for things that melt in the mouth, like candy. Still another verb is used when bread, in the broad sense, is being eaten, and yet another for the consumption of meat, mushrooms, and chilli. Finally, there are two verbs the use of which depends on the texture of the matter being eaten. One verb applies to mushy, gelatinous, overripe, and overcooked things, of which brains, bananas, and avocados might be examples. The other verb is appropriate for discrete, firm objects, among them young maize, popped maize, beans, and squash seeds. A food such as avocado might move from one category to another as it ripens or according to how it is cooked, and could thus partner either of the two verbs.

Other Maya languages treat the comestible universe in roughly the same manner; and the phenomenon may also be observed in some other cultures.   SC

ECCLES CAKES small English cakes similar to BANBURY CAKES, except that they are normally round in shape and the filling has fewer ingredients; currants, wheat flour, brown sugar, butter and vegetable fat, milk, and salt are standard.

The cakes take their name from the small town on the outskirts of Manchester where they were first made and named. Mrs Raffald (1769), herself from Manchester and the author of one of the best cookery books of the 18th century, had given a recipe for 'sweet patties' which may well have been the confections from which Eccles cakes evolved. Mrs Raffald's filling included meat (from a calf's foot), apple, candied peel, and currants, an assemblage compatible with what the term mincemeat (see MINCE PIE) used to mean.

The first mention of Eccles cakes by name seems likely to have occurred at the end of the 18th century when a certain James Birch was making them. An apprentice of his,

William Bradburn, had set up a rival operation by about 1813. Evelyn Vigeon (1993), in her brilliant and comprehensive history of these cakes, describes the confrontation:

James Birch advertised that he was the original Eccles cake maker *removed from across the way*, while William Bradburn retaliated with an advertisement claiming that his shop was *the only old original Eccles Cakes Shop. Never removed.* This rivalry was to the advantage of both manufacturers over the following century since visitors would often buy cakes from both shops to be sure they had indeed tasted the *original* one.

The same author traces the later history of these and other Eccles cake establishments, and provides details of some recipes published in the 19th century. She believes that early Eccles cakes may well have differed from those known now, both in shape (some at least were sold cut in squares) and the nature of the pastry (puff or flaky pastry is now used), and ingredients for the filling. She points out that the fact that Eccles cakes were being exported abroad by 1818 suggests very good keeping qualities, 'so they may well have included spirits such as brandy and rum in the same way as the nineteenth century Banbury cake'.

Chorley cakes are a variation of Eccles cakes, usually somewhat plainer.

ÉCHAUDÉ a French term whose basic meaning is 'scalded' but which is also the name for a kind of cake made by cooking the dough twice, first by scalding it and then by baking it. It takes various forms. Savoyard bakers, for example, produce *riouttes*; these unusual items of patisserie are very hard and dry, shaped in a ring so that they can be carried on a stock or hung on a string. They are dunked in red wine or hot breakfast drinks before being eaten.

According to Berkenbaum and Mahoux (1994), *échaudés* (which were mentioned in a 13th-century document as 'panes qui dicuntur [breads which are called] eschaudati') were one of the medieval ancestors of the PRETZEL.

ÉCLAIR a small pastry made by piping choux PASTRY in fingers; when baked, the pastry is split in half. French *éclairs au chocolat* are filled with chocolate-flavoured *crème pâtissière* and iced with chocolate fondant ICING; a similar version flavoured with coffee and topped with coffee glacé icing is also made. English éclairs are more likely to be filled with whipped cream, often vanilla flavoured, and the top dipped in melted chocolate.

Éclairs are used to make a *religieuse* ('nun'). A base of the sweet pastry which the French call *pâte sucrée* (see under shortcrust

in PASTRY) with a mound of *crème Chiboust* (*crème pâtissière* with egg whites) or chocolate MOUSSE in the middle is surrounded with chocolate and coffee éclairs propped vertically, and stripes of whipped cream piped between them. The whole is topped with a cream bun, and vaguely resembles a short, plump nun in a habit.

A number of pastries closely related to éclairs are made from choux pastry. See, for example, CREAM PUFF and PROFITEROLES.

There is also a savoury cheese éclair, baked with a grated cheese topping, then filled with a cheese-flavoured cream sauce. Unlike a sweet éclair, this type may be eaten hot.   (LM)

ECUADOR inserted like a wedge between COLOMBIA and PERU, and known as the 'Republic of the equator', is influenced more by the high Andes that split it from north to south than any tropic. 'It is always wise to judge people by their altitude,' the traveller Paul Theroux was counselled, and in Ecuador the *tierra caliente* of the sea coast, where Panama hats are made, and bananas are a chief export—supplanting COCOA when that crop was ravaged by disease at the turn of the century—has a tropical character distinct from the cool, high sierra and volcanic mountains where the capital Quito lies. A third region is the jungle beyond the Andes, source of the Amazon, occupied by the Jívaro Indians, and subject of long border disputes with Ecuador's neighbours, and a fourth, the Galapagos (annexed in 1832), whose TORTOISES were the common fare of American whalers in Darwin's time, and whose IGUANA were acceptable meat, 'for those whose stomachs soar above all prejudices' (*The Voyage of the Beagle*).

There are many common factors between Peru and Ecuador, not least the heritage of INCA rule and Spanish administration. Ecuador was part of the viceroyalty of Peru, and the Inca Atahualpa had his capital in Quito. Quecha is the dominant Indian language of both republics, although the Inca never managed wholly to absorb the coastal zone.

The similarity extends to their food and cooking: recipes like CEVICHE have equal currency, and Elisabeth Lambert Ortiz (1984) suggests they are distinguished from the other Latin American versions by their use of Seville orange juice. It is often served with corn (see MAIZE) and SWEET POTATO.

Ingredients, too, are common to both. On the coast, there is great dependence on BANANAS and green PLANTAINS. They are turned into crisps; banana flour is used in breads and cakes; and leaves are used as wrapping for TAMALES of soaked, dried corn. POTATOES, by contrast, have spread outwards from the Andes, and various *causas* and *ocopas* (*causas* made with mashed potatoes, *ocopa* with boiled) are as common here as they are in Peru. *Llapingachos*, potato cakes stuffed with cheese that are served with fried eggs in the sierra, may come with fried bananas on the coast, or with a sauce made from ground peanuts (see GROUNDNUTS) and TOMATO—a recipe also found as accompaniment to flank beef baked with potatoes. Typically, a LOCRO in Ecuador is made not with corn or wheat, but potatoes. Peanuts are used to give texture as well as taste.

The varied cuisine of the tropical coast is often contrasted to the sparer style of the sierra, Elisabeth Lambert Ortiz speaks of its 'combining foods not usually put together, pork stuffed with shrimps, for example', as well as benefiting from the rich luxuriance of materials and a taste for nuts other than peanuts. Almonds, well known in many S. American countries, are thought to be especially good in Ecuador, where almond sauces tend to be served with almost everything, including eggs and shrimp.

The importance of the GUINEA PIG in Ecuador has been the subject of a survey by Archetti (1997), which is a model example of the anthropological approach to food, relating its consumption at feasts to, among other things, Ecuadorian beliefs in the realm of hot/cold opposition and humoral theory (see FOUR HUMOURS).

Ecuador shares with Peru an affection for *ají* (CHILLI), though Ecuadorian cooking is not as fiery as that, for example, of S. Peru. It has taken from its northern neighbour Colombia a taste for using ANNATTO to flavour lard or oil.   TJ

EDAM a cheese named after a small port on the Ijsselmeer north of Amsterdam, is for many people the archetypal Dutch cheese. It is always spherical. The cheeses for export are coated with red wax, which makes them instantly recognizable. The inside is pale yellow.

Edam, GOUDA, and Friesland cheese all date back to the early Middle Ages. It is said that Edam was exported to England in the 8th century AD; but the first certain information is that by 1250 cheeses were a major manufacture and commodity all over the green grasslands centred on the markets at Gouda and Alkmaar (near Edam) and at Harlem. Cheeses were becoming a major export at that time, by land via the Rhine, and by sea through the ports.

At some stage Edam became distinguished from Gouda cheese by its texture, shape, and later its colour, although not its fat content which was the same until the 19th century. The pastures around the village of Edam are said to give the milk special properties, and perhaps encourage the formation of a firm

curd early in the making, which can be moulded into a ball. For this reason, flat wheels of Gouda and round wooden-moulded Edams (made in the helmet-shaped mould called a *kaaskop*) were distinguished in the famous and picturesque Alkmaar market where they were already being sold in the 16th century. Later, merchants started rubbing the round cheeses with rags soaked in vermilion dye to distinguish them yet more clearly for export.

Modern Edam, now a semi-skim milk cheese, is not just the one, young and bland, cheese which is so widely known, but a whole family of cheeses. There is a green-waxed Edam (with FINES HERBES); a mahogany-coloured one (with peppercorns); and a cumin-flavoured one in orange wax. Mature Edam (kept six months before sale) comes in a black wax jacket and is dryer and firmer than the others. There is an 11% fat type and a vegetarian one, both in the familiar red jackets.

Edam is made today all over the Netherlands and accounts for a quarter of cheese production. The standard-sized export Edams are 13 cm (5") in diameter and weigh 1.65 kg (3.5 lb). There are also larger sizes: Commissie and Middlebare.

EEL a name primarily applied to fish of the genus *Anguilla*, which are born and die in the oceans but pass most of their lives in fresh water, as explained on the next page. However, the term is also properly applied

to various marine fish which belong to the same order and have similarly shaped bodies: see CONGER EEL and MORAY EEL. The term also crops up in the names of some fish of other orders, e.g. the eel-pout (mutton-fish in the USA, quite good but not much eaten) and SAND-EEL, which share some of the characteristics of true eels. (Cusk eels and catfish eels are not true eels, but species of fish which bear some resemblance to eels, although more to CUSK and CATFISH respectively.)

Freshwater *Anguilla* eels, of which there are 15 species, are thought to have originated in the warm waters of the Indo-Pacific, but now occur in all five continents. The species differ in minor respects: size, disposition of fins, feeding habits, rate of growth, etc. But the two Atlantic species, which are the ones which have been most extensively studied, may be taken as typical, and this entry is focused on them. A few of the others are:

- *A. japonica*, which occurs in the temperate regions of E. Asia, although its spawning ground has not been established;
- *A. australis*, the short-finned eel of Australian waters;
- *A. reinhardtii*, the long-finned eel of Australian waters;
- *A. nebulosa*, the African mottled or Indian long-finned eel.

Anguilla anguilla is the species of Europe, N. Africa, and the Mediterranean. *A. rostrata*, a smaller eel, is found from the

EELS IN JAPAN

Eels have been eaten in Japan since antiquity, and they have always been regarded as a particularly nutritious food. It is recorded that a celebrated thief called Nihonzaemon, who was executed in 1747, was able to see in the dark and that he attributed this to a large consumption of eels. Since they are rich in vitamin A, the claim may have been true.

Most of the eels consumed in Japan are farmed. When farming began, towards the end of the 19th century, the eels were raised in artificial ponds, but now they are kept in indoor tanks under controlled temperature, and are given factory-made compound food.

Eel farmers have to contend with yearly fluctuations in the catches of elvers as they come up from the sea. There was a serious shortage of elvers in 1969, since when elvers of the European species have been imported from France.

By far the most popular way of eating eels in Japan is *kabayaki*. Indeed it is so popular that it has ousted all other methods that existed in the past and has come to be practically a synonym of eel. Opinions vary as to the origins of *kabayaki* but it seems to have been made in the late 18th and early 19th centuries, and to have been firmly established as a method of preparation by the mid-19th century. This is a dish prepared only by specialists and never at home. In Japan restaurants which serve nothing but eels, especially *kabayaki*, are common. The liver is made into a special dish, and there is a special eel soup.

Smoked eel is not prepared in Japan, partly because smoking is a method rarely employed in Japan (this is explained by the fact that traditional Japanese architecture does not have a chimney), and partly because *kabayaki* is so successful that it has virtually ousted all other methods.   KA

W. Indies to Newfoundland. Both species spawn in the vicinity of the Sargasso Sea; that is where the eggs hatch out and the resulting larvae commence their westward or eastward journeys. Those of *A. rostrata* have the shorter, westward journey, whereas the larvae of *A. anguilla* have a three-year eastwards voyage across the Atlantic ahead of them. So far as is known, none takes a wrong turning, presumably because their spawning grounds are situated in the right places for catching the right currents.

When the European eels arrive off the European coast they are transparent ELVERS and it is in this form that they ascend the chosen rivers. They will usually spend between six and twelve years in their new freshwater home (although some may live there for several decades). At a certain point they will change colour from grey to dark yellow, and then subsequently from yellow to silver. It is as silver eels that they proceed downstream towards the sea on their last journey, which takes them out into the Atlantic and back to the Sargasso Sea, where they spawn and perish.

This is a surprising lifecycle, the details of which have been well described by Moriarty (1978), who also records much information about the various methods of catching eels (spears, combs, wicker traps, wooden box traps, nets, etc.), their habits (which include resting in burrows, unlike most other fish), and the remarkable legends which have gathered around them. Some tales which might appear to be legends have a foundation in fact. Thus there is no doubt about the existence of 'eel balls', spherical clumps composed of scores of small eels knotted tightly together; nor about the perambulations on dry land of eels looking for a meal of peas, confirmed in these terms by a writer whom Moriarty cites:

Further observations on the eel's liking for green peas were provided by the Dowager Countess of Hamilton early in the nineteenth century. The eels from Lake Hedenlunda wandered into the fields at night and ate pea pods, making a smacking sound with their lips. Close investigations showed that they ate only the soft and juicy outer skin of young pods and did not gnaw through them.

The farming of eels is carried out in various places, including Italy (especially at Comacchio) and on a large scale in Japan (see box).

Appreciation of eels varies enormously from country to country. For example, they are little appreciated in N. America, except where French influence is important, whereas in Britain, Belgium, the Netherlands, Denmark, and Italy they are highly esteemed. In Japan there is such remarkable enthusiasm that a description of Japanese ways with eel is given in a box.

The flesh of the eel is rich in fat, too much fat for some people although the problem is

less if smoked eel (best from the Netherlands) is eaten. For dishes of fresh eel, there are various popular favourites: Jellied eel (England), *Anguille au vert* (Belgium), *Hamburger Aalsuppe* (Hamburg eel soup), etc. Less well known are Danish recipes for baking eel on top of a loaf of bread, so that the bread balances the fat meat of the eel. A similar tradition in Zeeland calls for bread rolls to be baked with eel inside, the result being called *paling broodjes*.

EGG (*see page 270*)

EGYPT has a recorded history which stretches back for millennia, further than CLASSICAL GREECE. The records which survive and which throw light on Egyptian food in ancient times include written documents, wall-paintings, and reliefs in tombs. Many tomb paintings showing food production and preparation were intended to ensure a plentiful supply for the deceased in the netherworld; the service which they render to food historians thousands of years later has been a by-product of religious attitudes. All this is well explained by Darby, Ghalioungui, and Grivetti (1977) in their aptly named book *Food: The Gift of Osiris*. The conclusions to be drawn from this mass of evidence are well summarized in a slim volume by Hilary Wilson (1988).

Wilson's book is particularly good reference for checking on basic questions such as what use was made of game animals and birds; what evidence about the species of fish available in Dynastic (3050–332 BC) and Pre-dynastic (before 3050 BC) times is available from archaeological sites; what cooking oils were used (the oldest royal food list, from the 6th dynasty Pyramid of Unas, included five kinds of oil); what was done with dairy foods in ancient times; what spices seem to have been in regular use; and what an Egyptian baker tending his bread oven looked like. In addition, Wilson has a particularly interesting chapter on the 'many surviving representations of Egyptian kitchens, notably in the Sixth Dynasty tomb of Ti and Saqqara, the tomb models of Meket-Re from the Eleventh Dynasty and the Twentieth Dynasty tomb of Ramesses III'. It is clear that, as one would expect, most domestic cookery was carried out in the open air or on a roof (practices which continue) and that the basic apparatus was a sort of concave pottery hearth in which a fire could be got going to heat various utensils placed above it. Wilson's paragraph on these utensils serves to show how much is known about them:

The usual domestic stove was cylindrical and of clay, with an arched stoke-hole, a shape so familiar that it was used as the hieroglyph for the

consonant G. The butchery model from Meket Re's tomb includes a stove with a crenellated top which allowed smoke to escape around the edges of a pan resting on it. Several cooking pot shapes may be identified from relief and painting. 'Frying pans' were wok-shaped with lug or loop handles. Pots for braising, or preparing such dishes as porridge, curved inwards at the top to reduce loss through evaporation. Large stew pans, shown full of joints of meat, had straight sides and flat bases. In ordinary kitchens of all periods, cooking pots were made of unglazed Nile clay, sometimes with a burnished slip coating. Wealthier households might use copper vessels or, in later periods, bronze.

If one turns from these works about ancient Egypt to an account of food in 19th-century Egypt by Lane (5th edn 1860), and then to a book of more recent times, notably that by Claudia Roden (1985), one thing stands out: there has been a remarkable degree of continuity in Egyptian foodways. A further lesson from the last-named book is that Egyptian foodways are connected by multiple strands with those of the Middle East generally (see ARABIAN FOOD, LEBANON AND SYRIA, JORDAN). This reflects in part the Arab and Turkish conquests, which did so much to establish the general repertoire of Arab and Middle Eastern food in Egypt, as elsewhere. It was in the 7th century that Islamic influence became dominant, bringing with it inevitably some changes in the cuisine, which became even more noticeable later when the Arabs introduced Persian-style dishes (e.g. meat stews incorporating fruit). When the Turks conquered Egypt early in the 16th century they introduced many more new dishes, including those using FILO pastry and many sweet items. However, these introductions mainly affected the upper and middle classes, and their impact on the mass of the population was negligible; the latter remained faithful, perforce, to a diet closely resembling that of their forebears in Pharaonic times. Breads, for example, have little changed. *Eish baladi*, the everyday Egyptian bread, is a round flatbread forming a pocket in the centre. It is often sprinkled with the characteristic spice mixture DUQQA. (The more expensive *eish shami*, 'Syrian bread', differs from it in being made partly of refined flour.)

A list of national dishes of Egypt would certainly include two items: FUL MEDAMES and the soup MELOKHIA. These and FALAFEL (the broad-bean version) are particularly Egyptian, as is pickled turnip, coloured pink by beetroot. So are PIGEON dishes; every Egyptian village has its pigeon tower and pigeons are perhaps more prominent in Egyptian markets than in any others. Some might add to the list one or more of the egg dishes which are of great antiquity. Claudia Roden (1985) has a charming passage about

(*cont. on page 271*)

Egg

The astonishing and unintentional gift from birds to human beings, the acme of food packaging, and a prime resource of occidental and oriental cooks alike. It is also the ultimate measure of ignorance and incompetence in the kitchen; 'he/she can't even boil an egg,' she/he will say, whether fondly or resentfully.

A reference to 'an egg', with no qualification, is assumed almost everywhere to mean a hen's egg, which is what this essay is about. For other eggs, see DUCK, OSTRICH, QUAIL. The hen's egg is usually the one which carries symbolic significance (the renewal of life, e.g. in spring festivals and EASTER FOODS). Symbolic meanings and folklore and associated topics are admirably dealt with by Venetia Newall (1971).

EGGSHELLS

Whether they are white or brown or speckled is immaterial to the cook. What does matter is that they are porous. One consequence of this is that eggs may absorb unwanted odours, a risk to which textbooks often call attention but which in practice seems to be slight. Another is that the carbon dioxide which begins to be formed within the egg as soon as it is laid can get out. Loss of carbon dioxide increases alkalinity and causes a slight diminution in the protein content of the egg. Egg processors prevent this by dipping their cleaned eggs in a special colourless and tasteless machine oil which seals the pores of the shell. By this means they also prevent another undesirable development, which is a gradual loss of moisture from within the egg and a corresponding increase in the size of the air pocket. They also, no doubt unwittingly, make it impossible to execute some kinds of egg cookery which are typical of the Middle East, notably 'hamine' eggs, in which whole eggs are simmered overnight, very gently, with oil and onions, whose flavour permeates the contents. A more exotic example is provided by *Œufs à la constantinopolitaine*, a recipe given by Mrs Leyel and Olga Hartley (1925), which calls for cooking eggs in their shells very slowly for at least twelve hours in a mixture of olive oil and Turkish coffee. The mixture eventually penetrates the shells, making the whites amber and the yolks orange and imparting a flavour of chestnuts.

There is one recipe which is unusual in that it involves the consumption of the eggshells. It is given by Dr Fernie (1905), in the guise of a tonic:

For delicate persons of all ages, the following preparation, which will contain egg shells in solution, has been found most singularly useful. Take six fresh eggs, six lemons, half a pound of castor sugar, and half a pint of white rum. Put the eggs in their shells inside a jar, without injuring the shells, peel the lemons, and, after removing their pith, squeeze the fresh juice over the eggs, then lay above them the rind and the pulp. Cover the jar lightly, and put it in a cool place for seven days, not forgetting to shake it well on each day. At the end of that time strain through muslin, when it will be found that the lemon juice has dissolved the eggshells. Add the sugar, and the rum; then bottle and cork it tightly. A wineglassful taken each morning before breakfast is the full dose, but at first it may be desirable to give only half this quantity.

Since the shell of an egg, surprisingly, constitutes a tenth of the whole, and since it contains a lot of calcium and even a little protein, this can be represented as an economical procedure for those with access to a free supply of rum.

EGG PROTEINS

These are what make an egg so important a source of nutrition, and such a versatile ingredient for the cook. Consider the composition of an egg, as shown in the table.

	Water	Protein	Fat	Ash
White	87.77%	10.00%	0.05%	0.82%
Yolk	49.00%	16.70%	31.90%	1.9%

It will be apparent that the white, apart from its large water content, is almost pure PROTEIN; and that the yolk contains proportionately less water, more protein, and much more fat. White and yolk can therefore be expected to, and do, behave differently when cooked. Moreover, the proteins in the yolk are not the same as those in the white, and coagulate at a distinctly higher temperature.

(Many books refer to egg white as 'albumen', which has the same meaning. However, this term can be confusing because there is also the word 'albumin' which refers to a class of proteins, all soluble in water, which includes albumen and others too.)

The protein in egg whites starts to coagulate in the temperature range 55–60 °C (131–40 °F) and definitely coagulates at about 65 °C (150 °F) or a little less. Those of egg yolks begin to thicken at 65 °C (150 °F) and coagulate at just over 70 °C (158 °F). Thus the yolk always sets after the white, whether an egg is being boiled (when this would be bound to happen anyway because the heat reaches the yolk later than the white) or being fried.

METHODS OF COOKING EGGS

The **poaching** of eggs is a subject best introduced by the eccentric Dr Kitchiner (1818) who has this to say as a preface to the mysterious 'Moost Aye's receipt to Poach Eggs': 'The Beauty of a Poached Egg, is to have the yolk seen blushing through the white, which should only be just sufficiently hardened, to form a transparent Veil for the Egg.'

However, 'Moost Aye', if there was such a person, omitted one important step in the preparation of an aesthetically satisfying poached egg. A little vinegar must be added to the boiling water before the egg goes in. The reason for this is that the acid promotes coagulation and reduces the tendency for long streamers of egg white to form. It is also helpful to whirl the water round and then break the egg into the centre of the whirlpool.

(Many people have 'egg-poachers' which consist of one or several shallow metal containers, each of a size to take one egg and fitting into a larger container in which water is boiled. The small containers are buttered and the eggs broken into them. The results are quite pleasing but are not, strictly speaking, poached eggs. Indeed it is hard to know how to classify them. They are really closer to fried eggs, although steaming plays a part in their cookery.)

Boiling eggs calls for little comment, except for the admittedly fundamental one that it is best not to boil them. If they are put in simmering water, just below boiling point, the risk of overcooking the white (to which the heat penetrates first) before the yolk (to which it passes later) is done is reduced; and so is the risk of the shell cracking owing to the egg being bumped around by violent agitation of the water.

If **hard-boiling** (American hard-cooking) eggs, do not choose absolutely fresh eggs, in which the white adheres closely to the shell, making it more difficult to remove the latter. The eggs should be rinsed under cold water after removal from the pan; this halts the cooking process, which would otherwise continue for a while and leave a disfiguring dark green colour where the yolk meets the white.

The **frying** of eggs (in a shallow pan, in butter, bacon fat, or oil) presents one problem. Since the heat is all coming from below, the upper parts of the white and the yolk will be last to cook, and in the meantime the lower parts may become overcooked. Putting a metal lid over the pan, to reflect heat downwards, is one solution and should produce an evenly cooked 'sunny-side-up' effect. Flipping the eggs over, to produce American 'up-and-over' eggs, is another.

Since the addition of liquid to an egg mixture raises the temperature at which the protein coagulates, the **scrambling** of eggs (or making an OMELETTE) will call for a higher temperature. However, scrambled eggs are best cooked very gently, and it is advisable to remove the pan from the heat just before the mixture reaches the desired final consistency; to halt the cooking at that point by adding a few knobs of cold butter or a little cream; and then to stir some more.

This curious piece of Sèvres porcelain in the Wallace Collection in London is probably an egg-perfumer (the base section housed the dish in which pastilles could be burned, and the egg was perched in the section above)

these and about the hard-boiled eggs which Egyptian picnic parties would take to public gardens or sacred places on festival days and which they would settle down to enjoy while watching the antics of conjurors and dancers or listening to recitals of tales such as those which are known in the western world as *A Thousand and One Nights*. *Beid hamine* (hard-boiled eggs) and *Baid mutajjan* (fried hard-boiled eggs, following a medieval recipe still used in MOROCCO as well as Egypt) are examples of what would be in the picnic baskets.

ELAND *Taurotragus oryx*, the largest African ANTELOPE, has some importance as food; attempts have been made to farm small domesticated herds in S. Africa (and have been successful in the Ukraine). An adult male eland may measure 1.75 m (just under 6') in height up to the throat, and weigh around 600 kg (1,350 lb). The eland, which has distinctive spiral horns, thrives under conditions (as regards supplies of food and water, and also tsetse fly infestation) in which cattle cannot survive.

Also, an eland can be milked, and its milk keeps very well.

The flesh of the eland, especially the hump, is savoury and tender. Pot-roasting is favoured, but other recipes suitable for beef can be used.

ELDERBERRY AND ELDERFLOWER, borne by elderberry trees, of the genus *Sambucus*, are found almost everywhere in Europe, W. Asia and N. America. The trees bear white flower clusters and abundant black berries, both of which are edible and widely eaten. Neither flowers nor berries are good when raw. In this state they contain small amounts of a poisonous alkaloid, and have a sickly, unpleasant smell and taste. Cooking alters the taste and destroys the alkaloid.

Elderflowers have been made into teas or TISANES in Europe and by N. American Indians, largely for medicinal use and especially as an antidote against colds. The flowers are also used to flavour cooked fruit and jam, which is achieved by stirring the panful with a spray of flowers until the flavour is judged strong enough. They provide, in a more substantial role, the basis of elderflower FRITTERS, sometimes claimed to be an invention of N. American Indians but having a lineage in Europe which goes back to medieval times (cf Hieatt and Hosington, 1998); these now enjoy a wide popularity. Elderflowers also go into MUFFINS and PANCAKES to lighten and flavour them.

In cookery, elderberries are often added to other fruits, especially apples. Elderberries combine with CRABAPPLES to produce an excellent and pretty jelly. They can be used in the same way with scarlet SUMAC berries. The elderberries need the additional PECTIN provided by these other fruits to produce a good gel.

The dried berries can be made into CHUTNEY, and an old British ketchup called poulac, now forgotten, was made from them. Scandinavian mixed fruit soups often include elderberries.

Elderberry cordial, an unfermented and non-alcoholic concentrate, makes a delicious summer drink. Elderberry wine, which is alcoholic, is a traditional country product.

Elderberry vinegar is made in various countries.

The common elder of the Old World is *Sambucus nigra*. American species include *S. canadensis* in the northern half of N. America and *S. mexicana* in the south-western states. The buds of the former have sometimes been pickled to make imitation capers. Fernald and Kinsey (1943) note a lack of interest in the use of elderberries of the species *S. canadensis*, and refer to a note by Clute (*American Botanist*, 1905) who suggests that:

Elderflowers with berries

The trouble is not so much in the pie itself as the way it is put together. Pies made of fresh elderberries are scarcely likely to appeal to many palates. The fruit still retains some of the rank eldery flavor possessed by the entire plant and made evident when the stem is broken; but if one will collect the berries when fully ripe and dry them in flat trays in the sun or in a warm oven he will have a cheap and appetizing material from which to manufacture pies all winter—and pies that are not inferior to huckleberry pies in flavor.

ELECAMPANE *Inula helenium*, a large plant, related to the SUNFLOWER, which grows wild in Europe and has become naturalized in N. America. Its rhizome and root ('white within and full of substance, sweet of smell and bitter of taste', as Gerard, 1633, put it) have many traditional uses in medicine, often mentioned in Saxon herbals and the Middle Ages. The plant used to be cultivated, mainly for such purposes; but the candied root was also regarded as a sweetmeat.

Fernie (1895) records that in the mid-19th century candy made from elecampane was still being sold in flat round cakes in London, and that this was eaten at night and in the morning as a cure for asthma, and

nibbled on journeys which exposed a traveller to 'poisonous exhalations'.

ELEPHANT the only survivor of the zoological order Proboscidea, which formerly included the mammoth and the mastodon, known from cave paintings and fossils.

The two principal species of elephant are *Loxodonta africana*, the sway-backed African elephant, and *Elephas maximus*, the Asian elephant. The latter, which is somewhat smaller than the former (4 tons as opposed to 6) is an endangered species, and the African elephant is now also in need of conservation. This need is not an entirely new phenomenon. There were elephants in ancient Egypt, where their meat was regarded as a delicacy and King Ptolemy Philadelphus (308–245 BC) forbade killing them; but they did not survive.

The idea of eating elephant flesh is now of little more than historical interest. However, there is considerable evidence of how it was eaten in the past, and some of this has been collected by Faith Medlin (1975). The greatest praise was bestowed by LeVaillant (1790), who in describing his travels in the interior of Africa gave this account of a breakfast of elephant's foot baked by the Hottentots:

It exhaled such a savory odor, that I soon tasted and found it to be delicious. I had often heard the feet of Bears commended, but could not conceive that so gross and heavy an animal as the Elephant would afford such delicate food. 'Never,' said I, 'can our modern epicures have such a dainty at their tables; let forced fruits and the contributions of various countries contribute to their luxury, yet cannot they procure so excellent a dish as I have now before me.'

Elephants' feet also feature in the very detailed account given by the explorer Sir Samuel Baker (1884) of how to dig a suitable oven in the ground and then prepare and cook a foot. He said that when, after 36 hours, the hot oven is opened, 'the elephant's foot will be deliciously cooked. The horny sole will detach like a shoe from a human foot, exposing a delicate white surface like a silk stocking. This is thoroughly good eating when hot; and with oil and vinegar when cold; it is far better than the well-known Oxford brawn.'

ELEPHANT GARLIC one of the various forms of *Allium ampeloprasum*, is also called giant or Levant garlic. It is more closely related to the LEEK than to GARLIC. However, it has large bulbs and cloves resembling those of garlic in shape and structure, and a mild garlic flavour, and these similarities account for its common name. One cultivar bears the official name

Elephant, and it can produce heads weighing as much as 450 g (1 lb) each. The plant originated in the Levant, and can be grown in the same conditions as garlic. It is cultivated commercially in the USA.

Elephant garlic can be baked as a vegetable, or sliced into salads.

ELEVENSES a colloquial expression which entered the English language in the late 18th century, meaning a light refreshment taken at about 11 o'clock in the morning. Although the timing is flexible and the extent of the refreshment, especially the food element, has proved to be highly variable, the institution has retained its place in the daily schedule of most British people. Nor are they alone in this. Of the many corresponding institutions in other parts of the world, the most important is probably the Mediterranean MERENDA or merienda. However, the *zweite Frühstück* (second breakfast) eaten in various German-speaking regions is an important northerly counterpart of this meridional institution.

In Chile there are *salas de onces* (Spanish for eleven), where EMPANADAS, cakes, and snacks can be bought; and according to Elisabeth Lambert Ortiz (1984) the name was derived from the 'English custom of having tea or coffee and biscuits at eleven in the morning' and has become, 'by some extraordinary transmutation, afternoon tea, so that a *sala de onces* is a tea shop'. Under MALTA is a description of the refreshments taken by Maltese office workers in mid-morning. These examples could be multiplied, since the need for some refreshment between BREAKFAST (especially if early and/or light) and LUNCH or its equivalent is widespread, although not universal, among human beings.

In this connection it is necessary to heed the warning given by the expiring Henry King, that elevenses or for that matter other light refreshments punctuating the day should not be allowed to attain the status of MEALS.

READING: Palmer (1952).

ELK a name which is applied to some members of the DEER family, Cervidae, but with a certain inconsistency between European and American usage. The European elk, *Alces alces*, is found in forests and marshes of N. Europe and Asia. It is a large animal but smaller than the animal known as elk in N. America, *Cervus canadensis*, which stands over 1.5 m (5') at the shoulder.

The American elk is one of the large deer which may also be called wapiti; the name is used of *C. elephus* or its subspecies in Asia. However, there is some doubt about the taxonomy; for example, it seems that the 'tian shan wapiti', one of the Asian ones, is almost exactly like the American one.

Pollard (1926) gives a good appraisal of elk meat:

The flesh is fine flavoured, but differs from all other venison. It is more nutritious than any other meat of which I have knowledge. A hungry labouring man is satisfied with about half the amount which would be required of beef. This nutritious quality of the elk is first alluded to by Lewis and Clark (ed Thwaites, 1904–5), and is fully confirmed by my observations.

Theodore Roosevelt, writing in the last year of the 19th century, displayed particular enthusiasm for elk tongue: 'Elk tongues are most delicious eating, being juicy, tender and well flavoured; they are excellent to take out as a lunch on a long hunting trip.'

ELVERS the young of EEL, at the stage where they reach land after a journey of two or three years from the spawning ground where they began life as larvae. They are still transparent, but have assumed the typical cylindrical shape of an adult eel.

Elvers can be caught in vast quantities as they enter the rivers which they propose to ascend. Those caught may then be sent alive to waters far upstream, where they would not normally penetrate; or exported to another country or continent (e.g. from W. Europe to Japan) to build up stocks there; or cooked and eaten.

The cooking of elvers is a completely different matter from the cooking of adult eels. Given their small size, it is a simple business, but techniques vary from place to place and provide a number of regional or national specialities. In England, especially Somerset (where millions of the elvers which come up the Bristol Channel arrive), they may be cooked in a loose mass, like whitebait, in a frying pan, then eaten with bread and butter. An alternative recorded by Dorothy Hartley (1954) is to season the cooked mass with herbs, and a touch of onion and of hot bacon fat, and press it into a 'cake' which is allowed to become cool before being sliced and eaten. In Spain, *angulas* (as they are called, adults being *anguillas*) are usually served in earthenware recipients after being cooked by a brief immersion, with chilli and garlic, in boiling oil. In Italy, around Pisa, there are interesting dishes which include *ce'e alla salvia*, using sage as the flavouring herb.

Dorothy Hartley has an intriguing tale of a woman who was accused of witchcraft because she produced a hot fish dinner from what had appeared to be a pail of clear water (the elvers which filled the pail being transparent until cooked).

EMBLIC or emblic myrobalan, *Emblica officinalis*, is a prized fruit in tropical Asia. Commercial growing takes place mainly in the Indian subcontinent, but the tree is also cultivated in S. China and parts of SE Asia. It is regarded as sacred by Hindus, whose religion prescribes that the fruits be eaten for 40 days after a fast in order to restore health and vitality.

Burkill (1965–6) states that the Malay name *melaka* is Sanskrit in origin, and that Malacca received its name from the tree.

The fruit is round, and almost stemless: light green when underripe, and ripening to a whitish or dull yellowish-green, or occasionally red. There are six and sometimes eight faint ridges extending from the base to the apex, which give the appearance of it being in segments, and it is hard to the touch. The skin is thin and translucent, the flesh crisp and juicy. The firmly embedded stone is ridged and contains six seeds.

The fruit is so sour that anything drunk after it will seem sweet. However, it can be stewed with sugar, made into jams and relishes, or candied. It has a very high vitamin C content; during the Second World War Indian troops were issued with emblic tablets and candies.

EMMENTAL the familiar Swiss cheese with large holes, takes its name from that of the Emmen valley near Bern. Genuine Swiss Emmental is marked 'Switzerland' in red on the rind. French Emmental came into being when some Swiss cheese-makers crossed the border into France, taking their skills with them; it is not the same as the Swiss kind, but closely similar. Imitations of Emmental, which is widely regarded as the archetypal 'Swiss cheese', are produced in other countries.

Although cheese was being made in the Emmen valley in the Middle Ages, it is only since the 16th century that Emmental has been made in its present large size: around 84 cm (33") in diameter and weighing up to 90 kg (200 lb) or even more.

The way in which Emmental is made is broadly similar to that of GRUYÈRE. However, maturing is carried out in a warmer cellar, with lower humidity; and there are other differences. All this favours the growth of the propionic acid-producing bacteria which give to many Swiss cheeses their characteristic flavour and (by giving off carbon dioxide) the holes or 'eyes' which are characteristic of some of them. The eyes in Emmental are numerous and may be as large as a walnut; whereas those of Swiss Gruyère are few and small.

Unlike Gruyère, Emmental has a dry rind free from micro-organisms. It is usually younger and milder tasting but saltier. The

normal maturing time is about four months, but may be substantially longer if a full-flavoured cheese is required.

Carr (1985) gives a good summary of the complex factors involved in making Emmental and adds:

It is not surprising therefore that Emmental is generally considered to be one of the most difficult cheeses to make successfully, nor that the Swiss, with their centuries of experience, remain unimpressed by their innumerable would-be competitors elsewhere. 'Anyone can make the holes,' they say, 'but only the Swiss can make the cheese.'

EMPANADA a Spanish and Latin American savoury TURNOVER. 'Empanada' means 'covered with bread'; and bread dough may be used, but the usual covering is shortcrust PASTRY. Often the semicircular seam is decorated by twisting it at regular intervals. The pastry may be baked or deep fried.

Fillings vary from one country or region to another. In Spain a mixture of minced meats and sausage is common, but in writing about empanadas in Galicia Janet Mendel (1996) lists no fewer than 18 examples of fillings, ranging from clams to rabbit, sardines to pigeon, and octopus to ham. In S. and C. America and the south-west of the USA a similarly wide range of fillings are used. Mexican fillings are highly seasoned with chilli peppers.

Empanadillas are small empanadas.

EMPERORS the puzzling name given to the various species of fish in the family Lethrinidae, which are distinguished by features, such as elongated scaleless snouts and cheeks, of which none seems to be imperial in character. In general, they resemble the GRUNTS. Apart from one on the W. African coast, the score or so of species all belong to the Indo-Pacific. Some of them bear the name **capitaine** in islands of the Indian Ocean.

Species which grow to a fair size and are of some commercial interest include:

- *Lethrinus chrysostomus*, called **sweetlip emperor** by some, well known on the northern coasts of Australia and a valuable food fish. Maximum length 90 cm (35"). The coloration is striking, especially the blood-red patch around the eyes.
- *L. nebulosus*, the **spangled emperor,** sometimes called mata hari, ranging from E. Africa and the Red Sea to the W. Pacific islands, attractively coloured (each scale picked out with a pale blue spot, and three light blue bands radiating from the eyes). To 75 cm (30"). Capitaine rouge in the Indian Ocean. The flesh is slightly

pinkish and is appreciated by the Japanese.
- *L. miniatus*, the **long-nosed emperor** (or, again, mata hari), to 90 cm (35"), another good fish.
- *Gymnocraneus griseus*, pleasingly called the **gingko fish** (but grey bare-nose in S. Africa). To 50 cm (20"), silvery-brown with three violet-blue bars on the head. Capitaine blanc in the Indian Ocean.

The name emperor is also given to a SNAPPER, *Lutjanus sebae*, the one which also has the distinctive name 'government bream'.

EMU *Dromaius novaehollandiae*, a non-flying bird of the family Dromaiidae, is indigenous to Australia and is now farmed there (and, more experimentally, in a few other parts of the world). Low (1989) draws attention to the enthusiasm, almost an obsession, displayed by one of the foremost early explorers in Australia, Leichhardt. It is recorded that this intrepid sampler of wild foods used to eat a kilo of emu meat for breakfast, the same for lunch, and almost another kilo for tea. But he did not only eat the meat, for he wrote:

the bones, heads and necks were stewed: formerly, we threw the heads, gizzards, and feet away, but necessity had taught us economy; and, upon trial, the feet of young emus was found to be as good and tender as cow-heel.

Generally speaking, emu meat can be substituted for beef in beef recipes, but its texture is softer and care must be taken not to overcook it. Smoked emu is marketed, and the meat also appears in sausages. Emu eggs are eaten, but are perhaps better known for their decorative quality; the shell is deep green in colour and thick enough to be carved.

EMULSION a blend of two liquids where one forms tiny droplets which are evenly dispersed in the other. It is not strictly a mixture, because the two liquids do not actually mix. The technical term for combinations of this kind is a COLLOID. The blend may be stable, although in practice—and especially in cookery—emulsions often separate.

Common emulsions used in cookery are MILK, CREAM, and BUTTER, and made SAUCES such as MAYONNAISE. Butter is not usually thought of as a liquid, but it is a genuine emulsion. To understand why, it is necessary to examine the structure of these substances in some detail.

In emulsions found in foodstuffs the two liquids are usually an oil or fat of some kind, and water or a watery liquid. There are two ways the liquids can combine. The oil may form droplets suspended in water, or the water may form droplets suspended in oil. Technically, the liquid which forms droplets is known as the disperse(d) phase, and the liquid in which these drops are scattered is known as the dispersion medium. Milk is an obvious example of an oil-in-water emulsion, with a small amount of semi-solid butterfat dispersed in a larger amount of water. (It also contains proteins which are dispersed in the water.) Cream is similar but with much more oil; very thick cream contains almost 50% fat.

There is a limit to how much oil an oil-in-water emulsion will hold. Thick cream is close to this limit; it is therefore not very stable. When cream is churned to make butter, the agitation breaks up the water into droplets. Quite suddenly—if you are using a hand churn you can feel it happening—the droplets of butterfat merge together; the result is a blend in which droplets of water are dispersed in continuous butterfat. The disperse phase and the dispersion medium have changed places, a process known as phase inversion. The new emulsion cannot hold as much water as the original cream did. The extra water separates out as BUTTERMILK. Butter is about 80% fat.

When an emulsion is formed (or, as above, reformed), an essential part of the process is mechanical work. One has to stir hard to make mayonnaise. Milk as it comes from the cow is not a totally stable emulsion; the butterfat slowly rises to the surface to form 'top of milk'. It can be made completely stable (at least, until bacteria make it 'go off') by putting more work into it—by the process of homogenization, in which it is forced through tiny holes which break the fat droplets into smaller droplets which are held more firmly in place and do not float upwards.

What holds the droplets in place in an emulsion? Oil and water do not mix because they are fundamentally different substances, not only in their obvious characteristics but also on a molecular scale. The molecules of water are 'polar': they have an unequal distribution of electric charge, one side of the molecule being positively charged, the other negatively. Many other substances also have polar molecules with unbalanced charges. Oil molecules, in contrast, are not polar; their charges are evenly balanced.

A positively charged object attracts a negatively charged one and vice versa, but two objects with similar charges repel each other. When two polar molecules are brought near each other, they tend to align themselves so that the positive side of one is facing the negative side of the other. Non-polar molecules such as those of oil do not feel these forces, but they are slightly attracted to each other by 'van der Waals forces', the very weak forces which attract all molecules to each other (they are named after J. D. van der Waals (1837–1923), a Dutch physicist). Polar molecules also feel van der Waals forces, but these are easily outweighed by the much stronger forces stemming from their electric charge.

If an attempt is made to blend water and oil, no matter how hard they are stirred together to mix them, the polar water molecules will tend to move together because of their electrical charges, and the non-polar oil molecules will tend to move together because of van der Waals forces. The two liquids will therefore separate.

Something else is needed to hold an emulsion together; this is known as an emulsifier. It is a substance whose molecules have one polar end and one non-polar end. The polar end is strongly attracted to a water molecule; the non-polar end is weakly attracted to an oil molecule. These molecules can form a layer at the boundary of a region of oil and a region of water, with their polar ends facing the water and their non-polar ends facing the oil. If, in a blend of oil and water, a droplet of oil is completely surrounded by a layer of emulsifier in this way, it will be able to stay suspended in the water and will not merge with other oil droplets.

Emulsifiers belong to a group of substances called 'surfactants', short for surface active agents. The best-known surfactant is soap, whose molecules surround particles of greasy dirt and hold them suspended in water, so that they float away out of the article being washed. Many foodstuffs display surface action to some extent and may be used as emulsifiers. Egg yolk contains a powerful emulsifier, lecithin, and a less strong one, cholesterol. The grains of some finely powdered ingredients also have this property, including mustard powder—which is why, when making mayonnaise, mustard is added to the egg yolk before mixing in the oil.

The food industry uses many other emulsifying substances, usually derived from natural foodstuffs. These include ALGINATES, made from seaweed; GUMS and PECTIN extracted from various plants; and various modified kinds of CELLULOSE. Their purpose is not only to bind emulsions but also to retain water in food, so that it does not go stale quickly. In foods sold in the EU emulsifiers are given E numbers beginning with 3 or 4.

The making of mayonnaise also demonstrates another fact about the formation of emulsions, the 'seeding' effect. As soon as a small amount of emulsion has formed, the remainder of the ingredients will blend much more easily. At first the oil is added drop by drop, but once the emulsion has started to take one can trickle it in in a thin stream, as long as one keeps stirring hard.

Because emulsions depend on the attraction between polar molecules, they can fail to form or break down if their watery component contains dissolved substances that carry a lot of electric charge. For example, ACIDS provide large amounts of positively charged hydrogen atoms. Adding vinegar to mayonnaise can make it curdle, unless it is dribbled in gradually while the mixture is stirred so that no regions of high acidity can form. ALKALIS (such as bicarbonate of soda) and excessive amounts of salt can also destroy emulsions. The breakdown of emulsions, and what to do about it, are described under CURDLING.

                                                        RH

ENGLAND a country which has been inhabited by successive waves of different peoples, a long list with which schoolchildren are more likely to be familiar than their parents: Celts, Picts, Romans, Vikings, Saxons, Angles, Normans, and that only takes us up to 1066. All these, some of them in ways which are too indistinct to perceive at this distance of time, have left their marks on the English kitchen. In more recent times the beneficial immigration of W. Indians, and Asians, especially from Pakistan, has very obviously changed the culinary scene. This same scene has also been enlivened by numerous refugees in the mid-20th century (Jews, Poles), and by the arrival in its closing decades of smaller but influential groups such as Americans and Australians and people from the Middle East, mainly clustering in the London area, and new arrivals in the category of refugees (many from Africa). Nor is this all. For centuries both the Scots and the Irish have descended on England in large numbers, bringing not only their great talents in business, literature, etc. but also their foodways.

England has also been radically affected by factors such as an uneasy relationship, marked by shifting alliances and oppositions, with continental Europe; the Protestant schism from the Roman Catholic Church and the Puritan influence of Cromwell's Commonwealth in the 17th century; the acquisition and subsequent loss of one of the world's greatest empires; and the impact of the Industrial Revolution, which affected England sooner and to a greater extent than any other country.

In these perspectives it may seem astonishing that food and cookery in England, at least until the very recent past, have seemed to outside observers—and indeed often to the English themselves—to be lacking in variety, finesse, imagination, and innovation; in short, to be somewhat dull and conservative. Yet there is truth in this view. English food traditions have been surprisingly persistent and resilient, even through the 20th century. This truth is borne out by the enduring quality which they have shown in former British possessions, even when quite unsuited to the very different climates to which colonists took them; see AUSTRALIA; NEW ZEALAND; WEST INDIES; plus of course ANGLO-INDIAN COOKERY (the source of those 'curries' which have been an established part of English cuisine for a century and more). But this truth is likely to be invisible to anyone who simply contemplates phenomena such as the growth in number, diversity and quality of restaurants in England, which constitutes so to speak a surface froth above what have been deep and almost still waters.

The three immediately following articles on ENGLISH COOKERY BOOKS, read in sequence, throw some tangential light on the gradual evolution of cookery in England by showing what sorts of books were, in successive centuries, deemed likely to find a market. But until recent times these books were concerned mainly or exclusively with food for affluent tables (farmer William Ellis, 1750, was a refreshing exception) and bore little relation to what most English people were eating. A more realistic impression can be had from reading Dorothy HARTLEY (1954), C. Anne Wilson (1973), and Christopher Driver (1983), among other works. The first of these authors covers English traditions, while the others take the whole of Britain as their canvas. On a smaller scale, such studies as that by Peter Brears (*Traditional Food in Yorkshire*, 1987) are of great value. Morever, these studies of particular counties (or areas such as the West Country) can now be related to an overarching structure created under the auspices of the European Union, a wide-ranging and systematic survey of traditional British foods, notably those of England; see Laura Mason (1999). Now that this new resource exists, it might seem surprising that it was not created long ago. However, the concept of defining and thus helping to preserve a 'national culinary heritage' is not one which readily occurs to English minds; it is more at home in countries of continental Europe, especially France.

Looking at the several hundred items which Mason identified and described, one sees a considerable emphasis on baked goods, which fits in with the widespread tradition of HIGH TEA and the socially more restricted one of AFTERNOON TEA. There are also many specialities which exemplify economical ways with meat (with vegetables in a Lancashire HOTPOT, with plenty of potato in SHEPHERD'S PIE) or OFFAL (see for example HASLET, TRIPE). English cheeses also come into prominence, far fewer in number than, say, the several hundred cheeses of France, but having a really important place in the diet and, at their best, achieving unsurpassed excellence (e.g. farmhouse WENSLEYDALE, and STILTON).

Yet it may be by their PUDDINGS that the English have achieved most fame. Even in the first half of the 18th century collections of pudding recipes numbering a hundred or more could be published, with no unnecessary repetition. A sort of zenith was reached in 1923 when the indefatigable author of *May Byron's Pudding Book* proclaimed on her title page the presence of 'one thousand and seventy recipes for puddings plain and rich, baked and boiled'. YORKSHIRE PUDDING, traditional accompaniment for roast beef, is but one of this host, as is black pudding (see BLOOD SAUSAGES), which is often featured in another source of English fame, at least in the eyes of foreign visitors, namely the English cooked BREAKFAST. The fact that this sort of breakfast, offering bacon and eggs with all the trimmings, or KIPPERS, has migrated from the home to hotels, cafés, railway trains, etc. does not diminish its importance in the English scheme of things.

Yet to refer to a 'scheme of things' may mislead. There is no 'scheme'. English foodways present an amorphous appearance. They have evolved in a somewhat random fashion and English people have consistently (but making a partial exception for the period of the Second World War) shown resistance to homilies about what they should or should not eat. In particular, they are resistant to being told that foods which they and their parents before them, and their grandparents too, have been eating should now be 'off' the national menu. Some controversies of this nature have even threatened to provoke lawlessness on the part of a traditionally law-abiding nation.

Some firm favourites on English tables have already been mentioned. For others, of varying degrees of antiquity, see FISH AND CHIPS, TOAD IN THE HOLE, TRIFLE, and numerous items in the territory of baked goods. For a further illustration of the tenacity of firm favourites, see the aptly titled book by Simon Hopkinson and Lindsey Bareham (1997), *The Prawn Cocktail Years*, in which the authors reveal that over a period of several decades the same three items (Prawn Cocktail, Steak Garni, and Black Forest Gateau) have constituted the favourite British (including English) meal out. Quite how this trio won their place in English affections would be hard to determine and is anyway irrelevant. There has always been something chancy—as though chaos theory was at work behind the scenes—in the way in which the English pick up dishes from abroad and then cling to them.

By common consent, the last quarter of the 20th century has seen a greater ferment in the realm of food preferences—in England as elsewhere in the western world—and any previous quarter of a century. Explanations, including the influence of television and of travel, the exponentially increasing numbers of 'celebrity chefs', etc., are not hard to find; but it will be left to people writing in about 2050 to make a considered assessment and to note which of the new trends turned out to have staying power and which, so far as English people are concerned, made little lasting impression.

The whole of this entry invites one question which was engaging the attention of one of the finest English food writers of the 20th century, Jane GRIGSON, just before her untimely death in 1990. The question is this: is one to take the phrase 'English people' as referring just to what might be called 'ethnic English', people whose ancestry lies in England, or should it indicate all the people who live in England? The question is not just about the use of words; it involves, obviously, issues of political and social importance.

In a food and cookery context, most people would until recently have taken the first interpretation; and many still would. It is certainly possible that the second, with its far-reaching implications, could end up by causing confusion and obscuring worthwhile traditions. However, Jane Grigson was moving in that direction, and planning to introduce into her highly esteemed work *English Food* (1974, but also in later editions and a posthumous one of 1992) dishes which belong to Asian and Caribbean immigrant communities in England. Given the extent to which English cookery absorbed foreign influences in the past, and considering the history of foodways in the USA and Australia (to take only two of many relevant examples), this would seem logical. Also, the same question has been settled in this way in other (e.g. sporting) contexts.

ENGLISH COOKERY BOOKS

OF THE PERIOD 1500–1700
English cookery books and books on food in this period offer an understanding of domestic life that increasingly defined the activities of men and women in the household as different in kind and in value. The word 'oeconomy', prior to the 17th century, denotes household economy: the preparation of domestic medicine and many household products, the preservation and conservation of food throughout the year, and the planning and implementing of family diet. Indeed, household economy centred around food and was recognized as the single most important factor in the survival of any family. As the 17th century moves through the Commonwealth period (1640–60) to the Restoration, husbandry turns into the economically visible work of farming and agriculture, while housewifery becomes the invisible labour of domestic women. The shift is documented by the books on food in subtle and intimate ways rarely available to the social historian.

The first printed book in English relating to cookery is probably *A Noble Boke of Cokery* (1500), which may have been published for the glory of the feudal estate but which provides good examples of a wide range of aristocratic eating habits: what was eaten, by whom, and how. It is closely followed by *The Book of Kervynge* (1508) which is also concerned not only with the techniques of cookery, but with the etiquette of preparation and serving. But for the first 60 or 70 years of the 16th century books related to food are usually part of more general enquiries. For example, there is Laurence Andrew, *The Noble Lyfe and Natures of Man* (c.1521), combining some recipes with natural history; there is Thomas Elyot, *Castel of Health* (1539), which could be called gastronomy; and F. Seager, *The School of Vertue* (1557), or Thomas Twine, *The Schoolemaster or Teacher of Table Philosophie* (1576), which are books on manners for young people.

By far the most dominant genres of writing on food during this early period are books of secrets, dietaries, and books on husbandry. Books of 'secrets' combine arcane alchemical experiments with receipts for household dyes, cleaning agents, perfumes, and medicines, and with receipts for wines, spiced hippocras, distillations, sugar cookery, the decorative use of gold leaf: examples include Conrad Gesner, *The Treasure of Euonymus* (1539), Albertus Magnus, *The Book of Secrets . . .* (c.1550s), and *The Secrets of the Reverend Maister Alexis of Piedmont* (1562), and these transform into books largely on food by way of the author (? John Partridge) of *The Treasurie of Commodious Conceites and Hidden Secrets* (1584, possibly 1573). Books on husbandry were largely concerned with the management of the country house. By the 1560s and especially during the 1570s these works begin to include more receipts; examples would be **Thomas Tusser,** *A Hundreth Good Pointes of Husbandrie, . . . with Huswifry* (1557 with many editions into the 17th century), or J. Fitzherbert, *Fitzherbert's Husbandry* (initially 1523, with many editions 1570–1600), or Leonard Mascall's many works.

Possibly the most interesting group of books on food are the dietaries, which were both preventive and curative. These writings indicate a sophisticated awareness of the interconnection between food and health, and offered substantial advice on domestic medicine which would have been essential not only because traditional practice was limited but also because the 16th century witnessed the incorporation of surgeons and physicians (apothecaries in 1617) into guilds, with such protective control over treatment that the new medicine was put outside the reach of most people. The 1530s and 1540s, which saw a huge increase in literacy, also saw the publication of Roger Bacon, *Beste Waters Artyfycialles* (c.1530); William Langham, *The Garden of Health* (1533), *The Treasure of Pore Men* (1539), and *This is the Glasse of Healthe* (1540), all of which address domestic medicine through diet.

Andrew Boorde's book on curative diet, *The Breviary of Healthe* (1552), became the forerunner of books which were increasingly moving into food and plant remedies and of the more specialized books on domestic medicine and professional pharmaceuticals in the 17th century. For example John Hollybush, *Homish Apothecarye* (1561), *Soveraigne Approved Medicines and Remedies* (1577), *The Poore Mans Jewell* (1578), Peter Levens, *Pathway to Health* (1582), and Thomas Coghan, *Haven of Health* (1584). Boorde also wrote *A Compendous Regryment or a Dyetary of Health* (1542) which became a much copied work on cookery and diet, followed by for example T. Phayre, *The Regiment of Life* (1545), and eventually leading to rather more specialized works such as Henry Buttes, *Dyets Dry Dinner* (1599), William Vaughan, *Naturall and Artificial Directions for Health* (1600), and John Harrington, *The Englishman's Docter or, the School of Salerne* (1607).

The books that present food as providing a regimen of preventive medicine, or remedies to sustain health, combine in the 1570s with those interested in the techniques of food preparation (which seem to have had a circulation in manuscript at least since the early exemplar of *The Noble Boke of Cokery*) in a book that focused on cookery itself: *A Proper Newe Booke of Cookerye* (1575 or earlier). During the 1580s many books including this kind of cookery were published: **John Partridge,** *The Widdows Treasure* (1585) and *The Treasurie . . .* attributed to him which went into many editions, with the latter becoming *The Treasurie of Hidden Secrets* (1600); and **Thomas Dawson,** *The Good Huswifes Jewel* (1584), which was much reprinted and copied, for example in *The Good Huswives Handmaid* (1594), and *The Good Houswives Treasurie* (1588). Several of these books claim to be from manuscripts by women and are openly addressed to women readers, with their lack of dedicatees possibly indicating their low status. Yet only slightly later **John Murrell,** using Dawson, published *A Newe Booke of Cookerie* (1615), *The Second Booke of Cookerie* (1620s), and *A Daily Exercise for Ladies and Gentlemen* (1617), in which the dedications consistently address patrons whose names changed as the books were republished through to 1640.

The sharp change that occurred from the 1580s in published writing to do with food can be brought into focus by studying two named writers with very different careers: **Hugh Platt** and **Gervase Markham.** The well-educated Londoner Sir Hugh Platt wrote widely on food technology and supply, on famine, and on new modes of food technology. He calls his receipts 'inventions' and 'experiments' rather than 'secrets' in *The Jewel House of Art and Nature* (1594). Significantly his *Delightes for Ladies* (1602) gave receipts for cookery, cosmetics, distillation, housewifery, and preservation; while his next book, *A Closet for Ladies and Gentlewomen* (1608), which also included the fashionable sugar cookery, contained only confectionery, distillation, and medicine: the three areas being developed by contemporary aristocratic ladies in their country estates. Gervase Markham was a completely different character who made his early name translating many European works of husbandry into English, aimed at the landed gentry rather than the aristocracy or urban entrepreneur. In 1615 he published *The English Hus-wife* which became the third part of his mammoth six-volume work *A Way to Get Wealth* (1620s). It is interesting that in 1616 he edited and added to Richard Surflet's translation of Charles Estienne, *Maison Rustique or the Countrey Farme*, and the differences between the two indicate an intelligent and perceptive editor adapting the book for English purposes yet not adding any cookery. Markham's work indicates a growing distinction between what men and women do in the household and how it is valued.

From 1600 three important genres of food writing coalesce:

- the cookery book which would comprise to a greater or lesser extent recipes with readily available ingredients, and fashionable cookery and carving (Dawson, Murrell);
- the gentry housewife's book related to household activities, cookery, and domestic medicine (Markham); and
- the aristocratic, or aspiring, lady's book concerned with preservation and conservation, usually sugar and stillroom work, but sometimes including medicines, experiments, and some specialized cookery (Plat).

All three genres were aimed at women, and the books of the Commonwealth period

(the silence in the 1640s is perhaps not so strange, given the war) largely maintain this audience. Examples are Ruthven, *The Ladies Cabinet Opened* (1639); W.J.'s version of the **Countess of Kent's** recipes *A True Gentlewoman's Delight* (1653) often bound with *A Choice Manual* (1653); her sister Alethea, Countess of Arundel, *Natura Exenterata* (1655); and recipes attributed to the exiled Queen Henrietta Maria in *The Queen's Closet Opened* (1654) containing *The Queen's Cabinet, A Queen's Delight*, and *The Compleat Cook.*

Books for either a general or male audience such as *A Book of Fruits and Flowers* (1653) or **Jos Cooper's** *The Art of Cookery* (1654) also emerge during this decade, along with the books by professional chefs often with French training (France being the home of the exiled royalists), such as La Varenne, *The French Cook* (1653); M. Marnette, *The Perfect Cook* (1656); and Robert MAY, *The Accomplisht Cook* (1660). Other writers focusing on men were those associated with Gresham College and later on with the Royal Society; examples include Thomas Mayerne, *Archimagirus AngloGallicus* (1658); Kenelm DIGBY, *The Closet of the Eminently Learned Sir Kenelm Digby* (1677); Denis Papin, *A New Digester or Engine for Softening Bones* (1681); John Houghton, *A Collection of Letters for the Improvement of Husbandry and Trade* (1681); and **John Evelyn,** *Acetaria: A Discourse of Sallets* (1699).

With the Restoration of 1660 the three main genres addressed to women remained viable but were transformed in response to the diversification in the social class of the readers as well as the writers in ways indicated by the writing of Hannah WOLLEY. Wolley's *The Cook's Guide* (1664) laid the basis for the small but important audience of professional women working as cooks, servants, confectioners, and teachers of the same, a genre added to by *The True Way of Preserving and Candying* (1681) and by Mary Tillinghast's *Rare and Excellent Receipts* (1690). Wolley's book for ladies, *The Queenlike Closet* (1670), combines the sense of occupation for the leisured lady, also provided by Geoffrey Hartmann, *The True Preserver and Restorer of Health* (1682), with the new sense of fashionable accomplishment for the upwardly mobile, exploited perhaps most successfully by John Shirley, *The Accomplished Ladies Rich Closet of Rarities* (1687). And possibly Wolley's most interesting work for the housewife, *The Gentlewoman's Companion* (c.1670), shifts the focus firmly from the self-sufficient community of the country house to the private home of the urban middle class: the former world finds echoes in the housekeepers' books of the 18th century such as SMITH, *The Compleat Housewife* (1727),

and the latter in books of direction for a family household such as *Salmon's Dictionary* (1696). In between lies the modern cookery book: works such as **William Rabisha,** *The Whole Body of Cookery Dissected* (1673).

The one area of food writing that remained substantially the same was that concerned with books addressing diet as preventive. Following Harrington's work on the *School of Salerne* (1607), there was R.H., *The Schoole of Salerne Regiment of Health* (1634), Thomas Muffet, *Health's Improvement*, translated and rewritten from the 1588 original by Christopher Bennett (1655), with Thomas Cocke, *Kitchin-Physick* (1676), a rather eccentric rewriting for the common people. Yet by the 1680s John Chamberlayne writes in a similar vein but distinguishes cookery and food appropriate to men in *A Treasure of Health* (1686), having already written on issues appropriate to women in *The Manner of Making Coffee Tea and Chocolate* (1684). Later he wrote *A Family Herbal* (1689). By 1691 Thomas Tryon, the great doctor to the poor, is also publishing gender-specific advice: *Wisdom's Dictates* (1691) to men, and *The Good House-wife Made a Doctor* (1692) to women. Perhaps it is appropriate to end the period with Tryon's *The Waye to Health* (1698), which opens with a praise to the author from Aphra Behn and proceeds to advise all men and women on 'meats, drinks, air, exercise', 'English herbs', the 'cheats and abuses of chymicall pretenders', plus a conversation with an Indian philosopher on the virtues of vegetarianism. LH

ENGLISH COOKERY BOOKS OF THE 18TH CENTURY

What follows could better be headed 'Cooks and Cookery Books and their Readers: Culinary Styles in the 18th Century'.

Cookery-book production in England during the first thirty years of the 18th century was dominated by the professional cooks who worked for the aristocracy and even, in the case of Patrick Lamb, for royalty. The most important names are those of Lamb (*Royal Cookery*, 1710), Henry Howard (*England's Newest Way*, 1703), John Nott (*The Cook's and Confectioner's Dictionary*, 1723), and Charles Carter (*The Complete Practical Cook*, 1730). These male authors saw themselves as purveyors of the art to noble patrons, and their works tend to reject the more mundane aspects of household management, in order to place due emphasis on the prestigious dishes of the 'court style' of cuisine which was now fashionable amongst the élite in Britain. This style owed much to the influence of the French, who had developed court cookery following the revolution in flavours (separating sweet from savoury) inaugurated by LA VARENNE. In England, the most influential French author was Massialot (see FRENCH COOKBOOKS): his *Cuisinier roïal et bourgeois* (1691) was translated into English in 1702 under the title *The Court and Country Cook*. The key elements of this court style were the *grosses entrées*, the OLIOS, the BISQUES, the TERRINES—all complicated dishes involving several meats with a strong, broth-based sauce and an elaborate garnish. This style is clearly part of a baroque aesthetic of the table which corresponds to a highly codified system of manners, in which protocol and precedence reigned supreme.

One male author who did not fit into this court and professional framework but displayed a pleasing eccentricity, a readiness to collect recipes from numerous different sources (and acknowledge them), and an ability to make his work a pleasure to read by introducing agricultural and other background information, was an amateur, Richard Bradley, the first professor of botany at Cambridge University. His book was *The Country Housewife and Lady's Director*, in two parts, first published as a whole in 1736.

However, in spite of the domination of male cooks, the ladies were not inactive. The tradition of 'good housewifery' found in MS receipt books and printed works produced during the 17th century was maintained by authors such as E. SMITH (*The Compleat Housewife*, 1727) and Mary Kettilby (*A Collection of above Three Hundred Receipts*, 1714). Both of these authors rely on manuscript collections for their receipts, thus perpetuating the mode of diffusion of receipts via the publication of MSS which was so prevalent in the 17th century. They also sought to incorporate into their works an adaptation of the court style, offering simplified versions of the key dishes, and adopting the separation of sweet and savoury which characterized the French culinary revolution of the mid-17th century. But while the tone of these two authors (whose works ran into far more numerous editions than those of their male rivals) implies a continuing interest in the kitchen on the part of women of the gentry class, many other works aimed at young ladies, whether devoted to cookery or more general, were deploring modern trends in education which were leading those young ladies to neglect the culinary arts in favour of more frivolous pursuits. All the evidence points to the abandoning of the female skills of cookery, first by the aristocracy, and then gradually amongst the gentry and its imitators.

After 1730, the male cooks were a minority amongst the authors of cookery books, and women now became the dominant force. This is partly due to the decline of court cookery, which, among élite circles

(especially the Whig politicians) was replaced by French NOUVELLE CUISINE, as exemplified by the works of Vincent La Chapelle (*The Modern Cook*, 1733), Marin, and Menon. In England, the most famous practitioner of the new style was Clouet (often known as 'Chloe'), who worked for the Duke of Newcastle in the 1730s and 1740s. Clouet's work is known to us through the receipts published by one of his assistants, William VERRAL, who brought out his racily written *Complete System of Cookery* in 1759. The new style was lighter and simpler, abandoning elaborate garnishes in favour of concentrated sauces in which one single ingredient dominated.

But although the new style found favour with a small group composed of members of the governing élite, it never caught on lower down the social scale. The books by Verral or his contemporary Martha Bradley (one of the few women cooks to have understood the new style) failed to sell. The great bestseller of the mid-18th century was the book by Hannah GLASSE (*The Art of Cookery, Made Plain and Easy*, 1747), which was overtly hostile to French cuisine while simultaneously plagiarizing its receipts. Mrs Glasse also appealed to potential buyers of her book by informing them that her aim was to instruct ignorant servants: the mistress was expected to buy the book, not to use it herself, but to teach her cook. Increasingly, women authors appealed to their female buyers by emphasizing how much the cookery books would release the mistress of the house from the drudgery of having to take an active role in supervising her domestics. Unfortunately, the reality of gentry-class women's lives often failed to conform to the image of the lady of leisure. Contemporary diaries and letters are full of the difficulties of hiring and retaining the services of a competent cook, and the mistress of the house was frequently obliged to roll up her sleeves and join in.

So, hardly surprisingly, underlying the emphasis on more or less authentic versions of the fashionable French cuisine, traditional English cookery continued. This continuity is especially visible in the areas of baking and sweet dishes, where one can follow a single line of development from the late 16th century to the very end of the 18th century. By the 1760s, English cookery books were offering a bastardized version of French dishes, using short-cut ingredients such as gravy browning and lemon pickle as substitutes for well-reduced broths and wines, and adding universal garnishes which hark back to the earlier French court style. But in more 'English' areas of excellence, in the pies and tarts and cakes, the traditions continued vigorously. Such are the strong points in *The Experienced English Housekeeper* (1769), by Elizabeth RAFFALD, a

work which sold very well and whose receipts were copied into their MS notebooks by gentry and middle-class women, and plagiarized by other authors, most notably John Farley (*The London Art of Cookery*, 1783, the most extensive piece of plagiarism in the whole century, containing only one very short recipe, for beef tea, which was not copied from earlier authors).

During the last quarter of the 18th century, there was a tendency to return to the encyclopedic works typical of the late 17th century. Under the influence of the Evangelical movement, the ladies wanted to know how to make nourishing soups and medicines to take on their charitable visits to the poor, and the sections on remedies which had died out from cookery books in mid-century (neither Glasse nor Raffald offered medical chapters) now returned. Another contributory factor was the ever-increasing emphasis on feminine delicacy: by doctoring themselves, women would be spared the need to reveal embarrassing details to a doctor. But whereas at the beginning of the 18th century the source for remedies had been family receipt books, with frequent remarks on the known efficacy of such receipts, by this time the authors raided the works of physicians for their medical sections. The most frequently used source was Dr William Buchan, whose immensely popular *Domestic Medicine* (1769) was used, for instance, by Mary COLE when compiling her *Lady's Complete Guide* (1788).

In the closing decades of the 18th century, two groups of authors stand out: the male tavern cooks, who boasted of working for places such as the prestigious London Tavern, which had a three-star reputation, and the female professional cooks or housekeepers. The women now presented the names of their employers to establish their credentials, just as the male chefs had done at the beginning of the century. But there was very little difference between the culinary styles of the two groups of authors: the cookery is generally very similar to that of Elizabeth Raffald, with simplified and bastardized French dishes alongside the developing repertoire of English items in the category of 'made dishes' (e.g. curry) and the continuing tradition of baking and sweet dishes.

A final development of the end of the century was the increasing number of small, cheap books, priced between 2s. and 6d. Such works were often abridged and simplified versions of the more luxurious works, offering a limited number of receipts in each chapter, but covering the same territory as the bigger books, including medical sections as well as culinary receipts, bills of fare, and instructions for marketing. Some were clearly aimed at the servants as buyers as well as readers; others offered a mix of receipts and more frivolous elements, such as songs, suggesting a readership of women from less well-off households seeking an initiation into the basics of gentility. At the very end of the century, one finds works offering moralizing advice combined with receipts for nourishing soups, enabling the charitable lady to fulfil her obligations without excessive expense: works addressed directly to the labouring classes would not appear until the middle of the 19th century.   GL

ENGLISH COOKERY BOOKS OF THE 19TH AND 20TH CENTURIES

These are exemplified for the general public by that of Mrs BEETON (1861) and for almost as many people by the work of her illustrious predecessor, Eliza ACTON (1845). Both belong to the mid-century and there are interesting things to be said about the decades before and after their books appeared.

The first half of the century was dominated, at least in terms of number of copies printed, by Mrs Rundell (1806), whose book *A New System of Domestic Cookery* had run into scores of editions by the 1860s. It began modestly enough as a relatively short compilation of recipes and surprised John Murray, the publisher, by its extraordinary success. It did not include many novel features, although it did have one of the first English recipes for tomato sauce; but it was evidently perceived as a highly practical work, neat in size and not encumbered by masses of obsolescent recipes such as weighed down many of the late 18th-century books with which it was competing. It must also have seemed less intimidating than a potential rival, the cookery book by the eccentric Dr Kitchiner (1817), entitled *The Cook's Oracle*, festooned with footnotes and digressions, full of cookery lore but aimed more at people with a literary bent than at ordinary cooks. Kitchiner was perhaps the first English writer to be strongly influenced by GRIMOD DE LA REYNIÈRE, but he claimed also to have studied a very large number of earlier English cookery books, which he lists.

Not much is known about Mrs Rundell herself, but the publishing history of her book has been charted and shows how much it was changed in the course of half a century. Indeed one of the main changes, the inclusion of much additional material, notably Anglo-Indian recipes, in the revised 1841 edition by Emma Roberts, was largely reversed later on when material of hers, which had been identified by the addition of her initials, disappeared. For collectors who would like to have the 'important' editions of the book, but not the numerous others, it is quite a problem to sort out requirements,

especially as there were pirated editions.

Emma Roberts was not alone in showing interest in the Indian subcontinent. One of the most remarkable books of the period, still very little known, entitled *Domestic Economy and Cookery for Rich and Poor; Containing an Account of the Best English, Scotch, French, Oriental and Other Foreign Dishes . . .*, was described as having been 'composed with the utmost attention to Health, Economy and Elegance, by A Lady'. It is a very substantial book, of almost 700 pages, but distinguished by a vigorous style and a profusion of knowledgeable footnotes. Who the 'Lady' was is not known, nor is it known how she acquired her arresting ideas and information; for example, recommending the making of bread as the Laplanders make it, from pine bark, and the statement that a physician of one of the embassies of China had told her of seeing very small children 'lying upon the sides of tanks, gathering every thing that had life, and putting what they had collected into little boxes formed like mouse-traps, to prevent their escape. The produce was put into the rice-pot.'

The appearance in 1846 of *The Jewish Manual* (see Raphael Chaim, 1983), a work that contained much material about Jewish cookery, marked a further innovation: writing about ethnic cookery.

It was also in the mid-19th century that specialized cookery books of another sort began to appear. One such was the work of William Hughes, a lawyer who was an enthusiast for fish. Under the pen name Piscator he published in 1843 a book entitled *Fish: How to Choose and How to Dress*, which seems to have been the first book entirely devoted to fish cookery to be published in Britain. It is a fine work, suffused throughout by first-hand knowledge and infectious enthusiasm. It can be regarded as a prototype for all those books on meat cookery, game cookery, etc. which abound in bookshops at the end of the 20th century.

The interest in India developed steadily during the 19th century. A wonderfully thorough book by Dr R. Riddell, who had previously written a manual of gardening for W. India, was published in Calcutta in 1849 (and thereafter in many further editions). A fair proportion of this was devoted to the Anglo part of ANGLO-INDIAN COOKERY, but much space was given to 'oriental cookery' and Hindustani names were given in romanized form. Other books of a similar kind followed, but it could fairly be said that all these were overshadowed by the work of an army officer, Colonel Kenney-Herbert, whose first publications came out under the pen name 'Wyvern'. Stationed in India, he contributed articles to the *Madras Athenaeum and Daily News* and then built around this material a book called *Culinary*

Jottings for Madras. This is a splendid volume. The colonel believed in surrounding his recipes with historical material, etymological explanations, amusing anecdotes, and, above all, every detail that seemed relevant to him about the choice and purchase of ingredients as well as the preparation of the dish itself. He went on to write other cookery books, including a series of the 1890s that began with *Fifty Breakfasts* and ended with *Fifty Dinners*—titles which represented another new genre of cookery writing.

Not all English cookery books of the 19th century were by English authors. Queen Victoria's chef, Francatelli, wrote several which enjoyed a vogue, and the ebullient Alexis Soyer was responsible for several interesting titles including *The Gastronomic Regenerator* and several recipe books for poor people. His reputation was enhanced by his activities in Ireland during the famine of 1847 and by his attempts to improve the food of the British army in the Crimea in 1855—plus his patented equipment (e.g. the Soyer stove) and preparations. To his discredit, he represented himself as author of a major historical work, the *Pantropheon*, which had apparently been written by a French teacher, Adolphe Duhart-Fauvet, resident in London, who received money for it but not the credit which he rightly expected; see McKirdy (1988).

As the 19th century wore on, what might be called 'gastronomic writing' began to appear, e.g. in the form of *The Thorough Good Cook* (1895) by George Augustus Sala.

The dilettante and literary tone of Sala's and kindred works was far removed from the nature of the 'blockbusters' of the last quarter of the century, beginning with *Cassell's Dictionary of Cookery* (1st edn 1875–6—see Elizabeth Driver, 1989—and on and on, well into the next century, and containing towards the end over 10,000 recipes). In the 1880s the prolific Mrs Marshall, the highly organized founder of a successful cookery school in London, brought out the first of her books on ices (again, see Driver, but also Barbara Ketcham Wheaton, 1976), to be followed by *Mrs A. B. Marshall's Cookery Book* (first edn c.1888) and *Mrs A. B. Marshall's Larger Cookery of Extra Recipes* (from 1891), which was a very large book indeed, contrasting with the specialized nature and easy-to-handle format of her ice books. Also around 1891 came the first version of a monumental work edited by Theodore Francis Garrett, whose credentials alone take up several hundred words. This was *The Encyclopaedia of Practical Cookery: A Complete Dictionary of All Pertaining to the Art of Cookery and Table Service*. Garrett's work appeared in 24 parts, to be bound up as two, four, or eight volumes. It represents by far the greatest compilation of its kind, then or indeed later, and may still be used to good advantage.

Garrett and Mrs Marshall between them provide a convenient bridge into the 20th century. There are far fewer landmark items in the period up to and including the Second World War. Mention should be made of the diligent May Byron, if only for *Pot-Luck* (her first book, 1914) and *May Byron's Pudding Book* (1923), a book well calculated to appeal to the very strong British taste for puddings and the like, witness the extensive subtitle: 'one thousand and seventy recipes for puddings plain and rich, baked and boiled: pastry dishes large and small: fritters, pancakes, fruit dishes, custards, creams, junkets, jellies, and sweet dishes of every kind'. The approach in these and kindred works was a simple one, to provide a lot of straightforward recipes with only a minimum of introduction (although May Byron's few pages of introduction to puddings are brilliant in their way—see PUDDING). A very different approach was now to be exemplified by authors such as Florence White, whose *Good Food in England* (1932) is a classic and a source of inspiration to all who have studied the history of English food. She believed in a deeply historical approach and drew on many sources, including folklore. This was an area where the resourceful Lady Gomme had been at work, dispatching questionnaires all over the country to correspondents of the English Folklore Society in order to elicit information about traditional local dishes, with some remarkable results which were saved for posterity and recorded in part by David Holbrook, 1990. All this activity reached a sort of culmination in the magnificent post-war book *Food in England* by Dorothy HARTLEY (1954).

The years of the Second World War were for obvious reasons bleak in this, as in other contexts, but produced a number of collector's items on how to make do with small rations and substitutes, and also saw the publication of the first instalments of *A Concise Encyclopaedia of Gastronomy*, edited by André Simon, the 'grand old man' of wine studies and gastronomy in England for many decades.

Then came radical change. The early work of Elizabeth DAVID sounded the keynote for a new style of writing about food and cookery, with attention focused on new themes. The books by Jane GRIGSON provide the other outstanding example of this. However, there were many other authors at work in a similar spirit, and, although it would be an exaggeration to refer to anything like 'a school of cookery writers', drawing inspiration from Elizabeth David and displaying the coherence of a 'school' of painters in Renaissance Italy, such

phraseology would not be too wide of the mark. Typical of the new movement were authors such as Claudia Roden (*A Book of Middle Eastern Food*, 1968 and later editions), and Patience Gray (*Plats du Jour*, written with Primrose Boyd, 1957, and *Honey from a Weed*, 1986). Typical of the editors whose selection and guidance were important for these authors was Jill Norman at Penguin Books. Typical of the whole process of change was the leading role taken by these and other women, together with the growing importance of the paperback editions of the books, and the influence of television.

ENOKITAKE *Flammulina velutipes*, a mushroom which looks different in its cultivated form from its appearance in the wild. This is because cultivation is of young specimens, which have a small convex cap on a long thin stem. The sticky, yellow to orange-brown cap is seldom more than 1 cm (0.3") wide, while the stem is typically as much as 12 cm (5") long. This mushroom is usually known by its Japanese name, since it is mainly the Japanese who cultivate it and who are the most eager consumers. Its distribution is, however, worldwide. It occurs in Britain and N. America, and has textbook English names: velvet shanks or velvet foot.

Wild specimens, which grow in clusters on deciduous logs, develop a much less delicate shape. Their velvety stems are thicker and less elongated, and the mature caps spread out quite wide. The season is late

autumn to early spring; warm spells in the winter bring them out. They are thus available when few other edible fungi are to be had, and are often referred to as winter mushrooms; they are regularly eaten in Germany, where their sweetish taste is appreciated, at this season.

The enokitake is so called because in Japan it grows wild on the stumps of the enoki (Chinese HACKBERRY) tree. It was originally cultivated on wet logs, but most of the cultivation is now done on a sawdust base in bottles fitted with stiff collars to hold the delicate stems upright as they grow. Cultivation can be carried out almost anywhere in the world, and some is done in the USA; but the main market and the main centre of production is still Japan.

The Japanese use enokitake in soups, stews, and so on, and also grill them with chicken etc. They have a mild flavour. The gelatinous layer on the caps should be removed from fresh wild specimens, and the stems discarded.

In western countries wild specimens have been used in soups, or preserved in vinegar. Cultivated enikotake (eniko in the USA) appear in salads and as a garnish. Fresh enokitake can be exported, since they keep for a time in sealed plastic packets. Canned enokitake are marketed from Taiwan as 'golden mushrooms'.

ENSAIMADA a sweet, airy yeast bun of Majorca. The name comes from *saim*, Mallorquin for the LARD of highest quality which is a main ingredient. This bun is one

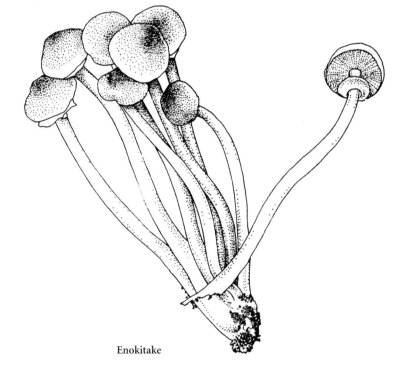

Enokitake

of Majorca's most famous products and in former times was not made anywhere else in Spain. It is said to have originated with the Moors, for its coiled shape resembles a Moorish turban. It comes in a standard form, plain with just a sprinkling of icing sugar, popular with morning coffee; and in various sizes filled with cream, confectioner's custard, or ANGEL'S HAIR jam. Large filled ones are sold by all bakers on Sundays and *fiestas*.   EC

ENTRÉE ENTREMETS, a couple of French terms which no doubt retain interest for persons attending hotel and restaurant courses conducted under the shadow of French classical traditions, but have ceased to have any real use, partly because most people cannot remember what they mean and partly because their meanings have changed over time and vary from one part of the world to another. Forget them.

ENZYMES are present in all living creatures: animals, plants, algae, fungi, and bacteria. They regulate the complex chemical reactions of life. Enzymes are catalysts: that is, they take part in chemical reactions without themselves being permanently changed by the reaction. Thus one molecule of an enzyme can work successively on many molecules of other substances, so enzymes are effective in tiny amounts. And effective they are: the artificial catalysts used in industry usually need high pressures and temperatures to work, but enyzmes operate quite happily at ambient pressure and body temperature.

All enzymes are PROTEINS. They are very diverse in nature. Some work in combination with other substances, which are termed coenzymes (several vitamins are coenzymes).

The substance on which an enzyme operates is known as its substrate. Many enzymes are highly specific in their action. They may work on any of a class of substrates; or produce any one of a limited number of effects; or be capable of producing only one effect on one substrate. Their names usually end in '-ase' added to the name of the substrate. Thus pectinase is an enzyme which acts on pectin. (Some of the first enzymes to be discovered do not have names of this type, such as the digestive enzymes pepsin and trypsin; but even these belong to the larger class of proteases, enzymes that act on protein.)

The one-to-one relationship of an enzyme with a substrate is often described as 'lock-and-key'. It is a useful way of thinking about enzymes because, like a real key, an enzyme depends on its shape to work. Its molecule is almost exactly the right shape to fit closely against a molecule of the substrate. Electrical forces on the surface of the enzyme pull the substrate towards it. But because the fit is not quite perfect, when the enzyme and substrate come together they become distorted. This sets up stresses in both molecules which can break bonds in the substrate, causing it to separate into two new and different molecules. That causes a further change in shape, so that the enzyme no longer fits against the new molecules. It comes unstuck and floats away, immediately springing back into its original shape so that it can attach itself to a new substrate molecule; only substances which can spring back in this way can work as enzymes. Other enzymes have the right shape to attract two other molecules and join them together.

Enzymes, despite their complexity and the precision of their action, are not in themselves living things. They can thus continue to work after the death of the creature they belong to, though of course no new supplies of enzyme will be produced, so the reactions will proceed more slowly.

From a cook's point of view enzymes can have useful effects. For instance, fruit continues to ripen after it is picked. Meat becomes more tender when it is hung. In these examples the enzymes break down the larger molecules of carbohydrate and proteins into smaller pieces, resulting in a softer texture, better flavour and greater digestibility. However, if such enzyme action is allowed to proceed indefinitely it will result in the food becoming too soft and finally rotten. And many enzymes have actions that are purely deleterious; they turn fruits and vegetables brown, and fats rancid (enzymes that work on fats are called lipases). It is therefore important in preserving foods to limit or exclude the action of enzymes.

Enzymes, like other proteins, are affected by heat; a few can recover if not too strongly heated, but most are permanently denatured. Cold inactivates them but does not destroy them.

Enzymes need water to be active. As food is frozen the watery fluids in it turn to pure ice, expelling all the substances dissolved in them into the remaining liquid, which eventually becomes such a concentrated solution that it cannot freeze. Thus there is always a little liquid in the food in which enzymes can continue work. Where possible, foods that are to be frozen are first blanched—briefly cooked—to destroy the enzymes.

Where blanching is not appropriate, as in the case of fruits to be eaten raw, there is another possibility. Many enzyme-regulated reactions need oxygen; so, if the foods are frozen under vacuum or in an inert gas, the enzymes will be inactivated. A strong sugar solution can also be used to fill the spaces between the cells and thus exclude oxygen.

Enzymes may also be inhibited by the presence of chemicals which interfere with the reactions they regulate. Strong solutions of SALT or SUGAR have this effect. So do high levels of ACID. Some plant enzymes stop working when acidity reaches the moderate level of pH 6.5 (pH 7 is neutral); others can hold out as far as pH 4, but that figure can easily be exceeded in a strong vinegar pickle. Animal enzymes mostly work only in the limited range from pH 6.5 to 8.

When food is fermented, many of the changes that occur in it are due to the action of enzymes. Sometimes these enzymes are naturally present in the foodstuff, as in the preparation of black TEA. Sometimes they are provided by micro-organisms which take part in the fermentation; for example, the *Penicillium* MOULDS which form the white rind on Camembert cheese produce proteases which soften the texture of the interior of the cheese.

Enzymes may also be taken from foods and used by themselves: papain (another protease) is extracted from unripe papayas and used as a meat tenderizer.   (RH)

EPAZOTE *Chenopodium ambrosioides*, is a plant of Latin America, in the GOOSEFOOT family, Chenopodiaceae. In food contexts it is best known by this, its Spanish name, derived from the Aztec (Nahuatl) *epazotl*; but it may also be called PIGWEED, Mexican tea, worm weed (because it is supposed to rid people of hookworm), bean herb (because anti-flatulence), etc.

Epazote has been described as one of the three 'secret ingredients' of Mexican and Caribbean cooking, the other two being *cilantro* (fresh CORIANDER leaf) and *comino* (ground CUMIN). Despite this reputation, epazote has not been made welcome in N. American or European kitchens. Its

Epazote

unpleasant aroma, which is enough to distinguish it from all related species, may account for this.

It is indeed notorious for its smell. In the spring, however, leaves are tender with only a faint smell, and can be used as a pot-herb, especially when mixed with other greens. By the beginning of summer the leaves become coarse, gain a stronger aroma and taste, and add a good but not overpowering flavour to soups, bean, and other dishes of southern Mexico, C. America, and the Caribbean. In the autumn the leaves turn red and develop a very strong aroma and an assertive taste. At this time it is possible to dry and bottle leaves, blossom, and seeds for use over the winter.

The related *C. berlandieri* is a cultivated annual grown around Mexico City where it is a popular vegetable. It is called *huauzontle*, and resembles a tall epazote.   (RB)

EPICURE a term derived from the Greek philosopher Epicurus, who declared happiness to be the highest good, which came to mean, in a food and wine context, a person of refined tastes. In the latter half of the 19th and the first half of the 20th centuries in Britain it was a designation to which many aspired. Nowadays it would be hard to find anyone so aspiring, and the term is half forgotten, or used in a humorous way, as in the well-known limerick:

> An epicure, dining at Crewe,
> Found quite a large mouse in his stew,
>   Said the waiter, 'Don't shout
>   And wave it about,
> Or the rest will be wanting one too.'

It may be thought a pity that the name of Epicurus, whose views had much to commend them, is not associated, in the English language, with something of greater import. On the other hand, if the contemplation of any surviving epicures provides amusement, it may be adding, slightly, to happiness.

ERINGO ROOT the root of the sea holly, *Eryngium maritimum*, which was widely eaten in candied or pickled form in England, and in other European countries, in the 17th and 18th centuries.

Boiled or roasted, the roots are said to taste something like CHESTNUT or PARSNIP; but they were more commonly used in sweetmeat form than as a vegetable. Candied, and sometimes called 'kissing COMFITS', they had a reputation as an APHRODISIAC, and it was for this reason that Shakespeare had Falstaff demand that the sky should 'hail kissing comfits, and snow eryngoes'. Belief in the aphrodisiac power of eringo root has been traced back to Pliny by

Ivan Day (1996a) who provides fascinating information on this and other aspects of the root in a major essay.

ESCABECHE a preparation of fried fish which has been allowed to cool and is then soused with a hot MARINADE of vinegar and other ingredients. The dish may be served hot, but it is more commonly kept and served cold. Indeed, the technique may well have originated as a means of preserving fish. The term occurs not only in its Spanish form, as here, but also in French (*escabèche*), Italian (*scapece*), Algerian (*scabetch*), and so on; and it appears in 17th- and 18th-century English cookery books as 'caveach', a word which could be either a noun or a verb.

Barbara Santich (1985) gives a good account of the probable etymology of the term (from the Persian/Arabic *sikbaj*, meaning 'vinegar stew', vulgarized into *iskebey*) and of the medieval ancestors of the dish. One of the earliest mentions in Europe is in the Catalan treatise *Sent Sovi* (14th century), where there are several recipes for *scabeig, escabeyg*, and *esquabey*. The simplest of these calls for a mildly vinegary and spicy sauce, thickened with toasted bread, onion, etc.; but others require nuts and raisins and fall into the category of sweet and sour. Santich points out that they correspond closely to some medieval English dishes with names like egurdouce (*aigre-douce*, SWEET-AND-SOUR). Indeed escabeche can be found, in past centuries and now, lurking under other names in various countries and contexts. In Italy there are many regional variants of the name *scapece*, but perhaps the most famous of all Italian versions of the dish, the Venetian *Pesce in saor*, is under a quite different name.

Escabeche has migrated, under the same name, to the Philippines, where Doreen Fernandez (personal communication, 1995) comments that 'it is always fish, fried first. When it is taken out of the pan, vinegar, onions, ginger and garlic (the latter two in strips) are added, sometimes soy bean curd [*tokwa*, see TOFU] slices, often mushrooms and red bell pepper strips or quarters. The sauce is thickened with flour mixed in water. It may also have soy sauce and potatoes. But always it is a fish fried then sauced to be sweet-sour.'

This last point is all the more interesting because, as Santich points out, what has happened in Europe is that escabeche has lost its medieval sweet-and-sour aspect, shedding the sweet ingredients such as sugar, raisins, dates, and becoming more 'streamlined'. An example is the simple modern Catalan *Sardines amb escabetx* (grilled sardines served cold in a vinaigrette with thyme, bay leaves, parsley).

The essay by Santich ends with a suggestion that the term CEVICHE may be derived from escabeche. Certainly, if it could be established that the two terms are directly and closely related, and not just coincidental lookalikes, this whole subject area would be greatly clarified.

ESCOFFIER AUGUSTE (1846–1935), the most famous chef of the period from 1890 to 1920. He worked for the first part of this time in partnership with César Ritz, the gifted hotel manager. They took over the new Savoy Hotel in London in 1890. They were dismissed together in 1897, in circumstances distressing for Escoffier, who was aware that the owners had built up a dossier of evidence that he took an illegal 'cut' of 5% on supplies for the kitchen; but after only a short break they continued their joint work at the Ritz Carlton Hotel, and Escoffier remained there, famous and revered, until his retirement in 1920. His book *Le Guide culinaire* (1903), on which more than one other professional chef had worked with him and which reflected essentially the cuisine of a grand hotel in the 1890s, became the bible of chefs trained in the classical French tradition. His later work *Ma Cuisine* (1934) was for domestic cooks rather than professional chefs.

It has been customary to credit Escoffier with the achievement of greater simplicity in his cuisine. Certainly, if one compares his menus and dishes with the worst excesses and extravagances of the 19th century, one sees a change of this kind. Yet to late 20th-century eyes and tastes his own work now seems extravagant and irredeemably old-fashioned. Likewise, he is rightly credited with a humane attitude towards his kitchen staff, which was unusual in his time (and cannot be taken for granted even 100 years later); but the contrast between what one writer has called 'the gilded creatures of high society posturing in the over-decorated rooms upstairs' and the underlings toiling desperately in the kitchen below is still striking and tends to bring up, implicitly, questions such as whether the top end of the restaurant trade then (as now, for that matter) does not genuflect too readily to snobbism and wealth. Yet, allowing the pendulum to swing back again in his favour, is it not endearing and amusing that Escoffier dedicated many of his culinary inventions to people such as opera stars (Dame Nellie Melba) or beautiful demi-mondaines (as his biographer notes) as well as to the Mr Bigs of his day (e.g. King Edward VII)? His career, dedicated but opportunistic, is rich in paradox, brilliantly brought out by Shaw (1994) in the following anecdote. When the Norwegian explorer Nansen visited the Savoy in 1892 he was planning an Arctic expedition which would take into account the fate of an earlier American expedition, whose ship, the *Jeannette*, broke up in the ice, with only one group surviving of the three which left the wreckage.

It was the wreckage of the *Jeannette*, drifting for years in the ice, which caught the creative imagination not only of Nansen, but also of Escoffier, to whom it suggested *Suprêmes de Volaille Jeannette*; a cold dish in which poached escalopes of chicken breast, decorated with tarragon and laid on layers of foie gras mousse and chicken jelly, were placed in a dish which was closely imprisoned within a sculpted block of ice so as to represent the ship held fatally by the drifting floes. The item was first served in June 1896 to celebrate Nansen's meeting with a British expedition. It was a Sunday night, there were three hundred people in the Savoy restaurant, and the *suprêmes* were a great success. It is only to be hoped that the *maîtres d'hôtel*, explaining the story to attentive clients, did not upset them by dwelling too long on the sufferings and deaths of most of the *Jeanette's* crew!

At Escoffier's birthplace, Villeneuve-Loubet (formerly called Villeneuve-sur Loup), there is a small museum in his honour, permitting one to step back in imagination into the world where he once reigned.

READING: Escoffier (1985); Anne Willan (1977).

ESPAGNOLE the name given in classical French cuisine to the 'mother sauce' from which are derived many of the sauces described under BROWN SAUCES. The name has nothing to do with Spain, any more than the counterpart term *allemande* (see VELOUTÉ) has anything to do with Germany. It is generally believed that the terms were chosen because in French eyes Germans are blond and Spaniards are brown.

Some authorities prefer to regard demi-glace (see GLACE DE VIANDE) as the parent of the group of brown sauces, and would say that espagnole is the penultimate stage in producing demi-glace. However, what is certain is that for people outside France as well as inside the term espagnole is widely understood to mean the basic brown sauce, and indeed one which can be used on its own although it normally has added flavourings and a new name.

The arduous procedure for making an espagnole on traditionally approved lines is now rarely followed.

ESSENCE a term which, in a culinary context, is neatly defined by the *NSOED* as 'A distillate or extract from a plant or medicinal substance, having its active constituents or characteristic properties in a concentrated form, . . . especially as an alcoholic solution of volatile substances.' There are instances, e.g. essence of vanilla,

where reputable firms market a product corresponding to this definition, but cheap imitations are also sold which do not.

Essential oils are not quite the same thing, but close. An essential oil is defined as a volatile oil obtained by distillation and having the characteristic odour of the plant etc. from which it is extracted. Familiar examples are oil of spearmint, oil of citronella.

ESTONIA northernmost of the three Baltic states, is the closest in culinary traditions to the Nordic countries, since it has FINLAND as its neighbour and developed largely under the domination of DENMARK and SWEDEN until conquered by Peter the Great of RUSSIA in the early 18th century. The upper citadel of Tallinn, the capital, still bears witness to the early 13th-century period of Danish domination. The Estonian language, along with Finnish and Hungarian, is one of the few surviving languages in the Finno-Ugric group.

Even in pre-Christian times, the two staple foods of Estonia were bread (mainly RYE, as throughout this region) and salted fish (the Baltic HERRING and SPRAT). Writing about the importance of the Baltic herring in particular, Pamela Davidson (1979), after a visit to Estonia during which she learned that the kippering of Baltic herring had been pioneered in Estonia in 1959 (and that 'Estonians consume their kippers chopped up, fried in a batter of egg, milk, flour, a little grated cheese and a touch of sugar, and served with tomato sauce'), recorded the existence of an entire book on the preparation of this fish. This is *Zakuski iz sel'di* (Herring Appetizers), published in 1961, and it contains 160 recipes 'ranging from the humdrum to fairy-tale fantasies, such as that which bids you hollow out sections of cucumber, stuff these with a salted herring salad, cap them with tomato slices dotted with mayonnaise, and proclaim the result to be cucumber mushrooms'.

The same author continues with a description of *kiluvol*, sprat pâté, made with what is probably the best-known and most typical Estonian fish, *kilu*, the Baltic sprat.

Kilu is exported in bright blue tins decorated with a picture of old Tallinn. Inside, the little silver fish lie tightly packed, curled in a circle, with a bay leaf on top. They are preserved with thirteen different spices and the flavour is strong, sweet and fishy. Head and gut are not removed, the fish being so small.

However, these are the de luxe version of *kilu*; the pâté is best made with plain salted *kilu* and butter plus salty fish juices, and served with hot boiled potatoes.

Otherwise Estonian cuisine is simple, incorporating many milk soups and milky sauces. Among sweet dishes are a rye bread

soup with apples, other apple dishes, and a rhubarb pudding.

ETHIOPIA is a country of staggering diversity. Two hundred miles south of one of the world's hottest deserts, the Danakil Depression—116 m (380') below sea level—mountains up to 4,500 m (15,000') often bear snow within 10 degrees of the equator. The geography is dominated by a massive knot of mountains and plateaux of still-active volcanic origin, heavily dissected by river valleys up to a mile deep and separated into eastern and western highlands by the Great Rift Valley, which to the north of Ethiopia becomes the Red Sea.

During the rainy season, which lasts from mid-June to mid-September, the highlands receive heavy rain from the monsoon, half of it leaving the country as the Blue Nile. The upper highlands, above 2,400 m (8,000'), and the lowlands, below 900 m (3,000'), are mostly suitable for pasturage; more than half the country is grassland. The bulk of the population lives in the *weynadega*, the 'zone between', where an unusually wide variety of crops may be available at a given time because of the different climates of the different elevations.

Isolated by this mountainous environment, and the surrounding deserts of the Horn and N. Sudan, the highlands have developed distinctive crops. Ethiopia has its own species of OATS (*Avena abyssinica*), and may be the original home of finger MILLET (*Eleusine coracam*). BARLEY and hard WHEAT are also ancient crops.

The highland grain par excellence is grown nowhere else; TEF (*Eragrostis tef*), the smallest of all grains, 2,500–3,000 seeds to the gram. Weeding this fine-stemmed grass is very laborious and the crop is subject to loss by the shattering of the seed heads, but it is disease and insect resistant, will grow in the cracking volcanic clays of the plateau, and produces a quick crop without irrigation. It is high in iron and, as a result (fortunately for people living at these high altitudes), anaemia is one of the few nutritional deficiencies that is rare in Ethiopia. Tef is also the preferred grain for INJERA, the sour flatbread of the highlands. Just under half the grain acreage in the country is in tef.

The other distinctive staple crop is ensete (*Ensete edulis* or *ventricosum*), also called false banana. It is grown at lower elevations than tef and is the principal crop of the southern highlands; there is evidence that the ancient Egyptians knew of ensete. The nutritious part of the plant is the root, which is dug up and scraped. The wet scrapings are buried in a pit for a period of weeks or even months to ferment and soften, and made into a flatbread called *wesa*.

Together with flatbread and dairy products such as cheese and butter, pulses (split peas, chickpeas, and lentils) and Ethiopian kale (*Brassica carinata*, also called Abyssinian cabbage or mustard) play a large part in the diet. Cattle and chickens are the principal sources of meat in the highlands, goats and sheep in the arid regions. Neither Christians nor Muslims eat pork; the Danakil, Oromo, and Somali avoid chicken and eggs as well.

Ethiopian food uses the largest variety of spices in sub-Saharan Africa: ginger, coriander, nigella (see BLACK CUMIN), clove, FENUGREEK, mustard, dill, cumin, caraway, and above all red pepper and Ethiopian CARDAMOM (*Aframomum corrorima*). The latter makes its way into virtually every stew in the highlands. Bishop's weed (see AJOWAN) and common basil are the favourite herbs. Mead (*t'ef*) and the turbid sour beer *t'alla* are flavoured with the leaves and stems of *gesho*, a buckthorn (*Rhamnus prinoides*).

In a country of great physical diversity where at least 70 languages are spoken, a few culinary features are widespread. Onions (or rather shallots) are fried without oil, giving a distinctive flavour to Ethiopian stews. Food is often served on, and picked up with swatches of, flatbread. Butter is usually clarified and flavoured with spices (*nit'r qibe*). Many groups serve some form of the dish called *k'itfo* in the highlands: diced raw beef mixed with spiced butter.

The dominant people of the western highlands are the Amhara and the Tigre, Coptic Christians who speak S. Arabian dialects brought to Ethiopia beginning about 3,700 years ago. Dialects much changed in the new surroundings, needless to say—in Amharic, the ancient Semitic word for 'almond' now refers to the African GROUNDNUT (*Voandzeia subterranea*).

Together they account for about a third of the population. The Tigre and Amhara have a large repertoire of vegetarian dishes based on kale and pulses because their Church observes 208 days of abstinence a year. Among them are *qolo* (paste of toasted grain); *ilbet*, broad beans boiled with sunflower seeds, garlic, and ginger; *wat's* (stews/sauces) made from ground safflower, rape, or cotton seed; and *ye-shimbra asa*, a fried 'fish' of chickpea flour.

Their meat dishes, apart from *k'itfo*, fall mostly into two classes: red stews (*wat'*), which include red pepper in the complex spice mix, and green stews (*alich'a*), which do not. *T'ibs* is a sort of hash or dry-fried meat dish. A dish is often made by crumbling *injera* with butter or *wat'*. The Amhara and Tigre avoid eating fruit.

The original population of the highlands spoke languages of the Cushitic family, distantly related to the Semitic languages, and most Ethiopians are still Cushite speakers. Among the largest groups are the Gurage and the Sidamo of the south-western highlands and adjacent lowlands. Unlike the Tigre and the Amhara, who live in villages, these ensete cultivators mostly live in individual homesteads. The Gurage are about equally divided among Christians, Muslims, and animists. The Sidamo, who have a highly developed agriculture including ploughing with oxen and terracing of fields, produce the famous Ethiopian coffee of their name. They are mostly animists.

Wesa, the staple bread, is often tough (even when made from ensete rendered less fibrous by long fermentation) and cannot be eaten without a moist accompaniment such as milk, butter, cheese, or *zamamojat*, a mixture of cheese, cabbage, and spices. There is also an ensete porridge. *K'itfo* is known, often under the name *brendo*. The wealthy eat millet *injera* and *wat'*, much like the Amhara and Tigre. Gurage and Sidamo living in higher elevations grow cereals and potatoes, rather than ensete. The Gurage believe that without butter, food 'has no taste', and even put large quantities of butter in coffee.

The largest group in Ethiopia, sometimes estimated at 40% of the population, are the Oromo (Galla), relative newcomers from Somalia. They overran the country in the 16th century, nearly obliterating the Amharic kingdom of the western highlands. Today they dominate the smaller eastern highlands and are found throughout most of the southern part of the country, those in the west being Christians and those in the east mostly Muslims. Even when continuing to live as nomads, they have begun to assimilate to their neighbours' way of life. The Arsi of the Rift Valley now grow their own maize (their staple food, from which they make an *injera*-like flatbread), millet and *t'ef*, and at harvest time they make *injera*, but as yet vegetables scarcely figure in their diet.

The original diet of the Oromo presumably resembled that of their former neighbours in the arid east, the Somali and Danakil (Afar). The latter eat a typical nomad diet of grain (usually millet) and dairy products, spiced with red pepper.

In a narrow strip on the western border of Ethiopia live the only people in the country who speak neither Semitic nor Cushitic languages. These Nilo-Saharans are culturally close to the people of southern Sudan, and their diet includes non-Ethiopian ingredients such as cowpeas.   CP
READING: Selinus (1971).

EUGENIA FRUITS a collective name sometimes applied to a large group of tropical fruits borne on trees classified in, or formerly classified in, the genus *Eugenia* of the family Myrtaceae. Fruit-bearing species are found in S. America, India, SE Asia, and Australia. The best known have their own entries: see JAMBOLAN, PITANGA, and ROSE-APPLE. See also JAMBU. This entry lists a few of the less well-known members, which mostly belong, as in these examples, to S. America, or to the Philippines.

Myciaria (formerly *Eugenia*) *cauliflora*, the **jaboticaba,** is a Brazilian species which is often cultivated, e.g. in the region of Rio de Janeiro. It is a large tree, remarkable in that it bears its fruits directly on the trunk, main limbs, and branches. The fruits are round and about 2–3 cm (1") in diameter, maroon or purple in colour, and not unlike a grape, but with a thicker skin. The white or pinkish pulp is translucent. The fruit is popular in the south of Brazil as something to eat fresh, and can also be made into a good jelly.

E. brasiliensis (formerly *E. dombeyana*) is a tree of S. Brazil and Peru which bears a crimson, cherry-sized fruit, the **grumichama** of Brazil, sometimes called Brazil cherry. This has a thin skin and soft flesh of a mild flavour, which prompted Popenoe (1924) to compare it with a bigarreau cherry, and makes it suitable for eating fresh and for making into jellies, jams, and pies. The grumichama exists in several varieties, distinguished by the colour of the flesh (dark red, vermilion, or white) but of equal merit; and it has half a dozen or more close relations which are less good to eat. The best of these is *E. luschnathiana*, the **pitomba,** another native of Brazil. Its small fruits, orange in colour and reminiscent of apricots, are little known outside Brazil, but may deserve wider attention.

EULACHON *Thaleichthys pacificus*, a fish of the SMELT family (Osmeridae) with a distribution in the NE Pacific from California to the Bering Sea. Its common name is taken from the Chinook language, and in Alaska has been transmuted to hooligan.

The eulachon is anadromous, ascending freshwater streams in the spring, when it is adult, to spawn. Average length is 20 cm (8"), but specimens nearly twice as long have been taken. The flesh makes fine eating. It is rich in oil, so much so that the fish used to be dried and fitted with wicks to serve as candles; hence an alternative name, candlefish. Smoked eulachon, golden-brown in colour and of excellent flavour, are a delicacy.

EVE'S PUDDING is the modern name of a baked pudding with a lower layer of chopped APPLES and an upper one of a

SPONGE mixture flavoured with lemon and vanilla. This is really a descendant of a grander pudding of the 18th century, Duke of Cumberland's pudding, which was boiled. The apples were therefore inside rather than underneath. The surrounding pudding was made of a very highly egged suet mixture. It was served with melted butter, wine, and sugar. The name 'Mother Eve's Pudding' appears in a 19th-century verse recipe for a boiled pudding which is like the Duke's, but without suet and with currants. The name of the Duke, who was the bloody victor of Culloden, may have been suppressed to suit Victorian sensibilities; but the anonymous poet is none too tender-hearted: 'Six ounces of bread (let your maid eat the crust . . .).'

Dunfillan pudding is a Scottish pudding, similar to Eve's pudding but made with blackberries instead of apples.

EXPLORATEUR usually l'Explorateur, a French *triple crème* cheese which is made in a thick disc shape and has a white bloom on its rind. It has a creamy texture and flavour, and contains 75% fat. Much of it is exported to Belgium.

This cheese is made in the Île-de-France. So is *délice de Saint-Cyr*, another *triple crème* with a white rind, but bearing reddish spots. *Magnum* is a similar cheese from Normandy, known as *Brillat-Savarin* when aged.

EYES of certain animals and fish are considered a delicacy in some culinary cultures but regarded as horrifying morsels by most people in the western world. In tales about the ordeals of western visitors who for reasons of courtesy have to adjust their behaviour at table to match that of their host in, say, the Middle East, the climactic moment is likely to come when the visitor is invited to eat a sheep's eye.

In Laos the eyes of the giant catfish of the Mekong are among the most highly esteemed parts of this highly esteemed fish.

Examples could be multiplied, but the practice of eye-eating (even if cornea, lens, and iris are removed, as in one unusual French recipe for *Yeux de veau farcis*) seems likely to contract rather than spread as the centuries roll by.

FADGE the N. Ireland version of potato cake. Fadge dough is prepared with mashed boiled potatoes and a little white flour and baked in rounds or FARLS on a pan or GRIDDLE. The cakes are often baked in bacon fat to impart additional flavour.

The dish was well established in Ulster counties by at least the early 19th century. Referring to the diet of the inhabitants of the parish of Ballymartin in County Antrim in 1838, an Irish writer gave a pithy description: ' "Fadge", a very good kind of bread made of potatoes and flour and baked on a griddle in large cakes or "scones".' Fadge is an indispensable part of the 'Ulster fry', a breakfast dish of bacon, fried egg, sausage, and black pudding.

In some parts of N. Ireland fadge cakes are known as tatties or parleys.   RSe

FAEROE ISLANDS far to the north of SCOTLAND and a little closer to ICELAND in the west than to NORWAY in the east, constitute a 'self-governing community within the Kingdom of DENMARK'. It is thought that the first people to arrive in the islands, of which there are 18 in all, came from S. Norway and Orkney, in the early 9th century AD. The existence of a Faeroese parliament dates back almost as far; and there is a long-established Faeroese language. The economy depends almost entirely on the fishing industry and the outlook for this in the 1990s seems to preclude for the present any prospect of the Faeroes moving to the complete independence which they enjoyed in the remote past.

Over the centuries a distinct Faeroese culture, including culinary culture, has evolved. Originally, this depended heavily on methods of preserving fish and meat (sheep brought from the mainland). The parallel problem in Iceland was largely solved by much use of sour whey, but the Faeroese managed almost entirely by the use of their fresh air, i.e. wind-drying. The drying shed (*hjallur*) is a feature of many Faeroese homes.

One of the two national dishes of the Faeroese is *rast fisk* (*rastefisk*), semi-dried and cooked fish (fully dried fish is *tørfisk*). The other—perhaps the more important in Faeroese estimation—is dried mutton, which again comes in two forms: semi-dried, which is *rast kjøt*, and produces the much loved *rastkjøt* soup; and fully dried, which is *skerpikjøt*. The fully dried products can be eaten as they are, without any cooking.

It is not surprising that there are echoes in the Faeroes of food in Norway, Iceland, and ORKNEY AND SHETLAND. The Faeroese fish balls (*knettir*) and the use of whale meat compare with Norwegian practice. Their proficiency in utilizing every part of a sheep or a fish matches that of Icelanders and Shetlanders; the Faeroese sheep's head dish, *seyðar høvd*, is an example.

The soil and climate of the Faeroes are not propitious for growing crops. In recent times the Faeroese have been able to import 'missing' items of food, and their traditional foodways have been to some extent overlaid by modern ones, especially Danish, and by attendant phenomena such as supermarkets and fast food. However, the community is a conservative one and much of the past survives, including consumption of the PUFFIN and other seabirds. Johannesen comments that roast puffin or guillemot, served with potatoes, a gamy gravy, jam, and other ingredients, 'is hardly to be distinguished from the finest roast grouse'.

However, his greatest enthusiasm is reserved for two other dishes: puffin soup, 'a little sweet, with raisin dumplings'; and 'puffin stuffed with sponge cake dough, boiled and served with potatoes'.

FAGGOT in Britain, is a term for a simplified form of SAUSAGE, easier and quicker to make at home than a proper one. A mixture of pork OFFAL—liver, lungs, spleen, etc.—fat, breadcrumbs, onions, and flavourings to taste is parcelled in squares of CAUL (the fatty membrane around the intestines). The parcels are packed into a tin and baked, and may be eaten hot or cold. Faggots have also long been made commercially: it was an accident with a batch of faggots at a shop in Pudding Lane which started the Great Fire of London in 1666.

Since faggots are made from cheap ingredients they have always been a popular food of the poor, especially in the north of England. They are also called 'savoury ducks' because of the resemblance of the little packages to small birds. The same idea is behind the name of the French equivalent, *caillettes* (little quails) or (more commonly now) *gayettes*. These are made of liver, fat bacon, and sometimes sweetbreads or other offal or lean pork, with garlic, sometimes shallots, and herbs and spices—but not with breadcrumbs or other cereal. They are baked in the same way as faggots, sometimes interspersed with tomatoes.

See also CRÉPINETTE.

FAIRY FOOD in the sense of food eaten by fairies, is, evidently, delicate fare. Fairies of different ethnic groups have developed differing diets and foodways and the research which is no doubt being done on the origins of these does not seem yet to have found the original source from which these evolved.

Katharine Briggs (1976), concentrating on fairies of the British Isles, remarks that according to one authority the fairies of the Highlands and Islands of Scotland borrow oatmeal from human beings and return double measure, but in the form of barley, which seems to be 'their natural grain'. One food offered to the fairies in Ireland was CHAMP, and it has been suggested that BOG-BUTTER may sometimes have been intended for them. Fairies are also said to drink the milk of red deer and goats, and to consume large quantities of weeds. These weeds can be made to look like sumptuous fare, a trick which would be convenient for human cooks but which involves the use of glamour in the original sense of the word (magic, enchantment). A converse, negative, technique enables the fairies to extract the essential goodness from human food, leaving it bereft of nutritional qualities.

Many foods have names with 'fairy' in them, especially in Scotland. However, these names do not normally imply any real connection with fairies; they are often given simply because the food in question is light and delicate. Examples are fairy cakes (small, usually iced, sponge cakes, not unlike QUEEN CAKES); fairy pudding and fairy cream; and fairy toast, which is just another name for melba toast. Fairy butter can be traced back a long way, e.g. to Hannah Glasse (1747), who says that it is 'a pretty Thing to set off a Table at Supper'. Her version, one of many, calls for egg yolks, sugar, and orange-flower water, as well as some normal butter.

FAIRY RING MUSHROOM *Marasmius oreades*, a small, common, edible mushroom which is also called champignon (the general French name for mushroom, transferred in English to this one species), champion (in the north of England), and Scotch bonnet.

The cap is cream or very pale brown, conical, and seldom much more than 3 cm (a generous inch) in diameter. Under it the gills are distinctively wide spaced and paler in colour. The stem, also pale, is thin and tough. The mushroom resists drought by shrivelling up (the meaning of its generic name is 'shriveller') and filling out again when it rains. It grows in open fields from summer to autumn. It is found in N. America and Australia as well as throughout Europe.

A close relation, *M. scorodonius*, which is known in Germany as *Küchenschwindling*, and in Russia as *chesnochnik* (little garlicky mushroom), smells of fresh garlic.

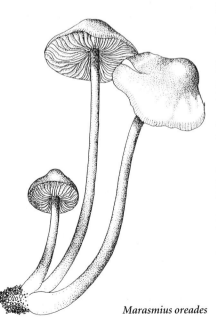

Marasmius oreades

The 'fairy rings' of darker green grass in fields are caused by successive generations of the mushrooms spreading out from an original small clump. These mushrooms are found in large numbers; just as well because they are so small.

Their flavour is excellent. They may be eaten raw; or cooked in a little olive oil with seasoning; or used in stews or soups. They can also be dried by discarding the stems, stringing the caps on a thread, and hanging them up for a few days. Once dried, they keep for a long time. In the middle of the 19th century it was the practice of the French 'à la mode' beef shops in London to use dried 'champignons' to heighten the flavour of that dish. And they are traditionally the mushrooms which are added to English steak and kidney pies.

FALAFEL (occasionally spelled felafel) are small, fried patties, croquettes, or rissoles popular in the Middle East mainly as a snack or a MEZZE. Their origin cannot be traced and is probably extremely ancient. It is, however, generally accepted that falafel originated in Egypt, where these tasty snacks have become one of the national dishes. The Christian Copts, who are said to be pure representatives of the ancient Egyptians, claim them as their own.

Falafel are called *ta'amia* in Egypt, except for Alexandria, where, as the rest of the Middle East, they are called falafel. Egyptians make them with the dried white broad beans called *ful nabed*. In the Lebanon, Syria, and Jordan they are more usually made with chick peas and/or dried broad beans. They are also popular in Israel, where they are sometimes called the 'Israeli hot dog', and are often served with a hot fenugreek relish called HILBEH brought to Israel by the Yemenite Jews. Some regard falafel as a national dish of Israel.

In making falafel, a special tool ('*aleb falafel*) is used to give shape to the puréed beans. This also has a lever which when released causes the falafel to pop out into the hot oil.

Falafel are made for religious festivals, especially among Christian communities during Lent when meat is forbidden. HS

FALSE MORELS a group of mushrooms in the genera *Gyromitra* and *Helvella*. They belong to the same family as the MORELS but need to be treated with caution. None of them has a cap which is both pitted and integral with the stem, like a true morel; but there is a family resemblance and casual inspection could lead to mistakes.

The need for caution applies especially to *Gyromitra esculenta*, whose fruiting body is markedly irregular in form, looking like a brain or a tangled mass of twine (or an untidy turban). It is widely distributed in Europe and N. America, and has been the subject of much puzzlement. In certain countries, for example Russia, it is marketed and eaten on a large scale. Elsewhere it has a documented reputation for being toxic, even fatally so, and is not eaten; it is forbidden as a market mushroom in Germany and Switzerland. In yet other countries it is eaten by some people with impunity, but proves harmful to others.

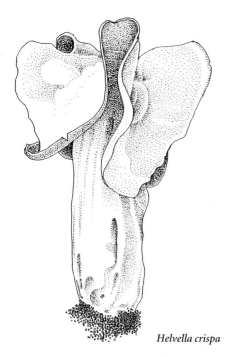

Helvella crispa

Various explanations have been offered. Some have thought that the mushroom exists in a number of varieties, of which only one or some are toxic; others have supposed that different races of human beings respond to it in different ways; others that it can be rendered safe by drying or boiling or both. The truth has emerged as a by-product of the American space programme. It seems that the toxic principle of this mushroom, gyromitrin, breaks down into another called monomethylhydrazine which is used as a rocket fuel. Investigations into sickness of rocket fuel handlers showed that at certain low levels this toxin has no effect, but that higher doses or a series of small doses will produce bad effects. If several people eat *Gyromitra* together and only one falls ill, that will be the one who ate most or who had had some the previous day. However, the toxin is soluble in water and readily evaporates, so it can be largely dissipated by thoroughly boiling the mushrooms, taking care not to inhale the vapours, and discarding the water. This explains why in countries where the mushrooms are so treated they can usually be eaten with impunity. However, the

dissipation may not always be complete, and it is safer to avoid these mushrooms. (See Marteka, 1980, for a lucid account.)

Mushrooms of the genus *Helvella* are generally regarded as safe, provided that they are picked when young and have been dried or cooked before they are eaten. (Some contain small quantities of helvellic acid and, if eaten raw, may produce symptoms like *Gyromitra* poisoning.) The best seems to be *H. crispa*, sometimes referred to as the 'common helvel' in English, which has a small cap of convoluted lobes (hence the French name *oreille de chat*, and the Spanish *oreja de gato blanca*) perched on a thick, vertically ridged stem. 'It gives me the idea of a piece of old kid glove crumpled up and stuck on the top of a worm-eaten cabbage stalk. The stem is here the principal part in regard to flesh.' Thus Delisle Hay (1887), who went on to term it an edible 'of first-class quality'. Other authors have praised it, but some describe it as merely edible, or 'inferior'.

Helvella gigas, the snow mushroom, is a chunky N. American species of coniferous regions, commended by Smith (1977) on the basis of his experience in Michigan and westwards, including the Rocky Mountains.

FAN SHELLS of the family Pinnidae, are among the largest edible BIVALVES and occur in most parts of the world, in shallow water. They are shaped like a half-opened fan and live upright in the sand, with the pointed end out of sight and anchored by a byssus to a stone, and the other projecting into the water. The Mediterranean species, *Pinna nobilis*, may reach a length of 75 cm (nearly 30").

The byssus, given the size of the shell, has to be long and substantial and is capable of being woven into a golden fabric from which gloves and stockings used to be made at Taranto in S. Italy. The special apparatus called a *pernonico*, by which fishermen hauled up fan shells for this purpose, was described by an 18th-century author, Aufrère, in writing about his travels in the region of Naples; he is quoted at length by Lovell (1884). It is typical of this eccentric and erudite author that he should not only know of Aufrère's work and quote it, thus preserving in perpetuity the full details of an unusual marine activity, but also add comments from sources such as the lost Roman parodist Matron which show that the fan mussel was greatly appreciated as food in classical times, besides being known as 'the silkworm of the sea'.

Another unusual feature of the fan shell is that it has the ability to repair damage to its shell, the projecting part of which is vulnerable. Almost every specimen shows signs of repair.

P. fragilis is a species which occurs in British waters. It has occasionally been fished in Devon, but is generally ignored.

In the Indo-Pacific region there are various species such as *Atrina pectinata*, whose Burmese and Thai names mean spade or mattock shell.

The size of the fan shell makes it desirable to remove the stomach and other organs, which is unnecessary when dealing with small bivalves. The muscular meat which remains is of good quality. In Europe it is usually prepared in the ways suitable for large SCALLOPS. In SE Asia it is used in soups or fried and served with coriander.

FARINA a word of Latin derivation which in both English and Italian just means FLOUR. However, in some places or contexts it may have a more precise meaning, e.g. hard (but not durum) wheat flour, or potato flour.

Potato flour can be used as a thickening and binding agent, and as part of the flour content of cakes. Its high capacity for absorbing liquid helps to give cakes a moist texture and to enable them to keep well. Italian *farina dolce* is likewise an ingredient of cakes, but is made from chestnuts, not potato.

FARL as explained by Ayto (1993), 'is a thin usually triangular cake made of oatmeal or wheat flour. Its name reflects its shape: for originally it was *fardel*, literally "fourth part", from *ferde*, "fourth" and *del*, "deal, part". As the oatmeal hints, it comes from Scotland ("an farls bak'd wi' butter", Robert Burns, *Holy Fair*, 1787).'

See also FADGE.

FARMER FANNIE (1857–1915), one of the best known American cookery writers. Disabled by a paralysing illness in her teens, which halted her education and left her with a permanent limp, she seemed unlikely to become a public figure. However, at the age of 30, in 1887, she enrolled in the Boston Cooking School (see LINCOLN, Mary) and only five years later became its principal, a position she held until she resigned in 1902 to open her own school, Miss Farmer's School of Cookery.

Farmer's approach to cooking was scientific. She recognized the relationship between sound nutrition and health, and insisted on precise measurements (she was the first to introduce the concept of level measurements in recipes). Her major work, often dubbed 'the Bible of the American kitchen', is *The Boston Cooking School Cook Book* (1st edn 1896). The book was considered a risk by its original publisher, but by the time of the 13th revised edition

(1990) almost 4,000,000 copies had been sold. A comprehensive, lucidly written, and well-organized manual, it begins with the chemical constituents of different foods, and progresses through the chemistry of cooking processes to the recipes themselves.

Although she prefaced her book with a quotation from Ruskin, her attitude to cookery was robust rather than romantic. On Boston baked beans she remarked that their reputation had often been attributed to 'the earthen bean-pot with small top and bulging sides in which they are supposed to be cooked', but observed drily that equally good beans had been prepared in a five-pound lard pail used to replace a broken pot. Hard work was no deterrent. 'The prejudice of thinking a frozen dessert difficult to prepare has long since been overcome. With ice cream freezer, burlap bag, wooden mallet or axe, small saucepan, sufficient ice and coarse rock salt, [and, she later reveals, some newspapers or a piece of carpet], the process neither takes much time nor patience.'

The book also contains menus, household hints, and a glossary of culinary terms. One chapter addresses the food needs of the sick, a subject in which she took a special interest. She was the author of *Food and Cookery for the Sick and Convalescent* (1904) and some other works. However, her fame rests entirely on her main book. This has so often been brought 'up to date' that it now differs greatly from the original; but a facsimile reprint of the 1st edition was published in the 1970s.

FAST FOOD a label which came into being in the USA (see entry thereon) early in the second half of the 20th century, when drive-in eating places were flourishing; Mariani (1994) refers to an example of its use in 1951.

The notion of being able to go into a public eating place and order something which would come almost at once and could be consumed quickly is, obviously, not a new one, but the proliferation of places, in N. America and globally, which proclaim their ability to provide fast food is a new and striking phenomenon. Fast food overlaps with STREET FOOD, but street food was always fast and new-style fast food is usually bought and often consumed under a roof. It need not be limited to such well-established items as HAMBURGERS, French fries (British chips) or PIZZAS, but it is typical of a fast-food establishment or outlet to offer only a few items, of proven popularity.

The antithesis of fast food is the movement known as 'Slow', which advocates dishes which benefit from long and slow cooking, and consuming them in a leisurely way.

FASTING an almost universal practice, is undertaken for various reasons but is more often than not connected with religion. The founding or leading figures in many major religions have been celebrated for, among other things, famous fasts; and all the religions stipulate or at least make provision for fasting at certain times or in certain circumstances.

It is necessary to distinguish between abstinence and fasting. Abstinence is to abstain from particular foods at particular times, whereas fasting is to do without food altogether (or, going to the extreme, without even water) for a particular period, often one day. However, the distinction has been blurred, at least for people in English-speaking countries, by the use of phrases such as 'fast days' to indicate when abstinence from meat is practised.

The whole history of abstinence and fasting in the various churches of Christianity is complex and shows a pattern of flexibility and evolution which is perhaps most apparent in Europe, where the practice of the Roman Catholic Church has become more liberal in some respects; the Eastern Orthodox Church has remained relatively conservative. The common feature in the main Christian churches is the observance of abstinence during LENT.

Abstinence was responsible for the practice in medieval times and later of calling 'maigre' those dishes or versions of dishes which could be eaten during a period of abstinence. The term is French but is so convenient that it was adopted into English from the 16th century onwards.

'Abstinence' meant principally abstinence from meat, but could be interpreted in other ways. In recent times some Christians mark LENT by simply abstaining from one or more of their favourite foods, for example chocolate, or from alcohol.

The Muslim institution of RAMADAN has an interesting structure. Zubaida (1991) remarks:

Every ritual fast ends with a feast. Lent is followed by Easter and its special foods. The supper after the fast of Yom Kippur turns into a special feast. Ramadhan has the special distinction, however, of repeating the fast-feast cycle each day for a lunar month.

The fasting during the period of Ramadan is the only 'compulsory' fast for Muslims, but there are days when a voluntary fast is appropriate, e.g. Ashura.

From the medical point of view, limited abstinence would rarely be harmful and often beneficial. The same applies to fasting for a short period, so long as water is taken, but fasting for more than a day without water and any form of prolonged fasting is likely to lead to trouble.

The 11th edition of the *Encyclopaedia Britannica* quotes with approval the view of a Protestant writer who rejected the idea that fasting is a thing meritorious in itself, and doubted its value even as an aid to devotional feeling.

Of course, when bodily health and other circumstances require it, it becomes a duty; and as a means of self-discipline it may be used with due regard to the claims of other duties, and to the fitness of things. In this last aspect, however, habitual temperance will generally be found to be much more beneficial than occasional fasting. It is extremely questionable, in particular, whether fasting be so efficient as it is sometimes supposed to be in protecting against temptation to fleshly sin. The practice has a well-ascertained tendency to excite the imagination; and in so far as it disturbs that healthy and well-balanced interaction of body and mind which is the best or at least the normal condition for the practice of virtue, it is to be deprecated rather than encouraged.

However, for those who see fasting as an obligation to their deity, these words would have seemed largely irrelevant, since they would see the obligation as overriding, not subject to health considerations.

FAT HEN *Chenopodium album*, also known as lamb's quarters and white goosefoot, a plant of the GOOSEFOOT family whose young leaves make an acceptable green vegetable.

This plant thrives on muck heaps, and remains of it have been found in neolithic middens; many of the local common names used in England reflect this, e.g. dungweed, muckweed, and dirty dick. The name 'fat hen' seems to have been given because barnyard hens could grow fat by eating this plant; and the French name *grasse poulette* matches the English one.

In N. America this is one of the plants commonly referred to as PIGWEED and is the one particularly referred to by Fernald and Kinsey (1943) in one of their most evangelical passages. Having explained what an enthusiastic reception this pigweed received from people who ate it without knowing what it was, they continue:

Another incident in the experience of the senior author illustrates the prejudice against not too attractive or conventional foods. Planning for a meeting of botanists in his study, he set to work on the menu to follow the business meeting: purée of dried Fairy-ring mushrooms, escalloped canned Purslane, salad of cooked blanched Pokeweed and Sorrel from the cellar, etc. A bread of Pigweed-seeds was decided upon. Proceeding in January to the border of a frozen truck-farm, a peck of seeds with husks and other fragments was quickly gathered. Winnowed by pouring back and forth from containers out-of-doors so that the lighter husks and debris blew away, a yield of a full quart of the black and drab fruits was left. When supper was served, Mrs Fernald brought in the soup which found favor, with thin biscuits of Jack-in-the-Pulpit flour, then the Purslane and salad, with a plate of intensely black muffins. I explained that, having no cook, I had volunteered to make the muffins. The plate went around the table, regularly to receive a polite, 'No, I thank you', until it reached the late Emile Williams, half-French and with more than usual Yankee consideration for others. Everyone else having declined my black muffins, Williams took one, put on his eye-glasses and inspected it, then sniffed at it. 'Ah, *Chenopodium album*' was his immediate diagnosis. Asked how he guessed, he replied: 'I've just been reading Napoleon's Memoirs. Napoleon at times had to live on it.' The plate was promptly cleared and returned to the kitchen for more, to nibble with the Beach-Plum preserve.

The same authors point out that fat hen (which, like spinach, loses much of its bulk when cooked) is a comparatively dry pot-herb which it is good to mix other greens of a mucilaginous nature; and that the seeds can be ground to produce a dark-coloured flour and bread of good flavour, tasting something like BUCKWHEAT products.

FATS AND OILS (*see page 291*)

FAT-TAILED SHEEP an important breed, seem to have come into existence around the 4th millennium BC. The earliest depiction of a fat-tailed sheep is on an Uruk III stone vessel of 3000 BC and fat- and thin-tailed sheep appear together on a mosaic standard from Ur dated around 2400 BC. The fact that fat-tails are now universal in the Fertile Crescent, where sheep were originally domesticated, while thin-tailed sheep predominate in peripheral areas— Europe, W. Africa, S. India, Tibet—suggests that the first domesticated sheep were thin tailed and the fat tail was a later development.

The tail may be a wide, beavertail-like flap, or a long kangaroo's tail with fat deposits along its length, or any intermediate shape. Among the world's hundreds of fat-tail breeds there are many odd curls, S-shapes, and wedges.

Herodotus had noted the existence of both kinds of tail in the 5th century BC:

There are in Arabia two kinds of sheep worthy of admiration, the like of which are nowhere else to be seen. One kind has long tails no less than four and a half feet long which, if they were allowed to trail on the ground, would be bruised and develop sores. As it is, the shepherds have enough skill in carpentry to make little carts for their sheep's tail. The carts are placed under the tails, each sheep having one to himself, and the tails are then tied down upon them. The other kind has a broad tail which is at times 18 inches across.

Altogether, about 25% of the world's sheep are fat-tailed. The type is found from the W. Sahara to Manchuria, from the Atlantic to the Pacific. It predominates in N. Africa (although the fat-tailed Barbary

sheep, predominant in Tunisia, is gradually replaced by the thin-tailed Maghreb variety as one moves west in Algeria and Morocco), the eastern half of the Sahara and all of sub-Saharan Africa except for W. Africa and the Congo Basin. It is universal in Egypt, the Fertile Crescent, and Arabia. More than 80% of Turkey's sheep are indigenous fat-tail varieties. The sheep of Madagascar, C. Asia, W. China, and Mongolia are fat-tailed, and fat-tailed sheep predominate in N. India.

The fat in the tail is a store of food, and it would seem reasonable to consider it a natural adaptation to a harsh climate, like the camel's hump. However, all wild sheep varieties are thin-tailed. The tails of fat-tail lambs have been docked experimentally, and the result was that the fat that would otherwise have been deposited on the tail was distributed elsewhere on the mature sheep's bodies. This shows that the tail is not essential for storing fat, and that the fat tail is a characteristic that humans bred sheep for, not a natural adaptation.

Why a fat *tail*? This takes some explaining. An animal can only metabolize its fat in liquid form. The inevitable consequence of this is that fat stored near the surface of the body, where it is influenced by ambient temperatures which are usually lower than the body's own temperature, has a lower melting point than fat stored deep in the body.

Such 'soft' fat was more desirable for cooking than interior fat because it melted quicker (it is unlikely that nomads took into account the aesthetic consideration that hard lamb or mutton fat leaves an unpleasant tallowy coating on the mouth). Unlike hard fat, however, which might be deposited in large, convenient lumps in the interior of the carcass, most soft fat was scantily dispersed all over the body subcutaneously. Sheep sometimes deposit larger lumps of soft fat in other places, such as the neck and throat.

Those deposits have limited value, however; there might be cool ambient temperatures on one side of the lump but warm body temperatures on the other.

Fat deposited on the tail turned out to be the solution. Surrounded as it is by cool temperatures, the tail can be home to a substantial slab of fat with a texture somewhat like bacon, though of course with a muttony aroma.

The extent to which early Arabic cookery books called for tail fat, and the various purposes for which is was used, has been discussed by Perry (1995*b*). In brief, the prominence of tail fat in medieval recipes, including those in the two 16th-century Persian collections which survive, varies considerably. What is clear is that, although it does appear in a handful of recipes for sweet dishes, this fat was primarily used for meat cookery; many such recipes begin with an instruction to 'melt the tail fat'.

It is also clear that the use of tail fat has been in marked decline in recent times. On the other hand, the numbers of fat-tailed sheep do not seem to be dwindling. There is thus a curious situation in which an ingredient appears to be disappearing from the kitchens and tables of the world although it continues to be produced, with no sign that production will be halted. A part explanation may be that the demand for lean meat has been growing, and the meat of these sheep, precisely because they store their fat in their tails, is lean. Also, these sheep are good milkers and some are prolific breeders.

Margaret Shaida (1992) confirms that this special tail fat has gone out of fashion in Iran, as elsewhere, but comments that:

it is infinitely more delicate in flavour than body fat, and gives a pleasing fragrance and richness to many Persian meat dishes that is difficult to

(*cont. on page 293*)

Fat-tailed sheep

Fats and oils

Fats and oils are chemically the same. Conventionally the word 'fat' is used for something that is solid at normal temperatures, and 'oil' for a liquid. COCONUT and PALM OILS, however, are liquid in the hot climate of their lands of origin, but generally solid in temperate climates, their melting point being between 21 and 26 °C (70–9 °F). Furthermore, the melting and solidification of fats and oils is a gradual process; they are not fully liquid above or fully solid below a given temperature.

Further details of individual fats and oils are given in the articles on the various nuts and other sources from which they are produced.

ARE FATS ESSENTIAL?

Fats and oils are to some extent a luxury both in cooking and in diet. Fat contributes to the palatability of food, making it more agreeable by increasing the smoothness and tenderness of the texture. Fat also carries much flavour, though in a pure state it has no flavour of its own. Many flavouring substances are soluble in fat but not in water. The flavour of meat, for example, is largely in its fat. If every trace of fat is excised from a piece of beef and a piece of mutton, it is almost impossible to distinguish between them. Fat also increases the satisfying quality of food. It takes a certain time to digest, so it increases the time that food remains in the stomach, giving a feeling of comfortable satiety.

In terms of the strict necessities of diet, hardly any fat is needed. The body requires fat as part of its own composition, but it can make fat from other foods. (This is in contrast to protein, which can only be had from protein—or its component substances—in the diet.)

However, a few grams of fat are necessary every day to carry the necessary vitamins A, D, E, and K, which are soluble in fat but not in water; and to provide certain substances found only in fat, the essential fatty acids. At least one of these is certainly needed: linoleic acid. Two others, linolenic and arachidonic acid, can probably be made by the body; although if they are eaten there is no need to make them.

Vegetable oils are much richer sources of these essential fatty acids than are animal fats, but in practice this is not very important because of the small quantities involved. Most diets, especially western ones, contain far more fat than the basic requirement. The traditional Japanese diet, for example, has only a fraction of the fat of a western one, and the Japanese remain perfectly healthy on it. Dietitians generally consider that the amount of fat eaten in western countries is excessive and unhealthy. Part of the reason for this is that fat is much higher in energy value than any other food, twice as much as sugar; 9 calories per gram or 255 calories per ounce. A diet rich in fat is therefore concentrated and calorific, and tends to lead to obesity.

Even if it were desirable, a completely fat-free diet would be impossibly bulky. If an active, grown man lived entirely on potatoes, which contain very little fat, he would have to eat about 4 kg or 9 lb of them every day to supply the 3,000 or so calories he needed.

Dietitians also pay attention to the nature of the fat which is eaten. In order to understand the statements they make, for example about the undesirability of consuming much 'saturated' fat, it is necessary to consider the chemical nature of fat and the various ways in which fats can be classified.

LIPIDS AND ESTERS

Fat is one of a class of substances called lipids. These include not only fats but also waxes (naturally found in plants); phospholipids, such as lecithin in egg yolk; and steroids, such as CHOLESTEROL, also found in egg yolk, and ergosterol, the chemical name of vitamin D.

Lipids belong to a larger class of chemical substances: esters. Esters are also important in food as flavouring compounds, some of which are oils and some are not. Esters which act as flavourings have an aromatic quality (in common language, not in the restricted chemical sense of 'aromatic'). An example of ester fragrance is ethyl acetate (now called ethanoate), the chief component of the smell of strawberries. Esters with small, light molecules are fragrant because the molecules are light enough to drift about in a vapour. But the esters which make up the bulk of fats have rather large molecules, so that they form liquids or solids with no smell.

FATTY ACIDS

An ester molecule is a combination of several smaller molecules linked together: an acid or acids with an alcohol. In fats the alcohol is glycerol, more familiar under its common name of glycerine. The glycerol molecule has three sites for connecting to fatty acids, and in a fat all three are filled. The fat molecule is therefore called a triglyceride molecule.

There is a wide assortment of fatty acids, and all fats and oils contain a mixture of them. Fatty acids can exist on their own, and may be detached from the glycerol which holds them. Their molecules vary considerably in length and weight. Those with the shortest molecules are volatile and have strong smells, noticeable when a fat breaks down and releases them, as happens when the fat becomes rancid. The shortest are butyric acid, one of the main smells of rancid butter; caproic, caprylic, and capric acids, which all smell 'goaty'; and lauric and myristic acids, which are components of the smell of bay and nutmeg. Longer, heavier molecules are not volatile and have no smell. A fat with a majority of short and medium length acids is liquid at normal temperatures; one with predominantly long acids is solid.

SATURATION

Another distinction between fatty acids is whether their molecules are saturated, monounsaturated, or polyunsaturated. A fatty acid molecule consists of carbon, oxygen, and hydrogen atoms arranged (at least in most of the fatty acids in foodstuffs) in a straight chain. Each carbon atom, except those at the ends of the chain, may have two hydrogen atoms linked to it. If two adjacent carbon atoms lack these attached hydrogen atoms, they link to each other in a 'double bond', which is less stable than a normal single bond. A double bond is therefore a weak link in the chain, which may easily be undone in a chemical reaction.

A fatty acid with no double bonds is said to be 'saturated'—totally filled with hydrogen. If it has one double bond it is 'monounsaturated'; if it has two or more it is 'polyunsaturated'. The more double bonds in the chain, the less stable the fatty acid. This effect is noticeable in the stability of the fat as a whole.

Generally, vegetable oils contain a higher proportion of monounsaturated and polyunsaturated acids than do animal fats, but there are exceptions: coconut and palm oils are highly saturated, and fish oils largely unsaturated.

COMMONLY USED EDIBLE OILS

Oil or fat	Ratio		
	S	M	P
Corn	14	26	60
Cottonseed	25	20	55
Groundnut (peanut)	20	41	39
Olive	15	82	3
Palm	51	38	11
Palm kernel	88	12	0
Rapeseed type A	7	59	34
Rapeseed type B	8	64	26
Safflower	9	9	82
Sesame seed	16	39	45
Sunflower seed	13	25	62
Walnut	10	19	71
Beef dripping	56	40	4
Chicken fat	31	48	21
Goose fat	27	62	11
Pork lard	42	47	11
Butter (fat)	58	38	11

Note: The proportions of the three kinds of acid in common oils are given under S (saturated), M (monounsaturated), and P (polyunsaturated).

Most of the longest fatty acid molecules are saturated, while unsaturated acids tend towards the shorter end of the range (although the very shortest acids are saturated). Thus increasing the proportion of saturated acids in a liquid oil tends to turn it into a solid fat. No fat is completely saturated, but full saturation has been produced experimentally. It results in a solid as brittle as china.

An industrial process, hydrogenation or 'hardening', is used in making hard MARGARINE from liquid vegetable or fish oils. The oil is heated with hydrogen. The hydrogen atoms attach themselves to carbon atoms at the weak double bonds, turning these into strong single bonds. Hardening a

fat not only makes it solid, but also more stable and less likely to become rancid. It is sometimes done for this reason alone, for example in the making of commercial peanut butter.

Soft margarine described as 'high in polyunsaturates' is made by a different process, from oils which would normally be liquid. These are made into an EMULSION which depends for its stability on chemical emulsifiers.

The proportion of saturated acids in a fat can be found by testing with iodine, which reacts with the double bonds. The result is expressed as the number of grams of iodine that are taken up by 100 grams of fat. This 'iodine number' or 'iodine value' runs from 0 for total saturation to nearly 200 in the edible oils highest in polyunsaturates. Coconut oil has an iodine number of 7, butterfat 32, olive oil 84, and soya oil 140.

EXTRACTION AND REFINING

Extracting fats and oils from their sources may be a fairly simple process or a complex one involving several stages.

The best oils from a gastronomic point of view are those extracted simply. The simplest process is cold pressing, as used for 'virgin' olive oil and for the best nut oils. The olives or nuts are pressed, and the oil left in the state in which it emerges, with many plant substances present which give it flavour and colour. Unfortunately, these substances include enzymes which attack the oil, so these natural oils do not keep well. However, they are valued for their flavour. Another example of a fat prepared by a natural, simple process which leaves it full of flavour but prone to spoilage is butter.

Cold pressing alone cannot remove all the oil from any fruit, nut, or seed. After the first pressing the crushed mass is heated to make the oil more liquid and readier to emerge. After this, solvents are sometimes used which wash the oil out of the plant tissue in the same way as dry cleaning removes the grease from clothes (in fact similar solvents are used). The solvents are then evaporated and recovered for reuse, leaving the oil. One other method, used for soya beans, is a centrifugal expeller which removes oil in the same way as a salad spinner removes water.

Animal fats and fish oils are extracted from meat trimmings or fish by 'rendering' them with steam to melt out the fats. For example, beef yields oleo oil for margarine and oleostearin (tallow) for solid cooking fat.

Some oils, such as cottonseed and rapeseed oils, are highly impure and inedible in their original state, whatever method of extraction is used, and any oil or fat extracted by any method other than cold pressing will contain impurities which are nearly always unwelcome. So the next stage is refining.

The oil is treated with steam to remove gum, and then with alkali to neutralize free fatty acids which might contribute unpleasant flavours. The alkali causes slight saponification: that is, it splits up some of the triglyceride molecules into glycerol and soaps. (Ordinary soap is made from fats and alkalis.) The glycerol and soap are washed out with water and the oil left for a while so that the water settles to the bottom and can be drained off. Next it is bleached with fuller's earth and given a final deodorization with steam. What emerges is a nearly pure oil containing a blend of saturated and unsaturated fatty acids. It has almost no taste or smell. Ordinary cooking oil is of this kind.

KEEPING FATS AND OILS

Even refined oils, devoid of enzymes, are subject to deterioration. Highly unsaturated ones are the least stable, especially those which contain appreciable amounts of linolenic acid (e.g. soya oil), which is the most troublesome of the common fatty acids.

Oils react with oxygen from the air. This can cause oxidative rancidity: a series of chemical reactions which releases compounds with an unpleasant smell and taste. Fish oils, which are highly unsaturated, and again soya oil, are especially prone to this spoilage.

Professional bakers and other food processors add antioxidants—substances which retard rancidity—to their goods. Sugar is a good antioxidant: biscuits with sugar remain fresh over four times as long as those without. Some herbs and spices are effective, including allspice, cloves, oregano, rosemary, sage, and thyme. The essential oils in these are often mildly antiseptic, restraining the growth of micro-organisms which cause rancidity. Many of the spices used in curry powders contain such oils.

EFFECTS OF HEAT

Fats and oils are not much changed by heating to moderate temperatures; they do not become 'cooked' in the same way as proteins or carbohydrates. (Butter is changed by heating because it includes water, which boils away, and protein, which cooks.) If an oil is heated excessively it begins to break down; a sign of this is that it gives off smoke. Soya oil, one of the most heatproof oils, has a 'smoke point' of 256 °C (492 °F). It does not actually catch fire until it reaches about 350 °C (662 °F). If flour particles fall off food which is being deep fried and float in the oil, they lower the smoke point considerably.

Oils used for deep-frying tend to deteriorate from repeated heating to near their smoke point. Some of the molecules break up and release free acids and other compounds which give the oil a rancid taste. Others polymerize—clump together—which causes the oil to become heavy and sticky.

Oil can also be affected by low temperature. If it is kept in a cold place, some of the heavier molecules may fall below their solidification temperature. The oil clouds and a solid deposit forms at the bottom of the bottle. This does no harm, and the oil will reliquefy if warmed.

Solid fats melt gradually, slowly becoming softer until finally they are fully liquid: this is different from, say, water melting to ice. Even apparently solid fats are not entirely solid. They consist of crystals of solid fat made up of the heavier molecules surrounded by liquid fat (or oil) made up of the lighter ones, which have a lower melting point. As the temperature changes, increasing numbers of molecules pass from one state to the other, according to their individual melting points. It is a curious feature of fats that once melted, they have to be cooled to well below their melting point to resolidify them. Butter, for example, melts at about 35 °C (96 °F) but has to be cooled to about 23 °C (73 °F) to solidify it.

TEXTURE OF FOODS

The presence of crystals in solid fats accounts for the pleasant, crumbly texture of pastry. The crystals force the starch particles in the flour apart and retard the formation of elastic gluten (as in bread), so the pastry stays 'short'. If the pastry becomes warm in making, the crystals melt, gluten forms, and the pastry becomes tough. Using too little fat also allows gluten to form. Fats with large crystals make good pastry. One such fat is LARD, whose molecules tend to have a particularly large acid in the centre of each triglyceride trio, which helps large crystals to form. Small crystals, such as those in vegetable cooking fats, make better creamed cake mixes. The fat spreads evenly throughout the flour and lubricates the surfaces of starch and gluten particles, so that they slide together when eaten and the cake has a tender texture.

emulate. As recently as thirty years ago, housewives in Iran would always ask the butcher to add a piece of *donbeh* to their purchase of lamb, and many Iranians recall how, as a child, they relished a sandwich of the crispy remnants of the tail after rendering.

Even more recently, similar practices have continued in Afghanistan and C. Asia, and also the use of pieces of the tail fat alternating with pieces of meat in kebabs. In the Arab countries of the E. Mediterranean region the principal surviving use of the tail fat seems to be in connection with the preparation of QAWARMA. It is noteworthy, however, that a bit of rendered tail fat added to the clarified butter is the secret ingredient

in many BAKLAVA recipes.
READING: Jill Tilsley-Benham (1987).

CP

FEASTS a feature of human foodways which is found in virtually all cultures and can be treated at various levels. The simplest one is that of enjoyment of the combination of ample and delicious food with congenial company (the term being rarely used of just one or two people eating, and applying more often to a company of, say, 10 to 1,000). At what might be considered to be a deeper level, feasts have attracted much attention from sociologists and anthropologists, who consider their symbolic significance, whether

this is explicit or not, and discuss the role which they can play in cementing human relationships etc.

Instances of feasting are, obviously, uncountable; but the same could almost be said of categories of feasts, since there are so many. A Symposium held at Oxford University in 1990, on 'Feasting and Fasting', served both to highlight the connection between these two antithetical activities and to illustrate, by providing numerous examples, the diverse character of feasts. Admittedly, the symposiasts failed to draw attention to what for many people, at least in Britain, must be the most memorable of all feasts: the 'midnight feasts' enjoyed by children, which are of particular interest because they are unusual in being illicit and clandestine, whereas virtually all other feasts are at least public and probably also publicized. However, despite this cardinal omission, the papers submitted illuminated many patches of what is a vast canvas. Thus Bjorn Fjellheim gave an account of the three-day Norwegian peasant wedding feast ('as a social mirror'); Rose Arnold commented on Emma's wedding feast in Flaubert's *Madame Bovary*; Professor Phyllis Bober had a paper on 'black' banquets (including not only the notorious one offered by GRIMOD DE LA REYNIÈRE but also the more creatively 'black' funeral feast devised by the hero in Huysmans's novel *A rebours*); Nevin Halıcı dealt with 'white foods in Anatolian feasts'; Professor Nicholas Kurti described among other things a feast at an Oxford college; Charles Perry summed up the main elements of medieval Arab feasting (hospitality, conviviality, and 'gourmet display', supplemented in his essay by a 10th-century Egyptian rhymester's comic ode on a village feast to which an army of uninvited guests poured in from several continents); Jo Marie Powers described how Samuel de Champlain initiated the first formalized feasting and social club in the New World in the winter of 1606–7, bringing together two widely differing cultures, the French and Micmac, at the common ground of the feast table; Alicia Rios described and interpreted the ritual of the 'First Communion Banquet', while Sami Zubaida wrote on the feasting involved in the celebration of Ramadan by Muslims; and Paul Stokes, delving in the remoter past, discussed what evidence for prehistoric feasts could be uncovered by archaeologists.

READING: Walker (1991); Bridget Ann Henisch (1976); Davidson (1988c).

FECULA is a general term for a STARCH which has been rendered more or less pure by washing in water, as opposed to a FLOUR or FARINA, which contains protein and other substances from the original plant. Most ordinary starches such as TAPIOCA and cornflour are feculas. So is 'ground rice', which is purified rice starch and is more accurately called *crème de riz* by the French. SEMOLINA, on the other hand, contains much protein.

Some French recipes call for 'fécule', e.g. to thicken soups. This is understood to mean potato starch, which is available everywhere in France and in some shops in other countries. It is effective in very low concentrations.

FEET of animals, consist mainly of skin, bones, and cartilage, but are normally edible

in that they yield some meat. Also, in most instances, they provide GELATIN when boiled; boiling calves' feet in particular used to be an essential step in making a JELLY.

In many cultures feet are not seen as repulsive or unsuitable to eat, but in the English-speaking world there has been a tendency, especially in recent times and urban environments, to disdain them unless they are disguised in some way (e.g. appearing in a BRAWN) or bear some more other name (e.g. trotters), perhaps with a traditional ring to it (e.g. cow-heel).

Feet vary greatly in size, from those of a chicken to the feet of the ELEPHANT, which in the past have constituted an exotic delicacy for travellers in Africa. In practice, however, the feet which attract the attention of cooks in the western world are usually those of sheep or lamb, pigs and calves. If these feet are deboned, singed, and cooked in a COURT BOUILLON they are ready for various final treatments.

Dorothy Hartley (1954) has characteristically precise and vivid information about some dishes traditional in England. One was Sheep's Trotters with Oatmeal, on which she says:

Sheep's trotters are the ceremonial part of the Bolton Wanderers football team dinners. Only the heavy types of mountain sheep, such as the Pennine Range sheep, can make this dish well. (I don't think a sparrow could make a meal off a Welsh trotter, but in the larger breeds of sheep, the trotters are almost as meaty as a pig's.)

She also explains the special merits, for people who are out at work from dawn to dusk, of Battered Trotters. Before going off at 6 a.m., one would set the trotters to stew very slowly with onion trimmings etc. One would also make a stiff batter to be put in the pantry. In the evening the trotters would be taken out, boned, dipped in the batter and fried. Meanwhile the cooking liquor would be boiled down to make a thickened gravy. Dorothy Hartley comments that this made a substantial 'tea relish' (see HIGH TEA). Economical too; 'trotters was cheap and t'trimmings cost nout'. She concludes with a very wise comment: 'When you find some people making some dishes over and over again, and specially well, you can nearly always see *why*.'

Generally, the treatment of feet in Britain reflected a desire to use up all of an animal, rather than gastronomic aspirations. No trace of the latter is to be found in the basic British method of brining pig's trotters and boiling them for several hours, to be eaten cold with vinegar. Prepared thus in S. Ireland, they are known as crubeens, and have been described with enthusiasm by Monica Sheridan (1966), who explains that:

The hind feet are made up entirely of tiny bones and gristle and are used only to give setting

strength to a brawn or a galantine. The front feet are the true crubeens, which have succulent bits of meat concealed around the bones. At one time they were a great favourite in the pubs of Ireland on a Saturday night, when they were consumed in large numbers. . . . I am very proud of the fact that I have been elected the first and only woman Member of Cumann Crubeen na h-Eireann, an exclusive, crubeen-eating club that meets every Saturday night in Tramore, County Waterford.

Boiled cow-heel is another traditional food of the poor in Britain, and may be eaten as it is or added to beef stews. In Scotland, sheep's trotters are added to Powsowdie (sheep's head broth, see HEAD).

Pieds et paquets is a well-known Provençal dish, involving 'packets' of stuffed sheep's TRIPE which are simmered lengthily with aromatics, together with sheep's trotters.

Pig's trotters are dealt with in various ways in France; the preparation *à la Sainte-Menehould* (with a mustard sauce) was celebrated by Alexandre Dumas (1873) in an anecdote which has the French king Charles VII, famished after a battle with the English, supping on the dish, which had been improvised for him and his companions by a woman in the little town of Sainte-Menehould. The coating of crisp breadcrumbs provides a contrast with the soft gelatinous meat.

Meat from feet is often one ingredient in a dish incorporating others, notably many sorts of BRAWN. In England, the title of 'pettitoes' was given to a highly seasoned RAGOUT made from the feet and internal organs of a sucking pig. Many dishes combine feet with meat from HEADS; there is a famous soup which has this combination and is known from Turkey (where it is *Kelle-paça*) through the Middle East to Afghanistan. Also, pig's feet may form part of the mixed meats served with SAUERKRAUT, and are made into a pig's feet and sauerkraut soup in Poland.

Poultry feet are more valued in the Far East than elsewhere. In China chicken feet are served in a much appreciated soup, and the webbed feet of ducks liked for the gelatinous texture they contribute to soups and braised dishes.

See also ZAMPONE.

FEIJOA *Feijoa sellowiana*, a small evergreen tree with grey-green leaves, is a native of S. America where it is found at high altitudes in parts of Argentina, Uruguay, S. Brazil, and W. Paraguay. It has been grown in other warm temperate zones of the world, usually as an ornamental; but it bears edible fruit and is sometimes grown commercially for this purpose, e.g. in New Zealand, where the flavour and keeping qualities of the fruit have made it popular.

The fruit is oval in shape, not more than 7 cm (3") in length, with a green, bloom-covered skin which may be blushed with red. The granular whitish flesh surrounding a pulp containing many tiny seeds has a flavour somewhere between pineapple and strawberry. The aromatic appeal of the fruit increases as it ripens.

The earlier part of the feijoa crop is best marketed as fresh fruit. The fruits which ripen later are mostly used to produce canned feijoa juice. Feijoa may also be stewed, or made into jams and jellies.

FENNEL *Foeniculum vulgare*, a plant of the parsley family (Umbelliferae), with feathery leaves and yellow flowers. It has been used in Europe since the beginning of the classical era, and probably earlier, both as a source of seed for flavouring and as a vegetable, in which case the stalk is the part eaten. It is now grown in moderately warm regions worldwide, mainly for seed.

There are three principal sorts of fennel: bitter and sweet fennel, both used as herbs, and Florence fennel, which provides a vegetable in the form of the swollen base of its stem.

Bitter fennel, the original wild form, is native to S. Europe and is now grown mainly in C. and E. Europe for seed. It is a tall, relatively thin-stemmed plant. The seed has a slightly bitter flavour rather like that of celery seed. This is not like the flavour of the other two kinds, which are better known in W. Europe, America, and elsewhere, so if the latter are used in C. or E. European dishes the wrong effect will be produced. Celery seed is a better substitute.

It is probable that bitter fennel was the only type in use in the classical world, since there is no mention of there being more than one kind until much later.

Fennel had an honoured place in Greek mythology, for it was in one of its hollow stalks that Prometheus is said to have hidden the fire he stole from the gods and, by bringing it to the human race, to have raised them from their former state of brutish ignorance. Incidentally, the ancients had another cause for being grateful to this mythical hero. The reason for the gods' withholding fire from mortals, so that it was necessary to steal it, was that Prometheus had tricked Zeus, the king of the gods, into accepting fat and bones as the gods' portion of animal sacrifices, while the humans kept and enjoyed the meat.

Spoerri (1982) observes that the Greek author ATHENAEUS stated that fennel (*marathon* in Greek) was put with brined olives in pious memory of the battle of Marathon. Not so; Athenaeus was quoting a joke from a 5th-century BC comedy, the joke being based on the fact that there is no connection whatsoever between the herb and the battle.

Roman cookery made much use of fennel, which is often mentioned by APICIUS. The seeds were included in seasoning mixtures of herbs and spices, and the chopped stems were used in mixed stews and in pickles.

Sweet fennel is first distinguished in an edict of Charlemagne, in the 9th century, ordering it to be grown in the south of France. Presumably it originated in Italy. Sweet plants have a tendency to revert to bitterness when old, showing that they are not a separate species. The seeds and stems have a mild ANISE flavour which the bitter variety totally lacks. (Anise also comes from an umbelliferous plant.)

Sweet fennel gained popularity rapidly. It was spread by Arab traders all over the Middle East and to India, whence it reached China. In the East it is mostly used for its seed. Flavourings of the anise type were already in favour here and the prolific fennel plant made a convenient source. The fresh leaf is also used. It can be dried, but with some loss of flavour; while the seed keeps very well. Indians chew fennel seed as a breath freshener. Sweet fennel is one of the ingredients in gripe water, the soothing drink given to babies.

Sweet fennel became firmly established in medieval European cooking, mostly as a flavouring but also as a vegetable. A special type with comparatively thick stalks is a traditional salad vegetable in and around Naples, where it is called *carosella*. The taste of fennel goes well with fish, and many old and new fish recipes combine the two. There is a Provençal dish, fish grilled *au fenouil*, in which dried fennel stalks are burned under the fish to give it a smoky aroma.

Florence fennel or finocchio is a vegetable. The short, stumpy plant has the bases of its leaf stems greatly thickened into a solid, overlapping mass which may be as large as a fist. This is earthed up as it develops, to blanch it. It is often eaten raw and thinly sliced, when it has an attractive crisp texture; but it may just as well be sliced thickly and braised or fried, or steamed, to be served as a hot vegetable. Either way, it has a delicate anise flavour.

The name *finocchio* is simply the general Italian word for fennel, but has been used in other countries to distinguish this special type, which was developed in Italy in the 17th century.

FENUGREEK *Trigonella foenum-graecum*, a leguminous plant related to CLOVER, is native to S. Europe and Asia and is widely cultivated as a condiment crop. In classical times, it was much better known in Europe than it is now. It was then grown both as a fodder crop and for the supposed medicinal properties of its seeds. The botanical name for the species and most of the common European names mean 'Greek hay'.

Fenugreek seeds, which are yellowish brown, are frequently used in India as a flavouring in curries. They need slow heating to bring out the full flavour, but overheating makes them bitter. Their aroma resembles that of celery. Since fenugreek is present and noticeable in most sorts of commercial CURRY POWDER, it constitutes, for many people in western countries, the specific aroma of curry.

Fenugreek

In S. India the seeds 'are the second ingredient after mustard seeds to be fried in hot oil for a few seconds before the other ingredients are added. They are also used roasted and powdered along with red chilli and other spices in a condiment known as muligapuri, to be eaten with idli and dosas' (Camellia Panjabi, 1994). The seeds are also used as a flavouring for pickles and, in Kerala, in fish cookery.

If sprouted to provide a salad vegetable, the seeds have only a slight and pleasant bitterness. The young leaves, however, a popular vegetable in India and often used to flavour PARATAS, are always bitter. They may also be cooked like spinach and served as an accompaniment to a main dish. Dried leaves are used as an ingredient in tandoori chicken or fish.

Uses in other countries vary. Thus fenugreek greens are a staple food in Yemen, and both Yemeni and Ethiopian cooks use much fenugreek in their sauces (see HILBEH). In Afghanistan, fenugreek seeds, which are rich in vitamins and sugar, are used not only for flavouring spinach, but also in a sweet rice dish called *Shola-e-olba*, and in some pickles.

An Australian plant sometimes called 'sweet fenugreek' but better known as Cooper clover, *T. suavissima*, is eaten by the Aborigines and said to have a good flavour. Tim Low (1989) quotes an early explorer, Major Mitchell:

The perfume of this herb, its freshness and flavour, induced me to try it as a vegetable, and we found it to be delicious, tender as spinach, and to preserve a very green colour when boiled. This was certainly the most interesting plant hitherto discovered by us.

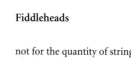

Fiddleheads

FERMENTATION a word used loosely to describe desirable changes brought about by living micro-organisms (YEASTS, MOULDS, and BACTERIA) in food and drink. Examples are making bread rise and turning milk into cheese. The term is often extended to changes caused by non-living ENZYMES, for example in the 'fermentation' of black TEA. When micro-organisms or enzymes cause undesirable changes, for example making food go bad, what happens is called spoilage rather than fermentation.

There are two main reasons for subjecting food to fermentation. One is to convert it from a form which will not keep, such as milk, to one which will, such as cheese. The other is to make foods which are indigestible in their original state, such as wheat or soya beans, digestible by turning them into products such as bread or TEMPE. As well as these practical benefits there are other gains, such as improvement in flavour.

While many fermentations of food are familiar, it is often not realized that the process plays a part in the preparation of COFFEE, COCOA, VANILLA, and many kinds of SAUSAGE.

For more detailed information on particular fermentations, see the articles on the fermented foods themselves.

FERNS provide, from their young shoots and sometimes their roots, a minor vegetable food in many parts of the world.

One fern product constitutes a wild delicacy in the northern USA and Canada. This is **fiddleheads**, the young shoots of the ostrich fern, *Matteuccia struthiopteris*, and the cinnamon fern, *Osmunda cinnamonum*. The common name refers to the

resemblance between the tightly curled shoots and the scroll on a violin head. The practice of eating them is said to have been introduced by French settlers, taking their cue from American Indians. Fiddleheads, which can be had canned or frozen, are usually boiled; the flavour has been described as resembling a blend of broccoli, asparagus, and globe artichoke.

Common bracken, *Pteridium aquilinum*, which grows abundantly in temperate northern regions all around the world, has generally been eaten in Europe and America only in times of famine; but in Japan it is esteemed as an oriental equivalent of fiddleheads, under the name of *warabi*. The part usually eaten is the very young, coiled shoot as it breaks through the ground in spring. It is covered in brown scales which have to be scraped off. After that it may be boiled quickly in at least one change of water to remove bitterness; the texture is then crisp and the flavour nutty. Very young shoots may also be grilled, peeled and eaten without further preparation.

Bracken root is also edible, indeed often preferred to the shoot. It is made into *warabi* starch in Japan, and has also been a traditional source of farinaceous meal in the Balearic Islands and the Canaries.

New Zealand is sometimes called the 'land of ferns', and a variety of *P. esculentum*, known as *aruhe*, was the most important source of food for the Maori before white colonists introduced sweet potatoes and maize. Crowe (1981) has collected opinions about its taste from early explorers. These range from reported resemblances to ship's biscuit or newly baked bread to Sir Joseph Banks's fuller description:

a sweetish clammyness in it not disagreeable to the taste; it might be esteemed a tolerable food was it

not for the quantity of strings and fibres in it which in quantity three or four times exceeded the soft part; these were swallowed by some but the greater number of people spit them out, for which purpose they had a basket standing under them to receive their chewed morsels, in shape and colour not unlike Chaws of Tobacco.

The fern most prized by the Maori was *Asplenium bulbiferum*, the hen and chicken fern, so called because of its habit of producing new plants on the old fronds. Recent New Zealand authors have described them as palatable.

Low (1989) contributes an interesting item for Australia:

In Moreton Bay the semiaquatic fern called bungwall (*Blechnun indicum*) was the mainstay of local tribes. Early settler Constance Petrie described how the starchy rhizomes were 'first roasted, then scraped and cut up finely with sharp stones on a log, when it was ready to eat. "Bangwall" was generally eaten with fish or flesh, as we use bread, though also eaten separately. In a camp, my father says, one would hear the chop-chop continually all over the place as their food was prepared.'

Bungwall is found in coastal swamps throughout E. and N. Australia, but is nowhere as much as in Moreton Bay; only there was it served as a staple food, although it is not eaten at all now.

Finally, the **maidenhair fern**, *Adiantum capillus-veneris*, which grows in moist shady places in Europe and N. America, has several uses. Its delicate fronds were used in Victorian Britain as cake decorations. A mucilaginous liquid made by boiling them down was, and occasionally still is, made into a sweetened soft drink called *capillaire*. This is usually given other flavours, as it has little of its own. It was popular in the 18th century. Dr Johnson used to add it to port.

Bracken and several other ferns are suspected of causing cancer. Thus the shoots and raw roots of bracken are considered to be carcinogenic, although the Maori methods of preparation eliminated this quality from the roots and reduced it in the shoots. Statistical evidence from Japan, where bracken is often eaten, is suggestive, and it is noticeable that farm animals avoid eating it. At least one other kind of fern is immediately poisonous, so such plants are not to be tasted at random.

FESENJAN a rich savoury dish which belongs to the cuisine of IRAN and nearby countries. Its distinguishing characteristics are the use of WALNUTS and POMEGRANATE in the sauce. The main element of the dish is usually DUCK, but other birds or meats or even meatballs may be used.   HS

FETA the best known of Greek cheeses, is now also made in other countries and continents (e.g. Denmark, America, Australia). The home region of feta includes Bulgaria as well as Greece, and some people think that Bulgarian ewe's milk feta is the best of all.

Feta is traditionally made from sheep's milk or sheep's and goat's milk mixed, but cow's milk is now often used. It is made in large blocks which are salted, sliced, and salted again, and packed into containers in which the cheese matures for about a month in the salty whey. The taste is sharp and, of course, salty. *Teleme*, made in several Balkan countries, is very similar.

FIBRE a term for the undigestible constituents of food. Among the most important of these is what is called roughage. This term is almost synonymous with fibre but refers particularly to undigestible CARBOHYDRATE material, for example CELLULOSE, in plant foods. The BRAN in cereals is roughage.

Roughage passes through the system unchanged, but absorbs and holds water, so acts as a laxative.

FIDDLER CRAB the name given to any of a large group of crabs of the family Ocypodidae, notably those of the genus *Uca*, which have one claw much larger than the other. Their habit of 'sawing' the large claw up and down in the air accounts for 'fiddler'; and a bevy of these crabs standing on a river bank and sawing away like a small orchestra is a quaint sight.

The African fiddler crab, *Uca tangeri*, is familiar to the inhabitants of Cadiz. Large numbers of these crabs inhabit holes in mud

banks near the salt pans in the vicinity. Fishermen remove the large claw from males and then return them to the water to grow another for next season. The claws, which are sold as *bocas de la isla*, contain particularly good meat.

Other fiddler crabs are exploited in other parts of the world. The survival strategies of these little musicians must be a successful one, for they have a wide distribution and have even warranted publication of a book on 'fiddler crabs of the world'.

FIELD MUSHROOM *Agaricus campestris*, for many people the 'only' wild mushroom to be eaten, is common in spring and autumn in grassy fields, especially where cattle graze, in Europe, N. America, China, Australasia, S. Africa, and temperate zones generally in northern and southern hemispheres. It is highly edible, and serves as the archetypal mushroom for this and other purposes in occidental countries. The cap, measuring up to 10 cm (4"), is white to pale brown; the stem relatively short; and the gills at first pink and later brown.

Field mushrooms may be eaten raw or cooked, whether they are at the button stage or are at the large flat stage with chocolate-coloured gills. (Later, when the gills are turning black and viscous, the only thing to be done with them is to make mushroom ketchup.) Dorothy Hartley (1954) commended the practice of country folk, who make brown bread and butter sandwiches with fine slices of field mushroom and a few drops of lemon juice as the filling.

Close relations of the field mushroom include *A. arvensis*, the HORSE MUSHROOM; *A. silvaticus*, the WOOD MUSHROOM; and *A. augustus*, the PRINCE. To this list must be added *A. bisporus*, the now relatively rare

ancestor of the common cultivated mushroom (which is usually classified as *A. bisporus* var *hortensis*: see MUSHROOM CULTIVATION). This always grows on rich soil, for example in gardens or on manure heaps. It has a pale brown cap, fibrous and scaly.

FIG *Ficus carica*, a fruit with many extraordinary features. The lifecycle of some sorts of fig depends on the efforts made by a tiny insect, the fig wasp, to reproduce itself: efforts which have a pathetic aspect, since they often fail in their main purpose, and lead to the production of more figs instead of more wasps.

In consumption as well as in generation, the fig is unusual. In the warm countries where it grows easily it is a cheap and staple food. Elsewhere fresh figs are a luxury and the fruit is better known in its dried form, whose characteristics are quite different.

The fig tree is the descendant of a wild tree, the caprifig (goat fig). This had spread from W. Asia into the Mediterranean region in prehistoric times, and then out to the Canary Islands and northwards as far as Germany. Wild figs may be eaten, but they are small and dry. The process of selection and cultivation, necessary to obtain palatable fruit, began in remote antiquity and continued in classical times. Over two dozen kinds of fig were known to the Romans.

The fig, already peculiar, became stranger still as it evolved from a wild to a cultivated plant. The mature fig fruit is botanically not a single fruit but almost 1,500 tiny fruits, which are normally what are thought of as the seeds. These are fixed to the inside of a vase-shaped structure, termed a 'syconium', which is the outer part of the fig. Earlier, at the flower stage, the syconium is the same shape but much smaller. It contains all the

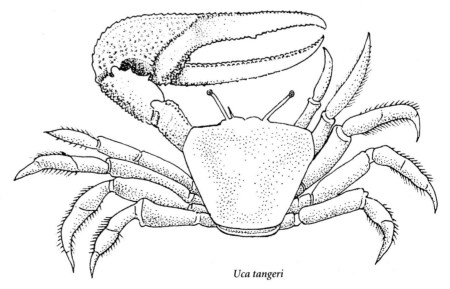

Uca tangeri

flowers and is completely closed except for a tiny hole at the opposite end from the stem.

The syconium of the wild caprifig contains both male and female flowers, but these are unable to fertilize each other because the female flowers mature some time before the male flowers produce pollen. Fertilization depends on a tiny, gnat-sized insect, the fig wasp, *Blastophaga grossorum*, which inhabits the syconium. Only the female wasp has wings. She develops over the winter inside a female flower, and is impregnated by the male in the spring. She then crawls around the inside of the syconium, thus becoming covered with pollen from the male flowers which surround it, until she finds the way out through the little hole. She leaves and flies to another syconium which, with luck, will be at an earlier stage and contain fertile female flowers. Entering it through its little hole, she finds a female flower and tries to lay her eggs down its style, ready to produce another generation of wasps. But the other female flowers nearby are pollinated as the wasp brushes against them, and will form fertile seeds.

The fertile fruits will give rise to a new generation of fig trees (even if they are eaten by humans or birds, for they pass through the body of either undamaged) and these trees in turn will depend on the caprifig and the wasps to help them have fruits of their own.

Cultivation started in Egypt or possibly Arabia, probably between 4000 and 2700 BC. There is a painting on the wall of an Egyptian tomb of the 12th dynasty, about 1900 BC, which clearly shows cultivated figs being harvested from a tree. By about 1500 BC figs were being grown in Crete and by 800 BC in mainland Greece. This was the age of Homer, who mentions them several times. The fig may have come to Greece from Crete, but the Greeks themselves thought that it had arrived from Caria in Asia Minor; hence the species name *carica*. At the same time the fig became established all over the Near East. It is mentioned repeatedly in the Bible.

The ancients discovered through experience that cultivated Smyrna figs would fruit only if there was a caprifig tree nearby. They would hang bits of caprifig branch in the boughs of the cultivated figs to encourage fertilization. (This is still practised, and is known as 'caprification'.) It is remarkable that in the 4th century BC both Aristotle and Theophrastus realized the need for the flower to be visited by the tiny fig wasp if the fruit were to form and not merely fall off.

The Romans used to eat large amounts of both fresh and dried figs. The finest fresh ones were an expensive delicacy, while cheap ones were described by Pliny as the food of slaves. Dried figs were used mostly as a sweetener and to make sweetmeats, their high natural sugar content being particularly valued in an age when sugar was an exotic rarity. Figs were used also in savoury dishes, and a Roman would not be surprised by the modern Italian habit of eating fresh figs with prosciutto.

During the period of the Roman Empire, new kinds of fig appeared which had less or no need for the fig wasp. The most important was what is now called the 'common fig', which produces two crops annually, neither of which needs to be caprified. So figs could increase their range, previously confined to the rather narrow band of climates which suited the wasp. This expansion of range achieved its greatest success much later, in the Americas. After an introduction to Haiti and Mexico in the 16th century, and then to Virginia, the fig found its real N. American home in California. In 1769 the Franciscan mission at San Diego was founded and began to grow a Spanish black common fig which (under the names of Mission or Franciscana) came to be a leading variety. American growers, who for long regarded the traditional European caprification process as a mere superstition, eventually learned how to grow Smyrna figs too.

In considering all the different sorts of fig, it is helpful to remember that there are four main botanical categories of fig (see table); and that within these are many commercial varieties (hundreds of them) of which only the most important are mentioned in what follows.

Type	Method of fertilization	Number of crops annually
Caprifig	by fig wasp	three
Smyrna	by caprification (fig wasp needed)	two
Common	parthenocarpic (no fig wasp needed)	two
San Pedro	parthenocarpic (1st crop) by caprification (2nd crop)	two

- **Caprifigs** or wild figs are cultivated for caprification of Smyrna figs and as part of the breeding of new varieties. However, an unusual variety appeared at Croisic in France in 1882, and has been given the name Croisic. It produces an unusually succulent fruit and is fully fertile without the mediation of the wasp. It is being used to generate new breeds which, it is hoped, will combine the good points of Smyrna and common figs.
- **Smyrna** (Calimyrna in the USA) figs still resemble the original cultivated in Asia Minor for more than 2,000 years. Much grown in Turkey, Greece, N. Africa, and California (where they are the main variety). Smyrna figs are larger than most, amber in colour both inside and out, and have the excellent nutty flavour which is characteristic of fertilized figs. They are often held to be the best of figs to eat fresh, which is normally possible only in the growing regions. Most are dried. The best ones are partially dried and left more or less in their natural shape.
- **Common figs** are grown mainly for eating fresh or for canning.

  Mission or Franciscana figs are a deep purple black outside and red inside. The texture is rather coarse but the flavour sweet and good.

  Dottato figs in Italy (Cadota in the USA), yellow-green on the outside, amber or violet inside, and medium to large in size, are the most important variety of common fig; usually eaten fresh, although they may be canned.

  Another common fig variety called Verdone in Italy and White Adriatic in the USA is particularly good fresh. It is green outside and pink or violet inside.

  Bardajic is the main common fig variety of Turkey. Californian names for locally grown figs of this type are Brown Turkey and Brunswick (but the latter covers two kinds, and these names mean the same only in California). Brown Turkey figs are eaten fresh or canned. They are medium sized, reddish-brown outside, and amber-pink inside.
- **San Pedro** or San Pietro figs, now grown less than the Smyrna or common types, are intermediate in flavour between them.

FIGGY PUDDING is nowadays more sung about, in a well-known Christmas carol, than eaten. There is a traditional Yorkshire figgy pudding whose density approaches that of CHRISTMAS PUDDING, and which may be allowed to mature in the same way. It consists of dried figs, chopped apples, carrot, breadcrumbs, flour, butter, eggs, brown sugar, black treacle, and lemon juice and rind; and it requires five hours' steaming. There are also lighter versions.

The original figgy pudding may merely have been a 'plum' pudding—that is, with any dried fruit—for in Cornwall, the word 'figgy' is still used for raisins. Figgy pudding is sometimes eaten on Palm Sunday, possibly in memory of Christ's cursing of the barren fig tree on that day.

FIGPECKER (or beccafico), any of various small birds in the group known as warblers, in the Mediterranean region, especially S. Italy and Cyprus. The capture of these tiny songbirds for consumption, entire, as delicacies offends the sensibilities of bird-lovers and efforts are made periodically to end or diminish the practice.

Amaranth Sitas (1968), writing of Cyprus, observes that the birds, which were commonly taken in September and were subsequently visible in grocers' shops in jars of vinegar, had been famous since medieval times. She draws attention to the following interesting passage by a certain John Locke (not the 17th-century philosopher), who visited Cyprus in 1553:

they have also on the Island a certaine small bird much like unto a Wagtaile in fethers and making, these are extreme fat that you can perceive nothing else in all their bodies: these birds are now in season. They take great quantities of them, and they use to pickle them with vinegar and salt, and to put them in pots and send them to Venice, and other places of Italy for present of great estimation. They say they send almost 1,200 jars or pots to Venice, besides those which are consumed on the island, which are of great number. These are so plentiful that when there is no shipping, you can buy them for 10 Carchies which coine are 4 to a Venetian Soldo, which is a penny farthing the dozen.

FILÉ also called filé powder or gumbo filé, consists of SASSAFRAS leaves, dried and reduced to a powder which is used to thicken, and also to flavour, dishes such as soups, stews, and gumbos (see OKRA).

In using the term, the Louisiana French have adapted to a new purpose the past participle of the French verb *filer*, meaning to spin thread. The thought is that the thickening effect produced by filé when added to hot liquids resembles the spinning of threads.

FILO is the Greek name for a dough of many paper-thin layers separated by films of butter. This structure is not obtained by repeatedly folding and rolling a single slab of buttered dough, as for *pâte feuilletée*, but by buttering and stacking separate paper-thin sheets (the method of BAKLAVA, BÖREK, and *spanakopitta*) or rolling up one paper-thin sheet around a filling to create many layers (the method of STRUDEL, *rétes*, and *zavín*). The sheets may be made thin by stretching the dough by hand (holding it by the knuckles, rather than the fingertips, to avoid tearing it) or by rolling a sheet (or for convenience a stack of sheets, separated by cornflour) until paper thin.

Although known to Europeans and N. Americans by a Greek name, the dough is clearly of Turkish origin. The medieval nomad Turks had an obsessive interest in making layered bread, possibly in emulation of the thick oven breads of city people. As early as the 11th century, a dictionary of Turkish dialects (*Diwan Lughat al-Turk*) recorded 'pleated/folded bread' as one

meaning for the word *yuvgha*, which is related to the word (*yufka*) which means a single sheet of filo in modern Turkish.

This love of layering continues among the Turks of C. Asia. To the Tatars, *yoka* means 10 or 12 sheets of very thin (although not paper-thin) dough which have been fried, buttered, and stacked up. Wedges are cut out of it, pie-fashion, and served with tea. The Uzbek *yupqa* is made by frying a thin sheet of dough on both sides in the bottom of a pot; sprinkling fried ground meat and onions in it; covering the filling with a raw sheet of dough; turning this 'sandwich' over to fry the raw side; and then repeating the process to build up a sort of cake 10–12 layers thick.

The idea of making the sheets paper thin is a later development. The Azerbaijanis make the usual sort of baklava with 50 or so layers of filo, but they also make a strange, archaic pastry called *Bakï pakhlavasï* (Baku-style baklava) using ordinary noodle paste instead of filo. It consists of eight layers of dough separated by seven layers of sweetened ground nuts. This may represent the earliest form of baklava, resulting from the Turkish nomads adapting their concept of layered bread—developed in the absence of ovens—to the use of the oven and combining it with the usual Persian pastry filling of nuts.

If this is so, baklava actually pre-dated filo, and the paper-thin pastry we know today was probably an innovation of the Ottoman sultan's kitchens at Topkapi palace in Istanbul. There is an established connection between the Topkapi kitchens and baklava; on the 15th of Ramadan every year, the Janissary troops stationed in Istanbul used to march to the palace, where every regiment was presented with two trays of baklava. They would sling the trays in sheets of cloth from a pole and march back to their barracks carrying the baklava in what was known as the Baklava Procession (*baklava alayi*).

Before the First World War, it was the custom for the great houses of Istanbul to keep two filo-makers on staff: one to make the filo for baklava, the other to make a stronger sort of filo for börek. Nowadays filo, and its European counterparts such as *Strudelteig*, are usually store-bought.

Given all the effort expended to make this dough capable of being baked into ethereally crisp layers, it seems odd that in Turkey filo is sometimes cooked with milk into a sort of pudding, *güllâç*. But *güllâç* is much admired for its delicacy. In Egypt, filo is even known as '*agin gullâsh* (*güllâç* dough), rather than as baklava dough.   CP

FINES HERBES the convenient French term for a mixture of chopped fresh herbs

used in cooking. A minimalist interpretation would be PARSLEY with any (or all) of: CHERVIL, TARRAGON, CHIVES. However, the number of different herbs to be used is far from fixed; and the range includes thyme, rosemary, burnet, and marjoram.

The mixture is used to flavour meat, fish, and salads, and (most common in Britain) to flavour omelettes.

FINGER-LIME the fruit of a shrub or small tree, *Microcitrus australasica*, found in the rainforest regions of NE Australia. It belongs to the citrus family, Rutaceae, but is not a true lime.

The near-cylindrical fruits are about 6 cm (2.5") long and may remain green even when ripe, although they can also be purple or blackish. The Australian author Cribb (1975) comments with enthusiasm:

If the fruit is cut across, the turgid pulp cells expand and separate, pushing out of the five or six longitudinal segments as a cluster of small glistening balls. For anyone who likes sour fruit these pulp cells are delicious; they burst pleasantly at slight pressure from the teeth and provide a most welcome refreshment. The fruits also can be made into marmalade which not only has a pleasant flavour and distinctive perfume but is ornamental as well, the sliced rings of fruit looking like miniature cartwheels.

FINLAND a country of enormous extent (only France, Spain, and Sweden are larger in Europe), a relatively small population (fewer than five million), and two languages (Finnish and Swedish). The Finnish language is of special interest because it, together with Estonian and Hungarian, is one of the few surviving examples of the Finno-Ugric linguistic family. About 6% of the population speak Swedish as their native tongue, whereas for all the rest it is Finnish; but just about everyone speaks both.

Of the many vigorous culinary traditions, some are focused on hunting, some on fish, others on gathering wild fungi, and several on particular enthusiasms which are shared with other Nordic countries, for example RYE BREAD (also BARLEY BREADS), the SMÖRGÅSBORD (*voileipäpöytä* in Finnish), CRAYFISH feasts, pickles of many kinds, and the golden CLOUDBERRY, which is found especially in the far north, within the Arctic Circle.

The parts of both Sweden and Finland which are in the Arctic are known as Lapland, and inhabited by Lapps, who traditionally provide Father Christmas with his home territory and training grounds for the reindeer. They have their own culture and foodways, with a strong emphasis on REINDEER—roast and smoked, in a stew (*Poronkäristys*), as a soup, in sausages, and (a rarity) smoked tongue. Reindeer meat is well partnered by many sorts of vegetable (but especially buttery and slightly lumpy mashed potato), lingonberry (see CRANBERRY) purée, and sour cream.

In Finland as a whole, ELK, BEAR, and HARE as well as reindeer are hunted and eaten. Finns are great hunters, but perhaps even greater at fishing. They have huge expanses of fresh water, noted for the excellence of BURBOT, among many other species. As for sea fish, there is inevitably a great interest, shared with Sweden and the Baltic states, in Baltic HERRING; this accounts for nearly three-quarters of the Finnish catch. What is more striking is the catholic nature of Finnish interest in other fish ROES (especially SALMON, WHITEFISH (including vendace), trout, burbot), as well as true (sturgeon) CAVIAR. All these things are beautifully displayed in the covered and open-air markets at Helsinki, for which the pistachio, apricot, and mushroom colours of Engel's classical buildings at the head of the harbour provide a superb backdrop. Fish bought in Finland come with a free helping of DILL.

Anna-Maija and Juha Tanttu (1988), in their survey of regional specialities, point to the influences affecting food from the west (Sweden) and from the east (Russia) and remark that:

At one time it was easy to draw a 'bread and buttermilk line' through Finland, since in the west, people baked rarely, but a lot at a time, and their buttermilk was long and stretchy. In the east, people baked at least once a week and made pasties in addition to bread, and the buttermilk was 'short' and more clotted.

It is also true that Karelia in the east of Finland and next door to Russia is the home of Finnish pasties, filled with rice or potatoes and bearing a recognizable resemblance to Russian pasties and pies (e.g. *kulebiyaka*— see COULIBIAC). However, the well-known fish 'pasty' *kalakukko*, like an edible lunch box with a filling of fish (perhaps perch) and pork fat enveloped in rye bread dough and baked thus, belongs to Savo, west of Karelia; and may have rutabaga (swede) inside instead of fish. Savo is also the province where vendace (see WHITEFISH) is prominent, cooked plain or in a stew or (again) baked in a shell of rye bread.

Like Danes and Swedes, Finnish people have fruit and other dessert soups as well as savoury ones, but what they like best are the hearty savoury ones. One of the most hearty belongs to the province of Häme. This is a meat soup which has a name which means 'lump soup', the lumps being potato dumplings which float in it. Finns love potatoes in many forms, including a potato porridge made in the province of Uusimaa, but they love especially tiny new potatoes served with dill.

Among desserts which foreigners find attractive are fruit pies or tarts, using northern berries, and also the oversize lacy PANCAKES (*muurinpohjaletut*) which are sprinkled with sugar in the sweet version— they can also appear with a savoury filling. And among desserts which only some foreigners find attractive is the interesting sweet dish prepared for Easter and known as *mämmi*. This is prepared from rye flour and malt. After boiling, the cold mixture is put in a birch bark basket (delightful items, typical of Finland) and baked. It is always served cold with cream and sugar.

READING: Beatrice A. Ojakangas (1964).

FIRETHORN or pyracantha, *Pyracantha coccinea*, an evergreen shrub native to S. Europe and Asia Minor. It bears copious small, round, bright red berries, and is often grown as an ornamental plant.

The berries are edible, although sour, and can be made into an agreeably sharp sauce or jelly for serving with meat. Raw berries can also be squeezed and a little of the juice added to sweet orange juice. The two flavours complement each other.

FIRNI (phirni), a sweet milky dessert, to be eaten cold, made either with cornflour or rice flour or sometimes both and usually flavoured with rosewater and/or ground cardamom. The dish is decorated with chopped or ground almonds or pistachio nuts. Firni and variations thereof can be found all over the Middle East (where what is essentially the same dish is generally called MUHALLABIA), Iran (*fereni*), Afghanistan, and India (often as *phirni*).

As one would expect with something so widespread, the history of firni goes back a very long way; it seems to have originated in ancient Persia or the Middle East; and to have been introduced to India by the Moghuls.

Firni belongs to an extensive family of sweet dishes, all based on milk with rice flour or cornflour. Other members of the family include KESHKUL-E-FUQARA, the Iranian *yakh dar behesht* (which translated gives the delightful name of 'ice in heaven'). KHEER (a milk pudding, but made with whole rice or semolina, vermicelli, etc.) is a slightly more distant relation.

Firni is a popular choice of dessert for festive occasions. Sameen Rushdie (1991) says that in India 'firni is a very popular choice of dessert at weddings and other large social gatherings where it is traditionally served as individual portions set in shallow bowls of unbaked clay, which have always been used in India as disposable crockery. Unfortunately that special flavour of unbaked earthenware that is so easily

absorbed by the firni is lost to us in the West, but the delicate fragrance of rose essence and cardamoms still makes it well worth having.' HS

FISH (*see opposite page*)

FISH AND CHIPS may fairly be said to constitute one of the national dishes of ENGLAND (and SCOTLAND), but does not have a very long history. The combination, in its familiar form, is thought to date back to the 1860s, in Lancashire or in London. However, the two component parts had existed separately for more than half a century before then, and it would be a rash historian who would deny the possibility that they had joined forces, somewhere, somewhat sooner.

Fried fish, sold in pieces, cold, must have been established as a standard street food in London by the 1840s or earlier. As Picton (1966) remarks, Dickens mentions a 'fried fish warehouse' in *Oliver Twist*, published in instalments 1837–9. At that time the fish was sold with a chunk of bread. Mayhew, who wrote his famous survey of London Labour and the London Poor in the 1850s and early 1860s, painted a lively portrait of a fried fish seller, stating that there were about 300 of them in London, and that one of them had been in the trade for 17 years. As Claudia Roden (1996) observes, there was a strong Jewish tradition of frying fish in batter and eating it cold. And it was 'fried fish in the Jewish fashion' which Thomas Jefferson discovered when he came to London and which was included in the first Jewish cookbook in English (1846). Roden also remarks that the National Federation of Fish Friers presented in 1968 a plaque to Malin's of Bow in London's East End as the oldest fried fish and chips establishment still in business; and speculates that the combination represented a coming together in London (or wherever) of E. European Jewish immigrants (for the fish) and Irish immigrants (for the potato).

Chips had an earlier history, probably from the late 18th century. However, potatoes as street food in the early 19th century mostly took the form of hot baked potatoes and these were a seasonal trade. It is not clear when chips achieved real popularity, nor whether it was in London or the mill towns of Lancashire that this happened.

The marriage of fish and chips, wherever it was consummated, gained popularity swiftly and spread, for example to Ireland; Darina Allen (1995) says that it was Italian immigrants (who had become prominent in the fish and chip trade in Scotland) who brought the combination over to Ireland

(*cont. on page 303*)

Fish—and seafood generally—represent the planet's largest stock of 'wild' food. Indeed, the term 'wild' applies to all seafoods except for the small (but growing) proportion which are 'farmed'. Yet the term is rarely so used. This might be because 'wild' may mean ferocious as well as non-domesticated, and many fish are perceived as gentle of habit. The Roman poet Ovid praised the grey mullet for its blameless life, browsing on vegetation and never partaking of flesh. But most fish gobble up other fish relentlessly, as the dialogue between the Third Fisherman and the First Fisherman in Shakespeare's *Pericles* makes clear:

Master, I marvel how the fishes live in the sea.
Why, as men do on land; the great ones eat up the little ones.

No one can know for sure how far back the **history of fish as food** for humans (or, earlier, hominids) stretches. Consumption and appreciation of seafood certainly date back to what are called 'the earliest times'. Two highly readable sources for the subject are Radcliffe's *Fishing from the Earliest Times* (1921) and *Ancient and Modern Fish Tattle* by the Revd C. David Badham (1854), which has more ancient than modern material in it.

The earliest evidence is mute: the middens of empty sea shells which have been uncovered on many prehistoric sites and which reveal, for what it may be worth, that primitive people in Scotland feasted on limpets and periwinkles, and Australian Aborigines on certain clams. Harvesting such foods, which conveniently sit waiting to be gathered in the intertidal zones, needs no technology. Catching fish, on the other hand, needs some. But it can be very simple, as techniques still used in Africa and Oceania demonstrate.

In fact, however, the art of fishing and the scale of consumption developed rapidly in early historic times. The works of early Chinese writers and of classical Greek authors, although some survive in mere fragments, exhibit a sophisticated range of specific fishing techniques and considerable discrimination between the species. Commenting on the more recent history of fishing, Radcliffe observes that techniques have changed less over the centuries than have corresponding techniques in, say, hunting (changed by the introduction of the gun); and that the spear, the line and hook, and the net have remained pre-eminent.

Classical Roman authors yield the first evidence of certain phenomena which are still evident 2,000 years later, namely gastronomic gush and undue emphasis on the merits of this or that particular species. It is odd that the Roman admiral Optatus should have taken pains to introduce the PARROT-FISH (Latin *scarus*) from the Carpathian Sea to the west coast of Italy. No one in the Mediterranean pays much attention to this fish nowadays, although it is known in the Aegean and (as *marzpan*) in Malta. Perhaps its vivid colouring, often bright green, attracted the admiral's eye. Roman enthusiasm for another fish, the RED MULLET, is easier to understand,

although the extreme financial greed and morbid practices which sometimes attended its consumption have puzzling aspects.

In medieval times, when the pomp and luxury of the Roman Empire had vanished, attitudes were more practical. This was the age when the demand for fish, stimulated by the Christian Church's insistence on meatless days, began to have a perceptible influence on the political and economic history of the western world. This development was linked with the realization that stocks of such fish as cod, in northerly waters, were truly enormous.

So, at least in Europe, the whole business of fishing and trade in fish took a new turn as the Dark Ages came to an end and northerly peoples such as the Scandinavians emerged from relative obscurity. The powerful Hanseatic League, centred on the Baltic Sea, was based to a considerable extent on its near monopoly of the trade in salted and dried fish; and these fish came from the huge stocks of the N. Atlantic. Indeed, the subsequent colonization of N. America was certainly stimulated—some would say largely caused—by the search for ever more effective ways of exploiting these stocks and by the competition between the maritime powers for them.

The effects of all this activity and of the fish cures which were then developed are still visible, because techniques devised to preserve fish, in the period before refrigeration, produced results for which people acquired a taste; and the products therefore continue in being. See, for example, herring cures under HERRING, and the separate entry for KIPPER; also LUTEFISK. Similar ones are now used for other species such as mackerel, marlin, swordfish and tuna.

In recent times, developments such as canning and freezing, in conjunction with the emergence of steam- and then diesel-driven fishing vessels, have wrought and are still wreaking great changes. Episodes such as the Anglo-Icelandic 'cod war' and the tangle of problems associated with fishing limits and quotas echo the manœuvres of the Hanseatic League and the era of colonization and serve as a reminder that food is the very stuff of which politics are made. This applies in both western and eastern hemispheres.

In another respect, however, there is a clear difference between East and West. The Chinese have a consistent record, stretching back for more than 4,000 years, of recognizing the nutritional (and often the medical) value of most seafoods, and of honouring fish. As Bernard Read remarked:

Owing to its reproductive powers, in China the fish is a symbol of regeneration. As fish are reputed to swim in pairs, so a pair of fish is emblematic of connubial bliss. As in water fish move swiftly in any direction, they signify freedom from all restraints . . . Their scaly armour makes them a symbol of martial attributes, bringing strength and courage; and swimming against the current provides an emblem of perseverance. The fish is a symbol of abundance or wealth and prosperity.

In the West, the fish was a symbol of Christianity and pre-scribed as Lenten fare; but opinions were divided on its merits, even on its suitability, as food. In Britain, for example, the evidence of 18th-century cookbooks indicates increased consumption of fresh fish from the sea, but the literature of dietetics shows a strong counter-current flowing from some medical authorities. As recently as 1835 Graham, in the sixth edition of his treatise on *Modern Domestic Medicine*, de-clared that fish 'affords upon the whole, but little nourish-ment, and is, for the most part, of difficult digestion, and this appears to be the general sentiment of intelligent medical men'. If this would raise eyebrows now, what of the book *On Leprosy and Fish-Eating* by Jonathan Hutchinson (1906) whose avowed intent was to demonstrate, in 400 pages, that the fundamental cause of leprosy was 'the eating of fish in a state of commencing decomposition'? These examples re-mind us that it is only in the present century that fish and other seafoods have been fully accepted in the western world as an admirable source of nourishment.

In their role as food for humans, fish have **several unusual aspects.**

- If fish are compared with land animals or birds as a source of protein, they have one great advantage. Because the water supports their weight, they need a less elaborate skeleton and therefore provide more flesh in relation to weight.
- A comparison with land animals and birds yields an-other point of interest. Humanitarian considerations are only applied selectively to sea creatures, in contrast to the land animals (especially mammals) and birds. It has recently become unseemly for anyone except the Inuit (Eskimos) to eat marine mammals, and concern is often shown over how to kill lobsters and crabs painlessly; but compassion has rarely extended to fish, although there are signs of growing concern over how they meet their death.
- Despite the prevailing view that fish do not really 'feel' pain etc., there has been a tendency to attribute human charac-teristics to them. This attribution may be implicit rather than explicit. Thus it has been maintained by some that fish from cold waters are somehow better to eat than those from subtropical or tropical seas. This notion could be based on the fact that fish keep better in cold climates, but there seems to be lurking under the surface a vague purit-anical idea that fish which swim in chilly waters acquire merits which are unattainable by those which laze among warm coral reefs. (Be that as it may, there is one clear dif-ference. It is characteristic of warm waters that there are very numerous species present, but each in relatively small numbers; whereas in cold waters one typically finds fewer species but in huge quantity.)
- The number of edible species of fish, especially in warm waters, is so great that no one has tasted them all; and per-haps no one ever will. Even Norwegians and Singaporeans,

who head the league table in per capita consumption, can only expect to sample the range.

- This multitude of species is quite enough by itself to cause confusion over names. But the confusion has been com-pounded by muddles over common, vernacular names. These muddles are far, far worse than those which afflict, say, fruits and vegetables.

Of the two main sorts of fishy confusion, one may be re-garded as natural and viewed with tolerance. This is the con-fusion caused by the fact that even within one language, indeed sometimes within one dialect, the same fish will have a range of different names. These reflect local practice in small coastal communities, which were often isolated from each other in the past by poor overland communications. In Italy, for example, the common grey mullet, *Mugil cephalus*, has more than 40 different names.

The other sort of confusion applies to European lan-guages, especially English, and is a by-product of coloniza-tion. Its effect is to make it seem that there are fewer families or species of fish in the world than there really are. Early English colonists, to take the main culprits as an example, applied familiar but inappropriate names to the species which they encountered in the New World, Australasia, and elsewhere. Of the fish which have been dubbed 'salmon' in Australia and New Zealand, none is a salmon, and some of them are not even related to each other. The MURRAY COD of Australia is not even a sea fish, let alone a close relation of the true cod.

Fish cookery

This is, to a large extent, a global subject. In whatever hemi-sphere, fish tend to fall into broad groups from the point of view of the cook, according to their size, shape, and fat con-tent. A Chinese cook has no problem in the fish markets of, say, Naples or New Orleans; and cooks from the western world can find fish close to their requirements in the Orient. Substitutions rarely present a problem. And any given fish can usually be cooked by any of several of the standard tech-niques available: grilling (US broiling), poaching, steaming, pan-frying (or stir-frying), deep-frying, stewing, braising, etc. (There are also a few specific techniques for fish such as AU BLEU, applied mainly to trout.)

There are also categories of fish dishes which are gener-ically although not always specifically transferable between the hemispheres. Fish balls are an example; those of Norway (*fiskeboller*) and their polymorphous relations in Malaysia (see Davidson, 1977) are both made with great finesse. And there is no reason why the fish puddings of Scandinavia (e.g. the Norwegian *fiskepudding*) should not have their parallels elsewhere. Equally, the fish soup/stews of Europe (such as BOUILLABAISSE, the *Cacciucco* of the Livornese coast, the *Cotriade* of Brittany, the *Marmitako* of Galicia) may claim justifiably to be, in their several ways, unique, but the principles on which they are constructed can be followed wherever there are fish.

Nonetheless, there are some interesting contrasts between East and West. Some spring from differences between the supporting casts of ingredients. For example, fish coated in an English batter and fried in beef DRIPPING is very different from the same fish fried in a wok in peanut oil. And there is a world of difference between fish simmered in a court bouillon flavoured with Mediterranean herbs and the same fish cooked in coconut cream with lemon grass and other SE Asian aromatics. Again, comparison is hardly possible between plain steamed fish, traditional fare for Anglo-Saxon invalids and convalescents, and something like *Haw mok* (Thai curried fish steamed in artichoke containers).

However, wherever one is and whatever range of other ingredients one uses, the same question is likely to come up, namely **how to calculate cooking time.** For the majority of cooks, practice has removed the need to calculate; but those who do calculate usually do it wrong.

A fish is cooked when its innermost parts have reached a temperature of about 63 °C (145 °F). In conventional (not microwave) cookery, heat travels from the outside to the inside. So the determining factor is the distance to be covered. Since the shape of fish varies greatly it is obvious for a start that the weight of a fish is not a good guide. It could not possibly work for both a long, thin eel and a chunky grouper. Realization of this prompted the promulgation of the so-called 'Canadian method', which calls for basing the cooking time on the maximum thickness of a fish. That is right. But if it is going to work, it has to be applied in accordance with the relevant law of physics, which is this:

The time taken for heat to penetrate an object is not in simple proportion to its thickness, but to the square of the thickness.

One might think that a piece of fish two inches thick would take twice as long to cook as a piece one inch thick. Not so; if the heat has to go twice as far, it will take four times as long. That many people are unaware of this explains why a thin piece of fish is often overcooked and a large fish risks being partly undercooked. It also explains the importance of scoring the sides of a fish, a practice which is found worldwide but is done with particular care in China. If the scoring is done at the correct intervals, and deeply enough, the result may be to halve the maximum distance which the heat must traverse to reach the innermost part, and therefore to reduce cooking time to a quarter of what it would have been.

The same principle applies to all foodstuffs. This was made clear in an extensive discussion at the Oxford Symposium on Food and Cookery 1997, when a statement about it was circulated under the signatures of Professor Nicholas Kurti (Emeritus Professor of Physics at the University of Oxford) and Harold McGee (the most authoritative writer on science in the kitchen). See Walker (1998), especially to learn what qualifications apply to the principle in respect of irregularly shaped or disproportionately thick items. Fish cookery is an area which is relatively free from any such complications, which is why it provided the context for discussing the principle at the Symposium, and why the principle is explained here rather than under HEAT AND ITS TRANSMISSION.

Finally, the fundamental question: does seafood need to be cooked? The Japanese, with their SASHIMI, have demonstrated that really fresh seafood is very good when eaten raw (especially so if it is presented with Japanese artistry). And the famous CEVICHE of Latin America provides a method of 'cooking' without cooking, applicable in particular to seafood. What happens here is that the marinating of seafood in lemon or lime juice causes the denaturation of the protein in much the same way as the application of heat in conventional cooking would do.

Both sashimi and ceviche are in the process of spreading round the world, and the former in particular seems sure to modify habits of seafood consumption; both directly and indirectly too, for the Japanese conception of what is a fresh fish in the market is gaining ground, and slowly tightening up lax standards elsewhere. (Not always so lax. In the 19th century, fish merchants kept cod alive in floating wooden chests for the London market. And even now it is possible, indeed customary, to buy live cod in Bergen in Norway, and live plaice in Denmark.)

A **fish kettle** is a specially designed cooking utensil for poaching whole fish, now almost always made of aluminium although examples in tinned copper survive. It is typically long and narrow, to match the shape of a normal fish, and has a removable grid which permits the poached fish to be lifted out without damage. Some antique fish kettles are relatively wider, presumably because they were intended to take two or more fish side by side. However, flatfish such as TURBOT would not fit into even a wide oblong kettle, so a lozenge-shaped sort, called *turbotière* in French, is made for them.

---

and who still have a secure hold on the business in Dublin. The number of fish and chip establishments grew steadily until the Second World War. Although variations on their standard fare, and various gimmicks, were often introduced, the basics never changed: fish (usually cod, haddock, skate, dogfish); malt vinegar; salt; perhaps a piece of lemon. There was also the traditional wrapping of newspaper, but that was already being phased out on hygienic grounds in the 1960s.

READING: Shipperbottom (1998).

FISHER M. F. K. (Mary Frances Kennedy) (1908–92), one of the finest American writers of the 20th century, devoted a substantial amount of her writing to food and cookery and in doing so created a new genre, of which her own work remains the outstanding example. As Davidson (1988*c*) put it when introducing an essay she had written on the nature of people who 'love to cook':

Among the famous writers on cookery in North America one stands apart, a star with her own share of the sky, a star whose luminosity differs in kind from all the others: this is M. F. K. Fisher. A quick look through her books will give the impression that they are about food—as indeed, in a sense, they are. But reading them reveals their transcendent quality; they are really about life itself.

In fact some of her books do not even appear to be about food. She was born in California in one environment, which she vividly described in *Among Friends* (1970), spent much of her life in France and Switzerland (see *A Map of Another Town*, 1964, for her time at Aix-en-Provence), and her last years back in California, in a one-storey house which exactly matched her needs—one huge room with a glorious view was kitchen and living area, another was bedroom and writing space, while the third room doubled as bathroom and art gallery.

The books which are of special food interest are mostly collections of essays: *The Gastronomical Me*, 1943; *Here Let us Feast*, 1946; *An Alphabet for Gourmets*, 1949; and *With Bold Knife and Fork*, 1968. In addition, however, she was largely responsible for the prose in the Time-Life volume on *The Cooking of Provincial France* (1969); and produced a translation (1949), with numerous notes, of *La Physiologie du goût* by BRILLAT-SAVARIN. This last item was a major achievement, blending harmoniously the thoughts of an idiosyncratic author with those of an idiosyncratic translator/editor.

Mary Frances, as she was known to her friends and admirers, was a passionate woman, not least in her discrimination about food (balanced by a total rejection of all forms of food snobbery) and about what might be called the 'fabric of life'. Some of her finest writing has to do with the environment in which food is chosen, prepared, enjoyed, and perceived, all these activities meshed in almost seamlessly with the other activities which make life a pleasure (or, sometimes but only temporarily, sad).

FISH PASTES AND FISH PASTE PRODUCTS. The former are English and the latter mainly Japanese.

Fish pastes (and kindred items such as bloater paste and shrimp paste) have figured at either high tea or afternoon tea in England, most often in delicate sandwiches. In the mid-20th century they were highly visible, in characteristic small jars with a bulging shape; but by the end of the century they were much less common. The paste consisted of a certain percentage of minced fish flesh, with additional spice (light) and colouring (muted).

Fish paste products of Japan are a different matter—big business, which accounts for something like 20% of the huge Japanese fish catch. As a group, these products are called *neri-seihin* (literally, 'kneaded products'). They are made of fish meat, usually a combination of two or three species of white fish reduced to a paste, to which salt and other secondary ingredients (various forms of starch, egg whites, flavourings, preservatives, etc.) are added. This paste is then shaped and heated so as to solidify it.

Documentary evidence suggests that this type of food existed in Japan already in the Heian period (794–1192). Originally fish paste was moulded round bamboo sticks (in the manner of Middle Eastern *kofta-kebab*, see KEBAB) and grilled over a fire. Present-day *chikuwa*, described below, retains this form.

There are endless local varieties, the chief differences consisting not only in the kinds of fish used (which depends largely on what the main catch is in the given locality) but also in shapes and in the way heat is applied (whether the paste is steamed, grilled, fried, boiled, etc.). Four common varieties are as follows:

Kamaboko is often, but not always, mounted on a rectangular piece of wood, and then either steamed or grilled. It is usually eaten sliced, with SOY SAUCE and WASABI (Japanese horseradish).

Chikuwa, literally 'bamboo tube', is of a tubular shape. It is grilled on a stick and so has a hole in the middle (hence the name). It is usually used in *nimono* (see JAPANESE CULINARY TERMS).

Satsuma-age is smaller (bite size) and takes many shapes, sometimes like a beef olive, with some stuffing such as a piece of *gobo* (BURDOCK), squid, shrimp, etc. It is deep fried in oil. When freshly made, it is commonly eaten as *nimono* or grilled.

Hanpen is squarish, cushion shaped, and of a spongy consistency because it contains grated *yamanoimo* (YAM). It is often used in *suimono* (see JAPANESE CULINARY TERMS), diced small.

The expression 'fish sausage', sometimes used as a general indicator of these fish paste products, is inappropriate, since, with a few relatively recent exceptions which are direct imitations of meat sausages, *neri-seihin* are neither stuffed into casings nor of a tubular shape—two conditions which the word 'sausage' seems to imply. In fact, Japanese *neri-seihin* are more often related to French *quenelles de poisson* and Scandinavian fish puddings. They are, however, usually firmer in texture than their French and Scandinavian counterparts.

FISH SAUCE an essential part of the diet in SE Asia and an essential ingredient for SE Asian cookery, is made by fermenting small, whole fish in vats of brine and drawing off the supernatant liquid, which is then matured in the sun before being bottled. The product is *nuoc mam* in Vietnam and *nam pla* in Thailand.

This product is closely related to the GARUM and liquamen of CLASSICAL GREECE and CLASSICAL ROME. However, in Europe other methods of preserving fish were introduced and their use for fish sauce was discontinued. It is of interest that this happened, since it is not uncommon for a mode of preservation, if it produces a distinctive flavour (such as fish sauce has), to outlive the introduction of new technology. (One English firm was marketing a product called 'garum' in the 19th century, for an advertisement appears in an English cookery book of the period; but this seems to have been an isolated survival or renascence.)

The protein content of fish sauce is high, and its composition resembles that of SOY SAUCE; indeed, its role in SE Asia is equivalent to that of soy sauce in China and Japan. The types of fish used vary from region to region. A mixture of marine and freshwater fish may be used.

This type of fish sauce can be the basis of a sauce incorporating other ingredients, for example the *nuoc cham* of Vietnam, made with *nuoc mam*, garlic, chilli, and lime juice. READING: Mackie, Hardy, and Hobbs (1971).

FISH SAUSAGES are a relatively rare commodity, although they were made in Europe in the past for fast days. British fish sausages, which enjoyed a small market until the end of the 19th century, were made of haddock, mackerel, kipper, etc., with the addition of cereal, in normal British sausage fashion.

The term 'fish sausage' is sometimes applied to Japanese textured fish products. It does not suit them, for reasons explained under FISH PASTES AND FISH PASTE PRODUCTS.

FISNOGGE an unusual culinary term in the Jewish kitchen, refers to calf's foot jelly (see VEAL), but literally means 'foot foot' in two languages, Yiddish and Russian. Because Lithuanian Yiddish speakers could not distinguish in their pronunciation between two Yiddish words, *fish* meaning fish and *fis* meaning foot, they were in a fix when they wanted to indicate the latter (as in 'would you like *fis* for supper?' meaning calf's foot jelly) and solved the problem by tagging on *nogge*, which is the Yiddish pronunciation of the Russian word for foot. An example of how an apparent confusion can have a logical explanation.

Hebrew speakers say *pecha* which is an adaptation of the Turkish word *paça* (meaning sheep's trotters or a dish made of them). RuH

FITWEED or culantro, *Eryngium foetidum*, a plant with edible leaves which originated in tropical America but was introduced successfully to parts of E. and SE Asia and is now of some importance there too. The unpleasant buglike smell which it gives off, reminiscent of CORIANDER, has earned it other names such as stinkweed (*stinkdistel* in Dutch) and false coriander. The name culantro, being also and originally the Spanish for (true) coriander, can itself be a source of confusion. Morton (1976) points out that it is for this reason that 'West Indian cooks tag the name *culantro* with *de burro, del monte, de coyote* or *de cimarron*'.

The roots provide a good condiment for soups and other dishes. The leaves, despite the smell, are eaten raw (in Java, for example), or steamed. They are liked as a relish with rice, or for fish dishes.

FIVE GRAINS OF CHINA In China, in antiquity, five grains or staples were recognized as the most important foods. Most were cereals but, as Francesca Bray (in the section 'Agriculture' in Needham, 1984) explains:

The Chinese term for grain, *ku*, was applied not only to the main cereal crops but also to such field crops as hemp and beans, also cultivated for their grains. Thus *wu ku*, the 'five grains', an expression commonly found in the classical texts, was understood to comprise *chi* (setaria millet), *shu* (panicum millet), *tao* (rice), *mai* (wheat and barley) and *shu* (legumes), though some commentators substituted *ma* (hemp) for rice. Other classifications referred to the 'six grains' (*liu ku*) or the 'nine grains' (*chiu ku*) making up the numbers by using more specific names for wheat, for barley, or for large or small beans.

Other lists of the five (or more) grains have been current, some including even the CHINESE WATER CHESTNUT, but this only serves to underline the point made above, that the Chinese term *ku* is not adequately translated by the English word 'grain'. The main point is that in the Chinese tradition rice, millets, wheat, and barley were of fundamental importance.

FIVE SPICES (Chinese), a Chinese ground spice mixture sometimes sold as 'five-fragrance powder'. It is golden-brown in colour and consists of STAR ANISE, FENNEL, CLOVES, CASSIA (Chinese cinnamon), and SICHUAN PEPPER (or GINGER and/or CARDAMOM); so there may be six rather than five ingredients. It is used sparingly, e.g. in marinades for meat, fish, or

poultry. The flavour of star anise is the strongest in the mixture.

This mixture is also used in parts of SE Asia.

FLAME used as a verb (equivalent to the French *flamber* which, in the form of its past participle, flambé, has entered the English language, oddly, as a transitive verb), is an instruction sometimes found in recipes involving ALCOHOL, and exploits the property of this substance to burn at a low temperature. Spirit or fortified wine is heated gently (in a ladle or small pan) until the alcohol it contains begins to vaporize, then ignited, poured over the food, and allowed to burn. The process removes most of the alcohol leaving behind a distinctive, concentrated flavour. Brandy is commonly used, principally in meat dishes; rum is used in CREOLE cookery, and with some desserts; calvados in Norman cookery, and so on.

Flaming is usually carried out at the end of cooking, as a piece of restaurant showmanship, the conflagration taking place immediately before the dish is served, usually in front of the customer. Elizabeth DAVID (1951, 1960) was by no means alone in expressing reservations about this practice.

The origin of the various flambé dishes prepared at the customer's table is mysterious, although most appear to be relatively recent, and probably derive from late 19th and early 20th-century grand hotel or restaurant practice, when rich and elaborate recipes were devised and named for the beau monde.

Setting light to CHRISTMAS PUDDINGS in English homes is a different matter. Here the flame lends emphasis to a winter festive dish. The custom goes back at least to the mid-19th century, when Mrs BEETON (1861) mentioned it as the mode of bringing them to the table. LM

FLAN a term with two meanings. The one most familiar in Britain, as neatly given in the *NSOED*, is: 'An open pastry or sponge case containing a (sweet or savoury) filling.' A typical flan of this sort is round, with shortcrust PASTRY. It is either baked blind before the hot or cold filling is added, or baked with the filling. The filling, especially if it is a sweet one, may incorporate CUSTARD.

In France the term *flan* carries the first meaning described above, but often has the second meaning: a sweet custard which is baked in a mould in the oven until set, when it may be served in the mould or turned out. See also *crème* and CRÈME CARAMEL.

The second meaning is the one which is used in Spain and Portugal, where *flan* is a

standard dessert, and in many countries, e.g. Mexico, where either language is used.

This second and very widespread meaning is the one which corresponds to the etymology of the term. The Old French *flaon*, derived from the Latin *flado*, had as its principal meaning 'a custard'. From the same Latin root came the Middle English word *flathon* and *flawn*, from which much later came flan.

In the USA what bears the name flan in Britain (the first of the two meanings above) is likely to be called TART or PIE. (HS)

FLAOUNES Easter cheesecakes which seem to be exclusive to Cyprus, where they are prepared, especially in Greek Orthodox homes, during the Easter feast days; this partly as a religious tradition but increasingly because they are very well liked. Bakeries now make them, often in a small size, at any time of the year.

Special *flaouna* cheeses, made from ewe and goat milk, are used; Gilli Davies (1990) explains that they are fresh, lightly pressed, cheeses, and have a tall cylindrical shape derived from the reed containers in which they are moulded. The same author writes:

Traditionally eaten to break the Lenten fast, Flaounes are, to me, the very best of Cypriot cooking. Cheesy buns with a soft rich filling and a crisp crust, just the thing to eat with a cup of coffee at breakfast or a glass of wine later in the day.

The cheesecake-like filling combines grated cheese, eggs, yeast, mint, and sesame seeds. The pastry dough, which may incorporate a very small amount of pounded mastic, is rolled out into thin rounds, which, once filling has been placed in the centre of each, are folded up to form a square shape, brushed with beaten egg, and sprinkled with sesame seeds before being baked.

FLAPJACK a term usually denoting a thick chewy BISCUIT made from rolled OATS, sugar, butter, and GOLDEN SYRUP baked in a flat tin. The mixture is cut into squares or fingers while still warm.

The name is also used in Britain and the USA for a griddle cake like a DROP SCONE. In this sense it is close to PANCAKE. Indeed the terms seem to have been synonymous in the past. 'Pancake or fritter or flap-iacke,' wrote John Taylor (1634). Gillian Edwards (1970), who cites this reference, has an interesting paragraph about the origin of the term:

Flap-jacks were so called because it was the custom to 'flap' them, or throw them up and catch them in the pan. Flap here means 'to toss with a smart movement; to throw down suddenly,' the sense being an echo of the sound. Halliwell records as a dialect phrase in 1847 'Flap a froize, to turn in the pan without touching it.' This general flapping and tossing added much to the fun of the feast.

FLATFISH the general term used to denote those fish which start life with one eye on each side of the head, as usual, but then adapt to their future way of life by having either the left or the right eye migrate round to the other side of the head. They are right-handed (dextral) or left-handed (sinistral) according to whether they finish up with two eyes on the right side (the SOLES) or two on the left (PLAICE and TURBOT).

The reason for this arrangement is the strategy which such fish have adopted in order to eat and avoid being eaten. This requires them to lie flat on the seabed, retaining full vision upwards but minimizing their own visibility to possible predators above them. The latter requirement is met by camouflage; the coloration of their backs matches the seabed with uncanny exactness, and they are in any case often half-buried in the sand. They can 'disappear' in this way with remarkable speed. Buckland (1883) described what happened on the coast of Kent when a seine net full of plaice rolled over and the plaice began to escape.

A fisherman cried, 'Look out, they'll sand!' a capital expression for I found that the fish sunk into the sand with such rapidity that the operation must be seen to be believed. The plaice lifts up its head and the upper third of its body and then brings it down on the sand three or four times with sharp, quick raps; a small cavity is thus made in the soft, wet sand, which at once fills with water; the fish then works its fins on each side of its body with such a rapid motion that they seem almost to vibrate. These combined efforts enable the fish to conceal itself almost quicker than the eye can follow, and nothing can be seen but its eye, which is of a lovely emerald colour.

The peculiar structure of flatfish is, for fish cooks, generally convenient. Flatfish cook quickly and evenly, being thin bodied. They are easily filleted. And their bones are rarely troublesome.

The largest flatfish is the HALIBUT. The best is the (true) SOLE. The centre of excellence for flatfish is the NE Atlantic; other regions are less fortunate.

FLATHEAD the usual English name for fish in the family Platycephalidae, a name which itself means 'flat-headed ones'. These are bottom-dwelling fish with flat, wedge-shaped heads and large pectoral fins which help them to move about on the seabed. Their backs are usually brownish, but they can change colour to match their surroundings. They spend most of their time half-buried in the sand, and are thus

particularly liable to be taken by trawls. Some are quite small, but others can reach weights of 3 to 5 kg (7 to 12 lb) or more.

Of the many species in the Indo-Pacific, *Platycephalus indicus*, which has a distribution from the Indian subcontinent to the southern part of Japan, and the northern parts of Australia, is the best known, and widely marketed.

Of the numerous other species of flathead found in Australian waters, several are important food fishes, e.g. the tiger flathead of New South Wales, *Neoplatycephalus richardsoni*. It and the relatively large northern dusky flathead, *Platycephalus fuscus*, and the even larger southern dusky flathead, *P. speculator*, make particularly good eating.

Australians may be the greatest enthusiasts for flatheads, but the Chinese also rate them highly.

FLAT LOBSTER slipper lobster, and flathead lobster are all English names for CRUSTACEANS of the family Scyllaridae, species of which are found in warm or temperate waters all round the world. Many of the European names mean something like 'cricket of the sea'; this because they make cricket-like noises in the water.

The flat lobsters all have the same shape—flattish, and with shovel-shaped feelers at the front—and general characteristics, but vary in colour and size. *Scyllarides latus*, of the Mediterranean, may be up to 45 cm (18") long, while *Scyllarus arctus*, the principal species of the E. Atlantic, is only half that size. In the Indo-Pacific, *Thenus orientalis* is the main species and it has a length up to 25 cm (10"); a slightly smaller relation, *Ibacus ciliatus*, is distinguished by having a bright red back.

They offer palatable meat, but have not been sought after in the same way as true LOBSTERS or PRAWNS. In the Mediterranean they are usually consigned to fish soups. However, in some places in the south of France and Italy, large specimens of *Scyllarides latus*, which may weigh up to 2 kg (4.25 lb), are esteemed almost as highly as the SPINY LOBSTER and are prepared in similar ways.

In recent decades, *Thenus orientalis* has achieved fame in Australia under the name Moreton Bay bug, or bay lobster, while a more southerly species, *Ibacus peronii*, has gained an almost equal reputation as the Balmain bug (or, in S. Australia, prawn killer). The former has the better flavour of the two.

FLAVOUR best defined as the combined effects of the TASTE and aroma of food, is a matter of practical concern to all cooks and to the food industry, and a challenge to scientists. The activities of cooks in adding or modifying flavours in the kitchen are referred to in numerous articles about spices etc. This one is rather about the theoretical aspects.

Although many flavours can be described effectively for everyday purposes, usually by referring to some other flavour ('it tastes a bit like strawberries'), a full scientific description or analysis is virtually impossible. The flavour of a single spice, which may be just one of numerous ingredients in a given dish, may embody hundreds of elements, of which some may not yet have been finally identified. For all the miraculous technology of spectroscopic analysis, there are mysteries here which will defy resolution for some time to come.

If only for this reason, the artificial and exact replication of flavours achieved by using natural ingredients is not possible. If the chemical identity of the dominant flavouring elements in, say, a spice is known, and if these can be synthesized, a close approximation can be achieved, but that is all.

The subject of flavour is thus of almost infinite complexity, and so is that of flavourings, both natural and artificial. Nor does it have a vocabulary which would make the task of grappling with it easier. It is fortunate that no difficulties of this sort impede our enjoyment of flavours; that they cannot be fully analysed or described in words is of little moment to the vast majority of the world's population.

Even an attempt to classify aromas (one constituent of flavours) leads to immediate difficulty. A typical classification of categories of aroma, from the 1940s, looked like this:

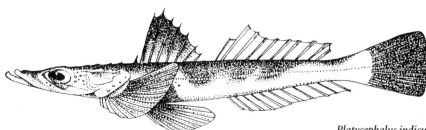

Platycephalus indicus

Ethereal
Aromatic
Fragrant
Ambrosial
Alliaceous
Empyreutic
Hircine
Repulsive
Nauseating

This list is partly opaque to the lay person (even if it is explained that hircine means goaty and that alliaceous has to do with the onion family) and partly too vague (fragrant and repulsive). There were simpler classifications. The great Swedish naturalist Linnaeus had a list of seven. Hans Henning, a German physiologist, produced a list of only six fundamental kinds of aroma:

Spicy
Flowery
Fruity
Resinous
Foul
Burned

These are understandable terms, but it can be objected that a short list like this is incapable of covering all the aromas we experience, or so general as to be useless. It does seem that, although Linnaeus gave us a practical and comprehensible system for the taxonomy of plants and animals, the achievement of a corresponding taxonomy of aromas is not within sight. And if this is beyond our present horizon, a taxonomy of flavours (and therefore flavourings) is necessarily even further out of sight.

However, someone who is dealing with a particular group of flavours and addressing a sympathetic audience may manage quite well. Thus Joan Morgan (Morgan and Richards, 1993) uses the following vocabulary in her useful survey of categories of apple flavours: refreshing and savoury (of summer apples); strawberry; vinous; densely fruity; aromatic (the most prized); sweet and scented (the German *Edelborsdorfer* is 'the perfect example'); honeyed; aniseed; russet; nutty; pineapple; fruit/acid drops. As a whole, this list will be an effective piece of communication for most people. It is interesting to see that the author thought it necessary to add explanations in only a few instances, notably 'russet'. Here she had to explain that russet is normally taken to refer to the colour of the skin; that possession of a 'russet' flavour is linked to that but not coextensive with it; and that what some of the greatest apple authorities—Bunyard (1925), Shand (1934), and Hogg (1851)—have said on the subject gives useful guidance. This illustrates an important point: in the absence of an agreed 'flavour language', it will often be necessary to amplify, in one or both of two ways, a term used: first by giving

examples of what the term is applicable to (vinous is now usually applied to McIntosh, aniseed develops in Ellison's Orange, etc.); and secondly by referring to fuller explanations, possibly in different and especially illuminating contexts, from other people.
READING: Jaine (1988); Walker (1993); Lake (1989).

FLOATING ISLAND a cold dessert consisting of a round, flattish, baked MERINGUE 'island' floating on a sea of CUSTARD. In France a similar dish is called *Île flottante*. Another French dish called *Œufs à la neige* (snow eggs) is made by forming beaten egg whites into small rounds (not one large one) which are then poached and placed on top of a light egg custard. In either case the islands may be topped with CARAMEL or grated almond or the like.

Hannah Glasse (1747) seems to be the earliest English reference in print, although she calls it Flooting Island and her long recipe differs from the above description, her island being made with thin slices of French rolls, jam or jelly, etc., rather than meringue.

Marian McNeill (1929) has a Scottish version which is different again; the egg whites are whisked with quince or raspberry jelly then piled on top of cream beaten with wine and sugar and a little lemon peel.

FLORENTINE as a noun refers to a biscuit (see NUT BISCUITS).

Historically, the term 'Florentine' applied in Britain to a PIE or TART containing meat or fruit or possibly both. Why the name was used in this way is not clear, although it probably reflected some French usage. At least four English cookery books of the first half of the 18th century give an almost identical recipe for A Florendine Of Veal, involving veal kidney and various spices in a

pie. Wright's *English Dialect Dictionary* shows that in Scotland it was usually a dish of veal baked in a plate with a cover of paste; and that in Bedfordshire an 'Apple Florentine' was served at Christmas. The use of the term 'florentine' for the big, round dish in which special apple pies were baked survived in the Yorkshire Dales until well into the 20th century.

The word, in its most common French meaning, refers to the city of Florence in Italy from where cooks are said to have introduced spinach into the French diet in the 16th century. The French call any dish which includes spinach, e.g. fish or eggs served on a bed of buttered spinach, or with spinach and a cheese sauce, *à la florentine*. In Italy, *alla fiorentina* means dishes, and ways of cooking, of Florence and the surrounding region.

FLOUNDER a name which originally referred to *Platichthys flesus*, a FLATFISH of the E. Atlantic, ranging from the White Sea down to the Mediterranean. This is a dextral flatfish (i.e. both eyes are on its right-hand side), but it occurs not infrequently in reversed form (i.e. eyes on the left-hand side). Reversed specimens can cause considerable puzzlement in the fish markets, although not as much surprise as the appearance of a completely albino flounder, white on both sides and equipped with pink eyes and fins, such as was once taken on the coast of Norfolk.

The flounder is common in estuaries and the tidal waters of rivers, and especially abundant in the Baltic Sea. It is more important as a food fish in N. Europe than in Britain, where its reputation is relatively low. Further south, however, on the coast of Galicia, the flounder is both abundant and highly appreciated.

The name 'flounder', like so many other names of fish familiar to people in Britain,

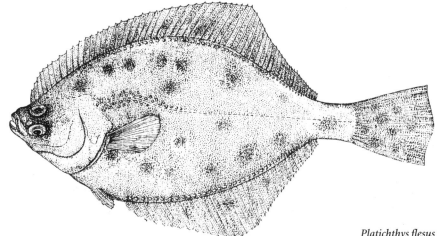

Platichthys flesus

was exported by English-speaking colonists and applied to fish in other parts of the world. The most important non-European flounders are:

- *Pseudopleuronectes americanus*, known as winter flounder or common flounder, the thickest and meatiest flatfish of the eastern seaboard of the USA and Canada. Maximum length over 60 cm (24"). Colour of the eyed side variable but often reddish-brown. Range from Labrador to Georgia; especially abundant in New England waters. In the southern part of its range this fish comes inshore in search of warmer waters during the winter, which accounts for the name winter flounder. The flesh is white and firm, well suited to grilling (US broiling) or pan-frying. McClane (1978*b*) remarks that: 'in waters off Montauk Point, New York, and around Block Island, Rhode Island, there exist populations of extra large flounders, locally known as snowshoes because of their shape and size.'
- *Paralichthys dentatus*, the summer flounder, so called because it comes inshore during the summer months. Maximum length almost 1 m (40"). Colour varies according to the bottom on which the fish is lying but is usually grey, brown, or olive with some noticeable dark spots. Range from Maine to S. Carolina. Another good eating fish.
- *Limanda ferruginea*, the yellowtailed flounder, has become an important commercial species on the eastern seaboard of the USA and Canada from Labrador down to Virginia. Maximum length 55 cm (22"). Colour variable, often grey-green or reddish-brown with large 'rusty' (hence *ferruginea*) spots, and a yellow tail. This species is also found in the NE Atlantic, but its English name on that side is yellowtailed dab rather than yellowtailed flounder. Also a good fish.
- *Pseudorhombus arsius*, an Indo-Pacific species in the family Bothidae. It is of some importance in SE Asia and is known in Australia, where it is only one of a very large number of species which are referred to as flounders—indeed, Australians use the name both for some sinistral (i.e. both eyes on the left-hand side) flatfish and for some dextral (both on the right-hand side) ones. See the next item.
- *Rhombosolea tapirina*, the greenback flounder, is important, commercially, in southern Australian waters, and is regarded by Australians as one of their best eating fishes. Of a diamond shape and with a maximum weight of 600 g (1.3 lb) it is best cooked whole.

FLOUR (*see page 309*)

FLOWERS the source of HONEY, have numerous culinary uses, as explained below.

Many common flowers are edible (although some are toxic). Historically, the use of flowers in food shows the links between CONFECTIONERY, pharmacy, and perfumery. The skill of the confectioner would be required to preserve flowers—such as roses—considered to have medicinal virtues; the resulting confection would have the pleasant side effect of perfuming the breath when eaten. When and where the preservation of flowers began is not known, although the Islamic world, with a love of flowers and a working knowledge of sugar confectionery, probably played a part. Perry (1993) quotes Moorish recipes from the 13th century requiring syrup flavoured with rosewater.

Of all flowers with a culinary application, the most widely used and valuable is probably the ROSE: made into fragrant waters, vinegars, conserves, and jams, candied, crystallized, and used fresh or dried, it serves as a paradigm for many other perfumed flowers, especially VIOLETS. CLOVE GILLIFLOWERS and orange flowers (see ORANGE FLOWER WATER) formerly had similar applications, but are now more restricted.

The practice of using flowers as food decoratively and for flavour varies from culture to culture. It is seen as charming and old fashioned in Britain, by those who are aware of it, but is little regarded (except in confectionery and drinks) in S. Europe. Further east, flowers become a more integral part of culinary practice, and the lines between cookery, pharmacy, and perfumery become as blurred as they had been in Europe until the 18th century. Florence White (1934) quotes a mid-19th-century lady writing from Beijing to a cousin in N. America: 'The Chinese, like the Near Easterners, are far too utilitarian to live in a flowery kingdom and not make a practical use of flowers.'

Whole fresh flowers can be cooked, **as a vegetable.** In this category fall CAULIFLOWER, BROCCOLI, and globe ARTICHOKES, all of which are, technically, immature flowers. The use of ZUCCHINI flowers in savoury dishes is well known in Europe. Other flowers can be dipped in light batter and fried, to make delicate sweet FRITTERS: elderflowers, apple blossom, acacia flowers, and lilacs can be used in this manner.

Examples from other continents include curried BANANA FLOWERS, stewed blossoms of WATER HAWTHORN, WATER HYACINTHS, stir-fried GOLDEN NEEDLES, and steamed YUCCA or AGAVE. See also CHRYSANTHEMUM, much used in Japan and TOPITAMBO.

The 'vegetable' aspect of flowers extends to their **use in salads,** to which they contribute colour, flavour, and texture and an attractive ephemeral touch. In Europe, the British appear to be most interested in this aspect, although there may be other localized examples. NASTURTIUMS, VIOLETS, CLOVE GILLIFLOWERS, and MARIGOLDS are all cited in this context in English recipe books; the blossoms of many herbs, such as ROSEMARY, BASIL, DILL, and CHIVES, can be added. Although the habit seems to have peaked in the 17th century, it has undergone periodic revivals. Another way of adding a 'flowery' note to a salad is to use a dressing based on a vinegar infused with flowers; rose, violet, clove gilliflower, and ELDERFLOWERS can all be used in this way. A method for flowers preserved as pickles—in layers in a jar, with sugar in between and vinegar to cover—was given by Gervase Markham (1615), with instructions for making them into 'strange sallets'. Nasturtium buds and seeds and broom buds were pickled in vinegar in the past. Less romantic, but much better known in a modern context, is the use of pickled CAPERS.

Another common and important use of flowers is as an ingredient **in beverages.** Fresh, they add decoration and delicate flavours, for instance WOODRUFF in German wine-cups, or make soothing hot drinks. In practice, because of their seasonal nature, and the close overlap between this area and pharmacy, preserved flowers—dried or as flavoured SYRUPS—are more important. Many flowers retain their perfume when dried, and release it in hot water. They can be used alone, as TISANES, such as camomile, lime, or lemon-balm; or added to TEA, the best-known examples of this in the West being rose or jasmine. (Gardenias, peonies, and *gwei-hua*, which has a peachlike scent, are also used in China.)

Cold flower-based drinks are often based on syrups. Compared to their importance in the past, these are little used in modern Europe, where, in the Middle Ages, they were a means of preserving flowers for flavour and for medicinal purposes. Later, they were simply fashionable drinks, such as *capillaire*, which in the 19th century meant syrup flavoured with orange flower water (the 18th-century original was based on an infusion of maidenhair fern). SHERBETS, syrup-based drinks, can be flower flavoured; Claudia Roden (1968) describes these as sold on the street:

The vendors carried a selection of sherbets in gigantic glass flasks, two at a time, held together by wide straps and balanced on their shoulders. The flasks glowed with brilliantly seductive colours: soft, pale sugary pink for rose water, pale green for violet, warm, rich dark tamarind.

A New World drink of this type is the Mexican syrup based on 'Jamaica flowers' (*Hibiscus sabdariffa*—see ROSELLE); dried,

(*cont. on page 310*)

Flour

The term 'flour' which used to be spelled 'flower', originally meant the finest product (i.e. 'the flower') of the process of bolting meal from cereal grains. In modern times, when the term is used by itself, it is taken to mean WHEAT flour. There are, however, many other cereal flours (CORNFLOUR is one example) and also numerous kinds of flour made from nuts (e.g. CHESTNUT flour) or starchy vegetables (e.g. CASSAVA flour, POTATO flour) or pulses (e.g. BESAN FLOUR).

In western countries the principal use of flour, understood as wheat flour, is in baking, especially BREAD. Numerous different grades of flour may be had for this purpose:

- **Wholemeal flour,** which contains all the bran and germ, is therefore more nutritious than white flour, from which they have been removed.
- **Wheatmeal** or brown flour is intermediate.
- **White flour** which has had all the bran and wheatgerm removed but may be 'enriched' with synthetic vitamins to make up for the loss. White flours are differentiated by their hardness. In the USA there are three degrees:
    1. bread flour, which is made from blends of hard wheat only and contains 12 to 14% or more of protein;
    2. all-purpose flour, made from a blend of hard and soft wheat, with 10 to 12% protein; and
    3. cake flour entirely of soft wheat, with about 9% protein. A high level of PROTEIN is associated with a high level of GLUTEN.

In Britain two grades only are normally available: strong flour, that is moderately hard bread flour; and flour just described as 'flour'; which is nearly as soft as American cake flour. Usually soft flour is bleached and hard flour is left its natural cream colour. Hard flour has a distinctly gritty texture when rubbed between the fingers.

- **Self-raising** (US: self-rising) flour contains BAKING POWDER. It has a limited keeping time because the baking powder absorbs atmospheric moisture, its ingredients react, and it loses its raising power.

Types of flour on sale include wholemeal and various shades of brown, from which some of the bran and germ has been extracted. Often the degree of extraction is stated; 81% is a typical figure. (The percentage refers to what remains, not what has been removed.) A flour described as 'wheatmeal' without a figure is likely to be paler, and 'brown' usually means very pale indeed. Coultate (1989) explains:

The bread-making properties of a flour are much improved by prolonged storage. Autoxidation of the polyunsaturated fatty acids of flour lipids results in the formation of hydroperoxides, which are powerful oxidising agents. One consequence is a bleaching of the carotenoids in the flour, giving the bread a more attractive, whiter crumb.

However, the most important of the beneficial effects of ageing are on the loaf volume and crumb texture. Over the first twelve months of storage of flour there is a steady increase in the loaf volume and the crumb becomes finer and softer.

Having explained the main meaning of 'improving' in relation to flour and that the principal improvements occur naturally if the flour is kept in store, Coultate goes on to explain how these natural processes can be replaced by similar but more rapid changes—brought about by chemical improvers.

For over 50 years it has been common practice to simulate the ageing process by the use of oxidising agents as flour treatments, at the mill or as additives at the bakery. The agents used have included:

- chlorine dioxide (applied as a gaseous treatment by the miller);
- benzoyl peroxide;
- ammonium and potassium persulphates;
- potassium bromate and iodate;
- azodicarbonamide.

The first two of these are usually described as bleaching agents, and the others as 'flour improvers', but there is no clear distinction between the two types of activity.

MILLING

To make wheat flour the wheat must be ground by one means or another. The evolution of grinding and milling techniques began with the earliest known pestle and mortar, dating from about 10000 BC; this came from the Azilian culture of S. France, where it was used to grind pigments. No doubt pestles and mortars were subsequently used for grains, but the result they produce, although adequate for a GRUEL or POTTAGE, does not really produce flour for bread.

In most places where a series of early food-grinding implements has been found, development can be seen to have proceeded in one of two ways. One was the larger mortar worked by two or more people pounding alternately with long-handled pestles, as is still seen in Africa. This is quicker, but does not give a finer grind. The other is a device in which the top stone, or pestle, rubs against the lower stone, or mortar, with a shearing effect on the grain which can produce flour as we know it. A large surface area is needed for efficiency, so the original bowl shape of the mortar is opened out into a flat form, generally at first with raised edges. This is set in front of the kneeling operator, sloping away from the body. A smaller, flat-bottomed stone is rubbed back and forth across the grain. The flour collects at the far end, where there is often a hollow.

Such devices, sometimes called saddle stones, are represented in ancient Egyptian paintings and tomb models and on Assyrian reliefs. Actual examples are found both in the old world and in America, where they were used for MAIZE. Early equipment of this type has also been excavated in the Balkans. A saddle stone grinds well but is slow, as well as exhausting.

Developments of the saddle stone, still manually operated but capable of greater output, appear to be concentrated in the E. Mediterranean; excavations on the Aegean island of Delos have yielded particular treasures. The lower stone was flattened, enlarged, and placed above waist height on a bench. One end of the upper stone was fixed to a pivot and both stones were 'dressed' with small diagonal grooves which crossed each other at an angle as the upper stone swept across the lower in an arc. Grooves were maintained in all subsequent mills.

From a reciprocating arc, the motion of the upper stone was converted to fully circular by placing the pivot at its centre, allowing it to rotate on the lower stone. To keep it centred, the lower stone was made conical. Grain was fed through a hole in the centre of the upper stone, and the action was driven by a handle that could be turned by two operators, usually women, sitting each side of the device ('two women grinding at the mill': Matthew 24: 41).

The small household quern (as this new device came to be called) grew into the classical world's 'hourglass' mill, so called because of its shape. The bottom was the conical grinder; its top was an extension of the upper stone to make a big funnel filled with grain. The upper stone was suspended on a pivot just clear of the lower one so that there was less tendency for the flour to be spoiled by stone dust and the stone was easier to turn. An hourglass mill was a big machine, at least as large as an oil drum, and was turned by slaves or a donkey.

Later progress in milling with stones depended on harnessing extra power. Once achieved, the stones could be enlarged and flattened, but the principles remained identical. Water power was perhaps first mentioned by Strabo in 150 BC, certainly by Vitruvius in 13 BC. It spread throughout W. Europe, bringing the potential of fine flour to most communities. Wind power was harnessed around the year AD 1000, allowing mills to multiply still further.

Such mills could grind any grain, which could be subsequently sieved or bolted. The Egyptians had used papyrus for sieves, later cultures horsehair or linen. Thus, from very early times, bread was ranked not only by its original ingredients (wheat, rye, or a mixture of various grains), but by its exclusion of unwanted bran.

The conventional stone mill, even when powered by steam engines and placed in series or groups in early industrial units created for the supply of large towns, for example in Paris, had a relatively low output. This was the case even though the French developed a system of twice grinding called *mouture économique* which greatly increased the extraction of white flour from stone mills. The problem was solved by the efficient, fast roller mill, first tried in Hungary in the 1820s, perfected in Switzerland in 1834, then quickly adopted all over Europe and America. Its multiple steel rollers not only ground the grain, but also separated the various fractions (bran, germ, endosperm) without the need for bolting. For the first time, truly white flour was available at a low price.

Objections to roller milling have been and are still raised, on various grounds. It is said that since it operates at high speed, it generates heat which damages enzymes in the flour. The very presence of metal is considered by some to be deleterious to the flour's original constitution. Others maintain that it creates a characterless, and nutritionally inert, flour by excluding important components, particularly the germ; or that it makes a nonsense of the concept of 'wholemeal' by removing the various fractions, then adding them back in at the end of the milling process. Stoneground flours are often preferred by people who take their bread seriously or are anxious to maximize flavour.

---

these flowers contribute colour and a tannic note to many packaged herbal 'teas'.

Since flowers are often associated with strong perfumes, they have many applications **as flavouring agents,** verging on the category of SPICES. CLOVES and SAFFRON are both derived from flowers as are rosewater and ORANGE FLOWER WATER. The last two act as traditional breath-sweeteners in DRAGÉES and sugar-paste CACHOUS. A very English use for rose and violet flavours is in FONDANT for the centres of chocolates (lily of the valley and wallflower are other examples, now little used); the candied petals are used to decorate the finished sweets. Thick, syrupy conserves of rose, violet, or orange flowers have featured in the cuisine of various countries, or flowers can be added to fruit as flavourings—for instance, elderflowers in gooseberry jam. GERANIUM flowers provide an attractive flavour, and YLANG-YLANG is an ingredient in SE Asian confectionery, together with SCREWPINE essence.

Finally, there is the simple **decorative aspect** of using flowers for colour. Susan Drury (1985) observed that the essentially medieval practice of serving coloured food at the table was retained in England, 'and nowhere was this more apparent in the use of flowers, either fresh or crystallised, which were used as decoration or ingredients in salads, pottages and tarts'.						(LM)

READING: Claire Clifton (1983).

FLUMMERY a name derived from the Welsh *llymru*, originally meant a dish made by soaking fine oatmeal (see OATS) in water for a long time and then boiling and stirring the liquid until it was almost solid (see SOWANS). It could also be made with oat bran. C. Anne Wilson (1973), in thus describing it, goes on to give a quotation from Gervase Markham (1631) which gives the impression of a peasant dish beginning to climb up the social scale. Markham praised flummery for its 'wholesomeness and rare goodness', and remarked that 'some eat it with honey, which is reputed the best sauce; some with wine, either sack, claret or white; some with strong beer or strong ale, and some with milk'. The climb continued, and towards the end of the 17th century the name flummery began to be used for something different: a sweet JELLY made with cream or ground almonds, set in moulds by means of calf's foot or ISINGLASS or HARTSHORN, and resembling the earlier leach, which was a kind of BLANCMANGE.

Ayto (1993) comments that in Britain 'flummery is a dish of yesteryear' although Mrs Beeton (1861) still offered a recipe for Dutch flummery, 'a sort of jellified custard made with generous amounts of sherry or Madeira'. The term survives in N. America meaning a berry dessert dish thickened with cornstarch, or the like.

FLY AGARIC the name given to a poisonous mushroom, *Amanita muscaria* (fly amanita), because its juices were traditionally used in fly-papers to kill flies. It belongs to the same genus (see AMANITA for a description) as the fatal death cap, but its toxic properties are different, less strong and seldom fatal. It is even doubtful whether they are fatal to flies; according to controlled experiments, it is possible that they merely make flies ill.

The fly agaric is instantly recognizable: it is the pretty red-capped, white-speckled 'toadstool' shown in traditional fairy pictures. It grows up to 15 cm (6") tall and wide. (The variety *regalis* may be larger still.) The red cap often turns brownish. It grows abundantly all over Europe and N. America, in Japan, and also in Australia (probably as an immigrant from the northern hemisphere) and N. Africa, its preferred habitat being woods in autumn.

The mushroom contains a substance, mycoatropine, which causes hilarious intoxication and hallucinations, preceded by vomiting and followed by strong pains and diarrhoea. It is thought to have been used in pre-Christian religious rituals in many parts of Europe, including Britain in the time of the Druids. The use of the mushroom has continued up to the present day in parts of Lapland and Siberia, where it is dried and chewed or made into an intoxicating drink. See also HALLUCINOGENIC MUSHROOMS.

FLYING FISH of the family Exocoetidae, do not really fly, but glide, using their very large pectoral fins like wings. By launching themselves upwards from the surface of the sea at maximum swimming speed, they have been known to attain a glide path more than 5 m (16') above the water and to remain airborne over a distance as great as 100 m (110 yards). Usually, however, they cover much shorter distances, skimming the waves.

A puzzling feature of this gliding is that the fish have been seen to accelerate in the course of it. The explanation is that they allow themselves to lose height until their tail fins are just in the water, then vibrate these as rapidly as they can, which causes them to gather speed. Maximum speed, as measured by an expert in SE Asian waters, is in the region of 65 k.p.h. (40 m.p.h.); see Davidson (1977).

Although the gliding is done as part of their strategy for evading predators, it may result in their dropping into the boats of human predators, who will in all probability have been fishing for other species; flying fish are in general counted as inferior food, although W. Indians relish them and incorporate them in dishes such as flying fish pies. The flesh resembles that of the HALF-BEAK.

In the Mediterranean, *Hirundichthys rondeletii*, whose wings are black, has a market length of around 20 cm (8") and may be met in some fish markets. In SE Asia, *C. oligolepis* is a common species. It is known as *bolador* (from the Spanish) in the Philippines, where it enjoys some popularity.

Flying fish belong to the tropical and subtropical waters of the world; their way of life does not suit colder climates.

FLYING SQUID a general name applied to SQUID of the family Ommastrephidae, which constitute about three-quarters of the commercial catch of squid in the world. Flying squid do not really fly, but can propel themselves out of the water, to escape predators, and glide for some distance. See SQUID.

FOCACCIA or fougasse, a flat bread which belongs essentially to the northern shores of the Mediterranean and has its origin in classical antiquity. In ancient Rome *panis focacius* denoted a flat bread cooked in the ashes (*focus* meant hearth). Thence came the term *focacia*, *focaccia* in modern Italian, *fougasse* in the south of France, and *fouace* in the north of France.

P. and M. Hyman (in the IPCF volume on Provence, 1995) remark that in France this form of bread had become a luxury item by the end of the Middle Ages. It could be, as at Amiens, a simple white bread; or it could be enriched as in Provence, where 14th- and 15th-century documents equate it with *placentula*, i.e. a sort of 'cake'. This enrichment made the product so different from plain bread that in at least one place it escaped a tax on bread. For many centuries it has had an association with Christmas Eve and Epiphany (cf the *gâteau des rois* described under GALETTE—a type of fougasse could fill this role in Provence).

However, what figured as one of the 13 desserts on Christmas Eve was a variation called *fougassette*, a sweetened version with orange flower water.

In an Italian context one thing is obvious, namely that the addition of a topping to a plain focaccia would result in a kind of PIZZA. However, apart from this aspect, Italian focaccia has branched out in various directions, both savoury and sweet. The term can now mean a dish called *torta* made by alternating layers of dough with savoury layers. It can also mean sweet confections made with raised pastry. Numerous regional specialities such as the *fitascetta* of Lombardy, the Tuscan *stiacciata*, and the *schiacciata* of Emilia are all descendants. Also, a focaccia may be made with flavourings such as onion and sage or anise, or honey, etc.

FOIE GRAS 'goose or duck liver which is grossly enlarged by methodically fattening the bird', as the *Larousse gastronomique* sums up the product. The enlarged liver has been counted a delicacy since classical times, when the force-feeding of the birds was practised in CLASSICAL ROME.

It is commonly said that the practice dates back even further, to ancient Egypt, and that knowledge of it was possibly acquired by the Jews during their period of 'bondage' there and transmitted by them to the classical civilizations. However, Serventi (1993), in his magisterial survey of the history and all other aspects of the matter, casts doubt on this legend, while agreeing that Jews played an important role in diffusing through Europe knowledge of the techniques for successfully 'cramming' the birds and processing the livers.

In modern times the foie gras of the south-west of France and that of Strasbourg have been the most renowned, although much of what is now consumed in France

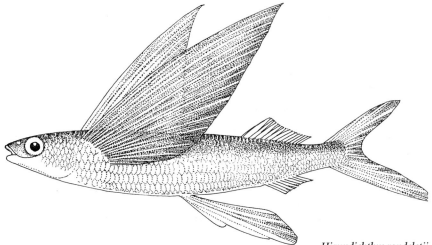

Hirundichthys rondeletii

has its origin in E. Europe or Israel, and the high value of the product may add other areas of production as time goes by. It seems unlikely, however, that France will be displaced from its position as principal consumer; and almost equally unlikely that opinion there will swing against the practice of force-feeding, despite rumblings of opposition to it elsewhere. The French, while acknowledging that the practice is carried to quite unnatural lengths, are apt to say that the birds themselves grow to like their additional daily rations of maize, pushed down their throats through a special funnel. An additional argument, that the (gastronomic) end justifies the means, is exemplified in a quotation given by the *Larousse gastronomique* from an author writing about traditional foods and dishes of Alsace: 'The goose is nothing, but man has made of it an instrument for the output of a marvellous product, a kind of living hothouse in which there grows the supreme fruit of gastronomy.'

The season for producing foie gras is in the winter. Opinions differ as to whether that of the goose or that of the duck is preferable. There are very precise French regulations about the marketing of all foie gras products. (These are among the aspects treated comprehensively by Serventi.)

FONDANT is prepared by dissolving SUGAR and GLUCOSE syrup in water and boiling to the soft ball stage (see SUGAR BOILING). When fondant is hand made, the syrup is poured out onto a cold surface and worked, first with a spatula until it turns from a clear liquid to a white, crumbly solid. It is then kneaded by hand until smooth, and finished by being left to ripen in a cool place for at least 12 hours. (This working process is mechanized for large-scale production.) The object is to produce minute crystals in a supersaturated solution of sugar, giving a 'creamy' texture to the finished product.

It is a confection which will keep almost indefinitely, given suitable conditions. Correctly made fondant can be melted and will maintain its creamy texture during this process; it can then be used for coating suitable fillings, rather in the same way as chocolate is. Fresh fruit, such as grapes or strawberries, can be dipped to make confections for immediate consumption. A fondant coating has an attractive, soft gleam and takes colours as pastel shades. The very sweet taste of the confection is offset by the addition of acid fruit flavours, coffee, mint, or chopped nuts. Fondant can also be cast in moulds and allowed to set; and soaked in sugar syrup to crystallize the exterior. It can be used to make a satisfactory ICING for cakes.

Fondant is a relatively recent development in CONFECTIONERY. It appears to have originated in the middle of the 19th century, probably in France. A variety of fondant which had cream amongst its ingredients was popular in the late 19th and early 20th centuries under the name of 'Opera Caramels'. Today, fondant has been reduced to a supporting role in confectionery, largely as a filling for chocolates. When used in this way, it is often referred to as crème, or cream filling; this is a statement about the texture, rather than a reference to the ingredients. A popular way of consuming fondant in the late 20th century is in a mint-flavoured, chocolate-coated form intended to be eaten after dinner. LM

FONDUE the French for 'melted', is the name of a Swiss dish made of melted cheese. Those partaking are provided with cubes of bread which they spear on forks and dip into the pot of cheese, which is kept hot over a spirit burner. (The name is also used for a quite different French dish, *Fondue bourguignonne*, in which the communal pot is full of heated oil and the eaters cook cubes of beef steak in it.)

There are many recipes for cheese fondue, including that given by BRILLAT-SAVARIN (1826) which has been condemned by Swiss authorities as being for scrambled eggs with cheese rather than a true fondue. Eggs do not appear in the classic Swiss recipes.

Most Swiss would agree that a proper fondue is made with a blend of cheeses—of GRUYÈRE, EMMENTAL, and a softer local cheese such as RACLETTE or APPENZELL—white wine, a little kirsch, a spoonful of flour to prevent curdling, salt, pepper, nutmeg, and nothing else.

Fonduta, the Italian version of fondue, is made with FONTINA cheese (see below). There is also a similar Dutch dish called *Kaasdoop* (cheese dip).

Fromage fondu is a different term, referring to a class of liquefied and blended cheese products, a few of which can claim a long history and special merit; Cancoillotte is one such, and Rance (1989) records that it is so important in its region, the Franche-Comté, that there was a special ration card for it during the Second World War.

FONTINA a mild Italian cheese from the Val d'Aosta. It has been produced since the 15th century, is made from whole cow's milk, and comes in wheels which weigh anything from 8 to 18 kg (18 to 40 lb). The texture is smooth, usually pitted with tiny holes, and the cheese melts well; it is used for the famous Turin dish *fonduta* (see FONDUE above) and in cooking. Older cheeses can be grated.

FOOD CHAIN or food web, the natural succession in which one organism eats another and is in turn eaten. The first term is more usual but the second is more accurate, given that these sequences involve all living creatures in the world and are massively interrelated.

The *NSOED* defines 'food chain' as 'a series of organisms each dependent on the next for food, especially by direct predation'. It equates 'food web' with 'food cycle' and defines the latter term as 'the system of interdependent food chains'.

To take a simple example of the kind often cited, plants take nutrients from the soil; cows eat plants; some humans eat cows. Nothing (usually) eats humans, so they are said to be 'at the top of the food chain' or 'top predators'. But the number of 'chains' leading upwards from plants is, for practical purposes, infinite, and so is the amount of criss-crossing between the 'chains'. So long as this is understood, the chain simile can be illuminating and it does help to focus attention on what happens to the organisms higher up a chain if one of the lower links in it becomes unavailable or extinct.   (RH)

FOOD HISTORY is not widely recognized as a discrete subject for academic work, in the same way as women's history and cinema history (to take but two examples). A few institutions, for example the Centre des Hautes Études in Paris, provide for study of aspects of it, but most such work in the English language has been conducted outside an academic framework, by amateurs. The volume of published work in this field has increased enormously, from a small nucleus, in the last quarter of the 20th century.

Many aspects of food history depend on written source material, for example old cookery manuscripts, cookery books of the distant and more recent past, and allusions in literature to meals and foodstuffs. In response to growing interest, a large number of old cookery books, in many languages, have been reprinted in the last decades of the 20th century. Those who work with them become aware that their content often reflects the practice of a previous generation, and that there are many instances of plagiarism, which can give a misleading impression. If, however, allowance is made for such factors, these books can yield valuable information. Some of this is statistical, as in studies by French and other scholars of the frequency with which certain ingredients occur in particular collections of medieval recipes.

Archaeology makes indispensable contributions to the study of ancient (and, sometimes, not so ancient) food history. The recent development of new techniques, for example in analysing food residues in excavated utensils (see, in this connection, Delwen Samuel, 1996), has greatly increased the already substantial importance of the archaeological contribution.

Cultural studies is perhaps the best phrase to use in order to indicate a range of scholarly activities which, unlike 'food history', do have their places in academe. These focus on subjects such as:

- the ritual aspects of food, including wedding and funeral food;
- the role of meals in structuring the day;
- the symbolic value of certain foods;
- food taboos, and food eaten for religious reasons;
- food as a means of asserting identity or group membership;
- the influence on foodways of fashion, social organization;
- communal eating, feasts, hospitality, food exchanges, and food as a means of bonding, courtship, etc.;
- the effect of class or caste systems, where applicable, on foodways;
- gender differences in relation to food.

There was a time when this sort of array of topics would have been apportioned between groups of scholars bearing labels such as 'anthropology' (now subdivided into 'cultural anthropology', 'social anthropology', etc.—the phrase 'culinary anthropology' has also come into use), 'sociology', 'ethnology', etc. Times change, and these 'disciplines' are now less sharply defined, more prone to overlap and coalesce, and subject also to amiable 'invasion' by writers bearing none of the familiar labels but discussing the same subjects.

To some extent these cultural studies are concerned to record what has happened or is happening, i.e. history, but in addition they often seek to elaborate the significance of what is recorded. Thus they go in for comparing, collating, seeking to trace or build patterns or frameworks; and here there is more scope for discussion or controversy—is it or is it not helpful and illuminating to try to fit foodways into the sort of general cultural framework proposed by the 'structuralists', for example? (The difficulties which have been encountered in trying to squash everything into a given framework would be alleviated if all concerned were to recognize that many of the meals consumed by the population of the world on a given day are to a greater or lesser extent dependent on chance factors, so that some element from chaos theory has to be accommodated in any theoretical model.)

Studies of food can be and are conducted on quite different bases. It would be reasonable to say that the fundamental information about foodstuffs comes from

fields of study which have not been mentioned above, especially biology in its various aspects: **botany, zoology** (including ichthyology), **microbiology** (see MICRO-ORGANISMS and connected entries), and **chemistry.**

FOOD POISONING a general phrase that covers a wide range of different illnesses caused by eating a food or something thought to be a food. Some foodstuffs may cause no harm when eaten in small quantities or occasionally, but serious effects when taken in large amounts or regularly.

Harmful substances can be in the form of nutrients, contaminants, additives, or natural toxicants.

Clearly, nutrients are normally beneficial. However, what are known as micronutrients—VITAMINS and trace elements (see MINERALS)—can poison if taken in excessive quantities. Such cases are very rare, and are generally considered the result of bad diet rather than 'food poisoning'.

Contaminants which have entered the food from the environment, but which should not normally be present in it, may be inorganic, organic, or microbial. Inorganic contaminants include compounds of metals such as lead, mercury, and cadmium; for example, acid foodstuffs may dissolve and take up lead from the soldered seams of cans. Organic contaminants include residues of pesticides and other agricultural chemicals. Microbial contaminants include a host of micro-organisms, of which the most important are discussed under BOTULISM, LISTERIA, and SALMONELLA.

ADDITIVES that have been implicated in food poisoning include MONOSODIUM GLUTAMATE; and the artificial colour tartrazine, said to cause hyperactivity in children.

The natural toxicants are numerous, surprisingly so to those who think of 'natural foods' as pure and beneficial, and who forget that the survival strategy of many living things includes harbouring toxins to deter predators. A common example is OXALIC ACID (or its salt, calcium oxalate), present in many plants such as spinach and rhubarb. READING: Albert (1987).

FOO-FOO the most common name for the starchy pastes popular in most of W. Africa, may be made from any of numerous vegetables. YAM foo-foo is said to be the best, but it takes time and hard work to make it since the boiled yam must be vigorously pounded for 20 minutes or more before the correct texture is obtained. The large mortars and double-ended pestles used

are an image which many retain in their memories of Africa. Foo-foo may also be made from PLANTAIN, CASSAVA, TARO, SWEET POTATO, or MAIZE.

Traditional foo-foo, because of the work involved, is a special occasion dish and is often supplanted in everyday life by pastes made from dried vegetables or flours. The slightly elastic freshly pounded foo-foo loaf is torn by hand, rolled into balls, and dipped into the sauce/stew which is served with it. Any seasoning is added to the stew, not to the foo-foo. Traditional foo-foo eaters swallow it without chewing unless the sauce or stew needs it.

Starchy pastes are the staple food of most Africans south of the Sahara. Other names include *ugali*, *nsima*, and *posho* in E. Africa, *funge* in Angola, and *putu* in S. Africa.   JM

FOOL a simple mixture of mashed fruit, raw or cooked as appropriate, with whipped cream, has long been a popular British dessert. It is a dish particularly suited to being made with acid northern fruits: gooseberries, raspberries, rhubarb, damsons, etc.

The name 'fool' is thought to be derived from the French *fouler* (to mash). So it is reasonable to suppose that the idea of mashed fruit was there from the start. However, one of the earliest fools, Norfolk fool, popular during the 17th century, contained no fruit. It was a rich boiled CUSTARD made with cream, eggs, sugar, and spices. (The dish known as 'white pot' was a variant of this, which might be thickened with breadcrumbs as well as egg and often contained currants. It was often called 'Devonshire whitepot', Devon being a principal dairy farming county.)

Norfolk fool may have been an exceptional instance of the name 'fool' being applied to a dish without fruit, for similar dishes with fruit were also being made at the time. The ancient fear that fruit was unhealthy was still strong, and it was customary to boil it to a pulp to make it 'safe', after which the fool was a good way of using the resulting pulp.

Either boiled cream or fresh might be used. In early fools the fresh cream was usually left unwhipped. Whipping was a long and difficult process before the general adoption of the fork in the late 17th century. In the 18th century oranges were added to the list of fruits which were used in fools. Eggs were still used in some fools, but this practice became less usual and has now disappeared.

In C. Europe there are plenty of recipes for fruit with cream, but always with some added refinement. No doubt simpler mixtures are made without benefit of recipes. One vernacular dish made all over

C., N., and E. Europe is *rote Grütze* (German) or *rødgrøt* (Scandinavian)—'red porridge'. This is a purée of red berry fruits thickened with cornflour or semolina and often mixed with cream. A Russian variant with cranberries is called KISEL. It is usually thickened with potato starch and served with a liberal amount of cream.

Something very like a fool which has a 'respectable' French name is *Crème printania*, made with puréed strawberries flavoured with kirsch and mixed with CRÈME Chantilly (sweetened whipped cream). Pellaprat's *L'Art culinaire moderne* includes a dish in its foreign recipes section which must have puzzled many French readers. It is there called 'Eaton mess'. This is in fact a primitive fool popular at Eton School under the nickname of 'strawberry mess'. It consists of roughly mashed strawberries with a modicum of whipped cream not fully combined with them. The same thing is made with bananas when strawberries are not in season.

FORME OF CURY(E) the title of the most famous and extensive recipe collection of the 14th century, means 'the proper method of cookery'. This compilation proclaims itself to have been made by 'the chief Master Cooks of King Richard II'. There are numerous manuscripts, best collated and explained in the edition by Constance Hieatt and Sharon Butler (1985, in the book entitled *Curye on Inglysch*). Earlier editions were those of Pegge (1780) and Warner (1791, reprinted in facsimile 1981). Although there are other such compilations (see MEDIEVAL CUISINE: THE SOURCES) this gives the fullest and best impression of Anglo-Norman cuisine.

The recipes, if they are to be used in modern times, require a full glossary, such as is provided by Hieatt and Butler, and some general background information about medieval cookery. Although they come from the royal kitchen, they are not all 'grand' or complicated.

FOUR HUMOURS is probably the most convenient phrase to indicate a system of thought about medicine, food, and diet which was of fundamental importance in Europe from classical antiquity until the development of modern scientific ideas in the 17th and 18th centuries.

This system of thought is especially associated with the name of GALEN (2nd century AD) who gave it what was regarded during the succeeding 15 centuries as its definitive expression. However, much of it came from earlier Greek authors, notably the medical writer HIPPOCRATES (5th/4th centuries BC) and the philosophers

Empedocles (5th century BC) and Aristotle (4th century BC). Empedocles contributed the idea that there are four elements: fire, air, water, and earth. A follower of his called Philistion connected each of these elements with a certain 'quality': to fire belonged heat; to air, cold; to water, moistness; and to earth, dryness.

These four qualities could be found in various combinations and could be predicated of other substances, such as foods or human bodies or parts of them. Indeed, the four qualities related to the four body fluids or 'humours', namely blood, phlegm, yellow bile, and black bile.

The theory went further in its listing of quartets. Human beings could be distinguished from each other by their 'complexions', four in number but, again, susceptible to various combinations. The term 'complexions', at least as used in the English language long after the time of Galen, was ambiguous; it could be taken literally (the aspect of a person's face) or in a general way as referring to temperaments or constitutions (see a typical scheme, in the table below).

Elements	Qualities	Humours	Complexions
Air	hot:moist	blood	sanguine
Water	cold:moist	phlegm	phlegmatic
Fire	hot:dry	yellow bile	choleric
Earth	cold:dry	black bile	melancholic

Galen believed that the proportions in which the four qualities were combined was very important, and that a good blend produced good health. He also attributed the varying characteristics of individuals to the various mixtures to be found in them of the four qualities. It was fundamental to his system that all foodstuffs could be described in terms of mixtures of the four qualities and that human beings should select foods which provided the appropriate mixture to complement their own 'complexions'.

Galen's views about the four humours and the importance of food for health were translated into Syriac, Arabic, Hebrew, and finally Latin. They permeated Arabic thinking (e.g. Arabic pharmacology) and, through the Latin translation, that of western Europeans. Jane O'Hara May (1977), in a work which has become a classic for this whole field of study, focused on the manifestations of Galenic doctrines in Elizabethan England, but the tale she tells could be applied, *mutatis mutandis*, to other European countries and cultures.

O'Hara May gives numerous examples of the ways in which Galen's teaching was applied to diet in England by food writers (and their readers) of the 16th century. Such application could become almost unbelievably complex. Thus it was necessary

to consider not only the qualities of foodstuffs but also the degree to which a particular food had a given quality. Degrees could go on a scale of 1 to 4, thus ripe strawberries were cold and dry in the first degree, whereas dates were hot in the second degree and moist in the first degree. Pheasant, a paradigm of 'middle of the road' foods, was temperate in all qualities, whereas hare was hot and dry in the second degree. Many dishes would contain a dozen or more ingredients in larger or small quantities. Assessing the effect of these combinations on diners who would themselves almost invariably represent a different mixture of 'complexions' would tax the powers of a computer, let alone a human brain working in a busy kitchen.

Echoes of the Galenic system may be found worldwide. It may be that in some parts of the world similar systems arose independently; see, for a possible example, ECUADOR. However, in many places the systems locally adopted clearly owe their origins to the writings of Galen, as in the case of the Persian SARDI/GARMI.

FOURME the French word for 'mould' (in the sense of a shaping mould, not a micro-organism), appears in the name of some cheeses moulded to shape. The best known is Fourme d'Ambert, a tall, cylindrical, semi-soft blue cheese with a yellow or brownish rind; quite like a small STILTON. Fourme des Monts du Forez is a general name for this cheese and its close relations, of which one other, Fourme de Montbrison, has a protected name. These fourmes come from the hilly regions (Loire, Puy-de-Dôme) west of Lyons.

The cheese generally known as CANTAL is officially called Fourme du Cantal.

The French word for 'cheese', fromage, is connected with the idea of moulding to shape. A similar link is made in Italian where *formaggio* (the ordinary word for cheese) is made in a *forma* and *una forma* is used to mean the whole cheese, as opposed to a cut piece.

FRAISE (or frawsey or froise), a medieval term referring to something of the general nature of a PANCAKE, made with batter and fried. Most versions were thick, and could incorporate small pieces of meat or bacon, vegetables, or fruits, sometimes with cream, ground almonds, or breadcrumbs, and usually sweetened. Sometimes the fillings were enclosed between two layers of batter; sometimes they were mixed in. Fraises survived into the 20th century. Later forms were almost all sweet, and were like fried or baked fruit BATTER puddings. See also TANSY.

FRANCE NATIONAL AND REGIONAL CUISINES The heading is deliberately in the plural. In France, cuisine is not simply a source of pleasure but a multifaceted discipline. For centuries, French gastronomes have articulated opinions in their writings and woven historical, sociological, and biological elements into personal philosophies of taste. A true 'Science of the table' has developed with its grand masters, heroes, and even its martyrs all serving the cause of *la gastronomie française.*

The development and growth of French cuisine owes much to the fact that, unlike many other western countries, France has historically had a gastronomic capital, Paris. Culinary resources are concentrated there: the best ingredients and the most sensitive palates were all to be found in one place. For centuries, observers marvelled at the diversity and abundance of foods available to Parisians. The provinces have long paid a gastronomic tribute to the capital in the form of hams, sausages, cheeses, and fish.

But a concentration of resources, a receptive environment do not alone explain the growth and development of French cuisine; one needs chefs. In France, cooks are respected but chefs are revered. Like soldiers and statesmen they are decorated and glorified; streets are named after them and schoolchildren can recite their names. French chefs do more than cook. They often feel a duty to improve upon the past, to 'advance' the art of cookery by renewing attitudes and exploring new tastes. Indeed the periodic formation of a 'nouvelle cuisine' is characteristic of French cuisine and one of its greatest strengths.

Since the 17th century, French chefs have been expressing their desire for 'reform' in the cuisine they inherited from the past. As time passed, they became more and more articulate in their criticism of the 'ancient cookery' and boastfully dogmatic about the virtues of 'modern cookery'. In 1733, for example, Vincent La Chapelle wrote: 'If a great lord's table were served today as it was twenty years ago, it would not satisfy his guests.' His *Cuisinier moderne* announced the birth of a 'nouvelle cuisine', a new way of cooking that was to be adopted by several generations of French chefs—until CARÊME challenged it in the early 19th century. In our own time, French chefs have once again 'rebelled' and the 'nouvelle cuisine' that revolutionized cooking during the 1970s has led to a new respect for vegetables, lighter sauces, and the 'discovery' of regional specialities (notably foie gras). Indeed, perhaps more than anything else, it is the French chefs' willingness to question and build on the past, to innovate, to revise, that has kept French cuisine pre-eminent among

western cuisines and one of the great cuisines of the world.

Not only does French cuisine have its heroes (the innovative chefs) and its great men (the gastronomes who encourage and criticize the chefs), but its martyrs as well. The best known is Vatel, who preferred death in 1671 to the shame of serving a flawed meal (he promptly committed suicide when he learned that the fish he ordered for a banquet had not arrived). Vatel's gesture is symptomatic of the physical and mental distress chefs endure. Today the pressures stem from their annual re-evaluation by the authors of a reputedly neutral, and anonymous, authority: the *Michelin Guide.* In order to maintain their coveted Michelin 'stars', chefs have been known to go into debt and toil gruelling hours at the expense of their health; these days, however, they generally prefer early retirement to the self-sacrificing gesture of Vatel.

Today, as in the past, chefs are grouped into 'schools' with debates raging between the partisans of one and supporters of another. French Cooking is a monument in a permanent state of renovation. French cuisine remains dynamic, integrating new products, thriving on trends, and rejuvenating itself through periodic purges and, at least once in each century, a 'nouvelle cuisine' is born. If French cuisine 'belongs' to the chefs and is a professional cuisine par excellence, it can also boast a score or more of distinctly regional cuisines whose names are generally derived from the old pre-Revolutionary division of the country into provinces. Although these regional cuisines are now a source of pride, the distinctive cooking of the provinces did not attract the attention of French gastronomes until a relatively late date. Indeed, no truly regional cookbooks appear in France until the 1830s when Nîmes gave us its *Cuisinier Durand* and Mulhouse its *Cuisinier du Haut-Rhin.* GRIMOD DE LA REYNIÈRE did much to whet the appetite of his fellow gastronomes for regional produce—and regional recipes—in his *Almanach des gourmands* (1803 to 1812) which was, among other things, a veritable catalogue of regional specialities. He never tired of praising artisans who shipped the finest duck liver pâtés to Paris or excelled in the preparation of a regional mustard. He was constantly calling attention to the gastronomic wealth of the provinces, which inspired the anonymous author of the *Cours gastronomique* to go one step further and publish the first Gastronomic Map of France in 1808. As never before, one could now visualize the wealth and diversity of the regions. Though drawn in an extremely stylized manner, one can recognize the inlets of the Atlantic seaboard where the famous *sel de Guérande* is made, and the oysters from Cancale are clearly visible along the

Normandy coast, as are the large white beans from Soissons, north-east of Paris. Hundreds of other delicacies figure on the map which leaves virtually no region barren. There is no caption, but the reader is invited to imagine his own: 'This the land of Milk and Honey, with turkeys as big as cows and strings of sausages as long as rivers, where pâtés are the size of wine barrels and every meal will be a feast. This is *La France Gastronomique.*'

Despite the enthusiasm of writers like Grimod and the publication of the *Cours gastronomique*, the century's most famous food writer, BRILLAT-SAVARIN, has literally *nothing at all* to say about regional cuisines in his *Physiologie du goût* published in 1826. Perhaps his attitude accounts for the mid-century silence that can be observed when it comes to French regional cookery. Nevertheless, by the end of the century there is a new manifestation of interest in the cooking of at least a selected number of regions, particularly in the south and east. Regionalists become active in places like Provence (Reboul publishes his famous *Cuisinière provençale* just before the turn of the century), Lorraine (the cuisine of Metz is documented in 1890 by E. Auricoste de Lazarque), in Alsace (Charles Gérard writes the first history of a regional cuisine in 1877, *L'Ancienne Alsace à table*), Bordeaux (in 1898 Alcide Bontou publishes the first book claiming to be about the cuisine of Bordeaux)—not to mention Marcel Herbet in Dax, south of Bordeaux, who already in 1858 had published a small *Cuisinier gascon*, reviving a title from the 18th century that, unlike its predecessor, actually contained recipes from the region! In short, when the 20th century begins, there seems to be a new-found interest in the foods of the provinces.

This burgeoning curiosity will get a tremendous boost with the advent of paid vacations in the 1930s and the spread of automobiles in the early years of this century. The coastal regions, in particular, benefited from the institution of paid vacations since many people headed toward the sea and Provençal cooking (which had been 'on the rise' since the early 19th century) found itself with yet more numerous adepts. Two influential food writers, Curnonsky and Austin de Croze, also made an important contribution to the growing awareness of regional food about this time. Their most important work, from a historical point of view, is *Le Trésor gastronomique de France*, published in 1933. This 388-page volume is a survey of French specialities. No recipes, just an immense list. Region after region, a never-ending gastronomic roll-call of sausages, fruits, candies, soups, fish, mushrooms, cheeses, virtually every food the French are known to eat parades by. The French reader could only swell with pride and admiration as he turned the pages and discovered the 'Douceurs' of Picardy or the seven (!) different cassoulets of the Languedoc. Like the *carte gastronomique* of 1808, *Le Trésor* was saying to him, 'you live in the richest country on earth, the pleasures of the table are at your doorstep, every province is a gastronomic paradise with a wealth of sausages, cheeses, candies, fruits, and more'. If France was not the richest country in Europe from a gastronomic point of view, it wasn't going to be easy to convince the French!

In addition to such gastronomic chroniclers as Curnonsky and Croze, French anthropologists, sociologists, and historians have all taken an interest in regional foods in more recent times. Some have tried to divide France into areas based on the use of three basic cooking fats: butter, lard, and olive oil. A map was drawn showing the entire Mediterranean coast covered with dots representing the use of olive oil; Brittany, half of the Atlantic coastline, and the Loire Valley were all covered with horizontal lines representing the use of butter; the south-west and much of Alsace had vertical stripes over them meaning that in these areas the preferred fat was 'lard'. The rest of France looked like a chequerboard indicating that both lard and butter were used, except for the Rhone Valley which also had a sprinkling of dots to indicate that all three were employed! But despite the fact that this map called attention to some basic distinctions of taste and culinary practice, it nevertheless lacked nuance—no mention was made of goose fat (important both in the south-west and Alsace) or walnut oil (important in the south-west and in central France), undoubtedly because neither is as 'basic' a fat as the lard or olive oil by which these areas were characterized.

In the not-so-distant past, one could have divided France along different lines. There were, of course, many regions where wheat was 'the staff of life' but for centuries, people living in south central France survived on a diet of chestnuts, not bread, and further south, toward Spain, cornmeal served a similar purpose. In the east of France, cornmeal was equally important. Indeed, in the Franche-Comté, it is called *gaudes* and used to make a porridge of the same name that was so frequently consumed by the people there that they were known as 'yellow bellies'. Today, *gaudes* is little more than a curiosity; the old folks make it on Sundays now and again but they have become 'bread-eaters' like everyone else in France. What bread are they eating? Baguette, of course. This would not have been the case at the turn of the century when 'white bread' was a perishable luxury only city dwellers could afford. A dark loaf, made with a mixture of

rye and wheat, was the only bread country folk consumed then and it was not until some time after the Second World War that the fragile baguette spread from Paris to the rest of France. Now it is the 'national loaf' just as camembert, in the course of this century, has become the 'national cheese'.

In the 1990s, the products and cuisine of one region in particular are more visible than any other—those of the south-west. Shops selling only products from the old province of Gascony have sprung up from Alsace to Provence and cassoulet has become a national dish. One can purchase jars of cassoulet virtually everywhere and some companion products such as confit and foie gras are equally available throughout the country in shops with names such as 'Duc de Gascogne'. More obscure products such as smoked duck ham or preserved duck gizzard (once considered oddities) are now familiar to everyone.

This is not the first time that regional specialities have been 'popularized' and entered the national diet. In the 19th century Alsatian sauerkraut (*choucroute*) spread throughout France via a new kind of restaurant, the brasserie, and in the 1920s *crêperies* did the same for Brittany's crêpes. But the biggest difference between today and the past is that today, people are willing to recognize that each region has its own full-fledged 'gastronomy'. Nowadays, books are written about the foods of virtually every region of France. Indeed, the French authorities are taking regional food seriously enough to have lent their support to an official inventory of regional foodstuffs which, when finished, will count no fewer than 26 volumes (one for each administrative region of the country); see under IPCF in the Bibliography. Deemed 'national treasures' by the Ministry of Culture, hundreds of regional foods are being described and studied for the first time. In short, today the foods of France are less of a mystery than ever before and, thanks to this new-found interest in the provinces, chefs can no longer monopolize the term 'cuisine'. HY
READING: Barbara Wheaton (1983).

FRANGIPANE a culinary term now well established in English as well as in French, which has an interesting history and various applications.

Claudine Brécourt-Villars (1996) observes that the variant form *franchipane* appeared in a French cookery book of 1674, meaning a custard tart flavoured with pounded almond and pistachio; and that it appeared with the usual spelling in a dictionary of 1732 as a name used by confectioners. She and other authors record the story that the name comes from an Italian aristocrat, Don Cesare

Frangipani, who became famous as the inventor of a perfume used to scent the gloves of Louis XIII. Her view is that frangipane originally meant a 'cream' flavoured simply with almond and used in the construction of various cakes; but later, by a natural extension, the confections made with the cream. Hence the similar modern meaning of products such as a tart or tartlet filled with an almond-flavoured mixture (whether of the consistency of custard or more solid).

The perfume was evidently based on the plant sometimes known as 'red jasmine', but also as 'frangipani'. This plant is now classified as *Plumeria rubra*, and its flowers are edible. Various authors have sought to ascertain what connection there could have been between the plant, the perfume derived from it, and the frangipane which we eat. Ayto (1993) may be consulted on this point. It has to be noted that Goldschmied (1954), in his authoritative dictionary of Italian culinary terms, mentions the 'perfumed gloves' story but gives *frangipane* as having two meanings: one a cream (but flavoured with vanilla—no mention of almond), and the other a panada used for stuffing fish and poultry.

FRANKFURTER a long, slender smoked SAUSAGE with a very soft fine texture. They are scalded before sale and parboiled in simmering water, so belong to the sausage type known in Germany as *Brühwurst* (see SAUSAGES OF GERMANY). As their name suggests, the sausages originated in or near the city of Frankfurt in Germany—according to E. Lissner's exhaustive *Wurstologia* (1939), in the mid-17th century.

Genuine frankfurters are made from lean pork mixed with bacon fat made into a paste and smoked, although similar sausages of beef or veal and pork, spiced and smoked, are made in the area. TRIPE, pig's HEART, and small amounts of cereal in the form of flour or breadcrumbs also find their way into some frankfurters; salt, saltpetre, sugar, mace, pepper, coriander, garlic, and onion are used in various combinations for seasoning. The saltpetre gives a pink colour. The 'franks' sold in the USA often contain a mixture of beef and pork; kosher types, consisting entirely of beef, are also made.

In 1904 the butcher Johann Georg Lahner, who produced frankfurters in Frankfurt, moved to Vienna, where he began to make similar sausages, likewise slender and smoked, and made from mixtures of pork and beef. These quickly became popular under the name *Wiener* or *Wienerwurst*; they are simply known as *Würstel* (or sometimes Frankfurter) in Vienna or 'wienies' in the USA. Some *Wiener* have a more coarsely chopped filling than frankfurters but, especially in types made abroad, there is usually no real difference.

In Prague sausages similar to frankfurters are sold in twos and referred to as *párky* (pairs). The French *saucisse de Francfort* is not unlike a frankfurter but is not parboiled before sale; *saucisse de Strasbourg* is much the same.

A frankfurter (or, sometimes, a wienie or other type of sausage) served hot in a finger-shaped bread roll is known as a hot dog. The connection between hot dogs and dogs, the animals, is at one or two removes. The name is thought to stem from newspaper cartoons of around 1900 by T. A. Dorgan, which portrayed talking frankfurters; these were also known as 'dachshund sausages' because of their shape.

The originator of the bun-and-sausage idea is unknown. It was not a major innovation, as sausage sellers everywhere would offer bread of some kind with their wares, as well as mustards and other relishes. However, the shape of the bun made it easier to hold than a greasy sausage, with or without a slice of bread. All that can be said with any certainty is that in the closing decades of the 19th century frankfurters and wienies were being sold in buns in various cities in the USA. Some sources credit A. L. Feuchtwanger, a small-scale sausage vendor in St Louis, Louisiana, in the 1870s, with the introduction of the bread roll; others cite Charles Feltman, a German butcher on Coney Island. Whoever had the idea first, and whether it was a frank or a wienie in the roll, it was an employee of Feltman, one Nathan Handwerker, who popularized them, opening his 'Nathan's Hot Dogs' stand on Coney Island in 1916 and undercutting his former employer's prices.

Since then the frankfurter, accompanied by ketchup, mustard, or pickles (or all of these), has become a favourite N. American street snack, and is firmly established in many other parts of the world.   (LM)

FREEKEH (also fereek), roasted green WHEAT, a speciality of certain Arab countries, notably Syria, Lebanon, Jordan, and Egypt, is exquisitely good. The green wheat stalks are harvested and gathered in bunches, then roasted in the fields over an open wood or charcoal fire. When cool, the ears are shucked and the grain is either kept whole or cracked. Of the two main kinds, that which is coarsely cracked and brownish-green in colour has a markedly smoky taste. The other, brown in colour, with the grains whole, is blander.

Chicken with freekeh, the latter swollen with the chicken stock in which it is cooked, is a remarkably good combination.

Dagher (1991), surveying traditional foods of the Near East for the FAO, observes that freekeh is normally eaten in place of rice, to which it is nutritionally superior. In the same context he refers to a product which has a similar sounding name, *frik*, but differs from fereek in several respects. It is made by parboiling or steaming, and then drying, immature grains of BARLEY; and is mainly used in N. Africa. It is also known as *mirmiz*.   (AH)

FREEZING among all the processes for PRESERVATION of food, has the advantage of causing relatively little change in the food.

It is thought of as a recent innovation, but has been used since antiquity, although only in places where the climate is cold enough for it to be possible by natural means. The Inuit (Eskimos) and other peoples of the far north have always stored food by simply burying it in the snow. This natural freezing has been practised in the northern parts of Russia, China, and Japan.

In more clement regions, ICE could be brought down from the mountains to assist in preserving food; but the use of ice by itself was not freezing and is dealt with separately—see also REFRIGERATION. It was not until the early 16th century, in Italy, that the discovery was made that if enough salt is mixed with ice its temperature falls to −18 °C (0 °F), and that this mixture can be used to freeze things. For a long time this technique was used only to make ICE CREAM and the like, not for preserving food.

The first food other than such desserts to be frozen artificially for sale was fish, in the 19th century. Dr Kitchiner (1817), mentioned frozen fish, presumably prepared in an ice and salt mixture, but the first patent for this method of freezing fish was not granted until 1842, to Henry Benjamin and Henry Grafton in Britain. The first mechanical freezing plant was built in Sydney, Australia, in 1861. By 1870 chilled meat—that is, a couple of degrees below freezing point, but not deep frozen—was being shipped from the USA to Europe in insulated holds cooled with ice and salt; 1880 saw the first successful shipment of chilled meat on the longer voyage from Australia to England.

By the end of the century the method was being applied to fish and poultry, and early in the 20th century experiments were made in freezing fruits. These were at first unsuccessful; the fruits were mushy when thawed, since they had been frozen too slowly so that large ice crystals formed which disrupted their delicate tissues. Similar troubles were encountered with vegetables, the more so since the need for initial blanching to destroy enzymes was not realized. Animal products generally emerge better from a process of slow freezing because of the greater elasticity of their tissues.

The problem was overcome by Clarence Birdseye, an American who lived in Labrador between 1912 and 1916. There, in the intense winter cold, he observed the effect of very rapid freezing not only on meat and fish, which the inhabitants customarily froze, but also on vegetables. He began experiments with artificial quick freezing and in 1923 set up a company to prepare and sell frozen fish. This soon went bankrupt, but he did manage to develop the first specially designed quick freezer for vegetables and fruits. In 1929 he was bought out by General Foods and the era of frozen food began in earnest.

At first only shops had freezers. At home, people kept frozen foods in the ice-making compartment of a refrigerator, which is just cold enough to store them for a few days. The home freezer came in gradually during the 1930s as an expensive luxury, at first mainly in the USA.

EFFECTS OF FREEZING

The preservative effects of cold are described under REFRIGERATION. When food is frozen rather than merely chilled, other effects come into play. The liquids in food are not pure water, but solutions of salts and sugars; so they are still liquid at 0 °C (32 °F), and only begin to freeze at lower temperatures. The stronger the solution, the lower the freezing point. Once the liquid starts to freeze, pure ice forms and the dissolved substances pass into the remaining liquid, which thus becomes a stronger solution with a lower freezing point. The liquid therefore freezes little by little, and no water solution ever freezes completely, even in the coldest freezer—there is always a residue of very strong solution. At a certain point, however, the solution will have become too strong for micro-organisms to function, with the exception of some troublesome moulds which can grow very slowly in a freezer.

Freezing does not stop the action of ENZYMES, which continues slowly in the residual unfrozen solution. However, the blanching of fruits and vegetables before freezing destroys the enzymes. If foods are frozen completely raw, they will still have a respectable freezer life, but less long than if blanched. There are some exceptions such as crustaceans, whose enzymes are so active that cooking before freezing is essential. Fruits that are to be eaten raw, and so cannot be blanched, are often packed in sugar or dipped in syrup before freezing, to exclude air and thus inhibit enzyme action.

Freezing does little damage to the nutritive value of food. Fruits and vegetables lose some vitamin C, mostly in processes such as blanching before they are frozen. But frozen peas—which are often frozen within minutes of being picked—still have more of the vitamin than 'fresh' peas which have been hauled to a wholesale market and then left sitting in a shop. Meats lose a certain amount of vitamin B1, again mostly in initial processing.

FREEZING METHODS

Quick freezing processes are designed to take food through the temperature range from 0 °C to –5 °C (32 °F to 23 °F) in a few minutes, since this is when most ice crystals form. The less time they have to form, the smaller they will be and the less damage they will do to the cell structure of the food. The smaller the pieces of food, the faster they freeze. Several methods are currently used for items of different sizes.

Air blast freezing is the most used technique. It freezes smallish objects, such as packets of frozen vegetables, quickly and uniformly. The food is frozen on refrigerated trays by a blast of chilled air at –12 °C (10 °F), after which it can be cooled more slowly to the storage temperature of a commercial freezer, –20 °C (–4 °F). A variant used for very small objects, such as loose peas, is fluid bed freezing, where the food travels along a belt pierced with holes through which chilled air is blown, lifting the food so that it is frozen in mid-air.

Contact or plate freezing is suitable for larger items that do not have to be frozen very quickly, such as fish fillets. These are frozen between refrigerated plates which press lightly against the food.

Immersion freezing is used for very large things such as whole chickens and turkeys. These are immersed in a very cold liquid—brine, sugar solution, or propylene glycol (a chemical also used as anti-freeze). After the food is frozen it is centrifuged to remove the liquid. A related technique is spray freezing, where food is sprayed with cold liquid as it travels on a wire mesh conveyor belt.

Luxury foods that are easily damaged by freezing, such as soft fruits, are sometimes frozen by dipping them in liquid nitrogen at –196 °C (–321 °F). Freezing is more or less instantaneous, so only tiny ice crystals are formed.

FREEZE-DRYING

This method can produce foods that are almost as well preserved as by straight freezing, but do not need cold storage. It exploits the fact that ice can 'sublime', or change straight from a solid to water vapour without passing through a liquid stage. (Sublimation is a familiar phenomenon in a home freezer: the frost that forms on the inside of bags of food comes from water vapour that has sublimed out of the food and then refrozen.)

Freeze-drying of a kind has been practised for centuries in cold, mountainous areas. If small pieces of food are left to freeze out of doors and hung up in the wind, the moisture will gradually sublime. The low air pressure at high altitude speeds the process. Products prepared in this way include CHUÑO, the dried potatoes of the Andes; and freeze-dried TOFU in Japan. (See also DRYING.)

Modern freeze-drying is used for small items such as peas and prawns, and also for liquids such as coffee. It is a relatively expensive technique and therefore used mainly for high-value products. The food is quick frozen by an appropriate method, then put in a vacuum chamber and very slightly warmed to encourage sublimation. The final product may have a moisture content as low as 2%. It is packed in an airtight container such as a foil pouch to prevent it from absorbing moisture.

The nutritional value of foods is scarcely more affected than in conventional freezing.
(RH)

FRENCH BREAD is made mainly with soft (low-protein) European wheat, which gives a sweeter flavour than the hard N. American wheat used in e.g. Britain. It also absorbs less water, giving a drier loaf, and rises less. It is not meant to be buttered, as most English breads are.

The bread which is regarded as a symbol of France is the **baguette,** a long thin loaf, whose crisp gold crust encloses a characteristic open crumb with large holes and which can be seen standing in racks in all *boulangeries*. This is, however, a relative newcomer. French loaves were already taking on a long shape in the 18th century (a development which was criticized by some authorities as pandering too much to the love of Parisians for crust), but the very thin long baguette was only introduced in the 19th century and did not penetrate the provinces until the 20th century. (Oddly, as provincials took to this urban bread, city people started to demand rustic country breads.)

A mixture of about 80% soft and 20% hard wheats is used for baguette flour. The other ingredients are water and salt. After preliminary processing, the dough is shaped into long thin loaves and allowed to prove for a while. Before baking, the tops of the loaves are slashed with a thin curved blade. A special oven, into which a jet of high-pressure steam is injected at the commencement of baking, is required. This causes the dough to expand rapidly, the cuts on top opening to give the leaf-shaped scars typical of these loaves. After the steam is turned off, the dry heat aids gelatinization of the crust, giving the characteristic golden sheen. As baguettes stale quickly, several batches are made daily.

Breads which represent older traditions are the round *miche, pain de campagne, pain de ménage, pain paysan*, and *gros pain*, everyday family loaves, now mostly based on wheat. A piece of SOURDOUGH kept from the previous baking is the traditional method for raising these. Working slowly, it gives a distinctive flavour. (The use of sourdough has persisted longer in France than in England. The English were fermenting their bread with yeast in the form of ale-barm as early as the 14th century, whilst the French used sourdough for all but the finest white bread well into the 18th century.) Most of these breads have a coarse crumb and a thick crust and will keep for several days.

Various sorts of ring loaf (*couronne*) are common, and loaves of many other kinds, representing regional traditions and ably listed by Poilâne (1981), are still made, but in decreasing variety and quantity. For an interesting flat bread of the south, see fougasse (under FOCACCIA). For certain enriched breads of France, see BRIOCHE; CROISSANT.   HY

READING: IPCF vol for Île de France (1993); Elizabeth David (1977).

FRENCH COOKBOOKS Unlike the literature of cookery in other countries, French cookbooks were penned almost exclusively by men up until the 19th century. Prior to then, not only were cookbook authors males, but mainly male professionals—that is to say, chefs. This does not mean that their public was exclusively masculine or exclusively professional since women no doubt read their books (or had recipes read to them) long before they published recipes themselves. We find proof of this in the 14th century when an elderly Parisian copied recipes from existing manuscript sources into a compendium for his young bride—proof that she could read (and cook—or at least govern the kitchen). The collection, called the MENAGIER DE PARIS (The Goodman of Paris), includes many recipes from TAILLEVENT's famous *Viandier* and the Goodman takes care to warn his bride that certain recipes are too complicated for his household or too expensive for his purse!

Taillevent's book had the privilege, around 1490, of becoming the first printed cookbook in French and though it seems to be addressed to professionals, we cannot exclude some non-professional (and feminine) readers from among its first purchasers. The book was an immediate 'best-seller'—remaining in print for over 100 years. In the course of the 16th century, a first book dedicated to 'ladies' also appeared, the *Excellent et moult utile opuscule* written by Nostradamus, a celebrated astrologer/doctor whose prophecies are much better known than this collection of beauty formulae, home remedies, and culinary recipes. The latter, for sweets (*confitures*) and syrups, are part of a much larger literature of confectionery which would be developed in the 16th century and afterwards become a feminine 'speciality', although no feminine author will appear in this domain for several centuries.

Though the 'ladies' would be addressed in books dealing with 'their' speciality (sweets), cookery books throughout the 17th century were written by male cooks for male cooks (*les cuisiniers*). The first and most important of these, *Le Cuisinier françois*, appeared in 1651. Signed by LA VARENNE it bore witness to changes in taste which had occurred since the last Renaissance cookbooks were published, most notably in the abandonment of medieval spices in favour of native herbs for seasoning. The 1660s saw the first 'culinary encyclopedias' with titles such as the *Ecole parfait des officiers de bouche* (1662), and *Ecole des ragouts* (1668). At the end of the century Massialot introduced another innovation by publishing his famous *Cuisinier royal et bourgeois* (1691) in dictionary form with folding plates devoted to table settings.

But it is not until the 18th century that French cookbooks become truly grand productions. The most spectacular was undoubtedly the second edition of Vincent de La Chapelle's *Le Cuisinier moderne* (1742), a full five volumes with 13 folding plates, one of which, for a table of 100, measures more than a metre long when fully deployed! This is the century of the first NOUVELLE CUISINE when French chefs took to publishing multi-volume treatises on the 'new' art of cookery.

It was in the midst of all these 'revolutionary' tomes that a lone, slim volume on cookery—*La Cuisinière bourgeoise*—finally addressed itself specifically to women, teaching female professionals employed in middle-class households how to prepare economical and fashionable meals. The book, unsigned but attributed to a certain 'Menon' (his name appears in the royal 'privilege'), was an immediate success and became one of the best-selling cookbooks of all time. First published in 1746, *La Cuisinière bourgeoise* was to go through more than 120 editions and its recipes would remain in print for over 150 years, being pirated in its sixth year by a Brussels publisher who made a fortune with his own editions, far more numerous than the Paris originals he was copying!

Despite the success of Menon's work, no other author addressed a feminine public until the Revolutionary period when a tiny volume appears addressed to *La Cuisinière républicaine*. This work, printed in 'l'an III de la république' (1795), has the distinction of being the only cookbook attributed to a woman in the pre-1800 period in France. It is a small treatise of 42 pages entirely devoted to only one food: the potato. The author, Mme Mérigot, caught up in the revolutionary fervour for a plant which, it was hoped, would provide an alternative to wheat, here provides 34 recipes for preparing the humble tuber.

After the Revolution, numerous *ménagères* (housewives) followed Mme Mérigot's lead and seized their pens, starting with Mme Louise-Auguste-B. Utrechte, 'widow of P. J. Friedel . . . famous confectioner in Berlin' (or so the title page of her first book proclaims). Devoted to a traditional 'feminine' subject but one which women had never written about before, *L'Art du confiseur* (The Art of Confectionery) was published by the author herself in Paris in 1801, and was still in print 24 years later. In 1805, Mme Gacon-Dufour became the first woman to sign a complete cookbook addressed to women, the *Manuel de la ménagère à la ville et à la campagne et la femme de la basse-cour* (A Household Manual for Women in the City and the Country with Advice on Managing Barnyard Fowl). In the first quarter of the 19th century an impressive collection of small cookbooks appeared, signed by hitherto unheard of 'Mesdames'; then a first 'Mesdemoiselle' signed a book in 1820. Suddenly all the Mesdames seemed to go into retirement, leaving the feminine author field exclusively to the Mesdemoiselles until the end of the century: Mesdemoiselles Françoise, Magdeleine, Marion, Jeanette, Marianne, Sillette, Thérèse, Marguerite, Madeleine.

Male chefs were far from inactive during this same period. The most important of these writers during the early years of the century is Marie-Antoine (Antonin) CARÊME (1783–1833). A pastry chef at the outset, not only did his cooking break new ground but his books did as well. Never before had cookbooks been so elegantly illustrated with delicately engraved chapter headings and tail-pieces, not to mention the carefully rendered plates depicting the monumental constructions that characterize Carême's cuisine and pastry. It fell to one of his students, however, to have the honour in 1867 of doing something his master no doubt dreamed of doing—using colour illustrations. Jules GOUFFÉ included 25 chromolithographs in his *Livre de cuisine* published that year. Gouffé's book, which separated *grande cuisine* recipes from simpler, 'home cooking' recipes, was to remain in print for over 50 years. But the true 'successors' to Carême are a duo, Urbain Dubois and Émile Bernard, who first published their influential *La Cuisine classique* in 1856. This book, which never included colour illustrations but which contained a frontispiece and up to 77 engraved plates in its later editions, remained faithful to Carême's classic form of illustration but adopted a much larger format, growing to two volumes in its third edition of 1869 and remaining in print into the early 20th century.

As the 19th century neared its end, the French cookbook market was crowded with books of all shapes and sizes. Not only had chefs been actively writing for each other, but the ladies could now choose among books written for them by men and by women. By the 1880s, cooking was being taught in some French public schools, and the first private cooking schools, like the Cordon Bleu, opened in Paris in the 1890s. Cookbooks were becoming much more didactic but, despite the early use of colour by Gouffé, illustrations were generally in the form of black and white engravings, photography being only rarely used at the turn of the century.

The early 20th century in France was the 'Age of Escoffier' (see ESCOFFIER), a chef whose influence still goes far beyond France. Starting with its appearance in 1903, his *Guide culinaire* quickly displaced Dubois and Bernard's *Cuisine classique* on professional chefs' bookshelves around the world. Escoffier's was the voice of the 'new' century, a true successor to Taillevent, La Varenne, and Carême. But strangely, unlike his immediate predecessors, Escoffier took no interest in illustrating his work: it never included engraved plates or drawings of any kind, and he eschewed the new medium of photography as well!

A contemporary of Escoffier, Prosper Montagné, wrote an equally monumental tome with Prosper Salles in 1900, this was *Le Grand Livre de la cuisine* which, enlarged in 1929, is still one of the major 20th-century cookbooks. But Montagné's most important contribution, in partnership with Alfred Gottschalk, was the *Larousse gastronomique*, first published in 1938. Larousse was already one of France's most prestigious dictionary publishing firms and the Larousse name on a dictionary guaranteed the reader of its seriousness. Indeed, this was a monumental tome: 1,087 pages of relatively small type dealing with everything which, in 1938, rhymed with French cuisine. The book has been reissued and updated on several occasions, but these succeeding editions do not replace the 1938 edition which, like Escoffier's *Guide culinaire*, is a reference book on classic French cookery that has yet to be surpassed.

In the 1970s, no new *Guide culinaire* having been written, the young chefs who rallied to the cause of NOUVELLE CUISINE all began writing their own books and although some, like those of Michel Guérard or Alain Chapel, were to become 'stars', their books will never attain reference status. Today's masters, like Joël Robuchon or Alain Ducasse, have produced highly personal volumes that in no way codify the cuisine of the late 20th century. Indeed, it is the collection of chefs' books that has become 'a reference' more than any individual work.

Now, as the 20th century comes to a close, French chefs are as active as ever, publishing both glamorous volumes in the great Carême tradition that one dare not take into the kitchen, and smaller, more accessible works with an eye to a broader reading public which they hope to seduce as well (*à la cuisinière bourgeoise*). An interest in regional cooking, which began in the 1920s and 1930s (see FRANCE: NATIONAL AND REGIONAL CUISINES), has grown during the latter half of the century as has interest in 'foreign cuisines', a novelty in France 50 years ago, but now a permanent fixture in the cookbook department of any bookshop in France.

Though women writers now have immense importance 'at home' and no doubt outsell the chefs on the domestic market, it nevertheless remains true that, as in the past, the most visible French cookbooks internationally are those written by chefs. These books give us a glimpse of the heights to which the French culinary arts aspire. Nevertheless, thanks to cajoling editors, some chef-authors make their recipes easier to follow and simpler to execute, adapting their know-how to the constraints of the housewife, or should we say the 'home cook' who, they know, will be reading them just as before with a practical eye. Today, with more women cooks rising to chef status in France, old distinctions (home cooking=women writers, great chefs=men) are less and less true. Women chefs are writing about their professional experiences for the first time and though 'Madame le chef' is still a recent phenomenon (Madame is more likely to be a humble *cuisinière*—cook), their number is growing. The masculine monopoly of French professional culinary writing, dating back at least 600 years, is on its way to becoming a thing of the past.   HY

FRIANDISE a French word meaning a dainty or delicacy, usually a small item of sugar CONFECTIONERY or a little CAKE eaten from the fingers. This word, having been out of fashion in English for some centuries, recently came back into vogue for describing PETITS FOURS and sweetmeats taken with coffee after dinner.   LM
READING: Annie Perrier-Robert (1986).

FRICANDEAU a term which came into vogue in English in the early part of the 18th century in the context of meat cookery. It is ultimately derived from the French verb *fricasser* and thus closely related to FRICASSÉE. The essential meaning seems to

have been a slice or slices of meat fried or braised, with a sauce or on a bed of something such as sorrel purée. The English translation by J.K. (1702) of two important cookery books by the French author Massialot contained a helpful glossary for English readers. This gave the following explanation of 'fricandoes': 'a sort of Scotch collops [see COLLOP], made of thin slices of Veal well larded and farced, which are afterwards to be dress'd in a Stewpan, close cover'd, over a gentle Fire.' The term was fairly common in English cookery books in the 18th century, but seems to have more or less disappeared from them during the first half of the 19th century. In France, however, ESCOFFIER was still giving a recipe for fricandeau of sturgeon in 1921 (in the 4th edition of his *Guide culinaire*).

FRICASSÉE a French term which long ago passed into English, at first meaning 'any meat fried in a panne', as Cotgrave (1611) succinctly put it. Although another 17th-century source declared it to mean 'varieties of Meat boiled together in a Broth', the term usually indicated frying (often small pieces, later to be enveloped in a thickened sauce) up to fairly recent times, when it began to fall into disuse. In France it is now used particularly of dishes based on white meat (chicken or veal) and clad in a creamy sauce.

FRIGATE MACKEREL (or bullet mackerel), a fish of the TUNA family in the genus *Auxis*. There are believed to be two species, *A. thazard* and *A. rochei*, both cosmopolitan in warm waters but not identical (although nearly so) in physiognomy and distribution (e.g. it is only *A. rochei* which occurs in the Mediterranean). The common names for them are confusing, often reflecting doubt whether they count as mackerel or tuna.

A. thazard may be over 50 cm (20") long, *A. richei* slightly less, but the usual size of either is around 35 cm (14"); so they are small in relation to most tuna. The pattern on their backs consists of dark bars or wavy lines.

The flesh of these fish is reddish and has a reputation for being indigestible. They are not in great demand.

FRITTER the English word for a small portion of deep-fried BATTER, usually but not always containing a piece of fruit, meat, fish, or vegetable. Fritters are generally eaten immediately after cooking, as, like all deep-fried foods, they taste best hot and fresh.

Many kinds of batter or dough are used to make fritters. An egg, milk, and flour batter is most usual in Europe; mixtures similar to

that used for choux PASTRY are also popular. In English the latter are known as BEIGNETS (the French word carries both the English meaning of fritter and a specific culinary meaning of deep-fried choux pastry). Runny yeast-leavened batters are used in some areas, making fritters akin to DOUGHNUTS. Some fritter-like confections are made in twisted shapes, for example, the various kinds of CRULLER. Others are closer to deep-fried stuffed pastries of the SAMOSA type.

Fritters are often sold at fairs, freshly cooked at special stalls. In several countries they are made as part of the carnival binge of rich foods, eaten before the fast of Lent begins; in Portugal, they are Christmas foods.

In Indian cuisines a mixture of BESAN FLOUR, water, and spices is used to coat vegetables for fritters; see PAKORA. Plain flour and water, or flour and egg-based, batters are used in China and Japan to coat meat, vegetables, and fish before deep-frying, for instance when making Japanese TEMPURA. Rice flour is not normally suitable for making fritters because it contains too little gluten to hold together.

HISTORY

The Roman *scriblita*, described by Cato in the 2nd century BC, was probably a precursor of both fritters and DOUGHNUTS. Lumps of a moist dough (leavened with SOURDOUGH) were spooned into hot fat, and allowed to stream in random shapes. Medieval 'cryspeys' were described in the Harleian MS of 1430; a liquid yeast batter using the whites of eggs only was run down the cook's fingers so that five narrow streams entered the hot oil, where they set into a tangle. They were served sprinkled with sugar. The modern Indian JALEBI also uses a streaming method to form spirals.

Most medical writers considered that fritters were indigestible, but they were too good to refuse and have been popular ever since. They appeared regularly in menus, usually as part of the last course. C. Anne Wilson (1973) quotes John Russell, who observed that 'apple fritter is good hot, but the cold ye [should] not touch'. Apple fritters have remained consistently popular through the ages. Other fruits, small pieces of meat or fish, slices of root vegetables (PARSNIP and SKIRRET were much liked for their sweet flavour), almonds, small balls of mixed herbs, pieces of fresh CURD, and fragrant FLOWERS were all used for fritters in the medieval kitchen. A 14th-century recipe used apple blossom mixed with white breadcrumbs and egg yolks, white wine and spices. In the 17th century herb fritters developed into delicate small fritters of individual leaves or pieces of leaves. Spinach, lettuce, and vine leaves were also used. Flower and leaf fritters survive, for example in Italy, where zucchini flowers and small young globe artichokes are dipped in batter and deep fried.

Most medieval fritters were yeasted with ale-barm, the froth on the fermenting drink. This continued to be added to batter until, at the beginning of the 18th century, it was realized that a better lift could be produced by separating the egg whites, beating them, and folding them back in.

Medieval batters for sweet fritters, like those for PANCAKES, contained wine or ale, sometimes cream, and more eggs than are usual today. Choux paste mixtures were in use for making fritters in France by the end of the 16th century. New varieties of fritter introduced in the 18th century were of flavoured ground rice; a thin type in the shape of a true lover's knot (as in a pretzel) was piped with a forcing bag. This shape survives in the old French *bugne* and the American CRULLER.

A few types of fritter from around the world are described below, merely to exemplify the ubiquity and variety of forms which this item displays.

Apple and **banana fritters,** a popular dessert in Chinese restaurants in the West. A light batter containing whisked egg whites is used to encase the prepared fruit, and the fritters are coated with CARAMEL and sprinkled with sesame seeds after cooking.

Churro, a Spanish fritter shaped like a long, curled sausage. The dough is made by boiling water and adding flour; sometimes an egg is added to enrich it. The soft batter is piped through a star nozzle into hot oil. When cooked, churros are sprinkled with sugar and served hot. Eaten with coffee or hot chocolate, they are a popular breakfast dish in Spain, Portugal, and Latin America. Flavourings such as vanilla, lemon, or rum may be added.

Filho, one of various Portuguese types of doughy fritters, often made for Christmas (*filhós de Natal*). Aniseed and orange juice are popular flavourings.

Flädli, a German fritter made from flour and egg dough and fried in lard; eaten at Easter. *Kücheli* is a similar type.

Poffertje, a Dutch term for small round fritters, which are dusted with icing sugar after frying. See Witteveen (1995).

Sel, a Nepali ring-shaped fritter made from pounded, soaked rice, banana, sugar, and ghee mixed with water to a soft batter, which is poured in a circle into the hot oil to make the shape. It is eaten especially at weddings and festivals.

Sirnik, a Russian fritter made from curd cheese, egg yolks, and a little flour and sugar, used as a breakfast or supper dish. The mixture is worked into balls and fried. They may be served with jam or sugar, or, flavoured with nutmeg and herbs, dished up with melted butter or sour cream, as a savoury.   LM

FROG an amphibian perceived by the English as a staple of the French diet, is indeed eaten in France but also in many other parts of the world, whether previously under French influence (as in Louisiana and some islands in the W. Indies) or not. Normally, it is only the hind legs which are cooked and eaten.

The frog most favoured in France is *Rana esculenta*, found over much of Europe, larger than the common frog and usually greenish, but with black markings. However, there are numerous other species in Europe and in other continents; many of the frogs' legs eaten in France come from elsewhere. There are frog farms in some countries and frozen frogs' legs may reach Europe from as far afield as Japan.

They have a delicate flavour and are customarily said to resemble chicken meat. Why the idea of eating frog should be repellent to the English in particular is mildly puzzling. It may have something to do with the ugly (to human beings) appearance of the creatures, or the thought that they emerge all slimy from evil-smelling ponds, or possibly (as ESCOFFIER seems to have thought) from the sound of their English name. Escoffier's English biographer (Shaw, 1994) has done a service in printing a translation of what that eminent chef had to say about the name, and about one of his ways of serving the legs:

Frogs or Nymphes à l'Aurore
For various reasons, I thought it best in the past, to substitute the mythological name 'nymphs' for the more vulgar term 'frogs' on menus, and the former has been universally adopted, more particularly in reference to the following 'Chaud-froid à L'Aurore':

Poach the frogs' legs in an excellent white-wine *court-bouillon*. When cooled, trim them properly, dry them thoroughly in a piece of fine linen, and steep them, one after the other, in a chaud-froid sauce of fish with paprika, the tint of which should be golden. This done, arrange the treated legs on a layer of champagne jelly, which should have set beforehand on the bottom of a square, silver dish or crystal bowl. Now lay some chervil *pluches* and tarragon leaves between the legs in imitation of water-grasses, and cover the whole with champagne jelly to counterfeit the effect of water.

Send the dish to the table, set in a block of ice, fashioned as fancy may suggest.

FROMAGE FRAIS or fromage blanc, two names for what is essentially a single range of products: a fresh white CHEESE, lightly fermented and of varying fat content. The texture is smooth and creamy, sometimes almost of pouring consistency. Fromage frais is intended for immediate use. It combines happily with fresh fruits such as strawberries and is the basis of some delightful French desserts such as *Cœur à la crème* (when it is combined with beaten egg white and sugar

and served in heart-shaped moulds). It also has many uses in dishes where a creamy effect is desired but without too much fat content (as in certain sauces and some stuffings for potatoes and other vegetables). Versions which are either unsalted or so lightly salted as not to be noticed are best for sweet dishes.

FRUIT CAKE a British speciality, is a close, rich, heavy cake made by the creaming method, raised with baking powder and beaten egg. Up to half the weight of the finished cake may consist of dried fruit. In earlier centuries it was called plum (or plumb) cake, 'plum' denoting all kinds of dried fruits. Today the name plum cake survives (in the English form) on the mainland of Europe, though here it often means a sadly dry product without much fruit.

Fruit cakes are used as part of celebrations, such as weddings; see WEDDING MEALS AND CAKES. They also loom large among CHRISTMAS FOODS and may make an appearance at christenings and birthdays. Many families have their own favourite recipes. Decoration is important; festive fruit cakes are usually topped with MARZIPAN and covered with royal ICING, suitably embellished with piping, cut paper, and little figures.

Lighter cakes, made with less fruit, to be eaten at teatime or for snacks, include Genoa cake (not to be confused with GÉNOISE). DUNDEE CAKE is a medium-weight species of fruit cake.

The fruit in these cakes may be any or all of currants, raisins, sultanas, and candied peel. CANDIED FRUITS, particularly cherries, are usually added, as are ground almonds.

Alcohol, usually brandy, is sometimes mixed into the batter for rich fruit cakes before baking. Some prefer to add it afterwards, by making small holes in the base of the cake with a skewer and dripping in a little liquid. This process may be repeated several times, as a fruit cake keeps for months when correctly stored; it is quite normal for it to be made well in advance of the event for which it is required, and most people consider it improved by keeping.

The fruit cake as known today cannot date back much beyond the Middle Ages. It was only in the 13th century that dried fruits began to arrive in Britain, from Portugal and the E. Mediterranean. Lightly fruited breads were probably more common than anything resembling the modern fruit cake during the Middle Ages. Early versions of the rich fruit cake, such as Scottish BLACK BUN dating from the late Middle Ages, were luxuries for special occasions.

Fruit cakes have been used for celebrations since at least the early 18th century when 'bride cakes' and 'plumb cakes', descended from enriched bread recipes, became cookery standards. The relationship between fruit breads and fruit cakes is obvious in early recipes, such as those given by Eliza Smith (1753) which include yeast.

Prodigious quantities of ingredients were required. Relatively modest plum cake recipes given by Eliza Smith called for 4 lb (1.8 kg) of flour to be mixed with sugar, spice, eggs, sack, cream, currants, and candied lemon, orange, and citron. Her 'Great cake' required among other things 13 lb (6 kg) of currants, 5 pints (2.8 litres) of cream and 4 lb of butter, 20 egg yolks, and 3 pints of yeast. Surprisingly little sugar was called for: only 1.5 lb (700 g). This probably reflects the cookery practices of the late 17th century, as Smith wrote her book at the end of her career.

Making a rich fruit cake in an 18th-century kitchen was a major undertaking. The ingredients had to be carefully prepared. Fruit was washed, dried, and stoned if necessary; sugar, cut from loaves, had to be pounded and sieved; butter washed in water and rinsed in rosewater. Eggs were beaten for a long time, half an hour being commonly directed. Yeast, or 'barm' from fermenting beer, had to be coaxed into life. Finally, the cook had to cope with the temperamental wood-fired baking ovens of that time. No wonder these cakes acquired such mystique.

By the mid-18th century the use of yeast as a cake leavener was dying out. In the 19th it seems to have been more or less forgotten, except for regional specialities such as BARA BRITH. Mrs Beeton (1861) made the observation that for leavening cakes: 'As eggs are used instead of yeast, they should always be very thoroughly whisked.' Yeast-raised cakes may have lost popularity because they did not keep as well as egg-raised cakes. By the late 19th century BAKING POWDER had replaced YEAST entirely as a leavener for cakes.

The hallowed formula of fruit cake with marzipan on top and icing on top of that was first put into print by Mrs Raffald (1782) and has held its place until now. (How this formula was reached is described in detail in an appendix to Bridget Ann Henisch, 1984.) Fruit cakes, rich or plain depending on the means of the household, were regarded with great affection by the British middle classes for most of the 20th century. They went into the tuck boxes of children at boarding schools, and were much used for picnics and shooting parties. Most people regarded them as robust, nutritious, comforting food. This was a complete change in attitude from that displayed by Eliza Acton in *Modern Cookery for Private Families* (1845), who said that 'more illness is caused by habitual indulgence in the richer and heavier kinds of cakes than could easily be credited by persons who have given no attention to the subject'. LM

FRUIT JELLY a dessert made from fruit SYRUP and GELATIN, allowed to set in a cool place. Valued for its clear, sparkling appearance, it was originally based on a gelatin-rich stock made from calves feet (or, sometimes, ISINGLASS). This type of JELLY demanded time and technical skill during preparation. Eighteenth-century jellies were served in glasses, sometimes presented as 'ribbons'—layers of jelly in different colours. Nineteenth-century jellies were often set in elaborate copper moulds, giving tall castellated and other shapes when turned out.

Nowadays a fruit jelly is mainly perceived in Europe as a treat for children, and is easily prepared from blocks of coloured, flavoured gelatin dissolved in water. In N. America, under the trade name Jell-O, it was used to a remarkable extent in the mid-20th century, mainly for the benefit of adult women.
READING: Brears (1996).

FRUIT PASTES FRUIT CHEESES, FRUIT BUTTERS: fruit sweetmeats made by puréeing fruit to give a homogeneous mass; sieving (if necessary); and mixing with an equal weight of sugar before drying over heat. The result is rather solid and has good keeping qualities. The basic principle of applying heat to fruit and adding sugar as a preservative is used to produce a wide range of related sweetmeats, including JAM, JELLY, and MARMALADE; bottled and canned fruits; and CANDIED FRUITS.

A variation is to dry the paste in thin layers to give a sheet of fruit 'paper' or 'leather'. Sugar is not always used in these, as

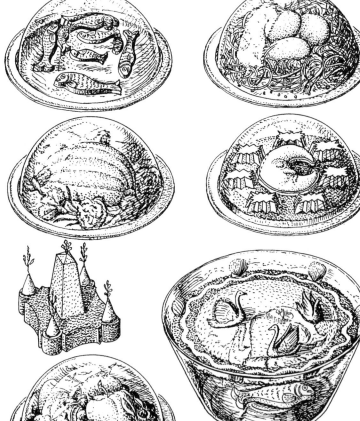

Elaborate jellies were a speciality of Mrs Raffald in Manchester, c.1769, including (*L to R*) a fish pond, a hen's nest with lemon zest 'straw', a flummery melon in a garland of flowers, the moon and stars, and (*bottom L*) a globe of fruit and vine leaves. John Bell's 1817 fishpond jelly (*bottom R*) has gold and silver fish, swans, and surrounding sugar banks. Solomon's Temple, c.1769, has a flummery base supporting towers, tipped with flower sprigs. (Artist: Peter Brears)

they are usually based on very sweet fruits such as APRICOTS. They are made mostly in countries which have reliably hot and sunny summers. The Middle Eastern *armadine* or *armadeu* is an example. Another variation on fruit paste is to use dried fruits such as apricots, DATES, or PRUNES, finely chopped and mixed with sugar, to give a very simple uncooked sweetmeat. CARROTS occasionally provide the raw materials for sweet pastes.

Fruit pastes provide an unsophisticated method of preservation in the sense that the integrity of the fruit is completely lost during the process (in contrast to candying, in which every effort is made to preserve the appearance of each item). The raw materials can be irregular, blemished, or can be trimmings from larger pieces. HONEY may have been used in the past in place of the sugar. The Romans preserved fruits in jars of honey; and must surely have known that fruit reduced to paste and dried would keep well, although no records of this have survived.

Numerous recipes for fruit pastes occur in 17th- and 18th-century cookery books. They are based on many different kinds of summer fruit, particularly stone fruits such as PEACHES and PLUMS; and PEARS, APPLES, and QUINCES. The words 'paste' and 'marmelade' (and sometimes 'preserve' or 'conserve') are used interchangeably to indicate a solid mixture of sugar and fruit purée. Sometime during the 18th century these developed into the substances we now know as jam and marmalade; strained juice was used for jellies, and concentrated to make flavourings. The use of the word 'cheese' to describe a solid fruit confection crept in.

In the CONFECTIONERY industry today, fruit pastes appear to have been reduced to a minor role as centres for FONDANT, CHOCOLATES, and DRAGÉES. Fruit pastes are made at home, and many countries have at least one version of a fruit paste-based sweetmeat. The home-made English version—apple paste or butter—which was fairly common in the past, is now almost forgotten except on the island of Jersey where a spiced 'black butter' is made from slowly reduced apple pulp.

Further east, many fruit paste recipes become complex and develop into HALVA-type confections. Fruit pastes are also made in the New World; for example, Fannie Farmer quotes peach leather as a speciality of Charleston in S. Carolina.

See also QUINCE PRESERVES.   LM

FRUIT SALAD an item which has adorned millions of menus in the western world, was first recognized as a dish in the mid-19th century. Mariani (1994) treats it as a precursor of the modern American term

'fruit cocktail' and says that American recipe books of the 1850s referred to 'fruit salad'. Ayto (1993) says that the term seems to have been first mentioned (in Britain) by Mrs Beeton (1861).

Whatever its history, fruit salad is a simple concept. Fresh fruit is chopped up (unless already very small) and mixed together with the possible addition of wine or a little liqueur or other ingredient designed to enhance flavour or (as when a sprig of mint is placed on the salad) appearance.

It is of course possible to have a 'salad' of dried fruits and nuts, as in the Middle Eastern *khoshab*; and, further east, Indonesia offers the spicy fruit salad *rujak*, which is patently different from anything in the western world.

See also COMPOTE.

FRUIT SOUPS especially popular in Germany and Nordic countries, are something of an anomaly. The category of SOUP is one of almost exclusively savoury dishes. Fruit soups, however, although they may be served at the beginning of a meal, are essentially sweet dishes. They may be thin and delicate or thickened and substantial. Riley M. Fletcher Berry (1907) made interesting comments about this distinction. He observed that, for the prosperous readers whom he was addressing, fruit soups would be served in very small glass or china bowls or bouillon cups; very delicate. However, he admonished these same prosperous readers, one should not forget that fruit soups 'are *foods* and as such are used in many countries by even the peasants, though they may lack dainty table appointments'.

One outstanding example of a dish which occurs on both sides of the dividing line, but predominantly as a 'solid' moulded dessert dish, is KISEL. It is quite closely related to another, which is more commonly met in liquid or near-liquid form; this is *rødgrøt*, the red berry soup popular in Denmark and other parts of Scandinavia (also in Germany as *rote Grütze*), which may be thickened with semolina but remains a soup rather than a moulded dessert.

Other fruits commonly used to make soups include cherries and apple, also gooseberries or blueberries, rose-hips, rhubarb, and even lemon; *Sitruunakeitto* is a creamy lemon soup of Finland. Dried fruits can also be the basis of a soup, with results similar to the Middle Eastern *khoshab*.

Persons obsessed with the categorization of dishes meet some perplexing problems in this area. The apple soup proposed by Eliza Acton (1845) is basically mutton broth but it does have a large amount of apple in it. The *Ash-e-meeveh* popular in winter in Iran contains lots of fruit (mostly dried) but also vegetables and the sort of seasoning which

belongs to savoury dishes. How are these to be classified? One can only say that fruit plays an important role in many soups which would not usually be called fruit soups.

FRUMENTY a 'porridge' made from WHEAT. The name is derived from the classical Latin *frumentum* meaning corn (in the general sense of the word). In the Middle Ages it seems to have been a staple food but as time progressed the dish appeared only on special occasions and with slight regional differences.

In the preparation of frumenty, new wheat is shelled, cooked slowly in milk, and flavoured and sweetened. This glutinous mass, which is known as creed (past participle of the verb 'to cree') wheat, used to be available ready dressed. Modern recipes which include butter, cream, sugar, rum, or brandy to produce something like a liquid Christmas pudding have little in common with the traditional forms of frumenty.

Frumenty appears to have been used formerly as an accompaniment to animal food, as 'venison with frumenty' and 'porpoise with frumenty' formed part of the second course served at the royal banquet given to Henry IV at Winchester on his marriage with Joan of Navarre. At the present day it is usually boiled with new milk and sugar, to which spices, currants, yolks of eggs, etc. are sometimes added, and is occasionally eaten as a dinner sweet at various times of the year—at mid-Lent, Easter, and Christmas. In the north of England, however, it is always exclusively a part of the Christmas fare, and is eaten hot.

There is evidence that in the past, frumenty was eaten at secular feasts, in celebration of harvest home, for instance. Before the 1860s it seems unlikely that frumenty was an everyday food for the rural poor; wheat was an uncommon grain at this time. In the Victorian age, however, records show that it was common workhouse fare.

There are many regional variations. In Somerset, it is known as furmenty or furmity.

FRYING the process of cooking food in hot fat or oil in an open pan. The FATS AND OILS used vary from place to place. All share the quality that they can be heated to a much higher temperature than boiling water. The surface of food cooked by frying therefore coagulates quickly; further cooking induces flavour changes and the result should be an attractive, crisp-textured food.

Deep-frying, in which the food is submerged in oil, LARD, or DRIPPING heated to a high temperature in a deep-sided pan, is something of an art. Many foods, including chips (French fries), DOUGHNUTS, and FRITTERS, are cooked this way. Careful temperature control is necessary for optimum results: too low, and the food will emerge pale and greasy; too high, and the exterior will scorch and toughen. If the temperature is correct, the outside cooks instantly, forming a seal, and the water inside the food converts to steam, from the surface inwards. This has the dual effect of cooking the food very quickly, and preventing fat from entering, as much of the steam escapes outwards through the surface. The fat or oil should not be allowed to burn ('smoking hot' fat is too hot—it smokes because it is burning). A frying thermometer is useful here. Otherwise a small cube of bread can be dropped into the oil and observed; it should take about a minute to brown, in which case the temperature is satisfactory.

Foods destined for deep-frying may be prepared by coating them with batter or egg, substances which form effective seals when they come into contact with hot fat; alternatively they may simply be dusted with flour, or blotted with paper or cloth, to remove surface moisture. After frying, they are allowed to drain briefly, then served up quickly, as fried food which has gone cold becomes unattractive. An exception to this rule is a tribe of fried confections and biscuits, many of Middle Eastern and Indian origin; see JALEBI for the best-known example.

Shallow-frying, using smaller quantities of oil or fat in a low-sided pan, is used for many foods, including eggs, fish, and steaks, which are allowed to brown on one side and are then turned. The residue left in the pan after meat has been shallowfried is often used as the basis of a sauce (see DEGLAZE). The method is sometimes called 'pan-frying' in English.

Both shallow- and deep-frying are popular methods of cooking, but deep-frying has also developed into a specialist craft. The speed with which the food cooks, and the appetizing smell produced make it a favourite method for cooking snacks and street foods around the world. Many festival foods are deep-fried, an echo of times when fats were in shorter supply and were reserved for special occasions. (LM)

FUDGE a sweetmeat made from sugar, milk, and butter boiled to the soft ball stage (see SUGAR BOILING) and then beaten, to produce a characteristic grainy texture. This is due to the presence of small sugar crystals in a supersaturated sugar solution. If the mixture is beaten whilst still hot, the crystals are relatively large; if the mixture is allowed to cool before beating, the crystals formed are much smaller and more even, giving a

smooth texture. A slightly different method is employed when fudge is manufactured on an industrial scale: here a proportion of FONDANT is added to 'seed' the mixture with crystals. Finally, the mixture is poured onto a surface and allowed to cool and set before being cut into small pieces.

Fudge is a favourite confection for home sweet-makers, as it is simple and can be flavoured with many different ingredients. Vanilla, coffee, chocolate, peppermint, nuts, and coconut are frequently encountered; fruit essences are sometimes used. Brown sugar or MAPLE SYRUP also provide variations.

The Scottish confection TABLET is similar in flavour and texture to fudge. The name 'praline', which is properly applied to a crisp confection of nuts and sugar (see PRALINE), is sometimes given in the USA to a soft fudge with nuts, often made with brown sugar or sometimes CORN SYRUP or light molasses (see SUGAR). Plain white sugar is also used. Some types are flavoured with chocolate or orange.

Penuche or *panocha* is a Mexican fudge with nuts, and sometimes coconut. *Panocha* is the name of a coarse Mexican sugar and this is used in the authentic sweet. As *penuche*, it is also popular in the USA, where conventional brown sugar, sometimes with corn syrup, is used.

Confections which taste fudgelike, based on milk reduced over heat combined with cereal cooked in oil, or on milk curd, plus boiled sugar are also made in the Indian subcontinent. BARFI is a good example. See also MILK REDUCTION and INDIAN SWEETS.   LM

FUGU the Japanese name for some species of BLOWFISH which are regarded as a great delicacy in Japan. The best known are *Fugu rubripes* (*torafugu*), and *F. porphyreus* (*mafugu* or *namerafugu*).

Shimonoseki, in the westernmost corner of Honshu Island, is specially celebrated for its fugu dishes. There it is called *fuku*.

These fish have to be prepared with great skill to avoid any possibility of the fatally toxic parts being eaten or contaminating the flesh. The lethal poison is tetrotoxin and it is found in the fish's gut and also in the liver, ovary, and skin. There are whole books devoted to the necessary technique, and only cooks who have qualified in this are allowed to deal with the fish. Even so, instances occur of Japanese dying from fugu poisoning, usually because someone without the necessary skill has attempted to prepare the fish.

For SASHIMI the flesh of fugu is sliced so thin as to be almost transparent, and the slices are arranged on a large round dish like flower petals. They are eaten with a dipping sauce usually containing some citrus juice and SOY SAUCE.

The flesh of fugu, milt, bones, head are cooked with tofu, vegetables, etc. in DASHI in an earthenware pot at the table. This is called *Fugu-chiri*.

The fins of fugu are grilled until they are slightly burnt and steeped in warmed SAKÉ. The resultant beverage is called *hire-zake* and drunk by the diners while eating fugu.

FULACHTA FIADH or fian, outdoor Bronze Age cooking sites, presented under their Irish name because Ireland possesses so many examples. The term *fulacht*, derived from Old Irish, means 'a pit used for cooking' and *fiadh* can be interpreted as either 'of the deer' or 'of the wild', while *fian* refers to a mythical band of Irish warriors known as the Fianna, hence 'the cooking pit of the Fianna/deer/wild'. They are the most numerous archaeological monument in Ireland; over 4,500 sites are known and 2,000 of these are in the County Cork region. Similar sites, known as boiling mounds or burnt mounds, are found in the English Midlands, the Orkneys, the Isle of Man, and along the N. Atlantic coastline.

In the field the fulacht fiadh is a distinctive crescent-shaped mound and the site is located near a water source, often a stream, natural well, or marshy area. The mound surrounds the cooking place, which consists of a rectangular stone or wood-lined trough and fire area. When cooking, the trough was filled with water and stones were heated in the nearby fire. Red-hot stones were toppled into the trough and the water was brought to the boil. Meat wrapped in cloth or straw was then immersed in the water for boiling. Experiments (see O'Kelly, 1989) have shown that a trough containing 450 litres of water can be brought to the boil in 30 to 35 minutes and the meat is cooked at a rate of 20 minutes to the pound. After each boiling the trough was cleared of the shattered stone debris, which was thrown aside and over time built up into the mound area.

Many fulachta fiadh have associated hut sites, many containing roasting ovens. These have been interpreted variously as hunting camps, butchering and meat-cure houses, and meat stores, interpretations which would suggest that fulachta fiadh were complexes designed for the large-scale butchering and preservation of hunted animals.

In Irish mythological literature the sites are used by the legendary warriors, the Fianna, for cooking the produce of the hunt, usually deer. A 12th-century text, *Acallam na Senórach* (The Colloquy of the Old Men), suggests that song birds may have been cooked in the pits: 'Birds out of trackless oaken woods would find their way into the Fianna's cooking pit.'

One theory suggests that the sites functioned as both cooking places and saunas. Both activities are mentioned in the following extract from Keating's history of Ireland (Dinneen, 1908).

However, from Bealtaine until Samhain, the Fianna were obliged to depend solely on the products of their hunting and of the chase as maintenance and wages from the kings of Ireland; thus, they were to have the flesh for food, and the skins of the wild animals as pay. But they took only one meal in the day and night, and that was in the afternoon. And it was their custom to send their attendants about noon with whatever they had killed in the morning's hunt to an appointed hill, having wood and moorland in the neighbourhood, and to kindle raging fires thereon, and put into them a large number of emery stones; and to dig two pits in the yellow clay of the moorland, and put some of the meat on spits to roast before the fire; and to bind another portion of it with súgáns [hay or straw ropes] in dry bundles, and set it to boil in the larger of the two pits, and keep plying them with stones that were in the fire, making them seethe often until they were cooked. And these fires were so large that their sites are today in Ireland burnt to blackness, and these are now called Fulacht Fian by the peasantry.

As to the Fian, when they assembled on the hill on which was the fire, each of them stripped off, and tied his shirt round his waist, and they ranged themselves round the second pit we have mentioned above, bathing their hair and washing their limbs, and removing their sweat, and then exercising their joints and muscles, thus ridding themselves of their fatigue; and after this they took their meal; and when they had taken their meal, they proceeded to build their hunting tents, and so prepare themselves for sleep.   RSe
READING: O'Drisceoil (1993).

FULMAR *Fulmarus glacialis*, a cliff-dwelling, gull-like bird of northern seas and coasts; it belongs to a group of seabirds commonly known as petrels and shearwaters.

Francesca Greenoak (1979) remarks that:

The most famous Fulmars are those of the island of St Kilda, where they have probably lived and been hunted for nearly a thousand years. The ornithologist William MacGillivray visiting the island in 1840 reported that the Fulmar 'forms one of the principal means of support to the islands, who daily risk their lives in its pursuit.' There is, however, strong evidence to show that the present great Fulmar spread is not of St Kildan birds, but a population overspill from Iceland.

The same author tells us that 'Fulmar' is from *Foul Maa*, meaning Foul Gull, because a sitting bird, if provoked by the near approach of a hunter, will 'eject a stream of oily secretion and half-digested food at the attacker, forcibly enough to be on target for about a metre and a half'.

The eggs of the fulmar are large, white and beautiful. They are prized as food.

FUL MEDAMES (or *mudammes*), often described as Egypt's national dish, certainly occupies a place of primacy in that country, and has done so for a very long time.

Jill Tilsley-Benham (1989) points out that it is a standard dish for breakfast (including the evening 'break-fast' of RAMADAN), but is also eaten as a snack (MEZZE) or a main meal. Egyptian immigrant workers in the Persian Gulf have been responsible in recent decades for spreading its currency eastwards. Lane (1860) had referred to the practice of leaving the beans to cook overnight in a pear-shaped earthenware pot which was 'buried, all but the neck, in the hot ashes of an oven or a [Turkish] bath, and having the mouth closely stopped: they are eaten with linseed-oil, or butter, and generally with a little lime-juice'.

The etymology of *Ful mudammes* is not entirely clear. Perry (1993), contributing to a learned discussion of the matter by four authorities, writes:

Fûl is the Arabic word for fava beans, cognate with the Hebrew *pûl*. *Mudammas* looks like the passive participle of a verb derived from the noun *dims*, which means 'ashes' in the Egyptian dialect of Arabic; the sense would be 'cooked over coals'. As we know, the beans are traditionally cooked overnight in a big pot set over coals.

Anyway, the word *ful* certainly means bean(s). However, the question arises: what beans? It seems abundantly clear that they are a variety, or varieties of the broad bean (*Vicia faba*, fava bean), but that leaves the question of defining or naming the varieties. Jill Tilsley-Benham explains that, in Egypt itself there are two kinds, of which the first is the more esteemed and more expensive:

• *Ful baladi sa'idi*, the local Upper Egyptian bean, is about 15 mm (0.6") long, plump, oval, and buff coloured.
• *Ful hamam* (meaning 'pigeon beans'), only about 7 mm (0.3") long, is peanut shaped and light mahogany in colour.

There is another variety called *ful rumi*, 'Greek' or 'European' beans. These are larger, about 20 mm (0.8") long, almost circular, very flat, and pale. They are rarely used in Egypt for making *Ful mudammes*, but appreciated by devotees in Syria.

The same author's detailed description of how *Ful mudammes* is made and presented is the basis of that given in the box.

MAKING FUL MEDAMES

The basic recipe calls for the well-soaked beans to be placed in a special pot called *damassa* with plenty of cold water. Some cooks add a small proportion of split red lentils, which helps to thicken the sauce and improve the colour. Carrot/onion/tomato (alone or mixed) can be added for extra flavour. Those who wish to eat their *ful* with hard-boiled eggs sometimes add them at this stage. Bicarbonate of soda is another common addition—the bean skins are invariably tough—and (in the Gulf) slices of lemon are sometimes added as well.

The beans are boiled, then left to simmer gently for 8–10 hours. If oven baked, the *damassa* lid is generally sealed with dough to conserve all possible moisture. Hot water is added when necessary to beans left on top of the fire. Although older strains of *ful* would have taken longer to soften than those used nowadays, the habit of such extended simmering probably evolved from their use as a breakfast food—it being simply more convenient to cook them overnight. Nowadays, although the traditional earthenware pots are still used in the villages, cooking methods in towns have changed, the hot ashes being replaced by modern stoves. Specially designed low-wattage hotplates are used and 'the latest style (aluminium) *damassa* is equipped with a rod-shaped heating element which keeps the beans simmering perfectly all night'.

Next, the *ful* are mixed (and sometimes mashed) with oil (cottonseed, linseed, olive, or corn) together with fresh lime juice. Alternatively they are simply mixed with *samneh*, a type of clarified butter, see GHEE.

The most common additional ingredients for the mixture are garlic (crushed), white or red onions (grated, chopped, or thinly sliced), spring onions (chopped), tomato (diced, juiced, or paste), hot pepper, and ground cumin seed. The fenugreek- and pepper-flavoured sausage *bastirma* is sometimes added.

Common accompaniments are chopped parsley, spring onions, fried or hard-boiled eggs, limes, olives, and assorted pickles. Country people relish a whole onion with their *Ful mudammes*, and this they divide into sections by a powerful blow with the heel of the hand. *Salatet tehina*, a creamy sauce of sesame paste (see TAHINI), garlic, and vinegar, is another favourite addition.

Ful mudammes is accompanied in Egypt by thin discs of the local wholemeal bread, *aysh baladi*, and in the Gulf by the similar *khubz tannour*, or *nan*.

FUMET a French term referring to a concentrated reduction of the stock obtained when cooking fish or vegetables in a liquid, often wine. It occurs most often in the fish version, as *fumet de poisson*, an important ingredient in many of the sauces which accompany seafood in European cookery. It is only rarely applied to vegetables except in the case of mushrooms (*fumet de champignons* being common enough).

FUNERAL FOOD is a subject which does not appear to have had any books devoted to it so far, although studies have been published of the customs prevailing in certain cultures or communities. Generally speaking, efforts are made to provide those attending a funeral with attractive, palatable fare, although sometimes the theme of frugality and moderation is prominent. The nature of the relevant religion and the general attitudes to food of the people practising it have an effect here.

Certain foods are perceived as connected with death and may be served at a funeral feast for that reason. For an example, see BROAD BEAN, which gave rise to the old English expression 'beano'.

In many cultures a funeral is a finite event, occupying a relatively short period on one day, and the provision of funeral foods, if any, is temporally adjacent, i.e. immediately after the funeral or (less often) immediately before it. However, in other cultures it may be inappropriate to focus attention on this short timespan, since the actual funeral is only a part of a larger ceremonial occupying several days (which in turn may be seen as only part of a much longer period of mourning). The burden undertaken by the bereaved family of providing food for mourners can be considerable if they have to cope with a period of several days rather than a single meal or refreshment. In the Middle East for example families can easily be ruined by having to provide food for large numbers of mourners who come for days rather than hours.

Certain foods or dishes are normally prepared only for funerals. An example which has been the subject of a study by Brears (1984*b*) is the category of funeral biscuits in Yorkshire. In fact his essay has a wider scope and incorporates a quotation from Nicholson (1890) as follows:

Before leaving the house for the grave-yard, the mourners have refreshment served to them—cheese, spice bread and beer for the men; biscuits and wine, both home-made, for the women. On returning to the house, a funeral feast is prepared, the like of which is only seen at these times . . . the expence was so great that families were impoverished for years.

This shows that the burden of expense can be crushing even when the timespan is limited. It also illustrates the practice of food before plus food afterwards, and makes an interesting distinction between spice bread (or cake) and biscuits. These biscuits were often provided in special wrappers, but frequently with a more chilling message such as:

When ghastly Death with unrelenting hand,
Cuts down a father! brother! or a friend!
The still small voice should make you understand,
How frail you are—how near your final end.

The biscuits could be what would now be called sponge fingers (see BISCUIT VARIETIES), or might be rounds of SHORTBREAD flavoured with CARAWAY seed and often stamped with a design including a heart (symbol of the soul, now departed). Brears records that the provision of funeral biscuits waned considerably in the first half of the 20th century and seems to have disappeared entirely thereafter.

Whereas the Yorkshire funeral biscuits were just for funerals, the special funeral food which is almost ubiquitous in the Balkans could be used for other occasions such as weddings or saints' days. This is VARENO ZHITO, described in its separate entry. The symbolic value of the wheat which is the basic ingredient is clear.

The complexity of funeral rites (Hindu, Buddhist, etc.) in Asia makes it difficult to single out any particular funeral foods; but Asia does provide one charming custom which deserves mention in this context. In Thailand a person is likely to compose a small cookbook before her or his death, so that it can be distributed as a keepsake to the mourners attending the funeral. These little books can be of beautiful design, such that they would be welcome additions to any library. It is, however, the content which is the true gift, and this reflects the dead person's taste in food, probably offering favourite recipes, which may be for simple or sophisticated dishes and may or may not be embellished by anecdotes and reminiscences. They constitute in effect a sort of symbolic 'food' which has the merit of being everlasting in that the mourners can use the recipes for the rest of their lives (and no doubt, if they wish, include them in their own funeral cookbooks, and so on ad infinitum).

FUNGUS in the scientific sense, means any of a group of simple plants which include MUSHROOMS and similar plants, YEASTS, MOULDS, and the rusts which grow as parasites on crops. Unlike more advanced plants, fungi lack chlorophyll and so can only grow as saprophytes (from dead plants or animals); or as parasites (on living plants);

or in a mycorrhizal relationship (symbiosis between fungi and the roots of trees).

Fungi vary in size from single-cell micro-organisms, too small to be seen by the naked eye, to the giant PUFFBALL, which may measure 1.5 metres (5') across. Edible fungi, exemplified by the common FIELD MUSHROOM and its cultivated relation, mostly fall between the two extremes.

The importance of fungi for human food is not limited to those which are eaten as such, or are visible. Many which are micro-organisms play an important part in making or processing human food. Yeasts are an obvious example, and are regarded as beneficent because of their role in, for example, the making of bread dough. But moulds, although generally regarded with suspicion, are also of importance.

This applies in both the western and eastern hemispheres, although there is a striking difference between occidental and oriental usage. In the West, fungi of this category are mostly used for milk products, notably in the manufacture of certain cheeses. In the East, their principal use is in the processing of SOYA BEANS (although they are also set to work on rice, groundnuts, cassava, fish, and other foods). See the entries on MOULD, SOY SAUCE, MISO, and TEMPE. The long history of cultivation of the soya bean in the Orient, its high protein content (of especial value in a region where protein has always been in short supply, dairy products are little used, and some religions prohibit meat), and the fact that it is hard to digest the beans unless they have been fermented are all factors which contribute to the different emphasis.

So far as the directly edible fungi are concerned, there is less of an East–West contrast, but something of a North–South one. 'Mushrooms', to use the term loosely as applying to edible fungi in general, are far better known as food in the northern than in the southern hemisphere.

FUNISTRADA a rare example of a 'ghost food', recorded by Bryson (1991). 'The U.S. Army in 1974 devised a food called funistrada as a test word during a survey of soldiers' dietary preferences. Although no such food existed, funistrada ranked higher in the survey than lima beans and eggplant.'

FUNORI *Gloiopeltis furcata*, one of the red SEAWEEDS which is used as food in China and Japan. This is a relatively small seaweed, whose branches form a characteristic shape, giving rise to one Chinese name which means 'antler vegetable'. Chinese commonly use it fresh as a vegetable, e.g. stir-fried. In Japan, much is processed to make a starchy food thickener, but some of the harvest is eaten fresh, or dried and subsequently reconstituted with dilute rice vinegar.

FUSILIER a name used for fish of the SNAPPER family, in the genus *Paracaesio*.

P. caeruleus, also known as the Japanese snapper, is an important food fish, although known only from S. Japan; it reaches a length of 50 cm (20"). *P. xanthurus*, the southern fusilier or yellowtail blue snapper, is a little smaller but has a wide distribution in the tropical Indo-Pacific, and from E. Australia up to S. Japan.

Tweedie and Harrison (1970) comment that these species are among the few economically important fish of the coral reefs.

They are taken by an exciting operation involving the positioning of a net by the reef and the driving of the fish into it by a team of swimming men, each holding a long string weighted at the bottom and flagged at intervals in its length with pieces of white cloth. These strings are jerked up and down and the moving flags scare the fish and drive them into the net. This strenuous mode of fishing is of Japanese origin and is still called by its Japanese name 'muro ami'.

FUTURIST MEALS as recommended by the Italian Futurists, especially Marinetti and Fillìa (1931), were one of the rare attempts to alter the fundamental design of a cuisine, indeed to achieve a full-scale culinary revolution. This was to be part of a much wider revolution, intended to overturn established patterns and conventions in all the arts as well as in politics and social organization. It is noteworthy that, while almost every feature of the proposed revolution could be criticized as unlikely to gain support, still less be achieved, it was the culinary aspect which from the outset seemed most clearly to be doomed.

Among the more sensational items on which critics immediately fastened were:

- No more spaghetti for the Italians.
- No more knives and forks.
- The principal feature of Futurist cuisine was to be the rapidity with which dishes, often containing but one mouthful or even less, would succeed each other.
- In fact the ideal Futurist meal would include some dishes which would not be eaten at all but merely passed beneath the nose of the diner to excite his curiosity.

So far as the Italian public were concerned, the salient item was the first of those listed above and their reaction was negative. The Futurists protested that there was far more to their plan than a simple ban on pasta, but protests had little impact. This was, in some ways, unfortunate, since some of their ideas—even if they took too extreme a form—merited consideration. One example was the banishment of music from meals, except for the express purpose of complementing a particular food or dish. The exclusion of normal condiments and 'a consistent lightening of weight and reduction of volume of food-stuffs' are other ideas which Marinetti advocated and which do not sound so very strange today.

Science, according to the Futurists, should play a greater part in cookery; but in general the scientific content in Futurist thought about cooking and foods was subordinate to artistic considerations, which were applied not only to the preparation and presentation of foods but also to the architecture of the restaurants, or rather 'cultural centres', in which the dishes would be served; for their consumption was to be attended by aesthetic experiences such as poetry recitals, art exhibitions, and fashion shows. (This was a fairly tame idea compared with the mock aircraft in which people were to have their appetites stimulated by the vibration of motors, their accustomed ideas shaken by tilted seats and tables, and their senses assaulted by weirdly composed dishes listed on aluminium menu cards.)

READING: Lesley Chamberlain (1989).

GABON NUT borne by the tree *Coula edulis*, which grows in W. Africa from Sierra Leone to Angola. It is not cultivated, but the nuts are an important part of the diet of the people in some regions, e.g. the Cabinda district of Angola.

The tree is not related to the true WALNUT, but its fruits and their kernels look like walnuts, so are sometimes called 'African walnuts'. The flavour is milder, between that of HAZELNUTS and CHESTNUTS. The kernels are eaten boiled or roasted, sometimes mixed with meat and sometimes fermented by being buried in the ground. They yield an oil which can be used for cooking.

GACHE a speciality of the island of Guernsey, is a semi-sweet fruit bread (see TEA BREADS AND TEA CAKES) highly enriched with butter, milk, and eggs, sweetened with brown sugar, sultanas, and candied peel, and baked in a cake tin. If rich Guernsey milk and butter, with their characteristic yellow colour, are used, the gache is especially good. The earliest written recipes are of the 18th century; but it had been made for some time

previously. The name 'gache' is also known in Normandy, where it applies both to a flat, plain bread and, in the Ille-et-Vilaine area, to a richer type similar to that made on Guernsey.   LM

GADWALL *Anas strepera*, a WILD DUCK which often associates with the MALLARD but is smaller and more slender. Although rare in the British Isles, it has a wide distribution across Europe, Asia, and N. America and exists in large numbers in many regions. Its breeding range is further south than those of other surface-feeding ducks, and some specimens have even reached tropical areas. Its diet consists mainly of vegetable matter and its flesh is described as delicious at any time of the year.

GALANTINE a culinary term in both English and French, whose derivation presents complicated questions which have been summarized by Ayto (1993).

In early English cookery books, the term referred to a sauce, previously written as 'galandine' and before that as 'cameline'.

Even in the late 17th century it is clear from the recipes of Robert May (1685) that galantine then was a dark-coloured sauce made with vinegar, breadcrumbs, cinnamon, and sometimes other spices.

Further back still, before developing into the name of a sauce, galantine had meant simply the jellied juices of fish or meat. This sense lingered on in France and eventually, in the 18th century, crossed the Channel to England and assumed there, as in France, its current meaning of a preparation of white meat, 'boned, cooked, pressed, and served cold with aspic' (*NSOED*).

GALEN (AD 129–199), a Greek physician who was born in Pergamum, once the capital of a kingdom, but at that time a provincial capital within the Roman Empire and still a centre of culture and learning. He studied philosophy and medicine there, proceeding to Smyrna and eventually to Alexandria as his studies advanced. He settled in Rome in 164. There he practised, lectured on anatomy and medicine, and wrote voluminously. He wrote on philosophy and literature as well as medicine, but it is the medical works that have largely survived. He moved in the highest society, and was appointed personal physician to the future emperor Commodus.

Correct diet was essential for health, in the ancient view. Galen's medical works therefore include several on food and nutrition, notably *On the Properties of Foods*. This is a systematic survey of foodstuffs. Each is rated hot/cold and dry/wet: a physician was thus enabled to prescribe a diet that would keep an individual's bodily 'humours' in balance and maintain health. See FOUR HUMOURS. As the earliest such manual that survives, Galen's work can be seen to have had a strong influence on all later ones, not only in medieval times but down to the present day in those parts of the world where humoral theory still helps to determine diet. But it is also a fascinating source of food history, for Galen was a fluent writer who never lost the opportunity to reminisce on country ways in Asia Minor, on student life in Alexandria, or on fine foods and wine-tastings in Rome.

Several other works by Galen, such as *On Good and Bad Juices* and his commentaries on HIPPOCRATES' dietary books, include interesting references to food and wine. What is difficult is to track them down. The only full index is in Latin, in the final volume of C. G. Kuhn's edition of his writings (20 vols, Berlin, 1821–33).

Galen tried to write from observation and decried all earlier authorities (except Hippocrates). Ironically he became the authority par excellence for medieval doctors, many of his works being translated into Syriac, Arabic, Hebrew, and finally Latin. Many also survived in Greek in the Byzantine Empire, where commentaries, adaptations, and abridgements continued to be produced. There are still not many translations of writings by Galen into English or other modern languages.   AD

GALETTE a flat, round cake; the word being derived from *galet*, a pebble weatherworn to the shape that is perfect for skipping. Buckwheat or maize crêpes are also called galettes in some regions, e.g. Brittany, as are various cookies. 'Flat as a pancake' is just as graphic in French: *plat comme une galette*.

As a cake, a galette is made of flour, sugar, butter, and eggs in infinite variations, or simply of puff pastry. The glowing *galette des rois* found in Paris, Lyons, and generally north of the Loire is fashioned almost exclusively from the latter, the classic *feuilletage*. The 'kings' they honour are the three Wise Men come to pay homage to the newborn King of Kings in Bethlehem. They appear around the Feast of Epiphany. (See also TWELFTH NIGHT CAKE.)

The traditional way of eating this galette, at dinner in a French home in January, goes something like this: the warm galette is brought to table where its fragrance and beauty are admired briefly before it is cut into the proper number of wedges. A child, usually the youngest, is sent to hide under the table, there to act as oracle. To the summons 'Phoebe' (or 'Apollo') he replies in Latin, 'Domine' (master). As he indicates each portion, the 'master' asks, 'For whom is this piece?' and the child calls out the first name that pops into his head, without regard to age or station, until all are served and begin eating in an air of anticipation. For someone is about to find the Bean in his cake and thereby become King (or Queen) of the festivity.

All this has virtually nothing to do with Epiphany, the Adoration of the Magi, etc. It is a cheerful pagan rite that can be traced at least as far back as the Saturnalia and Kalends of Roman times, as Bridget Ann Henisch (1984) informs us. The *magister bibendi* (or toastmaster) of these winter revels was chosen by means of a bean (which had served as a voting token earlier for the Greeks). Thus when the Church, in 336, decreed 25 December as Christ's birthday, with the clear intention of co-opting these immensely popular holidays, it was already the season to be jolly. By the end of the century, Epiphany joined it twelve days later on the liturgical calendar. The Wise Men were soon elevated to kings, to divest them of any occult connotation. The ancient ritual of bean, cake, and kingship, with its powerful, if vaguely similar, symbolism, was brought into the fold.

Although the *galette des rois* is much the most famous of all galettes, there are many others. The *Larousse gastronomique* (1984) has a useful list of those which are well-known regional specialities.   JBa
READING: Bauman (1987).

GALINGALE (or galangal), a spice consisting of the dried rhizomes of plants of the genus *Alpinia*, especially *A. galanga* (greater galingale) and *A. officinarum* (lesser galingale), in parts of India and E. and SE Asia. Greater galingale grows in the tropics, while the lesser can be grown in warm but not tropical climates. They are members of the GINGER family, and the spice, in the form of dried rhizomes or powder, has a general resemblance to ginger. The flavour is like a mixture of ginger and pepper; aromatic and pungent.

Galingale was known to the Arabs at least as early as the 9th century; Flückiger and Hanbury (1879) cite two Arab writers of that time who referred to it, and say that the name galingale came from an Arabic word which in turn came from a Chinese name which meant 'ginger of Kau-liang', the ancient name for a part of Guangdong. This is interesting because it seems to imply that the Arabs knew where it came from (China) long before Europeans did. The same authors, whose writing on this and other subjects abounds in erudite and often obscure references, note that it was known to Welsh physicians early in the 13th century. Certainly, it became a popular spice in medieval Europe, although its region of origin was at that time unknown to Europeans; see Redgrove (1933) for the tale of the 'discovery' of *A. officinarum* in Hainan in 1867, several centuries after it had more or less disappeared from European kitchens (despite a residual export trade from China to Russia, where Tatars used it with tea).

The rhizomes of the lesser galingale are reddish and smaller than those of the greater, and give a different and stronger flavour. The greater is the one most widely

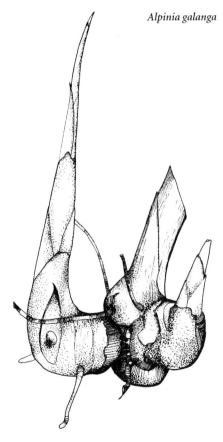

Alpinia galanga

used in Thai, Malay, and Indonesian cooking and known as *lengkuas*, it is sometimes used in stews and curry-type dishes, sometimes sliced as a garnish or to season sauces or flavour baked goods.

The rhizomes of *Kaempferia galanga*, known as *kencur* in Indonesia, have uses similar to those of galingale, and are also cultivated in tropical Asia.

GALLIMAUFREY (gallimaufry, and other variant spellings), an obsolete culinary term, corresponding to the French word *gallimaufré*, meaning a dish of odds and ends of food, a hodge-podge.

The obscurity surrounding the origin of this word, whether in the French or English version, prompted Dallas (1877) in *Kettner's Book of the Table* to compose one of the most elaborate and far-reaching essays in culinary etymology which has ever been written. He devoted over 14 pages to the matter, treating also several other words (galimatias, salmagundi, salmi, etc.—even Hamlet's 'miching malicho' and the Anglo-Indian mulligatawny) which he perceived to be connected by the root 'ma', meaning in his opinion a small bird or chicken and serving as an important piece of evidence for the previous existence of a language, possibly older than Sanskrit, which had already been lost in medieval times but which was the source of numerous words used in the kitchen.

Although the term itself is of little consequence, the fact that it engendered this towering edifice of etymological speculation is more than enough to warrant giving it an entry.

GAME in the culinary sense, is the flesh of wild animals, birds, or fish now or formerly hunted for food or 'sport'. Use of the term in modern times varies considerably according to the environment. Thus in Africa the term would embrace just about all edible animals and birds; whereas in Britain it would normally apply only to the small number of species which are the subject of game laws. In most parts of the world many species which were formerly hunted as game are now protected, at least in theory, either completely or by prohibitions on killing them during their breeding time.

Although, as noted above, fish can be classed as game, the terminology for them is rather different. 'Game fish' would normally be very large fish such as the MARLIN which human beings who take Ernest Hemingway as a role model pursue in powerful motor boats with sophisticated equipment. Smaller species for which anglers (role model Izaak Walton) lie in wait may be termed sporting fish (all the more so if they make really strenuous and persistent efforts to free themselves from the angler's hook, thus supposedly demonstrating a willingness to engage in a sporting contest with human beings), but would not normally be referred to as game.

The principal game birds of Britain are GROUSE, PARTRIDGE, PHEASANT, plus WOODCOCK, PIGEON, QUAIL, and various WILD DUCK and marsh fowl.

European game animals include various DEER, WILD BOAR, HARE, and RABBIT.

In N. America the range of game birds resembles that in Europe quite closely (with the addition of wild turkey), but there are more animals, especially in the category of 'small furred game' (which includes MUSKRAT, BEAVER, WOODCHUCK, RACCOON, and OPOSSUM).

The concept of game has from early times been somewhat blurred by the practice of rearing animals or birds in protected environments in order to provide a stock of game. This conflicts with the general notion that game is wild. The blurring has become more noticeable in recent times as a result of a considerable extension in the practice of 'farming', for example deer, pigeon, and quail, even the OSTRICH.

It is no doubt pedantic to ruminate about what can be classified as 'genuine' game and what has crossed the dividing line into the territory of domesticated races. There is, however, a practical point. The flesh of truly wild animals, birds, and fish is often deemed to be better, nutritionally and for health-giving qualities, than that of the farmed equivalents.

GAMMELOST a hard Norwegian cheese of exceptional mouldiness and sharp flavour. It is not, however, old, seldom being matured for longer than a month. The word *gammel* ('old') refers to the starting process by which it is made from skimmed milk. Instead of being curdled with rennet as most cheeses are nowadays, the milk is soured with lactic acid-producing bacteria and left to separate naturally. The curds are then literally boiled in whey for several hours, killing the bacteria and leaving a clear field for the formidable combination of moulds which will develop the flavour. After drying, the cheese is inoculated by piercing it with needles carrying *Penicillium roqueforti*, *Mucor ramosus*, and several species of *Rhizopus*. (Some farm-made cheeses are allowed to be infected naturally by their surroundings.)

The moulds grow fast, inside and out, developing a furry coating which is rubbed into the cheese every few days. When mature, the cheese is brown rather than blue, and has a crumbling and decayed appearance. Sometimes it is given a last-minute treatment with juniper flavouring: purists, however, prefer its putrid splendour unadulterated. The cheese is drum shaped, usually about 15 cm (6") high and weighing about 3 kg (7 lb).

GAMMON an English term used in the BACON industry and by butchers, originally meant the hindquarters of a PIG or swine,

but in the course of time came to apply only to cured meat, still from the hindquarters and usually the upper part of the leg. It is sold uncooked, to provide gammon steaks or rashers, both of which are moderately thick, not like rashers of bacon.

Gammon is, essentially, the same part of the pig as HAM. However, whereas in England ham (except for some imported specialities) is sold after being both cured and cooked, gammon has only been cured.

GAPER a name given to various edible BIVALVES which lack the ability to close their two shells tight together. The result, so far as human beings are concerned, is that they cannot be kept or transported for long distances alive, in the manner of oysters or mussels, but must be consumed, or shucked and preserved, shortly after being caught. Well-known bivalves to which the name gaper could be applied are the RAZOR CLAM, and the SOFT-SHELLED CLAM; but the latter is something of an exception in that it can survive for some time without water (indeed without oxygen).

One bivalve is regularly referred to as the gaper: *Tresus nuttalli*, which is large (up to 20 cm/8", with a weight of over 1.5 kg/4 lb), common on the Californian coast, and highly esteemed.

GARDEN MACE a name applied in Britain to a herb, *Achillea decolorans*. This has long, thin, prettily serrated leaves used for flavouring soups and stews. Their flavour is thought to be reminiscent of MACE, the spice.

GARFISH *Belone belone*, a fish of the Mediterranean and E. Atlantic which is remarkably thin, with a needle-like beak, and capable of planing along the surface of the water and even leaping over low rocks. It has a maximum length of 75 cm (30") and its body is thick enough to yield good fillets of flesh, suitable for poaching or frying. However, its bones are green, not just greenish but a good strong viridian, and this puts many people off eating it, although it is perfectly wholesome.

The Indo-Pacific harbours several species of garfish, of which *Tylosurus crocodilus* may be taken as typical. It is longer than *Belone belone*, but otherwise similar and an equally fast swimmer.

GARLIC (*see page 331*)

GARUM a condiment whose use was fundamental to cookery in classical times. It (*cont. on page 332*)

Garlic

Allium sativum, the most powerfully flavoured member of the ONION family, and an indispensable ingredient in many cuisines and dishes. Its cloves, of which a bulb contains six to more than two dozen, have little smell when whole but release a notoriously strong one when crushed. The question whether it is socially acceptable for people to give off this smell, as they do when they have eaten garlic, has been controversial in various parts of the world since the beginning of historical times.

Garlic's English name is partly from 'gar' meaning spear (cf GARFISH), referring to the spearlike leaves. The second syllable is from 'leac', leek.

Several species of wild garlic exist, and the cultivated species may have evolved from one of these in C. Asia and the E. Mediterranean region. De Candolle (1886) points to the very wide variation in common names as evidence that the plant has been familiar in most regions of the Old World for a very long time. It has been known in China since antiquity, and was an important article of diet in ancient Egypt and in classical Greece and Rome.

Garlic, already developed to a form hardly distinguishable from that we know today, is commonly found in Egyptian tombs, sometimes left as an offering like other items of food, sometimes playing a role in mummification. The Israelites, as they set off on their exodus, looked back with longing at the garlic of Egypt (Numbers 11: 5).

Garlic was an important vegetable to Greeks and Romans. Theophrastus (*c*.300 BC) remarked that several kinds were grown; and a section of the market at Athens was known simply as *ta skoroda* (the garlic). It was considered a strengthening food, ideal for workers, soldiers, and oarsmen, and often prescribed by dietitians; but some upper-class voices were raised against its smell. The Roman poet Horace wrote of 'garlic, more harmful than hemlock', that could drive one's lover to refuse a kiss and to retreat to the far side of the bed. It may be for this reason that garlic appears only twice in the recipes of APICIUS, one of these being for invalid food.

So far as the ancient civilizations are concerned, one could say that in general garlic was esteemed for its medicinal qualities, and eaten by the populace; but often disdained by the aristocracies and even the subject of taboos by priests.

CHEMISTRY OF GARLIC

Although garlic has been used therapeutically for thousands of years, its efficacy has been little understood until quite recent times. Its 'power to cure or alleviate' was attributed, in great part, to 'magic'.

In the 1940s scientists found that a substance in garlic called alliin was the 'parent' compound that must be broken down before antimicrobial effects are possible, and before the characteristic odour of garlic is evident. This catalytic breakdown is accomplished with the enzyme allinase, which is also naturally present in garlic. Alexandra Hicks (1986) wrote:

Simply stated, when a clove of garlic is cut or crushed, its extracellular membrane separates into sections. This enables an enzyme called allinase to come in contact and combine with the precursor or substrate alliin to form allicin, which contains the odoriferous constituent of garlic.

(A similar process takes place in an onion when it is cut. The cut allows an enzyme already present in the onion to start working, and it brings out the tear-producing element of onions.)

This is not all. The molecules released by these means are highly reactive, changing of their own accord into other organic compounds (always involving sulphur), which then in turn undergo further transformations.

Out of all this complex and sequential activity come the molecules which have the various medicinal qualities for which garlic is famed, including antibacterial, antifungal, and anti-thrombotic (preventing blood from clotting, important in the context of heart problems, for example). A wealth of scientific information on these and related matters has been provided by Koch and Lawson (1996), whose bibliography of over 2,000 items testifies to the amount of interest in and work on the subject.

Generally, garlic is a food rich in minerals, containing within the chemical complexity of its primary minerals a relatively high amount of sulphur compounds (allyl sulphides). These sulphur compounds occur in greater amounts in the genus *Allium* than in other vegetables; and they are higher in garlic than in its relations such as leeks, onions, etc. And it is these sulphur compounds which underlie the processes described above.

In addition garlic contains trace minerals such as calcium, phosphorus, iron; and is rich in vitamins B_1 and C.

Generally, it would be fair to say that the health-giving properties of garlic are well attested and have probably not yet been fully explored.

These properties doubtless depend to some extent on the variety or cultivar being used. These differ in various parts of the world, e.g. there are marked contrasts between French and Californian varieties. California Early is the white garlic most commonly seen in the US markets, although California Late is a better keeper (it will keep from one harvest to the next). Silverskin is another very fine white garlic. Carpathian is well known in C. Europe. The name Italian is loosely used of small, strongly flavoured varieties, and among these Italian Red is favoured by connoisseurs. A plethora of varieties, many of local fame only, thrives in the huge area extending from the Mediterranean to E. Asia. See also ELEPHANT GARLIC and HEDGE GARLIC.

Well-known garlic sauces or similar preparations in the Mediterranean region include AÏOLI, PESTO, SKORTHALIA, *persillade*, and also *gremolada*, the parsley and garlic mixture traditionally sprinkled on *Osso bucco* (see VEAL).

In Asia, garlic is important in cooking, but there seem to be no parallels to the special Mediterranean dishes which are centred on garlic; for Asians garlic is just something which is used all the time to add flavour to savoury dishes, with no special fanfare attending it. Exceptions to its general popularity occur, whether partial (as in Iran, where use is relatively rare and light) or total (as among the Jains, for whom the onion family is forbidden—see JAINS AND FOOD).

To say that by the end of the 20th century garlic had conquered the world would be something of an exaggeration. There are still ethnic and cultural groups (some in Britain and N. America, for example) who view it with dislike and distrust or who simply do not use it. But it is coming close to complete penetration of the kitchens of the world. And, if folklore is correct, its spread must be bringing ever closer the extinction of the vampire. For folkloric and light-hearted aspects of the subject, often emanating from California, see L. J. Harris (1980, 1986).

was made by fermenting fish, as the SE Asian FISH SAUCES, which closely resemble it, are still made.

From the numerous allusions to garum by classical authors, and in particular the descriptions of it given by Pliny (1st century AD) and in the *Geoponica* (10th century), it is clear that there were many methods of manufacture. Sometimes the entrails of large fish were used; sometimes small fish, whole. Such small fish were often of the genus *Atherina* (see sand-smelt under SILVERSIDE), which abounds in the Mediterranean and Black seas, or ANCHOVY or small GREY MULLET or SEA BREAM, or the like. The larger fish ranged down from the TUNA to MACKEREL.

The liquid drawn off after the salted fish had fermented for about two months was garum or liquamen; *allec* or *allex* was the name of the solid residue, which also had culinary uses.

Garum production was a commercial undertaking, not normally a domestic activity. Indeed in Byzantine times garum manufacture, like cheese-making, was banned from towns and villages because of the smell.

Archaeologists have found fish salteries and garum factories from the time of the Roman Empire along the coasts of Spain, Gaul, and Italy, and along the northern shores of the Black Sea. They have also found amphoras which had once contained garum of various qualities; at least one find, at Pompeii, still smelled distinctively of garum when excavated. The best quality of garum was *garum sociorum* (literally 'partners' garum', a name for which a parallel in modern times would be that used for the principal kind of Roquefort cheese, *de la Société*).

Some Roman recipes call for garum mixed with wine, or olive oil, or water. However, Roman use of garum may be compared, in a general way, to modern use of SALT, or that of SOY SAUCE in China and Japan, besides the aforementioned fish sauces of SE Asia.

Garum continued in use in early medieval times in both the W. and E. Mediterranean regions. The West may have lost the taste for

it first; at least, when Bishop Liutprand of Cremona visited Constantinople in 949 he remarked unenthusiastically on its presence in dishes served to him.

Although garum then fell into desuetude, some kindred products have survived in the Mediterranean, notably peï salat; and a product called 'garum' was advertised in a 19th-century English cookery book, *The Household Manager* (1868), as having been made according to the Roman method, 'the recipe for which has so long been lost, but has lately been found in the Island of Sicily'. The apparent lack of other such references to this product, which was made in Wandsworth near London, suggests that it was not a success.

In more recent times the relationship between garum and SE Asian fish sauces has become apparent to those who are interested in recreating Roman dishes, who therefore simply substitute Vietnamese *nuoc mam* or the like for garum. The German gastronomic writer RUMOHR (1822) was possibly the first in modern times to show awareness of the relationship. (AD)

GATEAU French for cake. The word is derived from the old French *guastrel*, which gave medieval English the word *wastrel*, meaning fine flour and loaves or cakes made from it. The word 'gateau' crossed the Channel to England in the early 19th century (*le cake*, meaning a pound cake containing dried fruit, crossed in the opposite direction, to France). In Victorian England cookery writers used 'gateau' initially to denote puddings such as rice baked in a mould, and moulded baked dishes of fish or meat; during the second part of the century it was also applied to highly decorated layer cakes. Judging by the amount of space given to directions for making these in bakers' manuals of the time, they were tremendously popular. Their prices varied according to the quality of the ingredients, their size, and the amount of decoration. Most were probably rather sickly, made from cheap SPONGE filled with 'buttercream' (butter and icing sugar beaten together), and

coated with fondant ICING. Elaborate piped decoration was added. Many fanciful shapes were made, such as trefoils, horseshoes, hearts, and butterflies, all using these basic mixtures. The primary meaning of the word 'gateau' is now a rich and elaborate cake filled with whipped cream and fruit, nuts, or chocolate.

French gateaux are richer than the products of British bakers. They involve thin layers of sponge, usually GÉNOISE, or MERINGUE; some are based on choux PASTRY. Fruit or flavoured creams are used as fillings. The latter are rarely dairy cream; instead *crème pâtissière* (confectioner's custard—milk, sugar, egg yolks, and a little flour) or *crème au beurre* (a rich concoction of egg yolks beaten with sugar syrup and softened butter) are used.

Gâteau has wider applications in French, just as 'cake' does in English. Apart from a conventional sweet cake it can mean a savoury cake, a sweet or savoury tart, or a thick pancake. A *gâteau de semoule* is essentially the same as English semolina pudding, but it is enriched with eggs, butter, and rum-soaked raisins, chilled in a mould, and turned out and served with fruit purée or jam. Sweet gateaux are popular for *goûter* (afternoon tea), birthdays, and Sunday lunch, and are usually bought from the *pâtissier*. The name given to a gateau can be descriptive, indicating a flavour, e.g. *gâteau au citron* (lemon cake) or *gâteau moka* (coffee); or a place of origin, such as *gâteau Pithiviers*. Some specialities have more fanciful names, such as *gâteau Saint-Honoré*. These last two are among the better-known gateaux of the Paris region listed below.

Paris–Brest, a ring of choux pastry, sprinkled with almonds, split, and filled with praline flavoured cream or *crème au beurre*. Named after the Paris–Brest bicycle race of 1891. A *pâtissier* in a Paris suburb, whose shop was close to the route of the race, was the first to make it, choosing a wheel shape for the obvious reason. It became popular and is now visible at Brest also.

Pithiviers, a pastry confection which is a speciality of Pithiviers, a town south of Paris. It is composed of two rounds of puff pastry enclosing a filling of ground almonds, sugar, butter, and egg yolks, flavoured with rum.

Saint-Honoré, a confection of two kinds of pastry with a cream filling. Shortcrust pastry provides a firm base for the soft and flexible choux pastry piped round it on top. Glazed PROFITEROLES are stuck to the ring of choux. The centre of the ring is filled with a creamy mixture (*crème chiboust*) stiffened with GELATIN and lightened with stiffly beaten egg whites. This cake is sometimes said to have been named after St Honoré, the patron saint of bakers, but others say that it owes its name to the rue Saint-Honoré in Paris, where it was created (possibly as a development of some existing product) in 1846 by a *pâtissier*, Chiboust. The learned authors of the Île-de-France volume listed under IPCF (1993) explain why they regard the matter as an unsolved 'mystery'.

GAZPACHO a Spanish term whose meaning has evolved over the centuries. It is now most familiar in the form of Andalusian gazpacho, which is typically a cold soup with various vegetable ingredients, notably garlic, tomato, and cucumber. However, a gazpacho may be served hot during the winter; and in its original form, derived from the Arabs who occupied much of Spain from the 8th to the 13th centuries, the essential ingredients were bread, garlic, olive oil, vinegar, salt, and water. These ingredients were pounded in a mortar, and the result was very similar to *Ajo blanco* (*ajo* meaning GARLIC and *blanco* meaning white) or *Sopa de ajo* (garlic soup), two other ancient dishes which have survived into modern times.

Garlic was and remains the dominating flavour element. Bread is used to provide thickness and heartiness. (In some very early gazpachos the bread is left in small pieces and not blended in with the other ingredients. If the bread is pounded in the mortar, it blends with the water and oil.) Vinegar is important for the refreshing qualities of those gazpachos that are particularly associated with warm weather; and it provides a link to Roman culture, as it was the Romans who popularized throughout their empire the use of vinegar for refreshment purposes.

Gazpachos can thus range in consistency from very liquid to almost solid. The internationally famous Andalusian gazpacho, which is said to have been introduced to France by Eugenia de Montijo of Granada, the wife of the Emperor Napoleon III, is of the liquid kind, and kitchens in the south of Spain always have a supply on hand, ready to pour into glasses as a refreshing summer drink, or to serve as a

cold soup with various finely chopped ingredients as garnish.

Ingredients from the New World, notably tomato, were not incorporated into gazpachos until comparatively recent times. Thus the recipe for gazpacho given by Juan de la Mata (*Arte de reposteria*, 1747) had none of these 'new' ingredients.

Less common types of gazpacho may include ingredients such as little pieces of fish or ham, hard-boiled (US hard-cooked) egg, green grapes, raisins, etc. Blanched almonds figure in the gazpacho of Antequera; red peppers and cumin seeds in that of Granada; and so on. The name *gazpachuelo* refers to an interestingly different gazpacho from Malaga; it may incorporate both angler-fish and small clams, potato, and mayonnaise, and is commonly served hot in winter. It is only one of numerous gazpacho derivatives which would probably not be recognized as gazpachos in the sense in which the term has entered the international culinary vocabulary.   (AR)

GEFILTE FISH an item of Jewish food which has changed considerably from the original version, which involved taking a fish such as pike or carp, cooking it, carefully extracting everything from inside the skin, mincing the flesh (freed from bones), and stuffing it back into the skin. This made it suitable for use on the sabbath, when Jews are not supposed to pick over their food, as they would have to do if the fish still contained bones.

Nowadays gefilte have become something like fish balls or the French *quenelles de brochet*. To make them, the fish (which could still be carp or pike but are now, at least in many Jewish communities, more often sea fish) are cooked, then freed of skin and bone, chopped, mixed with other ingredients (e.g. onion, and always including MATZO meal), formed into balls or torpedo-shaped patties, and poached. The chilled cooking liquid is used to coat the balls, like aspic. The dish is usually served cold with the accompaniment *chrain*, a beetroot and horseradish sauce.

If one thing is certain it is that there is no fish whose name is 'gefilte' (which means 'stuffed' and refers to the traditional version). This assurance may seem otiose; but there could still be people who were deceived by the famous spoof television programme in which the disappearance of gefilte fish from New York state waters was lamented, for example by fishermen who declared that they hadn't seen even one in a long while—a worthy counterpart of a notorious British programme which showed the spaghetti harvest taking place in Italy.

GELATIN (sometimes gelatine) is derived from collagen (present in skin, CONNECTIVE TISSUE in meat, and in BONES, particularly those of young animals) when it is heated. It is extracted commercially with hot water and acids or alkalis. Transparent and almost colourless, gelatin is sold in dehydrated form, as a powder or in thin fragile sheets. These are used as required, mixed with liquids and flavourings, to 'set' savoury ASPIC, desserts such as JELLY and MOUSSE, and stabilize commercially made ICE CREAM and other foods.

Gelatin is important in cookery and the food industry because of this ability to transform large amounts of liquid into an apparently solid substance or gel. The molecules of which it is composed have special properties that make this possible. They are hydrophilic (i.e. attractive to water), and have a long, threadlike structure. When liquid is added to gelatin and the mixture heated, the gelatin first swells, as the water is absorbed, and then dissolves. At this stage the mixture is known as a sol, and contains sufficient energy for the molecules to move freely in the mixture. On cooling, the molecules lose energy and form a mesh in which water is held both by chemical bonds on their surface, and physically in the three-dimensional network. In this form the mixture is known as a gel. If the mixture is beaten whilst viscous but before it is fully set, the gelatin is sufficiently elastic to stretch around and hold air bubbles; the result is then a foam (such as a mousse). Frozen, the mixture becomes ice cream, in which the gelatin also interferes with the formation of large ice crystals, allowing a smoother texture.   LM

GEM in American usage, a small 'muffin' popular in the 19th century. Gems were cooked in a gem pan. They bear little resemblance to an English MUFFIN. The same applies to New Zealand gems, claimed by Burton (1982) to be an invention of that country; they are made in gem irons, which typically hold a dozen.

In Britain the term is used for various small items of commercially produced flour or sugar confectionery; thus 'iced gems' are small biscuits with rosettes of coloured icing piped on top.

GENDER/SEX AND FOOD not just one topic but many, often treated by those numerous anthropologists and sociologists whose professional as well as personal interests include food. The overlapping of the two terms, 'gender' and 'sex', already means that the topics fall into two overlapping groups.

So far as gender is concerned, it may be sufficient to observe that men and women do differ physiologically, and that on these differences depend some differences in dietary requirements. It is therefore not surprising that in most cultures in most parts of the world, although most foods or dishes are perceived as suitable for both genders, some are seen to be more appropriate for men and some for women.

This principle may be unobjectionable, but the ways in which it has been put into practice do evoke criticism and protest, and not only from women, or from feminists. Generally speaking, practice has put men first and women second in the allocation of nourishment or of particularly appetizing titbits—or of temporal priority, who eats first and who takes what's left? On this last point see the entry on SUDAN (not that that country is any worse than many others in this respect, it is just an example).

There is a different aspect, that of food preferences. In an ideal world, perhaps, Jack Sprat would eat no fat and his wife would eat no lean, so there would not be a problem. For this kind of reason, there often isn't a problem. But, it may be asked, how come that Jack Sprat would eat no fat, that his wife would eat no lean, etc.? Were these truly personal preferences, or may there have been discriminatory factors at work in the culture of which the Sprats were part? Perhaps. Once one begins to unravel the influences which shape food preferences one is indeed being borne rapidly towards 'white waters'. Hence no more on these matters in this book.

Sex (meaning sexual activity) and food have often been linked. Each is the subject of appetites. Each represents a fundamental urge, transcending ethnic and gender boundaries. Each can give great pleasure (or dissatisfaction). Etcetera. So linkages in thought and in writing (and occasionally in deed, as when sexual partners anoint each other with edibles such as whipped cream) are not surprising. Whether they are approved or disapproved is another matter. Male gastronomic writers of what might be termed the 'old school' (e.g. GRIMOD DE LA REYNIÈRE and BRILLAT-SAVARIN) were apt to compare an early strawberry to 'a timid virgin' and to make assertions such as: 'A dessert without cheese is like a lovely lady who lacks an eye.' Persons seeking to defend these writers may say that they were the prisoners of the then prevailing culture; but the more serious gastronomic writer RUMOHR, their contemporary, managed very well without saying anything like this.

The deliberate fabrication of foods which resemble male or female sexual organs is a practice which probably goes a long way back into prehistoric times (cf BABA), but which has been on the wane in the 20th century. June di Schino (1995), in her remarkable essay 'The Waning of Sexually Allusive Monastic Confectionery in Southern Italy', puts a spotlight on one small area of such activity, but in doing so illuminates the whole subject and provides a bibliography which serves well as a basis for further studies. The instances which she lists of sexually allusive confectionery include several belonging to the category of virgin's breast cakes (honouring the martyrdom of St Agatha) such as *minni chini*, described by a Sicilian ethnologist as 'a kind of breast shape filled with cassata with sugar icing topped with a cherry', and the smaller *minnuzza di Sant'Agata* from Catania, which were small pastries shaped like an immature girl's breasts. On the male side, phallic breads used to be commonplace and some survive. In this domain, it often seems that great antiquity, and the presence of specimens in museums of popular art, confers respectability.

The nomenclature of food and dishes is more of a problem area. However, some Levantine titles for dishes, such as those which evoke ladies' thighs or breasts, no longer sound right (except, no doubt, in the countries where they have been used, unchallenged, for a century or more); and a question mark may be gradually forming over 'lady's fingers' (for biscuits or for okra).

People who wish to avoid both the Scylla of being labelled priggish or hypersensitive and the Charybdis of being perceived to endorse sexist language in connection with food are advised to choose their own words carefully but to abstain from criticizing those of others who have a more lewd disposition. In the company of persons who remark on, say, the phallic appearance of an asparagus spear, they may give an amiable (but faint) smile, to show that they take the point and are friendly towards the speaker; but they should not match guffaw with guffaw.

These sparse comments do not attempt to encroach on the topics covered under APHRODISIACS.

GENIPAP *Genipa americana*, also known as 'marmalade box' in some formerly British W. Indian islands, the fruit of a tall tree native to tropical America.

The fruit is 9–15 cm (3–6") long, oval shaped, but with a rounded middle. It has a thin, brown, leathery skin, within which there is a thin layer of grainy flesh, which turns yellow on exposure; and below this are many flat, round seeds encased in a brownish-yellow pulp. The fruit is only edible when overripe, and the flavour, likened by Popenoe (1932) to that of dried apples, is very pronounced. Its main use is for soft drinks, in the Philippines as well as in C. America, but it can also be made into preserves or pickles.

GÉNOISE a type of SPONGE CAKE (which may be called Genoese, in Britain, but is not to be confused with Genoa cake, which is really a type of light FRUIT CAKE). Whole eggs are beaten with sugar until thick, and the flour then folded in. This type of sponge may be simply dusted with icing sugar and eaten plain; or split and filled with jam and cream, or butter ICING. The top may also be iced. Sheets of génoise are used to make SWISS ROLLS.

Génoise-type mixtures are also made into sponge fingers (see BISCUIT VARIETIES and BOUDOIR BISCUITS) and French MADELEINES.

See also SAVOY.

GEODUCK *Panope generosa*, the largest burrowing clam in the world, is found on the Pacific coast of N. America from Vancouver Island to California. Its common name, thought to be of Indian origin, may appear as gweduc or goeduck or even gooeyduck, the last version being closest to the usual pronunciation of the name. According to another story, aired in the correspondence columns of the *Tacoma Daily Ledger* in July 1917, the Indians in the neighbourhood of Puget Sound knew the creature by a name which was pronounced

Geoduck

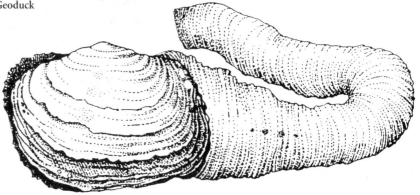

'hyas squish-squish'; and it was a certain John F. Gowey whose own name supplanted the original one. Mr Gowey was an ardent duck-hunter. On one occasion, when no ducks were to be seen, the volatile marksman fired at the jets of water emitted by these huge clams and 'bagged' several of them. Hence Gowey's ducks, later corrupted to gooeyducks. This story is not supported by Webster's dictionary.

The hinged shells of the geoduck are relatively small and quite incapable of meeting over the plump, orange-red body; still less of accommodating the lengthy neck or siphon, which is ivory in colour. A large geoduck may weigh 5 kg (11 lb). A mature adult, perhaps 15 years old, will hang down for a length of 60 or 70 cm (over 2') when held up by the end of its siphon; and its body will resemble that of a trussed hen in size and shape.

Geoduck meat is delicious. That of the siphon is best used in a CHOWDER, after it has been scalded and peeled and the horny tip discarded. The enlarged mantle of the clam, known as the 'breast meat', can be sliced into thin escalopes and prepared in a variety of ways.

Baby geoducks can and do swim; but they settle in the mud at an early age and stay put thereafter. Their favoured habitat is around the line of the very lowest tides, so that it is only on certain days of the year that fishermen on foot can get to them. Even so, it has been found necessary, since the 1920s, to accord them protection by regulating the methods and scale of the catch.

Efforts were made in the 19th century to establish geoducks on the Atlantic coast, but they failed. No one seems to have tried to transfer them to another continent.

GEOPHAGY means eating earth, especially certain kinds of clay. It is a widespread practice, often but not always connected with the special dietary needs of pregnant women.

In recent times geophagy has most often been referred to in the context of the black population in the southern states of the USA. Attention has been drawn to imports of special clay from Africa for the benefit of black women descended from the slaves who originally came from Africa. However, Laufer (1930), in the masterly survey which he published while Curator of the Department of Anthropology in the Field Museum of Natural History in Chicago, recorded examples from many parts of the world and drew instructive parallels between practices in the various continents. The following quotation serves both to illustrate his main point, that geophagy has been widespread, and to exhibit the pleasant style in which he wrote.

The fact that clay is eaten in India was known in Europe early in the nineteenth century. Curiously enough, the edible clay of India was then designated 'clay of the Mogol'. G. I. Molina (*Saggia sulla storia naturale del Chili*, 1810), therefore, wrote at that time that the Peruvian women are in the habit of eating pottery sherds as the Mogol women eat the dishes of Patna. The Indic pottery is described as being gray in color with a yellow tinge, known under the name 'earth of Patna' and found principally in the environment of Seringapatam. From this clay were manufactured vases so light in weight and so delicate in shape that 'a breath from one's mouth was sufficient to turn them upside down on the table.' Water poured into these vessels assumed a pleasant flavor and odor; and the ladies of India when they had emptied them would break them to pieces, swallowing the sherds with pleasure, especially in the period of maternity.

The clay consumed by the women of Bengal is a fine, light ochreous-colored specimen fashioned into thin cups with a perforation in the center and then baked in a kiln. In other words, it is ready-made pottery which they consume and which emits a curious smoky odor. It is this particular odor which makes it such a favourite with delicate women. The cups are strung on a cord and sold by the potters at so many pieces for one price. Formerly these cups were hawked about in the streets of Calcutta, but this is no longer customary. Such a street vendor of baked clay cups once figured in a Bengali play staged in a Calcutta theatre; she recommended her ware in a song, pointing out that her cups are well baked, crisp to eat and yet cheap, and that delicate ladies about to become mothers should buy them without delay, as eating them would bless them with sons.

GEORGIA the northernmost country of the Caucasia, shares with its neighbours (TURKEY, ARMENIA, AZERBAIJAN) a Mediterranean-type climate. Geographically, it can be divided into W. and E. Georgia, with the Suram Gorge marking the division. So far as food is concerned, Turkish influence prevails to the west and Persian to the east. Pokhlebkin (1984) points out that maize flour bread is eaten in W. Georgia, whereas wheaten bread is preferred in E. Georgia; and there are other differences, e.g. in the choice of animal foods. Taken as a whole, Georgia is perceived as having had a significant and beneficial influence on the food and cookery in RUSSIA. It was for long part of the Russian Empire, and then of the Soviet Union.

Georgian soups are typically thick, often thanks to the addition of a mixture of eggs or egg yolks with something acidic such as fruit juice. Fruit juices are also important in many of the distinctive and famous Georgian sauces, which also often incorporate crushed nuts. *Satsivi* sauce, probably the best known, uses WALNUTS and is usually served with cold chicken or other poultry, although suitable for fish etc. *Tkemali* is a sauce made from tart wild

plums. Others feature one or several of tomatoes, garlic, BARBERRIES, grapes, POMEGRANATES, and yoghurt. Similar preparations are found elsewhere in the Caucasus, but incorporated in dishes rather than served separately as a sauce.

Walnuts are liberally used. Georgia is almost the only country in the world where this rich, oily nut is used as an integral part of daily cooking and not just as a garnish for salads and cakes.

Meat is often cooked in chunks on skewers, i.e. as the *shashlyk* or *shish kebab* (see KEBAB) which is ubiquitous in the region; or in the stew called *Chankhi* where a little meat is cooked with a lot of vegetables and often with rice too; or cooked by frying to go into the sort of stew called *chakhokhbili* (often made with chicken).

Among vegetables, there is a noticeable enthusiasm for beans, especially lubia (LABLAB BEANS). These are prepared with plenty of spices and herbs, e.g. the following collection: cardamom, parsley, celery, leek, mint, basil or dill, coriander, cinnamon, cloves or saffron, and black pepper. Liberal use of such flavourings is characteristic of Georgian cuisine generally.

The numerous rice dishes called *plov* are patently related to PILAF, and equally variegated. However, although rice is important, there is no doubt about what is the real staple for Georgians, and that is bread. It has been said that for all Caucasians a meal without bread is unthinkable. The oldest bread is the thin, crisp, cracker-like bread known as LAVASH baked in a TANDOOR (known as *toné* to Georgians). The numerous other breads include *peda* (like PITTA bread), and Georgian specialities such as *mchadi* (a round flat corn bread), *kachapuri* (bread stuffed with cheese before being baked), and *deda's puri* (meaning mother's bread).

Cheeses in great variety constitute another strength of the Georgian kitchen. *Brynza*, a brine cheese, is popular and may be fried and served with the corn bread mentioned above and herbs. However, most cheese is probably eaten in the form of ZAKUSKI.

GERANIUM the common and familiar name of popular garden plants of the genus *Pelargonium* (there is a genus *Geranium*, to which some small-flowered plants like the cranesbill geranium belong, but most garden geraniums are *Pelargonium* spp).

Geraniums, which are native to southern or tropical Africa, were introduced to Europe in 1690. The leaves (not the flowers) of a number of species, especially *Pelargonium capitatum* and *P. odoratissimum*, have a roselike scent. This is because they contain the same essential oils, geraniol and citronellol, as attar of roses (see ROSES). The proportions of these vary with the strain of the plant, soil conditions, and degree of maturity; and other essential oils are often present. So the scent of geraniums may be lemony, or like orange, apple, or nutmeg, besides resembling rose. Since the mid-19th century the rose-scented geranium has been cultivated for the production of 'rose geranium oil', which is used in perfumes but also for flavouring and scenting food, in the manner of rosewater. In Tunisian confectionery geranium water largely replaces rosewater.

The addition of geranium leaves, in small quantity, to fruit desserts or to confections such as creams and sorbets is effective.

GERMAN CHEESES viewed collectively, are a disappointment. Before the reunification of the country, W. Germany alone ranked fourth of the countries of the world in cheese production; but the originality and variety of German cheeses does not match this lofty position.

Many German cheeses have external inspiration, like the EMMENTAL which has been made with success ever since Swiss experts were summoned in the 1840s to give advice on it to the cheese-makers of the Allgäu region. The same applies to LIMBURGER, the best known of the strong-smelling cheeses for which Germans seem to have a special liking; it had its origin in Belgium (although ROMADUR, its odoriferous partner, came from Bavaria). And the German Münster is a version of the French MUNSTER. The origins of TILSITER are more confusing. It was first made at Tilsit, when that city was in E. Prussia, but by Dutchmen.

The strong points in the German cheese list are HAND CHEESES, of which they have many varieties, including the multiple forms of QUARK, by far the most popular cheese in Germany.

One way in which German cheeses have been important is in their influence on American cheeses, which has been greater than one might expect; this is mainly due to the large numbers of farmers of German descent who have played a prominent part in the American dairy industry of the Mid-western States.

GERMAN COOKERY BOOKS have a distinguished history. From the late 15th to the 17th centuries they were more numerous and impressive than French ones, and rivalled those of Italy. The earliest and possibly the most famous is the *Küchenmeisterei*. This was first published in 1485 and, amazingly, had appeared in more than a dozen editions by 1500. No other printed cookery book of the 15th century had

such an impressive record. And this book continued to sell well for more than a century afterwards. Uta Schumacher-Voelker (1980), in her admirable essay on printed German cookery books up to 1800, relates it to the political and economic context in which it was compiled, and explains why it seems almost certain that the compilation was first made in a S. German monastery, citing the importance placed on Lenten food and other relevant features:

the complete lack of hare despite other game recipes (hare was regarded as unchaste); the lack of almost all saltwater fish (as monasteries mainly used their own products); the lack of sugar, which was very much in fashion at the time for the rich, and its substitution by honey (for whose production monasteries were famous); and the use of home-grown herbs rather than an abundance of expensive spices.

About a century later came Max Rumpoldt's *Ein neues Kochbuch* (1581), a finely produced and extensive work which contained something like 2,000 recipes, intended mainly for the upper class. Only one other cookery book of the century (Frantz de Rontzier's *Kochbuch*, 1598) displayed a comparable wealth of ingredients.

In the 17th century there was a period, corresponding to the Thirty Years War, when book production almost ceased. However, even before the end of the war some translations of foreign cookery books began to appear, including several from France and works by Sir Kenelm DIGBY and Hannah WOLLEY from England. The especially important work by Massialot appeared in German translation in 1739, and Menon followed in 1766. By this time many foreign culinary terms were being used in German works. Also, the first books with a regional emphasis had begun to appear. Maria Schellhammer (1692) was from N. Germany, while Conrad Hagger's book of Saltzburg cookery embodied recipes from what is now Austria. And there were many others in the 18th century; Schumacher-Voelker lists a selection of 15, in which Hamburg, Berlin, Nuremburg, Augsburg, Leipzig, and Magdeburg were among the cities represented.

Regional cookery books have continued to be important up to the present time. During the 19th and 20th centuries the appearance of cookery books in new genres matched what was going on in other European countries rather than, as in this instance, anticipating. A tribute must, however, be paid to the pioneering aspects of the gastronomic work by RUMOHR (1822).

GERMANY notoriously divided into two states for most of the second half of the 20th century, had only been a single entity since

1871 when the first unified Germany was formed by Prince Otto von Bismarck. Previously the region was a collection of small independent states, with the separate German-speaking kingdoms of Prussia in the north and east, Saxony in the centre, and Württemburg and Bavaria in the south.

In a rough sort of way, these ancient divisions are reflected in what may be termed the three culinary regions of Germany today. There is the north, where food preferences and customs reflect the proximity to Scandinavia and to the seas (North and Baltic). The central region, an area of rolling hills with wide expanses of forest and numerous spas (dear to German hearts), has a rich and filling cuisine. In contrast, the south offers lighter food, with a strong Italian influence in the Alpine region.

Given this variety, reflecting the wide range of climates and geographical features in this large country, and the various historical influences which have been at work on the different regions, it is hard to generalize about German cookery. However, it would be fair to say that it is perceived as being hearty, and based on wholesome family-type dishes, albeit with baroque decorations in the form of pastries. Features which are seen as typical of Germany include:

- Soups. The thick soups of Germany can be made from potatoes, dried peas, or lentils, robustly flavoured with sausage and onion, and thickened with flour.
- HERRING, found in such familiar forms as *Rollmopse* (rollmops in English, although this name is the singular of the German name), but also in lots of other guises such as *Bucklinge* and Bismarck herring (herring fillets soaked in vinegar with onion rings and seasoning).
- HAMS and other meat products including sausages (see SAUSAGES OF GERMANY). It has been well said that 'Meat is the cornerstone of German cooking, and the *Braten*, or roast, is the country's national dish.' Pork, fresh or cured, is the most common and most widely used of all meats in German cookery. The FRANKFURTER and the HAMBURGER have spread right round the globe.
- GOOSE and DUCK. These are the favoured German poultry. Duck provides dishes such as duck braised in beer or wine, stuffed with apples and prunes, served with red cabbage, etc. Goose is even more popular. Its blood and giblets may be combined with dried pears, prunes, and apples in the famous *Schwarzsauer*, a stew.
- Sweet and savoury combinations, reminiscent of medieval cookery, are met more often in Germany than elsewhere in Europe. Fish, meat, potatoes, and vegetables are often cooked with vinegar and sweetened with sugar to make the

piquant sauces the Germans love. Fruits are used to give the sweet-and-sour effect. Dried apples, pears, prunes, and apricots are part and parcel of the national diet. Such fruits are combined with pork in a dish named *Schlesisches Himmelreich* or (Silesian paradise), from the former province of Silesia. *Himmel und Erde* (heaven and earth) is another dish prepared with apples and potatoes. *Sauerbraten* is a famous beef dish which involves marinating the meat in a sour (wine, vinegar, buttermilk) marinade, braising it, and serving it with a sweetened sauce. Of the numerous variations, that of the Rhineland includes raisins. In many versions some sour cream is stirred in just before serving.

- SAUERKRAUT is described in detail in its own entry. It is used extensively as a vegetable (or garnish) and changes its name to *choucroute* in the region of Alsace, where the German language and culinary traditions overlap with French counterparts.

- POTATO COOKERY is as prominent in Germany as in IRELAND and accounts for specialities such as DUMPLINGS and PANCAKES made with potato and the special German potato salad (*Kartoffelsalat*).

- DUMPLINGS. The River Main, on which stands the city of Frankfurt, forms a culinary frontier between north and south. Here the language of the kitchen changes as northern *Klösse* (dumplings) change into *Knödel*. German love of dumplings, under whichever name, is a national characteristic. In Bavaria they are especially popular: liver dumplings, bread dumplings, bacon dumplings, yeast dumplings. Large dumplings are served with roast meat dishes. Small dumplings are used to reinforce soups. The tiny dumplings called *Spätzle* belong to the region formerly known as Swabia (now in Baden-Württemberg). Yeast dumplings are served with fruit or a sweet custard sauce.

- *Eintopf*, meaning 'one-pot', dishes (see ONE-POT COOKERY) are not unique to Germany but have been developed there to a greater extent than in many other countries. They are economical in fuel (and for WASHING UP) and can also be economical and filling when they combine a little meat with lots of vegetables. Their appeal to German housewives needs no further explanation, but their political significance in modern Germany does; and this is supplied by Bertram Gordon and Lisa Jacobs-McCusker (1989).

- Baked goods, of which many of the fancier kinds are linked to the German custom of afternoon coffee. All over Germany there are Konditorei famous for their TORTE

AND KUCHEN, fruit tarts and pastries. Details of other well-known German baked goods will be found under BISCUIT, DOUGHNUT, KUGELHOPF, LEBKUCHEN, PANCAKE, STOLLEN.

See also BLACK FOREST GATEAU (for an item of international fame but doubtful ancestry) and GERMAN CHEESES.
READING: Hannelore Kohl (1996).

GHEE clarified and evaporated BUTTER, made from cow or WATER-BUFFALO milk, used for cooking in India, especially the north. (The full name is *usli ghee*, and the spelling *ghi* is sometimes used.) The butter is melted and then simmered long enough to boil off all the water, during which time it takes on a nutty taste. It is used especially, but not exclusively, for cooking meat, and it is essential for many Indian dishes.

Ghee has considerable religious importance, being so pure that the addition of a bit of it is often enough to upgrade the status of food.

The original reason for making ghee, a name derived from the Sanskrit *ghrta*, was to make butter keep in the Indian climate. Ghee remains good for several weeks at room temperature, and for months in the refrigerator.

Vanaspati ghee is a vegetable shortening, made from highly saturated oils (e.g. coconut, cottonseed, rapeseed, palm), hydrogenized, and processed to look, smell, and taste like *usli ghee*.

Samneh (*samn, samna*) is the name given to clarified butter in the Middle East and the Arab world generally. Anissa Helou (1994) describes how it is made in the Lebanon:

Samneh is made from butter that has been boiled until the fat in the pan is as transparent as a tear (*dam'at el-eyn*). It is then taken off the heat and left to settle before being carefully strained through a fine sieve into sealed containers where it will keep for a year or more.

It turns up in N. Africa as *smen*, sometimes flavoured with herbs, or spiced, and/or aged. Ethiopia also has a spiced version, *nit'r k'ibe*.

GHERKIN a word derived from a diminutive form of the Dutch name for CUCUMBER, has two meanings. The first, which is the more general, indicates a small variety of cucumber (or an immature specimen of a larger variety), suitable for pickling. The second meaning refers to a separate species, *Cucumis anguria*, a small vegetable related to and resembling a cucumber, which belongs to the Caribbean; this is much used for PICKLE and is often referred to as 'West Indian gherkin'.

Those who are most enthusiastic about gherkins (mainly Russians, E. Europeans,

Ashkenazi Jews, including the large populations of these groups in N. America) would insist that both texture and flavour differ significantly between these various possibilities, and display connoisseurship in selecting their gherkins. They like 'dill pickles', i.e. gherkins etc. pickled with DILL, to go with many sorts of cured meat such as PASTRAMI. Paul Levy (1986) gives a precise and eloquent recipe for what he regards as the ideal dill pickle.

In W. Europe gherkins are a traditional accompaniment to a plate of PÂTÉ or a French, Swiss, or Belgian *assiette anglaise* (mixed cold meats). The French for gherkin is *cornichon*.

GHORAYEBAH a Middle Eastern BISCUIT made from a pastry dough of flour, butter, and sugar. There are two traditional shapes: discs, with a blanched almond on each, or 'bracelets' (made from long sausages of dough) decorated with chopped almonds or pistachios. Moroccan *ghoriba* are made from a similar mixture, but with semolina replacing the flour. The traditional shape for these is a flattened sphere, and they are dredged with sugar after baking.

Much the same product occurs in Greece, as *kourabiethes*, half-moons or round, sprinkled with icing sugar. They used to be special to the Christmas season, for which their snowy aspect was suitable, but now are made the year round. Blanched almonds, cloves, and rosewater may enhance their appearance and flavour; and their texture is like SHORTBREAD (or SHORTCAKE in N. America).

GIANT CLAM *Tridacna gigas*, the largest bivalve in the world, found in tropical waters of the Indo-Pacific region. It can measure well over 1 m (the record is 1.4 m/4' 6") across, weigh several hundred kg (more than 500 lb), and is reputedly capable of living for centuries. Half-shells of this huge creature have been imported to Europe to serve as decorations, fountains, or washbasins.

T. gigas has a small relation, *T. elongata*. The Thai name for the former means tiger's claw clam; for the latter, cat's claw clam. Tales are told of divers being trapped between the shells of the true giant, and drowned. This has no doubt happened, but by accident. The giant clam is not anthropophagous, nor indeed carnivorous. On the contrary it is a kind of marine 'farmer', obtaining most of its food from minuscule marine plants which grow along its mantle edges and are exposed to light and water whenever the shells are open.

The meat on the border of the shells is good to eat, especially if its rather strong fishy taste is partly masked by the use of curry paste and chilli peppers, as in Thailand. The huge adductor muscle may be boiled and dried and then used in soups.

GIBLETS a word derived from the OF *gibelet*, meaning a stew of game birds, now refers to the edible internal organs of a fowl, notably heart, liver, gizzard. The term has been in use in this sense since the mid-16th century, and sometimes had particular application to the goose.

Giblet pies are made, but the main use of giblets in modern times is probably to produce a good stock for giblet soup or GRAVY. Dorothy Hartley (1954) provides characteristically knowledgeable and detailed guidance on how best to make this broth.

GILT-HEAD BREAM *Sparus aurata*, generally regarded as the finest SEA BREAM in the Mediterranean (where the family of sea bream, Sparidae, is most strongly represented) or indeed anywhere else. Maximum length 70 cm (28"), average market length half of that. This beautiful silvery fish has a golden spot on each cheek and a crescent-shaped golden mark on its brow. In classical times it was sacred to Aphrodite, the goddess of love, either because it is itself hermaphrodite or because of its beauty.

The excellence of this species and its ability to thrive in waters less salty than the open sea have made it a strong candidate for fish 'farming', and this is now being practised in, for example, Greece. Fish bred in this way sometimes exhibit small deviations from the norm in things like scale counts, and are held by some to have a flavour and texture which compare unfavourably with those taken from the wild. However, there would seem to be no reason why, in 'farms' where space is ample and general conditions optimal, fish of the highest quality should not be produced.

The flesh of a gilt-head makes fine neat fillets, but the fish are often cooked whole, after being cleaned, since their size and relatively narrow bodies lend themselves to this very well. *Dorada a la sal* (the cleaned but otherwise whole fish is cooked in a thick 'jacket' of sea salt—and when the jacket is broken the skin peels off with it, leaving the succulent flesh exposed) is a well-known dish of Andalusia in Spain.

GINGER the name of the plant *Zingiber officinale*, and of its rhizomes. These are mainly consumed in the fresh ('green') state in the countries where they grow, but are also dried to provide an important spice; preserved with sugar to constitute a

sweetmeat; and processed to yield an oil used for flavouring.

The ginger plant is unknown in the wild state, but is thought to have originated in SE Asia. It has been cultivated since ancient times, and was among the most highly prized of the eastern imports to the Roman Empire. However, Romans used it relatively little in cookery, prizing it rather for medicinal purposes.

The fall of the Roman Empire did not stop the trade of ginger to Europe. It was in use in England in Anglo-Saxon times; and in later medieval times it was almost as common in England as pepper. By that time it was also being imported in preserved form for use as a sweetmeat. The history of GINGERBREAD goes back to the same period.

India produces about half the world output of ginger. Other important producers include Jamaica (whose dried ginger, pale and of delicate flavour, is highly esteemed), China, Taiwan, Thailand, and Nigeria. In recent times Australia too has developed production, specializing in preserved ginger.

The degree of pungency (caused by certain non-volatile compounds called gingerols) and the aroma and flavour of ginger vary according to many factors (region of origin, cultivar, conditions in which grown, stage at which harvested).

Fresh ginger and dried ginger differ noticeably in their flavouring effects. Both are used in Asian kitchens, but with the emphasis on fresh (sliced to the thickness of a coin), whereas in western countries it is more usual to find the dried, commonly in powdered form. European cookery in medieval times, at least in well-to-do households, made free use of ginger in all sorts of dishes, but by the 18th century use had become more narrowly focused, on baked goods such as biscuits and cakes; it has stayed there ever since, although the growing influence of oriental cuisines in Europe has brought about a certain revival of use in savoury dishes.

In Burma, where freshwater fish are preferred to sea fish, ginger has been used to mask the marine tang of the latter; used in a fair quantity, it will mask just about anything.

Fresh young ginger is used to make a delicious and subtle ginger drink called *khing sot* in Thailand. The ginger tea of Kashmir is famous. Ginger oil is used to flavour ginger beer (alcoholic to a varying degree) and ginger ale (non-alcoholic).

Shoga, *Zingiber mioga*, is a Japanese ginger, a milder species grown in Japan, and used fresh or pickled; see MIOGA GINGER.

GINGER BISCUITS including 'ginger snaps' and gingernuts, are the British representatives of a much wider group of

European spiced biscuits, and are closely related to, indeed sometimes overlap with, GINGERBREAD.

Most recipes rely on the old method of melting TREACLE, GOLDEN SYRUP, and brown sugar with quantities of butter, before adding flour. Originally the biscuits would have been based on melted HONEY (a substance which still gives a special flavour and texture to some spiced biscuits such as LEBKUCHEN), mixed with flour and spices.

The German name for a biscuit of the same general nature is *Pfeffernüsse*; while in Scandinavia, ginger or similarly spiced biscuits, often cut into heart or star shapes and decorated with icing, have names like *pepparkaka* or *peppernott*. All such names apply generally to any of the numerous spiced sweet cakes and biscuits made in C. Europe and Scandinavia. Although a literal translation is 'pepper cake', the names do not refer directly to pepper, but rather to the 'Pfefferländer', the eastern countries from which spices came. The selection of spices used in continental Europe is much wider than in Britain, and includes cinnamon, cloves, aniseed, nutmeg, and, in Scandinavia, cardamom, as well as ginger.

See also the Dutch speciality *speculaas* under BANKETBAKKERIJ.   LM

GINGERBREAD a product which is always spiced, and normally with GINGER, but which varies considerably in shape and texture. Some modern British gingerbreads are so crisp that they might qualify to be called GINGER BISCUITS. Others are definitely cake-like.

In the recent past many British towns had their gingerbread specialities whose recipes are still known. Examples are Ashbourne (a 'white' gingerbread) and Ormskirk (a 'dark' one). Some Scottish gingerbreads resemble SHORTBREAD, e.g. the Edinburgh speciality which was known as parliament cake (or 'parlies') in the 19th century. A thin crisp gingerbread, it is made with treacle and brown sugar, cut into squares after baking; it is thought to be so called because it was eaten by the members of the Scottish Parliament.

Grasmere gingerbread, from the Lake District, also has a shortbread texture. Originally it was based on oatmeal, as were broonie, an Orkney gingerbread recorded by F. Marian McNeill, and PARKIN.

Late medieval gingerbread in England had been made from a thick mixture of honey and breadcrumbs, sometimes coloured with saffron or sanders (powdered SANDALWOOD, a spice still called for in Zurich Leckerli—see NUT BISCUITS). Cinnamon and pepper were added for flavour. Made into a square, the confection was decorated with box leaves nailed down with gilded cloves.

Gingerbread was also ornamented by impressing designs within wooden moulds. The moulds were sometimes very large and elaborate and beautifully carved. In England, such confections were bought at fairs and, together with other sweet treats, were known under the collective name of 'fairings'. The habit of shaping gingerbread figures of men and pigs, especially for Bonfire Night (5 November), survives in Britain.

In the 17th century white gingerbread became fashionable. This was an almond paste confection resembling spiced MARZIPAN. Its surface was ornamented with real or imitation gold leaf, from which comes the expression 'gilt on the gingerbread'.

Generally, during the 16th and 17th centuries, gingerbread became lighter; breadcrumbs were replaced by flour. Treacle was used instead of honey from the mid-17th century on. Butter and eggs became popular additions, enriching the mixture; and raising agents were added to lighten it further.

In France the closest equivalent to the English gingerbread is probably *pain d'épices*, associated especially with the city of Dijon. It continued to be made with honey after English gingerbread switched to treacle.
(LM)

GINKGO *Ginkgo biloba*, the sole survivor of a group of primitive trees. Such trees grew all around the world in the very distant past; the 'petrified ginkgo forest' near Ellenberg in the state of Washington is estimated to be 15 million years old. This single species was saved by cultivation in N. China and has been reintroduced to Europe and Asia as a garden tree. (Western plant nurseries usually sell only the non-fruiting male ginkgo plants, because of the highly disagreeable smell from the fallen fruits of the females.)

The fruit is round, plum sized, and brown, with scanty flesh. The nut, freed of its putrid-smelling flesh, has a smooth buff-coloured shell and a thin brownish inner skin (both to be removed) enclosing a soft pale-yellow kernel, which becomes pale

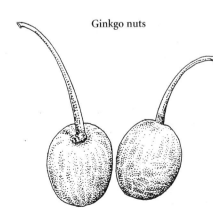

Ginkgo nuts

green on being cooked. The traditional practice in China was to leave the nuts until all the flesh had rotted away, and then roast them.

The Chinese like to eat the cooked kernels, which have a pleasant and mild flavour, as nuts. They also paint them red, the colour of happiness, and string them in festoons for wedding decorations. The nuts, after being roasted, boiled, or steamed, often appear in combination with other foods, and in sweet soups.

The Japanese, besides roasting or boiling the nuts, deep-fry them on pine-needle skewers. The nuts are also customarily added to certain dishes such as *Chawan-mushi* (savoury custards) and *Sazae-no-tsuboyaki* (turban shells, *Turbo cornutus*, baked in their own shells).

Ginkgo trees are common in Japan. Fresh nuts appear in the markets in the autumn. Canned ones, according to Tsuji (1980), are a poor substitute.

GINSENG *Panax ginseng* and other species, more a medicine than a food, grown extensively in Korea, N. China, and Japan. Its white branching roots, which sometimes resemble the trunk of a man, have to grow for five years before they are marketable, which makes it an expensive commodity. However, its reputation as an invigorating agent is such that very high prices are willingly paid for ginseng of the best quality, in various forms including a powder. Ginseng tea is drunk both for invigoration and as a pleasant beverage.

P. quinquefolius is American ginseng, less esteemed.

GIRAFFE *Giraffa camelopardalis*, an animal of Africa whose appearance is familiar to all and which is now protected by game laws, since it had been wiped out in parts of its range (by hunters who wanted giraffe hides rather than giraffe meat). Even if it would be permissible to eat giraffe, there would be little that is palatable to be had from its carcass. However, Leipoldt (1976) says that 'the long succulent tongue, properly cooked, is not only eatable but delectable'. He also anticipates any speculation that the remarkable well-developed bones of the animal would yield good marrow; they do not.

GLACE (DE VIANDE) and **DEMI-GLACE,** two French culinary terms which are less closely connected than might be supposed but which can conveniently be treated together.

Glace de viande is meat glaze, a greatly reduced meat stock which has a syrupy

consistency and can be used to impart its flavour and a shiny surface to appropriate savoury dishes, and to give additional flavour and body to sauces. References to this meat glaze at the beginning of the 19th century include Viard (1806), who describes how a veal stock which has been reduced to the consistency of a sauce can be used as a seasoning, and Beauvilliers (1814), who uses a little brush of chicken feathers to brush his meat glaze (*glace, ou consommé réduit*) over foods which will benefit from a 'glazed' appearance. Meat glazes are now rarely used, since their preparation is expensive and arduous.

Demi-glace is not a glaze of lesser or greater concentration, as one might suppose, but a sauce. To be precise, it is an ESPAGNOLE sauce to which has been added a little meat glaze. The distinction is made quite clear by Escoffier (1921), who has glace in his chapter on 'Basic Preparations' and demi-glace in his chapter on 'Basic Sauces'.

In the course of the 20th century certain French chefs 'revised' the classic demi-glace, making it in simpler fashion. However, like the espagnole, it has now virtually disappeared from French restaurant kitchens, where 'NOUVELLE CUISINE' chefs have abandoned the range of 'all-purpose sauces' in favour of a simple *jus* or buttery emulsion. No longer a 'basic sauce', the demi-glace is now considered to be a relic of an archaic form of cookery referred to respectfully as *cuisine classique* but no longer practised.
HY

GLASSE HANNAH (1708–70), probably the best-known English cookery writer of the 18th century, owed the fame which she and her principal work (*The Art of Cookery Made Plain and Easy*, 1747) acquired to a strange concatenation of factors: in part, to chance; in great part, unscrupulous plagiarism; in almost no part, to innovations in the style and organization of recipes, for which she claimed credit; and, to a small but significant extent, to her marketing abilities.

As for chance, who could have foreseen that England's greatest lexicographer, straying unwisely into a field with which he was unfamiliar and pontificating on the matter after the lapse of a quarter of a century, would have denied her authorship of her book? (It was Dr Johnson who thus erred.) And who would have supposed that the catchphrase 'First catch your hare' would have become firmly attached to her book, although the words do not occur in it?

The plagiarism was first revealed in this instance by Jennifer Stead (1983) in a pioneering essay which was the fruit of many months of patient research, and was later supplemented by further labours on the part of Priscilla Bain (1986). It emerged that 263 recipes (out of a total of 972) had been taken virtually word for word from one single earlier source, *The Whole Duty of a Woman* (1737, republished in 1740 as *The Ladies Companion*), while a further 90 or so were taken from other sources. It is commonly supposed that plagiarism in this field was near universal in the 18th century, and Jennifer Stead herself points out that the first Copyright Act of 1709 had no effect on cookery books and the like and that recipes were repeatedly copied by one author to another. However, this was not the universal pattern by any means. Some authors wrote in their own words, for example Richard Bradley (see ENGLISH COOKERY BOOKS OF THE 18TH CENTURY) and William VERRAL; others did not pretend to be doing anything more than repeating recipes already published (for example the compilation of John Nott, 1726); and there is one shining example (Mrs Mary COLE) of an author who did copy from other works but who acknowledged the source at the end of her recipes—sometimes going so far as to acknowledge two or three sources for a single recipe. Outright copying, accompanied by protestations that all the material was new and 'never before published', was not so widespread. Nor was Hannah Glasse the most culpable author, that dishonour being held by John Farley— and the female detective who exposed him, to the tune of 797 (out of 798) recipes stolen from other authors, was Fiona Lucraft (1992/3).

The innovations which Mrs Glasse claimed to be making in her book were mostly illusory. Some commentators have pointed to certain recipes in her book as examples of a new, vigorous, and direct style such as would enable the author to communicate effectively with the common herd of cooks and housewives; but most of these recipes turn out to be ones which had been composed a decade previously by the (presumably male) author of *The Whole Duty of a Woman*. Mrs Glasse professes to banish French extravagances and kitchen tricks, but then includes some recipes which exemplify the very faults she denounces.

Despite all this, there is something about her book which does represent a sort of hesitant advance in the direction of producing a popular cookery book which would be more accessible than earlier works. Certainly, some part of its success must have been due to a generally favourable reaction on the part of the public. But her vigorous marketing may have been just as important in this respect; it seems to have been a real innovation that she arranged for her book to be sold at Mrs Ashburn's china-shop at the corner of Fleet-Ditch (in London).

Hannah Glasse's life seems to have been largely an unhappy one; she was born illegitimate, married the wrong man, was declared bankrupt only seven years after her main book was published (and thus lost all control over it), and tragically lost six children in infancy out of 11 live births and one other (lost at sea) later on. But one thing stands out and that is a certain indomitable spirit which caused her to try a series of commercial ventures to prop up her financial position (one of these was her book, another was the production and marketing of patent medicine, and the last was setting up a 'habit warehouse' or clothes shop in fashionable Tavistock Street). Also, she wrote two later books, *The Compleat Confectioner* and *The Servant's Directory*. The former, as Fiona Lucraft (1997–8) has demonstrated, showed her pursuing her practice of plagiarism. On this occasion the principal victim was Edward Lambert, whose modest book on the same subject, published in 1744, was purloined almost in its entirety.

GLAZE as a verb and in the kitchen, means to give food a smooth, shiny, often transparent finish.

This can be achieved in various ways, one of which is to apply a coating of something which has these qualities, for example ASPIC, often used over fish.

Other examples of cold glazes are coating a cake with a suitable jam such as apricot; or applying a fruit syrup glaze (made by reducing the syrup in which fruit has been poached and then thickening with arrowroot) to, say, a cooked pastry shell.

Many kinds of glaze require heat to be effective. Thus, if vegetables are cooked with butter and sugar they will emerge with a shiny finish. Loaves of bread or buns may be coated with beaten egg or milk, or the like, before being baked; and the process of baking turns the coating into a glaze (using white of egg alone gives a clear glaze, whole egg gives medium brown, and yolk alone a rich brown). Similarly, if a dessert has sugar sprinkled on it and is then put briefly under a hot grill, it will acquire a shiny glaze, which will be brown underneath a transparent surface.

In the Orient, some other forms of glaze are used. When the Japanese cook things in teriyaki style (*teri* meaning gloss, see JAPANESE CULINARY TERMS) they use a sweet glaze based on SOY SAUCE. See PEKING DUCK for an example of Chinese glazing, using maltose.

Meat glaze is a special case. It is made by prolonged reduction of a meat stock, resulting in a syrupy liquid. See GLACE (DE VIANDE).

GLIKO or *glyko*, the Greek name for a preserve of fruit in syrup, to be served with a spoon. In Greece, Cyprus, Turkey, and the Balkan region this is the standard offering to a newly arrived guest or to a traveller needing refreshment. Patience Gray (1986) evokes a typical scene:

[*Gliko*] often greets the traveller after a laborious journey on foot across the mountains, served with ice-cold water from the village fountain and sometimes followed by a dose of *raki*, a powerful spirit distilled from pressed grapeskins, akin to *marc* or *grappa*.

The *glikó* is presented on a saucer with a spoon and is consumed under a fig tree in the courtyard. The lady of the house provides you with a rush-seated chair to sit on, and another on which to rest your legs. She sprinkles the courtyard floor with water from a water jar to lay the dust and cool the air, and presents you with a sprig of basil and a glass of spring water while you despatch the *glikó*.

There are many different kinds of *gliko*, for example made with muscat grapes, immature green walnuts, bitter oranges (or any citrus fruits picked when they are still small and green), small unripe figs, and sour or sweet cherries. Perhaps the best of all is made with, not fruits, but lemon blossom or acacia—just the petals, shaken from the tree. Rosemary Barron (1991) recommends also the blossoms of grapefruit, jasmine, honeysuckle, and rose; and suggests as well the prickly pear fruits which are so common in the E. Mediterranean region.

A *gliko* may also be prepared with almonds, and small vegetables like cherry tomatoes, baby carrots, and tiny aubergines (eggplants).

Terms such as *slatko* (Macedonian, Serbo-Croat) and *sladko* (Bulgarian) refer to the same sort of preserve.

GLOUCESTER CHEESE named after the English county where it has been made for three centuries or more, is made in two forms, single Gloucester and double Gloucester. The difference between them is mainly one of thickness. Both are 41 cm (16") in diameter, but while double is 10 to 12 cm (4 to 5") thick, Single is just over half as thick. A double Gloucester weighs around 11 kg (24 lb). It is always coloured red with ANNATTO; Single is usually uncoloured. The process by which either kind of Gloucester is made is similar to that for CHEDDAR, but with less severe pressing, so that it remains lighter, moister, and crumblier. It keeps well and after six months maturing has a mild, nutty flavour.

GLUCOSE as a scientific term, is a synonym of dextrose, the name of a simple sugar or monosaccharide which forms part of other, complex sugars and also of starch; see SUGAR. Glucose is the form in which the human body uses sugar; and the digestion of other, more complex, sugars, and of starch and other carbohydrates, is a process of reducing them to glucose. The sugar in the bloodstream, which forms a store of quickly available energy, is glucose.

A Russian chemist, Kirchoff, published a paper in 1811 which described his discovery that starch, treated with mineral acid, yields a sugary substance. A few years later a French chemist, de Saussure, showed that the reaction was hydrolytic and that the end result was glucose. This happened at a time when, because of the English blockade of France during the Napoleonic wars, rich rewards were available to anyone who could produce sugar in Europe from indigenous plant resources. The factories which produced 'starch sugar' in France ceased work when the blockade was lifted and cane sugar became available again; but production of glucose continued in Germany and was established in the USA later in the century. The glucose industry has become a substantial one.

However, most of the 'glucose' produced industrially does not correspond to the scientific use of the term. As explained under CORN SYRUP, the name 'glucose' is commonly applied to a syrup (produced from maize starch) which is by no means pure glucose, but contains an appreciable amount of dextrin.

Refined 'glucose powder', close to being pure glucose, is sold as a dietary supplement. It is useful for invalids because glucose requires no digestion, but goes straight into the bloodstream; and it is also less sweet than ordinary sugar. Pure glucose drinks may be used as a source of instant energy.

GLUTEN a substance found in WHEAT, which gives BREAD its texture. It consists of two PROTEINS, glutenin and gliadin. Wheat also contains two other proteins, albumin and globulin, which are soluble in water and dissolve when the flour is wetted.

The molecules of glutenin are in the form of long chains, those of gliadin shorter. When dough is kneaded, the long glutenin molecules are pulled out straight. The shorter gliadin molecules make links across the strands, so that the gluten forms an elastic network. The change in texture as this happens can be felt. When the bread is baked the gluten coagulates and becomes firm, giving the distinctive fibrous structure of bread.

Several minutes' kneading are required to 'develop' or draw out the strands of gluten; but excessive kneading must be avoided because it would overstretch and break the strands, so that the dough would lose its springiness. Adding fat to dough lubricates the strands of gluten so that they slip and do not become fully stretched. This gives a softer, 'cakey' texture. In making pastry it is important to knead as little as possible, to avoid developing the gluten. Leaving raw pastry to 'relax' allows any stretched strands to return to their original shape.

Different types of wheat contain differing amounts of gluten. The largest amounts are found in the durum wheat used to make PASTA; it requires long kneading to achieve the required springy texture. The 'hard' wheat used for bread flour contains smaller but still substantial amounts. 'Soft' wheat contains the least, and is therefore used for cake flour.

Other cereals do not contain gluten, though they do have other proteins. That is why RYE, BARLEY or MAIZE bread never has the texture characteristic of wheaten bread.
RH

GNETUM an Asian genus of tropical trees, none of which has an English name. The trees are elegant, usually small, and they bear bunches of small fruits; these are dark red when ripe, with seeds whose edible kernels constitute nuts and which have local importance as food in various parts of SE Asia. Other parts eaten include the leaves and flowers.

The most prominent species is *G. gnemon*, grown and used to some extent in Malaysia, Indonesia, and the Philippines. In Java, the nuts are 'abundantly sold either fresh or prepared by boiling, or better still by removing the outer coat, roasting in an iron pan, husking, moulding into cakes by beating and subsequently drying' (Burkill, 1965–6). The dried cakes, known as *emping*, are fried in coconut oil before being eaten.

GNOCCHI essentially a kind of DUMPLING, are distinguished from other dumplings by being Italian and having a close link with PASTA. They are made either from a pasta dough or from a mixture of POTATO flour and WHEAT flour, or from SEMOLINA or MAIZE (POLENTA). In form they are about the size of a thimble and are usually given a special shape by rolling the dough against a fork or the back of a grater, or forcing it through a wicker sieve, or in other ways. An illustration to the 16th-century macaronic poem 'Baldus' shows the Muses eating gnocchi the size of northern dumplings; but this may be a joke. Some of the numerous local varieties of gnocchi are described below.

The origin of gnocchi is inescapably tied up with that of pasta, partly because at first a similar mixture was used to make both, and partly because many old works called both 'm'caroni'. (The confusion persists in modern Padua.) It has been suggested that the macaroni mentioned in the *Decameron* (1351) as being rolled down a mountain of grated Parmesan by the inhabitants of the mythical land of Bengodi were actually gnocchi or they would not have rolled. The original flour and water mixture for gnocchi is still used in some parts of Italy, but mostly they are now made of potato flour with a little wheat flour. This usage dates only from about 1860, but the curious Mantuan gnocchi made from PUMPKIN are two or three centuries older than that.

Gnocchi are boiled and served with a sauce in more or less the same manner as pasta. They may be bought ready made, or made at home. The dough is formed into small balls and given a special shape or pattern in one of the ways referred to above. Miniature gnocchi for putting into soup can be made by pressing the dough through a coarse sieve or a perforated spoon. Since potato gnocchi were introduced in the 1860s they have become the dominant type; but in Genoa *trofie* (made by rolling a strip of dough around a stick) and *corzetti* (moulded by hand into a figure of eight shape) are made from pasta dough. *Trofie* are an alternative to *trenette* (thick pasta of a roughly square cross-section) for serving with the famous PESTO sauce.

Also made from pasta dough are the *strangulapreti* ('priest chokers') of Lucano. The idea of priests choking on gnocchi seems to be a favoured one: there are also *strozzapreti*, made with spinach dough, in Tuscany; and *strangulaprievete*, made from a conventional potato mixture, in Naples. In Mantua *gnocchi di zucca* are made from pumpkin with a little wheat flour to help the dough to bind. They are of an attractive golden colour, and are usually served plain with a little butter and cheese.

Other gnocchi include the Roman home-made kind, made from a boiled potato farina and egg mixture and cut into flat rounds with a glass; and the Sicilian *malloreddus*, made from a very plain flour and water dough and pressed with the thumb against a textured surface so that when cooked they curl up into the form of giant woodlice.

GOA although now part of INDIA, was a Portuguese possession—and the gateway to Portugal's empire in the East—for 450 years. During this long period its culture was an interesting mixture of Latin influences with those of the Hindus and Muslims who represented the indigenous population. This whole mixture was overlaid for a long time by the importance of the East–West trade conducted through Goa, an importance quite disproportionate to the small size of the territory.

All this was reflected in Goan foodways, which presented an interesting blend of

Portuguese and Indian cookery. The best-known example is probably VINDALOO, originally a pork stew imported from Portugal but 'Indianized' by the addition of various spices. However, there are many other hybrid dishes. The local sausages are *chouricos*. Fish dishes (of which there are many (Goa being essentially a strip of coastline) include *Quisade de peixe*. This is another name modelled on the Portuguese, but the fish (probably POMFRET, unknown in Portugal) is dressed with an oriental spice paste before being fried. Small coconut cakes are called *Bolinhos de coco* (after the Portuguese *bolo*, a cake). Coconut, which is almost ubiquitous in the Goan kitchen, appears again, with cashew, jaggery, and cardamom, in special Goan pancakes, *alebele*. And all accounts of Goan food mention *bebinca*, an extraordinary cake made for Christmas, consisting of five or more layers of coconut-milk pancakes, although without attempting to explain what relationship, if any, they have with the *bibingka* which is one of the RICE CAKES OF THE PHILIPPINES.

GOAT meat is taken from the adults of the species *Capra hircus*, closely related to sheep. Adapted to mountain habitats, goats are sure-footed, able to climb steep cliffs to find food, surviving on tree bark and thorny scrub—browsing habits which often destroy shrubs and trees. They complement SHEEP, which prefer grass, and the two animals are often herded together in lands around the Mediterranean and throughout the Middle East and C. Asia. In this area, goat meat and MUTTON are used interchangeably in cookery, as available.

The term 'wild goat' may refer either to a feral specimen of *C. hircus* (protected in many places) or to members of several other related species. These include the ibex (*C. ibex*), ranging from the Iberian peninsula to N. Africa, the Caucasus and C. Asia); the chamois (*Rupicapra rupicapra*), ranging from the Pyrenees through the Alps and Apennines to Asia Minor; and the mountain goat (*Oreamnos americanus*) of W. Canada and the western USA. All these have been hunted for food, but have a strong gamy taste.

Whilst goats are farmed in Europe (including Britain) they are of minority interest, and are principally used for milk, and milk products such as cheese and yoghurt, in this area. They are not native to the Americas, but have been imported by European settlers, and are farmed in Latin America, where they are well adapted to poor land in Mexico and the Andes.

Kid is the English name for the young of the species, which is more commonly eaten, and has tender, mildly flavoured flesh. (As

with mutton, our ancestors would probably have preferred an older animal. The author of MENAGIER DE PARIS (14th century) said, 'the meat of a spayed goat of six or seven years is reckoned the best; being generally very sweet and fat. This makes an excellent pasty.')

Goats were probably domesticated at about the same time, and in the same region, as sheep; that is, in SW Asia during the 8th millennium BC. Studies of the relative importance of goat and sheep bones at various sites indicate that the goat may initially have been more important as a meat animal. Their remains have been found at neolithic sites in China, and both goat and mutton were eaten in the ancient kingdom of Sumer (Iraq). In India, the Rig-veda mentions goat and sheep as food, and there is also evidence of these animals being eaten by Indus Valley civilizations. JEWISH DIETARY LAWS refer to them: 'thou shalt not boil a kid in its mother's milk.'

Goats probably came to Britain in the neolithic, and have been present ever since, but were never as important as cattle, sheep, and pigs. In medieval and early modern Britain, goats were kept on steep, scrubby land and used for meat, which was roasted, stewed, or made into pasties and pies up until the start of the 17th century, when it went out of fashion. Another use for goat was to make 'hams' of the haunches by salting and drying. Such hams came to be known in Wales as 'hung venison'. In the 18th century, goats were either looked on as 'the poor man's cow' or viewed, like deer, as game; feral goats (still to be found in most upland areas of Britain) were hunted and cooked like venison.

In contemporary Britain, goat meat finds favour with immigrants from Jamaica, where curried goat, cooked with onions, curry powder, and chillies, is a national festive dish. Two separate cultures are probably responsible for the presence of this exotic item on the Jamaican menu. These are the Spanish who were responsible for introducing goats to the New World in the first place; and secondly, influence from E. Asian indentured workers, present on the island from 1842 onwards. Apart from this, goat is little used in Jamaica, although other Caribbean islands, notably the French Antilles, have developed several recipes.

Roast kid is a festive dish in Mediterranean countries, spit-roast kid being found throughout the Balkans and the Middle East. In this region and in C. Asia goat or kid meat can be used in any recipe for lamb or mutton, although there are relatively few specific recipes for cooking it. Portugal is something of an exception; *Cabrito assado* (roast kid, preferably an animal about one month old) is popular over much of the country, and there are

other favourite recipes including *Chanfana*, a goat stew prepared for festive occasions.

Among Asian countries the Philippines stand out as the home of many interesting goat dishes. There are many goat restaurants in Manila, mostly offering *Caldereta* (derived from a Spanish stew for lamb or kid), a tamarind-flavoured soup similar to SINIGANG, and other specialities such as the various forms of KINILAW which incorporate goat meat and are often known as *kilawen* or *kilawin*. These last items are especially interesting in their Ilocano (of the Ilocos Islands) versions, flavoured with a fresh bitterness provided by bile or partly digested grass from the innards of ruminant animals.

GOAT'S MILK CHEESES are made in every country where there are significant numbers of goats; but they are almost always made on a small, local scale and few are exported.

The most diverse selection is that to be found in France, whence a few varieties are sent abroad. A *plateau de fromages de chèvre* (tray of goat's milk cheeses) may offer types ranging in size from barely larger than a walnut, as with **broccio** from Corsica or **rigottes** from the Rhône valley, to the weight of a Camembert or more.

Flavour ranges from mild and fresh, as in **Saint-Claude** from the Jura and numerous minor local varieties, to exceedingly pungent and perhaps even blue, as in the ancient and probably extinct **Tignard** from Savoie. Shapes may be round, as in the small **crottin** ('dropping') **de Chavignol**; pyramidal, as in **Livroux** and **Valencay** from the Indre; or long and cylindrical, as in **Chabichou** from Poitou or **Saint-Maure** from the Indre-et-Loire, which is stiffened by a straw passed through it from end to end. Nearly all are soft varieties. Some are covered in leaves or grape marc (debris from wine-making); most are ripened by surface moulds.

Local goat cheeses may be spotted in Italy by the generic name *caprino*; in Germany *Ziegenkäse*; and in Switzerland *Gaiskäsli*. Goat cheese is always dead white, with none of the yellow tinge that comes from the carotene pigments in cow's and sheep's milk.

GOBSTOPPER the vulgar British term for a huge, spherical, hard-boiled sugar sweet, impossible to crunch up so that it has to be sucked. It is often made with concentric layers of different colours, so that it changes colour as it dissolves. It is really a giant COMFIT or DRAGÉE.

GOBY any of numerous small fish of the family Gobiidae, whose diminutive representatives are found all round the world, in inshore waters, tidal pools, estuaries, etc. They are mostly of blotchy coloration and can change patterns and shades to accord with their surroundings, a factor which has helped to make them in terms of survival a highly successful family.

In the Mediterranean and adjacent waters of the Atlantic there are about 50 species, of which a few attain a size which makes them worth eating. An example is *Gobius niger*, the black goby, which may be 15 cm (6") long and which is not uncommon in the markets of Italy and Turkey; and another is *G. cobitis*, larger still. Discrimination among and appreciation of gobies is greater in Turkey than in any other European country.

The Indo-Pacific species include one which is, by goby standards, a giant: *Glossogobius juris*, maximum length 50 cm (20"), known in Malaysia as *ikan ubi* (meaning 'potato fish') and of interest as food to Filipinos (who in this respect may be counted as the Turks of the Pacific) and others.

However, a relatively large size is not a necessary condition for edibility in this family. The French name *nonnat* applies to the tiny 'transparent goby', which even in adult life does not exceed 5 cm (2") in length. 'Transparent' is not quite the right word ('colourless' would be better), but gives the right idea. These little fish are often associated with POUTINE, and are used in similar ways by people in Provence. Although their range extends from the Black Sea to Norway, they seem to be unmolested by human beings in most of the countries in whose waters they lurk.

GOLD AND SILVER LEAF are both used to decorate foods, and have been so used for many centuries. Surprisingly, both are harmless as long as they are consumed as pure metals, though many silver compounds are poisonous. They are on the EC list of approved colourings, having the numbers E175 and E174. Usually they are applied in the form of very thin sheets known as gold or silver leaf. Narrow ribbons and powder are also sold. All are tasteless and odourless.

Gold leaf is made by rolling the gold into a foil, placing it between skins of vellum or intestines until a multi-layered sandwich is formed, and then hammering it until the gold is seen to exude from the edges. The gold is then quartered and the process is repeated until the leaf has attained the desired thinness, which is very very thin indeed. It is often sold in books of 25 leaves, separated by thin tissue. Released from the book it is a most wayward material and the handling of small pieces demands care. In *An Ordinance of Pottage*, an edition of the 15th-century culinary recipes in the Beinecke MS 163, there is a recipe (138) in which a sweet pie is ornamented with blanched

Gobius niger

walnuts, wetted with saffron water, and impaled on a pin or needle for ease in handling. The needle is held in one hand and gold foil is laid on

with that othir hond with a thyng made therfore, & blow theron esyly with thy mouth, & that shall make thy gold to abyde. & and so thu may gylt them over, and florich thy bakyn meat therewith.

This is a precise description of how to use gold leaf, for if it is touched before it is fixed it will cling to the fingers and cannot be removed intact. The 'thyng made therfore' was possibly a fine brush made of a single line of hairs—a gilder's tip. The gentle breath upon the gold flattens it into place. One way of gilding gingerbread was to paint it with egg white when hot and dab on the gold.

Axioms and quotations warn us that appearances can be deceptive and all that glisters or shyneth is not gold, and the enticing gold of gingerbread on sale at fairs could not have been genuine for the high price would have ensured a restricted sale. It would often have been Dutch metal, an alloy of copper and zinc in proportions of about 80 : 20.

Elizabeth RAFFALD (1782) describes her Gilded Fish in Jelly. She used clear 'Blomange' to fill two fish moulds, turned them out and gilded them with gold leaf, laid them in a soup dish and filled it with clear thin calf's foot jelly; 'it must be so thin as they will swim in it'. (See drawing on p. 322.)

An easy way of applying gold is to use Danziger Goldwasser, a brandy-based liqueur which contains small flakes of gold leaf. A receipt for a similar drink is given by E. Smith (1734) where it is called 'The Golden Cordial' and is a blend of brandy, alkermes, oil of cloves, sugar, spirit of saffron, and leaf gold—two leaves to every bottle. Soyer (1847) used Goldwasser in the form of jelly cubes to add sparkle to his 'Peacock à la Louis Quatorze'.

Silver leaf is used in India (under the name *vark* or *varaq*) to decorate various foods, especially in MOGHUL CUISINE. It is

made by heating and beating silver until it resembles a sort of floss, of which a very thin layer is then compressed between two sheets of paper. Scraps of silver (or gold) leaf may sometimes be seen at Indian and Pakistani weddings, tossed casually on heaps of rice or wrapped around cakes. The brightly coloured condensed milk confections in Indian sweet shops are not usually covered with real silver, which would be too costly; aluminium is used to give the effect.   RSh

GOLDEN NEEDLES the long, thin, dried buds or withered blooms of *Hemerocallis fulva*, a lily which grows abundantly in N. China and has become naturalized (indeed grows as a weed) in N. America, where it is known as the tawny day-lily. The flower blooms only for one day. It develops from a long thin bud, and withers to a long thin shape again.

The buds (fresh or dried) and flowers, as well as the withered blooms, are used in cookery, especially in Chinese stir-fried and steamed dishes, and are appreciated for their delicate flavour and interesting texture. The flowers can be incorporated in omelettes.

The dried products are soaked before use. Knotting them in the middle prevents them from unfurling when cooked.

Other lilies furnish buds which can be similarly used, e.g. those of *H. aurantaca* in Korea.

GOLDEN SYRUP best known in Britain but also a standard item of the larder in some other countries which have been under British rule or influence, is a pale syrup which is a by-product of SUGAR refining. The term first appeared in the mid-19th century, when it applied to the thick sticky liquid obtained as a by-product of boiling down sugar-cane syrup to produce sugar; see also TREACLE, but bearing in mind the observation by Stobart (1980) that 'the world of treacles and syrups is one where there is almost total confusion in older books'. The same author states that the colour and taste of the product are provided by impurities deliberately left in it. He gives the basic analysis as 24% glucose, 23% fructose and 33% sucrose, with 'small amounts of inorganic compounds of calcium, iron, and phosphoric acid. The high sugar content makes it impossible for any spoilage organisms to grow.'

Golden syrup is used as a sweetening ingredient in, for example, biscuits and cakes, but its most popular use may be as a topping for pancakes, porridge, and various puddings (for example suet or sponge pudding) and desserts.

Comparable products in N. America are CORN SYRUP and MAPLE SYRUP.

GOOD KING HENRY *Chenopodium bonus-henricus*, otherwise known as allgood, a plant of the family Chenopodiaceae, whose members include also QUINOA, EPAZOTE, and several kinds of GOOSEFOOT. It is found widely in the temperate zones of Eurasia and serves mainly as a potherb, although the flower clusters are eaten and young shoots can be prepared like ASPARAGUS.

The English name comes from the German one, which had a complicated origin involving another, related but toxic, plant which was called *böser Heinrich* (bad Henry) and from which the good plant had to be distinguished. The 'King' in the English name is an interpolation made in England. Names such as Allgut come from the Latin *tota bona* of the early herbalists, but it is not clear why they gave such a flattering name to a plant which is of no great culinary or medical distinction.

Colonies of the plant, sometimes referred to as wild spinach, may be found on medieval sites in England and Wales. Its cultivation was still being carried on in some parts of Europe in the 19th century. Couplan (1983) records that it was traditionally eaten in spring and at the beginning of the summer in the Haut-Pays Niçois (inland from Nice), where its local name was *sangarrigous* and it was used in green GNOCCHI.

GOOSE a female bird whose male is a gander and whose young are goslings. In its wild form the goose (or rather geese, since the birds of several genera answer to this name) belongs to Europe, N. Africa, and C. Asia. The species to which the common domesticated goose belongs, by descent, is *Anser anser*, the greylag goose, still common in Europe as a wild bird.

Domestication took place late, since geese take 30 days to hatch their young and more to rear them, and that was too long for nomads. However, there are records of domesticated geese in ancient Egypt, and

wall-paintings show them being crammed to enlarge their livers. They were well established by classical times, witness the well-known story of how their cackling saved the Capitol at Rome from a surprise attack in the 4th century BC. Despite this good turn, and the fact that the goose was already sacred to the goddess Juno, the Romans ate them; Pliny observed in the 2nd century AD that the goose was chiefly prized for its liver, alluded to the practice of cramming, and remarked that soaking the liver in honey and milk made it even larger. Roman breeding of geese produced a relatively small, white bird; and the Romans exported this to the areas which they conquered. Such geese are still to be seen in the Balkans and C. Europe. In France, however, the Gauls needed no encouragement from the Romans; they were already producing plump geese, fed on barley or millet gruel. It may well be that it is the French who can claim the longest and most faithful devotion to the goose; and it is they who have become the acknowledged (although not the only) experts in producing FOIE GRAS.

As one would expect, the famous gastronomic raconteur Dumas (1873) relates the Roman anecdote mentioned above. But he also gives less familiar, and even more remarkable, tales to illustrate the bird's prudence and intelligence. Dumas quotes the 16th-century Italian-born French scholar Jules César Scaliger as saying that: 'Geese lower their heads in order to pass under a bridge, no matter how high its arches are.' Also, and even stranger:

They have so much foresight that when they pass over Mount Taurus, which abounds in eagles, each goose will take a stone in its beak. Knowing what chatterboxes they are, they ensure, by thus constraining themselves, that they will not emit the sounds which would cause their enemies to discover them.

The goose had a special importance in the Middle Ages because its feathers were needed for arrows. It also provided other useful things, including quills for pens; and its fat was especially prized. Dorothy Hartley (1954) points out that it has always been called goose grease in the countryside because it is the softest fat in its category, liquid at 44 °C/111 °F (compared with duck fat, melting at 52 °C/126 °F—which explains why a roast duck 'needs a quick strong heat "to start it", compared with goose'). By way of preface to a list of its numerous roles in a farmhouse, she observes that:

Goose grease is always treasured by country people as very useful. Well beaten to a cream, with vinegar, lemon juice, finely chopped onion and chopped parsley, it is used as a filling for sandwiches. It is more appetising than it sounds, having the creamy white consistency of thick

mayonnaise. Where the more sturdy Teuton element has remained in Britain, it is eaten on bread, seasoned only with salt and pepper.

These tales are capped by the observation of a French chemist, who, according to Dumas, 'saw a goose turning a spit on which a turkey was roasting. She was holding the end of the spit in her beak; and by sticking out and pulling back her neck, produced the same effect as the use of an arm. All she needed was to be given a drink from time to time.'

There used to be in England an established pattern whereby geese were fattened and eaten twice a year, at Michaelmas when they were plump from eating stubble, and as 'green' geese around Whitsuntide. The goose has also been a favourite bird for the Christmas table, whether roasted whole or prepared in pies in advance.

The goose has a special place in the gastronomic calendars of other European countries, where the traditions associated with it as a table bird are numerous. Geese also provide some famous oriental dishes, e.g. the marinated and roasted goose of Shantou in the north-east of Guangdong province in China.

GOOSEBERRY the fruit of bushes of several species of the genus *Ribes*, of which *R. grossularia*, the European gooseberry, is the principal cultivated species. Gooseberry bushes grow wild in most of the northern temperate zone, flourishing in cool, moist, or high regions where many other fruiting plants do not thrive.

Most wild species are thorny. The berries are 12 mm (0.5") or more in diameter, dark or pale green (the latter often called 'white'), yellow, or red, with firm skins which may be either hairy or smooth. The flavour is often sour.

Gooseberries were late to be taken into cultivation. The earliest record is said to be a fruiterer's bill from the court of the English King Edward I, dated 1276, for gooseberry bushes imported from France. However, the fruit has never been widely popular in France. It is traditionally used in northern parts of the country to make a sauce for fish, which explains its French name *groseille maquereau* (mackerel currant). As for the English name, Johnson (1847) has a theory:

Dr Martyun considers the name was applied to this fruit, in consequence of its being employed as sauce for that bird. It is somewhat unfortunate for this derivation that it has never been so used. It seems to me most probably to be a corruption of the Dutch name Kruisbes, or Gruisbes, derived from Kruis, the Cross, and Bes, as Berry, because the fruit was ready for use just after the Festival of the Invention of the Holy Cross; just as Kruis-haring, in Dutch, is a herring, caught after the same festival.

The *OED*, however, adheres to the derivation from goose, in favour of which it may be said that the sharpness of the gooseberry goes well with a fatty or oily meat (e.g. goose or mackerel). Dallas (1877) in *Kettner's Book of the Table* observes that the older herbalists always insisted that gooseberry was so called because it was used as a sauce for goose. He concedes however that there could be an alternative derivation linked with the Scottish name for the berry, groset or grosart, and continues:

The Scotch, it must be remembered are great in gooseberries. It is a northern fruit. When there was not a tree nor a shrub to be found in the Shetland islands and the Orkneys, there were goosberry bushes in abundance; and it was an old joke against the Shetlanders, that when they read their Bibles and tried to picture to themselves Adam hiding among the trees of the garden, they could only call up in vision a naked man cowering under a grosart bush. The gooseberries of Scotland are the perfection of their race, and for flavour and variety far beyond those of the south—just as English gooseberries are better than those of the Continent. On the Continent they are little prized, and not very well known. The French have no name for them, distinct from that of red currants.

It was in England that the popularity of the gooseberry led to improved, larger and sweeter varieties being bred. A distinction was made between dessert gooseberries, for eating raw, and cooking gooseberries, which are sour but have a superior flavour when cooked. From the late 18th century and throughout the 19th amateur 'gooseberry clubs' were set up in the Midlands and the north of England. These held competitions for the best-flavoured and, more particularly, for the largest fruit. Johnson (1847) points out that extraordinary results were achieved, especially in the vicinity of Manchester, by 'the lowest and most illiterate members of society, [who] by continual experience and perseverance in growing and raising new sorts, have brought the fruit to weigh three times as much as before and that, too, under the greatest disadvantages, not having the privilege of soil, manure, situation, &c. like the gardeners of their more wealthy neighbours'.

A few similar clubs existed in N. America. In England, in the 1980s, fewer than 10 such clubs survived, mostly in Cheshire. But the best known is the Egton Bridge Old Gooseberry Society, in Yorkshire. This was founded around 1800, and has held annual competitions (except for one or two years in the First World War) ever since. The sole criterion is weight. A new Egton Bridge record was established in 1985 when the champion berry, of the yellow variety Woodpecker, weighed 30 drams 22 grains (1.925 oz); but the world record (58 g/2.06 oz) was still held at that time by a Woodpecker shown at Marton in Cheshire

in 1978. Giant gooseberries are produced by removing all the growing berries but one from a plant.

In 1905 a mildew disease was accidentally introduced from America, wiping out the whole crop of European gooseberries. The plant was re-established by crossing with American species resistant to mildew, but the gooseberry has never fully regained its earlier popularity.

'Gooseberry' is a long-standing British slang term for an unwanted third person at a lovers' meeting; and of disparagement generally. But a good, ripe gooseberry can stand comparison with most other soft fruits. Gooseberry FOOL, a frothy purée with whipped cream, and gooseberry TANSY, a rich, firm dessert with eggs and butter, are renowned.

The eating quality of gooseberries cannot be predicted from their colour or hairiness. Some thornless varieties of the plant have been developed, for ease of picking.

In N. America gooseberries were eaten by Indian tribes throughout the wide area where they grew. There are many species, much like those of the Old World. One of the best is *Ribes divaricatum*, a cultivar of which is known as the Worcesterberry; with small, very dark, almost black berries. Another wild species, which is now also cultivated, is *R. cynosbati*, which produces berries suitable for pies, jellies, and preserves.

In Asia, especially Siberia and the Himalayas, wild gooseberries are gathered for local consumption, but not cultivated.

The 'Chinese gooseberry', described under KIWI FRUIT, and CAPE GOOSEBERRY are fruits of different kinds.

GOOSEFOOT the common name of plants of the genus *Chenopodium*. Both the English and the generic name were bestowed because the plants have leaves shaped like a goose's foot. These plants resemble and are related to SPINACH, and were in common use in Europe as green vegetables before spinach, which arrived from the east during the Middle Ages, superseded them. They are now little used, and rarely cultivated. One exception is QUINOA, a S. American species grown for its seeds. Common goosefoots whose leaves are eaten are described under GOOD KING HENRY, FAT HEN, and ORACH.

Most goosefoots are available all the year round, and their somewhat bitter taste can be dispelled by cooking the leaves in one or two changes of water, after which the flavour is mild and spinach-like.

GOOSE-NECKED BARNACLE *Mitella* (formerly *Pollicipes*) *cornucopia*, best known under its Spanish name, *percebes*, is a marine

delicacy which is unknown in many countries but appreciated with enormous enthusiasm in others. It is a CRUSTACEAN (not a MOLLUSC, as one might think at first glance), but very different from creatures like crabs and prawns. Its classification as a crustacean was belated, since its internal structure was for long not understood. It is indeed puzzling; Huxley (1877) described the barnacle (not just this one but any) as 'lying on its back, holding on by its head, and kicking its food into its mouth with its heels'.

This barnacle consists of what might be called a tube, as thick as a finger, with a dark parchment-like skin bearing tiny scales. On this is mounted a sort of hoof—a pair of white bony pads, from between which emerge the creature's feet.

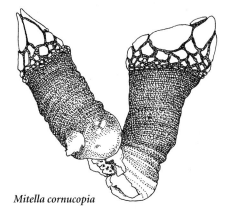

Mitella cornucopia

What one eats is, so to speak, the 'inner tube'. If the outer skin is pinched near the hoofs, it can be prised off, revealing a stalklike protuberance which is bitten off entire. *Percebes* may be eaten raw, but are usually boiled briefly before being offered in Portuguese and Spanish bars. They are particularly appreciated in the summer when they carry eggs.

The distribution of this creature extends on the coasts of the eastern central Atlantic from the Bay of Gascony down to Dakar, plus the N. African coast as far east as Algeria, but it is mainly known in Portugal and Spain.

Gathering these barnacles is a difficult and sometimes dangerous task, since they are typically attached to rocks at the foot of cliffs on rocky coasts.

More or less similar barnacles exist on other coasts, but are rarely gathered for food. The outstanding exception is *Megabalanus psittacus*, the giant barnacle of the west coast of S. America, known as *picorico* or *balanido gigante* in Chile and as *balanus* in Peru. This is a bigger creature, usually about 10 cm (4") long, but not infrequently twice that size. It is highly esteemed in Chile.

READING: Heron-Allen (1928).

GORAKA the fruit of a small tree, *Garcinia cambogia*, is used as a flavouring, thickening, and souring agent in Sri Lanka. It is related to the Malay *asam glugur* (see CARAMBOLA).

The fruits are about the size of an orange, yellow or orange in colour, and fluted on the outside. The interior is divided into segments, and it is these which are sun dried and stored. They turn black as they dry.

Chandra Dissanayake (1976) has interesting comments:

It is interesting to note that in rural homes the goraka is stored away above the open hearth with the result that it becomes quite soft and the acid improves with keeping. In the maritime provinces of Ceylon goraka is seldom ground but is soaked in salt water, crushed and added to curries. In modern homes where the open hearth is not available the tendency is to use the ground goraka as freshly dried goraka cannot be crushed. Goraka is also a thickening agent and as an acid can be used in the preparation of some meat curries. Goraka is also used in the washing of fish to remove the strong fish odour.

GORGONZOLA which it is reasonable to count as one of the three great blue cheeses of the world (the others being STILTON and ROQUEFORT), takes its name from the village of Gorgonzola near Milan, where it was first made.

It belongs to the STRACCHINO family of cheeses, which is to say that it is a whole milk, white, 'uncooked' cheese. It may properly be called *stracchino di Gorgonzola* or *stracchino verde* (green stracchino). The blue (or greenish) veins which distinguish it are produced by a *Penicillium* mould. The cheeses were traditionally ripened in cold, draughty caves near Gorgonzola for a full year. Modern methods of manufacture are quicker, but Gorgonzola remains an expensive product.

A distinction is made between young cheeses (*dolce* or *nuovo*) and older ones (*piccante* or *vecchio*). A white Gorgonzola is also available in Italy; it may be sold under the name *panerone*.

Because the veins in Gorgonzola are so often green, London's old green-marbled Stock Exchange was known as Gorgonzola Hall.

GOUDA called after the city of that name in S. Holland, is the principal Dutch cheese, accounting for over half the total production of cheese in the Netherlands. It is made from whole milk, and produced in a wheel shape with a markedly convex edge. Size and weight vary considerably; the weight is usually between 4 and 10 kg (9–22 lb).

The city of Gouda retains its Kaaswaag, the weigh-house for cheese, and

wagon-loads of cheeses are still sold there every Thursday.

A Gouda cheese has a higher fat content than EDAM, but is made in much the same way and has a similar flavour. Like Edam, it is pale yellow inside, has a smooth and elastic texture, and a mild, salty flavour which is sometimes varied by the addition of CUMIN. The manufacture of Gouda is now widespread, but the best cheeses are still those made by farmers in the vicinity of Gouda. These may be distinguished by appellations such as Boeren Gouda or plain *boerenkaas* (which just means farmer's cheese, but is usually Gouda).

A special excellence is also attained by Gouda cheeses which are allowed to mature. Some matured cheeses are encased in black wax, but others are left in their natural pale brown. The effect of ageing is to make the rind very hard and to sharpen the flavour. Gouda which has been kept for several years has a highly distinguished flavour, but is not commonly available outside the Netherlands. Young Gouda can be used in cooking, when a melting cheese is needed. Old Gouda is suitable for grating.

Stolwijksekaas is a related cheese, from Stolwijk, which has a fine reputation.

GOUFFÉ JULES (1807–77), one of the most famous French chefs of the 19th century, wrote one of the finest French cookery books.

His father Louis Gouffé was a pastry chef in Paris, whose three sons all entered the profession. At the age of 16, Jules was sufficiently accomplished to be making the presentation pieces for the window of his father's shop. One day, his constructions caught the eye of a passer-by, the famous CARÊME, who at once recruited Jules for his *brigade de cuisine*. Gouffé spent the next seven years working under Carême, learning the general art of cookery as well as that of preparing pastries. He later wrote: 'A good pastry chef can become an excellent cook, but one rarely hears of a man trained as a cook who goes on to master pastry.' He was fortunate in mastering both arts himself while so young, thus paving the way for a distinguished career as chef in important households.

Towards the end of his life Gouffé wrote a number of cookery books which were an attempt to sum up all of his own experience and make it available not only to other chefs but also to housewives. His first and most successful book was *Le Livre de cuisine* (1867), a comprehensive work which ran to nearly 900 pages and was distinguished by a number of innovations. The typographical design was clear and spacious, and the book was beautifully illustrated with nearly 200 engravings by Laplante and with colour

lithographs by Ronjat. (Mrs Beeton's great *Book of Household Management* had included such lithographs seven years previously, but Gouffé's was the first French cookery book to have them.) The content matched the presentation. Gouffé wrote in a limpid style, comprehensible by all and exhibiting a standard of literary craftsmanship which equalled the author's skill in the kitchen. This was, moreover, the first French cookery book to give metric measurements and cooking times in a systematic way. Gouffé wrote that the book was composed 'with a clock before my eyes and a scale always at hand'.

Le Livre de cuisine was divided into two parts: one on 'Grande Cuisine' and the other for more everyday preparations. It was a great success, not only in France, where many later editions were printed, but also in other countries. It was translated into several languages.

In 1869 Gouffé published *Le Livre des conserves*, followed in 1873 by *Le Livre de pâtisserie*. The three volumes together represented one large opus, treating all aspects of French cookery. All of them, and also his last publication, a small volume on soups (1875), have been reprinted in facsimile in the 20th century.

GOULASH probably the best known, outside Hungary, of Hungarian dishes, calls for a precise account. We must ask: 'What is goulash?' In Hungary, the word 'goulash' today refers to the cattle driver, the 'cowboy'. The only place on a Hungarian menu where you would find goulash (*gulyás*, as it is written in Hungarian) would be among the soups, and it would be called *gulyás leves*, meaning 'the soup of the cowboy'. What is known all over the world as 'Hungarian goulash' is called in Hungary *pörkölt* or *paprikás*. *Pörkölt* contains no sour cream. It is called *paprikás* if sour cream has been added to the *pörkölt*. Incidentally the *pörk* in *pörkölt* has nothing to do with the meat of a hog.

The dish of goulash is in fact relatively new under either of its names. Hungarian cattlemen, shepherds, and pigherders cooked cubed meat with onion and spices (with a 'short sauce', meaning a very small amount of liquid) for at least 300 to 500 years. But the dish could not be called *pörkölt* or *paprikás* because this spice, PAPRIKA, today considered the most Hungarian of all spices, is relatively new to the Hungarian cuisine. It was not known in Hungary until the 1820s when it became extremely popular and practically eliminated black PEPPER and GINGER from the average Hungarian kitchen.

Black pepper was used not only to give flavour and aroma to the food, but also as a preservative. Raw meat was rubbed and practically covered with ground pepper to keep it fresh longer. The pepper was used with salt, with sugar, or alone. When people in Hungary were experimenting with the new spice, they attempted to use paprika as a preservative and rubbed it on the raw meat. When this raw meat rubbed with paprika came in contact with the heat from the frying kettle, the paprika-covered meat formed a brown crusty surface with a pleasantly different taste resembling that of meat roasted over an open fire to the point of almost burning.

To get a piece of meat to this point is described by the Hungarian verb *pörköl*, which means to slightly burn the surface. The meat treated with paprika reaches this taste without the actual burning. That's why the new dish—the meat fried in small cubes with fat and onion—was called *pörkölt*. After beef, the same process was applied to pork, rabbit, veal, and poultry. Each one of these dishes can be called *pörkölt*.

The characteristic behaviour of the ground, dried red pepper (called paprika) during heating in high smoke-point fats (such as lard or rendered bacon fat) provided a new taste and required a new technology. Meat cubes and strips have been cooked with onions over a high heat over open fires for ages all over the world, e.g. in a Chinese wok. But the addition of paprika at the beginning of the searing of the meat, and a second time just before the dish was finished, gave an extremely appealing fragrance, a desirable deep red colour, and a taste which was pleasing to most.

In the middle of the 19th century, the new dish, *pörkölt*, became as popular as chicken, veal, or pork similarly prepared with paprika. Because these had been holiday dishes served on special occasions to guests, they spread much faster than more commonplace dishes. Because visitors from Austria, Bohemia, Poland, and Switzerland were treated as honoured guests and had been fêted with *pörkölt* or *paprikás*, those dishes found their way quickly into the cookbooks and the restaurants of the neighbouring countries.

What does all this have to do with 'goulash'? The difference between the Hungarian *pörkölt*, known all over the world except in Hungary as 'goulash', and goulash soup, is in the amount of liquid added to the meat, and whether potatoes and pasta are included. In the real Hungarian *pörkölt* or *paprikás* (in English 'goulash') there are no other ingredients except beef, pork, veal, or chicken, shortening (almost always from pork), paprika, onions, and once in a while selected herbs, spices, or condiments.

'Goulash' became so popular in N. America that many American cookery books list as an integral part of American cuisine such items as 'Hungarian goulash', 'beef goulash', 'pork goulash', and 'szekely goulash'.   LS

GOURD a name applied loosely to some or all CUCURBIT plants, especially in Asia and Africa. In N. America the term is applied particularly to varieties with hard-shelled fruits which are grown for ornament or to provide utensils. British use of the word is less exclusive, matching the French *courge* and the German *Kürbis*, which can refer to all cucurbits. Edible species belong to a number of different genera and are used in a variety of ways. See BITTER GOURD; BOTTLE GOURD; IVY GOURD; RIDGED GOURD (also called luffa); SNAKE GOURDS; WAX GOURD (also called winter melon).

Round gourd is a name sometimes applied to the tinda, a very small kind of WATERMELON.

Gourds present an interesting field of study for historians and anthropologists as well as for botanists. They are the plants which raise in the most acute form the controversy over pre-Columbian contacts between Africa and S. America (see BOTTLE GOURD). And the uses to which the hollow shells have been put are innumerable and often surprising. Many such uses are related to the storage of drink or food. The rounded bottoms are no impediment to this. Gourds can be induced to acquire a neck by the simple means of tying a cord round the young, still soft fruit. They can then be suspended on cords. Or a three-legged stand can be provided, as by the Maori for their gourd pots of birds preserved in their own fat (see CONFIT). Gourds are lighter than clay pots.

Gourds also provide a wide range of dippers, cups, and spoons. The outstanding examples are the decorated matés of S. America, described under MATÉ.

It is beyond the scope of this article to consider gourds as components of musical instruments, as supports for rafts, as homes for Chinese cricket champions, or as articles of clothing. The last category includes the extraordinary penis sheaths of New Guinea and other parts of the world, often fashioned from exceptionally long and thin gourds. Heiser (1979) has provided an excellent survey of the mysteries surrounding these 'phallocrypts' and of the uses and decorations of gourds in general. Organ (1963) also has good material on uses, besides a thoughtful passage on the possible transoceanic dissemination of gourds in ancient times.

A curious sidelight on gourd-growing emerges from the reminiscences of Kinau Wilder (1978), the niece of the botanist Gerrit Parmile Wilder. She records that At the bottom of his large garden he once grew some gourds. Without explaining to the outstanding socialites just why he wanted one stocking from each, he raised a lovely crop of most unusually shaped gourds, all labelled in large letters easily read from the street. There was the Agnes Galt, the Molly Wilder, the Sarah Wilder, the Ida von Holt, the Helen Carter, and many others. The stockings had been used to train the growing gourds and the results were extraordinary! My mother had awfully skinny legs but some of the others did not, and the display caused a near riot.

GOURMAND a term of French origin which usually indicates a person who is overfond of eating; greedy, a glutton. However, it is sometimes used in a milder sense, simply designating someone who loves good food (like GOURMET, see next entry).

In France the term has parallel meanings, but generally with fewer censorious overtones.

GOURMET a word which came into the English language from French as a noun, meaning somebody who takes a discriminating and informed interest in food. Since then, especially in N. America, it has become an adjective; a 'gourmet food' is one which will supposedly appeal to such a person. This development has probably had the result that fewer of the people who might have been glad to be called 'gourmets' 50 years ago are now willing to be so described. The word may eventually cease to have any real significance, except in a historical context.

In the French language, the word originally designated an accomplished wine-taster. For a long time now it has acquired a much more general meaning—like the English one, but retaining more respectability and significance. It is however met less often than the all-encompassing GOURMAND, see above.

GRAINS OF SELIM (also known as kimba pepper), the seeds of a shrubby tree, *Xylopia aethiopica*, found in Africa. The seeds have a pleasant musky flavour and are used as a pepper substitute. The pods are crushed and added whole to soups or stews, then removed before serving. The spice may be called Guinea pepper, African pepper, and Ethiopian pepper, thus potentially confusing it with *Piper guineense* (see ASHANTI PEPPER) and MELEGUETA PEPPER.
JM

GRAM an Indian term which refers to PULSES which are whole rather than split; the latter are called DAL.

The word is of Portuguese origin, from *grão* (grain, from the Latin *granum*), but is not, as one might expect, applied to cereal grains.

The term gram by itself, without an epithet, is taken to mean CHICKPEA (channa). Similarly, 'gram flour' means BESAN FLOUR, which is made from chickpeas. Other kinds of gram are listed below, with references to the articles in which they are described.

- Bengal gram is a name used in the south of India for CHICKPEA.
- Black gram, see URD.
- Green (or golden) gram, see MUNG BEAN.
- Horse and Madras gram, see HORSE GRAM.
- Red gram, see PIGEON PEA.
- Turkish gram, see MOTH BEAN.
- White gram, see SOYA BEAN.

GRANA the generic name of the group of hard, grating cheeses made in Italy. The most famous of these, **grana Parmigiano Reggiano**, is treated separately under PARMESAN, since it is so well known outside Italy under that name.

Grana cheeses take their name from the grainy texture which they all exhibit, even before maturity. They are all made by much the same process, using partly skimmed cow's milk and involving the usual sequence of a starter, curdling with RENNET, heating, pressing, and brining, followed by a lengthy maturing. They are produced in the form of large wheels, typically weighing from 20 to 50 kg (45 to 110 lb).

Besides the geographical classification, explained below, grana cheeses may be distinguished by the season of manufacture. Those made between April and June, called *di testa*, are considered the best. They may also be classified by age. All are matured initially for a period of 6–12 months, after which they are distributed to dealers for further maturing: a process which may continue for up to three years. Cheeses which are more than a year old are *vecchio* (old). Later they graduate to being *stravecchio* (extra old) and *stravecchione* (super extra old). As they grow older, grana cheeses acquire an ever sharper taste and become progressively more expensive. They keep for a long time, because of their low moisture content, but eventually turn powdery.

The history of grana cheeses can be traced back at least as far as AD 1000, which seems to have been roughly when monks in the Po Valley succeeded, by a system of irrigation, in starting the intensive farming of dairy herds and the production on a large scale of milk for cheese. During medieval times grana cheese acquired great importance because it kept so well and was easy to transport.

The principal varieties, defined by their districts of origin, are as follows:

Grana Bagozzo, known also simply as Bagoss, a minor variety from Bagolino in the province of Brescia. It is made by a process which differs in some respects from the standard one, and was the favourite cheese of Garibaldi. It used to be called grana Bresciano, but that name now applies generally to cheeses from the province of Brescia.

Grana Lodigiano, a type with a larger grain than the others, a sharper taste, and a stronger yellow colour which turns green after the cheese has been cut open. Cutting it also produces characteristic 'tears', small drops of moisture which are exuded. Once the rival of Parmesan in European fame, this variety is now rare and may risk becoming extinct. It is handicapped by the fact that it takes longer to mature than do its rivals.

Grana Padano, the product of a large area in the Po Valley and the Trentino, but excluding the inner region of Parmigiano Reggiano. A subvariety is grana Mantovano, from the district of Mantua.

Grana Piacentino, the pride of Piacenza and a cheese which was already being praised in the 15th century, and by Montaigne in the 16th, is now classified as a grana Padano, but formerly bore its own specific name. The people of Piacenza and those of Parma both claimed that their grana was the original one.

These appellations, excepting those which have been superseded, are all protected.

The correct method of cutting up grana cheeses is interesting. The wheel is first divided into 16 portions by vertical cuts of which each passes through the centre point. These portions are then sliced into two horizontally, yielding a total of 32, all of which should be equal in weight.

The use of grana cheese outside Italy is almost entirely confined to grating, usually in connection with Italian PASTA dishes, POLENTA, and MINESTRONE. Within Italy, this familiar use is augmented by consumption of young grana cheeses at table, but is still dominant. Di Corato (1977) attributes to the eminent gastronome Massimo Alberini the following succinct and eloquent statement:

It is, without doubt, the most typical Italian cheese, not only for its intrinsic value but, more important, for the contribution which it makes to the flavour and nutritive value of many dishes, from minestrone to pasta, from polenta to certain vegetables. [It] enriches without suffocating, gives vigour without overwhelming, and, in particular, confers an Italian character to [each such dish].

GRAPE the fruit of vines of the genus *Vitis*, has been celebrated as both food and the source of wine since antiquity. Wine, as such, is not within the scope of this book, although there is an entry for WINE as an ingredient in cookery. The present entry deals principally with the history of the grape and the use of table grapes.

The outstanding grapevine is *V. vinifera*. In its original form it was indigenous to the area stretching from the south-east coast of the Black Sea around the south of the Caspian Sea to Afghanistan, and is still found there. Like its cultivated successors, the wild vine is a climbing plant which needs to grow up some support.

Various cultures have left clues to the early cultivation of the vine. Paintings on the walls of Egyptian tombs of the 4th dynasty, around 2440 BC, show the growing of grapes, including obviously improved, large-fruited varieties as well as smaller ones like the Zante grapes from which currants (see RAISINS, SULTANAS, AND CURRANTS) are made. The Bible mentions vineyards from the time of Noah (Genesis 9: 20). From Asia, the Phoenicians, a trading and seafaring people, brought the vine to Greece not long after 1000 BC. It flourished in the Mediterranean climate and spread throughout the classical world.

THE GRAPE IN ANTIQUITY

The Greeks and Romans grew grapes not only for making wine and for eating fresh, but also for grape products.

Sugar syrups, made by boiling down must (fresh unfermented grape juice), were an important ingredient in Roman food. The difference between the various syrups is not fully known but, according to Pliny, *sapa* was more concentrated than *defrutum*, being boiled down to one-third of the original volume. *Defrutum*, used in savoury sauces, was reduced to only half the original volume. Another kind, *passum*, made from raisins and must or wine, was used as a sweetener. Grape syrup is still made in the Levant, where it is called DIBS (or, in Turkey, PEKMEZ).

VERJUICE, the juice of unripe grapes (or sometimes of other fruit such as CRABAPPLES), is another grape product of ancient origin. It was much used as a souring agent in cooking in Europe until it was ousted by cheap vinegar. (Good VINEGAR, of course, may itself be a grape product.)

Grape cultivation spread through the Roman Empire as its frontiers advanced and did not stop when the empire fell. The grape was already known beyond the boundaries of the empire, in regions with a cool enough winter for the vines. Indeed it had reached N. India from Persia as far back as the 7th century BC, and China around 100 BC.

In Asia and America, and in S. Africa too, other *Vitis* species existed, some producing grapes of reasonable eating quality and potentially suitable for cultivation. The

Vikings who were exploring the eastern seaboard of N. America long before 1492 evidently met at least one American species, probably *V. labrusca*, the fox grape (the other good one, *V. rotundifolia*, the muscadine or scuppernong grape, belongs to the south-east). After European colonization of the Americas began in earnest, following the voyages of Columbus, numerous expeditions of settlers took seeds of *V. vinifera* across the Atlantic. Some plantings were successful, but the plants failed to prosper in the cold winters of Massachusetts, and all over the north-east settlers were obliged to turn to native species, which they cultivated and improved. For example the black Concord grapes popular in the USA are a variety of *V. labrusca*. (There are also many *V. vinifera* × *labrusca* and other hybrids.)

While the European grape was becoming established in the climatically suitable parts of the Americas, the Dutch took it to S. Africa (where also a native grape of fair quality, *V. capensis*, existed) in 1655. Australia had no native grape, but provided suitable environments (New South Wales, Victoria, S. Australia) for the European grape when it arrived there.

Thus the empire of *V. vinifera* had spread round the globe by the mid-19th century. Then, in 1860, came a disaster which came close to wiping it out in its home base, Europe. An aphid, *Phylloxera vastatrix*, lives on the roots of some native American vines without harming them particularly. But once it gets onto the roots of *V. vinifera*, it soon kills the plant. Somehow *Phylloxera* was accidentally introduced into France and within a few years had ravaged all European vineyards.

Fortunately, it was noticed that American vines, a few of which were grown in Europe as exotics, were not affected. *V. vinifera* was saved by grafting it onto American rootstocks. Now all *V. vinifera* vines are grafted, save in a few places where it has been possible to maintain plots of ungrafted vines.

Towards the end of the 20th century the leading producers of table grapes were Italy, Turkey, Bulgaria, the USA, Greece, Portugal, and S. Africa. The main varieties are listed below.

More than 8,000 varieties of grape have been named and described, but only 40 or 50 are commercially important and most of these are purely wine grapes. A few varieties are grown to produce RAISINS, SULTANAS, AND CURRANTS. The most important hybrids and varieties of table grape (all belonging to *V. vinifera*, unless otherwise indicated) are the following:

Alicante, a black grape of French origin also grown in California, and elsewhere.

Almeria, a medium-large white grape of mild flavour, grown in Spain and the USA. A useful export variety, since it keeps well.

Baresana, an amber-coloured Italian eating grape, not very sweet but well flavoured.

Cardinal, an American cross between Tokay and Ribier, which has very large, red fruits of neutral flavour.

Catawba, an American hybrid of the native fox grape, *V. labrusca*, which has been cultivated in Kentucky since 1802. The large, purplish red fruits have a distinctive flavour, and are sometimes eaten as table grapes, but the variety is grown mainly for wine and juice.

Chasselas (or Golden Chasselas), a yellow French table grape of superior quality. It exists in several forms and may be the oldest known cultivated variety, to judge by Egyptian tomb paintings at Luxor.

Concord, a *V. labrusca* hybrid. It is the principal bluish-black grape of the north-eastern USA simply because it will grow there, being resistant to cold. The large fruits, which have a rather coarse flavour, often described as 'foxy', are sometimes eaten as dessert grapes, but most of them go for juice, wine, and jelly. The curiously bright purple American grape juice whose colour and flavour leads Europeans to suppose it to be synthetic is in fact a natural product of this variety. Some varieties are seedless.

Delaware, another native American variety (a *V. aestivalis* × *vinifera* × *V. labrusca* cross). It is small, dark pink, soft skinned, and has a sweet flavour. It is used both as a table grape and for making wine. It is popular in Japan and grown in Brazil.

Emperor, the second most widely sold table grape in the USA (more because of durability in transport and storage than for eating quality). It is red and thick skinned.

Gamay, the black grape from which Beaujolais is made. It is unusual for a wine grape in being of excellent eating quality.

Hanepoot ('honey pot'), the very sweet, meaty Muscat of Alexandria grape grown in S. Africa and often exported. It is an ancient variety and known as a table or raisin grape rather than a wine grape.

Italia, another Muscat variety, highly popular in Italy, whence it is exported to other European countries. It is also grown in the USA. A large, white grape with a thick skin and a heavy, sweet flavour.

Kishmish(i), see Thompson seedless.

Malaga, originally a vaguely used American term for large, white Spanish grapes of the same type as Almeria, which were imported from Malaga. However, there is also an American-grown Red Malaga with large pink or red grapes, crisp but lacking in acidity.

Muscat, a general term for a group of varieties. They are all large, ranging in colour from pale yellow to deep, black with thick skins, sweet and aromatic. Muscat grapes are among the best for eating fresh. They are also made into the large, flat 'muscatel' raisins (and sweet dessert wines such as Muscat de Beaumes-de-Venise).

Niagara (Concord × Cassady), a large, pale, yellowish-green grape of native American *V. labrusca* stock, is the principal white American table grape of that type, though less popular than *V. vinifera* white grapes. It has a tangy, slightly 'foxy' flavour.

Perlette, a very early white, seedless table grape, firm, crisp, juicy, and thin skinned, which has a mild but pleasing flavour. It is grown in California.

Regina, a variety with elongated, amber, sweet, crisp grapes, deservedly popular for table use in Italy. There are similar varieties in Greece (Rozaki) and Bulgaria (Bolgar).

Ribier, a European variety grown in the United States, which comes on the market very late in winter. The grapes are large, round, and purple-black, neutral in flavour and lacking acidity.

Thompson seedless, also called Sultanina or Kishmish(i), and widely grown. It is the leading American table grape, being firm, tender, and sweet, though without strong flavour. It is also grown, both in the USA and in Australia, for making sultanas, light-coloured, seedless raisins.

Tokay or Pinot Gris, grown both as a table grape and for making white wine. In California, where it is called 'Flame Tokay', it is grown for eating fresh and is second in popularity to Thompson seedless. The large, oval red fruit has a firm texture, tough skin, and a mild flavour.

Zinfandel, a reddish-black grape, grown in California both for eating fresh and for making wine.

The use of fresh grapes in cookery is limited, but essential to a few well-known dishes such as Sole Véronique.

GRAPEFRUIT *Citrus paradisi*, the refined descendant of a bigger and rougher fruit, the POMELO or shaddock. It has the distinction of being the largest CITRUS FRUIT commonly available, although a newcomer on the fruiterer's shelves.

The first mention of the grapefruit is in 1750, by an author who called it 'forbidden fruit' and said that it grew in Barbados. Around 1820 a French botanist, the Chevalier de Tussac, wrote in his *Flore des Antilles*:

I have had the occasion to observe, at Jamaica, in the botanical garden of the Government, a variety of shaddock whose fruits, which are not bigger than a fair orange, are disposed in clusters [French 'grappes']; the English in Jamaica call this the 'forbidden fruit' or 'smaller shaddock'.

It may be the clustering habit which gave the new fruit the name 'grapefruit'; certainly this explanation is more plausible than the suggestion that it tastes like grapes.

The grapefruit was introduced to Florida in 1823 by a French count with the ambiguous name of Odette Phillippe. It was slow to achieve popularity despite its beautiful appearance. The rather bitter flavour is an acquired taste and the fruit is difficult to peel in the way that one might peel an orange. However, trial consignments sent to Philadelphia and New York in 1885 sold well, and within a few years the industry had grown to a large size. Later, cultivation spread to California, Arizona, Texas, and then abroad. Israel, Argentina, and S. Africa are now major producers.

There are two main varieties of grapefruit: **Duncan,** which has a lot of seeds but a good flavour, and **Marsh,** which is seedless but has less flavour. Duncan is a direct descendant from a seed planted by Phillippe. Marsh originated as a chance seedling in about 1860, but was not used for propagation until 1886. The variety universally used for canning is Duncan.

In 1907 a pink variety of Duncan was found, and in 1913 a pink Marsh appeared. The latter is the ancestor of all the pink grapefruits grown today. Pink grapefruit cannot be canned, since they discolour.

About half of the world grapefruit crop is made into juice. The flavour of grapefruit juice is less impaired by processing than that of the other citrus fruits. Frozen concentrated juice is the best. Of the remainder of the crop most is eaten fresh, and the rest canned.

Grapefruit is more suitable for use as a dessert fruit than in cooking, since its flavour is assertive and tends to swamp anything else. However, grapefruits make good marmalade.

Fruits which are a cross between a grapefruit and a tangerine (mandarin) are called tangelos. See UGLI for a description of two such fruits, whose resemblance to a grapefruit is clear. Several other tangelos, which take after the other parent, are described under MANDARIN. Orangelos (orange × grapefruit) also exist. These are of minor commercial importance except in Japan, where the highly acid **Natsudaidai** is popular.

GRASSHOPPER the name used for insects of the families Acrididae and Tettigoniidae, with legs adapted for jumping and an ability on the part of the males to make chirping sounds. The first of these families is that in which the species bearing the name LOCUST occur; this name applies to those grasshoppers which are capable of swarming in immense numbers, and is used

of them while they are so swarming. The second family includes some but by no means all of the insects which bear the name CRICKET.

Discussions of the extent to which grasshoppers provide food for human beings overlaps, inevitably, with information about consumption of locusts and crickets. Indeed the terminology for the whole category of orthopterous insects is confusing; see also, for example, CICADA. However, it is not uncommon to find references to the eating of 'grasshoppers', such as the following from Bodenheimer (1951), quoting a missionary who was writing about the Shoshoco tribe in N. America:

The principal portion of the Shoshoco territory is covered with *Artemisia*, in which the grasshoppers swarm by the myriads, and these parts are consequently most frequented by the tribe. When they are sufficiently numerous they hunt together. They begin by digging a hole, 10 or 12 feet in diameter, by 4 or 5 feet deep; then, armed with long branches of *Artemisia*, they surround a field of 3 or 4 acres, according to the number of persons who are engaged in it. They stand about 20 feet apart and their whole work is to beat the ground, so as to frighten up the grasshoppers and make them bound forward. They chase them toward the centre by degrees—that is, into the hole prepared for their reception. Their number is so considerable that frequently 3 or 4 acres furnish grasshoppers sufficient to fill the hole. The Shoshocos stay in that place as long as this sort of provision lasts. Some eat the grasshoppers in soup, or boiled; others crush them, and make a kind of paste from them which they dry in the sun or before the fire; others eat them en appalas—that is, they make pointed rods and string the largest ones on them; afterwards these rods are fixed in the ground before the fire, and as they become roasted, the poor Shoshocos regale themselves until the whole are devoured.

GRATIN GRATINER two French terms, noun and verb respectively, which have entered the international culinary vocabulary, as has the expression *au gratin*.

Originally, back in the 16th century or beyond, the noun referred to that part of a cooked dish which stuck to the pot or pan and had to be scraped (*gratté*) off if it was not to be wasted. Since the 19th century the meaning has changed to the effect deliberately created by cooks when they cook a dish so that it has a crisply baked top. This is often achieved by strewing grated cheese or breadcrumbs on top, and the phrase 'au gratin' is often taken to mean 'with grated cheese', although the gratin effect can be produced without adding anything on top; as Ayto (1993) points out, the *gratin dauphinois* is correctly made of sliced potatoes baked in cream with no added topping. The gratin effect can be applied to a dish under the grill, or uncovered in a hot oven, or by using a SALAMANDER thereby

giving it a crust. Either this crust or the dish as a whole may be called 'gratin'.

GRATING CHEESES very hard cheeses made primarily for grating rather than as table cheeses, include most notably the GRANA group, especially PARMESAN, and the more aged types of PECORINO and ASIAGO. That these are all Italian is no coincidence, for the Italians are the principal users of grated cheese in their cooking. Cheeses of other nations which are used for grating include the Swiss SCHABZIGER and SBRINZ; old, dry Jack in the USA (see AMERICAN CHEESES); CHEDDAR in Britain, the USA, and elsewhere; and KEFALOTYRI in Greece. Much grating cheese is sold in grated form.

GRAVLAKS (or gravlax) a Scandinavian preparation of SALMON (*laks* in Danish and Norwegian, *lax* in Swedish) which differs greatly according to whether it is made in the traditional way, dating back to medieval times, or by modern methods. Astri Riddervold (1986, 1990a) has described both and pointed out the earliest mentions of the former.

The word gravlaks can be traced back in Scandinavian history to 1348, when a man from Jämtland, called Olafuer Gravlax, is mentioned. In 1509, another man, called Martin Surlax is mentioned in the annals of Stockholm. The words gravlax and surlax (buried fish and sour fish) are used as synonyms, buried fish describing the technique, sour fish the result—the fermented stinking fish. According to the old custom of giving people surnames in Scandinavia, both were probably professional producers of buried salmon.

Riddervold explains that the technique, which has been used in many circumpolar regions round the world, was not applied only to salmon, but also to HERRING and other oily fish, including some species of SHARK. Burial of the fish, whether in barrels or in holes in the ground which were covered with birch bark and stones, results in a fermentation which leads to a softening of the flesh and a sour taste. Short-term burial (4–6 days) makes salmon edible while still uncooked and is the precursor of modern gravlaks. Long-term burial (for months) was intended to preserve the fish for winter consumption (when ice and snow made fishing difficult) and yielded a product which was usually very smelly and which is now called RAKEFISK in Norway and *surfisk* in Sweden.

Making gravlaks in modern times does not involve burial. The salmon is cleaned, scaled, bisected lengthways, and deboned. A fillet is placed in a suitable recipient, skin side down, and strewn with fresh dill, crystallized salt, a little sugar, and white peppercorns. A matching piece, skin side up,

351 GREECE

is placed on it, followed by a board and a heavy weight. This whole arrangement is kept in a cool place for three days or so, the fish being turned every 12 hours and basted with the juices which exude. The preparation of gravlaks is customarily one of the household duties allocated to men.

Gravlaks is drained and brushed clean before being served. It is sliced very thin and eaten as a first course, usually with a special mild mustard sauce and perhaps some fresh dill, or with a potato salad.

GRAVY in the British Isles and areas culturally influenced by them, is . . . well, gravy, a term fully comprehensible to those who use it, but something of a mystery in the rest of the world.

Ideally, gravy as made in the British kitchen is composed of residues left in the tin after roasting meat, deglazed with good STOCK, and seasoned carefully. (Many cooks incorporate a spoonful of flour before adding the liquid but this practice is frowned on by purists.) Gravy varies in colour from pale gold-brown to burnt umber, and in thickness from something with little more body than water to a substantial sauce of coating consistency. In French meat cookery, *jus* is roughly equivalent to honestly made thin gravy in the British tradition.

Should gravy be classified as a kind of sauce? Simon (1983) thought not; gravy was distinguished from sauce by being 'made in the same pan in which meat or fish has been cooked, and almost, if not entirely, from the juices extracted during cooking', but thickening with flour or egg yolks made it a sauce (and no longer a gravy). If this ruling is accepted, then the 'red-eye gravy' which is famous in the American south must qualify as gravy. Evan Jones (1981) describes how it is made:

To enhance ham with red-eye gravy, put the fried slices aside and add one-half cup of ice water to the drippings, letting it bubble until it turns red. Some cooks use strong black coffee; others stir in one teaspoon of brown sugar until it caramelizes, then add the ice water.

The etymology of the word gravy, which probably comes from an Old French culinary term, has puzzling aspects. However, it seems clear enough that in the 14th and 15th centuries 'graue' meant sauces of broth, almonds, and spices used for white meats, fish, and vegetables. Ayto (1993) suggests that it was only in the late 16th century that

the critical change between obtaining this [the gravy] in the form of broth, from boiling the meat, and in the form of juices, produced by roasting, seems to have taken place. . . . In the seventeenth century, the practice was to make cuts in a joint when it was part-roasted, to allow the

juices to escape (a special press was invented to squeeze them out). Later, it became more usual to make gravy separately from a different, inferior cut of meat—typically from gravy beef, part of the leg used for that purpose (Hannah Glasse has a recipe which calls for laying 'a pound of gravy beef over your chickens', 1747).

From the 18th century onwards, however, there was something of a downhill trend. Dallas (1877) said gloomily that the gravy served with roast meat in England was often a mockery.

While the sirloin is turning before the fire, the cook takes a boatful of boiling water which she colours with caramel and seasons with salt. She pours this gradually over the sirloin, she catches it again in a dish below, takes off the fat; and this is what she calls 'its own gravy'.

Kitchen tricks involving burnt onions, caramelized sugar, 'gravy browning', and stock cubes are modern descendants of this practice. Indeed, numerous 'gravy mixes' or 'granules' (dehydrated compounds of colourings, flavourings, and thickeners) are to be had, for use with the meat residue, or in its stead. Yet in many homes in Britain a true gravy is still made; and this remains the most delicious accompaniment for the meat from which it comes and an essential feature of a meat dish. Should it be lacking, and especially in the north of England, the voice of the chief male at table will be raised in that most terrible and touching of remonstrances: 'Where's t'gravy, then?'

GRAYLING *Thymallus thymallus*, a European freshwater fish of the SALMON family, Salmonidae. Its range extends from S. France up to Scandinavia and from England to the Ural and Volga rivers of Russia. It may be found in lakes, but prefers clean, cool, swift rivers. Maximum length is 45 cm (18"); weight can be over 2 kg (5 lb). The silvery sides bear delicate horizontal stripes, violet in colour. These and the characteristic long and high dorsal fin make it easy to identify.

This is a good fish, worthy of the distinguished family to which it belongs. There is also an Arctic grayling, *T. arcticus*, which grows somewhat bigger and is an important food fish for communities in the Arctic regions.

The so-called 'Australian grayling', of the genus *Prototroctes*, belongs to a different family, is smaller, and is a species in decline.

GREECE is a small country on the southern shores of Europe, exposed almost in entirety to the Mediterranean and Aegean seas. Inevitably, this has been a major influence on its food and cookery.

However, it is also true that there is a large part of inland Greece traversed by often

inhospitable mountain ranges which provide another important influence. The only notable plains are in Thrace, Macedonia, and Thessalia. Otherwise the terrain is rocky and steep, mostly terraced and planted with trees which will withstand the heat and aridity. One is the queen of the Mediterranean, the OLIVE, relied upon for nourishment and to add flavour to the cuisine. Vine cultivation has also been of great importance, for fruit, but even more for wine-making.

In general terms the food is frugal and relies on fresh ingredients and dexterity to transform them. The freshness of the fish even if it is tiny *atherina* or *maritha*—both of the PICAREL family—is of enormous gastronomic importance to the islanders. Dishes are mostly enhanced with lemons and fresh or dried mountain herbs such as thyme and oregano. Spices—cumin, allspice, cinnamon, and cloves—are used sparingly but more prominently in the south of the Aegean, where Arab influence has left its mark, particularly in Crete and the Dodecanese.

Greek food traditionally centres round vegetables, fish, seafood, olive oil, and a plethora of fruit. Meat is less a centrepiece, more often used to enrich primarily vegetable dishes such as MOUSSAKA, stuffed vegetables, and stuffed vine leaves—the *thria* of the ancient Greeks who might originally have used young fig leaves rather than vine.

There is an astonishing continuity in culinary matters from ancient Greece through to the modern era. (In this connection see also CLASSICAL GREECE.) The modern trahanas (see TARHANA)—cracked wheat boiled in milk, dried in the sun, and stored for soup-making in the winter—is the ancient *tragos*. SKORTHALIA, the garlic and bread sauce which often accompanies fried fish and vegetables, is the *skorothalmi* of ancient Athenians. And modern *Fava*—a purée of yellow split peas dressed with raw onion, olive oil, and lemon—sounds very similar to the ancient *etnos* which was sold in the streets of Athens. Bread- and pie-making have been a long tradition. Sweets centred round all kinds of nuts, sesame seeds, and honey abounded in ancient Greece as they do now. Although it is fruit that is offered at the end of a meal, cakes and puddings are consumed with coffee.

There are dishes that are common to the whole country despite differences of terrain and history: winter and Lenten soups of beans, lentils, and chickpeas, *Fava*, stuffed vegetables and vine leaves, as well as traditional relishes of olives—often home grown and home cured—and preserved salted fish. And for the important religious celebrations a capon was stuffed for Christmas; but that has been replaced by turkeys. For the New Year a sucking pig roasted was a delicacy worth waiting for and for Easter the paschal baby lamb or goat roasted whole on a spit is universally loved.

For Christmas and the New Year large quantities of traditional cakes are made. *Melomarkarona* or *finikia* are the traditional honey-dipped biscuits made with olive oil and orange juice and *kourabiethes* are the little shortbread cakes studded with almonds and dusted with icing sugar. For New Year's Eve a large brioche-type cake is made which is called *vasilopitta*—St Basil's cake.

For Easter large quantities of hard-boiled eggs are painted bright scarlet. Also small and large cakes are made, some of the shortbread variety—*koulourakia*—and others of the brioche type—*tsourekia*. These are often decorated with the scarlet-painted paschal eggs and matriarchs will often make individually shaped ones—hens, rabbits, or simply plaited ones—for each child in the family.

Small cups of freshly made Turkish-style coffee are the national drink, as are ouzo—the aniseed-flavoured alcoholic drink—and retsina, the resinated wine, which are kept mostly for the evening and always accompanied by food.

However, there are also major variations between regions. There is the Greece of the sea and that of the land, with a sprinkling of history to account for further variations here and there.

Folklore reflects this gastronomic dichotomy not least through celebrating at least one hero who chose explicitly to move from one world to another. The Prophet Elias—a sailor by profession—got so fed up with being shipwrecked that he decided to start a new life. He took one of his oars and started walking, swearing that where he met people who did not recognize this implement he would settle. Finally, up on a mountain, the locals said that what he was carrying was a shovel for removing loaves from the oven. The Prophet had arrived at his desired spot and ever since his churches have been built on hills and mountains. And it is often in the mountain regions that one finds the most delicious breads and cheeses, and the traditional *paximathia* (twice baked barley bread slices, quite often with aniseed seeds in them—see PAXIMADIA).

Coastal and island Greece has on the whole a lighter cuisine relying mainly on vegetables and seafood. There is a daintiness and playfulness about it, needed if sea urchins (*ahini*), sea anemones (*galipes*), or limpets (*petalithes*) are on the menu. There is a natural concern with colour and appearance. Think of the pretty picture of a round large roasting tin filled with stuffed tomatoes, peppers, aubergines, and courgettes. A light fish soup finished with the much loved AVGOLÉMONO—egg-and-lemon sauce—is a universal dish there even

if it is only made with *petropsara*—rockfish which are the humblest and smallest of the catch.

Inland Greece—the interminable plains and the mountains—has more robust tendencies. Too arid or too cold for the olive tree, animal farming is the norm. Olymbos, Pindos, Roumeli, and Parnassos have a wealth of pies made with meat, cheese, and butter and delicious home-made FILO pastry. Of course pie-making has been traditional in Greece since ancient times. Artemidoros (2nd century AD) in his *Dream Translations* refers to *plakountas tetyromenous* and the medieval Greek *Lexika* to *plakountas entyritas*, all cheese pies.

However, the cheese pies in the Zagorohoria or in the village of Metsovo up on the Pindos mountains in NW Greece are different from the much lighter ones made on the islands, where the cheese used is mostly fresh white cheese, the *tyrovolia* of Mykonos or the fresh *myzithra* elsewhere. Mountain cheese pies are made with hard yellow (cow's) cheese, quantities of butter and quite often *trahana*. This kind of pie might as well have come straight out of the Byzantine kitchen where it would have been known as *trahanopitta*. As for the celebratory or MEZZE dishes they are almost of Homeric proportions and some of them little known elsewhere in Greece. They come under obscure names such as *tziyerosarmas*, *bohtsas*, *kolosafas* which are all of an intestinal or CAUL variety stuffed with rice, liver, lights, heart, kidneys, parsley, and hefty spicing—primarily black pepper and allspice. Dishes made for cool weather and strong stomachs. *Yiouvetsi*—baked lamb or goat with pasta and tomatoes—is a more familiar dish elsewhere in Greece. Other *mezze* dishes under the more descriptive names of *splinandero*, *kokoretsi*, and *garthoumba*—which are made with coarsely chopped liver and lights, wrapped with lamb intestine, and spit roasted or baked in the oven—although originating in inland Greece, are now found everywhere, though perhaps not so readily on the islands.

To trace some of the elements in common between the cuisines of Greece and her Balkan neighbours and Turkey, see also, especially, TURKEY and BULGARIA. Links with Italy are only noticeable in the Ionian islands, Corfu, Cephalonia, etc.   RSa

READING: Rosemary Barron (1991); Patience Gray (1986); Aglaia Kremezi (1993); Rena Salaman (1993*a*).

GREEN CHEESE of which the moon was thought to be composed until the contrary revelations of American spacemen in the 1970s, has never meant the same as blue cheese. In medieval England it seems to have meant 'new' cheese, for Andrew Boorde

(1542) stated that 'Grene chese is not called grene by ye reason of colour, but for ye newnes of it, for the whay is not half pressed out.'

However, in more recent times the term has referred to a cheese, of the COTTAGE CHEESE type or DERBY, coloured with sage (see SAGE CHEESE) and spinach juice.

The term has also been used for the Swiss green cheese SCHABZIGER, and for a cheese of Friesland in the Netherlands. An old Friesian saying is: 'bûter, brea en griene tsiis, hwa dat net sizze kin is gijn oprjuchte fries.' This means: 'butter, bread and green cheese; who cannot pronounce that, is no genuine Friesian.' The point is that only real Friesians can pronounce the first words correctly.

GREENGAGE the English name for a group of especially good green or yellow plums whose origin and classification are uncertain but which are generally classed in or with the species *Prunus insititia*.

The original type is thought to have come from Armenia to Greece and thence to Italy, where it was called *Verdocchia*. The fruit reached France during the reign of François I (1494–1547) and is still known there as *Reine Claude* after his wife. It may have reached England direct from Italy (it was originally known in England by its Italian name), but certainly at an early date, since stones of the fruit were identified along with those of other plums recovered from the wreckage of the *Mary Rose*, Henry VIII's flagship, which sank in 1545 and was raised in 1982.

The fruit later received its present English name after Sir Thomas Gage, who received stocks from his brother in France early in the 18th century. This honorific gesture is said to have been made by Gage's gardener when he discovered that the labels on the trees had been lost and that he would have to give them a name.

One famous old variety is the Transparent Gage, which was raised in the early part of the 19th century by Lafay, a Parisian nurseryman. Its qualities are vividly evoked by Bunyard:

If there is a better gage than this, I know it not, and certainly there is none more beautiful. Its French name, Reine Claude Diaphane, exactly describes its clear, transparent look; a slight flush of red and then one looks into the depths of transparent amber as one looks into an opal, uncertain how far the eye can penetrate.

Thomas Rivers brought it to England where it became the seed of a worthy line of gages propagated in his nursery at Sawbridgeworth.

Greengages, considered by many to be the finest of dessert plums, are best enjoyed in their natural state. However, they also make the most luxurious of plum jams.

The **mirabelles,** which are another group of mainly yellow plums, are also hard to classify with confidence but placed by some authorities as varieties of *P. insititia*. The kind known as *Mirabelle de Nancy* is believed to have come from the east to reach France in the 15th century and is still rated highly. The *Mirabelle de Metz* was first recorded in 1675. France is where the mirabelles are most highly esteemed.

GREENSAUCE owing its colour to green leaves, especially of SORREL, has a very long history, and an international one. Something of the sort may well date back to classical times and was apparent in medieval cookery in various parts of Europe.

In England, the earliest recipes or descriptions for the sauce call for a complex mixture of green herbs. Constance Hieatt (1982) cites the 12th-century *De Utensilibus* of Alexander Neckham, who includes among the ingredients sage, parsley, dittany (see DITTANDER), thyme, garlic, salt, and pepper. Jennifer Stead (1979) refers to various others, from the 14th century onwards, including Henry Buttes (1599), who said that greensauce was 'made of sweete hearbes . . . a clowe or two, and a little Garlicke', and Hannah Glasse (1747), whose recipe for roast 'green' (young) goose has sorrel as the only or main greenstuff for the accompanying 'green Sauce'. Jennifer Stead also shows how widespread in England was the use of 'greensauce' as the name for sorrel, observing that Geoffrey Grigson (1955) lists eleven English counties where this name was used. In addition, she quotes Yorkshire dialect dictionaries of the 19th century to good effect, e.g. Easther (1883):

Greensauce: the plant Sorrel, *Rumex acetosa*, called also by some *saar grass* (sour grass), much used formerly as a sauce with meat, especially veal. When the Rev. J. Paine entered on the occupancy of Woodlands Grove, Dewsbury Moor, about 1829, there was in the garden a long row of cultivated sorrel of a superior quality. In the dining room . . . was a box seat, or locker which contained a large heavy ball. This was pointed out to the incomers as to be used for crushing the *greensauce*, which was customarily placed in a large bowl, and the ball rolled about upon it. One of my informants says, 'About fifty years ago every garden had its greensauce. It was very common then to have *cofe* [calf] feet boiled, and the *greensauce* was used with them; also "amang sallit".'

An example of what is essentially the same thing in other cuisines is provided by Germany. The *Grüne Sosse* of Frankfurt, known in the local dialect as *grie Soessche*, is a famed speciality which is enjoyed in early spring when the herbs are young and fresh, especially on 'Green Thursday' before Easter (although nowadays the herbs are available all the year round, from greenhouses). The seven herbs traditionally used are CHERVIL, SORREL, CHIVES, PARSLEY, garden CRESS, salad BURNET, and BORAGE. Mimi Flögel (personal communication) emphasizes that it is important to have balanced quantities of the herbs, of which a small amount should be chopped and the rest put through a blender to bring out their liquid content. The green liquid is then combined with a mixture of sour cream, plain yoghurt, chopped hard-boiled egg, and flavourings, and the chopped herbs sprinkled on top. The sauce is served with boiled potatoes, fillets of fish, or thin slices of beef. Goethe belonged to Frankfurt and when he was away in Weimar he had his mother send him seeds so that he could grow the herbs for the *Grüne Sosse* which he liked to serve to guests.

GREY MULLET so called in Britain to distinguish them from RED MULLET, are just plain mullet for Americans and Australians. They are beautifully streamlined fish, which exist in a number of genera and species in tropical and warm temperate waters around the world. One species, *Mugil cephalus*, has a circumglobal distribution.

Of the numerous other species, some commonly caught and eaten are:

- *M. chelo* (=*Crenimugil labrosus*), the thick-lipped grey mullet, the most common European species, found from the Black Sea through the Mediterranean and up the Atlantic coast as far as Scotland.
- *M. saliens*, the leaping grey mullet, of the Mediterranean and the E. Atlantic coast from the Bay of Biscay southwards. Liable, because of its leaping habit, to be caught in surface nets.
- *M. auratus*, the golden grey mullet, which has a similar range and is also a leaper. It has a gold blotch on each gill cover.
- *M. curema*, the white mullet, of the W. Atlantic coast from New England to Brazil; also on the E. Pacific coast.
- *M. argenteus*, the tiger or jumping mullet, of southern Australian waters.
- *Liza subviridis*, the greenback grey mullet, is one of the most common in Asian waters.
- *Valamugil seheli*, the blue-spot grey mullet, another Indo-Pacific fish, has blue spots where the pectoral fins join the sides.
- *V. buchanani*, the bluetail mullet (bloustert-harder in S. Africa), a large one (1 m/40"), whose tail is a brilliant blue. 'Once an explosion that caused many hundreds to leap out of the water at Ponte Torres . . . produced a huge shimmering sheet of blue' (Smith and Heemstra, 1986).

The vegetarian disposition of these fish excited the admiration of the Greek poet Oppian, who thought them the most gentle of fish, 'harming neither themselves nor any other creatures, never staining their lips with blood but in holy fashion feeding always on the green seaweed or mere mud'. Oppian was also impressed by the gallantly amorous attitude of male grey mullet, observing that if a fine plump female was trailed through the water a throng of admiring males would pursue her (and thus be caught).

In fact, the food of the grey mullet includes, besides diatoms and algae, minute animal material which they extract from mud, so they are not strict vegetarians.

At their best, grey mullet are fine fish to eat. But Oppian's reference to mud can serve as a warning that those who have been browsing in unattractively muddy water may taste of mud. Subject to this proviso, grey mullet can be bought with enthusiasm, to be steamed, baked, grilled, or fried.

The eggs of the female, removed in their intact membrane, salted, washed, pressed, dried in the sun, and encased in wax, make the Mediterranean delicacy known as BOUTARGUE in France.

GRIDDLE a heavy metal plate heated over the fire (or by gas or electricity) and used for cooking small items of food. In Scotland, this is known as a 'girdle'. A heavy frying pan can be used instead. Foods cooked this way include various griddle breads, BANNOCKS, OATCAKES, PANCAKES, and SCONES. For all its apparent simplicity, in skilled hands the griddle (or girdle) can be used to produce an enormous range of delicacies. Important points are that the method is successful with flour derived from grains other than WHEAT (BARLEY, OATS, and BUCKWHEAT; POTATOES can also be used); leavening is not always necessary for mixtures used on griddles; and the method requires little or no fat to grease the surface—Marian McNeill (1929) observed that 'the girdle is floured for dough and greased for batter'. An improvised cover also extends the possibilities for baking on a griddle.

The idea probably grew from the use of flat stones heated beside the fire: versions of this survived in places, such as the 'bakstone', used in the English Midlands and Yorkshire for making oatcakes, and the 'planc' of S. Wales; by the 20th century, metal plates, similar to griddles but fixed in place, had usually replaced the original stones. The portable metal griddle developed as a handy item of cooking equipment, known by the Middle Ages, and possibly before. It is a device which was vital in houses without an oven, where, suspended over the fire, it formed the main means of baking flour products, and was found useful in larger ones when the oven was cold. It was too useful an idea to discard, and survived in areas where grains other than wheat were important, where poverty prevented the addition of a range or oven to houses, and because people liked the products from it. It may simply be coincidence that, in the British Isles, these were also areas of strong Celtic influence, or there may have been cultural factors involved.

The 20th-century strongholds of griddle baking in Britain are S. Wales and Scotland. In the former, many teatime specialities, including jam-filled pasties, are still baked on it at home. Thick Welsh pancakes (see DROP SCONE) are made on it and so are the smaller items known as Welsh cakes (whose Welsh name, *pice ar y maen*, literally means 'cakes on the stone'). These are typically small and round, fairly thin (1 cm/0.4"), biscuity on the outside and moist inside, enlivened with currants and spices; there are many variations but all Welsh authors seem to agree that these delicacies may be eaten hot or cold, with a sprinkling of sugar, or buttered. In Scotland, numerous types of scones and bannocks are baked on the girdle, also for teatime. In England, griddles are still used for making oatcakes in the W. Midlands, and the industrial baking of PIKELETS, MUFFINS, and CRUMPETS is based on the same principle. In Ireland, griddle baking is used for soda breads and potato breads. The buckwheat PANCAKES and GALETTES of Brittany, and the BLINIS of E. Europe, can also be regarded as forms of griddle bread.

In the Americas, corn breads, such as TORTILLAS, and CASSAVA breads are cooked this way. CHAPATIS and numerous other breads of Asia are also cooked on a hot metal sheet which is called a *tawa* (in Turkey *sac*).

Sometimes items such as bacon, steak, or eggs are cooked on a metal hotplate, and are also said to be 'griddled'. (LM)

READING: Minwel Tibbott (1976); Catherine Brown (1990); Bobby Freeman (1996).

GRIGSON JANE (1928–90). This highly influential food writer was active from 1967 right up to the time of her death, that is to say over almost 25 years. After an upbringing in the north-east of England and studies at Cambridge, she had worked in art galleries and publishing houses and as a (prize-winning) translator. It was because she had taken to spending part of each year working in France that she turned to writing on food. The transition, which was to have momentous results, was retrospectively described by Elizabeth DAVID when she wrote an introduction to a posthumous anthology of Jane Grigson's writing:

The first I ever knew of Jane Grigson was a typescript sent to me by Anthea Joseph of Michael Joseph, my own publishers.

For us in England, Jane's *Charcuterie and French Pork Cookery*, published in 1967, was a real novelty, and a wonderfully welcome one. Now that the book has long since passed into the realm of kitchen classics we take it for granted, but for British readers and cooks in the late 1960s its contents, the clarity of the writing, and the confident knowledge of its subject and its history displayed by this young author were new treats for all of us.

The subject had been little dealt with in English culinary textbooks—and for that matter it was, and remains, one seldom written about by the French—but here was a writer who could combine a delightful quote from Chaucer on the subject of a pike galantine with a careful recipe for a modern chicken and pork version of the same ancient dish, and who could do so without pedantry or a hint of preciousness. Jane was always entertaining as well as informative.

Jane Grigson's next books were *Good Things* (1971), a collection of essays from the *Observer*, for which she was now writing regularly; and *The International Wine and Food Society's Guide to Fish Cookery* (1973). The following year saw publication of *English Food*, essentially an anthology of recipes from other sources, meticulously acknowledged, but prefaced by one of the author's characteristically robust statements on what was wrong with food and cookery in England and how it might be put right. She was always a crusader.

She turned to categories of food, starting with edible fungi in *The Mushroom Feast* (1975) and going on to what many of her admirers consider to be her finest books, *Jane Grigson's Vegetable Book* (1978) and *Jane Grigson's Fruit Book* (1982). Both these books exemplified admirably the particular merits described by Elizabeth David above. In between them came *Food with the Famous* (1979) which gave her full scope for writing about some figures of the past whom she admired, including Parson Woodforde, Jane Austen, Thomas Jefferson, Émile Zola, and Marcel Proust.

The Observer Guide to European Cookery (1983) and *The Observer Guide to British Cookery* (1984) reflected further work for the magazine of the *Observer*. *Exotic Fruits and Vegetables* (with paintings by Charlotte Knox) took her further afield, but *The Cooking of Normandy* (1987), the third of the small cookery books which she wrote for Sainsbury's (the supermarket chain), brought her closer to both her homes, that in Wiltshire and that in France, to which she and her husband Geoffrey repaired annually. Geoffrey, the poet, had been the author of *The Englishman's Flora* (among many other works), which was and remains an invaluable reference for any student of traditional English foods. Geoffrey himself was so widely read that he constituted a sort of walking encyclopedia of English literature and his contribution to Jane's work in the form of general inspiration and particular suggestions was considerable right up to the time of his death, only a few years before hers.

In an obituary for the *Independent*, the present author wrote:

Jane Grigson left to the English-speaking world a legacy of fine writing on food and cookery for which no exact parallel exists . . . She won to herself this wide audience because she was above all a friendly writer . . . the most companionable presence in the kitchen; often catching the imagination with a deftly chosen fragment of history or poetry, but never failing to explain the 'why' as well as the 'how' of cookery.

READING: Isobel Holland, Lynette Hunter, and Geraldine Stoneham (1991).

GRILL to cook by direct exposure to radiant heat, as when a piece of meat is placed on a grill (a device, typically of parallel metal bars, to support it above or below the source of heat) or gridiron with heat from a charcoal fire or other source of heat playing directly onto it. The N. American word for the verb grill is broil.

The modern grill is a plainer device than the old gridiron, which was designed to go over a fire and which could be elaborate and elegant.

Similar or simpler kinds were in use throughout the western world so long as open-hearth cookery continued. They have been revived in a form suitable for the BARBECUE.

GRIMOD DE LA REYNIÈRE
ALEXANDRE-BALTHAZAR-LAURENT (1758–1837). Grimod de la Reynière lived during the crucial years during which the *ancienne cuisine*, exemplified in such works as *Les Soupers de la cour* by Menon (see FRENCH COOK BOOKS), was supplanted by *la cuisine moderne* of CARÊME and Plumerey. Grimod, as he is generally referred to, did not play a direct role in this transformation, but was rather an observer and chronicler of the cuisine practised in Paris in the first decade of the 19th century. He is generally credited with being the first food critic in the modern sense of the term, and for creating a new form of publication, the restaurant guide.

Grimod's first love was not food but the theatre, and it was primarily as a theatre critic during the last years of the *ancien régime* that he first appeared in print. His writing went relatively unnoticed until he called attention to himself by organizing a dinner at his home in Paris, frequently referred to at the time and thereafter as the *souper scandaleux*. The 'scandalous' aspect of this dinner, held on 1 February 1783, was presaged by the invitation he sent out announcing it. This was exceptionally large, 52 × 40 cm (20.5 × 15.75"), and printed to look like a death notice. Grimod is said to have welcomed his guests to a dining room hung with black cloth, with a coffin in the middle of the table, and the room full of candles (one for each day of the year). The dinner itself was said to be admirable, but the setting caused more of a stir than the food; and the event was so talked about that Grimod felt compelled to repeat it three years later. This made him a celebrity and established his association with the table, but his behaviour, at the scandalous dinner and otherwise, caused his family to insist that he be sent to the country 'for his own good', and he had to spend two years in a monastery near the town of Domère.

His interest in food must have been growing steadily, for an inventory of the books in his possession in 1795 (cited by Rival, 1983) shows that he owned almost all of the famous cookery books printed in the 18th century. By 1803, when Grimod's first book about food, *L'Almanach des gourmands*, appeared, he no doubt felt that he had accumulated enough expertise to pass judgement on the efforts of cooks and purveyors of food in all forms. The timing was good, since food shops and restaurants were proliferating in Paris at an extraordinary rate.

The *Almanach* was not just a guide to the best food shops and restaurants in Paris but also a collection of essays devoted to the serving, choosing, and preparing of food in general. Grimod's writing was full of hyperbole, with the merits of certain preparations described in extravagant terms but always with the utmost seriousness. Although he was not the first to write lyrically about food, Grimod was the first, at least in France, to devote a book to the critical appraisal of the food then available to his readers: where to buy food and where to eat out. The *Almanach* of 1803 was an enormous success, and was followed by seven others (1804, 1805, 1806, 1807, 1808, 1810, and 1811–12).

A feature of each *Almanach* was an account of the deliberations of a *jury de gustateurs* (tasting panel) whose function was to taste and evaluate pastries, hams, jams, or anything else submitted by shops throughout Paris, anxious to receive endorsement for their products. The jurors, twelve in number, would meet each Tuesday and could expect to spend at least five hours at table. Originally, only men were invited. In 1806 Grimod began to invite women too, on condition that they would not express views unless asked and that their votes would anyway not count. Among these underprivileged jurors was Émilie Contant of the Comédie-Française, to whom credit is due for changing the system of serving soup.

Grimod's 'jury' seems to have been the first such instrument for making awards of

excellence in the food trade. The institutions which have succeeded it have been as influential as the guidebooks which followed his *Almanach*. However, modern tasting panels are dull affairs by comparison with their exemplar, which maintained a standard of ceremony and mystery which has never been matched. Although Grimod's own elderly housekeeper, Hélène, was allowed to clear the dishes away from the jurors' table, they were otherwise quite insulated from the servants who prepared the food. Communications with the kitchen were maintained by Grimod through a speaking tube on which was mounted the head of a female cook; a head to which he bent his lips or his ear, according to whether he was speaking or listening.

1808 saw the publication of Grimod's *Manuel des Amphitryons*, a self-contained book which enlarged upon and treated systematically subjects such as the choice and serving of food, touched upon in the *Almanach*. This book was Grimod's main work in gastronomy.

The year 1812 was calamitous. Everything went wrong for Grimod, who had made many enemies and who did little to conceal his anti-Napoleonic sentiments. Obliged to leave the capital, he played another sinister joke. A notice was sent out announcing his death, and that the funeral procession would leave his house in the Champs-Élysées at 4 p.m. on 7 July. Only a few faithful friends responded by coming to the house at this hour. They found a bier in the hall and candles burning, and were taken into an inner room to murmur condolences. Suddenly a door was opened and they saw with stupefaction a table prepared for dinner with Grimod sitting at the end, fully alive and noting with satisfaction that he had correctly estimated the number of his true friends: there was a place laid for each, and none to spare.

His time in Paris thus terminated in his own strange style, Grimod passed the rest of his life in retreat in the country. He died on 25 December 1837, at the age of 80, at table and after finishing his Christmas dinner.

Although the *Almanach* had opened the way for other publications in which foods and restaurants would be evaluated on a regular basis, these did not start to appear at once when Grimod retired from public view. A very long time was to pass before tasting panels were revived and guides to restaurants became commonplace. On the other hand, books dealing with the appreciation of food started to proliferate almost immediately (see, for example, BRILLAT-SAVARIN), which suggests that his writing was a spur to such productions.

His own interest in food lay in the pleasures to be derived from it. In his writings, however, he went beyond mere

lyrical praise of dishes or the writing of recipes, and sought to instruct and guide the consumers and gastronomes. He thus created for himself a position of authority, to be occupied by many thereafter, as an arbiter between the producers of food and the public; and the consequences of this novel activity have been far-reaching.　　　HY

GRISETTE the French and also the English name of *Amanita vaginata*, a delicately flavoured mushroom found in the autumn in woods of many parts of Europe and America. It stands 10 to 15 cm (4 to 6") high and measures about 8 cm (3") across the cap when fully grown. The colour of the cap is usually grey (whence 'grisette') or brown, but some varieties (or closely related species—the taxonomy is uncertain) have orange or even whitish caps. The gills are white or creamy.

Grisettes are edible, but care needs to be taken to distinguish them from other, dangerous members of the genus *Amanita*. The grisette differs from other *Amanita* species by having no ring on the stem. It also has short radial marks around the top outer edge of the cap, like marks made on a pie crust by a fork.

Jordan (1975) comments that the flavour is pleasantly strong, and the texture delicate. Roux-Saget and Delplanque (1985) dub it the 'chop suey' mushroom, fit to be added to a mixture of fungi as its own flesh is scanty.

GROATS AND GRITS are terms which come from the same root and are almost synonymous. The former is more used in Britain and usually refers to OATS which have been husked (hulled), and crushed rather than ground; while the latter is used in N. America, especially the southern states, where HOMINY grits (see also MAIZE) are important.

Groats are not necessarily of oats and grits need not be of corn (maize), but if other grains are meant these have to be specified (as in BARLEY groats). Grits used alone would normally be taken to mean hominy grits (and hominy used by itself would usually refer to a more coarsely ground product than grits).

Grits for breakfast, or served as a side dish, are long-established dishes of the southern states. A speciality of Louisiana is 'grillade and grits', beef or veal braised with seasonings and served with buttered grits.

GROUND CHERRY a name applied to various plants of the genus *Physalis*, which bear fruits about the size of a cherry in a papery husk or calyx (like the CAPE GOOSEBERRY). There are many in

N. America, where they were eaten extensively by N. American Indians, and where the culinary writers Cora, Rose, and Bob Brown (1938) summed them up thus:

There's a lot of confusion about these homely little bundles of luscious flavor that grow about the size of cranberries, each enclosed in a tissue husk that looks like a Chinese lantern. Some say they taste like cherries, others like tomatoes. We've eaten them ever since we were kids and don't yet know which they resemble most. When preserved in syrup they taste like figs.

The two principal species, for each of which there are several cultivars available, are:

- P. pubescens (formerly P. pruinosa), whose fruits vary in colour and flavour according to the cultivar, but with a marked tendency to pineapple or strawberry flavours. Indeed the name strawberry tomato has been used. Besides the usual range of uses in jams, in pies, as ice cream toppings, and so forth, the fruits can be dried in sugar and then used instead of raisins in cakes.
- P. philadelphica, purple ground cherry (sometimes called wild tomatillo), popular in C. America for use in place of tomatoes and in hot chilli sauces. Cultivars include Purple de Milpa (small, sharply flavoured fruits) and Zuni (sweet, cultivated by the Zuni Indians since before the tomato).

See also CAPE GOOSEBERRY and TREE-TOMATO (tomatillo).

GROUND ELDER

GROUND ELDER *Aegopodium podagraria*, a plant of the umbelliferous family which grows in temperate Europe. The leaves have some resemblance to those of elder; hence the name. An alternative name, goutweed, alludes to the supposed medicinal properties of the plant.

Generally, this plant is perceived as an annoying weed which is notoriously difficult to eradicate. Gerard (1633) noted that ground elder 'is so fruitful in his increase that where it hath once taken roote, it will hardly be gotten out again, spoiling and getting every yeere more ground, to the annoying of better herbes'. However, it has enjoyed a limited use, mainly in N. Europe, as a pot-herb or salad ingredient, and has elicited praise from Pamela Michael (1980), who recommends it as a spring or early summer vegetable. She writes:

It is impossible to describe the entirely original flavour of ground elder when cooked. Don't be deterred by the horrible pungent smell when you pick the leaves which, if you have the plant growing as a weed in your garden, will be all too familiar. This smell entirely disappears in the cooking, and you are left with one of the most delicious wild vegetables.

GROUNDNUTS

GROUNDNUTS often called peanuts (and, in the past, monkey nuts), are not, in the eyes of botanists, true nuts. The plants which produce them, notably *Arachis hypogaea*, are LEGUMES like PEAS or BEANS, but have developed the habit of thrusting their flower stems into the ground after flowering and pollination, so that the fruit pods develop underground.

The groundnut, which thrives in both tropical and subtropical climates, was first grown in pre-Inca times in ancient Peru, and ranks among the half-dozen most important New World foods which were made available to the Old World as a result of Columbus' voyages at the end of the 15th century. Its importance was quickly perceived, and from S. America it spread rapidly around the world, being taken to both W. and E. Africa by the Portuguese, to the Philippines and E. Asia across the Pacific from Mexico, and to N. America from Africa. It is now one of the world's major food crops, vital to the nutrition of some peoples and to the economy of some countries. Although India is the main producer, and China lies second, the USA has become the principal exporting country and has provided some of the most picturesque personalities and marketing ploys associated with the nuts.

Groundnuts are grown both for use in solid foods and for oil. They are rich in protein (about 30%) and oil (up to 50%), but the amounts depend on the variety being grown and perhaps also on climate.

The ordinary groundnut or peanut, *Arachis hypogaea*, exists in several varieties, which fall into two main categories: the upright forms with the nuts all growing near the main roots, and the trailing form whose nuts are scattered along the creeping stems. The former are easier to harvest. The skin covering the kernel may be white, cream, brown, brick red, or even piebald—red and white. The number of kernels in a pod is only two or three in some varieties, but as many as five to seven in others. A few of the leading varieties are:

- **Virginia** (also called Virginia Bunch), providing most of the peanuts which are eaten in the USA as whole nuts (roasted and salted, or from the shell—the latter being known as 'ballpark peanuts'). It is an upright plant, and its pods usually contain two large seeds.
- **Florunner,** a new variety, an example of the trailing form, which has become dominant in the south-east of the USA; and most of it goes into peanut butter.
- **Spanish,** another upright variety, with smaller seeds which are rich in oil, so it is used principally for that.
- **Valencia,** with small and rich kernels, well liked for roasting in the shell.

Groundnuts are eaten in many forms. In western countries they are most familiar as roasted or salted peanuts, or in peanut butter (see below) or incorporated in confectionery.

Groundnuts are of prime importance in the cooking of Indonesia and Malaysia. Roasted and ground to a paste, they make the famous SATAY sauce for meat grilled on skewers. They also provide a salad dressing, *gado-gado*, and a kind of savoury peanut brittle, *rempeyek kacang*.

In W. Africa groundnuts are also an important food. Groundnut 'chop' is a favourite food in most parts of the region. This is a kind of stew, usually made with chicken, in which a groundnut paste features prominently.

Although both India and China produce large amounts of peanuts, these are mostly used for oil. The oil is extracted from the nuts simply by pressing. Oil made locally for local use is generally not deodorized or otherwise treated, so is somewhat gummy and has a noticeable peanut taste; this is acceptable in, for example, African regional dishes. Refined groundnut oil, which is tasteless and suitable for export, can be used as a bland alternative to olive oil for use in dressing salads. It is also a good cooking oil, well above average in its resistance to heat. Although relatively high in polyunsaturates, it does not go rancid quickly.

Peanut butter is a favourite food in N. America where peanut butter and jelly sandwiches have a hallowed place in the diet. It is made by roasting peanuts and grinding them to a paste, usually with a little salt. The minimum peanut content in peanut butter is 90%. Oilier varieties of peanut form a paste by themselves; others may need a little extra oil. Grinding may be stopped before the nuts are completely crushed, to make 'crunchy' peanut butter.

Rosengarten (1984) has a particularly informative and readable essay on the history of peanuts and peanut products in the USA.

OTHER SPECIES

Two other species of groundnut are also grown, although they have been largely supplanted by *A. hypogaea*:

- the **Bambarra** groundnut, *Voandzeia subterranea*, in tropical Africa, Madagascar, Brazil, and parts of Asia; and
- the **Hausa** or Kersting's groundnut, *Kerstingiella geocarpa*, in many parts of W. Africa.

Both have seeds which are starchy and contain less oil than the ordinary groundnut, but they have local importance as foodstuffs.

Bambarra groundnuts must be cooked before being eaten. Boiled fresh, they make a good vegetable, like LIMA BEANS in flavour.

In W. Africa they are often prepared by boiling and then crushing them into cakes or balls. If these are fried in palm oil, they keep relatively well.

The seeds of the Hausa groundnut are somewhat flattened and kidney shaped, dark brown or black in colour, and are prepared in various ways. The Dagomba tribe of the Gold Coast boil the kernels, add salt and SHEA BUTTER, and eat the mixture.

GROUPER the common name usually applied to fish of the genus *Epinephelus* and some close relations, seems to have come into English, in the 17th century, as an adaptation of the Portuguese *garoupa*, which in turn may have come from a SE Asian name such as *kerapu*. (The explanation that these fish, although normally solitary, sometimes congregate in large groups does not seem plausible.)

The variant 'groper' has been in use, especially in Australasia, since the late 19th century. Confusion may be caused by the fact that Australians often use the name 'groper' for certain WRASSES and PARROTFISH and apply the inappropriate names 'rock cod' or 'coral cod' to some groupers. For some species the name 'coral trout' is in use, for example *Plectropomus leopardus*, the leopard coral trout, a relatively large fish (maximum length 1.2 m/48") which has a variable but always striking coloration—the body is light red, or even orange, and largely covered with dark-edged blue spots.

Whatever the origin of the name, these fish occur in warm and tropical waters worldwide. They are heavy bodied and some species grow to a great size. The largest of all, *Promicrops lanceolatus*, has a maximum length of about 3.5 m (nearly 12'), and may weigh as much as 500 kg/1,100 lb. Adult specimens are dark brown, almost black, and must make a terrifying spectacle when they rush out of their hiding places to attack fishermen, as they reputedly do.

Coloration of groupers varies, being generally such as to camouflage the fish and therefore depending on habitat. The lifestyle is generally solitary, and a given fish will probably stay in its own territory throughout its life. There are records of groupers being regularly visited in the same spot by divers, and even of their making friends with these divers and learning to perform tricks for them. Many divers, however, seek them out to kill them, since they make impressive trophies; and most groupers are excellent to eat, with firm, flaky, flesh of a fine flavour.

The very numerous species include five in the Mediterranean (not counting a couple of Indo-Pacific species which have penetrated the E. Mediterranean via the Suez Canal). All five, which have maximum lengths of a

metre (40") or more, are also found in the E. Atlantic. Within the Mediterranean most of them are more common in the south and centre, and do not occur in, for example, the Gulf of Genoa or the N. Adriatic. But the most common and best-known species, *Epinephelus guaza*, is present throughout.

Groupers are numerous in the Caribbean region. *E. striatus*, the Nassau grouper, is one marked by distinctive bands. It was a fish of this species which was recorded as picking the pockets (full of crayfish tails) of a Nassau underwater photographer (Böhlke and Chaplin, 1968, a work in which the various Caribbean groupers are well catalogued). The largest of the family in the Caribbean, *E. itajara*, has been known to reach a length of 2.4 m (8'). It is known as jewfish or giant sea bass.

Several of the Caribbean groupers are also found in the E. Pacific. The main collection of Indo-Pacific species is most strongly represented in the Indian Ocean, SE Asia, and N. Australia, but there are several in Japanese waters.

The polka-dot grouper, *Cromileptes altivelis*, is among the most expensive fish in Hong Kong, although it has an unattractive Chinese name meaning 'rat grouper'. This is a grouper of medium size, with a maximum length of 60 cm (24"), and the superb quality of its flesh bears out the general principle that in this family it is the medium-sized fish which offer the best eating.

Epinephelus akaara is even more expensive at Hong Kong, where it is known as *hung-paan*. In the Pescadores Islands (west of Taiwan), special measures are taken to capture this species alive and to keep it alive until it is sold thus in the Hong Kong market. It is referred to as the 'red grouper', but is really a brownish fish with red spots.

There are many ways of preparing grouper. Small ones can be cooked whole, after cleaning; but it is more common to buy steaks cut from larger fish, which can be grilled, fried, or poached.

GROUSE a name which has a fairly wide application, hither and yonder, to various birds in the family Phasianidae, but which usually refers to the species *Lagopus lagopus*, in which the most important subspecies are *L. l. scoticus*, the red grouse of Britain, and *L. l. lagopus*, the willow grouse (or, in N. America, willow ptarmigan). The word is also part of the names BLACK GROUSE (*Tetrao tetrix*, Europe to Siberia); hazel grouse (*Bonasa bonasia*, Scandinavia and C. Europe to the Orient); and ruffed grouse (*Bonasa umbellus*, important in N. America). See also CAPERCAILLIE.

Grouse, plump and chicken-like, are chiefly ground-dwelling birds. However, at least in Britain, 'sport' requires that they be not shot on the ground. Thus grouse-shooting calls for beaters, whose task is to advance through the terrain where the grouse lurk, beating the heather or bushes, and making a commotion sufficient to frighten the birds into the air, where they present a legitimate target for the shooting party. The season begins on 12 August, which for grouse-shooters is therefore called 'the Glorious Twelfth'. (The subspecies of the human race which, in this setting, is the chief predator of the grouse used to be readily recognizable, whether male or accompanying female, by its raiment of heathery tweed; but in the course of the 20th century increasing numbers of foreign predators came upon the scene, often of a different and less appropriate coloration, yet still to be identified by the tell-tale guns which all carry.)

Grouse, whose dark flesh has a distinctive flavour, are excellent to eat. Young birds are suitable for roasting or braising; older ones for the casserole. In general, a recipe which is good for PHEASANT will suit grouse too. Eliza Acton (1855) advises that, when a grouse (or other similar game bird) is being roasted, a buttered toast should be introduced under the bird in the dripping pan about ten minutes before roasting is complete. Noting that there are few

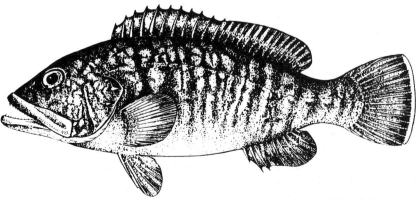

Epinephelus guaza

occasions when it is appropriate to bring the contents of the dripping pan to table, she claims not only that this is one, but that the toast 'will afford a superior relish even to the birds themselves'.

GRUBS of various insects come into the category of INSECTS AS FOOD.

However, grub is an imprecise term, meaning LARVA, especially but not exclusively of beetles. It is the grubs of beetles which are dealt with here. (For the larvae of butterflies, see CATERPILLARS and SILKWORM; and for those of certain Australian moths see WITCHETTY GRUBS. Bee grubs are also eaten in some places.)

An outstanding example of consumption of beetle grubs is given in the entry for COCKCHAFERS (which are scarabeid beetles). There are, however, numerous other examples, some involving advance preparations of a kind sufficient to demonstrate that the grubs are counted as a delicacy. Thus in Japan the grubs of a longhorn beetle are marinated in soy sauce before being grilled (broiled). And Schwabe (1979) records that in Samoa beetle grubs are fed on coconut shavings for a day or two, then wrapped in a banana leaf and roasted over charcoal.

GRUEL is a variation of PORRIDGE, made from finely ground oatmeal, which is mixed with water or milk, allowed to soak, and then cooked. Eventually the solids are strained out of the mixture; there is some disagreement as to whether or not this should take place before or after cooking. The result is smooth, and jellies when cold. It was prepared as suitable and nourishing food for invalids; tiresome Mr Woodhouse in *Emma* by Jane Austen seemed to eat little else. Salt, sugar, honey, or 'with the medical man's permission, a dessert-spoonful of brandy, or a table-spoonful of wine may be added', according to Delamere and Delamere (1868).

The name gruel is derived from the French *gruau*, which means finely ground flour. Medieval gruels might contain vegetables, herbs, or meat, such as 'drawn gruel', which contained the juices drawn from cooked beef, or 'forced gruel', mixed with pounded pork. Other versions were sweet, containing dried fruit, sugar, and butter; or medicinal, with herbs to purify the blood. The Scots regarded gruel as good for coughs and colds.   LM

GRUNT (besides referring to an American dessert, for which see SLUMP) is the common English name used for several species of fish in the family Haemulidae (until recently,

Pomadasyidae). These are Indo-Pacific fish, mostly of medium size (a typical maximum length would be 75 cm/30"), with fairly deep, narrow bodies and thick lips. Indeed the name 'sweetlips' is applied to many of them, e.g. *Plectorhynchus pictus*, which wears a bright livery and is also called 'painted grunt'. It is a popular fish in Malay markets, as is *Pomadasys hasta*, the silver grunt. In the W. Atlantic, the largest grunt is *Haemulon album*, the margate, greyish in general colour and an important food fish.

The large lips of these fish are used by some species for mutual display, 'facing one another and with wide open mouths pushing one another, an act often referred to as kissing, but its significance to the fishes is not really understood' (Wheeler, 1979).

The grunting noise which is characteristic of the family is audible when they are in the water, but most noticed when they are caught. It is produced by grinding their teeth, a natural reaction to capture, and the sound is magnified by the air bladder, which acts as a resonance chamber.

GRUYÈRE the finest and best known of all Swiss cheeses, has been made since the 12th century. Its reputation as one of the great European table cheeses was established by the 16th century; and 19th-century chefs gave it further renown as one of the world's great cooking cheeses (see e.g. FONDUE).

Within Switzerland, the use of the name Gruyère is strictly controlled, as are its other specifications and the manufacturing process. Compared with EMMENTAL, the other well-known Swiss cheese, Gruyère is smaller; usually 35 to 40 kg (77 to 88 lb) in weight and 50 cm (20") in diameter. It has fewer and smaller (little larger than pea size) 'eyes'. It is subject to a certain amount of surface ripening during its long maturing period (typically a year), which gives it a more nutty flavour.

Real Swiss Gruyère has 'Switzerland' stamped in red all over the flat faces of its broad 'wheels'. This is a necessary precaution; rivals and imitations are made elsewhere.

The French have good reason to call some of their own cheeses Gruyère, since they have been making them under that name for many centuries and the village of Gruyère, whence the cheese took its name, is only just on the Swiss side of the Franco-Swiss frontier—a frontier which, as Maggie Black (1989) points out, was hardly noticeable in the Middle Ages:

Whether you lived in French Haute-Savoie or Franche-Comté or in one of the neighbouring Swiss cantons, you battled with the same land of steep mountains and deep river valleys, snow-bound in winter and beset by gales. You spoke the same language when you met, but that might not

be often; the narrow mountain tracks were rough, and most farms were isolated. You grew and raised the same foodstuffs, and you made the same basic cheese, with some regional differences.

In these conditions both Swiss and French farmers chose to make a firm, condensed, long-maturing cheese which could be stored until the opportunity arose to take it over the mountains to market.

However, French Gruyère cheeses are not quite the same thing as the Swiss ones. The two main French types are *Gruyère de Comté* (or just *Comté*) and BEAUFORT (sometimes referred to as *Gruyère de Beaufort*). The former, which has a fruitier and saltier taste than might be expected, contains relatively large (cherry-size) holes; while the latter has virtually no holes at all.

The propionic acid bacteria which give these cheeses their distinctive acid taste also form bubbles of gas, which are what cause the holes; but this function of the bacteria is either inhibited or encouraged by various circumstances, so producing various results; and the degree to which the cheese is pressed also affects how holey it is. Swiss Gruyère is the hardest pressed and driest of all Swiss-type cheeses.

GUARANA a beverage made in Brazil from the seeds of the guarana tree, *Paullinia cupana*. As Emerson (1908) writes: 'The seeds are roasted and pulverised, after which the powder is moistened and formed into cakes and rolls of different sizes and many shapes. These are then dried in the smoke of green wood or, if the sun is hot enough, in the sun and become almost stone-like in their hardness. To make the beverage, all that is necessary to do is to scrape off with a knife about a teaspoonful of powder and pour it into a glass of water and the drink is ready. Sugar may be added.' The drink is sometimes known as 'Brazilian cocoa'.

GUASCAS (or huascas), *Galinsoga parviflora*, a herb of tropical America, especially the Andean region and Colombia, which has found its way by one means or another to parts of N. America, Europe, and Asia. It belongs to the family Compositae, is of erect habit, and may grow to a height of well over 1 m (say, 50").

Although in countries where it is naturalized the leaves are sometimes used as a vegetable (for example, writing of Java, Ochse, 1980, comments that the plants 'grow incredibly fast' and very densely, on roadsides and similar sites, and states that the young 'tops' constitute 'a much relished and savoury *lalab* [side dish of greens or fruit] which is eaten, steamed, with rice'), it is more usually regarded as a weed (sometimes called quickweed) and it is only in the lands where it originated that it has real culinary importance.

Elisabeth Lambert Ortiz (1984) remarks that: 'It is sold in jars, dried and ground into a green powder, in Colombian food shops. Though it has no relationship whatsoever to Jerusalem artichokes, its smell is reminiscent of that vegetable. It adds a delicious flavour to soups and stews, particularly those made with chicken.'

GUAVA the fruit of the small, shrubby tree *Psidium guajava*, native to C. America and the W. Indies, is now grown in tropical and subtropical regions around the world, especially India, SE Asia, and Hawaii. There are several other species in the genus with good fruits, and the name 'guava' is applied loosely to most of them.

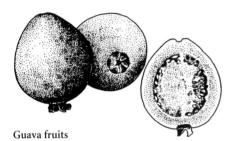

Guava fruits

The oldest known traces of guava as a human food date from about 800 BC, from archaeological sites in Peru. The tree was probably first cultivated there, but had spread as far north as Mexico by 200 BC. Europeans first met the fruit when they made their earliest voyage to Haiti, where the local name for it was *guayavu*. Spanish and Portuguese mariners soon spread the tree and its name to other regions. In the 17th century it was well established in India and SE Asia, and has remained popular there ever since.

Guava fruits vary in size, shape, and colour, even within the principal species, *P. guajava*. They range from the size of an apple to that of a plum, and may be round or pear shaped, rough or smooth skinned, and greenish-white, yellow, or red in colour. Large, pear-shaped, white ones are considered the best. The fruit has an outer and inner zone, the latter with many small gritty seeds (except in seedless varieties).

The taste is acid but sweet, with an unusual aromatic quality partly due to eugenol, an essential oil found also in cloves. Unripe guavas are astringent, but if picked when nearly ripe they are soon ready to eat.

Besides being eaten fresh, guavas can be used to make custards, ices, and beverages; or a delicious jelly, for which small, sour

fruits are preferred; or a stiff paste known as 'guava cheese'.

Morton (1987) observed that 'A standard dessert throughout Latin America and the Spanish speaking islands of the W Indies is stewed guava shells (*cascos de guayaba*), that is guava halves with the central seed pulp removed, strained and added to the shells while cooking to enrich the sirup. They are often served with cream cheese.'

Of the other species *P. cattleianum*, the Cattley or strawberry guava, is the best. It is a native of Brazil, produces round reddish-green fruits, and is now widely cultivated. The variety *lucida*, known as the Chinese strawberry guava, bears yellow fruits which are particularly good.

GUDGEON *Gobio gobio*, a small freshwater fish of C. and N. Europe and W. Asia, typically found in shoals on clean river bottoms. It has a roundish body with a series of dark blotches down the side, and reaches a maximum length of 20 cm (8"). A good food fish, eaten with appreciation in some European countries.

GUÉPINIE the French name for an edible fungus which falls in the category of JELLY FUNGUS. It is unknown in Britain, although it does have the English name 'apricot jelly' in the Pacific north-west region of N. America. It is *Phlogiotis* (formerly *Tremiscus* or *Guepinia*) *helvelloides*, a mountain species which, as the drawing shows, has a remarkable shape, difficult to describe. Its height ranges from 3 to 12 cm (1.5–5"); its colour is rosy orange or coral red; and its texture gelatinous, translucid, and elastic. A French author has described it as looking like a piece of candied fruit without the coating of frosted sugar. It is to be eaten raw in salads, e.g. with chopped hard-boiled eggs, chives, and capers, and a suitable dressing. It has little flavour of its own.

Phlogiotis helvelloides

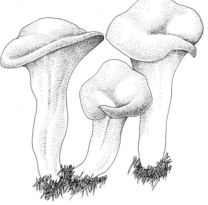

GUILLEMOT *Uria aalge*, a salt-water diving bird of the family Alcidae, known on various European coasts. It is not normally eaten, but its large eggs are gathered for food in some regions.

GUINEA-FOWL birds of four or five species, all in the family Numididae and all indigenous to Africa. Most of them have the speckled or pearl-like plumage which can readily be identified in ancient representations of the bird, and very noticeably and beautifully in a painting by Pisanello (or one of his associates) which is often reproduced. The most important species by far, *Numidia meleagris*, is the bird there depicted.

In Africa the various species of the guinea-fowl have ranges which collectively extend over the greater part of the continent south of the Sahara. They occupy a wide range of environment from the edges of the desert to savannah lands (favoured by *N. meleagris*) and high forests. They have always had a reputation as crop robbers and this habit, bringing them into close contact, albeit of a competitive kind, with humans may have contributed to their domestication. This probably took place in Africa and is likely to have been associated with the introduction of keeping the domestic HEN. Diffusion to Europe first took place from E. Africa, but there was subsequently a strong connection in this respect between Guinea in W. Africa and Portugal, which had a noticeable effect on the vernacular names given to the guinea-fowl in various languages. The Italian *faraona* is one of the few linguistic vestiges of the old connection with Egypt.

Guinea-fowl were certainly known in ancient Egypt and in classical Greece and Rome. They appear quite often in Roman mosaics. However, comments by such authors as Varro and Martial suggest that up to the 1st century AD or later guinea-fowl were 'still something of a rarity and the meat a special delicacy'. The quotation is from Donkin (1991) whose monograph on guinea-fowl is a model of its kind and covers the historical aspect, all the way up to the 16th century, with remarkable thoroughness.

The classical world was also responsible for the legend which provides the specific name of the guinea-fowl, *meleagris*. The sisters of Meleager, the prince of Macedon who met an untimely death, are said to have wept so freely that they were transformed by a goddess into the birds, the pearl-like spots on their plumage being the tears. The sisters then settled in the island of Leros, off the coast of Caria; and it is in fact this island which, according to Donkin, provides the first clear evidence of guinea-fowl outside Africa. The generic part of the scientific name, *Numidia*, refers to the N. African country of that name in Roman times. Some species of guinea-fowl had probably been established there from very early times.

The guinea-fowl took part in the COLUMBIAN EXCHANGE between the Old World and the New World. In this there were only three successful animal travellers from Africa to the New World: the ass, the cat, and the guinea-fowl. Although showing a tendency to become feral, the guinea-fowl was admitted to poultry yards and has been an item of domestic poultry there, as in Europe, ever since. Its limited success in this role, in both America and Europe, is probably the result of effective competition from the turkey and chicken. Donkin comments: 'The guinea fowl has tended to remain, in Edward Balfour's words, "the bohemian of the barnyard".' (A curious echo of this is the occasional use of the name 'Bohemian pheasant' for guinea-fowl on menus.)

GUINEA PIG (also known as cavy), *Cavia porcellus* in its domesticated form, and also existing in numerous wild species, acquired its name from Guiana, where Europeans arriving in S. America found it. Its original home was in the highlands of Peru and Bolivia.

The guinea pig had already been domesticated by the Inca of Peru, for whom it was an important food. Sophie Coe (1994) writes of them thus:

Domesticated and widespread by 2000 BC in the highlands, their squeaking and rustling still enlivens Indian dwellings today. They are fed specially collected wild plants and, because they cannot climb, a simple sill is enough to keep them inside the house. Notorious for quick multiplication, two males and twenty females are said to be able to provide a family with a *cuy* a day.

The Indians eat this little animal with the skin on, only removing the hair as if it were a suckling pig. For them it is a great delicacy, and they cook it whole, gutted, with much chilli and smooth pebbles from the river. The stones they call *calapurca*, which in Aymara means 'stomach stones', because in this dish they put the stones in the belly of the *cuy*. This dish the Indians consider a greater delicacy than anything the Spaniards can make. (Cobo, *Historia del Nuevo Mundo* (1890–93), ii. 306).

The stones Cobo describes were heated before they were put into the belly of the *cuy*. Roasting and boiling using heated stones were important in Andean culinary technology, and had other applications as well. During the siege of Cuzco, when the rebelling Inca had a force of Spaniards bottled up in the town, the thatched roofs were set on fire by hot stones hurled by the Inca. Putting a few heated pebbles in the body cavity of a *cuy* would have posed no problem. Other recipes for cooking *cuy* suggest stuffing it with mint and *Tagetes minuta*, a Mexican species of New World marigold. . . . The entrails of the *cuy* could be cooked with potatoes in a soup, or made into sauce.

A guinea pig may weigh as much as 1 kg, although the normal weight is only half that. In Peru and some other S. American countries breeding projects have been under way, producing 'super guinea pigs' which may weigh as much as 2 kg. It is not only in S. America that guinea pigs are prized as food. In W. Africa and the Philippines they are bred for the table.

Of the close relations of the guinea pig, the Patagonian cavy (or mara or pampas hare), *Dolichotis patagonum*, is perhaps the most interesting. This is a relatively large animal whose appearance is reminiscent of the hare and which may weigh as much as 15 kg (33 lb). A specimen which Charles Darwin shot in Patagonia (when he was spending time ashore in the course of the voyage round the world in HMS *Beagle*) weighed more than 9 kg (20 lb) and won very high praise from him; he said that it 'affords the very best meat I ever tasted'.

READING: Archetti (1997).

GUITARFISH *Rhinobatos rhinobatos*, one of the few species of fish which are intermediate between sharks and rays. The shape explains the common names. Maximum length 1 m (40"). Range: the Mediterranean and the E. Atlantic from Portugal down to Angola. A fish of only moderate quality, not prominent in the markets.

In the Indo-Pacific there are species of similar shape, notably *Rhyncobatis djeddensis*, known as the shovel-nose ray or sand shark and occasionally referred to as a guitar fish. It may reach a length of 3 m (10') and is an important game fish in parts of southern Africa and Australia. It makes much better eating than the Mediterranean species.

GULAB JAMUN a favourite among INDIAN SWEETS, is prepared from *khoya* (see MILK REDUCTION) or milk powder mixed with a little flour, warm milk, and GHEE. The dough is made into small balls which are deep fried gently in ghee, then lengthily soaked in rose-flavoured syrup (*gulab* means rose) before serving. They are also eaten hot.

LM

GULL the common name for a very large tribe of seabirds, of which many are edible but few are eaten, except locally in coastal communities where there is a tradition of doing so. It is more common for their eggs to be eaten.

Three of the best-known species are: *Larus canus*, the common gull; *L. ridibundus*, the black-headed gull; and *L. argentatus*, the herring gull. In England, in earlier centuries,

gulls were among the birds recorded as being kept in poultry-yards and fattened for consumption. Thus Robert MAY (1685) explained how to keep herns, puets (thought to be young black-headed gulls), gulls, and bitterns. One purpose of this was 'to furnish the table at great feasts'. Although nobody would think of doing this now, the elaborate measures suggested by May seem to show that in his time one could make the birds highly palatable. He explains that:

the manner of bringing them up with the least charge, is to take them out of their nests before they can flie, and put them into a large barn, where there is many high cross beams for them to perch on; then to have on the flour [floor] divers square boards with rings in them, and between every board which should be two yards square, to place round shallow tubs full of water, then to the boards you shall tye great gobbits of dogs flesh, cut from the bones, according to the number which you feed, and be sure to keep the house sweet, and shift the water often, only the house must be made so, that it may rain in now and then, . . . [the birds loved being rained on] . . . but if you feed her for the dish [i.e. especially for the table], then you shall feed them with livers, and the entra[i]ls of beasts, and such like cut in great gobbits.

GUM a word which originally referred only to sticky secretions of certain trees and shrubs which (unlike RESIN, another such secretion) are soluble in water. Nowadays, the meaning of the term includes some chemical products which have similar properties to those of the natural gums. These properties are of great use to the food-processing and catering industries. Commercially produced foods have to be protected, during the interval between production and consumption, from undesirable changes; emulsions must be kept from separating; dispersed particles must not settle to the bottom or top of a liquid; jellies must not dry up. Gums are used to stabilize the foods and prevent such changes.

In addition, gums can be used to thicken products such as sauces, giving any desired degree of viscosity or stickiness, or producing a gel; and as binders in cakes and similar items, where they can give a firm texture without the use of strong flour or more expensive binding agents such as eggs.

Gums are derived from a very wide range of sources. Some, such as GUM ARABIC and GUM TRAGACANTH, are exuded from the gashed bark of trees. Others, like gum guar (obtained from the CLUSTER BEAN), or locust bean gum (from the locust bean, see CAROB), come from seedpods. Some, like AGAR-AGAR, ALGINATES, and carrageenan (see CARRAGEEN), are derived from seaweeds; the Japanese use of KOMBU is an outstanding example.

Gums may also be made by the treatment of starch and cellulose in factories. And some, such as dextran, are even produced by bacteria.

All gums are CARBOHYDRATES with long molecules consisting of many sugar molecules linked into chains. These molecules disperse in water, and the shape of the chain, and the other molecule groups attached to it, influences the properties of the gum. When straight, linear chains disperse in water they take up a lot of space, making the liquid viscous in the same way as does starch which has a similar molecular structure.

Some of the molecules are chemically neutral, others have carboxyl groups (arrangements of atoms conferring acid properties). The neutral chains make liquids thick but not tacky; they do not gel but dry to a coating film. Acid types are affected by the acidity of the foodstuff in which they are dispersed. In highly acidic foods they precipitate (solidify and come out of suspension) and the smooth texture disintegrates. In moderate acidity they are stable and form a gel. Gelling is helped by the presence of calcium, a common element in foodstuffs and in hard water, which forms cross-links between the chains.

Gums with branched chains such as the gums arabic, tragacanth, karaya (from *Sterculia urens*, of tropical Asia), guar, and locust bean, form tacky dispersions and in favourable conditions, strong gels. They do not form coatings on food.

Most gums contain chains of both types in differing proportions so that they display mixed characteristics. In the food industry, gums are often chemically treated to alter the proportions and give them particular properties. Any one chain may include groups which are attractive to water and others which have an affinity to oil. Such a gum can be used as an emulsifier to hold oil and water together stably. Many gums are good emulsifiers.

The best gum for thickening, stabilizing, and emulsifying is gum arabic. Effective substitutes are gum tragacanth (often used in thickening salad dressing and brown sauce and also in ice cream and confectionery) and gum karaya (which will in addition prevent crystals from forming in ice cream). Gums ghatti (from *Anogeissus latifolia*, the ghatti tree of India) and guar (which has largely superseded locust bean gum, on which see CAROB) are used in salad dressings and ice cream as stabilizers and thickeners. So is carrageenan, which also serves to suspend cocoa particles in chocolate-flavoured milk, and stabilize other dairy products. Dextran can perform the same functions.

For gelling, gum furcellaran is most commonly used, not only in marmalades and jams, but also in jellied fish and meats.

(RH)

GUM ARABIC sometimes called Senegal gum or acacia gum, is a product of *Acacia senegal* and other trees of the family Mimosoideae. *A. senegal* grows in N. Africa, Arabia, and NW India. It is a small tree and its branches are protected from browsing wild animals by hooked thorns. The tree is now planted for gum production in other regions. For more general information, see GUM in the previous entry.

Gum arabic was one of the first gums to be used. The Egyptians of 2000 BC were already employing it in food as well as for binding paint (a role in which its effectiveness is demonstrated by the survival of Egyptian wall-paintings). It has been part of the pharmacist's stock in trade since the Middle Ages in Europe, and for much longer in the Middle East.

Legends ascribe almost miraculous powers to its value as a food. It was said that a man could live on nothing but 170 g (6 oz) of gum arabic a day. The truth is that in composition gum arabic is an ordinary CARBOHYDRATE of no special nutritive value. It is, however, a superior gum, effective in small concentrations, tasteless and odourless. It gives great viscosity to liquids due to its branched molecules, forms stable durable gels, and may be used to strengthen gelatin jellies. It is particularly useful in preventing sugar from crystallizing, and it also makes a strong, water-soluble adhesive.

The gum is harvested between January and March, when the fruit is ripe. Cuts are made in the bark and strips torn off, allowing the gum to ooze out in 'tears' which are then pulled off when dry, bleached in the sun, cleaned, and often sold without further processing. They are sometimes reduced to powder.

Traditionally the chief uses of gum arabic are in sweetmeats and as an adhesive used, for instance, to stick decorations onto cakes. Gum drops (well known from the phrase 'goody, goody gum drops!') used to be made with gum arabic which provided their tough gelatinous texture and prevented sugar from crystallizing. Now these sweets are often made with cheaper ingredients. In the Middle East sweetmeats are still made with gum arabic.

GUMS confections of fruit or other flavourings such as LIQUORICE, mixed with sugar syrup, set with GUM ARABIC. Better-quality versions still use this, but GELATIN is now mixed with the gum in some formulae, giving a cheaper product. Modified starches are also used in these sweets. Gums are dried out after manufacture to a much lower moisture content than JELLIES (which in principle are similar confections), and thus have a chewy, tough, texture. Wine gums,

midget gems, and fruit gums are popular 20th-century representatives of this group in Britain.

Gum-type sweets, and the related PASTILLES, have inherited the long tradition of confectionery as a vehicle for medicine. The use of gum as an ingredient gives a sweet which dissolves slowly in the mouth, useful for the treatment of throat infections. Medicated gums contain liquorice, honey, menthol, eucalyptus, and aniseed amongst their ingredients. (LM)

GUM TRAGACANTH a secretion from the tree *Astralagus gummifer*, which grows in parts of Turkey and the Middle East. For more general information, see GUM.

Gum tragacanth is still used by craft confectioners for making SUGAR PASTE. The gum, which is very expensive, must be soaked before it is added to the sugar mixture. It absorbs 15–20 times its own weight in water, and makes the paste malleable, subsequently drying to a porcelain-like hardness. As with GUM ARABIC, gum tragacanth has long been used in pharmaceutical applications; its use in confectionery dates back to at least the 17th century, when it was sometimes called gum dragon.

GUR CAKE a type of fruit slice, associated particularly with Dublin city, and made with stale bread and cakes. The stale ingredients are mixed with raisins and water and spread over a puff pastry base and baked on a large baking sheet. After baking a layer of icing sugar is placed on top and the cake is cut into squares.

The cake was popular amongst young Dublin children and is remembered fondly by the well-known Dublin celebrity Éamonn Mac Thomáis, in his book *Gur Cake and Coal Blocks*.

As we came out of the shop we were stuffing ourselves with the Gur Cake. It was only gorgeous, steaming hot, with sugar-coated pastry and the juice oozing out of the large currants and the other soft brown stuff. We could feel our bellies heating up.

The eating of gur cake became synonymous with Dublin children and the term 'Gurrier' was established in Dublin dialect, describing 'one who eats gur cake; a tough street urchin'.

In other regions of Ireland the cake is called Chester cake, Donkey's wedding cake, and Donkey's gudge/gunge. RSe

GURNARD the common name for fish of the family Triglidae, which is well represented in the temperate and warm waters of the Atlantic and Mediterranean and also includes a few Indo-Pacific species. These fish all have relatively large and conspicuously bony heads. It is rare for them to reach a length of more than 45 cm (18") and many are so small as to be suitable only for fish soups.

In N. America, where the name sea robin is often used, the gurnards are little used for food. In Europe, the larger species are brought to market. The most common are *Eutrigla gurnardus*, the grey gurnard, and *Trigla lucerna*, the tub gurnard, the largest of all.

Of the Indo-Pacific species, *Chelidonichthys kumu*, one of several which are red in colour, is reputedly best.

Gurnards tend to have rather dry flesh, but it is firm and white and yields good fillets. These may be fried or baked. A large gurnard may be stuffed and baked. It used to be the practice to preserve fried fillets in vinegar, but they cannot have been greatly esteemed if we are to judge by Shakespeare's Falstaff, who said: 'If I be not ashamed of my soldiers, I am a soused gurnet.'

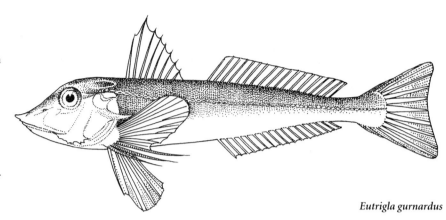

Eutrigla gurnardus

GUYANA, SURINAM, FRENCH GUIANA
These three countries—two republics and an integrated département—were colonies of England, Holland, and France respectively, although their administration has ebbed and flowed with the tides of W. European wars and diplomacy. Their history and development are more closely linked to the W. Indies than to Spanish or Portuguese possessions in Latin America. The French reached Cayenne in 1604, and the Dutch arrived in 1616, but Britain did not gain a permanent toehold until 1796. The fact that Demerara sugar and Cayenne pepper have both entered the language is some sign of their original importance.

The Amerindian population is tiny, long overtaken by African slaves brought in to work the sugar and spice plantations, and by the Indian and Indonesian indentured labour that succeeded them. The cooking of this region reflects strongly the preferences of the imported labour as well as local resources and colonial influences.

Evelyn Waugh, writing in 1934 after a visit to British Guiana, was not the first visitor to wonder at the tedium of a diet that depended largely on manioc meal (see CASSAVA), though had he kept to the coastal regions he would have benefited more from the wealth of CRAB, SHRIMP, and other seafood, and if his wanderings had taken in settlements of Bush Negroes, former runaway slaves, he might have encountered dishes that recalled an African past, such as *coo-coo*, a mush of OKRA and cornmeal (see MAIZE).

The stew called PEPPER POT originated in Guyana. It took its flavours both from spices that were grown in the new colonies, and from cassareep, a syrupy reduction of the juice expressed from grated bitter cassava root, sugar, cloves, and cinnamon. Cassareep (see CASSAVA) is used as seasoning in many meat dishes, and pepper pot, which is a substantial stew of mixed meats, depends more on this decoction for flavour than it does on pepper.

Other dishes of common currency may be naturalizations of European imports like the *rijsttafel* (RICE became a vital staple as the Indian and Indonesian populations increased), the Dutch split-pea soup (*Erwtensoep*) adapted to tropical conditions by the use of chillies and reflecting Portuguese influence by its use of SALT COD; or direct translations of Indonesian dishes such as SATAY or *gado-gado*; or Indian curries.

Okra and SWEET POTATOES are important vegetables, and CALLALOO figures as often as it does in the W. Indies. Tropical fruits in abundance, including the PAPAYA and PLANTAIN, have been commonplaces of the diet since long ago.

There is strong affinity between the cooking of the Guyanas and that of NE BRAZIL, if only because of their joint dependence on *farinha* (CASSAVA meal) and a common natural larder. There have also been borrowings of dishes such as blood pudding and other ways of dealing with pork.   TJ

GYPSY MUSHROOM
Rozites caperata, an edible fungus of Europe and N. America, which has a prominent ring on its pale, stocky stem and a distinctive, wrinkled, yellow-orange or tawny cap with a 'frosted' appearance. The cap, often with a darker boss in the middle, may measure up to 15 cm (6") across.

Light is cast on the nocturnal sartorial habits of elderly Finnish ladies by the Finnish name, which means 'granny's nightcap'. The species is often also called chicken of the woods in English (but see SULPHUR SHELF). The origin of the name 'gypsy' may be the German name *Zigeuner*, but why this was bestowed is not clear.

The distribution of the species in N. America is extensive, from Canada to Mexico; and it also occurs in Japan. In Europe it seems to be restricted to northerly or mountainous regions; thus it is known in the Highlands of Scotland but rare in England. It is often found in pine forests or where oaks and pines grow together. The fruiting season is midsummer to early autumn.

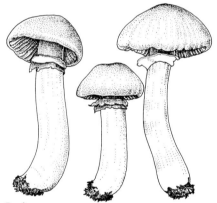

Rozites caperata

The flesh, which is whitish with an ochre tinge, has no special aroma but is delicious, and may be prepared in any way suitable for mushrooms generally. Smith (1977) rates it among the top 50 edible species of N. America. A French survey likens the flavour of its tender flesh to that of choice rabbit meat, and speaks lyrically of its appearance in wooded mountain terrain, where moss and rocks and bilberry abound.

GYUVECH
the Bulgarian name for a kind of earthenware casserole or the dish cooked in it. The name comes from the Turkish *güveç*, which has the same meaning. (It is

djuveč in Serbo-Croat, *gjuveç* in Albanian, and *givech* in Moldova).

The casserole is fairly shallow with a large surface area allowing maximum evaporation. It comes round or oval, lidless and sometimes earless, most often with vertical sides, though in the round version the sides could slope to a small flat base. The outside is normally unglazed because it was originally designed for cooking directly over embers. When glazed on both sides, the casserole is meant for oven cooking only.

Gyuveche, the diminutive form of gyuvech, is an individual-sized earthenware bowl, which sometimes has a domed lid topped with a knob.

These vessels are found all over the Balkans and are used for cooking almost anything of a savoury nature, including fish as well as meat, poultry, and game dishes.

MK-J

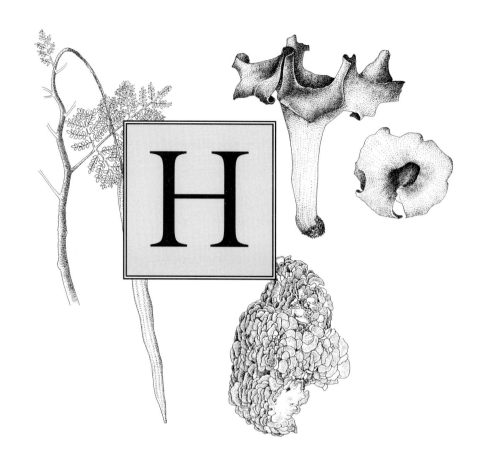

HACKBERRY also called sugarberry or honeyberry, is the fruit of the nettle tree, of the genus *Celtis*. The trees are quite large, but belong to the same family as the ordinary nettle. *C. australis* is native to N. Africa, but has been grown in Europe from ancient times, mainly for shade or to provide fodder for cows. Where it grows, the fruit is often eaten, raw, but it is not seen in many markets.

The fruit, which is sweet, resembles a small cherry: it may be yellow, brown, purple, or black. It has been suggested that it was the lotus eaten by the indolent lotus-eaters of Homer's *Odyssey*; but a more plausible candidate is the JUJUBE.

C. occidentalis, a similar tree, native to the south and west of the USA, bears fruits which have a better reputation than those of the Mediterranean species.

C. sinensis is the Chinese hackberry, also with edible fruits (and leaves).

HADDOCK *Melanogrammus aeglefinus*, a fish of the cod family which is of commercial importance on both sides of the N. Atlantic. Its range descends as far as the

Bay of Biscay in the east and New England in the west, but it may venture a little further south in the summer. Specimens over a metre (40") in length have been recorded, but the normal maximum is 80 cm (32") and the market length 40–60 cm (16–24").

This fish has a dark greenish-brown or purplish-grey back, with a black lateral line and a 'thumbprint' on each side. In this last particular it resembles the JOHN DORY, and there are traces in popular names and traditions of its being thought to be the fish which St Peter picked up; which it could not be as it is not found in the Mediterranean, still less in the Sea of Galilee.

For culinary purposes, the haddock and the COD are close competitors. Some prefer one, some the other. Icelanders, who are in a particularly good position to judge, rate haddock above cod. In the north of England there is an odd dividing line between Lancashire, where people prefer cod for their fish and chips, and Yorkshire, where they choose haddock (although a few places in Yorkshire, like Huddersfield, are in a grey area, where a tendency to favour cod may be noted).

Haddock does not take salt as well as cod, so the traditional ways of curing it are by drying and smoking. 'Rizzared' haddock in Scotland were simply sundried. 'Finnan haddies' (from the fishing village of Finnan, near Aberdeen) used to be smoked over a peat-reek, but achieved such renown that they are now prepared by less traditional methods elsewhere, including the USA (where the eminent ichthyologist Goode, in a moment of aberration, referred to them as 'Finland haddocks').

Smoked haddock has become popular in France. When the French refer to 'haddock', which has become a French word, they mean smoked haddock.

In practice, smoking is preceded by cleaning, splitting, and brining. What are called 'Glasgow pales' are small haddock which have been given this treatment but removed from the smoke when they have acquired no more than a pale straw colour. 'Arbroath smokies' are haddock (or, sometimes, WHITING) which have been beheaded, cleaned, dry salted, tied by their tails in pairs, and then hot smoked. The fish are then coppery-brown on the outside, creamy white inside, and of a mellow salty-smoky flavour. They are best eaten 'hot off the barrel', but the cure permits keeping them for a while.

The history of Arbroath smokies includes several points of particular interest. The process was originally carried out in the cliff-top fishing village of Auchmithie, which was largely populated by families of Norse origin. The fish—originally any surplus fish, but latterly haddock almost exclusively—used to be smoked above the domestic fires, but the need for more facilities led to the construction of numerous 'smoke-pits' set up with half whisky barrels on ledges in the cliff face. These would be covered with layers of hessian sacking. Early in the 19th century, some Auchmithie families settled in Arbroath and took their habits with them, building smoke-pits in their back gardens to continue their way of curing. By 1900, output from Arbroath exceeded that from Auchmithie, and the smokies began to be called Arbroath smokies rather than by their original names (Auchmithie 'lucken' or 'close' fish or 'pinwiddies'). Much of the production is now effected by modern plants; but it does not produce quite the same results.

Although salting is unsuitable as a long-term method of preserving haddock, very light salting is carried out in some places, producing for example the 'green-salted haddock' of Denmark and the 'night-salted haddock' of Iceland: both being products intended for early consumption.

HAGGIS often regarded as the national dish and exclusive property of Scotland, is the archetype of a group of dishes which have an ancient history and a wide distribution. All of them are relatively large parcels of OFFAL mixed with cereal and enclosed in some suitable wrapping from an animal's entrails, usually the stomach.

The concept of haggis is based on preservation. When an animal was slaughtered, the perishable offal had to be eaten at once or preserved in some way. Salted, packed into a stomach, and boiled, its keeping time was extended to a couple of weeks. Similar considerations produced blood puddings, some of which include offal as well as blood.

The first people known to have made products of the haggis type were the Romans, who were notably interested in foods of the SAUSAGE family. They made theirs of pig offal, enclosed in the cleaned CAUL of a pig (the caul is a membrane surrounding the intestines). Less often, sheep and goat were used.

The Scottish haggis may be an entirely indigenous invention, but in the absence of written records there is no way of knowing;

it could be an adaptation of a Roman recipe to the local MUTTON and OATS. The classic recipe, which has remained almost unaltered since a very early date, uses the large stomach of a sheep filled with the minced lungs, liver, and heart, plus fat, oatmeal, stock, salt, and pepper. Modern haggis generally has beef suet rather than mutton fat, and cayenne pepper or nutmeg are usual additions. The original way of fastening the stomach around the filling was with wooden skewers, but now it is generally sewn. The haggis is boiled for three hours. It swells considerably and has to be pricked with a needle to release the internal pressure and avoid bursting.

Since Robert Burns praised the haggis as the 'great chieftain o' the pudding race', this humble food has been served on Burns Night (25 January) with bashed neeps (mashed SWEDES), whisky, a piper, and an admixture of ceremony.

There are other types of haggis with a Scottish pedigree. Meg Dods's *The Cook and Housewife's Manual* (1826) has one made with leg of mutton, suet and marrow, breadcrumbs, egg yolks, anchovies, red wine, and cayenne pepper, wrapped in a veal caul and baked, not boiled. There is also a history of meatless haggis, sometimes called sweet haggis.

Although some English people are apt to treat the Scottish haggis as a joke, preparations of the haggis category have long been made in England, e.g. the West Country 'hog puddings', also made in Wales and Ireland. Conventional sausage casings rather than stomach were often used for the wrapping; but the filling of liver, heart, and lungs, mixed with cereal (oats, barley, or rusk), was like that of the haggis.

The traditional cooking of Russia includes dishes of the haggis variety. *Sal'nik* is a large parcel of sheep's caul enclosing liver, BUCKWHEAT, dried mushrooms, and sour cream. *Nyanya* is made in a sheep's stomach with meat from the head and feet, and buckwheat.

HAIRMOSS or hairweed, also sometimes called 'cowhair', freshwater algae of NW China and Inner Mongolia, identified by Dr Yan-Kit So (1984) as *Borgia fuscopurpurea*. The product is sold in dried form, looking like a mass of fine tangled black hair. It has to be reconstituted by adding water, when it turns dark greenish-brown. It has no taste of its own, but is prized for the slippery and bouncy texture which it possesses. Chinese refer to it as the 'treasure of the Gobi [desert]'.

HAKE is the name originally given to *Merluccius merluccius*, a member of the cod

family which ranges from the Mediterranean to Norway.

The N. American species *M. bilinearis* is silver hake. Two members of the genus *Urophycis* in N. America also bear the name hake: *U. tenuis*, the white hake (or Boston ling), and *U. chuss*, the squirrel hake. They resemble the true hakes in having two dorsal fins and one anal fin and no barbel.

The mouth of the European hake is grey-black inside; that of the silver hake dark blue. The silver hake, in accordance with its name, has a silvery iridescent sheen when freshly caught.

Enthusiasm for the consumption of hake runs highest in Spain (where it is *merluza*, but *legatz* in Basque) and Portugal (where it is *pescada*).

HALEEM (or *Halim*), an important and unusual dish which appears to have originated in the region of Iran and Afghanistan, is also known by the name *Harissa* (meaning 'well cooked') in certain Arab countries; but see HARISSA for a different meaning of that term. *Haleem* features either BARLEY or WHEAT with meat in a porridge-like soup. Margaret Shaida (1992) says the following about it:

It is said that this dish, like many others, was invented by the sixth century Persian King Khosrow and that when the Moslems conquered Persia a century later, it became a firm favourite of the Prophet. Its fame and popularity were thus assured and it spread all over the Middle East.

In many Arab countries today it is known as *harriseh* [harissa], and is indeed still sometimes called that in the southern regions of Persia, where it has long been regarded as the finest winter breakfast dish. The specialist restaurants that make barley porridge start their preparations in the evening and stir the porridge through the night to ensure the right consistency. Their first customers arrive well before dawn.

Claudia Roden (1985) describes it as an 'ancestral soup' symbolizing the diet of the mountain Kurds, and says that it is traditionally served on Assumption Day in Syria and Lebanon and as a breakfast dish in northern Iraq. Anissa Helou (1994), spelling the name *h'reesseh*, observes that in the Lebanon this is an alms dish, traditionally made in large quantity and distributed to the poor in churchyards.

Haleem, which is also made in Afghanistan and parts of India, is usually made with wheat and lamb, but in the past and to some extent nowadays with barley. Chicken is sometimes used instead of lamb. Each country has its own variations, especially with regard to accompaniments: in Iraq, Iran, and Afghanistan people sprinkle sugar and cinnamon (to which Lebanese are likely to add a pinch of cumin and one of ground cloves) on the porridge;

in India the porridge is cooked with the addition of various 'hot' spices. It is usual to provide some sort of fat to serve with the haleem, which could be oil or melted butter.

HS

HALF-BEAK the English name for a whole tribe of Indo-Pacific fish in the genus *Hemiramphus*. They are closely related to the GARFISH, but instead of having two long pointed jaws they have only a long lower jaw. This is not, strictly speaking, a jaw, but a bony projection from the jaw, and it is equipped with a sensitive fringe of tissue which serves for the detection of food. This tissue at the end of the half-beak is either red or green, and there are separate names in the Philippines for the two kinds.

The half-beaks, like the garfish, are capable of sustained gliding above the surface of the water, which accounts for the Thai name, *pla kathung heo*, meaning water-beetle. The largest species is *H. marginatus*, which attains a maximum length of 45 cm (18"). *H. far* is a spotted species with a range from the Red Sea to the Pacific. The flesh is delicate but bony, and can be baked, fried, or poached. That of *H. sajori*, a Japanese species, is considered to be good enough for use as SASHIMI (or *sunemono*, see JAPANESE CULINARY TERMS).

HALIBUT *Hippoglossus hippoglossus*, the largest of the flatfish, has been known to reach a length of 2.5 m (8') and a weight over 300 kg (650 lb). It is a fish of the N. Atlantic, ranging from the cold waters of the Arctic down to New Jersey and Scotland. The colour of the eyed side is greenish-brown or dark brown.

The Pacific halibut, *H. stenolepis*, does not attain quite the size of the Atlantic species, but may still be huge. It ranges from C. California through Alaska to N. Asian waters.

The name used to be spelled 'holibut', and 'holy' forms part of its name in several languages. The reason for this is not clear. The flesh of the halibut tends to be dry, and in large specimens coarse.

In the N. and NE Atlantic region, especially Norway and Greenland, halibut (including dried strips of the flesh) has consistently been an important element in the diet. In contrast, the reputation of the halibut in W. Europe has fluctuated. Nineteenth-century authors generally describe it as a fish which could only be sold when nothing better was available. However, a Mr Rowell, writing in *Land and Water* (16 July 1881), said that at Newcastle upon Tyne the halibut was prized, and that it cost more than twice as

much as COD and LING. As if to defend this unusual preference, he continued: 'Let any one get a piece of halibut from a small one, season it with nutmeg, pepper, and salt, and bake it in the oven, and I know nothing so fine.' This comment anticipated a change in the fortunes of the halibut, for which demand increased during the 20th century.

HALLUCINOGENIC MUSHROOMS some anyway, are eaten by some people. They include the well-known FLY AGARIC and certain species in such genera as *Psilocybe* and *Stropharia*. Research by the Wassons (1957, 1967, 1969) and a review of the subject by Gray (1973) have given some clarity to the vague ideas previously entertained about the antiquity and extent of this practice.

So far as Europe is concerned, Wasson (1969) effectively dismisses any idea that hallucinogenic mushroom cults existed in the past. Supposed evidence of ancient mushroom cults in Egypt and the Middle East has likewise been scouted. Nor are there any surviving traces of a mushroom cult in the Indian subcontinent, although some believe that the plant 'soma', deified by the Aryans in the Indus Valley in times BC, was fly agaric.

Mexico and C. America is the region where the evidence of mushroom cults is clear. The ritual use of hallucinogenic mushrooms there is recorded since the time of the Spanish Conquest. Although the fly agaric exists there, it does not seem to have been used. The species concerned, which were regarded as sacred, seem to have numbered just over a dozen, all belonging to the genera *Psilocybe*, *Stropharia*, and *Panaeolus*. The representation of mushrooms in stone, especially in Guatemala, was at its zenith between about 200 BC and AD 300. Gray (1973) lists the factors which point to these images having a ritual significance. (At the same time, he observes that in the 20th century there has been a marked tendency, for example in N. America, to produce such things as ceramic versions of the fly agaric, for use as salt shakers or simply as decorations, and that remains of these could mislead future archaeologists, who would seek to read into their existence something more than a passing fad in the gift shop business.) The same author cites evidence of a mushroom cult in Mexico in the 16th century, and of its persistence to the present time in conjunction with Christian practices, and refers to the first recorded occasions when white people took part in the 'sacred mushroom' rites. These experiences are of great interest, as the following quotation shows:

On June 29, 1955 Wasson and Richardson, along with about 18 Indians participated in the mushroom-eating ritual at Huautla in Mexico. The ceremony began about 8:00 p.m., the atmosphere was friendly but solemn, and it was conducted by a woman, the curandera or shaman. In some ways it resembled a communion, with chocolate first being served ceremonially. At about 10:30 p.m. the curandera cleaned the mushrooms and with prayers passed them through the smoke of resin incense. While doing this she sat before a table with Christian images. She then gave the participants mushrooms in pairs, keeping thirteen pairs for herself (the sacred mushrooms are small ones and do not compare in size to *Amanita muscaria*). Wasson was given six pairs which he chewed over a period of half an hour. He described their taste as acrid and their odor as rancid.

Before mid-night the curandera extinguished the light and about 30 minutes later both Wasson and Richardson started having visions which became quite intense late in the night and remained so until about 4:00 a.m. Wasson stated that the visions emerged from the center of the field of vision, were vivid in color, and always harmonious. They began with art motifs and evolved into palaces with courts, arcades, and gardens. Later he saw a mythological beast drawing a regal chariot, camel caravans, and mountains. The visions were not blurred but were sharply focused. In the meantime the curandera was singing and waving her arms rhythmically and at one time began a rhythmic dance. Both white participants fell asleep about 4:00 a.m. but woke at 6:00 a.m., rested and with clear heads but considerably shaken by their experience.

This account does not include any reference to the unpleasant side effects, such as vomiting, which often accompany the hallucinations, and which may be severe and dangerous.

Two compounds responsible for the hallucinogenic effect have been identified as psilocin and psilocybin. It seems possible that they will eventually have a beneficial application in the study and treatment of schizophrenia; but it seems unlikely that any mushrooms containing them will ever have any normal use as food.

HALO-HALO (literally 'mix-mix') is a speciality of the Philippines: a cooling snack of mixed fruit and beans, topped with finely crushed ice and milk or ice cream, which sometimes is taken for dessert. The mixture (from three to twelve items) may include: banana, JACKFRUIT, coconut, sweet potato, red MUNG BEANS, chickpeas, sugar palm fruit (see PALM SUGAR), purple YAM jam, leche flan (CRÈME CARAMEL), gelatin, and in recent times sweet corn or corn crisps.

Halo-halo used to be sold by Japanese vendors in halo-halo parlours or from street stalls before the occupation of the Philippines in the 1940s. It is the fanciest of a range of popular refreshments with crushed ice which have their counterparts in other SE

Asian countries, e.g. the Malaysian *ice kachang* and the Vietnamese *xung sa hot Luu* as well as the extensive array of Indonesian '*ijs*' drinks. It is reasonable to suppose that they grew up spontaneously as a reaction to hot weather and the availability of ice. It has been suggested, however, that the Japanese summer drink, a shaved-ice cooler called *anmitsu*, may have been the model for some or all of them, including halo-halo itself.

DF

HALOUMI a hard, salty, sheep's milk cheese, variable in character, which is well known in Cyprus and used as a cooking cheese in many Middle Eastern countries. It melts well, and is sometimes grilled on skewers with pieces of vegetable.

The name (which occurs in many variant forms and transliterations) is one of the few words of the ancient Egyptian language which have survived; in Coptic, it was written *ialom*; the modern pronunciation is *hâlûm*. Egyptians eat the cheese either fresh, under that name, or in conserved form, when it is known as *mishsh*; the latter has been flavoured with red pepper, brined, and stored in a sealed container with salted milk. *Mishsh* often becomes infested with tiny worms, which can be eaten without harm but are considered a nuisance. The Egyptian proverb '*Dûd il-mishsh minnu fî*' (the *mishsh* worm arises from it; namely from the cheese) means, roughly, 'The problem is inherent in the situation.'

CP

HALVA name of a hugely varied range of confections made in the Middle East, C. Asia, and India, derived from the Arabic root *hulw*, sweet.

In 7th-century Arabia, the word meant a paste of dates kneaded with milk. By the 9th century, possibly by assimilating the ancient Persian sweetmeat *afroshag*, it had acquired the meaning of wheat flour or semolina, cooked by frying or toasting and worked into a more or less stiff paste with a sweetening agent such as sugar syrup, date syrup, grape syrup, or honey by stirring the mass together over a gentle heat. Usually a flavouring was added such as nuts, rosewater, or puréed cooked carrots (still a popular flavouring). The finished sweetmeat could be cut into bars or moulded into fanciful shapes such as fish.

Halva spread both eastwards and westwards, with the result that it is made with a wide variety of ingredients, methods, and flavourings.

Halva has struck deep roots in India, and in the northern part of the country it has given its name to the caste of confectioners (the halvais). Semolina provides the base for many easily made Indian versions of halva.

The simplest recipe requires semolina to be fried in GHEE, mixed with spiced syrup and raisins, and cooked until fluffy. Ghee is added spoonful by spoonful until the mixture will not absorb any more, and the mixture is often served still warm from cooking. 'Bombay' halva uses this base with addition of spices (saffron, cardamom) and nuts (almonds, pistachios). 'Madras' halva is similar, but substitutes poppyseeds and coconut for the flavourings.

Indian halvas may be made without grain, using other basic ingredients. Thus *sathi* (ZEDOARY flour) may be used instead of semolina; or vegetables such as carrots, potatoes, beetroots, winter melons, yams, and squashes may be cooked in cream to a dense, pasty consistency and used as snacks or desserts. Fruit halvas are heavily sweetened purées, made from such fruits as bananas, unripe papayas, or oranges, and served with fried biscuits or breads. Puréed lentils, mung beans, and peanuts are also used as halva bases, as is curd or thick egg custard stiffened with coconut. Nuts, dried fruits, coconut, rosewater, and spices such as saffron, cardamom, cinnamon, and nutmeg are freely used for flavoring these sweets.

In Nepal, where the carrot and flour types of halva are usual, there is an unsweetened dish made of pounded barley, ghee, water, and salt only. This is no more than a consolidated porridge, but though unsweet is locally considered a type of halva.

Semolina halva is the usual type in the Middle East, where it is diversified by the addition of nuts, dried fruits, coconut, yoghurt, honey, and spices and other flavourings.

Some Turkish and Greek halvas, however, are made without grain and derive their texture from the combination of cooked egg (yolk or white) and solidified syrup. Nuts are always included, whether whole, chopped, or ground, and sometimes dried or candied fruit.

The halva best known in Europe and N. America is another non-grain type, sesame halva. This is a by-product of sesame oil production, made by grinding the solid remains of the sesame seeds finely, sweetening them with sugar syrup or honey, and pressing the mixture into a solid cake. Sometimes it is embellished with whole almonds or pistachios.

Between the Levantine sesame confections and the Indian vegetable pastes lie a rich variety of halva recipes from Syria, Iraq, Iran, Afghanistan, Pakistan, and C. Asia. *Halawat tamr*, an Iraqi sweetmeat, is a mixture of dates, almonds, and walnuts, chopped and kneaded together. A Syrian version of semolina halva, called MA'MOUNIA, is a speciality of Aleppo, where it is a popular breakfast dish. *Basbousa* is the name given to a similar dish made in Egypt.

Karachi halva, made from sugar syrup, cornflour, and ghee, produces a result a little like TURKISH DELIGHT. To western palates, almond versions of halva such as *halawah bil loz*, made in Iraq, are reminiscent of MARZIPAN.

In addition to the usual semolina paste, there are in C. Asia such varieties as *halwa-i tar*, a liquid variety served in bowls; *badråk halwa*, made from maize flour, honey, and walnuts; and *maghiz halwa*, a sort of BRITTLE made by pouring hot syrup over nuts.

HAM (*see page 368*)

HAMAGURI meaning 'beach chestnut', is the Japanese for CLAM, but is used in a much more limited way than the English word, being applied only to one particular BIVALVE, *Meretrix lusoria* (which has a shape like that of a chestnut), and to a close relation, *M. pechaliensis*, which is known as *shinahamaguri*.

Hamaguri have been prized and eaten in large quantities by the Japanese from time immemorial. In the numerous prehistoric 'shell mounds' discovered all over the country, hamaguri shells occur most frequently (followed by oyster shells).

It is said that each pair of hamaguri shells has a slightly different shape from any other and that, therefore, a single shell fits only its original partner. For this reason, hamaguri is considered to symbolize marital harmony and is often served at a wedding feast.

Hamaguri are thought to be at their best from late autumn to early spring, and are traditionally associated with the Dolls' Festival, which is celebrated on 3 March. Among the dishes in which they figure are: *Ushio-jiru*, a clear soup made by boiling clams and a piece of kelp in water; *Sakamushi*, steamed clams, sprinkled with SAKÉ; *Yaki-hamaguri*, clams grilled over a charcoal fire.

Although the Japanese do not apply their clam-word to other bivalves, they do eat with appreciation several species which would be called clams in English-speaking countries. Prominent among these are:

- *Ruditapes philippinarum*, known as *asari*. This is a member of the family Veneridae (see VENUS SHELLS) present also in Korean and Chinese waters and recently introduced to Spain. Maximum width 4 cm (1.5"). Eaten mainly in the spring. The pattern on the shells varies but is usually black on a light ground, giving an impression of a texture like woven cloth. Used in Japan for MISO soup and for *nimono* (see JAPANESE CULINARY TERMS) and *tsukudani* (salt-sweet preserves).

(*cont. on page 369*)

Ham

Ham is the hind leg of a PIG above the hock joint, cut from the carcass and cured by salting and drying, and sometimes smoking, so that it will keep for months at room temperature.

GAMMON is the same joint as ham, but is left attached to the side during BACON curing, and cut from it afterwards. It is milder in flavour.

'Ham', in its more general meaning of the hind leg, is applied to cured meat made from other animals, including WILD BOAR, MUTTON, GOAT, VENISON, and even BADGER.

The first records of hams come from the classical world. The Romans knew hams made by the Gauls in the last few centuries BC, cured by brining and smoking.

Cato described how, in the 2nd century BC, the inhabitants of N. Italy made hams by layering legs of pork with dry salt, followed by drying and smoking.

In medieval times, hams were made all over Europe. Every cottager kept a pig, which was killed in autumn and preserved to provide food through winter.

Europeans took pigs and the art of curing meat to the Americas, where several types of ham developed. Another area of expertise in the curing of pork meat is China, especially the region of Yunnan.

Combinations of factors such as pig breed, feeding, curing recipe, and storage method gave rise to many varieties of ham.

The process of curing all hams begins with SALTING. This may be done with dry salt or brine, or a combination of the two. Wet cures penetrate the meat more quickly. Saltpetre or nitrite (see SALT) is added in small quantities to improve penetration and give a pink colour.

After curing, which may take from a few days to several months, the ham is removed from the salt and dried. This operation may consist of hanging the ham in cool air, or may be aided by smoking. Some woods are particularly favoured; oak and hickory have a high tannin content which helps to preserve the meat, and aromatic woods can be used for a special flavour. Peat was used in Ireland. Certain European hams are finished over pinewood smoke, which forms a black, flyproof, resinous layer and flavours the ham slightly. During smoking, the hams lose about 25% of their weight.

Some of the most important types of hams are listed below, first those intended for eating raw, and then those which have been or will be cooked:

HAMS FOR EATING RAW

- *Jambon d'Ardennes*, the best-known Belgian ham, smoked dark brown.
- *Jambon de Bayonne*, French smoked ham with a smoky flavour and brown exterior, made around Orthez, to the east of Bayonne.
- *Jamón iberico*, Spanish ham from the native Iberian pig which is reared in woodlands of S. and W. Spain; also known as *pata negra*, as many of these pigs have black trotters. Salting, drying, and ageing (the last two in natural conditions) culminate in an artisanal product of high quality, accounting for little more than 5% of Spain's large production of hams.
- *Jamón serrano* ('mountain ham'), a term formerly used of all Spanish hams produced in the mountainous south-western region, including those from the Iberian pig (see preceding item), but now covering only the hams from white pigs, especially Large White, Landrace, Belgian White, and cross-breeds thereof. The region for these hams straddles the provinces of Extremadura and Andalusia. Local varieties differ slightly, but curing is mainly by dry-salting, and ageing (without smoking) for a year or more. *Jamón de Jabugo* is one of the best.
- *Knochenschinken* ('ham on the bone'), a hard, heavily smoked German ham, almost black.
- *Landrauch*, 'country smoked', heavily smoked and dry German ham.
- Parma ham, *prosciutto di Parma*, the most famous of raw hams, is dry salted with sea salt for up to a month, then dried without smoking for at least eight months and sometimes two years. The finest Parma ham comes from Langhirano near Parma, but other sorts of *prosciutto crudo* (raw ham) made elsewhere can be almost as good.
- *Prosciutto di San Daniele*, one of the best Italian raw hams of the general Parma type, made near Friuli.
- *Westfälische Schinken* (Westphalian ham), a notable German ham, first dry-salted then brined, scrubbed with clean water to reduce its saltiness, and gently smoked with beech and juniper wood with occasional additions of juniper berries.

HAMS WHICH ARE COOKED

- Bradenham ham, a delicate English ham, lengthily cured in molasses with juniper berries and spices to give a sweet flavour and a perfectly black outside. This ham has been made since 1781 at Chippenham in Wiltshire, not Bradenham, which is in Buckinghamshire.
- *Braunschweiger Schinken* (Brunswick ham), a mild German ham.
- *Jambon*, the French word for ham, which gives *jambon de campagne* ('of the country'), a general French name for minor local hams of various types.
- *Jambon de Paris* (also *jambon glacé* or *jambon blanc*), a lightly salted, unsmoked French ham, which is presented in various forms (of which the officially approved one is parallelepipedic, neither rolled nor on the bone). It has a very mild flavour, and is usually bought sliced and eaten cold. (Note: a *jambonneau* is a pig's forehock, cured by a method similar to ham.)

- *Jambon de Vendée*, called 'bacon' in medieval times, a boneless ham dry salted with sea salt, slightly dried, flavoured with *eau de vie* (of pear or plum) and aromatics such as rosemary, sold raw and ready to be cooked. Among the best of its class.
- Jinhua ham, made in the Zhejiang province of China from the Jinhua breed of pig. It has a rosy colour.
- Kentucky ham, a notable American ham, dry-salted and smoked with hickory and apple wood, which gives it a delicate flavour.
- *Pragerschinken*, meaning Prague ham, which comes from the Czech Republic. It is given a long brine cure, smoked with beech wood, and well aged. It is usually cooked and served hot.
- Smithfield ham, the best Virginia ham, which takes its name from the small town on the James River estuary in Virginia, where the hams are cured. However, the razorback pigs from which it is made are raised in N. Carolina as well as in Virginia. The hams are dry salted with salt and pepper, smoked with hickory and apple wood, then aged for at least a year. This ham is always cooked, often baked with a sweet glaze, and eaten hot or cold.
- Virginia ham, a class of fine American hams of which the foremost is Smithfield ham (see above). Their essential feature is the leanness of the meat.
- York ham, the name of a curing method which gives a superior product suitable for cooking and eating cold. It is dry-salted and smoked (lightly or heavily), and then matured for several months. The flavour is mild and the colour light. 'York hams' are made in countries other than England, not always as well as the original.

- Yunnan ham, the finest of Chinese hams, is made by a supposedly secret process, but is similar to a Virginia ham in its relative leanness.

Hams which are meant to be eaten raw (see above) are cut in very fine slices, and served, depending on the region, with curls of unsalted butter, fresh figs, or melon.

The usual method of cooking a whole ham is gentle simmering in a large container, An old practice is to add hay to the cooking water, which is supposed to help reduce saltiness and certainly imparts a delicate flavour. Alternatively, a ham can be partially simmered, then baked; or, exceptionally, baked from the start.

The English method for dealing with hot boiled ham is to glaze it with brown sugar and mustard or fruit juice, and decorate by scoring the fat in a lozenge pattern and studding it with whole cloves. Sweet glazes are also popular in N. America, and fruit such as pineapple or peaches are used as a garnish. Creamy sauces flavoured with wine or mustard are favoured in continental Europe.

English boiled ham to be eaten cold has toasted breadcrumbs pressed over the fat to make a coating.

Ham goes well with eggs and pulses, as in the English combinations of fried ham and eggs, and pea and ham soup. Variations on these themes are to be found in most European countries. A little ham goes a long way; thus some stock, bones, or a little meat are sufficient to flavour hefty amounts of dried peas or lentils. Small pieces of ham are also added to some potato dishes. In Italy, it is used in sauces and garnishes for pasta, and numerous S. European recipes begin with chopped onions and ham lightly fried together.

(LM)

- *Mactra chinensis*, called *bakagai* or *aoyagi*; the first name means 'idiot shellfish', referring to the way in which the red foot hangs out of the shell like the lolling tongue of an idiot (another noticeably red bivalve eaten in Japan is listed under ARK-SHELL).
- *Spisula sacchalinensis*, which is *ubagai* or *hokkigai*, for SASHIMI, TEMPURA, and *sunemono* (see JAPANESE CULINARY TERMS).
- *Tresus keenae, mirugai*, or *mirukui*, whose common name is given as 'horse clam' in some English-language books. The long projecting siphon is used for SUSHI.

(KA)

HAMBURGER one of the principal forms in which BEEF is consumed in the western world, has but a short history as a name (it first turned up in print towards 1890), although it is obvious that consumption of things like hamburgers, i.e. cooked round patties or rissoles of meat, dates back a very long way, and not only in Europe.

Ayto (1993) and Evan Jones (1981) provide good discussions of the way in which the port of Hamburg, via seamen from there, came to have its name applied to a particular version of this ubiquitous item. It seems that 'Hamburg steak' (in a Boston newspaper in 1884) preceded the snappier 'hamburger'; and that the St Louis World Fair of 1904 was a significant launching pad for the hamburger in a bun as we know it, although its growth to the status of a global food item required another four or five decades of the 20th century for completion. It also involved intense competition between the competing hamburger 'giants' in the USA, well described by McDonald (1997).

Ayto points out that the many other terms (such as cheeseburger) which followed hamburger were based on a misapprehension that a burger was a thing in itself which could be made of ham or of something else.

HAMMERHEAD SHARK *Sphyrna zygaena*, a remarkable member of the SHARK family whose most noticeable characteristic is the T-shaped head, with eyes at the extremities. This is a very large fish (maximum length 4 m/160") and a viviparous one; the mother may give birth to two or three dozen infant hammerheads, each already about 50 cm (20") long. The species has a circumglobal distribution, including the Mediterranean, the E. Atlantic from Senegal to the English Channel, western parts of the Indian Ocean, and temperate waters in the Pacific.

The existence of several other species of hammerhead, mostly also occurring right round the world and one even larger (*S. mocarran*, maximum length just over 6 m/240"), testifies to the efficacy, in evolutionary terms, of the special position of the eyes, which is unique to this genus.

Hammerheads are good to eat. The present author once had the experience of cooking a whole small hammerhead in a COURT BOUILLON, and noted that the English ladies who ate it were unanimous in declaring it to be delicious.

HAND CHEESES so called because they were originally moulded to shape by hand. They are of German origin and the German name *Handkäse* has the same meaning, as does the Spanish name used in S. America, *queso de mano*.

Hand cheeses come in lots of different shapes, with a wide range of flavours from delicate to strong, and variously coloured rinds. One can say, however, that they all have similar nutritional characteristics, being low in fat and high in protein.

The German *Handkäse* are by far the most important hand cheeses, and these are all made from sour milk curds. Among the scores of different sorts are *Weinkäse*, the 'wine cheese' which goes well with Rhine or Moselle wine, and *Bauernhandkäse*, an example of a cheese named for a place.

See also QUARK.

HAPUKU *Polyprion oxygeneios*, a huge fish of New Zealand and (formerly, at least) Australian waters. It belongs to the GROUPER family and is a relation of the WRECKFISH. Its maximum length is 2 m (80") and it can weigh over 100 kg (220 lb).

Ayling and Cox (1982) have written well of this remarkable and trusting (too trusting, alas) creature:

Hapuku normally swim slowly, but if they are disturbed they accelerate so rapidly using powerful beats of their large tail that cavitation around the fin makes an audible boom with each beat. When alive these fishes are a beautiful blue tinged grey on the back with a whitish belly, but this colour fades to a dull dark grey after death.

Hapuku live in loose herds containing anything from less than ten to over a hundred individuals that usually stay around a single rock reef for some time. They seem to prefer pinnacles of rock that are home for abundant populations of smaller fishes, and that have some suitable shelter site such as a large cave or crevice. . . . They are often seen by divers . . . around offshore islands . . . The huge fish show little fear and mill curiously around the intruders, sometimes coming so close that the diver can run a hand along their flanks as they glide slowly past. There is no sight more impressive for a diver than a group of hapuku moving against the blue-black backdrop of deepwater and steep rock pinnacles.

The flesh of hapuku is delicious and therefore in strong demand. Stocks of the fish have declined, and, since they seem to grow slowly and live to a great age, there is no quick means of reversing this trend.

HARDTAIL the common English name for *Megalaspis cordyla*, a fish of Indo-Pacific waters. Like many other members of its family (Carangidae) it has a streamlined body, adapted to swift swimming; and the resemblance to the shape of a torpedo is so marked that the name 'torpedo trevally' is sometimes used. The tail is thin and stiff.

This is not a very large fish (maximum length 40 cm/16"), nor an outstandingly good one. But it is widely available in SE Asian markets and makes palatable fare when fried, steamed, poached, or grilled.

HARE indicates, in English, various species in the family Leporidae, which is also the family of the RABBIT. As far as the cook is concerned, they differ from the latter by having dark, strongly flavoured flesh. In appearance, they are larger than rabbits, have longer ears, a notched ('hare') lip, and powerful hind legs. Young hares are called leverets in English until they are a year old.

Hares are a widespread and successful group. The brown, or European hare, *Lepus europaeus*, is native to and common in the British Isles, and the varying hare (*L. timidus scotius*) whose coat changes to white in winter, is found in Scotland. Hare of various species also range through Europe, China, and India, and across the African grasslands. In the New World, animals which would be considered hares in Europe are commonly called rabbits, e.g. the Californian jack rabbit (*L. californicus*) and the snowshoe rabbit (*L. americanus*). The European hare has been introduced in N. America, Chile, and Australasia.

Hares have never been domesticated. As small, common game animals, they must have played a role in the diet of man since remote antiquity. Dalby (1996) mentions that bones were found among the discards of the inhabitants of a cave in the Argolid in Greece, dated at 20,000–15,000 BC; and observes that the hare became the best-known game animal in the settled parts of Greece in historical times. The Romans also ate hare.

In medieval England hare dishes included 'hare in worts' (cooked with leaf vegetables), and hare cooked in sauces thickened with blood and bread, seasoned with pepper and ale. Roast hare stuffed with bread, suet, and herb forcemeat, had evolved by the 17th century; and CIVET of hare, a highly seasoned wine-based stew, came into fashion, probably under French influence. Jugged hare appeared in recipe books in the early 18th century, the meat and blood placed in a jug and cooked within a larger kettle of water. (When a hare is 'drawn', the blood is usually reserved, and added to the liquid in which the meat is cooked, as a thickener.) Nowadays this dish is usually cooked in a casserole, the sauce incorporating port or claret, redcurrant jelly, and the blood. Hare meat is also the basis for an old-fashioned English hare soup. The Scottish *Bawd bree* (*bawd* meaning hare and *bree* meaning gravy or cooking liquid) is a cross between a soup and a stew; Catherine Brown (1985) notes that Lady Grisell Baillie aptly described it as 'Hare soup with Hares in it'.

Hares are relatively large and one will feed six to eight people adequately. The flesh is lean and dry (sometimes tough), the flavour strong and rich, especially in older animals; these benefit from being marinated and/or cooked in a casserole, slowly with plenty of liquid. Hare should always be well cooked.

Roasting is used for young animals. In France, there are several recipes for roasting the saddle with *marc* and grapes or cream, juniper berries, and mushrooms; noodles are served with the latter version in Alsace. France also has a number of complex DAUBE and civet recipes for hare. *Civet de lievre à la royale* is the grandest version.

The German *Hansenpfeffer* is a highly seasoned casserole dish similar in conception to English jugged hare and French civets. Belgians use beer and chestnuts or prunes in their hare stews. S. Europe has a number of interesting hare dishes; there are both Italian and Spanish recipes which use chocolate in hare stews, e.g. the sweet-sour *Lepre in agrodolce* of Italy.

In N. America, most recipes for hare are based on dishes of European origin. Applejack may be an ingredient (instead of *marc*) in New England; civets appear in the French-influenced CREOLE cookery of the south. (LM)

HARICOT BEAN *Phaseolus vulgaris*, is a native of C. America, where several varieties with small, black seeds (beans) still grow wild, but has become the most important LEGUME cultivated in Europe and N. America. It is also grown in other temperate and subtropical regions of the world.

The plant was first domesticated more than 5,000 years ago. By the time the Europeans arrived in America numerous varieties of different sizes and colours were being cultivated in both S. and N. America. The first samples of the new beans to reach Europe, in the 16th century, were of a dark red, kidney-shaped variety, so giving rise to the common English name **kidney beans**.

In France their Aztec name, *ayecotl*, was soon corrupted to haricot, a name which already had another meaning (a meat RAGOUT) and another derivation (from *harigoter*, to cut up). This usage spread to England, with curious consequences; in the 18th century a dish might be called 'arrico of kidney beans', an apparent tautology but legitimate. The French still use haricot as the general name for a bean; whereas in English it signifies the small white beans of *P. vulgaris*, usually dried.

VARIETIES

Haricot bean plants show two distinct patterns of growth: pole beans which develop into vines and need support, and bush or dwarf beans which are low growers. There are many varieties of both, adapted to various climates, countries, market requirements, etc. There are four main ways of consuming beans: either they can be picked early and the tender pods eaten; or the beans can be 'popped'; or the fresh green beans can be eaten without the pods; or the beans can be dried before consumption. Generally speaking, any given variety is best used in one of these four ways; and the simplest method of categorizing varieties is by end use. However, the dividing lines are not clear-cut; it must be remembered that many beans in the third group are also available in dried form and many in the fourth group are eaten fresh in season.

1. **French** (or snap) **beans** are the usual names for the varieties classed as 'edible podded' and grown mainly with the intention that the immature or mature green pods be used as a vegetable. Depending on the variety, they may also be **green** (or wax or slicing) **beans**. The strings and other elements of toughness have largely been bred out of these beans, so the pods break or snap easily; hence the term 'snap'. (However, in the USA these snap beans may be called 'string' beans; unjustly because the really stringy green bean is the RUNNER BEAN, which is of a different species.)

The **haricots Beurre** are a subgroup of varieties with pale yellow pods; the beans inside are of various colorations.

2. The so-called **popping beans**, known in the Andes as *nuñas*, are a type of *P. vulgaris* which burst out of their seed coats when heated with a little oil: 'they open like small butterflies spreading their wings. The resulting product is soft and tastes somewhat like roasted peanuts.' The authors of *Lost Crops of the Incas* (National Research Council 1989) further explain that *nuñas* were developed for use at high altitudes where water boils at too low a temperature to permit cooking ordinary dry beans.

3. Of the varieties which are grown for the mature beans, which are extracted from the fully grown but not dry pods, many are likely to be called **shell beans** (or shelly beans), *haricots à écosser* in French, meaning simply that they are shelled before consumption. They include:

- The best known, **flageolet beans,** which are typically white or green, but may also be red. These are normally harvested just before the pods reach maturity, and may be cooked fresh, or dried. They are a true delicacy and go especially well with lamb.
- Some beans which are splashed or streaked with red and consequently bear names like

cranberry bean. Examples occur in Argentina and Chile (where the name of one sort is *porotos*).

4. The fourth category is that of varieties grown to produce fully mature beans which are found in dried form in the markets. Here we have:

- **Pea** (or navy) **beans,** seeds less than 8 mm (0.3") long, not kidney shaped. Navy beans are so called because they were part of the rations of the US navy in the 19th century. They are cultivated in the USA and Canada for use in the canning industry.
- **Medium haricot beans,** seeds 10–12 mm (0.5") in length, thickness less than half the length, a subgroup of which the mild-flavoured Pinto beans, mottled red and white, are typical. The **Borlotti bean,** the type most popular in Italy, is similar in colour, size, and flavour.
- **Marrow beans,** seeds medium to large, 10–15 mm (0.4–0.6"), thickness exceeding half the length.
- **Kidney beans,** of which **cannellini beans** are typical, seeds 15 mm (0.6") in length, more or less kidney shaped, may be shades of white, red, or purple, sometimes mottled.
- The **(Mexican) black bean** (*frijol negro, feijão* in Portuguese), sometimes called **turtle bean,** most nearly resembles the original haricot bean. The mature seeds, eaten fresh in season and dried at other times, are popular throughout Latin America and Spain. Their flavour is strong and full, and has been likened to meat or mushrooms. Black bean soup is exceptionally good.

Consideration in detail of all these numerous sorts of beans is greatly aided by the informative lists of varieties and cultivars provided by Facciola (1998).

PROCESSING AND COOKING

Black, pinto, and red kidney beans are canned successfully (see CANNING).

BAKED BEANS are produced commercially from navy and pea beans grown in the USA. The dish which inspired the canning of this product was Boston baked beans.

Although a preliminary soaking is a common procedure when cooking haricot beans, it is not universal. Mexicans often omit this step and start the cooking in hot water. Soaking and cooking times vary widely, depending on the age and size of the beans.

Some cooks add a pinch of BICARBONATE OF SODA to the soaking water to render dried beans more digestible and to shorten cooking times. The latter aim is met, since the bicarbonate helps to dissolve the cell walls, a process which also speeds the exit of 'the flatulating oligosaccharides' (as the substances causing flatulence are known)

from the beans. Unfortunately, however, loss of desirable nutrients also occurs.

Most agree that haricot beans should be cooked without salt, which tends to harden them, or that salt should only be added after cooking has made the beans tender. Earthenware pots are used wherever these beans are widely eaten and it is claimed that this enhances their flavour. The use of aromatics during cooking may also have a beneficial effect.

The greatest variety of bean dishes is found in S. America. In C. and S. Mexico, black beans are always seasoned with EPAZOTE. They are traditionally served after the main course in small bowls. Black beans play an eponymous role in *Feijoada completa*, national dish of BRAZIL, but they are supported by numerous meats and other important ingredients; see Elisabeth Lambert Ortiz (1979). See also REFRIED BEANS.

There are numerous regional dishes using haricot beans in France, and it is noticeable that when they are cooked as main dishes this is usually in areas where pork or goosefat is the preferred medium, e.g. Languedoc, Périgord, Alsace-Lorraine. See also CASSOULET.

HARISSA a word with three meanings in the kitchen. First, it is a red paste of CHILLI pepper used in Tunisia, Morocco, and throughout N. Africa as a fiery hot ingredient. A common brand in cans bears a picture of an erupting volcano. This harissa, as traditionally made at home, consists of chilli peppers which are soaked and then pounded with coriander, caraway, garlic, and salt, and moistened with olive oil. As Gobert (1940) remarks, this is 'always present and ready' in a Tunisian household.

Secondly the name is applied to a Tunisian dish consisting of seared green peppers, tomatoes, and onions, which are peeled, pounded, and flavoured with coriander, caraway, and garlic.

Thirdly, harissa is the name used in some Arab countries, notably Syria, the Lebanon, and Iraq, for a porridge-like soup of wheat and lamb which is described under HALEEM, which is the name used in the countries where the dish probably originated.

HARTLEY DOROTHY (1893–1985), widely seen as the writer who has made the greatest single contribution to the history of popular food in England. The phrase 'popular food' is chosen deliberately because the foodways which she recorded were those of the populace, not of court circles or the aristocratic and wealthy classes. She wrote other books about rural England, including

Water in England (1964) and *Made in England* (1939), but it seems likely that *Food in England* (1954) will be her most enduring achievement. She illustrated it herself (her normal practice) and furnished it with many apt quotations and anecdotes, often from obscure sources, as well as from her own lifetime of experience in the kitchen and as an insatiable, curious researcher. Looking back at her earlier life, one can see the significance for *Food in England* of several experiences, in particular: that she started cooking for her family when she was only 12 years old; that she became an art student in 1919, and was a prize pupil (and, later, a teacher of art); that she spent much time during the 1920s in the British Museum Reading Room; that in the 1930s she spent years travelling by bicycle or on foot around the UK with pen and camera, producing weekly articles on rural life for a national newspaper; and that after a spell in the Women's Royal Air Corps in the Second World War she was involved in teaching and lecturing on the history of food in various colleges. It can thus be seen that she was almost ideally equipped to take on her unique and pioneering role.

Miss Hartley made clear in the introduction to her book that it was written for cooks, not for historians, and that it was to the numerous cooks all over the country who were happy to talk to her that she owed much of her material. Perhaps thinking of these good ladies, she chose to reproduce on her title page a quotation from Gervase Markham (1615):

Your English housewife must be of chaste thought, stout courage, patient, untyred, watchful, diligent, witty and pleasant, constant in friendship, full of good neighbourhood, wise in discourse, but not frequent therein, sharp and quick of speech, but not bitter or talkative, secrete in her affairs, comfortable in her consailes, and skilful in all the working knowledges that belong to her vocation.

Many of the numerous readers who have become acquainted with her charming and vigorous personality through *Food in England* will have reflected that Markham's words could well have been applied to herself.

READING: Mary Wondrausch (1996).

HARTSHORN AND HARTSHORN-JELLY. Hartshorn was formerly the main source of ammonia, and its principal use was in the production of smelling salts. But hartshorn shavings were used to produce a special, edible JELLY used in English cookery in the 17th and 18th centuries. In her recipe for 'Hedge-Hog', Hannah Glasse (1747) assumes that her readers will know how to make this jelly, and suggests taking wine and sugar with it.

HARUSAME a Japanese term meaning 'spring rain', referring to the appearance of a vermicelli-like product made from various kinds of starch: MUNG BEAN (this kind, the best, is imported from China), SOYA BEAN, SWEET POTATO, cornflour (Japanese style). Although they may be found under names such as 'cellophane noodles' or 'bean thread noodles' or 'bean vermicelli', the Japanese do not count these as real NOODLES and never eat them on their own (as they do proper noodles). Harusame are commonly chopped and used as an alternative to batter for coating TEMPURA.   HS

HASH a term which has greater use in N. America than in Britain. It comes from the French *hacher*, meaning 'to chop', and entered the English language in the 17th century. Mariani (1994) remarks that it was found in America soon thereafter as a 'form of shepherd's pie or other melange of meat and vegetables'. This remains its general meaning. It has often had a derogatory sense, thus explained by Mariani:

By the middle of the nineteenth century hash became associated with cheap restaurants called 'hash houses' or 'hasheries' (an 1850 menu from the Eldorado Hotel in Hangtown, California, lists 'Low Grade Hash' for seventy-five cents and '18 Carets Hash' for a dollar) and the workers in such places were called 'hash slingers'. By the turn of the century 'corned beef hash' was being ordered, sometimes called 'cornbeef Willie.'

Although a hash was thus perceived as a dish of low quality, it has not lacked supporters who give generous praise to well-prepared hash, counting it as a dish which is outstanding for its tastiness as well as economy. John Thorne (1996) is one such and his book is the best resource for a historical conspectus of hash in the USA, for lyrical prose on the topic, and for a highly detailed recipe for 'Maine boiled beef hash', unrivalled in his view.

'Hash browns', a relatively recent abbreviation of fuller phrases such as 'hashed brown potatoes', refers to small rissole-like fried cakes of cooked and finely chopped potato.

HASLET (or harslet) was defined by Dr Johnson in 1755 as 'heart, liver, and lights of a hog, with the windpipe and part of the throat to it'. Nowadays, the term refers to a dish which is associated with the Midlands and north of England. This usually takes the form of a meat loaf made from OFFAL, usually from a pig, which has been chopped finely, placed in an oven dish of loaf form, preferably covered with a piece of flead (kidney fat) or CAUL fat, and baked.

HASTY PUDDING the simplest of all PUDDINGS, if it can be called a pudding at all, for it is no more than a PORRIDGE of flour and milk. Such a pudding could be made in little more time than it took to boil the milk, and it has no doubt been a popular emergency dish since the Middle Ages, if not earlier. Sweetened, flavoured with spice or rosewater, and dotted with butter, hasty pudding can be quite palatable; and in fact in the 18th and 19th centuries in England it was esteemed as a delicacy. Before 1800, an egg was often added to the mixture, though after this time mixtures with egg were given other names.

A hasty pudding hybrid is Malvern pudding, made of alternate layers of hasty pudding with egg and of sweetened cooked apple; it is baked.

In the far north of England, and in Scotland, at least as early as the 18th century, the name came to be applied to a plain porridge of oats and barley, made with water as often as milk. In Victorian England, too, hasty pudding was sometimes made with oatmeal, or with SAGO or with TAPIOCA. Milk was always used. This pudding evolved into what are called 'nursery milk puddings' in Britain; the name 'hasty pudding' is no longer used, but it is agreeable to reread what May Byron (1923) had to say about it while it still bore its old name:

There are certain traditional puddings which have never lost their high repute. Of such is the celebrated hasty pudding with which Jack the Giant-killer filled, not his mouth, but the bag beneath his doublet. 'Ods bobs!' cried his Welsh antagonist, 'hur can do that hurself,' and, unwarily swallowing an immense bowlful of the dainty, he was rent as by some high-explosive. Now, hasty pudding is the very meekest and mildest of all its tribe: butter (literally) won't melt in its mouth, unless it be scalding hot out of the saucepan. It is a tame, colourless, flavourless affair *per se*; yet, look you (as the Giant would have said), it has proudly survived, on this one noble achievement, the wear and tear of centuries. Still puddings run deep.

HAUSA POTATO the brown or black tuber of *Solenostemon* (formerly *Coleus*) *rotundifolius*, a plant indigenous to tropical Africa, possibly Ethiopia. It was probably taken to India by the Arabs and onwards to the E. Indies by the Portuguese. (It is also found in Madagascar and Mauritius.)

The Hausa potato is eaten both raw and cooked; and the plant has edible leaves.

Three close relations, of which the first and third belong to Asia and all are also eaten like potatoes, are: *Coleus parvifolius*, the African or (again) country potato; *C. blumei*, sayabana or Jacob's coat; *Plectranthus esculentus*, Livingstone potato, daju, or rizuka. However one calls them, these vegetables are of some importance regionally as cultivated crops, capable of playing understudy to the true potato in climates where the latter would not thrive.

HAWAII'S food today is a confusing mixture, a palimpsest of the foods of a dozen different ethnic groups. But one can make sense of it by taking note of two salient facts: first, that before the arrival of the first humans, probably around the 3rd century AD, Hawaii, one of the most isolated sets of islands in the world, contained essentially nothing edible on land. Very few species had managed to cross those staggering distances; those that did had speciated to provide a fine natural laboratory for evolutionary biologists. But apart from a few birds and a few ferns, there was nothing to eat; most important, there were no edible carbohydrates. Second, since the arrival of the first humans, Hawaii has been the terminal point of three diasporas: the great marine diaspora of the Pacific islanders; the great voyages of discovery of the Europeans and the Americans; and the end of the road for Koreans, Chinese, Japanese, Filipinos, and, lately, SE Asians. From these diverse influences, a CREOLE food is now being created, known in the islands as Local Food.

When the Hawaiians arrived in the islands, they brought with them some 27 or so edible plants, as well as pigs, dogs, and, as stowaways, rats. The most important plants were TARO and SWEET POTATO. The terrain and the climate in Hawaii proved particularly suitable for growing wetland taro and the Hawaiians constructed massive systems of ditches and patches (paddies) for this purpose, quite the most extensive in Polynesia. In dry areas where taro would not grow, sweet potatoes were the staple. Also important were BREADFRUIT, various YAMS, SUGAR CANE, and COCONUT, though, perhaps because this is at the limit of its range, the coconut played less part in Hawaiian culture than in other parts of SE Asia and the Pacific.

The staple of the diet was POI. This was usually made with taro, but sweet potato or other starches were used when necessary. The taro was baked in an earth oven (an *imu*), then pounded with a stone pounder on a large wooden poi board. It was then mixed with sufficient water to make a paste that would adhere to the fingers. Vegetables and fruits were in short supply, being largely confined to the leaves and stems of the taro plant and to the mountain apple.

The major protein was fish. Both pigs and dogs were eaten but they were largely reserved for the nobility. So too were the fish that were cultivated in the large salt and freshwater ponds that the Hawaiians constructed. For the bulk of the population,

protein was provided by wild fish and shellfish from the streams, the reef, and the ocean. The fish was eaten both raw (often living) and cooked. It was preserved against the periods of stormy weather that, particularly in winter, can make fishing impossible for days or weeks, by drying and by salting. This adequate, if bland, diet was spiced up by the salt that was collected from shorelines around the island, by an extensive array of seaweed, and by the roasted and ground nuts of the kukui (CANDLENUT) tree.

CONTACT TO ANNEXATION
In 1778, Captain James Cook sighted the Hawaiian Islands. Within a matter of years they had become part of the world trade. A succession of European and American drifters fetched up on the shores, followed in the 1810s and 1820s by forceful Congregational missionaries from New England. From the start, new animals and plants were introduced; cows, horses, and goats, and a bewildering variety of plants. The Hawaiian monarchy and subsequently the descendants of the missionaries quickly realized that apart from salt the islands had no exportable mineral resources and apart from sandalwood, which was quickly exhausted, no exportable vegetable ones either. Hawaiian food and haole food (the latter being the food of the white incomers) continued side by side with occasional input from the Chinese who also ended up in the islands. The Hawaiians added salt meat and salt salmon from the north-east to their diet; the haoles clung to the food of New England so far as they could, substituting taro for potatoes and bread, and mangoes for apples. On ceremonial occasions, there would be luaus at which largely Hawaiian food was served: poi, of course, and dried fish and shrimp, kalua pig baked in the *imu*, seaweed, sweet potatoes, chicken baked with coconut and taro leaves, and a dessert made of coconut milk thickened with Polynesian arrowroot. Given the mountains, many haole foods could be grown—Irish potatoes were sold to the forty-niners in California, for example—but even so the demand for European/American foods meant that the factors flourished.

THE PLANTATIONS AND ETHNIC FOOD
The food landscape of Hawaii began changing dramatically once the sugar plantations began to flourish following the signing of the Reciprocity Treaty with the United States in 1876. The Hawaiian population (like so many after contact) had declined precipitously and the planters turned to wherever they could find labour. Depending on the condition of the United States immigration laws and on the attitudes of foreign governments they hired contract workers from elsewhere as best they could.

In order, substantial numbers of Chinese, Japanese, Okinawans, Koreans, Puerto Ricans, Portuguese from the Atlantic Islands, and Filipinos arrived in the islands between the 1880s and the 1930s. By that time, the population was dominated by the Japanese. Each of these groups demanded their own food on the plantations and the plantation stores went quite some way to accommodate them. In addition, flourishing small farms, market gardening, and fishing operations sprang up as well as enterprises to make SAKÉ, TOFU, NOODLES, and other essentials. In the early years of the 20th century, rice was Hawaii's third largest crop. The Japanese had largely taken over fishing from the Hawaiians.

All these ethnic groups are still to be found in Hawaii and most (not the Puerto Ricans) have their own array of grocery stores, bakeries, restaurants, and spiral-bound cookbooks. Considerable back influence has resulted from the multicultural movements of the last ten years and from the pride many groups have taken in the 100th anniversary of their first arrival in the islands. Even so there are notable differences from food in the home country; almost all groups eat more beef, everyone eats white rice, and there is a certain irony in the sequences of fund-raising cookbooks from Buddhist temples with their lengthy sections on meat of all kinds.

LOCAL FOOD
Beginning in the 1920s and 1930s, certain forces began to produce a creole food, Local Food. (It is worth setting this in the context of other sugar islands in the Caribbean, also Mauritius and Fiji.) One was the arrival of home economists at the university, in the electric and gas companies, and in the extension services. Trained largely at the Columbia Teachers College in New York, these women recorded the diet of the Japanese, established the food values of Hawaiian foods and a range of tropical fruits, and trained large numbers of home economics teachers and school cafeteria managers. Surprisingly sympathetic to the different ethnic foods of the islands, they urged brown rice (a complete failure), milk (successful though at the expense of the digestive systems of the Asian adults who do not tolerate lactose), and ensured that the food in the public school system was an all-American diet of hamburger, meat loaf, Salisbury steak, and mashed potatoes. This exposure to American food was reinforced for the many who joined up following the bombing of Pearl Harbor in the Second World War. Although their quartermasters in Italy tried valiantly to find substitutes for rice (vermicelli), the Japanese, for example, had no option but to eat standard army K-rations. Back in the islands, the necessity

to show allegiance to America meant that many ethnic customs—costume, religious observances, language schools, and food—were dropped.

Now, at least in public, most of the population of Hawaii eats Local Food much of the time (as well as retaining some ethnic food and American food). The centrepiece of Local Food is the Plate Lunch available from lunch wagons and from numerous small restaurants and restaurant chains. It consists of 'two scoop' (scoop from the ice cream scoop used to dish it out, and in the singular to accord with the pidgin/creole that everyone speaks) sticky rice (Japanese japonica rice, that is), a large helping of meat, usually cooked in an Asian style, a portion of macaroni salad or potato salads, and perhaps a lettuce leaf or dab of KIMCH'I on the side. The rice is Asian; the style of cooking the meat (*katsu, teriyaki, kau yuk*, Korean barbecue) is Asian; the quantity of meat is haole; the heapings on the plate are haole. And it is eaten with chopsticks (Asian).

Certain other foods have made it into the Local category. Rice is without doubt the staple in the islands. *Poke* (pronounced pokey) is the Local fish dish, raw fish cut in small chunks dressed simply with salt and seaweed, or more ambitiously with chilli peppers, sesame oil, or SOY SAUCE. *Teriyaki* (see JAPANESE CULINARY TERMS) is the most popular way of treating all meats, including SPAM which is an island favourite. Soy sauce (called *shoyu*) is the universal condiment. Hard tack (see SHIP's BISCUIT; here called saloon pilots) is popular. Among ethnic foods which have come to be considered Local are: Hawaiian *laulau*, Okinawan and Portuguese donuts (*andagi* and *malasadas*—see DOUGHNUT), Chinese preserved plum (CRACK SEEDS), Asian noodle soup (*saimin*), Chinese *char sui bao* (*manapua*), and Filipino LUMPIA.

Local Food functions as a language. Locals in Hawaii regard mainland food as dull and boring and look on those who do not regard raw fish with relish with amused scorn. They cart rice cookers and rice when they go to the mainland. They are amazed that McDonald's on the mainland has neither rice nor *saimin*. Politicians distribute cookbooks with carefully chosen cross-cultural recipes as campaign gifts; they offer lavish public 'bashes' at the opening of the Legislature with heavy *pupus* (snacks) from all ethnic groups.

Creole languages typically de-creolize as the people become more integrated into mainstream society. Whether that will happen with Local Food or whether it will continue transmuting into something characteristic is unclear. But at the moment, Hawaii offers a fascinating example of the dynamics of food change.   RL

HAWTHORN or may or whitethorn, *Crataegus oxyacantha*, symbol of spring; the best-known member of a group of small, thorny trees of the rose family. Species of the genus grow throughout Europe, Asia, and N. America. 'Haw' comes from an Old English word which can mean both hedge and berry.

The common hawthorns, whitethorns, or may trees of Europe, *Crataegus oxyacantha* and *C. monogyna*, have small, red berries which are very sour and have not been much used as food except in times of famine. They are sometimes made into a sharp jelly for serving with meat. The flower buds are, or were, eaten by country children under the popular name 'bread and cheese' (or, in Welsh, 'burra cause') and make an interesting addition to salads.

The flowers were much used in English medieval cookery; there was even a special term, *spinée*, for dishes made with them, and the FORME OF CURY, compiled by the cooks of King Richard II, has a recipe for such a dish. The flowers, when open, have a strong almond scent.

The species with the best fruit is the AZAROLE (or azerole), *C. azarolus* (sometimes called Naples medlar but no relation to the ordinary medlar).

The Chinese thornapple, *C. pentagyna*, another fruiting species which has been esteemed since early times, is cultivated in China. The fruits are eaten stewed, candied, in sweetmeats, and in a jelly.

N. American haws and hawthorns of the genus *Crataegus* exist in a bewilderingly large range of species; hundreds, according to one recent authority, who declined to identify any of them on the ground that the whole subject was incomprehensible even to professional botanists. Some of these were acknowledged by early European settlers to have better fruit than European species. Wood, in his *New England's Prospect* (1634), declared that the 'white thorne' bore fruit as big as English cherries, 'esteemed above a Cherrie for goodnesse and pleasantnesse to the taste'.

Delicious jellies and marmalades can be made from these American haws. The flowers used to be a flavouring for mead and still are in Canada.

The numerous literary references to the hawthorn or May tree attest its many associations. It is everywhere taken as the first sure sign of spring, and in England it is used to decorate the traditional maypole. In traditional English beliefs, it was unlucky to bring into the house; to do so meant imminent death in the household.

HAZEL-HEN *Tetrastes bonasia*, a bird of the GROUSE family, Tetraonidae. Its range extends from C. and N. Europe to Japan and its preferred habitat is mountainous and wooded. Of moderate size (average total length 36 cm/14") and grouselike shape, it feeds on berries and has white flesh which is highly esteemed.

The hazel-hen is best roasted or prepared in other ways usual for grouse.

HAZELNUT the fruit of hazel trees, of the genus *Corylus*, called *noisette* in French and *nocciola* in Italian. British and American nomenclature differ here. In Britain the term hazelnut can be applied whether the tree is wild or cultivated, while the names cob and filbert indicate two sorts of cultivated hazelnut. Americans, in general, reserve the name hazelnut for their wild species, and call their cultivated nuts, which are almost all descended from European species, filberts.

The common wild hazel of Britain, most of Europe, and SW Asia is *Corylus avellana*. It is a low, shrubby tree, up to 6 m (20') tall, which often forms part of a hedgerow. Its small nuts with their hard, brown shells are borne in clusters of one to four, within a husk whose fancied resemblance to a helmet accounts for the name *Corylus*, from the Greek *korys* (helmet). 'Hazel' itself comes from the Anglo-Saxon *haesil* (headdress).

Towards the south of its range in Europe, the common hazel is joined by, and hybridizes with, the giant hazel (*C. maxima*), a more robust tree. From these wild species (and others such as *C. colurna*, of Asia Minor) have come numerous varieties and cultivars, many of which are hybrids. Indeed there has been so much hybridization that 'pure' examples of the original species would be hard to find in commercial orchards.

Cultivation of hazels probably began in classical times in Europe. Theophrastus (late 4th century BC) and Pliny (1st century AD) refer to trees having been brought from Asia Minor, and Pliny derives the Latin name *avellana* from Abellina (possibly Damascus in Syria). Since wild hazels were common in Greece and Italy, these imported trees were presumably of superior quality and intended for cultivation.

Cultivation ended for a while with the fall of the Roman Empire, but had restarted by the early 17th century in Italy. A centre of cultivation was Avellino in the Campagna, from which some suppose that the name 'avellana' was derived; but in view of Pliny's earlier attribution of the name this must be a coincidence.

Cultivation also began in England, mostly in the vicinity of Maidstone in Kent, where conditions are ideal. There were already two main alternative English names for hazelnuts, and these began to be used for cultivated varieties. One was 'cobnut' or 'cob', from the Old English 'cop' (head), which was applied to round nuts with short husks leaving the end of the nut visible. The other, 'filbert', was used for longer nuts completely covered by their husks. (This has led some to suppose 'filbert' to be a corruption of 'full beard': in German there is a comparable name, *Bartsnuss*, meaning 'beard nut'. However, it may refer to St Philibert, a canonized king of Normandy around whose day, 22 August, hazelnuts ripen.)

There are now in England numerous named varieties of both cob and filbert. It is a source of confusion that the variety of filbert most commonly displayed by English greengrocers bears the name Kentish Cob; it should correctly be styled Lambert's filbert.

Early American settlers were unimpressed by the small native hazelnuts which were eaten by Indians. In 1629 the Massachusetts Company sent to England for better English nuts for planting, so that organized hazelnut growing began more or less simultaneously in both countries. Although most American cultivated nuts are of European origin, there are some hybrids with the American wild hazel, *C. americana*, which are hardier than pure strains.

The most important commercial variety in the USA has been Barcelona, although Ennis bears larger nuts and has been gaining in popularity. The best variety in Italy is probably Tonda Gentile delle Langhe, from the part of Piedmont whose hazelnuts are famous. Whiteskin is another popular variety.

Turkey is now the largest producer of hazelnuts.

Hazelnuts are not difficult to process. The husk splits and falls off by itself a few days after picking. Both unshelled and shelled nuts are sold. The latter keep better than most other shelled nuts. The brown skin around the kernel need not be removed but if the nuts are lightly toasted, which often improves their flavour, the skins begin to peel away and can be removed by rubbing. Similarly, if the nuts are blanched by pouring boiling water over them and leaving them for a few minutes, the skin is easily rubbed off.

In most countries, hazelnuts have traditionally been eaten fresh ('green'). Their flavour varies from the milky, juicy, almost sharp taste of the nuts in autumn to the extreme sweetness which they attain after several months of ripeness.

The nuts are also used in cooking, generally in cakes and confectionery; there are many German and C. European recipes for hazelnut cakes. In Turkey they go into *lokum* (TURKISH DELIGHT) and in Italy into some kinds of *torrone* (the equivalent of NOUGAT). In Spain hazelnuts are also often used in savoury dishes, and are an ingredient of the famous sauce of Tarragona, *salsa*

ROMESCO. In French cuisine *beurre noisette* is butter heated until it is the colour of hazelnuts.

Hazelnut oil is a delicate product, whose profile in terms of composition and flavour is generally like that of walnut oil and which is similarly expensive. Jane Grigson (1981) visited a French nut oil factory and found that it was using hazelnuts imported 'from Avellino behind Vesuvius where Europe's best hazelnuts grow'. She recommends the oil for various purposes, e.g. in cake-making.

HEAD a part of animals which provides a range of foodstuffs which vary considerably in the uses to which they are put and the ways in which they are prepared. There is a great difference between delicate brains, for example, and strong cheek muscles. Individual parts of heads are treated under BRAINS, CHEEKS (including BATH CHAP), EARS, MUZZLE (snout), PALATE (with lips and noses/muzzles), TONGUE. This article deals with whole heads. See also COD.

Symbolically, heads, carrying much of an animal's identity, may represent more than simply meat, and have some deeper, cultural significance. Despite a sharp decline in the use of whole, undisguised heads on British tables, a few symbolic dishes survive. A pig's head, cooked and suitably adorned, can be a centrepiece 'boar's head' for a feast (although if this is intended to be purely ornamental, it may just be a raw head under a decorative aspic glaze piped with lard curlicues).

The most basic way of cooking a head, common in all European and many Asian cuisines and probably of ancient origin, is to boil it until the meat falls off the bones. This becomes either a soup (in hot climates) or a jellied concoction of highly seasoned chopped meat (in colder regions). And there have been other uses; thus calf's head used to be, in England, a standard source of meat for MOCK TURTLE SOUP.

Sheep's head broth is a well-known Scottish dish, known there as Powsowdie. Meg Dods (1826) gives a remarkably explicit recipe for it ('Take out only the glassy part of the eyes . . . '), and has an anecdote about a Scottish professor who had been away from his native land for many years and on his return made haste to procure a sheep's head and send it to the blacksmith's to be singed. At the hour of dinner, 'the chops of the learned professor watered with expectation when, lo! to his disappointment and horror, the fleshless skull was presented'. The labour involved in polishing the skull cost the professor sixteen shillings. This was an extraordinary misunderstanding in a country where sheep's head broth was a national institution and there were indeed sheep's head clubs dedicated to its consumption.

In many countries of the Middle East, including Turkey, Iran, and Afghanistan, a dish of broth and meat of slowly simmered sheep's head and trotters is made. In Iran and Afghanistan it is called *Kallah pacheh* (*kallah* meaning head and *pacheh* trotters). In Iran and Turkey it is eaten mainly as a breakfast dish. The version in Turkey is called *Kelle-paça* (head-trotter). Nevin Halıcı (1989) has the following to say about sheep's heads in Turkey:

If a sheep's head is served whole, the meat is eaten, then the brain is extracted and offered first to a guest or to the head of the household, and then passed round for others to help themselves.

Cold sheep's head has become so popular that you will find it being sold on street corners and at railway stations in every Anatolian town. In Diyarbakir in south-eastern Anatolia the menfolk usually have a dish of sheep's head and trotters for breakfast at the market before starting work.

Leipoldt (1976) vividly describes the impact made by a baked ox head in South Africa:

One's first emotion, on seeing this immense and horrific roast—in which, if the head happens to be that of an Afrikaner ox, the horns appear to stretch the whole length of the dining table, while the baked eyes stare with an expression that is ludicrous as well as baleful, and the lips are drawn back to show the teeth in a sort of snarl that no living ox ever shows—is one of profound shock. Indeed, on the first occasion when I assisted, as General Botha's guest, at a party where this gruesome dish was the main and only item on the bill of fare, two of my fellow gourmets were so overcome that they had to leave the table.

HEART an organ which is in almost all instances an edible part of an animal. Among the various sorts of OFFAL, it is unusual in that it consists almost entirely of muscle. Moreover, the nature of the organ is such that the muscles are in constant use, pumping blood around the body, while the animal is alive; and hearts of older animals are therefore likely to be tough and to need marinating before being cooked. Hearts also have to be trimmed of fat and 'pipes' beforehand.

Large ox hearts may be sliced and then grilled (broiled) if they are sufficiently tender; or, as more commonly happens, subjected to slow moist cooking, e.g. braising or stewing. Smaller ones are suitable for stuffing and then being baked. The smallest of all, such as hearts of rabbits, are apt to turn up with the edible meat in a casserole dish or the like.

Hearts of poultry and game birds count as GIBLETS.

HEART SHELL *Glossus* (*Isocardia*) *humanus*, a bivalve which has the shape of a human heart. Linnaeus, observing this, called it *Cardium humanum*, and its common names in most languages reflect the resemblance. However, the Dutch are out of line with *zots-kappen*, meaning fool's cap, and English fishermen are recorded as having used the names Torbay nose and oxhorn cockle.

The heart shell is akin to a cockle, and is sometimes called heart cockle, but it is not a true cockle. Its size can be as much as 10 cm (4"); and its range is from Iceland and Norway to the Mediterranean.

Although Lovell (1884) recorded enthusiasm for this bivalve on the part of English fishermen, and above all the wife of a coastguard at Brixham, who had 'often luxuriated in a dish of these delicious shellfish', the heart shell is not much sought after now. The same applies to related species in the Indo-Pacific region.

HEAT AND ITS TRANSMISSION are fundamental to cookery. In the most substantial, and most readable, modern treatise on the scientific aspects of cookery, McGee (1984) puts the point thus:

Cooking can be defined in a general way as the transfer of energy from a heat source to the food. Our various cooking methods—boiling, broiling, baking, frying and so on—achieve their various effects by employing very different materials—water, air, oil—and by drawing on different principles of heat transfer.

An assumption that the cook will have access to fuel, devices for generating and controlling heat, and supports or containers for the food during cooking is implicit in the concept of a recipe. Geography and technology dictate availability of fuels; in turn, these have intrinsic characteristics which have influenced the development of cuisines. They may burn fast (dead wood) or slowly (dried cow dung); hot (charcoal) or cooler (peat); be easily controlled (a gas flame) or require skill in their management (coal and other solid fuels). Electricity is one step removed from fuel, but is also important for generating heat for cooking. Fireplaces, ovens, and stoves have evolved in different traditions to deliver optimum heat using available fuels.

There are three basic ways in which heat can be transmitted:

- radiation, represented by grilling (broiling), spit-roasting, barbecuing, and, in a specialized form, by the microwave;
- conduction, an important consideration when choosing cooking utensils; and
- convection, through a medium such as water, air, or oil, as in boiling, steaming, and frying.

Radiant heat is a form of pure energy known as the infrared to physicists, and found on the electromagnetic spectrum at wavelengths between microwaves and visible light; atoms in a substance absorb microwave energy and then release it in the form of increased motion, which we sense as heat. To cooks it means a naked flame, glowing coals, or a hot electrical element. Food is cooked by being close enough to the source to absorb energy across the intervening space. Fire, the most basic source of radiant heat, has been known to man for many thousands of years, and was probably used to roast meat spitted on green wood far back into prehistory. Although an inefficient method of transmission, radiant heat is still utilized for grilling (broiling) and barbecuing. This is partly because it is very intense (coals and electric elements heat up to about 1090 °C/1994 °F; gas flames to 1650 °C/3002 °F), catalysing browning reactions which give attractive flavours on the surface of the food. This method is also utilized in a TANDOOR and in old-fashioned bread ovens, whose linings take up heat from fires lit inside, and radiate it back to the food being cooked.

Radiant heat is energy travelling at a wavelength which makes all molecules vibrate and so heat up. Microwave ovens (see MICROWAVE COOKING) also use radiation, but at a longer wavelength, and make only polar molecules (carrying a strong positive/negative charge) such as water, vibrate, heating it up. Since water only heats up to boiling before becoming a vapour, the food is cooked at less intense temperatures than those from conventional radiant sources, without the browning reactions and the flavours produced by them. This is why some microwaved foods have a soft, pallid appearance. But microwaves penetrate much further into the food, cooking it on the surface and to a depth of 2–3 cm (1") simultaneously.

In **conduction** the item to be heated is placed in contact with a heat source and heat moves directly from one atom to another. An example is an electric griddle heated by an integral element to give a hot surface, which in turn heats the molecules of, say, oatcakes placed upon it. The hotplates of electric or 'Aga'-type stoves heat pans placed upon them by conducting heat from one surface to the other. Conduction is also exploited by cooks who skewer potatoes before baking them; the skewer heats along its length and helps to cook the potato from inside. In practice, conduction is most important when considering cooking utensils, as some of the various materials involved (e.g. copper) are much better conductors than others (e.g. ceramics). In cookery, transmission by conduction is mostly used in combination with convection, the third way of delivering heat to food.

Convection requires a fluid medium and can be divided according to this into moist heat (using water, stock, milk, wine, or other liquid) and dry heat (relying on air or oil). As molecules in the medium heat up they become less dense and rise, lose energy as they cool, then fall again. The same principle applies to hot air in an oven (where a fan may be used to force the air to circulate and to even out the temperature) and hot fat in a frying pan or deep-fat fryer.

When moist heat is used, the temperature achieved can be no higher than boiling point (100 °C/212 °F, or slightly less at high altitude), so browning reactions do not occur, and boiled foods lack the intense flavour of grills; but it is an efficient method of heating, as liquids provide a dense medium directly in contact with the food. Thin liquids heat faster than thick ones, so consommé heats more quickly than thick soup. Poaching is a gentler version of boiling, using water at just below 100 °C.

To STEAM food, it is held over boiling liquid and the heat is transmitted by water vapour surrounding the food, and condensing on it. The temperature is effectively no higher than that of boiling water, although a tightly lidded pan has the effect of raising the pressure inside very slightly. Only a specially designed pressure cooker can take the temperature of water vapour much higher, say up to 120 °C (248 °F), when it will cook food much faster than conventional boiling.

Baking using the conventional (western) ovens relies on transmission of dry heat by convection, the air inside the oven heating up from elements in the oven walls and circulating around the food. It is an inefficient method of transmission, and fans are sometimes added to force the movement of air around the oven and even out cold spots. A relatively high temperature can be achieved, giving a pleasant brownness and flavour to many foods cooked this way.

In practice, all methods of cooking involve combinations of heat transmission methods: for instance the base of a pan of water over a low gas flame is heated by a combination of convection (through the air) and radiant heat; the heat is transmitted by conduction through the fabric of the pan itself, with an efficiency depending on the material of which the pan is made; and the water it contains heats by convection.

There is a final point. One could say that the objective of most acts of cooking is to raise the temperature of the innermost part of the food being cooked to a certain level. The question then arises: what is the relationship between distance to the innermost part and time required for cooking? The answer is that the time required does not vary in correct proportion to the distance but in proportion to the square of the distance. This is explained at greater length under FISH COOKERY since that is a subject where it is particularly relevant and where it has attracted recent discussion.   (LM)

READING: McGee (1985).

HEDGE GARLIC also known as Jack-by-the-hedge, *Alliaria petiolata*, an upstanding plant of European hedgerows, also known as garlic mustard. The leaves do smell slightly of GARLIC if chopped or bruised. Grigson (1955) gives a characteristically fine description:

In a brilliant sunshine, in May, one is always freshly struck by platoons of this familiar plant, at starched attention, the starch-white flowers above the new green leaves and against the green bank.

Some of the local names show that kitchen use of the leaves has a long history. Turner (1538) mentions it with the name 'sauce alone', since it was used by country people as a condiment, especially in the spring. Gerard (1633) observed that some people ate it, pounded, as a sauce for salt fish, in the same way that they would use ramsons (see WILD GARLIC). In the 19th century it was recommended as a boiled accompaniment to boiled mutton or as an addition to salads.

HEDGEHOG a small insectivorous animal, *Erinaceus europaeus*, found throughout W. and C. Europe. It is best known for a defence mechanism which consists of rolling up and exposing a spiny back to the world, a method which fails against the threat of road traffic. It is nocturnal in habit, and hibernates from October to April.

There are related species in other parts of Europe, and in Asia; but the PORCUPINE, although similarly protected by spines, is an animal of a different genus.

Hedgehogs are not normally sold or hunted for food, except by gypsies, whose traditional method for dealing with them is to encase the animals in clay and roast them, after which the baked clay is broken off, taking the spines with it. The meat is said to be tender and well flavoured, resembling chicken or sucking pig. Fernie (1905) provides alternative methods of cooking, and cites the *Tramp's Handbook* (1905) as evidence that hedgehogs are nice and fat at Michaelmas, when they have been feeding on windfall crabapples. He adds, but without giving a source, that in France the foresters of the marquis de Cherville were given to concoct a delicious stew of hedgehog with MORELS.

The 'hedgehog pudding' which formerly enjoyed some popularity in England, notably

in the 18th century but also in the 19th, was so called because of the slivered almonds which were stuck into its upper surface, where they resembled spines. (See TIPSY CAKE.)

HEINZ HENRY J. (1844–1919). Heinz started work at the age of 8 in his father's brickyard in Pennsylvania. He also helped cultivate the family garden and sell its produce. When he was 12 he had 3.5 acres (1.5 hectares) and a horse and cart and began to learn bookkeeping. The family horseradish patch provided his first convenience food; his horseradish was offered for sale, scrubbed and scraped or grated in vinegar, in clear glass bottles which revealed the purity of the product. He remembered this when evolving his eight 'Important Ideas', one of which was that housewives would pay someone to take over tedious kitchen work, while another held that a pure article of superior quality, properly packaged and promoted, would find a ready market on its merit.

In 1868, the year before his marriage to Sarah Sloan Young, Henry joined L. C. Noble in brick-making and food production. However, after initial success the under-capitalized business failed and Henry, as an undischarged bankrupt, could no longer own a business. So his brother John and cousin Frederick set up the F. and J. Heinz Company, in 1876, with Henry as their manager.

In 1882 a new site in Pittsburgh (still the site of the US complex) was bought, and two years later Henry had paid off all his creditors. In 1886 he travelled to Europe to meet his German relations, went also to England, and sold seven varieties of his goods to the famous British food store Fortnum & Mason. A new 'important idea' emerged: 'Our market is the world.'

Henry bought out John and Frederick in 1888 and launched the H. J. Heinz company. He was a master of publicity and promotion; he had the largest outdoor electric sign in New York, 200 black matched horses for deliveries, and, although he had over 60 products at the time, he found the number '57' to have a magical quality and advertised '57 Varieties'. The Heinz pickle symbol was made into a souvenir pin and over one million given away at one exhibition.

Another 'important idea' was that good food, well processed, did not need preservatives or colouring matter; Henry campaigned for the Pure Food and Drug Act, to the dismay of many of his competitors in the food industry. In the cognate field of food hygiene, the Heinz company internal manual on the subject became the standard work for the entire food industry. Nor were these the only good

causes which he promoted ahead of his time. His factory complex was organized so successfully on paternalistic lines, with a previously unimaginable range of facilities and benefits for employees, that he was hailed in some quarters as the man who had finally found the solution to the conflict between capital and labour.

The fine biography by Alberts (1973) conveys a vivid picture of this energetic and engaging man:

His blue eyes sparkled, his reddish muttonchop whiskers bristled, and he seemed always to move along at a half trot. . . . He had overpowering enthusiasm: for work and success, for travels, for his family, for religious pursuits and kind deeds, for good horses and bad paintings.

He was one of five famous Pittsburgh millionaires (the 'Lords of Pittsburgh', in Edith Wharton's phrase). Three of the other four—Carnegie, Frick, Mellon—showed greater flair in choosing paintings, but in other respects Heinz was surely as good as any.   (RSh)

HEMICELLULOSE a CARBOHYDRATE which occurs in the cell walls of plants. In composition it is intermediate between STARCH (used by plants as an energy store) and CELLULOSE (which plays a structural role). It is, however, difficult to define satisfactorily. In general, it differs from cellulose in being non-fibrous; in being more readily soluble in alkali and more readily hydrolysed by dilute acids; and in having fewer monosaccharide units per molecule.

Hemicellulose in wood has been studied more than hemicellulose in edible plants. Some is present in such things as fruits and wheat flour. It is indigestible by humans and of use only as roughage.

HEMP *Cannabis sativa*, is cultivated mostly as a source of fibre for rope-making and illegally for various narcotic products; but it also has edible seeds which are not narcotic and from which an oil can be pressed. Its leaves are occasionally grown as a vegetable.

Hemp grows wild in C. Asia, and was first cultivated in China from 3000 BC for its fibre and seeds. The plant has males and females. The males are taller and provide better fibres from their stems, while the females are stronger in narcotic substances; these are concentrated in a gummy resin which exudes from the flowers and are present in smaller amounts in the top leaves.

The narcotic and hallucinogenic element is referred to as cannabis and by numerous other (including slang) terms: ganja or *bhang* (crushed dried leaves of Indian wild hemp), grass, marijuana, pot, etc.

The ancient Greeks used to eat fried hempseed, and it has continued to be used as food until the present day in Poland and the Volga region of Russia, where oil pressed from the seeds was also used for cooking. The seeds (*asanomi*) are eaten in Japan in fried TOFU burgers. The leaves are used as a green vegetable and added to soups in parts of SE Asia, including Laos and the province of Aceh in N. Sumatra.

Cannabis is also made into narcotic foods such as the 'hash brownies' in the *Alice B. Toklas Cookbook*, where she spells it 'canibus'. Another example is the Moroccan candy called *majoun* which has been entertainingly described by Paula Wolfert (1973); she takes care to distinguish this from a different *majoun*, which belongs to Tetuán and is a marmalade with AGAR WOOD and AMBERGRIS.

The effect of the drug is similar to that of alcohol but it is probably less toxic. The main after-effect is a sharp hunger.

HEN/CHICKEN BREEDS domesticated versions of the species *Gallus domesticus*. Their wild ancestors are thought to be several species of jungle fowl, of the same genus, native to the Indian subcontinent and SE Asia. Remains from Chinese sites indicate that the birds could have been domesticated as early as the 2nd millennium BC. However, their diffusion westwards was a long process. They probably reached Britain, for example, with Celtic tribes during the 1st century BC. They had arrived in Greece, probably from Persia, about 500 years before that, and there are numerous references in classical literature, for example to their being served as food at symposia.

The Romans bred hens for their meat, selecting docile, heavy birds. Columella (AD 47) described a heavy type of hen with five toes (most breeds have four); similar hens still exist in N. Italy. An old English breed, the Dorking, also shares these characteristics, leading to speculation that ancestors of these birds flourished in Roman Britain. They may be the only birds in Britain with such a long history, because in the last 200 or so years, in Britain as well as in other countries, the situation has changed greatly.

In 1815 Bonington Moubray was able to specify 12 hen breeds (in his *Practical Treatise on Breeding, Rearing and Fattening all Kinds of Domestic Poultry*, a book which formalized the husbandry of poultry in Britain). Poultry breeding in N. England had now become a hobby of the industrial working class. Judy Urquhart (1983) says that by the beginning of the 19th century 'there were three distinct divisions of poultry. The south produced fat fowl for the London market, the north their fancy varieties, and everywhere else there were dung-hill fowls picking a living around the farmyard.'

At this time, as now, Londoners preferred fowl with fine-grained white flesh. Hens which fulfilled this requirement were raised mainly in Sussex and Surrey, a point illustrated by early breed names such as the Dorking, Kent, Surrey, and Old Sussex. Other areas had their own types, such as the Scots Grey, a good layer developed in the early 19th century by Scottish 'egglers' (egg-merchants), and the Cornish 'Indian Game Fowl'.

The arrival in Britain of various Asian breeds of poultry during the mid-19th century revolutionized attitudes to hens. Queen Victoria's Cochin fowl, which she placed on exhibition, made poultry breeding a fashionable pursuit. The decorative appearance of Asian breeds, their egg-laying capacity (winter as well as summer), and the eggs themselves (large and brown, practically unknown in Europe until then) stimulated interest in poultry generally, and led to the establishment of standards. Numerous fowl of Asiatic origin came into Britain, often acquiring names which had little to do with their origins: Cochins may actually have come from Shanghai; and Brahmas came to England via N. America, possibly from China. Birds of Mediterranean origin, such as the Minorca, a noted egg-layer, were also imported and developed.

In the mid-19th century, many developments in breeds took place in N. America, which has no indigenous hens. Here, the Indian Game Fowl was further developed and renamed the Cornish Game. The Leghorn (an important egg-producer) was developed from Mediterranean stock. Crossed with Asiatic breeds, it gave rise to a utility bird which eventually evolved into the Rhode Island Red, a commercial breed of great importance. The latter is an example of a 'composite breed', one of the strains of commercial poultry which were the foundation of the industry for the next 80 years. Imported birds were crossed to see what happened. The Plymouth Rock was developed from Cochin, Dorking, and Malay stock; the Wyandotte, a utility bird, had Cochin, Hamburgh, and Sebright bantam genes.

Composite breeds were brought to Britain and joined the Orpington (developed by breeder William Cook from regional breeds in the south-east) and the Light Sussex. The black strain of Orpington developed further in the southern hemisphere to become the Australorp. Meanwhile, continental European breeders produced breeds such as Barnvelder, Maran, and Welsummer; all of these, which were of N. European origin and arrived in Britain between the wars, were valued for their dark brown eggs. The French Faverolle is also a composite breed.

By the early 20th century, fowl for the table in England had to fulfil several requirements: most of their flesh was to be tender white breast meat; the bones should be fine and light; legs should be white rather than yellow; and the birds should be early maturing. All these points were met by Sussex breeds. In SE England, these birds were hand crammed with oatmeal to supply luxury table poultry for the London market until the time of the Second World War.

Most table fowl and eggs in Britain now come from the intensive systems of the poultry industry. The bird which populates broiler farms is known as a Cobb. Developed in N. America using stock from Plymouth Rocks, New Hampshire Reds, and Cornish Game, it is specifically bred to grow fast and early, and to have the maximum amount of white meat.

The aristocrat of modern table poultry is the French poulet de Bresse. These birds are from Gauloise stock, a blue-legged breed found elsewhere in France. Chickens raised in the Bresse region are identified with leg rings at an early age, and retailed with the ring in place to show their status.

'Bantams' are not a separate breed but dwarf hens or miniature strains of conventional breeds (the name may derive from the port of Bantam in Java).

See also CAPON, CHICKEN (DISHES). READING: Smith and Daniel (1982).

HEN OF THE WOODS *Grifola frondosa*, is probably the best of the edible fungi which belong to the group of POLYPORES. It has numerous caps, which cluster and overlap in a manner reminiscent of a hen's feathers. The underside of the caps is white, and its pores are plainly visible. These fungi, known

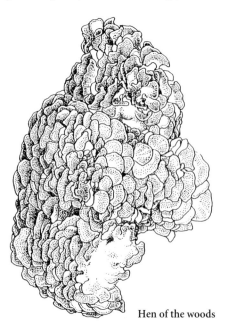

Hen of the woods

both in Europe and in N. America, usually form on the ground, attached to the roots and lower stems of hardwood trees, in which they are apt to cause rot. They may grow to a very large size. Ramsbottom (1953) cites a record from Hungary of a specimen which filled a two-horse cart. The common size is about 30 cm (1') across.

The Japanese name, *mai-take*, means 'dancing mushroom' and is given because this fungus is thought to resemble the waving hands and kimono sleeves of dancing girls.

Polyporus umbellata, a close relation which fruits earlier and has smaller, round caps, is of equally fine quality; see POLYPORES.

One hen of the woods will provide more than enough for a meal for a family. All the parts through which a knife will pass as though through butter are tender enough to be eaten. Any surplus can be pickled or frozen. The species is unusual among mushrooms in that it can be frozen without prior cooking, and will retain its pleasant flavour when thawed. Although its name is given because of its appearance rather than its taste, its meat is recommended as a chicken substitute.

HERB a word which has its origin in the Latin *herba* meaning a grass or other green plant. Botanists use the term to refer to a plant with a stem which is not woody (as that of a tree or shrub is); but the general use of the word is now in its culinary sense, indicating a plant whose green parts (usually leaves, sometimes stalks) are used to flavour food. However, it is still also used to indicate a plant of medicinal importance.

Until the 19th century the word was pronounced with a silent 'h' on both sides of the Atlantic; but this usage now survives only on the American side.

Although a plant which is a herb may yield a spice (e.g. coriander, whose leaves are a herb and whose seeds are a spice), the definition offered for SPICE shows that there is a clear enough distinction in practice, largely based on the part of the plant to be used. Most herbs can be used in dried form, although there is a general preference for using them fresh. Spices, on the other hand, are almost always, although not invariably, used in dried form.

The noun 'herbal' usually reflects the botanical or medicinal senses of the word and is applied to books which catalogue and illustrate herbs. Some herbals are referred to very frequently in food history contexts: e.g. that of Gerard (1597, rev edn 1633).

The term pot-herb is defined by the *NSOED* as 'a herb grown or suitable for growing in a kitchen garden' (which rather invites the question how one determines whether a herb is suitable for a kitchen garden and the potential answer 'if it is a pot-herb'). Ayto (1993) does better in remarking that the term 'denoted from the sixteenth to the nineteenth centuries any plant whose leaves and stalks could be boiled as greens'.

For herbal teas, see TISANE.
READING: Lesley Bremness (1994); Jill Norman (1997); Eleanour Rohde (1936).

HERMIT CRAB *Eupagurus bernhardus* and others, an eccentric creature which is edible although rarely eaten outside France. Alexandre Dumas, in his *Grand Dictionnaire de cuisine* (1873), wrote a felicitous entry:

A species of crab whose meat is regarded as a delicious morsel. It is usually grilled in its shell before being eaten.

There is nothing more comical than this little crustacean. Nature has furnished him with armour as far as the waist—cuirass, gauntlets and visor of iron, this half of him has everything. But from the waist to the other end there is nothing, not even a nightshirt. The result of this is that the hermit crab stuffs this extremity of himself into whatever refuge he can find.

The Creator, who had begun to dress the creature as a lobster, was disturbed or distracted in the middle of the operation and finished him off as a slug. This part of the hermit crab, so poorly defended and so tempting to an enemy, is his great preoccupation; a preoccupation which can at times make him fierce. If he sees a shell which suits him, he eats the owner and takes his place while it is still warm—the history of the world in microscopic form. But since, when all is said and done, the house was not made for him, he staggers about like a drunkard instead of having the serious air of a snail.

HERON any one of several stork-like wading birds in the family Ardeidae, but especially the grey heron, *Ardea cinerea.*

A large bird (average total length just under 1 m/3'), the heron used to be bred for the table in special heronries, recorded in the Netherlands as far back as the 13th century. Young ones, as soon as they were fully developed, would be shaken out of their nests, a spectacle much commented upon by travellers. Herons were eaten in Europe throughout the Middle Ages, often (along with other 'great birds' such as the STORK, CRANE, and PEACOCK) as items at important banquets, when they might be presented in dramatic fashion, with their bodies gilt.

Falcons could be trained to 'hawk' for herons, and sport of this kind was a feature of the age of chivalry. The glamour of this activity doubtless made herons taste better. The grey heron was anyway considered to be the best of a group of birds with similar lifestyles, to wit other herons and night herons, egrets, BITTERNS, and cormorants. All these counted as edible, although the cormorant was only suitable for the lower classes.

Witteveen (1986–7), in the only survey of the subject available in English, points out that in the Netherlands herons were eaten from late May to early July, being the earliest of the game birds to be available for the table. They could be roasted and served with a sauce. Maestro Martino, the 15th-century Italian cook who provided most of the recipes for PLATINA (1475), gives the earliest known recipe. He stuffed his herons with garlic or onions before roasting them entire.

The heron figured in books offering dietary advice up to the 17th century, but thereafter lost popularity. However, some were still on sale in English markets in the 19th century and there is at least one 20th-century recipe—that given by May Byron (1914) for a Heron pudding.

HERRING *Clupea harengus*, of all fish probably the one which has had most influence on the economic and political history of Europe.

The species is distributed right across the N. Atlantic, down to the north of France on one side and Chesapeake Bay on the other. Within the species it is possible to distinguish certain 'races' which have their own special characteristics. Thus the Baltic herring is smaller than the Atlantic and has a lower fat content. The maximum length of Atlantic specimens is 40 cm (16"), but the common adult length is 20–5 cm (5–7").

Herring typically swim in enormous shoals, but the size and abundance of these shoals have been difficult to predict for as far back as records go. Fluctuations which were attributable to biological reasons have been worsened in recent times by overfishing. The North Sea stock, for example, declined by 50% from the 1950s to the 1960s. Efforts have been made by governments, unilaterally or by international agreement, to restrict the herring fishery in a manner which would permit stocks to grow again, but the intrinsic unpredictability of the species makes it difficult to discern results with certainty.

Herring are relatively oily fish, but not so oily as to preclude frying them. In this case, the best plan is to coat them with oatmeal first, as in Scotland; and they should be served with boiled, not fried, potatoes. Grilling or baking are suitable techniques, whereas poaching or steaming are inadvisable.

What is most striking about the use of herring as food is the very large number of herring cures, mostly traditional and often dating back to medieval times, which are practised. Of this multitude the KIPPER, the supreme example of curing herring by cold-smoking, has its own entry. Cures which use hot-smoking (when the temperature of the smoke rises above 29 °C (85 °F) and the fish begins to cook) and various methods of pickling herring are briefly described below.

Red herring are fish which have been first soaked in brine with saltpetre added, then hung up to dry before being subjected to a heavy smoking—for several days and ideally over oak, beech, and turf. The history of the 'puissant red herring, the golden Hesperides red herring' (as Thomas Nashe referred to it in his book *Lenten Stuffe, or the Praise of the Red Herring*, 1567) dates back to the 14th century and has attracted much interesting writing. Samuel (1918) commented:

This fish is not gutted until it reaches the kitchen. The Yarmouth red herring may be eaten, uncooked, during the months of October, November and December. The skin should be peeled off, the head removed, and the fish gutted and cut across into four pieces, dusted with pepper, and eaten with bread and butter. The Yarmouth red herring is locally sometimes called a 'militiaman'; *per contra*, the vulgar Norfolk term for a militiaman in his red tunic . . . was a 'red herring', much as the red herring sold in the south of Scotland are sometimes known as 'Glasgow magistrates'.

An echo of the colloquial names is found in France where a corresponding product known as *hareng saur* has been made since the 12th century or earlier; it has *gendarme* as one of its names.

Bloaters also have a long history. The name may derive from a Scandinavian term, but may equally well just refer to the fact that fish cured in this way are relatively plump, so look 'bloated'. The similar French product, a speciality of ports in the north of Normandy, is called *bouffi*, also meaning swollen or bloated. The earliest references were to 'bloat fish'. Bloaters are made from whole fish, slightly salted, washed and dried and briefly smoked. They end up with only a faint flavour of smoke and almost no colour change, i.e. they remain silver. They can be eaten raw, in the same fashion as the red herring; or grilled and served with butter, or made into bloater paste. They have a slightly gamy flavour, due to the enzymes or ferments from the gut.

Buckling (*Bucklinge* in German) are hot-smoked herring which may or may not have had head and gut removed before treatment. In Germany they are usually eaten with a dark rye bread, or something similar, and butter, or served with scrambled egg and fried potatoes.

Rollmopse (which are called rollmops in English, although this name is the singular of the German name) are herring which have been beheaded, gutted, split open, deboned, and left in the form of double fillets, which are rolled up round pickled cucumber and kept in vinegar or wine and vinegar solution.

Bismarck herring are herring fillets which have been marinated in vinegar with onion rings and seasoning.

Sweet pickled herrings, with additions such as mustard sauce, are common in Denmark and are exported from there.

Sürstromming, a speciality of Sweden, are whole herring fermented by the action of salt and (in past times) natural summer heat. They develop a notorious smell, even in the canned form. Davidson (1979), recounting the lore which attends this remarkable product, writes:

Cans of sürstromming bulge slightly, to accommodate the fermentation. A Swedish naval officer told me that when they ate sürstromming on board his ship the cans were always opened on deck, because of the smell. The procedure thereafter is to drain and rinse the fish; to sprinkle some chopped, small red onion over them, to reduce the smell; and to lift off the fillets. These are then served with the small oval potatoes which the Swedes call almond potatoes; thin slices of a special bread, tunnbröd, which the northerners carry about in their wellington boots; and butter.

Apart from cooked herring dishes and cured herring, there is also the attractive possibility of eating *nieuwe haring*, the first herring of the season, as the Dutch do. Many stalls in the Netherlands offer fillets which can be lowered straight into the mouth with or without any accompaniments. This was formerly a ritual which took place during a few weeks only, at the start of the season; but the presence of some tiny nematodes in the fish has made it necessary to freeze all *nieuwe haring* (thus killing the nematodes), and a benefit from this requirement is the availability, from frozen stocks, of the delicacy at all times of the year.

READING: Hodgson (1957); Cutting (1955); Seumenicht (1959); Astri Riddervold (1990*a*, 1990*b*).

HICKORY NUTS from trees of the genus *Carya* in the walnut family, include the outstandingly good PECAN. Although none of the other species has commercial importance, there are several whose nuts are edible. Three are listed below, all N. American; the hickories of Europe did not outlive the last Ice Age.

- The **shagbark hickory,** *C. ovata*, so named because its bark is shaggy in appearance, is the most abundant and popular. The yield of nuts is low, but the kernels have a good, sweet flavour akin to that of the pecan.
- The **shellbark hickory,** *C. laciniosa*, also has a distinctive bark, and bears larger fruits. Its nuts are regarded by some as the best of the hickories. It is the lowland counterpart of the upland shagbark.
- The **mockernut,** *C. tomentosa*, may also be called white hickory or bullnut. Its nuts

have such thick shells that a hammer (for which 'mokker' is the Dutch word) is needed to deal with them and reach the sweet kernel.

Hickory nuts are still in demand in parts of the USA, but are now little cultivated. In earlier times they were more esteemed. White settlers found that they were a good food and would keep in the shell for a year or two in a cool store. The Algonquin Indians, whose name for the nut, powcohicora, was adapted by the settlers to pohickory and then hickory, had produced from ground kernels and water a strained 'hickory milk', which made a rich, creamy addition to soups, cornmeal cakes, and HOMINY, as well as a favourite beverage, POHICKORY.

HIGH TEA is a substantial late afternoon or early evening meal. The term has been in use since the mid-19th century and distinguishes it from the lighter, more elegant AFTERNOON TEA; and yet, to those who take either, they are simply tea. This is shown in the way Arnold Bennett manipulates the word in this quotation from *Anna of the Five Towns* (1902), a novel set in the Potteries district of Staffordshire:

The tea, made specially magnificent in honour of the betrothal, was such a meal as could only have been compassed in Staffordshire or Yorkshire—a high tea of the last richness and excellence, exquisitely gracious to the palate, but ruthless in its demands on the stomach. At one end of the table, which glittered with silver, glass, and Longshaw china, was a fowl which had been boiled for four hours; at the other, a hot pork pie, islanded in liquor, which might have satisfied a regiment. Between these two dishes were all the delicacies which differentiate high tea from tea, and on the quality of which the success of the meal really depends; hot pikelets, hot crumpets, hot toast, sardines with tomatoes, raisin bread, currant bread, seed-cake, lettuce, home-made marmalade, and home-made hams. The repast occupied over an hour, and even then not a quarter of the food was consumed.

'Teas' similar to the one described above crop up over and over again in English fiction and diaries from the mid-19th to the early 20th centuries; the constants are abundance and variety of food, the presence of ham or pie, salad, the choice of baked goods, preserves, and a fine display of table ware. Tea also became strongly linked in popular culture with abundant Yorkshire hospitality. Brears (1987) gives an account of a substantial Yorkshire tea which actually took place. It was

held by Miss Maffin in her small Wharfedale cottage about the 1860s. The round cricket table in the centre of the room, although barely a yard across, had been laid with her best china, a seed cake, bread and butter, ham sandwiches, and a salad of lettuce, cress, radishes and onions. Tea cakes regularly replaced the lid of the kettle, to become hot and moist in its steam, while muffins were toasted on a toasting-dog before the fire.

When her friends arrived, they arranged themselves around the table. It was *de rigueur* on state occasions like this for the ladies to sit fair and square to the table in the ordinary manner; but the gentlemen were allowed more latitude. Indeed, among the older generation, the correct claim to dignity seems to have been to sit with your chair sideways to the table, and your back to your hostess, your bread and salad or your ham sandwiches on your red spotted handkerchief spread across your knees, and your cup and saucer on the edge of the table. Seated in this manner, the company then proceeded to do full justice to the fare set out before them, the conversation flowing just as freely as the hot tea laced with rum.

The eating of tea, and the existence of two forms, afternoon tea and high tea, provides a lesson in British social history. Habitual consumption of either (it is not the custom to take both in any given day) says much about an individual's background and daily life. Afternoon tea, eaten after a light lunch and before a larger mid-evening dinner, is considered an indicator of a leisured, comfortable existence. High tea, eaten on arrival home from work, is popularly associated with old-fashioned households, rural or urban working-class backgrounds; although not invariably so, as Michael Smith (1989) points out, quoting from an unnamed earlier author:

High Tea. In some houses this is a permanent institution, quite taking the place of late dinner, and to many it is a most enjoyable meal, young people preferring it to dinner, it being a movable feast that can be partaken of at hours which will not interfere with tennis, boating or other amusements.

At high tea, the means and desires of the household and demands of the occasion dictate exactly what goes on the table. Cold cuts, meat pies, salads, pickles, crumpets, muffins, teacakes, preserves, honey, fruit loaves, cakes and sponges are all considered suitable foods, participants selecting according to tastes and appetite. Tea (Indian) is drunk throughout the meal, although coffee or cocoa may be served if preferred.

The origins of high tea are uncertain, but evidence indicates they are different from those of afternoon tea, and that meals of the high tea type were well established by the mid-19th century. 'High' seems to have been added to the name by people less familiar with it—those from a wealthy urban background, who adopted it as a novelty, or because it was conveniently timed for children, or as a cheaper, less formal alternative to dinner—from which the meal may actually have descended.

(LM)

HIJIKI *Hizikia fusiforme*, one of the brown SEAWEEDS, may be used fresh, but is more commonly dried and then rehydrated before use. The flavour is described as nutlike, and the texture is crisp.

HILBEH (or hulba or halba), an Arabic word which always indicates FENUGREEK but can mean anything from just that (the spice) through a foamy preparation made from the soaked and ground seeds to a thick soup-like dish based on this foamy preparation but including other ingredients. Of these other ingredients the most important in the YEMEN, where hilbeh/hulba counts as a national dish, would be the spicy chilli-hot paste called *zhug*.

Hilbeh is known throughout the Gulf region, but seems to be more important and better known in the Yemen than anywhere else.

In the north of the Yemen hilbeh is called hulba; not always just a difference of pronunciation, since methods of preparation and use also vary.   HS

HINDUISM AND FOOD Hinduism is not a single faith but a vast complex of beliefs and practices that have developed over some 4,000 years and an extensive land area, a highly complex system of interacting elements. Therefore, generalities about it are likely to be unsatisfactory. However, it has a certain geographic unity, being more or less confined to the subcontinent of INDIA, and its fundamental principles are common to all its followers. Several of these principles have deeply affected its attitudes to food: the underlying unity of all being; the high value placed on non-violence; belief in reincarnation leading ultimately to release from the illusion of individual existence; the extreme respect shown to cows; and the division of human society into *varna* or castes. Closely linked with the caste system is the concept of physical and ritual purification, by water or fire, and the need to maintain barriers between the self and anything that might contaminate it. Hinduism has a place for everything, and also a time.

At the root of Hindu foodways is the concept of sacrifice. Staple foods, especially grains, have always been offered to or shared with the gods before they are eaten. What the gods leave, *prasad*, is the purest food for man's spirit. Many plants, including food plants, are sacred to particular gods: for example, *tulasi* (holy BASIL) to Vishnu. GHEE (clarified butter) is used for anointing images and for purifying ritual items as well as being a medium for the most esteemed method of cooking. Traditionally, a Hindu eats twice a day, after morning and evening

worship. Fasting is not encouraged for non-ascetics, except on the eleventh day of each (lunar) month, but many sects forbid certain foods at certain times.

Hindu sacred texts emphasize that a man is what he eats, and rules are given for right foods, right ways of cooking, and right times to eat for every stage in life. The concept of 'hot' and 'cold' foods which in China reflects the contrast of YIN-YANG, and which is found in many cultures (see also SARDI/GARMI), can be traced back to early times in India. 'Hot', exciting food (including honey) is to be avoided by those who need to avoid lustful thoughts—students, widows, and ascetics. The 'twice-born'—initiated members of the three upper castes, Brahmans, Kshatriyas, and Vaisyas—should avoid garlic, onions, turnips, and mushrooms. Camel's milk, and milk from a cow that has recently calved, are forbidden.

The *Bhagavadgita* (17. 8) defines three types of people and the foods they like. The *sattvika* type, being wise and pure, enjoy healthy but rather bland food (milk, yoghurt, ghee, green vegetables, rice, wheat, beansprouts, pulses): these lead to long and, supposedly, zestful life. The *rajasika* are passionate and demand strong flavours, sourness, and pungency (spices, dal, pickles, chutneys, wine). At the bottom of the heap are the *tamasika*, lazy and ignorant, and given to eating potatoes, meat, aubergines, tomatoes, and putrid or stale foods, not to mention other people's leftovers. Foods, likewise, have personality. Those in which *rajas* (energy) or *tamas* (inertia) predominate make it hard to achieve the mental tranquillity necessary to worship effectively or achieve enlightenment. Even foods ideal for these purposes should be eaten in moderation. Alcohol is tolerated, but one should avoid it if possible.

The caste system started to fragment almost as soon as the four main castes established themselves, and there are now over 3,000 castes and subcastes, many of them limited to small areas or particular occupations. Every caste has its own council, which makes the rules for all its members' activities, including their diet; it is said that the lower the caste the better organized is its conciliar government. To give food is more blessed than to receive it. The oldest Vedic text, the Rig-veda, says that one should always eat with a guest. In practice, although guests at a feast are regarded as privileged and their caste can to some extent be ignored, the general rule is that hosts outrank guests. Therefore, if you refuse to accept food when it is offered, you claim in effect to be of a higher caste than your host; and low-caste villagers are said to use great ingenuity to persuade neighbours of slightly higher caste to accept food from them. If one person of the higher caste accepts, the lower caste has then leapfrogged over *all* members of its former superiors.

The higher one's caste, the more careful one has to be with one's diet. One can safely accept food only from members of one's own or a higher caste, so a top-ranking Brahman can only accept food cooked and served by persons of his own group, while the food itself (though vegetarian) is so easily polluted that he must eat at a safe distance from everyone else. Cooked foods themselves have a caste system. *Pakka* food is fried in ghee, *kacca* food is boiled in water. The act of cooking, the use of fire, makes food sacred and puts it at risk, by moving it from the natural world to the human; as a rule, uncooked food may be handled by anyone, and cow's milk is by definition pure and undefiled, so *pakka* food enjoys a certain protection from pollution and is more easily transferred between members of different castes than *kacca* food. A Brahman, however, will not accept milk from a low-caste person in case it has been polluted with water. Water itself cannot be ritually defiled if it is in a reservoir or a flowing stream, but it is at risk in a well or a small container. Because saliva pollutes, a water-drinker should pour the water into the mouth without letting the rim of the glass touch the lips. A cook must never taste what is being cooked. Always, what is impure will overcome what is pure; only the sacred can cleanse it.

The veneration of the cow dates from the earliest days of the Vedas, *c.*1800 BC—long before the evolution of Hinduism in anything like its modern form. In those days, herdsmen regarded all their beasts as more or less sacred, but the cow or bull was the preferred animal for sacrifice. Attitudes towards animal sacrifice fluctuated, but seem to have finished up in ambivalent fashion; such sacrifices were good in principle but impractical because of popular sentiment against them.

Modern writers link these changes to the rise (from the 5th century BC) of Buddhism (see BUDDHISM AND FOOD) and Jains (see JAINS AND FOOD) as creeds which offered freedom from the shackles of caste and a fast route to nirvana, escape from the cycle of rebirth. Although there are now few Jains and almost no Buddhists in India, the high status of VEGETARIANISM has remained, helped no doubt by the urge towards purity. The career of the Emperor Ashoka (reigned 268–231 BC) may also reflect a popular movement towards non-violence. However, when large numbers of people are seen to be making a virtue of a meatless diet, one may speculate that economic causes are partly responsible.

The Indian farmer does indeed have good reasons for not investing heavily in animals for slaughter, and for keeping but not slaughtering cows. In densely populated countries, it makes more sense to use the available land for growing crops, especially food grains, vegetables, and pulses, than for pasture—unless the pasture is for cows. Dairy cows transform fodder into calories and proteins in the form of milk much more efficiently than beef cattle (or any other animals) transform it into meat. They also provide dung for manure and fuel, and they pull ploughs and carts. There is roughly one cow for every four people in India, but by and large they do not compete with humans for food resources or space, except when they stand in the middle of a main road. Overall, they give far more than they take, and for that alone they qualify as sacred.

RO

READING: Achaya (1994).

HIPPOCRATES of Cos, universally venerated as the father of medicine, was apparently an older contemporary of Plato (thus *c.*400 BC) but absolutely nothing is known of his life from contemporary Greek sources. Much later writings suggest that he was the founder of the medical school of Cos, which had a distinctive philosophy opposed to that of neighbouring Cnidos, and was the author of an uncertain number of authoritative works on anatomy, surgery, medicine, dietetics, and medical philosophy. However, the substantial collection of medical writings of all kinds that goes under Hippocrates' name was really written by many different authors (some of whom followed Cnidian rather than Coan teachings) at different dates. It is a kind of library. Clearly, from a very early date, the tradition was to collect medical writings under the honourable name of Hippocrates, and there is no way of knowing whether any were really written by a person of that name.

Hippocratic writings were later translated into Syriac, Arabic, Hebrew, and Latin, and were the subject of commentaries in these languages and in Greek. Bolstered by the later authority of GALEN (see also FOUR HUMOURS), they have exerted an almost timeless influence over medicine and its practitioners, and even beyond. The Hippocratic collection includes the famous *Oath*, which enshrines medical confidentiality—and the separation between medicine and surgery. A sequence of *Aphorisms* begins with the well-known 'Life is short, the Art is long'. The medical notebook *Epidemics* 6 advises: 'Work, food, drink, sleep, sex: all things in moderation,' advice of which only the last phrase is usually quoted.

The Hippocratic collection often refers to food and the importance of diet. The subject is central to the treatises known as *Regimen in Acute Diseases, Nutriment and Regimen in Health*, but the most interesting is *Regimen* (or *On Diet*), a work probably of the 4th century BC which is a useful early source for the food and drink of Greece and for early ideas of nutrition. The anonymous author claims to have discovered a principle for prescribing diets that are suited to individuals' constitutions. Book 1 explains the philosophy and theory; book 2 sets out the characteristics of each food item and of various forms of exercise; book 3 applies the theory and gives a range of examples of diets and regimes of daily life intended for given human types and to combat given health problems. Book 4 advises on the use of dreams in diagnosing illnesses and dietary requirements.

AD

HIPPOPOTAMUS *Hippopotamus amphibius*, an African animal which is distantly related to the pig but very much larger (up to 4.2 m/14', and weighing up to 4 tons). As its name (meaning river horse) indicates, the hippopotamus lives in and out of water. It counts as being basically an aquatic species, but it comes on land to feed, usually during the night.

As with other large African mammals, the numbers of this species and the extent of its range have been seriously depleted; but it has been eaten in the past and it has been said that the breast and back muscles, pot roasted with spices and herbs, were regarded as 'the greatest delicacies that the hunter can provide' (Leipoldt, 1976). The same author comments that hippopotamus meat, which was formerly on sale at the Cape Town market, always tends to be greasy and needs the addition of wine or vinegar.

HOGMANAY traditionally the most important holiday of the year in Scotland, celebrates New Year's Eve. As a marker between the years, the celebration dates back to antiquity, but the name Hogmanay was not in use until the early 17th century. It seems to be derived from the Norman form (*hoguinané*) of the Old French *aguillanneuf*, meaning the last day of the year and also being a cry for a gift on that day. The gift which prudent householders kept available for the occasion used to be OATCAKES. Gillian Edwards (1970) has a fascinating discussion of the etymology and of the connections with earlier New Year rites. She explains among many other points that the name 'noor cake', sometimes used for the kind of oatcake or biscuit baked for this day, is simply a contraction of 'New Year's cake', and that some of the girls and boys who would go round soliciting these from bakers would wear aprons with numerous large pockets to accommodate them.

Catherine Brown (1996), who gives good descriptions of Hogmanay celebrations from her own experience, points out that up to the time of the Second World War the Scots did not observe Christmas Day as a holiday; its observance had been banned by the Church authorities in 1649, and Hogmanay had evolved into an occasion which did duty for it and for Yule and for Twelfth Night, as well as for the New Year.

HOGWEED *Heracleum sphondylium*, a biennial/perennial herb of Europe, Asia, and N. America, also called cow parsnip.

Mrs Phoebe Lankester, 'the English student of plant-lore', is cited by Fernald and Kinsey (1943) as having observed that pigs were fattened on hogweed, as the name suggests, and having further stated:

In Siberia and Russia the stalks are dried in the sun, when a sweet substance exudes from them, which resembles sugar, and is eaten as a great delicacy. A spirit is distilled from the stalks thus prepared, by first fermenting them with water and either mingling bilberries with them or not. . . . The young shoots and leaves may be boiled and eaten as a green vegetable, and when just sprouting from the ground resemble asparagus in flavour. The experiment is, however, seldom tried, owing to the ignorance of those to whom such an addition to the table would be a benefit and luxury.

Efforts to dispel the ignorance have not made much headway in the 20th century, although Phillips (1983) followed Mrs Lankester's advice, and pronounced hogweed shoots to be 'unequivocally one of the best vegetables I have eaten'.

HOJA SANTA (also *hierba santa* and many other versions), *Piper sanctum*, a plant whose large leaves are described as having an ANISE flavour (or resembling SASSAFRAS) and are used in the cuisines of various parts of MEXICO and CENTRAL AMERICA, e.g. to provide a wrapping for fish, or in soups.

HOKI *Macruronus novaezelandiae*, a fish which belongs to the family Macrouridae, close to the HAKE family, but has a much more tapering body than do regular hake of either the northern or southern hemispheres. Ayling and Cox (1982) make the interesting observation that, since the hoki is a fish of deep waters, where darkness prevails, the tapering body may serve to provide it with a longer lateral line, the instrument by which it and other fish detect the low frequency sounds produced by other fish (whether prey or predators). The maximum length of the hoki is indeed considerable: 1 m (40"). Its flesh is palatable, and distinguished by having large flakes.

A similar species, *M. magellanicus*, is found round the southern parts of S. America.

HOKKAIDO an island in the far north of JAPAN, has only been part of the country for about 100 years; colonization did not start until late in the 19th century. The original inhabitants were the Ainu. Because their foodways survived into recent times almost untouched by 'civilization', these have been zealously studied by anthropologists, with the result that the Ainu are mentioned more often in the literature than the relatively small population would seem to warrant. One remarkable feature of the indigenous culture is that there are striking and inexplicable resemblances between the language and that of the Basques in Europe.

Unlike the rest of Japan, which is mountainous, Hokkaido is flat, with much scope for dairy production, so consumption of butter and cheese is more common here than in the rest of the country.

HOLLANDAISE one of the most prominent sauces in the group of those which are thickened by the use of egg yolk. The fact that such a sauce will curdle if heated beyond a certain point is largely responsible for their reputation of being 'difficult'.

McGee (1990) has investigated both the history and the chemistry of the sauce. He reports that one of the earliest versions which he found, '*sauce à la hollandoise*, in the 1758 edition of Marin's *Dons de Comus*, calls only for butter, flour, bouillon, and herbs; no yolks at all'. On the chemistry, he observes that the use of egg yolk in hollandaise is not essential in order to produce the desired emulsification; this could be achieved by the butter, unaided, surprising though this may seem. He also explains that if egg yolks are used, it is by no means necessary to use the quantities found in most recipes; that there are disadvantages in using the traditional technique of cooking the yolks as a first step; and that on balance it is better to leave the cooking stage until after the butter has been added to (merely warmed) yolks. His findings and recommendations are best studied in his own book, where they are accompanied by much relevant detail.

Sauces which are derived from, or can be regarded as variations of, hollandaise include:

- *sauce aux câpres*, with the addition of drained capers;
- *maltaise*, with blood orange;
- MOUSSELINE (may also be referred to as *sauce Chantilly*), with whipped cream;
- *moutarde*, with Dijon mustard.

HOMINY dried and hulled MAIZE kernels, coarsely ground and prepared for consumption in various ways, including puddings and breads. The term is most commonly met in 'hominy grits', for which a finer grinding or a double grinding is used; see GROATS AND GRITS. Mariani (1994) says of hominy that:

It was one of the first foods European settlers readily accepted from the Native Americans, and the word, from one or another Algonquian words, such as *rockahominie* ('parched corn') or *tackbummin* ('hulled corn'), was used as early as 1629. Different terms describe hominy that has been treated or ground in different ways. 'Great hominy,' also called 'whole hominy,' 'pearl hominy' (from its pearly appearance), and 'samp' (from the Narraganset *nasàump*, 'corn mush'), is coarsely ground and prepared by scalding shelled corn in water and wood ash to separate the hulls, called the 'eyes'.

HONEY (*see page 384*)

HONEY CAKE a general term for cakes, biscuits, and breads using HONEY in the recipe.

The category of 'honey cakes' overlaps considerably with GINGERBREAD, since a gingerbread made with honey (e.g. French *pain d'épices*), could also be called a honey cake. The same would apply to the LEBKUCHEN of German-speaking countries, which are sweetened with honey and may be regarded either as soft biscuits or as thin cakes. Thus the familiar problem of distinguishing between CAKE and BISCUIT afflicts discussion of honey cakes.

If for these and similar reasons the usefulness of the category 'honey cakes' is questioned, the answer may come down to this, that the subject of what are called 'honey cake moulds' is an interesting one and that it does depend on this category. As Piroska Weiner (1981) points out, ordinary cake doughs prepared with a raising agent and having a light texture do not lend themselves to shaping; whereas a flour and honey dough is capable of retaining a sculptured form. The same author provides a detailed history of honey cake moulds, explaining that examples have been recovered from numerous archaeological sites (Egypt, the Middle East, classical Greece and Rome), but that the relatively crude effects achieved in ancient times with clay moulds were eclipsed in C. Europe in recent centuries, after carved wooden moulds came into use in the 16th century.

Mould patterns were highly traditional as a genre, carrying symbolic or seasonal meanings of the kinds one would expect. Popular engravings and lithographs often provided models. However, the patterns did change, in accordance with both popular

(cont. on page 385)

Honey

Honey is the sugary nectar of flowers gathered, modified, and stored in a honeycomb by honey bees (*Apis melifica* and *A. dorsata*). From the plant's point of view the purpose of nectar is to attract insects which pick up pollen and transfer it from flower to flower. As the bee swallows the nectar, its saliva hydrolyses (splits) the sucrose (ordinary sugar) in the nectar into the two simple sugars, dextrose (GLUCOSE) and fructose. The bee takes a little nectar for its own nourishment but gives up most of it when it returns to the hive, regurgitating it into one of the hexagonal wax cells of the honeycomb which has been built by the bees with other substances gathered from the plants. Each cell is an incubator for a young bee, which feeds on the honey as it grows.

Nectar turns into honey by evaporation. The finished product consists of 35–40% fructose, 30–5% dextrose, lesser amounts of other sugars and gums, 17–20% water, and traces of pollen, wax, acids, proteins, enzymes, vitamins, minerals, and pigments. Most of these substances come from the original nectar, and the composition of the honey depends on the type of flowers visited by the bees in the area. Bees visit flowers several hundred yards from the hive. As each bee returns it performs a wriggling 'dance' at the entrance to the hive. The angle at which it moves shows the direction of flight to the flower, in relation to the current position of the sun; the enthusiasm with which the bee wriggles shows how good a source of nectar the plant is.

VARIETIES

The flavour and colour of honey are highly variable. Much of the honey on sale in most countries is from clover and similar field crops. Its flavour is mild and its taste sweet. Although honey can be nearly one and a quarter times as sweet as the same quantity of sucrose, owing to its high fructose content, it tastes less sweet to the palate because of the other flavouring substances it contains. This applies particularly to honeys made from scented flowers which include heather, citrus blossom, raspberry, gooseberry, and other fruits, wild flowering herbs such as sage, thyme, and fireweed, scented trees such as acacia, lime (basswood in the USA), eucalyptus, and numerous other plants. Each has a distinctive flavour thanks to aromatic substances from the flowers. Colour is due to plant pigments, and ranges from white through red and green to black. Texture also varies with the relative amounts of dextrose and fructose. Dextrose crystallizes more rapidly than fructose, making for a more granular honey, such as that from clover, alfalfa, and buckwheat.

Honey may be eaten straight from the comb. The wax is not nutritious. It imparts a pleasant texture but little flavour. Usually the honey is extracted by crushing the comb and letting the honey drain out, often helped by extra pressure from a centrifuge. It may also be strained to remove particles of wax. The resulting honey is usually a moderately viscous, cloudy liquid. Some honey, such as that made from heather (*Calluna vulgaris*), has so much gum in it that it is almost a jelly and will not pour. When stored, honey gradually crystallizes and solidifies. It may be liquefied by gentle heating, which also makes cloudy honey clear. Heat 'inverts' the small amount of remaining sucrose, splitting it into dextrose and fructose.

HISTORY

Honey has always been a prized food in all parts of the world, not only for humans but for many animals. Bears and badgers, which are thick skinned and not troubled by stings, raid wild bees' nests in hollow trees. These animals can be a problem for commercial beekeepers, and in some places hives have had to be hung in the tops of trees to keep them out of reach of bears. A neolithic rock painting in the Araña cave at Bicorp near Valencia in Spain shows a man collecting wild honey. The oldest written reference to the use of honey is thought to be Egyptian, of about 5500 BC. At that time Lower Egypt was called Bee Land while Upper Egypt was Reed Land. By the 5th dynasty (c.2600 BC) apiculture was well established and is shown in several reliefs in the temple of the Sun at Abusir. Honey was a valuable commodity used widely in trade—in the accounts of Seti I (1314–1292 BC) 110 pots of honey were equivalent in value to an ass or an ox. In 1450 BC Thutmoses III is recorded as receiving tribute from Syria of 539 lb (244 kg) of honey.

The use of honey was taken to India by its Aryan invaders and became associated with religious rites. The ancient Indian Laws of Manu, dating from 1000 BC, set the 'tax rate' at one-sixth of the beekeeper's production.

Honey is also mentioned on ancient Sumerian clay tablets, possibly even older than the Egyptian reference. Later Babylonian tablets give recipes for 'electuaries'—medicines based on honey. An electuary mentioned in the 1st century AD by the Roman writer Pliny the Elder included powdered bees. It was said to be a cure for dropsy and bladder stones.

The earliest hives were hollowed out of tree trunks, and this practice still survives in some societies. If a colony of bees can be found while it is swarming—that is, gathering in a dense clump as a preparation for establishing a new nest—the whole swarm may be picked up and transferred to an artificial hive, where the bees will settle. The original method of gathering honey, whether from the wild or from a hive, is still employed. Smoke is used to drive out the bees so that the honey can be taken. They return to the depleted hive and stoically set about making more honey.

USES

Extravagant claims are made to this day for the healthful properties of honey, and recently also for royal jelly, a refined food made by worker bees in small amounts to feed the queen bee and which, it is said, preserves the youth of those who eat it. Before dismissing such beliefs as superstition it should be appreciated that honey is a highly complex substance, and contains compounds about which there is still much to be found out.

Fermented drinks have traditionally been made from honey, such as the old English mead, which is still available as a curiosity. Mead was also an important drink in medieval Russia. The word derives from the Sanskrit word for honey, *madhu*. A similar drink popular in Ethiopia is called *t'ej*.

The flavour of honey is volatile and easily destroyed by heating. There is little point in using an expensive fragrant honey in cooking. Honey used in place of sugar in a recipe darkens the food because the single sugars in it caramelize readily. These sugars are also strongly hygroscopic (moisture absorbing), and make the finished product keep well.
READING: Eva Crane (1975).

interest and artistic fashions (Gothic, Baroque and Rococo). Thus Renaissance rose, tulip, and pomegranate motifs, coaches and horses, the Adoration of the Magi, ladies in fashionable 18th-century dress, storks bringing babies, and hussars on horseback were all popular. Portraits of saints were produced for religious holidays (St Nicholas is still produced for Christmas), and heart shapes were made for lovers' gifts. In the 19th century the shapes were enhanced with piped sugar lines, names, and proverbs; paper pictures of angels, doves, or roses were stuck on, and mirrors embellished the hearts.

The art of carving honey cake moulds went into decline in the 20th century, and production ceased by the Second World War. Items for which honey cake moulds would have been used in the past are now likely to be decorated with icing, pictures, and mirrors.
READING: Sarah Kelly (1985).

HONEYDEW a sticky, sugary liquid exuded by some insects, especially aphids such as the common greenfly, which suck plant sap. Wherever these insects infest a plant thickly, there may be enough honeydew produced to drip onto the ground. This is one explanation given for the mysterious arrival of the MANNA on which the biblical Israelites fed in the desert. A car parked under a lime tree (*Tilia*, not *Citrus*) in summer will soon become covered with honeydew.

A few insects produce so much of the substance that it can be gathered and used as a sweetener. One such is the sugar-cane leaf-hopper, a pest of the sugar-cane crop in Hawaii.

There is no connection between this honeydew and the Honeydew MELON.

HONEY FUNGUS *Armillariella mellea* (and other *Armillariella* spp), an edible fungus named for the colour of its cap, usually grows on or around the trunks or stumps of trees. It is a harmful parasite, capable of killing trees. Its long, thin black rhizomorphs enable it to spread underground from tree to tree. Their appearance is responsible for the alternative common name 'boot-lace' fungus and (in the USA) 'shoestring mushroom'.

The honey fungus, which is also found in India and the Orient, is an autumn growth, and is closely related to the MATSUTAKE.

Honey fungus has an acid smell when fresh, but this disappears when it is cooked. The flavour can vary from mild to strong, even spicy. Jordan (1995a) expresses maximum enthusiasm for the species, and suggests that the best treatment is to pan-fry it gently in butter with a little chopped shallot. (Jaccottet, 1973, remarking that it is sold in Swiss markets, strikes a less positive note by stating emphatically that the fungus should be well boiled before its final cooking and the water discarded out of reach of pigs, who may be fatally poisoned by it.)

Another fungus which grows in clusters on tree trunks has the promising name of poached egg fungus (or porcelain fungus) because of its glistening translucent white cap, which may have a hint of yellow in the centre. It used to be assigned to the same genus as the honey fungus, but is now classified as *Oudemansiella mucida*. It is one of the few mushrooms which has to be washed, to rid it of gluten, after which it is edible.

HOPPER a curious English word formed from the Tamil word *appam* (also *appa*, *appe*), itself thought to be derived from the Sanskrit *apupa*, meaning fried dainty. The name hopper, one of a number of Anglo-Indian adaptations of Indian words, refers to a pancake-like speciality of both S. India and Sri Lanka, but was particularly prevalent in the latter country.

Madhur Jaffrey (1985) gives the following vivid description:

I have often said that if a French crêpe were to marry a crumpet or an English muffin, they would probably become the proud parents of appams. Appams are a special kind of pancake made out of a leavened rice batter. They are thick, soft, white and spongy in the centre and crisp and lace-like along their golden edges.

Hoppers are cooked in a pan resembling a Chinese wok known as a *cheena chatti* (literally 'Chinese pan') which gives them their characteristic bowl-like shape.

Hoppers are often eaten for breakfast, but Jaffrey emphasizes their versatility, and also their pleasing ability to sop up all sorts of juices and savoury or sweet flavours.

Another similar pancake served on festive occasions is known as the string hopper. The dough is extruded by a special implement into fine 'strings' and steamed. The result can be served with hard-boiled eggs, nuts, peas, chilli sauce, etc.   HS

HOPPIN' JOHN a dish of COWPEAS (black-eyed peas), cooked with fat pork, and rice with some seasoning. Craigie and Hulbert (1938–44) spell it 'hopping John', the form used by their two earliest citations (1838 and 1856). They define it as: 'a highly seasoned stew of bacon, peas, and sometimes rice'. Everyone seems to agree that the indisputable basis of the dish is cowpeas, fond memories of which the black slaves brought with them to N. America. John Thorne (1996) gives a generous amount of space to the subject, in the course of a chapter about the various forms which 'Rice and Beans' have taken in the Americas and especially in the southern states of the USA. He emphasizes, rightly, that to write about the slaves bringing with them cowpeas or any other item of what has since become known as SOUL FOOD is misleading. The slaves came with no physical possessions whatsoever, but they did have their habits, memories, and skills to help recreate their native dishes in the New World.

The origin of the name is uncertain. Thorne cites several theories which have been advanced by etymologists and cookery writers, none of which is irresistibly plausible.

HOP SHOOTS from the hop vine, *Humulus lupulus*, are a popular food in Belgium and the north of France around late March, when they thrust up from the ground. They are cooked in water, just long enough to make them tender, and then often served with scrambled eggs, or incorporated in a salad. Their sweet and aromatic flavour is set off by a slight touch of bitterness.

Hop shoots have been eaten in England also. Dorothy Hartley (1954) gives them as a Kentish dish—'boiled in broth and eaten like asparagus with butter toast'. There are also recipes for using them in sauces and soups.

HOREHOUND often called white horehound, *Marrubium vulgare*, a plant native to Mediterranean Europe and C. Asia, and naturalized in N. America. Its leaves make a tea, described by Grieve (1931) as 'an appetizing and healthful drink, popular in Norfolk and other country districts'. It is also used in candies.

HORN OF AFRICA taken here to mean the strip of coastal land which extends round the north-eastern tip of Africa from the Somali Republic through Djibouti to Eritrea.

The traditional food in the Somali Republic is RICE (*brees*) with meat (*hibbib*) and CHILLI. *Anan geil* is a dish of MILLET gruel with CAMEL milk and HONEY, which sounds like something which must have been there since the year dot. There are other dishes which reflect Arab—or even, in some instances, Italian—influence.

Paice (1994) ingeniously introduces Eritrea (a modern state since 1890, independent in its present form since 1993) with a poetic quotation from a classical Greek tragedian:

One of the earliest known references to the name Eritrea, derived from the Greek word for red, is in Fragment 67 of Aeschylus: 'There the sacred waters of the Erythrean Sea break upon a bright red strand, and at no great distance from the Ocean lies a copper-tinted lake—the lake that is the jewel of Ethiopia—where the all-pervading Sun returns again and again to plunge his immortal form, and finds solace for his weary round in gentle ripples that are but a warm caress.'

Staple foods in Eritrea include INJERA (as in neighbouring ETHIOPIA); and, as another bread, *kitcha*, which is thin and unleavened and prepared from wheaten flour. A menu might include *frittata*, an OMELETTE-type dish of eggs with peppers etc., reflecting Italian influence, which also shows up in the term *arrosto* for roast meat.

HORN OF PLENTY *Craterellus cornucopioides*, an edible fungus related to the CHANTERELLE but brown, grey, or bluish in colour, and almost black when wet. The stem and cap form a continuous structure which may be 12 cm (5") high. The fungus grows in the late summer and autumn,

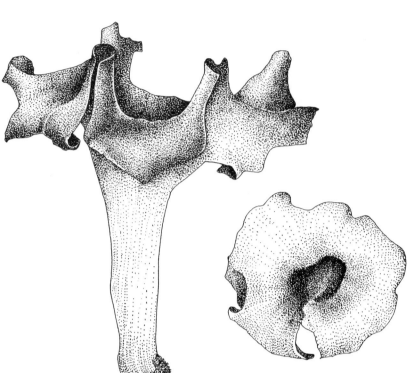

Horn of plenty

typically in the midst of hazel or beech trees. It is found in China as well as Europe and N. America.

The reputation of the horn of plenty varies from country to country. Most British authorities are unenthusiastic about it, except perhaps for use as a condiment after being dried and powdered, a procedure also recommended in France. In Scandinavia, however, it is given a higher rating; and in the USA McIlvaine (1902) described it as first class and said that several other species of the genus found there were equally good.

These ambivalent attitudes seem to be reflected in the common names in Romance languages. The French call it both *corne d'abondance* and *trompette des morts*, and there are corresponding pairs of names in Italian and Spanish.

HORN-SHELL *Cerithium vulgatum*, an edible mollusc inhabiting a single shell which is shaped like an ice cream cone with its open end bent over sideways. Size up to 7 cm (2.5"); colour of the shell usually brownish or greenish; distribution, the Mediterranean and E. Atlantic coasts.

The name is also applied to some Indo-Pacific species belonging to different families, notably *Cerithidea obtusa* and *Potamides telescopium*. Both are larger: up to 9 cm (3.5").

The Mediterranean horn-shell is eaten in a number of countries, and provides the

basis for a special Italian soup, *Zuppa di garagoli*, in the Romagna.

HORS D'ŒUVRES a French term which has been current in a food context since the 17th century (in England, only from the 18th), indicating minor, usually cold, items of food served at the beginning of a meal. In the 20th century, until quite recent times the hors d'œuvres trolley was a familiar sight in restaurants, incorporating up to several dozen little recipients containing the various delicacies on offer. Typical items would be ANCHOVIES, SARDINES, slices of smoked fish, olives, radishes, sliced tomato (or other salad vegetable), various sorts of SAUSAGE and other CHARCUTERIE, etc. Hot hors d'œuvres could be miniature savoury pastries or tiny fritters or other similar titbits; but these do not belong to the mainstream hors d'œuvres tradition.

See also TAPAS; MEZZE; and, on a somewhat different plane, SMORGASBORD; ZAKUSKI.

HORSE GRAM *Macrotyloma uniflorum* (formerly *Dolichos biflorus*), is also known as Madras gram, and as *kulthi* in India. The plant is widely cultivated in tropical Asia and Africa as a fodder and cover crop. The beans are smaller and flatter than peas and are usually kept whole rather than split. They are among the cheapest of the LEGUMES.

HORSE MACKEREL fish of the genus *Trachurus*, found in the Black Sea, the Mediterranean, and the E. Atlantic from Iceland and Norway down to S. Africa. Their maximum length is around 50 cm (20") and they have greenish-blue backs and prominent 'stepped' lateral lines, marked by a set of lozenge-shaped scutes (bony plates like especially large scales). In this respect they resemble many other members of the family Carangidae, to which they belong. The family, which is more important in the Indo-Pacific than in the Atlantic, is notorious for the confusion in English vernacular names (see JACK); horse mackerel may also be called SCAD, a name more often used for carangid species in the Indo-Pacific.

The three main species are *Trachurus mediterraneus*, *T. picturatus*, and *T. trachurus*. There is little to choose between them, and none enjoys a high reputation as food. The first two belong mainly to the Mediterranean. The third is the one with the more extensive range, down to S. Africa, where it is called maasbanker because of its supposed resemblance to a freshwater fish of the River Maas in the Netherlands.

HORSEMEAT the flesh of the horse, *Equus caballus*, is similar to BEEF, and eaten in many countries. In continental Europe, both horse and donkey, *Equus asinus*, are sold as 'horsemeat'; the flesh of the mule, a hybrid of the two, can also be sold under this title.

All these animals are, however, considered unsuitable for human consumption in English-speaking cultures, and the idea of eating them often arouses distaste. As animals which do not have cloven hooves or chew cud, horses and donkeys are prohibited for both Jews and Muslims.

In continental Europe, horsemeat is eaten with varying degrees of acceptance; the French, Belgians, and Swedish appear to be the most enthusiastic consumers. The meat is also consumed in parts of C. Asia, China, and Japan, and by some lower-caste groups in India, and generally seems to be acceptable in S. America. In N. America, the Anglo-Saxon prohibition against it is strong, although it has been eaten.

Theories advanced to explain the English aversion to horsemeat include the perception of horses as noble creatures, their role as pets, their value as draught animals, and dislike of the flavour. It is generally accepted that at the root is a religious prohibition inspired by the spread of Christianity.

There is a particularly good discussion in Simoons (1994), who surveys the subject on a global basis. In Europe, he believes, the Roman Catholic Church, inheriting from classical Rome a distaste for eating horsemeat, was the principal force of opposition to the practice, striving to suppress pagan rituals which involved sacrificing and eating a horse; but this was not easy and they even had to give a dispensation to Icelanders to continue. Simoons's study dispels any idea that attitudes to horsemeat have been consistent either geographically or temporally, except for a markedly consistent strength of feeling, on one side or the other.

Evidence indicates that prehistoric Europeans had few inhibitions about using horses for food. Horse bones, sometimes cracked open for extraction of marrow, are recorded at archaeological sites in England and elsewhere. At Soultré (Burgundy) there is evidence for hunting horses by deliberately stampeding them over a cliff—the first evidence of a long-standing relationship between the inhabitants of France and horsemeat.

In more recent times the French attitude towards horsemeat was affected in the mid-19th century by a campaign in favour of eating it, culminating in a spectacular *banquet hippophagique* in Paris in 1865, the menu for which included horse consommé, horse sausages, Horse à la mode, and several other presentations. Reception was mixed: Edmond de Goncourt described the meat as 'watery and blackish-red'; and Alexandre DUMAS doubted if it would ever become an article of daily consumption. Since much horsemeat was derived from horses too old to work, it is not surprising that it was tough. Special horse butchers' shops were established so that the cheap meat would not be passed off as more expensive beef.

In 20th-century France horsemeat is still principally consumed by the urban working classes, among whom it has a reputation for healthiness. Some specialist breeding of horses for meat is now undertaken, using Ardennes and Postier Breton horses, so meat from younger animals of more reliable quality is available.

Horsemeat is lower in calories than beef, and has a higher content of glycogen. It is considered good for dishes such as Steak TARTARE, which require raw meat, as the animal carries neither tuberculosis nor tapeworms. However, the meat spoils faster than beef, and poor handling of horsemeat was the cause of a serious outbreak of salmonella poisoning in France during the 1960s, which adversely affected the business of horse butchers. Root (1980) remarks that horsemeat shops were already an increasingly rare sight, although of striking aspect: 'with a gilded horsehead over the door and splendid fat carcasses displayed within, artificial roses running like buttons down their spines and bright ribbons fluttering along their flanks.'

Horsemeat is lean and similar to beef, but closer in texture with an underlying sweetness of taste. To balance this, some authorities recommend the use of garlic or herbs. No specific dishes based on horse appear to have developed in Europe; cookery books which allow discussion of the matter simply say that any method suitable for beef can be applied to horsemeat.   (LM)

HORSE MUSHROOM *Agaricus arvensis*, a large edible mushroom which is found in pastures or thickets in the autumn. Its distribution is wide: Europe, N. America, Japan, China, Australia, S. Africa.

The convex cap may measure 20 cm (8") across, twice the size of the common FIELD MUSHROOM. The gills are white at first, then pink, and finally brown. Like many other mushrooms in the genus *Agaricus*, this one smells of aniseed. It is good to eat, and may be cooked in any of the usual ways. The size and shape of the cap are suitable for stuffing.

HORSERADISH *Armoracia rusticana*, a potent condiment. It is not a kind of RADISH; both plants, however, belong to the crucifer family which also includes turnip, cabbage, and mustard. The pungent odour and 'hot' taste of horseradish are due to a substance called sinigrin which, when it is decomposed by the action of enzymes, liberates a volatile oil, similar to mustard oil, containing sulphur. The release of these properties only occurs when the root is cut or bruised; an unbroken root has no smell.

Horseradish is a native wild plant of E. and SE Europe and W. Asia. Once established, it is an ineradicable weed and it is now naturalized all over Europe and in the USA. But its westward movement seems to have been relatively recent. There is no certain reference to it in classical literature.

Much later, the 13th-century writer Albertus Magnus describes a 'raphanus' (radish) used for medical purposes in terms which fit horseradish well. But the German Fuchsius, in his *Historia Stirpium* (1542), gave the first unmistakable description of horseradish root used as a condiment, and this was repeated soon afterwards by Italian and English authors. An early English name was 'red cole'; this cannot have referred to the colour of the root, which is yellowish-brown outside and white within; but may have been given because the fiery taste was like red-hot coals. The name 'horseradish', which is also old, means a radish which is 'hoarse', or coarse and strong. The French name 'raifort' also means 'strong root'.

Horseradish is most popular in N. and E. Europe and Russia; in Britain; to some extent in France; and also in the USA thanks to European immigrants. The appearance of the Russian and Slavonic name *khren* in several W. European languages (in variant forms) shows that its use is at least partly adopted from E. Europe.

Horseradish is most often used in sharp relishes served with roast beef in Britain and with meat, fish, or eggs in other countries. For the strongest and most biting taste, fresh, grated horseradish may be used undiluted, as it is in some N. European countries with fish; but normally the bite is toned down in some way. Fresh horseradish may be mixed with apple or made into a sauce with emollient ingredients such as cream and egg. The French prefer to include horseradish in delicate cream mixtures, often with lemon juice. Elsewhere, vinegar has been and remains a common ingredient in horseradish preparations. Coles (1657) said that horseradish was served 'thinly sliced and wittily mixed with vinegar'.

Horseradish sauces are usually uncooked or only gently warmed. Heat destroys the pungency, and when whole horseradish roots are cooked as a vegetable, which they are occasionally in E. Europe, the flavour is quite mild.

In Norway the grated root is mixed in with whipped sweet-and-sour cream, vinegar, and sugar; this sauce is called *pepperrotsaus* and is served with cold boiled fish, in particular salmon.

A whole horseradish root is large, about 45 cm (18") long. Not all of it is usable; the outside has an unpleasant flavour and is scraped off, and the tasteless core is usually discarded. Even so, a whole root usually provides much more horseradish than anyone would want at one time, and the usual practice is to buy it in a prepared, preserved form. Preservation is important, because once horseradish has been sliced or grated and the flavour has developed, it quickly deteriorates. The traditional horseradish vinegar and pickled horseradish are two solutions.

Related plants in different genera have roots resembling horseradish and are similarly used. The most important is the Japanese WASABI. In India and E. Asia horseradish is almost unknown, but it has an understudy in the roots of the so-called HORSERADISH TREE.

HORSERADISH TREE

Moringa oleifera, a small tree of India now grown also in the W. Indies and other tropical regions. Europeans in India discovered that its root 'so exactly resembles horse-radish as scarcely to be distinguished from it by the nicest palate', and used it with their roast beef. However, the main reason for its cultivation is that its seeds are the source of ben oil, used in perfumery and for lubrication; and

the next most important reason is that the pods and leaves are edible.

The long, narrow pods or fruits contain a whitish mass in which three-winged seeds are embedded. These pods, when still young, are cut into short lengths and used in Indian curry dishes. The outside of the pod remains inedible and is discarded, but the mucilaginous inside and the immature seeds have a pleasant, slightly hot taste. As Ochse (1980) remarks: 'The stewed fruits cannot be eaten whole, but one sucks their contents and throws the tough valves away.'

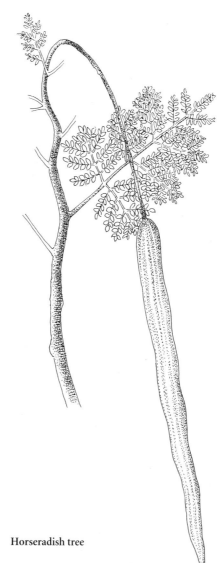

Horseradish tree

The leaves are also cooked as a green vegetable or used as a pickle or flavouring agent. Malini Bisen (1970) gives a whole range of recipes for 'drumsticks', as the fruits are known in India. She states that in Maharashtrian and Gujerati houses drumsticks are often used in a DAL, in a *kadhi* (buttermilk soup, *chaach* in Hindi,

that is flavoured chiefly with turmeric), and as a vegetable.

The Wealth of India sums up uses thus:

The tender pods are esteemed as a vegetable. They are cut into slices and used in culinary preparations: they are also pickled. Flowers and tender leaves are eaten as pot herbs. Seeds are consumed after frying: they are reported to taste like peanuts. The roots of the tree are used as a condiment or garnish in the same way as those of true horseradish.

The same source might have added that the fruits have a reputation as an aphrodisiac (no doubt because of their shape) and are for this reason fed to bridegrooms in S. India.

HORSESHOE CRABS

creatures of great antiquity, in the family Xiphosuridae. They bear a large and rounded outer shell, and have a formidable spike projecting behind, as means of protection. An alternative name for them is 'beetle crabs'. They are caught—in regions where people bother to catch them—in special nets or bamboo traps set in shallow inshore waters.

These crabs have small black eyes, but the males are reputedly blind and depend on the females, to whom they cling while moving around. Dozens of males may be 'in tow' from a single female. The Thai name for this crab means 'pimp' and was presumably bestowed because of this habit.

In SE Asia there is one species, *Tachypleus gigas*, which achieves a great size (even 40 cm/16" across the outer shell) and has correspondingly large eggs. The eggs are regarded as the delicacy and, mixed with the light blue blood which can be collected from the crab's body, are fried in Thailand.

HOSPITALITY

to judge by what one reads or experiences about the folkways and foodways of all the innumerable ethnic and other groups in the world, is everywhere 'traditional', 'unstinted', 'unrivalled', and often 'legendary'.

It would be good to think that all this is so; and it is certainly true that there is a very general disposition among the peoples of the world to give and to enjoy giving hospitality. The matter could well be the subject of a large book of global scope.

However, there has been a downside, brought to attention in a very reasonable manner by Mrs G. M. Culwick (1955):

A very real difficulty in safeguarding the shares of the women and children is the paramount obligation of hospitality. It is unthinkable that food should be withheld if any food is there, and in a community which does not live at the ends of telephone lines or have three postal deliveries a day, the majority of guests arrive unheralded. It is a matter which cannot be forced, it must take its time, but it is to be hoped that once they become alive to its importance some of the men will give a lead in devising some way of safeguarding their families without outraging local feeling.

No doubt the problem will tend to go away, in the Sudan (about which Mrs Culwick was writing and where she had been working) and other countries with similar traditions. No doubt also the gradual disappearance of the problem will involve the loss of some things of value. One must hope that the impulse to give hospitality is indeed almost universal and that it will continue to find expression, but with fewer untoward results for women.

HOTCHPOTCH sometimes hodgepodge, a term which in its culinary meaning, a mixed stew, dates back to the 16th century and has an obvious connection with HOTPOT. It also occurred in earlier forms in medieval times, for example, the recipes 'Gees in hoggepot' and 'Goos in hochepot' reproduced in Warner (1791).

A dish of this sort, which is almost infinitely variable, naturally occurs in many places. As Marian McNeill (1929) explains, the same thing is known in Scotland as *Hairst Bree* (harvest broth), and 'is made only when the kail-yard is in its prime, and the soup is fragrant with the juices of young growing things'.

However, the term hotchpotch was also well known in Scotland and Meg Dods (1826) has recipes for both Scottish and Winter hotchpotch. For the former, she too emphasizes the importance of having young vegetables, 'full of sweet juices'. She recommends sweet white turnips or 'the small, round, smooth-grained yellow kind peculiar to Scotland, which is almost equal to the genuine *Navet* of France'.

HOTPOT a word having different applications in the western and eastern hemispheres.

In the Orient, there is a cluster of dishes centred on the Mongolian hotpot, which may or may not have originated in MONGOLIA. A contrivance intended to sit in the middle of the table, within reach of the diners, embraces a heating apparatus and a circular 'moat' of simmering broth, into which the diners briefly dip thin slices of meat or morsels of vegetable. The Japanese SHABU-SHABU is a close relation.

In the west it is usually Lancashire hotpot, a dish of NW England and in particular of Lancashire. The main ingredients are lamb or mutton chops and potatoes, and the cooking is done slowly in a covered pot or casserole. A Lancashire hotpot dish is tall, round, straight sided, and has a lid. The dish is filled with layers of browned lamb or mutton chops and layers of onions and thickly sliced potatoes. Other ingredients sometimes added are kidneys and black puddings; oysters, when cheap, were also included.

The top layer is always an arrangement of overlapping potato slices, sometimes surrounding small circles made from the rounded ends of the potatoes. Stock is added and the dish slowly cooked in the oven. The lid is removed towards the end of the cooking to brown the edges of the potato slices. A Hot Pot Supper is a community event in Lancashire. The dish is invariably accompanied by pickled red cabbage.

Very large earthenware hotpots survive which some claim were necessary to fit the long chop bones of Pennine sheep ignoring the fact that the bones can be chopped or snapped and bent back. It may be that local cheap coal (used in locally made kitchen ranges) and the fact that the potato came early into use in Lancashire combined to make this dish popular. Also, it was a great advantage that hotpot could be left to cook while the family were at work. A variation using beef instead of mutton was recorded in a newspaper on Boxing Day (26 December) 1889:

Yesterday over 30,000 poor people in Liverpool were provided with 'hot pot' dinners. Each hot pot weighed ten pounds. There were used 13,000 lbs of beef, 15 tons of potatoes and a ton and a half of onions.

Ayto (1993) remarks that in the 18th century the term 'hot-pot' referred to a sort of hot punch and that the first writer to use it in print in the sense of a meat stew was Mrs Gaskell, who (in *North and South*, 1854) had a northern mill-owner enjoying a share of his mill-hands' hotpot. However, the term HOTCHPOTCH, now largely obsolete, had been used in a similar sense in earlier times. It meant a mixed dish, typically a meat and vegetable stew, and was derived via the form hotchpot from the medieval French *hochepot* (a term which survives, referring in modern times to a stew of N. France and S. Belgium, in which oxtail and often other meat ingredients figure). The Dutch *hutspot* belongs to the same family of dishes.   (RSh)

HOUGH (also hoch, haugh), a term used mainly in the north of England and Scotland for that part of an animal which corresponds to the human ankle; i.e. the hock, or to another hind-leg joint of meat such as shin. Potted hough is a Scottish delicacy which remains highly popular. Dorothy Hartley (1954) quotes a recipe which was clearly given to her orally by a Scotswoman and has an arresting start and finish. 'Take a hough and bash it well with an axe. No' just break it, but have at it, till the pieces are no bigger than a wee hen's egg.' She then describes how the pieces are stewed for at least four hours with the brown papery skins of onions, peppercorns, and a blade of mace. The meat comes away from the bone, and the strained liquid is allowed to 'gallop' while the meat is picked off the broken bones and pressed into a basin which, when full, is topped up with the liquid. 'It should set stiff. If it n' sets stiff, you must reduce again for it should be as stiff as glue.' The woman who provided the recipe is revealed as 'the mother of four champion blacksmiths', i.e. someone who knew about strengthening foods. If only for this reason it is worth recording her comments on the reception by her family of the dish.

All o'mine want no more than twa-three slices of potted hough, and a well of baked taties, and a fresh lettuce and mustard—maybe twa-three pickles would go wi'it well—and a tankard of ale—'twill fill them fine—'tis all guid meat.

Another word for hough or hock is skink; see CULLEN SKINK.

HUCKLEBERRY *Gaylussacia baccata*, a name made familiar by Mark Twain's *Huckleberry Finn*, is as American as the hero of that book. The plant is related to the CRANBERRY and BLUEBERRY (or bilberry). Its name is a corruption of 'hurtleberry', an old name for the blueberry; and the two plants are broadly alike, growing in the same regions, and being used in the same ways. However, the fruit of the huckleberry is different in structure; it is not a true berry, but a drupe, a fruit with a hard stone.

The black huckleberry, *G. baccata*, is the most popular, but Fernald and Kinsey (1943) aver that the dangleberry, *G. frondosa*, is just as good and will 'make one of the most luscious of desserts, being remarkably juicy and with a rich, spicy and sweet flavor'. The stones, however, make both species less attractive than the blueberry and they are not commercially gathered or cultivated. Berries gathered from the wild may be used in pies and conserves with or as a substitute for many other berries.

Other berries in N. America which may misleadingly be called 'huckleberries' are the 'red huckleberry', *Vaccinium parvifolium*, of the north-west, and the 'California huckleberry', *V. ovatum*. What is sometimes called the 'squaw huckleberry', *V. stamineum*, of the north is better called 'deerberry' and is evidently worth gathering; Facciola (1990) remarks that when cooked and served cold their flavour is like 'a combination of gooseberry and cranberry sauce, with the slight bitter taste of grapefruit marmalade'.

HUFFKINS a speciality of Kent in England, are small yeast-leavened cakes/rolls, shaped into ovals, each with a hole in the middle. They have been known since the late 18th century but are rarely made now. Annie Hood (1993) records various forms of the tradition; she says that the dough was often enriched with butter, egg, or fruit; that the hole in the middle would take jam; and that huffkins were latterly associated with the end of the hop-picking season. The origin of the name is unknown, and some of the various recipes suggest an affinity with TEA BREADS.

HUITLACOCHE is the maize smut fungus, *Ustilago maydis*. This is a disorganized greyish mass, glossy outside and black inside when overripe, which grows on MAIZE plants. It is edible and counted as a delicacy. Supplies are exported from Mexico to the USA.   SC

HUMBUG a small sweet made of a pulled sugar mixture, typically with a mint flavour. It has a traditional shape like a twisted cushion, made by chopping the rope of soft mixture into short sections and turning it through 90 degrees between cuts.

HUNDREDS AND THOUSANDS are tiny DRAGÉES, made by coating individual sugar crystals with sugar syrup. (If the coating process is carried on to build up large sweets, the result is a GOBSTOPPER.) A characteristic of hundreds and thousands is the bright mixture of colours—red, orange, pink, yellow—in which they are produced. These little sweets are scattered over icing to decorate cakes, or sprinkled over ice creams.

The corresponding French term, *nonpareille*, sometimes occurs in the Anglicized and archaic form 'non pareil'.
                                           LM

HUNGARY as a nation and a culinary entity, may be said to have begun at the end of the 9th century, when the Hungarian tribes, which had been moving west and south-west for centuries from Asia, accomplished the conquest of what is now their country. (Their linguistic brethren, the Finns, had chosen to move north-west and take up a position distant from them, thus separating the two surviving examples of the Finno-Ugric language group. Whatever culinary links there may have been between the two seem to have disappeared as a result of this divergence.)

Medieval Hungary rose to its zenith of wealth and power during the long reign of King Matthias I (1458–90), and the extant records of royal feasts reveal many aspects of modern Hungarian cuisine already in being. The association of gypsy music with meals, perhaps too inevitable and intrusive in 19th- and 20th-century Hungarian restaurants, was apparent at the wedding feast of the young King with Princess Beatrice of Naples. The influence of Italy, for example in the use of pasta; the love of game; highly embellished dishes of freshwater fish; the use of sauces made with the food's own juices; the supremacy among vegetables of the newly arrived onion—all these can be clearly seen at a distance of five centuries.

The death of King Matthias brought on a period of decline and then defeat by the invading Turks. For the greater part of the 16th and 17th centuries, Turkey ruled the central region of Hungary (while the western and northern parts were under Habsburg domination, and Transylvania was an independent principality). The long period of Turkish presence had fundamental effects on food and cookery. It was the Turks who introduced PAPRIKA, FILO pastry (which evolved into the STRUDEL), rice PILAFS, PITTA bread (to become *langós*, a sort of forerunner of PIZZA), the practice of stuffing peppers and aubergines (previously the Hungarians had only stuffed cabbage), the tomato, cherries and sour cherries, and corn. Although these benefits may seem slight by comparison with the serious disadvantages of being under Turkish rule, these disadvantages themselves, insofar as they impoverished ordinary people, helped to maintain in a pure state the simple food traditions which existed. By contrast, the prosperous people of Transylvania became more sophisticated in their commerce and their cuisine and showed the effects of, for example, French influences.

The next major period in Hungarian history, that of the Habsburg Empire of Austria-Hungary, was less inspiring for Hungarian cooks. The imported influences were now Germanic, although some of the aristocratic families managed to hang on to their French chefs. However, by 1867, when the Austro-Hungarian dual monarchy, giving Hungary much more independence, was established, various beneficial developments were already well under way. The famous pastry shops of Budapest were there, the foundations of the city's reputation for fine hotels had been laid, and a small but steady stream of Hungarian cookery books had begun to appear (the first had been published in 1695).

From the 1870s onwards the stream of cookery books accelerated (with the result that Hungarian cuisine is the best documented of any C. European country) and the activities of the Gundel family (especially Károly, 1883–1956) and others gave new glory to the restaurant and hotel business. From this era date some of the famous creations such as Dobostorte (see TORTE AND KUCHEN).

The cuisines of Hungary continued to flourish during the first half of the 20th century, suffered severely from the inhibiting influence of the communist regime after the Second World War, and have rebounded vigorously since then. This applies to all the regions: the area 'beyond the Danube', in the centre of which is Lake Balaton (the largest in C. Europe); N. Hungary, where live the Palóc, descendants of hunting tribes which were established there before the Middle Ages; the Great Hungarian Plain, containing the area known as the 'orchard' of Hungary. As always, the outstanding Hungarian dishes for foreigners are those known as GOULASH (*gulyás*). However, the entry for this last item explains in detail that the name is only used in Hungary for a soup, and that the dishes which go under the name outside Hungary correspond to various Hungarian stews with names such as *pörkölt* and *paprikás* and *tókany*. Other Hungarian specialities include the fish soups and other fish dishes of Lake Balaton, especially those involving *fogas* (ZANDER).

Some ingredients which have particular importance in Hungary are onions (carefully fried), cabbage, caraway seeds, and potatoes. DUMPLINGS and some forms of PASTA and NOODLES figure in various dishes. HONEY is important for the famous Hungarian honey breads and honey cakes.

However, by common consent the greatest glories of the Hungarian table are the pastries. Lang (1971) combined in his masterly survey the whole history of Hungarian cuisine with heartfelt praise for all its various glories, but reserved his greatest paeans for the pastries. He points out that, as a result of a beneficent piece of bureaucracy: 'The only places you won't be able to order pastries in Hungary are the restaurants.' It is to the pastry shops and espresso bars that one must go for the pleasures thus described by Lang:

There are few delights more enchanting than sitting down at a charming little lace-covered table and drinking espresso or hot chocolate with whipped cream, accompanied by a delicately decorated slice of *torta* or an endless variety of dainty *mignons* which make the Western petits fours seem like five-and-ten-cent gewgaws next to Tiffany's diamonds and precious stones.

HUSH PUPPY a small sausage-shaped FRITTER made from white cornmeal, milk, water, and chopped onion, fried in fat which has been used for frying fish. Its origins are obscure, but it seems to have originated in Florida before 1920. According to legend it was devised by hunters, who would throw an occasional fritter to their hunting dogs to keep them quiet. However, public outdoor fish frying sessions were common in Florida, and it is plausible to suppose that the hush puppy came into being at these, whether or not it owes its name to an ability to quieten hungry dogs.   (RH)

Huss a vernacular name for some DOGFISH which has been a source of puzzlement. Dawn and Douglas Nelson (1980) may have been the first to work out just how the name came into being.

The English common names of the small sharks known as dogfish are confusing. Living in Kent and having the opportunity to talk with old French fishermen, we think that we have a little light to shed on the matter, so far as the mysterious name 'huss' is concerned. In . . . *North Atlantic Seafood* (1979) . . . Davidson links it with the larger-spotted dogfish, *Scyliorhinus stellaris*. In our examination of Kent catches over the years we have concluded that both *S. Stellaris* and *S. caniculus* (the lesser-spotted dogfish) were simply called 'dogs', but that the 'spur-dog', *Squalis acanthius*, was known because of its viviparous habits as a 'nurse dog', This was shorted to 'a Nurse', which was pronounced in the markets as 'a Nuss', which the fishmongers thought was 'an Uss', with the result that they labelled the fish simply 'Uss'. When these fish got to London the highly educated Billingsgate porters assumed that the ignorant Kentish men had dropped an 'h', which they restored by changing 'Uss' to 'Huss'. We think that this is the origin of the name. In the last 20 years or so, however, we have noted that, while most of the dogfish sold in the market at Folkestone are still labelled 'Uss', and later, when sold in the shops, 'Huss', these are often lesser-spotted dogs (*S. caniculus*) and not spur-dogs. So the name may have been moving from one species to another as their abundance in the catch changes.

HYDROGENATION or 'hardening' of fats, a process in which liquid oils are turned into solid fats, so that hard margarine can be made from vegetable or fish oils. The oils are heated in a container with hydrogen and a nickel catalyst, converting some of the unsaturated fatty acids to saturated ones, which are more solid (see FATS AND OILS). Any possible health benefits from the original unsaturated fatty acids are lost.

The oils used to make soft margarine are not hydrogenated; instead, the spread is stiffened with emulsifiers (see EMULSION).
                                                                RH

HYDROLYSIS literally 'splitting by water', a chemical reaction in which the large, complex molecules of PROTEINS and CARBOHYDRATES are broken into smaller molecules. This is one of the fundamental processes of both cooking and digestion.

The single SUGAR molecules of which carbohydrates are composed, and the AMINO ACIDS which make up proteins, are linked end to end by a comparatively weak bond involving just one atom on each side. The linking force is electric: one of the atoms has a positive charge, the other a negative one. Opposite charges attract each other, holding the bond together.

Charged atoms or groups of atoms are known as ions. A molecule of water, which consists of two atoms of hydrogen and one of oxygen, can be split into two ions: a hydrogen ion, which has a positive charge; and a hydroxyl ion, which consists of one hydrogen and one oxygen atom and carries a negative charge. In hydrolysis these two ions are forced into the bond between the large molecules. The positive hydrogen ion links to the negative end of one molecule, cancelling out its negative charge. Similarly, the negative hydroxyl ion links to the positive end of the other molecule, cancelling its positive charge. There is now no difference in charge between the two larger molecules, so they no longer attract each other and can move apart.

Hydrolysis does not happen by itself; it needs some input of energy. It can be brought about rather slowly by putting proteins or carbohydrates in water and heating them. The reaction can be speeded up by adding an acid or alkali, whose built-in chemical energy helps to break the bonds. The strongly acid conditions in the stomachs of animals are an aid to hydrolysis; other examples are the use of acids such as lemon juice in marinades to tenderize tough meat, and the disreputable practice of adding BICARBONATE OF SODA (a mild ALKALI) to the cooking water of vegetables, which breaks down the cell walls and gives the food an unpleasingly mushy texture.

In digestion, most of the work of hydrolysis is carried out by ENZYMES, which can perform it without the aid of acids, alkalis, or heat.

When a living creature makes carbohydrates or proteins it performs the opposite of hydrolysis. Two sugar molecules of amino acids are linked by removing a hydroxyl ion from one and a hydrogen ion from the other. These ions combine to form a molecule of water.   RH

HYSSOP *Hyssopus officinalis*, originally from Asia Minor and the Mediterranean, is a small shrub which has been used for culinary and medicinal purposes since pre-Christian times. The plant has woody stems, whorls of lance-shaped leaves, and long dense spikes of tubular-shaped light blue, purple, pink, or white flowers from which bees make wonderful HONEY.

The flavour of the leaves is similar to THYME, and they can be eaten, fresh, with meat, fish, in salads (as can the young shoots), in soups, stews, and in fruit dishes;

Hyssop

or ground up as an ingredient in stuffings, pies, and sausages. Hyssop aids the digestion of fat and so makes a particularly good accompaniment to greasy meat dishes. The aromatic qualities of hyssop show to good advantage if a syrup is made using water in which sprigs of hyssop have been boiled and if this syrup is then poured over slices of fresh fruit or used in a fruit salad; Pamela Michael (1980) points out that the combination is particularly effective with plums, apricots, or peaches.

The flavour is strong so the plant should be used sparingly.

The names anise hyssop and Mexican (giant) hyssop have often been applied to *Agastache foeniculum* and *A. mexicana*, from the north central USA and N. Mexico respectively. As Julia Morton (1976) remarks, these large and highly aromatic hyssops 'are extremely attractive to honey bees and are often grown by bee keepers', besides being used for infusions of tea and occasional culinary purposes.

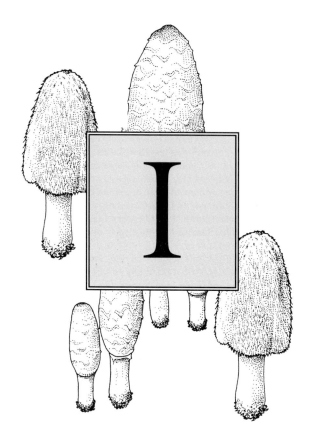

I

ICE not a food but an important adjunct to food and constituent of certain dishes, has been occurring naturally on the planet ever since freezing temperatures were first reached. Its use for culinary purposes certainly dates very far back in China, in cold regions where foods can be frozen by simply leaving them out of doors. Such use in W. Europe can be traced back to medieval times; and in the tropics to the time when advances in maritime transport made it possible to transport ice for long distances by sea (e.g. in the 19th century when ice from New England lakes was taken to the Caribbean, and also to England).

Stobart (1980), who gives an admirable and succinct account of the physics of ice, describes one architectural phenomenon brought about by its use:

Before the invention of refrigerators, winter snow was stored in pits or ice-houses insulated with straw for use later in the year. There is even a huge ice-house in the middle of the great Persian salt desert, a building the size (and rather the shape) of a tennis stadium, where snow was once packed to help people survive the summer's awful heat.

In the 20th century ice has come to be taken for granted in most parts of the world

as an available resource, and ICE CREAM has been added to the common currency of foods worldwide. The use of WATER ICES is less widespread but has an interesting history; see also SHERBET.

Although she did not live to complete the work which was eventually published under the title *Harvest of the Cold Months*, Elizabeth David had assembled for it a wealth of interesting information and the chapters which she had drafted invest the whole subject with the romantic spirit in which she approached it.
READING: Cummings (1949); Elizabeth David (1994).

ICE CREAM one of the most spectacularly successful of all the foods based on dairy products, has a comparatively short history. The first ice creams, in the sense of an iced and flavoured confection made from full milk or cream, are thought to have been made in Italy and then in France in the 17th century, and to have been diffused from the French court to other European countries. However, although the French did make some ice creams from an

early date, they were more interested in WATER ICES.

The first recorded English use of the term ice cream (also given as iced cream) was by Ashmole (1672), recording among dishes served at the Feast of St George at Windsor in May 1671 'One Plate of *Ice Cream*'. The first published English recipe was by Mrs Mary Eales (1718).

Stallings (1979) has described fully the extant evidence for the early history of ice cream, and has also drawn attention to some of the paradoxical features of this history. One such is that the English, although they were consistently influenced by the French in adopting iced desserts and the techniques for making them, stubbornly kept to their preference for ice cream over the water ices which were more in vogue on the Continent. Another is that, while they preferred ice creams, the English had remarkably few recipes for them. Mrs Eales was a pioneer with few followers; ice cream recipes remained something of a rarity in English-language cookery books (except for two which were translations from the French) until the end of the 18th century. Some authors gave no recipe; while others gave but one (e.g. Hannah GLASSE, in editions of her famous book from 1751 onwards, but with Mrs RAFFALD's recipe of 1769 substituted from 1784). The one notable departure from this pattern was by the little-known Mary Smith (1772), who gave ten recipes for ices, including Brown Bread Ice (which was in fact an ice cream) and Peach Ice Cream (which was really a water ice), thus illustrating the imprecision with which these terms were then used.

As for America, Stallings observes that:

ice cream is recorded to have been served as early as 1744 (by the lady of Governor Blandon of Maryland, née Barbara Jannsen, daughter of Sir Theodore Jannsen, Bart and sister-in-law to Lord Baltimore), but it does not appear to have been generally adopted until much later in the century. Although its adoption then owed much to French contacts in the period following the American Revolution, Americans shared 18th century England's tastes and the English preference for ice creams over water ices, and proceeded enthusiastically to make ice cream a national dish. In 1900, an Englishman, Charles Senn, would write: 'Ices derive their present great popularity from America, where they are consumed during the summer months as well as the winter months in enormous quantities. The enormous quantities of which he wrote were of ice cream.

This phenomenon has had a curious side effect in Britain and on the Continent. In our own century the term ice cream came to mean, for many people on both sides of the Atlantic, a dish of American origin; to such a point as to reinforce the failure of antique dealers, and even of some museums, to identify their ice cream moulds for what they are.

This 'phenomenon' constitutes perhaps the greatest paradox of all in the history of ice cream in the English-speaking world. However, ice cream has acquired its own histories in many other regions, quite enough to fill a book but here exemplified by just a few paragraphs.

In the Indian subcontinent, where the art of MILK REDUCTION has been highly developed, ice cream is called *kulfi* and is made with *khoya*, i.e. greatly reduced milk. It is traditionally made in cone-shaped receptacles, to which Achaya (1994) refers in citing a 16th-century document about the preparation of ice cream in Emperor Akbar's royal kitchens (with pistachio nuts and saffron). The same author suggests that the Moghuls had been responsible for introducing this frozen dessert to India, possibly bringing it from Kabul in Afghanistan, a country famous for being a crossroads between East and West. (This is perhaps the place to mention the theory that early iced dairy products developed in China before AD 1000 could have travelled westwards, although not by the hand of Marco Polo, who is associated with so much CULINARY MYTHOLOGY. The matter is discussed by Caroline Liddell and Robin Weir (1993), but without reaching any dogmatic conclusions.)

In SE Asia, the prize for interesting ice creams must be awarded to the Philippines. Ice cream must have arrived there from Spain, because the old-fashioned ice cream (*helado*) was made in a grinder called *garapinera*, with rock salt and ice packed round a central container of milk etc. In modern times American-style ice creams have been dominant, but often with 'native' flavours such as *ube* (purple YAM) and *macapuno* (see COCONUT), but also corn (MAIZE) and cheese—all these being sold by vendors from exceptionally colourful carts.

In the Near and Middle East there are a number of outstanding ice creams. In Iran an ice cream flavoured with SALEP, sprinkled with pistachios, and laced with rosewater is particularly popular although commercial production does not date back further than the 1950s. This may well have come from Turkey, where *salepli dondurma* (salep ice cream sometimes with MASTIC added) is a traditional delicacy. Salep and mastic turn up again in *booza ala haleeb*, the 'milk ice cream' of Lebanon, where another remarkable ice cream is made with apricot 'leather' (see APRICOT).

It might be thought that in the cold climate of N. Europe there would be less enthusiasm for ice cream, especially in the winter. However, the history of ice cream in Russia belies this idea. Lesley Chamberlain (1983) writes that:

Ice cream has been immensely popular in Russia since it was introduced in the eighteenth century as a delicacy for the aristocracy. By the end of the nineteenth century it was possible to buy as a piece of standard household equipment a morozhenitsa, consisting of a deep metal receptacle fitted inside a bucket filled with ice and salt. The receptacle contained the ice cream mixture and was fitted with a lid and a long stirring tool which dislodged mixture as it froze at the sides. But it probably remained something of a treat until in an immensely popular move in the 1920s Anastas Mikoyan set up the first Soviet Russian ice cream factory. That industry never looked back. Ice cream parlours are as popular in Russian cities as they are in the Mediterranean, and the product sold is of a purity and creaminess that constantly astounds Western visitors.

A world tour of ice creams could be continued indefinitely, but would probably lead always to the same conclusion, that Italy is the top country for this product. Certainly, the prevalence of ice cream parlours and vendors with Italian names, worldwide, is remarkable. However, a distinction must be drawn between the excellence of ice cream at good establishments in Italy and the quality of products sold with the benefit of Italian names outside of Italy. The latter may be good, but has often been greatly inferior.

The 'hokey pokey' which Italians sold to children in Glasgow (for example) at the turn of the century sounds fun and poses interesting etymological questions but, to judge by some contemporary descriptions, was of lamentable quality.

ICE CREAM CONES

Mariani (1994) writes as follows about the origins of the ice cream cone:

The ice cream cone is equally as confusing as to its origins. It seems clear that the cone (a wafer rolled to hold a scoop of ice cream) became popular at the 1904 St. Louis World's Fair, but there are several claims as to just who started hawking it there. Some authorities credit a Syrian immigrant named Ernest A. Hamwi with the invention, which was actually a Persian pastry, zalabia, that Hamwi rolled to hold ice cream when another concessionaire ran out of ice cream dishes.

For 'zalabia' see JALEBI, which may have been involved in the impromptu invention, as suggested. However, it seems simplest to suppose that the cone was derived from the European traditions described under WAFER. As for the immediate origin of the cones, Mariani cites Dickson (1972), whose view is that 'the most creditable claim is that of Italo Marchiony, an Italian immigrant who once offered documentary evidence that he took a patent on an ice cream cone as of December 13, 1904, but had made them since 1896'. Whether or not this is so, it remains true that the cones made their effective debut at the St Louis Fair of 1904. However, Caroline Liddell and Robin Weir (1993), in a full treatment of the subject including an illustration of the Marchiony patent and of the cornets featured in Mrs Marshall's book *Fancy Ices* (1894), suggest that the latter has a good claim, although her cornets were apparently to be eaten with a spoon and fork rather than out of hand.

See also BOMBE; CASSATA; PARFAIT; and the two immediately following entries.

ICE CREAM SODA 'made with milk, a flavored syrup, and a scoop of ice cream', is recorded by Mariani (1994) as making its first appearance at Philadelphia in 1874. Its importance became such that it was responsible for the name 'ice cream soda fountain', applied to an establishment where the whole range of ice creams and derived preparations could be had.

Mariani remarks that the small town soda fountain survived the Depression years better than the more opulent pharmacy fountains, and that in the 1940s 'Hollywood movies pictured ice cream soda fountains as oases of innocent Americana'. They were then trysting places of choice for teenagers. Decades later, such fountains are rare, except as nostalgic re-creations, but ice cream sodas remain standard items for Americans to order as refreshments.

ICE CREAM SUNDAE a dish which celebrated its centenary in 1981. Hachten (1981), recapitulating previous studies of the origin of the dish and the term, attributes the former to Ed Berners, 'owner of a modest ice cream parlor in Two Rivers [Michigan]', and a customer called George Hallauer. One day in 1881, Hallauer invited Berners to pour some chocolate syrup, which was on hand for making sodas, over his ice cream. Berners demurred, then assented. 'Chocolate-topped ice cream became the rage at Berners' store, and Berners began experimenting with other flavors. His delicious concoctions carried fanciful names like Flora Dora, Mudscow, and Chocolate Peany, which contained peanuts. A generous slurp of apple cider was also a popular topping.'

However, the new genre had still to acquire its name. This was achieved in nearby Manitowoc, where another ice cream parlour, owned by George Giffy, began to serve the embellished ice creams on Sundays. 'But one weekday, a little girl ordered a dish of ice cream "with stuff on it". When told he only served it on Sunday, the child is supposed to have said: "Why, then, this must be Sunday, for it's the kind of ice cream I want." Giffy gave it to her, of course, and henceforth called the dish a Sunday.'

The transition to sundae remains a mystery, but a minor one. Settlement of the major question was given concrete form when the State Historical Society of Wisconsin erected a marker at Two Rivers in 1973, recognizing it as the birthplace of the ice cream sundae.

The original ice cream sundae glass was canoe shaped, set on a pedestal. Glassware manufacturers are thought to have done much to spread the sundae in their enthusiasm for selling this new item. It is now usual to serve a sundae in a tall glass.

ICELAND a country which consists largely of lava fields and glaciers, and which has a long dark winter because of its northerly position, is not a great place for agricultural produce. However, the LAMB and dairy products are excellent. It is tempting to think that the latter may have been influenced by the Irish monks who migrated to Iceland in early medieval times, coming from a land already very rich in milk and everything that comes from it. One thing which the monks would not have brought with them is SKYR, which Icelanders perceive as unique to themselves (although pedants might point to products elsewhere, e.g. India, which appear to be the same).

In Iceland, as in other countries of the far north, the art of preserving food for the winter has had great importance. Icelanders had a special month known as the 'month of sour things' which came in the middle of the winter and was a time when people met in special gatherings to feast on preserved foods. Some methods of preservation were quite strange. The flesh of the huge Greenland SHARK, *Somniosus microcephalus*, could not be eaten in the normal way because it contained cyanic acid, but if it was buried and allowed to ferment, the acid was leached out and the flesh became safe to eat, although very smelly. It is perhaps not surprising that *hákarl*, as the product is known, is sold in fairly small pieces. These are shaped like a side of bacon, with the crinkled black skin looking like a fragment from one of Iceland's lava beds. Other fish, e.g. HALIBUT, are dried and eaten raw, with a little butter. However, the truly great story about dried fish involves a controversy about dried CODS' heads, which surpasses in interest and entertainment any similar debate anywhere else in the world. In 1914 a banker called Gunnarsson boldly attacked this cherished tradition as being uneconomical if the full true cost of drying one head was considered. The whole nation was shocked but 11 years passed before the Director of the National Library, Guðmundur Finnbogason, was ready to deliver the massive and crushing response which he had prepared, deploying mathematical, social, political, moral, linguistic, historical, and hygienic arguments.

Although little has been written in other languages about food in Iceland, there is an interesting literature in Icelandic. One which was published in 1800, the title of which in translation is *A Simple Cookery Notebook for Gentlewomen*, appeared to have a female author but was in fact written by her brother-in-law, Magnus Stephensen. He was a judge, and seems to have written the book while stormbound in Norway; but he thought it unsuitable for a cookery book to be presented as the work of a man. However, the greatest Icelandic cookery writer, Helga Sigurðardóttir, was a real woman writer and one in whom a romantic and classical beauty was united with unremitting industry. Her score of books constitute the best source material on traditional Icelandic cookery and its development from the 1920s to the 1950s.

ICEPLANT *Mesembryanthemum crystallinum*, one of the better-known edible members of a group of succulent plants, with fleshy leaves, from the tropical regions of the southern hemisphere. The leaves of the iceplant are covered with silvery spots

resembling frost, and have a pleasantly acid flavour. The plant was introduced to Europe and N. America in the 18th century as a substitute for SPINACH, capable of resisting very hot weather. It was not successful in that role, but flowering garden species of *Mesembryanthemum* remain popular.

In the same family, which bears the long name Mesembryanthemaceae, are *Carpobrotus* spp, including the Hottentot fig of S. Africa, *C. edulis*, which owes its common name to the resemblance between its fruits and figs. Several close relations occur in Australia, where they are generally known as 'pigfaces' (nothing to do with pigs or faces, it seems, but possibly a corruption of the Afrikaans name *big-vys*). Aborigines harvested the fruits of these. Low (1989) says that 'The juicy pulp, sucked from the base of the fruit, tastes delightfully like salty strawberries' and quotes a 19th-century clergyman on them:

The size of the fruit, is rather less than that of a walnut, and it has a thick skin of a pale reddish colour, by compressing which, the glutinous sweet substance inside slips into the mouth. When it is in season, which is from January to the end of summer, a comparatively glorious life begins for the Aborigines; hunger can never assail them as, this fruit is abundant all over the grassy part of the country, and they never tire of it; the men gather only as much as they want to eat at the time, but the women bring great quantities of it home to the camp, to be eaten at night.

ICING is the sugar-rich coating used to embellish cakes, buns, and pastries. The fondness of the British for this substance is illustrated by the fact that confectioner's sugar, a fine white powder, is known as icing SUGAR in Britain.

The simplest mixture for the purpose is a syrup or glaze of sugar and water, or sugar and milk, boiled and then brushed over the tops of yeast-raised goods whilst they are still warm. It dries to an attractive shine.

Simple water icing is a paste made from water and powdered sugar. It is mostly used for the plainer and more homely cakes such as VICTORIA SANDWICH CAKES. A more complicated variation is glacé icing, which requires the icing sugar to be added to a boiled sugar syrup and beaten. The result is very glossy. These types of icing are often coloured and flavoured with orange, lemon, coffee, or chocolate.

Cakes topped with water or glacé icing are often cut in half and sandwiched with butter icing (sometimes called buttercream) made from one part butter to two parts icing sugar creamed together, with any desired flavouring, to a fluffy consistency.

Cakes covered with these relatively simple icings are often further decorated with the addition of glacé cherries, ANGELICA, silver DRAGÉES, HUNDREDS AND THOUSANDS, etc.

FONDANT icing is literally fondant warmed with a little syrup, flavoured, and coloured. It is used principally for small fancy cakes, and is poured over to cover them entirely, setting to a soft, satiny sheen. Transparent icing is prepared from a boiled sugar syrup, mixed with liqueurs or fruit juices, and stirred to make it grain.

Sugar paste, home made or bought, is sometimes erroneously called fondant icing. It is prized by amateur and craft confectioners for the way in which it can be moulded and shaped. Since the 1970s it has become popular for decorating large celebration cakes made from sponge mixtures, or rich FRUIT CAKES. The icing can be rolled into a sheet to cover the cake, and coloured and modelled to make flowers, figures, and other ornaments.

Royal icing, the traditional covering for Christmas and wedding cakes in Britain, is made from icing sugar beaten with egg whites and a little lemon juice or ORANGE FLOWER WATER, to give a stiff, opaque white mixture. In the hands of a skilled confectioner, this can be used to produce perfectly flat, smooth surfaces, or piped into intricate borders, patterns, and trellis work, which are fragile but very hard when set. The confectioner may exhibit further skill by making 'runouts', flat shapes of icing which are allowed to dry and then mounted onto the cake as collars, plaques, or free-standing ornaments.

This icing is usually left white, although sometimes a colour appropriate to a specific event, such as a warm yellow tint for a golden wedding, may be used. It may also be silvered or gilded. It is always applied over a layer of MARZIPAN or almond paste. This is a pleasure to eat, but also serves to provide a smooth surface to work on. The combination acts as a seal; a cake covered in royal icing will keep in good condition for several months.

Davidson, in Henisch (1984), surveys the evolution of icing in England in the 18th and 19th centuries and identifies Mrs RAFFALD (1769) as the first author to provide for the combination of cake, marzipan, and royal icing. Her cake was a 'bride cake', which had also been known as a 'great cake' and only acquired the name 'wedding cake' in the 19th century.

However, until the late 19th century, icing was reserved for special cakes. An 18th-century icing was usually made by beating the ingredients together in a mortar, spreading the mixture over the cake, and drying it in a low heat. Mrs Glasse (1747) wrote: 'with a Brush or Bundle of Feathers, spread it all over the cake, and put it in the oven to dry; but take Care the Oven does not discolour it.'

In N. America the term 'frosting' has a slightly longer history than 'icing', but the two terms became interchangeable and 'icing' has now become the preferred usage.

LM

IDLI a speciality of S. India: these are small, round breakfast cakes/dumplings, greyish-white in colour, made from a dough of ground rice and URD dal and then fermented overnight. Idli are steamed in a special pan which has several smoothly rounded indentations. They are often eaten with coconut chutney or sometimes dipped into a spicy mixture called *milagain podi* which consists of coarsely ground toasted spices and DAL.

Idli may be flavoured with garlic, other flavourings such as COCONUT, or spices.

A sweet idli is made with urd dal, SEMOLINA, and jaggery (see SUGAR). Idli may also have a sweet stuffing—sugar, coconut, cashew nuts, almonds, raisins and so on, with flavourings such as cardamom and nutmeg.

HS

IGUANA any of several species of LIZARD. The arboreal lizard of C. and S. America, *Iguana iguana*, is the archetype but other members of the New World family Iguanidae bear the name. (The name is also applied to the Nile monitor, *Varanus nilotica*, a large aquatic lizard of Africa which is mentioned under MONITOR.)

Sophie Coe (1994) describes the importance of iguanas (both the green iguana, *Iguana iguana*, and the black iguana, *Ctenosaurus pectinata*) for the Maya people (see MAYA FOOD) and for the Spanish conquerors who took over C. America. The Maya had relatively little animal food available, so appreciated this resource. As for the Spaniards, they were delighted to find that these creatures could be designated as fish (given the fact that the green iguana spends much time in or around the water, although the generally preferred black iguana is much more terrestrial in habit); and that bishops of the Roman Catholic Church were prepared to endorse this and permit the eating of iguanas during Lent and on Fridays. Coe comments that these reptiles could be captured 'and kept for long periods of time without feeding, a convenient way to have a supply of fresh meat on hand. They also produce delicious eggs, leathery-shelled oblong capsules consisting entirely of yolk.' These eggs are about the size of table tennis balls.

Dr Nègre (1970), whose book about food in the French W. Indies deserves wider recognition as a classic, derives the name iguana from the Arawak word 'Ioana'. He has what is probably the most eloquent passage anywhere about eating iguana:

[Iguanas] feed themselves only on young vegetal shoots (that is why they regularly spoil the unfrequent attempts at farming made by the inhabitants from 'Saintes') and on hibiscus flowers: no edible animal can boast of such a delicate food; man himself, if compared to this animal, eats filthy food, comparatively speaking.

I used to enjoy such animals when I was in Guiana, where people regularly and rightfully eat them; even in France, in Paris, I have been told that a 'Banquet de l'Iguane' (an iguana feast) takes place every year; and there, some gourmets, whose palates are thoroughly educated, and who do not worry about stupid prejudices, taste these delicious reptiles recommended by the Larousse dictionary.

But in the 'Saintes', in Guadeloupe and in Martinique, where people easily swallow some piglets that paddle all their life among the dirtiest, muddy places of the island, and where people really enjoy eating ducks that have been unceasingly floundering in stagnant pools or in noxious ponds, where people also taste those chickens that feed themselves on 'ravets' (that is to say enormous cockroaches), there is nevertheless an aversion to iguana and people pretend to be deeply offended when you speak of saddle of iguana prepared with a 'chasseur' sauce.

Nègre goes on to cite early 17th-century writers, one of whom wrote that the iguana's flesh had the same whiteness, tenderness, exquisite taste, and delicacy as that of chicken, a comparison which others have often made. Thus Sir Osbert Sitwell, writing in *Wine and Food*, declared iguana to be '*very* good' (his italics). He admitted that 'it presents at first sight a somewhat case-hardened exterior, and that its saurian countenance bears an unpleasing expression, both sarcastic and ferocious'. But he declared that 'The saddle is white and tender as the best capon, and the eggs, too, are a suitable, and even delicious, concomitant.'

In S. Africa the French term *l'iguane* has been corrupted to *leguan*, under which name iguanas were formerly sold to Chinese customers. Recording how the Chinese roasted them (cutting the white flesh into thick strips, using spices and soy sauce), Leipoldt (1976) described the meat thus cooked as excellent, 'rather like chicken meat though of a more robust quality'.

ILAMA the principal Mexican name (derived, via Spanish, from the native Mexican name *illamatzapotl*, which translates as 'old woman's sapote') for the fruit of the tree *Annona diversifolia*. This is native to Mexico but found elsewhere in Latin America, in regions of low elevation. It resembles the CHERIMOYA, but the fruits are, according to some, even better.

The elongated fruits may be 15 cm (6") long and weigh close to a kilo (just over 2 lb). The skin is commonly rough, but sometimes smooth; the colour may be anything from green to pink, with a white bloom. The flavour of the pink varieties has a pleasant acidity like that of the cherimoya, while that of the green varieties is sweeter and closer to the SUGAR-APPLE.

The ilama, despite its excellence, had not been identified as a separate species, or introduced to other parts of the world, until the 20th century.

The name ilama is also applied, in Mexico, to a related C. American fruit, *A. purpurea*, generally known as the **soncoya** or *cabeza de negro*. This is common in the region, and is cultivated, at least on a small scale, as an alternative to the cherimoya. It is about the same size as the ilama, grey-brown in colour, with hard protuberances on the skin. The orange flesh within tastes something like that of the PAPAW or MANGO.

ILLIPE NUT a name of Tamil origin, is a commercial term for the oily seeds of a diverse collection of E. Indian and SE Asian trees. These trees belong to several genera and an indeterminate number of species; so the name is a vague one and the quality of the 'illipe butter' produced from the seeds varies.

However, *Madhuca* is certainly the most important genus. *M. indica*, a N. Indian tree, is the well-known mahua tree of Bengal, sometimes called 'Indian butter tree'. *M. longifolia* is its counterpart in S. India and Sri Lanka, and the two species are used in similar ways.

Illipe butter can be used to adulterate GHEE and COCONUT oil, both of which it resembles in texture, being liquid at tropical temperatures and solid in temperate conditions. Some illipe butter, which may also be called 'mowra butter' (a corruption of mahua—see above), is exported to western countries. The better grades of this have sometimes been used in MARGARINE or as a substitute for cocoa butter (see CHOCOLATE IN THE 19TH AND 20TH CENTURIES).

In their lands of origin, these fats or oils are often used as cooking fats. In Malaysia and Indonesia the name *tengkawang*, or other names ending in -*kawang*, are used for the product.

The genus *Madhuca* belongs to the same family (Sapotaceae) as the SAPODILLA, and some species have edible, although poor, fruits. In India, their flowers (to be exact, the tubelike corollae) are more highly valued for food. These are dried, and may then be eaten raw as sweetmeats, or boiled with acid leaves, or turned into a sort of sugar. Keeping qualities are good. Watt (1889–96) quoted a former magistrate of Monghyr as saying: 'Before leaving India, I had a ton [of the flowers] shovelled into sacks and put on board a vessel in Calcutta. They were gathered in April 1876, and, after being kept

for nearly two years, are as good as when first dried.' How the magistrate consumed his ton in England is not stated.

IMBU (or umbu), the fruit of the tree *Spondias tuberosa*, which grows wild in NE Brazil and is occasionally cultivated. It is described by Popenoe (1932) as the best of the genus (other members of which are the AMBARELLA and the MOMBIN).

Some trees are so productive that the fruit, when allowed to fall, forms a carpet of yellow upon the ground. In general appearance the imbu may be likened to a Green Gage plum. It is oval, about 1½ inches in length, and greenish yellow in colour. The skin is thicker than that of a plum, and quite tough. The flavor of the soft, melting, almost liquid flesh is suggestive of a sweet orange. If eaten before it is fully ripe, the fruit is slightly acid. . . . In its native home the imbu is eaten as a fresh fruit, and also furnishes a popular jelly. It is used besides to make *imbuzada*, a famous dessert of northern Brazil. This is prepared by adding the juice of the fruit to boiled sweet milk. The mixture is greenish white in color and when sweetened to taste is relished by nearly every one.

INCA FOOD The Inca, inhabiting much of what is now PERU, had only recently established their empire when the Spaniards arrived in force in the 1530s and toppled them. In this respect and in their more southerly location they were different from the ancient Maya and the Aztecs, with whom it is natural to compare them (see AZTEC FOOD and MAYA FOOD). Among other differences, one of the most important was that, whereas the Aztecs had no large domesticated mammals, the Inca had two; the LLAMA and the alpaca; and they also had available for food the vicuña and the guanaco (relations of the llama), various deer, and the domesticated GUINEA PIG.

The geographical setting provided a further and fundamental contrast. The Andes as a whole are a tangled skein of mountain ranges, but in the north of C. Peru, the stronghold of the Inca, there are only two: the Black Cordillera overlooking the Pacific and the White Cordillera further inland (with slopes running down eastwards to the Amazon). A high plain lies between parts of them. This remarkable region provided an enormous number of ecological niches. Given that for every 1,000 feet one ascends the temperature drops three or four degrees Fahrenheit, and adding to this all the possible differences in soils, sunny slopes or shady ones, good or poor drainage of water and frost, and protection or exposure to damaging winds and hail, the number of available micro-climates is astronomical. It makes plausible the claim that it is here that the largest array of domesticated plants has

been developed; and the Inca were well ahead in this process.

Their main food plant was MAIZE, but QUINOA was a close runner up. The POTATO, whose homeland this is, was also of great importance and, with its related tubers OCA and ULLUCO, provided crops which being underground were protected from the frost, hail, and storms typical of the mountain climate.

Greens were also available in wide variety. Indeed, one early Spanish observer said:

It is difficult to list all the greens, because there are so many of them and they are so small. It is enough to say that the Indians eat all of them, the sweet and the bitter alike. Some of them are eaten raw, as we eat lettuces and radishes, some of them cooked in soups and stews.

The same observer noticed that the Inca ate 'even the algae and water worms'. He could have added that they also consumed mayfly LARVAE, CATERPILLARS, beetles, and ANTS.

The Inca were sophisticated in techniques for preserving food, and had a remarkable system of warehouses and a complex organization for distribution from them. Plenty of SALT was available in Peru, both from the sea and from salt springs in the highlands. It was certainly a highly valued condiment, because one of the simpler stages of fasting consisted in eating without salt or CHILLI. However, there is some doubt about the extent to which salt was used for preservation. Salt fish was certainly known, but drying, and especially freeze-drying, may have been the preferred technique for preservation. What does seem clear, at least according to Cobo (a Jesuit missionary in Peru between 1609 and 1629), is that the Inca had a strange way of dealing with salt as a condiment. Each person would have a lump of salt to hand and would lick this in the course of eating; and if there was only one lump available they would pass it around, taking turns to lick it. They would also use a dissolved mixture of salt and a special clay (*pasa*, 'white with a few brown spots like soap') as a sauce for their root foods, 'moistening them in this mud as if it were mustard'.

Maize was the main staple, but NIXTAMALIZATION was unknown. Some maize was taken in a mildly alcoholic beverage called *chicha*, some was boiled, and some toasted, and maize products often went into stews. Maize and meat were the food of the gods.

In an Inca kitchen, the maize was ground by putting it on a flat stone slab and then rocking another stone shaped like a half-moon over it. A mortar and pestle took care of grinding lesser quantities of smaller things. Every house had a tiny clay stove with a little opening for stoking the fire and two or three holes where the pots could be put to heat.

According to one source (Bartolomé de las Casas—Dominican priest, later Bishop of Chiapas—defender of the Indians against the excesses of the Spanish conquistadores and settlers), the 9th Inca was responsible for a novel eating custom, whereby a plaza (with a large house beside it which could be used if it rained) was where everybody should eat, including himself:

After a brief time for chatting, and as the usual meal hour approached, the wives of all who were there came with their food in their little jars, already cooked, and a little container of wine on their backs, and if the lord was there they began with serving him, and then they served the rest. Each one was served and given to eat by his wife, and the lord the same, even if he was the Inca himself, who was served by the queen, his principal wife, with the first dishes and the first drinks, the rest of the serving was done by the male and female servants. Each woman sat back to back with her husband, she served him all the rest, and then starting with the first dish she ate of what she had brought in a separate place, being, as I have said, back to back.

(SC)

Reading: Sophie Coe (1994).

INCA WHEAT or quihuicha, *Amaranthus caudatus*, a species of the large group of AMARANTH plants and one of the most notable of those which have been used to provide grain food. It was food for the Inca in ancient times, lapsed into oblivion after the Spanish Conquest, and is now experiencing a revival.

Inca wheat and its relations are not true cereals, a term which applies only to the cultivated grasses of the family Graminaceae; but, like other plants whose fruits and seeds can be ground into flour with uses like those of the cereals, they are accorded the status of 'para-cereal'.

The characteristics of amaranths grown as grain crops are that they grow fast and produce high-protein grains in large, sorghum-like, seed heads. The protein includes lysine, usually deficient in plant protein. The grains (seeds) are contained in lidded capsules, one seed to one capsule, and arranged in dense spikes.

An excellent description is given by the authors of *Lost Crops of the Incas* (National Research Council 1989).

A staple grain of the Incas, Aztecs, and other pre-Columbian peoples, amaranth was once almost as widely dispersed throughout the Americas as corn. The most important Andean species is *Amaranthus caudatus*. In Quechua, the ancient Inca language that is still spoken in the Andes, it is called 'kiwicha'.

Kiwicha is one of the prettiest crops on earth; the beautiful colors of its broad leaves, stems, and flowers—purple, red, gold—create fiery fields that blaze across the mountainsides. The plant grows vigorously, tolerates drought, heat, and pests, and adapts readily to new environments, including some that are inhospitable to conventional grain crops. Nonetheless, it is little known outside the highland regions of Ecuador, Peru, Bolivia, and northwestern Argentina.

Kiwicha's grains are scarcely bigger than poppy seeds. However, they occur in huge numbers—sometimes more than 100,000 to a plant. Like other amaranth grains, they are flavorful and, when heated, they pop to produce a crunchy white product that tastes like a nutty popcorn. Light and crisp, it is delicious as a snack, as a cold cereal with milk and honey, as a 'breading' on chicken or fish, or in sweets with a whisper of honey. The grain is also ground into flour, rolled into flakes, puffed, or boiled for porridge.

These seeds are one of the most nutritious foods grown. Not only are they richer in protein than the major cereals, but the amino acid balance of their protein comes closer to nutritional perfection for the human diet than that in normal cereal grains.

Another amaranth, *A. hypochondriacus*, has been a staple grain food in Mexico since about 4000 BC. The Aztec emperors exacted an annual tribute of this grain from their subjects. The Spanish Church sought to eradicate amaranth cultivation because of the pagan Aztec ceremonies centred on it; and it anyway tended to be displaced by grains with larger seeds, such as MAIZE.

INDIA one of the largest and most populous countries in the world, has a great diversity of cuisines. Madhur Jaffrey (1985) put a dramatic spotlight on this diversity when she pointed out that India is larger than the whole of Europe (excepting Russia), that it embraces at least five major faiths, 15 major languages, and over 1,500 minor languages and dialects; and that the 17 states which were created within the country after it achieved independence were based on existing linguistic and cultural regions. What this means, she points out, is that the foods in these 17 states differ from each other as much as the foods in the various countries of Europe. The simple facts of geography are of course responsible for many differences; India has a wide range of climates, from the snowy Himalayas to the coconut palms of the tropical south, and the indigenous foods in the regions vary accordingly.

'India' used to refer to the whole subcontinent, whereas now it refers to the country called India, occupying most, but by no means all, of the subcontinent. The most important early centres of agriculture and civilization generally were in the Indus Valley, now mainly in Pakistan. This does not mean that what happened in that valley many millennia ago cannot be regarded as ancestral to current Indian foodways. It can.

But the ambiguity in the term 'India' has to be kept in mind when considering food history, among many other subjects.

Indian civilizations, like those of the Middle East and China, extend very far back in time. Thanks largely to Achaya (1994), who has brought together evidence from archaeology, etymology, ancient religious texts, and other literary sources, the study of Indian food history in the context of these successive civilizations, and also in relatively modern times, has recently become more rewarding.

The Harappan civilization flourished in the general area of the Indus Valley from about 3200 BC for 1,000 years or a little more. WHEAT and BARLEY were its staples and much archaeological evidence has recently come to light about the many other foods which were then in common use, the huge granaries built for storage, the ovens, and various cooking utensils. At a site in Rajasthan, dated to before 2800 BC, excavations have disclosed a ploughed and abandoned field, described by Achaya as being certainly 'the earliest ploughed field to have been found anywhere in the world'.

The next phase involved the arrival from C. Asia of the Aryans and associated groups. Whereas the Harappan civilization had been largely urban, that of the Aryans was predominantly agricultural and pastoral; and it was the Aryans who were the main inspiration behind the formation of the Vedic culture (centred on the Vedas, religious texts of which the earliest example was the Rig-veda, written in old Sanskrit). The various Vedas yield a lot of information about foods, and study of the Sanskrit and other languages, both earlier and contemporary, yields more; for example the occurrence in Sanskrit of names which clearly come from the 'aboriginal' (Munda) language, such as *vatingana* (aubergine), indicates items which were already well established in pre-Aryan times. Sanskrit also, in due course, marked foods of Chinese origin by giving them the prefix *chini*; thus *chinani*, peach.

There are thus many windows through which glimpses may be had of food in ancient India. In more recent times, the historical record is writ large, especially for the legacies of successive intrusions by other cultures. It was mainly in the north that these intrusions occurred, as natural barriers and great distances impeded migration to the south. For the most important culinary immigration of all, see MOGHUL CUISINE. There is also the Portuguese influence (see GOA) to be taken into account, and the emergence of ANGLO-INDIAN COOKERY in the period of British rule, often referred to as the Raj. The British influence made its impact throughout the country, although more so in some regions than in others.

The effect of these intrusions was to increase considerably the diversity, referred to above, of foods and foodways within India (and its neighbours—see BANGLADESH; NEPAL; PAKISTAN; SRI LANKA).

However, there are **common factors** and ways of thinking which give a measure of underlying unity to Indian foodways. The main component of the meal is CEREAL, with savoury dishes added as accompaniments and to provide flavour. LENTILS and PULSES generally, and vegetables, will always be important. Spices—especially GINGER and GARLIC, but including many others—are used everywhere with great discrimination and care. The general liking for milk products such as GHEE, YOGHURT, and PANIR is a prominent feature.

There is also the **conception of a meal,** which has as its focus the platter (*thali*), with its central pile of rice or bread surrounded by small containers of savoury accompaniments. Those eating help themselves to the various items, mixing them with rice or folding them up in pieces of flat bread. Sweet dishes are an exception. They are usually taken at the end unaccompanied by rice or bread.

Perhaps, however, the most important feature of Indian cookery is the existence of several clearly distinguishable **vegetarian cuisines.** VEGETARIANISM, as a widely prevalent social practice, derives from the doctrine of *ahimsa* or non-violence first propounded in the Upanishads (*c.*9th century BC) and further developed in the Buddhist and Jain religions (see BUDDHISM AND FOOD and JAINS AND FOOD). Jains and a large proportion of Hindus in S. India, Gujarat, and the Hindi-speaking heartland remain vegetarian. See also HINDUISM AND FOOD. However, even in non-vegetarian Kashmir, Punjab, Bengal, Orissa, Assam, and Kerala, *ahimsa* is observed in nutrition. Yamuna Devi (1987) has put together in a single enormous book a remarkably broad and detailed survey of Indian vegetarian dishes.

Although strict in matters of food prohibitions, Hindus take delight in food. Their spirituality and the objections which some have to worldly pursuits have never precluded culinary pleasures. Dandin, a 7th-century author, thus describes a homely meal:

She stirred the gruel in the two dishes, which she set before him on a green plantain leaf . . . He drank it and felt rested and happy. Next she gave him two ladlefuls of the boiled rice, served with a little ghee and condiments. She served the rest of the rice with curds, three spices, and fragrant and refreshing buttermilk and gruel. He enjoyed the meal to the last mouthful. When he asked for a drink, she poured him water in a steady stream from the spout of a new pitcher—it was fragrant with incense, the smell of fresh trumpet-flowers

and the perfume of full-blown lotuses. He put the bowl to his lips, and his eyelashes sparkled with rosy drops as cool as snow; his ears delighted in the sound of trickling water; his rough cheeks thrilled and tingled at its pleasant contact; his nostrils opened wide at its sweet fragrance; and his tongue delighted in its lovely flavour, as he drank the pure water in great gulps.

This charming quotation, used by Hashi and Tapan Raychaudhuri (1981) to illuminate an important essay on food in India, strikes an agreeable and positive note. However, while Hindu enjoyment of food is unquestionable, it is also true that the existence of the **caste system** has imposed handicaps on them in this respect. Shanti Rangarao (1990), in her lively book on food in India, comments:

Orthodox Hindus have been known to starve on a long journey rather than eat unfamiliar food cooked by strangers, or carry food in the 'polluted' railway carriage. Polluted it certainly is for them, when occupied by lower castes and Untouchables. . . . The Brahmin was condemned to eternal damnation if he ate food cooked or touched (even water) by people of other castes. Nor must they even *see* him eating. Foreign travel and crossing the ocean meant complete loss of caste for him, and the life of the excommunicated Brahmin could be made hell even before he got to the next world!

The same author gives as her opinion that caste and religious restrictions have been largely responsible for preventing the emergence of anything like a national Indian diet. She would no doubt agree about the common features shared by most Indian kitchens (see above), but lays more emphasis on the differences which she had herself encountered:

In my own university, the college I went to had a 'hostel' which catered for ten eating 'Sections', each with its own separate kitchen and dining-room labelled:

1. European
2. Non-vegetarian Hindu
3. Non-vegetarian Malayaele-Hindu
4. Tamil-Telugu-Christian
5. Syrian Christian
6. Brahmin
7. Thiyya
8. Nayar
9. Non-Brahmin Vegetarian
10. Cosmopolitan

The second last being for those students who could only eat Brahmin-cooked food but could not eat it with Brahmin students in their dining-room. And all this was for the students of just one part of India!

Apart from such differences in kitchen practice as were brought about by the caste system and other such factors, there were differences across the country which had arisen in a more natural way. For example there is the prevalence of steaming in the south of India, and the absence of it in the north. On the other hand the *dum* technique is widespread in the north but not elsewhere; this is the procedure whereby a partly cooked dish of rice and meat with many aromatic flavourings is put in a lidded pot,

sealed with dough, and left to cook with fire above and below for a long time.

However, so far as the outside world is concerned, the tremendous variety in Indian food, whether brought about by geographical and climatic differences (wheat and breads in the north, use of COCONUT in the south) or arising from religious dietary laws (no pork for Muslims, no onions for Jains) or from the caste system, or other causes, has been obscured to a very large extent by a coincidental factor. Most of the Indians who operate or cook in restaurants, inside or outside India, are from Punjab. (Bangladeshis are active in this business too but they are not 'Indian' in the sense used here.)

Madhur Jaffrey (1985, again) and Camilla Panjabi (1995, in a lecture at Oxford) are among those who have explained the historical background to this Punjabi dominance. The prime factors were the lack of any restaurant tradition in India, and the inhibitions which prevented members of various castes and religious groups from becoming professional cooks. Thus, in the upheavals which followed the division of the subcontinent into India and the two Pakistans in 1947, it was displaced Punjabis (numerous, eager to work, and relatively free of inhibitions) who could most easily become entrepreneurs and operators in the restaurant business. They took on these roles, and it was natural that they should subsequently staff the catering colleges set up to ensure part of the necessary infrastructure for tourism. Moulds were thus established whose influence will necessarily continue far into the 3rd millennium. (The wide popularity of TANDOOR cookery is, incidentally, one of a number of things for which Punjabis have been responsible—the villages of Punjab had communal open-air tandoors where housewives would bring their dough to be rolled into ROTIS and baked by the *tandooriya*.)

If it is true of India, as of some other countries, that the finest food is in homes rather than public places, then few foreign visitors have the opportunity to enjoy authentic Indian dishes at their best. But the authentic ingredients are more and more widely available, so there is an alternative: to recreate the dishes in one's own home, guided by the rapidly growing collection of really good books on the subject, of which a few are listed below.

See also three entries of a general nature: KASHMIR; PARSI FOOD; INDIAN SWEETS. In addition, see AMCHUR; BESAN FLOUR; BIRIANI; CHAPATI; CURRY; DAL; DOSA; GULAB JAMUN; HALEEM; HALVA; IDLI; JALEBI; KACHORI; KHEER; KHICHRI; KOFTA; KORMA; LADIKANEE; LASSI; LUCHI; MASALA; MILK REDUCTION; NAN; PAKORA; PARATA; PAYASAM; PILAF; POORI; POPPADOM;

RASGULLA; SAMBAR; SAMOSA; SEV;
SHRIKHAND; PANCH PHORON; TAMARIND;
TIFFIN; VINDALOO.
READING: Chitrita Banerji (1997); Minakshie Das
Gupta *et al.* (1995); Camellia Panjabi (1994);
Julie Sahni (1980, 1985).

INDIAN ALMOND (or tropical almond), the kernel of the fruit of *Terminalia catappa*, a tree which occurs in both wild and cultivated forms in S. and SE Asia, and has been widely planted in other tropical regions, mainly for ornament and shade. It is tall and handsome and has leaves which turn red in the autumn—unusual for a tropical tree. It is not related to the true ALMOND.

The fruits have a tender skin, beneath which is a thin layer of edible, subacid flesh. The nuts enclosed in this have thick, corky shells, which are difficult to crack; but the slim kernels, white inside a pale brown skin, have a good, delicate flavour and repay the effort of extraction. They are eaten raw or roasted. About half the kernel, by weight, consists of a pale oil similar to true almond oil; and this also has a pleasing flavour.

Besides the names cited above, the nut may be called Bengal, Singapore, or Fijian nut, and sea almond.

For other fruits and nuts of the same genus, which is an extensive one, see MYROBALAN and OKARI NUTS.

INDIAN SWEETS are based on a different tradition from that of European confectioners. Sugar is an important ingredient, but the Indian confectioner, or *halvai*, also uses substantial quantities of cereals, pulses, and milk products in a manner completely alien to European CONFECTIONERY. *Halvais* have produced as many variations on their themes as European confectioners have on boiled sugar sweets. The results run from simple BRITTLE and TOFFEE-type sweets through HALVA, BARFI, and SANDESH, to the family of confections based on RASGULLAS. All these are found all over the subcontinent.

The distinction between 'sweetie' and 'pudding' is less marked than in Europe. The term *mithai*, meaning sweet, has various applications, including approximations to the English categories of puddings and sugar confectionery. Many sweets find a place in the Indian diet as snacks or offerings of hospitality, as well as playing a role in more formal meals.

Regional variations can be seen in the use of certain ingredients; for instance the wheat-growing north of India is rich in recipes for sweet breads and biscuits whilst the use of COCONUT is a distinctive feature of the confectionery of W. and S. India.

Bangladesh (Bengal) is the part of the subcontinent acknowledged to produce the finest sweets, but many other places have their own specialities, such as *pak*, a fudgelike sweet made in the southern city of Mysore by adding toasted gram (see BESAN FLOUR) to a sugar syrup, giving a frothy mixture which has a crumbly texture when set.

Sweetmeats have a special significance in Hindu religion. They are considered as highly suitable offerings for the gods, and desirable spiritual states are described in terms of sweetness or NECTAR.

Mixtures of honey, milk, GHEE, sugar, and water, known as *panchamrita* (literally 'five nectar', i.e. the five foods which make nectar, food of the gods), are used for libations and in purification rituals. Sweets are an important part of the festival of Divali, which is celebrated in November according to the European calendar. This marks the beginning of the Hindu New Year, when sweets are sent to neighbours, friends, relations, and business acquaintances; they are also piled high in temples as religious offerings.

A distinguishing feature of the Indian tradition of confectionery is the use of milk products. *Halvais* reduce fresh milk by boiling to give a creamy substance called *rabadi*, used in Indian ice cream, kulfi. As explained under MILK REDUCTION, *rabadi* is further reduced to a pastelike semi-solid called *khoya*, which is used in barfi and many other sweets. It acts as a base and a binder and provides flavour and sweetness, derived from the slightly caramelized milk sugar, lactose, present in the reduced milk.

Milk is also used as a sweetmeat ingredient, especially for sandesh and rasgullas, in the form of fresh curd cheese (*chhenna*).

Sugar is used as a sweetener, measured by volume, usually in the order of one-quarter of the quantity of base ingredient. Poorer-quality confections use a higher proportion of sugar. Unless the sweetmeat is required to be white, refined sugar will not necessarily be used by the *halvai*. The Indian unrefined sugars, jaggery or gur (see SUGAR), which are brown and aromatic, may be employed to add their own distinctive flavour to barfi and toffee-type sweets. Boiled sugar syrup, important to the texture and appearance of much W. European confectionery, has a relatively minor role in Indian confectionery. It is used for cooking and soaking sweets of the rasgulla family, and plays an important part in making *pak*. Boiled sugar sweets such as *gajjak*, a type of brittle, are made and enjoyed throughout India, especially in winter as they are considered to be warming.

Nuts, particularly almonds and pistachios, add flavour and texture to Indian sweets. Together with edible GOLD OR SILVER LEAF,

they are much used for decoration. Common spices such as cardamoms, nutmegs, cloves, and black pepper are used for flavouring sweets. Rosewater (see ROSES) and SANDALWOOD essence are also used. Less familiar to western palates are *kewra* (see SCREWPINE), and *khus*, obtained from the roots of vetiver (see KHUS KHUS), both used by Bengali *halvais*.

A final distinguishing feature of Indian confectionery is the frequent use of deep-frying: JALEBI, GULAB JAMUN, PANTUA, and the many kinds of little dumpling called *pithe*, a speciality of Bengal, are all deep fried before being soaked in syrup. Alternatively, sweets may be cooked by gently boiling them in sugar syrup.

To the European palate, many Indian confections taste FUDGElike, due to the flavour of ghee or khoya, and the use of flours which give a grainy texture. Included in this category are barfi, sandesh, *mesu* (an aerated gram flour sweet), *vadi, beveca, pera,* and many of the sweets known collectively as LADDU—a word which designates shape rather than recipe. Confections which include a high proportion of chopped nuts such as pistachio barfi represent eastern variations on the ancient theme of sweet nut pastes, known to Europeans as MARZIPAN.

Indian sweets lack the long-keeping qualities of western sugar confectionery. The milk-based ones provide a method of short-term storage for a perishable food in a hot country which has never developed a tradition of hard-cheese making, but the sweets are generally intended to be eaten within a few days of manufacture. They are highly nutritious, and specific items are used as invalid food, or offered to new mothers. The traditions of the *halvai* transplant successfully with Asian migrants, and many of the sweets are now on sale in e.g. British cities.   LM

INDONESIA the fourth most populous nation of the world, covers a vast area of SE Asia. Its people are unevenly distributed among more than 15,000 islands, many of which are too small or too barren to offer a settled living to anyone. The islands vary enormously in size, climate, soil, and population density. Kalimantan (Indonesian Borneo) is roughly the size of France, and has about as many inhabitants as Paris. Sumatra is comparable in size with Spain or Queensland. Sulawesi (Celebes) is rather less than half as big, Java scarcely as large as England—yet Java supports over 80 million people, nearly half the total population. Dozens of smaller islands are still big enough to contribute to the country's food resources, and in E. Indonesia a few tiny islands for centuries supplied the Old World with its most treasured SPICES.

A map of Indonesia suggests the outlines of three of earth's major tectonic plates that lie beneath it. These are all subduction zones, where one plate is being gradually drawn under the edge of its neighbour, creating lines of weakness through which the molten rocks and gases of the earth's crust can burst to form volcanoes. A chain of active volcanoes follows the island arc through Sumatra, Java, and Nusatenggara, doubling back in a tight curve through Banda and then swinging north-east through Ternate, Tidore, and Halmahera. A little cluster of volcanoes occupies the NE tip of Sulawesi, but the rest of this island, along with all of Kalimantan and Irian Jaya, is free of volcanic activity (though subject to earthquakes). Although in the short term a volcanic eruption is highly destructive, and although even in the long term not everything that comes out of a volcano is good for the surrounding soil, many areas have been greatly enriched by minerals ejected from these unpredictable objects. The extraordinary fertility of W. Sumatra, SE Bali, or Java—whose population has been able to multiply roughly thirtyfold in the past two centuries—is in part due to volcanic soils. But these areas benefit equally from high rainfall, and a social system geared to the efficient production of staple crops, above all RICE.

Rice was probably brought to the islands at least 2,000 years ago by immigrants from the SE Asian mainland; the oldest surviving evidence of its cultivation is in Kalimantan, but it may have been grown earlier in Java, where intensive farming has long since obliterated all ancient traces of it. Rice has still not been accepted as the most-favoured staple in all the islands; TARO, CASSAVA, and SAGO still hold their own in E. Indonesia and are still popular even in prosperous W. Java. But the government's transmigration policy, moving complete rural communities from Java and Bali to under-populated areas elsewhere, plus official encouragement for rice farmers, mean that rice is likely to become a standardized basic food for almost all Indonesians within the next generation, provided yields can keep up with population growth and erosion of soils suitable for rice-growing can be checked.

The real staple food of Indonesia is FISH: sea fish from the deep water of the Indian Ocean on the south and west or the warmer, shallower water of the S. China Sea; freshwater fish from the lakes, rivers, tanks, and flooded rice fields of inland areas. Indonesians have necessarily always been sailors, traders, and fishermen, and much, or most, of the protein they consume comes from tuna, milkfish, anchovies, squid, shellfish, catfish, carp, gurami, and a great number of other species. When fish could not be eaten fresh, they had to be dried in the sun and/or salted, and fish spread out to dry are still a common sight in Indonesia today. The basic diet of many Indonesians is plain boiled white rice, with a little fish, some *lablab* (raw or plainly cooked vegetables), and a few hot chillies. CHILLI peppers were of course introduced from the New World after the voyages of discovery in the 16th century; they are now so universally popular, not to say addictive, that it is hard to imagine how Indonesians got along without them.

Mere hotness, however, is not all that people demand in their food. Most Indonesian cooking gives evidence of a love of sourness delicately balanced by sweetness. The latter is derived largely from COCONUT milk, which is often used as a cooking medium, or raw sugar. In some areas, notably C. Java, sweetness dominates, but most outsiders will agree that the sour notes offer more subtlety and much greater range. TAMARIND, LEMON GRASS, various fruits, GALINGALE, TURMERIC, bitter cucumber (see BITTER GOURD) are among their sources. The other contrast to sweetness, saltiness, is provided not only by salt itself but by various fermented products, particularly SOY SAUCE, introduced by the Chinese, and a strongly pungent shrimp paste called *terasi* (see BLACANG). *Terasi* may have links with the old Roman GARUM, a somewhat similar product.

What the world at large understands by 'Indonesian food' is principally the food of Java and Sumatra, with the additions of a few well-known dishes from Banjarmasin (S. Kalimantan) and N. Sulawesi and other regions, and one or two dubious classics adapted from Chinese and Dutch models. *Nasi goreng*—fried rice—is perhaps the most widely known, though not the best loved, of all the products of an Indonesian kitchen, especially when it is served with a fried egg on top. The fried egg is Dutch, the fried rice Chinese. Dutch also is the unhallowed custom of serving up a huge range of dishes all at once in a *rijsttafel*. This is based on the lavish feasts that used to be, perhaps still are, communally cooked in a village to celebrate a good harvest. If every dish is well cooked and retains its individuality, the *rijsttafel* may justify its presence at a really big party; but served to two or four people in an average restaurant, with every dish tasting more or less the same and everything kept for hours in a hot cupboard, it is a parody of Indonesian cooking and should be avoided.

The usual family meal, in a reasonably well-off household, consists of rice with one or two meat or fish dishes, some vegetables, and some soup to wash everything down—many people will not drink even water with a meal. Many savoury dishes are variants on a few basic ideas; for example, there are innumerable versions of *sambal goreng* (see SAMBAL), in which a mixture of spices, onions, garlic, and chilli is fried in a little oil and then added to the main ingredient to flavour it while it cooks. There are many stuffings and marinades, and many recipes for meat or fish wrapped in leaves (usually banana leaves) or cooked in some other container to retain juices, food value, and flavour. Such containers include sections of a large bamboo, and the hard sheath of a coconut inflorescence.

Cooking times are often very short, because much time has been spent on preparing and cutting up the food; no one expects to have to cut up meat at table, and knives are hardly ever provided. Many Indonesians still prefer to eat with their fingers (of the right hand only); a whole chicken may be torn in pieces and shredded, but any chopping or carving must be done in the kitchen beforehand. Most dishes are boiled, steamed, fried, grilled, or barbecued over charcoal. In the past, the only way to bake food was to wrap it in leaves and put it for several hours in a trench lined with hot stones. Later, a kind of metal oven was developed, with trays of glowing charcoal slotted in above and below the food. This met the demand for sweet pastries, biscuits, and layer cakes, which were first introduced by the Dutch; but oven-baking did not really catch on until gas and electric ovens became available to middle-class city dwellers.

Dessert is usually fresh fruit. Sweets and cakes are eaten in the afternoon, especially when visitors call. Ninety per cent of the population are Muslim (making this the largest Islamic nation in the world), and the end of RAMADAN, the fasting month, is marked by at least two days of social visiting, when junior family members (or employees) visit senior ones (or bosses) to ask forgiveness of the past year's trespasses, drink sweet black tea, and eat cakes of steamed glutinous rice flour and coconut.

Many regions of Indonesia have a colourful and reasonably well-documented history. For food, however, this history is largely a blank. This is the more surprising when one considers the extraordinary heights of sophistication reached by literature, music, painting, and metalworking in the courts of many rulers, above all those of central Java and Bali in the 18th and 19th centuries. Surely they must have cared for gastronomy as well? Yet there are no records of great feasts (except drinking bouts), no manuscript cookery books such as the Arabs and Chinese compiled so lovingly, no surviving traditions of a court cuisine. Nor is there a tradition of restaurant-going. The 'classic' dishes of Indonesia (for example, RENDANG) are all, as far as we know, of peasant and village origin.

In short, much research into Indonesian foodways remains to be done, and done soon, as food habits are changing swiftly, driven on by economic and industrial development and the rush of people from the countryside to the cities. Some changes are good, others may not be. Most people are far better nourished than in, say, the 1960s; some are even becoming obese, a condition formerly rare. Fast food is inevitably gaining ground over traditional dishes that took hours to prepare. US and Japanese food chains are taking over the custom that formerly belonged to street food stalls. (However, Indonesians have always taken for granted the availability everywhere of ready-cooked cheap food, so this is not really a change of habit, only of customer choice.) Despite Indonesia's success in growing enough rice to feed itself and distributing it fairly, the fashionable trend is to eat less rice and more bread, meat, and dairy products. One of the world's largest flour-milling complexes is located in E. Java. Great quantities of beef are flown in from Australia and the USA to supplement local produce. There appears to be little foundation here in Indonesia for the belief that Asians lack the enzymes needed to digest milk, and milk bars attract crowds of young sophisticates in the big towns. Supermarkets—clean, bright, and with fixed prices—are replacing the sociable confusion and haggling of the local market place. Cookery books and cookery journalism, unknown a generation ago, flourish. Hotel and catering schools have an estimated total of 100,000 students, and a professional chefs' association is doing much to raise the formerly low status of the cook in Indonesian society.

SO

INJERA the staple food or bread of ETHIOPIA which is leavened with YEAST or SOURDOUGH. It can be made of TEF, BARLEY flour, cornflour (see MAIZE), RICE flour, SORGHUM, or WHEAT. It is central to the Ethiopian consciousness. 'Have you eaten *injera* today?' is a standard greeting. 'He has no *wat*' (sauce) on his *injera*' means 'He's desperately poor'.

RH

INK CAP shaggy cap, shaggy mane, and lawyer's wig are all names for *Coprinus comatus*, an edible mushroom common in Britain and generally in temperate zones of the northern and southern hemispheres. The distinctive cap is shaped like a tall bell or (some say, less plausibly) a British judge's wig, and is notably scaly. The whole fungus grows up to 25 or even 30 cm (10–12") tall, singly or in clumps on dung heaps, lawns, bonfire sites, and roadside verges. Its main season is in the autumn, but it appears from early spring onwards.

The ink cap, whose delicate flavour is said to go particularly well with fish, should be gathered when young and white, and while its gills are still white or pale pink. Older specimens turn brown and black, then disintegrate into an inky mass. As one authority puts it: 'gills progressively white, pink, black and auto-digesting'. This progression can be very quick, occupying but half a day at normal temperatures (longer under refrigeration), so gathering and consumption must be accomplished rapidly.

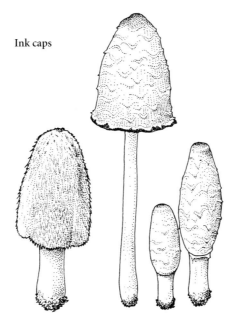

Ink caps

It seems likely that Shelley had an ink cap in mind when he wrote his uncomplimentary description of fungi:

> Their moss rotted off them, flake by flake,
> Till the thick stalk stuck like a murderer's stake
> Where rags of loose flesh yet tremble on high,
> Infecting the winds that wander by.

Warning Any ink cap which is of a greyish colour and is not shaggy is likely to be *Coprinus atramentarius*. This species contains a substance almost identical with the active agent in the drug 'Antabuse', given to alcoholics to make them violently sick if they drink the smallest amount of liquor. It is, however, an excellent mushroom, so good that some people in France are said to be willing to forgo their wine for a day in order to enjoy it.

INSECTS AS FOOD Historically in global terms, eating insects has been the norm for human beings. It is only in the western world, and in recent times, that it has been viewed as a strange or even revolting practice. However, even in the western world, people of almost all

cultures eagerly eat insect secretions: HONEY.

Insects are ubiquitous in the world and exist in enormous numbers. They have been described as the most successful class of living organisms. Of the countless species, it is generally, and for obvious reasons, the larger ones which have been eaten by human beings. See ANTS; CATERPILLARS; CICADAS; COCKCHAFER; CRICKET; GRASSHOPPER; GRUBS; LARVAE; LOCUST; MANNA (in part); SILKWORM; SPIDERS; TERMITES; WASP; WATER BUGS; WITCHETTY GRUBS.

Any consideration of the use of insects as food requires knowledge of the various stages in the lives of insects, most species of which undergo a process of metamorphosis, commonly following the sequence egg > larva > pupa > adult. The consumption of insects as food includes examples of insects in each of these stages.

A larva is an insect in a state of development (displaying little or no similarity to the adult form) lasting from the time of its leaving the egg until its transformation into a pupa, e.g. a grub or a caterpillar. A caterpillar is the larva of a butterfly or moth (or, loosely, of various other insects). A grub is the larva of a beetle, but this term too is used loosely. A pupa is an insect in the intermediate stage between larva and adult; the term chrysalis is used of a butterfly or moth in this intermediate stage.

There are few categories of food of which it can truly be said that a single book provides the basic survey to which all other studies inevitably refer. However, Bodenheimer (1951) fulfils this role for insects. Although his book has done much to spread information about the worldwide consumption of insects, it remains true that this consumption is hardly ever reflected in official statistics. This is partly because a single insect, although it may provide useful protein, fat and carbohydrate, furnishes only trivial amounts; partly because there are no sophisticated marketing arrangements for insects, such as would bring them within the scope of data on imports and exports; and partly, perhaps, because the class of data-compilers hardly overlaps at all with the class of insect-eaters.
READING: D. G. Gordon (1988).

INUIT COOKERY (Inuit being more or less equivalent to the old name Eskimo, and applying to peoples in the northernmost inhabited parts of the earth, e.g. Greenland) is, in its traditional form, subject to the limitations imposed by a very cold climate and a sparse range of fauna and flora. In this respect it is not unlike ANTARCTIC cookery. However, there is a big difference; the indigenous inhabitants of the Arctic regions (e.g. in the southern parts of Greenland, Labrador, Alaska, the Northwest Territories of Canada, Labrador) are relatively numerous whereas the Antarctic, being basically an uninhabitable icecap, has none.

The Inuit diet has attracted much attention because of its high proportion of meat and fat, as well as fish. The Inuit have subsisted mainly on:

- game animals, notably CARIBOU, MOOSE, polar bear;
- sea mammals, especially WHALE and SEALS;
- fish such as live in the Arctic Sea;
- berries of the far north;
- PEMMICAN, incorporating meat and berries.

Various studies of their diet and the extent to which they can thrive on it have suggested that they can manage well. A classic and readable study is that of Stefansson (1946).

IRAN ancient Persia, deserves a geological introduction. In prehistoric times, the land mass that is now Iran forced itself up to divide the oceans, splitting the Caspian Sea off from the Indian Ocean. Since then, it has formed a natural land bridge across these two seas, separating the cold northern plains of Russia from the hot southern deserts of Arabia, and connecting the Middle East with the Far East. The ancient Silk Route from China to Syria went through N. Iran, while the Afro-Arab-Indian trade routes crossed its southern regions. The centrality of its location in the ancient world meant that the Persian Empire, more than 2,500 years ago, extended from Russia in the north to Egypt in the south, and from Greece in the west to India in the east.

At the time of the Persian Empire, the Iranians carried their own produce—particularly SPINACH, POMEGRANATES, SAFFRON, and rosewater (see ROSES)—as well as their culinary skills to the far corners of the known world. At the same time they adopted produce and ideas from their colonies. Iran has also served as a conduit for many other products. LEMONS, ORANGES, AUBERGINES, and RICE were brought from the East (India and China) to Iran and were then carried west first to Greece and Rome; and later, by the Arabs, to N. Africa and S. Europe. During the transit, names were changed and passed on leaving a clear etymological trail. Later still, Iran was the source of much of the produce (rosewater and spinach, for example) and ideas such as endoring (gilding, see KOFTA) and ALMOND milk that the Crusaders brought to western Europe. The most recent influence to be felt in Britain has been the arrival in the 20th century, via India and Pakistan, of much of the vocabulary of Persian food (for example,

BIRIANI, *garam masala*, KEBAB, *murgh*, NAN, PILAF, tikka).

The mountains encircling Iran form a high, arid central plateau that is bitterly cold in winter and searingly hot in summer. Despite the aridity of the soil, it is fertile when watered, and the surrounding high altitudes serve it as both a water tank and an ice box. The Iranians developed a unique system of carrying water in underground channels from the mountains (which receive copious amounts of snow each winter) to the fields and orchards of villages scores of miles away in the central plateau. A simple system of mountainside natural or man-made caves, carefully fed by cool spring water and frozen in winter, resulted in ice being available throughout the summer months from ancient times.

The regions outside the mountain fringe as well as the mountain valleys to the north and west of the country are naturally fertile and productive, and it is here that viticulture has flourished for thousands of years. The Caspian littoral to the north has a temperate climate, warm and humid. There are also fertile oases in the southern regions where date trees and sweet oranges abound.

Thus the climate range, from the warm Persian Gulf to the high snowy mountains, is huge and results in a long growing season of great divergence. Fruits include the indigenous melons, grapes, MULBERRIES, peaches, apricots, nectarines, and POMEGRANATES, as well as MEDLARS, PERSIMMONS, oranges, melons, and sweet lemons.

As for **fish**, the Caspian provides marine fish which are suited to its relatively cold waters (from small SPRATS and HERRING up to the spectacular beluga STURGEON), while the warm waters of the Persian Gulf nurture SWORDFISH, TUNA, and SHRIMP. Fresh fish is mainly eaten on these coasts. Dried and salted fish is traditional for inhabitants of the central plateau, although the introduction of refrigeration has brought fresh fish there too, notably for the spring festival of No Ruz (New Year).

The food and cooking of Iran has much in common with that of the Muslim Middle East. The staple diet is WHEAT; much use is made of LAMB and poultry, and of YOGHURT and aubergines; there is a wide range of stuffed vegetables and of sweet pastries; and the diet is non-alcoholic. However, it can be distinguished from its neighbours by its fine rice dishes, and by its meat and fruit sauces. Most savoury dishes have a distinctive SWEET-AND-SOUR or sour flavour.

Of the numerous regional **breads**, six are acclaimed nationally: *barbari*, which is thick, crusty bread made in an oven (*tanoor*, see TANDOOR), is mostly consumed at breakfast; *sangak*, a thinner bread, baked over a bed of stones, is used as a sandwich bread (to wrap

round kebab, or cheese and herbs, etc.); LAVASH, a pliable, thin bread cooked on the wall of a tandoor, keeps well and is used to eat food by hand (instead of cutlery); *taftun*, a medium soft bread, is a popular accompaniment, especially dropped in thin soups and broths; *sheermal* is a thick, crusty sweet bread; and *nan-e qandi* a sweet, crisp, biscuit bread. All the breads are flat but leavened; and all are made with wheat.

The **rice** dishes are particularly striking, many of them prepared in a unique three-step method, by first soaking, then boiling, and finally steaming to produce a mound of light, dry rice dressed with butter and saffron (and formerly with GOLD AND SILVER LEAF). They come in two forms: *chelow* is plain white rice, while *polow* (see PILAF) is rice mixed with various ingredients, ranging from herbs, pulses, vegetables, or nuts to meat or poultry which may be grilled, poached, or stuffed and roasted. *Shireen polow*, for example, is saffron rice mixed with carrot shreds, orange peel, almonds and pistachios, and dried fruit, the whole encased in caramelized sugar, garnished with BARBERRIES and toasted almonds, and served with saffron chicken. It is known as the 'King of Persian Dishes'.

A third type of rice preparation, known as *katteh*, is cooked by the simple absorption method. This is very popular in the Caspian littoral which is the only region in Iran where rice is grown and where it is the staple diet. In this region, rice is eaten for breakfast, lunch, and dinner. Of the kinds of long-grain rice grown and eaten in Iran, Sadri (which resembles basmati) is the most popular. Round-grain rice, called *gerdeh*, also has its uses, e.g. in puddings.

Plain rice (*chelow*) is accompanied by a variety of meat or poultry sauce/stews (*khoresht*) combined with, for example, mixed herbs and LIMES; aubergines and tomatoes, split peas and limes, walnuts and pomegranates, oranges and carrots, QUINCE and split peas, parsley and mint with RHUBARB, and so on.

The use of **herbs** has always been prolific in Iran. Every meal is accompanied by fresh bread and a bowl of fresh herbs—*tarkhun* (TARRAGON), *shahi* (COSTMARY), *marzeh* (MARJORAM), *rayhan* (lemon BASIL), *na'na* (MINT), *tarreh* (garlic CHIVES), and *torobcheh* (radishes). Many dishes are cooked with herbs. One of the most popular meat sauce/stews referred to above is *Qormeh sabzi*, which is made with PARSLEY, CORIANDER, garlic chives and DILL. An interesting group of similar sauce/stews from the Caspian region is made with parsley and mint and one other single ingredient, such as rhubarb, sour green plums, or celery.

Many soups are herb based, and herbs figure in several kinds of *polow*, in all sorts of stuffing (see below), and in one or two kinds of mixed pickle.

Meat is scarce and expensive and is eaten sparingly. Sheep and goat meat are the most common. Beef is little eaten since the plateau is too dry to sustain herds of cows. Camel meat is also eaten, but it is poultry and game that offer most variety. Roast or grilled meat in large pieces is eaten only on festive occasions, although a wide variety of KEBABS, ranging from the thin, leaf-like *Kabab-barg* to the chunkier lamb *tikkeh*, appear on the table frequently. Both are marinated in finely chopped onion and lemon juice and basted with saffron and butter. All kebabs except *Kabab-barg* are eaten rolled in *sangak* or *taftun* bread and accompanied by herbs and/or *torshi* (pickles). *Kabab-barg* is served with plain white rice, flavoured with saffron, and mixed with butter, egg yolk, and SUMAC to result in what is generally accepted to be the 'national dish'—*Chellow kabab*.

The traditional cooking medium was *donbeh* (the rendered fat of the FAT-TAILED SHEEP), or *roghan* (clarified butter), but rising population and political upheavals in the 20th century have led to an increasing use of vegetable, particularly SUNFLOWER, oils.

Iranian **soups** are mostly of the thick vegetable sort, based on pulses and herbs. Like most savoury Iranian dishes, they are given a distinctive sour flavour, which is achieved by adding the juice of lemons, limes, or sour oranges, or other sour ingredients such as barberries, rhubarb, pomegranates, or unripe plums and grapes. One or two thin, broth-like soups are thickened with pieces of dried bread. This category includes the most popular soups, *Ab-goosht* and *Dizee*, which are made with lamb bone, onions, chickpeas, and limes— the solid ingredients are beaten into a paste and served separately while the broth is served with dried bread.

There is a summer soup (*Mast-o kheeyar*) made with yoghurt, cucumber, and mint, which is found also in many neighbouring countries. However, in Iran, the addition of chopped chives and mint, raisins, and walnuts gives it an added dimension. Generally, yoghurt features prominently in the Iranian kitchen. Strained yoghurt mixed with various cooked ingredients (spinach, shallots, aubergines, or beetroot) or prepared ingredients (shallots or cucumber) form a light summer meal with the name of *borani* (see BURAN).

Noodles (RESHTEH) have given way to rice over the centuries, and only a few noodle dishes remain. Each dish retains much symbolism; the word *reshteh* also means the reins or threads of life in Persian. *Ash-reshteh* (noodle soup) is served at prayer meetings and also during the spring festival

of No Rooz, as is *Reshteh polow* (rice with noodles)—significant items for an occasion when it is hoped that the tangled reins of life may be organized.

Stuffed meats and pastries were features of the cuisine of ancient Iran. In this century, stuffed meats and vegetables remain popular. Stuffed lamb and chicken are roasted in a *tanoor* or grilled over charcoal, while the stuffed vegetables are baked in sauces which can be sweet (grape syrup—see PEKMEZ and DIBS) or sour (lemon or sour grape juice) or savoury (TAMARIND). Only one stuffed (sweet) pastry (*qotab*) now remains popular. Its old Persian name, *sambusak*, has now passed to Britain as SAMOSA.

Various **desserts** are made with sugar (*qand*—the origin of candy), rice or rice flour, dates, wheat starch or chickpea flour, variously flavoured with rosewater, saffron, and/or cardamom and garnished with almonds and pistachios. Ice cream made with *sa'lab* (salep) and fruit sorbets are popular in the summer. However, the most popular dessert is fresh fruit followed by tea and sweetmeats. Traditional Iranian sweetmeats include *nokhodchi* (made with roasted chickpea flour and grape syrup); *noql* (almond slivers rolled in sugar syrup); *nan-e berenji* (rice shortbreads); *qotab* (almonds and pistachios encased in pastry); BAKLAVA (layers of filo pastry, ground almonds, pistachios, and syrup); etc. In the early years of the 20th century, these old favourites were augmented by many French-inspired pastries; thus the French mille feuilles was adopted, flavoured with rosewater and renamed 'Napoleon', while the French profiterole was adapted to become a tiny confection filled with rosewater-flavoured cream and sprinkled with cardamom sugar, to be called *nan khame'i*.

Drinks are non-alcoholic, although vine cultivation and wine production and consumption were common in pre-Islamic Iran. After the advent of Islam, *sharbat* (SHERBETS or iced fruit cordials) were developed and are still popular, particularly *sharbat-e limoo* (lime cordial), *sharbat-e beh-limoo* (quince and lime cordial), and *sekanjebeen* (mint and vinegar cordial). Yoghurt is also used to make a refreshing summer drink with mint, salt, and mineral water called *doogh* (see AYRAN).

COFFEE was introduced to Iran by the Arabs and remained popular for centuries. In modern times, however, coffee ('Turkish' style) is served only at memorial services. It was superseded in the 20th century by TEA, which is grown in the Caspian region. Tea is served in small glasses (without milk) throughout the day in all regions and at all social levels.

The ancient cuisine of Persia has had an influence, the full extent of which has still to be measured, on Ottoman cuisine (see TURKEY), ARAB CUISINE, the cuisines of W. Europe, and those of Russia, C. Asia, and the Indian subcontinent.   MS

IRAQ as it exists today, reflects the same natural division as ancient Mesopotamia, which consisted of Assyria in the arid northern uplands and Babylonia in the marshy south. Al-Jazirah (the ancient Assyria) grows WHEAT and crops requiring winter chill such as apples and stone fruits. The south, Al Iraq (Iraq proper, ancient Babylonia) grows RICE and is responsible for Iraq's position as the world's largest producer of DATES.

As one would expect, the north cooks rather like neighbouring Syria (see LEBANON AND SYRIA), while the south, even when it cooks dishes of the same basic type, produces quite original results because of its reliance on rice, fish, and dates. The difference goes beyond the ingredients, however. In Mosul, the cultural capital of the north, *mutabbaqa* (literally, 'layered') is a sort of flaky bun of puff paste, but in Basra in the far south the virtually identical word *mutabbag* means a dish of fish or meat smothered in rice.

The ancient civilizations of Mesopotamia subsisted largely on wheat and barley, and grain still dominates Iraqi cookery. Even more than Syria, Iraq tends to combine meat with grain in a single dish. There are far fewer of the small savoury pies beloved by the Syrians, but more varieties of meat porridge, meat and bread dishes, and the meat and grain paste called *kubba* (see KIBBEH). The porridges include the universal Muslim dish *harissa* (meat stewed with whole wheat, often overnight in a cool bread oven after the baking, see HALEEM). Another meat porridge, flavoured with dried lime and cumin and coloured with turmeric or tomato juice, is known as *Kashki* in Mosul, where it is the favourite food on the picnics—jovial occasions where by tradition respectable women could dispense with the veil in public—held near the tomb of the Sufi saint Qadib al-Ban. At times other than picnics, Qadib al-Ban's tomb is mostly visited by women who have been treated harshly by their in-laws. As they circumambulate his tomb they sing a traditional refrain which coincidentally contains the words: 'O Qadib al-Ban, bereave me of my mother-in-law and of the cooking of *kashki*.'

The dishes consisting of meat and broth or gravy mixed with bread are known as THARID or *tashrib*. In Baghdad, the distinction is that *tharid* is made with crumbled bread, while *tashrib*, a usual breakfast dish, is whole pieces of bread soaked in broth with meat on top, like the Syrian dish *fatta*. In Mosul the name is *tashghiba* and the dish is more elaborate, including such ingredients as lentils, noodles, and pomegranate as well as layers of meat and bread.

Iraqi *kubba* does not usually contain onions like its Syrian cousin KIBBEH, and in the north it is a more rugged product made with wheat groats (*jshishi*) pounded together with the meat and the BURGHUL wheat. Iraqi tradition claims that *kubba* originated in Mosul. The variety of *kubba* for which Mosul is famous today is quite distinct from the egg- or lozenge-shaped Syrian variety. It is a rather flat loaf the size of the hand or larger, stuffed with meat, almonds, raisins, and spices, and it can be either fried or poached. In the south, the *kubba* paste is made with boiled rice in place of wheat, and often with the tail fat (*liya*) of the FAT-TAILED SHEEP in place of meat.

Iraq also has a unique meat and grain speciality known according to dialect as '*uruq* or '*ghug*, a name which is perhaps the same as a word meaning the texture or 'grain' of wood. Meat, cut small and often fried, is mixed with the leavened dough and flavourings such as green onion and celery leaf, and the resulting loaves are baked like ordinary bread. The Marsh Arabs of the south simply call it *khubz lahm* or 'meat bread'.

Fermented wheat products are also known, such as *tarkhina* (bulghur and yoghurt mixed together and dried—see TARHANA) and *kushk* (bulghur boiled with beetroot stems, leavened, and allowed to ferment for a week—see KASHK). *Kushk* is eaten raw or cooked, and the juice of macerated *kushk* is added to the meat stew as a flavouring along with ingredients like quinces, eggplant, and mint.

Despite this great repertoire of wheaten dishes, however, and the fact that some of them can be traced back to Assyrian times, the high-status grain of Iraq, even in the north, is rice.

In an old folk-tale of Mosul, a man asks: 'O people of the Garden [Heaven], o people of the Fire [Hell], what do you eat?' They respond respectively, 'Apricots with rice' and 'Bulgar with tomatoes.'

The southern word for rice, *timman*, is a curious one, used nowhere else. Dates, the other great southern speciality, are used in a surprising number of ways, for example to coat broiled fish. Dates are also made into syrup and vinegar.

The cooking of Basra has had considerable influence on that of the Persian Gulf. A peculiarity common to Iraq and the Gulf is that meat on a skewer in chunks is called TIKKA rather than *kabab* (see KEBAB). Except among the non-Arab Kurds, the word *kabab*

in Iraq always means skewers of ground meat which are elsewhere known as *kofta kabab*.

In both north and south, beef—from cattle or water-buffalo—is far more common than in most of the Arab world, often more common than mutton. The presence of year-round rivers also provides Iraq with freshwater fish such as catfish and members of the genus *Barbus*. The best known is *shabbut* (*B. gripus*) which is the preferred fish for the national dish *Samak masquf* (in the southern dialect, *Simach mazguf*). Six or seven of these large fish are split and gutted and suspended around a fire on stakes inserted into holes pierced in their backs. When the fire has died down and the fish are nearly done, they are laid on the coals on their backs to finish cooking, and flavourings such as spices, onions, tomatoes, lemon juice, and vinegar are sprinkled on them.

North and south are also united by a freer use of spices than prevails in Syria or TURKEY, and a tradition, perhaps Persian inspired (see IRAN), of cooking meat with fruit. A number of strictly Persian dishes are known, among them candies, pastries, and a few stews intended to be served over rice in the Persian manner, such as *Fisinjan* (fowl stewed with walnuts and pomegranate—see FESENJAN). Persian influence is also shown in the names of various herbs and spices and the habit of calling sesame paste *rashi*, as it was in medieval cookery books, rather than by its Arabic name *tahina*. Herbs such as dill, tarragon, and peppergrass (see CRESS), relatively rare elsewhere in the Arab world, are as popular in Iraq as in Iran.

A number of Turkish dishes have been accepted, including the universal Turkish strudel pastries. Stuffed vegetables may be called by the usual Turkish name DOLMA, but they are more commonly known as *yapraq*, the Turkish word for leaf, whether they are leafy in nature or not. Turkish-style clotted cream, usually made from water-buffalo milk, is known as *gaymar*, a form of the Turkish word *qaymagh* (see KAYMAK). Some ingredients have been learned from the Turks in relatively recent times; thus, beside the ancient range of sour flavourings—VINEGAR (made from cider, wine, or dates, depending on the region), TAMARIND, and LIMES (fresh or dried)—the Iraqis use citric acid crystals under the Turkish name *limon duzi*.

Two great minority groups are found in the north-east: the Kurds, who speak a language related to Persian, and the Assyrians, a Christian (mostly Nestorian) group speaking a modern dialect of Aramaic. They both cook the usual northern dishes, particularly the heavy meat and vegetable stews suited to their cold winters. It is in Kurdish territory around Suleimania that

MANNA is gathered. A rice and vegetable soup flavoured with dill and yoghurt is known throughout Iraq as 'Assyrian soup', and the Assyrian women of the villages around Mosul are famous for their skill at making strudel sheets and pastries such as *baqlawa* (see BAKLAVA). CP

IRELAND unlike the rest of W. Europe, remained free of Roman influence in the early centuries of the 1st millennium AD, and thereby clung to vestiges of an earlier Iron Age Celtic culture for far longer than her European counterparts. With the arrival of Christianity in the early 5th century, aspects of Ireland's unique tribal, rural, oral, and hierarchical society, with its peculiar foodstuffs, were committed to writing within the scriptoria of the great monastic foundations. From at least the 7th century onwards, Irish monks turned out an unrivalled body of secular texts, the oldest extant vernacular sources in W. Europe, and it is these sources that provide an invaluable insight into the range of native Irish foodstuffs. Literary traditions are especially strong in Ireland, and the Irish have an unrivalled wealth of written material about their foodways, often romantic/tragic/of extraordinary dramatic impact.

The staples of the early Irish diet were cereals and dairy produce. OATS, BARLEY, WHEAT, and RYE were used in the preparation of PORRIDGE, gruel, boiled and roasted grain dishes, meal pastes, and coarse flat breads. The palatable qualities of wheaten flour and its potential for producing raised loaves rendered it a luxury and the food of festivals and holy days. More commonplace were cakes of oats and barley, baked on a flag or griddle over the open fire and taken with a variety of condiments and relishes. These are alluded to in the 7th/8th-century legal tract *Uraicecht Becc* (Small Primer) which details the proper rules of hospitality, stating that, should the noble (*aire desso*) call at one's door, he and four of his retinue are legally entitled to: 'four cakes to each man with their condiment, and their seasoning . . . four stalks of fresh onions to each cake, or honey, or fish, or curds; or a salted joint with every twenty cakes'.

Dairy produce was prevalent in the diet between the two Celtic festivals of Beltane (1 May) and Samhain (1 November). Between these two festivals, the lush upland pastures were grazed by cattle which in turn supplied milk in abundance for use in the preparation of sour milk drinks (which were preferred to fresh milk), curds, soft and hard cheeses, and of course fresh and salted butter.

The indigenous CHEESE-MAKING tradition is everywhere apparent in the sources and CURD CHEESES and soft and hard ones are regularly mentioned. Unpressed curds was a summer subsistence dish that was enlivened with the flavours of HAZELNUTS, WILD GARLIC, WOOD SORREL, HONEY, or salted butter. The diversity of shape and texture of both pressed and unpressed cheeses was enthusiastically interwoven into the imagery of many of the medieval tales. Thus for example, in the 9th-century *Togail Bruidne Da Derga* (Destruction of Da Derga's Hostel), there is mention of a warrior whose buttocks were each the size of a large soft cheese (*maothal*).

Likewise the soft unpressed sweet curd cheese *millsän* is referred to in the 11th-century tale *Aislinge meic Con Glinne* (Vision of MacConglinne): 'Each oar we plied in the new-milk lake would send its sea-sand of cheese curds to the surface.' So is the hard 'swollen' cheese (*tanach*): 'a bristling rubble dyke of stone, of swollen hard cheeses'.

As with most medieval societies, meat was a luxury, enjoyed only as an occasional indulgence. In Ireland this trend was complicated by the fact that wealth and social standing were calculated by the extent of one's dairy herd. Thus, the socio-economic value of cattle militated against the emergence of a beef-based meat diet. Consequently, PORK, but more usually smoked, salted BACON and MUTTON, were the most popularly consumed meats, along with their associated offal products. In particular, fatty streaky bacon enjoyed notorious popularity, served with at least an inch or two of fat; indeed, the general consensus was the fattier, the better. This defined taste for fat is also apparent in the Irish love of salted butter. Indeed, regardless of era, salted bacon, especially rashers of bacon, and salted butter have endured as favourite foodstuffs. Butter, when available in the past, was and still is served at all mealtimes and is used to enrich anything from oatcakes to potatoes to sweet currant cake.

In medieval Ireland large expanses of deciduous woodland dominated the landscape and, together with the great inland waterways, made a valuable contribution to the diet. VENISON (fresh and salted), WILD BOAR, hazelnuts, berries, haws, CRABAPPLES, WATERCRESS, wood sorrel, and wild garlic are alluded to frequently as highly regarded wild foodstuffs. In addition, freshwater fish and salmon were savoured in fresh or pickled form.

Overall, oats and dairy produce and salted meats continued to dominate the diet of most of the Irish until the widespread adoption of the potato in the 18th century. However, from the 12th century onwards it is clear that the Irish diet was undergoing significant changes, under the impact of conquest and colonization. In 1169, the Anglo-Normans arrived and established a presence in the southern and eastern

regions. Here, under their influence, the cultivation of wheat, PEAS, and BEANS increased substantially. Accordingly, somewhat of a regional diet based on maslin breads of wheat and rye, and pea and bean POTTAGES, became an established feature of Anglo-Norman districts. The popularity of wheat and maslin loaves was also facilitated by the introduction of the built-up oven by the Anglo-Normans and the new monastic orders who came to Ireland in the wake of the conquest.

Over time the process of colonization, consolidated during the Tudor and Stuart eras, saw the emergence of an Anglo-Irish gentry class with distinctively rich and varied cuisines. Expansive estate lands, kitchen gardens, and walled orchards offered up many novel ingredients, and, as Fynes Moryson (1617) comments: 'some lords and knights and gentlemen of the English-Irish, and all the English there abiding, having competent means, use the English diet.' The same author describes in contrast how the native Irish:

eat cakes of oats for bread . . . they feed most on white meats, and esteem for a great dainty sour curds, vulgarly called by them 'bonaclabbe'. And for this cause they watchfully keep their caws [cows] and fight for them as for their religion and life; and when they are almost starved, yet they will not kill a cow, except it be old and yield no milk.

By the early 18th century the rich cream and cheese diet, alluded to by Moryson, was on the decline due to the development of the extensive export trade in Irish beef and salted butter. As the exportation of butter soared throughout the 18th century, cheese-making, once so widespread, now became the prerogative of those with dairy stocks extensive enough to support a surplus of milk and cream. These commercial developments also coincided with an upsurge in the cultivation and consumption of potatoes. Amongst the poorer classes increased reliance on a diet dominated by copious quantities of potatoes and milk, and to a lesser extent oats, discouraged culinary innovation and paved the way for the disastrous Great Famine of the 1840s (see the next entry, IRELAND AND THE POTATO).

In some ways the post-famine diet displayed a noticeable continuity with pre-famine food traditions. Self-sufficient rural communities relied on the old-time staples of oats, bacon, and of course the potato. Native Irish food traditions were and are still markedly 'peasant' in origin and character. One reason is that until well into the 19th century, and indeed beyond, standard kitchen utensils were limited, through economic necessity, to the open cooking pot, the bastible pot (cast iron pot oven), and the griddle. Cooking was therefore confined to the open fire, with boiling and baking the

most usually employed cooking methods. By consequence, what are recognized as national dishes, such as Irish mutton stew (see IRISH STEW), bacon and cabbage, CORNED BEEF, BOXTY, CHAMP, COLCANNON, SODA BREAD, oatmeal PORRIDGE, and OATCAKES, are the products of this fundamental and unsophisticated approach to cooking. Both it and they have survived with great tenacity because their roots run so deep.

However, changes did come. In the late 19th century, the increased emphasis on grazing and dairy farming, facilitated by the post-famine reduction in population, enabled many farmers to take advantage of the sharp upward trend in the price of cattle and butter. This climate of general agricultural prosperity saw an upsurge in the consumption of animal fat, taken in the form of dairy produce and meats, particularly poor-quality imported bacon. These changes also coincided with improvements in the retailing and distribution of food. Thus, by the early 20th century, easy access to shop-bought goods diversified the range of the rural diet. In particular, tea, sugar, and white baker's bread became indispensable household items. In addition, access to these goods became symbolic of economic comfort and tea and white bread were held in great esteem, gradually displacing home-made breads, buttermilk, and milk drinks. Furthermore, as commercially produced goods became ever more apparent, a sort of stigma of inferiority attached itself not only to home-made foods but also to food from the wild (which evoked memories of the Great Famine, when they had been exploited by the poor and destitute).

Against this background it is understandable that fish, including many coarse fishes and shellfish, were considered objectionable outside coastal communities. Shellfish were viewed with definite suspicion, since eating improperly prepared or poor-quality molluscs had caused severe illness and even deaths in the past. In general, fish-eating was further tainted by its association with the Roman Catholic philosophy of fast and abstinence. Until well into the 20th century fish appeared on most dinner plates on the fast days of Wednesday and Friday, and during Lent. Boiled salted fish, served with a rudimentary white sauce, was the invariable choice on such occasions, truly penitential fare!

As the 20th century progressed, a good square meal of plain food became increasingly symbolic of economic comfort and security. Until well into the 1960s the average Irish dinner was the immutable trio of meat, vegetables, and potatoes, bulked out with white buttered bread and washed down with lashings of strong sweet tea, which was always drunk with the meal and not after. Although, during the economic boom of the 1960s, various ethnic cuisines began to make inroads into the diet in urban areas, thereby introducing a more cosmopolitan air to Irish foodways of the late 20th century, these foodways still bore the hallmark of their peasant origins, and the 'immutable trio' still reigned over many tables.

It is important, however, not to overemphasize the peasant nature of Irish foodways at the cost of blurring other elements of the wider picture. Irish society, regardless of era, has always maintained a complex social hierarchy, further diversified by outside settlers bringing their own food patterns and providing influences which trickled both laterally and downwards. At the upper echelons of society, the refined food culture of the Anglo-Irish gentry not only represented the economic affluence of the 'Big House', but also was perceived to be that of a foreign and decidedly more sophisticated culture; it thereby stood as the model for an aspiring Irish middle class, who sought to transcend the simplicity of their indigenous cuisine instead of embracing and building on it. It is good news that by the late 20th century the Irish have developed a more mature and independent set of attitudes to food, and that they are now ready to exploit the full potential of the island's natural resources. RSe

READING: Cathal Cowan and Regina Sexton (1997); Theodora FitzGibbon (1983); Florence Irwin (1949); Maura Laverty (1946, 1966); Biddy White Lennon (1990); A. T. Lucas (1960); Bríd Mahon (1991); Regina Sexton (1998); Monica Sheridan (1966).

IRELAND AND THE POTATO How and when the potato was first introduced to Ireland remains the subject of much conjecture and debate. Of the stories which have been current, the most plausible states that it was introduced to Ireland from Virginia by Sir Walter Raleigh, who owned estates in County Cork and was mayor of the town of Youghal in 1588 and 1589. In any case, the potato was certainly in Ireland by the late 16th century, and an established feature of the Irish diet by the end of the 17th. So successful was its assimilation into Irish food patterns that by the end of the 18th century it had displaced the older staples of cereals and dairy produce as the dominant item in the diet of the cottier (cottager) class and the landless agricultural labourers. Indeed, on the eve of the Great Famine in 1845, over one-third of the Irish population relied almost exclusively on the potato for their sustenance.

Potato cookery was ideally suited to the limited range of Irish cooking utensils. Even the most materially impoverished kitchen

was equipped with a cauldron and a griddle, and these were used imaginatively to create a variety of potato dishes. Most often potatoes were simply boiled in a cauldron or a three-legged pot over the open fire. In coastal regions it was commonplace to boil potatoes in sea-water, which prevented the skins cracking and thus ensured little mineral loss; this according to Florence Irwin (1949). After boiling, the potatoes were strained in a shallow wicker basket and delivered to the table ungarnished. The faster the eater, then the more potatoes could be snatched from the basket in the centre of the table. Olive Sharkey in her book *Old Days Old Ways* (1994) recalls her father's memories of his potato dinners:

the potato dinner was always the favourite meal in his home years ago, with everyone reaching hungrily for the spuds the moment my grandmother placed them in their basket on the table. It was essential that everyone learn to peel their potatoes quickly or they might miss out, the greedy, skilful peelers hoarding up little caches of spuds on their plates before actually tucking in.

Boiled potatoes were eaten mostly with salt and milk or buttermilk. For those who could afford it, a herring boiled in milk or water, or a piece of salted bacon, proved a tasty accompaniment. In lean times, a meal of 'potatoes and point' was popular. This humorous appellation refers to the practice of eating potatoes, whilst simultaneously pointing to the bacon smoking in the rafters overhead, which was enjoyed only as a treat on festive or holy days.

Potatoes roasted in hot ashes, *bruthóga*, were a relished dish. A Belfast man writing in the early 19th century who is quoted in Bourke (1993) highlights the association of roast potatoes with young children. He states that in every small cabin, children are to be seen engaged in the roasting of their own private stocks of potatoes: 'As you ride by a cabin you frequently see a group of children run to the door, each holding in his hand a roasted potato.'

In pre-famine Ireland the average cottier consumed anything between 7 and 14 lb of potatoes per day. Arthur Young notes that 'six people, a man, his wife and four children, will eat eighteen stone of potatoes a week or 252 lb'. These extraordinary consumption rates were accompanied by an explosive increase in the population; between 1780 and 1845, it rose from four and a half million to eight and a half. So the already high demand for potatoes was steadily growing.

These factors, and extreme poverty, forced many to concentrate potato cultivation on varieties that returned the most abundant yields. In the years leading up to the Great Famine the variety Lumper, a heavy yielder although of inferior cooking quality and taste, had become dominant except in the

north. Unfortunately it proved to be highly susceptible to a potato blight which had appeared in Belgium in the late 1830s and arrived in Ireland, with devastating consequences, in the mid-1840s. This blight was caused by a fungus, *Phytophthora infestans*, and its effect, where it took hold, was to destroy crops almost completely, leaving farmers with nothing but stinking black rotten remains of the tubers. In a country which had become so heavily dependent on a single crop, and on a single variety of this crop, the result was havoc. By 1851 about a million Irish had died and about a million had had to emigrate.

The tragedy gave the world one of the clearest lessons it has ever had in the necessity to maintain diversity of crops and of genes.

Some of the distress was alleviated by the British government through financial aid and food relief, starting in 1845 with the delivery of 'yellowmeal' (MAIZE). However, a change of government in Britain in the following year, coupled with a failure to grasp what was happening and a belief that 'market forces' would set things right, resulted in direct aid of this sort being discontinued.

Recurrent bad harvests in 1847 and 1848 then accelerated the suffering. In the absence of food, the starving resorted to the wild foods of the countryside and seashore. More consumed carrion and rodents. Others tried to squeeze the pulp from dank and rotting tubers in vain attempts at making boxty bread. The description of the ongoing catastrophe by Cecil Woodham-Smith (1962) is famous; and Austin Bourke (1993) has more recently presented, in a brilliant work, the results of his lifelong study of the episode.

Death through starvation, disease, and weather exposure ravaged the peasant population. Voluntary humanitarian intervention, in particular from the Quakers, saw the establishment of soup kitchens. The government followed suit by implementing what was known as the 'Soup Kitchen Act' in the spring of 1847, and Alexis Soyer (see ENGLISH COOKERY BOOKS OF THE 19TH AND 20TH CENTURIES), the famous French chef of the Reform Club in London, was entrusted with the task of creating a sustaining soup for the starving Irish. His recipe No. 1 called for 4 oz (115 g) leg of beef to 2 gallons (7.5 litres) of water, 2 oz (56 g) of dripping, 2 onions and other vegetables, 8 oz (225 g) of second-rate flour, 8 oz (225 g) pearl barley, 3 oz (85 g) of salt, and 0.5 oz (14 g) of brown sugar.

Ireland lost over a fifth of its population and suffered severe social scarring, all as the result of a potato-dominated diet. Yet the potato continued to feature as an important item in the post-famine diet of the Irish. To some extent its place on Irish plates was safeguarded by the introduction of spraying against disease. In any case, the Irish remain (in 1995) the highest per capita consumers of potatoes in the European Union.

See also BOXTY; CHAMP; COLCANNON; FADGE; FARL; POTATOES IN COOKERY.   RSe
READING: Regina Sexton (1998, for further detail on some aspects).

IRISH STEW is a celebrated Irish dish, yet its composition is a matter of dispute. Purists maintain that the only acceptable and traditional ingredients are neck mutton chops or kid, potatoes, onions, and water. Others would add such items as carrots, turnips, and pearl barley; but the purists maintain that they spoil the true flavour of the dish. The ingredients are boiled and simmered slowly for up to two hours.

Mutton was the dominant ingredient because the economic importance of sheep lay in their wool and milk produce and this ensured that only old or economically non-viable animals ended up in the cooking pot, where they needed hours of slow boiling. Irish stew is the product of a culinary tradition that relied almost exclusively on cooking over the open fire.

It seems that Irish stew was recognized as a national dish as early as about 1800 since it is the subject of a contemporary English broadsheet ballad.

then hurrah for an Irish Stew
That will stick to your belly like glue.

RSe

IRN-BRU a Scottish soft drink which is important for its symbolic value as well as for its refreshing qualities.

Under the less puzzling name 'Iron Brew', this was one of the patent bottled drinks developed in Scotland in the early part of the 20th century. The impetus towards commercial production of such drinks lay partly in the strength of the temperance movement, and derived some inspiration from the tradition of tonics and health drinks prepared by herbalists.

In the early days 'iron brews' were produced by several manufacturers, and often contained no iron. During the Second World War, they all disappeared (as a result of the rationalization of the soft drinks industry); and after it legislation was passed which made it compulsory to add 0.125 g of iron per fluid ounce to any beverage bearing the name 'iron-brew'. There was also some doubt about the future legality of calling something a 'brew' if it was not brewed in the traditional manner.

A. G. Barr, one of the main producers (and now the only one), accordingly

changed the name to Irn-Bru. Their product, heavily and wittily advertised (e.g. with images of iron girders which were supposedly dissolved into the brew), became so successful that it has now taken the title of 'Scotland's other drink', carried around the world by nostalgic Scots, and particularly to football matches at home and abroad where Scotland's number one drink is not allowed.

Irn-Bru does contain 0.002% of ammonium ferric citrate, besides caffeine, sugar, flavourings, and colouring. It is orangey-golden in colour and has a sweet-spicy flavour with a citrus tang.   CB

IRRADIATION is subjecting an object to radiation; and a short, powerful blast of radiation will sterilize foodstuffs by killing bacteria and other micro-organisms, as well as any larger creatures infesting the food. It does not make the food radioactive. Various kinds of radiation can be used: in order of increasing energy, electrons, X-rays, and gamma rays. The last two will sterilize food inside packaging.

Irradiation is routinely used on foods for hospital patients in intensive care whose immune systems are damaged so that they constantly risk infection. It is also used on meals prepared for astronauts.

The United Nations Food and Agriculture Organization (FAO) and the World Health Organization (WHO) have approved the use of irradiation for foods sold commercially, but there has been noticeable hesitation to apply the technique in Britain.   RH

ISINGLASS consists of COLLAGEN, which, when heated with water, yields a pure form of GELATIN. Isinglass is obtained from the swimming bladder (also known as 'sound') of certain fish, especially the STURGEON (from which 'Russian isinglass' is obtained), but also a large CATFISH of S. America (yielding 'Brazilian isinglass'), some species of Asian waters, and (in N. American waters) HAKE and COD.

The sounds, once removed from the fish and cleaned, are dried, and treated to acquire various shapes (e.g. 'book' when folded like the leaves of a book, 'pipe', 'ribbon').

A main use of isinglass has been for clarifying liquids, including wines and beers. Its fibrous structure apparently gives it this capability, which is not possessed by ordinary gelatin. Isinglass used to be equally important for culinary purposes, especially CONFECTIONERY and desserts such as FRUIT JELLY and BLANCMANGE; but its cost by comparison with competing products has virtually ended this practice.

ISRAEL a country whose foodways are diverse and in some respects perplexing. Schwartz (1992) has written with brilliance and sympathy about the diverse strands which have come together to form the present tangle. Underlying it is the simple fare which native inhabitants of the region have eaten for many centuries, even millennia: wheat products, lentils, broad beans, fruit and nuts, raw vegetables, flat breads, some lamb or kid, and—very prominent—dairy products. JORDAN offers a point of comparison for this stratum.

However, the earliest Israeli settlers, once the country had been established in 1948, tended to come from colder climates and to have established food preferences which were not suited to the warm Middle East. Schwartz explains that pioneering nutritionists and cookery writers in Israel, especially Lilian Cornfeld, had to work hard to familiarize incomers with such foods as the tomato and the aubergine and to lead them towards salads of raw fruit and vegetables and dairy foods. They succeeded, aided by the impact on the incomers of the outdoor life and hard physical work. For many of them this was quite novel, since the culture from which they came prized a thin, pale, scholarly appearance and all this stood for more than strength and robust looks. However, as Schwartz comments:

The physical image of the Israeli Jew was transformed. The weak, thin, small, bent Jewish immigrant managed to raise a new generation of people bearing similar physical characteristics to those born American or Australian.

Attitudes which are considered characteristic of the kibbutz movement were helpful in this respect. The kibbutzim who were already there before the Second World War had no problems in co-operating with Arabs in this and other respects, and even in the 1970s their food was very simple and reflected local resources. They had not had to grapple to any significant extent with JEWISH DIETARY LAWS.

However, the increasingly variegated flood of new settlers who were pouring into the country were bringing with them dishes and food customs from their lands of origin, and thus changing patterns of food consumption. One very marked influence has been that of the Jews from the YEMEN; but a survey of street foods in Israel now provides a mosaic of many other cuisines, sometimes adapted to conditions in Israel but often surviving in a pure state. Claudia Roden (1981) listed the numerous items which she found at snack bars and food stalls, explaining that foods of the Arab world were prominent, e.g. *Ful medames*, *shawarma* (see QAWARMA), TABBOULEH. There were also dishes brought from C. and E. Europe: schnitzel (see VEAL), GOULASH,

GEFILTE FISH, and chopped LIVER. And that was not all. Roden continues:

It was exciting to find 'hamine' eggs sold in the street and that 'bourekas', the old 'ladino' Turkish savoury pies, are so popular a snack that their name has been given to the type of film where people shout and hiss at the villain. A grated carrot salad with orange juice, honey and raisins from Morocco was offered at a kibbutz for breakfast, and I found that Moroccan 'cigars' (meat-filled pastries) are the most popular items at Barmitzvahs. Stuffed vine leaves, cucumber and yoghourt salad, 'hummus', aubergine and spicy mixed salads are sold ready-made in supermarkets, and Iraqi 'kubba' and 'sambusak' are frozen convenience foods.

Chicken soup and 'kneidlach', 'knishes' and 'kreplach' and carrot 'tzimmes' are still made in the houses of those who came from Eastern Europe. 'Latkas' and 'blintzes', 'pirochki' and 'kugel', 'lox' and 'beigels' are served in tourist hotels, but for the young Israeli-born Sabras they are nostalgic 'soul foods'. Picked up in Russia, Poland and Germany 'Yiddish' food once served to reaffirm a Jewish identity in later homelands.

(To learn more about some of these items, see JEWISH COOKERY, BÖREK, *pirog*, BAGEL, BLINI, KIBBEH, KREPLACH, SAMOSA, TZIMMES. *Kneidlach* are a sort of DUMPLING, *latkas* are potato FRITTERS, *lox* is SALMON.)

The contrast between its Ashkenazi and Sephardi branches is explained under JEWISH COOKERY. One way of looking at the cuisines of Israel is to see the country as an arena in which now one and then the other has been to the fore. In approximate terms, Ashkenazi food was in the lead until the 1950s, but was subsequently overtaken by Sephardi food; in 1949 the Sephardi accounted for just over 20% of the population, but in the early 1960s the proportion had risen to almost 50%. Now, at the end of the 20th century, further changes in the pattern of immigration appear to be restoring leadership to the Ashkenazi. All this depends simply on the provenance of the majority of immigrants at any particular time.

The situation with regard to dietary laws in Israel is paradoxical. The proportion of the whole population which adheres strictly to the laws is small, but the influence of this minority on explosive questions such as the availability and marketing in Israel of forbidden foods is greater than their numbers would lead one to expect. It can, however, be said that hitherto just about any food (including pork, sometimes described as 'white meat') has been available in Israel for those who are willing to seek it out.

In this complex situation it would be understandable if it proved impossible to identify a national dish. However, FALAFEL is widely regarded as fulfilling this role.

ITALIAN COOKERY BOOKS in the early centuries, were of considerable importance for the history of European cookery. A separate account is given of the work of PLATINA (1475), the first printed cookery book, but the story should begin with the manuscripts which antedated that. Platina deserves praise for several reasons, one of which was that he set a good example for all subsequent cookery writers (and one which some of them have followed) in stating clearly the source of most of the recipes which constituted the latter part of his book. This source was 'Maestro Martino, former cook to the Most Reverend Monsignor Chamberlain Patriarch of Aquileia', as his 15th-century manuscript, only discovered in the 1930s, describes him.

In her essay about Martino, Anne Willan (1977) remarks on the extent of Martino's kitchen skills, fully apparent in the manuscript, and the breadth of his knowledge:

Martino mentions the sausages of Bologna, the rice dishes of Lombardy, the crayfish of Venice and Rome, and the vegetables and fried dishes for which Florence was so famous. His easy familiarity with them all shows that by the fifteenth century a recognizably Italian style of cooking had already developed. Indeed, there are already signs of common methods and recipes in the few cookery manuscripts that antedate Martino, but none of them is nearly so well organized or complete as his work.

The same author describes the position of pasta in this early work and the role of feasts in Italian court life of the time, observing that although Martino by virtue of positions he held must have been entirely familiar with dishes of the utmost sophistication he chose in his manuscript to give relatively simple ones such as would suit the household of a well-to-do merchant. She praises Martino for discarding 'outmoded purées and porridges' and for being free of the old tendency to disguise foods: 'On the contrary, Martino tries to bring out the flavor of a single ingredient by careful seasoning and moderate cooking.'

It would be difficult to overestimate the influence of Martino. Because Platina's book was so successful and so widely disseminated (over 30 editions in its first 100 years and translations into several other languages), Martino's recipes were everywhere. One should perhaps add 'except, perhaps, in England', since an English translation of Platina did not appear until the second half of the 20th century. However, Martino's recipes were also embodied in another printed Italian cookery book, *Epulario*, which did appear in English at an early date and was often reprinted.

Another notable book in the same tradition, *Banchetti* by Cristoforo da Messisburgo (1548), was the work of a household steward who paid particular attention to the serving of dishes and to the *credenza*, which then meant an elaborate course of many cold dishes and only later came to mean a sideboard on which dishes were laid out.

The next landmark was publication in 1570 of the first edition of the *Opera* of Bartolomeo Scappi, a beautiful book which provided not only a full complement of recipes which marked many advances from those of Martino but also contained amazingly fine plates depicting all the equipment which a leading cook of the time would have in his kitchen. The plates have continued to be used right up to the present time, because there is no other resource available which gives such a clear visual impression of a major kitchen in Renaissance Europe.

There followed a lull in the production of important cookery books, although one or two interesting volumes on carving (especially *Il trinciante*, by Vincente Cervio, 1581) were published.

Vincenzo Corrado (1738–1836), a lay monk in the region of Naples, who became a teacher after the suppression of the religious orders in 1809, wrote numerous cookery books. Two of these are outstanding and ran to many editions: *Il cuoco galante* (Naples, 1773) and *Il credenziere di buon gusto* (Naples, 1778). Many of the others were of limited scope (e.g. potato cookery) or of a routine character; but *Del cibo pittagorico ovvero erbaceo* (1781) remains of considerable interest as an early vegetarian cookbook.

Corrado's recipes lacked the detail which anyone but a professional cook would need. Generally his ideas reflected the dominant French influence, but with material on the regional cookery of Lazio and Campania.

A more important work was the ambitious *L'Apicio moderno* (1790), a vast work in six volumes by the eminent cosmopolitan chef Francesco Leonardi, who worked at Naples when that city was at the height of its elegance, and also for Catherine the Great at St Petersburg. The book resembles an encyclopedia, with 3,000 recipes from five other countries in addition to Italy. However, despite its international flavour, the book is focused on Italy and there is some adaptation of foreign recipes to suit Italian tastes and ingredients. Leonardi was strong on pasta and could claim to be the first cookery author to record the combination of pasta and tomato which is so characteristic of Naples. His recipe for tomato sauce (*sugo di pomodoro*), as Anne Willan observes, is exactly the same as the recipe still in use. Naples and Neapolitan cookery, with dialect terms, were featured again by CAVALCANTI (1837), who can be regarded as the first regional cookery writer of Italy.

In the latter part of the 19th century there was one outstanding author, Pellegrino Artusi, whose book *La scienza cucina e l'arte de mangiar bene* (Science in Cookery and the Art of Eating Well) quickly became the best loved of all Italian cookery books, running to well over 100 editions by the end of the 20th century. The first edition (*c.*1890) was published by Artusi himself, because he could not find a commercial publisher for the book—perhaps because it was long and contained not just a large number of fine recipes but also guidance on diet and nutrition, background information, folklore, and anecdotes, i.e. all the elements which go to make a classic cookery book, but which were not perceived in this way in publishing circles in 19th-century Italy. Artusi was born in Romagna, but spent his life in Florence and Viareggio.

Lord Westbury (1983) compiled a fine bibliography of earlier Italian cookery books, reflecting his own great enthusiasm for research in this field and for collecting.

ITALY a country which had been all of a piece in the Roman Empire, indeed the centrepiece thereof, led a fragmented existence from the early Middle Ages until the 19th century, when under the auspices of Garibaldi it took its present political form. This fragmentation did not prevent it from being the cradle of the Renaissance in the arts, including the culinary ones. While the civilizations of France and Spain were still in bud, those of Italy (plural because of the numerous city states which shared the credit) were already flowering.

The first printed cookery book was that of PLATINA (1475). It was preceded by many important manuscripts, especially that of Maestro Martino, and followed by many other books (see ITALIAN COOKERY BOOKS), a publishing cavalcade which was rivalled by those in Germany and England but ahead of what France produced. Indeed Italy was clearly in the vanguard, so far as the culinary arts were concerned, of the whole of Europe. Whatever view one takes of the contribution of Catherine de' Medici (see CULINARY MYTHOLOGY) to the development of cookery in France, it is indisputable that Italy was leading the way during the Renaissance. By the end of the 16th century, however, the genius displayed by Italian artists working in many fields, including the kitchen, showed signs of fatigue, even exhaustion. As Anna del Conte (1987) observes, it was around then that 'the leadership of European

gastronomy moved over the Alps into France'.

One may speculate about the underlying reasons for this change. Were the city-states of Italy now too small to provide the base for even greater artistic advances than they had already achieved? Were questions of political and economic power involved? No doubt a full explanation would be highly complex. And it may be that this whole concept of gastronomic leadership does not represent the most fruitful way of looking at these matters. If the French went on to create their haute cuisine, which flourished so noticeably in the 19th century and tended to dominate the world of expensive hotels and high-class restaurants until quite recent times, are they to be envied and the Italians to be seen as losers in some sort of inter-cultural competition? The answer is surely not, for although they have not occupied the commanding heights of haute cuisine (a phrase for which they have no equivalent) they have succeeded better than any other European country in developing and spreading over most parts of the world a cuisine which has the enormous merits of being cheerful, tasty, varied, inexpensive, and unworrying (no need to worship international star chefs or quail in front of snooty head waiters or act as though the cost of some pretentious dish is no problem—on the contrary, all one has to do is enjoy the food, whether cooked at home or ordered in a restaurant). It will be for people in the imminent 3rd millennium to decide which countries or cultures have made the greatest contribution, in terms of food, to human happiness, but it seems safe to predict that the Italians will be up there at or near the top of the list.

One other matter to be settled in the 3rd millennium concerns a speculative prediction advanced by Fortey (1998) in his excellent 'unauthorised biography' of *Life* (on earth), where he muses on the size of the pepper mills wielded by Italian waiters, suggesting that the evolutionary phenomenon of 'larger and larger', familiar from examples such as the giraffe's neck and the peacock's tail, could apply here. He has already noted that the mills have been growing in size with the passage of time, and has observed 'tiny waiters struggling with vast black grinders, all the while trying to smile and keep up the banter'. What if there is an accelerating and runaway further increase? 'In my scenario,' he writes, 'the process continues until the pepper-grinder becomes so large that the waiter staggers around on wobbly legs, unable to lift it.' Such gigantism usually leads to some form of extinction. One must hope that in this instance it would apply to the grinders rather than to the restaurants or the waiters, whose tendency to bring elements of comic

opera into the gastronomic scene is to be applauded.

Applause is due also to the writers of various kinds who have done much to record the wealth of Italian foodstuffs. The exceptionally numerate di Corato, whose *451 formaggi d'Italia* (1977) and *928 condimenti d'Italia* (1978) are but two of a series, is one example. The works sponsored by the Ministry of Agriculture and bodies such as INSOR (the National Institute of Rural Sociology), producing works such as 'atlases' of typical food by category (cheeses, cured meats, and so on), are another. Thirdly, there are the books devoted to the wide range of different cuisines within the frontiers of Italy and the consequent wealth of different recipes which are a characteristic of Italian cookery as a whole. A compilation such as that of Anna Maria Gosetti della Salda (1967), with more than 2,000 regional recipes, is tangible evidence of this. It may be true that, once again, the political and economic history of Italy is the root cause of this astonishing array of local culinary traditions. It could have been the fragmentation of Italy up to the time of its unification which ensured that these local traditions were kept alive; and that a new overarching tradition came into being, namely the tradition of maintaining traditions.

In Sicily, where the cuisine was renowned in the time of classical Greece and during the Roman Empire, there was a strong Arab influence in early medieval times and this is still highly visible. The market in Palermo, La Vuccirìa, displays many sweet items of Arab origin, using almonds and dried fruit; and on one view of the history of PASTA some of the kinds on display would have their origin in items introduced by the Arabs when they occupied the island from the 9th to the 11th centuries. Sicilian savoury dishes often include tell-tale ingredients such as raisins, almonds again, and so on.

Naples, one of the three most historically important ports of Italy (the others being Venice and Genoa), was in medieval times a gateway for the entry of CATALAN COOKERY into Italy, and has continued to play a lively and pioneering role (one thinks of the TOMATO and above all of PIZZA) in Italian foodways, helped by the extraordinary degree of animation—high even by Italian standards—with which Neapolitans conduct their lives.

A calmer spirit prevails in Tuscany, famed for its traditional breads and olive groves, and part of the region which the Etruscans dominated before their civilization succumbed to the Romans. Parenti (1972) has pieced together the tantalizingly sparse information which survives about Etruscan foodways; but how much may have been owed to these by the Romans, and by those who in turn were the heirs of the Roman kitchen, remains uncertain.

In the far north of Italy, in the provinces bordering on Austria and Switzerland (gateways to the north), the picture is strikingly different. NOODLES resembling those of C. and N. Europe, rather than the kinds of pasta familiar in the rest of Italy, are present, and in Lombardy the consumption of pasta was negligible until quite recent times, its place having been occupied by POLENTA and RISOTTO. There is a similar north–south difference over the use of fats and oils, OLIVE OIL having been used in the south, LARD (pork fat) in the centre, and BUTTER in the north.

The frontiers of Italy are by no means the frontiers of Italian foods. PASTA and PIZZA are world conquerors. Italian ICE CREAM vendors are found in all continents, trading on the reputation which Italy deservedly gained for making ice creams of unrivalled quality. Parma HAM and PARMESAN cheese are two other invaders of foreign territory. Italian culinary influence spreads far and wide and is particularly noticeable in the USA.

See also CLASSICAL ROME.

READING: Elizabeth David (1967); Burton Anderson (1994).

IVY GOURD *Coccinia grandis*, or scarlet-fruited gourd, a CUCURBIT vine which occurs from the Sudan through India to SE Asia and is occasionally cultivated. The leaves are cooked as a green vegetable, and the fruits, which look like small plump gherkins, are also edible. The green (unripe) fruits are used in curry dishes in India.

JACK a general name often used for species of fish in the extensive family Carangidae. These are surface swimmers, with a coloration designed to help them evade detection by predators: blue-green backs and silvery undersides. They almost all inhabit tropical or subtropical waters. Size varies considerably, but relatively narrow bodies are standard. See also HORSE MACKEREL; SCAD; TREVALLY; POMPANO; AMBERJACK.

The reason for the name is unclear, and it does not translate directly into other languages. The name jack is also applied in a more specific way to some of the carangid species, notably:

- *Caranx hippos*, crevalle jack, a circumglobal tropical fish which has commercial importance in SE Asia. Maximum length: 1 m (40").
- *C. ignobilis*, yellowfin jack, slightly larger, called *maliputo* by Filipinos, who esteem it greatly (especially those caught in the volcanic Lake Taal, whose flesh is said to be delicately flavoured by the sulphur in the lava rock).

JACK BEAN the best-known name for a group of closely related beans which are now cultivated throughout the tropics. The principal species are *Canavalia ensiformis* (a New World plant) and *C. gladiata* (from the Old World). Strictly speaking, the former is jack bean or horse bean and the latter is sword bean, but in practice the names are intermingled and there is little difference between the two species. Both the botanical species names mean 'swordlike', a fair description of the long, flat pods.

Jack beans are especially popular in India, where the young pods, which have a flavour like French beans (see HARICOT BEAN), are eaten. The beans themselves, when mature, have tough seed coats which are removed, after soaking, before consumption. They are like BROAD BEANS in appearance and flavour.

In Africa the young leaves are eaten as well as pods and seeds. Flowers and young leaves are steamed as a condiment in Indonesia.

These plants can adapt to a wide range of climates. Provided that certain toxins which inhibit growth in animals and humans can be bred out of them, or removed in processing or cooking, the *Canavalia* beans could be an increasingly important source of protein in regions where other pulses do not thrive.

JACKFRUIT also known as jak, *Artocarpus heterophyllus*, and its close relation *A. integer*, the champedak (or chempedak), belong to the same genus as the BREADFRUIT. They are thought to be native to S. India, whence they spread to Sri Lanka and over the mainland of SE Asia, keeping to a more northerly habitat than that of the tropical breadfruit. Although cultivation of the jackfruit is greatest in India and Sri Lanka, it is practised in many other countries.

The fruit itself is enormous, occasionally reaching 40 kg (90 lb) in weight, which makes it the largest of tree-borne fruits. It grows directly from the trunk of the tree on a short stem. It is a composite fruit with a structure like that of the pineapple, but less tidy; the sections are clustered in irregular clumps. The fruit is elongated, its green skin fissured by the hexagonal boundaries of the sections and covered with spikes. Each fruit contains up to 500 large, starchy, edible seeds which are sometimes known as 'breadnuts', although the true BREADNUT belongs to a different species. Where the chempedak, a slightly smaller but similar fruit, is grown, it is usually as a source of these 'breadnuts'.

A general distinction is made between those jackfruits which are classed as 'soft' and those which are considered to be 'hard'. The latter are preferred. Some hold that the *peniwaraka* (honey jak) of Sri Lanka is the best of all.

Inside the jackfruit, the seeds are enclosed in large 'bulbs' of yellow, banana-flavoured flesh.

Jackfruit

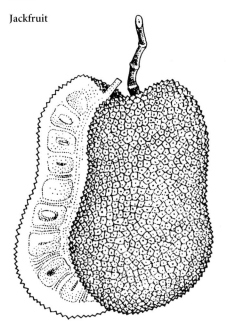

The flesh of the unripe fruit may be used as a starchy vegetable, or dried, or pickled. As the fruit ripens, it is covered with a bag, not to keep away birds or insects directly, but to encourage ants to swarm around it and thus repel other creatures; this according to Burkill (1965–6). It is ready for consumption as a fresh fruit when its skin is stretched out, with the spikes standing clear of each other, and as soon as it starts to give off an aroma; when the smell of a fresh jackfruit fills a room, it is already overripe. The smell of a ripe fruit, before it is opened, is disagreeable; but the aroma of the pulp inside is akin to those of the pineapple and banana. The pulp is firm, thick, and sweet, not slippery or fibrous. It will continue to ripen even after being peeled. All this is true of the champedak also, except that its odour before it is opened is even more potent.

The seeds resemble chestnuts. After being boiled in a change of water, to remove a slight bitterness, they can be made into a flour, or candied. The young shoots and flowers are sometimes eaten as a vegetable.

A related tree, *Artocarpus odoratissimus*, bears the fruits known as *marang*, which resemble those of the jackfruit, but are smaller (although still large by comparison with other fruits) and markedly superior as a dessert fruit. Indeed, it has been described by Coronel (1983) as 'one of the best native fruits of the Philippines'. The white flesh is very aromatic, sweet, and juicy. Doreen Fernandez (1997) relates the charming legend according to which a chieftain had promised the hand of his lovely daughter the Princess Marang to the son of another chieftain. However, when Marang fell in love with a merchant in the market place, where she was shopping for pearls, her father relented, reneged on his vow, and presented to her the man she truly loved. Then he died, but a strange tree was found growing by his grave, 'bearing fruits that were sweet, smelled heavenly, cured the sick, and made the old feel young—because it was the gift of a golden-hearted father'.

Of minor related species, *A. lakoocha*, the monkey jack or *temponek*, yields smaller, edible fruits.

JAINS AND FOOD The Jains are a religious sect in India, comparable in certain respects with Buddhists, who practise VEGETARIANISM and who are prohibited from taking life, even in its smallest forms. Thus Jain monks sweep the paths in front of them, to avoid treading on insects, and may wear masks to avoid inhaling tiny flying creatures. Jain lay persons not only abstain from obviously prohibited occupations such as fishing, but are also debarred from agriculture, where the risk of inadvertently taking life (e.g. when tilling the soil or gathering crops) would be high. They have therefore tended to engage in commerce, with the result that they are on the whole a prosperous group.

The influence of Jains on diet in the Indian subcontinent has been distinctly limited, partly because they are not very numerous and partly because parts of their own practice overlap with that of the enormously more numerous Hindus (see HINDUISM AND FOOD). Marie-Claude Mahias (1981) has nonetheless indicated a number of distinctive features in the rhythm and composition of their daily meals. She also points out that in declining to eat at night (when the smaller forms of life are more difficult to see) and in rejecting parts of plants, such as roots, which are essential to the life of the plants, and counselling avoidance of fruits with numerous seeds (fig, aubergine), they may be implicitly setting an example to others whose conception of the sanctity of life is less all-embracing. Jains do not eat any members of the onion family, Alliaceae, including garlic.

JALEBI an Indian sweet composed of whorls of BATTER, deep fried and soaked in SYRUP. The batter is usually based on plain flour, baking powder, and water, but may include other ingredients (e.g. YOGHURT, BESAN flour, SEMOLINA, rice flour, colouring). After being allowed to rest for a while, so that it ferments slightly, it is forced through a nozzle to form loops in hot GHEE. As soon as the shapes have set the jalebi are lifted out of the fat and dropped into hot syrup scented with saffron and rosewater (see ROSES). After a few seconds' soaking they are drained and served.

Achaya (1994), who gives a good account of regional variations in India, remarks:

According to Hobson-Jobson, the word jilebi is 'apparently a corruption of the Arabic zalabiya or Persian zalibiya'. If so, both the word and the sweet, syrupy article of food that it connotes must have entered India quite early. A Jain work of about AD 1450 by Jinasura has a reference to a feast which includes the jalebi.

Similar confections are made all over the Middle East. In neighbouring Afghanistan jalebi are traditionally served with fish during the winter months, in an association which is so close that the jalebi appear in mounds on the fishmongers' stalls.

In Iran jalebi are known as *zoolabiya* (or *zulubiya*, there are many variant spellings) and are still often made for special occasions, given to poor people at RAMADAN, etc. A pastry called *zellabiya* is made in the Lebanon but this also varies in shape as it is made into 'fingers' rather than whorls.

In the Middle East this item has interesting romantic and poetic associations. It is mentioned in stories of the *Thousand and One Nights*. A poem quoted by Forough Hekmat (1970) says:

Of sweet Zolo-biya chain I hung a necklace around her neck.
From its delicious loops I made a ring on her ears.

Some believe that the somewhat similar Arabic *luqmat el qadi* (meaning the judge's mouthful) may be the original version of this confection, dating back to early medieval times; there is a recipe in al-Baghdadi's cookery book of the 13th century. The dough for *luqmat el qadi* is a plain yeast one, and the method much as described above; a syrup made with honey and including rosewater is preferred by many. The finished articles may be heaped in a pyramid as the syrup sticks them together. They are sold by street vendors during festivals. This name lives on in Greece and Cyprus as *loukoumathes/ loukoumades*, which are so popular in Cyprus that in towns and large villages there are small shops which sell nothing else.

JAM a mixture of fruit and sugar boiled together, poured into jars, and sealed to give a long-keeping preserve with a wet semi-solid consistency, known to a food scientist as a gel. Jams, and related preserves such as FRUIT PASTES, JELLIES, and MARMALADES, are based on widespread and ancient methods of preserving fruit. Similar confections are made throughout Europe and the Middle East.

Successful jam depends on the interaction of three things in the correct proportions: SUGAR, PECTIN (long chainlike molecules occurring in the cell walls of plants), and ACID. Fruit contains all of these, but the jam-maker always adds more sugar, and sometimes pectin and acid.

Sugar is usually added to the mixture in the proportion of 1 : 1 by weight sugar to fruit pulp. It has two functions: it sweetens the fruit, and it plays an important part in gel formation. Sugar is highly attractive to water molecules and 'binds' them in solution. This leaves less water available for the *pectin* to form bonds with. Instead, the pectin molecules link to each other, forming a network which traps the sugar and fruit pulp. **Acid** encourages this process: normally pectin molecules carry a small negative electrical charge in water and therefore tend to repel each other. The function of the acid is to reduce the electrical charge. So when a jam mixture cools, the chainlike pectin molecules bond to form a network, holding the sugar solution and fruit pulp in what appears to be a solid mass.

Certain fruits are recognized by jam-makers to need additional acid or pectin to produce a satisfactory result. Strawberries are a good example: they contain little acid and weak pectin, and are notorious for a 'poor set'. Extra pectin, extracted from apples or citrus fruit, can be added; and home jam-makers are usually instructed to add lemon juice as well.

The optimum conditions for producing a good jam are: a sugar concentration of 60–5%; a pectin content of 0.5–1.0%; and a pH of 2.8–3.4. Stated like this it seems remarkable that anyone should produce jam successfully outside a laboratory; but centuries of trial, error, and experiment with gluts of acid fruit such as gooseberries have fixed jam firmly in the affections of the British. However, the preserve we now recognize as jam is a relatively modern descendant of all the rather solid fruit and sugar conserves, preserves, and marmalades of the 17th and 18th centuries. Even the word *jam* is a relative newcomer to our language, making one of its earliest appearances in *Mrs Mary Eales' Receipts* (1733). The development which took jam from a solid confection to a soft spreadable paste was the increased understanding of hygiene, such as the necessity for clean processing and for sealing the jars, that developed in the 19th century.

Even then, jams were a luxury, as sugar was not cheap: Mrs Beeton (1861) observed,

'It has long been a desideratum to preserve fruits by some cheap method . . . The expense of preserving them with sugar is a serious objection; for, except the sugar is used in considerable quantities, the success is very uncertain.'

In jam, fruit retains some of its form and texture (unlike pastes which are homogeneous). A sharp division is made in Britain between jam, and marmalade, which refers in the modern English-speaking world exclusively to preserves based on citrus fruit. Apart from this rather artificial distinction (which is not made elsewhere), jam can be made from more or less any fruit; vegetables such as carrot or marrow are sometimes incorporated as well.

In modern Britain, jam is cheap and commonplace, and is usually eaten as part of a meal such as breakfast, or a snack, with bread or toast. It is also used as an ingredient in baking, for instance: spread between layers of CAKE; used as a glaze on open fruit TARTS; as a filling in jam tarts and DOUGHNUTS; and as a layer in some puddings, for instance, BAKEWELL TART.

Other European countries produce jams which are generally used in similar ways to British jams. The fruits on which they are based vary from country to country, depending on climate. Thus Scandinavian countries make preserves based on CLOUDBERRIES or LINGONBERRIES; Poland and Hungary make CHERRY jams; and S. European countries make APRICOT jams. PEACH jams are a speciality of Apt in Provence.

Distinctions may be made between different jams according to their consistency; for instance the Russians recognize three types, discussed by Lesley Chamberlain (1983). These are '*varen'ye*, which should contain large chunks of fruit or whole berries and has plenty of syrup to spare, *dzhem* (from English *jam*), which is firmer, often set with pectin, and made of puréed fruit, and *povidlo*, fruit jelly or cheese'.

Varen'ye is used in baking, and as a dessert on ICE CREAM, and on CURD CHEESE. It is also taken with tea, being served in a small dish and eaten with a spoon. This use of jam as an accompaniment to drinks is also common in the Middle East. Claudia Roden (1968) describes the use of jams in Levantine rituals of hospitality. Pastries and jams, in crystal or silver bowls on trays,

were arranged around the spoon stand, next to which was placed a glass of water . . . The trays were brought round to each of us in turn as the coffee was served, for us to savour a spoonful of each jam, or more of our favourite one, with one of the little spoons, which was then dropped discreetly in the water.

Jams were also used as desserts, or to flavour a glass of drinking water.

See also *gliko*.   LM

JAMBOLAN the fruit of the tree *Syzygium cumini*, which grows wild in India and much of SE Asia and is cultivated in some countries of the region. It may also be called Java plum and black plum, or by the more general (Sanskrit) name JAMBU (see below).

The fruit is cherry sized, and either white or purple in colour. The taste is mildly acid and always astringent, sometimes very strongly so. The white variety is sweeter than the purple one. A further disparity between the two is revealed if the fruit is made into JAM or JELLY. The white fruits have twice as much PECTIN as necessary, while the purple ones have almost none; so an equal mixture of the two should be used.

In many countries the fruit is rubbed with salt to remove the astringency before being eaten. It may also be cooked in savoury dishes. In India the unripe fruit is made into a vinegar of an attractive purple colour and a pleasing aroma. Jambolan juice is an excellent source of SHERBETS and SYRUPS for making cool drinks.

The tree and its fruits have religious significance for both Buddhists and Hindus. The latter believe that the god Krishna holds the fruit in special regard.

JAMBU a name of Sanskrit origin, which is applied in Malaysia and Indonesia to several quite different kinds of fruit. In Malaysia it bears the general meaning of a cultivated, as opposed to a wild, plant; but it is most commonly used to refer to the JAMBOLAN (see above) and various sorts of ROSE-APPLE. The same is true of Indonesia, although here it may refer also to several plants of other genera. Examples include *jambu batu* (stone jambu), also known as GUAVA (*Psidium guajava*); and *jambu met*, which is the CASHEW fruit (*Anacardium occidentale*). See illustration overleaf.

JAPAN Japanese cuisine is world renowned for its meticulous preparation and refinement in presentation. The food is served in small, carefully arranged portions, with emphasis on visual appeal—the interplay of colours, textures, shapes, and overall design. This applies particularly to food in restaurants and in the households of what might be called loosely 'the upper classes', but it is a feature which is also apparent in the daily fare of ordinary people.

Because the islands that comprise the Japanese archipelago are mainly mountainous, very little land is available for agriculture, and, even with the most modern technology, harvests are frugal. The Japanese have traditionally learned to husband their food resources and to appreciate quality over quantity.

They have also developed a sensitivity to the individual foods as they are processed for eating. Unlike the Chinese and other Asians, who blend herbs, spices and main ingredients into a bouquet of flavours, the Japanese prize the particular properties of each ingredient and emphasize the equal importance of their individual flavours and textures.

The historic insularity and xenophobia of the Japanese have perpetuated a style of cooking relying on the indigenous ingredients of the country. With a comparatively limited assortment of foodstuffs from which to draw, a culinary tradition developed that emphasizes variety in methods of preparation, and skill in presentation.

To show off this versatility in treatment and to compensate for the small range and amount of food being served, presentation is all important, much in the same way that NOUVELLE CUISINE, while reducing the richness and quantity of the food and the complexity of the sauces, now emphasizes its visual appeal. Japanese food arranged on a plate resembles a carefully composed painting. And there is another dimension; a dish will convey a message—for example, a reminder that it is autumn.

Like the culinary habits of all nations, those of Japan reflect the geography, history, climate, ethnic inheritance, and culture of the people. The earliest inhabitants of the islands were probably immigrants from the barren lands of Siberia and the peninsula which later become Korea. They found a country infinitely more hospitable than their homelands. The islands were covered with vegetation, the climate was benevolent, and the seas stocked with an abundance of fish. They developed a deep appreciation for all forms of nature, which grew into a cult of worship for the fertility of the land and the spirits of the countryside. Later migrations of invaders from S. China, using the Bonin island chain and the Ryukyus, merged their clan worship with the nature worship of the earlier peoples to produce Shintoism. Shintoism, for so long the principal religion of Japan, is a direct outgrowth from and formalization of this nature worship (animism). Although it has been largely supplanted by later forms of religion, it can still be traced in the many festivals of Japan devoted to celebrations of the harvest and various aspects of nature, and to the reverence with which the Japanese regard forms of plant life and their incorporation into their foods.

The diet of the early Japanese was simple: fish, vegetables, fruits, SEAWEED. Occasionally, when it was available, meat or game was added. Unlike the Asian nations of the mainland, whose cultures and food styles became intermingled with those of their

Jambu batu (see p. 413), one of many forms of GUAVA, and often so called

neighbours, this simple regime descended down through the centuries virtually unchanged.

The Japanese are an island people and, until fairly recently, were somewhat insular in accepting influences and imports from the rest of the world. Throughout its long history, Japan would occasionally open its shores to foreigners and alien ideas, only to change its policies and shut them off again.

During periods of receptiveness, both SOYA BEANS and TEA were introduced from China, and indeed it is from Chinese cuisine that Japan has derived most of its major culinary influences.

Between the 6th and 9th centuries AD, when China was enjoying the full flowering of the T'ang dynasty, Japan opened up to the full range of Chinese cultural and religious influences, including Buddhism. In the middle of the 9th century, when the T'ang dynasty disintegrated, Japan again closed its doors to outside influence, refining the ideas, customs, and foods which it had adopted.

Tea, which was first imported from China around AD 800, only became a widespread beverage in the 15th century, partly through the Japanese court's adoption of the Buddhist tea ceremony. This ceremony has now become formalized and stylized into a cornerstone of Japanese culinary culture (see JAPANESE TEA CEREMONY).

By the middle of the 16th century, the Portuguese, then the world's foremost sailors and navigators, had already infiltrated a large part of Asia. They arrived in Japan and began trading. Although the Japanese despised them for their barbaric appearance—their beards, clothes, lack of bodily cleanliness—they nonetheless were willing to foster the relationship with the strange Europeans and gradually absorbed some of their practices. This is when the technique of dipping fish and other foods in batter and frying them originated. This technique, called TEMPURA by the Japanese, stems from the Latin word *tempora*, referring to the Ember Days, or *Quattuor Tempora*. During these days, the Roman Catholic Europeans were forbidden by their religion to eat meat and so substituted seafood, which they fried in batter.

After another long period of isolation, the Japanese were forced in the 1850s to recognize the outside world and to embark on industrialization. At the same time that they began to industrialize, they also borrowed from the western diet. The Buddhist tenets of vegetarianism were gradually abandoned and beef, pork, and poultry began to make an appearance in Japanese dishes.

Fish, SOYA BEAN products, seaweeds, vegetables, RICE, and fruit are still the pillars upon which Japanese cuisine is built, the first two staples providing the main sources of protein in their diet.

To understand Japanese cuisine, one must grasp the important role that seafood plays. Fish or other seafood is eaten at every meal, and it is unthinkable to prepare a Japanese meal without any of these. The coastal waters around Japan have always supported a rich marine life, which has more than compensated for the paucity of agriculture in the mountainous islands above them.

The Japanese tend not to have 'seafood restaurants' such as are found in the western world. Fish is naturally part of the fare served at every meal. There are, however, food houses that specialize in one category (e.g. fish from the 'Inland Sea') or species (e.g. EEL) or in one style of preparation (e.g. tempura).

SUSHI and SASHIMI are the names for two styles of serving uncooked fish, both of which are typically Japanese and may disconcert foreigners (especially those who are unaccustomed to the sight of really fresh fish, such as Japanese consumers demand). Briefly, sushi is seafood (usually raw, but in the case of e.g. OCTOPUS and CONGER EEL cooked) in combination with lightly vinegared rice garnished also with strips of seaweed, vegetables, and egg. Sashimi consists of cuts of the finest raw fish and seafood garnished with crisp shreds of *daikon* (see RADISH) and dipped into soy sauce and the hot, green Japanese horseradish called WASABI.

The three main soya bean products—MISO, TOFU, and SHOYU—are the second largest source of protein for the Japanese. Miso is a savoury paste made from fermented soya beans and, in its many varieties, provides a distinctive flavour to hundreds of dishes. Tofu, bean curd, is a white, custard-like curd made from soya bean milk. It can be incorporated in dishes either in its original state or pressed and compacted to extract more moisture. Shoyu (SOY SAUCE), an extract of soya beans, wheat, salt, malt, and water, is used to flavour Japanese food, as well as the dishes of many other nations of Asia (although in some, FISH SAUCE assumes this role).

In addition to fish and soya beans, seaweed is commonly eaten by the Japanese—as a wrapper for fish and other foods, as a garnish, and in a variety of snack foods, including tiny crisp rice crackers. Many edible types of seaweed are harvested off the coasts of Japan. The two principal ones are NORI (laver), which is rich in vitamins A, D, and B12, and KOMBU (kelp), a vital ingredient in the Japanese soup stock called DASHI, and also a source of vitamin C and iodine.

The main starch in the Japanese diet is rice, which requires a paragraph to itself. The word *gohan* means a meal as well as cooked rice, thus emphasizing the essential nature of rice in a Japanese meal. Hosking (1992) has done well to clear away a common misconception, that the Japanese always eat glutinous (sticky) rice.

This is not the case, Japanese rice is a short grain rice which is always cooked so that the grains cling to each other, but the Japanese sharply distinguish between glutinous rice (*mochigome*) and non-glutinous rice (*uruchi mai*). Essentially glutinous rice is kept for special occasions and for use in confectionery. It is always steamed, never cooked in the way that regular, non-glutinous rice is cooked,—a combination of boiling and steaming in which all the water is absorbed.

Apart from rice, wheat noodles (UDON) and buckwheat noodles (SOBA) are well liked, not only in soups, but also hot or cold with a variety of accompaniments and dressings. See NOODLES IN JAPAN.

Besides soy sauce, other flavouring agents—used sparingly to preserve the distinct character of the main ingredients—help to give Japanese food its special quality. These include rice vinegar, SAKÉ, MIRIN (an alcoholic liquid sweetener), and sesame oil. GINGER, both pickled and raw, members of the onion family, and dried mushrooms are all frequently used.

Turning to methods of cookery, there are two general points to be made. First, timing is the most important factor in Japanese cooking. Foods are cooked to the exact point of perfection—not a second more or less. The Japanese, like other Asians, rarely bake or roast, so most cooking takes place on the stove or range top. As in Chinese cuisine, the ingredients are cut into small pieces and are fried, grilled (broiled), or steamed.

The second important point is that the Japanese have a very precise and comprehensive categorization of their cooking methods (see JAPANESE CULINARY TERMS), and that within each of these there is ample scope for changing the main ingredient. For example, something in the category of *agemono* (deep-fried foods) which uses beef can be made with chicken, fish, or just vegetables without losing its essential character.

The Japanese, like most other Asians, do not usually serve meals in courses but set all the dishes on the table at the start of the meal.

Saké or tea are the usual beverages that accompany a meal. Saké is the brewed rice wine which is often heated and served warm. It is served from small porcelain carafes and drunk not in a glass but in a little decorative china cup. Green tea, *nihon-cha*, is the tea drunk daily in Japan, before, after, and during any meal.

The Japanese select their tableware very carefully. The dishes may be round or rectangular and are made of pottery, porcelain, or decorated lacquer. The food to be served dictates the size, shape, and material of a dish, tray, or platter. Food is eaten with chopsticks, which differ from the Chinese ones in that they are shorter and have slender, tapered ends rather than square. They are generally made of wood.

Dishes are garnished with a single chrysanthemum leaf or a spray of pine needles—the season dictates the choice. The importance of presentation is equally apparent on a smaller scale, in the famous Japanese BENTO box (for a lunch or picnic).

See also OKINAWA; HOKKAIDO. (JB)
READING: Keys (1966); Richie (1985); Elisabeth Lambert Ortiz (1986); Hosking (1994, 1996).

JAPANESE CULINARY TERMS in alphabetical order.

Aemono, Japanese for 'dressed (harmonized) things', is one of the two Japanese terms for a salad (the other being *sunomono*). The distinction between *aemono* and *sunomono* is not always clear.

Aemono salads may include fish, shellfish and seaweeds, poultry, and cooked vegetables or may be made of only one ingredient. There is no standard dressing for *aemono*. Sauces are often based on vinegar and SOY SAUCE, mixed with other ingredients, such as TOFU, MISO, or toasted and ground SESAME seeds.

Indeed, the role of sesame seeds in dressings for *aemono* is of great importance. For these purposes roasted sesame seeds are either roughly chopped with a knife or, more commonly, ground to varying degrees by means of a *suribachi* (a giant earthenware mortar, often measuring over a foot in diameter) and a *surkogi* (a correspondingly large wooden pestle, looking like a truncheon). Egg yolk may also be used. Other ingredients for the dressing include fish roe, *kinome* (leaf buds of SANSHO), mustard, WASABI, grated daikon (see RADISH), poppyseeds, and peanuts. These basic materials are mixed with soy sauce, vinegar, dashi, saké, sugar, water, etc.

Two of the best-known examples of *aemono* are *Horenso no goma-ae*, which is spinach with sesame seeds, and *Shira-ae*, vegetables with a dressing made from tofu.

Agemono, the term for something deep fried. Deep-frying in a light batter (TEMPURA) is the best-known technique, but some foods are deep fried with no more than a dusting of flour and some without any coating. In the second category are tiny fish skeletons from which the flesh has been removed for separate cooking; these are reputedly delicious. The third category includes halves of small eggplants, and other small vegetable items.

Mushimono, the category of steamed dishes (*mushi* means to steam). Chicken, fish, other seafoods, and vegetables are steamed; also glutinous rice, after having been soaked in water. They are often treated first with SAKÉ, and standard Japanese ingredients such as daikon (see RADISH) and KOMBU play a supporting role.

By far the most popular example of *mushimono* is *Chawan-mushi*. (*Chawan* means a teacup, though nowadays lidded cups specially made for this purpose are used.) This is basically a steamed CUSTARD. Small pieces of poultry, fish, shellfish, vegetables, fungi, etc. are put at the bottom of a cup, and beaten eggs mixed with DASHI are poured into it. The whole thing is then steamed slowly. This is especially popular with children, and is the only dish in the whole repertoire of Japanese cookery to be eaten with a spoon. Another well-known steamed dish is *Tamago dofu*. This is egg TOFU. A block-shaped, firm, savoury egg custard is made with dashi. It is usually chilled and served with soy SAUCE thinned with dashi.

Nabemono, the category of one-pot dishes (*nabe* means a pot or pan), many of which are cooked at the table by the diners. The typical pot used in *nabemono* cookery is an earthenware one called *donabe*. Its body is glazed inside only, the lid on both sides. The Japanese one-pot dish best known in western countries is *sukiyaki*.

A popular example of *nabemono* is SHABU-SHABU, a Japanese adaptation of the Mongolian hotpot. After describing the platter of freshly cut vegetables, with fish, poultry, or meat, which is ready for the guests, Tsuji (1980) observes:

This sort of dish puts into practice the Japanese culinary principle of eating the freshest food just lightly cooked and beautifully presented. On the table is a cast-iron pot or earthenware casserole, filled with broth, set on a heating unit. The meal begins, and with chopsticks everyone slides morsels of fresh food into the pot, fishes them out just as they are cooked, usually a minute or so, and dips them in a seasoned sauce in individual dipping bowls.

The broth is water flavoured with KOMBU; or it may be chicken stock. Anything to be cooked which would take a long time is parboiled beforehand. This way of cooking and eating is very popular in Japan, especially in winter, and most households have a portable gas or electric ring to serve as the heating unit.

Nimono, simmered dishes, a method of cooking which is applied to fish, octopus, meat which calls for slow cooking, chicken, vegetables, beans, chestnuts, etc. The term may also be used for a dish which is steamed over a simmering liquid. Thus octopus is first rubbed with grated RADISH, then steamed over a simmering liquid which includes DASHI and SAKÉ for as much as 10 hours, after which it emerges tender and with an undamaged skin.

Okashi, a Japanese culinary term which indicates small items of what can loosely be described as confectionery, such as are served to visitors with tea.

Okashi are also taken with the special whisked powdered tea at the end of a formal meal, but they are not part of it. A Japanese meal has no sweet course corresponding to western dessert, except for the fruit with which it always ends. Only after it has ended come tea and any accompaniments of the tea.

The name *okashi* comes from a word meaning fruit, and refers back to the time when fruit or dried fruit was commonly eaten between meals, as a snack and a sort of forerunner of confectionery. Traditional Japanese confectionery also has an after-runner in the form of western cakes and sweetmeats. These originally arrived under Portuguese and Dutch auspices at the end of the 16th century, and at first did no more than influence Japanese confectionery but have recently begun to supplant it.

Okashi are made from various ingredients, but the majority of them are based on sweet bean paste (most often made with AZUKI BEAN). They fall into various categories, determined by the method of manufacture, keeping qualities, precise purpose, etc.

Shirumono, a term which may apply to all soups or to thick soups in particular; in the latter case it contrasts with *suimono* (below), clear soups.

Suimono, the Japanese name for clear soups. (*Suimono* means, literally, 'a thing to sip' as the Japanese do not use a spoon for their soup but drink it directly from the bowl.) Other soups are classed as *shirumono*. (Nomenclature is not clear cut here. Sometimes the word *shirumono*, which means 'a liquid thing', covers all soups, including delicate, clear soups as well as substantial, thick ones. *Suimono* is then a subcategory of *shirumono*.)

Suimono are usually based on DASHI. They take their place at an early stage in the meal. One of the most popular is *Kakitama-jiru*, a beaten egg soup with a tang of GINGER, related to the Egg drop soup of China. Another is *Tori no suimono*, a clear chicken soup which may incorporate CHRYSANTHEMUM leaves and SHIITAKE mushrooms.

Sukiyaki, see *nabemono*, above.

Sunomono literally means 'vinegared things' and refers to salad-like items which have been given a vinegar dressing. This dressing may be of various kinds; there are at least a dozen and a half well-known ones, with various flavours provided by other Japanese ingredients.

Teriyaki, a term which refers to a special glaze applied to fish, meat, or fowl in the final stages of grilling or pan-frying. This glaze is sweet and is based on a trio of favourite Japanese ingredients: SOY SAUCE, SAKÉ, and MIRIN. *Teri* means gloss and *yaki* (as in *yakimono* (below)) refers to grilling or pan-frying. The glaze is called *teriyaki* sauce and may be bought in a commercially prepared form or made at home.

Tsukemono, the Japanese term for PICKLES, covers one pickled fruit (see UMEBOSHI) and an exceptionally wide range of vegetables. The traditional method of home pickling was in rice bran in large barrels, and salt pickles have also been used extensively, but there has been an increasing tendency towards buying commercially prepared pickles. These include many regional and local specialities. Generally, the display of pickles in Japanese food shops outshines anything to be seen in western countries; and this reflects the special place which pickles occupy in a Japanese meal. Although younger people now perceive them as optional, older Japanese regard them as indispensable to the closing stage of a meal (cf cheese in France and something sweet in Britain).

The vegetables most popular as pickles include daikon (see RADISH), cabbage, cucumber, eggplant, and radish greens. Western vegetables introduced to Japan are pickled in just the same ways as indigenous vegetables.

A link has been seen between the heavy consumption of pickles of all kinds by Japanese and their unusually high rate of stomach cancer, but it is not clear whether one particular category of pickles is implicated more than others.

Yakimono, the name for a grilled dish in Japan. Such dishes are normally placed towards the end of a meal and do not involve large helpings.

The grilling may be done over the flame or indirectly, the food being shielded by a flameproof metal mat, or in a pan. In the latter case the western culinary term would be 'pan-frying' rather than 'grilling'. However, the Japanese term has a meaning which extends to pan-frying and to baking in an oven (rather as 'roasting' in England has come to mean baking in an oven or 'roasting' in a pot, as well as the original form of roasting, in front of an open fire).

When grilling is done over charcoal, Japanese cooks do not prefer an aromatic charcoal which gives a smoky flavour, but rather 'one that burns smokelessly and odourlessly and emits a very hot heat so foods grill quickly. The best hardwood charcoal, called *bincho*, is made of oak, which came, traditionally, from Wakayama Prefecture. *Bincho* was named after a wholesale charcoal dealer. This charcoal is so hard and shiny that when poured from its sack it looks and sounds like large obsidian chips' (Tsuji, 1980).

Foods which are grilled are threaded onto skewers more often than in western countries; and it is also common for them to be cut up and marinated beforehand. Skewering foods so that, after being grilled, they will look good and be crisp outside but moist inside is an art which is practised earnestly, with excellent results.

Zensai, a Japanese term for what are called appetizers or HORS D'ŒUVRES in western countries, ZAKUSKI in Russia, etc. The correspondence is close in terms of position in the structure of a meal, although the choice of items and the delicacy of presentation are different.

JAPANESE TEA CEREMONY The tea ceremony, *chanoyu* (literally tea's hot water), was brought to Japan as a Buddhist ritual by the Japanese priest Eisai (1141–1215), who had learned about it in China while he was studying Buddhism there. He also brought back seeds of the tea plant.

From its earliest days, the ceremony was associated with Zen Buddhism and was practised as one of the Zen 'ways', as those disciplines are called. In this context it was the 'way of tea'. The great Zen monk Ikkyu (1394–1484) thought that tea produced greater enlightenment than long meditation. And indeed the very high caffeine content of powdered green tea (*matcha*) was certainly taken advantage of to keep the monks from dozing off during religious exercises.

The tea ceremony is still an important practice in Zen temples. However, it needs neither temples nor priests, so it often seems to the unenlightened observer purely social. It certainly has an established place in Japanese society as a social activity. No doubt this is connected with the fact that Zen is more a mystical philosophy than a religion, and in any case the link with Zen can be weak.

The meal served at a full-scale tea ceremony (*chaji*) is called *cha kaiseki*. It came into being because it is not desirable to drink strong *matcha* on an empty stomach and some sort of preceding meal was therefore indicated. *Cha kaiseki* is highly refined, with a menu which subtly reflects

the seasons. It has an important place in the sphere of Japanese food. It has had a surprisingly strong influence on the West as inspiration for nouvelle cuisine and *cuisine minceur*.

Apart from *chaji* there is a simplified version called *chakai* (tea party), when no meal is provided, merely tea made from the powdered green-tea leaves. Some kind of sweetmeat is served beforehand.   RHo

JARLSBERG a Norwegian cheese, semi-hard, bearing a likeness to EMMENTAL with its large holes and cream colour. It is round in shape, and some 10 cm (4") high, with a dry rind. It has a nutty flavour which is slightly more creamy than that of Emmental.

Although not christened, widely manufactured, or exported until 1959, this cheese is thought to have been made on Norwegian farmsteads for a considerably longer period. It is named after an old estate once settled by the Vikings, and a large-holed cheese of similar type has certainly been made since the beginning of the 19th century.

JAVA OLIVE the name given to the seeds of *Sterculia foetida*, a tall tree common from Africa through India and SE Asia to Australia. The tree is called 'fetid' because of the smell of its flowers. The seeds themselves smell and taste pleasant, although they are only safe to eat after being fried or roasted. They are the size and shape of olives, dark brown, and borne in a big, red, flat pod with lobes arranged like the blades of a propeller.

S. foetida is the commonest tree of its genus throughout the region, but there are others. In Latin America, *S. chicha* has seeds which are used as a substitute for COLA 'nuts' and are also reputed to taste like CHOCOLATE—not surprising since these trees belong to the same family as the cola nut and the cacao tree.

JELLY a word applied to items made from flavoured solutions mixed with a setting agent, and then allowed to cool. They can be sweet or savoury, and range in texture from soft, ephemeral desserts to chewy CONFECTIONERY. In scientific terms, they are substances called gels. In everyday language, the term jelly is used in three main ways.

Jelly sweets are confectionery items which use gelling agents such as GELATIN or PECTIN to maintain syrups in a rigid form. These sweets are produced in bright colours and soft textures, and include children's favourites such as jelly babies. They have a relatively high water content for confectionery, about 15%, which means that they do not keep as well as many sweets.

They may also be set with AGAR-AGAR, or a STARCH. TURKISH DELIGHT is an example of a jellied sweet using starch as a setting agent.

Jelly desserts, as made in Europe and N. America, are mostly flavoured with fruit; see FRUIT JELLIES.

Jelly preserves are like JAM, but use strained fruit juice rather than fruit pulp. In N. America, however, jelly is a general term for jam. In any case, pectin acts as the gelling agent.

The **history of jelly,** chronicled by Brears (1996) in a major and pioneering essay which won the Sophie Coe Prize for food history essays of that year, is complex. Generally, it would seem that confectionery-type jellies, and jelly preserves, developed from attempts to conserve pectin-rich fruit extracts; see, in this connection, the various marmalade-ancestors mentioned under MARMALADE. Modern dessert jellies, on the other hand, appear to be descended from medieval dishes based on calves' feet or other meat stocks, carefully clarified and flavoured.

A wide range of gelling or setting agents was known to medieval cooks. The animal kingdom was represented by GELATIN in the form of meat stock; ISINGLASS; and HARTSHORN. Plants provided pectin-rich juices from quinces or apples; and various kinds of gum (see GUM ARABIC and GUM TRAGACANTH).

Late medieval and 16th-century cooks made savoury (or savoury/sweet—many had an ambivalent character) jellied dishes using meat such as capon, chopped fine, mixed with cream or almond milk, flavoured with spices, sugar, or rosewater. These were known as *cullis*, *gellys*, or *brawn*. Another 'set' dish was a leach, made from cream or almond milk with isinglass. A sweet 'crystall gelly' was made with calves' feet stock, highly spiced (ginger, pepper, cloves, nutmeg), sweetened, and further flavoured with rosewater. These dishes, which are recorded in early 17th-century cookery books such as Sir Hugh Platt's *Delightes for Ladies* (1609), were ancestors of sweet confections such as BLANCMANGE as well as of the explicitly savoury ASPIC dishes which proliferated in the 19th and early 20th centuries.
READING: Brears (1996); Sally Kevill-Davies (1983, for moulds).

JELLYFISH not thought of as food in western countries, are valued as such in the Orient. Only some species yield edible matter, and of these *Rhopilema esculenta* is a good example. Discs taken from the umbrella part are dried, then marketed to be soaked, cut into strips, and scalded before use. This preparation causes the strips to form curls, the texture of which is described as 'tender, crunchy and elastic'. The curls may be served in a dressing of sesame oil, soy sauce, vinegar, and sugar. *Miang maeng kaphrung* is a Thai dish of jellyfish and green leaves.

Hosking (1996) observes that the Japanese name for jellyfish is *kurage* and that two species, identified by place names, are enjoyed: *bizen kurage* (the above-mentioned *Rhopilema esculenta*) and *echizen kurage* (*Stomolophus nomurai*), which may be as much as 1 m/40" in diameter, about twice the size of the *bizen*. 'Jellyfish is salted and then dried in the sun. It is mostly used in *sunomono* [see JAPANESE CULINARY TERMS] after the salt is soaked out. Having little if any flavor, *kurage* is enjoyed for its crunchiness.'

JELLY FUNGUS a name applied to FUNGI of the order Tremellales, which have a texture ranging from soft and gelatinous to hard and rubbery. The best-known species are described under WOOD EAR.

Generally, fungi of this sort have little or no flavour but are of interest for their texture. An example is *Tremella mesenterica*, witches' butter, which grows up to 7 cm (3.5") across and consists of yellow or yellow-orange convoluted lobes and folds, which look like brains or (the meaning of *mesenterica*) intestines. It can be added to soups.

Arora (1979), in the semi-humorous vein characteristic of his excellent book, recommends *Pseudohydnum gelatinosum*, the toothed jelly fungus, which has tiny 'teeth' under its cap. Commenting that it is said to be good with honey and cream ('what isn't?' he asks), he adds that it can be marinated and used in salads.

The apricot jelly, *Tremiscus helvelloides*, is described under GUEPINIE.

JERKY a name derived via Spanish from the native Peruvian *charqui*, meaning dried meat. The noun spawned a verb. Jerking meat consists in cutting it up into long strips and then drying these in the sun or at a fire. The practice was widespread among American Indians and among colonists in pioneering days. In modern times jerky occupies a niche in the nostalgic realm of 'trail foods'.

For the S. African equivalent, see BILTONG. For purely air-dried meats, see BINDENFLEISCH; BRESAOLA. For a similar but more complex product, see PEMMICAN.

JERUSALEM ARTICHOKE *Helianthus tuberosus*, a plant which does not come from Jerusalem and has nothing to do with the globe ARTICHOKE, nor with the CHINESE ARTICHOKE. The Jerusalem artichoke is a

N. American relative of the SUNFLOWER, itself native to Peru. Its tubers, and those of related species, were eaten by Indians, especially in what is now Canada, where other edible tubers would not grow. It was noted there in 1603 by the explorer Samuel de Champlain, who himself started the whole confusion by writing of 'roots which they cultivate, and which taste like an artichoke'.

The plant was soon brought back to Europe, at first to France. There, in 1613, six Brazilian Indians, members of the Topinambous tribe who had been brought back by an expedition, aroused much popular interest. Some enterprising hawker of the new vegetable appropriated their name, which is why the French name for the tuber is *topinambour*. In 1616 the root was introduced to England, from Terneuzen in Holland; it is possible that the name of this place was corrupted to 'Jerusalem', although the usual explanation is that 'Jerusalem' is a corruption of *girasole*, the Italian name for the sunflower.

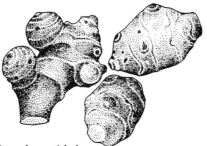

Jerusalem artichoke

The Jerusalem artichoke at first had an enthusiastic reception in Europe, where its curious, sweet taste was a novelty. It was used in sweet dishes more than as a savoury vegetable, but it soon palled and lost favour. By 1621 the writer John Goodyer, revising Gerard's Herbal, was writing:

which way soever they be dressed and eaten, they stir and cause a filthy loathsome stinking wind within the body, thereby causing the belly to be pained and tormented, and are a meat more fit for swine than men.

So the tuber lapsed into its present minor status. It retains some popularity in France; less in Britain; and is almost ignored in its native USA.

The sweetness and the 'filthy loathsome stinking wind' (an exaggeration) are both due to the same substance: inulin, a carbohydrate related to the simple sugar fructose. Unlike normal sugars, inulin is largely indigestible.

The tuber of the Jerusalem artichoke is typically branched, knobbly or segmented, and up to 10 cm (4") long. There are now more than a dozen popular varieties, including Fuseau, which has no knobs and is

thus easy to clean or peel. Colour of the tubers may be white, silvery, light tan, red, or purple. Some need not be peeled.

Jerusalem artichokes are good raw and grated in salads, with a taste like Brazil nuts. They must be fresh and crisp. Boiling is the usual way of cooking them. They are also good roasted, and make unusual and excellent chips (US: French fries). A traditional British soup made with them is called 'Palestine soup', a pun on Jerusalem.

JEWISH COOKERY like the Jews, has been spread around the world as a result of the Diaspora, the dispersion of the Jews, from biblical times to the present, outside their homeland. It has, to some extent, been reconcentrated in ISRAEL (but cookery in that country is not equatable with Jewish cookery as it comprises other elements also).

All Jewish cookery, naturally, is influenced to a greater or lesser degree by JEWISH DIETARY LAWS.

Jewish cookery of the Diaspora can be divided into two main branches: Sephardi and Ashkenazi.

The term **Sephardi** refers primarily to the Jews of the Iberian peninsula and their descendants. The Jewish community in Spain represented one of the finest flowerings of Jewish culture until 1492, the year when the Jews were expelled from that country (and shortly thereafter from Portugal). Following this, many Jews from Spain and Portugal joined Jewish communities already existing in Italy, the Netherlands, England, and parts of the New World. All these are called 'Western Sephardim'. Those who settled in the Balkans and the Mediterranean areas are 'Eastern Sephardim'. However, the term Sephardi has an even wider scope, covering Jewish communities in the Near East (e.g. Iraq, Iran); in the Yemen and Ethiopia; and in N. Africa.

Schwartz (1992) remarks that:

Sephardi Jews share the fact that the majority of them lived in countries which were at one time or other under the influence of Islam. Islam and Judaism have a lot in common; both sprang from a Middle Eastern nomadic pastoral culture.

The cookery of the Sephardim, broadly speaking, exhibits much evidence of the long period when the Sephardi community flourished in Spain. For much of this period most of Spain and Portugal were under Islamic occupation, which has in turn meant that the Spanish and Portuguese cuisines show a strong Arab influence, reflected in that of the Sephardim. Thus two streams of influence converged, both proceeding originally from the Near East, the region embracing the original homelands of both Jews and Arabs. This circumstance helps to account for the harmonious nature of

Sephardic cooking. It developed in a natural way in a geographical and cultural climate which was compatible with the Bible and the foods mentioned therein.

The term **Ashkenazi** refers to Jews belonging originally to the area of the Rhine Valley and the Elbe River and subsequently settling further east, in various parts of a broad territory extending from Alsace to Smolensk and from the Baltic to the Black Sea. Jews from Germanic lands are called 'Western Ashkenazim', and those from Slavic territories 'Eastern Ashkenazim'. Their vernacular tongues are Western and Eastern Yiddish. Yiddish was one of the strongest manifestations of European Jewishness.

In contrast to the Sephardic cuisine, the Slavic and Germanic cuisines which provide the setting for Ashkenazi food are very far removed from the biblical landscape and climate. Without any disrespect to Slavic and Germanic cultures, it could be said that by comparison with the sunny and vibrant Mediterranean and Near Eastern cultures, they present a less sparkling appearance.

One feature of Jewish culture is that much Jewish humour is food related. Traditional jokes often concern overeating, and may be linked with the reverence felt in Jewish families for 'mother's cooking'. Jews are far from being alone in this respect, but their attitudes, at least in the Ashkenazi culture, are more noticeable.

Under Jewish dietary laws no cooking (or other work) may be done on the Sabbath. Sokolov (1989) gives the necessary precision:

The general prohibition against work on the Jewish Sabbath (which runs from sundown Friday until Saturday evening) includes cooking. Warming is, however, allowed if (1) the source of heat was kindled before the beginning of the Sabbath, covered with a special tin plate or blech, and not adjusted once it has been lit; (2) the food to be reheated must have been previously cooked; and (3) liquids must not be brought to a boil. This greatly restricts the Sabbath diet. Even the Friday night meal must be set to cooking in the afternoon, before sundown.

The requirement thus imposed on observant households to prepare food in advance points towards some sort of one-pot stew. The terms cholent, hamin(e), and dafina (meaning 'buried') refer to this category of dishes. Cholent is Yiddish (Ashkenazi) while hamin and dafina are the Sephardi equivalents. None of these terms, it is to be noted, refers to a single specific dish. All are terms for a category, which according to Sokolov constitutes 'the most diverse and intellectually interesting of all Jewish foods'.

Claudia Roden (1996) explains that:

Cholent has deep emotional significance. The smell exhaled when the lid is lifted is the one that filled the wooden houses in the shtetl. In the old days in Central and Eastern Europe, the pot was hermetically sealed with a flour-and-water paste

and taken to the baker's oven, and the men and children fetched it on their way home from the synagogue. . . .

The basic traditional cholent is meat, potatoes, barley, and beans. The traditional accompaniments which are cooked in the same pot, are of German origin. They include kishke (a sausage filled with a flour-and-onion stuffing) and various knaidlach—all part of the dumpling family of foods.

Whatever the fascination of its intellectual content, this is heavy, filling food (whose stodgy nature has inspired a number of Jewish jokes), and Roden tells us that the Sephardi dafina, although it takes very many forms, is also 'usually stodgy and heavy on the stomach'. It may contain veal, beef, or lamb, sliced calf's foot, chickpeas or beans, potatoes or sweet potatoes, green vegetables such as spinach, and always hard-boiled eggs.

The distinction between Ashkenazi and Sephardi food, emphasized in what is said above, is important, but it should not be thought that it is rigid and all pervasive. The first Jewish cookery book in the English language (published in 1846: see Raphael, 1983) contained (along with English, French, Italian, Dutch recipes) both Sephardi and some Western Ashkenazi dishes. However, after the influx of E. European Jews later in the 19th century the Sephardi element in England was submerged under the weight of Ashkenazi food; and it is broadly true that in any given country or region one of the two eventually comes to be dominant, to the virtual exclusion of the other.

See also CHALLAH; BAGEL; GEFILTE FISH; KREPLACH; TZIMMES; MATZO; PASSOVER.

JEWISH DIETARY LAWS These resemble a building of marvellous complexity and great size, soaring towards the sky, yet resting on a few slender bases—like some of the marvels of modern architecture.

The bases are those passages in the Torah (Pentateuch, i.e. first five books of the Bible) which embody, according to the Jewish faith, the commands of God on dietary matters, as conveyed directly to Moses and passed on by him to the children of Israel.

Because the commands are brief, they have invited interpretation and amplification, which have been supplied on a generous scale, and over several thousand years, by rabbinical commentators, notably in the Mishnah and the Talmud. The ratio in size between the original sentences in the Bible and the accretion of the commentaries with which they are now encrusted must be something like one to several hundred thousand.

The biblical injunctions may be summarized thus as follows.

1. *What may be eaten.* Leviticus 11 and Deuteronomy 14 restrict consumption to:

(*a*) animals which both chew the cud and possess cloven hooves;
(*b*) birds not on the prohibited list;
(*c*) fish (and other aquatic creatures) which have both scales and fins.

Leviticus 11 also specifically bars 'every creeping thing which creepeth upon the earth', thus ruling out crustaceans such as lobster, prawn, and crab (all of which are also banned under 1c above), and frogs and snails, and all insects. (Nevertheless, in a passage which is difficult to interpret with certainty, some species of locust or grasshopper, even a beetle, are allowed, apparently on the basis that although they creep they do have legs which enable them to jump. Also, honey, despite being an insect product, is looked on with favour, being part of the biblical 'land of milk and honey' formula.)

Leviticus 17 prohibits consumption of the blood of any animal or bird. It also prohibits eating animals or birds which have died from natural causes or been mauled by predators.

Genesis 32 states that Jews do not eat the ischiatic nerve, which runs through the hindquarters of quadrupeds. This item is unusual in two respects. First, it is presented more as a custom than as a divine command. Secondly, an explanation is given, that the ischiatic nerve touches on the thigh bone and thus recalls the famous occasion when Jacob's thigh was put out in a wrestling bout with a stranger who, he discovered, was God incarnate.

2. *How must slaughtering be done?* The Torah itself provides no guidance. However, oral traditions (which some Jews believe go all the way back to Moses), subsequently put down in writing, supply a great deal of information about the correct procedures. In brief, domesticated animals must be slaughtered in a ritual manner, by an officially authorized and supervised slaughterer (*shechet*). Poultry do not need a trained slaughterer, but are still subject to rules. The animal or bird must be conscious when its throat is cut with a single stroke of the knife.

Animals and birds must be opened and inspected after slaughter, and must be found free of significant blemishes. Some Jews are stricter than others in determining what are significant blemishes.

3. *What rules apply to cooking?* The commandment recorded in both Numbers and Deuteronomy that no work is to be done on the Sabbath obviously includes cookery. So sabbath meals have to be cooked before the Sabbath.

Three separate passages in the Torah (two in Exodus and one in Deuteronomy) affirm that 'Thou shalt not seethe [boil] a kid in its mother's milk.' The idea that anyone, whether a Jew or not, would literally do this has struck many readers of the Bible as strange, and it is natural to suppose that the command carries a wider significance, such as rabbinical interpretations have in fact given it. These interpretations have led to the current situation, in which observant Jews separate cookery involving milk or milk products from cookery involving meat or meat products. Moreover, they separate consumption of the one from consumption of the other and have separate sets of kitchen equipment for them, to guard against cross-contamination.

4. *Special occasions.* These may be marked by established food customs, whether involving fasting or feasting, or may be governed by a dietary law. The prime example of the latter is PASSOVER. The command not to eat leavened food during Passover is in Exodus 12 and 13. Conforming with this is only one part of the complex Passover ritual, which constitutes for Jews an important way of recalling what they see as a fundamental feature of their history, namely the flight from Egypt.

COMMENTARY

Some commentators, including Jewish ones, have sought to find a rational basis (e.g. reasons of hygiene, or benefits to the economy) for at least some of the dietary laws. The results are not impressive. In any case, some rabbis deem it improper to subject the rules, which are the will of God, to any such analysis. Indeed it has been proposed that a Jew should not say that he detests the flesh of swine and therefore abstains from it; better to say that he finds bacon attractive but does not eat it because God has commanded him not to.

On doctrinal matters, Jews (not everywhere but in the USA and Britain, to take two examples) fall into three broad categories: the Orthodox, the Conservatives, and the Reform Church. As Jacobs (1995) makes clear in his description of where the three groups stand on dietary matters, there are plenty of exceptions to any generalization. Subject to this proviso, the Orthodox tend to take the dietary laws literally and follow them in full rigour; Conservative Jews interpret them more liberally; and Reform Jews, although many of them follow at least those rules which are actually stated in the Torah, attach less importance to them and may indeed ignore them.

As long ago as 1888, a number of Reform rabbis in the USA produced the 'Pittsburgh Declaration', in which they said that Mosaic and rabbinical rules about diet and dress originated 'under the influence of ideas entirely foreign to our present mental and

spiritual state' and were more likely to hinder than promote spiritual elevation. (In this connection it is relevant to note that the dietary laws which were passed on to the children of Israel by Moses were only a relatively small part of the divine commands which he conveyed. To judge by the amount of space devoted to various topics in the Torah, God was more concerned at that time with having Moses explain in detail what rules were to be followed about animal sacrifices to him, plus a whole lot of other matters such as property laws, penalties for marital infidelity, etc. Many of these non-food laws have been allowed to lapse, presumably because the context in which they had seemed appropriate had vanished. For example, Jews no longer sacrifice animals, although Leviticus abounds in instructions on exactly how they should do so, and some Jews pray that the practice can be resumed in the future.)

Despite the different tendencies described above, the dietary rules are perceived by many Jews as having had, and continuing to have, an important defining effect; they help to define the Jewish community, or a particular Jewish sect, in the awareness of its own members and of outsiders. Also, by discouraging social intercourse with outsiders, they may tend to slow down the rate at which marriage between Jews and non-Jews has been increasing.

See also JEWISH COOKERY.

KOSHER

THE key word for the subject of the dietary laws. It comes from the Hebrew *kasher*, meaning to make fit. In the English language it has acquired a wide meaning and many applications: correct, genuine, authorized, legitimate (in almost any context). In the narrower sense it refers to articles of food which are permitted to Jews and have been prepared in accordance with the dietary laws. It can also be used of a restaurant or a cookery book, and appears in the expression 'to keep kosher'.

JIAOZI are Chinese meat DUMPLINGS (see also DUMPLINGS OF ASIA), which constitute a meal on their own and are always eaten during Chinese New Year, reinforcing family reunions which take place at that time. Dr Yan-Kit So (1992) remarks: 'It has often been said that they are the best peacemakers for, in the rolling of the skins followed by the stuffing of them and then the cooking, the ice is bound to be broken and peace made between feuding parties in the family.'

Thinly rolled-out dough is usually stuffed with minced pork and chives or cabbage. The dumplings are then either poached or fried, and eaten with dipping sauces, SOY SAUCE, or other side dishes.

Each region of China has its own special version. In some southern areas of China they are made in the shape of the gold and silver ingots (*yuan bao*) that were used as money in ancient China; this augurs good fortune as well as good eating. Muslims in N. China use minced lamb or beef rather than pork.

See also MANTOU and WONTON.   HS

JICAMA the underground tuber of *Pachyrhizus erosus*, a leguminous plant of Mexico which was taken to the Philippines by the Spanish in the 17th century and has since spread across Asia and the Pacific. It is not, however, prominent as a vegetable except in Mexico and (since recently) the

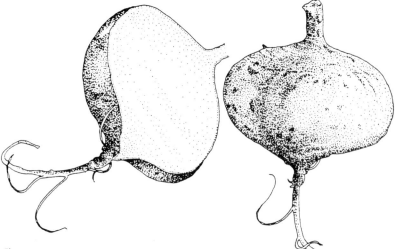

Jicama

south of China and the USA. Elizabeth Schneider (1986) expresses surprise that it has not been written about more.:

It has crunchy, juicy ivory flesh (the texture of water chestnuts) and a sweet, bland flavor that suits everything from fruit cup to stir-fried shrimp. It could not be easier to prepare, requiring only the peeling of its thinnish, sandy-tan, matte skin. Jicama is marketed in a useful range of sizes, from ½ pound to as much as 6 pounds. It can be eaten raw or cooked—and is very low in calories for so starchy-seeming a vegetable.

The name jicama is used in Ecuador and Peru for what is better called YACON.

JOBFISH the name given to fish of the SNAPPER family in the genera *Aphareus*, *Aprion*, and *Pristipomoides*. These small to medium-size fish are found in tropical waters around the world, especially the Caribbean and the Indo-Pacific, and are important food fishes in some regions. A few of the species are:

- *Aprion virescens*, the green jobfish, *aochibiki* in Japan, maximum length 1 m (40"), widely distributed from E. Africa to the Pacific islands, a good eating fish which is usually marketed fresh but may also be dried and salted. It is highly rated in Hawaii, where frying (of fillets) is recommended by local authors.
- *Pristipomoides filamentosus*, the crimson (or rosy) jobfish, maximum length 80 cm (32"), with a range from S. and E. Africa to Hawaii, is of good quality, and is important (as *opakapaka*) in Hawaii.
- *P. sieboldii*, the lavender jobfish, maximum length 60 cm (24"), marketed in, for example, Japan (as *himedai*) and Hawaii (as *kalikali*).

JOHN DORY *Zeus* spp, fish of remarkable shape, deep and thin in the body, which occur in the Mediterranean and eastern N. Atlantic (*Z. faber*) and also in Australasian waters (*Z. australis*) and in the NW Pacific (*Z. japonicus*).

Maximum length of these fish is around 60 cm (24"), and a large specimen may weigh as much as 3 or 4 kg (7–9 lb). Market size is usually about half as large.

The thin body serves a purpose. These fish cannot swim very fast, so are unable to catch their prey by speed. Instead they use stealth, approaching with an almost invisible profile and then shooting out the huge, retractable jaws to engulf the victim.

The black marks on each side are responsible for many of the common names such as *Saint-Pierre* in French and *pez de San Pedro* in Spanish; these signify an association with St Peter, whose fingers are supposed to

have left the marks. One tale is that this is the fish which he took up on the instructions of Christ, to find in its mouth the silver which he was to pay as tribute; but this cannot be so, since the incident took place at the Sea of Galilee (fresh water) and the John Dory is a marine fish. The alternative story is that St Peter threw a John Dory back into the sea after it had engaged his sympathy by making distressed noises.

Despite being so thin, the John Dory yields excellent fillets. It is prized in the Mediterranean and in Australian waters (especially New South Wales). In Britain, its reputation was low in the distant past, but was given a boost by the 18th-century actor Quin, who had a passion for it and who was reported to have settled the question of what sauce suited it best by announcing the banns of marriage between 'delicate Ann Chovy, and good John Dory'.

JOJOBA *Simmondsia chinensis* (formerly *californica*), a common shrub of the desert region of the south-western USA and Mexico, whose nuts were a foodstuff for American Indians. The name 'jojoba', most generally used for these, is a Cahuilla Indian one, but they may also be called goat nuts, deer nuts, or pig nuts.

The nut resembles a HAZELNUT in size and appearance, but is more pointed and has slightly flattened sides, giving it a triangular cross-section. It has a bitter taste, something like that of the ACORN.

The jojoba is unusual in that it contains a wax, which is liquid at normal temperatures. This has been used as a hair restorer. Another use suggested for it is in the preparation of 'slimming' foods. Wax is to oil as cellulose is to starch, i.e. it can be eaten and satisfies appetite, but is not digested and provides no nutrition. It therefore seems possible that the plant will acquire some minor and paradoxical importance as a source of non-food for the food industry.

JOLLOF RICE whose name comes from the ancient kingdom of the Wolof people of Senegal and surrounding countries, is one of the most common W. African dishes sold in chop houses, cookshops, and restaurants. It is regarded as a festival dish or one for special occasions and is, in effect, a W. African version of PILAF with as many variations as that dish. It is not usually as chilli-hot as most W. African cooking but contains a huge amount of tomato paste or PALM OIL, so the dish is always red.

Any meats, chicken, ham, smoked fish, and shellfish may be used to go with the rice, plus any or several of various vegetables (potatoes, pumpkin, aubergine, cabbage,

beans, dried peas). Spices and flavourings can be drawn from a wide range: e.g. curry powder, nutmeg, cloves, mint, thyme, garlic, and sugar.

Jollof rice is made wherever W. Africans have settled and is possibly the best-known African dish outside Africa. The Senegalese call it *benachin*.   JM

JORDAN like the other countries in the Fertile Crescent and the Arabian Peninsula, is a new state in an old territory, linked by geography, history, and demography to its neighbours. Its food production traditionally reflected the nature of its different soil conditions and its water resources; and its food transformation and preparation—its cuisine—reflected the skills of its inhabitants in adapting their tastes to the foods available to them.

Traditionally—until the political changes in the region, and in particular the influx of three successive waves of Palestinian refugees and displaced persons since the creation of Israel in 1948—Jordan's food production and its cuisine were products of the three micro-climates of its space: the Jordan Valley, the high plateau, and the desert: citrus, bananas, and vegetables from the Valley, cereals, pulses, olives and olive oil, and other fresh and dried fruits from the plateau, and dairy produce from the sheep and goat herds of the desert.

Until recent times the predominant food culture was that of the villages and the desert, which were not distinct areas but which complemented each other and exchanged their products. The growth of large urban centres such as Amman and Irbid introduced new food cultures from areas such as Palestine, LEBANON AND SYRIA, but did not replace the traditional cuisine, rather adding to it to produce what could now be described as a specifically Jordanian cuisine.

The staple diet of the Jordanian villages was, and still is, a combination of cereals and pulses with the many varieties of wild herbs which grow after the rains of autumn, winter, and spring, and with both the fresh and preserved dairy products of the sheep and goat herds which grazed between the desert and the town. Lentils and CHICKPEAS with wild herbs and yoghurt combined with cracked wheat (see BURGHUL) form many varieties of a basic dish. The rains of spring bring the wild artichoke—*aqoub*—truffles, and mushrooms, once the food of the people but now the delicacies of the new urban middle class. Similarly the traditional village food of *freeki* (see FREEKEH), corn picked when still green and roasted on wood, is now a speciality of the urban table.

What could rightly be called the national dish of Jordan—the *Mansaf*—which it shares with Iraq, Saudi Arabia, and Syria, is also a product of the combined resources of the village and the desert. Before the availability of cheap rice from Egypt, later from the Far East, the cereal base of *mansaf* was burghul; and what distinguishes the Jordanian *mansaf* from the Lebanese or Syrian *Qouzi* is the use of *jameed*, a dried and pumicestone form of yoghurt, instead of the fresh *laban* (see YOGHURT) or AYRAN which would accompany a *qouzi*.

Because both the village and desert populations were poor, often living on the margin of starvation, meat in the form of a whole or half-sheep was a luxury for special occasions, such as marriage or the arrival of a guest, or even a funeral; with the greater availability of meat, and the rise in income of the middle-class urban population, the *mansaf* is now no longer considered a luxury, but rather as the national dish which forms an element of the Jordanian identity.

CH

JOSHPARA an ancient form of Iranian RAVIOLI (or, to be exact, capelletti, meaning 'little hats') made by folding a square of paste over a filling to create a triangle and then wrapping the two acute angles toward each other. This creates a compact shape which is sometimes likened to the hat worn by 18th-century grenadiers because of its tallness, sometimes to an ear because of its impression of convoluted folding.

It is quite an ancient product. The Arabs adopted it with the pronunciation *shushbarak* or (through a folk etymology connecting it with *shish*, 'skewer', and BÖREK) *shishbarak*, which indicates that it was borrowed before the 10th century when it was pronounced *joshparag*. The first part of the name, *josh*, means 'to boil', but the second element is obscure, possibly meaning 'bit'. Iranians have felt the absence of a clearly analysable meaning, and the word is now pronounced *gosh-e-barreh* in Iran, literally 'lamb's ear'. The Turkish nations who have borrowed joshpara have done even more violence to the word: Azerbaijani *düshbara*, Uzbeki *chuchwara*, Uighur *chöchürä*.

The usual Iranian or Arab version is filled with lamb and onions and cooked in yoghurt. In C. Asia it is usually served without its cooking liquid and may have such fillings as meat, wild greens, dried tomatoes, mashed potato, or eggs and onions.

Medieval Iranian merchants trading flour for furs in W. Siberia taught it to Finno-Ugrian peoples such as the Udmurt, who coined their own name for it: *pelnan*, literally 'ear-bread', because of its shape. In the 17th century the advancing Russians adopted *pelnan*, eventually Russianizing the

pronunciation to *pel'meni*, and PEL'MENI in chicken broth is now a classic Russian dish.

CP

JUG a verb referring to a method of cookery which involves putting what is to be cooked (e.g. pieces of HARE) in a jug or jar, or something of similar shape, with liquid and simmering it therein. The jug or jar may be stood, for this purpose, in a pan of boiling water. Cooking by this method is usually long and slow.

It is also possible to jug a kipper by lowering it into a jug or jar which is then filled with boiling water and left to stand for a few minutes.

JUJUBE the name commonly given to the fruit of various small spiny trees in the genus *Zizyphus*. The most important is *Z. jujuba*, which grows in mild to temperate, dry areas of both hemispheres. It has been known in China since antiquity, and its fruit is often called Chinese date. Whether it originated in China or Syria is not clear, but it is cultivated for its fruits right across this range: in Japan, China, Afghanistan, Iran, and westwards to the Mediterranean region.

Z. mauritiana, the Indian jujube, is adapted to warmer climates. It is grown commercially only in India.

Generally, these fruits are candied, but they may also be eaten fresh. 'Ripe jujubes, when eaten raw, are amusing rather than delicious, and have a crisp, sprightly flavor different from other fruits.' Thus wrote Fairchild (1938) who recalled meeting them for the first time in candied form on a boat leaving Shanghai. The long, pointed seeds and caramel-like texture reminded him of the dried dates which he had eaten in the Persian Gulf region, but he knew they were not true dates and was puzzled by the scratches he saw on their surface. Later, the mystery was solved when he was sent one of the scoring knives with which the Chinese slash the tough skins of the fruit before stewing them in honey or sugar syrup. He recommended the honeyed kind.

Iddison (1994) has given a useful survey, based on his finding the fruit of *Z. jujuba* available for eating fresh in markets of Majorca, of both the jujubes described above and some other closely related species. Generally, the fruits of the other species, which are about the size of cherries and red, purple, or black in colour, are

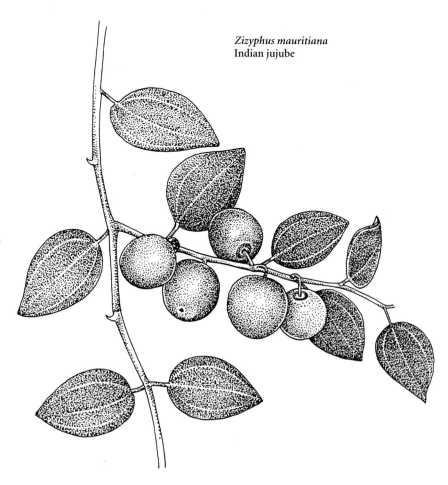

Zizyphus mauritiana
Indian jujube

considered too dry and mealy to be eaten fresh.

The jujube is noteworthy in one other respect. It is the leading candidate, in a field of dubious entrants, for having been what the 'lotus-eaters' described by Homer in the *Odyssey* had been consuming when they were afflicted by lethargy and forgetfulness. There is nothing narcotic about the jujube in its natural state, but it has been pointed out that it would have been easy enough to ferment it into a strong wine.

See also JUJUBES.

JUJUBES confections of sugar syrup and fruit flavourings, set with a high proportion of GUM, and falling into the general category of fruit GUMS and fruit LOZENGES, often with a medicinal application, e.g. good for sore throats.

Jujubes have been made since at least 1830 when Gunter wrote in his *Confectioner's Oracle* that 'Jujubes are very much in vogue abroad,—but it would be exceedingly difficult to say *wherefore*:- they are at best very little better than a sweetish sort of *India-rubber*!!' This was a harsher criticism than could fairly be made of good English jujubes, such as could readily be obtained until quite recently.

JUMBLES sometimes called knots, a type of biscuit popular in the 17th and 18th centuries. They were made from a light mixture of butter, sugar, eggs, and flour, flavoured with rosewater and aniseed or caraway seed. The mixture was made into thin rolls and shaped into rounds or knots before baking; the name derives from *gemmel*, twin, here referring to a double intertwined finger ring.

Cookies called jumbles (or jumbals) began to appear in N. American recipe books early in the 19th century. They often included chopped nuts which made some people think that they owed their name to the 'jumbling' of this ingredient in the dough.   LM

JUNIPER coniferous shrubs or trees of the genus *Juniperus*. The berry-like fruits are often used for flavouring purposes.

The common juniper, *Juniperus communis*, is found throughout Europe and N. America and in the Himalayas, growing as a scrubby bush on chalky hillsides. All parts of the plant are fragrant. The berries which are up to 1 cm (0.4") in diameter, take three years to mature, and are at first dark green ripening to a deep purple. Specimens at various stages of development exist on the tree simultaneously.

The berries are used throughout Europe to flavour meat and pâtés and in marinades for game. They are usually crushed before use to allow the oils to escape. In Germany they are used to flavour SAUERKRAUT.

JUNKET according to the *NSOED*, comes from an Old French word *jonquette* (spelled various ways) meaning a rush basket but also a kind of cream cheese made in such a basket. From the latter meaning it came to have its modern one: a dish of sweetened and flavoured CURDS (produced by the action of RENNET on milk). It can also mean a banquet or festive gathering.

Dorothy Hartley (1954) has the following to say, starting with a very precise admonition:

Junkets are made best in the peat country in the west of England.

In modern making, the milk is heated blood-warm and set with rennet. Rum is a usual flavouring, and clotted cream a usual accompaniment; often a powdering of nutmeg or cinnamon, covers the top.

The older junkets were usually made with the milk warm from the cow, and apparently curds and whey were sometimes listed as 'junkets' in old cookery books.

JUNSAI *Brasenia schreberi*, is a perennial aquatic plant of the same family as the water lily. Its young shoots are enveloped in a clear, jelly-like substance and are prized as food in Japan.

Junsai grows wild in ancient ponds with a thick layer of silt at the bottom. *Mizorogaike* in Kyoto (the name means 'deep-mud pond') is said to produce the best junsai in Japan. If junsai is transplanted artificially, the shoots will be bereft of the gelatinous covering and lose their culinary value.

Junsai is a summer food, available from May to August. It is first blanched and used for *aemono* or *sunomono*; see JAPANESE CULINARY TERMS. It is also put into soup.   KA

KACHORI (kachauri) are often described as stuffed POORI, and may also be compared with SAMOSA. They are made with a dough usually based on wheat flour, and come in two types: flat patties about 4 cm (1.5") in diameter and 6 mm (0.25") thick, popular for TIFFIN snacks and as travellers' food; and thinner ones (which may be called *dal poori*). Shapes vary (round, crescent, etc.).

Fillings are usually savoury, but can be sweet (for example *besan kachori* contain a sort of chickpea fudge with finely chopped dried fruits and nuts in it). Savoury examples are *matar kachori* (stuffed with a spicy mixture featuring green peas and served on special occasions); *aloo kachori* (seasoned potato, good for travelling); and *radhaballabhi kachori*, popular in N. India in the cold winter months, filled with a spicy lentil mixture. (HS)

KAFFIR an epithet which has been used, especially in southern Africa, of certain plant foods, for which it is now preferable to use names less likely to cause offence.

The term was originally an Arabic word meaning non-believer or infidel; and in this role it could be simply descriptive or derogatory, depending at least in part on the point of view of the speaker. (The same word, spelled with one 'f', was used to denote certain people in NE Afghanistan who were not included in the early medieval wave of conversions to Islam; but their descendants have in the main been converted and therefore do not like being called by this name.)

In southern Africa the term came to mean what would now be called 'black African', sometimes applying to a particular group and sometimes in a general sense. In most contexts it now has a pejorative sense, to such an extent that its use can be actionable in S. Africa. As a term in the English language, it is therefore falling into disuse. In future there are likely to be fewer and fewer references to 'kaffir corn' (a kind of sorghum), 'kaffir plum' (*Harpephyllum caffrum*, a tart red fruit cultivated in S. Africa), 'kaffir orange' (*Strychnos spinosa*, also known as Natal orange, not a true orange), and the more important 'kaffir lime' which is described under MAKRUT LIME, the name which it now seems better to use, in line with the recommendation of Saunt (1990).

The last instance is particularly interesting because the term 'kaffir lime' seems to have only a very short history in the English language and may be all the easier to eradicate for that reason. Since the fruit in question is of some importance in a number of SE Asian cuisines, it is in books about them that one is most apt to find references to it. Such evidence as had been amassed in the 1990s, when the usage came under scrutiny, suggests that the first occurrence in print may have been in the early 1970s, in Thailand. But it would be a reasonable assumption that the term had its origin in southern Africa and may have reached Malaysia and Indonesia from there through the Cape Malays, and then travelled westwards to Thailand. In the language of each of these countries the fruit had its own name, and there had been little reason until very recently for it to have an English name.

KAHK meaning bracelet, an Arabic term which usually refers to a bread ring, which may be seasoned with cumin and coriander and coated with egg and sesame seeds. A

Moroccan variation adds allspice and a pinch of chilli to the dough.

In the Lebanon *kak bil-Semsum* is a thick, small PITTA bread that is dipped in sesame seeds on both sides before being baked. It is either shaped as a small round pitta bread or made into a small handbag-like loaf with a thick round handle and a flattish round body. It is eaten as a savoury snack with a sprinkling of ZAATAR on the insides. Kahk is also made into a sweet breakfast sandwich, the bag end of the bread being cut open and filled with *knafeh* (see QATA'IF).

Lebanese Christians use a version of the dough, sweetened, enriched with milk, and flavoured with MAHLAB (black cherry stone extract), aniseed, and marjoram, to make Easter biscuits, *kahk bi Halib*; these are stamped flat with a wooden die bearing a religious motif.   HS

KAKI *Diospyros kaki*, a cultivated fruit of the PERSIMMON family whose wild ancestor grew in China. It has also been called 'Japanese persimmon' and a variety of it (cultivated in Israel) is extensively marketed as 'sharon fruit'.

It has for long been a popular fruit in China, Japan, and Korea, and has recently ousted the American persimmon in popularity in the USA, where it is cultivated in California. Its introduction there is credited to Commodore Perry in 1856. But Sir Joseph Banks, the botanist who accompanied Captain Cook on his first voyage round the world, is believed to have brought a specimen to Europe much earlier. In western countries it is often called the Chinese or Japanese or oriental persimmon.

The kaki fruit has many shapes (conical, round, flattened, or almost cubical), colours (yellow-orange to red, with a general resemblance to tomatoes), and sizes. The largest can weigh 450 g (1 lb) and measure 8 cm (3") in diameter. The thin skin encloses an orange-coloured pulp within which there may or may not be seeds. A kaki, like other persimmons, may be sweet or highly astringent. The astringency is the result of tannins which are normally present (although not in some cultivars) when the fruit is green and hard and which may still be present when it is ripe (although fortunately they are usually absorbed, during the process of ripening, by carbohydrates with which they are associated). The content of vitamin C and of sugar varies but is generally high.

Americans regard the kaki as a fresh fruit to be eaten out of hand, or used in e.g. persimmon ice cream. In E. Asia, however, the custom has been to dry them for storage and use during the winter and early spring. Whether a kaki is eaten fresh or dried depends on whether it is sweet or astringent.

Both are very common in Japan. They may be strung up to dry in the sun and wind, or sliced and laid out on rooftops to dry. When dried, the flesh has turned blackish and a fine coating of sugar, like confectioner's sugar, has appeared on much or all of the skin. One very exotic foodstuff consists in this sugar, scraped off the surface of the dried fruits and pressed in moulds to make ornamental tablets. Such tablets could be given by couples to people who had sent them wedding presents. Also, according to an authority who is referred to as 'S. Y. Hu', they were 'one of the eight comestibles offered with tea during the first course of traditional Chinese banquets'.

Dried fruits, which become flattened if suspended on a cord while drying or which may be flattened mechanically after drying, are known as pressed persimmons; these are packed in boxes in Japan, while in both China and Japan they often are stored on cords. Jane Grigson (1982), who writes with her usual charming erudition about the kaki and the Japanese (especially the great poet for persimmons, Shiki), offers her readers this charming titbit about persimmons in China:

> According to one thirteenth-century play, they sold candied persimmons in the street, crying 'supple-supple-soft, quite-quite-white, crystal-sweet, crushed flat candied persimmons from Sung-yang'.

The same author (1986, with Charlotte Knox) provides further poetic prose about the kaki from Japan, and also refers to what can be a puzzling sight for winter visitors in Piedmont, to wit:

> the brown skeleton of a [persimmon] tree, all leaves fallen, hung with huge orange-red globes. A glory often set off by snow and a blue sky. At first glance it seems as if someone had put up Christmas decorations a fortnight early, and that at night they would glow in the darkness.

Dried kakis are eaten out of hand or stewed much the same way as dried apricots and prunes. In China they are a particular favourite during the New Year celebration in February. (Once the spring rains begin and atmospheric humidity increases, the surface sugar liquefies, and the dried fruits are no longer considered edible.)

Oriental relatives of the kaki include *D. blancoi* (formerly *D. discolor*), a native of the Philippines or Malaysia which has been taken to other parts of SE Asia and the W. Indies. It is sometimes cultivated. The fruit, known as 'mabolo' or 'butter fruit', is relatively large, hairy, brown or purplish-red with a white pulp, and with a sweet and pleasing flavour. There are many other relations in Asia and in Madagascar.
READING: Julia Morton (1987).

KALE *Brassica oleracea* var *acephala*, is a different species from CHINESE KALE, *B. oleracea* var *alboglabra*, but the two plants have several features in common. Both are rather coarse and strongly flavoured in comparison with the more delicate CABBAGES of their respective regions; both have tough stems and are good only when young.

Kale and cabbage are varieties of the same species, and both are descended from the same wild ancestor. Kale is the more primitive of the two, and was the ordinary greenstuff of country people in most parts of Europe until the end of the Middle Ages, when the 'headed' cabbages were bred. In England kale was known as cole or colewort. Kale (or kail) is the Scottish name, and its continued prevalence is significant. Kale can grow in hard climates where the more delicate cabbages cannot, and still remains in common use in northern regions. There was even a 'Kailyard school' of Scottish writers, of whom J. M. Barrie was one. They were so called because they described Scottish rural life and a kailyard (kale field) was a typical feature of this. Indeed, the word 'kail' became generic for 'dinner' in Scotland; thus

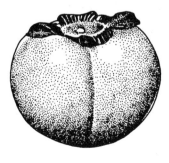

Kaki fruits
variety Hachiya on the left
Fuyu on the right

the 'kail bells' were those which chimed at dinner time, whether or not kail was on the menu.

Other names for kale include the Dutch *boerenkool* (farmer's cabbage) and 'collards' (a corruption of colewort and the usual name in the USA). All derive from the Greek *kaulos*, meaning stem. An interesting passage in Bradley (1736) illustrates the original primacy of the word 'cole'. He says that the Greek word 'Brassica' is 'in English Cole and Colewort', and refers to 'the sort of Cole which makes an Head, which we call Cabbage', and to 'the Cole so remarkable for its Flower, which we call Cole-Flower, or more commonly Cauly-Flower'. He continues:

The Coleworts are of many Kinds, some of which have their Leaves beautifully cut and curl'd of various Colours, such as Reds of all Sorts, Purples, Yellows and Greens, and also White. I have seen a Bed of these as beautiful as ever I saw any Thing of the Garden.

One advantage which kale had over cabbage until recently was that the season of some varieties extended over the January to April period when there was no cabbage. Hence the name Hungry Gap which one variety has.

Kale

Curly leaved kales such as Scottish kale (Scotch kale in the USA) are less coarse and rigid than the plain kinds, and it is they which are still popular as food. The others are now grown mainly for animal feed.

In the USA the principal kale-growing states are Virginia, Maryland, and New Jersey.

RAPE kale belongs to two different species: *Brassica napus* (rape and colza); and *B. rapa* ssp *campestris* (Indian rape and Indian colza). Common names are applied in accordance with the uses to which the plants are put: rape usually for cattle feed, and colza for oil from its seed. (The name colza comes from the Dutch *kool zad*, meaning kale seed.)

SEAKALE belongs to a different genus. Seakale beet, along with other SUGAR BEETS and CHARDS, belongs to the SPINACH family.

Both resemble true kale in having thick, tough stems and in needing to be well cooked.

KANAKA PUDDING a highly idiosyncratic dish of Hawaii. Rachel Laudan (1996) explains that kanaka, an obsolescent term, was much used in the 19th century to mean Hawaiian, and this PUDDING, which is indisputably Hawaiian, remained popular up to or beyond the Second World War.

The tradition of eating plain biscuits, (CRACKERS, sea biscuits, or 'pilots' as they are called locally) is a vigorous one in Hawaii; sugar is a Hawaiian product; and canned milk has been a leading staple. These ingredients are all that is needed to make kanaka pudding, by softening the crackers in hot water and taking them with sugar or condensed milk and possibly a little butter.

Laudan comments that this is 'one of those simple, homestyle desserts that seldom makes it into the cookbooks'. She does, however, give a recipe for Niihau pudding (named for the island of that name), which is recognizably both a form of kanaka pudding and a relation of bread and butter pudding (see BREAD PUDDINGS), and which involves soaking crackers with milk in a roasting pan, then spreading them with butter, adding raw brown sugar on top and baking all this in the oven until the sugar has melted and a crust formed.

KANGAROO APPLE also known as *poro-poro*, the fruit of an Australian shrub of the nightshade family, *Solanum aviculare*. The berries are shiny, elliptical, orange-red or violet when ripe, with a soft pulp and numerous seeds. They can be eaten raw or cooked, but must not be used until fully ripe.

KANGAROOS belong to the small number of marsupial species, all unique to the ancient assemblage of countries known to scientists as Gondwana and including S. America and New Guinea. They are characterized by giving birth to very immature young which complete their growth and development attached to a nipple in the mother's pouch.

In Australia 'kangaroo' is used as a generic term covering different species of kangaroo, wallaby, and wallaroo of large and medium size. All belong to the family Macropodidae and most to the genus *Macropus*. The distinction between species is mainly one of size, itself a function of habitat. Largest and fleetest are the red kangaroos (*Macropus rufus*) of the wide open plains of inland Australia. Somewhat smaller are the western and eastern grey kangaroos (*M. fuliginosus* and *M. giganteus*). The wallaroo

(*M. robustus*) and the agile wallaby (*M. agilis*), relatively common in N. Australia and S. New Guinea, inhabit more rugged, rocky terrains. Another widespread species is the swamp wallaby, *Wallabia bicolor*.

Kangaroo was (and still is) a favoured food of Aborigines. Margaret-Mary Turner-Neale (1996), of the Arrernte language group of C. Australia, has described how kangaroos are prepared and cooked:

They shoot them or spear them and then gut them. The milk guts are pulled out and a wooden skewer is used to close up the carcase. Then it's tossed on top of a fire to singe the hair which is scraped off, and then it's [put in a hole] and covered up with hot earth and coals to cook it. The tail and both feet are cut off before cooking. These are put in together with the rest of the carcase.

The kangaroo is chopped up so that a lot of people can eat it. The warm blood and fluids from the thighs and the hollow of the chest are drunk. Kangaroos are cut up in a special way: into the two thighs, the two hips, the two sides of ribs, the stomach, the head, the tail, the two feet, the back and the lower back. This is the way that Arrernte people everywhere cut it up.

According to R. J. May (1984), wallaby is commonly hunted in New Guinea and can sometimes be bought, lightly cooked, in Port Moresby markets. May reports that the flesh is tough and a little like rabbit in taste.

Kangaroo was also eaten by white settlers in the early colonial period, selling for sixpence a pound in Sydney in 1796 (when imported salt pork cost one shilling per pound). It was the principal source of fresh meat in Van Diemen's Land (Tasmania) for its first years, and in the 1840s could still be readily purchased in Hobart Town. Explorers and adventurers relied on kangaroos to supplement the minimal provisions they carried, while colonists occupied in clearing land, erecting shelters, and building up livestock herds regarded them as a ready source of fresh meat.

In 19th-century Australia the kangaroo was not only hunted for food but also for sport. The choice of kangaroo as the object of the ritualized, English-style hunt may have had something to do with the exhilaration of the chase, but kangaroos were also plentiful, offered a large target, and were easy to shoot and skin. In addition, kangaroo meat had a close resemblance to familiar meats and was said to be more tasty, more palatable than that of other indigenous animals; early recipe books have more recipes for kangaroo than other game. It was usually likened to hare or venison, which may explain why the most popular kangaroo dish, the steamer, originated as a variant of the English jugged hare.

The kangaroo steamer was essentially a simple dish of kangaroo meat, minced or finely diced, plus fatty bacon, salt, and pepper. These ingredients, sometimes with a small quantity of liquid added, were placed in a pot which was covered tightly and set on or near the hearth where it simmered or 'steamed' for several hours, until the meat was tender. It was first recorded in 1820 and seems to have been eaten throughout most of the 19th century.

Kangaroo tails were invariably made into kangaroo tail soup, while steaks were often grilled over open fires. Both these dishes could be found in hotel dining rooms until about the turn of the century. With increased production of cheap mutton and beef, 'bush foods' disappeared from many tables, especially in the cities where people were more likely to adopt the new trend of 'dainty dishes'. Even in rural Australia, however, kangaroos may have been less plentiful in the face of systematical destruction by pastoralists. For these landowners, kangaroos were not a source of food, as they had been to the early settlers, but were seen as competition to the production of 'real' food (mutton or beef) and income.

There were no absolute prohibitions on its sale or consumption in the 20th century, but food regulations made it difficult or impractical for retailers and restaurants to offer kangaroo and it virtually disappeared from Australian tables until the late 1970s. It is now available in all states. Its modern acceptance is, in part, a corollary of the environmental movement and its recognition of the damage done to fragile natural environments by the introduction of hard-hoofed animals such as sheep and cattle, but also coincides with renewed awareness of national identity and the development of interest in Australian culinary culture.

Kangaroo is very low in fat and cholesterol and may be cooked in similar ways to beef. It is often cured and smoked and served in salads. When grilled or roasted it is best served rare, having been allowed to rest after cooking.   BS

READING: Barbara Santich (1996).

KAPOK-TREE FRUIT from *Ceiba pentandra*, the large kapok tree of the tropics. The young leaves, buds, fruits, and seeds are edible. They are mucilaginous and may be eaten like OKRA. The green fruits may measure 14 cm (5.5"). A variety of this tree is important in Indonesia, as Ochse (1980) explains, with a thought-provoking display of reticence at the end of his explanation.

During three fourths of the year the tree stands leafless; in that time it flowers and bears ripe fruits. These fruits furnish the celebrated wool generally known under the name of capok, which is used, besides for filling mattresses and cushions,

Fruits of kapok-tree

for a great many other purposes. But on this matter I will be silent.

He goes on, however, to say that the very young fruits are eaten uncooked as 'lablab' (a plate of raw or lightly cooked vegetables, to be dipped in a SAMBAL before being eaten) and that the seeds are also edible. The light brown seeds from half-ripe fruits are eaten raw as a dainty. Ripe seeds are put in the ground for a week to germinate, then incorporated in 'lablab'.

KARABIJ finger-shaped pastries of the Middle East, similar to MA'AMOUL. They are traditionally served with a brilliant white cream called *naatiffe* (natif) which is made from the root of BOIS DE PANAMA. The karabij are dipped into this frothy cream and may then be arranged in a pyramid shape with the remaining cream poured over them.   HS

KARAKA *Corynocarpus laevigata*, an evergreen tree of New Zealand, bearing elliptical fruits, orange in colour when ripe, which were formerly one of the most important foods of the Maori.

Although the flesh of the fruits is palatable, with a distinctive flavour which has been compared to that of apricots or dates, and despite the presence in the kernels of a powerful alkaloid poison, it was the kernels which the Maori ate. Preparation, to make them safe, was elaborate. The whole fruits were first poured into an earth oven (see NEW ZEALAND) and steamed, then placed in a running stream, trampled on, left

to soak for a considerable time, and finally dried. The recorded opinions of Europeans on their edible quality are mixed, but generally unenthusiastic.

The Maori must occasionally have failed to render the kernels safe, since they had a treatment for anyone who was poisoned. This involved binding the victim's arms and legs straight, in anticipation of convulsions which would have left his limbs permanently distorted, gagging him, and burying him up to his neck in the ground until symptoms abated.

KASHA a Russian term which is an approximate equivalent to GROATS. It refers to a wide range of (mostly stiffish) PORRIDGE-like dishes, of which the best known are those made with BUCKWHEAT. Their versatility is explained by Lesley Chamberlain (1983): 'The various forms of kasha give it a place at every meal of the day—sweet in the morning and before bed, savoury to accompany soup or fill pies or pad out the main meal of the day.'

The same author describes how the washed grains are cooked in salted water until the liquid is absorbed, the technique resembling that for making a RISOTTO, and that the traditional way of serving such kasha is with plenty of butter. She also mentions a way of serving it which Urbain Dubois, the famous 19th-century French chef and author who worked in Moscow for a time, devised; this involves nutmeg and Parmesan cheese. Other ways of presenting kasha include with fried chopped bacon, or fried onions, or chopped hard-boiled eggs. A version with cooked mushrooms and sour cream was called *Dragomirovskaya kasha* after General Dragomirov who helped defend Russia against Napoleon.

KASHK and *kishk* are the two most usual vocalizations of the same word current in the Middle East. As Françoise Aubaile-Sallenave (1994) puts it, at the beginning of a detailed and authoritative essay, these 'occur in several cultural areas—Iran, Iraq, Greater Syria, Egypt, south Caucasia and Turkey—and represent very different language families: Indo-European, Semitic, Altaic, Caucasic'.

As if that were not already more than enough complexity, the word has several quite different meanings.

By origin the word *kashk* is Persian and it seems to have meant originally a BARLEY product. The meaning 'barley flour' is found in the *Shahnameh*, the Persian 'Book of Kings' by the 10th-century poet Firdausi.

Another, and more usual, meaning is 'mixture of cracked wheat and cracked barley' (also found in the *Shahnameh*).

Nowadays it is more commonly used for a Middle Eastern preserved food made from wheat and/or barley mixed with either sour milk or yoghurt. It can also mean a dish in which *kashk* or *kishk* is mixed with vegetables and/or meat; or it can mean dried yoghurt/buttermilk/curds on their own.

In the wheat-growing areas of Lebanon, Syria, Turkey, and Armenia *kishk* is the name usually given to a preserved food made of yoghurt and BURGHUL. At the end of the summer, just after the harvesting of the wheat crop, burghul is made by boiling, drying, and crushing the ears of wheat into small grainlike particles. The burghul is mixed with the yoghurt and spread on to a wide tray with edges and left for several days. As the burghul soaks up the liquid it is stirred and rubbed between the palms of the hands every morning. Eventually all the liquid is absorbed and the tiny grains called *kishk* are spread out on to clean cloths and left to dry in the sun. A final rubbing of the grains is done just before storing which reduces the grains to a powder. This is then put into bags for storage.

Anissa Helou (1994) gives a detailed description of how *kishk* is made in the Lebanon:

In my family, where *kishk* is made by hand at home, we use one portion of burghul to eight of salted yoghurt. The burghul is put into a wide crock and covered with two parts yoghurt. It is left to soak for 24 hours, during which time the rest of the yoghurt is salted and put in a cloth bag to drain its excess water. The next day the strained yoghurt is divided into three parts, one of which is mixed into the burghul/yoghurt mixture and the other two added on successive days. After all the yoghurt is included, the mixture is left for a week to ferment until it becomes quite sour. It is then spread, in small lumps, on clean cloths laid over straw mats and put out to dry in the sun. The dried lumps are then rubbed between the palms of the hand until they separate into a coarse powder. The powder is filtered through a coarse sifter and put away in canvas bags.

Kishk can be made into a hearty breakfast or soup or added to soups to thicken and add flavour. It is also added to other dishes including meat and rice dishes.

In modern Iran the word *kashk* does not seem to refer to grain at all; it means dried buttermilk. The buttermilk is dried in the sun and when beginning to harden is formed into small round balls. These balls can then either be stored as they are or they are crushed into a powder ready for use in winter months when milk is scarce and yoghurt cannot be made. This *kashk* is added to soups or stews to enrich and thicken them; it can also be reconstituted with water, making a rich sour sauce. (A similar product to this *kashk* is QUROOT).

See also TARHANA. (HS)

KASHKAVAL the Bulgarian and Romanian name for a hard yellow cheese made from sheep's milk in the Balkans. Throughout that part of the world, the name recurs in many versions. It has been suggested that the origin of these names may be the Italian CACIOCAVALLO.

For a Greek cheese of this type see KEFALOTYRI.

KASHMIR deserves consideration separately from INDIA and PAKISTAN. Its climate and the fertility of the soil make it uniquely blessed, in the Indian subcontinent, with food resources of the sort associated with the temperate regions of the world. The activities of the British, in past times, in introducing temperate fruits and vegetables has enhanced this natural wealth—besides other important beneficent influences such as that of MOGHUL CUISINE.

It has been said that Kashmir is a land of MILK and HONEY, and it is true that Kashmiris enjoy both, sometimes adding to milk or yoghurt a sprinkling of SAFFRON. The quality of the saffron grown there is regarded by some experts as being equal to the best which can be had from Iran or Spain. There are many other crops which are either best of their kind or different in interesting ways from the same things grown in other parts of the world; for example, the distinctive Kashmir shallots (*praan*), sometimes referred to as 'Kashmir onions', are exceptionally good. The landscape of the rich agricultural areas exhibits several dominant themes. There are dramatic yellow fields of MUSTARD, and mustard oil is the standard cooking medium. More important, perhaps, is RICE, providing rectangles of various shades of green and gold, depending on how far the crop has progressed in each. Gita Samtani (1995) observes that: 'It is here on the fields that salt tea is served in abundance. A special leaf is boiled together with water, milk, salt, and cooking soda until an almost pink colour permeates through the tea.' (Here there is an echo of the *qymaq chai* of nearby AFGHANISTAN.)

Kashmir is famous for its lakes, their surface often covered with the pink water lilies which spring up from the rhizomes of the Asian LOTUS, often referred to as 'lotus roots' and prominent in Kashmiri cuisine. The lakes are also home to the famous houseboats and to the floating vegetable gardens, built up with reeds and mud to provide fertile beds for many different vegetables.

The population of Kashmir includes not only Hindus and Muslims but also Buddhists; see HINDUISM AND FOOD, MUSLIMS AND FOOD, and BUDDHISM AND FOOD. Madhur Jaffrey (1985) explains that

Many of the Hindus in Kashmir are Brahmins, the high priestly class, where the men go by the title of 'pandit' (hence Pandit Jawaharlal Nehru). While the Brahmins of the rest of India abhor meat, Kashmiri pandits have worked out quite a different culinary tradition for themselves. They eat meat with great gusto—lamb cooked with asafetida [see ASAFOETIDA], dried ginger, fennel and lots of ground red chilles (rogan josh)—but frown upon garlic and onions. Garlic and onions, they say, encourage base passions.

KASUTERA (sometimes spelled castera), is the 'Castella cake' of Japan. This sponge cake, usually very sweet, was introduced to Nagasaki in the 16th century by the Portuguese and is only made by specialist bakers, some of the oldest established of whom are still in Nagasaki. The ingredients are white wheat flour, eggs, and sugar. The texture resembles that of a steamed cake, the result of its being baked in a confined, closed space with coals above and beneath. RHo

KATSUOBUSHI a prominent ingredient in Japanese cookery, is dried fillets of SKIPJACK flesh. These are treated by steam and then dried so thoroughly that they become as hard as wood, and indeed look like thick wooden boomerangs.

Traditionally, a special implement (like a plane set upside down on a box) is used to shave off very thin slices, usually destined for the preparation of the basic Japanese soup stock, DASHI. However, the shaving is a slow business which requires a certain expertise, so time-saving katsuobushi products are available, including ready-prepared shavings, and 'instant' katsuobushi granules.

KAYMAK the Turkish name for a product also prepared all over the Middle East, Iran, Afghanistan, and in India; this is a rich clotted cream, traditionally made from WATER-BUFFALO milk (and less good when made from cow's milk and cream). The milk is brought slowly to the boil in a wide, shallow tray, then simmered over a very low heat for a couple of hours, after which the heat is turned off and the cream left to stand for several more hours. It is then chilled. A thick layer of cream will have formed which can be cut with a knife.

Ayla Algar (1991) says:

it was once so popular and widespread in Turkey that special shops were devoted to it. The most famous of these were located at Eyub, where they appear to have functioned, at least in the sixteenth century, as trysting places, with the result that a decree issued in 1573 prohibited women from frequenting them.

Kaymak is enjoyed with some pastries and desserts and used as a filling for QATA'IF. It is often eaten with sweet preserves or honey;

see AFGHANISTAN for the ways it is used there.

Thick English clotted cream (see CREAM), as made in Devon and Cornwall, is often an acceptable substitute for kaymak.   HS

KEBAB now an English culinary term usually occurring as şiş (or *shish*) kebab, meaning small chunks of meat grilled on a skewer. *Shashlik* is a term which means essentially the same as şiş kebab but belongs to the countries of the Caucasus (ARMENIA, AZERBAIJAN, GEORGIA) and has also become common in RUSSIA, where many cities now have *sashlychnayas* (shashlik cafés). The word kebab percolated into the Balkans in the form of *ćevap* (diminutive *ćevapčići*).

The word kebab has an interesting history. In the Middle Ages the Arabic word *kabab* always meant fried meat. The compendious 14th-century dictionary *Lisdan al-'Arab* defines *kabab* as *tabahajah*, which is a dish of fried pieces of meat, usually finished with some liquid in the cooking. The exact shape of the pieces of meat is not clear. However, since there was a separate class of dish called *saraih*, which consisted of long and thin strips of meat, and since most modern dishes called kebab call for more or less cubical chunks, it seems likely that kabab was chunks rather than strips.

Kabab/kebab is not a common word in the early medieval Arabic books, because the Persian word *tabahajah* (diminutive of *tabah*) provided an alternative which was considered more high-toned. It is because of this original meaning that one still finds dishes such as *tas kebab* (bowl kebab) which are really stews. In the Middle Ages the Arabic word for grilled meat was not kabab but *siwa*. It was only in the Turkish period that such words as *shishkebab* or *seekh kebab* made their appearance.

However all this may be, the custom of roasting meat in small chunks on a skewer seems to be very ancient in the Near East. Part of the reason for this may have to do with the urban nature of the civilization there. In Europe the population was largely agricultural and people would butcher a farm animal and roast whole joints from it; but in the Near East they would go to a butcher's shop and buy smaller cuts. However, a more important reason, and the basic one, was surely that fuel has long been in short supply in the Near East but used to be superabundant in Europe, as deforestation proceeded. This made it natural for Europeans to do much more baking than Arabs (or Chinese or others with a lesser wealth of fuel), and likewise to be more disposed to roast large pieces of meat.

It is often assumed that the Syrian dish *kibbeh* (spelled *kubbah* in Arabic, and so pronounced in Iraq), a meat-loaf base of pounded lamb, onions, and bulghur, is related to kabab; but this is doubtful.

The well-known *kufta kebab* (see also KOFTA), a sort of meatball on a skewer (usually called *luleh kebab*, meaning 'rolled kebab', in Persian, because it is formed in a long sausage shape around the skewer), shows clearly that in Iran *kabab* came to have the basic meaning of meat on a skewer. (In Arabic *kufta kebab* is usually called by a name meaning 'kufta on a skewer'. The Persian word *kufta*, incidentally, completely ousted the native Arabic word *bunduq*, which at one time was lively enough to have given rise to the Spanish *albondiga*.)

Doner kebab, thin slices of marinated lamb packed tightly onto a vertical spit to form a solid mass and thus roasted, pieces of meat being cut off the outside as it browns, has become a familiar sight in western countries wherever Turkish immigrants have become established.

See also TIKKA.   (CP)

KECAP the Indonesian word (pronounced 'ketchap') applied to the dark brown SOY SAUCE of that country. This differs from the Chinese or Japanese kind in being made basically from SOYA BEANS and PALM SUGAR only, and in its short intense fermentation. Gentle heating for about five hours produces a sauce which is thick and viscous in consistency. Ninety per cent of soy sauce produced in Indonesia is called *kecap manis*; highly sweetened with palm sugar and flavoured with star anise and other combinations of herbs and spices. *Kecap asin* is less sweet, being made with only half as much palm sugar, and is also less dark and viscous. *Asin* means 'salty' and both these types are noticeably so.

In Java one also finds *kecap ikan*, a thick dark sauce, hardly distinguishable from *kecap manis*. The name indicates that fish flavouring (*sari ikan*) has been added to the *kecap manis*. There is another product which is also called *kecap ikan*. This is real FISH SAUCE in the SE Asian sense; it is produced mainly in W. Kalimantan and is not widely used in Indonesia. (*Kecap ikan* may also refer to a dish: fish cooked in *kecap manis*.)

Kecap manis is often used as a condiment for foods such as fried chicken (*ayam goreng*) and will be served in a small dish on the side, while *kecap asin* will be sprinkled on dishes of Chinese origin.

Kecap was originally produced in the home and is now largely made in cottage industries typical of Indonesia. However, large factories are now producing it and this has prompted attempts to preserve production at village level; if not in the home, then in village co-operatives. The making of kecap is laborious and requires skill, but need not involve complex technology.

The word 'kecap' has passed into the English language as catchup or catsup and then as KETCHUP, which now means something quite different.

KEDROUVIE NUT an intriguing mystery. The only reference found is in Emerson (1908), but it is sufficiently intriguing to deserve quotation:

There is one custom in certain parts of Siberia that I fear will not find many advocates, especially among the young ladies of America. At their risgovorki, or social gatherings, the young ladies that attend are, of course, expected to come attired in their finest clothes and dresses, but instead of participating in any of the conversations it is expected of them that they sit along the side of the room for the purpose of ornament and show. There is, however, one palliating feature for the young ladies about these gatherings, and that is that they are given plenty of kedrouvie nuts, in order to keep their mouths busy. These nuts have a very fine flavour and are considered a great luxury, but they have one drawback, which consists of an innumerable number of small figlike seeds, which are thought to be unhealthy and consequently are not swallowed. Therefore, in order to eat the kedrouvie nut, strict attention must, of necessity, be paid to the business of the moment.

KEFALOTYRI a salty, hard Greek ewe's or goat's cheese which is used as a table cheese when young, and for cooking (e.g. in a fried cheese recipe) when more than half a year old, and which is excellent for grating when it is even more mature. The name means 'hat' (or head) cheese because it is roughly the same shape and size as a brimless hat. The colour is pale yellow.

KEFIR originated in the Caucasian mountains and is one of the oldest known cultured milk products. It differs from other such products in that its fermentation is sustained by what are known as kefir grains. When immersed in milk, these yellowish, gelatinous granules swell and turn white, and initiate the fermenting process.

The kefir grains vary in size from something like a wheat grain to something large enough to be described (quite incorrectly, it need hardly be said) as a 'mushroom'. In fact, they are not single organisms but conglomerations formed from the sediment which is created in kefir by the active micro-organisms. This sediment contains bits of coagulated milk protein, with live cultures of various *Streptococci* and *Lactobacilli* and a yeast described as *Saccharomyces kefir*, and other miscellaneous detritus. It is apt to clump;

thus, when kefir is made in a skin bottle or round-bottomed container which is agitated (as by being attached to a nomad's saddle) the sediment rolls into balls.

The grains are added to the milk and it is left overnight until a CURD has formed. The milk is then strained and the grains recovered for reuse. The kefir is best consumed when chilled and should foam and fizz like beer.

KELP a name applied both to certain large brown SEAWEEDS and to the ash (a source of iodine and potash) obtained by burning them. The industries devoted to producing the ash were important in the 19th century, but then declined as cheaper sources for the two end products were discovered.

The species sometimes called 'edible kelp' is *Alaria esculenta*, whose long fronds (up to 3.5 m/12') are found on cold and rocky N. Atlantic shores around the low-tide mark. Midribs have been eaten like celery or chopped into salads in N. America; and various cooked kelp dishes have been recorded from such places as Greenland, Iceland, the Faeroes, and Orkney.

It is said that *Alaria* spp gathered in the N. Pacific region is sometimes marketed as WAKAME. It is in the Pacific that giant kelp, *Macrocystis pyrifera*, occurs; its fronds may be as much as 25 m (say, 80') long. Most of the commercial kelp preparations available in N. America come from this species.

In Japan, powdered kelp is used to make kelp tea, known as *kobucha*.

KENDAL MINT CAKE a confection of hard crystalline sugar heavily flavoured with MINT and shaped into slabs, has been made in Kendal in the English Lake District since at least the mid-19th century. It is promoted as an energy-giving food for polar explorers and mountaineers. LM

KEPAYANG the Malay name of a tree, *Pangium edule*, which is common in Malaysia, Indonesia, and the Philippines. It produces rough, brown fruits up to 15 cm (6") long with a yellow, sweet, aromatic pulp containing several flat, oval seeds the size of large coins.

The seeds are eaten in Malaysia and Indonesia after the removal of toxic substances (hydrocyanic acid) by repeated boiling and soaking in running water. Alternatively, the use of fermentation produces a strong flavoured condiment.

Burkill (1965–6) remarks that the antiseptic properties of the glucoside in the seeds is brought into use when pounded seeds are used, in the fashion of crushed ice,

to preserve fish on their way to market; this in Java.

A cooking oil is obtained from the seeds.

KERMES a deep purple-red dye used since ancient times as a food colouring. Its name is derived from the Arabic word *qirmiz*, which has the same meaning.

Kermes has a curious source. It is made from the dried, pulverized bodies of a scale insect, *Coccus ilicis*, which is a parasite on an ilex (or evergreen) oak, the kermes oak. After mating, the female insect settles on the oak and becomes attached to it, losing all her limbs, and swells into a round, featureless lump. For this reason it was long thought that the 'grains' which appeared on the tree were vegetable rather than animal. They are not the same as oak galls, which contain an insect larva but consist of woody vegetable matter produced by the tree itself in response to the irritation caused by the parasite.

During the Middle Ages kermes was gathered and prepared in Portugal, an old name for it being 'grains of Portugal'. A related insect native to Poland, *C. polonicus*, was also harvested for 'grains'.

Kermes was widely used as a food colouring in the medieval period, red being the favourite colour for decorated dishes. It was and still is added to a sweet, spicy alcoholic cordial, alkermes, which survives in France and Italy.

However, in the early 16th century COCHINEAL, a brighter dye made from an American scale insect, began to be imported into Europe. At first cochineal was used to adulterate kermes because it was cheaper. However, it was soon seen to be a superior product, and was sold on its own. Kermes declined in importance thereafter, but is still available.

KESHKUL-E-FUQARA The name of this rich milk and almond pudding, which is flavoured with rosewater, ironically means 'beggars' bowl'. There are many variations of the same dessert found all over Iran and the Middle East, and in Afghanistan.

Keshkul is the Persian word for an oval bowl made either of wood, metal, or coconut—or the very valuable COCO DE MER. These bowls were carried suspended by a chain from the shoulder by paupers or beggars called *fuqara* (the plural of *faqir*).

Faqirs, who called themselves 'the paupers of God', travelled from house to house begging for food. Donations of food (and sometimes money, although the faqir could not ask for money directly) were placed in the *keshkul* which would eventually be filled up with different kinds of food. Hence the name of this dessert—it is sprinkled and

decorated with various blanched nuts (almond, pistachio) and coconut, symbolizing the *keshkul* being filled with a variety of food. HS

KETAMBILLA the fruit of *Dovyalis hebecarpa*, a small shrub native to Sri Lanka, resembles a deep purple cherry but is covered with fine hairs. It is sometimes called 'Ceylon gooseberry'. Being quite acid, the fruit is generally used to make jams and jellies, but is also an ingredient in some meat and fish dishes. It is now cultivated in a few other tropical countries including the Philippines, and is known in Hawaii, California, and Florida.

A related African species, *D. caffra*, is commonly called kei apple or umkokolo. It occurs in both wild and cultivated forms in SW Africa, near the Kei River. It has been introduced to the Mediterranean region, and is grown in the Philippines as 'umkolo'. The fruit is soft, golden yellow when ripe, bearing a resemblance to the apricot. It is similarly used for jam, as are those of several minor African species of the same genus.

KETCHUP a general name for a range of salty, spicy, rather liquid condiments. These belong to the cuisines of the western world, but all are descended from oriental ancestors. The word 'ketchup' comes from the Chinese (Amoy dialect) *kêtsiap*, meaning a fermented fish sauce, probably via the Malay word *kechap*, now spelled *kecap*, which means SOY SAUCE. The word was brought back to Europe by Dutch traders who also brought the oriental sauce itself. The sauce has changed far more than has the word, although the name has appeared in a large number of variations such as catchup and catsup.

Tomato ketchup is the best known and almost the only ketchup left nowadays although formerly there were many different kinds, the only common features being their salty taste, their concentrated texture, and the fact that they kept well. Although tomato ketchup contains and indeed tastes principally of sugar and vinegar, mushroom ketchup contains neither, and is nothing other than a salted mushroom extract, differing also from tomato ketchup in its liquid transparent consistency. C. Anne Wilson (1973) believes that mushroom ketchup was the first kind in Britain; people used to pickle mushrooms, intending to use the mushrooms, but then started using the pickle too, and finally took to using the pickle by itself.

Oysters, mussels, walnuts, and many other ingredients have been used to make ketchup, and could be blended with spices, garlic or onions, wines, and spirits to vary the flavour. Stobart (1980) cites from the 19th century a host of ketchups including oyster, mussel, Windermere (mushrooms and horseradish), wolfram (beer, anchovies, mushrooms), and pontac (elderberries).

READING: Andrew Smith (1991, 1996).

KHEER is the Indian name for sweet milk puddings usually made with rice, although it can also be made with fine noodles called SEVIYAN, or SEMOLINA, CARROTS, or SAGO. It is sometimes called *sheer*, which means milk in Persian. It probably originated in Persia where a similar dessert is known as *sheer birinj* (rice pudding).

There are many variations in the flavourings which can include raisins, cardamom, cinnamon, almond, pistachio, saffron, kewra essence (see SCREWPINE), or rosewater, etc. For special occasions it is customary to decorate the chilled kheer with edible silver or GOLD LEAF.

The Persian version, *sheer birinj*, according to Hekmat (1970), was originally the food of angels, first made in heaven when the Prophet Muhammad ascended to the 7th floor of Heaven to meet God and he was served this dish.   HS

KHICHRI a popular Indian dish of rice and lentils with spices. It is the origin of the rather different dish known as kedgeree (see ANGLO-INDIAN COOKERY). In addition, as Zubaida (1994) points out in an interesting passage about the diffusion of foods and dishes, it has a further history:

A good example of imperceptible diffusion is the Cairo kushuri, an ever-popular street food, a dish of rice and lentils, often bulked up with the even cheaper macaroni, served with a garnish of fried onion and spicy sauces. I have not been able to find any satisfactory accounts of the origin of this dish in Egypt. I can only assume that it is the Indian kitchri, also made from rice and lentils and spices. And it must have reached Cairo through the British forces. Long before the hamburger and the fried chicken, colonial circulation spawned a popular staple which Cairo made its own.

KHOSHAB a traditional Near Eastern beverage-cum-dessert, served as a digestive. It is typically made from dried fruits and nuts (e.g. apricots, prunes, raisins, almonds, pistachios) simmered with sugar and rosewater. It is served cold. A drop of aromatic oil (e.g. musk, sandalwood, rose, or ambergris) may be added.

Ingredients and nomenclature vary considerably. In Persian, the name means 'good (*khosh*) (or agreeable) water (*ab*)'. In Egypt, *khushaf* is the name. In Turkey, the name *komposto* has come into use, marking the resemblance to the Balkan COMPOTE.

KHUS-KHUS *Vetiveria zizanioides*, also known as vetiver and Botha grass and sometimes spelled cuscus, belongs to the family Gramineae. It is a large bushy grass found in tropical India and cultivated throughout the tropical world.

Khus-khus has been used for centuries in India as an incense or perfume, and medicinally. The roots are a source of an essential oil which makes a stimulating tonic drink or is added to sherbets and other fruit drinks. It is thought to have a cooling effect on the body. Morton (1976) observes that in the food industry it is added to canned asparagus to enhance the flavour.   HS

KIBBEH a versatile paste of grain, onions, and meat that forms the basis of many dishes in LEBANON AND SYRIA, EGYPT (*kobeiba*), ISRAEL (*cubbeh*), IRAQ and extreme SW IRAN (*kubba*), the Persian Gulf (*chabâb*), and southern TURKEY (*bulgur köftesi*). It is known among the western Armenians as *kuefta*. (See also KOFTA.)

The grain is BURGHUL (bulgur wheat) in most places but often rice in Iraq, particularly in the south, where fish may replace lamb. In some places the grain predominates over or even supplants the meat. The mixture is traditionally pounded in a large mortar (*jurn*) carved into a block of stone several feet high with a correspondingly large pestle (*mudaqqa*) held vertically in both hands. The aim is to achieve a perfectly smooth mixture in which none of the ingredients may be detected. Making it by the traditional process can take several hours and in villages the sound of *kibbeh* being pounded can be heard throughout the afternoon.

Kibbeh is most often made into *aqrâs kibbeh*, which are thick patties or torpedo-shaped balls. These are always given a filling, perhaps a lump of fat but more usually a mixture of fried meat and onions, optionally flavoured with nuts and raisins. The *aqrâs* may be deep fried (*maqliyya*) or grilled (*mashwiyya*), and for these purposes the cook tries to form the *kibbeh* mixture into the thinnest possible crust around the filling, so that it becomes crisp in cooking but does not break. Mastering this difficult skill has traditionally been one of the great tasks of a prospective bride in Lebanon and Syria.

Aqrâs kibbeh are also cooked in liquid. In Egypt, Lebanon, and Syria this is usually a yoghurt sauce (*kibbeh labaniyya*), but in N. Iraq and S. Turkey the liquid may be lightly salted water (for a traditional large, flat patty made in Mosul and the torpedo-shaped Armenian *Harput kuefta*) or a stew of meat, onions, and vegetables such as tomatoes, chickpeas, cabbage, and aubergine, made sour with lemon or bitter orange juice.

In Egypt, Lebanon, and Syria, *kibbeh* is also baked in a round pan used for BAKLAVA, and cut into the same lozenge shapes as baklava or other geometrical designs. The cake has the same sort of filling as *aqrâs kibbeh*. Particularly in Aleppo, in northern Syria, balls of *kibbeh* may be roasted on skewers alternating with chunks of vegetables such as aubergine. The *kibbeh* mixture may be served raw (*kibbeh nayyeh*), and because this requires the highest grade of meat, completely free from sinews, it is a traditional hospitality dish for showing honour to the guest.

Kibbeh is the most characteristic dish of the eastern Arab world, but there is no evidence of it in medieval cookery writings. Possibly this is because the diluting of meat with grain made it food of the common people, not worth recording, but it may also be a dish that only originated in recent centuries. Iraqis say *kubba* was invented in Mosul, and this may be the case. Another Mosul and N. Iraqi speciality, '*urûq* (in the south of the country called *khubz lahm*), shows the same idea of combining roughly equal quantities of grain and a meat and onion mixture, in its case bread dough rather than bulgur or rice. The Iraqis also have a proverb concerning *kubba*: *Habbâya ysawwûha kubbâya*, or 'They make a grain into a *kubba*', meaning 'to make a mountain out of a molehill'.   CP

KICKSHAW a word derived from the French *quelque chose* and meaning a fancy dish, a 'little something'. In the 16th century the term denoted an 'elegant, dainty dish', but later it was often used in a derogatory sense. Thus Addison, writing in the *Tatler* in 1709, referred to 'That Substantial English Dish banished in so ignominious a manner, to make way for French Kick-shaws'. On the other hand, Hannah Glasse (1747), although she professed to be generally and hotly opposed to what she called 'French Tricks', gave a straightforward recipe for Kickshaws; in this instance small fruit pies.

The term fell into disuse, except as a deliberate archaism, in the course of the 19th century.

KIDNEYS which come in pairs, have a distinctive shape (rounded on one side, concave on the other) which is reflected in terms like kidney bean and kidney potato. The kidneys in animals have the task of removing waste matter from the bloodstream and excreting it as urine. This role puts some people off eating them, especially in N. America; but in most parts of the world those of cattle, sheep, and pigs are eaten with relish, especially those of a calf or lamb.

Kidneys are encased in a thick coat of creamy fat; this is generally removed before sale (although a calf's kidney can be cooked inside its fat). Kidneys should be bought and cooked very fresh. Those of adult animals, which will be less tender and often smell of urine, need careful preparation and relatively long cooking, e.g. braising; alternatively they can be chopped or sliced small and then stir-fried, as in China. Very small kidneys, e.g. of cocks or rabbits, cook rapidly and may be of use as garnish.

Kidney soups are found in N. and W. Europe (Russia, Poland, Germany, England). Grilled kidneys used to be offered at English country-house breakfasts; and STEAK AND KIDNEY PIE is a well-known English speciality. Braised kidneys are liked in France, and kidneys grilled on skewers are popular in the Near and Middle East.

KIMCH'I a fermented vegetable and fish relish which is one of the most important foods in KOREA. A little is eaten at every meal as an accompaniment to rice.

Most Koreans make their own kimch'i. The commercial product sold in jars is inferior. The main ingredient is usually CHINESE CABBAGE, but there are many variants based on other vegetables, e.g. the oriental radishes which are ubiquitous in E. Asia, or on CUCUMBER. *Tongkimch'i*, the normal cabbage-based version, differs in its composition in summer and winter according to what is available. A typical winter recipe includes, besides the cabbage: small quantities of salted fish, other vegetables such as leek, garlic, ginger, and chilli pepper 'threads', with many optional additions.

The minor ingredients are sandwiched between squares of cabbage leaf wilted by salting to make it more pliable. The bundles are tightly bound with string, then close packed in a jar of brine. Fermentation begins quickly and is usually complete within a few days, depending on the temperature. It is the normal lactic acid fermentation which occurs in any vegetable pickled in brine (see PICKLE).

Kimch'i keeps for some time if the jar is buried out of doors in the cold Korean winter, so it is a means of preserving vegetables for that season. When the jar is opened there is an unpleasant smell, but this soon dissipates and kimch'i itself has a pleasant if strong taste.

KINGFISH a name best reserved for two fish of the W. Atlantic, *Menticirrhus saxatilis*, the northern kingfish, and *M. americanus*, the southern kingfish; but the name is often used in a loose way of other species; see AMBERJACK, including yellowtail and

WAHOO. These fish are closely related, within the family Sciaenidae, to the CROAKERS and DRUMS, but lack an air bladder so cannot make the noise which their cousins produce. The northern kingfish has irregular dark bars on its sides, which the other species lacks. Maximum length 40 cm (16").

The northern kingfish is most common between Chesapeake Bay and New York; although its full range is from Florida to Cape Cod, it is only a summer visitor in the north and is largely replaced by the southern kingfish in the south.

These are excellent table fish. The white flesh has a fine texture, making it suitable for salads, and responds well to all the standard ways of cooking fish.

KINGKLIP *Genypterus capensis*, a large fish of interesting appearance; it is mottled, of variable coloration, and may reach a length of 160 cm (64").

The kingklip (called *koningklip* in Afrikaans) has a limited distribution along part of the S. African coast. It is described by Smith and Heemstra (1986) as 'one of South Africa's most sought after table fish; taken mainly by trawlers or deep line boats'. They quote earlier authors as saying: 'as it is nowhere abundant, far more fish named "kingklip" on menus is eaten than is ever caught.' The liver is said to be an outstanding delicacy.

KING MUSHROOM *Catathelasma imperialis*, a large mushroom which grows on the ground in mountainous woods in western N. America and in Japan. The olive brown, sticky cap measures 15–40 cm (6–16"), and covers buff gills which extend down the stalk a short distance. The stalk bears a double ring, and bulges just below this. Texture and flavour are good, and 'it will freeze well. Many people make pickled mushrooms from this fungus since it stays very crisp and crunchy' (Miller and Miller, 1980).

Not to be confused with the king boletus (see under CEP).

KINILAW a culinary term of the Visayan language in the Philippines, becomes *kilawin* or *kilawen* in other languages. It refers to fresh, uncooked fish briefly marinated in vinegar so that it is transformed from rawness to the very next stage while retaining translucence. It is thus fish 'cooked in sourness' (technically, in acetic acid) and then enhanced with such condiments as onions, ginger, and chilli.

On either side of this delicate edge between the raw and the cooked exist other variants of kinilaw: fish, crab, shrimp, or sea

urchin plucked fresh from the waters, dipped in vinegar (with chilli, or chilli seeds, or onions and ginger) and eaten raw; cucumbers or crunchy young papaya dipped in vinegar; banana 'heart' (i.e. BANANA FLOWER) blanched slightly and dressed with vinegar; pork, beef, goat, shrimp, or fowl cooked or half-cooked in vinegar. Kinilaw may also be made with flowers, insects, and seaweed—all fresh.

Archaeological evidence has proven kinilaw to be about 1,000 years old, and therefore indigenous to the Philippine Islands. The Balangay excavation in Butuan City (carbon-dated to the period of the 10th–13th centuries AD) uncovered fishbones cut the way they are today, in association with halves of the fruit known locally as *tabon-tabon*, also cut the way they are today for kinilaw. This fruit (*Hydrophytune orbiculatum*) is known locally as *tabon-tabon* and used in Mindanao both to remove the fishy, raw taste from kinilaw, and to prevent stomach upsets.

Variations on the theme are found throughout the islands. The fish may be washed in *tuba* (coconut toddy) before being marinated and served with *tuba* vinegar (fermented from the toddy). Others may add such condiments as wild onions or shallots, and ginger sliced, grated, or squeezed into juice. Chillis may be added whole, chopped, mashed, or marinated in the vinegar. Vinegar—usually made from sugar cane, coconut, or other palms such as *nipa* (*Nypa fruticans*), sugar palm (*Arenga pinnata*), or fishtail palm (*Caryota rumphiana*)—may be used as the marinade or kept separate as a dip. Lime juice may be used instead of or added to the vinegar. Sour fruit like green mango, *kamias* (*Averrhoa bilimbi*, see BELIMBING ASAM), green *siniguelas* (*Spondias purpurea* or 'Spanish plum'—see MOMBIN), and *balimbing* (*Averrhoa carambola*, CARAMBOLA) may be added to enhance the tartness. Grated *tabon-tabon* or *bakawan* (*Rhizophora* sp) bark may be used to neutralize the fish taste or smell. Coconut milk may be added at the last moment to sweeten the mix, or the coconut may be toasted before squeezing, to add a different flavour. A more exotic last-minute addition is *papait* (bile juice or juice squeezed out of partly digested grass from the digestive tract of GOAT, or cow), a speciality of the northern Ilocos Islands.

Kinilaw is thus an island-born cuisine, predicated on food absolutely fresh, 'cooked' in an acid medium.

See also CEVICHE.   DF

READING: Edilberto Alegre and Doreen Fernandez (1991).

KINKAJOU *Potos flavus*, an unusual animal of Latin America (S. Mexico to the

Mato Grosso in Brazil) which lives in tropical forests and has a long prehensile tail which enables it to hang from the branches of trees. Its maximum weight is under 5 kg (10 lb). Its diet features fruits but also includes insects; its long tongue enables it to suck nectar from flowers as well as to catch the insects.

The kinkajou are eaten but are not an important food resource, given their small size and shy habits.

KIPPER now usually a noun but formerly also a verb, meaning a method of curing HERRING (formerly also salmon) by splitting open, salting, and smoking.

The kipper is a British institution and is perceived as part of what a gastronomic writer of the French sort would call 'Britain's culinary heritage'. However, in its present form, as applied to herring, it only dates back to the first half of the 19th century. It was in the 1840s that a Northumbrian curer, after years of experiment, launched his kippered herring on the London market. He borrowed his term from a cure applied to salmon, but how far that went back is not clear. (References to 'kippered salmon' are known from as early as the 15th century, but there is room for doubt in interpreting them since 'kipper' was a term for a spent salmon, i.e. one which had done its spawning and survived in poor, emaciated condition. It may be, as Cutting (1955) suggests, that such salmon were made more readily saleable by the kippering process, and that this was how the process got its name.)

The best kippers are produced on an artisanal basis in Scotland, the Isle of Man, and a few places (such as Craster in Northumberland) in England. Those made on a larger scale may be quite acceptable, but suffer by comparison with the best and will have been treated with an artificial dye (permitted but undesirable).

Kippers are easily cooked, by frying or grilling (US broiling) or 'jugging' (see JUG).

A stir was caused in the 1990s by the publication of a French official work which seemed to suggest, while acknowledging the existence of British kippers, that a similar product made in the north of France was the original or dominant version; but the suggestion disappeared from the next printing. The incident does, however, point to the need to acknowledge here that there is such a thing as a French kipper.

KISEL sometimes spelt kissel, a Russian fruit dessert, is a type of FRUIT SOUP which has been thickened with ARROWROOT, CORNFLOUR, or POTATO flour. The dish is an ancient one, and the original thickening was obtained by a process of souring and

pounding cereals. The word *kisel* means sour. It is still made with oats in Belorussia, where it goes under the name *zhur*, i.e. sour.

Any fruit may be used to make kisel, e.g. plums, gooseberries, rhubarb, raspberries, etc., but kisel is at its best when cranberries or other tart berries or currants (red, white, black) are used.

A layered fruit and milk kisel, resembling BLANCMANGE, is also sometimes made.

Kisel is similar to the Scandinavian *rødgrøt* and the German *rote Grütze*.

KISSES a word used in Britain and N. America to describe various items of sugar confectionery or kindred items. The *NSOED* gives, from the early 19th century, 'a small cake or piece of confectionery; a sweet, a chocolate'. Craigie and Hulbert (1938–44), dealing with N. America, give, from 1825, 'a term applied to different kinds of candy, as a small ball of taffy or a confection made of sugar and egg whites'.

In more recent times, the best-known use of the term in this sort of sense has been for the Hershey Kiss, a kind of milk chocolate drop, brought up to a peak. It was first marketed in 1907 (and followed by the Hershey Hug in 1993).

The word is also applied to some confections with a hard exterior and a soft filling, such as chocolate-dipped marshmallows; or two small biscuits sandwiched together with a soft icing. There are corresponding terms in other countries: thus little almond biscuits filled with fruit preserves are called *bocconetti di mandorla*, 'almond kisses', in Italy.

Malini Bisen (1981) describes various forms of the Indian sweet delicacy called 'cool kiss', which typically involves fruit, sugar, potato flour, and cream.

KITCHEN and kitchen equipment, including ovens, pots and pans, the myriad culinary devices which have been employed around the world in the course of three millennia, and weights and measures for kitchen use, are topics which it would be pertinent and pleasant to explore in the present book. But no; they need, in the opinion of the present author, a separate volume, an 'Oxford Companion to the Kitchen'.

In the meantime, reference may be made to: *The Cook's Room* (1991, ed. Davidson); and *The Cook's Companion* (1985, by Susan Campbell).

KIWANO sometimes called African horned cucumber or jelly melon, *Cucumis metuliferus*, is a cucurbit whose fruit has a golden orange skin, with protuberances

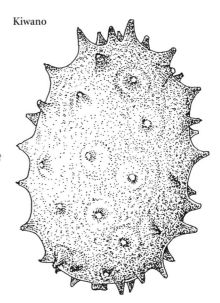
Kiwano

which give it the appearance of a small space craft. The flesh inside is of a rich green.

Generally, this fruit is more decorative than flavourful.

KIWI the national emblem of New Zealand, any one of several flightless and tail-less birds, about the size of domestic fowl, of the genus *Apteryx*.

For a long time now there has been no question of eating any of these rare creatures. However, an account by Charles Edward Douglas (a pioneer New Zealand explorer who wrote about birds among other things) survives (with his spelling) from the very end of the 19th century of its edibility:

As for eating a kiwi. Just before they commence breeding they are very fat and good eating. Still I must confess it requires some considerable practice to get the acquired taste. They have an earthy flavour, which to many would be disagreeable. The best definition I ever heard about roast or boiled kiwi, was a man, remarking it tasted as he should imagine a piece of pork boiled in an old coffin would be like. The egg has slightly the same flavour, but is not to be dispised. One egg makes an excellent fritter, covering an ordinary frying pan.

KIWI FRUIT (or Chinese gooseberry), *Actinidia deliciosa*, was first grown commercially on a large scale in New Zealand, but originated in E. Asia, where several other species of *Actinidia* grow wild and bear small fruits.

Seeds from the Yangtze Valley were taken to New Zealand early in the 20th century, and commercial cultivation began just before the Second World War. The fruits ripen slowly after being picked, and keep well, so there were possibilities for exporting them to Europe. The first shipment reached

England in 1953. When NOUVELLE CUISINE blossomed in France and elsewhere, the kiwi fruit quickly assumed a star role as an exotic, decorative ingredient in fruit salads and in many other dishes besides; the thin slices which can be cut from it to serve as a garnish had become a cliché by the 1970s.

The fruit, which is the size of a large egg, has a thin skin, brown and hairy on the outside. Inside is a firm, green pulp containing tiny, black, edible seeds. The taste is sweet and slightly acid.

Kiwi fruit are rich in vitamin C, ten times more than the equal weight of lemons would be. They also contain an ENZYME similar to that in PAPAYA or PINEAPPLE, which has a tenderizing effect on meat.

Once kiwi fruits had become popular in Europe and N. America, growers in the south of France and California began to cultivate them. New Zealand remains the principal grower and exporter but has lost what was effectively a monopoly.

A mystery to which Jane Grigson (1982) has drawn attention is why the Chinese did not perceive the possibilities of this fruit. There is little evidence of their having shown any interest in it, except as a tonic for children or women after childbirth.

KNOT *Calidris canutus*, a bird which appears in English recipe books of the 17th and 18th centuries but which was already losing its position in the markets by the beginning of the 19th century and has since dropped out of sight almost entirely as a table bird. The knot is also called red sandpiper or, when in its winter plumage, 'grey plover'. It appears on British coasts at the end of the summer and in the autumn, but has its breeding grounds in the Arctic.

The same applies to a few other sandpipers, which are smaller than the knot (whose average total length is 25 cm/10").

If a knot is prepared for the table, this can be done in any way suitable for a SNIPE.

KNOTWEED or knotgrass, a name referring to the knotted roots of plants of the genus *Polygonum*, including BISTORT and SMARTWEED, and *Fallopia*, but with special reference to Japanese knotweed, *Fallopia japonica*, an edible oriental herb which has been introduced to N. America; and *Fallopia sachalinensis*, giant Japanese knotweed, also edible.

Japanese knotweed is a vigorous plant which has made itself at home throughout the USA where its jointed, hollow stems (like bamboo, hence another name sometimes used, flowering bamboo) reach a height of 2 metres (7'). Gibbons (1962) indicated many uses for it. The young shoots make a pleasant vegetable, whose acidity can be

tempered by the addition of a little sugar in the cooking. Or, they can be steamed and made into a purée, which can in turn serve as the basis of a sweetened cold soup. The mature stems, peeled, can be treated like rhubarb; and it is even possible to make a jam or pie from them.

KOCHOJANG (kocho chang, kochuzang), a fermented hot pepper and soya bean sauce or paste, a product of Korea which has some resemblance to chilli pepper sauces of the Caribbean region. It is used to add flavour to savoury dishes.

Besides SOYA BEANS and CHILLI peppers, both fermented and ground, and salt the brew may include ground glutinous rice, JUJUBE flour, dried beef, SOY SAUCE, etc. Production, including time for maturing, is a lengthy process.

KOFTA is the common English form of a term which has currency all the way from India through C. Asia to the Middle East, the Balkans and N. Africa. It refers throughout its range to RISSOLES, MEATBALLS, CROQUETTES, DUMPLINGS, and so on, usually made of ground or mashed meat, well kneaded and often mixed with other ingredients such as rice, BURGHUL (bulgur wheat), or vegetables and spices to form a smooth paste. They are sometimes made, e.g. in India, with fish or just vegetables rather than meat.

Kofta often have a spicy stuffing, typically of nuts, cheese, or eggs. They can be cooked in numerous ways: grilled or barbecued; fried; steamed or poached, very often in a rich sauce.

Margaret Shaida (1992) says that the word kofta is derived from the Persian *koofteh*, meaning pounded meat; and that the first evidence of Persian meatballs appeared in one of the early Arabic cookery books They then consisted of finely minced, well-seasoned lamb, made into orange-sized balls, which were cooked and glazed in saffron and egg yolk three times. This method was later adopted in the West under the name of gilding or endoring.

In Iran there are again numerous variations on the preparation of *koofteh*. Perhaps the most famous and well known are the *koofteh Tabrizi*. According to Shaida they are the largest dumplings in the world with an average size of 20 cm (8") diameter but they are often much larger and she goes on to say:

These enormous dumplings are the pride of housewives from Tabriz and the whole north-western province of Azarbaijan.

Previously, considerable strength and stamina were required to pound the ingredients together into an adhesive mixture. One lady from Tabriz

told me to knead the mixture until my arms fell out. The other great joy of a Persian meat dumpling is the treasure hidden in its centre. In the case of a Tabriz meat dumpling, boiled eggs and fried onions, or prunes and walnuts are inserted into the centre of the dumpling. Occasionally . . . a whole chicken, itself stuffed with dried fruits and nuts, is concealed in its depths. Such inner delights elevate the Persian dumpling to a rare height of sophistication.

From Persia the kofta migrated to India with the Moghul emperors, and so did the hidden treasure version. On special occasions at the Moghul court *nargisi kofta* (narcissus meatballs) were served. The mixture of spiced meat is wrapped round hard-boiled eggs before being cooked. When served, they are cut open, and their yellow and white centres remind people of the narcissus flowers which bloom in the hills in the spring time. Here may be the origin of SCOTCH EGGS.

Many other countries, from the Mediterranean to C. Asia, have their own variations of kofta. The word can also be spelled in a number of ways: *kefta* (Morocco), *kyutfte* (Bulgaria), *qofte* (Albania), *kefte* (Greece, plural *keftethes*), *kufte* (Armenia), *köfte* (Turkey), and *kofta* (Afghanistan and India).

See also KEBAB, KIBBEH, and MEATBALLS.

HS

KOHLRABI *Brassica oleracea* (*Gongylodes* group), a bizarre form of the common CABBAGE in which the base of the stem swells into a globe the size of an orange while the leaves remain comparatively slight. The globe, which forms just above the surface of the soil, is the part of the plant of most interest to the cook. When young, this has

Kohlrabi

the texture of a good turnip and a flavour which has elements of both turnip and cauliflower. However, the stems which spring from the globe, and their leaves, are also palatable and resemble cabbage.

The plant is a biennial; and there are two principal varieties, white and purple. The origins of kohlrabi are as mysterious as its shape. In the 1st century AD Pliny the Elder mentioned a 'Corinthian turnip' which grew above the ground, but gave no further useful facts about it. The first reliable evidence shows it to have been grown in France in the 14th century. It is now popular in Germany and C. Europe (also to some extent in Israel, India, China, and SE Asia), but less so in Britain, where it is still a curiosity or used for animal feed. The name comes from a mistaken belief that it is a cross between cabbage or kale (German *Kohl*) and turnip (species name *rapa*). Its curious Latin variety name *gongylodes* refers to a type of small red turnip resembling the purple kohlrabi and common in C. Asia, where its Kashmiri name is gongolou.

Lesley Chamberlain (1989) remarks on the popularity of kohlrabi as a root vegetable in C. Europe, emphasizes that 'its flavour . . . is only fully released when it is as tender as soft fruit, so there is no merit in undercooking it'—or in eating it grated and raw in a salad, as some do.

KOJI the Japanese name for a product which consists of steamed cereal (usually rice) or legumes, fermented for several days, to provide a starter for preparing other fermented products, including SOY SAUCE, MISO, and SAKÉ. A flat yellowish-green cake in appearance, it is not edible itself but is rich in the enzymes needed for making these edible end products. The mould *Aspergillus oryzae* is the most prominent of the fermenting agents which produce koji, but many others may be involved, depending on the precise results to be achieved.

Koji is said to have originated in China and appears there and in Korea under various names; but it is generally known by its Japanese name because of the extensive uses to which it is put by the Japanese. Different kinds of koji are distinguished by epithets indicating a particular end product, or colour, or substrate: thus soy sauce koji, red or black koji, barley koji.

KOKAM *Garcinia indica*, a tree of the Asian tropics which produces round, purple fruits the size of a small orange. These have a variety of uses, the best known being the production of 'kokam butter', extracted from the kernels, in SW India. The description of this by Watt (1889–96) is not enticing. 'Kokam butter, as found in the bazaars of India, consists of egg-shaped or concavo-convex cakes of a dirty white or yellowish colour, friable, crystalline, and with a greasy feel like spermaceti.' He adds, however, that the product, when fresh, has a smell which is 'not unpleasant', and melts in the mouth like butter, leaving a sensation of cold on the tongue.

The fruits themselves have also been eaten in SW India as a semi-medicinal food. They are acid, and considered by some to be better than tamarind for the preparation of acidulous drinks. Joe Roberts (personal communication, 1990) says that a refreshing syrup is made from the juice for a fairly common drink in S. India; that the acidic flavour enhances certain curries and DALS; and that in Kerala kokam is used in fish cookery and is called 'fish tamarind'. In curry recipes tamarind and kokam may be used together.

KOMBU (or more correctly *konbu*), the Japanese name for many of a large and important group of brown SEAWEEDS, mostly in the genus *Laminaria*. In terms of annual production this is the second largest group in Japan, outranked only by WAKAME. Among the most prominent species of kombu are:

- karafuto kombu, *L. saccharina*, sweeter than the others because of the presence of mannitol;
- ma-kombu, *L. japonica*;
- mitsuishi-kombu, *L. angustata*, also called dashi-kombu since used for making the soup stock called DASHI;
- naga-kombu, *L. longissima*;
- Rishiri-kombu (after the island Rishiri), *L. ochotensis*, preferred for making soup stock because of its refined flavour.

Closely related species in the Atlantic may be referred to as oarweed or more loosely as kelp or wrack (sugar wrack in the case of the fourth).

The uses of kombu in Japan are manifold. It is found in many dishes and preparations as a main or subsidiary ingredient. It is, incidentally, very rich in MSG (see MONOSODIUM GLUTAMATE).

KONA CRAB *Ranina serrata*, the most delicious crab of Hawaiian waters according to Hosaka (1973), lives in sandy holes among the coral, a short distance offshore.

KONNYAKU also known as devil's tongue jelly, a food extracted from the starchy root/corm of *Amorphophallus rivieri* (formerly *A. konjac*), an Asian plant known as konjac. Konnyaku is a perennial plant of the arum family, said to be indigenous to India and Ceylon. In its native countries and also in China it has been grown since ancient times. It was first brought to Japan by way of Korea during the Nara period (710–94) as a medicinal plant. Its cultivation as a food plant started about 400 years ago in Ibaragi prefecture in C. Japan.

This is an important ingredient in Japan. The root/corm itself is never seen in the markets, not for reasons of propriety (the generic name means 'shapeless phallus', a horrifying concept) but because considerable processing is needed to turn it into anything edible.

Corms of konnyaku are first ground roughly and then made into refined flour. When mixed with water, it turns into a paste because of its main constituent, a polysaccharide called mannan. It is then solidified by adding limewater. It can then be moulded, cut into squares, boiled to remove the alkaline smell, and drained in baskets. The finished product is brown or grey in colour, dense and gelatinous in texture, and neutral in flavour. Fresh cakes are sold from tubs of water, and may be unrefined (dark) or refined (light).

The same foodstuff is sold in filament form. In thin filaments called by the poetical name *shirataki* (white waterfall) it is an indispensable ingredient for *sukiyaki* (see JAPANESE CULINARY TERMS). Thicker filaments are known as *ito konnyaku* (string konnyaku). *Shirataki* are sold in cans or refrigerated plastic tubs, and are believed to have a healthy cleansing effect on the intestines.

In any form, konnyaku is parboiled before use.

Konnyaku is generally treated like a vegetable (though there is a kind which is eaten uncooked, as SASHIMI). In itself konnyaku has little flavour, but is liked for its firm, jelly-like texture and for its ability to absorb the flavours of things it is cooked with. Two of the most typical dishes using konnyaku are: *nikomi oden* (vegetables, FISH PASTE, TOFU, konnyaku cooked together in DASHI, SOY SAUCE, and MIRIN) and *miso oden* (boiled konnyaku served with sweetened MISO).

A. variabilis, a close relation, is also used for the production of konnyaku. For another relation, see SURAM.

KOREA a country with a long history, a rich culture, an ancient court, and an elaborate system of etiquette. Korean food is hearty, boldly flavoured, and highly nutritious.

The Koreans like to say that they are descended from a single race, and, indeed, they are primarily Mongolian, slightly more stocky than the N. Chinese, but taller than the Japanese. Around the time of Christ, there were three kingdoms in ancient Korea,

Koguryo to the north, Paekche and Silla in the south. These kingdoms were culturally advanced and boasted royal courts, nobility, class systems, and centralized governments. It was around this time also that Buddhism was introduced to the area, becoming the preserve of royalty, while Confucianism flourished among the minor aristocracy. With the aid of the Chinese, Silla conquered the other two kingdoms and established a unified country with elaborate palaces and imposing monuments.

In later centuries, despite incursions from the north and the west, hostility from Japan, and some intrusive activity by Europeans, the Koreans maintained their autonomy. They lost it in 1910, when the country was annexed by Japan, but regained it after the Second World War.

The political division of the country into N. and S. Korea, which began with the Korean War of the 1950s, corresponds to a large extent with geographical and climatic factors. The mountainous north produces less food than the fertile and warm plains of the south.

Various things can be held to be prerequisites for the formation of a distinctive cuisine: the structure of a social system, to provide special occasions for the development of special foods; a long and prosperous court life (or the equivalent), to evolve refinements in the cuisine; and the establishment of a solid religion, to provide rituals and occasions for festivals and feasts. Korea has had all these. Its cuisine developed into two distinct types of cooking: the home cooking of the common people, developed within the traditional family and as the province of the housewife, and the complex and elegant cuisine of the royal courts, using a wider variety of seasonings and spices, more intricate cooking methods, and elegant presentation of food.

Throughout Korea, the main meal of the day is still breakfast, which evolved to fortify the men before a hard day's work. Lunch, even in the royal courts, was, and still is, a light meal: noodles or rice, mixed with red beans, nuts, and seeds for protein. Dinner in the courts and homes of the wealthy families was an elaborate affair of nine to twelve dishes accompanying a central bowl of rice. Everyday dinner in the home usually consists of between three and seven dishes, depending on the size of the family. Special occasions, such as the celebration of a wedding or a 61st birthday (any birthday after 60 is considered as a victory over death), or a birth or memorial anniversary, will all have their appropriate foods and table arrangements.

Koreans have always believed that good health is maintained by sensible eating and a good nutritional balance. They also follow the oriental rule of Five Flavours: salt, sweet,

sour, hot, bitter. Salt, soy sauce, and salty bean paste provide the first; beet sugar, honey, and sweet potatoes are used to sweeten food; chilli peppers and mustard provide heat; vinegars are used as souring agents; and ginger is regarded as a bitter flavour. In addition to the Five Flavours, the Koreans also try to follow an arrangement of five traditional colours: red, green, yellow, white, black. The last does not easily occur in nature, but such foodstuffs as dried cloud-ear mushrooms (see WOOD EAR) provide a semblance. Seaweed is not widely used in the cuisine, as it is in Japan.

The predominant elements characteristic of the cuisine are garlic, green (spring) onions, sesame seeds (toasted and used whole or ground), ginger, dried red chilli peppers. Ground cinnamon, hot mustard, and black pepper are also used. Meats and other foods are often marinated in mixtures of chopped green onions, sesame seeds, and oil, vinegar, and soy sauce before being cooked. Dips and combinations of condiments for sauces, such as hot bean paste, vinegar, and soy, accompany such dishes as barbecued or broiled (grilled) meats, deep-fried vegetables, etc. Dishes are often garnished with eggs, cooked into a thin omelette and then rolled, before being sliced into strips.

Beef is the most commonly used meat, in soups, barbecues, and hotpots. Offal (variety meats), such as tongue, heart, liver, and tripe, is also included in many dishes such as soups and stews. KIMCH'I, pickled vegetables, accompany most meals. These pickles compensate for the scarcity of fresh vegetables during the long winters, but summer pickles are also popular.

Korean meals are eaten from bowls. Rice and soup demand spoons. Chopsticks are used only to take portions from the serving dishes. The meals are presented on dinner trays, rather in the manner of the Indians or the Thai. Small trays are used for one or two people; a large, round tray, called a *kae-ryang sang*, is used for a crowd.

Firepots, the bronze or brass utensils with a bowl surrounding a central chimney that houses charcoal to cook the food or keep it warm, are used for special dishes and for some soups. The Mongolian barbecue, where various ingredients are diced into small pieces and then stir-fried on a convex iron griddle shaped rather like a Mongolian helmet, is rather a hybrid and, because of its association with an ancient enemy, is not a common item in Korea, although many Korean restaurants outside the country do feature it. JB

KORMA a polymorphic cookery term of the Near East and W. Asia, which also appears as *qawurma/awurma*, *qawarma*,

ghourma, *qrma*, *qorma*, etc., all of which forms are variations on the Turkish *qawurmah* (sometimes written *kavurma*, from the verb meaning to fry).

In Turkey, the term has two meanings: fried slices of meat; and meat conserved in fat and salt. In other parts of the Middle East the word has this second meaning (see QAWARMA). In Turkey, Syria, and Lebanon there are various dishes cooked from this conserved meat and called *qawurma*. In Iran, although this meaning is known, the derived word *ghourma* has come to mean primarily *ghourma sabzi*—meat and herbs braised in butter or GHEE with dried limes and some kind of bean.

The home territory of the korma family is an arc stretching from the Middle East through Afghanistan to N. India. In Pakistan and India, the term refers to a dish in the category of BRAISE (i.e. a dish in which the main ingredient is cooked slowly with a minimum of added liquid) or of STEW (a dish in which the main ingredient is cooked slowly in a relatively large amount of liquid). In the latter case it would normally be the sort of stew which finishes up with a thick rather than thin sauce.

Korma (*qorma*) in Afghanistan may be made either as a braise or as a stew; and it was probably from this pivotal region that the dish gradually spread to N. India with the Moghul conquerors (see MOGHUL CUISINE). Indians often enrich their kormas with nuts, yoghurt or cream, and butter.

KOUMISS or kumiss, a drink of some, but varying, alcoholic content, prepared by fermenting mare's milk. Its existence in an only slightly alcoholic form and its value as a 'food' combine to justify its inclusion in the present volume.

Koumiss is still a popular drink in C. Asian countries such as Tajikistan, Uzbekistan, Kazakhstan, and in Mongolia, where it is known as *ayrag*. It probably originated with the Turkic nomadic tribes who wandered throughout the steppes of C. Asia and China in ancient times. It was, and still is, considered to be strengthening and fattening.

Emerson (1908), who explores the subject with characteristic thoroughness, describes as follows how koumiss is made:

Take of mare's milk, not cow's, six parts and of warm water, one part, put this into a bag made from the skin of some animal in which there is a little sour cow's milk or a piece of rennet from the stomach of a calf, colt or lamb. This will induce fermentation and soon a thick scum will rise to the top. When this has ceased gathering, the bag is shaken for some minutes and is then allowed to remain quiescent for several hours, when it is again stirred by a sort of churning motion. It is only necessary to do this three or four times in order to have the beverage complete and perfect.

Marco Polo was one of the early travellers in the Orient who remarked on koumiss. Another was William of Rubruck, a Franciscan friar, who travelled across C. Asia in the 13th century and gave his own description of the making of koumiss, reporting that the churning went on sporadically for about three or four days, which is the length of time favoured by the Kazakh peoples who continue to make kumiss in Russian Turkestan in the 20th century. When William of Rubruck arrived at Karakoram, he was impressed to discover that a far-ranging French goldsmith had built for the Mongol prince, Mangu Khan, a silver fountain with four spouts which dispensed, respectively, koumiss, wine, mead, and rice wine, of which the first was the most honoured.

So far as China is concerned, people have tended to think of koumiss as a drink belonging to the north of the country (and Mongolia). Yet Chang (1977), writing of the Sung dynasty (960–1279), points out that 'it was a well established item in the Sung diet: the emperor had a special office for its production, some restaurants specialised in serving it, and it occurs many times in the lists of banquet foods'.

The range of koumiss, as noted above, also extended westwards from China. Mountstuart Elphinstone (1839) has this to say about koumiss when describing the food of the Uzbeks.

The national beverage is kimmiz, an intoxicating liquor, well known to be prepared from mare's milk. The milk is put in the afternoon into a skin, such as is used in India for holding water, and is allowed to remain till within two or three hours of day-break, when it is beaten and rolled about till morning at least; but the longer the better. The liquor thus made is of a whitish colour and a sourish taste: it is only to be had in plenty during the two last months of summer, and those who can afford it are generally drunk for the greater part of that period; but kimmiz is not sold, and those only can enjoy it who have mares enough to make it in the house.

Enough mares, in the right condition, were not always and everywhere available. The Kublai Khan had 10,000 pure white horses and mares at his disposal, and the milk of these mares was reserved for the royal family, so there was no shortage of koumiss in his palaces. But he was uniquely fortunate. Elsewhere, people might have to make do with a similar beverage made from sheep's milk, or from camel's milk or milk from the dri (see YAK). A similar beverage made by Laplanders, called *pima*, is made from reindeer's milk.   HS

KREPLACH small filled PASTA of JEWISH COOKERY. It is made at home from egg noodle dough, usually filled with minced meat or chicken, and often added to chicken broth. There are also cheese kreplach, which can be a main dish in 'dairy meals'.

The word is believed to come from the French *crêpe*, presumably via the German *Krepp*. Its odd appearance is due to the fact that it is plural in form; Yiddish, like Irish and Welsh, has a lot of novel plural suffixes such as -*lach* that have arisen from phonetic decay and analogical levelling.

However, a *crêpe* and a kreplach are certainly quite different. Presumably this was a Jewish development substituting noodle paste for crêpe batter, or a fancy foreign name applied to a dish with a different origin.   CP

KRILL the general name for the small shrimplike CRUSTACEANS which abound in polar waters, especially *Euphausia superba* in the Antarctic, and which are eaten in prodigious quantities by whales. In the latter half of the 20th century scientists and technicians, especially in Germany and Russia, have experimented with harvesting krill and producing from it foodstuffs for human beings.

The matter is of some importance because krill have the potential to be a food resource of unusually high quality; the nutritional content, which includes a balanced kit of amino acids and important trace elements, is almost ideal. Moreover, the resource would be a huge one. It was estimated in the 1980s that the annual catch of krill could be greater, in weight, than the whole annual catch of fish worldwide at that time. And it seemed that technical problems had been overcome by the elaboration of processing methods which could be carried out on board ship immediately after the krill (which spoil rapidly) had been caught. They are pressed to yield a juice full of protein. The presscake is set aside for animal feed. The juice is then heated to coagulate the protein, and this is formed into blocks of paste which are frozen. In the former Soviet Union this krill pâté was marketed as 'Ocean paste'; this was highly nutritious and quite tasty but not a popular success.

KRUPUK the Indonesian/Malaysian name for a thin, usually savoury CRACKER, popular in many parts of SE Asia and with many local variations. In some areas, they are called *keripik* (with a very short e). The basic material is flour—WHEAT, RICE, MAIZE, or CASSAVA—which is mixed with other ingredients to provide flavour and then dried in the sun to make something resembling a thin, dense, and exceedingly hard biscuit. When put into very hot oil, this more or less doubles its length and width in a few seconds, and when it has cooled it has a most satisfying crunchy texture.

The obvious comparison is with a Chinese PRAWN CRACKER; indeed, krupuk are often flavoured with prawn or shrimp, but tastier than the Chinese product. The best of these *krupuk udang*, or shrimp crackers, are considered to be those made in the town of Sidoarjo, near Surabaya in E. Java; these are widely exported. Another popular type is flavoured with chillies. Sweet krupuk are made in some places.   RO

KUBILI NUTS come from a tree, *Cubilia blancoi*, which grows mainly in the Philippines and also in the Moluccas and Sulawesi. The oval fruit is covered with spikes and about 5 cm (2") long. It contains a single, starchy nut resembling a chestnut, but with a less interesting flavour, although highly nutritious. The nuts have been sold in the Philippines under the name of *castañas* (chestnuts), and eaten boiled or roasted, but their future is uncertain; the tree has been classified as potentially needing protection.

KUDZU the Japanese name (more correctly rendered as kuzu) for a leguminous plant, *Pueraria lobata*, which is native to Japan and the Orient but has been widely cultivated in the south-east of the USA, and has become an aggressive weed. It is mainly grown as animal fodder, but is also the source of a valuable starch.

The starch, which is called *gok fun* in China and *ko fen* in Japan, comes from the root. Tsuji (1980) describes its good properties thus:

As a thickener, kuzu starch—extracted from the root of the vine—is excellent: it produces a sparkling, translucent sauce and adds shiny gloss to soups. It has a gentle pleasant aroma, and does its work at fairly low temperatures. Because it is an alkali, it balances acidity, such as found in sweets. Dusted over foods to be deep fried, it yields a light, crisp, almost crystalline snow-white coating.

A tropical species, *P. phaseoloides*, is native to SE Asia and has been introduced to Africa.

KUGEL a term often met in JEWISH COOKERY, meaning PUDDING. It may be either sweet or savoury.

Lokshen kugel, one of the most popular, itself exhibits this ambivalence; there is a savoury version made with noodles, curd cheese or sour cream, and a pinch of nutmeg, and a sweet one without the nutmeg but with the addition of sugar, lemon or orange zest, and raisins.

Best known of all is potato kugel. Claudia Roden (1996) introduces this with a quotation from the German poet Heinrich Heine, who addressed the editor of a Jewish magazine in what must have seemed like discouraging terms: 'Kugel, this holy national dish, has done more for the preservation of Judaism than all three issues of the magazine.' He meant potato kugel, no doubt made in the traditional way with eggs, chicken fat, onion, and grated potato.

The German word *Kugel* means ball or something round, and is evidently the origin of this term, as of KUGELHOPF, see below.

KUGELHOPF a rich, light, delicate yeast cake, made from flour, eggs, butter, and sugar, is related to BRIOCHE, BABA, and SAVARIN. It contains raisins, and may be flavoured with lemon peel or decorated with slivered almonds.

The identifying characteristic of kugelhopf is its tall ring shape. This is derived from the mould in which it is baked, round and deep, with a central funnel, and fluted with decorative swirls. After baking, the cake is turned out and dusted with icing sugar which catches in the pattern, like newly fallen snow.

Kugelhopf is one of the best-known C. European bakery products, but spelling and pronunciation vary, tending to be *kugelhopf* at the western edge of its range, and *gugelhupf* in the east. It is made in a wide belt from Alsace (where the small town of Ribeauville holds a fête in its honour every June); through parts of Germany (notably the Black Forest) and Poland; and into Austria, where a rich version of it is served for *Jause*, afternoon tea. The traditional pattern in C. Europe was for kugelhopf to be baked for Sunday breakfast, when the village baker had his day off.

It is also popular with Jewish communities who have settled in these areas. Lesley Chamberlain (1983) draws attention to the link between the name kugelhopf and the Jewish KUGEL, a kind of round, firm, sweet or savoury pudding. Both terms refer to something round; and both seem related to the German *Kugel*, meaning a ball or something round.							(LM)

KULCHA are small Indian breads made of leavened white flour dough, pressed into rounds and deep fried. Often they are filled with spiced vegetables or curd cheese before being fried.

In Afghanistan *kulcha* means biscuit.

KUMQUAT of the genus *Fortunella*, a fruit resembling a miniature ORANGE, seldom more than 3 cm (1.25") across. Until recently it was placed with the orange in the genus *Citrus*, but has now been assigned to a genus of its own because of the simpler structure of its fruit. In particular, its attractive golden rind is not a distinct, pithy covering like that of a true citrus fruit, but is thin, soft, and pulpy. This is all to the good because the rind is therefore edible, and the fruit can be eaten whole, although the taste of most kinds is rather too sour for the average palate.

Kumquat trees are all small, seldom exceeding shrub size. They are native to SE China, where they still grow wild, and the name is a corruption of the Chinese *chin kan* (golden mandarin). Two main kinds exist: the oval, *Fortunella margarita*, the best known and the one most often cultivated; and the round, *F. japonica*, with larger, sweeter fruits.

There are various natural hybrids, one of which, *F. crassifolia* (*F. margarita* × *F. japonica*), is unusually sweet and the best variety for eating fresh. This kind is cultivated in China and Japan, and there is one variety with striped fruits.

The kumquat can also form hybrids with true *Citrus* species. One fruit which is thought to have originated in this way is the calamondin 'orange' or CALAMANSI, whose parents may have been a MANDARIN and a kumquat. Since the kumquat is more resistant to cold than ordinary citrus fruits, growers have experimented with *Fortunella* × *Citrus* hybrids (orangequats, limequats) and *Fortunella* × *Poncirus* (trifoliate orange) hybrids (citrangequats), hoping to find edible fruits or useful hardy rootstocks for grafting. One citrangequat, Thomasville, has smallish golden fruits which are pleasantly flavoured.

Kumquats and calamondins have been cultivated in China since early times. Two kinds of kumquat are described in Han Yen-chih's *Chu Lu* (Monograph of Citrus) of AD 1178. Later, cultivation was taken up enthusiastically in Japan, where the cold winters made citrus growing difficult. The kumquat also spread further afield. Curiously, what may be the first reference to it, antedating the *Chu Lu* by almost three centuries, is in the Iraqi writer Ibn Wahshya's *Book of Nabatean Agriculture*, completed in 904. He describes a grafting method to produce 'very small citrons, of the size of an olive' but warns that

it must be done . . . at the time of a certain conjunction of sun and moon. [and the tree must be] fumigated with certain substances whilst a formula is uttered. The branch which is to be grafted must be in the hand of a beautiful damsel, whilst a male person has disgraceful and unnatural sexual intercourse with her; during intercourse the woman grafts the branch into the tree.

The kumquat was brought to London in 1846 by the plant collector and explorer Robert Fortune, after whom the genus is now named. By 1850 it had also reached the USA. The most popular way of treating kumquats in China has been to preserve them in honey, or more recently sugar. Sometimes the rind alone is preserved.

Shortly after their introduction to the West, kumquat plants would be placed on the table at fashionable dinners so that guests could pick the fruits. The main uses of the kumquat in western countries now are as an ornamental shrub and for making marmalade.

KVASS a Russian beverage which is just eligible for inclusion in this volume both because its alcoholic content is very low and because it appears as an ingredient in a number of dishes, including many of the items in the classic Russian cookery book by Molokhovets. Joyce Toomre (1992), the translator of this work, provides the following excellent description in one of her numerous Translator's Notes.

Kvass is a lightly fermented sour-sweet beverage that is commonly made of black bread or grain with yeast and somewhat resembles beer in flavor. Both grain *kvass* and beet *kvass* are used for soup. Other more delicate varieties of *kvass* are made from fruits or berries. *Kvass*, along with mead and beer, has been drunk since Kievan Rus'. Whereas the nobility in earlier times preferred mead, the common people drank *kvass*. It was the most popular drink in nineteenth-century Russia, consumed by the rich as an occasional refreshment and by the peasantry on a daily basis. Like the gathering of mushrooms and berries, the eating of *prjaniki*, and the consumption of *shchi*, the drinking of *kvass* in late Tsarist Russia had become a culture-laden act that helped to define one's Russianness. Although *kvass* was easily made at home, the itinerant *kvass* peddler was a common figure in the streets and markets. Even today, it is not unusual to see a *kvass* truck parked at the curb while the driver dispenses drinks to a crowd of customers. *Kvass* is a relatively healthy drink, having a low alcoholic content (0.7 to 2.2%) and a good proportion of readily assimilable proteins and carbohydrates.

There are also versions of kvass in neighbouring countries. Jean Redwood (1989) states that the Polish version is with lemon juice, and that the Lithuanians add raisins in addition, while cinnamon is a flavouring in the Ukraine. Added flavours in Russia include caraway, mint, or (further north) blackcurrant leaves.

LABLAB BEAN *Lablab purpureus* ssp *purpureus*, a LEGUME of African or Asian origin which has been grown in India since very early times. It is now cultivated in tropical and subtropical regions worldwide for human food and also as animal fodder. It has many merits: a high protein content; a high yield; the ability to stay green during droughts; and easy harvesting.

Other common names for the lablab bean include bonavist(a) bean, Egyptian bean, and hyacinth bean.

In modern Arabic, the general word for a bean, *lubia*, is taken to mean the lablab bean unless otherwise indicated.

Lablab comes in two main forms: a bushy plant, or one which grows like a vine. Pods vary from 5 to 20 cm (2 to 8") long and may be straight or curved. The beans are usually black or nearly so, but white in some varieties. The fresh mature seeds (especially dark-coloured ones) must be boiled to become edible; they contain a trypsin inhibitor that is broken down by heat and a toxic cyanogenetic glucoside that is soluble in the cooking water. The hardness of the seed coat necessitates a long cooking time.

Young pods make an excellent table vegetable. Dried seeds are a wholesome, palatable food, either cooked and eaten directly, or processed into bean cakes or fermented to produce a sort of TEMPE. Leaves and flowers are cooked and eaten like spinach. The sprouts are comparable to soya bean or mung bean sprouts.

LACHSSCHINKEN (salmon ham), a German product, not actually a HAM, for it is made from PORK loin. This is lightly salted, smoked, rolled, and encased in bacon fat. It has a pink colour, as its name suggests, and is eaten raw. Similar products are made in Poland, and in France, where it is called *filet de Saxe* (Saxon fillet).

LACTIC ACID produced by many kinds of BACTERIA in the fermentation of MILK and of some vegetable products, is mainly responsible for the sour taste of most milk products, and of other products, including SAUERKRAUT, GHERKINS, OLIVES, and cocoa.

Lactic acid-producing bacteria, often more simply called lactic acid bacteria, change the degree of acidity in (to take the main example) milk. When this process reaches the point at which the proteins are precipitated, the first step in CHEESE-MAKING has been accomplished; the CURD which will eventually become the finished cheese has been formed. The differing characteristics of the various lactic acid bacteria are one important factor in bringing about the wide variety of characteristics in cheeses.

LACTOSE INTOLERANCE an inability to digest lactose (milk sugar), so that drinking milk causes a digestive upset. Among white Europeans and a few other groups it is an unusual disability. But in the rest of the world, especially Africa and Asia, it is usual for the ability to digest milk to be lost as a person grows up. It seems likely that human beings originally had the capability to produce lactase in infancy and for as long as they needed mother's milk, but not thereafter, when the capability would have been superfluous. However, at some time after human beings in C. and N. Europe had begun to use the milk of domesticated animals and were in a position to benefit considerably from a prolongation of their ability to produce lactase, a new gene which provided for such prolongation would have been favoured by natural selection, so that this portion of the human race became able to digest lactose in adulthood and even into old age.

Lactose is the main and almost the sole sugar in milk. It is a disaccharide (double sugar) composed of the simple sugars dextrose and galactose. Splitting lactose into these two sugars is the first stage in digesting it, and is done with the aid of the enzyme lactase. A supply of lactase is therefore essential for digesting milk or milk products, unless they have been treated, before they are ingested, by some process which anticipates the requirement. Just about all Indians, for example, eat lots of yoghurt because the changes effected in milk by turning it into yoghurt make it digestible without the aid of lactase.

Most statements about lactose intolerance require qualification, since it is not an absolute condition. Those who are affected by it are usually able to digest small amounts of milk—say, a small glass of milk, taken with other food, as opposed to a large glass taken by itself. In many milk products, including YOGHURT and cheeses (especially hard types), much of the lactose is consumed during fermentation and changed into lactic acid, so that the result is more digestible.

LADDU (sometimes ladoo), the Hindi word for 'a spherical sweetmeat', a category of Indian confectionery defined by shape rather than ingredients, which vary to an almost infinite extent. These confections are typically based on a cereal or pulse flour or meal (e.g. semolina, rice flour, soya or MUNG BEAN or BESAN FLOUR). These basic ingredients may be fried in GHEE; may be enhanced with small pieces of dried fruit, nuts, CARDAMOM seeds, or grated coconut; and are usually mixed with sugar or syrup and formed into balls while still warm. Some laddu are made from a mixture of *khoya* (see MILK REDUCTION) and sugar formed into balls without cooking. Laddu are often quite large, with a diameter of 3–4 cm (1.5"), but others are relatively small. A yellow colour is popular. Some laddu have special significance as festive sweets, e.g. at weddings.

READING: Malini Bisen (1981).

LADIKANEE is Lady Canning, transformed into an Indian term by the *moira* (professional sweet-maker in Bengal) who created it. Chitrita Banerji (1997) explains that Lady Canning, who was 'Vicereine of India' at that time (shortly after 1858 when Lord Canning became the first Viceroy of India), challenged Bhim Chandra Nag, a prominent *moira*, to create a new sweet for her birthday. He did, and 'this new product, large, spherical, succulent and fragrant, became known as the ladikanee'. It remains very popular. See PANTUA.

Lady Canning was one of a very small number of titled British personages whose names passed into the culinary vernacular of other cultures. Lord Nelson and Lady Hamilton (see POLAND) are two others.

LADYFISH a surprising name for *Elops saurus*, a silvery fish of tropical waters which has poor flesh, full of small bones. It is sometimes called 'giant herring', since it has a superficial resemblance to a herring, but is larger (up to 90 cm/35" in length); and sometimes 'ten-pounder', in allusion to the weight which anglers expect it to have. It is related to the TARPON and MILK FISH.

In many places the ladyfish is better known to anglers than to commercial fishermen, but it does appear in the markets in SE Asia, for example. An author in Hawaii (Rizzuto, 1977) observes optimistically that the *awa'aua* (its local name) can be used in fish cakes if the bones are first 'kneaded out', a laborious process.

LAGOON CRAB a name given in various parts of the world to crabs inhabiting lagoons or living a mainly terrestrial life on the banks of lagoons. Generally, these are of little importance as food. However, one W. African species, *Cardiosoma armata*, especially plentiful in the Nzima country of Ghana, is accounted the best crab to eat in that country. The carapace, which is dark blue above, may measure 15 cm (6") across. The legs are bright red and covered with stiff black bristles.

LAKSA a term which derives from the original Persian word for NOODLE, *lakhsha* (meaning 'slippery'). Although Iran has not been a heavy consumer of noodles, it has an ancient history of noodle-making; indeed, there has been speculation that the Chinese learned the idea of noodle-making from the same Persian merchants who introduced the flour mill to them during the Han dynasty (206 BC–AD 220). The term *lakhsha* was certainly used in medieval Arabic and has shown considerable powers of survival. It is still used in E. Europe (Hungarian *laska*, Russian *lapsha*, Ukrainian *lokshina*, Lithuanian *lakstiniai*) and in Afghanistan (*lakhchak*).

Also, it is known that Arab traders or Indian Muslims had spread the use of pasta to Indonesia in perhaps the 13th century.

The old Indonesian and Malaysian name *laksa* shows that this pasta originated in Persia, not from a Chinese source (as in the case of the modern Indonesian name *mie*).

A quaint Persian tale retold in a 10th-century Arabic recipe collection has King Chosroes I offhandedly inventing *laksha* during a hunting expedition in the course of a discussion of how to flavour a soup of wild ass's meat. However, by the 13th century, RESHTEH ('string') had supplanted it, and this is now the usual word for a flat, sliced noodle in the Near East.   CP

LAMB (*see opposite page*)

LAMINGTON a small cake covered with chocolate icing and rolled in coconut. They are an Australian speciality believed to be named after Baron Lamington, governor of Queensland from 1896 to 1901, or his wife. It cannot be proved that they were invented in the kitchens of Government House, although the interest Lady Lamington appears to have taken in household matters may support the claim. A letter she wrote to thank the cookery writer Hannah MacLurcan for her most recent book in 1898 expresses an awareness of the advantage of clear practical instructions in the writing of recipes. However, the book contains no reference to the cake.

Some sources credit Amy Schauer, instructress in cookery at Brisbane's Central College from 1897 to 1938 and a renowned authority on culinary matters who was reputedly very fond of rich cakes and puddings. She wrote a cookery book, *The Schauer Cookery Book* (1909), which by the time of its 1935 edition had almost 200 cake recipes. However, the first known printed recipe for lamingtons appeared earlier, in 1902 in the cookery section of the *Queenslander*, a weekly newspaper, credited simply to 'A Subscriber'. From this time onwards recipes for the cake proliferated.

Fund-raising Lamington Drives are a thriving institution in Australia and attest to the enduring popularity of the lamington.

LAMPREY *Petromyzon marinus*, a very primitive fish, of the family Petromyzonidae. It is adapted to living as a parasite on larger fish, to the undersides of which it attaches itself by means of a suctorial toothed pad, through which it can suck the blood of its victim. This unattractive lifestyle is matched by an unappetizing appearance: slimy, jawless, a single nostril on top, and seven little gill openings on each side.

Although it counts as a sea fish, the lamprey goes up rivers to spawn and is

(*cont. on page 442*)

Lamb

Lamb is the meat of the young domestic SHEEP, *Ovis aries*. The age at which a lamb ceases to be 'lamb' and becomes a young sheep, technically yielding MUTTON, is not entirely clear. Biologically, this happens when the animal grows its first pair of permanent teeth. In culinary practice, two types of lamb are recognized.

First, there is the sucking lamb, fed only on its mother's milk. Formerly this was popular in England, and, known as house lamb, was bred especially for the Christmas market. It is now unusual to see very young lamb for sale in Britain, but it is still a delicacy in other countries. In France it is known as *agneau de lait*, or *agneau de Pauillac* (Pauillac is a town near Bordeaux); the Italians, Spanish, and Portuguese also hold such meat in high esteem, and young lambs are eaten in the Middle East. The flesh of a sucking lamb is very pale and tender, but lacks flavour.

Secondly, the meat of the weaned animal, between four months and one year old, is also called lamb, and forms the bulk of the sheep meat now sold in Britain. Older animals (from about one year) are properly called 'hogg', or 'hoggett' and their meat has to count as mutton, but it will not have developed a good mutton flavour until quite a bit older.

JOINTING LAMB

SUCKING lambs are often cooked whole, or cut into quarters, a leg of baby lamb providing two servings. Older lambs are still relatively small creatures, and there are none of the complex patterns of jointing associated with beef; similar cuts are found in Britain, the USA, and France. The animal is split down the backbone and cut into fore and hind quarters. The former yields the shoulder joint, containing the blade bone; the rest of the quarter is split into the breast; the 'scrag end' (the neck closest to the head); and the 'best end', which lies further back. This last cut, which contains an 'eye' of good meat, is much exploited. It can be separated into individual ribs to give cutlets or left in one piece and roasted as a 'rack'; this is what is called *Carré d'agneau* in French, a famous dish. Two racks, with the ends of the ribs exposed and arranged to intersect, make a 'guard of honour'; sewn together to make a circle with the meat on the inside and the curved bones radiating outwards, they make a 'crown'. If the two racks are cut from the carcass without splitting the backbone, they equal a 'chine'.

A hindquarter, of course, provides a leg. In France the lower part of this is known as a *gigot*, a word also used in Scotland, where it is pronounced *jiggot*. Further forward in the animal lies the loin, which can be cut into chops, or left whole; two loins with the backbone intact equal a 'saddle'. In England, a chop cut from a saddle is called a 'Barnsley chop'. The 'chump' is the rear end of the loin, above the leg; it contains a high proportion of bone. A leg and loin together comprise a 'haunch'.

French *pré-salé* (salt meadow) lamb is that grazed on salt marshes. It has a distinctive and highly valued flavour, as has Welsh lamb similarly grazed.

In haute cuisine, lamb does not have the primary importance of beef. Although the meat is the foundation of a number of classic dishes, it is little used for stock, and the fat has a distinctive flavour which is not liked in the western world. (Traditionally, it was used for making tallow candles.) Further east, both lamb stock and fat are used, and the fat from FAT-TAILED SHEEP was of great importance in medieval Persian cookery, and continues to be used in the Near and Middle East and C. Asia.

Lamb is a fatty meat, and most cuisines recognize the need for some kind of acid ingredient or sauce to 'cut' this. In England, mint sauce, composed of chopped fresh mint, sugar, and vinegar, has been the accepted accompaniment for roast lamb since the mid-19th century. In Spain, wine or wine vinegar is frequently used as a cooking or basting liquid. Around the N. Mediterranean, including Spain, the Balkans, and Greece, sauces for lamb are thickened with egg yolks beaten up with lemon juice. In N. African and Persian cookery, fruit such as apricots or quinces are often combined in stews with lamb or mutton.

Another approach to lamb cookery is to use strongly flavoured seasonings. Garlic and aromatic herbs such as thyme, rosemary, and oregano are used to flavour French roasts of lamb; paprika is favoured in Spain and Portugal, rosemary or anchovy and garlic in Italy, and tarragon flavours lamb stews in Romania and Hungary. (The combination of mint with lamb also occurs in the Middle East and India; either chopped fresh mint is used as an ingredient, especially in minced lamb dishes, or it is served alongside in a yoghurt sauce.) Vegetables which have some sweetness, such as turnips, are used as ingredients of French lamb stews. Alternatively, the lamb may be cooked with potatoes or rice, the fat cooking out to enrich and flavour the starchy accompaniment.

For some other European lamb dishes, see EASTER FOODS; HOTPOT; IRISH STEW; LOBSCOUSE; NAVARIN; SCOTCH BROTH.

It is in the Arab world, and in areas influenced by it, such as N. Africa, that mutton and lamb are most exploited in cookery. They are also much used in the cuisine of Pakistan, C. Asian countries, and N. Indian MOGHUL CUISINE.

Over much of this area, a whole roast lamb (or sheep) is the principal festive dish. Claudia Roden (1968) comments on one important Islamic tradition:

Although the poor can rarely afford meat, there is one day at least when all are assured of eating it. This is at the *Eid-el-Kurban* [the tenth day of the last month of the Muhammedan year, a festival in commemoration of Abraham's sacrifice].... By ancient custom, well-to-do families sacrifice a sheep or lamb on this day ... It is then roasted on a spit, and the meat is distributed to the poor. These offerings are also made after a death, a birth, and on other important occasions such as moving house, the start or end of a long journey, or the arrival of an important guest.

Fat-tailed sheep (of lamb age or older) are highly valued, and are often roasted with the tail intact, curved over the body to display it and to help baste the meat. KEBABS are a popular way of using smaller pieces of lamb and mutton. Kofta kebabs are made from minced meat, mixed with onion, egg, and spices, made into sausage shapes threaded on skewers and grilled (in Morocco, these are called *brochettes*). Indian moist dishes of lamb are usually quite highly spiced in combinations which depend on the region and the tastes of the cook. Root ginger, fresh chillies, and garlic are all used as the basis for sauces; ASAFOETIDA replaces garlic in Kashmir. Cinnamon, cloves, cumin, coriander seeds, and numerous other spices are used to flavour stews of lamb and potatoes or turnips, or *dupiazas* (which are dishes characterized by a garnish of onions fried until very crisp), or put into mild almond, cream, or yoghurt sauces.

Complex dishes of spiced rice in the category of PILAF, which may include lamb are also found throughout the Middle East and C. Asia. Recipes which originated in the area of Iran are particularly fine. The meat is often combined with fruit to give SWEET-AND-SOUR combinations, such as a *polo* (pilaf) of lamb and dried apricots. *Plov* (the Russian version of pilaf, their recipes deriving from the Caucasus and C. Asia), is flavoured with saffron and onion, incorporating fruit such as raisins, pomegranate, or sour plums, or, in the Uzbek version, dried barberries. BIRIANIS may also be based on lamb.

Instead of rice, COUSCOUS is the usual N. African base for lamb and mutton dishes.

See also: HEAD; KIBBEH; KOFTA; TAILS; MEATBALLS; MINCE; MOUSSAKA.   (LM)

indeed most often met in estuaries or the lower reaches of rivers. It reaches a maximum length of 120 cm (48"), but is commonly half that size. The river lamprey or lampern, *Lampetra fluviatilis*, is a smaller fish, and so is the Arctic lamprey, *L. japonica*.

Despite their striking lack of visual appeal, lampreys are edible and are greatly appreciated in some regions, for example Galicia and the north of Portugal. Galicians usually eat them in a pie (EMPANADA) or cooked in their own blood and served on a bed of rice. The latter dish, *Lampreia a la cazuela*, is more or less the same as the Portuguese *Lampreia à moda do Minho*. The Bordeaux region of France offers *Lamproie à la bordelaise*. Smoked lamprey is a delicacy in Finland, especially at Pori and Rauma, and is also eaten in Japan (*L. japonica*).

In England, lampreys have suffered a decline. Cookery books of the 17th and 18th centuries featured various ways of cooking them, but the recipes had almost disappeared during the 19th century and little has been heard of them since—although Davidson (1979) gives particulars of the Queen's Jubilee lamprey pie of 1977 from the city of Gloucester.

An unusual book in French (Lise Chapuis *et al.*, 1994) is devoted entirely to the lamprey, its natural history, lore, and recipes from an interesting range of sources.

LANCASHIRE a mild English cheese which used to be a farmhouse cheese made only in or around the county whose name it bears. Much of it is still consumed there. Its character derives from a technique known as the 'two-day curd' process, in which a portion of curd is retained from the previous day and added to freshly made curd (some fresh curd first being kept back to add to the next day's cheese). This gives a special flavour.

Lancashire melts well and is one of the best cheeses for making WELSH RABBIT.

LAND CRABS less well known than marine CRABS, are nonetheless a moderately important food resource in certain tropical and subtropical regions, notably the Caribbean.

The largest, and one which is greatly prized as food, is the so-called robber crab (or coconut crab), *Birgus latro*, measuring up to 15 cm (6") across the carapace and with a front leg span of as much as 90 cm (3'). This crab is common in islands of the Indo-Pacific. Early writers gave currency to the idea that it clambers up coconut palms to gather coconuts, then cracks them open and feeds on the contents; but Street (1966) casts doubt on this:

In recent years, however, several naturalists have investigated the habits of the robber crabs, and their findings do not substantiate the earlier reports. The occasional individual has been observed to remove a little of the husk, but none has stripped a nut completely, while the majority show no interest whatsoever in the complete nut. Even when provided with husked nuts, none of them proved able to open them. . . . As to their tree-climbing habits, they are capable of ascending the trunk of a tree if disturbed, but there is no evidence that they do so for the purpose of gathering food.

In the W. Indies, the land crabs most commonly eaten are *Gecarcinus ruricola* and *G. lateralis*. Chace and Hobbs (1969) state that in Dominica no distinction seems to be made between them, although the former (carapace width up to 9 cm/nearly 4") is almost twice as large as the other. Either will gladly be used for 'crab-back' or other local dishes based on crabmeat. Although they are terrestrial creatures, these crabs descend to the sea to spawn, and their larvae live in salt water for a time.

LAOS is the country, Laotians are the inhabitants, Lao are the principal ethnic group; so Lao cookery is not the same as the cookery of Laos, something which is shared with 56 other ethnic groups, some of them very small hill tribes. Most Lao live outside Laos, in China or N. Thailand.

The Lao are almost omnivorous and have many unconventional sources of protein, such as insects, which do not find a place in the statistics compiled by international authorities. So they are apt to be described as less well nourished than they really are. What is certain is that they are among the most beautiful people in the world, that their disposition is of great amiability, and their habits agreeably relaxed. At its best, life in Laos must have been almost paradisiacal.

The country is of breathtaking beauty, and, given the small number of inhabitants and its large size, food supplies adequate to support the population in good health could be produced with comparatively little effort. This suits the Lao, who like to have time to spare for festivals and whose natural tendency is to be unworried and relaxed about time, relating their activities only to the natural rhythm of the dry season and the rainy season and to the movements of the sun and the moon and the revolutions of the Buddhist calendar.

The Lao are also relaxed about their meals. If some official, notebook in hand, asks how many meals a family eats daily, the question will be greeted with surprise. Naturally, the number varies. It depends on what people are doing and how hungry they are. Sometimes one meal is enough; sometimes two; or three may be eaten.

The meals too are relaxed. What normally happens is that all the prepared foods (or fresh ones—the Lao eat a lot of fresh fruit) are laid out at once and people help themselves. Cutlery, chopsticks, and even plates are usually unnecessary, for morsels of meat, fish, or chicken can be wrapped up in edible leaves, along with any accompanying vegetables; and a ball of sticky rice (of which each person has a little basket) is used instead of bread as a 'pusher' or to mop up juices. However, some Lao dishes which are really soups—and there is always a pot of soup ready in a Lao house—call for soup spoons, which until recently would have been of the Chinese type, or made of wood.

DIET
The Lao are not bread-eaters, and do not normally use dairy products. Their staple foods are RICE (especially sticky or glutinous rice), fish (of which they have a very abundant supply in their rivers, ponds, and irrigated fields), PADEK (a kind of fermented fish sauce with chunks of fish in it), meat of all kinds (including, for example, that of water-monitors), ducks, chicken, vegetables, and fresh fruits. They enjoy feasts, but generally eat in moderation. In the countryside they can garner almost everything they need, and need only to cultivate rice. For many Lao, such items as meat, ducks, and chicken are luxuries. But nutritional requirements which would be satisfied by these foods are partly met by their use of *padek*, an important supplementary source of protein.

EATING CUSTOMS
The relaxed atmosphere of a Lao meal even invests procedures which are surprisingly formal. These have been described by Doré (1980), who explains that in Lao life the concept of *piep* (which may be loosely translated as 'prestige') is of importance. Similarly, the concept of *lieng* (feeding, giving nourishment) is a basic one which includes what might be called contractual obligations. Whenever a Lao eats a meal he must do so in a manner which respects the first of these concepts; and whenever he eats outside his own home he must respect them both. This means, in practice, that at a family meal the father and mother (being the persons of highest rank in the family unit) take the first mouthfuls, followed by the other family members in descending order of age. Once this 'first tasting' has been accomplished, the meal appears to be free for all, but in fact is still subject to rules; for example, that no one should help himself at the same time as anyone else or go in front of a person of higher rank, which would cause that person to lose *piep*.

LARD is PIG fat, obtained by rendering down the deposits which exist between the flesh and the skin and around the internal organs of pig carcasses. It is bland and white, and its ubiquity in an age when pigs were kept by all those who could afford them made it very important in the traditional cookery of Europe, the Americas, and China. The fat of the pig was an article of almost as much value as the meat. Lard contains much saturated fat, and this, combined with an image as poverty food and the increased availability of butter and oils, means that it is less important than formerly in the developed world.

There are several fat deposits in pig carcasses. The *flare* is found inside the loin and around the kidneys; it produces the finest lard, sometimes called leaf lard. The *back fat* is a hard layer between the flesh and the skin, which also yields good-quality lard. Softer lard is extracted from the fat around the internal organs, and fat belly pork contains layers of both types. These fats can also be used before rendering; the hard back fat is cut into cubes and preserved by salting for addition to stews in much of S. Europe. In French cuisine it is employed for LARDING lean meat and wrapping PÂTÉS; the CAUL, which contains some of the soft fat, is also used for wrapping.

Because of differences in quality, and the rate at which it melts, the fat from different parts of the carcass was prepared separately and used for different purposes. However, the general principle of rendering lard is simple: the fat is freed from flesh and membrane as far as possible, minced, soaked, and heated gently until it can be strained off the residue. The old-fashioned method for storing the best lard was to pour it into the well-cleaned pig's bladder and hang it in a cool place; the poor-quality lard from around the internal organs was always used quickly. Lard is sometimes seasoned; paprika is used for this in Spain, and chopped parsley in Italy. Modern packaged lard is produced by heating the fat with steam; it may be treated with bleaching and deodorizing agents, emulsifiers and antioxidants, or modified to improve creaming properties.

In keeping with the tradition of not wasting any part of the pig, the bits of membrane left in the pan, cooked by the action of heat on the fat, are used as salty snacks or eaten on bread; see CRACKLING.

Lard has many uses, especially in areas where plant oils and dairy fats are scarce. It acts as a spread, a preservative, a shortener, and a cooking medium. In both Europe and N. America, it was formerly much used on bread or toast. William Cobbett wrote in *Cottage Economy* (1823) that country children were badly brought up if they did not like sweet lard spread upon bread, and

recorded that he had eaten it for luncheon at 'the houses of good and substantial farmers in France and Flanders', whilst lamenting that the habit was declining as 'now-a-days, the labourers, and especially the female part of them, have fallen into the taste of *niceness* in food'. It is now uncommon to find lard as a spread in Europe and the USA, but, salted and flavoured with paprika, it is still used on toasted bread in country areas in Spain.

The use of lard as a preservative is best illustrated by the CONFITS of pork or goose made in SW France. These rely on cooking pieces of meat gently in large amounts of fat and then leaving the whole to cool so that the lard sets, covering the food. As this has been sterilized by the heat and the lard forms an airtight seal, the meat keeps for several months, and pieces can be removed at intervals provided the rest remains well covered. Although such methods are no longer necessary with modern storage techniques, they are still a part of the cuisine of this region, and the meat is used alone or as an ingredient for CASSOULET.

Like all fats, lard is composed of crystals. These are relatively large (compared to those found, for instance, in butter) and make it a poor creaming fat but an effective shortener for PASTRY. Thus there are few cakes which use lard, but many pastries. Even the English LARDY CAKE is really a bread dough enriched with lard by rolling and folding the dough around the fat. In the past, lard was the favoured fat for shortcrust pastry in the English kitchen, but modern shorteners are slowly replacing it. A mixture of lard for good shortening and butter for fine flavour were mostly used. It is also used for hot water pastry, setting as the paste cools, allowing for the traditional method of shaping the dough for raised pies by hand and baking them without the support of a mould. A little lard is often included in bread and pastry recipes both in Britain and continental Europe, and it is used to shorten many traditional Spanish biscuits, such as the fragile Christmas *polverones*. Lard is also used in the Latin American kitchen for enriching breads, pastries, and dough for fritters; and in China for making pastries and biscuits.

The use of lard for frying has been in decline in western countries, eroded by vegetable oils with their healthier image. As a cooking medium, it had been popular because readily available, and also because it has a relatively high smoke point (205 °C, 400 °F). Thus it was much used for traditional fritter recipes in Europe and America, and the collective German name for these is still *Schmalzgebackenes*, meaning 'something fried in lard'. According to Chang (1977) lard is still a preferred cooking fat in parts of China, notably the Fukien coast and the far west; in these areas, pigs are specially bred to be fat and display maximal separation of lean meat and fat in the carcass, allowing for easy separation of the two. (LM)

LARDING the process of introducing thin strips of pork fat (lardoons) into meat which lacks fat and would otherwise cook dry (e.g. venison, veal, pigeons). Fat, usually back fat, is cut into strips, pinched into the clip of a larding needle, and gently inserted into the meat.

Stobart (1980) comments that the popularity of the technique in France had the result that: 'In French cookery books of the last century almost every joint looked like a hedgehog.' He adds, on a modern note, that a gadget is available, on the lines of a surgeon's trocar (a tube cut diagonally and sharpened at one end), which permits 'larding' with frozen butter; and that cooks wishing to do something similar with polyunsaturated oils can manage with a large hypodermic syringe.

LARDY CAKE a traditional English tea bread popular in country areas. It is made from bread dough enriched with lard and sugar and, usually, spices and dried fruit. The dough is rolled and folded several times to give a layered texture.

Lardy cakes were originally intended as special celebration cakes, made only at harvest time or for family festivals. Elizabeth David (1977) remarks that 'It was only when sugar became cheap, and when the English taste for sweet things—particularly in the Midlands and the North—became more pronounced, that such rich breads or cakes were made or could be bought from the bakery every week.'

In the days when ovens were fired only once a week, and in some households only once a fortnight, for the baking of a very large batch of bread and dough products, any dough not used for making the daily bread was transformed into richer products such as lardy cakes, which thus earned the alternative name 'scrap cakes'. They might also be called 'flead cakes'—flead is a light kind of lard scraped off a pig's internal membranes. The high fat content in such cakes would prevent them drying out as much as ordinary bread.

LARK any of many species of songbirds in the family Alaudidae, but especially the skylark (to which Shelley addressed his famous ode), *Alauda arvensis*, and the somewhat plumper crested lark, *Galerina cristata*. The former is familiar in Britain, but the latter only appears there as a vagrant.

Larks are now protected species in the countries of the European Community, and the practice of eating them, roasted on lark-spits or made into PÂTÉS (such as the famous ones of Pithiviers in France) or with POLENTA, is dying away elsewhere too. In former times they were eaten on a large scale and their delicate flavour was appreciated, especially in France—although it was a Frenchman who said that the tiny carcase, stripped of wings, feet, and gizzard, resembled nothing more than a bundle of toothpicks. Another French writer, Favre (1883–92), anticipated the feelings of a century later by remarking on the usefulness to farmers of the larks' feeding habits and the charm of their songs, and by deciding that in his great dictionary the entry for larks should begin with quotations from poets and only then proceed to describe the range of French recipes for preparing them.

LARVAE the larval forms of insects, but also of certain other creatures which undergo the process of metamorphosis in reaching the adult form. Thus there are larvae of certain fish and crustaceans. However, it is the larvae of insects which are important as human food (where insects are acceptable in the diet—see INSECTS AS FOOD). Of the innumerable examples which could be cited, the most striking is perhaps that quoted by Bodenheimer (1951) from Bristowe (1932). The latter relates how a certain tribe in Thailand, near the Burmese border, would shoot a long-tailed monkey, gut it, stuff it with makrut lime leaves and other herbs, sew it up, smear it with a paste from the inside of a termite heap, and hang it up from a tree. After a supposedly delicious 'monkey sauce' has slowly dripped from the corpse into a bowl below, accompanied by some small 'maggots', the corpse is opened and a few large larvae (belonging to some species of beetle) are found within. Each of these is placed inside a specially treated coconut, and the hole made for this purpose is stopped up with termite paste once the larva is inside. Three weeks later the coconut is split open and a white grub (i.e. larva), 'the size of a tangerine, is found practically filling the interior of the coconut'.

For other, less startling, examples, see GRUBS.

LASAGNE probably one of the earliest forms of PASTA, is listed with other forms of the same sort in PASTA SHAPES. It consists of fairly thin flat sheets of pasta, typically interleaved with a savoury mixture and baked in the oven (*al forno*).

Some believe that its remote ancestor was the classical Greek *laganon*; this was a flat cake, not pasta as we know it now, but capable of developing in that direction. In classical Rome this was cut into strips and became known as *lagani* (plural). Cicero (1st century AD) was known to have been particularly fond of *lagani*. So was the Roman poet Horace, of the same century. He cited them as an example of simple peasant's food while boasting of his simple way of life. 'Then I go home to a dish of leeks, chickpeas and lagani,' said he (*Satires* 1. 6).

Although *lagani* were no longer, at this stage, a cake, it would be unwise to assume that they had become a product used like modern lasagne. More generally, as Perry (1981) has pointed out, it is an error to suppose that ancestors in classical times of modern forms of pasta were used then in the ways now familiar. It seems likely that they were usually treated as 'extenders' of savoury dishes, pieces of fried dough which could be added to dishes in the same sort of way as dumplings in recent times.

So, Horace's simple dish would have been a vegetable stew or pottage, and it is most likely that the *lagani* added to it were small squares or strips of fried dough.

However, something which could be called lasagne in the modern sense had appeared in Italy by the 13th century, since Marco Polo, recounting his travels in the Orient, said that he ate in Fanfur 'lasagne' made with flour of the breadfruit, implying clearly that he was already familiar with lasagne made of ordinary flour.

Since medieval times, lasagne have been a popular feature in the range of pasta products. Recipes have changed over the centuries, but the advantages of a pasta which comes in sheet form, for certain dishes which cannot otherwise be made, have been a constant in the kitchen. Lasagne verdi are coloured green with spinach.

LASSI an Indian YOGHURT drink of which there are two versions: salted and sweet. In both versions, it is a popular street food as well as being made in homes.

The quality of the yoghurt is very important for a good lassi. It should be slightly sour so that when diluted with water it still retains a strong yoghurt flavour. It should also be creamy otherwise the lassi will taste watery.

The sweet version is known as *metha lassi*. It often just has sugar added, but is sometimes flavoured with rosewater; and in Bengal a squirt of *gondo lebu* (scented lime) may be added. The salted version often contains spices such as roasted cumin seeds or black pepper. In S. India the spices added may be a paste of ground green chilli, ginger, coriander leaves, and garlic.

The diluted yoghurt with its flavourings is whisked until frothy and usually served with ice cubes.

See also AYRAN.   HS

LATH lathyrus, or grass pea or chickling vetch, the usual names for a leguminous plant, *Lathyrus sativus*, related to the PEA, BROAD BEAN, etc. It survives in dry, poor soil where better plants would die; and is now grown mainly in India as a source of cheap and inferior PULSE, known as *khesari dal*.

The plant is of W. Asian origin and was cultivated in S. Europe in the classical period (when *lathyros* was its Greek name). It is still grown there on a small scale as a fodder crop.

Lath has one mysterious and dangerous feature. From time to time there is an outbreak of a paralysing disease, lathyrism, among people and animals that consume it. The sufferer's legs become suddenly and permanently paralysed. HIPPOCRATES, the Greek physician of the 6th century BC, mentioned lathyrism, as did many writers after him. However, the poor of Europe continued to eat chickling vetch and other vetches, often mixed with cereal flour, and there were occasional epidemics. Lathyrism still occurs sporadically in India; and there was an outbreak in Spain in 1940–1.

LATVIA central of the three Baltic states, resembles ESTONIA to the north and LITHUANIA to the south in having an unusual language. But, whereas Estonian belongs to the Finno-Ugric group, Latvian and Lithuanian are rarities, sole survivors of an ancient group, closely related to Sanskrit within the Indo-European family of languages.

A favourite dish, perhaps the national dish, is *putr(a)*, described as a kind of vegetable/cereal porridge with suet or pork fat to which fish or smoked meat or whatever may be added. This can be made with barley, a popular cereal in this region, along with rye for the dark bread which goes with many of the numerous Latvian cold dishes, which are often assembled on the 'cold table'.

A taste for sour and salty produce is noticeable; and there is slightly more spicing evident than in Estonia. Dairy products, including some simple indigenous cheeses, are prominent, as are bacon, smoked fish, and pickles.

Fish dishes, such as may be enjoyed in Riga (the capital city), include a kind of Latvian fish soup (*Zivju supa*) which incorporates whole pieces of cooked fish with plenty of potato as well as the broth, and also—a distinctive touch—onion rings and grated carrot, both fried. Another is

Cepts lasis ar plumju kompotu, which is fried Baltic salmon with plum compote.

Besides some desserts introduced or adapted from Germany, there is *Kisels*, a sour-sweet dish of fruit juices (red, white, black currants and various berries) thickened with potato flour; see KISEL.

LA VARENNE FRANÇOIS PIERRE DE (*c*.1615–1678). La Varenne was the founder of French classical cooking. Ever since it appeared in 1651, critics have both acclaimed and belittled his book *Le Cuisinier françois*, but no one has questioned its importance. It was the first French cookbook of any substance since *Le Viandier* almost 300 years before; and it ran to 30 editions in 75 years. The reason for its success was simple; it was the first book to record and embody the immense advances which French cooking had made, largely under the influence of Italy and the Renaissance, since the 15th century.

Some characteristics of medieval cookery are still visible in La Varenne's book, but many have disappeared. New World ingredients make their entrance. A surprising number of recipes for dishes still made in modern times (*Bœuf à la mode*, *Œufs à la neige*, omelettes, beignets, even pumpkin pie) are given. The watershed from medieval to modern times is being crossed under our eyes in La Varenne's pages.

La Varenne was scarcely 35 when *Le Cuisinier françois* first appeared. At that point he had already been a master cook for ten years to the Marquis d'Uxelles, after whom he named his most famous creation, the DUXELLES of mushrooms seasoned with herbs and shallots, which is still a favourite flavouring for fish and vegetables. Beyond that, little is known about La Varenne himself, except that his name was a pseudonym, taken for some reason from a disreputable cook of an earlier generation who did a little pimping business for his master, Henri IV, and 'gained more by carrying the *poulets* (love letters) of the king than by larding them in the kitchen'. La Varenne died in relative obscurity, having benefited little from his success as a best-selling author.   HY

LAVASH a thin crisp bread usually made with wheat flour made in a variety of shapes all over the the regions of the Caucasus, Iran (where it is often so thin as to be like tissue and can be almost seen through), and Afghanistan. It is leavened and baked in a TANDOOR. Lavash is served with kebabs and is used to scoop up food or wrap round food before being eaten.

The Turkish *yufka* is similar, but is unleavened and cooked on a GRIDDLE, called

a *saj*. Its origins are ancient and it is also known as *lavaş* depending on the region. As in the other countries of this region large batches of this bread are made and stored for long periods. In Turkey they are stored on a board suspended by all four corners from the ceiling. The bread becomes dry and is restored by sprinkling with water and reheated as and when needed.

Yufka is also used in the same way as FILO pastry to encase various fillings.

LAVENDER *Lavandula angustifolia* (English lavender) and *L. latifolia* (spike lavender), both native to the Mediterranean region, is mainly used in perfumery, but has culinary uses also. The essential oils can serve to flavour foods; and the leaves and flowers of *L. angustifolia* can be incorporated in salads, vinegars, jellies, ice creams, and soft drinks; also, less commonly, in savoury stews. Bees which have an opportunity to visit lavender flowers give a particularly good flavour to their honey.

Crystallized lavender flowers are used for decorating confectionery and cakes. The small bluish leaves are most often used in dried form.

LAVIGNON or lavagnon, the French name for an edible BIVALVE, *Scrobicularia plana*, which is a local speciality of the Charente-Maritime. The species has a distribution extending from Norway to the Mediterranean and beyond, and is abundant in British waters, but seems not to be generally eaten. An English name, mud-hen, used to be current, suggesting some consumption in the past in England. Now it is sometimes named 'furrow shell' in technical works.

The lavignon has a maximum width of 6–7 cm (2.5"). It has a slightly peppery taste and is good when eaten raw, especially as part of a seafood salad to which it contributes its own particular flavour.

LEAVEN a noun denoting a raising agent for BREAD or other baked goods, is also a verb meaning to use such an agent. The word is derived from the Latin *levamen*, something that lifts or lightens. Strictly speaking, it refers to any raising agent, for example YEAST or BAKING POWDER. But it is most commonly used to mean a SOURDOUGH culture, a piece reserved from a previous batch of dough and used to 'infect' the current batch with natural yeasts and other micro-organisms that will both raise and flavour it.

Leaven has important symbolic significance in the Bible. When the Israelites left Egypt they abandoned their old way of life entirely, not even taking a piece of old dough. At the festival of PASSOVER Jews eat unleavened MATZO to commemorate this fresh start (Exodus 12: 15, 18–20, 34; 13: 6–7). Leaven is mentioned in the New Testament as a symbol of the kingdom of Heaven spreading through humanity (Matthew 13: 33; Luke 13: 20–1), but also of the corrupting influence of the old religion (Matthew 16: 6; 1 Corinthians 5: 6). RH

LEBANON AND SYRIA are neighbours on the eastern coast of the Mediterranean. Although both enjoy a favourable temperate climate, there are big geographical differences between them. Lebanon is small and mountainous with a long coastline while Syria has a relatively short coastline, but is vast, with huge areas of desert land.

The Phoenicians, who are thought to have reached this prize territory around 3000 BC, were among the first important settlers. They established a chain of city-states and safe anchorages along the coast and became the first great commercial mariners, trading in spices, grains, dried and preserved foodstuffs, and wines. Their position at the ancient crossroads of Europe, Asia, and Africa, their bountiful land, and their prosperous trade made them prey to constant invasion. These invading powers included the Egyptians, the Persians, the Greeks, the Romans (who merged all the states that lay between the Taurus mountains and the Sinai desert into one province they called Syria; it was not until 1942 that Lebanon became independent), the Crusaders, the Ottomans, and finally the French.

Lebanese and Syrian cuisines have evolved through the successive invasions, with each culture leaving its mark, even if it is now rather faint after the passage of many centuries. The clearest influence, as throughout the E. Mediterranean, is Ottoman. The French refining influence on the food of Lebanon also remains noticeable.

The basic ingredients are the same in both countries: fresh herbs, vegetables and fruit, dried pulses, BURGHUL (cracked wheat), rice, nuts, olives, yoghurt, TAHINI (sesame paste), spices, fish (often with TARATOR sauce), and meat in the form of lamb or chicken (boiled, grilled, or stewed); plus rose and orange blossom waters.

The most famous of the dishes which they jointly prize is KIBBEH (a paste of very finely minced lamb with burghul, onion, and basil or mint). The entry for this dish describes some of the ways in which it is prepared in the two countries. Especially notable are the geometrical designs incised on *kibbeh bil-saniyeh*, a form of *kibbeh* baked in a round shallow pan; the surface may be divided into

quarters, each of which will display a different pattern.

Other typical savoury dishes are stuffed vegetables, meat and vegetable stews, as well as charcoal-grilled meats; all these, by the subtle use of herbs and other flavourings, are given the Lebanese/Syrian hallmark. Less subtle than some of the other practices is the very emphatic taste for hot pepper in Aleppo.

Lebanese and Syrian versions of MEZZE coincide to a large extent, although it is generally held that the Lebanese mezze table is the best. However this may be, it is certainly appropriate that it is two dishes which indisputably belong to Lebanon and Syria and always adorn the mezze table, namely hummus and TABBOULEH, which have conquered much of the world in recent decades—almost as thoroughly as pizza made its conquest earlier in the 20th century.

Both countries have a strong tradition of preserving seasonal produce. Vegetables are dried or pickled and fruits are also dried, candied, or made into jams. Mutton or lamb is cut into small pieces and preserved in the form of a CONFIT (QAWARMA) and burghul is left to ferment in yoghurt, then dried and ground by hand to produce *kishk* (see KASHK). *Kishk* is used with qawarma to make a thick soup, or is mixed with tomato paste and chopped onion to make a filling for savoury pastries or a topping for bread.

Although most of the mainstream dishes have the same names, their preparation may be distinctly different from one country to the other. The Lebanese, unlike the Syrians, use fat sparingly. They have a greater variety of vegetarian dishes mainly because of the Lenten restrictions of their large Christian community. They also use a great deal of artistry in garnishing dishes and in fine-tuning the balance of flavours among the ingredients of a dish.

A good example is the salad called *fattoosh*. This is composed of parsley, mint, tomatoes, cucumber, spring onions, and bread, all seasoned with sumac, salt, and olive oil. Here, the Lebanese version has toasted bread, whereas this is fried in the Syrian version. Also the Syrians add small pieces of white cheese which affect texture as well as taste. The Syrian *lahm bi-ajine* (flat bread topped with minced meat) is also different. The Lebanese topping of minced meat is Armenian in origin and is mixed with tomatoes, chopped onion, and lemon juice. The Syrian is a drier mixture and only chopped onion and pomegranate syrup are added to the meat. Examples could be multiplied.

It should not be thought that Syrian food is inferior. On the contrary Aleppo is considered the Near Eastern capital of haute cuisine. Nevertheless, Lebanese food is

universally accepted to be more refined and more varied. One of the categories where the Syrians surpass the Lebanese is in their sweets. These are significantly superior and, oddly, much lighter. Their BAKLAVA are renowned throughout the Near East. Some (called *kol wa shkor*) are made with extremely thin layers of filo pastry and have different shapes. Others are made with a type of 'bird's nest' pastry, shaped in cylinders, and called *borma*; cf the description of *kunafa/knafeh* under QATA'IF. All are filled with a mixture of nuts (pine nuts, hazelnuts, walnuts, pistachios can all be used), sugar, and rose or orange blossom water, baked, and then coated with sugar syrup. *Baraziq*—small round biscuits dipped in pistachio nuts on one side and sesame seeds on the other—provide another example. The Syrian ones are thinner than others and have a lot more sesame and pistachios, which makes them lighter and more delicious.

A few dishes are particularly Syrian such as *karabeege Halab*, pistachio-filled semolina fingers, with accompanying *natef*, a sweet BOIS DE PANAMA mousse; see MA'AMOUL. Candied green walnuts and fruits as well as *qamar el-deen* (dried sheets of sweetened apricot purée—cf Turkish 'apricot leather' under APRICOT) are other Syrian specialities.

The Lebanese on the other hand can boast such dishes as *kibbeh bil-saniyeh* (mentioned above), *burghul bi d'feeneh* (a kind of 'risotto' of burghul, chickpeas, and meat), and *hindbeh bil-zeyt* (boiled wild chicory which is sautéed in olive oil and garnished with caramelized onion).

In fact, such specialities are often found in both countries and there are many over which both the Lebanese and the Syrians claim proprietary rights. More research is needed before such debates can be settled (if ever); and, as these two cuisines are the distillation of so many culinary influences over 5,000 years, the research will be arduous, although the fieldwork should be pure pleasure. AH

READING: Helen Corey (1962); Anissa Helou (1994); Aïda Kanafani-Zahar (1994, on traditional food preservation).

LEBKUCHEN a famous German speciality, belong to two broad categories of baked goods (HONEY CAKE and GINGERBREAD) and have a history which stretches back to medieval times. They then had a religious aspect, being often prepared in monasteries (where bees to provide both wax and honey were kept), and including seven spices in memory of the seven days in which God created the world.

In the 16th century production developed rapidly in the area around Nuremberg, which lay at the meeting point of important

European trade routes and was also a centre of the spice trade. A German recipe of this period calls for honey, sugar, cinnamon, nutmeg, ginger, pepper, and flour. (Eggs, butter, nuts, candied peel, and raising agents were added later.)

Closely related confections are also made in Switzerland, Austria, Poland, and Hungary. The number of versions is thus considerable. Sarah Kelly (1985) gives a useful summary:

[There are] . . . Lebkuchenzelten (simple Lebkuchen); Honigkuchen (honey biscuits—which can be spiced or not); Pfefferkuchen (heavily spiced gingerbread); Leckerli (Swiss gingerbread with mixed peel and nuts), to name a few. All of these contain honey and are made according to a standard formula: the honey is heated with the sugar (if called for) and butter or lard (if called for), before being mixed with the dry ingredients and then the eggs.

The one exception is *Nürnberger Elisenlebkuchen*—perhaps the most famous Lebkuchen—which are made by a different ('whisked egg') method, without flour and without honey.

Shapes and decoration also vary considerably. *Lebkuchen-Herzen*, heart-shaped honey cakes, are sold all over Germany in regional fairs, and at Christmas. The elaborate *Hexenhäuschen*—a gingerbread witch's house, iced and decorated with sweets for Christmas—is made from Lebkuchen dough. So are Christmas pigs, *Glücksschweinchen*, made in Germany and also sold at the annual Christmas market of Strasbourg. (These shapes recur in Scandinavia, where spiced biscuit mixtures are made into tree decorations and iced houses; and gingerbread or parkin pigs are traditional English autumn specialities.)

Switzerland is perhaps second only to Germany in enthusiasm for Lebkuchen. *Berner Honiglebkuchen* are moulded or iced with figures of bears, the symbol of the city of Bern. *Zuri-Tirggel*, a Christmas speciality of Zurich, are thin, pale Lebkuchen with an embossed pattern which is lightly browned. Lebkuchen dough is also baked with marzipan fillings to make *Biberli*. The best-known types are the St Gallen and Appenzell *Biber*; these are baked in large slabs and embossed with figures or decorated with marzipan plaques.

Most Lebkuchen are glazed after baking.

LECITHIN a fatlike substance found in the membranes of cells, and particularly abundant in egg yolk. Its scientific name is phosphatidyl choline. Lecithin is a powerful emulsifier (see EMULSION), a fact exploited in the making of MAYONNAISE and other sauces containing egg yolk. In the food industry lecithin, usually extracted from SOYA BEANS, is widely used as a general purpose emulsifier.   RH

LEEK a member of the ONION family distinguished by its mild, sweet flavour, is beset by the problems of classification which seem to affect the whole family. A traditional and simple solution is to say that *Allium ampeloprasum* is the wild leek, ancestor of *A. porrum*, the cultivated leek of Europe. (Note, however, that there are also cultivars of *A. ampeloprasum* itself, such as the ELEPHANT GARLIC group.)

European and Middle Eastern cultivated leeks differ from each other, and, although some authorities would disagree, it is convenient to classify the latter as *A. kurrat*; the Arabic name for leek is *kurrat*. The Middle Eastern leek has narrower leaves than the European kind and a distinct, often subdivided bulb. Nevertheless, it tastes like a leek and is used in the same way except that, because its green leaves are less coarse than those of a western leek, these too are eaten.

The leek, presumably the Middle Eastern species, was taken into cultivation by the ancient Egyptians, who bred improved varieties with thicker stems, represented in their tomb paintings. On the northern side of the Mediterranean, both the Greeks and the Romans of classical antiquity were partial to leeks, none more so than the Emperor Nero, who apparently believed that eating them would improve his singing voice, of which he was vain. He consumed such quantities that the people nicknamed him *Porrophagus* (leek-eater).

Whether because of or in spite of the Emperor's foible, the Romans considered the leek a superior vegetable, unlike onions and garlic which were despised as coarse foods for the poor. This can be seen from the works of APICIUS, who gives four recipes for leeks as a vegetable in their own right, while onions are relegated to the role of a minor flavouring and garlic, in tiny quantities, is mentioned only twice. Green leek leaves were used in salads; the bulbous base was cooked; and the plant was also used as a flavouring. The classical leek, even the thicker kind, was thinner in the stem and more onion-like at the bottom than a typical modern leek.

Some have suggested that the Romans may have introduced the leek to Britain and therefore to the Welsh, who subsequently made it their own special vegetable. There is an unverified tradition that Welsh warriors wore leeks in their hats to show which side they were on in a victorious battle against the Saxons in the 7th century, and that that is why the leek is the symbol of Wales. However, all this is highly dubious. In Saxon times the word *leac* was the generic term for any kind of onion or garlic (*gar-leac*), and even the more particular name *bradeleac* (broad leek) was also applied to ramsons (WILD GARLIC). So, if 7th-century Welsh warriors were wearing something called *leac* it may well have been something different from and much thinner (and more practical as a hat adornment) than the modern leek. The doubt is compounded by statements in early botanical works that the (true) leek did not reach Britain until much later. Whatever the true date was, Gerard (1633) was able to say that the leek was then in common use in England. It was certainly popular all over continental Europe and the Middle East by that time.

The straight white stem of a cultivated leek is produced by earthing it up, which compresses the leaf bases into a cylinder and keeps them white. It is possible to grow very large stems by this method, the limit being about 30 cm (1') tall and 7 cm (nearly 3") thick. Very large leeks are grown in Britain, especially in NE England, for competition purposes. For cooks, smaller, more tender leeks are preferable. Apart from their use as a vegetable, leeks are widely used as a base or essential ingredient for soups (such as VICHYSSOISE and the Scottish COCK-A-LEEKIE) and stews, for example the French POT-AU-FEU). Apart from its mild flavour the leek, being slightly mucilaginous, helps to thicken the liquid.

Although the leek will not grow in the hotter parts of Asia, it is grown and used in N. China. Karen Phillipps and Martha Dahlen (1985) remark that in Peking (Beijing) cuisine, the heart of the leek is served as a condiment for Peking pancakes; 'it is chopped in thin strips 2–3" long and rolled with filling and sauce in pancakes to make a meal'.

Raw sliced leeks are sometimes used in salads, to which they give an agreeable taste, milder than onion.

LEGUME any plant which belongs to the family of Leguminosae, characterized by seed-bearing pods; or the seeds themselves, usually called BEANS or PEAS.

The word, which entered the English language in the 17th century, has tended to oust the older word PULSE, although the older term is still current.

Legumes grow throughout the world and were amongst the earliest food crops cultivated by man. The patterns established then have come down through history and it is striking that particular legumes have an overriding importance in individual countries. The HARICOT BEAN is associated with C. and S. America, the SOYA BEAN with E. Asia, LENTILS with India. See also the list of entries at the end.

As well as being of great importance as food plants, in their contribution to world supplies of protein (8%, according to FAO figures), legumes play a major role in agriculture through their nitrogen-fixing capability.

However, the protein in legumes is 'incomplete', and if it is to give full value it has to be complemented by foods, notably cereals, which supply the missing elements. Eating patterns evolved spontaneously along these lines in many parts of the world, and many of the most traditional and popular ways of preparing legumes, e.g. maize and beans in Mexico, show the principle at work. See also PROTEIN; AMINO ACIDS.

Despite their nutritional value, legumes have been the subject of many disparaging references in literature. Thus the 'mess of pottage' which Jacob offered Esau in exchange for his birthright was made of red lentils, and the point of the story is that Esau obtained something of little worth. Aristophanes (in his comedy *Plutus*, early 4th century BC) has a character remark of a nouveau riche: 'Now he doesn't like lentils any more', and this seems to have been a proverb in classical Greece. The development of eating habits in modern Italy may show the tenacity of this attitude. The consumption of legumes has halved there since the Second World War, in the face of growing economic status and corresponding improvements in the standard of living. The situation is different in most of Asia and in C. and S. America. There, it is more usual for wealthy and poor alike to eat legumes regularly. The high esteem in which the soya bean and its products are held in China is well known.

Their fibrous seed coats may or may not be removed from dried legume seeds. Removal increases digestibility and improves keeping qualities, but may cause a nutritional loss, e.g. of thiamine content.

Ways of preparing legumes for consumption, with or without decortication, include boiling, roasting, fermentation, and germination. Individual entries deal with particular ways of preparing and cooking them, and in some instances with products obtained from them. See ACACIA AND WATTLE; ALFALFA; AZUKI BEAN; BEAN; BEAN SPROUTS; BROAD BEAN; CAROB; CHICKPEA; CLUSTER BEAN; COWPEA; DAL; FENUGREEK; FUL MEDAMES; GRAM; GROUNDNUT; HARICOT BEAN; HORSE GRAM; JACK BEAN; KUDZU; LABLAB BEAN; LATH; LENTIL; LIMA BEAN; LUPIN; LIQUORICE; MOTH BEAN; MUNG BEAN; PEA; PIGEON PEA; PULSES; RICE BEAN; RUNNER BEAN; SOYA BEAN; TAMARIND; TEPARY BEAN; TREE BEAN; TONKA BEAN; URD; VELVET BEAN; VETCH; WINGED BEAN; WINGED PEA; YAM BEAN.

LEICESTER also known as red Leicester, is the reddest of all English cheeses, simply

because the vegetable dye ANNATTO is added liberally to it. Made from whole milk by a process like that of CHEDDAR but retaining some moisture, it is hard and crumbly but very mild in flavour. It matures faster than Cheddar and may be sold at any age from two months onwards. A whole cheese has a flattish drum shape and weighs about 18 kg (40 lb).

Leicester is regarded as one of the best cheeses with which to make WELSH RABBIT.

LEIDEN (or Leyden) cheese, sold as *Leidse kaas* or *Komijne kaas* in the Netherlands, is wheel shaped with a greyish-yellow rind. The sides may bulge or be straight, and the cheeses all bear a mark of the two crossed keys which are the symbol of the City of Leiden. The weight of a whole cheese varies from around 5 kg (11 lb) to 8 kg (18 lb) or more. Leiden cheese resembles GOUDA, but is made on a much smaller scale, has a lower fat content, and a sharper taste; often incorporates some BUTTERMILK; and is always spiced. Some handbooks on cheese say that CUMIN is used; others mention CARAWAY. The truth is that both are normally added. There is also a version with CLOVES, made in Friesland and called *nagelkaas*.

The spices impart a greenish tinge to the inside of a Leiden cheese, besides giving it an interesting flavour. This use of caraway and cumin is echoed in some Scandinavian cheeses, e.g. Swedish Riksost.

LEMON (*see opposite page*)

LEMON GRASS *Cymbopogon citratus*, a perennial grass of tropical Asia and other warm climates, which grows abundantly in suitable conditions. It is valued for the lemony flavour which its stalks release when crushed and chopped, and is often used in fish cookery and curry dishes. Its alternative name is citronella.

Dried lemon grass stalks are available, as is lemon grass powder. These can be used but fresh stalks are much better.

A popular dish in Thailand consists of crabs steamed in a special earthenware pot, with lots of lemon grass. Those who have become accustomed to using it lavishly in SE Asia find it hard to believe that it has not come into wider use in those parts of N. America and Australia, and elsewhere outside Asia, where it grows.

LEMON SOLE *Microstomus kitt*, a left-handed FLATFISH of the family Pleuronectidae, thus not a true SOLE (true soles being right-handed). It is nonetheless a

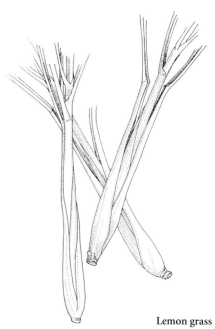

Lemon grass

fine fish of commercial importance. Maximum length 65 cm (26"), colour of the back generally dark brown but with varied and irregular markings of yellow, orange, etc. Widespread on the coastal banks of Europe from Iceland and Norway down to France.

Salted and dried lemon sole, prepared so as to yield strips of flesh which can be peeled off and eaten as they come, are (or used to be) known as *Schotse schol* ('Scottish sole') on the Belgian coast.

This lemon sole is not the same fish as the American winter FLOUNDER, although the name has occasionally been applied to the latter.

LEMON VERBENA *Lippia triphylla*, a small deciduous shrub with yellow green leaves and pale lavender flowers, was introduced to Britain from Chile in the 18th century. It belongs to the same family as Mexican oregano, *L. graveolens*, see OREGANO.

It can be grown in Britain, France, and Spain where it is used to make health-giving lemon-flavoured teas. It has a lemon scent and flavour. The leaves can be used in drinks, salads, fruit dishes, and desserts and in sauce recipes which call for a lemon flavour.

LENT one of the two most important periods in the Christian year, defined in the *NSOED* as 'The period of 40 days from Ash Wednesday to Easter Eve, devoted to fasting and penitence in commemoration of Jesus' fasting in the wilderness.' As such, it

(*cont. on page 450*)

Lemon

The fruit of *Citrus medica*, a tree whose original home may have been in the north of India. It only reached the Mediterranean towards the end of the 1st century AD, when the Romans discovered a direct sea route from the southern end of the Red Sea to India. Tolkowsky (1937), adduces complex arguments in favour of this view (as against the earlier view that the lemon did not arrive until the 10th century), and refers to frescos found at Pompeii (and therefore prior to AD 70) which show what he regards as indisputably lemons; also a mosaic pavement probably from Tusculum (now Frascati) of about 100 AD in which a lemon is shown with an orange and a citron.

Thus the fruit which can reasonably be regarded as the most important for European cookery was a comparatively late arrival. Nor was its use in cookery, as an acid element, appreciated at once. Nor, indeed, was there a Latin word for lemon. It seems likely that in classical Rome the fruit was treated as a curiosity and a decoration, and that lemon trees were not grown successfully in Italy until later.

The Arabs seem to have been largely responsible for the spread of lemon cultivation in the Mediterranean region. By the beginning of the 4th century AD, a fully indigenous orchard production had been established in S. Europe. It flourished in Sicily and Spain and parts of N. Africa, and the Mediterranean is still the source of many of the lemons consumed in Europe.

Arab traders also spread the lemon eastward to China. The Chinese name *li mung* is clearly an imported derivation. Lemons are first discussed in the texts of the Sung period (960–1279 AD) although it seems likely that some had been cultivated earlier.

During the Middle Ages lemons were rare and expensive in N. Europe, and available only to the rich. In the Near East, the lemon's wide range of culinary uses was explored. *The Treatise of the Lemon*, which was written by Saladin's physician, Ibn Jamiya, gives recipes for lemon syrup and preserves. His work was translated into Latin and published in Venice in 1583. At this time in Italy lemons were becoming plentiful enough to be important in the kitchen. The use of lemon slices as a garnish for fish was widespread. The archbishop of Milan's chef Christoforo di Messisbugo (a name with many variations in spelling), whose important culinary treatise, *Libro Novo . . .*, came out in several editions in the middle of the 16th century, gave recipes for marinated brill with lemon slices and candied citron and orange peel.

The lemon reached the New World (where there are no native citrus species) in 1493, when Columbus, on his second voyage, established a settlement on Haiti. Within 20 years there were abundant crops of good quality. The Portuguese introduced the lemon to Brazil before 1540 (and it was from Rio de Janeiro that the captain of the 'First Fleet' of colonists bound for Australia obtained the first lemon trees to be planted in that continent in 1788). In 1565 the Spanish set up their first colony in Florida, San Agostino (now St Augustine), and almost certainly planted lemons among many other Old World varieties. While lemons had been grown in California since the time of the early Spanish missions of the 1730s, it was not until after their dissolution in 1833 and particularly during the sudden increase of population caused by the 1849 gold rush that they were cultivated on a larger scale. Since 1950 California has apparently produced more lemons than all of Europe combined.

There is irony in the reflection that the crews of the ships responsible for spreading the lemon would have been at risk from scurvy, without realizing that they were carrying the fruit which was to prove an effective cure for the disease. The finding was obscured by a mass of quack curers until the British naval surgeon James Lind endorsed it in his *Treatise on the Scurvy*, written in 1753. Even so, it was not until the end of the century that the Royal Navy began to issue lemon juice to its sailors.

However, in modern times it is the well-known **culinary uses** of the lemon which are important. It is the most common accompaniment for FISH and other seafood dishes. But it is equally important as a souring agent; its pleasant acidity is crucial to the taste of many dishes. It acts as a flavour enhancer for other fruit when it is cooked or used with other ingredients. Certain tropical fruits, such as papaya, guava, and avocado, need its sharpness.

It is perhaps in the cuisines of the Middle East that the use of the lemon is used to the maximum extent. Not only fresh, but also dried or pickled/preserved lemons are common in Arab kitchens; see, for example, Perry (1995*a*).

Lemon is interchangeable with vinegar for many sauces and salad dressings and may give a more delicate result. The Greek AVGOLÉMONO sauce, which is embodied in several famous Greek soups, demonstrates the affinity between eggs and lemons, a theme which recurs in some versions of MAYONNAISE.

Stobart (1980) advocates a wider appreciation of the zest of the fruit, which contains the essential oil and thus acts not just to flavour but to perfume food. This can be important in

---

LEMON HYBRIDS

THERE is a hybrid, *C. × limetta*, of which various cultivars exist with common names such as limetta and sweet lemon. These non-acid lemons are grown on a small scale mainly in India and around the Mediterranean.

The Meyer lemon, first imported into the USA from China by F. N. Meyer, in 1980, is described by Saunt (1990) as 'probably a hybrid between the lemon and either an orange or a mandarin'. It has less acidity than true lemons, and indeed resembles a small orange more than a lemon. It provides excellent juice and is growing in popularity.

many of the sweet dishes for which lemon is a vital ingredient. Lemon CHIFFON pie, lemon meringue pie, lemon MOUSSE, and lemon SOUFFLÉ are just a few of scores of examples.

Lemon, a valuable source of PECTIN as well as of flavour, is important in making many JAMS and JELLIES. And every cook knows that when something acidic is needed to prevent enzyme BROWNING (as with cut apples) a dash of lemon juice may be the best solution.

Home-made lemonade (lemon juice, water, sugar, ice) is as fine a **beverage** as any in the world, and particularly refreshing in hot weather; this is *citron pressé* in France. In the Middle East and India, lemon SHERBETS are essentially the same thing. The carbonated drinks sold as 'fizzy lemonade' or 'lemon soda' or the like may or may not have a true lemon flavour, but in any case constitute a different sort of drink.

---

constitutes one of the major instances of FASTING (or abstinence) in the world. Details vary between the various Christian churches, but the following list of special pre-Lenten and Lenten days which have traditionally been observed in England may be taken as typical.

It comes from Constance Cruickshank (1959), a work of particular charm, and needs to be prefaced by the author's own observation that the whole pre-Lenten period is almost universally known as carnival, but not in Britain where it is simply Shrovetide. The list shows how almost all of these special days have been marked in England by something special in the way of food.

- Saturday before Lent—Egg Saturday;
- Monday before Lent—Collop or Peasen Monday;
- Shrove Tuesday—Pancake Day;
- Ash Wednesday—Fritter Wednesday (and the next day can be Fritter Thursday);
- Mid-Lent Sunday—Mothering Sunday, Refreshment Sunday, Fig Pie Sunday;
- Fifth Sunday in Lent—Passion Sunday, Carling or Carlin Sunday;
- Palm Sunday—Pudding Pie Sunday, Fig Sunday;
- Maundy Thursday—Shere Thursday;
- Good Friday;
- Holy Saturday—Easter Eve.

The following day, the first after Lent, is of course Easter Sunday.

See also EASTER FOODS.

LENTIL *Lens culinaris*, a legume which originated in the Near East. It has been cultivated since antiquity in Egypt and remains of it have been found in many prehistoric sites in Europe. Asia is where most cultivation is carried out, and India is the chief producer.

The plant is an annual, around 40 cm (16") tall, whose edible seeds develop in short pods, each typically containing two seeds. The seeds come in various sizes, from tiny to small. They also vary in colour in both the husked and unhusked state. The two main types noticeable among lentils of the Near East and Asia are: first, those which are

relatively large and light coloured or yellow; and second, the small ones, which are brown, pink, or grey. In India, it is the pink lentils which are mainly eaten by Muslims in the north, especially in Bengal; and the same applies in Pakistan.

The best-known cultivar is Red (also known as Egyptian or Masoor), salmon in colour when husked.

However, attempts to list lentils run up against a fundamental difficulty; the use of the word in an Indian context is much looser, spilling over from *Lens culinaris* into other species, as though lentil had much the same meaning as DAL (split PULSE). So, to take but one example, the seeds of *Cajanus cajan*, PIGEON PEA, may be called 'yellow lentils'.

In Europe, some kinds of lentil have achieved the status of a delicacy, e.g. the French variety *Verte du Puy*, very small, green, and relatively expensive. But lentils, like other pulses, figure more often in hearty dishes than in delicate and costly ones. Lentil soup is filling, and so are various winter dishes which combine lentils with sausages or other pork products.

Next to SOYA BEANS, lentils have the highest protein content of all vegetables (just on 25%). They are valued for this reason in Asia, and it may also account in part for their being a favoured food during Lent in Roman Catholic countries. (This has led some to suppose that there is a connection between the names. Indeed, in parts of England 'lentils' was turned into 'Lent tills' and then shortened to 'tills'. However, the true derivation is from the Latin *lens*, through the diminutive *lenticula* and the French *lentille*.)

Lentils have the distinction of being the subject of one of the most eccentric, and endearing, food books of the 19th century: *Food for the People; or, Lentils and Other Vegetable Cookery*, by Eleanor E. Orlebar (1879). The author, who had previously written a book on *Sancta Christina*, displays classical scholarship, a gift for rhetoric (evidenced by her letters to *The Times*), and an unerring eye for quaint details (for example in describing scenes in people's cafés and the haunts of Danielites). The temptation to reproduce pieces of her prose

can only be resisted on the assumption that the whole book will be reprinted before long.

LESLIE ELIZA (1787–1858), perhaps the most popular and prolific cookery writer of the 19th century. In her classic bibliography *American Cookery Books 1742–1860* (Worcester, 1972), Eleanor Lowenstein lists more entries for Miss Leslie than for any other author. There are 72 listings for works in various editions by Miss Leslie compared to those for her nearest rivals in popularity, Sarah Josepha Hale and Lydia Maria Child, who have 27 and 26 entries respectively. This is a remarkable preponderance.

Typical of many of America's most influential culinary writers, Miss Leslie was more than simply a cookbook author. She was involved with numerous other literary and social pursuits. She was, in fact, a bit ashamed of the fame and fortune she received from her cookbooks, considering them 'unparnassian', and assumed that her reputation would survive based upon her novels, children's books, and stories. By and large, however, Miss Leslie's prose writings have long been forgotten; her reputation rests on her culinary works.

Much of our information about Eliza Leslie's early life is derived from a charming autobiographical letter which is included in J. S. Hart's *Female Prose Writers of America* (1852). In this we hear of her Scottish descent, that her father was a friend of Franklin and Jefferson, that she had read an extraordinarily wide range of books by the age of 12, and that her father's early death in 1803 left her mother, herself, and her four younger siblings in an awkward financial situation. They seem to have operated a boarding house, and Eliza attended at some point the cooking school in Philadelphia run by Mrs Goodfellow, for she mentions that her first book was compiled from a 'tolerable collection of receipts, taken by myself' while a pupil of that school. This first book, *Seventy-five Receipts for Pastry, Cakes and Sweetmeats* (1828), does not repeat the acknowledgement of indebtedness to Mrs Goodfellow, but in his introduction to a recent reprint of the book culinary historian

W. W. Weaver carefully traces the recipes therein to Mrs Goodfellow and indicates that the success of the book was probably based on a combination of two remarkable talents, 'Miss Leslie's as a writer and Mrs Goodfellow's as a cook'.

In her preface, Miss Leslie stresses the fact that her recipes are 'in every sense of the word, American'. Miss Leslie's next cookbook was, however, decidedly not American. In 1832 she published *Domestic French Cookery, Chiefly Translated from Sulpice Barué*. This book went through at least six printings in 23 years. The mysterious Sulpice Barué turns out to have been editor of the 6th, 7th, and 8th editions of Louis-Eustache Audot's gastronomic classic *La Cuisinière de la campagne et de la ville*, first published in Paris in 1818 and reprinted, under varying titles, until the appearance of an 87th edition in 1887.

Miss Leslie's most influential cookery book appeared in 1837, *Directions for Cookery*. It was the most popular cookbook printed in America during the 19th century and was followed by several more recipe books. However, the autobiography (written in 1851) records that in terms of what she calls 'pecuniary advantage' her three books on domestic economy brought her the greatest benefit.   JL

READING: Jan Longone (1988–9).

LETTUCE *Lactuca sativa*, is by far the most popular of the leafy salad vegetables. The lettuce belongs to the very large family Compositae, which includes cultivated species such as CHICORY AND ENDIVE, and various wild plants with edible leaves, all more or less tough and bitter, e.g. the DANDELION and some THISTLES. The original wild lettuce, *L. serriola*, is still common in Europe and temperate Asia, and is as harsh as any of these. It is also called 'prickly' or 'wood' lettuce, an unpromising plant for cultivation.

The original reason for cultivating lettuce was probably medicinal. Wild lettuce and, to a lesser extent, its cultivated descendant contain a latex with a mildly soporific effect. This resembles and smells like the latex of the opium poppy, but the plants are not related.

Lettuce has a long history in the kitchen, beginning in the Near East. Ancient Egyptian tombstones of about 4500 BC show a plant which appears to be lettuce. It is impossible to be sure because early varieties were tall, spindly plants with a lot of stem, comparatively small leaves, and no proper head; and there are other plants of the lettuce and chicory group which have much the same form. (For this reason wild chicory has sometimes been called 'wild lettuce' in England). The Greeks themselves, who

called it *tridax*, were certainly using it not long afterwards. About 400 BC its dietary qualities were assessed in the Hippocratic text *Regimen*, and since it is mentioned by the other Greek writers on food it is clear that it was widely cultivated and eaten.

The Romans ate a lot of lettuce. The Latin name *lactuca* is connected with *lac*, milk, because of the milky sap or latex which oozes out of the cut stem. In the early Roman period lettuce was eaten at the end of a dinner to calm the diner and induce sleep. Later it was eaten at the beginning to stimulate appetite. This change would have coincided with the development of improved varieties which, selected for lack of bitterness, would have contained less of the narcotic substances. In the 1st century AD Pliny describes nine varieties including a purple and a red one. All these were still loose, headless types. The usual Roman way of serving lettuce was as a salad with a dressing, but APICIUS also gives a recipe for a purée of lettuce and onions and Columella described how lettuce was pickled in vinegar and brine.

By the 5th century the plant was being cultivated in China, where it has always been treated as a vegetable to be cooked. Because of this different approach the lettuces which have been developed in China and the Far East have different characteristics.

Following the Dark Ages, lettuce does not appear again in European literature until the late 14th century, in the prologue to Chaucer's *Canterbury Tales* where we read: 'well loved he garlic, onions and lettuce.' However, it seems that during the Middle Ages it was the wild *L. perennis*, perennial lettuce, which was eaten in salads by peasants; while the ancestral prickly lettuce continued to be used medicinally, and as a soporific. Later, in the 16th century, the cultivated plant began to take on the forms known today. Both the round-headed lettuce and the cos type were then described for the first time.

Seventeenth-century writers also mention minor varieties: cut leafed, oak leafed, and with multiple heads like BRUSSELS SPROUTS. Colours included light and dark green, red, and spotted. Some of these fancy plants have been revived.

Seeds of European lettuces were taken to the Americas as early as 1494. All American cultivated lettuces are of European ancestry, although there are wild American species, e.g. the Canada wild lettuce, *L. canadensis*. The wild plants are as harsh as their European relatives, and are not normally eaten.

By 1600 the narcotic effect of lettuce had been much reduced. It seems that the only known cases of lettuce having actually sent people into a stupor (unless one counts the Flopsy Bunnies, cited by Jane Grigson, 1978)

are when, in times of shortage, they have been reduced to eating large amounts of the stems of lettuces which have 'bolted' or gone to seed.

VARIETIES
These have been classified in various ways, mostly according to shape. The following main categories are recognized:

- **Butterhead** lettuces have soft, pliable, rounded leaves which overlap to form a head. They may be small, such as **Bibb**, the improved Summer Bibb, and Tennis Ball (one of the oldest surviving varieties) or large, such as Big Boston and the voluptuous Grosse Blonde Paresseuse (which is of course French and sounds like someone sitting for a portrait by Renoir).
- **Crisphead** 'cabbage' lettuces have crisp leaves which form tightly compacted heads, as in the case of the well known **Iceberg**, or may be long leaved without heads.
- **Long-leaved** lettuces, such as those in the **Cos** group, also called **Romaine,** have crisp leaves, but theirs are long and narrow. Cos lettuces are probably not named for the island of Cos but from the Arabic word for lettuce. The name Romaine may have been given because these lettuces reached W. Europe through Rome (the name *lattuga romana* has stuck in Italy, as has *romaine* in France). This type of lettuce is near universal in the Middle East because of its tolerance of hot climates.
- **Loose-leaved** lettuces spread out in rosette form, which makes it easy to cut leaves from them as needed (hence the French term *laitues à couper*). Oak-leaved and red/brown varieties are found in this group, as are varieties popular in the Far East, where the plants may be used as a cooking vegetable.

A special type of lettuce (*L. sativa*, Angustana Group) grown mainly in China is called 'celtuce' in English. The word is a combination of 'celery' and 'lettuce', given it because of its shape. Another, flattering, name is 'asparagus lettuce'. The fleshy stem is the part eaten, usually cooked. The lower leaves, which are tough and unpalatable, are stripped off before the plant is sold, leaving only the tender leaves at the very top.

The Indian lettuce belongs to a different species, *L. indica*, and has been developed separately from *L. sativa* varieties. It is rather coarse, and has reddish leaves, or leaves with a red midrib.

In Japan a common type of lettuce, *tsitsa*, has been independently domesticated from a different wild lettuce. It is sometimes referred to by the botanical name *L. tsitsa*, although this has not been officially recognized.

So-called 'miner's lettuce' is PURSLANE.

USES

For the principal use of lettuce, see SALADS.

In the 17th century, as French works of the period testify, the cores of full-grown lettuces were candied to make a prized confection known as *gorge d'ange* (angel's throat).

Cream of lettuce soup is popular, but cooked lettuce is not generally favoured in western countries, although it is common practice to cook peas with a little lettuce.

In China lettuce leaves are shredded and stir-fried. Celtuce stems are peeled and finely sliced crosswise before cooking; the tops are used like ordinary lettuce.

LIBYA a country which became independent in 1951, had previously been ruled by Spain (in the 16th century), the Ottomans, and (for 40 years in the 20th century) Italy. This history has left some marks on the cookery and foodways of Libyans; but the effect of increased prosperity (from oil) and the consequent expansion of food imports, in the last part of the 20th century, has perhaps made a greater impact.

As Merdol (1992) has put it: 'Libyan people eat three meals a day. But one may say that they set the table just for lunch. Other meals are light and not given too much consideration.'

The dishes commonly served for lunch, the main meal, are COUSCOUS and its accompaniments; macaroni with meat and vegetables in a tomato sauce; and *bazin*, which is distinctively Libyan. This last dish centres on a preparation of barley flour, boiled in water and then beaten with a special stick (*magraf*) into a hard dough. When the dough has been shaped into a pyramid, a thick meat and potato stew is poured round it and decorated with whole hard-boiled eggs.

Since most of Libya is desert and the climate is extremely hot, the scope for agriculture is limited. Potatoes, pumpkins, onions, have for long been grown; and are now being joined by aubergines, cucumbers, etc., which can be grown with the benefit of new technology. Legumes, of which the most popular are chickpeas, are imported, and so are most fruits except for dates.

The meat which is commonly used in cooking is *gargush*, another Libyan speciality. This is meat which has been cut into long strips, salted, sun dried, chopped up, fried (usually in olive oil imported from other Mediterranean countries), cooled, and stored in its own fat.

Libyans like their food to be quite hot and spicy. Hot red pepper, black pepper, cinnamon, and cumin are much used.

Tea is drunk in large quantities, having been prepared in Libyan style. This involves boiling tea for some time in a large kettle, then straining it, sweetening it, and pouring it to and fro to achieve a fine foam. Finally, it is reheated and served in very small glasses with foam on top.

Although, as noted above, there are some interesting Libyan specialities, very little has been written about food and cookery in Libya.

LICHENS occasionally provide human and animal food. Some of these are popularly called 'moss', but lichens are different from mosses and only the former are edible.

Lichens are biological curiosities. What appears to be a single plant is two, a fungus and a green or blue green alga. The two plants co-operate with each other to cover bare rocks, often in hostile (for example Arctic) regions where nothing else can grow. The alga can use photosynthesis to gain food from the air with the energy of sunlight, something no fungus can do.

The two lichens of economic importance are Iceland moss, *Cetraria islandica*, and reindeer moss, *Cladonia rangiferina*. Both are used as animal food in Arctic regions, and the latter is of vital importance to the Lapps. Iceland moss is also made into bread, especially in Iceland; and its virtues were extolled by, for example, Norwegian writers on food and diet around the end of the 18th century. It is processed by a series of soakings, which remove the bitter taste, after which it can be boiled to make an edible jelly or dried and ground to a flour for bread-making.

Iwatake, meaning 'rock mushroom', is the Japanese name of a lichen, *Umbilicaria esculenta*, which is an expensive delicacy in Japan and China. The high price is due to the difficulty of collecting it from the cliffs where it grows. According to Hosking (1996) collectors abseil down the cliffs in order to collect the lichen. After a thorough wash, it is soaked for two days and then made into TEMPURA or *sunomono* (see JAPANESE CULINARY TERMS).

Manna lichen, *Lecanora esculenta*, has been thought by some to be the MANNA of the Bible; but there are better candidates for that role. Nevertheless, it has long been, and still is, used for making bread by the Tatars of W. Asia and by tribesmen in arid parts of Africa. It is torn up by desert winds, which carry it long distances to fall in a mysterious rain. Some other *Lecanora* spp also behave in this way, and are similarly used. Other European species furnish traditional fabric dyes, usually purple but including the edible red food colouring CUDBEAR (from *Rocella tinctoria*, which also provides litmus, the chemical indicator of acidity) and crottle which produces the ginger colour of Harris tweed.

A N. African (and European) lichen, staghorn oakmoss, *Evernia prunastri*, is edible and suitable for making into bread. Baskets of this were found in ancient Egyptian tombs; but it is not clear whether it was there as food or for some other purpose.

N. American lichens include a desert species which blows around as manna. This is dark crottle or puffed shield lichen, *Parmelia physodes*. Other kinds are horsehair lichen, *Alectoria jujuba*, which is traditionally cooked with CAMAS. All these also grow in the Old World, but are not used there. In very hard times Indian and white settlers alike have sometimes eaten the bitter Arctic lichens collectively called 'rock tripe' (*Umbilicaria* and *Gyrophora* spp).

LIEDERKRANZ an American cheese developed at the end of the 19th century by Emil Frey, a dairyman of Swiss origin working in New York State. Confronted by a strong demand for the German cheese *Schlosskäse*, which almost always spoiled while being shipped across the Atlantic, he spent some years experimenting and finally produced a cheese which was similar but better. The Liederkranz singing club in New York, whose members had been prominent in stimulating the invention, received packages of the new cheese as a gift and the name of the club, which means 'garland of song', was bestowed on the cheese. It has since gained wide popularity throughout the USA. The centre of production was long ago moved to Van Wert, Ohio, in more productive dairy-farming country.

Liederkranz is an orange-skinned, surface-ripened, soft cheese with a pronounced aroma, akin to but less strong than that of LIMBURGER. It is packed in small rectangles. It should be eaten promptly, at its peak, since it does not keep for long. The taste is mellow and the centre should be creamy in consistency. It is now much better known than the *Schlosskäse* ('castle cheese') of Germany and N. Austria which it originally emulated.

LIMA BEAN *Phaseolus lunatus*, a plant of Peruvian origin, dated back to 7000 BC by discoveries in archaeological sites. Cultivation spread slowly northwards to Mexico and the Caribbean. European slave traders took it thence to Africa, and eventually it reached Asia.

The lima bean is a popular vegetable in the USA. American varieties are often sold fresh or frozen. All these are light-coloured types, pale green when fresh, pale yellow when dried. The lima bean is also a staple food in many parts of tropical Africa and Asia, including Burma.

One of its varieties is the large, flat, white butter or Madagascar bean, sold dried or in cans, which is the kind familiar in Europe. Dried butter beans are usually very large, especially the fat sort sometimes called 'potato beans'. They therefore need a preliminary soaking and lengthy cooking. The flavour is good.

No lima beans should be eaten raw. Certain varieties, especially those with a red or black testa, have been associated with high levels of cyanogenic glucosides, but there is no reliable correlation between seed colour and cyanide content. Environmental factors may also influence the degree of toxicity. These substances have been reduced to safe levels, by selection, in the USA and elsewhere. Proper preparation, including the changing of the soaking and cooking water, eliminates the poison.

LIMBURGER a strongly flavoured cheese which originated in the Belgian town of Limbourg (east of Liège, close to the German frontier), was thus presented to the British public in Garrett's *Encyclopaedia of Practical Cookery* (*c*.1895):

Limburger cheese is chiefly famous for its pungently offensive odour. It is made from skimmed milk, and allowed to partially decompose before pressing. It is very little known in this country, and might be less so with advantage to consumers.

Nonetheless, Limburger has demonstrated strong powers of attraction. It was, in effect, taken over by German cheese-makers in the 19th century, and is now generally perceived as a German cheese. It is also made elsewhere, notably in the USA.

It is a surface-ripened, semi-soft cheese, usually made from whole milk. It is drained by gravity, or only light pressure, and therefore remains very moist. Ripening is effected in a cool room by yeasts, moulds, and the characteristic micro-organism, *Bacterium linens*, which is chiefly responsible for the pungency. The cheeses, typically small and rectangular, are classified in Germany according to their fat content, which varies from 20% to over 50%.

The American cheese LIEDERKRANZ is of the same breed, but smaller and milder. The same applies to the German ROMADUR. READING: Maggie Black (1989).

LIME an important CITRUS FRUIT which seems to have originated in the region of Malaysia. While lemons are the major acid citrus fruits in the subtropics, limes are the most prominent in tropical regions. This is true of the lime in its familiar, very acid form (it has one and a half times as much acid, weight for weight, as a lemon); but, as

explained below, there are various kinds of lime, including sweet limes.

It is hard to judge when the lime was first taken into cultivation, since the oldest surviving documents do not distinguish it clearly from other citrus fruits. An Indian medical work of *c*. AD 100 refers to both lemon and lime as *jambira*. The later Arabic and Persian word, *laimūn* and *līmūn* seem also to have been used for both; and most modern names for either come from this root. The lime seems not to have been known in classical times.

Although the westward path of the lime in early medieval times is hard to trace, it seems safe to assume that it was carried to Europe by the Arabs; that it was cultivated to some extent in Italy and Spain; and that, because it is better suited by a hotter climate, such cultivation did not last for long. What is sure is that, soon after the discovery of the New World by Europeans, the lime was introduced there along with other citrus fruits, and that limes quickly became abundant in the W. Indies and C. America, especially Mexico. These were the ordinary, small, acid limes. Consideration of the further spread of the fruit requires a survey of the other kinds.

The species and varieties of lime have been well surveyed by Saunt (1990), who provides the following information and more besides:

- *Citrus aurantifolia*, the archetypal species, the one which originated in Malaysia, which commonly bears the names West Indian, Mexican, or Key lime (the last name refers to the Florida Keys), but is sometimes referred to as the 'true lime'. Given its original provenance, these common names are surprising. The explanation is simply that the first two of these names represent principal areas of production (most of the world production of limes is of this species, with Mexico as the leading producer, the W. Indies and Egypt coming next), while the third, as Professor Julia Morton (1987) explains, is a historic relic of the brief period (roughly 1913–23) when there was commercial production in the Florida Keys, after one hurricane had put paid to pineapple-growing there and before another hurricane more or less ended the cultivation of limes. The fruits of this lime have seeds, and propagation is usually from these seeds. It is this fruit which is the *kaghzi nimbu* of India, the *Gallego lime* of Brazil, the *limun baladi* of Egypt, and the *doc* of Morocco. This (not the so-called Persian Lime) is the lime grown in Iran, where it is known locally as Shirazi.
- *C. latifolia*, believed to have originated as a hybrid between the *C. aurantifolia* and the CITRON, probably came from the Orient by

way of Persia and the Mediterranean, then possibly via Brazil and Australia to Tahiti, and finally to California. Against this background it is comprehensible that its common names are Persian or Tahiti Lime. But in California itself it is referred to as the Bearss Lime. The fruit, which is almost always seedless, is the only lime cultivated in the USA.
- *C. limettoides*, the sweet lime, often referred to as Palestine or Indian Sweet Lime, is thought to be another hybrid by origin. It has a somewhat lower sugar content than the acid limes listed above but qualifies to be called 'sweet' because it is almost completely devoid of acidity. A juicy fruit which enjoys popularity in the Near and Middle East and India, it is *limun helou* or *limun succari* in Egypt and *mitha nimboo* in Hindi.

The acid limes are thought of as green fruits (as the phrase 'lime green' testifies). This is because, although they would ripen to orange and then yellow if left on the tree, they are deliberately picked at the green stage, perhaps partly in order to ensure that they are not confused with lemons.

The use of fresh limes in beverages and to flavour sweet items such as a sorbet or a mousse, or in Key lime pie in the USA, is well known and becoming more familiar as the availability of fresh limes in temperate countries increases. Less familiar is the use of limes, sometimes fresh but more often dried, in savoury stews and the like in the Near/Middle East and S. Asia. In Iran, for example, dried limes are indispensable in stews (*khoresht*) to which they give a pleasantly musty, tangy, sour flavour. Sometimes they are split open, the pips removed, and the rest ground up into a fine powder to be sprinkled into stews and soups. They can be dried for a short time when they remain pale in appearance for light-coloured stews; or for a long time when they become very dark for use in dark-coloured stews. They are known as *limoo amani* (Omani limes), while the name in Oman itself, as mentioned under ARABIAN FOOD, is *loomi*.

For other limelike fruits, see CALAMANSI (= calamondin), and MANDARIN LIMES.

LIME FLOWERS borne by the European lime or linden tree, *Tilia platyphyllos*, and other *Tilia* spp (including *T. americana*, the linden or basswood tree of N. America), are dried to make lime tea, popular in France, Spain, and elsewhere for its relaxing properties, but are also used sometimes to flavour dessert creams and similar confections.

A French chemist, Missa, discovered that a paste made from the fruits and flowers of the linden was a 'perfect' substitute in taste and texture for chocolate, except that it would not keep; an episode about which Fernald and Kinsey (1943) provide interesting details.

Lime flowers are liked by bees, and the excellence of the honey produced from them is the greatest benefit they offer, although an indirect one.

LIMPET the familiar MOLLUSC of sea shores around the world. Its typical conical shell has earned it the name *chapeau chinois* in France.

Most limpets are edible, and Stone Age middens in such places as Orkney show that in the distant past they were consumed in huge quantities; but few are now marketed.

Lovell (1884), with his unquenchable enthusiasm for mollusc-eating, collected some interesting traditional ways of preparing *Patella vulgata*, the common European species. Thus at Herm, 'limpets were placed on the ground, in their usual position, and cooked by being covered with a heap of straw, which had been set on fire, about twenty minutes before dinner'. And in more recent times the Scots used to mix limpet juice with their oatmeal. (Limpet juice is palatable, and can be used to make a limpet sauce which goes well with seafood; but it is hard work to prise a sufficient quantity of limpets off the rocks to which they cling with such tenacity.)

An Asian limpet, *Cellana nigrolineata*, has the reputation of being as good as ABALONE (which is itself a limpet, if the term is applied in its broadest sense). The giant owl limpet, *Lottia gigantea*, is praised even more highly by Ricketts and Steinbeck (1978). 'The Mexicans justly prize the owl limpet as food. When properly prepared, it is delicious, having finer meat and a more delicate flavor than abalone. Each animal provides one steak the size of a silver dollar, which must be pounded between two blocks of wood before it is rolled in egg and flour and fried.'

LIMU the Hawaiian term for edible SEAWEEDS, merits its own entry because of the extraordinary concentration, in a relatively small population, of knowledge and skill in preparing seaweeds as food, and also because Hawaiians have used an appreciable number of species which are not consumed elsewhere, for example *Grateloupia filicina*, *huluhuluwaena*, pubic hair limu because of its hairlike branches. Rachel Laudan (1996) explains:

The Hawaiians had names for over 80 seaweeds, of which 32 can be equated with scientific names. Limu was one of the few vegetable foodstuffs that was available to the first arrivals in Hawaii and it played an important role as a seasoning,

equivalent to the herbs and spices of Europe and Asia. It was especially important for women. Their diet consisted primarily of poi (pounded taro); pork, coconut, and all but three varieties of banana were denied them. The women picked limu, gossiping as they cleaned it, glad of the seasoning it brought to their foods. With the arrival of the Europeans and the changing of the Hawaiian diet, the number of species that were commonly eaten gradually declined. The reefs have been picked clean of many of the more popular forms of edible seaweed. Limu pickers have become rarer. No longer do women and children search for limu in the debris thrown up by storms on Waikiki Beach as once they did.

READING: Heather Fortner (1978).

LINCOLN MARY (1844–1921), American cookery author and teacher. Born in Massachusetts, she graduated as a teacher from the Wheaton Female Seminary in 1864, and married David Lincoln the following year. Her teaching career did not really begin until 1879 when she was asked to replace Miss Sweeney, one of the original teachers with Maria Parloa at the fledgling Boston Cooking School. Mrs Lincoln taught there until 1885, and in 1884 published *Mrs Lincoln's Boston Cook Book*, a text based on her courses at the school. According to the preface, the book was prepared 'at the urgent request of the pupils of the Boston Cooking School who have desired that the receipts and lessons given during the last four years in that institution should be arranged in a permanent form'. The recipes themselves were drawn from a wide range of contemporary authorities in Europe and the USA, including Soyer, Mrs Beeton, Marion Harland, and Miss Corson; and Mrs Lincoln stressed the science of cooking and its relationship to sound nutrition.

In 1885 Mrs Lincoln began teaching at Lasell Seminary in Auburndale, Mass., and in 1887 published *The Boston School Kitchen Textbook*, a text for public schools. Her other books include *The Peerless Cook Book* (1886), *Carving and Serving* (1887), and *What to Have for Luncheon* (1904). In 1894 she began to contribute a column, 'From Day to Day', to the *American Kitchen Magazine*, becoming its culinary editor in 1895, and became an active member of the New England Women's Press Association.

Mrs Lincoln's talents were more organizational than creative. She helped put cooking on a secure scientific basis. One of her public lectures was entitled 'Art and Science, versus Drudgery and Luck'. A popular speaker, she was invited by Sarah Tyson RORER to give a guest lecture at the annual Philadelphia Exposition in 1902. Mrs Rorer, an acknowledged leader in the domestic science movement, later referred to 'the three pioneers Miss Corson, Mrs Lincoln, and I

who started domestic science in this country'. See also AMERICAN COOKBOOKS.

LING *Molva molva*, a large fish of the COD family: maximum length 2 m (80"), market length about half of that. This is an Atlantic species, being taken mainly around Iceland and to the west of the British Isles; and only occasionally reported from the W. Mediterranean. It is considered to be close to fresh cod in merit; and in dried or salted and dried form it is almost as highly esteemed as the corresponding cod products. The dried and salted roe (*huevas de maruca* in Spain) is a delicacy.

The **Mediterranean** (or blue) **ling**, *M. dipterygia*, is somewhat smaller and less good.

LINNAEUS CAROLUS, the Latinized name of the great Swedish naturalist Carl von Linné (1707–78), who transformed the study of natural history by devising the binomial system of nomenclature. This provides for every species to have a name consisting of two Latinized words, the first indicating the genus to which the species belongs and the second being the specific or species name. The entry above on LING provides two examples, and there are hundreds of others elsewhere in the book.

This system is applicable to all living things, including all those members of the plant and animal kingdoms which provide food. Without them, and having to rely instead on the vernacular names in various languages, food studies (and many other kinds of study) would often fall into confusion.

The home of Linnaeus at Uppsala is a modest and charming place to visit, where one can combine saluting his memory and enjoying the simple and scholarly environment in which he lived and taught.

LINSEED comes from the flax plant, *Linum usitatissimum*, which is cultivated chiefly for the production of linen. Most of the seed is made into linseed oil, largely used in connection with paints, and cattle cake. Nevertheless, linseed itself is sometimes used as a food grain in India, where the species originated and where flax has been cultivated since earliest times. Linseed was also eaten in classical Greece and Rome.

In more recent times there are various instances of the use of linseed for human food. Thus Smith and Christian (1984) note that linseed oil was one of the vegetable oils which was important during fasts in medieval and post-medieval Russia. 'Hemp and flax seeds . . . were used in dishes with peas, for instance, or gave oil which was either an element in various dishes or the medium in which they were cooked.' They quote a Russian source to show that linseed oil was among those used for making fish dishes for the table of the Tsar in the 17th century.

Lane (1860) mentions the use of linseed oil for dressing FUL MEDAMES.

The German *Leinsamenbrot* is a dense, black bread containing whole linseed which is intended mainly as a health food, to relieve constipation, but is quite agreeable to eat.

LION *Panthera leo*, the 'king of beasts', nowadays having difficulty in surviving and therefore not to be recommended as food, has nonetheless been eaten with pleasure by peoples of the regions in Africa and Asia where it flourished. Leipoldt (1976) states that he had been told by African hunters that lion meat was as good as venison and that he had verified this by preparing the meat in various ways. Fried steaks, previously marinated in wine and vinegar, scored top marks, and lion meat also produced excellent BILTONG. However, he indicates, there was a very strong prejudice on the part of everyone except black Africans against using lion meat.

LIPTAUER the most widely used name for a mild, fresh, soft cheese popular in Hungary and other parts of Europe. It is made from whole sheep's milk, sometimes with cow's milk added, and was originally home-made by farmers.

Liptauer is distinctive not for its flavour, which is unremarkable, but for the way in which it is served: on a plate surrounded by little heaps of salt, paprika, mustard, butter, chopped chives, or caraway seeds, which are mixed with the cheese as desired.

LIQUORICE (or licorice), *Glycyrrhiza glabra*, a small leguminous plant whose thick roots, up to about 1 m (40") long, and underground runners contain a very sweet compound called glycyrrhizin. In its pure form this is 50 times sweeter than ordinary sugar; but the plant also contains bitter substances which partly mask the sweet taste. The name 'liquorice' is a corruption of the original Greek name *glycorrhiza*, meaning 'sweet root', which is also an old English name.

The plant, in one form or another, grows wild in parts of Asia and in S. Europe. Pieces of root or runner, cut into sticks and dried, provide a natural sweetmeat for chewing and are still widely sold in Asia, where liquorice has had a high reputation since ancient times for medicinal purposes.

Cultivation in W. Europe seems to have begun on a significant scale in the 16th century. An extract is prepared from the roots, for use in various ways. Liquorice was used as a flavouring and colouring in a number of sweet foods including GINGERBREAD; in stout and other dark beers.

However, it is probably in **confectionery** that liquorice has found its most extensive and attractive culinary use. For this purpose, the extract from the roots is combined with sugar, water, gelatin, and flour to give a malleable black or brown paste, which is tough and chewy. These attributes are used to great effect by manufacturers who mould it into pipes, cables, and long strips or 'bootlaces'; or combine it with brightly coloured soft SUGAR PASTE to make **liquorice allsorts.** These sweets, very popular in Britain, are of diverse and striking appearance, mostly made of layers of black refined liquorice combined in various ways with brightly coloured paste imitating marzipan. Some are lumps of liquorice rolled in coloured sugar vermicelli. Thanks to the liquorice in them, the flavour of these sweets is more interesting than that of most cheap confectionery.

Another traditional British liquorice confection goes by the name of **Pontefract cakes,** or Yorkshire pennies, little shiny black liquorice sweets, about 2 cm (1") in diameter, stamped with an impression of a castle and an owl. These small, round Pontefract cakes are still made in Pontefract, in Yorkshire, which has been the centre of liquorice-growing in England for many centuries. The origins of liquorice-growing in Pontefract, popularly attributed to the monks of a local monastery, are unknown. However, liquorice was being grown there on a large scale by the mid-17th century; and the available evidence has been effectively marshalled by the anonymous author of the essay published in *PPC 39* (1990).

The essayist remarks that Pontefract cakes may have been made as early as 1614, this being the date on a die-stamp bearing the Pontefract 'trade mark' of a castle and an owl. These cakes would probably have been medicines rather than sweetmeats. In 1760 a local chemist, named George Dunhill, first had the idea of mixing liquorice extract with flour and sugar to give the familiar sweets. A number of small concerns processed locally grown liquorice in Pontefract throughout the 19th century. Eventually, towards the close of the 19th century, demand outstripped supply, and the British confectionery industry imported liquorice juice from Spain and Turkey, perhaps the origin of the Yorkshire dialect term 'spanish' for liquorice sticks. Another dialect term, this time Scottish, is 'sugarallie', a shortened version of the 16th-century term *sugar alicreesh*. Before the advent of mass-

marketed soft drinks, children made 'liquorice water' by soaking a stick of liquorice until it dissolved in a bottle of water.

In other European countries, for example Denmark and the Netherlands, liquorice is a popular ingredient for sweets, of which the children in each country have their favourites.

LISTERIA a bacterium which can occur in food and cause listeriosis, a serious illness. Its full name is *Listeria monocytogenes*, and it was named after the famous 19th-century surgeon and pioneer of hygiene, Lord Lister. Listeriosis was first found in a rabbit in 1926, and a few years later in a human adult. It was not until the 1980s that investigations and experiments led to the conclusion that most outbreaks of listeriosis have been due to contaminated food.

These bacteria occur widely in the environment. They are destroyed by high heat and do not survive pasteurization, although normal reheating of foods will not kill them. But they have the unusual property of multiplying at low temperatures, even as low as 0 °C (32 °F), and for this reason pose a special problem.

Listeriosis hardly ever strikes healthy adults. Those most at risk from it are the unborn babies carried by pregnant mothers who have been infected; the elderly; and persons with an impaired immune system, such as transplant patients.

Foods which have been known to cause listeriosis include prepared salads and processed meats kept under refrigeration for too long; soft cheeses, possibly contaminated after production; and so-called 'cook-chill' foods, which are sometimes contaminated by careless handling or storage.

LITHUANIA southernmost of the Baltic states, had a relatively large territory in the Middle Ages, first by itself and later in a dynastic union with neighbouring Poland. The territory extended at one time to the Black Sea, and Lithuania had close trading links with the Mongol-Tatars, the Ottoman Empire, etc. (whence, probably, some traces of C. Asian influence on Lithuanian food and the presence of pomegranate in some dishes). These influences, however, affected the aristocracy more than the general population.

The Polish-Lithuanian state declined in the 17th and 18th centuries, and a continuing history of wars and other commotions in the 19th century and up to the Second World War led to Lithuania becoming a republic within the Soviet Union from 1945 to 1991.

Thus Lithuanian cuisine has been exposed to numerous influences, especially those of

POLAND, GERMANY, and RUSSIA. Yet indigenous traditions, many with medieval origins, survive. These reflect the agrarian nature of the country, and also its 96 km (60-mile) Baltic coastline, which yields the Baltic herring which are so well loved in all three Baltic states.

Other features which Lithuanians share with LATVIA and ESTONIA are excellent rye breads; a considerable emphasis on dairy products (including sour cream, buttermilk, cottage cheese, and hard cheeses which may be flavoured with caraway seeds); and a great liking for potatoes in many forms. Besides the ubiquitous plain boiled potatoes, Lithuanians enjoy a potato sausage, a potato pudding, potato pancakes, and dumplings made with grated potato, of which the most intriguing are called *cepelinai* (meaning zeppelins, referring to their shape) and are stuffed with meat, mushrooms, cheese, etc.

As in the other Baltic states, pork is the favoured meat, but among the most popular meat dishes are Lithuanian versions of the Polish *zrazy*, using beef. The bird most esteemed for the table is the goose. Among numerous items which have a Russian connection are beet soup (enjoyed cold in summer, see BORSHCH) and *kiselius* (a fruit dish—see KISEL).

LIVAROT a soft cheese made in and around the village of that name in the Calvados region of Normandy in France, may be one of the most ancient French cheeses, although the first record of it under the name Livarot dates back to the end of the 17th century (Rance, 1989). Best made from the milk of Normande cows, in this instance partly skimmed, it is slightly larger than its relation CAMEMBERT, and differences in the ripening process give it a much more pungent aroma and flavour.

Brown (1955) notes that Livarot has been characterized as a 'decadent' among cheeses, 'the very Verlaine of them all'. His free translation of a verse by the French poet Victor Meusy neatly evokes an image of an over-runny specimen:

> In the dog days,
> In its overflowing dish,
> Livarot gesticulates,
> Or weeps like a child.

LIVER a relatively large organ in most animals, birds, and fish, usually edible and in some cases delicious, although it has the unattractive function of secreting bile. Livers are appreciated in most parts of the world, although consumption is low in N. America.

Calf's liver is generally accounted the best among animals, because of the smooth texture and delicate flavour. Lamb's liver is smaller but also delicate. Both these mild types of liver are suitable for being quickly sautéed, sliced or in larger pieces. *Fegato alla salvia*, calf's liver cooked with sage, is well known in Italy, as is *Fegato alla veneziana*, with onions.

Pig's liver is widely eaten. It and ox liver tend to be coarse. The flesh of both is dark red and has a strong flavour which can be mellowed by long braising. Slices of either may be soaked in milk to soften the flavour before they are cooked.

Livers lend themselves well to the making of pastes, stuffings, sausages, and the like. Liver dumplings, made from calf's liver according to any of several good C. European recipes, are a real delicacy. The German and Austrian ones, called *Leberknödel*, are the best known.

Many game animals yield good livers, which are usually among the first items to be consumed. Deer liver, generally speaking, is excellent.

Among the other ingredients which go well with animal livers are bacon, oatmeal, sour cream, sharp apples, onions, shallots, garlic, marjoram, and sage.

Chicken livers are the most widely eaten of poultry livers, but the most famous are the specially fattened livers of goose or duck (see FOIE GRAS). Various game birds provide good livers, which may be served as special titbits on toast.

Some fish livers are delicacies, e.g. those of red mullet; and there are some places, notably Shetland (see Davidson, 1988*a*), where the art of using fish livers has been developed by a fishing community to an extent which is unimaginable for persons in non-coastal urban environments. However, certain fish livers are too rich to be eaten in more than tiny amounts.

LIZARD any of the reptiles which have four legs, a long tail, and a scaly or granulated skin, in the order Lacertilia.

For information about cooking and eating the larger lizards, see IGUANA and MONITOR. However, there are lots of smaller lizards in tropical and semi-tropical regions around the world, and many of these are eaten locally, although they yield relatively little meat. Sophie Coe (1994), recalling a storehouse full of dried lizards which was discovered by a Spaniard on an island off the Peruvian coast in 1532, draws attention to the careful description of such lizards and the techniques for catching, drying, and eating them, by Holmberg (1957). Her distillation of this description serves as a good indication of general practice in lizard-eating communities:

Dicrodon holmbergi, the lizard, lives in holes in the ground under *guarango* trees, and the fruit of these trees is the only thing that the lizard eats.

The tree is also called *algarroba*, *mesquite*, or *Prosopis juliflora*, and human beings eat the pods as well. From April to November the lizards hibernate, and we presume that the tree has no ripe fruit. As the fruit matures, the lizards emerge from their holes and sometimes even climb the trees to get it. The lizards are trapped, and their front legs and backs are broken to paralyze them. They are then thrown on the embers of a fire and scorched until their scaly skins may be removed by hand. Once skinned, they are buried in a shallow depression in the heated sand and covered with hot ashes. Ten minutes of cooking, followed by cooling off and gutting, makes a product that may be stored for a year or consumed immediately. Holmberg said that it could be eaten in *seviche* [see CEVICHE], the dish of fish marinated in lime juice, as well as in soups, stews, and omelets.

LIZARD FISH *Saurida tumbil* and close relations, fish of Indo-Pacific waters which have lizard-like heads. Maximum length 45 cm (18"). These fish are moderately good to eat, but tend to be dry, so unsuited to grilling. In Thailand (where *S. undosquamis* is the preferred species) they are usually boiled, or made into fish balls, or conserved by canning or salting.

LLAMA *Lama glama*, a S. American mammal, a member of the same family, Camelidae, as the Old World CAMEL. The llama, which was domesticated thousands of years ago, was one of two such species (the other being alpaca, *L. pacos*) which were of great importance to the Inca of Peru.

When the Spaniards arrived in S. America, they were impressed by the usefulness of the llamas as a source of clothing and transport and also food. Commenting on this third role, Sophie Coe (1988) cites an isolated mention of llama milk being used, but explains that, besides titbits such as the tongues and brains, it was the muscle meat which was important. Modern sources suggest that this has a resinous taste, in animals older than two years, because of their diet, but that the taste disappears if the meat is dried to make *charqui* (JERKY).

A third species, *L. guanicoe*, the guanaco, provided much fresh meat for Charles Darwin and the crew of HMS *Beagle* when they spent some months in Patagonia in 1833, before resuming their voyage round the world.

LOACH a fish of numerous genera and species in the family Cobitidae, occurring in rivers and lakes in Europe and Asia, especially SE Asia. Generally speaking, these are small fish, adept at concealing themselves by burrowing at high speed into a muddy or sandy bottom. Only a few of them are regarded as food fishes, notably *Botia hymenophysa* and *Acanthopsis choirorhynchos*.

These two species are eaten with some enthusiasm in Laos, for example; larger specimens of the former species may be grilled, while fish of the latter species are regarded as good for pickling or cooking in fish stews. (An unusual 'no smoking' rule accompanies the pickling process; the Lao believe that even a tiny shred of tobacco ash in the mixture will turn it bad and make it harmful.)

LOAF CHEESE is not a variety: the term describes factory-made cheeses which, for convenience, are made in a rectangular shape rather than the traditional round one.

LOBSCOUSE the English name for a dish, or rather group of dishes, which almost certainly has its origin in the Baltic ports, especially those of Germany. In all its forms, the name refers to a seaman's dish; and in England it is particularly associated, in recent times, with the port of Liverpool, which is why Liverpudlians are often referred to as 'scouses' or 'scousers'. The dish has, however, a long history in other nearby parts of England. Thus Hone (1826) relates that at what were called 'Merrynights' in N. Lancashire and Cumberland and Westmorland, lobscouse was served after the dancing.

As with many similar dishes, there are numerous and fiercely disputed variations. However, the following account may be taken as typical. Lobscouse is made in a single pot and begins by frying or 'sweating' in DRIPPING, sliced onions, carrots, and turnips. Stewing steak or mutton or corned beef is added; plus, when the meat is browned, salt, pepper, and water. Sometimes a cow-heel or pig's trotter is put in to give a gelatinous body to the dish. Chopped potatoes are always included. At this stage it can be put in the oven to cook for a long time.

Some insist that SHIP'S BISCUIT should be crumbled into the dish, while others maintain that pearl BARLEY is an essential ingredient.

A Liverpool street chant parodies 'The Charge of the Light Brigade':

Half a Leg, Half a Leg, Half a Leg of Mutton,
Into the Pan of Scouse rolled the six onions.

Labskaus, the German version, may be made with either fish (*Fischlabskaus*) or meat; in either case, preserved rather than fresh.

In Denmark the dish, traditionally made with salt beef, is known as *skipperlabskovs*

and is supposed to be thick enough to eat with a fork but not so thick that the fork can stand up in it. (Some Liverpudlians agree and say that it should be firm enough for a mouse to be able to trot over it but mushy and capable of being spread on bread to make a 'lobby butty'.)   RSh

LOBSTER *Homarus gammarus* and *H. americanus*, the outstanding CRUSTACEANS of N. Atlantic waters (see illustration overleaf). The two species are very similar; the situation is that what is essentially the same creature, the lobster, has developed in slightly different forms on the two sides of the N. Atlantic, and the differences have been judged great enough to warrant classifying them as two species, not one. One difference is that the American lobster grows slightly larger than its European brother. It is, however, difficult to give maximum dimensions. In the past, before the lobster fisheries became intensive, some lobsters lived to a great age and attained extraordinary sizes. For example, one which was taken off the coast of Virginia in the 1930s was well over a metre (39") long and weighed about 20 kg (45 lb). Nowadays a lobster half that size would be considered a giant.

The colour of the live lobster varies according to its habitat, but is usually dark blue or greenish. After being cooked, when the red pigment in its carapace is, so to speak, 'released', it turns bright red; 'like a cardinal's hat', as one French writer put it.

The range of the European lobster is from the far north down to the Mediterranean. The American lobster occurs as far south as S. Carolina. Their habits are such that they can only be caught in special lobster pots, and the fishery for them is relatively expensive and arduous. Partly for this reason, the lobster has become one of the most costly seafoods in the world. In N. America it is the Maine lobster which is most famous; but this fact seems merely to reflect the hard work put in by Maine publicists. The Canadian catch is more than twice the size of the United States one, and the southern part of the Gulf of St Lawrence is the richest lobster-breeding ground in the world.

Most sea creatures have worse enemies than man. Whales are an exception; so are adult lobsters. Baby and small lobsters fall prey to predators of their own element; but those which reach a respectable size are able to defend themselves very well. The stalked eyes give the lobster good warning of impending danger. The powerful abdomen, snapped down, will propel it backwards at an astonishing speed into a rocky crevice. The claws are formidable weapons in combat; and the shell (properly exoskeleton) is an effective armour. However, since the

shell is rigid, it has to be shed periodically as the lobster grows. Immediately after moulting, the lobster is a sorry sight, and as defenceless as a medieval knight who has doffed his armour. The body is soft and the claws shrunken and shapeless. Although the lobster quickly swells to its new size and starts to develop a new exoskeleton, it is not good to eat at this time. The swelling up to the new size is largely accomplished by absorbing a lot of water; the meat is therefore watery and not at all like the firm flesh which lobster-eaters expect.

Lord (1867) tells a strange tale about canned lobster.

The popularity of the Lobster extends far beyond the limits of our island, and he travels about to all parts of the known world, like an imprisoned spirit soldered up in an air-tight box. It has been said that during the Indian war a box of regimental stores belonging to our forces fell into the hands of the enemy, who thinking that a great capture of some kind of deadly and destructive ammunition had been made, rammed the painted tin cases, with goodly charges of powder behind them, into their immense guns, laid them steadily on the devoted British troops, and then with a flash and a thundering roar, preserved lobster, from Fortnum and Mason's, was scattered far and wide over the battlefield.

The NORWAY LOBSTER is a true lobster; but the SPINY LOBSTER, which exists in various species in tropical and subtropical waters around the world, is not.

LOCRO a characteristic vegetable stew of S. America, sometimes enriched with pieces of beef, salt beef, pork, or fish, and always containing a cereal element, as explained in an interesting passage by the Brown family (1971):

Locro is one of those flexible dishes of everyday country life that can be made with almost any meat or combination of meats, depending on the momentary resources of the kitchen. It resembles Arabian couscous, from which it probably originated, traveling to the Spanish colonies by way of the mother land. Out on the wheat-growing plains of Argentina the main ingredient of locro is most often whole grains of wheat, but coarsely milled corn resembling our hominy is equally good. Yellow corn is preferred in many localities because it is supposed to be sweeter, and one asks in the country store for maiz para locro (corn for locro).

Locro is very well known in ECUADOR, where one of its variant forms includes coconut milk.

LOCUST an insect which is proverbial for the ruthless manner in which it can devour crops, descending on and denuding huge tracts of agricultural land, but which is itself welcome food for human beings in many

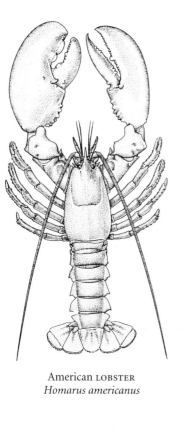

American LOBSTER
Homarus americanus

NORWAY LOBSTER
Nephrops norvegicus

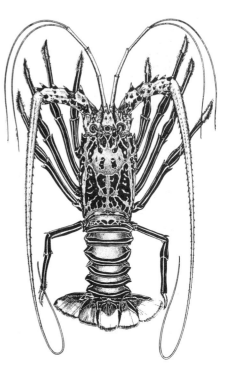

Painted SPINY LOBSTER
Panulirus versicolor

Lobsters,
large and small,
true ones with claws,
and others without,
from all four
hemispheres

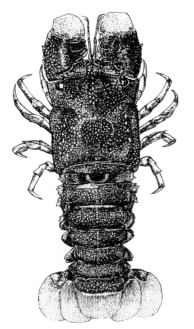

Mediterranean slipper lobster
Scyllarides latus (see FLAT LOBSTER)

Bay lobster of Australia
Thenus orientalis
(see FLAT LOBSTER)

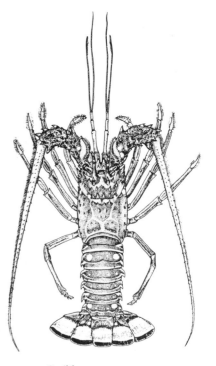

Caribbean SPINY LOBSTER
Panuliris argus

parts of Africa. The principal species, *Schistocerca gregaria*, known as the desert locust (in French, *criquet pèlerin*), ranges all over the continent, reproduces ten or more times a year, and may be encountered in flights of several billion individuals. The two contrasting aspects of the locust, by which people can 'enjoy not only the agreeable flavour of the dish, but also take a pleasant revenge of the ravagers of their fields' (Barth, 1857), are neatly expressed in the song attributed by Pringle (1851) to 'the wild Bushman' of Australia:

> Yea, even the wasting locust-swarm
> Which mighty nations dread,
> To me nor terror brings nor harm;
> I made of them my bread.

Bodenheimer (1951), as so often where edible insects are under discussion, provides a remarkably full survey of locust-eating which includes details of a dozen or so ways of preparing them. One point which stands out is that the females are better than the males, especially just before their migratory flight, 'at a time when their wings are short and their bodies are heavy and distended with eggs'. Legs and wings are discarded, either before or after roasting or boiling. Of the numerous personal accounts cited, this from an observer in S. Africa in 1782 is typical.

Joy showed itself suddenly on all faces when a cloud of advancing locusts was sighted, composed of millions of these insects. They passed not much above our heads on a front of almost 1000 m. continuing for over an hour in such a dense stream that they did fall like hail upon us. Those of my men who were accustomed to wild life, enjoyed them and boasted so much about the excellence of this manna, that I ceded to the temptation to eat them. My prejudices were certainly stronger than any real cause for aversion, as I could not detect any disagreable flavour, and they actually taste like the yellow of a boiled egg.

There are also accounts of drying the bodies of locusts and turning them into a paste or a flour which can be stored; and to a soup prepared with locust eggs. However, the last words should perhaps be allotted to the lively S. African author Leipoldt (1976):

Fried locusts. Nip off their wings, heads and legs, after you have plunged them into boiling water mercifully to kill them. What remains are the thorax and abdomen, which are the only parts that interest the epicure. You dust them with a mixture of pepper and salt (to which for some absurd reason that I have never been able to understand, some people add a little powdered cinnamon) and shallow-fry them in fat till they are crisp and brown. They taste not unlike whitebait that, somehow, have been stuffed with buttered toast.

See also GRASSHOPPER, a wider term which covers the family of bush-crickets as well as that of locusts.

LOCUST TREES *Parkia biglobosa* and *P. filicoidea*, are native to tropical W. Africa and bear pods which have some importance there and in the Sudan as a source of food.

The pods of *P. biglobosa* contain a sweet yellow pulp which is made into drinks and sweetmeats.

A traditional method of preparing the seeds in W. Africa requires the seeds to be repeatedly boiled, then husked and placed in leaf-lined baskets or similar containers to be fermented over a period of several days by a whole battery of micro-organisms which are naturally present. The fermented seeds may have wood ash mixed into them to reduce the smell. After fermentation they can be pounded into a paste or kept loose; and in either event may be formed into balls or pyramids and partially dried for storage. The product is used as a condiment, to flavour soups and stews, and is also a good source of protein.

The technique of production and the appearance of the product varies from place to place, as do its names. The principal name is perhaps *dawadawa* (in Nigeria), with variants such as *daoudawa*, but well over a dozen others are in common use, including *soumbara* (francophone W. Africa), *kinda* (Sierra Leone), and *netetou* (Senegal).

For a related tree of SE Asia, see PETÉ. The locust trees are also broadly similar to the CAROB.

LOLLIPOP a large, hard, boiled sweet mounted on a stick so that it can be sporadically sucked in a convenient way. The term 'lolly' is an 18th-century one for 'mouth', so a lollipop was something that one popped into one's mouth. It did not necessarily mean a sweet with a stick, as became usual later. A few old-fashioned boiled sweets sold by British confectioners are still called 'lollies' though they are stickless. The diminutive name 'lolly' has become the usual one for ice lollies. In the USA the other end of the word has been used as the basis for the new term 'popsicle'.

LONGAN *Dimocarpus longan*, is a slightly smaller and less well-flavoured relative of the LYCHEE, native to the same region and also of long-standing cultivation. Its fruits ripen later than the lychee, it withstands lower temperatures, and is less exacting about growing conditions.

Like the lychee, the longan has a rough and brittle shell, easily removed. The flesh within is whitish and translucent, enclosing a shiny black seed; hence the name 'dragon's eye'.

In China much of the crop is canned. The Chinese also dry the pulp, which acquires a

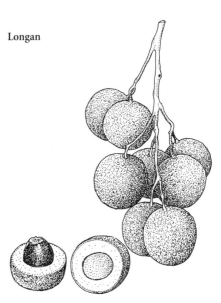

Longan

rich, smoky taste and can be used in cookery or added to tea for special occasions.

LONG PEPPER a spice which was much more widely used in classical and medieval times than now, comes from two species of plant in the pepper family. *Piper longum*, Indian long pepper, grows wild at the foot of the Himalayas and in S. India. *P. retrofractum*, Javanese long pepper, is found throughout Malaysia. The latter is the more pungent and generally held to be the better. It is certainly the longer; its fruit, a dark catkin-like spike made up of tiny seeds, may measure 6 cm (2.5") long.

When Theophrastus wrote about pepper in the 3rd century BC, he listed only two kinds, black pepper (*P. nigrum*) and long pepper: 'One is round [he describes the

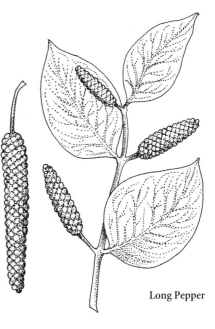

Long Pepper

reddish fruit of *P. nigrum*] . . . The other is long, black, with poppy-like seeds. This is much stronger.' Nearly 400 years later, Pliny described three sorts of pepper: black, white, and long. The last cost twice as much as white, which in turn cost much more than black.

Long pepper was still prominent in European recipes of the 16th century, and Bailey (1588) noted that 'long pepper is to be seen in every shop'. But the price differential was reversed. In 1607 black pepper cost 12 times as much as long pepper in France. This change may have indicated a decreasing demand, for it was about then that long pepper started to disappear from European recipes. By 1702 a French writer could write: 'I have nothing to say about long pepper since it is no longer used as food.'

Use of long pepper in India and other Asian countries has been more consistent. It even pre-dated the use of black pepper, and continues on a substantial scale, although much long pepper has to be imported. Linguistic evidence suggests that long pepper was also the first to be used in Europe. Its name in Sanskrit was *pippali* (corresponding to the Hindi *pipli*), and it is from this word that the classical names (Greek *peperi* and Latin *piper*) and modern terms for pepper have come.

P. and M. Hyman (1980) speculate that the decline of long pepper in Europe may have been caused by the introduction in the 16th century of CHILLI pepper. Gerard (1633) said of long pepper: 'It is in taste sharper and hotter than black pepper, yet sweeter and of a better taste.' If it had been prized for its hot quality, then it would have been natural for chilli to oust it, especially as the chilli was cheaper and, unlike long pepper, could be grown in the hotter European countries. Moreover, the chilli kept better. Long pepper, according to Bailey (1588), was 'moister than any other kind and it will sooner mold and waxe mustie than any other'.

If the above is correct, it would remain to explain the continued use of long pepper in Asia. The answer may be that Asian cuisines, unlike European ones, have room for three hot peppers; and that long pepper was a local product for Asians and less apt to spoil. In India there is some cultivation of long pepper, but most is gathered wild in the north. It is used generally as a spice, and also in pickles and preserves.

The hotness of long pepper is partly due to the presence of piperine, as in black pepper, but also to other alkaloids with numbing properties.

LOQUAT *Eriobotrya japonica*, a medium-sized, evergreen tree of the rose family. Its

Loquat

yellow/orange/apricot-coloured fruit (a pome, i.e. a fruit of the same type as the related apple or pear) is oval or pear shaped and up to 8 cm (3") long, with large, hard seeds. The flesh can be either apricot or, less often but more delicious, cream coloured. The fruit looks slightly like the related MEDLAR, and the two are often confused; indeed, the loquat is sometimes called 'Japanese medlar'.

The species had its origins in China, where it has been cultivated for over 1,000 years. Tolerant of both tropical heat (although preferring hillsides in very hot regions) and of a certain degree of winter frost, it gradually spread through E. Asia and India, and reached Europe in the 18th century. It is now grown on a small scale all around the Mediterranean, and also in Australia, and S. and C. America.

There was a time when the loquat claimed attention by being the first soft fruit to mature, ahead of apricots and peaches, but new precocious varieties of these have done away with this advantage, leaving the loquat with the handicap of spoiling quickly after picking. It has never become important commercially. However, when fully ripe, the loquat is quite sweet and luscious. Good jams and jellies may be made from unripe loquats; and if the seeds are included these give an almond-like flavour.

LOTUS *Nelumbo nucifera* of Asia and *N. lutea* of N. America, extraordinary plants of the family Nelumbaraceae which offer edible leaves, 'roots', seeds, and flowers.

Neither of them was the lotus of the fabled lotus-eaters of Libya; see JUJUBE. However, *N. nucifera* was certainly known in classical antiquity; there is an unmistakable illustration of it in a mosaic in the 'House of the Faun' at Pompeii.

The Asian lotus is much more important than the American one, and is prized mainly for its roots and seeds.

ASIAN LOTUS

The lotus has special significance for Buddhists. It is for them a symbol of purity, undefiled despite its muddy origin. The Buddha is often depicted holding a lotus flower, or seated upon one. It is said that he compared his fellow men to lotus buds in a lake—springing from mud and striving to reach the surface in order to blossom. The lotus also has mystical significance for many non-Buddhists.

The root, properly described as a subaqueous rhizome (swollen stem), resembles huge sausage links, a large string of which may easily measure more than a metre (say, 4'). The 'links' are reddish-brown, and have internal tunnels, as shown in the drawing. They are sliced to provide the ingredient of crisp texture and lacy pattern which is familiar in Chinese stir-fry dishes. The Chinese also candy the slices, for use on special occasions.

Roots can be cut into chunks for use as a vegetable, after the ends and the thick outer skin have been removed. Whole sections of root can be cooked in soups; or stuffed, typically with mashed mung beans, and braised with pork.

The root is also ground into a starchy paste, for use as a thickener; but this is an expensive item, not commonly found outside China.

Lotus roots

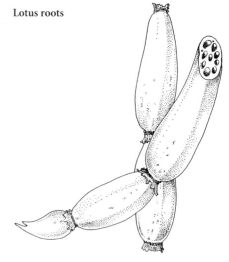

The seeds develop visibly in the top surface of the lotus pod as it ripens and are a pale buff colour when ripe. They split easily into two and are cylindrical, about 1 cm (0.4") long. They can be mistaken for shelled peanuts, and also have a nutty flavour, which is why in Thailand their chief use is in sweets, and why they are candied for festival fare. They also have savoury uses; being sold dried and needing lengthy cooking they are then mainly used in dishes such as stews.

Ground, they produce a starchy meal. If first preserved in a sweetened soy sauce mixture, and then ground, they constitute lotus jam, described by Hawkes (1968) as a favourite filling for certain oriental pastries and desserts.

The leaves, when young, can be cooked as pot-herbs. Older and larger ones are used as wrapping for foods to be steamed, to which they impart some additional flavour.

Unlike the Chinese, the Japanese did not develop the habit of nibbling lotus seeds. The only part they eat is the rhizome, which they call *renkon*. As a food it is prized chiefly for its characteristic crisp texture and peculiar shape. When it is peeled, *renkon* easily turns brown, so it has to be soaked in vinegary water before being used. If pickled in sweetened vinegar it is called *subasu*.

THE AMERICAN SPECIES

N. lutea, known as water-chinquapin, water-nut, duck acorn, and nelumbo, is a native of the eastern parts of the USA (but rare in the north) and of the south from Florida to Texas. It was valued as a food by American Indians. The rhizomes were baked, when they become mealy and somewhat like sweet potatoes. The seeds, which are still sometimes available as a speciality food, and have a pleasant nutty flavour, were prepared in numerous ways, including being ground for use in bread-making.

LOVAGE *Levisticum officinale*, an umbelliferous plant which grows in S. Europe and as far north as England. It resembles wild CELERY in appearance, and was formerly used in the same way, but is milder and sweeter with a distinctively warm, spicy fragrance.

Lovage was popular as a flavouring herb in classical times, and is often mentioned in APICIUS. The Romans called it *ligusticum* because it grew abundantly in Liguria. The altered form *levisticum*, common in late Latin, was the origin of the English and other modern names, and was later adopted as the botanical name. The hardier and coarser-flavoured plant which is sometimes called 'Scotch' or 'black' lovage, but whose correct name is ALEXANDERS, was given *Ligusticum* as its generic name (but has since lost it in favour of *Smyrnium*).

Lovage continued to be grown in medieval kitchen gardens. The leaves were used as a flavouring and to make a cordial; the stems were cooked like celery; and the roots were made into a sweetmeat. The suggestion of 'love' in the name is also seen in German: the plant had a reputation as a love potion.

The eclipse of wild celery by the cultivated type also led to a decline in the use of lovage,

Lovage

which is now little known anywhere. This is a pity, because the flavour is distinctive and, used with discretion, very good in soups, salads, and meat dishes alike.

LOVI-LOVI *Flacourtia inermis*, a low, fruit-bearing tree related to the RAMONTCHI and the RUKAM. It is cultivated in Malaysia, Indonesia, and Sri Lanka both for its fruit and for its decorative foliage.

The fruits are round, the size of small cherries, and dark red when ripe. Most are sour and astringent, and are normally reserved for purposes such as making jellies, preserves, and syrups.

LOZENGES a name commonly applied to small diamond-shaped pieces of sugar confectionery, particularly perfumed SUGAR PASTE; also, a tablet containing some kind of medicinal preparation (for instance, throat lozenges, for coughs). 'Lozenge' refers primarily to the shape, a square or diamond, into which a larger sheet of paste is cut. Thus other items such as biscuits, marzipan, and even preparations of meat may be cut into lozenges.

The word 'lozenge' has puzzled etymologists for years; one hypothesis, stated persuasively by Professor Maxime Rodinson in 1956, is that it derived from Arabic *loz*, almond, via *lauzinaj*, an almond cake known in the Levant from early medieval times. Recipes show this to have been a marzipan-like confection, which was cut into small

pieces for serving. 'Lozenge' first appears in Europe in 14th-century cookery manuscripts as 'losanges', shapes cut from a spiced pasta-like dough, sometimes made with almond milk. By the 16th century it referred to medicinal sweetmeats, and has retained this meaning ever since.   LM

LUCHI is a deep-fried bread made in Bengal, similar to the POORI of N. India. The main difference is that luchi are made with the finest plain white flour, while poori are made with coarser flour which retains a portion of the husk from the wheat.

In appearance a luchi is a round golden disc, 12.5–15 cm (5–6") in diameter and puffed up, although there are many variations in size. The flour is mixed with water and some GHEE, and then kneaded. However, if a larger amount of ghee is added to the dough whilst kneading, the luchi when fried in the oil will become flaky instead of puffy as it also absorbs a lot of oil in the course of frying. It is then known as a *khasta luchi*.

LUDERICK the official name, derived from an Aboriginal name, of an Australasian fish, *Girella tricuspidata*, which is also called blackfish, black bream, and sweep in Australia, and parore in New Zealand. It is especially abundant in the estuaries of New South Wales. Anglers prize it as a game fish, and commercial fisheries for it have some importance.

Doak (1978) has described these fish as 'swift and wary herbivores [which] more resemble deer than grazers such as sheep'. The three cusps (whence *tricuspidata*) on their close-set teeth enable them to crop the seaweeds which are their diet (but, it has been noted, always supplemented by the minuscule animal life found on the seaweed—fish fed with pure seaweed soon fall into a decline).

The name sweep is applied also to related species of Australasian waters, notably *Scorpis aequipinnis*; and the Maori name maomao is given in New Zealand to another relation, *S. violaceus*, a small fish but one which makes good eating.

The opaleye of the S. Californian coast, *Girella nigricans*, is a close relation and another fish which attracts anglers. The small and incidental commercial catch is marketed as 'perch'. The fish is generally perchlike in appearance, with bright blue eyes and an olive green body.

LUMPFISH *Cyclopterus lumpus*, a species with many remarkable features. The flesh is prized much less than the roe, and is sometimes quite inedible. And the fish has a strange 'lumpy' appearance and is equipped with a ventral suctorial disc. The colour of the thick skin is highly variable; blue-grey, yellow-green, and yellow-brown are common, but spawning males are to a large extent red. For some reason it has names in French and German which mean 'sea hare'.

However, the most remarkable and puzzling aspect of the lumpfish is its edibility (or inedibility), which varies by gender and season. Davidson (1979) wrote as follows:

The lumpfish, however, causes puzzlement, at least in countries where it is not familiar. An agreeable perplexity is induced by studying opinions of it expressed by British authors in the past. Sir Thomas Browne, in 1662, recorded it as 'esteemed by some as a festival dish, though it affords but a glutinous jelly, and the skin is beset with stony knobs after no certain order'. Parnell said that: 'The flesh, when cooked, is soft and very rich, and is considered by some of the inhabitants of Edinburgh as a luxury.' The force of the word 'some' is revealed by the additional comment that 'there are few stomachs with which it agrees, in consequence of its oily nature.' Buckland is more critical: 'I do not like the flesh at all myself; it is like a glue pudding.'

Festival dish or glue pudding? The answer is both. There is a considerable difference between the edibility of male and female; which is why there are separate names for them in countries where the lumpfish is well known, such as Sweden and Iceland. And the female is edible at certain seasons but not at others. An Icelander told me that when females with roe were taken and the roe had been extracted, to make lumpfish caviar, what was left was really no more than a glutinous mass, unsuitable even for making fish meal. It goes over the side. The male, on the other hand, provides good eating.

The same source provides detailed information about how people on the northern coast of Iceland, where lumpfish are plentiful, prepare both male (poached with vinegar to become *sodinn raudmagi*) and female (head and tail off, gutted, hung in a cool place until yellowish in colour, when they become *sigin grásleppa* and can be poached before consumption).

The range of the lumpfish is from the Bay of Biscay up to Iceland and the Baltic in the E. Atlantic; and from waters of the far north down to New Jersey in the W. Atlantic. The collection of roe for processing to become 'lumpfish caviar' is practised mainly by Denmark. Although its flavour and feel in the mouth cannot be compared with those of real (sturgeon) CAVIAR, it presents a somewhat similar appearance when spread on small biscuits or little bits of toast.

LUMPIA a pervasive phenomenon of the SE Asian food scene, which has colonized some other parts of the world, e.g. the Netherlands. Whatever it is called—lumpia in Indonesia and the Philippines, *popiah* in Singapore, egg roll for Americans—it is patently part of the SPRING ROLL family based in China. Members of this family all consist of ground or chopped-up food wrapped in a very thin wrapper, usually made of flour and water, with or without egg.

Lumpia have their own entry because they have, so to speak, acquired a life of their own and from one of their power bases, in Indonesia, they have colonized the Netherlands.

In the **Philippines**—to take as an example the country where lumpia-making has been carried to a high pitch of excellence—lumpia can be served in their natural state, or fried; and they can either be part of a meal or eaten as a merienda (snack), see MERENDA.

The filling varies. In the Philippines it can be a mixture of vegetables, sometimes sprinkled with peanuts, and a sweetish sauce with chopped fresh garlic served on the side. This is called *lumpiang sariwa* (fresh lumpia), and may be lined with a leaf of fresh native lettuce. Sometimes the mixture is served unwrapped, and called *lumpiang hubad* (undressed lumpia).

If it is filled with the heart of palm (*ubod*, the pith of the coconut tree, sautéed with shrimps and pork), as it is in Silay City, Negros Occidental, it is called *lumpiang ubod*. In Silay, the coconut trees are cut down for *ubod* the morning of the making, so as to have the *ubod* at its sweetest. A fresh scallion (spring onion) is tucked in for accent.

If the filling is chopped pork, Chinese style, it is usually made in slender cylinders then cut into 1 cm (2") portions, and called *lumpia Shanghai*. This usually comes with a sweet-sour dipping sauce. *Lumpia* may also be filled with fish, with cheese, with shrimps, with sautéed bean curd, with chicken, etc.

If filled with cooking bananas and jackfruit, it is called *turron*, not *lumpia*, and is a sweet snack.

In **Indonesia** a filling of meat and prawns is again used, but one of vegetables is more common. Bean sprouts are popular, again perhaps because of the crisp texture, and because they are cheap, though the original Chinese spring rolls never contained beansprouts. Lumpia are considered snacks, not part of a meal, and they are therefore quite small.

The Dutch picked up the idea and took it back to the Netherlands, where loempia became a popular one-dish meal. They also changed size, turning into giant loempia, many times the size of the originals. See DUTCH COOKERY.

LUNCH an abbreviation of 'luncheon', is the current term in English for a light meal taken in the middle of the day; colloquially, it indicates anything from a quick SANDWICH to an elaborate, leisurely, and sociable meal. In many cultures, the early afternoon is still considered a suitable time to eat the main meal of the day, and there are few foreign equivalents to lunch.

In its modern British form, lunch dates back to a period of social change in the early 19th century, as the time between BREAKFAST and dinner lengthened in the daily routines of the leisured and wealthy. Emerging to fill this gap, lunch was flexible in composition and often informal in nature, to cope with the ever-present possibility of guests—for these hours were also a time of day during which ladies were accustomed to call on their friends and acquaintances (French *déjeuner*, in contrast, began its career as a breakfast meal and moved through the day to occupy a noontime slot, allowing the evolution of the light *petit déjeuner*, now equivalent to breakfast). Subsequently, lunch has been defined by its relationship to other meals, and by the aspirations of those who wish to join the lunch-eating classes. This extends to the form of the word: lunch, as a synonym for luncheon, was considered vulgar in the mid-19th century, but during the 20th century the longer word has become confined to formal occasions and indeed is now obsolete.

Refreshment between breakfast and dinner was not a new idea, nor was it exclusive to those with time on their hands. C. Anne Wilson (1994) discussed various precedents which existed for light meals, showing that down the years these made confusing leaps in timing as they adjusted to alterations in the dinner hour. One such meal was 'nuncheon' or 'bever', ale or beer, accompanied by bread. Nuncheon, a word now confined to dialect usage, is derived from an Anglo-Saxon term meaning 'noon drink' (*bever* derived from the Latin *bibere*, to drink).

The word 'luncheon' itself is older than the meal to which it is now attached. In the 16th and 17th centuries it meant a lump or gobbet of food such as bread, cheese, or bacon. Wilson remarks that these were 'in fact the materials for a light meal' but continues, 'It was still to be some time before luncheon, in our sense of the word, came to the fore.'

In the early 19th century, lunch in the modern sense was mostly partaken of by women, the men (especially those in business and the professions) eating large breakfasts and large dinners, and little in between. There was also a significant social and age distinction, in that poorer people and children continued to eat their main meal in the middle of the day, calling it 'dinner', a habit which has persisted (when a midday meal is provided for schoolchildren it is still referred to as 'dinner'). This gave Geoffrey C. Warren (1958) a problem when defining terms. Considering the Mid-day Meal, 'which practically everyone has in one form or another', he remarks that:

Opinion is divided in an interesting way on what this meal should be called. Roughly, two-thirds call it 'dinner' and one-third 'lunch'. There appear to be two factors that govern the choice of word—the weight of the meal and the degree of sophistication of the person.

He discovered that there were few rules; that some people called it lunch regardless of what was eaten, whereas others made a distinction between a light lunch on working days and a heavy Sunday dinner, despite the fact that both were eaten at midday.

Against this background, it is not surprising that a British lunch has generally lacked gastronomic interest. Many 19th-century lunches appear to have been collations of leftovers, often roast meat, served cold or hashed, supplemented with salad, poultry, or game, plus bread, cheese, and puddings, as the household could afford and required. There are few items specifically associated with the meal, the most notable being plain fruit cakes, recipes for which appear under the title 'luncheon cake' in late 19th-century cookery books. Perhaps these developed from recipes similar to those for the solid yeast-leavened cakes with a sprinkle of currants which, served with beer, composed a mid-morning and mid-afternoon 'bever' in British public schools until the end of the 19th century.

Lunches do, however, vary widely in nature. The concept of a 'ploughman's lunch' of cheese, pickles, bread, and beer seems to have been the product of 1930s ideas about what was appropriate in a rustic context, rather than something based on a survey of what farm labourers actually eat at midday (or, one should add, a survey of classical literature, for that would have brought to light a description by Pseudovirgilius, in the poem called *Moretum*, of the earliest recorded ploughman's lunch being prepared and would thus have legitimized the concept in an unexpected way). A 'proper lunch', i.e. a full meal eaten at leisure, may be viewed in different ways, e.g. as a means of ensuring that one's loved ones absorb adequate nourishment during the day, or alternatively as a maddening interruption to the day's activity, which would be far better punctuated by a light snack. The latter view was eloquently expressed by Elizabeth von Arnim in a passage quoted by Fernie (1905), with which all enthusiastic gardeners and diligent writers (she was both) must surely agree:

Luncheon is a snare of the tempter, and I would fain try to sail by it like Ulysses (tied to the mast) if I only had a biscuit to comfort me; but there are babies to be fed, and the man of wrath, my

husband . . . So I stand by them, and am punished every day by that two-o'clock-in-the-afternoon feeling to which I so much object . . . It is mortifying after the sunshiny morning hours at my pond, when I feel as though I were almost a poet, and very nearly a philosopher, and wholly a joyous animal in an ecstasy of love with life, to come back, and live through those dreary luncheon-ridden hours when the soul is crushed out of sight, and sense, to take up with cutlets, and asparagus, and revengeful sweet things.

(LM)

READING: C. Anne Wilson (1994).

LUNGS often called lights, are the pair of organs used to draw air into the body and bring it into contact with the blood in man and most vertebrates. They often form part of the PLUCK (an expression which covers heart, liver, lungs, and windpipe) and are cooked as part of this item in various dishes, mostly stews. It is rare for them to be prepared on their own for human consumption, although some cuisines have specialized dishes of this nature. It is more usual for lungs to be eaten as an invisible ingredient of meat products such as sausages or pâtés.

LUPIN an annual or biennial leguminous plant of the genus *Lupinus* in the PEA family. Many lupins are grown for their flowers, but the seeds of certain species, although bitter and toxic when fresh, can be treated to make them edible and then roasted for eating or for use as a coffee substitute.

Anissa Helou (1994) has described the lengthy preparation needed to make the seeds into a snack food in the Lebanon. She believes that this food has been part of the diet there since several centuries BC.

Since the discovery in the 1920s of low-alkaloid, 'sweet' lupin plants, cultivars have been developed whose seeds can be used without preliminary preparation. The Saccharatus group of *Lupinus albus* are outstanding in this respect. The cultivar Ultra in this group has been used to produce flour for making lupin pasta.

Toasted and salted seeds, especially of *L. albus* and *L. mutabilis* (Andean lupin or *tarwi*) are served as a snack food or appetizer. *Tarwi* seeds are remarkable for their high protein content (almost 50%) and are also the source of an oil which has culinary uses.

LUTEFISK a speciality of Norway and Sweden, also the Swedish-speaking part of Finland and the Norwegian and Swedish communities in N. America. It consists of STOCKFISH (dried COD, usually, but LING and POLLACK have been used) which has been soaked, steeped in a LYE solution, and then

rinsed lengthily under running water before being boiled. This treatment gives the fish a jelly-like consistency. It is served with boiled potatoes and flatbread. Pepper and melted butter are necessary accompaniments. Regional variations of this standard service exist in both Norway and Sweden.

Whether the origin of lutefisk was in Norway or Sweden is debatable, and debated. What seems clear is that its history goes back to the early 16th century or earlier; and that speculations about how it first came into being (most of these postulate a series of accidents befalling medieval fish curers and/or housewives) lie far outside the boundaries of possible verification.

It is, however, possible to explain its limited geographical distribution. Lutefisk was, and is, eaten in winter, when it is very cold in the Nordic countries. If one postulates as necessary conditions for the emergence of lutefisk (*a*) a strong tradition of fishing and of drying the catch, (*b*) a climate so cold as to permit use of the technique in the days before refrigeration, and (*c*) forests or woods to supply wood ash to produce the lye; then the best candidates in Europe would be Norway and Sweden.

'Lye' is a term which has changed meaning over the centuries. It always indicates an alkaline product, and it is the action of ALKALI on the flesh of the fish which produces the distinctive result. But lye in late medieval times, when it was an all-purpose cleaner, would have been what is also called potash, K_2CO_3, easily prepared for kitchen use by boiling wood ash (ideally beech for lutefisk, but usually birch) in water and straining the result. More recently it would be caustic soda, NaOH, which is stronger; and this is what is currently meant by the term 'lye'. Ordinary washing soda, Na_2CO_3, produced by boiling ash from burned seaweed, has also been used. The addition of lime helps to make the fish whiter and may help in other ways. Both the history and the chemistry of lutefisk have been ably explored by Astri Riddervold (1990*a*).

The same author provides interesting information about the importance of lutefisk as a cultural symbol, especially for Norwegian and Swedish immigrants in N. America. Historically, lutefisk was eaten for supper on Christmas Eve, usually in association with rice pudding, and on Good Friday and Easter Day, and more generally during the whole period from Advent to Easter. At the end of the 19th century, however, came change; roast rib of pork began to usurp the place of lutefisk as the main dish for Christmas Eve supper, while lutefisk moved to another day of the Christmas season and rice pudding, in this particular context, began to disappear.

There might have been further, and more drastic, changes in the last quarter of the 20th century, when statistics showed that both in the countries of origin and among the immigrant communities in N. America the consumption of lutefisk was declining steeply. However, a public relations campaign in the USA halted and reversed the trend there; and it was followed shortly afterwards by a similar campaign in the home countries. Riddervold reproduces samples of the bumper stickers which played an important role in the campaigns, and shows how some of the slogans tended incidentally to create a new myth, that lutefisk is an APHRODISIAC.

LUVAR or louvar, a remarkable and beautiful fish, the only species in its family, Luvaridae. A cosmopolitan species of tropical and subtropical waters, and a loner, it is rarely seen in any fish market, although making an occasional appearance in those of the W. Mediterranean and California, usually because it has been taken incidentally in the course of fishing for TUNA or has stranded itself on a beach. Its diet is unusual, consisting largely of jellyfish. The beauty of its coloration—a pale pink body, blue above, with scarlet fins—attracts immediate attention; and a fully grown adult may be as much as 1.75 m (70") in length and 140 kg (310 lb) in weight. The flesh is reputedly excellent and not unlike that of tuna.

LUXEMBOURG Covering a scant 1,000 square miles, and with a population of less than 400,000, the Grand Duchy of Luxembourg was created by the Congress of Vienna, and became an independent state in 1867. Landlocked by BELGIUM, FRANCE, and GERMANY, it is a green country, traversed by three rivers (and three languages), and ranging in terrain from the Ardennes at its northern border with Belgium to the flatter Gûtland in the south.

In common with many small countries, Luxembourg defends its nationhood fiercely. In spite of this the influence of its neighbours, particularly Belgium, can be clearly detected in its cuisine, with additional, more contemporary, influences coming from Italy and Portugal. Betraying its history of poverty (in stark contrast to its present status as an international banking centre) many traditional dishes reflect a focus on vegetables, especially potatoes and *choucroute* (see SAUERKRAUT), and preserved foods, particularly pulses and smoked hams. This is demonstrated in the typical *Judd mat Gaardebounen*, often cited as the Luxembourg national dish: boiled, sliced smoked pork served with a thick preparation of fresh or dried broad beans flavoured with sage, and boiled potatoes. According to Nosbusch (*c.*1990), *Kermesse* (Christmas) used to be a welcome excuse for more festive fare, with dishes such as the *Kiirmeskuch* (a plain yeast-raised cake with raisins, eaten spread with butter and often topped with a thin slice of smoked ham), and an interesting soup, *Gehäck*, made with pork offal, and finished with prunes soaked in local Elbling wine.

The suffix *à la luxembourgeoise* seems to be used, even by the Luxembourgeois themselves, to cover a multitude of sins. Often denoting a fried piece of meat served with a sauce made with any combination of gherkins, shallots, or capers, it can simply mean the addition of some Luxembourgeois wine such as Riesling to a stew or fish dish. The *Alice B. Toklas Cookbook* (1954) characteristically caps all other contenders with Mashed Potatoes à la Luxembourgeoise: simply replace the milk or cream more usually added with a similar quantity of red wine.   JEL

LYCHEE *Litchi chinensis* (formerly *Nephelium litchi*), is the best and best known of a group of tropical fruits native to China and SE Asia. The name is sometimes spelled 'litchi'. Others in the same genus are the LONGAN, RAMBUTAN, and PULASAN.

Lychees are borne by a large, evergreen tree which has been cultivated in S. China since the 1st century BC, or even earlier. The tree will fruit only in a subtropical or tropical climate where there is a distinct dry season. So it has always been an exotic import for the N. Chinese. During the 1st century AD a special courier service with swift horses was set up to bring fresh lychees from Canton north to the imperial court. The fruit was considered the finest of southern delicacies, and Ts'ai Hsiang, in his *Li chih pu* (Treatise on Lychees), testified to the great demand for it during the Song (Sung) dynasty (AD 960–1279). Growing the fruit was at that time and later a large and ruthlessly competitive business. A lighter aspect is provided by the unusual nomenclature of what were considered to be the finest varieties, including 'glutinous rice dumpling' with its tiny 'chicken-tongue' seeds and 'imperial concubine's laugh'. This last, according to Karp (personal communication, 1997) drawing on Groff (1921), 'commemorates the celebrated Lady Yang, whose passion for lychees, fetched at great cost by the imperial courier service, helped cause the downfall of her lover, the emperor Hsüan Tsung, in 756 AD'. The same author describes how 'clubs of devotees met in temples and gardens to consume hundreds at a sitting' during the later period of the Ming dynasty.

Lychee cultivation now spreads along a narrow belt of suitable climate through Thailand to Bangladesh and N. India (especially Bihar). The Bengal region is especially productive and its crop has become larger than that of China. S. Africa is another major producer, and lychees are also grown in Hawaii. The main N. American area of production is Florida. The fruit travels well if picked just before it is fully ripe, so fresh lychees are available in western countries.

The round fruit is about 3 cm (1") in diameter with a tough, knobbly skin which is red in the ripe fruit but turns brown a few days after being harvested. Inside is a delicate, whitish pulp surrounding a single, large, shiny, dark brown seed (although some varieties contain tiny, abortive seeds). Only the pulp is eaten. It has a flavour reminiscent of the muscat grape.

There are more than a dozen important cultivars of lychee worldwide, with varying characteristics. Thus, of the two main US varieties, the Mauritius is much crisper and less sweet than the Brewster.

Lychees can be dried whole. The skin then becomes distorted and the contents rattle around when the fruit is shaken. The pulp takes on the character of a raisin. The term 'lychee nut' for the dried fruit is a misnomer. The hard nut (seed) within the dried pulp remains inedible.

Canned lychees are peeled and stoned. The industry is a large one, and the product pleasing, but the subtlety, texture, and exquisite perfume of the fresh fruit are largely lost in canning.

LYE a term now used in N. America to denote a dilute solution of caustic soda. In earlier centuries it meant an impure solution mostly of caustic potash, made by boiling wood ash in water. This was of considerable importance, since it and lime were the only alkalis available for tasks such as making soap. The culinary uses of lye (of either kind) include removing the bitterness from green olives and preparing the remarkable preserved fish known in Scandinavia as LUTEFISK.

Ma'amoul are little stuffed pastries traditionally made at Easter in the Middle East, particularly Syria, Jordan, and the Lebanon. They are usually made with SEMOLINA flour but come in various shapes and with a variety of fillings including walnuts, pistachios, almonds, or dates. Very often they are made in special moulds called *tabi* which can be oblong or round and which have indentations which form a pattern on the top of the ma'amoul. After baking they are sprinkled with icing sugar. KARABIJ are similar pastries. HS

Maas an African beverage, favoured by the Zulus and sometimes called *amass* or *amasi*, resembles a pourable YOGHURT.

Emerson gives a pleasing quotation from the book *Zululand* by the Revd Lewis Grout:

Their *amasi*, or thick milk, is made by pouring sweet milk into the *igula*, a large bottle-shaped calabash, where it soon undergoes a kind of fermentation, or acidulous chemical change, from being leavened, as it were, by a little which was left for the purpose when the previous mess was poured out. The whey which is generated by the process is first drawn off and used as a drink, or as

food for the little folks; then comes a rich white inspissated substance, which is neither curd nor bonny-clabber, nor buttermilk, nor anything else but just that light, acidulated, healthy, and to most persons very acceptable, dish which the natives call *amasi*.

Mabolo *Diospyros discolor*, a small SE Asian tree of the ebony family (to which PERSIMMON and KAKI also belong), grown mainly in Malaysia and the Philippines. It has been introduced to India, and is also occasionally cultivated in tropical America.

The round apple-shaped fruits, about 7 cm (3") in diameter, have a velvet-like skin, covered with fine reddish hairs, which encloses cream-coloured, sweet, and aromatic flesh, whose qualities have prompted at least one name meaning 'butter fruit'. Before they are ripe they can be enjoyed as crisp fruit or sliced and fried as a vegetable. Fully ripe fruits are eaten fresh for dessert. The juice can be used in drinks or to make jellies.

The fruits have an unpleasant smell, which accounts for derogatory names such as *caca de chat* (Réunion) and puts some people off them.

Macadamia nuts from the trees *Macadamia integrifolia* and *M. tetraphylla*, indigenous to Australia, are among the finest nuts in the world and are remarkable, historically, in several respects. They were not 'discovered' until the second half of the 19th century; they are unique among Australian food plants in achieving international renown; yet they have, in a sense, been purloined from Australia by Hawaii.

The trees are native to the vicinity of Brisbane in Queensland in NE Australia; and the nuts used to be called Queensland nuts. They were no doubt eaten by Aborigines, as a minor foodstuff gathered from the wild, but remained otherwise unknown until two eminent botanists came upon the trees. One of them, von Mueller, described the tree botanically, and the other, Dr Hill, named it for his friend Dr John Macadam.

Soon afterwards the good edible quality of the nut was discovered (according to one tale by a small boy in Brisbane, said to have been the first person to eat a macadamia nut), and commercial cultivation began on a small scale in the 1880s. Around 1882 the macadamia was introduced to Hawaii, and flourished. Growers there developed new strains, so successfully that Hawaii now accounts for something like 90% of world production. The nuts have become Hawaii's third most important crop and a major export.

Three principal species of *Macadamia* are found in the wild: *M. integrifolia*, with smooth-shelled, edible nuts; *M. tetraphylla* with rough-shelled, edible nuts; and *M. ternifolia*, with small, bitter, inedible nuts. These species interbreed and there used to be confusion about them, so that most older books describe one or both of the edible species as *M. ternifolia*. Improved, thin-shelled cultivated varieties have been bred, mostly from *M. integrifolia* stock with some crossing.

The nuts are borne by the tree in clusters, each nut being encased in a thick, fleshy, green husk. At maturity, the nuts usually fall to the ground and the husks split open, revealing the brown shells, round with pointed ends and up to 2.5 cm (1") in diameter. These are harvested from the ground. The nuts have a high moisture content when gathered, and must first be dried. They will then keep well for several months, but commercial nuts are usually shelled, and the white kernels further air dried; they will keep thus for a year or more. The nuts are often sold in vacuum packs after being roasted, and usually salted too. Roasting develops their pleasantly sweet flavour.

Most are sold to be eaten as they are; but they can also be used in cooking, for which purpose unsalted nuts are preferred; and in confectionery and ice cream, etc. They are recommended as a substitute in Indonesian recipes for CANDLENUTS, which are more difficult to obtain in the West.

Oil and nut butter can be extracted from macadamia nuts. These are of high quality but are not often manufactured, since it is more profitable to sell the nuts whole.

MACARONI the Anglicized version of the Italian *maccheroni*, a tubular form of PASTA which was among the earliest forms to be developed. The term is probably connected with an extinct word, *maccare*, meaning 'to pound'. A trace of the same root survives in modern Italian as *macarie* (rubble)—and also in the MACAROON, an Italian confection of pounded almonds. Be that as it may, the importance of macaroni was such that for a long time, in both Italian and English, the name could be used as a generic one for pasta (excluding only sheet pasta such as LASAGNE and filled pasta such as RAVIOLI).

In Italy *maccheroni* is made in various ways according to the general regional preferences for dressing pasta, thus,

maccheroni alla napoletana (with a tomato sauce) and *alla siciliana* (with aubergines or broccoli). Large-sized *maccheroni* are used for *maccheroni al forno*, a baked dish, and also for *maccheroni ripieni alla Toscana*, for which the maccheroni tubes are filled with a meat stuffing besides having a tomato sauce and grated cheese. A Roman favourite is *maccheroni alla carbonara*, a ham and egg mixture with a creamy sauce.

In England, the fashionable status of pasta in the 18th century was reflected in the slang term 'macaroni' for a dandy, referring in particular to a fantastic type of wig whose white powdered curls were thought to resemble tubular pasta.

There was a tendency in England in the 19th century for macaroni to appear as a sweet dish, reflecting the English fondness for puddings. (In fact there is a respectable tradition of sweet pasta dishes dating back to classical times, and it would be hard to draw a line between a sweet dish of baked lasagne and a pudding. The first puddings called 'puddings' to use pasta had been made in the 17th century with vermicelli, the thinner version of SPAGHETTI, before the arrival of tubular macaroni.) Mrs Beeton (1861) drew on information obtained from a traveller in Naples to explain, twice over, how macaroni is made and eaten, but her two explanations are inconsistent and suggest that she was a victim of the terminological confusion which for long surrounded 'vermicelli' and 'macaroni'. In contrast, Eliza Acton (1845) was completely clear about the tubular form of macaroni and the different sizes available, and even gave different cooking times for Naples and Genoa macaroni, for the smaller *macaroncini*, and for the very large and ornamental 'celery macaroni' (cut in short lengths). Her directions for cooking macaroni as a savoury pasta dish (including some English cheese with the Parmesan, not from patriotism but because she believed the results to be better) and for Sweet macaroni are models of their kind.

In recent times macaroni pudding has been one of the British nursery MILK PUDDINGS, the macaroni being used in the same way as rice or semolina in sister puddings. The usual procedure has been to cook the macaroni in milk and then add eggs, sugar, and flavouring and bake until set. Well made, and subtly flavoured, this is an admirable dish.

Another top favourite dish in England is macaroni cheese, rather different from what an Italian would find acceptable, but well liked in the British Isles.

Elbow macaroni is an American term for short, curved macaroni.

MACAROONS until the 20th century, referred exclusively to small domed biscuit-

like confections composed of sweet ALMONDS, finely chopped, mixed with sugar and beaten egg whites, and baked lightly. They were home made or bought, as skill and necessity dictated. Mrs Beeton (1861) remarked at the end of her recipe for them that it did not cost much more to buy them from a good confectioner. RATAFIAS were similar but usually contained a proportion of bitter almonds.

Macaroons were often served with wine or liqueurs as a light refreshment in the 18th and 19th centuries. They were also used in cookery, to provide texture and flavour in desserts and cakes. Typically, they were crushed and used in TRIFLES; and used whole, as decorations and accompaniments for creams and SYLLABUBS. Almond macaroons are in this way.

Macaroon recipes have appeared in cookery books since at least the late 17th century. These early recipes are sometimes identical to recipes for baked MARZIPAN, including the use of a WAFER underneath the confection. A much wider range of flavourings have been used with the mixture in the past than nowadays; Jarrin (1827) gave eight recipes, some using flavourings of chocolate, vanilla, cinnamon, lemon or orange peel.

Amaretti are small Italian almond macaroons, typically flavoured with bitter almonds or apricot kernels. *Amaretti di Saronno*, from Saronno in N. Italy, use the latter.　　　　　　　　　　　　　　LM

MACE one of the two spices produced by the nutmeg tree, *Myristica fragrans*. This bears a fruit containing a single, nutlike seed. NUTMEG is the kernel of the seed, while mace is the dried aril or 'cage' which surrounds the seed. Like nutmeg, mace is used for both savoury and sweet dishes. Both are ingredients of the English 'pudding spice' (often called 'mixed spice').

Botanical particulars of the two spices and their history are described under nutmeg. Mace is prepared by detaching it from the nut, flattening it, and drying it. Simply dried, it retains most of its natural red colour, and Indonesian mace is usually exported in this form. That from Grenada is first stored in darkness for some months to 'cure' it, takes on a paler, orange-yellow colour, and commands the higher price. Mace from either source normally reaches the consumer in powdered form, but can be had in whole 'blades'.

The properties of nutmeg and mace are not dissimilar, since they derive from the same essential oils, but mace is considered to have the finer flavour.

In Britain the name 'garden mace' is also used of a herb, *Achillea decolorans*, whose leaves are used for flavouring soups and stews. See GARDEN MACE.

MACEDOINE a French term, which came into use towards the end of the 18th century, indicating a salad mixture of fruits or vegetables in small pieces; by analogy with Macedonia, the empire of Alexander the Great, composed of numerous disparate territories. The term is useful and has spread to other languages.

MACEDONIA bears the name given in antiquity to the region which was the heart of the empire of Alexander the Great and has survived in various shapes and sizes, and under various sovereignties, until in 1992 it left the Yugoslav Federation to become an independent state. Here, living side by side, are Turks, Greeks, Gypsies, Albanians, Jews, Vlachs, Serbs, as well as the Macedonians who form the greater part of the popu-lation. The ethnic mix has given rise to the French culinary term MACEDOINE, see above.

The long hot summers of the region herald the Mediterranean climate found fur-ther south; the early mild springs boost the production of early fruit and vegetables—some of the earliest in the Balkans.

Apart from raising quantities of WHEAT and MAIZE, the area is a great centre for GRAPES and many other fruits, RICE, SUNFLOWER (the preferred cooking oil), SESAME, and ANISE.

Sheep breeding is the main object of livestock farming, and Macedonians hold dear their exquisite sheep's milk yoghurt, *ovcho kiselo mleko*, especially that made by shepherds in alpine submontane dairies. This mountain yoghurt is extremely thick, rich, and delicately flavoured under a pale-golden crust of cream. It may be presented together with a bowlful of freshly cooked cornmeal porridge (*bakrdan*), glistening with sheep's milk butter.

Macedonian food is typically Balkan (see BALKAN FOOD AND COOKERY). Old Slavic dishes mingle freely with adaptations from Greek and Turkish kitchens, though often supplemented with hot red chillies or CHILLI powder which give Macedonian country fare its characteristic fiery tang.   MK-J

MACERATE a verb meaning to soften by steeping in a liquid, either cold or hot. It occurs most often, in a culinary context, when fruit is to be softened by steeping it in spirits. It has occasionally been used of steeping foods in brine.

The softening effect can be achieved in various ways. To macerate a hard dried substance in water will cause it to absorb water and swell and become softer. Or the softening effect of the liquid may be achieved by its removing gummy substances which cement cells together. Equally, there may be chemical processes at work, if the liquid is acid or alkaline; or the softening can result from the liquid activating micro-organisms or ENZYMES already present in the substance.

MACKEREL *Scomber scombrus*, a common fish of N. Atlantic and Mediterranean waters. With its brilliant greeny-blue back marked with dark curving lines, its metallic sides, and white belly, it is a handsome fish. One might almost describe it as flashy in appearance, noting that the French name *maquereau* also means pimp and that in the past mackerel was a term for dandy in England.

Mackerel are oceanic fish, which normally swim in very large shoals. Their range extends from the Black Sea and the Mediterranean to Norway and Iceland; and from Labrador on the American side down to Cape Hatteras. Their maximum length is 55 cm (22") or a little more, but the common market length is around 30 cm (12").

The chub mackerel, *Scomber colias*, is common in the Mediterranean and is also found on the Iberian and French Atlantic coasts, and in New England waters. It is smaller and has more delicate markings and bigger eyes (hence the Sicilian name *occhi-grossi*), but fishmongers have little reason to distinguish it from its better-known relation.

There are several mackerel in the Indo-Pacific, of which *Rastrelliger kanagurta*, the rake-gilled mackerel (length up to 45 cm/18"), and *R. brachysoma*, the short-bodied mackerel (up to 35 cm/14"), are the most common. They provide the most important fishery in the Gulf of Thailand, and are the favourite marine fishes of the Thai people. The latter is one of the most important food fishes in the Philippines.

Mackerel have a relatively high oil content, and spoil quickly. This is why, since the end of the 17th century, there has been a special dispensation to sell them in England on Sundays. It also explains why a tart acid sauce is recommended to go with the fish. GOOSEBERRY is the best known, but unsweetened CRANBERRY or RHUBARB are also good. The flesh of a fresh mackerel has an excellent flavour, and is easily separated from the bones.

Hot-smoked mackerel, which needs no further cooking, is popular in western countries. Dried mackerel may be had in SE Asia.

See also FRIGATE MACKEREL and SPANISH MACKEREL.

MADAGASCAR (Malagasy Republic), the fourth largest island in the world, could almost count as a continent, since, as one of the guide books points out, it 'occupies its own tectonic plate', so that the indigenous species, plant and animal, evolved separately from those in Africa. What humans choose to eat in Madagascar must take account of the threat which wholesale consumption would pose to species which exist only in this huge island.

The Malagasy, as the inhabitants of the island are known, are mainly descended from the Malay/Indonesian and Polynesian seafarers who were the first arrivals somewhere around 500 AD. It is on the west coast that people of African (Bantu) descent are found. Half the population count as Christians and almost the whole of the other half profess 'traditional beliefs'. The virtual absence of Muslims and Hindus (although there are a few Indians and Chinese on the island) minimizes food taboos. French influence is noticeable, reflecting the period when the island was a French colony (1896–1960).

RICE is the staple. For breakfast it appears in *sosoa*, a soupy version, otherwise in the usual 'dry' form, *apangoro*. Rice is often cooked in an earthenware pot, the centre portion eaten and the rest caramelized or 'burnt' to make *apango*. This is mixed with boiling water to make *ranon'apango*, rice water, which is drunk with meals.

CASSAVA is another staple food, often supplementing rice in filling the need for carbohydrate. Where bread is used it is called *mofo* and is mostly baked in baguettes (see FRENCH BREAD).

Savoury dishes are, on the whole, not highly spiced, though a paste of chilli, ginger, and garlic, called *sakay*, is used in some. There is also a Malagasy version of PIL-PIL, and another sauce with chilli in it (plus tomato, onion, lemon, ginger) called *rougaille*. As an accompaniment to savoury dishes there is, as elsewhere in E. Africa and India, the spicy pickled vegetable confection known as *achards* (see ACHAR).

The national dish is *Romazava*, a soupy stew of beef, pork, and chicken with tomatoes and BRÈDES.

The 'national dessert' and often the only dessert on a menu is *banane flambée*. However, there are also coconut sweets, and yoghurt has become popular. VANILLA is an important crop in the island, so this import-ant flavour occurs readily in sweet dishes.

MADEIRA the beautiful Atlantic island which belongs to PORTUGAL and has long been famous for its Madeira wine, a fortified wine which has appealed to British palates over the centuries and also has many uses in cookery besides being associated with

MADEIRA CAKE (see below).

The food of the island has several interesting features, not least of which is the predominance in the fish market of TUNA and black SCABBARD FISH, *Aphanopus carbo*. It is the basis of several particularly good fish dishes.

A balmy climate ensures a plentiful supply of fruits and vegetables, remarked upon by many famous voyagers (e.g. Charles Darwin aboard HMS *Beagle*) who called at the island en route for more distant destinations. This climate is conducive to the cultivation of MAIZE, and the cuisine of the island, especially in some of the rural areas, includes interesting survivals of breads and dishes made with maize.

MADEIRA CAKE a rich cake made by the creaming method, flavoured with lemon zest, and decorated with a thin slice of candied CITRON; some recipes are similar to POUND CAKE. Jane Grigson (1974) remarks:

This cake was served with Madeira and other sweet wines in the nineteenth century, hence the name. Although it is now a popular cake at tea time, to enjoy it at its best serve it with Madeira in the old style.   LM

MADELEINE a small French cake associated with the town of Commercy in Lorraine. The true *madeleines de Commercy* are made from egg yolks creamed with sugar and lemon zest, with flour, noisette butter, and stiffly beaten egg whites folded in before baking in little shell-shaped moulds.

Legends about the origin of the name are critically discussed by Claudine Brécourt-Villars (1996). Madeleines have earned themselves an immortal place in literature, as the taste of one dipped in limeflower TISANE provided the basis for Marcel Proust's celebrated reference to them, and the phrase 'a madeleine of Proust'.

As Ayto (1993) observes, the name 'madeleine' has also been applied, for reasons which are obscure, to an English product: 'a small individual sponge cake in the shape of a truncated cone, covered in jam and desiccated coconut, and surmounted with a glacé cherry.'

MADIA 'nut', the seed of *Madia sativa*, a plant of S. America and the western seaboard of N. America. It is sometimes called Chile tarweed.

The seeds are edible, raw or roasted, and can be used to make PINOLE. They are also the source of madia oil, a sweet oil which has occasionally been used in place of olive oil. The plant is said to be cultivated for these purposes.

MADRAI (pronounced mandrai) is the Fijian word for BREADFRUIT, and also for a fermented product found in various of the Oceanic Islands.

The traditional way of using breadfruit in Fiji was to make the fermented product, which was also to be found in Samoa. Slightly unripe breadfruit was packed into a pit lined with leaves and covered with soil. After a fermentation of four or five weeks, the breadfruit had turned into a doughlike paste, which was then kneaded, deseeded, formed into patties and baked in coconut-smeared leaves in an earth oven (see NEW ZEALAND). The food which emerged was not unlike bread. Breadfruit has been known to ferment for up to a year in one of these Polynesian pits.

MAHLAB (mahleb, mahaleb), a spice obtained from kernels of the black (or mahaleb or St Lucy's) CHERRY, *Prunus mahaleb*. This tree is native to Asia Minor but now grows wild or in gardens throughout Europe. The stones of the fruits contain kernels, which are a beige colour and about the size of a peppercorn. These are quite soft and have a nutty chewiness. They are ground and used to give a sweet and spicy flavour to biscuits, cakes, and breads of Turkey, Lebanon, and elsewhere in the Middle East. The spice has also gained a foothold in Greece, perhaps via Cyprus; and it occurs in Armenian recipes.   HS

MAHSEER the most famous angling fish of India, belongs to the group of fish known by the general name BARB. However, not all authorities assign it to the genus *Barbus*; some would place it in *Tor*. In any case, one should refer to 'them' rather than 'it', because there are two main species.

- *Barbus tor*, the tor mahseer, is the better known of the two, and an important food fish. It may reach a length of 1.2 m (4') and is widely distributed in the rivers of the foothills of the Himalayas. It is easily recognized by its bright coloration: golden-green back, golden sides, silver belly, and orange-red pectoral fins.
- *B. putitora*, the putitor mahseer, may be twice as long and has been the subject of many tales by 'sport fishermen' in India. It is less common than the other, and somewhat less bright in its colours.

MAIDENHAIR BERRY the fruit of a trailing plant, *Chiogenes hispidula*, which occurs principally in Canada, but also in the state of Maine where it is known as 'moxie-plum'. Another Canadian name for it is 'capillaire'; and it is also called 'creeping snowberry'. The ivory-white berries are juicy and:

pleasantly acid, with a mild suggestion of checkerberry, but when eaten with cream and sugar they are one of the greatest delicacies of the northern woods, having, in addition to the mild, lemon-like acidity and the checkerberry-flavor, a suggestion in their aroma of heliotrope.

Fernald and Kinsey (1943), whose eulogy this is, go on to exemplify by this plant the 'danger to the uninformed which lurks in colloquial names'. In France and francophone Canada the name *capillaire* refers to the maidenhair fern. A certain Sir Richard Bonnycastle, having visited Newfoundland and no doubt tasted the famous preserve, published an account of Newfoundland plants in which he confounded the fern with the berry-bearing plant, observing that the former bore luscious little white berries. This error was then taken over by an encyclopedia, and the myth of the fern which bears berries became established: a dreadful warning to the compilers of works such as the present one.

MAIDS OF HONOUR are pastry tartlets filled with a white CURD, which is usually made with renneted milk and cream, butter, sugar, almonds, eggs, and lemon juice and zest. They have a historical association with Richmond and Kew in Surrey.

Various stories associate them with Tudor royalty but no one has been able to establish whether the maids of honour were themselves the main consumers or simply used them to please royal palates. The first reference in print, according to Ayto (1993), is 1769 in the *Public Advertiser*.

MAIZE (*see page 470*)

MAKRUT LIME *Citrus hystrix*, a member of the CITRUS family which is important in SE Asian cookery, is known as *makrut* in Thailand. In English, it has been called 'makrut lime' by several authorities, notably Saunt (1990); and this name is preferable to 'kaffir lime', for reasons explained under KAFFIR.

The fruit itself, which is knobbly and bitter, is used for its acrid juice, but the leaves are a more common ingredient and appear in SE Asian dishes with a frequency bordering on automaticity. They have a figure of eight shape, and it is usual to tear them into halves or small pieces before adding them to dishes, removing them when cooking is completed. In this and other respects they are similar to the BAY LEAVES used in European cookery. The flavour which they impart has the same general

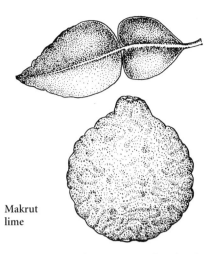

Makrut
lime

character, and substitution can therefore be practised when necessary.

MALABAR GOURD

Cucurbita ficifolia, is also called zambo or Malabar melon or ivy-leaved gourd. This perennial CUCURBIT vine is cultivated on a minor scale and enjoys some popularity as a vegetable in Latin America from Mexico, its probable region of origin, down through the highlands of the Andes to C. Chile.

The fruit, which may weigh as much as 11 kg (24 lb), is white, green, or white and green striped. It has black seeds and white flesh, whose uses have been well summarized in *Lost Crops of the Incas* (National Research Council, 1989):

The young fruit are used like zucchini. The mature fruits are prized especially for desserts, usually cooked and served in sweet syrup. . . . Mature, they are commonly stored (kept dry, but without any special care) for two years, and yet their flesh remains fresh and actually gets sweeter with age. They are eaten boiled or in preserves.

MALANGA

(or yautia, or tannia), the names used respectively in Cuba, Puerto Rico, and the English-speaking W. Indies for plants of the genus *Xanthosoma*, which provide edible corms and leaves. The third name is a corruption of the original Carib name *taia*. These plants belong to the arum lily family, as does the better-known tropical root crop TARO. But taro and other members of the species are native to the Old World, while malanga comes from the W. Indies and the adjoining region of tropical America.

Malanga corms may be 30 cm (1') long and are brown or yellow-brown outside and ivory or yellowish within. The skin is thick and often exhibits a pattern of rings towards the apex. Unlike taro, they have a blunt, potato-like shape. But the two have many characteristics in common: a tendency to produce small, secondary cormels around the central corm; sometimes the presence of acrid, irritating calcium oxalate crystals, especially in the skin, which have to be neutralized by peeling and cooking; and a texture and flavour superior to that of most starchy tropical roots.

In view of these similarities it may seem strange that, following the arrival of European settlers in America, taro has been grown in the W. Indies; while malanga has been introduced in Africa and, on a small scale, in SE Asia. The reason is that the two are complementary. In regions with a suitably warm climate malanga grows best in dry places and taro in wet ones, so that they may be cultivated respectively on hillsides and in valleys. In W. Africa, where both taro and malanga are staple foods, next in importance only to CASSAVA and YAMS, they are known as 'old' and 'new cocoyam'.

Species grown mainly for their tubers are: *Xanthosoma sagittifolium* (yellow yautia), whose small cormels around the central corm are called 'nut eddos' in the W. Indies; and *X. violaceum* (primrose malanga).

Species cultivated mainly or exclusively for their leaves are: *X. atrovirens* (dark-leaved malanga); and *X. brasiliense* (belembe). The leaves, generally consumed in the same ways as spinach, are a frequent ingredient of the popular Caribbean soup CALLALOO.

MALAYSIA, SINGAPORE, AND BRUNEI

politically separate but geographically united, are here dealt with together. Malaysia itself falls into two large parts (W. and E. Malaysia, with Singapore adjoining the former and Brunei the latter) and possesses a trio of principal cuisines (Malay, Indian, Chinese). Of Malaysia's population of close to 20 million, over half are Malays and Muslim; a third are *Peranakan* (Straits Chinese, mostly in Penang, Malacca, and Singapore, with roots in S. China); and 10% Indians, many from S. India.

W. Malaysia (the Malay peninsula) is part of mainland Asia and its northern states are influenced by its Thai neighbours. E. Malaysia (formerly the states of Sabah and Sarawak in the north of the huge island called Borneo, now mostly belonging to Indonesia) is a melting pot of tribes, traders, and adventurers, an island with a frontier mentality.

The fact that Indian and Chinese influence is so strong in Malaysia (stronger than in Indonesia) is the result of mass movements of labour during the colonial period. Even before that time, however, the under-population and under-development of peninsular Malaya attracted immigrant élites from E. and S. Asia and eventually from Europe. Every group brought its religion, but Islam has been dominant in the peninsula and in the coastal towns of Borneo since the 16th century or earlier. All these traditions have left their marks on cooking and eating.

An example is nonya (or nyonya) cooking. It is associated with Chinese immigrants who settled in Malacca in the 15th century, Penang somewhat later, and Singapore any time up to the Second World War. In former times, the men were addressed as 'Baba' and their wives as 'Nonya'. Daughters of well-to-do families were trained from earliest childhood in all the skills needed to run a household, and were expected above all to be expert cooks. Nonya cooking uses chillies, shrimp paste, coconut milk, and aromatic roots and leaves as in the Malaysian and Indonesian traditions, but it has retained the use of pork and noodles from its Chinese past. It values hotness and sourness, using tamarind more often than lemon grass.

The above shows that the culinary scene is a complex one. That said, one may nonetheless make generalizations. The staple food is RICE. This is called *beras* (or *nasi* when cooked) by the Malays, *fan* by the Chinese, and *arisi* (Tamil) or *chawal* (Hindi) by Indians. Rafi Fernandez (1985) describes the various ways of cooking rice in Malaysia and points out that 'in many homes it is cooked for all the three main meals'.

The secondary staple is seafood, which, like seafood everywhere, involves numerous species, of which the POMFRET is the most prized. Prawn/shrimp pastes (BLACANG/ *terasi* or the milder Chinese *hei-ko*) are a marine ingredient used in a very large number of dishes, as is dried ANCHOVY and FISH SAUCE. Besides rice and seafood, NOODLES are prominent, especially at hawkers' stalls, offering dishes such as fried

(cont. on page 471)

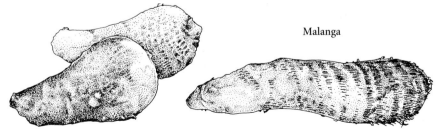

Malanga

Maize

Zea mays, one of the most important cereal crops in the world, has another name: CORN. This other name is used in N. America to refer to the sweet kinds of maize (sweetcorn) suited to human consumption; and in numerous familiar words and phrases such as POPCORN, 'corn on the cob', etc.

Like MILLET and SORGHUM, maize is a kind of grass, but it is readily distinguished from its relations by the large seed heads (cobs), and by the relatively short time which it takes to mature.

It is generally agreed that maize, although it exists in a bewildering variety of forms, is a single species and that this species originated in C. and S. America, probably as a result of a wild ancestor (which disappeared in prehistoric times) crossing with the related plant teosinte. No present form of maize is capable of self-propagation; and wherever it grows it is grown by man.

The oldest known remains of the wild ancestor of maize are grains of pollen found in an archaeologist's drill core—a way of sampling soil layers—taken in the excavations for the foundations of a new building in Mexico City. These remains are about 70,000 years old, and so date from a time before there were human beings in that region. Another archaeological dig in Tehuacán, Mexico, revealed the very small cobs, about 2 cm (0.75") long, of a wild maize which, judging from other remains found at the same site, seem to have been sown deliberately, not just gathered from wild plants. The date of this site is reckoned to be about 5500 BC. Bat Cave in New Mexico, inhabited since 4500 BC, has produced similar remains. This primitive maize had about 50 grains and was similar in type to a very small popcorn.

The oldest S. American remains come from Peru and date from about 1000 BC, by which time the whole continent was well inhabited and people were moving from one region to another, so that the development of maize became a matter of human selection and dissemination rather than botanical accident.

Maize plants bear seed heads ('ears') which are larger than those of any other kind of grass; modern varieties may have heads which, exceptionally, measure up to 60 cm (24") long. The grains are set in rows on a solid central 'cob'. There is always an even number of rows, 8 to 32, and there may be as many as 1,200 grains on a cob. In all modern varieties, the whole ear is covered by a few modified leaves which form the husk, which prevents the grains from falling off when they are ripe. This feature, although convenient for human beings, is what prevents the plant from reproducing itself naturally; if left on the plant, the ears simply rot away.

Another peculiarity of the maize plant is that the stem bears male and female flowers some distance apart from each other. The male flowers form a 'tassel' at the top of the tall stem. The female flowers are a considerable distance below them. These have a 'silk' or hairy plume at the tip which catches pollen blown off neighbouring male flowers by the wind. One hair extends from each undeveloped grain. Once pollinated, the female flowers become mature ears. Each plant may have one or two ears. The grains may have a hard or relatively soft coat of any of a large range of colours: white, yellow, orange, red, brown, purplish-blue, or nearly black, or with spots or streaks of several colours. Most modern varieties have white or yellow grains.

The greatest single dissemination of maize, transforming it from an American staple into a global one, is discussed in the box.

Whatever the truth may be about global dissemination, it took place after the main types of corn suitable for direct human consumption had been developed. These types (each of which is now represented by numerous varieties and cultivars), are as follows.

- Flint corn has relatively small grains, hard skins, and a good flavour. American Indians like the flavour and did not find the hard skin a disadvantage since they usually dried the ears before using them, so that any type of corn would need to be softened to make it edible.

DISSEMINATION

THE generally accepted view has been that Columbus discovered maize in the New World in 1492 and brought it back to Spain, whence it was taken with great rapidity to other parts of Europe, to Africa, and through the Middle East and India to China. Proponents of this view acknowledge as a difficulty that the earliest recorded references to maize in Europe give it names such as 'gran turco', but suggest that this was mere confusion, of the same sort which resulted in an American bird receiving the name 'turkey'.

An alternative school of thought holds that maize must have arrived in Asia, Africa, and Europe before 1492. The early names which it had in these three continents are cited as evidence that the plant had a Middle Eastern (Balkan, Turkish, Arabic) centre of distribution in the Old World; and the already strong argument from nomenclature is fortified by accounts of early travellers in Africa and elsewhere (all this being ably set out, with a multitude of references, by Jeffreys, 1975) and by pointing to the inherent improbability that a plant which first reached Spain in 1492 could have been under cultivation in the E. Indies in 1496 and in China by 1516. (Also, there seems to be archaeological evidence of its having reached Papua New Guinea (via Polynesia) 1,000 years ago. Once there, it could have travelled westwards through SE Asia and S. Asia, and then have been carried by Arabs to Africa.)

The controversy, for those who admit that there is one, is alluring, not least because acceptance of the second hypothesis would imply that other New World plants could have reached the Old World in pre-Columbian times.

- Flour corn, also called 'soft' or 'squaw' corn, has larger (sometimes huge) ears with big, starchy grains. This type was spread northwards from Mexico by Indians. One of the principal kinds of corn grown by the Hopi and nearby tribes is the variety Hopi Blue, a flour corn with blue grains. Various flour corns are used for the large-scale production of cornmeal in S. America.
- Dent corn is so named because the grain has a hard coat only around its sides, and the top—the side facing outwards on the ear—has a collapsed dimple in it when the corn is ripe. The grains are fairly large and starchy. This type spread north only after the arrival of the Europeans. It was the type on which the 'corn belt' of the south central United States was founded; but here it was always used more as animal fodder than for human consumption.
- Sweetcorn has kernels which are easily recognized by their wrinkled exterior. As Facciola (1990) puts it: 'their sweetness is the result of a genetic defect in metabolism which prevents the sugars in the kernel from being completely transformed into starch.' Sweetcorn is mostly used as 'corn on the cob'.
- POPCORN has its own entry.

As a staple food, maize is less good than wheat or rice in respect of its PROTEIN content and the quality of that protein. However, the diet of the ancient American Indians, which in most parts was mainly of maize, beans, and squash with a little animal food as available, was a sound one, since the beans made up the missing factors of the maize. Even now in much of Latin America a similar diet is followed.

Moreover, the adoption by the Aztec and Maya civilizations of the process known as NIXTAMALIZATION, which is essentially treatment with an ALKALI, improved the quality of maize protein considerably. Betty Fussell (1992) explains the process and the chemistry by which it affects this improvement; essentially it 'unlocks' important AMINO ACIDS which are present in maize but would not otherwise be 'available'. N. American Indians for whom maize was and is the staple have continued to use the process; but its import-ance has never been generally realized in the other continents to which maize travelled.

Besides being food for the stomach, maize has been of considerable importance as food for the imagination and for myths. Betty Fussell has an admirable chapter on myths involving maize. On a smaller scale, Janice B. Longone has produced a booklet prepared to accompany an exhibition on 'Mother Maize and King Corn: The Persistence of Corn in the American Ethos' (Ann Arbor, 1986), in which she pulls together such themes and literary references, with lore of all sorts; Aztec material rubs shoulders with a glossary of Narragansett Indian terms involving corn, quotations from the poet Carl Sandburg, a thumbnail history of popcorn, and a complementary section on the liquid corn of Kentucky ('where the corn is full of kernels and the colonels full of corn').

Some **maize products** have their own entries: see CORN-FLOUR (a fine form of cornmeal), CORN SYRUP, and HOMINY. The use of maize to produce certain BREAKFAST CEREALS is another matter. HUITLACOCHE (maize smut fungus) is not a maize product but rather a by-product.

Maize is used to produce various sorts of PORRIDGE or cornmeal mush.

Baked goods are numerous and varied. Maize is widely used in the production of CORN BREADS. Cornmeal may be used in conjuction with other flours (wheat, rye, etc.) to produce hybrid loaves; see, for example, Boston brown bread under BREAD VARIETIES. In addition there are kinds of bread which may be made from cornmeal or may be based on another grain; American ashcake (see again BREAD VARIETIES) is an example. For corn pone, johnny cake, and spoon breads, see CORN BREADS.

Maize has been used as the basis for many sorts of dishes in the continents to which it emigrated from America. One example is *Kenkey*, a Ghanaian dish of fermented maize balls, steamed in maize husks and served hot with pepper fish. It has also made a reverse migration to the Caribbean where it appears as Kanki, Conkie, or (in Jamaica) 'Tie-a-leaf'.

For other dishes based on maize, see ATOLE; HUSH PUPPY; MAMALIGA; POLENTA; SUCCOTASH; TAMALES; TORTILLAS. For scrapple, see PENNSYLVANIA DUTCH.

---

kway teow, a common sight in market areas, 'five-foot paths', and night stores. Generally, street food is wonderfully good. Singapore offers one of the most striking examples of that excellent arrangement whereby what is a parking lot during office hours is transformed, with amazing rapidity, in the evening into a ring of food stalls with a communal eating area in the middle.

Other characteristic items include SATAY, now widely adopted in the western world in its usual chicken or beef versions and of which an elaborate seafood version was recorded by Davidson (1977); RENDANG; and the elusive *rempah*—elusive because it is a spice mixture (often fried before use) which is constantly called for but varies considerably in composition. Singapore, incidentally, is one of the world's greatest entrepôts for spices, so has unrivalled resources in this respect.

SAMBAL and ACHAR (*acar*) are two more food terms which one meets everywhere; and they are among those which have been taken by Malay emigrants to S. Africa; for the human traffic has not all been one way, into Malaysia and Singapore—many have gone out as well as in.

MALDIVES islands in the Indian Ocean, to the south-west of the southern tip of INDIA and to the west of SRI LANKA. These islands, which now constitute an Islamic republic, were thought by Marco Polo to number over 12,000, but the modern count is close to just 1,200, of which 200 or so are inhabited. The republic is unique in having far more than 99% of its extensive territory be sea; the land area adds up to only about the same as Singapore.

The sea and the lagoons provide the dominant feature of the diet, which is fish. It is likely to come with RICE, onion,

COCONUT, CHILLI pepper, and lime juice; and it is likely to be either one of the numerous reef fish or a species of TUNA. Some tuna is sold fresh in the islands; some is canned; and much is either smoked (*valhoamas*) or smoked and sun dried (*hikimas*). This is the 'Maldive fish' which is such an important feature of cookery in Sri Lanka, usually finely ground, to become a potent flavouring and thickening agent.

The tuna theme appears in other ways. What might be called the national dish of the Maldives is a soup (*garudhiya*) with chunks of tuna in it. There is also a tuna paste, *rihaakuru*, which has been likened to Marmite. And tuna will be in the filling of the 'short eats' called *gulha* and *bajiyaa*.

Tropical fruits are plentiful for dessert, and there are also confections made with coconut, honey, rice flour, palm tree sap, banana, etc.

MALLARD

MALLARD *Anas platyrhynchos*, a wild DUCK which may fairly claim to be the most important of its kind, given its circumglobal range in cold and temperate zones of the northern hemisphere, the fact that it is the ancestor of most domesticated ducks in Europe, and its good eating qualities. Indeed, the term 'wild duck' is an alternative name for it.

It is a surface-feeder, quite large (average total length nudging 60 cm/24"), and highly adaptable; it is at home in almost any wet lowland countryside, in urban and suburban environments, and in marine areas outside the breeding season.

A mallard need not be hung before being cleaned and eaten. It is best when roasted or braised. Accompaniments include bitter orange, and there are several ways of enriching the gravy, e.g. with port wine. The breasts are much the best parts. The quality of the birds is said to be at its best, in Britain, in September; and the same is more or less true in N. America.

MALLOW

MALLOW the name of various plants in the family Malvaceae which because of their mucilaginous properties have a role in the herbal medicines of many countries. Many authors have attested to their virtues, but none more sweepingly than Pliny in the 2nd century AD:

About these [mallows and marshmallows] many other amazing things are said, but the most striking is that if anyone takes daily half a ladleful of the juice of any of them, he will be free from all diseases.

Mallows are, however, sometimes eaten as pot-herbs. Those of the genus *Malva* are treated here. The MARSHMALLOW, of the genus *Althaea*, has its own entry. For musk mallow, see MUSK.

The common and largest European mallow is *M. sylvestris*, typically found on roadsides and bearing pale reddish-purple flowers. Scalloped, disc-shaped fruits develop from these, and are likened in many countries to cheeses. In England they used to be called 'bread and cheese', and the 19th-century peasant poet John Clare wrote of 'Picking from Mallows . . . The crumpled seed we call a "cheese" '. A popular name in France for the plant is *herbe fromage*, and the Germans refer to the smaller *M. pusilla* as *Käsepappel*. Geoffrey Grigson described the 'crisp and slimy' cheese-like discs as having a taste like that of monkey nuts (see GROUNDNUT).

The immature fruits of *M. neglecta*, the common or dwarf mallow, are likewise referred to as 'cheese' or 'biscuits'; and *M. parviflora* has been called 'cheese weed'. Charlotte Clarke (1978) gives several interesting recipes for the latter species, including a creamed soup.

The leaves of *M. sylvestris* were eaten as a green vegetable in classical times by the Greeks and Romans, and this use has continued on a small scale. It is more common in the Orient, where *M. verticillata*, whose seeds are also used as a condiment,

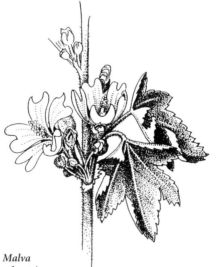

Malva sylvestris

are those most often used. The elegantly curled leaves of the cultivar Crispa of this species make a handsome addition to salads. Lucian, writing in the 2nd century AD *On Salaried Posts in Great Houses*, explains that the Romans used mallow leaves as a garnish for dishes and that, if you were among the last to be served, you risked having nothing but mallow.

The family also includes some shrubs and trees (see KAPOK; ROSELLE). Insofar as the whole group has common characteristics,

these are a tendency for edible parts to have a sour taste caused by the presence of malic acid (named for the apple, Latin *malus*, not for the mallow) and for other parts to be fibrous; many species are grown as a source of textile fibres.

MALT

MALT or malted grain, is grain which has been induced to germinate. It can be had either whole or in milled form. In the West most malt is made from BARLEY, and is chiefly used in making beer and whisky, and for the production of malt VINEGAR; but it is also important in BREAD-making, and a little is turned into malt extract.

Malting is the task of maltsters, and its technology is now far advanced. In summary the process involves steeping the grain (selected for its malting quality) until it 'chits', which means that rootlets burst through the seed coatings; letting germination proceed for a limited time, the length of which depends on end use, and then killing the embryos by heat; kilning the 'green malt' to varying degrees of dryness and colour; and milling it, if appropriate.

The purpose of all this is to bring about chemical changes, of which the most important is the secretion by the growing embryo of an ENZYME, amylase, which converts STARCH in the grain to maltose, a SUGAR. Dextrins, which are gummy CARBOHYDRATES with a slightly sweet taste, are also produced. The resulting malt is suitable for fermentation. If beer or vinegar is to be made from it, the milled malt is 'mashed' in hot water to produce a filtered liquid which is the 'wort' of brewers.

For bread-making, the milled malt is not mashed, but added directly to the flour. Besides being a direct source of sugar, the malt is able to convert starch in the flour to sugar. The sugar thus doubly provided feeds the yeast, helping the bread to rise well, and also provides an attractive flavour.

Much ordinary white bread, at least in Britain, contains a little malt. 'Granary bread' is made from a malted meal, with whole grains of cracked wheat scattered through it. There are also, in Britain, sweet, sticky 'malt loaves' commonly made of wheat flour and barley malt.

Malt is nutritious, providing energy from its sugar plus some B-group vitamins and minerals. During the 19th century it had a reputation in Britain as a restorative food for invalids and sickly children, and was added to their diet in various forms. *Law's Grocer's Manual* (*c*.1895) remarks that:

malt would seem to have become a boon and a blessing not to babes alone but to speculators as well. Besides malt bread, malt coffee, and malt sugar, there are various other preparations designated as malted: malted cocoa, malted marmalade, malted preserves, malted jellies, etc.

One result of this fad was the invention of malt extract. If the brewer's wort, referred to above, is not fermented but instead evaporated in a partial vacuum, the result is malt extract, a brown, sweet, and sticky concentrate. This is sometimes used in bread-making.

Malt extract, although its reputation as a health food has diminished, is still sold in dried and powdered form for making malted drinks.

See also MIZUAME.

MALTA and Gozo are the largest of a group of islands in the C. Mediterranean. One of these islands, Comino, is said to derive its name from CUMIN, which may have been grown there.

The Maltese cuisine is influenced by its physical closeness to ITALY and is largely based on PASTA and vegetable dishes, while the Gozitans have developed some local dishes, mainly rich pies using RICE, PUMPKIN, and soft cheeses called gbejniet.

Malta was first occupied by the Phoenicians. Succeeding occupations have left their mark, though perhaps the strongest influence, as regards eating habits, has been that of the Roman Catholic Church which has held sway in Malta since St Paul was shipwrecked there in AD 60; the Knights of St John, in whose hands Malta was for many centuries, were drawn from the nobility of Catholic Europe. A number of people retain the custom of eating fish on Fridays and a favourite 'cake' called qwarezimal is eaten during Lent. It contains neither fat nor eggs, so it is considered suitably penitential.

There is another factor. Since Malta belonged to Britain for 150 years, the restaurants, when they came into existence, were biased towards English food; and the development of tourism, geared as it was to include a high proportion of British visitors, tended to keep them that way in the early decades of independence. This has unfortunately given the Maltese restaurant cuisine a bad name. However, the demand for, and interest in, Maltese dishes, hitherto confined to Maltese homes and consequently invisible to the outside world, has been growing.

Many Maltese dishes depend on local food resources. Thus the strikingly beautiful DOLPHIN FISH (lampuki to the Maltese) occurs in unusual abundance in Maltese waters and is the main ingredient in lampuki pie and in other dishes during the season which lasts from August to November.

Malta is also blessed with fine fruit, for example the famous Maltese oranges, specially the blood oranges which give sauce maltaise its name. Apropos of oranges, Joseph Chamberlain, then Colonial Secretary, in a letter of early 1902 to Lord Grenfell wrote: 'Thank you for your welcome present of oranges, which are as good as usual, and, I am almost inclined to say, the best thing that Malta produces.'

Two special dishes deserve mention. The first, Ross fil-forn, a baked rice dish, contains meat, tomato sauce, eggs, and saffron. The use of this last ingredient may have a Phoenician origin. The second, Timpana, a mixture of macaroni, tomato sauce, meat, eggs, and cheese baked in a flaky pastry case, is probably Sicilian in origin.

As for soups, two unusual ones should be mentioned. Soppa tal-armla (widow's soup) is made with only green and white vegetables and garnished with a poached egg and a piece of ricotta or a small soft cheese. Aljotta is a light fish soup relying heavily on garlic and marjoram for flavour.

Most authentic Maltese dishes have Maltese names; and these are both attractive and puzzling. Maltese is a Semitic language, with heavy borrowing from Italian and French in vocabulary. The application of the name 'soufflé' to what is really a Maltese trifle is an etymological mystery.

Snack foods include the ubiquitous pastizzi, translated as, but not resembling, cheesecakes. They are covered tartlets, filled normally with RICOTTA, but the filling can also be made of peas, onions, and anchovy. The pastry for pastizzi is unique, and making it is an art. Even experienced pastizzi-makers say that they still strive for perfection after 20 years of practice.

A common mid-morning sight until recently in Kingsway (now Republic Street), Valletta, used to be that of young waiters emerging from the numerous small bars, carrying trays of pastizzi and tall glass tumblers of coffee and tea, elevenses for office workers. Pastizzi must be eaten fresh and hot. Some people like to eat the ricotta ones with sugar.

A & HCG

READING: Anne and Helen Caruana Galizia (1997).

MALTOSE sometimes referred to as malt sugar, a disaccharide (double SUGAR) formed when starch is broken down by ENZYME action, as when BARLEY is malted (see MALT), and also in the process of DIGESTION. Maltose is only one-third as sweet as sucrose—ordinary sugar—but its energy value is the same. The enzymes that form it belong to the group known as amylase or diastase; an example is ptyalin, found in saliva. Another enzyme, maltase, splits maltose into two molecules of glucose. Brewers and bakers classify grain by its 'maltose figure', a measure of how much maltose it will produce.

The name 'Maltose' is also given to a type of brown, sticky confectionery bar made with malt extract, which is popular in Japan.

RH

MAMALIGA an important dish in ROMANIA, closely resembles POLENTA, being a mush of cornmeal (see MAIZE) cooked until solid and then cut into pieces which can be served in any of various ways.

The name 'mamaliga' is derived from malai, now referring to a kind of cornmeal bread but originally meaning MILLET, which had been a staple food in Romania.

Lesley Chamberlain (1989) writes with eloquence on this subject and comments that 'In Romanian folk history the tools for making mamaliga—the iron kettle, the fire, the wooden stirring stick—are hallowed objects.' The stick in particular had symbolic significance, being often carved with the name of the family and with decorations. Chamberlain adds the pertinent comment that 'Mamaliga perfectly complemented the three or four flavours most prominent in Romanian cuisine: sour cabbage and pickles, bacon, sour cream and cheese.'

Klepper (1997) gives various contemporary mamaliga recipes, introduced by a charming quotation from Tereza Strătilescu (1907), whose book described Romanian country life.

The plainest kind of food, the real national dish, is the mamaliga with branza (cheese, sheep cheese). The mamaliga takes the place of bread, which is considered a luxury in a peasant's house; the mamaliga is always made fresh for each meal and eaten warm; cold mamaliga can be eaten too, but if a fire is at hand, it is cut into slices and fried on the embers. The table, of white wood, is milk-white with scrubbing; the mamaliga is turned out in the middle of it from the ceaun (iron kettle for mamaliga) and stands like a golden cupola smoking there until everybody has set down round the table.

In the same or a slightly different spelling (e.g. mamalyga in MOLDOVA), mamaliga is prominent in many neighbouring countries.

MAMEE Mammea americana, a fruit native to the W. Indies, which is now cultivated there, throughout tropical America, and to some extent in SE Asia, takes its name from the Spanish mamey. Its other names include mammee apple, and San Domingo or South American apricot; but it belongs to the same family as the SE Asian MANGOSTEEN, and is related neither to apples nor to apricots.

The large tree produces a round fruit the size of an orange or larger. The tough rind, pale russet in colour, is very bitter, as is the covering of the three seeds. The pulp between is firm, has something of the flavour of an apricot, and is of the same golden colour. This is eaten out of hand; stewed; or made into jam or jelly.

MAMONCILLO or genip(a), the fruit of *Melicoccus bijugatus*, a large tropical/subtropical tree which is native to Colombia and Venezuela and nearby areas and is related to the AKEE. The fruit is also known as honeyberry (a reflection of the generic name, *meli* meaning honey and *kokkos* meaning berry).

The cherry-sized green fruit looks like a small lime and is sometimes also called Spanish lime or (in the Dominican Republic) limoncillo. It has a single seed, large and hard, or two seeds flattened together so that they look like one. The sweet, gummy pulp surrounding the seeds is orange-pink in colour and has a refreshing flavour, reminiscent of grapes. The seeds may be roasted like chestnuts; and were eaten in this way, as a substitute for cassava, by the Indians of Orinoco.

This fruit is widely available in the markets of tropical America.

MA'MOUNIA a Middle Eastern sweet which is the ancestor of other types popular all over the region and in India. The original version and its variant *basbousa* may be classed as puddings; but another descendant, HALVA, has become so concentrated and rich as to enter the realm of confectionery.

Ma'mounia was probably named after the Caliph Ma'moun who reigned in the 10th century. Originally it was made from a thin sugar syrup thickened with rice cooked in fat. Now SEMOLINA is used, and the preferred fat is butter. A modern Syrian version which is a speciality of Aleppo is flavoured with lemon juice. The sticky, soft dessert is served warm, sprinkled with powdered cinnamon and spread with *eishta* (clotted cream, see KAYMAK).

Basbousa uses the same syrup and semolina basis, but the solid ingredients and the butter are usually more thoroughly cooked to consolidate them before combining with the syrup. There is a version with almonds which are simply fried with the semolina, but in others with almonds and yoghurt, and with coconut, these are baked before the syrup is poured over them. The simple almond version, which is at first soft enough to pour, is shaped in individual moulds and served when set but still warm.

LM

MANCHEGO the principal cheese of Spain, takes its name from the dry plateau of La Mancha, south of Madrid, where it is made from whole sheep's milk, the sheep themselves being of the Manchego breed. The best is said to come from around the city of Ciudad Real.

Manchego cheeses are pressed in moulds of a standard design which were originally of plaited straw, leaving a characteristic pattern on the surface. The pattern is now imitated with metal moulds. The shape is a flat disc (25 cm/10" in diameter and 8–12 cm/about 4" high) and the weight about 3 kg (7 lb). Manchego may be sold fresh (*fresco*) or slightly aged (*curado*) or older than three months (*viejo*); *Manchego en aceite* will have been immersed in olive oil for a year or so and will have developed a grey to black rind. As the cheese ages the flavour strengthens.

This is a full fat cheese with a yellow rind, and a creamy white, firm interior with few if any eyes. It is much used by cooks as a grating cheese.

MANDARIN was originally no more than a nickname given to a small, loose-skinned orange-like fruit, *Citrus reticulata*, which was brought to England from China in 1805. The word also denotes a Chinese official or the form of Chinese spoken by such officials and other educated people. However, it is not a Chinese word (their word for official is *kwan*), but came to English through the Portuguese form (*mandarin*) of a Malay word for 'counsellor' (*mantri*), itself derived through Hindi from the Sanskrit *mantrin*, also meaning counsellor and based on the root *man* which means 'to think'.

Despite its strange origin, the nickname stuck, and has become the most useful general name for a wide range of similar fruits. **Tangerine,** the alternative, is another nickname which seems to have originated towards the end of the 19th century in the USA, when mandarins supposedly from Tangier in Morocco became common. It is less useful as a general term because in the USA it is often applied only to dark-coloured kinds, and in Britain to an old-fashioned Mediterranean variety. Moreover, its usage excludes **satsumas,** which are an important kind of mandarin (see below).

The botanical classification of mandarins may eventually make matters clearer; but not yet, since there are several rival systems of classification in existence. The simplest arrangement puts all mandarins together in one species, *Citrus reticulata* (*reticulata* meaning 'netted', because of the fibrous strands of pith under the loose rind). This is considered an oversimplification by many, but at least distinguishes them from ordinary oranges.

The distinctive features of mandarins are that they are smaller, sometimes much smaller, than oranges; of a flattened shape, except for some hybrids described below; loose-skinned; easily separable into segments; and less acid than oranges. They normally contain more water and less sugar than oranges, and are often darker in colour. They may have no, few, or many seeds.

The original wild citrus from which mandarins are descended probably grew in NE India, where a wild mandarin, *C. indica*, is still found. It was taken into cultivation at an early date in S. China, as were other kinds of orange. However, mandarins were more highly esteemed than common oranges, partly because ancient varieties of the latter were dry, thick skinned, hard to peel, and seedy. The mandarin was prized as much for its fragrance as for its flavour, perhaps more. A poem by Liü Hsün (AD 462–521) describes its arrival at a banquet:

On the morning of the first frost,
The gardener plucks and presents it;
Its perfume extends to all the seats of the guests;
When opened, its fragrant mist spurts upon the
    people.

Of the many varieties of mandarin, that most admired by the Chinese in ancient times was a little reddish one from Nanking which fashionable women would hold in their hands so that they were scented by it.

Mandarins were not taken to the West along with the other citrus fruits, which had all reached Europe by the 16th century. And when they did come it was through an odd route. The first cultivars (probably of the ponkan type, see below) were brought to England in 1805, and it was apparently the descendants of these which were introduced into Italy in the following decade and which had become well established there before 1850. From Italy, cultivation spread quickly to other Mediterranean countries.

Meanwhile, mandarins had been taken direct from China to Australia in the 1820s. But it was not until the 1840s that the first mandarin was grown in the USA, by the Italian consul in New Orleans. Cultivation soon spread to Florida, California, and other states, and the new fruits were at first (despite their Italian provenance) called 'Chinas'. Later, when different, darker varieties were brought in from N. Africa they were called 'tangerines', a name which became general.

Mandarins, and most of their hybrids, are almost always eaten fresh, since the delicate flavour of both the fruit segments and the juice are lost in cooking. In Chinese cuisine, the peel of selected, fragrant mandarins is dried and used as a flavouring.

Saunt (1990), whose survey of varieties at the end of the 20th century is unsurpassed, finds it convenient to consider mandarins in three groups, plus a fourth miscellaneous one to accommodate some hybrids, etc.

1. **Common mandarins,** the most widely grown kind in China, SE Asia, and the USA, include numerous varieties. The leading one

in Florida used to be Dancy (named for a famous 19th-century grower), a largish, deep orange fruit with a sprightly flavour; but after long service as the dominant Christmas tangerine it has now given way to rivals. In California, Texas, and Arizona, the popular choice has been **Clementine,** which originated in Algeria in about 1900 and came to America shortly afterwards. **Ponkan,** a large, pale fruit with a mild flavour, is the mandarin most grown of all, globally. It grows well in hot climates and is much cultivated in Asia.

2. **Mediterranean mandarins** ('tangerines' to the British but not to Americans) were derived as explained above from English specimens. They are typically light in colour, often with a small, unobtrusive navel, and of mild but good flavour; and were for long the main Christmas mandarin in much of Europe. They are still grown around the Mediterranean, but have been partly ousted in commerce by the satsumas and clementines.

3. **Satsumas** were developed in Japan in the 16th century. Some botanists now assign the satsuma to a separate species, *C. unshiu.* Apart from the YUZU, the tree is more tolerant of cold than any other tree citrus. The fruit is seedless, bright orange in colour, less acid than other mandarins, and keeps well. Many varieties are now grown, mainly in Japan but also in parts of the USA where the winters are too cold for other citrus.

4. The fourth group, of **hybrids** and oddballs, most notably contains the **Tangors,** hybrids between a mandarin and an orange, and tending to be intermediate in flavour, size, and other characteristics between the two. For example, they are less flat in shape than pure mandarins.

Tangelos are hybrids between a mandarin and a POMELO or its descendant, GRAPEFRUIT. They are fairly similar to mandarins—though they do not have the typically flattened shape. Well-known examples grown in the USA are **Orlando,** a mild-flavoured, light-coloured fruit; and **Minneola,** darker in colour, with a rich, sharp flavour and a distinctive shape with a neck or knob on the stem end. Large tangelos, of grapefruit size, are described under UGLI, the best known.

The **King mandarin,** or King of Siam, is classified as *C. nobilis* by some. The fruit is large, medium orange in colour, and has a thick and knobbly, but peelable, skin. It may be a 'natural tangor', i.e. a hybrid which occurred spontaneously, and was one of the earliest fruits to be distinguished in Chinese descriptions of the citrus family.

One indubitable tangor is the **Temple orange,** a large, dark, sweet but rich-flavoured fruit. It is named for William

Chase Temple, a Florida grower on whose plantation it appeared in around 1910. Another, the **Ortanique,** has a peculiar mustard-coloured rind irregularly marked with brown specks. The rind is very hard but fairly easily separable, and has a fine 'Seville orange' fragrance. The flesh is pale orange and relatively acid.

See also MANDARIN LIMES, below.

MANDARIN LIMES a group of three or more similar fruits.

Rangpur, *Citrus × limonia,* a lemon × mandarin hybrid, originating in India. The fruit resembles a MANDARIN, and is grown in India, California, Australia, and Hawaii. The juice is added to mandarin juice in India to improve the flavour, but the rangpur is best known for the fine marmalade it makes, reputedly even better than that made with Seville oranges.

Kusaie is probably a form of rangpur, but is more limelike in aroma. It fruits almost continuously, and is common in Hawaii and Trinidad, though little known elsewhere.

Otaheite, known also as Otaheite Rangpur, is a non-acid form of rangpur. Its origin is unknown, but it was introduced to Tahiti from France, via England, and thence to San Francisco. The fruit is spherical and 4–5 cm (1.5–2") wide. The plant has fragrant purple flowers and is sold as a pot plant at Christmas in the USA, when it flowers and fruits at the same time.

MANGO one of the finest and most popular tropical fruits, has been cultivated in India since 2000 BC or earlier. The Indian mango, *Mangifera indica,* is the descendant of a wild tree still found in NE India. It is only one of over 40 (60, say some authorities) *Mangifera* spp., which grow in the region from India east to the Philippines and Papua New Guinea, and of which nearly half have edible fruits. But of all these *M. indica* is indisputably supreme; indeed, the judicious Purseglove (1968) has called it 'king of all fruits'. It thrives only in regions where there are clearly defined seasons, and is thus more often found in the northern part of SE Asia than in Malaysia and Indonesia where local species of *Mangifera* have evolved to adapt to growing conditions (see below).

The mango is much loved wherever it is found, and appears in many myths and legends. In Indian Vedic literature it is spoken of as a transformation of the Lord of Creatures, Prajapati, who later became the Lord of Procreation. A legend relates how Surya Bai, daughter of the sun, became a golden Lotus in order to escape the persecutions of an evil sorceress. When the King of the land fell in love with this lotus,

the sorceress burnt it to ashes. However, from its ashes sprang a mango tree, and the flower and the fruit both enchanted the King and won his love. When the ripe fruit fell to the ground, Surya Bai stepped out from it and was recognized by the King as his long-lost wife.

The mango was first made known to the outside world, it is said, by the Chinese traveller Hwen T'sang who visited India in the 1st century AD, after which cultivation of the mango generally spread eastwards. He used the name *an-mo-lo,* a phoneticization of the Sanskrit *amra.* Other names for the fruit in most Indo-European languages derive from the original Tamil *man-kay* or *man-gay.*

By the 10th century AD cultivation of *M. indica* had spread as far west as Persia, where it stopped, although the Egyptian climate would have been suitable.

By this time the mango had become a status symbol in India. The Moghul ruler Akbar (1556–1605) planted an orchard of mango trees at Darbhanga in Bihar, called *Lakh Bagh* because the number of the trees was supposedly one *lakh* (100,000). For a long time the cultivation of mango orchards in India remained the prerogative of rajas and nawabs.

From S. India the mango was spread by the Portuguese, who took it to Africa in the 16th century. It reached Brazil and the W. Indies in the 18th century, and Hawaii, Florida, and Mexico in the 19th century. However, although large numbers of mangoes are now grown in all these areas, India remains the world's largest producer, meeting not only the demands of an international market, but also her high domestic one.

Named **varieties** of mango, of which there are now many, are propagated vegetatively, a technique introduced in 16th-century Moghul India, because the tree, an enormous and handsome evergreen, does not grow true from seed.

Fruits vary in length from 5 cm (2") to over 25 cm (10") and in weight from under 100 g (4 oz) to over 2 kg (4.5 lb). Some kinds are almost round, others long and narrow, but they generally have a slight ridge on one side. The skin may be yellow or orange with a red flush, or else greenish-yellow (in the 'white' varieties) through to a rich golden-yellow. The large stone is covered with fibres which are small and short in good varieties but thick and extending right through the pulp in bad ones.

The fruit is highly aromatic. At its best the scent has a pleasant resinous quality; at worst it smells strongly of kerosene which it actually contains. Referring, evidently, to the better sort, Abul Fazl, author of the *Ain-i-Akbari* in the reign of Akbar, wrote of the mango:

This fruit is unrivalled in colour, smell, and taste; and some of the gourmands of Turan and Iran place it above muskmelons and grapes. In shape it resembles an apricot . . . a young tree will bear fruit after four years. They also put milk and treacle around the tree, which makes the fruit sweeter.

The variety of mango most acclaimed, and most often exported, is Alphonso, an Indian cultivar. In her survey of other leading varieties (there are hundreds of them) in various parts of the world, Morton (1987) makes the interesting point that in India most of the preferred varieties have yellow skins, while Europeans prefer yellow turning to red, and Americans (in Florida, at least) go for red skins. The Haden variety is exceptionally large.

Mangoes ripen satisfactorily if picked before they are fully ripe, so they can be exported fresh. Indeed, if left to ripen on the tree, they are apt to be invaded by worms. They are often canned in syrup; or pickled; or dried, for example to make AMCHUR in India and a similar chutney in Jamaica. Another form of dried mango in India is *amavat*, a leathery sweet sold in small rolls.

The unripe fruit is used extensively in India and elsewhere in SE Asia for making chutneys, pickles, and relishes of various kinds. Also, Patricia Arroyo Staub (1982) remarks that Filipino women like to eat green mangoes between meals; they use salt or soy sauce to mitigate the tartness.

Mango chutney is well known. It is to be noted, however, that Indians make non-sweet chutneys from the fresh fruit; these are quite different from the more jam-like product which they export. Their mango pickle is often highly spiced and may be extremely hot. Mangoes are also used to make vinegar. Other products in India include mango cereal flakes, mango custard powder, and mango toffee.

The related species *M. altissima* bears clusters of tiny fruits which have a place of their own in Philippine food culture, as Doreen Fernandez (1997) observes, pointing to the numerous vernacular names (of which *paho* is the most common) in the Philippines. The lack of an English name attests to its unfamiliarity outside the Philippines. The fruits are sour and are mostly eaten in pickled or brined form. They are sometimes used as a substitute for olives in sauces for pasta.

MANGOSTEEN the fruit of a small tree, *Garcinia mangostana*, native to Malaysia and Indonesia, much cultivated there and wherever else conditions are favourable, e.g. parts of Vietnam (which once had the largest mangosteen orchard in the world), Thailand, Cambodia, Burma, Sri Lanka, and the Philippines.

The tree is slow growing, and difficult to propagate, whether from seed or cuttings. It is also exacting about conditions, needing a hot, wet climate; fertile, well-drained soil; and shade while it is young. However, the reward for successful cultivation is great, witness the following meticulously observed and beautifully written eulogy from Fairchild (1930, as quoted in Popenoe, 1932):

This fruit is about the size of a mandarin orange, round and slightly flattened at each end, with a smooth, thick rind, rich red-purple in colour, with here and there a bright, hardened drop of the yellow juice which marks some injury to the rind when it was young. As these mangosteens are sold in the Dutch East Indies,—heaped up on fruit baskets, or made into long regular bundles with thin strips of braided bamboo,—they are strikingly handsome as anything of the kind could well be, but it is only when the fruit is opened that its real beauty is seen. The rind is thick and tough, and in order to get at the pulp inside, it requires a circular cut with a sharp knife to lift the top half off like a cap, exposing the white segments, five, six, or seven in number, lying loose in the cup. The cut surface of the rind is of a moist delicate pink colour and is studded with small yellow points formed by the drops of exuding juice. As one lifts out of this cup, one by one, the delicate segments, which are the size and shape of those of a mandarin orange, the light pink sides of the cup and the veins of white and yellow embedded in it are visible. The separate segments are between snow white and ivory in colour, and are covered with a delicate network of fibres, and the side of each segment where it presses against its neighbour is translucent and slightly tinged with pale green. The texture of the mangosteen pulp much resembles that of a well-ripened plum, only it is so delicate that it melts in the mouth like a bit of ice-cream. The flavour is quite indescribably delicious. There is nothing to mar the perfection of this fruit, unless it be that the juice from the rind forms an indelible stain on a white napkin. Even the seeds are partly or wholly lacking, and when present are very thin and small.

The fruit is usually eaten raw. However, in the Sulu Islands (between Kalimantan and the Philippines) a more acid variety is grown and made into preserves with brown sugar. (The flavour of the usual mangosteen would be overwhelmed by this treatment.) In Malaysia the unripe fruits are used for a preserve, *halwa manggis*.

There are many other wild and cultivated *Garcinia* spp, some providing sweet fruits, others tart seasonings, medicines, dyes, the artist's pigment gamboge, substances used for tanning leather, and timber. Of those with edible fruits, KOKAM has its own entry.

MANGROVE CRAB an English name applied in both a general sense, to more or less any crabs inhabiting mangrove swamps, and more specifically, to *Scylla serrata* (described under SWIMMING CRABS) and *Sesarma meinerti*. The latter is a smallish crab, with a blackish-purple carapace measuring no more than about 6 cm (2.5") across, and with hairy legs, whose most notable ability is that of climbing trees. The second word in the Thai name *pu samae* refers to a kind of tree found in mangrove swamps. Fishermen catch the crabs, usually at night, by picking them off the trees with gloved hands, then covering them with salt and keeping them for consumption the following day. They may be bought pickled in Thai markets, but can also be prepared in other ways.

MANKETTI NUT or mugongo nut, borne by trees of the genus *Ricinodendron*, especially *R. rautanenii*, in tropical Africa. The nuts are about the size of hazelnuts, and the nutritious kernels may be eaten raw or roasted (when they resemble roasted cashew nuts). The fruit pulp may be eaten raw, when it is like dates, but less sweet; or be boiled when, as noted by Facciola (1990), it turns maroon in colour and tastes like apple sauce.

The manketti nut is remarkable for the fact that it is often collected from elephant dung. Elephants are good at picking the fruit and eat them greedily, but their digestive processes do not affect the very hard nuts. When these emerge after a week inside the elephant, their seeds are ready to germinate; people then collect, clean, and crack the nuts, and eat them.

MANNA a sweet substance appearing at certain seasons on a wide range of plants, from trees to grasses. Manna is associated with infestation by scale insects, but it is often unclear whether the manna is exuded by the plant as the result of insect wounds or is, like HONEYDEW, a secretion of the insects themselves. Because of the multiplicity of sources, the identity of a given manna is often debatable. Donkin (1980), in a book-length monograph on the subject, has made the greatest single contribution to such debates.

Three mannas have importance as food. The best known is tamarisk manna, a white, honey-like substance which appears on the desert tree *Tamarisk mannifera* when infested by insects such as *Coccus manniparus*. This manna is known in Arabic as *mann*, in Persian as *taranjabin* (literally, 'fresh honey', because unlike bees' honey it is not enclosed in a comb but drips off the plant in hot weather), and as *gezo* (from *gez*, tamarisk) among the Kurds of N. Iraq, in whose region it is commercially gathered.

By the time tamarisk manna enters commerce it is a grey, sticky mass, about 10% of which is glucose and fructose, the remainder being sucrose and several other non-reducing sugars plus inedible residue. It is traditionally prepared by boiling in water and clarifying with eggs. The resulting syrup is most often made into a sort of HALVA (in Kurdish, *helwa-y-gezo*) with more eggs and perhaps the addition of almonds.

The second important manna appears on two spiny-branched shrubs known as camel's-thorn, *Alhagi maurorum* and *A. pseudalhagi*. It dries readily and is harvested by shaking the branches of the shrub over cloth. The highly descriptive Persian name is *tabashir taranjabin* (chalk manna). Camel's-thorn manna is primarily sucrose.

The third important manna is not produced by insects. It is a light or dark brown lichen, *Lecanora esculenta*, which can be dislodged from rocks by high winds and blown through the desert, sometimes raining on human settlements. Syrian Bedouins, whose name for it means 'earth fat', mix two parts of it with one part meal and make bread. A sort of jelly is also made. The Turkish word for lichen manna is *tıgala*, which provides the scientific name for the sugar present in it, trehalose.

Most other mannas are primarily of medicinal importance. Such is ash manna, produced by the flowering ash, *Fraxinus ornus*, which is the source of the laxative mannitol, although also used as a sweet confection.

The manna of the 16th chapter of Exodus is a miraculous food, intended not only to sustain the Hebrews during their wanderings in Sinai, but to teach faith and obedience. Moses commanded the people not to gather more than they needed for one day, and those who doubted that Providence would send manna again on the morrow, and therefore gathered more than they needed, found that the excess rotted and bred worms. Conversely, a double portion was sent on Fridays so that it could be baked or boiled for consumption the next day without violating the sabbath. This 'bread of Heaven' cannot be safely identified with any known vegetable manna, even though the Hebrew word is borrowed from the Arabic *mann*.

CP

MANTIS SHRIMP a CRUSTACEAN which is the marine counterpart of the insect known as praying mantis. The layman would be apt to compare it to PRAWNS and LOBSTERS, despite some obvious differences; but scientists group it with crabs. Of its five pairs of legs, the front ones are extensions of the mouth and those immediately behind are powerful ones with a jack-knife action which permits them to be used for seizing and slicing up prey.

Mantis shrimps are found in warm or temperate waters around the world, but are ignored in some regions. The main

European species is *Squilla mantis*, matched on the eastern seaboard of the USA by *S. empusa*. Both have a maximum length of 25 cm (10"), and the same applies to *Harpiosquilla harpax*, the most common of the various species in SE Asia. The largest Indo-Pacific species is *H. raphidea* (up to 35 cm/13").

There is a limited demand for mantis shrimp in the Mediterranean, just sufficient to ensure that they are brought to market. The Romagna is one part of Italy where they are esteemed. In W. Europe and N. America they are rarely seen. But they are more in demand in the Orient. The Japanese eat them with rice. Chinese soup stalls in SE Asia often have pickled mantis shrimp on hand. They are also to be had in Hawaiian markets.

MANTOU or mantu, a name which in one form or another is found all the way from Turkey to Japan, denotes what might be called a C. Asian equivalent of RAVIOLI, a whole family of items which fall in the category of DUMPLINGS OF ASIA.

In Turkey and Armenia, *manti* is a tiny boat-shaped pasta, open at the top, which is stuffed with ground lamb. A baking dish will be filled with these, topped up with broth and set in an oven to poach.

In Iran, Afghanistan, and C. Asia, it is a closed (or almost closed) ravioli-like pasta (sometimes as large as a fist) which is usually cooked in a special steamer known as *manti qasqan*. However, *suw manti* are poached, and in Uzbekistan, *qåwurma manti* are browned in oil and then either steamed or poached. The C. Asian *manti/mantu* may be filled with meat and onions, diced pumpkin, mashed potato, mung beans, radish, or a mixture of sugar and mutton fat. It is served with yoghurt or vinegar. In Afghanistan, the accompaniment to steamed, meat-filled *mantu* is yoghurt, chopped coriander, and a little tomato sauce, or a stew of carrots.

The Tibetan *momo*, which are also steamed meat dumplings, are remarkably similar and are so important to Tibetans that they are always served at a formal meal or a celebration, and are the subject of a proverb: if someone is a scold or talks too much, Tibetans say 'Kha momo nangshin dhe', meaning 'keep your mouth like a momo [i.e. closed]'. People fold them in different shapes to fit the various occasions, some plain and some fancy, and some 'with a tiny hole left in the top so the juice can be sucked out before the momo is eaten' (Dorje, 1985).

In wheat-growing N. China, *mantou* is a steamed leavened bread without a filling, eaten as a staple in place of rice. It is always made with light, white flour, rather than wholewheat flour, and the dough is slightly sweetened with sugar.

In Korea, *mandu* is a beef ravioli (the soup *mandu kuk* vies with *bulgogi* for the title of the national dish). The Japanese *manju* is a steamed bread made with wheat or rice flour with a curry or pork filling.

The origin of the word is obscure. One would presume that it is Chinese, except that the name *man tou* (which literally means 'barbarian heads') was originally spelled in several different ways, suggesting that the Chinese were trying to accommodate a foreign word to their non-phonetic writing system.

See also WONTON.   CP

MANUS CHRISTI an interesting term used in sugar CONFECTIONERY, mainly in the 17th century, when it usually referred to a sugar sweetmeat, often perfumed with rosewater and sometimes having gold leaf mixed in. Laura Mason (1998) describes several sorts and records successfully making one according to an early 17th-century recipe. She also explains that by the 18th century manus christi had become a cordial of sugar and rosewater or violets, administered to those of weak health.

Used in the phrase 'manus christi height', the term indicated a degree in SUGAR BOILING, which one would supose to be the right degree for making manus christi. Karen Hess (1981) mentions a suggestion that a gesture made in testing sugar syrup was thought to resemble that made in the blessing of the host and chalice, and that this gave rise to the name; but she points out that the stage referred to as 'manus christi height' was not in fact the stage appropriate for making manus christi (the sweetmeat). The same author remarks on earlier use of the term, in medieval times, when manus christi may have been a somewhat different product with a clearer religious connection. Elements of mystery still surround this term.

MAPLE SYRUP AND MAPLE SUGAR, specialities of the east of Canada and the north-east of the USA, are both produced by boiling down the sap of maple trees, notably the N. American sugar maple (*Acer saccharum*) and the black maple (*A. nigrum*). The process produces syrup first, while the sugar needs further boiling down. Up to the latter part of the 19th century, the sugar was the primary product. However, with the introduction of cheap cane sugar, demand switched to the syrup and is now almost exclusively for it. These sequences may be somewhat obscured by the traditional terminology in which 'sugar', 'sugar-tree', 'sugar-house', and 'sugaring off' are all terms which have tended to be applied to production of both syrup and sugar.

One tree, tapped at the right time of year (late winter/early spring), can produce several gallons of sap annually and does not seem to be harmed by the loss. This was well known to the Indians of NE America. Their original method of concentrating sap into syrup was to heat it with hot stones to evaporate some of the water. Another method was to leave the sap to freeze; the water would freeze to pure ice, leaving a sugar concentrate.

Early European settlers adopted the process, but found less cumbrous methods. They also found that the sap could be boiled down sufficiently to crystallize to a sticky fondant-like sugar which would set in moulds. (It is impossible to make dry sugar crystals because the sugar consists partly of dextrose and fructose, which are highly reluctant to crystallize.)

Maple syrup has a wonderful flavour, and is ideal for pouring over WAFFLES and for use as a flavouring for FUDGE and ICE CREAM. Since it is inevitably expensive, because of the low yield from the sap (40 gallons are needed for one gallon of syrup) and the laborious production process, imitations are sold, e.g. cheap corn syrup with just a tiny proportion of maple syrup added to give 'maple-flavoured syrup'. Nothing of this sort can match the real thing, and true maple syrup of N. American origin bears a controlled maple leaf mark as protection and guarantee.

READING: H. and S. Nearing (1950); Dorothy Duncan (1993); Bonnie Brown and David Segal (1981).

MARBLE CAKE made of two differently coloured cake mixtures briefly stirred into each other at the last minute before cooking. When cut the cake has a marbled appearance. Any light cake mixture can be used; usually a white or ANGEL FOOD CAKE mixture is combined with a chocolate version of the same thing.

It appears to have originated in the USA; the first cited recipe was in 1874 in Harland's *Common Sense in the Household.*   LM

MARGARINE was invented in France in 1869. At this time, during the crisis which led up to the Franco-Prussian War, BUTTER was scarce and expensive. The Emperor Napoleon III therefore instituted a competition for a cheaper substitute, which was won by a certain Mège Mouriès. His theory was that butter fat was formed in an animal's udder from its own fat and milk. So he mixed oleo, the oil obtained from beef fat, and skimmed milk and water and added a strip of udder to mimic the way in which milk is curdled with a strip of calf's stomach. He found that if he chilled, stirred, and

worked the mixture it formed a white, buttery mass with a pearly sheen, for which reason he is said to have named it 'margarine' after the Greek word for pearl, *margarites.*

While Mouriès's biological reasoning was almost completely wrong, he had in fact produced a substance very like butter, although his primitive product lacked flavour and colour. Margarine was an immediate commercial success despite the disdain of those who regarded it as a cheaper and inferior substitute. Many people still prefer butter, but margarine has now come a long way from the early, white, tasteless types. Moreover, the emergence alongside margarine proper of 'low-fat spreads' of many kinds has become a major factor in the situation.

In America, margarine has retained the ungainly title oleomargarin(e), often abbreviated to oleo. Artemas Ward (1923) has an interesting passage on this etymological point, offering an interesting alternative to the 'pearly sheen' explanation referred to above.

The clumsy title 'oleomargarin' was not devised, as one might suspect, by the enemies or defamers of artificial butter. The 'oleo' is of course self-explanatory. The 'margarin' perpetuates an error of French chemists who long held that olein, 'margarin', and stearin (as the glyceryl derivatives of oleic, 'margaric', and stearic acids) were the essential constituents of animal fats, and olein and 'margarin' of the fat of milk (i.e. butter). The so-called 'margaric' acid was in reality a mixture of palmitic and stearic acids, and 'margarin' of milk has totally disappeared from the language of the subject. Nor was the title 'oleomargarin' first applied to animal-fat butter—it had been given fifteen or sixteen years before to a solid substance obtained yet earlier from olive oil. Thus it happened that the *original* 'oleomargarine' was a fruit product!

Margarine, of the kind intended to resemble butter, can be among the most realistic of 'imitation' foods. A good-quality hard margarine spreads, melts, and combines with other ingredients in just the same way as butter. Only a slight deficiency in flavour and a small difference in texture or 'mouth feel', discernible when it is eaten as a spread on bread, give it away.

Margarine of this quality is nutritionally much the same as butter. It yields the same amount of food energy. Both are high in saturated fat. Margarine is fortified with added vitamins A and D to bring their levels up to those naturally present in butter.

Hard margarine may be made from varying mixtures of animal and vegetable fats and oils blended with milk; or it may be a purely vegetable product. Kosher margarine is of the second type. Vegetable oils used in hard margarine include PALM, GROUNDNUT, COCONUT, SAFFLOWER, SUNFLOWER, COTTONSEED, and SOYA BEAN,

the last two being much the most used in American brands. Animal products include lard, oleo oil (made by rendering beef fat), and fish oils of various kinds. Skimmed milk and whey are the other main ingredients, plain water being used instead for purely vegetable brands.

Soft margarine contains more unsaturated oils, so that its melting point is lower and it spreads easily when taken from the refrigerator. It may be deliberately made as high as possible in 'polyunsaturates' (oils whose molecules are unsaturated at more than one site: see FATS AND OILS) for those who see a health advantage in this.

The name 'margarine' is not used for 'low-fat spreads' which have extra water and air whipped into them, thus reducing their fat content; nor for various special products such as those made with olive oil. The range of what might be called 'butter alternatives' has widened and the terminology has become more complicated.

The process by which the traditional kind of margarine is made is interesting because it shows how difficult it is to copy a simple, natural food such as butter.

First the oils are degummed by heating them with 5% water to 90 °C (194 °F). Impurities such as carbohydrates, proteins, phospholipids, and resins are hydrated (combined with water) and blended into an oil-insoluble gum which is removed by centrifuging.

The oils are then neutralized to remove free fatty acids which might give unwanted flavours. They are heated in 25-ton batches with caustic soda at 75 to 96 °C (167 to 203 °F) for half an hour, which changes the acids to soap. The soap is washed out with water and the oil subjected to a vacuum to evaporate any water that remains in it.

The next stage is to bleach out any plant pigments—chlorophyll and carotenoids—by adding 1% of fuller's earth, a strongly absorbent powder, and heating the oil to 90 to 110 °C (194 to 230 °F) for a while under vacuum, afer which it is filtered.

The oil is then hydrogenated: that is to say, treated with hydrogen to saturate and harden it to the required degree. The process is carried out in a sealed, gas-filled vessel at a high pressure and a temperature of 180 °C (356 °F). It may also be interesterified: a process which rearranges the fat molecules and raises the melting point. Both hydrogenation and interesterification produce side products, so the oil has to be neutralized and bleached again. It is also deodorized by passing superheated steam at 180 °C (356 °F) through it in a very high vacuum to prevent oxidation (chemical reaction with the oxygen in the air, which would produce off flavours.)

The refined oils are then blended. Liquid oils and hard fats are combined in proportions that will give the required solidity. There must be some oils with a melting point below 34 °C (93 °F) so that the margarine will melt in the mouth when eaten as a spread.

Meanwhile, the aqueous phase—the watery part—of the emulsion is being prepared. For animal margarine, this is mostly skimmed milk, some of which is cultured with lactic acid-producing bacteria such as *Streptococcus lactis* to develop a natural 'buttery' flavour. The bacteria convert citrates in the milk to diacetyl, an important element in the flavour of butter and margarine alike. The skimmed milk is pasteurized to remove unwanted bacteria and enzymes, then a small amount is inoculated, kept warm, and allowed to sour. This is used as a starter for a larger batch, until enough milk has been sufficiently flavoured. The soured milk is cooled and blended with plain pasteurized milk. In the case of vegetable margarine using water, diacetyl has to be added later with other flavourings.

Now the oil phase is given vitamins A and D; colour, which may be natural or synthetic annatto or beta carotene; flavourings, including delta lactones, small amounts of butyric and caproic acid, and diacetyl if necessary (all flavourings naturally present in butter); salt; and up to 0.5% of emulsifiers such as lecithin (made from soya beans) and monoglycerides (made from organic acids and glycerol).

Then the oil and aqueous phases are emulsified in a rotator. This is a metal tube chilled by a cooling jacket to −18 °C (0 °F). Inside it metal blades revolve, churning the contents and scraping the walls. As the margarine solidifies it is scraped off by the blades and thrown into a 'tempering tube' 18 cm (7") wide and 3 m (10') long. It takes two minutes to travel along this tube, during which it is pressed and slightly warmed to consolidate it. Finally, the margarine is extruded and packaged.

Cooking with hard margarine presents few problems. It may be used exactly as butter, and will perform in the same way; although some of the cheaper sorts tend to spatter when used for frying.

Soft margarine is essentially a spread. It is not a substitute for butter or for hard margarine. It contains different proportions of ingredients, and is not good either for frying or as an ingredient in cakes and the like (excepting certain cake recipes formulated specially for it).   (RH)

MARIGOLD the common name of one group of garden plants in the Old World and another in the New World.

Calendula officinalis, a familiar garden plant in Britain, is a native of C. Europe, and its petals have been used since ancient times to colour food yellow and to give it a slightly bitter, pungent flavour.

In England the petals were used to colour cheese until ANNATTO was introduced from America. They have also been used, by infusion, to colour milk destined for cake-making, thus giving the cake a richer colour. Marigold puddings and marigold wine were made. Petals are still sometimes added to fish soups, e.g. conger eel soup in SW England. This is but a flickering survival of what was once a vigorously established practice, to judge by the comment of Gerard (1633):

The yellow leaves of the floures are dried and kept throughout Dutchland against Winter, to put into broths . . . in such quantity that in some Grocers or Spice-sellers houses are to be found barrels filled with them, and retailed by the penny more or lesse, insomuch that no broths are well made without dried Marigolds.

The petals, and occasionally the leaves, are chopped as a garnish for salads. As in the distant past, the petals can still be used as a cheap substitute for SAFFRON (only for the colouring effect, not for flavour) and indeed as a dye for other purposes. Turner (*c*.1560) observed disapprovingly that 'some use to make their heyre yelow wyth the floure of this herbe not beyinge content wyth the natural colour which God hath gyven them'.

The association with the Virgin Mary, arising from the first part of the English name, is the result of a linguistic confusion and is not echoed by the common names of any other languages. Originally marigolds were just 'golds', and emblematic of jealousy. Thus Chaucer: 'Jealousy that werede of yelwe guldes a garland.'

In the New World, various species have marigold as their name, or as part of it. Some of these are:

- *Tagetes lucida*, Mexican tarragon, sweet marigold (also sweet mace, pericón), whose leaves are used as a substitute for tarragon in seasoning various dishes. 'Bundles of the dried leaves and flowering tops are widely sold in Latin America for making an anise-flavored tea which is a popular and stimulating beverage' (Morton, 1976).
- *T. minuta*, 'Muster [*sic*] John-Henry' or Mexican marigold; the dried leaves are used as an aromatic seasoning for soups, broths, meats, and vegetables. Morton (1976) says that this species is called stinkweed or kaki weed and that it is often grown as a culinary herb in parts of S. America and southern states of the USA. The dried leaves have an aroma like apples. There is limited use of the essential oil in ice cream, candy, and soft drinks.
- *T. lemmoni*, an interesting herb found from Arizona to C. America. It has a very strong aroma, which has been described as being 'redolent of lemon, marigold and mint, besides resembling Mexican tarragon' (see *T. lucida* above). The aroma becomes less prominent in cooking.

It is likely/possible that the plant referred to by some food writers as *huacatay* or *yakatay* is one or more than one of the above species, or a close relation.

MARINADE MARINATE the noun and verb respectively which indicate the familiar procedure of letting a foodstuff, especially meat or fish, soak in a flavoured liquid before being cooked. The liquid may be wine or vinegar or lemon juice or olive oil or any of numerous alternatives, and the flavours are commonly added by herbs or spices. The time needed for successful marinating will depend on the size of what is marinated and also on its texture, since both these factors govern the speed with which the marinade will penetrate to its centre. However, it must also depend on the purpose. Stobart (1980) lucidly explains the various, often overlapping and complementary, purposes which marinating achieves. An oily marinade will give unduly dry and lean meat the fat needed to make it appetizing. An acid liquid will tenderize tough meat; or, in the case of lemon or lime juice for small fish, will achieve effects like those of cooking. Salt and various flavouring ingredients will have a preserving effect. When tenderizing is the chief aim, it is not uncommon to marinate overnight.

MARJORAM is an important culinary herb; but there are many marjorams, and their classification and nomenclature can be confusing. Part of the problem is that *Oreganum* is the generic name for the principal plants which are called marjoram; but oregano, oreganum, and similar names are applied in an unsystematic way to some (only) of these plants and to many others which have in common a single characteristic, namely exhibiting an oregano flavour. A further aspect of this whole complex of problems is that in N. America the name marjoram is largely replaced by oregano.

The plants which bear the name marjoram are relatively easy to list, as is done below. As for the name oregano and its numerous variants, current opinion among botanists is that the term should be treated as indicating a flavour rather than a defined group of plants. The plants which exhibit the flavour belong to several genera. This point is explained here because the present entry would seem defective if read by itself, without reference to OREGANO.

Four main species are recognized in the genus *Origanum*:

- *Origanum majorana*, sweet or knotted marjoram, is an annual plant, native to a region extending from S. Europe and N. Africa to W. Asia. It grows to a height of 30–60 cm (1–2'), forming characteristic 'knots'; and has a flavour similar to that of thyme, but more sweet and scented. This, one of the most important species for the cook, has been cultivated since ancient times. Although perennial in warm climates, it is at best half-hardy elsewhere. A hybrid between it and *O. vulgare*, which has been introduced in the USA, is hardier.
- *O. vulgare*, wild marjoram or common oregano, has a wide distribution in N. Europe and also flourishes in parts of the USA. A perennial, it grows as high as 70–80 cm (2' 6" or more) and has relatively large leaves. There are numerous cultivars, including Dark, Dwarf, Golden, Variegated, White. It is this species and its subspecies which are the starting point for any discussion of the term OREGANO.
- *O. onites*, pot marjoram, also perennial, less tall than *O. vulgare* and with smaller leaves, belongs to the E. Mediterranean region. It is sometimes called Cretan or Turkish oregano, or Cretan dittany (see however, DITTANDER). Less sweet than its larger relation, it is suited to strongly flavoured dishes, e.g. those with plenty of garlic or onion.
- *O. heracleoticum*, winter marjoram, is much used as a flavouring in Italy and elsewhere, and has several cultivars: Greek, Italian, Sicilian.

Several other species were formerly recognized: *O. tytthantum*, Kirghiz or Russian oregano; and *O. kopetdaghense*. But these are now regarded as synonymous with *O. vulgare* ssp *gracile*.

Comment on the flavouring characteristics of the various species is complicated by the fact that plants of one and the same species will differ noticeably according to the climate in which they are grown. Deni Bown (1988) states that in Greece, for example, there is enough light and warmth to permit *O. vulgare* to develop the essential oils (containing thymol and carvacrol, as in thyme) which provide its full flavour; whereas in the south of England the plant will grow but without developing these oils properly.

Despite the various ambiguities and complexities, it is safe to say that sweet marjoram was used extensively in classical times and is now a favoured culinary herb in virtually all European countries and N. America. It can be used fresh or dried with delicate vegetables, with tomato-flavoured dishes, and in stuffings, forcemeats, sausages and other preserved meats. Because of its delicate flavour it is best added shortly before the end of cooking or even by adding chopped raw leaves.

Pot marjoram is reputed to have originated in Sicily and was introduced to Britain in 1759. It is easier to grow and lasts longer. Although used in the same way, its flavour is less sweet and may even be slightly bitter. It is more suitable for adding to dishes that include other powerful flavours (onion, wine, garlic).

MARKETS for food are, obviously, worldwide phenomena and generally very pleasant ones. According to climate, they may be covered, open, or shaded. They may function daily or just once a week; be primarily for wholesale or for retail activity; serve a small locality or a wider area; be exclusively for food, or even for one category of food, or be mixed up with other things. They usually offer food at lower prices than prevail in shops, since the overheads are small. A good recent survey, intercontinental in scope, is that of Mimi Sheraton and Nelli Sheffer (1997).

MARLIN or spearfish, the name for several large BILLFISH, in the genera *Makaira* and *Tetrapturus*.

All marlin are large, powerful swimmers and are sought after as game fishes and also because they make good eating. The best known are:

- Atlantic blue marlin, *Makaira nigricans*, length around 3 m (10'), maximum recorded weight 580 kg (1,300 lb). Found throughout the warm waters of the Atlantic. Common names, such as the Spanish *aguja azul*, mostly mean 'blue marlin'.
- Atlantic white marlin, *Tetrapturus albidus*, up to 2.5 m (8'), known throughout the W. Atlantic from Nova Scotia to Brazil and probably also in warm waters of the E. Atlantic.
- Mediterranean spearfish/marlin, *T. belone*. It may reach a length of nearly 2.5 m (8'), has a relatively short bill, and is taken incidentally in the course of fisheries for swordfish and tuna. *Aguglia imperiale* in Italian, *pastardella* in Malta.
- Striped marlin, *T. audax*, up to 3 m (10'), the most important member of the family in the Indo-Pacific. Bears 15 or so white or pale blue stripes on its dark steel-coloured body. *Makajiki* in Japan.
- Black marlin, *Makaira indica*, a common Indo-Pacific species, which used to be called white marlin, a direct translation of the Japanese name *shirokajiki*, which was in turn bestowed because the dark colour of this fish changes to white after death.

- Indo-Pacific blue marlin, *M. mazara*, one of the largest (maximum weight over 900 kg/2,000 lb), blue-black over silver, with the 15 or so pale vertical stripes which so many of these marlins sport. Known in Japan as *kurokajiki*, which means 'black marlin' and resulted in the species being known in English for a time under that name (cf. the confusion over white marlin noted above).

See also SAILFISH; SWORDFISH.

MARMALADE in Britain, refers to a jam-like preserve made from the bitter, or Seville, ORANGE. The inclusion of the orange peel, cut into thin 'chips' or shreds, is characteristic of this preserve. 'Marmalades' based on other CITRUS FRUITS, such as LIME or LEMON, are made as is GINGER marmalade. However, orange marmalade is perceived as the archetype (although not the prototype), and orange marmalade, with toast, is part of the 20th-century concept of the traditional English breakfast.

The evolution of marmalade is a complicated story, well told by C. Anne Wilson (1985a). *Marmelada* was the Portuguese name for a sweet, solid, quince paste (see QUINCE PRESERVES). This luxury good was imported to Britain by the late 15th century, to be used as a medicine or a sweetmeat. Clear versions were known as cotignac (France) or quiddony (England). Recipes for quiddonies and thick quince marmalades of this sort are frequent in 16th- and 17th-century English cookery books.

Lemons and bitter oranges had also been imported to medieval and Tudor England. These (sometimes mixed with apple paste or jelly) were pulped into stiff 'conserves' and were called, by analogy with the Portuguese product, 'marmalades'. They were set in wooden boxes, or moulded in fancy shapes, to form part of the dessert or banquet course. Other fruits, such as damsons, apples, pears, and peaches, were also made into marmalades. All these marmalades were relatively solid confections, to be cut into slices and eaten from the fingers, not at all like modern marmalade.

The 18th century saw a new development; this was a transparent 'jelly' containing a little finely cut peel, the precursor of the modern product. There is a strong traditional belief that Scotland was responsible for the creation of the new jellied orange marmalade. If some of the tales told in support of this belief tax credibility, never mind, it 'feels' right. At this time marmalade was still perceived as a suitable item for dessert in England; but Scottish recipes of the mid-18th century used a higher proportion of water, giving a 'spreadable' consistency. In fact marmalade does appear to have been used as a breakfast spread at a much earlier date in Scotland than in England.

Meanwhile, and well into the 19th century, thick quince marmalades continued to appear in recipe books, so at this time the term 'marmalade' was used in a wider range of senses than it is now. It is illuminating to read what Mrs Beeton (1861) had to say:

Marmalades, jams and fruit pastes are of the same nature and are now in very general request . . . Marmalades and jams differ little from each other: they are preserves of half-liquid consistency, made by boiling the pulp of fruits, and sometimes part of the rinds, with sugar. The appellation of marmalade is applied to those confitures which are composed of the firmer fruits, as pineapples, or the rinds of oranges; whereas jams are made of the more juicy berries . . . Fruit pastes are a kind of marmalade.

It was during the latter part of the 19th century that the JAMS to which Mrs Beeton referred became the subject of a rapidly growing industry, mainly because sugar became much cheaper. Bread and jam became a cheap source of nourishment for the working classes. And marmalade received a boost, since the jam factories could produce orange marmalade in winter at not much greater cost than that of jams made with home-grown fruits during the summer.

Marmalade, however, had more of a luxury image than jam, and was exported to be used on breakfast tables throughout the British Empire; marmalade recipes also followed the flag, and became naturalized in many countries where supplies of citrus fruit and sugar were to be found. The range of different marmalades now being made in Britain, including some based on combinations of several citrus fruits, dark and light ones, chunky ones, and some with just slivers of peel in a clear jelly ('silver shred' for lemon, 'golden shred' for orange) is vast; and it seems safe to assume that in the 3rd millennium Britain will continue to lead the world in the production of marmalade (in the British sense of the term). A minor but interesting facet of this British attainment is that, among all the numerous culinary operations carried out in British domestic kitchens, marmalade-making is one which is quite often performed by men.

MAROILLES used to be the principal cheese of what is now the north of France. It is named after an abbey in that region, around which it and its predecessors have been made since the 10th century. Since the Second World War, however, it has been in severe decline (a shrinking market; different cows now used; deterioration of the pastures; etc.).

Maroilles, whose standard size is 800 g (1 lb 13 oz), is a flat and square, surface-ripened, semi-soft cheese with a strong smell. It is repeatedly washed during several months ripening to keep the surface organisms under control. Inside its pungent reddish rind, the yellow cheese is rich and mild.

A special version, *puant de Lille* ('stinker of Lille', from the smell) or *gris de Lille* (from its colour), is matured for longer; its smell is too much for many people.

MARRON *Cherax tenuimanus*, a CRAYFISH of W. Australia, related to the YABBY, but larger, in fact the third largest crayfish in the world. It is black when mature. Olszewski (1980) writes:

The marron has the largest tail, in relation to its body, of all freshwater crayfish. The tail constitutes 41 per cent of the marron's total body weight. This, together with its large overall size—up to 40 cm (15") long and weighing 1.8 kg (4 lb)—makes it *the* superior table crayfish. Its flesh is internationally renowned as the sweetest and finest crayfish meat available. Farmers are experimenting with commercial marron cultivation. In 1970 Americans attempted to introduce the marron into Louisiana, but it failed to adapt to American conditions.

Olszewski goes on to explain that the marron occurs naturally only in rivers and streams of the Jarrah forest area of south-western W. Australia. Since, unlike the yabby, it does not burrow, it will not tolerate semi-permanent water sources. However, it can be successfully introduced into man-made lakes and reservoirs, which has increased its range.

Morrissy (1978), the acknowledged expert on Australian crustacean cookery, recommends adapting E. and C. European recipes for crayfish, involving sour cream, for the marron.

MARRONS GLACÉS a French confection made from whole CHESTNUTS, peeled and steeped for several days in sugar solutions of increasing concentration until the sugar penetrates to the centres of the nuts, thus preserving them.

The principle is similar to that employed in the manufacture of CANDIED FRUIT, in which more sugar is added to the syrup daily. In the manufacture of candied chestnuts, the concentration of the syrup is very carefully controlled by temperature. The syrup, with the chestnuts, is gently heated each day to boiling point. Then the chestnuts are removed and the syrup allowed to boil to a higher temperature to increase the concentration very slightly (see SUGAR BOILING) before the chestnuts are replaced in it. The entire process takes about a week and is completed by giving the candied chestnuts a final coating of sugar syrup which dries to a smooth clear gloss.

The manufacture of marrons glacés on a commercial scale was started in the Ardèche, an area long associated with chestnut-growing, at the end of the 19th century. To keep up with demand, chestnuts now have to be imported, and marrons glacés are made in several other areas of France. The time and skill required in production, and the high quality of the chestnuts used, ensure that the results are always expensive.

Marrons glacés have, in Britain and elsewhere, a particular association with Christmas. LM

MARSHMALLOW the name of both a plant and a confection. The former, *Althaea officinalis*, a common plant of Europe and Asia, is related to the common MALLOW but looks more like the hollyhock. Although its leaves are edible, the chief use of the plant lies in its roots, which yield a mucilaginous substance which is the traditional basis for the sweet confections known as marshmallow but has now been almost entirely replaced by GUM ARABIC.

The sweet confection is made from syrup cooked to the hard ball stage (see SUGAR BOILING), then combined with a GELATIN or gum arabic solution, often with colouring and flavouring (mint, strawberry, orange flower water, etc.), and whisked into beaten egg whites. The mixture, dusted with icing sugar, is left to set, then cut into cubes or rounds.

A marshmallow has a distinctively chewy texture. It is a versatile substance, which displayed its versatility to maximum (some would say excessive) extent in the USA in the 1930s to 1960s, when it occurred surprisingly often in recipe books, for example as an ingredient for SALADS, in fillings and toppings for cakes and desserts, and as toasted marshmallows, crisp outside and melting soft within.

A similar product, *pâte de guimauve* (flavoured with rose or vanilla), is made in France.

MARZIPAN at its simplest, is a paste of crushed ALMONDS and SUGAR. It is sweet and has a rich, luxurious texture. A small proportion of bitter almonds are often added to almond paste; they add flavour and have a preservative effect. Two main types are recognized by confectioners: German and French.

For German marzipan, a speciality of Lübeck and Königsberg, whole almonds are mixed with the appropriate weight of sugar and then ground coarsely. The mixture is dried over heat, cooked for a short time, then poured onto a slab and spread thinly to cool.

French marzipan is made by combining ground almonds with sugar syrup boiled to the soft ball stage (see SUGAR BOILING), giving a finer and more delicate paste, with less flavour and a paler colour. This gives a malleable paste which is firm when cool.

In Britain a paste made of almond, sugar, and egg is often made at home and sometimes referred to as marzipan. This is used uncooked to make simple sweetmeats.

Marzipan has applications in all types of CONFECTIONERY. It is used as a filling for chocolates and chocolate bars. In sugar confectionery, it may be used alone, or in simple confectionery such as dates with rolls of marzipan inserted in place of the stones. These are often made at home as Christmas sweets. Marzipan is also used, by both amateur and professional confectioners, to make sweets in the shape of miniature fruits and vegetables. Colouring, and sometimes flavourings, are added to produce pretty results which are popular in Britain as cake decorations. It can also be used to make more ambitious figures, as the artists skill and imagination dictate.

As an ingredient in baking and flour confectionery, marzipan is an integral part of several traditional recipes, for instance STOLLEN and SIMNEL CAKES. It can also be baked lightly to make small biscuits and PETITS FOURS, akin to MACAROONS. Finally, marzipan is the essential substrate for the ICING of traditional rich FRUIT CAKES, made for celebrations such as weddings and Christmas teas.

Marzipan has a long history and an uncertain origin. The NSOED observes that the word came from the Italian marzapane via the German form marcipan (itself based on the misapprehension that the Italian word should be taken as coming from a Latin phrase, Marci panis, meaning the bread of St Mark). Ayto (1993) lucidly explains what superficially plausible, but unconvincing, efforts have been made to construct a complicated derivation (involving coins, weights, and boxes) for the Italian word.

Marzipan, which was known to the English in the past, and as recently as the early 20th century, as marchpane, has a pliable, easily moulded nature such that it could be sculpted into anything from fruits to coats of arms. It was used for making 'sotelties' (SUBTLETIES), spectacular models brought on at the ends of courses at medieval feasts. During the 16th century, subtleties went out of fashion, but marzipan remained important and became part of the BANQUET course, in the form of a large, circular cake. Sir Hugh Platt, in Delightes for Ladies (1609), makes it clear that marzipan was popular for modelling, and gives these

instructions for decorating a large marchpane, baked on a base of wafers, and iced with rosewater and sugar:

garnish it [the marchpane] with prettie conceipts, as birds & beastes beeing cast out of standing moulds. Sticke long comfits upright in it, cast bisket and carowaies in it, and so serve it; gild it before you serve it: you may also print off this marchpane paste in your moulds for banquetting dishes. And of this paste our comfit makers at this day make their letters, knots, Armes, escocheons, beasts, birds and other fancies.

Variations on plain marzipan included the use of pistachios, which gave a pale green colour; and spices such as cinnamon or cloves, to introduce an additional flavour.

The large marchpane continued to be made in England into the 18th century, mainly for wedding feasts. During this century, a change in fashion led to the evolution of the wedding cake in the form now familiar to us, a rich fruit cake with a layer of marzipan covering the dark, crumbly interior, and forming a smooth base for a layer of sugar icing. Small marzipan confections continued to be made; for example, 'rout biscuits' (a rout was a party); these were made in fancy shapes and decorated with candied fruits, nuts, and a glaze. A late survival of the large marchpane, in modified form, was 'Dublin Rock', a sweet dish of the 1890s. It was made from ground almonds, melted butter or thick cream, sugar, and brandy, beaten together vigorously and then allowed to set. Then it was broken into irregular lumps and piled up to resemble a cairn of rocks. 'Grass' and 'pebbles', in the guise of candied angelica and split almonds were used to decorate it.

Whilst marzipan still has a place in British and French confectionery, the practice of eating it as a dish in its own right has more or less ceased. In other parts of Europe, and the Middle East, marzipan and nut pastes remain popular. In Germany and C. Europe marzipan is still made into large cakes at Christmas, and decorations for the Christmas tree.

In S. Europe, too, marzipan is exploited for its sculptural qualities. The Italians make model fruit from it. The mixture is also shaped into larger figures, such as marzipan lambs for Easter, and little 'cakes' filled with chocolate or liqueur-soaked raisins. Other almond paste sweets are popular in Spain and Portugal: the figuritas de mazapán, little abstract shapes, toasted light brown, made at El Convento de Toledo; and the almond paste sweets of S. Portugal, filled with a mixture of egg yolk and sugar.

Almond paste is used as a component in N. African pastries such as cornes de gazelles. Numerous small macaroon-type cakes with almonds amongst their ingredients are popular items in pastry shops and cafes of the Maghreb. A taste for nut confectionery

extends round the shores of the E. Mediterranean, where it is shaped into small model fruits and other sweetmeats, into Iraq, where, as lowzina, flavoured with rosewater and cardamom, decorated with gold leaf, and cut into diamond shapes, it is made for Iraqi wedding celebrations. Indian confectionery also includes pastes made from almonds or pistachios and sugar, decorated with GOLD AND SILVER LEAF.

In Mexico, the Spanish taste for marzipan has been adapted to local materials and sweets of this type are based on items such as ground pumpkin seeds.   LM

MASALA means spice mixture in India. The word masala comes from the Arabic word which originally meant 'interests', hence 'necessities', hence 'seasonings'.

The blending of spices is the essence of Indian cookery and there are many different types and combinations of spices which suit particular dishes, regional specialities, and taste preferences. Masala can be ground or whole spices; mild or strong; bland or sharp; 'dry' or 'wet'. Every different version imparts its own distinctive flavour. The combination selected depends on what kind of dish is being prepared, e.g. whether it requires a strong 'hot' flavour or a subtle, aromatic flavour.

Generally speaking, a masala in N. India is made with dry spices pounded to make a powder, which keeps well, rather than being ground with a liquid to make a paste. S. India, on the other hand, tends to prefer fresh or green spices, ground with water, lime juice, coconut milk, or vinegar, to make 'wet' masalas or pastes. These vary in consistency according to the amount of liquid used, and in keeping quality according to the nature of the liquid. The range of possibilities is almost infinite. A few examples are given below.

The best-known masala is **garam masala**. It is the principal spice mixture in N. Indian cookery. Garam comes from the Persian word garm, meaning 'hot' in the special sense explained under SARDI/GARMI. A classic garam masala will therefore include some of the spices which are 'hot'— cinnamon, cloves, black pepper, and black CARDAMOM. Nowadays, however, garam masala usually includes some 'cooling' or more aromatic spices such as green cardamon, coriander, cumin, and tejpat leaves (Cinnamomum tamala, much used in the north of India, often called 'Indian cassia').

Blends of garam masala vary enormously, according to local or regional tastes. Other ingredients used include cassia, fennel, even dried rose petals, to take but a few examples.

The spices of garam masala are usually dry roasted before use. The mixture is then added to the dish as a final flavouring, just before it is served. *Garam masala* is mostly used with meat; to a lesser extent in poultry and rice dishes, such as PILAFS and BIRIANIS; and only rarely in fish or vegetable dishes, for which its aroma is considered too strong. *Garam masala* is in any case always used sparingly.

Chat (sometimes *chaat*) *masala* is a tart and salty spice blend which gets its unique taste from AMCHUR, the sharp, lemony seasoning made from ground, dried, unripe mangoes. The other elements in the mixture are variable; they can include ground ASAFOETIDA, mint, ginger, AJOWAN, cayenne, black salt, black pepper, cumin, coriander, and dried POMEGRANATE seeds. *Chaat masala* is used to flavour the salad-like dishes known as *chaats* (the most popular ones are made with shredded cooked chicken and mixed fruit) and as a seasoning when a sharp, hot, and tart flavour is required.

Dhansak masala is a 'hot' Parsi spice mixture used for DHANSAK dishes.

Gujerati masala is another 'hot' spice mixture with the addition of chillies, sesame seeds, fennel seeds, and ajowan seeds.

Kala masala (or black masala—*kala* means black) consists of pepper, clove, cinnamon, and other black spices.

Kashmiri masala is closely related to *garam masala*; its flavour is milder, being dominated by the fragrant green cardamon. It is used in the far north of India and, of course, in Kashmir. It is particularly used to flavour dishes cooked by the *dum* method, i.e. baked in a sealed pot.

Sambar masala, also known as *sambar podi*, is a special spice mixture of the Parsis and of S. India, widely used in vegetarian Brahman cooking, see SAMBAR. It is a tart mixture made up of toasted ground split peas (DAL), coriander, cumin, black peppercorns, and FENUGREEK powder.

Taaza (or *green*) *masala* (*taaza* meaning fresh or new) is a green spice paste based on fresh coriander leaves, mint, garlic, and ginger. It is added to meat or fish stews or vegetable dishes to give extra flavour.

Xacutti (or *shakuti*) *masala* is a speciality of Goa. Spices such as coriander seeds, cumin, black peppercorns, fenugreek, and chillies are blended with coconut, roasted until quite dark in colour, and then fried giving a toasted nutty taste and lending a dark colour to curries.

Char masala, a blend of spices used in Afghanistan, is closely related to the Indian *garam masala*. *Char* means 'four' in Persian and this spice mixture can be a combination of any four spices such as green cardamom, black pepper, cumin, cloves, black cardamom, and cinnamon.

See also SPICE MIXTURES.   (HS)

MASCARPONE a fresh Italian cheese made from cream coagulated by citric or tartaric acid, and therefore a kind of CREAM CHEESE.

This product does not keep, and is mainly produced in the autumn and winter. It is usually sold in small containers and is eaten by itself or in various mixtures with cocoa, coffee, liqueurs, etc.

One such confection is the Venetian dessert tiramisu, meaning pick-me-up, which involves first creaming the mascarpone with yolks of egg and a little fresh cream, and then incorporating whipped whites of egg. Layers of this mixture are alternated with layers of sponge fingers soaked in strong coffee and liqueur, and cocoa powder is sprinkled liberally between the layers. The whole is chilled before serving.

The name is not to be confused with, although possibly derived from, *Mascarpa/Mascherpa/Mascherpin/Mascherpina*, which refer to a kind of RICOTTA.

MASTIC an aromatic resin obtained from plants of the genus *Pistacia*. The best known is *P. lentiscus*, common on Mediterranean hillsides from Syria to Spain, and the source of the Chios mastic of commerce. Bombay mastic comes from *P. cabulica*, the terebinth pistachio tree.

When the stems of the bushes are wounded, even slightly, mastic exudes as a clear sticky substance. In cultivation, which takes place particularly in the Aegean island of Chios, vertical incisions are made in the stems during the summer, and the oval 'tears' of dried resin, ranging in size from 0.5 to 2 cm (0.25–0.75"), are collected shortly afterwards. The best grade is taken directly from the plant; a second grade is scraped from flagstones arranged around its base.

In its natural form, mastic is chewed for pleasure, like the CHEWING GUMS made from the New World gum chicle; our word 'masticate' probably derives from this practice, via the Latin verb *mastico* (I chew). The fruity and resinous aroma of mastic was greatly appreciated in medieval Islamic cookery, but mastic is now less used as a spice. The usage survives in parts of the Middle East and in Egypt, where mastic tears are often used to flavour stews; in Morocco, where mastic is the usual flavouring of ground almonds; in Greece, e.g. for an alcoholic drink like ouzo, and for flavouring Greek breads (see EASTER FOODS); and in Turkey for TURKISH DELIGHT; and in some places to flavour ICE CREAM.

In parts of Turkey a mastic 'jam' is made. It and aubergine jam are delicacies of which a teaspoonful is offered, with a glass of water, to guests. For numerous other Turkish uses, see Nevin Halıcı (1993).

The harvest of mastic in Chios takes place from July to September. A number of picturesque villages devoted to the cultivation of the small trees have existed in the arid south of the island since medieval times. Pyrgi, with architecture betraying a 13th-century Genoese influence, is one such. Rena Salaman (1993*b*) has described the *mastichochoria*, 'mastic villages', of Chios.

(CP)

MATÉ is a drink made from the dried leaves of the yerba, *Ilex paraguariensis*, indigenous to Paraguay and other parts of Latin America. Its use appears to go back to pre-Columbian times; later, it was adopted by the Spanish settlers. The name comes from the Inca word for a calabash: traditionally, GOURDS were used to make vesssels for the tea. Emerson (1908) writes:

The maté, speaking now of the vessel, is among the natives a small gourd [*Crescentia cujete-cuca* or *Curcurbita lagenaria-cabaco*] usually about the size of a large orange, the tapering end of the gourd serving as a handle. The top of the gourd is cut off, leaving a hole about an inch or so in diameter, through which the tea is sucked by means of a tube called a bombilla. These vessels are often silver-mounted and handsomely carved, and are prized accordingly. The bombilla is a tube seven or eight inches long and is either metal—silver— or a reed. At one end it is equipped either with a finely woven basket-work bulb or one of metal perforated with minute holes, so as to prevent the particles of the tea leaves from being drawn up into the mouth. The native method of serving it is to place a small quantity of the powdered leaves in the vessel and then pour boiling water upon them till the gourd is filled. It is necessary to drink the tea while it is hot, and until one learns how to manipulate the *bombilla* he runs a good chance of burning his lips and mouth, which of course furnishes much amusement for the spectators.

Early methods of production involved drying the twigs on frames called *barbracuras* erected over fires, which were kept going for 36–48 hours. The process completed, the dried substance was then pounded and packed in hide bales, still moist, which dried to form a compact packaging. Emerson explains how these early techniques were replaced in the course of time by more efficient ones, leading to a better product. Cultivation on a large scale was begun by the Jesuits, which is how maté came to be known as Jesuit tea. The cultivated plant is a small shrub with numerous stems (not a tree with a rounded head as it grows in the wild).

Maté is usually drunk *amargo*, i.e. bitter, without sugar, but can be taken like ordinary tea. Burnt sugar or orange peelings are sometimes added.

MATELOTE a kind of fish stew of which the best-known manifestations in France, its home territory, are those made with CARP or EEL. Generally, it is made with freshwater fish.

The term had migrated into English by the first half of the 18th century, and for a time had a wider meaning, e.g. a stew in which the main ingredient could be something other than fish.

The term patently derives from *matelot*, sailor; so it is odd that it is rarely used to mean a stew of sea fish.

MATSUMO *Analipus japonicus*, sometimes called fir needles, is an interesting member of the group of brown SEAWEEDS. The fresh young plants may be used in soups or as garnish for SASHIMI. When dried/salted/made into sheets, it serves other uses; salted matsumo can be layered with mushrooms to help preserve them. The protein content is higher than for most seaweeds.

MATSUTAKE a Japanese name meaning 'pine mushroom'. This fungus, *Tricholoma matsutake*, is so named because it grows in Japanese red pine forests in the autumn. It is dark brown in colour, with a meaty stem, and may measure 25 cm (10") in both height and width.

T. ponderosum, the 'white matsutake' of NW America, a close relation, is also known as the pine mushroom since it too is found under conifers in the autumn. It is slightly smaller, has a sticky white cap with small yellow-brown scales in its centre, white gills, and an aroma resembling that of the true matsutake. Marteka (1980) records that:

each year in the large Japanese-American community in Seattle, a contest is held to find the largest white matsutake . . . The window of Sagamiya's confectionery shop on Seattle's South Main Street displays the brownish-white mycological contestants that compete for top honor. Specimens weighing 1 or 2 pounds are not infrequent.

The Japanese consider the matsutake the finest of all mushrooms. It has a more distinctive flavour than its European relations, the ST GEORGE'S MUSHROOM and the BLEWIT. Specimens gathered in undisturbed stands of red pine are said to have a particularly fine and piny fragrance. Autumnal expeditions to gather and cook them in such a habitat are a popular form of outing. Hosking (1996) remarks that:

There is a certain ribaldry about young men and women going hunting for *matsutake*, since it is quite phallic in shape, and the chances of getting lost in the woods of red pine where it grows are quite high.

Fresh matsutake, packed in sawdust, are available seasonally in certain Japanese food stores outside Japan, but are very expensive. Canned matsutake are regarded by Japanese expatriates as better than no matsutake, but markedly inferior to fresh ones.

Matsutake should not be washed or severely trimmed; it is enough to wipe the caps with a damp cloth and to remove the very bottom of the stems. They should be sliced thickly and cooked briefly. In Japan they are often treated as a dish in themselves.

MATZO a word which has now entered the English language from the Hebrew *matzah* (plural *matzos* or *matzot*), refers to the Jewish unleavened Passover 'bread', which is like a large oblong water biscuit.

To Jews, these are invested with special significance, and are the only flour products allowed at PASSOVER (Pesach). The matzos are baked in memory of the flight of the children of Israel from slavery in Egypt (Exodus 12):

And they baked unleavened cakes of the dough which they brought forth out of Egypt, for it was not leavened; because they were thrust out of Egypt and could not tarry, neither had they prepared for themselves any victual.

In the same chapter, the Lord instructs Moses that Passover should be commemorated with special foods, including: 'Seven days shall ye eat unleavened bread; even the first day ye shall put away leaven out of your houses: for whosoever eateth leavened bread from the first day until the seventh day, that soul shall be cut off from Israel.'

Thus matzos play a special role in the ceremonial, symbol-laden Passover meal, or Seder. Before Passover, the whole house is cleared of any trace of *chametz*, leavened food, even the crumbs being swept up by the father and children, armed with a candle and goosefeather. When the house has been declared clean, blessings are called upon it. Three matzos are set out on the Seder table, concealed in the folds of a linen napkin or in a special *matzah dekke* (also known as an *afikoman*). They represent the three hereditary 'orders' into which Jews are still divided: the Kohanim (the priests), the Levites (their assistants), and the Israelites, the remainder. The meal cannot be finished until all the matzos are eaten.

Evelyn Rose (1985) says that the flour used is:

very special flour whose production has been strictly supervised—in the case of the special 'Shemura' matzot eaten by very Orthodox Jews, from the moment that the sheaves of wheat are gathered in the field. This is to ensure that at no stage can either the grain or the flour become damp and ferment, causing the dough to rise and thus leavening the bread—which is, of course, strictly forbidden. For the same reason, once the water has been mixed with the flour to make the dough, no longer than 18 minutes must elapse before the baked matzot are brought out of the oven.

Matzos are also used as an ingredient, in the form of 'matzo meal', crumbled matzos. They are used as a thickener in JEWISH COOKERY much as breadcrumbs are elsewhere; and are also made into dumplings to serve in broth or soup (*kneidlach*, or 'matzo balls'). Soaked, squeezed matzos serve as a basis for puddings, mixed with eggs and dried fruit and baked or made into fritters.

MAUKA *Mirabilis expansa*, a food plant which had some importance in the Inca empire but was then 'lost' until it was discovered in the 1960s to 1980s that it was still in use as a foodstuff in three widely separated localities in Bolivia, Ecuador, and Peru.

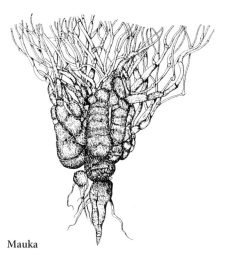

Mauka

The edible stems and tubers have a high protein content. The tubers can be grown to the size of a human forearm, and have a pleasing flavour. The experience of the Maukallajta Indians of Bolivia, for whom the plant is a staple food, suggests that it has considerable potential.

When freshly harvested, the mauka roots grown in Bolivia contain an astringent chemical that can burn the lips and tongue. Exposing them to the sun, however, replaces the bitterness with a pleasant, sugary flavor. Traditionally, the sun-sweetened tubers are chopped, boiled, and mixed with honey or brown sugar and toasted grain. The combination makes a hearty meal, and the cooking water makes an especially flavorful drink.

Lost Crops of the Incas (National Research Council, 1989) from which the above quotation is taken, goes on to say that the mauka grown in Ecuador is reputedly free of astringency, and is prepared in either salty or sweet fashion (*de sal* or *de dulce*).

Survival of the plant in three small areas separated from each other by great distances is thought to be a result of the Inca policy of transplanting, complete with their favoured crops, large communities within their empire.

Interest in future use of mauka is heightened by the fact that it will grow in places where no other root crops are viable.

MAURITIUS a volcanic island way out in the Indian Ocean (about 800 km/500 miles east of the very much bigger island formerly called Madagasgar and now the Malagasy Republic), has a relatively short history so far as human beings are concerned. Although there is evidence that Arab sailors had seen it earlier, it was the Portuguese who 'discovered' the island in 1510; and it was not colonized until the end of the 16th century, when the Dutch established themselves there and stayed for over a century. The French succeeded them in 1715, colonizing the island under the name 'Isle de France' and lasted for almost another century until ousted by the British, who restored the Dutch name 'Mauritius' (after a prince of the house of Nassau) and retained the island until it became independent in 1968.

Thus colonialism brought three separate European influences to bear on the island and its foodways; and geographical factors ensured that these were supplemented by influences from the Arab world, the Indian subcontinent, and the Orient. Jones and Andrews (1980), remarking that Robin Howe (1958) had said that there are three great kitchens in the world—French, Chinese, and Indian—comment thus: 'Mauritians would welcome this opinion, but frown at its limitations. All three cuisines flourish on the island, which of course makes Howe's choice highly acceptable. But the exclusion of Creole cuisine from the top league table wouldn't meet with local approval.'

CREOLE cookery is a concept which may be most familiar in the Caribbean area and the Mississippi Delta, but which finds application all over the world. Here it refers to a blend of black African and European (French, Dutch) and Indian cuisines. The black African element derives partly from the slaves imported by the Dutch and French colonists, mainly to work in the sugar plantations. Indians, from the south of India, had come to do construction work and also (after the emancipation of the slaves) to work in the sugar industry. Mention should also be made of the Chinese who came from mainland China and Hong Kong, mainly in the 20th century, and became prominent as retailers and businessmen.

So Mauritius has been a culinary melting pot. The official language is English, but the most common spoken language is a creole which reflects the mixture of peoples and provides the names for many of the foods which come out of the melting pot. This creole, to quote Jones and Andrews again,

is largely French-based but borrows freely from Portuguese (*camarons*, freshwater prawns), from Malagasy (*tandrac*, hedgehog), from Chinese (*min*, flour noodles) and from the Indian languages (*gadjak*, snack; *farata*, Indian bread; *masala*, curry powder; *dekchee*, cooking utensil etc.).

Vegetables include BRÈDES (leafy greens or a dish of the same), *palmiste* (hearts of PALM), and *chou chou* (CHAYOTE). Fish and seafood also have interesting names, often echoing those of other islands in the Indian Ocean: *capitaine* (see EMPERORS), mourgate (flying SQUID), etc. Other names in this category come straight from European languages: rouget (red mullet), camaron (shrimp, prawn). Mauritian flavourings deserve another quotation from Jones and Andrews:

Vindaye is what happens when mustard, saffron, chillies, garlic, oil and vinegar, amongst other things, come together and gently seep into the firm flesh of fried tuna. The longer the fish is allowed to soak up the spices, the riper and more potent the *vindaye* becomes. Octopus, known locally as *ourite*, can be subjected to the same battery of ingredients with equally devastating effect. . . .

It is believed that the name *vindaye* owes its distant linguistic origin to *vin d'ail*—garlic sauce [see also VINDALOO]. Similarly, *rougaille* hails from *roux d'ail*—also garlic sauce! Despite etymological connections, and the assertive presence of garlic in both dishes, *vindaye* and *rougaille* are in fact very different even to the innocent palate. A *rougaille*, always served piping hot, has a flavour dominated by the presence of tomatoes—in our case a small tasty variety called *pomme d'amour*. This ingredient, a *force motrice* in most Mauritian Creole cooking, is noticeably absent from *vindaye*.

The *pomme d'amour* is also the central flavouring and colouring agent in the famous Creole sauce—a sauce almost as international as vinaigrette or mayonnaise. Creole sauce poured over barbecued steak or fried red mullet or boiled prawns or even eaten on its own with Creole rice, immediately brings a blast of equatorial sunshine to a meal. Adding Creole sauce to an omelette is like turning a funeral cortège into a carnival.

MAY ROBERT (b. 1588), author of *The Accomplisht Cook* (1660), which has been described as 'the first full-scale English cookery book'. By its sheer size (over 450 pages and more than 1,000 recipes) and comprehensive scope this book eclipsed its predecessors, none of which had treated all branches of cookery.

May was a professional cook, from the age of 13 or 14. Marcus Bell, in the introduction

to the 1994 facsimile reprint of the 1685 edition of May's book, lists his various eminent employers, starting with Lady Dormer, who sent him over to France to work and study there for five years. Then and later his career progressed in Roman Catholic and royalist households. It is likely that his book would have been published earlier if he had not had to wait for the propitious circumstance of the Restoration of the monarchy in 1660. However, it would be a mistake to view his work as a Catholic cookery book, since it has less emphasis than corresponding books published in continental Europe on fast days, feast days, Lent, etc. It would also be wrong to suppose that it was dominated by material from May's French experience or from French sources. Such influences are apparent in his book (especially the section on eggs where he borrowed 35 recipes from the French author LA VARENNE), but in general his borrowing from other authors, English or French, was light and the flavour of his book is English.

READING: Introductory material to the reprint referred to above.

MAYA FOOD was that of a civilization which, unlike those of the Aztecs and Inca (see AZTEC FOOD and INCA FOOD), had been in severe decline for many centuries before the voyages of Columbus opened the way for the Spanish Conquest. However, the Maya remained an important ethnic group in SE Mexico and C. America, and their history is an important part of American history. Were it not for the fact that all their books but four have perished, and that until very recently it had not been possible to decode their hieroglyphics, much more would be known and written about them.

First contacts between Spaniards and the Maya were sometimes peaceful and permitted the newcomers to sample Maya fare, accounts of which survive. With the addition of archaeological and other evidence, all carefully weighed by Sophie Coe (1994), there is enough information to reconstruct with fair confidence their traditional diets; diets in the plural because of variations both over time and by region. The Maya territory included terrains of such varied characteristics that there were considerable dietary differences between, for example, the inhabitants of the limestone plateau, just above sea level, of Yucatan, and the people living in the pine-forested uplands of Guatemala.

MAIZE was the staple food and had great cultural significance, figuring in all important rites such as those attending births and deaths. It was consumed in many ways: in liquid form, as POSOLE or ATOLE (also spelled posolli and atolli); as a gruel;

and as breadstuff, in TORTILLAS and TAMALES. Little equipment was needed for these purposes, but hard work might be necessary. The first requirement was often the complex process described under NIXTAMALIZATION, which not only facilitates peeling and grinding the grain but also improves its nutritional quality. However, breadstuff made from young green maize did not require this, nor did it need a preliminary soaking or boiling; at the right point of ripeness it could be ground and shaped and baked without further ado. The baking could be done on a *comal* (flat clay griddle) or slab of suitable stone or simply in the embers of a fire. It was the grinding which was laborious.

Among flesh foods, the TURKEY was important. It seems that both available species were eaten, the domesticated one now familiar worldwide and also the ocellated turkey. IGUANA meat was appreciated and the bones of that animal from at least one archaeological site are darkened, suggesting that it was roasted, possible on a *barbacoa* (see BARBECUE). There is evidence of numerous other animals such as ARMADILLO, TAPIR, MONKEY, and the manatee (a marine mammal—see DUGONG) being eaten, plus various insects, and also of some ritual cannibalism. Fish and seafood were much consumed in coastal areas, and there is also evidence of trade in conserved fish and consumption of small freshwater fish. In short, a wider variety of foods were eaten then than in modern times; and it should be mentioned that the range of herbs and spices used as flavourings was similarly extensive, including those now regarded as typical of C. and S. America and others which have fallen out of use.

Beekeeping (stingless bees of *Melipona* and *Trigona* spp, which were indigenous) and HONEY production were important features of Mesoamerican life; the Maya certainly used honey to sweeten some maize drinks, but it is not clear whether they used it for preserves or confectionery.

Chocolate, one of the great gifts of the New World to the Old, is often thought of as an Aztec thing. The Maya, however, were familiar with it many centuries earlier, using cacao beans as currency and drinking chocolate (although it is not known whether they reserved the beverage for ceremonial occasions or had it regularly).

For an interesting point about Maya vocabularies, see EAT. For what can be inferred about their eating habits, and further information generally, see Sophie Coe (1994). (SC)

MAYONNAISE a famous sauce which is, essentially, an EMULSION of olive oil and vinegar (or lemon juice) stabilized with egg yolk and seasoned to taste (usually with salt, pepper, mustard). There are many theories about the origin of its name. For example, Stobart (1980) listed four principal theories. However, as Ayto (1993) puts it:

the explanation now generally accepted, based on the early spelling *mahonnaise*, is that it originally meant literally 'of Mahon', and that the sauce was so named to commemorate the taking of Port Mahon, capital of the island of Minorca, by the duc de Richelieu in 1756 (presumably Richelieu's chef, or perhaps even the duke himself, created the sauce). English borrowed the word from French in the 1840s (its first recorded user was that enthusiastic gastronome, William Makepeace Thackeray).

As a French word mayonnaise, meaning the sauce, first appeared in print in 1806. However, an interesting curiosity is its appearance in the phrase 'mayonnaise de poulet' in a German book of 1804—see Höfler (1996). Certainly, the word has appeared as both an adjective and a noun since the early 19th century, and still does. As an English noun, it has been prominent in the phrase Egg mayonnaise, a dish popular in Britain in the decades after the Second World War.

See also AÏOLI; GREENSAUCE; RÉMOULADE; TARTARE.

MAZURKA the Anglicized form of the Russian and Polish word *mazurek*, one meaning of which is a particular kind of cake/pastry. Their varied nature is clear from the fact that no two books seem to be describing exactly the same thing; and even one book (for example, the famous work of Molokhovets translated by Joyce Toomre, 1992) may give numerous widely different recipes.

Mazurkas can be in the form of small squares cut from a flattish meringue-like confection. These may be decorated on top with nuts and dried fruits or icing, sometimes with jam. Traditions vary between Russia and Poland and no doubt also by region, but a connection with Easter, Christmas, carnival week, or other special occasions is common.

The origin of mazurka cakes and the name is not known. The name seems not to have any connection with mazurka, the dance (where the name relates to a woman of a particular part of Poland, Mazovia). One theory is that they may have been inspired by the sweet pastries of Turkish cuisine. Lesley Chamberlain (1989) cites the Polish food historian Maria Lemnis to the effect that a visit by the Turkish emissary in 1778 turned into a festival of sweetmeats and left a permanent mark on Polish confectionery. The adoption of oriental techniques in cake-making coincided with the arrival of chocolate, coffee, and sugar

and together these two events inspired a minor revolution in Polish eating habits and social manners, which may have included the introduction of mazurkas. (HS)

MEADOWSWEET *Filipendula ulmaria*, a common wild herb of temperate climates in the northern hemisphere, whose fragrant clusters of creamy flowers and leaves have been used for flavouring various beverages and stewed fruits, besides having traditional medicinal uses and being much used for strewing purposes in medieval times.

MEAGRE *Argyrosomius regius*, a large fish of the Mediterranean and central E. Atlantic which belongs to the sciaenid family (see also CROAKER; DRUM; KINGFISH). Maximum length around 2 m (80"); usual market length half that or less. Although its Atlantic range is given as being from Denmark down to the Congo, and it used to be commonly taken in the region of Cadiz, it seems now to be caught mainly by Turkish fishermen. Their name and the Italian (*bocca d'oro*) both refer to the golden throat.

For the cook, the meagre may be treated like a particularly large SEA BASS, which it resembles in having firm white flesh, relatively free of bones, and good to eat cold as well as hot.

There are two other notable fish of the sciaenid family to be found in Mediterranean fish markets:

- *Umbrina cirrosa*, French *ombrine*, Spanish *verrugato*, Portuguese *calafate*, Italian *ombrina*. Maximum length 1 m (40"), marked with distinctive diagonal wavy lines (blue bordered with black) on its yellowish sides. Present also in the E. Atlantic.
- *Sciaena umbra*, the corb (and in French), Spanish *corvallo*, Italian *corvo*. Maximum length 70 cm (28"). One of its Turkish names means 'miller', referring to the relatively large otoliths ('stones' in the ears), which are thought to resemble a miller's grinding stones, and which can be made into necklaces.

The meagre is not called croaker, but it can and does make the noise which gives their name to croakers. Buckland (1883) records an interesting experiment in this connection:

The maigre is said to be able to make a noise under water. This has been described as grunting, or purring. On placing my hand and arm down the throat of a maigre, I discovered that the inner side of every gill-arch was studded with little pyramid-shaped projections, placed alternately, so that they would lock into each other like two combs. On drying and examining a specimen of these under a glass, I find that this roughness is caused by a vast number of very minute needle-pointed teeth, set as close together as the hooks on a teazle-head. There are also two sets of teeth (very much in the shape of a sheep's kidney) on the upper surface of the oesophagus. This plateau of oesophagal weapons is composed of teeth, some long and pointed, others very minute, feeling like sand-paper to the touch. The idea struck me that these teeth in the gullet might possibly be the instruments by which the fish produces his purring noise. Upon causing the room to be kept perfectly quiet, and grating them together, a noise was produced, reminding one forcibly of a mouse gnawing at a board; but most probably the fish in life could sing his own song better than we could, and I believe his teeth are musical instruments.

MEALS vary in number per day, relative sizes, and nomenclature around the world. As regards number, one thing was made quite clear by Hilaire Belloc (1940), applying the wisdom which he had acquired in an Anglo-Saxon environment to the rest of the world, in his poem about Henry King, whose chief defect was chewing bits of string. The doomed child, on the verge of expiring in front of the horrified physicians who had declared his case hopeless, issued this succinct warning:

> 'Oh my friends be warned by me,
> That breakfast, dinner, lunch and tea
> Are all the human frame requires.'
> With that the wretched child expires.

See BREAKFAST; ELEVENSES (also MERENDA); LUNCH; AFTERNOON TEA; HIGH TEA; DINNER (which includes supper).

MEAT (*see page 488*)

MEATBALLS have been the subject of an eccentric and enthralling book by Spoerri (1982), but neither he, nor any other author, has succeeded or could succeed in treating the subject comprehensively. There are too many manifestations, around the world, of this item, which is essentially just minced meat (of any edible animal) formed into a ball and cooked in any of various ways. For some of the best versions, in S. Asia, the Middle East, the Balkans, and N. Africa, see KOFTA.

Some of the general names in other languages for meatball are: *albóndiga* (Spanish); *keftédes* (Greek); *kötbulle* (Swedish); *Klopse* (German); *frikadeller* (Danish). There is great diversity among these, for the other ingredients and flavourings vary considerably. In Greece, for example, meatballs may include flat-leaved parsley, Greek oregano, thyme, mustard seeds, wine, breadcrumbs, olive oil, and salt and pepper. The result is unmistakably Greek and could not conceivably be confused with a meatball from one of the

Nordic countries. Traditional sauces or accompaniments also serve as lines of demarcation. Dill sauce or sour cream and spring onion sauce would label meatballs Russian, as Lesley Chamberlain (1983) indicates in an interesting passage about the oval *kotlety* and round *bitki* of that country. (She also implies what are patently insoluble riddles about the points at which meatballs become meat patties or HAMBURGERS or RISSOLES as their shape diverges from the purely spherical. Such questions abound. May one call a torpedo-shaped KIBBEH a meatball?)

Meatballs may be small, designed to go into soups or to be part of a dressing for pasta, or large enough to be the main element of a savoury dish. In the latter case they would often be a humble, inexpensive dish, ordering which in a restaurant would not have impressed American waiters of the mid-20th century, if one may be guided by the song about the man who ordered a single meatball and hankered for some bread to go with it, but was embarrassed to hear the waiter's voice come echoing down the hall: 'We don't serve bread with one meat ball.'

MEAT EXTRACTS is a term covering various products which claim to contain all the 'goodness' and flavour of meat in concentrated form. They are called extracts, or, more properly, 'extractives', because they are soluble substances extracted from meat when it is put into water. Chemically, they include soluble inorganic salts, lactic acid, and various nitrogenous compounds which are not proteins. Manufacturers add flavourings and other ingredients according to their own formulae. Best known in Britain are Bovril (a thick, syrupy dark brown substance), and Oxo (the crumbly 'stock cube'); both were originally intended for dilution as drinks. Their role as a dietary supplement is less than early advertising implied, but they contain B-group vitamins, and stimulate the secretion of saliva and gastric juices, a property derived from the smell and flavour of compounds produced during cooking meat. They are still used for drinks, as flavouring agents, and are added to meat dishes, soups, and numerous savoury snacks.

Commercial meat extracts have a complex history. When, in the late 18th century, scientists began to study the composition of meat, they claimed to have discovered a substance, held to be responsible for the good flavour of meat-based soups and sauces and the brown crusts of roasts, which they called 'osmazome' (from Greek, *osme* = odour, and *zomos* = soup). Through popularizing works by scientists and gastronomers in the first half of the 19th century, its retention came to be considered

a very important part of meat cookery. (Later, it became apparent that osmazome was a complex mixture of chemicals produced by browning reactions when meat juices were concentrated over heat.)

Nutritional theory also contributed to the development of meat extracts. The French physiologist Magendie, in the early 19th century, discovered that foods containing nitrogen are essential to human growth. This attracted much attention. Osmazome was known to be rich in nitrogen, and the German chemist Baron Justus von Liebig, experimenting with the broth from boiled meat, noted that this too contained appreciable amounts of the element. In the 1840s, he undertook experiments to discover how nitrogen contributed 'flesh-forming' properties. He concluded that some nitrogen-containing foods were more valuable than others. These experiments laid the basis for future work on PROTEIN.

This work led to speculation that water in which meat had been steeped or cooked yielded a soluble substance of great value as food. Meat bouillon was already a traditional medicine; the scientific discoveries enhanced this and led to a vogue, now disproved but not forgotten in folklore, for jellied broth and beef tea (made by infusing scraped raw beef in hot water for some hours) as invalid food. These substances were popularly considered to be strengthening, palatable, easily digested, and stimulating to the appetite.

A domestic precedent for preserving bouillons was provided by PORTABLE SOUP, strong meat broth boiled until it became syrupy, at which stage it was allowed to set and dry out. This had been available since at least the early 18th century.

Liebig eventually took the view that GELATIN, nitrogenous compounds in broth, and 'osmazome' were not flesh formers. This conclusion did not prevent him from entering commerce with a product for which extravagant nutritional claims were made. In the 1850s he had described a process for manufacturing a meat extract, and decided there was a market for such a product, based on a glut of meat available in southern hemisphere countries. In 1865 Liebig's 'Extractum Carnis' reached Britain from Fray Bentos in Uruguay. Later this was renamed 'Lemco', and was finally reformulated to become Oxo (first marketed in 1900).

Bovril originated in the 1870s when Scottish butcher and entrepreneur John Lawson Johnston emigrated to Canada and became involved in food processing. One of his inventions was 'Johnston's Fluid Beef', first manufactured in Quebec in 1874, and promoted with free samples at ice carnivals in Montreal. Re-established in London, (*cont. on page 490*)

Meat

Meat had a very general meaning, more or less equivalent to food, in early medieval times. So did the equivalent French word, *viande*; the first French cookery book, *Le Viandier*, was not so named because of any emphasis on animal flesh. 'White meats', in medieval English, were dairy products such as milk and cheese. Gradually, however, the meaning of 'meat' became more restricted until, with the exception of a few terms and phrases such as 'sweetmeat' and 'meat and drink', it came to refer solely to the flesh of animals used as food.

Most often, the word applies to the skeletal muscle of mammals; it would not include OFFAL (although many 'meat products' may contain offal). Of the several dozen mammals used for food on a regular basis, those yielding BEEF, VEAL, PORK, and LAMB are dominant in the western world, while WATER-BUFFALO has importance in Asia and GOAT retains some importance in the numerous parts of the world where goats thrive.

THE NUTRITIONAL AND MORAL DEBATE

A piece of meat is central to the definition of a proper meal for most Europeans and N. Americans. And it is an important source of high-quality protein in their diet. It supplies many of the AMINO ACIDS required by the human body for good health. It is also a good source of iron (see MINERALS), vitamin A and some B vitamins (see VITAMINS).

A less desirable component of the diet which is also supplied by meat is fat, especially saturated fatty acids (see FATS AND OILS), present in relatively high proportions in red meats. Neither cutting visible fat off the meat nor breeding very lean animals are entirely satisfactory responses, since the fat makes a valuable contribution to flavour and texture. The answer would seem to be to eat less meat generally.

The VEGETARIAN movement points out that there is no necessity for meat in human diet, as all the nutrients which it provides can be obtained from other sources. The arguments that killing for food is morally wrong and that raising food animals is a prodigal and wasteful way to use land are both frequently advanced; objections are also raised to modern methods of intensive animal husbandry. Yet people continue to eat meat; frequently in wealthy countries, and whenever they can in poorer ones. Meat on the plate is often an indication of status and wealth. Also, most people enjoy the taste and texture, so some meat substitutes, such as textured vegetable proteins (see PROTEIN), are textured and flavoured in ways which attempt to imitate meat.

Meat, more than any other food, is hedged around with taboos and notions of uncleanliness. Meat-eating peoples display puzzling anomalies over which species they consider 'clean'. There are no clear reasons why one animal should be perfectly acceptable food in one culture and not at all in another. Ancient ethnic and religious divisions, and the special hygiene problems provided by handling meat, have been suggested. The meat taboos best known to Europeans are the Jewish and Muslim prohibitions on pork and BLOOD, and the Hindu prohibition on beef. The British find the idea of eating HORSEMEAT distasteful, although it is used in much of continental Europe. Few Europeans would consider eating DOG except under the most extreme circumstances; yet dog meat is consumed in parts of China and was an important source of protein in ancient Mexico. Amphibians and reptiles, such as FROG, LIZARD, and SNAKE, are eaten in some areas. Animals which have a carnivorous diet are not generally considered suitable for food, and the meat of uncastrated adult male animals is often shunned. The strongest prohibition is that on CANNIBALISM, the consumption of human flesh.

The 'moral debate' referred to above has helped to precipitate lively discussions about the diet of early ancestors of humans, in an effort to establish what humans 'naturally eat'. These discussions seem unlikely ever to be fully concluded. However, it can be said that early in human history the invention of stone weapons and the development of hunting skills allowed for more meat in the diet, and the discovery of how to make fire enabled meat to be cooked and thus rendered more palatable. At the end of the last ice age (about 10,000 BC), Europeans were hunting on a large scale and meat, at that time always in the form of GAME, was important in their diets.

The domestic animals familiar today were developed from wild ancestors in prehistoric times. The chronology is uncertain, but it is thought that sheep, goats, cattle, and pigs were all undergoing domestication in the Middle East by 7000 BC. The dog was domesticated in both Eurasia and N. America, and the GUINEA PIG in S. America. The horse (thought to have been domesticated in Russia around 3000 BC) and the chicken (India, about 2000 BC) came late to the scene. All this was important for the history of meat-eating. It should be noted, however, that while domestication and herding meant that meat was close at hand and easily caught, it did not necessarily mean that it was eaten in large amounts, for animals were also valued for milk, wool, and draught.

Another important advance was the invention of fireproof metal and pottery containers, which made it possible for meat to be simmered in liquid as an alternative to roasting in front of the fire. A more ancient, but less convenient, method for cooking it in a liquid had been to place it in a stone-lined pit filled with water, and drop fire-heated stones in to warm the water; see FULACHTA FIADH, dealing with this in Ireland.

Cooking meat is touched on further at the end of this article. Meawhile it is appropriate to consider more closely just what is being cooked.

THE STRUCTURE OF MEAT AND ITS COLOUR

Physically, skeletal muscle consists of long bundles of very thin fibres, each fibre representing an individual cell. Collectively, these bundles give the 'grain' apparent when muscles are cut across. The basic chemistry of meat exploits the properties of two proteins which allow voluntary movement in animals. These are *actin* and *myosin* which exist as long molecules lying parallel to each other in muscle fibres. When muscles contract, electrical impulses cause the two proteins to slide past each other and bond, forming a complex molecule known as *actomyosin*, shortening and holding the position. The fibre bundles are supported by fine sheets of CONNECTIVE TISSUE and are attached to the bones by tendons; the protein COLLAGEN is important in these tissues. Protein accounts for about 18% of the total weight of lean raw muscle, water represents about 75%, and fat 3%. Most of the water is held mechanically within the structure of the muscle, although a small proportion is chemically bound to the protein. Proportions vary according to species, and joints of meat usually include more fat in the form of visible layers.

These properties contribute to the taste and feel of meat on the palate. Long, slender muscle fibres are associated with tenderness, and juiciness with the capacity of the muscle to hold water. High proportions of connective tissue increase the toughness of meat. Reticulin and elastin are not affected by heat, although collagen is, and on heating becomes GELATIN. Most meat produced by western animal husbandry also includes deposits of fat, both as a solid layer under the skin and around internal organs, and as marbling, tiny flecks within the muscle. Marbling also contributes to tenderness, as the pockets of fat melt and lubricate the muscle fibres during cooking.

The red colour of meat is derived from two pigments, both of which contain iron which combines reversibly with oxygen. Haemoglobin, the red pigment in blood responsible for oxygen transport, accounts for about one-quarter to one-third of the pigment. The rest is myoglobin which holds oxygen within the muscle, ready for metabolic purposes. The harder a muscle has to work, the more oxygen it requires and the more myoglobin it contains. HEART muscles, which work non-stop, are a deep red. Age and species also affect the amount of myoglobin; thus beef is a deeper red than veal, and lamb is redder than pork. WHALE meat, which has to hold large amounts of oxygen when the animals make prolonged dives, contains so much myoglobin that it is almost black.

Chemical changes in myoglobin produce the colour changes in fresh meat. After death, the pigment changes from the bright red oxygenated form in living tissue, oxymyoglobin, to purplish, deoxygenated myoglobin. If the meat is cut, the surface turns bright red again for a short time, as oxygen from the air combines with the myoglobin to give oxymyoglobin once more. Fresh meat sometimes shows a brownish discoloration due to denaturation of myoglobin to a form known as metmyoglobin. This reaction is also partially responsible for the brown colour of cooked meat. Traditional meat cures usually turn the meat a pink colour which is heat stable. A reaction between myoglobin and sodium or potassium NITRATES, present in minute quantities in many recipes for preserving meat, is responsible for this. Meat fat also varies in colour, a creamy white being considered most desirable.

The texture and flavour of beef benefits from hanging or ageing the carcass after slaughter. The lean part of beef which has not been aged for long is bright red. Beef which has been aged for some time is a darker red.

FACTORS INFLUENCING THE FLAVOUR AND TEXTURE OF MEAT BEFORE COOKING

The most obvious influence is that of species; other factors are the breed, age, nutrition, sex, and activity level of an animal. Domesticated animals, particularly cattle, have long been bred for specific purposes, and those intended for beef generally provide better meat than dairy cattle. Younger animals have tenderer muscle but less fat than older ones; this is why veal has a rather dry texture. Flavour, too, is milder. Castrated males have a different distribution of fat and muscle from uncastrated ones. A well-nourished animal is fatter, and one which has had little more to do than graze in a field will be tenderer than one that has spent its life pulling a plough. Exercise increases the number of filaments in the bundles of muscle fibres; the larger the bundle, the tougher the meat tends to be. Feedstuffs, too, make a difference to flavour, and certain substances may actually taint the meat.

The condition of the animal at slaughter and the treatment of the carcass afterwards are also important. Indeed, the physiological state of an animal at the time of slaughter is extremely important to the quality of the meat. A calm, well-rested animal is desirable, for in this state the muscles contain their full complement of glycogen (a form of carbohydrate found only in animal tissue, the substance which provides energy for instant action). On slaughter, the glycogen undergoes a series of chemical changes which eventually result in the formation of LACTIC ACID. In a live animal the acid is removed by the bloodstream, or broken down further. In a dead one, it accumulates and lowers the PH of the muscle from about 7 to about 5.5. The increased acidity enhances tenderness (because it aids denaturation of the proteins) and, by making the meat less hospitable to BACTERIA, allows it to keep better. If the animal is struggling or exhausted, the glycogen content of the muscles is lower, and the acid content of the meat correspondingly less, with bad, even disastrous, consequences for the quality of the meat. Rigor mortis, however, is a temporary and inevitable consequence of death, in which the actin and mysosin bind in response to changes in the chemical conditions within the muscle; it passes within hours as the changes continue. If meat is cooked while it persists, it will be too tough.

Domestic animals killed for meat in Britain are first stunned and then bled; removing the blood decreases the risk of spoilage. Generally, after dressing (removal of the hide, head, feet, and internal organs), rigor is allowed to pass and the carcass is hung or aged by suspending it in a temperature of 1–3 °C (34–7 °F) under controlled humidity for a length of time which varies according to species. Lamb is aged for up to a week, pork for about 10 days, and beef can be aged for up to six weeks. Veal requires no ageing. For kosher meat (see JEWISH DIETARY LAWS), Kashrut law stipulates that all meat must be consumed within 72 hours of slaughter. Offal is consumed very soon after slaughter.

During ageing further slow changes leading to increased tenderness occur in the meat. These are poorly understood, but are probably due to ENZYMES acting within the muscles. It is now unusual for meat to be aged for very long, principally for economic reasons: a large quantity of meat in store represents a considerable amount of inert capital; the storage itself is expensive; the meat loses some weight due to evaporation; and the surface of the carcass has to be trimmed after hanging, representing further loss.

An independent limiting factor in ageing meat is the fatty acid content. Unsaturated fatty acids are prone to rancidity. Beef, however, has a high saturated fatty acid content, which means it can be hung for a long time.

JOINTING MEAT

Patterns of jointing meat vary between countries depending on the methods favoured for cookery. In England, meat tends to be cut with two main methods in mind: roasting, for the tenderer parts with a high proportion of muscle, and stewing, for areas with more connective tissue. The various roasting joints are cut across bones and groups of muscles, and the fat left in place. Areas such as the forequarter, less suited to this treatment, are cut into chunks for stewing. N. Americans follow a simplified version of the same principle, with more emphasis on yielding small pieces such as STEAKS and CHOPS suitable for grilling (broiling) or barbecuing; meat unsuitable for such methods is often minced (ground). French butchery methods rely more on dissecting out muscles. Freed from bone, fat, and connective tissue, the meat is rolled and tied to give neat compact joints suitable for cooking with wine or stock.

At this stage, the tenderness of meat can also be influenced by breaking it down physically. Chopping, mincing, or grinding, which breaks the fibres into small pieces, is a common response to tough meat, from the American HAMBURGER to the Middle Eastern KIBBEH. Some cheaper cuts of steak are beaten or tenderized mechanically, but this also affects the water-holding capacity of the muscle, to the detriment of juiciness in the cooked meat. Even tender meat is cut in slices across the grain, making it easier to chew, as the fibres are shorter. Most cuisines have examples of this, for instance, the American T-bone steak, the French escalope (see VEAL), the Middle Eastern KEBAB, and the thin slices cut for STIR-FRYING in Chinese cookery.

The cook may also influence tenderness and flavour in the kitchen. One way of doing this is to add fat by LARDING or barding (as when small birds are wrapped in thin sheets of fat). Another is using a MARINADE. For marinating, meat is soaked in mixtures of herbs, spices, oil, and acid ingredients such as wine, vinegar, or fruit juice. Acid does denature the surface proteins of the meat, but has a limited effect on the interior and tends to make the meat dry. Chemical TENDERIZERS, using enzymes which break down proteins, can also be rubbed over meat before cooking.

COOKING MEAT

Meat is rarely consumed raw, although some cultures include the practice and one or two western dishes, notably steak TARTARE, do call for raw meat. There are several good reasons for cooking meat. Safety is one; raw meat may carry pathogenic organisms.

Cooking also enhances flavour and makes meat easier to chew and digest. It affects the structure of meat in several ways. It acts on the muscle fibres, in which the proteins coagulate, becoming shrunk and dense under prolonged heating. Collagen dissolves slowly at a low temperature, faster at a higher one. SEARING or surface browning enhances flavour (but does not form a juice-retaining crust, as was thought in the 19th century). Cooking denatures the myglobin; it retains its red oxymyglobin form in rare meat, but oxidizes and turns greyish-brown on further heating.

Methods for cooking meat fall into two basic categories: dry, which means to ROAST, GRILL, or FRY; and wet—to BRAISE, STEAM, POACH, or BOIL. Dry methods, in which heat reaches the meat by convection through the air or conduction through the surface of a pan, are generally used for tender cuts; wet methods, which rely on liquids for heat transfer, are suitable for tougher cuts with more connective tissue.

For more information on meat cookery, see BEEF; LAMB; PORK; VEAL; and BARBECUE.

See also MEAT PRESERVATION.

Johnson began to manufacture a stronger product marketed under the brand name Bovril (from Latin, *bo* = ox; and vril, from *vrilya* = life force, a word coined in a novel by Bulwer-Lytton).

Inspired advertising implying that a small amount of meat extract contained the concentrated equivalent of much larger weights of meat, and a belief in the essential 'goodness' of this, ensured success for the products. Especially notable was a picture of an ox sadly regarding a pot of Bovril, captioned 'Alas! my poor brother'. Such claims, including that by Liebig's company, that a pound of extract contained the concentrated essence of 36 lb (16 kg) of meat, were rubbished by doctors and others. *Law's Grocer's Manual* (*c*.1895) remarked that 'Most of these preparations form pleasant stimulants, but of very *doubtful* nutritiveness', a statement which did not prevent a mass of imitations, including Borthwicks Fluid Beef, Hipi Mutton Essence, Bonovin's Exox, CWS Silvox, Foster Clark's

Ju-Vis, Viskor, Verox, Beefex, Vimbos, Vigoral, Hugon's Torox, and Valentine's Meat Juice. Bovril and Oxo survived, Liebig merging with Brooke Bond in 1968 to form the multinational Brooke Bond Oxo.

The manufacture of meat extracts and essences is a trade secret, but seems likely to follow Liebig's original principles of steeping raw, pulped beef in water, heating the mixture, then straining it under pressure, boiling, and evaporating the liquid to a pasty consistency. Current brands have hydrolized vegetable protein and other ingredients included in the lists on their labels.   (LM)

MEAT LOAF a dish whose visibility is considerable higher in real life, especially in N. America and Britain, than in cookery books. This situation might be changed if it had a French name (*pâté chaud de viande hachée, préalablement marinée dans du vin de pays et des aromatiques*), but it does not. In the USA the term was only recorded in print from 1899, in Britain not until 1939 (although liver loaf and ham loaf occurred earlier). The use of 'loaf' is particularly appropriate as most recipes include bread, usually in the form of soft breadcrumbs. Also, it is shaped like a loaf and may indeed be baked in a loaf tin or something similar. A worthy dish, which can embody the sort of rusticity which the word 'peasant' evokes, but can also exhibit the kind of refinement associated with bourgeoise cookery. Its range, however, does not extend into the realm of haute cuisine.

The editors of the *OED* assert that meat loaf is usually eaten cold in slices.

MEAT PRESERVATION is one ancient and important part of the art of food PRESERVATION in general, a topic also discussed under CANNING, DRYING, FREEZING, PICKLE, REFRIGERATION, SALTING, SEALING, and SMOKING FOODS.

Raw meat putrefies because it is an ideal food for micro-organisms. BACTERIA and MOULD spores are easily introduced during processing, and they metabolize the surface of the meat, discolouring it and producing breakdown products with a foul smell. Storage processes are designed to inhibit this. Several methods are employed. They depend on controlling temperature, excluding oxygen, salting, and dehydration.

Dehydration is probably the most primitive method. At the simplest level, hanging thin strips of meat in a dry, draughty atmosphere is sufficient; this is how JERKY is made. Smoking meat probably originated from efforts to dry meat over the fire; smoke contains chemicals which have a preservative effect. At the far extreme of technology, meat is dehydrated by freeze-drying to provide lightweight military rations. Drying radically alters the texture of the meat, making it hard and chewy.

Until the mid-19th century, by far the most important preservation method was salting. This method was known in Britain as long as 2,000 years ago, and some types of salted meat, notably those based on pork, are still popular today. Salt acts as a preservative by combining with the water in the muscle so that it is unavailable for bacterial growth. Over the centuries several different methods or cures for meat have developed. One principal difference is whether the meat is dry salted or soaked in brine. Spices and sugar are sometimes added to give extra flavour, but the most important addition is saltpetre or NITRATE, which, in tiny quantities, helps the salt to penetrate the meat and produces a stable pink colour in the muscle.

Microbial growth in meat can also be prevented by SEALING, excluding oxygen. This principle was known, but imperfectly understood, by the Romans, who preserved meat by placing it in containers and covering it completely with honey. It is also the principle underlying English POTTING and the French method of making CONFIT of GOOSE or DUCK, in which the meat is cooked and stored in copious amounts of melted fat.

One problem with these relatively primitive methods is obtaining a truly airtight seal. This was solved in the early 19th century. In France, Nicholas APPERT was awarded a prize for his method of sealing jars in 1804. In England in 1810, a method for sealing meat in iron canisters was patented by Robert Durand. Meat and fat was placed in an airtight tin box, the top soldered on, and the whole container then heated to sterilize the contents. The art of CANNING developed rapidly in N. America, and by the latter part of the century, large amounts of canned meat were being imported to Britain from the USA, Australia, and Argentina. The basic method for canning remains the same today, with refinements in the shapes of the cans, the materials used, and a finer judgement of the time and temperature involved.

From the late 19th century onwards, meat-preservation techniques have concentrated on controlling low temperatures. Bacteria do not grow at temperatures below freezing (although they are not killed). It was common knowledge that meat kept well when very cold or frozen, but few people were able to exploit this. Ice houses, insulated pits filled with ice cut from frozen rivers and ponds in the winter, were only for the rich. It was the invention of mechanical refrigeration during the mid-19th century and its installation in steamships that made the difference. The first cargo of frozen beef from Australia arrived in London in 1880, and after that became a regular import. Frozen meat is kept at a temperature of −18 °C (0 °F). It is preferable for meat to be frozen quickly, as this forms small ice crystals. If large crystals are allowed to form, they damage the structure of the meat physically, and on thawing some of the water is lost in the form of 'drip', the thin red fluid which defrosting meat releases. Chilling, too, in which the meat is held at temperatures between 1 and 4 °C (34–9 °F), can also be regarded as a short-term method of meat preservation at low temperature.

Other methods of meat preservation, products of 20th-century technology, are still largely at the experimental stage. IRRADIATION, treatment with ionizing radiation at doses which kill spoilage organisms, has encountered problems with consumer acceptability, and produces flavour changes within the meat. The economic and social importance of meat in the diet of the developed world means that work on new methods of preservation is likely to continue.

MEDIEVAL CUISINE a phrase which usually refers to western, or Christian, Europe and to the 13th, 14th, and 15th centuries. There is good reason for this; almost all we know of medieval cuisine has been derived from written sources, and the oldest surviving culinary manuscript from Christian Europe (written in old Danish, and mentioned in MEDIEVAL CUISINE: THE SOURCES) was most likely composed in the first half of the 13th century.

The noticeable evolution of cuisine over these three centuries suggests that a developed, if undocumented, cuisine must have already existed before the first written recipe. It was certainly not a direct continuation of Roman cuisine (see CLASSICAL ROME), nor even of the later BYZANTINE COOKERY, both of which showed a fondness for the highly flavoured fish sauce GARUM (or *garos*). More likely the origins of medieval European cuisine were in the simple roasts and one-pot stews of meats and vegetables which became progressively more sophisticated as they were infused with spices and accompanied by elaborate sauces. For the culinary development of the post-1000 period must be seen in the context of the growth of towns and the increase in trade which occurred, especially after the First Crusade of 1099.

The twin revival of trade and towns had two corollaries particularly relevant to the development of cuisine: a gradual shift from self-sufficiency to a money-based economy, and the rise of the urban bourgeoisie. People were no longer solely dependent on what their patch of land produced but could buy what the market offered—and as trade expanded, so the market offered an increasing diversity of goods. But trade also brought contact with other civilizations, in particular the Arabs who controlled the spice trade from the East. In the 11th century the Genoese had trading enclaves in S. Spain, which had been conquered by the Arabs in the 7th century, and the guild of spice merchants of Montpellier had branches in N. Africa in the 13th century. Sicily, which was such an important centre for the diffusion of knowledge through translation of works from Arabic to Latin, was an Arab colony from the 9th to the 11th centuries. What the Arab civilization offered was a general model of a refined lifestyle in which food had a respected place, and specific examples of the use of ingredients which had hitherto been unknown (such as SUGAR) or little used in cuisine (such as ALMONDS).

Incidentally, the Arab link also provided a theoretical foundation, in the form of medicinal and dietetic writings, for the later European culinary texts. Around the 11th century Latin translations of many of the most important works of medicine—usually commentaries on the Hippocratic corpus by such respected doctors as Rhazes and AVICENNA—began to reach Europe. Alongside these, and similarly derived from Arab sources, was a popular and practical genre of 'health handbooks' which typically set out a code of healthy living, including dietary recommendations; while they did not necessarily give detailed recipes, they often described how an ingredient should be prepared, or which ingredients went well together. Certain medieval recipes (e.g. for *romania*, discussed by Rodinson in Perry, ed, 2000) have been shown to have made their way from dietetic texts to culinary compilations. Further, the dietetic text provided the model for the early written recipes, typically succinct and summary. By the end of the 15th century the art of recipe-writing had progressed as much as had the art of cooking; no longer a sequence of telegraphic instructions, the written recipe became the expression of individual (and identified) master chefs who recorded their own practices and experiences.

The authors or compilers of the medieval culinary manuscripts, insofar as they are known, worked for kings, other nobles, and wealthy merchants. Indeed, many of the surviving manuscripts—over 130, scattered amongst libraries in Europe and America— began their lives in the libraries of the rich, though cookery books were not common in medieval libraries. Inventories record herbals, books on medicine, dietetics, and agriculture, and books relating to the accepted leisure activities of the well-born rich (hunting, chess and other games, music), but mention of cookery books is infrequent. Nevertheless, most of the texts

were written in the vernacular, which suggests that they were intended for practical reference and instruction. And while they might have originated in noble and wealthy households, they included recipes for simple dishes as well as complex, costly ones.

Rich people, of course, could choose whether to eat simply or elaborately. The author of *Le* MENAGIER DE PARIS (1393) gives recipes for '*Potages communs san espices et non lyans*' ('ordinary dishes without spices and unthickened') which are typically soups or purées based on dried peas, fresh and dried broad beans, beet leaves, onions, and cabbage, sometimes with the addition of a piece of salted pork. Few of these 'ordinary' dishes, however, feature in his suggested menus for dinners to which guests would be invited, except those proposed for Lent. On the other hand, vegetable dishes formed the daily fare of resident students at the College of Trets in S. France in the mid-14th century, and for about six months of the year it was cabbage soup every second day! For the poor, whether living in the city or in the country, there was no alternative to these one-pot meals based on vegetables or pulses; they could not afford fresh meat, except perhaps on Sundays, and what they could afford were the cheaper meats and cuts which needed to be boiled to be made palatable. In any case, even had they been able to afford a joint for roasting, they lacked the necessary equipment. Studies of household inventories in France have shown that only rich households possessed roasting spits and grills; ordinary households had just a cauldron for boiling.

This soup or gruel, accompanied by breads, was the sustenance of the poor all over Europe, with minor variations from region to region. Dried peas and broad beans were commonplace in N. Europe, while in Mediterranean regions chickpeas and lentils augmented the options. Cabbages, beets, spinach, turnips, onions, leeks, and garlic were similarly prevalent, but southern gardens (at least by the 15th century) also yielded gourds, melons, aubergines, and cucumbers. It is significant that some of these 'newer' vegetables, introduced or popularized by the Arab culture, were prepared in more flattering ways than simply boiling with a piece of salt pork; they were puréed, enriched with eggs, flavoured with spices, in dishes which probably reflected an Arab influence. This variety of vegetables characterized the Mediterranean diet as much as did the predominance of white wheaten bread, the use of olive oil, eggs, and fish when possible, an abundance of wine, and meat typically in the form of mutton, lamb, and kid; pork tended to be eaten in salted form. In N. Europe, by contrast, bread was also made from rye and barley; dairy foods were more

common, beef was preferred to mutton, and fresh pork was more frequently eaten. Techniques of salting and curing pork differed between N. and S. Europe; these different traditions are still evident today in York-style cooked hams and the dried prosciutto-style hams common to Italy, S. France, and Spain. Salads were rare in N. Europe, but relatively common in Mediterranean regions, especially in spring and summer; they were made of a diversity of young salad greens and herbs, dressed with oil, salt, and vinegar.

Social differentiation added another dimension to this depiction of medieval food and eating. For those workers paid wholly or partly in kind, the quantities offered of bread and of 'companage' (literally, 'with bread', typically the meat component of the ration) varied in accord with the status of the work. As one moved up the scale from labourer to brother to preceptor in a monastery or similar establishment, so did the quantity and quality of the companage, and so did the quantity or the quality of the wine. In royal households where a whole retinue of courtiers was employed, more and more varied dishes in total, and dishes of higher status, were offered to those of higher rank and standing in the household. Medieval dietaries explicitly listed those foods appropriate to labourers (cow meat, salted meats), and those more suitable to persons who practised a more leisured lifestyle (chicken and other poultry, lamb, veal). The medieval recipe collections reflect the foods of this latter category.

Not surprisingly, this hierarchical cuisine made much use of social markers, and spices were ideally suited to this purpose. Expensive and instantly recognizable, they marked the status of a dish and of the household in which it was offered. Simple, homely vegetable dishes tended to avoid spices, apart from pepper (which by the medieval period had become quite cheap), while sophisticated meat dishes used imaginative combinations of the different spices then available: pepper, long pepper, ginger, cinnamon, nutmeg, saffron, mace, cardamon, cloves, grains of paradise, galingale, cubeb. Certainly, spices added flavour interest to a dish, but their fascination resided primarily in their symbolic value. There is no evidence that spices were used to camouflage the undesirable flavours of stale—not to say rotten—meat in refrigerator-less days, nor that spices served to enliven a monotonous diet of salted meats and fish. The standard accompaniment to salted beef or pork was either mustard or a similar condiment made from the seeds of the rocket plant, *Eruca sativa*. Salted meats and fish were considered low-status ingredients, appropriate for labourers but not for nobles, and certainly not worthy enough to be treated with spices. Nor were spices used as preservatives; the common methods of preserving food then, as now, were salting, pickling (with vinegar), conserving with sugar or honey, and drying, and all these are described in medieval recipes. Spices may often have been added in the preserving process—especially with fruits and vegetables cooked with sugar or honey—but they were not, *per se*, the preserving agents.

The evidence of cookbooks shows that spices were a distinguishing mark of medieval cuisine on more than one level, differentiating rich from poor, town from country, special feasts from ordinary meals. Spices marked the religious festivals of Christmas and Easter, an association which is retained to the present day. Christmas was a busy period for the spice merchants; the 13th-century Provençal poem of *Flamenca* evokes an image of spices

> giving such sweet and fragrant smell,
> As at Montpellier, where they sell,
> And pound the spice at Christmas tide.
> 'Tis then that their best trade is plied
> In spices.

Spices were not necessarily a standard ingredient in every dish, and could hardly have retained their image of luxury and rarity if they were ingredients of everyday usage. However, in those dishes which did call for spices, they would have been used in such amounts as to make their presence unmistakable.

One important role of spices was in sauces which were the obligatory accompaniment to roast meats (and, to a lesser extent, to boiled meats). While certain sauces were specific to certain roasts, others could partner a variety of meats. Cameline sauce, in which the dominant spice was cinnamon, could be served with roast lamb, veal, kid, sucking pig, venison, chicken, pheasant, partridge, and rabbit; GREENSAUCE (*salsa verde*), typically a purée of herbs and garlic with the addition of ground nuts or breadcrumbs, went with mutton, kid, and lamb; a simple blend of lemon or orange juice, salt, and spices with roast partridge and pigeon. The dark and heavily spiced *poivrade* or *piperata* sauce was a standard accompaniment to game.

Similar sauces entered into the composition of *brouets* (to use the French term; bruet or browet in England), the ancestors of the later RAGOUTS. The medieval *brouet* was a dish of meat (or poultry, or fish) in a spiced and thickened sauce. It usually required three culinary operations, the most common sequence being parboil–fry–simmer in a sauce. *Brouets* were dishes of high status, their complexity no doubt appreciated by discriminating diners. The ingredients employed to thicken

the sauce (and similarly, sauces for roasts), singly or in combination, varied from simply dried or toasted bread, often soaked in vinegar, wine, or VERJUICE then pounded with the spices, to almonds or almond milk, hazelnuts and walnuts, ground meat or fish, ground liver, and eggs or egg yolks, cooked or raw. In some sauces, particularly those made with almonds or almond milk, the sourness of the vinegar or verjuice was tempered by the addition of sugar or other sweet ingredients such as honey or, in Mediterranean regions, concentrated grape must (*sapa* in Italian manuscripts, *arrop* in Catalan ones).

In medieval Europe Christianity imposed an obligation to refrain from eating meat and other animal products such as milk and eggs during Lent, Ember Days, and on Fridays and Saturdays; in total, for about 150 days of the year meat was proscribed. Thus many of the meat dishes, in particular *brouets*, have Lenten or fish-day counterparts in which the meat is replaced by fish, stock by almond milk or a vegetable stock (the liquid from boiling peas, for example), lard by oil. Nevertheless, there were other ways of preparing fish which did not borrow from the carnal repertoire. They could be fried, for example—and often were in Mediterranean regions, where frying in olive oil was the most common procedure with small and medium-sized fish. Fried fish was accompanied by the juice of bitter oranges or lemons or by greensauce. Grilled fish was also served with lemon or orange juice, or with verjuice, or with the oil-and-vinegar marinade with which it was basted during cooking. Larger fish could be roasted (grilled), poached, or cooked in a sauce; such sauces, unless they were fish-day equivalents of meat dishes, tended to rely less on spices and more on herbs for flavouring.

Meat and fish could also be baked in pies. Some pies, consisting of whole chickens or joints of meat wrapped in a thick and presumably inedible pastry, were a means of short-term preservation; Maestro Martino (see ITALIAN COOKERY BOOKS) suggests that such pies keep for 15 days, or as long as a month. Recipe books rarely give recipes or instructions for making pastry (merely 'make a crust'), but by the end of the 15th century progress in culinary techniques produced a primitive type of edible shortcrust pastry using flour, olive oil, and water or flour, eggs, and butter. Since this required only a short cooking time, pie fillings were also modified by being sliced or chopped and partly cooked. The *torte*, which probably originated in Italy and became very popular in N. Europe in the 16th century (as a *tourte*), was generally a double-crusted pie with a soft filling based on fresh cheese and eggs with herbs, mashed vegetables, or meat

hash; unexpectedly perhaps, it was liberally strewn with sugar and sprinkled with rosewater. There were also single-crusted tarts with similar fillings and tarts of apples and other fruits.

The logic of medieval menus was not such as to discriminate separate savoury from sweet dishes, which could appear in almost any service. Nevertheless, the final course, prior to the spiced wine and COMFITS, most often consisted of sweet dishes—fruit tarts, custard tarts, baked apples, WAFFLES (*gaufres*), and FRITTERS. Fritters were perhaps more customary in S. Europe, where oil was more plentiful (though many recipes imply that the fritters are a winter dish, to be made when the pig is killed so that they may fry in the rendered fat). Some consisted of soft fillings, similar to those for *torte*, wrapped in pastry and fried; others were made of fresh cheese blended with egg white, flour, and flavourings. Commonly, they were sprinkled with sugar or drizzled with honey (even batter-dipped slices of mild cheese received this treatment in Catalan cuisine).

In the popular perception medieval cuisine is light years away from today's post-NOUVELLE CUISINE. Like an Egyptian mummy, it is seen as having curiosity value but little relevance to the present. Yet many dishes said to be 'traditional' have their origins in medieval cuisine, and many others have persisted, almost unchanged, for hundreds of years (a good example of this is the dish of spinach with currants or raisins and pine nuts found around the Mediterranean coast from Barcelona to Genoa, which is very similar to one described in a 15th-century Catalan recipe). The Christmas MINCE PIES and the sweet, spiced *petits pâtés de Pézenas* both have medieval origins; the German *Pfeffernüsse* and the *pan pepato* from Bologna use spice combinations that could have come straight out of a medieval cookbook. The GREENSAUCE served with boiled beef in Italy is virtually no different from the *salsa verde* of medieval texts; the Catalan ROMESCO can be described as a medieval sauce of pounded garlic, almonds, and bread, with the addition of pounded red peppers. A lemon wedge is a standard accompaniment to fried sole, and icing sugar is sprinkled on apple fritters, exactly as in the 14th and 15th centuries.

It might be rash to claim that modern cuisine is a direct descendant of the medieval, but it would be equally foolish to ignore the role of medieval cuisine in the evolution of European cuisines.

See also MEDIEVAL CUISINE: THE SOURCES.

BS

READING: Bridget Ann Henisch (1976); Constance Hieatt (1988); Bruno Laurioux (1997); Odile Redon, Françoise Sabban, and Silvano Serventi (1998); Terence Scully (1995).

MEDIEVAL CUISINE THE SOURCES.

Scholarship in this field made great advances in the last decades of the 20th century. The known sources are now more numerous and variegated than they used to be; and much new work has been done on elucidating and comparing them. For some notable examples, see Flandrin and Mary and Philip Hyman (1983), Rudolph Grewe (1979), Constance Hieatt (1988), Carole Lambert (1992); Bruno Laurioux (1997), Barbara Santich (1995*a*), Terence Scully (1988, 1995).

'Medieval' is here taken as referring to Europe, and to mean the period from the 13th to the 15th centuries, for reasons explained in MEDIEVAL CUISINE.

The oldest surviving culinary manuscript from Christian Europe was most likely composed in the first half of the 13th century. It is written in old Danish, and forms part of a family of four related manuscripts, of which an edition and translation by Rudolf Grewe and Constance Hieatt is forthcoming. Its content is such that it may well have originated in what is now Provence.

Following this and preceding the era of printed cookbooks are something like 150 other surviving manuscripts in various languages. Many of them can be grouped into 'families', where it is clear that some early compilation of recipes (which may itself not survive) was the ancestor of numerous later versions which display different degrees of adaptation or expansion (and different copying errors, which serve as clues for scholars trying to construct a 'family tree'). Among those of special interest are:

- For N. France and environs, the *Viandier* of TAILLEVENT, the basic early manuscript for the history of cooking in those parts; the unique document usually referred to as the MENAGIER DE PARIS (in which a wealthy Parisian of the 14th century gives a brief on running his household to his young bride); the 15th-century manuscript called *Du fait de cuisine* (with some recipes hinting at familiarity with Mediterranean practices) by Master Chiquart, head of the kitchens of the Duke of Savoy.
- For England, the FORME OF CURY, thought to be the manuscript record of the cooks of King Richard II; the manuscript in the Beinecke Collection at Yale University which has been published as *An Ordinance of Pottage* (ed. Constance Hieatt, 1988).
- For Italy, the work of Maestro Martino, which was drawn on heavily by PLATINA for the first Italian, indeed first ever, printed cookery book (1475).
- For Spain and Portugal, the important Catalan manuscript known as *Sent Sovi* (see CATALAN COOKERY); and the

Portuguese manuscript of the Infanta Dona Maria (see PORTUGAL).

MEDLAR *Mespilus germanica*, a small tree

of the rose family and a cousin of the APPLE. It bears an apple-like fruit, but this is open at the bottom end, exposing the five seed boxes.

The medlar, native to Persia, was grown by the ancient Greeks, then by the Romans from the 2nd century BC. It was a useful addition to the then scanty range of late-ripening winter fruits, and it subsequently spread throughout Europe. It is hardy and flourishes even in Scandinavia.

Several varieties have been cultivated including a seedless one, but it is more common as a wild tree. The medlar can be grafted onto quince or pear stock, but does best on hawthorn stock, as Gerard (1633) noted:

The medlar-tree oftentimes grows in hedges among briars and brambles: being grafted on a white-thorn, it prospers and produces fruit three times as large as those which are not grafted at all, and almost the size of small apples. We have divers sorts of them in our orchard.

Medlar

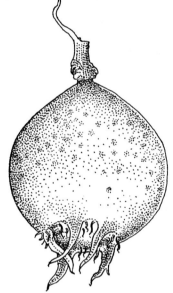

Among these sorts were the 'Neapolitan' variety and a dwarf medlar from the Alps and the hills of Narbonne and Verona.

Phillips (1823) commented that in his time the Dutch medlar was the only one in demand for planting.

The fruit has a notable peculiarity. Even when fully ripe in autumn, it is hard, green, astringent, and inedible. It is picked at this stage and stored in moist bran or sawdust until it browns and softens, a process called 'bletting'. Internal fermentation gives the fruit an acid, aromatic taste which appeals to

some and not to others. The result moved the poet D. H. Lawrence to refer to them as 'Wineskins of brown morbidity, autumnal excrementa', giving off an 'exquisite odour of leave taking'.

The strange taste of the medlar was popular in Victorian Britain. The fruits were brought to table in their bran or sawdust in a dish, and, for a dessert, the brown pulp was scraped out and mixed with sugar and cream. They could also be briefly stewed with sugar. Medlar jelly was made. But a better conserve, acceptable even to those who disliked medlars, was medlar cheese, made with eggs and butter like the more familiar lemon curd.

Medlars have now fallen from favour, except in a few areas such as Piedmont where they are known by the dialect name *puciu*. In the USA they are virtually unknown.

The name 'Naples medlar' has been used for the AZAROLE.

'Japanese medlar' is another name for the LOQUAT. (The Japanese name is *biwa*.)

MEGAPODE a general name applied to

birds in the family Megapodiidae, which belong to Australasia, New Guinea, and various islands of the S. Pacific. These are remarkable in that they do not hatch their young, but after laying the eggs pile up over them mounds of earth or vegetation which serve as incubators. Some megapodes hang around these 'nests' until hatching is complete, but normally the chicks are left to struggle out when they hatch and to fend for themselves, never seeing their parents.

Two groups within the family are formed by the scrub-fowl and the brush turkeys. In the former group *Megapodius freycinet*, the common scrub-hen, is best known. Of its many subspecies, *M. f. nicobariensis*, the Nicobar scrub-hen, has been accorded high praise, e.g. by one author in the 1930s, who declared it to be unsurpassed as a game bird, with white, sweet, juicy, fat flesh.

Brush turkeys, which do look something like turkeys, are mostly Australian. The species *Alectura lathami* is found in many parts of the continent.

MEGRIM *Lepidorhombus whiffiagonis*,

a FLATFISH of the W. Mediterranean and E. Atlantic. It is fished from relatively deep waters and attains a maximum length of 60 cm (24"); so, although its market length is much less, it is a sizeable fish. It enjoys moderate esteem in Spain but is generally regarded as unexciting, tending to be dry, and best fried with plenty of fat.

Alternative names for this fish are sail-fluke and whiff. The latter is a mystery, but the former is explained at length by, for example, Yarrell (1859), who states that in the Orkneys it is observed to use its tail fin as a sail to speed its progress across the surface of the sea. He quotes an interesting communication, dated 1849, from a correspondent in N. Ronaldshay:

In the winter and early spring a pair of Black-headed Gulls take possession of the Bay, drive away all interlopers, and may be seen at daybreak every morning beating from side to side, on the wing, and never both in one place, except in the act of crossing as they pass. The Sail-fluke skims the ridge of the wave towards the shore with its tail raised over its back, and when the wave recedes is left on the sand, into which it burrows so suddenly and completely, that though I have watched its approach, only once have I succeeded in finding its burrow. The Gull, however, has a surer eye, and casting like a hawk, pounces on the Fluke, from which by one stroke of his bill it extracts the liver. If not disturbed, the Gull no sooner gorges this luscious morsel, than it commences dragging the fish to some outlying rock, where he and his consort may discuss it at leisure. By robbing the Black-backs I have had the house supplied daily with this excellent fish, in weather during which no fishing-boat could put to sea. Close to the beach of South Bay a stone wall has been raised to shelter the crops from the sea-spray. Behind this we posted a smart lad, who kept his eye on the soaring Gulls. The moment one of the birds made its well-known swoop, the boy rushed to the sea-strand, shouting with all his might. He was usually in time to scare the Gull away and secure the Fluke, but in almost every case with the liver torn out. If the Gull by chance succeeded in carrying his prey off to the rock, he and his partners set up a triumphant cackling, as if deriding the disappointed lad.

MEHLSPEISEN literally 'foods made with flour', is a C. European overarching category of foods, some savoury and many sweet, which has been well described by Lesley Chamberlain (1989):

What the Austrians call Mehlspeisen, and which are eaten throughout their old empire, are those savoury or sweet dishes of dumplings, yeast pies, noodles, pancakes and other mixtures of grain with milk, sugar, cream and curds, which constitute more than a pudding and less than a meal. These dishes are deep tureens of nursery memories. As they literally translate, 'foods made with flour' can be sweet, semi-sweet or savoury, with more or less sugar and/or salt, depending on availability, or nowadays on taste. New dishes have evolved in every direction from the basic conjunction of coarse flour/meal and water.
. . . The various doughs and pastes combine with vegetables or fruit or soft cheese, cream, butter, bacon, nuts, jam, poppy seed and honey.

MELEGUETA PEPPER the spice from a W. African plant, *Aframomum melegueta*. Where Spanish influence is at work, the spelling in English has sometimes been malagueta or malaguetta. The spice has also

been known as grains of paradise or Guinea grains or pepper.

The plant itself is a tall, reedlike herb which bears red or orange fruits 5–10 cm (2–4") long. Each contains 60–100 brownish seeds, which are aromatic and pungent and which constitute the spice.

Melegueta pepper was unknown to the classical world, but acquired popularity in Europe from the 13th century onwards. This interest, for a long time so strong that the part of W. Africa from which it was shipped was known as the Grain Coast, was already declining in the 18th century and is now slight. However, the seeds continue to be used as a spice and for medicinal purposes in W. Africa, and the pulp surrounding them in the fruits is chewed as a stimulant.

A. granum-paradisi, a related species which also grows in W. Africa, is not, despite its scientific name, regarded as the true grain of paradise. Both species have served as CARDAMOM substitutes.

MELOKHIA (or molokhia), *Corchorus olitorius*, a plant related to and named after the MALLOW (for which *melokhia* is the Arabic word). It belongs to the same genus as the jute plant and is grown worldwide as a source of fibre; but the use of the dark green leaves as a vegetable is also widespread, from W. and N. Africa and the Mediterranean islands through the Middle East to Malaysia, Australia, the Pacific islands, S. America, and the Caribbean.

Melokhia

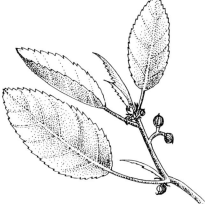

It is in EGYPT that the leaves, which are not unlike sorrel, have the greatest culinary importance. They are made into a soup, also called melokhia, to which they impart a mucilaginous/glutinous quality. This is one of the national dishes of Egypt and has acquired a symbolic importance as the typical dish of the populace, in contrast to more expensive dishes prepared in wealthier households. It is traditionally eaten with rabbit (or chicken or other bird) as a treat.

Generally, the leaves are cooked and eaten like SPINACH. They can be dried and stored; these make a fair substitute for fresh ones, and can be found in Middle Eastern food shops.

A few other plants in the genus provide edible leaves, and one (*C. trilocularis*) is cultivated in parts of Africa for use as a pot-herb.

MELON *Cucumis melo*, a fruit whose history, varieties, and nomenclature perplex even experts. All forms of the species hybridize readily with each other, or indeed with other family members; the French have traditionally taken care to avoid 'incestuous intercourse' by keeping melons and cucumbers well apart.

The melons familiar in western countries are eaten as dessert. In the Orient cooking melons, eaten as vegetables, are equally familiar. These two broad categories are treated here together. Neither includes the WATERMELON, which belongs to a different genus.

HISTORY

The wild ancestors of *C. melo* seem to have been native to the region stretching from Egypt to Iran and NW India. This fits the belief of many people that the finest melons of all in modern times come from Afghanistan and Iran and adjacent areas.

There is little clear evidence of melons being eaten in ancient times. References from classical Greece and Rome are sparse and lack the enthusiasm which one would certainly have expected if they had really good melons on their tables.

After the fall of the Roman Empire the rising Arab civilizations began to cultivate melons. Ibn Al Awam (d. 1145), the agricultural writer of Andalusia, lists six kinds of melon (none, according to his editor, recognizable as a variety known now).

The first unmistakable reference by a European writer is by Albertus Magnus (13th century), who distinguished between the watermelon and the 'pepo', describing the latter in terms which fit the modern cantaloupe (as the term is used in Europe, not as it is used in the USA). Melons were introduced to England in the 16th century, but had to be grown under glass bells or in glasshouses or 'steam-pits'. The same will have been true of most European countries except for those in the Mediterranean region.

Meanwhile the melon had reached China, where it began to develop into cooking varieties. And in 1493 it reached the New World, when Columbus took melon seeds to Haiti on his second voyage. The new fruit was adopted with great enthusiasm by the

Indians of C. and S. America; and the diffusion of melons into parts of N. America followed, although it was not until the last two decades of the 19th century that commercial growing and varietal development began in earnest.

DESSERT MELONS

These fall into three main categories, but there are also hybrids of an intermediate kind.

Cantaloupe melons are named for the town of Cantalupo near Rome, where they are supposed to have been first grown in Europe. They are among the most fragrant and delicious of melons, typically small, round, with a rough surface fissured into segments. The French Charentais is very small, has a yellow skin and orange flesh. The Ogen, named for the Israeli kibbutz where it was developed, has a yellow skin with green stripes rather than fissures, and green flesh. Galia is a related variety. Sweetheart has bright scarlet flesh. Besides varieties with green or salmon-coloured flesh, there are several with creamy-white flesh.

However, the name Cantaloupe is often used in N. America for melons in the next category

Netted (or musk or nutmeg) **melons** vary greatly but have one feature in common: a light network pattern which overlies and stands out from the surface. This was indicated by the word *reticulatus* in the former botanical name *C. melo reticulatus*. The flesh is usually but not always orange. Size varies from small to quite large. The skin may be whitish, yellow, or green; and it may or may not be segmented.

In N. America these are the most important melons of commerce. The best-known types are known as 'cantaloupe' and Persian. The latter is globular in shape, may weigh 3 kg (6 to 7 lb) and has a distinctive aromatic flavour. It is thought to have been introduced to California by Armenians.

Winter melons are so called because they ripen slowly and are not ready until late autumn. If picked before fully ripe, they will ripen slowly in storage, a procedure which is only possible to a very limited extent with the other categories of melon. Winter melons are slightly elongated, like a rugby football, and their skins are finely ribbed. The melons of Cavaillon were thought to be the finest by Alexandre DUMAS, who traded a complete set of his books (well over 300 volumes) for a lifetime supply.

However, the best known of the winter melons is the Honeydew, which has a yellowish, relatively smooth, skin and pale green flesh. Casaba melons, named after a Turkish town and in the same group, usually differ from Honeydews in having a rough skin. They have green or green and yellow skins and pale yellow flesh. Some connoisseurs believe that the finest fruits in this group are the long oval ones, with white flesh, of the cultivar Jharbezeh Mashadi in Iran.

The difficulty of knowing in advance whether a melon will be good or not is notorious. A French writer quoted by Leclerc (1925) declared pessimistically that it was necessary to try 50 to be sure of finding one really good specimen. However, the ripeness of a melon may be gauged by pressing the end opposite the stem. If the melon is ripe, it will yield quite noticeably. Cantaloupes and netted melons do not ripen much after being picked, so should not be bought if they are definitely hard.

The common practice of chilling melons before eating them makes them more refreshing, but diminishes the flavour. A good melon should not need sugar. Some people add a sprinkling of pepper or ginger, or salt.

COOKING MELONS

These are grown in India, China, Japan, and SE Asia. They are not sweet and are used for cooking like other vegetable gourds. Oil may be pressed from the seeds. See also WAX GOURD.

The best known of the 'cooking melons' is the pale, elongated variety called **pickling melon** or Chekiang melon, which is grown from Thailand through SE China to Japan. As its name suggests, it is pickled as well as being eaten fresh. The most important melon of this kind grown in India is known as *kakhi/kakri* and used to be classified as *C. melo* var *utilissima*, the last word of which name is borne out by a passage cited by Watt (1889–96):

This appears to me to be by far the most useful species of [the genus]; when little more than half-grown, they are oblong, and a little downy; in this state they are pickled; when ripe they are about as large as an ostrich's egg, smooth and yellow; when cut they have much the flavour of the melon, and will keep good for several months, if carefully gathered without being bruised, and hung up; they are also in this stage eaten raw, and much used in curries.

Melon seeds are a common snack food wherever melons are grown. They are also used in cookery for certain dishes, e.g. in C. and S. America and in China.

MENAGIER DE PARIS *Le*, the title of a late 14th-century treatise which has survived in several copies, giving remarkable insights into the organization of a noble household of that time. Until recently, the identity of the author was unknown, but Nicole Crossley-Holland (1996), after some diligent detective work, has argued cogently that the author was a certain Guy de Montigny, a 'knight' in the service of the Duke of Berry, who had residences in both his native Champagne and in Paris.

De Montigny (supposing that it was indeed he) composed the book when he was in his fifties, for the benefit of his young bride (an orphan, who was at most 15 years old when married), for whom it was intended to be a full brief on manners and deportment, and also morals and attitudes to marriage, plus a great deal of practical advice on management of the estate and its gardens, on running the household, and on organizing the purchase and preparation of food. It is this last feature which has given the book a special fascination for food historians. There are many compilations of recipes from medieval times (see MEDIEVAL CUISINE: THE SOURCES), and much may be learned from them, but Guy de Montigny provides much more, with everything set in the context of a real, functioning household.

This work has another feature which makes it exceptionally interesting. Most medieval compilations of recipes contained a certain amount of 'dead wood', because the processes of compiling and copying led naturally to the retention of at least some obsolete material from earlier times. Guy de Montigny, in contrast, was patently selecting for his youthful bride precisely those recipes which he expected to be used in his own house in the immediate future. By looking at the nature of the dishes he explained— including several kinds of POTAGE; coloured STEWS (white, green, yellow); PANCAKES, FRITTERS, and RISSOLES; CRAYFISH, CUTTLEFISH, PLAICE, RAY, SALT COD, and two or three dozen other fish; PARTRIDGE, WILD BOAR, and other game—one can form a vivid impression of the meals served at his table.

The *Menagier* may be studied in its first printed edition (Pichon, 1846, and reprinted several times in the 1960s); in the part translation by Eileen Power under the title *The Goodman of Paris* (1928); and in the edition by Georgine Brereton and Janet Ferrier (1981).

MERENDA also *merienda*, an Italian and a Spanish word with similar but not identical meanings.

La merenda is an important institution in Italy, thus described by Patience Gray (1986):

The Italian word *mero* stands for wine which has not been tampered with. But as such wine is bound to go to one's head if not accompanied by something to eat, it is ritually accompanied by a *merenda*. *La merenda* cannot be confused with the modern snack. The snack is snatched, la merenda is shared. The word implies conviviality and if anything is to be seized it is time by the forelock, an event insinuated between laying off work and the return to the polished anonymity of that little prison of perfection which is every Italian's home.

It comprises food in its simplest form—good bread and a plate of local mortadella or salame.

In Spain, the term *merienda* has a similar but somewhat wider meaning; not just (afternoon) snack, but also outdoor meal, picnic.

The Catalan term *refrigeris* (meaning refreshment) corresponds more narrowly to the Italian *merenda*. A standard Catalan *refrigeris*, echoed elsewhere, is *pa amb tomàquet*, ripe tomato crushed onto bread with sea salt and olive oil, with wine. An engaging and amusing book by Pomés about the theory and practice of this item, sustaining for so many people, was published in 1985.

Whatever the terminology, and whatever particular foods are favoured in one place or another, the pattern in the European countries bordering on the Mediterranean, from Turkey to Spain, is similar. A refreshment is taken in the fields or at work, usually of great simplicity and using local ingredients, among which bread and olive oil will figure, plus wine.

It is noteworthy that the Spanish version was exported, notably to Mexico and the Philippines. In the Philippines a meal called *merienda cena* is a late, heavier than the usual *merienda*, which counts as a full meal (what we would call supper).

MERGUEZ a sausage of N. Africa, especially Tunisia and Algeria, which is made from beef to comply with Islamic dietary law. They are heavily spiced with HARISSA, which gives them their characteristic hot flavour and red colour. They are eaten grilled and are often one of the ingredients of or accompaniments to COUSCOUS. Merguez have been adopted by the French, who eat them as a snack or with couscous.

MERINGUE an airy, crisp confection of beaten egg white and sugar. The word probably entered French from German, as did many other French words ending in -ingue. It first appeared in print in Massialot (1691), although earlier recipes for the same thing but without the name had been published. The name travelled to England almost at once and first appeared in print there in 1706. Legends to the effect that the origin of the name is connected with the activities of a Swiss chef in the 1720s may be disregarded. The same applies to the more pleasing notion advanced by Thudichum (1895) that the name came from the Merovingian kings of France, whose dynasty began in AD 481.

It seems to have been only in the 16th century that European cooks discovered that beating egg whites, e.g. with a whisk of birch twigs (in the absence of any better implement), produced an attractive foam. At first the technique was used to make a simple, uncooked dish called SNOW, made from egg white and cream. However, cooking such a foam would not have resulted in meringue, for any fat in the mixture, as represented by the cream, prevents the egg whites from taking on the proper texture. (This is why when meringue is made, the fatty yolks have to be carefully separated.) Even if the cream had been omitted, there would have been technical problems. The presence of any particle of sugar larger than a tiny speck causes absorption of moisture and the problem known as 'weeping', drops of sticky syrup. The sugar has to be ground very fine and added gradually. Furthermore, the light texture of meringue makes it such an efficient heat insulator that anything more than the thinnest layer of meringue must be cooked very slowly—more dried than baked—or the centre remains raw and collapses in a gummy mass. Nevertheless, snow was a beginning.

When true meringue made its appearance in the 17th century, it still lacked its name and was often called 'sugar puff'. Sometimes these were flavoured with caraway seeds. (Such practices have continued and multiplied. The addition of some other ingredients or flavourings to meringue can create an almost infinite number of variations. One modern example is *japonais*, where ground almond is added to the egg white.)

Small meringues are easier to make than big ones because of the problem of making heat reach the centre. Very small ones are termed *meringuettes* or *croquignoles* in French, and are used as a kind of PETIT FOUR. Modern Dutch *schuimpjes* are similar, but variously coloured. Medium-sized meringues were found suitable for splitting and filling with flavoured cream; and a layer of meringue continues in use as a topping for various sweet items, e.g. the many sorts of American meringue pie.

The problem of large meringues was solved in the 18th century with the invention of the VACHERIN, a large meringue case made to contain fruit and cream, or some other sweet mixture. In this connection see PAVLOVA; and, for an even more ingenious use of meringue, see BAKED ALASKA.

MESQUITE *Prosopis juliflora* and related species, American plants which are well known for their use as a fuel for barbecues (to which it imparts an attractive aroma), but also providing food from its pods. These may be ground into a meal (flour) which can then be used to make a beverage, or used as a kind of PINOLE, or as material for bread-making. It is exceptionally nutritious.

Medsger (1972), writing about *P. glandulosa*, remarks that it is often called honey pod because of the sweetness of the pulp surrounding the seeds. Also, the flowers provide nectar for bees, and this makes a delicious honey. The mature pods may be 15 cm (6") long. When the pods are still green they may be gathered and cooked whole.

METABOLISM the total activity of a living creature, including respiration, the uptake of energy from food, and the expenditure of that energy in the processes of life. The speed at which this happens is known as metabolic rate; basal metabolic rate is measured when the organism is at rest, and thus shows how efficiently it uses energy.

The study of metabolism has fascinated researchers for centuries. In the 1580s the Italian physician Santorio (or Sanctorius) began a 30-year experiment in which he tried to measure all the inputs and outputs of his own metabolism. He had a chair, bed, and table placed on a platform suspended from a large but accurate balance, and kept scrupulous records of his weight. More significant findings had to wait till the mid-19th century, when chemistry was far enough advanced to tackle the problem properly. The German researcher Jacob Moleschott (see Jane O'Hara-May, 1984) measured the daily intake of protein, carbohydrates, salts, and water by a man of average size and activity, and weighed and analysed body wastes. From these findings he drew up a balance sheet of the metabolism of carbon, oxygen, hydrogen, and nitrogen; this was influential well into the 20th century, when modern biochemists were able to provide more accurate and detailed figures.

Metabolic rate varies considerably from person to person; a matter of concern in the anti-fat culture of the West. A person with a low rate needs less food than someone with a high one in order to remain at the same weight. Many people with a high rate can actually eat more than they need and still not gain weight; their metabolism speeds up to burn off the extra energy. While they cram themselves with food and remain as slim as ever, plump people with a slow metabolism can only watch in envy. Nicotine increases metabolic rate, which partly explains why more and more young women are taking up smoking despite its well-known harmful effects. Amphetamines also speed up metabolism and, despite laws curbing the use of these risky drugs, are widely prescribed as 'slimming pills'.   RH

METAL UTENSILS have both physical and chemical effects on foods. These relate mainly to the preparation and enjoyment of food; but small amounts of metals can also be transferred from utensils into the food itself. All metals except gold and the platinum group corrode in air to form a layer of oxide on the surface, which is sometimes rubbed off into food. Neither pure metals nor their oxides dissolve in pure water, but acidic foodstuffs can react with them to form compounds, some of which are extremely poisonous.

Small amounts of some metals are required in the diet (see MINERALS). However, excessive amounts of these can be seriously harmful.

ALUMINIUM

This is a good conductor of heat, though not as good as copper. Aluminium pans should be fairly thick to allow the heat to travel from the centre to the outer rim; cheap, thin pans burn food easily. Modern aluminium pans have a non-stick interior coating of Teflon or some tougher composite material. Formerly they were made of bare metal, and it was assumed that any aluminium compounds accidentally formed in cooking were harmless. Although these substances came under suspicion of involvement in Alzheimer's disease, this idea is no longer current (see, for example, McGee, 1990). It is, however, best not to cook acidic foods such as fruit in a bare aluminium pan, as this will form substantial amounts of aluminium salts.

Pure aluminium metal was not made in useful amounts until 1845, and was at first extremely expensive. At dinners given by Napoleon III the most honoured guests had aluminium cutlery; the others got gold or silver.

BRASS

An alloy of copper and zinc. It is seldom used in western cooking vessels but sometimes seen further east, for example in the *ibrik* used for making Turkish coffee (some of these are tinned on the inside). It conducts heat well, but less well than copper.

BRONZE

A hard alloy of copper and tin, occasionally used for cutlery. As with other copper alloys, there is a risk of poisoning if it becomes tarnished.

COPPER

This conducts heat extremely well, making it ideal for cooking vessels. It is covered by a layer of brownish oxide—pure copper is salmon pink, but the colour of a freshly cut surface darkens in minutes. All copper compounds are poisonous; some of them, though not the oxide, dissolve in water and

so are particularly dangerous. Most copper pans are coated inside with tin, and the coating should be renewed as soon as it begins to wear off. Untinned copper is traditionally used in 'preserving pans' for making jam, which should be well scoured before use. There have been cases of poisoning from unlined copper vessels, especially when vinegar or other liquids containing acetic acid have been allowed to stand in them, forming copper acetate.

Copper is toxic to bacteria. A copper water jug actually disinfects the water in it to some extent. Naturally it must be kept scrupulously clean.

It is traditional to beat egg whites in a copper bowl. Experiments conducted at Stanford University by Harold McGee, Sharon Long, and Winslow Briggs have shown that a copper bowl does produce a lighter, stiffer foam than a glass one— though the foam begins to form more quickly in a glass bowl (reported in *Nature*, 308/596, 1984). They attribute the effect to interaction between copper and conalbumin, a protein in egg white.

GOLD

This soft, extremely heavy metal is always alloyed with varying amounts of silver and copper. Pure or not, it is not corroded at all either by air or any of the substances in food. The only danger from gold cutlery comes from dropping it on your foot.

For the use of gold leaf as a food decoration, see GOLD AND SILVER LEAF.

IRON

Cast iron is a hard, brittle metal containing large amounts of carbon. (Wrought iron is almost pure and quite soft; it is no longer manufactured, and any modern implement that appears to be made of it is actually of mild steel.) Cast iron is a good conductor of heat, so that thick iron pans cook evenly. Rust, iron oxide, is harmless but tastes unpleasant. Iron frying pans become coated with an impervious layer of oxidized fats which have become linked to one another in a polymerized, plastic-like solid. So they are not a problem in this respect. And iron casseroles are enamelled, so they should also be problem-free.

LEAD

A soft, heavy metal with a low melting point. It quickly forms a thick layer of white oxide, powdery and easily detached. All lead compounds are highly poisonous. Lead is a cumulative poison: the body mistakes it for calcium and uses it to make bone, so that large amounts build up. Poisoning causes colic and damage to the nervous system, as well as learning difficulties in children. The ancient Romans suffered severely from it, since their drinking water was carried in

lead-lined aqueducts and stored in lead tanks; they had lead cooking vessels; and they ate *defrutum*, a sweetener made by boiling down figs in a lead pan, so that the fruit acids leached lead into the mixture. In the 1st century AD the Greek physician Aretaeus described the symptoms, and the Roman architect Vitruvius correctly attributed them to lead in water. Edward Gibbon suggested that chronic lead poisoning was (along with Christianity) one of the causes of the fall of the Roman Empire.

Lead has continued to be a problem, especially in old houses with lead pipes; it is wise to run the taps for several minutes first thing each morning to drain away the water polluted by standing overnight. Early food cans were sealed with thick seams of lead solder, which caused slight poisoning when they contained acidic foodstuffs. See also 'Pewter', below.

Herefordshire cider, traditionally made in lead-lined presses, was identified in the 18th century as a cause of colic. Even more dangerous was sweet German wine faked by storing cheap, sour wine in lead vessels, forming intensely sweet 'sugar of lead', lead acetate. A partial cure was provided by the fashionable practice of 'taking the waters' at a spa, which involved floating in a bath for several hours a day. The effectively weightless conditions caused loss of calcium from bones, taking some of the lead with it. As long as enough new calcium (but no more lead) was provided in the diet, the poison would gradually clear from the body.

PEWTER

A soft alloy of variable composition, but always with a very low melting point—a pewter dish placed on an electric cooker ring will melt. Old pewter was composed mainly of lead and tin and, especially when used for acidic food and drink, deposited dangerous amounts of lead. Modern pewter is almost entirely tin with a little antimony to harden it, and is safe enough.

SILVER

An excellent conductor of heat; it is easy to burn your fingers when stirring a pan with a solid silver spoon. The 'silver' skillets used in expensive restaurants to prepare flambé dishes at the table are usually silver-plated copper; the coating lasts better than the usual tin.

The metal is quickly corroded by sulphur compounds in vegetables and egg yolks, forming a black tarnish of silver sulphide. This, like all silver compounds, is moderately poisonous. Red wine drunk from a silver goblet would have an unpleasant metallic taste; so the inside of such a goblet is gilded.

Silver, like copper, is toxic to bacteria, and a silver water jug purifies its contents.

For the use of silver leaf as a food decoration, see GOLD AND SILVER LEAF.

STEEL AND STAINLESS STEEL

Ordinary steel consists of iron (see above) with a little carbon added to harden it. 'Mild' steel is fairly soft, and is used in sheet form for baking trays and other utensils. 'High carbon' steel is harder and is used for good-quality cook's knives.

Steel is much more prone to rust than either cast or wrought iron and, except in knife blades, is always given a protective coating of tin, zinc, or enamel. When bare steel comes into contact with the complex chemicals in foodstuffs unexpected things can happen, often caused by CHELATION of iron atoms. The red anthocyanin pigments in fruits and red cabbage turn dark blue or grey, and off flavours may form. If a fruit pie is baked in a chipped enamelled steel dish, the filling will discolour around the chip.

Ordinary steel is a fairly good conductor of heat, and enamelled steel pans will cook evenly if the base is thick. Stainless steel, on the other hand, conducts heat poorly. High-quality stainless saucepans have a base made of a thick sheet of copper encased in thin steel, to ensure good heat transfer.

Stainless steel is an alloy of iron with 8% to 25% chromium and usually some nickel. It does not rust, but most kinds discolour quite easily. Only the '18–8' alloy is genuinely stainless; this is used for most utensils but is too soft for knife blades. If any kind of stainless steel is severely overheated it will discolour irreversibly.

TIN

A soft metal with a low melting point, mainly used as a coating on steel to prevent it from rusting, and inside copper pans. The metal wears away rapidly, so that foods prepared in tinned vessels contain appreciable quantities of pure tin and tin oxide. These, and tin compounds formed by reactions with foodstuffs, are not poisonous—though some organic tin compounds are deadly. Tin bleaches some plant pigments, and used to have unexpected effects on tinned fruit. Modern cans are lacquered inside. The milk pails used for hand-milking are tinned, rather than galvanized (see 'Zinc' below) like ordinary buckets. So, usually, are the metal parts of old-fashioned food mills and graters.

See also 'Pewter', above.

ZINC

Zinc, a soft metal which corrodes to form a rough layer of grey oxide, can be used to galvanize (i.e. coat) iron or steel to prevent it from rusting. However, care is needed in using galvanized utensils for food. Although zinc is an essential mineral, an overdose of it (or indeed of any metal, including tin) can be seriously harmful.   RH

MEXICO is a big country, eight times the size of Great Britain, for example. It stretches from the arid borderlands with the United States in the north to the tropical jungles of the Yucatan in the south, from the humid coastlines on the Gulf of Mexico in the east to the drier Pacific coast on the west. The high central plateau, where much of the population lives at an elevation of 1800 m (6,000') or more, is separated from the coasts by massive mountain ranges, passable only in a few places. Many parts of the country are still largely Indian with ways of life and culinary customs little changed by the Spanish Conquest; Mexico City, by contrast, is the largest city in the world, subject to the same international influences as any large metropolis. Does it then make sense to speak of Mexican food?

The answer is yes, and one way to see why is to consider the scene just after daybreak in the towns and villages across the Republic. Along the nearly empty streets, women walk slowly but purposefully, brightly coloured plastic buckets hefted on their shoulders. They are on their way to or from the mill, about the business of getting their MAIZE ground for the daily bread (TORTILLAS). Each night, they boil dried maize with water and lime, leaving it to soak overnight. In the morning, they drain it and rub the skins off the grains, before placing it in a bucket to take it off to the mill. There it is ground into a coarse wet flour (*masa*, or *nixtamal*). Once home again, they will shape it by hand or by hand press into flat cakes (tortillas), some 18 cm (7") in diameter and 2 mm (0.08") thick. These tortillas are cooked in seconds on a griddle (*comal*) and, even in the poorest families, carefully wrapped in a hand-embroidered napkin to keep them hot. The making of tortillas (as well as the roasting of onions, garlic, tomatoes, and chillies prior to their incorporation in sauces) is so central to Mexican cooking that stoves come ready equipped with griddles, in the same way that stoves in Europe and the United States come equipped with grills.

The plastic buckets and the mills appeared in the second half of the 20th century. So too did small neighbourhood tortilla factories for families that did not wish to make their own (though the consensus is that hand-made tortillas are cleaner and softer than those from the factories). Before that the grain was laboriously ground by hand on a grinding stone (*metate*). But these recent innovations are minor variants on a procedure that goes back centuries before the Spanish conquistadores first set foot in the country in 1519. It was the peoples of Mexico and its southern neighbour Guatemala who domesticated maize. How they did so is the subject of much scholarly debate but the achievement produced the world's third most important crop (following wheat and rice), a crop so thoroughly domesticated that it cannot reproduce without human intervention. It was they, too, who happened on the technique of soaking and boiling with wood ash or lime (NIXTAMALIZATION) which archaeological evidence suggests was already in place by 1500–1200 BC. This innovation, which unlike the plant itself was never transferred to the Old World, simultaneously makes it possible to remove the skin of the grain, allows the grain to be ground to a flour that produces a flexible bread, and renders the protein in the grain more accessible.

Maize remains the foundation of Mexican cuisine, eaten in all areas and by all classes (though the poorer the class, the heavier the consumption). It may be eaten in the form of tortillas, either to accompany other dishes, or stuffed with some combination of beans, meats, vegetables, and cheese. It may be eaten in the form of TAMALES, the dough stuffed with savoury or sweet mixtures and steamed in maize or banana leaves. It may be shaped into small cakes of myriad shapes and names, stuffed or topped with a variety of savoury mixtures. Or it may be taken as a thick drink, a kind of gruel, ATOLE, made by mixing the dough with water and flavourings, a favourite for breakfast and supper.

As well as maize, the pre-Hispanic inhabitants of Mexico had a rich variety of vegetable ingredients, still used today. Of particular importance were BEANS and chillies (CAPSICUMS). The vegetable protein of the beans complemented that of the maize, the chillies provided vitamins and seasoning. Aside from these, there were TOMATOES, AVOCADOS, SQUASHES, a rich array of tropical and subtropical fruits, and some exotics which we still value greatly, VANILLA, one of the few edible orchids, and CHOCOLATE. The lakes and rivers and coastline provided fish and shellfish, as well as edible algae. There were TURKEYS, GUINEA PIGS, and a varied range of game. The detailed recording of the foods of pre-Hispanic C. America by the early conquistadores, and, even more important, by the Franciscan Friar Bernardino de Sahagún in his *General History of the Things of New Spain* compiled in the mid-16th century, make it clear that the diet of the country was satisfying and varied. Again, most of the ingredients that supplemented the staple, maize, and the ways of preparing them remain central to Mexican cuisine; a main meal is incomplete without a serving of beans, usually simply boiled and served in their broth, and an enormous variety of chillies are cultivated to be chopped and added fresh to foods, or pickled in vinegar, or dried prior to being soaked and ground to flavour and thicken sauces.

With the arrival of the conquistadores in the 16th century, a whole range of new ingredients became available without causing the abandonment of older foods. The Spaniards brought with them wheat for bread, rice, almonds, sesame, sugar, spices such as cinnamon and nutmeg, raisins, capers, and olives. Many of these ingredients, and the methods of preparing them, have a distinctly medieval, Arab touch, reminding us that the Moors were finally expelled from Spain in the same year that Columbus discovered America. Besides this, Spanish cattle, pigs, sheep, and goats introduced European meats and fats, milk, butter, and cheese to the Mexican diet. To this day, Mexican food is a mestizo mixture of pre-Hispanic and Spanish, with the preponderance tipping to the Spanish in the higher social classes.

The major Mexican meal is taken between two and four, though this is somewhat under threat in large cities where distances make midday travel home impossible. In its full form, it consists of five courses: a soup (often of vegetable or noodles); a so-called dry soup (perhaps best understood as the equivalent of the Italian pasta course) of rice or noodles; a meat or fish dish accompanied by tortillas; beans; and a fruit or dessert with coffee. This is preceded by an early breakfast of coffee, milk, or atole with fruit and pastry and perhaps a later breakfast mid-morning of eggs, bacon, tomato and chilli sauces, and tortillas. The evening meal, except for a special occasion when it can be quite elaborate, is a simple matter of a pastry, a cup of chocolate, fruit, or perhaps some leftovers. The excellent rolls and sweet breads are usually attributed to the strong French influence, both cultural and political, of the second half of the 19th century.

The main courses that anchor the meal can be divided into a variety of types in addition to the simple grills and roasts that are as popular in Mexico as anywhere else. There are the MOLES, regarded as the national dish, and essential on festive occasions. A mixture of chillies, nuts, seeds, garlic, and spices is ground on the stone *metate* (or less satisfactorily if more expeditiously in the blender that almost every Mexican household possesses) and fried in hot fat (lard or cooking oil), water is added, and the whole simmered to make a thick aromatic sauce. (Sometimes a small amount of bitter chocolate is included, leading to the common misconception that Mexicans cook meat in chocolate sauce.) Pre-cooked meat or poultry is then added to

the sauce. Then there are the stews of Hispanic origin, the *tingas* and *almendradas* for example, made by the more familar technique of sautéeing onion and garlic and then simmering the meat in the sauce. Also enormously popular are a range of dishes made with mildly hot chilli peppers stuffed with meat or fish or beans, dipped in an egg batter, and fried.

Mexico is not the home of elaborate vegetable dishes, although the consumption of vegetables is enormous. They are eaten as soups, sliced raw and stirred into soups (radishes and avocados, for example), made into fresh sauces that are on the table for every meal, in stews, or piled on top of street food. Sweets in Mexico are just that, sweet. The classic ones are universally attributed to the nuns who sold them to raise money for their convents. Like certain other dishes, they have a medieval, Mediterranean air: glossy globes of crystallized fruit, thick pastes of quince or guava, milk boiled down to the consistency of toffee, things to be nibbled, crossing the N. European boundary between candy and dessert.

Mexico has an extraordinary range of drinks, both alcoholic and non-alcoholic. Apart from the atoles, there are the *licuados*, liquefied fruits and vegetables often with the addition of milk or a raw egg, that can be bought for a quick breakfast or pick-me-up on any street corner in a Mexican town. There are the *aguas frescas*, mildly sweet infusions of fruit or vegetables in water, sharpened with a little lime juice and quaffed in quantities with meals; tuna (cactus fruit), tamarind, cucumber, pineapple, melon, and another of those Arab legacies, *horchata*, an infusion of ground rice and almond. There are a range of bottled fizzy fruit drinks and hot fruit punches for Christmas as well as coffee, chocolate, and herbal teas galore. Pulque is the most famous mildly alcoholic drink, made from the sap of the agave plant which ferments readily without the addition of yeast, and sold in *pulquerias*, a Mexican male preserve with a folklore all their own. These, though, are now vanishing as beer, first introduced by German immigrants in the 19th century, gains in popularity. Tequila, made from the heart of a certain kind of agave, is now heavily promoted and perhaps the best-known alcoholic drink outside the country. It was the Spanish who introduced distilled liquors of this kind, and tequila is in fact just one special kind of *mezcal*, the generic name for agave liquors, and they in turn are just one of the series of liquors and liqueurs from cane sugar, pineapple, and other less well-known sources.

No account of Mexican food would be complete without mentioning its street food, candied sweet potatoes, roast ears of corn with chilli and lime juice, plastic cups of

gelatin and flan, bags of green chickpeas cooked in the pod, boiled peanuts, huge sheets of *chicharron* (fried pork rind, see CRACKLING) with hot pepper sauce, plastic bags stuffed with cut watermelon, cantaloupe, JICAMA, and coconut, glass jars of *aguas frescas* in pale green and white and crimson, but particularly the tacos (rolled, stuffed TORTILLAS), TAMALES, and *tortas* (stuffed bread rolls). These latter three can be prepared at home, but most often picked up from stands under the arcades in town squares, at the crossings of country roads. They can be filled with vegetables or cooked meats or any of the specially prepared meats that are usually also found in the market place such as *barbacoa* from the centre of the country (lamb wrapped in aromatic leaves and steamed) or *carnitas* (chunks of pork cooked in their own fat) or *pibil* from the Yucatan (pork wrapped in aromatic leaves and cooked in an underground oven).

These are the shared foods of Mexico. But the geographic diversity and wide spread of incomes means that within these general categories, foods are sharply distinguished both regionally and with respect to class. Veracruz on the Gulf Coast is famous for black beans and fish, the Yucatan peninsula for its seasonings of *achiote* and sour orange, Puebla and Oaxaca for their moles, Sinaloa for charcoal-grilled chicken, the northern states for their flour tortillas, and on and on. So too, in a country where religious (syncretic Catholic/Indian in many instances) and national holidays are celebrated with gusto, where food distribution remains sufficiently uneven that it does not swamp out the seasons, where freezers are still rarities, food varies with the seasons and with the festivals.

Mexicans are proud of their culinary heritage which they regard as one of the richest in the world. From the publication of *El cocinero mexicano* in 1831 (revised as *Nuevo cocinero mexicano en forma de diccionario* in 1872), there have been a series of recipe books, histories of food, celebrated traditional restaurants, and culinary organizations in the country. Although 'international' food (hot dogs, pizza, rotisserie chicken, and imported popcorn) is consumed, the tradition of Mexican cooking remains not simply alive and well, but dominant.   RL

MEZZE (sometimes spelled meze), an interesting word which came originally from the Persian *maza*, meaning 'taste, relish'. One of the few authors who has shown awareness of this Persian origin is Ayla Algar (1991):

I have traced the possible origin of meze to ancient Persia, where wine was the center of an emotional and esthetic experience that also included other forms of enjoyment, notably food and music. The original meze of Persia appear to have been tart fruits, such as pomegranates, quinces, and citrons, designed to alleviate the bitter taste left by unripe wine. Later nuts and small pieces of roasted meat were added to the spread of the wine drinker.

The mezze tradition extends westwards from Turkey into the Balkans, including Greece and southwards to the Lebanon and Egypt, and through N. Africa to Morocco; but in other Muslim countries the prohibition of alcohol has had sufficient force to prevent the mezze tradition from taking root (or, in the case of Iran, continuing in modern times).

Even in those Muslim countries where mezze survive or flourish, it is noticeable that they tend to be part of the structure of a main meal. In Greece and the Balkans, on the other hand, their function more closely resembles that of TAPAS in Spain, i.e. they are nibbles to be taken while drinking, or more particularly gossiping.

It has been well said that 'no Greek drinks without eating', and mezze are certainly important in Greece as food to be eaten with alcohol. Indeed, it used to be the case that mezze were served free with the ouzo.

Typical mezze found all over Greece, Turkey, the Middle East, and N. Africa include a range of simple snacks such as olives or cubes of cheese, more complicated dips such as TARAMOSALATA, *tsatsiki* (cucumber and yoghurt), *baba ghanoush* (aubergine purée), hummus, and more substantial salads and snacks of TABBOULEH, FALAFEL, DOLMA, and KEBAB.

It is generally acknowledged that Lebanese mezze are second to none, not only in variety and flavour but also in appearance. Anissa Helou (1994) has written:

The colours on the table were quite wonderful. Many of the dishes were served in Lebanese slipware bowls decorated with lovely brown and cream glazes. Inside them the food ranged from delicate shades of beige, a light ivory *hommus* (chick pea purée) to a raw silk like *baba ghannooge* (aubergine purée), each decorated with a sprinkling of red paprika interspersed with fresh green mint leaves. There were bright colours too, purple pickles, a glossy green *tabbooleh* (parsley salad) dappled with tiny red tomato cubes and light brown burghul grains and pink *habrah nayeh* (pounded raw meat). Then there were the savoury pastries, mini black thyme breads, light brown meat pizzas dotted with roasted pine nuts, dainty golden triangles and so many other colourful dishes.

MICRO-ORGANISMS a general term for single-celled living creatures. These include BACTERIA, YEASTS, and MOULDS, which are described under those headings.

Another group is the protozoans, single-celled animals. These include amoebae, some of which cause a severe form of dysentery; and marine dinophytes, which can suddenly multiply in enormous numbers to produce the 'red tides' that make shellfish poisonous. Algae include both single-celled and multicellular types, such as SEAWEEDS. Only one group of single-celled algae, *Chlorella*, has anything to do with food: it has been suggested that this should be grown in space stations to renew the oxygen in the air and to provide a raw material that could be processed into human food. Viruses are not usually classed as micro-organisms, for they are not truly alive and can only operate by hijacking living cells. They are relevant to food only insofar as they cause diseases in plants and animals.

Micro-organisms play varied and important roles in food, from useful fermentations to spoilage and FOOD POISONING.

Raw foodstuffs usually contain several kinds of micro-organism. These may feed on different substances and so be able to coexist, or they may compete for the same substance. An example of the first type is CAMEMBERT cheese, inside which lactic acid-producing bacteria live on lactose (milk sugar), while on the surface a mould digests protein, in the process softening the texture of the whole cheese. Examples of the second type are the 'alcoholic yoghurts' such as KEFIR, in which lactic bacteria and yeasts compete for sugar. In this case the two manage to grow side by side for long enough to achieve the finished product. More often, one organism will outgrow and overwhelm the other.

Some micro-organisms succeed by creating conditions in which their rivals cannot live. Again, the lactic bacteria are an example, making their surroundings so acidic that no other organisms can function; this is how they preserve foods. In fact these bacteria are usually themselves of several species able to tolerate different levels of acidity: low-acid types begin the fermentation and continue until they poison themselves with their own waste products; then more acid-tolerant species take over.

Micro-organisms, like any living things, grow best in certain conditions. Some can tolerate only a small amount of salt or sugar, while others thrive in quite salty or sugary foods. Some grow only where there is air, others where there is none—these are known as 'aerobic' and 'anaerobic' organisms. A few can switch modes to suit conditions: brewer's yeast, in the airless conditions of a brewing vat, produces mainly alcohol and a little carbon dioxide; while in airy conditions, as in bread dough, it produces a lot of carbon dioxide and a little alcohol. Most organisms grow best in moderate warmth, but there are many exceptions. Some moulds can grow in a deep freeze. Some bacteria can live at temperatures near boiling point, and some can form spores that survive prolonged boiling and grow into new bacteria when the temperature falls (see BOTULISM).

When a micro-organism is stopped from growing by being outnumbered, or by being frozen, or by excessive sugar, salt, or acid, it usually remains alive and will restart growth if conditions change. Thus the moulds which grow on top of jam will, if they infect a carelessly cleaned pot, be unable to grow in the strong sugar solution of the jam. But if the jam exudes a little moisture, which is a less concentrated solution, they will start growing in the little pool of liquid on top of the jam. Similarly, if dried foods become damp, organisms of several kinds will start growing.

Traditional methods of food PRESERVATION often work by creating conditions in which desirable organisms can grow while others give up. Thus salt added to shredded cabbage favours the salt-tolerant lactic bacteria which turn the vegetable to SAUERKRAUT. In the making of YOGHURT the milk is kept at a temperature slightly above blood heat, the preferred conditions of the bacteria that bring about the fermentation. Such methods are generally too hit-or-miss for the modern food industry, where the usual method is to kill all micro-organisms—or most of them, as in pasteurization (see MILK)—and introduce a pure culture of the desired organism.   RH

MICROWAVE COOKING a technique in which electromagnetic radiation is used to heat food. All radiation is a form of energy, and energy can be converted from one form to another. In this case the radiation absorbed by the food is transformed into heat. Microwaves are similar to radio waves but of higher frequency: in a domestic microwave oven this is 2,450 megahertz (MHz, millions of cycles a second), compared to around 100 megahertz for VHF radio. Radar also uses microwaves, so that in theory it would be possible to cook food by putting it at the focus of a radar dish.

Microwave cooking is quick, because the radiation penetrates the food more readily than the 'heat radiation' given off by the heating element in a conventional oven. (Heat is propagated by infrared radiation, similar in nature to microwaves but of much lower frequency.) It is also efficient, because radiation of a frequency around 2.5 GHz is strongly absorbed by the large organic molecules in food. This is apparent from the fact that the container in which the food is placed is hardly warmed at all, because its molecules are much smaller—they would need a higher frequency to be heated effectively.

Thanks to the efficiency of the process, microwave ovens use much less power than ordinary ones; typically they consume 600 to 800 watts, against 3,000 or more for an electric oven, and only for a fraction of the time needed for cooking by conventional methods.

A common misconception about microwave ovens is that they heat food 'from the inside'. This is not so: all the radiation is beamed into the food from a waveguide (a type of antenna) in the roof of the oven, and has to penetrate it like any other radiation. When using the oven to thaw a large piece of meat, it is possible to leave the centre frozen if the heating time is too short. Nor is the radiation evenly distributed throughout the cabinet: there are 'hot' and 'cold' spots. Most ovens have either an electrically driven turntable to revolve the food, or rotating 'stirrers' to deflect the radiation, so that heating is as even as possible.

A drawback of microwave cooking is that the food is not browned on the outside. This can be overcome to some extent by putting the cooked food briefly under an ordinary grill. Some microwave ovens have been made with a small conventional heating element inside the cabinet, which can be switched on to brown the food.

Some cooks scorn microwave ovens because they do not cook food 'properly'. But only a diehard traditionalist would deny that they are very useful for thawing frozen foods and reheating dishes made in advance and frozen.

Two spectacular accidents can occur. If food is put inside the oven in a metal dish, even a thin one made of foil, it will produce electrical discharges like a small thunderstorm in the cabinet. It is tempting to make a single cup of tea by using the oven to boil a cup of water and then putting in a teabag. The oven can 'superheat' the water above its normal boiling point, without the water actually boiling—there has to be some kind of 'nucleus' for the first bubble to form around, such as a speck of solid matter in the water. When the teabag is dropped into the superheated water it provides plenty of nuclei; the water boils suddenly and the teabag explodes with great force.   RH

MILK (*see opposite page*)

MILK CAP one of several names for edible mushrooms of the genus *Lactarius*, so named because all the species in it exude a 'milk'. Most are 'rusty' in colour. They have 'decurrent' gills, i.e. they are joined to and run some way down the stem.

L. deliciosus, which is common in autumn in coniferous woods in Europe and the northern parts of N. America, and also occurs in China, Australia, and S. Africa, is the saffron or orange milk cap. Its cap is up to 15 cm (5") wide, convex at the edges but depressed in the middle. It is of a pinkish saffron colour, sometimes marked with concentric rings of pale green. The rest of the fungus is also saffron, and when cut it exudes a milk which quickly turns to orange. (It later turns green but this is no cause for alarm. Nor is the fact that eating saffron milk caps results in reddish urine.) The somewhat bitter, spicy taste may or may not be liked. Jaccottet (1973) comments that in the opinion of many connoisseurs there is nothing delicious about it except its specific name. This paradox has been explained on the basis that the great Swedish botanist Linnaeus, who bestowed the scientific name, was for once confused and attributed to the saffron milk cap the superior culinary merit of one of its relations, probably *L. sanguifluus*.

L. sanguifluus is found in Spain and the south of France and Italy, where it enjoys high esteem. Its cap may be less red than that of *L. deliciosus*, but its 'milk' is redder (although without effect on urine).

An interesting curiosity is *L. glyciosmus*, a small coconut-scented milk cap with a relatively pale cap. The coconut aroma is unmistakable and use of this species in an omelette produces a surprising result.

Milk caps are best gathered and eaten when very young. They may be grilled over embers, or blanched and then baked or stewed, with a long cooking time. Sometimes they are pickled in vinegar.

Various less good *Lactarius* spp are edible but peppery; some are indigestible; and one or two are reputed to be toxic.

READING: Roux-Saget and Delplanque (1985); Jordan (1995*a*).

MILK FISH *Chanos chanos*, a fish of the order *Clupeiformes* (which also includes the herring family), found over a wide range in the Indo-Pacific, from E. Africa to the Red Sea, eastward to Japan and the Pacific coast of the USA, and down to the tropical waters of Australia. It is most prominent as a food fish in the Philippines and Indonesia, where large supplies for the markets are assured by catching fry at sea and then rearing them in fish-ponds, where they feed easily on a kind of sea moss and grow rapidly. They are silvery fish with greenish-grey backs; maximum length 180 cm (71"), market length usually under 100 cm (40").

Like other species in the same order, the milk fish has a dismayingly large number of fine, small bones. If it is to be enjoyed, some means must be found of dealing with these. One solution is to debone the fish by using professional techniques and equipment, as explained by Patricia Arroyo Staub (1982); but this procedure requires 10 to 20 minutes for each fish. Alternatively, it is possible to buy milk fish which have been cooked under pressure so that the bones have become soft and edible like the bones of canned sardines. In this case, it is advisable to cook the product, which by itself has a disappointing taste and texture, with other flavourful ingredients.

The skin of the milk fish is regarded as a delicacy in the Philippines, and it of course contains no bones.

Milk fish have in the past been called 'Moreton Bay salmon' in Australia, presumably in an effort to play down the bone problem; but these fish have never been marketed there on more than a small scale. In Hawaii, on the other hand, they are well liked; smaller specimens are considered to be suitable for eating raw, and the flesh of larger ones ideal for making fish cakes.

MILK PUDDINGS emerged in the 19th century as a feature of the British diet, associated especially with nursery food and invalid fare. These puddings are made with a bland starch such as sago, starch pastes, or gels, their texture derived from the thickening that is used. Their ancestors probably include BLANCMANGE and HASTY PUDDING. For details of some of them see MACARONI; RICE PUDDINGS; SAGO; SEMOLINA; TAPIOCA.

For other sweet dishes made with milk or cream, see JUNKET; CUSTARD; SYLLABUB.

It is fashionable in some circles to despise milk puddings. However, if they are well made of good ingredients, and subtly flavoured, they can be delightful, on their own or in partnership with poached fruits.

MILK REDUCTION As anyone who has ever boiled milk has learned, milk traps steam as it is heated, and if the heating continues past a certain point, a small explosion occurs in the pan. The milk suddenly 'foams up', as the cookbooks say, and overflows the pan. In order to overcome this problem when reducing milk over high heat, one should start off with a sufficiently large pan so that even foaming will not overflow the sides. After a while, when the milk has reduced and thickened, it becomes necessary to lower the heat very far and to keep stirring, both to prevent scorching and to stir back any skin forming on the surface of the milk.

Middle Eastern cooks carry this process to its ultimate. They reduce rich WATER-BUFFALO milk to a white solid called *eishta* in Arabic (see KAYMAK). When full reduction is done in the presence of sugar, the result is a

(*cont. on page 505*)

Milk

Milk is the most versatile of all foods. Fresh milk and products made from it (CREAM, BUTTER, BUTTERMILK, WHEY, all kinds of CHEESE, and innumerable soured milk products such as YOGHURT and SOUR CREAM) are widely used in the cuisines of large areas of the world. Milk has long been held in high esteem for its nutritious quality, which even in pre-scientific days was apparent from the fact that it provided complete nourishment for young animals and humans.

The oldest known record of animals being kept in herds and milked is a series of cave paintings in the Libyan Sahara, showing milking and perhaps cheese-making too, and possibly older than 5000 BC. The Sumerians, around 3500 BC, and the Egyptians a few centuries later used milk and have left reliefs and records showing that they prepared curdled milk products.

In contrast, the Chinese have seldom used milk: nor have peoples in a large part of SE Asia nor in any part of America before the Europeans arrived. It was also unknown in some parts of Africa. The inhabitants of these areas are usually unable, not merely disinclined, to take milk once they have grown up. Technically, they suffer from LACTOSE INTOLERANCE, which means they lose the ability to digest the lactose sugar in milk.

Before the techniques of refrigeration and pasteurization were introduced, milk would not stay fresh for long. It went sour, became rancid, or curdled. The whole range of milk products arose as a means of controlling this tendency and even turning it to advantage.

In composition, milk is mostly water. In cow's milk, the water content is 87% by weight. The next heaviest constituent, at about 5%, is milk sugar, which is almost entirely lactose. Its molecule is split in fermentation or digestion to yield the simple monosaccharide sugars dextrose and galactose. Fat content averages slightly under 4% but varies widely. The fatty substances include carotenoids (yellow pigments from plants which impart a creamy colour), free fatty acids which contribute to flavour, and the fat-soluble VITAMINS A, D, E, and K. Milk also contains useful amounts of the water-soluble vitamins (C and the B group). PROTEINS total about 3.5%, mostly casein, which is what constitutes the solid curd when milk is curdled. Traces of acetaldehyde, acetone, and formaldehyde contribute to the flavour of milk; and very fresh milk contains methyl sulphide, which gives it its 'cowy' smell.

Milks from different kinds of animal vary noticeably in composition. Thus human milk is more watery than cow's milk, has more sugar, less fat, and much less protein. This sort of variation can usually be related to the length of time which the young take to mature. Human babies grow slowly, calves quickly. The average figures for some animal milks are given in the table, in percentages by weight.

Animal	Sugar	Fat	Protein	Minerals	Water
Cow	4.9	3.9	3.5	0.7	87.0
Water-buffalo	4.8	7.2	3.8	0.7	83.5
Sheep	4.6	6.7	5.8	0.8	82.1
Goat	4.6	4.1	3.6	0.8	86.9
Mare	6.7	1.0	2.0	0.3	90.0
Human	6.9	3.8	1.9	0.2	87.2

But these figures are only averages. The composition of milk from the same kind of animal, indeed even from the same animal, is variable. Changes can be remarked according to the breed (for example Jersey and Guernsey cows give high-fat milk, Holstein low); the animal's diet, which itself changes with the seasons; the animal's age; the stage in its lactation period (see BEESTINGS); the time of day at which it is milked; and even the stage reached in one milking (the last milk to emerge has more fat than the first). Flavours vary, too; not only from species to species, as is patent from a comparison of cow, sheep, and goat cheeses, but also according to a particular animal's health (see STRACCHINO) and diet. Odd flavours can get into milk from strong-tasting foods eaten by the animal, and even from smelly substances in the air it breathes. And all this is before the milk even emerges. Many other factors can cause changes thereafter.

Raw milk fresh from the cow contains many kinds of ENZYMES, most of which are destroyed by pasteurization. The important enzyme actions which occur in the making of milk products are largely brought about by enzymes from outside sources. However, a few of the enzymes naturally present in milk survive and may do useful work. One of them, amylase, liberates sugar from the starch in flour, an effect useful in baking.

From the moment it leaves the udder, milk is subject to invasion by BACTERIA of many kinds. It is as close to being a perfect food for them as it is for human beings and animals. Some of these bacteria are harmful but others are beneficial, notably the LACTIC ACID-producing bacteria. It is these which have a souring effect on milk and are exploited in making fermented milk products. Although most of these bacteria are present naturally, it is usual in fermentation processes to add a starter culture of the preferred ones to give them a head start. Once these are in the majority they remain dominant and thwart the growth of others.

Physically, milk is a fluid, as all can see. It can be more precisely described as 'an emulsion, colloidal suspension and solution'. Its structure, in short, is quite complex. The casein (which constitutes most protein) and the fats are clustered separately in tiny micelles (groups of molecules—the closest lay term is 'globules') floating independently in water in which the sugar, salts, and other proteins are dispersed. This structure can break down when some chemical substance or physical event disturbs its balance. The casein and fat micelles then agglomerate into a curd, leaving the watery solution as whey.

When milk curdles, the long strands of the casein molecules tangle and link together. The extent to which this happens depends on what has caused the curdling. The fairly mild lactic acid produced in normal souring brings about only a light linkage, resulting in slight thickening of the milk without much separation of curds and whey. Enzymes such as rennin cause much greater linking and contraction of the network of strands, forcing out much of the whey so that there is a clearly visible clotting and separation.

Heating also restructures the proteins, and is a potent weapon in the battle to make milk keep longer than it naturally would. See the box on pasteurization, etc.

Milk may be **homogenized** to stop the cream from rising to the top. Separation occurs because the fat globules are just too large to remain suspended in the emulsion and, being lighter than water, slowly collect at the top. In homogenization, a process invented in France, the milk is forced through tiny holes which break the fat into smaller globules. Although homogenization is a purely mechanical treatment, it does affect the flavour of the milk, making it blander, and also increases its whiteness. Homogenized milk froths and boils over, and also curdles more readily.

Milk may also be **skimmed** to remove the cream, lowering the fat content of the remaining milk. This was formerly done by letting the cream rise to the top and then skimming it off. Now it is done in a centrifuge, which whirls the milk

MILK PASTEURIZATION AND PRESERVATION

VIRTUALLY all the milk on sale in western countries has been pasteurized to kill most of the bacteria naturally present in it and to make it keep longer. The least rigorous method of pasteurization uses a temperature below boiling point, and also below the critical temperature of 74 °C (165 °F) at which the compactly coiled molecules of the lactoglobulin proteins in the milk are irreversibly opened out, altering the flavour of the milk and giving it a 'cooked' taste. The milk may be heated to 63–6 °C (145–50 °F) for 30 minutes or, in a more modern process which, it is claimed, makes less difference to the flavour, to 72 °C (161 °F) for 15 seconds, followed by rapid cooling. HTST ('high temperature, short time') pasteurization of milk is done as the milk flows along a narrow pipe through a heat exchanger, so that heating and cooling can be very rapid indeed. 'Longlife' or UHT (ultra high temperature) is heated for only 1–2 seconds to as much as 138 °C (280 °F).

Sterilized milk, which may be given a preliminary UHT treatment, is bottled and then heated in the sealed bottles to 110 °C (230 °F) for 20 to 30 minutes. It tastes rather strange, stranger than UHT milk, since the prolonged heating has caused chemical reactions between the proteins and the sugars in the milk.

around rapidly in a circular vessel. The cream, which is lighter, collects at the centre. A little cream can be removed for 'partly skimmed milk'; or as much as possible may be extracted.

Evaporated and **condensed** milk are both made in the same way at the start: by heating milk moderately in a strong vacuum which lowers the boiling point so that most of the water evaporates. The resulting thick liquid is then either given a high temperature treatment to sterilize it, making evaporated milk; or sweetened to preserve it, making condensed milk. In both the flavour is much altered.

Powdered milk is made from skimmed milk. Whole milk is hardly ever made into powder because the fat in it becomes oxidized by exposure to the air and tastes unpleasant. Even skimmed milk suffers from this trouble to some extent. The flavour is altered both by oxidation and by the heat used in the process, which is usually spray-drying: the milk is sprayed into a large drum filled with hot air and the drops dry before they reach the bottom.

Powdered, evaporated, condensed, sterilized, and UHT milks all keep for a long time unrefrigerated, though the liquid ones usually begin to go off once they have been opened. Ordinary pasteurized milk lasts only three days in the refrigerator, or a week or so if held just above freezing. When it does finally succumb to bacteria it becomes very unpleasant. Rather than being soured by lactic acid-producing species, which prefer warmer temperatures and anyway have been almost wiped out by pasteurization, it is attacked by proteolytic (protein-destroying) bacteria which can work at low temperatures. These make the milk alkaline and smelly.

Yet another way of keeping milk has been described by Emerson (1908), in a chapter concerned mainly with myths but in terms which suggest that there is some historical record of what he relates:

When the European first visited India he found that the aborigines had for a beverage a drink which they called *dhy*, and on investigation it was ascertained to be dried milk. The method of drying it was primitive indeed. The milk of an ass, a mare, or a goat was put into a leather bag or skin and, tightly closed, this was then suspended beneath the belly of a horse. It soon became hard, greatly resembling chalk. When it was wanted for use a piece was broken off and dissolved in water, making a pleasant and invigorating drink. Its taste was slightly acid, but its odour was that of very sour milk. When and by whom this practice was inaugurated is not known; it is only one of the thousands of things that are lost in antiquity.

In cooking with milk the chief problems are with CURD-LING of one kind or another. This may be flocculation: separation at relatively low temperatures. At higher temperatures, above 70 °C (158 °F), COAGULATION occurs: this is the change in the proteins brought about by heat.

One of the commonest and most annoying instances of coagulation in milk is the formation of a skin when it is heated. Little pieces of denatured protein rise to the surface and join up into a layer which becomes increasingly coagulated and dehydrated, and thus tougher. It can be averted by stirring the milk; but as soon as stirring stops, the skin begins to form. It is no use trying to stir it back in to recombine it once it has formed: the only result is a mess of little bits of skin. There is no special type of milk which is immune from this problem, although semi-skimmed and skimmed milk suffer from it less. Skin formation can be reduced by heating milk only as hot as is needed—if possible not over 70 °C (158 °F)—and at the last feasible moment. In the catering trade milk may be heated with a jet of superheated steam from an espresso machine, which makes it froth rather than form a skin.

Milk sticks to pans when heated, for the same reason. A thin pan which does not spread the heat can cause fierce coagulation in the centre. The coagulated milk begins to 'burn'—that is, the proteins and sugar break down—producing brown specks and an undesirable taste. A thick pan, stirring, and moderate heating for as short a time as possible all help to avoid sticking.

Both flocculation and coagulation in milk are irreversible once they have occurred. There are no restorative measures as there are with mayonnaise or other emulsions.

Since milk and its products are among our most nutritious and delicious foods, it would be wrong to end this entry on a note of irreversible disaster. Rather should one remind oneself that milk is a great drink; it has built up its own 'culture' in many parts of the world—for instance, milk bars, the milk shakes of N. America, and the so far indestructible figure of the British milkman (milko in Australia)—and all this without taking into account the fabulously rich gallery of milk products.

See also MILK PUDDINGS; MILK REDUCTION.

---

coffee-coloured, spreadable solid that plays a traditional role in Hispanic American desserts, especially in Argentina, under the name *dulce de leche*. In N. America, an informal, folk/industrial version of this dish has evolved: a can of sweetened condensed milk is completely submerged under boiling water until the sugar in it caramelizes and the milk solidifies.

In the Philippines, to the north of Manila, it is traditional to reduce the milk of the carabao, the local water-buffalo, to a quarter of its natural volume and then to cook it with sugar until the mixture, still white, reaches the soft ball stage. Then these *pastillas de leche* are rolled in sugar and wrapped in white paper.

Reduced milk sweets reach their zenith as a genre in India. But it is India, before all nations, that has experimented most completely with reduced milk. It is not an exaggeration to say that Indian cuisine contains within it a minicuisine evolved around the various stages of thickness that milk attains as its water evaporates, its proteins coagulate, and its natural sugars turn a gentle brown.

Milk is the major source of animal protein for the millions of vegetarian Indians and a basic component of the daily diet of most of the rest of India. Buffalo milk, yoghurt, cheese, and the clarified butter called GHEE are universal in Indian food, and in their Indian versions, they have special qualities setting them off from their non-western analogues. The reduced milk dishes make up an even more special world.

Traditional slow boiling in an Indian *kadhai* (see WOK COOKERY) is a lengthy process made much easier and quicker in the microwave, but the result is the same.

Milk reduced to a quarter of its original volume is a light beige, aromatic liquid called *rabadi*. *Basoondi*, a cream pudding

dessert which is popular in Uttar Pradesh and Rajasthan, is basically a sweetened *rabadi* with the addition of pistachios and almonds.

Rabadi reduced further, by half (to an eighth of the volume of the original whole milk), is a fudgelike solid called *khoya*. There are also many dishes where whole milk and a solid ingredient are cooked together until the milk is absorbed and almost vanishes, leaving behind a richness of texture and taste. One of the most unusual of these, showing the cosmopolitan side of Indian cuisine, is a spicy dish whose basic element is corn kernels cooked in milk until the milk 'disappears'.

Rabadi, the thick but still pourable reduction, makes a rich sauce for desserts and fruit. A cheese precipitated from *rabadi* is the basis for the dessert cheese dumplings, Bengali *Ras malai*, and for the rich Indian ICE CREAM *kulfi*. *Rabadi* rediluted with some regular milk is served as a beverage sweetened with sugar.

From solid *khoya*, Indians make a broad variety of fudges (BARFI) flavoured with pistachio, cardamom, ground cashews, coconut, potato, ginger, mung beans, semolina, and pumpkin. *Khoya* is cooked with grated carrots to make a moist pudding called HALVA. The list could be extended because the Indian genius has applied the nutty richness of highly reduced milk to virtually every vegetable purée and flavouring. A particularly complex *khoya* dish is the pastry called *Khoya poli*, in which a thin, fried wholewheat puff (like the spherical bread called POORI) is stuffed with a paste of *khoya*, grated coconut, sugar, sultanas, ground cardamom, chopped almonds, and rosewater.

Perhaps the furthest that *khoya* cookery gets from a plain glass of milk is in the Kashmiri mock meat dish *Matar shufta*. This

is a vegetarian parody, as it were, of the ground meat and chickpea concoction called *Keema matar*. For *Matar shufta*, milk fudge grains are fried until they resemble ground meat.

Something like the same effect occurs in one of Italy's most celebrated dishes, *Arrosto di maiale al latte*, pork roast with milk, in which a boned pork loin is braised in milk. Eventually, the milk reduces to the equivalent of *khoya*, and then it cooks further, in the pork fat, until it browns in nutty, meatlike, and very delicious little flecks. No one will believe it began as milk—except perhaps an Indian guest willing to indulge in pork.   RSo

MILLE FEUILLES French for 'thousand leaves' and a term for any of several items made from several layers of puff PASTRY. Since one sheet of puff pastry, conventionally made, comprises 729 laminations, and mille feuilles may have two to five layers (1,458 to 3,645 leaves), this is an accurate description. The invention of the form (but not of the pastry itself) is usually attributed to the Hungarian town of Szeged, and a caramel-coated mille feuilles is called *Szegedinertorte*. CARÊME, writing at the end of the 18th century, cautiously stated only that it was of ancient origin.

The most usual kind of mille feuilles is made of three layers of pastry baked in a rectangular shape, sandwiched with a cream filling containing nuts, or some other cream or apricot jam, the top sprinkled with icing sugar. It is cut into smaller pieces with a fine serrated knife. Larger, round or oval ones are often made. One particular oval type consisting of two layers joined around the edge, containing the same almond filling as *gâteau Pithiviers* (see GATEAU) and iced with the same mixture diluted with egg white, is known in France as a 'Napoleon'—probably a corruption of 'Napolitain', from the Neapolitan habit of making layered confections. In the USA the name 'Napoleon' may be applied to any mille feuilles, and it is usual to top all kinds with royal icing.   HY

MILLER the common name of a mushroom, *Clitopilus prunulus*. Its distribution includes most of Europe, from the north down to Spain, and most of N. America, where it is called sweetbread mushroom. It grows in grassy areas in woods and parks from July to October, and is eccentric, which often causes the cap to be tilted (hence *Clitopilus*, meaning 'cap tilted over'). The cap, 5–10 cm (2–4") across, is grey or faintly plum coloured and convex in young specimens, then whiter and almost flat, with a 'kid-glove' texture. The gills, whose disposition gives mature specimens a trumpet shape, are first white and then pinkish. The white stem grows to 6 cm (2") high.

The naturalist who named the species in the 16th century had found his specimen under a plum tree; hence the specific name.

The flesh of the miller is white, soft, and fragile. It has an aroma of bread dough, which accounts for many of its common names (including the French *meunier*), and makes delicious eating.

MILLET the general name used for many similar cereals, notably of the genus *Panicum*. These bear small grains, yielding a coarse flour. They have been and in many places still are important staple foods, especially in dry, hot regions. Millet plants may grow up to 2 m (6') tall, with big seed heads bearing many small seeds.

Millets vary in flavour from thoroughly palatable to bitter and unpleasant. Many are grown mainly or exclusively as fodder crops for animals or poultry. Since most of them have many alternative common names the only clear way to list them is by their botanical names.

Panicum miliaceum is known as common, hog, or Indian millet, or as proso (its Russian name) or as broomcorn (because its untidy, spreading seed head resembles an old-fashioned besom). This species originated in the Near East, where it has been cultivated since prehistoric times. By the beginning of the 3rd millennium BC it had spread through Asia to China where, with *Setaria italica* (see below), it was one of the sacred 'five grains' (see FIVE GRAINS OF CHINA) which were ceremonially sown by the emperor and his family. The Chinese have always held it in lower esteem than rice, but it is still widely cultivated and consumed

in the north of China, away from the rice-growing areas. In the south maize has taken its place. The most usual way of eating millet in China is as a PORRIDGE.

Common millet arrived in Europe before 2000 BC. It was a staple food known to the ancient Greeks as *kenkhros* and to the Romans as *milium* (whence modern names). It was used for porridge and rough, unleavened bread.

Setaria italica is called foxtail millet, since the seed head resembles a fox's tail in shape and colour (though without the white tip). The flavour of the seeds is less good than that of common millet. This species shares its history with common millet, but grows better in warmer regions, for example, the south of China and Italy and Hungary in Europe, while common millet has been grown further north. It is the most important type of millet in Japan, and is also grown in India.

Eleusine coracana has the common names finger millet (referring to its five seed heads, which also account for the name birdsfoot millet), African millet, ragi (India). This species originated in E. Africa and was taken around 1000 BC to India, where it has become one of the principal millets eaten as human food. Ragi flour is made into the leavened pancakes called DOSA and the thinner, unleavened ROTI. Batloo is a flat millet bread cooked on a griddle and marked with depressions made by fingers. Another millet bread, popular all over India and particularly in Rajasthan and Gujarat is dhebra, which often has chickpea flour and wheat flour added for a lighter flavour and texture.

Finger millet is also widely cultivated in Africa, where it is made into a porridge, to be eaten with such other foods as are available. It is somewhat gritty, so the use of mucilaginous leaves such as MELOKHIA help it slip down. It is also used to some extent in China, Malaysia, and parts of S. America. The grain keeps well in storage. The flavour is pleasant but slightly bitter.

Pennisetum typhoides may be called bulrush or cattail millet (from its cylindrical seed heads), pearl millet (white seeded varieties), or bajra (in India, whither it was

taken from Africa around 1000 BC). It is made into unleavened bread in India, but is considered inferior to ragi (finger millet). In Africa it is generally made into porridge, but can be eaten like rice. It is a staple in the drier parts of tropical Africa, particularly in the northern territories of W. Africa and part of the Sudan, and in India.

Echinocloa frumentacea, Japanese barnyard millet (sometimes classed as a variety of *Panicum crus-galli*) is common in temperate regions of the Old World. It is *shanwa* in Japan, where it is eaten as porridge or mixed with rice, and *kheri* in India.

Digitaria exilis, 'hungry rice', is a genuine millet, not a kind of rice. It is grown in the drier parts of W. Africa, as is another species, *D. iburua*. In Nigeria the Hansa name for both is *fonio* or *fundi*.

See also TEF.

MINCE the verb, needs no explanation. Mince, the noun, has two meanings in Britain: meat which has been put through a mincing machine, or a savoury dish prepared by cooking such mince with water and a little onion and seasoning.

In the USA, the process is usually referred to as grinding, and the product as ground meat; or it may be called 'HAMBURGER', referring to the principal use of the result.

Any flesh can be minced, and this can be a convenient way of using the less tender or elegant cuts, and scraps left from cutting large joints. Naturally, the type of meat used depends on the favoured animal of the region; thus BEEF is especially favoured in Britain and N. America, and mixtures of beef and VEAL or PORK in much of Europe. LAMB is commonly used in the Muslim world.

Mince is relatively cheap, and can be 'stretched' by the addition of breadcrumbs, cornmeal, rice, or other grains. Many cuisines have dishes based upon it which reflect their culinary traditions in the use of flavourings and cooking methods. English SHEPHERD'S PIE is a method for using leftover roast lamb (cottage pie if the meat is beef). For KIBBEH in the Middle East minced lamb is usually the main ingredient. The

---

MILLET IN THE VENDÉE

Although millet is not much eaten in western countries, its consumption used to be much greater and little pockets of millet-eating survive. One such is in the Vendée (Pays de la Loire) where a millet semolina is used to make *meuille*, a sort of porridge; this, if allowed to become cold and solid, can be cut into slices and fried, or sprinkled with sugar to be *gâteau de mil*. The IPCF volume on *Pays de la Loire* (1993) records this, explaining that consumption of millet serves as a cultural marker, and is associated with agricultural festivals in the villages. Hongrois (1991) has provided much detailed information.

meat used for Middle Eastern mince dishes often has a very smooth texture obtained by prolonged pounding and kneading of the minced meat.

Approaches to the use of mince fall into a small number of categories:

- MEATBALLS;
- patties, for examples of which see HAMBURGER and KOFTA;
- PÂTÉS and their less glamorous relations such as MEAT LOAF;
- stuffings, as in filled pasta (RAVIOLI, WONTON, etc.) or larger items such as vegetables (DOLMA, etc.);
- sauces, such as the meat sauce which accompanies SPAGHETTI in Spaghetti bolognese; the fine texture of mince makes it suitable for such purposes.

MINCE PIE in Britain, is a miniature round pie, filled with mincemeat: typically a mixture of dried fruits, chopped nuts and apples, suet, spices, and lemon juice, vinegar, or brandy. Although the filling is called mincemeat, it rarely contains meat nowadays.

In N. America the pie may be larger, to serve several people. The large size is an innovation, for the original forms were almost always small. The earliest type was a small medieval pastry called a chewette, which contained chopped meat or liver, or fish on fast days, mixed with chopped hard-boiled egg and ginger. This might be baked or fried. It became usual to enrich the filling with dried fruit and other sweet ingredients.

Already by the 16th century 'minced' or 'shred' pies, as they were then known, had become a Christmas speciality, which they still are. The beef was sometimes partly or wholly replaced by suet from the mid-17th century onwards, and meat had effectively disappeared from 'mincemeat' on both sides of the Atlantic in the 19th century.

Mildred P. Blakelock (c.1932) wrote entertainingly of customs and superstitions associated with mince pies. She asked:

Is it lucky to eat as many as possible before Christmas, as says the dweller in London, or is the more elaborate custom found in Yorkshire more correct? The writer of this book, being a Yorkshire woman, is quite sure that it is not correct to eat mince pies before Christmas, but to eat one in a different house if possible on each of the twelve days of the season of Christmas. Anyone who does this ensures a happy year, as each mince pie so eaten is supposed to bring a happy month!

MINCHIN (also written as *mien chien*), a Chinese food item, made of fermented wheat GLUTEN.

After being kept in a covered container for several weeks, the gluten is overgrown with MOULDS (of as many as seven different genera) and BACTERIA. It is then salted and allowed to ferment for another two weeks before being cut into thin strips, like noodles, and used.

MINERALS a term loosely used to denote inorganic substances needed in the human diet. Not all of these are minerals in the sense of something that can be dug out of the ground. Another term used in this context is 'trace elements'; but this really means only substances that are needed in tiny quantities, and does not fit the first five items in the table towards the end of this article, for example the 4 g (0.15 oz) or so of sodium needed each day by an adult. Dietitians speak of 'macronutrients' and 'micronutrients' to mean things of which relatively large and small amounts are required.

We take in minerals in the form of various compounds, some of them highly complex. What the body actually needs is the pure elements in them—though these could not be got by eating the pure substance; sodium, for instance, is a dangerously inflammable metal. The daily requirement of sodium could be got by eating SALT (sodium chloride), BICARBONATE OF SODA (sodium hydrogen carbonate), or MONOSODIUM GLUTAMATE. Digestion will break all these down and take the sodium out of them. However, not all compounds can be broken down. Inorganic iron compounds such as rust (iron oxide) are very poor dietary sources of iron. The iron-containing compounds in meat, myoglobin and haemoglobin, contain far less iron but all of it can be absorbed, so they are much better sources.

Lack of minerals can cause deficiency diseases. The commonest is anaemia caused by lack of iron (but there are other causes of anaemia, such as lack of vitamin B12, which prevents the body from taking up iron from food). Calcium deficiency can produce the bone disease rickets in growing children, and osteoporosis in older people (again, this may also be caused by lack of a vitamin, in this case D). Some diseases are rare, such as goitre, a swelling of the thyroid gland in the neck caused by lack of iodine. This occurs in the few parts of the world where there is no iodine in drinking water. One of these used to be Derbyshire, and goitre was known as 'Derbyshire neck'.

Some minerals are known to be essential in diet, others are only thought to be. This is hard to ascertain: experiments on people, in which they were deliberately starved of some possibly necessary substance, would not be ethical; and it is no good using animals, as they often have different requirements. Nor are there any firm rules about how much of each mineral is needed. What is certain is that some elements that are essential in small quantities are poisonous in larger amounts, for example copper (see METAL UTENSILS).

These are the approximate daily requirements of minerals for an adult, stated in grams. The names given are not always those of the elements themselves, but of ions—electrically charged atoms of that element. For instance, chlorine is named as 'chloride'. Atoms of chlorine do not exist on their own, but go around in pairs. Only when chlorine dissolves in water and becomes ionized can the ions be considered singly. Phosphorus is named as phosphate, an ionized group of one phosphorus atom and four oxygen atoms; it is always found in this form in the body, for example as calcium phosphate in bone.

chloride	5.0
SODIUM	4.0
POTASSIUM	2.5
CALCIUM	0.75
phosphate (see PHOSPHORUS)	0.75
magnesium	0.25
iron	0.01
zinc	0.01
manganese	0.005
copper	0.002
molybdenum	0.0005
iodide	0.0001

It is possible that very small amounts of chromium, selenium, cobalt (other than that in vitamin B12), nickel, silicon, and tin are also necessary. Fluorine is beneficial because it strengthens children's teeth, but it may not be required for their survival, or necessary at all for adults.
                                                                                        RH

MINESTRONE an emphatic form of the Italian word *minestra* (one of two general terms for soup, the other being *zuppa*), refers to what is probably the best-known Italian soup, and certainly one of the most substantial. It has a high content of solid matter, including a range of vegetables, and PASTA or RICE, and may be regarded as a sort of Italian equivalent of SCOTCH BROTH.

As with most Italian soups, a sprinkling of PARMESAN cheese is almost obligatory, and helps to make the dish, taken with bread, a meal in itself.

The Genoese minestrone, as one would expect, has PESTO as an ingredient. Other regional versions also have their distinguishing characteristics.

MINNOW any of numerous species of small fish in the CARP family, belonging to genera such as *Rasbora*, *Esomus*, and *Luciosoma*. Minnows occur round the world, but are not normally consumed in Europe or N. America. In SE Asia, on the other hand, they are often eaten—scaled, gutted, and fried if large enough, or swallowed alive or cooked whole if small. In Laos, for example, *pa sieu* is the general name for various small minnows, which may be cooked whole in a banana leaf package with herbs and fish sauce. Another larger (up to 25 cm/10") minnow, *Luciosoma bleekeri*, has Lao names which allude to its being found in rice paddies.

Although almost all minnows are relatively small fish, and indeed the word 'minnow' is used in English to indicate something small, the family does include some large members; these are the squawfish found in the river systems of the Pacific north-west of the USA. *Ptychocheilus oregonensis*, the northern squawfish, is one such. These big minnows have some food value, and can be smoked successfully.

MINT the common name of most plants of the genus *Mentha*. There are about two dozen species, and many hundreds of varieties. As Deni Bown (1988) remarks in a graceful essay on mint, we are faced by 'a medley of hybrids and cultivars, often of uncertain origin, with characteristics of growth, flavour and aroma which may change according to conditions'.

A broad division, albeit with rough edges, may be made between spearmint and its close companions, the subject of this entry, and PEPPERMINT, which has its own special characteristics. See also PENNYROYAL, treated apart since it has its own distinctive common name.

Mint gave its name to a legendary nymph, Minthe, who attracted the amorous advances of the god Pluto and was changed into a plant by his jealous consort, Proserpina. The superstitions and beliefs associated with mint are often of ancient origin and vary with different cultures. In Greece, in remembrance of the nymph, young girls used to braid their bridal wreaths with sprigs of mint. In Rome, Pliny recommended that a wreath of mint was a good thing for students to wear since it was thought to 'exhilarate their minds'. Some modern research suggests that he was right.

The many sorts of mint have similar properties in varying degrees and may to some extent be used interchangeably. The main species and the principal hybrids, with some prominent varieties or cultivars, are:

- **Water mint,** *Mentha aquatica.*
- **Bergamot mint,** *M. aquatica* var *citrata.* Cultivars include several citrus-scented mints, such as Lemon Bergamot, Orange Bergamot, and Lime; also Eau de Cologne mint, which has small green leaves tinged with bronze-purple and a strong lemony scent (particularly good in orange jelly, according to Audrey Hatfield, 1964).

- **Field** (or wild) **mint,** *M. arvensis.*
- *M. arvensis* ssp *haplocalyx,* an **Asian mint,** used for scenting tea. Húng gioi in Vietnam.
- *M. arvensis* var *piperescens,* **Japanese mint,** important in Japan and as a source of menthol.
- *M.* × *gentilis* (*M. arvensis* × *M. spicata*), **red mint** or American applemint, often tinged with red, the main source of oil of spearmint (for CHEWING GUM). The cultivar Variegata has dappled golden leaves and a spicy aroma; it is known as **ginger mint,** and goes well with melon.
- **Horsemint,** *M. longifolia,* a highly variable species, commonly used in parts of India.
- **Corsican** (or Spanish) **mint,** also known as the crème de menthe plant, *M. requienii;* a creeping species with very small leaves.
- **Spearmint,** *M. spicata,* native to the Mediterranean area but naturalized in many other parts of Europe and in N. America. Very widely cultivated and used. This is '*the* mint' of cooks, the one commonly used for mint sauce and for flavouring new potatoes and peas, in Arab mint tea, etc.
- **False apple mint,** *M.* × *rotundifolia,* also known as woolly mint because of its hairy leaves, prized in the kitchen. The cultivar Variegata is an especially pretty plant, used to decorate salads and known as **pineapple mint.**
- *M. suaveolens,* round-leaved mint.
- *M.* × *villosa,* **applemint,** with lilac or pale pink flowers, is useful for salads and vegetable dishes.

Mint was grown and pickled in vinegar by the Romans, who introduced the plant into England. Throughout the Middle Ages, the herb was commonly grown in convent and monastery gardens and used extensively in cooking and medicine.

Mints, usually spearmint, are used, fresh or dried, to make jams, jellies, and sauces, to accompany meat, fish, or vegetable dishes. The leaves are also used to make teas, an Arab custom especially noticeable in N. Africa; the procedure is described under MOROCCO. Leaves are also added to fruit drinks and punches, e.g. the mint julep; and, in the Levant, often combined with cream cheese or yoghurt.

In England mint sauce is served with roast lamb. Gerard (1633) wrote that 'the smell of mint does stir up the minde and the taste to a greedy desire of meat'. Certainly the mint flavour is sweet and refreshing; and mint has digestive properties, so the habit of taking an 'after-dinner mint' has some foundation.
READING: Landing (1969).

MINTS a colloquial English term for any small sugar confectionery item flavoured with MINT, especially boiled sugar sweets. It is used to flavour DROPS; LOZENGES, or tablet-type sweets, based on SUGAR PASTE; mint chews; and various mint-flavoured DRAGÉES. As a favourite flavouring in Britain, it is used in many other species of confectionery, such as HUMBUGS and CHEWING GUM, which are not necessarily thought of as mints. It is also used extensively with chocolate, added as a flavouring, or in the form of FONDANT layers, or chips of boiled sugar. Mint has a long therapeutic history as an aid to digestion and a breath freshener.   LM

MIOGA GINGER *Zingiber mioga,* a close relation of GINGER but valued for its buds and stems, not the rhizomes. It grows abundantly in N. Japan, having apparently been introduced there from China.

The buds, thinly sliced and used as a garnish, are very fragrant but not hot like ginger. They are used, often in the form of

Mioga ginger

pickles, to garnish or flavour a wide range of dishes including soups, salads, TEMPURA, bean curd dishes (see TOFU), and SASHIMI. There is a popular belief in Japan that eating mioga ginger makes one forgetful, but this seems not to inhibit consumption.

MIREPOIX CHARLES-PIERRE-GASTON-FRANÇOIS DE LÉVIS, DUKE OF (1699–1757). Mirepoix was 'an incompetent and mediocre individual', writes Pierre Larousse at the end of the 19th century, 'who owed his vast fortune to the affection Louis XV felt toward his wife'. This same author informs us that the unfortunate Mirepoix had one claim to fame: he gave his name to 'a sauce made of all kinds of meat and a variety of seasonings'.

GRIMOD DE LA REYNIÈRE (1808) confirms the gastronomic pretensions of the hapless Duke when he cites a quail dish *à la Mirepoix* and claims that it was the invention of the deceased *Maréchal*. But what exactly, in the 18th century, constituted a dish *à la Mirepoix*? The answer is hard to supply since it is not until the 19th century that the term is encountered regularly in French culinary texts. Beauvilliers, for instance, in 1814, gives a short recipe for a *Sauce à la Mirepoix* which is buttery, wine-laced stock garnished with an aromatic mixture of carrots, onions, and a BOUQUET GARNI. CARÊME, in the 1830s, gives a similar recipe calling it simply *Mire-poix* and, by the mid-19th century, GOUFFÉ refers to a Mirepoix as 'a term in use for such a long time that I do not hesitate to use it here'. His mirepoix is listed among 'essences' and, indeed, is a meaty concoction (laced with two bottles of Madeira!) which, like all other essences, was used to enrich many a classic sauce.

By the end of the 19th century, the mirepoix had taken on its modern meaning and Favre, in his *Dictionnaire universel de cuisine* (c.1895, reprinted 1978) uses the term to describe a mixture of ham, carrots, onions, and herbs used 'as an aromatic condiment' when making sauces or braising meat.

Were he to observe cooks at work today, the Duke might be disappointed to discover that his would-be creation has been reduced to an 'aromatic condiment' but pleased to learn that his patronym has entered the French language and is pronounced daily in French kitchens from Paris to Bombay.   HY

MIRIN sometimes incorrectly described as a 'rice wine', is a spirit-based liquid sweetener of Japan, used only for cooking and especially in marinades and glazes and simmered dishes. The alcohol content, around 13%, is not always relevant; cooks sometimes burn off the alcohol, leaving only the special sweet taste which mirin imparts.

Mirin is normally sold in food shops rather than by wine merchants or liquor stores, and is normally available wherever oriental foods are on sale. Obtaining it in western countries used to be a problem; hence the advice in many cookery books to substitute sweet sherry if necessary (not a good idea, better just to use a little sugar syrup).

See also SAKÉ.

MIRLITON a French term for a small, sweet tartlet made of puff PASTRY usually with an almond filling. However, according to Theodora FitzGibbon (1976), a type particularly associated with Rouen have an egg, sugar, and butter filling, flavoured with ORANGE FLOWER WATER. English BAKEWELL TART is similar but larger.

MISO the Japanese name, now commonly used elsewhere, for what is also known as 'bean paste'. This is a fermented paste of SOYA BEANS and, usually, RICE or BARLEY or RYE. It plays an important role in Japanese cuisine. Similar products are used in SE Asia, especially Indonesia.

Miso was first made in China, where it and SOY SAUCE developed from a common predecessor, thought to have been a condiment prepared from meat, salt, and wine, fermented with a KOJI (starter culture) made from grain. A substance of this kind is mentioned in the *Analects* of Confucius. On archaeological evidence it is certain that by 200 BC a fermented condiment made with soya beans, rather than meat, was known in China. *Dou jiang*, the Chinese equivalent of miso, is familiar as an accompaniment to PEKING DUCK; but it is less important in China than miso is in Japan. The first Japanese written reference to miso dates from AD 701.

The Japanese use miso in many ways, notably for making miso soup, as a dressing for *aemono* (salads), in the cooking liquid of *nimono* (simmered dishes—see JAPANESE CULINARY TERMS), on grilled food, as an ingredient of pouring sauces, and as a flavouring for pickles.

Miso made from rice and soya beans (the usual kind) is *komemiso*; from barley or rye and soya beans, *mugimiso*; and from soya beans alone, *mamemiso*. There are also blended types and a kind made in Okinawa for which the stones of cycads are used. *Namemiso* (literally miso to be licked) is made by adding fish, shellfish, poultry, vegetables, seaweeds, nuts, sugar, etc. to miso, and is eaten as a relish.

Rice miso comes in a variety of colours, due to different ingredients and methods of fermentation. The light kinds are more quickly fermented and milder in flavour, the darker ones stronger and more mature. The colours range from that of 'white miso' (actually pale yellow) through red to brownish-black. Both sweetish and salty types are available, but the dark kind is always salty. A large amount of salt is needed in colder climates where fermentation is slow, to keep the beans from going bad before the fermenting organism takes hold. *Tsugaru-sannen miso* is fermented for three years. Barley miso may also be either sweet or salty. Plain soya bean miso includes one kind, *hatcho miso*, which may take up to two years to mature. Prepared miso keeps for up to a year when refrigerated.

In China, *dou jiang* also has yellow (sweet) and black (strong) varieties. The grain added to the beans is wheat rather than rice. A sweet wheat-flour version is called *tian mian jiang*. There is also a kind with chunks of soya bean in it, *dou ban jiang*; and a hot variety with red pepper, *la jiao jiang*.

Miso is fermented in two stages. First a mould, *Aspergillus oryzae*, is grown on steamed grain. This forms the koji (starter culture) for the eventual mixture. The soya beans are soaked, steamed and chopped, then mixed with the koji, salt, and water. The water contains YEASTS and lactic BACTERIA; in the past these were wild strains entering from the atmosphere, but now cultures are deliberately added. It is these organisms which develop the final flavour. The mixture is then left to ripen for as long as required.

When the fermentation of miso is complete the soya beans retain their original shape. Miso used to be ground daily at home with a huge pestle and mortar, but nowadays it is sold ready ground. Home-made miso is still ground by hand.

There is also a related dry product, hamanatto, a speciality of Shizuoka. This may be regarded as an early form of miso, similar to Chinese fermented black beans. It is made like miso but with the addition of toasted ground wheat to the beans. Dried in the sun, then mixed with pickled ginger, it is black and has a sweet taste. A similar product, *tauco kering*, has been introduced in Indonesia. NATTO is a different soya bean product, fermented by bacteria instead of moulds.

MITSUBA is the Japanese name of a perennial herb, *Cryptotaenia japonica*, which is cultivated almost exclusively in Japan. It is sometimes called wild chervil; and also has the names honewort (used of the closely related *C. canadensis* in N. America) and trefoil (but this last is used of other plants also).

Mitsuba comes in two principal varieties, *kansai* (green) and *kanto* (whiter); and the Japanese devote great care to their cultivation and to techniques such as winter and summer blanching to make them more tender. The leaf stalks look more like coriander than parsley, but have a milder flavour than coriander.

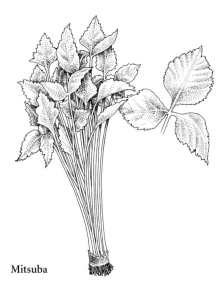

Mitsuba

Mitsuba has a role in Japan similar to that of parsley in western countries and coriander in most other Asian countries, but it has a wider range of uses. Joy Larkcom (1991) gives a good description:

Mitsuba has a delightful flavour, often described as celery-like, but to me has a unique blend of parsley, celery, and angelica, with angelica predominating. The leaves, the green stems and the highly prized blanched white stems are the main parts used.

Leaves and stems, fresh or blanched, are frequently used for seasoning clear and fish soups. The stems may be rubbed between the fingers until soft then tied into knots, which are dropped into the soup. Chopped blanched stems look beautiful scattered over soup.

Leaves and stems are also used to flavour a wide range of Japanese dishes, from savoury custards to *sukiyaki* and *ohitashi*: they should never be cooked for more than a couple of minutes or the flavour is destroyed.

MIZUAME a Japanese term which literally means 'water candy'. This is a very heavy syrup made by converting STARCH into SUGAR in one of two ways. In the first and traditional method, starch (usually from glutinous rice) is mixed with MALT, whose enzyme turns it into syrup.

In the second method, the starch used is usually from sweet potatoes or ordinary potatoes; and an acid (hydrochloric, sulphuric, or nitric) is used instead of malt. This second method is by far the more common nowadays, but the first method is said to produce a more flavoursome result, sometimes called 'barley mizuame'.

Mizuame has the consistency of GOLDEN SYRUP (or sometimes slightly thicker) but is completely colourless. It is eaten as it is, like honey; or is used as a sweetener in cooking, especially when glossy results are desirable; or may be the main ingredient of sweets.

MOCHA a Yemeni port (Moka) on the Red Sea, which gave its name to a fine type of COFFEE produced in that region, and then to a flavouring produced from this coffee, often with the addition of chocolate, for use in cakes and confectionery.

MOCHI a Japanese glutinous (sticky) RICE cake. The rice is steamed and pounded into a paste before being shaped into cakes. These may then be eaten while still soft or allowed to harden before being toasted and served with various accompaniments such as SOY SAUCE, sugar, NORI. As Hosking (1996) puts it:

They are one of the essential Japanese foods and, having a celebratory significance, are particularly eaten at New Year, when many people try to eat a lot of them. They are served in *zoni*, the special New Year soup. They are very soft and sticky and every year a number of people, usually old people, choke to death on them.

The pounding of the steamed rice can be quite a ceremony, calling for a huge mortar and pestle and strong sumo wrestlers. Rachel Laudan (1996), describing what happened to mochi when it migrated to Hawaii, gives a graphic description:

Two men, armed with long mallets somewhat similar to croquet mallets, stand on either side of a narrow vertical cylindrical tub, about 2½ feet tall. Into the hollow at the top a third man tips a pile of steaming hot rice. The first man raises the mallet over his head as if he were going to chop firewood with an ax and brings it down hard onto the rice. As he does so, the second man raises his mallet, so that the pounding is nearly continuous. The third man dodges backward and forward, first dipping his hand into a bucket of cold water so that it will neither stick nor burn in contact with the hot rice and then flipping the rice over so that it gets thoroughly pounded. From time to time, he shakes in a little water. After about 5–10 minutes, the rice is a glutinous mass. It is cut into chunks, formed into flat cakes, and allowed to dry. The texture of mochi made this way is supposed to be superb.

Mochi in Hawaii is in fact a subject on its own. The confection called butter mochi, which has evolved there along with other variants, is a mixture of sugar and butter and eggs with coconut milk and glutinous rice flour. Laudan speculates that its origin, given that it is not typically Japanese, was prompted by Hawaiian home economists pondering the uses to be made of ovens, when these became common in Hawaii; but she also thinks that it could be a descendant

of *bibingka* (see RICE CAKES OF THE PHILIPPINES). Recent versions include sweetened bean paste, or purple yam paste, or cocoa powder; and in an even more dramatic mutation (probably originating in California) of the 1990s mochi ice cream has come to the fore:

Bite-sized pieces of ice cream are covered with a thin skin of mochi. It retains its elasticity even though frozen and it insulates the ice cream. Which is better? Green tea ice cream covered with plain mochi or vanilla ice cream covered with espresso mochi? It's impossible to decide, so it's best to take both.

MOCK TURTLE SOUP a surprising item of English cuisine, celebrated in *Alice in Wonderland* (where Tenniel's illustration of a mock turtle encapsulates what would need several sentences of prose to explain). Real TURTLE dishes, including turtle soup, using turtles from the W. Indies, were expensive items which put a stamp of luxury on important dinners, from the mid-18th century up to recent times. So, almost as soon as such dinners began to be served, the search was on for an inexpensive substitute. The solution was to use calf's head, which has a texture like that of turtle meat, and to employ various little tricks to simulate the flavour and colour.

C. Anne Wilson (1973) points out that the process can be seen by comparing various early editions of Hannah GLASSE (1st edn, 1747). The first edition had nothing about turtle. That of 1751 included just a few additional recipes, of which To Dress a Turtle the West Indian Way was one (and this, interestingly, called for veal as a subsidiary ingredient). The sixth edition, of 1758, was the one in which mock turtle, using calf's head, made its bow.

Thereafter, for nearly 200 years, mock turtle soup recipes were frequently to be found in English recipe books. And, although the urge to imitate turtle soup has now just about disappeared, mock turtle seems assured of eternal life by its presence in the pages of Lewis Carroll.

MOGHUL CUISINE an important part of the cuisine of India, especially in the north.

Moghul is the Indian version of Mongol. The Mongol Empire was by far the greatest force in Asia in the Middle Ages. At its height, under the successors of the mighty Genghis Khan, it covered most of the known world. One enormous part of this empire was inherited by the leader Babur who ruled a region which included Afghanistan, much of Persia, and the north of the Indian subcontinent. His own favourite place was Kabul in Afghanistan, where he is buried, but the dynasty he founded, which reached its greatest magnificence under his grandson Akbar the Great, was based in India and drew its culinary inspiration(s) from Persia. Hence the introduction to India through the Moghul court, over a period of two centuries, of many highly refined and beautiful Persian dishes which were further developed and embellished in their new environment, often by chefs who had been trained in C. Asian or Persian styles of cooking.

Although the main culinary thrust of the Moghuls was to introduce Persian dishes to India, it was not a case of replacing what was Indian with what was Persian. Joyce Westrip (1997) gives an interesting description of the role of Abul Fazl, the philosopher poet and powerful courtier under Akbar the Great (1556–1605) and a meticulous recorder of the food served at the royal table. She points out that, from this and other sources, we know that the traffic was definitely two-way:

the emperor was subject to the influence of the numerous Hindu princesses who gained so great an ascendancy over him as to make him forswear beef, garlic, onion and the wearing of a beard. Akbar, a Muslim, went out of his way to introduce modified Hindu customs and heresies into the court assemblies to please and win over his Hindu subjects.

Thus what was achieved was an interesting blend of Persian and Hindu kitchen practices.

This legacy survives. Important categories of dishes which have a Moghul origin include: PILAF and BIRIANI dishes; KEBABS, KORMAS, and KOFTAS; TANDOOR dishes; SAMOSAS.

Rich dishes with almonds and pistachios are likely to be of Moghul origin, as are sweet rice dishes (flavoured with saffron). Among the most noticeable Moghul dishes are those decorated with GOLD AND SILVER LEAF (*vark*). The same applies to 'shahi' dishes (*Shah* means king), which are usually elaborate and rich with such things as cream, almonds, etc. The scent of rosewater may also betray a Moghul confection.

Some sweets which originated in C. Asia were developed under Moghul influence into the delicacies well known in India as BARFI, HALVA, GULAB JAMUN, JALEBI, etc. Persian fruit-based drinks called *sharbat* (see SHERBET), cooled with snow, were introduced to the court, some made with rosewater and almonds. Babur introduced many fruits from C. Asia, Afghanistan, and Persia including grapes, musk melons, pomegranates, peaches, and quinces; also nuts such as almonds and pistachios.

MOHINGA Small rice noodles called *mondi* or *mohinga*, made from slightly

fermented rice flour, are the basis of what is generally considered to be the national dish of BURMA, *Mohinga*. The noodles/vermicelli are bathed in a fish and creamy coconut curry sauce which is as thin as soup. This is accompanied by a number of side dishes ranging from hard-boiled eggs, limes, fried garlic, spring onions, chickpeas, chillies, bite-size patties made from shrimp or mung beans, and slices of the tender heart of banana palms. *Mohinga* is a popular street food and is available at nearly every street corner or market place where the itinerant vendors have set up their stalls.

MOJABAN *Sargassum fulvellum*, one of the brown SEAWEEDS. The Korean name is given because this species, although eaten in Japan also, seems to be most highly appreciated in Korea. The dried plant is soaked and drained, then cooked with garlic, spring onion, and spices.

MOLDOVA comprising much of what was formerly Moldavia, is situated between the UKRAINE and ROMANIA on what used to be one of the busiest trade routes between W. Europe and places further east. So its cuisine betrays historical connections with BYZANTINE COOKERY, GREECE, and TURKEY (which effectively ruled the Moldavians for 300 years), besides the two immediate neighbours.

An example of the Greek or Levantine influence is the popularity of MOUSSAKA (which is equally popular with a different spelling in Romania and throughout the Balkans), although in a modified form which involves having more vegetables (or being vegetarian).

Another resemblance to Romania is the ubiquity of *mamalyga* (see MAMALIGA). MAIZE is important in Moldova, although the bread is wheaten. Bread and *mamalyga* are the national staples.

In common with other Balkan countries, Moldova has its *givech* dishes (see GYUVECH), of which a typical one would include lamb or mutton with lots of different vegetables and some dill and parsley. And in common with the whole range of countries from the Adriatic Sea to C. Asia, Moldova has many sorts of *chorba* (a sour soup—see SHORBA). Standard ingredients are KVASS, SOUR CREAM, and a wide range of vegetables with dill and tarragon.

An interesting flavouring is *muzhdei/muzhdey* a concentrated mixture of garlic and strong beef stock. This is used, for example, with a purée of kidney beans and onion.

The use of apricots (or sour plums or quince) in meat or poultry dishes is no

doubt derived from the countries of the Caucasus.
READING: Notaker (1990).

MOLE the most famous Mexican sauce, takes its name from *molli*, a Nahuatl word meaning mixture or concoction; and it is indeed a mixture of many ingredients. The constant factor among the numerous different versions is the starring role played by CHILLI peppers and the fact that the mixture is always cooked.

Mole poblano de guajolote (Poblano is a synonym of Ancho, a cultivar of chilli pepper, and refers to the valley of Pueblo, where these peppers were first cultivated, while *guajalote* is wild TURKEY) or *Pavo in mole poblano* (*pavo* is the Mexican-Spanish word for turkey) is a dish of some antiquity and has achieved some fame for the inclusion of bitter chocolate in the sauce, although the quantity is small and the effect not separably discernible. Some have thought that the dish was made, with chocolate already added, in pre-Columbian times, but the lack of evidence for pre-Columbian use of chocolate as an ingredient in any food dish tells against this conclusively; and indeed the attitude of the Aztecs to chocolate was such that they would have been no more likely to use it in cooking than Spaniards would have been to cook with communion wine. Quite apart from this particular question, it is doubtful whether *mole poblano* dates as far back as the 17th century, as has been generally believed.
(SC)

MOLLUSCS a category of invertebrate animals including many important foods. Most are seafoods: CEPHALOPODS such as SQUID and OCTOPUS; BIVALVES, for example the OYSTER and the MUSSEL; and the single shells, including the PERIWINKLE. The last group is the least prized, but has a famous counterpart on land, the edible SNAIL; whereas there are no terrestrial cephalopods or bivalves.

Attitudes towards eating molluscs vary greatly. In countries far from the sea they may be unknown. But familiarity does not equate with acceptability. It is notorious that during their terrible famine of the 1840s those Irish people who lived in coastal areas and could have partly subsisted on food such as mussels ignored this resource. In some countries, a few molluscs are eaten and others shunned. Schwabe (1979), remarks that:

Traditional cultural prejudices about eating invertebrate animals vary in the extreme and generally without rhyme or reason. Mosaic food laws, for example, ban all creatures of the waters without fins or scales to orthodox Jews yet consider locusts to be a valuable food item. Similarly, it is not unusual to encounter Americans who will eat oysters alive but consider the very idea of eating cooked squid or land snails disgusting.

The general trend is towards increased consumption of molluscs. Economic factors play a part in this; and so does the fact that several outstanding cuisines (French, Chinese, Japanese) embody a wholehearted acceptance of molluscan food.

MOMBIN a name applied to some fruits of the genus *Spondias*.

The red mombin, or Spanish plum, *Spondias purpurea*, a native of tropical America, is a fruit of major importance in parts of Mesoamerica, and was long ago introduced to the Philippines by Spanish colonists. The fruits vary greatly in size, form, and palatability. They are commonly oval or roundish, from 2.5 to 5 cm (1–2") long and ranging from deep red to yellow in colour. Good ones have juicy flesh with a subacid, spicy flavour, not unlike that of the CASHEW fruit (another member of the family Anacardiaciae) but less pronounced. They may be eaten fresh, or boiled and dried.

In most Spanish-speaking countries this species is known as *ciruela* (plum), a name which has been corrupted in the Philippines to *siniguelas*. In parts of Mexico and in Guatemala it is known as *jocote* (from the Aztec *xocotl*). Common names in the French colonies are *prunier d'Espagne, prunier/ mombin rouge*.

The yellow mombin, *S. mombin* (or *S. lutea*), is native to Brazil and Costa Rica, where it is referred to as *caja* and *jobo*. Its yellow fruits are mildly acid, and juicy, but generally inferior to those of the red mombin.

The name hog plum, vexing because it is applied in various places to a host of different fruits, is sometimes used of both mombins, especially the yellow one (and also of the less important *S. mangifera*, amra or imra). It is not intended as a derogatory term, but simply refers to the food preferences of hogs. For other fruits of the same genus, see AMBARELLA and IMBU.

MONGOLIA is historically the homeland of Genghis Khan and his Mongol hordes (see also TATAR CUISINE) who swept westwards to Europe in the 13th century. This is a land-locked and thinly populated country perched between Russia to the north and China to the south. It is divided geographically into the arid south, including the Gobi desert, and the mountainous north, where there are pastures for cattle and some wheat is grown.

Mongolia is essentially a land of nomadic pasturalists, and large herds of sheep, goats, camels, and horses form the mainstay of the economy. The life of the Mongols is a constant cycle of seasonal migrations from flat open summer pastures to protected river valleys for the winter.

Sheep still provide the main staples: meat, milk, cheese, and rancid butter. The climate and way of life are not conducive to growing vegetables although some vegetables and fruit are now consumed and rice (imported from Vietnam), potatoes, and cabbage often now accompany the meat. Some Chinese flour noodles are also prepared. Mongolian bread is usually baked on a hot metal plate (*tava*) over the open charcoal or dried dung (*argol*) fire.

Meat is often cooked in a 'Mongolian firepot', the one item from the Mongolian kitchen which has become familiar in the western world. The device (which has its parallels in Japan and China, for example) has been described by Nicholls and Nicholls (1989) as resembling a small wok with a funnel through its centre, the whole being made of brass or tin.

A slice of meat can be cooked in the 'moat' of the firepot in just 20 or 30 seconds (and suitably prepared pieces of vegetable almost as fast), then taken out, dipped in any of various sauces, and eaten. At the end of the meal, when most of the meat is finished, the remaining vegetables are cooked for a few minutes, and then ladled with the resulting broth into individual bowls as soup, sometimes with added noodles.

Meat is also barbecued on a *tava*. Strips or slices of mutton are cooked on the hot plate which is first sprinkled with oil or fat. Fat of the FAT-TAILED SHEEP is popular, both rendered for cooking and for eating as a delicacy.

In the summer months, when flocks and herds are giving ample milk, the Mongol diet includes little else. Mare's milk (*ayrag*) is the most favoured and is drunk half-fermented, so that it has a sour and sometimes slightly fizzy taste; see also KOUMISS. Other milk products are butter, dried curds, and clotted cream. The butter is often made out of cow's milk, the remaining buttermilk is boiled until it curdles. The curds are then dried in the sun (cf *kashk*) and stored until winter-time when they are mixed with hot water and drunk as a substitute for fresh milk.

Horses not only provide the favoured *ayrag* but in fact they are the key to the nomad's existence and livelihood on the steppes. They are an essential element of daily life, transport, aid for tending the herds, and of course an asset for hunting. William of Rubruck, who travelled through this area in the 13th century, noted that Mongols made superb HORSEMEAT sausages which were eaten raw, and hung up thin strips of meat to dry in the sun (see JERKY). He also noted that raw meat would be placed under their horses' saddles or between their clothes to press out all the blood before drying and smoking it; a practice continued into recent times.

TEA is another staple food. Travellers were wont to give vivid but unenthusiastic descriptions of how this was traditionally prepared, using brick tea and employing a vessel which was never properly cleaned, only rubbed with dried dung. Salt water was used and, if the brick tea had to be softened before use, it was placed among glowing dung embers which gave it a characteristic added flavour. The tea was made with milk, and roasted millet might be mixed in to make it more substantial. A final touch might be the addition of a lump of raw sheep-tail fat.

The modern traveller in Mongolia fares better but still has the privilege of meeting a cuisine which generally remains faithful to ancient traditions and to the distinctive way of life of the nomads.

MONITOR any of various large tropical Old World lizards of the family Varanidae; they are called monitors because it was supposed that they gave warning of the presence of CROCODILES.

Monitor lizards are eaten in most SE Asian countries and often present a fearsome sight in the market, e.g. brought in whole to be butchered in front of the purchaser in countryside markets in Laos. In the Philippines a monitor is often trapped as it sneaks into chicken runs in search of the chickens which are its favourite food. 'It does indeed taste like chicken, except that it has a more intense taste and is less tender.' This comment by Doreen Fernandez (1994) is accompanied by the information that monitors are usually cooked in ADOBO style, e.g. *adobong matanda* (crisp, dry, with plenty of toasted garlic).

One of the biggest monitor lizards is *Varanus niloticus*, the Nile monitor, which may measure 2 m (over 6') in length. It has the ingenious habit of scraping out a hollow in a termite nest in which to lay its eggs. The termites repair their structure and the monitor's eggs are then protected by it. These eggs and the monitor's flesh are eaten with appreciation locally.

MONKEY is mentioned here for two reasons. First, there are various pieces of evidence about monkeys being eaten in the remote past or in primitive cultures in more recent times. For example, Sophie Coe (1994) records that two species (*Ateles geoffroyi*, the spider monkey, and *Alouatta villosa*, the howler monkey) were highly popular among the Lacandon of C. America, who ate them roasted; this in a situation where flesh foods were relatively scarce. Similar examples could be drawn from SE Asia.

The second reason for mentioning monkey is a horrifying story which has been current, to the effect that in recent times some Chinese have eaten monkeys' brains as a delicacy, scooping them directly from the head of the living animal. The victim's head was usually described as projecting upwards through the central hole (designed to take a steamboat) in the centre of a Chinese dining table.

The tale has been the subject of investigation by eminent food detectives from the English-speaking world. Derek Cooper (writing in the *Listener*, 1984) and Paul Levy (1986) concluded that it had no foundation. The former spoke with some authority since it was probably he who, by perpetrating a hoax, started the story off. The latter author was satisfied, from full enquiries of people in Hong Kong who could be expected to know, that it had never been a Chinese practice. However, he was made aware of the possibility that someone in Hong Kong, hearing the story, might have turned the myth into actuality; indeed he believes that an Italian film crew, working in Hong Kong, probably did just this.

Saunders (1995), belonging himself to the relevant hemisphere, took further pains to investigate and concluded that 'it was the obstinate lack of eye-witnesses that gave the story its air of urban myth. Like the tales of the vanishing hitch-hiker and the Gucci kangaroo, it was always something that happened to friends of friends.' However, he himself took on the 'friend of a friend' role in this scenario by admitting that he was on one occasion told by someone, unnamed, who purported to be an eyewitness, of preparations being made, in an unnamed SE Asian city, for such a gruesome rite.

It must be said in conclusion that the respected Anderson (1988) stated, unsurprisingly, that he had never witnessed such a scene, but added: 'though this is done in some places. It is a medicine rather than a food in any meaningful sense.'

MONOSODIUM GLUTAMATE (MSG). Marketed in Japan and elsewhere as *Aji-no-moto*, in SE Asia as *Ve-tsin*, in the west as Accent and under other trade names, MSG is a flavour-enhancing chemical compound, whose operation on the human nervous system is not well understood. It seems to make the tongue, and to a lesser extent the palate, more receptive to savoury, salty tastes. It therefore makes bland food more interesting, and has been widely used by the food-processing industry throughout the world, e.g. in canned soups. It is also used by chefs and cooks in some Asian and oriental-style restaurants, and in domestic kitchens in some Asian countries.

MSG is manufactured on a large scale in many countries—total world output is said now to be well over a quarter of a million tonnes per year. It is a white, coarse powder, with very little flavour of its own. Chemically, it is the sodium salt of glutamic acid. It is said to have been first isolated in the laboratory by a Japanese researcher in 1908; commercial production began in the following year. Nowadays it is usually manufactured from wheat GLUTEN or beet molasses by a fermentation process devised in the 1950s.

The effect of MSG has been known for centuries to the Japanese, who have long used *Laminaria* seaweeds (KOMBU) as a natural source of this mysterious substance. The broad, flat strands of this seaweed are often scored before cooking to help release it. Why the process of evolution should have endowed *Laminaria* spp in this way is not at all clear.

A pinch of MSG certainly helps to bring out (though it cannot create) the flavour of almost any soup, meat, vegetable, poultry, or fish dish. However, it acquired a bad reputation in the late 1960s when it was blamed for the 'Chinese restaurant syndrome'—a combination of discomforts in the head and chest suffered by diners in Chinese restaurants who had apparently absorbed too much MSG-laden food. The effects usually pass off quickly and without doing harm, but a sizeable minority of people are afflicted more severely and for a longer time. MSG is therefore forbidden in some countries as an additive to baby food and many food writers have advised against adding it to any food, although its natural presence in small amounts in certain foodstuffs seems to be non-controversial. It is identified in Europe by the number 621 but has no E-rating.   (RO)

MOONCAKES traditional Chinese 'cakes' consisting of a pastry shell with a sweetened filling, made specially for the Autumn Moon Festival. They are usually round, to symbolize the roundness of the moon, and are made with a special mould which imprints a chrysanthemum pattern and Chinese characters on them.

Mooncakes have various fillings such as a purée of red AZUKI BEAN paste or brown date paste. Along the Yangtze River and in the south the filling is LOTUS seed paste with whole preserved duck egg yolks, which represent the moon itself.

The moon has always held a special place in China, and this festival is a celebration of harvest time when a large, golden 'harvest moon' appears. Family and friends get together to view this full moon, poetry is written and recited, and thanks are given for the food being stored for the winter ahead. Mooncakes are eaten and exchanged as gifts, sometimes displayed in a pyramid of 13 to represent the number of lunar months in a year.

Legend has it that mooncakes were cunningly used by women to start a revolution against the hated Mongol rulers in the 14th century. They hid paper strips with secret messages inside the cakes, year after year during the Moon Festival, when sending mooncakes to neighbours, friends, and families, a procedure so traditional and universal that the Mongols never suspected what was happening.   HS

MOONFISH a name which belongs correctly to *Vomer setapinnis*, a fish of the carangid family (see JACK). This belongs to the tropical waters of the W. Atlantic but strays north during the summer as far as New England. Its silvery body is thin, and its maximum length 30 cm (1'), so there is not much of it to eat. However, it may be fried or baked, and there are records of its having been marketed in New York (as blunt-nosed shiner) and Massachusetts (as hump-backed butterfish). The high 'forehead' gives this fish a philosophical appearance.

A close relation, the lookdown, *Selene vomer*, is of less use as food, and has a more severe and discouraged look on its lofty head.

MOOSE the name used for the American counterpart of the European ELK. There are differing views about the taxonomy of this group of large animals in the DEER family. Many authorities consider that it is best to regard them all as belonging to a single species, *Alces*, but to recognize a number of subspecies. On this basis the moose of N. America would not be classified as *Alces americana* (sometimes treated as two species, the second being the Alaskan moose and classified as *A. gigas*), as in the past, but as a subspecies of *A. alces*.

The male of the species has the largest antlers in the deer family and may weigh almost 600 kg (1,350 lb). It is often found in areas where there are bogs or marshes, since aquatic plants are a favourite food.

The moose is valued for its meat. The part considered to be the finest tidbit of all (according to Vilhjalmur Stefansson, 1946, who lived among the Inuit (Eskimo) for many years, existing on a diet of meat and water) is the nose.

MORAY EEL *Muraena helena*, a formidable eel which reaches a considerable size (maximum length 150 cm/60"), presents a mottled appearance of varying coloration (e.g. whitish on brown), and lives in rocky crevices in the Mediterranean. It emerges at night to seek its prey, to attack which it is equipped with notably sharp and dangerous teeth. It has a reputation for cunning; Euzière (1961) believed that 'the moray likes to live near an octopus, of which when other food fails he will eat a tentacle, knowing that it will grow again'. This practice resembles the cut-and-come-again technique which human beings practise with some green salad plants.

The reputation of the moray as a table fish varies from indifferent to very good. Certainly, the bony tail-end is best avoided. However, if that precaution is taken, and if the fish is cut into sections, poached, and trimmed into neat bone-free pieces, it can be very good. Professor Giorgio Bini, the greatest 20th-century authority on Mediterranean fish, declared in a private communication (1962) that he thought the flesh of the moray to be 'perhaps the finest of all Mediterranean fish'.

MORELS edible fungi of the genus *Morchella*, considered a great delicacy in Europe and the USA, and also esteemed in China but poorly represented in the southern hemisphere (a deficiency which also applies to other good kinds of MUSHROOM).

A morel is noticeably different from a normal mushroom; instead of a cap, it has an upright fruit body, distinctively pitted and resembling a honeycomb or sponge. This is hollow inside, as is the stem. Only a few morels exceed 10 cm (4") in height, but the same species may grow to a larger size in America than in Europe. Most morels are ochre or brown in colour with a paler stem; but the black morel is taller and darker. They all grow in the spring in both fields and woods, reputedly preferring sites where there is ash from a fire. It is said that peasant women in Germany had to be restrained during the 18th century from lighting heath fires in order to encourage morels to grow; their activity had resulted in forests being burned down. (A similar tale is told of Provence.)

Morels are particularly plentiful in the Midwest of the USA, where morel festivals are held in the spring, notably at Boyne in Michigan.

The classification of morels is complicated by the occurrence of forms intermediate between the species traditionally recognized. The best-known species which are cited by authors are listed below. The notations E, NA, and OR indicate distribution in Europe, N. America, and the Orient (China and Japan) respectively.

- *Morchella esculenta* (=*M. vulgaris*) (E, NA), the common morel, has a pale yellow-brown head, but not pale enough to deserve being called white. However, specimens are found, especially young ones, which have lighter-coloured heads, and these are called *vraie morille blonde* in France.
- *M. deliciosa* (E, NA, OR) is distinguished by some authors on both sides of the Atlantic as being the finest morel. Others classify it as *M. esculenta*. Its head has whitish ridges and dark pits, and it is sometimes called white morel.
- *M. rotunda* (E) occurs in more than one form. The cap may be yellow-ochre to orange, or pale brown. The larger sort may be as much as 20 cm (8") tall.
- *M. crassipes* (E, NA, OR) is the thick-footed morel, which has a markedly thickened stem and fruits later than *M. esculenta*.
- *M. angusticeps* (E, NA, OR), the black morel, common in coniferous regions of N. America, is another choice species.
- *M. conica* (E, OR), *morille conique* in France, is relatively small (5–10 cm/2–4"). Its scientific and most of its common names proclaim the conical shape of its head.
- *M. elata* (E, NA, OR) is dark, usually blackish, in colour. In Europe it is much less common than a closely similar species, distinguished by its purple/green coloration, *M. purpurascens*.
- *M. hybrida* (E, NA), has a small pitted head which is joined to the stalk but has its margins free (hence the old specific name, *semilibera*, meaning half-free). It is the *morillon* or *morille bâtarde* of France, and has sometimes been classified separately from the true morels.

The pits or hollows of a morel are always clearly formed with prominent walls, which in some species have a prevailing vertical direction. If the structure is ill defined, looking rather like a brain or a tangled mass of twine, the fungus is probably one of those dealt with under FALSE MOREL, to be treated with great caution.

Morels would be a valuable crop if they could be cultivated. Attempts have often been made, with occasional success, as when the baron d'Yvoire, in 1889, grew some on an artichoke bed to which apple pulp had been applied. But each species has highly specific ecological requirements, and attempts at their cultivation are still of uncertain result.

Morels should be gathered in dry weather and carefully picked clean. All members of the group of fungi to which morels belong contain small amounts of helvellic acid. This is toxic, but is destroyed by cooking; so morels should not be eaten raw. They respond well to gentle stewing or simmering. The heads, being hollow, are suitable for stuffing; but, being expensive, they are often chopped up and used in sauces or as a garnish.

Morels dry well and are often sold in that form. They are also available in cans.

MOROCCO The N. African kingdom of Morocco lies alongside the Mediterranean Sea to the north and the Atlantic Ocean to the west and south. It is a country of fertile coastal and inner plains, high mountains, and desert land. Morocco is known as 'a cold country where the sun is hot'. Great extremes of temperature, both between winter and summer and between day and night, are the norm in most of the country. However, it still receives enough rain to allow for permanent cultivation of the basic ingredients of Moroccan food: WHEAT, MAIZE, vegetables, herbs, fruit, and meat in the form of lamb or chicken which are either boiled (COUSCOUS), steamed (*choua*), or stewed (TAGINES).

Berbers are the indigenous population of Morocco. The Arab invasion in the 7th century brought with it many Arab soldiers who settled there and who slowly Arabized the country and converted most of its inhabitants to Islam. This is not to say that Morocco did not come under other earlier influences. The Phoenicians established trading posts along its coast in the 12th century BC and the Carthaginians added their own in the 5th century BC. In the reign of the Emperor Claudius Morocco became a Roman province but when the Empire became divided Morocco passed first under Byzantine rule and later under the Arabs. Until then it was known as Mauretania and the official language was Latin.

Berber food must have absorbed some culinary influences from those early occupiers but it was the Arabs who had the longer-lasting effect on Moroccan cuisine. They brought with them eastern spices such as cinnamon, ginger, saffron, cumin, and caraway amongst others and the Moroccans adopted these to flavour their tagines and other dishes. It was also the Arabs who introduced the notion of SWEET-AND-SOUR cooking which they had taken from the Persians. Honey, sugar, or fruit, either fresh or dried, are often added to tagines or couscous sauces to impart that particularly delicate sweet and spicy taste which is so typically Moroccan.

One of the most effective ways to taste Morocco's most typical dishes is to attend a *diffa* (feast) where a succession of the best-known national dishes are served. Of course *diffas* are not daily events and are on the whole the reserve of the wealthy aristocracy and affluent middle classes. Most households will normally content themselves with one main dish for their daily meals. Often this will be a stew accompanied by a salad and bread, or a couscous or perhaps a substantial soup like *Harira* which is made with chickpeas (and/or lentils), meat, fresh herbs, and rice. *Harira* is usually the first dish which Moroccans eat to break their fast in the evening during RAMADAN.

A simple *diffa* will consist of half a dozen dishes whilst a larger one for a wedding or circumcision will include 20 dishes or more. The order in which these dishes are served is always the same. First comes the BESTILLA which is a round pie made with numerous layers of paper-thin pastry called WARQA (meaning leaf) inside which are separate layers of three different fillings, two savoury and one sweet. Stewed PIGEON and the spice mixture RAS-EL-HANOUT play important parts in the savoury ones, while the third is prepared with crushed sautéed almonds mixed with icing sugar and cinnamon. *Bestilla* is cooked on both sides and served sprinkled with icing sugar and cinnamon with the almond filling side up.

The second dish may be a *choua* of lamb (steamed shoulder and ribs of lamb) served with salt and cumin; or, in the countryside, a *mechoui* (barbecued lamb). Then come the tagines, fish, chicken or game, and lamb. The last tagine is always sweet and is customarily of lamb, onion, and honey. Finally comes a steaming couscous to make sure that no guest is left hungry. Traditionally guests are seated on cushions around a low table. The servants bring each dish on a large platter and place it in the centre. Everyone eats straight from it using their right thumb, index, and middle finger to scoop up the food. The bread, a rather flat white loaf, is used to soak up the sauces. The dishes follow each other until fresh fruit is brought in as a refreshing end to the meal.

Afterwards mint tea is served. Making it is an elaborate ceremony, supervised by the master of the house, who will have chosen the best green tea. Only fresh spearmint, *Mentha spicata* (of which a well-known cultivar is actually called 'Moroccan' and recognized as best for the purpose), should be used. The tea is brewed and heavily sweetened in a fine silver-plate bulbous-shaped teapot. At a *diffa* two pots of mint tea are brought to the table. The tea is poured simultaneously from both from quite high up over the narrow glasses.

Mint tea is served also at all other times. Everyone entering a home, shop, or office is at once offered a glass. Sometimes the tea is accompanied by the delicious crescent-shaped pastries called *qa'b el-ghazal* ('horns of the doe'); a thin layer of dough is wrapped around a moist almond and sugar paste which is flavoured with orange flower water.

                                          AH
READING: Mme Z. Guinaudeau (1981, 1994); Paula Wolfert (1973, 1989).

MORTADELLA the name used in English for a type of large and impressive pink pork SAUSAGE. Its chief distinguishing feature is its great diameter. Inside there is a mixture of minced pork (70% lean) and large flecks of white fat (produced by pushing strips of salt pork fat into the minced meat). The best are made from pure pork with peppercorns and (optionally) pistachio or olives. The finished sausage is served as a cold meat, in thin slices.

Mortadella originated in Bologna and has been much copied as 'Bologna sausage' or 'balony' (it is possible that the latter form was corrupted to give the word POLONY, but this may have other origins). It has been associated with the Italian city of Bologna, a place known for excellence in food since the Middle Ages. It was already being made in 1376 when the Bologna sausage-makers' guild was established.

There are also two other kinds of mortadella, described by Anna del Conte (1987). That of Amatrice in the Apennines differs from that of Bologna in being larded with only one piece of pork fat, flavoured with cinnamon and cloves, and smoked rather than steamed. The other kind is *mortadella di fegato*, featuring pig liver.

The name of the sausage is thought to derive from the use of a mortar (*mortaio*) to pound the meat to the necessary fine texture; but both the *OED* and Lissner (1939) cite the Latin term *farcimen murtatum*, a sausage seasoned with MYRTLE berries.

The attractive, reasonably long-keeping sausages are much copied outside Italy. However, the general conception in other countries of what a Bologna sausage should be like was not necessarily close to that of the original mortadella. Various meats were used, sometimes cooked in advance and often, in foreign copies, flavoured with anchovies. The sausages were smoked and then, usually, boiled. The one feature on which all were agreed was the pink colour, which could be achieved by adding saltpetre to the curing mixture.

The name Bologna for copies of mortadella is now almost obsolete except in the USA. American Bologna is usually made mainly from beef with some pork, and mildly spiced, then smoked and steamed.

In the vicinity of Bologna itself, mortadella is often put on the table at the beginning of a meal in irregular cubes, rather than thin slices. Eaten with rustic bread, these nuggets are highly effective in keeping any hunger pangs under control before the meal proper begins.

MORWONG *Nemadactylus douglasii*, and close relations in the family Cheilodactylidae, a sea fish which has assumed some importance in SE Australia from the time when the steam trawling industry in New South Wales was set up, around 1915, and substantial quantities began to be landed. It is likewise popular in New Zealand, where names such as *moki*— but see also TRUMPETER—are used.

The jackass fish, *N. macropterus*, is a close relation, which may be distinguished by a black band extending from the dorsal fin to the gill cover. It is grouped for statistical and commercial purposes with the morwong. Roughley (1966) observes that by no stretch of the imagination could this fish be likened to the jackass (an alternative name for the kookaburra), a bird renowned for its boisterous 'laugh', and that use of the inappropriate name provoked public indifference. The name 'sea bream' was therefore allowed, although it too is not really suitable. (It might have been better to adopt the New Zealand name *tarakihi*.)

These fish have a maximum length of about 60 cm (24") and make good eating.

MOSTARDA DI FRUTTA DI CREMONA, a preserve of candied fruits in a sugar or white wine and honey syrup and flavoured with mustard oil, a speciality of the Italian city of Cremona. It is eaten with cold boiled meat such as ham.

It is made of whole fruits such as cherries, little oranges, figs, plums, apricots, and slices or pieces of pear, melon or pumpkin. Elizabeth David (1965) remarks that 'this confection has an absolutely original flavour. Its origin goes back to the honey, mustard, oil and vinegar condiments of the Romans, who also preserved roots such as turnips in these mixtures.' Another such item is *mostarda di Carpi* (in Emilia) which is restricted to pear, apple, and sometimes quince, cooked in grape must.

A similar preserve is known in Austria as *Senffrüchte*; a speciality of Vienna, it is served with cold meats, hot roasts, and fried meats. Like *mostarda di Cremona* it involves many different kinds of fruits which are preserved by boiling and soaking in a sugar syrup which is heated up every day. Dry mustard is added at the end of the process, before bottling.

MOTH BEAN *Vigna aconitifolius*, a low-growing, mat-like plant which is cultivated as a PULSE in India, especially in dry regions such as Rajasthan, takes its common English name from the Hindi one. The young pods, containing tiny seeds, make a delicious and nutritious vegetable. In India the seeds, either whole or split, are used to make a DAL (*dal moth*).

MOULD a kind of FUNGUS, is generally thought of as an undesirable growth, but among the thousands of species of mould there are many useful kinds. Two examples are the white mould which grows on the outside of certain soft cheeses (*Penicillium candidum* or *P. camemberti*, or *Monilia candida*), and the blue mould inside blue cheeses (*Penicillium glaucum*, or *P. roqueforti*, or *P. gorgonzola*). Both soften the texture of the cheese, by producing ENZYMES which break down the milk PROTEINS. They also develop the flavour by depositing products of their metabolism. In all this, moulds collaborate with other micro-organisms, namely YEASTS and BACTERIA.

Moulds have other uses, not all to do with food. *P. notatum* is famous as the mould which drifted in through the window of St Mary's Hospital, Paddington, and colonized a culture of bacteria in a Petri dish, leading Sir Alexander Fleming to discover penicillin. Reverting to food uses, SOYA BEANS, widely used as a staple food in many Asian countries, are indigestible in their natural state, so various mould fermentations are used to produce enzymes which break down the protein in the beans and make it more accessible. Indonesian TEMPE is treated with the moulds *Rhizopus orizae* or *R. oligosporus*. TOFU, the bean curd of Japan and China, is fermented with various *Mucor* species. There is an aged version of tofu which bears some resemblance to blue cheese.

The furry growth which mould produces is the mycelium of the fungus, a filamentous growth by which it spreads. As the fungus feeds and grows it produces waste products which generally have a noticeable flavour. The furry growth is usually unwanted and the flavour disliked. But it may not be necessary to discard food which has 'gone mouldy', if the mouldy part can be cut or scraped off.

Mould spores drift on the wind and may settle on anything and grow if the conditions suit them. Most prefer slightly damp surroundings, and will not grow on dried food as long as it remains dry. Most, but by no means all, need a good supply of air, which is why they tend to grow on surfaces. This is the reason for piercing blue cheeses, as they ripen, with needles; the needle holes supply ventilation.

Some moulds can tolerate very adverse conditions, growing even on dry salt fish and in pickles. Most moulds, however, are prevented from growing by strong concentrations of salt or sugar, which interfere with their absorption of liquid. The mould which grows on top of the jam in pots can live only on the little pool of exuded liquid on the surface, not in the jam itself. (The very top of the jam may acquire a bad flavour from the mould, but the rest remains unaffected. Jam mould is easily prevented by sealing the surface from the air, e.g. by a layer of paraffin wax, the usual method in the USA.)

MOUSSAKA OR MUSAKA, often written as *musakka*, is a meat and vegetable stew, originally made from sliced AUBERGINE, meat, and tomatoes, and preferably cooked in an oven. This is the version current among the Turks and Arabs, who may also substitute courgettes (see ZUCCHINI) for the aubergines.

In the Balkans, more elaborate versions are found. The Greeks cover the stew with a layer of beaten egg or BÉCHAMEL sauce. Elsewhere in the Balkans *musakka* has become a much more various oven-baked casserole, admitting many more vegetables than aubergine or courgette, often dropping tomatoes and even meat. Bulgarian and Yugoslav versions emphasize eggs, and a given recipe may consist of eggs, cheese, potatoes, and spinach, or eggs, cheese, sauerkraut, and rice. In Romania, which considers *musaca* a national dish, the vegetables may be potatoes, celery, cabbage, or cauliflower—or may be replaced by noodles.

The name *musakka* is a curious one. It is the Arabic word *musaqqâ*, which means 'moistened', referring to the tomato juices. When the Turks used the Arabic alphabet, they spelled the name in good Arabic form as *musaqqâ*; however, the dish is not of Arab origin and it seems certain that the name was coined in Turkey. Few if any Arabs call this dish *musaqqâ*; the usual Arabic form is *musaqqa'a*, which reflects an attempt to render the Turkish pronunciation of *musakka* complete with its word-final accent. CP

MOUSSE a French term meaning 'foam', is applied to dishes with a foamy texture, usually cold and often sweet but also savoury and sometimes hot. The term was in common use in France by the 18th century. Menon (1758) has recipes for frozen mousses. Some confections are naturally foamy; others may need beaten egg white or whipped cream, and possibly GELATIN, to achieve the desired texture.

It will be seen that, although a cold SOUFFLÉ cannot be distinguished from a mousse, the latter name is used for a wider range of dishes.

Chocolate mousse is well known internationally. Other mousses, such as those incorporating ham (*mousse de jambon*) or fish or asparagus, are more likely to be found in a French context.

MOUSSELINE both the name of a sauce (a variant of HOLLANDAISE, incorporating whipped cream) and a culinary term of wider application, which is used to draw attention to the delicacy of various preparations such as whipped potato or QUENELLES.

The primary meaning of this French term is 'muslin' or 'chiffon' (see CHIFFON CAKE for American usage).

Sauce mousseline is considered to be an especially good accompaniment for turbot, and for asparagus.

MOZUKU *Nemacystus decipiens*, one of the most delicately formed of the brown SEAWEEDS. The thin gelatinous stems can be eaten fresh or blanched, or brined or salted, in which case they need to be rinsed or soaked before use. In blanched form they are a common accompaniment to SASHIMI.

MOZZARELLA a soft, fresh Italian cheese traditionally made with buffalo milk and dating back at least as far as the beginning of the 15th century, when it was called simply *mozza*. It is now prepared almost exclusively from cow's milk, in which version it is sometimes distinguished from the true mozzarella by the name fiordilatte. It melts well and is used in cookery besides being eaten at table. Its popularity extends outside Italy; it is made in the USA and Denmark.

A mozzarella cheese is small, seldom weighing more than 500 g (1 lb), and usually egg shaped (although Danish mozzarella is rectangular).

MUESLI a Swiss dish of cereal, fruit, and nuts, eaten with milk, made its first appearance in Britain as early as 1926, but until the 1960s its consumption was largely restricted to the health-food fringe. Since then, however, high fibre has been transformed from a fad to a multi-million pound business.

Muesli is a Swiss-German diminutive form of *mus*, 'pulpy food, purée'; it is related to an Old English word for 'food', *mōs*. When it was first introduced into Britain it was often called *Birchermuesli*, after its proponent Dr Bircher-Benner, who served it to patients in his 'natural health' clinic in Zurich. JA

MUFFIN a term connected with *moufflet*, an old French word applied to bread, meaning 'soft'.

The **English muffin** is round and made from a soft yeast-leavened dough enriched with milk and butter. It is usually cooked on a GRIDDLE, which gives it a flat, golden-brown top and bottom, with a white band around the waist and a light, spongy interior. For serving, muffins are toasted back and front and then split with the fingers by easing them apart at the joint all the way round. Some butter is placed inside, and the two halves put back together and kept warm. This method appears as early as 1747 and was recommended by Hannah GLASSE, who said that the inside of muffins should be like honeycomb. Writers on the subject of muffins agree that they should not be cut with a knife, as this makes them heavy.

Muffins were most popular during the 19th century, when muffin men traversed town streets at teatime, ringing their bells. In the 1840s the muffin-man's bell was prohibited by Act of Parliament because many people objected to it, but the prohibition was ineffective. In recent times, muffins have regained some popularity; in common with CRUMPETS and PIKELETS, they provide a physical base and a pretext for eating melted butter.

The word 'muffin' first appeared in print in the early 18th century, and recipes began to be published in the middle of the 18th century. There has always been some confusion between muffins, crumpets, and pikelets, both in recipes and in name. 'Muffin' usually meant a breadlike product (sometimes simply made from whatever bread dough was available), as opposed to the more pancake-like crumpets.

The **American muffin** is generally a small, squat, round cake which may be yeast leavened, although baking powder is used in many recipes. It is usually sweetened with a little sugar. These muffins may be plain, but are often flavoured with fruits, nuts, or savoury ingredients. Blueberry muffins are common. American muffins, still extremely popular, are oven baked in muffin pans or cups and are served primarily for breakfast or as an accompaniment to dinner.   LM

MUGWORT *Artemisia vulgaris* and a few close relations, large perennial herbs which grow wild in temperate zones of the northern hemisphere. Their use as a food flavouring is minimal in most regions, but of some importance in Japan.

The **European mugwort**, *A. vulgaris*, enjoyed a high medicinal reputation for curing certain complaints, as a spring tonic, and to prevent fatigue. Cole, in his *Art of Simpling* (1656) said: 'If a footman take Mugwort and put it into his shoes in the morning he may goe forty miles before noon and not be weary.' But it has also had culinary uses: the young shoots and faintly aromatic leaves, which are green above and white below, are used as a flavouring herb for goose and pork, and other fatty foods, in various European countries. In this respect, mugwort has been compared to TANSY.

This species occurs also in the Indian subcontinent, where it is sometimes known as Indian wormwood; this because the leaves contain the same bitter principle as the related plant WORMWOOD. Its use in W. and C. Asia is largely medicinal.

The plant was introduced to N. America and already flourishing there in the 17th century. Americans sometimes take advantage of its lemony aroma and bitter taste to add flavour to such meat dishes as benefit therefrom.

Japanese mugwort, *A. princeps*, bears leaves which, after being debittered, are used in soups and salads and for the preparation of mugwort MOCHI (rice dumplings), a traditional rural dish which is now widely available both in Japan and the USA. Green mugwort bread is also made in Japan.

MUHALLABIA a creamy milk dessert of the Middle East, usually made with cornflour, ground rice, and milk and flavoured with ORANGE FLOWER WATER or rosewater, see ROSES. Chopped almonds and pistachio nuts decorate the top. It is a similar dessert to FIRNI and KESHKUL.   HS

MULBERRY *Morus nigra* and *M. alba*, the black and white mulberries respectively, are fruits of Asian origin. The white mulberry is native to the central and eastern mountains of China and has been cultivated there for at least 5,000 years, mainly for rearing SILKWORMS which are fed on its leaves and will eat nothing else. The black mulberry may have originated in the mountains of Nepal or the Caucasus and is the species usually grown for its fruits.

Mulberries were referred to in the Bible in connection with King David and were also described by Pliny (1st century AD). Pliny, evidently speaking of the black mulberry, remarked that it had not been improved by horticulturists in the same way as other fruits.

It is likely that the Romans introduced the mulberry to Britain, as well as to France and Spain. Roach (1985) points out that since a tree can live for over 600 years (e.g. the mulberry planted when the Drapers' Hall in London was built, in 1364, which lived until 1969) and comes true from seed, Roman introductions could have survived into Anglo-Saxon times, when the tree was called 'mon-beam'.

In the 16th and 17th centuries attempts were made to establish silk industries in Europe, including England. James I had 4 acres (1.6 hectares) of mulberry trees planted where Buckingham Palace now stands. According to Roach (1985):

For a brief period there seemed a hope that Britain might be able to produce at least some of her requirements of silk. The king and the whole royal family so persevered in feeding their silk-worms and preparing thread that the Queen had enough silk, which she wound herself, to make some yards of taffeta, which were used to make a complete set of clothes in which she appeared at court on the occasion of the king's birthday.

It seems, however, that the trees imported for this purpose were of the wrong species, so the project failed.

The mulberry tree is of medium size and attractively untidy in appearance. Although the fruit superficially resembles a BLACKBERRY it is a different type of growth: a cluster of small berries, each with an individually lobed surface and each formed from one of a cluster of flowers. Such a composite fruit, of which another example is the pineapple, is called a 'sorosis'.

The fruit must be allowed to ripen fully before being gathered. Then, rather than being picked, it is allowed to fall off the tree, for which reason the tree is generally planted on grassy ground. A ripe mulberry is soft and easily damaged. Its purple juice stains the face and hands of the eater.

In Afghanistan where the black mulberry has the name *shah tut*, meaning 'king mulberry', mulberries are dried and powdered and mixed with flour to make bread called *talkhun*. Dried mulberries are also sometimes mixed with crushed walnuts and then called *chakidar*.

There are several other mulberries native to Asia and the Americas. All have edible fruits but only those of the red mulberry, *M. rubra*, in the eastern USA, stand comparison with the black mulberry. The black mulberry itself is naturalized in clement parts of the USA as a garden tree. The Indian mulberry is *Morinda citrifolia*. Its edible leaves may be eaten raw or used to wrap fish being cooked; unripe fruits are used in curries and SAMBALS; ripe fruits yield a beverage.

MULLOWAY *Johnius antarctica*, an important Australian fish of the sciaenid family, closely related and very similar to the MEAGRE, and also to DRUMS and CROAKERS. This is a big fish, reaching a length of 1.8 m (6'), and one which is not too choosy about the waters in which it swims; although essentially a sea fish, it is very common in certain estuaries and can also be found far upstream in rivers. The mulloway feeds voraciously on other fish, and is itself a favoured prey of human anglers.

Young specimens make good eating; older and larger ones are coarse and have a poor flavour.

A smaller (up to 125 cm/50") relation, *Atractoscion aequidens*, the teraglin, lives its adult life in offshore waters. It is considered to be a finer food fish. In S. Africa, where it is also present, it is known as Cape salmon or *geelbek*.

MUNG BEAN the seed of the plant *Vigna radiata*, a native of India where it has for long been under cultivation. It has now spread to China, SE Asia, the USA, the Caribbean, and E. and C. Africa. It is used not only for human food but also as a forage crop and as green manure. Several crops a year are possible, since the plant grows quickly.

In India, mung beans are also known as green or golden gram, depending on their colour. Split and peeled, all kinds reveal a pale yellow inside.

Used as a dried PULSE, mung beans need no soaking, cook relatively quickly, have a good flavour, and are easily digestible: a collection of merits which few other LEGUMES can match.

There are two main uses for the bean in China: to make bean sprouts (the Chinese names for which mean 'pea sprouts', to distinguish them from soya bean sprouts); and as a source of starch for mung bean vermicelli (cellophane noodles, *fen si*—see NOODLES OF CHINA). These noodles are a popular ingredient in Chinese cooking.

The name 'wild mung' is used of a plant treated under COWPEA.

MUNSTER despite its name, is a French cheese, from Munster in the Vosges mountains of Alsace near the German frontier. Its origin is attributed to Irish monks who settled in Alsace in the 7th century. The name Munster is from the same root as 'monastery'. A similar cheese is also made in Germany (where it is spelled 'Münster').

Munster is a surface-ripened, semi-soft, whole-milk cheese, best made (and supposedly only made) from the milk of the old Vosgienne breed of cows. The cheeses are ripened by surface BACTERIA in a cool cellar. These produce a less pungent smell than do the diverse organisms which infect many surface-ripened cheeses. The flavour is tangy but not strong.

Munster is almost always round and flat, and ranges upwards in weight from about 450 g (1 lb); some factory-made cheeses may be loaf shaped.

MUNTJAC *Muntiacus muntjak*, a small DEER with a wide range in Asia from India through much of SE Asia to China, Japan, and Formosa. Various races are recognized over this range. Both coloration and size vary. An adult male may measure between 50 and 75 cm (20–30") and is likely to weigh around 23 kg (50 lb). The antlers are small and are set on bony hair-covered ridges which extend down each side of the face; hence the name rib-faced deer which is sometimes used. The muntjac has a call which sounds like the bark of a dog and accounts for another common name, barking deer.

The muntjac provides good meat and is hunted for this throughout its range. Phia Sing (1981) is an outstanding author on the cookery of this animal, since he gives a number of highly detailed recipes from Laos.

MUREX a Latin name which is used in default of anything more convenient to denote the gastropods of the family Muricidae. These are best known as the source of purple dyes in antiquity. Purple was the imperial colour, used for Caesar's robe and for the sails of Cleopatra's warship; and its production was an important industry, carried out at Tyre and Sidon and other places in the Mediterranean.

However, the creatures inside murex shells are edible and are consumed in some parts of the world. The best Mediterranean species is *Murex brandaris*, whose shell may measure 9 cm (3.5"), but there are others. *M. trunculus* (French *rocher pourpre*) and *M. erinaceus* (French *perceur*) are, or used to be, popular foods in the Adriatic region. Vernacular names for these shells echo those of antiquity. The Provençal *burez* is evidently derived from murex; and the name *porpora*, used on the Italian Adriatic coast, comes from the classical (and modern) Greek *porphyra*.

MURRAY COD *Maccullochella macquariensis*, is not a cod, nor even a marine fish. If one looks for a reason why early settlers in Australia mistook it for a cod, one can only suppose that they were influenced by the mottling on its sides.

This is a large fish, up to 1.8 m (6') in length and possibly 90 kg (200 lb) in weight. It is widely distributed in the continent, not just in the Murray River system from which it takes its name. Generally good to eat when small, but less appreciated now than in the past. Large specimens tend to be coarse and fatty.

MUSHROOM (*see opposite page*)

MUSHROOM LITERATURE has distinctive features which deserve mention, not least the fact that by comparison with other kinds of plant life it is of very recent origin.

To be sure, fungi were mentioned by classical authors; but their nature was not understood. The fact that the fruiting bodies (the part of the plant which is observed, gathered, and eaten) spring up so quickly led early authors such as Dioscorides to produce fanciful theories about spontaneous generation. (These ideas lingered on well into medieval times and beyond. Lyly, writing in the 16th century, could still declare that snails crept out of their shells, turned into toads, and then, feeling the need of something to sit upon, fashioned toadstools for themselves.)

It was only in 1729, when Micheli published his *Nova Plantarum Genera*, that the subject began to have a scientifically acceptable basis. Linnaeus, the great Swedish natural historian of the mid-18th century, at first failed to absorb fungi into his scheme of things; indeed, he created a genus with the defeatist name *Chaos* to accommodate fungal phenomena for which he could not provide a better home. But in his *Genera Plantarum* he created the class Cryptogamia in which they were more suitably accommodated. It was another Swede, Fries (1794–1878), building on the work of a Dutch citizen of German origin, Persoon (1761–1836), who perhaps did most to establish further the classification which is still used.

Early authors distinguished between edible and poisonous fungi, but Paulet (1793) was the first to to write a book which combined a scientific description of fungi with detailed information about their edibility and the manner of cooking them. His lead was followed by other authors during the 19th century. The outstanding example is the work of Roques (2nd edn, 1841); his manual is still among the best guides to mushroom cookery. But few authors attained the standard set by him. Many of them lacked direct experience of cooking or even eating their subject matter and yet—conscious of the curiosity which their readers might have on this aspect—felt bound to include at least some comments on consumption. Such comments tended to be copied from one book to the next. It is prudent to examine such books for evidence of experiments by the author, such as can be found in the vast work by Charles McIlvaine and the slighter volume from the Revd Charles Badham (1863).

McIlvaine (*One Thousand American Fungi*, 1902) was a supreme optimist. Whereas many authors of mushroom books, haunted by visions of readers collapsing in

(*cont. on page 522*)

A term of uncertain derivation, first recorded as an English word in the 9th century; it seems likely to have come from *mousseron*, a French term which nowadays applies only to various small mushrooms. The *Grete Herbal* of 1526 said of 'mussherons' that: 'There be two maners of them, one maner is deedly and sleath them that eateth of them and be called tode stoles.' Thus at that time mushroom was, as now, a wide meaning and could embrace toadstools too.

Scientists now use 'mushroom' in the strict sense to denote only the fruiting body of a fungus of either the order *Agaricales* (in which falls the common field mushroom and others—see AGARIC) or the order *Boletales* (in which the CEP or king BOLETE is best known). But in everyday usage the word can be used very generally, applying to any edible fungi; and is certainly taken to include any edible fungus of the same general shape as a mushroom proper, having a round cap and usually a stalk. Some kinds of mushroom which grow out of the side of a tree trunk have almost no stalk. For example the oyster fungus, often called the OYSTER MUSHROOM, has a very short, offset stem. And there are also stemless fungi attached directly to a tree trunk and known collectively as BRACKET FUNGI. But even these can be called mushrooms. Any fungus of obviously non-mushroom shape, such as the PUFFBALL, MOREL, or TRUFFLE, is usually referred to under its own name; but the general remarks on mushrooms here refer to these equally.

Mushrooms and other large varieties of FUNGUS have been eaten since earliest times, as traces of puffballs in the prehistoric lake dwellings of Switzerland, Germany, and Austria show; but not by everyone and not everywhere.

The rarest and finest mushrooms, such as the truffle and the ORONGE, were highly esteemed in classical Greece and Rome, and have always been expensive. Some mushrooms are still among the most costly of foods, more expensive weight for weight than any of the spices except saffron. Cultivation, now under way for 300 years, has ensured that mushrooms are a common urban food as well as a feature of rural diet.

It is, however, easy to muster opinions hostile to mushrooms. To take examples from English only, Gerard, in his *Herbal* (1633), declared that 'Most of them do suffocate and strangle the eater.' Venner (*Via Recta ad Vitam Longam*, 1620) was only slightly less admonitory. 'Many phantasticall people doe greatly delight to eat of the earthly excrescences called Mushrums. They are convenient for no season, age or temperament.' And John Farley (*The London Art of Cookery*, 1784) referred to them as 'treacherous gratifications', emphasizing the need 'that those employed in collecting them should be extremely cautious'.

The knowledge that some mushrooms are highly poisonous, accompanied by a vague and justified impression that old wives' rules of thumb for telling the safe ones apart from the dangerous are not to be trusted, probably accounts for the persistence of these negative impressions. But there may also be an element of fear of the supernatural at work. Mushrooms and truffles are indeed mysterious things, as explained under HALLUCINOGENIC MUSHROOMS and TOADSTOOL. Their ephemeral nature, exemplified by the INK CAP, and their apparent lack of roots lend credence to the idea that they are 'unnatural'.

Wild mushrooms grow in most parts of the world and form part of the diet of most peoples, being eagerly gathered in most countries where they occur. The inhabitants of the British Isles, in company with the Dutch and most Arabs, are exceptions. British woods, and fields in the less intensively farmed regions, have plenty of varied and delicious fungi. But most British people recognize only the field mushrooms as edible and shun other species as 'toadstools'. This tendency is even more noticeable in Ireland, where large crops of precious morels may go unharvested. The Russians, Scandinavians, and Swiss, in contrast, all gather wild mushrooms with great enthusiasm, thronging the woods every autumn.

On the whole, the best varieties of mushroom grow in wooded areas, whether deciduous, as for the cep and GRISETTE, or coniferous, as for CHANTERELLES and the Japanese MATSUTAKE and some kinds of boletus.

In the world of plants generally, it is common for a species to occur in only one region, with related but different species in other regions. Species of mushroom tend to have a wider distribution, no doubt because their spores are so tiny and light that they can be carried from one continent to another, by the wind or on birds' feet. For example, one common variety of cep, *Boletus reticulatus*, occurs in Europe, N. America, Japan, and Australia. It does, however, seem to be true that the northern hemisphere is richer in fungi than the southern.

EDIBILITY AND NUTRITIONAL PROPERTIES

Most mushrooms are edible, but only a small proportion are worth eating; the rest are tasteless or unpleasant. A few are indigestible enough to cause stomach-aches, especially if eaten raw. And a very few are toxic, even fatally so. See the *Warning* below.

Mushrooms are not very nutritious in terms of energy value, since they are about 90% water, very low in fat, and have most of their carbohydrates in the form of indigestible chitin. But they do contain useful protein (1–3% depending on the species), and vitamins of the B group and certain others. For example, cultivated mushrooms have a little of vitamins C and K. The chanterelle owes its yellow colour to carotene, which yields vitamin A, and also contains vitamin D.

The Chinese, as is their wont, consider some mushrooms to be APHRODISIACS. But neither they nor anyone else seem to have speculated on the possibility that by eating mush-

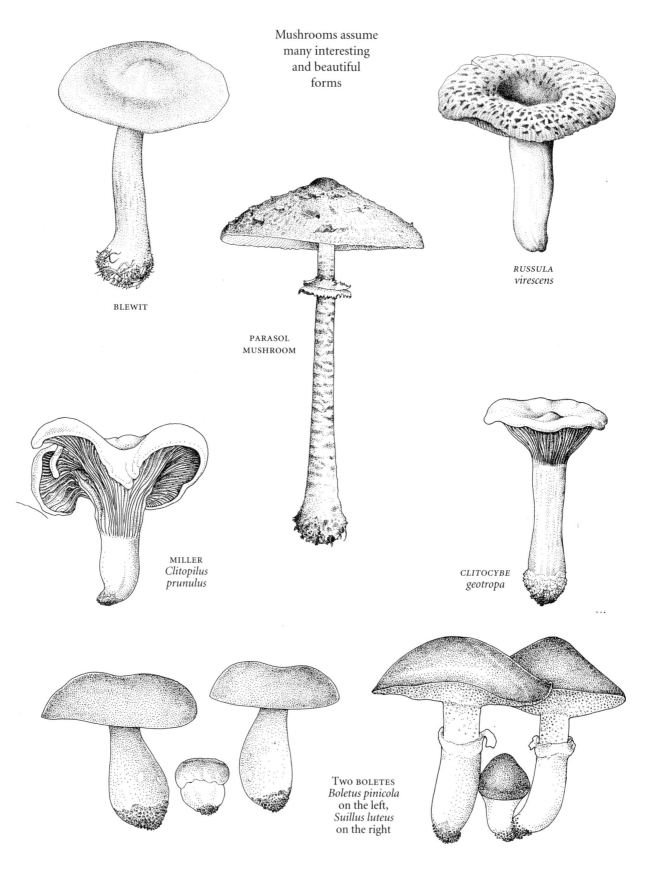

Mushrooms assume
many interesting
and beautiful
forms

BLEWIT

PARASOL
MUSHROOM

RUSSULA
virescens

MILLER
Clitopilus
prunulus

CLITOCYBE
geotropa

Two BOLETES
Boletus pinicola
on the left,
Suillus luteus
on the right

rooms one might somehow absorb their remarkable physical force. Tales of paving stones caused to rise from their bed by a few small mushrooms are familiar. An experience which befell Sir Joseph Banks in the 18th century was even more dramatic. He left a cask of wine in his cellar for some years. Returning, he found that a fungal growth proceeding from the wine had completely filled the cellar and had become so hard that it had to be hacked away with an axe; and that the cask, now empty of wine, was firmly pinned against the ceiling by it.

PRESERVATION, PREPARATION, AND USE

The poor keeping quality of most fresh mushrooms has given rise to various methods of preserving them. They may be pickled or brined, canned, or made into KETCHUP, but the most usual way is to dry them. Strong-flavoured species preserve their taste remarkably well, and last for years if kept away from damp. The Chinese WOOD EAR and the Japanese SHIITAKE are both dried on a large scale. In Europe the most favoured species is the common cep: German dried *Steinpilze* and Italian *funghi porcini* are both the common cep.

Mushrooms shrink greatly when dried, so the flavour is concentrated. They may be added direct to soups and stews, or first soaked in water if they are to be used in dishes which cook quickly. A few dried ceps are an effective means of adding flavour to cultivated mushrooms.

Many people peel mushrooms before using them. However, a wash, after which the mushrooms are to be shaken free of excess moisture, is less wasteful; and most mushrooms are better not washed at all but simply brushed clean.

The chief risk in cooking fresh mushrooms is of over-cooking them, so that they become unduly limp. True *Agaricus* mushrooms need very little cooking: indeed, they are excellent raw, in salads. The tougher species such as chanterelles are best braised very gently until just softened.

Warning. Toxic mushrooms exist in many genera which include well-known edible species. Thus the blewit, cep, and even the common field mushroom have harmful relations. There is therefore some danger for amateurs in mushroom-gathering; but mushroom poisoning is, fortunately, rare. Most countries operate rigid controls over what may be sold in markets where wild mushrooms are offered. Anything which could even be confused with a toxic species is banned. Some countries even insist that there should be an inspection of mushrooms which amateurs have picked for their own use. One such is Norway, where there is a 'sopkontrol' (mushroom checkpoint) at Holmenkollen railway station in the hills above Oslo, a favourite place for gatherers.

The most notorious toxic species belong to the genus AMANITA, which includes the terrible death cap (as well as the edible and excellent oronge, grisette, and blusher); but there are others, including a small parasol mushroom, and several of the numerous cobweb-caps.

Certain species, in addition to being mildly toxic, induce hallucinations. The best known of these is the fly agaric, the familiar white-spotted red toadstool of fairy pictures.

The amateur mushroom gatherer should eschew any mushroom which cannot be positively identified as belonging to a safe species. The risk of trouble should then be negligible.

The principle of positive identification is all the more important because the possibilities of confusion are often so great (the colour of the cap may vary, fragments of veil may be washed away by rain, the volva may be eaten by slugs) that it would be wrong to rely on any summary guidance, or old wives' tales (like the silver spoon test), or negative impression ('it doesn't really look like a death cap') for distinguishing the edible from the dangerous species. It is appropriate here to mention some further advice given by Fernald and Kinsey (1943): one should never gather wild mushrooms in the 'button' or unexpanded stage of growth; nor gather any which are beginning to decay.

Mushroom cultivation

This accounts for most mushrooms eaten, especially in western countries. However, many of the most desirable types of mushroom are not grown commercially, because it has so far been impossible to reproduce in a nursery the specialized conditions which they require. Many cannot feed simply on rotting vegetation but have a complex parasitic or symbiotic relationship with living trees. All one can do is plant trees of the right species, scatter some spores of the mushroom or other fungus, and hope. This is done with TRUFFLES, but with only limited success.

However, some mushrooms have been successfully cultivated for a long time. In classical times both Greeks and Romans grew the small *Agrocybe aegerita* (see PHOLIOTA) on slices of poplar trunk. The Chinese and Japanese may have been growing the SHIITAKE on rotting logs for even longer.

Modern European cultivation goes back to 1600, when the French agriculturist Olivier de Serres suggested a method in his work *Le Théâtre d'agriculture des champs*. In 1678 another Frenchman, the botanist Marchant, demonstrated to the Académie des Sciences how mushrooms could be 'sown' in a controlled way by transplanting their mycelia (filaments which spread through the soil underneath them like fine roots). John Evelyn (1699), in a cautious assessment of the worth of mushrooms in the 'sallets' (salads) about which he was writing, gives an interesting account of the information then available.

But besides what the Harvest-Months produce, they [mushrooms] are likewise raised Artificially; as at Naples in their Wine-Cellars, upon an heap of rank Earth, heaped upon a certain supposed Stone, but in truth, (as the curious and noble Peiresky tells us, he found to be) nothing but a heap of old Fungus's, reduc'd and compacted to a stony hardness, upon which they lay Earth, and sprinkle it with warm Water, in which Mushrooms have been steeped. And in France, by making an hot Bed of Asses-Dung, and when the heat is in Temper, watering it (as above) well impregnated with the Parings and Offals of refuse Fungus's; and such a Bed will last two or three Years, and sometimes our common Melon-Beds afford them, besides other Experiments.

Melon-beds, as Evelyn suggests, had been found to be good for mushroom-growing, and in the mid-17th century melon-growers in the Paris region had started to take advantage of this to cultivate mushrooms: the first *champignons de couche*. It was this which led later, in the 19th century, to the practice of growing mushrooms in 'caves'. Many of these were really quarries, in the Paris region again and in the Loire Valley, from which rock had been taken for building purposes. The quarries of the Loire Valley are still in use, but mushroom-growing in Paris has almost ceased. However, because it was around Paris that the cultivation of *Agaricus bisporus* began on a large scale, this species, the ordinary cultivated mushroom, is often called *champignon de Paris*. The mushrooms which bear that city's name are now cultivated all over the world, for example in Taiwan, but France remains a principal grower and exporter. The advantage of a cave is that it provides a stable environment, sheltered from sudden climatic changes. The same effect can be achieved artificially in the mushroom 'houses' which are now widely used.

Numerous other mushrooms are now cultivated, including: the OYSTER MUSHROOM (production of which has grown rapidly); ENOKITAKE; SHIITAKE; the STRAW MUSHROOM; WOOD EAR; and, tentatively, TRUFFLES. However, production of the common cultivated mushroom is still dominant. In the mid-1970s the total weight of commercially cultivated mushrooms, worldwide, was approaching a million tons annually, and of this nearly 700,000 tons were the common cultivated mushroom.

The flavour of the common cultivated mushroom, if it can be detected at all, falls short of that of its wild relations. The same may be true of other cultivated mushrooms; but complaints about them are less often heard.

agony after eating toxic species, pile warnings and cautionary tales upon each other to such an extent that their works seem to be funerary rather than culinary, he tends in the opposite direction and positively spurs on the hesitant. 'Reputed to be harmful,' he will observe, 'but never did me any harm!' And even species of moderate merit excite him to lavish praise; there must be many scores of mushrooms which he declares to be 'second to none'. His enthusiasm is infectious, and he makes clear that he has himself experimented with a high proportion of the 1,000 fungi he describes.

Charles Badham, the clergyman referred to above who wrote *A Treatise on the Esculent Funguses of England*, was a man in whom caution and enthusiasm were agreeably mingled. The purpose of his book was to introduce the ultra-suspicious English to mushrooms which they were neglecting (and continue to neglect). Mushrooms, he declared, were to be eaten 'with discretion not *à discrétion*'. Here is a sample of his prose:

I have indeed grieved, when I reflected on the straitened condition of the lower orders this year [1847], to see pounds innumerable of extempore beef-steaks growing on our oaks in the shape of *Fistulina hepatica*; . . . Puffballs, which some of our friends have not inaptly compared to sweet-bread for the rich delicacy of their unassisted flavour; *Hydna* as good as oysters, which they somewhat resemble in taste; *Agaricus deliciosus*, reminding us of tender lamb-kidneys; the beautiful yellow Chantarelle, that *kalon kagathon* of diet, growing by the bushel, and no basket but our own to pick up a few specimens in our way; the sweet nutty-flavoured *Boletus*, in vain calling himself *edulis* where there was none to believe him.

Badham's eloquence, fortified by the assurance that in a single summer he and his friends had eaten 31 species, must surely have won over some of the hesitant. And, although 31 was a creditable number, it was soon to be outdone. William DeLisle Hay, whose *Elementary Text-book of the British Fungi*—the unexciting title conceals a rich store of culinary information—was published in 1887, reveals by his personal comments on various species that he had tried about 200 of them. (But all such figures are overshadowed by a recent Italian author who claims to have sampled over 1,250.)

In the 20th century, outstanding contributions have been made by Roger Heim (*Les Champignons d'Europe*, 1969, and *Les Champignons toxiques et hallucinogènes*, 1978), John Ramsbottom (*Mushrooms and Toadstools*, 1953, a highly readable survey), and R. Gordon Wasson. Wasson began to write about mushrooms after completing a successful career as a banker, and with his sister Valentina produced a remarkable ethnobotanical work, *Mushrooms, Russia and History* (1957); see MUSHROOMS IN RUSSIA. Subsequently, Wasson maintained, in his controversial work on *Soma, the Divine Mushroom of Immortality* (1969), that soma, the mysterious object of an Aryan cult, was the FLY AGARIC. Whatever criticisms may be made of Wasson's work by mycologists, there is no doubt that the beauty and literary qualities of his books has done much to restore 20th-century mushroom literature to the elevated level which had characterized it in the 19th century.

Twentieth-century works on the cookery of mushrooms include two notable books, by Ramain (1979) and Jane Grigson (1975). American authors such as Arora (1979) and Marteka (1980) have made serious contributions. Roux-Saget and Delplanque (1985) have performed a useful service in summarizing the views of other, earlier French authors on the subject.

The most comprehensively illustrated work on European mushrooms is that of Phillips (1981).

It is remarkable that there is no work which treats edible fungi worldwide, with full attention to Asia and Africa; and how many people suppose that those familiar in Europe, for example, do not occur elsewhere.

MUSHROOMS IN RUSSIA

exceptionally, require a separate entry. This is partly because of the special place which mushroom hunting and eating occupies in Russia, and in Russian literature; and partly because the whole subject has been explored, in a unique manner, by Valentina and Gordon Wasson in *Mushrooms, Russia and History* (1957), a brilliant work lavishly produced in a manner which precludes, intentionally, any reprint. As they point out: 'When the Russian child learns his alphabet, he sees by a picture that "g" stands for *grib* [mushroom]; this has been habitual at least since the 17th century.' The Wassons also draw attention to the children's marching song 'Panic among the Mushrooms', in which the general of the mushrooms summons his hosts to war, but finds that most of them have excuses, cleverly framed to reflect their characteristics—the *smorchki* (morels), for example, cry off on the ground that they are elderly grey-heads. Finally, the *gruzdi* (explained below) rally to the flag and march off to do battle.

For Russians, familiarity with mushroom names is taken for granted from childhood onwards; and the first chapter of the Wassons' work contains many illuminating comments on the extent and importance of the vocabulary of mushrooms in the Russian language.

- With the sole exception of *Amanita muscaria* (the FLY AGARIC), toxic or otherwise harmful mushrooms have no common names.
- All merely tasteless or insignificant mushrooms are dismissed as *poganki* (little pagans).
- A miscellaneous group of gilled mushrooms, including the common FIELD MUSHROOM, are classed together as *syroezhki* (indicating that they can be eaten raw).
- Of greater consequence are the *smorchki* (MORELS).
- Mushrooms which flourish on dead tree stumps are *opjonki*. These are highly esteemed, including the INK CAPS and HONEY FUNGUS.
- One step upwards on the scale of excellence come the *masljonski* or *masljaniki*, meaning the buttery ones and referring to those species which would be called slimy in other countries.
- Alongside these, or perhaps even higher up the scale, are the *lisichki* (little foxes) and *ryzhiki* (rusty ones). The former are the CHANTERELLES, charmingly described as looking like 'yellow parasols, blown inside out'; but, we are told, less favoured in Russia than in Norway and Sweden. The latter are the MILK CAPS.
- Ascending the scale of values further, we come to the BOLETES; and here we find that the Russian names are linked to the trees with which these mushrooms have a symbiotic relationship; the *berjosovik* with the *berjoza* (birch), and the *podosinovik* with the *osina* (aspen).
- But the finest of all are the *belye griby*, meaning white boletes. These are the *cèpes de Bordeaux*, the best of the CEPS. Russians call them white to denote excellence rather than colour; and Valentina Wasson points out that the Basque name is similar. She also speculates that 'whiteness' of this kind may be associated with divinity, drawing attention to *The White Goddess* of Robert Graves.

MUSK a glandular secretion of the musk DEER and certain other animals, has a strong smell; so strong that 'the beautiful Hagia

Sophia in Istanbul still smells of the musk which was mixed with the mortar when it was built more than a thousand years ago' (Stobart, 1980). In appropriately discreet quantity or diluted form, musk was formerly used in the kitchen with rosewater to flavour such things as pies but this practice seems to have died out.

Musk deer do not all belong to a single species but to a family Moschidae, within which the Siberian musk deer, *Moschus moschiferus*, is prominent in the present context. Hunting these deer and trading in their musk is now subject to prohibitions or controls.

Other musky creatures in the animal world are not confined to land animals such as the MUSKRAT; there is also a species of octopus whose specific name, *moschata*, indicates a musky smell.

Smell-alikes in the plant world often have common names incorporating 'musk' or 'musky'. The musk melon (see MELON) is one example; and there are also the musk cucumber and the musk lime. The musk mallow, *Abelmoschus moschatus*, is a different matter, in that its seeds provide a musky spice (French, *ambrette*), sometimes used to flavour coffee.

MUSK OX *Ovibos moschatus*, a horned and hairy animal of the far north, whose range is now restricted to the Arctic regions of Canada and Greenland. In size it is comparable with a large goat or sheep. It provides meat for the Inuit (Eskimos) and for Arctic wolves, more or less the only other predator, but has no special claim to fame as food. The smell of MUSK which males emit during the mating season accounts for the common name.

MUSKRAT *Ondatra zibethica*, the largest of the voles, has a natural range all over N. America, wherever a suitable habitat (usually a marsh, freshwater or salt) exists. It is also known as marsh hare or marsh rabbit. An adult's head and body length is about 38 cm (15") and the weight may be 900 g (2 lb).

The muskrat has been introduced into Europe and the Soviet Union, mainly for its dark brown fur, which is also the chief reason for trapping it in the USA, e.g. in the bayou region of Louisiana. It lives in an elaborate system of burrows, and its burrowing activity can cause considerable damage to river banks.

Although not widely perceived as a source of edible meat, the muskrat does provide this. If properly cleaned (including the immediate excision of the two scent glands near the base of the tail) and prepared, muskrat meat is fine grained and tender, and according to some authorities (e.g. Hall and

Hall, 1980) better than beef in flavour and in nutritional qualities. It can be roasted or stewed. Ashbrook and Sater (1945) remark that it 'is eaten by all classes of people. It is a favorite dish at dinners given by church societies in Delaware, Maryland, and New Jersey, and an annual muskrat banquet is a fixture with certain gun clubs in both the East and the West.'

MUSLIMS AND FOOD Islam is the faith of nearly 15% of the world's population. It has a certain underlying unity, springing from the simplicity and straightforwardness of Muhammad's message and the basic tenets of the faith, even though these have been richly elaborated over the centuries. This simplicity is evident in Muslim dietary laws. Muhammad knew Judaism well, but the Qur'ān (which was not his own work but was revealed to him by the messenger of God over a period of many years) avoids many of the prohibitions and prescriptions of the Jews (see JEWISH DIETARY LAWS).

The Qur'ān mentions food often, praises it as one of God's gifts to humanity, and states that all food is permitted to the faithful with four exceptions: blood; pig meat; any animal that has not been purposely slaughtered as food; and any animal that has been slaughtered in the name of a pagan deity. These last two prohibitions are reflected in the law that any living creature intended as food for human beings must be slaughtered by the cutting of its throat while conscious and after the slaughterer has spoken the words: 'In the name of God; God is most great.' Meat killed in this way is *halal*, lawful. *Haram*, a term which has perhaps not quite entered the English language, is the opposite of *halal*, i.e. illicit. (*Makrouh* is an intermediate category found in Shia Islam, and indicates something which is somewhat frowned upon although not prohibited. Examples are shellfish and some birds, on which Shia Islam seems to share Jewish attitudes, as do some Sunni Muslims in Anatolia and elsewhere.)

Alcohol is forbidden (although wine had some favourable mentions in the Qur'ān). It must not even be used in cooking.

See also RAMADAN, the month in which the first revelation of the Qur'ān is said to have come to Muhammad, and the annual occasion when the special beliefs of Muslims about foods and fasting are most noticeable.

(RO)

MUSSEL *Mytilus edulis* and allied species, an edible BIVALVE with worldwide distribution and importance. Their dark blue or blackish shells are a familiar sight at the seaside, and 'wild' mussels (if one can use the term for a creature of sedentary habits which feeds innocuously on the nutrients which it can filter out of sea water) have been gathered and eaten since remote antiquity. But the introduction of myticulture, as the culture of mussels is called, in France in the 13th century raised the consumption of mussels to a new plane; and the development in Spain of a new method of rearing mussels on ropes suspended from rafts has transformed the industry in the latter part of the 20th century.

Mussels grow in clusters, attaching themselves by means of a 'byssus' (numerous threads, produced by the mussel itself) to rocks or other supports such as jetties or gravel beaches. They can also attach themselves to the hulls of ships, and it is by this means that the main European species, *M. edulis*, has been spread all over the northern hemisphere. Other species important as food, or potentially so, are:

- *M. galloprovincialis*, the Mediterranean mussel, which differs but little from *M. edulis*;
- *M. barbatus*, the bearded mussel, so called because it has a more noticeable 'beard'; it has names such as *cozza pelosa* (Italian);
- *M. californianus*, a slightly larger species of the Pacific coast of N. America;
- *Perna viridis*, the principal mussel of SE Asia, which has a greenish-black shell which turns yellow after exposure to the sun, and is larger still (maximum 20 cm/8", common market length only half as great);
- various 'horse mussels' which mostly belong to the genus *Modiolus* and are less good fare than mussels proper.

The **fan mussel** (see FAN SHELLS) belongs to another family.

There are certain localities where 'wild' mussels of exceptional quality are found; but in general these mussels tend to be skimpy and their consumption is sometimes risky for reasons explained below. The overwhelming majority of mussels brought to market are cultured, and these should always be both plump and safe to eat. Their size, appearance, and flavour vary according to species, age, and place of culture. More than one place claims to produce 'the best mussels in the world'. One such is Wimereux, near Boulogne in France, where the mussels are relatively small but have an excellent flavour and remarkably clean and pretty indigo shells. But myticulture is practised in so many places that it is doubtful whether anyone has ever been able to make a systematic comparison of all the competitors.

There are three principal methods of mussel culture. The most ancient, which is still the main method in France, involves fixing poles, known as *bouchots*, upright in marine mud flats and growing the mussels on these. The story has often been related of how an Irishman called Walton was shipwrecked in the Bay of l'Aiguillon on the French coast in 1235; how he decided to stay and make a living by trapping seabirds in nets held up by poles; and how his quick Irish wit led him to change vocation when he observed that the poles were soon covered with infant mussels. The same bay is still studded with *bouchots*, and they are also used on the French Mediterranean coast. This technique has the disadvantage that the mussels can only feed when the tide is in and they are covered with water.

A second method, used in the Netherlands and Denmark, consists in creating sheltered mussel 'parks'. Forming these in flat and low-lying littoral zones such as the Wadden Zee is easy, and the mussels can be first reared in dense beds, then thinned out over a wider area to give them better feeding. Protection can be provided against predators, and the mussels benefit from being able to feed continuously. Harvesting is highly mechanized.

The third method, which now accounts for a very high proportion of the total output of mussels, is to anchor rafts in suitable bays, notably those in the north-west of Spain where conditions are ideal, and suspend from these numerous ropes on which the mussels can grow.

Consumption of mussels varies greatly from country to country, and is remarkably high in Belgium, for example, where *Moules et frites* (mussels and chips) are a national dish, although low (so far) in the USA.

Mussels can be eaten raw, but cooking is usually preferable. They play the main role in the French dishes *Mouclade* and *Moules marinière*; in the Italian *Zuppa di cozze*; and in Turkish dishes of stuffed mussels. They are used in the Spanish PAELLA.

Although, as indicated above, mussels are safe if they have been professionally cultured and marketed, wild mussels must be treated with caution. They are by no means alone among shellfish in their capacity to harbour toxins, but they do present a somewhat greater risk than other bivalves, and they do from time to time cause PSP, paralytic shellfish poisoning. This typically occurs after there has been an abundance of a certain dinoflagellate planktonic organism in the water, an abundance which is often visible as the so-called 'red tide'.

MUSTARD the name of several species of plant in the CABBAGE family. The seeds of three of them provide the condiment mustard. Several also have edible leaves: see MUSTARD GREENS and CRESS, for mustard and cress. Some yield a culinary oil.

The three plants grown for their seed are *Sinapis alba*, usually known as white or yellow mustard, a small plant whose large seeds are tan or yellowish; *Brassica nigra*, usually called black mustard, up to 3.5 m/12' tall with small brownish-black seeds; and *B. juncea*, known as brown or Chinese mustard, with small, usually reddish-brown seeds. The first two are native to Europe, the third originally Asian though now widely grown. The first and third now provide virtually all commercial mustard; *B. nigra* was formerly used in many European mustards, but it is too tall and its seeds drop too easily for mechanical harvesting.

The sharp taste of mustard is due to the presence of various glycosides: black mustard contains sinigrin and white mustard sinalbin. They are sulphur compounds, also found in other members of the cabbage family. There is also an enzyme, myrosinase, sometimes called thioglycosidase. When the seed coat is broken and the contents come into contact with water, the enzyme breaks down the glycoside, forming allyl isothiocyanate and other compounds, which are oily, highly volatile, and sharp flavoured. They reach a peak of strength in about 10 minutes, but then break down in their turn unless something is done to prevent this. An acid such as VINEGAR will stop the reaction, as will heating. If either is applied to mustard seed as soon as it is ground, the reaction never starts; but if the flavour is first allowed to develop, the addition of vinegar preserves the pungency and flavour. Wine must or VERJUICE may be used instead of vinegar, though this is not common.

Mustard cultivation is ancient; witness remains of seeds at a Mycenaean site in Greece, and in the prehistoric Swiss lake village of Morigin. The Greek writer Herodotus mentioned mustard as a cultivated plant in the 5th century BC, and around AD 42 the Roman agricultural writer Columella described a method of preparing the condiment which is not unlike modern practice. The Romans brought *S. alba* and *S. nigra* to Britain, where both now grow in the wild.

Mustard has always been important in Europe because it grows locally and is therefore the cheapest of spices. Medieval European courts often employed a mustardarius, an official who supervised the growing and preparation of mustard. The first sizeable commercial mustard businesses grew up in the mid-14th century in France, around Dijon. The British mustard industry arose in Tewkesbury in the 16th century, and Tewkesbury mustard became famous for its strength. The seed was ground, blended with HORSERADISH, and formed into balls which would keep fairly well until broken up and mixed with vinegar, verjuice, wine, or other liquid. The mixture was often sweetened.

In Italy, from early times, mustard came to be used to flavour MOSTARDA DI FRUTTA, a fruit relish made from quinces or grapes. The Italian word *mostarda* refers to this, rather than the condiment itself, which is called *senape* and which is not in common use at table.

Since the Middle Ages there have been some developments of technology which have affected ways of using mustard, especially in Britain.

Mustard seeds are oily, so that when they are crushed they form a paste. Until the 18th century no one had found a way of drying the seeds enough for them to be milled into a powder. The first successful process was developed by Mrs Clements of Tewkesbury in 1720. Although this discovery paved the way for the dominance in Britain of mustard powder, 'made mustard' (i.e. mustard ready for use, the commodity found almost everywhere else in Europe) remained popular, one of the best known brands of the time being made by Keen & Sons of London; hence the phrase 'as keen as mustard'. The emergence of mustard powder as the most popular form in Britain was largely due to Jeremiah Colman, who from 1804 developed a mixture of white and black mustard seed, with turmeric for colour, and wheat flour to improve the texture when the mixture is made up. (Since the Second World War only white mustard has been used in the product; black mustard is now cultivated only in the Mediterranean region, on a small scale.)

The strength of English mustard, when it is made from the powder (and sometimes when it is 'made mustard'), is a surprise for foreigners. Strong mustard does occur elsewhere as a speciality, but it is rare, whereas in Britain it is the norm.

French mustard falls into three principal categories, all 'made mustards' (mustard powder has never been popular in France, and what is bought there is usually English). Bordeaux mustard is mild and brown, with a slightly vinegary taste and containing sugar and herbs, often tarragon. Dijon mustard is generally a paler yellow, stronger, and with less extra flavouring. (It was in Dijon, in 1853, that Maurice Grey invented a steam-driven mustard mill. He founded the famous firm of Grey, now Grey Poupon, and Dijon is the city primarily associated with mustard in French eyes.) Meaux mustard, also called *moutarde à l'ancienne*, is made from unmilled, crushed grains and is usually fairly mild.

German mustard, an essential accompaniment to German sausages, is mostly of the Bordeaux type. A serious sausage stall will have two kinds, mild and medium strong.

American mustard, as applied to hot dogs (see FRANKFURTER), is generally very mild and coloured bright yellow with turmeric.

In Argentina mustard is an indispensable accompaniment to beef. Preferred brands are British but made in local factories: both the ordinary kind made from powder and a milder made mustard called Savora, which is also sold in France.

Mustard seed is much used in Indian cookery, often being fried whole before it is added to dishes. The application of heat in the frying stops the enzyme from working, giving a mild nutty flavour.

The chief use of mustard in Chinese cuisine is as a vegetable in the form of mustard greens, which come from *B. juncea* as well as other species.

Mustard oil is made from *B. juncea* and other species, including *B. rapa*, the source of European rapeseed oil. It has a slight mustard flavour and is also an effective preservative, so is used in pickles as well as for cooking.

READING: Rosamond Man and Robin Weir (1988).

MUSTARD GREENS primarily *Brassica juncea*, come from a wide range of wild and cultivated mustard plants, almost all belonging to the genus *Brassica*, that of the cabbage. They are of minor importance in western countries but are eaten on a large scale in China.

Two wild **European mustards,** ancestors of the cultivated species, have edible, although bitter, leaves. The first is field mustard, *Brassica rapa* ssp *campestris*, whose cultivated varieties include Indian colza and Indian rape. In its wild form this is called kalewort or summer rape in England. The second is charlock, *Sinapis arvensis*. This plant, also known as wild or corn mustard, often used to be eaten, especially in Ireland, the Hebrides, and Sweden.

Traditional British mustard and cress (see CRESS) does not involve mustard greens of the kind dealt with in the present entry, but uses seedlings of the common white mustard, *Sinapis alba*, the source of mustard seed.

In N. America a number of wild brassica mustards have been used as pot-herbs, but are now overshadowed by the increasing popularity of oriental mustard greens, often referred to as leaf mustard.

Oriental mustard greens are consumed in much greater quantities. In China *gaai choy, B. juncea* var *integrifolia*, for example, exists in many forms available at different times of year. Most kinds have thick, fluted leaf stalks almost like those of celery but with the leaf extending along most of the length of each stalk. The taste is bitter, and it is usual to blanch and discard the water before continuing cooking.

Within this group, there are many important cultivars, for example:

- In Sichuan province, the type known in Cantonese as *daai gaai choy*, and in English as Swatow mustard greens or Swatow mustard cabbage, is particularly pungent, and relatively coarse and tough. Most of the crop is preserved by salting to make *haam suen choy*, which resembles sauerkraut. When not pickled, it is usually suitable only for soup, for which purpose other types of mustard greens are often preferred.
- Sow cabbage, the Cantonese *jiu la choi*, has a very good flavour. It may reach 45 cm (18") in height, and is the basis of a popular Cantonese dish in which it is braised with fermented black beans and pork.

Mustard greens are also much used, both fresh and pickled, in SE Asia, e.g. Thailand. The Hmong (Meo) people of Laos are especially partial to one short-stemmed, twisted variety, which is called *phak kad Meo* for that reason.

In Japan, mustard greens are eaten boiled, with SOY SAUCE. *B. campestris* is popular in Japan, where it is known as *komatsuma* and cooked in the same ways as spinach.

There are other mustardy greens outside the genus *Brassica* but belonging to the same family, Cruciferae. These include *Sisymbrium officinale*, hedge mustard, which is a tough, sharp-tasting plant: and garlicwort, garlic mustard, or 'sauce alone', *Alliaria petiolata*. The latter derives its names from its strong garlic flavour, which makes it a good accompaniment to meat and fish.

MUTTON is the meat of domestic SHEEP over one year old. It has a stronger flavour and deeper colour than LAMB. Formerly it was much liked and eaten in Britain; Mrs Beeton (1861) commented that it was 'undoubtedly the meat most generally used in families'. It was taken from animals between three and five years old, among which wethers (castrated males) were considered to yield the best meat.

Mutton production has, however, dwindled during the 20th century, as sheep were bred to grow and fatten quickly. Now it is a rarity.

In many countries where sheep and goats are important domestic livestock, lamb, mutton, GOAT, and kid are used more or less interchangeably, with adjustments for cooking time. This is true for the Iberian peninsula, the Balkans, the Middle East and C. Asia, and parts of Latin America. In

China there is a single word which does duty for all these animals. Since, broadly speaking, there are few specifically mutton recipes in such other countries, and since the history of mutton cookery in Britain is of interest, it is the latter which is mainly described in this entry.

A mutton carcass is larger than that of a lamb, but the pattern of jointing is the same. Mutton should be aged for longer than lamb; two to three weeks were common in the past.

Because mutton is now largely a thing of the past in Britain, recipes for it have either transferred themselves to lamb, or become items of historical interest. Plain spit-roasting or boiling were, no doubt, methods used from early times; but what one finds in early English cookery books are complex and highly flavoured mutton recipes. Thus Sir Hugh Platt (1609) gave a recipe 'To boyle a Legge of Mutton in the French fashion', which required the cook to hollow the meat out of the leg, chop it with beef suet and marrow, and work it into a mixture of cream, egg yolks, raisins, dates, and bread, stuff the mixture back in, and boil the joint. Similar recipes, becoming steadily simpler, reappeared over the next two centuries, eventually transforming into Mrs Beeton's stuffed leg of mutton, in which the bone was replaced by a plain forcemeat and the joint roasted.

Sharp ingredients, such as VERJUICE, vinegar, and lemon, were frequently called for in sauces and gravies for mutton during the 17th century. Carbonadoes (see CARBONADE, CARBONADO), thin slices of mutton cross-hatched with knife cuts, were grilled and served with onions and vinegar, or cooked with white wine and lemon. Many mutton dishes were spiced with cloves, cinnamon, and nutmeg, and cooked with aromatic herbs and lemon or orange peel. Sugar appears in some recipes, notably pies.

In the 18th century, the spices, apart from mace, nutmeg, and pepper, largely disappeared, as did the sourer ingredients. Oysters, anchovies, and mushrooms took their place, being put into the gravy or served under the meat as a 'ragoo'. Sliced lemons were a common garnish, and BARBERRIES enjoyed a vogue during the early 18th century. Cucumbers, cooked in sauce or gravy, were also popular with mutton. Capers (or pickled nasturtium seeds) were intermittently used from the 17th century onwards, and by the mid-19th century had become the accepted accompaniment for boiled leg of mutton. Redcurrant jelly was served with mutton from the late 18th century onwards.

Harico (from the French *haricot*, stew) came to England during the 17th century, a stew of mutton, turnips, and carrots; it remained a dish of English home cookery well into the 20th. In the 17th and 18th centuries, hashes of mutton were made from partially roasted joints cut in thin slices, and heated with gravy and seasonings. By the 19th century this had become a method for using up cold mutton, by reheating it in gravy with onions. One elaborate version of a HASH was given by Charles Carter (1730) as 'Shoulder of Mutton disguis'd'; it involved cutting all the meat off a shoulder without piercing the skin, cooking the meat with seasonings, and then placing the blade bone in the middle of the mixture and covering it over with the skin. This curious recipe resurfaced from time to time, notably as Mrs Raffald's 'Hen and Chickens', and made a late and surprising appearance in Mrs Beeton (1861) as 'Hashed Lamb and Broiled Blade Bone'.

Mutton (or lamb) was a popular pie filling from the 17th century until the 19th century. Two distinct types of pie seem to have existed. First, there were sweet mutton or lamb pies, whose history probably stretches back much further into medieval cookery. These involved raisins, dates, sugar, candied peel, cinnamon, and cloves, as well as the meat, and must have been well liked, for they appear in recipe books well into the 18th century, long after sugar had vanished from other meat dishes. Secondly, savoury mutton pies, usually filled with cutlets and forcemeat, or with CAUDLES of eggs, or ragoos (see RAGOUT) of oysters added after cooking, were also made. These continued to find favour well into the 19th century. Scottish mutton pies were apparently well liked by Dr Johnson, although it is not obvious whether they were sweet or savoury. More recent Scottish recipes for little hot mutton pies call for seasonings of salt, pepper, and mace or nutmeg, and a crust made with beef suet by a hot-water method; such pies remain very popular.

In the hilly sheep-farming districts of Britain, a boiled mutton pudding, encased in suet crust and very similar to the better-known (beef) steak and kidney pudding, used to be made. It included sheep's kidney, onion, and flour. Other additions were rowan-berries in season, or pickled damsons, or pickled capers.

Mutton was sometimes used to mimic venison, and there were also recipes for converting it to 'hams'. 'Braxty' mutton was meat from a sheep which had died from natural causes or met with an accident. Not everyone was willing to eat this.

Mutton seems to have been a popular choice for 'exotic' dishes. Recipes for a 'Persian Dish', a type of RISSOLE or kofta KEBAB, or a 'Turkish Dish', which was a PILAF-like mixture of mutton, onions, and rice, are also given from the first half of the 17th century and carried on well into the 18th, after which they are replaced by the curries of ANGLO-INDIAN COOKERY. 'China chilo', a dish (often highly spiced, e.g. with curry powder) of minced mutton stewed with onions, lettuce heart, and young peas with a border of rice, also appeared in 18th- and 19th-century cookery books; China presumably indicated an oriental origin while *chilo* would seem to come from *chelow/chalau*, the word for plain white rice in Iran and Afghanistan respectively.

Using up the remains of joints has for long been a preoccupation for British cooks (witness books with titles like '50 Ways of Using up Cold Mutton'). This version of 'Vicarage Mutton' was quoted by Dorothy Hartley (1954): 'Hot on Sunday, Cold on Monday, Hashed on Tuesday, Minced on Wednesday, Curried on Thursday, Broth on Friday, Cottage pie Saturday.' For cottage pie see SHEPHERD'S PIE. This, when it first appeared under the now familiar name in the latter part of the 19th century, was a mutton dish. Mutton also appeared in IRISH STEW and Lancashire HOTPOT, and in other dishes on British tables up until the Second World War, although it became less and less common, and was finally replaced by the meat now referred to as 'lamb'.   LM

MUTTON-BIRD any of various species of seabirds, especially shearwaters (*Puffinus griseus*, *P. tenuirostris*), of the southern oceans, whose flesh is thought to taste something like mutton. Such birds were a popular food of the Maori in New Zealand, who used to pot them in their own fat, thus making a sort of antipodean CONFIT. In the Seychelles, 'salted wedged-tail shearwaters' used to figure in certain traditional dishes, no longer made because the birds now have a measure of protection.

MUZZLE the projecting part of an animal's face, including the nose and mouth; may also be called snout. Beef or ox muzzle (*museau de bœuf* in French) can be prepared in the same way as for ox tongue, but is more often served cold, seasoned with oil and vinegar dressing, as an HORS-D'ŒUVRE.

Muzzle can also be boiled in a stew with other ingredients. One example is the Brazilian *Feijoada* which has pig's snout boiled with feet and ears, black beans, and Portuguese sausages.

MYROBALAN a name which is or was used of various astringent Asian fruits, notably EMBLIC (*Emblica officinalis*), which are not suitable for eating raw but have some food uses in pickled form or in preserves. The name is also given to the fruits of some trees of the genus *Terminalia*, which have similar uses, e.g. the belleric myrobalan, *T. bellerica*.

The name myrobalan plum was formerly applied to the fruit of *Prunus cerasifera*; see CHERRY PLUM.

MYRTLE *Myrtus communis*, a fragrant shrub which bears white flowers and blue-black berries, is native to S. Europe and the Near East, where it has long been cultivated in gardens.

The ancient Greeks considered it sacred to Venus. However, this did not inhibit them from eating the berries, which are pleasantly acid and sweet with an aromatic quality slightly resembling that of juniper. They make a pleasant jelly, and can also be boiled to produce a beverage, but the main traditional use has been to dry them and use them as a spice. The flower buds may be used similarly.

Myrtle leaves are used in Mediterranean countries to flavour roast pork and small birds. As the flavour is strong, the leaves are not cooked with the meat, but used as a wrapping or stuffing after cooking; this is enough to impart a delicate aroma.

BOG MYRTLE is a quite different plant.

NAMEKO the Japanese name for a small mushroom, *Pholiota nameko*, which grows wild in beech woods. It is also cultivated, formerly on wetted beech logs and now on a substrate of sawdust and rice bran. *Nameko* means 'viscous mushroom' and its salient characteristic is an unusual slimy coating. The cap is yellow or amber and shaped like that of a cultivated button mushroom. See illustration opposite.

The flavour is pleasant and slightly aromatic. Nameko are used extensively in Japanese cooking, e.g. in soups such as MISO soup, and stews, and cost less than the more famous SHIITAKE and MATSUTAKE mushrooms. They are sold fresh (although they do not keep well) and in cans and preserved in brine in jars.

P. nameko, although recorded from Taiwan, is essentially a mushroom of Japan only, where its distribution coincides almost exactly with that of the Japanese chestnut tree, *Fagus crenata*. For related species see PHOLIOTA MUSHROOMS. Although one, *Kuehneromyces mutabilis*, is a candidate for cultivation, none has so far rivalled the nameko.

NAMNAM a leguminous fruit, *Cynometra cauliflora*, apparently native to a region stretching from Thailand to E. Malaysia.

The fleshy pods are about 10 cm (4") long, wrinkled, with yellow flesh and a single large seed within, which is discarded during preparation. There are two varieties, a sweet one which is eaten raw and a sour one which must first be cooked, when its flavour is reminiscent of quince.

NAM PRIK the most popular sauce in Thailand, without which Thai food would be very different. (Since CHILLI peppers are an essential ingredient, it is clear that Thai food was in fact very different before the chilli arrived in SE Asia from the New World.)

Nam prik is on the table at every Thai meal, but exists in many versions. The essential features are, apart from chopped dried red chilli peppers (including their seeds), lime juice, Thai FISH SAUCE (*nam pla*), garlic, and a little sugar. Chopped dried shrimps are often added, and so are the smallest of all AUBERGINES (*makeua puong*—pea sized).

Nam prik is simply made, by preparing and mixing its ingredients. For *nam prik pao* (roasted *nam prik*) some of the ingredients, especially unpeeled garlic cloves and unpeeled small onions or shallots, are first heated in a heavy iron pan, without added fat. Shrimp paste (*kapee*) is similarly treated. Peanuts may also be roasted and included.

NAN is the Persian word for bread, now also in common use in India, Pakistan, Afghanistan, several C. Asian republics (particularly Uzbekistan) and Xinjiang province, China. In several Finno-Ugrian languages of W. Siberia, it is the general word for dough and dough products. In Afghanistan, it is used as the name for food in general.

People in western countries are likely to know nan, if at all, as something they have in Indian restaurants. However, its distribution in Asia and the various forms which it takes are a complex subject.

The original sense of the term was 'ashcake', a bread cooked on the hearth, as related words in Pashto and Armenian make

Nameko
mushrooms

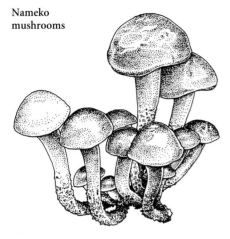

clear. Nowadays, the basic nan is a wheat-flour bread leavened with a starter of the SOURDOUGH kind, cooked in a clay TANDOOR. The clay and the smoke in the tandoor combine to produce a characteristic flavour. The bread is flattish and has a crisp crust.

Nans prepared in Iran include:

• *Nan-e-barbari*, a large oblong leavened bread made from finely ground wholemeal flour. Grooves are drawn with the fingers along the length of the flat loaf before it is baked in the tandoor. This bread is often sprinkled with sesame seeds.
• *Nan-e-sangak*, a leavened wholemeal bread which is indented by the fingers. It is called *sangak*, pebble, because it is baked in a tandoor on hot pebbles.
• *Nan-e-shir*, made with plain flour, baking powder, and milk, and sweetened with sugar, is often flavoured with vanilla.

The Uzbeks are known for their nans, which are nearly all round, rather than oblong, like a PIZZA with a thick ridge around the edge. They ornament their breads with geometric patterns of crimping and slashing on this ridge and concentric punch marks, made with a special punch called *chekich* (the subject of a study by Perry, 1994), on the flat centre of the loaf. Particularly beautiful breads are sometimes hung in hotels as art works. One has the impression that when the Uzbeks gave up nomadic life, the artistic impulses that had gone into the traditional nomad activity of carpet-making were channelled into baking. Their nans include some unusual items:

• *Goshtli nån*, a round bread containing ground meat (*goshtli* meaning 'meat').
• *Jizzali nån*, enriched with the cracklings of rendered mutton fat. (In Afghanistan there is a similar bread called *nan-e-jijek*).
• *Jirish nån*, a bran bread.
• *Shirmåy nån*, made with chickpeas and ANISE. Sometimes made in a long shape

known as *zabångåw*, cow's tongue, rather than round.
• *Zåghara nån*, not a wheaten bread but a mixture of grated pumpkin and maize flour, leavened and shaped into a hemisphere with a hole punched in the middle with the finger.

The Uzbeks also make a bread, *Qashqari patir*, said to have come to them from the Uighur city of Kashgar. It is made with onion juice in the dough, and the debris of squeezed onion shreds, mixed with sour milk, is smeared on the flat centre of the loaf, pizza-style.

The Uighurs of Xinjiang province, China, make the following nans:

• *Qaymaq nan*, enriched with cream; see KAYMAK.
• *Qatlima nan*, a coarsely layered bread made by smearing a thin sheet of dough with melted butter or fat, rolling it up tightly, cutting slices from it, roly-poly fashion, and rolling them flat.   CP/HS

NARANJILLA *Solanum quitoense*, a member of the nightshade family, bears fruits which resemble a little orange, as its common name, from the Spanish *naranja* (orange) indicates.

The shrub is believed to be indigenous to Ecuador, Peru, and Colombia, where it is grown commercially, chiefly for the production of juice, although the fruit is pleasant to eat. A brown hairy coat covers the fruit until it is fully ripe, when it rubs off. The fruit is about 6 cm (2.5") across, and divides easily into four sections. The yellowish-green pulp has an acidly sweet

taste, some say like a mixture of pineapple and lemon; and lots of tiny, thin seeds.

See also COCONA, of the same genus but bearing fruit with different characteristics.

NARAS *Acanthosicyos horridus*, a wild vine of the CUCURBIT family, common in the Kalahari and Namib deserts of southern Africa, which bears round, prickly, melon-like fruits. Local tribes, especially the Hottentots, depend on these fruits for a large part of their diet. During several months of the summer the fruits are eaten fresh. They are juicy, with a pleasant, slightly acid flavour. Fruits are also preserved.

The flat, oily seeds are kept for food in winter. They have a soft, nutlike texture and a buttery flavour, and are sometimes referred to as 'butterpits'. Besides eating them, the Hottentots extract a cooking oil from them. Butterpits used to be sold as a substitute for almonds in S. Africa.

NASTURTIUM *Tropaeolum majus*, a S. American plant, is best known as an ornamental; but the leaves of most kinds are edible and the buds and seeds may be pickled to produce a substitute for capers. The flowers are also edible and make a decorative element in SALADS. *T. minus*, the dwarf nasturtium, has similar properties.

Young nasturtium leaves taste something like WATERCRESS. (Indeed the name *nasturtium* is Latin for cress, and means 'twisted nose', with reference to the plant's pungency. In botanical nomenclature *Nasturtium* is the generic name of watercress.) They should be used sparingly.

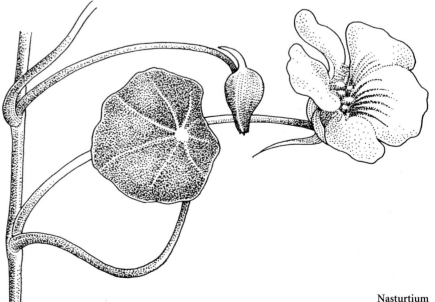

Nasturtium

A further idea was supplied by General Eisenhower in an exceptionally full and detailed recipe for vegetable soup which he contributed to *Celebrity Cook Book* (2nd edn, ed Lady Appleton, 1969):

As a final touch, in the springtime when nasturtiums are green and tender, you can take a few nasturtium stems, cut them up in small pieces, boil them separately as you did the barley, and add them to your soup.

A near relation of some importance is YSAÑO (or mashua, *T. tuberosum*), which is valued mainly for its tubers but whose leaves and flowers are also edible.

NATA a tough, jelly-like dessert made from COCONUT or PINEAPPLE trimmings, popular in parts of C. and S. America.

It is not a GELATIN or PECTIN jelly, but is composed largely of CELLULOSE, which is deposited by acetic acid-producing BACTERIA, *Acetobacter xylinum*. In fact it could be described as an unusually solid 'mother of vinegar' (see VINEGAR). The nata forms as a mat on the surface of a sugar solution in which the fruit trimmings are steeped. It is lifted off, washed, and sun dried; then cooked in syrup before serving. It is almost completely non-nutritious and has only a faint taste of the original fruit.

NATTO a Japanese fermented product made of SOYA BEANS, unusual in that it is fermented by BACTERIA (*Bacillus subtilis*) not by the MOULDS used for Indonesian TEMPE and other fermented soya bean products.

The bacteria give the beans a whitish coating and a flavour and texture which not all Japanese appreciate and which most other people find disconcerting. The flavour is strong, musty, and faintly ammoniac, and the bacteria develop on the beans a sticky slime which forms 'strings'; the longer these are, the better the natto, according to those who like the product.

Natto was often made in the home. Cooked soya beans were wrapped in rice straw, which supplies the necessary *B. subtilis*, and were left in a warm place for one or two days. However, commercially produced natto, for which the beans are inoculated with a pure culture of the bacteria, has largely replaced domestic production; and frozen natto is now available.

Natto is often used as an accompaniment for rice, and is itself accompanied by SOY SAUCE, mustard, and *negi* (Japanese onion); or by raw quail eggs (broken into and mashed with the natto). It is most popular in the eastern part of Japan.

NAUTILUS or pearly nautilus, *Nautilus pompilius*, unique among CEPHALOPODS in retaining an external shell, is sometimes called the chambered nautilus because this shell is built up, as it grows, by the addition of one chamber after another until there may be as many as three dozen. The animal's body is always accommodated in the last, outer, and largest chamber, and is equipped with several score of small arms. The shell contains a gas which makes it semi-buoyant, permitting the nautilus to change depth and to swim. It is not easy to catch, but Burma is one country where it is taken in quantity, perhaps because the shell, polished down to the 'pearl', can conveniently be carved into the shape of a peacock, the national emblem, and will then fetch a good price.

Although the shell may measure up to 25 cm (10"), its occupant is considerably smaller. It needs little preparation beyond removing the eyes, and may be cooked like any small SQUID.

NAVARIN a sort of stew of LAMB or MUTTON containing vegetables. During the winter months these will standardly be potatoes and onions, but in the spring the new season's vegetables (carrots, turnips, beans, peas, etc.) are used to make a *navarin printanier* ('spring navarin'). The French for 'turnip' is *navet*, which is probably the source of navarin. E. S. Dallas's comment in *Kettner's Book of the Table* (1877) suggests that the term was not of great antiquity: 'Navarin is a stupid word which has arisen from a desire to get rid of the unintelligible and misleading name Haricot de mouton, without falling back on the vulgar phrase, Ragoût de mouton.' JA

NECTAR besides meaning the sweet liquid which bees gather from flowers to produce HONEY, refers to the drink of the gods in classical mythology and, by extension, any particularly delicious drink. Nectar has thus a more restricted meaning than AMBROSIA, which can refer to both the food and drink of the gods, although commonly used of the food alone.

In the Homeric poems nectar is imagined as red (like wine) and as being served to the gods by Hebe, the divine wine-waitress ('cup-bearer' is the more traditional term). The 'nectar of bees', meaning honey, is a term first used by Euripides in the play *Bacchae* (c.400 BC).

NECTARINE *Amygdalus persica*, Nucipersica group, a variety of PEACH with a smooth skin and a flavour so fine that the fruit is named for NECTAR, the legendary drink of the classical gods. The flesh of modern cultivars is generally yellow and the skin red and yellow (although until about 1940 most nectarines, at that time smaller and with a sharper flavour, had greenish-white flesh). Like other peaches, nectarines may be 'clingstone' or 'freestone'. Their smooth skin means that they lack the protective 'fuzz' which is a feature of other peaches.

The origin of the nectarine is a mystery. It is a true peach, not a cross between a peach and a plum as some have supposed. Peach trees sometimes bear nectarines, and vice versa. In early literature from the time of the peach's origin in China to medieval times there is no clear reference to a nectarine. In France, however, the term *brugnon* was in use in late medieval times or soon afterwards for 'fuzz-less peaches', and in the 16th century at least one French writer gave a clear description of a nectarine.

The fruit soon reached England where by 1629, according to John Parkinson, there were six varieties and the name 'nectarine' was already in use. The nectarine was a latecomer to the USA. The first mention in print of cultivating nectarines was in 1722, in a book about Virginia, but cultivation in the eastern states only started in earnest in the early 19th century. Then, from about 1850 onwards, it became established in California, where the climate suits the nectarine perfectly. Since 1973 the production of nectarines in California, now embracing more than 150 varieties, has surpassed that of freestone peaches. In the 1990s Summer Grand and Mayglo have been the most important commercial varieties.

Nectarines are now grown in most areas where peaches are cultivated, although there are some where their lack of fuzz leaves them too vulnerable to disease. They are usually grown for eating fresh; if canned, they lose their special qualities. (Experts say that the special qualities of even fresh nectarines are less special than they used to be; cross-breeding with other peach varieties has left them with a less clearly distinctive flavour and texture.) Dried nectarines, of an attractive amber colour, are available.

NEPAL is a landlocked, mountainous country in the Himalayas perched between INDIA to the south-west and TIBET to the north-east.

Nepal, almost isolated from the rest of the world until the 1950s, is a mosaic of peoples of Indo-European and Tibetan stock with a wide range of cultures and religions. These factors are reflected in the cuisines; these are noticeably diverse and still heavily marked by their former almost complete reliance on the ingredients available in each small locality. But many factors, including the influx of tourists in the last decades of the 20th century, have set in train processes of change which are smudging the old culinary frontiers.

The main external influences in the cooking of Nepal come, naturally, from its two neighbouring countries, India and Tibet. Religious wars between Muslims and the old Indian principalities caused Indian Brahmans (priests) and Kshatriyas (warriors) to escape to the remote Himalayas, bringing with them their caste system and culinary customs and traditions. From the Chinese side there has been a steady infiltration of pure Tibetans which continues to the present day.

The Newars, who today mainly live in the lush Kathmandu Valley region, are one of the main ethnic groups of Nepal. Their ancestors ruled Nepal from about 700 BC to AD 100 and they have influenced Nepalese cuisine in many ways. They are renowned for their rich mythology, their traditions telling of the creation of the world, their numerous religious festivals and feasts, and their skill in growing the fruit and vegetables which are prominent at the feasts.

The Newars have in their turn been influenced by the hunting Ranas who, during the 19th century, virtually took over the Himalayan mountain kingdom and brought with them many culinary tastes and dishes with them from India, including recipes for venison and pork. Their rich, sumptuous food contrasted with the simple and plain food prepared by the ordinary people of Nepal.

Other groups with their own traditions and culinary tastes include the Gurkhas and the Sherpas. The Gurkhas, of course, were influenced by their service in the British army. Sherpas, well known as mountain guides and porters, live in the high mountains of E. Nepal. Their religion forbids them to kill animals but they nevertheless cook many meat dishes. Butchers from Tibet come especially to slaughter YAKS whose meat is then dried and smoked.

MAIZE is one of the few crops grown almost everywhere in the country. WHEAT and RICE are grown in the Kathmandu Valley, and in the fertile Terai region which is mentioned below. Further north root crops (such as turnip) and potatoes are cultivated.

The main food of the Nepalese is rice (*bhat*) usually served with DAL and one or two vegetable dishes which are either fried or made into a stew. Potato (*alu*) dishes are very common. Pork, lamb, buffalo, goat, and chicken (and duck) are included in the diet when affordable but beef is considered sacred and is not eaten. Chickens, like goats, are often used for sacrifice to the gods. The Nepalese are, however, a frugal people and, having made the sacrifice, the family may then cook and eat the remainder of the

animal. (At one of the more important temples—Dakshinkali—braziers are kept burning all day so that worshippers of Kali can have their meat cooked immediately after the ceremony and picnic on the spot.)

Kabaf is a particularly Nepalese dish. Although the word may have the same origins as KEBAB, *kabafs* are unlike the usual small pieces of barbecued meat; they are large pieces, cooked in their own juice.

Although Nepal is landlocked there are many rivers flowing down from the Himalayas and lakes providing plenty of freshwater fish. Fish farming has also been started in some places, producing carp and trout.

Noodles (*chau chau*) are popular in Nepal, as are the meat-stuffed dumplings called *momo* (see MANTOU); these reflect the Chinese influence mediated through Tibet. GHEE or MUSTARD oil (which gives a characteristic pungency to the food) is used for cooking. On the whole, food is, in general, bland but the use of various hot and spicy pickles (ACHARS) and CHUTNEYS with the rice adds flavour and piquancy. Ginger, garlic, onion, and chives are commonly used in Nepal.

There are two words for bread in Nepal: *roti* (Nepali) and *mari* (Newari). Besides making many of the breads common in India (CHAPATI, ROTI, PARATA, POORI, etc.) the Nepalese make some breads from rice, maize, MILLET, BUCKWHEAT, SOYA BEAN, and PULSES. Some of these are steamed breads, once again reflecting the influence of N. China; these may have a stuffing and are sometimes referred to as 'dumplings'. *Yomari* is one such, a steamed rice-flour dumpling made by the Newari people to celebrate Yomari Punhi, the festival of the full moon in December/January (a feast day of Lakhshmi, goddess of wealth), and also for the even (but not odd) numbered birthdays of children. Usually it is made in a conch shape and filled with roasted sesame seeds and brown sugar.

Of the numerous festivals in the Nepalese calendar, some involve fasting but the great majority call for festival food, for example, *Kwati*, a bean dish made with many sorts of beans at the Newari festival of Gumpuni. All the festivals feature sweet specialities, mostly the counterparts of Indian ones such as KHEER and JALEBI (although some seem to be distinctively Nepalese, e.g. *sel*, which are 'slimline' rice FRITTERS). An especially wide range of sweets is on offer during the Festival of Lights in the late autumn, and they also turn up at wedding feasts.

Yoghurt or curds are considered a delicacy and an important food for health. LASSI is also drunk, as are fruit-based drinks called *sherbats* (see SHERBET). Oranges and tangerines grow in the hilly regions of Nepal; mangoes in the Terai, the plain in the south

of the country. Pineapple is cultivated in E. Nepal. *Sherbats* are made from all these fruits and also from BAEL (*bel* in Nepali) fruit and other fruits.

Generally speaking, food taboos and habits in eating correspond to those of the same religious beliefs in India, but there are some interesting variations. Indra Majupuria (1980–1) observes that:

Among Tharus, when women serve meals for their husbands, there is a peculiar custom. The wife kicks her husband's dish of food with the toes of her leg. This is to symbolize the subjugation of men by the women.　　　　　　　　　　　HS

NESSELRODE PUDDING the best-known CHESTNUT pudding. Chestnuts lend themselves naturally to rich puddings. This one (known in France as *pouding à la Nesselrode*) was named for a Russian count who was a prominent diplomat in the mid-19th century. It is made from cooked, sieved chestnuts combined with a rich, sweet custard lightened by separating the eggs and adding the beaten whites later. The mixture is poured into a buttered mould, ornamented with glacé fruit, steamed, and served with fruit syrup. (There is also a cold imitation made with broken macaroons instead of chestnuts.)

Another chestnut pudding in the grand style is Mont Blanc, which is made from chestnuts cooked in milk, sieved, flavoured with vanilla and a liqueur, and mounded on a plate, then topped with sweetened whipped cream to represent snow on a mountain.

A Chinese pudding, *li tzu tan kao*, is nicknamed 'Peking dust' because it resembles a little heap of brown dust swept up by a street cleaner in that dusty city. The chestnuts are cooked in brown sugar and puréed, then sprinkled all over the outside of a mound of very stiff whipped cream. The edge of the mound is ornamented with fried, sugar-glazed nuts.

NETTLES of the stinging kind, notably *Urtica dioica* which has a range from W. Europe to the Himalayas, are gathered wild and used as a green vegetable in many parts of the world. Only the young shoots and tops of the plants are eaten, and they have to be cooked in order to destroy the formic acid which gives them their sting. Nettle soup is the only European dish in which they play a leading role; but they are also used in the production of nettle and ginger beer, and are an ingredient of the herb puddings made in the north of England (see DOCK PUDDING). The Scottish version of nettle soup is Nettle kail. The term kail means not only the vegetable KALE but also, in a more general way, greens or a soup made from them. This Nettle kail was in some regions a traditional dish for Shrove Tuesday, or to celebrate the arrival of spring. It would incorporate a little barley meal or fine oatmeal and a boiling fowl or cockerel stuffed with oatmeal, onion, and wild garlic.

Stinging nettles are used for food in Asia. Tibetans say that Milaraspa, their world-famous poet and saint, lived solely on *satuk*, nettle soup, for many years, until he turned green. One of his meditation caves lies above Kyirong (Happy) Valley, in surroundings which 'are completely barren, except for a long strip of nettles which starts at the cave and goes all the way down to the valley. People say that Mila accidentally dropped his soup pot one day, and that this strip marks its path as it rolled downhill' (Dorje, 1985).

The European purple and white dead nettles, *Lamium purpureum* and *L. album*, look like and may be used like true nettles but do not sting and are more closely related to mint. They used to be a popular food in Sweden, and have been introduced to N. America, joining an indigenous relation, the henbit, *L. amplexicaule*. The 'flame nettles' of the genus *Coleus* are also related to mint.

NEUFCHÂTEL is a mould-ripened, whole-milk soft French cheese named after a town in the north of Normandy—not to be confused with the Swiss canton of Neuchâtel, also a cheese-producing area but not possessing a variety named after it. Cheeses of the Neufchâtel type are manufactured not only in the area of origin but widely elsewhere, including the USA. They are always small, seldom much over 100 g (4 oz) in weight, and shapes vary widely: square (*carré*), heart shaped (*cœur*), a small loaf (*Bondon*), or a flattened cylinder (*Gournay* and *Malakoff*, the latter being rare now).

Neufchâtel is made by a variant of the usual French soft cheese process used for CAMEMBERT and similar varieties. The preparation is prolonged and complicated. Ripening takes place in a cool, damp cellar infected with several species of moulds and bacteria: strains of *Penicillium candidum* are prominent in a complex crew of micro-organisms.

Unlike many soft cheeses, Neufchâtel can be (and usually is) eaten when still relatively young and barely ripened: in this state the surface bloom is pure white and velvety. Such cheeses are very soft, with less flavour than later, but they have an agreeable tartness. When the cheese is allowed to ripen fully, the mould becomes blackish, the cheese hardens slightly, and the flavour develops considerably.

NEW ZEALAND one country in the world where the crucial date for its culinary history sticks out a mile. As David Burton (1982) puts it:

On 20 October 1769 the *Endeavour* anchored at Anaura Bay, south of East Cape. During the crew's brief spells ashore, wild celery was, on Captain Cook's orders, regularly collected and boiled with potable soup and oatmeal for the crew's breakfast. Probably the ship's cooks did not realise that this first crude marriage of local food and British cookery had laid the foundations for modern New Zealand cooking.

The Maori, the inhabitants of New Zealand when Cook arrived there, were descendants of the Polynesians who arrived in the islands around AD 800. They found plenty to eat, especially birds (including the now extinct moa); indeed, Gwen Skinner (1983) describes their avian larder as comprising 'an overwhelming choice of winged, flightless, foraging and wading birds'. They would have been less surprised by the wealth of inshore fish and other seafood (see, for examples, TOHEROA; TUATUA; PIPI). But the wide range of edible plants included some welcome novelties such as the bracken fern (see FERNS) which they came to cultivate besides eating it from the wild, and bulrush, see CAT-TAIL. However, they brought with them their own food plants, notably TARO and the SWEET POTATO (*kumara*) as well as things like the BOTTLE GOURD. The sweet potato was outstandingly successful in New Zealand soil and became their most valuable crop in the pre-European period.

Maori cooking methods included the 'hot stones' technique (see FULACHTA FIADH for a European version) with large wooden containers as recipients rather than pits. However, pits were the basic requirement for their most important cooking method, the *umu* or *hangi*. Earth ovens are familiar in the other islands of the S. Pacific, but there they are constructed on the surface of the ground or in shallow depressions. The Maori dug theirs deep down and what was cooked in them was actually cooked by steam. Skinner has a particularly fine quotation describing the building and operation of a *hangi* in olden times, but the practice continues and she is also able to describe and provide photographs of a *hangi* for 700 people in 1983. There is an obvious parallel with the New England CLAMBAKE. The other Maori cooking method, grilling—whether by fastening fish or birds to sticks leaning over the embers of a fire or by placing foods (such as clams) directly in the embers—was better suited to small meals, for just a few people.

The study in many volumes by Elsdon Best (1977) of the Maori includes much material about their foodways and is a shining example of how work of this kind should be done.

The arrival of European settlers brought new foodstuffs, some of them destined to become very important. The Maori did not give a big welcome to European vegetables such as carrots and turnips, but they were quick to grasp the advantages of the pig, which yielded more meat than any other animal they knew. They also, later, came to like mutton—of which large quantities were available very cheaply during the long period when sheep were being raised in New Zealand more or less exclusively for wool (in the absence of the technology needed to make possible export of the meat). And they enthused over the potato. Potatoes and wheaten bread cooked in the Maori style began to replace fern roots in their role as a staple.

The incoming settlers often had to resort, in times of hardship, to unfamiliar foods such as the Maori ate. Burton has a number of apt quotations about a soup made from SEA ANEMONE, a pudding made from fuchsia berries, the processing of the cabbage tree (TI, *Cordyline* spp) to produce sticky brown sugar crystals, and the reaction of hungry travellers in the bush to eating native rats (on the whole favourable—the rats had a wholesome vegetarian diet). However, generally speaking, the settlers were British in their attitudes to food, i.e. tending to be conservative and trying to reproduce on the other side of the world the fare to which they had been accustomed in Britain. Since the climate of New Zealand is comparable to that of Britain, although milder, this aspiration was not as inappropriate as it had turned out to be in various British colonies in the tropics (or, for that matter, in most of Australia). If this conservatism deterred the incomers from learning to appreciate some of the fermented foods which were a speciality of the Maori, they could nevertheless adapt their own ways of cooking birds and fish to the different birds and fish which they found in New Zealand. On some of them they bestowed unsuitable names (e.g. 'blue cod' for *Parapercis colias*, which belongs to a quite different family, but is, incidentally, of excellent quality, so that if one takes the term 'cod' to mean simply 'a good fish', as opposed to one with taxonomic significance, these early settlers got it right); but this was no impediment to cooking them successfully. Nor was there a problem over enjoying New Zealand oysters, clams, and cockles.

The arrival of some Italian and Greek immigrants, in small numbers in the 19th century but larger numbers later, did something to variegate the culinary scene. So did the introduced deer (a complicated story, which has culminated in deer meat being a major export of the country), and rabbits; and the discovery that subtropical fruits such as tamarillo (see

TREE-TOMATO) and KIWI FRUIT would flourish in the New Zealand climate. The latter fruit in particular made some fortunes during the period when it was in heavy demand, especially for NOUVELLE CUISINE purposes, in Europe and before horticulturists in the Mediterranean region had discovered that their climate too was suitable for it.

New Zealand may claim to provide a better example than most other ex-colonial territories of a cuisine which successfully incorporates what was indigenous with what was introduced. It can also claim, without necessarily designating them as national dishes, some original contributions to the world's repertoire. One is PAVLOVA. Another is toheroa soup, which Burton describes as:

the most celebrated and the rarest of all New Zealand soups, said by one romantic to have the flavour of oysters which have been fed an exclusive diet of asparagus tips. The more mundane truth is that toheroa feed on plankton, the green chlorophyll of which builds up in the toheroa's liver and produces the soup's asparagus-like colour.

Another, for which see BISCUIT VARIETIES, is the Afghan, which despite the mystery surrounding its name can stand as representative of the strong baking tradition in New Zealand.

NEW ZEALAND SPINACH *Tetragonia tetragonioides*, not a relation of ordinary spinach, but a creeping perennial with flat, thick, bright green leaves, which belongs to the same family as the ICEPLANT. The seed pods float and are borne naturally for long distances on ocean currents. Thus, besides growing in New Zealand and Australia, the plant is found in the Pacific islands, Japan, and S. America.

In New Zealand it is a coastal plant, eaten by the Maori; names in use there include *kokihi*, *vengamutu*, and *warrigal cabbage*. It has become less plentiful since the introduction of sheep into the country, but is now cultivated in many vegetable gardens. Captain Cook, when he was exploring New Zealand in 1770, realized its importance as a green and anti-scorbutic vegetable, had it gathered in quantity, and persuaded the ship's company to eat it by having it served to the officers in cooked green pottages or salads. It was Sir Joseph Banks, his botanist, who took the plant back to England where it was grown in Kew Gardens. By the 19th century New Zealand spinach, known also as 'Botany Bay greens', had become a popular summer spinach in England and America. An incidental but interesting point is that Botany Bay was originally going to be called Sting-ray's Harbour, since several large sting-rays had been caught and eaten there. But, as Banks recorded in his diary: 'We had

New Zealand spinach

with it a dish of the leaves of tetragonia cornuta [the then name for New Zealand spinach] boil'd, which eat as well as spinage or very near it.' This and other botanical discoveries prompted the change of name.

The great 19th-century French writer Alexandre DUMAS *père* committed what has become a notorious anachronism when he had d'Artagnan, one of his Three Musketeers, be offered in the 17th century a dish of 'tetragon', this vegetable whose discovery lay a century ahead.

New Zealand spinach differs greatly from true spinach, but has a somewhat similar flavour. A tendency to bitterness can be countered by changing the water while cooking it.

Other edible *Tetragonia* spp occur in S. Africa.

NGAPI NUT the edible 'nut' of a leguminous tree of SE Asia, *Pithecellobium lobatum*, commonly eaten in Burma (where its name indicates that it smells like the Burmese fermented fish paste, *ngapi*) and Indonesia. The wine-red young shoots and the flowers are also eaten.

The 'nuts', which are seeds borne in large pods, are served as a side dish in Java. Their offensive smell is dispelled when they are cooked. A popular treatment is to cook ripe seeds and then pound them into flat cakes which are sun-dried, fried, sprinkled with salt, and served as one of the side dishes called emping (see GNETUM).

NIGER SEED the oil-yielding seed of *Guizotia abyssinica*, a plant of the same family as the SUNFLOWER, but smaller, about the size of a Michaelmas daisy. A native of E. Africa, tolerant of poor soil and low rainfall, it is cultivated in Ethiopia and also in India (under the Bengali name *ramtil*).

The seeds are eaten fried or incorporated in CHUTNEYS or made into little cakes. The

oil they yield is similar to that from sunflower seeds, with a pleasantly nutty taste. It may be used as a substitute for GHEE.

NIGHTSHADE an ominous name, because of the ill repute of *Atropa belladonna*, the deadly nightshade, which indubitably contains toxins. Although the genus *Solanum*, home of most other nightshades, includes many edible species such as the POTATO and AUBERGINE, and counts the TOMATO as a close relation, the shadow cast by belladonna caused the whole tribe to be viewed with suspicion when they first became known to Europeans. However, several species which are called nightshades have berries which can be used as food.

- *Solanum nigrum*, black-berried nightshade, a bushy herb found in many parts of the world, bears small, black, many-seeded berries. These are sometimes called morelles, and have a reputation for toxic properties, but are used as a cooked fruit or in pies and preserves. It seems that the green, unripe berries do contain a harmful substance, but that this disappears as the fruits ripen. Bessey (in *American Botanist*, 1905) disarmingly recounts how:

I was lecturing on the properties of the plants constituting the Solanaceae, and, as a matter of course, said that the berries of the black nightshade were poisonous. A young fellow from Fort Dodge, Iowa, spoke up and said that the people in his neighborhood made them into pies, preserves, etc. and ate freely of them. I answered him, as became a professor of botany, by saying that as it was well known that black nightshade berries are poisonous, the student must have been mistaken. After a while, however, I learned that the people in central and western Iowa actually did eat black nightshade berries, and they were not poisoned either. Later, I learned the same thing in Nebraska for this species. The leaves of the plant are also edible, and are consumed like spinach.

With regard to his last sentence, Gwen Skinner (1983) has an interesting passage about use in the Pacific Islands, particularly Niue, where the plant is called *polo* and the leaves are used in, for example, a baked fish dish.
- *Solanum scabrum* is sometimes cultivated in the USA under the inappropriate name garden huckleberry. Facciola (1990) observes that the cultivar Schwartzbeeren counts as an 'heirloom cultivar brought by Volga German immigrants to Kansas and Nebraska in the 1880 to 1920 period'; that thoroughly ripe berries can be eaten raw, although it is usual to cook the berries with baking soda first, to remove the bitterness; and that the leaves are used in Africa as a pot-herb.
- *S. aethiopicum*, whose red fruits are eaten as a vegetable and whose common names

include Ethiopian nightshade, is treated under AUBERGINE.

- *Solanum* × *burbankii*, the wonderberry (or sunberry), has smallish blue berries with an intense flavour. Although the wonderment excited by this hybrid arose many decades ago, it must be maintained to some extent, since a cultivar is still listed, under the disarming name Mrs B.'s Non-Bitter.

NIPA PALM *Nypa fruticans*, a palm of the region stretching from E. India to Australia. Its various parts serve almost as many uses as the coconut, from fuel and roofing through cigarette papers to sugar and toddy. When the inflorescence is growing, there is a flow of sweet sap containing sucrose up the stalk towards it, and this can be, and in former times was, tapped as a source of sugar. However, it begins to ferment at once, so that it becomes toddy almost immediately and VINEGAR within a couple of weeks.

The fruit is spherical, about 30 cm (1') in diameter, with heavily protected diamond-shaped sections within. The starchy seeds are used by the Chinese to make sweetmeats. In Malaysia they flavour a commercial ice cream. In the Philippines, nipa vinegar is used to prepare chicken ADOBO and PAKSIW.

NITRATES AND NITRITES, chemical compounds used in the curing of meats, for example to make ham, bacon, some sausages, and silverside of beef. The type traditionally used is saltpetre, potassium nitrate. So-called Chile saltpetre, sodium nitrate, is also employed; it is cheaper and slightly stronger.

As the curing process continues, BACTERIA decompose a little of the nitrate into nitrite. Nitrites react with myoglobin, a PROTEIN in the meat, turning it pink and producing the characteristic colour of cured meat products. At the same time, even smaller amounts of compounds known as nitrosamines are produced. These are suspected of causing cancer. There are strict limits on the nitrite content of cured meats, intended to keep nitrosamines down to safe levels. RH

NIXTAMALIZATION is a process discovered by the Aztec and Maya civilizations of Mesoamerica (see CENTRAL AMERICA), but not by the Inca in S. America, which transformed the MAIZE which they had already domesticated into a truly superior foodstuff.

It is a complex process that starts with soaking the ripe maize grains and then cooking them with lime or wood ashes. This enables the transparent skin on the grain, the pericarp, to be removed, and of course makes the grain easier to grind. But the major contribution of nixtamalization is that it much enhances the protein value of the maize for human beings. So superior is nixtamalized maize to the unprocessed kind that it is tempting to see the rise of Mesoamerican civilization as a consequence of this invention, without which the peoples of Mexico and their southern neighbours would have remained forever on the village level. When and where this discovery was made is unknown, but typical household equipment for making nixtamal out of maize is known on the south coast of Guatemala at dates between 1500 and 1200 BC.

The Europeans accepted maize immediately, but unfortunately for them they accepted it as another grain, to be used like European grains, that is to say ground and then made into mush or bread. They ignored nixtamalization, probably thinking it unnecessary with their more powerful and efficient mills. Because of this, maize-dependent cultures away from the New World suffer from dietary deficiencies like pellagra and kwashiorkor, which do not exist where nixtamalization is used. Nor did the Europeans take back home with them the nutritionally superior combination of maize and New World beans, although the two ingredients made the trip separately. SC

NOAH'S ARK presents many problems for the literal-minded, not least, the food problem. It is indeed difficult to imagine how the logistics could have been handled. Bridget Ann Henisch (1967) devoted a charming and witty book, *Medieval Armchair Travels*, to the subject, and the rest of this entry is a quotation from that book.

Whatever the tragedies outside, the commentators kept Noah and his family much too busy to notice them. Their main job was to see that everyone was happy, clean and well-fed, the men looking after the animals, the women caring for the birds. This division of labour is remembered in a picture of the disembarkation in the *Bedford Book of Hours*, where it is a woman who is gently setting free a duck. No one is straining himself; indeed, Noah is having a nap, perhaps exhausted by the very thought of the strenuous timetable drawn up for him. In a Jewish story, no animal was prepared to be accommodating. Each expected to eat its favourite food at its accustomed meal-time, and so Noah raced up and down, one moment with buckets of vineshoots for elephants, the next with broken glass of which, as all agreed, ostriches were inordinately fond.

Christian commentators were less indulgent to these fads and fancies. A uniform diet of figs and chestnuts was favoured by many, led by St. Augustine, who remarked with brisk optimism:

> Hungry animals will eat almost anything and of course, God . . . could easily have made any food pleasant and nourishing.
>
> The City of God, Book 15, Chap. 27

Those who felt certain animals must have meat and could not be allowed to eye their neighbours, developed the theory that a special supply of sheep was loaded for them. This ingenious arrangement brought psychological as well as nutritional benefits: as the sheep were eaten, the Ark became roomier, and the irritations of close quarters were smoothed away. A Jewish storyteller partially solved the problem by making his lions seasick and unable to face more than a scrap of grass throughout the voyage.

Others dismissed the preoccupation with meat as irrelevant, in the belief that men and animals alike were vegetarians before the Flood. This was a popular idea, despite the unkind comment of Procopius that, if this were so, Abel had been wasting his time as a shepherd. After the Deluge vegetables were found to be less nourishing than before, and so God said that meat might be eaten instead, as a compensation and a reminder of the sin that had spoilt the world.

All worried about the vast quantities of food needed, and the consequent problems of storage and waste disposal in an already over-loaded Ark. Artists were much more relaxed, few bothering to squeeze in more than an occasional Lilliputian sack. Some tastefully arranged trays of fruit and vegetables lie unjostled in the larders. Under these, and inconsiderately far from the living quarters, are the *stercoraria* for dung and refuse.

NOODLES (*see opposite page*)

NORI or laver, an important group of SEAWEEDS in the genus *Porphyra*, especially *P. tenera* (Japan), *P. perforata* (N. Pacific), and *P. umbilicalis* (Europe). Of all the edible plants which grow in the sea, these are the most valuable and the most widespread; but their importance is obscured by the fact that they pass under various English names in different places. Laver is the name in England and Wales. In Scotland and Ireland it is sloke. The Japanese name nori has been largely adopted in N. America.

Laver is a reddish seaweed, of relatively small size and distinctive shape, which is harvested and dried before use. It may be sold in the dried form or, as happens in Wales, it may first be boiled which turns it into 'laverbread', a green mush rather like spinach purée in appearance. It can be warmed in a pan and served on toast with a little lemon juice. Or it can be mixed with a little oatmeal and fried in patties. (Welsh cookery books usually bid one make the patty of the laverbread and then coat it with oatmeal; but in practice this is difficult to do, the laverbread being too mushy to hold its shape.)

However, although the consumption of laver in Wales is of great antiquity, having been noted in medieval times, it is completely overshadowed in terms of quantity by the Japanese consumption, which amounts to many billions of sheets (cont. on page 539)

A difficult term. It has two main current meanings in English. First, it denotes certain types of occidental PASTA, especially those which are in the form of narrow strips and are served in soups (cf. *OED*). This meaning has a tendency to be expanded in respect of E. European pasta. Secondly, it refers to most of the numerous kinds of Asian pasta.

Usage in other languages differs somewhat. Thus the French term *nouilles* is used in a more general way than the English 'noodles' in the first sense; but it may refer specifically to the Alsatian dish known as *nouilles* (tagliatelle). The German *Nudeln* denotes any kind of pasta served as a dish in its own right, but also has the English meaning of 'noodles' when served as a soup ingredient.

Noodles are of major importance in many Asian countries, but attain their fullest glory in the cuisines of China and Japan. As will be apparent in these entries Asian noodles can be categorized according to their major ingredient: wheat-flour noodles; rice-flour noodles; and the vegetable starch group, including bean and pea starch, potato starch, and cornstarch noodles. There are, naturally, many different sorts within these three categories (see the sections that follow).

Noodles of Asia

These (including those of China and Japan, dealt with on pages 536 and 538) present an interesting pattern.

One salient point is the relative lack of noodles in the Indian subcontinent. It is hard to explain this on a simple basis such as lack of suitable cereal crops in the subcontinent, since noodles can be made from so many different and basic ingredients. The phenomenon seems to be more of a historical one. It may be that the kitchen territory which might have been occupied by noodles of certain kinds was already devoted to dishes in the DAL category. There is, however, one kind of Indian noodle which has achieved a moderate degree of prominence; see SEV, SEVIYAN.

Looking northwards at the huge arc of territory which extends from China and Mongolia in the East all the way to Iran and the countries of the Middle East, there are two aspects which deserve comment. One is that, again, there are large areas where noodles are of minor importance—Iran itself and the Arab countries at the eastern end of the Mediterranean. This is something of a mystery, since there are grounds for believing that noodles may have begun in what is now Iran (Perry, 1981), and they were certainly of importance in medieval Arab cookery. It seems possible that what happened was that PILAF in Iranian territory and COUSCOUS in N. Africa gradually encroached on the role played by noodles in ancient times. In fact, the 'mystery' can be resolved by postulating gradual changes in area-wide eating patterns.

A further interesting point is that in the noodle-using areas between Mongolia and Turkey there is great emphasis on what would be called filled pasta in western countries, items which are often in practice referred to as dumplings (see DUMPLINGS OF ASIA). A prime example is MANTOU. Also important in this category are JOSHPARA (with its strong Iranian connection) and PEL'MENI (familiar in Russia), and it would be true to say that filled pasta has proved less-vulnerable to encroachment by pilaf etc. than ordinary noodles.

A simple, perhaps too simple, explanation of the prevalence of mantu etc. could be that the combination of a meat or similar filling and a cereal envelope was convenient for nomadic cultures and more generally for people with very simple cooking facilities. One cooking pot would do, and the filling could be varied according to what was available—e.g. the vegetable filling in the *ashak* of Afghanistan (like ravioli) stuffed with *gandana*, which are Chinese CHIVES, or a filling of curd, or whatever.

However, the prevalence in the region of stuffed items has not excluded noodles which resemble vermicelli or have a ribbon shape; see RESHTEH; LAKSA, for two examples.

The picture is rather different when one looks at noodles in SE Asia. There, the stuffed noodles are less common and the influence of Chinese noodles of the thin ribbon type, and especially rice noodles, is far more apparent. It is dominant in what used to be called Indo-China. In Laos, *khao pun*, the national dish, is based on rice vermicelli. In Vietnam rice vermicelli are also prominent (*bun*, or the ultra-thin kind called *banh hoi*), and so are the flat thin rice noodles (*banh pho*), often referred to in English as 'rice sticks'. Vietnamese also relish the so-called 'cellophane noodles' (*mien/bun tau*, also called 'bean threads' in English, because made of mung bean), and egg noodles (*mi*) are prominent in some areas. The situation in Cambodia is similar but shows a closer relationship with some of the nuances displayed by the food of neighbouring Thailand. In Thailand a strong Chinese influence is evident, particularly in the north, but many of the wares offered by Thai street hawkers (e.g. *mi* or *mee*, a term which just means noodles but can also indicate a wonderfully complex dish of noodles with various seafoods—so good that it turns up as *mi Siam* in Malaysia) represent an evolution away from Chinese originals. This is true also of the noodles of Malaysia and Indonesia; they too reflect a strong Chinese influence, but modified by the impact on their cuisines of influence from the Middle East and the Indian subcontinent, conveyed in the Muslim culture which is dominant in these countries.

Further east, in the Philippines, one finds the greatest and most intriguing mixture of noodle dishes from other cultures.

To round off the survey one could continue eastwards to HAWAII, another outstanding example of mixed culinary cultures.

NOODLES OF THE PHILIPPINES

ALTHOUGH Filipinos have developed their own highly interesting ways with noodles—hence this special box for them—their debt to China (and to a lesser degree Spain) is obvious. The generic name for noodles is *pansit* (also spelled *pancit*), which comes from the Hokkien *pian+e+sit*, which means 'something that is conveniently cooked'. The names of the different types of noodle are still the Chinese names, or derived from them: thus, *bihon* (rice vermicelli), *miswa* (fine, dried wheat noodle), *sotanghon* (bean thread), *miki* (fresh wheat noodle with egg), Canton (pre-cooked wheat noodle with duck's egg).

The ways of cooking use Chinese and Spanish techniques, indigenized by local combinations. The most common way is to sauté noodles with garlic, onions, tomatoes, shrimps, pork, and vegetables: *guisado* in Spanish, thus *bihon guisado*, *sotanghon guisado*, etc. Other additions might be meat or fish balls, Chinese parsley (cilantro, coriander), mushrooms, etc. Another way is to cook it in broth (*pansit mami*), or to shake the noodles in boiling water in a bamboo skimmer (*luglug*) and then add a shrimp-based, annatto-coloured sauce (*palabok*), thus *pansit luglug* or *pansit palabok*, which is prevalent in Luzon. This may then be garnished with flaked smoked fish, crumbled pork crackling, sliced *kamias* (BELIMBING ASAM), sliced hard-boiled eggs, and CALAMANSI halves, then sprinkled with fish sauce (*patis*).

Some dishes are named after the towns of origin: *pansit Malabon* has oysters and squid, since that is a fishing town; *pansit Marilao* has crumbled rice crackers, since this is in rice-growing Bulacan. *Pansit molo* is not in noodle shape, but is rather pork-filled wonton in a broth originating in the town of Molo, the Chinese section of Iloilo city. *Pansit habhab* is from Lucban in Quezon, where it is eaten from a banana leaf without hands or forks, 'habhab' style.

Pansit is served at birthdays for 'long life', and is also the universal party dish and food gift.

The earliest restaurants in the Philippines were called *pansiterias* by the Spaniards. The name has persisted but now refers to the numerous noodle shops in the Philippines. At these economical and quick shops, one can buy a wide range of cooked noodle dishes.   DF

Noodles of China

To understand the history of noodles in China, it is necessary to know something of the history of the various cereals from which noodles can be made, and to realize that, originally and now, Chinese noodles have fallen into two distinct categories.

The earliest cereals used by the Chinese were MILLET and RICE, and the pair were known as *mi*. They were eaten primarily in the form of grains. However, either flour or starch could be produced from them; these, known as *fen*, were originally used mainly for cosmetic purposes, but from the 6th century onwards for food preparation, including the making of noodles. When this development occurred, the noodles so made were also called *fen*, and the term subsequently acquired an even wider meaning, embracing for example MUNG BEAN flour and SOYA BEAN flour (which provide two of the numerous non-cereal noodles which are popular in China).

Meanwhile, however, BARLEY and WHEAT had come into use. The collective term for them was **mai**. These two cereals were not normally eaten as grains but in products made from their flour. Once they had been processed to become flour, they were known as *mian*. This latter term became familiar later on (from the 12th century) as a general name for noodles, which it still is.

Wheat products were particularly esteemed and favoured when first introduced and were designated by the name *bing*. This name, which is often met in historical studies of Chinese noodles and the like, used to mean all wheat-flour products; but its meaning has now become restricted to pancakes and similar little round cakes or breads.

It is against this background that one must regard the hierarchy of noodles in China and the fact that those made from rice (in the south) and from wheat (in the north) are always in top place. It is noteworthy in this connection that *mian* (wheat noodles) can be made easily in the home, whereas *fen* (rice noodles) are nowadays always manufactured commercially.

Noodles were first popular in the north of China, where the climate favoured those cereal crops which are best adapted to noodle-making. The exact origins of noodles, however, are unclear; certain specialists think that they originated in C. Asia. However, once the concept was introduced to ancient China, it flourished because of its versatility—noodles are easily prepared from a variety of raw materials; they provide cheap and nutritious and filling food; they cook quickly; they may be eaten hot or cold; and in their dried form they may be stored for considerable periods.

It is likely that large-scale commercial production was already well under way in Han China, about AD 100, following the introduction of wheat-milling technology, probably imported from the Middle East. Noodles were first enjoyed by China's rulers, and then, as wheat became more widely available, by ordinary people. They acquired great importance in Chinese culture as they came to symbolize (by their length) longevity. It is for this reason that, in modern China, long noodles are always on the menu of a birthday celebration meal.

The diversity of Chinese noodles lies less in their shape (usually wide like fettucine (see PASTA SHAPES) or narrow like vermicelli) than in the number of food products they are made from, e.g. wheat, rice, beans, tapioca. Other ingredients are often added, particularly in making wheat noodles—e.g. egg, chicken extract, tiny shrimp or crab roe, spinach, LYE water (strong alkaline liquid, often rich in potassium carbonate from wood ashes).

A TRADITIONAL WAY OF MAKING NOODLES

MANY Chinese cooks, particularly in the northern provinces, have kept alive the traditional method of making long noodles by swinging them by hand. Yan-Kit So (1992) gives the following description of making noodles by hand:

The noodle master who knows the Way follows five distinct procedures. First, he adds cold water to strong flour, makes it into a smooth dough and leaves it for several hours or overnight. Second, he throws the dough on a hard work-top many times in order to strengthen the gluten before he rolls it out into a tubular dough. Third, with each hand holding one end of the dough, he picks it up as high as his own shoulder level and starts to stretch and elongate it horizontally, yet without letting it break in the centre. He puts it down, folds it back to more or less the original length, then takes it up again to repeat the rhythmic 'dancing' of the dough. This he repeats many times until he knows it is strong and elastic enough for him to proceed to the next step. Fourth, away from the work-top, he stretches the dough even longer, so long that it falls to form a semi-circle. Just as the onlooker holds his breath lest the dough fall to the floor, the noodle master, with one hand and great dexterity, swiftly passes one end of the dough to the other hand and, in the course of doing so, causes the semi-circle to twist into a rope hanging in mid-air. With both hands, he stretches out the rope again and repeats the rope-twisting several times until he feels that the dough is at last inherently strong and outwardly smooth enough for the splitting, the ultimate step that turns the dough into strands of noodles. Fifth, he places the rope back on the work-top and begins the splitting procedure. Magically, holding the ends in a special way and folding them back and forth, he splits the dough, doubling the strands every time. From 1 to 2, then 4, 8, 16, 32, 64, 128, 256; in eight splittings, he has a very impressive spread of individual noodles strands which he hangs across a thin bamboo pole to the thunderous applause of his audience. The action from dancing the dough to splitting it into noodle strands takes a consummate master about fifteen minutes, but it takes him about two years before he succeeds in harnessing the spontaneous energy to perform it.

This process gives the noodles a unique silky texture and they may be as fine as the 'angels' hair' grade (done by the most skilful operators). Noodles made by machine, of a coarser texture, are available in a great variety of shapes, either fresh or dried.

'LIKE NOODLES, BUT NOT NOODLES'

- **Gan si** (soya bean noodles). Made with SOYA BEAN curd pressed with a little wheat flour. Pale yellow in colour, the thickness of a wire coat-hanger, they are popular in vegetarian dishes as their protein content is very high. They are softened in a mixture of baking soda and water and then rinsed before serving, often in cold dishes.
- **Yang fen** (seaweed noodles). Quite similar in appearance to mung bean vermicelli, but thinner and more gelatinous and of a different nature, being 'threads' of AGAR-AGAR, a seaweed which occurs naturally in filamentous form.

- **Sha he fen** (rice noodles). Made from ground rice with water, these are popular in the eastern and southern provinces of China. They come in widths from 1.3 to 1.7 cm (0.5"). Fresh rice noodle sheets are used in DIM SUM.
- **Mi fen/lai fen** (rice sticks). Dry rice vermicelli in two thicknesses. *Lai fen* is the thicker variety, having a more chewy texture than the soft and delicate *mi fen*.
- **Fen si** (also fen-szu) (mung bean vermicelli). Mung bean starch is forced through a sieve to produce something like vermicelli; or processed to produce white translucent sheets of noodle which can then be cut or shaped in various ways (e.g. *fen pi* are round discs—semi-transparent and about 18 to 20 cm (7–8") in diameter—cut from the sheets). During the cooking process these mung bean noodles absorb a great deal of the cooking liquid and, being neutral in flavour, will take on that of the dish. They have various names in English, such as cellophane noodles, shining noodles, silver noodles, and glass noodles. One popular Sichuanese dish made with these noodles is called 'ants climbing a tree', a comical name characteristic of the Szechwan sense of humour. Tiny scraps of marinated pork cooked in a spicy sauce are arranged on top of the noodles and supposedly resemble ants in the branches of a tree.

Throughout China, noodles are now eaten as snacks and meals at almost any time of day. Fresh (wheat) noodles are made at home and both fresh and dried noodles can be purchased in most food stores. They can also be eaten in specialist noodle restaurants. Generally speaking, rice noodles are found in the south, wheat and BUCKWHEAT noodles in the north. In Guangdong egg noodles, uncommon elsewhere in China, are particularly popular.

Noodles are normally boiled first. They may subsequently be fried with other ingredients (see *chao mian* below).

The most usual way of eating noodles in modern China is, as it has long been, in soup. The combination is called *tang mian*. Small amounts of vegetables, meat, or seafood are usually added to the soup. An interesting version of noodles-plus-soup is *guo qiao mian* (crossing the bridge noodles), when the diner is given the noodles and the hot soup (with a

The following examples illustrate the numerous varieties and qualities of Chinese noodles:

- **Mian** (wheat noodles). These come in ribbons of various widths, sometimes as thin as vermicelli (e.g. *mian xian*, wheat threads, sold in skeins). They may be fresh or dried, and made with or without eggs. The name *mian* is often prefixed by a qualifying adjective denoting the type of noodle, i.e. how they are produced, their texture or flavouring. For example, *gan mian* means dried noodle and *xia mi mian* are noodles flavoured with shrimp. (Note that a qualifying adjective may also be used to describe how the noodle is prepared or served, e.g. *Dandan mian*, which is a Sichuan noodle dish prepared with a special sauce.)

layer of fat floating on the top which keeps in the heat) in two separate bowls. The origin of the name is the subject of more than one legend. It is said, for example, that in the days of the imperial court, when a bridge divided the emperor's palace from the rest of Beijing, the cook had to walk from the kitchen, which was outside the walls of the Heavenly City, over the bridge and into the palace, carrying a pot of hot water and the noodles. The noodles were dropped into the pot just as the cook reached the bridge. By the time the pot arrived at the emperor's table, the noodles were ready and still hot. However, the true explanation of the name seems to be that the diner makes a 'bridge' in passing the noodles from their bowl into the soup bowl.

Another soup-noodles dish is called *wo mian*, meaning nest noodles—there is usually a poached egg in the centre of the nest of noodles in the soup, and the dish is favoured for convalescents.

Previously boiled noodles are also stir fried with meat and vegetables. The Chinese term is *chao mian*, from which the English term CHOW MEIN comes.

The third common way of serving noodles is on a dish with meat, seafood, or vegetables, with some sort of sauce or dressing poured over the whole. The dish may be hot or cold. There is a popular sauce in Beijing called *tianmianjiang*, made by a complex process involving two fermentations, which yields a thickish brown product of a sweet and sour nature.

In addition there is the range of WONTON dishes. Wonton wrappers or skins, made from wheat flour and egg (sometimes treated with lye water), are thin, pastry-like wrappings, stretched like freshly made noodles, which can be stuffed with minced meat and other fillings and then either poached in bouillon, or (less often) fried. They are usually larger than western filled pasta (of which RAVIOLI are typical).

Noodles of Japan

Menrui is the collective term for noodles in Japan. When a particular type of noodles are referred to, they are called *men*, which derives from the Chinese word *mien* or *mian*.

It is generally accepted that *menrui* was first introduced into Japan from China during the Nara period (710–94). The original *menrui*, however, seems to have been more like sweet DUMPLINGS than what we call noodles. (These dumplings were called *konton*, the word whose original meaning is 'chaos', presumably because they had no definite shape. This is the same word as the Chinese *hun-t'un*, now familiar as WONTON. Later the name changed from *konton* to *undon*, and eventually UDON.) It is not known when the transformation from dumplings to noodles took place. In any case, it must have been a gradual process.

In time the custom of eating grain in pasta form spread throughout the country as a means of supplementing or, at times of famine, replacing boiled RICE as the staple food. This applied particularly to noodles made of BUCKWHEAT, which thrives in a cold climate where rice cannot grow. As for wheat noodles, their popularity may well have been partly due to the fact that the type of wheat produced in Japan, as in Italy, is not suitable for making bread.

Unlike the Chinese, the Japanese have almost never used rice for making noodles, although there is a Japanese term, *maifun* (the Chinese *mi fen*), for rice noodles. Plain boiled rice has always been so highly esteemed as a food that the Japanese have had no reason to turn it into anything else. Thus, while noodles have occupied an important place in Japanese diet, they have been mostly eaten in lieu of, or in addition to, boiled rice, never challenging the latter's supremacy. The role of noodles remains basically unchanged; they are popular snacks and light meals.

The Chinese practice of eating noodles on special occasions as a symbol of longevity is also found in Japan. A typical example is the custom of eating soba on New Year's Eve. Until not so long ago people who had moved house would distribute soba to their new neighbours by way of greetings.

There are now **five main types** of Japanese noodles, with many regional variations. These are as follows, the first two being the most important:

- SOBA, thin, buckwheat noodles, light brown in colour. Though it is possible to make soba purely of buckwheat flour (*kisoba*, or 'pure soba', preferred by connoisseurs), it is usual to add some wheat flour to the buckwheat in order to make the dough less crumbly.
- UDON, wheat-flour noodles, fairly thick, either round or square in section, and with a soft but slightly chewy texture. They are generally preferred in Osaka and W. Japan.
- *kishimen*, also called *himokawa*: like udon except that it comes in a flat, ribbon-like shape. The region around Nagoya, halfway between Tokyo and Osaka, is famous for this.
- *hiyamugi*, very fine, vermicelli-like noodles made of wheat flour.
- SOMEN, similar to *hiyamugi*, but in this case, the rolled-out dough is thinly coated with vegetable oil before being made into noodles.

Nowadays noodles are mostly machine made and are sold either fresh, boiled, or dried. (*Hiyamugi* and somen are always sold dried.) However, some noodle restaurants make a speciality of hand-made noodles, and in rural areas the art of making noodles at home is still alive.

There are two basic ways of serving soba and udon: *mori* and *kake*. In *mori* (literally 'to pile up') the boiled noodles are served with a cold dipping sauce (*tsukejiru*) made of DASHI, SOY SAUCE, and MIRIN. Soba is often served in this way but with small bits of NORI (laver dried like paper) sprinkled over it. Then it is called *zaru*. In *kake* (literally 'to pour over') the noodles are served hot in soup (*kakejiru*) similar to *tsukejiru* in a deep bowl. There are many variations on the theme of *kake*, depending on the toppings added to the noodles—prawn TEMPURA, *aburaage* (fried bean curd), pieces of chicken, a raw egg, etc.

Kishimen is eaten like udon.

Hiyamugi and somen are very much summer food. They are normally served chilled, often floating in iced water in a large glass bowl, and eaten with dipping sauce. Occasionally somen is eaten hot, in which case it is called nyumen.

CHINESE-STYLE NOODLES IN JAPAN

Any account of Japanese noodles is hardly complete without a mention of Chinese (or Chinese-style) noodles. It was chiefly after the end of the Second World War that they came to be eaten commonly in Japan, but they have now nearly surpassed the traditional Japanese noodles in popularity—in particular among the younger generations. There are two main types. One is *ramen*—thin, yellow, sometimes wavy wheat-flour noodles served in soup, with toppings like pieces of *ch'a-shiu* (Chinese barbecued pork). Instant *ramen*—fried noodles with a sachet of soup base that can be cooked in a few minutes—is extremely popular among the Japanese. The other type is *yakisoba*, similar to the CHOW MEIN of Chinese restaurants abroad.

Noodles are eaten perhaps more often in restaurants than at home—in urban areas, at any rate. Everywhere there is a restaurant which specializes in noodle dishes and which usually also delivers freshly cooked noodles. In the larger cities noodle stands are commonly found in railway stations, department stores, universities, etc. *Ramen* vendors who set up their stalls at street corners at night are also a usual feature of city life.

It is remarkable that, alone among Japanese foods, noodles are to be eaten in noisy, slurping fashion.

For products which are not considered by the Japanese to be true noodles, but are noodle-like and apt to be referred to by non-Japanese as noodles, see HARUSAME and *shirataki* (described under KONNYAKU).   (KA)

---

annually. The Japanese liking for nori can be traced back as far as the 8th century AD; and by the 17th century it was being cultivated in some of the inlets and estuaries which abound on the Japanese coasts. This, however, was a chancy business. In the last two months of the year, the plants grew to their maximum size, permitting a lucrative harvest in December and January. But no one knew what happened in the summer months, when all trace of nori disappeared; and no one could be sure that a seed-bed, rented from the owner as was the custom, would perform consistently. It might be very prolific in one year and barren in the next.

Without knowledge of the lifecycle of the plant, the nori farmers were unable to remedy this situation. Moreover, the increased pollution of the waters over the seed-beds was, by the late 1940s, threatening to extinguish the farming completely. Fortunately, a former student of Manchester University in England, Dr Kathleen Drew, had meanwhile been investigating what happened to the nori spores in the summer. She worked in Wales, being concerned to discover how laver reproduced itself. In 1949 she published a paper which contained the answer. The spores burrowed into the tiny pores and crevices of sea shells, where they grew into tiny pink, threadlike organisms. When the weather turned cold, these detached themselves, found a new anchorage and established themselves in readiness for the growing season. Dr Drew was also able to demonstrate that eggshells were just as suitable breeding places as oyster shells.

The Japanese were quick to follow up the discovery of 'Kassurine-San', as they knew Dr Drew, and had developed within a short space of time the system which is now followed for cultivating nori. Shells are suspended in nets in the water, and attract the spores which can develop safely in these artificial homes. As a result, production of nori in Japan increased tenfold from 1950 to 1980. Murray Sayle, in an essay on the subject, records the manner in which the Japanese do honour to the saviour of their nori. In 1963 a bronze monument was unveiled on a hill overlooking the Bay of Shimbara, which abounded in nori farms operating on the principle which she had discovered. 'On April 14 every year . . . Dr Drew is remembered in a touching ceremony in which the local nori farmers put her gown and mortar-board on her monument, hoist a Union Jack which has been made by local housewives . . . and place a tribute of nori from the current year's crop at her feet.'

In Japan nori is mostly sold in the form of thin paper-like sheets called *hoshi-nori*. Before being eaten, each sheet is held over fire for a few seconds so that it may become crisp and flavoursome (and turns dark green). Nori is sometimes eaten by itself (dipped in SOY SAUCE) or with rice; it can also be used for TEMPURA or cooked with soy sauce and made into a thick, black mush. But perhaps the two commonest ways of using nori are for *norimaki* (nori-roll—vinegared rice with some savoury morsel is made into a roll and wrapped in a sheet of nori) and *omusubi* (a rice ball with a pickled Japanese apricot inside is wrapped with a square of nori). These are typical picnic foods in Japan; when rice is wrapped with nori, you can eat it with your fingers without making them sticky. Nori also serves as a wrapper for SUSHI and the like. And it is often used to produce decorative effects on seafood platters. The Japanese rightly believe that, besides having a fine marine flavour and an interesting texture, nori is very good for them; it is a good source of iodine, calcium, iron, and other minerals which the body requires, besides providing a useful amount of protein which is of particular value in a vegetarian diet.

The name nori, as already noted, is used all by itself as an English-language name for *Porphyra* spp. In Japanese, however, nori refers to various species, some belonging to other genera, and therefore occurs with prefixes which tell one exactly what is meant. *Asakusa-nori* is purple laver (*P. tenera*), usually sold in sheet form. *Ogonori, funori, komenori* are all names for red algae of other genera. So is *tosakanori* (*Meristotheca papulosa*), an expensive product which may also be met in green form (having been treated with wood ash and then boiled) or white (bleached to make it look better with fish). AWO-NORI or *aonori* (green nori) is also a seaweed of another genus.

Some prefixes relate to form or use. *Yaki-nori* is toasted sheets; *sushi-nori* is the sheet used for SUSHI.

Cultivation of nori is mainly carried out in Japan, but it has also been established in N. America and a start has been made in W. Europe.

NORWAY is a mountainous country with only small areas of arable land along the coast and in the valleys. The coastline is long, with fjords cutting deep into the land. The Gulf Stream provides a better climate than could otherwise be expected in a northern country. Still, the growing season is short, and the soil unproductive during much of the year.

Transport along the coast and to inland areas used to be difficult for much of the year. This made it necessary to rely on conserving almost all food for later use. Farm animals were usually slaughtered in the autumn: the meat would keep better during the cold season. The harvesting of foods from the ocean, lakes, forests, and mountains was also seasonal. Fish, game, and wild berries had to be conserved for use during the rest of the year.

Cereals, milk and milk products were the most important elements of the older Norwegian diet. Barley and oats, better adapted to the climate than wheat, were the most common grains. Porridge and gruel were made from them, boiled with water or milk, or for special occasions with sour cream.

Bread, in the form of thin, crisp flatbread, was made from the same grains. It would keep for months and was baked only a few times a year. *Lefse* is softened before use, but otherwise similar to flatbread. More recent variations are *lompe* and *potetlefse*, both soft and made with potatoes. Leavened bread only replaced flatbread as the main type of bread by the end of the 19th century. The most common varieties in today's bakeries are *kneippbrød* (named after a German clergyman and doctor Sebastian Kneipp) and *franskbrød* ('French bread'), names that reflect its short tradition.

Different types of soured milk (usually cow's milk, sometimes goat's and sheep's) were used in the diet along with cheeses, butter, and whey. *Blande*, a soured milk mixed with water, was the daily drink. The cheeses were most often sour-milk cheeses: *pultost* is a ripened, unpressed curd cheese with a strong taste; GAMMELOST is a semi-hard cheese with a grainy texture, dark brown in colour. Several types of brown, sweet, whey cheese, *mysost*, are made, originally a way of conserving and using the whey. Nowadays milk or cream are often added.

The wide fertile valleys of E. Norway were best suited to the keeping of cattle. In the mountains and fjords sheep and goats were more common, but even the smallest farms usually had a cow or two. Salted and dried meat was eaten uncooked, while brine-salted meat was boiled. *Spekemat*, assorted cured meat, is used today as a snack, or as a party food. *Fenalår*, salted, dried, and occasionally smoked leg of lamb, is one of the more popular types. The most popular meat dish is *kjøttkaker*, minced beef patties, fried and served in a brown sauce. *Mors kjøttkaker*, the beef patties made by one's own mother, are always considered to be the best. Also highly regarded is *fårikål*, a mutton and cabbage stew.

Large uninhabited forests and mountain areas have supported a rich wildlife and provided opportunities for hunting (elk, reindeer, red and roe deer, hare, ptarmigan, black grouse, capercaillie).

There has always been a good supply of fish from lakes and rivers and from Norway's long coastline. COD and HERRING have been the most important species. Herring, called 'silver of the seas', has at times been eaten up to four times a day, although its availability has varied greatly. Herring used to be salted, dried, or (in the past) fermented in a light brine. Nowadays herring is most frequently encountered at breakfast tables and buffets, pickled and marinated in a variety of sauces. Cod was salted, dried, or both. *Klippfisk* (salted and dried, originally by laying it on cliffs) and *tørrfisk* (STOCKFISH, dried but not salted) are still produced in large quantities. Stockfish and *klippfisk* have been used in many ways, beaten till soft and eaten with butter, or boiled. One of the most popular dishes is LUTEFISK, stockfish softened in a solution of lye.

One of the greatest changes in the diet was brought about by the introduction of the potato in the middle of the 18th century. It could be grown successfully over larger areas than cereals, and in less than a century it was found on every dinner table. In the late 19th century Norwegians ate 144 kg (315 lb) of potatoes and 10 kg (22 lb) of other vegetables each per year, while the average in Paris was 22 kg (48 lb) of potatoes and 118 kg (260 lb) of other vegetables. Potatoes were mostly boiled, but also used in a variety of other ways. *Komler*, *komper*, or *raspeball* are potato dumplings, eaten with meat, or made with a filling of pork. After the Second World War potato consumption decreased, but many still feel that a dinner without potatoes is not a proper one.

The first Norwegian cookery book, written by Maren Elisabeth Bang (1797–1884), was published anonymously in Oslo in 1831. At this time the demand for cookery instructions and recipes was growing, and 30 editions of cookery books were published during the next 15 years. The household and cookery book by Hanna Winsnes (1789–1872), first published in Oslo in 1845, became the classic of the 19th century. These first books contained mostly recipes taken from foreign authors, as local dishes were familiar to everyone, and often not considered fine enough to be included.

Modern refrigeration techniques led to a decline in some of the old preservation methods and partly wiped out seasonal variations in the diet. Recently the interest in traditional foods has been renewed and some of the old dishes revived: the *lutefisk* already mentioned, RAKEFISK, and *smalahove* (sheep's heads). Popular seasonal foods are fresh lamb in September, fresh boiled cod in winter, fried mackerel and rhubarb soup in May, and fresh strawberries with cream in summer. It is interesting that almost all dishes considered truly Norwegian originated as peasant foods, and did not come from the upper classes.   OF

READING: Grøn (1927, 1942); Astri Riddervold (1990a, 1993); Notaker (1993); Osa and Ulltveit (1993).

NORWAY LOBSTER or Dublin Bay prawn (and *langoustine* in French), *Nephrops norvegicus*, a small lobster which is found from Iceland down to Morocco, and in the W. and C. Mediterranean, especially the Adriatic. Its maximum length, not counting the claws, is 24 cm (9–10"). Its carapace is pink, rose, or orange-red, often quite pale, and its claws are banded in red and white. It lives on a muddy sea bottom, in burrows, from which it emerges at night to seek food.

The name Norway lobster has a simple explanation: this CRUSTACEAN is abundant

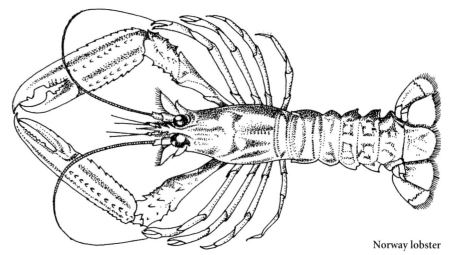

Norway lobster

on the coast of Norway. It owes its second name to the circumstance that fishing boats coming into Dublin Bay often had a catch of it on board, which was disposed of to street vendors and hawked as 'Dublin Bay prawns'; or, say some, because they were caught in Dublin Bay itself. Whatever the truth of the matter, the Irish were ahead of the British in eating the creature, since it was not until the 1950s that British fishermen began to think it worth while landing it. (It is nonetheless to be remarked that Lord, 1867, stated that many Norway lobsters were imported and that for every regular lobster sold at Billingsgate fish market, four Norway lobsters were sold. This suggests considerable interest and consumption in the 19th century.)

In the latter part of the 20th century the Norway lobster became a standard item on British menus, usually under the Italian name **scampi**. This reflects the fact that Italians in the Adriatic had for long appreciated it, and had many recipes for scampi cooked in this or that way, which became familiar to tourists.

The Norway lobster has several relations in S. American waters. The name 'lobsterette' is sometimes used for them.

Norway lobsters can be cooked like large prawns, e.g. by brushing them with olive oil and grilling them.

NOSTOC *Nostoc commune*, a mysterious food plant, whose name was invented, apparently out of the blue, by the 16th-century Swiss alchemist and medical writer Paracelsus. It is a blue-green alga, a primitive plant of the same class as SEAWEEDS or the green slime seen on rocks and jetties when uncovered by the sea at low tide. However, nostoc also grows inland, usually on rocks or soil made damp by fresh water. Its unexpected arrival and odd, gelatinous, beaded form have earned it a place among the heterogeneous substances which are called MANNA. It was viewed with horror in medieval Europe, where it was thought to be the 'stinking tawney jelly of a fallen planet, or the nocturnal solution of some plethorical and wanton star' (Lovelock, 1972). Old British names are 'star jelly' and 'will-o'-the wisp'.

The Chinese cultivate nostoc, since its gelatinous texture appeals to their palate. Besides the most common form of *N. commune*, which forms glistening, lumpy beads, there is a more stringy variety, var *flagelliforme*. Both these are also eaten in Japan and Java, while a different species, *N. ellipsosporum*, is eaten in C. Asia.

Nostoc is nutritious, containing fair amounts of protein and vitamin C. Like seaweeds, it contains a large amount of vegetable gum which gives it its texture.

NOSTRALE AND NOSTRANO are overlapping names for a large group of N. Italian cheeses which are generally of medium size, soft, round, and aromatic, with a relatively high fat content. They can be considered as members of the large family of ASIAGO/Vezzena cheeses. Nostrale is the name favoured in the NE Alpine region, and Nostrano is the common name of the region of Venice and Lombardy.

These cheeses exhibit many variations, but almost all are both eaten at table and used in cookery. Among the better known are *Nostrale di val di Susa* and *Nostrano trentino*.

NOUGAT the French and also English name, derived from the Latin *nux* (nut), for a confection of boiled honey and/or sugar syrup, mixed with beaten egg white, nuts, and preserved fruit. The ancestry of nougat can plausibly be traced back to medieval times and, beyond that, to early Arab sweetmeats.

Since the beginning of the 18th century, and possibly earlier, production of nougat has been particularly associated with the French town Montelimar (Rhône-Alpes); hence the occasional use of the word 'Montelimar' as a synonym for 'nougat' in English. This association has been the subject of a study by Durand (1993).

To make the traditional Montelimar nougat, honey and sugar are cooked to a temperature between 132 and 143 °C (270–290 °F) ('soft crack': see SUGAR BOILING) and whisked into the egg whites. Almonds (28%), pistachio (2%), and vanilla extract must be added at the end. The texture of the finished product—chewy or hard—is dictated by the temperature to which the sugar syrup is boiled, and the amount of sugar which is 'inverted' during this process (see SUGAR BOILING).

Italian *torrone* and Spanish *turrón* are, essentially, other forms of nougat. The similarity was recognized as long ago as 1607 when the anonymous author of *Le Thresor de Santé* bracketed together *nogats & torrons* as a pleasant confection.

See also BRITTLE; DIVINITY.
READING: IPCF volume on Rhône-Alpes (1995).

NOUVELLE CUISINE a recurring term in the history of French cookery. As explained in FRANCE: NATIONAL AND REGIONAL CUISINES, it first came to prominence in the 18th century, when Vincent La Chapelle described the simplified style of cooking recommended in his *Cuisine moderne* (1733) as a 'nouvelle cuisine'. This remained in vogue until the early 19th century. It was in the 1970s that the next 'rebellion' took place, producing the nouvelle cuisine which has, for better or for worse, altered the evolution of professional cooking in the western world during the closing decades of the century.

This latest nouvelle cuisine has its admirers and its critics, plus a lot of people who have mixed feelings about it, especially since it started to develop its own clichés, and a few aspects which look, perhaps, more like food for rebellion than rebels' food. Nonetheless, it is an important phenomenon and deserves to be defined here in an authoritative manner, by Henri Gault (1996), on the lines of a paper which he prepared for presentation at Oxford University in 1995.

Gault believes that he 'in all innocence produced a veritable manifesto' for the movement in the form of an article he wrote in 1973. At that time he felt that traditional French cuisine was in a rotten state. Yet there were grounds for hope. The kitchen floor tiles were beginning, just perceptibly, to crack and buckle under the influence of movements of the tectonic plates underneath; and Gault could foresee that these exciting tremors would soon shake up the whole culinary scene, thanks to some brilliant young chefs with new ideas.

Gault suggested that the revolutionary movement could be defined in ten points, here summarized:

- Cooking time reduced for most fish, for all shellfish, for poultry with brown meat and game, for roasts, veal, some green vegetables, pasta.
- New utilization of products. Our epoch of overproduction and bastardized technology had been poisoning or eliminating many valuable products. Instead of masking, with aggressive sauces, these asepticized and rigorously insipid foods, the new chefs were getting up early and going to the market in search of genuine material.
- Reduction of choice on menus. 'In Paris one is beginning to see less of those gigantic menus with a ridiculously varied choice, which necessitate huge stocks and a regrettable amount of cold storage.'
- Less use of refrigeration, which had been abused by the old school.
- Use of advanced technology. The young chefs, despite being cautious about refrigeration, would not 'let out cries like violated virgins at the sight of all the processes and machinery of cooking, conservation, cleaning and comfort' that are now available.
- A ban on obsolete and boring principles, such as rules about marinating game. 'The new chefs serve game hung but fresh and the spices that covered up the shameful fermentations have disappeared from their arsenal.'
- Banishment of terrible brown sauces and white sauces, 'these espagnoles, périgueux,

financières, grand-veneur, béchamel, mornay that have assassinated so many livers and covered up so many insipid pieces of meat'.

- Application of knowledge about dietetics. 'Without bowing to the inconsistencies of men in a hurry and women on a diet, they are discovering the pleasures of light dishes, of well made salads, of fresh vegetables simply cooked, of rare meat.'
- Avoiding the danger of deceitful presentations, 'of which the redoubtable [but now-to-be-reproached] Carême launched the fashion 150 years ago. In contrast, the new chefs like to adorn and embellish, but they understand the limits which must not be passed and the aesthetics of simplicity—as well as the vanity of sonorous nomenclature.'
- Invention. 'It has been said that for thousands of years and in particular during the 19th century, everything had been tried and established: all the equipment, the cooking methods, the successful combinations. Well, this is false. It is already sixty years since Jules Maincave, farsighted creature of genius, had the idea of replacing vinaigrette with a mixture of pork jus and rum, of marrying chicken with lily of the valley, of veal à l'absinthe. . . . There are millions of dishes that can be created and certainly hundreds of them that will survive.'

Such, in brief, was the 'manifesto'. Two decades later, it is interesting to consider which of the planks in the platform are now fully accepted, indeed perhaps taken for granted, and which are not. It is also necessary to take into account three further points which Gault himself made, looking back on his 'manifesto' and taking into account what had happened since.

- In addition to his 'ten commandments' he should have added an eleventh, the spirit of friendship and co-operation which animated the new chefs.
- He had forgotten to say anything about the need to preserve the achievements of the past and to keep alive traditional country cuisines. Alas, much had been lost, irrevocably.
- 'This nouvelle cuisine, wishing to be without roots and open to every influence, was the band wagon on to which jumped, along with the authentic cooks, a crowd of mountebanks, antiquarians, society women, fantasists and tricksters who did not give the developing movement a good reputation. Furthermore fashions, mannerisms and trickery attached themselves to this new culinary philosophy: minuscule portions; systematic under-cooking; abuses of techniques in themselves interesting (mousses, turned vegetables, coulis); inopportune marriages

of sugar, salt and exotic spices; excessive homage paid to the decoration of dishes and "painting on the plate"; and ridiculous or dishonest names of dishes.'

NOYAU the French word for a fruit stone, has also come to mean a liqueur or syrup which is used as a flavouring. This has been well described by Stobart (1980):

Noyau—To good peasants who do not like to waste anything, the kernels of apricots, peaches, plums and cherries present a challenge. Like bitter almonds they contain a glucoside which, when mixed with water (or the saliva in the mouth) is converted by enzymes into a mixture of benzaldehyde and deadly poisonous hydro-cyanic acid. Noyau (from the French *noyau*, a fruit stone) is a liqueur, cordial and useful flavouring, which consists essentially of a sugar syrup, usually with alcohol, flavoured with macerated kernels or sometimes with peach leaves or bitter almonds, which contain similar principles. Noyau had a reputation for being 'unwholesome'—naturally so, if there was cyanide in it. However, a quick boil will drive off the volatile poison, leaving only a delicate taste of benzaldehyde behind.

NUT BISCUITS are a large group within the multifarious category of BISCUIT.

In some of these biscuits ground-up nuts, usually almonds, replace some or all of the flour. The simplest are known in English as MACAROON or RATAFIA, made from ground almonds mixed with sugar and egg white and baked crisp. Baked nut mixtures appeared in English cookery books at the beginning of the 17th century when they were part of the banquet, a selection of sweetmeats and sweet wines taken at the end of a meal. They continued to be popular through the 18th century when a softer almond sweetmeat, called a rout biscuit ('rout' was an 18th-century term for a party), became fashionable. These were not really biscuits but little MARZIPAN shapes decorated with nuts, candied fruit, chocolate, and glaze. They were still being made at the end of the 19th century, shaped from a mixture of almonds, sponge cake crumbs, sugar, and egg yolks. They were the predecessors of the tiny biscuits and cakes to which the name PETIT FOUR applies.

A wider range of nut biscuits, many of which verge on being sugar CONFECTIONERY, are specialities of the Mediterranean littoral, where the Italians and Provençal French have made a particular speciality of them. 'Amaretto' (see MACAROON) is the generic Italian name for macaroon, usually almond based, sometimes flavoured with bitter almonds or apricot kernels (or pine nut kernels—*pinoccate*, pine nut macaroons, are a Christmas speciality of Perugia). An almond mixture spread on wafers and cut in a lozenge shape forms the basis of the softer,

more cakelike *ricciarello*, a speciality of Siena. The shape and wafer base of this confection relate it to the *calisson* of Aix-en-Provence, a soft, iced marzipan-like confection of almonds and candied fruit. Another nut biscuit is the *croissant de Provence*, crescent shaped and made from almonds, sugar, egg white, and apricot jam, coated with chopped almonds; a variation called *pignoulat* includes pine nuts as well as almonds.

Spanish and Portuguese nut confections related to marzipan and macaroons tend to be richer, mixed with whole eggs or egg yolks instead of whites. Many are shaped on wafer bases, such as the cinnamon-spiced *bollo Eulalia* of Spain, and the innumerable egg yolk and almond specialities of Portuguese convents and confectioners.

Italian nut biscuits which are richer and more elaborate than amaretti include the *bacio di dama* (lady's kiss), made of equal weights of ground almonds, flour, sugar, and butter, flavoured with sweet wine. The small, round biscuits are sandwiched together with chocolate. *Fave alla veneziana* (*fava* is Italian for broad bean, because of this small sweet biscuit's shape), traditionally sold in Venice during November, are based on a sugared pine nut paste. From Naples come diamond-shaped *mostaccioli* (moustaches) made from almonds and walnuts, with honey, cinnamon, pepper, and orange flower water among the ingredients.

Some nut biscuits are based on egg and sugar foams. Several of this type are made in Germany. Most famous are *Nürnberger Elisenlebkuchen* (see LEBKUCHEN).

Leckerli have been well described by Sarah Kelly (1985):

The word lecker, which in High German means 'delicious', becomes a noun in Switzerland, where it is applied to a wide variety of finger-length and rectangular biscuits that are baked for holidays. While many cities, including Bern and Zurich, have their own versions—each quite different and not necessarily spicy—the honey and spice version from Basel is certainly the most famous. In fact, one bakery in Basel produces nothing but Leckerli which are shipped all over the world in charming tin drum containers, symbolizing the Basel Fastnacht (carnival), a three-day pre-Lenten celebration, when the haunting music of pipes and drums, played by costumed Baselers, fills the air.

The Leckerli of Basle contain almonds but are not especially nutty. Those made in Bern (*Berner Haselnüssleckerli*) are based on hazelnuts and almonds with peel and spices. *Züri Leckerli*, of Zurich, are essentially marzipan biscuits, made with almond alone or almond and hazelnut. They come in four colours, corresponding to four flavours: white (rose water), pale beige (cinnamon), dark brown (chocolate), and rose red (powdered SANDALWOOD is the traditional colouring agent for these). All are decoratively moulded before being baked.

One nut biscuit which has developed in a slightly different manner is the FLORENTINE, which incorporates flaked almonds, candied peel, and dried fruit, and is coated with chocolate, 'brushed' to make wavy lines. These rich, chewy delicacies are not peculiar to Florence and are made everywhere.

Nut pastes also make fillings for many biscuits and pastries, from the BAKLAVA of the Near East to the Norwegian biscuits called *bordstabler* (stacks of planks) made from a rich whisked dough filled with almond paste, baked in thin oblongs, and presented in a square stack.   LM

NUTMEG one of the two spices obtained from the nutmeg tree, *Myristica fragrans*; the other is MACE. The tree is native to the Moluccas in Indonesia, and is also cultivated in Grenada in the W. Indies. The fruit which encloses the mace and nutmeg is itself edible; see NUTMEG FRUIT.

There is no record of nutmeg being known in classical Greece or Rome, but it had reached Constantinople by the 9th century AD, when St Theodore the Studite allowed the monks who lived by his Rule to sprinkle it on their PEASE PUDDING on non-meat days. By the 12th century it and mace were well known in Europe. When the Portuguese reached the Moluccas in 1514 they were able to acquire a monopoly in the trade, which they held for almost a century.

At the beginning of the 17th century the Dutch wrested control from them and laid the foundation of the Dutch E. Indian empire in the Bandanese island of Nehra, part of the Moluccas. They maintained their monopoly for over 150 years, but in 1770 a French expedition returned to Mauritius with nutmeg seedlings, and the first French nutmeg was picked eight years later. The British, who occupied the Moluccas from 1796 to 1802, planted nutmegs in Penang and

thereafter in other British possessions with seemingly suitable conditions, but it was not until the 1860s that cultivation of nutmegs in Grenada, which turned out to be the most suitable place for them, became significant.

The trees thrive in tropical conditions near the sea, and seem to prefer volcanic soils, as in the Moluccas and Grenada. They start to bear fruit between 10 and 15 years of age, and continue to do so for another 30 or 40. The nutmeg tree may be either male or female, and in the plantations one male tree is needed to ensure pollination of about a dozen females. Nutmeg is the brown kernel of the nutlike seed contained in the fruit borne by the female trees.

In **processing**, the sheath or aril surrounding the seed is first removed (to become mace). Then the seed, which has a hard shell and is usually referred to as a nut, is dried. After drying the kernel will usually rattle in the shell. The nuts are then cracked and the kernels extracted to be sorted into sound nutmegs and unsatisfactory ones. They are soft brown in colour and speckled like an egg.

The chemistry of nutmeg is interesting. Myristicin is one of the substances responsible for the 'warm' taste and special flavour of nutmeg. It has a narcotic effect, not noticeable in the small quantities used by cooks; but consumption of a large amount could produce a 'high'. (See also NUTMEG FRUIT.)

The **chemistry** of nutmeg is such that aroma and flavour disappear quickly once a nutmeg is grated. Hence the profusion of nutmeg graters, intended to be used immediately before the need arises. These graters are often made, felicitously, in the form of a mace.

Usage varies quite widely from one country to another. In Britain, for example, nutmeg is used for a number of milk dishes (RICE PUDDINGS, egg CUSTARDS, etc.) and in some cakes and beverages. In the

Netherlands and Scandinavia it is also used, much more freely than in Britain, for vegetable dishes, including mashed potato and spinach; and may also turn up with pineapple and some seafood items. In France and Italy it may appear in a BÉCHAMEL sauce, depending on the end use of the sauce.

NUTMEG FRUIT *Myristica fragrans*, normally thought of as just the receptacle from which the valuable spices NUTMEG and MACE are extracted, does have edible flesh, sometimes referred to as the 'fruit-wall'.

In Sulawesi the entire fruit is peeled and split into two and fruit halves (after the mace and nutmeg are removed) are spread out, sprinkled with palm sugar, and left for three or four days in the sun. After this treatment they have become translucent, with a pale brown tinge from the sugar, and are slightly fermented. They can be eaten as they are, as a snack food or at the end of a meal.

The dried fruit could be described as looking a little bit like crystallized pear or ginger, and the taste and feel in the mouth are a bit like crystallized ginger. The names used in Indonesia are *manisan pala* and *pala manis*, evidently two versions of the same name, *manis* meaning sweet.

Eating an unusually large amount of nutmeg can produce a 'high', and the same effect (no doubt attributable to the same chemical substance) occurs if much of the fruit is eaten. An incident in the 1990s, involving two young British visitors to Sulawesi who ate a substantial amount of the fruit, left them convinced that it had had an APHRODISIAC effect. This impression was heightened by the hilarity accompanying their consumption of the fruit in the market place. Consideration was subsequently given to their testimony by a London-based organization devoted to the study of spices, but no definite conclusion was reached. It was noted that Burkill (1965–6), who gives a characteristically thorough description of the processing and candying of the fruit, makes only the briefest of allusions to possible aphrodisiac properties. Nor has there been any suggestion that the jam made from the fruits in Sri Lanka has any special attributes of this sort.

NUTRITION the supply and uptake of nourishment, has been studied since ancient times. The Greek physician Hippocrates, who lived in the 5th century BC, and his followers over the next two centuries examined the connection between diet and health; many of their writings survive. Unfortunately they pursued the doctrine of the 'FOUR HUMOURS' (see also COMPOSITION

Nutmeg

Fruit cut open to reveal mace

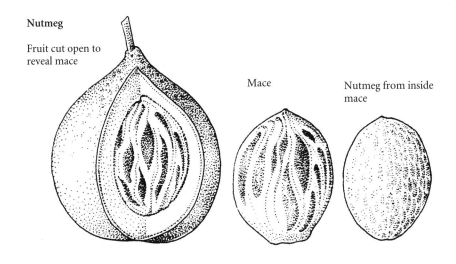

Mace

Nutmeg from inside mace

OF FOODS), which did much harm for many centuries afterwards. Chinese philosophers also studied nutrition, regarding all foods as having an influence on health so that there was no real distinction between foods and medicines; their beliefs live on in traditional Chinese medicine.

Only at the end of the 18th century did the science of nutrition begin to break free of the old theories. Gradually the basic constituents of food—PROTEINS, CARBOHYDRATES, and FATS AND OILS—came to be understood. This coincided with the Industrial Revolution, which over the following decades brought millions of people into towns, where they lived on foods increasingly impoverished by new techniques of food processing, and often heavily adulterated. The health of the working population declined. In Britain at the end of the 19th century, when large numbers of young men were called up to fight in the Boer War, they were found to be in such miserable condition that a commission of inquiry was set up. Its report (Watt Smith, *Physical Deterioration: Its Causes and Cure*, HMSO, 1907) recommended that schools should give instruction to both boys and girls in nutritional science. The School Meals Act of 1906 enabled local councils to provide meals for needy children.

At this time the role of VITAMINS and MINERALS in diet was becoming clear so that deficiency diseases such as rickets, once widespread, could be avoided. The British Medical Association produced the first recommendations for minimum requirements of nutrients in time for the food rationing imposed in the First World War to be organized on sensible lines.

After the war and at least until the slump of the 1930s, it was clear that public nutrition was much improved—though this was due more to prosperity than to ordinary people's knowledge of what constituted a healthy diet.

The first comprehensive control of public nutrition was in Britain during the Second World War. The nation was far from self-sufficient in food, but imports were now curtailed by submarine attacks on convoys. Basic foods were strictly rationed: meat including bacon and ham, eggs, fats of all kinds, cheese, sugar, even tea. Other foods were controlled by a system of 'points' to prevent hoarding. The Ministry of Food set up a Food Advice Division under Sir Jack Drummond, which issued information through advertisements, films, and the radio. Food advice centres in large towns gave practical demonstrations of how to make adequate meals from scanty supplies. All this sound guidance was mocked and resented, but reluctantly followed. In 1941 the Vitamin Welfare Scheme was set up to issue cheap milk, concentrated orange juice, cod liver oil, and vitamin A and D tablets to pregnant women and children under 5. The result, to everyone's surprise, was that, in spite of severe shortages of almost everything, public health improved to levels not seen before or since.

In western nations after the war, returning prosperity and the increasing availability of imported foods brought to ordinary people luxuries previously only for the rich. Ordinary people, too, began increasingly to suffer from the effects of overindulgence, and there was concern about the rate of heart disease. The public was increasingly bombarded with nutritional information from the Ministry of Health in Britain, the US Surgeon General, and pundits of all kinds. Much of this conflicted; for example, British and American lists of minimum daily requirements of vitamins and minerals were different, and still are.

Theories came and went. In the 1950s and 1960s people were encouraged to eat plenty of protein. Advertisements urged: 'Drinka pinta milka day,' and 'Go to work on an egg.' More recently, they have been supposed to follow a high-carbohydrate diet, eat eggs only occasionally, and drink semi-skimmed milk. It is small wonder that many become puzzled or sceptical as a result of all these S-bends and U-turns. But this is not a new phenomenon. Fernie (1905) observed that around the turn of the century one American authority advised that 'Computing cards should be put into requisition at each meal; then when the day is over you can find out whether you have taken too much of one kind of food, or not enough of another.' This prompted the *Chicago Tribute* to print a humorous verse of which the following is an extract:

Mother's slow at figures, so our breakfast's always late;
The proteids, and the hydrates make the task for her too great;
We never get a luncheon, since she figures on till noon,
And finds we've overdone it, and that nearly makes her swoon;
Mother's always tabulating every pennyweight we eat;
Except the meals we smuggle from the cook-shop down the street.

One reason for recent changes in the advice offered was the observation that people in the Mediterranean countries suffered less from heart disease. This was attributed to their diet: plenty of vegetables, fruit, and carbohydrate foods of all kinds, some fish, not much meat, olive oil, wine. The health statistics were impressive. At the same time people were being influenced by the ideas of Elizabeth DAVID and her followers, who were extolling the virtues of Mediterranean cuisine not for health reasons but because it was delicious.

A noticeable tendency in the West, especially in English-speaking countries, was a rise in VEGETARIANISM. It is perfectly possible to gain proper nutrition from a vegetarian diet, but it needs care in choice of foods. Vegetable proteins are 'incomplete' and need to be combined; it is striking how many of the traditional cuisines of peoples who eat little meat have instinctively developed dishes which combine cereals and pulses to 'complete' their proteins—for example, DAL and CHAPATIS in India, rice and peas in Jamaica, SUCCOTASH (maize and beans) in the south of the USA. Vegetarians risk deficiencies of some B-group vitamins and iron. These are particularly severe in the case of vegans, who eat no foods of animal origin at all, not even dairy products.

While Mediterranean influence was making itself felt in America, American eating habits spread to remote parts of the world, having a particularly striking influence in Japan, where the higher intake of protein caused children born from the 1960s onwards to grow several inches taller than their parents. Not all changes were welcome: heart disease, previously most uncommon, also increased.

At the end of the 20th century there was still no sign of an end to the division of the world into rich nations whose inhabitants ate too much and suffered the diseases of affluence and wondered how to dispose of surplus food, and poor nations whose people simply did not get enough to eat.

(RH)

NUTS are impossible to define in a manner which would be compatible with popular usage yet acceptable to botanists. In this book popular usage is preferred, so the GROUNDNUT (a LEGUME, also called peanut) and the CHUFA NUT (a tuber) are allowed to shelter under the umbrella word. (Incidentally, some other languages lack an umbrella word equivalent to nut. *Noix* in French looks like one, but just means WALNUT.)

Nuts are highly nutritious. Some contain much fat (e.g. PECAN 70%, MACADAMIA NUT 66%, BRAZIL NUT 65%, WALNUT 60%, ALMOND 55%); most have a good protein content (in the range of 10–30%); and only a few have a very high starch content (notably the CHESTNUT, GINKGO nut, and ACORN). The water content of nuts, as they are usually sold, is remarkably low, and they constitute one of the most concentrated kinds of food available. Most nuts, left in the shell, are also remarkable for their keeping quality, and can conveniently be stored for winter use.

The nutritional quality of nuts is evidently one factor which causes people to think of them as particularly health giving. But they also have a certain mystique, perhaps as a putative food of the hominoids who preceded human beings; and this may be one of the factors which make nuts a prominent food of vegetarians—in England, 'nut rissoles' have served as a symbol, for non-vegetarians, of vegetarian food. And the fact that they come in a sealed container provided by nature—and one more substantial than, say, an eggshell or banana skin—buttresses their reputation as a 'pure' food.

Nuts are also associated with festivities such as Christmas and Thanksgiving. Partly because they are such a concentrated food, they are not a staple item in any modern diet, although in past times the chestnut and the acorn were staples in some regions of Europe. Some of the best nuts, e.g. the macadamia nut, PINE NUT, and PISTACHIO, are and are likely to remain expensive, but the increasing tendency to use nuts in small quantity, often to provide texture and flavour for foods which would otherwise be bland, makes it feasible to enjoy them in this way.

OATCAKES made from OATS (in the form of oatmeal), salt, and water, sometimes with a little fat added, were the staple food of the inhabitants of the Pennines and the Lake District in England and of the Scottish Highlands for centuries. In these upland regions oats are the only cereal which will ripen in the cold wet climate. Oatcakes, together with BARLEY BREAD, were also of some importance in Wales and Ireland. They remain popular, and are now generally regarded as a Scottish speciality.

Scottish oatcakes include a little fat and are raised with baking soda. The old way to make them required the dough to be rolled out; one side was baked on the girdle (see GRIDDLE) and the other toasted before the fire (nowadays oatcakes are more likely to be baked in the oven). Cut in quarters, they were called FARLS. For storage they were buried among the dry oatmeal in the meal chest. Oatcakes had some importance as festive foods, especially at Beltane (1 May, an ancient Celtic festival) and Christmas.

Irish oatcakes were of a similar type, but cereals of all kinds declined in importance in Ireland when the potato became popular.

Bara ceirch, Welsh oatcakes, were pressed out into flat sheets by hand, and baked on heavy cast iron griddles.

Clapbread (which could be made from either barley or oatmeal) was the staple food of Cumberland. Meal and water were mixed to a stiff dough, rolled into a ball, and then 'clapped' or pressed out into a paper-thin sheet by hand on a board dusted with meal, then baked to make a stiff cake. This method, as well as conventional rolling, was also used to make havercake (from Old Norse *hafri*, oats), in the C. and N. Pennines, to a recipe not unlike the Scottish one. Bakestones, thin slabs of fine-grained sandstone which could resist heat, were used for cooking them; oatcakes were so important that many houses had a fixed bakestone, with its own separate hearth, to one side of the main fireplace.

Oatcake-baking developed into a distinct skill in W. Yorkshire, where the cakes were thin, soft, and moist. A batter made from fine oatmeal was used. This was lightly fermented, either by leaving it overnight to sour naturally, or with yeast. In its simplest form, the batter was poured onto a bakestone to make a rather thick oatcake. A finer type was called riddle bread, because a pool of batter was shaken or 'riddled' on a special board to make it spread thinly. The thinnest, finest type was thrown oatcake, which developed during the 19th century. The batter was transferred from the riddle board on to a sheet of paper or cloth and then thrown on to a hot bakestone to make a very thin, slender oval sheet which cooked in seconds. These were often made by commercial bakers, and late in the century an ingenious device consisting of a cloth belt mounted on a little trolley was used to deposit a long thin sheet of batter on the hot bakestone. Soft and very pale brown, they resembled lengths of wash leather when fresh. They were hung on a wooden rack or 'flake' to dry and harden.

Broken or crushed oatcake was mixed with broth, gravy or hot water, and butter to make browiss, a sort of savoury porridge, in Yorkshire. A similar gruel was made in Wales, either mixed with buttermilk to make shot (*siot*), or with breadcrumbs and bacon fat or DRIPPING and boiling water to make BREWIS (*brŵes*).

Staffordshire oatcakes are thicker and round, more like a thin CRUMPET or modern

PIKELET, and are fried with bacon for breakfast.   LM

OATS *Avena sativa*, a CEREAL which grows well in moist, temperate to cool climates, and will thrive in conditions which wheat or barley would not tolerate. Oats are therefore important as human food mainly in northern regions.

However, oats were a comparative latecomer to agriculture. Wild oats (just like those proverbially sown by young people) seemed unpromising. The small grains, borne singly on straggly seed heads, dropped off as soon as ripe; a useful feature for a weed trying to spread itself, but not for a cereal crop.

The first traces of cultivation, selecting from wild strains which kept their seeds long enough to be harvested, date from about 1000 BC in C. Europe. However, the Greeks and Romans of classical times were unimpressed, regarding oats as coarse, barbarian fare; and the Romans used them mainly as animal fodder, but did foster the growing of oats in Britain, where they were to become important as a food for human beings. Indeed, they became the principal cereal in Wales and, even more markedly, in Scotland.

This pattern lasted for a long time. In the early 19th century a survey showed that the Welsh ate more oats than all other cereals combined and that in Scotland the ordinary people ate almost no other grains. Thus Dr Johnson's dictionary definition of oats as 'a grain which in England is given to horses, but in Scotland supports the people', although unkindly meant (Johnson later confessed to Boswell, 'I meant to vex them', i.e. the Scots), was accurate. There seems to be an affinity between oats and people of Celtic origin. Elsewhere in Europe, oats are less important. The main regions where they have served as human food are Russia, and to some extent Scandinavia and parts of Germany and neighbouring N. European regions. Findlay (1956), having devoted his professional life in Scotland to the subject, gives a good survey of the varieties available and the conditions which suited them.

In the New World, oats did well, thanks to Scottish emigrants who took their tastes with them. They were first grown in Massachusetts in 1602. A number of local American recipes for oats are recognizably derived from old Scottish ones. And Quaker Oats, a means of making porridge quickly, are an American invention of the mid-19th century.

Oats are processed to produce **oatmeal** of various grades. These and 'rolled oats' are explained in the box. Oatmeal is generally unsuitable for making bread of the conventional kind, owing to an almost

---

OATMEAL GRADES AND ROLLED OATS

- Pinhead—used for haggis, oatmeal loaves.
- Rough—used for porridge or brose, sometimes rough oatcakes.
- Medium Rough—used by butchers for mealie puddings.
- Medium and Fine—both used for porridge, brose, skirlie, baking.
- Super-fine—used in baking and in oatcakes along with a coarser grade.

To make Pinhead oatmeal the whole kernel is cut in half with any floury meal sifted out. Medium Rough is also known as Coarse Medium. Medium and fine grades are the most popular. There is also Oat flour which is distinct from Super-fine, which still has a granule.

Rolled oats or Oatflakes were developed in America by the Quaker Oat Company in 1877 and are made by steaming and rolling pinhead oatmeal. While they have the obvious advantage of cooking more quickly than regular meal they have been specially heat treated with some loss of flavour and nutrients and this also applies to the other 'instant' oat porridges now on the market. Jumbo Oatflakes are made by steaming and rolling the whole groat.   (adapted from Catherine Brown, 1985)

---

complete lack of GLUTEN, the substance which holds bread together. However, as Elizabeth David (1977) points out, a very fine brown bread, with 'a wonderfully rich flavour', can be made with a mixture of three to four parts wheat flour and one of oatmeal. Catherine Brown (1985) has reported some successful experiments on similar lines in Scotland. But the characteristics of oatmeal are such that it is used much more for OATCAKES, a separate subject.

Oats are among the most nutritious of cereals, containing as much protein (16%) as the finest bread wheat, and higher levels of fat than any other common cereal. They make the best PORRIDGE of all, and it is commonly held that the disproportionately large measure of success and fame achieved by Scottish people on the world stage is partly or even primarily the result of a diet including oatmeal, especially porridge. Lockhart (1997) has neatly drawn together much information about *The Scots and their Oats.*

Besides its primary uses in porridge and oatcakes, oatmeal features in HAGGIS, in certain types of SAUSAGE, as a coating for HERRING, also for POTATOES, and sometimes for DUMPLINGS. There is also a range of semi-sweet oatmeal puddings which could be eaten either as part of a meat course or separately as a sweet dish. FLUMMERY was originally made with oatmeal.

For other traditional uses of oatmeal see BREWIS; BROSE; CRANACHAN; CROWDIE; GROATS AND GRITS; GRUEL; SOWANS.

OCA *Oxalis tuberosa*, an important food plant in S. America, especially in the region of the Andes, where it is second only to the POTATO as a root crop. The name comes from the Quechoa *o'qa* or *okka*. The plant is easy to propagate, and tolerates poor soil, high altitudes, and harsh climates.

The oca differs from other members of its genus, such as WOOD SORREL, in being grown mainly for its root tubers, although its spinach-like leaves and young shoots may also be eaten as a green vegetable. According to the National Research Council (of the USA, 1989), the tubers look like

stubby, wrinkled carrots. They have firm, white flesh and shiny skins in colors from white to red. Most varieties have a slightly acid taste—they have been called 'potatoes that don't need sour cream.' Others, however, give no perception of acidity. Indeed, some are so sweet that they are sometimes sold as fruits.

When freshly dug, some tubers have too strong an acid taste, but this disappears if they are left in the sun for a few days, when they become much richer in glucose and taste sweet.

Oca and some other *Oxalis* spp with edible tubers were introduced to Europe in the 1830s as a rival to the potato, but never became popular, partly because (as was originally true of the potato) there is a dearth of varieties with 'daylength requirements' which are compatible with any but equatorial latitudes. Oca has, however, been successfully introduced to New Zealand, where the tubers—sold under the misleading name 'New Zealand yam'—are commercially cultivated. The varieties which flourish in New Zealand could presumably flourish also in northern temperate regions.

Oca can be boiled, baked, or fried. In the Andes, the tubers are usually added to stews and soups, boiled or baked like potatoes, or served as a sweet, either plain or candied. In Mexico fresh oca is often sprinkled with salt, lemon, and hot pepper and eaten raw.

OCEAN QUAHOG *Arctica islandica*, a large edible bivalve of the N. Atlantic. It does not belong to the same family as the QUAHOG, but bears enough resemblance to it to justify the purloining of the name; and it earns the adjective 'ocean' by living only in relatively deep waters, from the latitude of Newfoundland down to that of N. Carolina. Until recently it was left undisturbed on both sides of the Atlantic. However, the decline in the stocks of the SURF CLAM caused American processors to look elsewhere for clam meat, and large quantities of the ocean quahog are now being landed on the American side, mainly for use in minced-clam products and stews.

The shells are almost circular and may measure 11 cm (over 4") in diameter. They have a periostracum (outer covering) which is brown or blackish; whence the alternative names of mahogany or black clam. The meat is also dark, so does not suit a New England-style clam CHOWDER, which is white, as well as it does the Manhattan version, which is not. And it seems to vary in quality according to the fishing ground. Specimens consumed in Orkney have been described as gristly, and those taken from certain beds have too strong a flavour of iodine or seaweed. But those from good beds in the W. Atlantic are excellent.

In Orkney and Norway respectively the ocean quahog is *coo shell* and *kuskjell*, *ku* being Norwegian for cow and the shells having formerly been used as 'the cow' in children's games.

OCTOPUS *Octopus vulgaris* and its relations, an edible MOLLUSC whose consumption has been inhibited, except in the Mediterranean countries and the Orient, by what is considered to be its alarming or repugnant appearance (a view not shared by the Japanese, who regard it as an amiable creature, as explained under CEPHALOPODS); by its largely undeserved reputation as a peril to divers—it is known as devil-fish in the USA; by the need (notorious but in fact not always applicable) to tenderize the flesh before cooking; and perhaps also by the unresolved difficulty of deciding what its plural form should be (a difficulty which must have caused at least some people who would otherwise have bought two to ask for only one).

O. vulgaris belongs to the Mediterranean, where it thrives to such an extent that it has greater commercial importance than squid or cuttlefish, and warm waters on both sides of the Atlantic (up to, for example, the English Channel and Bermuda, but not normally beyond). This is the octopus depicted on some ancient (Mycenaean, Minoan, Greek) vases, testifying to the appreciation with which it was eaten in

antiquity. Modern Greeks continue to eat it with enthusiasm, and import dried octopus from N. Africa, but their consumption per capita is less than that of the Spaniards, who rank first, as both consumers and producers, in Europe. Yet only a small proportion of the world catch is European, and the Spanish in turn are outdistanced by the Japanese who account for about half the world catch. The oriental and other relations of *O. vulgaris* are listed towards the end of this entry.

The octopus passes the winter in deep water but approaches the coast in early spring and spends the summer in inshore waters. It is a solitary creature, living in a crevice in the rocks or in a house fashioned for itself from an old pot or tyre or other piece of debris on the sea floor.

The housing policy of the octopus makes it vulnerable to fishermen who are willing to lend it suitable material. In the region of Naples, for example, the true octopus, which is reputed to have a special liking for the colour white, can be fished for by lowering to the seabed a white pottery amphora (*mummarella*) containing white pebbles. Once he sees this, an octopus will empty the pebbles out and install himself within; and the fisherman, seeing the pebbles scattered outside the amphora, will know that he can now haul this up with an octopus inside it.

The Japanese have also used this method. Akashi in Hyogo prefecture—a port on the sheltered sea between two of Japan's main islands, Honshu and Shikoku—is famous for its octopuses. There is a local legend that once upon a time a monster octopus living off the coast of Akashi stretched its tentacles onto the land and harassed a princess resting in a palace nearby. This prompted the people to devise the *tako-tsubo* (octopus-pot) method for catching octopuses. Long, narrow earthenware pots tied with ropes are lowered to the seabed and later, when octopuses are comfortably settled in them, lifted out of the water. The seabed along the coast of Hyogo prefecture is divided neatly into plots, and each octopus-fisher of the area is allowed to sink his octopus-pots only into his plot—an ancient right, jealously guarded.

The principal species of octopus, apart from *O. vulgaris*, are the following. For comparison, the usual market length, including tentacles, of *O. vulgaris* is from 50 cm to 1 m (say, 20–40"); and the maximum length three times greater.

- *O. macropus*, the lesser octopus, smaller than *O. vulgaris*, with relatively longer and thinner tentacles, is found in warm waters round the world. The Chinese call it *sui gwai*, or water ghost.
- *Eledone cirrosa*, the curled octopus, smaller still, is distinguished by having only a

single row of suckers on each tentacle. The common name comes from the way in which the body is curved back on itself. (An even smaller species, *E. moschata*, smells excessively of musk and is not recommended.)
- *Cistopus indicus*, the principal commercial octopus in Asian markets. Maximum weight about 2 kg (4.5 lb). The Chinese (in Hong Kong) call it *laai por*, meaning muddy old woman, whereas the names they give to other species liken them to birds and are poetical.
- *Octopus aegina*, weight around 0.5 kg (just over 1 lb). Has a wide range, from the Red Sea to W. Pacific. Known to the Chinese of Hong Kong as *saa lui* (sand bird).
- *O. bimaculoides*, a species of the Pacific coast of America, is eaten in Mexico and sometimes in California.

A baby octopus needs no special preparation, but can simply be deep fried or cooked briefly in boiling water.

Various methods of tenderizing a larger octopus are proposed. Some give an impression of folklore, for example the advice to add a cork to the cooking water. Others are known to be effective, but are tedious, such as beating the octopus on rocks. A Japanese method is to put the cleaned octopus in a bath of finely grated *daikon* (see RADISH) and to knead it with the fingers.

However, in Japan octopus is as often as not cooked without preliminary tenderizing. The two main ways of cooking octopus are boiling and *nimono* (see JAPANESE CULINARY TERMS). For the former technique, a live octopus is chosen, cleaned, boiled just lightly in order to prevent it from getting tough, and then sliced thin and eaten with a dip sauce made variously with SOY SAUCE, citrus juice, or mustard; or used for *sunonomo* (again, see JAPANESE CULINARY TERMS). When used for *nimono*, on the other hand, octopus is cooked for a long time—a few hours—to make it tender; it is often cooked with vegetables, *yaki-dofu* (see TOFU), KONNYAKU, etc.

OFFAL those parts of a meat animal which are used as food but which are not skeletal muscle. The term literally means 'off fall', or the pieces which fall from a carcase when it is butchered. Originally the word applied principally to the entrails. It now covers insides including the HEART, LIVER, and LUNGS (collectively known as the pluck), all abdominal organs and extremities: TAILS, FEET, and HEAD including BRAINS and TONGUE. In the USA the expressions 'organ meats' or 'variety meats' are used instead.

Offal from birds is usually referred to as GIBLETS.

Another, archaic, English word for insides, especially those of deer, was 'umbles', a term which survives in the expression 'to eat humble pie', meaning to be apologetic or submissive.

The taste and texture of offal depends on the particular organ, and on the species and age of animal from which it came. Generally speaking, offal from calves is held to be the best, providing large organs of fine flavour and texture. Lamb offal is also good, but sheep, pig, and ox offal tends to be coarse in flavour and texture.

Offal does not keep well so must either be prepared and cooked quite soon after slaughter or turned into a product which does keep (BRAWN, HASLET, PÂTÉ, some kinds of SAUSAGE).

The type of offal used in any given culture depends on the favoured meat animal, which may in turn depend on religious dietary laws. Muslim countries use much lamb offal. The Chinese have numerous ways of dealing with organs from pigs.

Offal is a good source of protein, and some organs, notably the liver and kidneys, are very valuable nutritionally. In most parts of the world, especially the less developed countries, it is valued accordingly. In the English-speaking world, however, the pattern is different. In N. America there has been and still exists a squeamish attitude which prompted the title *Unmentionable Cuisine* for the book by Schwabe (1979). In Britain, where there used to be no, or anyway few, qualms about eating offal, overt consumption has declined in the last half of the 20th century, although the offal is in fact still eaten in processed foods where it is not 'visible'.

Squeamish attitudes may be explained on various grounds. Heads and feet remind consumers too directly that the food is of animal origin. Ambivalence about eating certain bits of an animal's anatomy, such as TESTICLES, is expressed through the use of euphemistic names. Some internal offal has surreal shapes and strong flavours, which are not to everyone's taste. The meat of feet and ears is characterized by textures which are gelatinous and crunchy at the same time, a combination which is generally disliked in the western world, although appreciated in the Orient.

See also BRAINS; CAUL; CHITTERLINGS; CRÉPINETTE; FEET; HEAD; HEART; KIDNEYS; LIVER; BONE MARROW; OXTAIL; SPLEEN; STOMACH; SWEETBREADS; TAILS; TESTICLES; TONGUE; TRIPE; UDDER.

OGO the name in Japan, where use is common, of one of the more important red SEAWEEDS, *Gracilaria verrucosa*. The plants are bushy, relatively small (to 30 cm/12"), and purplish-red or greyish or brownish in colour.

This is widely used in the Indo-Pacific area, either fresh (young tender plants only) in salads; blanched as a garnish; or processed to yield a kind of AGAR-AGAR.

OIL PALMS the collective name for those palm trees which are a source of edible oils. The most important of these, *Elaeis guineensis*, is considered under PALM OIL.

The oil palms seem to have originated in widely separated parts of the world. *E. guineensis* is W. African. The American oil palm, *Corozo* (formerly *Elaeis*) *oleifera*, grows in southern C. and northern S. America and in the Amazon basin.

Other palms which yield edible oils include the COCONUT. In addition, the raffia palms, of which there are various species in the African tropics and a few in S. America, yield oil. The most important is the Madagascar raffia palm, *Raphia farinifera* (better known as a source of the raffia used by gardeners for tying up plants, and for having the largest leaves in the world—up to 20 m/65' long). The pointed, oval fruits, which may be sweet or bitter, yield an oil known as raffia butter.

The Babassú palm, *Orbignya martiana*, is common in C. and S. America, especially in the Amazon region. Its fruits resemble coconuts but are only the size of a large apple. They yield plenty of oil, but the shells are so hard that until recently (when new machinery was developed) it was impossible to exploit them commercially.
READING: Sokolov (1991).

OKA a purely Canadian cheese made by Trappist monks in the province of Quebec. It bears some resemblance to BEL PAESE or PORT SALUT.

OKARI NUTS the product of a tree, *Terminalia kaernbachii*, which grows principally in Papua New Guinea, can be almost as large as a tennis ball, and have large kernels which, because of the way in which the cotyledons (embryonic leaves) are wrapped round each other, look something like miniature cabbages.

The nuts, which have a mild flavour like that of almonds, are eaten both raw and cooked. 'Devilled in the fry-pan by the camp cook, these nuts go very well with the sundowner, when one is camped in the rain forests of Papua.' Thus wrote a correspondent to Menninger (1977), who collected a number of interesting comments on the species, all agreeing on the good quality of the nuts.

The related species *T. catappa* bears fruits with white kernels which also taste like almonds, so are called 'sea almonds'. According to Low (1989) the purple pulp of the fruits is also edible, and both fruit and nut are popular snack foods on the Torres Strait Islands.

OKINAWA The uniqueness of Ryukyu cuisine (Ryukyu is the ancient name of Okinawa, still often used, especially in a cultural context) must be attributable, first, to the historical fact that Ryukyu was once a tiny island kingdom maintaining precarious independence between China and Japan, and, secondly, to its geographical distance from the Japanese mainland and its position in the subtropics.

The influence of both China and Japan is clearly recognizable in the cuisine of Ryukyu as, indeed, in many other branches of its traditional culture. The great popularity of PORK is one of the salient points of Ryukyu cuisine and must be a Chinese influence. The people of Okinawa eat not only the meat but also various other parts of pigs, and this forms a striking contrast to the mainland Japanese, who started to eat meat as part of their normal diet only a little more than 100 years ago and are still rather squeamish about OFFAL.

A typical and well-known pork dish of Okinawa is *Rafutei*; shoulder and belly of pork are slowly stewed in SOY SAUCE, sugar, and *awamori* (the local spirit made from MILLET and used instead of saké). Other typical pork dishes include *Nakami-no-suimono* (soup of intestines and shredded stomach), *Mimikawa-sashimi* (*sunomono* of pig's ear), and *Ashitebichi* (stewed pig's trotters). Pork is used for making stock, whereas mainland Chinese use DASHI.

The people of Okinawa do not eat as much fish as the rest of the Japanese, but they make an extensive use of KELP. For example, *Konbu-irichii* is a regional dish in which shredded kelp and pork are stir-fried.

A seafood that is peculiar to Okinawa is the sea snake caught in the neighbouring subtropical waters. The Ryukyu name for it is *irabu*. It is sold smoked and comes in two forms—straight like a walking stick or coiled for easy portability. This is cooked slowly for as long as half a day with kelp and a pig's trotter and eaten with the soup.　　　KA

OKRA *Hibiscus esculentus* (formerly *Abelmoschus esculentus*), an annual plant of tropical and subtropical regions which bears pods which are eaten as a vegetable. It is the only member of the MALLOW family, *Malvaceae*, to be used in this way. The pods, which are typically ridged and tapering, but may be almost round, contain many small seeds and a gummy substance which gives okra its special character. The general appearance of the pods has resulted in their having the name 'ladies' fingers'.

ORIGIN AND SPREAD

Okra is generally regarded as native to Africa, and may have been first cultivated either in the vicinity of Ethiopia or in W. Africa. It is not known when it spread from Ethiopia to N. Africa, the E. Mediterranean, Arabia, and India. There is no trace of it in early Egyptian tombs, but it was recorded as growing beside the Nile in the 13th century.

Its westward migration to the New World seems to have been a result of the traffic in slaves. Okra had reached Brazil by 1658 and Dutch Guiana by 1686. It may also have arrived in the south of the USA during the 17th century, and was being grown as far north as Virginia and Philadelphia in the 18th century.

The spread of okra eastwards from India was slow. Its appearance in SE Asia may be assigned to the 19th century, and it arrived in China soon thereafter.

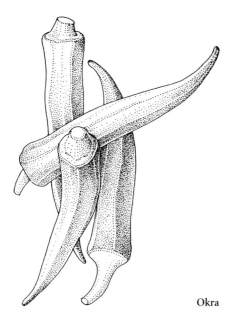

Okra

NAMES

Okra is itself an African name, as is the alternative name 'gumbo'. The local name in Angola was 'ki ngombo'. This was rendered by Portuguese slave traders as 'quingombo', and then shortened by slaves in the W. Indies to 'gombo' or 'gumbo'. This last is the name still used in the southern USA.

VARIETIES

There are many cultivars of okra. Pods range from under 5 cm (2") to 20 cm (8") long. They may be dark or light green, or (less common) bright red; the pods of some of the red-skinned cultivars remain red even after being cooked. The pods may be ridged or smooth. Their gumminess also varies.

There is a general preference in the USA for the gummier kind and for ridged pods of about 16–18 cm (7") long.

USES

In America the use of okra is one of the characteristics of CREOLE cookery and CAJUN FOOD. Sliced pods give a thick, glutinous texture to the famous 'gumbo soups', often referred to as simply 'gumbos'. FILÉ, a powder made from SASSAFRAS, may be used to add more gumminess. Okra itself can be dried and powdered to serve as a thickening agent.

Okra is only moderately popular in Europe, although it is eaten in the south of France and in Spain, and in other regions where it grows well and where N. African culinary influences appear. It is used much more extensively in the Middle East and India, as a vegetable. The gummy texture, which those who dislike it regard as slimy, was mitigated in Egypt in medieval times by cooking okra with meal. Modern methods include steeping the pods in acidulated water before cooking, and frying them even if they are later to be cooked in water. Care is taken not to break the pods and thus release the mucilaginous substance within. However, whatever one does, okra remains slippery, unless the pods have first been thoroughly dried. In India the dried, shrunken pods are cut into short sections and these are then fried and drained, after which they have the appearance of small CROUTONS and taste quite different from okra in its usual forms.

OLEASTER *Elaeagnus angustifolius*, the ancestor of the OLIVE, bears fruits which are eaten in Turkey and other Mediterranean countries.

The fruits are about the size of an olive and are usually marketed after being dried, when they are a pale brown and look something like small dates. Iddison (1994) writes:

The skin is thin and papery and peels off easily to reveal the buff-coloured, soft, mealy flesh which induces thirst. It is sweet with a flavour reminiscent of medlar and the flesh clings to the stone which is ribbed and striped brown. They are not used in cooking these days but their flesh was used in bread and also fermented to make a drink.

A variety which grows further to the east, e.g. in Afghanistan, bears red fruits, and there is now a cultivar of this. There are also other species in the genus which bear fruits in the Orient, Alaska, etc.

One such is the silverberry, *Elaeagnus argentea*, a shrub of northern N. America, especially the Hudson's Bay region, which bears edible fruits. These are too dry and mealy to be of gastronomic interest, but are consumed locally.

OLIO an interesting culinary term which enjoyed wide currency in English in the 17th and 18th centuries, and indeed for much of the 19th century too. It comes from the Spanish *olla* and Portuguese *olha*, both of which derive ultimately from the Latin word *olla*, meaning a pot. The English language also adopted, as far back as the 16th century, the Spanish term *olla podrida*, which literally means 'a rotten pot' (i.e. exactly the same as the French *pot pourri*) and in practice refers to a stew whose liquid element may be served as a soup separately from the meat and vegetables which it contains.

The English meaning of olio in its culinary sense is now given by the *NSOED* as: 'A highly spiced stew of various meats and vegetable, of Spanish and Portuguese origin; *generally* any dish containing a great variety of ingredients.'

The latter part of the above definition opens the gates very wide indeed, and it is true that the various sorts of olio which occur in old cookery books differ greatly in many respects but do have in common a large range of ingredients. Some have a remarkably large range, such as the 'Olio of Sturgeon with other Fishes' given by Robert MAY (1685). This called for sturgeon, eel, various herbs, bread, eggs, salt and pepper, nutmeg, gooseberries, potatoes, SKIRRETS, artichokes, chestnuts, BARBERRIES, grapes, butter, bay leaves, cloves, pistachios, orange juice and sliced lemons. But even this was eclipsed by his Olio Royal or 'extraordinary Olio' which seems to require not only a complex list of ingredients for making marrow pies (which themselves appear to constitute the olio) but a garnish consisting of two collars of pig BRAWN, 12 roast turtle doves (see PIGEON) in a pie, 18 QUAILS in a pie, 10 more pies, two salads, two jellies each of two colours, two forced meats, and two tarts.

By the time of Meg Dods (1826) the emphasis seemed to be on a variety of meats. Her recipe for an olio required 'a fowl, a couple of partridges, a piece of a leg of mutton, a knuckle of veal, and a few rump steaks; also a piece of good streaked bacon or ham'. This author adds that 'Spain as a nation is not eminent in cookery, though the *olio*, and a few more of its *omne-gatherum* stews of meat, pulse, and roots, are worthy of attention'. Her term *omne-gatherum* seems to be just right for this subject, although no one would now agree with her low estimate of Spanish cuisine.

OLIVES and OLIVE OIL (*see opposite page*)

OMELETTE a French word which came into currency in the mid-16th century but
(*cont. on page 553*)

Olives AND OLIVE OIL

The fruit of the olive tree, *Olea europaea*, and the oil which it yields, foods which originated in the Mediterranean region, are often thought of as symbolizing it.

The importance of the olive tree and the veneration which it has aroused since prehistoric times are widely attested, for example by the use of the olive branch as a symbol for peace. Biblical, classical, and other literary references abound. Lawrence Durrell wrote in *Prospero's Cell* that the whole Mediterranean 'seems to rise in the sour, pungent taste of these black olives between the teeth. A taste older than meat, older than wine.'

It is not only in literature that the trees and their fruits have been memorably portrayed. Maggie Blyth Klein (1994) remarks on the manner in which the Impressionist painters captured their spirit, and in how many different ways:

Renoir could not bear to paint a grey tree. He painted gold and, more exuberantly, pink, olive trees. Matisse, though a more abstract painter perhaps, preferred the olive's natural hue and painted grey olives at Collioure and Corsica. Cezanne, while loving his black cypresses and chestnuts as well, found a place for the grey-green olive in his rich landscapes. Bonnard painted the olive grey, but the grey did nothing to subdue the cheerful aspect of his St. Tropez. And the same could be said of Derain, a little later, who was able to capture the landscape of the Mediterranean with just a few, almost primary, colors.

It was van Gogh, however, who was most fascinated by the olive.

Van Gogh is said to have painted 19 pictures of olive trees, and Klein quotes a letter which he wrote from Provence, explaining how difficult but attractive he found this subject.

Olives from wild trees (oleasters) were sporadically gathered, in the Near East, by Neolithic peoples about 10,000 years ago. The small, bitter fruit of the oleaster contains more stone than flesh. The tree began to be cultivated, perhaps in Palestine or Syria, well before 3000 BC, and in the following three millennia olive farming gradually spread to Anatolia, Crete, Greece, Italy, S. France, and Spain—and also eastwards to C. Asia. Archaeologists find not only the discarded stones of the fruit but also the remains of olive mills and presses. Oil storage jars are found in large quantities: these often travelled long distances by sea.

To both Greeks and Romans the olive was a crop of the first importance. Athenians claimed the first olive tree, given to mankind by the goddess Athena and growing on the Acropolis. To destroy an enemy's olive trees was a sacrilegious act and a demonstration of ruthlessness in war. Cato's manual *On Farming*, the first Roman prose text (*c*.175 BC), devotes more space to olive-growing and oil-making than to any other topic.

The northern limit of olive cultivation remains a major landmark across Europe and W. Asia. However, in recent centuries olive-growing has spread far beyond these traditional regions. The Mission variety (as it is now called) was established at Spanish missions in California before 1800.

Major producers today include S. and C. Spain, Italy, Turkey, Greece, Tunisia, Morocco, and California. Smaller quantities are made in Provence, Syria, Australia, S. Africa, and several other countries. Three-quarters of the world's olive oil now comes from the countries of the EU, especially Spain and Italy.

CULTIVATION AND VARIETIES

The olive is an evergreen with foliage of a distinctive silvery-green. Deep rooted, it is slow to mature and very long-lived: olive-growing regions can show gnarled old trees reputed to be many hundreds of years old and still fruiting reliably. It is susceptible to severe cold: the frosts of 1870 and 1956 are blamed (along with foreign competition and cheap vegetable oils) for the steep decline of the olive industry of Provence. Olive trees are grown in valley meadows and on hillside terraces, an unmistakable feature of the Mediterranean landscape.

The fruit, a drupe with fleshy pulp and a high fat content, contains a glucoside which makes olives, especially unripe ones, very bitter. This has to be removed from table olives in the first stage of the preserving process, but it separates naturally from the oil when olives are pressed to produce olive oil.

Andalusia, in Spain, is the principal olive oil-producing region in the world. Numerous varieties of the olive tree are used, but one, Picual, is by far the leader (although this fact can be obscured by the use of different names for it in some parts of the region), and accounts by itself for something like 50% of Spanish olive production. It takes its main name from the shape of the fruits, which have a somewhat pointed tip (*pico* in Spanish). The chemical composition of its oil is admirably balanced. Of the other leading varieties for oil, Hojiblanca takes its name from the whitish underside of its leaves; and is used to some extent as a table olive. Lechin de Sevilla is grown mainly in the province of Seville. Picudo, another olive with a pointy tip, yields a delicate oil with flowery and fruity attributes, unmatched for certain purposes (GAZPACHO, warm salads, cake-making, etc.) and has excellent aroma and flavour

The other main olive oil-producing countries have their own favourite varieties, attuned to local conditions; Koroneiko, for example, is the major oil variety in Greece.

MANUFACTURE AND USES OF OLIVE OIL

Olives for oil must be gathered quite ripe. In the Mediterranean the harvest comes in late autumn and winter: in Provence, for example, it begins around 15 November, well after the grape harvest. Traditional harvesting methods of hand-picking and beating still compete with mechanical tree-shakers. The fruit must be gathered undamaged, then crushed without breaking the stones, spread on fibrous mats, and pressed. The fluid that is extracted, when allowed to settle, separates into oil and a bitter watery substance, *amurca* to Romans, which found numerous uses on old-fashioned olive farms.

Stone crushing mills, *trapeti*, powerful enough to crush the flesh effectively but sufficiently accurate in gauge not to break the olive stones, are among the most impressive examples of 2,200-year-old Roman farm technology—and some such mills are still used.

The hills of Tuscany are the source of some of the finest olive oils. Mrs Leslie Zyw (1981) has given an account of the procedures traditionally employed there; of the nutritional advantages of consuming cold-pressed extra virgin oil, uncooked; and of the gastronomic pleasure which it provides, whether cooked or not. She emphasizes that olive oils may vary as wines do, and that it is desirable to taste methodically and find what suits one best. She continues thus:

When the olive harvest begins, the first oil coming from the press is often very green, as the olives are less ripe than later on. Some people find this delicious. It is less bland and more piquant than the more mature oil. It also contains more vegetable residue than the oil which is sold later and which has therefore had more time in which to settle. A harvest time treat for the olive pickers is made by toasting bread over a wood fire, rubbing it with garlic and then pouring the fresh green oil over it. This simple food is quite superb. The very green oil becomes less green with time and eventually it looks much the same as the oil pressed later in the harvest.

Unfiltered oil has more and better flavour than filtered oil. But it is turbid and has vegetable residue. This *fondo* is characteristic of the best oil and is quite harmless. It can easily be used up just by shaking the bottle a little when using the oil.

Olive oil is variously classified for marketing. The International Olive Oil Council, with headquarters in Madrid, has ruled that 'Virgin' olive oil is 'obtained from the fruit of the olive tree solely by mechanical or other physical means, under conditions, particularly thermal conditions, that do not lead to alterations in the oil, and which has not undergone any treatment other than washing, decantation, centrifugation and filtration'. The corresponding US regulation, of 1982, defines 'Virgin' oil as 'resulting from the first pressing of the olives and . . . suitable for human consumption without further processing'.

For European olive oils the additional classification 'Extra Virgin' simply indicates a low acidity (less than 1%), a feature which is usually desirable for flavour.

The uses of olive oil need no explanation. Most of it is used in cooking, where it is important both for its contribution to flavour and also for its nutritional properties. Olive oil has one special virtue, unique among the commonly available FATS AND OILS. It is a predominantly monounsaturated oil, containing around 75% monounsaturated fatty acids. Moreover, it contains no cholesterol. It is considered one of the main constituents of the 'Mediterranean diet' whose effects on health are so widely praised.

TABLE OLIVES

Olives intended for preserving and table use (or use in cookery) are harvested at various stages of ripeness with very different results in texture and flavour.

Unripe olives are green, very bitter, and with firm flesh. Their flesh is often cracked, by a gentle blow with a mallet, to allow water and marinades to penetrate. As the olives ripen they become oilier, and their colour changes from green to purple. Fully ripe, black olives are oilier still, soft in texture, and relatively free of bitterness.

Methods of curing olives for table use vary considerably according to the degree of ripeness when the olives are harvested, and various other factors. Lourdes March and Alicia Rios (1988), in a remarkable essay with a considerable historical as well as technical content, has made the point that the various preparation and preservation processes have been carried out for a very long time in Spain by people who have no technical knowledge of the chemical phenomena which take place during them.

Nevertheless, the know-how acquired from their parents enables the country folk to recognize when the olive has reached the appropriate stage at any point in the proceedings, whether the process to remove the bitterness, the fermentation period or the seasoning procedure. They can also calculate the proportions of the ingredients without having to measure them, ending up with top quality olives which taste absolutely exquisite.

The complexity of this inherited wisdom is obvious from even a bare list of the techniques which may, separately or in combination, be applied:

- water-curing—repeated soakings and rinsings over many months;
- brine-curing, in a brine solution for anything from one to six months;
- dry-curing in salt;
- oil-curing, which may mean just soaking in oil for some months or may refer to dry-cured olives which are then rubbed with oil;
- lye-curing in a strong alkaline solution (wood ash or caustic soda).

The fermentation in brine, besides having a preservative function, breaks down the sugar that olives contain into lactic acid, thus contributing to their flavour. Flavour is also greatly improved by the use of herbs and spices which are usually added to the brine to form marinades of almost infinite variety.

After giving her list of curing methods (echoed above) Maggie Blyth Klein goes on to refer to the naming of the numerous sorts of table olive:

Most are sold by the name of the area or town of origin (e.g., Gaeta and Niçoise); several are named for the variety of olive from which they are made (e.g., Picholine and Salona); still others are sold according to the method of curing (e.g., Greek- and Sicilian-styles). Confusion arises when more than one olive comes from one place, as is possible with all olives, no matter how small the place of origin; when one variety is cured many different ways; when one person's Greek-style olive is another person's dry-cured.

The following are just a few examples, organized by country of origin, of well-known table olives:

- Spain is well known for Manzanilla, an important cultivar which is picked when green, and also for Hojiblanca and Gordal (and over a dozen other kinds).
- France provides not only the Picholine and Niçoise types mentioned above (both brine cured, the former green and of normal size, the latter quite small and often brown or darker), but also the Nyons olives, commonly black, dry salt cured, and on the bitter side.
- Italy has Gaeta olives, black and wrinkled, dry cured or sometimes brine cured, mild-tasting (the taste often enhanced by herbs).
- Greece is known both for Kalamata, black-purple and almond shaped, and also for the dark green, cracked, brine-cured Naphlion.

- USA, i.e. California, offers types with more general names such as Sicilian-style, Greek-style, or the self-explanatory 'black-ripe pitted'.

Stuffed olives are popular, and have a fairly long history. As early as the 18th century, producers of some of the olives of Aix-en-Provence, such as the famous Picholine variety, were stoning their olives and replacing the stone with capers, anchovies, tuna, pimiento (see CAPSICUM), etc.

Industrial methods of preparation result in olives that will keep longer, typically marketed in jars or tins. Olives in glass jars were first sold in 1898 in Oroville, California; Frederic Bioletti, also in California, developed olive-canning in the early 1900s. However, it was not until 1933 that a Californian mechanic, Herbert Kagley, built the prototype of the first mechanical olive pitter which could be used successfully to pit green olives for use in martini cocktails.

READING: Rosenblum (1997), Margaret Visser (1986: ch 7).

(AD)

had been preceded by other forms, e.g. *alumelle*, which are littered along a trail leading all the way from the Latin *lamella*, 'small thin plate', suggesting something thin and round. Cotgrave, in his dictionary of 1611, recorded its arrival in England in this entry: 'Haumelotte: f. *An Omelet, or Pancake of egges.*' He thus preferred the spelling which is used in N. America as opposed to the French spelling ending in -ette which is generally used in Britain. It is safe to assume that the word had been around for a while before 1611. It is anyway safe to assume that omelettes had been around in recognizable form in both France and England and elsewhere too from early medieval times, since the concept of frying beaten eggs in butter in a pan is as simple as it is brilliant.

Indeed, since so many dishes are now being found to have their origin in ancient Persia (see IRAN) or in early ARAB CUISINE, it is tempting to suppose that something like an omelette may originally have arrived from that region. If so, the Persian *kookoo* (or *kuku*) could be the best representation in the modern world of the original. A *kookoo* of the plainer sort involves mixing a generous amount of chopped herbs into beaten eggs, frying it in a round pan until it is firm and then (usually) cutting it into wedges for serving. Many versions have a very substantial filling. The same is true of the Middle Eastern *eggah*, to which Claudia Roden (1985) devotes eight pages, remarking that:

An *eggah* is firm and sound, rather like an egg cake. It is usually 2 cm (1 inch) or more thick, and generally bursting with a filling of vegetables, or meat, or chicken and noodles, suspended like

currants in a cake. The egg is used as a binding for the filling, rather than the filling being an adornment of the egg. For serving, the *eggah* is turned out on to a serving dish and cut into slices, as one would cut a cake.

The Spanish *tortilla* (not to be confused with the TORTILLA of Mexican cookery) resembles these ancestors in being relatively thick, cooked until firm, and often equipped with a generous filling, e.g. of potato. In this connection it is interesting that Sephardi Jews in a number of countries have made a speciality of potato omelettes. Claudia Roden (1996) states that this is referred to in N. Africa as an *omelette juive*. It could represent a milestone on the long trail from Persia to Spain. The trail could also have had a branch into Sicily leading to the Italian *frittata*, which again resembles the types already described.

Seen against this background, the light fluffy French omelette, with its runny interior and its non-existent or relatively scant filling, would be a diversion from the mainstream, a diversion which has of course gained wide currency in countries where French cuisine has enjoyed a period of ascendancy: e.g. Britain. It is perhaps not altogether fanciful to suppose that the remarkably large collection of omelettes brought together by the author of *Le Pastissier françois* (1653) and largely reproduced in translation by Robert MAY (1660, also 1685, reprinted 1994) contains within itself evidence of an evolution from a Middle Eastern past to a French classical future. It includes some omelettes to be fried well on both sides (the ancestral ones?) besides one which sounds perfectly suitable for a 20th-century French cook;

this last reads as follows in May's translation:

Break six, eight, or ten eggs more or less, beat them together in a dish, and put salt to them; then put some butter a melting in a frying pan, and fry it more or less, according to your discretion, only on one side or bottom.

Whatever their history and connections may have been, it is certain that omelettes of both basic kinds, when properly made, score remarkably high marks for being delicious, easy and quick to prepare, and nutritious.

It is also to be noted that in most of its manifestations the omelette may be sweet instead of savoury.

READING: Lallemand (1986).

ONCOM an Indonesian fermented food which resembles TEMPE in many respects. However, while tempe is usually made from SOYA BEANS, oncom (in the usual sense of the term—see below for another) is made from the presscake left over after oil has been extracted from GROUNDNUTS, or from okara (the residue from the production of TOFU or SOY MILK). The MOULD used to ferment it is *Neurospora sitophila*, whose spores give it a distinctive orange colour, whereas *Rhizopus oligosporus* is used for tempe. Another difference is that tempe, like Roquefort cheese, is inoculated throughout its mass, while oncom is inoculated on the outside only and is akin to Camembert in this respect.

Oncom is almost exclusive to W. Java, where a thousand or more shops purvey it fresh daily. The orange cakes, arranged on glossy green banana leaf, make a colourful display in the markets. Some of the vendors deal also in tempe, and a local linguistic confusion has arisen: tempe prepared from either groundnut presscake or okara, using *R. oligosporus*, may be termed oncom. Those who follow this usage are taking the substrate as the defining factor, whereas the general and more convenient practice is to go by the mould used and to reserve the name oncom for what has been fermented by *N. sitophila*. (This mould can, incidentally, be used to make a soya bean oncom. This is not done in Indonesia, but its feasibility has been demonstrated in the USA.)

To make oncom, the presscakes are first broken up, soaked and washed, then steamed and put in small moulds in a bamboo frame covered with banana leaf. The cakes in the moulds are inoculated with orange spores from a previous batch and left in a shady place until the fungus has penetrated them, after which they are cut into pieces and marketed.

Oncom is prepared in various ways for eating. It is usual to salt it and deep-fry it, with or without a batter. *Krupuk oncom* are a deep-fried snack with some resemblance to potato crisps (see KRUPUK). *Oncom goreng* is another snack food, in thin triangles. *Buras* is a steamed preparation, wrapped in banana leaf, with the oncom inside a ball of soaked white rice.

Peanut presscake oncom is a speciality of Bandung, so much so that it is often called *oncom Bandung*.

Oncom has a shorter life than tempe. When it is a few days old it can be further fermented to make a kind of DAGÉ.

ONE-POT COOKERY a vast subject, of particular interest to many groups: people with limited food-heating facilities (e.g. only one burner); those who have to cope with a shortage of fuel; anyone who has to produce a lot of hot food several hours hence with no supervision in the meanwhile; and also (perhaps on a trivial plane, yet not to be dismissed as an entirely negligible interest) those who seek to minimize WASHING UP.

A remarkable survey of the whole subject and its iconography by Bertram Gordon and Lisa Jacobs-McCusker (1989) begins with a list which includes the following items: the *Eintopf, Romertopf*, crockpot, stew pot, CHOWDER, CASSEROLE, *olla podrida, husepot* or *hutspot*, Lancashire HOTPOT and IRISH STEW, POT-AU-FEU, hochepot, CASSOULET, *puchero*, and COCIDO. Besides examples such as these, where various ingredients which might otherwise have been cooked separately all go into the one pot, there are of course innumerable other instances of a single ingredient being cooked in a single pot, e.g. porridge and its relations. But it is

the former category which is interesting; and the expression 'one pot' is normally taken to include in its meaning 'rather than the several which might have been used'. Gordon and Jacobs-McCusker devote special attention to the political and social importance with which the *Eintopf* was invested in Germany in the period between the World Wars, especially the 1930s. Hitler and the Nazi party in effect hijacked one-pot cookery for their own ends—fortunately with no lasting effects; no political stigma adheres to the practice, either in Germany or elsewhere.

Japanese culinary terms include one, *nabemono*, which refers simply to the category of one-pot dishes (*nabe* means a pot or pan), many of which are cooked at the table by the diners. A popular example is SHABU-SHABU, a Japanese adaptation of the Mongolian hotpot. In this connection it is interesting to note that in the English language the word 'pot' in 'one-pot cookery' has considerable force and cannot be replaced by 'pan'. Thus, a dish of meat and various vegetables stir fried in a wok is not one-pot cookery, because a wok is not a pot.

Moving to America, one finds that the category of food known as CHUCK to cowboys is rich in examples of one-pot dishes. One taken almost at random from Adams (1952) is 'Colorado stew with dumplings', made thus by the cook on the chuck wagon:

For this he cut bacon into pieces, covered it with water, and boiled until done. Diced potatoes and onions were then added and cooked some more. The dumplings were made the same way as baking powder biscuits, pinched off into small pieces, then placed on top of the stew and cooked until done. Here was a whole meal in one kettle.

One could also count CHILI CON CARNE as a one-pot dish.

The pot in one-pot cookery is normally covered, although a dish of numerous ingredients cooked in ancient times in an open cauldron would not be disqualified for its lack of a lid. Nonetheless, a lidded pot is normal. The dish called 'pot pie' or 'sea pie' not only has a lid but is sealed inside with a pastry top. (The history of SEA PIE, which had some puzzling aspects, was recently elucidated by food historians.)

There is an engaging description in Flora Thompson's *Lark Rise to Candleford* (1945), a rich source of information about rural foodways in Oxfordshire in the 1880s–1890s, of how the hot meal of the day was cooked in an English village a century ago:

Here, then, were the three chief ingredients of the one hot meal a day, bacon from the flitch, vegetables from the garden, and flour for the roly-poly. This meal, called 'tea', was taken in the evening, when the men were home from the fields and the children from school, for neither could get home at midday.

About four o'clock, smoke would go up from the chimneys, as the fire was made up and the big iron boiler, or the three-legged pot, was slung on the hook of the chimney-chain. Everything was cooked in the one utensil; the square of bacon, amounting to little more than a taste each; cabbage, or other green vegetables, in one net, potatoes in another, and the roly-poly swathed in a cloth. It sounds a haphazard method in these days of gas and electric cookers; but it answered its purpose, for, by carefully timing the putting in of each item and keeping the simmering of the pot well regulated, each item was kept intact and an appetising meal was produced.

ONION (*see opposite page*)

OPAH *Lampris guttatus* (formerly *regius*), is a large and beautiful fish which is met, very rarely, in the Mediterranean, and rarely in the Atlantic and Indo-Pacific. It is a fish of the deep seas, swimming in the midwaters; and since these have not been fully explored there is still something to be learned of its distribution. It has also been called moonfish and mariposa.

The opah, despite being toothless, and of majestic build, pursues and eats other fish and squid. On this diet it may grow very large, for example over 1.5 m (60") in length and over 1 m (40") in depth; the largest recorded weight is close on 75 kg (160 lb). Jane Grigson (1973) described its beauty well:

The aspect of its rounded eyes and rounded head is mild, almost dolphin-like. The huge, plump body, a taut oval up to 6 feet long, is softly spotted with white. The main blue-grey and green of its skin reflects an iridescence of rose, purple and gold. The fins are a brilliant red. The sickle tail has reminded people of the moon's shape; the ribs of its fins have seemed like the scarlet rays of the sun.

Relatively few people have eaten opah, but those who have agree that it is outstandingly good. The flesh is pink and firm, with an attractive flavour which has hints of salmon, tuna, RAY'S BREAM, and veal. It can be sliced very thin and eaten raw, Japanese style; or sliced more thickly and fried; or cut into steaks and grilled, or a whole 'shoulder' can be roasted.
READING: Parrott (1960).

OPOSSUM specifically the American opossum, *Didelphis virginiana*, a favourite game animal of the southern states of the USA, which figures prominently in the folklore of the region. A marsupial mammal (i.e. one whose young, when newly born, are carried in an external pouch), the opossum has a head-plus-body length of up to 50 cm (20") and may weigh 6 kg (13 lb). It has been compared for size with a cat or a sucking pig.

(cont. on page 556)

Onion

Onion is used both as a general term, applying to many members of the extensive genus *Allium*, and as a specific one referring to regular round (globe) onions of the species *Allium cepa*. The box shows what other entries there are, and how the botanical species relate to common names. Of the names shown in the box, the ones which constantly cause confusion are spring onions and scallions. Usage varies to such an extent that no generally valid definitions can be given.

The present entry is concerned with mature onions of the species *A. cepa*. The original wild ancestor of this, the common onion, has long since disappeared; but related wild species still grow in C. Asia. The whole diverse onion family evidently arose in this area, although it is now disseminated throughout the world.

Onions have been eaten and cultivated since prehistoric times. They were mentioned in records of the 1st dynasty of ancient Egypt (3200 BC), and constantly appeared in Egyptian tomb paintings, inscriptions, and documents from this time on. The even older civilization of Ur has left accounts (*c*.2100 BC) of onions being grown in gardens.

Attitudes to the onion in Egypt, as Darby *et al.* (1977) remark, had a dual quality; it seemed to be simultaneously the object of appreciation and reverence on the one hand and of taboos on the other. Priests were forbidden to eat onions. (Taboos on the eating of onions are not confined to Egypt; in India, Brahmans and Jains are also forbidden to eat them.)

What is certain is that in ancient Egypt as in ancient Greece and Rome the common people ate onions in large quantities, often raw. Ancient Egyptian onions were said to be large, white, and mild, ideal for the purpose. However, they would still have imparted a smell to the breath, which may have been the reason why the upper classes did not care to eat them. It is probably significant that recipes of *Apicius* gave them little importance; they are mentioned only as subordinate flavourings in mixed dishes and dressings.

Just as now, onions in the classical period varied in pungency, and there were recognized varieties. It seems to have been one variety of white onion which, in late Latin, bore the name *unio*, meaning a single white pearl, and leading to the French word *oignon* as well as the English 'onion'. The complicated etymology of words for onion in other languages has been deftly summarized by Ayto (1993).

Once the Romans had introduced the onion to Britain, it stayed put and has ever afterwards been an important part of the diet. Anglo-Saxon verse riddles often concern onions, including the following one (as cited by Lovelock, 1972), which sustains a double meaning with remarkable persistence:

ALLIUM SPP

ACEPA includes all the common western round (globe) ONIONS with single bulbs, which in their immature state are used as SPRING ONIONS in Britain; the 'aggregate' onions with multiple (underground) bulbs such as the SHALLOT, the 'ever ready', and 'potato' onions; and also the TREE ONIONS (also known as Egyptian or 'top-set' onions), which reproduce by forming miniature self-planting bulbs on top of the stem, e.g. the variety Catawissa. Both the last two groups can be referred to as 'multiplier' onions.

A. fistulosum is the most important in oriental countries; see ORIENTAL ONIONS. It is, however, known as the welsh onion (although nothing to do with Wales) in Britain and some other places. In N. America it is often called scallion, a name which is however used differently in the south where it is likely to mean green shallots.

Hybrids of *A. cepa* and *A. fistulosum* account for some of the hundreds of onion varieties/cultivars.

A. chinense, the Chinese *jiao tou* or Japanese *rakkyo*, is an oriental pickling onion.

A. porrum is best known as the LEEK, but includes a variety which is the bunching pearl onion.

A. kurrat is a species which fills the role of leek in the Near and Middle East.

A. scorodoprasum is the species usually called ROCAMBOLE; but that common name is of erratic application.

A. sativum is cultivated GARLIC.

A. ampeloprasum, the wild ancestor of the leek, is a species which exists in many forms. One of these is ELEPHANT GARLIC.

A. ursinum is the WILD GARLIC or ramsons.

CHEMISTRY OF ONIONS

THE 'bite' of raw onions, and the typical onion and garlic odours, are due to a complex of sulphur compounds. When an onion is cut, the crushing of the cells and the admission of air allows an enzyme to work on these substances. One effect is to develop pungency. Another is to release the volatile substance allicin, which irritates the eyes.

If onions are peeled and chopped under running cold water this washes away the allicin; but it may be inconvenient. A simpler method is to chill the onion in the refrigerator before working on it. The cold reduces the volatility of the substance.

Cooking onions transforms their 'bite' into the pleasing, slightly sweet flavour which is an asset to so many dishes. Some of the starch in the onion is transformed by heat into sweet-tasting dextrin and free sugar. The process is accompanied by the formation of brown compounds. Brown colours also come from reactions between proteins and sugars.

I am a wonderful thing, a joy to women . . .
I stand up high and steep over the bed;
Beneath I am shaggy. Sometimes comes nigh
A young maiden and handsome peasant's daughter,
A maiden proud, to lay hold on me,
She raises my redness, plunders my head,
Fixes on me fast, feels straightaway
What meeting me means when she thus approaches,
A curly haired woman. Wet is the eye.

The cultivated onion was introduced to the New World by Columbus on his second voyage to Haiti (1493–4), and thereafter by the early colonists. Although some minor wild onions are native to the Americas there was nothing to compare with the new kind, and American Indians took to it (and even more so to garlic) with enthusiasm.

VARIETIES

Over the millennia since onion cultivation began, many different types of round onion have been bred. Size varies, from small pickling onions about 1 cm (0.5") in diameter to huge specimens weighing more than 500 g (1 lb), sometimes more. (In 1980 for example, a new record was established by a Mr Rodger with an onion bulb grown in his council house garden in Scotland, weighing almost exactly 6.5 lbs). Colours may be white, brown, yellow, or red. Flavour ranges from very mild to strong, whether harshly biting or simply with a pronounced flavour.

Nomenclature among growers and in commerce is not internationally standardized, and the only advice which can be given is to 'know your onions' (a phrase from the 1920s) by the names used where you live. With this proviso, the categories or varieties most commonly on sale in western countries are as follows:

- Spanish onions are a large category of generally mild globe onions. (White Sweet Spanish, in contrast, is a cultivar name.)
- Bermuda onions are another category, including a number of varieties whose characteristics differ to some extent, although Red Bermuda, White Bermuda, and Yellow Bermuda are all mild.
- Hybrid onions include a couple of American favourites, both of the Yellow Granex type: Vidalia, named for the town in Georgia around which growing is concentrated; and Maui, named for the Hawaiian island in whose volcanic soil and cool climate this onion is at its sweetest. Not a hybrid, but often listed along with Vidalia and Maui, is the variety Walla-Walla Sweet, which was apparently brought to Walla-Walla in the state of Washington from Corsica at the beginning of the 20th century.

The above notes merely scratch the surface of a huge subject, which is continually evolving as growers and agricultural research stations develop new varieties.

The number of dishes in which onions play a supporting role, whether to add flavour or serve as a garnish, is vast. Those in which it is the principal ingredient are relatively few and are mostly European. Stuffed onion (popular in Britain), onion soup (whether French or not), and Alsatian onion tart are three examples. An example for Asia is onion *bhaji*.

The French term *soubise* (for an 18th-century prince of the family of that name) indicates the presence of onion, either in a sauce or in the form of a purée (often thickened with rice). Eliza Acton (1845) noted that the sauce was usually served with lamb or mutton cutlets; and while mutton was available in England there was certainly a preference for serving onion sauce with it.

Dorothy Hartley (1954) supplies an admirable coda to the subject:

The papery golden skins of onions should not be thrown away. They are good natural colouring for soups and stews. Broth should always be made golden and delectable by cooking the skins in it.

KEEPING ONIONS

THE keeping properties of onions vary inversely with the amount of moisture in them. Hard, dry, round onions keep for months. This property has had a considerable effect on commerce in onions, making possible, for example, the traditional practice of French onion-sellers from Roscoff and Saint-Pol in Brittany bicycling around English towns selling their wares. Alexander Dumas *père* relates one of his most charming (albeit improbable) anecdotes in explaining how this practice first arose. It was still flourishing in the 1970s, but Lindsay Bareham (1995) cites a press interview of 1994 with Jean Leroux, described as the last onion-man.

Although it is famed for what an Irishman would call its lifelike manner of feigning death (playing 'possum), recent studies suggest that this tactic is not now often used. However, opossums continue to be nocturnal animals and to display omnivorous tendencies, devouring not only fruits but also insects, small vertebrates, and, it is said, carrion. Despite this last item, its flesh is tasty and wholesome. The liver may be eaten. A favourite southern dish is 'possum and taters: the opossum is parboiled, then salted and peppered and roasted in a pan with peeled, roasted sweet potatoes.

ORACH *Atriplex hortensis*, a plant of the GOOSEFOOT family which grows wild throughout Europe as far east as Siberia and all around the Mediterranean coast, is also called mountain spinach. It is a tall, spindly plant with small, generally arrowhead-shaped leaves, which grows well in sandy or poor soil. Several of its closest relations, known as saltbushes because of the salty taste of the leaves, display similar characteristics in various parts of the world, but are rarely used for human food.

From the time of the rise of the Mediterranean civilizations orach was cultivated as a green vegetable, to be used as

557 ORGANIC FOOD

SPINACH now is. Its taste is like that of spinach but the leaves are less succulent.

There are varieties with red, white, and green leaves. Green orach was used in Italy to colour pasta. Another use was to mix orach and SORREL, thus alleviating sorrel's acid flavour.

Orach was used in England in the 16th century, but its popularity declined with the increasing use of spinach throughout Europe and it is now seldom grown.

ORANGE (see page 558)

ORANGE FLOWER WATER sometimes called orange blossom water, is produced by the distillation of ORANGE flowers of the bitter orange, i.e. the bigarade or Seville oranges. This produces an essential oil called Neroli (used in perfumery). The oil, rising to the surface, is drawn off, while the aqueous portion is used as orange flower water.

Orange flower water originated in the Middle East where it is still used to lend a delicate perfume to syrups, pastries, and puddings. It is often added with rosewater, or on its own, to *atr*, the sugar syrup of the Middle East, and used to soak or sprinkle over pastries and sweets. In Morocco, where it is known as *zhaar*, it flavours salads and certain TAGINES. The 'white coffee' of the Lebanon is made by adding a teaspoon of orange flower water to a coffee cup of boiling water with or without the addition of sugar. It is often added to flavour Turkish

coffee. A drop or two added to water with sugar is a popular soothing drink at bedtime for children.

As for Europe, there is evidence that in Sicily in the 14th century orange flower water was used, but as a perfume for bed linen etc. rather than in food. By the 17th century, however, it was widely used in Europe as a food flavouring. C. Anne Wilson (1973) says that:

the scented water was usually imported ready-made from France or Portugal. It became an alternative to rosewater, particularly in rich seed cakes, almond cakes and biscuits, and dessert creams. There is even a recipe of 1727 for orangeflower brandy. Both rosewater and orangeflower water continued as food flavorants all through the eighteenth century, though neither was in such constant use as rosewater had been during the century before.

In the south of France, from the 16th century onwards, there was a flourishing cultivation of the bitter orange for producing orange flower water—first for use in perfumery, later for flavouring. Its use was most widespread in the 18th and 19th centuries. (HS)

OREGANO a name applied in one place or another, but especially in N. America, to many of the aromatic herbs of the group treated at length under MARJORAM, and certain other plants. However, it is questionable whether the term oregano (or origano, as it is sometimes spelled) should

be treated as a plant name. Tucker (1994) has argued persuasively that oregano is best considered as the name of a flavour. He points out that:

vast confusion exists in popular and scientific texts on the correct identity of oregano. This is partly because a multitude of plant species have been called oregano or oreganum, and often these plants are substituted for each other. Most of these plants bear a unifying chemical signature: carvacrol and, to a lesser extent, thymol.

In Tucker's view it is this chemical signature which is intended when the term oregano is used.

Nonetheless, it is convenient to have a list of the numerous plant species involved in this nomenclatural tangle (see box).

The oregano flavour is widely used in the cuisines of Mediterranean countries and Latin America. So far as N. Americans (and many Europeans) are concerned oregano is an essential element in many kinds of PIZZA and has various other flavouring uses. See, however, MARJORAM.

ORGANIC FOOD a concept which has come more and more into prominence towards the end of the 20th century, is easier to define in general terms than in detail. The principle is that food should be produced by practising agriculture without the use of pesticides and artificial fertilizers, and (where livestock are concerned) by breeding and rearing animals and birds with due regard to their welfare and by methods which can be described as 'natural and traditional'.

Since the use of the term 'organic' in labelling foodstuffs is increasingly controlled (whether by governments or by organizations or producers), and since there is a general trend in the direction of buying such produce, there has been considerable debate about how exactly to define the term. In practice, in many places, it may not be possible to exclude small traces of pesticide that have been used in the past. Most systems of organic farming allow for inconsequential departures from the ideal. However, the question often arises: what allowances can properly be made to deal with this sort of problem, without prejudicing the integrity of the operation? For some foods, the scope for debate is greater than for others. Eggs are an example.

The production of organic foods and the degree of public support for the concept vary considerably from country to country. Denmark, for example, is much further advanced than Britain. A brief survey of the situation in the European Union and in other parts of the world is given by Lynda Brown (1998) in a book which is intended mainly as guidance for British consumers.

(cont. on page 560)

OREGANO SPECIES

- *Origanum vulgare* ssp *hirtum*, the common European oregano of commerce. Currently harvested in NW Turkey, where its local name means 'black' oregano. This is an E. Mediterranean ssp, which has a counterpart (ssp *glandulosum*) in the SW Mediterranean.
- *O. vulgare* ssp *vulgare*, wild marjoram, common in the northern regions of Europe and Asia and naturalized in N. America. The spp *gracile* is found in W. Asia. Ssp *virens* occurs in Spain and Portugal and their islands.
- *O. onites* (the species which the great botanist Linnaeus called *O. smyrnaeum*), the *rhigani* of Crete, found in the south of Greece and Turkey.
- *O. syriacum*, white oregano, called Lebanese oregano in the USA.
- *Thymbra capitata*: see THYME.
- *Lippia graveolens*, a member of the MINT family, Lamiaceae, and the species most commonly indicated by the term 'Mexican oregano' (other *Lippia* spp are also called orégano in Mexico and C. America).
- *Plectranthus amboinicus*, the herb described under SPANISH THYME.

The term oregano has also been used for species in no fewer than four other genera of the mint family and also for about half a dozen species in the family Verbenaceae. Some of these have only marginal qualifications for the name since their carvacrol content is relatively low. Tucker also notes certain anomalies. One example is *Satureja montana*, SAVORY, which is high in carvacrol but is not called oregano. Another is *Eryngium foetidum* (culantro, see SHADO BÉNI), which is not scented of carvacrol but 'has earned the dubious name of orégano de Cartagena'.

Orange

The most popular of the CITRUS FRUITS exists in two species: *Citrus aurantium* and *C. sinensis*. The former is the bitter (or Seville) orange and the latter comprises the vast range of sweet oranges, for eating out of hand or turning into juice. Their wild ancestors are thought to have grown in the region of SW China and NW India, but the growing of cultivated varieties has in modern times become concentrated in the Americas, where Brazil and the USA between them account for over two-thirds of world production.

Oranges seem to have been first used for the fragrance of their rind. They were valued as perfume or flavouring, and early Chinese documents mention them being held in the hand so that the warmth released their scent. Although the earliest oranges eaten in China seem to have been MANDARIN oranges, it does seem clear that some cultivation of ordinary sweet oranges began in the south several millennia ago.

SPREAD OUTSIDE CHINA
During the first centuries of the Christian era the orange began to spread beyond China, as the CITRON had done earlier. It reached Japan well before the earliest surviving Japanese literature was written (the 8th century), but it has always been less important there than fruits of the mandarin type. It also reached India in early times: a medical treatise of about AD 100, the *Charaka Samhita*, mentions it for the first time by what was to become its modern name, 'naranga'. This word is said to be derived from an older Sanskrit term *narunga* (fruit like elephants). 'Naranga' became *naranj* in Persian and Arabic, *narantsion* in late classical Greek, and *aurantium* (influenced by *aurum*, 'gold') in Late Latin, from which it is only a short step to the Italian *arancia* and French and English 'orange'.

However, the various questions which attend the etymology and the westward movement of the orange are complicated by the fact that it was the sour orange which first travelled westwards, with the sweet orange only following about 500 years later. The sour orange was apparently being grown in Sicily at the beginning of the 11th century and around Seville in Spain at the end of the 12th century, no doubt because the Arabs had introduced the fruit to these places. The sweet orange turns up in the Mediterranean area in the latter part of the 15th century. However, it is not always easy to know, from the common names then in use, which sort of orange was meant.

The earliest surviving description of the bitter orange in Europe was by the 13th-century writer Albertus Magnus, who called it 'arangus'. (Another name was 'bigarade', derived from Arabic. Bitter orange juice was used as a flavouring.)

The first mention of the sweet orange in Europe is sometimes said to be that in the archives of the Italian city of Savona, in 1471. Probably the seeds had come through the Genoese trade route, which had extensive connections with the Near East. However, PLATINA (1475, but having prepared his work in manuscript in the preceding decade) provides a better starting point. He says that sweet oranges 'are almost always suitable for the stomach as a first course and the tart ones may be sweetened with sugar'; which shows clearly that he knew both kinds.

Shortly after the Portuguese explorer Vasco da Gama returned from India after his discovery of the sea route around the Cape of Good Hope, in 1498, the Portuguese began to grow a superior kind of sweet orange which was said to be a direct import from 'China'—a vague designation which however came to be adopted as meaning the sweet orange. Thus the 'China' oranges which were an expensive delicacy in Britain from the late 16th century on were in fact from Portugal. And this Portuguese orange spread through S. Europe. The modern Greek for orange is still *portokáli*.

THE NEW WORLD
The orange arrived in the New World with Columbus, who took seeds of both kinds of orange (and of lemon, citron, and lime) to Haiti on his second voyage in 1493. The climate of the Caribbean proved ideal, as did that of the adjacent mainland. It is possible that in 1509 an early Spanish settlement in Darien (Panama) had oranges. More certainly, at some time before 1565 (when the first permanent Spanish colony in Florida, San Agostino, was established), early settlers planted oranges and started what was to be the enormous Florida citrus industry. The rival California industry did not begin until 1739, when missionaries began to grow oranges in lower California (the part now in Mexico). The first oranges in the northern (now USA) part arrived 28 years later.

Orange cultivation was subsequently established in many other parts of the world, e.g. southern Africa (1654), Australia (first seeds planted in New South Wales in 1788), and Israel (where the industry became really important after the emergence of the Jaffa orange in the latter part of the 19th century and the introduction of the late Valencia from the USA in the 20th century).

CULTIVATED VARIETIES
There are now six main categories of orange in cultivation.

Common sweet oranges exist in numerous varieties. Saunt (1990) explains that Valencia, the most important variety of all, is not an old Spanish one, as might be supposed, but 'first became of interest in the Azores and is almost certainly of old Portuguese origin'. It seems that it was sent from the Azores in the early 1860s to Thomas Rivers at Sawbridgeworth in England, who first named it Excelsior and sent it to the USA where it was renamed several times, finishing up as Valencia Late—this because a Spanish citrus expert visiting California thought it closely similar to a late-maturing variety grown in Valencia in Spain. This variety leads production in both California and Florida and in many of the main orange-growing countries, but not in Spain itself. Oranges of this variety have a thin rind, not difficult to peel at maturity, plenty of juice of a good colour, and usually two to four seeds.

Other varieties include Pera (important in Brazil) and Jaffa or Shamouti. The latter originated near Jaffa (then in Palestine, now in Israel) in the mid-19th century as a bud mutation on a local Beladi tree. Jaffa oranges have a very fine flavour and are almost seedless. Picked at full maturity, they keep very well. Jaffas are grown also in Cyprus and Turkey, but production declined somewhat towards the end of the 20th century.

Blood oranges are grown mostly in Mediterranean countries, especially Italy. The original mutation which produced the colour probably arose in the 17th century in Sicily. The earliest blood oranges were small and seedy but the better varieties which followed, notably Sanguinello, attracted international esteem. The best modern varieties include the round early-season Moro and the mid-season Tarocco (named for its resemblance to a child's toy top and renowned for its delicate flesh and well-balanced flavour). Sicily, especially the area around Catania, remains the best place for these oranges. A combination of cold winter nights and mild days favours the development of anthocyanins, the red pigments which give blood oranges their distinctive deep red colour. Connoisseurs of citrus fruits consider these oranges to be among the world's finest dessert oranges.

Navel oranges are unmistakable. Each has a rudimentary 'baby' fruit embedded in its apex. These oranges mature early, are typically large and seedless and easy to peel, and have a rich flavour which places them in the first ranks of dessert oranges. They thrive especially in subtropical climates such as the Mediterranean and are grown extensively in Spain, Morocco, Turkey, S. Africa, and Australia as well as California in N. America and Uruguay and Argentina in S. America.

As for the origin of navel oranges, Saunt (1990) explains that:

For some time it was widely believed that the navel orange originated as a limb sport near Bahia (now Salvador), Brazil, some time prior to 1822. There is now much evidence to disprove this theory, for navel oranges are known to have grown in Spain and Portugal for many years prior to 1822, and it seems more likely that they were first brought to Portugal from China and thence to Brazil much earlier than this.

It was certainly a Brazilian navel orange, called Bahia, which was introduced to the USA in 1870 to fill the need for a good early variety. Navels are seedless and can be propagated only by cuttings, so twelve young Brazilian trees were imported in tubs by the US Department of Agriculture in Washington. From here they were distributed among leading growers in California and Florida, thus acquiring the name 'Washington Navel'. The variety is now called either Bahia or Washington.

Acidless oranges, or sugar oranges, are another freak variety which enjoys a small popularity in Brazil, N. America, and Italy. They are almost without acid and therefore insipid in flavour.

Bitter oranges, *C. aurantia*, have declined in importance. They are grown mainly in Spain (hence 'Seville' oranges), and the bulk of the crop is exported to Britain where it is made into MARMALADE. Only bitter oranges can be used to make proper marmalade, which depends not only on their bitterness but also on the aromatic rind, which is quite different from that of the sweet orange.

These oranges have some uses as an acid element in cookery, especially in those areas where they are cultivated, including the Mediterranean. The dried rind is used to give its aroma to various savoury dishes.

KEEPING QUALITIES AND CULINARY USES

As with nearly all fruits, the flavour of a freshly picked orange is far better than that of a commercial grower's product. Modern oranges are robust and do not spoil quickly, a fact which unfortunately is exploited. An orange may undergo cleaning with detergent; 'degreening' with ethylene gas—which removes green but leaves the orange pale yellow, so that it has to be coated with orange dye; wax polishing to reduce moisture loss; and a long time in refrigerated storage before it reaches its eventual buyer.

The wax polish which nearly all oranges have on their skin has been described as harmful to health by several authorities, who recommend that orange rind should not be eaten, even after scrubbing. (Seville oranges, fortunately for domestic marmalade-makers, are left unpolished.)

The uses of bitter oranges have already been mentioned. Sweet oranges can be used to advantage in salads and sweet dishes, and generally for imparting a sweet orange flavour.

ORANGE HYBRIDS

THERE are also several citrus fruits called 'oranges' which are really hybrids between oranges and other citrus fruits. The popular **Temple 'orange'** is a tangor or mandarin × orange hybrid, as are the **King 'orange'** and the **Ortanique** (see MANDARIN). The **Poorman 'orange'** or 'New Zealand grapefruit' is an orangelo or orange × grapefruit hybrid (see UGLI). The miniature calamondin 'orange' grown as a decorative house plant is sometimes considered to be a mandarin × kumquat hybrid, and sometimes assigned to a species of its own.

One more orange needs to be mentioned here, since it may have originated as a hybrid of a bitter orange and the Palestine sweet lime. This is the **bergamot orange**, now classified as *C. bergamia*. Saunt (1990) points out that it would have been more appropriate to call it bergamot lemon. It is grown for making fragrant bergamot oil; see BERGAMOT.

The development of organic food production also varies according to the category of product. One area of particularly rapid growth is that of organic baby foods, notably in Germany.

ORGEAT a beverage which was originally made from BARLEY (Latin *hordium*, whence Provençal *ordi* for the cereal and *orji* for the drink) and later from ALMONDS.

C. Anne Wilson (1973) has described the sequence of drinks thus, starting with the thin drink of barley with pure warm water which Anthimus, in the 6th century AD, recommended for fever patients.

The later medieval version in France had the name tisane, was sweetened with sugar and seasoned with licorice and sometimes also figs. Adapted for English use it more often comprised barley boiled in water with licorice, herbs and raisins. It was still a licorice-flavoured drink in the first part of the seventeenth century, but soon afterwards was brought up to date by the substitution of lemon juice for licorice.

Another variant of barley water in France, called *orgemonde*, was flavoured with ground almonds. This too reached England during the seventeenth century, its name softening to 'orgeat' or 'ozyat'. Subsequently the barley dropped out, and English ozyat was made from ground almonds and sugar with orange-flower water or the juice of citrus fruits boiled with spring water. It was a cold drink similar to lemonade. Milk ozyat was boiled, spiced milk, cooled and mixed with ground almonds; and special ozyat glasses with handles were designed to serve it in.

ORIENTAL ONIONS used in China, Japan, and to some extent in SE Asia, are mostly varieties of *Allium fistulosum*: the species name means 'tubular'. These onions never form bulbs; instead, there is a cluster of thickened stem bases like a closely packed bunch of spring onions, which they resemble when young in both appearance and flavour. As they grow older, they keep the same shape, simply becoming larger and coarser.

A. fistulosum, as the senior member of the ONION family in China, has a name of a single character, *cong* (*chung* in Cantonese). These are general names for all onions, modified as suitable for other kinds: for example, the round European onion is called in Cantonese *yeung chung tau*, meaning foreign onion head. The Japanese name for the species is *negi*.

These oriental bunching onions are everywhere visible in the Orient. As Joy Larkcom (1991) puts it:

If the long loaf epitomizes the French shopper, the long white-stemmed onion epitomizes the Chinese. Tied to bicycles, peering out of panniers, it is the most ubiquitous of Chinese vegetables.

A. fistulosum spread westwards in early times, reaching Europe during the Middle

Allium fistulosum

Ages and England in 1629. It was called the 'welsh' onion: nothing to do with Wales, but from an old word, *welise* in Anglo-Saxon, *Welsch* in German, meaning 'foreign'. The French name *ciboule* comes from the same Latin source as the Italian and German names for the round onion. Although it has

the advantages of being perennial and very hardy, it has never been very popular in Europe; but it is sometimes used to provide spring onions.

Another onion species of Chinese origin, *A. chinense*, is known in China as *jiao tou* (in Cantonese *chung tao*) and in Japan as *rakkyo*. There is no western name other than the puzzling 'bakers' garlic' or the vague 'Chinese onion', so it is convenient to use the Japanese name. This species is grown in Japan, S. China, SE Asia, and to some extent in India. Rakkyo is another bunching type with clusters of very small bulbs, which are used mainly for pickling. In English, misleadingly, these may be called 'pickled scallions' or 'pickled leeks'; see also PICKLING ONIONS.

ORKNEY AND SHETLAND are often bracketed together as two distinctively different parts of SCOTLAND, lying to the north of the mainland; Orkney very close to it but Shetland closer to Bergen in NORWAY than to Aberdeen in Scotland. They do have some important features in common, notably the fact that they were both colonized by Scandinavians from the 9th to the 15th centuries (hence many culinary terms of Norse origin) and their strongly insular characteristics, but there are equally important differences between them, as the following comments by Catherine Brown (1981) show:

The gentle, undulating, green and fertile land of the Orkneys has more in common with the North-East Lowlands of Morayshire, Easter Ross and Caithness than with Shetland. This is fine farming country for rearing cattle, sheep and pigs as well as growing oats, barley and turnips. In Shetland, acid soils, a cool summer and frequent salt-laden gales restrict farming so that the people have turned much more towards the sea for a living than in Orkney. In this respect they belong more with the Hebrides and the West Coast. They were originally described as fishermen who had a croft, compared with the Orcadians who were farmers who kept a fishing boat. There are nearly four times as many fishermen in Shetland as there are in Orkney, but on the other hand Orkney farms are four times the size of those in Shetland.

So far as staples are concerned, it is noteworthy that a particular variety of BARLEY, from which BERE MEAL is produced (to make BANNOCKS, PORRIDGE, etc.), retains a prominent place, as do OATS. Likewise, KALE (the member of the cabbage family which has thrived in these northern parts for many centuries) continues to be important; it has traditionally been preserved in barrels with fat and oatmeal. Kale is often teamed with pork, another Orkney staple. Other popular vegetables are turnip/swede, potato, leek.

Fish which has been preserved in one or another of numerous ways, many of them shared with the Nordic countries, is certainly a staple, but, in the past at least, prime fresh fish has been gutted and dispatched to the mainland for sale there, leaving Orcadians and Shetlanders to make their range of distinctive dishes based on the heads, livers, and other innards which had been removed. Davidson (1988*b*) provides a survey of such dishes (e.g. muggies, krappin, stap) based on practical research in the kitchens of Lerwick (capital of Shetland).

Annette Hope (1987) gives an impressive description of the hardships endured by Shetlanders when engaged in the 'haaf' (deep sea) fishery in the summer; and Shetland publications give vivid details of this and other traditional practices.

Meat may be beef, mutton, or pork. Wind-dried meat is known as *vivda*. A special kind of preserved beef mince, spiced and salted, is known as *sassermaet* and is the basis for making the patties which are called *brönies*. However, the champion meat for Shetlanders comes from the Shetland sheep, which, as Catherine Brown (1981) explains:

are different from other breeds in Britain and have more in common with Norwegian, Swedish and Russian breeds which resemble the wild sheep of Siberia. It is a small, hardy, self-reliant sheep which lives mostly on exposed hills, feeding on coarse hill grass and heather but in severe times it also feeds on seaweed from the shore. All this combines to produce a mutton with a unique flavour which is stronger and faintly gamey compared with lowland mutton.

Returning to Orkney, one finds a fine range of griddle-baked goods, for example the Orkney pancakes made with oatmeal and BUTTERMILK, and the distinctive 'sour skons', flavoured with caraway seeds. 'Fatty cutties' are another griddle-baked speciality which resemble the Northumbrian 'singin' hinnies' (see SCONE) which 'sing' on the griddle because of their high fat content. Orkney is also famed for its SOUR MILK products and cheeses.

A sweet note at the end of this short survey is provided by whipkull, the ancient Shetland drink of egg yolks, sugar, and rum with which Yule (rather than Christmas) has traditionally been celebrated. This is one of many items which arrived from Norway, and bears an interesting resemblance to the Italian ZABAGLIONE (which is made with marsala rather than rum).
READING: Catherine Brown (1990); Margaret Stout (1968).

ORONGE the French name for a large, delicious and famous mushroom, *Amanita caesarea*, is also used in English. An alternative name is Caesar's mushroom.

The oronge, which grows in open woodland in many parts of Europe and N. America, and in China, prefers a warm climate. In France, for example, it is common in the south, but rare north of the Loire. It is the largest of the genus *Amanita*, sometimes reaching 25 cm (10") high and 20 cm (8") across the cap. The cap is a clear red or orange, becoming yellower with age, and all other parts are yellow.

The delicate and subtle taste has been highly esteemed since antiquity. It was into a dish of oronges, to be consumed by the Emperor Claudius, that the poisoner employed by his consort Agrippina introduced the juices of the deadly *Amanita phalloides* to bring about his death in AD 54.

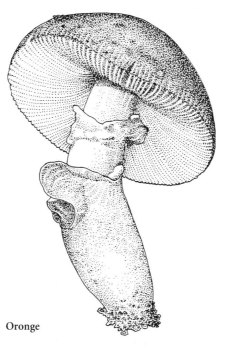

Oronge

(Wasson and Wasson, 1957, have shown that there was more to the Emperor's death than that, for Agrippina's fell purpose required that death should ensue more rapidly than this poison alone would have ensured. But the tale may be taken as broadly correct.)

A. ovoidea, the white oronge (French *amanite ovoïde* or *oronge blanche*), is a southerly species which may be even larger: up to 30 cm (12") across the cap, which is completely white. It has a floury exterior. Most authorities praise its quality, while drawing attention to the risk explained below.

A close relation in NW America is *A. calyptroderma*, the coccora. Its cap may be pale yellow instead of orange or red, and its gills are paler than those of *A. caesarea*, but the resemblance is very close and Italians in California, who recall the oronge in Italy, hunt it with great fervour. The name coccora (or cocoli or coconi) comes from the Italian word for cocoon, referring to the appearance of the young cap with its white, cottony patch of volval tissue still adhering to it.

Warning The oronge should be positively identified before being eaten. The common FLY AGARIC, which is poisonous, can look like a rather dark oronge if rain has washed the distinctive veil fragments off its cap.

ORTOLAN the French and gastronomic name for the little bird which the French fancy most in the genus *Emberiza*, whose members are known as buntings in non-gastronomic English. From beak to tip of tail they measure 12 to 15 cm (5 to 6"), and there is not much of them to be eaten; but they have aroused great enthusiasm among the likes of Alexandre DUMAS *père* (1873), who gave a lengthy account of a dialogue between a Pythagorean philosopher and a hunter on the propriety of killing 'one of these charming birds which afterall does no harm to anyone and whose looks and whose song bring joy to our eyes and ears'. The hunter's arguments are presented as more compelling than the philosopher's and Dumas concludes with a reference to *Ortolans à la toulousaine*. He explains that 'in Toulouse they have a special way of fattening ortolans which is better than anywhere else; when they want to eat them, they asphyxiate them by immersing their heads in very strong vinegar, a violent death which has a beneficial effect on the flesh.'

Most British people, and many in other countries too, would shrink from this notion. However, little more than a century ago Dallas in *Kettner's Book of the Table* (1877) said that the wheatears (Dallas insists on the final 's', which may be correct if the name was originally whitearse, but wheatear is now the 'correct' spelling) has been honoured with the name of the 'English ortolan'. The wheatear, *Oenanthe oenanthe*, used to be spit roasted, basted with good butter, and strewn with breadcrumbs. One of the erudite authors who contributed to the impressive survey of birds as food in Simon (1983) quotes the author of a history of birds in Sussex as confirming the comparison with ortolans and saying that wheatears 'are so fat that they almost dissolve in the mouth like jelly'. The Sussex shepherds who could earn up to £50 a year by supplying wheatears to poulterers in Brighton used to attend an annual celebration dinner, until about 1880.

OSMOSIS is the diffusion of liquids in one direction through a semipermeable membrane—that is, one which will allow small molecules through but not large ones. An example is a container of sugar solution divided in two by a sheet of cellophane. On one side the solution is strong, on the other it is weak. Water can get through the cellophane but sugar cannot. The result is that water flows through the membrane from the weak side to the strong side. This movement can generate considerable pressure, which is known as osmotic pressure.

Osmosis is important in food preparation because the cell walls of living organisms are semipermeable membranes. This is why bacteria cannot grow in strong sugar or salt solutions. Osmotic pressure removes water from their cells and prevents them from taking in nutrients from the solution. Osmosis is also at work when sliced cucumbers or aubergines are wilted by sprinkling salt on them, which draws water out of their cells so that they collapse. The opposite process is seen when blanched vegetables are 'refreshed' by putting them in plain water. In this case the solution is stronger inside the plant cells, thanks to the dissolved substances naturally present. Water flows into the cells and plumps them out, making the texture of the vegetable firmer. RH

OSTRICH *Struthio camelus*, the largest of birds, belongs to Africa, where its flesh and eggs have been eaten from early times. Now it has begun to be farmed elsewhere, and its meat is no longer as exotic an item as it used to be.

Its reputation had already had a boost in the 19th century by no less an authority than Charles Darwin. Voyaging round the world in the *Beagle* and pausing in S. America, he assured his womenfolk at home that he did not have to live on salt beef and biscuit, as they might have imagined, but enjoyed delicacies such as ostrich dumpling. There was also an unfortunate occasion when Darwin, who was particularly anxious to collect a specimen of a rare type of ostrich, smaller than usual, quite failed to notice that an ostrich shot by one of his colleagues in Patagonia was one of these rare creatures. 'The bird was cooked and eaten before my memory returned,' he wrote. However, it proved to be possible, using only the parts discarded as inedible, to reconstruct 'a very nearly perfect specimen'. Thus, one could say, Darwin and his companions were able to 'eat their ostrich and have it'.

As for the eggs, to judge by the comments of the poet and food writer Leipoldt (1976) they are disappointing except in dried form for cake-making and the like. Leipoldt counsels against even trying to make an ostrich egg omelette, describes how to make the best of a difficult job in preparing scrambled ostrich egg, and gives in outline an enticing recipe for 'Imitation Ostrich Egg', which sounds like something from

early Arabic cookery, and is probably better than the real thing.

OTAHEITE GOOSEBERRY *Cicca acida*, one of the few useful fruits in a large genus whose botanical name means 'leaf-flower'. This refers to the curious manner in which flowers grow along the edges of the leaf like branches; and, since the flowers develop into fruits, the fruits too occupy this odd position.

The origin of the plants is obscure but they are indigenous to Madagascar and have been cultivated for centuries in S. India and N. Malaysia and Indonesia, notably Sumatra. The fruit was introduced into Jamaica from Timor in 1793, and has been casually spread throughout the Caribbean islands. It has long been naturalized in S. Mexico and the lowlands of C. America, and is occasionally grown in S. America.

The tree is an abundant bearer, its branches being festooned with clusters of fruit, and it usually provides two crops a year, so the total quantity of fruit which it produces is very large. The fruits are grape-sized, green at first, and light yellow when ripe. They have a tart flavour which recalls that of the ordinary GOOSEBERRY (not a close relation). When cooked with sugar they become bright red and make excellent jams and filling for fruit pies. They can also be made into pickles and preserves, as is done in India. In Indonesia they are used to make a syrup.

OTHELLO the fanciful name of a sweet tartlet filled with chocolate cream custard. The name was given because Othello was a Moor and supposedly chocolate coloured. The conceit was then carried further; Desdemona is the same thing with white vanilla custard, and Iago with coffee custard.

OTTER SHELLS BIVALVES of the genus *Lutraria*, have minor importance as food in Europe and SE Asia. *L. lutraria*, the largest of several European species, is light in colour, may measure up to 12 cm (nearly 5"), and used to be called clumps or horseshoes in the Channel Islands. It can be steamed open and then fried.

A SE Asian species which is liked in Thailand for its tender meat is almost as large and has a purple shell which turns white when dry.

OXALIC ACID COOH.COOH, is naturally present in various foodstuffs, including SORREL, RHUBARB, SPINACH, and chocolate. It is toxic in large doses, at levels which are not reached in normal eating

patterns; but rhubarb leaves, if they were eaten, could deliver a harmful dose.

There is a persistent belief that the oxalic acid in sorrel is capable of softening the small bones of fish to such an extent that they 'melt away' or at least can be eaten without discomfort. Jaine (1986b) tested the hypothesis, using both sorrel leaves (which are traditionally used in cooking bony fish like shad) and various dilutions of oxalic acid, and established that any effect is insignificant. However, sorrel remains an excellent accompaniment to fish in the dishes where tradition calls for its use. The softening of fish bones can be and is achieved to some extent by prolonged cooking, whether with or without sorrel.

OXTAIL normally sold after being skinned and cut into chunks, has been a familiar sight in butchers' shops for centuries, but its sale was discontinued, at least in Britain, in 1997, in connection with BSE (see box under BEEF).

The dishes commonly made are oxtail soup, a long-standing favourite in Britain, but not only there; examples from other parts of the world include the oxtail soup of Sichuan which Yan-Kit So (1992) describes as a sophisticated rustic dish with chicken in it as well as oxtail, and including ingredients such as ginger, SICHUAN PEPPER, and dried CHINESE WOLFBERRIES. Apart from the soup there are various stews, e.g. the *Queue de bœuf en hochepot* of Flanders. These are rich but inexpensive dishes. The same applies to braised oxtail, and various forms of boned, stuffed oxtail. Generally speaking, wherever beef has been eaten there will be oxtail dishes, and they are likely to need lengthy cooking.

OYSTER of all marine MOLLUSCS the most prized and, until it was overtaken by the MUSSEL, the most cultivated. Almost alone among the molluscs, it has been the subject of a book at once scientific and poetic, Eleanor Clark's *The Oysters of Locmariaquer*. There is no better source from which to imbibe information about the manner in which oysters are reared and about their history in Brittany in particular.

All oysters begin their lives as 'spat', minuscule creatures which emerge by the million from the parent oyster and then look for something to which they can attach themselves. In nature this might be a rock, upon which the tiny oysters would grow (if not eaten by one of their numerous predators such as starfish, whelks, and slipper limpets) and eventually expire, after eight years or so spent filtering the sea-water and extracting nourishment from it. However, when man takes a hand, their lives are less sedentary, for they will be moved several times. First, if all goes according to plan, they will alight on specially prepared and positioned tiles (or other contrivances), on which they will spend eight months or so. These tiles will then be gathered up, so that the tiny oysters can be removed and redistributed in 'parks' or basins, incorporating some degree of shelter from predators, for what the French call the *élevage* stage. This lasts several years. Finally, the adult oysters are likely to be removed to five-star accommodation (the best of everything) for *affinage* (finishing).

Of the numerous species, the most important as food are described below.

The **European oyster,** *Ostrea edulis,* looks pretty, besides being delicious. Its shells are rounded and more regular in appearance than those of its larger cousin, the Portuguese oyster. There are many localities which have been famed for their oysters of this species, known as 'natives' in England and *plates* or *armoricaines* or *belons* in France. Although the Portuguese rival has taken over many breeding grounds, *O. edulis* continues to flourish in some, and has also been introduced to some places in New England and tried out elsewhere.

Colchester in Essex, where London clay underlies the estuaries, was the home of the renowned Pyfleet oysters. Whitstable in Kent had equal fame, and thanks to Charles Dickens (in his capacity as editor of *All the Year Round,* in 1859) we have a charming and detailed description of the Whitstable oyster fishery in the mid-19th century (quoted at length by Bolitho, 1960).

The Atlantic coast of France, and of Belgium and the Netherlands, is home to a number of other famous breeds; and the southern coast of Ireland is one of the most productive areas of all. In France, the European oysters now claim only a tenth or so of the market, but this fraction includes the famous belons of Brittany and some of the produce of famous *bassins* at Arcachon and Marennes-Oléron.

The **Portuguese oyster,** *Crassostrea angulata,* is, as its name indicates, a native of Portugal (and Spain and Morocco), although now considered to be the same as the giant Pacific oyster (see below). In Europe it has a maximum length of about 17 cm (6–7"), is usually whitish or dirty brown on the outside, and has one shell which is very noticeably concave. It is more robust than the European oyster, and has been introduced extensively into, for example, France and Britain. A story is told that a ship called the *Morlaisien,* carrying a cargo of these oysters from Portugal in the 1860s, took shelter from stormy weather in the Gironde estuary and there jettisoned its cargo, which was deemed to have spoiled; but that a number of the oysters were still

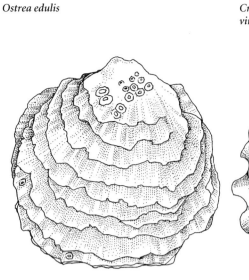

Ostrea edulis

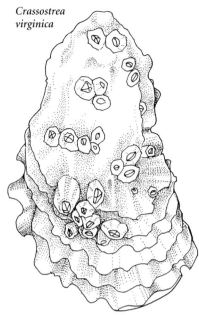

Crassostrea virginica

alive, found conditions in the estuary to their liking, and multiplied.

In France these oysters are called *huîtres creuses,* and dominate the market. Those from certain localities, for example the *fine de clair* from Marennes-Oléron, are especially esteemed, not because of their heredity (the spat often comes from elsewhere) but because of the qualities with which their environment during *élevage* and *affinage* endows them.

The **American oyster,** *Crassostrea virginica,* is larger than the European oyster, and about the same size (up to 17 cm/7") as the Portuguese oyster. The shell is rough and heavy, and usually of a greyish colour. The range of the species is the Atlantic seaboard from New Brunswick in Canada to the Gulf of Mexico. Early settlers in N. America were astonished by its abundance, and European visitors may still be surprised to find how relatively common and inexpensive the American oyster is. Its abundance has, however, decreased since the 19th century, which was for American oyster-lovers the period of supreme happiness. About 170 million pounds' weight were harvested in 1895. In the late 1920s the figure sank below the 100 million mark, and in the latter part of the 20th century to something like 50 million.

American oysters are marketed under a variety of names, mostly indicating whence they come. Among the most famous are the Cape oysters (from Cape Cod, especially Wellfleet, Chatham, and Wareham); those from Long Island (Blue Point, Gardiners Bay, Robbins Island); and those from the Chesapeake Bay area (e.g. Chincoteague Bay). It is not unusual for oysters to be transplanted to spend the last few months of their lives in these favoured habitats, where

they are thought to acquire special flavours characteristic of them.

If those who rate the Cape oysters best are correct, the reason may be this. In the colder northerly waters the oyster grows more slowly, taking five years to reach maturity compared with three in the Chesapeake region, and has a higher salt content. The slower growth rate results in the oysters forming smaller clusters and being more likely to have a pleasing shape for what is called 'the half-shell trade'.

There are several other American oysters, belonging to the Gulf States and the Pacific coast. The finest is probably the **Olympia oyster,** *O. lurida expansa,* a subspecies of the California oyster, *O. lurida.* This is a small (rarely up to 5 cm/2") and pretty oyster with an especially fine flavour.

Of **Asian oysters** the largest has already been mentioned above; it is the **giant Pacific** or oriental **oyster,** a form of *Crassostrea angulata,* formerly classified as *C. gigas,* which may be as much as 25 cm (10") long and (in normal growing conditions) has a markedly elongated form. The very large specimens, which would make an impossibly daunting mouthful, are not eaten raw, but cooked, or sun dried, or turned into 'oyster sauce'. Culture of this species is mainly for this last purpose. If, however, these oysters are harvested before they grow too big, they can be treated just like their other form, the Portuguese oysters familiar in Europe.

There are other smaller representatives of the genus in the region, but more interest attaches to *Saccostrea cucullata,* a species with one shell dimpled round the rim and the other equipped with corresponding protuberances, thus ensuring a very tight fit when the two close. This oyster is well known in Thailand, Malaysia, and Indonesia.

Australasian oysters include the Sydney rock oyster, *Crassostrea commercialis*, which is probably the most esteemed of all seafoods for Australians. This has a counterpart in the North Island of New Zealand, *C. glomerata*.

Oyster cookery flourished on both sides of the Atlantic in the 19th century, when oysters were plentiful and cheap in both Britain and N. America. Dishes such as oyster stews and soups, fried oysters, oysters on skewers with bits of bacon, and oyster fritters were common. But supplies began to dwindle in the 20th century and, as they became less common and more expensive, oysters were more likely to be eaten raw on the half-shell. Nonetheless, some luxury oyster dishes have survived, for example Oysters Bienville and Oysters Rockefeller, both with origins in New Orleans. Mariani (1994) has examined evidence about how these were originally prepared (the latter in particular supposedly having a secret recipe, dating from early in the 20th century), and he prefaces his account of these gastronomic peaks with illuminating general remarks on the earlier history of oysters (and oyster saloons and oyster houses) in the USA.

See also PEARL OYSTER.

OYSTER CRAB *Pinnotheres ostreum*, and *P. pisum*, pea crab, are remarkably small crabs (about 1.5 cm/0.6" or less) which live out their lives inside the shells of OYSTERS or MUSSELS. The female just stays there, but the male sallies out in search of a female, gets into the same shell as the female, copulates, and expires.

The pea crab is not normally eaten, but the oyster crab used to be regarded as a delicacy in the USA. Davidson (1979) records the following:

The *Washington Evening Star* of 21 September 1900 stated that there had even been a proposal to call it the Washington crab, since the first President of the United States had liked it so well, and said that 'we often see it floating upon the surface of an oyster stew'. It was usual to eat the little creatures whole, carapace and all, sautéed or deep-fried, with or without the oysters. They were also pickled. I am told, however, by a scientist at the Smithsonian that they ought to be eaten alive, that

they provide a welcome change of texture between oysters, and that they taste a little like celery. Few books contain a recipe for the oyster crab. An exception is *300 Ways to Cook and Serve Shell Fish* by H. Franklyn Hall, which was published at Philadelphia in 1901 and contains no fewer than sixteen.

OYSTER MUSHROOM or oyster fungus, *Pleurotus ostreatus*, is so named because it looks something like an oyster, and has a slippery texture. It grows abundantly on the trunks of dead or dying deciduous trees, and sometimes fence posts (or even, as a 19th-century observer called Plowright discovered, on the dry skull of a dead, stranded whale), in temperate regions throughout the world, from autumn to winter. It withstands cold, and even snow.

In shape it is like a distorted mushroom with a very short stem offset to the side and attached to the tree. Its gills are off-white, under a cap which is usually greyish-blue, turning pale brown with age. The fungus reaches 13 cm (5") in width. It is cultivated in China and Japan; also, on a smaller scale, in some European countries, of which Hungary was the pioneer.

The related species *P. cystidiosus* is cultivated in Taiwan and exported as the abalone mushroom. The name marks its resemblance to the large adductor muscle of the ABALONE.

There is also a white species, *P. porrigens*, sometimes called angel wings or 'savoury oyster', which is much smaller, and thinner, but otherwise similar. And some authors have distinguished as a separate species *P. evosmus*, the 'Tarragon oyster', of superior flavour and aroma. *P. cornucopioides* and *P. eryngii* are two more, both funnel shaped, and edible. The former may become one of the cultivated species in France (where it is known as *pleurote corne d'abondance*), and is found wild in Britain too. The latter, growing on the roots of certain flowering plants, is appreciated in the south of France, where it has many popular names, and esteemed in Spain as *seta de cardo*, but not found in Britain.

These fungi should be gathered only when young and tender, and the tough stems discarded. They can be fried, like oysters,

with results commended by McIlvaine (1902) as outstanding and by other authors as good enough to deceive an oyster-loving cat. They are juicy, may have an attractive peppery tang, and make a good addition to stews. Production and sales of commercially cultivated specimens are increasing, since growing them is easy.

OYSTER NUT the common name for the seed of either of two tropical African gourds borne by large vines, *Telfairia pedata* and *T. occidentalis*. The gourds themselves are inedible and are cultivated only for their seeds, which are large, numerous, and nutritious. A *T. pedata* gourd typically weighs 11 kg (25 lb) and has about 100 seeds, but it may be several times that size. The seeds are roughly circular and flattish (hence the name 'oyster nuts'), about 4 cm (1") in diameter and 1 cm (0.5") thick. *T. occidentalis* gourds, though not so large, have similar seeds. An E. African name for this species is *krobonko*. The seeds of both species are commonly called telfairia nuts. Other names for the plants are fluted pumpkin and Zanzibar oil vine.

The vines clamber up tall trees, and reach a great height. When the gourds ripen, they burst and the seeds are scattered, to be gathered, dried, and prised open (with difficulty, oyster fashion), revealing kernels with an olive-green skin and a soft but firm texture. The oil and protein content of these nuts is high (over 60% and around 27% respectively), they keep well, and their pleasant flavour makes them a good dessert nut.

Oyster nuts are eaten raw or boiled or roasted. Howes (1948) remarks that Africans will 'roast the nuts first, then extract the kernels and pound them to a paste by means of a mortar and the addition of a little water. This paste is then mixed with fish and cooked and wrapped in a banana leaf, affording a nourishing and toothsome dish.'

The kernels can also be pressed to yield a good cooking oil. The nuts are becoming increasingly important in international trade both for their oil and for use in confectionery; they are sometimes used as a substitute for Brazil nuts.

PACA *Agouti paca*, an American animal with a range from Mexico to N. Argentina, which is regarded by some authorities as the tastiest of all rodents. McGovern (*c.*1927) declared: 'I would trade all the beefsteaks and roast chickens in the world in order to banquet off one once more.' An observer among the Indians of Guiana in the 1880s had already declared that both the Indians and the colonists esteemed the flesh more highly than that of any other animal.

Adult pacas weigh from 6–14 kg (13–30 lb) and are approximately 60 cm (24") long with dark brown fur and four lines of white spots. In spite of being very fat animals they are astonishingly fast and agile and excellent swimmers. Their habits are nocturnal and they mostly feed on fruit, seeds, leaves, and roots.

Research is underway on breeding and raising them commercially but they do not seem to breed well in captivity.

PACAY a Quechua word used in Spanish to refer to a plant, *Inga feuillei*, which belongs to the upland areas of the Andean region of S. America and bears large pods, up to 70 cm (27") long, containing edible

white pulp. Some of the other plants of the genus with similar pods may be called guamá/guamo or ingá. Any of them, especially *I. edulis* and *I. paterno*, may also be called 'ice-cream bean'; the resemblance between the sweet, perfumed, white pulp and ice cream is striking.

The popularity of pacay pods, which offer a sweet snack food in a natural 'package', dates back to the times of the Incas, and persists among rural populations in the Andes. However, most of the numerous species in the genus are grown in lowland areas as shade plants, or for fuel. The nutritional value of the pulp in the pods is small. See illustration overleaf.

PACAYA the name used in C. America and Mexico for plants of the genus *Chamaedorea*, especially *C. costaricana* and *C. tepejilote*, which supply inflorescences which can be boiled as a vegetable, made into fritters, or used in salads.

PACIFIC ISLANDS are so numerous, especially if one includes uninhabited atolls, that a first glance at the map would suggest

that it would be impossible to organize them for the purposes of this book. However, for reasons involving geography, history, politics, and climate, they fall into three recognized groups; Melanesia, Micronesia, and Polynesia. The best-known islands in each group are shown in the box.

For various reasons there are separate entries for HAWAII, NEW ZEALAND, OKINAWA, and PAPUA NEW GUINEA.

Migrants from SE Asia began to move south into the islands of the W. Pacific and Australia about 30,000–40,000 years ago, and thereafter, over thousands of years, migrated into islands further east. Some of them eventually populated the huge area of what is now Polynesia. These peoples remained invisible to European eyes until the 16th century. Magellan, sailing round the southernmost point of S. America towards the end of 1519, was the first to sail into and across the Pacific Ocean and it was he who gave it its name.

The land area of the islands, compared to the vast area of ocean, is tiny. Indeed air travellers will perceive the islands as tiny specks in endless expanses of blue nothingness. But the world of the inhabitants of the small societies below is

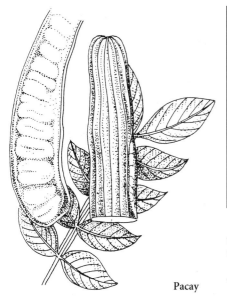

Pacay

BEST-KNOWN PACIFIC ISLANDS

Melanesia
Papua New Guinea, The Solomons, Vanuatu (New Hebrides), New Caledonia, Fiji

Micronesia
Northern Marianas, Guam, Western Carolines, Eastern Carolines, Marshalls, Nauru, Kiribati (Gilberts)

Polynesia
Tuvalu (Ellis), Wallis and Futnua, Western Samoa, American Samoa, Tonga, Niue, Cook Islands, Tahiti (Society Islands), Tuamotus, Marquesas, Australs, Hawaii (Sandwich Islands), New Zealand-Maori

much larger than mere terrestrial boundaries would suggest. A beach is for them the gateway to a different yet contiguous and familiar environment, a hunting ground which has been a perpetual source of sustenance. The fishing prowess of the islanders, acquired by culture, customs, and environment, is so great and so universal that it might seem to be a genetic trait.

It would certainly have been desirable for the early migrants to be good at fishing, since they would have found progressively less vegetation and fauna as they moved eastward and further into the Pacific. To be sure, they were able to take some of their own domestic animals with them, and to introduce some of their own crops. Even so, the range of edibles was limited, and the impact of the 'discovery' of the islands by Europeans was correspondingly great, since they brought new food plants and began depositing stocks of animals like the pig here and there for the benefit of future voyagers. (Tahiti, a prime example of this kind of implantation, has remained French throughout the era of 'decolonization' and shows many signs of French influence in its cuisine as well as in other respects. One benefit for food historians is that documentation of its food plants has been well carried out by French botanists.)

If seafood was the main staple and the main source of protein, one would certainly give second place to roots and tubers: notably TARO and SWEET POTATO, providing carbohydrate and forming in terms of volume the foundation of the diet. However, fruits and nuts were also important, especially the COCONUT; the liquid cooking medium throughout the area is coconut milk, providing a common denominator for all the diverse local cuisines.

Other points of interest which apply to the whole region or to much of it include these:

• SOY SAUCE is the standard condiment throughout the Pacific; households are equipped with gallon containers rather than little bottles.
• CORNED BEEF and SPAM have enjoyed remarkable popularity.
• The 'earth oven' is used (see NEW ZEALAND).
• Feasts were and are held on the slightest excuse—feasts of welcome to visitors, of parting and farewell, to honour new chiefs, new buildings, saints' days, births, marriages, and wakes (plus feasts laid on for the benefit of tourists!). The scene at a

typical feast is such a colourful one that it deserves a fuller description, provided by Jennifer Brennan in the box below.

PADEK a speciality of Laos, belonging to the family of FISH SAUCES but distinguished from most of them by the presence of chunks of fish in the liquid.

Padek has a very strong smell, and is usually kept in a special pot hanging outside the house. It is an ingredient in numerous Lao dishes. Sometimes the liquid element in it is used alone; this is called *nam padek*.

PAELLA to be precise the Valencian paella, universally known as a traditional

PACIFIC ISLAND FEASTS

THE sonorous echoes of a blown conch or the penetrating pounding of a wooden slit drum (the latter in Melanesia) cut into the evening air, alerting the participants and guests to the start of the festivities. With an air of subdued excitement and anticipation, clusters of people converge toward the feast site, drawn by lights hanging from the trees leading to a grassy clearing amid coconut palms by the sea. As the sun slips beneath the water on the horizon, a trio of musicians, heads crowned with wreaths of green ferns, softly beat on drums and pluck the strings of coconut ukuleles. All day long men and women have been moving to and fro, carrying bundles of food, baskets of fruit, sucking pigs slung by their feet from bamboo poles. Much laughter has been heard, with the staccato of chopping and the thud of pestles meeting mortars.

A long train of large, finely woven pandanus mats has been laid down the centre of the clearing. A four-foot-wide swathe of banana and TI leaves forms the 'table' surface down the centre of the mats. On the seemingly endless green expanse wooden platters jostle woven palm serving dishes, bamboo baskets, coconut bowls, and containers fashioned from banana leaves. Chunks of purple taro contrast with the bone-white sweet potato. Yellow yam slices punctuate green leaf cradles filled with young taro tops, steamed in coconut milk. Scarlet coconut crabs loom over dishes of the little, brown reef crabs; humble but no less delicious.

Whole, cooked reef fish, mouths agape, lie supine on banana leaves. Bowls display chunks of larger, white game fish, marinated until 'cooked' in lime juice, speckled with a confetti of green onions and scarlet chilli peppers, and dressed with coconut cream. Platters of chicken pieces lie alongside curved ribs of barbecued pork. Bound bundles of heat-browned banana leaves contain young taro leaves wrapped around a steamed filling of coconut cream, lemon, onions, shredded beef. Other leaf-wrapped 'puddings' feature taro, sweet potato, yams, plantains, all mixed in a melange of coconut cream and seasonings and steamed in the earth oven.   JB dish in Spanish cooking, takes its name from the utensil in which it is cooked and from the Spanish region on the shores of the Mediterranean where it had its origin. This dish symbolizes the union and heritage of two important cultures, the Roman which gave us the utensil and the Arab which brought us the basic food of humanity for centuries: RICE.

The etymological roots of the word are of interest. Going back a long way one finds in the Sanskrit language the word *pá*, which means to drink, from which were derived the Latin terms *patera*, *patina*, *patella*, meaning a chalice or culinary utensil to be used for various purposes including frying. In Castilian there existed a primitive form of denomination *paela* and also *patella*, so in an ancient dictionary we can read that 'patella is a pan or paella for frying'. There also existed old adapted forms of *padiella*, so we can read *paella* in the *Duties from Santander* of the 13th century and *paellon* in an inventory from Toledo in 1434. The name *payla* was also used and in the 16th century many classical authors mention these utensils in their works, among them Fray Luis of Granada who states in one of his works, 'the idols came to be unappreciated and were smelted down—as they deserved—to be made into paylas and caldrons'. This word, while it is not normally used in Spanish, can still be heard in Andalusia and Latin America. The etymological form *paele* or *payele* existed in French up until the 15th century and then became *poêle* which means pan.

The patina and patella which were used in Roman times were in principle of a concave base and, according to size, had one or two handles. This concave base gradually reduced its curvature until it became a flat, circular base of different diameters, taking full advantage of the heat from the fire, converting itself into the utensil called paella.

The types of cooking fires vary and depend on the natural environment. In the Mediterranean zone, the lack of forests, therefore of firewood, obliged the inhabitants to find some other form of combustion.

Along the coast where rice was first grown, the only firewood available was a branch or an odd log, vine shoots, or branches from the pruning of trees, etc. This firewood, because of its acid composition, has the advantage of contributing more calories and maintaining the embers at a regular heat.

The utensils began to adapt to the types of fires and from the different pans in the south of Europe sprang the art of frying. When this type of big pan or paella was used in the cooking of rice it was only natural that its diameter had to be in proportion to the

quantities of the ingredients and that its sides and circumference should be slight to make the evaporation easier, to cook the rice and to absorb the aroma of the firewood.

The size of paella pans is from 10 to 90 cm (4" to 35"), without any big difference in the depth which is approximately from 4 to 7 cm (1.5" to 2.5").

In Islamic Andalusia there were dishes based on rice with definite traditional and symbolic character, casseroles of rice and fish with spices which were eaten at family and religious feasts.

Later on, when rice began to take on the characteristics of an everyday dish, it was combined with vegetables, pulses, and also some dry cod, in this way forming a part of the menu during Lent. Along the coast fish always predominates with rice.

Perhaps as a hangover of these Islamic customs, in the orchards of Valencia, and as a special celebration, rice was cooked in the open air in a paella-pan with vegetables of the season, chicken, rabbit, or duck. With the sociological changes of the 19th century, social life became more active, giving rise to reunions and outings to the countryside. There also came into being the tradition, still very much alive, that men did the cooking of paella.

This rice for special days evolved into the Valencian paella. In 1840 in a local newspaper it was in fact given the name of Valencian paella. By natural process the tradition had already come into being.

The ingredients for the authentic dish are as follows: rice, chicken, rabbit or lean pork, green beans, fresh butter beans, tomato, olive oil, paprika, saffron, snails (or, a curious alternative, fresh green rosemary), water, and salt.

The ancient tradition was to eat the paella directly from its pan, so the round pan, surrounded by chairs, was converted into an admirable 'Round Table'.

The companions, with their spoons made of box wood with a fine finish, began to eat, each one drawing out his triangle and limit, then meeting in the geometrical centre of the paella. The respect and courtesy was worthy of the Knights of the Round Table.

This form of eating from the same dish is commented on in the *Book of Sent Sovi* when he mentions medieval habits which existed and still exist in the Arab world. It is probable that for this reason we hold on to these memories.   LoM
READING: Lourdes March (1985); Colman Andrews (1988).

PAIN PERDU (literally, 'lost bread'), a French method for using leftover bread or BRIOCHE. The sliced bread is coated in beaten egg and then fried in clarified butter and sprinkled with sugar. Pain perdu has

also been known in England since medieval times, and there are traces of something not very different in the recipes of APICIUS (1st century AD with later additions). Indeed it occurs in various forms and under different names in many countries, although it is convenient to treat the French version as the archetype (cf N. American usage—a name current there is 'French toast').

This sort of thing may often have represented a strategy for making the most of stale bread, but the use of expensive ingredients in many versions suggests that pain perdu was more frequently regarded as a delicacy. The Anglo-Norman versions of pain perdu sometimes used wine for soaking the bread, and almond milk for serving. Sugar or honey and spices were also poured over the bread before it was dished up.

In 17th-century England, pain perdu developed into a particularly rich dish known as 'cream toasts' or POOR KNIGHTS. In Spain, stale bread is soaked in milk, dipped in beaten egg, fried, and served with syrup or honey and spices, to form the basis of a popular dessert known as *torrijas* or *tostadas* (in Portugal, *rabanadas*).   (LM)

PAKISTAN a relatively new nation, created when India was partitioned in 1947. Until the secession of its eastern wing (now Bangladesh) in 1971, it covered those areas of the Indian subcontinent where the population was predominantly Muslim.

Although Pakistan is a new nation its cuisine has developed over centuries, and it is closely related to the cuisine of its neighbours, that of AFGHANISTAN to the west and INDIA to the east. Pakistan also shares a border with IRAN.

Pakistan is a land of contrasts. The Hindu Kush mountains lie to the north. In the south there is desert. In between there are areas of green valleys and fertile plains watered by the Indus and its four tributaries. The climate ranges from extreme heat to cold.

The staple grain is WHEAT and Pakistan is a predominantly bread-eating country. There is the flat leavened NAN, traditionally baked in a TANDOOR, and there is the unleavened wholemeal CHAPATI. Bread is used for scooping up food as it is the custom, as it is in most Muslim countries, to eat food with the right hand and not with cutlery. PARATA is a fried bread which is sometimes stuffed with DAL, or with vegetable or meat mixtures. PULSES are important and are widely used. BESAN FLOUR is used making PAKORA, which is a favourite snack food.

MAIZE is grown in Pakistan and a bread called *makai ki roti* is made from this. Pakistan also produces some of the finest RICE in the world, basmati, which is the preferred rice for preparing their special rice dishes such as BIRIANI and PILAF.

Pakistanis eat a great deal of meat (except for pork, forbidden to Muslims). Lamb is the preferred meat but chicken and beef are also consumed. The meat is prepared in three basic ways—as a KORMA, as KEBAB, or ground and made into KOFTA. These dishes are often highly spiced. A cooling minty yoghurt sauce called *burani* (see BURAN) is a common accompaniment to this spicy food.

Pakistanis have a sweet tooth and make a number of puddings, pastries, and sweets. As in other Muslim countries they are usually made with flour or mealy products such as semolina. HALVA, which means 'sweet' in Pakistan, is very popular; it can be made with flour or semolina but is sometimes made with nuts or even vegetables such as carrot or pumpkin. *Zarda pilau* is a sweet pilau (see PILAF) which is flavoured and coloured with saffron and cooked with pistachio, almond, and raisins. Rosewater (see ROSES) and kewra essence (see SCREWPINE) are common flavourings for sweets.

LASSI is a refreshing and cooling yoghurt drink especially welcome in the long, hot summer months. In winter, *kanji*, a semi-fermented drink, is made from black carrots.

The regions of Pakistan vary considerably. In the south there is Sind covering the area where the huge Indus River comes down to the sea—the area which was the cradle of the ancient Indus Valley civilizations. This is the one part of Pakistan where fish and other seafood are plentiful. To the west lies Baluchistan, largely pastoral, reflecting to some extent the influence of neighbouring Iran, for example in a KORMA (*Alu bokhara gosht*) which features PLUMS (of the species *Prunus bokhariensis*) and almonds as well as onion, green chilli, and meat.

To the north lies Pakistan's share of Punjab (the name means 'five waters', referring to five famous rivers), including the legendary city of Lahore and fertile land where exceptionally fine blood oranges, grapes, and sweet melons are grown. SUGAR CANE is also grown there and the whole region is known as 'the granary of the sub continent'. Westwards, towards Afghanistan, comes the North-West Frontier, a rugged area with famously warlike inhabitants. In terms of food, the emphasis is on meat and this is the home of one special kebab, *chappli kebab*, a minced meat KEBAB which has been formed into the shape of a sandal (hence its name), and which is exceptionally hot.

Further to the north comes Swat, presided over in former times by the Akond made famous by Edward Lear's poem. The first illustrated edition of this (ed. Jackson) was published in 1997. The illustrations by Ann Arnold include several food scenes, depicted in a manner both authentic and witty.

Further north still lies Baltistan, the improbable source of much of the restaurant cooking done in the British city of Birmingam; see BALTI. (HS)

PAKORA (pakaura) are batter-fried vegetables or fish, usually eaten as an appetizer or snack in India, Pakistan, and Afghanistan. They are a popular street food. The batter is usually made of BESAN FLOUR and water. They are flavoured with spices such as turmeric, coriander, and cayenne. Pakora are particularly popular with vegetarians.

A variety of vegetables can be used such as onion rings, cauliflower, cabbage, sliced aubergines, potatoes, carrots, cucumber, celery, and spinach. Pakora can also be made with cooked rice or semolina and also *panir* (cheese) and meat. They are usually served with a spicy chutney for dipping.

They are also known as *bhajis* or *bhajias*.
HS

PAKSIW a culinary term of the Philippines, refers to the process of cooking in vinegar, and also to the dishes so cooked. It is often fish, covered with vinegar, ginger, salt, and pepper and allowed to boil. Water and some pork lard may be added, and the dish then removed from the fire after a second boiling. It may be eaten hot or cold, and keeps without refrigeration.

Meats cooked in vinegar and spices are also called *paksiw*. Pork *paksiw* has soy sauce, a bit of sugar, garlic, and a bay leaf. When pork hock is used, BANANA FLOWERS and whole cooking bananas are often added. The most luxurious dish of the genre is *Paksiw na lechon*, made with what is left over after a feast of the whole, spit-roasted pig called *lechon*. This is cooked in vinegar, a sauce made from the liver, garlic, soy sauce, and other aromatic ingredients which sometimes include cinnamon and thyme. Many claim to prefer this to the original feast; and it is even said that roast pigs are sometimes bought for the sole purpose of making *paksiw*—an idea which stands on its head the traditional use of *paksiw* as a means of preserving food, including leftovers, in the days before refrigeration.

Lechon-makers prepare their own *paksiw*, or sell heads, feet, and other less popular cuts for home-made *paksiw*. DF

PALATE the roof of the mouth of a vertebrate. In human beings, this is regarded as the organ of taste; hence expressions such as 'she has a fine palate'. In certain other vertebrates, the palate is food for human beings. Beef palate (*palais de bœuf* in France, where it used to be popular—cooked in a

white COURT BOUILLON and dressed like calf's head) is nowadays almost unknown as a menu item.

Dried palate of WATER-BUFFALO is an ingredient in the kitchens of Laos (Phia Sing, 1981), but even there it is not always an ingredient of choice, being in some dishes a surprising substitute for the more expensive prawns which have to be imported from Thailand and would otherwise be preferred.

PALAVER SAUCE also called *plassas* (Sierra Leone), *ban flo* (Ghana), and palm oil chop, a dish which is widespread in W. Africa. It is based on large quantities of green leaves ('spinach'), including BITTERLEAF, and usually contains small amounts of meat and/or offal together with dried fish and shellfish. Often the thickening is of egusi seeds (see WATERMELON). It also contains what seems to the uninitiated like a very large amount of PALM OIL.

The name is thought to derive from the Portuguese *palavra* ('word'). JM

PALILLO *Escobedia scabrifolia*, a herb of the family Scrophulariaceae which is found in various countries of Latin America, sometimes also called *raiz de color* (colouring root) or (misleadingly, since it only resembles saffron in its colouring effect) *azafrán*. Elisabeth Lambert Ortiz (1984) writes:

Palillo is a Peruvian herb [of which the root is] used dried and ground to give a yellow colour to food. Since so many Peruvian foods are yellow or white, I'm sure it is a reflection of pre-Conquest Inca sun (and moon) worship. . . . I have found that using half the amount of turmeric gives much the same result.

PALM This subject has been given, by Corner (1966), a remarkably felicitous introduction:

Of all land plants, the palm is the most distinguished. A columnar stem crowned with giant leaves is the perfect idea, popular or philosophic, of what a plant should be. It suffers no attrition through ramification. In all the warmer parts of the earth this form stamps itself in grand simplicity on the landscape. It manifests itself in more than two thousand species and several hundred genera, every one restricted more or less by climate, terrain, and geographical history. The present distribution of palms resembles an immense chessboard on which we see the last moves of a great game of life. Kings and queens are Malaysian and Amazonian. The major pieces have moved into America, Africa, and Asia, and the pawns have reached the islands. There are fragments of the early moves in the Cretaceous rocks, dating back 120 million years. A fan-palm has been reported from the Triassic of

Colorado, and we do not know when the game began or whence it was derived. All we can say is that the palms are as old, if not older, than any other form of flowering plant and that they have endured while the rest have pressed forward into modern trees, climbers, herbs, and grasses, ramified, extended, twisted, and simplified.

Palm is now the general name for these trees, of the family Arecaceae, which have such an interesting history. It is a large family, belonging to the tropics and subtropics, and many of its members furnish important foodstuffs: the COCONUT, DATE, SAGO, PALM SUGAR, etc. See also OIL PALMS; PALMYRA PALM.

In addition, many palms provide edible leaves or shoots which are eaten as vegetables. In some, the whole central terminal shoot at the top of the stem is taken, giving a palm cabbage or heart of palm. This excision kills the tree, so it is normally a wasteful process and the product is expensive. Trees exploited in this way include the coconut palm, *Cocos nucifera*, and royal palms, *Roystonea* spp, which, if left alone, would produce coconuts and sago respectively. There are, however, palms which produce multiple shoots, from which some terminal shoots can be harvested without damage to the plant as a whole. Among these are *Guilielma gasipaes*, the peach palm or PEJIBAYE; *Sabal* spp, known as palmetto or in one instance 'swamp cabbage'.

Palm hearts (or hearts of palm, or palm cabbage) are available in cans, in stick-shaped pieces. These make a delicious salad, commonly served with a pinkish mayonnaise-type sauce and well liked in Belgium and France.

There is one other palm, *Euterpe oleracea*, which yields not only palm cabbages but also edible fruits, sometimes called acaí. It is cultivated in tropical America. Facciola (1990) observes that:

The pulp of the fruit is added to water to make a violet-colored beverage or juice. It is then consumed with tapioca and sugar, with cassava meal and grilled fish . . ., as a porridge cooked with cassava meal, or as an ice cream or popsickle flavoring.

This is not the only example of a palm producing edible fruit of this sort; there is also SALAK.

The rattan palm, *Calamus latifolius*, also bears edible fruits, brownish-yellow, imbricate, and apiculate (i.e. with a sharp little point projecting from the end and with overlapping 'scales', like the LYCHEE). The inner part of the shoots can also be eaten. In fact, other members of the extensive rattan family have edible parts including in some instances the 'cabbage'.

The pulp of the fruit of *Oenocarpus distichus*, bacaba de azeite, yields an oil comparable to olive oil; and *Orbignya*

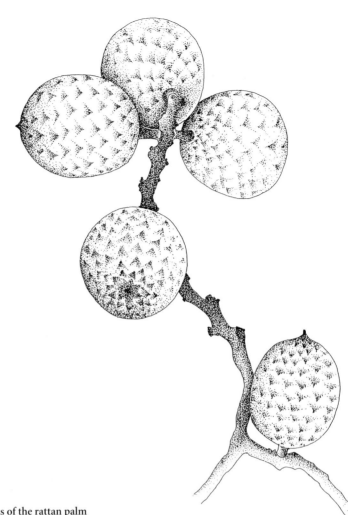

Fruits of the rattan palm

martiana, babassú, shows great culinary versatility, producing palm hearts, an edible oil, a flour which is mixed with milk and sugar to make a drink supposed to resemble chocolate, besides 'meat' which can be eaten as a snack or used to produce something like coconut milk; etc.

PALM OIL sometimes called palm kernel oil, an edible oil of great commercial importance and many uses. It is made from the nutlike fruit kernel of *Elaeis guineensis*, the most important of the OIL PALMS (under which head others are described) and the most productive of all plants supplying edible oil.

This is usually referred to as the oil palm. Originally it was only of importance in its native W. Africa, where it grows in the hot, moist region inland from the Bight of Benin and up the Congo Valley. The most common African name for its nut, from which the oil is taken, is **dende** (often written as dendé or dendê); and it is under this name that the oil is known in Brazil;

where it has been described (by Sokolov, 1991) as 'the heart and soul of one of the hemisphere's great postcolonial food cultures'. It had arrived there, in the region of Bahia, with slaves brought from W. Africa by the Portuguese, and enabled these Yoruba or Hausa slaves to recreate the essential smell and taste of their homeland in the New World. Even where dende oil is not available, people of African heritage have found ways of colouring their cooking oils red to resemble it.

This oil palm is now grown in tropical regions around the world and the production of palm oil (sometimes also called palm kernel oil) has become a major industry. Malaysia has become the main producer.

The tree is tall (up to 30 m/100') and long-lived (150 years or more). The fruit, the size of a small plum, is borne in large clusters of about 200, rather in the manner of dates. The outer skin is usually orange or yellow, in some kinds black at its pointed tip or all over. The fibrous pulp is very oily and unpalatable. The stone is the size of a nutmeg and has a hard, black case, sometimes thick, sometimes thin. Inside is a white, oily kernel.

Thus both the outer and inner parts of the fruit yield oils, which are different in character. Both are highly saturated, which means that they have a high melting point and are semi-solid in temperate conditions. Oil from the pulp is yellow and higher in free fatty acids, so that it has a pronounced flavour and easily becomes rancid. Kernel oil is paler, cleaner, and more stable.

The traditional method of extracting oil, practised by Africans for their domestic purposes, was to take a small amount of fresh fruit and to boil, pound, wash, strain, and reboil it, then to skim off the oil from the water. This yielded a good oil with a pleasant flavour. It did not keep long, but that did not matter, for only a little was made at a time. Kernels were cracked, and the oil extracted in a similar way.

It was not until the 19th century that there was any commercial interest in the palm as a source of saleable oil. At first European traders chose to leave extraction to the Africans, in order to save shipping costs on the fruit. However, the oil so produced was inferior; and around 1870 Europeans began to buy kernels separately so that they could extract the better kernel oil themselves, and apply new techniques to the pulp oil, making it edible. During the 20th century the growth of the MARGARINE industry magnified demand. Conventional hard margarine needs a semi-solid, highly saturated fat. Ordinary liquid vegetable oils, if used, have to be 'hardened' chemically. Palm oil needs less treatment, and has therefore been much used in margarine, with the result that during most of the 20th century world production of palm oil has been doubling every decade.

In 1848 four oil palms were taken from Mauritius to the botanical garden at Bogor in Java. Seeds from them were distributed around Indonesia and, by luck, a superior, high-yielding strain arose at Deli in Sumatra. It was short-stemmed, which made harvesting easier. The cultivation of this variety expanded rapidly in Indonesia, and later in Malaysia. Malaysia is now the world's largest producer; Indonesia has also outstripped the largest African growers, the Congo and the Ivory Coast.

New varieties, mostly bearing fruits with thin-shelled kernels, are gradually replacing older strains including the Deli. The average output in the world as a whole is 1,000 kg of oil per hectare (890 1b/acre), much more than that of any other oil plant.

PALM SUGAR commonly referred to as jaggery (or gur) in S. and SE Asia, where it is widely used, is obtained from the sap of various palm trees, notably *Arenga pinnata* and *Borassus flabellifer*, the PALMYRA PALM.

The sap is produced when the tree converts its starch reserves into sugar in preparation for the growth of inflorescences at the top of the stem. The procedure for obtaining the sap often involves maltreating the young inflorescence, e.g. by pummelling it with a wooden mallet over a period of several days, to bruise the tissue inside and set the sap flowing. The sap is collected in containers set to catch it as it flows out of incisions in the trunk. The flow may continue for two or three months.

The actual sugar content of the sap varies from 10% to over 15%. The product sold in the markets, often in a neat 'parcel' formed by a folded leaf, is brown and crumbly. In Malaysia it is called *gula melaka* (after Malacca, a centre for its manufacture), and in Indonesia *gula jawa* (for Java).

Palm honey (*miel de palma*) is a sweet product which sounds similar but is made by boiling down the sap of yet another palm, *Jubaea chilensis*, the Chilean wine palm (or *coco de Chile* or honey palm). The fruits of this palm have edible kernels which resemble small coconuts and are called *coquitos* or cokernuts or pygmy coconuts, occasionally available as an exported delicacy.

PALMYRA PALM *Borassus flabellifer*, a common palm of S. Asia, cultivated in India and Sri Lanka, mainly as a source of PALM SUGAR, but also for the extraction of SAGO and for its fruits and nuts. The palm, like the COCONUT and the NIPA PALM, also serves numerous other purposes. Indeed, if Watt (1889–96) is correct in referring to a Tamil poem which records 'some 800 uses to which the various parts are put', it may outdo its rivals in versatility. The leaves are used for writing material, thatching, etc., and are also a source of salt; the inflorescence provides juice, drunk fresh or boiled down to yield jaggery (sugar), or fermented to wine and vinegar.

The fruits grow in clusters like the coconut but are smaller (about 10–12.5 cm/4.5" in diameter), rounder, and slightly flattened at both ends. They have a dark purple skin, with green bracts at the base. Each fruit has three seeds, the fleshy part of which resembles the meat of the coconut and is eaten fresh. There is also a small quantity of liquid, which is taken as a drink.

This palm grows in most parts of the Sudan, where it is known as *doleib*, and is important as a famine food, besides providing palm sprouts.

PALOLO a strange marine delicacy of the South Sea islands, well described by Hornell (1950):

On the occurrence of one particular phase of the moon towards the close of the year, incredible numbers of a sea-worm, known as palolo in Samoa and Tonga and as mbololo in Fiji, rise to the surface of the sea from the submerged coral reefs which encircle these islands. This swarming is limited to two particular days, one usually in October, the other in November. The natives know from experience exactly when to expect them. . . . When the signs are recognized, every available canoe is manned and paddled out to the reef shortly after midnight; here they eagerly await the coming of the worms. If their calculation is correct, as it generally is, the swarm begins to appear on the surface about 2 hours before sunrise. Work is carried on with feverish haste. All are armed with hand-nets of some sort or other. Almost anything will serve, so dense are the writhing, wriggling masses of worms. Every canoe and receptacle must be filled before sunrise, for the moment the flaming rays of the sun strike the water, the worms, which are mere delicate-walled tubes filled with eggs or with sperm, burst and shed their contents into the water. Within a few minutes the swarms have vanished like smoke before the wind; no sign remains except a thin whitish scum floating on the surface.

Gwen Skinner (1983), giving the name as balolo, identifies the worm as *Eunice viridis*, the specific name being given because its colour is 'spinach-green', and

Palmyra palm fruits

states that balolo are eaten raw or fried in butter, sometimes with onion. She believes that, to be precise, what come to the surface are the detachable egg- and sperm-sacs of the worms, brownish and greenish respectively.

It has proved possible to freeze palolo, despite the delicate structure of the sacs.

PALOODEH a type of sweet dessert or drink which dates back to Zoroastrian times, is still made in Iran and also in Afghanistan and India where it is called *faluda*. The Middle Eastern *baluza, balusa* (and Turkish *palta*, for that matter) are all descendants of Persian *paludeh* in name, so that the geographical range of this item covers a very large area. The Persian word itself simply means 'sieved, refined'. But the meaning has been extended in various directions. Thus, to take just two examples, the word can mean cornstarch pudding or a kind of rosewater granita (see WATER ICES) containing a sort of vermicelli (described below) and sprinkled with lime juice.

To make the 'vermicelli', cornflour or wheat starch and water are blended together into a thick, white paste which is then cooked over heat until the mixture becomes almost translucent. The mixture is forced through a type of colander or pasta machine (in India called a *sev* machine, see SEV, SEVIYAN) into iced water (or snow, as in ancient times). The result is that tiny rice-like grains or small vermicelli are formed in the ice. (Nowadays the mixture is often piped into iced water which results in longer vermicelli.) The paloodeh is then served topped with one of a variety of toppings including fruit SHERBET; fruit syrup; FIRNI; or a kind of milk custard which is flavoured with SALEP or as a topping for ice cream (*kulfi* in India).

In Afghanistan these ricelike or vermicelli-like grains are often called *jhala*, which means hailstones, because of the resemblance to hail.

Mountstuart Elphinstone (1839) said that in the summer, when ice was to be had in Caubul (Kabul), fulodeh (faluda) was a favourite food, a 'jelly . . . eaten with the expressed juice of fruits and ice, to which cream is also sometimes added'.

The *balouza* of the Middle East is made from cornflour, water, and sugar which is cooked until thick and then flavoured with orange blossom or rosewater. Chopped almonds and pistachio nuts are stirred in. Claudia Roden (1985) says:

This pudding is like opaline encrusted with little stones. When it is served it trembles like a jelly. It is customary for an admiring audience to compliment a belly dancer by comparing her tummy to a 'balouza'.   HS

PANADA PANADE, an English and a French word which are both derived from the Latin *panis* (bread) and have similar but not identical meanings.

Panada, in English, dates back to the 16th century, and was often spelled panado. Its first meaning is a sort of bread gruel or soup, typically made by boiling some bread in water and then adding flavouring. With the addition of lemon, wine, and sugar, it was considered in the 17th century to be highly nourishing for invalids. Hannah Glasse (1747) thought so too but disallowed the wine in her version. The second meaning of the term is a paste made with breadcrumbs or any of various flours and water, milk, or stock, to be used for thickening or similar purposes.

Panade, the French term, can mean not only a bread soup or gruel of some delicacy, possibly enriched with egg and spiced, but also a similar soup in which the role of bread is taken over by potato or rice, for example.

PANCAKE means, to a western European or an American, a flat cake made from a BATTER of flour, eggs, and milk, and fried in a shallow pan or cooked on a greased GRIDDLE. It may be eaten flat, sprinkled with sugar; or rolled around a sweet or savoury filling, for example in many French crêpe dishes. Some pancakes of other regions fall neatly into this category, such as the Russian BLINI and Hungarian *palacsinta*. With others the distinction between a pancake and a griddle bread is not so clear.

Most pancakes or crêpes are thin. However, the excellent Scots pancakes and their counterparts in other Celtic areas (all treated under DROP SCONE) are thicker, and so are *Schmarren* (mentioned below).

The griddle method of cooking is older than oven baking, and pancakes are an ancient form. The first pancakes clearly distinguishable from plain griddle breads are sweet ones mentioned by APICIUS; these were made from a batter of egg, mixed milk and water, and a little flour, fried and served with pepper and honey.

An English culinary manuscript of about 1430 refers to pancakes in a way which implies that the term was already familiar, but it does not occur often in the early printed cookery books. It seems to have been only in the 17th century that pancakes came to the fore in Britain. They were made from a flour and egg batter mixed with milk, cream, or water. Gervase Markham (1615) favoured a batter made with water, because milk or cream made pancakes 'tough, cloying, and not crisp'. But cream had its advocates. Wine or brandy was also often added. By the next century the milk and cream faction had won. In 1737 *The Whole Duty of a Woman* gave four pancake recipes

(all subsequently copied without acknowledgement by the more famous Hannah GLASSE). One of these called for an extra rich batter with 18 egg yolks and ½ pint (250 ml) each of cream and sack. Another was a recipe for what was called 'A Quire of Paper', very thin pancakes fried on both sides, sprinkled with sugar, and piled in a flat stack; the name was given because in the 18th century a quire of paper consisted of 24 sheets folded in half.

Throughout Europe pancakes had a place among EASTER FOODS, especially on Shrove Tuesday (or Mardi Gras), the last day before Lent. Customs varied from country to country. Thus in the Netherlands WAFFLES as well as pancakes were eaten on Shrove Tuesday; in medieval Germany doughnuts were the Shrove Tuesday speciality, and pancakes were reserved for Easter days after Lent; while in Russia blini were sold by street vendors during the Maslyanitsa or 'butter festival' before Lent.

One peculiarly English institution is the pancake race. The oldest of these has been held at Olney in Buckinghamshire, in most years since 1445. Only local housewives can take part and they must make the pancakes themselves. The church bells warn when to make them and when to assemble for the start. Contestants, who must wear an apron and a hat or scarf, race over a course of 380 m/415 yards with the pancake in a pan, during which it must be tossed and caught three times. The winner and runner-up are presented with prayer books.

In the latter part of the 20th century the outstanding development in the world of pancakes has been the growth in the number of crêperies, not only in France but also elsewhere.

A small selection of interesting pancakes follows:

Bao bing (thin pancake), a Chinese pancake made simply of fine wheat flour and very hot water. The dough is kneaded and rolled thin; two layers at once, oiled to keep them separate, are rolled, cooked in this joined state on a dry griddle, and then peeled apart and stacked under a cloth. These are the pancakes which accompany the well-known PEKING DUCK, but they are also served with other dishes.

Crêpes Suzette, sweet pancakes rolled or folded with an orange sauce and flambéed (see FLAME) with curaçao or the like. Ayto (1993) dismisses the story that a French chef, Charpentier, invented the dish (by accident, in some versions) at Monte Carlo in 1896 for the then Prince of Wales, 'Suzette' being of the Prince's company at the time. He finds that the earliest reference in print is Escoffier (1903); and rightly comments that the dish was for the first two-thirds of the 20th century the epitome of luxury desserts, but is now less often encountered.

Dadar gutung, an Indonesian sweet pancake. Plain batter similar to the western type is used. The pancake is wrapped around a filling of fresh coconut meat cooked in water with brown sugar, and flavoured with cinnamon and lemon juice, with a little salt.

Palacsinta (in German-speaking areas *Palatschinken*—the word is derived from the Latin *placenta*; see CAKE), a thin Hungarian pancake similar to and used like a French crêpe; also popular in Austria as an alternative to the more solid *Schmarren*. There are plain and sweet versions, and also a light kind made with separated eggs, the beaten whites folded in just before cooking. The pancakes may be served flat with sugar, or rolled up around a filling.

Pannequet, a French term used for a crêpe rolled around a filling, savoury or sweet.

Potato pancakes are made in several countries. Irish BOXTY is a potato pancake. *Latke* is a potato pancake (sometimes described as a FRITTER) of Jewish cuisine, made from a mixture of raw grated and cooked mashed potatoes. The Polish *ratzelach* is a pancake based on grated raw potato but with several other ingredients, popular among Polish communities in N. America.

Schmarren, items which are popular in Germany and Austria, may qualify to be called pancakes although they are usually torn apart with forks before being served. The basic *Schmarren* are, or at least were, made of stale bread or sometimes buckwheat, soaked in water or milk, with no other addition than salt. They can be eaten on their own with a simple dressing of butter and sugar. Only the luxury recipes, for example *Kaiserschmarren*, have enrichments such as eggs.

Scots pancakes, see DROP SCONE.

See also POORI for an Indian item and QATA'IF for a Middle Eastern one.

PANCETTA salted belly of pork, an important ingredient in Italian cookery which is fairly closely related to BACON, and also to the Spanish tocino. It exists in many regional variations, with different periods of maturing, different aromatics, etc. The type called *guanciale*, which is taken from the 'cheek', in front of the belly, is very popular in C. Italy, especially Lazio.

Pancetta occurs in several famous pasta dressings, e.g. *Spaghetti alla carbonara* (see SPAGHETTI).

PANCH PHORON is a combination of five spices (*panch* in Hindi and in Persian means five). The most popular quintet is: MUSTARD seed, CUMIN SEED, FENUGREEK seeds, nigella seeds (see BLACK CUMIN), and

FENNEL seeds. However, alternatives include aniseed (see ANISE), CASSIA leaves, and red CHILLIES.

This spice mixture comes from the eastern coastal state of Bengal and gives a distinctive aroma and flavour to pulse and vegetable dishes. The spices, which are usually left whole, are fried in hot oil or GHEE, to which they impart their perfume, before the other ingredients are added. HS

PANDOWDY an old-fashioned deep-dish New England fruit dessert related to COBBLER, grunt, and SLUMP. Sliced or cut apples or other fruits are tossed with spices and butter, sweetened with molasses (see SUGAR), MAPLE SYRUP, or brown sugar, topped with a biscuit-like dough, and baked. Partway through the baking time, the crust is broken up and pressed down into the fruit so it can absorb the juices. This technique is called 'dowdying'. After the crust is baked, it becomes crispy. Pandowdies are served warm with heavy (double) cream, hard sauce (see SAUCE), or a cream sauce flavoured with nutmeg. CBI

PANETTONE an Italian yeast cake which is a speciality of Milan, is eaten throughout Italy on festive occasions such as Christmas and Easter. It is usually cylindrical and, like BRIOCHE, may range in size from an individual portion to a large cake to serve a number of people.

Panettone is made from a rich yeast dough containing flour, butter, eggs, sugar, and milk with raisins and candied peel.

Another similar celebration cake, more golden-yellow in colour and without fruit or nuts, is the pandoro of Verona.

PANIR and *peynir*, the Farsi (Persian) and Turkish words for 'cheese', which also occur in other related languages such as Urdu, sometimes appear as part of the names of cheeses made in the Near East and the Indian subcontinent. Examples are Turkish cheeses such as Beynaz and Kasar, which are often called *Beynaz peynir* and *Kasar peynir*; *panir kusei*, the 'pot' cheese of Iran; and *panir*, a popular Indian 'pickled' cheese.

PANNA COTTA also *crema cotta*, an Italian dessert made with CREAM (*panna*) and sugar mixed together and brought to a simmer with some added milk and a little gelatin, then moulded and chilled. If a flavouring is used, it should be delicate.

This preparation is particularly associated with Piedmont. Doglio (1995) states in his dictionary of Piedmontese gastronomy that the flavouring can be of rum (not delicate),

and that the mould into which the mixture is poured is lined with caramelized sugar. He refers also, without endorsing it, to a story that this dessert originated with a Hungarian woman living in the Langhe district of Piedmont in the early part of the 19th century. Her version apparently included egg, coffee, and vanilla.

PANTUA or *pantoah*, Bengali sweets made from dough based on flour and sugar mixed with other ingredients (milk powder, BESAN FLOUR, fresh curd cheese, coconut, sweet potato, green banana) and flavoured with cardamoms. The mixture is shaped into crescents or logs and deep fried in GHEE, then soaked in a rose-flavoured syrup. A sweet of this type, shaped into balls, each one containing a sugared cardamom seed or other candy, is known as a LADIKANEE or 'Lady Canning', apparently in honour of the wife of the 19th-century Viceroy of India Lord Canning. LM

PAPAW *Asimina triloba*, the fruit of a small N. American tree related to the CHERIMOYA, but with a distribution extending further north, into New York state. It has for long been cultivated by Indians and whites alike.

Papaw is among the fruits which are referred to by the general name CUSTARD APPLE; and is sometimes spelled 'pawpaw', a corrupted name which is, confusingly, often also given to the completely different PAPAYA.

The fruit has a smooth, yellowish skin without the knobs or reticulations which are characteristic of its tropical relatives such as the CHERIMOYA, SUGAR-APPLE, and SOUR SOP. The shape is slightly elongated and curved, and the average fruit is 10 cm (4") long. The pulp, like that of other annonaceous fruits, is yellow, soft, and smooth. It has a rich, sweet, creamy flavour evocative of both banana and pear, overlaid with a heavy fragrance, so that some find the whole effect cloying. Papaw is usually eaten raw, but can be baked or made into desserts of various kinds.

PAPAYA *Carica papaya*, one of the best tropical fruits, looks rather like a pear-shaped melon.

It is native to the lowlands of eastern C. America, but even before the arrival of Europeans it was already being cultivated well beyond this area. The Spanish and the Portuguese invaders took to it and quickly spread it to their other settlements. It was being grown in the W. Indies by 1513 and by 1583 had been taken from there to the E. Indies via the Philippines, taking with it its

Carib Indian name *ababai*, altered to 'papaya'. It also reached Africa at an early date.

It was spread through the Pacific islands as Europeans discovered them, and by 1800 was being grown in all tropical regions. Hawaii and S. Africa are now the main exporters.

The papaya plant is a very large, semi-woody herb shaped like a palm tree but with huge fingered leaves. It grows quickly from seed and bears fruit within a year. The fruits hang from the top down the central stem in large clusters. The plant continues to fruit well for another two years, after which it is cut down.

Its sexual habits are peculiar. Some strains, such as the South African Hortus Gold, have separate male and female trees. Seedlings are planted in threes and the males, which bear no fruit and are useful only for pollination, are thinned out when they flower and their sex becomes apparent. Others, such as the Hawaiian Solo, have fruiting hermaphrodites and females, of which the former are preferred and the latter thinned out. These two strains produce the majority of papayas in the West.

In regions where planting is less organized, different strains of papaya interbreed naturally and produce variable fruits, some pear shaped, some round, and ranging in size from smaller than an apple to a length of 30 cm (1') and a weight of 9 kg (20 lb). Very large papayas are inferior in flavour.

The preferred type of commercial papaya is generally up to 500 g (1 lb) in weight, occasionally twice as large. It is pear shaped, pale green when unripe and becoming blotchy yellow or orange when ripe. A fruit is ripe when it is mostly yellow and just beginning to soften to the touch. The pulp inside is of a creamy orange colour, soft, delicately scented, and sweet. The taste is slightly lacking in acidity, and is usually complemented by a squeeze of lime juice. At the centre is a mass of black seeds encased in a gelatinous coating. These are edible, although often discarded. They are crunchy and have a slightly peppery taste, like mustard and cress. Occasionally they are used, crushed, as a mildly spicy condiment.

Unripe papayas, especially of the larger kinds, are cooked as a vegetable, or made into pickles. Papaya fruits, especially unripe ones, and also the leaves of the plant contain an enzyme of a digestive character, papain, which has a powerful tenderizing effect on meat. This has been realized since early times and, wherever papayas are grown, tough meat is cooked in a wrapping of papaya leaves, or it may be left under a papaya plant whose unripe fruits have been cut, so that they drip a milky latex onto the meat, or is mixed with papaya in some other

way. Commercial meat tenderizer, available in powder form, is made from papayas. Papaya is also a great healer of upset stomachs, and the bitter leaves are often believed to prevent malaria, as the mosquito avoids people whose blood is not 'sweet'.

Papaya jam and canned papayas are produced on a small scale.

At least eight other species of the genus *Carica* bear edible fruits, including the BABACO, *C. pentagona*. *C. candamarcensis* is the 'mountain papaya' of the Andes, best eaten cooked, because of its high papain content. *C. quercifolia* is known in several S. American countries as *higuera de monte*.

Papaya is sometimes called pawpaw, a confusing name which is also used for the quite different fruit PAPAW.

PAPRIKA the familiar red spice, consists of the dried ground fruits of *Capsicum annuum*, the mild CAPSICUM fruit, often called pimento. Although this and all the other *Capsicum* species originated in the New World, the particular varieties used to make paprika were developed in Europe, especially in Hungary. The first paprika peppers to reach Hungary are thought to have been introduced from the east by Bulgarians, who had them from Turkey. The earliest reference to them in a Hungarian dictionary, according to Lang (1971), was in 1604, when the name used was 'Turkish pepper'. The name 'paprika', which is derived from the Latin *piper* (pepper) through Slavic diminutive forms (*pepperke, piperka*), did not come into currency until 1775.

Paprika has for long been an important ingredient in many Hungarian dishes, including what the Hungarians themselves call *paprikás*; see GOULASH. It has also acquired worldwide popularity as a mild spice whose bright red colour (for which the pigment capsanthin is largely responsible) enables it to enliven white or pale dishes.

Paprika peppers are now grown, to produce paprika, in a number of countries, including many in E. Europe but also Spain. Spanish paprika, known as *pimentón*, is made from round peppers about the size of a peach, of several varieties. It is a paler shade of red than Hungarian paprika, and differs slightly in flavour.

Although it exists in many varieties, some of which are very hot, paprika is normally mild and sweet and can be used more generously than most peppers. This has not always been so. It was only in 1859 that a process was invented which allowed for discarding the cores and seeds (which contain most of the pungent principle, capsaicin) thus reducing the pungency considerably. The commercial grades of paprika are given by Lang, best first, as

exquisite delicate (*különleges*), delicate, noble sweet (*édelnemes*), semi-sweet (*félédes*), rose (*rózsa*), and hot (*erös*). The two principal growing areas in Hungary are in the south of the country, one centred on the city of Szeged, the other on the neighbourhood of Kaloska, on the Danube.

Pimentón is a spice produced in Spain from the small round fruits of several varieties of *C. annuum*. It may reasonably be regarded as a Spanish version of paprika. It is almost sweet in taste and it is used both as a colouring agent and as a spice in itself. It is added to seafood, sausages, rice, and many other savoury dishes.

PAPUA NEW GUINEA a country about whose foods and foodways little had been written until recently, is the subject of one admirable book by May (1984). He observes that there is evidence of human settlements about 50,000 years ago, and also that some 9,000 years ago people in the highlands had established gardens, thus becoming some of the earliest known agriculturists. By 4000 BC, under the influence of successive migrations of people from S. Asia, agriculture had largely replaced hunting and gathering as a means of sustenance. Besides the indigenous food crops (SAGO, SUGAR CANE, some sorts of BANANA and YAM, BREADFRUIT, etc.), there were introduced species which the immigrants brought: TARO, more kinds of banana and yam, and perhaps COCONUT. The PIG and perhaps fowl also came with them, but the SWEET POTATO, now the staple crop in most of the highlands, was a later arrival.

The arrival of the sweet potato is of particular interest, since May asserts that recent archaeological discoveries show that it was being cultivated 1,200 years ago, and must therefore have arrived via Polynesia from tropical America. He says that the same seems to be true of MAIZE (which see for further comment on the question of how and when it travelled from the New World to the Old World).

Foods introduced since European contact include TAPIOCA, GROUNDNUTS, and a wide array of vegetables and fruits, plus cattle for beef, and deer.

Of the numerous aspects of food in Papua New Guinea which are of special interest, the following items represent no more than a small sample:

- Sago is prepared in three principal ways. In the first it is mixed with boiling water, stirred to produce a 'gluggy paste, at which stage it is removed from the pot (generally being twisted around a stick) and eaten'. A second method is to form the moist flour into 'cakes' to be griddle cooked over an open fire. May continues: 'Thirdly, the moist flour, sometimes with the addition of greens, may be baked in bamboo sections over a fire. As a variation on the second and third methods, in the Gulf and Western Provinces, the flour may be mixed with fruit, lotus seeds, green vegetables, sago grubs or diced meat, wrapped in palm spathe and placed over a hearth of hot embers; it is common to cook whole fish (in particular, catfish) in this manner. Sometimes leaflets are often used in lieu of palm spathe, to form a solid sago "stick" when cooked. Sago is also used in different parts of the country in a variety of soups. In the Sepik and elsewhere, it is mixed with coconut, banana and breadfruit and baked to form a solid "bread". In the highlands it may be mixed with *marita* [see below], and either cooked as a pancake with greens or wrapped in leaves and cooked in an earth oven.'

- SCREWPINE, *Pandanus* spp, is prominent. People of the highlands prize the fruits, which are eaten in three principal forms from various species in the genus. Describing all these, May devotes particular attention to what is known in Pidgin as *marita*. 'The marita is a lowland to middle altitude species (*P. conoideus*), which is cultivated, semi-cultivated, and occasionally gathered wild. It produces a long red or yellow fruit which may be more than a metre [3'] long and weigh up to 10 kg [22 lb]. It consists of a large number of small segments on a central core. Methods of preparation of *marita* vary but a common procedure is to cut the fruit into sections (the size of the sections depending on the method of cooking) and boil it for about half an hour. The red segments are then scraped off the core and their woody centres separated out (preferably strained) to leave a thin, oily paste which looks like tomato sauce and has a distinctive, mildly astringent taste. It goes particularly well with pork, but is also eaten with greens and other vegetables.'

- The number of 'exotic' animal foods which have been or are eaten is extraordinarily large. May believes that it can safely be said that all furry animals in Papua New Guinea are eaten in one part of the country or another, and instances tree kangaroo (*Dendrolagus* spp), cuscus (*Phalanger* spp), OPOSSUM (various species), bandicoot and bush rat (especially the giant rat *Melomys rothschildi*). Then, after a passage about CROCODILE eggs, LIZARDS, and SNAKES, he remarks that 'Any bird, it would appear, has a reasonable chance of ending up on the Papua New Guinean table.' He provides information about the cassowary (*Casuarius* spp, fine table birds, keenly hunted in parts of the highlands) and large fruit-eating and other PIGEONS.

- Information about INSECTS as food is also striking. The large sago grub (*Rhyncosphorus ferringinlus papuanus*), the larval form of a beetle, breeds in the rotting pith of palms. The grubs, which are about 5 cm/2" long and as thick as a man's finger, are 'harvested' and either boiled or roasted. In some markets they are sold spitted and grilled in SATAY style.

- Pitpit, *Saccharum edule*, is a close relation of SUGAR CANE (*S. officinarum*) and is, as May explains, 'cultivated for the unopened bud of its inflorescences. These inflorescences, which are about the size and shape of bullrushes, do not normally emerge from their grassy sheath, and in the market are usually sold in a bundle tied together by the top of the sheaths. Pitpit may be baked, steamed or boiled; occasionally it is eaten raw.' It should be noted that these remarks refer to what is called 'lowland pitpit', and that 'highland pitpit' is something quite different, *Setaria palmifolia*, also called New Guinea asparagus (from which the manner of consuming may easily be inferred).

PARAGUAY an inland republic of S. America which communicates with the world beyond by the rivers Paraguay and Parana which drain into the Rio de la Plata. Straddling the Tropic of Capricorn, it contains both jungle and more temperate grassland, including fertile alluvial plain that supports the growth and processing of MATÉ, Paraguay's most distinctive product and favourite beverage, from *Ilex paraguayensis*. Visitors used also to liken the colony to an orange grove, for that introduced fruit was grown all through the temperate ZONE, maintaining a tree being a legal obligation on householders.

Colonization by the Spanish was beset by problems, at one time solved by making the whole area over to the Jesuits, who were then expelled in 1768, and the Guaraní Indians have thus never lost their identity nor their language, which remains an official language in the republic.

Settlement by other European races, principally the Italians and Germans, has been relatively more important than in some Latin American countries and this has had its effect on national food preferences, for example for PASTA and dishes such as *Osso bucco* (see VEAL).

The chief staple is CASSAVA root or manioc which is a common accompaniment to rough stews (*locros*) of meat and corn. Cassava may also be made into *chipá*, or the more elaborate *chipá-guazu* (Guaraní), a cake of cassava, eggs, cheese, or meat. MAIZE is often part of a dish already involving cassava, or it can substitute for it. Cornmeal itself is the main ingredient of *sopa Paraguaya*, a corn bread with cheese and onions.

The grass plains have long been home to the rhea (*Rhea americana*), whose eggs are thought a delicacy, as well as the flesh, which is either jerked (see JERKY) or eaten fresh. TJ

PARASOL MUSHROOM *Macrolepiota* (or *Lepiota*) *procera*, a large, shaggy fungus, among the finest of edible mushrooms. The specific name *procera* means tall; a really large specimen may stand up to 30 cm (1') high and measure 25 cm (10") across the cap, which is shaped like a Chinese umbrella with a projecting boss in the middle. The gills are white or off-white. The stem bears a large, double ring but has no volva (torn sheath) at its base. It has a feltlike grey-brown covering which splits into vertical streaks as the stem expands. The cap is buff or grey-brown and scaly.

Lepiota rhacodes, the smaller shaggy parasol, is even shaggier and has flesh which stains red when cut. It is edible, but some people avoid it since there is a variety (*L. rhacodes* var *hortensis*) which can cause gastric upsets. It should always be cooked.

Both these species are common in Europe, growing on grass or on seaside cliffs and dunes in autumn, and are also found in N. America and Australia.

L. excoriata (in France *petite coulemelle*) is smaller still, with a whitish cap about 8 cm (3") across. It does not occur in N. America and is uncommon in Europe, but very good. *L. naucina*, esteemed in France as the *lépiote pudique* and in Italy as *bubbolina*, is reputed to make some people ill in N. America, perhaps because some forms of it found there are toxic. According to Arora (1979), one of its names there is 'woman on motorcycle', because of the shape and poise of its cap when it is young. This white or greyish cap may later measure 8–12 cm (3–4") across, with cream gills underneath which blush at maturity (hence *pudique*).

In the eastern USA, and as far west as Michigan, there is a common woodland variety, *L. americana*, up to 15 cm (6") tall and white except for the scales near the centre of the cap and the boss itself, which are brown. It makes good eating.

L. zeyheri is the S. African parasol mushroom.

Some small species of parasol mushroom are reputedly harmful, so it is best not to gather any which measure less than 8 cm (3") across the cap unless they have been positively identified.

Parasol mushrooms should be picked when they have just become adult, not so young that the cap is still closed and looks like a tambour stick. The stem below the ring is tough and is usually discarded. The ring itself and the cap may be eaten raw (save for *L. rhacodes*), or fried, or otherwise cooked. Large caps are suitable for stuffing. The flavour is good and reminiscent of hazelnut.

PARATA or **PARATHA**, an Indian flaky bread prepared by smearing the dough, which is unleavened and is also enriched with oil, with GHEE or oil and folding the dough three times. More ghee or oil is brushed over and the process repeated. The resulting packet of dough is then rolled out to the required size and fried in oil or dry cooked on a *tava* or GRIDDLE. The layers of pastry separate and flake while frying.

Paratas are often stuffed with spicy mixtures of meat or vegetables before frying. A similar bread is made in Afghanistan and Nepal.

PARBOIL is a verb with an odd history. Derived from Latin words meaning 'through' and 'boil', it originally meant 'to boil thoroughly'. This usage disappeared in the 17th century, ousted by the rival meaning 'to part-cook in boiling water', which also dates back to the Middle Ages and seems to have been based on a confusion between 'par-' and 'part'.

Parboiling is normally carried out in preparation for a continuation of cooking by some other means such as frying. Stobart (1980) explains why this familiar sequence is followed. 'Food is parboiled either because the higher temperature of the fat would dry it out or brown it too much before it was cooked through, or because it prepares the surface for the penetration of fat and flavour, as, for instance, when potatoes are roasted in meat juices.'

Parboiled rice (soaked and briefly steamed before milling) offers certain advantages over rice which has been milled without this treatment; see RICE AS FOOD.

PARFAIT a name properly used of a rich frozen dessert, similar to a BOMBE and often made in a bombe mould. A typical parfait is composed of two or several elements (a lining for the mould and a filling, which may itself be layered) and is flavoured with a liqueur, or with coffee, chocolate, PRALINE, etc.

In N. America, the term has come to mean something different, namely a combination of fruit and ice cream, served in a tall narrow glass which exposes to view the various layers of the confection. This sort of parfait is not a frozen dessert. However, the frozen dessert version can be frozen in individual parfait glasses, rather than in a single mould, so there is a relationship between the two different things.

PARKIN is peculiar to the north of Britain. It refers to two related types of GINGERBREAD, containing oatmeal (a traditional staple grain in this area—see OATS). Made by the melting method, with butter, beef DRIPPING or LARD, sugar, and TREACLE or molasses (see SUGAR), both were originally hearth or griddle cakes, and could be thin or thick. North of Yorkshire, the thin, biscuit, variety predominates, the Scottish term being perkins. The rarer, Scottish, thick variety is called broonie. The soft, thick, cakelike variety with a shiny, sticky surface is preferred in Yorkshire, where it seems to have become popular in the early 19th century, and from where it spread to most of its contiguous counties. In Lancashire, S. Yorkshire, and N. Derbyshire parkin was called tharf, thar, or thor cake.

Parkin may be derived from an older, honey-sweetened oatbread. Parkin was eaten especially at Celtic and Christian festivals from 31 October to 11 November. From the 19th century both types of parkin have been part of 5 November (Bonfire Night) celebrations, for which the biscuit type is often rolled thick and cut into parkin men or parkin pigs. JS
READING: Jennifer Stead (1991*b*).

PARMENTIERA a C. American tree, *Parmentiera aculeata*, which produces cucumber-shaped fruit, yellow-green and fluted. It is also known as the food candle tree and as *guachilote* (from an Aztec name), and has been cultivated in Mexico, Guatemala, and El Salvador. The fruit is sweet and can be eaten fresh, cooked, or pickled.

PARMESAN the English name of a hard Italian cheese which is properly called grana Parmigiano Reggiano, or just Parmigiano. The characteristics of the group of cheeses to which it belongs are described under GRANA. What is remarkable about the Parmigiano Reggiano variety is that, although the appellation is protected in Italy, the name Parmesan has become almost synonymous in other parts of the world with the whole group, meaning 'Italian grating cheese'.

Parma and Reggio Emilia used to have their own separate cheeses, but these were combined into the present joint name by a governmental decree of 1955 which established and defined the controlled appellations for grana cheeses. Although production in the vicinity of Reggio Emilia is now more important, Parma has retained the higher degree of fame which it had already enjoyed for many centuries.

Presciutto, in his *Gastronomia parmense* (1963), has collected an impressive series of tributes to 'Parmigiano', ranging from

classical authors (a little vagueness here) through medieval times to more recent eulogies. He cites evidence that Parmesan was among Napoleon's favourite foods; and that Molière, suddenly stricken by what proved to be a fatal illness, waved aside the conventional bowl of broth, called for Parmesan, and devoured it with such enthusiasm that it spilled over his deathbed. Although it failed to revive Molière, Parmesan has for long had, and retains, a reputation as good fare for invalids.

But the finest piece of publicity for Parmigiano was surely furnished by Boccaccio (*The Decameron*, novella 3, day 8), when he wrote of the imaginary country of Berlinzone and its village Bengodi (meaning enjoyment) where there was a mountain consisting entirely of grated Parmesan, on which there were people who did nothing but make macaroni and ravioli to be cooked in capon broth (and dressed with Parmesan). This tale developed into the familiar story of the Land of COCKAIGNE where everything is food ready to eat, and the mountain of Parmesan remained a central feature of the story.

Andrea del Sarto, the famous artist, is said by Vasari (*Lives of the Painters*) to have made a model temple with sausages as pillars, and Parmesan cheese providing their bases and capitals.

PARROTFISH the common name of fish of the family Scaridae, which are found in tropical, subtropical, and warm temperate waters around the world. Their teeth are configured somewhat like a parrot's beak, to facilitate their crunching of coral, from which they filter out the algae which they eat, excreting the sand. Their activity is thought to be a principal factor in the wearing down of coral reefs.

Parrotfish are related to the WRASSE family, and resemble them both in having bright coloration which varies with age and sex and in their habit of sleeping at night; but some of them grow to a larger size than any wrasse and they can be distinguished by the fusing of their front teeth into a 'beak'.

The one parrotfish present in the Mediterranean, *Sparisoma* (formerly *Euscarus*) *cretensis*, occurs throughout the eastern basin and all along the southern parts, but is rarely marketed except in Morocco, Cyprus, Turkey, and Greece; its range also includes the E. Atlantic from Portugal and the Azores south to Senegal. It is esteemed as a table fish, but not as much as in classical times, when Roman epicures thought so much of it that the Roman admiral Optatus transplanted some to the west coast of Italy in the hope of establishing a breeding population there. Roman taste in fish was influenced by colour, and it may be that the reddish colour of the females was thought to be especially attractive (males are usually grey-brown or purplish-brown).

The largest parrotfish are found in the W. Atlantic. Both *S. coeruleus*, the blue parrotfish, and *S. guacamala*, the rainbow parrotfish, may reach a length of 1.2 m (4'). These species apparently envelop themselves in a mucous 'envelope', like a sleeping blanket, at night before falling asleep.

In Asian waters *S. ghobban* is one of the larger species (maximum length 90 cm/3') and is sought after by restaurateurs at Hong Kong.

PARROTS AND COCKATOOS, belonging respectively to the families Psittacidae and Cacatuidae, a large range of birds among which there are some species which have been eaten, for example in Papua New Guinea, and also in past times in Australia and New Zealand. One can find traces of dishes such as parrot pie in early Australasian cookery books, but they attracted only lukewarm praise and were often the subject of jokes (cook a cockatoo with an old boot in plenty of boiling water until the boot is tender, then throw away the bird and eat the boot—that sort of thing).

PARSI FOOD The Parsis (Parsees) of W. INDIA are descendants of pre-Islamic, Zoroastrian, migrants from the region of AFGHANISTAN and IRAN. The main migration took place after the forces of Islam conquered Iran in the 7th century, and one of the most pleasing of all food-related legends explains how they arrived in India. Bhicoo Manekshaw (1996) describes what happened when a storm drove the refugees to Sanjan in Gujarat, and three Parsi dasturs (priests) approached the Rana (ruler) of Sanjan:

When he saw these tall, fair, well built men, the Rana tried to turn them away. Using typical inborn Indian politeness, he did not do so directly, but showed them a bowl full to the brim with milk, to indicate there was no space in the land. The senior dastur is said to have sprinkled some sugar into the milk and replied that the milk had been sweetened, but it had not overflowed. Thus the Parsis were allowed to land.

Thus began what was to be a fruitful interchange between Iranian and Indian foodways, later incorporating elements from ANGLO-INDIAN COOKERY, and culminating in the present delightfully varied Parsi cuisine. Parsis have few food prohibitions, indeed none of importance, and their periods of abstinence from animal meat are short. The Zoroastrian religion favours enjoyment of life.

Parsis like meat, and a Parsi meal normally includes a meat, fish, or chicken dish. Spicing is often complex, but moderate. The most famous Parsi meat dish is DHANSAK, for which the meat is cooked with lentils, other legumes, and vegetables such as spinach, aubergine, and pumpkin. This, according to Bhicoo Manekshaw, probably evolved from the Iranian *Khoreshte esfannaj*, and the same may be true of other meat and vegetable dishes. Fish, from the coast of Gujarat (including POMFRET, GREY MULLET, and BUMMALOW, otherwise known as Bombay duck), is much eaten and is regarded, along with the COCONUT and RICE, as a symbol of plenty. A group of CURRY-type sweet-and-sour fish dishes are known as *patias*. Other fish dishes show the influence of the cooks from GOA who worked for well-to-do Parsis in the early and mid-20th century.

Egg dishes are numerous. There are some special Parsi pickles, and the vinegars from Navsari and Valsad, made from SUGAR CANE, DATES, or toddy (see COCONUT), are famous. Sweet dishes and beverages reflect Iranian influence in, for example, the use of rosewater (see ROSES); but the same is true of India in general.

PARSLEY *Petroselinum crispum*, the most popular herb in European cookery. In the Middle East it is added so abundantly to various dishes that it takes on the role of a vegetable. Further east, it loses its pre-eminent place to the related plant CORIANDER (sometimes called Chinese or Japanese parsley, and similar in appearance although not flavour).

Parsley is an umbelliferous plant native to the E. Mediterranean area (Linnaeus believed that its origin was in Sardinia) and related to CELERY, with which it has occasionally formed hybrids. The ancient Greeks used the name *selinon* for both parsley and celery, and only occasionally bothered to distinguish parsley as *petroselinon*, meaning 'rock' celery or parsley. Later the Romans used the word *apium* in a similarly ambiguous way. Thus it is difficult to tell which is meant. However, the Greek writer Theophrastus, writing before 300 BC, describes curly-leafed and flat-leafed varieties of parsley similar to the two main modern types.

According to Pliny the Elder (1st century AD), the Romans held parsley fronds in particular esteem among seasonings. (Roman recipes often called for parsley seeds as well as the leaves, but the seeds are not now used.)

Parsley is more difficult to grow than other culinary herbs, because the seeds take so long to germinate—70 to 90 days. In medieval times there were superstitious beliefs about the seeds having to pay a series of visits to the devil before germination, and

so forth. Eleanor Sinclair Rohde (1936) gives an especially interesting collection of quaint beliefs about parsley. Many of these were taken from a correspondence in *The Times*, in which connections between parsley and women, and with Good Friday, recur often.

The numerous cultivars of parsley fall into two main categories: curly (or curly-leaf), and flat leafed. The former is preferred in English-speaking countries, partly because it is often used as a garnish rather than a flavouring, and has a more decorative appearance than the flat-leafed type. Champion Moss Curled and Forest Green are two favourite cultivars in this group.

If sprigs of curly-leafed parsley are quickly deep fried they emerge with their shape intact and a very pleasing dark green colour.

Flat-leafed parsley is dominant on the mainland of Europe, and universal in the Middle East. It is chopped and added to dishes as a flavouring, so there is no need for it to have a decorative appearance. The best flavour resides in the stems, and some recipes call for these alone to be used. In Middle Eastern salads such as TABBOULEH (whose other main ingredient is BURGHUL), chopped parsley is added by the cupful. Flat-leafed parsley looks like coriander but can easily be distinguished by smell.

Neapolitan parsley, much used in S. Italy, is in fact a group of cultivars (Gigante d'Italia, Celery-leafed, etc.) which are generally larger (almost 1 m/3' in height) than other parsley plants, with proportionally bigger leaves and thicker stems; indeed these plants can be grown and eaten like celery. The strong flavour of the leaves is prized by Italians.

Plain-leafed parsley constitutes the other group of flat-leafed parsleys, in which cultivars such as French and Italian Dark Green are found.

Many people think the flavour of curly-leaf parsley is always inferior to that of flat-leafed parsley. Certainly it is different; but variations in soil and climate affect the flavour of both kinds.

Parsley sauce has for long been a favourite in Britain. Rohde records that King Henry VIII liked it in the still customary form of a simple white sauce flavoured with parsley. In French cuisine a *persillade* (a mixture of parsley and garlic) is often used to flavour dishes.

Hamburg parsley, also called turnip-rooted parsley, originated in Germany in the 16th century. It is still popular in NW Europe. Although there was a vogue for it in Britain in the 18th century, it is now scarcely known there or in the USA, where it also penetrated briefly. It has an enlarged root resembling a small parsnip or a large, whitish carrot (although varieties with a round turnip shape are known). It is always eaten cooked, and is often used in soups. The flavour is between that of parsley and of celeriac (see CELERY).

PARSNIP *Pastinaca sativa*, an umbelliferous plant which grows wild in Europe and W. Asia and has been cultivated to produce an edible root. (The root of the wild parsnip is small, woody, and inedible, but sweet and with a distinct parsnip aroma; so it could originally have been used as a flavouring. Cultivation for this purpose would have improved its size and led to edible forms.)

The earlier ancient writers did not distinguish between parsnips and CARROTS. The first name for 'parsnip' was the Latin *pastinaca*; but even as late as the 1st century AD Pliny the Elder was using this to mean 'carrot' as well. Later writings such as those of Apicius suggest that the Romans cultivated parsnips, and held them in some esteem. The English name 'parsnip' comes, through French, from *pastinaca* with the ending 'nip' to indicate that it was like a turnip.

In medieval Europe there was a dearth of sweeteners; sugar was a rare, imported luxury, and honey expensive. Moreover the potato, prolific source of starch, had not yet arrived from America. So the sweet, starchy parsnip was doubly useful and became a staple food. Besides being eaten as a vegetable it could be used as an ingredient in sweet dishes. Dorothy Hartley (1954) observes that parsnip has 'the type of sweetness that mingles with honey and spice, so that some boiled plum and marrowfat puddings, flavoured with spice and sweetened with honey, were made with a parsnip base'.

As sugar became more readily available and with the gradual introduction of the potato, the standing of the parsnip in Europe waned. It is now eaten mainly in N. Europe, to only a moderate extent in Britain, and hardly at all in S. Europe. Nor has it gained much importance in other regions. Consumption in the USA is small. One of the reasons for such a generally half-hearted attitude is that the parsnip has a taste which, although not strong, is peculiar and not to everyone's liking. Its oddly semi-sweet quality makes it an awkward partner to other foods, although it goes very well with salt cod, for example. Large, old parsnips can be woody; even young ones tend to have a tough core which may be better discarded.

The parsnip is grown in colder climates, and is one of the few vegetables which is positively improved by frost. The effect of freezing the living root is to convert some of the starch into sugar. The plant can thus be left in the ground until needed.

Parsnips of modern varieties grow to 20–40 cm (8–15") long, and need lengthy cooking, although less than carrots. Most of the flavour lies directly under the skin, so peeling is to be avoided. They may be cut into large chunks, parboiled, and finished by baking or braising; or steamed and mashed. Baking produces a crisp, brown, slightly caramelized outside which is agreeable; and parsnip 'chips' (US: French fries) are good.

'Wild parsnip' is a name sometimes used for an unrelated root, *Cymopterus montanus*, eaten by the Indians of the south-west of the USA and Mexico, where it is called 'gamote'. The roots are peeled, baked, and ground into meal.

PARSON'S NOSE has been described with her usual lucidity by Theodora FitzGibbon (1976):

a colloquial English expression for the small fatty joint which holds the tail feathers of poultry. When well crisped after roasting, it is considered a tasty morsel by some people. When the bird concerned is a cooked goose or duck rather than a turkey or a chicken, the joint is called 'the pope's nose,' although, in a general way, Protestant communities are said to use the latter expression and Catholic communities the former!

The French term for the same thing is *sot-l'y-laisse*, meaning 'only a fool would leave it', reflecting the fact that this item used to be considered a delicacy in France too.

PARTRIDGE *Perdrix perdrix* in the family Phasianidae, an important game bird of Europe and C. Asia, often called **grey partridge** (to distinguish it from other partridges, of the genus *Alectoris*, described further on in this entry). The range of the species is from N. Spain up to the British Isles, Sweden, and Russia; and eastwards to Turkey and parts of W. and C. Asia. Thus it is known in most European countries, but in numbers which fluctuate and are in steady decline in regions, such as England, where modern agricultural methods are reducing the amount of suitable habitat.

The average total length of a partridge is only 30 cm (12"), but it has a plump, chicken-like shape and carries a fair weight—350 g (12–13 oz) for a good young bird. Coloration varies, generally brown above; males have a brown horseshoe mark on their undersides.

Young birds are best when hung for only a short time and then plainly roasted or grilled and served with their gravy (no strong sauce, such as would mask the birds' own flavour). Older birds respond better to being stewed or braised.

George Saintsbury, in his fine essay about partridge cookery in the *Fur, Feathers and Fin* volume on that bird (Saintsbury and Macpherson, 1896), observed that to his knowledge there were but two secondary methods of cooking partridge which deserve to be practised. One was the English partridge pudding (now rarely made—like steak and kidney pudding, but combining partridge with steak); the other was *Perdrix aux choux* (still in favour in France—partridge is braised with savoy cabbage and a little bacon, with spicing at discretion).

Other birds which may properly be called partridges include *Alectoris rufa*, the **red-legged partridge**, a bird best known in SW France, Spain and Portugal. As an introduced species, it is also common enough in SE England. In France, this bird is *perdrix rouge* (a name echoed in other languages) or *bartravelle*. It is larger than the grey partridge, and has lighter meat, tasting like chicken. *A. barbara* (the Barbary partridge, of Sardinia and N. Africa) and *A. graeca* (the rock partridge, of Italy and the Balkans) also have red legs.

In Asia, there are yet more species, including *P. hodgsoniae*, the Tibetan partridge. Partridges are appreciated as food in many Asian countries, from Iran and Afghanistan eastwards.

Besides this imposing array of what might be called true partridges there are in the same family, Phasianinae, many closely related birds which, naturally enough, tend to have English names consisting of 'partridge' plus an epithet. The largest such genus, which also has a very wide distribution around the world, is *Francolinus*, in which the best-known species, *F. francolinus*, may be known either as francolin or (especially in India) as black partridge. Eating quality varies considerably within this vast family.

PASKHA a rich, sweet type of CHEESECAKE/pudding, traditionally made at Easter in Russia (Paskha means Easter) to celebrate the end of Lent. It is made from cheese (curd, cream, or cottage), eggs, sugar, and dried fruits and is flavoured with vanilla. The sides of the paskha may be decorated with slivers of almonds, glacé cherries, and angelica, or left plain.

Paskha is traditionally marked with the orthodox cross. A special pyramid-shaped, perforated wooden mould called a *pasochnitsa*, lined with muslin, is used and it is this which leaves an imprint of the cross on the surface and often other decorations too.

The paskha are often taken to church to be blessed before being eaten on Easter Sunday and are traditionally served with another Russian Easter speciality, *kulich* (see EASTER FOODS).   (HS)

PASSION-FRUIT the best known of the fruits of various species of the genus *Passiflora*. This is a large group of climbing herbs and shrubs native to tropical America, SE Asia, and Australia. The names granadilla (or grenadilla) and water lemon are also used of the fruits of this group, overlapping with the name passion-fruit in a way which necessitates treating them all together. Granadilla is derived from *granada*, Spanish for pomegranate, and means 'small pomegranate'.

In S. America, the passion-flower became known *as Flor de las cinco lagas* (flower of the five wounds) because Jesuit missionaries used it in their teachings to illustrate the crucifixion of Christ. Each part corresponds to a particular emblem of the passion. Thus the three styles represent the three nails; the five stamens the five wounds (hands, feet, and side); the ovary, which is oval and set on a stalk, is taken to be either the sponge soaked in vinegar and offered on a stick, or the hammer used to drive in the nails; the spiky corona, prominently visible above the petals, is the crown of thorns; and the equal petals and sepals signify the ten apostles (Peter and Judas are not included).

Hence the name 'passion-fruit', most usually applied to *Passiflora edulis*, a plant native to Brazil. Since the 19th century it has been grown in Australia, New Zealand, S. Africa, and Hawaii; and now also in some other countries such as Israel. An alternative name is 'purple granadilla', referring to the deep purple rind of the main variety. There is also a yellow type, var. *flavicarpa*, which is the basis of the passion-fruit industry in Hawaii and Fiji.

The fruit, about the size of an egg, has a brittle outer shell which becomes slightly wrinkled when it is ripe. The soft, orange pulp is full of tiny seeds. These are edible, and liked by many, but others avoid them and prefer their passion-fruit in the form of jelly or juice. (Over a hundred fruits are needed to make one litre of juice, so it is a costly delicacy; but the juice has exceptional viscosity, because of its high starch content, and calls for considerable dilution.) Passion-fruit is also used in sherbets and confectionery, ice cream and yoghurt.

The flavour is of subtle composition and delicious. It is also very strong. Elizabeth Schneider (1986), writing in New York, rightly observes that many recipes from the countries where these fruits grow bid one take what would be impossibly expensive elsewhere, e.g. 'one cup of strained fruit pulp'; but that, 'fortunately, passion fruit works best as a flavoring. There is so much perfume and so little pulp that you can think of it as you would vanilla, or Cognac, or a spoon of dense raspberry purée—something to aromatize a dish.' In Australia passion-fruit icing is popular for cakes, especially for

sponge sandwich, and passion-fruit is used in the most traditional of various recipes for PAVLOVA.

The **giant granadilla** (or granadilla real), *P. quadrangularis*, is native to the hotter regions of tropical America. The fruit is larger, up to 20 cm (8") long, and greenish-yellow shading to brownish when ripe. It is popular in many tropical regions, including the hotter parts of India and SE Asia. In Indonesia it is made into a drink called *Markeesa* which is available in bottles. The flavour of the ripe fruit is inferior to that of *P. edulis*, but is eaten raw or used for juice or jelly. Unripe fruits are cooked as a vegetable in the same way as marrows.

The **sweet granadilla**, *P. ligularis*, is another tropical American species extensively cultivated in mountainous areas of Mexico and grown also in Hawaii, where it may be called water lemon, being very juicy. It has an orange shell when ripe.

The **water lemon**, *P. laurifolia*, sometimes called passion fruit, or Jamaica honeysuckle, is another tropical American species with yellow or orange fruits. The flesh is sweet, scented, and as good as that of *P. edulis*.

Curuba is the name in Colombia, where it is especially appreciated, of a yellow-fruited species, *P. maliformis*. It grows in other countries of the region, and the W. Indies, and has many other names: sweet calabash, sweet cup or conch apple (Jamaica), banana passion-fruit (New Zealand), and banana poka (Hawaii). The aromatic fruit, apple shaped with a thin yellowish-brown rind, is of high quality.

PASSOVER (Pesach), one of the most important religious holidays of the Jewish year, is the occasion for special foods. Its origin is explained in the Book of Exodus in the Bible. Bringing pressure to bear on the Pharaoh to let the Hebrews depart from Egypt, Moses cursed the Egyptians with ten plagues, of which the last and most horrific was that all the first-born males in Egyptian families were to die. To ensure that the deity invoked by Moses would not inadvertently cause the death of the first-born of Hebrew families on the night of carnage, Moses required all these families to place a sign of blood on their door posts. The blood was to come from a sacrificial lamb which had to be roasted and eaten with unleavened bread and bitter herbs. Schwartz (1992) points out that the origin of the paschal lamb tradition lay in the pagan habits of a nomadic past:

Past ceremonies are resuscitated every few generations and given a more contemporary meaning which answers the demands of a new understanding. Pesach was a spring thanksgiving festival when nomadic people settled down for a few months to enable the ewes to give birth and suckle their young. It was the only time of the year

when they had the opportunity to gather in fertile green enclaves, to tend their flocks, to meet friends and relatives, arrange marriages and conduct business. These gatherings were celebrated with joy and involved mysterious ancient blood rituals to ensure a prosperous year ahead.

Indeed the original meaning of 'pesach' is to skip or gambol, as young lambs and kids will do, while its other meaning is 'to pass over, to exclude', which is what had to be done for their dwellings on the night of the slaughter of the first-born.

The requirement to eat unleavened bread came from a different source, as also explained by Schwartz:

The holiday of the unleavened bread has its origins in the *fallahim* (settled cropgrowers') celebration of the beginning of the barley harvest when it was the custom to destroy all old leaven stocks. We do not know if grain was also destroyed, but the symbolic sale before Pesach of all Jewish grain stores, still practised now, indicates that symbolic destruction was practised in the past. This kind of practice is related to a global folk tradition of symbolically sacrificing leftovers of the previous year to guarantee a prosperous new year; a tradition which in modern times is probably echoed in 'spring cleaning'.

The requirement to make sure that there is no leaven or leavened goods or grains on the forbidden list (wheat, barley, rye, oats, and spelt—all considered to be potentially liable to fermentation) in the house and to do without leaven during Passover is essentially negative, but can be viewed as having positive results. The following two passages from Claudia Roden (1996) show how the search for stray or hidden leaven can be an occasion of fun for the family, and that the challenge of baking without leaven produces some fine results.

In Orthodox homes, only after total cleansing can the special Passover silverware, dishes, and utensils be taken out of storage and the 'kosher for Pesah' provisions, including matzos, be brought into the home. Part of my father's happy childhood memories was the 'search for *hametz*' the night before Pesah, when, armed with a candle, a feather, a wooden spoon, and a paper bag, he looked with his older sisters for pieces of bread hidden by his father, and the whole thing was burned.

As for the results of baking without leaven:

The demands of cooking without grain or leaven have produced a whole range of distinctive Jewish variants of dishes making use of ground almonds, potato flour, ground rice, matzo meal, and sheets of matzos to make all kinds of cakes, pancakes, pies, dumplings, and fritters. For instance, in the Arab world, kibbeh, usually made with cracked wheat and lamb, was prepared with ground rice. In Eastern Europe, matzo-ball or egg-drop soup replaced vermicelli. Stuffed neck was filled with mashed potato instead of the flour-based filling; sponge cake was made with ground almonds or potato starch. One of the gastronomic highlights was the splendid cakes made with ground almonds, hazelnuts, or walnuts. One of the most affectionately remembered is matzo-meal fritters.

The name Seder (meaning order) is given to the ritual Passover meal and the tray on which it is served. Claudia Roden kindly agrees to continue the story at this point:

The large Seder tray was one of the few things my parents brought with them to England. Every year we placed it in front of my father on a pile of telephone books and covered it with a small embroidered tablecloth. On it were placed six little dishes, containing three matzos under a napkin, to remind us of the Jews who had no time to let their dough rise when they fled, and five symbolic foods.

In Europe, a decorative ceramic Seder plate, which is divided into sections, carries the ritual foods: karpas, a green vegetable such as parsley or little Bibb lettuce, representing new growth, which is dipped in salt water, symbolising the tears of the slaves; maror, bitter herbs, which can be chicory, cress, or grated horseradish, to remind us of the bitter times of slavery; betza, a roasted egg, representing the sacrificial offering of a roasted animal to God in the Temple on each holiday (in my family we had one hamine egg for every member of the family); zeroah, a lamb-shank bone, representing the lamb sacrificed by the slaves on the eve of the Exodus and the sacrificial paschal offering in the Temple (in my family we had a boiled shoulder, which we ate); haroset, a fruit-and-nut paste recalling the color of the mortar made with Nile silt that the Jews used when they built the pyramids for the Pharaohs.

PASTA (see page 580)

PASTELE a small savoury pastry, a speciality of Sephardic Jews. The shape is that of a little, round raised pie. The pastry dough is a modified shortcrust, the same as that used for *sanbusak* (see SAMOSA) and the filling is either a minced meat mixture, often with pine nuts, or *khandrajo*, a mixture of aubergines, onions, and tomatoes, similar to RATATOUILLE.

PASTILLE a small confection of sugar syrup set with GELATIN or STARCH, and flavoured with fruit essences or medicinal ingredients. The composition of modern pastilles is closely related to that of GUMS and JELLIES. The name is derived from the Latin *pastilla* (little cake), and has been applied to several kinds of small sweets. This includes, in the 16th century, fruit paste confections, much reduced by boiling, and in the 18th century little round LOZENGES made with powdered sugar and gum, similar to sugar paste; they often contained medicines, or were flavoured with aromatics.

LM

PASTRAMI is a recent arrival in the English language; Mariani (1994) gives 1936 as the first appearance in print. However, the product has a long history. The name probably derives through Yiddish from Romanian or Armenian *pastrama*, a type of wind-dried beef. Lesley Chamberlain (1989) says that:

Wind-dried beef, pastrama, of Armenian origin, was observed to be a much-loved food among the poor [of Romania]. A nineteenth century traveller described it as 'thin, black, leather-like pieces of meat dried and browned in the sun, and with salt and squashed flies'.

Such products were widespread in the Levant and the Balkans. *Pastirma*, dried meat often seasoned with garlic and cumin, is the Turkish version, and it is under numerous variations of the Turkish name, e.g. *pasturma* in Bulgaria, that it is known in the Balkan countries. Maria Kaneva-Johnson (1995) explains that the meat can come 'from lamb, goat, calf or young water buffalo, cut into the thinnest possible slices and eaten uncooked or lightly grilled as meze'. She remarks that a version coated with a paste of paprika, fenugreek or cumin, and salt (to protect and add piquancy to the meat) is a speciality of the Anatolian town of Kayseri (Caesarea in Roman times).

The version which has become a feature of New York Jewish cuisine and is used for the famous pastrami on rye sandwich is adapted from these origins, but prepared in a somewhat different manner, which includes steaming the meat.

PASTRIES a collective name for items produced by the skill of the pastry-cook or *pâtissier*, usually based on short, puff, or choux PASTRY (hence the name), GÉNOISE sponge, or rich, yeast-leavened mixtures of the BRIOCHE type.

Exactly what is counted among pastries depends on the country concerned. In Britain, various yeast-leavened buns are included. In continental Europe, numerous STRUDELS and nut confections fall in this category. MERINGUES are considered pastries, and DANISH PASTRIES form a special group. Many sweet pastries may be used for dessert, but most people think of them in connection with mid-morning coffee or afternoon tea, when a selection might be made from a range of different pastries offered in a café.

Pastries are not necessarily sweet, although those falling in the savoury category are fewer. Most important are items such as VOL-AU-VENT, BOUCHÉE, and an English example, the sausage roll.

In making sweet pastries, a sound knowledge of baking and sugar confectionery is required. Authorities on pastry work lay emphasis on high-quality

ingredients, delicate handling, and cleanliness. The French, the Swiss, and the Austrians have a highly developed tradition of pastry-making, followed throughout much of the developed world. In this, sweet pastries are built up from several elements. The pastry or cake forms the basis; contrast in texture and flavour is provided by fillings of jam, cream, *crème pâtissière* (see *crème*), or CUSTARD, and embellishments of FONDANT, chocolate, or icing are frequently added. Attention is paid to uniformity of shape, colour, and decoration, as pastries are expected to make a fine display as well as being delicious.

In S. Europe, pastries rely less on dairy produce and more on nut mixtures. In several countries, nuns are recognized as making excellent pastries; many convents produce sought-after specialities. The Spanish and the Portuguese have donated a sweet tooth and skill in pastry-making to areas formerly under their control. Iberian-inspired pastries are often particularly rich in eggs. In E. Europe and the Middle East, a quite different, but very rich tradition of pastries based on FILO has developed: the best-known example is BAKLAVA. Here, too, the craft of the pastry-cook is a special skill. The Indian subcontinent has a wide repertoire of sweet items, some of which could be reckoned as pastries, although few are as complex as those from traditions further west. The Chinese have traditionally taken little interest in this area of culinary expertise; see MOONCAKES for an exception.

LM

PASTRY (see page 585)

PASTY nowadays a medium-sized or small PASTRY turnover, seldom larger than an individual serving.

The word pasty came into English, via old French, from the Latin *pasta* (dough). In the Middle Ages, pasties were often very large, and generally meant meat or fish, well seasoned, enclosed in pastry and baked (similar to modern *en croûte* dishes, see CROUTON). The differences between pasties and PIES seem to have been that the former was made without a mould and contained a single type of filling, whilst a pie contained a mixture and eventually became the name for the deeper, raised form. In both cases, the pastry was made to recipes and baked in a way which would make it inedibly tough, and was probably not intended to be eaten.

Medieval pasties often contained joints of meat or whole birds; C. Anne Wilson (1973) quotes an ordinance of Richard II in 1378 for prices charged by cooks and pie bakers, including those for capons and hens baked

(*cont. on page 584*)

A highly important and satisfying category of food which presents two paradoxical aspects. One is that it overlaps very extensively with the category of NOODLES. The other is that until very recently there was no adequate name for it. In Italy, where pasta had previously just meant 'dough', it was necessary to say *paste alimentari* to indicate what everyone now knows as pasta. In the English language it had been necessary to use the word 'noodles' or adopt circumlocutions such as 'macaroni products' (or even the offputting 'alimentary pastes', in direct translation from the Italian). It was only after the Second World War that 'pasta' started to establish itself in its present wide meaning. However, although the name in its present sense has but a short history, the range of products to which it refers has a long one.

In fact, no one knows how long a history pasta has. The origins of pasta (and equally those of noodles) are hard to establish, for two principal reasons. First, pasta is a product of such simple ingredients—essentially flour and water—that it is difficult to distinguish it from primitive, unleavened, flat griddle cakes which are made from the same ingredients. Second, pasta is largely a food of the common people of any nation where it is used, and is therefore less well documented than more luxurious foods.

There were, in the classical world, products which can be viewed as forerunners, e.g. the Greek *laganon* and *itria*, both of them terms which subsequently developed into pasta terms. But it is not clear that in Greece they were anything more than flat cakes. And although the Romans had *lagani* (plural, apparently *laganon* cut into strips) there is nothing to show that these were prepared like pasta.

An early piece of pictorial evidence, much debated, comes from an Etruscan relief of about the 4th century BC at Caere. This shows a set of tradesman's equipment which would be so well fitted for making hand-cut pasta that it is tempting to assume that it was for that. There is a rolling board with a raised edge to retain the ingredients, and a slim rolling pin to fit it. Both closely resemble types used today. There is also a small bag which might be a flour sprinkler; a jug; a ladle, perhaps for water; and an unmistakable wavy-rimmed pastry cutting wheel such as is used for making deckle-edged LASAGNE. Elsewhere, ancient slim metal rods have been found which closely resemble the 'ferri' around which medieval macaroni was moulded (see below), but these might have had a different use.

However, the question remains: what was done with the products of this equipment? There is no evidence that it was boiled, like pasta. The same question can be asked about classical *lagani* and *itria* in strip form.

The first hint that *lagani* or *itria* were being boiled comes from further east. The *Jerusalem Talmud*, a work of the late 5th century AD, contains a discussion on whether boiled dough can be allowed as unleavened bread under Jewish food law. Whether or not this reference bears directly on the pasta question, it is certainly probable that the boiling of pasta was an innovation made well to the east of Rome. In old Persian literature there are several references to *lakhshah* (see LAKSA). Details are not given, but from a 10th-century Arab recipe we know that at that time it meant a product like tagliatelle; strips cut from a thin sheet of dough. These were certainly boiled. *Lakhshah* means 'slippery'. The word entered medieval Hebrew and has emerged from it in Yiddish as *lokshen*. It also turned up as *laksa* in the Indonesian language in about the 13th century.

There was also a kind of stuffed pasta like RAVIOLI (more precisely, tortellini, for the packages were made as triangles with two of their corners curled around and joined). The name was 'JOSHPARAH', meaning 'boiled ? piece', a word which on linguistic evidence seems to date from the 9th century or before. Arabic texts of the 10th century mention *itriyah* (Greek *itria*), which was by now a strip-shaped, dried pasta bought from shops. (From the 13th century, the name RESHTEH, meaning 'string', was used for fresh tagliatelle, as it still is. Reshteh were made by rolling up the flat sheet of dough and cutting it into slices. From that time on, the name *lakhshah* was reserved for one dish only, wild ass meat broth with pasta.)

Evidence of the use of pasta in Europe during this period is almost totally lacking. The 9th-century Emir Abdurrahman II of Arab-occupied Spain employed a minstrel, Ziryab, some of whose songs mention foods which might be pasta. The first definite sighting in Europe is also by an Arab, the geographer al-Idrisi, who reported in the early 12th century that in Palermo, Sicily, people made strings of dough which they called *trii*. Al-Idrisi assumed that the name was from the Arabic *itriyah*, but it may equally well have come direct from the Greek *itria*. Sicily had been occupied by both Greeks and Arabs.

On the mainland of Europe, the first reference comes from the city archives of Genoa, and is dated 1279. It is a list of the estate of a dead man, Ponzio Bastone, including a 'bariscella piena de macaronis' (a basket full of macaroni). Clearly this was a durable item, or it would not have been listed. This means that it must have been dry pasta, professionally made, indicating in turn that macaroni was well established as a food.

Even if there were no earlier evidence for European pasta, this document would dispose of the theory that Marco Polo introduced pasta to Italy, having brought it back from China. See CULINARY MYTHOLOGY. Marco Polo did not arrive back in Venice until 1298.

The name 'macaroni', used in the Genoa document, was a general one, not indicating merely the tubular kind of pasta. Tubes were a S. Italian speciality, and were called *macaroni siciliani* to distinguish them. (The modern Italian spelling *maccheroni* is a later N. Italian idea.) Thus macaroni could then be any of the sheet or strip forms of pasta made in the early Middle Ages. In the later Middle Ages the general term vermicelli ('little worms') was introduced for strip forms alone. It was only in the 18th century that this came to mean the very thin strands now so described.

So when, in 1351, Boccaccio was writing in the *Decameron* of a fantastic, mythical land, Bengodi, whose inhabitants rolled macaroni down a mountain of grated cheese, he may well have been referring to a form of pasta which would not nowadays be called macaroni; it has been suggested that he actually meant GNOCCHI, which would have rolled better.

RAVIOLI are mentioned in some of the 140,000 preserved letters of Francesco di Marco, a merchant of Prato in the 14th century. They were stuffed with pounded pork, eggs, cheese, parsley, and sugar. In Lent a filling of herbs, cheese, and spices was used.

Platina's *De Honesta Voluptate* (1475) gives various pasta recipes, including the instruction that a type of pasta should be cooked for the time it takes to say three Paternosters. This is a remarkably short time, even for fresh pasta, and shows how early the Italians came to appreciate the *al dente* (chewy) texture still considered correct.

When in 1533 Catherine de' Medici went to France to marry the future King Henri II, and took her cooks with her, the wedding banquet included one dish of pasta dressed with the juice from roast meat and cheese, and one with butter, sugar, honey, saffron, and cinnamon; one savoury and one sweet.

During the Middle Ages and Renaissance the commercial making of pasta was controlled by guilds, and standards and prices fixed by law. The largest producers were Sicily, Sardinia, and Genoa. For an account of the successive devices which the Italians invented for processing the dough and shaping the pasta, see PASTA MANUFACTURE.

As the pasta industry grew, increasing amounts were exported to other European countries. Home-grown durum wheat was no longer sufficient and in the 19th century much was imported from the Ukraine. This was shipped through Taganrog, a port on the Sea of Azov which communicates through a narrow strait with the Black Sea. For years the best pasta was often marked *pasta di Taganrog* to show that it was not made from inferior types of wheat.

Russia continued to be the chief supplier well into the 20th century. However, in 1898, an American agronomist had brought back seeds of a superior Russian variety, which he began to grow in N. Dakota. The interruption of pasta exports from Italy to the USA during the First World War meant that pasta had to be made on a large scale in America. Because of this and of the collapse of Russian wheat-growing in the Revolution, America took the lead in durum wheat production; and even Italian pasta is now mostly made from wheat grown in N. and S. Dakota.

During Mussolini's rise to power between the World Wars, rumours circulated that he proposed to ban consumption of pasta and that he considered pasta responsible for the low state of the Italian people at the time. In fact,

PASTA IN BRITAIN AND AMERICA

AN English recipe for RAVIOLI appeared in the 14th century, while 'macaroni' with cheese appeared in cookery books from the Middle Ages onwards. At the end of the 16th century Sir Hugh Platt (1594, 1596) was recommending pasta as a food for the British navy and even showing a diagram (hard to interpret) of a piece of machinery for making it; see Thick (1992) for an excellent account of this and other matters to do with the early history of pasta in England.

From the late 17th century, 'vermicelli' (with a wider meaning than now) was often added to British soups. SPAGHETTI was introduced to the English language by Eliza Acton (1849 edn of *Modern Cookery for Private Families*). In general, however, pasta was an imported food of only minor importance in Britain until the second half of the 20th century. Towards the end of the century pasta had become a true staple in Britain, especially for the younger generation who appreciated its convenience and relatively low cost.

Pasta came to America with early Spanish settlers. In the USA the first notable introduction was due to Thomas Jefferson. During his stay in Paris in 1784–9 he ate macaroni and was much taken with it. ('Macaroni' is his own term, reflecting common French and English usage; it may have been pasta of any shape.) On his return, two crates of macaroni were among his effects. When his supply ran out, he had a friend send him an extruder from Naples.

However, it was really the massive late 19th-century immigration from Italy, and especially from Naples, which made pasta popular in the USA. Consequently, N. American ways of preparing pasta are essentially derived from Italian ones, although displaying variations such as spaghetti with meatballs. C. European and Jewish immigrants have brought their own (noodle) recipes.

these were scare stories put about by his opponents. The only real opposition to pasta came from the Futurists, who denounced it as 'a symbol of oppressive dullness, plodding deliberation, and fat bellied conceit', but this was ineffective; see FUTURIST MEALS. Rather than oppose the food, Mussolini actually tried to make Italy self-sufficient in wheat by a grandiose agricultural programme, which was none too successful. Nevertheless, a large acreage of wheat was and still is grown in N. Italy, especially on the Lombardy plain. The chief sufferer was the Naples pasta industry. Pasta manufacture shifted north.

It seems safe to predict that Italians will continue to be the leading consumers of pasta. Elsewhere in Europe the Swiss (partly due to the Italian element in their population) and French have, per capita, the highest consumption.

Pasta manufacture

This is a technical but interesting subject which includes both the choice of ingredients and the equipment needed in order to shape the results (see also the section on PASTA SHAPES below).

Pasta at its simplest is made from durum wheat and water. This special type of wheat is suitable only for pasta and SEMOLINA products, not for bread. Conversely, 'hard' bread wheat and 'soft' cake flour wheat do not make good ordinary pasta (although they are used for home-made fresh pasta, reinforced and enriched with egg, which overcomes what would otherwise be a weak, fragile texture).

Commercial egg pasta is made with durum wheat and about half the proportion of eggs to wheat of the richest home-made pasta (which can have ten eggs to a kilo of flour, i.e. four to a pound). Other possible additions are a little spinach for green pasta and, less commonly, tomato paste or beetroot juice for red pasta.

As for the instruments used to shape pasta, the oldest of these, scarcely a labour-saving device for it was very slow to operate, was the *ferro*, or iron rod, of Sicily, Calabria, and Apulia, used for making tubular macaroni. A flat strip of pasta was simply wrapped around the rod, pressed to seal it, and slid off. Sometimes a straight birch twig was used instead. In the Abruzzi a *chitarra* ('guitar') was and is still used to cut narrow strips (maccheroni alla chitarra). The device has many closely spaced wires, more like a zither than a guitar. A flat sheet of dough is placed on these and pressed through with a roller. In Romagna, a sharp comblike device is used to cut the sheet; the result is called garganelli. In Genoa a combined mould and cutter is stamped down on to a sheet of dough to form small, embossed *corzetti*.

The most important device of all is the extrusion press, without which it would have been impossible for round SPAGHETTI to be made, while tubular MACARONI would have remained a minor southern curiosity. This machine at its simplest is a piston and cylinder with holes at the far end of the cylinder. The piston pushes dough out through the holes. Enormous pressure is required, for the dough must be stiff enough to hold its shape when it emerges. The piston must therefore be moved by a screw.

Early machines had clumsy wooden screws, for the technical difficulties of making long metal threaded rods accurately made these uneconomically expensive until the 18th century. Extruded pasta was therefore rather a slow starter on the market. A small, primitive extruder, the *torchio* ('screw press'), which has a barrel about 30 cm (12.5") long and 7 cm (3") wide, survives in the Veneto region, where it is used for making bigoli, a thick (and therefore easy to extrude) kind of spaghetti made from wholemeal flour; it now has a mass-produced metal screw. The most recently introduced hand-operated device is the combined roller and cutter for homemade tagliatelle, now commonly available and quite unlike any traditional machine. Small, electrically powered extruders are also made for home use.

During the 18th century Naples gained the lead in the commercial manufacture of pasta. In 1700 it had 60 pasta shops; in 1785 there were 280. Part of this success came from the large-scale adoption of an improved screw press, which was known as *l'ingegno* ('the gadget'). The perforated die plate through which the pasta emerged could be changed to make spaghetti—at first a novelty—or macaroni, or any other simple shape. *L'ingegno* had a screw travel of almost 1.5 m (62") and could thus make spaghetti of that length, which was draped and folded in half on long racks in the street. It was broken at the bend when removed, giving the traditional long spaghetti with curved tips. Kneading was still done with the simplest of machinery, as was rolling. Fancy types of pasta continued to be hand made for many years. Cooked pasta was sold in the streets from mobile cookers, and eaten at its full length by hand, which involved raising the strands at arm's length and gradually lowering it into one's mouth.

In 1878 in Naples, production began to be mechanized. The first machinery—merely a set of semolina sieves—caused riots, but the trend was unstoppable. In 1882 British-made kneaders, extruders, and cutters were installed. In Toulouse in 1917, Féreol Sandragné invented the first extruder which worked continuously, due to an Archimedean screw feed like that of a modern mincing machine. It became very hot in operation, and required a cooling system. The device was adopted in one factory after another. The continuously emerging pasta was cut to length with a rotating knife whose speed could be varied. Thus, for example, macaroni could be made full length with a slow knife speed; short with a fast speed; and with a very fast speed the result was little rings.

In 1933, the firm of Braibanti installed the first completely mechanized continuous production line; it was during this same decade that Mussolini's agricultural policies caused the main spaghetti manufacturing industry to be transferred to the north of the country.

Manufacture of pasta is by no means confined to Italy. It was begun in the USA during the First World War, when supplies from Italy were interrupted. And it is practised in a number of other countries, including Spain, Greece, and Israel.

READING: Chenciner (1994); Julia della Croce (1989).

Pasta shapes

Pasta shapes, very numerous and still proliferating, include:

- Agnolini, a stuffed egg pasta of Lombardy and Emilia-Romagna, initially made in semicircular form, but with the corners of the semicircle bent round to form little rings; often eaten *in brodo*.
- Agnolotti, see RAVIOLI.
- Anolini, tiny stuffed pasta from Emilia-Romagna, half-moon shaped, with a stuffing which always includes meat.

- Bavette, bavettine, thin oval spaghetti.
- Bigoli, a thick spaghetti from Venice. Anna del Conte (1987) remarks that this is the only traditional form of pasta made with wholewheat flour; and that duck eggs are often an ingredient of the dough.
- Bombolotti, a short cylindrical form with a smooth exterior.
- Bucati, bucatini, very thin tubular pasta.
- CANNELLONI.
- Capelli d'angelo ('angel hair'), capellini ('little hairs'), the thinnest form of the SPAGHETTI family.
- Cappelletti, small stuffed pasta which are twisted into a shape something like a small three-cornered hat (cappelletti means 'small hats'). Cappellacci are similar but larger.
- Conchiglie, shell-shaped pasta with a ribbed surface, like cockles. Conchiglioni are larger and conchigliette are smaller.
- Elbow macaroni, an American term for short, curved MACARONI.
- Farfalle, resembling butterflies. Farfalloni are bigger butterflies, while farfalletti (stricchetti in Bologna) are intermediate in size.
- Fettucine, a ribbon pasta which is usually slightly narrower than tagliatelli, of which it is the Roman form. *Fettuccia* means ribbon.
- Fusilli, a spiral kind of spaghetti, twisted like a corkscrew. Fusilli bucati are similar but here it is a thin tubular form which is twisted.
- LASAGNE.
- Lingue di passero ('sparrows' tongues'), the smallest version of bavette. Linguine are in the same group, between bavettine and bavette in size.
- Lumache, like snail shells. (Chiocciole are also this shape.)
- Maccheroni (usually spelled 'macaroni' in Naples, whence it came, as in Britain—see MACARONI). Maccheroncini are smaller.
- Maccheroni alla chitarra, best described as 'square spaghetti', produced in Abruzzi by pressing a sheet of fresh pasta through the special cutting device called chitarra (meaning zither).
- Maltagliati, pasta shaped like long narrow triangles or diamonds, roughly produced (the name means 'badly cut').
- Mille righi, meaning 'one thousand stripes', one of numerous variations on the theme of rigatoni, see below.
- Orecchiette, meaning 'little ears', of the shape indicated by the name.
- Pappardelle, short pieces of broad ribbon pasta.
- Pastina perbrodo, a general term for the numerous kinds of small, quick-cooking pasta which are especially suited for serving in broths. These include alphabet pasta (*alfabeto*), especially popular with children.

- Penne, short pieces of macaroni cut diagonally at both ends like pen nibs or quills. Pennette are tiny, pennine are small, and pennone are the larger version.
- RAVIOLI.
- Riccie, meaning curly or rippled, is an adjective rather than a noun and can be applied as an epithet to many forms of pasta—thus lasagne riccie are lasagne with one or both sides ripple edged. Riccini are small 'curls' of pasta which may be both twisted and ripple-edged. Ricciolini are even smaller such curls.
- Rigatoni, tube-shaped pasta with a ridged exterior.
- Rotolo, a substantial form of pasta made by covering a flat sheet with filling and then rolling it up like a swiss roll. A speciality of Emilia-Romagna.
- Sedani, meaning 'celery', a S. Italian sort of macaroni, ridged like celery and often used in short pieces for soup.
- SPAGHETTI. Spaghettini (diminutive form).
- Tagliatelli, a popular ribbon pasta whose home territory is Bologna and whose counterpart further south, in the region of Rome, is fettucine (see above). Tagliolini and tagliarini are in the same family, as their names suggest.
- Tortellini, a kind of stuffed pasta which may be round or square; in effect cappelletti twisted in a different way (modelled, according to legend, on Venus' navel). Tortelli are larger.
- Tortiglioni, a tubular pasta with spiral ridges (hence the name used by some manufacturers, elicoidali.
- Trenette, a pasta from Liguria which is like tagliatelli (although the dough used is somewhat different) and is always dressed with PESTO.
- Vermicelli, a thinner version of spaghetti, especially in S. Italy. The word means 'small worms'.
- Zite/ziti, a tubular pasta (like maccheroni) associated particularly with Naples. Zitoni are a larger version.

A general point which aids comprehension of the diversity of forms of pasta has been well brought out by Stobart

---

SERVING PASTA, AND SAUCES

When pasta is served in soup or broth, it is *pasta in brodo*. Served as a separate dish with a dressing, it is *pasta asciutta*. A third category, *pasta al forno*, comprises various baked dishes, using plain or stuffed pasta.

One of the simplest and best dressings for pasta is of oil, garlic, and grated cheese. However, there are legions of others, for some of which see RAGÚ; tomato sauce for pasta appears in Ippolito Cavalcanti's *Cucina teorico pratica* of 1839. This book also includes dressings based on fish and one with clams resembling present-day *Spaghetti alle vongole*. (For other popular dressings, see SPAGHETTI and MACARONI.)

(1980), who explains that the 'surface-to-volume ratio is important', i.e. 'it takes less sauce to cover a piece of dough shaped into a ball than to cover the same piece rolled out into a large sheet, which has the same volume, but a bigger surface area. Even more sauce would be necessary if the sheet were cut into strips. Ribbed forms of pasta (*rigati*) trap more sauce than smooth ones (*lisci*).' Marrying a particular form of pasta to a particular sauce is indeed an art, instinctively acquired by Italians from an early age but needing to be learned by others.

in pasties. Beef, mutton, and game were also used; porpoise meat, which counted as fish, was made into pasties for fast days. Venison pasty was popular for many centuries, and was probably a status symbol, as beef was sometimes marinated in supposed imitation, a practice which appears to have gone on into the 17th century. Butter or beef marrow were often added to pasties generally, to help keep the meat moist.

Smaller, sweet pasties were also made; one medieval type was petyperneux (or pernollys), possibly meaning 'little lost eggs'. Containing whole egg yolks, currants and raisins, bone marrow, and spices in paste made of fine flour with saffron, sugar, and salt, these were fried. Later forms included the 'hat' (with the addition of pounded meat or fish), and, by the 16th century, a turnover shape known as a peascod (pea pod), whose filling included chopped kidney. Moulds in that shape, or in the form of a dolphin, were evidently used for making these. Large pasties were decorated with elaborate patterns cut out of rolled pastry.

The best-known pasty of modern times is the **Cornish pasty,** made in a pointed oval shape, with a seam of crimped pastry running the full length of the upper side. In the recent past, fillings varied. Cubed beef with root vegetables is now considered standard, but other meats or fish, or vegetables alone, were used. Theodora FitzGibbon (1976) recounts, 'It is said in Cornwall that the Devil never crossed the River Tamar into that county for fear of the Cornish woman's habit of putting anything and everything into a pasty.' The corners of the pasties could be marked with initials to identify the recipient. Sometimes very large pasties for a whole family were made. Some pasties contained two courses, so to speak; a savoury filling at one end and a sweet one at the other. Sometimes a very large family-size pasty would be made and taken to the local baker's shop to be baked.

Cornish miners who emigrated to the USA took their pasty tradition with them and Lockwood and Lockwood (1983) have described their subsequent evolution in Michigan, where they interbred, so to speak, with similar products brought by immigrants from Finland.

Other types of pasty are known in Britain. One which is still popular is the Scottish product, the **Forfar bridie.** Theodora FitzGibbon (1980) points out that Sir James

Barrie, who was born at Kirriemuir in Forfarshire, mentions the bridies in his novel *Sentimental Tommie*. The 'bridie' part of the name is of unknown origin; one legend attributes it to the first seller of the pasties having been a certain Maggie Bridie of Glamis, while Catherine Brown (see Mason, 1999) postulates that the shape was a lucky symbol eaten at the 'bride's meal' (i.e., the wedding feast). What is certain is that rump steak, cut into small strips or pieces, is the correct meat for the filling. Traditional recipes call for suet and chopped onions as well; the casing is of shortcrust pastry, and the bridie looks something like a Cornish pasty which has been put on its side.

Dorothy Hartley (1954) described a foot, a pasty traditionally eaten in Lancashire. The name comes from the form of the pasty crust. A piece of shortcrust pastry is rolled into an oval shape, then one end is rolled much thinner, so that it spreads out and the pastry assumes the form of the sole and heel of a shoe. Filling is put on the thick end, and the thin part wrapped over it and pressed down around the edge.

Something akin to the Cornish pasty is made in the county of Somerset; this is a **priddy oggy** (oggy is Cornish dialect for pasty) which appears to have been invented in the late 1960s. It is filled with pork, and the pastry contains cheese.

Other types of pasty include the BEDFORDSHIRE CLANGER (with suet crust enclosing a meat filling at one end and a sweet filling at the other), and the Yorkshire mint pasty, a large one with a sweet filling of raisins, currants, candied peel, brown sugar, and butter, liberally flavoured with fresh mint and lightly spiced.

PÂTÉ a French term whose meaning and use have both enlarged since early medieval times. The original meaning is best conveyed in English by the word 'pie' (or perhaps 'pasty' where the connection is more obvious). What was meant was a pastry case filled with any of various mixtures (meat, fish, vegetables), baked in the oven and served either hot or cold. Such things are familiar in other European countries, but the French term and French practice have become dominant.

By a natural extension, the term came to mean not only the whole 'pie' but also what was in the pie, especially if it was something

which could be served cold, in slices. At this point the meaning became much the same as that of TERRINE.

Once pâté had evolved in this direction, so that it was not thought of as being in a pastry case, there was a problem over what to call it when it was in a pastry case. The phrase *pâté en croûte* fills this gap.

The list of the various pâtés is almost endless. A few of the best known are:

- *pâté de campagne*, now ubiquitous but formerly a speciality of Brittany, pure pork pâté with onion and other flavourings;
- *pâté de gibier*, game pâté;
- *pâté de foie*, containing 15% pork liver and a lot of fat;
- *pâté d'Amiens*, of duck.

PÂTISSERIE the French word for a pastry-cook's shop. In English this has come to mean, by extension, the goods in the shop, particularly fine and fancy small sweet cakes. LM

PAVLOVA a type of MERINGUE cake which has a soft marshmallowy centre, achieved by the addition of a little cornflour and a teaspoonful or so of vinegar or lemon juice to the meringue mixture after the sugar is folded in.

When cooked, the meringue case is filled with fresh cream and fruit such as strawberries, raspberries, kiwi fruit. A version filled with a mixture of passion-fruit pulp and fresh cream is regarded as the most traditional.

The pavlova has been described as Australia's national dish, but it is also claimed by New Zealand. According to the Australian claim, it was invented in 1935 by Herbert Sachse, an Australian chef, and named by Harry Nairn of the Esplanade Hotel, Perth, after Anna Pavlova, the Russian ballerina who visited both countries in 1926. The built-up sides of the pavlova are said to suggest a tutu. The Australian author Symons (1982) concedes that the actual product had made a prior appearance in New Zealand, but suggests that its naming was an Australian act.

On the New Zealand side, however, Helen Leach (1997) has marshalled evidence to show that:

(cont. on page 587)

Pastry

A term with two main meanings:

1. a mixture of flour and (usually) fat and water with (sometimes) other ingredients, made into a DOUGH and cooked, and then used to cover, support, encase, or constitute dishes such as are described under PIE, TART, PASTY, and CROISSANT; and

2. a particular dish which consists partly or wholly of pastry in the first sense.

(1) is dealt with here, (2) under PASTRIES.

In this entry there are three interlocking and overlapping sections. The first gives a classification of the main types of pastry now in use. The second explains in a summary way the physics and chemistry of pastry-making. The third recapitulates briefly what is known about the history of the development of certain kinds of pastry.

TYPES OF PASTRY

The classification of these, if it is to be helpful, must embody the terms actually in use. If these terms corresponded to a logical categorization, whether by ingredients, technique of preparation, or purpose, that would be convenient; all the more so if the same categorization prevailed in different countries and languages. However, this is not the situation. The terms in use reflect various methods of categorization, and vary from place to place, including differences between British and American usage.

The first step is to distinguish five broad categories:

- **shortcrust,** the simplest and most common pastry;
- **rough puff** (or flaky), still simple, but layered (so it expands somewhat when cooked);
- **puff pastry,** which has very numerous layers and therefore expands (rises) noticeably when cooked;
- **choux pastry;**
- FILO **pastry** and the like (STRUDEL etc.), all distinguished by being paper thin and greatly stretched.

Shortcrust pastry (sometimes known as medium flake pastry in the USA) is made from flour; fat, usually lard or butter; water; and salt. The process is quick. The chilled butter or lard is cut into cubes and rubbed into the flour (already sifted and salted) to produce a mixture looking like coarse breadcrumbs. A well is made in this and iced water added little by little and stirred in until the dough coheres and can be formed into a ball. This is wrapped in foil or greaseproof paper and chilled for a short time before being rolled out and used.

Suet crust is the same, but made with suet as the fat. It has a very light texture.

Hot water crust (sometimes called short flake in the USA) has the same ingredients, but the water added is boiling. This causes the fat to melt. The result is a pastry which is strong in both the raw and cooked state, and therefore suitable for use in raised pies (see PIE).

Rich shortcrust involves a change in the ingredients. There is more fat in relation to the flour. Egg may be added, and sometimes sugar. The result is relatively soft, crumbly, and tender—and sweet, if sugar has been added. The French *pâte brisée* (meaning broken-textured pastry) is of this type. It is the classic pastry for flans and often has a little sugar, even when used for savoury dishes, but rarely egg. *Pâte sucrée* (sweet pastry) does include egg, and a larger dose of sugar; and it may also be called *pâte sèche* (dry pastry). The Austrian *mürbe Teig* (tender pastry) is a rich shortcrust with egg and sour cream or cream cheese; the latter ingredient gives it a special flavour. The same applies to the rich shortcrust used for *Linzertorte* (see TORTE AND KUCHEN) which includes ground almond as an ingredient. A further variation is found in the rich shortcrust used for the Russian COULIBIAC, which differs in being made with yeast, which makes it light and puffy. Indeed, it could be held that it really belongs in the next group.

Rough puff, flaky. Here we have a difference of technique rather than of ingredients. If rich shortcrust pastry is folded and rolled three or four times it becomes what is known as rough puff pastry. The layers of this partly separate and rise during cooking, although not nearly as much as in puff pastry proper. Rough puff is used for quickly made pie crusts. So is flaky pastry (sometimes known as long flake in the USA). It is made from flour with a high proportion of butter, and a little water. A quarter of the butter is added to the flour in the initial stage, resulting in a normal shortcrust pastry. Then the pastry is rolled, dotted with a further quarter of the butter, folded, re-rolled and allowed to rest in a cool place. The procedure is repeated twice more until all the butter is used. This pastry is finely layered with irregular inclusions of butter, giving a light but short texture midway between that of rich shortcrust and puff pastry. French *demi feuilleté* (half-puff) pastry is similar, but the butter left from the original mixing is added in a flat sheet at the first stage, so that the three turns and rolls spread it out more evenly between the layers. Its texture is closer to that of true puff pastry.

For genuine **puff pastry,** only about one-eighth of the butter is incorporated in the original mixture. The pastry is rolled out. Then the rest of the butter is spread over two-thirds of the area of the sheet of pastry, which is then folded into three in such a way that there are three layers of pastry enclosing two of butter. Folding and rolling is carried out six times in all, with rests between turns. The resulting pastry has 729 layers each separated by a thin smear of butter. Older methods called for folding in two and for nine turns, giving 512 layers. Either way, the pastry rises to a very light, laminated texture, crisp and frail. Puff pastry is used in delicate sweet and savoury articles of many kinds.

Yeast puff pastry is a richer kind, originally a speciality of Vienna and now used to make CROISSANTS and similar articles. The dough is made with yeast, milk, and eggs as well as flour and a mixture of butter and lard. Depending on the particular recipe, the dough is given up to four rolls and turns. The combined effect of the rolling and turning and the rise produced by the yeast is to give a pastry as light as normal puff pastry, but with a softer, richer texture and a more interesting flavour.

Choux pastry is made by melting butter in hot water, adding flour, and cooking the mixture until it is smooth and no longer sticky. Then eggs are beaten in one by one. The raw pastry is very soft, and is usually piped through a forcing bag. When cooked, it rises greatly and has a delicate, spongy texture which finds application in ÉCLAIRS and similar light delicacies. Barbara Maher (1982), remarking on its versatility, asked: who could guess that this pastry is the basis of products as apparently dissimilar as: CREAM PUFFS, *Herzogbrot* (Bread of the Dukes), Carolines, Salammbos, Mecca rolls, Paris Brest and St Honoré (for both of which see GATEAU), Lucca eyes, and Religieuses (see ÉCLAIR)?

FILO pastry is treated separately.

PHYSICS AND CHEMISTRY OF PASTRY

The striking differences in texture between various kinds of pastry have simple causes which lie in the nature of wheat flour and certain kinds of fat. Wheat flour, when kneaded into a plain dough made with water, develops strands of gluten, which are what give an elastic, tough quality to bread. In ordinary pastry, such a texture is undesirable; so a fat or oil is added. This retards the development of the gluten, mainly by physically interposing itself between the grains of flour so that the strands cannot tangle and be drawn out. A hard, solid fat such as lard or suet is most effective here. Lard in particular has a coarse, crystalline structure which makes a highly effective barrier. Butter is less effective, and shortcrust pastry made with butter alone has an inferior texture. If the fat is melted with hot water, or if liquid oil is used, the thin oily layer between the grains offers less obstacle to gluten formation and the resulting pastry is tougher. This is the effect deliberately sought in hot water pastry.

The fact that pastry made with solid fat is stiffer, both when raw and in the early stages of baking, is due simply to the solidity of the fat, and is unconnected with the previous phenomenon.

In puff pastry a certain amount of gluten formation is desirable, but all the strands of gluten must lie in one plane to give strength to the horizontal sheets. Thus the process is one of repeatedly stretching a mixture with only a little fat in it, but whose layers are separated by a barrier of butter. A good deal of air also gets in between the layers and it is partly the expansion of this, and partly the steam formed in cooking, which force the layers apart and make puff pastry rise in such a striking way.

In choux pastry, another notable riser, the preliminary cooking of a flour and fat mixture creates a smooth paste into which air can be beaten during the later stage of adding the eggs, which are themselves even better vehicles for air bubbles. The eggs are added after the cooking stage, simply to avoid hardening them prematurely.

In filo pastry, the gluten is developed to its full extent. The dough used is a mixture of flour and water only, which is thoroughly kneaded and then stretched so that the gluten strands are all horizontal. In this way it resembles a single leaf of puff pastry. When several layers of filo are wrapped around a filling they are brushed with melted butter to separate them, so that the resemblance to puff pastry is increased.

In strudel pastry, the reduction of gluten formation resulting from adding fat and egg to the dough is compensated for by the use of strong, high-gluten bread flour, and by adding a little vinegar to the mixture, which chemically assists the gluten to form.

In flaky, puff, filo, and strudel doughs, where gluten is formed, the process is assisted by giving the dough one or more 'rests' in a cool place. Ideally two hours in a refrigerator is required for each rest. During this time the gluten strands, which have been greatly stressed by the rolling or whichever process is used, draw themselves out a little more as the result of this tension, and thus become not only longer but also slacker. Once the gluten has 'relaxed' in this way, it is easier to stretch it further next time.

NOTES ON THE EARLY HISTORY OF PASTRY

Small, sweet cakes eaten by the ancient Egyptians may well have included types using pastry. With their fine flour, oil, and honey they had the materials, and with their professional bakers they had the skills.

In the plays of Aristophanes (5th century BC) there are mentions of sweetmeats including small pastries filled with fruit. Nothing is known of the actual pastry used, but the Greeks certainly recognized the trade of pastry-cook as distinct from that of baker.

The Romans made a plain pastry of flour, oil, and water to cover meats and fowls which were baked, thus keeping in the juices. (The covering was not meant to be eaten; it filled the role of what was later called 'huff paste'—see below.) A richer pastry, intended to be eaten, was used to make small pasties containing eggs or little birds which were among the minor items served at banquets.

However, the Romans were not strong on pastry. Like the Greeks, they cooked with oil. Pastry made with oil is palatable enough, but lacks stiffness in the raw state, and tends to slump during the early stages of baking. Pastry goods made with oil have to be small or flat, or closely wrapped around their contents. These forms are still noticeable in Middle Eastern dishes using oil pastry.

In medieval N. Europe the usual cooking fats were lard and butter, which—especially lard—were conducive to making stiff pastry and permitted development of the solid, upright case of the raised pie. This was made from coarse flour, usually rye.

No medieval cookery books give detailed instructions on how to make pastry; they assume the necessary knowledge (although some give incomplete accounts of ingredients). From later works (notably Gervase Markham's *The English Hus-wife* of 1615) it can be inferred that a stiff pie case or 'coffyn' (see COFFIN) for a tart was composed of coarse flour and a little suet amalgamated with boiling water, as hot water crust is made today. Raised pie cases were baked with their contents. The 'coffyns' for large open tarts were baked blind, that is, empty. The rough, grey pastry could be made to look quite pleasing by glazing the outside with egg yolk. But it was not intended to be eaten, except by servants after the meal. A similar coarse, stiff pastry was used to cover fowls and pieces of meat that were baked. A protective case of this kind was known as 'huff paste'. It not only sealed in the juice and flavour of the meat during cooking, but also acted as a barrier against contamination if the meat was not to be eaten at once. It was therefore left on until the last moment. Although it was not intended to be eaten, the pastry became well flavoured with meat juice and, outside the formal surroundings of a banquet, people would often gnaw the tough but tasty fragments.

However, not all medieval pastry was coarse. Small tarts would be made with a rich pastry of fine white flour, butter, sugar, saffron, and other good things, certainly meant to be eaten.

From the middle of the 16th century on, actual recipes for pastry begin to appear. The coarse rye pastry for raised pies, already described, remained as it was. For raised pies which did not have to be quite so durable, but might have to last a few days, there was a thick hot water crust of fine wheat flour and some butter. Sometimes meat broth was used instead of water. This pastry would be hard but fully edible. Fine pastry was made with the best wheat flour, which might be dry baked before use to give a short texture. It was mixed with plenty of butter, eggs, and cold water: in fact, it was a true rich shortcrust pastry such as is still made. Sugar, saffron, and the like would be added for sweet pasties.

Karen Hess (1981), who provides several important notes on the early history of pastry, points out that there is a difficulty in identifying the earliest references to puff pastry, since the Italian and French terms for this (*pasta sfoglia* and *pâte feuilletée*) also carry the more general meaning of 'leafed pastry', which has been known in the Mediterranean region since antiquity. She remarks that the first recipe for something recognizable as puff pastry is in Dawson (1596, but she cites an edition of 1586). An Italian–English dictionary of 1598, by Florio, seems to have been the first to use the English term 'puff pastry'.

- the name pavlova was being used in New Zealand as early as 1927, as the *OED* points out, but that this use referred to a different dessert, whose connection with New Zealand is anyway uncertain;
- the large soft-centred meringue cake which is the pavlova had been developed in New Zealand by 1934 (or possibly earlier), although it was not at first called pavlova; but
- the name and the dish were put together in New Zealand at some time before 1935, thus antedating the Australian activity.
(HS)

PAXIMADIA an exceptionally interesting Greek item in the frontier area between BREADS and BISCUITS. As Aglaia Kremezi (1997) explains in a fine essay on the subject, well equipped with historical references as well as contemporary observation, paximadia were originally barley biscuits, resembling RUSKS, which had to be soaked in broth to make them soft enough for eating. The fact that they were twice baked and very dry meant that they could be kept for long periods and were well adapted for use by travellers.

BARLEY had for many centuries been the staple food of the common people in Greece and neighbouring parts of the Mediterranean region. In more recent times a combination of barley and wheat flour has been used, producing lighter and crunchier biscuits. These appeal to Greeks who have met the traditional paximadia in the islands of the Aegean (and in Crete, supposedly the home of the best paximadia of all), and who wish to replicate the experience in a form adapted to modern requirements (i.e. no ritual of soaking before eating).

Paximadia do not belong only to Greece. Kremezi's essay and Dalby (1996) between them illuminate their wider distribution and the likely derivation of their interesting name.

PAYASAM a pudding traditionally served at weddings and other special functions in S. India. Most versions are based on beans or lentils. For example, *chirupayaru payasam* is made with lentils which are cooked with unrefined brown sugar, then simmered with coconut milk, CARDAMOM, and GHEE. The finished dish may be like a cream soup. The possible ingredients are legion: vermicelli, raisins, CASHEW NUTS, SAGO, ground almonds, etc. A vermicelli version is a favourite of the large S. Indian community in MALAYSIA.

Another payasam is made with rice which is cooked with milk, sugar and aromatic spices. This is prepared for the beginning of the festival of Dasehra, a ten-day festival celebrated all over India to commemorate the victory of the good Prince Rama over the army of the demon Ravana.   HS

PEA a LEGUME which originated in W. Asia, has been a staple food since ancient times. There are three main kinds: the first of these, the familiar garden pea, *Pisum sativum* ssp *sativum*, is by far the most important. A secondary form, the field or grey pea, used to be distinguished as *P. arvense*, but is now classified as a variety (*arvense*) of the above ssp. Third is the small, wild Mediterranean pea, ssp *elatius*, sometimes called the oasis or maquis pea.

Other legumes of different genera are popularly called 'peas'. See BUTTERFLY PEA; CHICKPEA; COWPEA; PIGEON PEA; WINGED PEA.

The earliest trace of the garden pea is in the relics of Bronze Age settlements in Switzerland, *c*.3000 BC. It was apparently grown by both Greeks and Romans in the classical period, spread quickly through India, where it is still a popular vegetable, and reached China in the 7th century AD. The Chinese gave it the name *hu tou* (foreign legume).

Both garden and field peas were eaten dried, and sometimes husked and split. Dried peas were one of the principal foods of poorer people throughout Europe in the

Middle Ages, especially in winter. They were cheap, filling, and a useful source of protein.

The old English name 'pease' is singular. The '-se' was dropped later under the wrong assumption that it was a plural form. (The modern Indian word *paisa*, meaning small coin, is from the same root.) Peas were made into thick broths and pease porridge; the old singular form survives in the name of the porridge and also in a related dish, PEASE PUDDING, which has its own entry. The old form also survives in the term PEASEMEAL.

Fernie (1905) records an interesting piece of history concerning the grey or field pea:

' "Hot Grey Pease, and a suck of Bacon," (tied to a string of which the stallkeeper held the other end,) was a popular street cry in the London of James the First.'

The garden pea was finally introduced to Europe in the 16th century and was grown increasingly thereafter. A sudden vogue for eating immature peas fresh, which was a novel procedure, reached a peak at the end of the 17th century. In 1696 Mme de Maintenon wrote from the court of Louis XIV: 'Il y a des dames qui, après avoir soupé, et bien soupé, trouvent des pois chez elles avant de coucher, au risque d'une indigestion. C'est une mode, un fureur.' (There are some ladies who, having supped, and supped well, take peas at home before going to bed, at the risk of an attack of indigestion. It's a fashion, a craze.) French peas were very expensive. Some of this glamour still attaches to the French petits pois, which are not a separate variety but ordinary peas harvested very young. The regions from which these come are the north and west of France, and Paris, where the towns of Saint-Germain and Clamart were so famous for the quality of their petits pois that their names came to be used as culinary terms for dishes incorporating petits pois.

One variety popular in England at the time was the sugar pea, also called snap pea and mange-tout. The pods of ordinary garden peas have a tough inner lining which makes them inedible, though they can be made into soup. (In pea-growing areas 'peascod' soup has long been a traditional harvest-time dish.) Sugar peas have a tender pod and, when young, the whole pod and the tiny peas in it can be eaten. Hence the French name *mange-tout*.

At the end of the 19th century, when canned vegetables began to be sold widely, peas were one of the most popular types. When peas are canned they become a dull khaki colour as their original chlorophyll green is destroyed by heating. French canned petits pois are this colour. However, in many other countries the change is unacceptable, and the peas are restored to their 'natural' green by being treated with a bright green dye. Most kinds of canned peas bear little resemblance to the fresh vegetable and may be considered as a separate food item. They include giant 'marrowfat' peas (seldom sold fresh) and, in the north of England, special 'mushy' peas. 'Processed' peas are treated with alkali to make them soft and starchy. The term 'garden peas' is used to distinguish unprocessed canned peas.

Peas were also among the earliest frozen vegetables in the 1920s and 30s, and here there is a real advantage. Fresh peas deteriorate noticeably in hours rather than days after picking. People without vegetable gardens or access to really fresh supplies will find that frozen peas, harvested at the ideal moment and frozen at once, are in effect the 'freshest' they can obtain.

Field peas are still grown extensively as a fodder crop or a 'green manure' ploughed back into the soil. For a special kind of dried field pea, whose use in the north of England for a Lenten dish survives, precariously, see CARLING.

Dried peas remain the main form in India, where they constitute several of the numerous types of DAL (split pulse). Size and colour vary greatly. All dried peas, especially field peas, are among the most difficult pulses to soften. They need soaking overnight, and even then cooking may take several hours. In contrast, fresh peas are easily spoiled by overcooking; indeed, they may be eaten raw.

PEACH *Amygdalus persica*, a fruit distinguished by its velvety skin, to which the Roman poet Virgil drew attention when he wrote of searching for 'downy peaches and the glossy plum'.

Like the PLUM and the APRICOT, the peach belongs to the rose family and is classified as a drupe, i.e. a fruit with a hard stone. Of all the fruits in this family, with the possible exception of the CHERRY, the peach is the most celebrated in literature, in the Orient as well as the West. It is a fruit of temperate but warm climates, which will not endure either tropical heat or severe cold. The NECTARINE, which has a smooth skin, is treated separately, although of the same species.

HISTORY

Wild peach trees still grow in China, the original home of the peach. Like their cultivated descendants, they are medium-sized trees, with handsome, pointed leaves; but their fruits are small, sour, and very fuzzy. Well before the 10th century BC (some authorities suggest very much earlier) improved varieties were being cultivated.

Peaches are easily raised from seed, and cultivation spread westwards through areas with a suitable climate, such as Kashmir, to Persia. It flourished there so well that it came to be regarded as a native Persian fruit; hence the specific name *persica*.

In classical antiquity Theophrastus (*c*.370–*c*.288 BC) was the first writer to mention the peach. Despite the lack of clear evidence, it is widely assumed that it was Alexander the Great who brought it to Greece from Persia. Pliny (1st century AD) mentioned half a dozen types, e.g. the peaches of Gaul (France) and the Asiatic ones, and declared the fruit to be particularly wholesome.

Generally, it seems to have been the Romans who spread the peach further north and west. Much later, in the 16th century, it was the Spaniards who took it to America. The 16th century used also to be thought of as the time when the peach reached England. However, as Roach (1985) points out, there is much evidence, including the supply of two peach trees to the Tower of London in 1275 and a reference by Chaucer (1372), to show that it was being grown there much earlier (and eaten even earlier, perhaps by Roman legionaries, for peach stones have been found in a 2nd-century site near the old Billingsgate fish market). But it seems that peach-growing was discontinued for a time, and that it was in the 16th century that the fruit was reintroduced from France and the Netherlands. Phillips (1823) gave to Wolf, the gardener of King Henry VIII, credit for this.

VARIETIES

There are two categories of peach, clingstone and freestone, distinguished by the ease with which the flesh comes away from the stone. Each includes fruits with both yellow and white flesh; and varieties of each were known from early times. Gerard (1633) described four varieties (white, red, yellow, and d'avant) and added: 'I have them all in my garden, with many other sorts.' Parkinson (1629) listed 21 varieties, and Rea (1676) 35. Many had names which indicated a French origin. Perhaps the most famous peaches of France have been those of Montreuil near Paris; but this was not an instance of a special variety, it was rather a special method of cultivation, using espaliers of a different design, to produce fruits of exceptional quality, packed by hand and internationally famed. The varieties used included l'Admirable tardive (=Téton de Vénus) and Gross Noire de Montreuil. Émile Zola admired their fine clear skin, like that of girls of the north of France, he thought, in contrast to the peaches from the Midi which were yellow and sunburned like the girls of that region. In 1993, however, there was only one lady orchardist selling genuine Montreuil peaches in the town.

Meanwhile, English nurserymen such as Rivers and Laxton in the 19th century were developing new, improved varieties. However, the English climate is not ideal for peaches, and English orchardists have to grow them in sheltered positions. The peach is much more at home in the Mediterranean region and in those parts of N. America which have a similar climate; and it is American growers, especially in California, who have done most in the 20th century to shape the pattern of world production.

Commercial cultivation in N. America had begun early in the 19th century, concentrated in the 'Chesapeake peach-belt' of the Eastern Shore of Maryland, Delaware, and S. New Jersey. Nowadays California produces about half of the American crop, with S. Carolina, Georgia, and New Jersey ranking next. The leading Californian varieties in 1996 were Elegant Lady and O'Henry. However, peach trees live only 10 to 20 years, and fashions change quickly, so—in N. America, and other regions too—each generation eats mostly new varieties.

One cultivar grown in S. Florida and the Caribbean, Red Ceylon, is of special interest. All peaches have a requirement for a certain number of hours at a 'chill' temperature while they are growing, and this requirement means that most varieties will not thrive in subtropical regions. The Red Ceylon is the big exception to this rule, because its 'chill requirement' is very low.

In the mid-1990s China was the world's largest peach producer followed by Italy, the USA, and Greece in that order.

PEACH FLESH

It seems to be widely recognized, writes a pomological correspondent in California, that the peach, of all fruits, most closely approaches the quality of human flesh, eventually reaching that state expressively described by William Morris as 'pinch-ripe'. No fruit is more laden with erotic metaphor. The pear is its nearest rival, but its cool, smooth skin cannot compare with the warm knap of a peach. The contrasting names of two varieties, Poire Cuisse-Madam and Pêche Téton de Vénus, express the difference. When the fruit-stealing episode which figures in the childhood section of so many autobiographies concerns peaches, the reference may be to 'kissing' rather than 'stealing' the fruit; and male fruit connoisseurs have written of 'stroking' peaches off the tree.

USE

To be at its best, a fresh peach has to ripen on the tree. Those which are exported over long distances are often picked long before they are ripe and make poor eating, may indeed be rubbery and tasteless or (worse still) have lost all their juiciness and become 'mealy' or 'floury' (usually because they have been refrigerated).

Fresh peaches are so good that it seems a shame to cook them, but they are good if poached in wine or made into pies. The most famous peach dessert, peach Melba, was created by Escoffier in 1893 to honour Dame Nellie Melba. It is less well known that when Mme Récamier, the famous beauty of the early 19th century, was ill, refusing all food and at death's door, she was tempted to eat and eventually recover by a dish of peaches in syrup and cream.

Peaches survive being canned better than most fruits. The flavour is altered, but still good. The canning industry, which started to grow towards the end of the 19th century, now accounts for nearly 30% of US peaches, and peaches are grown for canning in many other countries. Yellow clingstone peaches are the most popular for this purpose.

Dried peaches, in halves, are widely sold; and peach jam or marmalade is a delicacy.

In some Mediterranean countries the green or golden-green fruits (which never ripen fully) of so-called wild peaches are used in cookery and for preserves. These are not true wild peaches (only found in China), but escapes from cultivation. Patience Gray (1986) has written eloquently about *la persicata*, the wild peach jam made in S. Italy from these fruits.

PEACOCK the male of the PEAFOWL, *Pavo cristatus*, famous for its beautiful feathers, a bird which originated in India but was brought to Persia, and thence successively to Greece and Rome in times BC. It was so greatly prized in classical Rome as a bird to serve at banquets that Cicero (1st century BC) said that it was 'daring' to give a banquet without one. This statement provided a keynote which was echoed down the centuries until the 16th. After the fall of the Western Roman Empire the Franks and Ostrogoths kept up the tradition. The Emperor Charlemagne (in about 800) put it at the head of the list of birds which were always to be available at the places where he might stay. Records continue through the 10th and 11th centuries; and the *chansons de geste*, from the 12th century onwards (to the 16th), regularly depict the peacock as top bird for the banquet table.

Platina (1475), author of the first printed cookbook, gave it similar status for Italy. Thirty peacocks were served at the banquet given for Catherine de' Medici by the City of Paris in 1549. The French authors of a book known as *La Maison rustique* (1564) gave minutely detailed instructions on how they should be fed for the table. (Wild peacocks were known, and eaten, but those usually prepared for banquets were domesticated ones.)

Witteveen (1989, 1990), in an essay which is the best source of information on the subject, observes that peacocks seem not to have made good eating. He cites modern experiments which confirm the view expressed by some authorities in pre-medieval and medieval times that the flesh of a peacock is tough and needs to be hung and then given a prolonged cooking if it is to be edible. Implicit confirmation is provided by the fact that when the turkey arrived from the New World it rapidly displaced the peacock. The displacement was taking place in England before 1600. In Europe generally, peacocks were rarely on any menu after the late 17th century, nor did they continue to appear in cookery books, whereas there was abundant evidence of the growing popularity of their American rival.

The natural conclusion would be that the peacock had been used at banquets as a symbol, and for display, rather than because it was a pleasure to eat. (Indeed one recipe which called for stuffing the bird with a mixture in which pork predominated, thus sparing the assembled nobles from eating any peacock meat, rather gives the game away.) However, it may not have been quite as simple as that. It is true that there were occasions when peacocks made a wonderful display on the table, feathers fully fanned out, bodies gilded with real gold leaf, flames spitting from their mouths, a sight that would impress anyone. But there is plenty of evidence that peacocks were often presented in a much less showy way, cooked in a broth or made into a pie. A full explanation of its high status at banquets for 1,600 years and its subsequent eclipse within a century would have to take into account more factors than can be considered in this brief note.

PEACOCK-PHEASANT is the common name of handsome Asian birds of the genus *Polyplectron* in the pheasant family. It correctly indicates that these birds occupy a position intermediate between PHEASANT and PEAFOWL. There are several species, all apparently well regarded as food although varying in quality. *P. bicalcaratum*, the Burmese peacock-pheasant, exists in a number of subspecies of which one has a range extending to Hainan in the S. China Sea. Birds of this species are reputedly very easy to catch.

PEAFOWL *Pavo cristatus* and close relations, belong to the PHEASANT family and are found in the Indian subcontinent and (*P. muticus*) eastwards to Malaysia and Indonesia. In apparent contrast to the male of the species (see PEACOCK), these birds are considered to be fine fare when roasted, especially young specimens. Sala (1895) offers the mildly surprising advice that a roasted peafowl should be surrounded on the platter by roses or tulips.

PEAR *Pyrus communis*, *P. sinensis*, and other *Pyrus* spp; a fruit of which the connoisseur Edward Bunyard (1920) remarked that, while it is 'the duty of an apple to be crisp and crunchable, a pear should have such a texture as leads to silent consumption'. He meant pears of the western world, ignoring the crunchy Asian pears which in his time were gritty and inferior although the fine new varieties of them are no longer gritty.

The pear originated in the general region of the Caucasus, as did its cousin the APPLE; and both fruits were spread by the Aryan tribes from that area as they migrated into Europe and N. India. Both belong to the rose family, Rosaceae.

The original wild pear has been developed into what are now nearly 1,000 varieties, after a certain amount of interbreeding with other native wild pears of Europe and Asia. Of these last the two which are important in their own right are *P. pyrifolia* (Asian/nashi/apple/salad pear) and *P. ussuriensis* (Chinese white pear, Harbin pear). The former tends to have apple-shaped fruits; while the latter has fruits of a more typical pear shape. But there are so many cultivars and hybrids (falling into two groups, the so-called 'red pears' which have a brownish skin, and the pale green or yellow 'green pears') that no general statements about them are completely valid.

In ancient times the pear was generally considered a better fruit than the apple. Thus in China only one variety of apple was known until the end of the Sung dynasty (AD 1279), but there were many varieties of pear. In classical Greece and Rome a similar preference was evident. Around 300 BC the Greek writer Theophrastus discussed the growing of pears, including advanced techniques such as grafting and cross-pollination. Two centuries later, in Rome, Pliny the Elder described 41 varieties, whereas his parallel list of apples was much shorter.

During the Middle Ages the pear was especially popular in France and Italy, and most pears grown in Britain were from French stock. However, the famous Warden pear was of British origin; it was raised by Cistercian monks at an abbey in Bedfordshire. So important did it become as a cooking pear that it was regarded as a fruit in its own right; one finds references to 'wardens and pears'. Although pears for dessert were prized, it is noticeable that the balance between them and cooking pears was much more even in the past than it became in the 19th and 20th centuries.

The 16th century saw considerable activity by pear-breeders. At its end, two manuscripts detailing the fruits served at the table of the vegetarian Grand Duke Cosimo III of Florence listed 209 and 232 different

Pyrus pyrifolia

varieties which had appeared there alone. In 1640 Britain had a mere 64; but by 1842 this had risen to over 700.

In the 17th century pear-growing in France was at its height and many new varieties were developed. Louis XIV was particularly interested in fruit and vegetables and the pear was one of his favourite fruits. The introduction of espaliered trees, whose fruit ripened more evenly and was not so blown about as in open orchards, helped to promote the growing of fine pears in the Paris region.

The most notable pear-growers of the 18th century were both Belgian. Nicholas Hardenpont of Mons (Bergen) bred the first of the juicy, soft pears called Beurre (butter), and these were later developed by another famous Belgian breeder, Dr van Mons. Beurre varieties remain among the best of pears.

There are no native American pears. The pear was introduced into N. America in 1629, when the Massachusetts Company ordered pear seeds from England. Because the first American pears were raised from seed which, like that of the apple, does not breed true to variety, American pears became even more diverse than their European ancestors and many good, purely American strains arose.

In New England, during the 19th century, an extraordinary degree of enthusiasm for pears developed, so extraordinary that it deserved the name 'pearmania'. This phenomenon has been described, along with other remarkable features of the history of the pear, by Ian Jackson (1995).

Pears can be picked before they are fully ripe, though not too long before. They will ripen in a fairly cool place. Without this useful characteristic it would be impossible to market them, for a ripe pear is not only soft and easily damaged but also passes

through its period of perfect ripeness in a matter of hours, and after that quickly spoils (a process which can be slightly slowed by refrigeration).

A traditional way of preserving pears is by halving and drying. Also, pears are commercially canned on a large scale. The processors take care to avoid the development of a pink colour when the pears are heated in the can, whereas domestic cooks and professional chefs are pleased to achieve this effect.

The flavour of cooked pears is often improved by the addition of, e.g., red wine, almonds, or vanilla. Pears also go well with chocolate. In the dish Poires belle Hélène, whose name celebrates Offenbach's operetta about Helen of Troy, cooked pears are combined with chocolate sauce and vanilla ice cream. Italians eat pears with parmesan or pecorino cheese, a good marriage of flavours.

PEAR VARIETIES
Notable varieties of pear, past and present, include the following.

Abbé, a 19th century French variety, is a long, thin, greenish brown pear often with a red blush; a mid-autumn pear of good flavour and texture, used mainly for dessert.

Anjou; see Beurre, below.

Bartlett is the name used in the USA and Australia for Williams varieties (see below), after the American grower Enoch Bartlett who introduced them into the USA in 1817.

Beurre (which should really be spelled Beurré) varieties are particularly soft and juicy, with little of the gritty texture which some others exhibit. They include two good winter eating varieties: Beurre d'Anjou, broad, lopsided, and has a yellowish-green skin marked with russet; and Beurre Bosc, which is particularly aromatic in flavour, distinguished by a long, tapering neck, and coloured dark yellow with russet. Beurre Hardy is a harder kind often used for canning.

Clapp Favorite is an early ripening American dessert pear of fair quality, but rather granular. It is broad and dull greenish-yellow with some russeting.

Comice is short for Doyenné du Comice, which means 'top of the show'. Many would agree with this boast. It is a broad, blunt pear, greenish-yellow marked with russet or a red blush. The texture is unequalled, juicy, and not even faintly gritty. The flavour is particularly sweet and aromatic. The Comice is a purely dessert pear—in season from late autumn to midwinter.

Conference, a widely sold English winter variety, is easily recognized by its long, thin shape and russet skin.

Glou Morceau, a pear which dates back to the 18th century, is also called Beurre d'Hardenpont, after the Belgian priest the Abbé Nicolas Hardenpont of Mons.

Jargonelle, a fine old French pear dating from about 1600, is a dessert or cooking fruit with a distinctive aroma which is roughly imitated in the traditional British sweet called 'pear drops'. The main component of the fragrance is amyl acetate (which is also the smell of nail polish remover).

Josephine de Malines, a 19th-century pear of Belgian origin, is still grown commercially in the southern hemisphere. The pear was named by Major Espéren, an unsystematic but indefatigable grower, in commemoration of his wife; and it is the only important pear to have pink flesh. The scent is said to resemble that of the hyacinth.

Kaiser is a big, coarse, russet pear often on sale in continental Europe, but of no special merit.

Louise Bonne de Jersey is a pear to be picked towards the end of September, but not until it has what Brooke calls 'a painted, varnished look; the red must be shining red, and the greener portion must be turning yellow.'

Olivier de Serres, an old French variety often seen in S. Europe, is a good dessert pear which ripens very late. Dull greenish-brown, squat, and short necked.

Passe crasanne, a late winter pear suitable mainly for cooking, is common in S. Europe. It is big, broad, dull greenish-brown, and well flavoured, but rather coarse in texture. Coming from Italy, it bears the name Passacrassana.

Seckel, an American pear with a particularly good spicy flavour, but a rather granular texture. It is small, brownish-yellow, and russeted, often with a red blush. It is said that it was found as seedling by a trapper when he bought a piece of woodland in 1765.

Wardens, often referred to by Shakespeare and Parkinson, were cooking pears. For centuries Warden was the pear most commonly grown.

Williams, called Bartlett in the USA and Australia, now has several varieties. It was raised in 1770 in Berkshire by a schoolmaster called John Stair and was renamed Williams when it arrived in London. It was later taken to America by Enoch Bartlett and renamed again. All varieties are good dessert pears and good for cooking. They are also used for canning. The flavour is pleasantly musky. The season begins early, in late summer. The original variety, Williams bon Chrétien, is dull green with a red blush; there are now also clear green and red kinds.

Winter Nelis, a long-keeping pear in season from late autumn to late spring, has an excellent spicy flavour and a fair texture but lost popularity, partly because of its small size and rough skin, and partly because a high proportion of the fruits go bad in storage. The name is that of Jean Charles Nelis, a Belgian grower of the early 19th century.

PEARL OYSTER the common name of *Pinctada maxima* and *P. margaritifera*, edible BIVALVES of SE Asia. They are not true OYSTERS, but there is a general resemblance. *P. maxima* may measure 30 cm (1') and has shells which are at first yellow but later purplish-black. The inside is of a pearly brilliance; and there may be an actual pearl inside as well. *P. margaritifera* is dark inside.

The meat of the pearl oyster is delicious, and expensive.

PEASEMEAL a flour produced by processing yellow field peas such as are grown in E. England. They are roasted gently, a process which caramelizes some of the sugar, makes more starch and protein available for digestion, and darkens the colour. Then they are ground through three pairs of water-powered millstones, becoming successively finer with each set of stones, and packed into airtight containers for distribution.

The flour, which is produced and mainly used in Scotland, is brown-yellow in colour with a texture varying from fine and smooth to slightly gritty. The flavour is strong and earthy.

This flour and foods made from it, notably BROSE and BANNOCKS, have a long history in Scotland, especially as food for the common people. Marian McNeill (1929), explaining that pease bannocks are made in the same way as barley bannocks (the flour is mixed with water, milk, or whey, rolled thinly, and baked on a GRIDDLE), quotes an earlier reference to 'pease-scons'.

When peasemeal is used to make a brose, it is mixed with boiling water (or stock) for immediate consumption, eaten with butter and pepper or salt, or with sugar and raisins.

See also PEASE PUDDING.

PEASE PUDDING (alternatively known as pease porridge) is a peculiarly British dish, on account of the long-standing preference in Britain for PEAS over other pulses. It began its career in remote antiquity as pease POTTAGE, a thick PORRIDGE made from the dried mealy peas that were a staple food; this was the most usual way of preparing them. Pease pottage and, when available, bacon went together in the diet of simple country people. The bacon was heavily salted and the pease pottage, made without salt, balanced the flavour.

At the beginning of the 17th century the introduction of the pudding cloth allowed pease pudding, a more solid product, to be made. Usually the ingredients consisted only of peas (previously soaked, if dried peas are used), and a little flavouring: sugar and pepper, and sometimes mint, were commonly used. The ingredients were mixed and simply cooked in a pudding cloth in simmering liquid, perhaps alongside a piece of bacon, for which the pudding would be a fine accompaniment. Sometimes this very solid pudding was lightened with breadcrumbs, or a little egg or butter were used to enrich it. Pease pudding has now lost its importance in the British diet, but remains popular in the north. One can even buy it in cans.

It has been suggested that the old nursery rhyme:

> Pease pudding hot,
> Pease pudding cold,
> Pease pudding in the pot
> Nine days old

referred not to the inevitable appearance of the dish at all meals but to the making of a fermented product like a semi-solid version of Indonesian TEMPE, or a primitive form of Japanese MISO. Certainly, if the procedure in the rhyme were followed, boiling, cooling, and leaving for nine days, micro-organisms naturally present would have caused some kind of fermentation to take place, but unless some kind of starter had been used, the most likely result would have been spoilage.

The Chinese make a sweet version of pease pudding from cooked, puréed dried peas mixed with sugar and fried. This is more of a pottage than a real pudding. It is eaten hot as a dessert. There is also a cold cake made from the same purée with sugar and cornflour.

See also PEASEMEAL. A Scottish dish, pease brose, is mentioned in BROSE.

PECAN the most important native nut of N. America, is borne by one of the hickory trees, *Carya illinoiensis.* The hickories, which are related to the walnut trees, include several species with edible nuts (see HICKORY NUT), but the pecan is much the best. Its native habitat is the central southern region of the USA.

The name pecan comes from the Algonquin Indian *paccan*, which denoted hickories, including pecans. Rosengarten (1984) explains that:

A creamy liquid called powcohicoria or 'hickory milk' was prepared by the Algonquins: paccan kernels were pounded into small pieces, cast into boiling water, strained and stirred. This rich, nutty concoction was added to broth to thicken it, and to corn cakes and hominy as a seasoning.

Most pecans now come from cultivated trees, although many old, wild trees continue to produce nuts which are gathered and marketed. Cultivation is carried out in many states, especially Georgia and Texas. Since the time when Antoine, a slave gardener in Louisiana, achieved a breakthrough by 'topworking' some pecan trees and producing the variety Centennial, further advances have been made and there are now more than 500 named varieties.

Despite its excellence, the pecan is still little known outside N. America and Mexico, although it is now being grown in Israel, S. Africa, and Australia.

The nut shell, unlike a walnut shell, has a smooth surface. The kernel inside does bear some resemblance to that of a walnut, but is oilier and milder in flavour.

The main uses of pecans are in sweet dishes and confectionery, although they are also used in a stuffing for turkey. Pecan pie is one of the most famous American desserts. Pecan butter is also made.

PECCARY *Tayassu angulatus* and two other spp, American animals which look something like a small wild pig, and are sometimes so called, but which belong to a different family, Tayassuidae. This family is the New World counterpart of the PIG family in the Old World.

The peccary is one of the animals which exhibits a smell of MUSK, so is also called musk hog.

The range of the peccary is from S. Brazil to Arizona in the USA. It is eaten locally but is not accounted a delicacy. For the Maya people, however, it was a food resource of some significance. The region of C. America which they inhabited was not rich, in pre-Columbian times, in edible animals. READING: Sophie Coe (1994).

PECORINO the Italian name for a cheese made of sheep's milk. In this sense it covers a wide range of cheeses, many of which are produced locally and only on a small scale.

Pecorino cheeses may be young and fresh, or aged and suitable for grating. The latter feature has given rise to a second, more specific meaning of the name: hard cheeses made from sheep's milk in the central region of Italy and in Sardinia, where they play a similar role to that of the GRANA cheeses of N. Italy.

Many pecorino cheeses are small and disc shaped. With few exceptions they are heavily salted. Some have a patterned surface produced by a traditional mould of plaited straw, or by a metal copy designed to produce a similar pattern.

Pecorino Romano is the most famous. The classical author Columella gave instructions for making it which remain more or less valid. It is produced in Lazio and also in Sardinia, in weights varying from 8 to 20 kg (18 to 45 lb). It is salted and matured, and in its traditional form was given a protective coat of oil lees or suet, coloured dark. Another pecorino made in Sardinia is usually called **fiore Sardo,** because made with a RENNET derived from flowers.

Other well-known kinds of pecorino include:

- **Pecorino delle Crete Senesi,** a famous Tuscan variety, with an aromatic flavour derived from the presence of wormwood in the pastures. Its surface used to be coloured red with sheep's blood, but now tomato paste is used.
- **Pecorino dolce,** unusual in being only lightly salted, is for eating fresh. It is now usually made with a mixture of sheep's and cow's milk.
- **Pecorino Siciliano,** from Sicily, exists in various forms, of which the best known is probably **Canestrato.** This may be eaten fresh (under the name Tuma); or half-ripened (as Primusali, meaning that it has had its first salting); or mature, when it is much used for grating and cookery, especially as an ingredient for Sicilian stuffings.
- **Pecorino Toscano** is usually milder than the other pecorino cheeses, with an aromatic flavour which varies according to the type of pasture.

PECTIN the substance which causes jams and jellies to set, is a CARBOHYDRATE which exists in the cell walls of fruits and vegetables.

Unripe fruits contain a predecessor of pectin, called protopectin or pectose. As the fruit ripens, enzymes convert this into pectin, the quantity of which reaches its maximum just before the fruit is fully ripe.

Continuing enzyme action turns it into pectic acid. Neither pectose nor pectic acid has the setting power of pectin itself; hence the well-known difficulty of making jam or jelly with fruit that is overripe or markedly underripe.

It is equally well known that fruits vary in the amount of pectin they contain. Apples and citrus fruits have a lot. Cherries, figs, peaches, pears, pineapples, and rhubarb have much less. Strawberries and raspberries have pectin of inferior setting ability.

Pectin consists mainly of methyl pectate, which is a polysaccharide (a substance composed of long chains of sugar molecules). About half these sugar molecules are crosslinked to molecules of methyl alcohol. The nutritional value of these complex chains is negligible. Their value lies in the way they behave when fruit is made into jam or jelly.

The first step, boiling the fruit, causes the pectin to disperse through the mixture. The next, adding sugar and further boiling, crowds the chains of pectin together. The crowding effect is a simple consequence of the withdrawal of water, some of which is now occupied in holding the sugar in suspension and some of which evaporates. The crowded chains tangle. Then, when the mixture is allowed to cool and the molecular agitation within it diminishes, the tangled chains set into a continuous network with the remaining water trapped inside it. This is a gel.

The tangling effect, without which no gel can be achieved, will in this case only take place if the degree of acidity of the mixture is right, not much above or below pH 3.0. Mildly acid conditions are necessary to counteract small electric charges on the pectin chains which would otherwise attract water and maintain the pectin in solution. If the acidity is slightly too high, too strong a gel forms, giving a rubbery jam which shrinks and 'weeps', forcing out droplets of excess water. Strongly acid conditions prevent the pectin from setting at all.

Several other factors must be taken into account when making jams or jellies (see under JAM and JELLY). A familiar problem is that of making jam from fruits which contain little pectin, or pectin of low quality. One traditional answer is to mix fruits which have little pectin with others which have plenty. But one may not wish to add, say, apple to raspberry. Fortunately it is possible to obtain pectin as a liquid extract or in powdered form. These products are prepared from apple or citrus trimmings, preferably the former.

Special pectins used by the food industry include so-called low ester pectins which are capable of forming a gel in a sugarless solution, if a small amount of calcium salts is added to the mixture. These last pectins are used commercially to make aspic and to coat frozen foods with a protective layer of jelly.   RH

PEJIBAYE *Guilielma gasipaes*, also known as pupunha or peach palm, grows wild in Colombia, Ecuador, Peru, and Brazil. It was already being cultivated and distributed by Indians in prehistoric times. In C. America its presence is most noticeable in Costa Rica, where almost every Indian dwelling has a patch.

The palm reaches a height of 13 m (43'). The fruits grow in clusters of 50 to 300, and look like small peaches. As it ripens the fruit changes colour from yellow or orange to red or purple when fully ripe. The flesh usually contains a small seed, although some cultivated varieties are seedless. Both the fruit and the seed are edible.

In the Amazon basin it is one of the most popular articles of food, a position fully justified by its nutritional qualities. The authors of a survey of *Underexploited Tropical Plants with Promising Economical Value* (ed Ruskin, 1975) describe it as 'probably the most nutritionally balanced of tropical foods'. They point out that the fruit contains a finely balanced array of carbohydrates, protein, oil, minerals, and vitamins.

In one season, lasting from autumn to spring, a tree may produce 50 kg (110 lb) of fruits, borne in large clusters. Each fruit is about 5 cm (2") in diameter, with dryish, mealy, yellow or orange flesh surrounding the black seed. This is roughly pear shaped, and about 2 cm (0.75") broad. Once the fruit has been boiled, the flesh comes away readily from the seed. It is farinaceous in texture, with a pleasant flavour which has been compared to a mixture of chestnut and cheese. The seed has a thin, hard shell and an oily kernel, with a flavour like that of coconut.

The pejibaye has to be cooked (usually boiled, but also fried or roasted) before eating as it has a caustic effect (giving a burning sensation) if eaten raw. Both the young flowers and the palm hearts make good eating. The latter are of excellent quality, numerous (from the multiple shoots produced by the tree), and often canned for export.

PEKING DUCK a term most used for a special way of cooking duck which produces what is probably the most famous dish of Beijing (formerly Peking); and also the name for the variety of DUCK used in this dish, and now commonly bred in many parts of the world.

Chinese authorities do not attribute a very long history to the dish. Roast duck had

been recorded from the distant past, but this originally meant a Nanjing duck, of small size and black feathers, not artificially fattened. The story goes that the transfer of the capital from Nanjing to Peking brought unexpected results for the ducks which lived alongside the canal leading to the new capital, a canal used for grain supplies. These ducks, which like the Nanjing ducks were MALLARD ducks, were now able to feast on grains which fell overboard from barges, and they gradually became larger. In the course of time there evolved a new variety of duck, not only larger but plumper, and with white plumage. The plumpness was increased by the practice of force-feeding, mentioned in texts from the Five Dynasties in the 10th century AD.

This new variety of duck was appreciated outside China. In the 19th century it was introduced to N. America and became a firm favourite. It was also introduced to Europe and the famous Aylesbury duck of England is, if not exactly the same variety, a very close approximation.

However, it was only in China, and indeed for a long time only in Beijing, that the special dish known as *Beijing kaoya* (in China), Peking duck (in English), and *canard lacqué* (in French) was prepared. There was no single formula for the dish, but all versions have several features in common. First, the duck is a Peking duck, normally around two months old and specially fed, to reach a weight of 2 to 3 kg (5 to 6 lb). Second, after it has been killed and plucked, air is pumped in (usually by the cook, blowing hard) between skin and body, so that the bird is inflated. It is then gutted, hung up, blanched with boiling water, and coated with maltose to give it a dark amber colour. Third, the rear orifice is plugged and boiling water is poured into the inside of the bird, filling it to about 80%, to make it finally ready for roasting (preferably hanging, in a vertical oven built for the purpose, such as the specialist restaurants use, in which wood from fruit trees is burned).

The effect of roasting after this special treatment is to produce a cooked bird which has a shining golden exterior, attractively crisp, and a moist, succulent inside, the whole having a fine aroma and being free of excess fat.

Peking duck can be eaten in various ways. Perhaps the most common is to cut it into thin slices and then roll these up, with pieces of cucumber and Chinese chives (see CHIVES) or something similar, in fine pancakes, which have previously been brushed with sweet salted bean paste (*tianmianjiang*). There is some flexibility in the choice of added flavourings and in the sort of pancake used—sesame pancakes, for example, are recommended by some authorities.

PEKMEZ a molasses-like concentrate of grape juice used as a winter preserve and tonic in Turkey.

The equivalent of *pekmez* in many Arab countries of the Middle East is DIBS. Another example is Sicilian *vino cotto*; and a third is *mostarda* (not to be confused with MOSTARDA DI FRUTTA DI CREMONA), in which the concentrated grape juice is thickened with cornflour and flavoured with lemon, orange, nuts, and raisins.

The history of these products goes back to classical times. Before cheap sugar was available, unfermented grape juice ('must'), rich in naturally occurring sugar and richer still after being concentrated, provided an alternative source of sweetness to honey in grape-growing countries. Cooks in classical Rome used grape juice reduced by specified proportions as a sweetener; *defrutum* was must reduced to half the original volume; *carenum* was reduced by one-third; and *sapa* by two-thirds.

PELICAN'S FOOT *Aporrhais pespelecani*, an edible MOLLUSC inhabiting a single shell, found in the Mediterranean and also in eastern N. Atlantic waters; *A. occidentalis* is its counterpart on the western side.

The lip of the shell fans out into a shape like a webbed foot, indicating a relationship with the CONCH. But this is a smaller creature (up to 6 cm/2.25"), less well known, and consumed in only some of the countries on whose shores it occurs, notably Italy. It is abundant in the Adriatic, and has been the subject of a festival, the *sagra della crocetta*, in the summer in the Marche.

PEL'MENI a Russian equivalent of RAVIOLI, is often said to be derived from Chinese dumplings of the JIAOZI type spread through Siberia by Mongol invaders. However, it has been suggested that the Russian *pel'men'* is of Persian, rather than Chinese, origin, the name having been Russianized in the last 200 years from the original form *pel'n'an'* which Russian adopted from the Udmurts, a Finnish people of Siberia. In the Udmurt language, *pel'* means 'ear' and *n'an'* means anything made from flour: dough, bread, etc. The word *n'an'* is simply the Persian word NAN 'bread'; the Udmurts learned of flour from Persians.

Shapes of pel'meni vary; they may be curled like tortellini, square, or triangular. The traditional form is ear shaped. The dough is made with egg. The filling is of meat: traditionally a mixture of beef, pork, and elk.

Pel'meni are normally home made but have for some time been available ready made in Russian supermarkets. They are boiled and served with sour cream, butter and lemon juice, or oil and vinegar; or covered with sour cream and herbs and finished in the oven. Sometimes they are cooked and served in clear broth.

Ushki, a smaller version of pel'meni, are semicircular, shaped like little ears (which is what their name means). They are stuffed with chopped onion and mushroom, deep-fried, and, like their larger relations, eaten with certain soups.

Another fried member of the family is *chebureki*, a filled pasta of C. Asia, which is essentially the same as pel'meni except for being fried and not boiled.   (CP)

See also JOSHPARA; VARENIKI.

PEMMICAN a form of hard, preserved meat, used by N. American Indians. The name is derived from the Cree word *pemikân*, from *pimiy*, meaning 'grease'. The meat, from buffalo, deer, or other animals was air dried in strips until quite hard, then pounded to a powder and mixed with melted fat. It was usual to mix in berries also, especially cranberries. The resulting stiff paste was packed in skins, inside which it dried to a hard, chewy consistency.

Pemmican made in this way keeps mainly because it is dry (see DRYING). Salt played no part in the original drying process, though it might be added later for flavour. The berries were probably also added for flavour, but had a useful effect because of their content of benzoic acid, a natural preservative, which represses the growth of micro-organisms. The fat also helps preservation by sealing the meat from the air. The skin wrapping is not a sterile container because the food is not cooked in it—in fact, the only heating is the melting of the fat—but at least keeps the contents clean.

Pemmican was adapted by white explorers to suit their own needs and tastes. In the 1820s the Arctic explorer Sir John Richardson used the malting equipment of a brewery to make pemmican. The meat was dried in the malting kiln and ground in the malt mill. It was mixed with rendered suet, currants, and sugar, and packed in tin canisters. Soon pemmican was being canned in a conventional manner, which safeguarded its preservation and allowed it to be made in a slightly less dry and tough form. It could be chewed as it came, from the can, or made into a primitive stew. Canned pemmican remained a staple food of explorers and mountaineers.

PENGUIN a flightless bird of which there are many species in Antarctic waters. Although their appearance is so familiar (and people in the western world are often reminded of it by, for example, buying the paperback edition of a book or eating in a very old-fashioned restaurant or observing at social functions those few Englishmen who still dress up to look like either waiters or penguins—it is never clear which), the sight of a real penguin in its black and white livery is always exciting; and the study of the social behaviour of these birds is full of interest. Penguins are not often thought of as a source of food, but do provide edible meat. André Simon (1983) cites a description of the last Christmas Day dinner enjoyed by Captain Scott in the S. Pole ice pack, which included 'an entrée of stewed penguin's breasts and red currant jelly—the dish fit for an epicure and not unlike jugged hare'.

So far as food for humans is concerned the importance of penguins lies rather in their production of guano, a good fertilizer which has given its name to the Guano Islands off the S. African coast. It was in these islands and under official supervision that penguin eggs were, until 1968, collected and sold on a commercial basis. Bosman (1973) describes this trade and adds the following advice:

The penguin's diet consists exclusively of fish and other marine animals, and the flavour of its eggs is therefore totally different from that of poultry eggs, as it has a strong sea-food taste and smell. The egg is much larger than a hen's egg, the average length being approximately 7 cm, with a diameter of about 5 cm in the middle. . . . Gourmets who appreciate penguin eggs prefer to eat them after boiling them for 12 to 20 minutes. After the shell has been removed, the egg is mashed finely with a fork, and salt and pepper and vinegar (or lemon juice) are added, with perhaps also a little butter.

Another S. African source, Leipoldt (1976), agrees and, although he points to the possibility of scrambling or buttering penguin eggs, or combining them with flakes of fried fish, declares that no other treatment can compare with what he calls 'hard-boiling':

My old preceptress, who emphasised her injunctions with good-natured taps of her wooden spoon on my head, insisted that penguin eggs should be boiled in sea water, steadily for 15 minutes. That produced a clear, transparent jelly surrounding an opalescent green yolk that crumbled readily to fine primrose-yellow flaky fragments, for nobody ever ate them soft-boiled.

PENNSYLVANIA DUTCH cookery does belong to Pennsylvania (although the style spread widely, notably to Ontario, Ohio and parts of the Midwest), but is not Dutch in the modern sense of the term. 'Dutch' here is either a corruption of *Deutsch*, meaning German, or, possibly, a survival of the archaic use of 'Dutch' to mean, in effect 'Germanic' or 'German-speaking'. The influence of the Dutch themselves on N. American cookery way back can best be studied in the book by Peter Rose (1989).

Thus it may be more appropriate to use the phrase adopted by Weaver (1983) as the subtitle of his book on the subject: 'Pennsylvania-German Foods and Foodways'. This scholarly work, later complemented by the same author's book on *Pennsylvania Dutch Country Cooking* (1993), was based on a rare early cookbook in German, *Die geschickte Hausfrau* (1848), for use by the German-speakers of Pennsylvania, but ranges much more widely, setting the whole array of Pennsylvania Dutch kitchen equipment, ingredients, and recipes in their historical and cultural contexts.

Weaver observes that:

The central characteristic of classical Pennsylvania-German cookery was the interplay of sweet flavors against salty ones. The combination of fruit and salty meat in such Pennsylvania-German dishes as *Schnitz un Gnepp* (a stew of dried apples, smoked ham, and dumplings) or its older cousin *Gumbis* (apples, ham, bacon, and onions) . . . were typical of this classic arrangement of flavors.

Another dish is scrapple (*Panhaas*), a sort of savoury 'loaf' made with pork, cornmeal, and other ingredients, to be chilled and sliced, the slices then to be fried and served very hot. It is also known as Philadelphia scrapple, and is eaten as a breakfast or brunch dish, often served with apple slices and brown sugar.

The Pennsylvania Dutch repertoire includes a fine array of sausages, one-pot dishes, pickles, and baked goods.

PENNYROYAL *Mentha pulegium*, a perennial herb of the Near East, of prostrate habit, which has spread through Europe as far north as Finland. The 'penny' in its name is derived (by a tortuous route—see Grigson, 1955) from the Latin name by which it was known in the Middle Ages; this was *pulegium*, meaning flea plant. It then had a high reputation for driving away body lice and fleas, and is still valued for some

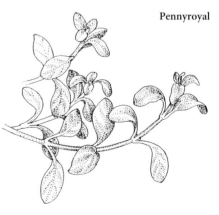

Pennyroyal

595 PEPPERMINT

medicinal purposes; but its use in the kitchen has been mainly as a savoury pudding herb, especially in the north of Britain, where it bears names such as 'pudding herb'.

Pennyroyal is commonly in use in Spain for a herbal tea.

PEPINO the fruit of *Solanum muricatum*, a small bush of about 1 m (3') in height which is native to temperate Andean areas of Peru and Chile and cultivated elsewhere in C. and S. America, and Australasia. The name *pepino* is Spanish for cucumber, and the Latin American name *pepino dulce* means sweet cucumber. (One variety, Rio Barba, is vinelike and its fruits do resemble a small cucumber.) However, since the pepino is usually more like a melon, it is sometimes called pepino melon or melon pear.

A typical fruit is about 7 cm (3") in diameter near the stem end, and 13 cm (5") long. Its skin is golden streaked with purple. It has little flavour, but can be used effectively in fruit salads.

The name pepino is used in parts of S. America for the CASSABANANA.

PEPPER the common spice, black pepper, *Piper nigrum*.

True peppers belong to the genus *Piper*, but the common name 'pepper' has been applied to very different articles; sometimes, as with capsicum peppers in the 15th century, this was done deliberately to cause confusion.

To summarize: the peppers that belong to the genus *Piper*—the 'true' peppers—are: white and black pepper, which are described below; LONG PEPPER; ASHANTI PEPPER; and CUBEB pepper. Other foodstuffs called 'pepper', for varying, sometimes not very obvious, reasons include SICHUAN PEPPER, RED PEPPERCORNS, MELEGUETA PEPPER, Jamaica pepper (see ALLSPICE), PEPPERMINT, CAPSICUM peppers, and CAYENNE (which also deals with Nepal pepper). The actual word 'pepper' comes from the Sanskrit *pippali* where it referred to long pepper.

Both white and black pepper are the dried unripe fruit of *P. nigrum*, one of the world's most important spice plants. *P. nigrum* is native to the forests of Tranvancore and Malabar and now extensively cultivated in tropical regions around the world. The pepper tree is a climber; on plantations it is usually grown on other trees—betel, palm, or mango—as its cordlike stems need support. The tree begins to bear fruit in its third year and continues for six or seven more.

To produce black pepper, the berries are gathered when they are turning red but before they are completely ripe. They are left in heaps for a few days to ferment and then spread out on mats in the sun to dry. As they dry the berries turn black and the skin and part of the pulp form a reticulated covering to the seed.

To produce white pepper, the berries are left for longer before harvesting. They are then soaked until the pericarp and pulp have become soft and loose, when the whitish seed can be easily removed. White pepper, although it contains more piperine than black pepper, is less aromatic and has a weaker flavour. It is usually used when dark specks would spoil the look of the dish, for example, in any white soups, in *blanquette de veau* (see BLANQUETTE) etc.

There is also a sort of pepper called decorticated black pepper which has had the skin of the peppercorn removed by machine and is therefore white. The flavour is between black and white pepper.

There are numerous references to pepper by classical authors. Pliny (1st century AD) describes black pepper minutely, complaining about the price and noting that white pepper cost almost twice as much as black. Pepper was a precious and expensive substance for the Romans and Gibbon lends his authority to the tale that Alaric the Goth demanded 3,000 lb (1,360 kg) of it as part of a ransom for Rome.

By the Middle Ages, pepper had assumed great importance in Europe where it was used by the rich as a seasoning, and also a preservative. The commonly accepted notion that its main use was to disguise the smell of tainted meat and other food has been largely exploded (e.g. by Gillian Riley, 1993, but there are many other refutations). The earliest reference to the pepper trade in England is in the statutes of Ethelred (978–1016) where it was enacted that 'Esterlings' bringing their ships to Billingsgate should pay a toll at Christmas and at Easter plus 10 lb of pepper. The first mention of the Guild of Pepperers, one of the oldest guilds in the City of London, is from 1180, when the guild was fined for not having obtained a royal licence. In 1328 the Pepperers were registered as 'Grossarii' from which the term grocer is derived.

Pepper has been one of the most important commodities of the SPICE TRADE. In Antwerp in the mid-16th century, for example, the price of pepper served as a barometer for European business in general. Singapore is now the most important centre of world pepper trade.

Green peppercorns are just the unripe seeds of *P. nigrum*. The berries are preserved by artificial drying or by bottling in vinegar, brine, or water. If bottled just as they begin to turn red, they may be termed 'poivre rose', but are not the RED PEPPERCORNS of commerce which are from a different plant altogether.

The seeds of *P. nigrum* are also a source of oil of pepper and oleoresin, used for flavouring sausages, tinned food, and drinks. The oils have the pepper aroma and flavour but lack pungency.

Indian black pepper is usually of a high quality. The main area of production is still the Malabar coast where the Alleppey variety comes from the south; Tellicherry from the north. The latter is the more expensive and is the sort used whole in Italian salami. Another Indian pepper is Mangalore; very dark with a good flavour.

The pungency of pepper is due to the active principles it contains—the volatile oil, piperine, and resin. The spice increases the flow of saliva and gastric juices and so improves the appetite. If consumed in sufficient quantities, it will have a cooling effect.

Pepper is available whole, cracked, coarsely ground, medium, or finely ground and has become, with the exception of salt, the most everyday spice in the world. In western cooking it is ubiquitous in the kitchen and as a condiment on the table.

PEPPERMINT *Mentha* × *piperita*, the member of the MINT family which has become a major horticultural crop, is thought to be a hybrid of *M. aquatica* (water mint) and *M. spicata* (spearmint). It is much more pungent than spearmint, and is the principal source of peppermint oil, which is extensively used in confectionery, and also in products such as chewing gum and toothpaste and by the tobacco industry. Menthol is the constituent to which it owes its distinctive odour.

Peppermint is grown in England, France, Germany, Italy, and other European countries. But N. American production is much greater. The main area of cultivation has moved several times in the last 100 years. Early in the 19th century it was in W. Massachusetts whence it moved to New York state, and then (after the introduction of the hardier Black Mitcham variety) to the Midwest. From there it has moved on to the states of Oregon and Washington. Control of quality of peppermint oil (and spearmint oil) has been carried further in the USA than anywhere else, partly no doubt because of the importance of these flavours in chewing gum. See Landing (1969) on the US industry.

A special French peppermint, stronger than the usual kinds, is *menthe de Milly*, grown and prepared for the markets at Milly-en-Gâtinais, a small town in the Île de France (i.e. not far from Paris) which has a long tradition of cultivating herbs with medicinal uses, a testimony to which is provided by Jean Cocteau's murals in the chapel of St Blaise. *Menthe de Milly* was formerly a special variety, Ameliorée de Milly, but since 50 years ago this has been replaced by Mitcham. The product is used as a flavouring in cookery and also for TISANES and in confectionery such as the famous *pastilles à la menthe*, as well as in various sweet or alcoholic beverages.

PEPPER POT (sometimes pepperpot) has two overlapping meanings. In the W. Indies it means a savoury stew, often highly seasoned, incorporating various vegetables and (for example) pieces of pig's tail and stewing beef. However, no one recipe can be identified as 'the recipe'. Connie and Arnold Krochmal (1974b) observe that 'each island has its own version of pepperpot'. And Norma Benghiat (1985), who counts it as a soup, gives an excellent historical survey, in which she says:

It is probably of Arawak origin, though it seems to have been more of a stew in those days. It is still prepared in the Amerindian way in Guyana, but in Jamaica it has changed over the years under the influence of cooks of different cultures. The ingredients have varied according to what has been available, and the dish has become more of a soup.

The second meaning, which goes back to the 18th century in the USA, was at first equally general and indeed may have migrated from the W. Indies to the mainland. Later, however, it referred to a particular version known as Philadelphia pepper pot, which apparently incorporated SEA TURTLE meat for a while in the 19th century but then adopted TRIPE as a less expensive substitute. In this sense the dish always lives up to its name by being highly seasoned with crushed peppercorns.

PERCH a name applied to various fish, notably *Perca fluviatilis*, a moderate-sized (maximum length 50 cm/20") Eurasian river and lake fish which has been widely introduced elsewhere for the benefit of anglers and because it is considered to be a good food fish. The yellow perch of N. America is almost indistinguishable from the European perch, but often classified separately as *P. flavescens*.

The name perch has been applied, by extension, to other species, freshwater or marine, which display characteristics (e.g. two distinct dorsal fins) similar to those of *P. fluviatilis*, especially members of the very large family Percidae. However, the English-speaking colonists who encountered fish in other continents and often had the privilege of bestowing common names on them were not, understandably, as systematic as ichthyologists would have been in their use of the name perch. Thus the climbing

perches of Africa and Asia would not, ideally, be called perches at all. And the name 'sea perch' has been bestowed in such a seemingly random fashion that it has little meaning except in a local context. *Morone americana*, called sea perch (or white perch) in N. America, belongs to the GROUPER family, Serranidae. On the other hand *Stizostedion vitreum*, which does belong to the family Percidae, is not called perch but walleye (although *S. lucioperca* is called pike-perch). Examples of such inconsistencies, inevitable since perchlike fish are so numerous, could be multiplied many times.

PERIWINKLE *Littorina littorea*, an edible MOLLUSC living in a small single shell (up to 2.5 cm/1"), widely distributed on both sides of the N. Atlantic. Periwinkles, or winkles as their vendors commonly call them, are now eaten much more in Europe than America, although the middens of American Indians testify to their use there in the past. Prehistoric mounds in Denmark, Scotland, and elsewhere show that they have been a popular European food for a very long time; and the diversity of vernacular names, such as *kruuk'ls* in Zeeland, points to continuing popularity in more recent centuries. Now, however, they are becoming a grander food, being served as *amuse-gueules* in expensive restaurants.

Species of *Littorina* are found around the world. Many of them live above the high-tide mark, knowing the waters of the sea only from splashes. It is thought that they may be on the way to becoming land snails. Their shells are usually dingy in appearance. Ricketts and Calvin (1968) discovered by chance a way of having these cleaned. He had occasion to feed a periwinkle to a sea anemone which required sustenance. The anemone swallowed it, but 'it was an intact and healthy *Littorina* that emerged, like Jonah, after a residence of from 12 to 20 hours in the anemone's stomach. It had

apparently suffered no harm whatever, but its shell was beautifully cleaned and polished.' The horny operculum with which the periwinkle, like other gasteropods, closes its shell had effectively kept out the anemone's digestive enzymes.

Periwinkles feed blamelessly by scraping detritus and organic matter off almost bare rock. It has been estimated that their grazing lowers the level of the rock at La Jolla in California by a centimetre every century.

It is usual to cook periwinkles for about 10 minutes in boiling, salted water, and then to pick them out of their shells with a pin. The cooked winkles can be eaten thus; but in some places they are dressed with a sauce, and in Wales they may be fried in bacon fat and then have an egg or two cracked over them to be left to fry or else scrambled.

PERLE JAPON a uniquely French product, with a superficial resemblance to TAPIOCA but based on potato starch. The small pearly grains, of regular size and round shape, are rehydrated before being cooked.

This product developed in a sidelong manner from tapioca. It became apparent that if the manner of producing tapioca was modified to make it come out in regular round 'pearls', the product had more attraction. So tapioca in pearl form competed with regular tapioca, both being made from CASSAVA starch, as tapioca still is. Then, towards the end of the 19th century, the pearls began to be made from the native product, potato starch, instead of the imported cassava starch. Thus the two products parted company.

Perle Japon is used in the west of France, for soups and for pâtisserie, especially on festive occasions. The one factory making the product is located at Nantes.

PERSIMMON or American persimmon, *Diospyros virginiana*, a fruit which used to be

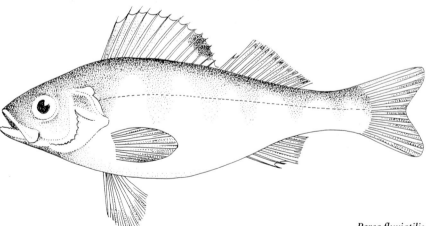

Perca fluviatilis

valued in eastern N. America but is now little eaten, partly because it has been eclipsed by a superior relative from the Orient, the KAKI (*D. kaki*). The DATE PLUM (*D. lotus*) is another close relative.

The name persimmon comes from 'putchamin', a phonetic rendering of the name used by the American Indians of the Algonquin tribe. They ate them when they were ripe and had fallen from the tree and dried them to be eaten in the winter. The first European to write about the fruit was probably the Spanish explorer Don Fernando de Soto, who learned about it from the Indians of Florida in 1539. Captain John Smith, in the 17th century, likened it to the MEDLAR, noting: 'if it be not ripe it will drawe a mans mouth awrie with much torment; but when it is ripe, it is as delicious as an Apricock.' Ripe persimmons were eaten by the settlers, or used in puddings, breads, preserves, etc. But the production of persimmon (or 'simmon') beer and wine and other alcoholic drinks was an equally important use.

American persimmons

A ripe American persimmon is usually yellowish-pink or orange to red in colour, but may be darker. In size it may be as small as a cherry or as large as a big plum. Shape varies, as does the degree of astringency (for a discussion of which see KAKI).

During the 19th century and the early years of the 20th there was considerable interest in the development of improved persimmons, based for example on the Early Golden cultivar which originated in Illinois; but this was largely stifled by the introduction of the kaki to California.

Artemas Ward (1923) has an interesting passage on the persimmon. Besides dismissing the 'old theory' that a touch of frost is necessary if the fruits are to achieve perfection, he has this to say:

As might be expected in a wild fruit, the specimens marketed vary greatly in value. The average fruit—though excessively astringent when green—is edible when 'dead ripe', but some trees

produce fruits which never become edible—their powerful astringency resisting every effort of the warmest southern sun. On the other hand, the best types become veritable sugar-plums at maturity. Among commercial fruits they are exceeded in sugar content only by the date. Their sweetness has indeed earned for them the nickname of the American 'date-plum', and the oddly wrinkled lumps of richly concentrated sugar-flesh hanging among the varicolored leaves of autumn are as eagerly sought by 'possums' and other wild creatures as by human beings.

The American persimmon is particularly good for preserves and fresh cooked in many ways—in cakes, puddings, and muffins. Those who are not sufficiently familiar with the fruit to be sure that it has lost its astringency will do well to add half a teaspoonful of bicarbonate of soda (baking powder) to each cupful of persimmon pulp, as heat accentuates the astringency.

There is one other persimmon native to America, *D. texense*, known as the chapote, or black or Mexican persimmon. Its range includes C. and W. Texas and parts of Mexico. The fruits, which are small, hairy, and black, are sweet when ripe but of no great merit. Since they leave an indelible black stain on everything they touch, they are perhaps best reserved for dyeing sheepskins black, as in the Rio Grande Valley.

D. digyna is another 'black persimmon', often called 'black sapote' (*zapote negro* in the Philippines), but no relation of the true SAPOTA. It is native to Mexico, where it is popular in the markets; and has been introduced elsewhere, but without noticeable success. The fruit is round, about the size of an orange, and ripens from a shiny green to a brownish-green colour. Inside, the flesh is glossy, dark brown in colour, soft, mild, and sweet. It can be made into desserts (the addition of orange or lemon juice is advised), milk shakes, and fruit drinks.

PERU like its neighbour, ECUADOR, is divided into three natural zones which have become cultural frontiers. The arid coastline, fertile only in oases of irrigation, washed by the cool Peru current, is largely mestizo with the small minority of Europeans concentrated on the capital Lima. Here has developed Peruvian *criollo* (creole) cooking. The Andes, home of the Incas, remain predominantly Indian, the language Quechua spoken more often than Spanish. Beyond, is the *montaña* (jungle), thinly populated, its borders disputed with Ecuador, its wealth on the increase with the discovery of oil.

The country is large enough, and communications have been tenuous enough, for marked regional differences to arise. Hence dishes from Arequipa are often

extremely fiery, and the cooking of Piura leans much on BANANAS, PLANTAINS, and peanuts, see GROUNDNUT.

On the coast, the Spanish Conquest may have destroyed much of the careful agricultural infrastructure of irrigation and terracing, but ultimately the colonial haciendas, maintained by slaves, replaced the Indian achievement and supported an expressive cuisine that combined produce from a fertile soil and equable climate, recipes and foodways from Spain and the Mediterranean, and Inca ingredients such as POTATO and CAPSICUM fruits.

Indian culture was more resistant to Spanish influence in the mountains, where the population had survived in greater number, though reduced to serfdom either on haciendas or in copper and silver mines. In food terms, pre-Columbian survivals are more common. The *montaña* has had relatively less impact on Peruvian diet and cooking methods.

The clearest Indian survivals are dishes involving potatoes, for instance *papas a la huancaina*, from the mountain city of Huancayo, which consists of boiled yellow-fleshed potatoes sauced with cheese, cream, olive oil, and *ají*, served with hard-boiled eggs, olives, and corn. The dish is coloured yellow with the flavourless herb PALILLO whose leaves are dried and powdered. *Ají*, the Peruvian term for CHILLI (also used in Ecuador and Chile), is complex in meaning and use, both elucidated by Jean Andrews (1984), in dealing with *Capsicum baccatum* var *pendulum*. Here it will probably indicate the fresh yellow Ají Amarillo pepper, of which the dried form (Cusqueño) is the principal condiment for many traditional Peruvian dishes. The predominance of yellow in such dishes led Elisabeth Lambert Ortiz (1979) to draw parallels with Inca sun worship. Other potato dishes—some called *ocopa*, others *causa*—where the potato is often mashed, often qualified by the town of origin or currency (e.g. *causa a la Limeña*, *ocopa Arequipeña*) take the basic material and dress it with more or less elaboration. Complexity is not invariable: in mountain districts a plate of boiled potatoes with nothing more than *ají* will often suffice.

Corn (see MAIZE) is an important staple, just as RICE has become through Spanish influence. Peruvian TAMALES are wrapped in banana leaves and given a slightly sweet edge with ingredients such as meats, boiled peanuts, or olives. A porridge of corn is added to fried meat, onions, and *ají* to make *tamal en cazuela* (casseroled tamale) which solidifies on cooling and may be sliced.

The Humboldt or Peru Current has the same beneficent effect on seafood here as in Chile and Ecuador. Seviche (see CEVICHE) is as commonly encountered as further north, often using the corvina, a relative of the sea bass, or *conchitas* (Peruvian scallops), ABALONE, or large and succulent prawns. The irrigation ditches and small rivers of the coastal region also support a healthy population of freshwater CRAYFISH. These are also made into *chupe*, a soup-stew containing potatoes and cheese or cream, which is popular along the whole Pacific seaboard, or a Mediterranean-influenced *Arroz con mariscos* where a variety of shellfish is cooked with rice in a shrimp stock and finished with fresh coriander. Fish may also be more simply fried, using ANNATTO oil or a dressing of peanut oil, and served with onions and *ají*.

Peru is less pastoral than, say, URUGUAY; thus large joints of meat (which will be roasted with a crust of lard, garlic, pepper, and herbs) are less common than dishes involving rich sauces and shredded or small cut meat. Unless, of course, the people eat *cuy*, the Quechua word for GUINEA PIG, widely available in the sierra, and most commonly either roasted over charcoal, or stewed with potatoes, garlic, and *ají*.

Another Quechua word is *anticuchos*, meaning 'a dish from the Andes cooked on sticks', which refers to the common Peruvian *entrada*, often served as street food, of ox heart marinaded in vinegar, skewered over charcoal, and brushed with a hot sauce of chilli and ground annatto seeds. Other meats, offal, and seafood are treated in like manner.

The colonial diet of Spanish Lima and the haciendas was rich, and mealtime customs elaborate. The *piqueo* is a preliminary buffet served before either banquet or *pachamanca* (the Quechua word for earth oven, similar to a clambake, called *curanto* in Chile), which is the most enduring form of public feast. The main midday meal was many-coursed, from *entradas*, through soup, a potato dish, meat or roast, before sweet dishes that joined once more indigenous ingredients with Spanish techniques. The reduction of milk, sugar, and vanilla, called *dulce de leche* in Argentina, is *manjar blanco* (meaning BLANCMANGE) here. A variant, *natillas Piuranas*, from the city of Piura, has an addition of indigenous ground walnuts. *Mazamorra morada* is a fruit compote, the syrup thickened with purple corn, *maíz morado*, to give it an unexpected hue. This corn is also used to colour a fruit drink, *chicha morada*. *Picarones*, sweet fritters of pumpkin and sweet potatoes, flavoured with aniseed, are also popular. TJ

PESTO the pride of the great Italian sea port of Genoa, is a thick sauce which is excellent with pasta or fish. It does not require cooking, but is one of those recipes where you have to add olive oil carefully and gradually to a mixture which you have pounded with a mortar; the pounded ingredients are garlic, PINE NUT kernels, grated PARMESAN cheese (or Sardo from Sardinia), salt, and fresh BASIL leaves. The flavour of basil is dominant.

PETÉ the Indonesian and most commonly used name for the edible seeds of *Parkia speciosa*, a tree native to Indonesia and Malaysia. It is cultivated, e.g. in Java.

The seed pods are long, up to about 30 cm (12") or even more, and characteristically twisted. The seeds vary in size, but may be 3 cm (1") long. Because of their strong aroma, which lingers on the breath like that of garlic, the Dutch gave them the name *stinkboon* (stink bean). For Indonesians, however, they are among the most prized vegetables and demand usually outstrips supply.

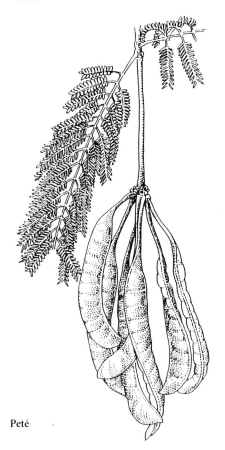

Peté

The seeds, young or ripe, raw, cooked, or roasted, are eaten in many ways, with rice. They can be conserved by drying them in the sun either in the raw state or after steaming them.

Fresh peté is taken out of the pod and the skin peeled off each bean before cooking. However, as Sri Owen (1986) explains:

A favourite way to cook young ones is to top and tail the pod, trim off the stringy edges and slice the pod very thin with the beans still in it. Crisp-fry

the pod, and the beans remain soft in the middle of the slices.

Mature beans are pickled in brine and known as *peté asin* (salted peté). They have a flavour which is bitter and nutty, rather than salty, and slightly reminiscent of garlic. This product is exported and is available in food speciality shops in the West, usually spelled *peteh asin*. The pale green beans look rather like shelled broad beans.

A related tree, *P. javanica*, is larger but yields peté of inferior quality. For trees of the same genus in Africa see LOCUST TREES.

PETIT FOUR any of the little biscuits and cakes to which this name is applied; for example, cigarette russe, langue de chat, miroir (for all of which see BISCUIT VARIETIES), MERINGUE, MACAROON, and TUILE. The name means 'little oven'; small ovens were used in the 18th century for baking such confections, and this may be the origin of the name.

PETRONIUS author of a picaresque Latin novel called *Satyricon*. In medieval Europe this was a secret Latin classic, known to a few fortunate scholars. Even fewer boasted of knowing it, for this work was sexually explicit and amoral in tone. By the 15th century, when classical texts began to be printed, no complete manuscript of the *Satyricon* survived, but there were several collections of extracts from which modern editions have been lovingly pieced together. What we can read today seems to come from books 14 to 16 of an original of considerable, but unknown, length.

It tells of the escapades of a group of disreputable friends as they travel from city to city in the Roman Empire. The rediscovery and excavation of Pompeii gave added interest to the *Satyricon*, for most of the surviving episodes are set very close to Pompeii not many years before it succumbed to the eruption of Vesuvius.

The longest scene, the one that makes the *Satyricon* so fascinating to the food historian, is the 'Dinner of Trimalchio'. A rich, boastful former slave is the host: his slaves, his guests, their conversation, their behaviour, are seen through the cynical eyes of the narrator Encolpius. Amusing details of the novel, such as the mosaic of a barking dog that startled Trimalchio's guests as they crossed his threshold, can be illustrated from actual finds at Pompeii. The menu, showy rather than elegant, gives Trimalchio the opportunity to display his vast wealth and allows the author to satirize the pretensions of 1st-century AD Roman society. Thanks to this scene, dormice rolled in honey and sesame seeds will forever be associated with Roman cuisine. Trick dishes, such as the eggs that turn out to be pies and the pig stuffed with birds, evidently formed conversation pieces at lavish dinner parties such as this.

The author, Petronius Arbiter, is generally thought to be the same Petronius who was the Emperor Nero's courtier and 'Arbiter of Elegance'. His fame and suicide (in AD 66) are described in two brilliant chapters of Tacitus's *Annals*. Whoever he was, the author of the *Satyricon* was not only able to write urbane, stylish, witty Latin but also—in the conversation at Trimalchio's table—to recreate the 'Vulgar Latin' of slaves and freedmen, the colloquial language of the Empire.

There has, however, been at least one instance of major confusion over the identity of Petronius. Mary Ellen Meredith (1851), after making some thoughtful comments on the feast of Trimalchio, recorded an amusing tale:

Petronius was held in such esteem by the learned German Meibonius, that seeing in a letter from Bologna the words *Habemus hic Petronium integrum* ('we have here Petronius, entire'), he took it for granted the complete manuscript of Petronius was there, and posted off in search of it; when he arrived, he asked where Petronius was to be found, and on being informed he was kept in the church, he expressed surprise at such a place being chosen to deposit him in; upon which his informant asked what fitter place could be found for a sacred body than the church; and the discomfited scholar found he had travelled with such infinite diligence only to discover the mummy of Saint Petronius!

AD

PHALSA *Grewia asiatica*, a large, scraggy shrub of the Indian subcontinent, which is cultivated commercially in the Punjab and around Bombay, also on a small scale in the Philippines.

In the spring the shrub bears small berries in pendulous clusters from slender, drooping branches. These need to be continuously harvested as they ripen at different times. As they ripen, the outsides change from green to almost black, and the flesh from whitish-green to purplish-red. They have a sweetish acid taste, can be eaten as a dessert, and are used for fresh drinks and in the soft drink industry.

pH FACTOR a measure of the acidity or alkalinity of a solution. It is always spelt with a small p, which stands for 'potential', and a capital H, the chemical symbol for hydrogen. ACIDS are substances which liberate hydrogen ions (charged atoms) when they dissolve in water. pH was originally defined as the logarithm to base 10 of the reciprocal of the concentration of hydrogen ions; now, however, it is defined by comparison with a

standard solution. What all this means in practice is that pH values lie on a scale from 0 to 14. Values from 0 to 7 represent acidity; 7 is neutral; from there up to 14 the solution is alkaline.

Foodstuffs are slightly acidic or neutral; even the slightest alkalinity causes an unpleasant 'soapy' sensation in the mouth as the ALKALI reacts with fats. The gastric juice in the stomach is extremely acid, and makes food acid as it is digested; this acidity is neutralized when food passes out of the stomach into the duodenum, where the pancreatic juice is slightly alkaline.

Foodstuffs are variable, so the pH values given here for foods are approximate.

human gastric juice	1.5–3.0 (strongly acid)
lemon juice	2.1
wine vinegar (weak)	2.5
orange juice	3.0
yoghurt	4.0
fresh milk	6.6–6.9
pure water	7.0 (neutral)
human blood	7.4
human pancreatic juice	8.0
1% bicarbonate of soda solution	8.0
1% caustic soda solution	13.0 (strongly alkaline)

(RH)

READING: McGee (1984).

PHEASANT *Phasianus colchicus*, a game bird indigenous to the Caucasus and Caspian region. The name *colchicus* refers to Colchis in the Caucasus from which Jason and the Argonauts returned with the Golden Fleece, bringing back also, according to the legend, the pheasant. This historic site is now in Georgia, where there are even now particularly good dishes of pheasant braised with walnut, orange, grapes, pomegranate juice, etc. (cf. FESENJAN).

The pheasant's range extends eastwards to Siberia and China, and it has been widely introduced in Europe since early times. There is a recipe for boiling it with spices in the FORME OF CURY (14th century).

The pheasant, with its close relations, is possibly the most important game bird of the world and great efforts have been made to maintain artificially large populations in those parts of Europe where natural conditions are favourable to the species. Without human help, the pheasant's presence in Europe would dwindle greatly.

Pheasants are handsome birds, especially the cocks, which are larger than the hens. The cock's long tail accounts for just over half its average total length of 30–5 cm (12–14"); and its coloration defies description, although the red wattle round

each eye is a standard feature. The hen tends to be of a more uniform brown.

Although smaller, hens are likely to prove more plump and tender than cocks. Birds should anyway be hung before being cooked. Roast pheasant is generally the preferred dish, the bird being first equipped with what one author calls a tight waistcoat of bacon, to make up for the dryness of the flesh. Older and tougher birds are best braised (to be served with green cabbage as in France) or in stews, while very old birds will make a delicious pheasant soup.

Dorothy Hartley (1954), with dry wit, recommends 'poached pheasant' as a dish, explaining that a cottager can poach the pheasant by smearing the inside of a paper bag with treacle, adding a few raisins and then propping the bag up among a row of peas. A cock pheasant will come along in search of the peas, stick his head in the bag, be unable to see where to go next, and stand patiently waiting until the cottager comes out to snaffle him.

Several pheasants, including one known as silver pheasant, are prized in the Indian subcontinent.

Other birds which are grouped with the pheasant include PEACOCK-PHEASANT and PEAFOWL.

READING: Marchington (1984).

PHILIPPINES an exemplary melting pot of cuisines.

Philippine cookery draws from definite and visible roots set in history. The Malay matrix goes deepest, and from it come dishes with native names (*laing, sinigang*) quite similar to those in other SE Asian cuisines. The Chinese influence, brought by traders from about the 11th century, is responsible for *pansit* (see NOODLES OF ASIA), LUMPIA, and other dishes also found elsewhere in SE Asia in a similar process of acculturation. The Spanish colonial regime brought with it as well Mexican inputs like TAMALES (since the islands were under the administration of the viceroyalty of Mexico), and the dishes now enshrined as fiesta food (PAELLA, *morcon*), and a name that came to be attached to a native dish: ADOBO. The American influence is chiefly felt in convenience and fast foods, such as sandwiches and salads, hamburgers and pizza. There are also strands of Indian and Arab influences, especially among the Muslim peoples of Mindanao.

The indigenous food pattern, however, is what nutritionists consider eminently healthy: a lot of rice (high carbohydrate) with some fish or seafood and vegetables, or a noodle dish with meat and vegetables. Meat is expensive, and often featured in the dishes derived from Spain, thus part of élite or special cuisine.

RICE is the basis of all meals, the assumed accompaniment of all food, and its mildness is shaper and foil to the tastes of viands (salty, sour, spicy, bitter). The Filipino preference is for rice to be halfway between the 'sticky rice' of, for example, Laos and the hard rice of India. It is usually washed in several changes of water, then water is added to the pot (the native way of measuring is to put the middle finger in, and add enough water to reach the knuckle) and brought to a boil. The heat is then lowered and the pot kept simmering till the rice is cooked. A little crust which often forms on the bottom of the pot called *tutong* is desired, and is eaten, or moistened and fried the next day for breakfast. Lining the bottom of the cooking pot with banana leaves is used as a means of preventing the formation of *tutong* and also adds a flavour which many Filipinos like. The clay pot (*palayok*) may be lined with banana leaf or screwpine for aroma and flavour. In the Visayas and Mindanao, rice is cooked in little handwoven leaf baskets, called *pusu*, which hang in bunches in the markets for sale and for taking on journeys.

Of the many native varieties of rice (including the sticky *malagkit*, the violet *pirurutong*, etc.), the ones most valued are those that are aged (and thus fluff up when cooked), fragrant, or have tiny grains (e.g. *milgrosa*). Wag-wag is another popular variety. Immature rice is pounded and roasted into *pinipig*, which is used in cakes, or sprinkled on drinks or on hot chocolate. Mature rice grains are soaked overnight and ground into a wet flour called *galapong*, which is the basis of the many rice cakes (see RICE CAKES OF THE PHILIPPINES) and snacks (*palitaw, bilo-bilo*) for both daily use and festive occasions.

The COCONUT is another Filipino dietary constant. The pith is used as a vegetable, as is the blossom. The florescence yields a sap that is fermented into a toddy (*tuba*) or into vinegar, or distilled into a coconut brandy called *lambanog*. The translucent flesh of the young coconut (*buko*) is scraped into the water for a drink; when it is slightly more mature (*malakanin*, or like the texture of rice) it is made into sweets and pies. The mature flesh is grated and squeezed for coconut milk/cream or used in cakes and sweets. The leaves wrap many of the rice cakes in every region. The Philippines are the largest producer in the world of coconut oil, which is the edible oil most used in their cookery, and of margarine, shortening, etc. The meat of the coconut, copra, is used in a very large number of Filipino recipes.

Seafood is dominant in the diet, for one because the 7,100 islands have a lot of shoreline as well as a lot of rivers, brooks, canals, and flooded ricefields that are sources of fish, crustaceans, and other sea animals. All kinds of seafood are eaten—rays, sharks, annelids, sea cucumbers, sea urchins—though sometimes not in all regions. Among the favourites are the *lapu-lapu* (GROUPER) and *banqus* (MILK FISH), the latter most available because commercially raised. A marine fish, its fry are transferred to fish ponds and reared in protected conditions. It is a bony fish, but is now often deboned by hand, although the bones 'dissolve' in certain cooking processes. Commercially 'farmed' seafoods include oysters, prawns, and certain seaweeds.

The availability of fresh seafood (because of the proximity of sources) is responsible for KINILAW, which is fish/shellfish/crustacean/annelid (or, less often, meat) briefly marinated in vinegar or lime juice to transform it from its raw state, then seasoned with onions, ginger, chilli peppers, etc. to retain its original translucent freshness. It is one of the oldest of Philippine dishes, archaeological evidence showing it to be at least 1,000 years old.

Two especially important seafood products are *patis* and *bagoong*. Each is a fermented FISH SAUCE, the latter being prepared mainly from anchovies or shrimps.

PORK is the most popular meat, and the spit-roasted pig, *lechon*, the most popular fiesta food. GOAT is popular in certain provinces, and many special dishes are made of its flesh, especially the Spanish *caldereta* and the Ilocano *pinapaitan*, which is flavoured with bile, to give it a bitter-sweetness. Chickens and ducks are raised for the table, the latter especially for the eggs. The native ducks, known as *itik*, are smaller than imported breeds but lay relatively large eggs. But they are not good mothers and do not hatch their own eggs, which must be done in a home-made batchery called *balutan*. BALUT is a fertilized duck egg with a partially grown chick inside, and is considered by Filipinos as a highly nutritious and tasty snack, although foreigners do not take to it readily. The native ducks eat seafoods and consequently their eggs have a fishy taste. For this reason they are often mixed with other ingredients or salted (in brine, in mud or clay jars) and coloured bright red.

Filipino ways of preserving eggs, making 'century' eggs, 'mosaic' eggs, etc., are numerous and interesting.

Vegetables, which are varied and abundant throughout the year, include leaves, tendrils, seeds, roots, flowers, fruits (e.g. young jackfruit, bananas). Many regions have all-vegetable stews that combine different textures: a leaf, a bole, a pod, a fruit, etc. Many dishes combine meat/fish and vegetables, most prominently SINIGANG, *tinola, nilaga*, and *putsero* (from the Spanish *pochero*).

Mushrooms gathered from the wild include *tengang daga*, WOOD EARS (literally mouse ears); and the kinds now cultivated, besides the ubiquitous 'button mushrooms', are SHIITAKE, STRAW MUSHROOMS, and abalone mushrooms (see OYSTER MUSHROOMS).

The abundance of fruits is especially remarkable in Mindanao. The BANANA is the most common fruit in the Philippines and the Filipinos are great connoisseurs of the different varieties. The favourite ones are: *lakatan* (yellow, also called ladyfingers); *latundan* (white); and *saba* (cooking bananas, used in stews and sweets). Cavendish bananas, grown for export, are not favoured by Filipinos. Mangos and durian are perhaps the most prized fruits, pineapple one of the most easily available. The range of citrus fruits includes many varieties of orange, pomelo, mandarin, and CALAMANSI (a limelike fruit, a frequent ingredient in Filipino recipes).

Filipinos eat noodles of the Chinese type on quite a big scale. The word for noodle is *pansit*. Any dish beginning with that word is a noodle dish. This is a large subject; see NOODLES OF ASIA.

Although rice is the staple food, wheaten bread has been established since the Spanish regime, and the typical bun, called *pan de sal* (bread of salt), is the usual breakfast bread. Many local breads have Spanish names: *pan de leche, pan de coco*, etc. The western-type loaf is called *pan Americano*, indicating its origin.

Evidence for the Filipino sweet tooth is seen in the sweet rice and cassava cakes cooked daily and for feasts. There are few native desserts, however, except for fruits cooked in syrup. Most of the candies, cakes, and desserts are Spanish in origin, and often retain the Spanish names: *leche flan* (crème caramel), *pastillas de leche* (milk pastilles), *brazo de Mercedes, mazapan de pili, ensaymadas, tortas reales*, etc. HALO-HALO may be had as dessert, but is more usually eaten in the afternoons, as a refreshment.

Alcoholic drinks are made from rice (*tapuy, baya*), sugar cane (*basi*), nipa palm (*laksoy, tuba*), and coconut (*tuba, lambanog*). These do not usually accompany meals, but have distinct importance in connection with food, since they are accompanied by *pulutan* (literally, food that can be picked up) in great variety; see Alegre (1992).

Outside authorities have pointed out (what could less easily be said by a Philippines author) that the Philippines are blessed with a culinary literature, mostly in English, which is remarkably extensive, lively, and well researched. This literature is infused by a spirit combining an attractive mixture of enthusiasm and lightheartedness (unmatched elsewhere in Asia and perhaps owing something to American influence) with an underlying seriousness of purpose.

The national heroine Maria Y. Orosa (1970) must be mentioned as one of the earliest of these writers, who exemplifies particularly the last aspect. (DF)

PHOLIOTA MUSHROOMS a genus widely represented in the northern temperate zones. One, the NAMEKO, is a well-known edible. Of the remainder, none has acquired a genuine English vernacular name, although 'pholiota' is used, and few are regarded as worth eating.

Most *Pholiota* mushrooms grow on trees or stumps or buried pieces of wood. The edible species in N. America include *P. squarrosa*, which won praise from McIlvaine (1902) and others, and which appears in Michigan in a form which has an aroma of garlic; but it enjoys less esteem in Europe, and recent American authors rate *P. squarrosoides* as better. Both have markedly scaly caps, the former dry and the latter slimy.

The genus used to be of greater gastronomic interest. At least three edible species formerly assigned to it have now been reclassified; these are *Kuehneromyces mutabilis*, *Rozites caperata*, and *Agrocybe aegerita*. The first is considered good enough for cultivation, for example in Japan (commercially) and Germany (privately). The second is treated under GYPSY MUSHROOM. The third is common in Spain (*seta de chopo*) and the south of France (*pivoulette*). It has a preference for poplar trees (hence another French name, *pholiote des peupliers*); a long season from early spring to late autumn and even winter; and firm flesh with an almond-like flavour.

PHOSPHORUS a chemical element essential to life. In every cell of every living creature, a substance known as ATP (adenosine triphosphate) acts as a store of energy. In vertebrates, bones and teeth are a network of calcium phosphate and protein.

Pure phosphorus is a non-metallic solid which exists in three forms, one of them highly poisonous and spontaneously inflammable. In living things it is always in the form of a compound, usually a phosphate—a combination with one atom of phosphorus and four of oxygen.

Phosphates are plentiful in foods: dairy products, eggs, and cereals contain substantial amounts. There is a traditional belief that eating fish is good for the brain because it contains phosphorus. So it does, but since phosphorus deficiency is almost unknown, no amount of fish will have any effect on brain function.

Phosphoric acid is used as a preservative.
RH

PHYSALIS FRUITS sometimes used as an English name to refer to the various fruits borne by plants of the genus *Physalis*. These fruits are enclosed in a papery husk or calyx, resembling a Chinese paper lantern, which accounts for the occasional use of 'Chinese lantern' as a name (at least for *P. alkekengi*, the species which is familiar as an ornamental).

Of the eight or so species, distributed round the world in temperate and tropical zones, the following are most prized for their fruits and have their own entries:

- CAPE GOOSEBERRY, *P. peruviana*;
- GROUND CHERRY, *P. pubescens*;
- TOMATILLO, *P. ixocarpa*.

PICAREL an English name which serves for two Mediterranean fish of the genus *Spicara*: *S. maena* and *S. smaris*. Almost all Mediterranean languages have separate names for them, e.g. Spanish *chucla* and *caramel*, French *mendole* and *picarel*.

These small torpedo-shaped fish have a maximum length of 25 and 20 cm (10"/8") respectively. *S. maena* has a deeper body than the other, but in those places where picarel are eaten with enthusiasm (notably Greece, Yugoslavia, and SE Italy) it seems to be *S. smaris* which is preferred. Both species have a range which extends a little way out into the Atlantic.

Picarel may be fried. Salted young picarel are a delicacy, known as *slana gira* on the Dalmatian coast from Dubrovnik north to the island of Hvar. Yet Faber (1883) recorded that at Venice it was an insult to call someone a picarel-eater. And the reputation of *S. maena*, further west in the Mediterranean, seems to be equally poor; it is called *mata-soldat* (kill-soldier) at places such as Port Vendres.

PICKLE as a verb, to preserve foods, especially vegetables, fruits, meat, and fish, in a preserving medium with a strong SALT or ACID content; as a noun, either the product of the process or the liquid or paste which is the preserving medium.

Immersing foods in VINEGAR or brine, or a mixture of the two, is a long-established way of preserving foods. Highly acidic solutions and strong salt solutions prevent micro-organisms from growing and enzymes from working (see PRESERVATION). The acetic acid in vinegar has a disinfectant effect, so that vinegar is a better preservative than other acid liquids of the same strength.

Most pickled foods use vinegar, but there are exceptions. A few recipes use lemon or lime juice. Pickled cucumbers ('dill pickles' in the USA) are often prepared in brine alone, and fermented by bacteria naturally present which produce LACTIC ACID. A similar method is used for pickled OLIVES (among the pickles appreciated by Greeks and Romans in classical times), for the beetroots used for making Russian BORSHCH, and also for Chinese 'Sichuan preserved vegetable', Japanese pickled daikon (see RADISH), Korean KIMCH'I, and some other oriental pickles. SAUERKRAUT, not usually thought of as a pickle, also depends on lactic fermentation. The noun 'pickle' is also applied to the mixture of salt, saltpetre, and spices used to cure meats such as ham and bacon. 'Pickled herring' is a vague term that can apply to salted herring or to recipes in which vinegar is used, usually for immediate eating rather than keeping.

Any type of vinegar may be used. British pickles are usually put up in malt vinegar; strong distilled vinegar is used for watery foods which would otherwise dilute the acid excessively (acidity must not drop below pH 4.0), or for light-coloured mixtures whose appearance would be spoilt by the brown tinge of malt vinegar. In wine producing countries wine vinegar is used. Oriental pickles are made with rice vinegar.

Fruit preserved in alcohol or purely by sugar, as in jam, is not thought of as constituting a pickle, but there are many borderline cases in which sugar plays an important part as a preservative, e.g. sweet pickles and CHUTNEYS or RELISHES. Sugar is in any case often added to pickling solutions, both for its flavour and for its preservative effect. Mustard, ground or as whole seeds, is another common addition which helps to preserve the pickle. Piccalilli, a sweet mustard pickle of mixed vegetables, is an example (British piccalilli is much more chutney-like than the US variety, but both contain large amounts of mustard). The Italian MOSTARDA DI FRUTTA DI CREMONA is a curious sweet fruit pickle largely preserved by mustard.

Almost any spice may be used in pickling. A typical British mixture consists of whole black and white peppercorns, mustard seed, allspice, coriander seed, mace, and a clove, perhaps with a chilli pepper for extra bite. In continental Europe garlic is often added. Some pickles contain turmeric, as much for its colour as for its flavour. A small amount of alum is sometimes added to pickled vegetables to keep them from softening.

Most pickles, except for lactic varieties and a few others meant for immediate use, are heated to boiling point to sterilize them. Pickles intended to be kept usually need time to mature, typically six months. During this time the flavours of the spices infuse and blend.

In the Near East the pickle table features pickled turnip among many other items. Pickled eggs are a traditional speciality in

Britain and elsewhere. There is an American watermelon rind pickle. In India, limes are pickled in their own juice. And so on. But the top country for pickles is generally accepted to be Japan.

See also ACHAR; GHERKIN. (RH)

'PICKLED' CHEESES (or brined cheeses) are those which are matured in their own WHEY, mixed with salt, so that they remain moist and are very salty. These simple white cheeses, traditionally made from ewe's milk, are of great antiquity. The two best known are the Greek (and Bulgarian) FETA, which is now made in many other countries, and the Egyptian domiati; but 'pickled' cheeses are widely made and consumed all over the Balkans, the Near East, and N. Africa. The HALOUMI cheese of Cyprus and the Lebanon and brinza in Romania are two more examples. Russians call this type of cheese *brynza*.

Domiati is made from whole or partly skimmed cow's or buffalo's milk that is salted at the very start of the process, which otherwise resembles that for feta. The cheese may be sold at once or matured for up to a year, during which time it darkens and its mildly acid taste becomes strong and sharp.

Yerevansky syr (cheese from Erevan, capital of Armenia) is a pickled cheese, ripened in cans with removable stoppers to allow topping up with brine.

Lesley Chamberlain (1989) remarks that cheese of this kind is ideal for salads, for pie fillings, and for combining with spinach, potatoes, courgettes, and other vegetables.

PICKLING ONIONS are of various kinds. They may be small round onions (see ONIONS), or SHALLOTS, or rakkyo (see ORIENTAL ONIONS).

The **bunching pearl onion** is a variety of *A. ampeloprasum*, the species which is better known as that of the cultivated LEEK. Rather than having a leek's thick stem, this variety has a cluster of little round bulbs which are used for pickling: they are the small, mild-flavoured, pure white 'pearl' pickled onions which are used as a garnish for food and also as a constituent of the 'Gibson' cocktail (a martini containing a pearl onion instead of the usual cocktail olive or lemon zest).

PICNIC according to the *NSOED*, originally meant a social event for which each guest provided a share of the food. Later it was linked to an excursion, for example to a beach, or the countryside, where food would be taken to eat out of doors. For many people, contemporary picnics involve an element of simplicity, where uncomplicated food such as hard-

boiled eggs, sandwiches, pieces of cold chicken are eaten without ceremony.

But there is considerable variety. Claudia Roden (1981) describes the Japanese picnic which is frequently an aesthetic experience, organized to celebrate and admire such things as the blooming of chrysanthemums, or cherry blossoms, or viewing the moon.

The Chinese are, in general, no picnickers, but do feast by the graveside, to honour their ancestors. Here the food may include '100 year eggs' and whole previously roasted or boiled pigs which are consumed after the ancestors have extracted the spiritual content from the offering.

The earliest picnics in England were medieval hunting feasts. Hunting conventions were established in the 14th century, and the feast before the chase assumed a special importance. Gaston de Foix, in a work entitled *Le Livre de chasse* (1387), gives a detailed description of such an event in France. As social habits in 14th-century England were similar to those in medieval France, it is reasonably safe to assume that picnics in England would have been more or less the same. Foods consumed would have been pastries, hams, baked meats, and so on. George Tubervile (1575, in a work which echoes that of Gaston de Foix) records a new development. At the end of the hunt, the deer would be dismembered and cooked, thus providing the excuse for a duo of picnics on the same day.

Picnicking really came into its own during the Victorian era, and enters into the literature of that period. Dickens, Trollope, Jane Austen all found pleasure in introducing this form of social event into their fiction. One can see why: a rustic idyll furnished an ideal way of presenting characters in a relaxed environment, and also provided an opportunity to describe a particularly pleasant rural spot.

Painters have also been drawn to the subject. As Gillian Riley (1993) shows us, the Impressionists constituted one such group. Monet's *Le Déjeuner sur l'herbe* is dominated by a raised pie and bottles of wine. Renoir's *Luncheon of the Boating Party* again features wine bottles as well as fruit. Cezanne's *Déjeuner sur l'herbe* conveys the mood of the picnic without dwelling on the food, although again the near-ubiquitous wine bottles are centre stage.

The picnic as such does not appear to have fired the imagination of the musician greatly, unless one wishes to recall the tiresomely haunting 1930s 'Teddy Bears' Picnic' which can still occasionally be heard on the radio. In order to give a balanced view of this sort of gastronomic event, the reader may need to be reminded of the possible inclemency of the weather (rain or excessive heat), the presence of flies, bees,

wasps, and gnats, sand in the food, uninvited dogs, and (in N. Africa sometimes) intrusive and curious children.

The word picnic is suggestive of simplicity and ease. Thus it is fair to use the negative to demonstrate the opposite, as in the sentence: 'To write the *Oxford Companion to Food* has been no picnic.' JD
READING: Georgina Battiscombe (1951); Elizabeth David (1955).

PIDDOCK the common name for a group of BIVALVES, of the family Pholadidae, which bore their way into hard mud, clay, or soft rock. This habit protects them from any commercial fishery. However, many species are edible and some justify the trouble of extricating them from their burrows.

Most piddocks are large. The shell of *Pholas dactylus*, a European Atlantic species, may measure 15 cm (nearly 6"). The creature is luminous, to such an extent that one observer found that the immersion of a single piddock in half a pint of milk created a luminous glow sufficient to make faces recognizable in the dark; and that someone who chewed a piddock and kept it in his mouth would have luminous breath, as though breathing fire. The shape of the shells has produced some interesting local names, e.g. *religieuse* and *bonne-sœur* at Brest, where a resemblance was presumably seen to the headgear of certain nuns. Consumption of this piddock is desultory in most areas, but it has been eaten with enthusiasm in Brittany and the Channel Islands.

P. orientalis, a SE Asian species, is similar in size but black and white in coloration. It prefers burrowing into hard mud.

Of the several species on the Pacific coast of America, *P. chiloensis* (from the Gulf of California to Chile), is large enough (12 cm/5") to be of interest, and snow white. The equally large wart-necked piddock, *Chaceia ovoidea*, whose siphons are united into a single and lengthy protuberance with flecks of hard material scattered over it like the marks on a carrot, is worth eating (not 'warts and all', but after removing the skin of the siphons).

In SE Asia piddocks may be boiled and eaten with sauce and rice, or sautéed with shallots, or made into a curry.

PIE a word whose meaning has evolved in the course of many centuries and which varies to some extent according to country or even to region. Many languages lack a truly equivalent word, since pies, in the Anglo-American sense of the word, are indigenous to Europe, especially C. and N. Europe, and occur elsewhere only as introduced dishes. It is in N. America that their introduction has been most extensive.

The derivation of the word may be from magpie, shortened to 'pie'. The explanation offered in favour of this is that the magpie collects a variety of things, and that it was an essential feature of early pies that they contained a variety of ingredients. So they did. But this aspect of the meaning has been lost, and nowadays one can have pies with only one important ingredient, e.g. the Scotch pie which contains just minced meat; a chicken pie; an apple pie, etc.

Early pies were large; but one can now apply the name to something small, as with small pork pies or mutton pies. However, shape governs usage, and terms like 'pasty' remain in use to distinguish things which do not have what is regarded as the correct pie shape.

Early pies had PASTRY tops; but modern pies may have a topping of something else (e.g. the mashed potato topping of SHEPHERD'S PIE or cottage pie) or even be topless (as in the USA).

If the basic concept of 'a pie' is taken to mean a mixture of ingredients encased and cooked in pastry, then proto-pies were made in the classical world and pies certainly figured in early Arab cookery. But these were flat affairs, since olive oil was used as the fat in the pastry and will not produce upstanding pies; pastry made with olive oil is 'weak' and readily slumps.

The Egyptians have some claim to the greatest pie of all time. Emerson (1908) remarks that they have always been proud of their ability to prepare very large dishes, and goes on to quote the following description by Abdallatef (or Abd el-Latif), a physician and traveller who was born at Baghdad in 1162, of a pie which he saw while travelling and studying in Egypt towards the end of the 12th century. This enormous pie was made thus:

Thirty pounds of fine flour, being kneaded with five pounds and a half of oil of sesame, and divided into two equal portions, one of these was spread upon a round tray of copper about four cubits in diameter. Upon this were placed three lambs stuffed with pounded meat fried with the oil of sesame and ground pistachio-nuts and various hot aromatics, such as pepper, ginger, cinnamon, mastic, coriander-seed, cumin-seed, cardamom, and nutmeg, etc. These were then sprinkled with rose-water infused with musk; and upon the lambs, and in the remaining space, were placed twenty fowls, twenty chickens, and fifty smaller birds, some of which were baked and stuffed with eggs; some stuffed with meat, and some fried in the juice of sour grapes, or that of limes or some similar acid. To the above were added a number of small pies, some filled with meat and others with sugar and sweetmeats; and sometimes the meat of another lamb, cut into small pieces, and some filled with cheese. The whole being piled up in the form of a dome, some rose-water infused with musk and aloes-wood is sprinkled upon it; and the other half of the paste first mentioned was spread over so as to close the

whole; it was then baked, wiped with a sponge, and again sprinkled with rose-water infused with musk.

However, although the calculations are difficult, it seems that this pie was outdone in size by at least two examples of the famous Denby Dale pie, a giant version of the meat and potato pie made by housewives in the industrial areas of W. Yorkshire and E. Lancashire. The giant is made only for special occasions (e.g. the Repeal of the Corn Laws Pie (1846) and the Bicentenary Pie (1988). This last example weighed 9.03 tonnes. See Laura Mason (1996).

See also TART, which may be regarded as a sort of topless pie.

PIG (see page 604)

PIGEON a term largely interchangeable with dove, although usually referring to the larger species of bird in the genus *Columba*, while dove is more commonly used of the smaller ones in that genus and in the genus *Streptopelia*. All are plump birds which make characteristic cooing noises.

There are numerous species around the world. Of those commonly found in Europe, the woodpigeon, *Columba palumbus*, is the largest (up to 40 cm/16") and the best to eat. It used to be called ring dove, for the clasp of white feathers on its neck. Its range, including the subspecies, extends to N. India and N. Africa.

The stock dove, *C. oenas*, and the rock dove, *C. livia*, enjoy less esteem as table birds. The latter is the ancestor of domestic pigeons, and all those semi-tame pigeons which throng European cities, for example in Trafalgar Square in London and St Mark's Square in Venice.

The turtle dove, *Streptopelia turtur*, is smaller than the others and has the most melodious song.

A squab (*pigeonneau* in French) is a young pigeon and the dish called squab pie is a pigeon pie (although the name is occasionally applied to a different pie, of mutton or pork—Devonshire squab pie is a pie containing mutton cutlets and apple). If a pie is to be made of older pigeons, and a really filling dish is required, the recipe given by Dorothy Hartley (1954) for Pigeon Pie with Dumpling Crust ('very substantial') is appropriate.

It is in Egypt that the arts of raising and cooking pigeons have been most developed. Generally speaking, pigeons may be treated like small chickens. Their breasts need to be protected with strips of bacon or the like if they are grilled or roasted.

PIGEON PEA *Cajanus cajan*, a LEGUME which is probably native to tropical Africa,

although India is the centre of diversity. Wherever it originated, it is now grown throughout the tropical regions of the world. Its resistance to drought and its generally hardy nature make it suitable for being grown on poor land by small farmers.

The botanical name comes from *kacang*, the Malay word for a pea or bean of any kind.

Over 90% of the world crop of the pigeon pea is produced in India, and it is there that it has most importance as food. Some seeds are consumed as green peas, but most are turned into DAL (split pulse). More dal is made from pigeon peas than from any other legume except channa (CHICKPEA).

The Indians distinguish two main varieties, var *flavus* and var *bicolor*. The former is known as *tur* (also rendered as *tuar, tuvar*, etc.) and the latter as *arhar*. Old Sanskrit names for the pigeon pea are *tuvari* and *adhaki* so it seems likely that the distinction is of long standing. *Tur* plants are relatively small, mature quickly, have yellow flowers, and bear pods containing only a few light-coloured seeds. They are usually grown as annuals. *Arhar* types, which are larger and grow further north, take longer to mature but bear heavier crops and are perennials. They have flower petals with red stripes, and maroon pods containing four or five darker or mottled seeds. These are referred to as red gram.

The distinction between the two varieties is maintained in the W. Indies, where *tur* is called *gungo* or Congo pea and *arhar* is no-eye pea. The name Congo pea may be a distortion of *gungo*, adopted because the pigeon pea was taken to the W. Indies from Africa. The crop is now called *pois de Congo* and *ervilha do Congo* respectively in French- and Portuguese-speaking countries of non-equatorial Africa.

Pigeon peas have a slightly acrid taste, which resides mainly in the seed coat. Removing this improves the flavour.

In W. Africa, as in India, the immature green seeds are sometimes eaten as peas, or the whole young pods cooked like green beans. Ripe seeds are soaked and then boiled, after which they are used in e.g. soups.

PIGNUT a name applied to certain true nuts, especially one of the HICKORY NUTS; but also to some edible, tuberous roots with a resemblance to nuts (see CHUFA; JOJOBA).

In Britain the name is applied to the nutlike tubers on the roots of the N. European herb *Conopodium majus*. These are about the size of a chestnut and can be peeled and eaten raw, or cooked; but, although many authors refer to schoolchildren eating them, there is little evidence of this now.

Pig

Pig, *Sus scrofa*, is the domesticated animal. The wild form of the species is WILD BOAR. For 'wild pigs', other than feral specimens of the domestic breed, see also BUSH PIG and WARTHOG.

Strictly speaking, a pig is the young animal; it becomes a hog on reaching sexual maturity, between six to eight months old.

The natural habitat of wild pigs is woodland. They are omnivorous, capable of living on anything from acorns to carrion, and were no doubt attracted to the crops and refuse heaps of early farming settlements. Piglets are easily tamed, and domestication of pigs may have begun as early as that of sheep and goats (the 8th millennium BC), in the same area; the bones of domesticated pigs are found at sites from 7000 BC onwards in the 'fertile crescent' of SW Asia. Domestication may have taken place in the Orient at something like the same time.

Pigs are found throughout Europe and the Americas, and in many parts of Asia, but are not kept by Jews or Muslims, for whom they are unclean. They are important meat animals in China, SE Asia, and Polynesia.

The true usefulness of the pig lies in its ability to forage anything from household waste to grass, and thrive. Growing and breeding fast, it yields a substantial carcass all of which can be used, except, in the old country saying, 'the eyes and the squeak'. For poor people in many parts of Europe and China the annual pig killing was their only real source of meat.

PORK TABOOS

A certain ambivalence in attitude runs through the history of the pig. In religion it often has sinister connotations; for instance one manifestation of the Indian goddess Kali is as a black sow which consumes her young. Some peoples now refuse absolutely to touch it; but in prehistoric times, pigs were used as food animals in areas in which they are now strictly taboo. Their remains have been found at sites in Mesopotamia, where the Sumerians were keeping pigs and eating pork during the 3rd millennium BC. Similarly, pigs were used for food at the Indus Valley site of Mohenjo-Daro, disappearing after the arrival of Indo-European invaders. Egyptian peasants continued to keep pigs as late as 1350 BC, and pork was allowed as food on certain holy days. Yet only about 800 years later Herodotus remarked of the Egyptians: 'The pig is regarded among them as an unclean animal, so much so that if a man in passing accidentally touch a pig, he instantly hurries to the river, and plunges in with all his clothes on.' The Jews (see JEWISH DIETARY LAWS) and Muslims (see MUSLIMS AND FOOD) have shared this prohibition for many centuries, but not since the very earliest times, as archaeological remains testify.

Various attempts have been made to find a rational explanation for the institution of the pork taboo in much of the Near and Middle East. Thus some have argued that hygiene was the underlying reason (they variously point to the pig's indiscriminate eating habits, to the fact that pork taints quite quickly in a hot climate, and to the problem of trichinosis—although this was not identified and understood until the 19th century AD). Others have suggested that economic reasons were at the root of the matter, pigs being seen as competitors with humans and with more appropriate domestic animals such as sheep and goats for limited resources. In one of the best-balanced discussions of this subject, Simoons (1994) has demonstrated the difficulties which beset these ideas and has suggested that the simplest solution is to suppose that the taboo is no more nor less than an instruction from the Supreme Being, whose commands are not susceptible to analysis.

PIGS IN EARLY TIMES

In prehistoric Europe, pigs flourished in the woodland environment. Whether domestic pigs were introduced to Britain by early farmers or tamed from native stock is unknown; at any rate, there must have been much interbreeding between domestic and wild pigs, as they roamed the woods and were only caught when their meat was required. Under Celtic law, a herd consisted of twelve sows and a boar.

Archaeological finds show that two types of pig developed in Europe: the 'sty' pig, short legged and bred for keeping in small spaces; and longer-legged pigs roaming the woods with a swineherd, living on 'pannage' (wild foods, especially acorns and beech mast). Sty pigs were kept by the Romans, who studied their breeding, rearing, and fattening, cramming them with dried figs and honeyed wine. Pigs provided various luxury foods for Roman tables, including cured products. Hams were exported from Gaul (modern France) to Rome.

Similarly, in China, during the Han dynasty (206 BC–AD 220), the pig had great status. Poorer households were encouraged to raise pigs, and pottery models of pig houses are found in tombs from this date. Butchering took place annually, just before Chinese New Year (a practice which survived until the 20th century).

MEDIEVAL TIMES

Pigs continued to be important meat animals in W. Europe after the fall of the Roman Empire. Country pigs lived on pannage; indeed, in the Domesday Book, woods were valued according to the number of swine they could support. In towns, pigs lived in sties, or even in people's houses, scavenging domestic rubbish in the streets. In England, bacon was a popular food of the Anglo-Saxons. The Normans, as with cattle and sheep, appropriated the best parts of the pig, calling the meat by the French word *porc*, giving the English language 'pork'.

In Britain, pannage gradually declined and new foods were introduced for fattening, including waste from distilleries and potatoes grown for the purpose. Skimmed milk and whey were also used, and pigs were often kept by dairy farmers to consume these waste products from butter- and cheese-making. Most people continued to keep a few pigs to provide their households with pork, bacon, and ham, feeding them on household waste.

PIGS IN THE NEW WORLD

Pigs of Spanish, French, African, and English stock were all imported to the New World. British settlers introduced pigs to Virginia, where they adapted well. For a short time the settlers at Jamestown kept them confined on an island still known as 'Hog Island', eventually allowing the animals to roam freely in both country and town. They spread westwards with 19th-century settlers, and the Midwest became an important pig-farming area. Pigs were introduced to Caribbean islands by the Spanish, and escaped to become feral; on Jamaica, these 'wild' hogs were caught for their LARD which was sold to Cuba. Feral pigs of Spanish stock are also found in Mexico, where they are known as *javalinas*.

Pigs of the Chinese type have been present in Polynesia as long as humans. Sailors left pigs to breed on islands, to establish living 'larders' for future use.

PIG-KILLING: THEORY AND PRACTICE

Numerous depictions of killing and butchering pigs appear in W. European art of the 15th and 16th centuries, often as symbols of November or December in books of hours. Midwinter, when the weather was cold, was the season to kill pigs and preserve hams, bacon, sausages, and salt pork. This was the habit in much of Europe.

The poor had two general objectives in keeping pigs. The first was to rear, economically, an animal which they would kill to provide meat for the household. The second was to sell some of the meat and use the money to buy another pig and perpetuate the cycle. 'There is no savings bank for a labourer like a pig,' observed Samuel Sidney (Youatt, 1860), who expounded his theory of cottage pig-keeping thus: a piglet, bought for a sovereign in early summer and fed on household waste, which, when it reached adult size, was supplemented with potatoes, grains, or buttermilk to aid fattening, was killed at Christmas. 'The hams he can sell to buy another pig, and the rest will remain for his own consumption, without seeming to have cost anything.'

Pig-killing entailed much excitement, hard work, and a welcome feast. Flora Thompson (1945) describes the killing (which in her village always took place at night, since the 'pig sticker' was a thatcher by day) as 'a noisy, bloody business'.

After the pig had been bled, it was scalded or singed to loosen the bristles, which were scraped off. The offal was removed, and, said Cobbett, 'if the wife be not a slattern, here, in the mere offal, in the garbage, there is food and delicate food too, for a large family for a week; and hog's puddings for the children. . . . The butcher, the next day, cuts the hog up; and then the house is *filled with meat!* Souse, griskins, blade-bones, thigh-bones, spare-ribs, chines, belly-pieces, cheeks, all coming into use one after the other, and the last of the latter not before the end of about four or five weeks.' The pig was cut so that two sides of pork, flitches, remained; these were cured for bacon.

Pig-killing remained an event in the English countryside as late as the Second World War, and is still important in parts of continental Europe. The pannage system is also still used in some parts of Spain and Portugal, where the lean Iberian pig feeds in woods and produces a particularly fine kind of HAM.

BREEDS

The Iberian pig mentioned above is an interesting example of an ancient breed (perhaps descended from the original Mediterranean wild boar) which has survived into modern time and is prized for its characteristics.

The origins of breeds of pig further north in Europe are less clear, and few can claim great antiquity. In 18th-century Britain, pigs, like other domestic livestock, attracted the attentions of agricultural improvers. Two distinct types of pig existed at that time: a small foraging type, principally found in Scotland, and a larger, lop-eared English type which had developed into several breeds. These shared the general characteristics of being long in the leg and body, covered in wiry hair, and slow to fatten; similar pigs roamed in France and Germany, still kept at pannage with a swineherd. For crossing with English stock, the Neapolitan pig from Italy, dark, almost hairless, and swift to fatten, and the Chinese pig, which was small, quick maturing and light boned, were used.

Pigs have been bred to be fat or meaty, heavy or light, according to changing requirements at different periods. Two hundred years ago, pigs were fat and heavy on sturdy legs. At the end of the 20th century, the trend is towards lean animals.

British breeds which evolved from 18th- and 19th-century experiments were divided into white pigs, 'large', 'middle', or 'small' in size, named according to their county of origin, Yorkshire or Cumberland; and black pigs, of middle or small size, which were the Berkshire and the Essex. The similar Wessex pig evolved in the late 19th century, and the two were crossed to produce the British Saddleback, black pigs with white belt. Distinct breeds of white pig also evolved in Cornwall and Wales. Finally, there were red pigs, represented by the Tamworth, covered with ginger bristles, a hardy but slow-maturing pig.

Essex pigs were exported to the USA in the early 19th century and gave rise to the Hampshire breed. Other notable USA breeds are the Duroc, a red breed from New Jersey, and the Poland China from Ohio. In Denmark, native Landrace pigs and imported British stock were used as the basis of the Danish bacon industry during the latter half of the 19th century. This was scientifically developed to serve as a profitable by-product of the Danish dairy industry (itself producing butter for Britain); the pigs were fed on the excess skim milk. The Landrace was intensively selected for leanness and length of body specifically for bacon production. The basic difference between pigs destined for pork and those for bacon is the weight at which they are killed; bacon pigs are much larger.

In China, because of the topography and climatic variability, many different breeds exist, from those adapted to the cold and high altitudes of the Tibetan plateau to the roly-poly pigs of the subtropics. Various types have specific uses for products such as pork, salt pork, lard (which, used as a frying medium, is more important than the meat in some areas), and ham (especially in Yunnan).   (LM)

READING: Hedgepeth (1978); Youatt (1860).

PIGWEED a name commonly applied to various plants, normally for the obvious reason that pigs eat them even if human beings do not.

In Australia the name has been used for wild PURSLANE. In N. America it has applied to various species of GOOSEFOOT, but especially *Chenopodium album* (see FAT HEN). Elsewhere in the Americas it is one of the names used for EPAZOTE.

PIKE *Esox lucius*, a freshwater fish of circumpolar distribution in the northern hemisphere. A voracious carnivore, it lives among the marginal vegetation of lowland rivers and lakes and attains a considerable size; females, which grow larger than males, may reach 1.5 m (60") and a weight of around 35 kg (84 lb) in continental Europe. The body is greenish-brown with speckles or curved lines of lighter green.

The pike is prized as a game fish—the larger the better—and as food, when those of medium size are preferred. A pleasant passage in *A Description of the River Thames etc.* (1758) tells us that:

The great Lord Bacon, in his History of Life and Death, observes the Pike to be the longest lived of any of the fresh Water Fish, and yet he computes his Age not to be usually above Forty Years; others think it not to be above Ten Years. It is observed, that the very old and great Pike have in them more of Grandeur than Goodness; the smaller, especially the middle sized, being esteemed the best meat, and the thicker, the firmer is the Flesh.

Modern scientists would say that Lord Bacon was closer to the truth than the 'others' on age; a pike over 30 years old has been recorded.

Smaller members of the genus in N. America are known as little pickerel. The chain pickerel (with black, chainlike, markings on its sides), *Esox niger*, is larger. It has a patchy distribution across the USA, tending to occupy regions where the pike is absent. Although it has value as a game fish, it is outclassed by a far larger member of the genus, the muskellunge (maskinonge in Canada), *E. masquinongy*, of which the principal subspecies inhabits the Great Lakes region.

The Amur pike, *E. reicherti*, is an important food fish in what was the eastern part of the Soviet Union. For the fish often called pike-perch, see ZANDER.

PIKELET nowadays, in England, a yeasted PANCAKE with a holey surface, like a thin CRUMPET cooked without a containing ring. This has probably always been the main use of the word; but in some parts of England, it is applied to other yeast-raised, griddle-baked products (including MUFFINS).

The name pikelet, which only appeared in print at the end of the 18th century, is thought to have come from a W. Midlands corruption of the Welsh term *bara pyglyd*, 'pitchy bread', breadcakes formed from a leavened batter of flour and milk and baked on the GRIDDLE.

In Australia and New Zealand, pikelet means a DROP SCONE.   LM

PILAF or pilau, a Middle Eastern method of cooking rice so that every grain remains separate, and the name of the resulting dish. Usually a flavouring such as meat (usually

lamb) or vegetables is cooked along with it, but plain rice, known as *sade pilav* (Turkish), *ruzz mufalfal* (Arabic), or *chelo* (Farsi), can also be cooked by this technique.

The word comes from the medieval Farsi *pulaw*, now pronounced *polo*. Most European languages have borrowed the Turkish form *pilav*, which is clearly related to the Russian and C. Asian *plov* (a term which coexists in the C. Asian Republics with *palaw*). Since the word has no credible Persian etymology, it might be Indian. However, there is no evidence that rice was cooked by this technique in India before the Muslim invasions, and Indians themselves associate pilaf-making with Muslim cities such as Hyderabad, Lucknow, and Delhi.

In order for the rice to cook as perfectly separate grains, it is very thoroughly washed of all surface starch, often even soaked all night. Then it is cooked in an open pot until nearly done, whereupon the fire is reduced and the pot is covered, and the rice is steamed for half an hour or longer. Careful cooks place a cloth over the pot before putting on the lid to protect the rice from drops of condensed steam, which would spoil the fluffy texture (the same technique used in Ireland to ensure mealy potatoes).

The first descriptions of the pilaf technique appear in the 13th-century Arabic books *Kitab al-Tabikh* and *Kitab al-Wusla ila al Habib*, written in Baghdad and Syria, respectively. They show the technique in its entirety, including the cloth beneath the lid, and describe still-current flavourings such as meat, pulses, and fruit. The Arab name, *ruzz mufalfal*, means 'peppered rice', but not with any implication that it is flavoured with pepper. The 13th-century recipes say to cook

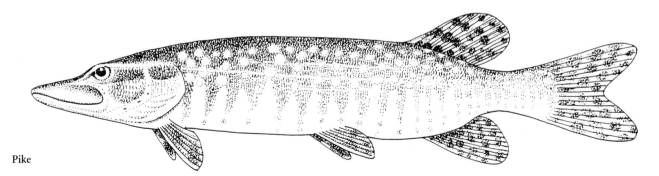

Pike

the rice 'until it is mufalfal', showing that the word refers to the appearance of the rice, plumped up in grains as separate as peppercorns. The pilaf technique is not mentioned in the 10th-century Arabic recipe collection, so presumably it spread in the Near East after the 10th century, and possibly as late as the 12th, because it is also unknown to the 13th-century Arabic books written in Spain and N. Africa.

One of the oldest recipes is *qabuli pulaw*, which means 'hospitality pilaf'. The original recipe is said to have been just meat and chickpeas, but almonds and raisins are found in most recipes today, from the Afghan *Qabuli palaw* to the Albanian *Kabuni*. There is also an Indonesian dish of chicken with rice cooked in its broth called *Nasi kebuli*, but it is not cooked by the pilaf method.

In Iran, the rice is removed from the pot and drained after its first cooking. Butter is then melted in the pot; sometimes bread or eggs (and often yoghurt) mixed with onions join the butter. The cooked rice is sprinkled over this, and the flavouring, usually a stew of meat with vegetables, fruit, or pulses, is added with the rice to steam along with it. The aim of this procedure is a golden brown crust called *tah dig* (literally the 'bottom of the pot'), which is highly relished, and ceremoniously offered to guests. A sort of tea is sometimes made by steeping *tah dig*. Curiously, given the cult of this crust in contemporary Iran, Armenia, and Azerbaijan, *tah dig* is not mentioned in the dozens of *pulaw* recipes given in the 16th-century Persian books *Karnameh dar Bab-e Tebakhi* and *Maddet ol Hayat*. The 16th-century recipes already show the Persian taste for elegant and imaginative fruit-flavoured pilafs, such as quince, barberry, sour cherry, pomegranate, and mulberry.

The C. Asian *palaw* (*plov*) is heartier and less elegant. According to the canonical recipe, a stew (*zirwak*, from the medieval Persian *zirbag*: 'that which is cooked underneath') is cooked in the cauldron-like pot *qazan*. When it is done, the soaked rice is sprinkled over it, covered with water to the depth of one finger joint, and boiled and finally steamed as usual. The stew always contains meat, onions, and the stubby yellow local carrot, which may be augmented with other ingredients such as pulses, vegetables, or dried fruits, but rarely are the added flavourings as flamboyant as one finds in a Persian or Indian pilaf. C. Asia is alone among pilaf-making regions in preferring short-grain rice.

In C. Asia, *palaw* is traditionally cooked by men, and burners for *qazans* are often provided at outdoor teahouses (*chaikhanas*), where parties of men sometimes even organize *palaw* contests. The dish is common at any meal, and essential for a banquet. The *palaw*-masters who cook for Uzbek weddings use gigantic *qazans* a metre and a half in diameter, because the ideal guest list for a wedding party is *yetti mahalla*, 'seven neighborhoods'.

In India *pulao* is associated with the cookery of the Moghul courts (see MOGHUL CUISINE) and extremely elaborate recipes with flowery Persian names (such as *Hazar pasand*, thousand delights) are current. The flavourings are such things as whole game birds, the yogurt- and cream-enriched stews called KORMA, and many combinations of fruits and nuts. Much about the spicy and extravagant flavourings may be characteristically Indian, but the pilaf cooking method contrasts with the local traditions of S. India, where the recipes do not aim at keeping the grains of rice separate. The typical indigenous rice dishes are porridges, puddings, and cakes made from ground rice.

There are some elaborate pilafs in Turkey, such as *perde pilav*, cooked with chicken, carrots, almonds, and currants and finally covered in FILO pastry and baked, and the C. Asian meat-and-carrot recipe (*Buhara pilavi*) is known. But these are not characteristic. In modern Turkey *pilav* is essentially a side dish, accompanying meat but not usually incorporating it. The common flavourings are pulses and vegetables (very often including the tomato, elsewhere in Asia quite rare in pilaf). The usual recipe is to cook the rice and any other ingredients together and then cover and steam, meaning that a Turkish cook must estimate how much liquid the rice will absorb more carefully than other pilaf cooks. The Turks are practically alone among Asian pilaf-makers in using fish and shellfish in pilaf, and, like their immediate neighbours the Syrians and Armenians, often make pilaf using bulgur wheat (see BURGHUL) instead of rice.

In the last 200 years, an interesting new school of pilaf has grown up in the Caribbean, based on the recipes brought by Indian labourers and merchants but much altered by the European and African culinary traditions of the region. A Caribbean pilaf may incorporate pork or bacon (unthinkable in the Muslim world), Worcestershire sauce, brown sugar, and olives or peanuts.   CP

PILI NUT the best known and commercially the most important of a group of nuts borne by trees of the genus *Canarium*. Most of these grow in or near SE Asia. Wild trees have three kernels in the stone. In the trees which are cultivated for their nuts, only one kernel develops, providing a large nut. Some species are grown for their edible fruits, but these are less important.

Pili nuts proper come from *C. ovatum*, native to the Philippines where 'pili' is the local name. They are rarely cultivated, but are an important food for Filipinos, who have a near monopoly in processed pili products. Production is centred in the Bicol region. They have also been introduced elsewhere in SE Asia and to C. America.

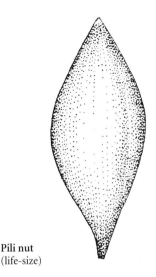

Pili nut
(life-size)

The entire nut with its shell is almond shaped, slender, pointed, and up to 6 cm (2.5") long. The shell is thick and hard to crack. The kernel is seldom more than 2.5 cm (1") long. It has the highest oil content of any nut (well over 70%), and a texture and flavour not unlike that of an almond but considered by some to be better. Doreen Fernandez (1997) has described uses as follows:

The nut is tender and crisp, its flavor mild and nutty. Most people know it only in the ways Bicolanos prepare it and sell it outside the region: nuts toasted, or toasted and salted, or fried, or sugar-coated or glazed; *pastillas de pili*; *turrones de pili*, *mazapan de pili*, *suspiros de pili*; pili brittle, chocolate-covered pili candy, sugar-coated candy with sesame seeds.

Bicolanos, however, also like the pulp, boiled and seasoned with salt, pepper, or *patis* [fish sauce], and the young shoots in salads. They also extract oil from the nut and use it for cooking.

In Malaysia and Indonesia *C. commune* (formerly *C. indicum*), the Java almond or **kenari nut**, is the most important species. It is native to the Moluccas, from which the name 'kenari', now used throughout these countries, originates. It reached Java through local enterprise before the 17th century, and in the 18th the British took it on to the Malay peninsula. It is now also cultivated in Sri Lanka where its name is kekuna and in the Pacific islands, where it is called galip nut in Papua New Guinea and ngali in the Solomons. The kernel is similar to that of the pili nut, but smaller. It has an equally high oil content and delicate flavour, and is used in similar ways, especially in baked goods and for cooking oil. Its flavour has been likened to a cross between a BRAZIL NUT and a MACADAMIA NUT.

The chief *Canarium* species cultivated for its fruit is *C. album*, grown in S. China and Indo-China. The sour, bitter, oily fruit, which is rather similar to pickled olive, is known as Chinese olive, or *kan lan* in China; it has been used there, sometimes preserved in honey, since at least the T'ang dynasty (AD 618–907), and valued as a breath freshener.

PILOTFISH *Naucrates ductor*, a cosmopolitan fish of tropical and sub-tropical waters which wears six or seven broad black vertical bands on its silver sides and has a maximum length of 60 cm (24"). This fish takes its name from its habit of accompanying ships, and large sea creatures such as sea turtles and sharks, as though piloting them. Wheeler (1979) writes:

The association has not been explained satisfactorily; amongst the suggestions advanced are shelter in the shade of the larger object, increased possibilities for foraging on waste scraps from meals, and even the shark's excrement. It is possible too that the pilot fish acts as a cleaner of parasites from its host. In any event the bond is evidently a strong one for *Naucrates* have accompanied turtles wandering as far as the inhospitably cold waters of England, far outside their normal range.

Pilotfish are not found in many fish markets. The Balearic Islands and Malta are two regions where they are obtainable. Their white flesh is suitable for grilling.

PIL-PIL also pili-pili and piri-piri, terms belonging originally to Africa, especially Mozambique (see ANGOLA AND MOZAMBIQUE), which refer to a small hot CHILLI pepper or to sauce or other preparation made from such peppers.

In francophone countries the versions with an 'l' are usual; the spelling piri-piri seems to belong rather to Portuguese-speaking countries.

Dishes which incorporate in their names any of these terms are likely to be very hot.

PINEAPPLE *Ananas comosus*, a tropical fruit of impressive appearance and attractive flavour, now grown in hot regions all round the world. The main producers are Hawaii and Malaysia. The bulk of the crop goes for canning.

This is a composite fruit formed of 100–200 berry-like fruitlets fused together, giving its outside a tessellated appearance. It grows on a short stem springing from a low plant with large swordlike leaves, small versions of which form the crown of the fruit. Fruits of normal size (there are miniature forms) average about 15 cm (6"). Weight ranges from around 1 or 2 kg (2 to 5 lb) to an extreme of 10 kg (over 20 lb); but only the Giant Kew variety reaches this extreme.

The original home of the pineapple was the lowlands of Brazil, where several *Ananas* species grow wild. Some of these bear edible but seedy fruits. No primitive form of the modern pineapple, which is almost invariably seedless, has been found, and the evolution of the fruit we know remains a mystery; but cultivation had certainly spread from Brazil to the W. Indies before the Europeans arrived. Despite being seedless, the plant is easily propagated by cuttings which may be taken from several places on the plant, including the crown of the fruit, and which remain viable for a long time even if they become dry.

In 1493 Columbus' expedition discovered the pineapple on Guadeloupe, and were astonished and delighted by its qualities. Later explorers were equally struck by what Sir Walter Raleigh called 'the princesse of fruits'. Sailors returning to Spain brought cuttings, and by the 1520s European gardeners had managed to grow fruit. One of the first was presented to Charles V (1519–29). He refused, with characteristic hesitancy, to touch it. Most people were more enthusiastic in their response, and pineapple cultivation spread quickly throughout the tropics. The main influence was that of the Portuguese sailors who traded to and from Brazil. This is why in most languages the word for the fruit is descended from the Brazilian Tupi Indian word *nana* or *anana* (excellent fruit), and not from the name *pina* (pine cone) which its first Spanish discoverers gave it because of its appearance.

By the middle of the 16th century the pineapple was being grown in India, and not long afterwards it had reached Java and China. But it was much later, in 1777, that the fruit was introduced to Pacific islands by Captain Cook.

Europeans, meanwhile, were captivated by the fruit and had tried to grow it in their hothouses, with varying success. The first English pineapple was grown in 1661 by John Rose, one of Charles II's gardeners. It seems likely that it was raised from crowns and suckers brought from Barbados; these can withstand desiccation and will resume growth when planted. A celebrated and mysterious painting of Rose presenting the fruit to the King alludes to his achievements with at least two pots containing young pineapple plants. Charles is said to have consumed it with relish, showing better judgement than his Spanish namesake. Fashionable enthusiasm for pineapples can be seen in the frequency with which they appear as a decorative motif in the buildings and furniture of the next hundred years.

Hothouse cultivation of pineapples as an expensive luxury continued in several European countries into the 19th century, and was developed into a fine art by the great Victorian gardeners of the 19th century in England. But when the varieties which they developed (Cayenne and Queen) were introduced to the Azores, which were just near enough for the perishable cargo to survive the voyage to W. Europe, the reason for hothouse cultivation disappeared.

Pineapple canning began in Hawaii in 1892 and in Malaya/Singapore at about the same time. It is now a big industry. It also became possible to send fresh pineapples for considerable, but limited, distances in refrigerated ships.

VARIETIES
Of the main varieties grown for eating fresh the two listed first are long-established ones, both of which are also used by canners:

- **Cayenne,** both acid and sugar contents high, moderately large, yellow flesh;
- **Queen,** an old variety, smaller, with less acid, a mild flavour, and rich yellow flesh, has given rise to the excellent modern variety Natal Queen;
- **Red Spanish,** mostly eaten fresh. It comes from the Caribbean and Florida, and has a

---

BROMELIN IN PINEAPPLES

IN its natural state pineapple contains bromelin, an enzyme which breaks down protein. It is similar to the enzyme papain (made from PAPAYA), which is used commercially as a meat tenderizer. The enzyme in the pineapple is so abundant and powerful that plantation and cannery workers have to wear rubber gloves to avoid their hands being eaten away. Meat marinated in fresh pineapple juice is not merely tenderized but likely to fall apart. Its activity is also responsible for the fact that a JELLY made with fresh pineapple juice and GELATIN will not set unless a gelling agent such as AGAR-AGAR is added. Bromelin is quickly destroyed by heating, so cooked or canned pineapple and juice have no active effect.

spicy, acid flavour. The principal variety grown for canning is a large one.

- **Sugarloaf,** sweet and with a mild flavour and yellow-white flesh.
- **Variegated,** with both skin and flesh of the ripe fruit 'albino white and sweet as honey' (Facciola, 1998).

In recent years several small varieties, whose core is edible, have come on the market.

EXPORT AND PROCESSING

A pineapple, unlike many other fruits, does not continue to ripen or sweeten after picking, since it has no reserve of starch to be converted into sugar. On the contrary, it will start gradually to deteriorate; and, at best, may be stored for no more than 4–6 weeks. So the trade in fresh pineapples, other than those consumed locally or exported by air, is a matter of nice calculation; fully ripe fruit cannot be used, but the fruits picked must be as near ripe as possible.

A fully ripe pineapple can be identified by pulling out a leaf from the crown; it will come away fairly easily. The smell should be pleasantly aromatic, not suggestive of incipient fermentation. When pineapple is canned, the fruit is trimmed severely to make the rings fit the can, and also to ensure that no little bits of skin are left in the flesh. The offcuts are used for juice. The harder core is also removed, and may be made into candied pineapple.

Another pineapple product is the jelly-like NATA made in Latin America by bacterial fermentation of the trimmings. Vinegar is sometimes made from cannery waste.

PINE NUT (or piñon, pinyon, pignolia), the names applied to the small edible seeds of many species of pine tree.

The finest pine nuts, which are most in demand for Arab, Spanish, and other dishes and confections, belong to the genus *Pinus* and to the northern hemisphere. Evidence of their use in the Middle East goes back to biblical times. The Mediterranean stone pine, *P. pinea*, grows at quite low altitudes, as anyone familiar with the landscapes of Provence, Italy, and the Middle East will be aware. Its nuts, imported to the USA, are the second most expensive nut on the market there, after the MACADAMIA NUT and in front of the PISTACHIO.

However, the pine nut trees of N. America are important too; the most important are *Pinus edulis*, *P. monophylla*, and the Mexican pinyon, *P. cembroides*. Lanner (1981) gives a masterly account of the first two, including history, distribution, and uses; but his book has a wider scope, since it offers an explanation of how in the course of 180 million years the original tall pines of N. Asia arrived as little desert trees in Mexico and the south-west of the USA. He also provides an illuminating account of how the piñon tree and a bird, the piñon jay, aid each other's survival, and indeed evolutionary progress. The nuts have no seed wings, with which to travel, and are not viable if they simply drop to the ground. The jay is an intelligent bird which harvests the nuts and stores them under the surface of the soil in a manner which permits those which it does not eat to germinate. The other side of the coin is that the jay is dependent on the nuts for food, and also for the stimulation of its courtship and mating procedures.

Pine nut trees have also evolved closer to the area where the first pines grew. *P. cembra*, the Swiss stone pine, has a range which extends eastwards from the Alps; and *P. gerardiana* is a native of the Himalayas. *P. koraiensis* bears nuts in Korea, as its name indicates, and in the north of Japan and China. The Chinese export its nuts, which cost less than the European ones.

The best pine nuts are of high value, but are difficult to cultivate commercially. As Woodroof (1979) puts it, the trees 'grow only under conditions that defy cultivation, fertilization, irrigation, and all kinds of mechanical spraying, harvesting and shelling. All operations are done by hand, in competition with rats, birds and insects.' This is still true for many species and regions.

Most pine nuts are sweet, with an attractive flavour and good nutritional and keeping qualities. The European nuts contain about 30% protein, of an easily digestible kind; American ones have less protein and more oil. The size is variable; 1,500 to the pound weight is normal in New Mexico and Arizona, but pine nuts of the southern hemisphere tend to be larger.

Spanish explorers in the 16th century found American Indians making meal from the nuts, besides eating them raw or roasted. They also mashed them up to make a nut butter, or for soups. The pattern continues. Some pine nuts are still eaten out of hand, raw or roasted, but most are used as ingredients in cooking, especially in the Middle East and the Mediterranean region. They make a good ingredient for stuffings, both savoury and sweet. The famous PESTO of Genoa cannot be made without them. Many sweet confections incorporate them; and the Tunisians, for example, add a few to their glasses of mint tea.

A product called pine milk is prepared by adding a little water to the kernels and pressing them. This keeps well and provides a fair substitute for meat in the diet.

The *Araucaria* pines, trees of the southern hemisphere, also bear edible nuts, e.g. *A. bidwillii*, the bunya-bunya pine of Queensland; *A. araucana*, the Chile pine or monkey-puzzle tree; and *A. augustifolia*, the para pine of Brazil.

PINOLE a meal (flour) made from the seeds of certain wild and cultivated plants, including parched MAIZE. The meal, which can be eaten dry or mixed with water to make a mush, was used by the Indians of Mexico and the south-western USA. Pinole made with CHIA seed is still famous in Mexico and was described by one author as 'the staff of life of the common people'. The bean of the MESQUITE tree is also made into pinole, and so are MADIA seeds.

PINTAIL *Anas acuta*, a surface-feeding duck with a slender long neck and pointed tail. The average length of the male is 66 cm (26"). It is one of the most widely distributed and possibly the most abundant (but not in Britain) of all the Old World migratory ducks. It is one of the best for eating, for despite its maritime habitat, much of its feeding is on fresh water.

Being so widely distributed, the pintail is called by a number of different names both in the British Isles and in America (e.g. sea pheasant, cracker, lady-bird, Harlan).

A related species, *Anas spinicauda* (known as Chilean, brown, or South American pintail), is among the commonest ducks of S. America, and one of the chief game birds in Argentina.

PIPI *Amphidesma australe*, a common edible BIVALVE of New Zealand. It is related to but smaller than the TOHEROA and TUATUA, and has smooth oval shells measuring up to 8 cm (3") across. It is widely consumed, although less esteemed than the New Zealand 'cockle' (see VENUS SHELLS) which often occurs on the same sandy shores, but lower down.

The name pipi (alternatively ugari) is also used in E. and S. Australia for *Plebidonax deltoides*, a kind of WEDGE SHELL which reaches a length of 5–6 cm (2").

PIROG the Russian word for PIE, together with its diminutive *pirozhki* (plural), comes from the word *pir* (meaning feast) and denotes something which, in the words of Darra Goldstein (1983):

is as ubiquitous in Russian life as it is in literature. Street corners are dotted with hawkers selling their pies hot from portable ovens; cafés offer meat pies along with bowls of soup. The importance of the *pirog* cannot be underestimated: in one of Gogol's *Dikanka* tales the narrator is alarmed to find that his wife has made off with half the pages of his book to use as baking paper for her pies, which, he confesses, are indeed the tastiest around.

The practice of enclosing all sorts of fillings, both savory and sweet, in an envelope of dough is an old one, and very characteristic of the Russian cuisine. The pies range from the complex and extravagant (the many-layered salmon *kulebyaka*, for instance) to the simple and plain (deep-fried half-moons of dough stuffed with leftovers). The large pies are called *pirogi*. They are usually square or rectangular in shape. Their diminutive cousins, the *pirozhki*, are pocket-sized and oval. All can be made from a variety of doughs—yeast, short or flaky pastry—depending on which suits the filling best.

Pirozhki (*pierogi* in Poland) come in a variety of shapes including small half-moons, and may be either fried or baked. They are a popular accompaniment to soups, especially clear broths and BORSHCH, or as part of ZAKUSKI.

Pyshki and *ponchki*, 'crisp-fried little patties with their endearing diminutive names', as Lesley Chamberlain (1983) says:

are made with the same raised dough used for *pirozhki* and using any of the fillings, but are always deep-fried and in the form of a square of dough containing a small quantity of stuffing. . . . Pyshki should be swollen, well browned and as light as air. Those filled with brains are considered the lightest and most delicate.   HS

PISMO CLAM *Tivela stultorum*, one of the best-known and most highly prized edible BIVALVES of the Pacific coast of N. America, occurs only in California. Its shells are triangular in shape; large, measuring up to 18 cm (7") across; and so thick that a big specimen can weigh almost 2 kg (4.25 lb); varying in colour 'from pale buckskin to deep chocolate'; and with a varnished appearance.

The clam takes its name from Pismo Beach. There, and at Moro Bay and in part of Monterey Bay, it is most abundant. Its preferred habitat is the intertidal zone of a flat sandy beach exposed to the Pacific surf. Its range does not extend beyond California.

Although a Pismo clam may lay 75 million eggs in one spawning season, very few of these survive and the tendency has been for the population to diminish under the impact of a heavy fishery, an impact which has for some time been ameliorated by various protection measures.

Weymouth (1920) describes the traditional procedure for digging:

At low tide the clam digger, in old clothes, slicker coat and pants and 'sou'wester' and armed with a potato fork, wades out to the [sand] bars. Here, he 'feels' for the clams, thrusting the fork into the sand very much as in spading with a spading fork and when a shell is struck it is lifted out. As the beaches are pure sand with very seldom a dead shell or stone, anything struck is pretty sure to be

a clam. In order to leave the hands free, the clams are carried in a sack fastened to the belt or over the shoulder, or what is now more common, a long netted bag or 'drag' with a light wooden hoop to hold the mouth open. This is usually fastened to the belt with a 'snap' as there often arise occasions where fifty to eighty pounds of clams are a distinct embarrassment and must be quickly cast off. . . . it is not uncommon to see the combers break over the shoulder or even the head of the digger, although at other times he may be only waist deep.

The Pismo clam belongs to the family Veneridae, as do other clams or cockles of the same region, such as the WASHINGTON CLAM.

Most Pismo clams finish up in city restaurants, where they are a popular dish; in chowders, fritters, or baked in the half-shell.

PISTACHIO *Pistacia vera*, a small tree native to parts of W. Asia and the Levant between Turkey and Afghanistan, bears nuts which have for long been highly prized. The earliest traces of pistachios being eaten in Turkey and the Middle East date back to about 7000 BC; and the species has been cultivated and improved during several millennia.

The genus *Pistacia* also includes the trees which produce MASTIC (an edible resin), and the terebinth tree (*P. terebinthus*, from which turpentine used to be obtained). These trees bear small fruits whose seeds (nuts) are used in the E. Mediterranean region to produce an edible oil. They have a resinous flavour of which there is also a trace in some varieties of *P. vera*, especially wild trees.

Pistachio trees were introduced from Asia to Europe in the 1st century AD, by the Romans. Cultivation of pistachios in the Old World now takes place mainly in Iran; countries such as Syria in the Middle East; S. Europe, from Turkey to Spain; and N. Africa. Crops are also gathered from wild trees in other countries, such as Afghanistan.

Cultivation began to be important in California in the 1950s, after the introduction of the cultivar Kerman, named after a district in Iran, but was only developed on a large scale in the 1970s. Australians grow pistachios on a smaller scale in Victoria, using the Kerman variety or an Australian selection, Sirora.

The pistachio tree generally produces a good crop only in alternate years. The nut is the kernel of the stone of a small, dry fruit which looks rather like an olive and grows in clusters. When the fruit is ripe, the shell usually gapes open at one end to expose the kernel, a condition which in Iran is termed *khandan* (laughing).

The kernel, which is about 15 mm (0.5") long in cultivated nuts, is unique among

nuts in being green, not just on the surface but all through. The green is due to the presence of chlorophyll, and varieties of pistachio differ markedly in this respect. Some kernels are more yellow than green, and some ivory. The dark green are the most highly valued. The shell of the nut is not green, but reddish. In the USA it is customary to dye imported nuts properly red, to mask blemishes and make them more attractive. But Californian pistachios, which are harvested and processed by more sophisticated means, are usually unblemished and left undyed.

The pistachio, with its unique colour and mild but distinctive flavour, has always been a luxury, costing three or four times as much as other nuts. It is generally eaten roasted and salted as a dessert nut. In cooking it is often used as a garnish or decoration, both in sweet and in savoury dishes. For example, it figures in some of the finest PILAF dishes and in European PÂTÉS and BRAWNS which are served in slices, so that the nuts appear as attractive green specks or slivers.

Pistachio ice cream is a beautiful green colour and, if made with genuine pistachio nuts, necessarily expensive. The green part of a correctly prepared CASSATA is made with pistachios.

PITANGA or Surinam cherry, the fruit of *Eugenia uniflora*, native to a region extending from C. America to S. Brazil. The shrub, or small tree, bears flowers singly or in groups of up to four, and these produce ribbed fruits up to 4 cm (1.5") wide, progressing in colour from green to orange to crimson and dark purple when ripe.

A number of cultivars have been developed, yielding delicious fruits with juicy, aromatic flesh. They are eaten out of hand or made into jams and jellies etc. Unripe fruits can be made into chutneys and in Brazil the juice is fermented to produce a vinegar.

PITAYA the Spanish name for the fruit of *Hylocereus undatus* and some other closely related cacti, is spelled in various ways and sometimes acccompanied by an epithet (e.g. *pitahaya roja* or *blanca* in Mexico and *pitahaya de cardón* in Guatemala). In English the fruit may be called 'strawberry pear' or, more recently, 'dragon's eye'.

The cacti bearing these fruits are indigenous to C. America, but are now cultivated also in the W. Indies, Florida, and the tropical regions of the Old World.

The oval fruit, up to 10 cm (4") long, may be bright red/crimson, peach coloured, or yellow. The pulp, which is sweet, usually white, and juicy, contains numerous tiny black seeds which give the impression of

Pitaya

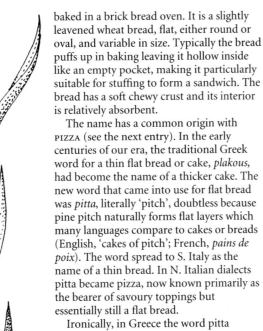

being scattered at random through it and which are eaten with it.

The juice makes a refreshing beverage. The fruit can be cut in half and chilled, then eaten with a spoon; the pulp is very faintly sweet, but so unassertive in flavour that the most favourable epithet which can be given to it is 'refreshing'. A syrup made from the fruit is used to colour confectionery.

PITTA the Israeli and western name for the Arab bread called *khubz 'adi* ('ordinary bread') or names meaning 'Arab, Egyptian, Syrian bread' or *kumaj* (a Turkish loanword properly meaning a bread cooked in ashes),

baked in a brick bread oven. It is a slightly leavened wheat bread, flat, either round or oval, and variable in size. Typically the bread puffs up in baking leaving it hollow inside like an empty pocket, making it particularly suitable for stuffing to form a sandwich. The bread has a soft chewy crust and its interior is relatively absorbent.

The name has a common origin with PIZZA (see the next entry). In the early centuries of our era, the traditional Greek word for a thin flat bread or cake, *plakous*, had become the name of a thicker cake. The new word that came into use for flat bread was *pitta*, literally 'pitch', doubtless because pine pitch naturally forms flat layers which many languages compare to cakes or breads (English, 'cakes of pitch'; French, *pains de poix*). The word spread to S. Italy as the name of a thin bread. In N. Italian dialects pitta became pizza, now known primarily as the bearer of savoury toppings but essentially still a flat bread.

Ironically, in Greece the word pitta eventually followed exactly in the footsteps of the word *plakous*, which it had replaced, becoming the name of a thick cake (e.g. *spanakopitta, tyropitta*). It retained its old sense in Turkey (*pide*) and Romania (*pita*). When Ben Yehuda was devising a modern vocabulary for Hebrew, a precondition for its revival as a spoken language, he borrowed the word pitta either directly from Romanian or via the Judaeo-Spanish spoken in Romania to refer to the bread he found being made in Palestine.

Pitta bread is eaten in a variety of ways. It is dipped in sauces or broken up in soups. Very often the pocket or flap is stuffed with any of various fillings. Small pieces of pitta are used for scooping up food.

In Lebanon and Syria, stale or toasted pitta is the basis for *fattoush*, the peasant bread salad, and for *fatteh* (see THARID). *Arais* is another Middle Eastern dish where the pitta bread is stuffed with savoury mince. *Khubz Abbas* is a special type of pitta where minced meat is incorporated into the bread dough before being baked. The book called *Recipes from Baghdad* (ed May H. Beattie, 1946) explains that:

A vow to make khubz Abbas as a thanks offering on the fulfilment of one's wish is generally taken at the time of acute anxiety, such as the illness of a beloved relative. In the event of recovery this savoury bread is prepared in vast quantities. Hot melted butter is also poured over rounds of plain khubz which are then sprinkled with sugar. The rounds of bread are arranged in great piles and are distributed in hundreds to the poor.

Khubz exists in many forms and with many epithets. Thus *khubz mbassis* is a Tunisian bread made of semolina, leavened, enriched with egg, fat of the FAT-TAILED SHEEP, and oil, flavoured with sesame seed and aniseed.

In Morocco the name comes out as *khboz*. *Khubz arabi* is two-layered pitta bread, at least in the Lebanon.

The early Arab cookery texts do not refer to *khubz*, since it was bought from specialists, not made in the home. However, it is safe to assume that its history extends far into antiquity, since flatbreads in general, whether leavened or not, are among the most ancient breads, needing no oven or even utensil for their baking.   (CP)

PIZZA a simple Italian dish associated especially but not exclusively with Naples, has become almost ubiquitous. After it had been taken to America by Italian emigrants it developed into an international food, and pizzerias have sprung up all over the world.

The name has a common origin with, and an obvious connection with, PITTA. A pizza consists mainly of a flat disc of bread. This is normally the base for various toppings, and it is safe to assume that since early classical times people in the general region of the Mediterranean were at least sometimes putting a topping on their flat breads (see FOCACCIA). Burton Anderson (1994), pointing to these precursors of pizza, goes on to say that the word pizza itself 'was used as early as the year 997 AD at Gaeta, a port between Naples and Rome'. He continues:

Abruzzi had something called pizza in the twelfth century. Calabria made *pitta* or *petta*, Apulia *pizzella* or *pizzetta*, Sicily *sfincione*. Tuscany's *schiacciata* (for squashed) was first roasted on stones by the ancestral Etruscans. Romagna's antique *piadina* is slim and crunchy like the crust of *pizza romana*, which also seems to have preceded the napoletana.

The *napoletana*, i.e. the pizza of Naples, can indeed be seen, and has been so seen for well over a century, as the archetype of modern pizzas. However, even in Naples itself one would not find complete agreement about what constitutes an authentic Neapolitan pizza. To follow Anderson again:

The most basic may be called *pizza all'olio e pomodoro*, though it is better known as *marinara* because its toppings of oil, tomato, garlic, and oregano could be stowed on voyages so that sailors (*marinai*) of this seafaring city could make pizza away from home. The more glorified *Margherita*, named in honor of Italy's queen on a visit to Naples just over a century ago, combines tomato with mozzarella cheese and fresh basil leaves to symbolize the red, white, and green tricolore of the Italian flag.

Defenders of these archetypes include the twenty-six pizzerie of the Associazione Vera Pizza Napoletana, whose members are pledged to uphold statutes that define ingredients, making of dough, and cooking. Each house carries a sign with an image of Pulcinella, the masked Punch of Neapolitan comedy, wielding a pizzaiolo's paddlelike peel.

To be authentic, pizzas should be made in a special wood-fired brick oven heated to a blistering 400 °C (750 °F). They have to be inserted and retrieved with a long-handled wooden peel (paddle). The sudden heat is necessary to melt and blend the topping, which very often includes mozzarella cheese, and to make the base puff up properly. This applies especially to versions with a thick topping, which acts as a barrier to heat.

Some pizzas have a filling enclosed in a folded over circle of dough. Such a pizza is properly called *pizza ripieno* or **calzone** (trouser leg), although a Palermo version, with a filling of meat sauce and salami as well as a cheese and onion topping moistened with wine, retains the name *pizza* (*di San Vito*). *Pitta maniata* ('kneaded') has a dough enriched with eggs and fat, thoroughly kneaded and enclosing a filling of hard-boiled eggs, ricotta cheese, salami, and chilli pepper. Small, individual-sized calzoni are made by folding circles of dough in half over the filling.

Pizzette are miniature pizzas which are often fried rather than baked. They are served as part of the ANTIPASTO table in Italian restaurants. Extra-large pizzas are often made rectangular and cut into portions of the same shape.

There are versions of pizza with no topping, sometimes called *pizza bianca* (white pizza). One such, the Tuscan *pan di ramerino* (rosemary bread), has no garnish save for a little rosemary. Other severely plain versions are found in Liguria, and there is a sweet but topless Easter pizza made in fancy shapes which is traditional in the Abruzzi. Such things are very close to pitta bread.

Other Mediterranean countries have traditional dishes resembling pizza. The *pissaladière* of Provence, topped with an onion-and-tomato mixture, a latticework of salt anchovy fillets, and olives, is sometimes made with pastry, but properly has a bread base. Incidentally, many recipes for QUICHE, which nowadays have a pastry base, began with one of bread. The Middle Eastern *lahma bi ajeen* has a base of a typical pizza dough, topped with a rich sauce of minced meat, onions, and various Middle Eastern flavourings.

In conclusion, it may fairly be said that the pizza of Naples has proved to be a world conqueror in the 20th century. To give the last word to Burton Anderson: 'It has been said that if Naples had managed to patent the pizza it would now be among Italy's wealthiest cities instead of one of its poorest.'

PLAICE *Pleuronectes platessa*, the most important flatfish of the European fisheries, has a range from the extreme west of the Mediterranean up to Iceland and Norway. The large red or orange spots on its brown 'back' (i.e. eyed side) make it instantly recognizable.

The maximum length is 90 cm (just 3'), but it is unusual to find a fully grown plaice measuring more than 50 cm (20").

The esteem in which this fish is held varies considerably, no doubt reflecting the fact that its quality as food depends not only on the season (spring is best) but also on the ground from which it is taken. Plaice from sandy bottoms are excellent, with firm and sweet flesh, while those from mud or gravel are likely to be poor fare. Danes and Swedes are among the greatest enthusiasts for plaice, and the former at least prefer to buy their plaice alive. It happens that the plaice is very tenacious of life (Day, 1880–4, records that one remained alive for 30 hours after being removed from the water), so this is not as difficult as one might think.

Plaice can be poached, or fried, or grilled.

PLANK a term for cooking fish in various ways which involve having it fastened to or placed on a suitable small wooden plank. A fish can be nailed to a plank which is then tilted up over an open fire; or nailed down (to prevent the heat making it curl upwards) to a plank under a grill; or cooked on a plank in the oven. In the last case, the plank should be as large as will fit into the oven so that there will be room for a decorative border of mashed potato around the fish. It should be of hardwood (e.g. oak, hickory, ash) cut across the grain. A good plank will improve with use and become a prized piece of kitchen equipment.

When a fish is cooked on a plank in the oven, it is often opened up down the middle, butterfly-fashion, and then fastened down before being anointed with lemon juice, parsley, melted butter, etc. The border of mashed potato would be added only about five minutes before the fish is ready. The fish is brought to table on its plank.

Planked SHAD is a well-known dish in the USA; but this is only one of many possibilities.

PLANTAIN (FRUIT) the name given to varieties of the BANANA which are only suitable for cooking. They are not botanically distinct, but for the consumer they are entirely different from eating bananas. They are most important as staple foods in E. and C. Africa, and to a lesser extent in SE Asia and the islands, S. India, and the W. Indies. Most varieties are longer and thicker than typical eating bananas, often rather angular in cross-section. There are pink, green, red, blackish-brown, and black-spotted yellow varieties.

A W. Indian plantain of unusual size is called the 'hundred pound plantain'; an exaggeration, but it can be about 60 cm (2') long.

The bluggoe, apple, or frog plantain is short, thick, and boxy. The horn plantain is long and pointed. All kinds are rigid and starchy, and only faintly sweet; they would be no more pleasant to eat raw than a potato. Cooked, however, they suit all kinds of savoury dishes, and some of them may be used in desserts. There is an expanding export trade in plantains to meet the needs of migrants from tropical countries to temperate ones.

Plantains are used much in the same way as any starchy vegetable. In E. Africa they are pounded and boiled to make FOO-FOO, a bland porridge, which may also be made with sun-dried plantain slices. But there and elsewhere they are also roasted or baked with more rewarding results. An excellent speciality of the Spanish-speaking Caribbean is *tostones*, for which slices of slightly unripe plantain are gently fried, squashed flat, and fried further until crisp. Plantain also makes successful chips (US French fries).

Plantains are often dried and powdered to make a light, digestible starch, which in the E. Indies is called *pisang* (Malay for banana) starch. This starch, and the otherwise useless fruits of a wild banana called *teparod* ('angel's food') in Thai and anglicized to 'tiparot', can be used in preparing sweetmeats.

PLANTAIN (PLANT) a name given to a group of small leafy plants, of the genus *Plantago*, long before it was applied also to the cooking varieties of BANANA (with which there is no connection, see previous entry).

The name comes from the Latin *plantago*, which itself comes from *planta*, meaning the sole of the foot and referring to the foot-shaped leaves. Another group of names, including the German name, is descended from the Anglo-Saxon *wegbreed*, meaning 'growing by the wayside', which turned into 'waybread' in the sense of food for travellers. Travellers would soon weary of a diet of plantain, although there are several species whose leaves, gathered when young and tender, are edible. One of them, *P. coronopus*, buckshorn plantain, qualifies as an element in the mixed salad of wild greens known as *misticanza* in Italy and has indeed been cultivated on a small scale in some European countries. Couplan (1984), the optimistic French authority on edible wild plants, avers that more than one species can be used either fresh in a salad or cooked in a soup.

Lovelock (1972) devotes a long and interesting passage to plantain, its local names and lore, and games played by children with it: the *locus classicus* for such information.

PLATINA BARTOLOMEO (1421–81). Platina was appointed Librarian at the Vatican in 1475, and in the same year published and dated the first printed cookery book, *De Honesta Voluptate* (a title which cannot be translated into either English or French without resort to a whole paragraph of explanation).

Platina was born Bartolomeo Sacchi, of an obscure family, and took the name Platina from his birthplace, Piadena, in the plains of Lombardy. He is known to have served for several years as a soldier and to have been tutor to the children of Ludovico Gonzaga, who gave him a letter of recommendation to the famous Cosimo de' Medici in Florence, when he went there to study Greek. It was probably in 1462 that he arrived in Rome, where he aroused papal wrath for supposed impieties and served two terms in prison before bouncing back into favour, and obtaining his librarianship, after writing some papal biographies.

That part of *De honesta voluptate* (books 6–10) which incorporates recipes came directly from the important *Libro de Arte Coquinaria* of Maestro Martino of Como. Of Martino's 250 recipes about 240 reappear in Platina, mostly in the same order but with some additional articles on fish, cereals, and vegetables. Platina's debt to Martino was acknowledged in the recipe for *biancomangiare* (a most important medieval dish, represented by BLANCMANGE in the modern world) in the following terms: 'What cook, oh ye immortal gods, could compare with my Martino, from whom I have learned most of what I write.'

Martino wrote his recipes in the vernacular, whereas Platina used Latin. He was one of the 'Roman humanists', who, as Gillian Riley, in her study of 'Platina, Martino and their Circle' (1996), puts it:

took a delight in conversing in the language of Horace and Virgil, of Cicero and Martial for its own sake; Latin tripped pleasurably and effortlessly off their tongues and pens, celebrating pagan themes and pagan activities. Dressed in togas, crowned with laurel wreaths, they re-enacted ancient ceremonies, of which feasting was one.

In line with this general approach to life, and with his own Epicurean beliefs (to be contrasted with those of the Stoics and the Peripatetics), Platina recommended moderation in the enjoyment of good things, and due regard for context. It was Epicurus who said: 'Before thinking what you have to eat and drink, seek around you with whom to eat and drink.'

Platina's book ran to a second printing in the same year as its first and subsequently appeared in at least 14 other Latin editions. The first French edition was published at Lyons in 1505. Meanwhile, the first two Italian editions had come out in 1487 and 1494 (from the hands of translators who did not realize that the recipes had originally been in Italian, in the Martino manuscript, and who consequently made some comical errors). The first English translation did not appear until 1967, when the Mallinckrodt Chemical Corporation in Saint Louis, Missouri, surprised its customers by giving them as a Christmas gift an English translation which was by, although not attributed to, Elizabeth Andrews. It was on paper stained by one of their chemicals to simulate antique parchment. Since then the authoritative translation by Mary Ellen Milham (1998) has appeared, with a full biographical essay on Platina.

Platina's work was of exceptional importance, and not only in transmitting to a very wide audience the admirable recipes of Martino. In the words of Leonard Beck (1984): 'The reader of *De honesta voluptate* is looking into the cocoon in which the modern cookbook is struggling to be born.' One could add a claim on Platina's behalf that he was the very first scholarly writer on food and cookery.

PLINY the Roman author of the *Natural History*, in full Gaius Plinius Secundus, is traditionally known in English as simply Pliny, or as 'Pliny the Elder' to distinguish him from his nephew and namesake. His vast work is a unique compilation from Greek and Roman sources, a kind of encyclopedia of the branches of knowledge now called 'scientific' and 'technical'.

Pliny was born in Como in AD 23/24 and had a distinguished military career, serving for some years on the Roman frontier in Germany, where he had the opportunity to explore the source of the Danube. His last posting was as commander of the Roman fleet at Misenum near Naples. From here, when Vesuvius erupted in 79, Pliny sailed to the aid of the people of Pompeii. Others escaped, but Pliny himself was overcome by fumes and died on Stabiae beach.

His death is described in a letter (6. 16) of Pliny the Younger addressed to the historian Tacitus. In another letter (3. 5) he lists his uncle's writings and describes his methods of work. He read, or was read to by a slave, during almost every leisure moment, even at meals and when being rubbed down after a bath. He went about Rome in a sedan chair so that he could go on reading. A second slave was always at hand to take notes. 'He left me', says his nephew, '160 scrolls full of extracts, written in a minute hand on both sides of the paper.'

From Pliny the Elder's only surviving work, the *Natural History*, both good and bad results of his research methods are evident. Astronomical numbers of 'authors consulted' are listed, classified, and totalled in a preliminary bibliographical section. Most of the statements that Pliny makes in his very long work evidently do go back to some one of these authors—but which author? How reliable? There is usually no way of knowing, for nearly all the texts he used are now lost. However, in botany, one of Pliny's major sources was the Greek scientist Theophrastus, whose work survives. Comparing Theophrastus' original with Pliny's (mostly unacknowledged) Latin versions, we can see that Pliny read too fast, often misunderstood difficult Greek turns of phrase, and tended to slant his report to fit a particular line of argument.

In spite of these problems the *Natural History* is a remarkable achievement in recording and classifying the knowledge available to an intelligent and inquisitive Roman in the 1st century AD. To the food historian the most useful divisions are books 8–11 (animals) and books 12–19 (plants), for Pliny gave special attention throughout to their uses to man. Book 14 deals with the vine and with wine; book 16 is devoted largely to the olive, and book 17 to fruit trees. The next major division, books 20–32, is also noteworthy: it deals with substances useful in medicine and diet, including important foods such as honey (22. 107), fruits again (book 23), milk, cheese, and butter (28. 123). Pliny is particularly informative on the spices, drugs, and other luxuries, many of them imported from the East, which were in so much demand on the Roman market. He, or an informant, had made detailed enquiries on prices and practices in this lucrative trade.

The *Natural History* was very popular in the Middle Ages. Its moralizing style has been less appreciated in modern times, but it remains an indispensable fund of information on many aspects of the Greek and Roman world.   AD

PLOVER the name generally applied to birds of the genus *Charadrius*, which also includes the dotterel. The family Charadriidae includes the lapwing.

The subject of plovers has been admirably dealt with in *Kettner's Book of the Table* by Dallas (1877), as follows:

The best are the golden plovers. They used to be, and often still are, roasted without being drawn—as were also turtledoves and larks; 'for,' says an ancient author, 'larks eat only pebbles and sand, doves grains of juniper and scented herbs, and plovers feed on air.' Later, the same rule was extended to the woodcock; and the general rule now is to dress the plover as a woodcock.

Plovers' Eggs must not be forgotten—delicious little things hard-boiled, exquisite in a salad, perfect in sandwich, most admirable of all set like large opals in the midst of aspic jelly. The chief supply comes from Holland. The first eggs that come over are sent to the Queen, and are worth 7s. 6d. apiece.

The golden plover preferred by this author is *C. apricarius*, whose names in various languages likewise refer to the gold spots on the upper part of its plumage (e.g. French *pluvier doré*). There is also the Asiatic and N. American golden plover, *C. dominicus*, which appears as a vagrant in W. European countries.

Plovers' eggs continue to please. Those of the common tern, *Sterna hirundo*, count as a tolerably good substitute.

PLUCK a term usually taken to mean the HEART, LIVER, LUNGS, and windpipe (or most of these) of a slaughtered animal, to be used as food.

See also the similar term GIBLETS.

PLUM the fruit of *Prunus domestica* and other *Prunus* spp. Other members of the genus include the APRICOT, PEACH, SLOE, and CHERRY. The relationship between plums and cherries is particularly close, the distinction being mainly one of size.

The word 'plum' has a long history of often ill-defined use. In the Middle Ages it seems to have meant virtually any dried fruit, including RAISINS, and this usage underlies names such as 'plum pudding' and 'plum cake'. Francesca Greenoak (1983), in her highly readable chapter on the plum family, discusses this point in relation to Christmas (plum) pudding, and suggests that raisins had already supplanted plums before Little Jack Horner (whose rhyme dates from the 16th century) 'stuck in his thumb'; so that what he pulled out was in fact a raisin.

Wild plums of several kinds are common throughout the temperate parts of the northern hemisphere. The earliest cultivation of plums, which took place in China, was of the species *P. salicina*, usually called 'Japanese plum' because it first came to the notice of western botanists in Japan.

It seems likely that *P. domestica*, the most important source of modern commercial cultivars, is indigenous to C. Europe; but the time and manner of its origin are uncertain. The plum does not seem to have been noticed by classical Greek authors, nor by Roman authors in the centuries BC. Pliny the Elder (1st century AD) commented with surprise that the earlier writer Cato (for example) had not mentioned plums and explains that by his own time there was a

'vast throng' of them; he enumerated a dozen distinct types.

Records survive which indicate that plums were cultivated in the gardens of medieval monasteries in England. Chaucer refers to a garden with 'ploumes' and 'bulaces'. The number of varieties had increased considerably by the time of Gerard (1633), who mentions having 'three score sorts in my garden and all strange and rare'. Two of his main groups are the common damson and the 'Damascen Plum' (see DAMSON; PRUNE). His account shows that new varieties were being imported from many European countries. Some of the best came from the Balkans and S. Europe; he praises those of Moravia in particular.

Plum cultivation became increasingly important in the 17th and 18th centuries, during which period the GREENGAGE was given its English name and the mirabelle plums so well liked in France were becoming firmly established. The most significant advances in the development of new varieties in England during the 19th century were made by Thomas Rivers. Early Rivers and Czar are two results of his work which are still esteemed. Many local varieties came into prominence during this period. Pershore was named after its place of origin and retains its importance in the Evesham area, where it is processed. Good marketing rather than inherent distinction assured the fame of the Victoria plum when it was first sold in 1844.

PLUMS IN THE NEW WORLD
American native plums are a mixed collection. Several good varieties of indigenous wild plum, which were eaten by the Indians before the arrival of white men, are still common and are often made into jam or jelly. Along the east coast, the BEACH PLUM is predominant. Inland the American wild plum, *P. americana*, sometimes called 'sloe' although the fruit is usually red or yellow, is widespread. In the south-east the chickasaw plum, *P. angustifolia*, often produces large, red fruit of good flavour. This and the previous species have sometimes been cultivated. In the north the hardy Canadian plum *P. nigra* is common.

Several of these native plums of N. America, edible even in the wild, have been the source of cultivated varieties, especially for the southern states of the USA where *P. domestica* will not thrive. However, the early colonists brought European plums with them to the east coast. The first kinds grown were a mixture of European and native plums, and some of these persist. William Prince, in 1790, planted the pits of 25 quarts of Green Gage plums. These produced trees yielding fruit of every colour, and out of them came the Imperial Gage (later brought to England as Denniston's

Superb), Red Gage, Prince's Gage, and the Washington plum. In 1828, the Prince Nursery offered for sale 140 different kinds of plums and to this nursery belongs the credit of having given plum-growing its greatest impetus in America.

During the 19th century, the growth of the plum industry (now fourth in importance of the tree fruit crops) began in earnest. The opening up of California coincided with the introduction of *P. salicina* varieties from Japan. Thus the Californian crop, by far the largest in N. America, is dominated by plums of oriental origin, among which the most important are the Burbank plums, named for their breeder, Luther Burbank. The most important variety in this group is Santa Rosa. Most Burbank plums are large, juicy, and red or purple.

Besides Santa Rosa, El Dorado and President, a large, purple, late dessert plum of good flavour, are major varieties. European species suitable for producing prunes are grown on a smaller scale.

USES
Plums can be picked slightly before they are ripe and will then reach perfect ripeness in a warm room. Refrigeration slows the process but does not stop it.

The best way of preserving plums is to dry them naturally, as with PRUNE varieties and also the Bokhara plum (*Prunus bokhariensis*), used in the cuisines of C. Asia and the northern fringe of the Indian subcontinent.

Plums are also candied to make 'sugar-plums', the most notable kind being Portuguese Elvas plums. Jams and jellies made from sour, wild varieties such as damsons are better than ordinary plum jam.

Apart from obvious uses in desserts, sharp-flavoured plums go well with fatty meats. They are used as a stuffing for goose and with pork in stews in C. Europe.

OTHER 'PLUMS'
Brazil, Hog, Jew, and Spanish plum are all names for the AMBARELLA and related species. Java plum and Malabar plum are fruits of the genus *Eugenia*. Date plum is an alternative name for the PERSIMMON.

See also DAVIDSON'S PLUM; and for Governor's plum see RAMONTCHI; LOVI-LOVI; RUKAM).

Japanese 'pickled plums' are really a kind of apricot (see UMEBOSHI), not connected with the species *P. salicina*, although that is often referred to as Japanese plum.

PLUM MANGO and gandaria are names applied to the fruits of two trees of the genus *Bouea*, native to the region of Thailand, Malaysia, and Indonesia. These fruits are like miniature mangoes. The better known of the two, *B. macrophylla*, is cultivated for its oval or round fruits, 4–6 cm (1.5–2.5") long, some of which have sweet, edible pulp. They are pickled and used in curry-type dishes, and can also be made into chutneys or jams.

POACH (and *pocher* in French), a verb which indicates a method of cooking which is generally taken to be in a liquid which is simmering (see SIMMER), i.e. just below boiling point, in the area of 90–96 °C/195–205 °F. But not all authorities agree on this. Some would keep the temperature markedly below boiling point—low enough to ensure that the surface of the liquid betrays no signs of movement, not even 'shivering'; others would permit some such motion (if only to ensure that the temperature does not fall too low, which it can easily do in the absence of any visible marker); others refer to 'a gentle boil'.

McGee (1990) has an interesting discussion of temperatures in relation to terms such as poach and simmer, bringing out the point that western kitchens are not well equipped for cooking at temperatures which might otherwise be seen as the most appropriate, e.g. 71 °C/160 °F or 82 °C/180 °F; ovens cannot be set low enough (one has to prop the oven door open with objects of varying thickness, having first carried out a calibration exercise), while cooks working on top of the stove have no surface motion to guide them and must resort to a thermometer or guess.

Poaching is normally applied to fish (in a COURT BOUILLON), dumplings, delicate meat products or offal, eggs, fruits (in a SYRUP), and anything else which it would be undesirable to subject to violent agitation, as when boiling. The lack of a precise and agreed-by-all definition of poaching is not a real problem, so long as one accepts that it is not the sort of term which can be defined exactly (as 'boil', for example, can be) and that the range of meanings which have attached themselves to it is a useful spectrum on which the cook, aided by common sense and experience, can draw. And the cook can recall that poach comes from *pocher*, which means pocket, referring to the 'pocket' of coagulated white within which the yolk of an egg is retained while it is being poached, so that the manner of poaching an egg (starting with boiling water and reducing at once to a simmer) may be treated as the archetypal act of poaching, from which other such acts are derived.

POCHARD *Aythya ferina*, a diving DUCK of Europe and Asia which favours still inland waters and has a largely vegetarian diet. Size is moderate (average total length 45 cm/18"). It is regarded as good table fare.

The pochard has close relations in N. and S. America, E. Africa, and elsewhere.

POHICKORY a favourite drink of American Indians, prepared wherever hickory trees grew. According to Emerson (1908), Governor's Island in the upper New York Bay was famous for its HICKORY NUTS, which were of the shellbark kind and well suited to making pohickory:

The method pursued by the Indians in making pohickory was to pound the nut, shells and kernels, in a mortar with a proper amount of water until a milky liquor was produced, when it was ready for use. . . . The Indians of New England as well as of the South used it freely and plentifully, for owing to the nature of the nut, which could be kept for two or three years without deterioration, the beverage could be made at any season of the year.

POI a sour, fermented paste made from the corms (underground swollen stems) of TARO (*Colocasia macrorrhiza*) in the Hawaiian Islands. It is the staple food of the region although it contains very little protein. The taro is boiled and pounded to a paste with water. Lactic acid bacteria from the natural environment invade it and cause a fermentation like that of any other vegetable pickle. Few non-Hawaiians find poi particularly appetizing.

POKEWEED a wild plant of the genus *Phytolacca*, which has edible, spinach-like leaves, wholesome and delicious when they are young. The plant is best known in N. America and its name derives from its common American Indian one, *pocan*.

The best species for use as a green vegetable is the American pokeweed, *Phytolacca esculenta* (formerly *americana*), which now grows wild in Europe. It thrives in adverse conditions. In the USA its distribution extends from the eastern states to Texas, and it has a special place in the folklore and gastronomy of several regions. Krochmal and Krochmal (1974*a*) write:

For generations, people of Appalachia have looked forward to the early spring harvest of poke greens or 'poke sallet'. Boiled in three or four changes of water, they are one of the first spring vegetables available for the taking. Ambitious youngsters in Kentucky used to earn a few cents of spending money by harvesting and selling poke greens. Now a poke sallet canning industry flourishes in northern Kentucky and southern Ohio.

Saunders (1976) remarks that the second water for boiling can have a bit of pork fat added and that the pokeweed is served with a dash of vinegar. Kavasch (1979) gives an Indian recipe from New England for the

young sprouts; wood ash, wild garlic, and bacon fat are added to the second water and the sprouts are served hot with nut oil or nut butter.

The whole young shoots may also be cooked as a substitute for asparagus. In Delaware some people preferred these to asparagus as an accompaniment to shad. In the Creole cookery of Louisiana pokeweed is called *chou gras*, and is used in soup. The young shoots are also made into pickles.

The purple berries are used to produce a red colouring, sometimes added to foodstuffs. In the 18th century certain Portuguese were found to be adding it to red wine, a practice which was viewed with such alarm that the King ordered all pokeweed to be cut before it produced berries.

Other species of the genus are leaf vegetables of minor importance in tropical America, India, China, and E. Africa.

POLAND has changed shape and size to a bewildering extent. At one time in the distant past the Polish-Lithuanian 'Commonwealth' stretched from the Baltic to the Black Sea and was larger than any other country in Europe. In 1831 what was left of this vast area was ceded to Russia; and then reduced to zero in the First World War. What is now Poland represents a mean between these two extremes and does correspond fairly closely to the area occupied by speakers of the Polish language. Its cuisine is best introduced in the wise words of Mary Pinińska (1990):

The shape and form of a nation's cuisine is at first wholly dependent on its soil and climate. In later years it may also be moulded and polished by its proximity to trading routes, and by war, foreign influences, economic prosperity, religion and so on, but its basic characteristics remain. The elementary ingredients of Poland's cuisine were dictated by the rich, dark soil and the harsh northern climate, which yielded cereal crops such as rye, wheat, millet, barley and buckwheat. From these came bread: from rye the beautifully dark, dense, moist loaves so typical of this part of Europe; and, from other grains, white bread with which soups were made and whose stale crumbs were used to thicken and bind stuffings and sauces. Fried breadcrumbs have long been used as a garnish in Polish cooking, and *à la Polonaise*, which means a garnish of fried breadcrumbs, often with diced hard-boiled egg, is part of international gastronomic vocabulary.

The basics also include the vegetables which grow readily in Poland, often in pickled form (SAUERKRAUT, pickled beetroot, cucumber, etc.). Hearty soups incorporating cereal and vegetable are important, e.g. *Grochowka*, yellow-pea soup with barley. Other soups are reminiscent of Russian or Lithuanian ones (sorrel soups; CHŁODNIK, cold beetroot soup). There are even dill soups, reflecting the position of DILL as the favourite flavouring. FRUIT SOUPS eaten in the summer in the north-west of Poland may well reflect an influence from Denmark and Germany.

Among the cereals, BUCKWHEAT ranks first in esteem; it appears in numerous forms, including an important role as a side dish for game or meat. Other staples include two dairy products. One is curd cheese, used for many purposes including *zakaski*, the Polish counterpart of the Russian ZAKUSKI; as a stuffing for *pierogi* (see PIROG); and for cheesecake. The other is *smietana* (like the Russian *smetana*, this product is usually translated as 'sour cream', although it is not quite the same: see SOUR CREAM).

Mushrooms (fresh or dried) have been a sort of staple since the 10th century, when the introduction of Roman Catholic fasts brought them into greater prominence as a substitute for meat. If European countries were to be ranked in enthusiasm for and knowledge about edible fungi, Poland would be up at the top. One could say the same about game. It abounds in Polish forests, and one of the most famous Polish dishes is *Bigos*, hunter's stew. Plentiful game suits the Poles particularly well because, as many foreign observers have noted, they have an inconveniently large appetite for meat (which often had to be satisfied with the beloved Polish sausages).

If the above paragraphs represent the basic foods of Polish territory, it remains to consider the intrusion of external influences. The Roman Catholic version of Christianity (contrasting with the Orthodox version in neighbouring Russia) has already been mentioned and continues to provide the great holidays and feasts in the Polish calendar. Another influence of a religious character arose from the arrival of large numbers of Jews in the 14th century. The Jewish community in Poland grew to be one of the largest in the world, and Poland may be regarded as the chief source of the Ashkenazi branch of JEWISH COOKERY.

Then, early in the 16th century, arrived the Italian princess Bona Sforza to marry the Polish King Zygmunt the Old. Unlike the non-impact of Catherine de'Medici on French cuisine (see CULINARY MYTHOLOGY), this was a significant occasion. To Bona Sforza's retinue is attributed among other innovations the introduction of salad items, and to this day these, indeed greens generally, are known in Poland as *wloszczyzna* (Italian things).

French influence was apparent at the court of the last king of Poland, Stanislaw Augustus Poniatowski, who came to the throne in 1764 and employed a chef, Tremo, who combined the refinements of French cuisine with indigenous traditions. Pininska remarks that he had a sense of humour, for on the title page of his collection of recipes (preserved at Cracow) he wrote: 'Not everybody thinks, but everybody eats.' It was during this period, the same author notes (citing Father Kitowicz, whose work of the 1780s on Polish food and other customs at that time provides a remarkable parallel to the work of Le Grand d'Aussy, 1782, in France), that the sinister dish called 'black goose' was relegated from banquets to funerals, and that the doughnuts which had been such that you 'risked having your eye blackened by one' could now 'be blown off a plate by the wind'.

The French influence was largely confined to the aristocracy and wealthy people. In any case, the Second World War and the consequent scarcities and hardships set the clock back to just about where it started; and Polish cuisine remains stubbornly Polish. It seems unlikely that the Polish predilection for simple and substantial dishes and for sweet things (among which one could cite MAZURKA and BABA) will ever be extinguished.

One curiosity of Polish cuisine is the existence of some savoury dishes (often or possibly always involving mushrooms and sour cream) named after Lord Nelson (*po Nelsonsku*), plus at least one sweet dish named for Lady Hamilton. An appeal to the Polish nation broadcast from Warsaw radio in the late 1970s, asking for an explanation, brought no response.

READING: Lesley Chamberlain (1989).

POLENTA a kind of thick MAIZE porridge, solid when cold, which is a staple dish in N. Italy. Its history as a maize dish dates back to when maize was introduced to the region by the Venetians from America in the mid-17th century. However, it is thought that even before then polenta was being made with CHESTNUT flour, and that in this form it goes back to antiquity. Moreover, since *polenta* in classical Rome meant pearl barley (Ayto, 1993), a barley version is probably lurking in the historical background.

The usual way of making polenta is to boil the cornmeal (polenta) in water, stirring constantly, then to simmer until it is so thick that the spoon will stand up unsupported in the pan. Once made it can be served at once with gravy, butter, and cheese, or a tomato sauce, but it is commonly spooned out while still hot on to a baking dish, spread into a thin layer and then cooled. Once cool it can then be cut into pieces, reheated by frying in oil, grilled or baked, and served with some kind of sauce or as an accompaniment to various savoury dishes, with which it is thought to go well.

Closely similar dishes exist in Balkan countries where maize was adopted as a staple food. The Romanian MAMALIGA is the best-known example.

POLITICS AND FOOD must have been almost coextensive subjects in prehistoric times. To the extent that 'politics' existed, they would have been about who got what to eat. This fundamental issue would have been the underlying one in territorial disputes. Even in modern times it would not be wholly unreasonable to proffer such an analysis. Many of the wars which have taken place during the historical period can be traced at least in part to such causes; and not a few governments or social systems have been overturned because of food issues.

However, in modern times writers about the politics of food, a new phrase, are likely to be addressing questions such as the relationship between governments and the food industry (national or, increasingly, multinational). Cannon (1987) is a striking example of this genre of food literature in Britain.

A related but somewhat different subject is that of 'ideologies and food'. Gordon (1988) presented a remarkable study about fascism and gastronomy, based on but not confined to Nazism in Germany and Fascism in Italy.

A lighter aspect of this whole complex of topics is provided by questions relating to the diet of prominent political figures through the ages. What did they eat? What did they wish people to think they ate? Did they wish others to adopt a similar diet, or were they anxious to maintain a contrast between their own diets (whether ascetic or luxurious) and those of the hoi polloi? What, in particular, was the diet of national leaders who introduced sumptuary laws, to prevent extravagant expenditure on food and wine? Such questions could be broadened to include 'lifestyle', not just diet; and the results of a global and historical study could be interesting.

POLKAGRISA a Swedish pulled candy, flavoured with peppermint and vinegar, coloured in red and white stripes.

POLLACK *Pollachius pollachius*, a fish of the COD family which has a range in the E. Atlantic from northern waters down to Portugal. Although its maximum length is well over one metre, specimens in the markets are likely to measure 50–80 cm (20–32").

This species is perfectly good to eat but is not caught in large quantities, so relatively uncommon in the markets. The French name is *lieu jaune*. It is not to be confused with the SAITHE, *P. virens*, a more important species which is *lieu noir* in French and pollock in the USA.

POLONY a SAUSAGE known throughout Europe and N. America. In England it is made of a pork and beef mixture, highly seasoned to suit various regional tastes. Other meats can be used. The mixture was formerly encased in a natural skin ('weasand', i.e. the gullet), but is now usually presented in an artificial skin; in either event the skin is dyed scarlet or pinkish-red. The sausage is hot smoked and cooked in water.

Polonies appear so often in early English cookery books, from the 17th century onwards, as to give the impression that they were for a long time the best-known sausages in England. The spelling varied. Rabisha (1682) had a recipe 'To Make Polony Sassages to keep all the year'. Hannah Glasse (1747) had Belony, but in later editions of her book this was changed to Bolognia. The name is usually said to derive from boloney, a corruption of Bologna, the city which has long produced sausages which were much admired and copied outside Italy (see MORTADELLA); but some suppose that it came from Polonia, the old name for Poland, also an area with a strong sausage-making tradition.   LM

POLYPORES a general name for a group of edible fungi which have tubes rather than gills under their caps, and thus resemble BOLETE mushrooms, but which differ in normally having a much firmer texture. Some have the capacity to go on producing new tubes; indeed many are perennial. Most of them have fused or multiple caps (instead of the one-cap-on-one-stem arrangement)

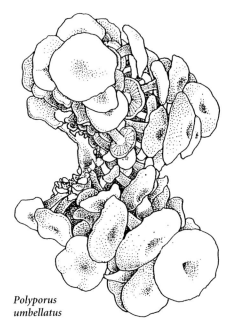

Polyporus
umbellatus

and grow directly from wood stumps or logs, whose decay they promote until no nutrients are left. As Miller and Miller (1980) remark, none of them contains a serious toxin (although many are inedible); all should be eaten cooked rather than raw; and all are fleshy and firm, and therefore (provided that they are edible at all) suitable for dishes in which bulk is needed.

The best-known species are described under BEEFSTEAK FUNGUS, SULPHUR SHELF, and HEN OF THE WOODS (not to be confused with chicken of the woods, an alternative name for sulphur shelf). For a rare and remarkable curiosity, see STONE MUSHROOM. Less well-known, but edible, species include the following.

Polyporus umbellatus, the umbrella polypore, is found on both sides of the Atlantic, at the base of tree trunks or on logs, especially oak. Its short main stalk divides into as many as several hundred branches, each bearing a small buff-coloured cap spotted with darker brown or grey. Of excellent quality when young, and with a floury aroma. It is said that in the Franche-Comté the species is so highly prized that people go out to water it in the woods when the weather is unduly dry during its season (around July).

P. squamosus, the scaly polypore or dryad's saddle, also occurs in both Europe and N. America. It grows on stumps and logs and damaged trees; has conspicuous brown scales on its cap, to which the stem is attached at the side; and fruits around May. Worth gathering when young; the tender edges of the caps are the best parts.

Albatrellus ovinus, the sheep mushroom (*polypore des brébis* in France), grows in the ground, usually in mountainous regions and under coniferous trees. It has a wide distribution in N. America, and in W. and N. Europe. Its edible quality was praised by Ramain (1979); and it is said to have an aroma resembling that of fresh almonds.

POMEGRANATE *Punica granatum*, the fruit of a small tree which is native to Iran and still grows wild there. The trees are small; evergreen or deciduous according to climate; and very long lived. The seed is distributed by birds which eat the fruit.

The pomegranate was well known in ancient Egypt. The Israelites in the desert regretted the refreshing fruit they had left behind them, so that Moses found it necessary to assure them that they would find it again in the Promised Land (Deuteronomy 8: 8). The fruit was known to the ancient Greeks and is mentioned in Homer, but it seems to have reached the Romans more circuitously via Carthage (Punis) in N. Africa. They called it *mala punica* (Carthaginian apple), whence comes

the generic name *Punica*. The species name *granatum*, the Spanish *granada*, and the name pomegranate itself all refer to the many 'grains' or seeds.

Although the pomegranate has been cultivated and appreciated since antiquity, these seeds and the fact that the fruit is laborious to consume have held it back from universal popularity. The pulp which surrounds the seeds has to be separated from the membranes which retain it. And the seeds, although edible, are intrusive and require a decision whether to swallow them down or spit them out. The problem is well illustrated by a classical legend concerning the fruit. Persephone, daughter of Demeter, goddess of fruit and fertility, was carried off to the underworld by its god, Hades (Pluto). Demeter, in her efforts to force her daughter's release, prevented earthly plants from bearing fruit (thus creating winter, a formerly unknown phenomenon). Persephone for her part, vowed not to eat while in Pluto's kingdom, but eventually succumbed and ate a pomegranate. She spat out all the seeds but for six, which she swallowed. When Pluto finally gave in to Demeter, he was allowed to keep Persephone for six months of every year because of those seeds; and this is supposed to be the origin of the alternation between winter and summer.

Pomegranate

Spanish sailors took the pomegranate from the Mediterranean region, where it had long been cultivated, to America. It was a useful fruit for sea voyagers since its hard skin helps it to keep well. It became established in the south of the USA and then, in the 18th century, in California. The fruit had also spread eastwards, to India and China. The first mention in Indian literature is of the 1st century AD, about the time when Laufer (1978) considers that it arrived there. Many authors, relying on late sources, state that it had already reached China around 150 BC, having been introduced from Samarkand by Chang Kien; but Laufer shows that its arrival was more likely to have been early in the period AD. In China the fruit was grown in the warm south and sent to colder regions as an exotic delicacy.

Pomegranates are now most popular around the Mediterranean and throughout the Middle East as far as India. They have until recently been largely ignored by the English-speaking world, although some are grown in California for sale to inhabitants of Hispanic origin.

The fruit varies considerably in size and quality. Trees do not grow true from seed, so good varieties are propagated by cuttings. The best eating pomegranates are as big as large oranges, sometimes yellow in colour but more often dark brick red. The colour of the pulp may be anything between white and deep wine red. In the east, seedless or almost seedless pomegranates are quite common. In 1860 cuttings of a seedless tree from Palestine were distributed in the USA, and some trees from those cuttings may still be alive. But in general there seem to be no seedless varieties in western countries, although types with soft seeds are often classed as 'seedless'.

Inferior pomegranates, especially those from wild trees, contain mostly seeds and membranes, and what pulp they have is very sour and astringent. Anyway, sour pomegranates have their uses, e.g. in India, where the seeds of the wild pomegranate (*daru* in N. India) are used as a sour condiment, ANARDANA. In the Middle East also, sour pomegranate seeds often appear as a condiment or garnish.

Good eating pomegranates have plenty of juicy pulp with a sweet, sharp flavour which is only slightly astringent. This can simply be eaten out of the half-rind with a spoon, or more luxuriously presented by carefully separating it from the yellow membranes around it and piling the glistening pulp and seeds into a dish.

Pomegranate juice makes a refreshing drink. When reduced to a thick, dark syrup (*robb-e anar* in Iran) it is used in cooking, for example in some traditional Persian poultry or game dishes such as FESENJAN, where walnuts in combination with the syrup provide the characteristic flavour. A similar use is found in the countries of the Caucasus, notably AZERBAIJAN; and it has penetrated northwards from the Caucasus into Russia.

The following quotation from Olearius (1669) in Laufer (1978) illustrates the antiquity of Persian practices with pomegranates:

Pomegranate-trees . . . grow there without any ordering or cultivation, especially in the Province of Kilan, where you have whole forests of them. The wild pomegranates, which you find almost everywhere, especially at Karabag, are sharp or sourish. They take out of them the seed, which they call *Nardan*, wherewith they drive a great trade, and the Persians make use of it in their sawces, whereto it gives a colour, and a picquant

tast, having been steep'd in water, and strain'd through a cloath. Sometimes they boyl the juyce of these Pomegranates, and keep it to give a colour to the rice, which they serve up at their entertainments, and it gives withall a tast which is not unpleasant.

Grenadine is a concentrated syrup made from the juice, but is suited to making a beverage, diluted, rather than for use in cooking. Commercial grenadine is usually very sweet.

Pomegranate jelly is also made.

POMELO or pummelo (as preferred by many authorities), or shaddock, *Citrus grandis*, the ancestor of the GRAPEFRUIT, continues to be widely grown in tropical areas (and California and Israel) and eaten, and many good new varieties have evolved or been bred, including those in three groups identified by Saunt (1990) as Thai, Chinese, and Indonesian. The varieties in the Indonesian group are larger than the others but vary considerably in other respects. (Some authorities would include here the UGLI, which is treated separately in this book.)

The origin of the pomelo was almost certainly in the region of Malaysia and Indonesia. Wild fruits, like the cultivated forms, are highly variable; predominantly sweet, sour, or bitter; juicy or overly dry; and with pale or pink flesh and yellow or greenish rind. The pomelo also grew wild in parts of China. It and the ORANGE are mentioned in the earliest Chinese documents which refer to citrus fruits. It is reasonable to suppose that the pomelo has been gathered and also cultivated by the Chinese for thousands of years.

A large pomelo is bigger than any other citrus fruit, measuring up to 30 cm (1') in diameter or even more (weighing up to 10 kg (22 lb), according to Saunt. Much of its bulk is taken up by the very thick skin, which is loose and easily removed.

The pomelo spread westwards in the wake of other, more prized, citrus fruits. In 1187 a pilgrim to Palestine encountered a 'fruit called Adam's apple whereon the marks of Adam's teeth may be right plainly seen'; this was a variety, with indentations in the rind, which is mentioned by later writers too.

The climate in Europe is too cool for the pomelo, except in Spain, whither it was brought by Arabs. However, Europeans were responsible for its common names. Their origin can be traced back to the Malay word *pumpulmas* (which may itself have been borrowed from another language). This became, almost without change, the Dutch *pompelmoes*; and the English then blurred it to pomelo, perhaps by confusion with the French *pomme* (apple). One quaint English name, closer to the Dutch, was 'pimplenose'.

It was probably in the mid-17th century that the pomelo was introduced to the W. Indies, where citrus cultivation was already well established, and acquired its alternative name shaddock. Sir Hans Sloane, in his narrative of his voyage to the W. Indies in 1687–8, asserted that the fruit had first been taken to Barbados by a Captain Shaddock, commander of an East-Indiaman; but the matter is doubtful.

What is certain is that the 'shaddock' thrived in the W. Indies, in various forms; and it seems likely that it was there, in the course of the 18th century, that it developed into the grapefruit. Tolkowsky (1938) quotes a French botanist of the early 19th century as saying:

I have had the occasion to observe, at Jamaica . . . a variety of shaddock whose fruits, which are not bigger than a fair orange, are disposed in clusters; the English in Jamaica call this the 'forbidden fruit' or 'smaller shaddock'.

Another source of the same period described the same variety and said that it was known as grapefruit, because its flavour resembled that of a grape.

The pomelo, whose flesh separates readily into segments, is usually eaten fresh. However, Valentin (1982) records that there were people in Réunion who, as recently as 1960, knew how to preserve a pomelo whole as *pamplemoussier confit*; a considerable feat. And preserved pieces of rind occur in jams or in candied form. Simoons (1991) remarks that in China 'pummelo rind is parboiled and cooked as a vegetable, for example in a meat or shrimp-egg stew'. The same author has a good passage on the importance of the pummelo in Chinese culture, observing among other things that: 'Pummelo leaves or skins are soaked in water to make a ceremonial bath to ritually cleanse a person and repel evil.'

READING: Julia Morton (1987).

POMFRET is a name mainly used for two deep-bodied narrow fish of Asian coastal waters. These have many characteristics in common, but belong to different families. The white pomfret, *Pampus argenteus*, is in the family Stromateidae; whereas the so-called black (brown-grey in reality) pomfret, *Formio niger*, is the one and only member of the family Formionidae. The pomfrets, when adult, have no pelvic fins; a characteristic which they share with the rather similar group of what are called butterfish (also of the family Stromateidae—*Peprilus triacanthus* is the outstanding one on the eastern seaboard of the USA, dubbed by Mitcham (1975) 'one of the most delicious treats which Mother Ocean provides, and one of the rarest').

The white pomfret is the larger, with a maximum length of 50 cm (20"); the black pomfret only reaches 30 cm (12"). In each instance, average market length is about half the maximum.

The white pomfret is the most highly esteemed fish for serving at honorific meals in Malaysia, where the excess of demand over supply makes it expensive. Indeed it is everywhere expensive. Its firm white flesh divides readily into fillets; and the soft anal fin and tail fin should be eaten too.

The black pomfret is also good. The Mediterranean pomfret, *Stromateus fiatola*, is considered less good.

POMOLOGY from the Latin for fruit (later apple), is the study of fruits, largely from the consuming point of view. Its concentration on the edible or useful aspects distinguishes it from the specifically botanical study, carpology (derived from the corresponding Greek word), which treats of the fruits that all flowering plants bear, whether eaten or not.

Pomology is often used loosely to refer to the practice of fruit culture and, although this meaning has no place here, but rather in a companion to gardening, the influence of horticultural methods on systematic description deserves attention. With improvements in pest control, for instance, certain small blemishes, once considered to be essential characters of the fruit, are now recognized as the incidental result of disease or insect nibbling. Modern methods of mechanical harvesting have attracted attention to the conveniently clustered arrangement of fruit on the boughs of certain clones, an aspect of pomology that scarcely interested an earlier age.

Indeed, whether the pomologist is a horticulturist or not is a significant point, for the gardener and the dinner guest are unlikely to look for precisely the same thing in fruit, and the pomologist who studies his subject on the tree will not produce the same monograph as he who knows fruit solely from the dessert plate. Although at least two English poets, Thomson and Coleridge, liked to bite suitable fruits directly from the tree, without the bruising intermediary of the hand, there is usually an interval, and sometimes a long interval, between picking and eating. It is thus possible to study fruit in isolation from the plant on which it grew, much in the way that gems or minerals were once classified without reference to geological time or strata, and to discuss fruits, as Charles Morren sourly observed of the dilettante pomologists of his day, just as one 'would praise the pas seul of a ballerina or a prima donna's fioritura'.

The history of pomology is therefore fundamentally the history of the fruit-eater. Descriptive pomology, attending to structure, writes the recipe book; systematic

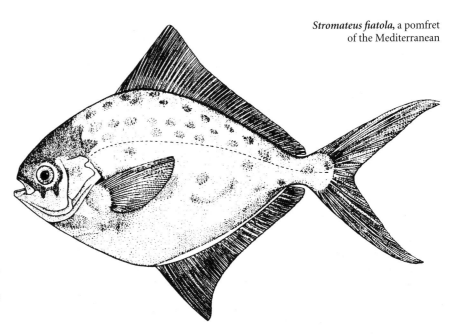

Stromateus fiatola, a pomfret of the Mediterranean

pomology, intent on classification, arranges the menu. The earliest systems failed only through no clear sense of audience or direction, as revealed in their final resort to disparate subdivisions. The oldest known scheme, for instance, devised by Theophrastus in the 4th century BC, divided fruits by season, flavour, origin, and use. Only at a time when how to grow fruit was more important than what fruit to grow could one ignore the overlappings and contradictions inherent in this unsatisfactory appeal to, respectively, the gardener, the diner, the philosopher, and the cook.

The earliest surviving pomological writings, Greek, Roman, and Chinese, give only slender details of the fruits themselves. Although it has always been tempting, particularly to French pomologists, to identify classical fruits with modern survivals, such exercises, like the reconstruction of Greek music, are more or less imaginative guesswork. Those few early pomologies that neglect cultivation in favour of connoisseurship of the fruits are hardly more satisfying for the systematist: the 12th-century Chinese treatises on the lichi (LYCHEE), for example, are essentially lichi club handbooks, rich in metaphor and indulging in the typical oriental conceit of enumerating pleasures.

Popular names, evocative of appearance, furnish in themselves a crude system of classification. To the Talentiaion pear of Theophrastus, so called from its resemblance to the metal weights of the balance, add the gourd-shaped Calebasse, the quoin-shaped or wedgelike Quining, the nippled Téton, the barrel-shaped Tonneau, the Sugarloaf pippin, the many egg plums and pears, the bagpipe-shaped Musette, the spindlelike Fusée, the Sheep's Nose apple, the

Bishop's Thumb, and the many Ladies' Finger fruits.

As these names indicate, shape is a more significant element in folk-pomology than colour, which to this day, in many minds, still runs to the old extremes of black and white with no shade in between. The blue and white peas of the pre-Mendelian experimentalists are the green and yellow of today, each colour having shifted by a degree. Yellow apples, cherries, and peaches as well as green figs are often referred to as 'white', while purple grapes or figs and deep red apples are said to be 'black'.

Not only was colour poorly conveyed in words; it was difficult to represent on paper, and before the 19th century was seldom adequately reproduced except in original paintings of private collections. The uncoloured wood engravings of the great herbals of the Renaissance attempted a rough grouping by species and then by form. The rude outlines of Costards, Pearmains, Bergamots, Calvilles, and Reinettes appear mingled in among the wild flowers, but varieties were few, for as both Clusius and Gerard explained, local differences might keep a botanist uselessly occupied until the end of his days. Every province had its distinctive varieties, but as these were seldom found at any distance from their original home, they were of purely local interest and beneath the notice of the botanist, who attempted instead the universal and eternal with his modern identifications of the classical flora of Dioscorides and Theophrastus. In pomology any similar effort was hampered by the vague and conflicting descriptions of the ancient authorities and their annoying custom of merely listing names, seemingly less as an attempt at a pomology than to serve as a social register, for many Roman heroes and patrician families proudly bore the names of fruits or vegetables, or bestowed their own on them.

The inconveniences to the systematist of local variation were eventually overcome in the 17th century by those vast collections of fruits, symbolic (like a royal bride) of good diplomatic connections, which were the pomological equivalent of (and often an adjunct to) the virtuoso's cabinet of curiosities. Fruits came to have a separate existence as natural artefacts, museum or market specimens which were only incidentally once attached to a tree. A 17th-century Italian treatise, G. F. Angelita's *I Pomi d'Oro* (1607), is evidence of this way of thinking: a modern work of this title would be devoted to the tomato, but the book is about figs, melons, and seashells.

The mycologist P. A. Micheli (1679–1737) catalogued the 695 fruits to appear in the course of a year on the table of Cosimo III, Grand Duke of Tuscany. Some of the nuts survived to be studied by Antonio Targioni-Tozzetti, who observed in 1850 that Micheli's distinctions 'were overly refined and often taken from accidental forms', exactly what one would expect of a pomologist in the curio-laden atmosphere of the Tuscan court, where individuals, both vegetable and human, were often elevated into types.

Some improvement in classification was made at the later court of Frederick the Great at Potsdam, where the royal architect H. L. Manger (1728–90) devised the first comprehensive arrangement of apples and pears. His first, and appropriately Vitruvian, division was by form, but finding this inadequate, Manger added rather less satisfactory subdivisions based on flavour, introducing such subjective categories as the disagreeably sweet or the pleasantly sour. Later systems made considerable improvements on Manger's scheme but none could altogether avoid incorporating that element of taste and personal choice so often expressed in the naming of fruits as Favourites, Pleasants, Nonpareils, or Seek-no-furthers, but so seldom leading to a consensus.

The development of systematic botany between the time of Linnaeus and Darwin is paralleled in pomology. The collection, description, and cataloguing of the natural world produced several regional pomonas to accompany the national floras and faunas of the late 18th century: Kraft's *Pomona Austriacae* (1787–96), Gallesio's *Pomona Italiana* (1817–39), and van Noort's *Pomologia Batava* (1830). The classification schemes for fruit, for all their crudity, had something of the Linnaean spirit, and in fact, when he dealt with edible plants, Linnaeus himself was inclined to think like a cook or kitchen gardener, distinguishing his alliums, for instance, according to their onion scent, just as Hieronymus Bock, two centuries before, had grouped mustards and cresses by the pungent flavour of their seeds.

Certain 19th-century pomologists, among them C. F. Willermoz, editor of *Pomologie de la France* (1863–73), and the Belgian botanist and politician B. C. Du Mortier (1796–1878), attempted to fashion a natural system of sorts from the classic French names already borne by the fruits, treating Beurré, Bergamot, Doyenné, etc. as general terms indicative of form, to which Bosc, Espéren, or du Comice could be added as epithets. Such terms, however, had been variously interpreted over a period of several hundred years; some, undoubtedly, such as the Reinette or Russet apple, referred to probable natural divisions within the species, but many names were too imprecise or insignificant to be useful. In view of this confusion in nomenclature, a bold elimination of all general terms was undeniably attractive, although it would leave pomology a tangled web of unrelated varieties. Such was already the state of popular pomology in N. America, where the names of foreign fruits, like the unpronounceable surnames of immigrants, were ruthlessly truncated upon arrival. The American Pomological Society gave official sanction to the tendency, pruning fruit names by legislation, although with a sparing hand. When, however, Joseph Decaisne, director of what is now the Jardin des Plantes in Paris, reduced the names of pears to single epithets in the *Jardin fruitier du Muséum*, his countrymen were outraged, and few forgave him his excision of the evocative Beurré.

The court, as a centre of pomological activity, did not survive the French Revolution—or should one say the Industrial (a word of sinister meaning in fruit-growing)? Mayer's *Pomona Franconia* (1776–1801) was the last of the court-inspired pomologies. The associations formed by wealthy amateurs in the early 19th century provided a sort of substitute—the collection of the Horticultural Society (precursor of the Royal Horticultural Society) at Chiswick formed the basis of Robert Thompson's succinct *Catalogue of Fruits* (1826), a landmark in the study of synonymy—but increasingly it was the nurseryman who took on the role of the grand duke or prince bishop. Already, for the last half of the 18th century, the nursery catalogue of the monastery of the Chartreux in Paris had served as the amateur's guide to varieties. Their collection furnished the basis not only of Duhamel de Monceau's *Traité des arbres fruitiers* (1768, several times reprinted and revised) but, after the suppression of the monastery during the Revolution and last-minute rescue of the trees, of Decaisne's official nine-volume *Jardin fruitier du Muséum* (1858–75).

Nursery stock formed the basis of many of the influential pomologies of the century, among them A. J. Downing's *Fruits and Fruit Trees of America* (1845), the standard American manual of the time, greatly revised and expanded in later editions by his nurseryman brother Charles, the greater pomologist of the two, and André Leroy's six-volume *Dictionnaire de pomologie* (1867–79), the most comprehensive French pomology ever published. The later studies of E. A. Bunyard, distilled into such deceptively insubstantial books as *A Handbook of Hardy Fruits* (1920–5) and the discursive *Anatomy of Dessert* (1929), deserve to be mentioned here, for he too was a nurseryman, whose antiquarian learning and Italian tastes, so like those of his friend Norman Douglas, allowed him to endure uncorrupted the progressive 'industrialization' of fruit-growing in this century. The traditional commercial inclination to dupe the ignorant purchaser with old varieties under a new name was altogether foreign to these scholarly nurserymen; if they had a fault it was the vainglory of displaying for the delectation of the fastidious enthusiast an absurdly large selection of fruits that might better have been amalgamated. Intoxicated by sheer number, they made but slight and half-hearted attempts at the essential task of winnowing.

With the rise of extensive commercial production a very different motive, state assistance to the orchardist, led to the formation of large government collections in the late 19th and early 20th century. The magnificent series of *Fruits of New York*, of which seven volumes were produced by S. A. Beach and U. P. Hedrick between 1905 and 1925, lavishly subsidized by that great fruit-growing state in its days of prosperity, are the finest pomologies that have yet appeared in the USA. Muriel Smith has recently published a comprehensive *National Apple Register* (1971), based on the collections of the (British) National Fruit Trials at Brogdale. And it seems to be a point of pride for a socialist republic to produce a national pomology to symbolize the transition of its natural resources from private to public ownership; the most recent and elaborate of these is the seven-volume Romanian *Pomologia Republicii Populare Romine*.

Modern state pomology, oriented towards the grower rather than the consumer, and tending to consider the orchard first, then the tree, the crop and finally the quality of the individual fruit, has turned pomology in new directions. Some aspects may be considered virtues. The old rules of the exhibition room, which allotted prizes to half a dozen exceptional specimens gathered from a tree which might have borne nothing else, admittedly provided a poor model for descriptive pomology. The productivity, vigour, health, habit, and hardiness of the tree are now more fully noted: no longer does mere quality dominate in the evaluation of a fruit. What little poetry once existed in picking fruit has largely disappeared and, with the glory of harvest-time thus somewhat diminished, the fruit tree can be contemplated the more readily in all its seasons. Such aspects of the tree as the flowers of spring or the dying colour of the leaves were once apt to be appreciated, when they were noticed at all, only as pleasing features unconnected with the fruit; not until this century was their value as specific characters fully recognized.

There are also drawbacks to this sort of pomological thought: it has no place for such subjective, elusive, and unquantifiable qualities as flavour. Moreover, what can be grown for the greatest profit commercially is not always, indeed is not usually, of the highest quality, and as a result the official study of existing fruits and the commercial breeding of new varieties often gives little consideration or satisfaction to the lover of fine fruit.   IJ

POMPANO *Trachinotus carolinus*, one of the finest fish in the large carangid family (see JACK), is a fish of the W. Atlantic, with a range from Brazil up to Massachusetts. Its name seems to be derived from the Spanish word *pámpana*, meaning vine leaf. (In SE Asia the name appears as *pampano* and is applied to the beautiful *T. blochii*, golden in colour.)

The pompano has a maximum length of only 45 cm (18"), but its body is deep and narrow, and its appearance aristocratic. Its colour, blue-green above, shading to silver below, is typical of its family. It is caught in abundance off the Gulf coast of Florida.

Related species found in the Caribbean area are the larger (occasionally much larger, even over 1 m/40") *T. falcatus*, known under the English name 'permit', and the somewhat smaller *T. goodei*.

The 'round pompano', *T. ovatus*, is found in the E. Atlantic and the Mediterranean.

The flesh of all these fish is firm and compact; and their shape and size facilitate taking good fillets.

POND APPLE *Annona glabra*, a tree which grows wild in the American tropics, especially the W. Indies and S. Florida, and also in parts of W. Africa, bears yellow fruits

which smell like oranges but have little flavour. These are edible when fully ripe and can be made into jelly, but Morton (1987) considers them merely a 'survival food'. The names 'custard apple' and 'alligator apple' are sometimes used in the USA and the W. Indies respectively.

PONT L'ÉVÊQUE one of the most notable French soft cheeses, is named after the town in Normandy around which it is made. It is a mould-ripened, whole milk cheese. Unlike Brie and Camembert, its two rivals, it is not imitated outside France.

The milk from which Pont l'Évêque is made should ideally be absolutely fresh and still warm from the cow. It is renneted at a rather higher temperature than that for a typical French soft cheese, sometimes as high as 35 °C (95 °F). The curd is drained on a straw mat before being packed into 10 cm (4") square moulds. When firm, the cheeses are removed, salted, and dried standing on edge; they have to be turned frequently to avoid sagging.

The cheeses become naturally infected with a mould endemic in the curing room. This is not the usual *Penicillium* type, but *Monilia candida*, possibly together with other organisms. Occasional washing with brine stops the mould growing too much. The result is a crust of a distinctive yellow-brown colour. Full ripening takes up to six weeks.

PONYFISH of the family Leiognathidae, are small fish of the Indo-Pacific which often shoal in estuaries and enter fresh water. In life they are coated with slime and on death exude mucus, unattractive characteristics which have earned them the names of 'slimy' or 'soapy' in S. Africa. A more attractive alternative name, 'silver-belly', is self-explanatory.

Ponyfish have a very protractile mouth, a phenomenon which can be demonstrated by squeezing the head, when the mouth will shoot forward. For this reason they are also called 'slipmouth'.

Two of the most common species are *Leiognathus splendens*, regarded in Thailand as the best of the family and probably the largest (maximum length 20 cm/8"), and *L. equulus*. In some areas ponyfish are very abundant; for example, in the Gulf of Thailand they have accounted for about 15% of the trawl catch.

Ponyfish can be bought either fresh or salted and dried in the markets. They can be fried, or used in fish soup. Despite their small size, they are widely used as food, but sometimes for ducks rather than humans, or in the production of fish meal.

POORI an Indian bread prepared in a similar way to CHAPATI, but deep fried in such a way that the pooris puff up.

Pooris are made with a variety of flours depending on the type of poori with a small addition of oil or GHEE and enough warm water to make a stiff dough which is then kneaded. The dough is then usually divided up into balls which are then flattened and rolled out into rounds. The frying is done in a utensil called *karhai*, using smoking hot oil or ghee.

Some pooris are stuffed, with various vegetables and spices. For these the dough is rolled out, the filling placed in the centre, and the edges folded up to enclose it completely. The dough is then carefully rolled out again before being fried.

The numerous varieties of poori include:

- *masala poori*, poori stuffed with spices and/or vegetables such as potato;
- *kadak poori*, a poori made with mixed wholemeal and besan flour and spiced with turmeric and chilli powder;
- *puran poori*, stuffed with sweetened lentils and flavoured with cardamom and saffron;
- *bhel poori*, thin, crisp-fried rounds of dough mixed with puffed rice, fried lentils, and chopped onions.

Madhur Jaffrey (1985) gives a description of *bhel poori* as follows:

But there is one equalizer in Bombay to which everyone succumbs—Parsi millionaires, movie stars and taxi drivers alike—and that is bhel-poori. Bhel-poori is a snack. The place to have it is Chowpatty Beach, the time sundown, when most of Bombay like to promenade by the sea to 'eat the air'.

A hissing hurricane lamp lights up the bhel-poori vendor's cart. All the ingredients for the snack are neatly laid out in an orderly fashion so his fingers can move with dizzying speed. Some puffed rice is put into a bowl. Then, some wheat-flour crisps are crumbled over it. Generous sprinklings of chopped onion and chopped boiled potato follow. The vendor cups the bowl in both hands and tosses its contents. Two chutneys are now spooned in: a tart, hot green one made with fresh green coriander and green chillies, and a thick sweet-and-sour one made with tamarind and dates. Some sev, fine, squiggly vermicelli made out of chickpea flour, are thrown in as well, followed by more of the two chutneys. The bowl is given a final toss and emptied into the saucers of waiting customers. Hot, sweet-and-sour and crunchy, the bhel-poori is now ready to be gobbled up.

The same author adds that 'it takes years of practice to make really fine, soft pooris. It is said in Benares that if twenty five pooris were stacked on a plate and a coin dropped on the lot, the sound of the coin hitting the plate should be heard with clarity.'

Gujjia is another type of poori which is crescent shaped and filled with a sweet stuffing of milk fudge, cream of wheat, coconut, and nuts. See also KACHORI.   HS

POOR KNIGHTS a late 17th and early 18th century English name for a rich dish of fried bread, similar to French PAIN PERDU. John Nott (1726) directs the cook to cut penny loaves into round slices, dip them in cream or water, and then in a mixture of eggs, cream, sugar, and nutmeg. The bread was fried in butter, with the rest of the egg mixture poured onto it, and served with butter, sugar, and rosewater. Less rich recipes called for the bread to be soaked in milk or wine, dipped in egg yolk, and served with jam or sugar and cinnamon.

The origin of the curious name, sometimes expanded to 'poor knights of Windsor' is a puzzle, although the Danish name *arme riddere* and the German *arme Ritter* may be earlier and may provide the explanation. After the 1730s, English cooks reverted to the name pain perdu.

POPCORN a snack made by roasting dried MAIZE kernels of a particular variety in a closed pan with a little fat. The starch in the maize swells as it cooks, and 'pops' audibly as it bursts the outer skin of the kernels. The resulting light, crunchy morsels are often enhanced by coating with TOFFEE or BUTTERSCOTCH; or eaten with salt. Popcorn is a popular street (and cinema) food in N. America.

Betty Fussell (1992) talks eloquently about the place of popcorn in the affection of N. Americans.

Popcorn is a truly indigenous fast finger-food that links all ages, places, races, classes and kinds in the continuing circus of American life. Popcorn is the great equalizer, which turns itself inside out to attest to our faith that colour is only skin deep and class superfluous.

The 'poppability' of maize kernels depends on the presence of a high proportion of a particular starch in the kernel, and on the moisture content. Particular cultivars of maize are grown especially for popping.

Archaeologists working in New Mexico uncovered quantities of corn cobs and kernels, including some (dating from early in the 1st millennium BC) that were popped. An experiment showed that the popping capacity of corn lasts well: some of the unpopped kernels, placed in hot oil, proved still capable of popping.

Popped or parched corn was noted by early European observers in many parts of N. America. Some tribes pounded it into meal to provide a lightweight portable food, a habit noted by Benjamin Franklin. The commercial history of popcorn begins in Chicago in the late 19th century, when Charles C. Cretors developed a machine for popping corn in large quantities.
READING: Smith (1997).

POPOVER an American favourite for breakfast and to accompany meat dishes, closely resembles a small YORKSHIRE PUDDING and is made with a similar BATTER (similar also to that used for PANCAKES). Popovers are baked in patty tins or custard cups in a hot oven. They earn their name (which first appeared in print in 1876) by a tendency to swell over the sides of the tins or cups while they are being baked.

POPPADOM (sometimes papadam, papadum) and **PAPAD**, Indian circular thin crispbreads often referred to by Indian writers as wafers (in the case of papads 'lentil wafers'). Poppadoms are usually made of BESAN FLOUR (chickpea flour). Both poppadom and papad, however, are sometimes made with tapioca, rice, or potato flour. In any case, they are fried in oil until crisp.

Some types are highly spiced. In the north they tend to be seasoned with 'hot' spices such as AJOWAN, pepper, and dried chilli flakes to contrast with the more mildly seasoned food which they accompany. The reverse applies in S. India, where a plainer wafer is preferred, to complement the highly spiced food of that region.

Poppadoms are particularly associated with the Malabar Coast in S. India. This fits in with what Ayto (1993) says: 'The word comes from Tamil *pappatam*, which is probably a blend of *parappu*, "lentil" and *atam*, "something cooked, cake".' *Hobson-Jobson* (1903; Yule and Burnell, 1979) had reached the same conclusion, but embellished it with additional etymological titbits, including the use of 'popper-cake' in Bombay and an interesting early (1820) quotation about 'papadoms'.

Poppadoms are, clearly, closely related to papads (or papar or appalam); but whether the relationship amounts to identity (with the names varying according to the region or language) or there are distinct differences between the two is unclear.

Those who make the distinction say that papads are usually larger than poppadoms (about 22 cm/9" in diameter, whereas poppadoms are usually about 8 cm/3" in diameter). Also, papads contain not much baking soda and a generous amount of salt, whereas poppadoms contain more soda and just a little salt. (The characteristic flavour of the poppadom is provided by the baking soda which also gives it its light, porous texture.) Again, papads are rolled out paper thin whereas poppadoms are rolled out a little thicker and puff up more.

How and when these wafers are eaten in India varies from region to region but generally speaking they are served with nearly all vegetarian meals at the end of the meal. In the West it has become common practice in Indian restaurants to serve poppadoms as a snack to nibble on before the meal is served.

POPPY the flower of various plants of the genus *Papaver*, of which *P. somniferum* ssp *somniferum* is notorious as a source of opium. The same species provides edible leaves and pleasantly flavoured seeds which, when mature, are not narcotic and are pressed to make a salad or cooking oil. The young leaves are also edible. The common poppy, *P. rhoeas*, is also grown for oil.

The opium poppy is related to a wild poppy, *P. somniferum* ssp *setigerum*, a native of the E. Mediterranean. The Greeks of classical times grew it both for its seed and for opium, which they used medicinally as a painkiller and sleeping draught. Cultivation spread eastwards to Arabia, Persia, and India, eventually reaching China in the mid-16th century. Opium is a latex exuded from small cuts made in the unripe seed capsules. It is collected when it hardens. It may then be refined to make morphine and heroin. A small amount is used legally to make these drugs for medicinal use.

When the poppyseed ripens, the narcotic substances change to harmless forms. The blue-grey seed of the cultivar Hungarian Blue-Seeded is the one most commonly used in Europe, especially in baked goods (such as the Silesian speciality *Mohntorte*—see TORTE AND KUCHEN) and they are commonly sprinkled on top of breads, biscuits, and cakes in Germany, E. Europe, and countries of C. Asia. Poppyseeds are also used as a flavouring in some egg, potato, and pasta dishes.

Indian poppyseed (usually of the cultivar White Persian) is much smaller and off-white, and serves to thicken sauces and curries. Roasted poppyseed, which has a nutty flavour, is often used in spice mixtures.

Poppyseed oil, made in Europe and India, is highly esteemed, especially in France.

PORBEAGLE or porbeagle shark, *Lamna nasus*, ranges in the E. Atlantic from the Murman coast south to Africa and (less frequently) the Mediterranean. On the American side of the Atlantic, where it is also known as the mackerel shark, it can be found from the Gulf of St Lawrence down to S. Carolina.

The maximum length of this shark is 3 m (120"). The flesh is of high quality and is particularly esteemed in Germany, where much of the European catch ends up. It is also appreciated in Galicia. There is little demand for it in N. America, and it is not rated highly by sport fishermen since its resistance is feeble (although the British naturalist Couch reported one surprising incident, when a porbeagle which had been caught leaped at the fisherman and succeeded in tearing his clothes). Sport fishermen have more interest in a close relation *Isurus oxyrhincus*, the mako, or sharp-nosed mackerel shark, a vigorous opponent and one whose flesh is comparable with that of the porbeagle.

Smoked porbeagle emerged in the latter part of the 20th century as a new delicacy.

PORCUPINE the name used of several species of animal, belonging to two families (Erethizontidae for New World porcupines, and Hystricidae for those of the Old World) and having in common the long quills (spines) which constitute their protection. In this they resemble the HEDGEHOG, but are not closely related.

The common or crested porcupine, *Hystrix crestata*, of the Old World is the largest, and may weigh 27 kg (60 lb). There are few records of its being eaten, save by gypsies and rural people who have nothing better, and insofar as one can establish anything about methods of preparing and cooking these seem to be as for the hedgehog. For the Canadian porcupine, *Erethizon dorsatum*, Faith Medlin (1975) has collected a number of conflicting pieces of advice about which bits to cook and how to do the cooking. Leipoldt (1976), for his part, is in no doubt at all on these points. He reproduces from an early manuscript directions for cooking porcupine crackling, which is to be sent to table with plenty of rice and lemons cut in halves. 'This out-of-the-way dish would have delighted Elia, for its sapid crispness far exceeds that of ordinary pork crackling.'

PORGY a general name applied in the USA to various species of fish in the family Sparidae, especially *Stenotomus chrysops*. This is a fish with a brownish back, silvery lower down, which has a maximum length of 45 cm (18").

The Narragansett Indians called it *mishcuppauog*, *pauog* being their name for fertilizer. This was shortened by the early settlers in New England to scuppaug; and afterwards to scup, a better name than porgy (or paugy, as it used to be spelled at New York), and one still in use as a common name. Another common name is northern porgy, since the range of this species is from Cape Cod southwards as far as the Carolinas only, below which *S. aculeatus*, the southern porgy, takes over.

The porgy is a fine fish with firm and flaky flesh.

There are other species, all found in the region of the south-eastern coasts of the USA and the Caribbean, to which the name may be applied. These include:

- *Calamus bajonado*, the jolthead porgy, a species which is also found off the Pacific coasts of C. America. Maximum length 65 cm (26"), coloration silvery with blue and violet tinges and sometimes brown blotches or bands.
- *C. nodosus*, the knobbed or Key West porgy, one the best in the group, with knobbly protrusions in front of its eyes above bright blue and yellow speckled cheeks. Maximum length 20 cm (8"), general coloration silvery blue.
- *C. leucosteus*, the whitebone or chocolate porgy, the most commonly caught member of its genus; appreciated as food, especially in the W. Indies. Maximum length 45 cm (18"), coloration silvery with brown markings.
- *Pagrus pagrus*, the red porgy, a species of the E. Atlantic and Mediterranean which, because its eggs manage to drift right across the Atlantic before hatching, occurs also in the W. Atlantic; see SEA BREAM.

PORK the fresh meat of the domestic PIG, *Sus scrofa*. The ease and economy with which pigs are reared has made pork an exceptionally important meat around the world, except amongst Jewish and Muslim communities who regard it as unclean. All of a pig can be utilized (indeed, the French have promoted the use of the entire pig carcass to a fine art, that of CHARCUTERIE), and the meat is preserved very effectively by traditional methods based on salting, smoking, and curing to produce hams, bacon, and other products which are useful both as meat and as flavourings.

There is a wealth of dishes for both fresh and cured pork. Fresh pork alone is considered here. For the meat of young pigs see SUCKING PIGS.

Pork was relished in classical times. Dalby (1996) draws attention to the highly differentiated Greek vocabulary for denoting pigs of varying ages and sizes, and observes that sucking pigs were a delicacy; the Greek cooks then leapfrogged two sizes up to 'substantial young pigs'. The same may well have applied in Rome; the Romans certainly liked sucking pig.

Medieval English pork recipes included PIES, BRAWN, and little RISSOLES. In the 17th and 18th centuries such recipes as are given for fresh pork imply sucking pigs or small pigs and give instructions for collaring and sousing, or baking in a highly spiced pie. Only in the 19th century do instructions for

plain grilled cutlets or chops become common.

Porkers, pigs intended to be eaten as fresh meat, are nowadays killed before the age of six months, and at a lower body weight than pigs used for bacon. Their lean meat varies from a light pink to almost white, depending on cut and breed, and, because the animal is young, is tender and mildly flavoured.

Most cuisines have their own fresh pork dishes which depend on the use of aromatic, acid, or fruity flavourings or accompaniments. Cream is sometimes used in sauces for lean fillet or chops, whilst fattier pieces are added to heavy dishes of pulses or preserved cabbage, adding richness and flavour. Sweet-sour flavour combinations are typical of some cuisines, notably those of C. Europe and China. Pork can also be marinated for several days in wine, vinegar, and herbs in imitation of wild boar, a method used across much of C. and S. Europe.

Joints of pork cooked by roasting or braising are popular as cold dishes in many countries. The stock which accumulates during cooking jellies when cold and is served chopped as a garnish. It is also interesting to note the presence of a small but widespread group of dishes using combinations of pork and seafood, especially clams and shrimp.

In Britain, roasting is favoured for large pieces and grilling for small ones. Most cuts are suitable for roasting, although those from the forequarters contain much fat and some connective tissue. Despite the fat content of the joints, the lean has a tendency to dryness, and a different strategy is required to that used for beef and lamb. Longer, gentler heat ensures thorough cooking, while sauces and stuffings help to preserve moisture. In Britain, the crackling is liked and usually left on roasting joints. It is a rare instance of the skin of a land animal being eaten. Herbs, typically sage and onion, are used to make stuffing for roast pork, and fruit is served with it in the form of apple sauce.

In Germany and E. Europe, caraway is a favourite aromatic for pork. Paprika, peppers, and onions are much used in SE Europe. Fresh red or white cabbage, sauerkraut, pulses, potatoes, or dumplings are common accompaniments.

In the French kitchen, favoured aromatics are garlic, rosemary, and juniper berries; some regional dishes combine pork with apples or prunes. Fennel, rosemary, marjoram, garlic, and juniper berries are variously favoured aromatics in Italian pork cookery. Distinctive dishes such as loin of pork cooked in milk, which reduces to provide a grainy sauce, appear in Italian and Spanish cooking. Generally, sweet peppers, paprika, and garlic are favourite flavourings for pork in Spain and Portugal.

American cookery was heavily influenced by English and German practices. Pork and beans, a traditional Saturday meal of New England, declined in popularity during the mid-19th century but gained a new identity when someone thought of canning it, to give the ancestor of modern baked beans. Molasses is used as a flavouring in this dish; it was also important as a condiment for pork in general. Sweet ingredients are characteristic of American pork cookery, including fruits or fruit juices such as apple, cranberry, peach, and pineapple which are used as sauces and garnishes.

A richer fusion of Old and New World ingredients has evolved in S. America. Pork is seasoned with Old World ingredients such as coriander, garlic, oregano, cumin, cinnamon, and cloves in dishes which also contain New World beans, hot peppers, and EPAZOTE. Both sweet peppers and chillies in all their forms are important in Latin American pork cookery, and plantains and avocado are sometimes incorporated. ANNATTO, as a spice or as oil expressed from it, is also used. Sweetness is provided by oranges, plums, or dried fruits, sweet potatoes, corn kernels, or pineapple; sharpness by vinegar or lime juice. Pork is used as filling for TAMALES, or topping for TORTILLAS, and larger pieces are wrapped in banana leaves for baking. 'Jerked' pork, in the Caribbean, indicates a whole pig smeared with spices and cooked over a slow fire on a grill made from newly cut allspice wood, another method thought to derive from Amerindian culture.

Although pork is by far the most important meat in China, it is little used in Japan. In SE Asia generally it is popular except in Muslim areas, such as much of Indonesia. In the Philippines, Spanish influence is highly evident; *lechon* (whole roast pig) is served on all special occasions, and ADOBO, a stew flavoured with vinegar and garlic, is often made with pork.

PRECAUTIONARY NOTE

Pork must always be well cooked since pigs may suffer infestation by parasites, notably *Trichinella spiralis*, a species of worm which develops cysts in the flesh of infected animals. If pork is inadequately cooked, the cysts remain viable and pass into humans. A serious illness, trichinosis, may then result. Properly cured raw pork products, such as *prosciutto de Parma*, are safe because the organism is killed by the curing process.

See also: ANDOUILLE; BACON; BLOOD SAUSAGES; BRAWN; CAUL; CHARCUTERIE; CHITTERLINGS; COLLOP; COPPA; CRACKLING, CULATELLO; EARS; FEET; HAM; HEAD; LACHSSCHINKEN; LARD; LARDING; LUNGS; OFFAL; PÂTÉ; PIG; PORK PIE; RILLETTES; SALT PORK; SAUSAGES; SMOKING FOODS; SUCKING PIGS; WILD BOAR.

PORK PIE The British pork pie and its relative, the veal and ham pie, are survivals of the medieval tradition of raised pies, and have changed surprisingly little. This particular pie, simply known as 'pork pie', is of a form distinct from other pies which merely happen to be made with pork. The filling is of fresh pork without other major ingredients, seasoned with salt, pepper, and a small quantity of herbs, especially sage.

At Melton Mowbray in Leicestershire, long famous for its pork pies, anchovy essence was added not only for its flavour but because it was thought to give the meat an attractive pink colour, while pies from other districts were brownish or greyish. In modern pies, which are always pink, the colour is achieved by the use of chemicals.

The case is made from a hot water paste of flour, lard, and boiling salted water, well kneaded to give it strength. A small hole is left in the centre of the lid. Traditionally there was a decorative rosette around the hole. Sometimes hinged metal corsets are used to stop the case of the pie from sagging during baking.

Present-day pies are almost always supported, so that they have sheer vertical sides, whereas those of former times used to bulge slightly. The support is removed towards the end of the baking to allow the pastry to brown. Once the pie is baked, and while still hot, rich stock made from trimmings is poured in through the hole by means of a funnel. When the pie cools the stock sets into a protective jelly.

Pork pies are circular when small or medium sized, and are also made as long, rectangular 'gala pies'—for a gala or miners' festival. Large pies used to contain eggs and sometimes also pickled walnuts; but now eggs are more usual in veal and ham pies, and walnuts are never used.

PORRIDGE has two meanings. One is a general descriptive term for any cooked mush of cereal, pulses, or vegetables. Many of these have their own specific names, such as FRUMENTY, made from WHEAT; TSAMPA, made from BARLEY; POLENTA, made from MAIZE; CONGEE, from RICE. These examples fit the term porridge quite naturally, but when it comes to a vegetable 'porridge' (or anything with meat in it, like HALEEM) many people would hesitate to use the term. Nevertheless, there is a clear relationship with such items as DAL, Indian spiced pulse dishes; Ugandan *matoke*, based on PLANTAINS; and POI, made from TARO. If the word is used in this way, the main ingredient is usually cited.

More specifically, the usual meaning of porridge in Britain is a hot mixture of oatmeal (see OATS) cooked slowly with water and salt (or, nowadays, made with 'quick porridge oats'). Marian McNeill (1929) gave 'The One And Only Method' for making porridge, recommending the cook to be 'very particular about the quality of the oatmeal. Midlothian oats are reputed to be unsurpassed, but the small Highland oats are very sweet.' Her instructions are to bring the water to the boil, and then add coarse oatmeal 'in a steady rain from the left hand, stirring it briskly the while with the right, sunwise, or with the righthand turn for luck—and convenience'. A special stick, known as a spurtle, or theevil, is used to stir. Once the porridge has returned to the boil, it should be allowed to cook slowly for 20–30 minutes. During cooking, the starch in the oats gelatinizes, resulting in soft but distinct grains in a thick, creamy textured mixture.

Having for long been a staple food in Scotland, porridge had many dialect names, such as *brochan* in the Highlands, and was subject to regional variations, e.g. the use of buttermilk or whey instead of water. It might also be poured into a mould (for instance, a drawer in the sideboard), and allowed to set, then sliced to take as rations when working distant from home during the day. Older folk would refer to it in the third person plural, as 'they' or 'them', and people stood to eat it, holding their bowls in their hands. Horn spoons were preferred for taking up the porridge, because they did not become as hot as metal ones. Each spoonful would be dipped in a cup of cold milk, cream, or buttermilk.

Quotations recorded by Marian McNeill (1929) suggest that the Scots did sometimes sweeten porridge, but mostly for children. Generally, however, the Scots think that only salt and milk or cream should be allowed as accompaniments to porridge, and it is the English who see sugar or another sweetener as appropriate additions. In Yorkshire, according to Peter Brears (1987), 'wherever possible the porridge would . . . be sweetened with a generous helping of treacle'.

Porridge is a descendant of POTTAGE, a thoroughly English institution, and in the past had some importance in the diet of the English labouring classes, for example the weavers who, in Leeds in the 18th century, called it 'water pudding' and ate it for both breakfast and their evening meal. But the English have forgotten all this and, being accustomed to buying porridge oats in cartons which bear a picture of a kilted Scotsman, those of them who take porridge for breakfast perceive it as Scottish in origin.

See also BROSE; CROWDIE; FLUMMERY; GRUEL; HASTY PUDDING; SOWANS.

PORTABLE SOUP a product which achieved some prominence in 18th-century English cookery books, was a precursor (and a relatively sophisticated and refined one) of 19th-century MEAT EXTRACTS and 20th-century stock cubes. Bradley (1736) explained in his agreeable prose the benefits of the product, describing it as:

[a] curious Preparation for the use of Gentlemen that travel; the use of which I esteem to be of extraordinary Service to such as travel in wild and open Countries, where few or no Provisions are to be met with; and it will be of no less Benefit to such Families as have not immediate Recourse to Markets, for the Readiness of it for making of Soups, or its Use where Gravey is required; and particularly to those that travel, the lightness of its Carriage, the small room it takes up, and the easy way of putting it in use, renders it extremely serviceable. This is what one may call Veal-Glue.

It was made by taking a lot of meat and boiling it lengthily, then reducing the liquid to a syrupy consistency, after which it would dry quite hard and keep well until the time came to reconstitute it with boiling water. Aromatics or other flavourings could be used in boiling the meat or added at the reconstitution stage.

Hannah Glasse (1747) gave two recipes, one lifted from an earlier work (as was her wont). Both state that a piece of the 'Glew' the size of a walnut is enough for a pint of water. The second recipe, listing the various dishes and ways in which it can be used, could be translated without great difficulty into 'tips on use' to be printed on a modern stock cube or 'instant soup' packet.

Portable soup in its original form survived, at least in recipe books, into the 19th century. How many travellers actually carried it around in their pockets or in little tin boxes, as recommended, is a question which seems unlikely ever to receive a satisfactory answer.
READING: Jan Longone (1985).

PORT SALUT a French cheese which had its origin, around 1815, in a monastery of Trappist monks at the abbey of Notre Dame de Port du Salut, in Mayenne. During the 19th century the reputation of this cheese spread, and production increased very considerably. The name was registered in 1874, but imitators multiplied. Since 1959, when the monks sold the name, it has been the property of a large commercial concern.

A Port Salut cheese, made from whole or very slightly skimmed milk, is 25 cm (10") in diameter and almost 5 cm (2") thick, weighing just over 2 kg (5 lb). It has a semi-soft but elastic texture, a natural orange rind, and a 50% fat content.

During ripening, which takes six to eight weeks, yeasts, moulds, and bacteria colonize the surface to give the combination of a pungent smell and a rather mild taste which is typical of a surface-ripened cheese.

Cheese made to the same specifications in other parts of France is called **Saint-Paulin.** This is often considered as a variety in its own right, but it is really the same as Port Salut. See also TRAPPIST CHEESE.

PORTUGAL The history of food and cookery in Portugal, as in neighbouring SPAIN, was successively influenced by being in the Roman Empire for seven centuries; by the Arab invasion and continuing presence in early medieval times; by having a leading role in the voyages of the early European explorers in pursuit of spices; to some extent by Portuguese colonization of parts of Africa and the orient; and certainly by the COLUMBIAN EXCHANGE which followed the 'discovery' of the Americas and which led to Portugal having important possessions there, notably Brazil.

Having Spain as a neighbour, and a more powerful one, also had its effect, and has even raised the question whether the Portuguese have their own cuisine or possess only a derived version of Spanish cuisine. In this connection, a Portuguese writer suggested that the earliest printed Portuguese cookery book, by Domingos Rodrigues (1680), was merely a copy of an earlier Spanish work, the *Arte de cocina* by Francisco Martinez Montiño (1611 and often reprinted). Remarkably, this claim was not challenged until an essay of which Eulalia Pensado (1992) was senior author showed conclusively that there was no basis for the allegation. The first Portuguese cookery book and Portugal's culinary heritage thus had their proper glory restored, courtesy of a Spanish historian.

In fact, there is one important Portuguese culinary text from an earlier period, a manuscript which survives at Naples and contains the recipes of the Infanta Dona Maria, taken by her to Italy in 1565, the year of her marriage to an Italian duke. These recipes have a more medieval flavour than those in the book by Rodrigues, but the two collections can be seen to be drawing on a common Portuguese tradition, which in turn can be seen to be different from the Spanish tradition reflected in the book by Montiño.

Although one can refer to 'a common Portuguese tradition', it is necessary to add that the topography of Portugal is such that the cuisine of Portugal is fragmented to an unusual degree. The contrast between coastal and inland areas is marked, and so are the differences between various coastal communities (which did not in the distant past enjoy easy communications with each other). One way of measuring the extent of the fragmentation is quickly apparent from a study of an important book on regional cookery in Portugal: María Odette Cortes Valente (1973). Another work, that of Olleboma (c.1936), is not specifically devoted to regional cookery, but includes much on it and served to spread knowledge of it outside Portugal when an English author subsequently published a lot of the recipes, but without attribution.

To take *bacalhau*, SALT COD, as an example, there are literally several hundred recipes for this, many of them belonging to particular places in Portugal. It is a valid generalization to say that this is one of the favourite foods of the Portuguese, wherever they live. And some of the recipes, naturally, are popular throughout the country. One example is *Bacalhau dorado*, salt cod scrambled with eggs and potato. Other seafoods which are high in popularity and are the subject of numerous recipes include SARDINES (the smell of which, as they are grilled over a charcoal brazier, pervades most coastal towns and villages). The standard high-class fish is HAKE, *pescada*. Squid, *lulas*, appear on every menu; and so do the small clams called *amêijoas*. Again there are many local recipes, but also some which are used throughout the country—in the case of the clams *Amêijoas à Bulhão Pato*, honouring a Portuguese poet and reminding everyone who sits down to eat it of the very strong literary tradition of the Portuguese people.

Among the other specialities of parts of Portugal are:

- a wealth of soups, including *Caldo verde*, made with the distinctive CABBAGE called *couve tronchuda* (classified as *Brassica oleracea*, Tronchuda group, also known as Galician or Braganza cabbage) and *Canja*, a chicken soup which goes back to medieval times; also bread soups, *açorda* (cf SHORBA);
- roast SUCKING PIG, especially associated with the province of Beira;
- goat stews and roast kid;
- dishes using the CHESTNUTS of the northern part of the country;
- various dishes using MAIZE;
- dishes of the *pudim* (pudding) category— it is appropriate that Portugal, often described as 'Britain's oldest ally' (since the 14th century), should be one of the very few countries to share with Britain a taste for, and expertise in making, puddings;
- anything using quinces, another British connection since the Portuguese were, in a roundabout way, responsible for English MARMALADE, which is descended from *marmelata*, Portuguese QUINCE PRESERVE;
- the rich dessert confections associated with convents and making great use of egg yolk—for some people the outstanding Portuguese delicacies .

In considering what influence the Portuguese have had on foodways in their former colonial possessions (including Brazil, the largest and most populous country in S. America), and vice versa, it is apparent that the Portuguese adopted some African ingredients and dishes on a limited scale; the liberal use of fresh CORIANDER and dishes incorporating the term *piri-piri* (see PIL-PIL) are examples. In the reverse direction, the Portuguese can take credit for introducing VINDALOO (*vino de alho*, i.e. vinegar) to India; the TEMPURA technique to Japan (a major contribution); the cake called KASUTERA, also to Japan. As for China, the two-way traffic which took place in or through Macau was of great importance. Annabel Doling (*c.*1995) says: 'For almost a century, Macau was the Venice of the East and arguably the most important entrepôt in the world.' Her detailed description of the interplay of Portuguese dishes with Cantonese cooking and also the indigenous Macanese cuisine abounds in interesting detail.

See also: ANGOLA AND MOZAMBIQUE; BRAZIL; GOA; MADEIRA.
READING: Edite Vieira (1988).

POSH-TÉ *Annona scleroderma*, a minor fruit of the family Annonaceae, is found in Mexico and Guatemala. The green fruits may be up to 8 cm (3") in diameter. The white pulp inside the thick peel is sweet and aromatic, but not so marvellously good that consumption of this fruit, despite its attractively odd Spanish name, is likely to extend beyond its native region.

POSOLE the current and Spanish name for the Aztec *pozolli*, an important MAIZE-based beverage of the Maya in classic Maya times (see MAYA FOOD), among the later Aztec, and still in modern times.

The maize used to make it was ground once only (compared with the two grindings needed for TORTILLAS), then mixed with water to make a dough which would keep for months in a container reserved for the purpose or wrapped in leaves that had been used for wrapping a previous batch of sour posole. Thus there would be present the right assembly of bacteria, yeasts, and moulds to sour the new batch. The soured dough has been found to have very good nutritional qualities. It was and is diluted with water to make the beverage. This was evidently a standard refreshment, since the Chamula, when bearing a corpse to the cemetery, filled the mouth of the dead person with *posolli* on the ground that the standard remedy for a tiring journey was to sit by the side of the road and drink *posolli*.

Additions which could be made to posole, to improve its basic pleasant but sharp taste, include honey, cacao, ground SAPOTA seeds, green maize. In modern times posole and greens are a popular combination, but are regarded by some as 'poor Indian food'.

The term *pozole* refers to a soup-stew which in various forms (there are white, red, and green versions) is popular in Mexico and parts of C. America. It contains a maize product of one kind or another, as well as some form of meat, but is not connected with posole.

See also ATOLE. (SC)
READING: Sophie Coe (1994).

POSSET in its earliest medieval form was a drink made from milk lightly curdled by adding an acid liquid such as wine, ale, citrus juice, to it. It was sweetened and often spiced. Sometimes the curds and whey were separated and the curds mixed with conventional JUNKET curds, breadcrumbs, and honey to make an 'eating posset' that was thick enough to slice. In the 17th century sack (like sweet sherry), claret, or orange juice were used in eating possets. There were rich versions containing cream and eggs. Later additions in the 18th century included almonds and crumbled Naples biscuits (sponge fingers, see under BISCUIT VARIETIES), and brandy might be added to the wine. By now the dish had more or less lost its identity, and soon lost its name; it developed into the early types of TRIFLE and into various 'creams', which contained fewer eggs or none and resembled a SYLLABUB or a fruit FOOL.

Sack posset, long the most popular type, became first 'sack cream' and then, when it was made with white wine in the 19th century and the reason for the name was forgotten, 'suck cream'.
READING: Moira Buxton (1993).

POTAGE a French term which has become international, denoting nowadays a thick soup. However, the word, which has an interesting history, originally meant in both French and English simply 'what is in the pot', often a 'meal-in-itself' dish of the POT-AU-FEU type. In English the term became Anglicized to POTTAGE and then developed its own history. In French it retained this original meaning up to the 18th century. Whole capons, *jarrets de veau*, shoulders of mutton, and so on could all be potages. In every such instance, there was solid matter (including grain) and liquid (sauce). What happened next was that the liquid sauce usurped the title of the whole dish, so that potage in French came to mean what would now, in English, be called SOUP.

Famous *potages* include *Potage Saint-Germain*, with peas. Favre (1903) had listed more than 170 others, most of which are now forgotten.

POTASSIUM a chemical element necessary to the working of living cells; it plays a role in the conduction of nerve signals. In the pure form potassium is an inflammable metal which combines readily with other elements, and it is always found in compounds such as potassium chloride, an impurity in sea SALT; and potassium NITRATE, saltpetre. The Latin-looking name of the element is actually a back formation from 'potash', potassium carbonate originally obtained by heating wood ash with water in earthenware pots (see LYE).

In the body it is essential to keep levels of potassium and SODIUM in balance; this can be upset by excessive use of salt, sodium chloride. Fruits and vegetables contain abundant potassium. RH

POTATO (*see opposite page*)

POT-AU-FEU a dish symbolic of French cuisine and a meal in itself. Pieces of meat (preferably of various kinds, some lean, some fat, some of gelatinous character) are cooked lengthily and gently in water with certain vegetables (onion studded with cloves, carrot, turnip, possibly parsnip, blanched cabbage) and a BOUQUET GARNI. Potatoes, cooked separately, may be included in the final presentation, which comprises: the skimmed bouillon (BROTH), probably with CROUTONS and grated cheese; then the meats, sliced, with the attendant vegetables and whatever is desired in the way of condiments and pickles.

Pot-au-feu can also mean the earthenware or metal pot in which this and kindred dishes are cooked.

See also POTÉE, a related French dish; and, for a couple of the comparable dishes outside France, COCIDO and OLIO. HY

'POT' CHEESES are not the same as POTTED CHEESES. The term has several applications. A traditional English pot cheese was a form of COTTAGE CHEESE kneaded and moulded into small balls, and served fresh. The name is misleading, since the only pot used in making the cheese was the saucepan in which the milk was heated.

A Greek whey cheese, Mitzithra, made in much the same way as RICOTTA with the WHEY left over from FETA, is sometimes known as pot cheese. There is also an Iranian pot cheese, *panir kusei*, which has greater claim to the name since it is enclosed in an earthenware pot, in which it is matured for several months.

Potato POTATOES IN COOKERY

The potato *Solanum tuberosum*, now a staple food in most parts of the world, has been developed from what were originally an unpromising group of food plants growing at high altitudes in S. America. Evidence shows that the potato was being cultivated 2,000 years ago in Peru.

These first potatoes had small, misshapen, and knobbly tubers, of many colours, and a bitter taste, but could be rendered edible by techniques which the inhabitants of the region now embracing Bolivia and Peru learned in antiquity. Selection and natural interbreeding combined eventually to produce tubers which would be recognized in modern times as potatoes. Selection continues in modern times, drawing on the very wide range of characteristics which wild potatoes display. Some can be found as high as 3,960 m (13,000'). Some are so resistant to frost that they can grow on, or very near, the snowline. Others grow better in a warmer and drier climate, some of them in a warmer climate than cultivated potatoes can tolerate.

Wild types continue to be eaten. These are known as *papas criollas*, native potatoes (*papa* being the general/common Indian name for potato in S. America).

The first Europeans to encounter the potato did so in 1537 in what is now Colombia. They belonged to the Spanish forces of Jiminez De Quesada. On entering a village from which the inhabitants had fled they found maize, beans, and 'truffles' which a later account described as 'of good flavour, a delicacy to the Indians and a dainty dish even for Spaniards'. These 'truffles' were potatoes.

The potato was introduced to Spain during the 1550s and it was also grown early in Italy. It was not a success. The potatoes used were small, watery and still rather bitter, and were anyway of a variety which had climatic requirements which could not be met in northern latitudes. Nor could they match the immediate appeal of other newly discovered tubers, for example the JERUSALEM ARTICHOKE and the SWEET POTATO.

The arrival of the potato in Britain, despite the best efforts of scholars, remains something of a mystery, with tales involving Raleigh and Drake. It is one of those subjects which must either be dealt with in a single paragraph (as here) or be allowed at least 50 pages. However, it is generally accepted that potatoes were introduced to the British Isles (including Ireland) during the 1590s. See also IRELAND AND THE POTATO.

Gerard (1633) had grown potatoes in his garden and championed their virtues, though his account is inaccurate and he seems to have muddled them with another American tuber, called openauk. However, except in Ireland, the potato remained in disfavour in Britain. In the north of Ireland (and in Scotland) the Protestants would not plant it, one objection being that it was not mentioned in the Bible. Catholic Irish who had qualms on this account dispelled them by sprinkling their seed potatoes with holy water and planting them on Good Friday. Like many new and expensive foods it had a reputation as an APHRODISIAC, in which context it is mentioned by Shakespeare in *The Merry Wives of Windsor*. It was also said to be poisonous, a common accusation against members of the *Solanum* genus, which includes deadly nightshade.

Elsewhere in Europe royal or governmental edicts promoted the cause of the potato. In Sweden there was a royal edict in 1764. In Prussia Frederick the Great ordered cultivation on a large scale in Silesia and Pomerania.

Official decree was one thing, genuine popularity another. In 1784 Benjamin Thompson, better known as Count RUMFORD, the famous American scientist, inventor, soldier, and adventurer, entered the service of the royal Bavarian government to reorganize the workhouse system. The inmates of these 'Houses of Industry' were fed as economically as possible on bread and thin gruel. Rumford contrived to make the gruel incredibly cheap by substituting potatoes for the barley which had been used before. Yet, despite the gnawing hunger of the workers, he had to conceal the presence of potatoes by boiling them behind a screen, until they disintegrated unrecognizably, to prevent the inmates from rejecting the gruel.

Other subterfuges were practised, including the one which is supposed to have persuaded the French to esteem the potato by popularizing it at the French court. Parmentier, a French army officer during the Seven Years War, was taken prisoner and kept in detention in Hamburg. There he became used to potatoes, which were part of the prison diet. After his release he brought the French King, Louis XVI, round to his way of thinking, and even persuaded the queen, Marie Antoinette, to wear potato flowers to ornament her dress. The potato became fashionable and part of French cuisine, where to this day dishes containing potato are styled *parmentier*. More important, he set up a large plantation of potatoes near Paris in order to make the potato more popular with the people. (The field was surrounded by ditches and patrolled by guards. Parmentier instructed the guards to make only a show of vigilance. The curious local peasants, wondering at what could be so valuable, sneaked in at night, stole the potatoes, and planted them in their own gardens.) The popularity of the potato steadily grew from then on. The French Revolution did nothing to stop it; in fact, in 1793 the royal Tuileries gardens were turned into a potato field. Parmentier himself wisely went underground like his vegetables and lived for many more years.

It was in the following century that the Irish, who had come to depend upon the potato almost entirely, suffered a disaster. A fungus disease which had originated in Belgium in the late 1830s spread to Ireland and, aided by the mild, damp climate, totally wiped out the crop during the 1840s. For more about this and its tragic consequences see IRELAND AND THE POTATO.

Aspects of the early history of the potato, of early perceptions of its nature, and of its wide distribution are evidenced by its many names. These fall into several groups. The original Peruvian Indian name *papas* has not spread widely except in South America and the Philippines. The name 'potato' and 'patata' in Spanish stems from the Caribbean Indian name for the sweet potato. Confusingly, the Spanish for the sweet potato is *batata* and the Italian *patata*. The potato's resemblance to a truffle is shown in the 16th-century name *turma de tierra* (earth truffle) and in early Italian names *tartufo bianco* (white truffle) and *taratufflo*. This was perverted in German to *Kartoffel*, which became the Russian *kartochki* and similar names in several Slavonic languages. The British slang 'spud' refers to a potato-digging spade.

Names of the 'earth apple' type, formerly used in Europe for other roots, are also widespread, and that name was once used in English. The modern French name *pomme de terre*, the Dutch *aardappel*, and obsolete German *Erdapfel* are among many variants. In Persia the name *seb-i-zaminee* also means earth apple.

The potato was introduced to India possibly as early as 1615, where it had a slow start but was gradually accepted as a palatable vegetable. Despite its value to a largely vegetarian population, it has still not become a staple food to compare with pulses and rice. It has been even less successful in winning a place for itself in oriental cuisines, although it is of course known throughout the Far East and SE Asia and has achieved local importance in some places, e.g. where the English and Dutch introduced it. (The Dutch, incidentally, had been among those Europeans who took to the potato rather slowly. A remarkable essay by Witteveen (1983) on early potato recipes in the Netherlands charts in detail the slow but steady northward progress of the potato from what is now Belgium to Friesland, at a rate of something like two and a half kilometres a year.)

Generally, in colonies populated largely by white settlers the spread of the potato kept pace with developments in Europe: that is, slowly. Irish immigrants took it to N. America in 1719, for it had failed to spread directly from S. America either among Indian or white colonists. The first plantation was at Londonderry, New Hampshire. In 1770 Captain Cook introduced the potato to Australasia, where it had become common by the middle of the next century.

Potato products are made from potatoes which have been reduced to powder in one of two ways. The first is simple cooking, drying, and grinding, which preserves the solid constituents more or less in their original proportions. This is the method used to make potato flour, a product which has a wide range of uses. Derivatives of potato flour include: instant mashed potato; various frozen potato products; and potato crisps.

Alternatively, the starch may be extracted from potatoes by a washing process. This is the method used to make the very light potato FECULA or starch, used as a thickener for delicate dishes.

POTATO VARIETIES

THE choice of potato varieties by potato growers varies by country or region, and also changes steadily over time. In Europe, it was in the mid-18th century that a range of varieties, adapted to the longer European growing days, began to be recorded and deliberately marketed as special and different. Before long there were scores of them, then hundreds. About 700 potato varieties are now held in a governmental reference collection in Scotland.

Commercial potatoes are classified as 'early' (these provide the small 'new potatoes') or 'maincrop', according to when they mature and are harvested. Wilson (1993) has provided an excellent survey of British and European varieties of both categories, explaining their origins, uses, and relative importance in commerce and the kitchen. This survey reflects the position in the 1990s, and covers among very many others:

- early varieties—Arran Pilot, Home Guard, Red Craig's Royal, and Maris Peer;
- maincrop—Desiree, Kerr's Pink, King Edward, Red King, Golden Wonder, Majestic, Maris Piper, Pentland Crown, Pentland Dell, and Redskin.

The lists would be different for France and Germany and even more so for, say, Oregon, Ohio, and Maine in N. America. The same applies to Wilson's useful recommendations on varieties suited to specific purposes, in Britain:

- for baking—King Edward;
- for roasting—Desiree (red skin);
- for chips (US French fries)—Maris Piper;
- for boiling/steaming—Wilja or Nicola (yellow-fleshed);
- for salad—Ratte;
- as new potatoes—Duke of York.

A specialized process for preserving potatoes in Peru is described under CHUÑO AND TUNTA.

See also POTATOES IN COOKERY (which in turn has pointers to items such as BOXTY, CHAMP, CLAPSHOT, COLCANNON, and STOVIES) and IRELAND AND THE POTATO.
READING: Wilson (1993); Salaman (1949).

Potatoes in cookery

This is a ramified subject since the potato is so versatile and has become almost ubiquitous in the world, thus exposing itself to a wide range of cuisines in all five continents.

Potatoes arouse strong passions, not the sort which the aphrodisiac properties which potatoes have been supposed to have but do not in fact possess, but partisan passions. Some think mashed potatoes with good milk and butter are incomparable, and so they are for certain dishes (bangers and mash). Others claim with justifiable confidence that plain boiled potatoes if done with the skilful techniques of the Irish (drain when cooked, leave to rest a few minutes in the pot with a clean teacloth on top, and shake slightly) are the best of all. Untold and unthinking hordes would assert that chips/frites/French fries have no real competition, although their assertions might falter if they were introduced to the golden-topped butter-and-cream enriched slices which are scalloped potatoes. So-called 'gourmets' may think that Parisienne potatoes have no equal (except, possibly, the most delicate croquettes), while Alpine skiers, comparing notes in mountain huts, will give the palm to Swiss *rösti*. In the few families where a Sunday roast is still served, highest praise would go to mother's roast potatoes, but her offspring might be silently thinking that they prefer jacket potatoes with a dash of yoghurt.

The truth is that all these ways of cooking potatoes produce admirable results, if done properly and for appropriate purposes. Also important, the choice of variety. For the cook, the most important distinction is whether the potato is of the waxy or floury type. Floury potatoes bake well and mash well and are fine for chips, but they disintegrate when boiled. Waxy potatoes remain entire when boiled, but do not mash at all well. In scientific terms, the difference lies in the amount and chemical composition of starch molecules.

Floury potatoes are the most popular in Britain. In continental Europe, waxy potatoes are generally preferred. These do not crumble when boiled, and their particular texture gives the best results in various continental potato dishes (e.g. *gratin dauphinois*, German or French potato salads). Some varieties, notably what are called Finnish in N. America, have yellow flesh, which is preferred for some purposes.

The same advice (choose an appropriate variety) applies to other dishes in which potatoes figure—OMELETTE, DUMPLINGS, PANCAKES, FRITTERS, RISSOLES, GNOCCHI, toppings and fillings for pies, such as SHEPHERD'S PIE and Cornish pasties (see PASTY), and potato pastry.

The nomenclature of potato dishes seems to encourage whimsicality. Besides some of the Irish and Welsh examples, there is a tasty and euphonious dish from Northumberland called Pan haggerty, and the Scottish Tatties 'n' herring have a pleasantly unruly ring to their name. *Aloo makalla*, the famous dish of the Baghdadi Jews of Calcutta, sounds sprightly to English ears, although perhaps not in Calcutta; it consists of potatoes which have been boiled briefly and are then fried in oil to cover until golden brown, crisp outside, and meltingly soft inside. Some would also see a whimsical element in the Finnish name *Imellettyperunasoselaatikka*, which (as Beatrice Ojakangas, 1964, explains) is a traditional potato casserole which is unique in that 'it undergoes what the Finns call a "malting" process wherein the starch of the potatoes breaks down to form a simpler sugar', a process which takes them some hours at the side of a large wood stove.

Sweet dishes containing potato are relatively rare, but do exist. Potato apple cake, for example, is a well-established speciality of Northern Ireland. It is composed of two potato cakes, rolled thin and sealed together round a filling of apple slices. The round is then cut into four triangular pieces or FARLS and cooked on a pan or baked in an oven. Once baked they can be moistened with a sweet buttery sauce. Traditionally baked on a griddle, potato apple cake was a festive Hallowe'en dish.

For some people, when choosing a way of cooking potatoes, it is relevant that advice to eat potatoes with their skins is soundly based. Although the skin itself is not nutritious the layer immediately under it, only millimetres thick, contains most of the potato's vitamin C content. It also holds most of the flavour.

See also: ALIGOTE; BOXTY; CHAMP; CLAPSHOT; COLCANNON; FADGE; HOTPOT; IRISH STEW; KUGEL; PANCAKE (for *latkes* and *ratzelach*); PUNCHNEP; STOVIES.

READING: Lindsay Bareham (1991); Gwen Robyns (1980).

POTÉE nowadays a POT-AU-FEU using pork as the meat and including not only the usual root vegetables but also haricot beans and often potatoes; a dish emblematic of rural France, simple, rustic, familial, claimed by various regions of France as their own speciality.

The meaning was broader in the distant past. Antoine Furetière (1691) gave this quotation, by way of definition and illustration: 'the contents of the marmite of an ordinary bourgeois. He arrived late to dine with me, he was content with my *potée*, we ate only the *potée*.' The potée then was a sort of antique POTAGE, of varying ingredients, belonging to the bourgeoisie rather than the peasants, and without any special regional connotation.

The provinces which now claim for themselves the 'true potée' include Auvergne and Champagne, as well as Alsace and Burgundy. Sausages, smoked bacon, even ham appear in some recipes, but such variations, reflecting local produce, are within the accepted framework. Less usual is the inclusion of beef in Franche-Comté; and of lamb or duck, or even conger eel, in Brittany.

In the francophone city of Liège, in Belgium, the potée is a dish of major importance. As elsewhere, the common factors among the numerous local recipes are a mixture of meat and potatoes with other vegetables, and slow simmering.   HY

POTTAGE the medieval term for a semi-liquid cooked dish, typically based on cereal, which in various forms was a mainstay of diet for many centuries.

The word comes from the French POTAGE meaning something cooked in a pot. It thus has a very wide application. It is no longer in use in English, its function having been largely taken over by PORRIDGE, which is the same word, slightly changed and now having a more restricted meaning.

Pottages were a universal feature of primitive kinds of cookery, but they developed at an early stage into quite sophisticated preparations. In Roman times, Apicius gave a recipe for a pottage (*tisana* was the name he used) made of barley with three kinds of pulses, eight kinds of leafy vegetables, four flavouring herbs, liquamen (fish sauce), and a garnish of chopped cabbage leaves.

In the Middle Ages, and especially in Britain, pottages were eaten by all, from the poorest to the richest. The simplest kinds were cereal pottages: oatmeal in the north, barley, rye, or wheat FRUMENTY in the south. To the rich these dishes were an accompaniment to meat; to the poor they were complete meals. Pease pottage, made from dried peas, and other pulse pottages were equally important. These dishes might be quite plain or contain herbs or other additions. Vegetable and meat pottages were thickened with breadcrumbs, oatmeal, eggs, or, for the rich, amidon (wheat starch). Most contained onions. One universal favourite was green porray, made from a large number of green vegetables and herbs which were boiled until thoroughly soft.

There were also luxurious pottages for those who could afford them. One such was rice pottage, made with rice imported from Lombardy, cooked in sweetened almond milk and coloured with saffron. Another thick pottage was blanc manger, originally a mild-flavoured blend of shredded chicken, almond milk, and sugar, and the precursor of BLANCMANGE.

Indeed, because the term pottage had such a wide meaning it could embrace many subcategories of dishes. Constance Hieatt's edition (1988) of an important medieval culinary manuscript, under the title *An Ordinance of Pottage*, is one of a number of works which illustrate this point. One could count as kinds of pottage: bruet, charlet, gravey, maumeny, mortreus, porre, etc.

Pottages had to be fairly liquid, and storable; otherwise what was in the bottom of the pot would burn. If a plain pottage seemed too liquid to be a satisfying dish, the problem could be overcome by pouring it onto a slice of bread to make a sop. The word 'sop', evolving to mean the liquid rather than the solid in this conjunction, is a precursor of 'soup', and the form is recalled in modern soups served with fried bread croutons, and in French onion soup with its floating piece of bread topped with cheese.

A further development came with the invention of baked, and later boiled, puddings in the late 16th and early 17th centuries. Many old pottage mixtures were adapted. The dried fruit plum pottage, a type with meat, dried fruit ('plums'), and breadcrumbs, became plum pudding; although the old pottage survived to the early 19th century (see CHRISTMAS PUDDING). Pease pottage became pease pudding. Bread and butter pudding and BLANCMANGE are two other examples of pottages which gained new roles.

Lest this account might seem unduly centred on Britain, it should be pointed out that pottages of the kind described were a peculiarly British food, just as puddings were later. In 1542, Andrew Boorde, the royal physician, explained: 'Pottage is not so much used in all Christendom as it is used in England.' In France the old pottages found their successors in soups (*potages*), some of the rustic varieties of which are almost as solid as their medieval predecessors. One might cite the Gascon *garbure*, a massively solid vegetable soup made from cabbage, dried beans, garlic, herbs, and a piece of CONFIT (potted meat). It is often thickened with chestnuts and poured over a sop in a thoroughly medieval manner.

POTTED CHEESE used to mean, and still sometimes does mean, a pounded mixture of more than one cheese, or of a cheese with other added ingredients, covered and sealed with a layer of clarified butter. This was an example of the well-established old technique of POTTING. Graham (1988) observes that British potted cheese (like the somewhat similar *fromage fort* of France) could be 'an excuse for using up odds and ends of stale cheese'; but that versions using fresh cheese have appeared in recipe books since the mid-18th century, and that those calling for mace as a flavouring (along with the standard ingredients, butter, and sherry or other wine) are perhaps the best. The same author has a vivid passage about the pungency of *fromage fort* ('the kick it packs is quite definitely *fortissimo*') and about some notable examples such as 'Gris de Lille, popularly known as Vieux Puant de Lille (Old Stinker of Lille)', which according to a by-law of that city may not be conveyed in a taxi. His conclusion is that the most 'devilish' of these preparations is that of Foudjou in the lower Ardèche, of which one specimen was kept going in a crock for 15 years.

In recent times the phrase 'potted cheese' has sometimes been used for various commercial products which can best be described as 'cheese mixtures', moulded into various shapes and packed in various ways. These verge on the territory of **processed cheeses,** convenience foods with no pretensions, which have been the subject of a nicely balanced description by Christian (1982):

Once described as 'a triumph of laboratory technique over conscience', processed cheese is essentially an emulsion of second-rate cheeses, flavou\red, stabilized, extended, sterilized and wrapped so as to impede any natural, enzymic or bacteriological action that might conceivably give some identity or flavour. Nonetheless, it is enormously popular with children and unsophisticated palates—probably because of its blandness—and is thus an important source of protein for millions of people.

POTTING has a wider meaning than merely putting things like jam or pickles into pots: it also denotes a method of preserving meat or fish in a pot sealed by a layer of fat to exclude air. (POTTED CHEESE is considered separately, see above.)

Potting is an old technique derived from that of the medieval PIE, which was often used deliberately as a way of conserving food rather than merely presenting it. The crust of the most solid raised pies was made from coarse flour. It was not intended to be eaten, except as a remnant thrown to the servants, but constituted a durable and airtight shell. The food inside it kept for quite a long time because, having been cooked in a sealed container, it was sterile. The explanation was not understood in the Middle Ages, but the effect was obvious in practice. Observation must also have shown that the weak point where decay began was the top of the filling which did not intimately touch the top crust, because the filling shrank in cooking; and which was exposed to the entry of air through places in the crust where steam had escaped. Therefore the top of the filling was sealed by pouring in, through a hole in the crust, boiling stock or melted fat, which luckily had themselves been sterilized by heating. When this addition solidified it sealed the filling effectively. Such pies were used, for example, for sending Severn lampreys from Gloucester to London, a journey of several days which could scarcely have been undertaken with any other of the primitive PRESERVATION techniques of the time.

Towards the end of the 16th century it was realized that the crust could be replaced with a pot which was reusable, so that there was no waste of flour. The meat or fish thus potted was sealed with a layer of melted butter. Sometimes a bladder or a piece of parchment was bound over the top of the pot, which sealed the butter from the air which would otherwise have turned it rancid.

During the 16th and 17th centuries potting was widely used both as a method of preserving foods at home and to protect it in transit. The lampreys which had once been sent to London in a pie now went in pots. Other delicacies were also dispatched to the capital in this way, such as small birds. BRAWN, which in the Middle Ages had been a POTTAGE and had later become a pickle of fatty pork with verjuice and wine, now became a potted dish. Potted meat or fish might be in large or small pieces, or pounded to a paste. Such foods were a fashionable item at the dinners of the rich, and a useful standby for anyone: one could broach a pot of pigeon (a popular variety) as easily as a modern cook would open a can. Potted foods were usually eaten cold. Estimates of keeping time ranged from a month to a year or more.

The French equivalents of the English potted foods have various names. CONFIT was and is made mainly in the south-west. RILLETTES are a speciality of the Loire region. A TERRINE is really a potted food, although seldom made for long keeping and therefore with only a thin layer of fat on top.

(These are often called pâtés: technically a terrine is anything made in the earthenware dish of that name, usually rectangular with a lid, and a PÂTÉ is enclosed in pastry (*pâte*). This distinction applies whether the mixture is coarse or fine and whatever it is made of: meat, game, fish, or other things. However, use of the term pâté has been irreversibly widened to include virtually any preparation resembling what is found inside the pastry case of a true pâté.)

Despite their popular success, potted foods had a potential weakness which the older pies and true pâtés did not. A food baked in a crust is sterile, and therefore keeps well. So is a food baked in a pot, provided that it is promptly sealed with adequately hot fat. Many potted foods were so baked: for example, Sir Kenelm Digby's recipe (1669) for potted pigeons involved baking them for eight or ten hours in claret and butter, followed by more butter as a seal. He confidently asserted that it would keep for 'a quarter of a year', and this seems reasonable. However, no need was felt to bake the food in the pot, and often recipes made it impossible to do so. The food might be cooked in a liquid which was drained off and replaced by butter for potting; or it might have to be pounded after cooking but before it was put in the pot. Since there was no notion at the time of the need for sterility in preserving, no one realized that this would let in bacteria and that the potted food would go bad, as it often did. Hannah Glasse has a direction in her *Art of Cookery* (1747) 'to save potted birds, that begin to be bad'. They were put into boiling water for half a minute only, then dried, seasoned with salt, pepper, and mace, and repotted under fresh butter.

This would not have worked. By the time it was realized in the 19th century—first practically by APPERT, then scientifically by Pasteur (see CANNING)—how food becomes contaminated, the vogue for potted foods was waning. The role that potting played in preservation has been taken over by canning or made unnecessary by refrigeration and improved transport. Those potted foods that are still made survive because they are delicacies: for example, potted shrimps in England, or French terrines or rillettes.

Humbler survivals are the British commercially made meat and fish pastes sold in jars for spreading on bread. During the heyday of potting other foods were treated in the same way. Potted cheese has been mentioned; this did not need to be sealed, as it was preserved naturally by the protective bacteria of the cheese. Attempts were made to pot fruits and vegetables. Although these seldom worked, they were stages on the way to the discovery of canning.

Potting has always been principally a European method of preservation. A couple of exceptions are mentioned under CONFIT. The Chinese have been preserving meat and fish in pots since several thousand years BC, but always by making it into a fermented pickle so that it protects itself without the need for sealing.

POUND CAKE a cake of the creamed type, is so named because the recipe calls for an equal weight of flour, butter, sugar, and eggs; in old recipes, a pound of each, making a large, rich cake. Beaten egg is relied on to raise the cake. Sometimes the eggs are separated, the whites beaten separately and folded in just before baking to enhance their raising power.

Pound cake has been favoured in both Britain and the USA for over two centuries. Recipes for it were already current early in the 18th century, for example that given by Richard Bradley (1736).

Barbara Maher (1982), in an elegant chapter on this class of cake, quotes a delightful passage from James Beard (1974):

I remember that when I was young, my mother always had a pound cake in the larder. One week it would be a caraway seed cake, with the little pungent flecks pushing through the smooth golden-yellow cake. Another week it might be a citron cake, with thin slivers of citron on the top (never mixed in, lest they sink to the bottom). Sometimes there were chopped walnuts in our cake, or ginger, which gave it an exotic, spicy flavour. Pound cake was our standby. We had it for tea, toasted for breakfast, and as a foundation for fruit desserts, with fresh or poached berries, poached plums or peaches, and slathers of heavy cream poured over everything.

The German *Sandtorte* is similar to pound cake; and a French cake, *quatre quarts* (four quarters), uses the same principles, elaborated by an initial beating of the egg yolks with sugar to help cake texture. Various flavourings are added to the basic mixtures, such as brandy, rosewater, spice, or orange rind.

Cherry cake, popular in Britain, is essentially a variation of pound cake. Glacé cherries are added to the mixture before baking. (They tend to sink to the bottom, but cutting them into halves makes this defect less likely.)

See also MADEIRA CAKE.   LM

POUTINE the name used in Provence for both the SARDINE and the ANCHOVY in their larval state. They are *poutine nue* (or *poutina nuda*) so long as they remain without scales, and *poutine habillée* (or *poutina vestida*) when the scales appear. These minute fish (hundreds to the pound) cannot legally be fished in other parts of France, but the Alpes-Maritimes is a region where the relatively permissive fishery regulations of Sardinia continued to apply for 100 years after the Comté de Nice was reincorporated in France in 1860. So the people of Nice and thereabouts could go on consuming large quantities of poutine when they appeared in the early part of the year. Since 1960 the fishery for poutine has been severely regulated but not eliminated.

The Spanish equivalent of poutine is *aladroch*; but that name applies to small anchovies only, whether larval or somewhat larger.

Poutine can be made into a soup, often with very fine pasta such as *cheveux d'ange*, or omelettes; or used in *pissalat*, a special condiment of Nice which in turn gave its name to *pissaladière*, an onion/anchovy tart now made with salted anchovy fillets.

Other tiny fish which are similarly appreciated in Provence are nonnat (see GOBY) and melet (see SILVERSIDE).

PRAIRIE CHICKEN *Tympanuchus cupido*, a N. American close relation of the GROUSE, is not unlike a PARTRIDGE in appearance. It makes good eating and has sometimes in the past been available in very large numbers from the Midwestern states. De Voe (1866) says that in his day they were usually brought to the New York market in frozen state, and that the flesh, which is moderately dark, is best from a young fat bird.

These birds, which can be divided into subspecies, including the greater and the lesser prairie chicken, have various other names, including prairie hen and greater pinnated grouse. The species was at one time almost extinct and is still uncommon but does survive in prairie regions of Canada and USA.

PRAIRIE DOG *Cynomys gunnisoni*, a burrowing rodent of the family Sciuridae found in the SW region of the USA. The name 'prairie dog' comes from its distinctive bark, like that of a dog. These animals construct systems of tunnels underground, so elaborate that they can be referred to as 'prairie dog villages' or 'prairie dog towns'.

WOODCHUCK, which are of generally similar appearance and size, are sometimes referred to, incorrectly, as prairie dogs. They make very good eating. The prairie dog itself, according to Schwabe (1979), 'is still commonly eaten by Indians and has a slightly "earthy" taste'.

PRALINE a combination of almonds and boiled sugar, is a popular confection with a long history. The name is originally French, and the *Dictionnaire de l'épicerie* (1898) gives this definition: 'PRALINE.—Bonbon formé d'une amande rissolée dans du sucre dont elle forme ensuite le noyau, et parfumé et coloré de diverses manières.'

The important points in this definition are that it refers to almonds which are whole and separate, each covered with boiled, grained sugar. This remains the primary meaning of the word in modern French.

According to an often-repeated but unverifiable legend dating back to the end of the 18th century at least, the name 'praline' is derived from the Duke of Plessis-Praslin (1598–1675). His cook is supposed to have invented a method for coating whole almonds in grained caramelized sugar, and later to have retired to the town of Montargis to produce the sweets commercially. Whatever the truth, pralines were well known, outside as well as inside France, by the 18th century, when recipes for 'Prawlins', or for 'Almonds Crisped' appeared in English cookery books. Borella (1770) observed that 'pralin' is 'French Anglicised, as there is no English word to express the real idea of the French in this sort of preserving almonds'. Eventually, however, praline, like many other French culinary terms, became an adopted word in the English language.

As an English word, praline now has the main meaning of a powdered nut-and-sugar confection, the nuts commonly (but not exclusively) used being almonds. The skinned nuts are cooked with a syrup boiled to the caramel stage (see SUGAR BOILING). The mixture is then poured onto a surface to cool, after which it is ground (finely or coarsely, depending on the end use. The resulting powder (referred to in French as *pralin* or *praliné*) is never used by itself, but always as an ingredient in other confections, whether desserts or chocolate products.

In N. America pralines are a speciality of several southern states. In Louisiana, especially New Orleans, the name applies to candies made with PECANS in a coating of brown sugar which used to be sold by Creole women known as *pralinières*.

In French-speaking Belgium and in German, the word praline simply means a filled chocolate; and this usage has also appeared to some extent in English.   (LM)

PRAWN a name linked to SHRIMP, under which heading the differences in usage between Britain and N. America are explained. The present entry deals with what British people call prawns, although all of them would be called shrimps by Americans.

The international trade in frozen prawns (or prawn meat) has grown to be very large and will no doubt continue to grow as methods of 'farming' certain species are perfected. This trade is not confined to just a few dominant species. The number of

different species which lend themselves, in different parts of the world and different conditions, to commercial exploitation is large; the comprehensive catalogue by Holthuis (1980) demonstrates this. Even a selective list of them is therefore bound to be long. The list given here has been split up by region, but it must be remembered that prawns, once caught and frozen, do not stay in their own regions but often travel halfway round the world to meet their destined consumers.

PRAWNS OF THE NORTH ATLANTIC AND MEDITERRANEAN

- *Palaemon serratus*, common prawn, a species of inshore waters with a range from Norway to the Mediterranean. Maximum length 10 cm (4"). Almost colourless when alive, of a fine orange-red when cooked.
- *Pandalus borealis*, northern or deep-water prawn, red when alive—but few people see it thus because it belongs to deep waters and is usually cooked at sea. Range: from Greenland down to Britain in the east and Martha's Vineyard in the west. Fished extensively in Norwegian waters.
- *Aristeus antennatus*, French *crevette rouge*. To 20 cm (8"). Light red with a mauve headpiece. (The slightly larger *Aristeomorpha foliacea* displays similar colours, but darker.) Mainly a Mediterranean species, as is the following one.
- *Penaeus kerathurus*, French *caramote*, Italian *mazzancolla*. To 22 cm (9"). Brown with reddish tints. Of a high reputation, especially in Italy.

PRAWNS OF THE CENTRAL WEST ATLANTIC

- *Penaeus aztecus aztecus*, brown shrimp (but not always brown, may be called 'golden' or 'red-tailed' shrimp); to 22 cm (9"); very important in commercial fisheries.
- *P. duorarum duorarum*, pink shrimp (but not always pink); larger than the brown shrimp; important in the Gulf of Mexico and the Caribbean.
- *P. setiferus*, white shrimp (usually translucent white, may also be called 'grey' or 'green-tailed' shrimp); to 20 cm (8"); important in the Gulf of Mexico.

PRAWNS OF THE INDO-PACIFIC

- *Penaeus monodon*, giant tiger prawn.
- *P. japonicus*, Japanese (king) prawn or kuruma prawn.
- *P. indicus*, Indian (banana) prawn or white prawn.
- *P. merguiensis*, banana prawn or white prawn.
- *Metapenaeus ensis*, greasy-back prawn or school prawn.
- *M. affinis*, sometimes called the jinga shrimp because of its name *jinga* in NW

India; of major importance in Pakistan, the west coast of India, Sri Lanka, and Malaysia.
- *M. monoceros*, the speckled prawn/shrimp and ginger prawn in SE Africa, commercially important from the E. Mediterranean to the Indo-West Pacific, including E. and much of SE Africa.

The part of a prawn which is eaten is often referred to as 'the tail'. Strictly speaking, the tail is the small fan of fins at the very end of the prawn. However, current usage is deeply rooted and will not change. Running along the top of what must, then, be called the tail is a dark thread like gut, which should be removed from all but the smaller specimens.

Prawn or shrimp cookery covers a wide range of techniques and recipes. Recipes range from the famous Prawn cocktail which symbolized British restaurant menus in the 1960s to exotic CURRY-type dishes in Asia, some involving coconut cream and most being served with rice, a happy combination. Once cooked, the tail meats can always be battered and deep fried; or used in a STIR-FRY dish; or featured in a salad. These are but a few examples from a very wide range of possibilities.

PRAWN CRACKERS are a product of SE Asia, well described by Charmaine Solomon (1996):

Large, crisp, deep-fried crackers popular in Indonesia and Malaysia, where they are called krupuk udang and Vietnam, banh phong tom. Sold in packets in dried form, they are made from starch (usually tapioca flour), salt and sugar, together with varying amounts of prawn or fish. They are sun dried and keep very well.

The same author goes on to say that the best prawn crackers are large ones from Indonesia, containing more prawn than their less expensive rivals. She regards those from China as a possible substitute; flavour and texture are less good but they come in an assortment of vivid colours.

PRESERVATION (*see opposite page*)

PRESERVE a word applied to foods treated by some means to achieve their PRESERVATION. Thus foods which have been chilled, frozen, pickled or treated with sugar are all preserved foods.

The words 'preserve' and 'conserve' are also used more specifically to indicate an (often expensive or unusual) JAM. Although this is generally regarded as pretentious today, both words were used this way at least a century before the word 'jam' became common.

Preservation

Preservation of food has been a problem and challenge for the human race since prehistoric times, since natural supplies of food run short in the winter and few foods keep for long without some preservative measures being taken. Those that do, such as nuts, are preserved by animals. But—apart from a few special cases such as bees—the only animal that treats food to make it keep is man.

All fresh foods begin to spoil at once, quickly or slowly. As soon as a plant is harvested or an animal killed, substances in it which were essential to its life begin to break down. It may also be colonized by micro-organisms coming from outside, or be acted on by those already present, such as the bacteria in the intestines of animals and the yeasts which form the 'bloom' on fruit.

Food spoilage may be caused by ENZYMES. Various MICRO-ORGANISMS, notably YEASTS and MOULDS and BACTERIA, are responsible for numerous other forms of spoilage. And some foods are spoilt simply by exposure to the air, without any intervention by enzymes or micro-organisms.

As will be clear from the following paragraphs, which deal in turn with each kind of agent of spoilage, they have beneficial aspects as well as harmful ones, and in many instances the beneficial aspects actually promote preservation of food. It would therefore be a mistake to think of them as 'the enemies' in this context; but they all can cause spoilage unless prevented and it is useful to know what measures of prevention are effective in each case.

Innumerable **enzymes** are at work in all living things. They control the chemical reactions of life processes, but they are not themselves alive; they can continue working after the death of their host.

Some enzyme action can have a beneficial effect up to a point, as in the ripening of fruit after picking and the increasing tenderness of meat when it is hung. But if these changes are allowed to go too far, the food softens and spoils. Some changes are purely deleterious, for instance rancidity in FATS AND OILS; or normally undesirable, as in the BROWNING of vegetables.

Enzymes can be destroyed by heating food, even briefly, to boiling point. They can also be prevented from working by simple preservative chemicals such as salt and acids. Cold slows their action, but even freezing does not stop it completely.

Yeasts and moulds may also have both good and bad effects. They release enzymes of their own into the food, breaking it down, and producing substances which cause 'off' flavours. But some yeasts and moulds cause useful FERMENTATION, as in BREAD and alcoholic drinks. Moulds are used in CHEESE and in the making of TEMPE from soya beans.

Yeasts and moulds can be kept out of food by hygienic precautions, controlled by chemical methods or killed by IRRADIATION—a controversial technique used mostly for spices. They can be slowed or stopped by refrigeration, freezing or drying—but some moulds can grow in a freezer at temperatures below –18 °C (0 °F).

Some **bacteria** are useful. To exploit them, while suppressing undesirable bacteria, it is usually necessary to create special conditions favouring their growth, and sometimes to introduce a starter culture of them. Both these practices have been carried out for millennia, long before anyone knew that bacteria existed. Procedures which gave a good result were presumably found out by trial and error. SAUERKRAUT provides an example: of the bacteria present on the cabbage leaves, those which produce the desired effect grow strongly in airless, salty conditions, which other bacteria cannot stand. Most milk products, including CHEESE, YOGHURT, and BUTTER, are produced with the aid of bacteria, as are SOURDOUGH bread and VINEGAR.

The fermentation in milk products, sauerkraut, and certain other foods such as olives and salami is a preservative process. It is brought about mainly by LACTIC ACID-producing bacteria, which also give pleasantly sour flavours to the food.

Bacteria can be suppressed or controlled without great difficulty, by drying, refrigeration, pickling, or cooking; but there are a few species which can remain active at –5 °C (23 °F), and some which can form spores that survive the heat of normal cooking. Irradiation kills all bacteria. But there remains the problem of the toxins produced by certain species, such as those which cause BOTULISM.

There are also changes brought about purely by chemical reactions; one of the most important is rancidity of fats caused by the **oxygen** in the air, or less often by water.

PRESERVATION TECHNIQUES

These are mostly ways of destroying enzymes or micro-organisms, or inactivating them (sometimes merely slowing down their activity very markedly); and of denying them access to the food, if they are not already present.

COOKING preserves food by denaturing protein—damaging its molecules by heat. Enzymes are proteins, and all are destroyed before the temperature reaches boiling point. Some bacteria can survive normal cooking temperatures by forming spores, which grow into new bacteria when the food cools. No moulds will withstand cooking.

SEALING food in a partial vacuum or an inert gas is usually done only after micro-organisms have first been killed by another method. It is a good way of preventing rancidity caused by oxygen in foods which otherwise keep well, such as nuts.

CANNING and bottling almost always involve cooking to kill micro-organisms. The contents of the container remain sterile until it is opened. Air is also excluded.

REFRIGERATION is seldom more than a short-term method. The low temperature slows all processes, including spoilage.

FREEZING can make some foods last for years. They must first be blanched to destroy enzymes and micro-organisms. Even the coldest freezers cannot arrest spoilage completely, because when watery liquids freeze they form pure ice, leaving dissolved substances in the remaining water which becomes a solution too concentrated to freeze. Fats continue to go rancid, though very slowly.

DRYING paralyses micro-organisms of all kinds, which need water to operate. In most cases these remain alive and will start growing again as soon as the food is moistened. Drying destroys enzymes, whose protein structure is denatured when it loses water. But traditional, slow drying methods allow a good deal of enzyme action before humidity falls to that point. Many dried fruits are darkened by enzymes. Drying does not halt rancidity caused by oxygen in the air; oily foods are seldom dried.

SALTING turns all water in food to a strong salt solution; it is often combined with drying, which further increases the strength of the solution. When salt—sodium chloride—dissolves in water its molecules split into electrically charged sodium and chloride ions, which interfere with chemical reactions and thus suspend the action of enzymes. The solution also creates a strong osmotic pressure (see OSMOSIS) on the cell walls of bacteria and other micro-organisms, which prevents them from passing substances in or out. Both enzymes and micro-organisms will restart when the salt is removed or diluted.

SUGAR creates an osmotic effect in the same way. It does not stop enzyme action; but most foods that are preserved by sugar, whether by bottling in syrup or by crystallization, are cooked, so that is not a problem. A sugar coating can also exclude air, an effect exploited in 'torrefaction', where COFFEE beans are given a sugar coating during roasting to keep their oils from going rancid.

PICKLE and pickling are loose terms covering preservation in a strong vinegar solution, fermentation by lactic acid-producing bacteria, and (sometimes) the salt curing of meats. In both vinegar and lactic pickling the preservative is an acid, which prevents enzymes from working (again by flooding the environment with ions). Most bacteria that cause spoilage or food poisoning cannot work in strongly acid conditions. In vinegar pickling the acid is added to the food, usually combined with salt and often sugar as an additional safeguard. In lactic pickling, lactic acid-producing bacteria make the acid on the spot, thus paralysing their undesirable competitors. They are helped to get a head start by adding a little salt, which they can tolerate better than their rivals can.

SMOKING is almost always combined with other preservation methods such as drying, salting, or, in hot smoking, cooking. It has a certain drying effect itself, but its most important outcome is to seal the surface of the food with an airtight, antiseptic coating.

IRRADIATION kills all micro-organisms by damaging their genetic material. The low doses used in treatment of food have little effect on enzymes. Food can be irradiated through a sealed container, sterilizing the contents.

(RH)

PRESSURE COOKING a way of cooking things at a higher temperature than is normally possible, by increasing the air pressure in the recipient and thus raising the temperature at which water boils.

Denys Papin can be counted the inventor of this, in the 17th century, but it is only in recent times that pressure cookers suitable for domestic kitchens have been available. By using them, cooks can reduce cooking time considerably; and may also be comforted by the thought that some bacteria are destroyed more readily at the temperature reached inside the pressure cooker.

Larger devices, which have important applications in industry and are known as autoclaves, have been available for longer.

PRETZEL a term which may refer to a small plain bread or to a whole range of biscuits, of which many are sweet, most with the characteristic knotted shape, but some in stick form.

The best-known pretzel is a hard, salt-strewn bread snack suitable for being eaten with beer, for example. It was in this form that it crossed the Atlantic into America, where the word first appeared in print around 1824. Mariani (1994) states in addition that the first commercial pretzel bakery in the USA was set up in 1861 in Pennsylvania. He gives an interesting account of the evolution of American pretzels:

Today pretzels come in a variety of shapes and sizes, from sticks, called 'thins,' to rings and saltless, hard, thick teething pretzels called 'Baldies' (because there is no surface salt and it appears 'bald'), a registered trademark . . . Especially popular in New York and the eastern cities are puffy yeast pretzels sold by street vendors and at candy stores. In Philadelphia these same pretzels are usually eaten with a squirt of yellow mustard or slathered with melted butter. So famous are Philadelphia's pretzels that the city is nicknamed the 'Big Pretzel'.

The sweet biscuits which are called pretzels because they borrow the pretzel shape are best known in Germany and Austria. They belong to the category of small butter biscuits and bear names indicating the principal ingredient with which the dough has been enriched or the kind of icing which has been added. Thus *Haselnussbrezeln*, with hazelnuts; and *Zitronenbrezeln*, with lemon icing.

PRICKLY PEAR also called Barbary pear, cactus pear, Indian pear, Indian fig, or tuna fig, is not a kind of pear or fig, but comes from any of numerous CACTI of the genus *Opuntia*. These are all native to the drier regions between C. America and the great deserts of the USA, but some have become firmly established in the Old World, especially around the Mediterranean, in India, and in Australia.

Their fleshy, spiny leaves take the form of flattish discs or pads stacked one on another.

The best fruits are said to be those of *O. megacantha*, which is at present found only in Mexico and the southern USA. The main species in the Mediterranean is *O. ficus-indica*, of which there are several varieties producing different fruits.

The prickly pear fruit resembles a small cucumber, but with seeds distributed evenly through its flesh and with rosettes of little spines on the outside. Size varies from tiny to 12 cm (5") long. Colour may be cream, yellowish-green, pink, red, or purple shading almost to black. The best USA types are the large purplish-red Cardona and yellow Amarilla, which have relatively few spikes. Around the Mediterranean the best are usually pale yellow, though there are also good red ones. In Sicily several large, sweet, almost seedless varieties are cultivated, the finest being called Surfarina and Bastarduni.

Prickly pear fruits are generally eaten fresh and raw. Good ones are tender and pleasantly sweet, though lacking in acidity, so a squeeze of lime or lemon juice helps. They need to be peeled and it is advisable to remove the spines from the peel first. The original N. American Indian way of doing this is to pick the fruits in the early morning while the spines are still wet with dew and soft, and rub them in sand to remove them. Otherwise, the fruit is best attacked with a knife and fork. The rind comes away easily. The seeds are no more troublesome than grape pips.

In Tunisia the fruits are often made into jam, and in the USA they produce a delicious jelly.

American Indians sometimes dried the fruit for winter use. They also boiled it to make a pulp resembling apple sauce. Spanish settlers boiled it down further to make a syrupy paste, *queso de tuna* (prickly pear cheese). The Indians did not waste the seeds. They saved them, dried them, and ground them into meal.

In Mexico, and elsewhere, the thick and fleshy young leaves (the 'pads' which, in Spanish, are called *nopales*) are used as a vegetable. They are stripped of their spines and peeled, then cut into strips and boiled. The boiled strips are rinsed to remove a gum which exudes from them before further use. Then they can be eaten by themselves, in mixtures of vegetables, in omelettes, or made into pickles. Canned *nopales* (plain, or in brine or a vinegar pickle) are available.

PRINCE a suitable name for *Agaricus augustus*, a large edible mushroom of great merit which occurs in most parts of Europe—for example, Germany, France, and Italy, and occasionally in Britain—and the north-west of N. America. It is not common anywhere, but sometimes grows in groups. The cap, which is light yellowish-brown covered with darker brown scales and may measure 20 or even 25 cm (8 or 10") across, is perched on a thick, relatively short, whitish stalk. The flesh bruises yellow. The aroma is of bitter almonds.

The prince is a meaty mushroom, with a fine flavour. Arora (1979) observes that it is found at all seasons, including winter if mild enough, and produces several crops each year:

Especially important since it fruits in the spring and summer, when edible fungi are scarce. It's like getting two mushrooms in one: sweet and almondy when young, strong and mushroomy at maturity. Unfortunately, maggots and sowbugs are crazy about it too.

PROFITEROLES miniature choux PASTRY buns which can be either savoury or sweet. In England they are a popular dessert, split and filled with whipped cream or *crème pâtissière* (see CRÈME), or sometimes ice cream, and served with hot chocolate sauce. Sometimes the tops are coated with caramelized sugar.

In France they are an essential part of wedding celebrations, made into a CROQUEMBOUCHE—a pyramid glazed with caramelized sugar. They are also used in *gâteau Saint-Honoré* (see GATEAU).

Savoury profiteroles exist; they have cheese or meat fillings.

The word is a diminutive of the French word *profit*, meaning profit or a gain. LM

PRONGHORN *Antilocapra americana*, an animal which has some characteristics in common with the ANTELOPE but differs in belonging to the New World (whereas all true antelopes are of the Old World) and in having hollow branching horns, such as no other animal possesses; so it is classified in a family of its own, Antilocapridae. It, and its family with it, almost became extinct at the beginning of the 20th century, when numbers had dwindled from 75 million to a mere 20,000; but it was saved and restricted hunting for it is now allowed in some states.

The pronghorn is the fastest animal in the Americas, capable of bursts of 70 m.p.h. Shoulder height around 90 cm (3'), colour buff to reddish-brown with a white face and black nose. The white throat bears two black bands and the underside of the body is white.

The knowledgeable de Voe, writing from his vantage point in the New York market in 1864, was already calling the pronghorn 'scarce', but was able to muster convincing testimony that its meat was tender and delicate, with a flavour superior to ordinary VENISON. It can be cooked in any of the ways suitable for venison, and makes excellent JERKY.

PROTEIN the principal material of which animals are made. Proteins also play an important role in the life of plants and other living things; for example, all the ENZYMES that control chemical reactions in organisms are proteins. Thousands of kinds of protein are known, and more are constantly being discovered.

Proteins are composed of carbon, hydrogen, oxygen, and nitrogen; it is the presence of the last of these which distinguishes proteins from the other materials of life. There is often also a little sulphur and phosphorus. Proteins are highly complex substances with huge molecules containing thousands or millions of atoms.

Each molecule is a long chain made up of smaller molecules known as AMINO ACIDS. These are joined by a link called a 'peptide bond', which is fairly weak and easy to break.

Plants make proteins from substances in the soil and the air. Nitrogen is in relatively short supply; although there is plenty of this in the air, plants cannot absorb it directly. Leguminous plants such as beans have nodules on their roots, containing bacteria which take in atmospheric nitrogen and make it available to the plant. Other plants have to rely on nitrogen compounds in the soil, which come mainly from decaying plants and from the action of lightning which turns atmospheric nitrogen to nitrates, and also from fertilizers made from nitrate rocks.

Animals need proteins to provide the vital materials for the growth and repair of their bodies, but they cannot make them in the way plants do. They therefore have to eat plants or other animals. Luckily it is not necessary to eat the exact protein that is needed to repair a particular organ. Digestion breaks proteins into their component amino acids, which the body then reassembles as required.

A moderately active adult man needs about 45 g (1.6 oz) of protein a day and a woman 38 g (1.3 oz), assuming the protein to be of high biological value. Any protein above this amount, and any amino acids that cannot be used because protein is 'incomplete' (see below), are burnt as fuel, providing the same amount of energy as sugar: 4.5 calories (18.8 kJ) per gram or 127.5 calories (534 kJ) per ounce.

COMPLETE AND INCOMPLETE PROTEINS
Of the 20 amino acids that play a significant role in the human body, 8 or 10 are an essential part of diet (the rest can be made by changing other amino acids). It is also necessary that there should be enough of each one, and that all should be eaten at the same meal, so that the body can have the full range to work on. This means that proteins which contain all the essential amino acids in the proportions in which they are needed are more valuable as foods than those which lack or do not have enough of a vital component. Foods of animal origin are, as might be expected, the most valuable. They are said to provide 'complete' proteins—though in fact this is an exaggeration, as is shown in the table.

Foods of vegetable origin provide 'incomplete' proteins, which are still useful but do not contain everything that is needed, or not enough of it. Cereals such as wheat, rice, and maize, which supply most of the protein in the diet of peoples all over the world, are notably low in the essential amino acid lysine. Legumes, in contrast, contain abundant lysine; and methionine, the amino acid they tend to lack, is plentiful in cereals. Thus cereals and legumes eaten together complement each other's protein, making it 'complete' and fully usable.

The availability of protein in legumes is further restricted by their indigestibility. This is especially true of dried beans. Soya beans, in particular, need to be treated in some way that breaks down their physical and chemical structure to make the proteins more available (see TOFU; MISO; TEMPE).

Protein foods can be assigned a 'biological value' showing how near they are to completeness. A more useful measurement is 'net protein utilization', which also takes into account how digestible they are (shown in the table published by the FAO in the 1970s).

Food	Biological value	Net protein utilization
Hen's egg	93.7	93.5
Cow's milk	84.5	—
Fish	76.0	—
Beef[a]	74.2	66.9
Soya beans	72.8	61.4
Potatoes	66.7	—
Wholemeal wheat flour	64.7	40.3
White rice	64.0	60 (approx.)
Peas	63.7	46.7
Groundnuts	54.5	42.7
White wheat flour	52.0	—
Lentils	44.6	29.7

[a] Other meats have similar values.

TYPES OF PROTEIN

From the cook's point of view there are two classes of protein, fibrous and globular. The difference lies in the way the long molecules are arranged. In a fibrous protein the chains lie lengthways like the strands of a rope. Examples are myosin, one of the chief proteins in muscles; and COLLAGEN, the main component of CONNECTIVE TISSUE such as cartilage. In a globular protein the chains are loosely bundled. Examples are ovalbumin, the main constituent of egg white; and casein in milk. All protein structures include a good deal of water, which makes up about three-quarters of the weight of muscle. A fibrous protein holds the water in a rigid network of strands. Globular proteins are dispersed in water, forming a thick liquid.

Proteins are also classed as 'insoluble' or 'soluble' in water. In fact, a 'solution' of protein is not much like a solution of (for example) salt in water, because the molecules are so enormous. It is more appropriate to think of it as a COLLOID system of small solid particles suspended in water. All enzymes are soluble proteins, and indeed can only work in a liquid environment. Globular proteins are always soluble, but fibrous proteins may be of either type.

PREPARATION AND DIGESTION

Protein is digested by digestive enzymes (themselves proteins) which can break the peptide bonds that connect the amino acid links. This can happen only if the enzyme can physically reach a link. In some proteins few or no links are exposed, so the protein is indigestible. However, proteins can also be broken up by HYDROLYSIS, the action of water, which proceeds more quickly at high temperatures and in acid conditions. Once the protein has begun to disintegrate, more links are revealed for the enzymes to work on. This is how cooking makes meat digestible. Hydrolysis also goes on in the strongly acid digestive juices of the stomach.

Some proteins are easily digestible in their natural state, but others need preparation if they are to provide any useful nutrition. Globular proteins are easy to digest. Raw egg is an excellent source of protein. Fibrous proteins are harder to deal with. Raw collagen is more or less indigestible. In muscle tissue it covers the strands of myosin, so that these cannot be digested either; therefore raw meat is a poor source of protein. This applies to the human digestive system; carnivorous animals are better equipped to extract nutrition from raw meat.

Cooking changes collagen into GELATIN, which is still not very nutritious. But it is soluble, and is quickly removed to reveal the much more valuable myosin underneath.

The unravelling of protein in cooking processes is known as 'denaturation'. Its effect varies with the type of protein and how far the process goes. When meat is cooked, hydrolysis frays and breaks the collagen. This begins at a temperature of about 60 °C (140 °F) and gets into full swing at about 70 °C (160 °F). Myosin behaves in a similar way at these temperatures; but if the meat reaches boiling point, myosin shrinks and coagulates into a tough, unyielding lump. That is why meat should be cooked gently. It is also important not to let it dry out, as hydrolysis can proceed only if water is present. Globular proteins partly unravel and become tangled, causing them to solidify, as when egg white sets. Again, overheating gives a tough, leathery texture.

Changes can also be made without cooking. Acids can cause hydrolysis without heating, as when tough meat is marinated in wine or lemon juice. Enzymes may also be used, as in the making of junket or cheese when milk is curdled by adding RENNET (a digestive enzyme obtained from the stomachs of calves). Some fruits contain proteolytic (protein-breaking) enzymes, for example papayas, pineapples, and figs.

Recipes from regions where tough meat is the norm often call for a marinade made with fruit or juice.

When egg white is beaten, the globular proteins are pulled out into strands which form a network of fibres to support the frothy result. Kneading bread dough pulls out the fibres of gluten, one of the proteins in wheat flour, in a similar way.

Gelatin is made by boiling down bones, skin, and meat trimmings, all containing collagen. The result is a protein that is still fibrous but has rather short strands and is soluble in water (in the limited sense already described). When hot water is poured onto gelatin the heat energy makes the strands vibrate, so that they loosen and the protein floats about freely. As the liquid cools, the strands move more slowly and eventually settle into a tangled mass, so that the liquid sets to a jelly.

Textured vegetable protein is a recent product, consisting of vegetable protein treated so as to simulate some natural animal food, such as the meat of chicken. As the 20th century drew to a close, one could not say that it was either a failure or a success.   RH

PROVOLONE an important cheese of southern Italy, closely related to CACIOCAVALLO. It is made from whole cow's milk and comes in a variety of shapes: cone or pear shaped, round like a melon, and cylindrical. The weight is typically from 1 to 6 kg (2 to 13 lb), but enormous cheeses to which the name *provolone gigante* applies are sometimes made.

There are three sorts of provolone: mild, sharp, and smoked. The smoked sort may be mild or sharp. All have a higher fat content (45%) than that of caciocavallo. Another difference between the two is that at an age when caciocavallo has already graduated from a table to a grating cheese provolone will still be suitable for table use.

Production of provolone is not confined to the south. There is also a *provolone Lombardo*, from the region of Brescia and Cremona. And cheeses of the same type and name are made in the USA.

PRUNE the French word for PLUM, means in English a dried plum. The word has been used in English in this sense since medieval times (although for several centuries it could also, confusingly, mean a fresh plum).

Prunes all come from a group of oval, black-skinned plums. Their special characteristics are a very high level of sugar, which allows them to be sun dried without fermenting (although nowadays the process is often speeded by drying machinery) and a 'free' or easily detached stone, which is uncommon among plums. Prunes turn completely black in drying as the result of enzyme action. This would be considered unacceptable in any other fruit, but is deemed normal in prunes.

Some dried fruits, when reconstituted with water, have an unmistakable resemblance to the original fresh fruit. However, just as raisins seem different from grapes, so do prunes appear to be distinct from plums. For the cook and the consumer they are a fruit in their own right, and a very good one; versatile, convenient, full of flavour. There was a time when the less knowledgeable people in the English-speaking world would snigger at the mention of prunes, which they associated with old age and laxative qualities, but such unsophisticates are nowadays rare.

The most famous prune plum is certainly Prune d'Agen, named after a town in Aquitaine in the south-west of France. In fact, Agen lies on the edge rather than in the centre of the prune region; the prunes were named d'Agen because the Canal du Midi passes through the town, which served as the main 'port' for dispatching them. In the singular, the name Prunes d'Agen denotes the variety of plum. The plural (*prunes d'Agen*) refers to the product, the prunes.

It was this same French variety that was taken to California by a Frenchman in the 19th century and is prominent among those used in the California prune industry. Californian production now dominates the international trade in prunes and indeed provides a high proportion of those sold in France itself.

Although the prunes of Agen are generally acknowledged to be the best, there are others whose rank is high, including:

- the *brignole*, named after the town of Brignoles, whose speciality it is;
- the *pruneaux de Tours* (also called *pruneaux fleuris* because of a whitish bloom caused by the crystallization of sugar), made from St Catherine plums;
- Carlsbad 'plums', which are prunes: large ones;
- the small Quetsch plums, made into prunes in C. Europe.

It takes approximately 1.5 kg (3 lb) of fresh plums to produce one of prunes, the loss of weight being accounted for almost entirely by the removal of water. Yet prunes in modern times are moist and succulent. The explanation is that their moisture content, reduced by the initial drying process to 23%, to ensure that they will keep satisfactorily in storage, is restored to a higher level (29% for *pruneaux secs*, up to 35% for *demi-secs*) before they are shipped to the markets. This 'rehydration' gives them an attractive softness and sheen.

The uses to which prunes can be put, and the further treatments which they may be given, are numerous. Those of Agen are produced in close proximity to Armagnac, so are sometimes sold in jars containing this brandy, or steeped in a little of it before use. They may also be steeped in wine, or in tea, or of course in water; and they need not be steeped at all if they are to be incorporated in a dish which contains liquid, especially if the dish calls for long cooking. There are a number of meat or game dishes of this sort, notably *Lapin aux pruneaux* (rabbit with prunes, a speciality in the Loire region and the north of France generally). See also COCK-A-LEEKIE.

On the sweet side, a former fashion for prune mousses or prune soufflés has been on the wane, but prune compotes, prepared by stewing prunes in red wine, are now more common, as are prune tarts. Prunes stuffed with marzipan make a good sweetmeat.
READING: Souyri and Glory (1986).

PTARMIGAN *Lagopus mutus*, a bird of high and stony mountainsides, whose choice of such an austere habitat tends to preserve it from the attention of predators. The fact that it is so little threatened has resulted in the ptarmigan behaving like a tame bird, often exhibiting no alarm at the presence of human beings; and, although shooting takes place and the ptarmigan is appreciated as a table bird, the numbers shot are not very high.

Parts of Scotland provide a suitable habitat for this bird, but its range in that country seems to be slowly contracting in a northward direction. The whole range of the species is circumpolar from the Nordic countries eastwards to the Bering Strait and then continuing to N. America (where the name is 'rock ptarmigan') and Greenland; plus outposts in the higher regions of the Pyrenees and the Alps and a few places in C. Asia and Japan.

The flavour of the meat varies according to which of the wild mountain foods a bird has been eating, but has sometimes been compared to that of the red grouse or the hare.

PUCHERO a mixed meat stew which is second only in importance in Spain to COCIDO, and is prominent in the Philippines (often spelled *pochero*); there, like cocido, it is a festive dish, served at family reunions, Christmas, etc. It often has a tomato sauce (usually on the side) and an accompanying aubergine or squash relish. This last feature is probably part of the indigenization of the Spanish dish in the Philippines, as is the use of saba bananas as one of the ingredients. However, the Filipino *pochero* remains quite

clearly a version of the Spanish original, which it resembles in using a luxurious combination of, e.g., beef, pork, chicken, ham, salt pork, chorizo (see SAUSAGES OF SPAIN AND PORTUGAL), chickpeas, cabbage. The same applies to the version of puchero which is important in ARGENTINA.

PUDDING Garrett (*c*.1895) points out what a difficult task it is to define the meaning of this word:

The term itself, which, according to Skeat, is of Celtic origin, is in culinary parlance extended so widely by the fancies and tastes of cooks that it is difficult to assign any limitation to its application. Webster describes a Pudding as a species of food of a soft or moderately hard consistency variously made, and this we are compelled to accept, having nothing more definite to offer.

Nonetheless, people constantly try to pin down a more exact meaning. The *NSOED* gives:

A cooked dish consisting of various sweet or savoury ingredients, esp. as enclosed within a flour-based crust or mixed with flour, eggs, etc., and boiled or steamed; a baked batter mixture. Now also, the sweet course of a meal.

This definition would eliminate e.g. SUMMER PUDDING, because uncooked. There is also an implication, perhaps unintended, that a MILK PUDDING is not strictly a pudding.

The final sentence of the *NSOED* definition calls for amplification. In Britain a pudding, narrowly defined, came to be seen as the principal or normal kind of sweet course at the end of a meal, and then by extension came to mean the sweet course; thus 'What's for pud, mum?'—a question to which the answer might be 'ice cream' or 'an apple'.

To focus attention on British usage is legitimate, since pudding may be claimed as a British invention, and is certainly a characteristic dish of British cuisine. Admittedly, the Portuguese *pudim* (and to a lesser extent the Spanish *púding*) are similar concepts. In general, however, few other languages have words which correspond to it, although the French *boudin* has survived from medieval times (see BLOOD SAUSAGES) and provides a clue to the etymology of pudding.

It seems that the ancestor of the term was the Latin word *botellus*, meaning sausage, from which came *boudin* and also pudding. Puddings in all their variety and glory may thus be seen as the multiple descendants of a Roman sausage. The HAGGIS, by its nature and the way it is prepared, illuminates the connection.

In the Middle Ages the black pudding (see BLOOD SAUSAGES) was joined by the WHITE PUDDING, which was also made in a sausage skin, or sometimes a stomach lining so that it was a larger, round item like the above-mentioned HAGGIS. White pudding was almost completely cereal in composition, usually containing a suet and breadcrumb mixture. It was variously enriched and flavoured, and there were sweet versions.

In diverging from these origins English cooks found two paths which could be taken to advance pudding cookery.

The first was to take advantage of the fact that by the 16th century many ordinary houses had small ovens built into the chimney breast, or at the side of the main bread oven where there was one. These ovens were not very hot. It was possible to bake a white pudding mixture or a cereal pottage slowly enough to suit it. Often, it was enclosed in pastry, wholly or partly. So this path led to baked puddings.

The second path involved finding a different container to replace the gut used for sausages, which was in many ways inconvenient. The breakthrough came when the pudding-cloth was invented, around the beginning of the 17th century. C. Anne Wilson quotes a recipe of 1617 for sweet SUET PUDDING called Cambridge pudding (or COLLEGE PUDDING), in which occurs the sentence: 'Let your liquor boil, and throw your pudding in, being tied in a fair cloth; when it is boiled enough, cut it in the midst, and so serve it in.' As she remarks:

The invention of the pudding-cloth or bag finally severed the link between puddings and animal guts. Puddings could now be made at any time, and they became a regular part of the daily fare of almost all classes. Recipes for them proliferated.

By the 1690s British puddings were attracting the admiration of foreign visitors, such as a French visitor, François Maximilien Misson, who felt obliged to inform his (presumably French) readers that a pudding was a very difficult thing to describe, yet very good, and that the English made them in lots of ways:

They bake them in an oven, they boil them with meat, they make them fifty several ways: blessed be he that invented pudding, for it is a manna that hits the palates of all sorts of people; a manna, better than that of the wilderness, because the people are never weary of it. Ah, what an excellent thing is an English pudding! To come in pudding-time, is as much as to say, to come in the most lucky moment in the world. Give an English man a pudding, and he shall think it a noble treat in any part of the world.

During the 18th century, suet mixtures were joined by the first SPONGE PUDDINGS, and boiled and baked BATTERS became common. Sweet puddings included all kinds of fruits, jam, spices, meringue, and other delicacies. Plain puddings remained important. Among savoury types, the first beef steak and mutton puddings appeared.

Sweet milk pottages made with cereals such as rice or barley persisted. As new kinds of starchy products began to be imported, for example SAGO and TAPIOCA, these were adopted for that purpose, and also used in boiled and baked puddings. These, at first usually rich and interestingly flavoured, were to be simplified into the bland 'nursery' MILK PUDDINGS of succeeding centuries.

At this point, towards the end of the 18th century, the nature of puddings was illuminated by Dr Johnson in a memorable passage, reproduced in the box.

Indeed, by 1800 the pudding was internationally renowned. Even a proud Frenchman such as Beauvilliers included a recipe for 'plumbuting' in his L'Art du cuisiner of 1814.

The disappearance of domestic servants in the 20th century brought further changes. The pudding-cloth was found to be difficult for housewives to use themselves. So, boiled puddings were now almost always made in basins covered with greased paper and foil and steamed partly immersed in water. Thus did the British **steamed pudding** come fully into its own. Roll-shaped puddings were either converted to basin format or baked. The general trend towards haste and fashionable aversion to 'stodge' led to the decline in popularity of many fine old puddings, especially the category of suet puddings. It is noteworthy that in the 1990s steamed and SUET PUDDINGS were being taken up again at the level of expensive restaurants. One influence tending to preserve the tradition of British puddings has been that of the Women's Institute; see the nursery classics section in Grace Mulligan (1995).

See also: BAKEWELL TART; BATTER; BREAD PUDDINGS; CABINET PUDDING; CHARLOTTE, CHRISTMAS PUDDING; DOCK PUDDING; FRUMENTY; NESSELRODE PUDDING; MACARONI (for macaroni pudding); PEASE PUDDING; QUEEN'S PUDDING; ROLY-POLY PUDDING; SAXON PUDDING; SUSSEX POND PUDDING; YORKSHIRE PUDDING.

PUFFBALLS edible fungi of Europe and N. America and temperate zones generally in both northern and southern hemispheres. They range in size from tiny 'buttons' to the huge *Calvatia gigantea*, which is commonly the size of a football or human head, and may look alarmingly like a discarded skull (*tête de mort* is one French name for it). It has been known to reach even larger sizes. In the USA specimens are sometimes found measuring 61 cm (2') across and weighing about 18 kg (40 lb): the record is held by a puffball discovered in New York state in 1877, which had a circumference of 15' 6".

All puffballs belong to the family Lycoperdaceae, including the genera *Calvatia*, *Bovista*, and *Lycoperdon*. In general, small puffballs, which are often pear shaped, are in the genus *Lycoperdon*, meaning 'wolf's fart', or *Bovista*; and large ones, usually round in shape, in the genus *Calvatia*, meaning 'baldness' and by extension 'bald head'.

Marteka (1980) gives a useful list of edible N. American puffballs of the large kind. He gives praise not only to *Calvatia* (now *Langermannia*) *gigantea* but also to *C. cyathiformis*, the cup-shaped puffball, so called 'because of the cuplike, papery base that remains after a spore eruption has blown most of the mushroom away'. Earlier, when suitable for eating, this looks like a loaf of bread inside, and may also resemble a loaf from outside, although its colour can range from white to pinkish tan. It has the 'fairy ring' habit of growth, and is commonly

---

DR JOHNSON ON PUDDINGS

LET us seriously reflect what a pudding is composed of. It is composed of flour, that once waved in the golden grain, and drank the dews of the morning; of milk, pressed from the swelling udder by the gentle hand of the beauteous milk-maid, whose beauty and innocence might have recommended a worse draught; who, while she stroked the udder, indulged in no ambitious thoughts of wandering in palaces, formed no plans for the destruction of her fellow-creatures—milk that is drawn from the cow, that useful animal that eats the grass of the field, and supplies us with that which made the greatest part of the food of mankind in the age which the poets have agreed to call golden. It is made with an egg, that miracle of nature, which the theoretical Burnet has compared to Creation. An egg contains water within its beautiful smooth surface; and an unformed mass, by the incubation of the parent, becomes a regular animal, furnished with bones and sinews, and covered with feathers. Let us consider—Can there be more wanting to complete the Meditation on a Pudding? If more be wanted more can be found—It contains salt, which keeps the sea from putrefaction—salt, which is made the image of intellectual excellence, contributes to the formation of a Pudding.

From Boswell's *Journal of a Tour to the Hebrides with Dr Johnson.*

found in September. *C. craniformis*, the brain puffball, is similar but has a top which is wrinkled like the folds of a brain. In the western USA there are two notable species: *C. booniana*, which is egg shaped, dull white to tan, and has a rough, later cracked, surface; and *Calbovista subsculpta*, which is covered with cone-shaped warts, prefers a higher, cooler habitat, and may appear as early as the spring. The same author gives details of various smaller American puffballs, of the genus *Lycoperdon*, but opines that since there is an abundance of large ones these are not worth collecting and can be left in peace to confuse golfers searching for their golfballs.

Lycoperdon perlatum, *vesse-de-loup perlée* in France and gemmed puffball in the USA, has been given the picturesque name of devil's tobacco pouch in Britain. It must be gathered very young if it is to be edible; and the same applies to *L. pyriforme*, the pear-shaped puffball, which is eaten in France and Germany. Both species occur in Australia.

The name 'puffball' is given because the inside of a mature specimen consists of dusty spores, which puff forth if the skin is burst open. The spores are numerous. A Canadian expert once calculated that a puffball 16 × 12 × 10" would produce 7 trillion (7,000,000,000,000) spores; and that, if each developed into a puffball of the size of the parent, the combined mass of puffballs would be 800 times the size of the earth.

For gastronomic purposes, however, puffballs must be gathered long before they have reached this stage. The inside should be white and homogeneous, resembling cream cheese. (If it is turning mustard yellow or brown, the spores have started to develop and the mushroom is inedible. If it is hard to the touch, and purplish, it is something different: an earthball, which is not edible (although specks of it are used in C. Europe to give an aromatic flavour to savoury dishes). If, when a supposed puffball is bisected, the outline of a nascent mushroom of conventional shape can be seen, it must be the 'button' stage of such a mushroom, and should be identified or discarded.

Dorothy Hartley (1954) has more to say than most authors about the preparation of puffballs.

Puff balls, to my mind, are the most delicious fungi. The little round ones should be gently stewed in milk, till you can pierce them easily with a skewer. Then pour off the milk, and use it to make a white sauce with butter and a dust of mace, some pepper and salt. Return the puff-balls to warm through and serve hot, with brown bread and butter. The Giant Puff-Balls, are exactly like sweetbread, both in texture and flavour. Slice and fry them, and serve with a squeeze of lemon juice. The giant puff-ball is a feast in itself, and I remember a huge one found by a shepherd of the

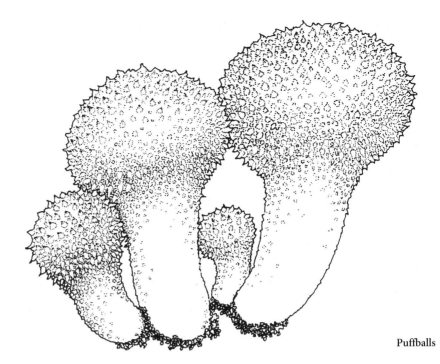

Puffballs

wolds near Loughborough. It was about twenty-four inches in diameter. We cut it in slices, egg-and-breadcrumbed them, and fried them; and one giant puff-ball served six people.

She goes on to explain that the giants should be cut with a breadknife, in slices about 1 cm (0.5") thick, and that they are best fried in hot bacon-fat, after which they should be drained, seasoned, and sprinkled with cider or vinegar. Turning to those of intermediate size, like hen's eggs, she is quite carried away by the decorative possibilities. Their virgin appearance, with skins like 'white kid', is emphasized by coating them with white flour and adding white pepper and salt before poaching them in milk delicately flavoured with a bay leaf and a scrap of onion. When the sauce has been made, and it and they are cooked, they are garnished with tiny bunches of scarlet BARBERRIES and sprigs of green parsley or cress.

Puffballs may be eaten raw in salads, sliced into strips or cut into chunks. They may also be used for sweet dishes. Hay (1887) proposes 'Puffball Fritters with Jam'.
READING: Jordan (1995a).

PUFFIN *Fratercula arctica*, a seabird of the auk family (Alcidae) which inhabits northerly coastal waters of Europe. Neither its appealing appearance nor its wealth of quaint common names nor the fishy and 'rank' taste of its flesh have preserved it from being snared and eaten. It is said that they could be made palatable by pickling them with spices. However, it seems to be only in the FAEROE ISLANDS that these birds are eaten to an appreciable extent.

PULASAN *Nephelium mutabile*, a fruit of the same region as the closely related RAMBUTAN, is similarly popular and much cultivated. It differs in having much shorter hairs on the skin, and it is usually dark red. In most kinds the seed is large and there is little pulp, but what there is is delicate and sweeter than that of the rambutan. In addition, the seed is more easily removed. The flesh of ripe fruits is eaten raw or made into jam.

PULLED CANDY The method and effect of pulling candy are described under SUGAR BOILING. Despite the labour of making it, pulled candy of various kinds is popular for making at home. This is because it is best made by several people at once, so that a whole batch can be pulled before it cools too much to be workable. Thus making it is an excuse to have a party. Commercial kinds are usually pulled mechanically. Pulled candy can be made from a plain sugar syrup, as in HUMBUGS. Often advantage is taken of the pulling technique to join strands of different colours, or opaque pulled and clear unpulled strands, as in British BULLSEYES, French BERLINGOTS, and Swedish POLKAGRISA. Some TOFFEE, or rather taffy, is pulled. So is all ROCK.

Pulled sugar sweets are most popular in W. Europe and N. America, but the technique is also known and used in the Middle East and Asia.

PULSES the edible seeds of any LEGUME such as BEANS, PEAS, or LENTILS. The name may be used for either fresh or dried seeds. They have been a major staple food in man's diet since earliest times.

The word derives from the Latin *puls*, meaning POTTAGE, and came into the English language at the end of the 13th century. It is still commonly used in Britain, although largely supplanted by the word legume, with which it is virtually synonymous; but it is not normally used in N. America.

Drying, the simplest way of preserving all food, is a technique particularly suited to pulses; their protein and fat content remains largely intact, while the flavour, although altered, remains good.

In India, where pulses of all kinds are especially important, a distinction is made between GRAM, which are whole, unpeeled pulses, and DAL, split, skinned pulses. Legume seeds are always double in form and split easily when the skin is rubbed off.

PUMA (also known as mountain lion, panther, catamount, cougar), *Felis concolor*, one of the 'big cats' with a remarkable range extending from W. Canada down through Mexico and C. America to Patagonia in S. America. A solitary animal, which is capable of astonishing leaps and preys mainly on deer, it has attracted little attention as food for humans. However, Charles Darwin, eating it in Patagonia and recording his impressions in the journal which he kept during his famous voyage on the *Beagle*, thought that its meat was good, 'very white, and remarkably like veal in taste'. (Indeed, misled by some remark which had been made, Darwin actually thought at first that he was eating a kind of veal, namely the flesh of a half-formed calf, long before its proper time of birth—which, he says, was one of the favourite dishes of the country.)

There is quite a lot of puma meat, since a puma may weigh up to 100 kg (225 lb).

PUMPERNICKEL a wholegrain RYE BREAD from Westphalia in Germany, is leavened by a SOURDOUGH culture. It is also known as *Schwarzbrot* because of the characteristic dark colour which results from the caramelization of the starch in the rye grain during the long, slow baking process.

According to the *OED*, the name pumpernickel, whose ultimate derivation is uncertain, originally meant 'lout' or 'stinker', and was then by transference applied to the bread (which was notorious for causing flatulence).

The bread is often sold very thinly sliced, in packets, and is good with smoked sausage or cheese.

PUMPKIN a large vegetable fruit, typically orange in colour, round, and ribbed, borne by varieties of the plant *Cucurbita pepo*, one of four major species in the genus *Cucurbita*; see CUCURBIT.

The name is thought to derive from an old French word *pompon*, which in turn came from the classical Greek *pepon*, a name also applied to the melon.

Fruits of the species *C. pepo* and its hybrids may have other common names, such as SQUASH (with various epithets); but it is within this species and its hybrids that we find the varieties known as Spirit, Trick-or-Treat, and Connecticut Field, which are among the traditional Hallowe'en pumpkins, and the others which have the distinctive shape and coloration which are particularly associated with the name pumpkin. However, the name 'pumpkin' is not a precisely defined one and it may be applied to certain varieties of related species, especially when they happen to resemble the true (Hallowe'en-type) pumpkins. Thus fruits of *Cucurbita maxima*, WINTER SQUASH, may be called pumpkins.

Pumpkins are eaten when fully ripe. They often grow to a large size: the unconfirmed record holder, grown by Ivan Peace of Suncook, New York, in 1962, had a claimed weight of 122 kg (268 lb).

Pumpkin flesh is rather fibrous and has an earthy taste which is not universally liked. It is used for both savoury and sweet dishes. The Argentinian method of cooking a meat stew in a hollowed-out pumpkin uses the extracted flesh of the vegetable to thicken the sauce.

The French use pumpkin almost exclusively for making soups (*soupe au poitron*); however, in uses in the Rhône-Alpes, especially in the south, a pumpkin-flavoured bread is made (*pain de courge*). Originally the pumpkin was a cheap wheat 'extender', but a premium is now paid for this speciality bread, which is eaten like BRIOCHE, for breakfast, tea, or a snack. *Citronillat* is a pumpkin pie from Berry. For an interesting pumpkin speciality in Majorca, see ANGEL'S HAIR.

When pumpkin is used in sweet dishes, spices such as ginger and cinnamon are commonly added. This practice goes back a long way. For example, American pumpkin pie, a main feature of the American THANKSGIVING dinner, may have been derived from old English recipes for sweet pies using 'tartstuff', a thick pulp of boiled, spiced fruit.

In Cyprus *kolokotes*, pasties (about the size of Cornish pasties) stuffed with pumpkin and crushed wheat, are popular in the winter, e.g. for a quick hot breakfast on a cold day. Nicolaou (1983) believes that this delicacy is unknown outside Cyprus. The use

of cloves, cinnamon, and sultana raisins to flavour the filling suggests an ancient origin.

In Spain and Mexico pumpkin seeds (*pepitas*) are eaten roasted, fried, or salted; and they are a popular snack in other countries too.

The tendency for the name 'pumpkin' to be used in a very wide sense, including what are more commonly known as squashes, is well illustrated by the following quotation from Lady Llanover (1867), whose comments on the use of pumpkins in Welsh kitchens are anyway of intrinsic interest.

Few vegetables are so little understood and consequently so much undervalued in Great Britain as pumpkins. Perhaps Gower in South Wales is the only part of the United Kingdom where pumpkins are grown as an article of diet by the rural population; and there they are to be seen, as on the Continent, hanging from the ceilings for winter store, and any little spare corner in the field or garden is made use of to place the small mound on which to sow a few pumpkin seeds. The varieties of this plant are so numerous that it would be beyond the limit of any cookery book to attempt an enumeration of comparative merits, from the vegetable marrow to the Turk's turban and the yellow pumpkin, which grows to such a size as to fill a wheelbarrow; but it will not be out of place to note shortly a few of the modes in which pumpkins are available. For white soup they can be used alone, with merely the addition of onion, celery and sweet-herbs for flavouring. They are excellent when boiled, sprinkled with salt and sweet-herbs; or fried in egg and crumbs like soles. Also plain, boiled in slices and served with brown gravy. In Gower they are added to hashed meat, made into pies with apples, and put into soup. Pumpkins have one peculiar quality in addition to a good deal of natural sweetness; they will absorb and retain the flavour of whatever they are cooked with. If stewed with plums it tastes exactly like them in puddings and tarts; the same with apples, rhubarb or gooseberries; and for savoury cookery it would be difficult to say in what dish it may not be used with advantage as an addition.

PUNCHNEP a Welsh dish of root vegetables cooked and mashed together, with a little butter or cream added for serving. Potatoes and baby white turnips have been the most popular mixture, but swedes, parsnips, carrots, or peas may all be used either together or separately with potatoes.

PURSLANE a name of wide and loose application, refers chiefly to *Portulaca oleracea*, a plant which originated in the Near East or C. Asia and has been eaten in those regions for more than 2,000 years. The well-known 19th-century horticultural writer Loudon wrongly thought that the plant originated in Latin America, and the hare which he, or possibly an earlier source which he failed to cite, thus set running may occasionally be seen scampering across the pages of more recent works.

Purslane was cultivated and eaten in ancient Egypt, and in classical Greece and Rome. The Romans called it *portulaca*, said to be the origin of the early French *porcelaine*, from which the English name is derived.

Gibault (1912) remarks that in medieval times the Arabs thought it so good that they called it 'the blessed vegetable'; and cites evidence of its cultivation in Europe in the 13th and 14th centuries. Although it is often said to have been a late arrival in England, there is evidence that it was known there at that early time.

The original wild plant had small green leaves and a sprawling habit. Cultivated varieties are mostly upright, with emerald green or golden, in some instances large golden, leaves. These are fleshy and mucilaginous, as is usual in their family, Portulacaceae; and mild in flavour. They can be cooked like spinach or—as in France—used raw as a salad vegetable.

In Australia the wild plant (or a very close relation), with its pretty yellow flowers has been known as munyeroo or purslane or by a name which has different meanings in N. America, PIGWEED. Low, in *Bush Tucker* (1989), explains its previous importance for Australians. He cites an early settler in Queensland, Rachel Henning, who wrote: 'We get along with wild vegetables till the tame ones see fit to flourish. We have a wild plant which makes a capital salad and which we seldom dine without. It rejoices in the name of pigweed.' The juicy leaves and stems are sometimes still cooked as a vegetable. The seeds were an important food for the Aboriginals.

Purslane is not much eaten in western countries, although it crops up here and there, for example in Mexican markets in the USA under its Spanish name. It is more popular in the Middle East and the Indian subcontinent.

Other species of the genus provide edible leaves in various parts of the world; and some other plants of different genera are commonly called purslane. Of these, the important one, declared by a leading British authority, Joy Larkcom (1984), to be her favourite winter salad plant, is *Montia perfoliata*, known as winter purslane, or Spanish or **miner's lettuce.** or just called 'claytonia' after its former generic botanical name. This plant, which bears two forms of leaf, both decorative, originated in N. America and can be grown as far north as Vancouver.

See also SEA PURSLANE.

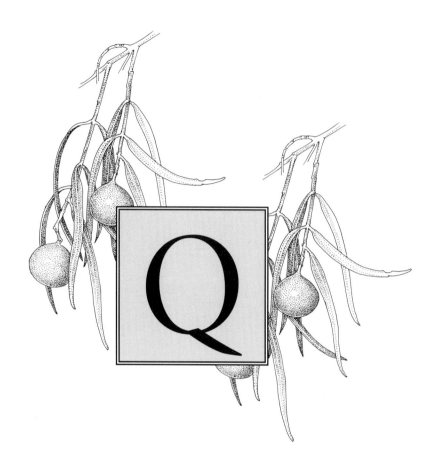

QATA'IF (*kadayif, kunafa, knafeh*), a family of Near Eastern PASTRIES which can take the form of PANCAKES or a sort of dry-baked vermicelli.

The original meaning was pancake, and this is still what *qata'if* (locally pronounced '*atâyif*) are in Egypt and Syria. A usual recipe is to pour leavened batter onto a greased pan and cook slowly on one side only, just until the batter is set. This half-cooked cake is folded over a sweetened cheese or nut stuffing; the raw side is tacky and the edges readily seal. The semicircular filled cakes are then deep fried. Stores sell both cooked stuffed '*atâyif* and the raw pancakes (crêpes) for stuffing and frying at home. This pastry is also found in Turkey, where it is known as *dolma kadayif*.

Medieval Arabic cookbooks record this recipe, and also describe *qata'if* which were served simply with honey and sesame oil. However, at least as early as the 9th century the most highly regarded medieval *qata'if* were crêpes, unleavened and as thin as possible, and the batter might consist of an ounce of cornflour (US cornstarch), an ounce of water, and an egg white. It was not fried in a greased pan but very slowly cooked on a sheet of polished metal (sometimes referred to as a mirror) wiped with a cloth full of wax and walnut meats. The resulting thin crêpes were wrapped around a sort of marzipan called *lauzînaj*, and by extension the crêpes themselves were sometimes confusingly called *lauzînaj*.

This paper-thin crêpe cooked on the 'mirror' was also known as *kunafa* in Arabic. The 13th-century recipes for *kunafa* do not wrap these crepes around a filling but serve them hot with butter and honey, pancake fashion. Some of the recipes call for the crêpes to be cut up with scissors 'the size of rose petals' or even 'as small as possible' first.

The modern Egyptian or Syrian *kunâfa* is clearly descended from this dish, but it is made in a different way. Instead of being cooked as a sheet, the batter is dribbled onto the heated sheet of metal from a perforated container (*kunafiyya*), making threads that look like vermicelli. The heated metal sheet dries them and they are subsequently baked or fried with plenty of butter in various forms, but always with a filling.

The filling is usually of walnuts, almonds, or pistachios—chopped or ground, perhaps moistened with a little rosewater and sugar. Or a filling of sweetened cheese or clotted cream (see KAYMAK) may be inserted after cooking.

Sometimes the threads are baked to form flat baklava-like cakes (*basma*), with the filling sandwiched between layers of dough.

More often the threads of dough are wrapped around the filling into small, individual rolled pastries, which are baked and then have syrup poured over them. This is the form commonly found in Middle Eastern pastry shops.

In the Arab countries, *kunafa* became the name for this dry-cooked vermicelli. In Turkey, the vermicelli pastry was called *tel kadayifi*, which literally means 'string *qata'if*', a nicely expressive term. This name, with, or more often without, the word *tel*, has passed into usage in neighbouring countries such as Iran (where it is *ghatayef*) and Greece (*kataifi*).

By extension, the Turks use the name *ekmek kadayif* (bread *kadayif*) for a rich sweet made by soaking bread in syrup and butter. In Egypt it is known as '*eish al-sarâya* (palace bread) and '*eish ekmek kadayif.*   CP

QAWARMA (or *confit d'agneau*) is minced lamb preserved in fat from the tail of the FAT-TAILED SHEEP (called *Awassi*). Until not so long ago it was the main winter meat-preserve of Lebanese mountain dwellers. Each family set aside one or two six-month-old, or younger, sheep—usually castrated males to safeguard the meat from bad smells during the sheep's period of heat, or else sterile ewes whose flesh is not as tough as that of fertile ones. The sheep are fattened during the summer months and force-fed by hand with grain and mulberry and vine leaves. They are butchered after 14 September (the Feast of the Cross) when the weather becomes cooler and the best cuts of meat and offal are moved and prepared for the feast which ensues the slaughter. The fat from the tail is chopped coarsely and set aside whilst the rest of the meat (a third meat to two-thirds fat) is chopped in 2 cm (1") cubes, salted, and also set aside.

The preparation of qawarma takes place in the afternoon after the family and guests have feasted on a variety of dishes made with the better cuts of meat and offal. The fat is put in a large pan called *dist* and placed over a medium-low heat. It is stirred until melted and golden before the salted chopped meat is added and cooked for 10 to 15 minutes. The qawarma is poured hot into earthenware jars and left to cool before being covered with a cloth on top of which go weighted lids. The jars are stored in a cool place and the stock of qawarma will last until the summer when fresh meat becomes more readily available. Qawarma is still prepared, though far less at home than commercially, and is now more of a delicacy than a winter preserve. It is cooked with *kishk* (see KASHK) to produce a hearty breakfast soup, or fried with eggs, or eaten plain with bread as with RILLETTES.   AH

QUAHOG *Mercenaria mercenaria*, one of the most popular CLAMS in N. America, is known also as littleneck, because the 'neck' on which its syphons protrude is much shorter than that of its principal rival, the SOFT-SHELLED CLAM; and as hard(-shelled) clam, because its shell is much stronger and thicker than that of the other.

The name quahog (pronounced co-hog), or quahaug, is of American Indian derivation. The species is a native of N. America, with a range extending from Canada down to Florida, but has established for itself (via the kitchens of ocean liners) English colonies in Southampton Water and Portsmouth harbour; and has also been introduced to the south of Ireland and the basin of the River Seudre in France. The French, in deference to its American origin, call it 'clam'.

A quahog may measure up to 13 cm (5"). The shell is dull in colour—dirty white, brown, or greyish, sometimes with zigzag red markings near the margins—and is purplish inside. Quahogs are marketed in different sizes, each with its own name. In New York the list runs thus, the numbers indicating how many to the bushel: littlenecks, 450–650; cherrystones, 300–25; mediums, 180; and chowders, 125.

The name wampum clam may also be met. Wampum was American Indian bead money, and the purple interior of the quahog shell was used for high-denomination wampum.

The manner of eating quahogs depends on their size. Those up to the size of cherrystones are best eaten raw. Mediums are to be steamed open and served on the half-shell, or used in a CHOWDER. The largest are also for chowders; but may be stuffed. Cap'n Phil Schwind (1967) relates the amusing tale of how Captain Ben Nickerson advertised for a bride, who had to be a good cook and a true Cape Cod girl; of how he gave each applicant a bucket of quahogs to cook, as a test; and of the nice discrimination shown by the winner in serving the small ones raw and the larger ones, minced, in a chowder.

The OCEAN QUAHOG is of a different family.

QUAIL *Coturnix coturnix*, the smallest of the European game birds, belongs to the same family, Phasianinae, as the PARTRIDGE and indeed looks like a very small partridge. Its numerous relations around the world include birds known as blue quails, brown quails, and bush quails; plus, in N. America, mountain quails, California quails, and the bobwhites, *Colinus* spp.

The derivation of the word 'quail' has been charmingly explored by Francesca Greenoak (1979) who points out that it is an imitative name, cognate with 'quack'.

This association becomes clearer when it is seen that it comes, via the Old French *Quaille* (a form used also by Chaucer), from the Latin *Quaquila*. The Quail's voice also gave rise to a number of imitative names in Britain and Ireland, which incorporate the three sharp notes. Among these are But-for-but, Wet-my-lip, Wet-my-feet and Quick-me-Dick. The cock may make this call over a wide area, ranging up to forty kilometres or more; which may be what earned him the name Wandering Quail. Alternatively, this name could be associated with Quail migrations. The Quail population appears over history to have varied a great deal in its size; sometimes the migratory flocks are sparse, sometimes quite huge, like those described in Exodus which twice saved the Israelites from starvation: 'and it came to pass that at even, the quails came up and covered the camp'.

The same author comments that quail were not eaten much in classical times,

apparently because they were thought to be unwholesome because of eating poisonous plants such as hellebore. Quail did not figure prominently in medieval menus in England, although they are regular summer visitors, familiar in hayfields and cornfields and sometimes called corncrakes for that reason.

Nowadays quails are appreciated as food, despite their small size, and in Europe are commercially reared, for both eggs and meat. In Pakistan they are prepared in curry-type dishes and they also appear further east, for example in Laos, as a popular food whenever available.

QUAKING PUDDING is a pudding with a light, frail texture which is halfway to being an egg CUSTARD. Most of what solidity it has comes from breadcrumbs. This is one of the oldest of the puddings made in a cloth. A recipe for it was recorded early in the 17th century, and it also appears in Samuel Pepys's diary; he recalls having eaten a particularly good 'shaking pudding'. This pudding is often served with a sweet white wine sauce.

QUANDONG the fruit of the S. Australian SANDALWOOD tree, *Eucarya acuminata*=*Santalum acuminatum*, known also as native peach or (in W. Australia) wolgol. This is round and red, as large as a small plum, and has soft, sweet, red flesh which is made into jam or chutney and used as pie filling. The stone is hard to crack, but yields a kernel which is rich and whose flavour when roasted ranges from somewhat bitter or pungent to acceptable.

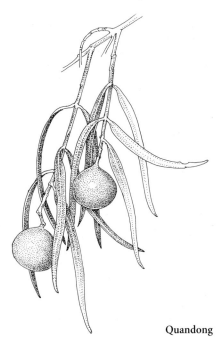

Quandong

The quandong is a parasitic tree, capable of attaching itself to any of numerous hosts and able to survive in very arid conditions. In the 1990s a start was made in cultivating it.

QUARK (pronounced 'kvahrk' and meaning curd) is a fresh CURD CHEESE made from skimmed milk and is consumed by Germans on a very large scale.

Various kinds of quark can be ripened to form a different cheese. Thus *Sauermilchquark*, which is made from SOUR MILK, is the basis for one of the best-known sorts of HAND CHEESE, *Sauermilchkäse*. A family tree showing all the varieties and products of quark would be extremely complicated. This is inevitable, given the extraordinary importance of quark; it accounts for about half the cheese eaten by Germans themselves, and has been spreading abroad steadily, helped by its reputation as a suitable food for slimmers (although its fat content varies according to the type) and by its versatility in the kitchen.

A version with some of the fat restored to it is called *Speisequark* (*Speise* means food). Quark with cream mixed into it is *Rahmfrischekäse* (see CREAM CHEESE).

Plain quark has a neutral taste which makes it suitable for use in sweet dishes. It is sometimes sold with fruit pulp already mixed into it.

The growing popularity of quark outside Germany is perhaps partly due to its name; to non-German ears, this is memorable, faintly mysterious, and suggestive of an invention by Lewis Carroll.

QUEEN CAKE a small rich cake made from a creamed mixture with currants, lemon zest, and sometimes chopped almonds, baked as individual cakes. They have been popular since at least the 18th century. Now usually baked in paper cases, traditionally little fluted tin moulds in fancy shapes were used; Eliza Acton (1845) said that heart-shaped moulds were usual for this mixture.   LM

QUEENFISH also called talang or leatherskin, *Chorinemus lysan* and close relations, are members of the carangid (JACK) family with a widespread distribution in the Indo-Pacific area; their range includes southern Africa and Australia. These fish, which have a maximum length of over 1 m (40"), are rated only fair for edibility. Some Chinese prefer not to eat them, believing that the dark blotches along their sides are marks left by the fingers of a god who claimed them for his own.

QUEEN'S PUDDING or queen of puddings, as the name of a pudding, seems not to have a very long history. As a dish, however, it apparently goes back to the 17th century. Sir Kenelm Digby (1669) gave a recipe for a dish like modern queen's pudding: breadcrumbs combined with milk and egg yolks, part baked, and then topped with jam and meringue made from the whites and baked until done.

What queen may have been involved or how is unclear. There is a recipe for 'Queen Pudding' in Garrett (*c*.1895); but it is not the same as queen's pudding above. This same book does, however, have a recipe for Manchester Pudding, which matches one given by Mrs Beeton (1861) and may provide a clue. A Manchester pudding has a layer of puff pastry at the bottom of the dish and does not have a meringue topping. Otherwise it is more or less the same as queen's pudding and indeed Helen Pollard (1991) says that it is simply a variation of queen's pudding. This evidence perhaps suggests that queen's pudding received its name at about the beginning of the 20th century; and at that time there was only one queen who could have inspired the name (no doubt after commenting favourably on a helping of Manchester pudding, possibly in the course of a royal visit to that city) and that of course was Queen Victoria.

Be this as it may, queen's pudding in its modern form is one of the best British puddings.

QUENELLES a French term which came from the German *Knödel*, meaning DUMPLING, refers to small dumpling-like items made of finely minced fish or meat with some bread and seasoning incorporated. The texture is fine, the shape is usually round or variations such as a short sausage shape. Cooking is done by poaching.

Among the best-known quenelles are those of VEAL and those of PIKE (*quenelles de brochet*).

QUESO the Spanish for 'cheese', forms part of some names of cheese of Spain and Latin America. In Portuguese the word *queijo* plays a similar role.

The Spanish cheese MANCHEGO is often referred to as queso Manchego. The same applies to numerous other SPANISH CHEESES. Other examples of the usage, from Latin America, are:

• *Queso Chihuahua* is a famous Mexican cheese made by the Mennonite communities around Chihuahua City. Quesillo is the diminutive form of *queso*, for example the Mexican *quesillo de*

Oaxaca, a soft and slightly acid cheese which melts well and is good in cooking.
• *Queso blanco* (white cheese) is much used all over South America. It varies from country to country, but in general it is a fresh cheese made from whole or skimmed cow's milk, crumbly in texture and rather heavily salted. If pressed to consolidate it, it is known as *queso de prensa* (pressed cheese). Some of this is aged until very hard and is used for grating.
• *Queso de crema* is either a cream cheese, often used as a spread in place of butter, or a soft, surface-ripened cheese resembling BRICK CHEESE.
• *Queso anejo* (aged cheese) is a dryish, salty, crumbly, Mexican cheese, made from skimmed milk and matured for six to eight months, which figures largely in Mexican cuisine, for example in *enchiladas* (see TORTILLA).

QUICHE a French term derived from the German word *kuchen* (see TORTE AND KUCHEN), most prominent in Lorraine and indeed the phrase 'quiche Lorraine'. It was only at the beginning of the 19th century that the term became current, and it then meant a tart with a filling of egg and cream. (In this connection see the IPCF volume on Lorraine, 1998.) The version now well known, which includes bacon (and sometimes cheese) in the filling, was originally a variant known as *quiche au lard*. Whereas the original could be eaten on meatless days, this variant—now known around the world as quiche Lorraine—could not. Nonetheless, a quiche Lorraine is perceived as something with only a slight meat content. This may account for the reputation it acquired in some English-speaking countries, where it only became familiar in the latter part of the 20th century, as a dish not suitable for 'he-men' or 'real men'.

At the end of the 20th century the quiche has become the subject of innumerable variations, which are usually and correctly given names which do not incorporate 'Lorraine'.

QUINCE *Cydonia oblonga*, a relative of the APPLE and PEAR, originated, as they did, in the Caucasus, where small, twisted quince trees still grow wild. The most usual type of quince resembles a large, lumpy, yellow pear. It has hard flesh and many pips and is too sour and astringent to eat raw; but it has a delicious fragrance and when cooked with adequate sweetening develops a fine flavour and turns pink. There are also round varieties. Quinces are nearly always used for cooking. However, a few are mild and sweet enough to eat raw; these include some new varieties being developed in the 1990s, e.g. one referred to as 'apple quince'.

The scent of quinces was greatly appreciated, and cultivation spread to the Levant and SE Europe before that of the apple. The fruit was known in Palestine around the beginning of the 1st millennium BC, and the 'apples' mentioned in the Song of Solomon were almost certainly quinces.

The ancient Greeks held the quince sacred to Aphrodite, the goddess of love. Indeed, the golden apple of Hesperides given by Paris to Aphrodite, leading to the downfall of Troy, is generally believed to have been a quince. Its first mention in Greek writings dates from just after 600 BC, when it figures in a marriage ceremony prescribed by the ruler Solon.

The common quince was called *strythion*. The Greeks successfully developed a superior variety from Kydonia in Crete, whence comes the generic name *Cydonia*.

The Romans, who also rated the quince highly, had a different name for it: *melimelum*, which comes from the Greek for 'honey apple'. This was not because the quince was supposed to be sweet but because it was preserved in honey to make an early example of the numerous QUINCE PRESERVES (see below).

The quince continues to be well liked in its native region, the Caucasus, and is important in Turkey. In Persian cuisine, with its tradition of meat and sour fruits cooked together, there are many recipes for meat and quince stews, and for quinces with meat stuffing. The combination is also common in Moroccan cooking and in parts of E. Europe such as Romania.

In Britain, quince sauce was a traditional accompaniment to partridge. However, the most usual use for quinces in Britain was in tarts and pies. Quinces were often added to apple pie, giving it a pink colour and interesting flavour. Quinces were also cored, filled with sugar, and roasted like apples; and quince marmalade and jelly remained popular until a decline in popularity in Britain during the 20th century.

There are no native American quinces but the quince was still at the height of its popularity when Europeans began to settle in America, and immigrants soon began to grow the fruit. Interest has since declined in N. America, but the fruit remains popular in many Latin American countries, especially Uruguay, where there are large plantations.

QUINCE PRESERVES are important because in their original forms they were the ancestors of modern JAM and MARMALADE. The various names derive from classical languages. In ancient Greece, quinces were known as apples of Cydonia, *mela Kudonia*.

The French *cotignac*, Italian *cotognata*, and Greek *kidonopasto*, along with the 17th-century English words 'quidony' or 'quidoniac', can be traced back to this Greek origin. The Portuguese word *marmelada* (from which the English word MARMALADE is taken) and the Spanish *membrillo* derive from Latin *melimelum* (honey apple, referring to QUINCE or a preserve thereof).

Thus modern European quince preserves can be traced back to two sweetened quince preserves known to the classical world, both of which were based on quinces stored in honey, sometimes with vinegar and spices added. This method was applied to other fruits (and vegetables such as turnips), which were placed uncooked into the honey. When kept for a year like this, they became soft. Observation taught the cooks that to produce a reliably acceptable result from quinces, it was necessary to cook the fruit first; if the raw quinces were the slightest bit under ripe, they remained extremely hard during storage. Hence the discovery was made that cooked quinces combined with sugar (in the form of honey), and acid (in this case vinegar) would produce a solid gel; and thus the properties of PECTIN were first exploited. The discovery that other fruits gelled when treated this way does not seem to have come until much later, as they softened on storage without cooking.

Quince preserves with honey were known in the medieval Arab world, and they reappear in Europe in an early French cookery book, *Le Menagier de Paris* (*c*.1394— see MEDIEVAL CUISINE: THE SOURCES). The tradition of quince sweetmeats appears to have been so strong because they were regarded as having medicinal properties, which could be varied by adding different spices. They were thought to be particularly good for the digestion. Their medieval English name was chardeqynce (flesh of quince).

In 16th- and 17th-century England many recipes for quince preserves were published under the names of quidoniac, quiddony, marmelade, or sometimes paste of Genoa. These pastes (by now sometimes made from other fruits) could be cast in fancy shapes, 'a Dog, or Dolphin, a Syren, or a Vessel full of Flowers' (G. Rose, 1682), and gilded, or set in little boxes. They seem to have gone out of favour in England in the late 18th century, but have remained popular sweetmeats on the Continent. The coarser quince pastes, such as *membrillo*, are served in Spain with cheese.

Cotignac d'Orléans is a superior form of *cotignac*, a clear jellied sweetmeat made of the juice of quinces boiled with sugar and poured out to set in little round wooden boxes. It has an attractive colour, likened by one French author to that of 'the most

beautiful rubies'. Larger pieces are moulded with figures such as Joan of Arc. *Cotignac* in this form has been associated with Orléans from at least the 16th century.

QUINOA *Chenopodium quinoa*, provided the principal grain crop in the region of the Andes before the conquest of America, and is still an important staple food there. It is not a typical cereal but is used as if it were. The plant has green leaves like SPINACH (a relative), grows to 150–160 cm (5'), and produces great quantities of tiny white or pink seeds in large sorghum-like clusters. These are typically white or pink, but among the numerous cultivars are many which display other bright colours, including black, yellow, and orange.

Quinoa, which is found in a belt stretching from S. Colombia to NW Argentina and N. Chile, can withstand extreme conditions and grows at altitudes too high for maize. It was a major agricultural commodity of the Aztec and Inca and has played an important ceremonial role, over long periods of time in both N. and S. America.

Much of the harvest is now gathered by machine. Processing involves threshing the seed heads to remove the seed, winnowing to remove the husk, and washing in an alkaline solution to remove bitter, apparently toxic, compounds that occur in the seed. Once processed, quinoa grain is used in the preparation of bread, biscuits, tortillas, stews, and soups. Its flour can be added to wheat flour for enriching baked goods. The leaves can be eaten as a green vegetable.

In recent times, the potential value of quinoa beyond its current range of cultivation has been widely recognized. The quality of its protein is roughly equivalent to that of milk, due to a high concentration of essential amino acids.

Huauzontle, *C. nuttaliae*, is a distinct species and resembles broccoli. It is native to Mexico, where its immature seed heads are eaten whole, fried in batter. The mature seeds of this and of other species in the USA, Australia, and Siberia have also been used as food.

QUROOT is a C. Asian dried curdled milk product similar to the KASHK of Iran. Yoghurt or buttermilk are dried and formed into hard pebble-like balls which are stored for winter use. The word *quroot* comes from the the Turkish word *qurumak* meaning to dry.

Quroot is a popular product in Afghanistan and they have a special bowl which they use to reconstitute the balls which is called a *targhora-e-qurooti*. The bowl, which is made from pottery, has small stones/pebbles embedded in the clay at the bottom. These form a rough surface over which the hard balls are rubbed while adding water until a thick creamy consistency is reached. The reconstituted quroot is used in a number of dishes, mainly as a sauce served with noodle, and *burani* dishes (see BURAN). It is also added to the soup called *mashawa* and a short-grain rice dish called *mastawa*. Afghans also prepare a simple dish, called *Qurooti*, by adding lots of crushed garlic and salt and pepper to reconstituted *quroot*, then boiling the result and enjoying it with NAN. It is often flavoured with mint.

Qara quroot is a strong-tasting dried black (*qara* means black) curdled product made from whey which is boiled down and then dried.

See also TARHANA.   HS

RABBIT the small mammal *Oryctolagus cuniculus*. Native to Morocco and the Iberian peninsula, rabbits are now found throughout W. and C. Europe, and have been introduced to the Azores, Madeira, S. America, Australia, and New Zealand. They inhabit grassland or open woodland, are mostly nocturnal in habit, and eat herbage and bark.

Rabbits belong to the family *Leporidae*, which includes the various species of HARE. Considered with reference to N. America, confusion arises. The cottontail rabbit (*Sylvilagus floridanus*) and marsh hare (*S. aquaticus*) would be considered rabbits by Europeans. On the other hand, the jackrabbit (*Lepus californicus*) would be thought a hare in Europe. From the cook's point of view, the important difference is that the flesh of rabbit is pale and mildly flavoured, while that of hare (the larger animal) is dark and often very strong. The two are treated differently in the kitchen.

Rabbit meat for the table can be derived from either wild or domesticated animals. Domesticated or 'hutch' rabbits are bred to be larger than wild ones; there are several varieties. Currently, the word 'rabbit' is applied irrespective of age. In the past, the animal was a rabbit up until the age of a year, and subsequently referred to as a coney.

HISTORY

The range of rabbits was restricted to the countries of the W. Mediterranean until about the 3rd century BC, when the Romans began importing live rabbits to Italy as a source of meat. They are said to have fattened rabbits in warrens or yards known as *leporaria*, using ferrets to catch them.

Most authorities support the theory that it was the Normans who brought the stock from which the modern British and Irish population is descended, some time after the conquest. Records for them in the Scillies and on Lundy Island date back to the late 12th century. Walled and paved courtyards, which forced the animals to breed above ground, were used, so that the young could be easily removed. This was important to the medieval dietary regime as *laurices*, unborn and newly born rabbits, were not considered 'meat' and could be eaten on fish days. They were also kept in warrens, enclosed areas of land in which they could feed and burrow, and from whence they were conveniently caught. But they began to escape and establish feral colonies shortly afterwards, being caught with nets and ferrets.

In the late 14th century in England, rabbits were an expensive luxury. Medieval cooking methods included serving them roasted, with the heads on, sauced with ginger and VERJUICE, or made into highly seasoned dishes known as civey or gravey, ancestors of modern French CIVET.

During the early modern period, the sailor's habit of releasing breeding pairs onto islands to provide supplies of fresh meat aided the spread of rabbit around the world. In Britain, the custom of keeping rabbits in warrens persisted well into the 18th century. A device called a 'tipe' (a trap sunk into the ground between two fields) was used to catch them. Warren-bred rabbits, and the carcases of animals used for fur, were readily available and cheap. The cook stuffed and roasted, or stewed them, or baked the meat in pies.

Although feral rabbits were known in central Scotland in the Middle Ages, they only reached the Western Highlands and Islands in the 19th century. At about the same time the warrens in England were abandoned in favour of other land uses. This and the development of sporting estates benefited the feral rabbit population, as the expansion of cultivated land provided more food, and their predators were now being hunted ruthlessly.

The rabbit population exploded in the 20th century; it was put at 100 million in the early 1950s, and regarded as vermin. Myxomatosis, a disease first noted in S. America, was then deliberately introduced into Australian and European rabbits, proving lethal. In Britain, the rabbit population fell to about 5% of its previous estimate and has remained at a reduced level ever since, despite a partial recovery from the mid-1970s onwards.

COOKERY

Domestic rabbits are killed for the table at about the age of three months. A young rabbit has ears which tear easily, and sharp teeth and claws. They require no hanging, and the meat is pale and tender; that of does (females) is considered better than that of bucks (males).

A MARINADE is sometimes used, e.g. for wild and older animals, which are less tender and have a stronger flavour. Barding (see BARD) or LARDING helps to keep the flesh moist during roasting.

Among the ingredients which are considered fitting to go with rabbits are mustard (widely used) and prunes (in Belgium and France). In general, recipes for rabbit are similar to those for chicken and reflect the various styles of national and regional cuisines (thus casseroles with ham, wine, brandy, and garlic in Spain and Portugal; and the use of sour cream sauces in C. and E. Europe). In S. America, where rabbits have superseded indigenous animals such as AGOUTI or PACA, they appear with e.g. peppers and coconut (Colombia) or peanut sauce (Chile) or other locally popular accompaniments.

Recipes for using rabbit meat in cold dishes such as BRAWN (England) or RILLETTES and GALANTINES (France) are also encountered. The meat is often augmented with pork.   (LM)

RABBIT FISH of the family Siganidae, were formerly described as belonging to Indo-Pacific waters where numerous species were listed. Now, however, following the gradual fall in the salinity of the Bitter Lakes which punctuate the Suez Canal, some Indo-Pacific fish have been able to swim through the Canal and establish themselves in the E. Mediterranean. Foremost among these is *Siganus rivulatus*, which has acquired local Mediterranean names as far west as Malta; but its path has been followed by *S. luridus*,

so two of them are now part of the Mediterranean fauna.

A rabbit fish, so called because its rounded head and general appearance is thought to resemble a rabbit, may also be called spinefoot. This is because it has sharp spines not only at the front of the dorsal fin, and in the pelvic fins, but also underneath in the anal fin. These spines can inflict painful wounds.

RACCOON *Procyon lotor*, a furry animal of N. America which belongs to the same family, Procyonidae, as the pandas of China. Typical measurements for a raccoon would be 75 cm (30") for head-plus-body length and 12–15 kg (27–34 lb), so there is plenty of it to be eaten. The bushy tail is marked by black rings, and the face by a black 'mask'. Indeed, the animal has an engaging and striking appearance, and it is not surprising that it quickly attracted the attention of early white settlers. Thus Captain John Smith, he whose life was saved by the Indian princess Pocahontas, referred to it as 'a beast they call aroughcun, much like a badger . . . living on trees, as squirrels do'.

The raccoon is well known for its habit of washing its food before eating it. In the absence of water, it will clean the food by rubbing it. Its largely nocturnal diet of both plant and animal matter is wholesome and it in turn provides good eating for human beings. The fat, however, is strong in flavour and smell and best removed before cooking. The lean meat is dark. Roasting is recommended and a number of recipes suggest sweet potatoes as stuffing or accompaniment.

Although raccoons are found just about all over the USA, often in the vicinity of water, their popularity as food and as the quarry in 'coon hunts' is most apparent in the southern states. They show ingenuity in devising ways of throwing pursuing dogs off their scent.

RACLETTE is the name of both a cheese and of a dish made from it, the speciality of the Swiss canton of Valais; see SWITZERLAND.

The cheese is high in fat and semi-soft, making it particularly suitable for melting. The flavour is mild and rich. A whole cheese is a flattish disc weighing about 6 kg (13 lb), with a reddish rind. It is matured for four to seven months.

Racler means 'to scrape'. The dish is traditionally made by exposing the cut surface of half a cheese to a fire and progressively scraping off the melted cheese onto a hot plate, to be eaten with baked potatoes and pickled white onions (and other accompaniments, as desired).

Nowadays there are special electrical devices which permit those who do not have blazing log fires in Alpine shelters to prepare the dish in the comfort of their own kitchens or on a restaurant table.

RADISH *Raphanus sativus*, a cruciferous plant related to, for example, TURNIP and HORSERADISH. The swollen upper part of its root has been used for food since prehistoric times over such a vast area of the Old World, from W. Europe to China and Japan, that the place and manner of its origin are obscure. Most botanists believe the place to be W. Asia and the main ancestral wild plant to be *Raphanus raphanistrum*, a type of charlock (see MUSTARD GREENS), but it is likely that other wild ancestors would have crossed with this.

The 5th-century BC Greek writer Herodotus, who had a weakness for tall stories but may here be relating the truth, said that there was an inscription on the Great Pyramid in Egypt recording the enormous amount of radishes (and also of onions and garlic) eaten by the slaves who built it. The inscription has not survived, but there are many pictures and records of radishes in slightly later Egyptian remains.

The Greeks knew three kinds of radish, corresponding to the modern long and round radishes, and to the Round Black Spanish variety. The ordinary Greek term for any radish was *raphanos* and the Latin name *raphanus*. The modern name radish is derived not from this but from the Latin *radix*, root. In the 1st century AD the Latin writer Pliny described a further kind of radish of immense size, as big, he said, as 'a boy baby' (boys were supposed to be larger than girls). Since radishes have about the same density as babies, this would have weighed about 3 kg (7 lb). Accounts of huge radishes continued to be told by later European writers, the largest weight claimed being 45 kg (100 lb) by the famous herbalist usually known as Matthiolus (1544, see Mattioli in the Bibliography). However, the home of the large radish is really in the Orient, as explained below.

The radish disappeared from European literature with the fall of the Roman Empire, though presumably it was still grown, and is not mentioned again until the 13th century, by Albertus Magnus. He described several types, including a giant radish, which he said had a tapered shape and a rather sharp taste. Large, elongated, but mild radishes became the most popular kind in Europe in succeeding centuries. These were slow-growing types which kept well after lifting in autumn, and provided a useful winter vegetable.

The radish did not reach Britain until the mid-16th century, only a short time before

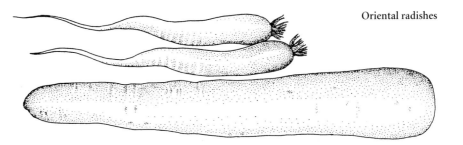

Oriental radishes

Spanish and Portuguese colonists introduced it to the New World, where nowadays Florida is the major producer. In Britain, Gerard (1633) mentioned four varieties, mainly 'used as a sauce with meates to procure appetite', but also 'eaten raw with bread'. This last phrase serves as a curtain-raiser for a later development, when the small, young, spring radish, with its slightly hot taste due to a glucoside substance similar to that in the related plant mustard, became the dominant kind, for salads or as a piquant hors d'œuvre. Perhaps the most satisfactory way to eat them is to hold what is left of the green stalk between one's fingers, rub the radish over a piece of butter, dip it in salt (as Evelyn, 1699, remarked, it brings its own pepper with it!), and eat it with bread and butter.

Radishes vary in shape—oval, round, turnip shaped, olive shaped, tapering from the top, and even tapering from the bottom; and in external colour—white, pink, red, purple, black. Internal colour also varies, most strikingly in the flamboyant fuchsia hue sported by some varieties such as Beauty Heart—see below.

The **black radishes** favoured in many E. European cuisines are of a more earthy, robust character. A full account of their uses is given by Elizabeth Schneider (1986), who explains among many other things that the use of a zester to pare off strips of the black skin will produce remarkable black and white striped effects, which even survive cooking.

There is also a wide variation in the size of radishes. The **oriental radishes,** also known by their Japanese and Hindi names, daikon and mooli, may reach a length of 45 cm (18") or more, and really constitute a different vegetable, almost omnipresent in oriental cuisines. Grated daikon is a garnish for SASHIMI in Japan. Ribbons and slices of daikon also make an attractive garnish; and slices are often included in stir-fry dishes. Pickled daikon is widely used, especially in Japan and Korea (see KIMCH'I).

Joy Larkcom (1991) draws attention to some Chinese radishes which have dramatically coloured flesh. One example is 'Xin Li Mei' (which translates as 'Beauty Heart'—see above) with red flesh, and others with green or purple flesh or internal crimson striping, suitable for oriental vegetable carving. She explains that in N. China the Beauty Heart radishes are treated as fruits, crisper than an Asian pear.

RAFFALD ELIZABETH (1733–81), author of one of the finest 18th-century English cookery books, *The Experienced English Housekeeper*. She was also a professional housekeeper, confectioner, shopkeeper, innkeeper; and she compiled and published the first three Manchester Directories.

She was born in Doncaster. Her father had been a schoolmaster and, after a reasonable education which included a little French, she entered service at the age of 15, gaining experience and skills in several Yorkshire families.

She wrote: 'the common servants [being] so ignorant in dressing meat, and a good cook so hard to be met with, put me upon studying the art of cookery more than perhaps I otherwise should have done.'

In 1759 she became housekeeper at Arley Hall, Cheshire, the seat of Sir Peter and Lady Elizabeth Warburton. It was a prosperous, well-managed estate and Lady Elizabeth was considerate and helpful to her housekeeper at a time when the house and gardens were undergoing considerable rebuilding and alterations.

The Head Gardener was John Raffald of the Stockport family of horticulturalists and he and Elizabeth married in 1763. They left for Manchester and opened a confectionery shop in Fennel Street which also sold made dishes, cold suppers, and elaborate centrepieces for the dinner table. The shop catered not only for the local gentry but also the growing numbers of manufacturers and merchants attracted by the business and trade of engineering and textiles. She added to her business a Register Office (an employment agency), and in 1766 moved to the Market Place where the goods on sale now included perfumes, cosmetics, and seeds. John Raffald's family had a stall in the Market Place supplied with produce from their own market gardens.

This apparently indefatigable woman was also during this time writing her cookery book and in addition had the responsibilities of a mother. Many accounts, copying the same erroneous source, state that she had sixteen children, all daughters; the church registers reveal six.

She made regular use of the advertising columns in, notably, the *Manchester Mercury*. In 1768 the goods for sale at her shop included

Canterbury, Shrewsbury and Derbyshire Brawn, Newcastle Salmon, Yorkshire Hams, Tongues and Chaps, Potted Woodcocks, Char and Potted Meats, Portable Soups for Travellers . . . fresh Mushroom Catchup, Walnut Catchup, Lemon Pickle and Browning for made Dishes, Pickled Mushrooms, Barberrys, Mangos, and other sorts of Pickles; dry and wet sweetmeats, Plumb cakes for Weddings and Christenings, and all sorts of Cakes, Mackroons and Biskets, Jellies, Creams, Flummery, Gold and Silver Webs for covering Sweetmeats, and all other decorations for cold Entertainments.

The list continues with what are clearly bought-in spices, imported foods, and fruit and goods for gardeners.

In 1769 she advertised her book,

an entire new Work Wrote for the Use and Ease of Ladies, House-keepers, Cooks, & c. entitled The EXPERIENCED ENGLISH House-keeper By ELIZABETH RAFFALD. Wrote purely from Practice, and Dedicated to the Hon. Lady Elizabeth Warburton, Whom The Author lately Served as House-keeper. Consisting of near 800 Original Receipts, most of which never appeared in Print.

First Part, Lemon Pickle, Browning for all Sorts of made Dishes, Soups, Fish, plain Meat, Game, made dishes both hot and cold, Pyes, Puddings, & c.

Second part, All kinds of Confectionery, particularly the Gold and Silver Web for covering of Sweetmeats, and a desert of Spun Sugar, with directions to set out a Table in the most elegant Manner, and in the most modern Taste, Floating Islands, Fish Ponds, Transparent Puddings, Trifles, Whips, & c.

Third part, Pickling, Potting and Collaring, Wines, Vinegars, Catchups, Distilling, with two most valuable Receipts, one for refining Malt Liquors, the other for curing Acid Wines, and a correct List of every Thing in Season in every Month of the Year.

The book was subscribed in NW England, Yorkshire, and London, five shillings to subscribers. She was encouraged by receiving over 800 subscriptions. In her preface she assured readers that the recipes were 'not borrowed from other authors, nor glossed over with hard names or words of high style but wrote in my own plain language and every sheet carefully perused as it came from the Press, having an opportunity of having it printed by a neighbour, whom I can rely on doing it the strictest justice, without the least alteration'.

The book sold swiftly, and a second edition soon appeared, including about 100 additional receipts, some from the collections of a 'noble generous-minded lady' and other 'worthy ladies'. She wrote 'Those I have tried, I found really valuable and those which I have not yet had such an opportunity of proving the goodness of, I have weighed them the best I could, and carefully examined their probable goodness, before I ventured to publish them. These are given genuine as they were purchased at a considerable expence from the inventers.'

Seven editions of the book were published in her lifetime when she sold the copyright to R. Baldwin of Paternoster Row for the reputed sum of £1,400. He asked that some northern words be changed but she refused; the 'wooden garth' or hoop in which she advised cakes to be baked was, and remains, nostalgically, a Manchester word for a child's hoop. The book continued in print well into the 19th century.

In 1772 she compiled and published her 'Manchester Directory', the town's first Directory and a necessary guide for the rapidly developing commercial and manufacturing centre. She produced a second Directory in 1773 by which time the Market Place shop was sold and the Raffalds had moved across the river to the King's Head, Salford, a commodious coaching inn. There they established various businesses (Florists Feasts, restarted the Card Assemblies, hired out chaises and funeral coaches) but adverse trade and pressing creditors compelled them to leave.

To maintain the family Elizabeth started a refreshment business 'during the strawberry season' at the racecourse on Kersal Moor, selling coffee, tea, chocolate, strawberries, and cream. John Raffald, who had been a good gardener and able botanist but was something of a spendthrift, then became Master of the Exchange Coffee House in Manchester and Elizabeth took over the catering, mainly soups. With unremitting industry she compiled and issued a third Manchester Directory and continued to sell her cookery book.

She died, 'of a spasm', in April 1781, 'lamented by a numerous acquaintance' (*Manchester Mercury*), and mourned by her husband and three surviving daughters.   RSh

RAGI the Indonesian name for the fermented and dried greyish balls of roasted rice flour which serve as a starter culture for many of the various fermented foods in which the region of E. and SE Asia is rich. There are special ragi for MISO, TEMPE, and TAPÉ and for rice wines as well as for NAN (bread).

Ragi includes MOULDS, YEASTS, and BACTERIA of the types required for a particular fermentation. It has been suggested that the name comes from the Hindi word *ragi* which means 'millet' and that this was the grain first used. Nowadays most ragi is made on a base of rice flour. The flour is mixed with garlic, pepper, galingale, and chillis, which help to discourage

unwanted organisms. The mixture is moistened, and then inoculated by sprinkling previously made ragi on it (although sometimes natural infection from the surroundings is sufficient). It is dried slowly to a crumbly ball or cake which keeps for several days.

Other starch crops may be used as the basis; versions of ragi in Africa have been prepared with MILLET or CASSAVA flours.

For a different although somewhat similar starter which is widely used in Japan, see KOJI.

RAGOUT a French term, adopted into English as ragoo in the 17th century, which indicates a stew of meat and vegetables, especially if a highly flavoured sauce is added to it towards the end of the cooking time. The verb *ragoûter*, from which the noun is derived, means 'to revive the taste of', i.e. 'to perk up', e.g. by this addition.

In the 18th century, when many English cookery writers held fancy French dishes in scorn (or professed to do so), the ragoo became a sort of symbol of what they disliked. Thus Thacker (1758), explaining why his own book was so good, contrasted it with some other books which were:

stuff'd with ragoos, and other dishes a-la-mode de France, as they call them; in which the mixture of spices is so great, and the expence so extravagant, that it frightens most people from using them; or, if any be so curious as to try them, and follow their rules punctually, instead of meats that are healthful, and agreeable to the palate, they will find a hotch-potch, destructive to an English constitution.

The term lingers on in French restaurant parlance, and one edition of the *Larousse gastronomique*, perhaps in a desperate attempt to counter English criticisms in earlier centuries, states that there is such a thing as a *ragoût à l'anglaise*, in which liaison is effected by the introduction of potatoes, the result being supposedly the same as what is called IRISH STEW!
READING: Thacker (1758).

RAGÚ the true name for the Bolognese sauce which has acquired international currency, especially in *Spaghetti alla bolognese*. In Bologna, the home of this sauce, it was first used for a baked pie of LASAGNE, not as the sauce for spaghetti or other *pasta asciutta* which is its commonest form today. The original ragú was made without benefit of the meat mincer, and the meat was chopped into smallish chunks. Nor did it contain tomato, which did not arrive in Italy from America until later, and even then was only grudgingly accepted; even now a correct *ragú bolognese* has only a light tomato flavour.

The principal ingredient is always minced meat, usually beef, cooked with chicken livers, unsmoked bacon, onion, celery, tomato purée, and wine. Debased forms of the sauce are frequently met; these lack the subtlety and roundness of flavour which characterize the authentic versions.

RAINBOW RUNNER (or just runner, as in Australia), *Elagatis bipinnulatus*, a fish of the carangid (JACK) family which is found in tropical or near-tropical waters in the Atlantic (both sides, but not in the Mediterranean) and many areas in the Indo-Pacific region. A pelagic fish, rarely found in coastal waters, it has a maximum length of just over 1 m (4'). Its back is the greenish-blue typical of deep-sea species; and it has a few blue and yellow stripes running along its sides, which account for 'rainbow' in its name, but tend to fade after death.

This fish is sought by anglers, and makes good eating, but is rarely available in quantity in the markets.

RAISINÉ (also called *vin cuit*, but that term has other meanings), a speciality of two Swiss cantons, Vaud and Fribourg, made out of old varieties of apples or pears or a combination of both. In the countryside, it is a tradition to make raisiné every two years (the preferred varieties of pears or apples give a substantial harvest only every second year), after the fruit harvest in autumn. First the juice is extracted by squeezing and then put into a large copper cauldron and simmered for about 48 hours. As it has to be constantly stirred—to caramelize, but not burn—it provides the occasion for a social gathering in the evening. Each member of the party takes their turn in stirring the raisiné until it has reduced to a tenth; the remaining liquid is very dark brown, with a thick consistency. It can be kept for a long time, and eaten as a dressing for boiled potatoes, as they do in rural areas, or mixed with some cream and eggs and used to fill an open tart. Ice cream is also made with this product.

Raisiné, made from grapes or a mixture of grapes and other fruits, is also known in parts of France.

RAISINS SULTANAS, AND CURRANTS, all terms meaning a dried GRAPE. Raisin can be used in a general sense, to apply to all such items, but is usually taken to mean a dried grape which is not a sultana or a currant. Sultana is sometimes a noun, sometimes a variety name (Sultana grapes), and sometimes an adjective (sultana raisins). Currant is a plain noun.

Raisins of most kinds originally came from the Mediterranean region, the Middle East (especially Turkey), and W. Asia (notably Afghanistan). They are still produced in these regions, but the leading producer is now California, where the main raisin varieties of grape are the following:

- California White Muscat. The grapes are amber to yellow-green in colour, thin skinned with firm, rich, moderately juicy, finely flavoured flesh. Grown especially for raisins as it is too tender to be shipped fresh.
- Thompson Seedless (or Oval Kishmish or Sultanina). The grapes are yellow with low acidity and entirely seedless.
- Sultana (or Round Kishmish) is grown in limited quantities. The grapes have a higher acid content than Thompson Seedless and occasionally develop seeds.

Other varieties are: Spanish Malagas (or Muscatels), large and delicious; Smyrna Sultana, seedless, pale yellow with a fine flavour; Corinthian raisins, a separate grade of sultanas, usually a little larger and darker than Smyrnas, but not to be confused with currants.

Sultanas are usually larger and paler than ordinary raisins.

Currants are tiny raisins made from drying a small, black variety of grape which was first grown at Corinth in Greece. Such currants have been used by cooks since classical times, sometimes in savoury dishes but most consistently in bakery goods and sweet foods. They often figure in English recipes of the 17th and 18th centuries as 'currans'. They continue to be indispensable ingredients for such items as SPOTTED DICK, ECCLES CAKES, and Scottish BLACK BUN. Cultivation of grapes for currants has spread to Australia and the USA.

Zante is a small, black grape originally grown in the E. Mediterranean area for drying into currants.

The so-called raisin-tree, *Hovenia dulcis*, does not bear raisins. It is a deciduous shrub grown from the Himalayas to Japan (where the name is *kenponashi*), whose thickened fruit stalks, when dried, bear some resemblance to raisins and can be used in similar ways.

RAKEFISK the Norwegian name for fermented TROUT (or other freshwater fish), notorious for their smell but well loved in rural communities where they have been an established tradition for centuries, and now also acquiring 'chic acceptance in urban society'. The phrase is from Astri Riddervold (1990*a*) whose book on this and similar Scandinavian fish products is as readable as it is authoritative.

Riddervold explains that the more famous product GRAVLAKS, when prepared in the old traditional manner, involves burying salmon for a short period. Rakefisk is made by the same technique, but the fish are buried for longer. So, whereas gravlaks has never had an offensive smell, the more fully fermented rakefisk is quite different in this respect. Riddervold cites an 18th-century Norwegian clergyman as writing 'that you would not dare ask a lady for a kiss when you have eaten this wonderful fish', but observed that despite this handicap farmers in some regions would eat it every day. It is perfectly wholesome.

The Swedish name for rakefisk is *surfisk*. A Swedish writer cited by Riddervold points out that the tradition of preserving fish by burying it in the ground is found all over the world in circumpolar areas, and that in the Nordic countries the practice is found mainly in those regions where the winter is longest and coldest. For an example of a very large sea fish being so treated, see *hákarl*, under ICELAND.

RAMADAN the ninth month of the lunar Muslim calendar. During these 29 or 30 days, from one new moon to the next, the faithful fast from dawn to dusk, abstaining from food, drink, tobacco, and sexual activity as long as there is sufficient light to enable the eye to distinguish between a black and a white thread held at arm's length. In practice, the fast is governed by the morning and evening calls to prayer. *Suhur*, the early morning meal, must be finished before dawn; most Islamic countries have traditional foods for *suhur*, but city dwellers nowadays tend to eat a normal breakfast, often made up from the previous evening's leftovers. Towards the hour of *maghrib*, the sunset prayer, food is made ready; cooks may taste, as long as they do not swallow. When the signal is given, by beating a drum, firing a cannon, or an announcement on radio and TV, everyone drinks a glass of water and eats something sweet before attending household or communal prayers and then launching into the evening meal.

Fasting is one of the five 'pillars of Islam' and is enjoined on everyone who has reached puberty. Certain groups are excused, notably travellers (which includes soldiers on active service), the very aged, and the sick (which may include pregnant women and nursing mothers). The very devout will not swallow their own saliva, but spit it out. Anyone who breaks the fast on one or more days can 'pay back' by fasting for an equal number of days after Ramadan is over, or make good the fault by distributing food to the poor, but this concession is intended principally for involuntary fast-breakers, for example women during menstruation.

The fast is a commandment of God, but it is not a penance or a commemoration of past events. The individual benefits by remission of sins and spiritual training, but a prime purpose is to strengthen the solidarity of the Muslim community. Fasting is not compulsory for anyone, but social pressures to observe it, for rich and poor alike, are strong.

The rules, of course, do not prevent people from eating as much as they like (or can afford) during the hours of darkness. During the day, lack of sleep and dehydration probably hit people hardest. Whatever apologists say, efficiency and productivity suffer. Because the lunar year is about 10 days shorter than the solar year, Ramadan moves gradually backwards against the cycle of the seasons, and daytime fasting is a severer challenge to Muslims in northern latitudes in June than it is in December.

Zubaida (1991), in a brilliant essay on Ramadan, points out that only a few special dishes for the occasion are common to all Muslim communities. Each region has its own Ramadan specialities. A tradition of the Prophet favours breaking the fast with dates, and this is widely observed in the Arabian peninsula and the Persian Gulf countries where dates are extensively cultivated. The drink called *gamar-eddin*, which is made from sheets of APRICOT paste (or apricot 'leather'), is also important as something with which to break the fast in many parts of the Arab world.

A popular feature of the Ramadan evening meal is a rich soup. Zubaida remarks:

There is the famous *harira* of Morocco, a soup of lamb broth with a variety of pulses, vegetables, fragrant herbs and/or meat, depending on season, region and level of prosperity. It is paralleled in Iran by a very similar *ash*, with the addition, for Ramadhan, of dried fruit.

A common genre of Ramadan dishes for breaking the fast is a paste of pounded meat and cereals with various flavourings: in Iraq, Syria, and Arabia it is known as *harissa*, in Iran, Afghanistan, and India it is HALEEM, and in Anatolia *keshkek*. There were formerly, in some countries, traditional dishes such as *kleiʔ* (mutton and/or camel meat preserved in fat) in Fez in Morocco to be eaten for *suhur*, but the trend has been to replace these by a normal Arab breakfast.

Consumption of sweetmeats is universal and may be carried on through the night. Popular items include BAKLAVA, QATAʔIF, HALVA, with nuts, dried fruits, syrups and honey, sweetened cheeses, and often the 'clotted cream' known as KAYMAK in Turkey.

Ramadan is certainly not a feared or gloomy month—just the opposite. Most Muslims fully appreciate its spiritual, social, and physical benefits. It is a time for mutual forgiveness and the settlement of debts and differences. And quite apart from the good food that can be enjoyed at night, usually in a celebratory atmosphere, there are the preparations for the feast of Eid or Idul Fitri that immediately follows.

To eat on the three days of this feast is a religious as well as a social obligation. A good supply of titbits is kept handy for visitors. Alms are given to the poor; this *zakat* is another of the five pillars of the faith. Entertaining is lavish and meals tend to be heavy.

In SE Asia, to draw examples from another region, rice made yellow with turmeric is served, because yellow has been the colour of royalty and celebration since long before Islam arrived there. Sticky rice, or rice that has been compressed so that the grains stick together, is also associated with the festival; in Malaysia and Indonesia people make *ketupat*, little packets woven from strips of coconut leaf in which rice is cooked. In Java a popular dish for Idul Fitri is *sambal goreng daging*, a highly spiced beef dish. In Sumatra they eat RENDANG (buffalo meat long-cooked in spiced coconut milk) with sticky rice. However, there is no 'classic' meal for Eid; what matters is that there should be the very best food and plenty of it.

See also MUSLIMS AND FOOD.   (RO)

RAMBAI the Malay name, also used in English, for the fruits of several trees of the genus *Baccaurea*, most of which are native to Malaysia and Indonesia. Two, which have sweeter and better fruits than others, are cultivated there, and a third in India, Burma, and Thailand.

B. motleyana, the most important of these, produces abundant clusters of fruit hanging in long strings. Each fruit is oval, about 4 cm (1") long, with a thin, velvety, pale brown skin. When ripe this skin becomes soft and wrinkled, which is one way of distinguishing rambai from the DUKU AND LANGSAT fruits which it closely resembles. A soft, translucent, whitish flesh surrounds a few flat, brown seeds. Cultivated varieties have a sweet, mild flavour and are refreshing when eaten raw. Wild trees produce fruits which are too acid to be eaten thus, but are suitable for cooking, making preserves, and alcoholic drinks. The sweet varieties are also used in these ways.

B. dulcis, with similar fruits, is grown in Sumatra and Java, and its large sweet fruits, called *tjoepa*, are sold in local markets.

B. sapida is cultivated for its fruits in India (as *lutuqa* or *lutqa*) and Burma, and in Thailand (where it is *mai fai farang*).

RAMBUTAN *Nephelium lappaceum*, a fruit native to the western lowlands of Malaysia, is now cultivated in many parts of

Rambutan

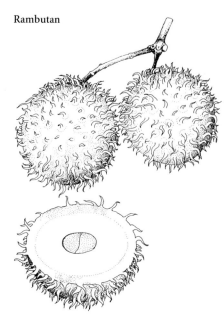

SE Asia, where it is highly popular; in Sri Lanka; and in Zanzibar, where it was introduced at an early date by Arab traders. It is closely related to the LYCHEE.

Fruits vary in quality and type; there are crimson, greenish, and yellow or orange varieties. The inner part of the fruit is smaller than a lychee, but the outside looks larger because of the long hairs which give it its name, *rambut* being the Malay word for 'hair'. It looks slightly like a sweet chestnut. The flavour is usually more acid than a lychee, but highly aromatic, and the seed has an almond-like flavour.

RAMEKIN and the corresponding French word *ramequin* are both derived, according to Graham (1988), from the Flemish *rammeken*, the diminutive of *ram*, meaning cream. Thus the basic meaning of the term is 'a little cream'. It seems always to have involved cheese, but Graham points out that it has:

been used over the centuries to describe almost anything from Welsh rabbit or a melted cheese sandwich to a cheese-flavoured egg custard, tartlet, soufflé, pudding or puff. It later came to be applied also, by metonymy, to the receptacle in which some types of ramekin were cooked.

This last is probably the sense most familiar to English-speaking cooks nowadays. A typical ramekin is of pottery or porcelain, round, small (about 5–8 cm/2–3" in diameter), straight sided, and able to accommodate a small CUSTARD or MOUSSE or SOUFFLÉ or PÂTÉ.

In France likewise, *ramequin* generally refers to the small pot, but *Larousse gastronomique* (1997) mentions two surviving examples of its meaning a savoury mixture such as could be served on toast.

RAMONTCHI *Flacourtia indica*, also known as Governor's plum, is a shrubby tree of the same genus as LOVI-LOVI and RUKAM. Native to India, it was introduced in the distant past to islands of the S. Indian Ocean and is now planted throughout the tropics.

The fruit is like a small red plum in shape, size, and colour. The pulp is yellowish-white, juicy, and usually acid; but some cultivated varieties are sweet enough to be eaten raw. Unripe fruits are good for making jellies, preserves, syrups, and similar products.

RAMPION *Campanula rapunculus*, was a popular vegetable in many European countries, including Britain, in the 16th and 17th centuries; Evelyn (1699) remarked that its tender roots, eaten in the spring, were comparable to the RADISH but much more nourishing. However, like many other root vegetables, the rampion lost popularity as the POTATO gained acceptance. It is still occasionally used in France and Switzerland, but is now largely forgotten. Indeed, some English-speaking people are likely to know of it only by its German name, because of the Grimm brothers' fairy story 'Rapunzel'. In this tale a witch imprisoned the daughter of a woman who stole rampion (*Rapunzel*); a sign of the regard in which it was once held.

Rampion is closely related to the harebell and resembles it when in flower. The root, which may be as long as 30 cm (1'), is tapered and narrow, with an agreeable nutty flavour. Both roots and leaves may be eaten raw in salads. Old recipes call for cooking either of them.

The BELLFLOWER ROOT of Korea (*toraji*), *Platycodon grandiflorus*, is a close relation.

RAPE *Brassica napus*, one of the most ancient members of the CABBAGE tribe, is a coarse but useful green vegetable.

Its main importance, however, is that its subspecies *oleifera* is the source of rapeseed oil, a product which is very widely used in cooking. There had been a problem which discouraged its use; it was high in erucic acid and glucosinolates, which have anti-nutritional properties. However, plant-breeders in Canada have in the last decades of the 20th century developed the variety Canola, which does not suffer significantly from this handicap. Some rapeseed oil is now sold as Canola oil. The names rapeseed oil or colza oil are, however, more common.

Tiny rape seedlings mixed with CRESS are sold for salads; a cheap alternative to the traditional mustard and cress, but one which lacks the sharp taste of the other. At a later stage of growth, young rape thinnings are sometimes sold as spring greens. Later still, the leaves can be used as a pot-herb, and the inflorescences cooked like BROCCOLI.

RAS-EL-HANOUT an important spice mixture (the name means, literally, something like 'top of the shop') found in varying forms in Tunisia, Algeria, and Morocco. It is one of the most complex such mixtures. Mme Guinaudeau (1958 and later editions) gave a list of 27 ingredients which has conveniently been echoed in an annotated English version by Paula Wolfert (1973, also with later editions). What seems clear is that standard ingredients are CUMIN SEEDS, CORIANDER SEEDS, TURMERIC, GINGER, CARDAMOM, and NUTMEG, but that many others, such as CINNAMON, CAYENNE PEPPER, rosebud (of the damask ROSE), OREGANO, are usually included, all in powdered form. Wolfert (1973) points out that certain supposed APHRODISIACS, including the 'green metallic beetles', cantharides, which are called 'Spanish fly' (*Lytta vesicatoria*) and are notoriously dangerous, have appeared in many Moroccan prescriptions; but these seem to be irrelevant for flavouring purposes. This last point is among those wittily brought out by Levy (1986) in a major essay on 'Spanish fly', based on research at Taroudan and Marrakesh in Morocco.

The ras-el-hanout of Tunisia typically includes rose petal and is relatively mild. That of Morocco is more pungent. Both are often used to flavour the accompaniments of COUSCOUS. In Morocco the mixture is often used in sweet lamb dishes such as *mrouziya* and always in the cooking of game. Guinaudeau explains that it is the spice for the festival Aid el kebir and also for certain winter dishes which heat the blood.

RASGULLA (Hindi), or *rasagolla* (Bengali) or *rasbari* (Nepali), a Bengali sweet popular throughout India. Essentially it is a small DUMPLING made of a mixture of *chhenna* (CURD: see also INDIAN SWEETS) and a little semolina which is boiled in syrup, and kept submerged in syrup until it is needed, so that it becomes soft and spongy. They are eaten cold, and can be served 'wet'—with syrup, or a creamy sauce—or 'dry', coated with sugar or nuts. The finest recipes omit the semolina, giving an extra spongy result. They have a curious 'squeaky' texture, derived from the curd. Rasgullas and related confections form the basis of a whole 'family' of Indian sweets. They may be filled with nuts and raisins; or stuffed with candied peel. There are giant stuffed versions, filled with pistachio BARFI, called 'rajah's dish' (double size) and 'nawab's dish' (four times ordinary size, with four different fillings).

Dry sweets based on rasgullas removed from the syrup include *raskadamba*, which are coloured red or yellow, and coated with powdered, dried curd; *rasamundi*, rolled in sugar; and *danedhar*, heavily sugar coated so as to appear like crystallized fruit. Other dry versions are *chum-chums*, which are diamond shaped, and filled or piped with an icing of reduced milk and almonds.

Rasmalai are another sweet based on *chhenna*, this time shaped into flat cakes. After cooking in syrup, the cakes are soaked in a mixture called *rabri*—cream plus thickened fresh milk, flavoured with pandanus (see SCREWPINE). Mrs Balbir Singh (1967) observes: 'This can truly be said to be the choicest of the Indian dishes. It is very delicious and is a treat for every tongue and every age.'

RASKARA an Indian sweet based on COCONUT. A mixture of sugar and coconut is cooked gently in a little GHEE until it forms a sticky paste. Bengali raskara is flavoured with black pepper and a tiny quantity of raw camphor; that from Uttar Pradesh uses the more common Indian flavourings of rosewater and cardamom. Raskara is much used as a filling for other sweets, or is sprinkled on puffed rice as a breakfast dish.

LM

RASPBERRY *Rubus idaeus* and other *Rubus* spp, a fruiting plant of which there are many varieties, grows wild in all the cooler regions of the northern hemisphere, and in some southern parts. The genus also includes the BLACKBERRY, CLOUDBERRY, DEWBERRY, and SALMONBERRY, and is part of the rose family.

Both raspberries and blackberries can be any colour from white through yellow, orange, pink, red, and purple to black, the difference between being one of structure. The fruit, though called berry, is technically an etaerio of druplets (a cluster of small fruits with stones). The etaerio grows from a core called a receptacle. When a blackberry is picked the receptacle remains inside the etaerio. When a raspberry is picked the etaerio comes away from the receptacle, which remains on the plant as an obvious white, conical structure. The absence of a core in the picked fruit makes raspberries softer and juicier to eat than blackberries.

The first people known to have cultivated raspberries were the ancient Greeks. Writing of them in the 1st century AD, the Roman writer Pliny the Elder explains that they called the raspberry *idaeus* because it grew thickly on the slopes of Mount Ida. (There are two mountains of this name, one in Crete and the other in Asia Minor, both still overgrown with wild raspberries.)

The Greek account differs slightly, according to Leclerc (1925), who describes it thus. Raspberries used all to be white, but one day, when the god Jupiter, still a child, was making the mountains resound with the echos of his furious screams ('à rendre sourds les Corybantes eux-même', comments Leclerc), the Nymph Ida, daughter of Mélissos, King of Crete, wished to pick him a raspberry to appease him. She scratched her breast on the spines of the shrub, staining the fruits a bright red for evermore. For this reason, raspberries are red, and the place where they grow called Ida.

WILD RASPBERRIES

R. idaeus is the modern botanical name of the chief species of both the wild and cultivated raspberry. The old English name for raspberry was 'raspis'. Its origin is obscure, but thought to be connected with the rough, slightly hairy, and thus 'rasping' surface of a raspberry, compared with the shiny, smooth blackberry. Another old name was 'hindberry', given because the fruit was eaten by deer. The common German and Danish names are forms of the same word.

The common European wild raspberry has a distribution which extends well to the north of the Arctic Circle, and grows also in W. and N. Asia. (Wild plants of this species in America are not native, but escapees from cultivation.) There are red, yellow, and white forms. The flavour of some wild varieties is outstanding, so 'canes' (cuttings with a piece of root) are often taken from wild plants and transferred to gardens.

Wild raspberries are abundant in N. India and the Himalayas. Many species are very dark red or black. One of the most common is the Mysore (or hill) raspberry, *R. niveus*, a native of Burma and India, which is grown in Kenya and elsewhere in Africa, and is the only member of the *Rubus* family which has been successfully grown in Florida. The small fruits, black when ripe, are covered in a fine white bloom.

Wild American species include *R. strigosus*, of wide occurrence and quite similar to *R. idaeus*. Most kinds are red. It has no common name more specific than 'wild red raspberry'.

In the eastern USA and Canada *R. occidentalis*, the black raspberry, is common. This is usually black, though yellow and red forms exist. It is more acid than most raspberries, which makes it particularly good for cooking.

The paler, often orange SALMONBERRY, *R. spectabilis*, is named not because of its colour but because American Indians in the north-west often ate it with salmon roe.

CULTIVATED RASPBERRIES AND HYBRIDS

Modern cultivated raspberries in Europe are mainly varieties of *R. idaeus*, often crossed with other species to improve yield and disease resistance. In N. America, cultivated raspberries include *R. idaeus*, *R. strigosus* (for red raspberries), *R. occidentalis* (for black raspberries), and hybrids between these and others.

The climate in parts of Scotland is ideal for raspberries and it is there that some of the finest crops (90% of which are eaten in Britain) are grown.

Raspberries and blackberries are to some extent interfertile, and hybrids exist. The best known of these is the **loganberry.** In 1881 Judge J. H. Logan of Santa Cruz, California, discovered this plant growing in his garden. It was an accidental cross between one of his own raspberries and a wild blackberry outside the fence. Loganberries are dark red and of a good size. The plants yield well, and the fruits are canned in large quantities.

Hybrids of similar parentage but much more recent origin are the **Tayberry** and **Tummelberry,** each named for a river in the east of Scotland.

Other recent attempts to achieve superior hybrids had already produced the **Boysenberry** and the **Youngberry**, both called after their inventors. The Youngberry is fairly good, with a large, deep red, sweet fruit. There is also a cross between the Youngberry and the loganberry: the **ollalie.**

USE

Raspberries have inspired flights of fancy in haute cuisine, most often in the guise of syrups and sauces used as an accompaniment to other fruits such as pears and figs. Raspberry sauce is an important ingredient in peach Melba (see PEACH). A more sober English alliance goes back to the 18th century, when 'creams' enriched with eggs and tinted pink with the fruit were a characteristic sweet dish.

Raspberry VINEGAR is one of the most popular flavoured vinegars. In Yorkshire, it used to be served with YORKSHIRE PUDDING, after the meat.

RAT any of a large number of species of long-tailed rodents, mostly considerably larger than the related mice (although there are some which are only mouse sized). Rats come originally from the Old World but are now found worldwide.

The two principal rats, so far as people in temperate climates are concerned, are *Rattus rattus*, the black rat, and *R. norvegicus*, the common, grey, or Norway rat. In the western world they are regarded as pests rather than as potential food. There are, however, records of their being eaten, and some notoriety attaches to the rat dishes which were consumed in Paris, when the city was besieged by Prussian forces in the Franco-Prussian War of 1870–1.

In W. Africa, rats are a major item of diet. The giant rat (*Cricetomys gambianus*), the CANE RAT (*Thryonomys swinderianus*), the common house mouse, and other species of rats and mice are all eaten. In some areas this group may provide as much as a half of locally produced meat.

In rural Thailand, particularly in Pathum Thani province, rice rats, which are quite small, weighing just 90 g (3 oz), are relished, especially when pork and chicken prices are seasonally high. In the Americas there are nearly 200 species known as rice rats, some no doubt appreciated as food.

Simmonds (1859) supplies some characteristically arresting information about rats being eaten by the Chinese:

In China, rat soup is considered equal to ox-tail soup, and a dozen fine rats will realize two dollars, or eight or nine shillings.

Besides the attractions of the gold-fields for the Chinese, California is so abundantly supplied with rats, that they can live like Celestial emperors, and pay very little for their board. The rats of California exceed the rats of the older American States, just as nature on that side of the continent exceeds in bountifulness of mineral wealth. The California rats are incredibly large, highly flavoured, and very abundant. The most refined Chinese in California have no hesitation in publicly expressing their opinion of 'them rats'. Their professed cooks, we are told, serve up rats' brains in a much superior style to the Roman dish of nightingales' and peacocks' tongues. The sauce used is garlic, aromatic seeds and camphor.

From the southern hemisphere comes an impressively detailed account by Elsdon Best (1977) of Maori ways with rats. He explains that the native rats ate many kinds of berries, beech mast, and other wholesome foods of the forest.

When rats were to be potted they were, according to my Matatua notes, put in a large wooden bowl or trough (*kumete*), and allowed to remain there for a while; if in good condition, as they generally were when taken, the fat would soon commence to exude from them, and when a quantity had so collected, then hot stones were put in it, and renewed occasionally. This caused more fat to collect in the vessel, while it also cooked the fat and rats together, or at least sufficiently so to please the Maori taste, never in itself any too fastidious. The rats were then packed in gourd or wooden vessels, and the melted fat was poured over them, this being the preserving agent.

RATAFIA a word whose three meanings are explained below. Its origin is obscure. According to Favre (1883–92), the word is derived from the Latin phrase *Res rata fiat*, which was pronounced when a treaty or other such instrument was ratified. Since the custom was to accompany the ratification by drinking a good liqueur, the phrase, abbreviated, became a name for such a liqueur. If this is the origin of the name, it would explain why there is doubt about whether the name applies to all liqueurs or only some and, if only some, which. (It is usually understood to apply to liqueurs made from brandy and any fruit juice, especially those made by a process of maceration; but some authorities regard a flavouring of bitter almonds as necessary.)

The three meanings of ratafia are:

1. Ratafia, a drink popular in the 17th and 18th centuries, probably of French origin. It was a cordial or a brandy-based liqueur flavoured with almonds, peach, cherry, or apricot kernels, or soft fruits; similar to NOYAU, a word which came into use in the late 18th century and largely supplanted ratafia.

2. Ratafia, an 18th- and 19th-century variation on the MACAROON, flavoured with bitter almonds (proportions ranging from 30 to 100% of total almond content), or sometimes with apricot kernels. These seem to have been first made in England in the early 18th century to recipes very similar to macaroons, and used similarly; ratafia biscuits may have acquired the name because they were eaten with the drink ratafia, or because of the use of bitter almonds as a flavouring in both items. Very small almond biscuits are still manufactured under the name of 'ratafias'.

3. The word is also used to describe a bitter almond flavour; for instance, 'essence of ratafia' (essence of bitter almond); or 'ratafea cream' (a dessert flavoured with apricot kernels—see Mrs Eales, 1736).

(LM)

RATATOUILLE an interesting example of a dish which achieved international currency during the 20th century, from a standing start as a local dish of the region of Nice, not recorded in print before Heyraud (c.1930).

In the late 18th century and the 19th the name was used in French to indicate a coarse stew. It apparently derived from *ratouiller* and *tatouiller*, two expressive forms of the French verb *touiller*, meaning to stir up. According to Ayto (1993), the word first appeared in English in *Cassell's Dictionary of Cookery* (1877), but in the misspelled form 'ratatouville'. It retained in that work the early French meaning of a meat stew.

What Heyraud and subsequent authors described in the 20th century was something quite different. Heyraud defined it as 'a ragoût of aubergine with tomatoes, courgettes and sweet peppers', and commented that it was much eaten throughout Languedoc and Provence. According to him, 'ratatouille' was the original name and belonged to Nice (as did the alternative name *sauté à la niçoise*); at Nîmes, however, the name *bourbouillade* was in use. Escudier (1964), shrewdly pointing to two reasons for its growth in international popularity, comments that the ratatouille of Nice 'is a summer dish which is becoming more and more popular. It is easy to make and has the advantage of also being able to be eaten cold.'

By the end of the 20th century the term has become so widely known that it is sometimes used as a generic term for any similar preparation made with other vegetable ingredients.

RAU RAM the Vietnamese and most commonly used name for *Polygonum odoratum*, a herb used in SE Asia. It is sometimes called Vietnamese coriander, since its strong smell has some resemblance to that of coriander. The narrow pointed leaves are used when young; they become too bitter, and reddish, when they grow bigger.

READING: Bond (1995).

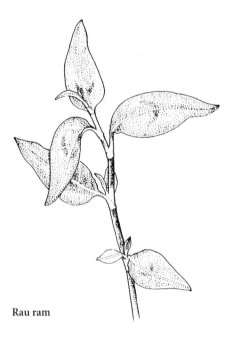

Rau ram

RAVIGOTE a piquant French sauce; the verb *ravigoter* means 'to perk up'. *Sauce ravigote* is usually met in its cold form, when it is in effect a variation of VINAIGRETTE, achieved by adding CAPERS, FINES HERBES, and chopped onion.

There is, however, a warm *sauce ravigote*, based on VELOUTÉ, with the addition of fines herbes and shallot butter, plus wine and wine vinegar.

RAVIOLI the archetypal stuffed PASTA of the western world, can be presumed to be Italian in origin but had started to appear as far away as England by the 14th century (when the FORME OF CURY gave a recipe for 'rauioles'), and was known in the south of France in medieval times.

So far as Italy is concerned, the earliest records of ravioli seem to be in some of the 140,000 preserved letters of Francesco di Marco, a merchant of Prato in the 14th century. They are described as being stuffed with pounded pork, eggs, cheese, parsley, and sugar; while in Lent a filling of herbs, cheese, and spices was used. There were both sweet and savoury kinds.

However, although this fortunate merchant could enjoy complex forms of ravioli, the basic and probably original kind were simply stuffed with spinach, or curd cheese. It is in relatively recent times that the filling for ravioli has become as varied as it now is: seafood, fungi, various kinds of meat—the form lends itself to almost infinite variety.

Agnolotti are similar but round or semicircular in shape. Both ravioli and agnolotti are normally accompanied by a sauce, such as tomato.

These are the western relations of well-known products of the Orient and C. Asia, such as, for example, MANTOU, JIAOZI, and PEL'MENI.

See also CALSONES; KREPLACH; VARENIKI.

RAW FOOD A diet consisting entirely of uncooked foods, as is sometimes advocated, would obviously require us to forgo many gastronomic pleasures. But it would be perfectly adequate and would include many such pleasures. We would not be restricted to salad vegetables, fruits and nuts, milk, raw fish, and steak tartare. Provided that the preparation of foods without heat was allowed, for example by marinating them or using the technique of fermentation, we could enjoy salami, prosciutto, cheese, and many other dairy products, and many alcoholic drinks (although neither beer nor spirits).

This diet would be expensive, since it would omit most of the cheap filling foods such as bread, potatoes, and the majority of legumes. But it would also avoid the wastage of certain nutrients which many acts of cookery entail.

Seizing on the point that it would be feasible to live on such a diet, and reminding us that our remote ancestors did just that, some authors have gone so far as not only to condemn cookery (treatment of food by heat) but also to eschew the use of artificially cold temperatures. Thus, Mr and Mrs Eugene Christian, in *Uncooked Foods and How to Use Them* (1904), claimed that 'nature has provided a diet that can be selected and eaten without changing its form or chemical properties by the application of either *heat* or *cold*, and which will be perfect'. They cited the perfect health of their own family as evidence, and dwelt with fervour on the emancipating effect which their 'natural diet' would have on women.

When . . . the woman who has dreamed of a true home has settled therein, it gradually dawns upon her that, instead of being a queen, she is an improved vassal. She finds that she must stand over a miniature furnace for an hour in the morning and breathe the poisonous odor of broiling flesh, and spend another hour among the grease and slime of pots and dishes . . . She soon realises that the fires of the morning are hardly out until those for the noon are kindled and the labors from luncheon often lap over into the evening, and those of evening far into night. The throne over which she dreamed of wielding the queenly sceptre has been transformed into a fiery furnace, gilded with greasy pots and plates, blood and bones, over which she has unfurled the dish-rag.

The authors are sufficiently ingenious to make provision for the general desire that some food should at least be warm; and for the appetizing aromas that emanate from heated foods more readily than from cold ones. Their recipe for Sweet Potato Soup, for example, allows for it to be slightly heated ('not enough to cook', they explain). And further examination of their recipe section reveals that quite a high proportion of the dishes are to be warmed to 'about 145 °F'. These concessions may be thought to weaken their case slightly, and they are not made in a number of later, less eloquent and engaging but more finely argued, books by other authors.

See also COOKING; and for a different view of one kitchen activity, WASHING UP.

RAY AND SKATE, a pair of names which can be used almost interchangeably for fish of the family Rajidae. No biological basis exists for using one name in preference to the other for any particular species; nor do dictionaries provide clear guidance. On the whole, however, the following practices are observed.

- The smaller species in the family Rajidae are rays and the larger ones skates, at least in reference books and for ichthyologists.
- In Britain, however, all of these fish are called skate when they are on the fishmonger's slab.
- Species of related but less important families, such as Myliobatidae and Dasyatidae, are always rays; thus 'eagle ray', 'devil ray', etc.

The unusual shape of rays is the result of their pectoral fins being greatly enlarged to constitute a more or less quadrangular 'body'. These enlarged fins are referred to as wings. Rays are greatly 'flattened', like true FLATFISH, as befits their bottom-living mode of life. They are cartilaginous, lacking true bones. Reproduction is achieved by the laying of eggs in horny capsules, which when found empty on the sea shore are referred to as 'mermaids' purses'.

The best ray for eating, and the one best known in Europe, is *Raja clavata*, the thornback ray. Its name reflects the fact that its back bears numerous prickles and thorns sticking up from button-like bases known as bucklers. An alternative name for this prize ray is roker. Others which are appreciated include *R. montagui*, which has a pale brown back prettily ornamented with dark round spots, and *R. radiata*, which is an Arctic species but ranges some way south on both sides of the Atlantic. Among the larger species which are usually called skate, *R. batis* and also *R. alba*, the white skate, are noteworthy.

Rays have an ammoniac smell which puts some people off eating them. However, it should not do so. Non-bony fish, such as rays and sharks, use urea, a chemical substance, to control their osmotic balance (stop water leaching out of them into the sea or vice versa). On death, the urea starts to break up, producing ammonia and the ammoniac smell. This is good, since one wants to be rid of the urea and all traces of the ammonia will anyway be dispersed in cooking.

Cooking rays or skates is simple enough (although it can be sophisticated, e.g. a topnotch *Raie au beurre noir*, ray with black (i.e. dark brown) butter). Once cooked, the long strands of flesh part easily from the cartilaginous 'bones'.

RAY'S BREAM named after the famous English naturalist John Ray (1627–1705), a deep-bodied fish which does not belong to the same family as the various kinds of SEA BREAM, but which has a general resemblance to them and may be cooked in similar ways. The flesh is delicious.

This is a brown-grey fish of relatively deep waters, found in many seas including the central and western parts of the Mediterranean. Of a solitary lifestyle, it is not common in the markets anywhere but seems to be least uncommon in Spain, where its name is *japuta*. Maximum length 70 cm (28").

RAZOR CLAM or razor-shell, any of a group of edible BIVALVES, mainly of the genera *Ensis* and *Solen*, whose shells resemble in shape the old-fashioned cut-throat razor. They are very brittle, usually covered by a glossy brown or yellowish periostracum (outer covering), and gape permanently at both ends. This last feature makes it impossible to market razor clams alive in their shells.

Its long and powerful 'foot' enables a razor clam to make its way through wet sand like a knife through butter, dodging danger by a swift descent. Hunting them in the intertidal waters where they lurk can be a frustrating business, and even perilous since the sharp edges of their shells can inflict severe cuts. In Orkney, where the cult of eating them has reached its apogee, they are known as spoots and their pursuit as spooting.

Opinions differ on how to make them emerge from their holes. Putting a teaspoonful of salt into the hole is said to work in some places but not in others. The comments of George Henry Lewes (1860) are apposite.

There is something irresistibly ludicrous in grave men stooping over a hole—their coat-tails pendant in the water, their breath suspended, one hand holding salt, the other alert to clutch the victim—watching the perturbations of the sand, like hungry cats beside the holes of mice.

However, Lewes did this himself, with varying results, and concluded that there was no certainty in the matter and that often, when a razor clam responds to a dose of salt by letting the tip of its syphon appear for a moment, 'it is merely to see what is the matter, and to indulge in a not altogether frivolous curiosity as to the being who can illogically offer salt to him who lives in salt water'.

The common species of European waters are *Ensis ensis*, which is curved; and *E. siliqua* and *Solen marginatus*, which are straight. Maximum lengths are around 15 cm (6"). On the eastern seaboard of N. America *Ensis directus*, the eastern razor clam (or Atlantic jack-knife—see below), is the main species; while on the western coast, from Alaska to California, *Siliqua patula*, the northern razor clam, is prized.

The SE Asian species *Sinovacula constricta* reaches a length of 10 cm (4") and has shells which are yellow and blue on the outside. *Solen grandis* is another Asian species which is widely eaten.

The name **jack-knife clam** is sometimes applied to certain razor clams in California and in Asian waters, but is perhaps better reserved for CLAMS of related genera, notably *Tagelus* (*T. californianus* being the Californian jack-knife clam).

If there is a useful distinction here, it seems to lie in a difference of proportion between length and breadth; the jack-knife clams being those which are shorter and broader and therefore less like a razor. Certainly the habit of 'jack-knifing' themselves down through the sand or mud is common to both these lots of clams and cannot itself constitute a distinction between them.

Razor clams, once removed from their shells, may be eaten entire. The meat is white and tender when cooked. Of the few dishes which specifically call for them, the Italian *Zuppa di cannolicchi* is noteworthy.

REBLOCHON is a surface-ripened, semi-soft whole-milk French cheese from the Haute Savoie and Savoie regions. It has a mild, subtly sour taste, and is made in a flat disc shape weighing about 600 g (1 lb 5 oz). There are also miniature versions.

RED COD *Pseudophycis bacchus*, a fish of New Zealand waters, especially around the South Island, is not a true cod but a member of the family Eretmophoridae, bottom-living fish of moderately deep waters. Its alternative common name is hoka.

Maximum length close to 1 m (40"); average length half that or less. A grey-pink fish above, more white below, with pink fins. There is some commercial trawling for the red cod, but it is rated acceptable rather than good as a food fish.

RED-COOK a term which occurs as a verb, signifying a method of cooking, in books about Chinese cookery. It usually refers to a meat dish prepared by stewing or braising, with a liberal amount of soy SAUCE to produce the reddish colour. Not all Chinese meat dishes which are red or reddish when finished are made in this way; some depend simply on the use of red colouring.

RED CRAB *Geryon quinquedens*, a deep-water CRAB of the W. Atlantic, from Cuba up to Nova Scotia. A fishery for this species, which had not previously been exploited, has been started in New England. The meat is good. Although the legs are thin, their meat slips out easily.

In the north of Spain a similar fishery has been begun for *G. affinis*, the corresponding species of the E. Atlantic. Normal weights of the 'cangrexo real' (as this crab is known in Galician) are 1 kg (2.25 lb) for the male (and much less for the female).

REDFISH a name which for obvious reasons has been applied to various species of fish around the world, is best used for fish of the genus *Sebastes* in the family Scorpaenidae, especially *S. marinus*. This is a bright red or orange-red fish, with a maximum length of 1 m (40") although it is commonly about a third of that. It belongs to the cold northerly waters of the Atlantic down to the Gulf of Maine on the west and the North Sea on the east, and is the object of a sizeable commercial fishery, for consumption in Scandinavia and also in

Germany, where it may appear on menus as Island Rotbarsch, since the supply comes mainly from Icelandic waters.

S. marinus is known as 'ocean perch' in the USA, and may also bear that name in Canada.

A smaller relation, *S. viviparus*, is its counterpart in shallower waters; and it is this species, if any, which may be called by the unsuitable name 'Norway haddock' in Britain.

In Australia redfish has become the official name of the nannygai (see ALFONSINO).

RED MULLET *Mullus barbatus* and *M. surmuletus*, are among the most prized fish of the Mediterranean, distinguished by their crimson colour and delicate flesh. They are also found in the Atlantic, *M. surmuletus* as far north as the south coast of Britain. A Black Sea version of *M. barbatus* is recognized as *M. barbatus ponticus*.

M. barbatus is smaller (maximum length 25 cm/10") and paler than *M. surmuletus* (maximum length 40 cm/16"). The latter often bears horizontal yellow stripes on its sides; and its common names usually mean 'of the rocks' (thus, French *rouget de roche*, Italian *triglia di scoglio*).

Into the western end of the Mediterranean another red mullet pokes its nose. This is *Pseudupeneus prayensis*, a species which belongs to the west coast of Africa, from Morocco to Angola. At the eastern end of the Mediterranean there has been a more interesting incursion. When de Lesseps built the Suez Canal, he was of course creating a passage for ships, not fish; and the salinity of the Bitter Lakes which punctuate the Canal was anyway too great to allow fish to pass through. However, a century or so later, the flow of water in the Canal had diminished the salt level considerably and Indo-Pacific species began to swim up from the Red Sea. These included two red mullet (or goatfish, as they are known in the Indo-Pacific), *Upeneus asymmetricus* (formerly *U. tragula*) and *U. moluccensis* (formerly *Mulloidichthys auriflamma*). These species are now established as breeding populations in the E. Mediterranean.

The Romans of classical times would have greeted these new arrivals, had they come 2,000 years earlier, with great enthusiasm. Many Roman authors testify to the red mullet fever which gripped their contemporaries in the first centuries AD. One symptom was an undue preoccupation with size, which caused the price of large specimens to rise to absurd heights, equivalent to many hundreds of pounds in the 1990s, for a really big one. Another was the habit of keeping red mullet in captivity and arranging for guests to enjoy the highly specialized aesthetic experience of watching the colour of dying fish change. The moralist Seneca attacked the practice with savage irony, claiming that a Roman would no longer attend the bedside of his dying father, however much he desired the father to die(!), if the rival attraction of a dying red mullet was on offer.

Red mullet may be grilled or fried. Their delicate but firm flesh needs no sauce or stuffing, although these are sometimes supplied. The liver is a delicacy.

RED PEPPERCORNS (or PINK PEPPERCORNS), which have enjoyed a vogue as a spice in the last decades of the 20th century, are not related to the common black PEPPER but come from a different plant, *Schinus terebinthifolius*. This is indigenous to Brazil, where it is known as *aroreira*, but since the 19th century has been widely diffused in other tropical areas. It is also called Brazilian pepper tree, Christmas-berry, and Florida holly. In the French island of Réunion it is known as *poivrier, sorbier,* or *incense.*

The plant can grow to tree size, and bears masses of ivory flowers. These are succeeded by small, single-seeded berries, which are glossy green and then bright red. When fully ripe, they become dry, with nothing inside except the seed. The flavour is slightly sweet at first, then peppery (with a hint of menthol) and pungent. Although the plant is common in parts of the USA, where it was first introduced for its decorative quality, it is from Réunion that the red peppercorns of commerce chiefly come. They are exported as 'baies roses de Bourbon', then processed and packed in France as red or pink peppercorns.

It was Alexandra Hicks (1982) who first dispelled confusion about the nature of these 'peppercorns'. She explained that there had been two reasons for it. First, the berries of *Piper nigrum*, the ones which become true peppercorns, do go from a green to a red stage as they ripen (although they are normally picked when green). So there do exist 'red/pink' berries which can properly be called pepper berries; but they do not occur in processed form or in commerce. Secondly, there is a plant, *Schinus molle*, known as the Peruvian pepper tree, which is closely related to *S. terebinthifolius* and which bears purplish-red berries which have long been used as a condiment in Peru; and this plant is now common in California.

Red peppercorns may be decorative, and serve to add pungency to a dish, but it is questionable whether they are entirely suitable for consumption. Persons handling the plants may develop rashes; children who eat more than a few of the berries, ripe or unripe, experience digestive upsets and vomiting; and birds which feed excessively on the ripe berries become intoxicated and unable to fly.

Most chefs who use red peppercorns are unaware of all this, and do not know what the peppercorns really are.

REFRIED BEANS is the misleading translation of a term very familiar in Spanish-speaking countries of C. and S. America: *frijoles refritos*. This refers to beans which have first been cooked in water and are subsequently fried. There is no question of their being fried twice, i.e. literally refried. Diana Kennedy (1986) has explained the matter:

Several people have asked me why, when the beans are fried, they are called *refried*. Nobody I asked in Mexico seemed to know until quite suddenly it dawned on me. The Mexicans have a habit of qualifying a word to emphasize the meaning by adding the prefix *re-*. They will get the oil very hot (*requemar*), or something will be very good (*retebien*). Thus refrito means well fried, which they certainly are, since they are fried until they are almost dry. I am glad to say that Santamaría in his *Diccionario de Mexicanismos* bears this out.

REFRIGERATION i.e. keeping foods at a low temperature, preserves them for a limited time. All the processes of life, indeed

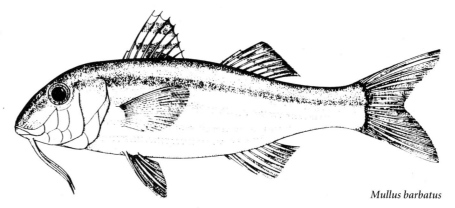

Mullus barbatus

all chemical reactions, take place more slowly at low temperatures.

Heat is a form of energy which manifests itself as a vibration of the molecules of which things are made. In a hot body the molecules move fast; in a cold one they move more slowly. That is why chemical reactions occur more slowly in cold conditions.

There is no such thing as 'cold'; a cold body simply contains less heat energy than a hot one. When two objects at different temperatures come together, heat flows out of the warmer body into the colder one until eventually they are at the same temperature.

When a substance changes state—that is, when a solid melts to a liquid or a liquid turns to a gas, or vice versa—there is a considerable transfer of heat energy. For example, when ice melts, a lot of heat has to pass into it to allow it to change to water. This heat is drawn in from the surroundings, so anything in contact with the melting ice loses heat and becomes colder. All the available heat is going into the melting process, so the ice and its meltwater remain at freezing point until all the ice has melted, and only then do things start to warm up.

Similarly, when any liquid evaporates to a vapour the process demands heat. The liquid can be made to evaporate by heating it. But it can also be made to evaporate without heating, by reducing the ambient pressure. In this case all the heat that is required has to come from the surroundings, which therefore become cooler. When water vapour condenses to a liquid it gives up the heat it has taken in, warming the surroundings.

ICE

The preservative effects of cold were observed early, even if the reason was not understood. The Romans used to chill perishable foods by packing them in snow brought from the Alps, using straw to insulate the snow and keep it from melting both on the journey and in use. The icehouse is another ancient invention, developed in the Middle East, taken up in Renaissance Europe, and familiar in N. America until recently. Ice is collected from lakes in winter, or from mountains, and stored in a heavily insulated building, usually sunk into the ground. With proper management there will still be some ice left by the time winter comes again.

Both these methods are strictly for the rich, who could afford to have ice transported and to build an icehouse. One other traditional method was available to all: the evaporation of water through unglazed earthenware. If water is stored in an unglazed pot, a little of it seeps through the clay and evaporates on the outside, cooling the pot and the water still inside it. Ideally the pot should be set in a shady spot exposed

to any wind, since the movement of air speeds evaporation. This method is still widely used to cool drinking water in India and elsewhere. The same principle is used in the modern earthenware cooler for milk bottles.

In Italy in the early 16th century it was discovered that if ice is mixed with salt the temperature of the mixture will fall as low as –18 °C (0 °F; in fact the zero point of the Fahrenheit scale was determined in this way). This phenomenon may seem surprising, but it depends on simple facts of physics. A solution of any substance in water always has a lower freezing point than that of pure water; in the case of the strongest possible salt solution this is that stated above. When ice melts, the temperature of the ice and the meltwater around it is always exactly that of the freezing point of the water, even if this is below the normal melting point of the ice. So if ice is floating in a salt solution, it will melt at the freezing point of the solution.

THE MECHANICAL REFRIGERATOR

In the 1830s some attempts were made to build mechanical refrigerators that used the cooling effect of evaporation, but these were unsuccessful until the British physicist William Thomson (later Lord Kelvin) worked out the principle of the heat pump in 1851. A liquid is made to evaporate by lowering the ambient pressure and without heating it, so that it becomes extremely cold. The cold vapour is piped through a closed container, and the heat of whatever is in the container passes into the vapour, so the contents are cooled. After this the vapour is led out of the container and compressed to reliquefy; this releases the heat that has gone into the vapour. The liquid is then vaporized, and thus cooled, again. The fluid travels in an endless cycle in a closed circuit of pipework, constantly taking heat out of the container and releasing it into the open air. All that is needed is some means of driving the fluid around the circuit—in most modern refrigerators this is an electric pump.

The first workable refrigerating machinery was built in 1857 by the Frenchman Ferdinand Carré. It used a variant of the principle just described. The refrigerant fluid is ammonia dissolved in water. The ammonia is made to boil out of the water by heating it—ammonia boils at a lower temperature than water. This creates enough pressure to force the ammonia vapour into another vessel, where it condenses into a liquid. Still driven by this pressure, the liquid flows through an expansion valve which greatly reduces its pressure, causing it to evaporate and become very cold, after which it passes through the food compartment and cools the food. From here it flows to another

vessel containing water in which it dissolves again, and thence back to the start of the cycle. The system could reach a temperature as low as –30 °C (–22 °F), and was soon in use for the FREEZING of meat.

Carré's refrigerator could equally well be used to keep foods cool without freezing them; but it was too big for home use. The domestic refrigerator had to wait until electric motors became small and reliable. The first practical model was the Kelvinator, launched in the USA in 1918. Since then the refrigerator has gradually become ubiquitous and indispensable.

An improvement came in 1931 with the invention of chlorofluorocarbons (CFCs), a group of inert gases which make excellent refrigerants. They do not need to be dissolved in water, and the cycle is the simple one described first. One other difference between the cycles is that the simple one needs a mechanical pump to drive fluid around the system; while (at least in a small machine without long pipe runs) the ammonia cycle can be powered entirely by the water heater and there need be no moving parts. This cycle is still used in small gas-powered refrigerators for caravans and boats.

In the 1970s it was established that CFCs were eroding the earth's ozone layer, and since then they have gradually been replaced by less harmful chemicals such as hydrochlorofluorocarbons (HCFCs) and butane. With this beneficial change, refrigerators regain in full their reputation as one of the great boons of the 20th century.

(RH)

REINDEER *Rangifer tarandus*, a large DEER inhabiting the northern regions of Europe and Asia, especially well known as a food in Sweden, Finland, and Russia.

The meat from a reindeer, which is better than that from its close relation the CARIBOU, is cooked and eaten in many ways (roasts, stews, etc.) in the countries where it lives in the wild. It has become increasingly available, often as smoked meat, elsewhere. Reindeer tongue is a delicacy. However, the praises of reindeer meat have been sung in the most melodious and informative manner by Anna-Maija and Juha Tanttu (1988):

The reindeer is a way of life in Lapland. It's both a pack animal and the tourist's darling. Its skins are made into boots and furs. Its horns are made into souvenirs. But above all reindeer are the Lapp's *cattle*. The Lapp lives on and from reindeer meat.

Reindeer meat is wonderful. It has a slightly gamy taste, is rich in nutrients but not too fatty. It's easy to digest and can be served in a variety of ways. The reindeer tastes so good because it eats good food itself: first it's fed on its mother's milk, later it forages for its own moss, in the unpolluted wilds of Lapland.

Reindeer dishes combine old Lapp folk traditions with modern meat technology, quality controls, and inspections.

You can make anything out of reindeer meat, from soup to stews. But Lapland has its own delicious specialities.

The Lapp serves smoked reindeer roast in thin slices as an appetizer and on sandwiches. Reindeer tongue is delicious cooked and also makes an excellent paté.

One of the simplest, tastiest, and perhaps most famous reindeer dishes is reindeer stew. The meat is cut into slivers while still frozen, put into a pot with a bit of water, and simmered until tender. Experts have different views of what 'real' reindeer stew should be. Some say that fatty pork should be added to the pot. It's a matter of taste. The stew is served with mashed potatoes, seasoned with butter and onions, and lingonberry purée. (Some purists leave that out, too.)

Reindeer meat has its own special taste and doesn't need any 'fancy' spices. The most common seasonings are green and black pepper, allspice, bay leaves, and salt. Suitable accompaniments are onions, carrots, celery, parsnips, and pickled cucumbers. Reindeer meat doesn't suffer if you cook it with cream or sour cream, either. It also gets along well with mushrooms and berries: lingonberries, cranberries, rowanberries.

See also KOUMISS for the slightly alcoholic beverage called pima which is made from reindeer milk.

RELISH as a noun and in a culinary context, refers to a CONDIMENT or highly flavoured item of food taken with plainer food to add flavour and interest to it. An English example would be a small serving of pickled vegetables taken with plain bread and cheese.

A condiment may be a relish. However, it is more usual to refer to a condiment, e.g. mustard, as a condiment. Condiments are normally taken in small quantities, whereas relishes often come in mouthfuls and can usually be taken in conjunction with the main food, not necessarily in or on it; no one would just eat a spoonful of mustard, whereas one might very well do this with a SAMBAL (corresponding closely to the meaning of relish) or CHUTNEY.

RÉMOULADE a French culinary term which usually refers to a mayonnaise-like dressing with mustard. It is thought to have been derived in the 17th century from a name used in Picardy for the black radish, whose piquancy is not unlike that of mustard.

In the past, the term designated a broth flavoured with chopped anchovies, capers, parsley, spring onions, garlic, and a little oil. Its modern sense (a mayonnaise-like emulsion) seems to have evolved in the 19th century. It is now rarely encountered in France except as an element of *céleri rémoulade*, a popular salad made of grated celeriac (șee CELERY) and MAYONNAISE that has been highly seasoned with Dijon MUSTARD.

When the term occurs as an English word, it may lack the accent.

RENDANG an interesting dish, perhaps unique in its cooking method, which belongs to the Minangkabau ('Victorious Buffalo') people of W. Sumatra, although it has latterly become common property for all Indonesians and has appeared elsewhere in adapted forms (to some of which the phrase 'dry beef curry', which would not be appropriate for the original, authentic version, can be applied).

The WATER-BUFFALO meat, or beef, should be of a flaky sort, with some fat; brisket is the best cut of beef to choose. Spices and flavourings are shallots and garlic; ginger, GALINGALE and TURMERIC; chilli peppers; turmeric leaf (*daun kunyit*) and salam leaf (see DAUN SALAM). The cooking medium is coconut milk and the technique is to cook the cubed meat, with its flavourings, in enough coconut milk to cover it for, say, an hour and a half, uncovered; then to let the now thick coconut milk bubble for another half-hour until it starts to turn into oil, becoming brown and even thicker. Stirring is now continuous, until the dish is almost 'dry'.

In this unusual sequence, the stage of simmering in the liquid coconut milk passes seamlessly into the final stage which, with the coconut milk now turned into oil, must count as a form of frying.
READING: Sri Owen (1986*b*).

RENNET is a substance used for CURDLING milk, either as part of CHEESE-MAKING or to make the dessert JUNKET. Most rennet is of animal origin, but vegetable rennet is used for making some cheeses, both of traditional and kosher or vegetarian varieties.

Animal rennet contains the digestive enzyme rennin, which curdles milk in the normal process of digestion. The usual source is the lining of the fourth stomach (the abomasum or true stomach) of a calf, though other young animals may be used. The animal should be unweaned, and thus with a high ability to digest milk, and abundant rennin. The gizzard lining of domestic fowls may also be used, giving a rennin which has a less powerful effect. Traditionally the linings, of whatever type, were salted and dried, which allowed them to retain their effect for several months. Only a small strip was needed. Modern rennet is a liquid extract or a powder.

The stomach lining of human beings, like that of calves and other animals, contains rennin, which exerts its curdling effect on milk which has been ingested. Thus, although we swallow milk as a liquid, we quickly turn it into a solid, like junket.

Vegetable rennet depends for its power on various plant enzymes which have a similar coagulating effect on the protein in the milk. Some traditional Italian CACIOTTA and PECORINO cheeses are made with fiore ('flower') rennet obtained from the wild cardoon, *Cynara cardunculus*. This plant is used for the same purpose in Spain and Portugal. The common British plant lady's bedstraw, *Galium verum*, is another source, which has the added advantage that it also supplies a yellow dye suited to colouring cheese or butter. Some other plant enzymes (ficin from figs, papain from the papaya, etc.) could be used but are not entirely suitable, since they tend to produce bitter cheeses.

RESHTEH a Persian word meaning thread or string, sometimes referring to a very fine NOODLE like 'angel's hair' but more often to a Middle Eastern fresh egg noodle of ribbon shape, often home made and hand cut.

Reshteh, as Perry (1982) points out, was 'the only word for noodle known in the several 13th century Arabic cookery books and in the poems of the 14th century Persian rhymester Bushaq'. And it has indeed become the general Persian name for noodles.

Claudia Roden (1985), writing about the present role of reshteh in the Middle East, remarks that, 'like rice, it has escaped the stigma of being a filling dish for the poor'. Indeed, although a common dish of the Arab world, it is considered suitable for special occasions. By standard practice the reshteh is broken up and fried brown, but nowadays it may be browned under the grill and added to rice.

Reshteh has more than one special significance in Iran. Margaret Shaida (1992) gives an example:

Dishes containing noodles are traditionally prepared at times of decision or change so that the 'reins (of life) may be taken in hand' and the future given direction. Reshteh polow is often served on the eve of the new year [Persian New Year—21 March] as its threads intertwine in the same way that the family bonds are tied together.

She also explains that reshteh is also made for occasions of thanksgiving, and appears in the soup *ash-e-reshteh* (sometimes called *ash-e-poshteh-pa* or pilgrim's soup), traditionally served on the eve of departure of a loved one going on the pilgrimage to Mecca or any long journey.

See also SHA'RIYYA; NOODLES OF ASIA.

(HS)

RESIN a sticky secretion of certain trees and shrubs; or any synthetic substance which has the property of naturally occurring resins. Resins resemble GUM in some respects although differing in others. Gums are soluble in water, whereas resins are not, although soluble in alcohol. Also, while gums are more or less devoid of flavour, resins contain essential oils which do have flavour and can be put to use in making flavourings.

Resins are often extracted by incisions in the bark of the trees or shrubs which yield them. Examples with food uses are MASTIC, obtained from plants of the genus *Pistacia*; BALSAM of various kinds; ASAFOETIDA (and the spice SILPHIUM of classical times).

RESTAURANT According to contemporary dictionaries, a restaurant is simply an eating place, an establishment where meals are served to customers. By this definition, restaurants—by whatever name they have been given—are almost as old as civilization. The ruins of Pompeii contain the remnants of a tavern which provided foods and wines to passers-by. For as long as there have been travellers there have been institutions offering food and accommodation (and the traditions of hospitality ensured that they were also welcomed into private dwellings). Indeed, the prime function of these early 'eating places' was to cater to the needs of people away from home who, unless they had brought their own food and cooks with them, were obliged to take whatever was available—or go hungry. From the second half of the 17th century there were cafés, public places where people could meet and talk, eat and drink. Serving only coffee, to begin with, they soon became established as meeting places for men of letters; some also provided newspapers for their clientele to read, or facilities for playing chess or billiards. In England there were also taverns which, catering to a socially superior clientele, employed well-known cooks and offered an extensive choice of dishes.

The restaurant, as it was conceived in Paris towards the end of the 18th century, had a different vocation. Its principal advantage was that it offered diners a choice: according to BRILLAT-SAVARIN, restaurants allowed people to eat when they wanted, what they wanted, and how much this would cost. The top restaurants of the day boasted a vast menu, with a choice of 12

soups, 65 entrées of beef, mutton, chicken, or game, 15 roasts, and 50 dessert dishes.

Prior to this, French catering was highly regulated and shared between various corporations, such as *traiteurs*, *rôtisseurs*, *pâtissiers*, *aubergistes*, and *taverniers/cabaretiers*. The regulations surrounding these trades gave each one certain privileges. The *rôtisseur*, for example, roasted meat but was not allowed to bake dishes in the oven, nor to make 'ragouts'; the *pâtisseur* could bake pies but was not allowed to sell roast meat; the *aubergiste* could offer wine but not food, unless it came from a *traiteur* or a *charcutier*. Nevertheless, around 1760 some Parisian *traiteurs-rôtisseurs* were offering diners a basic *table d'hôte*.

At this time the word 'restaurant' meant a restorative beverage, such as a thin soup. Places supplying such foods were known as 'bouillons'. In 1765 the owner of one of these, a man by the name of Boulanger, added to his menu a dish of sheep's feet— *Pieds de mouton à la sauce poulette* (a kind of white sauce enriched with egg yolks). He was immediately attacked by the corporation of *traiteurs*, who accused him of selling a RAGOUT, a dish they considered theirs by right.

A ragout is a dish in which the meat (or poultry or fish) cooks *in* a sauce, usually with vegetables, herbs, and other flavourings. In Boulanger's dish, the sauce was made separately and poured *on* the meat. The distinction is subtle, but it was enough to convince the court that the *traiteurs'* claim could not be upheld. This opened the way for the establishment of a new style of eating house and, incidentally, made sheep's feet *à la poulette* a kind of cult dish, which even appeared on the royal table. It could be said that the modern restaurant has its genesis in a legal technicality.

By 1771 the word 'restaurateur' was defined (in the *Dictionnaire de Trévoux*) as 'someone who has the art of preparing true broths, known as "restaurants", and the right to sell all kinds of custards, dishes of rice, vermicelli and macaroni, egg dishes, boiled capons, preserved and stewed fruit and other delicious and health-giving foods'. The restaurateur had total control of the wine and food service and was able to present one bill for all the foods eaten and wines drunk, whereas previously the *aubergiste* had been obliged to collect payment on behalf of the *rôtisseur* for roast meats, on behalf of the *pâtissier* for pies, and so on. The word 'restaurant', used to describe an eating house, first appeared in a decree of 1786.

While some restaurants were established in Paris before 1789 (the Grande Taverne de Londres opened about 1782 under the celebrated Antoine Beauvilliers, and at least three other famous restaurants appeared in

the next few years), the abolition of guilds and their privileges in the wake of the French Revolution, together with an influx of deputies into the capital and a surplus of unemployed chefs no longer in charge of aristocratic kitchens, laid the scene for an enormous expansion of the restaurant industry in the 19th century. Restaurants were thus an important consequence of the Revolution and concurred with its aims in contributing towards social equality and promoting egality around the table. Eating well was no longer the privilege of the wealthy who could afford to maintain a cook and a well-supplied kitchen.

While the new restaurants flourished in 19th-century Paris, it was evident that some of their customers were not necessarily eating at a restaurant simply because they were hungry but were choosing the restaurant as a place to meet (literary groups in Paris), to be seen, or because the restaurant offered something different. This was an urban phenomenon. Throughout the 19th century restaurants seem to have been very much associated with cities; the first (red) Michelin guide of 1900 recommended hotels in the country with good accommodation and good food, but no restaurants as such.

To follow the history of restaurants round the world during the 20th century would require another book, rather than another page. However, it may be noted here in conclusion that the USA would necessarily loom very large in any such extended account of the evolution of the restaurant. At first restaurants in America seemed to follow the French model, offering French cuisine and often employing French chefs. They also served French wines. However, the introduction of Prohibition in 1920 caused many of them to close their doors, at the same time opening the way for an expansion of quick-service, alcohol-free, female-friendly cafeterias, luncheonettes, and tearooms serving a different class of cuisine to a different clientele. These in turn led to the proliferation of fast-food chains whose stereotyped outlets, while fulfilling all of Brillat-Savarin's criteria, are a long way from the restaurants he knew and praised. It would also be true to say that for many people the word 'restaurant' now signifies something rather more pretentious than the inexpensive quick eateries which Americans have bestowed upon the world. However, the word continues to retain its wider meaning and there seems to be no reason to encourage a narrowing of its use to the more expensive end of the restaurant spectrum.

(BS)

RESURRECTION CHEESE a Welsh cheese to which the American author Bob

Brown (1955), whose taste for oddities was well developed, drew attention, citing the following passage from *The Story of Wales* by Rhys Davies (1943):

The 'Resurrection Cheese' of Llanfihangel Abercowyn is no longer available, at least under that name. This cheese was so called because it was pressed by gravestones taken from an old church that had fallen into ruins. Often enough the cheeses would be inscribed with such wording as 'Here lies Blodwen Evans, aged 72'.

RHINOCEROS a thick-skinned, horned animal which exists in five species, of which the most important are: the great Indian rhinoceros, *Rhinoceros unicornis*; the black or hook-lipped rhinoceros (*swartrenoster* in S. Africa), *Diceros bicornis*; the white or square-lipped rhinoceros (*witrenoster* in S. Africa), *D. simus*. All species are much reduced in numbers and it would be inappropriate to think of them as a food resource. However, they have been so used in the past. There are various references in early Indian texts to rhinoceros being a permitted food.

RHUBARB the edible stalks of *Rheum rhabarbarum* and two or three other species of the same genus, in the family Polygonaceae. Botanically, rhubarb is a vegetable; but the US Customs Court at Buffalo, NY, ruled in 1947 that it was a fruit, since that is how it is normally eaten.

Wild rhubarbs are all native to Asia. They prefer a cool climate and flourish especially in the general area of Mongolia and Siberia and in the vicinity of the Himalayas. The rhizomes and 'crowns' from which the leaf-bearing stalks grow survive readily in ground which is frozen during the winter.

Rhubarb was known in classical Greece and Rome as an imported dried root with medicinal qualities. Dioscorides (1st century AD) stated that the plant grew in the regions beyond the Bosporus.

There is some debate about how far back Chinese knowledge of rhubarb extends. Pen Khing's herbal, of about 2700 BC, listed it; but Laufer (1978) says the work is spurious. Others point out that in Chinese rhubarb has composite names (e.g. *ta hwan*, 'the great yellow one'), which are descriptive, whilst all genuinely ancient plants have a root word of a single syllable. It does, however, seem to be certain that it was known by the age of Han, 206 BC; that it was valued medicinally; and that it developed into an important article of trade from China to W. Asia during the 10th century.

In England, rhubarb became known, at first in a purely medicinal context, in the 16th century. The idea of eating the stem may have occurred to people, much later,

because of the resemblance between rhubarb and its smaller relation, SORREL. Ray, in his *Historia Plantarum* (1686), compared rhubarb stalks favourably with those of sorrel. However, it was some time before rhubarb recipes began to appear in English cookery books. One early example was in Mrs Rundell (1806). Other recipes for sweet pies and tarts followed during the first half of the 19th century.

Meanwhile, new varieties and hybrids were being developed. Early plants had mainly green stalks, and it was those with a red tinge which were selected to produce the modern red varieties. There are now numerous cultivars, varying in yield, colour, size, season, oxalic acid content, etc. Irish Giant is an interesting curiosity, with stems which may be as much as 1.5 m (5') long, and as thick as a man's arm.

Rhubarb is often forced, either by covering the plant with a pot to encourage early growth in the spring or by the modern method of hothouse cultivation. The practice has been observed in Afghanistan as well as in western countries, where the effect of forcing was accidentally discovered at the Chelsea Physic Garden early in the 19th century. In Britain the sweetest rhubarb, called 'champagne rhubarb', comes very early and has slim, tender stalks.

Rhubarb is mainly used for pies (hence its being known as 'pie-plant' in the USA) and similar dishes, but also for jams. The use of ginger to enhance the taste of rhubarb is traditional, especially in jam-making. Orange and angelica are used likewise.

In Britain the combination of rhubarb and CUSTARD is as irresistible to some as it is offputting to others; and rhubarb CRUMBLE, also with custard is deservedly popular.

Rhubarb may be cooked as a vegetable. For example, in Poland it is cooked with potatoes and aromatics. It is used in *khorest* (stew) in Iran and in Afghanistan it is added to spinach. In Italy it is used to make an aperitif, *rabarbaro*, which has a low alcoholic content and is regarded as a health drink.

RICE (*see the feature which begins on page 662, dealing with rice as a crop, and then with rice as food*)

RICE BEAN *Vigna umbellata*, an annual LEGUME of tropical Asian origin, so named

because its small seeds, when dried, are eaten with or instead of rice and are only slightly larger than rice grains. Colour of the seeds ranges from yellow through red and brown to black, and the beans are sometimes mottled. Light-coloured types are preferred.

Rice beans have been grown extensively in NE India and adjoining regions as far east as southern parts of China. However, the quantities grown have diminished, partly because of changed patterns of rice production which have eliminated the intervals between rice crops, intervals in which it was formerly the practice to insert a crop of rice beans. Nevertheless, the fact that the rice bean is one of the very best legumes for nutritional purposes has recently caused a renewal of interest in its use as food for humans.

One problem to be solved if this valuable plant is to be exploited more fully is that its vinelike habit of growth and the fact that the pods fall apart and scatter seed of their own accord make harvesting difficult.

RICE CAKES OF THE PHILIPPINES constitute an interesting group of rice dishes, which in the Philippines would most often be eaten at a merienda (light afternoon meal; see MERENDA).

Puto is the generic name for a rice cake made from *galapong* (rice flour), slightly sweetened and steamed. The rice for *galapong* is not ground dry, but soaked overnight and then ground wet, formerly in large stone grinders. Fermentation takes place during the soaking, and yeast is usually used. Almost every town or region has a typical *puto*, a distinctive recipe developed in it reflecting regional taste, or made for special occasions.

Among the best known are: *putong Polo*, from Polo in Bulacan, which are small (about an inch across), and come in two forms, *puti* (white) and *pula* (red-brown). *Manapla puto*, from Manapla in Negros Occidental, is steamed in banana-leaf cups. Malolos, in Bulacan, has a white *puto* fragrant with STAR ANISE. On Christmas Eve, Pampangos of San Fernando serve *putong sulot*, anise flavoured and cut in parallelograms, with *panara*, a vegetable-filled, peppery pasty. One of the best known is *puto bumbong*, made of the violet rice called *pirurutong*, steamed in a bamboo tube
(*cont. on page 665*)

> **M**ENTION of health at the end of the entry on rhubarb brings to mind purgative powers, plus questions about possible health risks if a lot of rhubarb is eaten. In fact the purgative principle in rhubarb is a group of substances allied to chrysophanic acid and is present mainly in the root. The stalks contain oxalic acid, which is harmful if eaten to excess, but the amounts are no greater than those in spinach and chard, for example. Rhubarb leaves contain much more, and are not edible.

Rice

Oryza sativa, a grain that is a STAPLE food for roughly half of humanity.

Rice has several advantages over most other staple foods. It gives higher and more reliable yields than WHEAT and BARLEY. The moisture content of the grain is low when it is harvested, and is further reduced by drying. It therefore keeps well in storage; in cool, dark, and reasonably dry conditions its quality declines only a little after three years and it should be quite eatable after as much as ten years. It is easy to transport, because it is not heavy with moisture and does not bruise. Most important of all, rice has a good flavour and texture when cooked, absorbing and setting off to advantage the flavour of any sauce or other cooking liquid.

Although most people associate rice with a hot, wet climate, it was not originally a tropical plant. It is descended from a wild grass that was probably first cultivated in the southern foothills of the E. Himalayas and the upper reaches of the Irrawaddy, Salween, and Mekong. Rice-farming presumably began only after someone had discovered the technique of rice-cooking (see RICE AS FOOD). The earliest known remains of cultivated rice have been found in the central Yangtze Valley and are about 8,500 years old. By now the number of varieties in existence may be as many as 100,000, of which 8,000 or so are, or have recently been, grown for food. The rest are 'wild' rices, but not to be confused with the long, black grains of WILD RICE (*Zizania aquatica*), a different plant.

Rice is now cultivated in over 110 countries, in many different climates and environments. This versatility is the result of a very long process. Rice extended its boundaries gradually, because it took time for early farmers to breed (through seed selection) new varieties that would tolerate heat, cold, drought, flood, and local soil conditions. Because different rices cross-breed easily, and because there are many 'wild' varieties, the genus still defies exhaustive botanic classification. For practical purposes, agriculturists count four main types: dry or 'upland' rice, which is grown mainly on hillsides, often by slash-and-burn cultivation in poor soil; rain-fed rice, grown in shallow water; irrigated rice, grown in shallow water fed from storage and drainage systems that make crops more or less independent of rainfall; and deep-water rice, grown in estuaries or other areas liable to flooding to a depth of as much as 5 m (16'). Different types predominate in different regions of the world. Mainland China grows irrigated rice almost exclusively; Latin America is about 75% upland rice; S. Asia as a whole is about one-third rain-fed, and rather less than one-half irrigated.

For agricultural purposes, rice varieties are also grouped by their growing characteristics. Some tolerate cold or heat, others drought or salt water. The time they take to come to maturity varies from 90 to 180 days or even longer, and they vary just as much in the number of tillers (grain-bearing stems) that each plant produces, in the height of their stems (from 0.5 m to almost 2 m/1.6–6.5'), and in their reaction to the length of daylight hours. Light-sensitive rices flower only when the day is exactly the right length to give them time to ripen their grain before the growing season ends.

The characteristics on which growers focus most attention overlap with but are by no means identical with those which are important to consumers. From the consumers' point of view the classification and nomenclature of rice is complex and sometimes perplexing—perhaps more so than for any of the other major plant foods.

Rice farming and breeding have passed, and are passing, through a continuing revolution, of which the 'Green Revolution' of the 1960s and 1970s was only a chapter. The most ancient techniques remain in use and still have much to commend them. All over S. and E. Asia, rice is grown in small terraced fields which can only be cultivated by hand. Outside the USA and Australia, the average size of a rice farm is between 0.5 and 2 hectares (1–5 acres), and small farmers obviously cannot afford sophisticated machinery. The most modern rice varieties are often farmed by old methods, sown in nursery beds, transplanted by hand, and reaped with a sickle or even, stem by stem, with a tiny blade concealed between the fingers so as not to offend the goddess of the growing rice. At the other end of the technological spectrum, pre-germinated seeds are broadcast by a low-flying aircraft, the flow of water through the fields is controlled by a computer, and a combine harvester gathers in the crop.

One advantage of the old methods was that every ricefield contained a wide range of genes, which protected the crop against total loss; whatever pest or disease struck, some, at least, of the plants would resist it. When no fertilizer or other chemical was used, the natural ecosystem of the flooded field supported fish, frogs, and waterfowl which enriched the soil and fed the farmer. A skilled reaper could also select, as she cut, the finest heads of grain to be set aside as next year's seed.

Modern varieties of rice, developed in great quantity in the search for higher yields, tend to be given initials and numbers, such as IR36, a variety bred by the IRRI (International Rice Research Institute) and believed to be perhaps the most-cultivated single crop in history; in the 1980s it was estimated that over 10% of the world's rice land was sown with this one variety.

Generally, however, the rice plant gives high yields in the right conditions, and early farmers soon realized that the best varieties were those that liked shallow, slowly moving water. In fact, irrigated rice can be grown year after year on the same land indefinitely, and may produce two or even three harvests a year; yields are low, but dependable. But the work of building and maintaining a system of fields, with the channels to supply and drain off water, is immense, and requires a close-knit, orderly community. This was a price that many societies were willing to pay in return for the benefits rice gave them. It is both a generous and a demanding crop.

Perhaps for that reason, rice spread slowly. It was established in N. India, in S. and C. China, and all over mainland SE Asia, by about 2000 BC. By about the 1st century AD it was grown in what is now Sarawak and Sulawesi, and probably in the Philippines, where the immense flights of terraced fields in the hills around Banaue are said to be over 2,000 years old. Much of the terracing that so takes the eye in Java and Bali, however, is of relatively recent date.

The next major advances were into the Middle East and Japan, sometime between 300 BC and 200 AD. It was not until 1900 that cold-tolerant varieties were bred capable of flourishing in the climate of Hokkaido, and by that time Japan was on the brink of a thoroughly modern programme of genetic improvement; rice had long been the country's staple, and indeed plays a leading role in the foundation myth of the Japanese imperial family.

In the Mediterranean, the Greeks and Romans knew about rice, but regarded it as an expensive import, to be used mainly as a medicine. It was probably brought from India to the Near East by the Persians, but they never thought of it as their staple diet, and it was not grown in Egypt until the 6th or 7th century AD. It is not mentioned in the Bible, although Coverdale's English Bible of 1535 translates the food that Jacob gave to Esau as 'ryse' instead of lentils (Genesis 25: 34).

Rice cooked in clarified butter is said to have been the favourite dish of the Prophet Muhammad. His followers certainly took rice to N. Africa, Spain, and Sicily, into Turkey and across the Sahara to W. Africa, where a different species, *O. glaberrima*, was already cultivated (and still is).

By the 13th century rice was being imported into N. Europe. The *OED*'s first citation of the word is from Henry III's household accounts in 1234. By the 15th century its attraction had been introduced to N. Italy, where it flourishes in the plains.

In the so-called 'COLUMBIAN EXCHANGE' of natural resources, rice was one of the Old World's finest gifts to the New. But it did not become established in America until almost two centuries after Columbus' voyages, another example of how slowly rice has moved to new homes. Many varieties were tried, and a certain amount of selective breeding carried out, before the crop could be adapted to the soils and climates of the Americas. In the north, the first successful crops are said to have been grown from seed brought to Charleston by a ship from Madagascar, while the knowledge of how to grow rice may have been brought from W. Africa by slaves selected for their farming skills; see Karen Hess (1992) for a discussion and much other information about rice in S. Carolina. A pioneer of genetic improvement of all natural products was Thomas Jefferson, who travelled to Piedmont to find out why Italian rice fetched a higher price in the Paris market than Carolina rice, and smuggled seed out in his pockets.

'Carolina gold', whatever its genetic origins, flourished in the freshwater tidal swamps around Cape Fear from the 1690s until competition from Mississippi valley rice in the later part of the 19th century. Shortly afterwards, Japanese immigrants to California set up the west coast rice industry. Some of the crop's most spectacular gains, in fact, have taken place in the past 100 years, in the Americas, N. Japan, China, E. Indonesia, and parts of Australia. At the same time, it has continued to move from being a subsistence staple towards becoming a commodity, a foodstuff traded on local and then on world markets.

Rice products. Rice is ground into rice flour (used for puddings, cakes, biscuits, etc.) or (even finer) rice powder, rolled into flakes, 'popped' by cooking it in pressure vessels which are then suddenly opened, and pre-cooked to make 'instant' rice. A modern rice mill exhibits an astonishing variety of high technology among the traditional noise and dust.

Rice bran, which is removed in the milling and processing of rice, is still used as animal feed, and can also be processed and sold as a beneficial garnish or additive for foods. In Japan, where it is known as *nuka*, rice bran is an important medium for pickling.

A major product of rice is the rice noodle of which many types are found in Asia and China (see NOODLES OF ASIA and NOODLES OF CHINA).

Rice is also fermented to make vinegars, rice wine, SAKÉ, and TAPÉ. In Latin America, especially in Ecuador, a little known but interesting fermented rice product (ARROZ FERMENTADO/*amarillo*, or Sierra rice) is made and consumed. READING: Grist (1953); Sri Owen (1993). (RO)

Rice as food

Considered as food, rice is perceived in different ways in different cultures. Attitudes towards the proper way to cook and eat it seem to depend on the role rice plays in the lives of the people. In many communities where it has long been established as the principal staple, it is revered as divine and is still cooked and served in the plainest possible way; the dishes that accompany it may be elaborate and exquisite, but the rice itself is too precious to be treated as just another ingredient. (Of course there are dishes such as Cantonese fried rice, and *Nasi goreng* (the Indonesian equivalent), which do not conform to this pattern.)

At the other extreme—the other end of the trade route— rice was in the distant past an expensive import, so rare that it was locked in the spice cupboard and carefully recorded in the household accounts. In medieval Europe it was made into MILK PUDDINGS with refined SUGAR (also very scarce); this is one of the origins of BLANCMANGE. In Elizabethan England it still had a little of the magic of strangeness; steeped in cow's milk with white breadcrumbs, sugar, and powdered fennel seed it was given to nursing mothers. In

Charles I's time rice boiled in milk with sugar and cinnamon was regarded, as most foods are sooner or later, as an APHRODISIAC. But then it became easier to obtain, and gradually opened the way towards general use and led to the wealth of English RICE PUDDINGS, Scandinavian rice dishes such as the rice porridge of Norway traditionally made for Christmas Eve, and delicacies such as the rice tart of Liège.

Meanwhile, a third attitude to rice had developed in regions where it was grown as a food crop, played an important role in most people's diet, but was not the only or a major staple food. In much of India, the Levant, the Middle East, and N. and W. Africa, rice became the basis of a huge range of savoury dishes, all of which may be regarded as variations on the PILAF.

Whatever approach is taken to cooking rice, it will be a valuable source of nutrients (see box) and the essential process in the kitchen will be the same: to break open the cell walls and release the starch inside. Boiling water or steam does this very effectively, and if the water is part of a sauce, or is flavoured in any way, the flavour will quickly be taken up by the rice itself. However, the individuality of each grain survives cooking. The grains expand greatly as they absorb the cooking liquid, of which they take in surprisingly large quantities.

Although the use of boiling water or other liquid or steam, at some stage, is essential to every form of rice cookery, the details vary greatly from culture to culture, as does the appearance of the finished dish. For examples, see PAELLA; PILAF; RISOTTO.

If rice is cooked in a constricting wrapper, e.g. of banana leaf or aluminium foil, the grains are forced together into a compact mass which can then be cut up and eaten or can be further cooked (usually fried). This 'compressed rice' is popular all over Indonesia (where it is called *lontong*) and in some other parts of SE Asia.

KINDS OF RICE: THE COOK'S CHOICE

All the above refers to rice as though it were a single ingredient. There are, however, many kinds of rice and, of all the major plant foods, rice seems to be the most perplexing in its classification and nomenclature. The problem arises from the fact that different systems of classification are adopted for different purposes. The main ones are as follows.

- By botanical variety or (more often) group of varieties such as Basmati. Arborio and Carnaroli are Italian varieties (both falling into the Italian category *superfino*—see below).
- By country or region of origin—not as often as one might suppose, since what used to be geographical terms have tended to be transferred out of their original environment, e.g. Carolina. But Camargue rice is still rice from the Camargue, and Dehra Dun is still from Dehra Dun Valley in India.
- By size/shape of the grains—the Basmati group are long-grained, while the kinds of rice favoured in Japan,

Italy, and Spain are short- or round-grained, such as the Spanish variety marketed as Bomba. The terms patna, rose, and pearl are still sometimes used to indicate long, medium, and short grained. In Italy the terms *comune*, *semifino*, *fino*, and *superfino* are used; *comune* being the shortest, *superfino* the longest.
- By degree of 'stickiness', indicated by terms like 'glutinous' rice and 'sticky'. This depends on the proportion of the two types of starch, amylose and amylopectin. The latter always makes up at least 70% of the starch, even in the unstickiest Basmati, but a really sticky rice may contain as much as 83% amylopectin. ('Glutinous' is a misleading adjective, as no rice contains any GLUTEN.)
- By a combination of the two preceding items, e.g. 'Indica' for long-grained, non-sticky types, 'Japonica' for short-grained, relatively sticky, and 'Javanica' for long-grained and again somewhat sticky.
- By colour, e.g. the purple rice of the Philippines (*pirurutong*) and the black rice of some other SE Asian countries (probably the same thing, unmilled rice with a very dark husk from which the colour leaches into the white grain when cooked). Red rice in Asia may be ordinary rice dyed red (as happens in China) or may just be unpolished rice (called 'red' to distinguish it from white, polished rice). Red rice of the Camargue in France is brownish-red.
- By some other characteristic, e.g. aroma, as in 'Thai fragrant (or jasmine) rice'.

RICE IN NUTRITION

A GRAIN of rice is about 80% starch. When rice is eaten and digested, this starch is converted stage by stage to glycogen in the blood stream providing an excellent supply of muscular energy.

Inside the rice grain, the starch occupies cells whose walls are made of indigestible cellulose (itself another form of starch). Between these cells are a number of useful proteins; a cupful of cooked rice supplies about 9% of an average adult's daily protein requirement, although several necessary amino acids are missing. These are made up, in most diets, by proteins from other sources, usually meat but often legumes (e.g. the rice and bean dishes of C. America and the Caribbean, and the *Risi e bisi* of Venice). Vegetarians often derive their 'complementary' proteins from soya beans.

Unmilled brown rice, regarded as a health food in western countries, is rarely eaten in rice-staple countries, where people value the whiteness of the milled grain, from which the brownish or reddish outer layers have been rubbed off. These bran layers are rich in fibre and in B-group vitamins. Milling these off reduces the food value of the rice, but other foods eaten in modern diets normally make good the loss. (If not, beriberi will become a menace, as it did in earlier times—see VITAMINS.)

and eaten with grated coconut and brown sugar. It is especially served at Christmas time.

There is also *puto* with topping or flavouring. In Meycauayan they mischievously call *puto* with egg *putong lalaki* (man's *puto*), with meat *putong babae* (woman's *puto*), and with cheese *putong bakla* (homosexual *puto*). There is meat-filled *puto* called *puto pao* (referring to the Chinese steamed bun called *siopao*).

Puto is thus round or in sheets, moulded or cut up, plain or filled, eaten with *dinuguan* (blood stew) or *pansit* (see NOODLES OF ASIA), or with grated coconut and sugar. Always, however, it is made from ground rice, and is steamed.

The *puto maya* of Cebu is not really a *puto*. It is, strictly speaking, a *suman*, since it is made from glutinous rice boiled in coconut milk, which is the basic *suman* recipe. *Puto seco* is not a puto either, but a dry crumbly cookie (*seco* means 'dry').

Suman is a Filipino dessert made of sticky rice. It may be cooked in pans and then topped with a sugar-and-coconut syrup. This is sometimes called *bibingkang malagkit* or *suman latik*, and may have *latik* (toasted grated coconut) on top. It may also be shaped into cylinders and wrapped in young coconut leaves, then steamed. This is sometimes called *suman sa ibus*, and is eaten with sugar, or with sugar and sesame seeds, or dipped in hot chocolate, or with ripe mangoes. It may also be made into flat banana-leaf-wrapped packets (about 2" × 5"), or trapezoidal leaf-wrapped packets, perhaps cooked with LYE, and called *suman maruecos* or *suman sa lihiya*. These may be eaten with sugar or with coconut syrup. *Suman* can also be made from grated CASSAVA or from corn, in which case it is called *suman cassava* or *suman maiz*.

Biko is a large rice cake of glutinous rice cooked with coconut milk, much like *suman*, often topped with fried coconut meal (*latik*).

Cuchinta (or *kutsinta*) is also a rice cake, but not porous like *puto*, and without the whole rice grains of *suman*. It is made from ground rice, sugar, and lye, then steamed. The lye brings about a light brown colour and a jelly-like texture. This is also eaten with grated coconut.

Bibingka is also made of *galapong*, coconut milk, sugar, eggs, and now baking powder. (It even comes as a boxed mix.) The batter is poured into a banana-leaf-lined container and baked in a clay oven (or a regular oven) on live coals. It may be topped with cheese made from the milk of the carabao (the local WATER-BUFFALO), slices of salted duck eggs, butter. It is served with grated coconut. In the nine days before Christmas, the dawn masses are the occasion for *bibingka* stalls outside churches, where the vendors give a free cup of *salabat* (ginger tea) with each *bibingka*.

Rachel Laudan (1996), dealing with *bibingka*-derived confections in Hawaii (see MOCHI), has remarked that the name *bibingka* may have come from Goa, where this item was a popular dessert in the 19th century; a book of that time gives two recipes for Portuguese Coconut Pudding, the second of which is headed 'Bibinca dosee . . .'.

Sapin-sapin means 'layer-layer', and it is a layered dessert made from fine rice flour (*galapong*), coconut milk, and sugar. It is usually layered in a flat round basket (*bilao*), each layer coloured differently. This is therefore a rice cake to cut in wedges.

These are only the best known among Philippine rice cakes. Almost all regions have their own specialities with their own names. Ilocanos make *tupig* and wrap it in young coconut leaves, and this is sold at cockpits and markets. They also pour *puto* mixture in bamboo tubes and throw them into a fire as they go off to midnight mass. When they return, the *tinubong* is cooked. The Maranaw *dodol* (white or glutinous rice, brown sugar, coconut milk) is cylindrical and leaf wrapped and sticky-chewy. Almost every region says: 'Try our *puto/suman/kutsinta*, etc. It is the best.'   DF

RICE PAPER is used to provide an edible base for sweet confections such as MACAROON, does not come from the rice plant but from *Tetrapanax papyrifera*, a shrub or small tree of China. The paper is made from the pith of the stem.

RICE PUDDING is the descendant of earlier rice POTTAGES, which date back to the time of the Romans, who however used such a dish only as a medicine to settle upset stomachs. There were medieval rice pottages made of rice boiled until soft, then mixed with almond milk or cow's milk, or both, sweetened, and sometimes coloured. Rice was an expensive import, and these were luxury Lenten dishes for the rich. Recipes for baked rice puddings began to appear in the early 17th century. Often they were rather complicated. In one, rice previously cooked in milk was combined with sugar, breadcrumbs, egg yolks, half the whites, BONE MARROW, AMBERGRIS, rosewater (see ROSES), NUTMEG, and MACE. There is a traditional Cumberland rich rice pudding, 'clipping time' pudding, with suet or marrow, raisins, currants, sometimes eggs, and cinammon. Plain boiled rice puddings enclosed in a cloth appeared in the 18th century. Usually they included raisins.

Nutmeg survives in modern recipes. It is now unusual to add eggs or fat, and rice pudding has tended to become a severely plain nursery dish. Nevertheless, it has its devotees. There is a curious ambivalence about the skin which forms on top: some consider it the best part, while others recoil from it. Advertisements for canned 'creamed rice' (which is only a degraded version of the pudding) state proudly that it has no skin. One point on which there is universal agreement is that it is vital to cook a rice pudding very slowly.

The Chinese eight jewel rice pudding is so named because it is made with eight different kinds of fruit preserved with honey. Eight was said by Confucius to be the number of perfection. The fruits are arranged on the bottom of the dish and cooked, sweetened glutinous rice poured on top. The pudding is then steamed for several hours so that the rice breaks down into a homogeneous mass. It is then turned out (it is only just strong enough to stand up, so this is tricky) and served hot.

See also KHEER; FIRNI; SHOLA; MUHALLABIA; RICE AS FOOD.

RICOTTA an Italian cheese which is by far the best known of WHEY CHEESES. The name, meaning 'recooked', refers to the process of manufacture.

The production of ricotta is an economical way of using the whey left over after the production of cheeses such as PROVOLONE. This whey contains protein which can be coagulated. The resulting cheese has little flavour but many uses; and it has become popular wherever Italian gastronomic influence has spread. It may be regarded as the Italian equivalent of

COTTAGE CHEESE, so long as it is understood that it is a different product, although with similar characteristics and uses.

Ricotta is usually made from the whey of cow's milk, but sheep's, goat's, and buffalo's milk whey are also used.

The 'recooked' aspect consists simply in the fact that the original milk has been 'cooked' once to separate curd from whey and the whey is then 'cooked' again, being raised to a high temperature, for the production of ricotta. A little sour whey or other coagulant is added after the heating to help form the second lot of curd, which is then skimmed off. It may or may not be salted at this stage. Light pressure is applied to the curd to produce fresh ricotta, which nevertheless remains crumbly and moist. The other type, dried ricotta, is always salted, pressed more heavily, and dried in a curing room.

There are nearly a score of distinct ricotta cheeses which are well known in Italy, some distinguished by regional names which show whence they come, e.g. *ricotta Romana*, although this is now produced elsewhere too.

In Italy fresh ricotta is often eaten as a dessert, seasoned with salt or sugar. However, it is also used in cookery, especially for stuffings (e.g. of certain kinds of CANNELLONI and RAVIOLI).

RIDGED GOURD

or (angled) luffa, *Luffa acutangula*, an Asian member of the GOURD family, distinguished by its long, thin shape and its 10 longitudinal ridges. The colour is light or dark green. Cultivation takes place in India, SE Asia, China, and Japan.

The ridged gourd is best eaten young, when still less than 10 cm (4") long and tender throughout, including the ridges. Chinese stir-fry it. Indians use it in curry dishes. It may be given any of the usual treatments for ZUCCHINI or SUMMER SQUASH.

Ochse (1980) remarks that in Indonesia the young fruits, cooked or steamed, serve as a side dish, *lablab*, or are cut into slices and cooked with coconut milk and other ingredients.

Herklots (1972) lists other culinary uses.

In Hong Kong very young fruits, unpeeled, are cut in small pieces, cooked for a short time and served with stewed mutton; the bright green, crisp fruit is in sharp contrast to the texture of the meat. In Jamaica pieces of young fruit, peeled, boiled and seasoned with butter, pepper and salt, are incorporated in curries. In Japan they may be sliced and dried before being cooked.

RILLETTE

an item of French CHARCUTERIE which is most commonly made of pork but may also be of duck or rabbit or other meat.

The term is derived from the word *rille*, a dialect form of the Old French *reille*, meaning lath, plank, rung, etc., and applied since the 15th century to (presumably long and flat) pieces of pork. The variant *rillette* appeared in early times. The rillettes of Tours and subsequently of Le Mans have been famous, and the term has become part of the English culinary vocabulary.

Rillettes, as sold in a *charcuterie*, do not look at all like flat 'planks' of meat. They have undergone a series of processes, an initial cooking, the addition of some bones and seasoning, further cooking followed by removal of the bones and fat and then, with the fat being gradually restored, the teasing apart of the strands of the meat, producing the characteristic moist grey fibrous appearance of the final product.

The people of the Sarthe region are renowned for their heavy consumption of rillettes; at 12.5 kg (27.5 lb) a year per person this is 100 times higher than the national average.

READING: Breton (1994).

RISOTTO

a celebrated and popular RICE dish which originated in the rice-growing areas of N. Italy. It has something in common with PAELLA and PILAF, in that rice is cooked in liquid with other ingredients whose flavour is absorbed by the grains, but the method is quite different; risotto is probably a peasant dish which has become sophisticated. The first recipes were published in the mid-19th century by Artusi, the first celebrated Italian cookery writer, and Vialardi, later chef to King Victor Emmanuel.

The rice must be medium to long grain, *fino* or *superfino*, and the liquid is normally a stock made from meat and/or vegetables. The rice is gently sautéed in butter, often with some oil and a little onion, and the stock is then added, a ladleful at a time, each ladleful being taken up by the rice before the next is added. Finally, it is *mantecato*—a knob of butter and some grated Parmesan are added, the risotto is left to stand for a minute or two, and then the melting butter and cheese are thoroughly stirred in. The result should be *al dente* with a rich, creamy consistency. The method requires more or less continual attention from the cook, and to make good risotto requires experience. The result should be eaten without delay, not kept waiting or reheated.

Towards the end of the 20th century a steady expansion of the concept of risotto was observable, especially in restaurants. Some sweet risottos (e.g. with melon) were already familiar in parts of Italy; now there were more. The range of added ingredients and flavours for conventional savoury risottos was expanded and, as risotto became a more prominent international dish, the role of a risotto was also expanded—it could now be the basis of a more complex dish.

RISSOLE

as a culinary term, has a simpler meaning in English than in French. An English rissole is normally composed of chopped meat, bound with something such as egg, flavoured to taste, shaped into a disc or ball or like a sausage, and fried in a pan. Around this basic formula there exists a penumbra of variations which permit making fish rissoles and vegetarian rissoles (even a fruit rissole, in the 14th century); adding other main ingredients, especially potato; coating with breadcrumbs before frying; and, of course, serving with a sauce if desired. Some authors have supposed that the Latin word *isicia*, which certainly meant something of the sort, could confidently been translated as rissoles, and have remarked that APICIUS declared peacock rissoles to be the best (followed by pheasant, rabbit, and chicken) and listed the ingredients for three different thick sauces which could be used.

However, although making rissoles can plausibly be traced back to classical antiquity (the technique being simple and obvious in any culture in which meats were roasted and facilities for frying existed), there is no necessary connection with the derivation of the actual word from Vulgar Latin (*russeola*, reddish) via Old French (*ruissole*).

In the French kitchen the verb *rissoler* means to brown, and a rissole is always encased in puff pastry or the like, usually fried, but sometimes brushed with egg and baked in the oven. Such rissoles may be savoury or sweet. The latter kind would typically be powdered with fine sugar and accompanied by a fruit-based sauce.

ROAST

as a verb, meant originally to cook by exposure to radiant heat in the open; but has more recently come to mean what would formerly have been called baking, namely cooking in the enclosed space provided by an oven.

The term, in either sense, is usually applied to meat. It can be used of fish or vegetables, but less commonly although it is familiar in certain uses, e.g. roast potatoes.

Meat roasted in the earlier sense was kept turning on a spit in front of a fire, with a dripping pan under it to collect the melting fat, and had to be basted almost continuously to avoid its being dried out. If it was cooked at the same fire, but by being held over it on a gridiron, that would be to GRILL (US broil) it.

Meat 'roasted' in the oven is being cooked in a moist heat and needs no or less basting. The term 'pot-roast' indicates doing much the same thing but in a covered cooking vessel, with a small amount of liquid, the meat being browned first and possibly accompanied by vegetables; see BRAISE.

Roasting meat was something at which the British were, indeed are, supposed to excel. An 18th-century visitor to England from Sweden, Per Kalm, remarked that 'the English men understand almost better than any other people the art of properly roasting a joint'. Admittedly, he qualified the compliment by observing that the English art of cooking did not extend much beyond roast beef and plum pudding, but still it was a compliment; and the French term *rosbifs* for Englishmen may also be taken as including at least a touch of affection, although usually derogatory.

ROCAMBOLE a name used erratically of more than one plant in the ONION family. It sometimes refers to a form of true GARLIC, *Allium sativum*, Ophioscorodon group (the cumbrous style of classification now recommended), which has only a small basal bulb and tiny bulblets forming from the flower head, and is prized for its chive-like garlic-flavoured leaves. But it may also refer to *A. scorodoprasum*, sometimes called 'sand leek', which grows wild throughout Europe, often in dry, sandy, or rocky places, with bulbs which can be used like garlic but have a milder flavour.

ROCK a British sweet made in large and colourful sticks. There are two types: ordinary rock, sold at seaside resorts and other places visited by tourists, and Edinburgh rock, which is the original form of the sweet but remains mainly a local speciality of Edinburgh. Ordinary rock is a sweet of the plain pulled candy type, which is always professionally made, since it demands very complex pulling techniques. Each cylindrical stick consists of a coloured outer layer enclosing a white core with lettering made of coloured candy ('A present from Llandudno' or something of the kind) which runs the whole length of the stick, so that each letter is actually a long strip whose cross-section is that of the letter, and wherever the rock is broken the exposed ends will show a legible inscription (though one of them will show the letters in reverse. The letters are made in a fairly large size from hot coloured sugar and surrounded by a white matrix and coloured outer layer; then the assembly is drawn out to great length so that it becomes quite narrow.

Sometimes the sticks are as long and thick as a child's arm.

Although the history of pulled sugar and pulled candy goes back to the Middle Ages, rock with letters in it is probably a recent invention. The first person who remarked on it was Henry Mayhew in the 1860s, in his study of the work of Londoners, where he noted that a sweet vendor had recently introduced short sentences into sugar sticks. Examples included 'Do you love me', 'Do you love sprats', and 'Sir Robert Peel'—the last remembering a then recently dead Prime Minister.

Edinburgh rock comes in much smaller sticks, pastel coloured and with a peculiar chalky consistency. It is made from a conventional sugar syrup in which little attempt is made to inhibit crystallization, so that during pulling a mass of very small crystals is formed. It is left exposed to the air for a day after making, during which it absorbs moisture and becomes quite crumbly. White Edinburgh rock is flavoured with vanilla, lemon, or mint; pink with raspberry or rose water; yellow with orange; and beige with ginger. Although the vast majority of Edinburgh rock is made professionally (still mainly in Edinburgh), it can be made at home.
READING: Laura Mason (1995).

ROCK CAKE (sometimes rock bun, as in some late 19th-century references cited by the *OED*), a fairly plain and solid small cake/bun, usually enlivened with RAISINS (or currants) and candied peel. Rock cakes take their name from their irregular craggy appearance, not from their consistency. They are made by baking uneven lumps of dryish dough on baking sheets.

Recipes dating back to the 1860s are recorded; a range of flavourings including mace, lemon zest, and brandy were used in early examples. Arnold Palmer (1952) has a reference to City gentlemen in London in the 1870s standing at a counter and lunching 'off a glass of sherry with a rock cake or a couple of biscuits'. The use of currants, which became standard in the 20th century, is attested from the 1880s.

ROCK CRAB the common name of *Cancer irroratus*, a W. Atlantic (Labrador to Florida) relation of the better-known European crab (see CRAB, COMMON) and DUNGENESS CRAB. The yellowish carapace, dotted with brown or purplish spots, may measure a little over 10 cm (4") across.

The rock crab in turn has a close relation, *C. borealis*, the **Jonah crab.** This is slightly larger, and has bigger claws. It has a similar range but is only found in a limited number of localities.

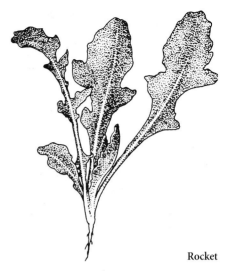

Rocket

ROCKET *Eruca sativa*, a plant which grows wild in Asia and the Mediterranean region, has been introduced elsewhere, including N. America (where it is known by its Italian name, *arugula*), and cultivated for use as a SALAD plant. Its flavour, akin to that of horseradish or some sorts of cress, is strong in mature leaves, so these are added to salads with discretion. Young leaves may be used freely. Their popularity as a smart ingredient in western restaurants may obscure the fact that they are grown and liked in some places, e.g. the north of Sudan, where cuisines are more basic and less susceptible to changes of fashion.

In classical Rome the plant was cultivated both for its leaves and for its seeds, used as a flavouring. The seeds can also be used to produce an oil.

ROCK-FISH a collective name indicating any of various fish which frequent rocky bottoms in the sea. Some fish which live among rocks are large (e.g. the groupers and the conger eel), but the collective term usually refers to the small species which are useful for going into fish soups etc. and which need not be precisely identified. The French term *poissons de roche* has the same meaning and is a label often seen on a pile of miscellaneous small fish for sale.

ROCKLING a name applied to several species of fish of the COD family, Gadidae, but in particular to the three-bearded rockling, *Gaidropsarus vulgaris*. This fish has a maximum length of just over 50 cm (20") and a relatively long body, the upper part of which is of a red or reddish colour, marked with brown blotches. The three 'beards' are not beards but barbels, used for groping around for food.

This rockling has a range in the E. Atlantic from Norway down to Portugal, and is present in the western basin of the Mediterranean. The smaller *G. mediterraneus* is another 'three-bearded' rockling with a similar range. But there are yet others with four or five barbels. None has commercial importance, but they have delicate flesh and *G. vulgaris* in particular is worth eating if obtainable and if really fresh.

ROCK-RABBIT *Procavia capensis*, a small rabbit-sized animal of the Middle East and Arabia and most of sub-Saharan Africa. Surprisingly, it is more closely related to the elephant than to the rabbit. Another name for it and close relations is hyrax. One of these close relations is probably the 'coney' of the Bible.

These small animals constitute a minor food resource in most countries in their range. They feed on a healthy diet of fruit and leaves which must be responsible for one feature of them, which is that their excrement contains a substance used in perfumery (although not, so far as can be discovered, traceable in the flavour of their meat).

ROE the eggs or spawn contained in the ovaries of a female fish, especially when ripe. These may also be called hard roe. Soft roe refers to the ripe testes (milt) of a male fish.

The roe of some fish is a delicacy. CAVIAR is the outstanding example. Other luxury products are BOUTARGUE and TARAMOSALATA. However, humbler, unprocessed, roes can also be delicious and may constitute a dish in their own right, e.g. fried slices of COD roe, SHAD roe in the USA, and soft HERRING roes on toast in Europe. Finnish people are outstanding connoisseurs of fish roe, e.g. of SALMON, WHITEFISH, TROUT, and BURBOT.

Roe is at least as good a source of protein as fish flesh, and often slightly superior.

ROLLS i.e. bread rolls. Most countries have versions of bread rolls as well as large loaves. Convenience and speed are probably the main reasons, as small rolls need much less proving and baking time than loaves, and so can be produced relatively quickly for breakfast. There is no precise delineation between rolls and BUNS, except that rolls are generally plain or savoury, made from ordinary or slightly enriched bread dough, and served with savoury foods. Buns are generally sweet.

The simplest rolls are round or oval in shape, such as English dinner rolls. One of the simplest variations is provided by the French and Belgian pistolet, which is a plain roll but split down the middle to give a two-lobed effect. Bakers may of course display their skill by shaping rolls into knots or other decorative shapes. One fancy shape is the French *tabatière* (snuffbox), a round, pouch-like roll with a 'flap' at one side.

The 'pocket' theme is echoed by what is perhaps the most famous roll in N. America, the Parker House roll. Mariani (1994) explains that this puffy yeast roll with a creased centre was created at the Parker House Hotel in Boston soon after its opening in 1855; and that they are 'sometimes called "pocket-book rolls" because of their purse-like appearance'. From this local beginning they have become a standard item on American tables.

Another American item described by Mariani is the kaiser roll (also called Vienna roll or hard roll), which takes it name from the German word for emperor, this because in shape it resembles a crown. It is believed to have originated in Vienna, and was brought to America by German and Jewish immigrants. Crisp and light, it can be made into sandwiches or eaten as a breakfast roll. It is often topped with poppyseeds.

Aberdeen rowies (also known as Aberdeen butteries or butterie rowies) are small breakfast rolls, enriched with butter by a process of rolling and folding similar to that employed for making CROISSANTS. The shape is roughly oval. A speciality of the Scottish city of Aberdeen, where they are eaten warm, usually for breakfast and spread with butter and marmalade.

A split, filled roll is the basis for some of the world's most popular snack foods, such as the sesame-topped bun enclosing a hamburger, and the soft white finger roll which forms the basis for a hot dog. Such breads are very similar to 'bridge rolls', a British party and buffet standby for many years. These small fingers of enriched white dough, baked closely together so that the sides almost touch, thus remaining soft, are usually split in half and served open, covered with some sort of topping.

There are many other baked items which verge on being rolls but are usually perceived as being in some other neighbouring category such as BUNS or TEA BREADS AND TEA CAKES. For two examples of these other items see ENSAIMADA; HUFFKINS.

ROLY-POLY PUDDING a widely used name for a SUET PUDDING made in a roll shape. The name is generally given to a pudding with a sweet filling such as jam, or treacle and breadcrumbs, or mixed dried fruits with marmalade; in each case spread over the flat sheet of dough and rolled up. However, there are also savoury types, for example bacon pudding (see BACON), which was often made in this shape.

The lasting fame of the name was conferred by Beatrix Potter's quietly horrifying book *The Tale of Samuel Whiskers or The Roly Poly Pudding* (1908) in which the stuffing of the pudding was a savoury one. The hero, Tom Kitten, was to be the stuffing, but fortunately he escaped.

Formerly roly-poly pudding was boiled in a pudding cloth; but the skill of enclosing a pudding of this shape in a cloth has now mostly been lost. Since it could not be adapted to a basin as could a round pudding, it is now almost invariably baked. However, the change of technique has been applauded by no less an authority than May Byron (1923), who also notes an interesting gender-related point about it:

Roly-poly pudding, however (also euphoniously known as dog-in-a-basket), appeals to the masculine appetite as nothing else can do. If you doubt this assertion, go into a City restaurant at midday, and scrutinise the customers' faces when they hear that 'jam roll is off.' It does not need to be accompanied by the gammon and spinach of the nursery rhyme. It is indeed sufficient unto itself. And when it is baked instead of boiled . . . then, as Humpty Dumpty said, 'there's glory for you!'

ROMADUR a German cheese made in Bavaria, is of the same type as LIMBURGER, but is cured for a shorter time at a lower temperature, emerging as a cheese which is generally smaller, milder, less salty, and less smelly than the other. Carr (1985) points out that the two cheeses have similar histories in that both originated in Belgium, where the ancestor of Romadur is called *remoudou*.

ROMANIA was born as a new state from the 19th-century union of the old principalities of Wallachia and Moldavia. The majority of its population are ethnic Romanians, descendants of Romanized tribes of the ancient Thracians and of Roman colonists after the Roman conquest in AD 106.

Although more than half of Romania is made up of lofty mountains, the country is still overwhelmingly agricultural. MAIZE is (or was until recently) the bedrock of the Romanian diet. The grain is milled into a fine flour which is used for making MAMALIGA, or ground coarsely for *păsatul*— two kinds of thick maize porridge which firm up when allowed to cool. These are eaten mixed with cheese, soured cream, or butter, or as a substitute for bread. Nowadays, however, there is a shift away from maize towards wheat, with an increasing urban consumption of bread and other wheat products.

Romania's most colourful crops are provided by the POPPY and the SUNFLOWER. The ripe poppyseeds are not narcotic, and are freely used to sprinkle over bread dough, or as a filling for confections such as *cozonac*—the traditional yeast cake baked on Good Friday in celebration of the Romanian Orthodox Easter. A high-quality edible oil is also extracted from the ripe, cold-pressed poppyseeds. The use of cooking oil obtained from sunflower seeds is gradually replacing animal fats for most culinary purposes.

Fruits make up a significant part of the diet: cherries, quinces, grapes, and apples are cultivated in higher areas, especially in the foothills of the Carpathians. Plums abound throughout the country.

Large herds of dairy cows graze on the pastures of the plains, water-buffaloes inhabit the low-lying regions of the Danube, and sheep are confined to the hilly and mountainous areas. The white brine cheese *telemea*, made from cow's, sheep's, or water-buffalo's milk, takes first place in the list of Romanian cheese; it tastes very much like FETA cheese but it is often spiced with aniseed. *Cașcaval* (see KASHKAVAL), as old as the Romans who probably introduced it, is a hard, yellow, full-fat cheese made from sheep's milk. *Brînză*, too, is a sheep's cheese, pale yellow and rather crumbly.

The most southern and extensive lowland region is **Wallachia,** meaning 'Land of the Wallachs or Vlachs' (from *Walh*, a Germanic word for foreigner, which has also given Wales its name). Wheat, maize, and barley are now widely grown here, with rice in the far south, and a great many walnut groves strung along the Danube. Bucharest, the capital, lies in this region.

Integrated life during the long era of Ottoman domination have helped to shape Wallachian cookery in the Balkan mould. A number of dishes, coinciding in name and, to a certain extent, in content with those to be found in other Balkan countries, are now national institutions in Wallachia and the province of Banat. BAKLAVA (*baclava* in Romanian), *chiftea* (burger), *ciorbă* (soup, see SHORBA), *dulceată* (fruit preserved in heavy syrup), *ghiveciu* (mixed vegetable casserole, see GYUVECH), *iahnie* (stew), *musaca* (MOUSSAKA), PILAF, *rahat* (TURKISH DELIGHT), *sarmale, mezelic* . . . all obviously derived from Turkish and Greek sources, have entered the Romanian national kitchen either via the Balkans, or directly during the Turkish occupation of the country.

Many Romanians still live in scattered pockets all over the Balkan peninsula. Often known as Vlachs, they speak Aroumanian, a dialect of the Romanian tongue. Many Vlachs are settled in **Dobrogea,** Romania's only maritime province lying in the north-eastern corner of the Balkans. This province already had a motley mixture of population, including Turks, Tatars, and Ukrainians. The Danube with its delta is where the best

fish are to be caught. The fishermen, many of Ukrainian descent, spit-roast or grill their catch over wood embers, or cook a Russian-Ukrainian fish soup called *uha*; in contrast to the Wallachian *ciorbă* (see SHORBA), this soup is not acidulated.

The food in the province of **Maramureș,** which borders on the Ukraine, also shows the influence of Romania's north-eastern neighbour. Local specialities include Russian BORSHCH, which is beef soup with beetroot and other vegetables; *kașa*, porridge made with food grain; *găluști* or dumplings, called in Russian *galoushki*; and *rasol*, a dish of boiled beef, its name derived from the Russian word for brine, *rassol*.

Beef constitutes the core of the cookery of Maramureș, and the province of **Moldova** (Moldavia) in NE Romania. The national emblem of Moldova is the head of an aurochs, the wild bull (*Bos primigenius*), the ancestor of all modern cattle, drawing attention to the long history of cattle rearing in the region.

Quite different from the rest of the country is the cookery of **Transylvania,** the largest of Romania's provinces, which lies within a crescent formed by the Carpathians and the Transylvanian Alps. Three national cuisines meet and cross-pollinate here: Romanian, Hungarian, and German. Saxon cookery in the region has retained much of its original character: *Auflauf*, baked pudding; *Knödeln*, dumplings; *Gewürzküchlein*, embossed spiced biscuits; *Rosenkranz*, a rich ring-shaped yeast cake; *Bratwurst*, beef or pork frying sausage—these are a few of the many dishes still prepared in the German tradition.

A distinct group in south-eastern Transylvania are the **Sekels**—a Hungarianized branch of the Bulgar-Turks, who had joined the Hungarians before the conquest (in AD 896) of their present-day homeland. Sekel food is considered by many Hungarians as the true, indigenous, Hungarian cuisine which has survived to this day relatively intact. *Székely gulyás*, for example, is thought to be of much older parentage than the modern Hungarian GOULASH.   MK-J

READING: Notaker (1990).

ROMBAUER IRMA (1877–1962), author of one of the best-loved and most used American cookbooks of any period, *The Joy of Cooking*. The child of a family of German origin in St Louis, Missouri, she came to cookbook writing in an incidental way, following the death of her husband. Her first book was published at her own expense in 1931 and was not transmuted into a commercial publication until 1936. Full success came in 1943 and thereafter the book became a best-seller. Anne Mendelson

(1996) has provided a brilliant history of the book and its author, and of her daughter Marion Rombauer Becker, who was co-author from 1951 and then solely responsible after her mother's death in 1962. She reckons that total hardback sales of the book from 1931 to 1996 amounted to almost 10 million copies. It seems likely that a comparable number of paperback copies have been sold.

In an illuminating comparison of *The Joy of Cooking* with its rivals of the decades from the 1930s to the 1970s, Mendelson highlights the special attractions of the book, which depended very much on its author's lighter and more personal touch. *The Joy of Cooking* was not devised to match the requirements of the market, as perceived by professional publishers, but as a direct and often breezy communication from an enthusiastic cook to whoever cared to be on the receiving end. That the number of people who elected to be on the receiving end was so vast reflects credit not only on Irma Rombauer's approach to the subject, but also on that of her daughter, who introduced a considerable amount of nutritional and other scientific material without weighing the book down unduly and who rivalled her mother's tenacity in holding out against unreasonable proposals by the publishers. (The degree of author/publisher strife was spectacularly great.)

The history of *The Joy of Cooking* sheds much light on the development of American tastes in food, and cooking methods, and cookbooks over a large part of the 20th century. Mendelson's biography brings this out clearly; and it would doubtless have been a source of gratification to both Irma Rombauer and her daughter to think that the story of their record-breaking and much-beloved book could be used so effectively to trace a larger piece of history.

ROMESCO (in full, *salsa romesco*), the name of an important Catalan sauce, whose ingredients are normally a pounded mixture of fried bread, garlic, grilled tomato, almonds, and hazelnuts, plus paprika and chilli powder, all made into a smooth paste with wine (if possible from the Priorat) and wine vinegar. But there are many different versions, as Patience Gray (1986) has attested:

The variations of this sauce are legion, secrecy surrounds the method and there is no common agreement among fishermen or cooks about its creation. The annual *romescada* at Cambrils near Tarragona is in fact a kind of challenge to fishermen to produce the 'best' *romesco*. Four thousand people may turn up to participate in the contest (as onlookers) and a white night is spent by restaurateurs to prepare for the multitude. The master *romesco*-makers set to work, crouching over their mortars, at little stands in the dazzling April light, engulfed by an excited throng.

ROOK *Corvus frugilegus*, possibly the only member of the crow family which is still eaten, although rarely, in Britain. The range of this bird extends across the boreal and temperate zones of Europe and Asia as far as China. It is known for its hoarse 'caw' and its habit of breeding in large colonies known as rookeries (one of which, in Aberdeenshire, comprised nearly 7,000 nests in the 1950s). Its reputation as food has never been high, but in some parts of the north of England, for example, rook pie has been an established dish. As so often, *Cassell's Dictionary of Cookery* (various editions before and after 1900) gives a balanced view, to accompany a detailed recipe:

The rook affords a dry and coarse meat. A pie made of young rooks is tolerable; at least, it is the best form for using these birds as food. . . . Rooks require long stewing, or they will not be tender. The breasts are the only parts of the birds which are really worth using.

ROOT BEER a beverage of which Artemas Ward (1923) gave a good description:

a refreshing beverage made by the fermentation of an infusion of roots, barks, and herbs, such as sarsaparilla, sassafras, spruce, wild cherry, spikenard, wintergreen, and ginger, with sugar and yeast. The flavoring or extract, is retailed in convenient packages, each sufficient for about five gallons of 'beer.' It is the action of the yeast on the sugar which gives the slightly exhilarating quality (from the small percentage of alcohol produced) and the effervescence (from the action of the carbon dioxide).

The alcoholic content, if any, of root beer is so small that it could be and was recommended by the temperance movement in N. America, and easily qualifies for inclusion in this book, along with KVASS and KOUMISS and the like.

ROQUEFORT one of the three most famous blue cheeses of the world, has a longer recorded history than either of the others (STILTON and GORGONZOLA). It is probably the cheese which Pliny, writing in the 2nd century AD, described as 'bearing off the prize at Rome'. It is certainly the cheese which the monks of St Gall offered to the Emperor Charlemagne in the 9th century. He first disdained and then, under their tuition, delighted in the veined parts, so much so that he was furnished with two whole Roquefort cheeses each year thereafter. St Gall is not far from the village of Roquefort sur Soulzon, after which the cheese is named.

The village, now almost a small town, lies on the side of a hill called Le Combalou in the region of Les Causses, limestone plateaux which prolong the westerly flank of the Cévennes mountains. It is a wild and arid area, not for lack of rain but because the porous limestone soaks it up and leaves the surface too dry for anything but the hardy box and other scrub. Sheep can graze there, but the land cannot be used for other purposes.

Le Combalou, like other hills in the area, suffered an internal collapse in the very distant past, which left it equipped with natural caves. These communicate through fissures (known as *fleurines*) with the open air above, and encompass an underground lake. The caves remain at a remarkably constant temperature, between 44 and 48 °F (7–9 °C), night and day, summer and winter, and always enjoy a relative humidity of 95%. Visitors, who are made welcome, see ample evidence of moisture. But they will not see the most important resident of the caves, the mould *Penicillium roqueforti*, although this micro-organism is present by the millions. Invisible themselves, these work on the cheeses with visible results, being responsible for the blue veins which gradually develop inside.

Three main factors contribute to the unique flavour and texture of a Roquefort cheese: the use of sheep's milk, inoculation with *Penicillium roqueforti*, and the special conditions which the caves offer for maturing the cheeses.

Until fairly recent times the sheep's milk which was used all came from sheep grazing in the vicinity. However, when production of Roquefort was stepped up in the 19th century the supply became inadequate. The rules were therefore adjusted to permit the use of sheep's milk from certain selected places such as Corsica and the Pays Basque, where conditions were deemed suitable.

The mould itself, which grows naturally in the cave and can be cultured on pieces of bread, is used elsewhere, e.g. in the production of Danish blue (see DANISH CHEESES. But the extraordinary conditions in the caves, maintained by beneficent currents of air through the *fleurines*, cannot easily be replicated; and Roquefort justly retains its protected status, since it has no peer. (It is fair to add, however, that the *bleu des Causses*, also made from sheep's milk, and with the same mould and techniques, but matured in caves of less repute, can come very close to the real thing.)

The curd for Roquefort is prepared at the dairies where the milk is collected, and is inoculated in advance with a little of the *Penicillium* when it is placed in its moulds. The infant cheeses, known as *pains*, are conveyed to Roquefort and enter the caves for a period of *affinage*, which lasts for several months and involves salting, brushing, piercing with needles, lying on one lot of shelves for weeks on end, being wrapped in tinfoil and transferred to cold storage, the use of a thin, hollow probe to check progress, and so on. The attendant human beings are dedicated to their work, and enjoy particularly good health as a result of sharing this strange environment with the cheeses.

A finished cheese weighs about 2.5 kg (6 lb), and is wrapped in aluminium foil and furnished with a stamped label to guarantee its authenticity. The Société Anonyme des Caves et des Producteurs Réunis de Roquefort, founded in 1842 and known to all simply as La Société, is responsible for 80% of the production. In all, about 1,600 tons are produced annually, most of it to be eaten in France. For obvious reasons, Roquefort is among the most expensive cheeses; but it is rich, so that a little goes a long way, and there is no waste.

This outstanding cheese is the subject of a whole book by Pourrat (1956), published by La Société and translated into English as *The Roquefort Adventure*. This is presented as a work which enables the reader to comprehend, by a study of what has happened at Roquefort, the history of mankind; and it bestows on the struggles which have taken place over protection of the name, and also between the dairymen and the cheese-makers, an epic quality not usually associated with such matters.

RORER SARAH TYSON (1849–1937), one of the most prolific and influential American cookery writers. Her biographer (Weigley, 1977) credits her with 54 cookery books or booklets, and cites much evidence of her important role in shaping the study of home economics and dietetics. She has been described as the first American dietitian. Mrs Rorer came late to the profession and had little formal instruction. Having enrolled for a cookery course at Philadelphia in 1879, and having completed it with distinction, she was asked to take it over when the teacher resigned. She did, and never looked back.

In 1883 she opened the Philadelphia Cooking School which, with the corresponding institutions at Boston (see Mrs LINCOLN and Fannie FARMER) and New York, was to play a central role in the formation of American ideas on cookery in the rest of the 19th and the early part of the 20th century. She was a woman of method, and of energy; a combination which enabled her to conduct a wide range of activities. Besides running her school, she took part in many pure food expositions, became a leading cookery journalist, travelled in Europe, and opened a restaurant in New York (which was, however, a failure). She was a considerable show-woman, and in her cookery demonstrations customarily wore a silken dress, to show that cooking need not be dirty work. A typical press comment was that 'in her biscuit-colored dress of India silk, her dainty cap set upon fair hair, her neat apron and arm shields, Mrs Rorer does present a very pleasant appearance indeed'. Relying on her presence and her reputation as 'Queen of American Cookery' and 'the nation's instructress in cooking', she was not averse to disconcerting her audience by condemning some of the very dishes she was teaching them to prepare ('There is nothing in a cake to give you brain and muscle unless you get the latter from beating the cake') or undermining established ideas ('When a man talks to you about his mother's cooking, pay no attention to him'). If something went wrong with a demonstration, her wit was quick enough to carry it off. Thus when, in boning a chicken (after an explanation of the need to know its anatomy precisely), her knife missed a joint, she commented briskly: 'Malformation of the joint.' Her principal books were *Mrs Rorer's Philadelphia Cook Book* (1886) and *Mrs Rorer's New Cook Book* (1902). These and her other publications revealed a certain development in her thinking as time passed, but certain themes were constant. A salad should be served 365 days a year. Desserts were bad.

ROSE-APPLE the unsatisfactory English name most commonly applied to any of a group of EUGENIA FRUITS (a name which has retained some currency although less appropriate after most of the species have been transferred from the genus *Eugenia* to *Syzygium*). Alternative names in English are no better, and it would be preferable to use the Indian/Malay name JAMBU, the meaning of which is explained separately, instead. The fruits do bear a superficial resemblance to apples, but do not eat like apples. Four principal species in the group are described below.

Syzygium jambos, the 'true' rose-apple, is native to the Malay peninsula. It is cultivated in that region, in India, and in the W. Indies (where it may be called 'pommerac' or 'rac apple'—or 'Malabar plum', a name sometimes also used for the related JAMBOLAN). The fruit may reach the size of a small apple and is yellow, often tinged with pink, or greenish in colour, with a waxy surface and a delicate aroma of rose. The flesh within is also rose scented, whitish, crisp, and juicy but lacking in flavour. They may be cooked with sugar or made into jams or jellies, preferably mixed with other fruits which have more flavour.

S. malaccense, the Malay (rose) apple, is the fruit of a tall and striking tree which is native to the Malay archipelago, but is now cultivated from India to S. China and Hawaii (where it arrived before the Europeans and is known as *ohia ai*). The fruits, which are roundish but slightly oblong and narrowed at the stalk end, measure about 6 cm (2.5") and have waxy skins, at first pale green and later of a rosy hue with faint white markings. The flesh, which is scented, is juicy and slightly sweet in flavour.

S. samarangense, the Java or Semarang (rose) apple, is cultivated in its native region, Malaysia and Indonesia, and occasionally in tropical America. The fruits are nearly round, or pear shaped, and measure about 5 cm (2"). They are commonly pale green or whitish, but sometimes pink or red. Betty Allen (1975) remarks that: 'The green forms are eaten with a little salt, and they make a pleasant sauce. The pink fruits on the whole are more juicy and less aromatic, but all of them are rather flavourless.'

S. aqueum, the watery rose-apple or water apple, originated in the south of India and grows wild there and in parts of Malaysia. It has an uneven shape, being wider at the apex than at the base. 'The colour of the fruit varies from white to bright pink, the skin is glistening, almost translucent and bruises easily. The flesh is crisp and watery, with a scented flavour, sometimes insipid' (Betty Allen). The fruits are good thirst-quenchers and, although they consist mainly of water, have fruit sugars and a lot of vitamin A in their skins. They make good additions to salads.

ROSELLE (sometimes rozelle), *Hibiscus sabdariffa*, also called flor de Jamaica or Jamaica sorrel or red sorrel, although it did not reach Jamaica until the beginning of the 18th century and is not a close relation of sorrel. It is thought to have its origin in Africa, but is now cultivated in many tropical regions, including SE Asia. Burkill (1965–6) infers from the nature of its names in India and Malaysia that it is a relatively recent arrival in Asia. It is grown mainly as a fibre crop, but its culinary uses amount to more than a mere by-product.

Roselle is a woody annual, with green leaves on stems which are usually red. There are two main types: *H. sabdariffa* var *altissima*, which is the more important economically because of the fibre for which it is cultivated; and *H. sabdariffa* var *sabdariffa*, which embraces the cultivars grown for their edible calyces (see below).

The young leaves and shoots are used in some regions, especially Africa, as a green vegetable. They are mucilaginous, and pleasantly acid, and have been compared to rhubarb. In the Philippines they are sometimes used to impart acidity to the dish called SINIGANG. The leaves and stalks are used as a curry seasoning in India and Sri Lanka.

The plant is unusual in that one of its edible parts is not the fruit but the calyx of the fruit. The calyx is what is familiar as the little green star on top of a tomato or

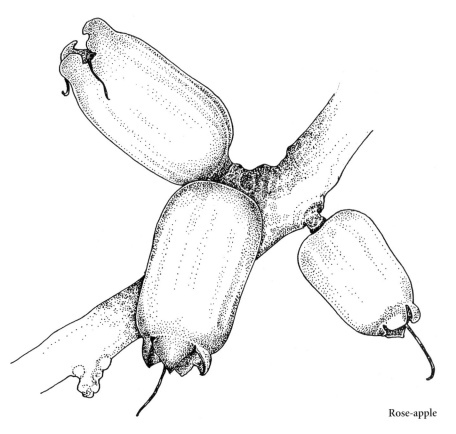

Rose-apple

strawberry. In this instance it is red, large and fleshy, and enwraps a small, useless fruit. It is made into a refreshing, sour 'sorrel' drink in the W. Indies and elsewhere, and is also used to produce jellies and jams. Gladys Graham (1947), writing from Panama, says of it:

Sorrel is such an important beverage and jam-jelly ingredient that highway crews widening Central American roads will cut down every other shrub and tree in their way, leaving the sorrel to blossom on the road shoulders. It comes at the end of wet season, or the beginning of dry, and the sorrel drinks of Christmas times are almost as important as the attendant ceremonies and fetes. The product will taste a little more like cranberries than cherries.

Roselle

The calyces are marketed dried as well as fresh, and are the source of a red food colourant. The Filipino author Maria del Oroso, whose collected essays on food were published in 1970, recommended a wide range of uses for them, embodied in 60 recipes. These included sauces and omelettes and cakes, as well as beverages. The roselle had been introduced to the Philippines in 1905, shortly after it arrived in Australia and the USA.

ROSEMARY *Rosmarinus officinalis*, one of the most prized culinary herbs, is a common wild plant of Mediterranean hillsides, but will also grow as far north as S. England, where the Romans introduced it originally (although it is commonly said that it had to be reintroduced by the Normans after 1066).

There is no doubt about the importance attached to rosemary in classical Greece and

Rome, but the situation with regard to ancient Egypt is less clear. An 18th-century archaeologist found and reported a specimen of rosemary in a garland adorning an Egyptian body. However, a later commentator remarked that the leaves were reported to be green, which seemed odd after thousands of years in a tomb, and speculated that the archaeologist might have been fooled by a practical joke carried out by his guides. On the other hand, Dorothy Bovee Jones (in Foley, 1974) records that:

In his 'Histoire Naturelle', Valmont Bomare (1731–1807) reported that when coffins were opened after several years, branches of rosemary that had been placed in the hands of the dead were found to have grown so that they covered the corpse.

Thus an element of doubt remains, which is perhaps appropriate for a plant whose 'Ancient Egyptian name was tentatively said by Loret . . . to be nkpty.'

In medieval times, and indeed throughout history, people have tended to attach more importance to the medicinal than to the culinary properties of rosemary. However, some of the supposed medicinal properties are important in the context of diet and doctrines such as that of FOUR HUMOURS, and deserve mention here. There was a general opinion that rosemary fortified the brain and memory (hence students wearing rosemary wreaths before taking examinations), and Gerard (1633) advised that to remedy weakness and coldness of the brain some rosemary should be boiled in wine and the patient should inhale the fumes through his nose, while Culpeper (1653) recommended it as a remedy for such 'cold diseases of the head and brain, as the giddiness and swimmings therein'. The list could be prolonged indefinitely, but space must be found for one more recommendation, that of Sir Thomas More, whose garden on the banks of the Thames was but a few hundred yards from where this article is being written; he wrote: 'I lett it runne all over my garden walls, not onelie because my bees love it, but because it is the herb sacred to remembrance and therefore to friendship.' He might have added 'and to love and fidelity', and that rosemary is unusual in having a traditional use at both weddings and funerals. To go by Dorothy Bovee Jones (again), he could also have referred to it being an ingredient in a famous medieval formula:

In the handwriting of Queen Elizabeth of Hungary, there may be seen today, in a library, formerly the Imperial Library of Vienna, a manuscript dated 1235. It contains the formula for the famous 'Hungary water,' a distillation of rosemary, lavender and myrtle. The Queen was paralyzed, and tradition says that this recipe was invented by a hermit especially for her. Rubbed with it every day, it did indeed effect a cure. The preparation became well-known, especially in

southern France, in the neighborhood of Montpellier, where it was widely used.

Its distinctive aromatic flavour is especially liked in Italy, for both sweet and savoury dishes (Italian butchers often dress meat with it before selling it, or hand out free bunches of it with the meat); and Provence. Rosemary is often used to good effect with roasts, e.g. roast lamb, or as a stuffing for fish to be barbecued. The use of some rosemary when wood is burned to smoke meat and sausages gives the products a flavour which is especially liked in Spain.

Pamela Michael (1980) describes some interesting sweet confections made with rosemary. These include a rosemary conserve, for which she found recipes from the 16th and 17th centuries and which is described as looking and tasting almost exactly like honey. Another is a kind of compote of oranges flavoured with rosemary. For effects which are both decorative and edible she cites crystallized rosemary flowers (small and fiddly to work with, but very pretty) and also a medieval edible centrepiece called Rosemary Snow: 'a large branch, or "bush", of rosemary was decorated with whisked cream, egg white and sugar, usually set in a loaf of bread.'

ROSES the well-known flowering shrubs of the genus *Rosa*, can be traced back to ancient Persia, Egypt, Babylon, and China. More than a score of species are recognized; and there are almost innumerable hybrids and cultivars. The petals of most species can be eaten or used to flavour food, either directly or in the form of rosewater (a fragrant flavouring obtained by the distillation of the petals); and the fruits (known as rose-hips or haws) of many species are edible. Species which are good sources of petals or rosewater include:

- *R. centifolia*, cabbage rose;
- *R. × damascena*, damask rose;
- *R. gallica*, French rose, rose de Provence;
- *R. moschata*, musk rose;
- *R. rugosa*, Japanese/Chinese/Turkestan rose.

PETALS

For the Greeks, from whom many of the relevant legends come, the rose was a symbol of love, beauty, and happiness. The Latin word *rosa* comes from the Greek word for red, *rodos*. The Romans, who associated the rose with Venus, goddess of love, scented their wine with rose petals.

Roses had probably first been cultivated, several thousands of years ago, in Persia. It is known that Persia was making and exporting rose wine from rose petals as long as 2,000 years ago. In Iran rose petals are still preserved in jams or dried to be used to perfume many sweet dishes. The dried petals are also added to the spice mixture ADVIEH used in flavouring savoury dishes.

In medieval England they were used to flavour butter (which can also be flavoured with rosewater). Rose-petal jams, conserves, and drinks have been and still are made in Europe. The French town of Provins in Champagne is famous for its rose-petal jam. In Turkey rose petals are boiled in water to flavour *loucoum* (TURKISH DELIGHT), and in India they are put into a heavy syrup to make *gulkand*, a rose-petal preserve which is used with betel leaf for cutting bitter aftertastes and refreshing the mouth. In China, flower heads of the red China rose, *R. semperflorens*, are sometimes cooked whole as a vegetable.

Crystallized rose petals used in western countries are more of a decoration than a flavouring.

ROSEWATER

The ancient Egyptians, Greeks, and Romans managed to extract fragrance from the rose by steeping petals in water, oil, or alcohol. And it is probable that the technique of distillation of rosewater evolved in the 3rd and 4th centuries AD in Mesopotamia.

By the 9th century Persia was distilling rosewater on a large scale. It is, however, usual to name AVICENNA, the famous physician of the 10th century, as being the person who discovered rosewater. It was in his time that the use of rosewater as a flavouring for food came into vogue in the lavish and sumptuous cuisine of the Arabs. It was used to flavour a variety of dishes and was even sprayed over the surface of the cooking pot.

The use of rosewater spread to Europe via the Crusaders. It was, for example, popular in medieval England. Rosewater was also a favourite flavouring of the Ottoman Turks and they in turn introduced it to Bulgaria, where the Valley of the Roses at Kazanluk is famous for its production of rosewater, oil of roses, rose-petal jams, and preserves.

Water distillation is the oldest method used to extract the fragrance, and rosewater is still produced in this way in many eastern countries. The technique has been summarized by Helen Saberi (1993), who points out that the same method can be used to obtain rose oil, known in English as attar or otto of roses, derived from the Persian *atr*, meaning perfume or essence.

Nowadays, however, steam distillation is the preferred method of obtaining attar of roses, as it produces a more delicate and fragrant oil.

Rosewater is still used extensively all over the Indian subcontinent and the Middle East. Famous rosewater-flavoured dishes include Turkish delight; the rosewater-flavoured desserts and sweets of the Middle East and India (see, for examples, SHOLA; BAKLAVA; FIRNI; HALVA). Rosewater also flavours beverages such as LASSI and SHERBET.

FRUITS

Rose-hips or haws, the fruit of the rose, have been eaten as a fruit in Europe and Asia and by the Indians of N. America. The vaselike receptacle of the fruit contains seeds covered with irritating hairs, so it has to be emptied before it is edible. Or the whole fruit can be boiled to make a sweet, slightly perfumed syrup. Species whose fruits are used both in Europe and Asia include the briar rose or dog rose, *R. canina*, which is made into tea or TISANE, and the eglantine, *R. eglantaria*.

Rose-hips are remarkably rich in vitamin C. When, during the Second World War, the British diet lacked fruits providing this vitamin, schoolchildren were sent to gather rose-hips, from which a syrup, issued as a dietary supplement for small children, was made. Rose-hip syrup is still sold, especially for babies.

ROTI a general Indian term for bread. In this sense it covers the whole amazingly diverse range of breads found in the subcontinent. However, it is also used in narrower senses, for example in some parts of India as an alternative name for CHAPATI and *phulka*, or as part of the names of particular breads.

The origins of roti, in the wide meaning of Indian breads, can be traced back 3,000 or 4,000 years, to the arrival of the Aryans in the Indus Valley. In this connection it is noteworthy that BARLEY was the major grain eaten by the Aryans. Although WHEAT was known from very early times, its widespread adoption for bread-making purposes came relatively late. Later still came corn (MAIZE), probably brought by the Portuguese and welcomed in the Punjab.

Numerous names of breads incorporate the term roti. These may reflect the method of cooking (*tandoori roti*); or something to do with shape and size (*roomali roti* is as thin as the scarf after which it is named). But more often they refer to the type of flour used; thus *besan ki roti* contains chickpea (BESAN) flour.

Roti in the wide sense have become an important element in the intercontinental culinary scene, mainly because so many of these Indian unleavened breads have spread to other parts of the world where Indians and their foodways have become established, including SE Asia, E. Africa, and some islands in the W. Indies, not to mention many cities in England.

The Trinidadian writer V. S. Naipaul, whose ancestors had migrated from the plain of the Ganges 100 years previously, recalled in one of his many books how important sacrifice had been to his people and that it made the cooking of food into a ritual: 'the first cooked thing, usually a small round of unleavened bread, a miniature, especially made, was always for the fire, the God.' The symbolism remained important although it could be pointed out that roti and other Indian breads in Trinidad differ significantly from the originals in being made, nowadays at least, with baking powder. If Trinidadian roti, made thus, are ripped apart to provide pieces which can be dipped into curry dishes, they are called 'buss-up-shut' because of a resemblance to the torn cloth of a 'burst up shirt'.

Finally, a noteworthy feature of the impact of roti on the British in the days of the Raj has been illuminated by Ayto (1993):

> The words for most Indian breads have only infiltrated English since the 1960s, but roti is an exception. Members of the British army serving in India in the late nineteenth century took it up as a slang term for 'bread', spelling it *rooty* or *rootey*: 'And the 'umble loaf of "rootey" costs a tanner, or a bob' (Rudyard Kipling, 1900). The long-service medal awarded to British soldiers in India in the early twentieth century was colloquially known as the *rooty gong*.

ROUGHY the name adopted in Australasia, and now widely used, for fish of the family Trachichthyidae, especially the orange roughy, *Hoplostethus atlanticus*. As the scientific name indicates, this species is not confined to Australasian waters, although that is where it has come to prominence as a commercial catch and from where it is exported to many destinations. It is also found off S. Africa (where the general common name for fish of this family is slimehead, or slymkop), and in the N. Atlantic, although its presence there has been little noticed. The body, deep and compressed in shape, is orange in colour, with silver tinges on the flanks. The skin is rough; a near relation is sometimes called the sandpaper fish. Maximum length 40 cm (16") in New Zealand waters. The flesh, which is good to eat, is usually available in fillets.

The smaller silver roughy, *H. mediterraneus*, has a similarly wide distribution but is of much less importance.

ROUILLE a French sauce which is typically orange or red in colour (from pounded sweet red pepper, paprika or the like), thick in consistency (bread is an ingredient), flavoured with garlic, and suitable for adding to Provençal fish soups such as *Aigo sau* and BOUILLABAISSE.

ROULADE something rolled up, for example in the manner of a SWISS ROLL. This French term gained increasing currency towards the end of the 20th century, when savoury preparations of this sort, as well as sweet ones, proliferated.

ROUX 'The various kinds of roux are used as the thickening agents for basic sauces, and their preparation, which appears to be of little importance, should actually be carried out with a great deal of care and attention.'

So begins August ESCOFFIER's article on *Roux* in his monumental *Guide culinaire*; almost an entire page is devoted to *roux brun*, though only short paragraphs deal with the preparation of the *roux blond* and *blanc*. Etymologically, and historically, all this makes perfect sense. *Roux* in French literally means 'reddish' (or 'orange') hence the first roux must have been *brun*. These early roux were made by cooking flour and butter together until a reddish tint was obtained then using this to thicken a sauce or broth. Its widespread use in French cooking seems to date from the mid-17th century. At that time, LA VARENNE (1651) described the preparation of a *liaison de farine* (flour thickener) made by cooking flour in lard and, by the end of the century, cooks are referring to this mixture as either *farine frit* or *roux*.

By the mid-18th century cookbook authors are advising that 'roux de farine' (flour-based roux) be cooked until the butter and flour are 'a nice yellow' and recommend that the resulting paste be stored for later use (cooks need only 'warm a piece in a little pot' with broth as needed). The roux had its critics, however, and some French gastronomes began complaining about the over-use of the roux in sauces as the 19th century approached. CARÊME came to its defence in the 1830s calling those who dared criticize the use of roux 'ignorant men'. 'How', he asks, 'can fresh butter and the finest flour, mixed and cooked over the embers, turn into the unhealthy menace some authors decry?' A roux, writes Carême, is as indispensable to cooks as ink is to writers but, he warns, just as a poor scribbler cannot produce a masterpiece simply by dipping his pen into that black liquid, a sauce is not necessarily improved if the roux has not been simmered with sufficient care.

In recent years the roux has once again come under heavy criticism and, with the advent of NOUVELLE CUISINE in the early 1970s, many chefs abandoned its use (preferring to thicken their sauces with vegetable purées or using emulsified butter instead). But, despite its chequered history, the roux remains one of the cornerstones of French cuisine and, when perfectly executed, imparts a slightly nutty flavour as well as an appealing unctuosity to sauces which use it as a base. HY

ROWAN AND SORB are, strictly speaking, two distinct species of tree in the genus *Sorbus* in the rose family; but the names tend to be used interchangeably. To compound the confusion, the sorb may also be called 'service tree' in Europe, whereas in America that name is given to a more distant relation (see SERVICE-BERRIES). All bear clusters of red or orange 'berries' (not true berries, but DRUPES), which are sour and astringent, unless exposed to the mellowing effect of frost, and most suited to making a sharp jelly which goes well with venison and other game or fowl.

S. aucuparia, the rowan or mountain ash, owes its specific name to the practice of bird-catchers in Germany and elsewhere who would trap small birds in hair nooses baited with rowan berries. It grows wild in Europe and N. Asia, especially in mountainous regions, and is matched by *S. americana* in the east of N. America.

S. torminalis, the one usually called sorb, tends to grow further south in Europe (in Britain, for example, rarely north of C. England). Because its fruits are larger than those of the rowan, green or brown rather than orange, and recognizably like small apples or pears, the name 'sorb apple' is sometimes used. In the south of Italy, the sun ripens the fruits sufficiently for them to be eaten raw. In Britain, where they used occasionally to be gathered for sale, it was usual to 'blet' them (as with the MEDLAR) to soften them and mellow their sourness, and then to use them in tarts.

RUE *Ruta graveolens*, a small shrubby plant of the European parts of the Mediterranean region, now cultivated elsewhere too. The leaves, blue-green and fleshy, have a strong and unattractive aromatic odour, and a bitter taste. They are used, fresh or dried but usually minced and in small quantity, for flavouring bread, meat dishes, and so on; and to impart bitterness to certain alcoholic drinks.

The plant has enjoyed a high reputation for medicinal properties. Another common name, herb of grace, arose because holy water used to be sprinkled from brushes made of rue.

R. chalepensis is Egyptian rue, less important but otherwise similar. What is sometimes called Syrian or African or wild rue is, however, a plant of another genus, *Peganum harmala*, whose seeds are used as a condiment, e.g. in Afghanistan as *ïspand* (or *ïsfand*) and in Turkey as *üzerlik*.

RUKAM the Malay name for the fruit of *Flacourtia rukam*, a tree of the same genus as the better-known RAMONTCHI and LOVI-LOVI. Native to Asia and long associated with Madagascar (as French and Spanish names, *prune malgache* and *ciruela de Madagascar*, testify), it has been introduced to the American tropics.

The roundish fruits are about 2 cm (1") in diameter, nearly black in colour when ripe, and with a juicy, acid, yellowish-white pulp. They vary in sweetness but some are good eaten raw when ripe. Like the ramontchi, they can also be made into jams and so forth when slightly unripe.

F. cataphracta, the paniala, is cultivated in the Far East and has also been introduced to the New World. Its russet-purple cherry-sized fruits resemble the rukam.

RUMFORD COUNT (1753–1814). Benjamin Thompson was born in the Commonwealth of Massachusetts. He came from farming stock but, with an eye on higher things, he studied experimental philosophy, chemistry, and medicine as well as French, and became a schoolmaster before the age of 20.

During the American War of Independence Thompson was a loyalist and spy working for the governor of Massachusetts. Later he raised and commanded the 'King's American Dragoons', a regiment known and hated for its atrocities on Long Island. His first 'British' career, spent partly in America and partly in England, during which he was knighted, elected a Fellow of the Royal Society, and became a full colonel, ended in 1784 when, at the age of 31, he left for Munich and entered the service of the Elector of Bavaria, first as aide-de-camp, then Minister of Police and Grand Chamberlain. The 15 years in Munich were very productive. In addition to his seminal contributions to the theory of heat he also designed the 'English Garden', a lasting memorial. He was created a count of the Holy Roman Empire and chose for his title Rumford, the original name of the town of Concord (New Hampshire).

In 1798 he returned to England and founded in 1799 the Royal Institution of Great Britain. He settled in Paris in 1803.

The Harvard University Press edition of Rumford's published work, in five volumes, covers a wide variety of subjects. Less than one-tenth of the approximately one million words are devoted to food. However, these passages are of great interest and demonstrate Rumford's great interest in topics as disparate as:

- the design of the ideal coffee pot;
- how to feed most economically poor beggars in Bavaria, while providing adequate nutrition;
- the design of kitchen ranges;
- the possibilities of cooking at lower temperatures than are usual;
- the transfer of heat in food by convection.

On the last of these items, it is often said and seldom contradicted that Rumford discovered convection by observing that hot stewed apples or apple sauce cooled more slowly than clear soup. This is cited sometimes as an example of observations in everyday life leading to discoveries in basic science. Rumford did indeed try to find the reason for the vastly different behaviour of a clear broth and a viscous pureé, and explains his puzzlement thus:

When dining I had often observed that some particular dishes retained their Heat much longer than others, and that apple-pies, and apples and almonds mixed (a dish in great repute in England), remained hot a surprising length of time.

Much struck with this extraordinary quality of retaining Heat which apples appeared to possess, it frequently occurred to my recollection; and I never burnt my mouth with them, or saw others meet with the same misfortune, without endeavouring but in vain, to find out some way of accounting in a satisfactory manner for this surprising phenomenon.

However, it was a chance observation in an entirely different field (examining the sand on the sea shore at the hot baths of Baia, near Naples) that gave him the clue to the nature of the transport of heat by convection and the reason for the difference between apple sauce and broth; in the apple sauce the circulation of the water is hindered by the fibrous material suspended in it.

The famous soup which Rumford devised for feeding the poor of Munich in the workhouse was 'a soup composed of pearl barley, pease, potatoes, cuttings of fine wheaten bread, vinegar, salt, and water, in certain proportions'. After much experiment he concluded that this was 'the *cheapest*, most *savoury*, and most *nourishing* food that could be provided'. He gave precise instructions on the preparation and specified, for example, stale little loaves of *semmel* bread (such as the bakers in Munich donated to the good cause) as being the most suitable for his purpose.

Each inmate of the workhouse was to receive 20 fluid ounces (560 ml) of this soup (whether as the only meal of the day or as the main meal or as one of two meals is not clear, although many commentators have adopted the first and worst interpretation). An analysis in the 1930s showed that the calorific value of such a meal would only be 960 calories. It would follow that unless the recipients managed to obtain quite a lot more food from other sources, they were on a starvation diet. This is not to say that there was no value in Rumford's work on his soup. It was indeed economical and nutritious, and it is significant that Rumford himself wrote of the advantages of adding a little minced red herring and grated cheese to it. On the assumption that some such supplements were often provided, and on the further assumption that one helping of the soup was not all that the inmates were given, they may have been getting just enough.   (NK)
READING: Sanborn Brown (1979); Rumford (ed. S. C. Brown, 1968–70, especially vols. i–iii); Kurti (1996).

RUMOHR KARL (1785–1843), often referred to by his title, Baron von Rumohr, one of the most unusual and impressive figures in the history of gastronomic writing.

His book *Geist der Kochkunst* (The Essence of Cookery) was first published in Germany in 1822, attributed to Rumohr's personal cook (*Mundkoch*) Joseph König. The profession of *Mundkoch* dated back to times when persons in high positions found it necessary to have a trusted employee to cook and taste (for fear of poisoning) all their food. König had accompanied Rumohr on two extensive trips to Italy, whither he went in his capacity as art historian, but taking a keen interest in the food. In the second edition, published in 1832, after the book had been established as a success, Rumohr acknowledged that it was his own work.

Rumohr was equipped to write his book (which preceded by several years the more famous work by BRILLAT-SAVARIN) by a scholarly knowledge of food and cookery in classical times and by much experience of cooking in his own household, plus a remarkably wide range of knowledge about British, Italian, French, and Spanish cookery and even such esoteric items as flavourings used in Indonesia, the diet of N. American fur trappers, and the cooking of food on heated stones in the South Sea islands.

The whole thrust of his work was not in the direction of grand dinners and expensive dishes but towards a resurrection of the native German traditions of cookery and towards increased understanding on the part of his readers of nutrition and of the scientific aspects of cookery. He saw his readers as women; his book was dedicated specifically to six women and in the more general sense to all those German women who had responsibility for feeding households. Such women would have been favourably impressed by his understanding of kitchen procedures and by his down-to-earth approach. In the vigorous and philosophical introduction to his book, Rumohr remarked severely: 'a certain over-refinement of the art of cookery is tending to appear among civilised people. This usually accompanies an affected taste in literature and art.' (This snippet illustrates how ready he was to perceive connections between the so-called fine arts—and for that matter religious, ethical, and political questions—and the art and science of cookery.) In another passage he denounced 'the habit of eating fussy snacks'. He explained that a 'nibbler' could be recognized immediately by his decaying teeth, swollen eyes, and dreamy appearance. However, with his customary analytical and precise approach, he conceded that there were special reasons for students having snack meals (while proposing that they should organize themselves to eat in messes, like English army officers, in order to avoid this necessity); he also observed that his criticisms did not apply with equal force to all the various regions of Germany. He said that 'the habit of eating between meals, with its characteristic "fast food shops", has so far established itself in a few provinces only. It is most entrenched in Upper Saxony.'

The excellence of Rumohr's writing and of the advice which he offers would have been more than sufficient, if he had been writing in English, French, or Italian, to assure him a very wide audience and enduring international fame. However, he is still little known outside Germany. His book was translated into Swedish some time ago, but no French translation is available and the first English translation, the excellent one by Barbara Yeomans, did not appear until 1993 (see Rumohr, 1993).

RUNNER BEAN *Phaseolus coccineus*, is so called because it is a climbing plant. It has a stronger flavour and more showy flowers than the green 'French bean' (see HARICOT BEAN) with which it is sometimes confused.

The runner bean originated in C. America, possibly Mexico. American Indians still eat the starchy roots, besides the young pods and dried seeds which are generally consumed.

The 'scarlet runner', named for its bright red flowers, was introduced to England by Tradescant, the gardener of King Charles I. At first it was grown for its flowers which were often used in bouquets. The flower colour is a sign of the colour of the seeds, which range from white through pink to a deep purple. Mottled seeds are common.

Some of the very numerous cultivars have round, stringless, pods. In Europe and

N. America it is usual to eat the pods when they are still young and tender. In Britain they are often allowed to grow on before being marketed and in this state are referred to by Jane Grigson (1978) as 'monstrosities'. In the same vein, Stobart (1980) remarks that when the beans have become old and tough they have to be sliced before use and that this practice is referred to in America as 'Frenching', although it would be abhorrent to the French.

When mature seeds are sold in the USA, they may be called snail beans, butter beans (white ones), or pea beans.

RUSKS are composed of bread dough incorporating sugar, eggs, and butter. It is shaped into a loaf or cylinder, baked, cooled, and sliced and then dried in low heat until hard. They have a low water content and keep well. Sharing a common origin with the modern BISCUIT, medieval rusks were known as *panis biscoctus* (meaning 'twice-cooked bread') and were used as a form of preserved bread to provision armies and ships at sea (see SHIP'S BISCUIT).

In many countries there are products which resemble rusks in that they are essentially oven-dried bread, whether plain (e.g. BRUSCHETTA) or of a sweet kind; but they may incorporate other ingredients such as spices or nuts, and are given individual names according to recipe.

In Britain, plain rusks are generally thought of in specialized terms, as an edible teething aid for babies, or as 'rusk crumb' (which acts as a meat extender in some sausages) but regional traditions of using rusks in place of bread survive, especially in East Anglia, where they are made in the shape of small rolls and called 'hollow biscuits' or 'knobs'.

In N. America the term zwieback is much used, referring to a sort of rusk made by toasting or baking until dry slices from a small loaf. Ayto (1993) suggests that the word, which is German and simply means 'twice baked' (i.e. the same as BISCUIT), crossed the Atlantic with German emigrants in the 1890s. (LM)

RUSSIA a country which has presented many different faces to the world—from the time of Mongol rule in the early medieval period through the centuries of the Tsarist Empire to being the core of the Soviet Union for most of the 20th century, to the Russian Federation of the 1990s.

Behind these various faces have always been the masses of ordinary Russians, mostly peasants. Their food, unlike that of the wealthy and privileged (whether at the Tsarist court or belonging to the upper reaches of the Communist Party), has been

consistently simple. A similar dichotomy between the food of the wealthy and that of the poor has of course been observable in many countries; but it has been especially noticeable in Russia.

Features of the standard Russian diet, hitherto, have been:

- sourness, apparent in the lavish provision of pickles; in the use of sour yeast doughs for the typical Russian breads (RYE BREADS, or rye and wheat, mostly brown or dark brown, the darkest of all being the black *Borodinsky*); and in KVASS, the beer-like fermented drink made from black rye bread.
- a fundamental range of vegetables, notably CABBAGE, BEETROOT, TURNIP, and SWEDE.
- much reliance on hearty soups, several of which (BORSHCH, SHCHI) achieved international fame.
- little meat until the 19th century, though it is now a central part of the main meal. Many edible fungi (where available); see MUSHROOMS IN RUSSIA.
- CURD CHEESE (*tvorog*) and SOUR CREAM (*smetana*); see also RUSSIAN CHEESES; 'PICKLED' CHEESES.
- onion, garlic, HORSERADISH, and DILL as the basic flavourings.

Lesley Chamberlain (1983), in a brilliant introduction to the whole subject of food in Russia, identifies the main influences which have successively been brought to bear on the underlying pattern.

Long ago it was the Mongol conquerors who were responsible for introducing, at least for the wealthier households, certain spices from Asia (e.g. ginger and cinnamon). But there were many later arrivals from the same direction, and these included some but not all forms of pasta; see box.

Tea arrived from the late 17th century in small amounts and then from the 18th century in larger quantity, as explained by Professor Robert Smith (1980) in an elegant essay on the samovar.

The Russian Orthodox Church calendar had a huge influence, specifying over half the days of the year as suitable only for 'Lenten' foods (vegetables, fish, fungi), while eggs, milk, meat could only appear on the other days. Russian Easter confections such as *kulich* (see EASTER FOODS) and PASKHA belong of course to the same calendar.

It was Tsar Peter the Great (at the end of the 17th century and the beginning of the 18th century) who was largely responsible for bringing Russia into a European (especially Scandinavian) cultural context, with repercussions in the kitchens of the well-to-do and for important items such as the ZAKUSKI table.

The 19th century saw the introduction of French chefs etc. to St Petersburg and Moscow, and the publication of the monumental cookery book by Elena Molokhovets of which an admirable edition in translation, with copious explanatory material, by Joyce Toomre (1992) is now available. The three famous French chefs who left their mark in Russia were CARÊME, Urban Dubois, and Olivier. The last of these three opened a restaurant called the Hermitage in Moscow in the 1880s, described by Lesley Chamberlain as 'one of the great historic restaurants of the world', and it was there that French-Russian cuisine was most fully elaborated. Although the French influence, at least at the top of the culinary tree, was great, one must beware of supposing that any dish with *russe* in the title actually came from Russia. Charlotte russe, for example, as explained under CHARLOTTE, seems to have been invented by Carême in France or England and was only rechristened by Carême later. It is *Sharlotka* in Russia. As for 'Russian salad', as interpreted in western countries (i.e. diced cooked vegetables in or with mayonnaise), it was essentially a French-Russian creation called *Vinegrety* which had a dressing of oil and vinegar (see VINAIGRETTE). The salad to which Olivier gave his name involves cold game (or

---

THE ARRIVAL OF PASTA IN RUSSIA

THE passage below is by Joyce Toomre (1992). She says that the eastern origin of noodles and ravioli-like preparations in Russia is well established by etymological evidence.

Both the words and the products show their Eastern roots. The Russian word for noodles, *lapsha*, comes from Turkic instead of the Germanic *nudel* from which both the English noodle and French *nouille* derive. According to Kovalev, the word for small Siberian dumplings, *pel'meni*, comes from Finno-Ugric while their shape and filling resemble the Central Asian *chuchvar* and *manti*, the Turkish *borek*, and the Georgian *khinkali*. Only *vareniki*, another type of filled dumpling, show their Slavic origins directly since the name derives from the verb *varit'*, to boil. *Vareniki* are prevalent in the Ukraine and are more likely to have entered Russia across the Polish border from Eastern Europe and Austria-Hungary. Vermicelli and macaroni were both later imports from Western Europe. Dal', the great Russian lexicographer of the nineteenth century, defined *vermishel'* (vermicelli) as *ital'janskaja lapsha* (Italian noodles) and *makarony* (macaroni) as *trubchataja lapsha* (tubular noodles) or *ital'janskaja trubki* (Italian tubes).

salmon in Lent) and has a more sophisticated dressing.

In thinking of Russian food and cookery, one naturally thinks of European Russia, but the Russian Federation extends all the way eastwards to Mongolia and China and includes regions (notably Siberia) with very different characteristics and different foodways. To take one example, the Buryats of S. Siberia (who may in turn be divided into the W. or Baikal Buryats and the E. Buryats who live on the other side of Lake Baikal) have distinctive foodways which are the subject of an award-winning essay by Sharon Hudgins (1997), based on pioneering culinary research among these people:

Placed in front of me was the sheep's stomach, which had been filled with a mixture of fresh cow's milk, fresh sheep's blood, garlic, and spring onions, tied up with the sheep's intestines, and boiled in the pot with the rest of the meat. . . . Our hostess leaned over and sliced the top of the stomach. The contents had not been fully cooked and blood oozed onto my plate. She took a large spoon, scooped out some of the semi-coagulated mass, and handed a spoonful to me.

A far cry from the dishes recommended by Mrs Molokhovets or those confected in St Petersburg by imported French chefs.

See also: BABA; BLINI; CAVIAR; COULIBIAC; PASKHA; PIROG; SERVICE À LA RUSSE; STURGEON.
READING: Darra Goldstein (1983); Jean Redwood (1989); Pokhlebkin (1981, 1984); Smith and Christian (1984).

RUSSIAN CHEESES are largely modelled on those of other countries, or have been developed on parallel lines.

The first cheeses to be imported into Russia on a substantial scale were Dutch ones, in the 18th century. The popularity of this type of cheese has been maintained ever since. In the 19th century wealthy Russians imported the English hard cheeses (Cheshire, Chester) which joined Dutch cheeses as a luxury on the ZAKUSKI table. As Lesley Chamberlain (1983) points out, the Russians never followed either the French practice of eating these matured cheeses as the penultimate course of dinner or the English way of eating them at the end of the meal.

Appreciation of semi-soft, soft, and blue cheeses developed later. No doubt tastes of this sort were restricted to the wealthier and more sophisticated Russians. It is interesting in this connection to examine the use of cheese in the greatest Russian cookery book, that of Molokhovets (1861). Joyce Toomre, her translator into English (1992), sums this up as follows:

Molokhovets used cheese extensively in her recipes. Those specified were Dutch

(undifferentiated), Parmesan, Stilton and Swiss. Limburger cheese was mentioned, but not used in a recipe. Despite the influence of French cuisine on the Russian kitchen, Molokhovets did not refer to French cheeses, either as a class or individually, not even Roquefort. The cheese most commonly used in these recipes is *tvorog*, made at home from curdled sour milk.

Russia did not have a native tradition of sophisticated cheese-making; but everywhere there was some sort of CURD or COTTAGE CHEESE. *Tvorog*, mentioned above, is the generic name for these. There were 'pickled' (brined) versions of them, such as *brynza* (see 'PICKLED' CHEESES). *Tvorog* and *brynza* did not qualify for the ZAKUSKI table, but were and still are often served as the first course of a simple meal.

Among the numerous Russian dishes which use *tvorog* are PASKHA, *pirozkhi* (see PIROG) with a cheese filling, and some kinds of cheese pudding.

RUSSULA a genus of mushrooms. It is surprising that the group has no common English name, except for 'russula', which is simply the scientific name laicized. The same applies in Italy, where the name is *rossola*, and in France, where all except one species (mentioned below) are *russule*. The very large number of species (over 100 in Britain and nearly 200 in Europe as a whole), the bright hues which many of them display, and the fact that many are highly edible could be expected to have yielded a whole crop of vernacular names.

Russulas have a wide distribution, from Russia to S. Europe, in N. America, China, and Australia. Most russulas are of medium size, up to 10 cm (4") across the cap, which in young specimens is convex but later acquires a depression in the centre. The gills are normally white or whitish, and so is the stem, but the cap is often brightly coloured. The relatively short stem has no ring or volva, and is noticeably brittle, snapping like a stick of soft chalk.

The best species for eating, and the one which does have vernacular names, is *Russula virescens*, with a green or greenish-grey cap, paler at the edges than in the middle, and with a surface which breaks into a characteristic pattern of cracks. A summer mushroom, found under oak and beech trees, it is a traditional favourite in the north of Italy (as *verdone*).

Other good species include:

- *R. xerampelina*; its specific name means the colour of dried vine leaves (purple or brown). The French call it *russule feuille morte*. It develops an aroma reminiscent of crustaceans, and is sometimes called shrimp russula in N. America.
- *R. aeruginea*, whose specific name means verdigris, also has a green cap, varying

from grey-green to verdigris to blue-green or even darker. It grows mainly under oak or hazel trees. Its slightly acrid taste is dispelled by cooking.
- *R. integra* has a cap which may be purple, chocolate brown, or brownish-yellow, or even present a bleached effect. This is because its pigments are soluble in water and may be changed or washed right out by rain. It may be eaten raw in salads. The flavour suggests fresh almonds.
- *R. obscura* may measure 6–10 cm (2–4") across the cap, which is wine red or purple-brown in colour. It develops a honey-like aroma and has a mild taste.
- *R. olivacea* has a cap which may be purple, olive green, or brownish. It prefers a mountainous habitat, e.g. the Vosges and the Jura in France. It is only occasionally found in Britain.
- *R. cyanoxantha*, the 'charcoal-burner' (French, *russule charbonnière*), has a purple cap which turns green with age. One of the best. Common in woods, especially after summer storms. Found in N. America, but usually infested by maggots.
- *R. paludosa* is a large species with a red cap which may measure 15 cm (6") across. It is more common in the Nordic countries than in W. and S. Europe, and likes a damp environment under conifers.
- *R. mustelina*, which is *russule belette* in France, flourishes in subalpine regions among spruce trees. Highly commended by certain French authors, and likened in appearance to the *cèpe de Bordeaux* (see CEP), except that it has gills not tubes under its cap.
- *R. claroflava*, with a clear yellow cap, is found in moist and marshy areas. Excellent, but uncommon.

All species of *Russula* which have a mild taste are edible; those with a bitter, acrid taste, some of which can burn the mouth severely, are to be avoided. It is prudent to take special care over the identification of those with red caps.

RYE *Secale cereale*, a cereal which came into cultivation later than WHEAT, BARLEY, and OATS. Rye was for centuries the principal bread-making cereal of N. Europe, and still is in eastern parts of the continent, especially in Russia. This is partly because it grows well in cold regions: well into the Arctic parts of Scandinavia and up to 4,250 m (14,000') in the Himalayas. It is not just a northerly substitute for wheat, since it has its own special qualities and is preferred by some peoples, but the amount grown is slowly declining.

The original ancestor of rye was a perennial grass, *Secale montanum*, common in N. Africa and mountainous regions of the Near and Middle East, and known as mountain rye. Probably around 3000 BC, somewhere in the highlands of E. Turkey, Armenia, and NW Iran, where the harsh climate is unsuitable for wheat or barley, this was developed into a cultivated annual plant.

Cultivated rye, *S. cereale*, is up to 1.8 m (6') tall. The seed head has two rows of narrow greyish-green seeds enclosed in large husks with stiff bristles.

Rye cultivation entered Europe from the east around 2000 BC and had spread westwards to Germany by 1000 BC, skirting the lands where the classical civilizations were developing. (It also spread eastwards to the Himalayas, but without entering the main part of India; nor did it reach China.)

The first mention of its cultivation is in the 1st century BC by Pliny, who describes it as grown in the Alps and an unpleasant grain fit only for the very hungry. However, the Germanic tribes valued it. When the Anglo-Saxons invaded Britain they brought rye with them and for a long time afterward more rye was grown in Britain than wheat. Bread was made both from pure rye flour and from maslin (rye and wheat ground together); the latter gives a more manageable bread dough. Lower grades of bread were made with mixtures of rye and barley and other grains.

Other Germanic tribes, such as the Franks, established rye firmly in France, where a dense, grey, rye bread remained the chief kind in country areas until the early 20th century, long after rye had faded into relative unimportance in Britain. In Germany, C. and E. Europe, and in Russia, RYE BREADS were dominant. The numerous kinds ranged in colour and solidity from the deep brown and dense German PUMPERNICKEL and the common Russian black bread, to the paler and lighter breads of Poland and Sweden.

Rye was first grown in the New World in 1606, when the French pioneer L'Escarbot sowed it in Nova Scotia. (The so-called 'giant wild rye' of the north-west, *Elymus condensatus*, also called 'bunch' or 'lyme grass' and eaten by Indians, is a native but not closely related plant.) Rye has continued to be grown on a small scale in the north of the USA and in Canada, where various kinds of rye bread have been made popular by E. European and Jewish immigrants and have indeed become indispensable for certain American kinds of sandwich, e.g. the Jewish salt beef and rye.

Apart from bread, rye is also used to make certain drinks, including the Russian KVASS.

RYE BREADS are most popular in continental Europe north and east of the Rhine; in Scandinavia; and in N. America where immigrants from these areas have settled. They are made from pure RYE, or rye and wheat mixed (a combination known historically as 'maslin' in Britain), and are often flavoured with caraway, aniseed, fennel, or cumin.

Because its seeds are greyish-green, it is impossible to make pure white flour from rye. Bread made from rye flour with all the bran removed is pale grey. Wholemeal rye flour gives 'black bread', which is really dark greyish-brown unless some colouring agent is added. Rye is low in gluten, the substance which gives wheat bread its light, elastic texture; so rye bread is always rather dense. However, its total protein content is only slightly lower than wheat, and rye bread keeps moist for longer than wheat bread, thanks to a small amount of natural gum in the grain which traps moisture, and which is also responsible for its characteristic stickiness.

A distinguishing feature of nearly all rye bread is that it is leavened with a SOURDOUGH culture, normally by keeping back a piece of dough from the previous batch. The culture contains yeast and lactic acid-producing bacteria which give the bread a special and delicious sour flavour. PUMPERNICKEL is made with a culture containing only bacteria, which is why it rises so little. In the highly baked, unleavened rye crispbreads of Scandinavia the faintly bitter natural flavour of rye comes through pleasantly.

The French still make rye bread (*pain de seigle*), especially in Brittany, the Massif Central, and the south-west.

ERGOT IN RYE

RYE suffers from a peculiar disease called ergot, caused by the fungus *Claviceps purpurea*. The organism invades the grains and replaces them with swollen black or purple lumps. Rye in this condition, which is quite easy to spot, is described as 'spurred'. Ergot is exceptionally poisonous. Eating even a small amount of it causes hallucinations, and even death. The outbreaks of 'dancing mania' and other aberrations which affected whole villages in the Middle Ages were generally caused by ergot. The active substance which produces hallucinations is lysergic acid, a form of which is the drug LSD.

SAANEN is the oldest cheese in the world, not in the sense of being the longest established variety (its manufacture dates back only to the 16th century) but because an individual Saanen cheese may be as much as 200 years old.

It is a hard cheese similar to SBRINZ, and is made in the Swiss cantons of Bern and Valais. It is always matured for at least three years, and sometimes seven. By this time it is very dry and keeps indefinitely. Ordinary Saanen is used for grating. It is made in flat wheels up to 40 cm (16") across and weighing up to 11 kg (25 lb).

When a child is born in a household, a special Saanen cheese is traditionally commissioned. That is his or her personal cheese, and small portions of it are eaten by all the family to commemorate his or her name day and other special occasions. The cheese may outlive its proprietor: the personal cheeses of notable people are ceremonially eaten—very sparingly—for decades after their death, until they are finally consumed.

SACHERTORTE a famous Austrian cake served on festive occasions in German-speaking countries. It is a rich chocolate sponge cake glazed in apricot, and iced with bittersweet chocolate.

It was first produced in 1832 by Franz Sacher, chef to Prince von Metternich, and is reputedly the only cake in the world that was ever the subject of a court case. Sarah Kelly (1985) describes how the dispute arose:

when Demel's, Vienna's most famous pastry shop, and the Sacher Hotel, owned by a branch of the same Sacher family, contested who had the right to call their product the 'genuine' Sachertorte. Demel's case was based on the fact that the shop had bought the right to produce the 'genuine' Sachertorte, stamped with an official seal of bittersweet chocolate, from Edouard Sacher, the grandson of the creator. . . . The Hotel Sacher based their case on the family connection with the cake's creator. The most discernible difference between the versions from the two establishments was in the placing of the apricot jam. . . . Seven years later, the courts decided in favour of the Hotel Sacher. Demel's, however, . . . announced that they would simply market their Torte as the 'Ur-Sachertorte', the very first version.

In Demel's version the cake is glazed on top then covered with icing, while in the Hotel Sacher's version it is split in half and the jam spread between the layers. Spread on top of the cake, the apricot glaze provides a glassy, smooth surface over which the warm icing, worked to exactly the right temperature and consistency, can flow smoothly and rapidly to give the cake its characteristically smooth coating. Viennese bakers' manuals recommend using a specially shaped cake tin to produce a smooth cake with rounded edges over which the icing can flow.

Sachertorte is properly inscribed on top with the word 'Sacher' in chocolate. In Vienna it is generally served with unsweetened whipped cream, which Sarah Kelly says 'cuts the sweetness and marries wonderfully with the rich chocolate cake'.

LM

SADDLE in the culinary sense (French *selle, râble*), is a joint of meat from lamb, mutton, or any species of deer. It is taken from the back, between the last rib and the hind legs. This gives a cut which consists of two loins and the vertebrae in between, plus the fillets (tenderloins) underneath; the 'skirt' (the thin flaps of muscle attached to the outer edges of the loins) can either be cut away or partially trimmed and folded underneath. A saddle of hare is a similar cut, but extends to the tail.

Saddles are usually roasted; those from game animals are often larded first (see LARDING). To carve, the meat is cut in long narrow slices parallel to the backbone.

An equivalent joint of beef is known as a baron.
LM

SAFFLOWER *Carthamus tinctorius*, a plant of W. Asia which is a member of the SUNFLOWER and THISTLE family, and resembles a thistle with deep orange flowers. These flowers yield orange and red dyes which were in use from very early times (witness a mention in an Egyptian inscription of 3000 BC).

Even in early times safflower was also used in cookery as an adulterant of, or substitute for, the much more expensive SAFFRON; hence many common names such as 'bastard saffron'.

In the second half of the 20th century safflower oil, extracted from the seeds, began to attract considerable attention. This was partly for health reasons (it has a higher proportion of polyunsaturates than any other commonly available oil), but it is in any case an excellent light cooking oil.

Safflower cultivation is now carried out in the drier regions of N. Africa, China, India, and the USA.

SAFFRON *Crocus sativus*, the most expensive of all spices. True saffron is contained in the orange-red stigmas of the crocus flower. The stigmas are dried and stored in sealed containers to avoid bleaching. The final product is an aromatic, matted mass of narrow, threadlike, dark orange to reddish-brown strands about 2 cm (1") long.

Originally from W. Asia, and particularly from Persia, the saffron crocus has also been widely cultivated in S. Europe since ancient times, to be used for its medicinal properties, in food, and as a dye.

The Moghuls brought the use of saffron, along with many other culinary practices, to India from Persia. The cultivation of saffron in KASHMIR, where some of the finest crops in the world are gathered, dates back to the 3rd century or beyond.

In the westward direction, the Arabs were cultivating saffron in Spain by AD 960, though it was not until the 13th century, when the Crusaders returned with corms from Asia Minor, that cultivation spread to Italy, France, and Germany. Throughout medieval times, saffron occupied a position of great commercial importance in Europe.

The plant is said to have been introduced into England in the 14th century by a pilgrim who hid a corm in his hollow staff. Certainly, by the 16th century the saffron crocus was being cultivated on a significant scale in England, particularly in Essex where the town of Walden was renamed Saffron Walden. Use of saffron was especially noticeable in the west of England, and some believe that it had arrived there long before the 14th century via the Phoenicians and their tin trade with Cornwall.

Saffron has been known to the Chinese since ancient times. Laufer (1978), who went into the matter thoroughly and took pains to demolish the myth that saffron ever grew in China, stated that as long ago as the 3rd century AD a Chinese writer referred to saffron-growing in Kashmir; and that it was from Kashmir that saffron was exported to China. It arrived via Tibet, so was called 'red flower of Tibet'.

The stigmas can only be picked by hand, and it requires 70,000 flowers to obtain one pound avoirdupois of saffron; or 0.5 hectares (1 acre) to yield about 4.5 kg (10 lb) of dried saffron. The cost of production is therefore high. A painting from Knossos in Crete of about 1500 BC is thought to represent a monkey, trained for the purpose, picking saffron flowers; but if this was the practice it has not been continued. Traditional practice in Spain has been described by Johnson (1992), who also draws attention in prose which itself has an amazingly graphic quality to a quintet of 19th-century paintings in the Museum of Fine Arts at Valencia, all on the theme of saffron (harvesting, processing, and the 'Saffron Exchange').

The maximum yield occurs in the third year after planting. In France (Gâtinais) saffron beds are uprooted and replanted after three years; in Spain every four years; in Italy (Piana di Navelli near Acquilia) every year; and in Kashmir every 10 to 15 years. The majority view among connoisseurs seems to be that the finest-quality saffron is that produced in SE Spain, but at least one eminent authority awards the palm to Iran.

Saffron has a spicy, pungent, bitter taste and a tenacious odour, so only a very small amount is needed to give flavour and colour.

In England, one of its uses was to flavour and colour cakes (see SAFFRON CAKE), particularly in Cornwall; and it is used for certain baked goods in various regions of N. Europe.

Saffron is an essential ingredient in the BOUILLABAISSE of Provence. It is used to flavour and colour many, but not all, rice dishes (for example, PAELLA) in Spain, and it is an essential ingredient of Milanese RISOTTO. The Portuguese also use it in rice dishes, and in various desserts.

Saffron is of great importance in Persian cuisine. It is used in many of their rice dishes including PILAF and SHOLA. The Moghuls, again, were responsible for introducing many of the dishes using saffron to India.

These include Indian pilaf and BIRIANI dishes; meat and poultry preparations such as *Shahi raan* (royal roast leg of lamb with saffron raisin sauce); and desserts such as KHEER.

Since saffron is such a valuable commodity, less expensive substitutes are sold, either openly as substitutes or in some instances by deception. Two of the most common are TURMERIC, which provides a yellow colour but has nothing of the saffron flavour (and should never be used in sweet dishes), and SAFFLOWER.

READING: Humphries (1996).

SAFFRON CAKE or saffron bread (as some would call it) has a long history. In earlier centuries, as Laura Mason (1999) points out, saffron buns and cakes were made in various parts of England, although they are now regarded as a Cornish speciality. Sir Kenelm Digby (1669) gives an early recipe. It is for a rich yeast bread with butter, milk, sugar, sultanas, currants, and other spices as well as saffron.

Saffron breads are also made in Sweden, especially on 13 December, the feast of Santa Lucia. Enriched and mixed with fruit, candied peel, and almonds, the dough is shaped into plaits, crosses, and buns called *Lussekatter*, St Lucia's cats. Traditionally, they are served by one of the daughters of the house, who dresses in a long white robe and a crown of lingonberry twigs and candles for the occasion.

SAGE *Salvia officinalis*, a perennial and evergreen herb of the MINT family. It belongs to S. Europe and Asia Minor, but is now cultivated for culinary use in most temperate regions of the world. That grown in Dalmatia, on the Adriatic coast, is considered to be among the best.

In the classical world and medieval times the uses of sage were medicinal. However, although it retains to this day a reputation for restorative powers, sage gradually lost its importance in medicine and acquired instead, by the 16th century, a number of uses in European kitchens.

Sage is commonly used in Italy, e.g. in *Fegato alla salvia* (liver with sage) and also with eel at Venice (a practice echoed in Germany), besides many other dishes. In England the combination of sage and onion to make a savoury STUFFING (for pork or goose or in sausages) is common. In N. America, according to Rosengarten (1969), sage was for a time the most favoured culinary herb of all.

Generally, the robust flavour of sage is better suited to hearty dishes than to subtle ones. But what is called (for the obvious reason) Greek sage, *S. fruticosa*, is milder than *S. officinalis* and can be used with greater freedom.

Of the many other species in the genus, *S. rutilans*, called pineapple sage because of its pineapple scent, is one of those used as a flavouring for food, especially desserts. Another is *S. lavandulifolia*, which has a lavender scent. *S. clevelandii*, the blue sage of western N. America, is a third.

See also CLARY; CHIA.

SAGE CHEESE is moderately well known in England; sage DERBY is marbled green as a result of adding juice obtained from SAGE leaves to the curds when the cheese is being made, while sage LANCASHIRE has chopped sage leaves added to the curds, producing a stronger flavour. These sage cheeses were formerly associated with festivals. See also GREEN CHEESE.

In the USA, there is more to be said about techniques for making sage cheese, and it has been well and amusingly said by Bob Brown (1955). His search for the 'real thing' was eventually successful and he noted his reactions on tasting 'genuine Vermont sage':

Oh, wilderness were Paradise enow! My taste buds come to full flower with the Sage. There's a slight burned savor recalling smoked cheese, although not related in any way. Mildly resinous like that Near East one packed in pine, suggesting the well-saged dressing of a turkey. A round mouthful of luscious mellowness, with a bouquet—a snapping reminder to the nose. And there's just a soupçon of new-mown hay above the green freckles of herb to delight the eye and set the fancy free.

SAGO a light, almost pure STARCH obtained from the stems of various PALMS, especially the sago palms, *Metroxylon sagu* and *M. rumphii*.

Sago is used to a minor extent in western cooking, e.g. to thicken soups or sauces. The only dishes in which it has played a leading role are the sago puddings referred to at the end of this article.

In S. India, SE Asia, parts of Africa, tropical America, and among the Australian Aborigines, sago is made into a thick but translucent paste which is nutritious but whose texture and taste, unembellished, lack interest. Methods of brightening up this food include making it into a kind of ravioli stuffed with pork, groundnuts, and onion, as in Thailand.

The naturalist Alfred Wallace (1869) observed the sago production and cooking process in the eastern islands of Indonesia in the mid-19th century, and described its use:

[the] starch . . . which has a slightly reddish tinge, is made into cylinders of about 30 lb weight, and neatly covered with sago leaves, and in this state is sold as raw sago. Boiled with water this forms a thick glutinous mass, with a rather astringent taste, and is eaten with salt, limes, and chilies.

Sago-bread is made in large quantities . . . The hot cakes are very nice with butter, and when made with the addition of a little sugar and grated cocoa-nut [*sic*] are quite a delicacy . . . Soaked and boiled they made a very good pudding or vegetable, and served well to economize our rice, which is sometimes difficult to get so far east.

The sago palms, which grow in the wetter parts of SE Asia, are the chief source of sago. But sago is also made from other palms whose main use is to produce such items as sugar, toddy (an alcoholic drink), dates, and 'palm cabbage'. The CYCADS (archaic plants intermediate in form between a giant fern and a palm) include one species, *Cycas revoluta*, which is called the Japanese sago-palm since used for this purpose. For so-called 'wild sago' in the USA, see Florida arrowroot under ARROWROOT.

Whatever the kind of plant used, sago is extracted from the stem in the same way. The plant is first allowed to grow almost to maturity (about 15 years for a sago palm). Just before it flowers, when it has built up in a large store of starch in its stem, it is felled. The stem is split, the pith scraped out, ground, and repeatedly washed and strained to purify the starch. One sago palm may yield up to 400 kg (900 lb) of starch.

When sago is exported to western countries it is mixed to a paste with water and rubbed through a coarse sieve to make small pellets, thus giving it the familiar 'frogspawn' texture which is visible in a sago pudding. This texture delights a few cognoscenti in Britain but is repellent to the majority and has no doubt contributed to the virtual disappearance of the pudding from British tables. Its decline in favour has

been a steep one. When sago was first imported around the beginning of the 18th century it was considered a superior substance, fine, delicate, and digestible. It was added to soups as well as made into puddings, and was also made into special dishes for invalids. Sago pudding may be baked or boiled, and its plainness relieved by adding fruit to it.

SAILFISH *Istiophorus platypterus*, one of the great game fishes of the world, is closely related to the BILLFISH, like which it has a bill, but is distinguished by its lofty, sail-like dorsal fin. It used to be thought that there were various species, but these have been reduced to one with a worldwide range: the whole of the tropical Atlantic; Arabia to southern Africa; E. Africa across to the Pacific coast of America; Japan down to Australia.

Sailfish are relatively light in weight for their length (up to 3.5 m/12'). They are good edible fish, but generally less esteemed than the related MARLIN.

ST GEORGE'S MUSHROOM *Calocybe gambosa*, used to be *Tricholoma* (or *Lyophyllum*) *georgii*, a name given because it often appears as early as St George's Day, 23 April. It is not unlike the common FIELD MUSHROOM in appearance, but the edge of the cap is wavier and less tidy, and there is no ring on the stem. The cap may measure up to 15 cm (6") across, but is commonly about two-thirds of this size. Both gills and cap are cream in colour. This mushroom

St George's mushroom

grows in rings like the FAIRY RING MUSHROOM. It is an excellent edible. Dr Badham, the Victorian authority on edible fungi, declared it to be 'the most savoury fungus with which I am acquainted'. His high opinion is echoed in continental Europe. It is not found later than July; but a close relation, the BLEWIT, appears in the autumn and is almost as good.

A related species, whose very different coloration is indicated by the English name 'plums and custard', is *Tricholomopsis rutilans*, common around conifer stumps in Europe and the east of the USA. McIlvaine (1902) opined: 'The flesh when cooked is gummy, like the marshmallow confection. It is excellent.'

Another close relation, esteemed in many countries including Sweden and France (as *clitocybe en touffe*, referring to its habit of growth in clumps), is *Lyophyllum connatum*, a white mushroom of excellent quality which has an aroma of clover.

SAINT-NECTAIRE is a surface-ripened, semi-soft, French cheese made from whole milk. It resembles a rich and superior MUNSTER, but is produced in the MONT DORÉ district of the Auvergne. Its shape is a flat disc, and its typical weight is from 1.75 kg (3.5 to 4 lb). The rind is brightly patched with white, yellow, and red mould which it acquires through ripening in cool, damp cellars in Clermont-Ferrand. Its taste should be faintly acid but no more.

SAITHE *Pollachius virens*, a member of the COD family which goes by various other names: coalfish or coley in Britain, and pollock (not the same as POLLACK) or Boston bluefish in the USA. With a maximum length of 120 cm (48"), this is a substantial fish. However, it is often caught much smaller and in places where it is especially appreciated there are special names for the juvenile sizes; for example, Shetlanders call the smallest sillack or sillock, while the larger year-old specimens are piltock. The species spans the N. Atlantic, descending to New Jersey on the west and the English Channel on the east. The catch on the east side is by far the greater.

For most people, fillets of the adult fish will be all that is available. These can be cooked like cod or haddock. However, the flesh is slightly grey in colour and less fine than cod, so cooks who are intent on a good presentation often use saithe, as in Norway, for fried fish balls or the like. Young saithe, where available, are highly esteemed, e.g. 'breaded' with oatmeal and fried, as in Shetland. In Orkney, where one-year-old fish are 'cuithes', these are traditionally split, salted, and dried over a peat hearth. Once

fully dried, they are like wood and slightly phosphorescent. In some houses, so many would be hanging from the rafters that people could read by their light.

One of the German names for saithe is *Seelachs*, meaning 'sea salmon'. Germans salt and smoke slices of it, so that they finish up with a salmon-like colour.

SAKÉ a well-known Japanese alcoholic drink, usually referred to in English as 'rice wine' (although this is something of a misnomer, given that it is brewed), is familiar wherever Japanese restaurants exist as something to be served, often warm, in small decorated china cups. In Japan, however, it has another role, as a major ingredient in the kitchen, ranked by Tsuji (1980) with SOY SAUCE, MISO, and DASHI as one of what he terms the Big Four. He comments that the effects of saké are to tenderize; to suppress unwanted strong smells; to tone down saltiness; to remove or tame fishy flavours; and (an intriguing property, not explained in terms of chemistry) to preserve in a state of animation certain delicate flavours which might otherwise disappear. Japanese cooks also make use of saké as a pickling medium.

Saké, which is slightly stronger than MIRIN, is used sparingly, even when the practice of some cooks, who burn off the alcohol before use, is followed.

SALAD a term derived from the Latin *sal* (salt), which yielded the form *salata*, 'salted things' such as the raw vegetables eaten in classical times with a dressing of oil, vinegar, or salt. The word turns up in Old French as *salade* and then in late 14th-century English as salad or sallet. At that time, in the medieval period, salads were composed of green leaves, sometimes with flowers. Later, at least in England, fruits such as orange and lemon were added (at least in a decorative role), and the 17th century was the era of what was called the grand sallet, which could have a multitude of ingredients. Thus Robert May (1685), in the first of no fewer than 14 grand sallet recipes, instructs as follows:

Take a cold roast capon and cut it into thin slices square and small (or any other roast meat . . .), mingle with it a little minced taragon and an onion, then mince littice as small as the capon, mingle all together, and lay it in the middle of a clean scoured dish. Then lay capers by themselves, olives by themselves, samphire by it self, broom buds, pickled mushrooms, pickled oysters, lemon, orange, raisins, almonds, blue-fits, Virginia Potato, caperons, crucifix pease, and the like, more or less, as occasion serves, lay them by themselves in the dish round the meat in partitions. Then garnish the dish sides with quarters of oranges, or lemons, or in slices, oyl and vinegar beaten together, poured on it over all.

Of the others, the 'grand Sallet of Alexander-buds' is relatively simple—just the named buds 'laid round about upright' with capers and currants, carved lemon, sugar scraped over all, oil and vinegar.

The 17th century was evidently ripe for a single-subject book devoted to salads and in 1699, with just a year to spare before the 18th, it came: Robert Evelyn's *Acetaria*, the first such book in the English language. Evelyn has evidently given much thought to definitions and categories. He announces that: 'we are by *Sallet* to understand a particular Composition of certain *Crude* and fresh Herbs, such as usually are, or may safely be eaten with some *Acetous* Juice, *Oyl*, *Salt*, &c. to give them a grateful Gust and Vehicle.' Roots, stalks, leaves, buds, flowers are what he is writing about; fruits, he says, belong to another class. Following him on these lines would deprive us moderns of having the anomalous tomato in our salad, but is yet in line with the clear distinction we make between 'salads' and 'fruit salads'. To compare him with May: the catalogue which he gives of salad ingredients does not include fruits as such, although the grated rind of oranges and lemons is welcome among the herbs; and there is no sign of any meat, unless one counts the small red worm which, he warns his readers, often lurks in the midst of celery stalks, but which is of course to be discarded not eaten.

Evelyn considers the question whether to begin or end the meal with salad. He seems to think that the French begin with it and that this is a good plan (the salad slips down through the system and does not create obstructions for what follows), but creates an atmosphere of puzzlement by quoting the Roman poet Martial:

> The *Sallet*, which of old came in at last,
> Why now with it begin we our Repast?

Evelyn also gives his attention to salad dressings, but only after giving precise instructions for picking, cleansing, washing, putting in the strainer, swinging, and shaking gently the herbs. These, 'spread on a clean Napkin before you, are to be mingl'd together in one of the Earthen glaz'd Dishes: Then, for the *Oxoleon* [his rather precious term for the dressing]; Take of clear, and perfectly good *Oyl-Olive*, three Parts; of sharpest *Vinegar* . . . *Limon*, or Juice of *Orange*, one Part; and therein let steep some Slices of *Horse-Radish*, with a little *Salt*.' He has more to say, but this is enough to show that little has changed in the three centuries since he wrote, except that adding horseradish to what we now call a VINAIGRETTE is no longer a common practice, and international hotel cuisine, under American influence, now offers alternative dressings: typically two, Thousand Island and Blue Cheese.

In the 19th century there is evidence enough in Eliza Acton (1855) and various gastronomic writers in the latter half of the century that salads and their dressing were taken seriously in England. Acton's recipe for 'French salad dressing' is a model of its kind:

Stir a saltspoonful of salt and half as much pepper into a large spoonful of oil, and when the salt is dissolved, mix with them four additional spoonsful of oil, and pour the whole over the salad; let it be *well* turned, and add a couple of spoonsful of tarragon vinegar, mix the whole thoroughly, and serve it without delay. The salad should not be dressed in this way until the instant before it is wanted for table.

However, the liveliest writing on the subject came from the pen of Alexandre Dumas (1873), who quotes at length the diverting anecdote in Brillat-Savarin (1826) about the Chevalier d'Albignac, who made his fortune in London by dressing salads as his profession, but also expressed his own views, with obsessive detail to match that of Evelyn, on the choice of ingredients and describes his own (complex) method—a description which culminates with the lofty words: 'Finally, I put the salad back into the salad bowl and let my servant toss it. And I let fall on it, from a height, a pinch of paprika.'

The 20th century has seen innovations in the treatment of salads in the western world, including the introduction of 'warm salads', an item of NOUVELLE CUISINE, but more lasting significance probably attaches to spreading awareness, for example in Britain, of salads from other countries, continents, and cultures. So-called 'Russian salad' (not really Russian—see Lesley Chamberlain, 1983, for a full account of this and of the different Russian perception of salads generally) was already familiar in the 19th century, but it is only more recently that the Middle Eastern salad TABBOULEH has begun to verge on ubiquity, while *Salade niçoise* (an infinitely refreshing and delicious mixture of, usually, lettuce, tomatoes, French beans, anchovy, tuna, olives, hard-boiled eggs with a vinaigrette dressing) is now a standard item hundreds and even thousands of miles away from Nice. American contributions such as Waldorf salad (apple, celery, and mayonnaise from 1896, and with walnuts from the 1920s) and Caesar salad had already become internationally popular in the first half of the century. Mariani (1994) has an exceptionally full entry on Caesar salad, invented at Tijuana in 1924 by Caesar Cardini. He explains among other things that Cardini did not approve adding anchovy to his original list of six ingredients: romaine lettuce, garlic, olive oil, croutons, parmesan cheese, and Worcestershire sauce; he thought that any faint aroma of anchovy emanating from the Worcestershire sauce would be quite enough.

Later, Asian dishes which have to be counted as salads although they may not bear the name have received a welcome in other continents. Examples are Japanese *aemono* and *sunomono* (terms meaning 'dressed things'—see JAPANESE CULINARY TERMS); *yam* (*yum*) from Thailand; and items such as Indonesian vegetable salads of great flexibility such as *urap*, which has a coconut dressing, and *karedok*, which has a peanut dressing.

See also FRUIT SALAD.
READING: Laura Shapiro (1986).

SALAK the Malay name for the fruit of several kinds of small, stemless palms which grow in Indonesia, Malaysia, Thailand, and Burma. The best is *Salacca edulis*. The fruit is shaped like but smaller than a pear, and has a shiny brown scaly skin. The yellowish flesh is described as being slightly crisp in texture, with a pleasant blend of sugar and acid in the flavour. These palm fruits are cultivated in Bali, where at least two cultivars are especially prized.

The young fruit may be pickled. According to Uphof (1968) fruits preserved in cans, with salt water and sugar, are eaten by Muhammadan pilgrims during their journeys to Mecca.

The fruits of *S. conferta* are exceedingly sour, and are used in cooking in the same way as TAMARIND. The Chinese make them into a candied sweetmeat.

SALAMANDER a noun but also as a verb, indicating the use of a salamander to brown the top of a dish, often giving it at the same time a crisp crust. The equipment consists of an iron disc mounted on the end of an iron rod, which is furnished with a wooden handle. The disc is heated red-hot, then passed to and fro over and close to the dish to be 'salamandered'. Susan Campbell (1985), discussing this technique, points out that it is particularly appropriate in making a CRÈME BRÛLÉE, although used in the past for many GRATIN dishes.

Use of the term in a culinary context derives from the mythical lizard-like animal of the same name which was supposed to be able to survive or even live in the flames of a fire.

SALEP a starchy powder made by drying and pulverizing the root tubers of certain plants of the orchid family, notably *Orchis latifolia*, *O. mascula*, *O. militaris*, and *O. morio*. The powder makes a beverage, either a cool and refreshing one in summer or a hot one for cold weather. Since it is an effective thickening agent, it has various food and medicinal uses; e.g. to thicken milk drinks and ice creams especially in the Middle East and parts of Asia.

The roots of the orchid have a testicle-like form, as the name orchid (Greek *orchis*, meaning testicle) suggests. Common English names include cullions, bollocks, dog's cods, etc. The name 'salep' itself is Turkish from the Arabic *thalab*, meaning fox; and one step further back leads to the Arabic *khusya th-thalab*, meaning 'fox's testicles'. Not surprisingly, the roots have a reputation as a powerful APHRODISIAC. (Yet, paradoxically, salep is also thought to be wholesome and beneficial fare for children.)

The drink enjoyed a vogue in England under the name salop or saloop in the late 17th century. C. Anne Wilson (1973) records that the powder was stirred into water until it thickened, then sweetened and seasoned with rosewater or orange flower water. 'At the height of its popularity salop was served in the coffee-houses as an alternative to coffee or chocolate; and salop-vendors peddled the drink in the streets, or sold it from booths.' This beverage was supposed to have great nutritional qualities, and a certain mystery surrounded it; witness the incorrect statement by Hannah Glasse (1747) that it was made from a hard stone ground to powder. (When imported, the roots had been baked until semi-transparent and dried in the form of oval pieces, always hard and horny, yellowish-white, and sometimes clear. So it was easy to suppose that they were some sort of mineral or animal horn.)

However, the true home of salep is in SE Europe, Asia Minor, and the temperate parts of India, where the plants from which it is made grow. The Turks like it as a drink, and used to import the powder in large quantities from Armenia for its preparation. They usually make it by adding a little of the powder and some sugar to milk, bringing to and keeping at a boil until somewhat thickened, and then serving hot with cinnamon or cinnamon and ginger sprinkled on it. It is sold thus from great brass or copper urns by street vendors.

In parts of the Middle East, Iran, and Afghanistan salep is used in the making of ICE CREAM, giving it an elastic consistency. The Persian (Iranian) version is the best known of all ice creams in that country and, according to Margaret Shaida (1992), is known as *Akbar Mashdi* after the man who first produced it commercially in Tehran in the 1950s. The corresponding ice cream in Syria is called *buza* (not to be confused with the Turkish *boza*, which is a fermented drink made from grains such as millet or BURGHUL and rice).

The Turkish version of this ice cream is *hakiki Maraş dondurması* of which Holly Chase (1994) writes:

consumption of . . . genuine Marash ice cream made with salep remains one of [Turkey's] more sensual gastronomic pleasures. Throughout Turkey in summer, Marash ice cream is widely sold by street vendors who stir their tubs of cool enticement with long wooden paddles. So strong is the association with Marash, which is both a province and a town in south-eastern Anatolia, that its vendors, even in Aegean resorts, are almost always folklorically dressed in costumes of the distant south-east—passementerie vests, baggy trousers and striped cummerbunds.

The same author makes four other interesting points about salep. First, the elastic quality of these 'stretchy' ice creams is not, as some writers state, due to the presence of MASTIC. It is true that mastic has elastic qualities and that it is often an ingredient of these ice creams. But it is there for flavouring purposes; the stretchiness of the ice cream is due to the salep which it contains.

Secondly, salep itself is almost tasteless and its thickening qualities are not readily distinguishable from those of arrowroot, potato starch, and cornflour. Indeed packets of 'instant salep' list cornflour as an ingredient, along with salep and sugar. The questions implicit in these observations leap to the mind; all the more so when one reflects that Claudia Roden (1985) considers that the substitution of cornflour for expensive salep is legitimate (and adds, incidentally, that Egyptians now commonly add grated coconut to the confection).

Thirdly, there are native purple orchids in England, whose roots were known in the past as 'dogstones', and the 1771 edition of the *Encyclopaedia Britannica*, which gives a good description of the selection and preparation of salep, suggests that British orchid roots are a reasonable substitute for the Middle Eastern ones.

Fourthly, there is a puzzle over the relationship between salep and the Egyptian drink called *sahleb* (sometimes given as *sahleb* or even *shahlab*). The orientalist Lane (1860), a meticulous observer, said that the vendors of sahlab would proffer 'a thin jelly, made of water, wheat-starch, and sugar, boiled with a little cinnamon or ginger sprinkled upon it; or made as a drink, without starch'. Emerson (1908) follows Lane. In modern times, however, Claudia Roden (1985) gives salep (=sahlab) as the most important and indeed eponymous ingredient of this drink. This is as one would expect; but a question is left in the air—has the drink changed, or did the earlier authorities misunderstand its composition, or have there been two different drinks of the same name?

SALIVA a secretion from three pairs of salivary glands in the mouth, has various components, including some sodium

chloride (common salt) and sodium bicarbonate. The two which help most to prepare food for its passage to the stomach are a protein, mucin; and the enzyme ptyalin, a type of amylase. The former lubricates the food; the latter hydrolyses starch to maltose. A human adult normally generates 1–1.5 litres (1.75–3.5 pints) of saliva daily.

The BIRDS' NESTS that are made into soup consist of dried saliva of birds.

SALLY LUNN a major enigma for food historians. It is not that there is doubt about what it actually is. It can be described as a round tea bread (or tea cake, the term some would prefer to use) made from a rich yeast dough containing flour, milk or cream, eggs, a little sugar, and sometimes a little grated lemon peel or mixed sweet spice. This may be made as one large or several small buns, and can be baked in a mould, or shaped by hand and baked on a sheet. A Sally Lunn is traditionally served very fresh, split into two or even three layers, with butter or clotted cream.

However, the derivation of the name is a subject which has excited many pages of prose. Ayto (1993) cites two references in print from the late 18th century. The earlier (from Philip Thicknesse's *Valetudinarian's Bath Guide*, 1780) tells of a fiddler who dropped dead after 'a hearty breakfast of spungy hot rolls, or Sally Luns'. The *Gentleman's Magazine* of 1798 also referred to them as hot rolls, 'gratefully and emphatically styled "Sally Lunns"'. The name Sally Lunn (Lunn is more usual than Lun) is said to commemorate a woman baker of that name who had a pastry-cook's shop and cried her wares in the street. Why not? A pleasant and plausible tale.

However, there is a complication. Eliza Acton (1845) has a recipe for a 'rich French breakfast cake' called *solimemne*. This name appears in various forms, including *solilem*, and is thought to come from *soleil et lune* (sun and moon [cake]), since the product is golden on top (being glazed with egg) and pale underneath (or, say others, because it is golden outside and white inside). Dorothy Hartley (1954) ingeniously combines this derivation with the existence of the woman baker, declaring that what the latter cried 'in her good west-country French was "Sol et Lune! Soleilune!"' (On this theory, the woman baker would not have been called Sally Lunn.)

Many authors remark that the French *solilem* is of Alsatian origin. It has, however, proved difficult to find corroboration of this in French books about Alsatian cuisine or French reference works generally. Favre (*c*.1905) does give a recipe for *Solilème*, which is indeed not unlike standard recipes for a

Sally Lunn, and says that it is of Alsatian origin (adding however that it is likewise known in Germany). He provides for making a large one (to be sliced horizontally into two or three layers, with lightly salted butter added between) or a number of small ones, all to be served hot. There must have been something to prompt this item in his encyclopedia, and indeed to prompt the meticulous Eliza Acton to give her recipe half a century earlier; but what? The earliest French reference which has come to light is in CARÊME (1815). This is long after the Sally Lunn was being cried in the streets of Bath, but just before Carême was in England (1816, working at the Royal Pavilion in Brighton). So the hypothesis that Carême 'discovered' the Sally Lunn when he was in England and decided to make what was doubtless a slightly adapted version of it, giving it a French name, does not work. *Kettner's Book of the Table* by Dallas (1877) includes, however, a memorable salvo fired against Carême on the basis of that hypothesis:

The greatest cook of modern times, Carême, came over to England to minister to the palate of the Prince Regent. He did not stay long, but he stayed long enough to appreciate the charms of Sally Lunn and her ever memorable cake. He was a great cook, but a fearful coxcomb—an immeasurabl egotist. If ever he made the slightest change in a dish, he vaunted the variation as an original idea, and thenceforward set up as the sovereign creator of the dainty. So it was that he dressed up Sally Lunn a little, and presented her to the Parisian world as his own—his Solilemne. The fact might well be forgotten, but there are stupid asses who will not let us forget it. They come over to England; they send up, among the sweets of a dinner, Sally and her teacake, rigged out in the height of the French fashion; and like an English dancer or singer who insists on Mademoiselle to her name, the good honest Sally that we know is announced as the incomparable Solilemne.

The persuasiveness of this prose is undimmed after more than 100 years. In default of further evidence, such as researchers in Alsace have recently searched for in vain, it is tempting to assume that Kettner had it more or less right, although a mystery remains: how did Carême learn about the Sally Lunn *before* he set foot in England?

SALMAGUNDI (or salmagundy), a term dating from the 17th century, has been defined in the *NSOED* as 'a cold dish made from chopped meat, anchovies, eggs, onions etc.'

In writing about salads of the 17th century, C. Anne Wilson (1973) explains the term thus:

Sometimes an egg and herb salad was further enhanced by the addition of cold roast capon, anchovies and other meat or fish delicacies. Late in the 17th century the name of salamagundi was applied to mixtures of this type, and was subsequently corrupted to 'Solomon Gundy'.

The latter name has survived in N. America. The earlier name was derived from the old French salmigondis, of unknown origin according to the *OED*.

Hannah Glasse (1747) has three recipes for Salamongundy, but sums up the essence of this dish at the end of the third recipe: 'but you may always make a Salamongundy of such things as you have, according to your Fancy.' She also says: 'if it is neatly set out it will make a pretty figure in the middle of the table, or you may lay them in heaps in a dish; if you have not all these ingredients, set out your plates or saucers with just what you fancy.' The reference to 'heaps' probably indicates a usual way of presenting this sort of salad; a series of overlapping layers based around a basin or deep saucer upside down in the dish.

The extreme permissiveness displayed by Hannah Glasse has also been at work in the field of spelling. 'Sallid magundi' is but one of numerous variants.   (HS)

SALMON of which there are six well-known species, in the family Salmonidae, all belong to the northern waters of the northern hemisphere. The fish which have been called 'salmon' in Australia and S. Africa are not salmon at all.

The most famous salmon is *Salmo salar*, the Atlantic salmon, whose range extended in times past from Portugal up to Norway and across by Greenland to N. America, probably down to the Hudson River. However, the lifecycle of this fish is such that it has increasingly come up against man-made obstacles in the last two centuries and is now not found at all in some places where it formerly abounded.

Every salmon starts life as a tiny blob in the deep gravel of a cold stream where the parent fish deposit their eggs. Out of the eggs come tiny alevins which soon emerge from the gravel and are called fry. As they gain in size, they become parr, a stage which lasts until they make their way down to the sea, undergo various changes designed to fit them for life in salt water, and acquire a new name, smolts.

Some salmon come back to their native rivers to spawn after only one year at sea. They are called grilse. Most, however, spend two to four years at sea, growing into fully adult salmon of 80–100 cm (32–40") before they make the return journey. Arriving full of food and vigour at their home rivers, they then make what is often an arduous journey up to a suitable gravel bed, and deposit their eggs. They are 'spent' by the effort and no longer a valuable prize for anglers; indeed many just die.

It is on this return journey from the sea, as they enter the estuaries and then make their way first upriver and then upstream that the traditional methods of catching them (nets at the river mouths, rod and line from the river banks) are used. The salmon were not in the past caught at sea because no one knew where they were. Now that they have been 'found', for example off the coast of Greenland, they can be caught there, and this has caused controversy. However, the depredations caused by sea fishing are of little importance by comparison with the harm done to salmon by the pollution or blocking of rivers. Similar problems have afflicted, to varying degrees, the five species of Pacific salmon which are listed in the box.

The mechanisms which enable salmon to return to the rivers from which they set out are complex and perhaps not yet fully understood, but amazingly effective. This 'magic' feature may help to account for the prominence of salmon in mythology.

Towards the end of the 20th century the 'farming' of salmon developed into a big business, with various results, some good and some undesirable. Farmed salmon can be marketed cheaply, and the supply has become so plentiful that there seems to be a risk of repetition of the situation which existed in some places in medieval times, when (to take one well-worn example) apprentices in the north of England stipulated that their free meals should not include salmon more than three times a week. There are also problems of pollution (caused by having huge numbers of fish in a confined space) and problems of quality

(fish farmed in inferior operations tend to be fatty and less flavourful, and may have problems with parasites and other health hazards).

Cooking salmon is never a problem. Its firm meaty flesh is suitable for any of the standard methods, including the ancient 'barbecue' method of American Indians in the Pacific north-west, who would split a fish open, impale it on strong green twigs and set these at an angle in the ground beside an open fire. Salmon poached in a COURT BOUILLON and served cold with mayonnaise and a garnish of cucumber is a traditional treat in Britain.

Salmon also lends itself to various interesting cures. The most widespread is smoked salmon, a product made in many countries but perhaps at its best when prepared in Scotland or Ireland with wild salmon (note, incidentally, that 'wild smoked salmon' is an inappropriate description—it should be 'smoked wild salmon'). See also, for the next most famous example, GRAVLAKS.

READING: Netboy (1968).

SALMONBERRY *Rubus spectabilis*, a relation of the BLACKBERRY and RASPBERRY, has a structure which resembles the latter more than the former, since the fruit, which is red or yellow-orange when ripe, pulls away from its conical receptacle.

The salmonberry is found in N. America, for example in SE Alaska and at suitable altitudes in the Pacific north-west. It is one of the numerous berries eaten by American

---

THE FIVE SPECIES OF SALMON IN THE PACIFIC

- **S**OCKEYE salmon, *Oncorhynchus nerka*, length to 84 cm/34", the most valuable commercial species. At spawning time the male is bright red and has developed a hooked lower jaw (a characteristic of salmon in this genus) and a somewhat humped back; the female is also red. The name 'sockeye' has nothing to do with the fish's eyes; it is a corruption of an American Indian name.
- Chinook, king or spring salmon, *O. tshawytscha*, length to 1.5 m/51", has dark spots on its dorsal and tail fins and on its back, and is second in importance commercially.
- Chum salmon, *O. keta*, up to almost 1 m/3'2" long, no dark spots on back or fins, particularly important in Canada; also called 'dog' salmon, because males have greatly enlarged canine-like teeth at spawning time.
- Coho or silver salmon, *O. kisutch*, up to 90 cm/35" long, a deep-bodied fish with some black spots on its dorsal fin and the upper part of the tail fin; the flesh cans well, but this species is of secondary importance.
- Humpback or pink salmon, *O. gorbuscha*, up to 75 cm/30" long, so the smallest of the group, of considerable value on the Asian side of the N. Pacific. This species has been introduced to the N. Atlantic.

These are the marine species. In addition, as Wheeler (1979) explains:

In several Canadian lakes there are landlocked salmon, which migrate from river to lake as if the latter was the sea. This is the ouananiche, a name borrowed from the local Indian dialect, and a famous game fish. Another landlocked salmon is the E. American sebago salmon, found in Sebago and other lakes and their associated rivers.

Indians and used by them in making PEMMICAN. The name salmonberry is said by Charlotte Clarke (1978) to reflect the practice of eating the berries with half-dried salmon roe.

SALMONELLA BACTERIA

SALMONELLA BACTERIA which are one of the commonest causes of FOOD POISONING. There are many species, most of which cause vomiting, diarrhoea, and abdominal pain, and often a fever that may last for a couple of days. Usually the symptoms, although unpleasant, are not very serious in healthy people; but in the very young and old, and people with impaired immune systems, salmonella infection may be fatal.

Salmonella often infect poultry. They are killed by proper cooking and, since they do not produce toxins, the poultry is then safe to eat. If, however, frozen birds have not been properly thawed before cooking, the inside may not reach a high enough temperature to kill the bacteria and trouble results.

The infection can also affect eggs. Usually the contamination is restricted to the outside of the shell, but sometimes the organism gets into the bird's oviduct and so affects the inside of the egg. Poisoning will then result if the egg is eaten raw or lightly cooked. A particularly troublesome species which achieved notoriety in the early 1990s is known as *Salmonella enteridis* phage type 4. This is often associated with infection from the contents of eggs.

The risks of salmonella poisoning from poultry or eggs seem to vary from virtual zero in some countries to quite substantial, notably in Britain.   (RH)

ŞALŞ

ŞALŞ an interesting Arabic culinary term which seems not to have been used since the 13th century, but which, by its use in that period, raises interesting questions about the culinary interchanges which took place between the Crusaders and their Arab adversaries.

Historians who study these interchanges look principally to Muslim Spain where Christians and Moors knew each other over a longer period and more peaceably than in the conflicts brought about by the Crusades. It is also commonly held, and correctly, that culinary influences passed from the Arab world to Europe, rather than in the other direction. However, Maxime Rodinson (1949) drew attention to a recipe in the 13th-century Arabic cookbook *The Link to the Beloved* for 'a bread which the Franks and Armenians make, which is called *aflāghūn*', and remarked that despite its Armenian name it resembled *pain d'épices* (see GINGERBREAD). In the same

book there is a recipe called 'Frankish roast' (*al-shiwā' al faranji*). In this dish lamb is basted with the usual Saracen combination of sesame oil and rosewater, and the Frankishness of it seems to reside in the idea of spitting the animal whole, rather than cut up into small pieces in the Near Eastern fashion.

The most interesting of the western influences Rodinson found in *The Link to the Beloved* was *şalş*. In addition to the recipe in *The Link* there are several more: in both manuscripts of another 13th-century work, *The Description of Familiar Foods*, and one manuscript of a text related to it, *The Book of Dishes*. Although none of the manuscripts describes *şalş* as Frankish, the word is undoubtedly the same as salsa or sauce, evidently treated by Arabic as a collective noun. No other etymology is remotely likely, and there is more evidence in the fact that all the *şalş* recipes in *The Description* are either in a section on fish dishes or explicitly associated with fish. Because of the religious requirements of fasting, the Europeans may have had a more developed repertoire of fish dishes than the Syrians.   CP

READING (and for bibliographical references): Perry (1987*b*).

SALSIFY SCOLYMUS, AND SCORZONERA

SALSIFY SCOLYMUS, AND SCORZONERA, a trio of European or Eurasian plants which it is convenient to treat together as they are closely related to each other within the family Compositae and are all used in similar ways as root vegetables.

None of the three is widely popular, but salsify, *Tragopogon porrifolius*, is the best known. It is a larger relative of the common wild plant goat's beard, *T. pratensis*. Indeed Tragopogon means 'goat's beard', a reference to the hairy seed 'clocks' of these plants. The meaning of *porrifolium* is 'leek-leafed', which is a fair description.

Wild salsify is native to the lands around the E. Mediterranean. It was probably eaten in classical times, but the earliest surviving mention of it is by Albertus Magnus in the 13th century. Cultivation began in Italy and France in the 16th century. In Britain the plant was grown first for its purple flower, attained a modest popularity as food in the 18th century, but relapsed into obscurity in the next. It has never been popular in the USA. Russia, France, and Italy are now the countries in which salsify is most grown and eaten.

The root of salsify, which resembles a long, white carrot, is not easily removed from the soil without damage. If it is broken it must be used at once, for it discolours and spoils quickly. Even when cutting up the plant for cooking it is advisable to drop the pieces into acidulated water to preserve their colour; a precaution which applies equally to scolymus and scorzonera.

Salsify root is usually baked or boiled, or made into a cream soup. To prepare it as a vegetable it is best to cook it unpeeled, but cut into large pieces, after which it is easy to remove the skin. Young salsify leaves are good in salads. Some gardeners grow the plant for its young shoot alone, earthing it up like Belgian 'Witloof' chicory to whiten it. In these circumstances the root will not develop, and is wasted. The smaller wild goat's beard is like a miniature version of salsify in every respect except that its flowers are yellow. The roots have been gathered and eaten like those of salsify. In Italy the young shoots are picked for salads.

Scolymus, *Scolymus hispanicus*, is also known as Spanish salsify or Spanish oyster plant, names which it shares with scorzonera (see below). Another name, golden thistle, indicates correctly that it is a kind of THISTLE. The root resembles that of salsify in flavour; but, unlike salsify, it is branched. It is usual to boil it, peel it, scrape the flesh off the woody and inedible core, and mash it or make it into croquettes. Some people prefer it to salsify, especially in Spain, where it is a popular vegetable; others dismiss it as tasteless.

Scorzonera, *Scorzonera hispanica*, is sometimes called 'black' or 'Spanish salsify'. Its name means 'black bark' in Spanish. The plant is native to a wider area than the previous two, and grows wild as far east as Siberia. Early uses were medical, but scorzonera gradually came to be accepted as a food rather than a medicine. In 1699 Evelyn wrote:

It is a very sweete and pleasant Sallet, being laid to soak out the Bitterness, then peel'd may be eaten raw or condited: but best of all, stew'd with Marrow, Spice, Wine. They likewise may bake, fry or boil them; a more excellent Root there is hardly growing.

Cultivation of the plant began in Spain and spread to the rest of Europe. It was usually cooked, though the leaves were eaten raw in salads like those of salsify.

The roots of modern varieties can be eaten raw without having to be 'laid', since

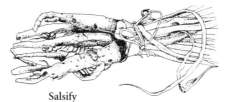

Salsify

Scorzonera

they are not bitter, but on the contrary slightly sweet. The flavour of scorzonera is generally considered superior to that of salsify, but the thin root is even more easily damaged. A very sweet variety of scorzonera, formerly classified as *S. mollis*, is grown in Sicily and used to make sweetmeats. Indeed, de Candolle (1886, English edn) said that in Naples he had tasted 'Scorzonera ices'; but he found them 'detestable'.

SALT sodium chloride (NaCl), is commonly said to be essential to life, and this is broadly correct although strictly speaking what is essential is the SODIUM which is present in some foodstuffs in one form or another.

Salty is a basic TASTE, which we are equipped to detect by some of the taste receptors in our mouths. Salt is also important in the PRESERVATION of food, especially by SALTING in PICKLES.

Since prehistoric times much effort has been devoted to obtaining salt for use with food. One main source is the existence of underground deposits of salt, from which it can be mined. Examples are the famous salt quarries at Nantwich in Cheshire, those at Lüneburg in Germany, and many others in various parts of the world. The other great source, which is inexhaustible, is the sea (or other naturally occurring briny waters), which is made to yield salt by a process of evaporation.

Rock salt is what the salt mined from underground is called, whether it is literally mined in solid form (a practice now rare) or pumped up to the surface and then evaporated, to be crystallized to the desired degree of fineness. In some countries rock salt is used only in crude form for preservation purposes and for use in ice cream machines etc. However, rock salt which has been processed to the extent necessary to make it edible is sold for use in the kitchen and in small salt grinders at table. Its flavour will depend on any impurities left in it, and these in turn depend on the source.

Sea salt is the category to which belong many of the kinds of salt specially prized by connoisseurs. These salts are presented in attractive flakes or crystals. Some of the finest are French, e.g. from Guérande in Brittany and Noirmoutier, and some places on the Mediterranean coast; from Trapani in Sicily; from the coastal salt pans in Tunisia; from the *salinas* of Majorca; and from numerous sites in other continents. That of Maldon in England is also renowned.

Much sea salt is evaporated by artificial means. However, there are many places, especially in the Mediterranean region, where traditional techniques are used, the sea water being drawn into large shallow 'basins' and left to evaporate by the heat of the sun. As this process takes place, the salt formed on the bottom of the pans will be affected, often in colouring, by the nature of the clay or other substrate forming the bottom. Higher up in the layer of salt will be crystals which have not come into contact with the bottom and remain pure white; and it is these which constitute in France the more expensive *fleur de sel*.

What is usually called **table salt** is what is most used in kitchens (but see the next paragraph) or at table. This is a mass-produced, refined product which comes in very small grains, has been treated to ensure that it pours easily even in slightly damp conditions ('when it rains, it pours' was a slogan for one brand), and is sometimes iodized (i.e. iodine, a trace element which is lacking in some diets, has been added).

Salt in the kitchen may be of various kinds, often the same as table salt but in large or professional kitchens likely to be something of coarser texture—or indeed a small selection of different salts, since the various purposes for which salt is used in the kitchen do not all call for the same kind. One overriding rule, especially important at a time when people are advised to lower their intake of salt, is not to use too much at any stage in the preparation of a dish; and to remember that what is prescribed in older recipe books may be too much by more recent standards. Otherwise cooks have to profit from the numerous explanations and tips given in cookery books and from their own experience. Examples of specific points to bear in mind are:

- Salt added to raw ingredients will draw out moisture from them (sometimes desirable, sometimes not).
- A very small amount of salt can be used to enhance the sweetness of, for example, pineapple and grapefruit; and improves the flavour balance in sweet bakery goods such as cakes.
- Salt added to a liquid which will later be reduced will have a much stronger effect after the reduction.
- When considering whether or how much salt to add in the course of cookery, take account of any salty ingredients already present or likely to be added later (e.g. soy sauce).

Although salt is now readily available and inexpensive, it was formerly in some places a costly commodity which loomed large in the economic and political fabric of many cultures. Ayto (1993), having explained that the word for salt in most European languages (French *sel*, Spanish *sal*, German *Salz*, Russian *sol*') come from a single Indo-European root, points out that:

Its cultural centrality is hinted at by such linguistic relatives as English *salary*, which originated as a Latin term for an allowance given to soldiers to pay for salt, Russian *khleb-sol*', 'hospitality', which means literally 'bread-salt', and of course the English expressions *salt of the earth*, 'admired person' (a reference to the Sermon on the Mount, 'Ye are the salt of the earth,' Matthew, 5: 13).

There is a considerable literature on these aspects, and much has also been written on the technology from prehistoric times to the present, and on salt in religion and folklore. Multhauf (1978), who, following in the footsteps of a 19th-century German author whom he admired, devoted an entire book to the subject, especially the scientific and technological aspects, while disarmingly stating that his 'attempt to cover the subject in all times and places must be taken with a grain of salt', has probably done more than any other recent author towards this laudable aim.

OTHER SALT TERMS

BAY salt, a term now little used, meant sea salt (which in practice does usually come from a bay) produced by natural means, i.e. salt produced by the heat of the sun playing on sea-water in shallow basins or reservoirs. See Webster (1861). The bay originally intended by the term was Bourgneuf Bay, south of the mouth of the Loire River, where salt production dates back to the 14th century.

Black salt (*kala namak*) is a salt used in India which is brownish-black in lump form but pinkish-brown when powdered. It is liked for its special taste and what has been called a 'smoky aroma'.

Block salt, now rarely made, was made by pouring freshly evaporated and still hot crystalline salt into moulds, where the crystals stuck together to make blocks. For use, salt was grated off the blocks.

Gros sel is a French term for bay salt/sea salt.

Kosher salt, so called because it meets Jewish requirements, comes in large irregular crystals and has no additives. Readily available in N. America.

Pickling salt is designed for the purpose, dissolving quickly.

'Salt upon salt', in England in the 18th century, was an interesting curiosity. Rock salt mined in Cheshire was sent to the coast to be heated and dissolved in brine and then recrystallized.

SALT COD is COD which has been salted, usually dry salted (as opposed to being steeped in liquid brine), and then partially dried. After the salting, the water content of the fish will be just under 60%; after the drying, around 40%. (STOCKFISH is cod which has simply been dried, to the point where water content is around 15% and it is hard like a stick.) Depending on the degree of treatment, salt cod may have a white 'frost' of salt on it, or be creamy in colour.

	FRESH COD	SALT COD
French	cabillaud, morue fraîche	morue
Portuguese	bacalhau	bacalhau
Spanish	bacalao	bacalao
Italian	merluzzo	baccalà

One point which stands out from the table is that in some languages the same word is used for 'cod' and 'salt cod'. These are languages of people who do not have fresh cod swimming in their waters and who have a long tradition of eating salt cod. So far as they are concerned, cod *is* salt cod! That goes for the Portuguese and the Spaniards. The French are in a different position, since they have a N. Atlantic coast as well as a Mediterranean one, and it is in French that the greatest possibilities of confusion exist. They use the word *morue* for salt cod, but also speak of *morue fraîche*, which is fresh cod, and in the north they have a completely separate and different name for fresh cod, 'cabillaud'. The French also possess one of the best known of all salt cod dishes, *Brandade de morue* (see BRANDADE).

The Portuguese are the greatest enthusiasts for salt cod. They call it *fiel amigo* (faithful friend) and display great connoisseurship when visiting their special salt cod shops (e.g. in the rua do Arsenal in Lisbon, near the waterfront). Each such establishment will offer about a dozen different grades, and each has a fearsome guillotine-like contraption built into the serving counter, so that the merchant can slice off exactly the amount of the stiff unyielding stuff that the customer (of any class—salt cod knows no social barriers in Portugal) might want.

The Portuguese are not without competitors, such as Italians and Spaniards, and people in various parts of France, and the Caribbean islands and parts of S. America and Africa. But in many parts of the world salt cod arouses no emotion whatsoever and no one eats it (except for any immigrants of Portuguese or Spanish or Italian descent).

There are interesting historical reasons for all this. To set them out in full would involve the history of international and trade relations in the N. Atlantic over several centuries, the history of the Roman Catholic Church and its fast days, that of the slave trade and colonialism, that of shipbuilding and fishing gear, and also to some extent that of food conservation and cookery.

To be brief, both salt cod and stockfish have their origins in early medieval times. Europeans, belonging to the Catholic faith and observing meatless days, needed a lot of fish, and stockfish from Norway was a valuable commodity as far back as the 10th century. Really large supplies of cod off the N. American coast, especially on the Newfoundland Banks, had possibly been located even at that time by intrepid fishermen from Iceland and Norway, but it was only after Cabot 'discovered' Newfoundland in 1497 that Europeans— with Portuguese, Spanish, and French fishermen in the lead—began to exploit this resource seriously.

This plenitude of American cod represented great wealth for anyone who could get it back to Europe. Methods of conserving fish at that time were (1) dry-salting and drying; (2) salting in brine; (3) just drying; or (4) smoking. Method (2) suited fatty fish, but not cod. Method (3), used for producing stockfish in Norway, would not work on the damp and misty shores of Newfoundland. Method (4), by itself, has only a marginal effect on keeping qualities. So method (1) was adopted. The cod were beheaded, split along the belly, cleaned, and rid of their backbones (except for a small piece by the tail). Then they were stacked with layers of salt between them, and the salt began to extract the water from them and replace it. Later, they would be dried and would become the salt cod of commerce.

Technological advances have been made since the 16th century; but the basics are still the same, and so are the procedures by which the product is prepared for consumption. There are many different views about how much soaking in fresh water is needed for this purpose; but a middle-of-the-road position would be that it should soak for 18 hours, with three changes of water. The pieces are then scaled and cooked in any of several hundred ways. (An examination of books pertaining to salt cod in the National Library in Lisbon brought to light a remarkable compilation, already including over 100 recipes, by Febrósia Mimoso; but she was outdone by an anonymous work of 1927 which declared 'more than three hundred'.)
READING: Cutting (1955); Burgess *et al.* (1965).

SALTING as a means of preserving food (see also PRESERVATION), has been practised since antiquity. The salt most used is common SALT, sodium chloride, but saltpetre (see NITRATES AND NITRITES, which consists of potassium nitrate and sodium nitrate, has similar effects. For some purposes 'dry-salting' is appropriate, for others the use of brine, which is salt in solution.

In its role in PRESERVATION of foods, salt operates mainly by its effect on osmosis, which is the passage of water through 'semipermeable membranes' such as the cell walls of plant or animal tissue, living or dead. A semipermeable membrane lets water through but blocks the passage of the bigger molecules of substances dissolved in it. When such a membrane has a strong solution on one side and a weak one on the other, water is drawn through it in one direction only, from the weak solution to the strong one, which it dilutes. This pull is called 'osmotic pressure'.

Plant and animal cells contain relatively weak solutions of natural salts, sugars, and other dissolved substances. BACTERIA and other micro-organisms live comfortably in weak solutions of this sort, drawing in nutrients through the cell walls. If, however, these micro-organisms are exposed to a strong solution, such as one containing a lot of salt, the outward osmotic pressure created by the strong solution prevents them from feeding, and thus from reproducing. They may remain alive, and can return to normal functioning if the outside solution is diluted; but while the strong salt solution is present their activity is inhibited and the decay which they would otherwise cause is thus arrested.

However, decay is caused by ENZYMES naturally present in foodstuffs as well as by living micro-organisms. Salt also stops the working of enzymes by upsetting the electrical balance of the liquid in which they act. So a salt solution, if strong enough, will also prevent decay due to enzymes, and this can be observed when sliced apple is put in brine to stop it from browning.

The strength of the salt solution is important. Some micro-organisms can tolerate quite strong solutions. Among these are certain LACTIC ACID-producing bacteria which, rather than causing decay, bring about beneficial fermentations. For this reason, only a moderate amount of salt is used in some preparations, allowing these bacteria to grow while inhibiting others which would cause decay and which are less tolerant of salt. Examples are SAUERKRAUT, the KIMCH'I of Korea, SOY SAUCE, and other similar condiments. The lactic acid produced by the 'good' bacteria will itself be a safeguard against the growth of the 'bad' ones. Eventually the acid becomes so concentrated that even the 'good' bacteria are inhibited: fermentation stops and the food keeps.

Osmosis caused by salt is also exploited in the preparation of dry-salted foods such as dry salt fish and meat. The applied salt draws water out of the cells of the tissue, so that salt both speeds drying and suspends decay while the food is still sufficiently moist to be at risk. (See also DRYING.) The same effect is used when fresh cucumber is salted to make it a less watery salad ingredient; and to collapse the cells of aubergines before cooking them in oil, so that they will not absorb an excessive amount of oil.

TYPES OF SALT USED FOR PRESERVING
Purity is important. For example, extra pure pickling salt is sold, so that impurities will not cause discoloration in the pickles.

From the Middle Ages until well into the 19th century, the only fully satisfactory salt for curing meat and fish was considered to be bay salt, made by solar evaporation from sea water on the coasts of France and the Iberian peninsula, and valued for its good flavour as well as for its purity. The preference for bay salt, which would now be called sea salt, had another reason. Because the process of solar evaporation is slow, large crystals tend to be formed. These dissolve relatively slowly in any curing process, avoiding the risk of what is called 'salt burn', an unwelcome phenomenon which occurs when fine salt is used; this dissolves quickly and produces a sudden high concentration, which at once dehydrates the outer layers of the food, making them relatively impervious and denying the benefit of salting to the inner layers.

SALT PORK which is simply raw PORK preserved either with dry SALT or in brine, is sometimes called pickled pork. It was formerly an important staple of European and N. American kitchens.

Canning, freezing, and chilling have made brine unnecessary for preserving pork; when it is now prepared, it is because people have acquired a taste for it. This is not surprising, as salt meat has been prepared in Europe for at least 2,000 years and was known to both the civilized Romans and the supposedly barbarian Celts.

A major use of salt pork in the recent past was for provisioning ships. Thomas Bewick (1807) observed that pork 'takes salt better than any other kind [of meat], and consequently is capable of being preserved longer: it is therefore of great use in ships, and makes a principal part of the provisions of the British navy.'

Any part of the pig can be preserved with salt, and some products are so altered by the process and sought after for their own sake that they are known under specific names, such as BACON or HAM. Pork fat, too, is salted and kept for adding to stews and soups, especially in S. Europe, a practice which was also followed in Britain in the last century.

When fresh pork was commonly salted for PRESERVATION, either brine or dry salt was used according to the preference of the curer, and the meat was treated as soon as it was properly cooled after killing. The meat was cut into pieces weighing about 1 kg (2.25 lb). As is common with cured meat, saltpetre was added to the cure, giving the meat a pink colour; spices were also used to taste. Bay leaves, onions, cloves, and allspice were called for in a recipe from the southern USA. After a few days dry-salted pork produced brine simply by the action of salt drawing fluid out of the meat. The pork was kept submerged in the brine, usually packed in barrels, and large quantities were generally prepared, to provide a supply of meat to last some time. It was considered ready to use after about 12 days, and would keep for one to two years, depending on climate and the skill with which it was prepared. To cook it, the meat was simply simmered gently in water. Saltiness was reduced by soaking the meat before cooking and changing it during simmering if necessary.

Even now, lightly salted pork is still used for its good flavour in European peasant cookery. The cooked meat is served with mashed potatoes, cabbage, purées made from dried pulses or other vegetables, or put into composite dishes such as CASSOULET or POT-AU-FEU.   LM

SALTS a wide range of chemical compounds including common SALT. The scientific definition of a salt is a compound formed when the hydrogen of an ACID has been replaced by a metal; a rule is that when an acid reacts with an ALKALI the product is a salt plus water. For example, the formula of hydrochloric acid is HCl—one atom of hydrogen and one of chlorine. The acid reacts with sodium, Na, to make common salt or sodium chloride, NaCl. The hydrogen has been replaced by sodium. In this case the hydrogen is released as a gas. For an example of a reaction between an acid and a base, one may again take hydrochloric acid, this time reacting with caustic soda or sodium hydroxide, NaOH—one atom each of sodium, oxygen, and hydrogen. The reaction is:

$$HCl + NaOH \rightarrow NaCl + H_2O$$

Again, common salt is formed, leaving two atoms of hydrogen and one of oxygen, which form water, H_2O.

Things are not always that simple. Often only some of the hydrogen of the acid is replaced. The result is an 'acid salt' with some available hydrogen which has an acid effect when the salt is dissolved in water. An example is CREAM OF TARTAR (potassium hydrogen tartrate), whose formula is $C_4O_6H_5K$. K is the symbol for potassium.

Salts are conventionally named after the metal and the acid that could be used to make them; for example the hard mineral in bone, calcium phosphate, could be made by a reaction between calcium and phosphoric acid. The ending '-ide' denotes a compound of two elements only (such as sodium chloride); '-ate' means that some oxygen is present; '-ite' means that there is a smaller amount of oxygen. Any other extras are added to the name (as in potassium hydrogen tartrate). Making this scheme uniform has involved changing some of the traditional names of salts.

Other salts used in the kitchen include saltpetre (sodium or potassium NITRATE), BICARBONATE OF SODA (sodium hydrogen carbonate), alum (aluminium potassium sulphate, a 'double salt' containing two metals), and waterglass (sodium silicate), formerly used to seal the shells of eggs to make them keep longer. Sea salt is mostly sodium chloride but also contains magnesium chloride, magnesium sulphate (better known as Epsom salts), potassium sulphate, calcium carbonate (dissolved limestone), potassium bromide, and sodium bromide, among many other salts.   RH

SAMBAL the Indonesian/Malaysian word for a wide range of side dishes and CONDIMENTS, mostly hot and spicy. Some are uncooked, others are cooked.

The term can mean, specifically, a hot CHILLI condiment or sauce. Or it can mean (as in the phrase *sambal goreng*, fried sambal) the mixture of chillies and other spices fried together as the basis of a highly spiced savoury dish. In the broadest sense it can indicate any side dish (of meat, fish or vegetables) to accompany rice.

Finally, it sometimes refers to a main dish, for example *sambal goreng cumi-cumi*, which is squid in a sauce of the fried sambal referred to above.

The basic Indonesian sambal, in the first specific sense listed above, is *sambal ulek*, an uncooked mixture made by crushing chillies, with a little salt and some lime or lemon juice or vinegar, in a mortar with a pestle. *Sambal udang* contains in addition prawns or shrimps, *sambal terasi* (see BLACANG) includes a pungent shrimp paste, *sambal bajak* a combination of spices and other flavourings, etc.

The sambols of Sri Lanka are parallel preparations, thus defined by Chandra Dissanayake (1976): 'Any type of uncooked mixture containing vegetable, coconut or fruits with seasoning added. Other condiments may be used. Usually onions, chillies and some form of acid is used.' The name crops up elsewhere too with slightly different spellings but always recognizable. The Cape Malays were responsible for introducing their sambals into S. Africa, where they are an important part of Cape Malay cuisine and have evolved into some new forms suited to the different range of produce available there.

SAMBAR the name of the soupy dish or stew which (with many variations) is eaten all over the south of India, using *sambar podi/masala* as the spice mixture, see MASALA. It is usually fiery hot, because of the presence of red CHILLI pepper in this. It also contains black PEPPER, TURMERIC, CORIANDER seeds, FENUGREEK, CUMIN SEEDS, and also—an unexpected touch in a spice mixture—small amounts of DAL (split pea), e.g. *chana*, *urd*, and *arhar dal*.

SAMOSA (samoosa) are small, crisp, flaky pastries made in India, usually fried but sometimes baked. They are stuffed with a variety of fillings such as cheese, cheese and egg, minced meat with herbs and spices, vegetables such as potatoes, etc. Sweet fillings are also popular. Samosas are usually eaten as a snack, often as a street food.

The Indian version is merely the best known of an entire family of stuffed PASTRIES or DUMPLINGS popular from Egypt and Zanzibar to C. Asia and W. China. Arab cookery books of the 10th and 13th centuries refer to these pastries as *sanbusak* (the pronunciation still current in Egypt, Syria, and Lebanon), *sanbusaq*, or *sanbusaj*, all reflecting the early medieval form of this Persian word: *sanbosag*. Claudia Roden (1968) quotes a poem by Ishaq ibn Ibrahim al-Mausili (9th century) praising *sanbusaj*. An ancient and widespread recipe for the dough in both India and the Near East is: '1 coffee cup of oil, 1 coffee cup of melted butter, 1 coffee cup of warm water, 1 teaspoon of salt. Add and work in as much flour as it takes.'

In the Middle East the traditional shape of *sanbusak* is a half-moon, usually with edges crimped or marked with the fingernails; but triangular shapes are also used. In India triangular and cone-shaped samosas are popular. In Afghanistan, where the name is *sambosa*, and in the Turkish-speaking nations, where it is called *samsa* (and variants), it is made both in half-moon shapes and triangles.

Sedentary Turkish peoples such as the Uzbeks and the people of Turkey itself usually bake their *samsas*, but nomads such as the Kazakhs fry them. Occasionally *samsas* will be steamed, particularly in Turkmenistan.

These pastries were still made in Iran as late as the 16th century, but they have disappeared from most of the country today,

surviving only in certain provinces; e.g. the triangular walnut-filled *sambüsas* made in Larestan. However, the Iranians of C. Asia, the Tajiks, still make a wide range of *sanbusas*, including round, rectangular, and small almond-shaped ones.

In India, savoury samosas are usually served with a chutney of some sort. Sweet samosas are also popular, as in the Middle East. The usual Arab *sanbusak* is filled with meat, onions, and perhaps nuts or raisins, but *sanbusak bil loz* is stuffed with a mixture of ground almonds, sugar, and rose or orange blossom water. In Iraq and Arabia dates are a common filling; while in Afghanistan HALVA or raisins are often used.

In C. Asia, the versions made with rough puff pastry (*waraqi såmsa*, *sambusai varaqi*) are filled with meat. Those made with plain dough (leavened or unleavened) may be filled either with meat or other fillings such as diced pumpkin, chickpeas, herbs, wild greens, fried onions, mushrooms, or dried tomatoes.

The 'patties' of Sri Lanka and 'curry puffs' of Malaysia also derive from samosa and are variations on the same theme. CP/HS

SAMPHIRE the name of two species of plant which are often confused although not closely related. They have, however, characteristics in common, especially in appearance, and both are pickled for table use. Rock samphire, *Crithmum maritimum*, is the important one. It belongs to the Umbelliferae family along with celery, fennel, etc. Marsh samphire, *Salicornia europaea*, is a chenopodium (of the beet family) and is more available but less prized. If one comes across a reference to 'samphire' in an old cookery book (or indeed a modern one), it is sometimes difficult to tell which sort is meant. As Jane Grigson (1978) observed, it would have been a great convenience if everyone had agreed long ago to call marsh samphire by its alternative name glasswort (given because it used to be burned to provide alkali for glass-makers).

Rock samphire, also known as sea or true samphire, originated in the Mediterranean. The name 'samphire' (and its earlier versions, sampere and sampier) came from a French name *herbe de Saint-Pierre*. The French called it thus because it grows among the rocks and shingle of sea coasts and on cliffs, and therefore seemed to belong to the fisherman saint called Peter (*Petros* in Greek, meaning rock).

Rock samphire is a small woody shrub with long, thin, fleshy leaves which have a powerful resinous aroma, variously described as being reminiscent of varnish or sulphurous, but are nonetheless wholesome and appetizing. (Any undesirable smell or taste disappears when samphire is pickled

and it then makes a tasty relish for cold meats or salads.)

Both the Greeks and Romans used it in salads and also lightly steamed it to be eaten as a vegetable. Pliny (1st century AD) wrote that Theseus had a meal with samphire before leaving to fight the Minotaur.

Pickled samphire was once so popular and saleable in England that men risked their necks to collect it from the cliffs. Robert Turner wrote of samphire gathering on the cliffs of the Isle of Wight, in 1664, that it was 'incredibly dangerous . . . yet many adventure it, though they buy their sauce with the price of their lives'. Pamela Michael (1980) cites a 17th-century eulogy: 'of all the sawces (which are very many) there is none so pleasant, none so familiar and agreeable to Man's body as samphire.'

Rock samphire's popularity declined by the end of the 19th century due to its scarcity. Very often the inferior marsh samphire (see below) or perhaps golden samphire, *Inula crithmoides*, would be substituted.

Crithmum maritimum

Samphire leaves are best in spring, until early summer, before the plant flowers and when it is bright green and fresh. The raw plant's strange aroma is too strong for salads so it is best boiled briefly in water, drained, and butter added. Prepared in this way samphire marries well with fish. Davidson (1979) describes a simply made purée of samphire with butter as a fish sauce of good green colour.

Marsh samphire, as noted above, is also known as glasswort from its former use in soda glass manufacture. It and some close relations (hard to tell apart) are found near the sea, particularly around estuaries where all the mineral and trace elements are washed down from the highlands above. They are abundant in soda and were harvested, dried, and then burnt. Their ash (sometimes called barilla, the common name for one of them, *Salsola soda*) was used in the production of glass; hence the name 'glasswort'. In N. America the colloquial name 'chicken claws' is used for these plants.

Jane Grigson (1978) tells us that in Norfolk and Suffolk marsh samphire is boiled and eaten as a vegetable and regarded as a summer delicacy. She goes on to suggest: 'Boil it until just tender—better still, steam it—and serve it with melted butter or an hollandaise sauce.'

Marsh samphire is more salty than rock samphire and does not have the same powerful aroma.

The current French name for marsh samphire is *salicorne*, while rock samphire is *criste marine*. But there seems to have been confusion in France (as well as in Britain—and no doubt elsewhere) between the two samphires. Indeed, as Philip and Mary Hyman point out in *Le Patrimoine culinaire de la France: Pays de la Loire* (1993), both of these plants may also be designated by the name *perce-pierre* (literally 'pierce rock') which logically should refer to rock samphire, and at least one 18th-century French author describes *criste marine* as growing on the edge of marshes! In recent times marsh samphire has been sold by fishmongers as a vegetable (confusingly presented as a kind of 'seaweed'), but traditionally both samphires are pickled; as long ago as the beginning of the 17th century the author of the *Trésor de sante* (1607) described how *criste marine* (*perce-pierre*) was to be preserved in vinegar, in much the same way as nowadays.   (HS)
READING: Tee (1983).

SAMSOE the best known of Danish cheeses, has changed much since the islanders of Samsö won a reputation for cheese-making in the early Middle Ages. Denmark has long been a major producer and exporter of cheese, and has had an eye on world markets. In 1800 a landowner, Constantin Bruun, invited Swiss cheese-makers to his estate to make an Emmental-type cheese, which they did; and this was the origin of modern Samsoe. Over the years it has become much more like a Danish cheese than a Swiss one—softer and milder than its original, although a properly matured Samsoe can have quite a well-rounded flavour. It is made in broad wheels weighing about 14 kg (30 lb), and has largish holes or 'eyes' like those of the original Emmental.

SANDALWOOD a name of Indian origin, refers to various small trees and shrubs native to E. Indonesia, the Pacific islands and N. Australia. Most are of the genus *Santalum*, but the Australian genus *Eucarya* furnishes wood with a similar fragrance.

The trees are best known as the source of aromatic wood and roots, used as incense and for religious and medicinal purposes. They have fruits which are edible, but mostly without merit, although in some species the seed kernels constitute excellent nuts. These have a normal flavour, without the heavy fragrance of sandalwood, which would be unwelcome in a food.

In medieval Europe, a red (or, sometimes, yellow) food colour known as sanders was extracted from the wood. It seems to have been used almost exclusively for its colouring effect. The practice has continued in C. Europe, for example in the red Christmas biscuits (*Wygützli*) of Switzerland, and also the type of marzipan known as *Züri Leckerli*. See also NUT BISCUITS.

The S. Australian sandalwood tree, *Eucarya acuminata*, bears the QUANDONG or Australian peach, a fruit of some importance.

SAND-BUG also known as sea cicada, *Hippa asiatica*, an engaging little creature which looks something like a crab, a prawn, a beetle.

The sand-bugs, considered a delicacy in Thailand, are whitish-yellow in colour and measure from 3 to 6 cm (about 1–2"). They are best sought after high tide, when the waters have swept them up onto the beach; but they must be sought quickly, for their habit is to dig themselves holes in the wet sand and it is difficult to extract them from these. The island of Phuket is famous for them and people there proudly tell visitors that the royal family of Thailand order them for state banquets, even 20,000 at a time.

The head is cut off and the carapace removed, then the bodies are deep fried and served as crunchy little morsels with a sauce or with 'jungle honey' (i.e. honey gathered from the wild).

SAND CRAB a name which can be applied to any of the numerous species of CRAB which in any part of the world have a sandy beach as their habitat, but particularly applied in W. Africa to *Ocypoda africana*. This crab, whose carapace may measure 5 cm (2") across, lives in burrows in the sand, chiefly around the high-water mark. It excavates the burrow by moving sideways in the desired direction, pausing every now and then to whisk the excavated sand out of the opening, and sometimes to flatten the mound of sand thus produced outside. It

emerges at night to forage for food. It is a very alert creature and a rapid runner, so not easily caught, but is in demand, especially for the red eggs which females may have on the underside of their carapace.

SAND-EELS small silvery fish of the genera *Ammodytes* and *Gymnammodytes*, are widely distributed and numerous in the northern hemisphere, but commonly destined to furnish food for other fish, or to be turned into fish meal, rather than for human consumption.

In the N. Atlantic, *Ammodytes tobianus* is the common inshore species, while *A. marinus* is its offshore counterpart. Most authorities distinguish *A. americanus* as the N. American sand-eel. It belongs to the eastern seaboard; the corresponding species of the Pacific north-west is *A. hexapterus*, with a range extending as far as Japan.

The main species in the Mediterranean, where it seems to be confined to the northern coasts only, is *Gymnammodytes cicerelus*.

It used to be the practice to call the smaller ones sand-lances. Whatever their size, these fish have one habit in common, which is to bury themselves in the sand for protection. Their lancelike form enables them to burrow rapidly downwards for a foot or more, often in the intertidal zone, and there they will stay for hours on end.

At one time there was a vogue for 'fishing' for them with special rakes at Portobello near Edinburgh and in SW England, where they abounded. Certainly, they were more often cooked in the 19th century than now. Eliza Acton (1855) observed that:

The common mode of dressing the fish, which is considered by many a great delicacy, is to divest them of their heads, and to remove the insides with the gills, to dry them well in a cloth with flour, and to fry them until crisp. They are sometimes also dipped in batter like smelts.

SANDESH a Bengali speciality, esteemed as the finest of INDIAN SWEETS. The name originally meant 'news', referring to the custom of sending sweets by messenger to one's friends and relatives when enquiring for their news, with which the messenger would return. The Bengali word *tattura* also means 'presents of sweets'.

There are innumerable types of sandesh, but all are made from the same basic mixture of pressed curd and sugar or syrup cooked together, sugar being preferred as giving a better flavour. The more curd in the mixture the finer the quality, so that the best sandesh, with four times as much curd as sugar, are less sweet than cheaper types with up to twice that proportion of sugar. The mixture takes on a texture like that of fudge.

It may be stuffed, for example with a mixture of *khoya* (condensed milk, see MILK REDUCTION) and nuts. Often it is pressed into decorative shapes in small wooden moulds; otherwise simply cut into pieces. Some kinds of sandesh are named for their shape: *gutke* (flat ended) or *badam takti* (*takti* means lozenge shaped; *badam*, the 'Indian almond'—see MYROBALAN—used in the mixture). They may be pressed in the shape of fruits, with which they are flavoured and whose name they bear: for example, *am sandesh* is flavoured with preserved mango and shaped like a mango, and there are also *ata* (custard apple) and *kamranga* (sour plum) sandesh. Other sandesh are stamped with, and named for, mottoes, proverbs, and the like: *sukhe theko* ('God bless you'), *pati param guru* ('the husband is the wife's guru') are examples. In British India English mottoes were common: 'forget me not' and even 'God save the King'.

SANDWICH a term, and indeed an object, whose origin is generally attributed to John Montagu, the 4th Earl of Sandwich, who according to the *NSOED* is 'said to have eaten food in this form so as to avoid having to leave the gaming table'. Ayto (1993) cites a work of 1770, *Londres*, by the author Grosley in support of this view, and remarks that the first use of the word in print occurs in the journal of Edward Gibbon for 24 November 1762, when he had dinner at an establishment which he regarded as 'truly English' and was able to observe numerous important contemporaries supping off cold meat 'or a Sandwich'.

Sandwiches take so many forms in the modern world, including double- and triple-deckers, the open sandwiches typical of Scandinavia (and their miniature versions known as CANAPÉS), and legions of toasted sandwiches, that a catalogue would be a book. Some which are of special interest, for whatever reason, are:

- The **Reuben sandwich,** a New York Jewish creation, combining CORNED BEEF and EMMENTAL with SAUERKRAUT on sourdough PUMPERNICKEL bread, the whole being grilled. Evan Jones (1981) discusses rival theories about its origin, one of which takes it back to 1914 (when an actress in a Charlie Chaplin film supposedly ate the first Reuben special, but with Virginia baked ham instead of corned beef) whereas the national Kraut Packers Association supports the view that a grocer called Reuben Kay, taking part in a weekly poker game in Omaha as recently as 1955, was the true inventor.
- A **club sandwich** (first appeared in print 1903, in a book called *Conversations of a Chorus Girl*) is usually a three-decker toast affair, with chicken, mayonnaise, lettuce, tomato, and bacon. Some believe that it was originally only a two-decker, perhaps matching the two-decker 'club cars' running on US railroads from 1895.
- The **BLT** (bacon, lettuce, and tomato) is another popular and long-established item in N. America, and also wherever Americans go, which is everywhere.
- The **Dagwood,** named for the sort of colossal over-stuffed and many-layered sandwich which the famous comic strip character of that name, in the strip called *Blondie,* favoured. From 1936 onwards, but in its early days not as huge as it became.
- The **submarine** of the southern states of the USA is a long and substantial cylindrical sandwich, consisting of a French bread generously filled with various savoury ingredients. It can be called just 'sub' or 'torpedo', or (especially in New Orleans) a 'poor boy' (because hearty fare for the impoverished).
- Hot roast beef sandwiches are a well-known example of the hot sandwich available in American delis.
- **Butties** and **sarnies** are English slang terms for sandwiches, the former north country and long established, the latter more recent. In terms of gentility a Liverpool chip butty is at the opposite end of the spectrum from the decorous and delicate little cucumber sandwiches which appear on British afternoon tea tables.

Fernie (1905) had a remarkable knack for picking up amusing and arresting anecdotes or quotations to enliven what he wrote about foods. Here are three examples from his entry on Sandwich.

- [From *The Pickwick Papers*] 'What are all them clerks eating Sandvidges for?' asked Mr Weller, senior, of his son, Sam, when they went together to the Will Office, at the Bank of England. 'Cos it's their dooty, I suppose,' replied Sam; 'it's a part o' the system: they're allvays a-doin' it here, all day long.'
- Some remarkable Sandwiches were lately recorded (by Dr J. Johnston) as having been made with satisfactory effect of cottonwool, for a patient who accidentally swallowed his false teeth through being struck in the face by a wave whilst swimming in the open sea. He was treated with Sandwiches containing a thin layer of cotton-wool in each, between the slices of bread and butter; and after a week, when a mild laxative was given, the dental structure, being now enrolled in cotton-wool, was passed without difficulty amongst the excrement.
- [From *Alice through the Looking Glass*] . . . the White Knight had a little box 'of his own invention,' to keep clothes and Sandwiches in, 'You see,' he told Alice, 'I carry it upside down so that the rain can't get in.' 'But the things can get out,' Alice gently remarked; 'do you know the lid's open?'

However, it may be that Sheila Hutchins (1967) has the honour of recording an even greater oddity:

Probably none . . . was so strange as that sandwich well-known in the early 19th century and invented by a 'frail, fair one—the famous Mrs Sawbridge, we believe—who to show her contempt for an elderly adorer, placed the hundred pound note, which he had laid upon her dressing table, between two slices of bread and butter, and ate it as a sandwich.'

SANSHO (or Japanese prickly ash), *Zanthoxylum piperitum,* a deciduous spiny shrub, grows wild throughout Japan and in N. Korea and parts of China. The Japanese also cultivate it at home for culinary purposes, especially the preparation of the spice called sansho. The orange-coloured berries are harvested and dried in the sun and ground to make this. The bitter, black seeds inside are better discarded before the grinding. Sometimes the powder is combined with ordinary black pepper.

The spice has been called 'Japanese pepper' but its flavour is tangy rather than hot, and it has a slightly numbing effect in the mouth. Sansho is used in Japanese cooking to add a sharp note to fatty foods, eels for example. Other uses include the preparation of *kiri-sansho,* the cake which is a speciality of Tsuruoka. The sansho powder is blended with flour and kneaded into a cake.

Pestles made of prickly ash are highly valued because the extreme hardness of the wood gives them a long life and does not impart any flavour to what is being ground.

In spring the young leaf shoots are used to garnish all kinds of food. The leaves may also be boiled with meat or fish to suppress strong smells; added fresh to various dishes as a flavouring; or preserved by boiling down with sugar, soy sauce, and water.

Two minor related species are also used as spices. *Z. armatum* (=*Z. alatum*) is winged prickly ash, whose seeds may be met in various parts of Asia, sometimes as 'Chinese pepper', and are used in Nepal as *timur* to impart a minty flavour to dishes. *Z. planispinum* has peel which is used as a spice. But the important relation is *Z. simulans,* which is SICHUAN PEPPER.

If only to forestall confusion, mention should also be made here of *Z. rhetsa,* often called Indian pepper, or lemon pepper, or, in Nepal, *timur,* whose bark and unripe fruits are used as a sharp flavouring which has citrus overtones. It is also necessary to note that this species and both Japanese prickly ash and the Sichuan pepper plant were formerly classified in the genus *Fagara*, and that this obsolete classification seems to have given rise to the use of a vernacular name 'fagara' for sansho or its relations. Such usage is now seen to be inappropriate but survives in some older books.

SANTOL *Sandoricum koetjape* (formerly *S. indicum*), a fruit tree of Malaysia and elsewhere in SE Asia, which also grows in Mauritius.

It grows fast and produces an abundance of round fruits which have a tough, yellowish-brown rind enclosing five segments of white pulp. This is eaten fresh, dried, or candied, or (as in Thailand) pickled. Filipinos seem to be the greatest enthusiasts for santol, and are breeding trees of superior quality.

SAPODILLA sapotilla, sapodilla plum, sopota, zapote, chico sapote, chiku/ciku, naseberry, and even tree potato, are all names for the fruit of *Manilkara zapota*, a medium-sized evergreen tree native to Mexico and C. America. The Aztec name *zapotl* gave rise to the whole group of names such as zapote and sapodilla, the wide use of which can be confusing: see SAPOTA.

The tree, which also produces the gum chicle, from which CHEWING GUM is made, was cultivated in the region long before the arrival of the Spaniards. Lintels made from its timber have been found in Mayan ruins dating from about AD 470. The Spaniards liked the fruit and introduced it to the Philippines, whence it spread gradually through SE Asia, reaching India in the 19th century. Cultivation began in Australia more recently.

The fruit is a round or oval berry between 5 and 10 cm (2–4") in diameter, with a rough brown skin. It must be eaten ripe, since latex and tannin present in the unripe fruit give it an unpleasantly astringent taste. As the fruit ripens, on or off the tree, its skin becomes less rough and hard, and reveals a yellow colour when scratched, instead of the green which unripe fruit would show. The flesh is also yellow-brown, or pinkish-brown, with a soft, translucent juicy pulp containing large, flat, black seeds which are easy to remove. The aspect of the interior resembles that of a pear, except for the seeds seeming bigger. The French botanist Descourtilz described it as having 'the sweet perfumes of honey, jasmine, and lily of the valley'. Another comparison is with brown sugar. The ripe fruit may also have a slightly granular texture, reminiscent of half-dissolved sugar.

The sapodilla is usually eaten raw, though in the W. Indies it may be boiled down to make a syrup. Some prefer to eat it when

thoroughly overripe, like a MEDLAR. This is reflected in the name 'naseberry' from the Spanish *níspola* (medlar) and in the French *nèfle d'Amérique* (American medlar).

SAPOTA or sapote, is the Anglicized form of the Latin American name *zapote*. These names are applied to numerous American tropical fruits, of which some but not all are related to each other within the family Sapotaceae. The word was taken up by the Spanish in Mexico from the local term *tzicozapotl* or *tzapotl*.

The best-known fruit in the group, SAPODILLA (see above), is sometimes called just 'sapote'. It belongs to the genus *Manilkara*.

Some other sapotes belong to the related genus *Pouteria*. *P. sapota* bears large fruit: generally oval in shape, from 8 to over 20 cm (3 to 8") long, with a rough, russet-coloured rind, and a soft, sweet, salmon-coloured pulp which is generally made into jam. The species is found in the wild from S. Mexico to northern Nicaragua, but has been brought under cultivation in a much wider area, including parts of SE Asia. There are a number of named cultivars.

This fruit is sometimes called 'mamey/ mammee sapote', 'mamey colorado', 'chicomamey', or plain 'mamey', but is not to be confused with the unrelated MAMEE.

The names 'white sapota', 'zapota blanco', and 'Mexican apple', are applied to *Casimiroa edulis*, not a member of the family Sapotaceae but distantly related to the citrus fruits. It is grown in C. America and Mexico. The small, pale yellow fruit has the flavour of a ripe pear.

Quararibea cordata, called 'sapote' or 'chupa chupa', is another unrelated fruit grown in Peru and Colombia. It is oval, about 13 cm (5") long, with a flavour between that of an apricot and a mango.

'Black sapote' is a name sometimes given to what is really a black PERSIMMON.

SAPPAEN an interesting cornmeal 'mush and milk dish' prepared for the evening meal by Dutch settlers in New York state, as vividly described in a manuscript notebook by Rufus A. Grider, a teacher and artist of the Mohawk Valley, quoted in Peter Rose's *The Sensible Cook* (1989) and here given in a slightly edited form:

Until about 1830 to 1840 the inhabitants of the rural districts of Schoharie—which were settled by the Dutch and Germans—ate their meals from a large pewter dish placed by the housewife in the center of a round top table [an example of such a 'top table' measured 20.5" in diameter]. . . Mush was prepared in the fall and winter of the year. It was boiled in the afternoon and about one hour before mealtime poured from the iron pot into the pewter dish and set in a cold place; cooling stiffens it. Near meal time the house wife made as many

excavations as there were guests—piling or heaping up the centre, and filling the hollows with COLD MILK . . .—as many pewter table spoons as milk ponds were supplied. After Grace was said by the head of the family, everyone began to diminish the bank and increase the size of his white lake by feeding on its banks and centre—but there were limits, and beyond those no one could go—if for instance any one tapped his neighbors milk pond it was ill manners—if children did so, the penalty was finger clips.

Rose quotes other sources to show how sappaen was an integral part of the Dutch/American diet, along with CRULLERS, Dutch pickled meats, TRIPE dishes and 'Kool Slaa Heet en Koud' (COLESLAW, hot or cold).

SAPS defined by the *NSOED* as 'the fluid, chiefly water with dissolved sugars and mineral salts, which circulates in the vascular system of a plant and is essential to its growth'. As one would expect, the sap of many trees and smaller plants can provide nutritious food for animals, birds, and humans. This is mainly in the form of sugar syrups, several of which may be made into beverages, non-alcoholic or fermented to become alcoholic (e.g. palm toddy).

MAPLE SYRUP is perhaps the most prominent example; this is obtained from at least half a dozen maple species. The black birch, *Petula lenta*, is a source of BIRCH SUGAR.

Many palm trees (see PALM; PALMYRA PALM; PALM SUGAR) are frequently tapped, using complex techniques which have evolved over many centuries, to yield their sap and the valuable products which are obtained from it. Corner (1966) comments that the Chilean wine palm, *Jubaea spectabilis*, has been so heavily exploited to satisfy the thirst for its *miel de palma* that stocks have been greatly depleted. (The same author provides a fascinating and detailed account of the mechanics of the sap flow in palm trees.)

SAPUCAYA NUT sometimes spelled 'sapucaia' and also called paradise nut, is among the best nuts in the world, but available only in Brazil and Guyana. It comes from trees of the genus *Lecythis*. The main species is *L. sabucajo*, but there are scores of others, all natives of the same region and generally known as monkey pot nuts (see below).

The genus is closely related to that of the BRAZIL NUT, and the largest trees are almost as tall as the huge Brazil nut tree. However, a significant difference in their containers has made it impossible to market sapucaya nuts commercially, despite their excellence. Like Brazil nuts they are encased in a big, round, woody container, but that of the sapucaya has a detachable base or 'lid'. Whereas the whole container of the Brazil nut falls bodily off the tree, only the lid of the sapucaya comes away, allowing the nuts within to fall out singly or to be picked out by monkeys and parrots, who also compete, indeed fight, for those which fall to the ground. Since monkeys can run faster than people, and parrots can fly, human collectors get only a few nuts. These are eaten locally, either as dessert nuts or in chocolate and confectionery.

Sapucaya nuts are almond shaped, and measure up to 5 cm (2") long. The frail, brown shell is marked with longitudinal ridges, sometimes having a whitish aril (seed coat) fixed to one end. The oil content is high, giving them a soft texture. The flavour is delicate and distinctive.

The nuts must be eaten soon after they fall from the tree, since otherwise they would turn rancid. The empty container will itself drop off the tree after a time. It is called a 'monkey pot', hence the name 'monkey pot trees'. The pots are used as monkey traps, having been baited with some grains of maize and then fixed to e.g. fence posts. The idea is that a monkey inserts its hand, clenches it around the maize, and then cannot withdraw its clenched fist. Rather than let go of the maize it panics and remains stuck until the farmer finds it and kills it.

Although there is no trade in sapucaya nuts, Brazilians with gardens often grow trees for their own use, or for that of bees; the flowers of the tree make good honey.

SARDI/GARMI literally cold/hot, refers to the Persian system (dating back at least to pre-medieval times and still current in Iran and Afghanistan) of classifying foods and human temperaments for the purpose of optimizing diet. This may be seen as a simplified version of the FOUR HUMOURS, the system associated with the Greek writer GALEN. It certainly seems to have reached Persians through Arabic translations of Galen in the 9th century AD.

Although sardi/garmi does not match the system of the four humours in all particulars, it has shown greater powers of survival. This may be partly because it is less complicated. Jill Tilsley-Benham (1986b), whose lively essay on sardi/garmi is the best exposition of the subject in English, looked outside Iran to see how the same tradition, transmitted from Arabic sources, had faired elsewhere. She writes:

How then, has the humoral system fared in Arab lands? The only concrete evidence that I could find was in Iraq and Morocco—two countries whose antique cuisines closely identify with pre-Islamic Persia. Many Iraqis still talk of certain foods in terms of *harr* (Hot), and *bared* (Cold), but it is folk memory rather than serious practical

application, that keeps the tradition alive. In Morocco, on the other hand, *es-sxun* (Hot) and *el-berd* (Cold), remain an integral part of daily life, and it was through Moorish-influenced Spanish and Portuguese physicians that humoral theory reached South America, where *caliente/frio* is still popular today. Spanish explorers are credited with having taken it to the Philippines as well, but it would seem more likely that Muslim missionaries, who converted the island people some three hundred years before, were those responsible.

To determine whether survivals of the humoral doctrine around the world represent the quaternary Galenic tradition or the binary Persian derivative may not always be clear, and is anyway a subject which awaits study. But it would be a reasonable hypothesis to suppose that it is normally the binary system which has survived, at least for practical purposes. If this is correct, it would give added significance to sardi/garmi, which would be seen to be the earliest and original binary system.

Jill Tilsley-Benham's paper is embellished by numerous real-life examples of how the sardi/garmi doctrine is followed in Iran and she also explains that although not everyone agrees on the division of certain foods into 'hot' and 'cold' there was a definite pattern:

Garmi foods appeared to be distinguished mainly by their sweetness, richness, warmth of aroma and high calorie content—qualities which can be present singly or in combination. Sugar, honey, fats and oils were top of our 'hot list', followed (but in no particular order) by dried fruits such as raisins, dates and white mulberries. . . . Then came nuts, and some of the sweeter fruits and vegetables—especially those from tropical lands, like bananas, yams and coconuts. This agrees, of course, with Hippocrates' theory that hot countries generate hot foods, hot people and hot diseases. After this we listed garlic and onions (but not the spring variety), spices (again the product of sultry climes) and such sweetly aromatic herbs as mint, tarragon, basil and fenugreek. (The only cold herbs mentioned were parsley and green coriander . . .) Meat, from the ultra-rich camel's hump to rabbit . . . is garmi too; with veal as the possible exception. . .

. . . Sardi . . . is characterised by sourness (vinegar and acidic fruits), blandness and, to some extent, pallor (milk, yoghurt, rice, white fish), high water-content (cucumber, water-melon, lettuce) and a low-to-moderate calorie count.

SARDINE a group of fish found all round the world, all belonging to one subfamily in the highly complex group of clupeoid fish (in which there are over 300 species altogether). As so often happens, the common name does not exactly match scientific classifications; but in this instance it is not far out. Most fish in the genera *Amblygaster*, *Sardina*, *Sardinops*, and *Sardinella* are called sardine (that is, if they are called by any English name); and the name is rarely used of any other fish.

There is sometimes confusion between sardine and **pilchard.** The short answer is that a sardine is a young pilchard and a pilchard a grown-up sardine. However, it is necessary to add that pilchard refers to a fully grown specimen of only one species, *Sardina pilchardus*, which has a range extending further north than other sardines, indeed not only to the south of England (where the pilchard fishery is important) but far beyond, even to Norway. However, as noted below, the name pilchard is also used of a Japanese species.

Sardines of the Mediterranean and Atlantic are:

- *Sardina pilchardus*, mentioned above; maximum length 25 cm (10"); some authors recognize two subspecies, *S. pilchardus pilchardus* and *S. pilchardus sardina*; range of the former from Gibraltar to Bergen, range of the latter from the Black Sea to Gibraltar and south to Senegal.
- *Sardinella maderensis*, the 'Madeiran sardinella', French *grande allache*; maximum length 30 cm (12"); range throughout the S. Mediterranean and down the African coast to Angola.
- *Sardinella aurita*, the 'round sardinella', French *allache*; maximum length 30 cm (12"); range from the Black Sea (occasionally) throughout the Mediterranean and in the E. Atlantic from Cadiz south to S. Africa; also in a slightly different form (classified by some as *S. brasiliensis*) in the W. Atlantic from Cape Cod down to Argentina; also in the W. Pacific from Japan to the Philippines.

The sardines of the Indo-Pacific are numerous and some of them have remarkably limited ranges, for example *S. hualiensis*, which is more or less confined to Taiwan and a small section of the coast of China. The strangest of all is *S. tawilis*, a freshwater species occurring only in Lake Bombon in the Philippines. The commercially important species include:

- *S. brachysoma*; the 'deep-body sardinella'; standard length 12 cm (5"); important in Indonesia, but found elsewhere also.
- *S. gibbosa*, the 'goldstripe sardinella'; standard length 15 cm (6"); has a thin yellow line along its side; range all the way round from E. Africa to NW Australia.
- *S. longiceps*, the 'Indian oil sardine'; standard length 20 cm (8"); the most important and abundant clupeoid fish in Indian waters, which may account in some years for 30% of the entire catch of marine fish.
- *Sardinops melanosticus*, the 'Japanese pilchard'; standard length to 24 cm (9.5"); one of the most important commercial fishes of Japan.

The name *poutine* in the south of France refers to larval sardines or anchovies.

Fresh sardines are excellent when grilled. They may also be fried, but possess plenty of oil themselves; so deep-frying is preferable to pan-frying. For a remarkable west of England dish which was originally made with pilchards, see STARGAZEY PIE.

Canned sardines are among the few canned products which have their own retinue of connoisseurs (and vintage years). Competition is intense between e.g. French, Spanish, and Portuguese producers. Elizabeth David (1984) has a fine essay on the subject, focused on the sardine-canning industry of Nantes in France. The book by Bonnadier (1994) provides a wider survey, covering both fresh and canned sardines and including almost 100 pages of history, lore, poetry, and so on; one of the most extensive treatments of its kind of any fish.

SARSAPARILLA an extract from the roots of various C. American plants of the genus *Smilax*, especially *S. officinalis* and *S. rotundifolia*, used as a bitter ingredient in soft drinks. The plants are prickly, creeping shrubs.

The name comes from the Spanish words *zarza* (bramble) and *parilla* (little vine). It was bestowed by the Spaniards when they arrived in C. America, found the product already in use, and took it up themselves, mainly for medicinal use. During the rise of the soft drinks industry in the USA in the second half of the 19th century, it was customary to claim health-giving properties for the drinks, and many of them were based on or named for sarsaparilla, which was thought to be beneficial. Research in the 20th century has established that sarsaparilla contains certain saponins, a group of substances of which some have medical significance, but that those present in sarsaparilla are responsible for the bitter flavour and do not promote health.

The related *S. china*, China root, provides a sarsaparilla in Asia; and other plants in the genus fill a similar role elsewhere or have other minor uses as food.

SASHIMI a Japanese term for a dish of sliced raw fish. The word is derived from *sashi* (to pierce) and *mi* (flesh), with no element specifying fish or seafood; and similar techniques can be used to produce dishes called sashimi chicken or beef, but these are rarities by comparison with the ubiquitous fish sashimi. Tsuji (1980) has declared sashimi to be 'the crowning glory of the formal meal' in Japan (by which he does not mean that it comes at the end, for it is usually served at an early stage), and emphasizes that its preparation is not just a

matter of choosing supremely fresh fish but also of taking into account the seasons at which the various species are at their best.

Sashimi is presented with great elegance in an arrangement which often incorporates a bed of shredded white RADISH (daikon) and a mound of finely grated WASABI, plus a dipping sauce (SOY SAUCE with added flavours) and further garnishes such as SHISO leaves, sprigs of prickly ash (the SANSHO plant), or thin curled strips of the red stems of CORKWING (*bofu*).

The slices of fish are normally around 1 cm (0.25–0.5") thick, but for certain species or presentations paper-thin slices are preferred. Factors such as the thickness of the slices affect other features such as the composition of the dipping sauce; a citrus fruit and soy sauce called *ponzu* is a favourite with very thin slices.

SASSAFRAS *Sassafras albidum*, a common tree of the eastern USA, from Maine down to Florida, which yields a fragrant volatile oil used as a flavouring and perfume. All parts of the tree have been used for flavouring, but the bark of the root contains the highest concentration of oil.

Before the arrival of European settlers in America, the Indians chewed the root. Spanish colonists arriving in Florida in 1512 attributed restorative virtues to sassafras and British colonists in Virginia (then including New England) also raved about its virtues. Euell Gibbons (1962) quotes extensively and entertainingly from such sources before going on to explain that, although sassafras was used as a lure to bring Europeans across the Atlantic in search of their fortunes, it was so common that it never attained a high value.

Sassafras tea, a brew of a deep red colour, was enjoyed in the southern states. Fernald and Kinsey (1943) cited from the *American Botanist* (1907) a powerful rebuttal of the idea which had evidently been aired by someone that during the Civil War sassafras tea was drunk in the south because ordinary tea was not available. Not so, declared the Alabama doctor who administered the correction:

it was used from choice and a taste long cultivated. Long before the war, both whites and Indians made sassafras tea during the spring when the sap of the sugar maples was running. They boiled the sap a while then added the sassafras roots and boiled them a while longer and the tea was finished and a drink fit for the gods was the result.

Sassafras jelly, made from the tea, is sometimes served with meat. Sassafras tea was also drunk in Britain in the 19th century.

Sassafras leaves contain not only sassafras flavour but also a gummy mucilage. They are dried and powdered to make FILÉ.

SATAY OR SATÉ, a dish of SE Asia, especially Indonesia, Malaysia, and Thailand, which consists of small strips of meat, chicken, or fish threaded on to thin skewers (usually bamboo) and grilled (US broiled). The loaded skewers are often marinated before being grilled. Marinades vary from place to place but typically include dark SOY SAUCE with lime juice, sugar, garlic, and other seasoning. The common accompaniment for satay is a dipping sauce based on peanuts, pale brown in colour. But other sauces may be used.

Balls of minced meat, appropriately spiced, can be used on satay skewers instead of the more common strips of meat.

Satay has achieved wide popularity in other parts of the world, which adds interest to the question of its origin. Jennifer Brennan (1988) says that:

Although both Thailand and Malaysia claim it as their own, its Southeast Asian origin was in Java, Indonesia. There satay was developed from the Indian kebab brought by the Muslim traders. Even India cannot claim its origin, for there it was a legacy of Middle Eastern influence.

In the 19th century the term migrated, presumably with Malay immigrants, to S. Africa, where it appears as *sosatie*.

SAUCES fall into various categories. What might be called 'composed sauces', i.e. composed in the kitchen and served with a dish, are essential to classical French cuisine and, more generally, are important in adding palatability to numerous dishes throughout the western world. But these sauces have few counterparts in the rest of the world; thus in Asia it is more usual to find that what fills the role of a sauce is part of the dish itself (e.g. curries), or that it is a condiment such as the SE Asian fish sauces.

Even within the category of composed sauces there are vast differences. Some are simple mixtures of ingredients (e.g. PESTO, ROMESCO, SKORTHALIA). Others require cooking, sometimes in two stages. Basics (STOCK, FUMET, GLACE DE VIANDE, ESPAGNOLE) are prepared first, and always on hand in professional kitchens on the French model. These lead to 'mother' sauces such as BÉCHAMEL and HOLLANDAISE; mothers because in a third stage they have offspring such as sauce mornay (cheese sauce) from béchamel and MOUSSELINE from hollandaise. Family trees can be constructed, into which all recorded composed sauces will fit, but contemplation of them is tedious.

English cookery of the traditional and simple sort is not strong on sauces. The Frenchman who alleged that there was only one, 'drawn butter', by which he meant melted butter with a dusting of flour in it, was exaggerating, but in a venial way. A tour of England in the mid-20th century would have revealed that bread sauce (for chicken), parsley sauce (for fish), and cheese sauce (for macaroni) were quite common. These are all delicious when well made; see for example Fernie (1905) on bread sauce. All are essentially versions of the WHITE SAUCE which had been an economical alternative for the more expensive drawn butter. On the sweet side, the British are partial to CUSTARD sauce. There is also the solid 'sauce' known as 'hard sauce' and associated particularly with Cumbria and with CHRISTMAS PUDDING. It is made with butter, sugar and (usually) brandy or rum, and has been adopted in the USA since the 1880s.

See also AÏOLI; AVGOLÉMONO; BÉARNAISE SAUCE; BORDELAISE; BROWN SAUCE; BROWN SAUCES; CHOCOLATE SAUCE; CUMBERLAND SAUCE; GRAVY; MAYONNAISE; MOLE; RAGÚ; RAVIGOTE; ROUILLE; TARATOR; TRAVELLING SAUCE; VELOUTÉ, VINAIGRETTE; WHITE SAUCE.

SAUERKRAUT because the name is German (although now adopted into English too), is usually supposed to be a German invention of considerable antiquity. In fact, it appears to have evolved gradually from earlier forms of pickled cabbage, and not to have attained its present style until the 17th century.

The history of PICKLES goes back to the 3rd century BC, but all early pickles were 'wet' types made with brine or other liquids. The distinguishing features of sauerkraut are that it is dry salted, all the liquid in the resulting product being drawn out of the cabbage itself by the salt, and that it is preserved and flavoured by fermentation. The Romans had introduced dry vegetable fermentation with their development of silage as cattle feed, but the process was not extended beyond this for many centuries.

So, although the Romans ate quantities of cabbage and liked pickles, they did not combine these two predilections into sauerkraut, but instead preserved cabbage in sour wine, vinegar, and VERJUICE, with the addition of salt, sometimes in very large amounts.

This continued into the Middle Ages. Medieval pickled cabbage often had to be rinsed to remove the salt to make it edible. In the highly acid and salty liquid, the cabbage was preserved but did not ferment. However, the German name *Sauerkraut* and the French *choucroute* (a corruption of the German) were already in use, and stuck when the technique changed.

The first description of a naturally acidified product is in *Le Tresor de santi* (1607), which describes it as German. The cabbage was shredded and packed in layers with salt, JUNIPER and BARBERRIES, PEPPER, and spices. The layers were pressed down firmly and the crock topped up with brine.

In 1772 the third edition of James Lind's famous *Treatise of the Scurvy* describes a Dutch method for producing *zoorkool*. Essentially it is the same as the German method, but no brine is added. The cabbage instead is kept under constant pressure by means of a weight so that its juice is squeezed out, and the salt also helps to extract it.

It is by this method that sauerkraut is made now. Berries and spices are usually omitted. However, there are some unusual Russian and Balkan sauerkrauts tinted amber with QUINCE and pink with BEETROOT. (Beets for making BORSHCH are also preserved on their own by a similar process.)

Since the classical period, cabbage had been credited with health-giving properties, and sauerkraut was no exception. It was, quite rightly, supposed to prevent scurvy, and we now know that acidity preserves much of the vitamin C originally in the fresh cabbage. At the same time as Lind was writing of *zoorkool*, Captain Cook was persuading his sailors to eat 'sour crout', though not without difficulty. He ate in their own mess, making a pointed show of appreciating the food, for he knew their instinctive dislike for anything 'out of the Common way, altho it be ever so much for their good', but that when 'their Superiors set a Value on it, it becomes the finest stuff in the World'.

At its simplest, sauerkraut is made with just two ingredients, hard white cabbage and salt. The dirty and damaged outer leaves are removed and the cabbage washed and sliced. The slices are then packed into a crock, which may first be lined with whole clean leaves. The shreds are packed in layers which are salted (other flavourings being added if desired) before the next layer is applied. Even distribution of salt is vital. There must be between 1.5% and 4% salt by weight in the mixture, 2.25% being ideal. When the crock is about two-thirds full a cloth is laid over the surface and covered with a wooden disc which is weighted to press it down. This arrangement presses the cabbage to help squeeze out the juice, which is also extracted by the salt, and the cloth also excludes air, for the fermentation is anaerobic (airless) and contamination by aerobic (air-breathing) organisms must be avoided. The crock is then set in a cool place to allow fermentation.

In a day or so, the extracted liquid covers the lid. Lactic bacteria naturally present in the cabbage begin to ferment the sugars in the extracted liquid: first *Leuconostoc mesenteroides* then, as the acidity rises, other species such as *Lactobacillus brevis* and *L. plantarum*. Full fermentation takes two months or more, depending on temperature.

A low temperature favours the growth of bacteria which create a good flavour. At 7 °C (45 °F) as much as a year may be needed but the results are excellent.

During fermentation in a crock or barrel the liquid which rises over the disc becomes covered by a layer of slimy dextran, a bacterial waste product which has to be skimmed off from time to time lest it become infected with unwanted organisms. (This problem is avoided by the equipment used in large-scale industrial processes.)

It is still possible to buy old-fashioned sauerkraut from the barrel in some shops. The bacteria are still at work and it must be used soon before it spoils. It may be too sour for some tastes, in which case it can be rinsed with cold water. Still completely raw and crisp, it needs half an hour's simmering or more to cook it. Canned or bottled sauerkraut has been pasteurized to kill the bacteria and make the product keep. The process partly cooks, so less cooking time is needed.

The most famous sauerkraut dish is the *choucroute garnie* of Alsace, which is sauerkraut with *lard fumé* (see BACON), SALT PORK, and pork sausages of Colmar or Strasbourg accompanied by potatoes. There are several other sorts of *choucroute garnie*, notably the German-style version using both Nuremberg and Frankfurter sausages, some different cuts of pork and apple. However, the extent of possible variations is almost infinite. An Alsatian journal once published a statement by Julien Freund, director of the Institute of Sociology in Strasbourg, which constitutes a particularly endearing example of the kind of gastrobabble associated with French gastronomy:

Sauerkraut is tolerant, for it seems to be a well of contradictions. Not that it would preach a gastronomic neutrality that would put up with all heresies. It rejects dogmatism and approves of individual tastes. It forms a marvellous combination with numerous spices, odours, or spirits: juniper berries, coriander seeds, peppercorns, cranberries, Reinette apples, stock, and wine; it even welcomes flakes of yeast or leftover Gruyère since it accepts being prepared *au gratin*. Its flavour sustains various potato dishes: boiled in their skins, crisps (potato chips), braised, sautéed, grilled, or simply cooked in water. It adopts many sorts of fat, including lard, butter, goose fat, or roast dripping. The variety of meats to which it consents is infinite: sausages of all kinds, such as knackwurst, white sausage, Lorraine, Montbéliard, chipolata, black pudding, hams, smoked or salted bacon, quenelles, pickled and smoked pork, goose, pheasant, etc. It makes excuses for red wine, although it has a weakness for beer and lets itself be spoilt by white wine. Each stomach may find its own happiness in it.

SAURY *Scomberesox saurus*, a pelagic, shoaling, fish of the Mediterranean and N. Atlantic, which also has a circumglobal distribution in temperate waters of the southern hemisphere. Its other common names include needlefish and skipper, the first because its jaws project in the form of a thin beak, the second because of its habit of 'skipping' out of the water when escaping from predators. It reaches a length of about 45 cm (18").

The saury has edible qualities similar to those of the GARFISH, but is mainly important because it provides food for tuna and other valuable large fish.

SAUSAGE SAUSAGES OF BRITAIN, SAUSAGES OF FRANCE, SAUSAGES OF GERMANY, SAUSAGES OF ITALY, SAUSAGES OF SPAIN AND PORTUGAL (*see page 698*)

SAUTÉ the past participle of the French verb *sauter* (to jump, hence to fry in shallow fat, while tossing, i.e. making to jump). The word is also a noun in French (meaning a dish thus prepared), and has succeeded in migrating into English in both forms, with the same meanings, and complete with accent. This causes a slight problem, since the infinitive (*sauter*) has not migrated. Thus in English, when the imperative is required, as often happens in recipes, only the past participle is available. The result looks odd ('Sauté the mushrooms . . .'), but works.

Originally, in France, a *sauté* was a dish of meat or poultry cut into pieces and cooked only in fat, but the French now also use the term for dishes which simply involve browning foods before adding a liquid. Hence a *sauté d'agneau* is not simply pieces of lamb quickly browned but a lamb stew. On the other hand, a *sauté de champignons* (sautéed mushrooms) may indeed be mushrooms cooked only in fat and served 'dry' with a few herbs or garlic.

A sauté pan resembles a frying pan, but is usually a little deeper and has straight sides, so that there is less risk of the food 'jumping' right out.

SAVARIN a dessert, is essentially an enriched yeast dough baked in a ring mould. A syrup laced with kirsch or rum is used to soak it when cool; and the central hole may be filled with fruit or cream. There is also a solid, holeless form, *mazarin*, which is split and filled with cream.

The savarin derived from the E. European BABA, as naturalized in Alsace in the 18th century. What happened was that in the mid- or late 1840s one of the brothers Julien, Parisian *pâtissiers*, experimented with the baba in a slightly different form. He used the same dough, but removed the dried fruits and soaked the savarin with his own 'secret' syrup. He named his new confection in honour of the famous gastronomic writer

BRILLAT-SAVARIN, although this name for it does not seem to have been recorded until the 1860s.

SAVORY herbs of the genus *Satureja*, in the MINT family, indigenous to S. Europe and the Mediterranean region. Summer savory (*S. hortensis*) and winter savory (*S. montana*) are the best-known species.

Classical Greeks, who knew it as *thymbra*, and Romans both made much use of savory in medicine and cookery. The several species known in Greece, including *S. thymbra*, were recognized by Roman writers on farming as being distinct from the Italian kind, which they called *cunila* or, colloquially, *satureia*; it is this that we now know as summer savory. It was used as a condiment and to flavour pickles and sauces. Virgil recommended it, along with thyme, for planting near beehives.

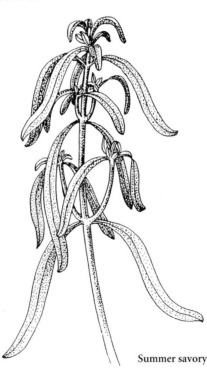

Summer savory

Savory remained important in medieval Europe. It occurs, as saetherie, in an Anglo-Saxon medical text of about AD 1000. By the 16th century its English name had become savourie, and it was an important ingredient in stuffings.

Summer savory has narrow dark green leaves, which are highly aromatic with a peppery flavour. It is a good flavouring for poultry, meat, soups, eggs, salads, or sauces and can be used, like parsley, as a garnish. In continental Europe it is often known as the 'bean herb' (cf. *Bohnenkraut*, the German name) as it brings out the taste of beans, peas, and lentils. The leaves also yield a spicy essential oil which has a sharp bitter flavour

and is used in the food industry as a flavouring.

Summer savory was one of the first plants introduced to N. America by the colonists. It is now grown commercially in California.

Winter savory, *S. montana*, is sharper and spicier than *S. hortensis*. It is also used in stuffings, marinades, and pickles.

SAVOURIES constituted during the 19th century and much of the 20th century a course at the end of an English dinner. Small items, often with fanciful names like 'angels on horseback', they were thought to provide a suitable closing note to the meal and to aid digestion.

The term goes back to the 17th century, when it could also refer to a savoury appetizer served at the start of a meal, but this usage dropped out of sight. Savouries made with anchovy were popular. VERRAL (1759) had anchovy fillets on fried fingers of bread, sprinkled with Parmesan cheese, placed under the grill and then given a squeeze of Seville orange juice—'a trifling thing, but I never saw it come whole from table'. Mrs Raffald (1782) had a similar savoury, but using plenty of Cheddar cheese and parsley. In the mid-19th century Eliza Acton (1855) proposed what she called 'savoury toasts', small squares of toast buttered and spread with mustard and then covered with plenty of grated cheese and seasoned ham before being fried and then being placed in a Dutch oven to dissolve the cheese. Her 'observations' illuminate the role of such things in her time:

These toasts, . . . may be served in the cheese-course of a dinner. Such 'mere *relishes*' as they are called, do not seem to us to demand much of our space, or many of them which are very easy of preparation might be inserted here.

So recipes certainly existed (and could incorporate various ingredients such as the caviar, conserved lamprey, and 'potted birds made high' offered by Mrs Rundell), but they were not prominent or numerous; it was only towards the end of the 19th century that Mrs de Salis published her collection of *savouries à la mode*.

Savouries still exist in time warps such as London clubs, or in nostalgia restaurants, but their heyday was the era of formal upper-class dinner parties such as flourished in late Victorian and Edwardian times. Apart from those mentioned above, the best known of them included:

- Scotch woodcock, another anchovy savoury, the desalted anchovies being chopped fine, placed between slices of toasted bread and the whole then covered with a thickened mixture of cream and egg yolk.

(*cont. on page 702*)

Sausage
SAUSAGES OF BRITAIN, SAUSAGES OF FRANCE, SAUSAGES OF GERMANY, SAUSAGES OF ITALY, SAUSAGES OF SPAIN AND PORTUGAL

Typically a chopped meat mixture stuffed into a tubular casing. The concept no doubt originated in antiquity, when it was desirable to find some way of preserving the blood and minor bits and pieces of a pig, rather than have to eat them immediately after the annual killing; see HAGGIS; BLOOD SAUSAGES. But the method has proved to be so adaptable and successful that sausages have come to take many forms, and questions of definition and classification are complex.

To take definition first, meat is not a defining characteristic. Fish sausages have been known since antiquity. Glamorgan sausages contain neither flesh nor fish nor fowl, but cheese and leeks. Nor is the familiar tubular shape essential; sausages may be spherical or ovoid or flattish; and tubular sausages may be straight or curved or even circular. Finally sausage casings, or 'skins' (see below), are unnecessary. If sausage mixtures are shaped into cohesive rolls, for example, these count as sausages because of their shape and composition. To exemplify two areas of flexibility in one product, Scotland has Lorne sausages, which are square (Glaswegian, 'squerr') in section and without a casing.

As for classification, we must give thanks that sausages are not in the realm of natural history; for, if they were, the arguments conducted by rival taxonomists would be endless. The evolution of species and subspecies and hybrids of sausages proceeds so fast, and they proliferate around the world with so little control over their nomenclature, that they must always outstrip classification.

However, one can discern three major categories. First, fresh sausages (such as dominate the market in Britain) which are intended for cooking; second, cured sausages, containing raw meat and intended for keeping and slicing (e.g. most forms of salami); and third, cooked or part-cooked sausages which are meant to be sliced and eaten cold (MORTADELLA) or heated and eaten hot (FRANKFURTER).

The first two categories had already emerged in classical times. In Aristophanes' satirical play *The Knights* (424 BC) the real Athenian demagogue Cleon is seen off by an imaginary sausage-seller, 'born and bred in the market, a brazen-faced rogue' but a comic hero and an ideal politician, since he was prepared to 'mince all policies, stuff (adding grease), dress up with butcher's sauce'. The playwright of Greek Sicily, Epicharmus (early 5th century BC), had even entitled a play *The Sausage*, but nothing else is known of it.

The ancient Greek sausage-seller represented a trade that made use of all that was left after prime meat (dealt in by butchers) had been eaten or sacrificed. Writing in the 2nd century AD, ATHENAEUS refers to the cooked-meat shops of Alexandria, which likewise specialized in sausages and all kinds of offal. There is little other evidence on how Greek sausages (*allantes*) were made, but we know that some, called *khordai*, were served sliced: perhaps these resembled salami.

In the Roman Empire two terms came into prominence that still survive. APICIUS gives a recipe for the first, *lucanica*, a spicy, smoked, beef or pork sausage named after a region of S. Italy from which Roman troops had brought the recipe back to the capital. *Lucanica* (it is a moot point whether the term is singular or plural) are referred to by the 1st-century Roman poet Martial and are frequently mentioned in documents from the 4th century onwards. Modern descendants of the term *lucanica* include *linguiça*, *longaniza*, and *luganega*; most such descendants seem to be long, undivided smoked sausages. The second term is *salsicia*, from which many modern names are derived. This occurs in word lists from the later Empire, but there is no early recipe.

Both words originated in Latin but were also borrowed into Greek, replacing the terms mentioned earlier: this suggests that Roman sausage-making skills swept the board. Certainly there were several other Roman kinds: PETRONIUS talks of *tomacula* sold hot at street stalls, but nothing is known of how they were prepared. An early Byzantine text, *The Miracles of SS Cosmas and Damian*, provides the first textual record of a string of sausages (*seira salsikion*).

The conversion of the Roman Empire to Christianity posed problems for some sausages. Not only did many of them contain blood, whose consumption was forbidden by the Bible, but they were associated with pagan phallic rites. Nevertheless, sausages survived and were a common feature of the diet of medieval Europe. In contrast, little use was made of them in the Arab world. This was no doubt due to their links with the pig, which neither Muslims nor Jews were permitted to eat. They could have been made from other meats but in practice were not, and even in the modern Arab world there are still only a few kinds (notably the N. African MERGUEZ), whereas there are countless varieties of RISSOLE and MEATBALL.

In medieval Europe pork was certainly the meat most used in sausages, and pepper was the most common spice. But national and regional divergences were already apparent, some depending on the range of ingredients readily available, others on climate.

Broadly speaking, sausages for cooking and eating hot were found in northerly countries more than in the warmer Mediterranean region. And traditions of cured sausages were strongest in areas where a dry wind could be counted on to help with the cure. This factor gave an advantage to mountainous regions, for example in Spain, or countries where prevailing winds blew from the north and were not damp. Here damp countries like England were at a disadvantage. This may account for the failure of the English to produce a range of cured sausages to rival those of the Continent, and for the preference they have shown for fresh sausages.

Sausages which are cooked before sale are spread fairly

evenly through the different climates of Europe, and indeed other parts of the world.

The divergences in the making and consumption of sausages were extended to the New World after Columbus. Spanish and Portuguese sausages invaded Latin America and the Philippines. In N. America the great sausage incursions took place later, with the arrival of German, Polish, Italian, and other immigrants in the 19th century. It would probably be true to say that in the latter part of the 19th century there was a wider diversity of sausages in the USA than anywhere else in the world, although for sheer number of types Germany would have been in the lead.

The 19th century also saw the rise of the mass production of sausages. A notable result of this was the introduction of bread into British sausages, a unique development (though a Roman recipe of Apicius also includes cereal).

THE SCIENCE OF SAUSAGE-MAKING

Little need be said about fresh sausages, except that an unexpected ingredient in many recipes is ice. This is added to the meat used for sausages before the mixture is placed in a 'bowl chopper', a bowl which has a set of revolving blades at the bottom. It prevents overheating during the intense mechanical chopping and, in British sausages containing cereal, provides water which moistens the product. Chopping devices are favoured over mincers because the latter tend to crush the meat, squeezing out the juices.

It is in the preparation of cured sausages, preserved by salting, drying, smoking, and often some degree of fermentation, that science comes more into the picture.

Dried sausages intended for long keeping rely on good hygiene and traditional methods of preservation, which are finely adjusted to encourage the growth of a particular microflora in the product. Raw meat is generally used; it is diced, minced, or reduced to a paste as the recipe requires; mixed with salt, saltpetre, spices, and sometimes alcohol in the form of beer, wine, or brandy; and stuffed into the casings which are tied to make links of an appropriate size. A period of drying, usually in cool moving air, but sometimes over heat, follows; the sausage may lose up to 50% in weight during this time. Most cured sausages are larger in diameter than fresh ones, since a very narrow sausage would dry excessively in storage. Some salami are bound with string, which may be tightened several times as the sausage dries and shrinks.

After several weeks of drying, the interior of a cured sausage will have undergone fermentation by lactic acid-producing bacteria present in the mixture; this gives the pleasantly acid flavour of many such products. The increased acidity, combined with the process of dehydration, and a fairly high salt content further raised by loss of water, take the sausage through a 'preservation barrier', from being a fresh, perishable product to a stable and durable one. A white 'bloom' of yeast cells is visible on the skin of certain varieties; they are harmless, and play a part in the maturing

process. The sausage may also be smoked, introducing further preservatives in the form of phenols, which inhibit microbial growth. Hot-smoking also cooks the product to some extent.

Saltpetre, potassium nitrate, used originally because it contains as an impurity potassium nitrite which reacts with myoglobin in the meat to give a stable pink colour, has an important role in sausage-making, inhibiting the growth of many bacteria. In the past, when preservation was less well understood, toxic organisms sometimes infected sausages. The long keeping time, absence of oxygen, and inadequate acidity of a badly prepared sausage made it ideal for the growth of *Clostridium botulinum*, an organism now more commonly associated with canned foods, but which was first identified in sausages in Germany in the early 19th century:

Sausage casings

THESE are generally lengths of intestine from various animals. The small intestines of sheep provide the narrowest, and also some wider ones. Pig casings are wider. Wider still are ox 'runners' (small intestines), and the widest of all are ox 'bungs' (large intestines), which may be over 10 cm (4") wide and are used for mortadella and the largest salami. The stomachs of sheep and pigs provide round casings for HAGGIS and hog puddings, and for their equivalents in other countries. In the past bladders and even wombs have been used. The CAUL or mesentery of a calf is a sheet of fatty tissue from around the intestines. With the fat left on, it can be used as a filling for ANDOUILLES, or it can be scraped to make a convenient flat sheet of casing which can be made into parcels around a FAGGOT or other items. Weasand (oesophagus or gullet) was used for POLONY (dyed red outside).

Fish guts provide casings for fish sausages. Only rather large fishes have wide enough guts.

The preparation of casings is a laborious business (soaking, turning inside out, scraping clean) but there are machines which do the job quickly. Natural casings are generally salted, and keep for several years in a refrigerator.

Natural casings are still extensively used, and always for high-class sausages. However, there are artificial casings. The earliest of these, made in the 1930s, resembled cellophane. Most are now made from COLLAGEN, obtained by boiling down hide, or from cellulose, a plant material. Fully synthetic plastic casings, which are not edible, are also in use, but only for cheap, large slicing sausages.

Natural casings are always slightly porous, allowing sausages to dry easily and to cook well without bursting. They can usually be distinguished by their curved form, except in large salami, which are straightened by their own weight and sometimes by a network of strings around the outside.

Artificial casings are apt to be non-porous, which hinders the blending of flavours in dishes where sausages are cooked with other ingredients. In addition, they are often tough, and tend to stick to the pan when sausages are fried.

hence its name, from *botulus*, a form of the Latin word *botellus*, sausage. Modern mass-produced sausages, especially fresh types, often contain extra preservatives such as sodium metabisulphite and ascorbyl palmitate.

See also the sections below on SAUSAGES OF BRITAIN/ FRANCE/GERMANY/ITALY/SPAIN AND PORTUGAL. There are of course many sorts of sausage in other parts of the world, but most of these are variations on themes displayed in these five sections.

Sausages of Britain

These are normally fresh types for cooking; they differ from the general run of such sausages in having a significant cereal content. This difference has only been visible since the latter part of the 19th century, when industrial production of sausages began and manufacturers, anxious to have a mass market, sought to keep costs down. The idea of combining meat with cereal in a sausage-like casing was by no means a new one. HAGGIS is an antique and excellent example of the combination. But up to this time English sausages had been like Continental ones in being made more or less entirely of meat of some kind.

British pure pork sausages, similar to the French or Italian ones, are still made on a small scale, but the great majority of British sausages are made with RUSK crumb or special 'sausage meal' (rather than the traditional breadcrumbs). The meat content of commercial sausages ranges from below 50% to 95% or more in the most expensive. Pork, or pork and beef, are considered best. Pure beef sausages are cheaper and are preferred in Scotland, where pork has been a less popular meat.

Traditional British sausages, all seasoned with pepper, usually black, and often with mace, include:

- Cambridge, with sage, cayenne, and nutmeg;
- Oxford, of pork, veal, and beef suet with sage, nutmeg, pepper, and sometimes herbs;
- Wiltshire, with ginger, and sometimes other seasonings;
- Yorkshire, with nutmeg, cloves, and cayenne;
- Lincolnshire, with sage and thyme;
- Manchester, with sage, cloves, nutmeg, and ginger;
- Cumberland, made of coarse-cut pork, and spicier than most, not twisted into links, but sold by length from a long coil;
- Epping, an extinct but interesting variety, skinless, made of pork mixed with beef suet and bacon, with sage and spices;
- Glamorgan, a sausage containing cheese and leek (no meat or fish). This too is skinless, consolidated with a coating of egg white;
- tomato, a peculiar local variety which remains popular in the Midlands. It is a normal British pork sausage coloured reddish with tomato purée.

Sausages of France

As one would expect in a country which stretches from the Mediterranean to the Pyrenees and the Atlantic coast, these are diverse.

A French fresh sausage is simply called *saucisse*, a term which often implies also a relatively small size. The commonest fresh types are *saucisse de Toulouse*, quite large, with an unusually high proportion of lean meat, and intended for grilling; and *saucisse de Strasbourg*, for poaching.

The general French term for large sausages, whether fresh, smoked, or cured, is *saucisson*. They are almost exclusively boiled. Indeed, the most common boiling sausage is simply called *saucisson à cuire*, although specific regional names exist in different parts of the country.

Small dried sausages (*saucisses sèches*) are less common than the larger ones (*saucissons secs*). Both are simply dried—never smoked—and eaten sliced without cooking. These, like the cooking sausages, are almost exclusively pure pork and are made throughout the country. Those from Lyons, and the neighbouring Beaujolais region, are particularly sought after. Several have surprising names. *Rosette* designates a *saucisson sec* made with the part of the intestine that terminates as the rectum (and is named because of its pinkish coloration). People in Lyons are also fond of *Jésus*, a fattish, banana-shaped *saucisson sec* which apparently derives its name from its resemblance to a baby in swaddling clothes.

Saucissons are rarely smoked, although fat *saucisses* sometimes are. The most famous smoked sausages in France are from the Franche-Comté, where numerous pork products are traditionally smoked. This is the *saucisse de Morteau*, a short but plump sausage which is to be poached and served hot with cabbage, lentils, or potatoes. It provides something of an exception to the general rule that a *saucisse* is smaller than a *saucisson*. It is roughly the size of a *saucisson à cuire* from Lyons.

See also ANDOUILLE, ANDOUILLETTE; CERVELAS.

Sausages of Germany

Reputed to number 1,000 or more, these deserve a book to themselves, and indeed have one famous one: Erich Lissner's *Wurstologia* (1939). In this and other works elaborate classifications are given, but in practice there are just three major categories.

BRÜHWURST

This term means a parboiled sausage, made from finely chopped raw meat, not intended for keeping, usually scalded by the manufacturer, sometimes smoked, to be heated before serving, always sliceable, often red in colour. Examples are:

- FRANKFURTER and *Wiener*, and the larger version, *Bockwurst*;
- *Bierschinken*, a large pork sausage studded with pistachio nuts;
- *Knackwurst*, pork and beef, flavoured with cumin and garlic;
- *Extrawurst*, fairly large and very finely chopped, mainly used in Austria;
- *Weisswurst* (white sausage), a speciality of Munich, which is made from veal only and is deathly white, with a flavour so slight as to be almost undetectable, and for which a special mustard has been designed, eaten only with it;
- *Bierwurst*, a coarse pork and beef sausage flavoured with garlic;
- *Schinkenwurst* (ham sausage), a Westphalian sausage made from flaked ham, smoked over a fire of beechwood and juniper berries.

ROHWURST

Raw sausage, for keeping, made from meat which has been cured, air dried, and sometimes smoked. A speciality of N. Germany. There are two types, spreadable and sliceable. The most common spreadable ones are:

- *Teewurst*, always a smooth, very fine textured paste. It is made from raw pork and beef or pure pork, highly spiced;
- *Mettwurst*, a raw smoked pork and beef sausage, often spreadable; but also available in a coarse-cut sliceable version.

Common sliceable ones include:

- *Cervelatwurst*, see CERVELAT;
- *Bratwurst* (grilling sausage), usually included in this category although they are not cured. These are pork or pork and veal sausages. There are many varieties, distinguished by their seasonings and size and usually named after the places with which they are associated: *Nürnberger, Coburger, Regensburger, Thüringer* (said to be the original kind), and *Fränkischer* (from Franconia).

KOCHWURST

Fully cooked sausages, not necessarily intended for keeping, constitute the third main category. Here the most important type by far is:

- *Leberwurst* (liver sausage).

The category also includes some sorts of BLOOD SAUSAGE:

- *Rotwurst* (red sausage);
- *Blutwurst*, of finer consistency.
- *Zungenwurst* (tongue sausage) is similar but containing large pieces of tongue and sometimes liver, often seasoned with paprika and nutmeg.

Sausages of Italy

These include one outstandingly large and important family, the salami. This name (the plural of the Italian word *salame*) applies to matured raw meat slicing sausages made to recipes of Italian origin, either in that country or elsewhere. Within Italy there are scores of types.

Salami are mostly medium to large in size, and those made in Italy are usually dried without smoking. Characteristically, when cut across, they display a section which is pink or red with many small to medium-sized flecks of white fat. Pork, or mixtures of pork and beef or pork and *vitellone* (young beef), form the basis; seasonings and fineness or coarseness of cut vary to regional taste. Names denote style, a principal ingredient, or place of origin. These include:

- *casalinga* (domestic, home made), of coarse-cut pork with plenty of black pepper, and not very large;
- *nostrano* (our own), usually quite coarse;
- *Genovese* (from Genoa), of pork and *vitellone*, strongly flavoured;
- *Milanese* (also known as *crespone* and *bindone*), mild types, mostly pork with beef or *vitellone*, with garlic—now mass produced, and probably the best-known type outside Italy;
- *Felino*, from the town of that name near Parma, an especially fine and highly regarded type containing wine and whole peppercorns;
- *Fiorentina* (Florentine), of various kinds, one variation being *fiocchiona*, a large, coarse-cut pork salame flavoured with fennel seeds;
- *cacciatorino* (from *cacciatore*, hunter), a small type from the region around Lake Como.

Salami made in S. Italy and Sardinia are distinguished by their spiciness. They include:

- *Napoletano* (Neapolitan), long, thin, pork and beef sausages seasoned with red and black pepper;
- *Sardo* (Sardinian), containing red pepper but not black;
- *Calabrese* (Calabrian), short and stumpy, containing large flecks of fat;
- *Peperone*, long, narrow, and highly spiced.

All these belong to the class of *salame crudo*, raw salame. *Salame cotto*, cooked salame, is made from highly seasoned pork, or a mixture of meats not suitable for raw salame. It is cheaper than and generally inferior to raw salame. But the category includes MORTADELLA, famous for being the largest of all sausages.

Of salami produced in other countries the most notable are those of Hungary; indeed the Italians themselves copy it as *salame ungherese*. It is a fine, hard, pork salame, lightly smoked and subtly spiced.

The Italian term for a small fresh sausage is *salsiccia*. This category includes *Luganega*, a famous fresh pork sausage of

Lombardy, flavoured with cloves and cinnamon. This is usually unlinked and sold by the length rather than by weight. Anna del Conte (1989) traces it all the way back to a recipe of APICIUS in classical Rome; but his recipe used different flavourings.

Sausages of Spain and Portugal

These two groups are treated together, because the sausages of the whole Iberian peninsula, and of the Balearics, can be regarded as constituting one family—and an important one, for representatives of it have become established in C. and S. America, parts of the USA where Spanish or Portuguese influences are felt, and the Philippines.

- *Chorizo* (Portuguese *chouriço*), the best known of all, is usually made of chopped or minced pork, with some fat, prepared with sweet and hot paprika or pulp from red peppers, giving it its characteristic red colour. Garlic and black pepper are among the other flavourings. *Chorizo* sometimes appears as a soft sausage to be cooked with beans etc. for soups, but much more commonly as a hard, cured sausage, of which slices are eaten cold or used as an ingredient; in Portugal, for example, a slice of *chouriço* is obligatory at the bottom of a bowl of *Caldo verde*, potato and cabbage soup.

- *Morcilla* is like black pudding, a kind of BLOOD SAUSAGE. Janet Mendel (1996) says that it is 'seasoned with cinnamon, cloves and nutmeg. Some regional types may contain onion, anise, fennel, rice or pine nuts. . . . *Morcilla* is usually stewed with pulses and vegetables.'
- *Salchichón* is a hard, cured sausage, called *longaniza* or *fuet* if long and thin. *Salchicha*, on the other hand, is usually a fresh pork sausage in links.
- *Butifarra*, *butifarró*, and *butifarron* are a family of names which cover a large range of sausages, including several of special interest. *Butifarra negra* is another blood sausage, while *butifarra blanca* is a white sausage made of minced pork and spices, cooked, a speciality of Catalan cuisine. Andrews (1988) draws attention to *botifarra dolça*, a sweet version which is a speciality of the Empordà region, cured with sugar and sometimes flavoured with cinnamon and lemon juice, to be eaten as dessert.
- *Sobrasada*, the most famous sausage of Majorca, is irregular in shape, soft, spicy, and a reddish-orange colour. It is a popular snack, spread on bread. Authentic *sobrasada* contains cuts of meat from the loin, fillet, and leg of pork, all finely chopped and mixed with salt and paprika (to be absolutely correct, *pimentón mallorquín*). Size varies according to the type of intestine used as casing. The sausage keeps for up to a year in a cool place.

- Angels on horseback, which are oysters wrapped in a thin slice of bacon, skewered, fried, and placed on a sippet of fried bread.
- Devils on horseback, as for the angels, but with stoned and soaked prunes instead of oysters.

See also WELSH RABBIT.

SAVOY (French *Savoie, biscuit de Savoie*), a type of SPONGE CAKE. This differs from the other main type, GÉNOISE, in having egg yolks and whites beaten separately rather than together. The yolks are beaten with sugar; then flour (in modern recipes, half wheat and half potato) is folded in, and the stiffly beaten egg whites. Vanilla and lemon rind may be added as flavourings. The result is a light and delicate cake, eaten without further adornment. The Italian *pan di Spagna* is similar but contains less sugar.

The same sort of mixture can be used to produce small biscuits. There can be confusion here, since the word biscuit has two senses in French. As noted above it can mean a cake. But in the plural it can mean much the same as English 'biscuits'.

The Savoy biscuit arrived in England early in the 18th century. However, it did not arrive alone. Other similar 'biscuits', named according to their supposed origins— Naples, Lisbon, or Spanish biscuit—also became popular in England at that time, and the differences between them, if differences there were, no doubt perplexed people then as they do now.

When Mrs Mary Eales gave a recipe for 'spunge biscuits' in her *Receipts* (1718), the situation became clearer, since this phrase conveys to British ears the correct impression, whereas terms such as 'Savoy biscuit' suggest something different. Moreover, Mrs Eales specified that the biscuits should be baked 'in little long Pans', which corresponds to the shape of modern sponge fingers (or BOUDOIR BISCUITS).

SAWFISH large fish of the family Pristidae, especially *Pristis pectinata*, which has a maximum length of 7.5 m (25') or even more. The 'saw' with which it is equipped for killing its prey is also capable of inflicting great damage on, for example, fishing nets. Indeed, since these fish are viviparous, the saws of baby specimens would lacerate the insides of their mothers if they were not provided with little sheaths which they wear until after birth.

The principal sawfish belong to the Indo-Pacific. Despite the obvious problems of catching them, they are sought after and highly regarded as food in certain countries of the region, notably Sri Lanka, Malaysia, and China.

SAXON PUDDING a steamed brown BREAD PUDDING made with milk and eggs, sometimes with chocolate, or with almonds and crystallized fruit. The name is the English and the French one (*pouding à la saxonne*) for a pudding which is genuinely German in inspiration. Its name in German-speaking areas is *Bettelmann* ('beggar'), and it is similarly made with dark rye breadcrumbs and eggs; but there are innumerable versions with different additions, rather than one kind specific to Saxony.

SBRINZ a cheese of Swiss origin, was named for Brienz, the lake and region where it was first made. *Spalen*, an alternative name, is the word for the wooden tubs in which it was dispatched. Strictly speaking the name *Spalen* refers to the young cheese, which has the texture of GRUYÈRE, while Sbrinz is used for the mature version, which is aged for two or three years, during which it acquires a strong, full flavour and becomes very hard. It is not unlike the GRANA group of cheeses in Italy.

Sbrinz was probably being made much as it is now in the 1st century AD, when the Roman writer Columella mentioned a hard cheese made in Helvetia. Besides being especially hard, Sbrinz is almost without holes or 'eyes', and excellent for grating. It also melts well; and is eaten as a table cheese—thin slivers shaved off it make a good appetizer.

A whole Sbrinz is a flat wheel up to 69 cm (27") across and weighing up to 45 kg (100 lb). Kindred cheeses are manufactured in Italy and Argentina under the same name or as Sbrinza.

SCABBARD FISH long, thin, and usually silvery fish of the family Trichiuridae, are found in many parts of the world. The English names which have been used for them include hairtail (for those species whose tail ends in a point, rather than being forked), cutlass fish and sabre fish, ribbon fish, and (in the southern hemisphere) frostfish. An interesting variation on these themes is provided by an alternative name in the Philippines: *bolungonas*, meaning sugar-cane leaf.

The maximum length of the various species varies from about 1 to 2 m (3–6'). The largest, *Lepidopus caudatus*, occurs on both sides of the Atlantic and in the Mediterranean. Another Atlantic species, *Aphanopus carbo*, is the dominant fish in the catch at Madeira, besides being taken frequently off the Portuguese coast; it likes deep water and is of a blackish colour.

In the Indo-Pacific there are *Trichiurus haumela*, a common species; *T. muticus* (tin white in colour, accounting for the emphatic Malay name *timah-timah*, meaning tin-tin); and *T. savala*, whose range extends to Australia. The frostfish of New Zealand, so called because often found washed ashore in large numbers on frosty nights, is *Lepidopus lex.*

From the cook's point of view, the rear end of one of these fish offers little; but sections cut further forward yield excellent flesh, which can be fried, baked, or grilled. In the western hemisphere there are signs of appreciation at Madeira (above all), in Portugal, and in certain Mediterranean countries. Interest in the Indo-Pacific is more widespread. These fish have occupied fourth place in importance in the marine fisheries of India, where they are mostly sun dried before being marketed.

SCAD one of several general names applied to fish of the family Carangidae. See also JACK and TREVALLY. The origin of the name scad is unknown, and it seems unlikely that anyone could ever establish why some species of the Indo-Pacific, which is where the name is most commonly in use, came to be scad while others took the name jack and yet others trevally. It is usual to attribute confusion in the naming of fish in distant waters to the vagaries of English-speaking colonists, whose naming of the species they met in other continents was often misguided by imagined resemblances between these 'new' fish and the ones with which they had been familiar at home; cf AUSTRALASIAN SALMON and MURRAY COD. But, in the present case, one is left wondering where the names scad, jack, and trevally came from.

Be these matters as they may, the Indo-Pacific species commonly called scad include:

- *Decapterus russelli*, which together with its close relation *D. macrosoma* provides the most important fishery in the Philippines. It may be called round scad or mackerel scad. It and the next species are of medium size (market length around 30 cm/12");
- *Megalaspis cordyla*, the hardtail scad, often just called hardtail;
- *Atule mate*, a relatively small fish, prized in Thailand and Cambodia.

SCALD As a culinary term, this verb has two meanings: to pour boiling water over; or, in the case of milk or cream, to heat to just below boiling point.

SCALDFISH small FLATFISH of the genus *Arnoglossus* in the family Bothidae. Their scales come off very easily, so that captured specimens have a 'scalded' appearance. *A. laterna*, which has a maximum length of just under 20 cm (8"), is found in the Mediterranean and E. Atlantic. *A. thori* and *A. imperialis* are slightly larger relations. None is important but all are acceptable fare.

SCALLOP an edible MOLLUSC which exists in many species around the world and is highly esteemed in almost all regions, although not in SE Asia. Scallops belong to the family Pectinidae, in which the principal genera are *Pecten* and *Chlamys*.

Scallops do not crawl or burrow, so do not have a large 'foot'. Instead, they have a highly developed adductor muscle, by means of which they can open and close their shells and so propel themselves through the water. The Japanese name for scallop means, literally, 'full-sail fish', from the manner of its movement with one shell raised. Not all scallops exercise this ability. Some remain anchored by a byssus to some solid object. Others start life thus and then become free rangers, swimming or resting on the sea bottom.

Most but not all scallops are hermaphrodites, equipped with both an orange roe (or coral) and a whitish testis. Europeans eat these as well as the adductor muscle, but in N. America they are usually discarded. Scallops are usually cleaned at sea, and only the adductor muscles (or muscles and roes) brought to market. But other parts, such as the mantle, are edible, and Canadian processors have canned scallop 'rims and roes', for use in CHOWDERS.

Some of the principal species are as follows:

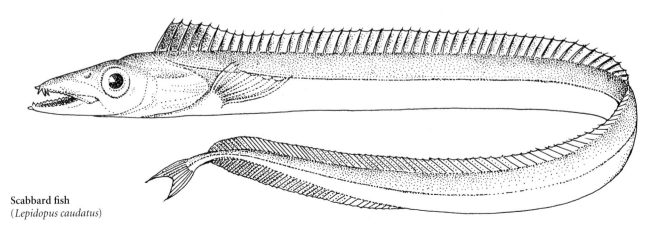

Scabbard fish
(*Lepidopus caudatus*)

- *Pecten maximus*, the 'great scallop' of the N. Atlantic (Norway down to the Iberian peninsula): maximum diameter about 15 cm (6"), 15–17 radiating ribs on the shell. These ribs are rounded.
- *P. jacobaeus*, the slightly smaller Mediterranean scallop; 14–16 ribs, which are flattened.
- *Chlamys opercularis*, the queen (scallop) or quin: maximum size 10 cm (4"), about 20 ribs. *Vanneau* in French, *volandeira* in Spanish. Colour of the shell may be anything from yellow through pink to purple or brown. A species of deeper waters, fishery for which is increasing.
- *Placopecten magellanicus*, the Atlantic deep-sea scallop, is the object of an active N. American fishery. Maximum size 20 cm (8"), shells relatively smooth.

A large and common species of the Indo-Pacific, *Amusium pleuronectes*, is known in Thailand as *hoy phat* (the traditional name) or *hoy shell*, a new name which has a curious explanation. The Shell Company, which is active in Thailand as in so many other countries, displays its scallop shell emblem there. Noticing the likeness, Thai people have taken to naming the scallop after the company.

SCHABZIGER known as Sapsago in the United States, is a Swiss cheese quite unlike any other. It is a hard, strong, almost fatless skimmed-milk cheese, coloured green with the aromatic clover *Melilotus cærulea* and pressed into small blunt cones weighing almost 100 g (4 oz). Schabziger is made in the Swiss canton of Glarus, and is sometimes called Glarner. It is usually eaten grated and diluted with butter, and is known as 'the poor man's cheese' because a little goes a long way.

The manufacture of Schabziger is also highly individual. Skimmed milk, sometimes mixed with buttermilk, is soured and heated almost to boiling. This causes the lactalbumin proteins in the milk, as well as the usual casein, to coagulate. The curd is pressed into large blocks and left to ferment. This process produces butyric acid (a characteristic flavour of rancid butter) in addition to the lactic acid from the original souring. After a few weeks the cheese is dried, ground to powder, mixed with clover, and pressed to shape. Sometimes pressing is omitted and the green powder sold in packets as a condiment or sandwich filling.

There is a mistaken belief that Schabziger is a goat's milk cheese. This is caused by confusion with the German word *Ziege* ('goat'). It is always made of cow's milk. It has a pronounced spicy flavour.

SCONE defined by the *OED* as 'A soft flat cake of barley meal, oatmeal or flour, baked quickly and eaten buttered'. The dictionary explains that it is originally a Scots word and may be derived from 'schoonbrot' or 'sconbrot', fine white bread. The pronunciation of the word shows a distinct regional divide, being 'skon' in Scotland and northern England, and 'skoan' in the south.

What is certain is that the term is mainly a British one, and covers a wide range of small, fairly plain cakes. Leavened with baking powder, or bicarbonate of soda and an acid ingredient such as sour milk, they are quickly made and best eaten hot with butter. Scone recipes are found in great variety up and down the British Isles but, together with the closely related BANNOCK, are particularly a Scottish speciality.

Scones may be sweet or savoury. Depending on the recipe and cooking method, they may be seen to be related to SODA BREAD, cake, or PANCAKES. Traditionally, scones are cooked on a girdle or GRIDDLE but nowadays they are usually baked in an oven.

Sweet scones served with jam and whipped or clotted cream have been a feature of AFTERNOON TEA served in British teashops throughout the country in recent times. Such scones are made from wheat flour sifted with baking powder, mixed with a small proportion of sugar. A little fat (usually butter or margarine) is rubbed in; eggs and milk are added to make a firm dough. Dried fruits such as currants or sultanas are frequently added to this basic mix. This is rolled into a thick sheet, cut into rounds and baked in the oven.

This recipe, so simple and excellent, should not be messed around with. However, some variations are permissible. Unsweetened mixtures can be flavoured with grated cheese or chopped herbs. Wholemeal or white flour can be used as the cook pleases. Bicarbonate of soda combined with buttermilk, yoghurt, or sour milk, will leaven the mixture effectively to give soda scones.

Instead of making small individual scones, the dough can be baked as one large flat cake and split into wedges afterwards. These large scones were probably the norm in previous centuries. A surviving example is a regional speciality of Northumberland, the **singin' hinnie**, a large unsweetened scone with currants, which has been celebrated by Maria Kaneva-Johnson (1979), with an explanation of the 'singing'. A similar but richer confection, more like a tea cake, is the Yorkshire fat rascal (see TEA BREADS AND TEA CAKES).

Singin' hinnies are correctly cooked on a girdle. Another type of scone which calls for

a girdle is the DROP SCONE (often called Scots pancake or by Welsh or Irish names).

Scottish housewives in particular were skilled at making scones and bannocks on the girdle. In the wetter Scottish climate oatmeal or barley flour usually took the place of wheat, and scones were sometimes flavoured with caraway. Vestiges of a tradition of yeast-raised scones and recipes using sourdough fermentation can be detected in recipes given by F. Marian McNeill (1929).

Mashed potatoes can be mixed with a little flour and milk to make potato scones, popular in both Scotland and Ireland; these were also made in parts of England such as the West Country, but are now seldom seen.

Scone-type mixtures are used, especially in N. America, as a thick dumpling-cum-pastry topping on a dish of stewed fruit; see COBBLER.

In the USA the term 'BISCUIT' may denote more or less what in Britain would be called a scone—though the term 'scone' has also come into limited use in N. America.   (LM)

SCORE a verb meaning to make cuts in something which is to be cooked. The cuts may be shallow or deeper and may form a grid pattern or be a series of diagonal incisions. In any case the purpose is usually either to facilitate the penetration of heat, thus shortening the cooking time, or to permit the penetration of added flavours. The rationale underlying the first of these two purposes is discussed in detail under HEAT.

Scoring is often applied to fish, especially when it is to be grilled (US broiled). Leaving a sizeable fish whole and grilling it risks having the outside overcooked by the time sufficient heat has penetrated the interior. The CRIMPING of fish is done for a different purpose.

SCORPION FISH mainly of the genus *Scorpaena*, occur all round the world, but it is in the Mediterranean and especially in Provence that they have achieved fame, mainly as an essential ingredient of BOUILLABAISSE. One of their number, *S. scrofa*, the largest (maximum length 55 cm/22"), is the *rascasse rouge* or (in the Midi) *chapon*; ideal for this purpose when small. It presents the formidable aspect which is characteristic of scorpion fish, mitigated perhaps by its cheerful red colour. Although it is considered to be an archetypal Mediterranean species, its range extends into the Atlantic, as far north as Brittany.

A large *rascasse rouge* (usually known by its French name outside as well as inside France) makes a fine dish on its own, baked with wine and aromatics and basted often enough to counter any tendency of the firm white flesh to dry out. A few smaller species of *rascasse* are also found in the Mediterranean; but their role is usually to disappear into the bouillabaisse, or similar dish, rather than make a solo appearance.

These fish belong to the family Scorpaenidae in the order Scorpaeniformes, the maily-cheeked fish, which include also REDFISH and GURNARD. They all have large heads and conspicuously spiny dorsal fins, and are well camouflaged by a combination of colour, markings and protuberances.

Leaving the Mediterranean and surveying scorpion fish in other parts of the world (where they have achieved less fame), one is soon lost among the host of species. In the western N. Atlantic, for example, there are over a dozen. One good one, *S. cardinalis*, turns up in Australia, where it was given the inappropriate name of red rock cod. In California, a solitary member of the genus, *S. guttata*, keeps company with over 50 species of the closely related genus *Sebastes* (which are often, along with various other fish, called 'rock cod').

A. J. Liebling once proposed in the *New Yorker* that efforts be made to compare N. American fish of this family with the *rascasses* of the Mediterranean. What he wanted to know was whether an authentic bouillabaisse could be made in N. America. No one seems to have responded to his challenge, nor does anyone seem to have surveyed the scorpion fish in other parts of the world from this point of view.

SCOTCH BROTH or barley broth, probably the best-known member of the BROTH clan, and one of the most famous Scottish dishes, is typically prepared by boiling beef and barley, adding vegetables (carrot, swede, onion or white of leek, parsley) and a very little sugar. When cooking is completed, the broth is served with more chopped parsley and chopped green of leek and seasoning; the meat may be still in it, or may be served separately.

There are, as is natural with a dish of this kind, many variations. One of the earliest recipes, that of Mrs Cleland (1755), used as vegetables just some heads of celery, with some marigolds; and the meat was provided by a boiling fowl or cock, not beef. Some recipes include potatoes, cooked with or separately, and according to Catherine Brown (1985) the broth 'is often eaten with a large mealy potato making an island in the centre of the soup plate'.

Marian McNeill (1929) provides a rich anthology of notes and quotations to exemplify the minor variations in this broth and the praise which has consistently been given to it. She chose the following from the

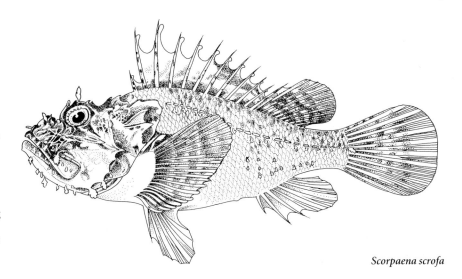

Scorpaena scrofa

account by Boswell (1786) of Dr Johnson's visit to Aberdeen:

At dinner, Dr Johnson ate several plates of Scotch broth, with barley and peas in it, and seemed very fond of the dish. I said, 'You never ate it before?'—Johnson, 'No, sir; but I don't care how soon I eat it again.'

SCOTCH EGG a hard-boiled egg enveloped in sausage meat and then fried. It is a popular cold snack, often eaten in pubs, or on picnics. Its origin is unclear although it could possible be a descendant of a form of Indian KOFTA, as suggested by Annette Hope (1987). Ayto (1993) states that the first printed recipe was in Mrs Rundell (edn of 1809), and suggests that the Scottish origin of the item was pointed up by its appearance in Meg Dods (1826), where it is described as being eaten hot with gravy, a practice also recorded by Mrs Beeton (1861).

SCOTCH PIE a small savoury PIE to be bought from bakers throughout Scotland. These small mutton pies, with their crust standing up round them about 1 cm (0.5") above the filling, were always a very popular fast food for working people in Glasgow. They are still to be found in all bakers' shops there, though they are not so easy to find now in some other parts of Scotland. The rim above the meat was often filled with hot gravy, peas or beans, and a spoonful of potato to make a complete meal. They are always served piping hot. Bakers keep them in a hot cupboard—they are not good cold.

CB

SCOTER *Melanitta nigra*, a European and N. American diving duck which used to be thought, at least in Normandy and parts of Britain, to be permissible fare during LENT. Their fishy taste seemed to absolve them

from counting as 'flesh'. However, they have rarely been considered a delicacy, either in Europe or in N. America, although Phillips (1922–6 quoted in Simon, 1983) said that in New England they were 'still very much appreciated by those who have the patience and the courage to stew them in the proper way'. Phillips also took the trouble to pass on a camp cookery method of cooking them in a 'backwards oven', after which they were said to be 'invariably tender, juicy and deliciously flavoured'.

SCOTLAND to venture an understatement, is not at all difficult to distinguish from England; the differences leap to the eye in many different aspects of the two cultures, including notably food and cookery. In these and other respects the people of Scotland have closer links with Scandinavia and France (as explained below), than do the English. Geographical differences have tended to give them different staple foods, especially in the northern part of the country; a lower level of prosperity in the past has imprinted a certain frugality on their kitchens; and the same genius which resulted in a quite disproportionate number of Scots being responsible for British achievements in medicine, engineering, philosophy, and the construction and administration of the British Empire flowered in a different way to produce some of the finest (and in the instance of Meg Dods most astonishing, even surreal) writing on food.

The best starting point from which to explore this fine writing is the classic work entitled *The Scots Kitchen* by F. Marian McNeill (1929). England acquired later a broadly comparable work, that by Dorothy Hartley (1954), but there are few countries in the world which possess an equally charming and scholarly account of their culinary history. Marian McNeill paid due attention to Gaelic terminology and to the underlying Celtic culture, and embellished her book with a truly remarkable wealth of quotations. She was perfectly prepared to quote English authors, not least Boswell (1786) recording the famous trip which he and Dr Johnson made to the Hebrides. Although Johnson, notoriously, defined oats as 'a grain which in England is given to horses, but in Scotland supports the people' (see, however, a gloss on this in OATS), he had many perceptive and complimentary remarks to make about the hospitality he received and the food he ate on this journey. See SCOTCH BROTH for his enthusiastic reaction to that dish. And, in a passage which is immediately comprehensible to any modern reader who has enjoyed a similar experience, he gave unstinted praise to the Scottish breakfast:

In the breakfast the Scots, whether of the Lowlands or mountains, must be confessed to excel us. The tea and coffee are accompanied not only with butter, but with honey, conserves, and marmalades. If an epicure could remove by a wish in quest of sensual gratification, wherever he had supped, he would breakfast in Scotland.

One might add that Johnson's hypothetical epicure would be equally successful in his search for sensual gratification if he or she were to enjoy a proper Scottish HIGH TEA.

The Scottish connection with France is known as the Auld Alliance. Marian McNeill, who provides an appendix of almost 150 Scots culinary terms which are of French derivation, takes care to explain that, despite the belief that Charlemagne (8/9th centuries) was at the origin of the Alliance:

Its authentic beginnings, however, go no farther back than the twelfth century. Later, when England, led by her Norman conquerors into a series of wars of aggression, had subdued Wales and partially subdued Ireland, she turned to Scotland and France, who were thus drawn to make common cause against a powerful enemy, and it was by this means that Scotland was able to maintain the national independence asserted at Bannockburn in the fourteenth century. The Scottish archers fought with distinction during the Hundred Years' War, one of their leaders, the Earl of Buchan, being created Constable of France. In recognition of their services Charles VII appointed as Royal bodyguard the famous Scots Guard of France, which consisted of a hundred gendarmes and two hundred archers. . . . After the Union of the Crowns of England and Scotland in 1603, the native element in the Scots Guard was gradually thinned, but the Guard persisted as part of the pageantry of the French court, until the latter went down, with all its pomps and vanities, in the maelstrom of the French Revolution.

The above-mentioned Meg Dods ('Mistress Margaret Dods of the Cleikum Inn', 1826) affords various glimpses of the French connection, remarking for example that the Scots howtowdie is a version of the Old French *hétoudeau*, both meaning young

hen. The book, purporting to be by a character in Sir Walter Scott's novel *St Ronan's Well*, is prefaced by a diverting and often incomprehensible introduction in which another character from the novel, Peregrine Touchwood, Esquire, commonly styled the 'Cleikum Nabob', descends on Mistress Dods and becomes involved with the 'celebrated Dr Redgill' in a curious blend of horseplay (as when the doctor is charged by a porker and turns a 'somerset') and gastronomic philosophy, punctuated by dour Scottish comments from Mistress Dods. In this zany framework sit hundreds of beautifully precise recipes, many of them equipped with weird footnotes to remind us to take any solemn expression off our faces.

Incidentally, the first Scottish cookbook, by Mrs McClintock (1736), had been a sober affair, short and practical; it was, surprisingly, unknown to bibliographers and food writers until Virginia Maclean (1973 and 1981) brought it to light.

The Scottish links with Scandinavia are most visible in Orkney and Shetland, but continue to be evident down to the Border Country (and indeed into the north of England, which has much in common with the Lowlands of Scotland). The contrast is heightened the further north one goes, partly because of changing geographical features. Annette Hope (1987) has an illuminating chapter about the wild parts of the Highlands and the enormous changes made by deforestation (starting already in medieval times) and other factors, leading to changes in mean annual temperature, patterns of rainfall, habitats for wild animals such as DEER, plus changes in the laws about GAME, the growth of poaching (she cites Alexander Davidson as the supreme poacher, emphasizing his reputation as a devout reader of the Bible, the generosity with which he disbursed his spoils to those in need, and his unusual diet of 'oatmeal saturated with whisky and rolled into sausage-shaped patties'). As for the Scots diet in more general and less eccentric manifestations, another writer, Maisie Steven (1985), has been responsible for a major study of the changes in this from medieval to modern times, and the consequences for health of the Scottish people. In this context the chapter on 'Glasgow Good and Bad 1940s and 50s' by Catherine Brown (1990) is highly illuminating and refers, as part of the 'good' side, to the famous Glasgow tearooms (especially that of Mrs Cranston) which distinguished the city in the first half of the 20th century and provided an excellent outlet for the innovative art nouveau architect Charles Rennie Mackintosh. The same author has described in the same book the work done recently to revitalize traditional Scottish cookery (with horror

stories of the occasional blunders committed by over-zealous and historically ignorant publicists). All these books testify to the importance which Scottish writers attach to Scottish food, and make a good introduction to any reflections about what is likely to happen to it in the 3rd millennium.

For other features of Scottish cookery, see BANNOCK; BAP; BLACK BUN; BROSE; CLAPSHOT; CULLEN SKINK; DUNDEE CAKE; HOGMANAY; KALE; STOVIES; HADDOCK (for Arbroath smokies and Finnan haddies); HAGGIS (not, as sometimes supposed, a purely Scottish item); MARMALADE; PORRIDGE; SWEETIES. See also ORKNEY AND SHETLAND, whose distinctive foodways called for separate treatment.

READING: Catherine Brown (1981, 1985, 1996); MacClure (1935).

SCREWBEAN a bean from the plant *Prosopis juliflora*, which is a shrub related to MESQUITE and which grows in the south-western USA. It is also called tornillo, screws, and screw pod mesquite, all its names having reference to the spiral seed pods. The pods are rich in sugar. The beans may be ground and then combined with water to produce a nourishing gruel. The Mojave Indians thought that the taste of young screwbeans was unsatisfactory and used to leave them to decay in a pit lined with arrow weeds for about four weeks, after which they would dry and grind the beans and then make the gruel.

Leaves and roots have also provided food for American Indians of the region, for example the Papago as well as the Mojave, but the plant has only been cultivated on a small scale.

SCREWPINE also often called pandanus, the common English name of many plants of the genus *Pandanus*, refers to the twisted stems which they usually exhibit. These plants, of which there are hundreds of species, grow in the tropics from India through SE Asia to N. Australia and Oceania.

Classification of the species is still uncertain. A principal species is *P. tectorius* (including what was formerly *P. odoratissimus*), the 'fragrant screwpine'. Its flowers are the source of keora/kewra essence, used in parts of India and in Sri Lanka as a flavouring. In Australia the fruit pulp was baked and eaten by Aborigines.

However, the most important use of screwpine for flavouring purposes is that of the young leaves of *P. amaryllifolius* in Malay and Indonesian dishes. *Daun pandan* (pandan leaf) is an important ingredient, whose use extends also to Thailand and

other SE Asian countries including Vietnam.
It is prized not only for its delicate fragrance
but also for the natural green colour which
can be obtained from the leaves by boiling
them and which is then used to colour
various sweet foods.

Many of the species have fruits which
count as edible although their appeal is
limited. One such is *P. spiralis* in tropical
Australia, which, according to Tim Low
(1991):

> bears enormous fruits the size of human heads,
> which crumble when ripe into wedge-shaped
> segments, the inner bases of which may be sucked,
> but only after roasting in the fire.

This sounds like hard work, but the reward
is said to be pulp tasting like apricot or
custard apple. The seeds, extracted from a
woody matrix inside the fruits, were once an
important Aboriginal food and probably
more important than the fruits because they
were more nutritious.

In New Zealand a plant of the same
family, *Freycinettia banksii*, called *kie kie* or
tawahara by the Maori, provides two edible
items: small fruits and large sugary white
flower bracts.

SCURVY a disease caused by lack of
vitamin C. It affects connective tissue:
symptoms include sore gums and loose
teeth, ulcers on the legs, and lethargy. It
takes several months without the vitamin for
the first signs to appear. The disease can be
quickly cured by eating foods containing the
vitamin.

Scurvy was a sailor's disease, brought on
by months at sea without fresh food. In the
time of the great European explorers at the
end of the 15th century it was the greatest
single cause of death in sailors, even in
wartime. Often ships would arrive after a
long voyage with only a quarter of the crew
alive, and they on the brink of death. On
land, much of the population of Europe was
at risk from scurvy every winter, thanks to a
diet largely of preserved foods and a
prevailing prejudice against fruit and
vegetables. The disease often appeared
among people in besieged towns.

The Chinese had discovered much earlier,
around the 5th century AD, that scurvy at sea
could be avoided by carrying live ginger
plants on board junks. But it took Europeans
until the early 17th century to discover that
green plants and fresh fruits cured scurvy.
Nobody had any idea why, and the discovery
brought little benefit to sailors. On long,
stormy ocean voyages in small, cramped
ships, no plant would survive. During their
rare landfalls sailors would gather any edible
green plants, of which several species became
known as 'scurvy grass' (see CRESS;
HORSERADISH; SEAKALE; SORREL).

Screwpine

One of the few preserved foods to contain
any vitamin C is SAUERKRAUT. This was
often carried in barrels on Dutch ships. By
the 18th century its effect against scurvy had
been noticed. Captain James Cook carried
sauerkraut on his voyages specifically to
prevent scurvy. However, he had great
difficulty making his men eat it.

In 1747 the British naval surgeon James
Lind conducted experiments on
antiscorbutic substances—that is, those able
to prevent scurvy. It had been noticed that
citrus fruits were highly effective, but the
Royal Navy considered them too expensive
to dispense to sailors. One theory was that
the acid in these fruits was the active
substance. Lind selected six groups of two
sailors already suffering from scurvy, and
gave each group a daily dose of one of six
reputed antiscorbutics: vinegar; a small
amount of dilute sulphuric acid; a quart of
cider; a pint of sea water; a medicine made
from nutmeg, garlic, and mustard; and two
oranges and a lemon. The sailors drinking
cider showed a slight improvement, but
those eating the citrus fruits got better
quickly. In 1753 Lind published his results in
A Treatise of the Scurvy.

By the end of the 18th century the Royal
Navy had reluctantly agreed to give lemon
juice to sailors, and the disease vanished at
once from HM ships. In the mid-19th
century lime juice, which was cheaper
because limes were grown in the British
W. Indies, was issued instead. This contains
much less vitamin C than lemon juice. The
disease returned briefly until the dose was
increased. British sailors became known as
'Limeys', a word still in use.

Vitamin C was still undiscovered, and the
dangers of scurvy were still not generally
recognized. Captain Scott would probably
have returned safely from the South Pole in
1912 if he and his men had not been crippled
by scurvy. Ironically, he died just as
researchers in Europe were making real
progress in the discovery of the vitamin (see
VITAMINS).

Scurvy is still seen, very occasionally,
among old people living alone who neglect
their diet.   RH

SEA ANEMONE the name for a group of
marine creatures which resemble flower
heads anchored to rocks and of which a few

are edible. The snake-locks anemone, *Anemonia sulcata*, the best known, appears in Mediterranean markets. After being cleaned and (optionally) marinated, they can be made into a soup or used in an omelette or fried.

A related creature, *Actinia equina*, lacks a real English name but is *tomate de mer* in French, being the size of a tomato and red in colour. It is less edible, but can play a minor supporting role in fish stews or soups.

SEA BASS

Dicentrarchus labrax and *D. punctatus*, remains one of the most prized fishes of Europe as it was in the times of classical Rome. Pliny (1st century AD) stated that specimens taken in rivers, which these fish penetrate some way upstream, were preferred; but nowadays those taken from the sea are counted best.

A silvery fish, with a maximum length of 1 m (40"), the sea bass has a range which extends from the Black Sea through the Mediterranean and in the E. Atlantic from Senegal up to the south coast of England (*D. punctatus*) or as far as Norway (*D. labrax*). It is a favourite fish for anglers, especially on the south coast of Ireland.

The flesh of sea bass is of a fine flavour. It is also relatively free of small bones, and firm; it holds its shape well after cooking. Thus a large specimen is an ideal fish to serve at a cold buffet, and the consequent demand from restaurants is a factor in the high price it fetches. So is the fact that the fishery for it has been on an artisanal scale, or conducted for sport. However, sea bass enter rivers and are prepared to live in saltwater lagoons, so are susceptible to fish farming, despite their slow growth rate, and this has made it easier to provide a controlled supply of 'portion-sized' fish.

See also BASS; STRIPED BASS.

SEA BREAM

mostly of the large family Sparidae, include numerous species which make fine eating. They are particularly abundant in the Mediterranean, where the DENTEX and GILT-HEAD BREAM are especially good; and in the W. Atlantic and Caribbean regions (see PORGY); and have many relations in the warm waters of the Indo-Pacific, where the name bream is applied not only to the family Sparidae but also to members of the families Lethrinidae (some are described under EMPERORS), and Nemipteridae (THREADFIN BREAM) and occasionally to a SNAPPER (thus 'government bream' for *Lutjanus sebae*). The present entry describes them generally and describes the species which seems to be the best qualified to bear the name 'sea bream' as its own.

The sea bream are generally oval in shape when viewed from the side and narrow bodied, with a single long dorsal fin. Most have a large mouth and canine-type teeth; but some species are equipped with other sorts of teeth, designed to deal with their chosen sorts of food.

Common names for these fish are confusing, and many have no real English name, if only because they dwell in non-English-speaking regions. The one species for which sea bream is the accepted common name is *Sparus pagrus*, of particular interest because it occurs both in the Mediterranean (and E. Atlantic) and in the Caribbean region. The explanation is that its eggs are carried westwards across the Atlantic by ocean currents, and their incubation period, of about 60 days, corresponds to the time which this voyage takes. So, after floating across deep waters in which the newly hatched fish would have no chance of survival they arrive at just the right moment among inshore waters of the Caribbean, where they emerge and can survive. This sea

bream (*pagre* in French, *pargo* in Spanish, *pagro* in Italian) is a sizeable fish (maximum length 75 cm/30").

See also RAY'S BREAM.

SEA BUCKTHORN

Hippophäe rhamnoides, a small tree which grows wild in Britain close to the sea, in the Alps, and in Russia and China. It bears clusters of orange berries, insipid in taste, but capable of being stewed and sweetened or made into jams, jellies, etc. Jane Grigson, writing in the *Observer* in 1988, found that with the addition of cream the berries would make an attractive pinkish-orange ice cream.

The spineless cultivar Novost Altaya, developed in Russia, and experiments elsewhere, including Scotland, suggest that these berries may become more important.

SEA CUCUMBER

is a mysterious creature which belongs to the class Holothurians. These creatures are quite distinct from fish, crustaceans, and molluscs. There are a lot of them (over 600 species) and they occur all round the world, but only a few species are used as food and only in some regions, notably the Orient (where the principal markets are at Hong Kong, which is by far the most important, and in Korea, Singapore, and Malaysia) but in recent times also in Barcelona and its environs, and to a small extent in Provence and elsewhere in the Mediterranean, e.g. Istanbul.

A sea cucumber does resemble a cucumber in shape. It is distinctly phallic in appearance, a feature which is underlined by its habit of ejecting sticky threads (Cuvierian tubules) when squeezed. It does not swim around, but moves sluggishly about on the sea bottom extracting modest nourishment from the sediment. This quiet life is

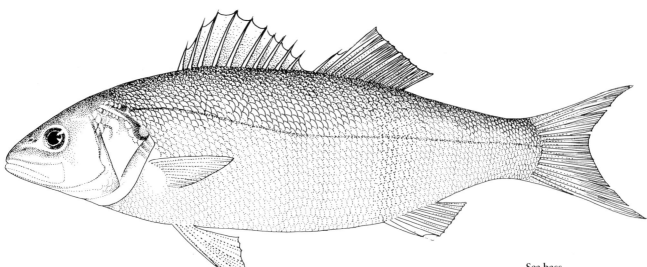

Sea bass
(*Dicentrarchus labrax*)

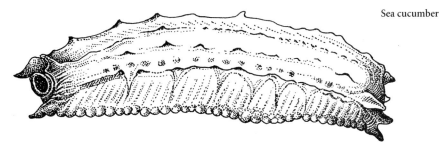

Sea cucumber

sometimes punctuated by a melodramatic piece of behaviour; if severely disturbed, the sea cucumber will eviscerate itself (i.e. eject its entire apparatus of stomach etc.) and then regrow the missing organs within the space of a few weeks.

One end of the sea cucumber is its mouth, recognizable by a fringe of tentacles. The other end houses the anus, and also, quite often, an unwanted guest in the form of a small fish which backs into the hole and lives there, feeding itself by nibbling at the host's gonads.

Sea cucumbers have a great appeal to the Chinese because of the interesting slippery texture which they acquire after being suitably prepared, and also for their flavour. The method followed in preparing them, often done in the Pacific islands where they are collected and processed as a cottage industry, is first to boil them in water until they swell; then to slit them open along the underside, wash them, and boil them again, to the point at which they are rubbery but not too hard; next, to remove the guts and then smoke and dry the creatures over a fire of mangrove wood or coconut husks; and finally to cure them in the sun for a few days. When the time comes to use them, they are soaked to soften them and make them swell in readiness for being cooked.

The species most prized by the Chinese is *Microthele nobilis*, which comes in two forms, white and black, depending on habitat. It is often called teatfish or mammy fish, the latter name being apparently derived from the native name *mama* in the Gilbert Islands. The white teatfish lives in moderately deep water, on clean sand and in or near turtlegrass; the black version likes shallower water and to be near living coral. Next in order of estimation come two somewhat smaller species, both of the genus *Actinopyga*: the blackfish and the deep-water redfish. The prickly redfish, *Thelenota ananas*, is of less value, although still considered to be worth exploiting and of generous size. Its 'prickles' are large teats which occur in groups of two or three all over the body.

In the 1970s an enterprising restaurateur in Barcelona noticed that fishermen on the Catalan coast had for long had the habit of collecting these creatures, of the species *Stichopus regalis*, and eating them themselves. He went into the matter and put them on his menu, since when they have graduated to being the most expensive seafood in Barcelona.

Apart from Barcelona, Japan seems to be the one place where sea cucumbers are marketed fresh. There, and also in Taiwan, it is *Stichopus japonicus*, a relation of the Barcelona species, which is most favoured. Everywhere else, and especially in places where there are ethnic Chinese communities, it is the dried product which is available.

SEA GRAPES *Caulerpa racemosa*, one of the green SEAWEEDS, with 'plastic-looking grapelike nodes borne on branches'. The green is not just green, but vibrant green. This seaweed is always eaten fresh, and should be consumed within hours of being harvested (although Patricia Arroyo Staub, 1982, comments that sea grapes can be kept successfully in a refrigerator for a few days, provided that they are not washed until taken out for consumption). In the Philippines it is usual to eat them with fresh onions and tomatoes. In Indonesia they may be coated with sugar; in China, added to noodle soup; in Taiwan, quick fried or boiled.

SEAKALE *Crambe maritima*, is a member of the CABBAGE family, Cruciferae, as its generic name suggests (*krambe* being Greek for cabbage), but it is not a type of KALE. Nor is it a relative of seakale beet (a kind of CHARD).

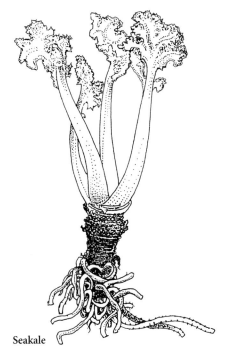

Seakale

Seakale grows wild around the shores of Europe from the Atlantic to the Black Sea. If it grows normally it is bitter and inedible. If, however, the wind covers a young plant with sand, it is cut off from the light and develops a thick, blanched leaf stalk with a tiny, under-developed leaf at the tip. The result is a tender, mild stem vegetable which can be eaten like asparagus, although it takes longer to cook.

It is a traditional sailor's specific against SCURVY, and is one of the various plants called 'scurvy grass'. Lovelock (1972) suggests that Pliny (1st century AD) was referring to seakale when he wrote of a kind of cabbage called 'halmyrides', which grew on the coast, always stayed green, and was taken as a provision for long sea journeys.

Seakale was forced under cover in Italy during the Middle Ages, and its use gradually spread. It reached England in the 17th century. Forced seakale was considered a great delicacy and enjoyed a vogue until the 18th century.

An Asian relative of seakale with large, edible roots, *C. tatarica*, is used in Siberia and as far west as Hungary as the 'Tartar (i.e. Tatar) bread plant'. The roots, which may be grated raw in salads or cooked like potatoes, taste mild and sweet. The plant also has an edible stem.

SEA LETTUCE *Ulva lactuca*, has a worldwide distribution and is possibly the most widespread of the edible green SEAWEEDS. Its thin, crinkled, lettuce-like leaves pass from pale to bright to dark green as they grow and age. They may be used raw in salads or cooked in various dishes and combinations, including soups.

SEALING excluding air from food, is a method of PRESERVATION used since early times. The Romans covered apples in clay to make them keep through the winter. The first systematic use of sealing was in medieval Europe, where it was discovered by trial and error that perishable foods would keep better if enclosed in a PIE. After the pie was cooked, hot fat was poured in through a hole in the crust. This solidified and sealed the contents from the air in the space under the crust. As long as the melted fat and the pie were more or less at boiling point when this was done, the contents would remain sterile and might last for several weeks.

Usually the pie crust, made of hard, dry 'huff paste', was thrown away or given to servants. It was realized that this waste could be avoided if the food was cooked in an earthenware pot rather than a crust—the origin of POTTING. As before, the top was sealed with hot fat; then the pot would be covered with a piece of parchment which would help prevent the seal from being broken. No one then knew of the existence of the micro-organisms that cause spoilage, or how they could be killed by heating, so mistakes were often made, such as allowing the food to cool before pouring on the fat.

Things like jars of pickles would also be 'sealed', often by covering them with a piece of bladder tied firmly into place. A leather top fastened over such a covering gave greater protection against possible assaults by mice and insects. However, this was still not a true seal. A layer of oil on the top of the pickling liquid would be a better solution.

Progress came at the beginning of the 19th century with the invention of what was later called CANNING—though originally glass jars sealed with a cork were used. For the first time the process of heating and sealing was so effective that perishables could be made to keep for years. In the 1860s the French chemist Louis Pasteur discovered how micro-organisms spoil food, so that it was possible to design really effective methods of destroying and excluding them.

Sealing is not restricted to completely sterile packages. Foods that keep reasonably well but develop off flavours when exposed to oxygen in the air, for example nuts and coffee beans, are now sealed in airtight packs. It is helpful to remove as much air as possible from the pack. Sometimes this is done by sucking out air through a small one-way valve to create a partial vacuum, a technique sometimes called by its French name of *fermeture sous vide*. Another method is to fill the container with nitrogen, a cheap and tasteless gas. (RH)

SEALS being marine mammals, attract sympathy from many people and there would be wide support for the proposition that they should not be killed for food except in those sparsely populated areas where they have traditionally been an important part of the diet of the indigenous peoples. Among such people are the Inuit (formerly called Eskimos) in the far north; see INUIT COOKERY. The same applies in the Antarctic, except that in the absence of indigenous populations, the privilege is reserved for explorers and research personnel; see ANTARCTICA for a few details about eating seals there.

SEA PIE (also known as pot pie) seems to have acquired its principal name because it was essentially shipboard food. It was a complete meal in a pan, cooked economically on top of a galley stove. It consisted of a good rich meat stew, with plenty of gravy. The boiled suet pudding which would have accompanied it on land, on shipboard became a suet paste layer laid on top of the stew to steam gently under a tightly fitting lid. Because of this top paste, it was called a 'pie' (sailing vessels did not generally have ovens until the 18th century, when navy ships carried ovens for officers' fare). Sea pie was made by Yorkshire keelmen's families who carried goods from the Humber Estuary onto the Yorkshire canal network, up to the mid-20th century. The keels were barges with huge square sails, which only occasionally ventured to sea. They had a little coal stove in their tiny cabins but no oven, so everything had to be fried or boiled. Harry Fletcher described sea pie in *A Life on the Humber* (1975):

Dad liked to make a sea-pie himself. We had a big oval iron pan into which he would put a rabbit, stewing beef and all the vegetables we had. It was cooked slowly on the fire, and then Dad made a suet dumpling the size of the pan, and we really gorged ourselves.

For the history of sea pie in N. America see Gary Gillman (1991) and Karen Hess (1991). JS

SEA PURSLANE *Sesuvium portulacastrum*, a reddish plant found in hot coastal areas around the world, which belongs to the family Aizoaceae. Its fleshy, succulent leaves may be rinsed to diminish the saltiness and eaten raw as a salad; or cooked; or pickled like SAMPHIRE (to which it has often been compared). American writers about wild food plants have remarked on its presence in the southern states of the USA, and on its usefulness both as a minor vegetable for human use and as animal feed. It is prized in its pickled version in the Philippines.

SEARING the process of cooking the surfaces of a piece of meat briefly at a high temperature until well browned, before reducing the heat and allowing cooking to finish more gently. There is one good reason for searing meat, which is that high temperatures concentrate the juices that do leak, and encourage a process known as the MAILLARD REACTION which gives a good flavour in the finished dish.

CULINARY MYTHOLOGY tells a different tale, and states that searing 'seals the juice' into the meat, thus producing a moister end result and avoiding the loss of flavourful and nutritious matter. There is, however, no truth in this plausible theory. As McGee (1990) has demonstrated by a series of simple and elegant experiments, juice (water, water-soluble proteins and other substances, and melted fat) leaks from meat during cooking whether it has been seared or not, and experiments in the 20th century have shown that seared meat loses rather more weight (through fluid drip) than that cooked at a moderate temperature from beginning to end.

Searing, as a culinary process, originated in the 19th century when German chemist Justus von Liebig postulated, but never demonstrated, that high temperatures coagulated proteins on the surface of meat and formed a juice-trapping 'shell'. Since 18th-century researchers thought they had isolated a water-soluble substance, which they called osmazome, held to be responsible for flavour and nutritive qualities of meat, preserving the juices was considered of prime importance (and played a large part in the development of MEAT EXTRACTS). Harold McGee remarks that Liebig's theory probably became popular because it offered a pseudo-scientific rationale for a new method of cooking, and thinks that the searing myth lives on because it offers a vivid and commonsensical picture of what happens to meat during cooking. Some of its persuasiveness may come from searing's resemblance to cautery, the time-honoured surgical technique of using boiling liquid, a red-hot piece of metal, a burning lens, or an electrical current to stop bleeding.

He notes that the myth has even seduced well-known experts in the field of meat science, but that cauterizing is not, in fact, a good analogy; the slow leaching of fluid from the surface of meat is very different from a steady flow of blood from a defined point. Meat proteins are arranged in bundles of long thin cells, contained in collagen sheaths; conventional methods for slicing meat usually run at right angles to these, allowing fluid to leak from the ends of innumerable cut cells. Under the influence of heat, meat proteins do coagulate from the surface inwards, but instead of welding into a watertight surface, they become shrivelled and disorganized, allowing juice to seep around the ends. After some experiments, McGee concluded that it is the thickness of the meat, and the degree to which it is done, that dictates final moisture content, and observed that fat content also influences the apparent juiciness of the meat when it is eaten. LM

SEA TROUT or salmon trout, *Salmo trutta trutta*, is the sea-going form of a species which also includes the brown trout of rivers and the bull or lake trout of larger inland waters. These other, freshwater, forms are described under TROUT. The sea trout, like the salmon, is a migratory fish, most often caught in rivers, which it ascends in order to spawn; but its middle life is spent at sea. Its natural range is from Portugal to Norway and Iceland. It is particularly esteemed in Wales, as **sewin**.

The maximum length of sea-run trout seems to be over 1 m (40"), but this is exceptional. The fish are usually grey or silvery with black or reddish spots. The flesh, like that of the salmon, is pink; this is because the diet includes crustaceans which contain a carotenoid pigment.

SEA TURTLES creatures which when adult are relatively immune to predators (apart from certain large sharks, whales, and human beings) but whose pattern of reproduction renders them vulnerable to extinction, belong to the order Chelonia (or Testudines) and have a very long history, stretching back to the time of the dinosaurs, 90 million years or so ago.

There are seven surviving species of sea turtle, of which six have a global distribution in tropical or subtropical waters. Many have well-defined feeding areas, such as shallow waters with a plentiful supply of marine grasses, and all have a limited number of 'rookeries' for reproduction. If only these creatures had been able to develop a viviparous capability, so that they could give birth to their babies at sea, they would have an assured future. Unfortunately, however, they stayed with the technique of laying eggs on land, specifically on beaches with certain characteristics, and this may spell their eventual doom. Where the beaches used by the various species have been identified, efforts may be made to prevent at least human predators from digging up the eggs; but in the case of mainland beaches it seems all but impossible to protect the eggs from raccoons and foxes. (It should not be thought that the turtles are careless about depositing their eggs. On the contrary, they go to great lengths to excavate deep holes in the sand—Bustard (1972) records finding dead turtles, stricken by a heart attack brought on by the intense physical effort, poised over the holes they were making— and to cover their traces afterwards. But several predators can detect the eggs by smell, even though they are buried deep.)

Early navigators who carried out the great voyages of exploration soon discovered the advantages of capturing live turtles and keeping them on board as a source of food when needed. As Carr (1967) wrote:

The vitamin hunger of sailors, which came from nowhere and made men's gums grow over their teeth, and could send a corpse a day sliding over the rail, practically disappeared in the Caribbean after the discovery of *Chelonia*, the green turtle. No other edible creature could be carried away and kept so long alive. Only the turtle could take the place of spoiled kegs of beef and send a ship on for a second year of wandering or marauding. All early activity in the new world tropics— exploration, colonisation, buccaneering and the manœuvrings of naval squadrons—was in some way dependent on the turtle.

Although the number who perished in this way in the Caribbean was great, what happened there only affected a small proportion of the world population. The same was, broadly speaking, true of the depredations which followed when, in the 18th century, the fashion for turtle soup began.

The earliest recipes for dressing sea turtle were given by Richard Bradley (1732), and ascribed by him to a Barbados lady. Bradley said that the sea turtle 'is a fine Animal, partaking of the Land and Water. Its Flesh between that of Veal, and that of a Lobster, and is extremely pleasant, either roasted or baked. There are some of these Creatures that weigh near two hundred Weight. They are frequently brought to *England* in Tubs, of Sea Water, and will keep alive a long time.' He did not mention turtle soup, but this soon became a standard feature of English cookery books; it appeared, for example, in the 4th edition (1751) of Hannah Glasse's famous book *The Art of Cookery Made Plain and Easy*.

Turtle soup, prepared from the calipee (flipper meat) was elevated in the 19th century to become a 'must' for civic banquets and suchlike occasions; and, since it was difficult and expensive to make, recipes for MOCK TURTLE SOUP, of which the first seems to have been in Hannah Glasse's 6th edition (1758), became increasingly frequent.

Calipee, incidentally, is adjacent to the lower shell of the turtle and contains yellowish gelatinous matter. Calipash is the meat adjoining the upper shell and it has green gelatinous matter. Calipash is sometimes used as the name of a dish prepared from this upper meat. When it has been dried (which is easy) it is very light and easily portable and almost indestructible.

Although developments of this sort contributed to endangering the survival of the sea turtles, it seems likely that the greatest threat has come from the consumption of and traffic in their eggs. These are not hard shelled, like hen's eggs, but enclosed in a flexible white membrane. It is usual to boil them, but they do not set hard; the white will remain quite liquid.

The species which have been exploited as food are as follows:

- *Chelonia mydas*, the green turtle, varies in colour from pale olive green through greenish-brown to almost black. The maximum length of its carapace, measured over the curve, is 1.5 m (between 4.5 and 5') and the maximum weight is something like 200 kg (240 lb), but most specimens are far smaller. The flesh of this species is the best for making turtle soup and for eating generally.
- *Eretmochelys imbricata*, the hawksbill turtle, has as its name indicates hooked jaws which enable it to feast on crabs and prawns. It is smaller than the green turtle (length of carapace unlikely to be more than 75 cm/30") and less sought after as food than as the source of tortoiseshell. It is, however, eaten, and its eggs are prized as a delicacy.
- *Caretta caretta*, the common or loggerhead turtle, may be 1 m (40") long, is brown in colour, and provides good meat which has been made into turtle stew in Malta, for example.
- *Dermochelys coriacea*, the leathery or leatherback turtle, is by far the largest, sometimes measuring almost 2 m (7') long. Its back is covered with a thick, leathery skin, rather than a true carapace, and has seven golden ridges running from front to rear. It is a truly pelagic species, given to wandering over the oceans (as opposed to making periodic migrations to reach rookeries). Its meat is not prized, but its eggs are; these may be as large as tennis balls and have a reputation—shared with the smaller eggs of the other species—as an aphrodisiac.

It is to be hoped that measures of conservation and the nascent industry of turtle farming will be successful in maintaining the sea turtles as a renewable food resource.

SEA URCHIN the common name for a sea creature (of the order Diadematoida) which provides the least amount of edible material for its volume; but that small part is a great delicacy.

The name sea urchin comes from an old English meaning of urchin: hedgehog. And the sea urchin does look like a small hedgehog, with spines sticking out in all directions from its 'shell' (correctly, 'test'). These spines break off easily and are very difficult to extract from, for example, the foot of an incautious bather. Their purpose is to make their owner an unattractive mouthful for predators.

Inside the more or less spherical test there is little edible matter: in fact nothing but the five orange or rose-coloured ovaries, also known as corals. These are revealed by cutting the sea urchin open horizontally, preferably using the French implement designed for the purpose and called *coupe-oursin*, the French name for sea urchin being *oursin*. The corals, which need no cooking, make a delicious mouthful, with no accompaniment save a drop of lemon juice. They can, however, be incorporated in certain cooked dishes, for example an omelette or scrambled eggs, and can also be used to make an excellent sauce.

The sea urchin of the Mediterranean, *Paracentrotus lividus*, is the best known, and the Mediterranean region is where these delicacies, marketed where they are landed, are most appreciated. This species may be found as far north as the south coast of Ireland. It measures up to 8 cm (4") in diameter.

In the N. Atlantic, all the way round from the English Channel to New Jersey, the species is *Strongylocentrus droebachiensis*. Indeed, it has a circumpolar distribution. However, it is not marketed in many places. In N. Europe, for example, it is largely ignored. It is abundant on the coast of Maine but is there called 'whore's eggs' and regarded with abhorrence. Some are fished in the Bay of Fundy, and the taste for them may spread, but the unwieldy nature of the creatures makes it uneconomic to transport them unless they are going to fetch a very high price at their destination. On the whole, it seems likely that they will continue to be exploited only locally, and only in certain places. Some evidence suggests that the number of such places may be diminishing. A clergyman called Wallace, writing about Orkney in the 1680s, said: 'The common people reckon the meat of the Sea Urchin or Ivegars, as they call them, a great Rarity, and use it oft instead of butter.' This practice has died out and Orcadians now call the sea urchin 'scarriman's heid', scarriman meaning a tramp or street child with unruly, spiky hair.

Further south in the W. Atlantic there are smaller species, little eaten except for *Cidaris tribuloides* in the W. Indies.

The giant sea urchin of California, *Strongylocentrus franciscanus*, has been declared by Euell Gibbons (1964) to be the best of all, and to be greatly appreciated by Californians of Italian descent. It is sometimes as much as 10 cm (5") in diameter. *S. purpuratus* is smaller but more abundant, and its corals also have a fine flavour.

SEAWEEDS marine algae which, insofar as they are used as food, might better be termed 'sea vegetables'; but this new term has yet to achieve wide currency, perhaps because the ways of preparing and serving seaweeds, and the quantities eaten, seem far removed from vegetable cookery. Japan is

undoubtedly the country in which consumption of seaweeds and knowledge about them is highest.

The main edible species, and indeed all seaweeds, fall into three groups, distinguished by their basic coloration (although this can vary according to several factors).

Green and blue-green seaweeds include:

- *Enteromorpha* spp (Japanese *aonori*/AWO-NORI);
- *Ulva lactuca* (SEA LETTUCE).

Brown seaweeds include:

- *Laminaria* spp (Japanese KOMBU);
- *Undaria pinnatifida* (Japanese WAKAME).

Red seaweeds include:

- *Porphyra tenera* and other *Porphyra* spp, NORI in Japan, laver in English;
- *Chondrus crispus* (CARRAGEEN);
- *Palmaria palmata* (DULSE);
- *Gelidium amansii* (Japanese TENGUSA).

Although numerous seaweeds are edible in one form or another, only a limited number are consumed on a large scale. In Japan, production of wakame has been by far the greatest, kombu and nori in second and third places.

Many seaweeds are processed, e.g. by drying, compressing into sheets, after being harvested. Some are available in powdered form, as a kind of seasoning.

Besides being consumed fresh or after being processed as described above, seaweeds also yield substances which are of great importance to the food industry and are consumed 'invisibly' in foods as diverse as biscuits and confectionery, ice cream, syrups, jams, and salad dressings. These are the so-called phytocolloids, naturally occurring in seaweeds and capable of stabilizing and emulsifying. The most important are algin (or alginic acid), agar, and carrageenan. These are all derived from red or brown seaweeds.

The nutritional qualities of seaweeds are impressive. They typically provide useful protein, easily assimilable carbohydrate, virtually no fat, generous helpings of minerals and other trace elements, plus vitamins.

SEED CAKE similar to MADEIRA CAKE, flavoured with CARAWAY seeds. Now considered an old-fashioned curiosity and rarely made, seed cake formerly enjoyed great popularity in Britain. Early versions contained caraway COMFITS; seeds alone came into use in the 18th century.

Seed cake probably had another meaning, as given in an account by Morris (1892):

Fifty years ago seed-time had also its festival, though on a lesser scale, as well as harvest. At the

backend, when the early sowing had been completed, the farmer made a sort of feast for his men, the principal feature of which was 'seed-cake', which was given to each of them. The cake did not get its name from anything that it contained, for it was in fact an ordinary sort of currant or plum cake, but from the occasion. On these minor festivals the men had as much ale to drink as they liked, and right well they enjoyed themselves. This old custom has, I believe, now quite died out.

This may be the sense Thomas Tusser (1557) intended, speaking of seed cake to which the village was treated when wheat-seed was put in the ground.   LM

SEMOLINA is usually made from the very hard durum WHEAT, a variety of Mediterranean origin which is now grown mostly in the USA and Canada. When coarsely milled, the brittle grains fracture into sharp chips, and it is these which constitute ordinary semolina.

The word 'semolina' is Italian, derived from the Latin *simila*, denoting fine flour. The use of the term in English for coarse chips therefore represents a departure from the original meaning. In fact, however, a finer semolina flour is available; this is used for making PASTA, so durum wheat is sometimes called macaroni wheat.

The main characteristic of semolina is that it is tough and will not turn into a starchy paste when cooked. Paradoxically, this causes it to produce a light texture, of an interestingly granular nature. Semolina is therefore used in making GNOCCHI and CROQUETTES, both of which can otherwise be heavy and stodgy.

British semolina pudding, being essentially just semolina cooked in milk (and therefore lacking the flavour which is developed when wheat products are cooked at higher temperatures, e.g. by frying), does not show off the product to advantage. However, properly used, semolina can be as delicate as any starch, tending to form a paste rather than a jelly. In this role it is a thickener in Middle Eastern dishes of the MA'MOUNIA type, and also, fried golden brown and then mixed with large amounts of sugar, gives solidity to most of the many kinds of HALVA.

Semolina continues to be used interchangeably with cornflour in some puddings of the general BLANCMANGE type. The German *rote Grütze* and Scandinavian *rødgrøt* ('red groats' in the sense of a fine grained PORRIDGE), which are thickened fruit purées, often use semolina. See also KISEL. So do the Italian *budino di ricotta* and the Russian *gurievskaya kasha*: see RICOTTA and KASHA.

Semolina cakes are made in some countries. The Greek *ravaní* calls for flour and semolina in equal amounts. After baking, the hot cake is cut into squares while still in the tin and soaked with a thin syrup.

Maize and rice 'semolinas' are also made, but are starchier than the genuine article.

SERVICE À LA FRANÇAISE See also SERVICE À LA RUSSE. The whole question of service *à la* this or that is of limited interest and, at the time when people were exercised about the matter, only affected a minuscule proportion of the human species. However, some understanding of the matter, especially the so-called service à la française which persisted in the aristocratic upper end of French and other European cuisines from medieval times until the mid-19th century, is essential for understanding many early cookery books, and in particular those which had to do with court cookery.

In former times the structure of a formal meal was not by 'courses' (as the term is now understood) but by *services*. Each *service* could comprise a choice of dishes from which each guest could select what appealed to him or her most.

- The first service could include soups, HORS D'ŒUVRES (somewhat different from what now bear that name), things to replace the soups (e.g. meat dishes), and things in the category of ENTRÉE (e.g. more meat dishes).
- The second service would include roast game and meats and any particularly impressive savoury dishes, e.g. a whole roast sturgeon.
- The third service called entremets (see ENTRÉE) would include a wide-ranging mixture of vegetable and other dishes (different from entremets in the more recent sense of sweet dishes).
- The fourth service would be DESSERT: fruits, compotes, pastries, and finally ices and cheeses (if served).

Except for the business of *relevés* ('removes'), which meant substituting one lot of dishes for another lot of dishes within a single service, the procedure for a meal of this kind would be to put all the items belonging to one service on the table together, for display. Then either the diners would help themselves as best they could from whatever was within reach or the dishes would temporarily be taken away to be carved up in portions and offered to the diners.

This system was, obviously, cumbrous and not at all conducive to the enjoyment of the foods. One has the impression that some of the ramifications of the system may have been invented for the greater glory of the masters of ceremony and chefs and cookery book authors, who were probably the only people to understand them. In short, the system may have been appropriate for state banquets and other formal occasions, when making an impression of wealth and power was the purpose, but it was inappropriate for other purposes.

Peter Brears (1994) has given a fine and well-illustrated account of the waning of this kind of service in Britain.

SERVICE À LA RUSSE is what replaced SERVICE À LA FRANÇAISE, in Britain and elsewhere in Europe (France, Germany), in the course of the 19th century. This new style of table service provided for dishes being served to guests at their seats by servants who handed them round. It therefore required more servants. There was also the need for table decorations to take up the spaces which the dishes themselves would have occupied under the old system.

Valerie Mars (1994) has drawn attention to the difficulty in discerning when the new system was first introduced and to the considerable controversy which it brought about in aristocratic or plutocratic circles in England, where some opposition and incomprehension persisted until almost the end of the century. She observes that Mrs Beeton (1861) 'advised against dinners *à la Russe* in households without sufficient resources', i.e. the sort of household for whose mistresses she was writing. A cartoon in *Punch* in 1863 shows a couple of baffled Englishmen dining à la russe in France. Says one: 'this is what they call à la Russe, isn't it?' Responds the other: ' "Allerouse" is it? Well there, I could a' sworn it warn't Beef or Mutton.'

Most commentators agree that, however closely the earliest W. European dinners à la russe may have been modelled on some (unidentified) paradigm, the relationship had become attenuated by the beginning of the 20th century. Comments by Russian visitors to Paris or London must have been recorded and would make interesting reading, but have not come to light in a food history context.

SERVICE-BERRIES fruits of N. American trees of the genus *Amelanchier* in the rose family. There are a dozen or so species and several hybrids. The purplish 'berries' (not true berries but drupes, i.e. fruits structured like apricots, with a single stone) have a general resemblance to blueberries and vary in edibility from very good to passable. Other names for some of them include sarvisberry, shadbush or shadbloom (because blooming when the shad are running in eastern rivers), juneberry, and saskatoon. This last name usually applies to *A. alnifolia*, which is evidently the best, since it has far more cultivars than the others. *A. canadensis*, apparently unique in that it is found also in E. Asia, ranks second.

The Indians in N. America used service-berries as fresh food and also beat them into a paste as an ingredient for PEMMICAN.

Where they are plentiful and good, or cultivated, they are well worth eating. 'To the European taste the berries are best when made into puddings or pies, the thoroughly cooked seeds giving a flavor suggesting sweet cherry pie. The berries, especially if cooked first, are splendid for berry-muffins, yielding a rich almond flavor.' In addition to this enthusiastic verdict, Fernald and Kinsey (1943) remark that some early travellers in the north of America, such as Sir John Richardson, considered that the dried berries, used in puddings, were almost as good as the finest currants.

SESAME *Sesamum indicum*, one of the first oil-yielding plants to be taken into cultivation, in Egypt or the Near East. Wild species, with one exception, are African; but there is a secondary 'source of diversity' in India, where sesame was introduced in very early times. The name sesame is one of the few words to have passed into modern languages from ancient Egyptian, in which it was *sesemt*.

Sesame is an upright annual herb, up to 2 m (6') tall and bearing its seeds inside small, sausage-shaped pods about 3 cm (1.25") long. The pods of primitive strains have a tendency to split abruptly open when ripe, allowing the seeds to scatter. This may account for the command 'Open sesame' in the tale of Ali Baba and the Forty Thieves.

The seeds are numerous, pear shaped, and no more than 3 mm (0.1") in length. They may be white, yellow, brown, or black, according to variety, with a white inside which is revealed when they are hulled. They have a pleasantly nutty flavour, which is developed by roasting. The oil produced from them, in the unrefined state, also tastes slightly nutty. Thus both the seeds and oil have a role in flavouring, besides providing a simple food or cooking medium.

Sesame is often mentioned by classical writers. The Greek authors Herodotus (5th century BC) and Strabo (1st century BC) both mention its being cultivated for oil in Babylonia, and this is confirmed by an entry for sesame oil on a clay tablet forming part of the accounts of Nebuchadnezzar's palace (6th century BC). Theophrastus (4th century BC) described sesame as being grown in Egypt. In the 1st century AD Dioscorides mentioned the sprinkling of sesame seed on bread in Sicily, a practice which has continued to the present day, e.g. on hamburger buns.

Further east, sesame had long been grown in Persia and India. It was probably introduced from Persia into China early in the Christian era, but the first firm evidence of it in China dates from the end of the 5th century AD; see Laufer (1978).

In Africa the cultivation of sesame dates back to early times not only in Egypt and Ethiopia but also further to the south and west. Other species of the genus, e.g. *S. alatum* (tacoutta), were also gathered from the wild by tribes in the regions of the Sudan and former Tanganyika. It was from W. Africa that slave traders took seeds to America. Substantial quantities are now grown in Guatemala, Venezuela, Mexico, and the south of the USA (where the W. African name 'benni' survives as 'benniseed'), although the main producing countries are China and India.

Considered simply as a source of oil, sesame has a low yield, on average 150 kg per hectare (135 lb an acre). Even the olive, whose yield is notoriously low, averages 200 kg a hectare, and the prolific oil palm more than 1,000 kg. However, sesame oil is of high value, free of unwanted odours, with good keeping qualities, and high in polyunsaturated fatty acids (oleic, linoleic); and sesame seeds are in strong demand for flavouring.

Sesame oil is important as a cooking oil in S. India. In Japan it is said to have been the only cooking oil used in the distant past, and is still the most highly esteemed (although nowadays frequently mixed with a less expensive and more neutral-tasting oil). The Chinese prize it highly; their name for it means 'fragrant oil'. In some regions it is used for general frying purposes; in others it will be added to dishes, both sweet and savoury, in small amounts just before serving, so that its fragrance is not lost.

In W. and C. Europe sesame seeds are not much used except for sprinkling on bread and cakes, but at the eastern end of the Mediterranean it becomes more common. Notable uses there are for TAHINI, a ground sesame paste, and in sweets such as HALVA.

In India, where the name *gingili* (Anglicized to gingelly) is used, the seeds have many roles in cookery: sprinkled on breads, pastries, and biscuits; used as an ingredient in a sweet called *tilkuta*; also in PILAFS, sauces, stuffings, and sometimes fried and sweetened. In China the seeds are used as a coating for small, deep-fried titbits, and in confectionery, practices now common elsewhere too.

However, it is probably in Japan that the use of sesame seeds has been most highly developed especially in *shojin-ryori*, i.e. the vegetarian cooking traditionally developed and practised in Buddhist monasteries and temples, whose influence on Japanese home cooking is considerable. Although sesame is cultivated in Japan, the demand for sesame seeds far outstrips the domestic production, and much is imported.

All three types of seeds are sold in Japan—black, white, and brown (or golden). There seems to be little or no difference in taste, and which type is chosen for a particular dish is largely a matter of habit based on aesthetics. However they are to be used, they are always lightly roasted in the first place. Roasting such tiny seeds evenly and without burning requires care. Traditionally this is done in a *horoku* (a shallow, oval, unglazed earthenware dish used for slow cooking) over a charcoal fire, but nowadays it is common to use a small frying pan.

The roasted seeds are often sprinkled over rice or other cooked foods as an added flavour. They are sometimes mixed with salt and placed on the table as a condiment (*goma-shio*, i.e. sesame-salt). Also, sesame seeds are one of the main components of various dressings, for *aemono* (see JAPANESE CULINARY TERMS) and dipping sauces.

It is rare for sesame seeds to become the chief ingredient of a dish, but one notable exception is *goma-dofu* (sesame TOFU). For this seeds of the white type are roasted, ground to a smooth paste, mixed with water and arrowroot, cooked slowly, and set in a rectangular mould. The result is eaten by itself or used as a garnish in a clear soup.

SEV AND SEVIYAN, Indian noodle terms. The Sanskrit name for noodles is *sevika*, which may derive from an unrecorded word meaning 'thread' connected with the root *siv*, which refers to sewing.

Sev are crisp, fried 'noodles' prepared from BESAN FLOUR. To make them a special press, a *sev*-maker, is used. They are a popular Indian snack food.

Seviyan (also *seviya/sivayya/shavayi*) usually refers to a sweet dish of vermicelli noodles. HS

SEYCHELLES an archipelago of more than 100 islands north of the Malagasy Republic in the Indian Ocean, was apparently described by General Gordon as the biblical Garden of Eden. Modern tourists, whose numbers are wisely limited by the government to 4,000 or so at any one time, might well agree so far as scenery and fauna are concerned, but the paucity of information about the diet of Adam and Eve (only the apple?) precludes any comparison between their cuisine and that of the Seychelles. However, there was no sea accessible to Adam and Eve. So, since the Seychelles diet is based on seafood (plus the COCONUT, RICE, BREADFRUIT, and numerous not-mentioned-in-the-Bible tropical fruits), there must be great differences.

Fish which are popular locally include various species which were almost unknown to Europeans 50 years ago but are now imported from the Indian Ocean to W. Europe—including, for example, several species of SNAPPER (such as *Lutjanus sebae*, called *bourgeois*, and JOBFISH), and of the huge family Carangidae (mostly called JACK in English), besides large fish such as TUNA, MARLIN, and SAILFISH. Fish dishes tend to incorporate a sauce or to be of the curry type, using coconut cream.

Coconut cream also appears with fried banana as a dessert. The many varieties of banana include tiny ones (mignons) and a giant red PLANTAIN. There are almost as many varieties of MANGO as of banana and when these are in season (October to January) they play a leading role in fresh fruit salads, usually dusted with cinnamon. Other fruits which are popular include PAPAYA, JACKFRUIT, and CUSTARD APPLE (locally *zat*).

Some of these fruits are popular also with the fruit-eating bats, which may themselves figure on a Seychelles menu as one of a number of exotic items. Seychelles menus do contain surprises, and unexpected combinations of ingredients or techniques from the various influences (African, French, English, Indian, Malay, and Chinese) which have played upon the islands since they first became inhabited in the 18th century.

SHABU-SHABU a Japanese one-pot dish inspired by the Mongolian hotpot. The name is supposed to indicate the swishing noise made by the morsels of meat as they are moved in the boiling broth. In Japanese restaurants, Shabu-shabu is often made in a shining brass recipient resembling a samovar in shape; it has a central funnel which contains live charcoal. The dish is always prepared at table, but a waitress may relieve the diner of the task of cooking the morsels.

The main ingredients are thinly sliced beef and an assortment of vegetables. These could include Chinese leaves (see CHINESE CABBAGE), welsh onion (see ORIENTAL ONIONS), and shiitake, possibly with the addition of TOFU or *shirataki* (see KONNYAKU). Everything is cut into bite-sized pieces which the diners, using chopsticks can swish back and forth in the boiling broth until cooked to their liking. The morsels are eaten with dipping sauces. This dish is a fairly recent introduction to Japanese cookery.

SHAD fish of the genus *Alosa* in the HERRING family, normally live in the sea but ascend rivers in the spring to spawn; and that is when they are caught and are at their best for eating.

The most famous species is the American shad, *A. sapidissima*. This abundant species was originally a poor people's food on the eastern seaboard but later achieved the status of a delicacy, as did its roe. Weaver (1982) has described the change in Philadelphia, where it was most noticeable. During the 19th century this shad was introduced to the Pacific coast. Its close relations in America include *Pomolobus mediocris*, the hickory shad.

In Europe, the principal species are *Alosa alosa*, the allis (or allice) shad, and *A. fallax*, the twaite shad. The former may reach a length of 60 cm (24") and has a range from the Mediterranean (where it is rare) to S. Ireland; the latter is slightly smaller and is more common in the Mediterranean, besides being found as far north as the Baltic.

Dallas in *Kettner's Book of the Table* (1877) observed that the best shad were at that time to be found in the rivers of Germany and France; and that these fish demonstrated their love of salt by following salt barges up the Seine to Paris.

There are also species in the Black Sea and its region, notably *A. pontica*. The Soviet cookery book which was published under Stalin's auspices in the 1930s, *The Book of Tasty and Healthful Foods*, refers to it as the Kerch herring (the Kerch Strait being what connects the Black and Azov seas) and asserts that it has a worldwide reputation as the best fish of its kind; an assertion in which some have detected the hand of Stalin himself.

Various fish in Indo-Pacific waters are referred to as shad, including the famous Indian hilsa, *Hilsa ilisha*, and a couple of species called 'gizzard shad' because they have thick muscular stomachs like the gizzard of a fowl.

Caught in their prime, shad are good to eat; but there is a notorious difficulty over their numerous small bones. A legend of the Micmac Indians explains that the shad was originally a porcupine which, discontented with its lot, asked the Great Spirit Manitou to change it into something else. The spirit responded by turning the creature inside out and tossing it into a river, where it had to begin a new existence as a shad.

There are various theories about how to 'melt' the bones before eating the fish. One is that very long cooking achieves this. Others believe that the oxalic acid in sorrel will do the trick; hence the numerous traditional recipes which call for cooking shad with sorrel, including *Alose à l'oseille* in France. There is some experimental evidence to support this practice. No doubt other experiments would show that a more expensive ingredient, cognac, is also

efficacious; this was asserted by M. Francis Marre, a *chimiste-expert* at the Court of Appeals in Paris, who came from Tressan, where shad fished in the Hérault have been given this treatment.

Well-known American recipes include Planked shad. An interesting one from Morocco calls for stuffing the shad with dates which have themselves been stuffed with a mixture of almonds, semolina, etc.

SHADO BÉNI the mysterious and highly variable name given in the W. Indies to *Eryngium foetidum*, a plant native to tropical America which is used as a flavouring herb. Other spellings which may be met include: shadon bené, shadow beynay, shado benni, and chadron beni. All seem to be descended from a French vernacular name, *chardon béni*, meaning blessed thistle. The plant is not a thistle, but has thistle-like leaves.

Among the places where it is much used are Trinidad, where it is commonly found growing wild in drainage ditches etc. It is a favourite herb for use in fish dishes.

Fit weed is a Jamaican name given in a W. Indian book, apparently because the herb is thought to cure people of fits. In this connection, see the separate and complementary entry under the headword FITWEED. Anyone supposing that the existence of two entries for a single plant, and a smelly one at that, must be due to some sort of accident will be absolutely right.

SHALLOT *Allium cepa*, Aggregatum Group, differs from the regular ONION in that instead of having a single bulb it divides into a cluster of small bulbs. These are smaller, more delicate in flavour, and less powerful in smell than ordinary round onions.

The subdivision into little bulbs is a characteristic which the shallot shares with some other species, all of which are known as aggregate or bunching onions. Unlike round onions, these aggregate onions are perennials, spreading themselves by means of the division process. Some sorts, milder than shallots, are usually called 'multiplier' or 'ever ready' onions. One, grown mainly in Ireland, is the 'potato onion', so called because its bulbs are broader than they are high, and resemble a potato in shape.

Amongst the several kinds of shallot, most have elongated brown bulbs. One variety is known in France as the *cuisse de poulet* on account of its golden skin. Other types have grey-brown or pink or (in SE Asia, for example) red skins.

The shallot was described before 300 BC by the Greek writer Theophrastus, who called it *askolonion*. In the 1st century AD

Pliny concluded that it was so named because it came from Askalon (now Ashkelon, in S. Israel), and the attribution has remained. In truth it originated much further east, probably in C. Asia, and reached India before it came to the Mediterranean.

The original Greek name has spawned all the modern names, as well as the term 'scallion', which has been used to mean a shallot, a spring onion (especially in the USA), or one of the small bulbs of any bunching variety of onion.

Shallots can be eaten raw in salads, but their special qualities are best revealed when they are cooked. Their contribution to French cuisine, and especially to certain sauces, e.g. BÉARNAISE, is well known; but they are of no less importance in the Orient. They also make excellent pickles, and are much used for this purpose in SE Asia.

Julie Sahni (1980) says that 'shallot is particularly savored by those vegetarians who are forbidden to eat garlic. The southern vegetable-and-lentil stew called SAMBAR, made with shallots as the only vegetable, is considered a delicacy around the entire country of India.'

SHA'RIYYA the usual term in the Arab world for vermicelli (see PASTA SHAPES). It is pronounced *sha'riyya*, as if from the word for 'hair'. This is a logical derivation, and the Turkish world *şehriye* reflects this pronunciation, but since its first appearance in the 15th century, the word has regularly been spelled *sha'îriyya*, as if from the word for 'barley'.

Menus written in a learned style of Arabic sometimes call vermicelli by an antique Greek name, *itriya*, and *itriya* is the modern Hebrew generic term for pasta. In the Middle Eastern region vermicelli is most often toasted light brown and cooked in a PILAF (*rizz bi-sha'riyya*).

N. Africans also make *sha'riyya* noodles, using the method described in the 13th-century Arabic recipes from Spain of rolling pellets of dough between the fingers until they become short strings. The noodles are sometimes steamed like COUSCOUS.

For the usual Arab home-made noodle, see RESHTEH. CP

SHARKS include many edible species, of which the best known are treated under ANGEL SHARK, DOGFISH, HAMMERHEAD SHARK, and PORBEAGLE. This entry deals with them in a general way, briefly describing some of their characteristics.

Sharks are not necessarily large; nor are they all dangerous. Some of the dogfish are quite small, and some big sharks are inoffensive. But in general they are large and voracious fish. Like the RAY AND SKATE and the STURGEON, they differ from the majority of fish in having no true bones. Instead they have a cartilaginous skeleton. In this respect they are a survival from the very distant past and count as 'primitive' fish; the fish with proper bones are a more recent development. Despite being primitive creatures in this sense, sharks have proved to be highly successful survivors. There are a lot of them. The FAO survey *Sharks of the World* (Compagno, 1984) is in two large volumes. The author states that approximately 350 species of living sharks are currently known. He adds that about 48% of these are to his knowledge of no use to fisheries; 25% are of limited use; 20% are of considerable importance; and 7% are major fisheries species.

SHARK'S FIN an ingredient greatly valued in China, comes—obviously—from a SHARK, but not just any shark and not just any fin. Of the numerous species in the Indo-Pacific only a few are especially sought because they yield fins with the qualities required; and distinctions are also made between e.g. the dorsal fin and the ventral fins and others.

Kreuzer (1974) listed what he thought were the most valuable fins, explaining that those of sharks shorter than 1.5 m (5') are preferred, and mentioning the pectoral fins of the sawfish shark (*Pristis pactinatus*) and, more generally, the upper lobe of the tail of all sharks. He additionally listed fins of one of the nurse sharks; and the more recent publication by Compagno (1984) draws attention to the use of one such shark, *Nebirus ferrugineus*.

The value of fins, which are always sold dried, depends also upon their condition and on the length of unbroken cartilaginous 'strands' which they will yield after the very elaborate processing which they undergo in professional kitchens. Some idea of the care which is lavished on them is afforded by the reflections of Cheng (1962) on the technique to be followed in keeping a fin in perfect shape during both the cooking processes which it will undergo. He explains that Cantonese cooks will use a 'net' made of bamboo to fasten the fin in its shape, and that this device is not used by cooks of other schools. But this device is not really ideal; for the bamboo net, however clean it may be, might, in the long process of cooking at the semi-final stage, leave, at least psychologically, a trace (however infinitesimal it may be) of the taste of the bamboo. Anyhow, such a net might hinder the juices of the ingredients cooked with the fin from permeating the fin thoroughly. Therefore a net made of fine silver wire should be used.

Shark's fin soup has a base of (usually) a rich chicken broth. The gelatinous quality of the fin gives the soup its remarkable texture. The Chinese appreciate the soup not only for this but also because shark's fin counts as one of the *pu* foods. These are foods with a reputation for strengthening and repairing the human body. Typically, they are rich in protein and easily digestible. Many are also 'exotic' in the eyes of foreigners and expensive.

Shark's fin can also be braised and served as a dish on its own; or, more economically, used in small quantities to give a 'special' character to dishes such as scrambled egg, stuffing for duck, filling for DIM SUM, etc.

SHCHI the famous cabbage soup of Russia. Pokhlebkin (1984) claims that it has been the basic hot soup of Russia since 1,000 years ago, and that over these many centuries 'an ever-present smell of shchi prevailed in every Russian peasant hut'. He points out that there are many different versions, but gives the following clear guidance on ingredients for the most traditional one.

In its most complete form shchi contains six ingredients: cabbage, meat (or in rare instances fish or dried or salted mushrooms), root vegetables (carrots, parsnips), spicy seasoning (onion, celery, garlic, dill, pepper, bay leaf) and tart or sour flavouring (sour cream, apples, sauerkraut brine). The first and last are the indispensable ingredients.

Jean Redwood writes (1989):

cabbage soup or shchi is to the Russians what minestrone is to the Italians. It is eaten by rich and poor and spoken of and longed for by exiles, referred to often in Russian literature and even evoked in poetry.

SHEA BUTTER sometimes called galam butter, is a solid vegetable fat prepared from the seeds of an African tree, *Butyrospermum paradoxum* ssp *parkii*, found in many of the drier parts of tropical Africa. The fat can be refined until tasteless and odourless, and is sold as baking fat under various trade names. It is an important article of local diet.

The trees produce oval fruits which enclose in their sweet but scanty pulp a single, oval, shiny brown seed almost 4 cm (1.5") long. The pulp is edible but is not usually eaten, since part of the traditional preparation process involves allowing it to rot away. In some districts the fruits are exposed in the sun, in others kept moist in jars. The kernels are then roasted and pounded to make the butter. Some peoples, such as the Hausa, prefer butter from unroasted nuts. This is pale yellow, while that from roasted nuts is greyish-brown. Both have a strong, somewhat rank smell.

The butter is sold in large loaves or balls from which a piece is cut off for the buyer. If properly made and not adulterated it keeps well.

For western consumption, the butter is extracted from unfermented nuts by boiling in water, either in the country of origin or in the importing country. Shea butter in refined form has been used for margarine and as a substitute for cocoa butter.

SHEEP animals of the genus *Ovis*. The meat of the domestic sheep, *Ovis aries*, is important in cookery as LAMB (when young) and MUTTON (when over a year old). Sheep are widely farmed, not only as providers of meat, but also for their MILK, which is made into yoghurt and various cheeses; their wool and hides are also important. Youatt (1877) declared: 'Among the various animals given by the benevolent hand of Providence for the benefit of mankind, there is none of greater utility than the sheep.'

The GOAT is closely related and in some parts of the world the two animals are herded together and their meat used more or less interchangeably in the kitchen.

Many species of wild sheep are dotted around the world. They include several mouflons (e.g. *O. musimon* of Sardinia and Corsica and *O. orientalis* of W. Asia) as well as the American bighorn or mountain sheep, *O. canadensis*. Of other Asian species, the Argali, *O. ammon*, lives in mountainous areas from Bokhara to Tibet and Mongolia and has remarkably massive curling horns (of which the longest are borne by what is called Marco Polo's Argali). The only wild sheep of Africa is the Barbary sheep or aoudad, *Ammotragus lervia*, which belongs to the mountainous parts of the Saharan region and is appropriately coloured pale brown.

Sheep can thrive on rough pasture in cold, wet, mountainous regions, and hot, dry climates. They can graze shorter grass than cattle. With goats, they have long been the principal meat animals of N. Africa, the Balkans, and a vast area stretching from the E. Mediterranean through the mountains and desert lands of C. Asia to the Mongolian steppes. In W. Europe their importance for meat has fluctuated over the centuries; their wool and milk were sometimes more valuable products.

The social system of and habits of wild sheep made for easy domestication. They did not wander far and had a predisposition to follow a dominant leader. By about 9000 BC sheep had been domesticated in N. Iraq, and in subsequent millennia they spread with early pastoralists into Europe and also eastwards, while retaining the Middle East as their base, so to speak, and also—for some time at least—as the centre of diversity for breeds. The importance of sheep to the people of the Middle East from early times can be gauged from the Bible, in which there are frequent references to them. Among the many breeds of sheep which are native to the area is one of particular importance and interest; the FAT-TAILED SHEEP which are now found in many parts of the world are thought to have originated in the Middle East, perhaps around 3000 BC.

Sheep and goats were probably introduced to Britain during the neolithic period with other domestic livestock. The geographical isolation of parts of the British Isles has meant that some breeds have survived little changed from when they were first introduced. The Soay breed, of the St Kilda group of islands in the Outer Hebrides, is probably a relic of breeds introduced between 4,000 and 2,000 years ago. Primitive breeds are also found on the Shetland and Orkney Islands (where one breed, kept on the foreshore for centuries, shows physiological adaptations to a diet of seaweed). It is possible that Romney Marsh sheep are descended from Roman imports.

It was in comparatively recent times, following the start of the Industrial Revolution and the consequent increase in the demand for meat, that the breeding of sheep for meat made important advances in Britain. In the late 18th and throughout the 19th centuries, improved Leicester and Southdown breeds were popular. The new Leicester was a small-boned animal which fattened quickly and carried a relatively high proportion of meat. Mrs Beeton (1861) considered that Southdowns had a better flavour, and noted that, for these, demand exceeded supply. Blackfaces were widespread in the Highlands of Scotland by 1800, and the various breeds of Welsh Mountain sheep were improved in the 19th century. Cheviots were developed from local Northumberland sheep, with the introduction of Lincoln and Leicester blood to improve meat quality. The Dorset Horn, which has an extended breeding season, was used to produce lamb for the London Christmas market until the mid-19th century. This was known as 'house lamb', born at Michaelmas and reared indoors, often by hand.

The coming of railways led to movement of sheep over long distances to urban markets, and began to erode strong regional preferences in the size and conformation of mutton carcasses. The 19th century also saw the beginning of a lively export trade of sheep for breeding from Britain (and elsewhere in Europe). New Leicesters went to Australia and the Americas; Romney Marsh sheep to New Zealand, Australia, and S. America; Cotswolds to N. America and Australia; and the improved Shropshire to many destinations.　　　　　(LM)

SHELLFISH 'Any animal living in water whose outer cover is a shell, whether testaceous, as an oyster, or crustaceous, as a crab' (*OED*).

On this basis it is correct to use the term for all single shells, BIVALVES (except the SHIPWORM, once it has passed the juvenile stage), and CRUSTACEANS; and also for the SEA URCHIN, for one CEPHALOPOD (the pearly NAUTILUS), and for SEA TURTLES. In practice the term is applied in a general way to the single shells, bivalves, and crustaceans. It is less satisfactory than the French *fruits de mer* (edible sea animals other than fish) but more convenient than the Italian *frutti di mare* (if lexicographers are correct in restricting the meaning of this to edible MOLLUSCS and sea urchins).

SHEPHERD'S PIE a savoury dish of minced meat with a topping of mashed potato (now almost universal) or pastry (in Scotland in former times). In keeping with the name, the meat should be mutton or lamb; and it is usually cooked meat left over from a roast.

The name of the dish conjures up visions of shepherds of long ago eating this simple fare, but the name does not seem to have been used until the 1870s, when mincing machines were developed. The dish itself doubtless dates back much further, and it is generally agreed that it originated in the north of England and Scotland where there are large numbers of sheep. So the common idea that shepherds ate the dish back in, say, the 18th century is probably right.

The term **cottage pie,** often confused with shepherd's pie but properly denoting a similar dish made with minced beef, has a somewhat longer history and is similarly effective in evoking a rural and traditional context.

Shepherd's pie, well made from good ingredients, is delicious, easy, and inexpensive. But sometimes a dreadful travesty of it is served. Jane Grigson (1974) exhumed for her readers a report from the *Pall Mall Gazette* in 1885, to the effect that the Eastbourne Board of Guardians had ordered a mincing machine for the use of 'aged and toothless paupers' in their care. Commenting on this, she writes:

with the first mincing-machines, prison, school and seaside boarding house cooks acquired a new weapon to depress their victims, with water, mince, shepherd's pie with rubbery granules of left-over meat, rissoles capable of being fired from a gun.

The dish also crops up in ANGLO-INDIAN COOKERY. Jennifer Brennan (1990) says that shepherd's pie was considered a great standby by Indian cooks and was often served for TIFFIN.

The equivalent dish in France is called *hachis Parmentier* in honour of the man who persuaded the French to eat potatoes.　　　HS

SHEPHERD'S PURSE *Capsella bursa-pastoris,* a small plant of the crucifer family, related to MUSTARD. It grows abundantly in temperate regions of Europe and Asia, and has also become common in N. America

---

SHEEP IN MODERN BRITAIN:
THE STRATIFICATION TECHNIQUE

THE breeding of sheep for meat in modern Britain aims to produce lamb carcasses with a minimum of fat and bone. It is a complex business which maximizes land use in the wet, cold uplands of the west and the north. It depends on a system of 'stratification', a close interplay between the hill and lowland farms, which developed in the second half of the 19th century. The 'improved' breeds from the 19th century and a handful of imported exotic breeds are used.

The process starts on mountain farms. First, flocks of pure mountain breeds—Swaledale and Dales bred in the Pennines, Herdwicks in the Lake District, Cheviots on the Scottish Borders, and Blackfaces in the Highlands—are maintained on moorland. A proportion of ewes (females) produced by these flocks are mated with rams from lowland breeds such as Leicester, Wensleydale, or Teeswater to produce a generation of cross-bred lambs. These combine the hardiness and good mothering qualities of their dams and the rapid growth of their sires. The female lambs are sold to lowland farms, where they are mated with rams from breeds bred especially for meat, such as Suffolk, Downland breeds, Texels, and French breeds. The progeny of this crossing form the bulk of the lamb sold in butchers' shops up and down the country. At all levels, flocks of pure-bred animals must be maintained to provide breeding stock for the future, and the excess lambs from these, plus all the cross-bred males, also enter the market as meat animals.

since the arrival of Europeans. The name refers to the heart-shaped seed capsule.

Shepherd's purse leaves, which have a mild mustard flavour, have been used as a green vegetable in many regions. They are sold in S. Chinese markets, sometimes wild and sometimes cultivated; but they do not seem to have been cultivated anywhere else. The wild plants are, however, of some importance in Korea, where they are sold complete with the long white tap-root. Koreans boil the leaf stems and dress them with a sauce including onion, garlic, and red pepper threads.

In China during the Sung dynasty (10th to 13th centuries AD) there was a movement in favour of natural food. Shepherd's purse and other wild crucifers figured in a famous vegetable soup, Tung Po's soup, about which the poet Su Shih wrote an essay and a poem, explaining that 'the recipe does not use condiments but has a natural taste'.

Both in Europe and America the seeds have been ground to make bread, and the hot tasting root used as a spice.

SHERBET (*see opposite page*)

SHICHIMI (togarashi), a Japanese spice mixture. The name means 'seven flavours' but is often translated as seven spices. The mixture is composed of: red CHILLI pepper flakes; SANSHO pods, roughly ground; black HEMP seeds or white POPPY seeds; white SESAME seeds; RAPE seed; *mikan* (MANDARIN orange) or YUZU peel in tiny fragments; and NORI (green seaweed) in small bits. The mixture is available in various strengths (i.e. degrees of hotness), and its main use is to be sprinkled on bowls of noodles, soups, or grilled meats.

SHIITAKE the Japanese and also the usual western name for a forest mushroom of Asia, *Lentinus edodes*, which grows on rotting wood. A crude sort of cultivation of this species dates back for many centuries in China and Japan. Scientific cultivation, which has developed into a major agricultural activity for a huge number of people in Japan, and for many in China and Korea, is a recent development. Shiitake are now so readily available in the Orient as to be the counterpart there of the common cultivated mushrooms in the western world; but they have the advantage of a better flavour. Cultivation of the shiitake has begun on a limited scale in parts of the USA and some European countries.

In the name shiitake, *take* means mushroom and *shii* is the name of one of the various Japanese trees whose dead wood serves as host to the mushrooms. However,

other deciduous trees such as certain oaks are better, and preferred by the shiitake, whose name is therefore not wholly appropriate.

A full-sized shiitake has a cap up to 10 cm (4") wide and occasionally larger, brown but fissured with a network of white cracks. The off-white gills are also split and torn, and run part of the way down the stem like fan vaulting. The stem, which is set eccentrically, allowing the mushroom to grow from a vertical trunk, is pale brown and has no ring.

In Japanese markets, shiitake are graded into two main qualities: **donko,** the preferred one, with thick, roundish, and only partly opened caps; and **koshin,** when the cap is fully opened and thinner. A similar distinction is made in China, where the donko type is known as 'floral', because the white patterns show more distinctly on it, or as 'winter mushrooms' (they are usually grown in the winter, when the cold slows down growth and the mushrooms can absorb more nutrients.

Several species of *Lentinus* grow wild in Europe and the USA. They are similar in appearance but tend to be smaller than the shiitake. Most are edible, even the one known in the USA as 'railroad wrecker' from its ability to destroy the wooden ties or sleepers on railroads.

A white species, *L. polychrous*, is common throughout SE Asia and S. India.

Shiitake have for long enjoyed a reputation for being health giving as well as delicious, and are sometimes called 'the elixir of life'. Recent research suggests that they contain substances which may ward off flu and lower cholesterol levels in the blood.

The flavour of fresh shiitake is strong, and a few are enough in most dishes. They are used for appearance and texture as well as for flavour, and the velvety caps are normally kept whole unless very large. The stems, which are tougher than the caps, can be used for soup. Dried shiitake, which are exported on a large scale from Japan, retain much of the original flavour.

SHIP'S BISCUIT or hard tack or sea biscuit, a type of unleavened bread which was baked, sliced, and oven dried. Thus it was 'twice-cooked bread', the meaning of the medieval Latin term *panis biscoctus*, from which comes the word BISCUIT.

This product was used for centuries as rations for sailors. In good conditions it would keep for a year or more in sealed barrels, but at sea it was often difficult to keep it dry, and it could become infested by weevils.

A special bakery at the royal docks at Chatham was devoted entirely to baking ship's biscuit for the Royal Navy. The method was unchanged for several centuries.

The *Encyclopaedia Britannica* of 1773 gave the following description:

Sea-bisket is a sort of bread much dried by passing the oven twice to make it keep for sea service. For long voyages they bake it four times and prepare it six months before embarkation. It will hold good for a whole year.

Sailors had various methods for making hard tack palatable, e.g. crumbling it into the dish called LOBSCOUSE.

Similar breads were made by other seafaring nations; for instance a *pain bateau* was made on the Atlantic coast of France for the fishermen going to Newfoundland.

See also CRACKER.
READING: Layinka Swinburne (1997).

SHIPWORM *Lyrodus* (formerly *Teredo*) *siamensis*, sometimes called teredo worm, is a strange MOLLUSC which starts life as a BIVALVE, in a double shell, but then, having established itself in a suitable piece of wood—often a floating log or the trunk of a 'sam' tree in a mangrove swamp—becomes long and wormlike, with the original two shells transformed into mere appendages at each end. All that one normally sees of the shipworm is the snail-like head peeping out of the bark.

As its name implies, the shipworm can do considerable damage to the timbers of boats, and it is usually thought of in this connection rather than as a foodstuff. Yet it is edible, although not often marketed, and may even have been the subject of some of the earliest experiments in 'sea farming'. Coastal dwellers in Thailand and elsewhere in SE Asia have for long cultivated the shipworm in logs anchored in the sea. They may be pickled in vinegar or *nam pla* (Thai FISH SAUCE), or fried and eaten with eggs. However, there is no need to cook them. Doreen Fernandez (1994) comments that the shipworm (known as *tamilok*) is picked from old wood, especially driftwood, in parts of the Philippines.

The wood is chopped up so that the worms, pink, six to eight inches long, may be extracted, washed a little, and deposited wriggling on one's tongue. The *tamilok*, its fans swear, has a fresh clean taste that sends shivers of pleasure down one's alimentary canal.

SHISO the Japanese name for a herb, *Perilla frutescens* (formerly *nankinensis*), whose cultivation and use is most prominent in Japan although also observable in China, Burma, the foothills of the Himalayas, and more recently in California too. 'Perilla' is sometimes used as an English name.

The half-dozen or so cultivars of this herb include both green-leaved and red- or

(*cont. on page 720*)

Sherbet

A sherbet, basically and historically, is a cold, sweetened, non-alcoholic drink, usually based on a fruit juice. The earliest recorded word for it seems to be *sharâb*, the classical Arab term for a sweetened drink. However, in the late Middle Ages this word developed its current Arabic sense (a sense prevailing in both Turkish and Syrian Arabic) of an alcoholic drink. A different word was therefore needed for a non-alcoholic sweetened drink, and this emerged as *sharbât*. The Turkish term *s(h)erbet* comes from this newer word.

The old word *sharâb*, before it changed its meaning and apparently at a very early date, passed into Spanish and Italian and thence became current in most of the European languages; obvious examples are the English word syrup and the French *sirop*.

The later Arabic word *sharbât* also entered European languages. In the late 16th century it appeared in Italian as the name of a beverage drunk in Turkey. Then the beverage itself entered Italian cuisine, under the name *sorbetto*. It took this form because the Italians assimilated it to their verb *sorbire*, meaning to sip. The Italian *sorbetto* gave rise to the French *sorbet*, the Spanish *sorbete*, etc. All these words begin with 's' not with 'sh'. English seems to be the only language which took the word sherbet directly from the Turkish, complete with its 'h'.

Recipes for the traditional Middle Eastern sherbets have not changed much over the centuries. There are two main categories of ingredient: a fruit (or vegetable) juice; and a sweetening agent (originally honey, although even in medieval times the then more expensive sugar occurs in some recipes). An optional third category would be spices. The sherbets were cooled by ice or, more romantically, snow.

In Turkey and the Middle East generally, sweetness is auspicious, so sherbet is served on auspicious occasions: at meals during RAMADAN, in place of water; at engagement parties; when someone enters a religious order. And, because of its auspicious nature, it is a standard offering to guests. It seems to have been the custom in Turkey to serve sherbets as refreshments between the courses of banquets or important dinners; but sherbets did not owe their existence to any such requirement—they were a part of daily life there, and in Egypt too.

The sherbet is served in coloured glass cups, generally called 'kullehs', containing about three quarters of a pint; some of which [the more common kind] are ornamented with gilt flowers, etc. The sherbet-cups are placed on a round tray, and covered with a round piece of embroidered silk, or cloth of gold. On the right arm of the person who presents the sherbet is hung a large oblong napkin with a wide embroidered border of gold and coloured silks at each end. This is ostensibly offered for the purpose of wiping the lips after drinking the sherbet, but it is really not so much for use as for display.

Commenting on this description, which is taken from the 1860 edition of Lane's *Manners and Customs of the Modern Egyptians*, Claudia Roden (1985) says that the same traditions have continued to be observed, as she remembers from her own childhood. These traditions, of course, only applied in well-to-do households. She does not neglect to explain how the ordinary people would obtain their sherbets from street vendors.

As the vendor went by, people would rush down from their flats to drink several glasses ... The vendors carried a selection of sherbets in gigantic glass flasks, two at a time, held together by wide straps and balanced on their shoulders. The flasks glowed with brilliantly seductive colours: soft, pale, sugary-pink for rose water; pale green for violet juice; warm, rich, dark tamarind; and the purple-black of mulberry juice. As they went through the street, the vendors chanted their traditional, irresistible calls of 'Arasous!' and 'Tamarhindi!', accompanied by the tinkling of little bells and the clanking of the metal cups which they carried with them.

According to the dictionary compiled by Foretière in the late 17th century, a sorbet in France at that time was also a drink, of sugar and lemon pulp. Diderot's great encyclopaedia of the 1750s suggests that it remained so during the 18th century. During the 19th century, however, a sorbet could be either a drink or a sort of ice more suitable for drinking than eating, and in the latter case had an alcoholic content. The distinction between an iced drink and a drinkable ice is a fine one, but it clearly existed for the French, and it was the drinkable ice which developed into the eatable sorbet (see WATER ICES) now found in French restaurants.

For English and American sorbets of the 19th century, the book on *Victorian Ices and Ice Cream* (1976) by Barbara Wheaton is a fine source. Part of this reproduces recipes from a famous English book, Mrs Marshall's *The Book of Ices* (1885). Wheaton explains how a protracted Victorian dinner—she is speaking of the upper classes—would be punctuated halfway through by a refreshing sorbet, usually a lemon water ice with spirits added and fruit for garnish.

The word sherbet did not pass into general use in America until the middle of the 19th century. Later on in that century, it and sorbet were used as synonyms. And a charming conceit had been devised whereby the cup in which the sherbet/sorbet was served was itself composed of ice. When Charles Dickens was in New York in 1867, he was honoured by a banquet at Delmonico's, at which ice cups (made by freezing water between two cup-shaped moulds) were used to serve a lemon and orange sorbet strengthened by American sparkling wine, kirsch, and prunelle. Mrs Marshall approved strongly.

In the 20th century the custom of serving a sorbet as a refresher in the middle of a large meal, normally a luxury meal in a restaurant, has been revived. And a sorbet, or a selection of sorbets of different flavours, is a standard low-calorie item on the dessert menu. Such sorbets are eaten, not drunk.

But in England there was a surprising development. It is not unusual to find that something appreciated by the upper classes either travels downwards, socially, if its nature is such that poorer people can afford it; or, in the contrary case, is imitated by some cheaper product. In England, the sorbet had the latter fate. A sherbet powder was produced which could either be made into a fizzy drink, or sucked into the mouth, where it would likewise fizz. The powder was composed of BICARBONATE OF SODA and tartaric acid (see CREAM OF TARTAR), plus sugar, and was cheap. Anyone could afford it.

This product had already appeared in the 19th century; an edition of *Law's Grocer's Manual* of about 1895 describes in detail how it can be made, and compares it to another powdered product, now less prominent but still surviving, lemon kali. Cassell's *Dictionary of Cookery* (also about 1895) gave a more refined recipe for use in the home.

But it was in the 20th century that this sort of sherbet really spread its wings. Three favourite kinds were: a tube containing the powder and furnished with a liquorice stick or 'straw', which was used to convey the powder to the mouth and was itself eaten in the process; a 'sherbet lemon'—a lemon sweet for sucking, with sherbet powder inside; and a 'sherbet bomb', shaped like a UFO, covered with RICE PAPER, and again containing the sherbet powder.

As for developments in the USA in the 20th century, it must be said that no two Americans will give exactly the same answer to the question: what is a sherbet? Differing laws in the various states have to be taken into account, as well as different local traditions and differing individual opinions. California is the state where the largest quantities of sherbet are made, and Californians will typically state that a sherbet certainly does not contain milk or milk products. In New York state, on the other hand, it seems to be a legal requirement that it should. An outsider can only rejoice in the thought that this Old World confection has proved to be so polymorphous in the New World.

READING: Davidson (1993); Laura Mason (1998).

purple-leaved forms. The former are used by the Japanese for garnishing and in salads. The cultivar Red, sometimes called beefsteak plant from the colour of the leaves, is best known as the colouring agent for their pickled 'plums' (see UMEBOSHI), ginger, etc., and as a beautiful wrapping for certain items of confectionery. The cultivar Curled is of an even darker purple colour and has an aroma described as 'peppermint-like'; other cultivars have aromas more like lemon or cinnamon or cumin.

The seeds are roasted and crushed to produce perilla oil; this was formerly put to local use only for culinary purposes, but has now attracted wider interest since of all edible oils it is said to have the highest level of polyunsaturates.

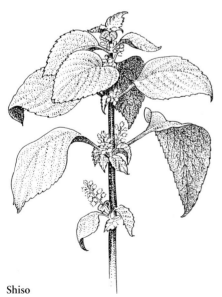

Shiso

SHOLA (or sholleh) is the name given to a number of dishes all over the Middle East, Iran, and Afghanistan in which short-grain rice is cooked until soft and thick, with other ingredients chosen according to whether the shola is to be savoury or sweet.

Margaret Shaida (1992) says: 'According to the culinary historian Charles Perry, *sholleh* was brought to Persia by the Mongolians in the 13th century. Three hundred years later, some 15 *sholleh* dishes, mostly savoury, were listed in the Safavid cookery book.' She goes on to say that nowadays '*sholleh* has all but disappeared from the cuisine of Persia, except for 2 or 3 soup dishes (*sholleh ghalamkar*) and one very celebrated dessert, *sholleh zard*'.

Shola-e-zard is a sweet saffron and rosewater (or orange flower water) flavoured rice dish cooked not only in Iran, but all over the Middle East and in Afghanistan. It has a religious significance, being made on the 10th day of Muharram (the Muslim month of mourning). *Shola-e-zard* is also made as a *nazr*, which is a custom of thanksgiving or pledge practised in Iran and Afghanistan. The *shola* is cooked and then distributed to the poor and to neighbours and relatives. In Afghanistan, at least, *shola-e-zard* is traditionally served with *sharbat-e-rihan* (SHERBET with basil seeds).

Similarly a savoury shola of Iran called *ash-e sholleh ghalamkar*, literally scribe's soup, which dates back to medieval times, was traditionally prepared to heal the sick. Claudia Roden (1968) remarks on the old belief that for the cure to be effective, the ingredients (mainly lentils and spinach, without rice in this instance, in the recipe which she gives) had to be bought with money begged in the streets. This dish is often chosen to serve at prayer meetings for the recovery of a sick child or the safe return of a loved one.

See also RICE PUDDING.   HS

SHOOFLY PIE a very sweet PIE (in the American sense—it would be a TART in Britain) with a filling of molasses and/or brown sugar. Mariani (1994) states that this was not recorded in print in the USA until 1926, and that it is believed to be of PENNSYLVANIA DUTCH origin. Some have thought that the name is a corruption of some German word, but the more likely explanation is simply that the exposed surface of the pie is so sweet that flies have to be shooed away from it.

The equivalent confection in Britain is TREACLE tart, which has a much longer history.

SHORBA In most Islamic countries, the word for 'soup' is *shorba*. This is not, as one might expect, a word related to 'sherbet' or 'sorbet'. It is a Persian rather than an Arabic word, compounded of *shor* (salty, brackish) and *ba* (stew, dish cooked with water).

The word *ba* is also found (in forms reflecting its pre-9th-century pronunciation *bag*) in the names of various medieval dishes such as *zirabaj* (cumin stew) and *sikbaj* (vinegar stew, the ancestor of ESCABECHE). It is perhaps unsurprising that the dictionaries have assumed that shorba was distinguished by a salt flavouring. But there is a more reasonable meaning than 'brackish stew' for a dish that has spread so widely. It is suggested by a recipe in a 10th-century Arabic cookbook which in turn purports to describe a dish prepared for the 6th-century Persian king Chosroes.

The instructions call for meat to be 'boiled lightly and taken out of the water. The water is thrown away and the meat is returned to the pot and water is poured upon it and salt and a stick of cinnamon and a stick of galingale are thrown in.' (The first step is clearly a way of getting rid of the scum that rises when meat is boiled, which would now be done by skimming the broth.) When meat is boiled in plain water, the results are boiled meat and nearly flavourless water; when it is boiled in salted water, it makes broth. This is no doubt how shorba got its name, from salt's chemical properties, its ability to change the ionic balance in the cooking pot, rather than from its use as a flavouring.

The awareness of the distinction salted/unsalted would have been strong in the Middle Ages because meat was regularly parboiled to tenderize it before roasting or frying.

Shorba is the spelling in both Arabic and Persian, but Turkish has çorba. In Moldova it is chorba, and in Romanian ciorbă, the version which has become familiar in N. America. In C. Asia forms such as shorpo and sorpa occur, also shulpa (Tatar). In Afghanistan, Pakistan, and bits of China and India, forms such as shorva are found. The wide distribution of the same name in these different versions testifies to the basic nature of this range of dishes.   CP

SHORE CRAB the English name commonly used for the small edible crab of European shores, Carcinus aestuarii and C. maenas. The first of the pair belongs mainly to the Mediterranean, and the second to the Atlantic; but they overlap in range. The back is greenish and the maximum width of the carapace 7 cm (3").

This is the crab which is the subject of the softshell crab operations which have been carried on in the Lagoon of Venice since the 18th century. Just after they have shed their old carapace, and while the new one is still soft, these crabs are known as moleche. They are in this desirable state for less than half a day, so timing is crucial; as the time for 'moulting' approaches the crabs are kept in special hatcheries where they can be inspected several times a day. The main season for moulting is the spring.

The shore crab is not alone on and in the vicinity of European shores. Apart from the SWIMMING CRABS, there are many other small or medium-sized crabs scuttling to and fro, and some of them are edible. Three notable ones are:

- the furry crab, Eriphia verrucosa—French ériphie, Italian favollo, Spanish cangrejo moruno—furry in appearance, with a fine flavour, perhaps the most sought after crab on the Mediterranean coast of France;
- the shamefaced crab, Calappa granulata—French crabe honteux, Spanish cangrejo real, Catalan cranquet dormidor;
- Pachygrapsus marmoratus—French crabe marbré, Spanish cangrejo de roca—brown with grey-green marbling on its back.

SHORTBREAD a biscuit whose origin lies in the 'short cakes' made in the 16th century (see BISCUIT). In Britain it is regarded as a particular speciality of Scotland, although similar biscuits, such as SHREWSBURY CAKES, are made elsewhere. The original Scottish shortbread is simply a thick layer of rich, sweetened shortcrust pastry, without any extra flavourings. The texture is delicately crumbly. It relies on the quality of the ingredients for its mild but satisfying flavour. The classic proportions of ingredients for a shortbread recipe are one part sugar to two of butter and three of flour. It may be slightly adjusted by varying the type of flour used; usually soft cake flour is chosen, which is further softened in some Scottish recipes by adding some rice flour.

There are many variations. The thick Pitcaithly bannock has peel and almonds in the mixture. Queen Victoria's Balmoral recipe for shortbread was seasoned with a little salt; egg yolk and a little cream are added for extra richness in Ayrshire shortbread; and demerara sugar in Dorset shortbread. Goosnargh cakes, named for the village in Lancashire where they achieved great popularity in the 19th century, contain ground coriander and whole caraway seeds.

Petticoat tails are Scottish shortbread biscuits, baked in a round, with a characteristic shape resembling that of an outspread bell-hoop crinoline petticoat. The shortbread is made of flour, butter, and sugar, bound with milk or an egg, and optionally flavoured with almond or caraway seeds. The centre circle should be marked and removed before slicing the main round.

Dorothy Hartley (1954) says:

These simple biscuits . . . date at least from the twelfth century. They were called 'petty cotes tallis'; that is, little cases, or 'cotes' (we have the word in sheep-cotes—small enclosures), made of pastry and cut into triangular pieces. 'Tallis' or 'tallys' were cuts made on sticks to count or measure by, so the word tally came to mean any sort of cut-out pattern . . . Every cook knows how the pointed ends of cut cakes and biscuits break off—so, after several centuries of broken tips, someone evolved the cure: they cut a circle out of the centre before baking. By then the filling had come out of the 'cotes' and they were biscuits only—'pettycotes tallys'.

Another theory claims that the name is a corruption of petites gatelles, small French cakes popular with Mary Queen of Scots, who brought them to Scotland in 1650. Marion McNeill (1929), quoting the Annals of the Cleikum Club, says, 'In Scottish culinary terms there are many corruptions, though we rather think the name petticoat tails has its origin in the shape of the cakes, which is exactly that of the bell-hoop petticoats of our ancient Court ladies.'

SHORTCAKE as Ayto (1993) observes, is 'a term of dismaying diversity. Its application varies widely from place to place and over time, and the only common factor is the use of shortening—butter or lard—to make it soft or crumbly.' In England the word was already in use in Shakespeare's time (he had a reference in The Merry Wives of Windsor to a character called Alice Shortcake, and a recipe book of 1594 had already included 'To make short Cakes'), but it was not always in the past—nor is it now—properly distinguished from SHORTBREAD.

In N. America, on the other hand, shortcake has become prominent as a dessert, traditionally consisting of a crumbly cake made of biscuit dough, split, filled with strawberries (and often whipped cream too), topped with more whipped cream and decorated with more strawberries. Sometimes a different fruit is used and some cooks may substitute SPONGE CAKE for shortcake; but no alternative version can match the excellence of the original. Harpers Magazine in 1893 remarked, 'They give you good eating—strawberries and short-cake—oh my!'—an exclamation which has been echoed many times since.

SHORTENING a N. American expression for any fat or oil used in baking to make the finished item short (tender) in texture. The type of fat used as shortening depends on individual recipes, and the term has the advantage of being neutral and non-specific. In the past butter and lard were the most important; oils were of less use to the home cook, as they tend to give greasy, mealy textures in baked goods. In the 20th century, margarine, and various compounds of lipids (often vegetable derived and partly hydrogenated), combined with emulsifiers and pre-creamed for easier mixing, have been designed for shortening particular bakery products in industry.

Although the word shortening is rarely used on the east side of the Atlantic, the concept exists, in the terms SHORTBREAD, SHORTCAKE, and short PASTRY, all of which require a high proportion of fat blended into flour giving a friable result. The common rationalization of the function of shortening is that the added fat breaks up gluten masses created when flour is made into dough. However, Harold McGee (1984) remarks that 'the role of added fats and lipids in doughs and batters is not so straightforward' and provides for scientifically minded bakers a much more complex explanation of what happens, insofar as it is understood.

(LM)

SHREWSBURY CAKES are a kind of BISCUIT (indeed occasionally known as Shrewsbury biscuits) of the SHORTBREAD type, made from flour, sugar, and butter, circular, fairly thin, and with scalloped edges. They are flavoured with spices, and sometimes rosewater.

A monograph on Shrewsbury cakes written by a Shrewsbury historian (Lloyd and Lloyd, 1931) throws light on their early history. Since the 17th century Shrewsbury cakes always appear to have been known for their crisp, brittle texture, which is referred to by one Lord Herbet of Chirbury, who sent his guardian in 1602 'a kind of cake which our countrey people use and made in no place in England but in Shrewsbury . . . Measure not my love by substance of it, which is brittle, but by the form of it which is circular.'

By the end of the 17th century, the cakes were sufficiently well known for the playwright Congreve, in *The Way of the World* (1700), to use the expression 'as short as a Shrewsbury cake', and for poets and musicians born in the W. Midlands to use them as motifs in their work. The earliest recorded recipe, given by Eliza Smith (1734), is for a sweet biscuit spiced with cinnamon and nutmeg.

A reference to the biscuits in the popular 19th-century series of poems *The Ingoldsby Legends* ensured their further fame. One of the poems therein mentions a maker of Shrewsbury cakes named Pailin; and a trade mark 'Pailin's Original Shrewsbury Cakes' was in use by the late 19th century.

Similar 'short cakes', of a crisp, friable texture, variously flavoured, were known in other parts of Britain. LM

SHRIKHAND (sometimes srikhand), a sweet Indian dish, particularly of the Maharashtra-Gujarat, made with strained YOGHURT (or CURDS), beaten until light, sweetened with sugar, enhanced with spices such as SAFFRON and CARDAMOM, and garnished with slivers of, e.g., PISTACHIO or charoli seeds (called CALUMPANG NUTS in English). It often incorporates fruit such as mango. This dish, a particularly attractive example of Indian uses of yoghurt, may be served throughout a meal in India, although for western palates its place is the dessert course. HS

SHRIMP a term which always refers to certain CRUSTACEANS, to wit those in the sub-order Natantia (swimmers) in the order Decapoda Crustacea (ten-footed crustaceans), but which, with the associated term 'prawn', is used in different ways on the two sides of the Atlantic—and in other parts of the world, depending on whether use of the English language has been influenced by the British or by Americans. Since the FAO (Food and Agriculture Organization of the United Nations) has taken the trouble to produce a comprehensive *Catalogue of Shrimps and Prawns of the World* (Holthuis, 1980), they may be allowed to explain:

we may say that in Great Britain the term 'shrimp' is the more general of the two, and is the only term used for Crangonidae and most smaller species. 'Prawn' is the more special of the two names, being used solely for Palaemonidae and larger forms, never for the very small ones.

In North America the name 'prawn' is practically obsolete and is almost entirely replaced by the word 'shrimp' (used for even the largest species, which may be called 'jumbo shrimp'). If the word 'prawn' is used at all in America it is attached to small species.

This entry deals with shrimp in the British sense. The first thing to be said is that there are unmanageably large numbers of species and that it is often both difficult and pointless to distinguish between them. The main use of these small shrimps in SE Asia is in the production of shrimp paste, a fermented product which goes under names such as *blachan* (Malaysia and Indonesia); see BLACANG. The fishermen who harvest and process the shrimps for this purpose are not likely to pause in their work to check the specific identity of each tiny creature.

There are, however, some species which deserve particular mention. In Europe *Crangon crangon* is the most common small shrimp, often called brown shrimp, and the one which is the object of important traditional fisheries in England (especially Morecambe Bay), the Netherlands, Belgium (where a traditional fishery at Oostduinkerke by men mounted on large horses may provide the absolute extreme in ratio of size between hunter and hunted), Denmark, and elsewhere, including the Mediterranean. *C. franciscorum* represents the same genus in the NE Pacific; it is known as California, bay, or grey shrimp.

These little shrimps are translucent (grey) when alive, but take colour (brown) when briefly boiled, which is all the cooking they need. This is one reason why they may be called either grey or brown shrimp, the other being that they can adapt their translucent colouring to their environment, matching the sand on or in which they live.

In the Indo-Pacific species described as having 'commercial importance', i.e. sought

by fishermen and regularly sold in the markets, are found in a few genera such as *Acetes* and *Caridina*, but the identification of all those which disappear into shrimp paste would be, as indicated above, an impossible task.

Potted shrimp is a delicacy in England, especially the north-west. It was well described by Dorothy Hartley (1954). Shrimp paste is also an English favourite; quite different from the fermented shrimp paste of SE Asia.

SICHUAN PEPPER *Zanthoxylum simulans*, is a pepper which, as the name indicates, belongs to the province of Sichuan in China and does much to give the cuisine of Sichuan its special character. The small fruits of the plant are dried to become reddish-brown 'peppercorns', and are subsequently sold either whole, or whole but seeded (best), or as a powder for use as a spice. It is one of the ingredients of the Chinese spice mixture FIVE SPICES.

Sichuan pepper has a pleasing aroma and a numbing rather than burning effect on the mouth.

Classification of Sichuan pepper in the genus *Fagara* and any use of the common name 'fagara' for it are respectively obsolete and inappropriate. See also SANSHO.

SILKWORM As is well known, the silkworm, *Bombyx mori*, is reared for the production of silk and its diet consists solely of mulberry leaves. It is less well known that the pupae (or cocoons) of the silkworm are edible and have a composition similar to that of shrimps.

The pupae are prepared for the unreeling of the silk thread by being placed in boiling water in what are known as reeling basins. The silk thread is then reeled out of them. The pupae are at this stage already cooked and edible after their boiling, but are usually further cooked by frying in fat and are then salted or seasoned with lemon leaves; or made into a soup; or pounded and then cooked with green leaves. Sometimes the cooked pupae are dried in the sun and then preserved. HS

SILPHIUM a spice which was greatly appreciated in classical Greece, and also in Rome, where it was called *laserpitium* or *laser*. It came at first only from the hinterland of Cyrene in Libya: it was resin or sap, tapped from the root and stem of a plant. The stem itself was also a delicacy, but probably little known outside the region of production.

The supply of silphium gave out in the first century AD: but meanwhile an alternative source had been found in Media (now Iran), where Alexander's soldiers had learnt to use 'silphium' to tenderize tough old meat. This supply (which, nearly all authors were to agree, was inferior) was called *silphion Medikon*, Median silphium, by Greeks and appears as *silfi* in the Roman recipes of APICIUS. It is certainly identical with what we now know as ASAFOETIDA, the sap of *Ferula asafoetida* and related species, as was first pointed out in modern times by Garcia da Orta (1563).

First mentioned in the poems of Solon, Athenian lawgiver, in the early 6th century BC, silphium, as a seasoning or as the dominant flavour of sauces, was to be present in almost every banquet narrated in the literature of the centuries that followed. It was also of great importance in medicine: doctors recommended its use in the diet, and it was prescribed as a constituent of many compound drugs in the Hippocratic texts of the 5th and 4th centuries BC.

The best description of the plant and the harvest is given in slightly inconsistent reports conscientiously summarized by Theophrastus, the Greek scientist and successor to Aristotle, writing his *History of Plants* in 310 BC.

Silphium has a big thick root, a stem as long as ferula and just about as thick, and a leaf (which they call *maspeton*) similar to celery; it has a flat fruit, rather leaf-like, called *phyllon* 'leaf'. Its stalk is annual, like ferula. In spring it puts out this *maspeton*, which purges sheep and fattens them greatly and makes their meat amazingly tasty; after that the stem, which they say is eaten all ways, boiled, baked. There are two kinds of sap, one from the stem, one from the root. The root has a black skin which they strip off. The harvesters cut in accordance with a sort of mining-concession, a ration that they may take based on what has been cut and what remains, and it is not permitted to cut at random; nor indeed to cut more than the ration, because the resin spoils and decays with age. Exporting it to Piraeus [for Athens] they prepare it as follows: after putting it in jars and mixing flour with it they shake it for a long time—this is where its colour comes from; and thus treated it remains stable. That, then, is how silphium is collected and treated. It is found over a large region of Libya: more than five hundred miles, they say. Its oddity is to avoid cultivated land, and to retreat as the land is gradually brought under cultivation and farmed—obviously as if, far from requiring husbandry, it is essentially wild. The Cyrenaeans say that silphium appeared seven years before they settled their city, and they have been there about three hundred years now.

That was what the Cyrenaeans say about it. We can add from others that 'the root grows to about eighteen inches or a little more, and has a head about the middle of its length, which comes higher, almost above ground, and is called "milk": from this in due course grows the stem, and from that the *magydaris* and the so-called *phyllon*, its seeds; in the first strong south wind after Sirius it detaches, and silphium grows from it. The ground must be dug annually: if it is left it does still seed,

and the stems do appear, but both stem and root are inferior, while if dug they are better because the soil was turned over.' This conflicts with the report as to its retreating from cultivated land. 'The root is eaten fresh, chopped, with vinegar. The leaf is golden in colour. In spring and winter sheep are driven into the hills and pastured on this and on another plant like southernwood.' We shall have to find out which of these reports is true.

In another passage Theophrastus says that 'the root sap is better: it is pure and translucent and more solid. The stem sap is more liquid, which is why they mix flour with it to set it. The Libyans know the time to tap it—it is they who are the silphium collectors.'

Dioscorides (1st century AD), writing his *Materia Medica*, treated Libyan and Median silphium under one heading but attempted to define the difference between them:

Silphium grows in the Syria and Armenia and Media region and in Libya . . . The juice is collected by making an incision in the root and the stem. High quality is shown in its being reddish and translucent, myrrh-like and powerfully scented, not greenish, not rough in taste, not readily turning white. The Cyrenaic, even if one just tastes it, at once arouses a humour throughout the body and has a very healthy aroma, so that it is not noticed on the breath, or only a little; but the Median and Syrian are weaker in power and have a nastier smell.

The Libyan harvesters were apparently contracted to sell all their silphium to the Greek-speaking kingdom of Cyrene, which grew rich in the trade. Some of the harvest was, however, smuggled to Carthage. The silphium plant, a sturdy umbellifer (though with some untypical features), was a regular Cyrenaic coin type for hundreds of years. A well-known 6th-century BC painting on a Greek vase in the Louvre is generally thought to show Battus, the King of Cyrene, supervising the weighing and packing of what are apparently sacks of silphium (but others have thought that it is wool).

Profiteering may have led to the final decline. The geographer Strabo (1st century AD) wrote: 'it came close to dying out when the natives, in the course of some dispute, erupted and destroyed the roots of the plant. They are nomads.' Two generations later, Pliny in his *Natural History* seems to tell the end of the story. In his time silphium was 'worth its weight in silver . . . For many years now it has not been seen in the [Libyan] region, although, sensing the chance of higher profit, countrymen who keep beasts there deprive their flocks of pasture. The single stem found within living memory was sent to the emperor Nero.'

After this Libyan silphium disappears from the record, with one exception. Lovers of mystery may turn to the 5th-century AD letter from Synesius, Bishop of Cyrene, to

his brother on the Libyan coast, complimenting the latter on a stem of silphium received from his garden!

No plant now known from Libya or N. Africa produces a resin that resembles asafoetida. Whether the last stem was consumed by Nero, by Bishop Synesius, or by some less-known gourmet, there can be little doubt that Libyan silphium, already vanishing in early Roman times, has now vanished. But the possibility of identifying silphium with *Laserpitium gummiferum* has recently been taken up again: this plant, not currently used for food, grows in Spain and the Maghreb and experiments are going on in Spain and France to see if its properties match up with silphium.

Cooks who currently recreate the Roman recipes of APICIUS use 'Median silphium', asafoetida, confident in the knowledge that this is exactly what the makers of those recipes must have used and that Strabo, at least, had judged asafoetida 'sometimes better' than silphium.   AD

SILVERSIDE the American and most suitable name for the small fish of the family Atherinidae. These shoaling fish, found in temperate and tropical waters around the world, willingly enter brackish waters, caring little how salty these are. They include several species for which there is a commercial fishery, notably *Menidia menidia*, on the east coasts of N. America. This fish reaches a maximum length of 14 cm (6"). Its back and upper sides are transparent green and there is a silver band, marked above by a dark line, running along the side. They are delicious. Larger specimens should be fried, while smaller ones may be treated like WHITEBAIT. Indeed, whitebait is one of the numerous alternative common names which are used of this fish, others being green smelt, shiner, spearing, and sperling (mostly names which belong to the true SMELT).

These are fecund creatures. They have been described, when spawning in hedge grass at the head of a bay, as rolling about and jumping out of the water in such numbers that the water was 'whitened with the milt, and the grass so full of eggs that they could be taken out by the handful'.

Silversides of the Mediterranean and the E. Atlantic coasts are often referred to as sand-smelts, but they are not smelts. The chief species is *Atherina presbyter*, with a maximum length of 21 cm (8.5"), so appreciably larger than the American silverside. How to classify its close relations in the Mediterranean, already a confusing question, has been further confused by the arrival of an Indo-Pacific silverside, *Pranesus pinguis*; it has immigrated through the Suez Canal and is now established in the

E. Mediterranean where it has acquired local names such as *zoubara* and *cachcouch.*

Mediterranean silversides are prepared as American ones. Small specimens are called *melet* in the south of France; while very small ones are called *muccu* at Syracuse and formed into small round cakes, with parsley and garlic, to be fried.

SIMMER a verb which means to cook something in a liquid which is just below boiling point, i.e. (at sea level) about 90–96 °C (194–205 °F). Such a temperature is more than sufficient to achieve the coagulation of PROTEIN, which is commonly the result desired in cookery, and is often preferable to boiling something, since it avoids undue agitation of the liquid and may be slightly more economical in the use of fuel. The surface of a liquid which is simmering shows occasional bubbles and some movement, but not much.

The term may also be applied to the liquid itself, as in an instruction to bring milk or broth to simmering point.

See also POACH and STEW.

SIMMONDS PETER LUND (1814–97), author of *The Curiosities of Food; or the Dainties and Delicacies of Different Nations Obtained from the Animal Kingdom* (1859). This is in all probability the first attempt to write a general worldwide survey of animal products.

Simmonds was born in Aarhus, Denmark. He became a writer on 'applied sciences', with a series of books on agriculture, food preservation, commercial foods and beverages around the world. He was in charge of the British exhibit at the Paris Exhibition of 1867, and the exhibitions at Amsterdam in 1869 and 1883, and seems to have been the director of some type of food and agriculture 'museum' in London.

SIMMONS AMELIA, author of *American Cookery* (1796), which is regarded as the first American cookbook. American housewives had previously been dependent on English cookbooks or American versions of English books. Although many of Simmons's recipes were based on English practice, she broke new ground by giving some recipes which used indigenous American vegetables like pumpkin, squash, corn, and Jerusalem artichokes. Her recipes for corn (maize) are thought to be the first printed recipes in English for that highly important foodstuff.

Her recipes include a traditional pumpkin pie; cranberry sauce to be served with turkey; and a cakelike gingerbread. Reflecting the transatlantic idiom she refers to emptins, slapjack, shortnin, cookies, and slaw (the last two terms both borrowed from the Dutch). The 1800 edition has a recipe for chowder, and such patriotic confections as Independence Cake, Election Cake, and Federal Pan Cake.

Another innovation in *American Cookery* is the first recorded use of an artificial raising agent in baking. This was pearlash, a precursor of modern baking powder.

Amelia Simmons's stated intention was to write recipes for all grades of life—a basic manual for American cooks. She was first published in Hartford, Connecticut, and refers to herself as an orphan. Apart from these clues, hardly anything is known about her. Her book has been reprinted in several modern editions. The Applewood Books reprint (1996) of the 2nd edition benefits from an editorial introduction by Karen Hess.

READING: Mary Tolford Wilson (1957); Jan Longone (1996*b*).

SIMNEL CAKE made for Easter, is a type of FRUIT CAKE, similar to Christmas cake. It is distinguished by the use of MARZIPAN or almond paste. Usually, half the raw cake mixture is put in the tin, covered with a sheet of marzipan, and the remaining mixture added. Towards the end of baking the top of the cake is covered with more marzipan, decorated with little marzipan balls, and browned lightly. Some omit the central layer of marzipan, and there is debate over the number of balls. Since they are said to represent the 12 apostles, some contend there should be 11 (thus excluding Judas); others say there should be 13 (to include Christ).

The marzipan is a late 19th-century embellishment of a food with a very long tradition, according to C. Anne Wilson (1973). Medieval simnels appeared to be a type of light bread boiled and then baked. Spices and fruit probably become features of the recipes during the 17th century. From then on, there is evidence for several regional simnels, mostly using fruited, spiced yeast dough. Sometimes this was encased in a rich crust of pastry or dough similar to SAFFRON BREAD, a form reminiscent of the Scottish BLACK BUN. The exception was on the island of Jersey, where the word 'simnel' meant a kind of biscuit until at least the mid-19th century.

Simnel cakes are particularly associated with the towns of Shrewsbury, which seems responsible for the cake as understood today; Devizes, which produced a star-shaped version without marzipan; and Bury, where a rubbed-in mixture, giving a result rather like a very rich scone, was baked in a long oval.

Originally simnel cakes belonged to Mothering Sunday (the fourth Sunday in Lent). Formerly marked by the population making pilgrimages to the mother church of their parishes, this became a day on which children working as servants and apprentices were given leave to visit their parents. Simnel cakes were taken as presents. Mothering Sunday has been eclipsed by the unrelated N. American custom of Mother's Day, and simnel cakes are now simply associated with Easter. There is, however, an isolated British survivor of a Mothering Sunday speciality, the 'mothering buns' made in the city of Bristol: these are rather plain yeast-leavened buns, iced, and sprinkled with hundreds and thousands, eaten for breakfast on that day.

(LM)

SINARAPAN a phenomenon peculiar to the Philippines, explained by Gilda Cordero-Fernando (1976):

Sinarapan, the smallest fish in the world, measuring one-half centimeter, are found swimming in Lake Buhi, Camarines Sur, in large thick schools. When dried, the fish stick together and look like patties of *ukoy* [a fried patty made of mung bean sprouts and shrimps], with only the heads visible. Sinarapan are wrapped in banana leaves and cooked with tomatoes in a clay pot, fried in cakes, or made into an omelet with slices of hot peppers.

SIN-EATING a curious practice by which a professional sin-eater was supposed to consume the sins of a person recently dead by consuming food before or at the funeral. Hone (1832) assembled evidence of this, largely pertaining to England but no doubt echoing similar customs elsewhere. His main English source, quoted both indirectly and directly, was John Aubrey (1626–97), from whom the two descriptions which follow derive.

Within the memory of our fathers, in Shropshire, in those villages adjoining to Wales, when a person died, there was notice given to an old 'sire' (for so they called him), who presently repaired to the place where the deceased lay, and stood before the door of the house, when some of the family came out and furnished him with a cricket (or stool), on which he sat down facing the door. Then they gave him a groat, which he put in his pocket; a crust of bread, which he ate; and a full bowl of ale, which he drank off at a draught. After this, he got up from the cricket, and pronounced, with a composed gesture, 'the ease and rest of the soul departed, for which he would pawn his own soul.'

In the county of Hereford was an old custom at funerals to hire poor people, who were to take upon them sins of the party deceased. One of them (he was a long, lean, ugly, lamentable poor rascal), I remember, lived in a cottage on Rosse highway. The manner was, that when the corpse was brought out of the house, and laid on the bier, a loaf of bread was brought out, and delivered to the sin-eater, over the corpse, as also a mazard bowl, of maple, full of beer (which he was to drink up), and sixpence in money: in consideration whereof he took upon him, ipso facto, all the sins of the defunct, and freed him or her from walking after they were dead.

There does not seem to be any record of what happened when a sin-eater, with his great accumulation of other people's sins, himself died. Perhaps the whole load was taken over by a younger member of the profession.

SINIGANG is a sour stew of the Philippines that is sister to other SE Asian sour stews (soups like the Thai *Tom yam*). It can be made of almost any fish (silver sea bass, grouper, etc.), crustacean, meat, or chicken; and the names of the dishes vary accordingly—thus *Sinampalukang manok* is the chicken version. It is always accompanied by vegetables—eggplant, string beans, WATER SPINACH (*kangkong*, swamp cabbage); and it is always soured with one or some of the many sour fruits and leaves of the country: green mango, TAMARIND (or young tamarind leaves and sprouts, specific to chicken), *kamias* (see BELIMBING ASAM), sour pineapple, the tropical Asian vegetable known in the Philippines as *alibangbang* (*Bauhinia malabarica*), tomatoes, and sometimes CALAMANSI.

The perfect degree of sourness is called by Tagalogs *katamtaman* (sour with an edge). The people of Cebu, who call their sour soup *tinola* or *tinowa*, prefer it only mildly soured with tomatoes.

Sinigang is flexible, adjusting to all budgets and to seasonal flexibility, accommodating fish large or small, or just the head, or, luxuriously, just milk fish bellies; different meat cuts, although a mixture of fat with lean and some bone is preferred; and almost any vegetables in season.

It is served at breakfast, lunch, or dinner—the broth as soup, the meat/fish/shrimp and vegetables with rice. The sourness makes it a cooling dish in the tropical heat.   DF

SIPHNOPITTA a honey and cheese pie which is a Greek Easter-time speciality. It is made on most of the Greek islands but as the name implies it is renowned on the island of Siphnos. A soft, fresh, unsalted sheep's cheese called *mizithra* is used in the making of this pie and the honey is thyme scented. It is sometimes called *melopitta Siphnou*.   HS

SKIPJACK *Katsuwonus pelamis*, a cosmopolitan fish of the TUNA family, common in the warm waters of the Indo-Pacific and Atlantic, but less so in the Mediterranean. It accounts for over a third of the world catch of tuna.

Normal length around 60 cm (24"), maximum just over 1 m (40"). The distinctive parallel dark blue stripes running along the sides of its belly account for many vernacular names, including the Australian striped tuna and, more picturesquely, watermelon (a name used also in the USA).

Skipjack swim in schools, which are often associated with floating driftwood, whales, and flocks of birds; and this behaviour has made possible some specialized fishing techniques for them including the use of man-made aggregations of flotsam.

Skipjack (*katsuwo*) is caught and eaten in huge quantities in Japan. Back in the Edo period (1603–1868) there was a fashion for eating the first skipjack of the season. In Tokyo (called Edo then) citizens of all classes vied in eating skipjack before anybody else in spring. As a result, early skipjack often fetched a prodigious price.

Skipjack is eaten in Japan in various ways including SASHIMI, or as *tataki*—the fish is filleted, grilled for a few moments only over (ideally) a straw fire, sliced like sashimi, and served with a special dip. It is among the fish which appear in the form of *shiokara*, a salt-cured preserve of the flesh and gut. Skipjack is also made into KATSUOBUSHI, and sometimes into *namaribushi* ('halfway katsuobushi', still sliceable).

SKIRLIE a Scottish speciality, is a fried mixture of oatmeal, onion, and suet, with seasoning. It can be used as a stuffing or served as an accompaniment to roast meat or game.

The name, which does not seem to have been used before the 20th century, is thought to be derived from 'skirl', to cry out or make a noise like bagpipes; this because of the noise made by skirlie as it is fried in the pan.

SKIRRET *Sium sisarum*, also called water parsnip, an umbelliferous and perennial plant whose root used to be eaten until the spreading popularity of the potato ousted it. The root is branched, like that of scolymus (see under SALSIFY), but unlike the other root vegetables in the family (carrot, parsnip, salsify, etc.). Each branch is about as thick as an early, forced carrot, grey outside and white inside, with a flavour resembling that of celeriac (see CELERY), but sweeter. Old roots have an inedible, woody core.

The plant is native to E. Asia, and has been eaten in China and Japan since early times. During the 16th and 17th centuries it also became popular in Europe. De Candolle (1886) surmised that cultivation of the plant spread westwards from Siberia to Russia and to Germany, where it was first described by Fuchsius in 1542. It arrived in England later in the same decade from Holland: the name skirret, originally skywort, is a corruption of the Dutch *zuikerwortel*, sugar root.

Skirret is cooked and eaten in the same ways as salsify and scorzonera. Commenting on this, Richard Bradley (1736) recommended boiling, peeling, and serving with a sauce of melted butter and sack. 'In this manner are they serv'd at the Table, and eaten with the Juice of [bitter] Orange, and some likewise use Sugar with them, but the Root is very sweet of itself.' The anonymous authors of *Adam's Luxury and Eve's Cookery* (1744) echoed Bradley's advice but also gave an interesting recipe for Skirret Fritters, made with 'Pulp of Skirrets'. However, mention of skirrets had largely disappeared from the recipe books by the end of the 18th century.

There have been signs of renewed interest in this vegetable in France in the 1990s.

A close relation of the skirret, *S. cicutaefolium*, occurs in N. America, where it is known as 'water parsnip'. It was described by the Arctic explorer Richardson in the mid-19th century as 'a small white root about the thickness of a goose quill, which had an agreeable nutty flavor'. The species name indicates that its leaves resemble those of the deadly beaver-poison (*Cicuta* spp), prompting Fernald and Kinsey (1943) to recommend that even those familiar with both plants should invite a rabbit or guinea pig to taste this root before doing so themselves.

SKORTHALIA a Greek GARLIC sauce which is made with almonds or walnuts, olive oil, salt, soaked and squeezed white bread, and of course garlic. It is one of those recipes where the olive oil has to be added drop by drop to the pounded mixture of other ingredients; a little wine vinegar is added at the end. As with many Greek recipes, there are regional variations. In Cephalonia for example mashed potato is used instead of the bread.

SKUNK an animal notorious for the horrible smell which it can emit, exists in a number of species, of which *Mephitis mephitis*, the striped skunk, is the best known. This animal has a range in N. America from Canada down to N. Mexico. Head and body length may be 45 cm (18") and weight up to 5 kg (11 lb).

The awful smell is a measure of self-protection. The jet of fluid emitted from the anus may travel nearly 4 m (12') and be smelled half a mile away. The glands responsible for this must of course be removed if the animal is to be eaten.

However, if this and other preparations are carried out properly, it makes good food.

Berlandier (1980) described an interesting meal:

At supper time we ate a small digitigrade carnivore known in the country as the zorillo, which is a species of skunk . . . they remove the anal glands and, having burned the hair, they cook it over coals. Despite the repugnance which I then had for that food, I was very soon convinced to the contrary, and I believed myself to be eating sucking pig.

SKYR a cultured milk preparation which has been made in Iceland since the first settlers arrived there in the 9th century. It seems likely that it was being produced elsewhere, e.g. in Denmark and Britain, at that time, but it was only in Iceland that production continued into and beyond medieval times. For Icelanders, skyr is a major element in their culinary heritage and is thought to be unique to their country. Nonetheless, Sigríður Thorlacius (1980) observes that 'a Dane, who had worked in a dairy in Iceland, brought the formula with him to Denmark and started making skyr in a dairy in Jutland with great success'. She also remarks that when her husband was given dinner by Prime Minister Nehru in India he discovered that the SHRIKHAND of that country was astonishingly similar to skyr.

Skyr is made using skimmed sheep's or cow's milk with bacterial cultures and rennet added. These curdle the milk. The curds become the skyr and the whey is put to other uses, including preservation of foods. It is served as a dessert with cream, sugar, and sometimes fruit.

SLIPCOTE also called slipcoat, is an antique and imprecise term used for any English soft cheese whose exterior or 'coat' becomes loose and easily slips off. Sir Kenelm Digby gave a recipe for it in 1669, treating it as a distinct variety. But the name most often refers to a COLWICK cheese which has ripened between two plates and has acquired a 'slip-coat'.

A slipcote may also be a STILTON which has gone wrong.

SLIPPER LIMPET *Crepidula fornicata*, a small N. American MOLLUSC which inhabits a single shell but does not otherwise resemble a LIMPET. It has a 'half-deck' inside its shell, and is sometimes called boat shell.

The slipper limpet preys on oysters. It was accidentally introduced to S. England along with some American oysters in 1890, and is now established there. The pestilential character of the species would be mitigated if it was more widely realized that it is good to eat, raw or cooked. Some were harvested and eaten in Britain and the Netherlands during the Second World War; but in normal times the difficulty of securing an acceptably high yield of meat from the creatures precludes their commercial exploitation, helpful though this would be to the oyster population.

SLOE or blackthorn, *Prunus spinosa*, a common wild hedgerow bush throughout Europe and W. Asia, is probably the only plum species native to Britain. Its small, black fruits are a byword for mouth-puckering astringency. Yet they make excellent jam, are infused to produce sloe gin, and are fermented to make other kinds of alcoholic drinks. Couplan (1983) writes that preserved in vinegar they are a good imitation of UMEBOSHI.

SLOVENIA formerly the northernmost and richest republic of YUGOSLAVIA, but independent since 1992, is a neighbour of ITALY, AUSTRIA, and HUNGARY. It is predominantly Alpine country, with less than 20% arable land, best suited to the cultivation of barley, rye, buckwheat, oats, maize, millet, and potatoes.

The Slovenes came early in their history under Latin and Roman Catholic influence, which was followed, on and off, by a millennium of Austrian domination. An astonishing fact is the determination which the Slovenes have shown in preserving their language, customs, and cuisine irrespective of alien rule. Many dishes, such as *kaša* (see KASHA), drawn from the ancient pan-Slavonic pool and typical of the food of the Slovenes from the 6th century onwards, have survived into the present. Other examples are *žganci* and *močnik*, types of PORRIDGE made from buckwheat, rye, maize, or wheaten flour, which run the gamut from almost solid to liquid mixtures.

The Slovenian *kolač* is the oldest Slavonic ritual leavened bread; it can be round, ring shaped, and often elaborately decorated (see *kulich* under EASTER FOODS). *Juha*, another ancient Slavic dish, is a meat and vegetable soup and an intrinsic part of the Slovenian meal. *Ded* and *vratnik* are conserves of chopped pork, packed into a pig's stomach, bladder, or large casing, poached or smoked or just air dried. *Ded* means 'grandfather' in Slovenian—the dried product has lots of wrinkles on its surface.

Štruklji, the pride of the Slovenian national kitchen, was derived from the Austrian STRUDEL, but through the centuries the Slovenes have developed, modified, and transformed the original into a series of new and disparate dishes. *Štruklji* can be made with stretched or rolled-out sheets of pastry, with yeast-raised dough, or with a lightly enriched dough of wheaten or buckwheat flour and mashed potatoes. The fillings are usually based on cheese, rice, potatoes, haricot beans, *kaša*, cracklings, fresh or smoked meat or pork, combined with eggs and pig's blood. Sweet fillings can be equally varied and may include apples, plums, cherries, pumpkin, bilberries, walnuts, poppyseed, or millet. The filled and rolled-up pastries are either baked, steamed, or boiled like an English pudding.

The Slovenes appear to be the only European people who still use MILLET in their traditional cookery; and, like the Russians and the Poles, they have a liking for BUCKWHEAT. The raw materials available to them are now far less limited than in the past, but people still cling to the old traditional ingredients and dishes which, for many, are a metaphor for national identity.

MK-J

SLUMP a culinary term immortalized by Louisa May Alcott, author of *Little Women*, who gave to her home in Concord, Massachusetts, the name Apple Slump and recorded a recipe for the dish. This is a dish of cooked fruit with pieces of raised dough dropped on top, the whole being then further cooked. The reason for the name is thought to be that the preparation has no recognizable form and 'slumps' on the plate. It is served with cream.

For related items, see PANDOWDY; COBBLER.

SMARTWEED *Persicaria* (formerly *Polygonum*) *hydropiper*, an annual herb of Europe and Asia which owes its alternative name water pepper to its pungency and the fact that it grows in wet conditions. In Europe it has had only medicinal uses, but in Japan (where it is known as *tade*) it is consumed on a large scale as a garnish and accompaniment for many dishes.

The plants are usually marketed at the seedling stage, only a few days after the seeds have germinated. The leaves, which may be purplish or green, broad or narrow, according to the variety, are very pungent.

Hamada (in Yashiroda *et al.*, 1968) remarks that the pungency of tade differs from that of WASABI and pepper, and that the fresh leaves are used as a garnish for such favourite Japanese dishes as SASHIMI, TEMPURA, and SUSHI. 'After a mouthful of a particular dish, one savours a tade leaf. Tade is a favourite herb in summer cooking. My father would often ask for some tade leaves to garnish any summer dish.'

Hosking (1996) explains that the green variety, *yanagitade*, an annual herb growing to a fair height and bearing willow-like leaves, is mainly used in fish cookery to remove the fishy smell. Benitade has small purple leaves, which have a peppery flavour and which are used as an accompaniment to sashimi and parched as an ingredient of soup.

The species *P. odoratum* is well known as RAU RAM in Vietnam.

SMELT the name for several species of fish in the family Osmeridae (and the less important family Retrospinnidae in the southern hemisphere). *Osmerus eperlanus*, which has a maximum length of 35 cm (14"), is found from the far north of the N. Atlantic (plus the Baltic Sea and many lakes in N. Europe) down to the Bay of Biscay (including the lower reaches of some rivers, such as the Seine in France and the Tay in Scotland). It has a silvery stripe along its sides, like the SILVERSIDE, and has a modest reputation as a food fish in some parts of its range.

The smelt of N. America, also called rainbow smelt, is *O. mordax*, which exists in several forms over a very wide area of the Arctic, stretching down to the N. Pacific and the NW Atlantic and as far south as, for example, New York. In the 19th century, New Yorkers used to enthuse over the 'green smelt' from Raritan Bay; 'green' because they were caught swimming, whereas a high proportion of the smelt brought to market had been naturally frozen in the winter ice.

Smelt have an unusual flavour, signalled in advance by the smell of cucumber (or violets, an alternative analogy) which they give off. They are to be eaten very fresh.

The **capelin** (*capelan* in francophone Canada), *Mallotus villosus*, belongs to the same family and also smells of cucumber. It is appreciated in Greenland. Generally, however, its importance in the scheme of things is as food for cod or other larger fish.

SMITH E. (*c.*1675–*c.*1732), one of the most important cookery writers of the first half of the 18th century. Her *Compleat Housewife: or, Accomplished Gentlewoman's Companion* appeared in 1727 and new editions followed until 1773. It was also the first cookery book printed in America: William Parks used the 5th edition as the basis for his 1742 publication at Williamsburg, and further editions appeared at Williamsburg in 1752 and in New York in 1751 and 1764. What little is known of the author comes from the various editions of her book: she states in her 1727 preface that she has been employed by 'fashionable and noble Families' for more than thirty years. Assuming that she went into service aged about 15, this gives a probable birth-date in the 1670s. The title

pages of the 5th and 6th editions (1732/3 and 1734) announce nearly 50 new receipts, 'communicated just before the Author's Death'.

Uncertainty also prevails over her full name: early editions are by 'E—S—'; after her death, the name becomes 'E. Smith'. The name Eliza has often been attributed to her, apparently on the basis of a letter from A. W. Oxford (the bibliographer) to Genevieve Yost, the author of a bibliographical study of the book: she asked him about the full name, and he said he thought the name Eliza might appear in one of the editions held by the British Library, but the present holdings of the library do not confirm Oxford's supposition.

E. Smith's book contains bills of fare (borrowed from Patrick Lamb), receipts for cookery, confectionery, and remedies, and plates illustrating table-settings. The culinary receipts belong to the tradition of 17th-century manuscripts: the flavours lean towards the wine-gravy-anchovy combinations of the late Restoration period; there are also a few receipts for scaled-down versions of the grand dishes of the French court style. The author states that her medical receipts come from family manuscript sources. The book was used as the main source for the culinary and confectionery receipts in a popular compilation, *The Complete Family-Piece* (1736), thus ensuring an even wider diffusion of Mrs Smith's work.   GL

SMOKING FOODS (*see page 728*)

SMÖRGÅSBORD the best-known feature of the cuisine of SWEDEN, is related to the Russian ZAKUSKI and also to HORS D'ŒUVRES and MEZZE, but less closely to TAPAS. It assumed something like its present form in the course of the 19th century, following old traditions of placing all foods on the table at once and of guests bringing their own contributions. Nowadays it is usually prepared by the hostess, without contributions, and consists in an assortment of cold dishes, sometimes supplemented by hot ones, served either as the preliminary to a meal (like zakuski) or as a full buffet meal.

The literal meaning of the term is 'buttered-bread table', which might lead one to expect an array of open sandwiches. In practice the various savoury items (cured HERRING in various forms, other seafood delicacies, cold meats, various salads, and cheeses) are presented with various Swedish crispbreads or the like, and only a few items, if any, would appear as miniature open sandwiches.

When smörgåsbord is a full buffet meal, a typical sequence of 'courses' would be

herring (always first); other seafood items such as GRAVLAKS; what are called 'small warm dishes' (*småvarmt*); cold meats and the like; cheese/fruit/light dessert.

The *smørbrod* of Norway and *smørrebrød* in Denmark sound as though they would be similar to smörgåsbord, but both terms refer to open sandwiches, as the names (buttered-bread) suggest. In Finland, where two languages prevail, smörgåsbord is the name used by Swedish-speakers, while Finnish-speakers use *voileipäpöyta*.

SNAILS gastropod MOLLUSCS which have an external enclosing spiral shell, especially the land snails in the genus *Helix*. (There are both land and marine snails, but the name snail by itself is usually taken to indicate the former.) The many different edible varieties of these include some which have been cultivated since earliest times. *H. salomonica* was eaten in ancient Mesopotamia. Ucko and Dimbleby (1969) believe that the Romans domesticated a species of large snail, probably *H. pomata*, keeping them in special vivaria and breeding for such characters as size, colour, and fecundity.

The best-known snails for the table are the above-mentioned *H. pomata*, which is *escargot de Bourgogne* in France, also known as vineyard or Roman snail, and *H. aspera*, the common or garden snail, *petit gris* in France. Though the former is larger, the latter is considered tastier by some connoisseurs, and both share a chequered history on French tables where their status has passed from favoured delicacy to outcast and back again over the centuries.

The first French snail recipe was given around 1390 (by the author of the MENAGIER DE PARIS), but was not echoed in other medieval French cookery texts such as the *Viandier* of TAILLEVENT. The only reference to snail-eating in the 15th century seems to imply that it was practised in Lombardy rather than in France.

In the 16th century there are numerous signs of a more positive attitude and it is clear that they were served at banquets. Of particular note is their inclusion in a little booklet published in 1530, whose title translates as *A Noteworthy Treatise Concerning the Properties of Turtles, Snails, Frogs, and Artichokes* by Estienne Laigue. The author criticized four foods that he felt were all equally bizarre but popular with his contemporaries. Of the four, he was kindest to the snail.

I know snails are ugly, but not so hideous as turtles, nor so vile, and nothing like as poisonous; I also know that the ancients ate them, but I can't accept people's eating them daily, since other foods are more nourishing and of better substance.

(*cont. on page 729*)

Smoking foods

Smoking foods helps to preserve them and also gives an attractive flavour. In the past it was important as an adjunct to SALTING and DRYING in the PRESERVATION of fish and meat; but even then it was used for other foods where it was not necessary to preserve them. Now that techniques of preservation have advanced, smoking remains in use for flavouring.

Wood smoke contains tarry substances which are deposited on the food, and whose flavour penetrates it to some extent. These substances contribute to preservation by killing BACTERIA. They form an impervious layer on the surface of the food, sealing it from the air. This averts rancidity of fat caused by exposure to the air; so smoking is especially useful for fatty foods such as HERRING or BACON. Smoking also helps preservation through the heat of the process, which dries the food. However, smoking is not generally used on its own as the only preservation method for a food, since it has a limited effect.

Cheese, fruits, and even nuts and hard-boiled eggs are smoked, but the method is associated particularly with fish and meat, and was probably first used for these. It is practised in many regions of the world, perhaps originating independently in several of them in prehistoric times. The discovery would have come when a fire was lit under fish or meat which was being dried, either to speed up drying or to keep away flies. The pleasant flavour and improved keeping quality would have been noticeable as an effect of the smoke. As early as 3500 BC the Sumerian civilization of Mesopotamia was smoking fish; and the Chinese may well have been practising it equally early, though there is no evidence of this until later, when smoked foods are mentioned as normal items. An unusual delicacy of China in the T'ang dynasty (AD 618–907) was black smoked APRICOTS, made in Hubei province.

The simplest method of smoking food, by hanging it over an open wood fire, is effective, but better results can be achieved by using an enclosure to concentrate the smoke. A mud kiln with a small hole in the top to let the smoke out slowly, another at the side for maintenance of the fire, and a few sticks across the inside for suspending the food works well. In modern Africa large oil drums are often adapted for the purpose.

The Romans had smoked CHEESE, both locally made and imported. The modern cheese CACIOCAVALLO, originally made in pairs tied together for hanging up and smoking, is of very ancient origin and may be a descendant of a Roman type.

Smoking **fish** in Europe goes a long way back. The remains of what seems to be a fish drying and smoking station have been discovered by the River Bann in Ireland. They are dated to about 2000 BC, almost 1,500 years before salting was introduced into W. Europe.

In classical times the fish of the Mediterranean and Black Sea were often preserved by smoking, and the Greeks were adept at the art. The Romans paid large sums for special products such as *salsamentum*, smoked Black Sea TUNA packed in jars. Tuna are oily fish for which, as noted above, smoking is especially suitable.

In medieval Europe smoked herrings were a common food, as important as dried white fish in the diet of the poor. An English document of 1349 mentions specially built smokehouses for herrings, showing that the business was carried on on a large scale. A smokehouse was simply a high, narrow building crossed by small beams between which sticks were laid from which the fish were hung. The roof was covered with tiles which were not cemented, and the smoke escaped through the gaps between them. The fire at the bottom was of oak if possible, ash being a second choice. The whole process took several days, with intermissions to allow the fish to 'rest'. Such smokehouses continued to be built with little alteration until recently: the first continuous kiln, with the fish carried through on chains, was not patented until 1883. In fishing districts fishermen's wives smoked their own fish in the chimney. This practice was very common in Scotland until the mid-19th century: the use of peat as a fuel made the process easy and successful.

HADDOCK, not an oily fish, was often smoked. SALMON, from early times and until the 19th century a common fish, especially in Scotland, was also smoked. Again, this was a salty, hard product, not like modern smoked salmon, which has a tender and slightly moist texture and in most instances a mild flavour (which will, however, be influenced by the kind of wood burned to produce the smoke, and can sometimes be strong).

The practice in English smokehouses was to treat fish at a reasonably low temperature, not normally above 29 °C (85 °F); this is termed cold-smoking.

In N. Europe a different process was developed in the Hanseatic ports: hot-smoking, in which the smoke temperature may be well above boiling point and the fish is wholly or partly cooked. Herring treated by such a method are known as *Bücklinge*, Anglicized to 'buckling'. The same process has also been used for other fish, such as mackerel, eels, salmon, and sturgeon.

Hot-smoking does not prolong the keeping time of the fish; it is used for its effect on the flavour and texture only. The combination of smoking and cooking is found in the Orient and elsewhere. For example, the Japanese cook mackerel, bonito, and tuna by steaming them before smoking, after which they are dried.

In Africa hot-smoking of fish is common. In Ghana a kind of shad called bonga is smoked and cooked (indeed, often burnt black) in simple kilns made from oil drums.

Smoking is also used for many kinds of preserved **meat.** The primitive dried meat strips of the *charqui* (see JERKY) or BILTONG type, which have been prepared by hunters since prehistoric times, would often have been hung over a fire to make them dry quicker. In medieval Europe BACON and HAM were always smoked as part of the preservation process needed to make them last through the winter. Unsmoked gammon (see BACON) preserved only by brining has a relatively short keeping time. As in any smoking process, the benefits were drying, coating, and flavouring; but the coating was often taken a step further. The peculiar black hams which are still made in several European countries are smoked over a fire of coniferous wood which gives them this thick, tarry coating. The purpose is to make them flyproof; another result is a strangely resinous flavour.

Pork was not the only meat that was smoked, and preserved meats similar to ham or bacon have been prepared from beef, mutton (especially popular in Iceland), goat, and wild boar. Turkey and duck are also smoked, as are some kinds of SAUSAGE, for example FRANKFURTER.

MODERN METHODS

During the 19th century improvements in transport, notably the building of railways, allowed less drastic methods of preservation to be used. When the use of REFRIGERATION became general, the tendency was reinforced. Smoked fish was one of the first types of food to benefit from this. Around 1835 a new type of lightly salted, lightly smoked bloater (see HERRING) was first made at Yarmouth.

In 1843 or shortly before, John Woodger of Northumberland invented a new kind of smoked herring which he called the 'Newcastle kipper', a name deliberately taken from the older 'kippered salmon'. Thus was born the famous British KIPPER, prepared by splitting and gutting, lightly salting, and smoking them overnight. In the next few decades these kippers almost completely took over the market from the old salty red herrings. At the same time the Scottish smoking of haddock became lighter, to produce the 'Finnan haddie', a golden-yellow split fish. (For this and similar products see HADDOCK.)

In continental Europe the trend towards lighter smoking, noticeable in the treatment of buckling (mentioned above), was slower to affect bacon and ham, which were often stored for a long time and needed greater protection. Now, however, 'smoked' bacon is barely smoked at all, and needs to be refrigerated.

The choice of wood for smoking has an important influence on the flavour. Hardwoods are best. Oak is preferred in Britain, hickory in the USA. Beech and birch are also good. Softwoods give a resinous, bitter taste which is generally unwanted. However, a small proportion may be added to give a dark colour. A small amount of an aromatic wood, for example apple, rosemary, or juniper, may be added toward the end of smoking for a special flavour.

Wood smoke contains some carcinogenic substances, and frequent consumption of heavily smoked food is thought to be a health risk. However, the trend in the 20th century has been towards lighter smoking.

The association of the three animals named by Laigue was no novelty or accident, and is of some importance. Already in the *Menagier de Paris*, snail recipes appear immediately after one for frogs; and, in the 16th-century cookbook mentioned above, the snail preparation, as well as one for frogs, was appended to a recipe for turtles. This association was to be a constant in French cookbooks virtually from then on, no doubt partly because there have always been people, like Laigue, who consider these foods unconventional, but also because all three were, oddly enough, considered 'fish' by the Catholic Church and therefore permitted on meatless days.

After 1560 snails went into a decline for about 90 years, culminating in a virtual banishment from refined tables for almost 200 years thereafter. The evidence for this is abundant. If a cookery book gave a recipe for snails, it would be with an apology for introducing such a distasteful foodstuff. The complete silence on the subject of GRIMOD DE LA REYNIÈRE is indicative, as is the fact that not a single one of the best restaurants in Paris in 1815 had snails on the menu.

There is, however, evidence that, although snails were absent from Parisian tables at the beginning of the 19th century, they were being eaten in the eastern provinces. A cookbook of 1811 from Metz in Lorraine included the following statement:

We imitate the Romans and fatten snails for the table, raising them in special enclaves that we call 'escargotières'. We feed them with herbs and bran until winter comes and they seal themselves up in their shells; in this way we can eat them all winter long, when there's too much snow to go hunting for them in the hedgerows.

Since there are various references to snails in the same context as oysters, which suggest that in French provinces far from the sea snails were a natural substitute for oysters, an enthusiasm for snails in Alsace and Lorraine is not surprising.

When the great comeback began, in the 1840s, and turned into what, despite the slow locomotive habits of snails, might be called a flood in the 1850s and 1860s, it could be seen to be linked to the spread of brasseries in Paris; and these were typically opened by Alsatians, neighbours who doubtless shared the taste of the snail-eaters in Lorraine. This was probably no coincidence. Certainly, the comeback was very noticeable and achieved so complete a reinstatement of the snail that it has stayed in place ever since.

The penetration of snails into the smartest restaurants of Paris prompted an English author, Hackwood (1911), to express vividly his prejudice against both the French and snail eating, thus:

It has been argued that the national food forms the national character; in proof of which have often been put forward the contrast between the smooth, slippery, volatile character of the soup-, snail- and frog-eating Frenchman and the heavy, stolid, and imperturbable character of our own beef- and pudding-eating countryman.

It is reasonable to hope, indeed suppose, that such confrontational attitudes have been going into decline in the course of the 20th century just as clearly as the snail went into decline in earlier centuries, but that there will be no ensuing comeback.
READING: Stobart (1980); Hyman (1986).   HY

SNAKE GOURD *Trichosanthes cucumerina*, an Asian CUCURBIT of typical vinelike growth, native to India (where it is known by names such as *parval* and *padwal*) but now also grown in other tropical regions. Of the various species in this genus, the snake gourd is the only one which has any importance as a food; others may be too bitter or even toxic. The fruits would be curved like snakes if they were not induced to grow straight by hanging small weights from their ends. They are elongated and can measure well over 1 m (4') in length,

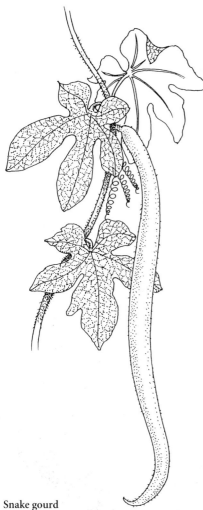

Snake gourd

those countries. The Chinese make a snake soup, and serve marinated snake meat with rice. The Japanese have a way of grilling marinated strips of meat which is reminiscent of their way of treating EELS. Generally, the obvious resemblance between eels and snakes makes recipes for the one suited to the other; but snakes are leaner.

Simmonds, in his comprehensive *Curiosities of Food* (1859), has nothing to say about snakes being eaten in Asia. He gives an extensive quotation from an author who had eaten snake in Australia and found it palatable, but rather fibrous and stringy, 'like ling-fish'. But he gives pride of place to an account in the *Penny Magazine* of a meal of 'Musical Jack' served to a traveller in Kaskaskia, Mississippi. The traveller thought that he was eating fried eels, but . . .

'Stop,' said the individual that occupied the bottom of the table, before I had swallowed two mouthfuls. 'You, Sir, I presume, have no idea what you are eating; and since you are our guest for the time being, I think it but right that you should have no cause hereafter to think yourself imposed upon. The dish before you, which we familiarly call "Musical Jack", is composed of rattlesnakes, which the hunter who accompanies us in our tour of exploration was so fortunate as to procure for us this afternoon.'

Arnold (1996) deals knowledgeably and thoroughly with the cooking of rattlesnakes in Colorado, which he has practised in his restaurant and on which he comments:

Truth is, the meat is rather like chicken, and after being braised for 90 minutes, it comes away from the bones in flakes, not unlike lump crab. I guess it's the thought of it that turns people off, but surprisingly, it's number one of all the appetizers at my restaurant, The Fort, near Denver. We serve some 200 snake portions a week, and 1200 pounds of rattlesnake meat a year.

Arnold deals also with some surprising minutiae of the complex economics involved; for example, 'one enterprising dishwasher collects the rib bones, cleans and bleaches them, then packs one to a glassine envelope, and staples these to a large card advertising "mountain man toothpicks".'

Gilda Cordero-Fernando (1976) has written in encouraging terms about eating a python such as one might meet in the jungles of Mindoro in the Philippines. She advises that, having overpowered the python, one should turn it into SINIGANG; and states that the 'delicious taste of snakemeat is a cross between chicken and tunafish'. These comparisons crop up frequently in connection with the meat of snakes and lizards and other such creatures (see also LIZARD, MONITOR, ALLIGATOR).

Snakes have been eaten on a small scale in various parts of Europe. The French refer to grass snakes as *anguilles de haie* (hedge eels). In Britain there is a tradition of eating viper soup, on which Jennifer Stead (1995*b*),

taking her cue from Simon Varey (also 1995), provides an essay which is now the *locus classicus*.

SNAPPER a name generally applied to numerous species of marine fish in the family Lutjanidae (although by no means all members of that family have the name). They are tropical fish, mostly of medium size, distributed around the world but sparsely represented in the E. Pacific. Their heads are usually long and pointed, and their jaws, the upper of which are equipped with canine-like teeth, can snap vigorously. Most of them are good edible fish, some outstandingly so.

If the use of the name snapper were consistent, and applied to all species in the family Lutjanidae, there would be a very large number of important species to list. In practice the species in certain genera within the family usually have other names and can be found under FUSILIER and JOBFISH. The name snapper is mainly applied to species in the genera *Lutjanus*, *Macolor*, *Ocyurus*, and *Rhomboplites*; and it is these which are dealt with here. Among them are numerous species; many of commercial importance; see the full catalogue edited for the FAO by Allen (1985). The short lists below simply provide some examples, grouped by region. (The Mediterranean and NE Atlantic have none; the SE Atlantic hardly any.)

WEST ATLANTIC
- *Lutjanus analis*, **mutton snapper:** from New England to Brazil; length to 75 cm (30"); coloration variable, often greenish-blue above, pink on the sides, with a black blotch above the rear part of the lateral line and red ventral fins.
- *L. apodus*, **schoolmaster:** to 60 cm (24"); greyish-brown with light vertical bars, and orange or yellow fins. The most common snapper of W. Indian coral reefs.
- *L. griseus*, **grey snapper:** tropical W. Atlantic; to 90 cm (3'); generally greyish with tinges of green or red.
- *L. mahogoni*, **mahogany snapper** (ojanco in Cuba): tropical W. Atlantic; to 48 cm (20"); grey/olive with a reddish tinge.
- *L. synagris*, lane snapper (villajaiba in Mexico); to 50 cm (20").
- *L. vivanus*, **silk snapper:** to 80 cm (32"); good quality, marketed.
- *Ocyurus chrysurus*, yellowtail snapper: to 70 cm (28"); common.
- *Rhomboplites aurorubens*, **vermilion snapper:** to 60 cm (24"); especially common off the south-east coast of the USA.

INDO-PACIFIC
Most Indo-Pacific snappers have a range which includes SE Asia, and usually extends

corresponding to a diameter of only 5 cm (2").

It is the young fruits which are eaten. Although the whole plant has an unpleasant smell, the prepared fruits do not, and those from cultivated plants should be free of the bitterness found in some wild strains. The peeled fruits are sliced or chopped into pieces and boiled for use as a vegetable, being suitable for incorporation in curry-type dishes or a stew or a SAMBAL.

SNAKES of just about every sort have been eaten in most parts of the world where they occur. Snake venom is in the head area only, and the flesh may safely be consumed. Australian Aborigines would bake snakes in the coals of a camp fire; and the Cribbs (1975) cite an old popular song based on this practice: 'If I knew you were coming, I'd have baked a snake.'

In parts of SE Asia snakes are regularly seen in the markets, but they do not constitute an important food resource. The same applies in China and Japan. But ways of preparing snake meat are better known in west to the Red Sea and E. Africa. In many instances the range includes N. Australia, and parts of Oceania.

- *L. argentimaculatus*, **red snapper** (or mangrove jack): tropical Indo-Pacific; to 90 cm (31"); grey to pink above, shading to pink below, sometimes with a silvery spot on each scale (hence alternative names, silver or silver-spotted snapper), the body turning darker red after death.
- *L. gibbus*, **humpback red snapper:** tropical Indo-Pacific; to 50 cm (22"); basic colour red or grey. Known in Australia as the paddle-tail because of the distinctively curved upper part of the tail fin.
- *L. johnii*, **John's snapper:** tropical Indo-Pacific; to 70 cm (28"); yellowish with a bronze sheen and a black spot on and above the lateral line.
- *L. kasmira*, **common bluestripe snapper:** tropical Indo-Pacific; to 35 cm (14"); yellow with four bright blue stripes along the sides.
- *L. malabaricus*, **Malabar blood snapper:** tropical Indo-Pacific, but not E. Africa; red or orange-red. Of excellent quality. One of the main commercial species in the Persian Gulf. Hamrah in Kuwait, scarlet sea perch in Australia.
- *L. guttatus*, **spotted rose snapper:** E. Pacific from Mexico to Peru; to 50 cm (21"); pink above, pale below, a black spot above the lateral line.
- *L. quinquelineatus*, **five-lined snapper:** to 38 cm (15"); a good eating fish, common in the markets.
- *L. rivulatus*, **blubberlip snapper:** to 65 cm (26"); tropical Indo-Pacific.
- *L. sanguineus*, **humphead snapper:** to 85 cm (34"); E. Africa to W. coast of India.
- *L. sebae*, **emperor red snapper,** also red emperor (Australia) and **bourgeois** (Seychelles): to 1 m (40").
- *L. vitta*, **brownstripe snapper:** to 40 cm (16"); has a brown or blackish stripe running along the side; common in the markets.

The name 'red snapper' is legitimately applied to several species in the family whose coloration is vermilion or red or rosy red, and which are particularly good to eat. Since the name has considerable appeal to customers, some fishmongers and restaurateurs have become overly generous in applying it, including some snappers whose hue may at best be described as tinged with red and which are of less good quality.

SNIPE *Gallinago gallinago*, a brownish bird with an unusually long bill, which accounts for very nearly a quarter of the average total length (just over 25 cm/10"). This enables it to probe for food in the mud of marshes and other watery haunts. The range of the species extends right round the globe in the northern hemisphere. Many but by no means all snipe migrate southwards for the winter.

There is not much of a snipe, since its average weight is only 120 g (4 oz), and shooting it for table use has declined, at least in Britain. It is, however, good to eat, and has been rated very high by certain authorities.

There are two close relations, of which the jack snipe is smaller and the great snipe very slightly larger.

SNOEK as it is called in S. Africa, or barracouta (the Australian name, not to be confused with barracuda, a different fish), *Thyrsites atun*, is a fish which exists in abundance in the southern hemisphere (Australasia, S. America, S. Africa). Maximum length 135 cm (54"). The coloration, steel blue over silver, is typical of pelagic fish.

Snoek is an important food resource, and its flesh is of good quality. During and after the Second World War it acquired an undesirable reputation in Britain, whither large quantities of it in cans were imported from S. Africa, largely because the British public were tired of being exhorted to eat things they did not really like, and especially things handicapped by quaint names like 'snoek', the offputting character of which had not been perceived by the civil servants charged with the task of promoting it.

Smoked snoek is a successful product.

The similar name snook applies to several species of American tropical waters, especially the Caribbean, in the family *Centropomidae*. The largest, *C. undecimalis*, is an important game fish. The maximum length is something like 1.5 m (4' 9"). It occurs not only in coastal waters and estuaries but also in some inland waters, and has well-flavoured white flesh.

SNOW the natural substance, occasionally occurs in recipes, e.g. as an ingredient in a certain type of PANCAKE, but when the term is met in cookery books it is more likely to mean a kind of dessert which became popular in England in the 16th century. This was simply a confection of egg whites and cream, flavoured with rosewater and a little sugar and whipped until stiff; or any of a number of variations on this theme. It could be served as a novelty at banquets, mounded over an apple and spread on the twigs of a branch of rosemary to look like real snow. Sometimes gold leaf was added for extra effect. This dish remained popular for a long time.

Karen Hess (1981) comments:

Snow cream is the English version of *crêmets d'Anjou*, those delightful heart-shaped desserts that one finds down river from Tours. Instead of being sweetened, they are served with sugar and fresh cream on serving. It seems likely that the Plantagenets brought the sweet to England.

In the 18th century cooked, whipped apple pulp was added to make apple snow. This dish, still current, is now a light egg white and apple purée mixture eaten cold. Elsewhere, hot versions exist; Lesley Chamberlain (1983) explains that a Russian dish whose name translates intriguingly as 'air pie' is made with fruit purée, sugar, and egg whites only, and served hot.

Also still current, in various European countries, are cakes based on whipped egg white, often called 'snow cake' or a similar name.

SNOW CRAB *Chionoecetes tanneri* in the N. Pacific and *C. opilio* in the N. Atlantic, crabs of polar waters which have become important commercially, indeed an important and valuable food resource. An alternative name for them is **queen crab** and, as one would expect, there is a **king crab** to match, in the form of *Paralithodes camtschatica*.

The most obvious characteristic of these crabs is that they have enormously long legs; so their meat is usually marketed frozen or in cans, since the great length of these relatively thin legs and the distance of the fishing grounds from the markets make any other procedure uneconomic.

As one moves up towards the North Pole, it is not only the species of crab found on the seabed which change, but also the methods of fishing for them. Whereas the more compact edible crabs of temperate waters are caught in pots, the only method which works on rocky or irregular bottoms, or by trawling, the specialized Russian and Japanese fishing boats which seek out snow crabs in the icy Arctic waters use tangle-nets. These are of considerable size, and constructed so as to form 'walls' on the seabed. The snow crabs become entangled in them as they try to move past; and the best catches are made at the time when the crabs are moving into deeper waters for breeding purposes. This has become a really big operation, with one lot of boats for laying the nets and another for picking them up and a factory ship equipped for freezing and canning attending each fleet.

In waters less far north there are other long-legged crabs which live in deep water and are at present under-exploited, but have commercial possibilities. The RED CRAB, *Geryon quinquedens*, is one such. Since the king crab is sometimes known as 'red king crab', there is a possibility of confusion here; the more so since another interesting red crab, the centolla or southern king crab, *Lithodes antarcticus*, is being fished in large quantities off the coast of Chile.

The meat in the legs of all these crabs, which is succulent and has a sweetish taste, may be used for any of the standard crab preparations.

SOBA the Japanese word for BUCKWHEAT, and for NOODLES made from buckwheat, which are traditionally preferred in the eastern half of Japan, especially in Tokyo.

Buckwheat has been eaten in Japan from early antiquity, but it was in the 17th century that soba became common, though it must have been known earlier. The increased popularity of soba at this time was encouraged by a rise in the production of buckwheat, in the wake of the period of peace and prosperity that followed the setting up of centralized government in Edo (present-day Tokyo) in 1603 after decades of civil strife.

Soba has always had a dual identity. In rural areas, where buckwheat was an important element in the daily diet, it tends to be made specially for festive occasions. On the other hand, it has always been readily available to city dwellers as a street food.

Soba is made by mixing buckwheat flour with water, kneading it vigorously (often treading it), rolling it out, folding it, and cutting it into thin strips. As buckwheat dough is inclined to be dry and crumbly, 20 to 30 per cent of wheat flour is usually added.

In the Edo period (1603–1868), when buckwheat noodles first became popular, coloured noodles were often made by incorporating various ingredients (e.g. mugwort, *Artemisia indica*; green tea (to make *cha soba*, green, subtly flavoured, a rarity); shrimps; eggs; chrysanthemum petals; sesame seeds; seaweeds) into the basic dough—in the same way that spinach is sometimes added to pasta dough. But these coloured varieties have almost completely disappeared.

There are numerous ways of serving soba, but the most basic are *mori*, with a dipping sauce, or *kake*, as a soup. (These words come from *moru*, to pile up, and *kakeru*, to pour.) There are a number of variations on these two themes. One of the most popular is *tempura soba*, which is a *kake soba* with prawn TEMPURA placed on top.

Yamaimo soba, lighter in colour and chewier in texture than the plain kind, are made by adding Japanese mountain yam (*Dioscorea japonica*) flour to the basic dough.

Most soba is commercially manufactured and sold dried, although soba restaurants in the cities make their own on the premises. The traditional techniques survive in rural areas.

SODA BREAD any bread raised with BICARBONATE OF SODA and an acid, often supplied by soured milk or buttermilk. Unlike yeast-raised breads, it is quickly made, and does not require strong flour.

The bread has been a particular speciality of Ireland since the late 19th century. In Ireland the use of bicarbonate of soda or bread soda in bread-making was commonplace by the 1840s and certainly by the second half of the 19th century soda bread had become an established feature of the Irish diet. Its popularity can in part be attributed to the fact that rural Ireland did not have a strong tradition of yeast bread manufacture. Until the late 19th century bread-making was considered an entirely domestic procedure and executed with a limited range of utensils; the pot oven or 'bastible' and the flat iron GRIDDLE. These utensils were ideally suited to soda bread preparation and the soda itself provided a convenient, storable, and predictable leaven regardless of the strength or weakness of the flour. In comparison to the more traditional oaten bread, soda bread was easily prepared and decidedly more palatable especially with hot melting country butter.

Soda bread or cakes were baked in the pot oven over the dying embers of the fire and covered with a few sods of burning turf. Traditionally a cross was cut into the dough, which helped in the even baking of the bread and assisted in the quartering of the loaf afterwards. The custom was emphasized especially on Good Friday in honour of the Crucifixion, but the everyday elucidation for the practice was 'to let the devil out'.

In Ireland soda bread is prepared with either white or wholewheat flour. Brown soda bread is popularly served with smoked salmon. A sweet version of the bread can also be prepared with the addition of sugar and currants, raisins, or sultanas; this is known by a variety of names including SPOTTED DICK, spotted dog, and railway cake.

SODIUM a chemical element essential to life. Communications between nerve cells depend on letting sodium ions (electrically charged atoms) in through the cell membrane, and cells contain a mechanism called the 'sodium pump' which constantly removes the excess. Up to a third of the energy used by the cell goes to keeping this 'pump' running.

Sodium in its pure state is an inflammable metal and it is always found in compounds or, in cells, as ions (charged atoms). The most abundant sodium compound, and the form in which most sodium is consumed, is common SALT, sodium chloride. Other compounds used in foods include BICARBONATE OF SODA (sodium hydrogen

carbonate) and Chile saltpetre (sodium NITRATE). Caustic soda (sodium carbonate), the most powerful of all alkalis, is used to clean and disinfect kitchen surfaces.

In the body, it is essential to keep levels of sodium and POTASSIUM in balance. Almost always, any imbalance is an excess of sodium due to eating too much salt. The body's attempts to correct this can damage the heart. Doctors prescribe a low sodium diet, which in practice means not adding salt to food; ordinary foodstuffs provide enough sodium to maintain normal levels in the body.   RH

SOFFRITTO and sofrito, the Italian and Spanish forms of a word which means much the same in both languages, always indicating a preliminary aromatic preparation which is basic to a very wide range of savoury dishes. For Italians it is a mixture of chopped onion, garlic, parsley, and probably tomato and other ingredients too, lightly cooked in olive oil. In Spain, cooks are likely to use paprika, and garlic is not always present; while in CATALAN COOKERY the *sofregit* is closer to the Italian soffritto. But these are general indications; all cooks have their own formulae, which may in any case vary slightly according to the use to which the soffritto will be put.

Oddly, there is no corresponding French term, although cooks in the south of France constantly do something very similar. The relevant instruction in their recipes is standardized, and reads almost like an incantation: 'Faites revenir à l'huile un oignon haché, des tomates épluchées, épépinées et concassées, deux gousses d'ail écrasées.'

The term is much used in Sephardic Jewish cookery, where it can often mean a whole dish incorporating meat or chicken braised with oil and a little water, and coloured and flavoured with saffron.

The soffritto emigrated with Spanish colonists to the New World and Elisabeth Lambert Ortiz (1973) remarks that it took a new form in Puerto Rico where salt pork, ham, and peppers are used. There and in other Caribbean islands it has the same function as in Europe and something like the same importance. Much the same applies in various Latin American countries, where, as one would expect, tomatoes and peppers are regularly used.

SOFT-SHELLED CLAM *Mya arenaria*, an edible BIVALVE found on both sides of the N. Atlantic, is greatly appreciated in Canada and the USA but less popular in Europe, where its range extends only as far south as the English Channel. It is large (up to 15 cm/6") and has a brittle shell which gapes

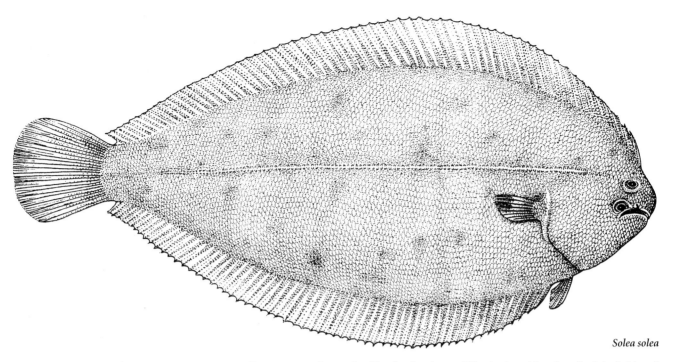

Solea solea

permanently at each end. Even so, it can survive for a long time out of water, and even without oxygen, so can be marketed in good condition. Its double siphon is long, accounting for an alternative common name, long-neck. (A third name, steamer, is bestowed because it is judged to be particularly suitable for steaming. There is no obvious explanation for the Irish names maninose, nannynose, and brallion; nor is it clear why it has been called old maid in England.)

The species was accidentally introduced to the Pacific coast of N. America in the 1870s, established itself there, and is the object of a sport and commercial fishery. It was at one time cultivated in the San Francisco Bay area.

Because they gape, these clams tend to be sandy and gritty. The first step is therefore to purge them by keeping them alive for a day or two in clean water, preferably with a little cornmeal. They are then ready for a CLAMBAKE, to become steamed softshell clams, or for use in certain clam CHOWDERS and clam pies. The reputation of this clam rests also on its excellence when battered and fried. It was the first clam to be so treated, an event said to have taken place in Essex, Massachusetts, in the early part of the 20th century. However, nearby Ipswich became the headquarters of the clam processors and soft-shelled clams therefore became known also as Ipswich clams. They remain the most popular clams for battering and frying in New England.

SOLE *Solea solea*, a FLATFISH of superb quality which ranges from the

Mediterranean to the north of Scotland and the south of Norway. The best fishing grounds for it are the North Sea and the Bay of Biscay. In Britain it is often distinguished from its less good relations (on which see below) by being called Dover sole. This is not because it congregates round Dover, but simply the result of Dover having in the past been the best source of supply to the London market of freshly caught specimens.

The name sole may also be correctly applied, but usually with a qualifying epithet (e.g. French sole), to other species of the family Soleidae. These all belong to the group of dextral flatfish (i.e. flatfish with both eyes on the right-hand side of their heads—see FLATFISH). The other true soles are dealt with at the end of this entry, where information will also be found about the occasional misuse of the name sole for fish which are not true soles.

The name *solea* is from the Greek, 'as the Greeks considered it would form a fit sandal for an ocean nymph' (Day, 1880–4).

The maximum length of this fish is 50 cm (20"). The colour of the eyed side is sepia, marked in life by darker blotches.

Wheeler (1979) has described the habits of the sole thus:

The sole is found on sand, mud, and even fine gravel. During daylight it lies buried with only the eyes and gill cover exposed. At night-time, or during very dull days it is active, and large specimens are not infrequently seen swimming at the surface of the sea. The best catches of soles are usually made at night.

The same author explains that the sole is to some extent migratory, moving into shallow water in spring and summer, and offshore when the sea cools during winter. The North Sea being at the northern end of its range, it may be driven during winter to seek refuge in the few deeps which this sea offers. The Silver Pits in the centre of the North Sea may have earned this name because of the concentration of soles there during really cold weather.

The sole keeps relatively well, and many authorities hold that it is at its best a day or two after death, when its excellent flavour has developed fully.

A whole sole, grilled and served with nothing more than lemon wedges, is as good

OTHER SOLES

These include:

- The sand sole (also known as French sole), *Pegusa lascaris*, ranges from the Mediterranean to Britain, length up to 35 cm (14").
- The thickback sole, *Microchirus variegatus*, is somewhat smaller but has a thicker body.
- Klein's sole (not a name which fishmongers would use, but the only available English name), *Solea kleini*, is a Mediterranean species of fine quality.
- The black sole, *Synaptura orientalis*, is a species of the Indo-Pacific.

a dish as one could have. However, it is a fish which is well adapted to being filleted, yielding cohesive, firm fillets of a good thickness, and many of the classic sole recipes are for fillets. These are sometimes masked by over-elaborate sauces and garnishes which could well be done without, but there are certain preparations, e.g. Sole Véronique (with green grapes) which enhance rather than obscure their intrinsic fine flavour and texture.

There are a number of true soles, of which examples are given in the box, but there are also a number of species which are popularly known as 'soles' but are not. One example is the LEMON SOLE of Europe. In N. America the name sole is applied to several species of FLOUNDER, including both left-eyed and right-eyed ones, but no true soles of the family Soleidae occur in American waters.

SOMEN Japanese NOODLES made from wheat flour and resembling vermicelli (see SPAGHETTI). The difference between somen and other types of Japanese noodles lies in the way it is made. Whereas all the other types of noodles are made by rolling out dough and cutting it into thin strips, somen is made by pulling dough. It is said to have been introduced from China at two separate periods—first during the Nara period (710–94) and second during the Kamakura period (1192–1333). It was not until the Edo period (1603–1868) with an increase in the production of wheat, that it came to be eaten widely.

Since making somen requires a high degree of skill, it is always made professionally and usually sold dried. To make somen, wheat flour is mixed with salt and water (the amount of salt varies according to the weather) and the dough kneaded first by hand and then by treading it. It is then flattened into a large disc, cut spirally into a long, flat belt, and pulled gradually at intervals, to give the dough time to rest and to 'mature'. When the dough has attained a certain length, it is hung on a horizontal rod and continues to be pulled to a greater thinness. Finally, when it is as thin as vermicelli, it is dried and cut to an even length and sold in neat bunches.

Connoisseurs say that the best somen is that which is made at the coldest time of the year (early February), and that it is at its best when it has passed at least two rainy seasons (June). In other words, somen made in February this year will reach its peak in the summer next year. This is because while the dough is being pulled, it is repeatedly painted with vegetable (usually cottonseed) oil so as to prevent it from drying up and becoming brittle. As somen

seasons, the smell of the oil gradually disappears.

Somen, like *hiyamugi* (see NOODLES OF JAPAN), is a summer food. It is eaten cold, often served floating in iced water in a large glass bowl, with a soy sauce-based dipping sauce. In every bunch of somen one or two coloured strands are included for visual effect. Dried *hiyamugi* and somen packed neatly in boxes are often used as gifts in the summer.

Special types of somen include: *cha somen*, which has green tea powder added to the dough; *tamago somen*, with egg yolk added to the dough, giving the noodles a warm yellow colour; and *ume somen*, noodles which are pink because SHISO (beefsteak plant) is used to colour the dough.

Somen is occasionally eaten hot in winter, cooked in a soup with vegetables, fish, etc. Cooked thus, it is called *nyumen*.

SONOFABITCH STEW a cowboy dish of unusual character. It contained various ingredients from a newly killed fat calf: heart, liver, tongue, pieces of tenderloin, sweetbreads, brain, and 'marrow gut'. This last item is explained by Adams (1952):

Marrow gut is not a gut at all, but a tube connecting the two stomachs of cud-chewing animals. It is good only when the calf is young and living upon milk, as it is then filled with a substance resembling marrow through which the partially digested milk passes. This is why only young calves were selected for a good stew. The marrow-like contents were left in, and they were what gave the stew such a delicious flavor.

For clarification of the stomachs of a calf, see TRIPE. What is being referred to here is evidently the passage leading to the abomasum (in fact, the fourth stomach) and the abomasum itself with its distinctive flavour of rennin-curdled milk.

The pieces of calf were added in order, the toughest first and the brain last. The dish was seasoned, and a 'skunk egg' (onion) might be added.

The name of the stew could be adapted to refer to anyone who was currently unpopular: thus, 'Cleveland stew' because the President of that name 'ran the cattlemen out of the Cherokee Strip'. Other names were Rascal stew and SOB stew.

SORGHUM *Sorghum bicolor* (formerly *vulgare*), a cereal related and similar to and sometimes confused with MILLET, is an important staple food of the upland, drier parts of Africa and India. In other parts of the world it is chiefly grown as animal fodder. It is native to Africa, and was probably first cultivated in Ethiopia between 4000 and 3000 BC. It spread thence to

W. Africa, the Near East, India, and China, and later to the New World.

In appearance sorghum is a typical grass with long, flat leaves and large, feathery seed heads. The main cultivated varieties vary considerably in the colour of the seeds and in the size of the plant. The tallest may reach a height of 6 m (20'); but dwarf varieties, low enough to be harvested by machinery, have also been developed.

Among the numerous cultivars, it is generally true that those with white grains (especially Black African and White Pearl, the latter being the most highly esteemed in India) are used for food, while the red-seeded kinds are for making beer.

The flavour of the better grain sorghums is robust and resembles that of buckwheat. The grains may be eaten whole or as a flour. Such flour is coarse and lacks gluten, so is more suited to making PORRIDGE than bread; but Indians make sorghum meal into CHAPATIS and similar unleavened breads.

The *saccharatum* group of cultivars are not grown for grain, but for the sap in their thick stems, the source of sorghum syrup. These sweet sorghums are sometimes called 'sorgo' or 'Chinese sugar cane'. The syrup is produced from them by methods akin to those used in the processing of sugar cane.

Sorghum is only suitable for making syrup, not for the production of solid sugar. The reason is that only a third of its sugar content is sucrose (common sugar), which crystallizes easily. The major part consists of dextrose and fructose, which do not readily crystallize, and some gummy dextrin.

In its usual form, sorghum syrup is a sticky, dark brown product which has only been partly refined and which has a flavour like that of sugar-cane molasses, see SUGAR. The dextrin can, however, cause it to set solid. And in China a technique of evaporation is used to turn it into dried strips, yellow-brown in colour.

In the USA, in the 19th and early 20th centuries, sorghum syrup was popular as a cheap alternative to maple syrup. Production, mainly in the southern states, was as much as 20 million gallons or more annually. It is still produced and used, but to a lesser extent.

SORREL the name of a number of plants of the genus *Rumex*. The sour taste of their edible leaves is responsible for the name 'sorrel', and all other European names for the plants also mean 'sour'. WOOD SORREL is not closely related, though its leaves have a similar flavour.

Sorrels grow wild throughout Europe and Asia. There are a few native American kinds, but the common species from the Old World are now naturalized. The main European wild species are common sorrel,

Rumex acetosa; and round-leafed or French sorrel, *R. scutatus*. These have been eaten as green vegetables since ancient times. Even in the 20th century English schoolchildren would eat 'sour dabs', sorrel picked from the wild.

At first common sorrel was the most used, and it was often cultivated. During the Middle Ages improved varieties of round-leafed sorrel were bred in Italy and France, and these became more popular. The new 'French' or 'Roman' sorrel arrived in England at the end of the 16th century, and was ousting the older species in popularity by the end of the 17th. It is now the most widely cultivated kind, and is much eaten in France and Italy. French sorrel, although it is the mildest kind, retains the typical sour and bitter taste, which is due to the presence of OXALIC ACID.

When sorrel is eaten as a vegetable it may be blanched first and the water discarded to reduce the acidity. One old practice was to mix it with ORACH, a leafy vegetable of mild flavour. Sorrel is added to salads and used as an ingredient in soups, purées, and sauces, as an omelette filling, and as a stuffing for fish where its sharp flavour is especially good. It also has a reputation for dissolving, by means of the oxalic acid which it contains, the tiresome small bones found in certain fish, such as the shad. However, experiments reported by Jaine (1986) suggest that there is little basis for this and that it is prolonged cooking rather than sorrel which achieves the desired effect.

An old English accompaniment to meat and fish was GREENSAUCE made from sorrel pounded to a paste with vinegar or lemon juice and sugar; and this name was also applied to the plant itself.

SOUARI NUT product of the tree *Caryocar nuciferum*, native to northern S. America. The first syllable of souari is pronounced to rhyme with 'how'.

Like its relation, the BRAZIL NUT, it is a large, wild tree whose fruits are gathered in the jungle and which has not proved amenable to cultivation. The fruits, about the size of a child's head, contain three to five nuts with heavy, warty (sometimes spiny) shells.

The kernels are soft and white, with a mild flavour which has been compared to those of the HAZELNUT and ALMOND, and a high oil content (*c*.60%). They may be eaten raw, roasted, or cooked in salt water. Also, they yield a good cooking oil or, cold pressed, a semi-solid cooking fat like butter, which explains the alternative name 'butter nut'.

C. villosum, the *pequiá* or *arbre à beurre*, also has fruits which yield edible seeds and oil.

SOUFFLÉ a French word which literally means 'puffed up', is a culinary term in both French and English (and used in many other languages) for a light, frothy dish, just stiff enough to hold its shape, and which may be savoury or sweet, hot or cold. There is no mistaking a hot soufflé; but cold ones are difficult to distinguish from a MOUSSE.

The basic hot soufflé has as its starting point a ROUX—a cooked mixture of flour and butter. This is cooled slightly and blended with egg yolks and savoury or sweet flavouring ingredients which are either already cooked or do not require much cooking. The result resembles a thick rich sauce. Stiffly beaten egg whites are then folded in. The mixture is baked in a high-sided dish. It rises mainly through simple expansion of the air in the egg foam.

This type of soufflé was a French invention of the late 18th century. Beauvilliers was making soufflés possibly as early as 1782 (though he did not publish his *L'Art du cuisinier* until 1814). Recipes for various kinds appear in Louis Ude's *The French Cook* of 1813, a work which promises a 'new method of giving good and extremely cheap fashionable suppers at routs and soirées'. Later, in 1841, CARÊME's *Pâtissier royal parisien* goes into great detail on the technique of making soufflés, from which it is clear that cooks had been having much trouble with soufflés that collapsed. The dish acquired a reputation for difficulty and proneness to accidents which it does not really deserve. Conversely, a successful soufflé has a certain glamour.

The unjustified reputation for frailty which hot soufflés have attracted may be partly due to nervous cooks who open the oven door while the soufflé is cooking to see how it is getting on. This lowers the temperature in the oven and disrupts rising. A soufflé has to be left undisturbed for the full cooking time and then served promptly. A soufflé will collapse if it is undercooked, or if it is kept waiting after cooking.

Most of the mixtures used in these dishes had been in existence for centuries under other names. Even the earliest CUSTARDS made with unbeaten eggs rose to some extent when cooked. However, beating as a method of lightening eggs or cream was not introduced until the 16th century (see MERINGUE).

There are some Ukrainian and Russian dishes of the hot soufflé type, independently evolved and slightly different in composition. The Ukrainian *drachena* is made from a mixture of egg yolks, cream or milk, flour, salt, and a little sugar into which the beaten whites of the eggs are folded. It is baked and served with melted butter and herbs.

The term is also applied, as an adjective, to other things, always indicating something puffed up. Thus an omelette soufflée is a light, usually sweet omelette given a foamy texture by beating the egg whites separately.

See also SNOW.

SOUL FOOD a phrase which came into use in the 1960s, expressing the idea that the 'soul' of African Americans would be fortified by the preparation and consumption of the foodstuffs and dishes which belong to their culture and traditions.

Typical items of soul food are hominy and grits (see GROATS); CORN BREADS; black-eyed peas (see COWPEA) and collard greens (see KALE); CHITTERLINGS, hog jowls, and pigs' FEET. The appeal of soul food stretches out beyond ethnic boundaries, appealing to many Americans as part of the American tradition, but especially in the southern states.

SOUP the most general of the terms which apply to liquid savoury dishes, embraces BROTH, CONSOMMÉ, BISQUE, POTAGE, etc. According to Ayto (1993), the word is derived from the same prehistoric German root which produced English sup and supper. From that root came a noun, *suppa*, which passed into Old French as *soupe*. This meant both 'piece of bread soaked in liquid' and, by extension, 'broth poured onto bread'. The word, with the latter meaning, entered English in the 17th century, joining the term 'sop', which had already arrived separately and was well established as meaning the bit of bread that was soaked. (Ayto also points out that the arrival of the word 'soup' fell in the period when people began to serve the liquid soup without the hitherto always present sops.)

Similar terms in other languages include the Italian *zuppa*, the German *Suppe*, Danish *suppe*, etc.

Of the various categories of dish which may be eaten, soup can certainly be counted among the most basic. Its role (in that small fraction of the world's population which eats western-style meals of several courses and is familiar with restaurant meals and 'dinner parties') as an appetizing first course should be viewed against the historical background, in which soups with solids in them were a meal in themselves for poorer people, especially in rural areas. Such soups can stray, over what is necessarily an imprecisely demarcated frontier, into the realm of stews. This tendency is noticeable among fish soups, for example; many of the best-known dishes which are referred to as fish soups, for example BOUILLABAISSE, display it.

The domain of soups is so vast that it includes several large categories. One is that of the FRUIT SOUPS which are popular in N. Europe and the northern parts of C. Europe. Another is the host of 'sour soups' which are important in N., E., and C. Europe. Lesley Chamberlain (1989) has interesting things to say about these, not only those with a fermented 'beer' base or using SAUERKRAUT but many with a subtler sour element, imparted by a dash of vinegar to finish, or pickled beet juice (see BORSHCH). She counts the Balkan sour soups, notably the many sorts of *ciorba* (see SHORBA), which are likely to use lemon or yoghurt as souring agents, as a subgenre, 'part of a different gastronomic world, more centred on Istanbul than on Vienna'.

One might postulate another category, that of which it could be said, giving only a slightly different focus to the nursery rhyme about the little girl who had a curl right in the middle of her forehead, that 'when they are good they are very very good, but when they are bad they're simply horrid'. Tomato soup is a prime example, often concealing its identity when of the inferior kind under the name 'soop doojoor', which is a near-ubiquitous legacy to the restaurants of the world of French gastronomy. Pea soup is another. Brown Windsor, now almost extinct, was another, of which Ayto writes:

Brown Windsor was the music-hall joke amongst British soups, an undistinguished meat broth—often the thinly disguised offspring of a stock cube—trotted out in seaside boarding-houses, train restaurant-cars and the like. The origins of the name are, perhaps deservedly, lost in obscurity—Mrs Beeton, for instance, does not mention it—but it may have some connections with a sort of transparent brown soap popularly known in the nineteenth century as brown Windsor.

A joke it became, but Garrett, editing his twelve-volume encyclopedia of cookery in the 1890s, took it very seriously, bidding the cook begin by boiling three calf's feet for an hour and finish—after adding Madeira wine along the way—by putting a dozen crayfish QUENELLES into what was evidently, for him, a luxury soup. This same author had a keen eye for the unusual (witness his Sanitary soup and Vocalist's soup), and gave over 120 soup recipes altogether. The longest entry was that for mulligatawny soup (see ANGLO-INDIAN COOKERY).

A list of exotic or strange soups would have to include the 'teakettle soup' of Wales (see BREWIS), and its C. Asian counterpart, the 'teapot soup' of Afghanistan (see Helen Saberi, 1992), and two renowned specialities of China, BIRD'S NEST soup and SHARK'S FIN soup.

Finally, the role of certain soups as invalid food has to be acknowledged, together with the importance attached in the 19th and much of the 20th century in England to 'soup kitchens' as a means of giving food to the needy or homeless (in which connection see the discussion under RUMFORD).

See also BORSHCH; CHLODNIK; COCK-A-LEEKIE; CONSOMMÉ; CULLEN SKINK; SCOTCH BROTH; MINESTRONE; MOCK TURTLE SOUP (also TURTLE and SEA TURTLE); PORTABLE SOUP; POTAGE; SHCHI; VICHYSSOISE.

SOUR CREAM an example of a dairy product in motion; its use has been steadily spreading westwards. It is a traditional and important ingredient in Russian, E. European, German, and C. European cooking, both in savoury and in sweet dishes. In the second half of the 20th century, however, it has started to become a staple in the western parts of Europe, N. America, and elsewhere.

The attractive sour (perhaps better termed acid) taste offsets the richness of the cream which might otherwise be cloying. Sour cream is thicker than fresh cream of the same fat content. This is a result of partial coagulation brought about by the acid created during the souring process.

Russian *smetana* and Polish *smietana* are often taken by translators to be 'sour cream', although the dictionaries give the meaning of the words simply as 'cream'. In fact *smetana* and *smietana* are mixtures of sour and fresh cream, and have a milder taste than sour cream alone.

Traditionally, sour cream was made by letting fresh cream sour naturally. Lactic (and to a small extent, acetic) acid-producing BACTERIA in the cream could normally be relied upon to give an acceptable taste. It was always a mixture of species that did the work: *Streptococcus* and *Leuconostoc* species producing a little acid and some diacetyl, a substance which gives a pleasant buttery flavour, while various species of *Lactobacillus* made a greater amount of acid. However, occasionally some unwanted micro-organism would grow and give an off flavour. *Smetana* had to be made immediately before use, since it took only a few hours for the bacteria in the sour cream to sour the fresh cream completely.

Modern cultured sour cream is made by pasteurizing and homogenizing light (English 'single') cream and inoculating it with a pure culture of selected bacteria. The cream is kept fairly warm to favour their growth until it is sour and thick enough, then repasteurized to stop the process. It is therefore 'dead' when sold, and cannot be used as a starter. Sour cream of whatever type must not be boiled in cooking, or its partly coagulated custard-like texture will be overtaken by complete coagulation and it will curdle. Nor can it be whipped. Otherwise, it has a wide variety of uses, amply demonstrated in the cuisines of E. and C. Europe.

Römme, a Norwegian sour cream, is made into *römmegröt*, a cream-enriched PORRIDGE.

SOURDOUGH BREAD strictly speaking, is bread raised with a leaven of flour and water in which wild YEASTS have been encouraged to grow, by keeping it warm and allowing it to ferment over a period of days. During this time it sours and develops a characteristic flavour. In practice, many sourdough breads made today include compressed or dried yeast, added to boost the action of the leaven and yield a lighter, better-risen loaf.

To make sourdough from scratch, there are three stages. First, a starter mixture is made. In its simplest form this is a flour and water batter, providing food and moisture for the yeast spores which the baker hopes are present. Milk, sugar, or mashed potato are sometimes added to the starter. Today, as they are usually made for the sake of their flavour, and not as a necessity, many sourdough recipes call for some baker's yeast at this point, to get the mixture working properly. Once this mixture has fermented, a portion of it is used to ferment a 'sponge' by adding it to more flour and water; this second mixture is then used to leaven a batch of bread. In the past, the common habit of kneading dough in wooden vessels which were never washed, just scraped clean, would have aided the baking process by supplying more yeast spores.

Once a batch of bread has been mixed with the leaven, there are two ways in which the system can be perpetuated. Either the reserved starter can be kept cool and fed periodically with more warm water and flour, to be used as needed; or a piece of dough is kept, uncooked, to add to the next day's bread. The latter is the basis for the *levain* system traditionally used by French bakers. (Using *levain* in the old-fashioned French manner was an elaborate and time-consuming process, calling for the reserved dough to be mixed with flour and water in instalments until it was working sufficiently to raise a batch of bread.)

Sourdough starters are especially popular for RYE BREADS in Germany, C. Europe, Scandinavia, and amongst Jewish communities (rye has a natural tendency to develop a sour taste). Wheat sourdoughs are very popular in N. America, particularly the San Francisco area. Here, where it is popularly believed that the environment contains an especially good strain of wild yeast for bread-making, they are started using flour and water only. LM

SOUR MILK an ambiguous term, which can mean either milk which has 'turned' by mischance or milk which has been deliberately soured in a controlled manner. Either can correctly be described as fermented milk; see FERMENTATION.

If raw, unpasteurized milk is left in a warm place, the LACTIC ACID-producing bacteria which are always naturally present in it will grow and will convert its lactose (milk sugar) into lactic acid. The process is a kind of fermentation. It produces a sour taste which may be pleasant if the fermentation is not allowed to go too far (when it would cause curdling).

In the days before pasteurization sour milk could be prepared simply by keeping milk in a warm place till it went sour. Now, however, pasteurized milk is almost universal, and this remains fresh until, finally, protein-destroying bacteria invade it and it goes bad rather than sour.

The natural souring of unpasteurized milk is a chancy business. Half a dozen or more kinds of bacteria are involved, but in varying degrees of dominance and with varying, unreliable results. So, in the controlled, commercial production of sour milk (and SOUR CREAM and other soured milk products, including CHEESE and YOGHURT) it is usual to wipe the slate clean by an initial pasteurization and then to add cultures of the desired bacteria in suitable proportions.

Sour milk has various uses, notably in making SODA BREADS and SCONES. The lactic acid in the sour milk reacts with the soda to produce gas, which raises the bread. Sour milk will also add a pleasant taste to mashed potatoes, and to some soups; but it curdles more readily than ordinary milk, so such soups should not be allowed to boil after its addition. Stobart (1980) has a useful survey of soured milks in Scandinavia and elsewhere. He gives a useful definition of the term 'clabber': 'thick, sour milk which has not separated into curds and whey. Clabbering is souring milk until it reaches this point.'

Acidophilus milk is a kind of soured milk which contains a culture of *Lactobacillus acidophilus*. The product was developed in the first half of the 20th century in response to the view then current that consuming live bacteria of the kinds used to ferment milk, and specifically to make yoghurt, reinforces the bacteria naturally present in the human intestine, with beneficial results. The bacteria associated with yoghurt, *Streptococcus thermophilus* and *Lactobacillus bulgaricus*, would have been favoured for this purpose but cannot survive in the human intestine, whereas *L. acidophilus* can although the flavour it imparts is inferior.

Douglas (1911) provided a serious and charming book about soured milk and its products, which still repays study. The frontispiece is a photograph of the oldest woman in the world (126) and her son (101), Bulgarian peasants. The title is: *The Bacillus of Long Life: a manual of the preparation and souring of milk for dietary purposes together with an historical account of the use of fermented milks, from the earliest times to the present day, and their wonderful effect in the prolonging of human existence*. The optimistic note struck here continues to be echoed more than 80 years later by many people, notably those who uphold the merits of yoghurt as a health-giving food, although some of Douglas's scientific material has been overtaken.   (RH)

SOURSOP *Annona muricata*, a tropical fruit native to the W. Indies and northern S. America, and now cultivated also in Mexico, India, SE Asia, and Polynesia. It is the most tropical and largest-fruiting member of the family of annonaceous fruits, which also includes CHERIMOYA, ILAMA, BULLOCK'S HEART, etc.

The name may come originally from the Dutch *zuurzak*, which is also used in the Netherlands Antilles and Indonesia, but the derivation is uncertain. The Malay name, *durian Belanda*, is interesting. Betty Molesworth Allen (1965) has the following to say:

The word *Belanda* (meaning Hollander) was used to indicate something which was foreign and made known by the Dutch, and the spiny fruit of this plant must have suggested that of the native Durian. This interpretation, indicating that the object is foreign but resembles something already known, has resulted in some interesting etymology: thus halwa Belanda is chocolate, and kuching Belanda (foreign cat) is the rabbit, which has been introduced into Malaya.

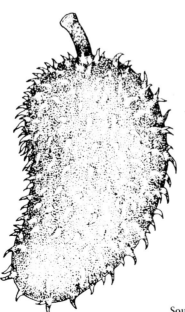

Soursop

The small tree bears its fruits indiscriminately on twigs, branches, or trunk. The fruits, which range from 10–30 cm (4–12") in length and up to a maximum of nearly 5 kg (15 lb) in weight, are ellipsoid or irregularly ovoid, one side growing faster than the other. The thin leathery-looking skin is dark green to begin with, later yellowish-green (and yellow when overripe). Because of the soft spines on the skin, the soursop is sometimes called the 'prickly custard apple' (it is closely related to the other fruits called CUSTARD APPLE).

Fruits are picked while still firm, and are said to be at their best if eaten five or six days later, after softening enough to yield to the pressure of a finger.

The white flesh of the fruit consists of numerous segments, mostly seedless. Quality varies from poor (one unkind writer likened it to wet cotton wool) to very good. At its best, it is soft and juicy with a rich, almost fermented character; pleasantly aromatic with an aroma reminiscent of pineapple.

The soursop, as its name suggests, is more acid than its relations, but the acidity varies and the pulp of some fruits can be eaten raw. Others have to be dressed with sugar to make them palatable.

The fruits are often so very juicy that it would be appropriate to speak of drinking them rather than eating them; and good soursop drinks, such as the Brazilian *champola* and *carato* in Puerto Rico, can be made by combining the juice pressed from the pulp with milk or water and sweetening if needed, plus pink or green colouring in the Philippines. Soursop ice cream is popular in many places. Morton (1987) draws attention to many other sweet confections, such as soursop custards, and adds that it is possible to cook immature fruits as vegetables. 'I have boiled the half-grown fruit whole, without peeling. In an hour, the fruit is tender, its flesh off-white and mealy, with the aroma and flavor of green corn (maize).'

SOUTHERN AFRICA This vast area, including S. Africa, Namibia, Botswana, Lesotho, and Swaziland, has some of the most beautiful and fertile country in the world, as well as two of its great deserts, the Kalahari and the Namib.

The great Portuguese navigator Bartolomeu Dias was the first European to sail round the southern tip of Africa, driven by a storm and unaware of what exactly was happening. In fact, by rounding what is now the Cape of Good Hope he had opened the sea route to India, which then came into use; but it was not until the middle of the 17th century that a victualling settlement at the Cape was established by the Dutch East India Company and began trading with the indigenous population. To make this outpost viable, a limited number of farmers from Europe were allowed to immigrate and establish themselves there. It was these people and their successors, mainly Dutch and German and later known as Boers (or Afrikaaners—the terms are almost synonymous), who were authorized to import slave labour from SE Asia; and it was the arrival of their slaves which laid the foundation for the Cape Malay cuisine which is such a prominent feature of S. Africa.

The British seized control of S. Africa in 1814 and sent out thousands of British settlers. It was this which prompted the Great Trek into the hinterland of the Boers. Meanwhile a new element was being added to the ethnic mix by the arrival of Indians to work in the sugar plantations of Natal. (The Indian spice market in Durban is still important.)

The early settlers—Dutch and German—brought with them a sense of orderliness, frugality, and a love of jams and preserves, *konfyt*, and of baked goods which remains evident even now. They founded huge, self-sufficient estates, often a day's wagon ride from any neighbours, and became cut off from developments in Europe. The French Huguenots who were also early arrivals were mainly responsible for founding the successful wine industry, whence comes some use by Europeans of wine in cooking.

However, most of the dishes thought of as particularly S. African have their origins in Indonesia, apart from the few that were developed during the Great Trek.

The early settlers apparently used both the fat of FAT-TAILED SHEEP and fish oil as cooking mediums.

One of the best-known Cape Malay dishes is *bredie*, a dish of spiced mutton ribs cooked with vegetables, which may originally have been greens (see BRÈDES for the likely connection of the names) but now vary over a wide range. Leipoldt (1976) cites a score of different *bredies*, including ones which use tomato, quince, parsnip, lentils, and cauliflower. *Bredies* are always eaten with rice.

Another dish is *sosaties*, related to SATAY; these are KEBABS of lamb or mutton, marinated with spices, barbecued then served with a curry sauce. Older recipes suggest that *sosaties* were also simmered in their marinade. Many *sosatie* dishes include fruit such as apricots. Yet another Malay dish is BOBOTIE which is made from minced meat, mixed with spices, sugar, milk, and raw eggs baked in the oven. Dishes such as *breyani* (BIRIANI) and *kerrie* (see CURRY), although the names are of Indian origin, are still regarded as part of the Cape Malay tradition.

Supplementary items of Malay origin include *atjars* (cf ACHAR, but the meaning here is items preserved in oil with spices); SAMBALS (side dishes of grated raw fruit or vegetables with chillies); and *blatjang*. This last item is not the same as the Indonesian BLACANG (which is a dried shrimp condiment), but consists of fruit pickled in vinegar with chillies. Van der Post (1977) has a particularly good passage on how these and other items were modified, sometimes radically, when transplanted from Indonesia or Malaysia to S. Africa.

The Malays were expert fishermen with experience of preserving fish in warm climates. *Ingelegte vis* or spiced pickled fish was one introduction which, together with dried fish, came to provide important provisions for ships visiting the Cape. The most popular fish for this were SNOEK, dried then usually reconstituted as *gesmoorde snoek*, something like a *brandade de morue* (see BRANDADE) with chilli. CATFISH, porpoise, and seal were all popular with the Malays. Early settlers, unused to such large marine creatures, cut them into dice called *mootjies* and simmered them with onions. GREY MULLET (*harder*) and HERRING were also salted and dried, when they were known as *bokkems*, used like Bombay duck (see BUMMALOW).

Foods associated with the Great Trek are dried fish of these kinds; *boerewors*, farmer's sausages, made from mixed meats, often including game; BILTONG, dried strips of salted meat, the best reputedly being made from kudu or other ANTELOPES or OSTRICH, which was important for its keeping qualities; and *potjiekos*, food such as VENISON, cooked in a *potjie* or *drievoetpot*, a three-legged cauldron suspended over the fire. The trekkers also planted MAIZE (which they called *mielie*, whence the African term 'mealies') wherever they settled, and this soon came into cultivation by the Africans.

A curious custom of the trekkers, possibly learnt from the Africans, was the use of old termite hills as bread ovens. The top would be cut off and a hole scooped in the side. A fire was lit in this and the *potjie* food cooked on the top. When this was finished the top would be plugged, the ashes raked out and sourdough bread baked inside after the opening was sealed with clay.

Another tradition is the *braai* (BARBECUE), which had been cooked on a wood fire, often including *sosaties* and *boerewors* as well as steak.

The traditional diet of the rural people remained similar to that of their E. African forefathers. However, there was one important change. Maize mostly replaced MILLET to make the staple PORRIDGE called *putu* in S. Africa or *bogobe* in Botswana. This was often enriched with dried pumpkin or melon and commonly fermented. Sour porridge in Botswana is called *ting*. Cattle were wealth and seldom eaten though much use was made of dairy products. Fat-tailed sheep were also raised. Pumpkin leaves and other greens were added to the relish. Beans were popular and might be cooked together with melon or pumpkin.

Insect-eating was and is popular with many S. Africans. Fried locusts were common before the advent of pesticides, and the brightly coloured mopane 'worms', which feed on the mopane tree, actually CATERPILLARS of the emperor moth, are much eaten in season. ANTS and their larvae, usually fried or roasted, have also been popular.

Desserts that have become 'national' dishes, mostly of Dutch or Cape Malay origin, include *koeksisters* or *koesisters*, which have nothing to do with sisters but are a sort of sweet, spiced DOUGHNUT based on an Indonesian original; *melktert*, a cinnamon-flavoured egg custard tart; and *mosbolletjies*, sweet buns, made in the wine-producing areas, leavened with grape must. Van der Post, again, has a wonderfully evocative passage about baked goods. JM

READING: Leipoldt (1976); Renata Coetzee (1982); Vida Heard and Lesley Faull (1975); Hildagonda J. Duckitt (1891 and numerous later edns); Veldsman (1999).

SOUTHERNWOOD *Artemisia abrotanum*, also known as old man, maid's ruin, lad's love, or kiss-me-quick-and-go, is a native of S. Europe, where it grows wild in Italy and Spain. It is a relation of TARRAGON, WORMWOOD, and MUGWORT, and is a tall and attractive plant, with feathery silver-green leaves and small yellow flowers (though it rarely flowers in northern climes).

It was grown in Britain in Elizabethan times, mainly for its medicinal properties; and has been used in minor ways in the kitchen in various European countries, e.g. Italy, where the young shoots flavour certain sweet dishes and the leaves may be included in stuffings for pork or goose, or to flavour vinegar. After being introduced to N. America around 1600 it became an occasional culinary ingredient there.

Southernwood has a strong, bitter lemon smell and taste, which comes from the essential oil contained in its leaves; these can be dried, and are sometimes used to protect clothes from moths and other insects. Pamela Michael (1980) gives an impressive list of other uses (protecting a judge in court from jail fever, keeping ladies awake during lengthy sermons in church, removing pimples, and—this from Coles, 1656—provoking carnal copulation); and recommends the bitter-sweet flavour of southernwood for use in a plain Madeira cake, besides endorsing the suggestion by Sir

John Hill in the 18th century that one should take southernwood tea three times a day.

(HS)

SOWANS the Scottish name for a type of GRUEL made from sids, the inner husks of the OAT grain. These are mixed with lukewarm water and left in a warm place until slightly fermented and sour, a process which takes, on average, a week. Then the liquid is strained, the sids being squeezed by hand to extract all the goodness before they are discarded. The liquid is allowed to stand for two days, at the end of which all solids it contains have sunk to the bottom. This sediment is the sowans. When required, the liquid is poured off. The sowans are prepared by heating them with salt and fresh water, and cooking gently for ten minutes until thick and creamy. They are served like PORRIDGE, sometimes accompanied by butter. Sowans were also thinned and used as a drink, sometimes laced with whisky.

A similar dish was made in Wales, where it was known as *sucan* in the south-west, but in the north was called *llymru*, a word which was Anglicized to FLUMMERY. This was popular in Cheshire and Lancashire, and also the West Country (where it was known as *wash brew*, according to Gervase Markham). Made by steeping oatmeal, or oat husks, until they soured, the liquid was strained and boiled until thick and creamy. According to Minwel Tibbott (1975) it would then be put in a bowl to cool and set, and subsequently: 'A large tablespoonful of this jelly-like mixture was usually served in a bowl-full of cold milk, and tradition has it that it should be swallowed without chewing.' The mixture could be sweetened and flavoured before setting.

These original oat-based concoctions were largely forgotten long ago in England, but lingered on in Scotland. Marian McNeill mentions that at Mafeking, during the Boer War, a Scottish soldier kept the garrison alive by making sowans with the contents of the horses' feed box. And for the ultra-frugal, sowans could be conserved, either by changing the water on top regularly, or by allowing the sediment to dry and cutting it in cubes.   LM

SOYA BEAN *Glycine maximus*, one of the great staple foods of the world, ranks with wheat and rice in importance and outstrips both in the richness of nourishment it provides. The peoples of China, Japan, and all SE Asia, who generally have little or no meat in their diet, are sustained by the soya bean's high content of PROTEIN: 35%, far beyond that of any other plant. Furthermore, the protein is more 'complete'

than other vegetable proteins, i.e. it supplies a full and well-balanced mixture of the essential AMINO ACIDS. The bean is also rich in oil (about 20% in dried beans) and is the world's main source of cooking oil.

The origin of the soya bean is shrouded in legend, but it may have been domesticated in China by the 3rd millennium BC. Cultivation of the bean soon spread from China to neighbouring countries, including Japan.

In 1692 Engelbert Kaenfer, a German botanist, brought seeds to Europe and various attempts were made to establish it as a crop plant in Europe and America. It achieved some success in India, where it is known as white gram. In the West, however, it aroused little interest until the Second World War, when American soya bean powder was used as a 'meat extender' in sausages and similar products.

Soya beans are now a major American farm product, grown for oil, for use in processed foods, and as animal fodder. Some of the numerous varieties are suitable for growing as far north as Canada. Seed sizes and colours vary from white through green, red, and brown, to black. The commonest kinds are smallish and pale brown.

There was a reason for the slow acceptance of soya beans in the West. Simply considered as beans, and cooked in the conventional way, they are extraordinarily tough, even after long boiling, and have a bitter, 'beany' flavour. They are also indigestible; and, if they are eaten whole, most of their protein passes straight through the digestive system and is lost.

In eastern countries, however, they do not eat soya beans in their natural state. Occasionally the immature pods are cooked as a vegetable, or raw beans crunched as a snack; but most of the crop is processed and transformed into greatly altered products. These include TOFU or bean curd in Japan, China (where it is called *dou fu*), and SE Asia; SOY SAUCE and KECAP of various kinds all over the region; Chinese fermented BLACK BEANS; Japanese MISO and NATTO and similar bean pastes; TEMPE in Indonesia; and a SOY MILK surprisingly similar to cow's milk. In all these some extraction or fermentation process has made the taste and texture pleasant and the protein more digestible. Tofu, miso, and tempe form a major part of the diet of the peoples who use them.

The first of these products to become known in the West was SOY SAUCE, which was brought back by traders from the 17th century onwards and became popular as a condiment.

During the 19th century western scientists realized how phenomenally nutritious the beans were. Attempts were made to prepare an acceptable product from them by a

mechanical extraction and powdering process yielding a meal resembling flour but much higher in protein. This meal was used to make all the early soya products, which were inferior and only acceptable in times of shortage. Soya bean meal is still used, e.g. as an addition to wheat flour in some baked goods. Research into soya bean production and the development of new varieties have been remarkably extensive.

In the 1960s manufacturers gained greater skill with soya products and the first reasonably realistic 'meat analogues' were introduced. Soya protein was forced through nozzles and stretched into fibres which were packed together to give a meatlike texture. The Japanese have brought the process to a peak of ingenuity, producing soya 'steaks' which are shaped, flavoured, and coloured with disconcerting realism.

However, the most striking development in western use of the soya bean has been the growing acceptance of the oriental fermented soya products. These are now made in western countries on a steadily increasing scale.

Soya beans are also used to make bean sprouts.

SOY MILK (soya bean milk) resembles cow's milk in many respects but is produced entirely from the SOYA BEAN (see previous entry). In its simplest form it is made by soaking soya beans, grinding them with more water, bringing to the boil, and then filtering. The result is nutritious and digestible but has a taste and odour which is generally disliked by people who are accustomed to dairy milk. The Chinese, who are not so accustomed, have drunk soy milk with pleasure since ancient times. For western people, however, and for the Japanese market, soy milk has to be treated so as to remove its characteristic taste and odour. This process may be accompanied by adding new flavours, often based on fruits, as has happened with yoghurt.

Soy milk is useful to people suffering from LACTOSE INTOLERANCE, who cannot drink dairy milk, and also to people who for whatever reason wish to avoid animal fats. The fat in soy milk is unsaturated and there is only about one-third as much of it as there is fat in regular milk (the comparison would be different with semi-skimmed or skimmed milk). The protein content of soy milk is about the same as that of cow's milk.

Soy milk can be used to make milkshakes, blancmange, custards, and sauces, but it would be wrong to assume that it can be used as a milk substitute in every situation, or that from the gastronomic point of view it is ever a completely satisfactory substitute. There are signs that calling it 'milk' (as opposed to something like 'soy bean beverage') will be ruled out as incorrect in at least some parts of the world.

SOY SAUCE the universal condiment of China and Japan, is also widely used throughout SE Asia. It is the main condiment in Indonesia, where SOYA BEANS are grown extensively. In Vietnam and the Philippines it competes with the FISH SAUCES of the region, which it resembles in composition. The ingredients are normally soya beans, WHEAT, and SALT.

Soy sauce is used in the Orient as freely as salt is in the West, and indeed often instead of salt, as it has a salty taste. This is but one element in its flavour, which is difficult to describe since it interacts with the flavours of the various foods to which it is applied. It can be described as having a sharp, tangy, almost meaty quality.

Although soya beans have been grown in China for at least 3,500 years, the sauce is a slightly more recent invention. It was developed during the Zhou dynasty (1134–246 BC), and probably evolved in conjunction with the fermented fish sauces, many of which involved both fish and rice. The moulds *Aspergillus oryzae* and *A. soyae* are the principal agents in producing soy sauce, and the enzymes which they provide are similar to those which ferment fish sauce. These organisms are common and could accidentally have got to work on soya beans, with results which would have been recognized as a 'fishless fish sauce'.

Early soy sauce was a solid paste known as *sho* or *mesho*. This developed into two products, liquid *shoyu* and solid MISO. In China the liquid sauce is used more than the paste, while in Japan both are of equal importance.

The European name 'soy' (similar in all languages) originates with the 17th-century Dutch traders who brought the sauce back to Europe, where it became popular despite its high price. Old silver bottle labels marked 'soy' occasionally appear in antique shops. The beans are called soya or soy after the sauce, not the other way round.

The traditional process for making soy sauce is still used for sauce of high quality. In Japan it starts in April and continues for a whole year, making use of the changing temperatures in the different seasons. There are several stages, and fermentation is carried out by many different moulds, bacteria, and yeasts which successively predominate in the developing sauce as conditions change to suit them. In outline the process is this. Defatted, steamed soya beans and roasted, crushed wheat are mashed together. The mixture is inoculated with *tane-koji*, a starter culture of the two necessary *Aspergillus* moulds, and is allowed to ferment, then mixed with a strong salt

solution and inoculated with another starter containing several kinds of bacteria and yeasts for a further fermentation which lasts from 8 to 12 months. The reactions in this last period create a complex blend of substances contributing to the final flavour. The chief elements are salt, amino acids, organic acids (lactic and acetic), alcohols, sugars, and numerous volatile aromatic substances including vanillin, the flavour principle of vanilla. When fermentation is complete, the mixture is filtered or racked to extract the sauce; and this is commonly pasteurized to kill the remaining organisms and arrest fermentation. (There are, however, some special sauces which have been allowed to go on fermenting for several years.) One ton each of defatted soya beans, wheat, and salt produce 5,000 litres of soy sauce.

Soy sauce is available in both light and dark varieties. The most extreme of the dark types is the viscous Indonesian KECAP made from black soya beans. In Japan the standard kind is the light one favoured in the Osaka region, amber in colour and saltier than the dark types.

Tamari is a soy sauce made without any wheat, from whole or defatted soya beans only, and is darker in colour than the standard kind.

Something very much like soy sauce, which apparently originated in much the same way from ancient Middle Eastern fish sauces, was made in the Arab world during the Middle Ages under the name *murri*. It was not made from beans but from mouldy barley, sometimes extended with wheat flour or bread; see BARLEY.

SPAGHETTI commonly said to account for more than two-thirds of the whole annual consumption of PASTA, is certainly its most popular form (among many—see PASTA SHAPES), but by no means the oldest. Indeed, until the introduction of extrusion presses, and especially of the powerful machines which were introduced in the latter part of the 19th century (see PASTA MANUFACTURE), its production was a laborious business.

MACARONI, tubular and hollow, was easier to make without modern machinery, and its name was sometimes used in a generic way for pasta. Spaghetti is solid and thin (the name means 'thin cords'), but not as thin as vermicelli, for example. The differences in diameter were what struck Mrs Beeton (1861), it would seem, since in one passage she implies that this is the only difference between macaroni and spaghetti. No doubt this was because spaghetti had only recently reached England. According to Ayto (1993), the first record of the word being used in print in English belongs to Eliza Acton

(edition of 1849), who also showed a lack of familiarity with the product by spelling it 'sparghetti'. Ayto goes on to point out that spaghetti only became a commonplace of the British diet after the Second World War, 'either in the somewhat travestied form of tinned spaghetti in tomato sauce (often produced in rings or hoops, to get round the problem of how to pick up the long wayward strings on a fork—always an embarrassment to the British) or as the perennial bed-sitter standby *spaghetti Bolognese*, spaghetti in tomato and beef sauce (often abbreviated half-affectionately to *spag bol* or *spag bog*).'

Returning to Italy, it becomes clear that Eliza Acton and Mrs Beeton were pardonably unsure in this matter. The earliest record of the word spaghetti (in an Italian dialect dictionary for the region of Piacenza) has been dated by Piccinardi (1993) at 1836. And the term was not recorded in mainstream Italian until 1846; this by the author of a domestic dictionary, who more or less equated spaghetti with vermicelli. Piccinardi explains that this dual nomenclature persisted, reflecting the practice of certain manufacturers, and exists even now; in some parts of S. Italy vermicelli is the preferred term for either or both.

Anyway, for reasons thus made clear, the names of the Italian spaghetti dishes which are now known worldwide are of relatively recent birth. It might be thought that spaghetti and tomato sauce, perhaps the simplest combination, would go a long way back. However, the first documented tomato sauce for pasta appears in Ippolito Cavalcanti's *Cucina teorico pratica* of 1839. This book also includes dressings based on fish and one with clams resembling present-day *Spaghetti alle vongole*. Another of Cavalcanti's dressings uses cheese and beaten raw egg. This is a precursor of the modern *Spaghetti alla carbonara*, one of the most popular pasta dishes, but of obscure origin.

Spaghetti alla carbonara is made with spaghetti which, when still as hot as possible from cooking, is liberally dressed with hot fried PANCETTA (the sort called *guanciale*), which resembles bacon, raw beaten egg, and grated cheese. The heat cooks the egg to some extent. Additions often made are a little wine, heated with the bacon, or cream. It has been suggested that this is a traditional dish of the *carbonari*, or charcoal burners, but that is implausible. A more credible explanation is that it was invented in 1944 as a result of the American occupation troops having their lavish rations of eggs and bacon prepared by local cooks. The name would then be from a Rome restaurant, the 'Carbonara', which makes a speciality of the dish.

SPAIN The cuisines of Spain, oddly, took up more space in Alexandre Dumas's *Grand Dictionnaire de cuisine* (1873) than those of any other country except France. But, despite so many pages to the subject, this illustrious writer did not try to convey the complexity and interrelationships of these cuisines; nor did he offer any analysis of their origins. Indeed, the task would have been difficult, if only because Spain includes within its frontiers two other cuisines; see BASQUE FOOD AND COOKERY and CATALAN COOKERY. Apart from these, and the cuisines of the BALEARIC ISLANDS, there are distinctive local and regional cuisines, notably that of Galicia in the north-west, which can be viewed as part of Celtic cuisine, in company with Ireland, Wales, Cornwall, and Brittany.

Any notion that there is a shortage of published material about Spanish food and cookery will be at once dispelled by turning to SPANISH COOKERY BOOKS, where it will be seen that the Spaniards themselves have produced outstanding gastronomic literature and have been pioneers in food history studies.

However, foreign observers have also played a part. A quarter of a century before Dumas's book was published, the English traveller Richard Ford had included in his book about travelling in Spain (best known in the version called *Gatherings from Spain*, 1846) a whole chapter and much besides about food. Much of what he wrote on the subject reads like commentaries on paintings by Velázquez, Murillo, and others (Spanish painting of the 16th and 17th centuries was extraordinarily rich in food scenes and still lifes of food). However, he offers many interesting historical insights, describing the enormously strong Spanish tradition of hospitality as 'an Oriental trait' inherited from the long centuries of Arab occupation, from the 8th to the 15th centuries. Scores of countries around the world lay claim to 'legendary' HOSPITALITY, but Spain is among those with a strong claim and Ford may have been right about its origin.

However, in looking for the roots of Spanish food traditions one must go back to the Phoenicians, who founded the city now called Cadiz in 1100 BC; the ancient Greeks, and the Carthaginians (who may have been responsible for starting wine production in Spain); and, more important, the Romans who used Spain as a major source of food, especially wheat and olive oil. Extensive planting of olive trees by the Romans laid the foundation for Spain's present position as a leading producer of both OLIVES AND OLIVE OIL.

Introductions by the Arabs were also of fundamental importance for Spain's future. They are particularly associated with the use of ALMONDS (the essential ingredient for so many Spanish desserts, baked goods, and confectionery items); with the introduction of CITRUS FRUITS (including the lemon and the bitter (Seville) orange, without which British marmalade would never have been born); SUGAR CANE and the process of refining sugar from its juice; many vegetables, among which the AUBERGINE was outstanding; and numerous SPICES such as cinnamon, nutmeg, sesame, coriander, aniseed, etc.

The Arabs introduced RICE to the tidal flatlands in what is now Valencia. Although, when the Arabs were driven out in the 13th century, rice production petered out and was only resumed in the late 19th century, this area is now under very intensive cultivation. PAELLA, which set out from its own territory, Valencia, to become Spain's most internationally famous dish, must be made with the local rice, which has special characteristics, if it is to be authentic. The use of SAFFRON in paella is also something which stems from an Arab introduction.

In the period of Arab rule, a large Jewish community prospered, enjoying a sort of 'golden age' for activity in philosophy, science, and medicine. They called their country Sepharad, so they were the Sephardi Jews who were dispersed elsewhere when expelled by King Ferdinand and Queen Isabella in 1492 and who have been responsible wherever they have gone for maintaining and developing the most attractive branch of JEWISH COOKERY. The same year saw the famous voyage by Columbus to the New World, opening the way for the Spanish Conquest of much of C. and S. America and the extension of Spanish cookery traditions throughout that vast area (plus parts of N. America and the Philippines). Thus in the field of culinary exchanges Spain has been a major recipient and a major donor. All these matters have been treated in his monumental *Historia de la gastronomía española* by Manuel Martinez Llopis (1981).

Spain has two long coastlines and seafood, as one would expect, is prominent, in the coastal areas and the big cities. Like neighbouring PORTUGAL, Spain displays great enthusiasm for and expertise with SALT COD. Another speciality is *percebes* (GOOSE-NECKED BARNACLE), which appears often in TAPAS bars (but not normally in the proliferating *tapas* bars outside Spain, since these creatures are difficult to obtain elsewhere).

Another favourite *tapas* item is *jamón serrano*, mountain HAM. The best hams are made in mountain regions, where the salt-curing is aided by a combination of cold winters and hot summers, and are served raw, sliced very thin. If made from the wild black Iberian pig, they qualify to be called *jamón Ibérico*, or *pata negra* (black hoof). Prize hams come from Andalusia and Extremadura, where Montánches is the ham capital and people talk, as did Richard Ford long ago, of a certain Duke of Arcos who fattened his pigs by shutting them up in places where they could eat an abundance of vipers. This may have given the pigs a special flavour, but it is normally considered that feeding on acorns in oak forests produces unsurpassed results.

The mountains and central plateau of Spain are an arid area, most of which is sparsely populated. Foods here are simple, hearty, and completely geared to the seasons.

SPANISH BREAKFAST

BREAKFAST happens twice in Spain. The worker, businessman or schoolchild has a first breakfast early, before leaving in the morning: bread or toast served with coffee with lots of milk and sugar, or cocoa with milk. People who do hard physical work might start the day with something more substantial: a garlic soup or thick porridge. . . .

Schoolchildren and workers alike set off with a bag containing a second desayuno, to eat between 10 and 11 o'clock in the morning. The businessman or office worker probably slips out to the corner café. This second breakfast may be *café con leche*, coffee with milk, with a sweet roll or biscuits, *galletas*, dunked in the coffee, or *una tostada*. A *tostada* is much more than a thin slice of toasted bread; it's usually a small roll split lengthwise and toasted on a grill, sometimes rubbed with garlic and tomato, then served with a plate of olive oil for dipping. . . .

The worker probably carries in his bag a *bocadillo*, a sandwich consisting of bread roll split and filled perhaps with *manteca*, paprika-flavoured lard, or sausage, canned tuna or maybe half a potato omelette. This repast is accompanied by coffee or a beer and may finish with a piece of fruit. Thus sustained, he can work until dinner at 2 o'clock.

Sunday breakfasts are more leisurely, with all the family at home. Papá might bring home *churros*, fritters, for the family to dunk in coffee or thick hot chocolate.

Janet Mendel (1996)

Jane Grigson (1983) may well have had in mind this part of Spain, among others, when she recorded her impression that Spanish foodways still had a medieval feel to them. This was a compliment. It reflects the high degree of continuity which has in fact persisted up to the present time from the Middle Ages. Changes are taking place, but against a background of stability and eating patterns which represent a natural evolution over long periods of time. Witness the description by Janet Mendel (1996) of the breakfasts eaten in contemporary Spain (see box).

If any one thing can serve as the symbol for the cuisines of Spain, it is probably the *olla*, the earthenware pot in which so many one-pot dishes, especially COCIDO and *olla podrida* (cf. OLIO), are made. Richard Ford put it nicely: 'Into this olla it may be affirmed that the whole culinary genius of Spain is condensed, as the mighty Jinn was into a gallipot, according to the Arabian Night tales.'

See also BALEARIC ISLANDS; CANARY ISLANDS; ESCABECHE; GAZPACHO; OMELETTE (for *tortilla*); SAUSAGES OF SPAIN AND PORTUGAL; SPANISH CHEESES.

READING: Pepita Aris (1992); Anna MacMiadhachain (1976); Alicia Rios and Lourdes March (1993); Marie José Sevilla (1992).

SPAM a canned meat product that came to the fore in the Second World War, having been devised by the Hormel Company in the USA in 1937. As Rachel Laudan (1996) informs us, a competition was held for a catchy name, and the $100 prize was won by the entry 'Spam' indicating spiced ham. The product consisted of finely ground pork spiced with salt, sugar, and other flavourings.

Spam has retained some popularity in various parts of the world, although regarded with disfavour by those who eschew processed foods or have pretensions to gourmet status. Perhaps because such people are thin on the ground in the PACIFIC ISLANDS, spam is highly regarded there. Writing of the situation in Hawaii, Laudan observes that spam is the subject of a whole cookbook, only partially tongue-in-cheek, and that it is prepared in many ways: spam and eggs, spam and rice, spam sushi, spam musubi, spam lumpia, and spam wonton (all delicious, as is spam tempura, akin to the British invention of carefully sliced spam fried in batter). She completes the picture thus:

Locals . . . understandably regard Spam as thrifty and tasty, a food of childhood, a food of family meals and picnics at the beach, a food of convenience. A food of convenience, moreover, with a certain status, harking back to the time when buying something canned conveyed

affluence and keeping up with the times. Even the fact that it can be carved is endearing because it makes Spam easy to shape for sushi and musubi. It is the motherhood-and-apple-pie of Hawaii, not specific to any ethnic group, and hence invoked by politicians to show just how deep their Local [the term has a special meaning when capitalized] roots go. . . . Shudders or not, in Hawaii Spam continues to be something to be reckoned with.

SPANISH CHEESES exemplified to the outside world by MANCHEGO, one of the finest sheep's cheeses to be found anywhere, exist in a bewildering number of forms, perhaps even rivalling the figure of 365 often quoted as being the number of French cheeses. The reason is that in most parts of Spain, and also to some extent in Portugal, there are very strong traditions of local, artisanal cheese-making which continue to display great vitality. The Spanish for cheese is QUESO, and the full name of many cheeses begin with that word, e.g. *queso Manchego*.

A high proportion of Spanish cheeses are made with sheep's milk or goat's milk or a mixture of the two. Many of them have interesting shapes, for example the last two in the short list of examples below.

- **Burgos** is a mild, white sheep's milk cheese, with a hint of saltiness, which must be eaten very fresh. Often eaten as a dessert, sprinkled with sugar or served with honey.
- **Cabrales,** one of the few blue cheeses of Spain, is made in the mountain farms of the Asturias from cow's milk, sometimes mixed with ewe's or goat's milk. It has been described as similar to ROQUEFORT. The dried curd is transferred to an *horreo* (granary or storehouse on raised stilts typical in NW Spain and N. Portugal) until the blue mould appears, when the cheeses are taken to the famous cave of Jouz del Cuevo to complete their maturation.
- **Cabreiro,** one of the mixed goat's and sheep's milk cheeses, smooth and white, comes from Castelo Branco near the Portuguese frontier. Eaten fresh or ripened in brine.
- **Roncal,** a hard cheese with a smokey, piquant flavour, is made from ewe's milk in the valley of Roncal in Navarra in the summer.
- **Cebrero** is a good example of the Galician cheeses, most of which are made from cow's milk. The shape, resembling a thick-stalked mushroom with a concave cap, is unusual.
- **Tetilla,** a name meaning nipple or teat, is another Galician cheese. It is also known as *perilla* because its shape, derived from the wooden mould in which it is made, could be likened to a flattened pear as well as to a breast. Has a clean salty taste.

SPANISH COOKERY BOOKS The first culinary documents in Spain appeared during the period of Arab rule, in the 13th and 14th centuries. These reflected the interaction between Spaniards and Arabs; and are of great interest.

One has been translated into Spanish by Miranda (1966) under the title *Manuscrito anónimo del siglo XIII sobre la cocina hispano-magribi*, and is featured in the excellent work by Lucie Bolens (1990) on the cuisine of Andalusia from the 11th to the 13th centuries.

The famous cookery book by Ruperto De Nola appeared originally in Catalan (see CATALAN COOKERY) but had great influence in Spain generally when it appeared in Castilian in 1525 (and subsequently had many more editions in Castilian than in Catalan).

Many authorities have pointed to a book published in Madrid in 1599, the *Libro del arte de cozina . . . a la usança española, italiana y tudesca, de nuestros tiempos*, by Diego Granado Maldonado, as the next landmark. Some of these authorities noted that Diego Granado (as he is usually known) showed a detailed knowledge of Italian cookery. However, until the important essay on him by Jeanne Allard (1987) was published, it was generally accepted that his book was a true reflection of Spanish cookery of the time; no one had realized that the great majority of his recipes were simply translated from one of the most famous early ITALIAN COOKERY BOOKS, that of Bartolomeo Scappi (1570). Allard showed that of the 762 recipes given by Granado, 587 came from Scappi, 50 from De Nola, and only 125 from sources still to be identified. She points out that plagiarism in this field was common, but that in this case 'we are faced with an unusual phenomenon, not just the usual "borrowing" but the borrowing of recipes from a foreign, though neighboring, cuisine, and from a different language'.

Various Spanish cookery books appeared in the 17th century. That by Francisco Martínez Montiño, the head cook of King Philip III, was first published in Madrid in 1611 and was still being reprinted over 200 years later. Montiño was highly critical of Diego Granado (without actually naming him), but on the ground that he was ignorant, not because he was a plagiarist, serving up to the Spanish public many hundreds of Italian recipes. (This episode, as Allard rightly points out, highlights the need for a proper comparison to be made between French, German, Italian, Spanish, and English recipe compilations of the period.)

Two prominent books of the 18th century were *Nuevo arte de cocina* by Juan Altamiras (1745, reprinted in 1994), a practical work which described how to prepare the kind of food eaten by ordinary people; and the more specialized *Arte repostería* by Juan de la Mata, dealing in a comprehensive way with confectionery, cakes, and other sweet things plus items like pickles and sauces. However, it was in the 19th century, and particularly during its later decades, that cookery books began to proliferate. The beginning of the 20th century saw the publication of several works of great interest such as the cookery book of Don Manuel María Puga y Parga, who wrote under the pen-name 'Picadillo' in La Coruña: an excellent book. A late 19th-century novelist, the Countess of Pardo Bazán, published *La cocina española antigua* (1913) and *La cocina española moderna* (1914).

All these and other works were described in a volume of essays (*Conferencias culinarias*, 1982) reflecting the proceedings of Spanish conferences concerned with history, anthropology, and cookery, and Spanish gastronomic writing. This followed on the heels of the very large and important book *Historia de gastronomía española* by Manual Martinez-Llopis (1981), the doyen of such studies. A similar efflorescence could be observed in other countries in the 1980s and 1990s, but it would be fair to say that Spanish writers were pioneers in this respect. See also the admirable bibliography by Maria del Carmen Simón Palmer (1977).

SPANISH MACKEREL a name sometimes applied to the chub mackerel (see MACKEREL) but of more importance as the principal English name for fish of the genus *Scomberomorus*. These are large fish, found in various tropical and semi-tropical waters around the world, especially in SE Asia and the Caribbean (but not at all in the Mediterranean), and in the southern hemisphere. They are greatly appreciated for their compact flesh and fine flavour.

The main species in the Indo-Pacific are:

- *S. commersoni*, the largest in SE Asian waters, is known also in Australia, as the narrow-banded Spanish mackerel (and providing great excitement for anglers in the region of the Great Barrier Reef). It is commonly just under a metre long but sometimes reaches almost 1.5 m (60"). The sides are marked by wavy vertical grey stripes, more noticeable on the lower part of the body.
- *S. guttatus*, the spotted Spanish mackerel, is smaller and has three rows of roundish spots on its silvery sides. Its range extends from India to Japan. Its Australian counterpart, *S. queenslandicus*, the school mackerel, is very similar.
- *S. lineolatus*, the streaked Spanish mackerel, is a little bigger than its spotted brother, and has rows of brownish spots on its sides, elongated so that they almost run into each other and form streaks.

- *S. niphonius*, which Australians call spotted Spanish mackerel, is another species of the southern hemisphere; and so is *S. semifasciatus*, the broad-banded Spanish mackerel of N. and W. Australia.
- *S. concolor*, the Monterey Spanish mackerel, is found in the NE Pacific.

Mention should also be made of a Caribbean species, *S. regalis*, the cero.

SPANISH NEEDLES *Bidens pilosa*, a herb of the daisy family which grows in warm regions worldwide; it is also known as cobbler's pegs, because of the shape of the flower, or as margarita. The barbed projections on the fruits, which catch readily in clothing and constitute an efficient means of distribution, are the 'needles' of the most common name.

The young leaves are cooked like spinach in some places, especially Africa and parts of SE Asia (e.g. Java). Generally, however, it is regarded as a tiresome and stubborn weed.

Julia Morton in an essay about Spanish needles as a wild food resource published in the *Journal of Economic Botany* (1962) investigated the potential of the leaves as food, and recommended them as cooked greens with butter or salt and vinegar. Her findings were endorsed by Martin and Ruberté (1975), whose survey of *Edible Leaves of the Tropics* provides further information.

SPANISH THYME *Plectranthus amboinicus* (formerly *Coleus aromaticus*), a herb of uncertain origin which is used in Asia and the W. Indies as a flavouring for savoury dishes. In the W. Indies it may be known as either Spanish or French thyme, but it is not a true THYME. It also goes by the name 'Cuban oregano' and is one of several plants which are referred to as Mexican OREGANO.

SPARROW *Passer domesticus*, criticized by Aristotle for being the most wanton of birds, i.e. taking every possible opportunity to breed. It was no doubt for this reason that sparrow's eggs enjoyed some popularity as an APHRODISIAC. There are various references to sparrows being eaten of which one, as noted by Simon (1983), is in the English edition (1654) of La Varenne's *The French Cook*: 'The Tourte of Sparrows is served like that of young pidgeons with a white sauce.'

SPATCHCOCK a culinary term, met in cookery books of the 18th and 19th centuries, and revived towards the end of the 20th century, which is said to be of Irish origin. The theory is that the word is an

abbreviation of 'dispatch cock', a phrase used to indicate a summary way of grilling a bird after splitting it open down the back and spreading the two halves out flat. See also, however, SPITCHCOCK.

SPICED BEEF a kind of preserved beef which is a traditional festive dish in many countries. In Ireland, for example, heavily spiced beef is an important part of traditional Christmas fare. The beef is soaked in brine, brown sugar, juniper berries, and spices which can include black peppercorns, cinnamon, cloves, ginger, mace, nutmeg, and pimento for any time between three weeks and three months. Beef is sometimes cured in cider casks to impart additional flavour.

Elizabeth David (1970) remarks that beef prepared in such a way has also been called Hunting Beef or Beef à l'Écarlate, and that various forms of the recipe have been known in England for at least 300 years. Her prescription involves brown sugar, saltpetre, sea or rock salt, black peppercorns, allspice, and juniper berries; she gives characteristically precise instructions for cooking the beef, commenting that it 'will carve thinly and evenly, and has a rich, mellow, spicy flavour which does seem to convey to us some sort of idea of the food eaten by our forbears'.

See also PASTRAMI.

SPICE MIXTURES or 'mixed spices', are commonly thought of as, and here taken to be, dry powders; but they are sometimes taken to mean spicy pastes such as are described separately, for example SAMBAL (Indonesia) and MASALA (India).

A spice mixture, in the sense of a mixture of spices, may be peculiar to one village, or family, or individual. Here the term 'spice mixtures' is used to indicate established mixtures, well known in a country, region, or ethnic group. However, even established mixtures are variable, not only in the proportions of ingredients but also in the ingredients themselves; it is notorious that there may be five, six, or seven spices in Chinese FIVE SPICE mixture.

Variations of a local kind are particularly common in Arab countries, where the composition of ready-made spice mixtures is variable even within a single neighbourhood, and the names vary widely. In Bahrain, for instance, the mixture might be called *bharat*, in other places one might hear *afawi*, *abazir*, or other names.

Spice mixtures should not be kept for long before use. This is true of individual spices also, once they have been ground, but the principle applies more strongly to mixtures since the various components will stay viable for different lengths of time, with the result that some elements in a mixture will stale before others and the balance will be upset.

Important mixtures, which are the subjects of separate entries, are: ADVIEH, COLOMBO, CURRY POWDER, DUQQA, FIVE SPICES, HARISSA, MASALA, NAM PRIK, PANCH PHORON, RAS-EL-HANOUT, SHICHIMI, TABIL, ZAATAR.

Other noteworthy mixtures include:

- *baharat*, a fiery preparation from the Gulf States, used to spice meats and vegetables (see ARABIAN FOOD); there are counterparts elsewhere in the Arab world, e.g. *sabe b'harat makhlootah* in Lebanon;
- *bebere*, a complex and variable Ethiopian blend, in which chillies, ginger and cloves are standard ingredients;
- *goma shio*, a simple Japanese mixture of sesame (*goma*) and salt, used as a condiment;
- mixed spice, as used in British baking, usually consisting of cinnamon, cloves, mace, nutmeg, coriander, and allspice. Also known as pudding spice;
- pickling spice, highly variable (often according to the material being pickled), with ingredients such as black and/or white peppercorns, mustard seed, coriander, ginger, allspice;
- poudre douce (or douce poudre), poudre fine, poudre fort, poudre lombard; four medieval mixtures, of which the first and third were sweet and strong respectively. These terms occur in many different spellings in medieval manuscripts. The MENAGIER DE PARIS gives a recipe for poudre fine, composed of ginger, cinnamon, grains of paradise (MELEGUETA PEPPER), cloves, and sugar;
- pudding spice; normally equals mixed spice, above;
- quatre épices, a French term which usually indicates a mixture of black pepper, nutmeg, ginger, and clove, but with cayenne pepper and cinnamon as alternative ingredients;
- *suwanda kudu* (meaning 'fragrant mixture'), prepared in Sri Lanka with cumin, black cumin, cinnamon, cardamom, cloves, coriander, and fenugreek.

Lesley Chamberlain (1983) mentions two interesting mixtures which she met in Russia:

- *khmeli suneli* (*suneli* meaning bouquet), a mixture containing crushed fenugreek, bay leaf, coriander, dill, celery seed, parsley, basil, thyme, saffron (or turmeric), and mint, in variable proportions;
- *adzhika*, 'a mixture of cayenne pepper, chilli powder, salt, black pepper, and crushed bay leaves'.

READING: Delaveau (1987); Lagriffe (1968); Landry (1978); Jill Norman (1990).

SPICES are difficult to define. 'One or other of various strongly flavoured or aromatic substances of vegetable origin obtained from tropical plants, commonly used as condiments, etc.' (*OED*). This needs two corrections and one rider. Some of the plants which produce spices belong to temperate climates (e.g. caraway seeds); and spices are more often used in cooking, not as condiments (at table, when cooking has already been completed). The rider is that there are some substances of animal origin, e.g. ambergris, which are often included in lists of spices, if only for want of any other category into which to put them. Otherwise, the *OED* definition may be regarded as helpful.

Several authors have demonstrated the possibility of writing a book about spices, or about herbs and spices (a popular combination in books, as in the kitchen) without attempting to say what a spice is. Redgrove (1933) is not one of these. He addresses the question squarely, pronounces it insoluble, yet hints at a solution: 'herbs' are the herbaceous parts of aromatic plants; 'spices' are their dried other parts—rhizome, root, bark, flower, fruit, seed; and 'condiments' are spices or other flavourings added to food at the table. Thus MUSTARD greens would be a herb, and mustard seeds a spice, while mustard in a mustard pot, at table, would be a condiment. This would be a convenient set of definitions, and has the merit of being as close to common usage as any rational definitions could be expected to come.

That complete coincidence is unattainable is a fact explained to some extent by the history of spices, which also explains why the *OED* declares that they have to be from tropical plants. The history of the SPICE TRADE, of great importance from remote antiquity to medieval times as a stimulus to voyages of exploration, is treated separately. Here it is relevant to note that this trade was with the Orient, and resulted in the term 'spice' (which comes from the same root as 'species' and originally meant a kind of merchandise) being applied to oriental products rather than to European ones. The meaning of the term widened when American spices came into the picture, and widened still further when it became convenient to use the term as one of gastronomic use rather than geographical provenance and value. But it has not yet been extended to include certain flavouring substances common in Europe, such as garlic, although logically it should; and there are other anomalies such as the exclusion of HORSERADISH (although WASABI, 'Japanese horseradish', is included by some authors).

The most expensive spices are saffron, vanilla, and cardamom, in that order. Some spices have a preservative effect on foods,

exercised by their essential oils. It is, generally, these same essential oils which provide the flavour. For an explanation of what they are, and their characteristics, see ESSENCES.

A separate survey is given of SPICE MIXTURES.

SPICE TRADE a subject of political and cultural, as well as economic, interest.

In commercial terms, PEPPER has always been the most important of the SPICES, followed usually by CLOVES and NUTMEG; but there are many others. Since their general characteristics are that they take up relatively little space, but are of considerable value, they have often been used as objects of barter against bulkier, less exciting but more necessary, goods such as rice and cloth.

In the early days of the trade, there was considerable mystery, fostered by those involved in the trade, about where some spices came from (usually S. or SE Asia). Their high value and this atmosphere of mystery combined to give these natural products something of the allure of precious metals. They were indeed sometimes used as currency.

Pepper from India was being traded in the Middle East before 2000 BC. It travelled along ways that were dictated by geography and have remained in use ever since, although shifts of power from time to time close some routes and developments in technology make others more attractive. Overland, the route went up the valley of the Indus, through the passes of the Hindu Kush, to join the great east–west Silk Roads. By sea, it was shipped from ports on the west coast of India to either the Persian Gulf or the Red Sea. Indian and Arab merchants handled most of the trade as far as the Mediterranean; redistribution to markets further north and west was controlled by the Phoenicians until Alexander the Great destroyed Tyre and set up his new entrepôt at the mouth of the Nile. The Greeks in turn gave way to the Romans, whose seapower allowed them to send ships directly to India. This round trip took two years, until Hippalus, a Greek seaman, rumbled the Arabs' 'secret' of the seasonally alternating monsoon winds, thereby cutting the return journey to only 12 months and precipitating an increase in Roman pepper consumption.

For the European importing countries, spices were very expensive, this because they came from afar, and changed hands so many times in the course of long and dangerous journeys. At their destination they could cost the western consumer at least 10 times and often 40 times as much as they had cost at source. But those Romans and Europeans of the later medieval period who could afford them willingly paid the high prices for various reasons. One was the obvious one; they liked their food spiced. Besides, spices were a good way to show off wealth and power. And they were thought to have valuable medicinal properties. (It used to be said that spices were needed to disguise the off flavour of spoiled meat; but this was a piece of CULINARY MYTHOLOGY.)

China, like the Mediterranean world, traded for centuries with S. and E. Asia, but without the long chain of middlemen. The key spices here were cloves and nutmeg, produced only on a few small islands in what is now the eastern Indonesian province of Maluku (the Moluccas). Cloves were being exported to China in the 3rd century BC, two centuries before they reached Alexandria. As Asian commercial empires developed, trade increased and Indian merchants, too, set up permanent bases in or near the spice islands, so that a network of trade routes brought these new communities and their products into the larger world. At the same time as the seaways were flourishing, the Silk Roads across C. Asia were regulated and policed by the Han emperors, so that Rome and China were in continuous, if indirect, contact. Trade prospects must have looked good in, say, AD 350.

But the Chinese, to secure their own borders, had displaced Mongol and C. Asian pastoral tribes. The quest by these tribes for new territory (besides being responsible for the fall of the Roman Empire in the 5th century) severed overland trade routes and reduced the spice trade to a fraction of what it had once been.

However, the invaders were horsemen, not sailors, and the seaborne links of the network survived. Spices, now including the first nutmegs seen in the West, found their way back into Europe along with other oriental goods as Christendom grew slowly out of the ruins of Rome and economic life re-formed with Constantinople as its centre. Then came the sudden expansion of Islam and the consequent disruption of all trade relations with the Orient.

In the long term, Islam was to bring lasting benefits to the West, including the supply of a wider range of goods and materials than Europe had ever been able to obtain before. From about 1100 onwards overseas trade revived strongly in Europe, where the resources of capital, know-how, and trade goods were at last sufficient to give the merchants of the N. Italian cities a chance to do business with Islamic states on something like equal terms. Their profits, partly from spices, sufficed to make Venice, Genoa, Florence, and other city-states almost as rich and powerful as the caliphate of Egypt. 'Arabic' (actually Indian) numerals made proper management of goods and money possible, and were the basis of

N. Italian banking and double-entry bookkeeping. These techniques, whether native to Italy or learned from Arab models, all assisted the growth of modern capitalism.

Muslims, who had at first been unwilling to do business with Christians, were happy to trade with Hindu India. Hindus had been very active in trade with the Far East. Although they were now becoming increasingly reluctant to travel, because they risked pollution or loss of caste if they mingled with strangers, Indian Buddhists and Jains travelled freely throughout the Far East to engage in trade by barter. So spices could flow from the Far East to the Arab world through India.

Eventually, as the Hindu presence in the Far East diminished, the Arabs were encouraged to extend their own voyages to Sumatra, Java, and the more distant spice islands, especially after they realized that Indian 'nutmegs' were inferior to those of Ambon and Banda.

This was, however, only one aspect of the long process by which Arab influence in Indonesia gradually replaced Buddhist and Hindu in all areas of life. There was no political conquest, but religion followed trade, local rulers were converted to Islam, and their subjects, of course, followed them. Because the change was slow and on the whole peaceful, it struck deep roots. Commercial continuity was largely unbroken, with inland villages of Java producing big rice surpluses for the sultans and merchants of the north coast, who then shipped it to Maluku, where rice and textiles were bartered for nutmegs, mace, and cloves. These spices then started their long journey, either north to China or west to India and eventually, perhaps, to Constantinople, or the Hansa ports, or England.

In Europe, the great days of the Italian cities were now ending and the future lay with nation states. As early as 1418 Prince Henry the Navigator set up a school of navigation and started sending Portuguese expeditions questing down the west coast of Africa. In the middle of the 15th century, Constantinople fell to the Turks, and in the course of the century pepper prices in Venice went up by a factor of 30. It was abundantly clear that maritime European powers now had good reason to look for a direct sea passage to the Indies. By the late 15th century, they also had the technology and the resources to do so with some hope of success. Following the voyage by Vasco da Gama in 1497–9, round the Cape of Good Hope to Calicut and safely back to Lisbon, the Portuguese set about their entry into the spice trade with a buccaneering zest from which other nations quickly learned. In only 13 years after da Gama's voyage, Portugal, one of the poorest countries in Europe, had not only annexed Brazil but also captured

the three principal stations on the route to the East: Ormuz, controlling the Persian Gulf; Goa; and Malacca, the hub of SE Asian trade in spices and many other goods. A few years later, a Portuguese *feitoria* (factory) in Ceylon established a monopoly in cinnamon that it held for more than a century.

In fact, however, this small nation had overreached itself; its rather primitive administrative systems could not develop fast enough to replace aristocrats with meritocrats, and it never managed to get firm control of the Red Sea route, or of the clove and nutmeg producers of Maluku. Crown agents and private adventurers got rich but sent as little as they could back home to the royal treasury, so the country as a whole profited little. And Portuguese successes naturally inspired strong reactions from trade rivals, notably the Muslims of Indonesia, who attacked European settlements frequently. In N. Sumatra, the Achenese drove the Portuguese out and kept control of pepper production until the second half of the 19th century.

It was the Dutch and the English who, towards the end of the 16th century, emerged as the principal competitors of the Portuguese. (The struggle might have involved the Spaniards too, but the defeat of the Spanish Armada in 1588 more or less ruled them out.) The British founded their East India Company in 1600 and the Dutch counterpart of this was set up only two years later.

The Dutch took the lead in the 17th century. By 1621 they had driven the Portuguese from Indonesia, created new monopolies in nutmeg and cloves, and set up a factory and port at what is now Djakarta. Dutch forces occupied Ceylon in 1636 and captured Malacca in 1641. By the 1680s the Dutch had established themselves unshakeably in Makassar, where their impressive Fort Rotterdam still stands. By 1700 they were fixing clove and nutmeg prices in almost every market place of the world.

The 18th century, however, brought serious problems for the Dutch. One was that they had to counter over-production of cloves and cinnamon. On a notorious occasion in 1760 they had to burn excess bales of spices in the streets of Amsterdam. A much more serious problem was the erosion of their stranglehold on production. As Rosengarten (1969) records:

Between 1770 and 1772 Pierre Poivre, the French administrator of the island of Mauritius [and perhaps a relation of the Peter Piper who picked a peck of pickled pepper], managed to smuggle clove, nutmeg, and cinnamon plants out of the Dutch-controlled Spice Islands. New spice plantings were established in Réunion, the Seychelles, and other French colonies. The blockage of Dutch East Indian ports by British ships in 1780 barred the export of spices to Holland.

In 1799 the Dutch East India Company, suffering from losses by piracy and the takeover by England of the Dutch ports on the Malabar Coast and many Dutch stations in the E. Indies, went bankrupt. This, perhaps, marked the end of what has been seen in retrospect, despite the ruthless and sometimes bloody struggles which took place, as the 'romantic' era of the spice trade.

Spices are now being traded in larger quantities than ever. The biggest importer is the USA, followed by Germany, Japan, and France. The greatest entrepôt is Singapore. The big exporters are India, Indonesia, Brazil, the Malagasy Republic, and Malaysia.

Much has changed, although much remains the same. The Banda Islands still export nutmeg and mace, but the mansions of former Dutch planters lie open to the rain or are converted into homestays for tourists, while the fine stone quay where the world's merchant ships once jostled for space lies tranquil and decayed.   (RO)

READING: Miller (1969); Rosengarten (1969, with very full bibliography); Schoff (1912).

SPIDER CRAB *Maia squinado*, a crab of the Mediterranean and NE Atlantic which takes its English name from the spider-like arrangement of its legs. It is reputed to hibernate, emerging in May (hence *Maia* in the scientific name: *squinado* comes from the Provençal name). The carapace is reddish-orange to brown and may measure 20 cm (8") across.

This crab's remarkable ability to camouflage itself gives it a high degree of protection, for it often looks like a small rock encrusted with natural growths. The naturalist Edward Step, who studied it in Cornwall, described in detail how Gran'fer Jenkin (a Cornish name for it) uses his nippers to break off bits of seaweed or other suitable items, 'kisses' these to coat them with gummy saliva, and then 'plants' them among the prickles and hooked hairs on his back. An extraordinary feature of this operation is that the crab selects items which will not merely stick to its back but will grow there, so that a little 'garden' is created which in turn attracts minuscule marine creatures which find it a good habitat and contribute by their presence to the effect of camouflage.

One other odd piece of behaviour has been noticed. Spider crabs will sometimes form themselves into conical heaps, just below low tide mark. The heaps may be several feet high and may comprise a thousand or so individuals, which are apt to stay in this posture for weeks on end. The smaller crabs are observed to have the inside

berths in this arrangement, and the whole procedure may be a defence against predators such as the octopus.

British fishermen used to disdain spider crabs, and were irritated by their presence in pots set for more valuable prey. However, despite the thinness of the legs this is an excellent edible crab, particularly appreciated in France and Spain, and at the northern end of the Adriatic, where *Grancevola alla veneziana* is a well-known dish. One very large spider crab serves two, but one per person is the norm. The female, slightly smaller than the male, is the better buy, especially in the early part of the year, when she is carrying eggs.

SPIDER HERB a common wild plant in tropical regions. Five-leafed spider herb, *Cleome gynandra*, is found in Asia and Africa.

The leaves contain an essential oil which resembles garlic or mustard oil, and have a strong taste, described as being between radishes and ASAFOETIDA. They are mainly used as a flavouring. In Malaysia, for example, they are salted, pickled, and eaten with rice. They are also cooked, which with other subsequent treatment makes the leaves less bitter, and eaten as a pot-herb in various places.

SPIDERS often thought of as insects but correctly considered to be part of the separate class Arachnida, are a remarkably

successful group of creatures which exist in many forms, some of them large enough to be worth eating and regarded as delicacies in certain, mostly primitive, societies. Hillyard (1995) has provided the most recent summary survey, in which he observes that the people who relish spiders include 'Indians in South America, the Bushmen of southern Africa, and the Aborigines or native Australians'. His own account draws on the detailed description by the English spider enthusiast Dr W. S. Bristowe (1924), who conducted some of his research in Laos, where he found that the giant orb-weavers (*Nephila* spp) were popular fare; the abdomen would often be bitten off and eaten raw, having a mild taste like that of raw potato mixed with lettuce. However, the favourite was a large blue-legged tarantula in the genus *Melopoeus*, which was described as being especially nutritious, with a 60% protein content.

The theme of tarantulas recurs in Hillyard's description of how the Piaroa Indians of Venezuela capture, cook, and eat them. The goliath tarantula (*Theraphosa leblondi*) has a leg span of 25 cm (10") and an abdomen the size of a tennis ball. The Piaroa twist off the abdomens using a leaf (to avoid touching the hairs which can cause urticaria), and squeeze the contents onto another leaf which is folded over and tied, then placed on the hot coals. When it is cooked the large fangs are detached and put beside the body (to be used as toothpicks). The white flesh which is found inside and the meat in the legs (also cooked) are said to

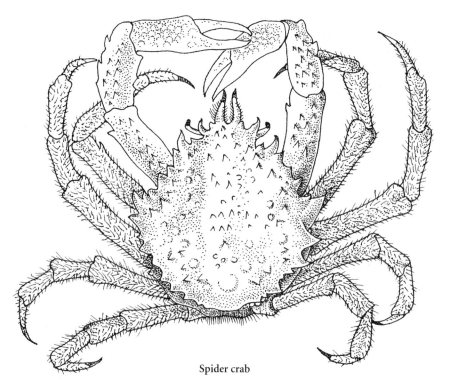

Spider crab

taste like prawns. The eggs of the female are also consumed.

Hillyard also quotes a traveller in New Caledonia who observed two children feasting on spiders whose remarkably strong webs had already been remarked upon by his party because impeding their progress in the woods. The prepared spiders were broiled on the embers and the children 'swallowed at least 100 of them in our presence'. The species is thought to be *Nephila edulis*.

SPINACH *Spinacia oleracea*, the 'prince of vegetables' according to the 12th-century Arab writer Ibn al-Awam, originated in Persia, where some inedible wild relations still grow, and where it was under cultivation in the 4th century AD or earlier. Its name in English and in many other languages derives, via Arabic, from an old Persian name, *aspanākh*.

The plant had travelled east to China via Nepal by the 7th century, but only reached Europe in the 11th century, when the Arabs who invaded Spain brought it with them.

Spinach was a better green vegetable than the GOOSEFOOTS, SORRELS, ORACH, and similar plants which were widely used in medieval Europe, and gradually usurped their place. However, it was still a novelty in Italy in the 16th century (according to Matthiolus) and did not become established in Britain until the middle of that century. Before being accepted as a food plant, it was used for medicinal purposes; it has a mildly laxative effect, due to the oxalic acid which it contains.

The nutritional qualities of spinach have been much lauded, in part at least because of its high content of iron. However, the availability of the iron is reduced because the OXALIC ACID combines with it making it less easily absorbed, and the same is true of the calcium it contains.

Spinach is valued as a vegetable cooked on its own, but is also conspicuously versatile as an ingredient in other dishes, providing delicate fillings for pastry and pasta, combining well with eggs, etc. Part of its appeal comes from its subtle, faintly bitter-sweet taste, but part also from its attractive deep green colour. This spreads readily into any mixture in which spinach plays a part. Spinach or spinach juice have often been used purely for colour, for example in making certain kinds of pasta. No other common plant gives such a strong green.

Medieval recipes, both European and Asian, often called for spinach as an ingredient for sweet dishes. For example, it could be combined with egg, honey, almonds, and spices, and used as a filling for a tart or flan. The habit of adding nutmeg to cooked spinach may be seen as a survival of these practices. Another such survival, as

Jane Grigson (1978) pointed out in giving the recipe, is the Provençal *tarte d'épinards au sucre*, often eaten on Christmas Eve. The same author gives, for the benefit of those who like to go back to origins, a Persian recipe for spinach *kuku* (an OMELETTE with spinach); and gives a full account of the remarkable ability of spinach to absorb butter (cf. the aubergine's absorption of olive oil).

Spinach is notorious for shrinking greatly when cooked. A large saucepan full of raw spinach soon reduces to about a tenth of the volume. This surprising reduction is of course avoided when fresh young spinach leaves are used in salads.

Spinach substitutes are numerous. The excellence of spinach has caused its name to be applied to many other leafy vegetables which reflect, even slightly, its characteristics and merits. That is why some unrelated plants have names such as NEW ZEALAND SPINACH, CHINESE SPINACH, vine spinach (see BASELLA), mountain spinach (see ORACH), and so forth.

SPINY LOBSTER the correct name for CRUSTACEANS of the family Paniluridae, is preferable to the name crawfish which is sometimes used but invites confusion with CRAYFISH. Needless to say, using the name crayfish or cray, as sometimes in Australia, is even more likely to cause confusion.

The spiny lobsters are indubitably lobsters, but they differ from the archetypal LOBSTER of the N. Atlantic in having no claws and in belonging to warmer waters. Indeed they are most abundant in the tropics, although their range extends into temperate waters, for example up to SW England, in some regions. Their size and the excellence of their meat ensures that they are in strong demand, although the question whether they are better than or inferior to the common lobster is and will no doubt for ever be debated. Such debate is complicated by the fact that the established recipes for the Atlantic lobster, generally speaking, have been those of classical French cuisine plus the more robust traditions evolved in N. America; whereas the spiny lobster, with its worldwide range in warmer waters, has attracted to itself a large number of recipes involving tropical or subtropical ingredients.

In the Mediterranean (mainly in the western basin and the central parts) and SW Europe the two species are *Palinurus elephas* and *P. mauritanicus*. They are brown or reddish in colour and have a maximum length of 50 cm (20"). There are certain places where they find a congenial habitat and are much more common than elsewhere, for example Minorca and the tiny (Tunisian) island of Galita.

In the Caribbean there are at least three species:

- *P. argus*, the most important commercial species in American waters, which can, exceptionally, grow to 60 cm (24") and 14 kg (30 lb). Colour varies. This is the *lagosta comun* of Brazil.
- *P. guttatus*, a smaller and darker species, sometimes called spotted crawfish or Guinea lobster. In French it is *langouste brésilienne*.
- *S. laevicauda*, of a bluish-green or purplish colour, with white spots on the sides of the tail; the *lagosta cabo-verde* of Brazil.

A larger number of species are found in the Indo-Pacific, especially in SE Asian waters, but also in Japan (*P. japonicus*), E. Africa, Australasia, and the Pacific islands. Among the best known are:

- *Panulirus polyphagus*, officially called 'mud spiny lobster' in English because of its liking for muddy substrates, important in the Bay of Bengal and the Gulf of Thailand, greyish-green;
- *P. homarus*, the most important commercial species in SW and S. India, dark green or reddish brown, spotted with white;
- *P. penicillatus*, a species of dark colour, brown or purplish, whose range extends all the way from the Red Sea to the Galapagos Islands;
- *P. versicolor*, the 'painted spiny lobster', which has a beautifully patterned green and white colour scheme;
- *P. ornatus*, also of very striking appearance. The legs are banded in cream and maroon, the spines on top of the body are orange at the base and green at the tip, and the general effect is like that of a delicately coloured butterfly.

The most important species of the American Pacific coast is *P. interruptus*. In California it is generally known as 'langosta'. It can (exceptionally) be huge: length to 90 cm (35"), weight over 13 kg (30 lb).

Finally, to illustrate yet further the extent to which different species of these beautiful creatures have evolved in response to different environments, there is *P. echinatus*, the 'brown spiny lobster', which is specialized for island habitats. It is found on one stretch of Brazilian coast, but otherwise inhabits Atlantic islands: Trinidad, Cape Verde Islands, Canary Islands, and even Ascension Island and St Helena.
READING: Holthuis (1991).

SPITCHCOCK an obsolete culinary term which applied to a method of grilling pieces of eel after dressing them with breadcrumbs and chopped herbs. But the matter is obscure (Hannah Glasse, 1747, spells the word 'pitchcock' and omits the herbs) and there is a suspicious resemblance between this term and SPATCHCOCK.

SPLEEN (or melt or milt), a spongy organ found near the stomach or intestine of most vertebrates, has the function of maintaining blood in good condition. Jane Grigson (1967) describes it thus:

In appearance it is a long flat oval of dark reddish meat, with a line of white fat running from end to end. It usually disappears—in England, as in France—with the rest of the pluck [heart, liver, lungs] into faggots, sausages and pâtés.

Although that sums it up well, the spleen may also appear in mixed OFFAL dishes and occasionally has a lead role, as in an interesting street food of Palermo in Sicily, *guastelle* (spleen sandwiches) of which Sokolov wrote in a 1994 issue of the *Natural History Magazine*:

Guastella is actually the name for a certain kind of soft roll with sesame seeds on top; it resembles a hamburger bun. You cut it in half and fill it with warmed ricotta, caciocavallo [a hard cheese made from cow's milk], and beef spleen, an organ meat that is much appreciated in Sicily. The spleen is sliced and cooked literally swimming in lard.

In Brussels a dish called *Chousels au Madère* (spleen and pancreas with a Madeira sauce) has customarily been served on Thursdays, the day of the slaughtering of the cows.

SPONGE CAKE a light CAKE made by the whisking method in which egg yolks are beaten with sugar, then flour and other ingredients added; see also CAKE-MAKING.

The term 'sponge cake' probably came into use during the 18th century, although the *OED* has no reference earlier than a letter Jane Austen wrote in 1808 (she evidently liked sponge cakes).

Two alternative methods of whisking are recognized. The first is usually called by its French name, GÉNOISE. The second method produces SAVOY cake/gateau/biscuit.

Sponge cake mixtures may also be used to produce what are often called 'sponge fingers'; see BOUDOIR BISCUITS.

Towards the end of the 19th century something called a 'sponge-cake pudding' began to appear, but then became simply SPONGE PUDDING.

For a curiosity in this field see KASUTERA.

SPONGE PUDDING is made with a mixture like that for a SPONGE CAKE. A simple sort of sponge pudding, made from equal weights of flour, butter, sugar, and eggs, and steamed in a basin, is known as canary pudding, perhaps because at some

time it was served with a sauce made with sweet Canary wine.

A similar mixture may be baked in small tins shaped like a bucket, so that, when turned out, they look like little sandcastles; these are called castle puddings. They usually have a jam sauce or a sweet wine sauce poured over them.

SPOTTED DICK AND SPOTTED DOG are both popular British SUET PUDDINGS which are 'spotted' with raisins. Strictly speaking, spotted dick is of the 'roly poly' type (see ROLY POLY) with raisins and sugar spread on a flat sheet which is rolled up; and spotted dog is a plain cylinder with raisins or currants and sugar mixed with the suet paste, so that it has visible spots on the outside. Both, correctly, should be boiled in a cloth, but are often now baked.

See SODA BREAD for another meaning of spotted dick.

SPRAT *Sprattus sprattus*, a small fish (maximum length 14 cm/5.5") of the HERRING family which abounds in coastal waters of the Mediterranean and NE Atlantic. It can survive in waters of low salinity, such as those of the Baltic, where it exists in the form of a subspecies *S. s. balticus*.

The Caspian sprat, *Clupeonella delicatula*, belongs to the Caspian and Black seas, where it evolved at a time when the Black Sea was not connected to the Mediterranean. It is slightly larger (to 17 cm/6").

The American writer Artemas Ward (1923), ever alert to the desirability of judging foodstuffs by their intrinsic merit rather than by how common or costly they are, observed that:

In England the sprat's prolific abundance socially offsets its fine eating qualities—it is a lowly fish under its own title (its participation in the comparative aristocracy of whitebait being of only recent knowledge)—but it has made its mark on the English language and English customs.

(Until late in the 19th century there was much debate about the identity of WHITEBAIT.) Lord Mayor's Day in London, 9 November, was known as 'Sprat Day' because that was when the sprat season was considered officially open.

The sprat's reputation is highest in Scandinavia and Germany. As Wheeler (1969) remarks:

In Norway conditions are ideal for a special sprat fishery where the fish are trapped in the long, narrow fjords by means of nets, then driven into keeping pens until required for the canning factories. The resultant sprats, seasoned and canned in oil, are sold as 'brisling'.

In Sweden these canned sprats are known as 'Swedish anchovies'. In Estonia, *kilu* are

regarded as the most typical fish of that country and are exported in round tins, within which they are curled up in a circle.

In Germany, the sprats smoked at Kiel, known as *Kieler Sprotten*, are an established delicacy. They are hot smoked, whole, and consumed like buckling (see HERRING). In the Netherlands and Belgium, bundles of lightly smoked sprats are offered for sale, to be skinned before being eaten. Kinds of sprat PÂTÉ are prepared in Poland and the Baltic States.

There is no true sprat in Asian waters, although the name sprat is sometimes loosely applied to certain small fish of the herring family which do occur there. In the southern hemisphere, there is the blue sprat, *Spratelloides robustus*, a smaller fish (maximum length 10 cm/4") common in the inshore waters of southern Australia. *Sprattus antipodum*, a sprat of New Zealand waters, is not fished for commercially.

SPRINGERLE pale, brittle BISCUITS, shaped in wooden moulds which are often quite elaborate, originated in the German province of Swabia as early as the 15th century. They were formerly baked to mark various holy days, but more recently became Christmas specialities.

Springerle are made from eggs beaten with sugar, with flour added to make a stiff dough, and flavoured with (usually) rum and aniseed. The dough is rolled out and the moulds pressed down on it to make the raised pattern (knights on horseback, lambs, rabbits, etc.). The moulds are removed and the shaped dough is allowed to rest and dry out for up to 24 hours, ensuring a smooth, unfissured surface when the biscuits are finally baked. After baking the biscuit has an underside which is slightly grainy, and a smooth white upper surface, which in former times was often painted in colour.

Recording all this, Sarah Kelly (1985) suggests that the name may be derived from the way the biscuits rise or 'spring' in the oven, or from a common mould shape which shows a leaping horse. She also explains that biscuits which are really the same thing under other names include the so-called *Würzburger Marzipan* (not, as one might think, a form of almond paste); *Eierzucker*, made in Nuremberg; and *Anisbrötli* in Switzerland.

SPRING ONIONS are known as 'green onions' in the USA, and also as 'salad onions' or 'scallions'. The last name is not exclusive, for it is also applied to the individual bulbs of aggregate onions such as SHALLOTS, and sometimes even to LEEKS. Most of the spring onions grown in the West are simply immature plants which, if left in the ground (and suitably thinned out) would develop into full-sized onions. Thus the same onion patch would produce spring onions, as thinnings, in spring, and large onions in the autumn.

Spring onions are now available all the year round, so the name has lost its original significance. Generally, white varieties of onion are chosen, purely for reasons of appearance. Spring onions from any variety of onion will, however, always be paler and milder flavoured than the fully developed bulb.

Spring onions can equally well be produced from the welsh onion, that is the oriental species (*Allium fistulosum*) which if allowed to develop further would simply become larger, rather than produce bulbs. See ORIENTAL ONIONS.

Spring onions are usually eaten raw in the West, in salads or on their own. There is no reason why they should not be cooked, except that they are more expensive than round onions. In Chinese cooking, where raw vegetables are rare, onions are normally cooked whatever their age.

SPRING ROLL

SPRING ROLL (plus egg roll and LUMPIA, which are sometimes the same thing and sometimes not, but always closely related), a snack or item of finger-food, usually consisting of a wrapper of very thin pastry or pancake around a savoury filling.

In the full Chinese name, which transliterates as *chun juan*, the third and fourth written characters mean literally 'spring roll', because the original filling was of lightly cooked spring vegetables, wrapped in a skin that was then quickly deep fried so that the crisp textures of wrapper and filling contrasted with and complemented each other. During the Tang dynasty, such *chun juan* or spring cakes were eaten to celebrate the sowing of the new year's corn in early February, though it was many centuries later that spring rolls adopted their modern sausage-like form and size—usually about 5 cm (2") long.

This highly convenient food has spread widely outside China in one form or another and is particularly visible in the neighbouring countries of Indo-China. The Vietnamese often use a rice-based wrapper, extremely thin, like paper. A typical filling would include pork and shrimp and various herbs of the kind favoured by the Vietnamese (e.g. coriander, Chinese chives, and mint). They make miniature rolls as well as normal-sized ones. Accompaniments to these rolls include peanut sauce with shredded carrot and daikon.

SPUN SUGAR

SPUN SUGAR sugar boiled to CARAMEL (160 °C/320 °F), and then 'spun' by flicking it in a fine stream off the end of two forks tied together. The thin trail of sugar sets instantly into a hair-like filament. In the classic method for spinning sugar, the filaments are caught over a wooden bar (such as a broom handle), and removed in a bundle at the end of the process. It must be used soon after it is made, as it rapidly softens and becomes sticky, especially in humid weather. Spun sugar was much used in haute cuisine for decorating desserts and fruit. In the 18th and 19th centuries, it was made into elaborate table decorations, spun into moulds shaped as vases, baskets, temples etc. This practice, largely discontinued, has been revived towards the end of the 20th century, e.g. by trailing thin streams of caramel over an inverted mould to form a 'net' which can be used to cover ice creams, etc.   (LM)

SQUASH

SQUASH the American name which embraces numerous members of the genus *Cucurbita* in the CUCURBIT family (*Cucurbitacae*). The name is derived from the Massachusett Indian word *askutasquash*, meaning 'eaten raw'. *Cymling* is also an American Indian word for a white, scalloped squash.

Because of their differing characteristics and uses, the squashes are best dealt with in several entries rather than one. These entries, which correspond more to popular names than to botanical classifications, are: SUMMER SQUASH, WINTER SQUASH, VEGETABLE MARROW, and ZUCCHINI (the last two of which are the same vegetable at different stages of growth). See also VEGETABLE SPAGHETTI.

SQUASHBERRY

SQUASHBERRY *Viburnum edule*, a shrub of Canada and the northern USA, which bears juicy red 'berries' (not true berries, as each contains a large stone). The fruits bear some resemblance to those of the CRANBERRY TREE, *V. trilobum*, but are smaller and less acid. They are used raw or cooked, in jellies, etc. An alternative name is 'mooseberry'.

SQUAWROOT

SQUAWROOT a name applied by European colonists to various medicinal and edible roots which they found being used by the Indians in N. America. As Quinn (1938) observed, 'There were countless "squawroots", for the colonists bestowed this convenient name upon any root they saw a squaw digging.'

Some tubers of the western USA which were important to the Indians and bore this name were also called yampa, Indian potato, wild caraway, and ipo. They are of the genus *Perideridia*, and are related to the CARROT. Their foliage, like that of the carrot, is referred to as Queen Anne's lace. S. and M. Thompson (1972) state that all have edible tubers, resembling carrots in texture and flavour, and that the most palatable is *P. gairdneri*; *P. bolanderi* has a spicier, radish-like taste. The whitish tubers measure up to 5 cm (2") long and under 1 cm (0.3") thick. They are best baked, and do not have to be peeled, as the skins are tender.

Yampa is now little known, but it was once an important food, as the naming of various western towns and valleys after it testifies.

SQUETEAGUE

SQUETEAGUE *Cynoscion regalis*, otherwise known as weakfish (because of the tender mouth, easily torn by a hook), a fish of the western N. Atlantic. It belongs to the family Sciaenidae and is thus a close relation of the CROAKERS and DRUMS; the males of the species share with their brother drums the capability to make loud noises in the water.

An impressive fish, which may attain a length of 1 m (40") and has a complex and

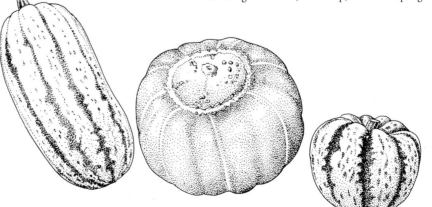

Squashes
from left to right: Delicata, Buttercup, Sweet Dumpling

attractive coloration. It ranges as far north as Massachusetts (in the summer only) and as far south as Florida, and counts as the most important sciaenid fish in N. American waters. Its quality is good, but that of its less common relation, *C. nebulosus*, the spotted squeteague, is considered to be even better. Both fish are liable to be called by such misnomers as 'trout', 'sea trout', etc. in the southern states.

One more relation, and a very good one, is *C. nobilis*, which belongs to California. It attended a different christening ceremony, since it came away with the name 'white sea bass' (see BASS).

SQUID one of the major food resources of the sea and probably the most important of those which are not yet fully exploited. Like other CEPHALOPODS, squid are eaten less than they might be because some people are repelled by their aspect and ignorant of how to prepare and cook them.

Squid occur in all oceans and seas, except the Black Sea. The world catch is huge. The Japanese market absorbs about half of it.

The architecture of squid is simple. The tubular body has two swimming fins projecting at the rear. At the front is the head, with two long tentacles and eight 'arms' projecting from it. Because squid swim near the surface and are vulnerable to attack from predators below, they are almost colourless.

There are numerous species, in a dozen families, two of which accommodate all the edible species. Members of the family Loliginidae are inshore creatures. Those of the family Ommastrephidae, on the other hand, are oceanic. They constitute about three-quarters of the world catch and comprise the so-called 'flying squid' (which do not really fly, but can propel themselves out of the water and glide for some distance).

The most important loliginid squid are as follows:

- *Loligo vulgaris* is the principal squid of the Mediterranean and of the E. Atlantic as far north as the English Channel. *Calamar* in Spanish, *calamaro* in Italian—names which often figure in restaurant menus.
- *L. forbesi* belongs to the NE Atlantic and is the most common edible squid as far south as the British Isles.
- *L. pealei*, an American species common from Cape Cod to Venezuela, is known in the USA as long-finned or bone or winter squid. The market for it in the USA remains limited, although Americans of Mediterranean descent buy it and others are gradually taking to it.

Ommastrephid squid of commercial importance include:

- *Todarodes pacificus* is the most important. Its range is from W. Canada to Japan and China.
- *Nototodarus sloani* is a species whose range in the Indo-Pacific is largely in the southern hemisphere.
- *Illex illecebrosus*, short-finned squid in the USA, occurs in slightly different forms on both sides of the N. Atlantic.
- *Todarodes sagittatus* is a species of the eastern N. Atlantic and the Mediterranean. It is this to which the French name *calmar* correctly applies.

All squid are remarkable in one respect. The processes of natural selection have operated on them in a manner which suggests that fitness for being stuffed by cooks in kitchens was a criterion for their survival. It is so easy to empty out the innards from the body, leaving a convenient receptacle. The head (minus eyes) and tentacles and arms can be chopped to form part of the stuffing, the rest of which can be rice, vegetables, sometimes meat (chopped ham is good) or whatever. Alternatively, the body can be sliced across to form rings, which, with tentacles and arms, can be deep-fried to form an element in the traditional Italian *Frittura mista*.

SQUIRREL a tree-dwelling rodent of the family Sciuridae, to which the WOODCHUCK and PRAIRIE DOG also belong. Squirrels have a global distribution. All species have a long bushy tail and strong hind legs; and eat nuts and seeds.

Squirrels can be cooked like rabbit or even chicken. In the United States, where wild squirrels are classified as game, their flesh is esteemed. Ashbrook and Sater (1945) offer an extensive collection of recipes (including two versions of the famous Brunswick stew) and declare:

Squirrel meat if properly prepared is truly delicious. The flesh is light red or pink in color and has a pleasing flavor. The slight gamy taste present in most game meats is not so pronounced

in the squirrel. The young ones can be fried or broiled the same as rabbits.

In Britain squirrels are not considered as game nor eaten to any significant extent.

SRI LANKA once known as Ceylon, a very large island situated off the southern tip of INDIA and close to the tropics, exhibits in its food most of the features which its situation would lead one to expect: RICE the staple (with BREADFRUIT, JACKFRUIT, and YAM as secondary staples), frequent use of COCONUT in curry-type dishes, some emphasis on seafood, discriminating use of many spices, use of jaggery (see PALM SUGAR) and toddy (see COCONUT), skill in making Indian-type breads and S. Indian specialities such as IDLI and DOSA (here *thosai*), heavy consumption of mango, banana, plantain, etc. But there are interesting differences and some surprises:

- Maldive fish, dried and grated TUNA fish from the MALDIVES, is used freely as an ingredient and a sort of condiment.
- Apart from its own versions of CURRY POWDER, Sri Lanka has at least one special spice mixture, called *suwanda kudu*, 'fragrant powder', comprising cumin, black cumin, cinnamon, cardamom, cloves, coriander, and fenugreek.
- The HOPPER (a sort of pancake made out of leavened rice batter, which also comes in the noodle-like string hopper version) is so prominent (along with idli and dosa) as to constitute a distinctive feature of the cuisine.
- The wide range of acidulating agents—the various fruits and acids used in the preparation of curries—includes GORAKA, mango, billing (see BELIMBING ASAM), besides limes, tomatoes, and vinegar.
- *Mallums* are distinctive vegetable dishes thus described by Chandra Dissanayake (1976): 'a preparation in which a fruit, edible root, leaf, vegetable or coconut may

---

SQUID DISHES IN JAPAN

THE Japanese name for squid is *ika*; cuttlefish, regarded as being in the same category, are *koika*.

The most lavish way of eating *ika* is probably *ika-somen*, said to have been started by *ika* fishermen and now popular in Hokkaido, the northernmost of the main islands of Japan, where large quantities of squid are caught. For *ika-somen* the flesh of squid is cut into long thin strips resembling SOMEN (thin vermicelli-like noodles eaten cold in summer), to be served raw in a deep bowl, and eaten with grated ginger and soy sauce, as if they were noodles.

Squid may be eaten as SASHIMI, but the thicker flesh of cuttlefish is generally preferred for this. Squid is also eaten in the preparations known as *yakimono, nimono, sunomono*, and *aemono* (see JAPANESE CULINARY TERMS); and as TEMPURA.

Dried squid is called *surume* and is eaten grilled, or cooked with other ingredients.

be finely shredded or grated and cooked until done with coconut.'

- The Sri Lankan range of CHUTNEYS and relishes shows some influence from further east, for example the use of *blachan* (a shrimp paste; see BLACANG) and *sambol* (see SAMBAL).

There is not much sign in the kitchens of Sri Lanka of the period when the island was a Dutch possession, nor of any British culinary influence. It could be said, however, that the British presence is mainly commemorated by the tea plantations which are so important for the economy, and that the Dutch were partly responsible for the great sophistication in the use of spices (besides leaving behind them a few Dutch terms such as *frikkadel*—surviving as fricadell).

STAGE MEALS by which are meant meals consumed or apparently consumed on the stage in the course of a dramatic performance, have received little attention in the literature, but have a *locus classicus* in the form of an essay by Osbert Sitwell (1963).

This makes the point that actors have sometimes counted upon receiving actual nourishment from stage meals. Sitwell cites some legal proceeding in France in the summer of 1841, when an actor called M. Clary was accused in court by his manager of impossible obstinacy and non-cooperation. His defence was that when he was playing the part of a prince or a marquis or other person of distinction on the stage he expected treatment in the matter of food and drink conformable to his temporary rank and the spirit of the part he was playing. Yet the manager starved the actors. They had to drink seltzer water instead of champagne and had even been given a pasteboard turkey which they were expected to pretend to consume.

It was this sort of situation which caused Sitwell to entitle his essay 'The Banquets of Tantalus'. He remarks that 'these cruel feasts where bread turns inevitably to a stone and every—or almost every—chicken to a property fowl could, no doubt, assume a dream-like quality of horror to those compelled every night to partake of them'.

Sitwell also points to the awkwardness caused by the fact that even make-believe food is apt to start saliva flowing and create appetites which might cause actors to fluff their lines. However, he does refer to some stage meals which went well. Sir Herbert Tree, playing the role of a penniless poet at the French court, had a meal suddenly bestowed on him, and had to react as a starving poet would have done. He believed in realism, so it was necessary for him to tackle a whole chicken, with his hands.

Potential difficulties were solved when he caused

to be constructed for himself a fine, plump, hollow pullet out of papier mâché, the breast being composed of two lids. He then filled it every night with real slices of excellent cold chicken and was thus able, when the moment came, to fling himself on the bird, tackle it with his fingers and eat it with a proper relish and abandon in front of an enthusiastic audience. In addition, he concluded this banquet with a whole bunch of genuine grapes.

Tree thus achieved realism without a degree of mess which would have been awkward on a London stage, although perhaps acceptable in a Sicilian setting. Sitwell interposes a recollection from 1909 of one of the famous Grasso family of actors playing in a disused church, under a shadowy roof and in the midst of plaster angels, his role being that of a worker in the sulphur mines, a part to which he added

a touch of sullen melancholy, alternating with a farouche and flaring gaiety, by eating macaroni, picking it out of an enormous bowl with his fingers, which he made to seem thick and swollen, and cramming the strands clumsily into his mouth. He would sit down, get up, walk about, still munching, still talking. Every word was audible.

However, apart from such exceptional feats, it is probably true that there is only one kind of stage meal which keeps clear of the problems described above, namely tea. The practical difficulties here are minuscule. A real tea can be served without great difficulty. Little sandwiches and cakes can be passed, even eaten, without disturbing the actors' lines. Indeed—as Sitwell suggests—the main influence of food on late 19th- and 20th-century English drama may be apparent in the tendency for playwrights, when faced by the need to make a social encounter on stage fully plausible by introducing the element of food which would be there in real life, to opt for tea.

STAPLE FOODS AND STAPLES are terms which carry various possible meanings, depending on the cultural and geographic contexts.

At the simplest level, in Britain in the 20th century, staples are what a family thinks necessary to have in their store cupboards; and these could range in importance from really basic items such as flour, sugar, and salt to less essential desirables such as HP Sauce or tomato ketchup.

Another meaning, which comes into play in discussions of the diet of given groups (local, ethnic, regional, national), is 'the fundamental items of the diet', which in one instance might be rice and fish; in another plantains, peanut oil, and coconut; and in yet another bread, root vegetables, and meat.

Further nuances emerge if one considers equivalent terms in other languages. Among those which Botsford (1990) cited in a paper delivered to an international symposium on 'Staple Foods' were:

- French, *un aliment de base*, a basic food;
- German, *Hauptnährungsmittel*, indicating 'the most important' item in a diet;
- Italian, *principali generi di consumo*, the principal articles of consumption;
- Czech, *hlavni plodiny*, main fruits (Slavic languages tie the concept of a staple to the idea of fruitfulness).

Returning to the English word 'staple', Botsford explained that it reached English from the Old and Middle French *estaple*, which came from the Low German *Stapel*, meaning a prop or support. From this meaning it came to indicate a heap or a stand for laying things on; then heaped wares or a storehouse; and then a market or entrepôt. A 17th-century dictionary stated clearly that: 'Staple signifieth this or that towne or citie, w[h]ither the Merchants of England, by common order or commandment, did carrie their woolles, wool-fals, cloathes, leade and tinne.' This meaning survived in the names of some English market towns such as Barnstaple and Whitstable.

From market the further meaning of goods (foods) in a market or in storage emerged naturally enough.

STAR ANISE a spice consisting of the small, star-shaped, dried fruits of *Illicium verum*, a slender evergreen tree of the family Illicaceae related to Magnoliacea. This is not known in the wild state, but is assumed to be indigenous to China. It is not a relation of ANISE, but shares with it the same essential oil, anethole, which is used for flavouring some drinks and confectionery; star anise is the principal commercial source of anethole.

The appearance of the fruit is remarkable. Eight (rarely, 9 or 10) carpels attached to a central column produce the starlike shape. These carpels, which can be over 15 mm (0.25") long and are often irregularly developed, are dark reddish-brown in colour; each normally contains one hard light brown seed.

Star anise

Cultivation, which is not easy, is almost entirely confined to S. China and parts of SE Asia.

Star anise is one of the ingredients of (Chinese) FIVE SPICES. Jill Norman (1990) observes that it occurs in some western recipes for syrups and jams in the 17th century; and that some western chefs now use it in, for example, fish stews. In China it has been associated with pork and poultry.

STAR APPLE *Chrysophyllum cainito*, a tropical fruit popular in the W. Indies and C. America. It was being cultivated long before the arrival of Europeans, and has always been prized for its ornamental value as well as for its fruits. The author Charles Kingsley once described it as being 'like an evergreen peach, shedding from the underside of every leaf a golden light'.

The tree is cultivated in tropical America as far south as Peru and north to Florida, but attempts to introduce it into Asia have had disappointing results, although it is appreciated, and fairly common, in the Philippines.

The fruit is the size of a small apple, white (*cainito blanco*) or purple (*cainito morado*), with a soft pulp containing a central 'star' of flat, brown seeds set in translucent jelly. The flavour is sweet. To be good, the fruit must be ripened on the tree. It is usually eaten fresh, but can be made into preserves, and is also used in a drink called 'matrimony', the pulp being mixed with bitter orange juice, in Jamaica.

Several other *Chrysophyllum* species, in Africa and Asia as well as America and the Caribbean region, have edible fruits.

STARCH a constituent of plants, is the most important form of CARBOHYDRATE in our food, and supplies most of the energy in the diet of most peoples. Pure starch, when cooked, is easily and almost completely digestible, turning to SUGAR. Actual plant starches contain a certain amount of CELLULOSE, another CARBOHYDRATE which is not digested by humans but supplies essential dietary fibre.

In plants starch acts as a food reserve. It is stored in various places: seeds, as in cereals; tubers, as in potatoes and yams; or stems, as in sago.

Even those vegetable foods which are rich in protein may contain large amounts of starch. Thus, if the water present is ignored, about 70% of wheat and 80% of rice is starch. Very starchy foods such as cassava contain virtually nothing but carbohydrates and water.

From the cook's point of view starch is important both as a constituent of starchy vegetables and flours, and as a relatively pure, refined product in powder form which is used as a thickener for liquids and as a stabilizer and emulsifier for various mixtures. Powdered starch is made by washing other substances out of various flours (wheat, maize, rice, sorghum), roots (tapioca, arrowroot, potato), and fruits (chestnut, banana). The same general chemical and physical considerations apply to starch in any form.

STRUCTURE AND BREAKDOWN OF STARCH

In chemical terms starch is a polysaccharide, i.e. it has large molecules composed of long chains of smaller sugar molecules joined end to end. About three-quarters of the total, depending on the source of the starch, is in the form of amylopectin; this consists of short, interconnected chains making up a many-branched mass comprising thousands of sugar units. The rest is amylose, consisting of single chains from 70 to 350 units long. The length of the chains, and the proportion of amylose present, both affect the performance of the starch.

Raw starch is more or less insoluble in water because the granules are tightly packed together inside the shielding cell walls. Even when a plant is ground into a powdered starch, breaking up the cells, the dense, compact surface of the granules themselves resists the penetration of water. For the same reason raw starch is highly indigestible.

Heating dry starch breaks up its structure, producing fragmented molecules called pyrodextrins (Greek *pyr*, meaning 'fire', and dextrin, the general term for what is produced when starch is broken down). Some pyrodextrins have brown colours and pleasant flavours; sweetness also comes from individual sugar molecules released by the disintegration of the starch. Pyrodextrins account for some of the colour and flavour in bread crust and toast. (They are also produced in starched clothing when it is ironed. Dextrin is slightly sticky, so the fabric stiffens with too much heat, and the brown colour of scorching appears.)

Dextrin and sugar are also produced by the action of ENZYMES on starch. This occurs in grain when it is malted, and in flour when it is made into bread. It also happens when starch is digested. Digestive enzymes break off more and more of the nutritious sugar until the layout of the molecule prevents them from going further, leaving an undigested 'limit dextrin'.

When starch is heated in water something quite different happens. Heat loosens the structure of the granules and they become porous, absorbing a very large amount of water. Swelling starts at about 60 °C (140 °F), and by the time the mixture has reached 85 °C (185 °F) the granules are up to five times their original size. These figures vary according to the source of the starch and other substances present. Starches from roots, such as potato and arrowroot, generally need less heating to start the process than do starches from cereals, including cornflour and sorghum starch. There are also differences in whole vegetables. Varieties of potato which are mealy when cooked have larger starch granules and a higher starch content than those which become waxy.

EFFECT OF COOKING

Cooking affects starch because in dry starch the molecular chains are folded tightly together. When water penetrates the starch the chains unfold and disperse, causing expansion of the granules. The molecules, forced into rapid movement by the hot liquid, collide and make the mixture viscous. This is noticeable when a white sauce thickens. There has to be enough starch in the mixture to bring the molecules close enough together for thickening to take place. Stirring is necessary to prevent a sauce from sticking, which is what happens when it dries and burns on the bottom of the pan. But excessive stirring, especially after a sauce has thickened, tears the molecular chains away from each other and reduces viscosity. Certain starches are particularly badly affected by stirring, for example tapioca.

If the mixture is allowed to cool, the movement of the molecules slackens. When the straight amylose molecules collide with each other they will now lock together firmly. Eventually they may connect into a rigid network throughout the liquid, and the starch paste sets into a gel. The effect is termed 'gelatinization', but has nothing to do with gelatin, which gels similarly but is a protein.

Lumps in a starch paste are caused by clumps of granules gelatinizing on their outsides and becoming impervious. A common cause is too rapid heating. The granules should be well separated by liquid, sugar, or fat before their temperature reaches 60 °C (140 °F).

Not all types of starch set to a gel. Potato starch has very long amylose chains in its large granules, and these do not readily lock. It makes a very viscous starch paste which remains a paste when cool. Since the gelatinization of starch is an important factor in the baking of bread and cakes (the starch swells and gels between the gluten strands and helps to support the structure), potato starch is not a good ingredient for breads and cakes, although some, such as certain brands of MATZO, are successfully made with a proportion of potato starch.

Other types of starch perform according to the length of their amylose chains and the relative amounts of each of the two types of molecule; the branched, amylopectin molecules have little tendency to lock together. Cornflour has an unusually high viscosity and gelling capacity. Sorghum, a common commercial starch, also performs well. Wheat starch is about average. Rice starch produces a rather frail gel. All these cereal gels are opaque. Root starches do not gel, and generally the cold paste remains comparatively clear.

If a setting paste is stirred while it cools, it may fail to gel. In the food industry, specially prepared 'thin boiling' starches are often used. These do not thicken when hot and remain easy to stir, but still set to a gel when cool.

Knowledge of the behaviour of different types of starch allows the cook to choose the right one for any desired result. Wheat flour used as a starch thickener needs relatively long cooking to remove its raw taste; and even after cooking it has a noticeable flavour. Thus it is unsuitable for dishes where the other ingredients would suffer from long cooking or have a delicate flavour. CORNFLOUR is more suitable in both respects, but if even more delicacy is needed the choice should fall on ARROWROOT, which has the shortest cooking time and the mildest flavour of all. It thickens liquids without making them opaque.

For thickening soups and sauces in European recipes where delicacy of flavour is important, RICE starch ('ground rice' in Britain, *crème de riz* in France) is a good choice. If short cooking time is the main concern, POTATO starch (*fécule* in French recipes) is preferable.

In Chinese and other oriental cooking the usual requirement is for a translucent soup or sauce with a rather glutinous texture. The Chinese themselves tend to use tapioca when glutinousness is required, and arrowroot or sometimes cornflour when it is not.

Recipes calling for CASSAVA starch (manioc) cause no problem, since ordinary TAPIOCA is simply a refined form of this. SAGO is also widely available. BANANA starches such as pisang starch (a Malay name) and PLANTAIN meal are less common; but, as banana starch is very light and delicate, arrowroot is a suitable substitute.
RH

STARGAZEY PIE a traditional British PIE made with small, oily fish, whose heads are left poking up round the edge of the pie. Pilchards (see SARDINE) were the species originally used by the Cornish and Devon fisherfolk who invented the pie, but it was later made elsewhere with herring.

The standard explanation of this odd pie is that the heads of pilchards are uneatable, but full of rich oil which it would be a shame to waste. If the fish are arranged with their heads resting on the rim of a circular pie dish and projecting out of the crust (their tails clustered at the centre), the slope causes the oil to run down into the body of the fish; and when the pie is cut up the now useless heads can be discarded. However, experiments have shown that the amount of oil thus 'saved' is close to zero, which suggests that the only valid rationale for the pie is an aesthetic one.

The pie had a thin bottom crust and a thicker top one, both of shortcrust pastry. The fish were gutted and stuffed with a spoonful of herbs, or mustard, apple, or SAMPHIRE.

The name 'stargazey' describes the star-shaped ring of fish heads peering out of the circumference of the pie, possibly gazing at the stars with the uppermost eye. In some versions the heads were grouped at the centre, dislocated to gaze upwards in a cluster, and the tails were set around the edge. The stargazey idea was also adapted into a straight form with the fish sandwiched between two strips of pastry. this could be divided into individual fish pasties and was suitable for sale from market stalls. Whoever devised this form had presumably abandoned the notion of precious oil dripping down.

STARLING *Sturnus vulgaris*, and numerous relations in Europe, Asia, and N. America, a small and somewhat impudent bird which is occasionally eaten. In the past, starlings have been available in London food shops, but the almost complete absence of recipes for them in cookery books suggests that they have never really been regarded as delicacies or eaten on a large scale.

STEAK a piece of meat (beef, unless otherwise indicated) or fish cut to be a convenient portion, usually a small slice about 2 cm (0.75") thick, for grilling (US broiling), frying, or cooking over charcoal.

The word itself comes from an Old Norse word *steikjo* which meant to roast on a spit, a method of cookery which was always popular in England. In the 15th century, beef steak 'griddled up brown' was sprinkled with cinnamon and served with sharp sauce. An alternative name for grilled steak, 'carbonado' (see CARBONADE, CARBONADO) enjoyed a vogue in the 16th century, but lost ground thereafter.

Cuts of steak vary from country to country, according to the various ways of jointing beef (see BEEF). In all cases, however, meat from the area where the ribs join the backbone, between the shoulders and the hip of the animal, is most important.

In Britain steaks are named according to the basic joints from which they are cut. These are the fillet (also known as tenderloin, or undercut), a long muscle located underneath the bones of the sirloin. This provides the leanest and tenderest meat. The sirloin itself, removed from the bone and cut into slices, also becomes steaks, less tender than fillet, but with more flavour. Finally, the rump, or aitch bone, a big piece of very lean meat, is usually sliced to give large steaks which have good flavour but are less tender than sirloin.

Steak terminology in the USA, where there has been a strong tradition of eating large steaks (a practice which carried associations of virility), varies to some extent from region to region and anyone looking for detailed information will do best to consult American sources.

In France, two cuts are particularly important. First, the fillet is divided to give, from the thick end, CHATEAUBRIAND (a large cut used for several people); *tournedos*, small compact round steaks cut from the centre or 'eye' of the fillet; and, from closer to the narrow end, *filet mignon*. The other cut used for steaks is the *entrecôte* (literally, 'between the ribs'). They are cut from just behind the shoulder. The French system of dissecting out muscles from a carcass yields other pieces of lean tender meat suitable for steaks. The *contrefilet* or *faux filet*, the lean eye of meat which runs along the top of the sirloin, is used in Britain and the USA as well.

Steak **cookery,** at its simplest, involves no more than grilling them under a fierce heat to a specified degree of 'doneness'. The terms used to indicate this are: blue (*bleu*), in which the outside of the meat is sealed and brown but the inside remains red; rare, in which the inside of the meat has heated up, but the fibres are soft and still very pink; medium (*à point*), where much of the pinkness has disappeared, and the fibres have started to congeal; or well done (*bien cuit*), at which stage the inside of the meat is uniformly brown-grey and has lost much of its juiciness.

In Britain, steaks are usually plainly grilled or fried. Less tender cuts of steak are braised with root vegetables, or made into stews, pies, or STEAK AND KIDNEY PUDDING OR PIE.

In N. America grilling, especially over charcoal, is the favoured method, but others are popular.

- A 'planked steak' is one which has been placed in a depression in a specially prepared wooden board, with butter or dripping and herbs, and put in a very hot oven.
- 'Swiss steak' is round (rump) steak, with flour and seasoning rubbed into it, fried with onions, and cooked by braising.
- A carpetbag steak (also popular in Australia) is a boneless steak stuffed with fresh raw oysters (possibly a development of old English dishes of steak and oyster sauce, or a pie).

In French cookery, *steak-frites* (steak and chips) is a standard dish, but higher up the gastronomic scale steaks are used as vehicles for various fancy sauces and garnishes. Some ways of serving tournedos are:

- *chasseur*, with shallots, mushrooms, and white wine;
- *Rossini*, with thin slices, sautéed, of FOIE GRAS and TRUFFLES;
- *Henri IV*, on CROUTONS, accompanied by ARTICHOKE hearts filled with BÉARNAISE SAUCE.

Entrecôte steaks also have their classic garnishes such as béarnaise sauce, and many other items (e.g. *à la bordelaise*: see À LA).

Steak au poivre is a steak coated with crushed peppercorns and fried, or one served with a sauce containing peppercorns.

In Tuscany, large tender steaks from the local Chianina cattle are made into *Bistecca alla fiorentina*, charcoal grilled with olive oil, and served with lemon wedges.

In Japan, a country which had little tradition of meat-eating until the 19th century, there is now a well-developed taste for high-quality steaks and a repertoire of Japanese methods for cooking and serving them.

When steak is minced and eaten raw, with various accompaniments, it is steak TARTARE. In Italy this has a parallel in *carpaccio*, while in France a similar dish is known as *Biftek à l'américaine*. (LM)

STEAK AND KIDNEY PUDDING or PIE, which counts as a British national dish, does not have a long history.

Beefsteak puddings (but without kidney) were known in the 18th century, if not before; Hannah Glasse (1747) gives a recipe, making clear that this was a SUET PUDDING. A hundred years later, Eliza Acton (1845) gave a recipe for 'Ruth Pinch's Beefsteak Pudding', named for a character in Dickens's *Martin Chuzzlewit* and rather more extravagant than what she called 'Small Beef-Steak Pudding'. Neither had kidney. Shortly afterwards, however, Mrs Beeton (1861) did give a recipe for steak and kidney pudding, and this has kept a foothold in the British repertoire ever since. It was, however, overtaken in popularity by steak and kidney pie, which was easier to make. The filling for the pie is cooked separately, so that one can tell when the meat is tender, impossible in a sealed pudding. Only then is the meat put into a pie dish and the crust set over it. Then the pie is briefly baked to brown the PASTRY.

For both pudding and pie, the filling includes onion, and often mushrooms or oysters. Dorothy Hartley (1954) offers compelling advice on the choice and use of mushrooms and some words of warning about oysters (which may become too hard—indeed she suggests that it might be better to use cockles and rather implies that omitting any such molluscs would perhaps be better still). Besides this advice she provides one of her characteristic sets of drawings to show exactly how the pudding version would be organized.

The crust of the pie is usually made from flaky pastry, though other kinds are quite common. For a large pie, the top crust is attached to a band of pastry stuck around the inner rim of the dish, to keep the crust from shrinking off the rim.

Cockneys call steak and kidney pudding 'Kate and Sydney Pud'.

STEAM is what water turns into at a temperature of 100 °C (212 °F), as explained under BOIL, and to steam foods is to cook them in this steam at that temperature in (necessarily) a lidded recipient.

This method of cooking has certain advantages. The food will not be bumped about by the agitation of boiling, or even simmering, water; and loss of water-soluble vitamins is less than when the food is immersed in boiling water. For this last reason, steaming vegetables is recommended. However, there are many other uses for the technique, for example steaming COUSCOUS in the upper part of a couscous steamer, while other ingredients (meat, vegetables) which will go into the finished dish are boiled in the lower part. Also, several dishes can be steamed at once, stacked in tiers above a pan of boiling water, a technique which has been exploited by the Chinese, of whose cookery steaming is a fundamental feature.

Steaming usually involves direct contact between the steam and the food; but the steam can be used indirectly, to heat the outside of a sealed vessel, which then conducts heat through its walls to cook food inside, as when English steamed PUDDINGS are cooked.

Cooking food *en papillote* (e.g. tightly enclosed in a wrapping of foil in the oven) is also a form of steaming; the moisture in the food is turned into steam as the food heats, and cannot escape through the wrapping. A similar technique comes into play, on a larger scale, in the earth ovens of the PACIFIC ISLANDS and the slightly different ones used by the Maori in NEW ZEALAND, and in the N. American CLAMBAKE.

STEPPE or **stepnoj** is a cheese first made in Russia by German immigrants, which is now manufactured also in Denmark, Germany, and Austria. It resembles a whole-milk TILSITER but is made at a slightly lower temperature, so that it is softer and milder. It is coloured yellow with a pigment such as ANNATTO. Unlike Tilsiter, Steppe is never given additional flavourings such as CARAWAY.

STEW as a verb, to SIMMER in a closed vessel; as a noun, the resulting dish.

The cuisines of most countries include some well-known stews, e.g. IRISH STEW and the Spanish COCIDO, since these dishes have many practical advantages. Meat (of fish or poultry or game) can be combined in one dish (see ONE-POT COOKERY) with vegetables; so there is no wastage of fuel and less WASHING UP. The mixture of ingredients in a thick and opaque sauce casts a veil of uncertainty over the proportions of expensive ingredients to cheap ones. The slow steady cooking enables the cook to be away from the kitchen before a meal.

See also for example PEPPER POT; SONOFABITCH STEW; WATERZOOI.

STILTON an English cheese of international fame and the only British cheese to have legal protection, is officially described as follows:

Stilton is a blue or white cheese made from full-cream milk with no applied pressure, forming its own crust or coat and made in cylindrical form, the milk coming from English dairy herds in the district of Melton Mowbray and surrounding areas falling within the counties of Leicestershire (now including Rutland), Derbyshire and Nottinghamshire.

The Bell Inn, a coaching-house inn on the Great North Road, in the village of Stilton, seems to have become in the first quarter of the 18th century the main outlet for what was known locally as Quenby cheese. Quenby was 30 miles away, but as travellers became accustomed to buying the cheese at the Bell Inn it took on the name of Stilton. So much seems clear, but it is much more difficult to unravel the actual origin of the cheese. Rance (1982) assembled the evidence and described the possibilities in a masterly way. He also provides the best account of the subsequent history of Stilton, of its manufacture, and of its characteristics.

Among the writers who took notice of Stilton at an early stage was Daniel Defoe, who passed through Stilton in 1722 in the course of his *Tour through the Whole Island of Great Britain* (1724–7), and Richard Bradley (see ENGLISH COOKERY BOOKS OF THE 18TH CENTURY), who in the early 1720s was the first to publish a full recipe (which he claimed to have received from the Bell Inn) for making the cheese. It is interesting that he included mace in the recipe, and that the cheese continued to engage his attention, for in a later book (1729) he made some additions to the recipe.

Few farmhouses maintained the tradition of making Stilton in the rest of the 18th century and the 19th century, and there have not been many producers in the 20th century, although in the year 1980 total production amounted to 8,000 tons, which is a lot.

One occasionally reads about the practice of pouring some port wine into a Stilton through an aperture at the top. This is a foolish idea (which may have had its origin in a misplaced adaptation of an old custom—legitimate but no longer relevant—of letting wine drip on to the outside of the cheeses to assist crust formation). Mrs Beeton (1861) mentioned it, adding that sherry, Madeira, or old ale could also be used, but then seemed to drop the idea, asserting that 'that cheese is the finest which is ripened without any artificial aid'.

The use of a traditional silver scoop for lifting out servings of the cheese can be followed in restaurants or institutions where consumption is rapid. In domestic situations it is better to cut it across, removing a whole round for immediate consumption and then fitting the upper part back on to the lower part to ensure that what is left will keep well and not dry out.

White Stilton is an unblued cheese, with pleasant characteristics.
READING: Hickman (1996).

STINKHORN the common name for FUNGI of the order Phallales. These are fungi whose reproduction is ensured by animals eating and dispersing their spores. The service is performed for stinkhorns by flies, which are attracted by the smell of rotting carrion which they emit and which accounts for 'stink' in their name. The scientific name Phallales was bestowed because of the strikingly phallic shape of these fungi. One

Phallus impudicus

of the most common, and one which shows this resemblance most obviously, is called *Phallus impudicus* (shameless phallus).

There seems to be no authoritative survey of the edibility of stinkhorns, nor any reason to suppose that many of them can be eaten by humans with pleasure and safety (except, perhaps, in the 'egg' stage, before they have burst out and the evil-smelling slime has formed). However, one at least, *Dictyophora* sp, is marketed in dried form in China and Hong Kong. The Chinese name for it means 'bamboo fungus'.

Arora (1979), with characteristic thoroughness, devotes several pages to these fungi. From McIlvaine (1902), whom he affectionately terms the 'mycophilic madman' and plenipotentiary of 'toadstool-testers', he gleans the information that in the 'egg' stage, when they are elastic, like bubbles of some thick substance, 'they demand to be eaten . . . Cut in slices and fried or stewed, they make a most tender, agreeable food.' He also quotes the following from Gwen Raverat's Victorian reminiscences, about how 'Aunt Etty' (who was related to Charles Darwin) would go hunting for stinkhorns and why:

armed with a basket and a pointed stick, and wearing special hunting cloak and gloves, she would sniff her way round the wood, pausing here and there, her nostrils twitching, when she caught a whiff of her prey; then at last, with a deadly pounce, she would fall upon her victim, and then poke his putrid carcass into her basket. At the end of the day's sport, the catch was brought back and burned in the deepest secrecy on the drawing-room fire, with the door locked, *because of the morals of the maids.*

STIR-FRY an almost self-explanatory verb which came into general use in English only in the second half of the 20th century, in line with a growing interest in oriental cookery techniques. To stir-fry is not much different from the French *sauter* (see SAUTÉ) but it is done in a WOK, not a sauté pan, and using a frying medium such as peanut oil, which is characteristic of oriental cookery, rather than butter or olive oil. Also, it lays greater emphasis on speed, which depends on having the ingredients cut up into small pieces or strips ahead of time.

The advantages of stir-frying, especially for a mixture including lots of vegetables, lie in this speed and the consequent minimizing of the loss of vitamins, colour, etc. Typical stir-fry dishes use just a small amount of meat or seafood with relatively large quantities of vegetable and noodles.

STOCK Theodora FitzGibbon (1976) gives a characteristically clear account of stock: 'The word covers many culinary preparations, but generally speaking a stock

is the liquid extracted from fish, meat, poultry or vegetables by slow cooking with water, or wine and water.' There are many familiar uses for this liquid, when strained; and, if boiled down, it will provide an essence or glaze.

STOCKFISH the name for COD and related fish which have been simply dried (as opposed to being salted and dried) until their moisture content has been reduced to around 15%, when they are stiff as a board and will keep well. Some say that 'stockfish' means 'stick-like fish'—though others say that the name was given because it is necessary to beat the product with a stick to help soften it up, and yet others think that the name refers to the poles or sticks on which the fish were hung to dry.

Stockfish was an important article of commerce in Europe in the 10th century and early medieval times. Later, when the salting of cod on a large scale became feasible (see SALT COD), that method became more popular, but stockfish has continued to be preferred in parts of Africa and of Italy. Some names for it in other languages are: *stockfisch* (French), *Stockfisch* (German), *stoccafisso* (Italian), and *stokkfisk* or *tørrfisk* (Norwegian).

Stockfish, it need hardly be said, has to be soaked to prepare it for cooking.

STOLLEN a rich fruit bread/cake from C. Germany, especially the city of Dresden. According to Ayto (1993) the name is derived from an Old High German word, *stollo*, meaning a support or post. The characteristic shape of Stollen—oblong, tapered at each end with a ridge down the centre—is said to represent the Christ Child in swaddling clothes, whence the name Christstollen sometimes given to it.

The Dresden Stollen, now known internationally as a Christmas speciality, is made from a rich, sweet yeast dough, mixed with milk, eggs, sugar, and butter, sometimes flavoured with lemon. Raisins, sultanas, currants, rum or brandy, candied peel, and almonds are worked into the dough. After baking, the Stollen is painted with melted butter and dusted with sugar. It may then be further decorated with candied fruits. There is some affinity between the Stollen and Scottish BLACK BUN.

Stollen may include a filling such as MARZIPAN.

STOMACH the organ or organs in which an animal's digestion of food begins. Ruminants (notably cows, sheep) have several. For the best-known uses of their stomachs as human food, see HAGGIS and TRIPE.

A pig's stomach, also known as hog's maw, is convenient for stuffing and was used thus in classical Rome. Such dishes are still to be found in various parts of the world, with other parts of the pig often providing elements for the stuffing. The Chinese also use pig's stomach as meat, in stir-fries, and soups.

STONE CRAB *Menippe mercenaria*, a brownish-red crab, mottled with grey, whose range extends from the Caribbean and the Gulf of Texas to the Carolinas, but which is especially associated with Florida. It may measure 12 cm (5") across and has relatively large claws, one bigger than the other, which are tipped with black. It lives in burrows in shallow water.

The association of this crab with Florida was emphasized by Damon Runyon, who stated (erroneously) in a Miami newspaper article of 1954 that it 'hangs out around the Florida Keys and nowhere else in the world', and went so far as to suggest that only established residents of Dade County in Florida deserved to enjoy it. He admitted, however, that it had been largely ignored there until 1920, when a visiting Harvard professor saw specimens being thrown away and pointed out how good the meat was.

Although the backfin meat of this crab is edible, the accepted view is that everything is 'waste' except for the claw meat; and it is only the claws which are sold. Fishermen remove the larger claw and toss the crab back into the water, since it will survive this amputation and grow a new claw.

STONECROP the general name for the numerous plants of the genus *Sedum*, common in temperate and northern regions of Europe and Asia. They have hot, bitter leaves. The milder kinds are eaten as vegetables; the medium ones used as condiments; and the strongest are inedible but have been used as emetics.

The common English names of the stonecrops are interesting but confusing. Grigson (1955) lists them in an illuminating way and explains how the French name *trique-madame* turned into the English 'prick-madam' and was used in the form 'trip-madame' by John Evelyn in a list which he drew up between 1688 and 1706 of plants for the kitchen garden. He was referring to *S. reflexum*, the yellow stonecrop, which in some places shares the name 'creeping Jenny' with *S. acre*, more commonly known as wall-pepper or golden stonecrop. *S. acre* has the distinction of possessing the longest vernacular name in the English language: 'welcome-home-husband-though-never-so-drunk'. However, *Sempervivum tectorum*, the so-called houseleek or sengreen, is a close

runner-up with the name 'welcome-home-husband-though-never-so-late'.

Stonecrops are now largely forgotten as a vegetable, although roseroot, *S. rosea*, a northern species, has continued to be a salad vegetable of value in the regions where it grows.

Orpine is also called 'livelong' because of its long lasting flowers. In N. America the names 'stonecrop' and 'live-forever' are applied to various species including *S. triphyllum*, on which Fernald and Kinsey (1943) comment:

Live-forever or Frog-plant is familiar to most children in regions where it occurs on account of the readily loosened epidermis of the leaf, loosened by holding the leaf between the tongue and the roof of the mouth; after which, by blowing into the opening, the loosened epidermis may be distended like a frog's throat. It is, therefore, surprising how few people are familiar with the delicious quality of the tender, young leaves and stems as a salad. If the plant is to be used as salad, it should be gathered very young, but as a potherb (of indifferent quality) it may be used until July. The rounded or finger-like tuberous roots are crisp and succulent and after some days pickling in a salted vinegar, best put on the tubers while boiling hot, they form a tasty relish. After midsummer the tubers become stringy and tough, but again in late autumn crisp tubers may be found. They often occur in enormous masses and then furnish an abundant and easily obtained food.

STONE MUSHROOM *Polyporus tuberaster*, an especially interesting species among the POLYPORES, is the *pietra fungaia* of (mainly) the central and southern parts of Italy. It occurs elsewhere in Europe but has been less noticed in other countries. Ramsbottom (1932) elucidated the mystery of its nature thus:

Since the earliest times there are references to a stone which, on being watered, gives rise to a mushroom. There are hints of it in many writers, and it is said to be mentioned by Strabo in 50 BC. It appears to have had some connection with the mysteries of the Lynx, and was regarded as the coagulated urine of wolves to be found on the summits of high mountains. The idea was seriously argued in the writings of the Renaissance period.

The stone, as a matter of fact, is a mixture of rock, earth, and pebbles bound together by the mycelium of the fungus *Polyporus tuberaster*. . . . The stone may be of different sizes and composition, occasionally weighing as much as fifty pounds.

The same author explains that the stone is, technically, a pseudo-sclerotium. A true sclerotium is a compact mass of fungus mycelium. This may be edible. If, however, the sclerotium is interspersed with earth etc. (in this instance, usually earth and pebbles of tufa), it falls into the pseudo category and it

is only the fruit-bodies, i.e. the mushrooms which sprout up from the structure, which are potentially edible.

The stone mushrooms were at one time prized delicacies for the tables of popes, kings, and dukes. They seem to have been found mainly in the vicinity of Naples, and were remarked upon by numerous writers of the 16th and 17th centuries. Micheli (1729) was the first scientist to describe the phenomenon correctly. It has become rare in modern times, and was already uncommon at the beginning of the 18th century, when Samuel Pepys tried in vain to obtain a specimen from Naples. Rymsdyk (1791) later described one at the British Museum as 'a kind of *Fossil*, extremely curious, for laying it in the earth, and a little earth on the top, then wetting it with water, *mushrooms* will shoot up in a short time'. (It is not clear whether the British Museum had allowed him to perform the experiment.)

It has now become possible to create the 'stones' artificially, to procure a continuous supply of mushrooms.

STORK any of a number of species of bird in the family Ciconiidae, which is represented in most parts of the world: in Europe by *C. ciconia*, the white stork, and *C. nigra*, the black stork. The long legs of storks are famous, as are their nesting habits.

Storks are protected species, at least in those parts of Europe where they nest (NW France, Germany, the Netherlands, and Belgium). They were, however, sometimes eaten in medieval times, although they do not appear regularly on the menus for banquets, as do the CRANE, HERON, PEACOCK, and SWAN.

STOVIES (known in full as stoved tatties), a Scottish dish of potatoes, onions, etc., often with mutton, stewed with very little added liquid.

Stovies make a delicious dish, but their main interest lies perhaps in the etymology of the term. Given the large number of French culinary terms which have been in use in Scotland for centuries, it is tempting to derive stovie from *étuvé*, a French word with just about the same meaning, i.e. something cooked in a closed recipient with very little liquid; of BRAISE. This was the view taken by Marian McNeill (1929). However, Catherine Brown (1985) prefers the theory that the use of the English word 'stove' as a verb meaning to stew has a history quite independent of the French term. She points out that Gervase Markham (1631) referred to 'letting a bird stove and sweate till evening', and suggests that the particular value of the verb to stove lay in its having a meaning between sweating and stewing 'since often, as in stovies, very little water is used'. She also remarks, as is generally accepted, that this use of the word 'stove' is particularly Scottish; but adds that it is not exclusively Scottish, since it has also remained in use in the north of England.

STRACCHINO the family name for a group of Italian cheeses which have been made in Lombardy since the 12th century.

The dialect word *stracco*, of which *stracchino* is a diminutive, means 'tired'. The cheeses were originally made in autumn from the milk of cows migrating south to avoid the winter cold; and the exertion of the journey made their milk thin, suggestive of tiredness.

Most of these cheeses are made from whole cow's milk, mixed with milk from the previous evening, but they vary considerably in other respects. The green-veined GORGONZOLA is quite different from the mould-ripened TALEGGIO. A distinguished member of the family is robiola, considered by some authorities to be one of the most ancient of all cheeses and to owe its name to the Latin word for red, referring to the reddish rind. Fresh stracchino is known as crescenza.

STRAWBERRY the fruit of plants of the genus *Fragaria*, is a symbol of the Virgin Mary and also of summer and of the delights of summer fruit. As Andrew Boorde (1542, also ed Furnivall, 1870) put it: 'Rawe crayme undecocted, eaten with strawerys or hurtes [whortleberry, bilberry, etc.] is a rural mannes banket.'

However, Boorde's strawberries were far removed from the fruits grown today (and still eaten with cream). In fact, the kinds of strawberry cultivated now date back only to the 17th century, as explained below.

The Latin name *fraga* refers to the fruit's fragrance. The English word 'strawberry' is due to the 'straying' erratic habit of the plant, which it shares with many other members of the rose family, such as the blackberry.

Wild strawberries are indigenous to both the Old and the New World. The small, wild strawberry of temperate zones in Europe and Asia is *Fragaria vesca*, of which an Alpine variety is recognized, and also an American one. *F. moschata*, the hautbois or musky strawberry, belongs to C. Europe. *F. virginiana* is native to N. America and known as scarlet or Virginia strawberry; and *F. chiloensis*, pine or beach strawberry, to S. America.

Wild strawberry varieties are little cultivated commercially because of their small fruits and low yield, but some of them are among the most delicious of all strawberries, and are much sought in the wild and sold for high prices.

Strawberry cultivation, using the European wild species, had begun by the 14th century, but progressed slowly until the colonization of the Americas and the discovery of *F. virginiana*, enjoyed both fresh and dried by American Indians. This species was introduced into Europe in the early 17th century, and was followed later by *F. chiloensis*, a larger and juicier species with a pineapple flavour, found on the west coast of N. and S. America but associated particularly with Chile. This was brought into France by a French officer, Frézier, who had found the plants growing at the foot of the Andes.

Eventually the two American species began to hybridize naturally, and the result was *F. × ananassa*, the modern cultivated strawberry. A major role was played here by the botanist Antoine Nicolas Duchesne, who published his *Histoire naturelle des fraisiers* in 1766, when he was only 19. However, the innovators of the 19th century were British. Thomas Andrew Knight pioneered large-scale, systematic strawberry-breeding, producing two famous varieties, the Downton and the Elton. On the crest of this wave, a market gardener called Michael Keens produced the 'Keens' Seedling', remarkable for size and flavour. It caused a sensation when it came into cultivation in 1821 and quickly spread to the Continent and to America. Virtually all modern varieties are derived from it.

In recent times, one of the most productive sources of new varieties has been the 'Universities program' in California. Commercial cultivation of strawberries in the USA had begun on the eastern seaboard, in the region from Boston to Baltimore. It then shifted southwards and inland, in tune with the development of railroads and refrigeration, and had reached the Pacific north-west before 1900. Later, within five years of the introduction of the 'University varieties' in 1945, California came to dominate the American strawberry industry in quantity of production and in length of season.

There is great and increasing diversity of flavour and other characteristics, including season, amongst the new varieties; and the general effect, worldwide, is to make fresh strawberries available for longer than in the past. Despite the excellence of well-made strawberry jam and such confections as strawberry SHORTCAKE, no one would deny that this fruit is most delicious when eaten fresh. Cream is the traditional accompaniment in England; elsewhere in Europe, sour cream is preferred. In France and Italy, red wine may be used instead (as also happened in England, for Thomas Hyall, writing in 1593, said that strawberries were 'much eaten at all men's tables in the summer with wine and sugar').

READING: Whiteaker (1985.)

'STRAWBERRY TREE' or arbutus, *Arbutus unedo*, originated in the Mediterranean region. It is an attractive tree which in favourable conditions grows up to 10 m (30') high. It is cultivated chiefly for ornament, since it has attractive white flowers, shiny leaves, and orange-red, strawberry-sized fruit.

These are edible, but somewhat acid and lacking in flavour. They are used for making jams and jellies; and in Turkey a kind of vinegar.

A couple of other species native to the E. Mediterranean region and the Canary Islands have similar fruits which can be eaten fresh or candied. The **madrona**, *A. menziesii*, of the Pacific coast of N. America has scarlet fruit which were eaten, fresh or dried, by local Indian tribes and early settlers.

STRAW MUSHROOMS *Volvariella volvacea*, sometimes called paddy straw mushrooms, have been cultivated for centuries in China and SE Asia. They are grown outdoors on bundles of wetted rice straw and are usually gathered while still young and small. A full-sized mushroom is up to 8 cm (3") across the cap, which is conical, white, and has a darker top. The stem may reach 12 cm (5") long and 2 cm

---

THE STRUCTURE OF THE STRAWBERRY

AN odd feature of the strawberry is its peculiar and unique structure. It is technically known as a 'false' or 'accessory fruit'. The seeds which, unlike those of any other fruit, are on the outside, are the true fruits of the plant. The fleshy 'berry' to which they are attached is an enlarged, softened receptacle, corresponding to the small, white cone which remains on the stem of a raspberry when the fruit is picked. (Both fruits belong to the rose family and have the same fundamental form; but the strawberry's cluster of dry fruit seeds is described as an 'etaerio of achenes', while the raspberry's cluster of juicy grains is an 'etaerio of druplets'.)

(0.75") thick, and is a streaky off-white. There is no ring, but there is a large volva (cup-shaped sheath) at the base. The gills, at first white, become pink when older.

Dried or canned straw mushrooms are available from Chinese food stores anywhere. Dried straw mushrooms soften quickly when soaked in warm water. The flavour blends well with chicken and other mild-tasting dishes.

STREET FOOD in a given place, is often far more interesting than RESTAURANT food. Generally speaking, wherever it is found it will be likely to represent well-established local traditions; and in some places a tour of hawkers' stalls may be the quickest and most agreeable method of getting the feel of local foods.

Among the factors which seem to determine how numerous and diverse street foods are in this or that country, one is clearly climate—a temperate or warm climate makes these operations much easier and also produces a larger number of passers-by who are not intent on getting to somewhere out of the cold. Another factor is the degree of economic development. Broadly speaking, developed countries have fewer street foods. However, there are many exceptions or anomalies. Singapore is highly developed yet rich in street foods. And in a developed country such as the USA the previous abundance of street foods may have been reduced or eliminated by new forms of competition (fast food restaurants, for example) in most parts, but may retain a toehold in some places where there are numerous immigrants from countries which have rich traditions of street food.

There are indeed few generalizations which can safely be made on the subject. Nor is there much literature available for study. Conventional recipe books often ignore street foods, especially if they are items which the local population would always buy ready prepared rather than cook at home. However, there are several useful sources listed under 'Reading' below. The work done by the FAO (Food and Agriculture Organization of the United Nations) in surveying street foods in some African countries reflect concern for hygiene and consumer protection but at the same time yield valuable information about local traditions. Some international meetings, e.g. the 1991 Oxford Symposium on 'Public Eating' (with essays describing street foods in Afghanistan, Hawaii, Hungary, Nigeria, the Philippines, etc., and an account of the American hot dog stand), contain useful surveys. And there are a number of specialized local publications which describe hawkers' food in places such as Penang and Bangkok.

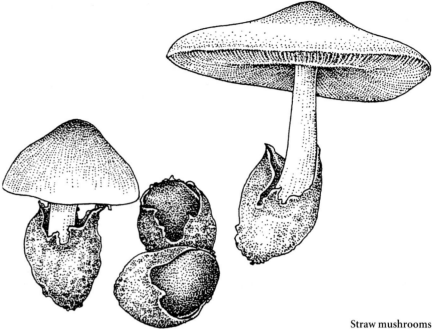

Straw mushrooms

A list of the most famous and widespread street foods would certainly include ICE CREAM, DOUGHNUT, HAMBURGER, and hot dog (see FRANKFURTER).
READING: FAO (1990); Kenny Yee and Catherine Gordon (1993); Lin and Har (1986); Mi Mi Khaing (1978); Walker (1992); Doreen Fernandez and Edilberto Alegre (1988); Doreen Fernandez (1994).

STRIPED BASS *Morone saxatilis*, a valuable inshore fish of the eastern seaboard of the USA, ranging from the Gulf of St Lawrence down to the Gulf of Mexico (and often called rockfish or just 'rock' in the southern part of its range). The species was introduced also to the Pacific coast in the 19th century. Its maximum length is more than a metre (over 40") but the market length is less than half that.

Cole (1978), in *Striper*, a book which takes its title from the most common of the vernacular names for the fish, has celebrated both it and the fishermen who pursue it. He explains vividly how voracious these fish are, and what carnage ensues when they descend on their prey:

When a school of three hundred or four hundred stripers receives its simultaneous feeding message from impulses not yet fully deciphered by humankind, the creatures detonate a group frenzy that shatters the water's surface with the violence of an erupting undersea geyser.

Everywhere the bait fish fly, as if some soundless, invisible tornado were sucking them up from beneath the sea. Broad bass tails smash the surface in white welts of foam; the turnings of the feeding fish start scores of swirling whirlpools, each a mark of the consummate energy a fish needs to reverse its course and swerve

open-mouthed through the very center of the mass of panic the bait fish school has become. . . . Sea birds scream of the carnage; their coarse signals carry for miles, attracting hundreds, sometimes thousands of their kin.

Anglers, as well as professional fishermen, seek the stripers, which make fine eating. Early settlers were quick to appreciate this. Wood (*New England's Prospect*, 1634) wrote:

The basse is one of the best fishes in the country, and though men are soon wearied with other fish, yet are they never with basse. It is a delicate, fine, fat, fast fish, having a bone in his head which contains a saucerfull of marrow sweet and good, pleasant to the pallat and wholesome to the stomach.

A close relation, *Morone americanus*, is much smaller, and is usually referred to as white perch or sea perch. An excellent pan fish.

See also BASS; SEA BASS.

STROOPBALLETJE a soft, sticky Dutch sweet made from a TREACLE, sugar, and butter mixture similar to that for TOFFEE but cooked to a much lower temperature, the soft ball stage (see SUGAR BOILING). The mixture is poured on to a slab, left to cool until it starts to set, and divided into balls.

STRUDEL is the German name for a PASTRY composed of thin sheets of dough around a soft filling (the word literally means 'eddy' or 'whirlpool'). German strudel is relatively dry, a long roll, holding raisins and chopped apples, bent in a horseshoe, baked, and cut across in slices. Similar pastries are popular in much of

C. and E. Europe, and are closely related to various Balkan and Middle Eastern confections also based on the same type of thin dough. This is known in English either as strudel pastry, or by its Greek name, FILO.

This pastry is very important to strudel and related dishes. All countries in which it is known take great pride in it, and several claim to have invented it, the Hungarians citing flour from hard Hungarian wheat as a contributory factor in support of their claim. It is true that high-protein flour is required for strudel pastry; but the method is widely known, not only in C. Europe, but throughout the Middle East, where it is used in BAKLAVA, and notably in Turkey, which may well be the place of origin. Made from flour, egg, and a little butter mixed to a dough with water, it is kneaded until silky and rested. The dough is then placed on a floured cloth on a large table, rolled a little, and stretched by placing the hands underneath and pulling it gently towards the edge of the table until it forms a huge, thin sheet. When properly pulled out, it is said that one should be able to read a newspaper through it.

To make the pastry into a long roll, it is brushed with melted butter, scattered with breadcrumbs, and the chosen filling placed at one end of the sheet of dough. The cloth is lifted so the pastry rolls up to the other end of the table; it is curved round, brushed with more melted butter and baked.

Strudels may be eaten hot or cold. Apple strudel, the best known to W. Europeans, is a special favourite in Germany and Austria. However, Lesley Chamberlain (1989) gives a sense of how much more widespread and varied strudels actually are:

From Germany in the north, through Austria, Hungary and Yugoslavia, to Bulgaria, Turkey, Greece and Lebanon, half the world has a passion for dishes of intricately folded pastry. The strudels of thin pastry enriched with fat are sweet in Central Europe, and sweet or savoury by the time they reach the Balkans.

Many other fillings are possible, based on different fruits, for example the cinnamon-flavoured cherry strudel, which is a Balkan favourite. Other mixtures use ground walnuts, or boiled poppyseeds, or sweetened, spiced curd cheese. (LM)

STUFATO and stufatino, its diminutive, are Italian terms for a STEW or BRAISE of meat cooked with wine in a tightly closed recipient. This passed into the French language and produced a family of French terms such as *estouffade* and *étouffe*, all with much the same meaning. *Étuvée* is a term with a different derivation but it too has this meaning. The cooking method indicated by all the terms means, in effect, that the meat

(or fish, or fowl, or vegetable) is cooked by STEAM.

STUFF and stuffing, the process of filling cavities in meat, fish, vegetables and fruit, and the substances used for this purpose.

In English, the use of the term 'stuff' in cookery emerged from a mass of generalized meanings to do with victuals (preserved in the expression 'foodstuff') and non-edible possessions, to become, sometime in the 16th century, attached to mixtures for filling pies. It developed, a little later, into the idea of 'stuffing' the cavity left by the removal of a bone before meat is cooked. The French word *farce* (still in use as their word for stuffing) also carries other meanings, including that of padding out. It is recorded in English from the late 14th century onwards and eventually gave English the term 'forcemeat', applied to fine-textured, elaborate mixtures used especially with meat and fish.

There are many practical reasons for stuffing food. These include using a rich mixture which contributes fat to dry meats, such as roast hare. Conversely, a plain starch-based substance can be used to absorb dripping and juice from rich meat, such as mashed potatoes inside roast goose. A small quantity of meat stretches further if used in stuffing, e.g. in vegetable marrow stuffed with minced meat.

Besides being of practical advantage, the use of stuffings and forcemeats sometimes carries the idea of a conceit, a hidden surprise in an apparently plain dish. This sort of practice has a long history. An example from the classical Roman world is the roast pig served at Trimalchio's feast, which was stuffed with sausages and black puddings. Medieval recipes, including many early Arabic ones, often called for some kind of stuffing, even if it was only an almond inside a meatball.

In 17th- and 18th-century English recipes, mixtures for stuffings and forcemeats of many types are recorded. Some were combinations of seasoned cereal and fat, such as the pudding used in the recipe 'to bake a Tench with a Pudding in her belly' by Murrell (1638). Others required veal, pork, or chicken meat with spices and herbs.

As with most culinary practices, the use of stuffings and forcemeats has varied according to current fashion and has sometimes gone over the top. Dallas in *Kettner's Book of the Table* (1877) remarked scathingly of late 19th-century French practice:

The French name for it [stuffing] is *farce*, and their use of it tends to farce . . . They swell out their viands, and surround them with farce, quenelles of whiting, quenelles of chicken . . . forcemeat shaped into balls, shaped into eggs,

shaped into corks, farce inside the meat, farce coating it and masking it, farce swimming around it; so that often a solid dish professing to be solid meat proves to be mainly farce.

The use of flavoured stuffings has survived up to the present in most cuisines. In England a bread-based mixture flavoured with sage and onion is traditional for goose or pork, and chestnut stuffing is used with turkey in many countries. Generally, poultry provide natural homes for stuffings, as do squid and various species of fish which have large stomach cavities. Rice or rice and meat mixtures are used in these ways, and also for stuffing vine leaves and vegetables, in Mediterranean countries (see DOLMA). Many Middle Eastern dishes such as KIBBEH are based on the idea of using stuffing.

The principle is not confined to savoury dishes. To take one example, MARZIPAN is often used to replace the stones removed from dates, and apricots are treated in a similar way. (LM)

STURGEON of the family Acipenseridae, are primitive fish. They have shovel-like snouts, equipped with barbels, for rooting about in search of food (the German name, from which many others are derived, is from the verb *störer*, to root about). On their sides they have rows of bony scutes.

The species—about two dozen, all in the northern hemisphere—vary markedly in their habitats. Some live at sea and spawn in freshwater, while others are purely freshwater species. They are a resource of considerable value, especially for their CAVIAR. The fact that culture of some species, at least to the extent of rearing young sturgeon in a protected environment, has proved possible increases their importance.

The most important species are:

- *Acipenser sturio*, the sturgeon of the Mediterranean and NE Atlantic, now relatively rare, although populations have lingered on in the rivers Gironde and Guadalquivir (until the 1980s, returning to the Gironde in the 1990s). This sturgeon has been known to reach a length of 4 m (13') although the usual adult length is about half that.
- *A. ruthenus*, the sterlet, which is essentially a freshwater species, although it does venture out to sea in the Black and Azov seas. It is known also in Siberia. Its common names are *çiga* or *çuka* (Turkish), *chiga* (Bulgarian), *cegǎ* (Romanian), and *sterlyad'* (Russian). Normal adult length only about 50 cm (20").
- *A. gueldenstaedti*, a larger sturgeon (adult length up to 1.7 m/5.5') of the Black, Azov, and Caspian seas. It has a short, blunt snout. Its common names are *koraca*

(Turkish), *Ruska esetra* (Bulgarian), *nisetru* (Romanian), and *Chernomorsko-azovskayi osëtr* (Russian). It is the source of *osciotr* caviar.

- *Acipenser stellatus*, the sevruga sturgeon, which is the main source of caviar in the Caspian, but also abundant in the Azov Sea and an occasional stray visitor to the Adriatic. Its common names are *mersin balığı* (Turkish), *pustruga* (Bulgarian), *pastruga* (Romanian), and *sevryuga* (Russian).
- *Huso huso*, the 'great sturgeon' of the Caspian and Black seas, largest in that region. It provides *beluga* caviar.
- *Acipenser mikadoi*, of N. Japan. Maximum length 1.5 m (nearly 5').
- *A transmontanus*, the white sturgeon of rivers in NW America, a very large fish indeed—it may reach 4.5 m (15').
- *A. oxyrhinchus* (which some authorities equate with *A. sturio* above), a sturgeon of the eastern seaboard of N. America.

The merits of the caviar obtained from these various species are discussed under CAVIAR. As fish to be eaten, they are all good. The quality of sturgeon meat has often been compared to that of veal, and the comparison offers a useful guide to cooking methods, e.g. frying thin escalopes, grilling thicker slices, and roasting 'joints'.

SUB-SAHARAN AFRICA is here taken to comprise W. Sahara, Mauritania, Mali, Burkina Faso, Niger, and Chad.

Much of this area, mostly former French colonies, is sparsely populated. Most of the people live in the less arid southern areas around the few rivers and lakes, notably the Niger and Lake Chad. The terrain is fairly flat with the exception of N. Chad. The Sahel, the strip between desert and savannah, which makes up most of the western countries, is mostly scrub.

The cooking is most influenced by that of N. Africa. Mauritania, for example, has a dish, *michoui*, stuffed leg of lamb with dates and raisins, which is very similar to Moroccan dishes. The staple foods are RICE and MILLET with *fonio* or hungry rice, *Digitaria exilis* or *D. iburua*, and wild grains being commonly eaten in some areas, often with a meatball and peanut (see GROUNDNUT) sauce. YAMS and PLANTAINS are also eaten, and BEANS and LENTILS are important. MAIZE porridge is widely eaten in the E. Sahel. Millet grains may be made into COUSCOUS or boiled with CASSAVA to a mush called *le tô*. For festive occasions this is served with two sauces, one made of minced meat, dried fish, and dried OKRA powder and the other of diced meat and tomatoes. These are usually combined before serving.

Combinations of meat and fish to make relishes or sauces are as common as they are in W. Africa. Noodles, called *kata* in Mali, are popular in the western countries. A baguette-type bread is common in the towns.

The herder peoples, such as the Fula, tend to live in the more northern parts. Red meat is a luxury for most but beef, goat, lamb, often cooked with okra, and CAMEL (there is a dish of stuffed camel stomach reminiscent of haggis) are all eaten as well as game such as antelope, ROCK-RABBIT, and CANE RAT, confusingly known as *agouti* in French-speaking countries. Near the Niger and Lake Chad, fish are an important part of the diet; they include Nile perch, *Lates niloticus*, and TILAPIA. Meat and fish are often dried, sometimes by choice rather than necessity. Many of the peoples are Muslim and pork is seldom seen. Chicken, GUINEA-FOWL, and PIGEONS are all popular. *Maafe*, a chicken and groundnut stew with sweet potatoes and tomatoes, is claimed as their invention by the Bambarra tribe of Mali, who also gave their name to the Bambarra groundnut (see GROUNDNUT).

SHEA BUTTER, PALM OIL, and groundnut oil are all used, though less liberally than in southern W. Africa. Chillies and tomatoes feature in many dishes. *Riz gras* is a common dish of rice with a thin stew of beef and tomato. JOLLOF RICE is a festival dish. Stews of cassava leaves with dried fish and palm oil or with okra are also served with COUSCOUS or rice. The Senegalese chicken dish *yassa* is popular as is *atik*, a dish of dried cassava porridge with smoked fish, tomatoes, and as many other vegetables as are available. Burkina Faso has a dish called *maan nezim nzedo* made with freshwater fish, okra, greens, and tomatoes. There is a special celebration pastry made in Mali, consisting of rice flour and honey, called *tsnein-achra*.

The traditional wood-burning hearth, made of three stones on which the pot sits, is still to be found in country areas throughout this area. Meat may be grilled on open fires but the oven is uncommon outside towns.

As almost everywhere in Africa, STREET FOOD is an important part of the culture. *Chichingas*, like kebabs, and *chawarma*, similar to a doner kebab, are popular street foods. Bean fritters, sweet pastries, and grilled sweetcorn are also common.   JM

SUBTLETIES While medieval diners ate, at formal meals, they observed the spectacle that was performed between courses. The course was called a met; the activities between courses were therefore the entremets (see ENTRÉE AND ENTREMETS). The contemporary English term was 'soteltie'. (The subjects, however, were not always subtle, as when a woman in childbirth was depicted as a soteltie for a wedding.)

There were two basic types: the plainer was a setpiece, made of anything from pastry or butter to wood and canvas; the more elaborate ones (*entremets mouvants*) included automatons or live participants. They were amalgams of song, theatre, mechanics, and carpentry, combined to convey an allegorical fantasy or even a political message.

The execution of a series of entremets for important festivities occupied large numbers of people. The preparations for the entertainments at the wedding of Charles the Bold brought craftsmen to Bruges for weeks at a time—painters, sculptors, carpenters, and wax modellers by the dozens. The banquet entremets displayed the ducal wealth; their imaginativeness revealed the mentality of a culture. At the Feast of the Pheasant, for example, Philip the Fair was trying, at least ostensibly, to induce his guests to join him on a crusade to rescue Constantinople from the infidel. Assuming leadership of a crusade, traditionally the role of the Holy Roman emperor, would have enhanced Burgundy's claims to higher political status. A programmatic entremet was enacted to stimulate enthusiasm. A giant Saracen entered, leading an elephant (the chronicle unfortunately does not tell how it was contrived). Seated on the elephant was that excellent knight, co-organizer, and later chronicler of the feast Olivier de La Marche, playing the role of the captive Eastern Church. He wore a long white gown and sang, in a falsetto voice, a moving plea to Duke Philip.

The line between entremets made to be eaten and for allegorical purposes was not strictly observed. At Charles the Bold's festivities a course at one meal consisted of some 30 pies, each enclosed in a silk pavilion and each bearing the name of a walled town under Charles's rule. The visual effect was that of a military encampment; the message was clearly a statement of Charles's military strength. A more pastoral, poetic conception appeared at the last of these wedding feasts. Thirty platters were made up to look like gardens, each with a golden hedge surrounding a different kind of fruit tree; each tree bore the name of a ducal abbey. Around the trees were figures of peasants harvesting the fruit while others held baskets with candied spices and fruit for the guests to eat. Other entremets at these festivities were more fantastic: a court dwarf rode in on the back of a lion and was given to the bride, Margaret of York, to whom he sang a song and presented a daisy (in French *marguerite*); they were followed by a dromedary ridden by Indians who released live birds to fly around the hall. There were also automatons and a whale containing musicians.

How are we to understand these festivities? Johann Huizinga, usually sensitive to the nuances of late medieval expression, wrote that it is 'difficult to regard these entertainments as something more than exhibitions of almost incredible bad taste', and he describes the feast as a 'barbarous manifestation'. I would suggest instead that the medieval banquet be regarded as would an illuminated manuscript page of the same period. The manuscript page is composed of several elements. The written text, the content of which gives rise to the illuminations, is likely to be plain or only moderately embellished; an elaborate initial letter is followed by legible, uniform script. The framed illustration puts the significance vividly before the reader, who, in the 14th century, may well have given more attention to the picture than to the written word. Smaller images elsewhere on the page may represent other ideas associated more or less appropriately with the principal subject. Further fantastic ornaments and drolleries seem to reflect free—often very free—associations in the illuminator's mind.

The medieval feast contains similar components. Food is analogous to the manuscript text: eating the meal was the occasion for the events that went on around it. As the lettering of the text was of subsidiary importance on the page to the beholder, so the dishes on the tables were only a modest part of the elaborate spectacle. The major *entremets mouvants*, such as the allegorical conquest of Jerusalem, are comparable to the formal framed scene on the vellum page. The lesser entremets—the fantastic creatures, the singing lions, the griffons spewing forth live birds—are similar to the more loosely related ornaments on the manuscript page. The plausibility of this analogy is supported by the fact that the same artists who were called upon to produce paintings and manuscripts also worked on the feasts. Among the artists who helped create the spectacles for Charles the Bold's wedding were Jacques Daret, who had been a student of Robert Campin, and Hugo van der Goes. Medieval manuscripts are a feast for the eye; medieval banquets addressed the other senses as well.   BW
READING: Bridget Ann Henisch (1976).

SUCCOTASH an American dish which requires cooking fresh corn kernels (see MAIZE) and LIMA BEANS, separately, in boiling water until tender, after which these ingredients are mixed with each other and with a little butter (or salt pork, say some) and cooked until ready. This description is broadly true, but glosses over the fact that, as Evan Jones (1981) puts it: 'there may be a dozen "authentic" ways to make succotash.'

He states, for example, that the oldest recorded recipe for succotash requires boiling two fowls as the first step and includes as ingredients turnip, potato, and corned beef and pork. Craigie and Hulbert (1938–44) give 1751 as the first reference in print ('Mo[the]r dined with us upon Suckatash and Ham'); and their next reference from 1778 is to Succotosh, being corn and beans boiled together with bear's flesh. The use of salt pork in early versions is well attested.

Jones explains too that views about the correct cultivar of the lima bean to use vary, unsurprisingly, from one part of the country to the other; thus some New England cooks prefer a kind with 'cranberry-sauce colored splashes on the pods'. However, what seems to be universally agreed is that the name succotash was formed from some Narragansett Indian words (notably *misickquatash, sukquttahash*).

There is a place called Succotash Point in Rhode Island, on Narragansett Bay; but succotash has come to be more popular in the south than in its region of origin.

SUCKET The name sucket has been used for various confections. It is derived from now extinct French and Italian terms, *succade* and *succata*, meaning 'juicy' (modern French *sucette* means 'lollipop' and Italian *succo*, 'juice'). It was first used in English for an imported sweet, candied orange or lemon peel. From the mid-16th century suckets were made in Britain from local fruits, vegetables, and roots of many kinds. At this time no one understood what caused things to decay, and there was no attempt to sterilize containers. Only a severe treatment, involving prolonged boiling in syrup to concentrate it, had any chance of success. Sometimes things which were made into suckets were salted before they were put into the syrup. Unripe fruits were used—a convenient way of saving fruits such as apricots or peaches which failed to ripen in a bad summer. Other things included citrus peel from fresh imported fruits, and later, as skill grew, pieces of citrus fruit; green walnuts; some vegetables such as ANGELICA stalks; and various roots including those of ALEXANDERS, BORAGE, ELECAMPANE, ERINGO ROOT (popular well into the 19th century), FENNEL, and PARSLEY. Many of these were credited with medicinal properties.

Wet suckets were kept in jars, covered with the cooking syrup, and lifted out with special forks when required. They were heavily sugared, quite unlike later types of bottled fruit in syrup. This tradition has almost completely vanished, apart from preserved ginger, and a handful of old-fashioned products made in the Philippines.

Dry suckets became the forerunners of modern CANDIED FRUIT.

SUCKING PIGS as the name implies, are young pigs fed only on their mothers' milk. They are killed at ages from two to six weeks old (best at three to four weeks), and are often roasted whole. The meat, as with all young animals, is pale, tender, and on the gelatinous side. The true delicacy is the skin, which, correctly roasted, becomes wonderfully good CRACKLING. Seasonings are added according to local tastes, but are generally kept to a minimum, for it is the textures that are important in this dish. The body cavity of the pig is sometimes stuffed, or the OFFAL made into a stew to accompany it. Sucking pigs are items for special occasions, and have been or are served at feasts in many parts of the world. In modern Europe, its strongest admirers are the Portuguese and Spanish; it is almost an obsession in the Coimbra area of Portugal, and a speciality of Segovia in Spain.

Sucking pigs are sometimes referred to as suckling pigs; this is incorrect, since it is the mothers who suckle and the young who suck.

Esteem for sucking pigs goes back to classical Greece and Rome. Later, they were widely used in medieval cookery. Later still, when pigs became animals farmed in enclosed sties (as opposed to the free-ranging medieval woodland pig), the numbers of piglets raised for pork or bacon was limited by available food, so a larger proportion would be killed and sold as sucking pigs. Eighteenth-century recipes for whole pigs detailed by Hannah Glasse (1747) included several which were clearly intended for sucking pigs, although not so named. Mrs Beeton (1861) still had one recipe for roast sucking pig (always the most favoured way of cooking them), but in recent times sucking pig has become less and less usual in England and the USA.   (LM)

SUDAN the 12th largest country in the world, exhibits a wide range of climates (from the south with its nine months of rainy season to the arid north), of food crops, and of diets.

A good survey of the food crops is given by Ferguson (1955). The main staple crop is *dura*, great or Indian MILLET (*Sorghum bicolor*), but other millets are grown, notably bulrush millet (*dukhn*, a staple for rural communities in the west of the country) and finger millet (*telebun*, the main staple cereal in the south-west). Other major food crops are *simsim* (SESAME, grown for its oil, which is the cooking oil preferred by the Sudanese), CASSAVA, SWEET POTATOES, and GROUNDNUTS. Others of considerable importance include COWPEA, OKRA (*bamia*), and MELOKHIA, the last two of which are typical ingredients in Sudanese cookery. A lot of ROCKET is grown in the north.

AMARANTH plants, whether wild or cultivated, provide a popular leafy vegetable, especially in the south, where they are known by a tribal name, *bedi bedi*.

The DATE is by far the most important fruit, but BANANAS and MANGOES flourish in the south, as do some other tropical fruits. The PALMYRA PALM grows in most regions and can play an important role as a famine food. The ROSELLE fruit (*kerkade*) provides the Sudanese with a distinctive and delicious drink, deep rose red in colour.

For animal foods, sheep and goats are most important. Mutton is the preferred meat, except in the south, where it is beef. The desert sheep is an interesting breed, well adapted to local conditions. In the southern areas, among non-Muslim tribes, pigs form part of the indigenous food resources. The form of dried meat which is most commonly eaten, although never preferred to fresh meat, is *sharmut*, made by salting and drying.

A substantial part of the Sudan is called 'the meatless region', because the prevalence of the tsetse fly prevents the inhabitants from keeping domestic animals. In those parts, any wild animal that can be caught is likely to be eaten, so into the cooking pot go snakes, bush rats, tortoises, etc.

The influence of traditions of hospitality and customs whereby men have priority for food over women are by no means unique to the Sudanese. However, a lucid essay by Mrs G. M. Culwick (1955) has drawn attention with great cogency to how these factors affect them:

The household does not eat until the men have finished, except that if the meal is much delayed small children may be given something to keep them quiet. The duty of hospitality is paramount and no one knows what guests may come before the men have finished eating. In accordance with custom, they must be invited to partake. So the men, whether at the 'diwan' or eating at home, often call for more food than originally sent to them and the family has to manage as best it can.

Though there are, of course, many individual exceptions, I cannot escape pointing out that in general the women are not as well fed as the men. Naturally I do not mean that all men are well fed and only the women underfed. They vary, but at any standard of living the scales are tipped in their favour. Except in the heyday of youthful married life, the women go short first and get the good things last of anyone.

SUET the hard fat from around the kidneys and loins in beef and mutton, which yields tallow and is used in cooking. It is used in SUET PUDDINGS and for the mincemeat in MINCE PIES.

SUET PUDDINGS a speciality of Britain, especially England, are traditionally based on beef SUET (see above). Its high melting point gives to suet puddings (and to suet crust and suet dumplings) a lightness not readily attainable with other fats. Among the oldest puddings in which suet was used were the ancient sausage-like WHITE PUDDINGS. Suet paste appeared in the Middle Ages in small dumplings of the COLLEGE PUDDING type; but it did not become really important until the introduction of the pudding-cloth at the beginning of the 17th century, which made large boiled puddings feasible.

Suet puddings (or DUMPLINGS—the terms are often interchangeable) might be absolutely plain, made only of suet and breadcrumbs and flour. Until the end of the 18th century, indeed until the early 20th century in some regions, it was customary in simple households to begin a meat meal with broth from the meat, followed by a plain suet pudding (boiled with the meat if appropriate), and only then, when appetite was largely satisfied by this filling combination, to serve the meat. Sheila Hutchins (1967), in introducing an admirable chapter on suet puddings, has a fine quotation from Mrs Gaskell's *Cranford* embodying the slogan 'No broth, no [suet] ball; no ball no beef'. She describes how in farmhouse kitchens in Essex and Suffolk, her part of England, a suet pudding was usually boiled in a cloth in a long roly-poly shape and cut into slices a short while before the roasted meat was ready. The slices would be laid in the dripping-pan for a minute or two and browned. However, people who could not afford a joint for roasting could still have their dumplings:

Boiled currant dumpling or meat dumplings cooked in cotton bags in large copper pans used to be sold in the streets of London till about 1860 at a halfpenny each. Plum duff too, either round or roly poly shape, was popular in the London streets in the early nineteenth century and was sold together with a batter pudding made with raisins.

Well-known savoury suet puddings include STEAK AND KIDNEY PUDDING, bacon pudding (see BACON), and Suffolk onion pudding, to which Sheila Hutchins would add a good dozen more including partridge or pigeon puddings from the Ashdown Forest where special pudding basins used to be sold for making them; a formidable item called pork plugger; Shropshire herb roll; and Kentish rabbit pudding.

Turning to sweet suet puddings, the same author comments:

The heavy boiled sweet puddings thought to be typical of English cooking were rare in polite homes before the second quarter of the nineteenth century and reached the height of their popularity in the Victorian era, very probably under the influence of the rather Germanic court, on the arrival of the Prince Consort. Those in Victorian cookery books have a surprising number of German names—Kassel Pudding, Kaiser Pudding, Royal Coburg Pudding, Pudding à la Gotha, and of course Albert Pudding among others.

It is true that George I was known as Pudding George, but it can be maintained that the Hanover monarchy did not so much impose suet puddings on England as adopt what they thought to be a good thing when they arrived. The tradition goes back to the aforementioned (Oxford and Cambridge) college puddings, and of course includes the ancestors of CHRISTMAS PUDDING (which does include suet although this is very heavily outweighed by the other ingredients.

Efforts have for long been made, by one means or another, to prevent suet puddings becoming too soggy. Thus, Eliza Acton's 'The Welcome Guest's Own Pudding' of 1855 was enriched and lightened by the use of eggs and a complicated blend of fresh and dried crumbs and crushed RATAFIAS.

Some English regional sweet suet puddings are baked, for example Tadcaster pudding, with mixed dried fruit and golden syrup, turned out after baking and covered with a spiced hot treacle sauce; and Cheltenham pudding, with fruit and crystallized ginger, served with brandy sauce. See Dorothy Hartley (1954).

As explained under PUDDING, the popularity of suet puddings and steamed puddings waned during the 20th century in Britain, but was having a well-deserved revival towards the end of the century.

SUET PUDDING SHAPES

Suet puddings come in two shapes: spherical and cylindrical. The spherical type is made by laying a pudding-cloth inside a basin, lining it with suet paste, filling it, and then adding a lid of more paste and knotting the cloth over the top—loosely, to avoid the rising paste bursting the cloth. The cylindrical type is made from a flat sheet of paste usually spread with filling and rolled up (see ROLY-POLY PUDDING), but it is less easy to tie the cloth around a pudding of this shape. Now that the pudding-cloth is obsolescent, spherical puddings are made in a basin covered with foil and greaseproof paper; and cylindrical rolls are often baked (a treatment which is anyway traditional for some).

Sugar SUGAR BEET, SUGAR CANE

Sugar is fundamental to the nutrition of plants and animals, and exists in one form or another in all living creatures. Sugars are CARBOHYDRATES, i.e. their molecules consist of carbon, hydrogen, and oxygen. (These molecules are relatively small. The more complex carbohydrates such as starch and cellulose are mainly composed of many sugar molecules joined together.) There are many different chemical forms of sugar.

The simplest sugars are termed monosaccharides, 'single sugars'. Of these, the fundamental one is **dextrose** (commonly called **glucose**), which occurs naturally in fruits and vegetables, and also in the blood of animals, where it provides a short-term store of energy. The digestion of all carbohydrates is essentially a process of reducing them to dextrose. That is why powdered glucose and glucose syrup, which consist mainly of dextrose, give quick energy. They need no digestion, but go straight into the blood.

Another common monosaccharide is **fructose** (sometimes called laevulose), also naturally present in plants, and abundant in HONEY. A third is **galactose,** one of the constituents of the sugar in milk.

All these monosaccharides have the same chemical formula. The difference between them is in the way the atoms are arranged. They have six atoms of carbon in each molecule and are therefore called hexoses. (Pentoses, with only five carbon atoms, also exist. Common ones are arabinose and xylose. They are widely found in plants, for example in pectin and other constituents of cell walls.)

Ordinary white sugar is a disaccharide, or 'double sugar'. Each of its molecules consists of two single sugar molecules joined together: one of dextrose and one of fructose. The chemical name is **sucrose.** Refined white sugar is 99% pure sucrose. Other disaccharides are **maltose,** found in malt extract and consisting of two molecules of dextrose; and **lactose** or milk sugar, found in milk and made up of one dextrose and one galactose molecule.

Not all sugars taste equally sweet. Pure fructose is almost one and three-quarters times as sweet as ordinary sucrose;

dextrose only three-quarters as sweet as sucrose; maltose one-third; and lactose one-sixth. Other sugars may be even less sweet and some actually taste bitter. But all the common sugars have the same food value. An ounce of any pure sugar yields 112 calories.

Differences in sweeteners result from the differences in arrangements of atoms, from which other consequences can flow. The atoms of natural sugars are all laid out in an asymmetrical manner, having a right-handed spiral twist. They are known as D or dextro (right) sugars as opposed to L or laevo (left) sugars. L sugars do not commonly occur in nature, since their shape makes them useless to plants and animals, and they pass straight through the digestive system unchanged, with a food value of nil. They can, however, be made in the laboratory by a difficult, expensive chemical process. This could turn out to be more than an academic exercise, since researchers have discovered that some L sugars taste sweet. If the new skills of genetic engineering can be used to breed bacteria or produce enzymes that will manufacture L sugars in quantity, the ideal sweetener is in prospect: something which is just like normal sugar but has no calories.

Incidentally, although dextrose is a D or dextro sugar, this is not the reason for its name. It was called dextrose to contrast it with laevulose (the alternative name for fructose). Nor should it be supposed that laevulose is an L or laevo sugar. It too is a D sugar. The explanation is that, quite apart from the L and D classification described above, sugars have been classified as 'right' and 'left' according to the direction in which a beam of polarized light is twisted when it is passed through a solution of each. This helps in the chemical analysis of sugar.

NATURAL SOURCES OF SUGAR

A wide variety of plants have been exploited for the sugar they contain. These may be present in stems or tubers where they function as a food store for the plant. Sugar is also formed in seeds when they germinate, to provide food for the young plant. Seeds are deliberately germinated to make MALT.

One of the first sources of sugar to be exploited was HONEY. This comes indirectly from plants, by courtesy of the bees. Having extracted the sugary nectar from flowers, bees use enzymes in their saliva to split the sucrose into dextrose and fructose. Fructose is the most abundant sugar in honey, which is therefore considerably sweeter than a sucrose syrup of the same concentration. However, because it is an impure and variable food containing other flavourings, subjective assessment of its sweetness varies greatly. Some of the best and most flavourful honeys seem less sweet than plain sucrose.

Various kinds of MANNA containing sugars have been used since ancient times for sweetening purposes.

Other sweet-tasting substances

IN addition to the true sugars, such as those mentioned above, there are many sugar-like and sweet-tasting substances. Some, although closely resembling sugars, are technically alcohols, such as mannitol (present in some kinds of MANNA); glycerol, the source of the sweet taste of glycerine; and sorbitol, used to sweeten diabetic confectionery. Any sweet taste in a natural food is almost invariably due to a sugar or sugar-like substance, apart from a few oddities such as the miracle berry (see SWEETENERS, both for this and for artificial sweeteners, which are quite a different matter).

Another ancient sweetener which is still prepared in the Levant is DIBS, a syrup made by boiling down raisins, sweet grapes, or locust beans.

In the Indian subcontinent and in SE Asia a crude, dark PALM SUGAR called **jaggery** or gur is used.

However, sugar cane has become much more important than any of the ancient sources of sugar. A plant native to E. or S. Asia, it too has been exploited for millennia. At first it was used whole or only partly refined into a crude product, practices which still survive in Asia. But methods of refining have been developed which now make it possible to extract 99% pure sucrose from sugar cane. The many forms which it takes in commerce are described below, while the botany and economic and technological history are in the section headed Sugar cane.

CANE SUGAR

There are many kinds of cane sugar and syrup, differing in their purity and degree of refinement. The least pure is **blackstrap molasses** (from the Dutch word 'stroop', meaning syrup) or black TREACLE, which is a residue from cane refining. Next is 'raw' dark brown sugar. The darkest of ordinary western sugars is Barbados or **muscovado.** (This was originally made in Barbados but may now come from elsewhere. The name muscovado comes from the Spanish *más acabado* (more finished), because it has been separated from the molasses with which it was originally mixed.) The crudest sugar of all brown sugars is known as foot sugar or foots because in early processes it settled at the bottom of the barrel.

There are various partly refined, lighter brown sugars. **Demerara,** originally made in Demerara (Guyana), has relatively hard crystals. However, much modern brown sugar, including 'London Demerara', is made not by partial refining but by adding a little molasses to white sugar. As a result, the taste is relatively feeble. Pieces, yellows, sand, or scotch is a pale, soft, sticky sugar which is a by-product of a late stage of refining.

Light **cane-sugar syrups** are used for cooking in Britain (much as CORN SYRUPS and MAPLE SYRUPS are used in the USA). One such is a medium brown treacle made by partial refining of black treacle. However, the pale yellow GOLDEN SYRUP which emerges from another stage of white sugar production is now more popular. This is technically known as an invert sugar syrup. Inversion is a process by which sugar is heated or treated with acid (or both), to split some or all of the sucrose into dextrose and fructose. These single sugars are much less willing to crystallize than is sucrose, and the syrup will remain liquid for years. The inversion process incidentally gives golden syrup a mild but distinctive flavour.

All partly refined sugar products have special flavours due to residual plant substances from the original cane, or created by the manufacturing process. They are not interchangeable in the kitchen; substituting one for another in a recipe is likely to alter the flavour of the dish.

Fully refined white sugars have virtually no flavour apart from a sweet taste. The difference between them is one of crystal size.

Preserving sugar is the coarsest. The big crystals do not stick together when stirred into a liquid, so they actually dissolve faster than granulated sugar. This reduces the risk of caramelization and burning. Otherwise preserving sugar is exactly the same as any other white sugar.

Granulated sugar has medium-sized crystals, as does lump sugar, which is simply granulated sugar moistened with syrup and pressed into blocks. An American term for this, 'loaf sugar', is a misnomer, since real loaf sugar is the cone-shaped product of an obsolete refining process. It is seldom seen in the West, but occasionally encountered in oriental countries. There is also a Colombian type of loaf sugar called *panela*.

Caster sugar is so named because it is of the right fineness for use in a sugar caster or sprinkler. (The spelling 'castor' is now quite common.) This is the same as 'superfine sugar' in N. America.

Icing sugar or confectioner's or 'powdered' sugar is the finest of all, made by mechanically crushing crystals. A little starch may be added to keep it dry.

Candy sugar is a special type made by growing large crystals in a strong sugar solution which is allowed to evaporate. The crystals are often grown on strings. Coffee sugar, which is naturally white but sometimes artificially coloured, is a candy sugar.

Barley sugar is not made from barley, but from ordinary white sugar. (The name was originally applied to a sweet flavoured with barley water.) To make barley sugar, white sugar is melted without water. At 170 °C (320 °F) it liquefies. It is then allowed to cool and harden, which happens so quickly that it does not manage to form crystals. Instead it sets to a hard substance for which the scientific term is supercooled liquid. (Other common supercooled liquids are ordinary glass and asphalt.) Barley sugar is slightly brown as a result of the formation of CARAMEL.

OTHER SOURCES OF SUGAR

Sugar beet (see below) yields a white sugar which is (to scientists although not to marmalade-makers) indistinguishable from white cane sugar. However, the partly refined products which occur during the refining process have a foul smell, as anyone who has been downwind of a beet sugar refinery will know, and a correspondingly bad taste. Consequently there is no brown beet sugar or beet molasses. The waste products are used for animal feed.

In the USA CORN SYRUP is an important sweetener. This is made by breaking down the long molecules of maize starch into individual sugar molecules.

The N. American maple also produces a syrup (see MAPLE SYRUP), with a delicious flavour. See also BIRCH SUGAR.

The sugar palms are a source of PALM SUGAR, such as the jaggery already mentioned, in regions where they grow. Sugar is made by boiling down the sap. Sweet varieties of sorghum, an important grain, are used to make SORGHUM syrup.

SUGAR AS A FOOD

As a foodstuff, sugar has attracted much criticism. This applies particularly to refined white sugar. Unrefined brown sugar is sometimes portrayed, in contrast, as healthful because of the nutrients which it retains. It is true that people who eat a lot of white sugar tend to have an unhealthy diet, may be obese, and are exposed to the risk of heart disease. This, however, is not the fault of the sugar, which contains no harmful substances; it is the fault of people who eat too much of it. Since sugar provides energy but nothing else (no vitamins, no protein, no essential fatty acids, virtually no minerals) it follows that a diet which is high in sugar will risk being short of necessary nutrients.

Brown sugar contains small traces of protein and common minerals which in a normal diet are freely supplied by other foods. There seems to be no good ground for regarding it as a 'health food'. There is, however, a reason for preferring it to white sugar; it has a more interesting flavour.

See also CONFECTIONERY; JAM; JELLY; PRESERVATION; SUGAR BOILING.

Sugar beet

The second most important source of SUGAR in the world, sugar beets, are certain cultivars of the plant now classified as *Beta vulgaris*, Crassa group. This group also contains the far more numerous cultivars of BEETROOT, the familiar crimson vegetable.

The root of the plant was originally small and disagreeable in flavour, but with a noticeably sweet taste. As early as 1590 the French botanist Olivier de Serres managed to extract a sugar syrup from it. In those days cane sugar was still very expensive, so his discovery might have been exploited, but nothing came of it at the time.

In 1747 the German chemist Marggraf extracted sugar from beet, and observed that the root contained up to 6.3% sugar in dry matter. Again, interest was slight. Later, however, one of Marggraf's students, Karl Franz Achard, was backed by Frederick the Great of Prussia in research which eventually led to the setting up of a small beet sugar refinery in Silesia in 1800.

The Napoleonic wars cut off supplies of cane sugar to France. In 1812, under direct orders from Napoleon, beet was cultivated and refined on a large scale for the first time. After the war, renewed imports of cane caused the industry to collapse, but it was revived and, after various vicissitudes, established itself and grew in France, Germany, and Britain. Much of the sugar eaten in northern countries now comes from beet.

Selective breeding has increased the sugar content of beet to 20% of which almost all is extractable. The modern sugar beet has a large, white root of a broad cone shape.

Only fully refined white sugar can be made from beet. Unlike sugar cane, which yields a range of agreeable semi-refined brown sugars and syrups, beet gives a malodorous crude extract. The smell which emanates from a beet refinery is notoriously disagreeable. Residue from the process is fed to uncomplaining farm animals.

To extract sugar from beets, they are washed, sliced, and boiled in successive changes of water, each stage yielding progressively less sugar. The sugary liquid is then treated successively with lime and carbon dioxide gas. The latter causes the lime to precipitate (solidify) as chalk, physically entangling much of the impurities as it falls out of solution. The chalk is then filtered out, after which the later stages of refining are exactly as for white cane sugar.

It is sometimes said that beet sugar 'is not the same' as cane sugar, for example in making jams and marmalades. Scientists retort that it is precisely the same, meaning that the chemist can detect no difference. However, the fact remains that the two sugars have different origins, and have undergone different initial refining processes. If, then, a difference in their performance is perceptible to ladies with expertise in making jam and marmalade, this should surely not occasion surprise, still less result in the ladies being denounced as ignorant; it should cause the chemists to reflect, humbly, that they are not omniscient in these matters.

Sugar cane

Saccharum officinarum, the source of most of the world's sugar, is the descendant of a now extinct wild plant which probably grew in New Guinea. (A reference is made under PAPUA NEW GUINEA to the consumption there of not only sugar cane but also the enclosed inflorescences of *S. edule*, locally called *pitpit*.)

The sugar cane is a giant grass looking rather like bamboo; but its stems, instead of being hollow, are filled with a sappy pulp. Nearly 90% of the weight of cane is juice, and this juice contains up to 17% sucrose (common sugar) and small amounts of two other sugars, dextrose and fructose. Sugar-cane juice is pleasantly sweet, although lacking in flavour. It is used as a soft drink in sugar-growing countries, and raw cane is chewed as a sweet.

Not surprisingly, cane was cultivated from an early date in many parts of Asia including India and China. The earliest known reference to it is in a love poem in an Indian sacred work, the Atharra-veda, where sugar cane is used as a symbol of sweetness and attractiveness. Herodotus, the Greek historian (5th century BC), knew of the plant, and in

327 BC Alexander the Great sent some back to Europe from India.

The fact that the juice could be boiled down to make solid sugar was discovered in early times. The first surviving account of solid sugar comes from a Persian tablet of 510 BC, which describes it as coming from the Indus Valley. This early product would have resembled the modern Indian raw, dark brown sugar called gur or jaggery.

During the 7th century AD the Persians improved the refining process, introducing the use of lime (see below) and other refining agents. Their product, an almost white loaf sugar, was soon being exported to the West, where hitherto the only sweeteners had been HONEY and occasionally MANNA. The exotic delicacy fetched high prices. Soon sugar cane was being cultivated in many regions to the east and south of the Mediterranean. For a while it was even grown in Spain, and Sicily, too far north for it to thrive. The Venetians set up an import and export trade supplying N. Europe.

Cane cultivation spread westwards to the Canaries and Madeira, and in 1493 Columbus took some plants to the Caribbean. It grew so well in that climate that it soon became the chief crop of the whole region. Mintz (1985), an anthropologist with much Caribbean experience, has written on the production of sugar in the region and, more generally, on the whole ramified process by which sugar was transformed from being a costly spice or condiment into a major foodstuff of the western world.

As cultivation spread and sugar became more plentiful, the price fell. By the beginning of the 19th century white cane sugar was no longer a luxury. During the Napoleonic wars the blockade of France stimulated the introduction of a rival plant, the sugar beet. Throughout the century refining methods for both became more advanced. Cane and beet sugar are now among the cheapest of foods.

A primitive and ancient process is still used to produce 'raw' sugar such as Indian gur or jaggery and Mexican *piloncillo*. The crop is burnt to remove the leaves, and then cut down close to the ground since the bottoms of the stems are richest in sugar. The stems are shredded and crushed in simple ox-driven machinery to press out the juice, which is then concentrated by being boiled in shallow pans. Lime is added to make the proteins in the juice coagulate and collect on their surface other impurities. These form a dirty scum which is skimmed off. Further boiling removes so much water that the sugar begins to crystallize. As it does so it is scooped out and set to drain. The solid crystals are moist, dark brown sugar, tasting strongly of molasses.

The earliest white sugar was made by boiling raw sugar with lime water and bullock's blood. The blood coagulated, absorbing more impurities and in doing so removing most of the brown colour. The scum was repeatedly skimmed off and the partly purified liquid filtered, boiled to concentrate it, and poured into conical moulds to crystallize and solidify. The conical loaves were then broken up, redissolved and repurified, this time with egg white. Finally, the 'double refined' sugar was reformed into conical loaves, and sold thus. Before use, the loaf sugar had to be smashed up with hammers, an exhausting process. The first kinds of lump sugar (which is still called loaf sugar in the USA) were made by sawing up loaves.

Modern sugar production is in its early stages a mechanized version of the primitive process. The cane may be harvested mechanically. The stems are smashed in hammer mills and the juice washed out in a diffuser, where hot juice is constantly circulated through the shredded cane. Heating with lime follows, and the partly purified liquid is evaporated in a series of vacuum pans. (The use of a partial vacuum makes it boil at a lower temperature, saving energy.) The concentrated juice is encouraged to crystallize by 'seeding' it with 'magma', a mixture of crystal and syrup. The result, known as 'massecuite', is a thick sludge of sugar and syrup. It is centrifuged to extract the syrup, which is dark blackstrap molasses and useful in its own right as a foodstuff, and for making rum, industrial alcohol, and citric acid.

The raw sugar is then purged of the last traces of molasses by washing it with clean syrup and centrifuging it again. It is mixed with hot water and partly decolorized with phosphoric acid, then neutralized with lime and further heated to coagulate a few remaining impurities. The liquid is again filtered, then run through beds of charcoal which absorb the last traces of colour. After a final filtration it is vacuum evaporated, 'seeded' with fondant sugar (whose tiny crystals make effective starters for crystal growth), centrifuged, and dried with hot air.   RH

SUGAR ALMONDS almonds coated with a layer of fine sugar, as for DRAGÉES. The sugar is often coloured, traditionally with pastels such as pink, blue, yellow, and mauve. Sometimes metallic coatings are applied, e.g. in the form of leaf silver. Sugar almonds with marbled exteriors are local specialities in several parts of France; they are called *cailloux de gave* or 'river pebbles'.

Sugar almonds play an important part in rites of passage, particularly christenings and weddings, at which they are offered as symbols of good fortune. This custom is strong in France, Greece, Italy, other Mediterranean countries, and as far east as Iran and Afghanistan where they are known as *noql*. Margaret Shaida (1992) explains that in Iran it is usual to coat slivers of almond with sugar, flavoured with rosewater, and that these are served at all festive occasions. As a New Year offering they are supposed to ensure that the mouths and lives of the recipients will remain sweet for the whole of the coming year.

Less sophisticated versions of almond dragées are sometimes made at home by cooking almonds, or other nuts, such as hazel, in sugar syrup and then stirring the mixture till it 'grains'. The almonds, with some of the sugar clinging to them, are separated and dried. Many 17th- and 18th-century PRALINE recipes are of this type. Such confections are still sold by street vendors in southern Spain as *almendras garrapiñadas*.   (LM)

SUGAR-APPLE the English name used in the W. Indies and America for the fruit of *Annona squamosa*, a small tree native to tropical America but now distributed in tropical regions around the world. It is also called sweet sop (in contrast to the SOUR SOP). The British in India called it CUSTARD APPLE, and it is also known more precisely as the 'scaly custard apple' (the scales which cover the greenish-yellow skin, under a whitish bloom, are also indicated by the specific name *squamosa*). The sugar-apple is grown elsewhere (e.g. SE Asia, Queensland, Réunion), but enjoys greatest popularity in Latin America, the W. Indies, and India. Its range in America extends from Mexico and the W. Indies down to parts of Brazil.

Sugar-apple

At Bahia in Brazil, where it is said to have been first introduced by the Conde de Miranda, it is called *fruta do conde do mato* (fruit of the woodland Count—but the related BIRIBA has a superior name, being called 'fruit of the Countess'). A Spanish author of the 17th century wrote of it:

The pulp is very white, tender, delicate, and so delicious that it unites to agreeable sweetness a most delightful fragrance like rose water and if presented to one unacquainted with it he would certainly take it for a blanc-mange.

The pulp may indeed be white, but is commonly creamy-white or yellowish, which helps to account for the first part of the name 'custard apple' (the latter part is only explicable on the assumption that the use of a single word in ancient times to mean both 'fruit' and 'apple' lingered on until recent times). The pulp is divided into numerous distinct segments, many of which may contain a black seed; this is poisonous and is spat out when the fruit is being eaten out of hand.

This is a delicate fruit, liable to come apart when ripe, unless carefully handled. Besides being eaten fresh for dessert, it is used to make SHERBETS and to flavour ICE CREAMS. The pulp ferments easily, so if a purée is made for these purposes (by sieving and thus separating out the seeds) it has to be used without much delay.

SUGAR BOILING is a multi-stage process by which many familiar types of sugar CONFECTIONERY are produced.

The principles of sugar boiling are simple. They depend on the chemical properties of common SUGAR (sucrose), when it is dissolved in water, to produce a syrup, and heated. Heating drives off some of the water, thus increasing the concentration and the temperature of the solution. Arresting this process at different temperatures and then cooling the mixture produces different textures. Texture and appearance can be further altered by the use of additional ingredients, and by the treatment of the mixture during cooling.

Since the late 19th century, specially designed THERMOMETERS have been used for measuring the temperatures of boiling sugar solutions, allowing accurate results. Modern sugar boilers and confectionery manufacturers also have the benefit of chemically pure ingredients. An older system for recognizing different sugar concentrations, relying on skill, observation, and experience, is still frequently quoted in manuals of home confectionery recipes. This gives the temperatures and terms for the stages of sugar boiling shown in the table; the associated confections are given in the third column.

Temperature	Term	Confections
106–13 °C (223–36 °F)	thread	
112–16 °C (234–40 °F)	soft ball	FONDANT, FUDGE
118–21 °C (244–50 °F)	firm ball	soft CARAMELS, TOFFEE
121–30 °C (250–66 °F)	hard ball	hard CARAMELS, TOFFEE, MARSHMALLOW, EDINBURGH rock
132–43 °C (270–90 °F)	soft crack	BUTTERSCOTCH, HUMBUGS, NOUGAT, BULLSEYES, seaside ROCK
149–54 °C (300–10 °F)	hard crack	BARLEY SUGAR, acid DROPS
160–77 °C (320–50 °F)	caramel	nut BRITTLE, PRALINE

For each stage there is a method of determining the state of the solution by observation. Before testing, the pan of hot sugar solution is taken from the heat and cooled by dipping the base in cold water. This prevents the mixture from boiling to a higher stage.

At the thread stage, a little syrup dropped from a spoon, or stretched between finger and thumb, will form a short, fine thread. The next five stages are all tested for by dropping a little syrup into iced water. At the soft ball stage, the syrup will form a ball

under water, but lose shape immediately in the air. At the firm ball stage the syrup will be firm but pliable; it will still lose shape fairly quickly at room temperature. When the syrup has reached the hard ball stage, it will mould easily into a ball; when removed from the water it will hold its shape and feel resistant to pressure. At each of these three stages, the syrup will feel quite sticky.

The next stage is known as soft crack. Some syrup is dropped into iced water, and then stretched gently between the hands. It should separate into hard but elastic strands, and only feel slightly sticky. At the hard crack stage, the syrup is removed from the water and bent. It should snap easily, have a yellowish tinge, and no longer feel sticky.

The final stage is caramel. This is determined by dropping a little syrup onto a white plate and observing the colour. A light caramel is a gold, honey colour; a dark caramel is a reddish amber. If the solution cooks beyond this point, it burns, turns black, and is useless.

Cooks and confectioners have known for centuries that sugar solutions boiled to 'heights' or 'degrees' or 'stages' have variable properties. It is possible that some of this knowledge arrived in Europe with sugar itself, during the Arab invasions of the 7th and 8th centuries AD. How much was known at that time about the properties of sugar is not clear; but the word 'CANDY' derives from Sanskrit *khanda* via Arabic *qand*. By the late 14th century references to penides, a barley-sugar type confection, show that some knowledge of sugar boiling existed in England. By the early 17th century, some of this specialized knowledge was given in cookery books and confectionery manuals.

Common terms from English 17th-century books are thin syrup; thick syrup; MANUS CHRISTI height; sugar boiled to sugar again; candy height, and casting height.

Manus christi, as a sugar boiling term, seems to have meant an approximation to the thread stage; and is only used in this sense in books from early in the century. The other 'heights' of boiling sugar continued in use in cookery books well into the 18th century, by which time it had been joined by a system of French origin.

The French author Massialot gave six terms which, in the 1702 English translation of his *Le Cuisinier royal et bourgeois*, appeared as: smooth, pearled, blown, feathered, cracked, and caramel. As Nott (1726) observed, each of the six degrees could be divided into the lesser and the greater, making twelve in all.

These terms, subject to minor variations, gradually came into general use and remained current through the 19th century. They look as though they more or less match modern terms, but the apparent resemblance conceals differences in practice.

'Caramel' in 18th- and 19th-century usage corresponded to what would now be considered the hard crack stage; it was then thought that sugar which was cooked until the colour changed to gold or amber was burnt and spoilt. Generally, confectioners of the past seem to have favoured caution, and sugar was not usually boiled to high temperatures. Most of the degrees formerly recognized appear to have been temperatures which would now be classified as thread or ball. Cooking beyond this stage would have been tricky when using heat sources such as open fires, controlled with difficulty. The soft ball stage is also the concentration at which a poorly managed sugar solution will show signs of recrystallizing whilst hot. This must have been a problem when the scientific principles behind sugar boiling were unknown, and may be the origin of the 17th-century expression 'sugar boiled to sugar again'.

Confectionery was expensive in the 17th and 18th centuries not only because sugar cost a lot but also because of the experience and skill which sugar boilers needed. Many sweetmeats which seem different in appearance and texture begin with the same process of concentrating sugar solutions over heat; but thereafter techniques for adding to and manipulating the sugar become crucial. Recipes which evolved by trial and error can now be shown to have embodied subtle control over the sugar as it cools. This retrospective understanding calls for modern knowledge of the physics and chemistry of sugar.

In chemical terms, common sugar (sucrose) is a substance which is crystalline, with an orderly structure of molecules forming a characteristic shape. This can clearly be seen in granulated sugar; each 'granule' takes the form of a cube.

Provided the proportion of sugar to water is suitable, sugar will dissolve completely in water at room temperature; once in solution, the sugar molecules move about freely (as do the molecules in sugar which has been rendered liquid by the application of heat). A solution which holds as much dissolved sugar as it can is said to be saturated.

Applying energy in the form of heat to a sugar solution allows more sugar to be dissolved in it; such a syrup, which is saturated at the higher temperature, is said, when cooled quickly, to be a 'supersaturated' solution. The amount of sugar in a solution also affects the boiling point. The more sugar there is in a solution, the higher the boiling point will be.

If a hot saturated sugar solution is allowed to cool slowly, the sugar comes out of solution and crystallizes on the bottom of the container. (This is how ordinary

crystalline sugar is solidified at the end of the hot refining process.) If the solution is cooled so quickly that it has no chance to crystallize, it forms a supercooled liquid. There is no fixed proportion of water in such a liquid. If there is only a slight excess of sugar over the normal saturation level, the supercooled liquid is a thin syrup. With increasing sugar concentration the syrup becomes thicker, then a sticky, flexible semi-solid, then a hard glass. Because cooling is fast, the sugar retains the disorderly molecular structure of a liquid.

The formation of a supercooled liquid sugar is encouraged by a process known as 'inversion' which takes place when sucrose is heated. As it boils, sugar syrup loses water; it gradually departs from the nature of a sugar in water solution and approaches that of melted sugar. Pure sucrose has a melting point between 160 °C and 186 °C (320 °–368 °F); but, due to the phenomenon of inversion, it is impossible to have pure molten sucrose. This is because during the heating process the sucrose breaks down ('inverts') to simple sugars: dextrose (melting point 146 °C, 293 °F) and fructose (melting point 102–104 °C, 216–219 °F). No matter how fast syrup is heated there will be some degree of breakdown. This phenomenon helps to prevent the boiled sugar recrystallizing. This is because the molecules of sucrose, fructose, and dextrose are different sizes, thereby 'interfering' with the formation of an orderly crystalline structure.

To encourage the breakdown of sucrose, a proportion of dextrose (glucose) is often included in modern commercial confectionery recipes. Acids, either in the form of tartaric acid (in CREAM OF TARTAR), or those naturally occurring in fruit are also used to aid inversion. (The interaction between sugar and fruit acids is also integral to the process of JAM- and JELLY-making).

In their simplest forms, boiled sugar sweets consist of sugar syrup boiled to the hard crack stage with the addition of substances to give flavour and colour, and to encourage inversion. The result is poured onto a cold surface and shaped. BARLEY SUGAR and acid DROPS are examples of this type of sweet.

Similar mixtures are used to make PULLED CANDY. The syrup is boiled to the soft crack stage and poured onto a cold surface. It is worked intensively, first with a scraper whilst still hot, and then by twisting and stretching it by hand or machine as it cools. Pulling is a process which requires some care to prevent the syrup recrystallizing; adding dextrose to the recipe is one precaution. As the syrup is worked, some air is incorporated into the mixture, giving it a distinctive satiny sheen Two colours of mixture may be worked together to give a striped or marbled effect.

Favourite sweets of past times, such as HUMBUGS and BULLSEYES, are produced this way.

A syrup boiled to the hard ball stage, pulled, and left to mature uncovered will start to recrystallize: this phenomenon is exploited in the making of Edinburgh ROCK, which has a distinctive, friable texture.

Various sweets are made by adding dairy products such as milk, cream, or butter to syrups. These form emulsions with the sugar and help to prevent recrystallization of the mixture when this is not desired. The hardness of the result is dictated by the stage to which the sugar is boiled; this ranges from firm ball to soft crack, giving progressively harder results. BUTTERSCOTCH is one type; others are known as different forms of TOFFEE. Also in this group are a type of toffee known as CARAMELS. These should not be confused with sugar boiled to 160 °C/320 °F; they gain their distinctive flavour from long cooking, and reactions between proteins and sugars in the mixture.

In some sweets, controlled crystallization is encouraged. The simplest example is FONDANT: this is a sugar and dextrose syrup boiled to the soft ball stage and poured onto a cold surface. Then the mixture is worked, gently at first, and then more vigorously. The object of this process is to allow the formation of small, even, sugar crystals in a supersaturated syrup. FUDGE is based on the same principle; the syrup is enriched with dairy products and flavourings, and beaten either hot or cool depending on the desired texture.   (LM)

SUGAR CANDY sugar in crystalline lumps deposited from a sugar solution. Formerly, when sugar was an expensive rarity, this was of great importance in the European kitchen and was regarded as a sweetmeat in its own right. A shortened version of the term has given the word CANDY, used in N. America to indicate sweets in general.

Both the etymology of the term 'sugar candy' and the methods given in early recipes for making it indicate an ancient origin. 'Sugar candy' can be traced back through Persian *qand* to Sanskrit *khanda*, meaning sugar in pieces. The fact that the word has such an ancient derivation shows just what a desirable and uncommon item sugar candy was as it travelled from culture to culture.

The method for making sugar candy given in early confectionery manuals required sugar syrup of a specified strength to be poured into earthenware jars with an arrangement of sticks or strings inside. Sometimes the syrup was coloured, or flowers were added. The jars were kept hot for some days, then drained of excess syrup and broken to extract the lumps of candy, which had crystallized around the sticks. This process seems arcane to the modern reader, but demonstrated an instinctive grasp of sugar chemistry, based on practical knowledge gained from centuries of trial and error. In Britain, this basic method was used into the 19th century.

The verb 'to candy' today indicates a method of preservation using sugar syrup; CANDIED FRUIT, MARRONS GLACÉS, candied GINGER, and candied ANGELICA all use this process.   LM

SUGAR PASTE a mixture of icing SUGAR, water, and GUM TRAGACANTH made into a malleable paste. Glycerine, GELATIN, and liquid glucose are sometimes added as well, for a more robust mixture. The paste can be rolled, shaped, coloured, and painted as the user's imagination dictates, and then allowed to set and dry, giving edible ornaments that will keep indefinitely, provided they do not get damp. Paste-type mixtures are also used for making sweets, especially mints. Variations on sugar paste, more or less inedible, include starch or plaster of Paris amongst their ingredients, and are intended purely for decoration.

In the modern kitchen, sugar paste has been reduced to a minor role as a medium for decorating celebration cakes. It is rolled into a sheet to cover the cake itself, and made into flowers and figures. Modern cake decorators value sugar paste for its clothlike qualities, and the way it can be draped, frilled, and worked to resemble embroidery. The relative ease with which sugar paste can be worked has made it a rival to royal ICING, which requires more practice and technical skill if it is to produce good effects.

This usage gives little clue to the historical importance of sugar paste as a sculptural medium for executing elaborate culinary fantasies. Sugar paste has long been valued by confectioners for the plastic qualities it displays, and the hard porcelain-like manner in which it sets. However, the date at which sugar paste first made an appearance in the repertoire of the confectioner is unknown. Primitive versions may have been employed in making medieval SUBTLETIES, elaborate and partially edible sculptures used in feasts. Recipes for *pastillage*, made from sugar and water-softened gum tragacanth, appear in the earliest French confectionery manuals, published by the quack doctors and alchemists Alexis of Piedmont and Michel de Nostradamus in 1555.

From then on, through the 16th and 17th centuries, sugar paste was a favourite device of confectioners for decorating the banquet table. It could be pressed into dishes and allowed to dry, and then unmoulded to give edible crockery, thinner and whiter than any products of the 17th-century European potters. It could be modelled and moulded to imitate fruits, or shaped into birds and animals. Sheets of paste were pressed into two halves of moulds, filled with COMFITS, and stuck together, to provide a surprise for the diners. Little scraps of paste were perfumed to make 'kissing comfits' to sweeten the breath, or cut into LOZENGES.

Throughout the 18th century, sugar paste enjoyed a vogue as a medium for making decorations from simple flowers to magnificent and costly sculptures for the dining tables of the rich. These were often designed to make flattering references to the abilities or interests of the guests. Jarrin (1827) described how, whilst working in Paris, he had made a group, 2' (60 cm) in height, of Napoleon 'led by Victory, attended by several allegorical figures, which were intended to express the various high qualities so liberally attributed to Napoleon by the French so long as success attended him'.

Sculpting in sugar paste was evidently a declining art in the early 19th century, for Jarrin complained that the technique had fallen into disuse and that residual fragments of the art had been transferred to the pastry-cooks. This state of affairs was shortly to be remedied by the great Antonin CARÊME, a chef whose influence extended far beyond his native France, and who is said to have remarked that 'The fine arts are five in number: music, painting, sculpture, poetry and architecture—whereof the principal branch is confectionery.' His interest in the 'architectural' possibilities offered by sugar paste established a lasting fashion for immense sculptural table decorations, ranging from a simple cornucopia to models of famous cathedrals. 'To the artistic confectioner Gum Paste has much the same meaning as clay and marble combined have to the sculptor,' gushed Garrett (c.1895). Sugar paste was augmented with pulled boiled sugar; ice, lard, and butter also provided materials for the cook-sculptor. This fashion for elaborate table decorations lasted until the demise of haute cuisine in the 1930s.

Confectioners continued to make paste sweets, initially using paste rolled into sheets and cut, later developing machinery for making 'compressed tablets' using paste mixtures. Some of these, such as medicinal lozenges and scented CACHOUS, have declined in popularity in the 20th century; but others, such as MINTS and SHERBET, are still consumed enthusiastically.

SULPHUR SHELF and chicken of the woods are the oddly contrasting popular names of a 'bracket fungus', *Laetiporus sulphureus*, which is found in Europe and N. America. It is a large, amorphous growth, yellow or orange, fluted on the upper side and with yellow pores underneath. It grows on dead stumps or logs, and sometimes on living trees (which it affects with a kind of heart rot) in late summer and autumn. Favoured hosts are eucalyptus and Douglas fir.

This fungus is popular in N. America but only in some European countries, notably Germany and to a limited extent France. Only the tender outer portions (soft to the touch) of young specimens should be harvested (they grow back, so further harvesting is possible). The taste is faintly acid. Texture has often been compared to that of chicken breast, but Arora (1979) draws a comparison between cooked sulphur shelf and tofu, and especially recommends sulphur shelf for use in omelettes. He judges specimens from eucalyptus to be the best.

SUMAC the name of certain shrubs in the genus *Rhus*, of which various species grow wild in the warmer regions of the northern hemisphere. The species used in Middle Eastern cookery is *Rhus coriaria*, Sicilian or elm-leafed sumac. Its hairy 'berries' (so called, but not true berries) are dark red to purple when ripe. The spice sumac is made from the dried, powdered berries.

The acid fruits are used as a sour flavouring. They were so used in classical Rome, before the introduction of the lemon; and their modern use in the Middle East is most noticeable in areas where lemons are rare, for instance the remoter parts of Syria and N. Iraq.

In medieval Arabic cookbooks, sumac entered into cooked dishes such as *Fakhtiyyah* (which gets its name from the Persian word for ring-dove, presumably because of the pale purple shade produced by the combination of sumac and yoghurt).

As a spice, sumac is sprinkled on KEBAB and PILAF in Iran, Iraq, and Turkey. In Iran, for example, a bowl of it is always served with *Chelo kebab*, to be sprinkled on the meat and/or the rice. See ZAATAR for the mixture of sumac and wild THYME which is sprinkled on fried eggs in the Middle East.

Sumac berries are also used in N. Africa, India, and the Orient. They are sold in dried form, either whole or powdered. Whole dried berries can be soaked in water to produce a sour refreshing drink.

Species of sumac in N. America include several which were used by Indians, and then by white settlers, to make drinks with a resemblance to lemonade; hence names like lemonade berry or lemonade sumac.

(CP)

SUMMER PUDDING a favourite English dessert which combines a mixture of summer fruits with bread. Redcurrants (see CURRANTS) and RASPBERRIES are the best fruits to use, but some varieties of GOOSEBERRY are suitable, and a small quantity of blackcurrants and a very few STRAWBERRIES may be included. In autumn, BLACKBERRIES can be substituted. In other countries, corresponding kinds of berry will do very well. In any case the fruit is lightly cooked with sugar.

The pudding is made by lining a buttered basin with fairly thin slices of good bread cut to fit exactly. The fruit and juice are then spooned in, and more bread placed over the top. The assemblage is then pressed down by a weight and left to stand overnight or longer. To serve, it is turned out, upside down. It is usually accompanied by cream.

In the 19th century this pudding seems to have been known as 'hydropathic pudding' because it was served at health resorts where pastry was forbidden. This name must have begun to seem unattractive or inappropriate early in the 20th century, when the new name summer pudding, which is now universally used, began to appear in print. Until recently it was thought that the earliest recorded use was by Florence Petty (1917) who, on the title page of her attractive book, styled herself 'The Pudding Lady' (and drew attention also to her qualifications as a Sanitary Inspector and a Horticulturist). However, it has now been established that a missionary in India, Miss E. S. Poynter (1904), had used the term much earlier, in her book; and that soon afterwards Miss L. Sykes (c.1912) used it as the title of a recipe which was even closer than Miss Poynter's to those now in use.

SUMMER SQUASH a name used for those kinds of SQUASH, mostly of the species *Cucurbita pepo*, which are eaten fresh in season, when they are immature and the skin is still soft, as opposed to WINTER SQUASH (mostly of the species *C. maxima*) which can be stored and whose skin hardens during storage.

The distinction is not always useful, since some *C. pepo* varieties, e.g. the Crookneck group, store well, while winter squash can be good eaten fresh. Nor is there a clear botanical distinction; there are some varieties of *C. pepo*, e.g. Acorn, which are mostly used as winter squashes, although if harvested when young they can be eaten as summer squashes.

Summer squashes tend to be watery, and care must be taken not to overcook them.

Some of the prettier varieties of summer squash, such as the Yellow Custard Squash, with its flat, scalloped shape, are among the numerous cultivars which can be dried and used for decoration. Sunburst, the first hybrid yellow scallop squash, is very attractive with creamy flesh of delicate flavour, and looks especially good when picked at the 'baby' stage with blossom still attached.

See also ZUCCHINI and VEGETABLE MARROW, both of which fall into the summer squash group.

SUNFLOWER *Helianthus annuus*, an annual plant of the daisy (Compositae) family, grown mainly for the valuable oil obtained from the seeds. These typically contain 35–45% by weight of oil; they are also a popular and nutritious snack food, raw or roasted and salted.

The sunflower is remarkable for its height (up to 3.5 m/12') and the size of its flower heads (the record is a diameter of 75 cm/30"). A flower head may contain several hundred (or even up to 2,000) seeds. The name sunflower (and the generic name *Helianthus*, which means the same) is probably derived from the resemblance of the yellow flower head to the sun; but it may have to do with the plant's habit of keeping its maturing flower head turned towards the sun, so that it faces east at dawn and west at dusk. The French name *tournesol* suggests this, as do the Italian, Spanish, and Chinese names.

The plant thrives in a sunny temperate climate, and withstands a wide range of temperatures. It is native to N. America, where several species are still common in the wild. *H. annuus* had been taken into cultivation, and the higher-yielding type with a single flower had been developed, long before Europeans arrived. The native Indians dried or roasted the seeds, then milled them into a meal which could be made into cakes or added to soup. They also extracted oil from the seeds by boiling them.

When the sunflower was introduced to Europe in the 16th century, at first to Spain, it was treated as an ornamental plant. However, in the early 18th century Peter the Great took it to Russia, where a chance circumstance caused it to become an important food plant. The Church banned the eating of oily plants on fast days, but the sunflower, being a recent introduction, was not on the list drawn up by the clerics. The laity, who were sharper eyed, took to chewing the seeds—raw, roasted, or salted—and, later, to extracting oil from them (a practice first essayed in Bavaria in the 1720s). Russia subsequently became the largest grower of sunflowers. In Europe, Romania and Poland also grow large amounts, as do Yugoslavia and Turkey.

Cultivation was started in Argentina in 1870, and greatly increased in the 1930s, when the Spanish Civil War made Spanish olive oil unobtainable. Argentina later became the second largest producer, overtaking the USA.

Most cultivation in N. America is carried out in the north of the Great Plains region, e.g. in Minnesota, the Dakotas, and neighbouring Manitoba in Canada. Since sunflower oil is high in polyunsaturated fatty acids (linoleic, oleic), the American sunflower industry received a boost in the 1970s when the movement towards polyunsaturated cooking oils gathered momentum. 'Sunoil', as it is known, also benefits from having no cholesterol.

Special varieties of sunflower have been bred to produce maximum yields of oil. It is the principal cooking oil in Russia; much used in E. Europe; and ranks about sixth as a cooking oil in India.

The seeds have a pleasant, slightly sweet taste. Besides constituting a snack food, highly nutritious and particularly well liked by Russians, they are used extensively in confectionery.

READING: Heiser (1976).

SUNSET SHELLS or sunset clams, are edible BIVALVES of the genera *Gari*, *Macoma*, and *Soletellina*, whose shells are tinged or rayed with sunset colours. They occur around the world, and are gathered for food in many places, but it seems to be only in the Philippines that they arouse real enthusiasm. *Soletellina* spp are there known as *paros* or *parosparosan*, and are highly valued, being steamed or parboiled in the shell to produce an excellent broth.

SUPRÊME as in *suprême de volaille*, a French culinary term applied especially to the breast, often with wing attached but boned, of a chicken (or game bird such as partridge); and, by extension, to a choice fillet of meat or fish. A suprême can be breadcrumbed and fried, but is most commonly met in 'white' form, poached and covered with a white sauce.

A vast range of French menu terminology (see À LA) may be used to indicate precisely how a suprême is prepared and served.

SURAM *Amorphophallus paeoniifolius* (formerly *campanulatus*), also known as elephant's foot yam (because the large rhizome is thought to resemble an elephant's foot) or telinga potato, is a root crop related to TARO in the arum lily family. Of the numerous species in the genus only two are cultivated: suram itself, mainly in India, but also in SE Asia; and *konjak*, *A. rivieri* (see KONNYAKU), mainly in Japan.

A curious feature of the scores of species in this genus is the highly disagreeable smell of the inflorescence, like that of rotting meat. This attracts flies, which pollinate it. The 'amorphous phallus' of the generic name, a horrifying concept, is justified by the crumpled, shapeless form of the spadix which projects from the inflorescence. (The spadix can be of awesome size; one inedible species found in Sumatra has a spadix 2 m/6' long.)

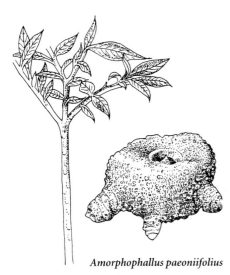

Amorphophallus paeoniifolius

Suram tubers, which have the advantage of keeping well, are eaten in India. Achaya (1994), who gives the name as suran rather than suram, mentions that one of these huge tubers can weigh as much as 10 kg (22 lb). Those found growing wild are acrid in flavour, containing needle-crystals of calcium oxalate, and are only edible (if at all) after tedious treatment. Cultivated varieties, whose flesh may be white or pink, are free of this problem and may be sliced and boiled or baked without special prior processing. They are, however, often pickled. Uses are also found for young shoots and leaves, e.g. in curry-type dishes in Thailand.

SURF CLAM *Spisula solidissima*, an edible species of great commercial importance in the USA, where it accounts for almost three-quarters of the CLAM harvest. It is a large clam, measuring up to 16 cm (6") across. It may also be called bar/hen/sea clam. It takes the names surf and bar clam from the circumstance that early settlers found it in the surf or on bars; but its habitat is in deeper waters, whence the apter name sea clam. It is especially abundant off the coast of New Jersey. South of Cape Hatteras, it is replaced by the smaller *S. raveneli*; and in Canadian waters by *S. polynyma*, which has a purplish foot which turns red in cooking and is accounted superior.

Surf clams are usually shucked raw and minced for use in clam CHOWDERS. The large foot is tough, but the twin adductor muscles, which are white and cylindrical, located just below the apex of the shell, are delicious morsels.

The name surf clam has also been used, in works written in English, for some Asian species which are found in the surf. The name has been happily applied to *Mactra mera*, which belongs to the same family as *Spisula* and is esteemed in the Philippines. This species has also been called trough-shell, and there is a Chinese tradition that intoxicated persons will revive if they eat them.

SURTOUT a term current in 18th-century recipe books, often meant a tureen; but it could also mean 'covered all over', as in 'Pigeons surtout' which were PIGEONS covered with slices of veal and breadcrumbs.

SUSHI perhaps the best known internationally of all Japanese specialities, consists essentially of 'fingers' of vinegared RICE with pieces of very fresh fish or other seafood laid along them, served with thin slices of vinegared GINGER (*gari*) and hot green tea. However, in this, the best-known form and the one which belongs to Tokyo, sushi is really an abbreviation for *nigiri-zushi*, the full name. There are other sorts of sushi, with names indicating whether the product is, for example, pressed in a mould, wrapped in a piece of toasted NORI seaweed, or even just a formless bed of vinegared rice with pieces of seafood scattered on top. This last item calls for no special skill, but the art of making *nigiri-zushi* is deceptively difficult and calls for a long apprenticeship.

Most of the popular seafoods may be used, provided that they are exquisitely fresh, but there are some, such as oysters, which do not 'work' in this combination.

SUSSEX POND PUDDING is so named because it has a large amount of butter in the middle which melts when the pudding is boiled, and soaks into the mixture. The original form of the pudding, as described in Ellis (1750), was made from flour, milk, eggs, and a little butter, so that it was a predecessor of the 19th-century SPONGE PUDDING. More butter entered the mixture as the 'pond' melted. It was not sweetened, and was eaten either with meat or by itself.

Later, a sweetened SUET PUDDING mixture lightened with baking powder became usual, and there was a further curious innovation. A thin-skinned lemon was placed, whole, in the centre of the 'pond'. It could be pricked all over so that the juice seeped out to flavour the mixture; but sometimes it was left unpierced, and exploded when boiled. This type of pudding was called 'lemon bomb'.

A variant made over the county border, Kentish well pudding, contains dried fruit instead.

SUSUMBER *Solanum torvum*, a tropical bush which is related to the AUBERGINE, but bears only small fruits the size of peas, sometimes known as 'pea eggplants' (eggplant being another name for aubergine). There is some cultivation in the W. Indies and in SE Asia, and the fruits have started to appear in N. American oriental markets.

Susumber

The fruits are bitter. They are used in Jamaica, when unripe, to give a puckery flavour to salt dried codfish (akee) or freshwater crayfish, or in soups and stews.

They are eaten in curry-type dishes in Malaysia, for example, again being preferred unripe. They can be added raw to chilli sauces such as the NAM PRIK of Thailand; and they are also pickled.

SWAN a bird which exists in three species in Europe, the most important for present purposes being *Cygnus olor*, the mute swan, which is relatively easy to domesticate. Its size, coloration and graceful appearance when it is swimming are familiar. Less familiar is the idea of eating swans. However, evidence marshalled by Witteveen (1986-7) shows that the practice was widespread in Europe from the 8th century AD until the 17th (and in some places even the 18th) century.

The French naturalist Belon (1555) summarized the general opinion: 'the swan is an exquisite bird and a French delicacy, eaten at public feasts and in the houses of lords.' Young cygnets were apparently the best to eat, especially if fattened with oats, so as to lose their fishy taste. C. Anne Wilson (1973) remarks that they were the costliest of all fowl in the London poultry market of the 14th and 15th centuries. In common with the other 'great birds' (CRANE, HERON, PEACOCK) swans were usually roasted; often served with a well-spiced medieval sauce;

and sometimes served in full display, with feathers arrayed and body gilded. Scully (1995), commenting on the fashion in the latter part of the 14th century for court cooks to present cooked animals in a lifelike pose, looking as though they had not been cooked, explains how the swan, for example, underwent an elaborate skinning procedure before being cooked, and would then be 're-dressed' in its skin and feathers just before being served. This fashion included having the animals (e.g. a boar) breathe fire in front of the guests. 'By soaking cotton in aqua ardens and igniting it at the right moment, the animal could continue for some time to do the impossible while it was paraded on a platter around the dining hall.' Scully rightly comments that it was rather bizarre to apply this technique to a swan, but that this was done by Chiquart, the chief cook at the Savoy court in the early part of the 15th century (whose treatise 'On Cookery' has been edited and translated by Scully, 1986).

One main factor which brought an end to serving swans at banquets was the arrival of the TURKEY, a formidable competitor from the New World which could be reared with less trouble.

SWEDE AND RUTABAGA two names for a root vegetable, *Brassica napus* ssp *rapifera*, which is closely related to but botanically and commercially distinguished from the TURNIP. Swedes differ from turnips in having ridged scars forming concentric rings around their tops. The 'root' is not a true root but the swollen base of the stem, and these marks are leaf scars.

The swede probably originated in C. Europe and reached France and then England in the 17th century. By the late 18th century it had become an important European vegetable crop; and by the beginning of the 19th century it had reached the USA.

Varieties with white flesh exist but the yellow-fleshed sort is the one which is usually marketed. Some kinds have purple outsides. 'Swede' is a general British term for all, whatever the outside colour.

Rutabagas, the name used in the USA, are always yellow, pale inside and darker outside. Yellow varieties become a deeper yellow or orange when cooked, in contrast to most vegetables which lose colour. The word 'rutabaga' is a corruption of the Swedish dialect term *rota bagge*—'red bags', referring to the bulbous shape. Swedes were grown in Sweden very early after their appearance, which explains their name.

In Scotland, swedes prevail over turnips, and are called 'neeps' (a contraction of 'turn-neeps', an early form of 'turnips').

Swedes have a milder taste than turnips. Some people find the taste of young swedes too mild, preferring old, large swedes which are more strongly flavoured. In this condition they are often served mashed. The texture is drier, which again is preferred by those who find turnips watery. Swedes have a good capacity for absorbing fat. One well-known dish in which they have a prominent part is the Scottish neep purry or bashed neeps which are traditionally served with HAGGIS.

SWEDEN the largest of the Nordic countries, has an interesting culinary history, in which native traditions have been overlaid, at least to some extent, by German and French influences. Swedish culinary literature includes one mammoth work, the great *Kok-konsten* (Arts of Cookery) by Hagdahl (1896), which serves as a monument to the French influence. But the charming work of Margareta Nylander (1822) had struck a less pretentious note with great charm, and there is no lack of interesting books in the 20th century; one might instance the *Prinsessornas Kokbok* (1945), so endearing in its homage to the young Swedish princesses of that time (who appear on the cover, be-pearled and set in oval gold frames with crowns on top, but reappear inside coiffed in white for kitchen work); and what is probably the most scientific of all works on fish cookery, *Att koka fisk*, by Gyllensköld (1963).

Among the marine delicacies for which Sweden is famous are *surströmming* (see HERRING) and the dish known as Jansson's temptation, based on what many books call anchovy, but which in Sweden (unless recourse is had to canned anchovy) must be SPRAT. Having tasted this in Stockholm's beautiful Saluhall (covered market), and then gone on to Gothenburg, Davidson (1979) wrote:

Fine though it is, the array of seafood in a Baltic city such as Stockholm would hardly satisfy a Swede from the west coast, accustomed to the greater variety of Atlantic species; and least of all someone from Göteborg (Gothenburg), Sweden's greatest fishing port. This is a sober and delightful city, in which the gentian and calico livery of the trams matches the blue overalls of the porters on the fish quays and the bleached wooden boxes in which they carry the fish; fish so revered that the retail market in which they are purveyed to Göteborgers is built like a church and is indeed called, in the local dialect, the *Feskekörka* or fish church. The atmosphere within, where a gallery overlooks the nave along which shoppers may process, and the merchants stand in stalls like box-pews, is suitably ecclesiastical. Nothing is lacking except organ music and perhaps a few votive candles flickering before whichever is the finest of the day's turbots, turbot being the particular predilection of Göteborgers.

Like the other Nordic countries, Sweden is a great place for CRAYFISH, in season; for the use of the numerous northern berries in preserves, cakes, etc.; for special Christmas dishes (here including *julgrot*, the traditional Christmas rice porridge); for LUTEFISK (especially on Christmas Eve); and of course for the SMÖRGÅSBORD.

When Jane Grigson (1983) visited Stockholm she had a characteristically vivid recollection when faced by the ubiquitous rye crispbread, *knäckebröd*:

I remembered a portrait I had seen of the great Gustav Vasa, the 16th century King of Sweden, dressed all in black with yellow slashes, like a regal insect, who encouraged his subjects to grow rye and make crisp bread. He is the Rye King of the packaged crisp breads sold in Britain.

She would also have enjoyed typically Swedish biscuits, *pepparkakor*, spiced in the Scandinavian way (not with pepper—see GINGER BISCUITS). Besides cinnamon and ginger, CARDAMOM is much used and the simple cardamom biscuits are among the best.

In the north, like neighbouring FINLAND, Sweden has a Lapp region, known for its REINDEER meat.

The Swedish word *husmanskost* means homely fare and strikes one of the keynotes of Swedish food. *Pytt i panna* (bits and pieces) is one of the best European ways of dealing with leftovers: cooked meat and potato diced and turned into a piquant savoury dish with the addition of good salty bacon and onion, topped with fried egg. The popular yellow pea soup (shared with Denmark) is another example. It should not be thought, however, that corresponding keynotes of elegance and sophistication are missing. Nor is the fine balance displayed by Swedish cuisine confined to the capital or expensive restaurants; on the contrary, as a study of various Swedish books on their regional specialities will demonstrate, it is a nationwide phenomenon.

SWEET AND SOUR (or acid), *aigre-doux* in French and *agrodolce* in Italian, a juxtaposition or blending of tastes which has been a feature of many cuisines. Sweetness and sourness are two of what are usually counted as the four primary tastes sensed through the mouth (see TASTE), and therefore operate at a basic level in helping to determine the FLAVOUR of foods. (Of the two other primary tastes: one, saltiness, is used in some cultures in preference to sweetness; the other, bitterness, although sometimes appreciated, is generally disliked and serves as a warning of inedibility.)

The sweet-sour combination has affinities with certain foods: sweet-sour ingredients enhance rich meats, some fish, and vegetables; and relishes based on the combination go well with cheese and pork products.

People everywhere enjoy the naturally occurring sweet-acid balance of ripe fruit, but deliberate production of sweet and sour by combining specific ingredients is more limited. A well-known modern use of sweet and sour is in meat and fish dishes from the Guangdong region of China. SE Asian dishes and Indian food have some sweet-sour items but generally tend towards the sour and salty. Further west, however, the use of sweet-sour combinations reappears in subtle forms in W. Asia, the Middle East, and N. Africa. Here the sharp-sweet qualities of fruits such as apricots, pomegranates, and quinces are exploited in meat dishes. Across the Mediterranean, in Sicily, *agrodolce* dishes employ vinegar and raisins with vegetables (sprinkled with pine nuts for texture), while in mainland Italy sauces based on similar principles are used with game. These may be of very ancient origin: a honey and vinegar sauce, with pine nuts, sultanas, herbs, and spices, was described by APICIUS. Sugar, redcurrant jelly, and sometimes chocolate are now used as sweetening agents in *agrodolce* sauces for meat.

In Scandinavia and C. Europe, sweet-sour combinations are basic to the cookery. To take a few examples: HERRING cures use sugar and vinegar; sweet-sour marinades are used in preparing meat for certain dishes; and red cabbage is cooked with sugar (or apples) and vinegar.

In the field of preserves, sweet (from sugar and fruit, especially dates) and acid (vinegar, lemon, green mango, or tamarind) appear in the chutneys and brown sauces popular in Britain. These are descendants of 17th- and 18th-century attempts to copy Indian sweet-sour preserves of ripe mangoes and other fruit. An earlier British taste for sweet-sour combinations can be glimpsed in sugar, fruit, and VERJUICE mixtures used in meat dishes in medieval times, a use which was then widespread in Europe.

In the recent past, British tastes in Britain, and perhaps elsewhere in the western world, seem to have tended towards sweet or salt dimensions in food, with less emphasis on sour, but this could be just one phase in the swings of a pendulum.   (LM)

SWEETBREADS a butchers' term which covers both the thymus gland and the pancreas of a young animal, usually a calf or lamb (although pig's can also be used). The roundish pancreas, located by the stomach, is larger than the elongated thymus (or throat) gland, and preferred by many. The name thymus comes from a supposed resemblance to the bud of the herb thyme.

All sweetbreads have to be prepared and cooked soon after purchase, since the soft gland tissue deteriorates quickly. Their white colour and delicate texture have conspired to give them a reputation as a food for invalids or convalescents.

Eliza Acton (1855) points out that preparation should always include a good soaking, and blanching them 'to render them firm. If lifted out after they have boiled from five to ten minutes according to their size, and laid immediately into fresh spring water to cool, their colour will be the better preserved.' She goes on to give characteristically precise instructions for stewing them, or slicing them into cutlets which can be egged, breadcrumbed, and fried and (a nice touch, this) served with a sauce poured *under* them. However, she makes clear that, along with brains, gristle (tendons), and ears, sweetbreads are a foodstuff of the second rank and require suitable added flavours if they are not to seem insipid.

The classic way of preparing sweetbreads in France is to cook them in butter and serve with sorrel purée.

SWEET CICELY the perennial herb *Myrrhis odorata*, is native to Europe and is widely cultivated there and in Asia. Both the generic and specific names (from Greek and Latin respectively) refer to the plant's fragrance.

The leaves of sweet cicely, like lacy ferns, are often flecked with white and have slightly downy undersides. They are light green turning purple in the autumn and taste of ANISEED. They can be used in spring salads; and their sweetness can be used to remove sourness from food, particularly fruit, so it is useful to add some when stewing rhubarb or gooseberries.

Fresh leaves can be added to soups, stews, omelettes or salads. Thomas (1992) remarks that the roots were formerly boiled as a vegetable and could be candied like angelica. Drinks and liqueurs, for example Chartreuse, can be flavoured with sweet cicely.

Although sweet cicely is used in many countries for particular purposes, its general use is most apparent in Germany, and in French cuisine where it is often partnered with tarragon.

SWEET CREAM and **SWEET CURD**, used respectively to make sweet cream butter and sweet curd cheese, differ from the more usual type in that they have not been pre-ripened by LACTIC ACID-producing BACTERIA to develop a sour flavour.

Sweet cream butter, rather tasteless compared with the normal kind, is used in preparing some very delicately flavoured baked goods. It is not the same as unsalted butter although it may be unsalted.

Sweet curd cheeses include BRICK, EDAM, GOUDA, MUNSTER, and (in the USA) a variant of Cheddar, rather soft and mild.

SWEETENERS other than SUGAR and substances containing sugar, have become important in the 20th century, especially in the western world, where an addiction to sugar and sweet foods often conflicts with a desire to avoid becoming fat.

Some natural substances have a powerful sweetening effect when present in small amounts. One of these is glycyrrhizin in LIQUORICE. In the actual root, or the black sweetmeat made from it, its sweetness is partly masked by other, bitter compounds.

Several tropical plants contain substances which, when eaten, have the bizarre effect of making everything else taste sweet for some time. The most notable of these is the 'miracle berry', *Synsepalum dulcificum*. Food scientists have not yet succeeded in bringing its active substance, miraculin, under control so that it bestows sweetness in a more selective or restrained way. If they do, it could become important.

The only non-sugar sweetener at present licensed for use in most countries is saccharin, a synthetic substance made from coal tar. It was accidentally discovered in 1879 at Johns Hopkins University by chemists working on the coal tar derivative toluene, one of whom licked his finger and noticed that it tasted sweet. A commercial manufacturing process was developed in 1894. Saccharin is now widely used not only as a sweetener for coffee and tea and for dieters' foods but also in many conventional processed foods and drinks. It is a cheaper means of sweetening these than sugar. Saccharin in pure form is 300 to 500 times as sweet as common white sugar. (This is not a record. Some substances taste up to ten times sweeter still.) It has an unpleasant, bitter aftertaste, although the principal kind used today, sodium saccharin, is better than older kinds in this respect.

Another sweetener which is powerfully effective in small concentrations is aspartame, made by chemical treatment of natural AMINO ACIDS.

Other artificial sweeteners were formerly used, especially cyclamates. These are only thirty times as sweet as sugar, which make them more controllable; have less of an aftertaste; and are resistant to cooking, which saccharin is not. However, they are thought to be potentially carcinogenic, so have been banned since 1969/70 in the USA and many other countries including Britain.

SWEETIES the general name used in Scotland for BOILED SWEETS, TOFFEES, and the like. Scottish people have indulged themselves with sweeties ever since the 15th century, when sugar began to be imported in quantity, and have acquired an international reputation for the quality of their products and also for the interesting names which many of them have. See also TABLET and some of the items described under TOFFEE.

According to Jenny Carter and Janet Rae (1989), the first manufacturing confectioner to set up trade in Edinburgh was an Italian who was given a licence in 1665 to make 'confeits'. When, later, Glasgow became an important centre for sugar-refining, the number of confectioners in that city multiplied. The same two authors continue:

the Sweetie Wives, who made their own confections, were a familiar sight in both the streets and the markets. The Border towns also had women who liked making sweets and some of the most familiar confections originated in that locality in the nineteenth century.

For some reason the Border towns (in Scotland the term 'border' refers to the region north of the border with England) showed particular prowess in making sweeties. One of their most famous products is Hawick balls, which are dark brown peppermint-flavoured boilings, with a hint of cinnamon, once called taffy rock bools. Some of the historical comments by Carter and Rae appear below; while the two following items are furnished with descriptions by Catherine Brown (1981).

- **Hawick balls.** 'Original recipes for the bools have been lost but it is known that two women, Jessie McVittie and Aggie Lamb, introduced the sweet for the first time in their shops in Hawick. Little did they imagine that the bools would become so famous; not only do Hawick Balls allegedly inspire prowess at rugby, a tin of the sweets has also been buried at the South Pole during an Antarctic expedition. . . . Jessie made the Rock Bools in her shop at Drumlanrig Square, Hawick, in the 1850s as well as Black Sticky Taffy and White Peppermint Taffy. It is said she stretched her Rock Bool mixture and hung it on a nail stuck in the wall, where she could keep an eye on it from her shop counter. As the mixture slowly slid to the ground, Jessie carried on with her housework and tended to customers, until such time as the mixture fell close to the floor when she would suddenly get hold of it, give it a twist and a stretch and hang it over the nail again. The method of "pulling" was repeated over and over.'
- **Soor plooms** 'are round, green balls with, as their name suggests, an acid, astringent tang. The plooms are said to commemorate an incident in local history when a band of English marauders were surprised and overcome while eating unripe plums.'

- **Berwick cockles** 'were originally home-made peppermint flavoured, white with pink stripes and shaped like the cockle-shells fished up near Tweedmouth harbour. They are now a commercial product as popular north of the Border as they are south of it. (Berwick-upon-Tweed, in the course of its lively history, has found itself both north and south of the border.)'

Border sweeties include some special kinds of toffee.

- **Jeddart snails** belong to Jedburgh. These are dark brown toffees, mildly peppermint flavoured. The name and shape were given to them by a French prisoner-of-war in Napoleon's day when he is said to have made them for a Jedburgh baker.
- **Moffat toffee** is a unique toffee, hard, amber and gold striped, with an intriguing tang, made in Moffat by a local family who have been making it for generations. Originally a sweetie shop product, it is now factory made with a wide distribution.

Other parts of Scotland have also contributed famous sweeties, for example the following three from the Glasgow region.

- **Cheugh jeans.** In the latter half of the 19th century a local character, known as Ball Allan—The Candy King of Glasgow, made a variety of sweetie known as cheugh jeans. Cheugh means 'chewey' and they were of many different flavours: clove, cinnamon, peppermint, ginger. The chocolate variety was very popular, and it is certainly cheugh.
- **Glasgow toffee** is made with GOLDEN SYRUP, plain chocolate, and vanilla essence.
- **Helensburgh toffee** is a more sophisticated and delicate confection, as befits the pretensions of this leisured and wealthy haven sited at a convenient distance from the industrial centres. More like a fudge than a toffee, it has a rich, creamy flavour and is now one of the most popular home-made sweeties.

Yet other traditional sweeties include:

- **curly-doddies** or curley-murlies, mixed sweets formed on a seed or other foundation such as caraway, clove, or almond, which have a gnarled exterior;
- **curly andra,** a white, coral-like sweet with a coriander seed in the centre. The name is a corruption of curryander, a Scots form of coriander;
- **black man,** the subject of a charming quotation attributed to 'a native of Kilmarnock' by Marian McNeill (1929): 'In the pan, in the little shop where we bought it, it looked like gingerbread, but when it was broken up, it was a crispy crunch, like

a petrified sponge, but once it was in the mouth, it melted into the most soul-satisfying, delectable sweet. (It was about an inch thick.) Even after sixty years, I can still taste it in my memory.'

For Edinburgh rock, see ROCK.

SWEET POTATO *Ipomoea batatas*, the most important of the tropical root crops, is the starchy tuber of a vine of the convolvulus and morning glory family. It is not related to the ordinary POTATO, although both plants are of American origin.

The sweet potato is the cultivated descendant of a wild plant, remains of whose tubers have been found in a cave in Peru inhabited before 8000 BC. It was taken into cultivation during the last centuries BC, well before the time of the Incas, and became a staple food all over tropical America as far north as Mexico and on the Caribbean islands.

It is likely that it was during the 13th century AD that the sweet potato was taken westward to Easter Island and Hawaii, and in the next century to New Zealand. These dates have been calculated from Hawaiian and Maori records. It could be that Peruvians aboard a raft were blown out into the ocean and made a lucky landfall on the sparse islands to the west. However, the voyage may have been deliberate; Thor Heyerdahl repeated it in his Kon-Tiki expedition of 1947, using a similar raft, to prove that it was possible. It had previously been supposed that the sweet potato must have been carried to the Pacific islands by Europeans, at a later time. However, the validity of Heyerdahl's demonstration is supported by the fact that the ancient Peruvian name for the sweet potato, *kumar*, is found with only minor variations (*kumala, gumala, umala*) in several Pacific island languages.

The first Europeans to taste sweet potatoes were members of Columbus' expedition to Haiti, in 1492. Later explorers found many varieties as they extended the range of their expeditions. Early accounts give various local names, *aji, camote, apichu*, and others; but the name which stuck was the first known Haitian one, *batata*. Later this name was accidentally transferred to the ordinary potato after its discovery by Europeans in 1537, causing a confusion which still persists.

Native American sweet potatoes in use at the time were not all sweet. Some were plainly starchy and others markedly fibrous, as were those which had been taken to the Pacific islands. But the European explorers were interested only in the sweet kinds, and it is these which have been spread by European influence while the others have largely died out.

The sweet potato was cultivated in the south of Spain from the early 16th century, and proved a popular novelty. Attempts to grow it further to the north were only partly successful. The plant is easily grown from roots or cuttings in hot countries; but in cooler regions it has to be started in a hothouse. Although for this reason it could never become a major food crop in Europe, it enjoyed two brief vogues in France during the 18th and early 19th centuries, since both Louis XV and the Empress Josephine, who was a Creole, were partial to it.

Sixteenth-century Spanish explorers took the sweet potato to the Philippines; and from there Portuguese traders spread it to the E. Indies and India. It is generally accepted that the sweet potato reached China at the end of the 16th century. There was a famine in Fujian province in 1593 and the governor sent an expedition to the Philippines to search for food plants. Next year the ships returned with sweet potatoes, which soon became a staple of that part of China. Early in the 18th century the sweet potato passed into Japan. The fact that it is called *karaimo* (i.e. Chinese potato) in the Ryukyu Islands (Okinawa), *ryukyu-imo* in Satsuma, and *satsumaimo* in the rest of the country is said to indicate the route by which it arrived.

It was probably slave traders who introduced the sweet potato to Africa, where it was called *igname* or *nyam*, which simply means 'yam'. Since that time the sweet potato has been steadily displacing the true YAM as a major carbohydrate food in tropical Africa.

On the N. American mainland sweet potatoes had long been grown by the Indians in Louisiana, where de Soto found them in 1540, and as far north as Georgia. By 1648 the colonists in Virginia were cultivating them. The sweet potato was especially valued during the war against the British and the Civil War, for it grows quickly and its underground habit makes it less vulnerable than surface crops to deliberate destruction.

There are numerous **varieties.** Most have tubers which are about the size of medium ordinary potatoes, and generally of an elongated, slightly pointed shape, though there are also round kinds. The skin may be white, yellow, red, purple, or brown, and the flesh white, yellow, orange, or even orange-red. The two main categories of sweet potato now grown are best distinguished as 'soft' and 'firm'; one becomes soft and moist when cooked, while the other remains mealy and relatively firm. The flesh of the soft ones is apt to be orange, and that of the firm ones white or yellow. In the USA the soft kind is sometimes called 'yam'; a misnomer, as the true YAM is a different plant.

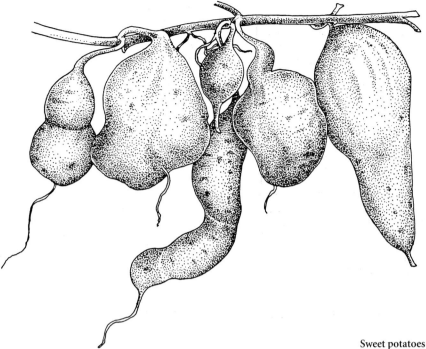

Sweet potatoes

The **boniato,** often regarded as a vegetable in its own right although correctly known as a cultivar of the sweet potato, is of the firm kind, with a brown or red skin and white flesh. It is outstandingly mealy when cooked, and has found its way from Cuba and the Antilles, where it has long been popular, to the USA.

Yellow flesh indicates the presence of carotene, a source of vitamin A. Sweet potatoes provide only half as much protein as ordinary potatoes, but contain much starch and a little sugar. The tubers do not store well. Traditional methods of preserving them have included partial drying of whole roots by the Maori, slicing and sun-drying in China, and candying in many countries. They can also be made into a starchy meal. Around 1766 such a product was being exported from Savannah, Georgia, to England. It never became popular, but sweet potato meal or starch is used by the food-processing industry. The tubers are sometimes canned.

Most sweet potatoes are used fresh: baked or boiled in their skins (after which they can be slipped out of their skins and mashed), or fried. They can also be used in baking breads or cakes; and chips (US French fries) can be made of them. In China and Japan, roasted sweet potatoes are sold by street vendors. Many find the flavour of sweet potato more attractive if it is further sweetened and spiced with cinnamon or nutmeg. It is often made into desserts in the USA, on the lines of pumpkin pie.

The most remarkable root in the genus *Ipomoea* is the manroot or man of the earth, *I. leptophylla*, which grows in the western

USA. This huge tuber, the size and shape of a fully grown man, is not very good to eat, and remarkably difficult to dig up; but Indians have reluctantly turned to it in hungry times. Other species with edible roots are of minor importance. See also JICAMA, a plant which was formerly classed in the same genus.

SWEETS in these sense being considered here, is a word which English children recognize as a collective term for diverse items of sugar CONFECTIONERY. Sometimes reduced to the diminutive 'SWEETIES' (especially in Scottish usage), it is roughly equivalent to the French term *bonbons* and N. American 'candy'. (In another sense, 'sweets' can be more or less equivalent to desserts, sweet courses at the end of meals.)

It is difficult to provide a satisfactory definition of sweets in the sense that children use the word. That they should have a high sugar content seems a logical assertion—but low-sugar sweets are made. Sweets should be sweet, but there are some very sour varieties (acid DROPS) and bitter types (LIQUORICE and cough sweets). Sweets are generally small—but there are also some very large ones, such as GOBSTOPPERS. Designed mostly to appeal to children, some find a ready sale amongst adults, who yet consider many sweets to be rubbish.

One qualification for a sweet to be truly appreciated by children seems to be that it should resemble anything but food. Ever since the price of sugar began to fall, nearly 200 years ago, and possibly before, confectioners have modelled childhood fantasies and fashions in sugar. Examples include 'Nelson's Buttons' in pink peppermint-flavoured sugar paste, hard sugar 'toys' shaped like horses or steam engines, boiled sweets striped like Victorian dresses, and moulded chocolate pipes, cigars, and cigarettes, packed in boxes as 'smoker's outfits'. Many items appear to be shaped and named to represent particularly unappetizing substances: bull's eyes, rifle shot (a type of DRAGÉE), false teeth (in boiled sugar or MARSHMALLOW), liquorice bootlaces, rats (in coloured gum), traffic light lollies, and SHERBET flying saucers are a few of the items which have been marketed.

Some sweets are equipped with surprising visual and flavour effects: gobstoppers change colour when sucked, sherbet fizzes in the mouth, and bubble gum is as much about bubbles as sweetness. Certain TOFFEES are enjoyed for their chewy or stretchy texture, and rituals develop around other sweets—such as biting the heads off jelly babies. The basic confections have a long history, and many were originally held in high regard as medicines or luxury goods. In the 20th century, these curiously flavoured, brilliantly coloured, and outlandishly named tooth-rotters are more likely to provide a lesson in observation of the physical world and a rite of passage for most British children. (LM)
READING: Laura Mason (1998).

SWIMMING CRABS a large category of crabs which swim in the water as opposed to just scuttling about on the sand or the seabed, and which include such important edible species as the BLUE CRAB of N. America. Swimming crabs can easily be recognized by the fact that their hindmost legs have developed into 'swimmerets', paddle shaped at the ends so that they can be used for propulsion.

The chief family of swimming crabs, Portunidae, is well represented around the world. In Europe it includes a number of small species, notably *Necora puber* (formerly *Macropipus/Liocarcinus/Portunus puber*), Spanish *nécora*, French *étrille*, Italian *grancia d'arena*. The largest crab of a small tribe whose members are usually consigned to the soup pot, this one may measure 7 cm (2.5") across the body.

In the Indo-Pacific there are larger swimming crabs, such as:

• *Charybdis cruciata*, the mask crab, so called because the markings on its back, which may measure over 15 cm (6") across, are thought to resemble a mask.
• *Scylla serrata*, the mangrove crab (but it shares this name with some other crabs which live in mangrove swamps). This crab is slightly larger and a full-grown specimen may weigh as much as 1 kg

(2.25 lb). Typically dark red or nearly black in colour. Similar crabs with somewhat different characteristics, especially colour, are regarded by many experts as varieties of the same species; but fishermen certainly have different names for them and it may be that there are other valid species such as *S. oceanica*, a pale green crab.

• *Portunus pelagicus*, another large swimming crab (carapace up to 20 cm/8" across), light blue with white spots (male) or brown with white spots (female). Makes good eating, also in the softshell state. The Thai name, *pu ma*, means horse crab; whereas the Thai call *P. sanguinolentus*, a close relation with three distinctive purple spots on a greenish-yellow carapace, *pu dao*, meaning star crab.

SWISS ROLL a confection made by rolling up a thin oblong sheet of SPONGE CAKE spread with jam to make a roll. When sliced the cake reveals a spiral of thick yellow sponge cake with a thin stripe of jam.

There are many variations on this idea. Some are rich confections, often using chocolate-flavoured sponge rolled up with whipped cream. A special variety is the French *bûche de Noël*. (See CHRISTMAS FOODS.)

In the USA they are called jelly roll. See also ROULADE.

SWITZERLAND a country whose gastronomic map has no capital, as Eva Maria Borer (1965) pointed out. Swiss cookery traditions are preserved in five different languages (French, German, Italian, and Switzerdeutsch, plus Romansch) and the 23 cantons of this mountainous and pastoral country. Many of the dishes commonly encountered correspond very closely to ones found in France, Germany, and Italy. However, the cuisines of Switzerland do have their own individual characters and are collectively distinguished by a certain emphasis on cheese cookery and an interesting range of baked goods.

In the realm of cheese cookery FONDUE and RACLETTE are well known internationally. The home of the former in Switzerland is the western part of the country. The best-known fondue is that of Neuchâtel, but the fondues of Waadtland and Geneva are also famous, as is the *fonduta* of the mountain valleys of the canton of Tessin (Ticino) near Italy.

Raclette has its home in the canton Valais. Borer (1965) has an evocative passage on this:

Johanna Spyri described the prototype of all Swiss national dishes made from melted cheese in *Heidi*, in a famous scene when the old grandfather fries

the cheese at an open fire. Basically, Raclette is just that—cheese fried in the fire; and in Wallis, and many restaurants all over Switzerland, this speciality is prepared at an open wood fire. A mature Gomser cheese is halved and the cut side held in the flames till the surface begins to melt. The melting cheese is scraped on to a warm plate—*racler* means to scrape—and eaten with small potatoes, salt cucumbers and onions pickled in vinegar.

One author, Sue Style (1992), has given an exceptionally clear account of Swiss history as the backdrop to the emergence and characteristics of the 23 cantonal cuisines. Among the perceptive observations which she makes are those applying to the people of Ticino (by the Italian frontier) and the francophone cantons:

• 'The Ticinese are proud of being Swiss, which is completely compatible in their view with having many favourite Italian dishes (mostly from Lombardy or Piedmont) and retaining the endearing Italian characteristic of being relaxed about food.'
• 'The French speakers of Switzerland, known by themselves as *les Suisses romands* and by the Swiss-Germans as *die Welschen* (meaning, literally, celtic—non-alemannic—and therefore foreign), are inevitably more influenced by the French culture of the table, not only from their proximity to France, but also for historical reasons—not for nothing are they descended from the Burgundians. Some of Switzerland's largest lakes are in the French-speaking part, and lake fish is frequently served.' Apparently *filets de perches* (fried fillets of perch) are the most popular dish of the region, ahead of the more famous fondue.
• 'The Swiss Germans in general have a less developed "culture of the table" than the French- or Italian-speakers. . . . Powerful soups precede pork dishes with cabbage (fresh and salted). . . . Sausages are legion, potatoes are practically *de rigueur*. Probably most representative of all is the wonderful *Rösti*, a sort of grated potato pancake seen as the quintessential Swiss-German dish by the French speakers. (The dish has even given its name to the river Sarine, otherwise jokingly referred to as the *Rösti-graben*, the deep dividing "ditch" between French- and German-speaking Switzerland.)'

Switzerland has been the home of many famous hotel schools, where chefs and hotel managers are trained, mainly on conservative lines so far as food is concerned; classical French restaurant cuisine has had a long shelf life in the Alpine climate.
READING: Sarah Kelly (1985, for baked goods).

SWORDFISH *Xiphias gladius*, a fish which ranges right round the world. Most of its common names refer to its 'sword'. This is not for driving holes through the bottoms of wooden boats (although there are many tales of this happening), but to be flailed around among banks of smaller fish, which are thus killed or stunned. Maximum length (including the sword) is 4 m (13').

Although so large, and so formidably equipped, the swordfish often lazes on the surface of the water and can be harpooned. In classical times, as now, this was a common method of capture. Swordfish are also taken in tuna traps.

A traveller in Sicily in the 18th century recorded that the Sicilian fishermen used a Greek sentence as a charm to lure the fish towards their boats; if the fish overheard a word of Italian he would plunge under water at once and make off. A possible explanation of this phenomenon is that the Sicilians, in whose waters swordfish abound, are notoriously skilful at catching them, much more so than Greeks.

The flesh of the swordfish is very compact, and is excellent grilled. It is consumed on a large scale in N. America. Smoked swordfish, which is prepared in Turkey and elsewhere, is a delicacy.

SYLLABUB (or sillabub), a sweet, frothy confection which was popular in Britain from the 16th to the 19th centuries, and has since been revived in a small way as a dessert.

The origin of the word 'syllabub' is a mystery. Lexicographers find no compelling reason to accept any of the explanations offered so far.

Originally syllabub was a drink with a foamy head, but the foamy part was the object of chief interest and later became the main element. It has often been said that the primitive method of making syllabub, ensuring a good foam, was to partly fill a jug with sweetened, spiced white wine or cider, and to milk a cow directly into it. When this technique was critically examined, and subjected to experiments, by Vicky Williams

(1996), it was found to be unsatisfactory; and it began to seem doubtful whether it had ever been a common practice. Ivan Day (1996b) crowned the debate on this particular question by a historical and technical survey of the whole subject of syllabubs, now the *locus classicus*. He acknowledges at the end of his essay help received (presumably on the particular question of direct milking) from cow 53 at Thrimby Manor Farm, Cumbria, as well as the illumination provided by the numerous 17th- and 18th-century authors whose recipes he cites.

SYR AND SIR are respectively the Russian and Serbo-Croat words for 'cheese', and form part of the names of some cheeses made in Russia, Yugoslavia, and elsewhere. For example, the Russians consume quantities of Edam-type *Gollandsky syr* ('Dutch cheese'—Russian has no letter H).

More genuinely Russian or Soviet cheese names are usually place names. Well-known types are *Moskovsky syr* (from Moscow) and *Altajsky syr* (from the Altai)—both hard; *Latvysky syr* (from Latvia) and *Volzhsky syr* (from the Volga)—both surface ripened; *Desertny syr*, which is mould-ripened; *Jerevansky syr* and *Cecil*—both 'PICKLED' CHEESES. These are only a handful from a vast collection including many regional cheeses made on a small scale by herdsmen or on collective farms.

Serbo-Croat cheese names frequently use a place name and *sir*, as in *Mjesinski sir*, a cheese made from ewe's milk and usually cured for a year in a sack or sheepskin bag. *Somborski sir* is made from sheep's and cow's milk mixed with water and fermented in a vat to give a curious bitter taste. Again, there are numerous other varieties, many of them hard 'pickled' types made, as FETA is, in conjunction with WHEY CHEESES to avoid waste.

SYRUPS are solutions of SUGAR dissolved in water, or solutions of fruit juice and

sugar. A knowledge of the properties of syrups at different concentrations and temperatures is basic to SUGAR BOILING and CONFECTIONERY, and they are also important in fruit PRESERVATION and in making soft drinks and cordials. Some substances which carry the name syrup, with qualification—GOLDEN SYRUP, glucose syrup, CORN SYRUP—are products of the sugar and starch industries and are bought from refiners or specialist producers.

Plain syrup of sugar and water is sometimes called 'stock syrup'; quantities are made up and stored for use in large kitchens, where it has many applications in dessert-making, especially as the basis for sorbets (see WATER ICES). It can be made up to whatever strength the cook requires, the optimum being somewhere around the proportions of 1650 g (60 oz) sugar dissolved in 1 litre (1.75 pints) water just at boiling point, and then cooled; this is strong enough to keep well, but not so heavily saturated that the sugar will begin to crystallize out again. Whilst the domestic cook can generally rely on using measured quantities of sugar and water to produce syrup for a given recipe, it is important for chefs and those in the food industry to know the precise strength, which is ascertained by measuring the density at a specific temperature using a hydrometer. Originally, this was expressed in degrees on the Baumé scale; now a decimal system is used.

The word syrup derives from the same Arabic root as the word SHERBET. They were known both in the kitchen and in medicine in Britain by the 14th century. Ever since then, syrups have been found useful as a vehicle for flavours, for cooking fruit or for preserving it by bottling or as candied fruit, for making up cooling drinks when diluted with water, and as a means of easing the passage of medicaments down a patient's throat; this follows a general European pattern of usage. Further east, syrups have an additional culinary role in the making of pastries such as BAKLAVA.

LM

TABASCO the trade name of a bottled hot chilli sauce made since the 1870s from Tabasco peppers, which are a variety of the species *Capsicum frutescens* and are very small, thin, and yellowish. The special flavour is produced by a fermentation process, carried out since 1868 at Avery Island in Louisiana, which is the projecting peak of a subterranean mountain of salt. The story of how Tabasco, a variety name, came to become a commercial one, the property of the McIlhenny family, and other interesting features of the sauce's environment and history have been described by Naj (1992).

Tabasco sauce is convenient as a source of 'bottled hotness', but has a number of rivals, also based on one or other variety of hot CHILLI pepper.

TABBOULEH a prominent item in Near Eastern MEZZE, is best described as a refreshing salad of PARSLEY, TOMATO, and BURGHUL (cracked wheat) with spring onion and mint plus oil, lemon juice and seasoning (and any of several optional ingredients such as ground cinnamon and allspice). The

proportions vary from place to place, and from family to family, some preferring a mixture which is almost purely green, others liking a greater proportion of tomato and burghul.

Anissa Helou (1994), describing its preparation in the Lebanon (widely perceived as its original home territory), emphasizes that the herbs should be chopped by hand, with a very sharp knife, not in a food processor (which would risk making them mushy). Tabbouleh is to be served with inner Cos lettuce (or young vine or white cabbage) leaves, with which it is scooped up to be eaten.

A comparable but different Turkish dish, *kısır*, is a golden, not green, mixture of burghul with tomato and onion etc.; it is usual to dress it with POMEGRANATE juice and add paprika instead of cinnamon. (Thus, although they have sometimes been confused in western countries, the differences between *kısır* and tabbouleh are considerable.)

TABIL a spice mixture specific to Tunisia, usually a blend of CORIANDER (fresh or the

seeds), CARAWAY seeds, garlic, and red peppers, both sweet and fiery, either ground or pounded to a paste.

TABLET a Scottish sweet made from sugar and milk or cream boiled to the soft ball stage (116 °C/240 °F; see SUGAR BOILING), and then stirred vigorously to make it 'grain' or crystallize. It is poured into trays and allowed to set before being cut into smaller pieces or 'tablets'. The texture of this confection resembles crisp fudge. It was known in the early 18th century when purchases of 'taiblet for the bairns' were recorded in *The Household Book of Lady Grisell Baillie* (1692–1733), and Mrs McLintock (1736) gave recipes for orange, rose, cinnamon, and ginger tablets in the earliest work on cookery published in Scotland.   LM

TABOO (or tabu), a word which in a food context (as indeed in others) means 'prohibited', especially for religious or other mysterious reasons. A prohibition overtly based on some fully explicable reason would not normally count as a taboo.

Some prohibitions which could be referred to as taboos (although not everyone would wish to use this term, which comes from Tonga in the Pacific Ocean) are mentioned in articles about particular religions and food, e.g. MUSLIMS AND FOOD, JEWISH DIETARY LAWS, or foodstuffs which have been prohibited for some people, e.g. PORK.

TAGINE meaning 'stew', is a category of dish fundamental to cookery in MOROCCO. The same word appears in the name of the special earthenware cooking recipient (*tagine slaoui*) with a distinctive pointed cover in which it is cooked. The recipients, for everyday use, are made of thick earthenware, but there are also finer ones with elaborate glazing and decoration.

Tagine dishes, which are prepared by long simmering over an open fire or a bed of charcoal, may be savoury or savoury and sweet. The latter combination was very frequent in early ARAB CUISINE and also common in medieval Europe (where it was an inheritance from the Arabs). Morocco is by no means the only place where it has survived to the present time, but is one of a few outstanding examples.

Paula Wolfert (1973), one western author who has made a study of Moroccan cookery, provides a wide range of tagine recipes. Many feature LAMB (for example with wild CARDOONS, a speciality of Tangier, or wild artichokes or fennel). Preserved lemons are a very frequent ingredient. Chicken tagines include one where the chickens are cooked with an extraordinary 'jam' made of tomatoes cooked with honey. Perhaps the most remarkable tagine cited by this author is 'tagine of lamb, quinces, amber and aga[r] wood', a speciality of Tetuán. The use of quinces, honey, and orange flower water exemplifies again the savoury and sweet combination. It is only on special occasions that the two most luxurious and expensive ingredients (see AMBER and AGAR WOOD), which clearly date back to very ancient times, are used. Wolfert comments:

A fingernail scraping of ambergris dissolved in water, then added to the sauce, is credited with aphrodisiacal powers—which might help explain its price of ninety dollars per ounce. An inch-long piece of aga[r] wood, pulverized in a brass mortar with some sugar and then added to the sauce, imparts a rich and musky aroma somewhat reminiscent of the inside of a Gothic church.

TAHINI (sometimes tahina), an oily cream (paste) which is extracted from SESAME seeds. The seeds are first soaked in water for 25 hours before being crushed with a heavy hammer to loosen the bran from the kernels. The crushed seeds are put to soak again in highly salted water—the salt content being enough to 'float an egg'—for the bran to sink while the kernels are skimmed off the surface and grilled before being sent to the mill to be ground and release the thick oily cream (paste). There are two types of tahini, a light ivory one and another darker one, the former being generally superior in both taste and texture. Besides being used as is, tahini can be embodied in savoury dips for mezze (e.g. TARATOR, *hummus*, *baba ghanoush*); used in making HALVA (with sugar syrup, essences, and BOIS DE PANAMA); or diluted with the juice of Seville oranges and stock and cooked to make a sauce for *Kibbeh 'arnabiyeh*.   AH

TAILLEVENT (*c*.1312–1395), the 14th-century chef of the French court who achieved enduring fame when an important collection of recipes, attributed to him (although many may have come from an earlier manuscript source), was published. This was the first printed French cookery book. Taillevent's career has been well summarized by Anne Willan (1977):

Taillevent—his real name was Guillaume Tirel, but many apprentices in those days picked up nicknames that they never outgrew—must have been quite a character, for a remarkable amount is known about him in an age when most craftsmen, like the builders of the Gothic cathedrals, passed forgotten into history. In 1326, when he was about fourteen, he was a *happelapin* (kitchen boy) to Queen Jeanne of France and was charged with the unenviable task of turning the great roasting spits before the open fire. By 1346 Taillevent had risen to *keu* (cook) to King Philip VI, and in 1349 he was granted a house 'in consideration of the good and pleasant service the king has received.' Soon after, he was raised to the rank of *écuyer*, or squire, and passed from household to household within the Valois family until, in 1381, he was at the top of his profession as master cook to King Charles VI. He probably compiled *Le Viandier* a few years earlier with the encouragement of King Charles V, known as Charles the Wise for his fine judgement and cultivated tastes.

Appraising the importance of *Le Viandier*, Terence Scully (1995) writes:

Though this collection undoubtedly inherited much of its material from previous generations of cooks and recipe collections, and grew by accretion through several generations of copies during its long lifetime, its subsequent influence can be sensed to a greater or less degree in most of the printed cookbooks of the late fifteenth and sixteenth centuries. The *Viandier* embodies late medieval French cookery. Only one major work in French manages to modify this standard French corpus, and that is the *On Cookery* of Master Chiquart where we can see how the court of Savoy, sitting astride the Alps, was able to combine the best of contemporary French, Italian and local cuisines.

And Anne Willan sums up by saying that:

deservedly or not, Taillevent was the most famous and important medieval cook; Le Viandier stands apart from other medieval writings on cookery in having been continuously recopied and reprinted from Taillevent's death in 1395 until the final edition of 1604. The rich harvest of French cookbooks did not begin until the 1650s and until then *Le Viandier* was the most successful French expression of the art.

The reference to the 'final edition' does not of course take account of modern editions, which began in the 19th century and of which a recent example is that by Scully (1995).

TAILS of mammals, are generally thin and bony and seem unpromising material, but have their uses. In European cookery, the most highly considered is the meaty, well-flavoured OXTAIL.

Pigs' tails, which are mostly gristle, are less popular. One use for them, at an old-fashioned pig-killing (see PIG), was to bake the tail in the oven and give it to the children as a crunchy snack. The tails can also be used to enrich gelatinous stews or stocks; or, if available in quantity, used as a main ingredient. As with other pig OFFAL, dishes have polarized into the fine and the robust. An elaborate example is stuffed pigs' tails, in which the skin is carefully removed to form a long bag, providing a container for fine pork forcemeat; conversely, an example of subsistence food is the Caribbean stew of pigs' tails and salt cod known as *Megatee*.

Sheep's tails or, more specifically, the tails of FAT-TAILED SHEEP are important in the cookery of the Middle East and C. Asia, where they are valued as a source of cooking fat. European sheep have thin tails, but, at least in the past, these were used enthusiastically. Lambs' tails were available in sheep-farming communities during the late spring, when certain breeds had their tails removed. Simon (1952) emphasized that the tails must be those docked from live lambs, as 'when stewed, they are very gelatinous and delicious; if cut from killed lambs they are shrivelled and useless.' One dish, which must have been fairly popular in Britain, as several recipes exist, was 'Lamb's Tail Pie'. Dorothy Hartley (1954) gave directions for making this: 'Instruct the shepherd to keep the docked tails warm, packing them in a sack, and let him bring them straight to the kitchen. Scald, removing the wool, joint the tails and stew.' The stewed tails, with root vegetables, barley, green peas, and hard-boiled egg, were covered with shortcrust pastry and baked. A more urbane dish was quoted by Florence White (1932) for stewing lambs' tails in clear gravy, to be garnished with capers and chopped shallot. Alternatively, the meatier parts of the tails could be fried, and the remainder used for stock.

Other mammals whose tails have been, or are still, valued are BEAVERS and KANGAROOS. Of cold-blooded creatures, LOBSTERS and CRAYFISH are particularly prized for their delicious 'tail' meat.　　LM

TAIWAN a beautiful island which was indeed so named (Ilha Formosa) by Portuguese sailors on their way to Japan early in the 16th century. Although there have been human inhabitants since 10,000 years or more ago, the history of the island can be said to have begun in the 17th century, since when it has been governed or ruled by a whole range of foreign powers or Chinese authorities. A huge change occurred in 1949, when the Chinese government forces, defeated by communists on the mainland, retreated to Taiwan. This brought in hundreds of thousands of incomers, including at least some from all the various regions of mainland China, bringing with them their own cuisines. It is commonly said that a better range of these cuisines may be enjoyed in Taipei, capital of Taiwan, than anywhere else.

The various cuisines of CHINA thus dominate the culinary scene. Among them, however, is the Taiwanese cuisine. This resembles the cuisine of Fujian on the mainland in various respects, such as the emphasis on seafood. The explanation is simple; most Taiwanese came from Fujian and the language spoken by Taiwanese is the same as that spoken in the southern part of Fujian. The cuisine of Taiwan also exhibits the influence of JAPAN (which occupied the island from 1895 until 1945). There are numerous Japanese restaurants.

The aboriginals of Taiwan (the 'natives' whose ancestors were there before anyone else arrived) number several hundred thousand. Their foodways, especially with regard to fish and fishing, have been studied but are much less prominent than those of the Hakka, who account for over a tenth of the population and have a distinctive identity. The Hakkas had been a persecuted minority in the north of China, who moved to the south and then across to the Pescadores Islands and on to Taiwan itself, where they were the first Chinese arrivals. Their cooking reflects their origins as an agricultural society, with considerable emphasis on the pig and its products and a down-to-earth flavour.

A particularly pleasing aspect of Taiwan is the large number of tea houses, some in Japanese style and all tending to be places where peace and quiet reign—in contrast to the intensely animated street-food scenes which are likely to provide visitors with their first impressions.

TALEGGIO a soft, mould-ripened Italian cheese of the STRACCHINO family. It takes its name, which is a controlled denomination, from the Taleggio valley in Lombardy. It has been made there only since the 1920s; but has a longer history, for it was formerly a local product of another district near Bergamo.

A Taleggio cheese is in the form of a quadrangular parallelepiped, with sides measuring about 20 cm (8") and a weight of 2 kg (4 lb). Of all Italian cheeses Taleggio is the one closest to a French soft cheese. It is made by a process akin to those used for CAMEMBERT and NEUFCHÂTEL. As with the latter, the white mould on the surface turns reddish after a while. The fat content is at least 40%, and the flavour mild and lightly aromatic.

TAMALES (the singular in Mexico is *tamal*, in English tamale) are an important feature of Mexican food and date back to pre-Columbian times. A specially prepared cornmeal dough, usually stuffed with something but sometimes cooked 'blind', is steamed inside little (or not so little) packages of carefully trimmed corn husks or similar wrapping such as banana leaf.

The dough is, ideally, made from a particular kind of ground nixtamalized (see NIXTAMALIZATION) corn kernels, and pure lard (which was not used, of course, in pre-Columbian times). It produces what could be described as an aromatic bun with the consistency of firm polenta.

Size and fillings vary widely. Diana Kennedy (1986) provides a good survey, and writes entertainingly of her search for giant tamales, reputed to be 1 m (3') long and called *sacahuil*, which is at the other end of the spectrum from the tiny tamales called *norteños*.

Sweet tamales are made as well as savoury ones. In considering fillings, it is important to remember that what makes tamales so wonderfully good is the flavour of the corn; the filling is just a relish, whether it takes the form of red or green salsa, MOLE, pineapple, coconut, or other sweet material.

Tamales are almost invariably eaten with ATOLE, corn gruel. They remain, as in the past, an important festival food. 'Are you going to make tamales?' is a common question before a festival (and a substantial question—a cook making them from the starting point of dried maize faces a lot of work, which will be less if commercial *masa harina* (a fine maize flour) is used, but will then yield less good results). Festival tamales are often tinted lurid colours, especially the sweet ones.

However, tamales have become much more than just a festival food, being available at all seasons; they can be bought

from street vendors for breakfast, for example.

Tamales in other places have developed along other lines. In the Philippines, for example, related products called tamales are popular snacks. However, they are not made from cornmeal but are basically a rice-flour preparation with the addition of crushed peanuts, chicken, pork, hard-cooked egg, and seasonings wrapped in banana leaves and boiled. (The chlorophyll of the banana leaves seeps into the rice during cooking and the finished product has a greenish colour.) The ingredients and spiciness vary from region to region. One version, from Meycauayan (Bulacan), is quite different. It is sweet, without a trace of peanuts, spices, or meat, and is about a quarter of the size of regular tamales, beautifully wrapped in banana leaf in a trapezoidal packet. Another provincial version of tamale might compete with the Mexican giants for which Diana Kennedy searched. It is large enough to serve as lunch for two or three, and luxuriously flavoured with pork ADOBO and with chilli.
　　　　　　　　　　　　　　　　(RL)

TAMARIND *Tamarindus indica*, a large and beautiful evergreen tree native to tropical Africa. It had already spread to India in prehistoric times, has for long been established in SE Asia and is now distributed throughout the tropical and subtropical regions of the world. Having strong and pliant branches and an extensive root system it can be grown in places exposed to high winds; and it is also resistant to drought.

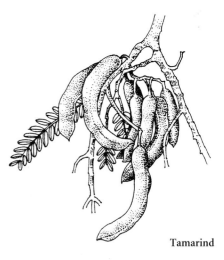

Tamarind

The tamarind is prized for its pods, which grow in clusters and contain very small beans, surrounded by an attractively sour/acid pulp. They are harvested when fully ripe, the shells and seeds are removed, and the pulp compressed into 'cakes'. In this form tamarind provides an acidifying agent widely used in Indian and SE Asian cooking.

The pulp can also be turned into a syrup, with the addition of sugar, and then diluted to make soft drinks such as the *tamarinade* of Jamaica and the *jugo* or *refresco de tamarindo* of Latin American countries.

In Thailand the pulp is eaten as a simple sweetmeat, dusted with sugar, as well as being squeezed with water to give a sour juice. The roasted seeds may be used as a flavouring for compotes of young palm shoots. The Chinese in Indonesia also eat the roasted seeds. Indonesians and others often use the leaves for flavouring purposes.

In the W. Indies, the ripe fruit is sometimes sugared and made into patties, sold in the markets of Jamaica, Cuba, and the Dominican Republic. Similar products in the Philippines, incorporating sweet potato in addition, are known as champoy. Filipinos also candy peeled ripe fruits.

The name tamarind is given to some unrelated plants. Among these are the 'native tamarind' of Australia, *Diploglottis australis*, whose yellow, lobed fruits contain an acid jelly-like pulp which is used to make a refreshing drink, and for jam. The so-called 'sweet tamarinds', of the genus *Inga*, grow in tropical America and bear fruits with edible pulp; see under PACAY. *Pithecolobium dulce*, a C. American tree mentioned under NGAPI NUT, has edible tamarind-like pods with edible pulp and is sometimes called Manila tamarind.

Tamarinds are an ingredient of WORCESTERSHIRE SAUCE.

TANDOOR the Middle Eastern clay oven, found from the Arab countries to India. The original Babylonian form of the name, *tinûru*, is probably related to *nâr*, the Semitic word for fire. In Hebrew, Aramaic and Arabic, but not Persian, the 'n' is doubled: *tannûr*. The pronunciation *tandur* or *tandir*, current in Turkey, C. Asia and India, reflects the emphatic Turkic pronunciation of the double n. In Egypt and N. Africa, where the tandoor has largely been replaced by the European-style bread oven, the name *tâbûna* is used instead of *tannûr*.

Unlike the European bread oven, which is made of brick, the tandoor is a piece of pottery (the Arabic *al-tannûr* has given Spanish its word for clay pipe, *atanor*). It is essentially a large clay jar with an opening toward the bottom for adding and removing fuel. Potters may sell ready-fired tandoors for installing in the home—in the wall or floor of the building, or outdoors, surrounded by more clay to make a beehive-shaped free-standing structure—or the pot may be built up *in situ* from soils of clay and fired from within.

In the European bread oven, loaves are set on the horizontal oven floor to bake. In the tandoor, the breads (necessarily flat in shape) are slapped onto the vertical wall, where they bake quite quickly by a combination of radiant heat and convection.

After the day's bread-making, casseroles and other dishes may be baked in a tandoor (as in a brick oven) to use the residual heat. In cold climates, the tandoor also heats the house, like the hearth in Europe. In Turkey, the word *tandir* can refer to a pan of coals set under the communal table to warm the feet.

In the Middle Ages, skewered meats were more often roasted in a tandoor than over burning coals, as they still are in C. Asia. Tandoor meat cookery has been popular in India since 1948, when a Kashmiri restaurant named Moti Mahal became a fashionable dining spot for politicians in New Delhi. As a result, Indian tandoori restaurants have sprung up all around the world. Ironically, in the Arab countries the tandoor has been steadily losing its prominence with the modern taste for brick oven breads, such as the 'pocket' bread known in Europe and America as PITTA.   CP

TANSY *Tanacetum vulgare*, a herb whose name is supposedly derived by abbreviation from 'athanasia', the draught which gave Ganymede immortality. A tall and umbelliferous plant of northern temperate zones, it stays long in flower, and this, according to Dodoens (1578), caused it to be associated with everlasting life. The flowers are pretty, like yellow buttons, and the scent is attractively refreshing and spicy.

Tansy was grown extensively in the past for both culinary and medical uses. It preceded MINT as an accompaniment to lamb, and was used to flavour puddings, cakes, and egg dishes, besides giving its name to a dish called 'a tansy', which was like a large flat OMELETTE or PANCAKE, associated especially with Easter. The connection between tansy and eggs was very strong in England. However, the ingredients of a tansy could vary considerably, as the quotations from 16th- and 17th-century sources given by Eleanor Rohde (1936) demonstrate. Although one 15th-century 'tansey' (see Hess, 1981) contained only eggs and tansy, other herbs such as spinach and SORREL were commonly used with tansy, and it is safe to assume that the quantity of tansy was relatively small, since its flavour is strong. Evelyn (1699) referred to 'its domineering relish sparingly mixt with our cold Sallet and much fitter (tho' in very small quantity) for the Pan, being qualified with the Juices of other fresh Herbs'.

Tansies were mostly sweet, but Izaak Walton's recipe for Minnow Tansies with cowslips or primroses exemplifies another and charming possibility; Elisabeth Ayrton (1974) gives a delightful summary of Walton's recipe and remarks that if you fish the MINNOWS in a little stream in April and walk home through flowering fields in which you gather your COWSLIPS and primroses, 'you will be eating the English spring'.

In the course of time, the dish known as tansy came to be made without any tansy at all. Ayrton presents other flower and fruit tansies from the 18th century, showing some of the directions in which tansies evolved after losing their eponymous ingredient.

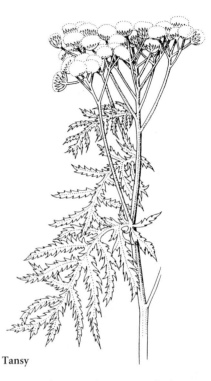

Tansy

Tansies began to disappear in the latter part of the 18th century, and are heard of no more. However, tansy puddings, which usually have many other ingredients but taste perceptibly of the tansy juice which goes into them, have shown greater staying power. Pamela Michael (1980) cites one from 1588 which translates easily enough into a modern recipe.

Tansy is the flavouring herb for the Irish sausage DRISHEEN, made with sheep's blood and milk.

TAPAS a Spanish institution which has spread not only to other Spanish-speaking countries but also elsewhere, in the form of tapas bars.

At the simplest level, tapas are titbits eaten with drinks at a bar and before proceeding to have a full meal. They thus fill a role similar to that of, say, HORS D'ŒUVRES or ZAKUSKI. If they were served in the home, as a prelude to a meal in the same premises, the resemblance would be close. However, their essential role is to be eaten in a bar, or rather a succession of bars. A remarkable essay by

Alicia Rios (1987) on what might be termed, in Spanish fashion, the philosophy of tapas provides a uniquely illuminating description, short extracts from which follow. She begins by explaining the meaning of tapeo.

Tapeo is a term used to describe the Spanish tradition of going out before lunch or dinner to mingle with friends while drinking an apéritif, and sharpening the appetite for the main meal ahead by choosing from the myriad of tempting appetizers on offer in the bars throughout Spain.

The art of *tapeo* represents the perfect marriage between food and drink, because, unlike the more well known concept of food supplemented by good wine, in the case of the art of tapeo, it is not the wine which lubricates the ingestion of good food, but quite the contrary; it is the food which really acts as an accompaniment to the series of sips of good wine.

The art of *tapeo* is like a baroque, sybaritic game, as it pleases the five senses by means of the multifarious smells, the friendly pats on the back, the sight of beauty on the streets. It induces states of inspiration and delight, it gives rise to witty banter on trivial topics and the interchange of snippets of juicy gossip. There is a kind of irony and philosophy peculiar to this custom, like a treaty of coexistence accompanied by elegance and a generosity of the spirit developed to the ultimate possibilities. The *tapeo* is a peripatetic art which takes the form of a route; a path paved with chance meetings and random conversations.

The drink stimulates the appetite and aids digestions, and the food palliates the ethylic effects of the drink. The combination of these factors results in a perfect balance which is supported by the concept of physical space, as the *tapeo*, by its very nature, inherently involves a plurality of settings. It is impossible to imagine the art of tapeo taking place in a single session with no element of sequence or spacing. However good a particular bar may be a good *tapeador* could never exhaust his possibilities in any one place. Movement is essential to the creation of the spacing concept and also involves physical exercise which, as well as aiding digestion, is really a trick, as the stimulating effect of the movement consequently leads to more changes of location.

Tapas can be divided into sections according to their different places of origin, and likewise the many kinds of bars can be classified according to their specialities.

Some of the most representative *tapas* come from the area of Castile which offers *montados de lomo* which are small pieces of bread with a slice of meat on top such as marinated loin of pork fillets, *chorizo a la plancha*—slices of spicy pork sausage cooked on the griddle, *morcilla*—a kind of black pudding sausage made with blood and rice or onion and served fried, *cazuela de callos a la madrileña*—the Madrid speciality of tripe casserole, and *patatas bravas*—medium sized chunks of fried potatoes coated in a hot, spicy sauce made from tomatoes and chilli peppers.

In Galicia, on the northern coast of Spain, we find a great variety of dishes related to the cephalopod family such as octopus prepared in the typical Galician way and many kinds of shellfish, also the Galician omelette made with potatoes, vegetables and chorizo.

As a prototype of the *tapas* available in Andalusia we could perhaps take the seafood group, which in this region is usually served fried or seasoned with a vinaigrette dressing.

Indeed there is an enormous range of diverse regional specialities, far too many to list here. Furthermore, many tapas are to be found nationwide, like for example the inevitable unpeeled prawns and *boquerones* (fresh whitebait) served in vinegar, which are to be found in display on the counters of bars everywhere, not to mention *tortilla española*, Spanish potato omelette.

It does not matter if the ideal *tapa* is somewhat large, but this volume must be distributed in terms of height, and not of surface area. For example the *montado*—a piece of fried *morcilla* on a small slice of bread, speared with a cocktail stick, or perhaps assorted pickles on sticks, can be piled very high because they do not conflict with the requirement for occupying a minimal surface area. This phenomenon has various explanations. Let us consider first the ethical reasons, which are always connected with the respect shown with regard to the meal awaiting in the home. Food with a large surface area is reserved for the more intimate atmosphere of meals enjoyed with the family or friends. There are also various other fundamental reasons. The individualization of the portions is an important factor as it renders cutlery virtually unnecessary. The fork, for example, is only needed to spear the bite-sized morsel, and the use of the knife is not considered correct form, even if only to cut a sausage up into pieces. Cutlery has no place in the art of *tapeo*, belonging to the environment of sit-down meals.

TAPÉ

TAPÉ is the Indonesian word for the products of a FERMENTATION using either CASSAVA or sticky RICE, the result in both cases being a sweet and faintly alcoholic food which is served as a snack. Cassava tapé (*tapé singkong, tapé ketela*) is made by peeling, splitting, and boiling mature cassava tubers, inoculating them with RAGI, and incubating them semi-anaerobically for 24 to 48 hours. Active agents in the fermentation include YEASTS and MOULDS. The result is a soft-textured, juicy length of cassava with a tangy flavour. It can be eaten straight, or put in drinks made of coconut milk and palm sugar such as the mouth-watering cendol, or may, as in E. Java, be baked as *tapé panggang*, where the compressed tapé emerges in a cake of a rather chewy, stringy consistency with a flavour reminiscent of apple strudel.

Tapé ketan is made from black or white sticky rice which has been steamed and inoculated with the mould *Amylomyces rouxii* and a combination of various yeasts. This is then incubated in an airtight container for 36 to 48 hours. *Tapé ketan* varies according to the type and quality of the rice used. White rice will come out greenish and have a sourish aftertaste; black rice should produce a juicy tapé. In W. Java they make a kind of cendol by boiling the

tapé ketan with palm sugar and serving it with a topping of water-buffalo yoghurt; the ketan in this case will resemble in taste and appearance a dish of stewed berries.

Most popular in C. and E. Java, *tapé ketan* is generally served on special occasions such as the end of the fasting month RAMADAN, known as Lebaran, or as a special treat for visitors. In Bali, tourists are often given a wonderful form of breakfast porridge called *jenang tapé*, where *ketan hitam* is boiled with coconut milk and palm sugar, and served with banana and grated coconut.

Tapé-like products are found elsewhere in SE Asia. In China, there is *chiu-niang* (*lao-chao* in Cantonese) which is served at New Year celebrations as a sweet, either alone, or prepared with eggs, chicken, and TOFU. The Chinese also use it in seafood preparations and encourage new mothers to partake of its highly nutritious properties.

TAPIOCA

TAPIOCA an important product of CASSAVA, and broadly speaking the only one which has a presence in western kitchens. Cassava flour is treated in such a way as to form what are called flakes, seeds, and pearls of tapioca, which constitute an article of commerce known under the name 'tapioca fancies'.

Cassava is an American plant, although the main producers are now in Asia and Africa. Ayto (1993) explains that the name tapioca comes from the Tupi-Guaraní languages of S. America, in which the word *tipioca* refers to the starch produced by processing the roots. Spaniards and Portuguese adapted this name to tapioca, in which form it became an adopted English word in the late 18th century.

Tapioca pudding is well known as one of the family of British MILK PUDDINGS. Like other members of the family, it is sometimes despised by the ignorant, that is to say persons who have no knowledge of how good they are when properly made. Also, when tapioca is cooked in milk it becomes translucent and jelly-like, causing children to detect a resemblance between it and frog spawn. This may have been an additional factor in inspiring distrust of tapioca pudding.

Pearl tapioca, rather than the quicker cooking flake kind, is preferred for tapioca pudding, and that available in N. America is usually the best.

Both boiled and baked puddings are made. A baked pudding can be substantially improved by adding egg, a little butter, cinnamon, and lemon rind. Tapioca also combines well with fruit, and a baked pudding made with plenty of apple and relatively little tapioca can be excellent.

Tapioca has other uses, such as thickening soups.

TAPIR the name for animals, of which species are found both in SE Asia (*Tapirus indicus*) and S. America (*T. terrestris*), belonging to the family Tapiridae which is related to the RHINOCEROS. These shy creatures, of nocturnal habit, live in tropical forests, preferably near water and the vegetation which they like to eat. Thus they are not often seen and are not widely known as food for humans, although they are hunted and eaten by the indigenous peoples of the countries where they are found. Their size (about the same as a donkey, with a maximum weight of 225 kg (500 lb), or even more in Malaysia) is such that one tapir feeds a lot of people.

The number of tapirs has been steadily declining in parallel with the destruction of tropical forests. In principle they could become a food resource if they were 'farmed'; and it is stated by Boitani and Bartoli (1986) that some S. American Indians capture the young and keep them in captivity until they mature. However, there is no reason to expect further developments on these lines.

TARAMOSALATA a savoury spread which is prominent among those Greek dishes which have acquired international fame. *Taramás* (*tarama* in Turkish) means salted fish ROE. In the past, and to some extent even now, the spread has been made with the dried roe of GREY MULLET, a product called *avgotáracho* in Greece but more widely known under the French name BOUTARGUE. When this became too expensive there was a transition to smoked cod roe, resulting in a spread which differs in flavour from the original but is not inferior to it.

In any event the roe is mixed with soaked white bread (sometimes mashed potato instead), olive oil, and lemon juice, plus a very little finely chopped onion. Recipes vary in detail, but the product is always pale pink in colour.

TARATOR a term with two meanings, depending on where it is met.

In BULGARIA (and in slightly altered form in neighbouring countries) it refers to a refreshing cold soup of yoghurt, cucumber, walnuts, garlic, etc. This is not far distant from the Greek cucumber and yoghurt salad called *tsatsiki*.

In TURKEY and the Middle East tarator is the name of a sauce which is made with TAHINI (sesame paste), lemon juice, and garlic. This has many uses. Grilled or baked fish served with tarator sauce is a common, and often a festive, dish in EGYPT, and also in LEBANON AND SYRIA.

TARHANA or trahana(s) (and other spellings), a family of grain products, extending from Iran to the Balkans and Hungary. The basic recipe is crushed WHEAT mixed with YOGHURT, allowed to rest and sour up to seven days and then formed into sheets or pellets which are dried in the sun. These dried sheets or pellets are crumbled at some point before use. The usual destination is soup, but it is also eaten by itself as a sort of PILAF, and often with crumbled cheese as a sort of breakfast cereal.

The first recorded literary reference seems to be the 14th-century poet Bushaq, where occur the lines:

'Asheq-e nânam; agar tarkhâneh nabud, gu mabâd.
Balkeh bâ nân niz, agar beryân nabâshad, gu mabâd.

which translate as

I am the lover of bread; if there is no *tarkhâneh*, so be it.
Nay—as long as there's bread, if there's no roast meat, so be it.

The Turks spread this Iranian culinary idea throughout Anatolia and the Balkans, including Greece. (For an explanation of why the name must have travelled from Persia to Greece and not vice versa, as some have suggested, see Perry, 1997.) There are many variations in the product and in its use. In Hungary, at the western extremity of the product's range, *tarhonya* was being made 400 years ago in the way described above, but in modern Hungary it is simply flour rubbed with egg, making it something like a dried cousin of *spaetzle*. In Turkey and the Balkans, flour-based *tarhana* is often flavoured with items such as tomato, pepper, onion (or herbs such as mint, thyme, dill). Such flavoured doughs are often cooked before being soured. In Turkey, sour cornelian cherry juice (see DOGWOOD) is sometimes used in place of yoghurt. Similarly, POMEGRANATE juice or VERJUICE may replace yoghurt in Iran.

Much the same product has been known in the Arab countries from Egypt to Iraq at least since the 9th century under the name *kishk* (see KASHK). It is sometimes eaten raw by itself as a chewy snack. (The word *kishk* comes from the Persian *kashk*, which originally meant crushed wheat or barley—it is related to the Russian word *kasha*—but in Iran, *kashk* has lost the grain component and the word now means dried WHEY.)   CP

TARO the most widely used name for members of a group of tropical root crops, mostly of the genus *Colocasia* and especially *C. esculenta*. Taro is native to the Old World, but has become an important source of food in tropical and warm regions worldwide.

The taro root is, botanically speaking, a CORM. Cultivated varieties are usually the size of a very large potato, roughly top shaped and circled all over their surface with rough ridges. There are many lumps and spindly projecting roots. The skin is brown and hairy. Inside, the flesh may be white, pink, or purple. Some sorts of taro produce small subsidiary 'cormels' of the same shape as the parent. In the W. Indies these smaller cormels are called 'eddos'—from the W. African word for any taro—and the main central corm 'dasheen', a creole name supposedly adapted from the French *de Chine* (from China, an erroneous attribution).

The family has a bewildering range of names. Other common names for the principal kind of taro are colocasia, which has also become the botanical name, and the corresponding Arabic name *qulqās*; old cocoyam, a name used in Africa to distinguish it from new cocoyam (see MALANGA); dasheen, and elephant's ear, because of its large leaves.

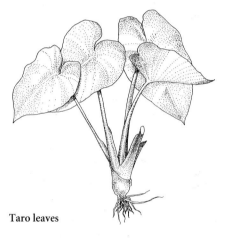

Taro leaves

The botanical name has been subject to change. At present it is considered that there is one species, *C. esculenta*, in which two main kinds of taro are recognized as var *esculenta* and var *antiquorum*.

Taro originated in India or SE Asia, and may have been first cultivated as early as 5000 BC.

It was well suited to primitive agriculture. If a root is dug up, and the top cut off in one piece to remove the leaves and thrown away, the discarded top sometimes survives and grows a new root. Also, taro grows quickly and in the right climate can produce three small or two large crops a year.

Cultivation of taro spread eastwards to China (before 100 BC) and Japan; and also westward, arriving in Egypt around 100 BC. There it came to the notice of the Latin writer Pliny, who called it 'the arum of the Egyptians'; and it also picked up the Greek name *kolokasia*, which had formerly been used for a lotus root. Cultivation spread through Africa, and by the early centuries of the Christian era the plant was a staple crop in W. Africa. Slave traders took it across the Atlantic, and it became an important crop in the W. Indies and tropical S. and C. America; it is now grown as far north as the southern USA.

TARO IN JAPAN AND THE PACIFIC ISLANDS

The type of taro commonly eaten in Japan is the small, round variety which is known as eddo in England. The Japanese name *satoimo* consists of *sato* meaning 'village' or 'hamlet' and *imo*, which is the generic term for edible, farinaceous tubers and tuberous roots. Since the sweet potato did not reach Japan till the 17th century, and the potato even later, the Japanese *satoimo* was the most important tuber for a long time. It has been widely cultivated in the southern half of Japan, where the climate is favourable, resulting in many local varieties (of which one of the best known is *ebiimo* of Kyoto).

Satoimo is eaten steamed in its skin (called *kinukatsugi*—'a lady in a veil'); boiled; cooked in e.g. DASHI, SOY SAUCE, or MIRIN; or put in MISO soup.

Moon-viewing in autumn, like cherry blossom-viewing in spring and snow-viewing in winter, is a time-honoured, elegant custom in Japan. Traditionally the moon on the 15th night of the 8th lunar month, which usually falls in September, is thought to be the most beautiful, and *satoimo*, which is at its best at this time of year, has a strong association with this annual occasion. It is customary to offer 12 *satoimo* (13 in a leap year) to the moon on that night.

The introduction of taro to the Pacific islands had major results for the diet there, since it rapidly became a staple of the region. It is especially important in HAWAII, where the prevailing creation myth states that taro was the first-born of Father Sky and Daughter Earth, humans coming next. Traditionally, the cultivation of taro in Hawaii has been men's work and its sacred character was such that women were not supposed to touch the plants. Indeed the most commonly produced red variety was in former times reserved exclusively for use by the chiefs.

Related root crops of minor importance include giant taro, *Alocasia macrorrhiza*, and the giant swamp taro, *Cyrtosperma chamissonis*. Unlike *Colocasia* spp, these can flourish on coral atolls, so are valued by many communities in the Pacific. As their common names indicate, they can grow to a huge size.

USES

The roots of wild plants are generally unpleasantly acrid in flavour on account of the presence of crystals of calcium oxalate, which are clustered particularly thickly under the skin. Selection, even in very early times, of the least acrid plants has led to modern cultivated strains, some of which are mild enough to eat raw. However, the calcium oxalate problem can be overcome by peeling and cooking.

When properly prepared, taro has a light, mealy texture like a delicate, floury potato. The flavour is pleasant, light without being insipid, sometimes slightly sweet. As a staple food it provides mainly carbohydrates; it has less protein than potatoes or yams.

Eddos have an advantage in that they last longer in storage than dasheen, because the tops are not cut off. Varieties which produce cormels are considered to have a superior flavour and texture.

Chinese use of taro varies and embraces two varieties. The large corms called *bun long wo tau* (betel-nut taro) are braised or steamed. Similar treatment can be given to the cormels known as *hung nga woo tau* (red-budded taro), but in Guangdong these are more commonly boiled, peeled, and eaten out of hand, including by moonlight at the mid-autumn festival.

In Hawaii and Tahiti taro is the root most often used for making the starchy fermented paste POI. Taro has also sometimes been used to make a powdered starch resembling ARROWROOT.

The large leaves and the tender parts of the leaf stalks are eaten as a vegetable in many regions. They also contain calcium oxalate, so thorough boiling in a change of water is necessary; after that they have a faint but pleasant flavour. In the W. Indies they are called CALLALOO and are a main ingredient in the popular dish of that name. In Mauritius the leaves are similarly used, but there called *songes*; and the corms of some varieties (large and with purple flesh, or smaller and green) are also eaten, under the local name *arouilles*. As in Mauritius, so in parts of continental Africa.

TARPON a name used for two closely related fish, *Tarpon* (formerly *Megalops*) *atlanticus*, and *Megalops cyprinoides*. The former is a large game fish of both sides of the central Atlantic (sometimes as far north as Nova Scotia on the American side); the latter is a relatively small fish, sometimes called small/ox-eye/Indian/Pacific tarpon, of the Indo-Pacific.

Young tarpon have the unattractive habit of lurking in stagnant or muddy inshore waters, where the lack of oxygen compels them to come to the surface and 'gasp' for air periodically. The explanation is that in such waters they escape the attention of potential predators.

The Atlantic tarpon, which may reach a length of nearly 2.5 m (8'), is prized by anglers, who are pleased and excited by the leaps which they make when hooked. However, it is little used for food; indeed in N. America it is not regarded as worth eating. The Indo-Pacific species is bony and disappointing, but nonetheless eaten.

TARRAGON *Artemisia dracunculus*, a plant indigenous to Siberia, S. Russia, and W. Asia, was virtually unknown in Europe in classical times and only began to turn up as an ingredient in Italian and French cookery in the late medieval period. It was introduced to England in the 16th century.

There is a distinction, important for cooks, between what is really the wild form of the plant, known as Russian tarragon, and *A. dracunculus* var *sativa*, which is French tarragon. The latter is greatly preferable; the former has a coarser flavour.

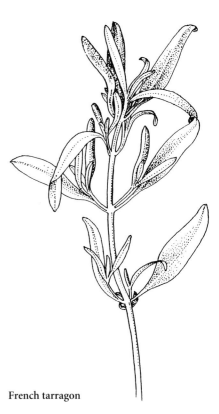

French tarragon

Tarragon is used, in discreet quantities, with tomatoes, fish, salads, meats, chicken, and lobster. It also gives its name to tarragon vinegar, one of the best-known flavoured vinegars. It is most strongly established in French kitchens. Not only is it one of the usual elements in FINES HERBES, but it also occurs as the chief flavouring in many French dishes, such as *Poulet à l'estragon*, and certain sauces. BÉARNAISE SAUCE is the best-known example.

TART a term which overlaps with FLAN, subsumes QUICHE and PIZZA, and is largely replaced in N. America by PIE. A tart is a flat, baked item consisting of a base of PASTRY, or occasionally some other flour preparation, with a sweet or savoury topping not covered with a pastry lid. Such dishes have been made for a long time. They include pizza and its ancestors and relatives, with a base of bread dough; and some ancient forms of tart are described under that heading.

The term 'tart' occurs in the 14th-century recipe compilation the FORME OF CURY, and so does its diminutive, 'tartlet'. The relevant recipes are for savoury items containing meat. A mixture of savoury and sweet was common in medieval dishes and typical of the elaborate, decorative tarts and pies which were served at banquets. There was, however, a perceptible trend towards sweet tarts. These usually contained egg custard and fruits of various kinds, which could be used to provide the brilliant colours of which medieval cooks were fond: red, white, and pale green from fruits; strong green from spinach, which was used in sweet tarts; yellow from egg, with extra colour from saffron; and black from dark-coloured dried fruits. There are many 16th-century recipes for coloured 'tartstuffs'.

Tourte de moy, so called in England in the 16th and 17th centuries, was a tart of bone marrow (*melle* in French, changed to moy in English).

Nomenclature in other languages is as complex as in English. In French *tarte, tartelette, quiche,* and *flan* have much the same usages as their equivalents in English. But see also CROUTON; TIMBALE; MIRLITON. Tourte is a vaguer term, applied rather to cakes, raised pies, or even a large, round loaf.

In German *Torte* usually means 'cake', but there are exceptions: for example *Linzertorte* is indisputably a jam tart. *Pastetchen* or *Törtchen* are names for tartlets. In Italian *torta* means cake or pie or occasionally tart; but the most usual term for a tart is (*torta*) *crostata*. A *timballo* is a peculiarly Italian type of pastry-cased tart with a filling including pasta. In Spanish *tarta* means tart, and *tartaleta* or *pastelillo* means tartlet.

The pastry now used in most tarts is *pâte brisée*, a type of rich shortcrust which is strong enough to support a slice of the tart when it is cut, but is not tough. It may or may not be slightly sweetened. For sweet tarts, the richer *pâte sucrée*, which contains egg and a fair amount of sugar, may be used. Simple jam tarts are outstandingly popular items in this category. For something a little more sophisticated see BAKEWELL TART.

TARTARE a French word which has been in use since the 13th century and refers to the Tatars (the name of one of the tribes of the Turco-Mongol peoples of C. Asia who were renowned for their fierceness). The term has two meanings in the kitchen, both involving piquancy.

Sauce tartare is a MAYONNAISE made with hard-boiled egg yolk and the addition of onion/spring onion/chives; or finely chopped GHERKINS, CAPERS, and FINES HERBES.

Steak tartare is raw steak (beef or horsemeat), chopped and seasoned and presented with accompaniments as described in the article on STEAK. (These accompaniments include items such as onion which occur also in sauce tartare.)

TARTE TATIN an upside-down French apple TART (or PIE, depending on how one looks at it). Into the baking tin goes first a layer of sugar, then slices of apple, pre-cooked a little in butter, and finally the pastry. After being baked, the whole is turned out upside down. The apple juices then soak down into the pastry and the sugar has caramelized, giving a lovely golden topping.

The *Larousse gastronomique* explains that the name commemorates the Tatin sisters, who popularized it in their restaurant at Lamotte-Beuvron, to the south of Orléans, in the early 20th century. Later in the century, chefs devised variations, using pear, pineapple, or rhubarb, to give but three examples.

TASTE is a component of FLAVOUR (flavour equals taste plus aroma), but is here dealt with separately, despite the tendency in common parlance to use 'taste' as though it were a synonym of 'flavour'.

Tastes are what we detect with the taste buds in our mouths. These are elongated cells which terminate in what are called gustatory hairs. They are extremely small. The greatest concentration of them forms a kind of V shape on the supper surface of the tongue, just visible as tiny nipple-like protuberances and officially known as the vallate papillae. However, such papillae occur elsewhere on the tongue; and on the soft palate, the pharynx, and the epiglottis. All of them are inside the mouth. None are to be found on the hairs of a man's moustache, for example (although this might be a convenient arrangement, for which a precedent is provided by the taste buds to be found in the barbels of a catfish, which enable this creature to 'pre-taste' foods before admitting them 'through the barrier of its teeth', as Homer might have said if he had paid attention to the matter).

The taste buds are specialized. Some respond to sweetness, others to an acid taste, and so on. At one time it was thought that the taste buds were arranged in groups, for example those responding to sweetness on the tip of the tongue. However, although there is some truth in this notion, the actual arrangement is much less tidy, and may even be subject to change with the passage of time.

A similar uncertainty attends the question: how many tastes are there? Some of the many answers to this question date back to the remote past. For example, the views of Yi Yin, who was both cook and prime minister to King Tang, founder of the Shang dynasty in the 16th century BC, were preserved in the writing of Lu Buwei (3rd century BC). He thought then, as Chinese cooks think now, that there are five tastes—salty, bitter, sour, pungent, and sweet—which correspond to the five elements (water, fire, wood, metal, and earth) which constitute one of the basic ideas in Chinese philosophical thinking.

In Europe, one of the most interesting theories of taste was that of Père Polycarpe Poncelet, whose *Chimie du goût et de l'odorat* was first published in 1755. The title of his book implies full awareness on his part of the distinction between taste and aroma, and he assumes that his readers will understand this. His desire to link tastes with musical notes, as shown in an ingenious illustration in his book, reproduced in Jaine (ed., 1988), led him to insist that there were seven tastes; but if his *fade* and *aigre-doux* are discounted (the first seeming to be a negative term, meaning only 'not enough taste', and the second meaning simply sweet and sour, i.e. a combination of two tastes), his figure comes down to five.

In fact, the view which has been most widely accepted, at least in western countries, is that there are four tastes: sweet, bitter, acid (or sour), salt. However, many people believe that one or some of the following should be added to the list:

- metallic;
- 'meaty' or (to use the Japanese term) *umami*;
- astringent;
- pungent (as in the Chinese list above).

These are all sensations which occur in the mouth, so on the basis that tastes are, together with texture, what you sense in the mouth area these might be admitted. If, on the other hand, tastes are to be defined by the existence of taste buds reacting specifically to them, then the basic four must remain the only ones.

This sounds neat, and works well enough for astringency and pungency. The effect of sour persimmons on the mouth, making it pucker, and that of chilli pepper, creating a 'burning' sensation, apply to all the fleshy parts of the whole mouth area, not just taste buds; so they are different phenomena.

However, *umami* and the supposed 'metallic' tastes are more difficult. Although it seems clear that there are no specific taste buds for either, it seems equally clear that the taste buds collectively play a part in *umami* sensations (especially if one takes as a test case the taste/flavour intensifying properties of MONOSODIUM GLUTAMATE); and it seems to be the taste buds collectively, or anyway more than one kind of them, which react with salts of iron, copper, and tin to produce the metallic taste. (This taste is, unsurprisingly, often associated with foods which have been stored in cans.)

Certainly, common sense and common parlance suggest that we should not deny that things can taste meaty or metallic; but we can nevertheless maintain that these are not primary, independent tastes.

There are various other points to be taken into account in considering taste:

- Not everyone has a complete and properly functioning set of taste buds. Tests show that people have widely differing abilities to detect tastes, and that some people are 'taste-blind' to some extent in the same sort of way that people can be colour-blind.
- The very young show most sensitivity to tastes, and the elderly progressively less.
- Temperature affects taste. Sweetness and bitterness cannot be detected at all in foods which are either very hot or very cold. Sweetness is most intense at around 35 °C/95 °F (as in a hot but not too hot pudding); bitterness thrives on a cooler temperature such as 18 °C/64 °F.
- The strength of a taste may be increased, surprisingly, by the addition of a contrasting taste; adding a little salt to pineapple, as many SE Asians do, makes it taste sweeter. (This is useful knowledge for those who like a sweet taste but do not wish to use more sugar.)

READING: Lake (1989); Jaine (1988).

TASTING (against poison), a practice not unknown in modern times, was much more common in antiquity and was notably visible at the tables of royal or other powerful personages in the Middle Ages. The annals of the 14th- and 15th-century European countries are full of instances where troublesome nobles were neatly disposed of by the agency of poison. Several potent drops expressed from monkshood or wolfsbane, or from hemlock—the umbelliferous plant, not our innocent evergreen tree—or black hyoscyamus, yielded by the herb henbane, could be depended upon to make quick and relatively quiet work of an enemy. Likewise the lethal

effects of mercury, arsenic, or antimony sulphide were well understood by the pharmacists—and others—of the day. Besides, the chances to instil a poison in food abounded: the formal procedures followed for serving food in noble households meant that numerous individuals handled a multiplicity of prepared dishes as they made their long way between a distant kitchen and the dining hall. The determined assassin with a proclivity to poison had a remarkably good range of choice, in the areas both of means and of opportunity.

It is entirely understandable then, that the aristocrats and even royalty of the period were usually anxious about the wholesomeness of all the dishes that were set before them to eat. Yet so great was the apprehension about deliberate poisoning that a whole system of checks and counter-checks had evolved and was continuously in place in noble households, to ensure that none of the foods served to the high table were in any way tainted. In no other area of a prince's life did the security of his person give rise to such a complex series of formal tests than in the matter of his food. Everything he ate was subject to two sorts of assays: by a piece of unicorn horn, and by a sample being consumed by one of his trusted officers. (In the first case the presence of poison in the food might cause the unicorn horn—usually a piece of narwhal tusk, of dubious provenance—to change colour or tremble or even exude a sort of sweat; in the second case, the poison's effect upon the 'human guinea pig' would be adequately manifest.) At some courts these tests were regularly carried out several times during the process of dishing out and serving.

The above, which is based on Scully (1995), refers to Europe in the Middle Ages. Procedures in other parts of the world and in other epochs were similar in principle although different in detail and in the degree of elaboration which was thought necessary or found feasible.

TATAR CUISINE is of particular interest because of the geographical location of Tatarstan, formerly part of the Soviet Union and now a semi-autonomous state within the Russian Federation. With its capital, Kazan, lying about 500 miles directly east of Moscow, it is the northernmost Muslim community. The Kazan Tatars (so called to distinguish them from several smaller Tatar groups) prepare many familiar Near Eastern dishes such as PILAFS and KEBABS using cold-climate ingredients, beef or goose often replacing lamb and chicken. They are known for their substantial meat pies, including the large, rectangular *belish*, the small, round *peremech*, and the large, round *gubadia*. *Peremech* has a distinctive appearance; there is a little circular 'window' on the filling, around which the dough is neatly pleated. It is often served with a topping of thick onion soup and a spoonful of yoghurt.

The use of BUCKWHEAT, HORSERADISH, and POTATOES gives Tatar cuisine a quasi-Russian appearance, and Tatar SAMOSAS (*sumsa*) are made with a puffy dough, like the Russian *pirozhki* (see PIROG). Tatars and Russians also subscribe to the same school of hospitality, centring around the samovar and large arrays of buttery pastries. *Pekhlewe*, the Tatar BAKLAVA, is not made with flaky strudel-type dough. It is simply seven or eight layers of NOODLE paste alternating with layers of sweetened nuts. *Chekchek*, a sweet consisting of pea-sized balls of fried dough bound into a flat loaf with honey, is also known in Uzbekistan and has affinities still farther east; the same dish is known in China under a Manchu name, *saqima* (*sachima*).   CP

TAUTOG *Tautoga onitis*, a fine fish of the WRASSE family which belongs to the NW Atlantic and is most abundant between Cape Cod and Delaware Bay, although its range extends further north and south.

The common name is a version of the American Indian name *tautauog*. It appears

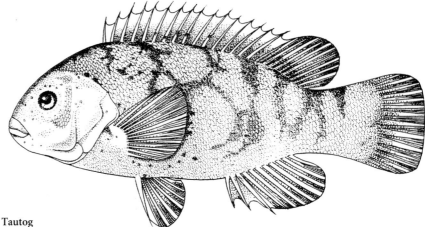

Tautog

also in French, where the fish is *tautauge noir*, referring to the dark coloration which also accounts for an alternative English name, black fish.

Although this fish has a maximum length of 1 m (40") its common length is up to half of that. It enjoys a healthy diet of clams, mussels, and small crustaceans, and has for long had a high reputation as a table fish. Making an interesting connection with the classical world, Davidson (1988*b*) remarked:

It is related that in the early nineteenth century a certain General Pinckney was so impressed by its merits that he imported a smack-load of tautog from Rhode Island and let them loose in the harbour of Charleston, South Carolina, where their descendants were still swimming about fifty years later. Whether true or not, it is an agreeable story, reminiscent of (indeed possibly inspired by, for the General may have been a classical scholar) the efforts which powerful Roman gourmets made to establish fish stocks, notably of other species of wrasse, where they wanted them.

TEA produced from the bush *Camellia sinensis*, is primarily important as one of the all-time great beverages of the world, a role which it first fulfilled in China and adjacent areas but which it has subsequently played (to packed tea houses one might say) in the rest of Asia, Europe (especially Britain), N. America, and Australia. Because of this role it has given its name to institutions such as HIGH TEA and the JAPANESE TEA CEREMONY.

Tea made as in TIBET, with butter, may be said to constitute a food; and of course nourishment is obtained from tea drunk with milk, as it often is in Britain. For an example of the eating of tea leaves as a sort of relish, see *lepet* under BURMA.

However, tea is also of some importance as a flavouring. Of the three main categories of tea (green, oolong, and black) the first and third are most commonly used for this purpose. Various sweet dishes, of which ICE CREAM is the most obvious example, can be given a subtle tea flavour, but some is also used in some parts of the world for savoury dishes. Thus in Vietnam there is a tuna and pork dish in which these main ingredients are simmered in tea—ideally lotus-flavoured tea but ordinary black tea will do. One effect of the tea in a dish of this sort is to balance the fat.

Tea terminology is a matter of concern to tea drinkers and also to cooks who are using tea as a flavouring. When tea is used as a flavouring for food, recipes often just say 'tea', without being more specific. In fact, the choice of tea would often be important and is best made with some knowledge of at least the main types of tea, as briefly indicated here.

Teas, like wines and coffees, are classified in many ways, for full details of which one of the major works on the subject has to be consulted, especially the venerable but unrivalled two volumes by Ukers (1935). Here is no more than a sketch map.

The first and fundamental classification is by the extent, if any, of fermentation. This produces the three main categories referred to above:

- Green (unfermented). The fresh leaves are dried immediately after picking. This prevents oxidization and inactivates the enzymes.
- Oolong (semi-fermented). Large-leafed teas, whose fermentation has been arrested before complete. The best come from Formosa, see below.
- Black (fermented). The leaves are wilted, bruised by rolling, and allowed to ferment in contact with the air, so that oxidization takes place. Then they are dried.

Another fundamental classification is by country or region of origin. Here there are:

- India. Most teas from India are black and two well-known examples are Assam and Darjeeling. Assam is full-bodied whereas Darjeeling, from the foothills of the Himalayas, is often called the champagne of teas and has a fine, delicate flavour.
- China produces both green and black teas. The best-known example of Chinese green tea is Gunpowder, a pale-coloured tea with a sharp distinctive taste. This tea is popular in N. Africa where it is flavoured with mint. Keemun is a well-known black tea from the Huangshan mountains.
- Formosa produces the best oolong teas which have a delicate fruity taste and are sometimes scented with jasmine, gardenia, or rose petals.
- Ceylon (Sri Lanka) produces a number of excellent teas and has been in the business for a long time.
- Kenya produces teas which have a quality something between the strong teas of India and the lighter teas of Sri Lanka.
- Japan produces almost exclusively green teas and tea plays an important part in Japanese social life and culture (see JAPANESE TEA CEREMONY). *Bancha* is the everyday green leaf tea; *matcha* is the more expensive powdered tea used for the tea ceremony.

Other terms, which also include classification by size of leaf, include:

- brick tea, made from coarse tea leaves, stalk, and dust, which are steamed and pressed together to form a brick to make it easily transportable. It is exported from China to Russia, and is used, for example, in Tibet and Mongolia where it is brewed with yak butter and salt. Brick tea was once used as a form of currency;
- Russian tea, which can mean either tea grown in Russia or tea drunk in the Russian style, i.e. in a glass with lemon;
- jasmine, tea flavoured with jasmine flowers. Tea can also be flavoured with other flowers, such as rose petals and orange blossom or fruits such as apple and mango;
- pekoe/orange pekoe/broken orange pekoe. Although pekoe was originally a Chinese word meaning 'white hair' (the white down on 'first flush' pickings) it is now a quality term for black leaf teas; and broken means that the leaves are broken in passing through rollers;
- Earl Grey, black tea which has been scented with oil of bergamot; one of the earliest blended teas, going back to the 18th century;
- English breakfast, which, according to Ukers, was a name originally applied to China black tea (Congou) in the USA, but subsequently used to include blends of black teas in which the China flavour is dominant.
- souchong (from the Chinese *siao-chung*, meaning larger leaves), which includes lapsang souchong which is described as having a distinctive smoky/tarry taste.

See also TISANE.
READING: Helen Gustafson (1996).

TEA BREADS AND TEA CAKES, collective terms of which the first is the more general. It applies to all the yeast-leavened baked goods considered suitable for AFTERNOON TEA or HIGH TEA in Britain, including many spiced, fruited, and enriched breads and buns. The latter term is applied especially to flat BUNS, about 15 cm (6") in diameter, often fruited, and lightly enriched with butter and egg; these are usually split, toasted and spread with butter. A few of the relevant terms used in Britain are listed below:

- **currant bread,** a general name for any fruited bread, from tea cakes to BARA BRITH;
- **fat rascals,** Yorkshire tea cakes containing sultanas and sweet spice, raised with baking powder, served hot, split, with butter;
- **fruit bread,** lightly enriched doughs containing dried fruit, favourites all over NW Europe. Many festive breads, such as PANETTONE, are fruit breads;
- **malt bread,** malt loaf, a soft cake-like bread sweetened with malt extract and sultanas. Served sliced and buttered for tea;

• **spice bread:** a term loosely embracing various enriched breads containing butter, eggs, fruit, and spices such as caraway or mixed sweet spice. The mixture was also made into small buns. These enriched spice breads may be counted among the forerunners of today's fruit cakes.

See also BARM BRACK; SAFFRON BREAD/CAKE; SALLY LUNN.

TEAL birds of the genus *Anas*, are a small kind of WILD DUCK.

The European teal, *A. crecca*, breeds in parts of Britain and has had a high reputation as a delicacy. Venner (1628) declared it to be the most pleasant and wholesome of all waterfowl. It is in season during the winter. In France a distinction is made between the *sarcelle d'été* and the *sarcelle d'hiver*, the former being the resident population while the latter are visitors.

There are several species in N. America. The green-winged teal, *A. carolinensis*, is the best known; but some prefer the blue-winged teal, *A. discors*, which is slightly larger and which attracted special praise from the ornithologist Audubon. Other species occur in S. America (one of them being known as pampas duck in Argentina), Hawaii, and parts of Asia.

TEF (or teff), *Eragrostis tef* (formerly *abyssinica*), is the native grain of Ethiopia (formerly Abyssinia). It grows about 75 cm (30") high on a stalk not much thicker than an oat straw, jointed at regular intervals. The flowering heads bear countless minute crimson flowers, which eventually yield seeds smaller than a pinhead.

The plant is prolific and is the most important food crop in Ethiopia, the only country which grows it as a cereal grain. (Elsewhere, as in Kenya, Australia, and S. Africa, it is occasionally cultivated for hay.)

In Ethiopia, where cultivation dates back to prehistoric times, the grain is ground into brownish flour and made into a soft, spongy bread called INJERA (or *ingera*). This has an agreeable acid flavour and is served with all kinds of dishes; it is eaten with the fingers.

TEMPE (or tempeh), a thin cake made by fermenting SOYA BEANS, is the Indonesian solution to the problem of making this indigestible vegetable into a nutritious food. It plays an important part in the cuisine of Java, and related products appear all over SE Asia, just as that other important soya bean product, TOFU, does further north.

Tempe is vital for the adequate nutrition of many Javanese, whose diet is rice based and contains little animal food. Rice is high in protein, but these proteins are low in the essential amino acid lysine. Soya beans have plenty of lysine, but even after the beans are cooked much of this protein is physically and chemically locked up and cannot be digested. The mould used in tempe fermentation produces enzymes which break up and 'pre-digest' the protein and make it accessible to human digestion. Indeed, as Sri Owen (1986) remarks:

Nutritionists and cooks must agree that tempe has a lot going for it. It contains about 40% protein—more than any plant or animal food—carbohydrates without starch, unsaturated oil without cholesterol, all eight essential amino acids, Vitamin A and several B-complex vitamins, iron, calcium, zinc, phosphorus and magnesium. It can be frozen at almost any stage in its manufacture or preparation.

Tempe is traditionally made from whole, dry soya beans which are washed, soaked until soft, partially dehulled, and boiled for a short time; this eliminates their pungent 'beany' flavour. The beans are then cooled to lukewarm, and inoculated with a starter culture of mould (*Rhizopus oryzae* or *R. oligosporus*). A small amount of tempe from a previous batch may serve as a starter, or a concentrated culture (RAGI, sometimes grown on hibiscus leaves) may be used. The beans are then divided into portions which are traditionally wrapped in banana leaves (preferable to plastic bags) and left to ferment until they have reached the required stage of ripeness.

The origin of tempe is unclear. It has certainly been made for centuries, possibly even millennia. One theory has it that Chinese traders visiting Java showed the inhabitants how to make soy sauce, whose starter, KOJI, is prepared from soya beans by a comparable process. It is only in the 20th century that tempe has become popular outside Java, and even now it is rarely found except where there has been migration from Java on some scale.

Tempe is now used in an increasing variety of ways by Indonesians. Its firm consistency allows it to be sliced, marinated in water and garlic, and then deep-fried. It may be boiled in a sauce, often made with KECAP; or steamed in banana leaves; or chopped small after being cooked and added to meat and vegetable stews or vegetable salads.

Tempe can be used at any of four stages in the fermentation process. *Tempe koro* is given four to six hours' less ripening time than normal tempe, giving a stiff underripe cake. Normal tempe (sometimes called *tempe murni*, pure tempe) ripens from 24 to 48 hours and is the most commonly used and the most versatile. *Tempe semangit* is two or three days older than this, and *tempe busuk* (rotten tempe) three to five days. The mould gives the tempe a flavour and texture reminiscent of cheese. *Tempe murni* resembles CAMEMBERT, while *tempe busuk* is like mature STILTON, being more crumbly and ammoniac in smell; its enzymes also have a marinating, tenderizing effect on other foods when it is combined in mixed dishes.

All kinds of tempe are kept in their wrappings until needed, as exposure to the air causes the mould to grow out of control and turns the surface black.

Tempe and similar products in Indonesia are also made from other vegetables. VELVET BEANS yield *tempe bengkuk*, WINGED BEANS *tempe kecipir*, wild TAMARIND seeds *tempe lamtoro*, and MUNG BEANS *tempe kacang hijau*. See also ONCOM, a product similar to tempe made from GROUNDNUT presscake.

The Javanese are very competitive about various tempes and their place of origin, but it is the *tempe murni* produced in the town of Malang in E. Java which is usually the most acclaimed, although the kind in C. Java which still uses banana leaves can sometimes be of comparably high quality.

Recent research in the USA has shown that tempe can be made successfully with a very wide range of both single and mixed legumes, grains, and seeds, including barley and soya beans; millet and soya beans; buckwheat; bulgar and wheat; oats; brown rice; okara, the presscake remaining when tofu is made. It is even possible to have noodle and pasta tempe. The nature of the end product varies with the choice of substrate. Not all are as versatile as the original soya bean tempe. But it is clear that tempe in an increasing number of varieties is capable of greatly extending food resources. READING: Shurtleff and Aoyagi (1985).

TEMPURA the name given in Japan to fish or vegetable fried in a light BATTER, in pieces of moderate size. This is the best known of three forms of deep-frying in Japan, which collectively provide the category of *agemono*, deep-fried dishes; see JAPANESE CULINARY TERMS.

The same sort of thing as tempura is prepared in many other places, but the manner in which it is done by the Japanese has given their version great renown. The history of tempura goes back about 400 years, to the time when Portuguese missionaries arrived in Japan. The Portuguese word *tempuras* means Ember Days, when meat was not eaten. It has been plausibly suggested that on these days the missionaries cooked fish and vegetables in the manner most palatable to them, by frying in batter, and that the Japanese adopted the technique and the name from them.

Since then tempura has come to be regarded as one of the most important Japanese dishes. There are many tempura restaurants: also tempura bars, where the customers are served the hot morsels in succession across the counter, the moment they have been cooked, and taste them at their best, are popular. Yabuki (*c*.1950), himself a tempura-restaurateur, explains that the Japanese characters which represent the word were chosen simply to produce the right sound, corresponding to what had been a foreign name, but that two of them happen to convey an appropriate meaning—flour like gauze, or a batter so delicate that it resembles a revealing dress. This batter is made with egg, water, and flour. The raw food is coated with the batter, and dipped in hot oil until golden brown, then served at once. The temperature of the oil should not be below 170° or above 180 °F (77–82 °C). Vegetable oil is usually used. Some say that sesame seed oil is ideal.

Any food that can be eaten deep-fried is used for tempura. Common materials include: *kurumaebi* (large prawn) and *ebi* (shrimp); *shirauo* (whitebait) and most kinds of white fish; vegetables, SHIITAKE mushrooms, fresh ginger, CHRYSANTHEMUM leaves, NORI, etc.

Sometimes two or three ingredients such as small shrimp, chopped tentacles of squid, chopped MITSUBA, diced BAMBOO shoot, or shredded carrots are mixed with batter and fried together by ladlefuls. This kind of tempura is called *kakiage*.

Tempura made entirely with vegetables is called *shojinage* (*shojin* means 'abstinence', but people usually make this version for economic rather than religious reasons).

Tempura is normally eaten dipped in *tentsuyu*, a mixture of SOY SAUCE, MIRIN (sweet cooking rice wine), and DASHI, into which one mixes grated daikon (see RADISH) and ginger.

(There is even an ice cream tempura—a Japanese version of BAKED ALASKA.)

TENCH *Tinca tinca*, a freshwater fish of the CARP family found throughout Europe. Length rarely over 50 cm (20"); coloration blackish-green with lighter and reddish underside. The flesh is soft but tasty and commands a high price in countries where it is appreciated, notably Germany. Tench are sometimes farmed in fish ponds, despite their slow rate of growth.

TENDERIZERS are used with MEAT, to make it more tender.

There are two ways of doing this. One is mechanical: breaking down the meat fibres by chopping or grinding. The second is to use a chemical agent. Marinades incorporating acid ingredients such as wine, vinegar, or fruit juice come into this category. The acid does act on the surface of the meat exposed to it, breaking down some of the links between proteins, but it also has a drying effect. Another chemical method is to add ENZYMES, extracted from plants, which break down proteins. Mixtures containing these are available from companies selling spices and seasonings. *Papain* (from unripe PAPAYA) is usually the active ingredient. *Bromelin*, extracted from PINEAPPLE, and *ficin*, from FIGS, have a similar effect.

The use of enzymes to tenderize meat sounds like a product of modern biotechnology, but is an ancient technique. Mexicans and others have, since antiquity, wrapped meat in papaya leaves before cooking.

However, the use of enzymatic tenderizers in meat cookery is attended by several limitations. These, and the experiments carried out to establish how and why they operate, have been well described by the three ladies responsible for some of the best work on experimental studies of food: see under Campbell (1979) in the bibliography. Briefly, these agents act only on exposed surfaces (including any exposed by pricking the meat); they are most active at temperatures between 55 and 75 °C (130 and 165 °F), i.e. far above room temperature; and they are deactivated at temperatures as high as boiling point. See also McGee (1984).

(LM)

TENGUSA the Japanese name for one of the red SEAWEEDS, *Gelidium amansii*. Widely used in S. and E. Asia for the production of AGAR-AGAR. In Japan, this seaweed ranks fourth in production, after WAKAME, KOMBU, and NORI.

The plants are dark red when fresh, but turn yellow if bleached by sunlight or soaked. The iodine content is high.

TENNIS CAKE an English Victorian cake made to accompany the newly invented game of lawn tennis. Some authorities say that the original recipe is by Mrs Beeton herself, although it does not appear in the first edition of her book. It is a creamed cake made light by reserving the egg whites, and also raised with baking powder, containing finely chopped glacé cherries, sultanas, and candied peel; it is flavoured with vanilla, cinnamon, and maraschino or noyau liqueur, and topped with almond paste, glacé icing, glacé cherries, and candied angelica. In the late 19th and early 20th centuries, tennis cakes, like other cakes and gateaux of the time, were very elaborate; one bakery textbook of the period gave 29 schemes for decorating the top of tennis cakes. By this time the cake had evolved from a round shape into an oblong approximating to the shape of a miniature tennis court.

TEPARY BEAN *Phaseolus acutifolius*, a relation of the HARICOT BEAN, is thought to be a native of C. America. It has a long history in Mexico; Purseglove (1987) states that it was first cultivated there 5,000 years ago. It has also been cultivated in Arizona since times BC. The variety cultivated is var *latifolius*.

The name may come from the Papago Indian name for bean, *pawi*. It has been suggested that when the Spaniards asked the Papago for the name of the bean, the reply was *t'pawi* (meaning 'it is a bean').

The tepary bean has been introduced into parts of E. and W. Africa where arid conditions are suitable for it. It is not, however, grown extensively outside its area of origin and even there its present range has become contracted as a result of the haricot bean replacing it.

The plant resists drought and disease well, and gives a small but quick yield of beans with a very high nutritional value. On the other hand, they are difficult to harvest, since the pods split open explosively, scattering the beans; and the beans themselves are small.

Tepary beans, which may be oval, flattish, or round, vary considerably in colour; Niethammer (1974) lists flesh colour, speckled brown, dark brown, reddish-brown, speckled yellow, purplish-black, clay colour with lavender speckles, greenish-yellow, and white. They measure about 8 by 6 mm (roughly 0.25" each way). They are shelled and dried before use. The combination which they offer of small size and outstanding nutritional qualities makes them highly suitable as travellers' provisions. They need longer cooking than haricot beans, but the flavour is equally good. In the regions where they are grown, they often turn up in soups.

Mary Kelsey (1990) states that the northern Pima Indians are specialists in growing teparies. She also records that the Hopi Indians still use white teparies to break a fast; they parch them in hot sand, then mix them with salt water, and beans thus prepared may also be used 'for observation of spiritual events'. Many Indian groups have also used the related *P. metcalfei*, cocolmeca or 'tepary bean of the brush' (Spanish *tepari del monte* or *frijolillo*). These are larger beans, and easier to harvest since they drop next to the plant.

TERMITE HEAP MUSHROOM a name applicable to various fungi which grow on termite heaps, but par excellence to *Termitomycetes titanicus*, the largest edible mushroom in the world and reputedly among the best. This giant, which is found throughout Zambia (and no doubt in neighbouring African countries), has a cap which may measure almost 1 m (say, 3') across. It was first scientifically described by Pegler and Piearce (1980), who commented: 'It is incredible that such a large fungus which is popularly known and common in Zambia should have remained undescribed until now.' It seems that the cap is the only part which is normally eaten.

TERMITES insects in the order Isoptera, are better known for eating timber (they have a remarkable ability to digest wood) than for being eaten themselves; but in many tropical regions they are eaten locally and even regarded as a delicacy.

Termites, often known as 'white ants', live in social groups with a complex caste structure which defines the tasks which any given specimen should perform. They inhabit termite mounds which can be of great size and always make their presence obvious to human or other predators. These mounds, incidentally, provide a habitat for some very large edible fungi (see TERMITE HEAP MUSHROOM) as well as for the internal 'plantations' of tiny fungi which the termites grow for their own use.

Examples could be quoted from many parts of the world of the methods followed in catching and cooking termites. Bodenheimer (1951) draws attention to the description of termite consumption in 'the astonishing account of *Termes bellicosus*' given in the *Philosophical Transactions of the Royal Society* (1781) by Henry Smeathmann and based mainly on observations on the Banana Island:

[The Africans] are content with a very small part of those which at the time of swarming, or rather of migration, fall into the neighbouring water, which they skim off with calabashes, bring large kettles full of them to their habitation, and dry them in iron pots over a gentle fire, stirring them about as is usually done in roasting coffee. In that state, without sauce or any other addition, they serve them as delicious food. And they put them by handfuls into their mouths, as we do comfits. I have eaten them dressed this way several times, and think them both delicate, nourishing and wholesome.

This recommendation is supplemented by the comment from Sparrmann (1789) that he had 'discoursed with several gentlemen [in S. Africa] upon the taste of the white ants' and met with the unanimous opinion that they are 'most delicious and delicate eating. One gentleman compared them to sugared marrow, another to sugared cream, and a paste of sweet almonds.' Another comparison, reflected in terms such as 'rice ants' and 'bushman's rice', is with grains of rice, which these ants are perceived as resembling.

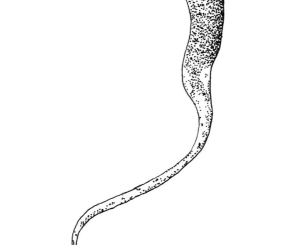

Termitomycetes titanicus

TERRINE a French term (dating back to medieval times) used also in English (since the 18th century) to denote either a type of oven-proof dish with a close-fitting lid or what is cooked in it. The word derives originally from the Latin *terra*, meaning earth and referring therefore to an earthenware dish. By extension a similar dish made of metal may be called a terrine.

The recipient itself is often but not invariably rectangular; it is straight sided and fairly deep. What is cooked in it has evolved in the course of time to its current form, a sort of 'loaf', suitable for being sliced, of minced meat, poultry, seafood, or vegetables (or even fruits). The terrine is often layered so that when slices are cut from it they present an attractive and multi-coloured appearance.

In practice, it is hard to discern any significant difference between terrine and PÂTÉ, except that the latter term does not have the additional meaning of the recipient.

TESTICLES appear on menus under various euphemisms which prevent the diner from confronting too directly the contents of the plate. Those from sheep are known as 'fries' in English, and are sometimes called *rognons blancs* (literally, 'white kidneys') in French. In N. American English, calf's testicles are called 'prairie oysters'. The old English term for testicles was 'stones', those of lambs and cocks being most frequently cited.

In many pastoral cultures, in areas as disparate as the hill regions of the British Isles and the pampas of S. America, lamb's or calf's testicles have probably always been a seasonal item of food in late spring. At this time of the year, the rightful owners are deprived of them during castration, a routine annual process in any meat-raising economy.

These general points aside, the history of using testicles for food is surprisingly obscure. In English cookery from the 17th to 19th centuries, recipes for lamb stones are occasionally given. They were put into spiced cream sauces or made into FRICASSÉES. They are also mentioned as ingredients of extraordinary and elaborate dishes of mixed offal and other titbits, such as (according to Robert May, 1685):

a dish of Oxe Pallets with great Oysters, Veal, Sweetbreads, Lambstones, peeping Chickens, Pigeons, slices of interlarded Bacon, large Cock-combs, and Stones, Marrow, Pistaches, and Artichocks.

These were all roasted or fried, and served heaped up on a dish garnished with slices of orange and lemon, according to Robert May (1685). This dish required both lamb and cock stones. Lamb stones were also listed amongst the ingredients of pies during the late 17th and early 18th centuries.

Testicles continue to be eaten in many countries, perhaps especially in Spain, Italy, the Middle East, and the Orient, and their identity continues to be disguised almost everywhere by euphemisms.   (LM)

TEX-MEX a term which first became current in the late 1940s, refers to certain Mexican dishes as they are made in Texas. The key note is struck by the use of CHILLI pepper, as in CHILI CON CARNE. Standard items of this hybrid cuisine include CORN BREADS, enchiladas, nachos, tacos, TAMALES, and TORTILLAS.

TEXSEL GREENS a relatively new green vegetable, is a cultivar developed towards the end of the 20th century from Ethiopian/Abyssinian MUSTARD, *Brassica carinata*, a plant indigenous to E. Africa. Older leaves and stems are cooked, and served like collards (see KALE) or like SPINACH (whose flavour they slightly resemble). The inflorescence can be treated like a head of broccoli. Young leaves are used in salads.

For nutritional purposes, it compares well with the other BRASSICA vegetables. The crop extends from late spring to autumn.

The name Texsel (also spelled TexSel or Teksel) was given because this is a cultivar developed at the University of Texas; but the name has now become the usual common name.

THAILAND performed an extraordinary feat in the last three decades of the 20th century by invading the cities and even towns of the English-speaking world and studding them with Thai restaurants. In speed and scope this feat is unique. It reflects in equal measure the attractive qualities of Thai cuisine and the entrepreneurial abilities which many Thai people have developed in recent times.

It is tempting to connect this striking success with one other aspect of Thailand's history which again makes the country unique in SE Asia; it was never colonized. Moreover, broadly speaking, the country has a remarkably long history of stability, to which the Buddhist religion, the social structure, and the monarchy have contributed. These features have combined with a wealth of indigenous produce to establish a coherent and highly developed cuisine. The royal court has not only helped generally to establish and enhance Thailand's cultural identity, but has also served in highly specific ways to promote (in the sense of 'bringing forward') Thai cuisine. The royal kitchens have been a forcing house for the talents of Thai cooks. Kings of Thailand have written cookery books; and the category of royal cookery books has overlapped occasionally with another and exceptionally interesting category which seems to be peculiar to Thailand, namely funeral cookbooks; see FUNERAL FOOD.

The population is Buddhist with minority groups of Muslims, Christians, and animists. Buddhism (see BUDDHISM AND FOOD) has not influenced the cuisine by creating a predominant vegetarian tradition, although there is a school of vegetarian food from the south derived from Chinese influence which skilfully mimics meat products. One can, however, see the impact of Buddhism in Thai attitudes to food—the way it is revered and has an important ritual role. A small offering will be made to the family's spirit house every day; food is given to the Buddhist monks as alms; weddings and funerals are celebrated with a feast. In connection with funerals see, again, the paragraph on Thai funeral cookbooks in FUNERAL FOOD.

Geographical factors conspire to make Thai cuisine pleasantly diverse. The long coastline around the Gulf of Thailand, central plains with major river systems, dry uplands in the east and mountains on the western and northern fringes of the country—all these foster different kinds of dishes.

The majority of the population is employed in agriculture. RICE dominates the economy and the landscape of the central plains where two crops of rice a year are the norm. CASSAVA, SUGAR, MAIZE, and PINEAPPLE are also major export items.

Rice is not only the mainstay of most meals. It also appears in noodles both fresh and dried. Rice flour is made into dumplings and finds its way into many sweet dishes. Sticky rice is favoured in the north and for some sweet dishes.

As in other countries where rice is the staple, it provides for Thai cooks a perfect basis on or beside which they can construct their complex and subtle pattern of flavour and visual appeal. The interplay of flavours will include sour, salt, sweet, and, most powerfully, the heat of CHILLIES. Of the salt elements, the most important are FISH SAUCE (*nam pla* in Thailand) and shrimp paste. Other prime flavouring agents include fresh CORIANDER leaf, lime juice, COCONUT milk, fresh BASIL, sugar including PALM SUGAR, MAKRUT LIME leaf, GARLIC, fresh GINGER and GALINGALE, TAMARIND, and

---

SOME THAI FOOD TERMS

GAENG, curries, generally very hot. There is plenty of liquid in *Gaeng khieo wan* (green curry) and *Gaeng ped* (red curry). *Gaeng mussaman* (Muslim curry) and *Gaeng phanaeng* (dry curry) have thicker sauces and are slightly milder.

NAM PRIK is a hot sauce with many variations, used to flavour plain rice or as a dipping sauce.

Yam are like salads and invariably contain a small proportion of meat or fish; they are based on vegetables, cellophane noodles, fruits such as the POMELO, and flowers such as the BANANA FLOWER. *Som tam* is particularly popular and has green PAPAYA as its main ingredient.

Larb, meat salads, are prepared from chopped or ground meat from any source, cooked or raw, and are a speciality of the north-east.

Gaeng chud are soups, the most popular being *tom yam kung* made with prawns and *tom khaa gai* prepared from galingale, chicken, and coconut milk.

Sen or *mee*, noodles, are made from rice, wheat, and mung beans, the first two being available in fresh and dried forms. They are used in a variety of dishes. *Kuiteow* are fresh large rice noodles usually fried with vegetables; *mee krob* are wheat noodles deep-fried and coated in sugar syrup as a savoury dish.

Khanom are the sweet dishes although they may have a savoury edge, for instance being flavoured with garlic. They are usually small individual items and many are prepared in banana leaf parcels.

LEMON GRASS. Besides dried chillies, several dried spices—notably cumin, cardamom, coriander and cinnamon—are in frequent use.

On the visual side, it is remarkable how even a simple dish will have its appearance enhanced and transformed with delicate vegetable carvings.

The first meal of the day will usually be a simple thick rice soup with accompaniments of chicken, dried squid, and pickled vegetables. Rural workers take a basket of cold sticky rice to the fields for lunch whilst city dwellers make use of the huge range of eating facilities from pavement noodle-sellers upwards. Casual consumption of street and snack foods, between formal meals, is a basic part of Thai eating habits.

Families reassemble for more formal evening meals. Steamed rice will typically be accompanied by a 'hot' curry, a cold salad, a vegetable dish, and a soup. Food is served tepid and eaten with a fork and spoon; there is no need for a knife as all food is cut small. A ball of sticky rice in the hand may be the chosen utensil in traditional northern meals.

Fresh fruit is typically served at the end of a meal. Mangoes, of which many varieties are available, are a particular speciality. They are eaten both ripe with sticky rice, *Mamuang khao niew*, and also when the flesh is still slightly green with a dip of salt, sugar, and dried chilli. (PI)

THANKSGIVING

A national American holiday centered around a family feast commemorating the first harvest of the Plymouth Colony in 1621 after a winter of great suffering and near starvation. The colony had been established the year before, and, in thanks to God for their survival, Governor William Bradford (1590–1657) declared a feast to be held between the settlers and the Indians of the region, led by Chief Massasoit of the Wampanoag tribe, which had signed a treaty with the Pilgrims. It is not known exactly when the feast was held, but it was most probably between September 21 and November 9.

Massasoit arrived at the feast, which probably lasted several days, with ninety-nine braves, bringing many of the dishes, including popcorn. Governor Bradford sent out four men to catch game, but it is not known for sure whether the fowl consumed on the first Thanksgiving included turkey, which has since become the traditional main course of Thanksgiving celebrations. It is known that oysters, eel, corn bread, goose, venison, watercress, leeks, berries, and plums were eaten, all accompanied by sweet wine.

The next recorded Thanksgiving in the Plymouth Colony was on July 30, 1623, at which turkey was definitely served, along with cranberries and pumpkin pie.

Mariani (1994), who wrote the above account, goes on explain the evolution of a local New England anniversary into a national holiday (from 1789), and the

manner in which the day of its celebration has fluctuated; since 1863, except for two years in the Second World War, it has been the last Thursday in November.

The concept of a feast held to give thanks for a happy event is, naturally, widespread in the world. However, whatever parallels may be found to this American occasion, it is indisputably the archetypal thanksgiving feast.

THARID

THARID or tharida, an ancient Arabian dish of bread mixed with stewed meat. It was praised by the Prophet Muhammad, who said of his favourite wife: 'Aisha surpasses other women as tharid surpasses other dishes.'

The Prophet's sanction has made tharid one of the tiny handful of Arabian dishes to have spread beyond the peninsula. It is prepared today from Morocco (*trid*) as far east as Xinjiang province, China (*terit*), in versions varying from the plain ancient dish of bread sopped in broth or stew to fairly elaborate ones. Most modern tharids involve alternating layers of stew and flat bread. The Syrian dish *fatteh* made by mixing toasted PITTA bread with yoghurt and stewed meat is essentially a tharid; however, some *fattehs* are mixed with chickpeas instead of meat.

In the Middle Ages, very elegant tharids were made. Crisp, thin bread was pounded in a special basin called *mithrada* to give a smoother texture when mixed with the stewed meat. In Moorish Spain, the bread crumbled for tharid was often a sort of puff pastry. The present-day Moroccan *trid* consists of layers of the paper-thin pastry WARQA alternating with stew.

Moorish Spain was particularly rich in tharids, including an odd one of eggplants stuffed with meat and bread crumbs. However, the everyday Spanish Arab tharid was apparently made with considerable broth. The Portuguese word for soup, *açorda*, derives from *al-thurda*, an alternative Moorish pronunciation of tharida. CP

THEOPHRASTUS

THEOPHRASTUS On his deathbed the Greek philosopher and scientist Aristotle was asked to choose his successor as head of the peripatetic school. He sent for Rhodian wine. 'This is indeed a good, sound wine,' he said as he sipped it. Then he asked for a cup of Lesbian wine. 'Both are excellent,' he said, 'but the Lesbian is the sweeter.' His followers took the gentle hint, passed over Eudemus of Rhodes, and appointed Theophrastus of Eresus on Lesbos as their head. Born about 371 BC, Theophrastus had come to Athens to study under Aristotle. He succeeded his teacher in 322 and died about 287.

His real name was Tyrtamos. Aristotle himself gave him the nickname

Theophrastos, 'divinely spoken', because of his eloquence. Both Aristotle and Theophrastus, in their serious writing, cultivated a special clipped style that demands intense concentration, lacking most of the recaps and repetitions that help the reader to assimilate normal prose. Theophrastus combined this feature skilfully with rhythm and euphony, a combination admired by his contemporaries but not by most later readers.

Few of his many writings survive. Of those that do, the most important are two botanical treatises which give a great deal of information about agriculture, gardening, and wild plants, and thus about the plant foods of Greece and neighbouring countries. They are traditionally called *History of Plants* and *Causes of Plants* (better titles would be 'Enquiry into Plants' and 'Plant Physiology') and follow the pattern of Aristotle's *History of Animals* and other zoological works. They aim to systematize the results of direct research and of enquiries made by students, in various parts of the Greek world, among farmers, 'root-cutters' (herbalists), and others with specialized knowledge. Students of the school of Aristotle and Theophrastus had accompanied Alexander the Great's expedition, crossing SW Asia to the banks of the Indus. They sent back information on the trees and the food plants of Persia, Afghanistan, and India: thus Theophrastus' writings contain the earliest reports in Europe of citrons, bananas, mangoes, JACKFRUITS, PISTACHIOS, JUJUBES, and TAMARINDS.

The researches of Theophrastus contributed directly to the botanical information in Pliny's Latin *Natural History* and were also incorporated in Greek and Roman dietary and pharmacological writings. The classification of plants developed in the *History of Plants* was not significantly improved upon until superseded by the system of LINNAEUS. AD

THERMOMETERS

THERMOMETERS measuring temperature, are found in some domestic kitchens and not in others; but are virtually omnipresent in large professional kitchens and food-processing establishments.

All thermometers of conventional design are descended from a device invented by the Italian scientist Galileo in 1592, and now known as a thermoscope. It was a narrow glass tube with a bulb at the bottom. This was filled with water, and the top was left open. If the temperature of the surroundings rose the water would expand, causing its level in the tube to rise. The amount of expansion was tiny, but the change in level was amplified by the fact that the bulb was much larger in diameter than the tube.

The word *thermomètre* was first used by the Jesuit Father Leuréchon in 1626. Soon it was realized that the device could be made more accurate by sealing it from the air so that the liquid would not evaporate. This was done by filling the tube completely, heating it till the water boiled, and then thrusting the top end into a hot brazier to melt the glass. As the water cooled it contracted, leaving a vacuum in the top of the tube. Later alcohol was used instead of water; this freezes at –114 °C (–173 °F), so that temperatures below zero can be measured. Normally it would boil at 78 °C (173 °F), but the pressure inside the tube caused by the expansion of the alcohol keeps it liquid, and alcohol thermometers can measure temperatures well above the boiling point of water. In 1670 mercury was used; this has the advantage of being much easier to see than water or alcohol, even if dye is added to these. But it freezes at –39 °C (–38 °F), so it is unsuitable for very low temperatures.

At first any scale marked on the thermometer was arbitrary. At the beginning of the 18th century the German physicist Carl Gabriel Fahrenheit built improved thermometers and devised the scale which bears his name. He fixed the zero mark (what we now call 0 °F, equal to –18 °C) as the lowest temperature he could achieve, by mixing ice and salt. The 100 °F mark was supposed to be blood heat, but he seems to have had a slight fever when he made the measurement, as normal human temperature is 98.6 °F (37 °C). In 1742 the Swedish astronomer Anders Celsius tried to produce a more rational scale, taking as the low mark the freezing point of water, and as the high mark the boiling point of water. In fact, he called the bottom of his scale 100° and the top 0°, but this was soon found inconvenient and reversed.

Glass thermometers are fragile. Where no great accuracy is needed, a bimetallic strip thermometer is often used. This contains a thin, flat strip made of a layer of iron and a layer of brass soldered together, and bent into a coil. The outer end of the coil is fixed, the inner end attached to a spindle carrying an indicator needle. Brass expands more when heated than iron does, so when the coil is heated or cooled its curvature changes, turning the spindle and moving the needle.

Thermometers are used for various purposes in cookery. The sugar thermometer is an alcohol type set in a brass holder which is designed for SUGAR BOILING operations, including jam- and marmalade-making. It can be lowered into the hot syrup or jam (or, conveniently, fitted over the side of the pan, with its bottom end in the syrup or jam), and will register up to 180 °C (356 °F), slightly above the caramel point of

sugar. It can also be used for other tasks where temperature is important, such as making yoghurt. Oven thermometers are usually of the robust bimetallic type, with a magnet on the back so that they can be fixed to the steel wall of the oven.

MEAT thermometers are used to tell whether the interior of a joint has reached a certain level, for example 60 °C (140 °F) for rare beef or 85 °C (185 °F) for well-done pork. One type has a sharp-ended, hollow metal probe filled with a liquid which conveys heat to a bimetallic strip thermometer at the outside end. Modern meat thermometers are electronic, with a piece of carbon inside the tip of the probe whose electrical resistance increases as it is heated. The instrument measures the resistance, converts it into a temperature, and shows the figure on a digital display.

RH

THISTLE the name for many plants, generally thought of as prickly rather than nutritious. However, many are eaten, notably the ARTICHOKE.

Some wild European thistles of the genus *Carduus* have stems which, once peeled, can be used like asparagus and have a good flavour. In France and Germany names meaning 'wild artichoke' are given to various thistles with edible heads, including the smooth carline thistle, *Carlina acaulis*, and milk thistle, *Silybum marianum*.

Many thistles also have edible roots, including *Onopordum acanthium*, the species which is the symbol of Scotland; the milk thistle; and Spanish SALSIFY.

Thistle leaves are used as a vegetable, mainly in Asia. Those with edible leaves include the Japanese blessed thistle, *Cirsium japonicum*; the meadow distaff, *C. oleraceum*, eaten in Russia and Siberia; and a host of others.

THREADFIN BREAM breamlike fish of the family Nemipteridae, most but not all of whose members have a long filament extending backwards from the tail fin. The species *Nemipterus japonicus* is a common one in SE Asian waters; its market length is around 20 cm (8") and its body, pink above and yellow below, bears longitudinal stripes. The white tender flesh makes good eating.

Two other species well known at Hong Kong are *N. virgatus*, *hung sam* (golden thread), a larger fish; and *N. bathybius*, *wong to* (yellow belly).

THREADFINS tropical fish of the family Polynemidae, are so called because the lower part of their pectoral fins consist of very long rays, sometimes longer than the body of the

fish. These serve as organs of touch, helping them to detect their prey.

Eleutheronema tetradactylon, a species which has a range from India through SE Asia, may reach a length of over 1.5 m (60"), but is usually much smaller. It is silvery-green above and creamy below. It is a fish of commercial importance in India, and is highly esteemed in Thailand—to be fried, boiled, steamed, roasted, pickled, or dried. The specific name means 'three-fingered', referring to the three long rays. Some related species have six or seven, but the one which costs most in Thailand, where it is in demand for some special fish soups, is *E. tridactylon*, which has three.

Polynemus indicus, a rather small species with a broadly similar range, is a golden fish, which enters estuaries. It is common on the west coast of Malaysia. *P. paradisius*, the tupsi fish of India and the mango fish (*nga-pon-na*) of Burma, is quite small (just over 20 cm/8") but is regarded as a delicacy in both countries. In Thailand its name is *pla nuat phram*, meaning the fish with a Brahman moustache.

The genus *Polydactylus* (many-fingered—they gave up counting) is represented in the E. Pacific (Peru to California) by *P. approximans*; and in the W. Atlantic by *P. virginius*, which is common in the W. Indies. Both of these are small fish.

THRUSH the common name of many species of bird in the genus *Turdus*, to which the BLACKBIRD also belongs. Best known in Britain and W. Europe are the beloved song thrush, *T. philomelos*, and the mistle thrush, *T. viscivorus*. These two were already distinguished from each other and from close relations in Anglo-Saxon times. The name 'mavis' (cf French *mauvis*) was used more or less interchangeably with thrush by Shakespeare, as Francesca Greenoak (1979) points out; but in more recent times it refers to the song thrush in East Anglia and to the mistle thrush in parts of Scotland.

Thrushes are among the numerous kinds of small bird which have been trapped and eaten in most of Europe. The practice has been dying out, partly no doubt in deference to bird-lovers. Traditional ways of cooking thrush included: with POLENTA in the north of Italy; roasted with JUNIPER berries in Belgium; grilled on a skewer, again in Italy; and made into a PÂTÉ or TERRINE.

THUNDER AND LIGHTNING a dramatically named sweet item, which has evidently taken various forms, all involving a contrast of dark and light. Fernie (1905) has much plausible detail built into his description:

About Devon, and Cornwall, Clotted Cream is eaten with every practical form of sweet thing, from stewed fruit to Christmas pudding, treacle and Cream being an approved combination. This is colloquially known as 'thunder and lightning;' and orthodox lovers, out for the day, order it with their tea, in Fuschia-covered cottages; then the correct and mystic practice is to smother a 'split cake' (a sort of small Sally Lunn) with some of the thick Cream, and to trace on its surface, in casual letters formed by the golden syrup, trickling from a spoon, the beloved one's name, or its initial letters.

On the other hand, Dorothy Hartley (1954) says that thunder and lightning consists of: 'Hot plain water-boiled rice (as for curry) served piled high and loose on a hot dish, with golden syrup handed separately.'

The term 'treacle' can be used correctly of either the dark, thick TREACLE which was more common in the 19th century than now, or of the GOLDEN SYRUP which is mentioned in both the above accounts and which is paler and runnier. It seems probable that, when the expression 'thunder and lightning' originally came into use in a food context, the dark treacle was meant. But the subject is one which calls out for further illumination.

THYME *Thymus vulgaris*, an important flavouring herb of the Mediterranean region and S. Europe, has been introduced to N. America and is widely cultivated. The principal culinary thyme, it is best known in the form of its cultivar English (also English Winter), but the cultivar French (also Narrow Leaf French, or French Summer) has a stronger flavour and is preferred in France.

There are many other species and some of them have cultivars, so the choice for the cook is extensive. A selection of minor species is shown in the box. More important are the hybrid *Thymus × citriodorus* (classification and terminology of thymes are confusing, this used to be *T. pulegioides × T. vulgaris*), lemon-scented thyme, of which there are several cultivars; and *T. praecox* ssp *arcticus* (formerly *T. serpyllum*), wild or creeping thyme, sometimes called mother of thyme, widespread, including N. Europe, also with a number of cultivars. Yet another species, which is important in the Middle and Near East, is *T. capitatus*, conehead thyme, which may (confusingly) be called 'Persian hyssop' although in Arabic it is *za'atar farsi* (Persian thyme). See also ZAATAR; this is probably the most common and the strongest ingredient in most of the spice mixtures which bear that name. Its flowers are the source of the famous Hymettus HONEY; and what is called 'Spanish origanum oil' is produced from it. It is one of the species which provides the well-known flavour called OREGANO.

OTHER SPECIES OF THYME

- *T. broussonetii*, a pine-scented thyme of N. Africa.
- *T. caespititius* (formerly *T. azoricus*), Azores thyme, with a tangerine scent.
- *T. herba-barona*, caraway thyme, has a cultivar, Nutmeg. The specific name was given because in past times it was thought suitable for rubbing into a baron of beef. The other names indicate the nature of the aroma.
- *T. mastichina*, mastic thyme or Spanish marjoram, is used in many parts of the Mediterranean region. Its distilled oil (in commerce 'oil of wild marjoram') has an odour of eucalyptus and camphor.
- *T. pulegioides*, broad-leaved thyme, has a number of cultivars including one bearing the name Oregano (also Italian Oregano), whose bright green leaves have an aroma similar to OREGANO.

Thyme is a standard component of a BOUQUET GARNI. Dried thyme, if not kept for too long, is an adequate substitute for fresh. The flavour varies according to species or cultivar, but is generally of a sharp and bittersweet taste with a strong and warm aroma. This is due to the presence of thymol, common to all true thymes.

The leaves of most kinds of thyme can be used to good effect with almost any savoury dish: vegetable, fish, poultry, meat. The essential oils produced from any of several species have many uses in the food industry.

In the W. Indies a plant of a different genus is known as thyme: see SPANISH THYME.

Ti *Cordyline fruticosa*, is a plant found in tropical Asia and Oceania. It is called *auti* in Tahiti and *ki* in Hawaii. The young shiny green leaves are eaten as a pot-herb. The Polynesians especially prize the plant for the large fibrous root which is high in sugar and when baked has a flavour a bit like molasses candy. Jennifer Brennan (forthcoming) describes the baking:

The Polynesian baked the ti tubers in large, communal earth ovens; similar to those used for cooking foods for feasts. However, these particular ovens were dedicated solely to the preparation of mass quantities of the tubers for community occasions and were generally dug in the bush areas outside the villages. As the preparation and cooking took two days and involved a number of people these 'bakes' were very social affairs.

The ti pits were circular in Samoa, with a raised earthen rim or berm. In Tahiti, the openings were rectangular. Similar ovens were constructed by the Maori in New Zealand but, although they were called *umu ti*, the plant baked was a different species, the New Zealand cabbage tree, *Cordyline australis*. The results were similar because the Down Under species has an equally high concentration of fructose.

This confection can be eaten or used to sweeten puddings and other foods. It is now seen less often than in the past.

TIBET by virtue of its high altitude and cold climate, requires substantial and warming foods. A lot of fat is eaten.

Generally speaking, staple foods of Tibetans have to be foods which themselves are adapted to the climate. The cereal most consumed is barley; toasted barley flour, TSAMPA, is the main staple. However, *tsampa* just means toasted flour, and may be prepared from wheat, maize, millet, oats, even soya beans. Popped grain, *yoe*, is another popular cereal product. Bread may be steamed or fried, using wheat flour. Pancakes are made of buckwheat.

Rinjing Dorje (1985) is an author the title of whose book, *Food in Tibetan Life*, indicates that its scope is much more than that of a recipe book. He explains the attitude of Tibetans to eating meat:

Where grains and vegetables are plentiful, people eat hardly any meat. This is because Buddhism does not allow taking the life of another. But for those, in many parts of the country, who have to eat meat for survival, one feels: 'It's permitted, for the sake of one's survival.' Thus, even though nomads have to get much of their food by slaughtering animals from their herds, their way of life is still religiously respectable. And people who live in other ways, even monks and nuns, welcome the dairy and meat products that the nomads provide.

Still, Tibetans do not eat the meat of small animals. Since a life is a life, no matter what size, people consider it better to take just one life, of a single large animal. It would take the lives of many small animals to produce as much meat.

Momo, steamed meat-filled dumplings (see MANTOU), are very popular. So are various dishes using OFFAL. If an animal is killed by other beasts or falls from a cliff, Tibetans will readily eat it and think it their duty, as well as pleasure, to utilize every edible scrap.

Meat, even fat, and cheese can be dried easily in the cold dry atmosphere. *Sha kampo*, dried meat, can be prepared in quite thick strips and will become dry like cork, and tender to eat whether cooked or not.

Most Tibetans abstain from fish, pork, and poultry. For all, dairy foods are important. The dri (female YAK) is used just for milk and milk products. There are also cows and there are animals called *dzos* (male) and *dzomos* (female) which are a cross between a yak and a lowland cow.

TEA has to be imported into Tibet, where a lot is drunk. Tibetan *boeja*, tea mixed in a churn with butter, salt, and cream, surprises those who are accustomed to drinking their tea in warmer countries.

Noodle dishes (see NOODLES OF ASIA), including one called *chow-chow*, are among those which have entered Tibet from China. Nepal has contributed split pea pancakes and pickled vegetable greens; and the influence of India is plain in some curry-type dishes and HALVA.

A traditional Tibetan kitchen is very simple. The fuel is wood or animal dung.

TIFFIN an Anglo-Indian term used in India for lunch or a light snack in the middle of the day or in the afternoon.

The word, which is not recorded in Indian usage until the beginning of the 19th century, may have its origin in a colloquial English word, tiffing, which according to Grose's dictionary of 1785 meant 'eating or drinking out of meal-times'. Yule and Burnell (*Hobson-Jobson*, 1979), who have a particularly full and charming entry in their dictionary, seem to think so and provide a wealth of examples of use of the term in the 19th century. These are well chosen to illustrate the flexibility in timing of this 'slight repast'.

In earlier centuries, Europeans in India had heavy, lavish meals in the middle of the day and a light meal in the evening, as Achaya (1994) points out; but by the turn of the 20th century eating patterns had changed and the luncheon, which became known as tiffin, was much lighter, the main formal meal being taken in the evening. As Jennifer Brennan (1990) remarks:

Tiffin, the midday meal, was a welcome break in the long Indian day; the pause for sustenance and prelude to a siesta. . . . *Tiffin* was a domestic meal, a chance for husbands and wives to eat together if they wished. Children were seldom present at the table, taking their tiffin . . . in the nursery.

The sort of dishes served for tiffin vary but curries were very popular and salads often served particularly in hot weather. Leftovers from roast dinners could be used up, cold with relishes or made into pies or minced into cutlets and meatballs. Fruit fools, jellies, and ice creams were popular desserts.

In the cities of India tiffin is delivered to homes and offices in tiered aluminium or enamelled tiffin containers which are balanced on wheeled frames. These containers hold separate dishes of rice or bread, curry, and dal.   (HS)

TIKKA a Hindi word which has been adopted into English. It means much the same as KEBAB, referring to chunks of meat, poultry, etc. cooked on skewers. Chicken tikka has become, in Britain, one of the most popular 'takeaway' dishes, rivalling pizza for the number one slot. It has achieved this prominence in a relatively short period of time.

TILAPIA a name applied to various species of freshwater fish in the genera *Tilapia* and *Sarotherodon*, especially *S. mossambicus* and *S. niloticus*. Both belong to E. Africa, but the natural range of the latter extends northwards to the Nile and to Israel and Syria.

Both species are good food fishes, not too bony, and have now been introduced to many other areas, especially in Asia, for culture in ponds. This kind of fish farming has acquired considerable commercial importance. *S. niloticus*, the larger and faster growing of the two species, can reach a length of 50 cm (20") and a weight of over 6 kg (14 lb).

These are herbivorous fish, with family instincts. The male makes a nest in the soft bottom of the pond or stream and swims round it, looking attractive, until a female comes and lays eggs in it. The male then fertilizes the eggs and the female keeps them in her mouth for a few days until they hatch, thus earning the epithet mouth-brooder.

TILEFISH *Lopholatilus chamaeleonticeps*, a deep-water fish of the NE Atlantic, which is one of the most brilliantly coloured species known outside the tropics. It may be over a metre long and weigh up to 15 kg (33.75 lb), but the usual adult length is 80 cm (32").

The specific name *chamaeleonticeps* is not quite appropriate. A chameleon can change its coloration at will, whereas a tilefish cannot; it merely exhibits a remarkable range of colours. Leim and Scott (1966) have described it as:

bluish to olive-green on back and upper part of sides, changing to yellow and rose on lower sides and belly, latter with white midline. Head reddish on sides, white below. Back and sides above lateral line thickly dotted with irregular yellow spots. Dorsal fin dusky with larger yellowish spots . . . anal fin pinkish with purple to blue iridescence; pectoral pale sooty-brown with purplish reflections.

The range of the tilefish extends from Nova Scotia to Florida, and even beyond. Its presence in the northern part of the range has fluctuated considerably. The band of temperatures in which these fish can live is relatively narrow, and an influx of cold water into their northerly haunts can kill off millions of them. This happened only a few years after the tilefish had been 'discovered', and had won almost instant approval as a table fish, in the 1870s. Its flesh is fine grained and has an excellent flavour. The advice usually offered to the cook is to treat it like cod.

The name tilefish has a wider application; it may refer to other species in the family Branchiostegidae. The Japanese tilefish is the other member of the family which has some culinary renown, and the Japanese distinguish three kinds, red, yellow, and white. The white is the best.

TILSITER (or Tilsit), a surface-ripened cheese first made by Dutch settlers in E. Prussia in the mid-19th century, is said to have been created by accident when some of their GOUDA-type cheeses became infected with moulds, yeasts, and bacteria in a damp cellar.

Tilsiter, which is ivory or pale yellow in colour, with very small holes, has a tangy flavour and a supple texture; just firm enough to be classified by Germans as a *Schnittkäse* (sliceable cheese). It is now produced in many places besides Germany; notably C. Europe including Switzerland, several Nordic countries, and the Soviet Union. It comes in wheels or loaves, with or without a rind, and may be made from

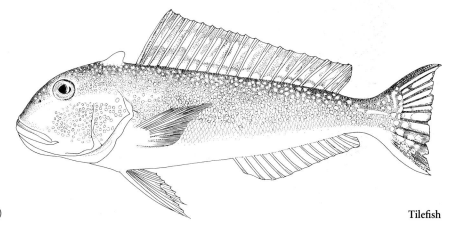

Tilefish

whole or skimmed milk. The latter version is sometimes flavoured with CARAWAY seeds.

TIMBALE a French term of which the original meaning is 'kettledrum'. In a culinary context it has entered the English language and is defined by the *OED* as: 'A dish made of finely minced meat, fish, or other ingredients, cooked in a crust of paste or in a mould: so called from its shape.' In practice, rice or pasta may provide the 'case', and there are various sweet timbales as well as savoury ones. Some of these approach the nature of a PUDDING.

TINAMOU the name for birds of the family Tinamidae, of which there are over 40 species ranging from Mexico to Patagonia. These birds are unusual in that the female courts the male, who then has charge of raising the fledglings. They live on grassy plains and seldom take to the air, so an attempt to introduce them to Europe as game birds was unsuccessful.

In size, tinamou resemble small plump chickens. The flesh is tasty and tender. The best known for table purposes seems to be *Rhychotus rufescens*, the Argentine tinamou.

TINOLA a Filipino culinary term which normally indicates a boiled chicken dish, in which the chicken is first fried with garlic, ginger, and onion, then boiled and given a distinctive flavour by the use of green PAPAYA, salt or fish sauce, and *sili* (chilli, hot pepper) leaves. In Cebu, however, it is a kind of SINIGANG, usually fish with vegetables, lightly soured with tomatoes.   DF

TIPSY CAKE a SPONGE CAKE or VICTORIA SANDWICH CAKE soaked with sherry syrup and decorated with cream. Popular since the late 18th century, it belongs to the British tradition of cake, cream, and alcohol puddings such as TRIFLE.

Eliza Acton (1855) gave Tipsy Cake the alternative name of Brandy Trifle. Florence White (1932) went one step further and combined what was known as HEDGEHOG cake with tipsy cake into a hedgehog tipsy cake.

Versions exist in other countries such as the Spanish *bizcocho borracho a la crema*, a type of sponge cake soaked in syrup flavoured with rum and orange liqueur, and filled with a lemon-flavoured custard.   (LM)

TISANE a fragrant herbal infusion drunk for refreshment or medicinal reasons or both. The history of the word is unusual. It began in classical Greece as *ptisane*, which

meant barley water, passed via Latin (*ptisana*) into 13th century French (*tisaine*), and 16th century English (ptisan, still meaning barley water). Later, it reappeared in English as tisane, 'a 20th century readoption from the French' (as Ayto, 1993, explains). See also ORGEAT.

The phrase 'herbal tea' has more or less the same meaning. It came into being not because herbal teas have anything to do with the TEA plant but because of the dominance of true tea among hot beverages made by infusing leaves. This has resulted in 'tea' being taken to cover any such beverage. The existence of flavoured teas (real tea, flavoured with herbs or fruits) is a further source of confusion. It would be preferable to retain 'tisane', which has a respectably long tradition as an English word, and to use 'tea' only for real tea.

Popular tisanes include camomile, MINT, rose-hip (see ROSES), VERVAIN, and various mixtures. Most tisanes are made from leaves, dried or fresh, but sometimes the flowers (e.g. lime blossom, French *tilleul*, or a floral mixture) or root (e.g. GINSENG) are used.

TOAD IN THE HOLE a traditional British dish consisting of something in the way of meat (now usually SAUSAGES) baked in a BATTER pudding, provokes historical questions of exceptional interest. What are the origins of the dish and how did it get its name?

Enquiries are best commenced from two starting points. The first is that batter puddings (whether baked in the oven by themselves or cooked under the spit or jack in the drippings falling from a joint—in the latter case they could be classified as YORKSHIRE PUDDING) only began to be popular in the early part of the 18th century. Jennifer Stead (1991*b*) has drawn attention to entries in *The Diary of Thomas Turner 1754–1765* (ed Vasey 1984) and points out that Turner had sausages cooked in a baking tin with batter poured in and around them; not called toad in the hole by him but precisely foreshadowing what is now the most common form of that dish. Incidentally, Jennifer Stead's essay is the best reference for studying the complex historical questions surrounding batter pudding and YORKSHIRE PUDDING in Yorkshire.

The second is that the earliest recorded reference in print to toad in the hole occurs in a provincial glossary of 1787, quoted by the *OED* as saying: 'the dish called toad in a hole meat boiled in a crust.' That gives the name, but the technique is different from that subsequently established. A slightly later citation in the *OED*, recording what Mme d'Arblay said in one of her letters, about Mrs Siddons and the Sadler's Wells, has a batter pudding (albeit of such enormous

dimensions as to be barely credible): 'as illfitted as the dish they called toad in a hole . . . putting a noble sirloin of beef into a poor paltry batter-pudding.'

Mrs Beeton (1861) describes the dish as 'homely but savoury'. Her recipe had steak and kidney cooking in the batter, but she said that leftover meat could be used.

TOADSTOOL an imprecise term which usually denotes an inedible or toxic FUNGUS, has a long history. As Ramsbottom (1953) points out, MUSHROOM and toadstool appear to have been synonymous terms in the 16th century. Thus we hear from Henry Lyte (*A niewe Herbal*, 1578) of someone being 'sicke with eating of Venimous Tadstooles or Mousherons'. But the very name toadstool suggests something nasty, and it is not surprising that of the two terms it was the one which, for English-speaking people, came to refer to undesirable fungi.

In earlier times there were variations of the name, for example toodys hatte and paddocstool (1450), of which the latter survives in the north-country paddockstool, while the former is still echoed in Brittany, where local names mean toad's hat or toad's bonnet. However, generally speaking, the toad is imagined as sitting on a toadstool, not sheltering under it; and it is always a toad, not a frog, no doubt because it used to be thought that toads were venomous.

The word has no validity for scientists.

TOAST as everyone in Britain knows, is made by placing a slice of bread in front of dry heat—a fire, a grill, or an electric toaster—until the surface browns and gives off an attractive smell. The attractive taste, smell, and colour of toast come from the thermal decomposition of sugar and starch molecules on the surface of the bread.

The true toast addict is fussy about its preparation, choosing day-old baker's bread to make it, and insisting it is eaten as soon as ready, for good toast must be consumed whilst hot. It is the smell of toast, and the sensations of the hot crunchy outside of the bread combined with the soft inner crumb and melted butter, that make it so appealing. Left to go cold, it becomes leathery and loses its aroma.

Toast is a standard part of a proper English breakfast, and together with a cup of tea, it forms a popular snack at any time. Butter is the most common accompaniment; other toppings include MARMALADE or jam or honey, especially at breakfast time. Toast is often used, rather in the style of a medieval trencher, to provide an edible base for, say, poached eggs, sardines, baked beans, and other, mainly savoury, items.

Why toast should have become such an English speciality is not clear. Possibly English wheat bread, which kept for several days, had something to do with it. It certainly lends itself more to toasting than the close-textured RYE BREADS, staple food in much of N. Europe. Elizabeth David (1977) says, 'I wonder if our open fires and coal ranges were not more responsible than the high incidence of stale bread for the popularity of toast in all classes of English household', and comments on the number of devices invented for holding bread in front of an open fire. These have now been replaced by the toaster, and the electric or gas grill.

Certainly, toast has a long history in Britain. 'Tost' was much used in the Middle Ages, being made in the ordinary way at an open fire. At this time sops—pieces of bread—were used to soak up liquid mixtures, and these were often first toasted, which reduced their tendency to disintegrate. Often toast was spread with toppings. 'Pokerounce' was toast with hot honey, spiced with ginger, cinnamon, and galingale. 'Toste rialle' was covered with a paste of sugar and rice flour moistened with sweet wine and including pieces of cooked quince, raisins, nuts, and spices, the whole thing covered with gilt sugar lozenges. A popular dish of the 17th century was cinnamon toast, which at that time was made by covering the toast with a paste of cinnamon and sugar moistened with wine. Early settlers in N. America retained their liking for it, and it became a traditional American dish.

Meat toppings for toast became fashionable during the 16th century. At first they were sweetened: for example veal toasts were made with chopped veal kidney and egg yolks, sugar, rosewater, cinnamon, and ginger. Various other 'hashes' based on finely chopped meat were served on toast. A trace of this practice survives in the serving of toast fingers with plain cooked minced meat, an adaptation made to the original dish in the 18th century.

The toast-and-something habit has a long precedent in England. Towards the end of the 16th century all kinds of things began to appear on toast, such as poached eggs (which had been previously served in broth); buttered (scrambled) eggs; ham or bacon; anchovies; and melted cheese. All of them have remained associated with toast. The last achieved existence as a separate dish known as WELSH RABBIT (or rarebit) which it has maintained until this day. Toast with toppings became very popular as 'savoury toast', beloved of the Victorians and Edwardians. This, remarked 'Wyvern' (Kenney-Herbert, 1894a):

belongs wholly to English cookery . . . savoury toasts of an ordinary kind ought to be favourably regarded by all thrifty housekeepers, inasmuch as

they afford an easy and pleasant way of working up fragments of good food that might otherwise be wasted.

Throughout the Middle Ages and early modern period, toast was often moistened in wine when making such dishes as toasted cheese, but at the end of the 17th century it became more usual to butter it. Hot buttered toast was eaten at breakfast. Later, when AFTERNOON TEA became the fashion, it appeared here too.

The 1890s saw the arrival of Melba toast. This is extraordinarily thin toast and a technique for producing it is often attributed to Escoffier and Ritz, who are supposed to have named it for Marie Ritz (who had been demanding thinner toast) but then renamed it for Melba at a time when her diet called for something of the sort. Elizabeth David (1977) found the story appealing but questionable.

Toast also has a slightly disreputable history as a basis for drinks. Amongst many coffee substitutes used in the 18th century, burnt toast soaked in water was the easiest to make. The result was not much like coffee; but then neither were any of the other drinks made from grains, roots, and herbs. However, towards the end of the century TOAST WATER (see below) was made as a drink in its own right.   (LM)

TOAST WATER an example of a whole category of supposedly health-restoring foods. Water in which cereals have been cooked or soaked plays a leading role in traditional folk medicine in many countries, and with good reason. Illness drains the body's energy and fluids. To counter this, water prevents dehydration and starch helps to restore strength. In the past, if you wished someone well, it seemed natural to drink his or her health in a liquid in which bread, the staple food, had been steeped; toasting and flavouring the bread, and substituting wine for water, made the wish more effective and the drink more palatable. We therefore still toast our friends on formal occasions. Rice water is still given to invalids in many parts of Asia and Africa. Barley water (usually flavoured and fortified with lemon—for vitamin C—and sugar) was a popular energy-giving drink in Britain until about 1980.

Toast water was made in most bread-eating households throughout the 18th and most of the 19th centuries. Boiling water was poured onto toasted bread and allowed to cool. It was then strained, and was ready to drink, though flavourings were often added—sugar and cream, lemon, dried orange peel, currant jelly, or roasted apples. Alexis Soyer (1849) gave precise instructions for making it, and insisted the toast must not be burnt, stating that:

the idea that bread must be burnt black to make toast water is quite a popular delusion, for nothing nourishing could come from it: if your house was burnt to ashes, it would be valueless; and the same with burnt bread, which merely makes the water black, but the nutriment of the bread, intended to relieve the chest, has evaporated in smoke by being burnt.

However, Dr and Mrs Delamere (1878) contradicted this, alleging that bread charcoal is an efficient water purifier, and that the toast should actually be set on fire. This issue is amusingly described by Helen Pollard (1993) in a well-researched exegesis in which she comments:

In support of Soyer and other writers, it is true that the brown colour of toast is partly due to the conversion of insoluble starch into soluble dextrins which would contribute a (negligible) amount to the nutritive value of the preparation. The main benefit from drinking toast water would, however, be the replacement of body fluids. The final word on toast water must belong to the Delameres. 'If the toast-and-water is required to appear in decanters, as "President's sherry", it should be poured away from the bread as soon as it has sufficient colour.'

The notion of toast water lingered into the late 20th century in a number of patent health foods, but the decline of protracted minor illnesses and the use of antibiotics have made these liquid diets less necessary.
(RO)

TOFFEE the modern British name for a sweet formerly called 'taffy'. The older name survives in the USA, but British toffee and American taffy are not quite the same.

Much toffee is still home made. The basic form of British toffee is made from a syrup of SUGAR and BUTTER with some addition to inhibit crystallization, such as SYRUP or TREACLE in place of part of the sugar, or an acid such as lemon juice. It is cooked to the soft or hard crack stage (for soft or hard toffee respectively; see SUGAR BOILING) with little or no stirring, and is poured straight out to set without pulling or other working. Many kinds of additions and flavourings are possible; treacle, nuts, chocolate, cream or sour cream, mint flavouring, and even whisky are among those used.

Welsh forms of toffee (variously called taffi, ffani, or cyflaith) are much more like American taffy. In particular, they are usually pulled, as is most American taffy (see PULLED CANDY), The agreeable custom of taffy-pulling parties has survived up to modern times in parts of Wales, while it is probably extinct in England. Not all Welsh or American taffy contains butter, though usually some honey or syrup is used in the mixture to reduce the amount of crystallization. Thus pulled taffy is not as hard as plain pulled candy. A popular

American sweet is salt-water taffy, a butterless type originally made with sea-water. Another pulled toffee—at least in its classic form—is Irish YELLOWMAN, a sweet still often sold at fairs by hucksters proclaiming its supposedly health-giving properties.

Scottish toffees are numerous and renowned. Those which are specialities of Glasgow and Helenburgh, and one or two others, are described under SWEETIES.

See also BRITTLE; CARAMEL; FUDGE; TOFFEE APPLE.

TOFFEE APPLE a popular confection in Britain, especially in the autumn, when they used to be prominent, with their vivid red colour, at autumn fairs. A whole fresh apple, on a thin stick, is dipped in high-boiled sugar syrup which has been coloured red; and allowed to set before being wrapped in cellophane.

The *OED* gives no quotations relating to toffee apples earlier than the beginning of the 20th century. However, the use of the term as soldier's slang for a type of bomb used in the First World War suggests that they were already well known, and probably have a longer history than the quotations allow.

In the phrase 'toffee apple' the word 'toffee' means simple boiled sugar, not the mixture of sugar and dairy produce which is what the word usually refers to. This may be another indication of an older origin of the toffee apple. See also TOFFEE.

There is some similarity between toffee apples and the Chinese dessert items which consist of pieces of banana or apple fried in batter and then coated in caramelized syrup. Whether there is any historical connection is not clear.

TOFU a white curd made from SOYA BEANS, originated in China as *tou-fu* (now *dou fu*). Tofu, the name commonly employed worldwide, is the Japanese adaptation of this. The product is also known as bean curd.

It has been said, with some justice, that tofu occupies a place in oriental cookery which corresponds to that of dairy products in other parts of the world. It exists in various forms which offer parallels to cheeses; and the similarity extends beyond appearance and use. The composition of tofu, a highly concentrated protein food, resembles that of cheese.

The proteins in soya beans, although abundant, are physically and chemically locked up in a manner which frustrates human digestion. Making the beans into tofu renders them more available. This is particularly important because tofu yields the essential amino acid lysine, which is lacking in the staple food of the region, rice.

The preparation of tofu, as practised now, begins with soaking the soya beans. They are then ground with added water, boiled, and filtered to produce a warm 'milk'. This is curdled by calcium sulphate, or by a traditional curdling agent called *nigari* in Japan; this is bittern, the lye left over after the crystallization of salt from sea water. The curd is then ladled into boxes and pressed to squeeze out most of the remaining 'whey'.

The similarity to cheese-making is striking. Indeed, some have thought that the manufacture of tofu was originally an adaptation of cheese-making, learned perhaps from the Mongols. However, questions about its origin are difficult to answer. Dr Yan-Kit So (1992) draws attention to work by a Japanese historian, with which many Chinese historians agree, which seems to establish that there is no significant mention of tofu in Chinese literature until the 10th century AD. This seems to rule out a traditional belief that the Chinese Lord Liu An of Hainan invented tofu in the 2nd century BC.

What is certain is that tofu arrived at an early date in Japan and has also been an important food in Korea since the distant past. The first recorded reference to tofu in Japan is from the 12th century AD, which was also the period when Zen Buddhism, with its vegetarian tenets, became popular there, a development which has no doubt favoured the use of tofu ever since. However, it was probably only during the Edo period (early 17th to late 19th century) that tofu became ordinary people's food in Japan and also came to be made much softer than the original kind.

Toftu is also important in other countries, e.g. the Philippines, where it is *tokwa*.

The number of different forms which tofu can take is very great. The book by Shurtleff and Aoyagi (1983) provides extensive information and explains the characteristics and particular uses of the various sorts. A few of them, including those most likely to be met and some of special interest, are listed below.

PLAIN TOFU
Plain tofu (doufu) in China is usually prepared in large squares, which are cut by the vendor to yield smaller squares of about 10 cm (4") and 4 cm (1.5") thick. This doufu, which is moderately firm, is often sold immersed in water in sealed containers.

Pressed tofu, *doufu-kan*, is also sold in squares, rather smaller, and has a meatier, more chewy texture. It may have added colour or flavour. The version called *wu-hsiang kan* is a sort of savoury pressed tofu, flavoured with five or more spices. It comes in various shades of brown and is described as resembling smoked ham.

The regular kind of tofu in Japan is *momendofu*, cotton tofu, with a surface marked by the weave of the cotton cloth in which it is wrapped to be pressed. It is less firm and contains more water than the regular Chinese doufu (to which Japanese pressed tofu is closer in these respects).

Kinugoshi, 'silk tofu', is a Japanese product which has a finer consistency, like silk (but neither silk nor cotton is used in its manufacture). It has its counterpart in China, *sui-doufu*. These are soft forms, usually too soft to be cut into pieces; instead they may be scooped into bowls, topped with a little soy sauce or sugar, and eaten with a spoon.

Freeze-dried tofu used to be made naturally, by taking advantage of freezing temperatures at high altitudes or night-time, but is now commercially manufactured. When reconstituted, it has a spongy consistency.

Tofu appears in numerous shapes: sheets of one kind or another, strips, shreds, knots, noodles, etc. Smoked tofu is also available, usually in small blocks of one form or another.

COOKED FORMS OF TOFU
Deep-fried tofu in China appears under names such as *doufu pok* and *cha-dofu*. *Abura-agè* in Japan are deep-fried thin slices of tofu suitable for slitting open and making into pouches. *Inari-zushi* are these pouches filled with SUSHI rice, vegetables, mushrooms, etc.—a favourite picnic dish.

Ganmodoki is the name used in the Tokyo region for deep-fried tofu balls (kneaded with other ingredients, including a binder such as ground yam).

Yaki-dofu, pieces of tofu which have been grilled to produce a surface mottled with brown, and a texture which holds together well, are another Japanese item.

FERMENTED TOFU
In China tofu is fermented to make various products, some of which are considered too smelly by western people (just as western blue cheeses are off-putting for people from the Orient). The generic term is *doufu-ru*. The most popular type is white *doufu-ru*, within which category are types spiced with minced chilli pepper or any of numerous other seasonings.

Red *doufu-ru* is deep red in colour and has a distinctive flavour, from the red fermented rice which is used in preparing it. It includes a variety flavoured with rose essence and sugar.

Tsao-doufu has an alcoholic aroma, betraying the rice wine and rice wine lees used in making it. A green version, *ch'ou doufu*, is popular in Taiwan, where it is considered a delicacy by those who like it, although others are repelled by its smell and appearance.

Chiang dou-fu are cubes of tofu fermented in soy sauce or Chinese-style miso. Reddish-brown and salty.

In the Philippines fermented soya bean curd is *tausi*.

MISCELLANEOUS

An example of pickled tofu and of the many specialities in Japan is *umesutsuke*, tofu pickled in plum vinegar, with a purple exterior.

One important Chinese speciality, hardly known at all in Japan, is *dofu nao*. This is a very soft form, sometimes referred to as 'smooth curds'. In fact, the Chinese name means literally 'bean brain', referring to the brain-like texture. It is treated like a sort of pudding, and vendors do a brisk trade in it from their carts. The scene is vividly described by Shurtleff and Aoyagi:

Customers seat themselves at stools around the cart and get ready for a hearty breakfast (costing less than 5 cents). The vendor ladles out scoops of custard-like curds into deep bowls, tops them with a warm syrupy sauce (*hung t'ang*) containing peanuts and brown sugar, and places them (together with porcelain spoons) on the edge of the cart, which serves as a table. In some areas the curds are mixed with *cha-t'sai* pickles, tiny dried shrimp, soy sauce, and a dash of sesame oil, then served as a thick soup. In others, they are mixed with sweet oil, vinegar, finely chopped meat, or spices.

In many of these forms tofu is made and bought daily. In Japan every village has its tofu shop, where work starts early in the morning, as in bakeries for bread in western countries. These shops may also sell SOY MILK, although there are often separate shops for that. YUBA, which may appear in cookery books as 'bean curd skin' or 'tofu skin', has its own specialist shops or stalls, at which it appears in an astonishing range of imitative forms: poultry, fish, tripe, etc. Another product is okara, the 'presscake' (pulped skins of the soya beans) left over when the milk is made; highly nutritious but not so tasty.

There are also special tofu restaurants, where a varied meal consisting entirely of tofu in different forms may be had. The scope for cooking with tofu is almost unlimited.

See also MISO; NATTO; SOY SAUCE; TEMPE.

TOHEROA *Amphidesma ventricosum*, the most famous of the edible BIVALVES of New Zealand. It is a large CLAM (record length over 30 cm/1', usual size half of that) with relatively thin and brittle shells, yellowish or grey. It is a relatively agile bivalve, capable of moving sideways through the sand and a strong burrower; its long twin siphons allow it to live about 25 cm (10") below the surface of the sand.

The toheroa occurs only in certain localities on the west coast of the North Island and in Foveaux Strait. Although it has been locally very abundant, it is subject to strict controls and the variable 'close season' sometimes extends right through the year.

The toheroa is large enough to require cleaning, after which it can be dealt with like any other large clam. Its best-known use is in toheroa soup, cans of which are marketed as a delicacy.

Two related New Zealand species are the TUATUA and the PIPI.

TOMATILLO *Physalis ixocarpa*, is a plant of many names, most of which reflect the resemblance between its fruit and that of a true TOMATO in the green state. Tomatillo means little tomato, apt because its size is usually no more than 2.5 cm (1") across, although some specimens measure more than twice as much.

Other names include green tomato, since it remains green even when ripe; husk tomato, since like other PHYSALIS FRUITS it grows inside a papery calyx or husk, in this instance brown; and sometimes Spanish tomato, not because it is known in Spain, but because it grows in Mexico. Another, better, name is Mexican husk tomato. (The plant abounds in Mexico and Guatemala, and was a staple in the Aztec and Maya economies.)

The fruit itself is thin skinned, and when ripe may vary in colour from green to yellow, or purple. The flesh is pale yellow, crisp or soft; acid, subacid, or sweet; and contains many tiny seeds.

Elisabeth Lambert Ortiz (1979) writes: 'The green tomato is very important in Mexican, and to a lesser extent Guatemalan, cooking, giving a distinctive flavor to the "green" dishes and sauces. The flavor is delicate and slightly acid.' Fresh tomatillos have to be cooked for a few minutes to bring out the flavour properly. They are an essential ingredient of guacamole (see AVOCADO).

The tomatillo fruits well in Queensland, Australia, and in S. Africa. It was introduced into India (Rajasthan) in the 1950s and is used to make a sweet CHUTNEY.

P. philadelphica, sometimes called wild tomatillo (or purple GROUND CHERRY), is also cultivated in some places.

TOMATO (*see page 800*)

TOMCOD *Microgadus tomcod*, a close relation of the COD but much smaller (maximum length 40 cm/15") and found only in the NW Atlantic, from Labrador down to Virginia. It may be distinguished from codling (young cod) by the long filaments of the ventral fins and the more rounded tail fin. Colour varies, but is usually olive-brown above with green or yellow tinges and darker mottling.

The tomcod frequents coastal waters and estuaries. An unusual winter fishery for it, through holes cut in the ice, has traditionally been carried out in the St Lawrence River. Brightly painted fishing cabins are erected on the ice and furnished with heating for the fishermen as they work their holes.

This fish can be fried, poached, or baked. In some places, including New York, it has been treated as a delicacy.

TOMME (or, less often, tome), a French word which means cheese and forms part of the name of certain French cheeses, especially in the Savoie. The best known is *tomme de Savoie*, but there are numerous others. Almost all are made from skimmed cow's milk, but *tomme de Beaumont* is made from whole cow's milk, and there is also *tomme de chèvre*, made from goat's milk.

The variety of tommes is such that it is difficult to generalize about them. But they typically have a grey, mouldy rind; a soft, pale interior; and a mild tang. *Tomme au marc* is an exception. It is coated with marc (grape pips and skins left over from wine-making) and has a strong taste and aroma. Some other tommes benefit from added flavours: brandy, or the spirit made from marc, or fennel, etc.

The Italian term *toma* and its diminutive *tomino* are evidently related to the French term although the cheeses they denote are not quite the same.

TONGUE possessed by most vertebrate animals, a fleshy muscular movable organ of the floor of the mouth which bears sensory taste buds and has special functions in tasting and swallowing food.

Tongues from the larger animals have 'roots' which are normally trimmed off, with other unwanted matter, before sale; and they have thick skins, which can be removed easily after parboiling. They may also be smoked, for example beef tongues in the Jura region of France.

Tongues in general need prolonged moist cooking, which often takes the form of braising, to make them tender, and may be eaten either hot or cold. In Britain cooked tongues, canned, are a popular item for eating cold with salad or in sandwiches. In France, hot cooked tongue is more

(*cont. on page 801*)

Tomato

The tomato, *Lycopersicon lycopersicum*, is an American plant which bears the familiar fruits (perceived as a vegetable because of their main culinary uses), and which is now grown and consumed worldwide. The plant is a member of the family Solanaceae and therefore a relation of the New World CAPSICUM peppers and POTATO, and of the Old World AUBERGINE. The presence of nightshades in the family may have made people cautious about using newly discovered members of it. This did not apply to capsicum peppers, since they were seen as providing a valuable new spice and spread like wildfire. The aubergine and the potato, however, were received with considerable reserve in W. Europe; and the same was true of the tomato.

Sophie Coe (1994) explains that the tomato originated in S. America, where the ancestor of our edible tomato was *S. pimpinellifolium*, which bears a long spray of tiny red fruits which split on the plant. The edible descendant travelled north to Mexico and was one of the Solanaceae cultivated by the Aztec. Now began a linguistic confusion. The Aztec word *tomatl* meant simply plump fruit. For them, our edible tomato was *xitomatl*, while the husk tomato (TOMATILLO) was *miltomatl*. Spaniards, not understanding the importance of the suffix in each name, used *tomatl*, which they turned into *tomate*, for both. As a result, it is often difficult, when reading early Spanish sources about Aztec use of the tomato, to know which fruit is meant. What does seem clear, however, is that there was a consistent linkage in Aztec cuisine between the tomato and CHILLI peppers.

This link snapped when the fruits were taken to Europe. The story of their reception when they reached Spain and Italy is a tangled one, unravelled by Grewe (1988). He postulates arrival at Seville, a centre for international trade, especially with Italy and the Low Countries, early in the 16th century. An Italian herbalist (Mattioli, 1544) referred to what must have been tomatoes as *mala aurea* (golden apples) and later (1554) mentioned a red variety. The Dutch herbalist Dodoens (1554) gave a fuller description and an illustration. Thereafter mentions and illustrations became fairly frequent, although there is little evidence to suggest that people had begun cooking or eating tomatoes except rarely and by way of experiment. A supposed connection with the mandrake, the suggestive form of whose root had earned it a reputation as an APHRODISIAC, led to the notion that the tomato had similar properties, which may in turn have prompted the Swiss naturalist Gesner to call it *poma amoris*. The fruit thus became linked with the Hesperides myth and acquired the string of names exemplified by *pomme d'amour* in French and *pomodoro* in Italian.

As Grewe (1988) pointed out, no printed recipes for using tomatoes appeared in the early period of Spanish culinary literature (1599 to 1611), and after that efflorescence no new cookbooks were published in Spanish until 1745 (when the book by Juan Altamiras had 13 recipes with tomato as an ingredient, out of a total of 200). However, it is reasonable to suppose that there was some activity with tomatoes in Spanish kitchens. The earliest known printed recipe, which occurs in a Neapolitan book, *Lo scalco alla moderna*, by Antonio Latini (1692/4) is for 'Tomato Sauce, Spanish Style' and calls for adding finely chopped parsley, onion, and garlic—with salt, pepper, oil, and vinegar—to the finely chopped flesh of previously seared and peeled tomatoes.

Grewe also draws attention to evidence from paintings that already, half a century before Latini's book, the tomato was becoming a familiar ingredient. The painting by Murillo which is popularly known as *The Angels' Kitchen* (1646), executed for the Franciscan convent of Seville, shows angels preparing a meal, with a tomato, two aubergines, and a sort of pumpkin visible in a corner.

Andrew Smith (1994) was able to marshal interesting evidence of use in English kitchens from about 1750 on, including a recipe in the 1758 supplement to Hannah Glasse (1747). He makes the point that Jewish families in England, many of whom were of Portuguese or Spanish descent, seemed to display more readiness than others to eat the strange fruit. Smith also remarks that an early edition of the *Encyclopaedia Britannica* (1797) announced that the tomato was now 'in daily use'. However, for most people in Britain the tomato remained an object of suspicion until the end of the 19th century, witness this passage from Flora Thompson (1945):

It was on Jerry's cart tomatoes first appeared in the hamlet. They had not long been introduced into this country and were slowly making their way into favour. The fruit was flatter in shape then than now and deeply grooved and indented from the stem, giving it an almost starlike appearance. There were bright yellow ones, too, as well as the scarlet; but, after a few years, the yellow ones disappeared from the market and the red ones became rounder and smoother, as we see them now.

At first sight, the basket of red and yellow fruit attracted Laura's colour-loving eye. 'What are those?' she asked old Jerry.

'Love-apples, me dear. Love-apples, they be; though some hignorant folks be a callin' 'em tommytoes. But you don't want any o' they—nasty sour things, they be, as only gentry can eat. You have a nice sweet orange wi' your penny.' But Laura felt she must taste the love-apples and insisted upon having one.

Such daring created quite a sensation among the onlookers. 'Don't 'ee go tryin' to eat it, now,' one woman urged. 'It'll only make 'ee sick. I know because I had one of the nasty horrid things at our Minnie's.'

Meanwhile, in Italy the large-scale cultivation and canning of tomatoes, especially in the region of Naples, had developed into a large industry, and Americans were also canning tomatoes on a large scale from the mid-century onwards. And in the 1830s the production of **tomato ketchup,** which was to become America's 'national condiment', besides invading tables in most other parts of the world, began in earnest.

Although tomato ketchup is by far the most important tomato product, **tomato paste** or concentrate is also a staple. It is now an industrial product but like so many other things it has its traditional domestically produced counterpart, known in most of the countries bordering the Mediterranean. Patience Gray (1986) gives a fine description of making it in the south of Italy, where it is '*la salsa secca*, probably the most healthy conserve in existence'. The same author also describes the making of *la salsa* (the regular, thick liquid kind), which could by a stretch of the imagination be regarded as an ancestor of tomato ketchup.

Among the most basic and simple tomato dishes of the Mediterranean region is one of which Patience Gray writes: 'Probably the most universal refreshment in summer among working men in Greece, Italy and Catalonia is a slab of bread onto which are crushed some ripe tomatoes with a garlic clove, sea salt, bathed in olive oil, most invigorating.' This is the Catalan *Pa amb tomàquet*, which is the sole subject of the book of that name by Pomés (1985), an outstanding example of the witty-but-serious approach to food topics of which good examples occur in California, the Philippines, and a few other favoured areas besides Catalonia.

The total number of dishes around the world in which tomato is the or a main ingredient must amount to thousands. For a foodstuff which has come up to the front from almost nowhere in under two centuries, the tomato has proved to have astonishingly vigorous penetrative qualities, so that it is as close to being ubiquitous in the kitchens of the world as any plant food. In part this is due to its versatility; the hundreds of varieties now popular (green, yellow, orange, red, tiny to huge, spherical to irregular, juicy or not, acid or sweet or balanced, strongly flavourful or not, suitable for stuffing, etc.) are capable between them of playing a multitude of roles in finished dishes. It is also relevant that the tomato is highly marriageable. Among its best-known mates are basil, garlic, onion, thyme, oregano, peppers (with a bow to the Aztec), cheese, egg, and meaty flavours.

Lest it be thought that the tomato has carried all before it, victorious on every possible front, it should be noted that there are certain dishes where continuing skirmishes are fought between those who would admit tomato and those who would exclude it; one such is clam chowder. In these instances it may be that the adversaries of the tomato unknowingly display some vestigial traces of the suspicion which greeted its first arrival in the Old World.

See also KETCHUP; RATATOUILLE; PIZZA.

commonly met, and characteristic dishes are: *Langue de veau, sauce piquante* (calf's tongue is considered the best); and *Langue de bœuf à l'aigre-douce* (or *sauce madère*). *Langues à l'écarlate* are tongues salted, trimmed, enclosed in a sort of sausage casing, cooked, coloured red, and used as an item of CHARCUTERIE. In the context of French cuisine, it is no doubt unnecessary to explain that langues de chat are not what they might seem, but biscuits (see BISCUIT VARIETIES); but some explanation is needed for the antique title *Langue d'Ésope*; this dish consists of sheep's tongues rearing up around a pyramid of chestnut purée, with whole chestnuts on top, and is mentioned here because chestnuts are generally regarded as one of the ingredients which go well with tongue.

Ox, calf, lamb, and pigs' tongues are all commonly eaten in Europe; whereas in N. American markets ox tongues only, and those rarely, are available.

The tongues of deer make a good dish; and REINDEER tongue, often smoked, is a delicacy in some northern countries. Hunters will eat bears' tongues. Rabbits' tongues, cooked, have been served in France as an hors d'œuvre or as a garnish for meat dishes. Proceeding even further down the scale of size, one finds that in Roman times the tongues of songbirds were regarded as a great delicacy.

In the world of seafood, various fish, such as cod, have tongues which are eaten with enthusiasm.

TONGUE CLAM not a clam, not even a mollusc, is a creature which mimics a clamlike bivalve in appearance but is really a brachiopod. The genus *Lingula*, to which the tongue clam belongs, is of extreme antiquity, indeed according to some authorities the oldest living genus of animals, having survived unchanged for 500 million years or more.

The greenish shell has a maximum length of 45 cm (18"), but with the long stalk (peduncle) extended the creature may be almost twice that length. It lives in a vertical burrow, with just three little holes or a tiny slit in the sand showing where it lurks.

Tongue clams are exploited locally in various parts of SE Asia. The stalks are boiled or steamed; or they may be pickled in vinegar.

TONIC WATER is a non-alcoholic drink based on sweetened, carbonated water flavoured with quinine. It is now probably best loved as one partner in the drink gin and tonic, a mixture considered by many to epitomize the British Raj; however, the combination does not appear to have been popular until well into the 20th century, when it joined a well-established range of other drinks based on gin and bitters.

Artificially carbonated water has been known since the mid-18th century, when a method for making it was invented by Dr Joseph Priestley. In the 1790s, a Mr Jacob Schweppe (amongst others) set up a small factory in London to produce sparkling waters. Many of these included blends of mineral salts, in imitation of naturally occurring spring waters, considered to have qualities beneficial to health. Quinine, as well as being used as a prophylactic against malaria, was also considered to be an appetite stimulant and a more general antidote to fever. Bayley (1994) comments that Schweppes added 'Indian' Tonic Water to their range in the 1870s as a commercialization of an already well-established Raj practice of adding anti-malarial quinine to soda water. This remains the best-known brand of tonic water, although a 'Quinine Tonic Water' had been patented in 1858 by one Mr Erasmus Bond.

LM

TONKA BEAN the fruit of a leguminous tree, *Dipteryx odorata*, native to the forests of Colombia, Venezuela, Guiana, and Brazil. The beans are mainly gathered from the wild in Venezuela, but there has also been some cultivation. The value of the beans has been due to their containing coumarin, which has an aroma between those of hay and of VANILLA.

The dried beans (one to each pod) are cured in rum and then dried again, when they become coated with a white deposit of coumarin. Until shortly after the Second World War they were in considerable demand as a source of flavour for liqueurs, confectionery, and chocolate. However, the use of natural coumarin in food was banned in the USA in 1954, and the use of tonka beans restricted to perfume. In other countries they have now been largely replaced by synthetic coumarin and vanilla.

TOOTH FUNGI also called teeth fungi, include several highly edible species. Many have 'teeth' which are long, like spines, and hang downwards. So their common names reflect their resemblance to hedgehogs, waterfalls, beards, or the shaggy heads of bears or monkeys. It is the pendent teeth which are edible. Others such as the hedgehog fungus have small teeth which are only visible when one looks under the cap.

The genus *Hericium*, whose members grow on deciduous trees and their stumps or logs, supplies some of the best. *H. coralloides* and *H. erinaceum*, which occur in many parts of the world including Europe and N. America, are of picturesque appearance, giving rise to names such as bear's head, coral, or waterfall in N. America.

Hydnum repandum

H. coralloides is a white growth, up to 30 cm (12") across, which can be of startling beauty. Marteka (1980) records that:

In 1806, Elias Fries, a renowned Swedish botanist who helped lay the groundwork for mycology by setting up a classification system for fungi, decided to devote his life to the study of fungi after spotting a coral hydnum while blueberrying with his mother as a child. Even when he wrote his autobiography *Historiola Studii Mei Mycologici* fifty years later, Fries still vividly remembered the emotion that seized him when he found an unusually large specimen of the coral hydnum.

Marteka also quotes Krieger (1947) as saying that 'its pure whiteness seen in contrast with the dark colors of some fallen, moss-covered monarch of the forest, will cause even the most callous to stop in wonder and admiration. It seems almost sacrilegious to recommend it as food for the camper who wishes to vary his diet with a taste of mushrooms.' However, other writers affirm that young specimens, firm and white, are so delectable that the sacrilege is justified.

H. erinaceum, satyr's beard in N. America, has much longer spines which do look like a beard. It is the famous monkey's head mushroom of China, where it is both gathered wild (found, typically on the trunks of an oak, *Quercus mongolica*) and cultivated on a modest scale. Both these species make good eating when young and fresh, but need to be carefully cleaned, blanched, and cooked long and gently.

The same applies to *H. clathroides* (formerly *ramosum*), a more compact growth with short spines which grow along the length of the branches rather than being clustered at the tips. Like the other two, this has a global distribution.

Hedgehog fungus, *Hydnum* (formerly *Dentinum*) *repandum*, is common in woods in Europe and N. America and China, in the autumn. Its cap, which is usually of a creamy colour and a suedelike texture, bends up at the edges (the meaning of *repandum*). The thick stem is often off centre. The area between it and the cap is covered with spines, whence two alternative names, rubber brush fungus and pig's trotter fungus.

The species *Sarcodon imbricatum* is not unlike *Hydnum repandum*, but can grow to a larger size (up to 25 cm/nearly 10" across the cap) and has large dark scales on its cap.

TOPITAMBO or lerén or sweet corn-root, common names for *Calathea allouia*, a close relation in the family Marantaceae of the W. Indian ARROWROOT plant. The boiled tubers, like small ovoid potatoes in appearance, have a crisp and unusual texture (provided that care is taken not to overcook them, when they would quickly turn to mush). They have some similarity to the JERUSALEM ARTICHOKE (or *topinambour*, a name with which topitambo is confused or for which it is substituted in some places); but the plants are not closely related.

The flower clusters are also cooked and eaten, and the leaves, used as a wrapping, give an agreeable additional flavour to tamales and other foods.

TOP-SHELLS a group of single shells so called because in shape they resemble spinning tops. *Trochus niloticus maximus*, a large SE Asian species, is familiar because its large shells (30 cm/1') are used for ornamental purposes. They are black and white, but successive polishings produce a reddish hue and then a pearly finish. In Burma the shells are thought to resemble a kind of pagoda dome, so the last part of the Burmese name, *kha-yu-zedi*, means shrine.

Top-shells are boiled to permit extraction of the meat, which can then be fried or used in curries or soups. It can also be dried, and

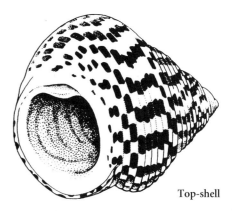

Top-shell

a product described as 'canned top-shell' is exported from China.

The top-shell of the Mediterranean, *Monodonta turbinata*, is much smaller: a mere 3 cm (just over 1"). It too is edible, and is usually eaten without further ado after being boiled for a while in sea or salted water with aromatics such as thyme. The small creatures are prized in various places, including the island of Murano near Venice where they are known as *bodoletti*.

TORTE AND KUCHEN. *Torte* is a German word which corresponds fairly closely to GATEAU. Its sister-word, *Kuchen*, can usually be translated as CAKE (large or of biscuit size); but in this connection see also QUICHE, a derived term. Torte appears in the title of many celebrated C. European confections, including SACHERTORTE. A few other examples are:

- *Engadiner Nusstorte*, a speciality of the Swiss canton of Engadine, is really a kind of pie consisting of two layers of rich sweet short pastry enclosing a filling of caramelized sugar mixed with cream and walnuts.
- *Dobostorte*, named after Dobos, a famous Hungarian chef who created it in 1887, is made by building up five or more thin circles of SAVOY sponge sandwiched with layers of a creamed filling, often flavoured with chocolate. The top layer of cake is covered with a layer of sugar CARAMEL, marked into portions.
- *Linzertorte* is a Viennese pastry made from a dough of flour, ground almonds, butter, and sugar, flavoured with lemon zest and cinnamon. Raspberry jam is spread over this base, and covered with a latticework of strips made from the dough, before baking.
- *Mohntorte* is a poppyseed cake, originally a speciality of Silesia. It is made from four layers of sweet short pastry, interspersed with a filling of ground poppyseeds (see POPPY) mixed with sugar, chocolate, raisins, candied peel, and almonds.

- *Zuger Kirschtorte*, a speciality of the canton of Zug in Switzerland, is made from three layers of *japonais* MERINGUE and a layer of Savoy-type sponge, sandwiched with pink-coloured kirsch-flavoured buttercream, and covered with toasted almonds.

Although Kuchen often refers to something less fancy than a Torte, one of the most famous Kuchen is very fancy indeed. This is the *Baumkuchen* (tree cake), which may be seen in the windows of specialist bakeries in Vienna and Berlin. Sarah Kelly (1985) has described it thus:

A metre or more in height . . . Baumkuchen is so called because of the concentric rings, like those of an ageing tree, which appear on a cross-section of the cake, and because of its tree-like shape, characterized by indentations which resemble the shaft of a screw. Unlike most cakes, Baumkuchen is grilled, not baked, on a rotating rod which turns horizontally in front of a red-hot grill plate. Each time a coating caramelizes, the baker applies a new layer of rich mixture—the process which produces the concentric rings. When the mixture runs out, he presses a long wooden 'comb' into the soft 'tree', giving it the characteristic indentations, before glazing it first with apricot and then with a clear or chocolate icing.

Baumkuchen is of particular interest because of its history. Barbara Maher (1982) traces its evolution in Germany from 15th-century monastery kitchens through the famous cookery book of Rumpolt (1581) to modern forms and to a remarkable eulogy by the German writer Theodor Fontane. She also notes that Dorothy Hartley (1954) had found an English manuscript recipe from the 14th century which provided what was essentially the same thing.

Streuselkuchen (crumble cake) can be a plain rubbed-in cake (see CAKE-MAKING) with a cinnamon-flavoured CRUMBLE topping. A more elaborate version, called *Apfelstreuselkuchen*, has a layer of apple (or other fruit) purée between two layers of crumble.

TORTILLA a round, thin unleavened bread made from ground MAIZE, a basic food of Mesoamerica. It is not known for how many millennia this has been a staple; but when the conquistadores arrived in the New World in the late 15th century, they discovered that the inhabitants made flat corn breads. The native Nahuatl name for these was *tlaxcalli* and the Spanish gave them the name tortilla.

Making the basic tortilla is simple, at least in theory. First a dough is made. To do this, the maize kernels are parched and cooked briefly in a mixture of unslaked lime and water. This step (see NIXTAMALIZATION) loosens the husks, increases the nutritional content of the grain, and ensures that a flexible flat bread can be made. Then the

corn is ground into a dough called *masa* in Mexico (a commercial product called *masa harina*, a flour made from the prepared kernels, can be mixed with water to make tortillas when corn is unavailable). The dough is shaped between the hands, or patted out on a flat surface, or stamped out with a special press. The tortillas are then cooked on a hot, ungreased GRIDDLE. They should be speckled with brown, and puff up when turned, but remain soft and pliable—rather like an Indian CHAPATI.

The art of tortilla-making was highly developed by the native Mesoamericans; one 17th-century Spanish observer, Francisco Hernández, remarked on the fine, almost transparent tortillas prepared for important people. The province of Oaxaca is known for the thinnest; those made in Guadalajara are thick, and the startling colour of blue corn is carefully preserved in tortillas made in the mountains of C. Mexico. Wheat flour, introduced by the Spanish, is used in the north of the country.

Fresh tortillas are eaten as bread, used as plate and spoon, or filled to make composite dishes such as *tacos* and *enchiladas*. These are described in their basic forms below, but their fillings may involve selections made from items such as shredded cooked meat, *frijoles refritos* (REFRIED BEANS), fish, scrambled eggs, or crumbled chorizo (see SAUSAGES OF SPAIN); cheese or sour cream; guacamole (avocado purée), shredded lettuce, sliced onion, other vegetables; and a *salsa* (sauce). This last item comes in two main fresh versions (each with many variations): *salsa roja*, onions, garlic, serrano CHILLIES all toasted on a griddle and then ground together with salt and herbs; and *salsa verde*, Mexican 'tomates' (green tomatoes) plus the same ingredients treated in the same way. Herbs used could be coriander or oregano.

A **taco**, in Mexico, is a fresh tortilla rolled around mashed beans, shredded meat, and sauce. It can be lightly fried after filling, and is eaten as a snack or an appetiser. In the TEX-MEX cuisine of the USA, a taco denotes a tortilla bent in half, deep fried to give a U shape, and filled with minced beef, shredded lettuce, and grated cheese.

An **enchilada** is also a tortilla rolled around a filling of meat, vegetables, or cheese; it differs from a taco in that the tortilla is fried and dipped in a piquant tomato sauce before the filling is added. Alternatively, the tortillas can be dipped in sauce and then fried. This is a main course for a main meal.

A **quesadilla** is a 'turnover' made by folding a fresh tortilla in half around a simple filling such as cheese, epazote (a pungent herb), and pepper, or potatoes and chorizo, and deep-frying it. This is just a snack.

Stale but not dried-out tortillas can be converted into *tostadas* by frying them and serving with some kind of topping—melted cheese, guacamole, fried beans, or shredded meat and salad. Or they are cut into wedges and fried until crisp to make *totopos* or *tostaditas*. Nachos are corn chips spread with cheese and Jalapeño peppers. Mexicans also cut dry tortillas into squares, fry them, and use in place of croutons in soup; or cut them into strips and make concoctions reminiscent of pasta dishes.

Tortilla dough is often used to make small snack items, collectively known as *antojitos* (little whims). These range from simple fried dough chips flavoured with chillies or cheese, to little balls filled with fried beans, and *chalupas*, little boat shapes with fillings (although in the north of Mexico, a *chalupa* is a *tostada*). The range is vast. Cooking may be on the griddle or by frying.

See also TAMALES; and see OMELETTE for *tortilla* in another meaning.   (LM)
READING: Diana Kennedy (1975); Sophie Coe (1994).

TORTOISE the common name for terrestrial species of reptiles in the order Chelonia; but see also TURTLE, since the usage of the names tends to overlap.

Tortoises are eaten less than turtles are, but are nonetheless consumed locally, and on a small scale, in many parts of the world.

So far as preparation and cookery are concerned, tortoises are much the same as turtles.

TRAPPIST CHEESE has to be defined in part by negatives. The name is given to any cheese of the PORT SALUT type which is not pretending to be real Port du Salut, or is not another named variety such as Saint-Paulin. The original Port du Salut was invented by Trappist monks, and many copies are also made by Trappists in other monasteries; but there are plenty of laymen making Trappist cheese all over Germany, Austria, and E. Europe. The first use of the name was in 1885, in a monastery near Banjaluka in Bosnia.

TRAVELLING SAUCE for which a detailed recipe was given by Richard Bradley (1736), who acknowledged it to a certain Mr Rozelli of The Hague, was a bottle or jar of concentrated sauce which travellers could take with them on journeys. The ingredients were variable, according to individual tastes, but the general procedure was to infuse a number of flavouring elements such as nutmeg, ginger, dried orange peel, shallots, and other herbs and spices in a suitable liquid (red wine, vinegar, VERJUICE). The product, in a well-stoppered container, could keep for up to a year if vinegar or wine had been used, but only three months with verjuice. Bradley assures us that it 'is a good Companion for Travellers, who more frequently find good Meat than good Cooks'.

This product occurs less often in recipe books of the 18th century than do recipes for another 'travellers' aid', namely PORTABLE SOUP. Since the sauce had to be carried in a bottle or jar, it was less convenient than the small dry cubes of 'veal glue' which constituted portable soup.

TREACLE a term which in Britain may be correctly applied to various SUGAR syrups including GOLDEN SYRUP obtained during the process of sugar-refining, ranging in colour from just about black to pale golden, is in practice used mainly of the darker syrups, brown or black, which are called molasses elsewhere.

Treacle TART is a favourite dessert in England. Treacle, of the dark sort, also appears in THUNDER AND LIGHTNING.

TREE BEAN the name given to leguminous plants—shrubs, trees, and climbers—of the genus *Bauhinia*. These grow widely in Africa, India, and SE Asia, and there is also more than one Australian species.

All the bauhinias have two-lobed butterfly leaves. These are commemorated by the generic name, which honours a pair of botanists, John and Caspar Bauhin. The bauhinias mostly lurk just inside the threshold of edibility. None is very good, but many have sufficient local importance to justify a mention.

The seeds of *Bauhinia reticulata* are eaten in tropical Africa, and the pods of *B. esculenta* are widely consumed, especially in S. Africa, where it is known as camel's foot (a name possibly imported from India, where it applies to *B. purpurea*).

The Malabar tree bean, *B. malabarica*, bears pods which are used as a flavouring in Thailand and Java and elsewhere in SE Asia. The leaves and pods of the 'Buddhist tree bean' (a name sometimes used, apparently because this species occurs often in Buddhist sculptures), *B. variegata*, are also eaten in India and its flowers pickled.

In Australia, at least one species has been used by the Aboriginals, who obtained sweet substances from the flowers or by making cuts in the bark. 'After rain they visit the scored trees and gather the *minni*, a thick sweet sap which exudes from the cuts like jellied honey-coloured gum; a great delicacy among the blacks, who eat it straight from the tree.' This from an early 20th-century settler, quoted by Low (1989).

TREE-COTTON *Gossypium arboreum*, a bushy treelike cotton plant, indigenous to Asia, which bears yellow or red flowers. When dried, these are dark brown and are used in Thailand in dishes such as *Gaeng kae*, a vegetable soup made with coconut milk.

The seeds of this plant yield an edible oil, but the main source of COTTONSEED OIL is *C. herbaceum*.

TREE ONION (or proliferous/top/ Egyptian onion), either a variety (var *proliferum*) of *Allium cepa* or (as in *Cornucopia*) *A. cepa* × *proliferum*. Perversely, the best-known strain is called the Egyptian onion. This plant, which is a hardy perennial, spreads itself in an odd way. The flowering top of the plant, which may reach a height of 1.2 m (4') or more, develops into a cluster of bulbils (miniature bulbs); and above these may develop a 'second storey' of more bulbils. As they grow, their increasing weight and the withering of the stem causes the cluster to keel over and plant itself at some distance from the parent plant. The underground bulbs also divide like those of aggregate onions. Both top bulbs, picked before they fall, and the underground ones are eaten. They are hot and strong. The little round top bulbs make good pickled onions.

TREE-TOMATO or tamarillo, *Cyphomandra betacea*, a fruit which resembles the tomato, but grows in bushes at high altitudes in tropical and subtropical zones. The plant was first cultivated by Peruvian Indians, but is now found

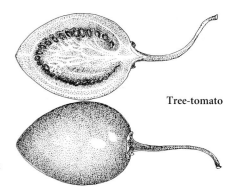

Tree-tomato

elsewhere, e.g. India, Sri Lanka, Malaysia, New Zealand, and California.

The fruits, 5–6 cm (2") long, with a smooth reddish-yellow skin, are borne in clusters of three or more. The succulent red or yellow pulp surrounds black seeds. The flavour is rich and sweet, allayed by some acidity. The fruits are eaten fresh; or stewed; or made into jam, preserves, or pickles, in much the same way as tomatoes. In Réunion, for example, they take the place of tomatoes for many purposes when the latter are out of season.

What has become the accepted commercial name, tamarillo, was adopted in New Zealand around 1970.

TREVALLY a name applied in an indiscriminate manner to various fish of the carangid family (see JACK). It sounds like a Cornish name, which would suggest that Cornish emigrants to the New World, and especially to Australasia, are responsible for its use; but it is thought by the *NSOED* to be a version of cavally, which in turn is probably derived from the Italian *cavalli*, plural of the Italian name for HORSE MACKEREL. The horse mackerel, another member of the same family, used to be taken in very large quantities in Cornwall.

The more important of the species to which the name has been applied include:

- *C. sexfasciatus*, sometimes called the 'great trevally', found in many parts of the Indo-Pacific; it may reach a length of over 1 m (4').
- *C. speciosus*, almost as large, a handsome but toothless fish which also has a wide distribution in the Indo-Pacific; may be referred to as golden trevally, kingfish, or cavalla.
- *C. georgianus*, sometimes called silver or white trevally, is well known in New Zealand and Australia; to be eaten very fresh, or smoked.
- *Alectis ciliaris*, threadfin trevally (and pennant trevally in Queensland), found from Indian waters to Australia and Hawaii; distinguished by very long 'trailers' from dorsal and anal fins.

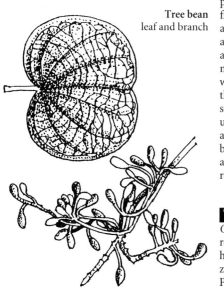

Tree bean
leaf and branch

TRIFLE a traditional English sweet or dessert. The essential ingredients are SPONGE CAKE soaked in sherry or white wine, rich CUSTARD, fruit or jam, and whipped cream, layered in a glass dish in that order. The cream is often decorated with, for example, slivers of almond, glacé cherries, ANGELICA.

The word trifle derives from the Middle English 'trufle' which in turn came from the Old French *trufe* (or *trufle*), meaning something of little importance.

Originally, in the late 16th century, the culinary meaning of the word trifle was 'a dish composed of cream boiled with various ingredients'. This is also the description one could give of a FOOL. Indeed Florio, in his dictionary of 1598, bracketed the two terms when he wrote: 'a kinde of clouted cream called a foole or a trifle.'

The first known recipe entitled trifle was in *The Good Huswife's Iewell* [i.e. Jewel] (1596) by T. Dawson, and there were many such recipes in the 17th century, including a 'Triffel' from the great cookery writer Robert May (1685), but these were little more than spiced and sweetened cream, latterly thickened by renneting.

It was not until the mid-18th century that something like the modern trifle began to emerge. Biscuits wetted with wine were then in place at the bottom of the bowl, and custard was on top of them, while the topmost layer could be achieved by pouring whipped SYLLABUB froth over all. When this froth was replaced by plain whipped cream, the process of evolution was virtually complete.

Helen Saberi (1995*b*) gave the first historical account to cover the evolution of the trifle up to this point; what happened to it thereafter, both in Britain and on emigration to the USA and elsewhere; and its relationship to things like TIPSY CAKE, whim-wham, and the Italian *zuppa inglese*.

TRIGGER FISH the common name for a larger number of species in the family Balistidae, notably *Balistes carolinensis*. They may also be called leatherjackets, in allusion to their thick and tough skins. The 'trigger' in the main name is a little spine on the back, just behind the solitary dorsal spine (and in fact representing a rudimentary second dorsal spine). This 'trigger' can be used to lock the dorsal spine in an upright position.

Some trigger fish may reach a length of 60 cm (24"), but they are mostly smaller. Nonetheless, as they are deep bodied, they have enough flesh to be worth eating, and it is good. They are often divested of their leathery skins before being sold.

Among the species brought to market are:

- *Balistes carolinensis*, of the W. and E. Atlantic and the Mediterranean;
- *Monacanthus cirrhifer*, the most common species in Japanese waters and the most appreciated, especially in summer;
- *Alutera monoceros*, a relatively large trigger fish of the Indo-Pacific, greyish-brown with yellow fins;
- *Abalistes stellaris*, another Indo-Pacific species which Maxwell (1921) said was preferred to all other fish by many Malay, including fishermen. The reason given was the likeness between its flesh and chicken meat.

TRIPE generally defined as the stomach of ruminants (even-toed, hoofed animals with a three- or four-chambered stomach such as the cow, ox, sheep, deer, etc.). Tripe from cow/ox/calf is much the most common. There are four types.

- The paunch or rumen (the first and biggest compartment of the stomach of a ruminant) provides what is called plain or flat or blanket tripe. It is also known as double tripe (French *gras-double*) because its smoothly seamed exterior and its inside lining are quite distinct. It may also be called thick-seam tripe.
- The walls of the reticulum (the second compartment) provide honeycomb tripe, so named because of its appearance. It is often attached to flat tripe, but is more tender than the other (French *réseau*; *millet*; *caillette*).
- The omasum or psalterium (third compartment) is known as leaf, book, or Bible tripe (French *feuillet*; *bonnet*).
- The abomasum is described as the 'true glandular stomach' but the least important for cooks (French *franche mule*).

For a use of the milk-filled abomasum of a calf, see SONOFABITCH STEW.

The term reed tripe may be used of the third or fourth types. The French name *gras-double* may be applied to any of the first three types.

All tripe from the butcher is very white, as a result of lengthy and tedious processing (soaking in lime, then in brine and boiling). In the north of England, and no doubt elsewhere, being a tripe dresser was a specialized calling.

Tripe generally needs many hours of cooking even after it has been prepared. In Normandy a beautiful honey-golden utensil called a *tripière* is used for cooking it. This is circular, wide, and shallow, with a small removable lid.

Well-known tripe dishes include *Tripes à la mode de Caen* (Normandy); American PEPPER POT soup; Tripe and onions (north of England); *Busecca* (tripe soup,

Lombardy); *Tripas à moda do Porto* (Oporto in Portugal).

However, pride of place should perhaps be given to *İşkembe çorbası*, Turkish tripe soup, in the light of the information provided by Nevin Halıcı (1989):

In Turkey tripe soup is usually drunk late in the evening. In large towns there are tripe restaurants—işkembeci—which remain open all night. People who have been out drinking make a final call at the tripe house before returning home. During the Kurban Bayramı, the religious feast of sacrifice, tripe soup is made without fail in every home where the ritual of sacrifice has been observed.

TRIPLETAIL *Lobotes surinamensis*, a fish which does not really have three tails, but whose extended dorsal and anal fins give this impression. It bears a general resemblance to SEA BASS, is brassy-brown in colour with blotches, and may grow to a length of 1 m (39"). Its extensive range includes the W. Atlantic (Virginia to Argentina, including the Caribbean, whence *surinamensis* in its name), the E. Atlantic (the Strait of Gibraltar to southern Africa), the W. Mediterranean (rarely), and many of the tropical or warm seas of the Indo-Pacific, including parts of Australia.

Wheeler (1979) remarks that young tripletails are quite common. 'They are found in shallow water inshore, where they have been known to mimic floating mangrove leaves, drifting at the surface in a gently curved posture with the head slightly lower than the tail. They are also frequently found in floating sargassum weed, which suggests that they are common offshore.' Adults are less common and have the reputation of being sluggish; indeed one of the Thai names for this species means 'sluggish snapper'. However, if trapped in a net, they may manage to make a big jump, accounting for the name 'jumping cod' given to them in parts of Australia.

This is a fish of good quality, to which all standard preparations may be applied. Small specimens can be grilled whole.

TRITICALE of the genus X. *Triticosecale*, a new kind of cereal grain created by man. Its development began in 1876 when a Scottish botanist, A. Stephen Wilson, first managed to produce seedlings of an artificial cross between WHEAT and RYE. The name 'triticale' is a combination of the botanical generic names of wheat (Triticum) and rye (Secale).

Such crosses occasionally occur naturally in the field, but the resulting hybrids are always sterile. Nevertheless, the prospect was attractive: a cereal with the superior bread-making properties of wheat and the hardiness of rye. Wilson's plants were also sterile; but in 1891 a German, Rimpau, managed to produce partly fertile side shoots on an otherwise sterile plant. It was not until the 1930s that further progress was made. By this time more was known about genetics, in particular concerning the experimental doubling of chromosome numbers in plants, which could be done by treating them with the chemical colchicine.

Briefly, a normal plant is a diploid: it contains two half sets of chromosomes (genetic material): half of each of its parents' chromosomes. Tetraploids, inheriting a full complement of chromosomes from each parent, and thus having double the normal allowance, occur in nature or can be induced. There are higher levels of 'ploidy': hexaploidy (three full sets), and octoploidy (four). All these polyploid plants have a tendency to grow to a large size: most cultivated wheats are hexaploids or tetraploids with seed heads far larger than their wild diploid ancestors. Furthermore, polyploidy is a way of overcoming the incompatibility of two insufficiently closely related plants whose chromosomes do not match each other, although it does not automatically result in a successful crossing with fertile offspring, as the early triticale breeding attempts showed.

By 1939, after seven years' work with repeated crossing of hexaploids and octoploids, a German scientist, Müntzing, was getting promising results, and by 1950 he had produced plants with 90% of the yield of wheat. From 1954 Shebeski and Jenkins at the University of Manitoba in Canada began intensive breeding. It became clear that the new grain was nutritionally as good as wheat and barley, and that it was possible to make bread with it. In 1970 the first commercial variety, Rosner, went on sale. Meanwhile, the International Centre for the Improvement of Maize and Wheat, in Mexico, produced new lines called Armadillo, which, when combined with Canadian strains, began to produce superior plants.

The latest kinds of triticale have good hardiness, very large seed heads, and are nutritionally better than wheat, having a higher content of lysine, an amino acid, in which wheat and other cereals are rather low. Triticale is a little weaker than wheat in GLUTEN (the substance which gives wheat bread its firm texture), but with slightly altered preparation methods it is possible to make triticale bread of satisfactory texture. The flavour is stronger than that of wheat, not particularly like that of rye, but with a characteristic 'nutty' quality. Triticale bread, flour, and breakfast cereals have been made available so that consumers can try the new grain.

TROUT a group of fish in the genus *Salmo*, which is where SALMON also belong. Because trout are a favourite of anglers and are food fishes of high value, they have been introduced from one continent to another on a large scale, and have also become a major subject of fish farming. Trout of one kind or another are now found in every continent except Antarctica, and some confusion over nomenclature has resulted. The three species of true trout, with their common names in English, regions of origin, present distribution, and maximum lengths, are listed below. So are two related fish to which the name trout applies, albeit less correctly.

- *Salmo trutta*, the brown trout in its freshwater version, sea trout or salmon trout in the migratory, sea-run version (see SEA TROUT). Originally a European species, found at sea in the NE Atlantic, and in fresh waters as far east as the Caspian Sea. Now introduced to N. and S. America, Australasia, S. Africa, E. Africa, India, etc. Up to 140 cm (55"). The sea-run fish, which migrate to sea at any age from 1 to 5 years and spend anything from six months to five years at sea before returning, grow larger than the freshwater fish.
- *S. gairdneri*, rainbow trout, also known in its sea-run version as steelhead. Native to NW America. Introduced to Europe, where it is farmed. Probably identical with the species known as *S. mykiss* in Asia. Up to 120 cm (4'). As with the preceding species, it is the sea-run specimens which are the largest.
- *S. clarkii*, the cutthroat trout. Native to NW America. In the headwaters of some American and Canadian rivers it is represented by a subspecies, *S. c. lewisi*, the yellowhead cutthroat trout. Up to 1 m (39").

Long usage has legitimized the use of the name trout for two of the fish in the genus *Salvelinus*, whose members are more correctly known as CHAR:

- *Salvelinus fontinalis*, the brook trout. Native to NE America. Widely introduced to rivers in temperate zones around the world; and occurs in a sea-run form in the NE Pacific. Up to 85 cm (34").
- *S. namaycush*, the lake trout. Native to much of N. America, including the far north and the Great Lake system. Its original range has been extended by introduction, for example to California. Up to 120 cm (4').

Cookery of trout is not a problem. Poaching or grilling (US broiling) are common techniques, as is cooking *en papillote* (in an aluminium foil package with flavourings and a little butter or olive oil),

and frying (as in *Truite aux amandes*). *Truite au bleu* is a special technique for trout; see AU BLEU.

TRUFFLE a fungus whose fruiting body grows underground and which constitutes a mysterious, costly, and delicate foodstuff.

One wonders whether President Truman ever received, and tasted, the largest truffle of which a record exists: a giant which registered over 2 kg (4 lb) on the scales. The Italian who dug it up in 1951 near Alba, in the heart of the Italian truffle country, sold it for 130,000 lire (equivalent, perhaps, to more than £3,000 now) and Goldschmied (1954) records that the businessman from Rome who bought it intended to offer it in homage to Truman. If he did, there would have been a pleasing contrast between gift and recipient; the simple eater from Missouri faced by a supreme example of the most expensive, subtle, and mysterious of the foods known to man. The Roman donor could also have reflected that he was giving to the leading personality of the New World the one Old World food which he could not possibly, at that time, grow on his own territory.

It is true that some species of truffle exist in N. America, including *Tuber texense*, an edible white truffle used by some restaurateurs. But no one has claimed that this, or any other truffle outside Europe, is a serious rival to the black truffle of Périgord, *T. melanosporum*, or the white truffle of Alba, *T. magnatum*.

The black truffle is probably at its best in Périgord, where conditions conspire to bring it to perfection, but it does grow in other parts of France, and also in Spain and Italy. The white truffle of Italy is found in a number of localities but mainly in the vicinity of Alba in Piedmont where the principal market is held. These two species stand alone, in excellence as in fame.

It was not always so. A Roman living 1,800 years ago who wished to honour his own emperor might well have offered him a specimen of *Terfezia*, the desert truffle which was brought to Rome from Arab lands, especially N. Africa. *Terfez*, as the Arabs know it (*faqqa* in the Gulf States), is still found and prized as a seasonal delicacy, especially after winter rains, in the region of Kuwait and the Persian Gulf. It is usually cleaned, sliced, and fried; but, since it is dug up from the sand, it tends to be difficult to clean completely. Perhaps partly because of this, its reputation and consumption have dwindled remarkably since classical times—to such depths that nowadays it would actually be illegal to offer it for sale as a truffle in France.

In ancient times, and indeed until about 100 years ago, no natural historian understood what truffles are and how they grow. Theophrastus thought that they (and other fungi) were produced by the rain of thunderstorms; Dioscorides that they were a kind of root; Pliny that they were 'callosities of earth'; and Plutarch that lightning was a necessary condition of their formation. Even in the 18th and 19th centuries, when some learned men were beginning to see the truth, others continued to uphold quite false theories.

In reality, a truffle is the fruiting body of a fungus which grows wholly underground. Truffles are not the only underground 'mushrooms', but they are the only valuable ones of this habit. The plant itself consists of an extensive web of filaments so fine as to be invisible. And these filaments, known as the 'mycelium', link up with the roots of certain trees and shrubs in what is called a 'mycorrhizal' relationship. This relationship benefits both parties. From the point of view of the tree, the filaments of the truffle become extensions of its own roots and enable it to draw up more sustenance, notably minerals, from the soil. For the truffle, the tree gives nourishment in the form of products synthesized by its leaves. This remarkable exchange is not achieved by mere contact between the mycelium of the truffle and the roots of the tree. They are organically bonded together by a special growth called a 'mycorrhizal'.

So it is clear that the cultivation of truffles, which for obvious reasons has long been attempted, is on the one hand difficult (how to reproduce a natural phenomenon of such complexity?) but on the other hand possible (since young trees in a mycorrhizal condition can be transplanted). The would-be cultivator has to remember that the system only works with some kinds of tree (notably, but not exclusively, certain kinds of oak), in a limited range of climates, and on certain types of soil (a limestone base being preferred).

Other factors are also relevant. Rebière (1967), the doyen of truffle experts in the Périgord, lived not far from the little truffle museum in the village of Sorges. One striking feature of the areas where truffles grow is the 'scorched earth' area round a tree which has a mycorrhizal relationship with truffles, especially the black truffle. Virtually no other plants, except for those which need no water, can grow in such soil and the underground progress of the truffle mycelium can be charted by the spread of this barren ground. Rebière recorded some intriguing information about the 'shock treatment' which will help restore a former *truffière* to productivity again. Roadworks help, especially if heavy bulldozers are used. And having a local basketball team use a piece of ground for their games is another favourable factor.

The mycelium of the black truffle starts active growth in May and continues until July. The fruiting bodies are white when they first begin to form, then successively greyish and reddish, by which time they have reached full size. Finally, when they reach maturity, they are nearly black and veined white inside. There is often a long pause, perhaps of several months, between the time when a truffle reaches its full size and the time when it matures. This accounts for the length of the season, extending over five winter months.

Most truffles remain well underground. Skilled hunters may be able to detect from signs on the surface that a truffle is below; but the aid of animals or insects has to be invoked to ensure a full harvest. The aroma of a mature truffle can be detected by a pig or a dog, and it is these animals which have traditionally been trained to do the work. The pig has some disadvantages, especially for the truffle-poacher, since separating it from a truffle it has found is awkward; dogs are nimbler and less possessive.

The insects which help belong to the species *Helomyza tuberiperda*, and may be seen hovering over the spot where a truffle lies concealed. They hover with the intention of depositing their larvae on the truffles, little realizing what an expensive baby food they thus provide for their tiny offspring.

Even with these various aids, truffle-hunting is a skilled business, and one which is closely regulated. Truffling rights in a piece of land may be separated from ownership of the land itself. This is not surprising since an expert hunter working in good terrain may gather the equivalent of six months' livelihood in a few weeks, if the summer weather has been right and the season a good one. The season runs from November to February, and even March, in the Périgord.

The supreme manner of enjoying truffles must no doubt be that described by Alexandre DUMAS *père* (1873), writing about the goings on at the house of one of the 'queens' of the Paris theatre of his time, Mlle Georges, when offering supper to intimate friends after the show.

. . . at the house of [Mlle Georges], she who embodied every form of sensuality, no mercy was shown to the truffle, it was compelled to yield every sensation which it was capable of giving.

Hardly had she arrived home when perfumed water in a shallow basin of the most beautiful porcelain was brought to Georges, in which she washed her hands. Then the truffles were brought, truffles which had already been subjected to two or three ablutions and the same number of scrubbings; and, in a separate plate, a little vermilion fork and a little knife with a mother-of-pearl handle and a steel blade.

Then Agrippine, with her hand modelled on classical lines, with her fingers of marble and her rosy fingernails, started to peel the black tubercle, an ornament in her hand, in the most adroit fashion in the world. She cut it in thin tiny leaves, like paper, poured on some ordinary pepper and a few atoms of Cayenne pepper, impregnated them with white oil from Lucca or green oil from Aix, and then passed the salad bowl to a servant, who tossed the salad which she had prepared.

A modern connoisseur might suggest instead that whole truffles, unpeeled, be wrapped in several layers of cooking paper greased with goose fat, and roasted gently under hot cinders. But this would be for the very wealthy. Most people must be satisfied with the slivers of truffle to be found in *pâté de foie gras truffé* or with putting a tiny amount of truffle in a recipient used for storing eggs, which will then acquire a wonderful truffle aroma and flavour.

Another delicacy known as 'truffle' belongs to the realm of chocolate CONFECTIONERY. This is a cherry-sized ball of soft chocolate paste, often encased in a harder chocolate coating. If dusted with COCOA powder, as they often are, these are thought to look like freshly dug real truffles. Hence their name which first became current in the 1920s.

TRUMPETER the name of some Australasian fish of the family Latridae, related and similar to the MORWONG. The best known, and best to eat, is *Latris lineata*, the Tasmanian (or striped) trumpeter; the next best are *Latidropsis ciliaris*, called blue moki in New Zealand, and *L. aerosa*, the copper moki.

Roughley (1966), whose views are highly authoritative in this matter, describes the Tasmanian trumpeter as one of the six finest food fishes in Australian waters; 'its flesh is white and firm, of splendid texture and delicious flavour.'

TRUMPETER a S. American bird, *Psophia crepitans*, related to CRANES, BUSTARDS, and rails; it and two other close relations in the same genus belong to the order Gruiformes. Trumpeters enjoy a wholesome diet of berries and insects and are appreciated as food, especially when young.

Tubby birds, about 50 cm (20") long in body, with long necks and long legs, trumpeters are gregarious, noisy, as befits their name, living mostly on the ground and nesting in tree holes. They are found mainly in the rain forests north of the Amazon, where destruction of their habitat has endangered their survival. However, they are easily domesticated and may be used to guard barnyard fowls in the same manner as GUINEA-FOWL.

In fact, according to Alexandre DUMAS (1873) an *agami* (as the French call the trumpeter) will gladly undertake a much wider range of duties, for example chasing dogs and cats out of the dining room and shepherding flocks of ducks and turkeys to their appointed places at the correct times. A friend of Dumas took two of the birds back to France, where they promptly assumed full control of his farmyard. Having their heads and necks, which are covered with short curly feathers, scratched was sufficient reward for them. However, Dumas relates that his friend lost one of the two agamis when it fell from a roof top and broke its back. 'His interest in gourmandise caused him to taste its flesh, which he found delicious and certainly better than most of our chickens. The meat of the agami is in fact very delicate, and very much sought after.'

TSAMPA is the main staple of TIBET. The word *tsampa* means flour made from toasted grain, and the grain most commonly used for the purpose in Tibet is BARLEY. However, *tsampa* can also be made from wheat, corn, millet, oats, even soya beans.

Tsampa is consumed in several different ways. The simplest is as a drink, made by adding it to cold water or, more commonly, to tea. A soup (*tsamtuk*) is also made, using butter, soya beans, and cheese (*chura*). In addition, Tibetans use *tsampa* flour to make 'cakes' such as *pag* and *sengong*. Dorje (1985) explains the first of these thus:

This is a very common food of the monks and nuns in Tibet. Each person mixes his own *pag* in a bowl or cup, but it takes some practice. This is how it is done. When people are served tea, they blow the butter that floats on top to one side and drink the tea. Then when there is just a little tea and the butter left, they add some *tsampa*. The *tsampa* is mixed in with one hand rubbing the flour, tea, and butter against the inside of the cup, while the other hand holds the cup and turns it in the opposite direction. When everything is mixed into a stiff dough, the *pag* can be rolled into little balls and popped into the mouth. Things can be added to make the *pag* fancy, but basic *pag* is just butter, tea, *tsampa* and sugar.

Dorje's mother is a Sherpa, so he speaks with good authority of the second 'cake', *sengong*, which is a Sherpa-style cake, mostly eaten in the southern part of the country and important in the Himalayas. The dough (of salted water, *tsampa*, and butter) is heated to thicken it, stirred a short while over a low heat, then served with a coating of butter and with hot tomato sauce. Tibetans pull off a chunk of the dough, roll it in the sauce and pop it in their mouths.

TUATUA *Amphidesma subtriangulata*, an edible BIVALVE of New Zealand beaches. It is related to the TOHEROA, but is smaller and has heavier shells of a more noticeably triangular shape. Its distribution is much wider than that of the toheroa, and it is particularly abundant on the eastern beaches of the North Island. Clam-diggers are allowed to gather up to 150 per person daily.

The tuatua, being more common, does not enjoy as high a reputation as the toheroa, but is of comparable merit and makes a good soup. See also PIPI.

TUILE (French for 'tile'), a kind of thin, crisp, sweet BISCUIT made of a light creamed mixture with egg whites, and sometimes ground or chopped almonds (in which case, *tuiles aux amandes*), flavoured with vanilla or grated orange or lemon peel. While the biscuits are still soft from baking they are laid on a curved surface such as a jam jar or rolling pin so that they take the shape of a typical S. European roof tile. Italian *tegolino* and Spanish *teja* are the same thing.

TUNA (or tunny), a group of large and medium-sized oceanic fish which are a food resource of primary importance.

The name tuna, like most general fish names, is not applied in a uniform way and does not always correspond to the scientific classification of these fish. With rare exceptions it is used only of fish in the family Scombridae, and within that family is reserved almost exclusively for members of the two genera *Thunnus* (all of whose members except one are always called tuna in English) and *Euthynnus* (where names such as little tunny, thonine, and kawakawa prevail). Within the same subfamily as these are two other genera, whose members are likely to be referred to in scientific works as tuna, but which have other common names and are the subjects of separate entries. These are *Katsuwonus* (one species only, often just called SKIPJACK rather than skipjack tuna), and *Auxis* (whose members are usually called FRIGATE MACKEREL). Close relations, with many of the same characteristics as tuna, include BONITO. For a catalogue of all these species see Bruce Collette and Cornelia Nauen (1983).

The principal tuna of the world, with their common names, maximum fork length, distribution, and special characteristics, are as follows (but see also SKIPJACK):

- *Thunnus alalunga*, longfin tuna or ALBACORE, to 127 cm (50"), worldwide in the Atlantic and Indo-Pacific, has long pectoral fins, has its own entry as there is much to be said about it.
- *T. albacares*, yellowfin tuna (warning: in French this is *albacore*, see preceding species), to more than 2 m (*c*.2.5'), record angling weight 176 kg (*c*.375 lb), worldwide in tropical and subtropical seas but not in the Mediterranean, dorsal and anal fins and finlets bright yellow.
- *T. atlanticus*, blackfin tuna, to 1 m (39"), occurring only in the W. Atlantic, from Massachusetts down to Brazil, most commonly taken in the Caribbean region, dorsal and anal fins dusky, the first dorsal fin especially dark.
- *T. maccoyii*, southern bluefin tuna, to 2.2 m (90"), around the world south of 30 degrees S., the southern member of a trio of similar species, the other two of which come next.
- *T. obesus*, bigeye tuna, to more than 2 m (*c*.2.5'), worldwide in tropical and subtropical waters but not in the Mediterranean, has relatively large eyes.
- *T. thynnus*, northern bluefin tuna, to 3 m (over 3'), record angling weight 679 kg (*c*.2150 lb), in the Atlantic and Pacific (at least two subspecies are recognized, one for each ocean), always north of the Equator and as far north as Norway, the largest tuna and the one most familiar to Europeans.
- *T. tonggol*, longtail tuna, to 130 cm (51"), from the Red Sea to SE Asia and Australia.

Tuna are warm-blooded fish, which are in constant need of oxygen. They can only obtain an adequate supply by swimming continuously at a fair speed (so that oxygen-rich water is incessantly rushing over their gills), and for this purpose they need very powerful muscles. It is this dark muscular meat, so different from the white flesh of most fish, that human beings enjoy eating. Large pieces of tuna may be braised like joints of meat. However, it is more usual to cut steaks which may be grilled (US broiled) or cooked in other ways; or not cooked at all, as when the Japanese eat choice fresh pieces of tuna as SASHIMI. So great is Japanese enthusiasm for tuna that they and N. Americans between them account for half the total catch. See also TUNISIA for a good dish which uses canned tuna.

TUNISIA a country whose culinary history embraces that of ancient Carthage (close to the city of Tunis), imperial Rome, the Ottoman Empire, and the Arab conquest of N. Africa, has also been exposed to strong Italian (especially Sicilian) influences, to even stronger French ones (during the period when Tunisia was a French Protectorate), besides showing traces (e.g. in the port of Sfax) of Greek influence. So it is a rich and complex cuisine. One of the best sources for studying it is a wonderfully erudite monograph by a French savant, Dr Gobert, which was published in 1940 in the *Archives de l'Institut Pasteur* in Tunis, but still awaits an English translator. In recent times, Mohammed El Kouki has done much to preserve the national repertoire of recipes in his huge compilation thereof.

The staple food is COUSCOUS, with lamb and MERGUEZ sausage, or chicken or fish, plus an ample provision of vegetables and a hot chilli sauce (HARISSA) as the standard accompaniment. A restaurant menu will often feature *Briq à l'œuf* as a first course to precede couscous. This is an egg cooked (by deep-frying) inside a triangle of paper-thin folded pastry (see WARQA), perhaps with a little tuna added. The trick is to lift up the triangle and consume it all in judicious bites without spilling any egg. A liking for *briqs*, once acquired, stays for a lifetime and inevitably draws *briq*-eaters back to Tunisia or to Tunisian restaurants.

Until the last two decades of the 20th century, Mediterranean fish and other seafood were in ample supply, landed from small fishing boats and sold in bewildering profusion in the markets of the coastal cities and towns. Various factors, notably the growing demands of tourist hotels (pleasantly landscaped and unobtrusive, but numerous) and pollution and overfishing in the Mediterranean, have replaced this happy situation by one in which short supply and high prices put seafood out of the reach of most Tunisians. The following description of going out for a fish supper in the 1960s is now nothing but a fond memory:

La Goulette, which takes its name from being the 'throat' of the ship canal which connects Tunis itself with the sea, is the site of a group of fish restaurants, which extend their tables far out over the pavements and the square during the summer. What pleasure it was to sup there, starting with a *chakchouka* and going on to eat a grilled daurade or grey mullet selected from the glass-fronted cabinet in front of the restaurant, with family parties of Tunisians all round, the men in their cool white djebbahs, jasmine-sellers brushing past one's elbow, the legion of La Goulette cats brushing past one's ankles, and primitive strings of coloured lamps switched on overhead as dusk fell. Here was no nonsense of complicated menus—just marvellously good fish charcoal-grilled and served with plenty of chopped parsley and lemon.

Tunisian sweetmeats, based on Arab traditions, are a delight. For those who find many of them too heavily laden with calories, there are the Tunisian DATES from the desert oases and elsewhere in the south, as well as numerous other fruits—oranges, lemons, grapes, etc.

Regional variations in the food include the presence of wild boar and many edible fungi in the north-west. The tiny island of Galita, which can be reached from Bizerta, is a great place for SPINY LOBSTER. The promontory of Cap Bon has traditionally been the scene of the annual TUNA fishery, which involves guiding the migrating fish by stages into a large trap, the 'death chamber', where they are dispatched. This is like the *matanza* of Sicily. Tunisian ways with tuna, apart from grilling fresh steaks, include a particularly enjoyable cold dish, *Salade meshouiwa*: a little canned tuna; seared sweet peppers, tomatoes, garlic, and onion; hard-boiled eggs; seasoning with caraway as well as salt and pepper; lemon juice and olive oil, and black olives to garnish.

READING: Kouki (1967); Gobert (1955).

TURBOT *Psetta maxima*, a FLATFISH with an extensive range: from the Black Sea through the Mediterranean and up the European Atlantic coasts as far as the Arctic Circle. It may reach a length of 1 m (just over 3'), but half this is a normal adult size. The colour of the back is generally greyish or sandy brown, and it is noticeable that most scales develop into tiny bony tubercles. In the Black Sea region, these tubercles become much more prominent, indeed larger than the fish's eyes, which accounts for the vernacular names there (meaning 'nail-head', for example, and has also caused scientists to distinguish the Black Sea turbots as a subspecies, *P. m. maeotica*.

The great breadth of the turbot's body accounts for an old Scots name, bannock-fluke (bannock being a round oatcake, and fluke a general name for left-eyed flatfish).

The main fishery for the turbot in Atlantic waters is in the North Sea. The numbers caught are not great, indeed very small in relation to the demand. The firm white flesh is highly esteemed, and is often honoured with an expensive sauce (e.g. lobster sauce, sauce mousseline) in restaurants. The French writer BRILLAT-SAVARIN has a memorable anecdote about the procedure devised for steaming a giant turbot; and this is a useful reminder that steaming is an excellent way of cooking it. However, slices cut across and fried, with the skin still on, are also delicious. Various authorities have urged the desirability of eating skin and (this from Jenny Wren, 1880) fins.

TURKEY with reference to birds, was originally a prefix to the terms cock, hen, and poult (a young bird), but now stands on its own and denotes the species *Meleagris gallopavo*. Native to N. America, these birds are now farmed and used for table poultry around the globe. A book by Schorger (1966) provides much historical information about the bird and its transformation into a global food item.

The nomenclature of turkeys in modern European languages and scientific Latin reflects confusion about the origin and nature of the birds on their arrival from the New World. They were confused in European minds with GUINEA-FOWL, and probably peacocks too. Linnaeus used *Meleagris*, the Roman name for guinea-fowl, when naming the genus to which turkeys belong. Europeans called turkeys by names reflecting a supposed eastern origin, including *coq d'Inde* (cock of India), later corrupted to *dinde* or *dindon* in French. The English, who may have had their first birds

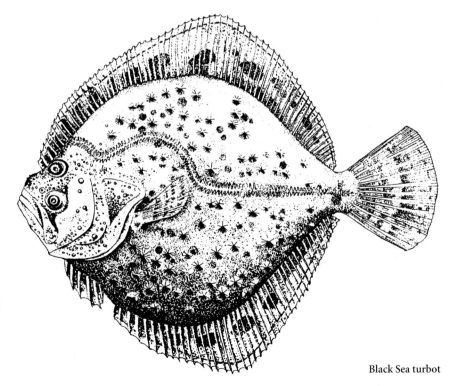

Black Sea turbot

through the agency of the Levant or Turkey merchants, settled on 'turkey-cock'.

Wild turkeys of N. America are much leaner and more streamlined birds than their modern descendants. In their natural state they live in flocks, roosting in swampy areas and feeding on woodland berries and seeds. They are awkward in flight but run fast. Two distinct races of wild turkey are known—one whose range originally covered eastern N. America from Canada to Texas, and another from further south, around the Gulf of Mexico. The Mexican variety may have been more important, as it appears to have been more adaptable and easily domesticated, but the pre-Columbian history of the turkey is obscure. It is thought to have been domesticated late in the 2nd millennium BC, somewhere in C. America. By the time of the Spanish Conquest, it was reared as a table bird and eaten by royalty. The earliest full description of turkeys in the New World was given by Bernardino de Sahagún (1529) who recommended the meat of the hen as fat and savoury, and recorded several modes of preparation, including in TAMALES.

When turkeys reached the Old World, they appear (unlike other foods from the Americas, such as tomatoes and potatoes) to have diffused swiftly and been consumed enthusiastically. In England in 1541, they were cited amongst large birds such as cranes and swans in sumptuary laws; their prices had been fixed in the London markets by the mid-1550s; and Tusser (1557) spoke of feeding turkeys on runcivall pease, and of eating them at Christmas.

Liliane Plouvier, in a learned paper (of the 1980s) about the early history of turkeys in Europe, found that, in France, Queen Marguerite of Navarre is recorded to have raised turkeys at Alençon in 1534; and 66 turkeys were served at a feast for Catherine de' Medici in 1549. In Belgium, turkey prepared in three different ways (boiled with oysters; roast and served cold; and in a pasty) was served in 1557 at a banquet held in Liège. Reasons for this speedy acceptance are not hard to find. The turkey would have been seen as similar to the domestic poultry familiar in Europe since ancient times, and confused with guinea-fowl; and there was anyway a firm medieval precedent for eating all sorts of fowl, wild and tame, large and small.

Amongst settlers in N. America, the turkey also proved popular. In 1609 the inhabitants of Jamestown, reduced almost to starvation, were kept alive by gifts of wild game, including 'turkies', from the indigenous population. Wild turkeys were served at the second THANKSGIVING dinner in 1621, and may have featured in the first, of 1620.

Describing how, during the 17th and 18th centuries, turkeys became established as farmyard fowls in England, C. Anne Wilson (1974) explains that great numbers of them would be driven to London on foot, starting in August at the end of the harvest, from as far afield as Suffolk and Norfolk.

Although poorly adapted to cold, damp climates, the turkey gradually displaced the GOOSE as a Christmas meat in Britain, and comments from 19th-century observers show that turkeys raised in Britain achieved a large size. At the end of the 19th century, the two main breeds were the Norfolk Black and the Cambridge Bronze. The former is a much leaner bird with less breast meat than turkeys now commonly reared, and lost popularity because after the black feathers had been plucked the skin was left with a pitted appearance. The bronze did not share this problem and was cross-bred for increased size with N. American stock to give a creature known as the American Mammoth Bronze; but eventually this was ousted by white types which owe much to American and continental European stock.

When it came to **cooking turkeys**, they were rapidly assimilated into various styles of cuisine contemporary with their arrival in Europe. Plouvier, examining early recipes, found that there were several for turkey in Italy by 1570 (e.g. in Scappi's *Opera dell'arte del cucinare*); besides being spit roasted, made into *paupiettes* or little poached QUENELLES, they could be stuffed, stuck with cloves, encased in a coarse crust with the head exposed, and baked. Recipes were published in Germany by the 1580s, but turkey recipes only appeared in France during the 'culinary renaissance' of the 17th century, when La Varenne gave several recipes, including one requiring a truffle-perfumed bouillon.

In England, turkeys were being made into pies during the reign of Elizabeth I, and soon afterwards Gervase Markham (1615) recommended that they should be roast, and served with a sauce of onions, flavoured with claret, orange juice, and lemon peel.

From the 18th century onwards, turkeys were firmly established in the European culinary mainstream. Originally associated with high status (although sometimes with a satirical turn, witness the 19th-century name 'Alderman in Chains' for a roast turkey garnished with festoons of sausages), they spread easily from the tables of the aristocracy onto those of the bourgeoisie, and then in more recent times onto everyone's table, at least as a food for special occasions, and nowadays as a year-round addition to the available range of 'white meats'.   (LM)

TURKEY a country whose history is mirrored in its food. Applying the archaeological concept of strata to Turkish cuisine reveals fairly distinct stages of evolution, successively superimposed on each other. One can discern Far Eastern, C. Asian, Iranian, Anatolian, and Mediterranean layers, each of them reflecting one stage in the long and complex history of migration that has enabled the Turkish people both to exert and to receive influence all across Eurasia.

The comparison with archaeology is particularly apt for the earliest period of Turkish history, one characterized by nomads, wandering in the marches of China; see box.

The recorded history of Turkish cuisine begins in about the 10th century, when the Turks came into contact with the Irano-Islamic culture and definitively entered the orbit of Islamic religion and civilization. They thus came to share a cuisine which had already evolved through a process of exchange between different ethnic groups; and they made their own contributions, including bulghur wheat (see BURGHUL) and BÖREK, plus the stew called *güveç* (see GYUVECH).

The first important literary monument of the Muslim Turks is a remarkable Turkish–Arabic dictionary, the *Diwan Lughat al-Turk*, composed in the late 11th century by Mahmud al-Kashghari. Replete

---

WHERE THE TURKS CAME FROM

THE earliest settled Turkish culture of note was that of the Uyghurs, who established their kingdom in the mid-8th century in what is now Xinjiang. The Uyghurs were under the strong cultural influence of China, and it is most likely during the period of their flourishing that *mantı* (see MANTOU) entered the diet of the Turks. A kind of dumpling still eaten with enthusiasm by virtually all the Turkish peoples, this dish may derive its name from the Chinese. It should not be thought, however, that culinary influences flowed in only one direction. The delight taken in stuffing not only pasta but also intestines and vegetables is so widespread and constant a feature in Turkish cuisine (see, for example, DOLMA) that it would be difficult to regard it as a mere borrowing. On the contrary the presence of stuffed dishes in the cuisine of N. China may well be a symptom of Turkish influence, although it is possible that the transmission took place in the era of Mongol dominion, some six centuries later.

with precious information on the material culture of the Turks, this dictionary demonstrates among other things the ancient lineage of much of present-day Turkish cuisine. Mahmud al-Kashghari lists terms relating to the preparation of bread and other dough products: varieties of bread such as *yufka* (see LAVASH), *ak ekmek*, *kara ekmek*, and *kevşek*; implements such as the *oklava* (rolling pin); and methods of cooking such as the use of the *tandır* (clay oven, see TANDOOR), and the *sac* (GRIDDLE), as well as burying the dough in warm ashes (*gömmec*). We also learn from this source that a fondness for milk products such as YOGHURT, AYRAN (yoghurt drink), and various types of cheese—something alien to the culinary traditions of China—was already well established among the Turks.

As the Turks moved westward through C. Asia toward the Islamic Middle East, they came into contact with the highly evolved and sophisticated urban culture of the Iranians. This was to leave an indelible Iranian imprint on the language and literature of the Turks as well as on many other aspects of their cultural life. But despite their far-reaching subordination to Iranian models, the Turks maintained to a large extent autonomy in culinary matters. This was particularly remarkable given the high prestige of Iranian cuisine in the early Islamic world; many of the words found in the most ancient Arabic cookbooks are Persian, and the caliphs of Baghdad always prided themselves on the consumption of elaborate Iranian dishes. The Turks, too, came to appreciate some elements of Iranian cuisine, for example, stews in which fruits and meats were combined. Vegetable stews, known as *yakhni*, were also absorbed from the Iranians into Turkish cuisine.

The fact that the word KEBAB is of Persian origin might suggest that the Turks learned something about grilling meats from the Iranians. However, Mahmud al-Kashghari informs us that the Turks were already acquainted with the art of cooking meat on skewers, which is indeed obvious (it stands to reason that nomadic Turks should have practised this convenient and easy method of cooking). So although the Iranians supplied the generic name for kebab dishes, there is no reason to attribute to them the numerous specific kinds of kebab which are characteristic of Turkish cuisine.

Similar remarks apply to *pilav* (see PILAF). The word itself is the Turkicized version of the Persian *polow*, and rice was cultivated in Iran, as well as elsewhere in the Middle East, long before the arrival there of the Turks, who had known nothing of it while they lived in C. Asia. But in early Iranian and Iranian-influenced Arab cuisine, rice was chiefly used in desserts and as a starch accompaniment to fish. The emergence of

pilaf dishes, in all their rich variety, seems to have accompanied the rise to prominence of the Turkish element in the Islamic world.

At about the same time that Mahmud al-Kashghari was compiling his dictionary thousands of miles further east, one branch of the Turkish peoples was beginning to settle in Anatolia. This was the start of a process that led to the Islamization and Turkicization of most of Anatolia and the triumphant installation of the Ottoman Turks in Istanbul, at the junction of Europe and Asia, where for centuries they determined the destinies of the Balkans, the Arab world, and much of the Mediterranean basin.

The chief predecessors of the Ottomans in the Turkicization of Anatolia were the Seljuqs, a branch of the great dynasty that had once ruled much of the eastern Islamic world. Their seat of rule was the city of Konya, a brilliant centre of culture that attracted scholars, poets and mystics from various regions of the islamic world. The cuisine was correspondingly lavish and cosmopolitan.

Much culinary information on the Seljuq period is to be found in the works of the great mystic and poet Mevlana Jalal-al-Din Rumi. Thanks to Mevlana, we know that a whole variety of vegetables, pulses, nuts, fruits, breads, buns, pastries, sweets, milk products, and pickles were available in Seljuq Anatolia. Further details are in an essay by Feyzi Halıcı (1988), who also describes Mevlana's cosmology and philosophy, his preferences and pleasures (SHERBET, HALVA, GARLIC, dancing the 'whirling dervish' dance), and mentions the tomb of his cook Ateşbazı-Veli, near Konya, one of the principal shrines in the world for gastronomic pilgrims.

The Ottoman period of Turkish history has its roots in the 13th century, but begins

blooming to full splendour with the conquest of Istanbul in 1453. Largely rebuilt by Sultan Mehmed the Conqueror after its capture from the Byzantines, the city became home to a great variety of peoples from within and without the Ottoman domains. The Ottomans subsidized the arts in huge ateliers, the culinary equivalent of which were the vast kitchens of the Topkapi palace. Within a generation, as the result of this previously unparalleled cultural mixing, there was a distinct Ottoman style in all the decorative arts, and also in cookery.

The Topkapi palace kitchen and its staff were greatly expanded in the course of time, especially under Sultan Süleyman the Magnificent. At one time the staff numbered 1370, a figure which is less astonishing if one takes into account the extraordinary degree of specialization in the kitchens. The preparation of soups, kebabs, pilafs, jam, drinks such as *hoşaf* (see KHOSHAB), sherbet, and *boza* (a fermented drink usually made from MILLET) each represented a separate skill to be learned as an apprentice and refined in a lifetime of labour. So high was the degree of specialization that by the mid-18th century each of six varieties of HALVA was assigned to a separate master chef, with a hundred apprentices working under him.

Further information about the scale of catering at the Topkapi palace (to feed as many as 10,000 people) and the importance of food during the Ottoman period for the corps of Janissaries and for the *tarikats*, the Sufi brotherhoods, is provided by Ayla Algar (1991).

The palace enjoyed, no doubt, an exceptional degree of culinary riches, but what is known about the food markets of Istanbul suggests that the general population also fared well. Evliya Çelebi, the celebrated 17th-century traveller, provides us with a detailed and vivid account of the

---

THE SPICE BAZAAR IN ISTANBUL

ENTERING the Spice Bazaar today is still a dramatic experience. With little transition from the street to the entrance, which is festooned with the gaudy displays of the newspaper- and magazine-sellers, one leaves behind the bustle and the often inclement weather of the outside world—heat and dust in the summer, rain and mud in the winter—to be enveloped immediately in a vast, dimly lit realm redolent with hundreds of scents. Apart from the often dazzling electric lights that highlight the displays in each shop, light is provided only by glass-covered apertures high in the vaulted ceiling that arches over the market. On each side of a walkway broad enough to take two lanes of traffic stand hundreds of shops offering the most varied kinds of foodstuffs. The Spice Bazaar is in fact like a permanent exhibition of Turkish foodstuffs. Here you will find not only every type of spice both familiar and unfamiliar but also dried roots and barks used for medicinal purposes; a great variety of cheeses; *sucuk* and *pastırma*; honey, both in jars and honeycomb; black and green olives; almonds, walnuts, hazelnuts, and pistachios; dried fruit and herbs; rice and other grains; clarified butter; rosewater and bergamot oil; and a host of other items the precise nature and use of which are a mystery to the uninitiated.

food-related guilds of Istanbul. These included bakers and butchers, cheese-makers and yoghurt-merchants, pastry chefs and pickle-makers, and fishmongers and sausage-merchants.

Some of the markets (especially the Egyptian spice bazaar—see box on page 811) are still functioning, and there is still a large presence of street vendors selling a great diversity of foods.

However, Istanbul has always been exceptionally fortunate. To keep a proper balance, one must look at the foodways of the huge rural population of Turkey. These have been remarkably stable over many centuries and are distinguished by simplicity.

Throughout Turkey, the staples are bread (*ekmek*) and yoghurt. Bread may be leavened or unleavened. An example of the latter is *yufka*, described under LAVASH. Everyday Turkish breads, which some people (not only Turks) count as just about the best in Europe, are well described by Ayla Algar (1991). They include the Turkish version of PITTA bread, called *pide*, which are soft, oval or round, bread 'pouches' which can be stuffed or simply used for mopping up other foods. Yoghurt was brought by early Turcoman nomads from C. Asia and is made from buffalo, cow, goat, or sheep milk. It can be dried into doughlike cakes and preserved for months, or drained to make cheese, or diluted to make the drink AYRAN. It is used raw or in cooking or as a sauce, sweet or savoury.

The use of OLIVE OIL is confined to the western parts. Edible fungi and wild food plants (see Evelyn Kalças, 1974) are eaten where they occur. WHEAT is grown almost everywhere, although on the Black Sea MAIZE flour is common and elsewhere MILLET, OATS, or BARLEY may be the predominant grain. The sweetening is provided variously by fruit, dried fruit, HONEY, or PEKMEZ. Either beans (to make *fasulya*) or CHICKPEAS are widely consumed. Other ingredients which are constantly used in Turkish kitchens are LAMB, AUBERGINES, NUTS.

Turks living in coastal regions, whether of the Mediterranean or the Black Sea or the Bosporus which connects them, have enjoyed the additional bounty of seafood and display considerable discrimination in selecting and cooking it. Their enthusiasm for *hamsi* (ANCHOVY) has inspired a number of interesting folk poems (see Davidson, 1981). Among larger fish, BONITO, BLUEFISH, TURBOT, and SWORDFISH are greatly appreciated. Annual migrations of many species through the Bosporus used to permit very large catches being made.

It is remarkable to reflect that Istanbul was already after the fall of the Roman Empire the hub of BYZANTINE COOKERY, of which few traces remain; that it served as one of the greatest entrepôts in the SPICE TRADE; that it then became the focal point of Ottoman cuisine, which exerted such a powerful influence on the Balkans and certain countries in C. Europe; and that a visitor to Turkey at the end of the 20th century will find everywhere, not only in this great city, evidence of enduring food traditions which involve most of Asia and much of Europe, symbolically joined by the Bosporus bridges.

See also: AŞURE; BAKLAVA; SHORBA; TUTMAÇ; TURKISH DELIGHT.   (AA)

READING: Ayla Algar (1985, 1991); Feyzi Halıcı (1988, and numerous other papers of the First International Food Congress held in Turkey in 1986); Nevin Halıcı (1989).

TURKISH DELIGHT as it is known in western countries, should really be known by its Turkish name, *lokum* (or *rahat lokum*, or *loucoum*). It is said to have been a Turkish invention, attributed to Hadji Bekir of Constantinople, is now a highly popular sweet throughout the Middle East, and is exported from Turkey and Greece.

Lokum is a delicate but gummy jelly made by cooking a mixture of syrup and cornflour slowly for several hours, after which the mixture is poured out, left to set, and cut into cubes which are rolled in icing sugar. Flavours vary, and many are family or trade secrets. Most are based on lemon or lemon and orange juice, and rose or orange flower water are usual. MASTIC is often used. Chopped nuts or puréed apricots, or both, may be added. A distinctly different flavouring is provided by crème de menthe or peppermint oil. Rose-flavoured *lokum* is usually coloured pink, and the mint type green.

TURMERIC a spice and colouring agent obtained from the rhizomes of *Curcuma longa*, a herbaceous perennial plant native to India or SE Asia. It is now widely cultivated in the tropics, but India remains by far the largest producer. The plant was taken into cultivation in very early times, probably in the first instance for its dye, and no longer occurs in its wild form.

The double role of turmeric in food preparation is matched only by PAPRIKA among the common spices. However, it is more often compared with, or substituted for, the expensive SAFFRON. When Marco Polo found turmeric in China in 1280, he described it as 'a vegetable which has all the properties of true saffron, as well the smell as the colour, and yet it is not really saffron'. This was an exaggeration, since aroma and flavour are not alike, but the yellow of turmeric does resemble that of saffron. This accounts for the French name *safran d'Inde* and other similar names.

Turmeric rhizomes, of which the central ones are bulbous and the others of 'finger' shape, are cured, dried, and cleaned before sale. Their interior is yellow, due to the presence of the pigment curcumin, and the exterior of rhizomes packed for sale may be coated with turmeric powder to enhance their appearance.

Although turmeric is used as a cosmetic, and as a dye for cloth and a simple colouring agent for food and drink, its main use in Asia is as a condiment. When thus used it always adds colour too; and it is often the principal ingredient of CURRY POWDER, to which it gives the dominant yellowish hue. Madras turmeric, the kind usually imported to Britain, is a mixture of cultivars suitable for this purpose. In N. America, turmeric is used more as a simple food colourant, and Alleppey turmeric from Kerala, which is a mixture of cultivars with a particularly high tinctorial power, is preferred.

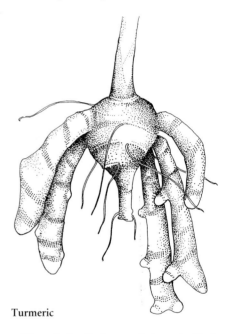

Turmeric

The volatile oil of turmeric is not itself of commercial importance but supplies most of the aroma, and therefore the flavour, of the spice. The colour is supplied by curcumin and other curcuminoid pigments.

Besides being an essential ingredient of curry powder, turmeric is often used by itself for colouring and flavouring foodstuffs, including fish dishes. It is used in mustard pickles, and sometimes to colour butter or cheese and certain sweetmeats.

Turmeric has close relations with similar properties: see ZEDOARY.

TURNIP *Brassica rapa*, one of the earliest cultivated vegetables, is thought to have

originated in N. Europe in about 2000 BC
from a variety of bird rape, *B. campestris*.
The 'root' (not a real root, but the swollen
base of the stem) of the wild plant is edible
but spindly. Selection over the centuries
would have produced larger turnips, of
which there were already many varieties in
the classical period.

Roman writers, e.g. Columella in AD 42,
distinguished between two main types of
turnips: 'napus', which was relatively
slender, pointed, and delicate; and 'rapa',
which was large and round. Ever since, there
has been confusion over how to classify
turnips. The current arrangement is to call
the common white turnip *B. rapa*; to assign
its relatives the SWEDE and rutabaga to
B. napus ssp *rapifera*; and RAPE, grown for its
oil-bearing seeds, to *B. napus*. But this is not
universally agreed.

From 'rapa' is derived the common name
'rape' which, however, is now given to other
species, notably *B. napus*. From 'napus'
comes the Scottish word for a turnip, 'neep'
(but Scots prefer swedes, so it is swedes
which they mean when they use the name);
the word 'turnip' itself; and the French *navet*
(via the diminutive *napetus* and the tendency
to turn a 'p' into a 'b' or 'v').

Turnips were an important food for the
Romans, especially in the time of the
Republic, before their Empire spread and
brought in rich agricultural lands. At the
beginning of the 3rd century BC the war hero
and consul Curius Dentatus was approached
by envoys from the hostile Samnites while he
was roasting turnips over a fire. They offered
him a large amount of gold to defect to their
side; but he preferred to attend to his
turnips. In this moral tale the turnip is
presented as a simple, rustic food.

The turnip spread from the classical world
through Asia to N. China, where it had
become a common vegetable well before the
medieval period in Europe, and it was taken
from China to Japan about 1,300 years ago.

The Chinese, like Curius Dentatus, have
traditionally cooked turnips by roasting. The
high temperature increases the sweetness of
the vegetable by converting some of the
starch to tasty, brown pyrodextrins in the
crisp outside. The Japanese use turnips
freely, especially in pickled form and carved
in a chrysanthemum shape.

In Europe, the French have devoted most
care to turnips, and there are various parts of
France which are famous for growing
specially good ones. The French pick turnips
young, in early summer, when no larger
than a small orange, and braise them or fry
and glaze them. They are the traditional
accompaniment to certain dishes, e.g.
Canard aux navets. The habit of serving
plain boiled turnips, often large and old
winter specimens, seems to have been
characteristic of English-speaking countries.

Turnip tops, like other brassica greens, are
edible and good. They appear briefly on the
market when the turnip crop is thinned in
March.

Pickled turnips have been immensely
popular in the Arab world, usually coloured
pink by putting a bit of beetroot in the
pickling jar. Turnips are also pickled in
Korea, for example. In China, they are sun
dried in strips, then salted or preserved in
soy sauce; and round turnips are sometimes
preserved whole.

In Japan the leaves and roots are used for
pickles, but the root is also boiled and eaten
with YUZU-flavoured MISO.

TURNOVER a general term for a PASTY
made by folding a sheet of pastry over a
lump of filling and sealing the edge. A circle
of pastry gives a semicircular turnover; a
square gives a triangular one. Turnovers
range in size from tiny to large enough for
several helpings, as in the family-sized
version of the Cornish pasty.

TURTLE a name which can be used
loosely of all the four-limbed reptiles in the
order Chelonia, but is best reserved for the
aquatic members of the order (TORTOISE
being the preferred name for those which
live on dry land). Of the aquatic turtles, the
marine species are described under SEA
TURTLES, while the present entry is devoted
to freshwater turtles and the general
question of turtle cookery.

Turtles which live in fresh or brackish
water occur in and are eaten in most
regions of the world. They are commonly
grouped into categories such as the
following:

- Snapping turtles, or snappers, which have
a reputation for being dangerous to handle
casually; they snap and bite—indeed the
largest of all, the so-called alligator
snapper, which weighs up to 100 kg
(225 lb), can easily snap through a broom
handle. These turtles probably account for
about half the turtle consumption in the
eastern USA. The common snapping turtle
in the USA is *Chelydra serpentina*.
- Soft-shelled turtles, whose shells are
leathery and which have long soft snouts.
They can remain under water for a long
time. They too need to be handled with
care.
- Terrapin, especially diamondback
terrapin, *Malaclemys terrapin*. This
terrapin and its eggs have been greatly
prized as delicacies in the USA and there
was a time when the species was in danger
of becoming extinct, although it has since
been revived to form an adequately large
population, and is farmed.

Turtles have posed a problem for those
who frame or interpret religious laws. They
could be eaten during Lent by Catholic
monks, anyway in some places. But they are
a forbidden food for Jews (Leviticus 11: 29).

So far as turtle cookery is concerned, the
one outstanding dish is, or was, turtle soup.
So far as England is concerned, this subject is
covered under SEA TURTLES, since it was
marine species which were used there. In
N. America, however, terrestrial turtles
could be used and the snapping turtle has
been described as the great soup turtle of the
Mississippi basin. Authorities on both sides
of the Atlantic agree that turtle soup should
not be attempted in the domestic kitchen
but bought from a specialist maker or
prepared by experts in a banquet context.
However, dried turtle meat was formerly in
demand for making the soup on a smaller
scale; it was said that 110 g (4 oz) of it would
yield soup for a dozen or more persons. The
important subject of MOCK TURTLE SOUP has
its own entry.

TUTMAÇ a Turkish word meaning
NOODLES which in one form or another is
found in the remotest corners of the
Turkish-speaking world, from the Tatars on
the middle Volga to the Salars in Gansu
province, China, and the isolated pagan
Turkish nationalities of the Altai mountains.

In his 11th-century dictionary of Turkish
dialects, Mahmud al-Kashghari recorded a
pleasant and quite unbelievable folk-tale
about how *tutmach* was invented at the
behest of Alexander the Great, whom he
refers to by his Koranic name, Dhu
al-Qarnain:

When Dhu al-Qarnain emerged from Zulumat
[the Land of Darkness where the sun disappears
when it sets, and the Fountain of Youth is to be
found], his people had little food and
complained to him of hunger, and said to him,
'*Bizni tutma ach*', that is 'Do not keep us here
hungry, let us go so that we can return to our
homes.' He consulted the wise men on that
subject so that this food might be produced,
tutmach. It strengthens the body, reddens the
cheeks and is quickly digested, and after the
tutmach is eaten, the broth is drunk several-fold.
When the Turks saw that, *tutmach* was named, its
root being *tutma ach*, that is 'Do not cause
hunger.'

In Xinjiang the modern Uyghurs tell the
exact same story about PILAF (specifying that
the wise men were Aristotle, Socrates,
Hippocrates, and Plato). This reflects the
fact that pilaf has assumed the role of the
grand dish of hospitality, which *tutmach* had
enjoyed in the Middle Ages.

In Turkey the noodle soup called *Tutmaç
çorbasi* survives in the folk cuisine of
Anatolia to the present day. The dough
(made from wheat flour, egg, and water) is

cut into squares which are then fried before being added to the soup. This had been a dish of the court cuisine of the Seljuqs and retained its high standing until at least the 15th century, but then lost its pride of place to PILAF and was not a dish incorporated into the classical Ottoman cuisine.

Other medieval Turkish noodles survive today in Turkey and C. Asia. *Salma* are small noodles in the shape of coins or shells and *ovmaç* (or *umaç*) are small pellet-like soup noodles.   CP

TWELFTH NIGHT CAKE a cake made for Twelfth Night, the last of the twelve days of Christmas. Now a celebration of Epiphany, the occasion when the three Kings visited the infant Jesus, this festival has inherited some of the pagan customs associated with Roman Saturnalia, when slaves were allowed many privileges including eating with and gambling against their masters. Dice were thrown to choose a 'king', and everyone had to obey his command. The two ancient traditions involving kings were interwoven to give the modern Twelfth Night custom of choosing a 'king' by dividing a cake containing a token—a dried bean or a china doll. The finder gains privileges or pays forfeits, depending on the custom of the country. Sometimes a dried pea, for a queen, is also included. (For the French Twelfth Night cake, and corresponding comments, see *galette des rois* under GALETTE.)

The custom of the 'Twelfth cake', complete with bean, flourished for centuries in England. During the late 17th century, the series of tokens included in the cake (at this time, a fruit cake leavened with yeast) expanded. Bridget Ann Henisch (1984) cites Henry Teonge, a naval chaplain, who wrote in 1676 that

we had a great cake made, in which was put a bean for the King, a pea for the queen, a clove for a knave, a forked stick for the cuckold and a rag for the slut. The cake was cut into several pieces in the great cabin, and all put into a napkin, out of which each took his piece, as out of a lottery; the each piece is broken to see what was in it, which caused much laughter, to see our Lieutenant prove the cuckold, and more to see us tumble one over the other in the cabin, by reason of the rough weather.

During the 18th century the tokens became a series of characters printed on paper which were cut out, folded, and drawn from a hat. The custom eventually declined in the middle of the century, though a vestige survives in the coins or tokens that are still put into a CHRISTMAS PUDDING. In 1794 the actor Robert Baddeley left £100 to be invested to provide a cake for all those acting at Drury Lane Theatre on Twelfth Night.

In France a little china token or a bean is included in the filling of the *galette des rois*; the person who finds the bean in their portion becomes king or queen for the evening. As early as the 13th century, the street cries of Paris included *gastel à fève orroriz*—the cake with the King's bean. There are similar old traditions elsewhere. In Spain, the *roscón de reyes* is ring shaped, decorated with candied fruit, and contains a *sorpresa*, a coin or a little ceramic figurine to bring luck to the finder, but in Mexico the finder of the china doll in the Kings' Day ring must give a party at Candlemas. A similar custom is observed in New Orleans, where King cakes are BRIOCHES iced in purple, green, and gold, containing a plastic baby; the finder of the baby is supposed to give the next party. The Portuguese also make a ring-shaped cake; mixed with port and stiff with candied fruit, the *bolo rei* is available throughout the Christmas season. In Portugal, the finder of the bean has to provide the next year's *bolo rei*. Swiss and German *Dreikönigskuchen* are wreaths or rounds of rich bread, each with an almond concealed in it to confer kingship on the lucky finder.

TZIMMES a Jewish culinary term thus described by Claudia Roden (1996) as:

a general term for a sweet vegetable or meat dish. Just as Oriental Sephardi Jews inherited a taste for meat with fruit from tenth century Baghdad, Ashkenazi Jews acquired similar tastes in medieval Germany.

Roden remarks that in Yiddish lore sliced carrots are associated with gold coins, and carrot tzimmes (glazed with honey) is a dish which is eaten as a symbol of prosperity at Rosh Hashana (the New Year). However, meat-and-prune tzimmes is probably the most popular. Roden states that S. African Jews of Lithuanian origin seem particularly fond of it, and that it is often eaten at a harvest festival. Because of the festive image of these dishes, the word tzimmes has acquired the colloquial meaning of 'a big fuss'.

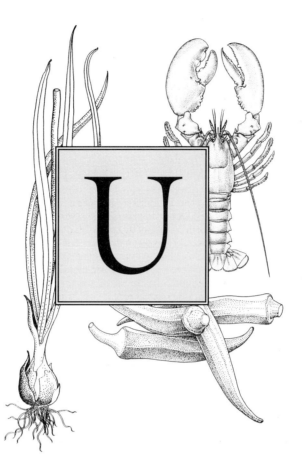

UDDER one of the foods which is doing a slow disappearing act, at least in western countries. Cow's udder, boiled to prepare it for consumption, counts as a form of TRIPE; it is called elder in Britain and *tétine de veau* in French *triperies*.

The term elder appears to be Middle Dutch, and was probably first recorded in Ray's *North Country Words* (1674). It was used mainly in the north and north-west of Britain, but appeared also in Scotland and Ireland.

Not surprisingly, little is known of its history. Though udder appears to be first mentioned as a food in 1474 (*OED*), its finest hour came on 11 October 1660, when Samuel Pepys in the company of his wife and Mr Creed, dining at the Leg in King Street, thought sufficiently of their 'good udder to dinner' to record it in his diary. That at least assured a place for it in posterity and the *OED*.

Since then, for the most part, it has been downhill all the way. Though La Varenne (1654) and Charles Carter (1730), for example, give recipes, and Hannah Glasse (1747) recommends both a roast and *forced* (stuffed) udder, udder is more often

conspicuous by its absence. Dallas in *Kettner's Book of the Table* (1877) notes that udder is no longer abundant in the market though it formerly had a recognized position in French cookery. *Cassell's Dictionary of Cookery* (1899) gives it, but of more recent authors only Escoffier and Prosper Montagné seem to include an entry of any significance.

Long gone from the daily diet of most people, udder is thus a vanishing food. It seems to survive, towards the close of the 20th century, almost exclusively in a small cluster of towns in industrial W. Yorkshire (Keighley, Halifax, Huddersfield, Dewsbury) and in E. Lancashire, especially in the market halls of places like Accrington, Bacup, Wigan, Burnley, and Colne.

A traditional tripe dresser in such places would be preparing dark and light tripe, cow heel, neat's foot oil, black pudding, and elder. Nothing was wasted; the copious quantities of fat produced as a by-product would be sold to the fish and chip trade.

Devoid of teats and skin, raw elder looks like a large, pink, amorphous blob. It has to be drained of any remaining milk which would otherwise taint the flavour, after

which it has to be simmered for six hours or so until tender. The final step is to 'dress' it so that it looks good. The finished product smells faintly of tongue and has something of the same softness, but is chewier. Many early recipes grouped the two together.

Elder is not an exclusively British phenomenon. The French connection has already been mentioned. In Belgium one may be offered smoked *pis de vache* and there must be many other such dishes. Barbara Kirshenblatt-Gimblett (1987) has drawn attention to a recipe for udder from the Jews of the Yemen. LB

UDO *Aralia cordata*, a plant in the family Araliaceae whose young stalks are eaten as a vegetable in Japan, especially in the spring. The flavour has a hint of fennel, and the texture is pleasantly crisp.

Udo stalks are usually peeled and steeped in cold water and then eaten almost raw. For example, they may be parboiled briefly, then cut into slices or strips and added to *sunomono* or *aemono* salads (see JAPANESE CULINARY TERMS); or slices may be added to soups just a minute or two before they are taken off the fire.

Udo is rarely available outside Japan, since it does not keep well.

UDON Japanese noodles (see NOODLES OF JAPAN) made from wheat flour. They are similar to spaghetti but softer in texture.

Udon are said to be of Chinese origin, introduced to Japan during the Chinese Tang dynasty (618–907). Contemporary documents suggest that the original udon was not noodles but pieces of rolled-out dough wrapped around fillings, like Chinese WONTON. (The words 'udon' and 'wonton' have a common root.) It is not clear when udon came to mean noodles as it does today. Udon as noodles seems to make its first appearance in the first half of the 14th century. According to some sources, it was eaten mainly by Buddhist monks and gradually spread amongst ordinary people. This is not unlikely, since there were close links between Buddhism and Chinese culture at the time.

Udon is made by mixing wheat flour with water (with or without salt, sometimes with vinegar to make the resulting noodles look whiter), kneading it into a fairly stiff dough, rolling it out, folding it, and cutting it somewhat thicker than SOBA. Much of udon consumed today is machine made.

Originally udon was eaten as *nikomi-udon* (stewed udon). For this, freshly made udon is added to MISO-based soup without preliminary boiling, and cooked with various vegetables. This is essentially a home-made dish to be eaten as a supplement to or substitute for *gohan* (cooked rice). There are endless local variations, and in a few areas the dough is not cut into noodles but into small squares—possibly reminiscent of the original form of udon.

It was probably as a result of the rising popularity of commercially prepared soba in the 17th century that udon, too, came to be served in specialist restaurants and stalls, in the same way as, and alongside, soba. In contrast to soba, which tastes distinctly of BUCKWHEAT, the flavour of udon is neutral, allowing any number of variations in the additional ingredients, such as vegetables, seaweeds, eggs, fish, shellfish, poultry. There is even udon with curry sauce.

UGLI a fruit of Jamaican origin, unkindly so named. It belongs to the category of citrus fruits called tangelos (see MANDARIN), which are hybrids of mandarin and GRAPEFRUIT, but markedly different from either parent. An ugli may be almost as big as a POMELO, over 15 cm (6") in diameter and 1 kg (more than 2 lb) in weight, but much of it consists in a thick, baggy rind. The rind has a

pulled-up appearance at the top, like a kitten picked up by the scruff of the neck. Despite its thickness, it is easily peelable and has a fine fragrance of CITRON (unlike any other mandarin, tangelo, or pomelo). The segments of flesh separate freely like those of the pomelo, but have a different flavour, more like that of a mandarin, barely bitter and with a faint overtone of honey or pineapple.

Another large citrus fruit which is usually classified as a tangelo, the New Zealand grapefruit or poorman orange, has the shape and size of a grapefruit, but is more orange in colour and slightly less acid. It is said to have been imported from Shanghai early in the 19th century, and may really be a mandarin × pomelo hybrid. Whatever the truth about its origin, it is used like the grapefruit in New Zealand, where it is the leading citrus fruit on the market. As this suggests, it can tolerate a cooler climate than the true grapefruit, and also ripens much earlier. For these reasons it is now being grown in N. California.

UKRAINE a vast country which used to be called the 'bread basket' of the Soviet Union. Its capability as a source of bread certainly impressed the French novelist Balzac, who had a Ukrainian wife and who referred to the Ukraine in a letter as 'this terrestrial paradise, where I marked 77 ways of preparing bread'. Savella Stechishin (1979), whose book on *Traditional Ukrainian Cookery* is of exceptional merit, writes:

To the Ukrainians, bread is one of the holiest of all foods. The older people consider it most disrespectful when leftover pieces of bread are thrown about carelessly. They pick up such pieces reverently, kiss them in apology, and then feed the bread to the birds or burn it on the hearth.

Besides conventional forms of wheaten bread, there are numerous rich and festival breads (and indeed cakes and the like). In this connection see PASKHA and BABA. There is also the ring-shaped plaited bread called *kalach* or *kolach*.

The national dish is said to be VARENIKI, a stuffed pasta, and *vushka*, miniature versions thereof. DUMPLINGS, for example *galushki*, also feature often, to be eaten on their own or in soups.

If bread is the main staple, then pork (especially fat bacon) and beetroot are not far behind in importance (and are in fact combined in a pork and beetroot casserole called *Vereshchaka*). Beetroot is not only a frequent choice as a vegetable but appears in the Ukrainian versions of BORSHCH, the national soup. Stechishin devotes much space to this, explaining how to make the beet KVASS which 'imparts a pleasant mellow flavour . . . unattainable with any other acid' and describing various finishing touches:

To finish borsch in a truly traditional way, most old country cooks mash together a little salt pork with some raw onion to a smooth paste. They claim that, without this final touch, borsch lacks character. Those who have a violent passion for dill, use it liberally in borsch. Some feel that a discreet use of garlic essence is just the thing to blend the borsch flavors together for a richly finished product. Unless the borsch is meatless for Lent days, a few tablespoons of sour cream are always added to it just before serving.

Since the Ukraine is so huge, it is not surprising to find some subcuisines within it. One such is that of the Hutsul highlanders in the Carpathian mountains. MAIZE is their staple cereal and they have a range of dishes such as cornmeal mush (*kulesha*) and a corn bread called *malay*. Cornmeal is also the basis of several kinds of spoon bread (see CORN BREADS). In some other regions MILLET continues to be important as a cereal.

It is sometimes said that a distinctive Ukrainian cuisine did not emerge clearly until the end of the 18th century or the beginning of the 19th. If this is so, it may have been in part because of a superabundance of neighbours (the list now reads: BELORUSSIA, POLAND, Slovakia (see CZECH AND SLOVAK REPUBLICS), HUNGARY, ROMANIA, MOLDOVA, RUSSIA) and other influences (German, Tatar, Turkish). The influence of Christianity has also been considerable.

ULLUCO *Ullucus tuberosus*, a minor root crop cultivated in the high Andes region of S. America, ranging from Colombia to N. Argentina. Although hardy and unaffected by high altitudes, it is not suitable for the far south or north, being sensitive to the length of the day; but it may be possible to develop cultivars which do not have this handicap. Where ulluco is cultivated it is an important part of the diet, sometimes second only to the potato, sometimes third after OCA.

The excellent description in *Lost Crops of the Incas* (National Research Council, 1989) reads thus:

One of the most striking foods in the markets, its tubers are so brightly colored—yellow, pink, red, purple, even candy striped—and their waxy skins are so shiny that they seem like botanical jewels or plastic fakes. Many are shaped like small potatoes but others are curiously long and curved like crooked sausages. (One of the bent types, splashed with maroon streaks, is known as 'Christ's knee'. A small, pink, curled variety is called 'shrimp of the earth'.) Their skin is thin and soft and needs no peeling before eating. The white to lemon-yellow flesh has a smooth, silky texture with a nutty taste. Some types are gummy when raw, but in cooking, this characteristic is reduced or lost. Indeed, a major appeal of ulluco is its crisp texture, which remains even when cooked.

Among the numerous varieties, some have tubers as large as normal potatoes, but most tubers are smaller and the smaller ones are most prized. Among the many different shapes and colours, the most common combination is roughly spherical and yellow.

Ulluco may be freeze dried to make *llingli*, a long-keeping product like the CHUÑO made with the potato. Ulluco are also canned for export; they keep their texture and flavour well.

Because of their high water content, ulluco are not suitable for frying or baking, but they can be cooked in many other ways—boiled (whole, or sliced and then served with vinegar), boiled and mashed, or added to stews and soups. They are preferred to the potato for thickening soups, because of their silky texture. In pickled form, they can be added to hot sauces.

The green leaves can also be eaten, in ways similar to the plant's relation BASELLA.

UME *Prunus mume*. This is a deciduous tree of the rose family, 5–10 m (16–30') high. Its original home is in China, though some wild specimens have been reported in parts of Kyushu as well as Taiwan.

Because of its highly fragrant, white or pink blossoms, which come out in February and March before any other blossoms, ume has been a popular garden tree in Japan since the earliest times. Its fruit are similar to apricots in shape; they are green at first and greenish-yellow when fully ripened, which is normally in June.

The ume fruits have a strongly acid and bitter taste, due to the high content of citric and malic acids, and are not suitable for eating raw. Moreover, when unripe, they contain amygdalin, which is also present in bitter almonds, and are toxic.

Most ume produced in Japan are made into UMEBOSHI (see below), but they are also used to make an interesting liqueur, *umeshu*.

UMEBOSHI Japanese salted and dried 'plums'. Umeboshi literally means 'dried ume'. This fruit, as explained above, is more correctly described as a sort of apricot; but the salted and dried version is plum coloured, the flavour is like that of a tart plum rather than an apricot, and the rendering 'plum' has stuck. The typical purple or red colour of umeboshi is produced by red SHISO leaves. Umeboshi have a wrinkled and shrivelled appearance with a sour and salty taste. Hosking (1996) explains that:

These apricots come large and small, soft and hard, and are an item of daily consumption. Usually colored red with red shiso leaves, they are mostly eaten as a pickle with rice, but the large soft ones, desalted by soaking in water, make very

good tempura. A cup of [green] bancha tea containing an *umeboshi* makes a good start to the morning. A bento with an umeboshi on top of the rice is called *hinomaru bento*, after the Japanese flag. Rice gruel (*kayu*), a breakfast food, is usually served with *umeboshi*.

This is one of the oldest and most important preserved foods in Japan. Many Japanese housewives still make their own umeboshi every year. Some families are proud owners of vintage umeboshi, which can be more than 100 years old, handed down from generation to generation.

It is generally believed that umeboshi has medicinal, antiseptic, and preservative properties. It is said, for example, that rice cooked with an umeboshi in it does not go bad in hot weather, or that an upset stomach can be cured by the juice obtained from ume in the process of salting. Umeboshi and plain rice porridge, referred to above, is valued as an invalid food as well as a breakfast dish.

A purée of umeboshi, called *bainiku*, is available in bottles or jars, for use in certain sauces which require its tartness.

UPSIDE DOWN CAKE or upside down pudding, as it is sometimes called, is a creamed cake (see CAKE-MAKING) which is turned out after baking so that the base becomes the top, displaying a decorative pattern composed of fruit; pineapple rings and glacé cherries are popular choices. It is usually eaten warm, with custard.

The name may also be used for finished cakes which are pressed with syrup and fruit in a mould and then turned out for serving, and a similar principle is employed in some ice cream desserts and TARTE TATIN.

Generally, the concept of upsidedownness has had only limited applications in the kitchen, but it is used quite often for savoury moulds, where the artificer desires a pleasing pattern of vegetables or prawns or whatever to appear on top of the item when it has been unmoulded.

URD (or urad, or black gram), *Vigna mungo*, the most important PULSE in India. It has ceremonial significance for Hindus, e.g. at birth and death rites. It is not known in the wild but is presumably a descendant of wild *Vigna* spp. It has now been widely introduced to other tropical areas.

Urd is closely related to *V. radiata*, the MUNG BEAN. Nomenclature adds to the possibilities of confusion. Thus it is urd which has the specific name *mungo*, which might be expected to belong to the mung bean. Moreover urd beans are not all black (as their alternative name 'black gram' would suggest), but may be green (the green ones are smaller and ripen later than the

black ones); and green gram is one of the alternative names for mung bean. However, any possible confusion is dispelled when the two small pulses are peeled and split, thus becoming DAL instead of GRAM, for the urd is then seen to be white inside while the mung is yellow.

Urd has a good flavour, but is a notably solid foodstuff, needing longer cooking than most other small pulses, and difficult for some people to digest. It is not soaked before being cooked. Ground urd makes the best POPPADOMS and is used in IDLI and DOSA.

Whole young pods may be cooked as a vegetable, but the principal use is of the mature beans.

The urd bean, or seed, is the reputed origin of the very small Indian weight known as *masha*.

URUGUAY Situated between the rivers Plate and Uruguay, with a short sea coast, this is a small country. It was colonized from ARGENTINA, whose governor sent 100 head of cattle to initiate development in the 17th century, and shares with that large neighbour culinary ingredients, likes and dislikes.

The last Indians had been swept away by the mid-19th century and modern Uruguay seems marked only by the pastoral agriculture of the pampas—sheep in the south and west, cattle everywhere else—and by the predominantly Spanish and Italian backgrounds of its European colonists, whose influence is manifest in the capital, Montevideo.

The pampas were where the gauchos, nomadic half-Indian herdsmen, roamed and worked. Darwin, in his account of the voyage of HMS *Beagle* (first published in 1839 as part of another work), described a gaucho supper which 'consisted of two huge piles, one of roast beef, the other of boiled, with some pieces of pumpkin; besides this latter there was no other vegetable, not even a morsel of bread.' The gauchos preferred beef to what was apparently rather dry mutton. Another British visitor, the Revd J. H. Murray, chaplain in Colonia and author of *Travels in Uruguay* (1871), explained how meat was always consumed fresh, due to the climate and lack of refrigeration, and that breakfast might be sheep killed then cooked, all in half an hour. 'Mutton thus killed is so excessively tough that it leaves us nothing to do for some time but to chew it in silence, which is anything but convivial.'

However, even if the mutton was unpalatable, the general diet at that stage of development was 'mutton and biscuits, and potatoes and vegetables where there is a garden'. The naturalist W. H. Hudson was of Argentine extraction. In *The Purple Land*

(1885) he wrote of supping in Montevideo on a stew of mutton scrag, with pumpkin, sweet potatoes, and milky maize, 'not at all a bad dish for a hungry man'. On the other hand, he recorded in the same book having meat from a fat, freshly killed heifer, which was the best roast meat he ever ate. Leonard (1970) refers to this meal, and to the setting:

the enormous kitchen of a Uruguayan ranch house, with a fire smouldering on a clay platform fenced with cow bones stuck in the earthen floor. Meat was boiling in a great iron pot hung by a chain from the roof, and more meat was roasting on a spit six feet long. Nothing was served except meat, which the diners carved from the roast with their knives.

Old ways have changed in some respects, and the wild gauchos are now but a memory. But many traditions remain, including the emphasis on meat. On the banks of the River Uruguay is the town of Fray Bentos, the home of the Liebig Company's meat-processing factories, described by one impressionable visitor as 'the kitchen of the world' and the source of much of the CORNED BEEF sold elsewhere in the world.

The River Plate is a source of fish, and of large frogs. The Browns (1971) noticed that Uruguay was addicted to frogs and used the whole body to make a soup.   (TJ)

USA a subject which is not amenable, in the area of food and cookery, to description in a short essay. It is a fine subject for a whole book, as Jones (1981) and Hooker (1981) and others have demonstrated. A broad canvas of the size which, say, Tintoretto liked to use and a fistful of broad brushes are suitable equipment, whereas a miniaturist's panel the size of a small postage stamp is not. The trouble is that there are so many climates and ethnic elements to be dealt with. It is like a jigsaw puzzle which has too many pieces, so that there is no way you can put it together. Three pieces of the jigsaw, as it happens, are described under CREOLE FOOD, CAJUN FOOD, and PENNSYLVANIA DUTCH; but there are many others which could equally well claim a share of the spotlight.

The spotlight would certainly have to play on the foodways of the indigenous N. American Indians, since they were there first and initiated many ways of utilizing the plant and animal foods of the continent. Many of their food terms and practices are mentioned in other entries (see, for examples, CAMAS; PEMMICAN; SUCCOTASH; WILD RICE).

However, what is more rewarding than listing the other ethnic or religious groups whose arrival and establishment in the USA have left lasting marks on the foodways (one thinks in the first place of the slaves from Africa and of SOUL FOOD, but also of the huge Jewish community in New York City, of the Scandinavians in the Midwest, of the Spanish and French in the south, and on a lesser scale of the Ethiopian and Afghan communities centred on the District of Columbia) is to step back, as it were, and consider what role the USA has played and is playing in the global gastronomic scene (taking gastronomic in its widest sense, and not as referring to the food of expensive restaurants and connoisseurs). In this perspective, several points stand out.

One role which N. Americans played, but only in part, was that of pioneer in exploring the uses of the new food resources which were available in the New World. TURKEY, yes; MAIZE, not much in the early days (Europeans were quicker off the mark); POTATO, slowly as in Europe; TOMATO, the same.

Another role which only N. Americans could have played (who else ever had the resources of land for raising CATTLE on the epic scale which they achieved?—not even Australians) lay in establishing a pattern of meat consumption whose scale dwarfed anything in earlier history and is unlikely ever to be rivalled. (In some other cultures wealthy people had eaten a lot of meat; but there had never previously been a large population in which virtually everyone expected to do so.)

A different sort of role was the one they played in adapting foodways to the advent of the motor car. It can be maintained that the motor car, whose mass production began in the USA, and the aeroplane have done more than any other new feature of life in the 20th century to transform human society. Americans have a gift for seeing opportunities where others might see only problems. Thus it was in the USA—with its numerous automobiles and enormous network of roads—that the whole subculture of roadside diners and drive-in eating places came into being and flourished on a scale unthinkable elsewhere. The Sterns (1984, 1986a) have chronicled the sorts of food which diners would offer, differing noticeably from one region to another although with common elements. Heimann (1996), in a work entitled *Car Hops and Curb Service*, has told the story of the drive-ins with the panache which it deserves. Studying his pictures of the buildings and the imaginatively costumed hops (see box), and recalling that the heartland of the drive-in included Hollywood, who can resist a frisson on hearing the tale of one hop who served Jean Harlow? Clad in a white costume, her platinum hair 'a dream', driving a white convertible, the star ordered a small orange juice and left the hop not only an indelible memory but also a big tip.

All this was part of the transformation of street foods, made necessary in America by the transition from a world of pedestrians to a world where everyone moved by automobile. Street foods had to be transformed into FAST FOODS, obtainable from or in buildings which were surrounded by ample parking space. The repercussions have been worldwide.

One major effect was the emergence of HAMBURGER chains. McDonald (1997) has described their early history and the commercial wars waged between them— White Tower, Burger King, Jack-in-the-Box, Wendy's, and McDonalds. These were major battles and—whatever view one takes of the

---

COSTUMED TO SERVE

DRIVE-IN chains were more successful if they had a theme, and if both their architecture and the costumes of the car-hops were immediately recognizable. It seems that none of them chose to have middle-aged males dressed like penguins and looking shifty, the European style of that period. Most had youthful females, and vied with each other for originality and daring in their costumes. Girl Robin Hoods, with feathers in their green caps, would be the lure at one place, while another would offer cowgirls with fringed skirts, and the hops at another establishment were costumed 'like the dandies of the Old Dominion—long tailed coats of blue material with gray collars and white bow ties; gray pants, white dickeys with standing collars; low crowned gray top hat worn at a rakish angle and a gold fob with a ribbon'.

California had no monopoly of new fashions. 'Deep in the heart of Texas, Sivils Drive-In dressed their hops in what would become the epitome of car hop fashion. Mrs. Sivil introduced to the drive-in world an abbreviated costume of satin shorts and bare midriff top crowned with a foot-high plumed [drum] majorette hat that caused a sensation across America.' There is a photograph of 52 of the majorettes lined up on the roof of and in front of the Dallas branch, the flags of the USA, of Texas, and of Sivils flying above.

The one item which was mandatory for all hops was a smile on the face. For, when women took over the profession of hop, as they swiftly did, 'a smiling feminine face became the drive-in's preeminent icon'.

hamburger—important ones. The scale of the McDonalds enterprise at the close of the 20th century is astounding and, together with Coca-Cola and Pepsi-Cola, it has become a principal standard-bearer of American culture around the world. Many Americans would rather that this were not the case. But it must be said that it was on American soil that these phenomena flourished initially, grew at dazzling speed, and poised themselves for a global role. The Sterns (again, this time 1992, in their brilliant survey of pop culture) have provided what is probably the best short history of Mcdonalds, analysing the factors which led to success and throwing into dramatic relief the crucial nature of decisions which they, or their successors, must make: crucial for them, and to some extent for others too.

The lesson which emerges from a study of all this is that the arts of salesmanship and advertising have acquired, in America and in recent times, a previously unimaginable importance for the present and future history of food. This importance stretches far beyond the frontiers of the USA. But it grew within them, and the ferment which keeps it alive and growing is unmistakably American.

No one would deny that there are highly talented chefs at work in the USA; that there are some restaurants of world class; that there is much excellent produce to be had and many delightful subcuisines to be sampled across the huge breadth of the country. But much the same can be said of other countries. What distinguishes the USA is not a collection of merit badges like these, which others too have deserved, but the uniquely exuberant, restless, and irreverent disposition which has made Americans hungry for novelty and experiment, coupled with the wealth (natural resources, money) which permits translating hankerings into actuality.

The 20th-century developments in the American food scene have not lacked chroniclers. See, for outstanding examples, Harvey Levenstein (1988, 1993) for the social history of food and its fashions; Sokolov (1981) for a nostalgic backwards look; J. and K. Hess (1977) for pungent criticism of the naïveté and inaccuracy displayed in some American writing about food; Schwartz (1986) for the American infatuation with diets; Laura Shapiro (1986) for turn-of-the-century activities; Anne Mendelson (1996) for the background to *The Joy of Cooking* (see Rombauer, 1931, Rombauer and Rombauer Becker, 1951); and many besides.

See also AMERICAN COOK BOOKS; CHUCK, CHUCK WAGON; WHITE TRASH COOKING; FISHER, M. F. K.

READING: as indicated above, also Mariani (1994) for all American culinary terms; Carolyn Niethammer (1974) on *American Indian Food and Lore*; Adams (1952) for cowboy cooking; Arnold (1985, 1990, 1997) and Jacky Williams (1993) for pioneer cookery in the West; Harva Hachten (1981) for the food history of Wisconsin, illuminating the whole Midwest; Sheila Hibben (1947) for a pioneering study of American regional cookery, and Betty Fussell (1986) for a later one; Sokolov (1991); Clark (1997) and Noël Riley Fitch (1997) for the culinary and cultural contexts in which James Beard and Julia Child exercised their influence on American cooks.

V

VACHERIN the name of several cheeses made in Switzerland or in the neighbouring region of France which have little in common except that they are made of whole cow's milk (as the name, derived from *vache*, meaning cow, indicates).

Vacherin (du) Mont d'Or, until recently, could be either Swiss or French, the name being shared amicably enough by cheese-makers in the Vaud (Switzerland) and Franche-Comté (France) The Swiss have now acquired exclusive legal right to the name, and the French product has to be called by another name, such as *vacherin du Haut-Doubs*. Rance (1989), who treats these cheeses at length and with particular affection, deplores this development. The cheese is soft and rich, a flat disc which may measure up to 30 cm (1') in diameter. It is bound by a strip of spruce bark and packed in a shallow spruce box which imparts a resinous fragrance to it.

Vacherin fribourgeois, made in the canton of Fribourg, exists in two principal forms: the winter cheese called *vacherin à fondue* and used for making Fribourg FONDUE; and a dessert cheese called *vacherin à main*.

Vacherin, in another sense, is a French **iced dessert** of MERINGUE, fruit, and ICE CREAM in various presentations, usually round and looking rather like a vacherin cheese, which seems to be how it came by its name.

VANDYKING a method of cutting off the top of a fruit or vegetable with a zigzag cut, so that it can be replaced. The technique is well suited to grapefruits and tomatoes. Its name alludes to the pointed beards which are familiar from the numerous portraits painted by the artist van Dyck.

VANILLA obtained from the cured pods of the plant *Vanilla planifolia*, is one of the few tropical spices indigenous to the New World, and one of the most popular flavourings worldwide for confectionery and other sweet foods.

V. planifolia, a plant of C. America where it grows wild on the fringes of the Mexican tropical forests, is a vine with thick, fleshy green stems and long leathery leaves. Its small greenish flowers open early in the morning, for at most eight hours, and are pollinated, it is thought, exclusively by humming birds and melipone bees. The fruits—yellow-green pods up to 30 cm (12") long—develop within four weeks, and it is these, also called 'beans', which are harvested and treated to produce the vanilla flavour.

V. tahitensis, which belongs to Tahiti, and is cultivated there and in Hawaii, may be descended from *V. planifolia* but has noticeably different characteristics. *V. pompona* is a less important species, yielding 'West Indian vanilla'.

Vanilla was first used by the Aztecs and its use recorded by the Spanish. Diaz noticed Montezuma drinking *tlilxochitl*, a drink made from cacao beans flavoured with vanilla; Sahagún, a Franciscan friar who arrived in Mexico in 1529, saw the spice on sale in the markets as an item of AZTEC FOOD.

In the second half of the 16th century, the Spaniards imported vanilla beans into Spain and made chocolate flavoured with the spice. Hugh Morgan, apothecary to Elizabeth I, suggested vanilla as a flavouring in its own right and gave some cured beans to the Flemish botanist Clusius who described them in his *Exoticorum Libri Decem* (1605). Plants were taken to Réunion in 1822 by the French, then to Mauritius in 1827 and to Madagascar in about 1840. But pollination of the vanilla vine is mysterious and only occurs unaided in Mexico—even there only a small percentage of the fruits set naturally. So it was not until Albius, a former slave in Réunion, developed a practical method of pollinating vanilla artificially that commercial cultivation of vanilla became possible. Madagascar, together with the Comoro Islands and Réunion, now produces about 80% of world output of the variety of *V. planifolia* known as Bourbon vanilla.

Vanilla pods are harvested before ripening and then plunged into hot steam at 70 °C (160 °F) before being left to ferment for up to four weeks. After this time the surface of the fruit will be covered in crystals of glucose and vanillin and the fruits themselves have become black from oxidization but are still flexible. Long and very slim, they are tied in bundles and packed into tin containers. They should keep indefinitely like this and may become covered with small crystals of vanillin. This 'frosted vanilla' is especially well esteemed.

Much of the vanilla entering western markets is used for the preparation of vanilla extract, a hydroalcoholic solution which contains the extracted aroma and flavour of vanilla. Pure vanilla extract will be labelled as such and must (by US regulations) contain at least 35% alcohol. That of the finest quality has a low sugar content, a rich perfumed smell, and is an amber colour. It needs to be kept in a dark place. It is always expensive, more so than less good products with labels such as 'vanilla flavouring'.

Vanillin, the chief flavouring principle in vanilla, has been the subject of much attention from flavour chemists. The first synthetic vanillin was produced by German chemists in 1874 from coniferin, the glucoside found in the sapwood of certain conifers. Synthetic vanillin can also be produced from other sources such as coal tar extracts. However, although synthetic vanillin is chemically pure and can be up to 20 times cheaper than the real thing, it lacks what Rosengarten (1969) described as the 'pure, spicy delicate flavour' and the 'peculiar bouquet' of natural vanilla; these depend on the conjunction of other flavouring elements with vanillin, and have so far proved to be unreproducible in the laboratory.

VARENIKI Ukrainian filled PASTA resembling RAVIOLI, usually made from an egg dough. A potato dough is used sometimes, especially for sweet versions. Of the numerous fillings, COTTAGE CHEESE is the national favourite.

Vareniki are boiled, drained, and traditionally served with *smetana* (SOUR CREAM) or chopped crisp bacon, or both.

Sweet *vareniki* filled with fruit, especially plum, are enjoyed as a dessert. In some parts of the Ukraine they go under the Czech name *knedli*.

VARENO ZHITO a Bulgarian boiled WHEAT dish with nuts, sugar, and lemon juice. Maria Kaneva-Johnson (1995) explains that *zhito* and the Serbo-Croat *Zhito* stem from the Old Slavonic *žita* meaning cereals or wheat, itself derived from *žit*, life (underlining the true significance of cereals, particularly of wheat, for all Slavic peoples).

She goes on to say:

This flavourful mixture of wheat grains, sugar and nuts has gathered unto itself a host of ritual functions and meanings. It is possibly of pre-Christian Slavonic origin, but was adopted by the Eastern Orthodox Church and introduced into the cult of the dead. It is offered at funerals, memorial services and on All Soul's Day to churchgoers, in small spoonfuls on clean paper napkins. Small bowlfuls are afterwards sent to all the neighbours.

In the recipe which accompanies this description the wheat used is *grouhana pshenitsa*, literally 'pounded wheat', i.e. wheat from which the coarse outer layers of bran have been removed. Preparation of the dish takes three days in all (and some of the liquid drained from the wheat on the third day can then be used in making AŞURE, if the cook has any energy left).

The same dish is found in Serbia, where, besides being offered on the day of the patron saint, it is sold (as *žito*) in most pastry shops in individual glass bowls or goblets.

VASILOPITTA a traditional Greek New Year bread, also known as St Basil's bread. New Year's Eve and New Year's Day are celebrated more elaborately than Christmas in Greece. The Greek equivalent to Father Christmas is Aghios Vasilis—St Basil—and he arrives on New Year's Eve when the children also receive presents. The *vasilopitta* occupies a prominent position on the table for the arrival of the New Year.

Rena Salaman (1993a) quotes from William Miller (*Greek Life in Town and Country*, 1905):

On the same night, too [New Year's Eve] takes place the ceremony of cutting 'St Basil's Cake'—a large circular mass of brioche with almonds and walnuts upon it, which is solemnly cut open, shortly before midnight, by the head of the house. Sometimes a franc or a gold piece is put into the cake, and the person receiving the piece which contains the coin, is supposed to be going to have a lucky year. In the country, after cutting the cake,

a fine pomegranate is thrown violently on the ground, so as to scatter the seeds.

A favourite flavouring for this cake is MAHLAB, but ANISEED is also popular and whole aniseed gives the bread an interesting texture and a pungent festive aroma. The traditional shape is a very large round loaf with a small loaf on top.   HS

VEAL (*see page 822*)

VEGETABLE HUMMING BIRD
Sesbania grandiflora, a leguminous tree native to S. and SE Asia, now cultivated in both Old and New World tropics. The tree has a remarkably rapid growth and represents a resource which could be exploited increasingly for many different purposes.

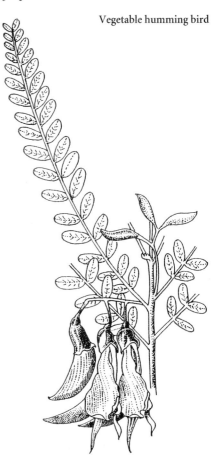

Vegetable humming bird

The young leaves, tender pods, and huge flowers are prized as food in SE Asia. The leaves, which are remarkably nutritious, are used in curry-type dishes, or fried or steamed. The pods (length about 30 cm/12") are also eaten as a vegetable, and the seeds they contain may be processed like soya beans (which they rival in nutritional merit).

The creamy-white flowers, whose supposed resemblance to humming birds

(cont. on page 823)

Veal

A name derived from the Latin *vitellus*, a calf, via Norman French, means the flesh of calves, young cattle of the species *Bos taurus*. National and regional variations in its consumption are strongly marked. In Europe it is important in the cookery of the Netherlands, France, Italy, Germany, and (to some extent) Spain; but less so in Britain, and hardly at all in Russia.

The influence of immigrants from veal-eating countries in Europe has given veal some limited popularity in both N. and S. America, but this too varies by region. It has never been important in Middle Eastern or Asian countries.

How much distinction had been made between the flesh of calves and that of mature cattle in the remote past is unclear. By classical Roman times, however, veal was being prescribed in some recipes. Later, in the Middle Ages, there are enough references to veal in France and England to show that it was known and appreciated; see, for example, the 15th-century recipes in *An Ordinance of Pottage* (ed. Constance Hieatt, 1988), including one for Veal bucnade which Hieatt thinks more or less the same as the modern French recipe for *Blanquette de veau à l'ancienne* (see BLANQUETTE). It is certainly clear that the gelatinous stock obtained from calves' feet was highly prized from early times—as it is now—for making jellies; and that veal roasts and stews were familiar fare in wealthy households. However, the British, having adequate pasture for mature cattle, have generally been able to indulge their preference for beef.

In the latter part of the 20th century consumption has been affected by moral and other scruples. Many people in Britain have looked askance at veal, mainly because they disapprove of methods for rearing calves in 'crates', restricted spaces, on an iron-deficient diet with no exercise or sunlight. This is not an entirely new worry. Mrs Beeton (1861) commented 'there was no species of slaughtering practised in this country so inhuman and disgraceful as that, till very lately, employed in killing this poor animal; when, under the plea of making the flesh *white*, the calf was bled day by day, till, when the final hour came, the animal was unable to stand. This inhumanity is, we believe, now everywhere abolished.'

In France, in the decades following the Second World War, a parallel move away from veal was caused by the practice of feeding hormones to calves, until this was made illegal. However, veal consumption by the French has remained high in comparison with that of, say, the British or N. Americans.

QUALITY AND CUTS

The best veal is considered to come from animals aged about two and a half or three months, especially if exclusively milk fed, giving the almost white meat prized in continental Europe.

France, Italy, and C. Europe are the home region of veal escalopes, thin round or oval pieces cut from the loin, leg, or best end. These were formerly known as COLLOPS in Britain. A schnitzel is an escalope under its German name.

The term 'fillet' when used of veal has two meanings: it may apply conventionally to the undercut from the loin, but is also used to mean a long narrow muscle from the leg, and both are used for escalopes. Italian *scaloppine* (US scallops) or *piccate* (and the smaller *piccatine*) are cut from the leg fillet. The *medaillons* (round slices) and *grenadins* (little steaks) of French cookery are cut from either the loin or the leg fillet.

The close texture and mild flavour of lean, minced veal makes it a valuable ingredient in many PÂTÉS, GALANTINES, and STUFFINGS, besides showing to advantage in such dishes as veal loaf. The value of the gelatinous stock which can be produced from veal bones, feet and trimmings, which has already been mentioned, accounts for the use of 'veal glue' in England in the 18th century; this was a precursor of the modern stock cube.

VEAL COOKERY

Perhaps partly because veal recipes owe so much to Italian cookery, there is considerable consensus amongst cooks from different countries about appropriate flavours and accompaniments. Broadly speaking, these fall into three categories: first, the use of sharp flavourings, especially lemon, which is a common garnish, or acid vegetables, such as sorrel, spinach, or tomatoes, or the use of paprika and sour cream which is typical of (for example) parts of Germany and Austria; secondly, the addition of salted meat in the form of prosciutto, ham, or bacon; and thirdly, cheese, either grated into a coating mixture, or as a slice melted on the meat. Eggs are also called for in stuffings and sauces, and a fortified, sweetish wine such as Marsala or sherry or Madeira is often chosen for veal cookery.

Recipes for veal in English cookery books, past and present, reflect this consensus and often show continental European influence. The veal and ham pie which came into prominence in the 19th century can be regarded as an English contribution to the repertoire. And there were others. Although GREENSAUCE is by no means exclusive to England, its use in England with veal is distinctive. 'Scotch collops' were thin slices of fried meat, usually veal, as in Hannah Glasse (1747). Nor did veal escape the popular 18th-century English treatments of collaring or potting. The paleness of the meat was valued in the latter method; potted veal packed in layers with potted tongue produced an attractive effect when cut and was known as 'marble veal'.

Whatever sort of recipe is used for veal, gentle heat is required, otherwise the meat tends to become dry. One interesting technique is for escalopes to be rolled around a filling and braised. English cooks were doing this in the 17th century and calling the result 'veal olives', a curious term whose origin is explained under BEEF OLIVES.

In Italy escalopes form the basis of some of the most famous dishes. *Saltimbocca* (literally 'jump in the mouth') consists of a very thin slice of veal and a leaf of fresh sage, covered with a slice of prosciutto, fried, and served with gravy made in the pan.

Costoletta alla milanese, a well-known Milanese dish, is a veal chop (or cutlet on the bone), dipped in egg and breadcrumbs, fried gently in butter, and served with lemon wedges. This bears a resemblance to but is not the same thing as the *Wiener Schnitzel* which is so popular on the other side of the Alps, in Austria and Germany; the Milanese cut the meat from the rib and fry it in butter, whereas the Austrians take the escalope from the leg, and fry it in lard. The Milanese version seems to be much the older of the two.

It is easy to be confused between *costoletta* and *cotoletta*. The former is a chop, or cutlet on the bone—a cut of meat with a piece of rib. *Cotoletta*, on the other hand, indicates not a cut of meat but a manner of cooking, to wit egg-and-breadcrumb treatment followed by frying in butter. The cut of meat used for a *cotoletta* of veal would be an escalope. *Cotoletta alla bolognese*, where the veal is topped with ham and cheese, or just cheese, is a famous dish of this sort. However, if prepared in a different way, the escalope would retain the name indicating its cut, e.g. *scaloppina* or *piccata*, as in *Piccata al limone*. Things other than meat (for example

mushrooms, slices of aubergine, fillets of fish, chicken breasts) can be cooked *a cotoletta*, meaning *cotoletta* style. All this is well explained by Anna del Conte (1989).

One of the most famous of Italian veal dishes is *Vitello tonnato*, which is braised veal, larded with anchovies, sliced, and marinated in a sauce of tuna, olive oil, lemon juice, and capers; the versatility of this recipe can be demonstrated by making it with white turkey meat. Another famous dish is the Milanese *Osso bucco*—sawn sections of veal shin (with the marrow left in) cooked with wine and tomatoes, sprinkled with a mixture of chopped parsley, garlic, and grated lemon peel, called *gremolada*.

As for the New World, Mariani (1994) observes that beef cattle were not plentiful in the USA until the 19th century and that even then the abundance of grass and fodder in the Midwest encouraged rearing them to full size.

It was only with the arrival of Italian and German immigrants in the late 19th and early 20th centuries that an appetite for veal developed in the eastern cities, with schnitzels and veal scallopine showing up on restaurant menus. Annual consumption of veal by Americans in the 1940s was nearly 10 pounds per capita, but, largely owing to the high cost of the meat, it had fallen to about one and a half pounds by the early 1980s. It is still mostly eaten in Italian and French restaurants, where adaptions of Old World recipes have resulted in dishes like 'Veal Parmesan' and 'Veal Francese', whose names are unknown abroad.

(LM)

accounts for the name, contain sugar and are used in Thailand in sour soups. (There is also a variety with red flowers, but these have little flavour, create a purple colour in dishes, and are used much less often.) In Indonesia they are used in *gado-gado*, a mixed vegetable salad, and similar dishes.

VEGETABLE LAMB so called, is really part of a tree fern, *Cibotium barometz*, of SE Asia. Fanciful thoughts by early travellers caused it to become known as the Vegetable Lamb of Tartary and to be the subject of many legends.

VEGETABLE MARROW a mainly British phenomenon. Specimens of the marrow/zucchini group of cultivars of the SUMMER SQUASH, *Cucurbita pepo*, are best eaten when young, as ZUCCHINI. In Britain, partly perhaps because of the competitive spirit in which amateur gardeners seek to grow vegetables of record size, some cultivars of these vegetables have traditionally been grown to extreme dimensions before being marketed or exhibited.

These huge marrows are very watery and their original flavour, never more than mild, will have been diluted to vanishing point; so

the best thing to do is to stuff them with a well-flavoured mixture.

VEGETABLE OILS are all dealt with separately, either in their own right (as olive oil, under OLIVES AND OLIVE OIL) or under the plant from which they come (as groundnut/peanut oil, under GROUNDNUT). See also FATS AND OILS for a general survey.

VEGETABLE SPAGHETTI originally (in the 1930s) an American cultivar of the SQUASH *C. pepo*; also known as spaghetti squash or noodle squash. The ripe fruits are

Vegetable spaghetti

ochre/light buff in colour, about 24 cm (9") long and 0.75 kg (1.5 lb) or more in weight. What is special about them is that the stringy fibres, which in a normal squash form a small layer between the flesh and the seeds, are over-developed so that they take up most of the inside and look and handle remarkably like spaghetti. The taste is bland, so this vegetable goes best with something which has a stronger flavour.

In the latter part of the 20th century several new cultivars of a hybrid of *C. pepo* were introduced, all having similar characteristics to the original vegetable spaghetti but mostly with fruits which are orange when ripe. Among these Orangetti is prominent. White Fall is larger and creamy white.

VEGETARIANISM as a term, only came into general use after the formation of the Vegetarian Society at Ramsgate in England in 1847. However, the phenomenon, that is to say the existence of significant numbers of people who as a matter of principle did not eat animal flesh, dates back to classical times or beyond. The Greek philosopher Pythagoras (6th century BC), best known for his theorem in geometry, gave his name to a diet which precludes meat, although it is not certain to what extent he followed this himself (e.g. whether he ate fish). An account of his teaching was published by Antonio Cocchi and translated into English by Dodsley (1745), serving to transmit a version of his doctrines to modern generations.

An account of what Pythagoras actually ate (honey for breakfast, millet or barley bread for dinner, and raw or boiled vegetables) is provided in one of the earliest books recommending vegetarianism, *On Abstinence from Animal Food* by the Greek author Porphyry (3rd century AD). This remains one of the most persuasive documents of its kind, and includes in moderate language and elegant prose most of what are now regarded as the main arguments for not eating meat.

Vegetarianism has not been confined to the western world, indeed it is more widespread in Asia where it is strongly linked to the main religions (see HINDUISM AND FOOD; BUDDHISM AND FOOD; JAINS AND FOOD).

The list of famous people who have been vegetarians (of one kind or another—see below) is a long one, including Voltaire, Shelley, Tolstoy, Wagner, Bernard Shaw, Gandhi. (The list stops here because if it went on it would juxtapose Hitler with Gandhi.)

The principal categories of vegetarians are:

- plain vegetarians, following the simple rule that they do not eat fish, flesh, or fowl (but there are gradations, e.g. some would eat fish);
- vegans, who abstain from all food of animal origin, which means no milk or eggs, for example;
- ovolactarians, like vegans, but including eggs and milk in their diet;
- lactarians, ditto but without eggs;
- herbivores, eating only plants;
- fruitarians, eating only fruits;
- granivores, eating only seeds and grain.

The nutritional adequacy of a vegetarian diet (of any of the above categories) has been called in question. It seems to be generally agreed that risks centre on protein (and especially the composition of the mixture of amino acids which result from the breakdown of protein taken at a meal) and vitamins, above all vitamin B12. A vegetarian risks having too little of certain amino acids, unless taking special precautions. These precautions consist mainly in taking foods in certain combinations (e.g. rice and beans) which provide corresponding combinations of complementary amino acids. The difficulty is never insuperable, but it is greater for those who practise the more extreme forms of vegetarianism. As for vitamin B12, which is crucial to well-being, it has traditionally been derived from animals (in the form of liver, eggs, milk, and cheese), but it has become possible to produce it synthetically, using no animal sources. Much fine print has been devoted to this whole area of study, but the general conclusion is that vegetarians and vegans can obtain all they need so long as they are willing to follow certain rules which people who have a more varied diet do not need to observe.

For their part, vegetarians and vegans can point to the health risks associated with heavy consumption of red meat and animal fats.

The proportion of the population in western countries which has adopted some kind of vegetarian-style diet, or which professes to be moving in that direction, has been increasing towards the end of the 20th century. However, this is a fluid situation, and any attempt to produce reliable statistics is hampered by potential confusion over terminology, especially when one considers groups such as those who no longer eat red meat but do eat everything else.

READING: Spencer (1993); Janet Barkas (1975).

VELOUTÉ meaning 'velvety', is the term used for a basic French sauce which is made with STOCK—veal, chicken, or (for a fish velouté) fish. First of all a ROUX is made with butter and flour; then plenty of stock is blended in and flavouring added. After prolonged simmering, the sauce will have acquired its velvety texture. A liaison of egg yolk and/or a little cream can be added at the end to enrich it and make it even more velvety.

Velouté, with the addition of various other ingredients, acquires new names. To take but two examples, adding egg yolk and chopped mushroom produces *sauce allemande*, while tomato turns *velouté* into *sauce aurore*. *Sauce Bercy*, based on shallots and white wine, is exceptional in that when it is used for fish it is made with a *velouté de poisson*, and when for meat with a concentrated meat stock.

Anne Willan (1989) points out that, apart from 'the classic velouté variations, free-form additions, such as saffron or a purée of spinach lead to some of the most innovative sauces in modern cooking'.

The term velouté may also be used of a soup.

VELVET BEAN a name applied to a large range of hairy-podded leguminous plants, of the genus *Mucuna*, which are native to tropical Africa and Asia and parts of Australia. Many are vines which climb high into the rainforest canopy and bear large flowers. Where they are grown, this is mainly for animal fodder, e.g. *M. deeringiana* as the Florida or Georgia velvet bean of the USA; but several species have been used for human consumption in Africa and Asia. These include *M. nivea* in India, about which Watt (1889–96) commented that the large, tender pods were valued as a vegetable by the Hindus and that the eminent botanist Roxburgh had said that they were, 'when dressed like French beans, a most excellent vegetable for European tables'.

Watt was careful to say also that the velvet-like skin should be removed before cooking; the hairs on the pods are troublesome. The worst are those of *M. pruriens*, the cowitch or cowage (not the same as New Zealand cowage, a spinach-like vegetable), whose name, derived from a Hindi word, is coincidentally apt since its itching quality drives cattle wild. A further problem is that the seeds may contain toxins and have to be boiled in several changes of water before consumption. However, Indonesians contrive to use them, often fermented to make a kind of TEMPE, in various ways.

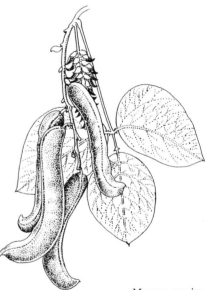

Mucuna pruriens

On the northern coasts of Australia the Aborigines used the rainforest velvet bean, or burney bean, *M. gigantea*. Noting this, Low (1989) quoted an explorer called Leichhardt:

I gathered the large vine-bean, with green blossoms, which had thick pods containing from one to five seeds. Its hard covering, by roasting, became very brittle; and I pounded the cotyledons, and boiled them for several hours. This softened them, and made a sort of porridge, which, at all events, was very satisfying.

VENEZUELA was given its name, meaning 'Little Venice', by the explorer Amérigo Vespucci when he encountered villages built on stilts above the water. The first territory on mainland S. America to be colonized by the Spanish, the home of Eldorado, it has long been the inspiration of explorers and visitors, from Sir Walter Raleigh to Joseph Conrad and beyond.

That impressive Caribbean coastline, punctuated by giant rivers and great islands, was the home of Indians who, Raleigh noticed, 'use the tops of palmitos [palm hearts] for bread, and kill deer, fish and porks for the rest of their sustenance, they also have many sorts of fruits that grow in the woods, and great variety of birds and fowl.' But first impressions mislead, for Venezuela is as much a highland culture, with settlement in the Andean valleys on the western side of the country. The tropical coast and the deep jungle towards GUYANA are relatively less favoured. There are also wide plains (*llanos*) where cattle herding is significant, but all, in Venezuela, has recently been dominated by oil, making it the richest (for a time) Latin American state, with the fastest moving and most urbanized society. The lack of a strong Indian presence has meant that most of the inhabitants are either Spanish, negro, or mestizo. José Rafael Lovera (1988) has shown how these latterday changes have affected traditional diet. WHEAT has displaced MAIZE as the universal staple, particularly in large cities, while CASSAVA (yuca) still rules through the province of Guyana in the south-east. Imports of foreign foods have reduced reliance on indigenous fruits and vegetables.

There are many features common to Venezuelan cookery and that of COLOMBIA. They concur in the use of ANNATTO, the enjoyment of CAPERS and green CORIANDER as flavourings, the universal employment of COCONUTS and BANANAS in cooking, as well as a reliance on the CORN BREAD *arepa*.

Distance from pre-Columbian Andean cultures has ensured that Venezuelan cooking leans more on Spanish and negro originals, or borrowings from Mexico and the Spanish Caribbean. Hence Spanish dishes like *Ropa vieja* are translated into *Pabellón caraqueño* (shredded flank steak with a tomato sauce, black beans, and plantains), while Mediterranean recipes such as stuffed cabbage (*Repollo relleno*) are current. Old World spices like cumin and capers are highly esteemed and supermarkets sell *aliño preparado* (or *criollo*), a ready-ground mixture of cumin, oregano, annatto, pepper, and paprika. There seems less dependence on CHILLI in many Venezuelan recipes by contrast to those of Colombia or Ecuador. Mexican originals have been suggested for the AVOCADO sauce *guasacaca*, which is similar to guacamole, and the *arepa* is similar in concept, if not shape (it is more bunlike), to the TORTILLA.

Nonetheless, substantial stews and soups called *sancocho* or *ajiaco*, as in Colombia, are common. These normally involve meat or seafood supported by cassava and green PLANTAINS (for a *sancocho*) or by MAIZE, potatoes, avocado, and chillies (for *ajiaco*).

Maize, bananas, and cassava are the three main foundations of popular cooking, and black beans are the fourth. Venezuelans call them *caviar criollo*, and they feature as accompaniments to many meats, or cooked as a substantial dish seasoned with cumin and served with *arepas*.

German immigration in the 20th century has meant that Venezuela is blessed with good cheeses (and beer).   TJ

VENISON the general term in English for the meat of DEER. Originally the word applied to any furred GAME, but it had assumed its current meaning by the late Middle Ages.

In Britain, three species of deer are commonly used for food: the red, which is the largest, now largely confined to the Scottish Highlands; the fallow; and the roe, the smallest of the three and the one considered best by cooks. For a description of these and of the main deer in N. America, see DEER.

The term 'venison' is often extended to the meat of other species in the deer family, including, in the USA, ELK, MOOSE, and CARIBOU. Various types of ANTELOPE and gazelle provide meat which might loosely be described as venison in parts of Asia, throughout Africa, and in N. America.

The season for venison in Britain lasts from late June until January. The deer are always bled and gralloched (gutted) immediately after killing. The carcass is hung for 12–22 days, according to the weather. Traditionally, the meat was rubbed with powdered ginger and pepper during hanging to discourage flies and prevent tainting. It is apparent that this did not always work, since methods for rescuing tainted venison were a common feature of old recipe books.

The meat is dark red and fine grained; such fat as it contains is high in polyunsaturates, but it is generally very lean and inclined to be dry. It is often marinated and larded (see LARDING) before cooking to alleviate this.

Generally, cookery of venison at different periods and in various parts of the world has followed national and regional preferences in meat cookery, and the trends of the time. One somewhat unusual dish which featured in English cookery from medieval times onwards to the 19th century was the venison PASTY. Venison, highly seasoned with pepper or ginger, was

enclosed in pastry. Gervase Markham, in *The English Hus-wife* (1615), instructed the housewife to use a sturdy rye flour crust for this dish, which was expected to last some time. Recipes for imitating it, using beef, were current. Samuel Pepys recorded that on 6 January 1660 he was entertained to dinner 'which was good, only the venison pasty was palpable beef, which was not handsome'.

Roasting has been the most favoured way of cooking good venison. The meat is generally larded for this, and many consider it is best slightly underdone. Accompaniments include rowanberry (see ROWAN AND SORB), redcurrant (see CURRANTS), SLOE, or CRANBERRY jelly.

VENUS SHELL or venus clam, the common name (albeit more common in conchological manuals than in market places) for a number of edible BIVALVES in the family Veneridae. The wider name COCKLE, although properly reserved for members of the family Cardiidae, is often applied to them (as indicated below), and it certainly falls more easily from the lips of fishmongers; but the two families are distinct. The venus shells which are eaten include a famous one, the QUAHOG, and the moderately well-known VERNI, which have their own entries. Many of the species are in the genus *Chione*.

On the Pacific coast of the USA there are several species, notably *C. fluctifraga*, the smooth chione, and *C. undatella*. They are also called hardshell cockle, mud cockle, and bay cockle; and are highly regarded as food. The same applies to *Protothaca staminea*, the common littleneck.

Asari is the Japanese name of *Ruditapes philippinarum*, a member of the family commonly eaten in Japan, especially in the spring, present also in Chinese and Korean waters, and now being 'farmed' in Galicia in Spain as *almeja japonesa*. Maximum width 4 cm (1.5"). The pattern on the shells varies, but is usually black on a light ground, giving an impression of ridges. The surface texture resembles woven cloth. In Japan, *asari* are used in MISO soup, and for *nimono* (see JAPANESE CULINARY TERMS) and certain other dishes.

In the southern hemisphere New Zealanders esteem *C. stuchburyi*, which is common on their beaches but nevertheless subject to regulations about maximum permissible catches. They refer to it as a cockle.

In SE Asia a number of venus shells are eaten, but these may be commonly referred to as a SURF CLAM (*Paphia undulata*) or as sand clams (the excellent *Circe scripta* and *Anomalacardia squamosa*) while *Meretrix lusoria* is called hard clam.

What this survey shows is that members of the family Veneridae are apt to be called by many names other than venus shell.

VERJUICE literally 'green juice', is an acid liquid obtained from CRABAPPLES, sour GRAPES, and other unripe fruit. It was much used in medieval European cooking, and lingered on until the 19th century. Theodora FitzGibbon (1976) remarks that its use in western kitchens was eventually superseded, almost completely, by the familiar instruction to add a dash of lemon juice (to whatever). However, it has continued to be an ingredient in certain condiments; and its use in Europe has been revived on a small scale towards the end of the 20th century.

Verjuice, under the name of *abghooreh*, is a common ingredient in the cuisine of Iran. It is made from tiny unripe grapes when the crop is thinned out at the beginning of the growth season; and is bottled for use throughout the year. In Lebanon verjuice is called *hosrum* and used as an alternative to lemon juice.

VERNI the French name (in the absence of an English one) of *Callista chione*, a relatively large CLAM—up to 9–12 cm (4–5") across. Because of its size, the French sometimes call it *grosse* or *grande palourde* (see CARPET-SHELL), although *verni*, referring to the varnished appearance which the reddish or pinkish brown shell presents, is the official name.

The *verni* has a range from the Mediterranean to the south of Britain. It is often eaten raw in the Mediterranean region. Lovell (1884) remarked that this species was not common in England but that Cornish fishermen sometimes took it, and knew it as 'cock' or 'cram'.

VERRAL WILLIAM (1715–61), one of the most engaging cookery writers of the 18th century, served his apprenticeship under a well-known French chef, M. de Saint-Clouet, who was for a time chef to the Duke of Newcastle, the greatest potentate in the eastern part of Sussex. When Verral took over the White Hart in Lewes in 1737, he practised cookery on French lines, as taught by Saint-Clouet.

In 1759, his book, *A Complete System of Cookery*, was published for sale in both Lewes and London, with a preface which must have aroused some astonishment by its racy style and the length of its principal paragraph (about nine pages in each of the two 20th-century reprints). This throws light on the equipment with which he worked and also on some tricks of the trade which he did not scruple to employ, as in the following excerpt from his description of a dinner which he prepared:

Now the two puddings (improperly called so) were made as follows: I took a few potatoes, boiled, and thump'd to pieces, with an egg or two, and a little sugar, for one; the other was a few old mackeroons I had in my house perhaps twenty years: I soak'd em well, and put them into a little milk and flour, instead of cream and eggs, seasoned it high with plenty of onions, &c., to which I added a large clove of garlick, which is enough for the dishes of a fifty-cover table served twice over, and covered it over with some good old Cheshire cheese instead of Parmesan; so that the colours were alike, and sent up, as said before. Well, neighbour, says the old gentleman, now for a bit of pudding, and then we shall have done pretty well, I hope: let's see, here's eight of us; so they were cut into so many parts, and every one took his share, and heartily they fell to, except one whose taste was not quite so depraved as the rest; he tasted, but went no farther. You don't eat, neighbour, says the opposite gentleman. I don't love sweet things, says he. Well, I do, says one that was gobbling down the highest dish that ever was. They vastly commended it, and swallowed it all down; but the beauty of it was, the mackeroon eaters eat it for a custard, and to this moment call it the best they ever tasted. But one of 'em said it had a terrible twang of bad egg, though there was neither egg or butter in it. Well, says my old friend, with such a sort of a groan as may frequently be heard in large peals at your great feasts in and about the metropolis of this kingdom. I say, I hope everybody has made a good dinner; but we may thank you for it, Mr Cook, says he, turning to me; why we should have cut but a sad figure to-day, if we had not had the apparatusses. Pray, Sir, says one of the most learned, what is an apparatus? Why, says my old friend, laughing at him, why a stewpan is one, a pot is another, a ladle another, and many other things down in my kitchen are called apparatusses; so I left them in the midst of their sublime chat, and went home.

See also COOK, for a further sample of Verral's prose.
READING: editorial matter in the two recent editions of Verral (1948, 1988).

VERVAIN *Verbena officinalis*, a European plant with greyish leaves and small lilac flowers, has enjoyed a medicinal reputation since antiquity. It is now used to make one of the better-known herbal teas or TISANES, which is slightly bitter but may be sweetened with honey.

VETCH a general name for about 150 species of leguminous plants of the genus *Vicia*, of which the best known is the BROAD BEAN. Other species are mainly grown for animal food, for example, French or Narbonne vetch, *V. narbonensis*, in the south of Europe.

In classical times both Greeks and Romans liked to eat the seeds of the bitter vetch, *V. ervilia*, remains of which have also been found in excavations at Troy. The species is, or was in the 19th century, cultivated in Afghanistan. Common vetch, *V. sativa*, includes a variety, 'bigpod' vetch, which has seeds as large as peas and is eaten in Algeria.

Chickling vetch is another name for LATH.

VICHYSSOISE a chilled POTATO and LEEK cream soup created by a French chef, Louis Diat, in New York early in the 20th century. Of those who identify 1917 as the year of its creation, none gives chapter and verse. Höfler (1996) gives as the first occurrence in print in French a reference in an issue of *La Revue culinaire* of 1923, where the dish is identified as an item of American cuisine.

Diat came from the Bourbonnais in France, not far from Vichy; and his new soup was based on recollections of one prepared by his mother, but served hot. The customary sprinkling of CHIVES on top was one of Diat's contributions to the new, chilled version.

Despite an attempt in 1941 by some French chefs in New York to change the name to *Crème gauloise* (because of their dislike of the wartime Vichy government in France) and although Diat (1946) did not use the name Vichyssoise in his own cookbook, the name has stuck and this soup continues to be internationally famed. Indeed, it is so well established that it is occasionally used as a generic term, e.g. in 'a vichyssoise of parsnip and runner beans'.
READING: Mariani (1994).

VICTORIA SANDWICH CAKE named after Queen Victoria, is a plain cake made by the creaming method (see CAKE-MAKING), closely related to POUND CAKE. Although sometimes referred to as 'Victoria sponge cake', it is not a true SPONGE CAKE in the sense that SAVOY or GÉNOISE are. Usually is is cut in half and spread with jam and/or cream to give a sandwich. The top is usually dusted with icing sugar.

VIETNAM has a cuisine which is delicate, complex, and sophisticated, combining the techniques of Chinese cooking with the indigenous ingredients, the light accents of French finesse, and, in the south, some of the herbs and spices of India.

Culturally and geographically, the country divides into three areas: the fertile Red River delta to the north; the long, mountainous, and rather barren highlands; and the lush Mekong River delta to the south. This tripartite division has also applied to the regional cuisines, with Hanoi, Hue, and

Saigon (Ho Chi Minh City) being the culinary capitals.

This same division is fundamental to the history and politics of the country. During the 1,000 years of Chinese rule and domination over Vietnam, from before 100 BC to AD 939, it was plainly visible. The three regions were: Nam Viet in the north, Champa in the centre, and Funan in the south. It was in Funan that Indian influence, through trade, was strongly felt and left a mark still visible in modern times.

The Chinese domination of Vietnam lasted until AD 939. When the Vietnamese threw off the colonial yoke, they retained the cooking techniques and eating methods of the Chinese; they still eat with chopsticks—the only SE Asian nation to do so.

Following the pattern in the rest of Asia, European countries began to establish spheres of influence in Vietnam, starting as early as 1516, when the Portuguese arrived in the country. Later it was the French who, convinced that they needed a base for colonial expansion, became masters of Cochin-China (their name for the south of Vietnam), and in due course of the north (then called Tongking), as well as the centre (Annam). By 1883, Vietnam was a French protectorate, a situation that lasted until after the Second World War.

Despite decimation during periods of war, the wildlife remained abundant. The forests supported tigers, elephants, wild boar, oxen, and deer, as well as wildfowl. Domesticated animals included WATER-BUFFALO, goats, pigs, ducks, and chickens. Coconut palms, jackfruit, mango, orange, lime, and rubber trees, as well as coffee bushes, were cultivated. Rice was grown in abundance in the paddy fields of the south. All kinds of fruits, including melons, and such vegetables and herbs as ginger, sesame, peanuts (GROUNDNUTS), mint, and basil, were plentiful.

The influence of China is seen in the Vietnamese STIR-FRY dishes, although the local vegetables and spicings make these subtly different from those of China. The use of FISH SAUCE produces a lighter accent in simmered dishes and soups than the SOY SAUCE of China. The Vietnamese habit of wrapping meats and snack mixtures in lettuce leaves and including fresh herbs in the little bundles is a vestige of the original civilizations that existed before the centuries of Chinese influence, and is practised with delicacy.

Translucent Vietnamese rice noodles, when softened, wrapped around a simple blend of filling ingredients and then deep fried, make SPRING ROLLS which are feather-light and superior to those of China. Other rice noodles (see NOODLES OF ASIA) are popular and an important staple.

The cuisine of the northern part of Vietnam is the one which resembles most closely that of China. Black pepper is used for spicing, as well as ginger. There is less variety of foods than one finds in the south.

In the centre of the country, the cuisine is more refined. Spicier dishes are in evidence and the use of chilli peppers (introduced by the Portuguese) is widespread. Thick, fermented fish sauce is incorporated in dishes as a seasoning, and game from the highlands is often included in the meals of those with access to it.

To the south, the cuisine is highly varied. Traces of Indian and French influence are seen in the Vietnamese curries, in the inclusion of potatoes and asparagus, and in the Vietnamese talent for making exquisite PÂTÉS from both meat and fish. SUGAR CANE is grown and is used in both sweet and savoury snacks. One of the latter, *cháo tôm*, is a delicious combination of shrimp and pork paste which is moulded around lengths of sugar cane, before being baked or fried.

When the Vietnam War ended in 1975, the food resources of the country were severely depleted. A major exodus of refugees was instrumental in a wide diffusion of Vietnamese food, especially in N. America and Australia.   (JB)

READING: Jill Nhu Huong Miller (1968); Nicole Routhier (1989).

VINAIGRETTE also known in Europe as French dressing, is probably the most common dressing for SALAD (barring commercial preparations) in the western world. It is essentially a 'mixture' (inverted commas because oil and vinegar are, strictly speaking, immiscible) of olive or other oil with vinegar (or lemon juice or the like or a combination of some vinegar and some lemon juice), plus salt and pepper and optionally plus herbs, shallot, mustard, etc.

The generally accepted proportion of oil to vinegar is 3 to 1, although some prefer 4 to 1. If lemon juice replaces vinegar, the proportion is closer to 1 to 1. Some authorities recommend that one should begin by dissolving the desired amount of salt in the vinegar, since it will not dissolve in the oil.

The main use of vinaigrette is for green salads, but it is also appropriate for other salads (e.g. a tomato or potato salad), as a dressing for avocado and for artichoke hearts; also with meat preparations such as *fromage de tête*/head brawn.

When a vinaigrette is destined for a green salad, it must be mixed immediately before the salad is served, and the salad should be tossed by hand without any delay. This is partly because of the problem posed by the immiscibility of oil and vinegar, and partly

because the green leaves will wilt after a while under the influence of the dressing.

VINDALOO a term which appears in the curry section of menus in Indian restaurants worldwide. It belongs to GOA and has been described by Madhur Jaffrey (1995) as Goa's most famous export to the western world. She points out that it is often taken to mean the hottest available curry, but that historically this is not so; and continues thus:

The correct spelling, *vindalho*, gives away the main seasonings of the original dish which was once a kind of Portuguese pork stew seasoned with garlic (*alhos*) and wine (*vinho*) vinegar. There were probably some black peppercorns in it as well, especially at the tables of affluent families. The vinegar acted as a preservative, allowing the stew to be eaten over several days.

The same author points out that in Goa, under the influence of the Portuguese colonialists, pork became the meat of choice, not only for themselves, but also for converted Hindus and mixed race Catholic Goans. The original recipe for *vindalho* acquired new ingredients: ginger, cumin, cloves, cardamom, and an enormous number of dried red chillies (with more colour than bite). Goa took to the chillies in a way Portugal never did.

VINEGAR has been in use for thousands of years and its origins are untraceable. One of the earliest references is from the 5th century BC, where Hippocrates recommended its medicinal powers. However, then as now, its main use has been as a flavouring and preserving agent.

There was no need to invent vinegar as it makes itself without difficulties. When wine or any alcoholic drink is exposed to the air it turns sour. Aerobic (air-breathing) bacteria invade it and oxidize (combine with oxygen) the alcohol to acetic acid. Before the invention of the wine cork this was a constant and unwelcome phenomenon. Flasks of wine were sealed with clay and wax which often cracked and let in the air, so that the wine soon went sour. Indeed the word 'vinegar' comes from the French *vin aigre*, meaning sour wine.

Sour wine is not, however, the same as fine vinegar made by a controlled process. Not all acetic acid-producing bacteria give a satisfactory taste. Ideally one needs a culture mainly of *Acetobacter aceti*, of which there are several strains which coexist and cooperate. Other creatures have a symbiotic (mutually beneficial) relationship with these bacteria and assist the fermentation. These include a nematode worm, *Anguilula aceti*, known as the 'vinegar eel', as well as some flies, mites, and lice. Modern factory processes are designed to eliminate these so-called parasites; but some of them still help to produce a superior flavour in vinegar made by traditional methods.

The presence of the right bacteria is ensured by adding vinegar from a previous batch to the wine to be fermented. It is important that this starter should contain 'mother of vinegar', a gelatinous scum full of living bacteria which forms on fermenting vinegar.

The best **wine vinegar** may be made from either white or red wine, the latter having an agreeable mellow taste. Sherry also yields a particularly well-rounded flavour.

Wine vinegars of the finest quality are made by a simple and ancient method known as the Orléans process. This requires the maker not to be in a hurry (the process takes months); to use small barrels (from which the heat engendered by fermentation dissipates quickly); to use wine of good quality; and to provide access to the barrels for air (which will contain acetobacters, bacteria naturally present in the atmosphere). When the vinegar has developed the required acidity some of it is drawn off and more wine added. This sequence can be repeated for an indefinitely long period.

Important elements in the flavour of good vinegar are esters, substances formed in the reaction between acids and alcohols. These continue to form in vinegar, slowly, so that the vinegar matures with keeping. One very fine kind of vinegar—not a wine vinegar, since it is made from must, not from wine—is the true BALSAMIC VINEGAR from Modena and Reggio in Italy; this is matured for decades, even centuries. Aged vinegar acquires an increasingly brown colour as enzymes discolour compounds from the original fruit.

Mass-produced wine vinegar is made from inferior wine, using techniques which save time but sacrifice quality.

Malt vinegar used to be called alegar which is a more appropriate name as it is made from an unhopped type of beer. It has a malty taste which may be disliked in salad dressing but appreciated in pickles. The natural faintly brown colour is usually darkened with caramel.

Malt vinegar may be distilled to make a very strong 'spirit vinegar' suitable, among other things, for pickling watery vegetables. This is usually left uncoloured, so may be called 'white vinegar'. (Sometimes a similar product is made not from natural vinegar but from a mixture of synthetically produced acetic acid and water. However, by law in Britain, the USA, and some other countries, this may not be called 'vinegar'; in Britain it is labelled 'non-brewed condiment'.)

Cider vinegar has long been a speciality of the apple-growing areas of the north-east USA, and of apple-growing regions in Europe such as Normandy. Its popularity has spread, partly because of its supposed health-giving properties, its good flavour, and its relatively low cost.

Rice vinegar, used in Chinese and Japanese cooking, is commonly a clear, light-flavoured vinegar, always relatively mild and sweet. Mildness also characterizes red and black versions, and indeed most Chinese vinegars whether based on rice or millet or any of a score of other kinds of plant material. The very finest Japanese rice vinegar, *genmai mochigome su*, is made from unpolished glutinous rice.

Other vinegars are numerous. It is not essential to start with an alcoholic beverage. Any liquid containing sugar or starch can be induced to ferment first to alcoholic liquor then to vinegar. Starting substances include trimmings and rejects from the fruit industry, such as citrus fruit, pineapples, plums, pears, peaches, and even dates and persimmons. Besides rice other cereals are used; a SORGHUM vinegar made in Quemoy (the island off the coast of China) is said to be of exceptional quality. Molasses and other sugar products are also used. The vinegars which Parsis like best, from the cities of Navsari and Valsad, are made from SUGAR CANE, DATES, or toddy (see COCONUT) and impart a special taste to Parsi pickles and chutneys etc.

Flavourings may be added to vinegars. Wine vinegar is often flavoured with herbs such as tarragon and basil, or with chillies. Vinegar readily takes up any flavouring. A drink which still survives in some rural areas is raspberry or other fruit vinegar. The vinegar was much diluted, flavoured with fruit and sweetened. Raspberry vinegar, which enjoyed a vogue in the latter half of the 20th century, has a long history in Britain, and not just at wealthy or sophisticated tables; it has traditionally been eaten in Yorkshire, for example, with YORKSHIRE PUDDING.

Vinegars vary in both flavour and strength, and are rarely interchangeable in recipes.

VINE LEAVES are consumed as a vegetable in various parts of the world. See DOLMA for the principal use, when the leaves are stuffed with a mixture based on meat or rice. They do impart something of their own pleasantly acid flavour to a stuffing, but in other respects they may be replaced, if not available, by other edible leaves.

A remarkable example of double replacement seems to have occurred in Vietnam and California. The story goes that the Middle Eastern practice of wrapping meat in vine leaves was taken to India by the Persians and subsequently introduced by the Indians to SE Asia. However, although the merits of the arrangement were recognized, there was a practical problem in that grape vines do not grow well in a tropical climate. So the Vietnamese started to use leaves of *Piper lolot* (called by them *la lot*) in much the same manner. The next instalment came when Vietnamese emigrated to the USA, taking with them *la lot* leaves for culinary use. They soon found that *la lot* is difficult to grow in the Mediterranean climate of California; so, little knowing that they were completing a full circle, they substituted the vine leaves which were easily available.

VIOLET the French name for a sort of edible sea creature which does not have a current English name, although it may sometimes be referred to as a 'sea squirt'. These creatures belong to the family Pyuridae in the order Stolidobranchiata, and occur in various species around the world, although not everywhere regarded as edible.

Microcosmus sulcatus

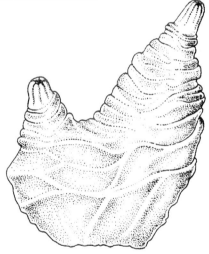

In the Mediterranean, *Microcosmus sulcatus* reaches a dimension of 20 cm (8") and is not uncommon in the markets, especially those of Provence. It is the yellow part inside which is eaten, raw, looking something like scrambled egg.

In S. America the smaller species *Pyura chilensis* is exploited and consumed locally.

VIOLET *Viola odorata*, a familiar garden flower, indigenous to Europe and N. Africa but introduced elsewhere, whose petals are sometimes used as a fragrant flavouring. In candied form they make good decorations for cakes, trifles, etc. The fresh petals are used in salads, as garnishes, and to flavour milk puddings and ice cream.

Claire Clifton (1986) in her essay 'The Search for the Blue Violet Salad' quotes M. F. K. Fisher:

I remember deciding once, long ago and I believe after reading Ellwanger's *Pleasures of the Table* for the first time, that the most exquisite dish I had ever heard of was a satiny white endive with large heavily scented Parma violets scattered through it. It meant everything subtle and intense and aesthetically significant in my private gastronomy, just as, a few years earlier, a brown-skinned lover with a turquoise set in one ear lobe epitomised my adolescent dream of passion.

She went on, under 'E for Exquisite' in *An Alphabet for Gourmets*, to say that when the salad was served to her it was a crushing disappointment.

VISCACHA *Lagostomus maximus*, an animal of the chinchilla family which lives in warrens on the pampas of ARGENTINA. It measures up to 50 cm (20") and somewhat resembles a rabbit, but has larger gnawing teeth, a long tail, and large digging claws on its front feet. When cooked, the meat is very white and good.

VITAMINS are important, indeed literally vital, constituents of foodstuffs, but were not discovered until early in the 20th century and have not yet been fully explored.

They betrayed their presence through illnesses befalling groups of people who for one reason or another were deprived of one of them. The prevalence of SCURVY, which results from a deficiency of vitamin C, might well have started the process of discovering the vitamins. But scurvy was a special problem that arose mainly on long sea voyages and seldom affected the population at large. In general it would be true to say that most people in Europe, up to the 19th century, obtained what vitamins they needed from their diets, even if these diets were rather monotonous. However, the advent of processed foods in the 19th century brought with it, along with some advantages, new risks of vitamin deficiency, and set the stage for serious and systematic work on the causes of such deficiency diseases as beriberi and pellagra.

The roller milling of flour was introduced in Hungary in the 1840s and soon spread all over Europe and N. America. For the first time it was possible to make really white flour at a low cost. The public took to the new inexpensive white bread with enthusiasm, and the extracted bran was fed to the animals. But the bran contained most of the valuable B vitamins of wheat, notably thiamin and niacin, the lack of which causes both beriberi and pellagra. Although these diseases seldom occurred in an acute

form in Europe, standards of health declined.

Gail Borden's invention of sweetened, condensed milk in the 1850s also caused problems. This product has lost most of its vitamins A and D, which are needed to ward off xerophthalmia (an eye disease) and rickets. Rickets became common in the cities, but the explanation was not immediately apparent. Nowadays condensed milk has vitamins added.

In Asia, the introduction of 'polished' rice, with the bran rubbed off to leave the grains attractively white, left many people exposed to beriberi, resulting from an inadequate supply of thiamin. An outbreak of the disease in the Japanese navy in the early 1880s raised a suspicion that some dietary deficiency was responsible for the disease. In 1886 the Dutch East India Company sent an expedition to Indonesia to find the cause, and this had good results. In 1897, after eight years' work, Christian Eijkman established that polished rice was deficient in some substance, though he could not find what this was. In 1901 his colleague Gerrit Grijns discovered that this substance existed in rice bran.

The substance was recognized as essential to health, in addition to the traditional trio of protein, carbohydrates, and fat. So it was at first called 'the accessory substance' or 'the accessory food factor', in the singular. Casimir Funk, in Warsaw in 1912, extracted it in an impure form; it was what we now call thiamin. By this time it was clear that more than one such substance existed. Funk mistakenly thought that all the accessory food compounds were amines, a type of nitrogen compound, and coined the term 'vitamine' for them because they were vital to health. When this was found to be wrong the final 'e' was dropped, and the modern word 'vitamin' was the result.

Scientists had still to take one important step; they had to advance from the knowledge that such things as vitamins existed, and in what they were to be found, to knowing what they actually were. By 1915 the Americans McCollum and Davis had proved that there were at least two, which they called A and B, and the process of isolating them began.

Vitamin C was proved to exist by a long series of experiments on guinea pigs begun in 1907 by the Norwegians Holst and Frölick. Actually they were trying to induce beriberi, but the animals went down with what was obviously scurvy. (This was a double fluke. Guinea pigs, apes, monkeys, and vampire bats are the only animals apart from humans which cannot make their own vitamin C.) The vitamin was isolated in 1925, by the Hungarian researcher Albert Szent-Györgi.

Vitamin D was discovered and named by McCollum in 1921; and vitamin E by Evans

and Bishop in 1922, though it was not isolated till 1935.

This system of identifying vitamins by letters has now lost its original neat pattern as a result of more recent discoveries. Vitamin B has been divided into B1 (thiamin), B2 (riboflavin), B6 (pyridoxine), and B12 (cyanocobalamin), the gaps in the sequence indicating substances which were thought to have been B vitamins and then found out not to be after all. Niacin or nicotinic acid, although a member of the B group, has no number; for some time it was confused with thiamin until it was shown that only niacin prevents pellagra. Folic acid, biotin, and choline also belong to the B group but do not have numbers. The former vitamin F has been reclassified as an essential fatty acid (see FATS AND OILS). The letter G was once given to riboflavin, now B2.

One other vitamin has a letter: vitamin K, a substance required for the clotting of blood. The letter stands for the German word 'Koagulation'.

Vitamin P is a name sometimes given by health food enthusiasts to rutin, a substance found in citrus fruits. Orthodox scientists do not believe that it is necessary to health.

Vitamins may also be classified into two groups: fat soluble and water soluble. Fat soluble vitamins are found in fatty and oily foods. They are vitamins A and D, both found in liver, oily fish, and dairy products; vitamin E, in many vegetable foods, especially wheatgerm, and milk; and vitamin K, widely present in many vegetable foods. Because these vitamins are insoluble in water, they tend not to be lost in cooking. Water-soluble vitamins are the B group, found in yeast, wheatgerm, cereal products, meat, and fish; and C, found in fresh fruits, vegetables, and milk. These are easily lost in food preparation; vitamin C is particularly evanescent, being destroyed by exposure to light, heat, or air.

Two vitamins can be acquired from sources other than those described above. Vitamin A can be made in the body from carotenes, the common yellow plant pigments found in leafy vegetables (and, of course, carrots). Vitamin D is made in the skin when it is exposed to sunlight. (RH)

VOL-AU-VENT a French term, recorded in its present form in print from 1800. It means 'flying in the wind', denoting a very light shell of puff PASTRY, usually with but sometimes without a lid, enclosing a filling of commensurate delicacy. That, anyway, is the idea. In the wrong hands, what emerges is a tough pastry case full of sticky goo with a few fragments of mushroom or whatever embedded in it.

A vol-au-vent case is made from two layers of puff pastry, cut into a circle or oval with a fluted pastry cutter. A smaller cutter of the same shape is used to remove the centre of one piece. The outer ring of this piece is placed on the other piece so that when the pastry rises during baking it forms a case with a base and a wall; while the removed centre is baked separately to make a lid. A very small vol-au-vent is a BOUCHÉE (mouthful). The filling is always bound with a sauce, e.g. VELOUTÉ.

The *Larousse gastronomique* states that CARÊME invented the vol-au-vent and that the most famous version is *financière* (with QUENELLES of chicken or the like and mushrooms in a Madeira sauce).

WAFER as a culinary term, belongs to the same group as WAFFLE and the French *gaufre*. All these terms refer to foods which are baked in heated irons: that is, the raw mixture is sandwiched between two pieces of metal whose heat cooks it. The iron has an incised pattern which increases its surface area and improves the transfer of heat to the mixture, and also gives it a decorative form.

Ayto (1993) explains that wafers were introduced to Britain in the 13th century by the incoming Normans, and that the word was taken directly from the Anglo-Norman *wafre*. He notes that in those early days a layer of cheese could be inserted into the wafer, making something like a modern toasted cheese sandwich; and that the Elizabethan waferers who sold wafers in the streets 'had the reputation of being go-betweens in clandestine love affairs'. Against this background he judges modern wafers to be 'less exciting'. However, they have for a very long time been useful in a situation where a crisp base or accompaniment to sweet things is required, notably ICE CREAM.

Better known, perhaps, is the role of communion wafers in various Christian churches. And the region where wafers have been and are particularly liked is that of the Netherlands and Belgium.

WAFFLE a light BATTER cake cooked in a waffle-iron or other device to give it its characteristic honeycomb shape. The word comes from the Dutch *wafel*, and the Netherlands and Belgium continue to be the part of Europe where most waffles are eaten. However, they have become even more important in N. America. Mariani (1994) comments that:

> The item was known to the Pilgrims, who had spent time in Holland before sailing to America in 1620, and 'waffle parties' became popular in the latter part of the eighteenth century. Thomas Jefferson returned from France with a waffle iron, a long-handled patterned griddle that encloses the batter and gives it its characteristic crispness and shape. A century later vendors on city streets sold waffles hot and slathered with molasses or maple syrup.

The same author comments that after the 1964 World's Fair in the USA, 'Belgian waffles', thicker than the usual ones and made with yeast, have become extremely popular; and that in the south waffles may be made with rice or cornmeal and called 'Virginia waffles'.

Although waffles have much in common with WAFERS, they are quite a different proposition when it comes to consumption. Their thickness and deep honeycomb pattern gives them an ability to support lots of butter, MAPLE SYRUP, or whipped cream, or alternatively various savoury preparations such as the kidney stew on waffles said to have been a favourite dish at Baltimore.

WAHOO *Acanthocybium solandri*, one of the finest game fishes in the world. It has an extensive range in the Indo-Pacific and is also found in the Caribbean region. A fast-moving predator, usually found singly or in small groups in open water, it is nowhere common and has little commercial importance, although good to eat. Its maximum length is 2 m (80") and the record weight 63 kg (139 lb).

WAKAME *Undaria pinnatifida*, one of the brown SEAWEEDS, of considerable importance in Japan. The broad brown fronds are typically about 1 m (40") long and 36 cm (15") wide, with a thick mucilaginous centre rib and lobelike projections at the sides. Sold fresh in the spring, but always obtainable in semi-dried or dried form. The texture is delicate and the taste pleasing.

In terms of quantity consumed, wakame is the dominant seaweed in Japan; in recent times it has accounted for over half of Japanese consumption. It is used especially in soups, but must not be simmered for more than a minute, if its abundance of nutrients is to be preserved. It can also be incorporated in salads. The calorie content is said to be zero.

Another brown seaweed which can be used instead of or with wakame is sugara, *Scytosiphon lomentaria*, whose form is quite different—more like strings of exceedingly thin long sausages. It is said to have a very high iron content and to taste of beans. Only suitable for use after being dried. May be bought in sheet form.

WALES The enjoyment of food in Wales has always been constrained by circumstances and limited resources; but that does not mean that life was always hard. Though much of Wales is upland, its soil thin and acid and its climate wet, there is still some good soil to grow cereals; good grass to fatten sheep and cattle in the hillsides and valleys; and rivers, lakes, and coasts to provide a great variety of fish.

Early Celtic society was still semi-nomadic, and transhumance persisted in parts of Wales almost into the 18th century, with flocks being taken up to the *hafod* in summer and brought down to the *hendre* for the winter. Chiefs and kings took their courts on perpetual circuit, and each tenant or community they visited paid for the privilege by providing quantities of food according to a minutely detailed tariff. The system can be glimpsed in the legal codes of medieval Wales, all of them claiming to be versions of the customary law codified by Hywel Dda in the mid-10th century. Food renders were paid in beer, bread, meat (usually on the hoof), and honey; oats, cheese, and butter were sometimes demanded as well. In good times, these were what most people ate, with the addition of more perishable items such as fish and shellfish, and a few vegetables—Hywel Dda's Laws mention only leeks and cabbages.

Even when society became more settled, cooking techniques remained basic. A large cauldron or cooking pot set or suspended above an open fire was in general use. It was in this that cawl, one of the most typical of Welsh dishes and often a meal in itself, was boiled—and probably reheated and added to over a period of several days. In the same cauldron or pot would be made various kinds of POTTAGE based on a mixture of oatmeal and water. One of these, a refined version, became known in England as FLUMMERY, the closest the English could get to the Welsh word *llymru*.

Another essential piece of kitchen equipment was a flat, round bakestone that could be heated evenly. It was used for a range of flat barley and wheaten breads; with a large earthenware pot inverted over it, the stone became a pot oven, *ffwrn fach*, suitable for baking small loaves and cakes, one of which, *bara pyglyd* or pitchy bread, became popular in the Midlands of England as pikelets. Another bread, BARA BRITH, is at least as good as any other fruit loaf or tea bread (a genre in which Celtic bakers excel). The small, spicy 'Welsh cakes' (see GRIDDLE) presumably developed when spices became available in the 17th century. It is an easy mistake to think of Welsh culture as isolated; Wales's openness to foreign products and influences has been both its strength and its weakness, as may be seen in the rush of the Welsh upper classes to adopt English habits, fashions, and even names in the centuries after the conquest.

Nevertheless, PORRIDGE, soup, and bread remained the staples of Welsh life for centuries in every household, regardless of rank; in good times, these foods could be richly elaborated, and in bad times they could be reduced to whatever was available. Gerald of Wales (Giraldus Cambrensis—though he was only half Welsh) describes his people as hospitable and occasionally over-indulgent in meat and strong drink, but more usually frugal and well able to go without supper if they had to. 'The whole population lives almost entirely on oats and the produce of their herds, milk, cheese and butter,' he wrote in 1188. 'You must not expect a variety of dishes from a Welsh kitchen, and there are no highly-seasoned titbits to whet your appetite.' He did not mention the Welsh fondness for toasted cheese, which according to an old story was once used as a means of decoying surplus Welshmen outside the pearly gates when even Heaven became overcrowded with them. For the Welsh, cheese was a more immediate problem, as a good WELSH RABBIT (*caws pobi*) requires harder cheese than is made in Wales, and they had to barter their sheep for imported hard Cheddar.

However, apart from its mountain lambs, excellent fish, and soft, subtle cheeses, Wales had, and has, several gastronomic specialities. The best known are the COCKLES of the Glamorgan sands and laver (see NORI), edible seaweed that is gathered around the south and west coasts. Both are collected and prepared for market at the village of Penclawdd and sold on Swansea market stalls, where supply is hardly equal to demand. Laver 'bread' is the green pulp produced by boiling the seaweed for up to six hours; it is then usually mixed with oatmeal and fried in bacon or sausage fat.

The good old days in Wales, insofar as there were any, seem to have survived the Norman-English conquest of 1282–4. The major component of any noble old-fashioned feast, the singing of praise songs to the harp by the household bard, died out quickly, killed off by English disapproval; but the food tradition, which came from the people rather than the aristocracy, continued vigorously until the 17th or 18th centuries. Then the determination of landowners, many of whom were themselves Welsh, to enclose the land and replace men and women by sheep led to something very like the Highland Clearances in Scotland and impoverished many families who had hitherto lived quietly but well on their own fields. The Industrial Revolution and the development of the iron and steel industries continued the proletarianization of Welsh society. In the absence of written records of traditional Welsh recipes and foodways, the scene might have been set for their disappearance. Yet, as Bobby Freeman (1996) explains, all was not lost because:

the traditional dishes were passed orally from mother to daughter, and since the Welsh have good memories for the spoken word, it would be seldom necessary to write the recipes and methods down. Mati Thomas prefaces her collection of very old Welsh recipes, a prize-winning National *Eisteddfod* entry of 1928, with the declaration that she wishes to make a written record of the old dishes of the latter part of the 18th century from the memories of old people, while they were still alive to recall them for her.

This manuscript collection, is as far as I know, unique as a record of traditional Welsh recipes, old cooking methods and comment upon the frugal lifestyle of the small independent or tenant farmers who characterised the Welsh rural scene from medieval times to practically the present day.

One celebrated exception to the lack of printed records of Welsh food traditions appeared in 1867, the work of Lady Llanover, who was born English but was brought up in Wales and throughout her adult life was a passionate champion of Welsh culture. Her book, *The First Principles of Good Cookery*, is one of the most eccentric in the whole history of culinary literature, and one of the most engaging. Bobby Freeman provided an illuminating introduction to it when it was republished in 1991, drawing attention to the Welsh elements in it, especially the Welsh recipes in the lengthy recipe appendix; these include one for Salt Duck which acquired a vigorous new lease of life towards the end of the 20th century. By this time others were hard at work, sifting authentic Welsh traditions from the English ones with which

they had often become entangled and ensuring their survival.   (RO)
READING: S. Minwel Tibbott (1976, 1991).

WALNUT one of the finest nuts of temperate regions. There are a dozen species of walnut tree with edible nuts, in a family which also includes the PECAN and other trees which bear HICKORY NUTS. The most important species is the Persian walnut, *Juglans regia*; sometimes called 'English walnut' in the USA. This large and beautiful tree is found wild over a broad area from SE Europe through temperate Asia, most of the way to China.

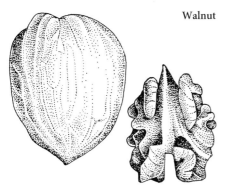

Walnut

The fruit is a green DRUPE, with flesh surrounding a hard-shelled stone or nut. Inside the nut is the edible kernel.

When the fruit is very young and green, the fleshy outside part can be eaten. (At this time the shell is undeveloped, so the entire fruit is edible, although sour in taste.) But as the fruit ripens the fleshy part becomes thin and leathery.

The shell consists of halves separated by a papery membrane, the division marked by a clear seam around the outside edge. This membrane is bitter and has to be removed when the nut is opened. The half-kernels within are convoluted like brains, and their shape has fascinated artists from early times. Indeed, the name for walnut in Afghanistan, *charmarghz*, means 'four brains'.

Wild walnuts have been gathered and eaten since prehistoric times. The practice of pressing oil from them is also of great antiquity, as is the use of walnut juice as a dark brown dye. The earliest mention of walnut cultivation comes from ancient Greece. The wild native varieties there bore small and dry nuts, which were not used for oil. But when a superior cultivated variety was imported from Persia, this yielded oil as well as being better to eat. The Greeks called it *karyon basilikon* or *persikon* (royal or Persian walnut).

The Romans were prepared to pay a high price for good walnuts. There was a tradition of throwing walnuts at weddings; and couples must have wished that something

lighter could have been chosen as a symbol of fertility. The Latin name for the walnut, which has become its botanical one, *juglans*, means 'Jupiter's acorn'. (Acorns were a traditional Roman food of longer standing.)

In Europe the walnut has been of particular importance in France. In so far as the French have an equivalent to the term 'nut', it is *noix*, but that word usually indicates the walnut. The walnut was not taken from France to Britain, where climatic conditions make its cultivation difficult, until the 15th century. Its English name may be derived from the old term 'welsh', meaning 'foreign' or 'from Gaul'. Recipes for pickling walnuts, green and black, abound in English cookery books of the 17th and 18th centuries, so it must have been grown extensively despite the difficulties.

The Persian walnut had reached China before AD 400. Cultivation became important in Sichuan province, and varieties with extremely thin shells ('papershells') were bred.

Early settlers in New England took the walnut to America. Although several good native species were already there, the Persian nut achieved and retains dominance. At present the largest producer is the USA, especially California, where cultivation is concentrated in an area east of San Francisco. Other large producers are Turkey, China, Russia, Greece, Italy, and France.

France, where walnut cultivation takes place mainly in the south-west, is the country where most attention is paid to named varieties. Corne and Marbot, and the group known collectively as Grenobles, are prominent. Noix noisette is a small variety,

no bigger than a hazelnut. Noix Cerneau rouge has a red kernel skin. Noix Coque tendre is outstandingly thin shelled.

The walnut-growing areas of Italy are concentrated round Naples, Salerno, and Sorrento. The soft-shelled variety Sorrento is dominant.

Walnuts may be picked at various stages of development, depending on how they are to be used. In large plantations the fruits are usually shaken off the tree by a large and violent device attached to a tractor.

Green walnuts are, as already mentioned, edible whole, but are extremely sour. They are made into pickles, ketchups, marmalade, and jam. There are both European and Asian preparations of these kinds.

Half-ripe walnuts, in which the nut is sufficiently developed to be extracted from the now inedible outside, are preserved in syrup in the Middle East: delicious.

Ripe walnuts are available in the shell, but most are shelled, producing either half-kernels or broken pieces (cheaper, but just as good for cooking). Walnuts in the shell, which are usually bleached to improve their appearance, can be stored for several months.

Ripe walnuts are mostly eaten as dessert nuts or used in cakes, desserts, and confectionery of all kinds, from ice cream to BAKLAVA. But they also have many uses in savoury dishes: French walnut soup, and walnut sauces with horseradish or with garlic and oil; Italian dressings for pasta (walnuts are often added to the pine nuts in PESTO, and there are other, similar preparations); and E. European and Middle Eastern meat dishes, such as the Persian

OTHER WALNUT SPECIES

OF the American species of walnut, cultivated on a smaller scale, the most important is the **American black walnut,** *J. nigra*, often regarded as the national tree of the USA, although its native range is confined to the eastern half of the country. The nut has a thick, hard shell, blackish-brown in colour, difficult to crack without breaking up the kernel. The flavour is stronger than that of a Persian walnut, but pleasant; and stands up better to cooking than that of the Persian walnut.

The **butternut** or American white walnut, *J. cinerea*, also grows in the eastern states, and also has a troublesome hard shell. As its name suggests, it is light in colour and the juice does not stain. The kernel has a strong but good flavour, which some prefer to that of the Persian walnut, and is more oily. Indeed, when white settlers arrived they adopted the practice of American Indians and used it as a source of oil. The **California walnut,** *J. californica*, is native to that state.

S. American species include the **Ecuadorian black walnut** or nogal, *J. neotropica*, whose rich kernels provide a sweetmeat called *nogada de Ibarra*.

Native Chinese species include one northern species which can stand the cold well, the **Manchurian walnut,** *J. mandschurica*; and the **Cathay** (or mountain) **walnut,** *J. cathayensis*. This last is a good source of oil, and is also eaten roasted, with salt, and in various kinds of confectionery.

The **Japanese walnut,** *J. ailantifolia*, bearing smallish nuts of fine flavour, is now also cultivated in the USA, sometimes (in the variety *cordiformis*) called heartnut because of its shape.

FESENJAN, a rich stew of duck, chicken, game, or lamb with walnuts and pomegranate juice.

Walnut oil is a traditional salad and cooking oil of France, Switzerland, and N. Italy. It is less used than formerly because it has become very expensive. Ripe nuts, of varieties selected for their oiliness, are stored for two or three months before pressing, during which time their milky juice turns to a light, clean oil with a marked and characteristic flavour. Some think walnut oil the supreme salad oil, others dislike it. It does not keep well.

WAMPEE (or wampi), the Malay name for *Clausena lansium*, a Chinese fruit tree which is cultivated there, in SE Asia, and in the W. Indies. It bears clusters of small yellow-green fruits which resemble miniature limes. These contain an aromatic, mildly acid pulp which is pleasant to eat when the fruit is fully ripe. Jams are made of it.

WARD ARTEMAS (1848–1925), author of *The Grocer's Handbook* (1919), *The Grocer's Encyclopedia* (1911), and *The Encyclopedia of Food* (1923). The third work, an expanded and revised version of the second, was his major achievement. It runs to nearly 600 pages and contains a thousand or so entries, from abalone to zwieback. Ward's criterion for inclusion was 'whatever seemed to be of practical use', and he did not restrict himself to American foods, although the emphasis is on these. The book has appendices of food names in six languages and a glossary of culinary terms.

Ward wrote for the general reader, with the stated intention of combating ignorance about nutrition. 'No-one', he asserted, 'can feel content with the haphazard, untrained, uncalculated dietaries of the past.' Accordingly, he included an eight-page section on food values, advocating an informed and rational approach to diet.

The style of the book is agreeable, giving the impression of a serious but charming personality; and Ward took care to include in his entries enough well-chosen anecdotes and quotations to ensure that it would be thoroughly readable.

Ward was a prominent New York businessman and philanthropist. As president of Ward & Gow, an advertising firm, he is credited with pioneering modern methods of advertising. He was also chairman of the board of numerous companies with interests in chocolate, dairying, orchards, and soap. He wrote a biography of his ancestor General Artemas Ward, a Revolutionary War hero, and presented to the town of Shrewsbury,

Massachusetts, a library and museum of Ward memorabilia in his memory.

WAREHOU the New Zealand name for several species of fish in the family Centrolophidae. These have moderately deep bodies and bear a general resemblance to species of the carangid family (see JACK and TREVALLY). *Seriolella brama*, the common warehou, has a maximum length of 75 cm (30") and is found in Australian as well as New Zealand waters. The same applies to the silver warehou, *S. punctata*, and the white warehou, *S. caerulea*, which are of comparable size but inhabit deeper waters and are known also off the southern coasts of S. America. These are good food fishes.

A fourth warehou, *Hyperoglyphe antarctica*, is considerably larger (maximum length 140 cm/56") and presents a surprising feature; although it is not related to the HAPUKU, it is often fished with it and resembles it and is marketed under that name rather than its own, which is blue-nose warehou.

The species *Centrolophus niger* belongs to the same family. It is the rudderfish in New Zealand, but called blackfish in the N. Atlantic and Mediterranean, where it also occurs. It is edible but fails to arouse enthusiasm.

WARQA a paper-thin N. African pastry resembling a somewhat stiff FILO. It is made by tapping a lump of dough on a heated GRIDDLE and removing the thin layer that sticks (hence its Algerian name, *malsuqa*, 'that which sticks'). Warqa is used in THARID, many pastries (including the elaborate squab pie BESTILA) and *brik*, the flat, triangular fried version of the Turkish BÖREK characteristic of TUNISIA.   CP

WARTHOG *Phachochoerus aethiopicus*, well described by Burton (1962) as a 'hideously grotesque long-legged pig'. His description continues:

Skin slate- or clay-coloured, naked except for a few bristly hairs. Mane of long bristly hairs on head continued along mid-line of back. Head long, broad, with long blunt warts (excrescences strengthened with gristle: no obvious function). Muzzle broad with upward-curving tusks.

This animal may attain a length of 1.50 m (5'), so there is plenty of meat on an adult specimen. This may be cooked in any of the ways suitable for pork, but it does not taste like pork.

WASABI *Eutrema wasabi* (formerly *Wasabia japonica*), a perennial herb which is

not related to HORSERADISH but resembles it in flavour, and is often referred to as 'Japanese horseradish'. It is found elsewhere in E. Siberia, but belongs essentially to Japan, where it is used extensively, providing one of the most important flavourings in Japanese cookery.

The plants grow wild in or on the banks of mountain streams and are cultivated in flooded mountain terraces. This cultivation requires great care, since the water temperature has to remain a constant 11–14 °C (51–7 °F) throughout the year. Nagano, Shizuoka, and Shimane are the main growing districts in Japan. The plants take several years to reach maturity.

Wasabi

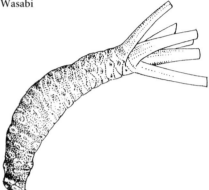

The Japanese name is said to mean 'mountain hollyhock'. The roots are sold in Japanese grocery stores in pans of water. Peeled and trimmed, they are grated into a fine paste, pale green in colour. This is used especially with SUSHI and SASHIMI (raw fish) and in soups, to which it adds considerable pungency.

A wasabi pickle is also made; the leaves, flowers, stalks, and rhizomes are chopped, brined, and then preserved in SAKÉ lees and (subsequently, before use) mixed with MIRIN and sugar.

Fresh wasabi can rarely be obtained outside Japan. Tins of wasabi powder (to be prepared like mustard powder) or tubes of wasabi paste may be used instead.

WASHINGTON CLAMS of the genus *Saxidomus*, are esteemed as food on the Pacific coast of N. America. They are large BIVALVES with thick shells, which bear numerous and finely spaced concentric lines but no radial ones. The northern form, *S. giganteus*, has a range from Alaska down to San Francisco. It may measure 11 cm (just over 4"). Its specific name seems to have been chosen without adequate reflection, since the other species, *S. nuttalli*, is much larger: up to 17 cm (nearly 7"). This is a purely Californian species, with a range from Humboldt Bay to San Quintin Bay in Baja

WATER
835

California, and may be distinguished from its smaller relation by purple markings on the inside of the shells. The fishery for it is extensive. The two species are marketed together and share the same common names, which include butter clam and money clam as well as Washington clam.

Weymouth (1920) explains these common names thus:

The name 'Washington clam' is also applied to the gaper, but its local use for *Saxidomus* is said to have come from its resemblance to *Venus mercenaria* of the Atlantic coast, as noted by Indian chiefs at the time certain of them were in Washington, D.C. conferring with government officials. The name 'money shell' came from the use of *Saxidomus* shells of pearly appearance and unusual thickness as money by the Indians of Bodega and Tomales bays.

The name butter clam simply indicates melt-in-the-mouth quality, and is applied in other parts of the world to bivalves which are thought to make especially tender eating. It is the preferred common name in Alaska and in British Columbia.

WASHING UP (or 'doing the dishes', 'faire la vaisselle', and so on) has in most cultures been seen as an activity which is not an intrinsic part of preparing, cooking, and consuming food. Nor has it been highly regarded, although the truth is that it is a skilled business calling for a natural aptitude, a discriminating attitude to the various means available, and considerable practice. However, the idea that it is somehow separate from the meal is the greater and more pervasive error. And it is not infrequently viewed, e.g. by Mr and Mrs Eugene Christian, as an intrinsically revolting operation; see RAW FOOD.

A better way of regarding it is as the climax of the whole cycle (gathering, preparation, cooking, eating) and as a piece of ritual which should have engaged the attention of anthropologists and the like to a much greater extent than the questions which have tended to preoccupy them, such as whether food is boiled or roasted. The purification of the utensils has to be the final, culminating stage of any meal, the stage which in effect sets the scene for the next meal and permits life's processes to continue.

It follows from this that the choice of person to do the washing up is no light matter, and that the person or persons chosen should be viewed as having a privilege. Whether they use traditional techniques or harness modern machinery to help them is immaterial; the responsibility has been given to them, and the honour of praise for a job well done awaits them.

The sight of a washer-up standing, dominant, at the sink while the other

celebrants of the meal, typically, loll in chairs recalls irresistibly the similar scenes enacted so often in places of worship—the priest standing before the altar, the congregation seated, the timeless ritual unfolding for the thousandth time but charged with as much significance as on the first. As the utensils begin to emerge in pristine purity, as the dancing mop-head and caressing linen cancel out any recollections of the grosser aspects of appetite and eating, even the proudest shoppers and cooks, exalted by witnessing the true climax of the meal, must acknowledge the precedence of these acts of completion.

WASP an insect which is normally thought of as something which stings human beings rather than providing nourishment for them. However, wasps' nests have been raided for food by Aborigines in Australia. A bundle of flaming grass would be held under the nest long enough to drive away the adult wasps, and the white larvae would then be picked out and eaten raw.

Another example may be taken from Japan. As Bodenheimer (1951) relates with relish, basing himself on first-hand information from a Japanese zoologist, Professor Tetsuo Inukai, the people of Nagano (an inland province, where fish is difficult to obtain) prized the pupae of wasps, especially those of the genus *Vespula*, and had devised ways of securing these without risk of being stung.

WATER after oxygen, is the principal requirement of the human body; this consists mainly of water, and water has a function in all its tissues and all chemical actions within it. The amount of water required by an individual in a day depends on many variables (size, level of activity, ambient temperature), but is generally more than one would suppose.

Most people think of their water intake as coming in the form of water itself or other liquids which, just because they are liquids, are recognized as being mostly water. However, the amount of water which people obtain from the 'solid foods' which they eat is again much greater than they would suppose. A water melon is 93% water, even bananas rate 76%, potatoes 80%, most other vegetables over 90%, eggs 75%, fresh meat/poultry/seafood 60–80%, and bakery products 25–45%.

Even in the very distant past people have valued purity in the water they drink or use for food preparation. There are many references in classical antiquity to particularly pure springs. However, it is clear that then, as now, not much can be done to control the purity of the water content of

naturally occurring foodstuffs such as, say, a peach, a sardine, a potato, or a glass of cow's milk.

In many parts of the world water is still what people obtain from a well or spring, and here there may be an element of choice (if there is more than one well or spring within reach). In the much more extensive parts of the inhabited world where water comes out of a tap, there is less or no choice. Here, if people want a different water, they move.

Overlaid on this general picture is the pattern of special commercially available drinking water. This pattern is becoming global. The survey by Maureen and Timothy Green (1985) of the world's best bottled waters, although in the nature of things it could not be comprehensive, included waters in 25 countries and three continents. It gives clear explanations of what is meant by terms such as mineral water and spring water, and throws incidental light on many interesting subjects such as national attitudes to water, here exemplified by a passage about China:

The Chinese have a traditional respect for the virtues of good water. Indeed, in Cantonese slang the same character stands for both 'money' and 'water' (rather as 'bread' means money in American slang). Early Chinese writings abound with praise of water. The writer Wang Chia of the Chin dynasty noted that 'The bubbling foundation of Pon Lai gives a thousand lives to those who drink it', while Prime Minister Chang Kun, describing a new spring to the Emperor of the Tang dynasty, observed, 'Chronic ailments of all kinds are cured in no time just by a draught of that water.'

Concern over the quality of bottled waters used to focus on their mineral content, and the consequent health-promoting or curative properties which particular waters, especially spa waters, were thought to have. Now, concern is rather for purity and flavour. And the signs are that, gradually, use of bottled waters will spread from direct consumption (where it is already used extensively in much of the world), to use in making tea and coffee etc. (a use already established to some extent), to use in the kitchen. (If this progression were to be carried to its logical extreme, one could envisage special water being supplied for all growing food crops and for domesticated animals used for food.)

The use of specially treated or selected water in the kitchen is foreshadowed by practices in the food-processing industry, where it can be important not only for water to be free of gross impurities but also to have either more or less alkalinity for various different purposes.

READING: Franks (1984, for the physics and chemistry); Dorothy Hartley (1964, for the history in England).

WATER BISCUITS thin, hard biscuits with a flaky texture and golden-brown bubbles all over the surface. They are made from soft wheat flour and water, with minimal amounts of other ingredients, and baked in a very hot oven to give a rapid rise. Those from Orkney have a high reputation.

Water biscuits are 20th-century British descendants of the very plain SHIP's BISCUITS and the very slightly enriched Victorian 'captain's biscuit'. Originally such plain biscuits were used in place of fresh bread when it was unobtainable; now they are popular with cheese.   LM

WATER-BUFFALO *Bubalus bubalis*, one of the most important animals of Asia, makes a contribution to food supplies both directly, when its milk is used or it is eaten as meat, and indirectly because of its role as a draught animal in agriculture. Its world population in the 1980s was estimated to be over 130 million.

There are two general types, the swamp buffalo and the river buffalo. The former is found from the Philippines to as far west as India and is primarily a work animal; it is also used for meat but almost never for milk. The river buffaloes are found further west from India to Egypt and the Balkans, even to Italy. They supply well over half of India's milk and their butterfat is the major source of GHEE.

The meat of the water-buffalo—at least of animals bred for the purpose—is fully comparable with beef. In one respect it is superior; the water-buffalo has a more efficient digestive system than cattle and can extract nourishment from coarser forage, so is a better 'converter' of vegetable matter into animal protein.

Water-buffalo milk has a higher content of both butterfat and non-fat solids than cow's, and is often in greater demand and more expensive for that reason. Whereas 8 kg (17 lb) of cow's milk is normally needed to produce 1 kg (2 lb) of cheese, 5 kg of water-buffalo milk would be sufficient. Its milk (which lacks the yellow pigment carotene which is in cow's milk) produces pure white soft cheeses, of which MOZZARELLA cheese is the best known—but there are many others in the Balkans and the Near East; and is the preferred milk for making KAYMAK.

The whole subject of water-buffaloes, their distribution and use in the various countries where they are to be found, and the possibility of increasing the already substantial debt of human kind to these animals has been particularly well explored by the Food and Agriculture Organization (FAO) of the United Nations, in publications which include several by the world authority W. Ross Cockrill.

WATER BUGS also known as water boatmen, insects of the family Corixidae, used as food by the Aztecs (see AZTEC FOOD).

The bugs themselves were collected in nets, ground, formed into balls, wrapped in maize husks, and cooked. The name for this food was *axayacatl*.

The bug eggs were called *ahuautli*, meaning 'water amaranth', probably because of their granular texture. They were collected on loosely twined ropes flung into the lake. They could be made into TORTILLAS or TAMALES or, again, wrapped in maize husks to be toasted. They were said to taste like fish, or caviar.

These foods have continued to be eaten. A characteristically thorough disquisition by Emerson (1908) begins with this quotation from 'that festive monk, Thomas Gage, who visited Mexico in 1625':

The Indians gathered much of this and kept it in Heaps, and made thereof Cakes, *like unto brickbats* . . . and they did eat this Meal with as good a Stomach as we eat Cheese; yea, and they hold opinion that this Scum or Fatness of the water is the cause that such great numbers of Fowls cometh to the Lake, which in the winter season is infinite.

Emerson goes on to say that the cakes of *axayacatl* were still being sold in the markets in the 20th century; and that the black heaps of *ahuautli* could still be seen dotting the mud flats, and, when made into a paste with birds' eggs, were a staple food in Lent.

Given the recent vogue in Mexico for reviving the eating of GRASSHOPPERS and other insects (see INSECTS AS FOOD), it seems likely that consumption of *ahuautli* will continue.   SC

WATER CHESTNUT a name applied to three water plants of the genus *Trapa*, whose strangely shaped fruits each enclose a large

white kernel bearing some resemblance to CHESTNUTS.

The water chestnut best known in Europe is *Trapa natans*, often called caltrop or Jesuit's nut. A caltrop, for which the Latin word is *trapa*, is a military device consisting of four metal spikes arranged so that, whichever way it falls, at least one spike points upwards. Caltrops were scattered in the path of charging cavalry to cripple the horses, and have been used more recently to burst car tyres. This water chestnut has a seed whose capsule bears four large spikes, one pair larger than the other. The kernel, of about the same size as an ordinary chestnut, has been eaten since prehistoric times in Europe; and in the 1st century AD Pliny described it as a staple food of the Thracians, who made it into bread. It remains in use in the regional cookery of Italy and France, e.g. in the Loire region.

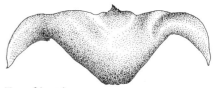

Trapa bicornis

The plant also grows in Asia and in Africa, especially on the shores of the lakes in Uganda, and has been introduced to N. America. The nut has a floury, chestnut-like texture and a flavour described by Sturtevant (1919) as being between those of chestnuts and of mild cheese. It is usually eaten boiled or roasted, since it is thought to be slightly toxic when raw.

In China, Korea, and Japan there is a different species (not to be confused with CHINESE WATER CHESTNUT, which is not a nut but a CORM). This is *T. bicornis*, sometimes called bull's head in English because of the two large, curved horns on

Water-buffalo

the capsule. It is about 7 cm (2") broad from tip to tip, and the Chinese name, *ling kok*, means 'spiritual horn'. This nut, which is very starchy and resembles the potato in several respects, has been an important food in China since antiquity. It has to be thoroughly cooked (usually boiled) and may be eaten as a vegetable, candied, or made into a pickle. It is traditionally eaten during the mid-autumn Moon Festival.

The singhara nut, *T. bispinosa*, is an important food in Kashmir. The name is Bengali. The plant is cultivated in fenced off sections of lakes. It also grows over a wide area from Africa to Japan, and is cultivated along the banks of the Nile, Zambezi, and Niger; not that much cultivation is necessary, since it grows freely and can be a bothersome weed. The nut is occasionally eaten raw, but is usually cooked—boiled or roasted. In Kashmir it is made into a kind of porridge, or dried and ground to flour.

WATERCRESS *Rorippa nasturtium-aquaticum* (syn *Nasturtium officinale*), a useful perennial plant with a long season, which in some regions extends right through the year. (The garden flower nasturtium belongs to a different genus, *Tropaeolum*.)

Nasturtium is Latin for 'nose twister', referring to the plant's pungency. Watercress shares membership of the crucifer plant family with MUSTARD, and both plants owe their pungency to substances of the same kind.

Watercress grows wild in Europe and Asia, and also in America since its introduction by European immigrants. Wild watercresses have been continuously popular since ancient times, not only for their pleasantly biting taste, but also for a wide variety of supposed health-giving properties. Thus the Greek general Xenophon made his soldiers eat it as a tonic. The Romans and Anglo-Saxons both ate it to avert baldness. Gerard (1633) recommended watercress as a remedy for that now forgotten disease, 'greensickness of maidens'. Francis Bacon advised that it would restore youth to ageing women; and so on. In fact watercress does contain useful amounts of vitamins A and C, together with iron and other minerals, but no one has identified any mysterious curative substances in it.

Irish belief in the virtues of watercress (*biolair*) is especially strong. Theodora FitzGibbon (1983) points out that it is often mentioned in early manuscripts and books, for example as a 'pure food for sages', the holy men who customarily lived like hermits and might eat little but dry bread and watercress. Growing wild in the pure and unpolluted waters of W. Ireland, the watercress is of exceptional quality. It is also cultivated, probably since long ago.

However, cultivation of the plant is commonly said to have begun at Erfurt in Germany, in the mid-16th century. It was not practised in England and the USA until the beginning of the 19th century.

Cultivars, whose appearance varies considerably, include hybrids, and a winter variety with attractively bronze-tinged leaves.

Watercress is usually eaten raw as a salad vegetable. The Romans ate it thus, dressed with pepper, cumin, MASTIC leaves, and GARUM. It can also be cooked, though this destroys its pleasant sharpness, and it makes a good soup; the French *Potage cressonière* is made from watercress and potatoes. Watercress is also much used as a garnish, especially for game.

In China, where it has a name meaning 'western water vegetable', watercress is commonly used in soup but is not eaten raw. Because both thrive in shallow water, it competes for space with rice in some areas.

Various other plants which are sometimes referred to as watercress or mixed with it or treated in the same ways include brooklime, *Veronica beccabunga*.

WATER DROPWORT *Oenanthe javanica* (formerly *stolonifera*), a water plant of the umbelliferous family, whose shoots, leaves, and roots are all eaten in the Orient and SE Asia as an adjunct to rice or an addition to soups and vegetable dishes. Their flavour tends to be too strong to permit eating them on their own. Hawkes (1968) remarks that in Hawaii it is common to find bunches of the pretty green leaves, often with roots attached, in the markets.

Hawkes also draws attention to the related *O. sarmentosa* of N. America whose small black-skinned tubers provided a delicacy for American Indians.

Water dropwort has its greatest importance in Japan, where it is called *seri*. Yashiroda *et al.* (1968) write:

Should you chance to be on the outskirts of Matsue, in western Japan, in winter—particularly before New Year's Eve—you would see many little flat-bottomed boats moving about in the shallow waters of seri plantations. The picking and cutting of seri shoots for shipment to Osaka, Kyoto and many other cities is an annual winter rite in Japan.

There is an ancient custom in Japan of eating *Nanakusa-gayu* (literally 'seven grass rice gruel') on 7 January. This is soft boiled rice to which seven, mostly wild, plants are added. The seven grasses (or herbs) are: *seri* (water dropwort), *nazuna* (shepherd's purse), *gogyo*, *hakobera*, *hotokenoza*, *suzuna* (young Japanese turnip), and *suzushiro* (young daikon—see RADISH). The custom is said to have started in the reign of Emperor Daigo, in the early 10th century. Since then, the last two on the list have attained the full status of vegetables, but the others are

regarded as essentially wild plants, though *seri* itself is commonly eaten and cultivated.

WATER HAWTHORN a name given to herbaceous water plants of the genus *Aponogeton*, whose flowers have a slight hawthorn scent. They belong to southern Africa but have only become semi-naturalized in parts of France and Italy (Aponus is the name of a warm-water spring near Padua).

The roots of *A. cordatus* are eaten in the Malagasy Republic; and the flowering spikes and leaves of *A. distachyos* are consumed locally in parts of S. Africa, with enthusiasm; indeed, it is the best-known and most highly prized wild plant of the Cape region. Leipoldt (1976) writes of its

beautiful white, strongly-scented flowers studding the surface of quiet wayside pools . . . It has a thick fleshy bulb which is edible, but is rarely used, the flower buds being much preferred. Bundles of these can still be bought on the Cape Town Parade and sometimes in the streets from itinerant hawkers, four bunches making a *kooksel*, or sufficient for an average dish. The flowers must be fresh, partly-opened, with the calyces bright green.

The same author explains that when the stalks have been removed the washed buds can be stewed gently with some added flavourings, including wild sorrel; or can be used with mutton in a *bredie* (see BRÈDES).

WATER HYACINTH *Eichhornia crassipes*, an aquatic plant of Brazilian origin, with beautiful blue flowers. It spreads rapidly and can form dense mats of vegetation in still or sluggishly flowing waters; in fact it is a menace to the health of the rivers, canals, and lakes which it invades.

American Indians used its young leaves, stalks, and flower buds as food, but their example has not been widely followed. In Malaysia, Burkill (1965–6) suggests that the plant is handicapped by the name *bunga jamban*, which refers to its luxuriant growth in the vicinity of latrines. Ochse (1981) observes that it is eaten in Java but that its tendency to cause itching when eaten raw is not entirely dispelled by cooking; and it seems that Indonesians would anyway prefer other herbaceous waterplants, such as *Monochoria* spp, which are free of problems. However, the buds of the water hyacinth are appreciated in parts of the Philippines, as Gilda Cordero-Fernando (1976) explains:

In May and June, the fresh waters of Pakil bloom with purple water hyacinths and the boatmen row to collect the buds (called *beno*) in them. Baptized 'sea peanuts' by tourists, inside the tough green peel, *beno* is white, and looks like a shelled peanut. Always eaten with salt, *beno*, when young, is soft and fresh-tasting, though some prefer it mature and mealy.

WATER ICES seem to have come into being, in Europe, at about the same time in the second half of the 17th century as ICE CREAM. The same technique is used for both products; see ICE.

It has been suggested that ices (whether water ices or ice cream) were made much earlier in China. This seems not impossible, and would be difficult to disprove. However, the further idea that they were introduced to Europe by Marco Polo, returning to Venice from China in the 13th century, is unsupported and is best counted as a piece of CULINARY MYTHOLOGY.

As for precedence in Europe, if the enquiries recorded by Caroline Liddell and Robin Weir (1993) and Elizabeth David (1994) may be assumed to have carried research as far as possible, no one can say whether true water ices were first prepared in Italy or France or Spain. Whatever the point of origin, their use spread quickly between the more sophisticated cities of Europe, although there is no sure evidence of when they first crossed the Channel to London.

A succinct description of water ices, with an important point about making them, was given in *Cassell's Dictionary of Cookery* (edn of c.1890): 'Water ices are made of the juices of ripe fruits mixed with syrup and frozen; and it must be remembered that if the juices are sweetened excessively they will not freeze.' Additional flavourings or a little liqueur may be added.

Water ices may be served as a stand-alone refreshment, as a dessert, or as a means of refreshing the palate about halfway through a meal of many courses. In the last case especially, they are apt to figure on a menu, even if it is in English, as 'sorbet', the French name. It and several more names in other languages, e.g. Italian *sorbetto*, and Spanish *sorbete*, belong to the SHERBET group. Another Italian term, *granita*, refers to a water ice with a more granular texture than the standard kind.

WATERLEAF a N. American marsh plant, which makes a pleasant wild salad vegetable. The most important species, hairy waterleaf or 'woollen breeches', is *Hydrophyllum appendiculatum* and grows in the eastern and southern USA. Early white settlers, following the Indians' example, made use of it, and it is still gathered each spring in Kentucky.

Virginia waterleaf, John's cabbage, Indian salad, or Shawnee (or Shawanese) salad, *H. virginicum*, is similar. *H. occidentale* is a species of the western states, where it has been eaten as 'western-squaw lettuce'.

WATERMELON *Citrullus lanatus*, a fruit quite distinct from the ordinary sweet

melons and with a longer history of cultivation. It is a native of Africa, where there were originally two species: the watermelon itself and the very bitter colocynth, which is inedible without being processed but has some food uses as well as some in traditional medicine.

Watermelons were eaten and cultivated in Egypt well before 2000 BC. Surviving wall-paintings clearly show the large green fruits. These are highly refreshing, and especially useful as a source of potable liquid where water supplies are polluted. This advantage encouraged its spread to lands around the Mediterranean and as far east as India and, eventually (10th to 12th centuries AD), China.

However, although the watermelon was in common use in nearby Egypt, the Greeks and Romans do not seem to have known it until well into the Christian era. It probably came to wider notice in Europe after the fall of the Roman Empire, through the Moorish invasion of Spain. The fruits can be grown in the hotter parts of S. Europe, but have never been as important there as ordinary melons.

In America it was another matter. The watermelon was taken there direct from Africa by slave traders, reaching Brazil by 1613 and Massachusetts shortly afterwards. American Indians, as well as the white settlers, took to growing it. Improved varieties were bred mainly in the New World. The tendency for bitter fruits to appear was eliminated, and very large ones, already known in Europe in the 16th century, were reliably produced. By 1822 there were reports of watermelons weighing 9 kg (20 lb); but nowadays 25 kg (55 lb) is common and 45 kg (99 lb) is reached in the larger varieties.

Numerous cultivars now exist, of various shapes, colours, and sizes. Small ones are generally round, one of the best known being Sugar Baby, a dark green, early variety. 'Baby' is a comparative term, for the fruits average 3–4 kg (7–9 lb) in weight: while wild watermelons may be only the size of an orange. 'Sugar' and 'sweet', names which are wished onto many varieties, are also ex-aggerations: no watermelon has more than a faintly sweet, insipid but refreshing flavour.

One of the largest and most common is Charleston Gray, an elongated fruit with a pale green, marbled skin. Striped varieties are also widespread. Most have pink or red flesh, although there are also yellow-fleshed kinds, e.g. Yellow Baby. The colour of the flesh is significant in some contexts. Julie Sahni (1980), writing of the Brahmans and Jains in India, says: 'Certain strict vegetarians won't eat food that resembles meat, such as tomatoes, red beets, and watermelon, because of their fleshlike colour.'

Special types are also grown. The 'citron' or 'preserving' watermelon, *C. lanatus*,

Citroides group, is grown for pickling. Only the harder flesh next to the rind is usually pickled. The **tinda,** a small variety grown in India, now classified as *Praecitrullus fistulosus*, is used as a cooking vegetable in the same way as any other GOURD.

Watermelon seeds are oily and edible. The Chinese are particularly fond of eating them, preferring black seeds. The outer coating of the seed needs to be removed, which can be done by rubbing or light scorching. In Africa the seeds of certain kinds of watermelon, known in Nigeria and elsewhere as **egusi,** are processed in various ways, including cooking in salt/fermenting/roasting/grinding; they often finish up in an egusi soup.

WATER SPINACH *Ipomoea aquatica*, also known as swamp cabbage and kang kong, a plant which grows in water and is a common vegetable in Asia. It enjoys especial popularity in the south of China and SE Asia.

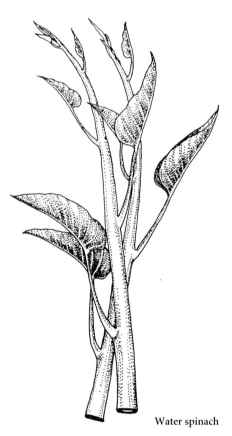

Water spinach

Despite its English names, this vegetable, which belongs to the family Convolvulaceae, is related neither to spinach nor to cabbage, although it can be used like the former for some purposes. When cooked, it offers an agreeable contrast: crisp stems and limp leaves. In Cantonese cuisine it is always stir fried, with garlic and fermented bean curd or shrimp sauce. Elsewhere, for example in the

Philippines, it is prepared in a greater variety of ways. There is a Filipino saying: 'Walang talong? mahal ang gabi? kangkong na lang!' (No eggplants available? Taro too expensive? Let's use swamp cabbage!) Sri Owen (1986a), who recommends serving it with a spicy sauce, remarks that in Indonesia it has been regarded as a lowly vegetable, unsuitable for pretentious purposes and very cheap, although its flavour and nutritional qualities are excellent. It provides a generous measure of protein and, because it grows in water, has a relatively high content of minerals such as iron.

Several varieties are cultivated. *Seu ong choi* has relatively thick stems and light green leaves. *Gon ong choi* has thinner stems and more numerous, narrower, medium green leaves.

WATERZOOI a Flemish dish of freshwater fish or chicken with vegetables, simmered in plenty of liquid, including white wine. Prepared with care, this is a delicate dish of great visual attraction, but also substantial. It is sometimes described as being in the 'soup-stew' category, and is certainly best served in deep bowls.

Waterzooi is particularly associated with E. Flanders and the city of Ghent. The unnamed but authoritative author of *Belgian Cuisine* (1981) says that the debate whether the first *Waterzooi à la gantoise* was made with fish or with meat is doomed to go on for ever, but that his impression is that most 'experts in gastronomy' believe it was fish. He also points out that there were plenty of freshwater fish in the rivers near Ghent in past centuries, but not now, so that it has become reasonable to use sea fish. He goes on to deplore the use of battery-bred chickens for the chicken version of waterzooi, stating that this important regional speciality can only be properly enjoyed if it is made with authentic free-range birds, as it used to be.

The broth element in waterzooi may be thickened with egg yolks to make a pale creamy soup; this is done for the chicken version rather than the fish one.

WAX CAPS a group of mushrooms whose gills turn into a waxy mass when ripe. Some have waxy or slimy caps.

Classification of the group is a problem; some authorities assign all these mushrooms to the genus *Hygrophorus*, while recognizing three 'groups' (*Camarophyllus*, *Limacium*, and *Hygrocybe*, established long ago by Vries) within the genus; others prefer to have two genera, *Hygrophorus* and *Hygrocybe*; or three, or even four. The older way is followed here, but with the species organized into the 'groups'.

CAMAROPHYLLUS GROUP

The best-known edible wax cap is probably *Hygrophorus pratensis*, the meadow wax cap. Typical specimens have a light (yellow to tawny) cap (hence the vernacular American name, buff cap), which is dry, not waxy or slimy; a white stem; and white gills which are only moderately waxy.

H. niveus, the snowy wax cap, a pure white species as its names indicate, occurs in both Europe and N. America. It is considered by many authorities to be the best to eat in the genus, despite its relatively small size. McIlvaine (1902) recalled it with particular affection:

In the West Virginia mountains, along grass-grown road-sides, their purity and exquisite perfume attracted me in 1881. I have them and a few others to thank for seducing me into becoming a mycophagist.

LIMACIUM GROUP

Limacium means 'of snails' and refers to the slime on the caps of mushrooms in this important group.

A fine woodland mushroom which belongs to it is *H. marzuolus*, which has a thick foot and a cap of good size (up to 10 cm/4" across). It is sometimes called *charbonnier*, because the cap of an adult specimen is normally black (though parts shielded from contact with the air, for example by a wet and fallen leaf, remain white). It prefers high altitudes; arrives early in the year (hence the French name *hygrophore de Mars*), growing just after the snow has thawed or even in the snow, and is well known in the Jura, the French Alps, and Switzerland. Jaccottet (1973) remarks on the need for human collectors to be keen eyed if they are to discern it in the moss and fallen leaves where it hides, and alert if they are to anticipate squirrels. A friend of his, contemplating from behind a tree trunk four specimens which he had come across after a long search, was frustrated to see a squirrel come forward and bear off the biggest and best. He had to make do with the other three, and was further discomforted by a qualified rebuke from Jaccottet, who considered that they too rightly belonged to the squirrel.

H. poetarum has an attractive name and is highly esteemed by some. It is a mountain species, liking calcareous soil, sometimes associated with beech trees and sometimes 'under very old fig trees, where it attains a size of 20 cm [8"] across the cap, white touched with rose' (Patience Gray, 1986, who recommends grilling sections, then dressing them with olive oil and pounded garlic).

HYGROCYBE GROUP

The mushrooms in this group typically belong to meadows and have bright colours,

for example the scarlet which makes *H. puniceus* so noticeable.

McIlvaine (1902), with characteristic enthusiasm, quotes a Professor Peck as saying of *H. miniatus*, a small species which occurs in both Europe and N. America and is typically yellow-red, that it 'is scarcely surpassed by any mushrooms in tenderness of substance and agreeableness of flavour'; and makes a point of saying that he himself often ate *H. conica* (one of a couple of slightly suspect members of the group) with impunity and pleasure. But few people nowadays exploit these less familiar species.

CULINARY USES
In general, slow cooking is recommended for wax caps. Several kinds are found suitable for being preserved in olive oil (*sott'olio*) in Italy, or for use in certain soups.

WAX GOURD *Benincasa cerifera*, is sometimes known as white or ash gourd. It is often referred to in a Chinese context as a winter melon (but see MELON) or, in a variety which has little hairs on the surface, fuzzy melon.

The species is thought to have originated in Japan or Indonesia; it reached China at an early date. The shape of most varieties tends to oblong, and the colour of the skin is dark green, with white flesh inside. This is the largest vegetable to be found in oriental markets; it may weigh as much as 45 kg (100 lb) and have a diameter of 25 cm (10"). It is normally sold by the slice.

The wax gourd is popular throughout SE Asia as a summer vegetable, being in season then despite its appellation; and it is also eaten as a vegetable in Japan. Where curry-type dishes are made, pieces will often go into them.

It is a favourite vegetable for preserves and pickles, and may be called 'pickling melon'; but it is not to be confused with the variety of MELON which is grown for pickling.

WEDDING MEALS AND CAKES vary widely around the world. In medieval Europe some of the greatest FEASTS, and those which were recorded in detail, were wedding feasts extending over several days. That type of extended wedding feast still exists in some Asian countries, but western celebrations are now usually focused on a single meal (quaintly termed 'wedding breakfast' in England, no matter at what time of day, on the ground that the bride and bridegroom are breaking their fast for the first time as man and wife).

In Britain, the most prominent single food item associated with a wedding is the **wedding cake.** This has been the subject of an admirable book by Charsley (1992), who not only records its history (pinpointing such crucial changes as the introduction of cakes which were not only in tiers but had the tiers separated by pillars) but also discusses the customs associated with it and its symbolic significance. The main focus of the study is Britain, but there is a highly interesting chapter on forms of wedding cake which have evolved elsewhere, frequently from a British model, but with what are sometimes startling variations. Thus in Japan there are tiered white wedding cakes which are completely inedible and furnished with a slot at the back into which the bridal couple can insert the knife, the sole purpose of this structure being to enable photographs to be taken of 'cutting the cake'. Charsley offers fascinating reflections on how features of an institution like the wedding cake undergo change, often in the form of a slow 'drift', sometimes more suddenly (as when the 'plastic icing'—plastic in the sense of being suitable for modelling, not made of plastic—invented in Australia began to oust within a few decades the traditional but brittle royal icing), and occasionally producing the phenomenon of 'marooning' when one type keeps rigorously to its traditional form, unaffected by the drift which is changing the other types.

WEDGE SHELL wedge clam, or coquina are any of a large number of species of the genus *Donax*, small but edible marine BIVALVES. The hinged, double shell is wedge shaped and small, and the creatures are best used to make a clam broth. *Donax trunculus* is the main Mediterranean species, and has been extensively consumed in certain regions, for example around the mouth of the Nile. *D. californicus* is gathered, without great enthusiasm, on the Californian coast. Another Californian species, *D. gouldi*, is more popular and has been abundant in some years; its shell has a slightly different shape which earns it the name bean clam (cf the French name *haricot de mer* for *D. trunculus*).

WEED a term applied to unwanted and troublesome plants. The classic definition is 'a plant in the wrong place'. This was amended by Celia Thaxter (1894) to read: 'a plant which has an innate disposition to *get* into the wrong place.'

What is a weed to some people may be a prized edible to others. The point was emphasized by Patience Gray (1986) when she entitled a book on food and cookery in certain Mediterranean regions *Honey from a Weed*, echoing a verse by William Cowper. The DANDELION is one of very many examples.

WEEVER any fish of the family Trachinidae, which is represented only in the NE Atlantic and the Mediterranean. All weevers have venomous spines on their back and on the gill-covers. Since they have the habit of burying themselves in the sand, they can be a hazard to barefoot bathers. It is usual, and prudent, to have these spines cut off when the fish are bought.

Trachinus draco, the greater weever, has a maximum length of nearly 40 cm (15"). It is called 'greater' in contrast to *Echiichthys vipera*, the lesser weever (always less than 15 cm/6"), with which it shares an extensive range from Norway to the E. Mediterranean. The other two species, which are only found in the Mediterranean, may also be about 40 cm long; these are *Trachinus araneus*, the spotted weever, and *T. radiatus*, the streaked weever.

The firm flesh of weevers gives them a useful role in BOUILLABAISSE and other fish soups. But large specimens can be cooked in various ways, e.g. grilled or filleted and fried. They are eaten in some countries, such as Belgium, France, and most Mediterranean countries, but not in others, such as Britain. (The fact that a surprisingly large number of weever recipes occur in an English cookery book of the early 18th century is not, as might be thought, evidence that they used to be eaten in England; these recipes were lifted straight out of a French cookery book to 'pad out' the English work.)

A closely related Mediterranean fish, with similar characteristics and uses, is *Uranoscopus scaber*, the **stargazer**, so called because its eyes look upwards even more markedly than those of the weevers. It is said to be the fish with whose gall Tobit recovered his sight, although it seems improbable that a fish of this species should have leapt out of the River Tigris. It has an interesting range of common names, including: *bœuf* or *rat* in French; *miou* or *muou* in Provence; and *kurbag balığı* (frog-fish) in Turkish.

WELS *Silurus glanis*, the largest European CATFISH, inhabits fresh waters in C. and E. Europe and further east to the Aral Sea. It may also be found in brackish coastal waters of the Baltic and Black Seas. In E. Europe it is a valuable commercial fish, which may be 'farmed', as happens in Hungary.

The normal market size is about 1 m (40"), but the official maximum length is 3 m (10'), and the record (an old one) is 5 m (16'), with a weight of just over 300 kg (660 lb). On this basis it would run a close second to the giant catfish of the Mekong for the title of world's biggest freshwater fish.

The wels is good to eat, although unattractive in appearance.

WELSH RABBIT a savoury which is normally understood to consist essentially in a piece of toast with melted cheese on it. This description would, however, have seemed quite inadequate to Lady Llanover (1867), whose own account of the matter, given the engaging and eccentric manner in which she annexed to herself the whole subject of Welsh cookery, must be given priority:

Welsh toasted cheese and the melted cheese of England are as different in the mode of preparation as is the cheese itself; the one being only adapted to strong digestions, and the other being so easily digested that the Hermit frequently gave it to his invalid patients when they were recovering from illness. Cut a slice of the real Welsh cheese, made of sheep and cow's milk; toast a piece of bread less than a quarter of an inch thick, to be quite crisp, and spread it very thinly with fresh cold butter on one side (it must not be saturated with butter); then lay the toasted cheese upon the bread, and serve immediately on a very hot plate. The butter on the toast can of course be omitted if not liked, and it is more frequently eaten without butter.

However, even if one accepts Lady Llanover's prescription as the most authentic, there remain perplexing questions of etymology and history. One thing which is not in doubt is Welsh fondness for cheese treated in some such way. In the 14th century Andrew Boorde wrote of a commotion in Heaven, where 'a grete company of welchmen . . . trobelyd all the others'. He explains how St Peter solved the problem:

He went outside of heven gayts and cryd with a loude voyce, 'Cause Babe! Cause Babe' [this would now be written *caws pobi*], that is as moche as to say 'Rosty'd chese!' Which thynge the Welchmen herying ran out of heven a grete pace . . . And when St. Peter saw them all out he sodenly went into Heven and lokkyd the dore! and so aparyd all the Welchmen out!

The real problem is to find a plausible explanation for 'rabbit'. This difficulty has caused some authorities to declare that the term should really be 'rarebit', meaning a choice morsel. However, this does not work. The 'rabbit' version has been found in print as early as 1725, whereas 'welsh rarebit' was first recorded 60 years later. Ayto (1993) believes that rarebit, a term previously unknown, was invented 'to reinterpret the odd and inappropriate sounding rabbit as something more fitting to the dish'.

One piece of evidence of which the significance is difficult to discern is that Hannah Glasse (1747) gives four of these rabbit-cheese recipes: one for a Scotch-Rabbit, one for a Welch-Rabbit, and two for an English-Rabbit. The first of these four was the simplest (toasted bread, butter, toasted cheese), while the second allowed the possible use of mustard, the third called for a glass of red wine to be soaked up by the toast before the cheese was put on it, and the fourth was really quite complex requiring white wine as well as red wine and the use of a chafing dish.

Graham (1988) is one recent authority who should definitely be consulted about these mysteries, to which he devotes several pages. He remarks that:

The French have always prized the Welsh rabbit. To the best of my knowledge, the dish first appeared in a French cookbook in 1814, when Antoine Beauvilliers published a recipe for *wouelsche rabette* (*lapin gallois*) in his *L'Art du cuisinier*. But it really came into fashion when Anglomania was at its height around the turn of the century. In *L'Art des mets*, published in 1959, the French gourmet Francis Amunatégui remembers the atmosphere, decades earlier, at the then very British restaurant, The Criterion, opposite the Gare Saint-Lazare in Paris. Anglophiles flocked there specially to order Welsh rabbit (by that time spelt correctly but usually abbreviated to *le welsh*) and wash it down with English ale in pewter mugs.

Bobby Freeman (1986) has an authoritative description of the dish, in which she points out that many English counties in the southern and western parts of the country had 'rabbits' like the Welsh one, thus rightly broadening the scope of the 'why rabbit?' question so that it ceases to be purely Welsh. She too draws attention to French and indeed international interest, quoting the following introduction to a recipe given in *Cassell's Dictionary of Cookery* (1885):

Rare-bit, Welsh.—Brillat Savarin, the famous French Gourmet, gives the following recipe taken from the papers of M. Trollet, bailiff in Meudon, in the Canton of Berne: . . .

Those who believe that the term Welsh rabbit was originally derogatory, indicating a cheap substitute, must marvel to see the humble dish so treated by the most famous French gastronomic writer—although the recipe that he took such pains to acquire and pass on does not include bread in any form and offers no guidance on the choice of cheese, two remarkable defects.

WENSLEYDALE a hard-pressed, whole-milk English cheese which is available in two versions: an expensive and prized blue kind which some consider superior to STILTON; and an almost unmatured white variety which is produced and sold on a large scale.

Wensleydale is an ancient cheese. The name is that of a Yorkshire valley where formerly there were two Cistercian abbeys whose monks made the cheese. At this time sheep's milk was used. After the dissolution of the monasteries the cheese was made on farms and from cow's milk.

The process of making Wensleydale differs from the typical CHEDDAR process mainly in that the curd is repeatedly wrapped in a cloth, pressed lightly, removed, cut up, and replaced in the cloth before it is

salted and put into forms. During this time lactic acid-producing bacteria work busily, giving the cheese a pleasant sourness.

Blue Wensleydale is unusually firm in texture for a blue cheese. Traditionally the blue mould infection occurs naturally in the curing room. The maturing period is at least six months for the blue type but only two or three for the white. Both kinds are made in a tall drum shape ranging in weight from about 7 kg (15 lb) for the largest blue cheeses to as little as 500 g (1 lb) for the smallest white ones.

WEST AND CENTRAL AFRICA The main common factor among the foods of the culturally and linguistically different peoples of this vast region is that the starch content of meals, whether it is RICE in the west, MILLET or MAIZE in the north, or PLANTAIN, YAM, or CASSAVA in the south and the east, is considered to be 'real food', while sauces or stews are there to help it down.

The coastal countries of W. Africa, from north to south, are Senegal, the Gambia, Guinea Bissau, Guinea, Sierra Leone, Liberia, Ivory Coast, Ghana, Togo, Benin, Nigeria, Cameroon, Equatorial Guinea, Gabon. The inland countries are the Central African Republic, the Congo Republic, Congo (was Zaire).

The diet of rural people, the majority of the population, is simple. Most exist on starchy vegetables, beans, especially black-eyed peas (see COWPEA), and an astonishingly varied range of greens; more than 100 species of leaves, both cultivated and wild, are common fare. Meat, even 'bush meat' (game), is a luxury, although available in the markets, where numerous exotic items can be seen—including MONKEY, CANE RAT, BATS, and giant SNAILS (*Achatina fulica*), besides more conventional game such as antelope and wild pig. The abundant fish of both coast and rivers is often salted and dried (when it is known as stinkfish). It is quite common for meat and fish, fresh or dried, to be used together in the same stew such as in the dish *Futu* which usually has twice the amount of meat to dried fish.

A liking for mucilaginous textures in food is shown by the popularity of OKRA, BITTERLEAF, and MELOKHIA (locally known as *crain crain*), usually cooked with fermented locust beans (see CAROB).

Most peoples, especially those of the south, like their food liberally seasoned with salt and hot pepper—also coloured and flavoured with palm nut oil, which gives dishes a red colour from its carotene content and is an important source of vitamin A.

Chicken (although commonly rather tough in this part of the world) is the most popular of all flesh foods but GUINEA-FOWL,

geese, muscovy ducks (see DUCK), and rabbits are also raised.

Popular flavouring ingredients include thyme, dried BAOBAB leaves and fruit, 'African nutmeg' (*Monodora myristica*), GRAINS OF SELIM, ASHANTI PEPPER, turmeric, the species of BASIL called partminger, ginger, chilli, lemon grass, bitterleaf, dried okra, potash, egusi seed (see WATERMELON), coconut, groundnuts, locust beans (CAROB), and SESAME. Stock cubes, particularly Maggi, are widely used. Chilli pepper, known simply as red pepper, has mostly replaced the traditional MELEGUETA PEPPER.

Various staples—yams, coco-yams (TARO), or plantains and nowadays cassava, sweet potato, or maize flour—are made into FOO-FOO, a starchy paste which is almost ubiquitous in this region.

What is said above about staples may be taken as applying to more or less the whole region. Obviously, however, there are differences within the region. For example, the most westerly countries show the influence of the Maghreb; they have COUSCOUS (often made from millet rather than wheat, and flavoured with dried baobab leaves) as a staple besides rice, and in some places a legacy of French bread survives. A second example is provided by the more arid areas, where SORGHUM and millet are still eaten as staples.

Reverting to generalities, a distinctive African keynote is sounded by the use of groundnuts as a sauce for staples and in stews. Groundnut (peanut) stew is common everywhere. It may be based on beef, chicken, fresh or smoked fish, crab, or mixtures of ingredients, but seldom pork or lamb. Sweet potatoes, potatoes, beans, or eggplant may be used as a thickener. The constants are peanut butter or fresh ground and pounded peanuts, chillies, tomatoes, and herbs.

Groundnut stew may be served with rice, and the many possible accompaniments include hard-boiled eggs, sliced fruit, cucumber, onions, chutney, roast nuts, bell pepper, and raw onions. It is usually made on the 'brown the meat after the water evaporates' principle.

PALAVER SAUCE, based on large quantities of green leaves, is also widespread. So is *Fréjon*, a traditional Good Friday paste made from black-eyed peas (see COWPEA), coconut milk, and sometimes carob or chocolate, said to be a Brazilian dish brought to Africa in the 19th century. It is served hot with fresh fish and *gari* (cassava meal).

The national dish of **Senegal** is *Thieboudienne* or *Chep-bu-jen*, meaning fish and rice in the Wolof language, usually served with vegetables. Other prominent dishes are shared with other countries. *Yassa*, found throughout W. and C. Africa, is chicken or fish marinaded in lemon or lime juice, grilled on a barbecue, and then fried with onions and simmered with the marinade. This is usually served with rice. JOLLOF RICE is known all over W. Africa and in most parts of the world where Africans have settled.

Ghana is said to have one of W. Africa's best cuisines, although the most highly regarded cooks come from Togo. The staple in the south of Ghana is fermented maize balls, called *kenkey*, steamed in maize husks; in the north, *tozafi* (*tz* for short), a millet porridge, is more common. *Gali foto* in its simplest form is a breakfast dish made from cassava flour. It is better known in the version cooked with tomatoes, sweet peppers, eggs, and spices. The favourite version has a tin of salmon or corned beef added (or a topping of lobster or shrimp). A famous party dish is *Akotonshi*, made from stuffed land crabs and served with fried yam.

Ponkie is the general name for pumpkin. This is often stewed with other vegetables and minced meat and served with a boiled starch vegetable. *Tatali* are fried cakes of cornmeal and plantains, flavoured with hot peppers, usually served with *yoyo* sauce (sprat and pepper sauce).

In **Nigeria,** a vast country with the densest population of any in Africa, starch pastes are often made from sweet potatoes or maize. Soupy stews or stewlike soups are popular. Examples are egusi soup, often made with offal, palm oil, carob (called *ogiri* when fermented and often likened to yeast extract in taste), partminger, and egusi powder, and the various okra soups. Soup made from goat is so important that it is usually served at the most important functions. A dish usually credited to Nigeria is *Moin moin* (or *Moyin moyin*), made from a ground paste of black-eyed peas (see COWPEA), hot pepper, and onion. It may be flavoured or thickened with eggs, tomato, dried fish, ginger, egusi seed, or corned beef. It is steamed, wrapped in leaves or in moulds, and served with a starch dish or cut up and served as snacks. In the north of the country polished millet, *jero*, is served with *taushe*, a thick broth of meat, pumpkin, greens, red pepper, and peanuts.

The cooks of **Cameroon** are regarded as the best in C. Africa. Most of the region is covered by dense rain forest and the peoples mostly follow the pattern of relying on starchy roots in the south and grains in the more arid north for staple foods, though a 'bread' is made from mashed bananas and flour in much of the area. *Atchu* is made from taro, *bobolo* and *miondo* from cassava. On the whole the food is blander than that of W. Africa. *Ntomba nam* is a peanut sauce eaten with meat. Sauces of pounded leaves are common. *Ndole* is made from BITTERLEAF and *kwem* or *saka-saka* from

cassava leaves. Most food is liberally seasoned with palm oil. *Aloco* or *dop* is plantain cooked in palm oil with onions and chilli.

The **Congo** (Zaire) is the world's 12th largest country, mostly rain forest in the north and savannah in the south. The national dish is *Moambé*, a spicy peanut sauce with palm oil served with meat or chicken and rice. Another dish of note is *Soso*, rich chicken stew. Game meat such as monkey, antelope, and PORCUPINE is common as are freshwater fish from the Congo basin.

Small chop (snacks) and **street foods** are a way of life all over the area. The most popular are spiced kebabs called *chachanga* in Ghana, *tsire agashe* in Nigeria, *coupé-coupé* in C. Africa, and *soya* in Cameroon. In the west *chawarma* (cf QAWARMA) is much liked and is similar to doner KEBAB. *Akara* (Sierra Leone and Nigeria) or *koose* or *akla* (Ghana) are fried bean balls, eaten everywhere (and the ancestors of the Caribbean *akkra*, fritters made with black-eyed peas, not to be confused with *accra* which are salt fish cakes of Trinidad.) There are a number of sweet snacks on sale at market and roadside stalls; *puff-puff* are a sort of doughnut and *chin-chin* are crispy morsels of sweetened dough. Various coconut 'biscuits' are also on sale and sweetened porridges, though these are mostly eaten for breakfast.

Despite its interesting features, and despite the huge influence which it has had in the Americas, wherever the slave trade reached, the cookery of W. Africa has attracted little attention from Europeans, and little of it has so far been offered to the increasing number of tourists who visit the region. (JM)

WEST INDIES a geographical term which the *NSOED* neatly defines as the chain of islands between Florida and Trinidad, is not synonymous with the Caribbean, but the two terms are often used alike; W. Indies cookery and Caribbean cookery would not normally be taken to be two different subjects. Anyway, they are here treated as one—a big one which could easily be the basis of half a dozen or more entries but is better treated as a unity, because of the recurring patterns to be found within it and the common ingredients which do much to mark the cuisines of the various islands.

The indigenous peoples, Carib, Arawak, Taino, all but disappeared under the impact of Spanish conquest. Traces may be found of their foodways, but these are scant. Cristine MacKie (1991) has written about archaeological evidence of their eating a wide range of fish and seafood, as one would

expect, and has drawn on accounts by early travellers such as Enciso (whose *Brief Summary of Geographie*, 1519, was translated for the Hakluyt Society in 1932).

There are two big islands, Cuba and Hispaniola (now the Dominican Republic and Haiti), and three of medium size—Trinidad, Puerto Rico, and Jamaica. The number of smaller ones is very large. All of them have at one time or another been colonial territories, belonging to one of five colonial powers, British, Dutch, French, Spanish, and the USA, all of whom have left their mark on foodways in the islands. Other marks were left by slaves brought from Africa and by indentured labour, especially the Indians who were prominent in Trinidad. Some of these links with other parts of the world are quite complex to unravel. For example, the Madeirans who were brought to some islands in the 19th century brought with them foodways which had something of a Mediterranean flavour, yet were not quite Mediterranean, Madeira being an Atlantic island which faces the African coast.

Generally speaking, the characteristic foods of the islands include CASSAVA, YAM, tannia (see MALANGA) and SWEET POTATO, PLANTAIN and BANANA (made into various delightful desserts), AVOCADO, SUGAR-CANE products, GOAT, IGUANA (in some islands), SEA TURTLE (to the extent permitted), LAND CRABS, large FROGS, and FLYING FISH (fried with banana). Also, SALT COD (locally referred to as salt fish) is widely eaten in the islands, with interesting variations of nomenclature; Elizabeth Lambert Ortiz (1973) cites Salt Fish and Ackee (see AKEE) in Jamaica, Trinidadian Accra, Barbados Codfish Cakes, Jamaica's Stamp and Go, the Bacalaitos of Puerto Rico, the Acrats de Morue of Martinique and Guadeloupe. Accra in Trinidad are traditionally served with 'floats', fried yeast biscuits.

The subject of fresh seafood in the region can well be approached through the two magnificent volumes by Ebroïn (1977b) who combines scientific knowledge of the species with expertise in cookery.

As for categories of dish, there is a noticeable emphasis on one-pot dishes, including the range of CALLALOO dishes; numerous versions of PEPPER POT; and CHOWDERS using local ingredients. As for other categories of dish, there are variations on the theme of ESCABECHE (*escovitch* in Jamaica); CEVICHE/seviche dishes, making generous use of lime; many spicy soups; various dishes using COCONUT cream; and a fair number of pies of one sort or another, savoury or sweet. Interesting use is made of various fruits and vegetables which are unknown or uncommon outside the region, for example the AKEE which can be served with salt cod.

There are some curious adaptations of European or other terminology. For example, the old English term SALMAGUNDI has been stripped of its first two syllables and appears by itself, 'gundy', in the sense of 'spread'—as in salt fish gundy. The term COLOMBO has been brought into use, at least in Guadeloupe, for various meat or other stews using colombo powder. Nègre (1970), perhaps the most idiosyncratic of the numerous entertaining and erudite authors who have written about food in the Caribbean, even declares that Colombo, brought by coolies from India in the 1850s and 1860s, 'has become a national dish in the West Indies'. He also states that the term has been used not only for a dish but also for an event:

In Guadeloupe, the radio announcements let you know that Mrs X or Mrs Z from Saint-François or from anywhere else cordially invites you to the colombo they are organizing for such or such a day, at their home. You can go there freely, for you will be charged for it . . . and most often, you will eat very well. There is a ball, of course, but you do not have to dance!

Other manifestations of Indian cuisines are noticeable, perhaps to the greatest extent in Trinidad. Cristine MacKie (1987) has some particularly good passages on this.
READING: Elisabeth Lambert Ortiz (1973, 1975); Connie and Arnold Krochmal (1974b); Ebroïn (1977a, for the cuisine of the French Antilles).

WHALE a term denoting a large category of marine mammals, notably the largest such. Until the 20th century it was generally accepted that whales could be hunted and utilized for various purposes, including the provision of food. In whaling communities it has been and remains a routine matter to eat whale meat when it is available. However, advances in the technology of whale-killing equipment, decreases in the stocks of certain species of whale, and changing perceptions of what is an appropriate relationship between human beings and whales have all contributed to create a new situation, in which eating whale meat has become a matter of controversy.

During the Second World War whale meat was used in Britain to supplement normal food supplies; and this prompted publication of various recipes for it. Generally speaking, it was not popular.

Bob Brown (1955) records a remarkable tale:

In *The Cheddar Box* [see under AMERICAN CHEESES], Dean Collins tells of an ancient legend in which the whales came into Tillamook Bay to be milked; and he poses the possible origin of some waxy fossilized deposits along the shore as petrified whale-milk cheese made by the aboriginal Indians after milking the whales.

READING: Fosså (1995).

WHEAT (see page 844)

WHEAT PRODUCTS AND DISHES. Among the products FLOUR is pre-eminent. Other wheat products include:

- **Amulum,** a thickening starch, was made by the Romans from emmer. 'Amulum' means 'unground'. Whole grains were soaked for several days and squeezed in a cloth to force out a fine paste which was dried to a powder. It continued in use into the Middle Ages, when it was known as 'amidon'.
- **Boiled wheat** is important in some regions. A popular Bulgarian boiled wheat dish with nuts, sugar, and lemon juice is VARENO ZHITO; see also the connected sweet dish AŞURE. A curious old Russian graveside ritual involving the Russian version of boiled wheat is described in BLINI. Special festive wheat puddings are made by the Lebanese Maronites (*Qamhiyya*), and by Sephardic Jews in the Balkans (*kofyas*).
- BURGHUL (bulgur) is cracked wheat; wheat which has been parboiled, parched, and coarsely ground. It has numerous uses in the Middle East and neighbouring regions. For example, it plays an essential role in TABBOULEH and can be the basis for a PILAF; it can also be used to make porridge, taking less time to cook and having a more tender texture.
- COUSCOUS.
- FREEKEH, roasted green wheat, is an exceptional delicacy of the Arab world.
- **Parched wheat,** wheat cooked by dry heat, which makes it more digestible and gives it a nutty taste. This has been eaten since very early times, before the invention of bread. It is often mentioned in the Bible. It may be eaten as it is or combined with liquid ingredients in various dishes.
- PORRIDGE is not, on the whole, a successful dish for wheat. Wheat porridges take a long time to cook and are relatively tasteless, greatly inferior to oat porridge. They have, however, been eaten in the north of China, like corresponding rice dishes in the south. There are various ways of making them more interesting. FRUMENTY is a wheat porridge enriched with milk and often spiced, which was popular in medieval Europe, and still is in some regions. See HALEEM for a wheat and meat 'porridge' made in Iran, Afghanistan, and India.
- SEMOLINA.
- **Sprouted wheat** is used to make a salad or cooked vegetable and is popular with modern vegetarians. In sprouting, it develops vitamin C which is not present in the original grain. *Samanak* is the sprouting wheat which is made into a

pudding at New Year (Nauroz, first day of spring) in Iran and Afghanistan.
- **Wheatgerm** and the wheatgerm oil which it contains are extracted and sold separately. Wheatgerm is often used as a dietary supplement (it contains vitamin B) and is added to some brown breads.

READING: Mangelsdorf (1953); Sokolov (1996).

WHELK is a large marine MOLLUSC, inhabiting a single shell. Whelks are widely distributed, but are commercially exploited in only some regions. They are carnivorous, scavenging among carrion or preying on other molluscs, using their extensible proboscis, tipped with a radula, to reach into and extract nourishment from their victims. In certain climatic conditions they can absorb toxin from their prey, and are capable of retaining this for several months; so their harvesting is best left to professional and knowledgeable gatherers.

The main European species, *Buccinum undatum*, the common or waved whelk or buckie, reaches a length of 10 or even 15 cm (4–6"). *Neptunea antiqua*, the almond or red whelk, is a more northerly species and larger.

In W. Atlantic waters, *Busycon carica*, the knobbed whelk, is larger still. The knobs on its shell are used for striking and breaking open the shells of its prey, held helpless by the large foot. The channelled whelk, *B. canaliculatum* is almost as big, and may be distinguished by the deep, channelled grooves which follow the whorls of the shell. It arrived on the Californian coast early in the 20th century.

Whelks are too big for the sort of culinary treatment given to the smaller marine snails. The large muscular foot is the part usually eaten cut into steaks and tenderized if need be. When whelks are commercially processed, as in the Canadian province of Quebec, they are first washed and steamed, then shucked and trimmed down to this muscular part, which is canned or packed in glass jars with a marinade of sugar and spiced vinegar.

WHEY the watery part of MILK which is separated from the solid CURDS in CHEESE-MAKING, is something of which the world has much too much. Yet, if better ways of utilizing it could be found, this surplus whey could be a valuable source of nutrition. Almost a third of the proteins in milk are left in the whey, as well as all the sugar.

The size of the problem is intractable. Ten kg (22 lb) of milk are needed, typically, to produce 1 kg (2.2 lb) of cheese. Between 6 and 9 kg (13–20 lb) of whey will be left over.

(cont. on page 845)

Wheat

A grass of the genus *Triticum*, wheat is the second oldest (after BARLEY) of cultivated cereals. It is now the most widely cultivated, exceeding RICE in the quantity grown; but, since some types of wheat are used as animal fodder, it remains true that more people rely on rice than on wheat as their staple food.

Numerous wild grasses of the genus *Triticum* grow, or once grew, over a wide area of W. Asia. The story of how certain of them evolved first by natural processes and later by informed selection and breeding into the wheats now available is a complex one; see items under 'Reading' at the end of this article.

The situation now is that most cultivated wheat, indeed virtually all the wheat which is made into bread, belongs to the species *T. aestivum*; that this exists in thousands of different cultivars; that the introduction of dwarfing genes in the second half of the 20th century marked the opening of what may well be called 'a new era' in the development of wheat; and that the present large range of cultivars makes it possible for wheat to be grown in many different climates, and to meet more desiderata in quality and characteristics than ever before.

The other important species of wheat which is cultivated is *T. durum*, which is especially suited to the manufacture of PASTA and has probably been so used since about the 1st century BC, which available evidence suggests is when it first appeared.

But a long history precedes the situation thus summarized. By the beginning of recorded history wheat had already become firmly established all over temperate Asia and Europe, its cultivation limited only by climate. And, almost everywhere it was grown, wheat was the most esteemed of cereals, comparatively expensive and not for the poor, who continued to exist on lowlier grains such as barley and MILLET. This is shown by the name 'wheat' itself, which refers to the prized whiteness of wheat flour.

The Romans were highly dependent on wheat, and imported vast amounts from growing regions in their empire, including Britain. (When the Greek explorer Pytheas visited Britain around 330 BC, long before the Romans arrived, he found much wheat grown in SE Britain. The Britons built huge barns for threshing it in, he said: the implication in this statement is no doubt the first reference in literature to the uncertain British climate.) By AD 360 the Romans had built up wheat-growing in Britain to such an extent that wheat was exported from there to feed the army on the Rhine.

Although the ancient Egyptians, the first advanced bread-makers, no doubt had preferences among the kinds of wheat available, the Romans were the first to clearly distinguish 'hard' wheat, suitable for making bread, from 'soft' wheat. The Romans also valued other wheats for particular purposes: for example APICIUS' recipes call specifically for spelt (see list opposite) in a recipe for crushed cooked wheat with mussels, and for stuffing fowl, and spelt was used for making POTTAGES and in soups and sausages. Emmer (see list opposite) was used for making amulum (see WHEAT PRODUCTS AND DISHES), the Roman equivalent of cornflour. Both emmer and spelt were made into the flat, unleavened sheets which were the forerunners of PASTA.

After the fall of the Empire the wheaten infrastructure created for it by the Romans tended to disintegrate. For example, the Saxon invaders of Britain, who preferred their native RYE, greatly reduced the amount of wheat grown.

During the Middle Ages wheat recovered somewhat. It was, however, used mainly for the delicate bread of the rich, both in Britain and in the rest of Europe. Coarse bread for trenchers (slices used as plates) was made from barley or rye. The common bread of most people was maslin: wheat and rye ground together, and sometimes grown together (although this was not very successful, for the rye ripened before the wheat was ready). Poorer bread was made from barley or rye alone, or from rough mixtures of these with bean or pea meal, or even acorns. The principal type of wheat grown in Britain was cone wheat (see opposite). Wheat became the predominant bread grain only in the 18th century.

Wheat was first properly established in the New World in 1529, when the Spaniards began growing it in Mexico. As the continent was opened up by European expansion the enormously productive wheat-growing areas of the Midwest, Canada, and Argentina came to outstrip anywhere in the Old World, rivalling even the vast wheat region of the Ukraine. The last major wheat-growing country to begin cultivation was Australia in 1788. The leading wheat producers are now the USA, the Russian Federation, and China.

As already explained, the most important kinds of wheat now cultivated are those for making bread, hard varieties of *T. aestivum*. ('Hardness' in wheat means that the proteins in it contain a large proportion of glutenin, the main protein that forms the GLUTEN which gives a good texture to bread. For the role of gluten, see BREAD.) Hard wheats are what are mainly grown in the wheat-producing areas of N. America, and other main regions including those of S. America and the former Soviet Union.

The other important species, *T. durum*, is hard in a different sense. It is literally, physically hard. When the grains are ground they splinter into chips of an almost glassy quality. These are SEMOLINA, the basis of N. African COUSCOUS, but most important in the making of PASTA. Durum wheat has been grown for centuries in Italy for this purpose, the best coming from Lazio, the province around Rome. However, local production is not sufficient. Up to the end of the 19th century much was imported from the Ukraine; it was known as 'Taganrog wheat' for the name of the port on the Sea of

Azov from which it was shipped. Nowadays, most of it comes from N. Dakota and Manitoba.

There are other species, listed below, in alphabetical sequence:

- *T. compactum*, **club wheat,** is still grown in C. Asia and China, and in parts of the north-western USA, and used for some breakfast cereals, crackers, etc.
- *T. dicoccum*, **emmer** descended from *T. dicoccoides*, wild emmer, now mostly fed to livestock although good bread and other baked items could be made from it.
- *T. macha* (and *T. vavilovi*) are still grown in C. Asia.
- *T. monococcum*, **einkorn,** the oldest cultivated wheat of all, is still grown in poor soils in Spain, France, E. Europe, Asia Minor, and Morocco, where modern wheats would not flourish.
- *T. polonicum*, the so-called **Polish wheat,** is cultivated mainly in Spain and warmer regions of S. Europe where the climate favours it.
- *T. spelta*, **spelt,** survives on a small scale in parts of C. and E. Europe, where the unripe grains are used in soup, under the name of *Grünkern*, German for 'green grain'.
- *T. sphaerococcum*, **shot wheat,** named for its almost round grains, is a drought-resistant strain important in N. India.
- *T. turgidum*, **cone** (or rivet or poulard) **wheat,** once the principal variety in Britain, is too soft for commercial bread-making, and has largely been superseded by *T. aestivum* varieties.

The **structure** of the ear and grains of wheat is similar to that of many other cereals and grasses. The ear has a tower-like structure consisting of 'storeys' called 'spikelets', each containing two to five flowers of which some but not all develop into grains. In einkorn (German for 'single grain', reflected in its botanical name *monococcum*) the grains are arranged singly. In emmer they have a paired arrangement. In more advanced wheats they are thickly clustered. Each grain is covered with a husk called the 'lemma' which may or may not have a long hair or 'beard' on the tip; modern wheats include bearded and beardless varieties. The beard is quite useful in making it harder for birds to get at the seeds; Indian farmers like bearded wheat for this reason.

When grain is threshed the seeds are separated from the husk and the rest of the ear. In former times **threshing** used to be quite laborious, particularly with the older, 'hulled' types of wheat with firmly attached husks, as opposed to the later 'free threshing' varieties. The freshly harvested ears were first given a time to dry, then any of several methods was used: flails to beat the ears; stamping on them; driving oxen around on them so that their hooves did the threshing; or dragging a spiked sledge over them. Then the chaff—the husks and debris—was 'winnowed' or blown off the heavier grain with the aid of the wind or with fans. Later, machinery was introduced, and now threshing is done instantly inside a combine harvester.

The threshed grain is still covered in a brown (or red) coat, the bran. The coat has several layers. At the tip there are sparse, fine hairs, and inside the base, where the seed is attached to the ear, is the embryo or germ, which will grow into a new plant if allowed to. Most of the inside of the seed is taken up by the endosperm, which is mainly starch and acts as a food store for the developing embryo. In a typical wheat grain 85% of the mass is endosperm, 13% bran, and 2% germ.

Wheat contains more PROTEIN than rice or most other staple cereals. Its protein, which is present with the starch in the endosperm, is important in two ways. First, it makes wheat the most nutritious of common staple grains. The protein supplies all the AMINO ACIDS which are needed in human diet, except that it is rather low in lysine and, not so seriously, in tryptophan and methionine. By a happy coincidence beans and other pulses are rich in lysine, so a diet of wheat products and pulses, common in many poor areas, is well balanced even if hardly any animal foods (whose protein is complete, with all the amino acids) are eaten. Secondly, the protein gives wheat its superior quality as a bread-making grain. Wheat contains proteins of five main groups; albumins, globulins, and proteoses, which are water soluble; and glutenin and gliadin, which are not. Wheat has much more glutenin and gliadin than do other cereals. It is these proteins which form gluten in bread-making, giving wheat bread its pleasantly elastic texture. Hard wheats, the kind for bread, contain more of them than do soft wheats.

The form in which wheat reaches the consumer, whether directly or through a baker, varies. It may be one of the products listed in WHEAT PRODUCTS AND DISHES (page 843). But it is most often flour, which is a subject on its own; see FLOUR.
READING: W. R. Aykroyd and Joyce Doughty (1970).

The state of Wisconsin alone was reckoned not so long ago to produce half a million kg of cheese annually.

The nature of whey makes the problem worse. If discharged as an effluent, it burdens the water system with its high demand for oxygen. A cheese factory can thus create requirements equivalent to those of a sizeable town of human beings. Moreover, whey is an ideal medium for the growth of micro-organisms and, consequently, the spread of pollution.

In some countries whey is drunk in its liquid form. It is nutritious and has often been prescribed for invalids. But its taste is generally regarded as insipid. The 'orange whey' to which Hannah Glasse (1747) and other 18th-century authors referred was made palatable by adding an acceptable flavour. In the Hebrides, on the other hand, unflavoured whey seems to have been the favourite beverage, known as 'bland'. It is well described by Emerson (1908):

The great universal non-intoxicating beverage of these islands is bland, and it can be had at almost any time or at any place, for it is a home-made article and therefore very plentiful. Bland is simply a preparation of whey, but owing to the quality of the grass or to the climate becomes here a truly palatable and nourishing potation and one that all travellers and visitors never fail to mention in their memoirs.

Whey is also used in cookery, but only to a small extent, because in many places it is difficult to obtain in quantities smaller than a road-tankerful and because cooks do not know about it. (Iceland is one country where they do.)

Whey may be dried. The sweet whey left over when cheese is made from whole milk is easier to spray-dry than the acid (sour) whey which is the residue of cheese-making with skimmed milk; but both can be so treated. Dried whey has been incorporated into dietary supplements for parts of the world where people do not have enough protein. Confectioners have also found some use for it. And some carbonated drinks including whey have been modestly successful in Switzerland (Rivella), Poland (whey KVASS), and Brazil (*tai*, the only one to contain whey protein).

But all such outlets, and production of WHEY CHEESES (below), account for only a tiny proportion of the whey which accumulates daily for disposal.

WHEY CHEESES which are made in many countries, are a useful way of using up the enormous amounts of whey left over from normal CHEESE-MAKING. The two main kinds are typified by RICOTTA and mysost. Sérac (see BEAUFORT) is another interesting example.

Mysost is a purely Norwegian cheese. *Myse* means 'whey' and *ost* 'cheese'. Standard mysost, *primost*, is made from cow's milk whey; *gjetost* is made from goat's milk whey; *flötost* is enriched with cream. All kinds are quite sweet in taste, and rather resemble cheesy fudge; a likeness increased by the colour, which ranges from very pale to medium brown. There are kinds which are sweetened further with brown sugar. Some others include spices: caraway, cumin, or cloves.

WHITEBAIT tiny fish, transparent or silver-white, were thought in the past to be a separate species of small fish, the subject of much argument among natural historians; the Frenchman Valenciennes even created a new genus, *Rogenia*, to accommodate the puzzling little creatures. However, they are now firmly identified, at least so far as Britain is concerned, as the fry of various fish of the HERRING family, but mainly of the HERRING itself and the SPRAT. In other English-speaking countries the term may be used for a similar mixture, for example the fry of SILVERSIDE or SAND-EEL in New England; or for a mixture of quite different fish, e.g. the young of freshwater fish, notably *Galaxias maculatus*, the inanga, in New Zealand. Incidentally, these galaxiid fish have an interesting lifecycle, which takes them out to sea and back again at the beginning of their lives, and are the object of special fisheries when they swim back,

tiny and transparent, to their native rivers; all this is admirably described by Peat (1979).

Whitebait used to be fished in huge quantities in the tidal waters of the Thames and elsewhere. They were and are deep fried, whole. Their size has always varied, but the figure of 180 to the pound weight may be taken as typical. As a dish enjoyed in England, they can be traced back to the early 17th century, but Buckland (1883) cites a claim that it was Richard Cannon of Blackwall (downstream from the City of London on the River Thames) who first persuaded local tavernkeepers to serve whitebait dinners. These became all the rage. The season ran from about February to August and not only engaged the attention of the well-to-do but would also provoke what one author called 'a vast resort of the lower order of epicures' to the taverns serving whitebait.

The thronging but inferior epicures were enjoying a wider variety of fish than they could have realized. Dr James Murie, in his *Report on the Sea Fisheries and Fishing Industries of the Thames Estuary* (1903) analysed the contents of boxes of whitebait and found 32 different species therein. The fry of 21 species of fish, including eels, plaice, and lumpfish, turned up from time to time, together with various shrimps, crabs, octopus, and jellyfish. However, the the tiny herrings and sprat were in the vast majority; and it seems safe to assume that nowadays any intruders are even less common than then.

WHITEFISH a general name for fish of the genus *Coregonus* in the SALMON family. These are mainly freshwater fish, but a couple of them come out into the Baltic Sea. All are of moderate size (a length of 25–50 cm/10–20" is typical) and live in relatively cold waters, although *C. lavaretus* has a range which extends down into Italy. Because of the formation of separate races in landlocked waters, the genus is rich in subspecies, the complexities of which are ignored here. The prominent species are:

- *Coregonus lavaretus*, known as houting in its purely freshwater form, or as powan (Loch Lomond in Scotland), skelly (the English Lake District), and *gwyniad* (Wales). A silvery fish with a greenish-brown back. Very good when smoked. The roe is used in Finland to produce a sort of orange caviar, salty but good.
- *C. albula*, the vendace or pollan; *muikku* in Finland, *siklöja* or *mujka* in Sweden. A rich little fish with a strong and interesting flavour. Very small vendace are called *naiolamuikku* (nail vendace) in Finland; only their heads are removed before they are deep fried. Vendace caviar,

again, is quite salty so best served with sour cream.

A couple of less important species which occur in the White Sea/Barents Sea/Arctic waters of N. America may be met under the name cisco.

The name whitefish is also used for *Lactarius lactarius*, a small fish (maximum length 30 cm/12") of the Indo-Pacific. It is not remarkable for being white, but is grey above and silvery below. It is in India, and in Thailand; but it is not popular in Malaysia and is disdained at Hong Kong. It may be fried or poached; and it can be bought dried.

WHITE PUDDING in modern British usage, a SAUSAGE filled with a mixture which would typically include white meat, fat, cereal (oatmeal, see OATS), and flavourings. As presented for sale, it is white, in contrast to the more common black puddings (see BLOOD SAUSAGES). According to Theodora FitzGibbon (1976), the traditional Irish version was shaped like a horseshoe and consisted mainly of lard mixed with toasted oatmeal. The French equivalent is *boudin blanc*; and in Spain there is *morcilla blanca*.

C. Anne Wilson (1973) refers to medieval antecedents such as the 14th- and 15th-century 'frawnchemyle', and mentions recipes of the Elizabethan period.

British white puddings have survived in some regions (e.g. the West Country) more than in others. For a Scottish product which falls into the same general category, see SKIRLIE.

WHITE SAUCE one of the most basic SAUCES, especially in England and N. America and other parts of the world where English traditions have influenced cookery. It is similar to the BÉCHAMEL sauce of France, although some versions of béchamel have developed on somewhat divergent lines.

This sauce is simply made by cooking a little flour in melted butter to make a ROUX, and then incorporating milk into the roux, after which a desired flavouring is normally added.

The other technique which is often used is the blending method. For this the flour is mixed with a little cold milk to a paste and then added to the rest of the milk and brought to the boil stirring continuously until thickened.

White sauce, like béchamel, is made in different consistencies, depending on what it is to be used for. A very thin white sauce is added to flavour and thicken soups; a pouring or coating consistency as an accompanying sauce; and PANADA is a very thick version of it used for binding (for example for CROQUETTES) and as a base for SOUFFLÉS.

Other thickening agents can be used, such as cornflour, or ARROWROOT, or butter with flour kneaded into it (*beurre manié*).

WHITE TRASH COOKING a cuisine of N. America which is important because of the large numbers of people who practise it, and because it has been so eloquently described by Mickler (1986, 1988):

If someone asked me what sets White Trash cooking aside from other kinds of cooking, I would have to name three of the ingredients: saltmeat, cornmeal and molasses. Every vegetable is seasoned with saltmeat, bacon, or ham. Cornbread, made with pure cornmeal is a must with every meal, especially if there's pot liquor. It's also good between meals with a tall glass of cold buttermilk. And many foods are rolled in cornmeal before they are fried. Of course nothing makes cornbread better than a spoon or two of bacon drippings and molasses. For the sweetest pies and pones you ever sunk a tooth into, molasses is the one ingredient you can't find a substitute for. And a little bit of it, used on the side, can top off the flavors of most White Trash food, even a day-old biscuit.

Commenting that equipment is the next most important thing after ingredients, Mickler affirms that only three utensils—a skillet, a Dutch oven, and a cornbread pan, all of black cast iron—are needed to produce 'that real White Trash flavour and golden brown crust'. He says that the black iron skillet is as special to this kind of cooking as is the wok to Chinese cooking. And he has interesting comments on the chameleon-like nature of White Trash recipes.

Another real common feature of White Trash cooking that sticks out in my mind is that the recipes, because of their deliciousness are swapped and passed around like a good piece of juicy gossip, and by the time they make it back to their source they might be, and almost always are, completely different. Raenelle, Betty Sue's sister-in-law, says, 'If I fry down three onions, she's gonna fry down four. If I put in one pack of Jello, she's gonna tump in two.' So with every cook trying to outdo the other one, and with all the different tastes, these recipes change so fast it's hard at times to catch them still long enough to get them down on paper.

WHITING a name for fish, the meaning of which varies from the Atlantic to the Indo-Pacific.

1. What might be termed the 'original whiting', the first fish to bear the name, is *Merlangius merlangus*, a fish of the COD family which has a range from the N. Atlantic through the Mediterranean to the Black Sea. Maximum length 70 cm (30"), market length about half of that. These are fish of variable coloration; the back may be brownish, bluish, or greenish. The flesh is easy to digest but lacking in flavour. It is considered to be very suitable for invalids, especially when steamed or poached.

The so-called 'blue whiting', *Micromesistius poutassou*, may be regarded as a deep-water version of the whiting; hence perhaps the fetching Greek name *prosphygáki* (little exile or refugee). It is *poutassou* in French, *blauer Wittling* in German, *bacaladilla* in Spanish, and *pichelim* in Portuguese. If landed very fresh, it may be cooked like whiting; but most of the catch is turned into fish meal.

2. Whiting is also the common English name applied to various species of fish in the Indo-Pacific, notably in Indian and Australian waters, although none of these fish is related to the whiting of the N. Atlantic.

Sillago sihama is the Indian whiting. It is an important food fish in the subcontinent and much of SE Asia; the flesh has a good texture and the flavour is delicate. It has a maximum length of 30 cm (12") and has a light grey or olive back with silvery sides and belly. These fish are caught in large numbers at the appropriate season (from May to December on the east coast of India), despite their ability to 'disappear'. Maxwell (1921) remarked that they: 'are very shy and instantly bury themselves in the sand on the appearance of any danger. Even a passing dark cloud leads to their immediate disappearance into the sand whence they emerge a few moments later.'

Of the species in this genus which occur in Australian waters, *S. maculata*, the trumpeter whiting, is important and is mainly caught in the winter months; while *S. punctata*, the spotted or King George whiting, is the most important food fish in the south from W. Australia to Victoria. Both are of moderate size and fine quality.

WHORTLEBERRY a name loosely applied, in ways which vary from country to country, to various sorts of BERRY. All or almost are of the genus *Vaccinium* to which the BLUEBERRY belongs. The name is best reserved for *V. myrtillus*, but allowable also for what is often called bog bilberry, *V. uliginosum*. These berries are relatively large and blue-black in colour, but less good to eat than the blueberry.

In Ireland whortleberries are called fraughans and were picked traditionally on the first Sunday in August, known as Garland or Fraughan Sunday. Communities gathered on hill tops and lake shores to collect the berries in specially designed rush and wicker baskets. Often the berries were used in courtship rituals. It was customary for young boys to present their sweethearts with the gathered fruit. Once the girl returned home she would make a fraughan cake, which was later enjoyed by herself and her boyfriend at the bonfire dance held on Fraughan Sunday night.

The name 'red whortleberry', when met, probably refers to CRANBERRY/lingonberry.

WIGEON or widgeon, a DUCK of the genus *Anas*. The European wigeon, *A. penelope*, has an arctic and boreal range in Eurasia, extending as far south as Britain, where it used to be known as the easterling. Its average total length is 45 cm (18"). The American wigeon, or baldpate, is *A. americana*. These are gregarious birds, reputedly lacking in intelligence and therefore an easy prey for wildfowlers.

Wigeons can make good eating. De Voe (1866) gives the curiously precise (or ironic?) guidance that a wigeon which has displayed enough intelligence to watch a canvasback duck diving for wild celery, to observe it coming to the surface again, and then to 'snatch the delicious morsel' and make off, is considered to have an excellent flavour.

WIGS (or whigs, or wiggs), small cakes of lightly spiced and sweetened bread dough, the basic ingredients being butter, sugar, flour, milk (or cream), and yeast. Some recipes contain eggs; some contain sack. Among the spices specified are ginger, nutmeg, mace, cloves, and saffron; caraway seeds seem always to have been included. Currants are occasionally added.

Wigs were made under that name from medieval times. Ayto (1993) says: 'They appear to have been introduced into Britain from the Low Countries in the fourteenth century, for the name is a borrowing of Middle Dutch *wigge* (which etymologically means "*wedge*-shaped cake").'

They were particularly popular in the 18th century; recipes range from the rich and varied ones given by E. Smith in 1734 to the single, plain version spiced only with caraway seeds given by Elizabeth Raffald (1769). Not one of the 18th-century recipes described their shape; it was assumed that everyone would know that they were triangular.

Caraway seeds were a very popular flavouring for English cakes, buns, and biscuits during the 18th, 19th, and early 20th centuries, and their use may have been symbolic of the spring sowing of wheat. This may explain the serving of wigs and other seed cakes during Lent. Wigs and ale were a Lenten supper in Pepys's day, and wigs were also eaten for breakfast.

Wigs more or less disappeared from cookery books in the 19th century. However, Florence White (1932) reported that 'whigs' were then still made at a restaurant in Bath, and at Hawkshead in Cumberland; she said that they were 'usually made into large round cakes, crossed so as to be easily divided into quarters'. (LM)

WILD BOAR *Sus scrofa*, found from Europe to C. Asia and from the Baltic to N. Africa, in various races and subspecies.

It features in many classical myths. For example, to kill the immense Boar of Erymanthus was one of the Twelve Labours set for Hercules. And perhaps the earliest hunting story to be written down was Homer's tale of the great boar ravaging the countryside of Calydon, eventually dispatched after Atalanta had wounded it with one of her arrows. The wild boar features in early British, Celtic, and Roman art and coinage.

Bridget Ann Henisch (1976), writing of medieval times, says that:

Wild boar was often the star attraction of a Christmas feast, and the head was brought in to the sound of its own special songs, ranging from the merely cheerful to brisk reminders of the season's doctrinal significance.

This tradition has lingered on, not necessarily in connection with Christmas. The annual Boar's Head dinner at Queen's College, Oxford, is one example.

For eating, a young wild boar (*marcassin* in French—*sanglier* is the term for older animals) is greatly to be preferred. Recipes such as those used for VENISON are often recommended, and may provide for accompaniments such as cooked prunes, apple, or chestnuts. The boar themselves will eat almost anything they find or dig up in the forests, but particularly food such as acorns. The meat has a strong taste, sometimes obscured by a MARINADE, standard treatment for all but the youngest animals.

Although wild boar were hunted to extinction long ago in Scandinavia and the British Isles, demand for the meat has resulted in their being re-introduced on a small scale, but not into the wild.

WILD DUCK a category of birds which includes a large number of species which are edible, but only a few which are regarded as really good to eat and which are likely to be found in appropriate markets during their seasons.

The family Anatidae includes geese and swans as well as ducks. Among the ducks, it is usual to distinguish between surface-feeding ducks, which feed by upending rear ends and dabbling for food in the water with their bills, and diving ducks which dive right down into the water in search of food. The former prefer marshes and ponds as a habitat, while the latter are likely to be found in open waters or the sea. The term 'duck' is not a precise one, and some birds which are ducks have names which do not include the term.

Some wild ducks maybe taken either from inland waters or from salty waters (whether the sea or estuaries). Generally, the former are preferred since the latter tend to have a fishy taste.

For the wild duck which are usually counted the best to eat see CANVASBACK; GADWALL; MALLARD; PINTAIL; POCHARD; TEAL; WIGEON.

WILDEBEEST a name applied to various species of ANTELOPE, for which the name 'gnu' is also used. The white-tailed gnu or wildebeest, *Connochaetes gnu*, is no longer found in the wild but has been preserved on farms. The blue wildebeest or brindled gnu, *Gorgon taurinus*, survives in larger numbers. Leipoldt (1976) wrote that 'its meat is tasteless and stringy, but its tongue, liver, brains and kidneys are considered delicacies'.

WILD GARLIC is a name which should apply to plants of true GARLIC, *Allium sativum*, growing in the wild; but in practice it is used of other plants in the genus which do grow in the wild and do possess at least some garlic-like characteristics.

In Britain the most important species to which the name applies is *A. ursinum*, also known as 'bear's garlic' (a name echoed in other languages) and more fittingly as **ramsons**. This name comes from *hramsan*, the plural of the Old English *hramsa*; so, as Geoffrey Grigson (1955) points out, ramsons is a double plural. Yet other names include badger's garlic, devil's garlic (cf the Swiss *Teufelschnoblech*), gypsy's onions (cf the German *Zigeuner Knoblauch*), and a quartet of hostile names from Somerset: snake's food, stinking Jenny, stinking lilies, and onion stinkers.

Wild garlic has its merits. Grigson comments:

Not to be despised, these white stars and viridian leaves because of a garlic smell. Gerard Manley Hopkins wrote of a wood 'curled all over with bright green garlic' (in his journal in 1871), and in blossom or leaf Ramsons is one of the most beautiful floorings. Gerard wrote that in the Low Country fish sauce was made from the leaves, which 'maye very well be eaten in April and Maie with butter, of such as are of a strong constitution, and labouring men.'

Europe has other species which may be called wild garlic. *A. vineale* (also known as field garlic, *ail des vignes* in French) is too strong for most tastes, although the tops of the young leaves, in spring, can be added to a green salad.

In N. America, the name wild garlic could indicate any of several species, but is most often used for *A. canadense*, whose other common names are Canada onion and meadow leek. This species has sweet and palatable bulbs and also bears clusters of bulbils at the flower head. These clusters can be pickled entire to make an attractive relish. The plants as a whole may be cooked like leeks. Gibbons (1962) provides both praise and cooking instructions.

More 'wild garlics' occur in S. Africa, in the form of *Tulbaghia* spp, whose bulbs are usually too strong for kitchen use but whose leaves have a good garlicky flavour.

See also HEDGE GARLIC.

WILD RICE *Zizania aquatica*, a cereal which grows in water, mainly in the central and southern states of the USA, parts of Africa, SE Asia and S. China. It is a tall plant (up to more than 3 m or over 9'), not closely related to ordinary RICE and not readily susceptible to cultivation. Hawkes (1968) describes the large terminal panicles as 'somewhat like airy candelabra, hung with the seeds', and observes that the seeds are relished by waterfowl as much as by man.

In the USA wild rice covers large areas of the Upper Mississippi Valley. Artemas Ward (1923), writing before it had achieved a reputation as a 'gourmet food', made approving comments on 'its peculiar, slightly smoky flavor', and described the harvesting.

In northern Minnesota it is gathered by Indians in canoes paddled slowly through rice-beds, the seeds being shaken into the bottoms of the canoes from the grass-heads pulled over and downward for the purpose. As the seeds do not all ripen at the same time, a 'field' is gone over again and again at suitable intervals. Harvesting is followed by parching to dry the hulls, which are then easily separated from the grain.

Wild rice is never 'pearled' to remove the seed coat, as is ordinary rice. So it is always brown (or greenish). It has an interesting 'grainy' taste, more marked than that of ordinary brown rice. Americans find it particularly good with game birds; and it is used as a stuffing for THANKSGIVING turkey in its home territory. Generally, it can be used in the same ways as ordinary rice, but for obvious reasons is much more expensive.

In China there are two species, *Z. aquatica* and *Z. latifolia*. The latter, sometimes called Manchurian wild rice or water grass, has broader leaves, which are used for wrapping dumplings. The plants are not exploited by the Chinese for the grains, but for their swollen young shoots, which are cooked and eaten like asparagus.

READING: Sri Owen (1993).

WINE (in cookery), a topic touched upon under ALCOHOL, has been clearly and specifically treated by Anne Willan (1989), who introduces it thus:

Wine can mellow to a remarkable richness when it is simmered in sauces, braises or stews. To avoid a raw taste, it must always be thoroughly reduced during cooking, red wine by half and white wine even more. First, the alcohol evaporates, then the wine concentrates so the finished dish is rich and mellow. This evaporation may be an integral part of the cooking process, as in the long cooking of a casserole or the simmering of a brown sauce. At other times the wine is reduced on its own, as when red wine is used to deglaze pan juices for a steak.

The quality of the wine used will be reflected in the result. It would not, however, make sense to sacrifice rare or expensive wines in the cooking pan. One quality which will not survive cooking is the sparkle of champagne or similar wines, although a little of the sparkle may survive in uncooked dishes such as a champagne sorbet (see WATER ICES).

The above refers to table wines. The role of fortified wines in cookery is different. They are typically added at the end of a cooking process, and the alcohol in them, which will not have been boiled off, remains potent. In fact, their use may be a case of 'wine in cooked dishes' rather than 'wine in cookery'. A spoonful of sherry added to a soup just before it is served is not subjected to cooking, although it certainly has its effect on the soup. The Italian fortified wine Marsala is sometimes the best choice for deglazing pan juices. The Spanish Malaga and Portuguese Madeira are also particularly suited to certain dishes.

Wines are also used as an ingredient of a marinade. The effect of the wine is then produced before cooking; if any wine survives (with other elements of the marinade) on whatever has been marinated, the effect of the cooking on this is not of significance for the finished dish.

WINGED BEAN *Psophocarpus tetragonolobus*, a tropical, climbing, leguminous plant, whose pods have four wavy ridges running along them from end to end. It is also known as Manila or Goa bean, and sometimes as princess or asparagus pea (a name also applied to the WINGED PEA, below). The pods may be 30 cm (1') long.

The plant is probably native to SE Asia. Indonesia and Papua New Guinea are centres of genetic diversity. Distribution now extends to W. Africa, the W. Indies, and other tropical areas; and much interest is being shown in the possibility that the plant, a good source of protein, could make a major contribution to world food supplies.

A remarkable feature of the plant is that all parts are edible: shoots, leaves, flowers, pods, seeds, and (although sometimes too small for use) tubers. The tubers of leguminous plants, such as this one, provide much better nutrition than other root crops. Whereas the latter are low in protein, tubers of leguminous plants benefit from nitrogen fixation and are consequently rich in protein.

In most of Asia it is usually the immature pods which are eaten; but in Java the seeds, roasted to make them palatable, are preferred, and are also used in the production of a kind of TEMPE. The tubers, raw or cooked, are eaten in Burma and Papua New Guinea (roasted in embers with a pleasant, slightly nutty flavour). In W. Africa the young leaves and tubers are eaten as well as young pods and mature seeds.

The flowers of the plant are added to dishes to colour them blue, and Duke (1981) says that the fried flowers taste like mushrooms.

WINGED PEA *Tetragonolobus purpureus*, a LEGUME native to the Mediterranean region of Europe and the Near East, is so called because its four-sided pods terminate in four 'wings'. It is an annual, of a trailing habit, and its pods are from 3 to 9 cm (1–3") long.

The plant is cultivated in warm temperate regions, and it is sometimes grown as a culinary herb. Its flavour is acceptable, but it is hard to discern any basis for the name 'asparagus pea' which is sometimes used. The young pods are pickled or cooked whole. There are other plants in the genus with similar characteristics.

Although the plants are not only unrelated but quite different, the winged pea has often been confused with the WINGED BEAN (above), no doubt partly because the English common names are confusing.

WINTERGREEN a wild plant of N. America, *Gaultheria procumbens* of the heather family. It has other common names, notably chequerberry. The name wintergreen has also been used for the unrelated plant *Mitchella repens*, which is better called partridge berry.

Both plants produce purple or red berries with a sour, aromatic flavour, but the former is preferred since its berries are juicier. American Indians ate them and made a tonic tea from both the berries and the leathery scented leaves. In the 18th century this tea was the subject of favourable comment by, among others, a French doctor whose friend Pehr Kalm, the Swedish traveller, named the genus for him.

Oil of wintergreen, a flavouring which is produced commercially for use in confectionery and cough drops, was originally distilled from wintergreen; but it is now made either synthetically or from the sweet/black or yellow birch trees, *Betula* spp, which contain what is virtually the same aromatic oil; see BIRCH SUGAR.

Salal, *Gaultheria shallon*, a plant of north-western N. America, bears dark purple berries of excellent flavour which are made into pies, jam, and jelly; see Charlotte Clarke (1978).

WINTER SQUASH a name which is applied to those kinds of SQUASH which are allowed to mature on the vine, then stored for use in winter. The skin is hard and inedible, while the inside becomes firm and is often superior in flavour to most sorts of SUMMER SQUASH.

The dividing line between summer squash and winter squash thus corresponds to differences in use. It does not correspond to divisions between the four principal botanical species of squash. Nor is it a firm dividing line, because there are some cultivars which can be harvested early as summer squash or kept to become winter squash.

Despite the above, it remains true that virtually all the principal cultivars are either summer or winter. How the winter squashes relate to the principal species is shown in the list below.

- *Cucurbita maxima* includes the larger kinds of winter squash, e.g. the cultivars Hubbard and Buttercup.
- *C. mixta* includes the Cushaw group of cultivars, of which Golden Stripe Cushaw is the best; Silver Edges, grown for its large and tasty silver-edged seeds; Japanese Pie (seems marked with what look like Chinese characters, so sometimes called Chinese alphabet squash); and the desert cultivar Apache Giant.
- *C. moschata*, a species which grows only in warm regions, provides some of the smaller sorts of winter squash, including the Butternut group of cultivars, the Winter Crookneck, and the Cushawsome; plus some sorts of PUMPKIN and improved cultivars of Calabaza, a word which just means squash in Spanish, but is also used for a group of large squashes with bright orange flesh which are very commonly used in C. and S. America and the Caribbean. Calabaza is referred to as WINTER SQUASH, because it has a hard shell and keeps well, but it is not a seasonal vegetable.
- *C. pepo* includes some cultivars of the Acorn group (but the great majority of cultivars of this species are always treated as summer squash).

Kabocha is a squash which is difficult to categorize. Elizabeth Schneider (1986) explains that the name is both a generic grouping and a more specific marketing name in the USA, applied to:

many strains of Japanese pumpkin and winter squash of both *Cucurbita maxima* and *Cucurbita moschata* species. Home Delite, Ebisu, Delica, Hoka, Chirimen, Hyuga, Hoka, and Sweet Mama are all varieties that might be called kabochas in a Japanese or American market.

Schneider adds that, with their flattened drum or turban shapes and deep green skins, they bear some resemblance to Buttercup; and that all have a fine flavour, rich sweetness, and almost fibreless flesh.

WITCHETTY GRUBS regarded as a delicacy by many inhabitants of Australia, past and present, are the LARVAE of various moths and cockchafers. The correct spelling is witjuti, and the term is properly reserved for the larvae of a large moth of the genus *Xyleutes*; but the Cribbs (1975) remark that it has come to be applied to any large white grub found in wood.

Witchetty grubs

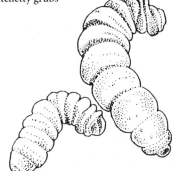

Presence of the grub could often be detected by a sawdust-like heap of excreta on the ground at the bottom of a gum tree. The hunter would then look for a hole about the size of a pea in the bark, chip it open with an axe and use a hook to extract the grub; a skilled hunter could remove the grub from its hole without damaging it and 'spilling the gravy'. Witchetty grubs can be eaten raw or roasted. The one thing to remember is not to eat the head, so the grub is held by that end and the remainder is nipped off. The flavour is rich, reminiscent of nuts, the latter, we are told, being due to the partly digested wood present.

WOK COOKERY as practised in China originally and now more or less all round the world, bears some resemblance to what the French do with a SAUTÉ pan, in that foods are cooked quickly while being tossed about, but it is nevertheless different (see STIR-FRY). The curved bottom of the wok makes it possible to cook with a very small amount of

oil, into which the ingredients fall back every time they are tossed up. They are always small enough, or cut sufficiently small, to ensure that a couple of minutes suffice to cook them. The heat used under a wok in professional Chinese kitchens is very intense—something outside the experience of western cooks.

A similar pan is called a *kadhai* (or *karhai*) in India.

READING: Yan-Kit So (1985).

WOLF-FISH *Anarhichas lupus*, a fine fish of moderately deep water in the N. Atlantic (from New Jersey up to Greenland and down to Scotland), which has a maximum length of 120 cm (47"). It belongs to a family referred to sometimes as marine catfish, which may be technically correct but is puzzling since the wolf-fish does not have the 'whiskers' which are characteristic of catfish, and its formidable teeth are described as being 'doglike'. However, the main point is that it makes excellent eating. It is appreciated particularly by the Dutch, who call it *zeewolf* (whereas in Scandinavia the cat theme is echoed with names like *havkat*, meaning sea cat; and the Icelandic name means stone-biter, referring to the teeth).

The wolf-fish was not widely consumed in earlier centuries, probably because it was not caught in quantity. It was sufficiently unfamiliar in the late 19th century for British ichthyologists to cite comments from people who had tasted it, e.g. Yorkshire fishermen who 'loved it'. On the other side of the Atlantic De Kay (the natural historian of New York state) had declared in mid-century that smoked wolf-fish was like salmon.

WOLLEY HANNAH, the first woman to author a cookery book in English. Other works had emerged in the 1650s with the names of aristocratic ladies featuring prominently on the title page, and there is no doubt that they carried out many of the recipes, but Wolley self-consciously wrote about food and domestic matters in order to publish, earn money, and address specific audiences. The different genres of book she constructed out of the old influenced the next 100 years of cookery publishing, and tell of a sophisticated understanding of the new social structures that came with the Restoration of 1660.

Wolley began her career with *The Ladies Directory* (1661), but her *Cook's Guide* (1664), filled with kickshaws and 'Ho-good' (*haut goût*) sauces to make the readers 'gratified in the Gusto's', formed the basis of her *Gentlewoman's Companion* (*c.*1670) addressed to professional cooks and to

housewives of the growing middle classes, as well as *The Queenlike Closet* (1670) addressed to 'all ingenious ladies, and gentlewomen'. The cookery book itself went into several editions until the end of the century, and versions of it were included in at least three related works: *The Compleat Servant Maid* (1671), *The Ladies Delight* (1672), and *The Accomplisht Ladies Delight* (*c.*1677). The latter two books, with the 1677 containing a lookalike portrait of Wolley, are similar and went into many editions; but they lack the flamboyant style of Wolley's own earlier writing with its claim to avoid 'vain expressions', 'multitudes of words . . . to little or no purpose', for 'the good of all the female sex', and are probably pirates.

The focus on women in her writing on food clearly defines the divisions in domestic lives at this time. She writes for the woman earner, as servant, as provisioner, and as teacher of cookery; for the upwardly mobile lady who combines serious occupation with fashionable display; and for the gentry housewife who is increasingly modelling housework on the private home of the urban middle class. LH

WONTON (or won ton), the Anglicized form of two Chinese words meaning a small 'dumpling' or roll consisting of a wonton wrapper (made from the same dough as egg noodle) with a savoury filling, especially of minced pork with seasonings. Sweet wontons, e.g. with a date and walnut filling, also exist.

Wontons may be steamed or pan fried or deep-fried; and are often served in soups, or as items in DIM SUM. One variation is to have open-faced steamed wontons, shaped to have a flat bottom so that they will stand upright; these are *shao mai*.

See MANTOU for a survey of the whole range of similar items which are found from China in the east to Turkey and Russia in the west. See also JIAOZI, dumplings of the same sort but with thicker wrappers.

WOOD APPLE the fruit of a small tree, *Feronia limonia*, found in most parts of the Indian subcontinent and eastwards to the China Sea. It is also called elephant apple, and formerly had the botanical name *F. elephantum*, because elephants like to eat it. So do monkeys, to judge by the Sanskrit name *kapipriya* (dear to monkeys).

The round grey fruits, the size of apples, have hard shells and contain a brown pulp which is used to make sherbets, jellies, and CHUTNEYS in India. The pulp is also eaten raw with sugar, or with salt, pepper, and oil. It is inconveniently full of small seeds.

The tree exudes a gum which closely resembles GUM ARABIC, but is whiter, more transparent, more expensive, and supposedly superior in viscosity.

WOODCHUCK *Marmota monax*, also known as groundhog (and, sometimes, incorrectly as 'prairie dog'). This animal of N. America is something like a squirrel and belongs to the same family, Sciuridae, but is larger than most squirrels with a head-plus-body length of 40–50 cm (16–20"). It has been well described by Ashbrook and Sater (1945), who remark that it is 'the legendary harbinger of spring weather calculations' and cite other interesting information:

Paul C. Estey, in *The Woodchuck Hunter*, writes:

There is no reason why woodchuck should not be splendid eating because they are one of the cleanest animals. People who have once eaten them invariably like them and stick to such a diet when they can.

Woodchucks are considered as a sport animal and can be hunted almost any time of the day, if the weather is good. They are sun worshippers and prefer a vegetarian diet. It is said a woodchuck can eat in one day as much clover as a full-grown sheep.

'The flesh of the young "chuck",' according to an article by Francis X. Lueth in the spring 1943 issue of *Illinois Conservation*, 'is delicious if the little red kernels or glands which are found in each foreleg, high up near the body, are cut out.' . . .

Young ones may be cooked in the same manner as cotton-tail rabbits. . . . The muscles of the woodchuck are dark and thick, but the meal is mild in flavour.

The woodchuck has two close relations, which are similarly edible and somewhat larger. *M. marmota*, known as the Alpine marmot, belongs to the Alps and the Carpathian Mountains, but has been introduced elsewhere in Europe, e.g. the Pyrenees and the Black Forest. *M. bobac* belongs to the steppes and some cultivated regions of C. Asia.

WOODCOCK *Scolopax rusticola*, a bird which is highly prized over its wide range, from N. Spain and Britain to Siberia and Japan. Its presence in the Mediterranean is more or less limited to Corsica. Its smaller namesake, the American woodcock, *Philohela minor*, is highly rated in N. America.

The woodcock eats a varied diet of wholesome foods and presents a plump aspect. One provides a sufficient helping for one person. It is usually roasted, without first being cleaned, since the entrail is accounted essential to full enjoyment of the bird's fine flavour.

The season for woodcock in Britain varies by region but is generally focused on the last months of the year. The numbers in Britain are considerably augmented during the winter by migrant birds, which depart again in the spring. A remarkable notion about 'the second home' of these birds has been described by Francesca Greenoak (1979).

There is a tradition that Woodcock arrive overnight, all together, on a change of wind to the easterly, some time near All Hallows. Several other migrants are said to 'pilot' the Woodcock flocks to their winter home . . . It used also to be thought that the months of absence were spent on the moon. (This theory continued to be promulgated until well into the eighteenth century, and by reasonably eminent people, though perceptive and intelligent men such as Sir Thomas Browne disbelieved it and supported the then rather off-beat idea of migration, put forward by Olaus Magnus in the sixteenth century.) Charles Morton in a tract in the *Harleian Miscellany* elaborates on moon migration, describing how the birds take two months to travel there and the same period to get back, spending three months in a lunar habitat. (There is a similar superstition about goose migration.)

Ruff (the cock) and reeve (the hen), *Philomachus pugnax*, is a bird which used to be highly esteemed, especially in Lincolnshire and adjacent areas of England, when fattened for the table, and which could be treated like woodcock in the kitchen.

WOOD EAR (or tree ear) mushrooms, of the genus *Auricula*, a staple ingredient of oriental cookery. They grow on trees, usually deciduous, in tropical, subtropical, and temperate climates, including Europe, N. America, and Australia. They are cultivated on a large scale in China, and also in Japan and Taiwan, and are available in dried form wherever oriental foodstuffs are sold. After being soaked and softened, they have a markedly gelatinous texture.

The main European species, occurring also in N. America and Australia, is *Auricularia auricula*, which is also one of the two main species used in China (where the general name for these fungi is *muer*). The other is *A. polytricha*, present in China and Australia but not in Europe or N. America. The distinction between the two species is imperfectly represented in common names, especially those translated from the Chinese, but it is generally thought that the Chinese name 'cloud ear' applies more to *A. auricula* than to the other.

WOOD MUSHROOM a name loosely applied to the numerous mushrooms which grow in woods, is sometimes used specifically of *Agaricus* (or *Psalliota*) *sylvicola* (or *silvicola*), the woodland counterpart of the common field mushroom of Europe. This has a white or cream cap which smells of anise, bruises yellow, and measures up to 10 cm (4") across. Found also in N. America, it is generally rated as inferior to the field mushroom, but still a good edible. Calonge (1979) praises its aromatic qualities.

The PRINCE, a related species, is sometimes called the large wood mushroom.

WOODRUFF *Galium odoratum*, a wild herb of Europe and W. Asia, now also found in N. America. It has sweetly fragrant flowers and leaves which, when dried, have a lasting scent of new-mown hay; so it is also called 'sweet woodruff'. The plant has a reputation for being invigorating.

Woodruff is used to flavour some N. European sausages and certain French jellies and puddings, but its main use is in drinks, especially of the cooling summer 'cup' type. It is particularly popular in Germany, where the young shoots are steeped in white wine, sometimes with the addition of brandy and sugar, to make *Maitrunk*.

WOOD SORREL *Oxalis acetosella*, a wild plant of Europe and N. America whose leaves are more bitter than those of true SORREL but are nonetheless eaten as a green vegetable, or added in small quantities to salads. There are numerous related species of which the same can be said; but the important member of the genus is *O. tuberosa*, prized for its edible tuber rather than its leaves, and known as OCA.

WORCESTER(SHIRE) SAUCE originated in the 1840s. The story goes that it was the result of an accidental oversight in a Worcester chemist's shop, Lea Perrin's. A barrel of spice vinegar, made according to an Indian recipe for a customer but never collected, was left for some years in the cellar. It began to ferment; possibly, some say, because one of the ingredients was soy sauce. The shopkeeper was about to throw out the spoiled barrel, but fortunately tasted the contents and discovered that they had undergone an intriguing change. He therefore bottled them, sold them as a sauce, and began to produce more.

Worcester sauce is now widely used not only in English cooking but all over the world, sometimes in locally manufactured versions. In Japan, for instance, soy sauce and Worcester sauce (known to the Japanese as *ustasosu*) are the two standard sauces to be found on dining tables; Hosking (1992) gives historical background for the latter and explains its particular appeal to the Japanese palate on the ground that it enhances the flavour known to the Japanese as *umami* (see TASTE). Yan-Kit So (1992) describes the corresponding phenomenon in China:

In many Cantonese kitchens Lea & Perrins Worcestershire sauce stands as a twin to the soy sauce bottle, and is used most popularly as a dipping sauce for deep-fried food such as spring rolls and prawn balls.

Being highly concentrated, Worcester sauce is employed mostly as a CONDIMENT or an ingredient rather than as a relish like the BROWN SAUCE which it superficially resembles.

The ingredients are supposedly secret, and it is said that no imitations of the original brand have achieved quite the same flavour.

WORMS in the class of creatures known as annelids, exist in various forms, all or most of which are likely to be edible, although rarely or never eaten.

A shining exception is provided by the extraordinary marine worms of the Pacific described under PALOLO. Another marine worm which is eaten with some enthusiasm is the SHIPWORM.

On land, earthworms are a prized item in the diet of many birds, and writers of the 'guess-what? school' have been able to produce some information about their being eaten by human beings in various parts of the world; but they are generally seen as being too repulsive. A children's rhyme, portraying such worms as the very last thing anyone would normally wish to eat, is significant, and became the subject of an anonymously initiated correspondence from 1995 onwards in the journal *PPC*. It begins:

Nobody likes me, everybody hates me,
Guess I'll go and eat worms,
Long fat curly ones, short fat wriggly ones,
I bite their heads off,
I suck their bodies out,
I throw the skins away.
Nobody knows how well I thrive,
On worms three times a day.

Simmonds (1859) gives an anecdote about a painting called *Luther at the Diet of Worms*. A child, having studied this, remarked: 'Mother, I see Luther and the table, but where are the worms?' This is but one of scores of jokes provoked by the curious title 'Diet of Worms'.

Many kinds of worm exist as parasites in animals, including human beings and some are ingested accidentally (for example the tiny nematode worms found in some fish), but there seem to be no instances of their being chosen as a human food.

'Mopane worms' are described under CATERPILLAR.

WORMWOOD *Artemisia* spp, herbs of a dark reputation as a source of the drink absinth, production of which has been banned since 1915 in France, its homeland.

There are three species: *A. absinthium*, the common wormwood of Europe and W. and C. Asia, and introduced to N. America; *A. pontica*, the more delicate 'Roman wormwood' of SE Europe and W. Asia; and *A. maritima*, a smaller plant which grows typically in salt marshes and coastal regions from W. Europe to Siberia. The first two yield oil of wormwood, a bitter substance containing toxins, and it was from the first species that absinth, notorious for its bitter and toxic content, was distilled.

The notoriety of absinth was greatest in 19th-century France. Alexandre DUMAS *père* (1873) remarked that any regimental surgeon would agree that absinth had killed more French soldiers in Africa than had Arab weapons; and that it had had equally dire effects on the ranks of poets: 'Some of our bohemian poets have called absinth the green Muse. Some others, not in this group, have died from the poisonous embraces of this same Muse.' He instanced the fatal passion of de Musset for absinth, 'which perhaps served also to give his verses such a bitter flavour'.

It seems, however, that absinth or wormwood were sometimes used, in very small doses, as a culinary flavouring agent. Landry (1978) speaks of German dishes involving fatty meats in which a 'mini-bouquet' of wormwood would be introduced but discarded before serving. However, as he points out, a similar effect could always be achieved with less or no danger by using related herbs, notably *A. vulgaris*, MUGWORT, or *A. abrotanum*, SOUTHERNWOOD. Indeed, another member of the genus is *A. dracunculus*, TARRAGON, well known in the kitchen and perfectly safe.

WRASSE the usual English name for fish of the family Labridae, of which there are hundreds of species around the world in temperate, subtropical, and tropical waters. Only a small proportion of them are marketed and eaten, and only a few of them have importance as food. The TAUTOG, which is described separately, is probably the most important.

The typical wrasse is a fairly small fish, brightly coloured, thick lipped, well toothed, and furnished with a single dorsal spine of which the spiny (forward) part is much larger than the soft (rear) part.

Features of their life style have been well described by Wheeler (1979).

Many species of wrasse have been found to act as cleaner fishes, picking external parasites off other fishes at recognized stations. This has even been reported in the temperate waters of England and New Zealand, although best known among tropical species. Wrasses also show most interesting breeding behaviour, the differential colouring of males and females leading to elaborate pre-spawning displays. Some species construct nests out of plant material which are guarded, once the eggs are deposited, by the male. As a group they are well known for their habit of sleeping at night, either buried in the sand of the bottom or wedged between rocks. Observation on sleeping wrasses in the Bermuda Aquarium have shown that they go through a period of rapid eye movement (REM) which, in higher vertebrates, is usually associated with dreaming. It thus suggests that some wrasses dream.

Four of the best-known European wrasses are *Labrus bergylta*, the ballan wrasse; *L. viridis*, French *labre vert*; *L. merula*, French *merle*; and *L. bimaculatus* (or *mixtus*), the cuckoo wrasse. The first of these belongs to the E. Atlantic and is usually recognizable by its profusion of white spots on a darker background. The second (normally green in colour) and the third belong principally to the Mediterranean; while the fourth is found in both the Mediterranean and E. Atlantic. The first three may reach a length of 50 cm (21") or so, while the fourth is somewhat smaller. All are eaten, as are a number of their smaller relations, although these are more likely to finish up in a fish soup than to be cooked by themselves. One other species which deserves mention, because popular as a food fish in the Balearics, is the cleaver wrasse, *Xyrichthys novacula*, which has an extraordinary pattern of vertical stripes on head and body; its Spanish name is *raor*.

In the W. Atlantic there are numerous species, mostly small reef fish, but including one larger fish, *Lachnolaimus maximus*, the hogfish, which may reach a length of 90 cm (3') and a weight of over 10 kg (25 lb) and is an excellent food fish.

Californian sport fishermen take quite large numbers of *Pimelometopon pulchrum*, the California sheephead. Fitch and Lavenberg (1971) record two large specimens, one of which weighed over 15 kg (36 lb) while the other, which was 53 years old, was almost as heavy. The flesh is said to be fine grained and mild in flavour.

In Asian waters, there are only a few wrasses which are highly rated as food fish. One is *Choerodon schoonleini*, known as *tsing yi* at Hong Kong, where it is an expensive delicacy if sold alive, and is usually steamed. Another is *Cheilinus chlorurus*, which has numerous red spots on its head which may form lines and anastomosed figures (i.e. in a pattern like that of branches of trees). However, the prize wrasse of SE Asian waters is undoubtedly *Cheilinus undulatus*, the species commonly referred to as Napoleon wrasse or hump-headed Maori wrasse, which is highly prized as a food fish and may grow to a great size (exceptionally, up to 2.3 m/7.5' and almost 200 kg/over 400 lb). Like certain kinds of GROUPER, these noble fish are amenable to human contacts if approached and handled in a friendly way. The pleasing impression which they thus create is heightened by their intellectual appearance.

WRECKFISH *Polyprion americanum,* a large (maximum length 2 m/80") greyish or dark brown fish of the family Perchichthyidae, related to the GROUPER family.

It takes its name from its habit of lurking in wrecked ships or similar debris. Its range includes the S. and N. Atlantic and the Mediterranean. It occurs as far north as Norway and Newfoundland, but rarely, and is indeed not common anywhere. It is prepared like groupers.

YABBY the Australian name for certain CRAYFISH, notably the semi-aquatic ones of the genus *Cherax*, and especially *C. destructor*, is a version of the Aboriginal name *yappée*. The term is not used in all parts of Australia, nor does it mean the same thing in all the parts where it is used; but the usage indicated is heavily dominant.

The range of the yabby covers something like a third of Australia, extending north from Victoria and S. Australia. Maximum dimensions are 16 cm (6") and 150 g (5 oz). Early settlers in Australia did not take to the yabby, although the Aboriginals could be seen eating them with enjoyment, but during the 20th century their popularity grew and they acquired a certain symbolic value. Olszewski (1980) compiled an impressive sampler of poems, cartoons, folklore, and jests to do with what he called 'the humble yabby'.

See illustration opposite, and also MARRON, a related species of W. Australia.

YACON *Polymnia sonchifolia*, a plant of the SUNFLOWER family which is indigenous to the Andean region of S. America. It is valued for its round or spindle-shaped tubers, which are usually eaten raw, but can also be boiled or baked. They have little nutritional value, but provide a pleasantly sweet and crunchy addition to salads, with a refreshing flavour; they have been compared to apples and watermelons in this respect.

Unlike the majority of roots and tubers, but like other relations of the sunflower, yacon stores carbohydrates mainly in the form of inulin. This consists largely of fructose. Humans have no enzyme for dealing with inulin, so it passes through their digestive tract without being metabolized and, as a consequence, yacon provides few calories and may have some potential as a low-calorie sweet diet food.

In its native region the plant is a popular item in family gardens, but not common in the markets. The tubers keep very well.

In Ecuador and Peru the name JICAMA is used; but this is better reserved for the species *Pachyrrhizus erosus*.

YAK the male of the species *Bos grunniens*, belonging to the same family as the bison, cow, water-buffalo, and eland. It is the female of the species, called dri, not yak, which is the well-known source of food in TIBET and nearby mountainous regions. It is uphill work trying to persuade Europeans and Americans to use the word 'dri', since in the English language yak has come to mean both genders. However, one should try, since writing about 'yak milk' is as absurd as writing about 'ox milk'.

Dri milk is richer than cow's milk because it contains more butterfat. It is readily turned into YOGHURT (*sho*) in Tibet and one way of making butter starts with this yoghurt. When butter is made, thin buttermilk will be left over and this can be turned into a soft cheese (*chura loenpa*) which is much used in Tibetan cookery.

YAM (*See page 856*)

YAM BEAN a name applied to several leguminous plants with swollen edible tubers. The most important is *Pachyrrhizus erosus*, a perennial vine native to C. and S. America which has in the last few hundred years been introduced to most tropical and subtropical regions of the world, including parts of Africa, India, SE Asia, and Hawaii (where it is said to bear the name 'chopsui potato').

The tuber is starchy with a crisp texture and a slightly sweet taste. It can be eaten raw; or cooked, e.g. in soups; or sliced and made into chips. The Chinese include it with stir-fried vegetables as an alternative to water chestnuts or bamboo shoots. They also pickle it. In Indonesia the tuber is used in making *rujak*, a sharp and spicy salad in which fruits are the main ingredients.

Young pods may be eaten whole, but mature pods and the seeds within them are toxic.

The African yam bean, *Sphenostylis stenocarpa*, is widely known by its Hausa name, *girigiri*, but has many others, e.g. *kulege* (Ewe), *okpo dudu* (Ibo), and *sese* (Yoruba). Its starchy tubers look like sweet potatoes but taste more like ordinary potatoes. It also has seeds which are edible if soaked before being cooked. This plant has a wide distribution in tropical Africa and is an important source of starch and protein for Africans.

As explained under WINGED BEAN, the tubers of leguminous plants are generally more nutritious than other tubers.

YARG a full-cream cow's milk cheese first produced in 1983 in Cornwall by a couple called Gray; hence the name, which is Gray spelt backwards. Maggie Black (1989) states that it is based on a Cornish prototype of the 15th century.

A wheel of Yarg, in its wrapping of (edible) nettle leaves, usually measures about 25 cm (10") across and 7 or 8 cm (3") high. After being mould ripened for three weeks, it has a white and downy rind over a creamy surface area containing a moist, crumbly interior. Fat content 30%, moisture content 40%: so midway between the cheeses called semi-soft and those called semi-hard.

YEAST has been used in the preparation of food and drink for as long as there have been leavened bread and beer, but it was only in the 19th century, thanks to the work of Pasteur, that its nature was understood.

Even now, yeast can understandably be treated as a sort of miracle. Elizabeth DAVID (1977), in a fine account of the history of yeast in English baking, remarks that:

In Chaucer's England one of the names for yeast or barm was goddisgoode 'bicause it cometh of the grete grace of God'. These words imply a blessing. To me that is just what it is. It is also mysterious, magical. No matter how familiar its action may become nor how successful the attempts to explain it in terms of chemistry and to manufacture it by the ton, yeast still to a certain extent retains its mystery.

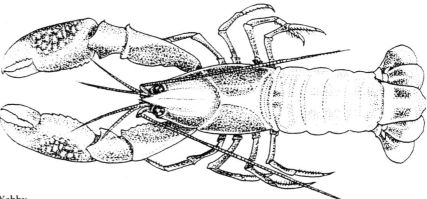

Yabby

Yeast is a single-celled fungus, of which hundreds of species have been identified. Those of the genera *Saccharomyces* and *Candida* are the most useful. The single cells are very small: hundreds of millions to a teaspoonful. Instead of feeding by photosynthesis, as green plants do, they feed on carbohydrates (and other nutrients— their dietary needs are remarkably extensive, considering how small they are) and excrete alcohol. They breathe air and exhale carbon dioxide.

Various species of yeast reproduce in different ways, some vegetative (by fission or budding) and some sexual. They survive but are inactive in freezing conditions. They grow slowly at cool temperatures; steadily at 24 °C (80 °F); and unrestrainedly at 38 °C (100 °F). They are killed by a temperature of 60 °C (140 °F).

Despite the simplicity of their structure, yeast cells can operate in alternative ways; one that suits bread-making and one that is right for brewers. Given plenty of air and some food, yeast grows fast and produces a lot of carbon dioxide. It is the pressure of this gas which makes bread rise. Only a little alcohol is formed. However, in a fermentation vat, where there is almost no air but an abundance of food in the form of sugar, the yeast cells change to a different mode, breathing little and concentrating on turning sugar into alcohol.

The same species of yeast, *Saccharomyces cerevisiae*, constitutes both baker's and brewer's yeast, and the connection between brewing and baking used to be intimate. A model of a combined brewhouse and bakehouse found in an Egyptian tomb of *c.*2000 BC is to be seen in the British Museum. Beer leaven, known as 'barm', was used for bread-making until quite recent times. The making of beer, black bread, and the alcoholic drink KVASS were traditionally linked in Russia. There are still some who believe that bread made with barm had an especially good flavour.

However, it is no longer true that the same yeast is used for brewing and baking.

Many different strains of *S. cerevisiae* have evolved or been selected, and those which are used for brewing are different from those which best suit the bakers, and are cultured on a different substrate. The various species and strains also differ in a way which has important consequences for flavour. The complex chemical reactions which the enzymes secreted by yeast bring about in the process of fermentation include the formation of minute quantities of organic acids, minor alcohols, and esters. These affect flavour, and they vary from strain to strain. The phenomenon is particularly noticeable in wine-making, where the yeast used is generally a strain of *S. ellipsoideus*.

Yeasts may grow and **work with other micro-organisms**. In SOURDOUGH BREAD the yeast, often of the genus *Candida*, is the partner of LACTIC ACID-producing BACTERIA. Yeasts also work with bacteria to ferment KEFIR and KOUMISS. The manufacture of SOY SAUCE, and of the Japanese drink SAKÉ, requires the presence of MOULDS which produce sugar for the yeast to consume. Many surface-ripened cheeses are worked on by a mixed culture which includes yeast, although always in a subordinate role to moulds (as on BRIE) or bacteria (as on LIMBURGER). Yeasts, moulds, and bacteria all co-operate in the fermentation of COCOA beans, to develop the flavour of chocolate.

There are three types of **commercial yeasts for baking** to be had.

• Fresh compressed yeast, best bought directly from a bakery, comes in moist cakes which are creamy or grey. The life of yeast in this form is limited, but may be prolonged by refrigeration or freezing.
• Dried yeast, called 'active dry (baking) yeast' in the USA, is in the form of dried granules, and keeps for a year or more, all the better if refrigerated. Weight for weight, it has twice the potency of compressed yeast.

(cont. on page 857)

Yam

Properly the name of an edible tuber of plants of the genus *Dioscorea*, 'yam' is often used in a general sense to embrace other tropical root crops such as SWEET POTATO, TARO, OCA, etc. The wider usage (although permitting the use of Soun's drawing of sweet potato as a decorative feature on page 854) is an inconvenience; all the more so since the genus *Dioscorea* itself comprises scores of species which are often difficult to distinguish from each other. However, one must not complain. The origin of the word 'yam' was such that its meaning had to be elastic. The story goes that Portuguese slave traders, watching Africans digging up some roots, asked what they were called. Failing to understand the question aright, the Africans replied that it was 'something to eat', *nyami* in Guinea. This became *inhame* in Portuguese and then *igname* in French, and yam in English.

The scientific name *Dioscorea* refers to the classical Greek writer on medicine, Dioscorides, and serves as a reminder that many yams have medicinal as well as culinary uses. Their reputation in making poultices is high. Some also serve as a source of steroid drugs, including a main ingredient of the contraceptive pill. An even more negative function is fulfilled by the few which produce toxins for arrow poisons, in Malaysia, and for fish poisons.

All edible yams have to be cooked before consumption, to destroy the bitter, toxic substance dioscorine which they contain in the raw state. When cooked they are starchy and bland, sometimes slightly sweet. No yams constitute a gastronomic excitement; they are just plain, filling food, providing plenty of carbohydrate and about as much protein as the potato.

In some regions yams are an important staple. This is true of Fiji and other Pacific islands; and also of Nigeria and other W. African countries, although the position of the yam there as the most popular staple food has been weakened by increased cultivation of the sweet potato.

The yam has one serious disadvantage; it extends deep underground, as far as 2 m (6'), and digging it up can be an exhausting business. Thus, although yams have been known in most parts of China since ancient times they have not been much eaten there except during famines. And, when a hardy variety of yam was introduced experimentally to Europe, to relieve the distress caused by the potato blights of the 1840s, it was grown successfully enough but failed to become popular.

PRINCIPAL SPECIES

Yams are so numerous that only the main cultivated species can be mentioned. Most of them are natives of the Old World, from SE Asia, nearby Pacific islands, and Africa; but there is also a small group native to S. America. Yams existed at least as far back as the beginning of the Jurassic era, when dinosaurs had not yet been succeeded by mammals and S. America and Asia were still joined. After the continents separated at the end of the Cretaceous era, the evolution of American yams proceeded separately, but they are still not much different from their Old World relatives. It is true that, as a group, they tend to produce clumps of small tubers rather than single huge ones; but they share this convenient habit with certain Old World yams. The differences between Asian and African yams, which were separated only in historic times by the drying up of the intervening land, Arabia, are also slight. The transfer of useful species by human agency has anyway confused the picture.

Even within the main cultivated species, yams vary to a remarkable extent in size, shape, and colour. The typical yam, if there be such a thing, is a large, oblong root which looks something like a mortadella sausage encased in a bark-like skin. It is this sort of yam which is seen in markets in industrial countries where there are immigrants from yam-eating countries. But where yams are indigenous and widely eaten the diversity is great. Some yams produce many small tubers, no larger than potatoes. Others produce single giants. The greatest recorded weight is 60 kg (130 lb), for a greater Asiatic yam dug up in Malaysia (source cited by Burkill, 1965–6). There are intermediate sizes and shapes, including some with branching 'fingers' and others which first develop downwards and then curve back up towards the surface of the soil. (The diversity of shapes can be illustrated by just a few of the many Malay common names for particular kinds: peaked-cap yam, elephant's ear yam, snake yam, buffalo-thigh yam.) The rind may be rough or smooth, pale in colour, or brown, or purple. The flesh is often white or yellow, but sometimes pink or purple, either just under the skin or all through.

- *D. alata*, the greater Asiatic yam or water yam, is the most important species in SE Asia and the nearby islands. A common name for it is 'ten months yam', since it takes that time for the tubers to develop. In Fiji, where this yam is the staple food, most of the names for the (11, not 12) months and seasons refer to the stages of its growth. Of all yams this species produces the largest tubers, though there are also smaller and branched ones. Some are white fleshed; others as purple as a beetroot. This species spread to Madagascar by AD 1000, the African mainland not long after, and was being grown in the W. Indies in the early 16th century, having been brought over by slave traders.
- *D. cayenensis*, the white or yellow Guinea yam, is the principal species of W. Africa, where its most usual African name is *allato*. The white and yellow varieties are sometimes called respectively 'eight months' and 'twelve months yam'. The former, distinguished as *var rotundata*, has moister and softer flesh than the latter, and also keeps better in storage. It is normally prepared as a boiled vegetable but widely used in the preparation

of FOO-FOO. Most W. African cultivars are considered to have a superior flavour and contain no toxic constituents.

- *D. esculenta,* the lesser Asiatic yam, has long been cultivated in India, the whole of SE Asia, and N. Australia, where one aboriginal name for it is 'karro'. Despite its designation as 'lesser', it can reach a large size. There are single and bunched varieties. The flesh is soft and, in most kinds, has a slightly sweet taste. It does not store well, and is generally eaten as a cooked vegetable.

- *D. batatas,* the Chinese yam, is a cultivated form of another species which still grows wild in China and Japan. It is more resistant to cold than most other yams. The tubers are very long, as much as 1.5 m (5.5'). This yam, the one most eaten in China and Japan, is also cultivated in SE Asia, where the climate is not too hot, and in America. A starch used in cooking, called Guiana arrowroot, is made from the tubers.

- *D. globosa,* the globe yam, is the species preferred for cultivation in India. All its varieties are white.

- *D. bulbifera,* the oddest yam, is the 'air potato', which has poor underground tubers but also bears small tubers above ground on its long, climbing vine. This SE Asian yam is also cultivated in tropical S. America, the Caribbean, and parts of the southern USA, but is nowhere a major variety. A few other species also have aerial tubers.

- *D. trifida,* the only native American yam which is cultivated to any extent, is known as the cushcush yam. This bears clusters of up to a dozen small tubers whose texture and flavour, by the generally undemanding standards applied to yams, are good. It is grown in the Caribbean islands and tropical S. America. It is baked or cooked as a vegetable and some cultivars have an excellent flavour.

- *D. opposita,* Chinese yam, a native of China, is widely grown in China, S. Japan, Korea, and nearby islands. The tubers are eaten as a vegetable, usually after slicing or grating and boiling.

- *D. japonica* is cultivated in several varieties in Japan. Its name there, *yamanoimo* (or *yamaimo*) means moun-

tain tuber. Since antiquity it has been highly prized as food. Its underground tuber has a long tapering shape, sometimes reaching 2 m (over 6') in length. The skin is brown; the flesh white. Because it is slim and brittle, digging it up without breaking it requires a high degree of expertise and once it has been successfully dug up, it is transported with great care, coddled in straw. *Yamanoimo* has traditionally been considered a particularly nourishing food whose energy giving quality is compared to that of the eel, and so it is sometimes called 'the eel of the mountains'. Some people even attribute to it an APHRODISIAC property. This is doubtful, but it is true that it contains a large amount of diastase and thus helps digestion. *Yamanoimo* is nearly always eaten raw, in the form of *tororo*.

USES AND CUSTOMS

Most yams keep well and were often used as provisions for lengthy sea voyages. Steaming, or boiling and mashing (or boiling and then grilling), or roasting, or frying (including fried croquettes of mashed yam) are recommended ways of cooking them. See also FOO-FOO.

Yams can be ground to make a kind of meal, which also keeps well.

Lovelock (1972) describes some unusual practices. In Fiji, the yam is 'grown in earth that is hard and unprepared in the belief that it is a sporting sort of vegetable that likes to feel resistance before it will show its strength (and therefore grow large)'. He continues:

In the D'Entrecasteaux Islands, off the east coast of New Guinea, there lives a gloomy and suspicious people who believe that yams travel underground from garden to garden. They therefore spend a good deal of time trying to entice their neighbours' yams into their own plots by magic; and yet are righteously indignant if someone else's superior magic (or husbandry) produces a crop better than their own. In the neighbouring Trobriand Islands there is a much happier and more open race. These make a parade of their wealth by constructing fairly open yam-houses in order that all can see the quality of their produce, putting roots of best quality well to the fore, of course. Particularly fine yams, however, are displayed outside the stores, often framed and decorated with paint.

- Instant yeast is a type of dried yeast formed into much smaller particles. It is intended to be mixed directly with flour rather than dissolved in water as usual. The small size of the grains gives it a large surface area, so that it can spring into action as soon as the flour is wetted.

For use in baking the amount of yeast should not exceed the correct proportion, usually given as 1 oz of yeast for 3½ lb flour. A higher proportion of yeast leads not to greater speed but to failure. A lower proportion results in a longer proving time, but possibly in a better flavour. Dried yeast

should not be used in bread recipes which call for a lot of yeast, for example for brioche dough, as they have a strongly 'yeasty' flavour which can spoil the finished product.

Yeasts as food. In addition to fermenting and flavouring other foods, yeasts themselves may be used as food. They contain much protein and all but one of the B vitamins (B12), and some of them will grow on the most unpromising material such as the waste products of wood pulp mills or even oil refineries. They are consequently used to provide dietary supplements for countries whose diets are deficient in protein. This is a new

development, but the consumption of yeast in the form of brewer's yeast pills and yeast extract dates back to the 19th century and these products still have a reputation as health foods.

Yeast extract is not, strictly speaking, an extract, since none of the various processes used to produce it is 'extraction'. The yeast is allowed to 'digest' itself with its own enzymes, breaking down its own proteins by HYDROLYSIS. It is then concentrated, and sometimes flavoured. If brewer's yeast is the starting point, it is treated to remove its unduly bitter taste. The product does not supply complete protein, as meat extract does, but is nutritious. In its common form it is dark brown and viscous, with a strong, salty tang.

Wild yeasts are everywhere, and may intrude where they are not wanted. If a dish of sugary food, or a fruit juice, starts to taste alcoholic, they are to blame; primitive wines were (and sometimes still are) fermented by the yeasts naturally present on the surface of grapes. Wild yeasts can also induce bloating and softening in home-made pickles. But they cause less trouble than the moulds to which they are related; and the same kinds of hygienic precautions are effective against both.   (RH)

YEHEB NUT (also yeeb, ye-eb, ye'eb), the seed of *Cordeauxia edulis*, a small leguminous bush of hot and dry regions, notably Somalia. The National Academy of Sciences (1979), noting that this is now regarded as an endangered species, explains its usefulness:

The ye-eb is such a hardy shrub that during drought it is sometimes the only food left for nomads. Its food value has at times enabled destitute Somalis to rely on it alone for subsistence. . . .

The seeds alone make an unusually nourishing and balanced diet. Although their protein and carbohydrate contents are less than those of most other pulses, the seeds contain both fat and sugar.

These nuts have not entered commercial trade and seem unlikely to do so, so few people outside their native region have tasted them. Some authors have suggested that their flavour and texture are comparable with those of the CHESTNUT or CASHEW nut.

YELLOWMAN is an Irish TOFFEE confection made of butter, brown sugar, vinegar, and GOLDEN SYRUP. These ingredients are melted and boiled at a temperature of 285 °C (545 °F). At this stage a quantity of sodium bicarbonate is added to the liquid causing it to foam spontaneously. This additional ingredient gives the confection its characteristic brittle and honeycombed texture. Production of the confection probably dates to the early 19th century when sodium bicarbonate was first introduced into Ireland.

The delicacy is popular in N. Ireland and has a particular association with the Lammas Fair in Ballycastle, County Antrim. Ballycastle, which is a sheep and pony fair, is held on the last Tuesday in August. Traditionally young boys attended the fair sporting delicately fashioned plaits of corn straw called 'Harvest Knots' in their buttonholes, designed to win the attention of the young girls. If successful they might then express their affections further, by treating

their new found love to some Yellowman. A popular traditional ballad recounts:

At the Ould Lammas Fair, boys, were you ever there?
At the Ould Lammas Fair in Ballycastle, oh?
Did you treat your Mary Anne to dulce and yellowman?
At the Ould Lammas Fair in Ballycastle, oh?

Yellowman is known colloquially as yellaman in N. Ireland. For 'dulce', see DULSE.   RSe

YEMEN The northern part of Yemen includes the highest part of the Arabian plateau with areas of the highest rainfall which comes with the summer monsoon. The terraced slopes grow principally SORGHUM, also qat and COFFEE. Wheat and maize are grown under irrigation in the high valleys. The oases of Shabwa, Ma'rib, and Nejran were once prosperous towns on the Spice Road leading to the Mediterranean.

The southern part of Yemen, formerly the British Colony of Aden, lies to the west of Oman in the southern part of the Arabian peninsula, on the rim of the Indian Ocean.

The culinary symbol, so to speak, of Yemen is HILBEH (or hulba), essentially a fenugreek paste, often beaten to a foam. This serves as a topping for *maraq*, the soupy stew. (The importance of the fenugreek paste is such that the whole dish may be called hulba.) Fenugreek also figures in the S. Yemeni recipe for the spicy sauce *s'hûg* or *z'hûg* (in N. Yemen, this word, more often in the plural, *sahâwig*, means a condiment of tomato, onion, and chilli). The peasants live on '*asîd*, a sorghum porridge which they dress with spiced butter or yoghurt.

The staple grains are MILLETS; 80% of Yemen's grain production is either sorghum or broomcorn millet. Breads, besides the usual Arab pocket bread *khubz* (see PITTA), include the tandoor bread *maluj* and *lahuh*, a sourdough crêpe cooked on one side only—essentially the same as the Ethiopian INJERA, but made from white sorghum, a grain unique to Yemen. On festive occasions, particularly in the region of Sanaa, the meal begins with *bint al-sahn* (daughter of the dish) a sort of flaky crêpe pastry. The egg-rich dough is formed into very thin leaves which are smothered with *samneh* (clarified butter, see GHEE) and placed on top of each other in layers forming a sort of cake, and then baked. The bread is served hot from the oven with more *samneh* and sometimes honey.

Because of the summer rains, Yemen supports an unusually large population for the Arabian peninsula. This, and the country's isolation from other Arab population centres (culinary influences are more likely to come from India and

Indonesia, because of Yemen's maritime tradition), have made for many distinctive features in the Yemeni kitchen. It is the only country which still regularly uses cookware carved from soapstone. Surprisingly, the frail-looking stone pans (*miglâ*), which rather resemble ashtrays, can survive years of hard use. Yemenis claim food tastes better cooked in stone than in metal.

MOCHA, named after Yemen's Red Sea port, al-Makhâ, is one of the world's finest varieties of COFFEE, which found its beginnings in the Yemen. Since shortly after the First World War, however, for various reasons production in the region of origin has been restricted. Curiously, coffee-drinking is little appreciated and in any case very few Yemenis can afford it. Instead they make *qishr*, a tea of ground coffee husks which has an aroma like unroasted coffee beans, possibly adding ground ginger (and sometimes cinnamon, cardamom, sugar). When real coffee is drunk it is heavily scented with cardamom and rosewater. Tea, which is sweetened with sugar (in the pot), is increasingly drunk, flavoured with the same spices as *qishr*.

The usual Arab hospitality prevails in the Yemen. Eating customs are that the men eat first and the women and children have their meal afterwards or in another room. Food is eaten off a cloth spread on the carpet and all the food is eaten communally from pots, platters, and bowls. Food is eaten with the right hand as in other Muslim countries.

Qat leaves, which come from the plant *Catha edulis*, and which are a mild stimulant, are often chewed after lunch or during the afternoon, especially in N. Yemen. They are not swallowed; instead, they are collected inside one cheek while being chewed.

Just as in western countries people may favour their 'local produce' or 'produits de la région', so do Yemenis esteem what they call *baladi* (i.e. indigenous) food. For certain purposes, e.g. nourishing a woman after childbirth, *baladi* food is obligatory.

Jews from the Yemen who have emigrated to Israel have had a considerable impact on the cuisine of ISRAEL.

YIN-YANG a concept of Chinese philosophy which can be described as the interaction of the two basic opposing forces of the universe, namely yin (female, dark, cold) and yang (male, light, hot). The sun is the symbol of yang, while the moon represents yin. This duality is all pervasive but has acquired (possibly as a result of influences from, or transmitted through, India) a specific application to food. The necessity to maintain a balance in the body and in the diet between yin and yang is a fundamental principle, often unspoken, which underlies the planning of diets and meals for the Chinese.

Yin foods include those which have a cooling effect, watery items such as fruits, and foods of mild flavour. Yang foods, representing strength and heat, include animal foods and hot spices. It is appropriate to think of all foods as constituting a spectrum from one extreme to the other, many of them inclining only slightly in one or other direction.

There are obvious parallels between this Chinese system and the SARDI/GARMI principle of Iran and Afghanistan, and the doctrine of the FOUR HUMOURS which was most fully expressed by the classical Greek writer GALEN. Indeed, philosophical ideas embodying duality and calling for a balance between opposing tendencies seem to be almost universal.

The relationship between yin-yang on the one hand and the Chinese system of the five elements on the other is not clear. No one seems to know which came first. However, as both are elements of the first importance in Chinese thinking about the cosmos, it does seem clear that neither should be considered without, at the least, some knowledge of the other. The five elements are earth, wood, fire, metal, and water.

YLANG-YLANG *Cananga odorata*, an Asian plant whose fragrant flowers yield by distillation an essential oil which is used for flavouring various confectionery goods and the like, and also coconut oil.

YOGHURT a remarkable example of a food from Asia which has succeeded during the 20th century in invading the diet of the western world to such an extent that it has become a staple.

Yoghurt is one of the fermented milk foods whose origins are probably multiple. It is easy enough to imagine how, in parts of C. or W. Asia, unintended fermentation of milk could have produced something like yoghurt, and that people would have noticed that this would keep for much longer than fresh milk, besides tasting good. There is another advantage which applies particularly to many Asians. Yoghurt is much more digestible than milk for those who suffer from LACTOSE INTOLERANCE—a common condition in Asia but rare among Europeans. The reason for this is that the fermentation which produces yoghurt converts most of the lactose in milk to LACTIC ACID.

The main role in the fermentation is always played by lactic acid-producing BACTERIA, and it is this acid which gives all yoghurts their characteristic sour taste. In many types of yoghurt the bacteria are

joined by YEASTS, making the product mildly alcoholic and sometimes slightly fizzy; see KEFIR.

Yoghurt is the Turkish name for the product, long since adapted into the English language, no doubt because yoghurt reached W. Europe through Turkey and the Balkans. The original yoghurts of Turkey and the Balkans are typically fermented by two species of bacteria, *Streptococcus thermophilus* and *Lactobacillus bulgaricus*. These are commonly employed in commercially made yoghurts in western countries, but do not produce results which taste like a farmhouse yoghurt in, say, BULGARIA. One reason, that they are not based on whole fresh milk, could in principle be surmounted. However, the other reason is that the special characteristics of the Bulgarian farmhouse yoghurt depend on certain micro-organisms which are naturally present in Bulgarian farmyards but cannot be replicated for use elsewhere.

Yoghurt can be made from many different milks; cow, goat, sheep, mare, water-buffalo, camel, and dri (female YAK). These all have different characteristics, and not only in features such as texture and flavour. Yoghurt from goat's milk is relatively stable when used in cooking, and sheep's milk yoghurt is also better from this point of view than cow's milk yoghurt, but any yoghurt can be helped by the addition of a little cornflour to remain stable in cooked dishes.

In the western world, yoghurt comes in various forms (e.g. strained, flavoured, 'live') but it is almost always just yoghurt, whereas in the regions where it has been important for centuries, or millennia, it is also available in the form of yoghurt products. These include yoghurt drinks (see AYRAN and LASSI); yoghurt cheeses, which at their simplest are made by putting yoghurt in a muslin bag and letting the whey drip out; and various other specialities which enable yoghurt to be kept for much longer, even indefinitely. These last products include KASHK and QUROOT, and also *lebne* (or *labne*, *laban*), about which Furugh Hourani (1984) wrote in most evocative fashion, explaining that in Lebanon yoghurt would be transformed into *lebne* by straining and adding salt, and that the *lebne* merchant would arrive with his donkey carrying on both its sides heavy white cloth bags of *lebne*. What he brought was no optional luxury, it was a necessary and major item for the larder. 'Three or four hundred kilos a year was not an exceptional intake for one family.' Once the man and his donkey had gone,

the women and girls of the family would gather around the table which had been scrubbed like their hands and arms to remove any dirt or dust which would cause the *lebne* to turn bitter and disintegrate; each one would cut off a small

portion from the large and solid mountain of *lebne* and roll it in the palm of the hands into small balls the size of a quail's egg, though some families preferred a larger ball the size of a ping pong ball. The balls would then be placed in rows on large trays, covered with a clean cloth, and placed in a cool spot to dry for about two more days. Finally they would be put into large jars and covered with olive oil. Preserved like this, *lebne* lasts until the following spring or even longer if kept in the refrigerator. In the mountains of Lebanon *lebne* balls in olive oil are the basic diet of many families: they take their place on the table morning, noon and evening along with the equally essential olive. Spread on the paper-thin loaves of mountain bread they are carried by children going to school to be eaten on the way or during the lunch break.

The importance of yoghurt in the Indian subcontinent is comparable, and it is freely used in cookery both there and in C. Asia. *Raita*, the dish of cucumber in yoghurt with mint, wherever it may have originated, is now met not only in India, the Near East (it is *mast-o khiyar* in Iran, made with very small and almost seedless cucumbers), and the Balkans (*tsatsiki* in Greece). Various savoury dishes such as BURAN are widespread, but it is noticeable that in many cultures there is a sort of rule that fish must not be combined with yoghurt (a topic explored by Davidson, 1988*a*).

Yoghurt is generally regarded as an important health-promoting food, and has been thought to contribute to longevity, notably in the Smolyan district of BULGARIA. Maria Kaneva-Johnson (1995) provides a useful survey of the factors promoting longevity in the Balkans, concluding that the frugal diet traditionally followed up in the mountains has been important in this respect, while making clear that yoghurt is but one feature of this diet.

See also SKYR; SHRIKHAND.

YORK an ancient and once well-known English variety of cheese, is also known as Cambridge, because the centre of its manufacture moved from York to around the city of Ely in Cambridgeshire, and to Bath. It is now almost extinct.

York is a soft, fresh, whole-milk cheese which is rectangular in shape and, in its most comely form, dramatically striped. A slice of curd, coloured orange by ANNATTO, is sandwiched between two uncoloured slices to produce this effect. York was often in the past flavoured with herbs.

YORKSHIRE CHRISTMAS PIE a huge raised PIE in the medieval tradition, which outlasted other kinds and became so popular in Yorkshire in the 18th century that pies were sent to London as festive Christmas fare. It was still being made in the closing years of the 19th century. It was one of those feats of 'Russian doll' stuffing which are better known as being made for Arab wedding feasts. A typical recipe is in Hannah Glasse's *The Art of Cookery* (1747). A very thick crust enclosed a turkey, which was stuffed with a goose, the goose with a fowl, then a partridge, then a pigeon. All these birds were boned. On one side of the turkey was a hare cut in pieces; on the other woodcocks, moorhens, or other small wild game. At least 2 kg (4 lb) of butter were also put in before the massive lid was closed and the pie baked. Not all pies were made with boned birds, so that some pies had to be dismantled and the various creatures removed to carve them, detracting from the pie's appeal.

YORKSHIRE PUDDING is made from an egg, flour, and milk BATTER cooked in a large shallow tin containing a layer of very hot beef DRIPPING. It is a popular accompaniment to roast beef in Britain, and the two together compose the 'traditional' Sunday lunch. Sometimes the batter is poured into smaller, round tins to make individual puddings but this is not the authentic Yorkshire method. Strictly speaking, the pudding, cut in squares, should be served with GRAVY before the meat, to take the edge off the appetite.

Batter puddings have a long history and exist in many forms, mostly sweet. According to C. Anne Wilson (1973) it would have been cooks in the north of England who devised the form for which Yorkshire became famous. She draws attention to a recipe for 'A Dripping Pudding' which was published in *The Whole Duty of a Woman* (1737):

Make a good batter as for pancakes; put it in a hot toss-pan over the fire with a bit of butter to fry the bottom a little, then put the pan and butter under a shoulder of mutton, instead of a dripping pan, keeping frequently shaking it by the handle and it will be light and savoury, and fit to take up when your mutton is enough; then turn it in a dish and serve it.

At this time, meat was roasted on a spit, or by suspending it from a jack in front of the fire, so the instruction to place the pudding under the meat meant that it was some inches below, not poured around the joint in the same baking tin. Hannah Glasse (1747) gave a similar recipe, calling it 'A Yorkshire pudding'. She makes it clear that it should be brown and dry, and remarks that: 'It is an exceeding good pudding, the gravy of the meat eats well with it.'

Jennifer Stead (1991*b*) discusses the origin and development of the dish. Commenting on the localized attribution of 'Yorkshire' attached to it, she notes that batter puddings were also known in the south of England;

Yorkshire batter puddings appear to have been distinguished by their lightness and crispness. This is obtained by introducing the batter into a pan containing fat which is smoking hot, thus starting to form a crust underneath straight away; as the pudding continues to cook, the air incorporated into the batter during mixing expands, making it rise, and the fierce heat dries out the top of the pudding leaving it crunchy. Stead relates the technique to the people:

This accords with their fabled brusque temperaments: the fact that they require spanking hot fat, explosions as the batter hits it, fierce heat, and crisp results, may explain why it has often been said that only Yorkshire folk—those possessing the Yorkshire temperament—can make a true Yorkshire pudding.

Such details had not escaped Hannah Glasse, who herself came from the north of England and who said that the dripping must boil before the batter is added.

Yorkshire people frequently castigate southerners for not being able to make proper Yorkshire puddings. Stead suggests that one reason for this is that cooks in the south are accustomed to making perfectly legitimate batter puddings of softer texture, which were never intended to be crisp and well risen. She thinks, however, that the main reason may be that throughout the 19th century cookery writers (mostly from the south) misunderstood and distorted the recipes for true Yorkshire pudding. As she says: 'it is clear that some writers had never clapped eyes on, let alone cooked, a Yorkshire pudding.'

New kitchen technology in the shape of the enclosed coal range, and later the gas or electric oven, changed the Yorkshire pudding in one essential. It was no longer possible to cook it under the roasting meat, and therefore it no longer received the juice dripping from the joint.

Yorkshire pudding was never eaten exclusively with beef. The early recipe for batter pudding mentions mutton; indeed, it could be served before any roast meat, in which case an appropriate sauce (mint, for lamb, or apple, for pork) might be served with it. Sugar, vinegar, jam, mustard, or golden syrup were other options, although the pudding was always eaten before the meat in Yorkshire, whatever was eaten with it.

For a Yorkshire pudding mixture with sausages embedded in it, see TOAD IN THE HOLE; this is but one of scores of variations on an outstandingly popular theme.

YSAÑO *Tropaeolum tuberosum*, a minor root crop cultivated since early times in the high Andes in S. America. Its history is unknown, but it has certainly been grown since early times. It is a climber and belongs

to the same genus as the nasturtium, all species of which are native to S. America.

The S. American name *mashua* is being used to an increasing extent as the English name.

The plant produces numerous small, knobbly, conical tubers weighing up to 100 g (3.5 oz) each. The wide variations in colour (black, red, yellow, white, spotted, streaked, etc.) are signalled by many different names in the countries of origin. Cultivated varieties, now numerous, also vary widely in colour, and in flavour too. Some are strongly bitter and acid, and edible only after treatment resembling that by which CHUÑO is prepared from potato in parts of S. America. The tubers are boiled, then allowed to freeze overnight, and pounded to powder. Other kinds are mild and when boiled in the ordinary way have a flavour similar to that of JERUSALEM ARTICHOKES, but a more mucilaginous texture.

The tubers are considered a delicacy in Bolivia and Peru and have intermittently engaged the attention of European horticulturists. Vilmorin-Andrieux (1885) observed that one had to use S. American methods of preparation if there was to be any hope of enjoying the vegetable. A century later, dealing no doubt with more recent varieties, a correspondent in the *Garden* (June 1989) recorded growing ysaño successfully in SW Scotland:

a highly perfumed vegetable with a distinct, robust flavour, good with butter, salt and pepper, or white sauce. It is a bit like Jerusalem artichoke, but with more character. Its strong flavour also adds character to a stew. However, it is not a vegetable you would want to eat every day.

YUBA the Japanese name for a delicacy consisting of the thin skin which forms on the surface of SOY MILK when it is heated in preparation for making TOFU. These 'skins' are lifted off as they form, in a procedure which has been described in detail by Yan-Kit So (1992) after witnessing it being done on an artisanal scale at Hong Kong. When the skins have dried, they may be used, after being softened by tepid water or stock, as they are, or as wrappers or in clear soups. Their popularity is greatest in China and Taiwan, but the product is well known in Japan, where it is a speciality of Kyoto. Hosking (1996) observes that it is 'highly nutritious, being the richest source of protein known (over 52%). It is also high in natural sugars (12%) and polyunsaturated fats (24%) and therefore very high in energy.'

When the 'skins' are dried in a rolled up form, they may be called 'bamboo yuba' because of a resemblance to bamboo shoots.

The Chinese display remarkable skill in making yuba resemble meat and meat products. Shurtleff and Aoyagi (1983) explain that:

Most of these imitation meat dishes are prepared by pressing fresh yuba into a hinged (wooden or aluminium) mold, then placing the well-packed mold in a steamer until the yuba's shape is fixed. In some cases the finished products are deep-fried or simmered in a sweetened or seasoned soy broth (in the same way the Chinese 'whole cook' many fish and other animals). Served at su-tsai restaurants which specialize in Buddhist vegetarian cookery, each has its own well-known name: Buddha's Chicken (suchi), Buddha's Fish (suyu or sushi), Buddha's Duck (suya), Vegetarian Tripe (taoto) or Liver (sukan), Molded Pig's Head (tutao), and Molded Ham (suhuo). The Sausage Links (enchan) are made of a mixture of fresh yuba, agar, and Chinese red fermented rice (ang-tsao) packed into real sausage skins.

YUCCA succulent plants of the genus *Yucca* in the family Agavaceae, which yield various foods and beverages. The common yucca, *Y. filamentosa*, is also known as Eve's thread or Adam's needle, since both threads and needles can be made from the leaves. The spiked leaves have also given rise to the name Spanish bayonet.

Yucca flower clusters were an important vegetable in C. America and the south-west of the USA, and are still eaten (rather like cauliflower, says one author). Those of, for example, *Y. glauca* (soapweed yucca) and *Y. elephantipes* (Spanish dagger, izote) can be used raw in salads, or boiled or battered and fried. Those of *Y. brevifolia*, the Joshua tree yucca, are best if parboiled first, to remove bitterness.

The fleshy fruits of *Y. baccata* and certain other species are sweet enough to be used as a filling for pies or made into sweetmeats; and it is said that mature buds of *Y. brevifolia* can be roasted and eaten as candy.

Young shoots of yucca, like large asparagus stalks, can be peeled, sliced, soaked, and fried. The roots of some species such as the Joshua tree are edible.

Another feature of the roots is that they contain enough saponin to serve as a soap (*amole*); hence the name soapwort (cf BOIS DE PANAMA). Saunders (1976) explains that the long-haired American Indians regarded an *amole* shampoo as a necessary preliminary to certain rites. He also gives a good description of Indian use of yuccas as food:

One of the most widely distributed is *Yucca baccata*, called by the Mexican population *palmilla ancha* or *dátil*—the former name meaning 'broad-leaved little date palm' and the latter 'the date fruit'. The fruit is succulent, plump, and in shape like a short banana, and is borned in large upright clusters, seedy but nutritious. Indians have always regarded the dátil as a luxury. As I write there comes vividly to mind a chilly, mid-August morning in the Arizona plateau country, where two Navajo shepherdesses left their straggling flock to share in the warmth of our camp fire and to pass the time of day. As they squatted by the flame, I noticed that one slipped some objects from her blanket into the hot ashes, but with such deft secretiveness that my eyes failed to detect what they were. Later as the woman rose to go, she raked away the ashes with a stick and drew out several blackened yucca pods, which had been roasting while we talked. I can testify to the entire palatibility of the cooked fruit (the rind being first removed), finding it pleasantly suggestive of sweet potato. Those fruits that morning were still green when plucked. Dr. H. H. Rusby informs me that the sliced pulp of the nearly ripe pods makes a pie almost indistinguishable from apple pie.

YUGOSLAVIA created in 1918 as a political union of the S. Slavs, broke up in 1992 and the Yugoslavia which remains is made up of only two federal republics, Serbia and Montenegro, and two provinces, Kosovo and Vojvodina, each with its own historic background and culinary heritage.

Serbian cuisine is an evolved form of Slavonic traditions moulded by the changes and influences it has experienced during the centuries of domination by Rome, Byzantium (see BYZANTINE COOKERY), and TURKEY. It is characterized by such ingredients as *kajmak* (clotted cream—see KAYMAK); *sir*, a generic name for various semi-hard porcelain-white cheeses made from sheep's milk and kept in brine (see SYR); *Kačkavalj* (see KASHKAVAL), and two types of YOGHURT: the liquid *jogurt* prepared from cow's milk, and *kiselo mleko*, the very best, luxury, sheep's milk yoghurt.

Slatko, a popular Serbian syrupy conserve, is made with every conceivable fruit or baby vegetable, fruit peel or flower petals. In more traditional households it is still offered to the afternoon visitor with a glass of water and a cup of Turkish coffee (see GLIKO).

Vojvodina lies to the north of Belgrade and shares a border with HUNGARY and ROMANIA. The province is the granary of Yugoslavia, as well as its main sugar supplier and stockbreeder for beef and pork, and has rich freshwater fishing grounds. It is settled by Serbs and other Slavs, plus large numbers of Hungarians, Romanians, Slovaks, and Ruthenians, each speaking and reading in their own tongue. So the cuisine is variegated, as food is prepared and eaten in more than five different cultural settings. C. European influences are quite pronounced, particularly in cakes and pastries which often echo famous Hungarian or Viennese confections.

South of Belgrade, the cooking of **Kosovo** is quite different. Most of the population is of Albanian origin. Many Albanian families in Kosovo still live in patriarchal communities of between 50 and 90 members, where food is cooked and bread baked collectively, and eaten in intimate commensality. Meals are served out of a huge cooking pot (*tenxhere*) or baking pan (*tavë*) on low, round tables (*sofër*). A feature of the Albanian and Turkish cuisines in Kosovo is that they have retained their national character virtually intact.

Montenegro (Crna Gora, 'Black Mountain') occupies the south-western tip of Yugoslavia. Less than 5% of its territory is touched by the plough. Along the Adriatic, the mountains are skirted with vineyards, citrus orchards, and olive groves, some of the olive trees being over 3,000 years old. In contrast, in the highlands of the interior, cultivation is limited to isolated pockets of fertile soil whose small harvests consist mainly of maize and potatoes.

Sheep are of greater importance here than cattle and, as of old, the summer surplus of milk is converted into cheese, butter, yoghurt, and clotted cream. Local specialities include *pršuta*, smoked mutton.   MK-J

YUZU a distinctive CITRUS fruit which was formerly recognized as a species, *Citrus junos*, but is now regarded as a hybrid, possibly between *C. ichangensis* and *C. reticulata*. It is one of the most cold

Yuzu fruits

resistant of the citrus fruits and grows wild in Tibet and the interior of China, where there is some cultivation of it. It is more commonly grown in Japan, where the acid fruit is a popular ingredient.

The fruit is the size of a mandarin orange, bright yellow when ripe, with a thick uneven skin and paler flesh containing many pips. It smells like a lime, and has a very sharp taste.

Although the yuzu is too acid to be eaten raw, it is used widely in Japanese cookery. For example, a small piece of the zest is often added at the last moment to a bowl of clear soup. A tiny heap of finely shredded zest will be placed on top of cooked vegetables or fish, or mixed with MISO to make a condiment. Or a yuzu cup, made by removing the flesh and keeping the skin intact, is filled with miso and baked.

The juice is also used, although never to make a drink. Its aroma is thought to enhance the delicate flavour of MATSUTAKE mushrooms. Grilled or baked matsutake is usually eaten with a dipping sauce made of soy sauce and yuzu juice.

Although the ways in which the yuzu are used in Japan often correspond to the use of the lemon elsewhere, its fragrance is quite different, unlike any citrus familiar in western countries (Tsuji, 1980).

The sight of ripe, golden yuzu suggests to the Japanese mind the approach of winter. However, earlier in the autumn, green, unripe fruit is also used. In summer a single blossom of yuzu—small, white, and fragrant—is sometimes floated in a bowl of clear soup.

There is a tradition in Japan to take a *yuzu-yu*, that is, a yuzu bath, on the evening of the winter solstice. This is a hot bath in which several whole fruit of yuzu, usually wrapped in cheesecloth, are floated. One sits in it, enjoying the rising scent and occasionally rubbing oneself with the softened fruit.   (KA)

ZAATAR (or za'atar or zahtar), the Arabic name for wild THYME, commonly denotes a mixture of that herb with SUMAC, usually but not always with toasted SESAME seeds. Another ingredient can be the ground seeds of *Pistacia terebinthus*, a relation of MASTIC.

In its simplest form zaatar is used to garnish *labneh* (see YOGHURT); and it is used throughout the Near East to flavour fried eggs.

The bread called *mana'eesh bil-za'tar* is popular in the Lebanon, especially for breakfast; the dough is spread with a mixture of zaatar mixed with some olive oil before being baked.

Tucker and Maciarello (1994) have drawn attention to the occurrence of zaatar as part of the names of several kinds of HYSSOP, thus:

- *za'atar rumi* or *franji* (Roman or European hyssop), *Satureja thymbra*;
- *za'atar hommar* or *sahrawi* (donkey or desert hyssop), *Thymbra spicata*;
- *za'atar farsi* (Persian hyssop), *Thymbra capitata*.

ZABAGLIONE is the Anglicized (and internationally current) form of the Italian word which is correctly spelled *zabaione* and which became at the beginning of the 19th century *sabayon* in French. It denotes one of the most luxurious of dishes of the CAUDLE type, and is generally supposed to have been invented in the early 16th century at the Florentine court of the Medici. Egg yolks, Marsala wine, and sugar are beaten vigorously in a double boiler until thick and foamy. There are later versions with cream, including a frozen one.

Lesley Chamberlain (1983) remarks that a version of zabaglione was popular among the Russian aristocracy in the late 19th century under the strange name of gogol' mogol'. This was at the height of Russian-French imperial cuisine, so gogol' mogol' presumably arrived in St Petersburg with a French chef who was accustomed to making sabayon.

In France the name *sabayon* is also applied to a sauce, which belongs with the sauce called MOUSSELINE and is often made with champagne, for serving with fish or crustaceans.

ZAKUSKI are perhaps the most distinctive feature of a Russian meal. The word, meaning 'little bites', originally referred to the sweet delicacies and pies served after a main meal. Now it has two meanings: either something relatively light served before a meal, usually with vodka, or by extension a snack, often eaten in a *zakusochnaya*—a stand-up bar.

The origin of zakuski is generally attributed to an enlightened 18th-century tsar, Peter the Great. As Lesley Chamberlain (1983) explains:

They came from Peter's fact-finding tours of the civilized world west of Russia and his conquests to the North. He began his Grand European tour in the Baltic port of Riga, and travelled west across what is now Northern Poland, through Berlin, thence to Holland and England. His long war with the Swedes gave him control of the Baltic and a brief hold on Finland. Gastronomically speaking, this Swedish-dominated world was rich in salted and pickled fish, apples, potatoes, pickled cucumbers, cheese and dairy products, sausage and other preserved meats and dark rye bread. These preparations still characterize the attractive cold buffet that the typical zakuski table is today.

Zakuski may be cold or hot or both. Cold ones will include, when possible, CAVIAR as well as the items indicated above. Hot ones are always items which are simple to serve and eat; *pirozhki* (see PIROG) are favourites.

In the 19th century, zakuski would be laid out very formally on a table, often in a room set aside especially for this purpose and adjoining the dining room. There is one such room in Pushkin's flat in Leningrad. The company would assemble round this table, propose toasts, clink glasses, down the first glass of vodka in a gulp, and quickly follow it with a bite of herring or a caviar canapé. This is an excellent sequence; the vodka cleanses the palate, leaving it fully prepared and stimulated for the taste of whatever follows. The company would then adjourn to the dining room, where they would embark on the meal proper.

Chekhov once wrote that 'the very best zakuska, if you would like to know, is the herring'. The various kinds of cured herring are also one of the simplest zakuski. It is fortunate that simplicity sometimes coincides with excellence. During the period of the Soviet Union, virtually all Russians had to settle for simple zakuski. Apart from anything else, they did not have the space for something grander. They would sit down at table straight away, in a room which usually acts as bedroom, living room, dining room, and study. The zakuski would simply be served as the first course. However, the tradition of zakuski lives on and is indeed inextinguishable.

ZAMPONE is an unconventional 'sausage', a speciality of Modena in the Emilia-Romana region of Italy. The skin is not a sausage casing of the usual sort, but a boned pig's trotter; the name 'zampone' literally means 'great paw'. A spiced mixture of pork and pork offal is used for the filling, and it is then subjected to a lengthy soaking and simmering, and served sliced with other boiled meats.

ZANDER also known as pike-perch (because thought to display some characteristics of both the PIKE and the PERCH), *Stizostedion lucioperca*, a large and carnivorous freshwater fish of C. and E. Europe, whose range has been extended westwards, even to East Anglia in England, by introduction. A fully grown pike-perch may measure up to 1 m (40") and will eat other fish voraciously; indeed, it has been praised as an instrument for the conversion of inedible fish into edible (itself). Its favoured habitats are large lakes or slow-moving rivers.

Appreciation of this species as food is most apparent in E. Europe, including Russia; elsewhere it tends to be valued more for the 'sport' which it affords to anglers.

ZEBRA any of several African mammals of the horse family, Equidae, which bear on their white hides the distinctive black stripes which have given the word 'zebra' wide currency in the English language.

The so-called Grévy's zebra, *Equus grevyi*, is the largest of these; adapted to living in a semi-desert or desert environment, it is found from N. Kenya to Ethiopia and Somalia. However, the common zebra of southern and eastern Africa, *E. burchelli*, is, as one would expect, the most common. Standing 1.25 m (50") high at the shoulder, it is often seen with other animals on the plains. An adaptable species (with several subspecies, but not as many as there were, for some have been exterminated), it may also be found in wooded terrain. An African name for it is *bontkwagga*.

Leipoldt (1976), speaking from S. African experience of eating many game animals, praises the zebra as 'a clean grass feeder' whose meat is outstandingly good:

Zebra flesh . . . I should without hesitation deem the tenderest, most savoury, and best flavoured of all game meat, especially when the animal is young. A zebra fillet, portioned into tournedos, is incomparably the finest meat that is obtainable in a Bushveld camp.

ZEBU *Bos indicus*, the hump-backed CATTLE of Africa and Asia, are important in those continents in various roles. They differ morphologically from European cattle in various respects besides the characteristic hump which is usually present, and are generally better adapted to a tropical environment. Juliet Clutton-Brock (1981) comments:

There is no general agreement on whether zebu cattle were first developed in south western Asia or on the peninsula of India but there is little doubt that the many breeds of humped cattle in Africa at the present day are of secondary origin and were first introduced from India or the Middle East.

Humped cattle are depicted on cylinder seals from the ancient civilizations of Mohenjo-Daro and Harappa in the Indus Valley which are dated 2500–1500 BC, whilst in southern Iraq on Sumerian and Babylonian sites they are also depicted from about the same period.

ZEDOARY *Curcuma zedoaria*, a perennial herb of NE India and SE Asia whose dried rhizome is yellow and provides a spice which has some resemblance to GINGER. It is musky and pungent, and was used in Europe, along

with its relation GALINGALE, in medieval times. In later centuries, however, both galingale and zedoary dropped out of sight in European kitchens, although continuing to be used by apothecaries.

The rhizomes of zedoary are rich in starch, which is extracted from them in India as *shoti* starch. This resembles ARROWROOT, is sold as a powder in cans, and is used for thickening purposes.

The leaves are said to have a flavour like LEMON GRASS, and are used as a flavouring for fish and other foods in Java. The hearts of the young shoots are eaten.

From the descriptions given by Ochse (1981) it seems that the general pattern, at least in Indonesia, for use of this herb and subspecies or varieties is for the hearts of young shoots and the young tops of rhizomes (and sometimes the inflorescences) to be eaten, as a cooked vegetable or in salads; that there are various medicinal uses; but that there is little or no use for flavouring purposes.

ZUCCHINI the Italian and American name for what the French and many English-speaking people call courgettes, any of several varieties of the SQUASH *Cucurbita pepo* which have been developed for this purpose and are still relatively small (around 8–10 cm/3–4") when mature, or small young specimens of other varieties of the same species which belong to the VEGETABLE MARROW group and would grow much larger if left alone.

This is one of the most attractive and delicious of the CUCURBIT vegetable fruits, but only became prominent in the 20th century. In the 1920s, when the learned Dr Leclerc was writing, the French still referred to *courgettes d'Italie*, and it seems clear that it was the Italians who first marketed vegetable marrows in a small size; and that it is therefore appropriate to choose their name zucchini rather than the French name courgettes as the adopted English name. The subsequent development of purpose-bred varieties intended to be nothing but zucchini and never growing much larger, has been conducted in several countries.

The 19th-century French author Vilmorin-Andrieux (1883, English edn) gave an illustration of the elongated variety of marrow grown in Italy (*courge d'Italie*), and commented that:

All through Italy, where this Gourd is very commonly grown, the fruit is eaten quite young, when it is hardly the size of a small Cucumber, sometimes even before the flower has opened, when the ovary, which is scarcely as long or as thick as the finger, is gathered for use. The plants, which are thus deprived of their undeveloped fruits, continue to flower for several months most profusely, each producing a great number of young Gourds, which, gathered in that state, are exceedingly tender and delicately flavoured.

The English translator added, more than half a century before the hour of the zucchini struck: 'This should be tried in England.' Vilmorin, incidentally, had given the Italian name as *cocozello di Napoli*.

That there is no true English name reflects the fact that, although courgettes were mentioned (in italic, to show that the word was a foreign one) in a few English recipe books of the 1930s, they only became popular in England after Elizabeth DAVID in the 1950s and 1960s had introduced them (not in italic) to readers of her books; and that as zucchini they had a similarly late arrival in the USA, where Italian immigrants made the introduction.

Zucchini may be poached; or blanched, stuffed, and baked; or cut into small sticks and very slowly and gently cooked with garlic in olive oil (exceptionally good) or deep fried. Courgettes or zucchini lightly cooked in butter are also a delicate dish. Their mild flavour can be complemented with herbs, parsley, chives, basil, etc.

The Italians and French took a lead, now followed in restaurants all over the world, in stuffing and deep-frying courgette flowers. Some varieties of zucchini are specially grown to be of miniature size when they bear flowers, the body of the fruit then being little more than a handle for the bloom.

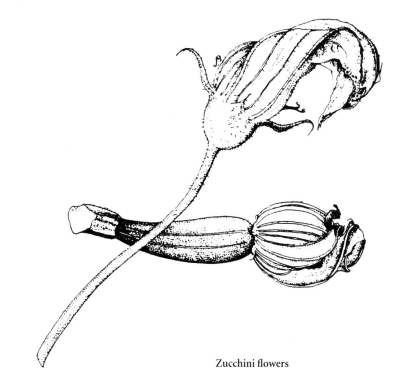

Zucchini flowers

BIBLIOGRAPHY

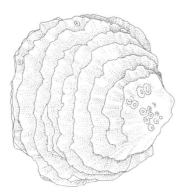

This is intended to help the reader find publications which have been referred to in the text of the present book as sources of quotations or information. It does not include books which have been mentioned in a less substantive way, for example as illustrations of the output of a particular cookery author or of the cookery books published in a given language or country. I have also omitted books such as novels from which perhaps no more than a phrase has been quoted.

Where possible, publishers are shown for works published after 1900; but sparingly for earlier ones.

PPC = the food history journal *Petits Propos culinaires* (in English); published since 1979 by Prospect Books Ltd, London (http://members.tripod.com/rdeh).

A Lady (1829), *Domestic Economy and Cookery for Rich and Poor*, London: Longman, Rees, etc.

ABDALLA, MICHAEL (1990), 'Bulgur . . . in the Cuisine of Contemporary Assyrians', in *Staple Foods*, Oxford Symposium on Food History 1989, London: Prospect Books.

ABRAHAMSON, ROY A. (ed) (1972), *The Cook Not Mad*, facsimile edn, Toronto.

ACCUM, FREDERICK (1820), *A Treatise on the Adulterations of Food*, Philadelphia.

—— (1821), *Culinary Chemistry*, London.

ACHAYA, K. T. (1994), *Indian Food: A Historical Companion*, Delhi: OUP.

ACTON, ELIZA (1845), *Modern Cookery for Private Families*, London: Longmans.

—— (1855), *Modern Cookery for Private Families*, rev edn, London: Longmans.

—— (1986), *The Best of Eliza Acton*, ed Elizabeth Ray, London: Penguin.

ADAMS, RAMON J. (1952), *Come An' Get It: The Story of the Old Cowboy Cook*, Norman: University of Oklahoma Press.

AITCHISON, J. E. T. (1890), *Notes on the Products of Western Afghanistan and of North-Eastern Persia*, Edinburgh.

AL AWAM, IBN (1977), *Le Livre de l'agriculture*, medieval MS; 3 vols, Tunis: Éditions Bouslama.

ALBERT, ADRIEN (1987), *Xenobiosis*, London: Chapman & Hall.

ALBERTS, ROBERT C. (1973), *The Good Provider: H. J. Heinz and his 57 Varieties*, Boston: Houghton Mifflin.

ALBERTUS MAGNUS (1969), *The Boke of Secretes*, facsimile edn, Amsterdam: Theatrum Orbis Terrarum.

ALCOTT, W. A. (1838), *The Young Housekeeper*, Boston: George W. Light.

ALDROVANDI, U. (1963), *Aldrovandi on Chickens* (1600), trans L. R. Lind, Norman: University of Oklahoma Press.

ALEGRE, EDILBERTO N. (1992), *Inumang Pinoy*, Manila: Anvil.

—— and FERNANDEZ, DOREEN G. (1991), *Kinilaw*, Manila: Bookmark.

ALGAR, AYLA ESEN (1985), *The Complete Book of Turkish Cookery*, London: Routledge &

Kegan Paul.

—— (1991), *Classical Turkish Cooking*, New York: Harper Collins.

ALLARD, JEANNE (1987), 'Diego Granado Maldonado', in *PPC* 25, London: Prospect Books.

ALLEN, BETTY MOLESWORTH (1965), *Malayan Fruits*, Singapore: Eastern Universities Press.

—— (1975), *Common Malaysian Fruits*, Kuala Lumpur: Longman.

ALLEN, DARINA (1995), Irish Traditional Cooking, London: Kyle Cathie.

ALLEN, G. R. (1985), *Snappers of the World*, Rome: FAO.

ALLEN, MYRTLE (1987), *The Ballymaloe Cookbook*, new edn, Dublin: Gill & Macmillan.

ALPERS, ANTONY (1960), *Dolphins*, London: John Murray.

AL TAIE, LAMEES ABDULLAH (1995), *Al-Azaf: The Omani Cookbook*, Oman: Oman Bookshop.

ANDERSON, BURTON (1994), *Treasures of the Italian Table*, New York: Willam Morrow.

ANDERSON, E. N. (1988), *The Food of China*, New Haven: Yale University Press.

ANDRÉ, JACQUES (1981), *L'Alimentation et la cuisine à Rome*, Paris: Belles Lettres.

ANDRÉ, TCHERNIA (1986), *Le Vin de l'Italie romaine*, Rome: École française de Rome.

ANDREWS, COLMAN (1988), *Catalan Cuisine*, New York: Atheneum.

ANDREWS, JEAN (1984), *Peppers: The Domesticated Capsicums*, Austin: University of Texas.

ANDROUET, PIERRE and CHABOT, YVES (1985), *Le Brie*, Evreux: Presses du Village.

Anon. (1910), *A Book of Simples*, London: Sampson, Low & Marston.

Anon. (1758), *A Description of the River Thames*, London.

Anon. (1744), *Adam's Luxury and Eve's Cookery*, repr London: Prospect Books (1983).

Anon. (1485), *Küchenmeisterei*,

Anon. (1662), *L'Escole parfaite des officiers de bouche*, Paris.

Anon. (1607), *Le Thresor de santé*, Lyons: Huguetan.

Anon. (n.d.), *Le Vray Cuisinier françois*, Paris: Pierre Mortier.

Anon. (1991), 'The Pontefract Liquorice Industry', *PPC* 39.

Anon. [by a lady] (1737), *The Whole Duty of a Woman*, London: T. Read.

ANTHIMUS (1996), *On the Observance of Foods*, trans and ed Mark Grant, Totnes: Prospect Books.

APPERT, M. (1810), *Le Livre de tous les ménages ou l'art de conserver*, Paris: Barrois.

APPLETON, Lady HELEN (ed) (1969), *Celebrity Cook Book*, Edinburgh: Dr Barnado's.

APULEIUS (1989), *Metamorphoses*, vols i and ii, ed and trans J. A. Hanson, Cambridge, Mass.: Loeb Classical Library.

ARBERRY, A. J. (1939), 'A Baghdad Cookery Book', *Islamic Culture*, 13.

ARCHESTRATUS (1994), *The Life of Luxury*, ed and trans J. Wilkins and S. Hill, Totnes: Prospect Books.

ARCHETTI, EDUARDO (1997), *Guinea Pigs*, Oxford: Berg.

ARIS, PEPITA (1992), *The Spanishwoman's Kitchen*, London: Cassell.

ARISTOPHANES (1980), *The Comedies of Aristophanes*, vol i, trans Sommerstein, Warminster: Aris & Phillips.

ARMSTRONG, JULIAN (1990), *A Taste of Quebec*, Toronto: Macmillan of Canada.

ARNOLD, SAMUEL P. (1985), *Fryingpans West*, Denver: Arnold & Co.

—— (1990), *Eating up the Sante Fe Trail*, Colorado: Colorado UP.

—— (1996), 'A Rattle in the Throat: The Unmentionable Cuisine', *PPC* 52.

—— (1997), *The Fort Cookbook*, New York: HarperCollins.

ARNOTT, MARGARET (ed) (1975), *Gastronomy*, The Hague: Mouton.

ARORA, DAVID (1979), *Mushrooms Demystified*, Berkeley: Ten Speed Press.

ARTEMIDORUS DALDIANUS (1975), *The Interpretation of Dreams, Oneirocritica*, trans R. J. White, Park Ridge, NJ: Noyes.

ASHBROOK, FRANK G. and SATER, EDNA N. (1945), *Cooking Wild Game*, New York: Orange Judd.

ASHMOLE, ELIAS (1672), *The Institution, Laws and Ceremonies of the Most Noble Order of the Garter*, London: Nathanael Brooke.

ATHENAEUS (1927–41), *Deipnosophists*, trans C. B. Gulick, Cambridge, Mass.: Loeb Classical Library.

AUBAILE-SALLENAVE, F. (1994), 'Al-Kishk', in S. Zubaida and R. Tapper (eds), *Culinary Cultures of the Middle East*, London: I. B. Tauris.

AUDOT, LOUIS-EUSTACHE (1818), *La Cuisiniere de la campagne et de la ville*, Paris: Audot.

AULAGNIER, A. F. (1839), *Dictionnaire des aliments*, Paris.

AYKROYD, W. R. and DOUGHTY, JOYCE (1970), *Wheat in Human Nutrition*, Rome: FAO.

AYLING, TONY and COX, GEOFFREY J. (1982), *Guide to the Sea Fishes of New Zealand*, Auckland: Collins.

AYRTON, ELISABETH (1974), *The Cookery of England*, London: Deutsch.

—— (1980), *English Provincial Cooking*, London: Mitchell Beazley.

AYTO, JOHN (1993), *The Diner's Dictionary*, Oxford: OUP.

BACHMANN, WALTER (ed) (1955), Continental Confectionery: 'The Pastrycook's Art', London: Maclaren.

BACON, JOSEPHINE (1988), *The Complete Guide to Exotic Fruits & Vegetables*, London: Xanadu.

BADHAM, Revd C. DAVID (1854), *Ancient and Modern Fish Tattle*, London.

—— (1863), *A Treatise on the Esculent Funguses of England*, 2nd edn (ed F. Currey), London.

BAILEY, WALTER (1588), *A Short Discourse of the Three Kindes of Pepper in Common Use*, London.

BAILLIE, Lady GRISELL (1911), *The Household Book of Lady Grisell Baillie 1692–1733*, Edinburgh: Scottish History Society.

BAIN, PRISCILLA (1986), 'Recounting the Chickens: Hannah Further Scrutinised', in *PPC* 23.

BAKER, Sir SAMUEL W. (1884), *True Tales for my Grandsons*, New York: Macmillan.

BANCROFT, H. H. (1882), *Native Races of the Pacific States of North America*, vol ii, San Francisco.

BANERJI, CHITRITA (1997), *Bengali Cooking, Seasons and Festivals*, London: Serif.

BANG, MAREN (1831), *Den norske huusmoder*, Christiania.

BARBEROUSSE, MICHEL (1974), *La Normandie*, France: Hachette.

BAREHAM, LINDSEY (1991), *In Praise of the Potato*, London: Grafton Books.

—— (1995), *Onions without Tears*, London: Michael Joseph.

BARKAS, JANET (1975), *The Vegetable Passion*, London: Routledge & Kegan Paul.

BARKER, WILLIAM (1974), *The Modern Patissier*, London: Northwood Publications.

BARR, ANN, and LEVY, PAUL (1984), *The Official Foodie Handbook*, London: Ebury Press.

BARRON, ROSEMARY (1991), *Flavors of Greece*, New York: William Morrow.

BARTH, H. (1857), *Travels and Discoveries in North and Central Africa*, London: Longman, Brown, Green etc.

BARTLETT, J. R. (1848), *Dictionary of Americanisms*, New York.

BATTISCOMBE, GEORGINA (1951), *English Picnics*, London: Country Book Club.

BAUHIN, J. (1610), *Historia Plantarum*.

BAUMAN, JAMES (1987), 'Les Galettes des Rois', in *PPC* 27, London: Prospect Books.

BAYLEY, STEPHEN (1994), *Gin*, London.

BAZORE, KATHERINE (1953), *Hawaiian and Pacific Foods*, New York: M. Barrows.

BEAN, LOWELL JOHN, and SAUBEL, KATHERINE SIVA (1972), *Temalpakh*, Banning, CA: Malki Museum Press.

BEARD, JAMES (1964), *Delights and Prejudices*, London: Victor Gollancz.

—— (1974), *Beard on Food*, New York: Alfred Knopf.

—— (1977), *Theory and Practice of Good Cooking*, New York: Knopf.

BEATTIE, MAY H. (ed) (1946), *Recipes from Baghdad*, Baghdad: Government Press.

BEAUVILLIERS (1814), *Art de cuisinier*, Paris.

BECK, LEONARD N. (1984), *Two Loaf-Givers*, Washington: Library of Congress.

BECKETT, R. (1984), *Convicted Tastes*, Sydney: Allen & Unwin.

BEETON, ISABELLA (1861), *Beeton's Book of Household Management*, facsimile of 1st edn, London: Chancellor (1982).

—— (1865), *Mrs Beeton's Dictionary of Everyday Cookery*, London.

BEHR, EDWARD (1992), *The Artful Eater*, New York: Atlantic Monthly Press.

Belgian Tourist Office (1981), *Belgian Cuisine*, Brussels: National Tourist Office.

BELLOC, HILAIRE (1940), *Cautionary Verses*, London: Duckworth.

BELON, PIERRE (1555), *L'histoire de la nature des oyseaux . . .*, Paris.

BENDER, ARNOLD E. (1965), *Dictionary of Nutrition and Food Technology*, London: Butterworths.

BENEDETTI, BENEDETTO (1986), *L'aceto balsamico*, Spilamberto: Consorteria dell'Aceto Balsamico.

BENGHIAT, NORMA (1985), *Traditional Jamaican Cookery*, London: Penguin.

BERKENBAUM, PHILIPPE and MAHOUX, FRÉDÉRIC (1994), *Biscuits*, France: Casterman.

BERLANDIER, JEAN-LOUIS (1980), *Journey to Mexico during the Years 1826–1834*, Austin, TX: Texas State Historical Association.

BERRY, RILEY M. FLETCHER (1907), *Fruit Recipes*, London: Archibald Constable.

BERSTEN, IAN (1993), *Coffee Floats Tea Sinks*, Sydney: Helian Books.

BERTHIAUME, G. (1982), *Les Roles du Mageiros*, Montreal: E. J. Brill and University of Montreal.

BERTON, PIERRE, and BERTON, JANET (1974), *Pierre & Janet Berton's Canadian Food Guide* rev edn, Toronto: The Canadian Publishers.

BEST, ELSDON (1977), *Forest Lore of the Maori*, Wellington: Government Printer.

BEST, R. I. (1910), 'The Settling of the Manor of Tara', *Ériu*, 4.

BEVERLEY, R. (1705), *The History and Present State of Virginia*, London.

BEWICK, THOMAS (1807), *A General History of Quadrupeds*, repr London: Ward Lock (1970).

BICKEL, WALTER (ed) (1977), *Hering's Dictionary of Classical and Modern Cookery*, London: Virtue.

BIGELOW, H. B., and SCHROEDER, W. C. (1953), *Fishes of the Gulf of Maine*, Washington: US Government Printing Office.

BINI, GIORGIO (1960–70), *Atlante dei pesci delle coste italiane*, vols i–viii, Rome: Mondo Sommerso.

BISEN, MALINI (1970), *Vegetable Delights*, Delhi: Wilco.

—— (1981), *Indian Sweet Delights*, Bombay: Wilco.

BITTING, A. W. (1937), *Appertizing or The Art of Canning*, San Francisco.

BLACK, MAGGIE (1989), *Paxton & Whitfield's Fine Cheese*, London: Webb & Bower/Michael Joseph.

BLACKMAN, GRANT (1980), *Catching and Cooking Australian Fish*, Melbourne: Pisces Books.

BLAKELOCK, MILDRED (*c.*1931), *Old English Cookery, 1775–1931*, London: Wells.

BLANCARD, E. (1927), *Mets et produits de Provence*, 3rd edn, Toulon: Bordato.

BLANCHARD, ÉMILE (1866), *Les Poissons des eaux douces de la France*, Paris: Baillière.

BLOOM, CAROLE (1995), *The International Dictionary of Desserts, Pastries and Confections*, New York: Hearst Books.

BODENHEIMER, F. S. (1951), *Insects as Human Food*, The Hague: Dr W. Junk.

—— (1960), *Animal and Man in Bible Lands*, Leiden: E. J. Brill.

BÖHLKE, JAMES E., and CHAPLIN, C. C. G. (1968), *Fishes of the Bahamas and Adjacent Tropical Waters*, Philadelphia: Academy of Natural Sciences.

BOISARD, PIERRE (1992), *Le Camembert*, Paris: Calmann-Lévy.

BOITANI, LUIGI, and BARTOLI, STEPHANIA (1986), *The Macdonald Encyclopedia of Mammals*, London: Macdonald.

BOLENS, LUCIE (1990), *La Cuisine andalouse, un art de vivre: XI–XIII siècle*, Paris: Albin Michel.

BOLITHO, HECTOR (1960), *The Glorious Oyster*, London: Sidgwick & Jackson.

BOLOTNIKOVA, V. A., et al. (1979), *Byelorussian Cuisine*, Minsk: Uradzai.

BOND, Dr ROBERT (1995), 'Rau Ram', *PPC* 51.

BONNADIER, JACQUES (1994), *Le Roman de la sardine*, Avignon: Éditions A. Barthélemy.

BONTOU, ALCIDE (1898), *Traité de cuisine bourgeoise bordelaise*, repr Bordeaux: Féret (1977).

BOORDE, ANDREW (1542), *A Dyetary of Health*, ed F. J. Furnivall, London: Early English Text Society (1870).

BORELLA, Mr (1770), *The Court and Country Confectioner*, London.

BORER, EVA MARIA (1965), *Tante Heidi's Swiss Kitchen*, London: Nicholas Kaye.

BOSMAN, HERMAN CHARLES (1973), *Mafeking Road*, Cape Town: Human & Rousseau.

BOSWELL, JAMES (1786), *Journal of a Tour to the Hebrides with Samuel Johnson*.

BOTKINE, FRANÇOISE, et al. (eds) (1993),

Cheeses of the World, London: Little Brown.

BOTSFORD, KEITH (1990), 'Some Considerations on the Nature of Staples', in *Staple Foods*, Oxford Symposium on Food History 1989, London: Prospect Books.

BOTTÉRO, J (1995), 'The Most Ancient Recipes of All' in *Food in Antiquity*, ed John Wilkins et al., Exeter: University of Exeter.

BOURKE, AUSTIN (1993), 'The Visitation of God?', Dublin: Lilliput.

BOWN, DENI (1988), *Fine Herbs*, London: Unwin Hyman.

BRADLEY, MARTHA (c.1758), *The British Housewife*, facsimile edn, vols i–vi, Totnes: Prospect Books (1996–8).

BRADLEY, RICHARD (1732), *The Country Housewife and Lady's Director, Part II*, London: D. Browne & T. Woodman.

—— (1736), *The Country Housewife and Lady's Director, Parts I and II*, facsimile of 6th edn in one vol, London: Prospect Books (1980).

BRAND (1859), *Hints for the Table*.

BREARS, PETER (1984a), *The Gentlewoman's Kitchen: Great Food in Yorkshire, 1650–1750*, Wakefield: Historical Publications.

—— (1984b), 'Of Funeral Biscuits', in *PPC* 18.

—— (1987), *Traditional Food in Yorkshire*, Edinburgh: John Donald.

—— (1994), 'A la Francaise. . .', in C. Anne Wilson (ed), *Luncheon, Nuncheon and Other Meals*, Stroud: Alan Sutton.

—— (1996), 'Transparent Pleasures: The Story of the Jelly, Parts One and Two', in *PPC* 53 and 54, London: Prospect Books.

BRÉCOURT-VILLARS, CLAUDINE (1996), *Mots de table, mots de bouche*, Paris: Stock.

BREMNESS, LESLEY (1994), *Herbs*, London: Dorling, Kindersley.

BRENNAN, JENNIFER (1988), *Encyclopaedia of Chinese and Oriental Cookery*, London: Black Cat.

—— (1990), *Curries and Bugles*, London: Viking.

—— (forthcoming), *Trade Winds and Coconuts*.

BRERETON, GEORGINE E. and FERRIER, JANET M. (eds) (1981), *Le Menagier de Paris*, Oxford: Clarendon Press.

BRETON, OLIVIER (1994), *Rilles, rillons, rillettes*, Paris: Du May.

BRIDGES, BILL (1981), *The Great American Chili Book*, New York: Rawson Wade.

BRIGGS, KATHARINE (1976), *A Dictionary of Fairies*, London: Penguin.

BRIGGS, RICHARD (1792) *The New Art of Cookery*, 1st US edn, Philadelphia.

BRILLAT-SAVARIN, JEAN ANTHELME (1826), *La Physiologie du goût* (1st edn), published anonymously by the author.

—— (1972), *The Physiology of Taste*, trans M. F. K. Fisher (first pub with illus. 1949, later edns with text only), New York: Knopf.

BRISTOWE, W. S. (1924), 'Notes on the Habits of Insects and Spiders in Brazil', *Transactions of the Entomological Society of London*, 3/4.

—— (1932), 'Insects and other Invertebrates for Human Consumption in Siam', *Transactions of the Entomological Society of London*, 80/2.

BROTHWELL, DON and BROTHWELL, PATRICIA (1969), *Food in Antiquity*, London: Thames & Hudson.

BROWN, BOB (1955), *The Complete Book of Cheese*, New York: Random House.

BROWN, BONNIE and SEGAL, DAVID (1981), 'Sugaring Off', in *National and Regional Styles of Cookery*, Oxford Symposium on Food History 1981, London: Prospect Books.

BROWN, CATHERINE (1981), *Scottish Regional Recipes*, Glasgow: Molendinar Press.

—— (1985), *Scottish Cookery*, Glasgow: Richard Drew.

—— (1990), *Broths to Bannocks*, London: John Murray.

—— (1996), *A Year in a Scots Kitchen*, Glasgow: Neil Wilson.

BROWN, CORA; BROWN, ROSA; and BROWN, BOB (1938), *Most for your Money Cookbook*, New York: Modern Age.

—— —— —— (1971), *The South American Cook Book* (first pub 1939) New York: Dover.

BROWN, LYNDA (1998), *Organic Food*, London: Fourth Estate.

BROWN, SANBORN C. (1979), *Benjamin Thompson, Count Rumford*, Cambridge, Mass.: MIT Press.

BROWNE, Sir THOMAS (1902), *Notes and Letters on the Natural History of Norfolk*, London: Jarrold & Sons.

BRUNETON-GOVERNATORI, ARIANE (1984), *Le Pain de bois*, Toulouse: Eché.

BRYAN, LETTICE (n.d.), *The Kentucky Housewife*, Paducah, KY.: Collector Books.

BRYSON, BILL (1991), *Mother Tongue*, London: Penguin.

BUCHAN, WILLIAM (1769), *Domestic Medicine*, Edinburgh: Balfour, Auld & Smellie.

BUCKLAND, FRANK (1883), *The Natural History of British Fishes*, London: SPCK.

BULTITUDE, JOHN (1983), *Apples*, London: Macmillan.

BUNYARD, E. A. (1920), *A Handbook of Hardy Fruits: Apples and Pears*, London: John Murray.

—— (1925), *A Handbook of Hardy Fruits: Stone & Bush Fruits, Nuts, etc.*, London: J. Murray.

—— (1929), *The Anatomy of Dessert*, London: Dulau.

BUONASSISI, VINCENZO (1976), *Pasta*, Wilton CC: Lyceum.

BURGESS, G. H. O., et al. (1965), *Fish Handling and Processing*, Edinburgh: HMSO.

BURKHARDT, BARBARA; McLEAN, BARRIE ANGUS; and KOCHANEK, DORIS (1978), *Sailors and Sauerkraut*, Sidney, BC Canada: Gray's Publishing.

BURKILL, I. H. (1965–6), *A Dictionary of the Economic Products of the Malay Peninsula*, vols i–ii, 2nd edn, Kuala Lumpur: Governments of Malaysia and Singapore.

BURNETT, JOHN (1966), *Plenty and Want*, London: Nelson.

BURTON, DAVID (1982), *Two Hundred Years of New Zealand Food and Cookery*, Wellington: Reed.

—— (1993), *The Raj at Table*, London: Faber & Faber.

BURTON, MAURICE (1962), *Systematic Dictionary of Mammals of the World*, London: Museum Press.

BURTON, ROBERT (1651–2), *Anatomy of Melancholy*, 6th edn, London.

BURUM, LINDA (1985), *Asian Pasta*, Berkeley: Aris Books.

BUSTARD, ROBERT (1972), *Sea Turtles*, London: Collins.

BUTTES, HENRY (1599), *Dyets Dry Dinner*, n.p.

BUXTON, MOIRA (1993), 'Hypocras, Caudels, Possets', in C. Anne Wilson (ed), *Liquid Nourishment*, Edinburgh: Edinburgh University Press.

BYNUM, CAROLINE WALKER (1987), *Holy Feast and Holy Fast*, Berkeley: University of California.

BYRON, MAY CLARISSA (1914), *Pot-Luck*, London: Hodder & Stoughton.

—— (1923), *May Byron's Pudding Book*, London.

CALONGE, FRANCISCO DE DIEGO (1979), *Setas (Hongos)*, Madrid: Ediciones Mundi-Prensa.

CAMPBELL, A. M., PENFIELD, M. P., and GRISWOLD, R. M. (1979), *The Experimental Study of Food*, Boston: Houghton Mifflin.

CAMPBELL, SUSAN (1985), *The Cook's Companion*, London: Chancellor.

CAMPBELL, TUNIS G. (1848), *Hotel Keepers, Head Waiters, and Housekeepers' Guide*, Boston: Coolidge & Wiley.

CANNON, GEOFFREY (1987), *The Politics of Food*, London: Century Hutchinson.

CARCOPINO, J. (1940), *Daily Life in Ancient Rome*, trans E. O. Lorimer, New Haven: Yale University Press.

CARÊME, ANTONIN (1815), *Le Pâtissier pittoresque*, Paris: l'auteur.

—— (1822), *Le Mâitre d'hôtel français*, Paris: l'auteur.

—— (1828a), *Le Cuisinier parisien*, Paris: l'auteur.

—— (1828b), *Le Pâtissier royal parisien*, 2nd edn, Paris: Didot.

—— (1833–5), *L'Art de la cuisine française au dix-neuvième siècle*, Paris: l'auteur.

CARNACINA, LUIGI, and VERONELLI, LUIGI (1966), *La buona vera cucina italiana*, Milan: Rizzoli.

—— —— (1977), *La cucina rustica regionale italiana*, vols i–iv, Milan: Rizzoli.

CARR, ARCHIE (1967), *So Excellent a Fishe*, New York: Charles Scribner's.

CARR, SANDY (1985), *The Mitchell Beazley Pocket Guide to Cheese*, London: Mitchell Beazley.

CARTER, CHARLES (1730), *The Complete Practical Cook*, repr London: Prospect Books (1984).

CARTER, ELIZABETH (1989), *Majorcan Food and Cookery*, London: Prospect Books.

CARTER, JENNY, and RAE, JANET (1989), *Chambers Scottish Food Book*, Edinburgh: Chambers.

CARTER, SUSANNAH (1772), *The Frugal Housewife*, Boston: Edes & Gill.

Cassell's Dictionary of Cookery (1899) (first pub 1875–6), London: Cassell.

CATO, MARCUS PORCIUS (1934), *On Agriculture*, trans W. D. Hooper, London: Heinemann.

CAVALCANTI, IPPOLITO (1837), *Cucina teorico-pratica*, Naples.

CAVANNA, G. (1913), *Doni di Nettuno*, Florence.

CERVIO, VINCENZO (1581), *Il trinciante*, repr Florence: Casa Editrice II Portolano (1979).

CHACE, FENNER A., Jr, and HOBBS, HORTON H., Jr (1969), *Freshwater and Terrestrial Decapod Crustaceans of the West Indies*, Washington: Smithsonian.

CHAMBERLAIN, LESLEY (1983), *The Food and Cooking of Russia*, London: Penguin.

—— (1989), *The Food and Cooking of Eastern Europe*, London: Penguin.

CHAN, W. L. (1968), *Marine Fishes of Hong Kong*, vol i, Hong Kong: Government Printing Office.

CHANEY, LISA (1998), *A Mediterranean Passion*, London: Macmillan.

CHANG, K. C. (ed) (1977), *Food in Chinese Culture*, New Haven: Yale University Press.

CHAPMAN, PAT (1993), *Balti Curry Cookbook*, London: Piatkus.

CHARALAMBOUS, G. (ed) (1994), *Spices, Herbs and Edible Fungi*, Amsterdam: Elsevier Science BV.

CHARSLEY, SIMON R. (1992), *Wedding Cakes and Cultural History*, London: Routledge.

CHAPUIS, LISE, et al. (1994), *La Lamproie*, Paris: Le Temps qu'il Fait.

CHASE, HOLLY (1993), *Turkish Tapestry*, Groton Long Point, CT: Bosphorous.

—— (1994), 'Suspect Salep', in *Look & Feel*, Oxford Symposium on Food History 1993, Totnes: Prospect Books.

CHAUVET, MICHEL (1988), 'Note about the History of Brèdes', in *PPC* 59, London: Prospect Books.

CHENCINER, ROBERT (1994), 'The Noodles of Samarkhand: Engineering Pasta', in *Look and Feel*, Oxford Symposium on Food History 1993, Totnes: Prospect Books.

—— (1997) *Dagestan: Tradition and Survival*, London: Curzon Press.

—— and SALMANOV, EMILE (1988), 'Little Known Aspects of North East Caucasian Mountain Ram and other Dishes', in *Taste*, Oxford Symposium on Food History 1987, Totnes: Prospect Books.

CHENG, F. T. (1962), *Musings of a Chinese Gourmet*, London: Hutchinson.

CHILD, REGINALD (1974), *Coconuts*, London: Longman.

CHIQUART, Maistre (1985), *De fait de cuisine*, edn of medieval MS, Sion: T. Scully.

CHRISTIAN, Mr and Mrs EUGENE (1904), *Uncooked Foods and How to Use Them*, New York: The Health Culture Company.

CHRISTIAN, GLYNN (1982), *Glynn Christian's Delicatessen Food Handbook*, London: Macdonald.

CLARK, ELEANOR (1959), *The Oysters of Locmariaquer*, London: Secker & Warburg.

CLARK, ROBERT (1997), *James Beard: A Biography*, London: Grub Street.

CLARKE, CHARLOTTE (1978), *Edible and Useful Plants of California*, Berkeley: University of California Press.

CLARKSON, ROSETTA E. (1972), *The Golden Age of Herbs and Herbalists*, New York: Dover.

CLAYTON, BERNARD, Jr (1973), *The Complete Book of Breads*, New York: Simon & Schuster.

—— (1978), *The Breads of France*, Indianapolis: Bobbs-Merrill.

CLELAND, ELIZABETH (1755), *A New and Easy Method of Cookery*, Edinburgh: printed for the author.

CLIFTON, CLAIRE (1983), *Edible Flowers*, London: Bodley Head.

—— (1986), 'The Search for the "Blue Violet Salad" ' in *Cookery: Science, Lore and Books*, Oxford Symposium on Food History 1984 and 1985, London: Prospect Books.

CLUTTON-BROCK, JULIET (1981), *Domesticated Animals from Early Times*, London: British Museum (Natural History) and Heinemann.

COBBETT, WILLIAM (1823), *Cottage Economy*, repr Hereford 1974; London: printed for the author.

COCCHI, ANTONIO (1745), *The Pythagorean Diet*, trans R. A. Dodsley, London.

COCKRILL, W. Ross (1976), *The Buffaloes of China*, Rome: FAO.

COE, SOPHIE (1985), 'Aztec Cuisine, Part II', in *PPC* 20.

—— (1988), 'Inca Food: Animal and Mineral', in *PPC* 29.

—— (1994), *America's First Cuisines*, Austin: University of Texas.

COE, SOPHIE, and COE, MICHAEL (1996), *The True History of Chocolate*, London: Thames & Hudson.

COETZEE, RENATA (1982), *FUNA: Food from Africa*, Durban: Butterworths.

COHEN, D.; TADASHI, I.; IWAMOTO, T.; and SCIALABBA, N. (1990), *Gadiform Fishes of the World*, Rome: FAO.

COLE, JOHN N. (1978), *Striper: A Story of Fish and Man*, Boston: Little, Brown.

COLE, MARY (1791), *The Lady's Complete Guide*, London: G. Kearsley.

COLES, WILLIAM (1656), *The Art of Simpling*, London.

—— (1657), *Adam in Eden*, London.

COLLETTE, BRUCE B. and NAUEN, CORNELIA E. (1983), *Scombrids of the World*, Rome: FAO.

COLLINGWOOD, FRANCIS and WOOLLAMS, JOHN (1806), *The Universal Cook and City and Country Housekeeper*, London.

COLLINS, DEAN (1933), *The Cheddar Box: Cheddar Cheese*, vol i of 2, Portland, Ore.: The Oregon Journal.

COLOMBIÉ, A. (1906–7), *Nouvelle Encyclopédie culinaire*, vols i and ii, Paris: Melun.

COLUMELLA (1934), *De Re Rustica*, trans H. B. Ash, London: William Heinemann.

COMBET, CLAUDE and LEFRÈVRE, THIERRY (1995), *The Tour de France des Bonbons*, Paris: Robert Laffont.

COMPAGNO, LEONARD J. V. (1984), *Sharks of the World, Parts 1 and 2*, Rome: FAO.

COOK, ALAN D., et al. (eds) (1983), *Oriental Herbs and Vegetables*, Brooklyn, NY: Botanic Gardens.

COOPER, ARTEMIS (1999), *Writing at the Kitchen Table*, London: Viking.

COOPER, J. (1654), *The Art of Cookery Refin'd*, facsimile edn, Ann Arbor: University Microfilms.

CORDERO-FERNANDO, GILDA (1976), *The Culinary Culture of the Philippines*, Philippines: GCF Books.

—— (1992), *Philippine Food and Life*, Manila: Anvil Publishing.

COREY, HELEN (1962), *The Art of Syrian Cookery*, New York: Doubleday.

CORNER, E. J. H. (1966), *The Natural History of Palms*, London: Weidenfeld & Nicolson.

CORONEL, ROBERTO E. (1983), *Promising Fruits of the Philippines*, Los Baños: University of the Philippines.

CORRADO, VINCENZO (1773), *Il cuoco galante*, Naples.

—— (1778), *Il credenziere di buon gusto*, Naples.

—— (1781), *Del cibo pittagorico ovvero erbaceo*, Naples.

COST, BRUCE (1990), *Asian ingredients*, London: Jill Norman.

COTGRAVE, RANDLE (1611), *A Dictionarie of the French and English Tongues*, ed William S. Woods, Columbia: University of South Carolina Press (1950).

COUCH, JONATHAN (1877), *A History of the Fishes of the British Islands*, vols i–iv, London.

COULTATE, T. P. (1989), *Food: The Chemistry of its Components*, 2nd edn, London: Royal Society of Chemistry.

COUPLAN, FRANÇOIS (1983), *Le Régal végétal*, Paris: Debard.

—— (1984), *La Cuisine sauvage*, Paris: Debard.

COUSIN, FRANÇOISE, and MONZON, SUSANA (1992), *Cuisines du monde: gestes et recettes*, Paris: CNRS.

COVARRUBIAS, MIGUEL (1937), *Island of Bali*, London: Cassel.

COWAN, CATHAL and SEXTON, REGINA (1997), *Ireland's Traditional Foods*, Dublin: National Food Centre.

COYLE, L. PATRICK (1982), *The World Encyclopedia of Food*, New York: Facts on File.

CRAIG, ELIZABETH (1953), *Court Favourites*, London: André Deutsch.

—— (1955), *Beer and Vittles*, London: Museum Press.

CRAIGIE, Sir WILLIAM A. and HULBERT, JAMES R. (1938–44), *A Dictionary of American English on Historical Principles*, vols i–iv, Chicago: University of Chicago Press.

CRANE, EVA (1975), *Honey: A Comprehensive Survey*, London: Heinemann.

CRIBB, A. B. and CRIBB, J. W. (1975), *Wild Food in Australia*, Sydney: William Collins.

CROSBY, ALFRED W., Jr (1972), *The Columbian Exchange*, Westport, Conn.: Greenwood.

CROSSLEY-HOLLAND, NICOLE (1996), *Living and Dining in Medieval Paris*, Cardiff: University of Wales Press.

CROWE, ANDREW (1981), *A Field Guide to the Native Edible Plants of New Zealand*, Auckland: Collins.

CRUICKSHANK, CONSTANCE (1959), *Lenten Fare and Food for Fridays*, London: Faber.

CULPEPER, NICHOLAS (1653), *The English Physician*, London.

CULWICK, Mrs G. M. (1955), 'Food and Society in the Sudan', *Proceedings of the Annual Conference of the Philological Society of Sudan*, 1953.

CUMMINGS, RICHARD O. (1949), *The American Ice Harvests*, Los Angeles: University of California Press.

CUTTING, C. L. (1955), *Fish Saving*, London: L. Hill.

DAGHER, SHAWSKY M. (1991), *Traditional Foods in the Near East*, Rome: Food and Agricultural Organization of the United Nations.

DAHLEN, MARTHA and PHILLIPPS, KAREN (1980), *A Guide to Chinese Market Vegetables*, Hong Kong: South Morning Post.

DALBY, ANDREW (1996), *Siren Feasts*, London: Routledge.

—— and GRAINGER, SALLY (1996), *The Classical Cookbook*, London: British Museum Press.

DALLAS, ENEAS SWEETLAND (1877), *Kettner's Book of the Table*, London: Dulau.

DANAHER, K. (1972), *The Year in Ireland*, Cork: Mercier Press.

DARBY, WILLIAM J., GHALIOUNGUI, PAUL, and GRIVETTI, LOUIS (1977), *Food: The Gift of Osiris*, vols i and ii, London: Academic Press.

DARROW, GEORGE M. (1966), *The Strawberry*, New York: Holt, Rinehart & Winston.

DAVID, ELIZABETH (1950), *A Book of Mediterranean Food*, London: John Lehmann.

—— (1951), *French Country Cooking*, London: John Lehmann.

—— (1955), *Summer Cooking*, London: Museum Press.

—— (1960), *French Provincial Cooking*, London: Michael Joseph.

—— (1965), *Italian Food*, 2nd edn, London: Macdonald.

—— (1970), *Spices, Salt and Aromatics in the English Kitchen*, London: Penguin.

—— (1977), *English Bread and Yeast Cookery*, London: Allen Lane.

—— (ed) (1980), *Cooks and Confectioners Dictionary* (see under John Nott, 1726), London: L. Rivington.

—— (1984), *An Omelette and a Glass of Wine*, London: Robert Hale.

—— (1994), *Harvest of the Cold Months*, London: Michael Joseph.

DAVIDS, KENNETH (1976), *Coffee: A Guide to Buying, Brewing and Enjoying*, San Francisco: 101 Publications.

DAVIDSON, ALAN (1975), *Fish and Fish Dishes of Laos*, Vientiane: the author.

—— (1977), *Seafood of South-East Asia*, Singapore: Federal Publications.

—— (1979), *North Atlantic Seafood*, London: Macmillan.

—— (1981), *Mediterranean Seafood*, 2nd edn (further rev in 1987 impression), London: Penguin.

—— (1984), 'Capirotada Lives On', Notes and Queries, in *PPC* 16.

—— (1988a), *A Kipper with my Tea*, London: Macmillan.

—— (1988b), *North Atlantic Seafood*, 2nd edn, London: Penguin.

—— (ed) (1988c), *On Fasting and Feasting*, London: Macdonald Orbis.

—— (ed) (1991), *The Cook's Room*, London: MacDonald.

—— (1993), 'Sherbets', in C. Anne Wilson (ed), *Liquid Nourishment*, Edinburgh: Edinburgh UP.

—— and DAVIDSON, JANE (trans and ed) (1978), *Dumas on Food*, London: Michael Joseph.

DAVIDSON, PAMELA (1979), 'Recipes from the Soviet Union', in Davidson (1979).

DAVIES, GILLI (1990), *The Taste of Cyprus*, New Barnet: Interworld.

DAWSON, THOMAS (1596), *The Good Housewife's Jewel*, repr Lewes: Southover Press (1996).

DAY, FRANCIS (1876), *The Fishes of India*, vols i and ii, London: Bernard Quaritch.

—— (1880–4), *The Fishes of Great Britain and Ireland*, vols i and ii, London.

DAY, IVAN (1996a), 'Down at the Old Twisted Posts', in *PPC* 52.

—— (1996b), 'Further Musings on Syllabub', in *PPC* 53.

DE CANDOLLE, ALPHONSE (1886), *Origin of Cultivated Plants*, 2nd English edn, London.

DE COURCHAMPS, M. le comte (1853), *Dictionnaire générale de la cuisine française ancienne et moderne*, Paris.

DE CROZE, A., and 'CURNONSKY' (1933), *Le Trésor gastronomique de France*, Paris: Delagrave.

DE DIJN, ROSINE (1992), *Belgium, Land of the Good Life*, Brussels: GEV and Lannoo.

DELAMERE, EDMUND, and DELAMERE, ELLEN (1868), *Wholesome Fare*, London: Lockwood.

—— —— (1878), *Wholesome Fare*, 2nd edn, London: Crosby Lockwood.

DELAVEAU, PIERRE (1987), *Les Épices*, Paris: Albin Michel.

DE LAZARQUE, E. AURICOSTE (1979), *Cuisine Messine*, Marseilles: Laffitte.

DEL CONTE, ANNA (1987), *Gastronomy of Italy*, New York: Prentice Hall Press.

—— (1989), *Secrets from an Italian Kitchen*, London: Bantam Press.

DELLA CROCE, JULIA (1989), *Pasta Classica*, London: John Murray.

DELLA SALDA, ANNA GOSETTI (1967), *Le ricette regionali italiane*, Milan: 'La Cucina Italiana'.

DE LUNE, PIERRE (1660), *Le Nouveau Cuisinier*, 3rd edn, Paris: Pierre David.

DE MOOR, JANNY (1995), 'Dutch Cookery and Calvin', in *Cooks & other People*, Oxford Symposium on Food History 1995, Totnes: Prospect Books.

DE RONTZIER, FRANTZ (1598), *Kochbuch*.

DERRICKE, J. (1581), *The Image of Ireland*, London.

DÉRY, CAROL (1996), 'The Art of Apicius', in *Cooks and Other People*, Oxford Symposium on Food History 1995, Totnes: Prospect Books.

DE VOE, THOMAS F. (1866), *The Market Assistant*, New York: Orange, Judd.

DEVI, YAMUNA (1987), *The Art of Indian Vegetarian Cooking*, New York: Bala Books.

DEWITT, DAVE and GERLACH, NANCY (1990), *The Whole Chile Pepper Book*, Boston: Little Brown.

—— and WILAN, MARY JANE (1993), *Callaloo, Calypso & Carnival*, Freedom, Calif.: The Crossing Press.

DICKSON, PAUL (1972), *The Great American Ice Cream Book*, New York: Atheneum.

DI CORATO, RICCARDO (1977), *451 formaggi d'Italia*, Milan: Sonzogno.

—— (1978), *928 condimenti d'Italia*, Milan: Sonzogno.

—— (1979), *838 frutti e verdure d'Italia*, Milan: Sonzogno.

DIGBY, KENELM, Sir (1669), *The Closet of Sir Kenelm Digby Knight Opened*, ed Anne MacDonnell, London: Philip Lee Warner (1910).

DINNEEN, D. (ed) (1908), *The History of Ireland*, ed G. Keating, London.

DI SCHINO, JUNE (1995), 'The Waning of Sexually Allusive Monastic Confectionery in Southern Italy', in *Disappearing Foods*, Oxford Symposium on Food History 1994, Totnes: Prospect Books.

D'ISRAELI, ISAAC (1817), *Curiosities of Literature*, London.

DISSANAYAKE, CHANDRA (1976), *Ceylon Cookery*, Colombo: Metro Printers.

DOAK, WADE T. (1978), *Fishes of the New Zealand Region*, 2nd edn, Auckland: Hodder & Stoughton.

DODOENS, REMBERT (1578), *A Niewe Herball, or Historie of Plantes*, trans Henry Lyte, London.

DODS, MARGARET (1826), *The Cook and Housewife's Manual*, Edinburgh: Oliver & Boyd.

DOGLIO, SANDRO (1995), *Il dizionario di gastronomia del Piemonte*, San Giorgio di Montiglio: Daumerie.

DOLING, ANNABEL (c.1995), *Macau on a Plate*, Hong Kong: Roundhouse Publications.

DONKIN, R. A. (1980), *Manna: An Historical Geography*, The Hague: Dr W. Junk.

—— (1991), *Meleagrides*, London: Ethnographica.

DORÉ, AMPHAY (ed) (1980), bulletin of Cercle de culture et de recherches Laotiennes, issue of Dec 1980, Saint-Germain en Laye: Copie Express.

DORJE, RINJING (1985), *Food in Tibetan Life*, London: Prospect Books.

DOUGLAS, LOUDON (1911), *The Bacillus of Long Life*, London: T. C. & E. C. Jack.

DOUGLAS, MARY (1966), *Purity and Danger*, New York: Frederick A. Praeger.

DOUGLAS, NORMAN (1952), *Venus in the Kitchen*, London: Wm. Heinemann.

DRIVER, CHRISTOPHER (1983), *The British at Table*, London: Chatto & Windus.

—— (ed) (1997), *John Evelyn, Cook*, Totnes: Prospect Books.

DRIVER, ELIZABETH (1989), *A Bibliography of Cookery Books Published in Britain 1875–1914*, London and New York: Prospect Books in association with Mansell Publishing.

DRUMMOND, J. C. and WILBRAHAM, ANNE (1939), *The Englishman's Food*, London: Jonathan Cape.

DRURY, SUSAN (1985), 'Flowers in English Cookery in the 17th and 18th Centuries', *PPC* 20.

DUBOIS, URBAIN, and BERNARD, ÉMILE (1856), *La Cuisine classique*, vols i and ii, Paris: E. Dentu.

DUCKITT, HILDAGONDA J. (1891), *Hilda's 'Where is it?' of Recipes*, London: Chapman & Hall.

DUKE, JAMES A. (1981), *Handbook of Legumes of World Economic Importance*, New York: Plenum Press.

—— (1985), *Handbook of Medicinal Herbs*, Boca Raton, Fla.: CRC Press.

Dumas, Alexandre (1873), *Le Grand Dictionnaire de cuisine*, Paris: Lemerre.

Duncan, Dorothy (1993), 'Maple Magic', in Walker (1993).

Durand, J. (1993), *Le Nougat de Montélimar*, Pont-Saint-Esprit: La Mirandole.

Eales, Mrs Mary (1736), *Mrs. Mary Eales's Receipts*, facsimile edn (same as 1st edn, 1718), London: Prospect Books (1985).

Ebroïn, Ary (1977a), *Art culinaire créole des Antilles Françaises*, Paris: E. Kolodziej.

—— (1977b), *Art d'accommoder les poissons, les crustacés et les mollusques des Antilles Françaises*, Paris: E. Kolodziej.

Edwards, Gillian (1970), *Hogmanay and Tiffany*, London: Geoffrey Bles.

Ellis, W. (1750), *The Country Housewife's Family Companion*, London: James Hodges.

Ellison, J. Audrey (ed and trans) (1966), *The Great Scandinavian Cookbook*, London: George Allen & Unwin.

Elphinstone, Mountstuart (1839), *An Account of the Kingdom of Caubul*, repr London: OUP (1972).

Elst, Rudy van der (1988), *Guide to the Common Sea Fishes of South Africa*, Cape Town: Bhb International.

Elyot, Thomas (1541), *The Castel of Helth*, facsimile edn, New York: Scholars' Facsimiles & Reprints (n.d.).

Emerson, Edward R. (1908), *Beverages, Past and Present*, vols i and ii, New York: The Knickerbocker Press.

Emmison, F. G. (1964), *Tudor Food and Pastimes*, London: Benn.

Escoffier, A. (1921), *Le Guide culinaire*, 4th edn, Paris: Ernest Flammarion.

—— (1934), *Ma Cuisine*, Paris: Ernest Flammarion.

—— (1979), *The Complete Guide to the Art of Modern Cookery*, trans H. L. Cracknell and R. J. Kaufmann, London: Heinemann.

—— (1985), *Souvenirs inédits*, Marseilles: Jeanne Laffitte.

Escudier, Jean-Noël (1964), *La Véritable Cuisine provençale et niçoise*, Toulon: Provencia.

Euzière, Jean (1961), *Les Pêches d'amateurs en Méditerranée*, Cannes: Robaudy.

Evans, E. Estyn (1957), *Irish Folk Ways*, London: Routledge & Kegan Paul.

Evelyn, John (1644), *Sylva*, London.

—— (1699), *Acetaria: A Discourse of Sallets*, facsimile edn, London: Prospect Books (1982).

Faber, George L. (1883), *The Fisheries of the Adriatic*, London.

Facciola, Stephen (1990, rev edn 1996), *Cornucopia: A Source Book of Edible Plants*, Vista, CA: Kampong.

Fairchild, David (1930), *Exploring for Plants*, New York: Macmillan.

—— (1938), *The World was my Garden*, New York: Charles Scribner's.

FAO (1977), *The Water Buffalo*, Rome: FAO.

—— (1988), *Traditional Food Plants*, Rome: FAO.

—— (1990), *Street Foods*, Rome: FAO.

Farga, Amando (1963), *Eating in Mexico*, Mexico: Mexican Restaurant Association.

Farley, John (1784), *The London Art of Cookery*, repr Lewes: Southover (1988).

Farmer, Fannie Merritt (1896), *The Original Boston Cooking-School Cook Book*, facsimile edn, New York: Plume (1974).

—— (1904), *Food and Cookery for the Sick and Convalescent*.

Favre, Joseph (1883–92), *Dictionnaire universel de cuisine*, 4 vols, Paris, Libr.-impr. des Halles de la Bourse et du Commerce.

—— (1903), *Dictionnaire universel de cuisine pratique*, 2nd edn, facsimile reprint Marseille: Laffitte (1978).

Fenton, Alexander (1977), *Scottish Country Life*, Edinburgh: John Donald.

—— and Kisbán, Eszter (ed) (1986), *Food in Change*, Edinburgh: John Donald.

—— and Owen, Trefor M. (ed) (1981), *Food in Perspective*, Edinburgh: John Donald.

Ferguson (1955), 'Food and Hospitality in the Sudan', *Proceedings of the 1953 Annual Conference of the Philological Society*, Sudan.

Fernald, M. L. and Kinsey, A. C. (1943), *Edible Wild Plants of Eastern North America*, Cornwall-on-Hudson, NY: Idlewild Press.

Fernandez, Doreen G. (1994), *Tikim: Essays on Philippine Food and Culture*, Manila: Anvil Publishing.

—— (1997), *Fruits of the Philippines*, Makati City: Bookmark.

—— and Alegre, Edilberto N. (1988), *Sarap: Essays on Philippine Food*, Manila: Mr & Ms.

Fernandez, Rafi (1985), *Malaysian Cookery*, London: Century.

Fernie, W. T. (1895), *Herbal Simples*, Bristol: Wright.

—— (1905), *Meals Medicinal*, Bristol: Wright.

Fiddes, Nick (1991), *Meat: A Natural Symbol*, London: Routledge.

Field, Carol (1990), *Celebrating Italy*, New York: William Morrow.

Fieldhouse, Paul (1986), *Food and Nutrition: Customs and Culture*, London: Croom Helm.

Finck, Henry T. (1914), *Food and Flavour*, London: J. Lane.

Findlay, William M. (1956), *Oats: Their Cultivation and Use from Ancient Times to the Present Day*, Edinburgh: Oliver & Boyd.

Fisher, Mrs Abby (1881), *What Mrs Fisher Knows about Old Southern Cooking*, San Francisco: Women's Co-operative.

Fisher, M. F. K. (1943), *The Gastronomical Me*, San Francisco: North Point Press.

—— (1946), *Here Let Us Feast*, New York: Viking.

—— (1949), *An Alphabet for Gourmets*, San Francisco: North Point Press.

—— (1968), *With Bold Knife and Fork*, New York: Putnam.

—— (1970), *Among Friends*, San Francisco: North Point Press.

—— (1978), *A Considerable Town*, New York: Knopf.

—— (1984), 'Loving Cooks, Beware!', *Journal of Gastronomy*, 1 (summer).

—— and the editors of Time-Life Books (1969), *The Cooking of Provincial France*, Amsterdam: Time-Life.

Fitch, John E. and Lavenberg, Robert J. (1971), *Marine Food and Game Fishes of California*, Berkeley and Los Angeles: University of California Press.

Fitch, Noël (1997), *Appetite for Life: The Biography of Julia Child*, New York: Doubleday.

FitzGibbon, Theodora (1967), *The Art of British Cookery*, 2nd edn, London: Cookery Book Club.

—— (1976), *The Food of the Western World*, New York: Quadrangle/New York Times Books.

—— (1980), *Traditional Scottish Cookery*, London: Fontana.

—— (1983), *Irish Traditional Food*, London: Macmillan.

Flandrin, Jean-Louis; Hyman, Philip; and Hyman, Mary (eds) (1983), *Le Cuisinier françois*, Paris: Montalba.

Fletcher, Nichola (1987), *Game for All*, London: Gollancz.

Floris, Maria (1968), *Bakery: Cakes and Simple Confectionery*, London: Wine & Food Society.

Flower, Barbara, and Rosenbaum, Elizabeth (trans and ed) (1958) *The Roman Cookery Book*, London: Harrap.

Flückiger, F., and Hanbury, D. (1879), *Pharmacographia*, London: Macmillan.

Foley, Daniel J. (ed) (1974), *Herbs for Use and for Delight*, New York: Dover.

Ford, Richard (1906), *Gatherings from Spain*, London: Dent.

Forster, Robert and Ranum, Orest (ed) (1979), *Food and Drink in History*, Baltimore: Johns Hopkins UP.

Fortner, Heather J. (1978), *The Limu Eater*, Hawaii: Sea Grant.

Fosså, Ove (1995), 'A Whale of a Dish: Whalemeat as Food', in *Disappearing Foods*, Oxford Symposium on Food History 1994, Totnes: Prospect Books.

Franks, Flex (1984), *Water* (rev edn of 1983), London: The Royal Society of Chemistry.

Freely, John (1974), *Stamboul Sketches*, Istanbul: Redhouse Press.

Freeman, Bobby (1986), *First Catch your Peacock*, rev edn, Talybont: Y Lolfa Cyf.

Freethy, Ron (1983), *Man and Beast*, Poole: Blandford Press.

Fries, E. (1821–9), *Systema Mycologicum*, E. Mauritius: Gryphiswaldia.

Furetière, Antoine (1691), *Dictionnaire universel*, 3 vols facsimile edn, Paris: Le Robert (1978).

Fussell, Betty (1986), *I Hear America Cooking*, New York: Viking.

—— (1992), *The Story of Corn*, New York: Alfred A. Knopf.

Gacon-Dufour, Mme (1805), *Manuel de la ménagère à la ville et à la campagne*, Paris: Buisson.

Gage, Thomas (1648), *Travels in the New World*, ed J. E. S. Thompson, Norman: University of Oklahoma Press (1958).

Galizia, Anne and Caruana, Helen (1997), *The Food and Cookery of Malta*, Totnes: Prospect Books.

Gantz, Jeffrey (1981), *Early Irish Myths and Sagas*, Harmondsworth: Penguin.

GARCIA DA ORTA (1563), *Colloquios dos simples e drogas*, repr Lisbon (1872).

GARRETT, THEODORE FRANCIS (ed) (*c*.1895), *The Encyclopaedia of Practical Cookery*, London.

GASKELL, Mrs ELIZABETH (1854), *North and South*, Manchester.

GAULT, HENRI (1996), 'Nouvelle Cuisine', in *Cooks and Other People*, Oxford Symposium on Food History 1995, Totnes: Prospect Books.

GELFAND, MICHAEL (1971), *Diet and Tradition in an African Culture*, Edinburgh: E. & S. Livingstone.

GÉRARD, CHARLES (1971), *L'Ancienne Alsace à table*, France: Alsatia-Colmar.

GERARD, JOHN (1633), *The Herbal*, New York: Dover.

GERBER, HILDA (1959), *Traditional Cookery of the Cape Malays*, 3rd edn, Cape Town: A. A. Balkema.

GIBAULT, GEORGES (1912), *Histoire des légumes*, Paris: Librairie Horticole.

GIBBONS, EUELL (1962), *Stalking the Wild Asparagus*, New York: David McKay.

—— (1964), *Stalking the Blue-eyed Scallop*, New York: David McKay.

—— (1967), *Beachcombers' Handbook*, New York: David McKay.

—— (1971), *Stalking the Good Life*, New York: David McKay.

GILLMAN, GARY M. (1991), 'Les Cretons and La Cipaille', in Notes and Queries, *PPC* 37.

GLASSE, HANNAH (1747), *The Art of Cookery Made Plain and Easy*, facsimile of 1st edn, London: Prospect Books (1983).

—— (1760*a*), *The Compleat Confectioner*, London.

—— (1760*b*), *The Servant's Directory or House-Keeper's Companion*,

GOBERT, Dr E. G. (1940), 'Les Usages et rites alimentaires des Tunisiens', *Archives de l'Institut Pasteur*.

—— (1955), 'Les References historiques des nourritures tunisiennes', *Cahiers de Tunisie*.

GODARD, MISETTE (1991), *Le Goût de l'aigre*, Paris: Quai Voltaire.

GOLDSCHMIED, LEO (1954), *Enciclopedia Gastronomica*, Milan: Ceschina.

GOLDSTEIN, DARRA (1983), *A La Russe*, New York: Random House.

GOODE, G. BROWN, and associates (1884), *The Fisheries and Fishery Industries of the United States: Section 1, The Natural History of Useful Aquatic Animals*, Washington: Government Printing Office.

GOODY, JACK (1982), *Cooking, Cuisine and Class*, Cambridge: CUP.

GORDON, BERTRAM M. (1988), 'Fascism, the Neo-Right and Gastronomy', in Jaine (1988).

—— and JACOBS-MCCUSKER, LISA (1989), 'One Pot Cookery and Some Comments on its Iconography', in *The Cooking Pot*, Oxford Symposium on Food History 1988, London: Prospect Books.

GORDON, DAVID GEORGE (1988), *The Eat-A-Bug Cookbook*, Berkeley, CA: Ten Speed Press.

GOSETTI DELLA SALDA, ANNA (1967), *Le ricetti regionali italiane*, Milan: Solares.

GOTTSCHALK, Dr ALFRED (1948), *Histoire de l'alimentation et de la gastronomie*, vols i and ii, Paris: Hippocrate.

GOUFFÉ, JULES (1867), *Le Livre de cuisine*, Paris: Hachette et Cie.

—— (1869), *Le Livre des conserves*, Paris: Hachette.

—— (1875), *Le Livre des soupes et des potages*, Paris: Hachette.

—— (1877), *Le Livre de patisserie*, Paris: Hachette.

GOWERS, EMILY (1993), *The Loaded Table*, Oxford: Clarendon Press.

GRAHAM, GLADYS R. (1947), *Tropical Cooking*, Panama: Panama American Press.

GRAHAM, PETER (1988), *Classic Cheese Cookery*, London: Penguin.

GRAHAM, SYLVESTER (1837), *A Treatise on Bread and Bread-Making*, Boston.

GRAY, PATIENCE (1986), *Honey from a Weed*, London: Prospect Books.

—— and BOYD, PRIMROSE (1990), *Plats du Jour*, London: Prospect Books.

GRAY, W. D. (1973), 'Hallucinogenic fungi and ethnomycology' in *The Use of fungi as food and in food processing*, pt II, Cleveland: CRC Press.

GREEN, MAUREEN, and GREEN, TIMOTHY (1985), *The Good Water Guide*, London: Rosendale Press.

GREENE, GRAHAM (1973), *The Honorary Consul*, London: Bodley Head.

GREENOAK, FRANCESCA (1979), *All the Birds of the Air*, London: André Deutsch.

—— (1983), *Forgotten Fruit*, London: André Deutsch.

GREWE, RUDOLF (ed) (1979), *Libre de Sent Sovi*, Barcelona: Barcino.

—— (1981), 'Catalan Cuisine . . .', in *National and Regional Styles of Cookery*, Oxford Symposium on Food History 1981, London: Prospect Books.

—— (1988), 'The Arrival of the Tomato in Spain and Italy', *Proceedings of the First International Food Congress in Turkey* (1986).

GRIEVE, Mrs M. (1931), *A Modern Herbal*, vols i and ii, repr, New York: Dover (1971).

GRIGSON, GEOFFREY (1955), *The Englishman's Flora*, London: Phoenix House.

GRIGSON, JANE (1967), *Charcuterie and French Pork Cookery*, London: Michael Joseph.

—— (1971), *Good Things*, London: Michael Joseph.

—— (1973), *Fish Cookery*, London: David & Charles.

—— (1974), *English Food*, London: Macmillan.

—— (1975), *The Mushroom Feast*, London: Michael Joseph.

—— (1978), *Jane Grigson's Vegetable Book*, London: Michael Joseph.

—— (1979), *Food with the Famous*, London: Michael Joseph.

—— (1981), 'The Nut Oils of Berry', in *PPC* 9.

—— (1982), *Jane Grigson's Fruit Book*, London: Michael Joseph.

—— (1983), *The Observer Guide to European Cookery*, London: Michael Joseph.

—— (1984), *The Observer Guide to British Cookery*, London: Michael Joseph.

—— (1987*a*), *The Cooking of Normandy*, Cambridge: Martin Books.

—— (1987*b*), 'Caul Fat as Cooking Medium', in *The Cooking Medium*, Oxford Symposium on Food History 1986, London: Prospect Books.

—— (1995), *English Food*, London: Penguin.

—— and KNOX, CHARLOTTE (1986), *Exotic Fruits and Vegetables*, London: Jonathan Cape.

GRIMOD DE LA REYNIÈRE, LAURENT-ALEXANDRE-BALTHAZAR (1805), *Almanach des gourmands*, 3rd vol, Paris: Maradan.

—— (1807), *Manuel des amphitryons*, repr, Paris: A. M. Métailié (1983).

GRIST, D. H. (1953), *Rice*, London: Longman.

GROFF, GEORGE WEIDDMAN (1921), *The Lychee and the Lungan*, New York.

GRØN, FREDRIK (1927), *Om Kostholdet i Norge indtil aar 1500*, Oslo: n.p.

—— (1942), *Om Kostholdet i Norge fra omkring 1500—tallet og op til ver tid*, Oslo: n.p.

GUÉGAN, BERTRAND (1980), *Le Cuisinier français*, Paris: Belfon.

GUINAUDEAU, Mme Z. (1958), *Fes vu par sa cuisine*, Rabat: J. E. Laurent.

GUINAUDEAU-FRANCE, Mme Z. (1981), *Les Secrets des cuisines en terre marocaine*, Paris: Taillandier.

GUNTER, WILLIAM (1830), *The Confectioner's Oracle*, London: Alfred Miller.

GUPTA, MINAKSHIE DAS, GUPTA, B., and CHALIHA, J. (1995), *The Calcutta Cook Book*, New Delhi: Penguin India.

GUSTAFSON, HELEN (1996), *The Agony of the Leaves*, New York: Henry Holt.

GYLLENSKÖLD, H. (1963), *Att koka fisk*, Stockholm: Wahlström & Widstrand.

HACHTEN, HARVA (1981), *The Flavor of Wisconsin*, Madison: State Historical Society of Wisconsin.

HACKWOOD, FREDERICK W. (1911), *Good Cheer*, London: T. Fisher Unwin.

HAGDAHL, Dr CH. EM. (1896), Kok-konstem, facsimile edn (first pub 1879), Sweden: Gastronomiska Akademiens Bibliotek (1963).

HAGEN, ANN (1992), *A Handbook of Anglo-Saxon Food: Processing and Consumption*, Pinner: Anglo-Saxon Books.

—— (1995), *Anglo-Saxon Food and Drink: Production and Distribution*, Hockwold cum Wilton: Anglo-Saxon Books.

HALE, SARAH JOSEPHA (1839), *The Good Housekeeper*, Boston: Weeks, Jordan.

HALICI, FEYZI (1988), 'Food and Kitchen Image in Mevlana's Writings', in *Proceedings of the First International Food Congress, Turkey, 1986*.

HALICI, NEVIN (1989), *Nevin Halıcı's Turkish Cookbook*, London: Dorling Kindersley.

—— (1993), 'Mastic in the Turkish Kitchen', in Walker (1993).

HALL, S. J. G., and CLUTTON-BROCK, JULIET (1989), *Two Hundred Years of British Farm Livestock*, London: British Museum (Natural History).

HALL, WALTER and HALL, NANCY (1980), *The Wild Palate*, Emmaus, Pa.: Rodale Press.

HAMBRO, NATHALIE (1981), *Particular Delights*, London: Jill Norman & Hobhouse.

HAMP, PIERRE (1932), *Kitchen Prelude*, London: Constable.

HARDIN, PHILOMELIA ANN MARIA ANTOINETTE (1842), *Every Body's Cook and Receipt Book,* Cleveland.

HARLAND, Mrs MARION (*c.*1844), *Cookery for Beginners,* San Francisco: Golden Age Bazaar.

—— (1874), *Common Sense in the Household,* New York: Scribner, Armstrong.

HARRIS, LLOYD J. (1980), *The Book of Garlic,* Los Angeles: Panjandrum/Aris Books.

—— (1986), *The Official Garlic Lovers Handbook,* Berkeley: Aris.

HARRIS, MARVIN (1978), *Cannibals & Kings,* London: Collins.

—— (1986), *Good to Eat,* London: Allen & Unwin.

HART, J. S. (1852), *Female Prose Writers of America,* Philadelphia.

HARTLEY, DOROTHY (1939), *Made in England,* London: Methuen.

—— (1954), *Food in England,* London: Macdonald.

—— (1964), *Water in England,* London: Macdonald.

HASSALL, ARTHUR HILL (1876), *Food: Its Adulterations and the Methods of their Detection,* London: Longmans, Green.

HATFIELD, AUDREY WYNNE (1964), *Pleasures of Herbs,* London: Museum.

HAWKES, ALEX D. (1968), *A World of Vegetable Cookery,* New York: Simon & Schuster.

HAY, WILLIAM DELISLE (1887), *Text Book of British Fungi,* London: Swan Sonnenschein etc.

HEARD, VIDA and FAULL, LESLEY (1975), *Our Best Traditional Recipes,* Cape Town: Howard Timmins.

HEDGEPETH, WILLIAM (1978), *The Hog Book,* New York: Doubleday.

HEIM, ROGER (1957), *Les Champignons d'Europe,* vols i and ii, Paris: Boubée.

—— (1978), *Les Champignons toxiques et hallucinogènes,* Paris: Boubée.

HEIMANN, JIM (1996), *Car Hops and Curb Service,* San Francisco: Chronicle Books.

HEISER, CHARLES B. (1976), *The Sunflower,* Norman: University of Oklahoma Press.

—— (1979), *The Gourd Book,* Norman: University of Oklahoma Press.

HEKMAT, FOROUGH (1970), *The Art of Persian Cooking,* 2nd edn, Tehran: Ebn-e-Sina.

HELLEI, ANDRAS (1973), *Les Coutumes alimentaires,* Khmères, Phnom Penh: Institut National de la Statistique et des Recherches Économiques.

HELOU, ANISSA (1994), *Lebanese Cuisine,* London: Grub Street.

HENDERSON, WILLIAM AUGUSTUS (n.d.), *The Housekeeper's Instructor,* London: J. Stratford.

HENISCH, BRIDGET ANN (1967), *Medieval Armchair Travels,* Philadelphia: Carnation Press.

—— (1976), *Fast and Feast,* University Park, Pa.: Penn State UP.

—— (1984), *Cakes and Characters,* London: Prospect Books.

HERKLOTS, G. A. C. (1972), *Vegetables in South-East Asia,* Hong Kong: South China Morning Post.

HERODOTUS (1858), *The Ancient History,* trans W. Beloe, New York: Derby & Jackson.

HERON-ALLEN, EDWARD (1978), *Barnacles in Nature and Myth,* London: OUP.

HERSEY, JOHN (1987), *Blues,* New York: Knopf.

HESS, JOHN, and HESS, KAREN (1977), *The Taste of America* (also new edn 1989), New York: Grossman.

HESS, KAREN (ed) (1981), *Martha Washington's Booke of Cookery,* New York: Columbia University Press.

—— (1991), 'La Cipaille and Sea Pie', in 'Notes and Queries', in *PPC* 38.

—— (1992), *The Carolina Rice Kitchen,* Columbia: University of South Carolina Press.

HEYRAUD, H. (*c.*1930), *La Cuisine à Nice,* Nice: Leo Barma.

HIBBEN, SHEILA (1947), *American Regional Cookery* (first pub 1937), Boston: Little, Brown.

HICKMAN, TREVOR (1996), *The History of Stilton Cheese,* Stroud: Alan Sutton.

HICKS, ALEXANDRA (1982), 'Red Peppercorns: What They Really Are', in *PPC* 10.

—— (1986), 'The Mystique of Garlic', in *Cookery: Science, Lore and Books,* Oxford Symposium on Food History 1984 and 1985, London: Prospect Books.

HIEATT, CONSTANCE (1982), 'Greensauce: Elderflowers', in 'Notes and Queries', in *PPC* 12.

—— (ed) (1988), *An Ordinance of Pottage,* London: Prospect Books.

—— (1995), 'Sorting through the Titles of Medieval Dishes: What is, or is not, a "Blanc manger"', in Melitta Weiss Adamson (ed), *Food in the Middle Ages,* New York: Garland Publishing.

—— and BUTLER, SHARON (1985), *Curye on Inglysch,* London: OUP.

—— and HOSINGTON, BRENDA M. (1998), 'From *Espinee* to *Sambocade*: Flowers in the Recipes of Medieval England', in *PPC* 59, London: Prospect Books.

HILLYARD, PAUL (1995), *The Book of the Spider,* London: Random House.

HIPPOCRATES (1978), *Hippocratic Writings,* ed G. E. R. Lloyd, Harmondsworth: Penguin.

—— (1923–), *Hippocrates,* ed and trans W. H. S. Jones, 4 vols, Cambridge, MA: Loeb Classical Library.

HODGSON, W. C. (1957), *The Herring and its Fishery,* London: Routledge & Kegan Paul.

HÖFLER, MANFRED (1996), *Dictionnaire de l'art culinaire français,* Aix-en-Provence: Edisud.

HOGG, R. (1851), *The Apple and its Varieties,* London: Groombridge & Sons.

HOLBROOK, DAVID (1990), 'A Treasury of cakes', in *PCC* 35.

HOLLAND, ISOBEL; HUNTER, LYNETTE; and STONEHAM, GERALDINE (1991), 'Bibliography of Jane Grigson's Books', *PPC* 38.

HOLMBERG, ALLAN R. (1957), *Lizard Hunts on the North Coast,* Chicago: Natural History Museum.

HOLT, VINCENT M. (1885), *Why Not Eat Insects,* London: E. W. Classey (7th edn 1978).

HOLTHUIS, L. B. (1980), *Shrimps and Prawns of the World,* Rome: FAO.

—— (1984), 'Food in Wartime Netherlands', in Notes and Queries, *PPC* 18.

—— (1991), *Marine Lobsters of the World,* Rome: FAO.

HONE, WILLIAM (1826), *The Every-day Book,* London.

—— (1832), *The Year Book of Daily Recreation,* London.

HONGROIS, CHRISTIAN (1991), *Si t'aimes pas l'meuille . . . Culture et consommation du millet en Vendée,* Aizenay: n.p.

HOOD, ANNIE (1993), 'Kentish Food', *PPC* 45.

HOOKER, RICHARD J. (1978), *The Book of Chowder,* Cambridge, Mass.: Common Press.

—— (1981), *Food and Drink in America,* Indianapolis: Bobbs-Merrill.

HOPE, ANNETTE (1987), *A Caledonian Feast,* Edinburgh: Mainstream.

HOPE, ROSE-ELLEN (1983), 'The Legacy of Western Camas', *PPC* 13.

HOPKINSON, SIMON, and BAREHAM, LINDSEY (1997), *The Prawn Cocktail Years,* London: Macmillan.

HORNELL, JAMES (1950), *Fishing in Many Waters,* Cambridge: CUP.

HOSAKA, EDWARD Y. (1973), *Shore Fishing in Hawaii,* Hawaii: Petroglyph Press.

HOSKING, RICHARD (1992), 'Pavement Food, Packed Meals and Picnics in Japan', in Walker (1992).

—— (1994), '. . . Appearance and Texture in Japanese Food', in *Look and Feel,* Oxford Symposium on Food History 1993, Totnes: Prospect Books.

—— (1996), *A Dictionary of Japanese Food Ingredients and Culture,* Rutland, VT: Charles E. Tuttle.

HOURANI, FURUGH AFNAN (1984), 'Cooking with Yoghurt', in *PPC* 18.

HOWARD, HENRY (n.d.), *England's Newest Way,* n.p.

HOWE, ROBIN (1958), *Cooking from the Commonwealth,* London: André Deutsch.

HOWES, F. N. (1948), *Nuts,* London: Faber.

HOWLAND, Mrs ESTHER ALLEN (1844), *The New England Economical Housekeeper,* Worcester, Mass.

HUDGINS, SHARON (1997), 'Raw Liver and More: Feasting with the Buriats of Southern Siberia', in *Food on the Move,* Oxford Symposium on Food History 1996, Totnes: Prospect Books.

HULME, F. EDWARD (1902), *Wild Fruits of the Country-Side,* London: Hutchinson.

HUMPHREY, THEODORE, and HUMPHREY, LIN (1988), *'We Gather Together': Food and Festival in American Life,* Michigan: UMI Research Press.

HUMPHRIES, JOHN (1996), *The Essential Saffron Companion,* London: Grub Street.

HUSSON, A. (1875), *Les Consommations de Paris,* Paris.

HUTCHINS, SHEILA (1967), *English Recipes and Others,* London: Methuen.

HUTCHISON, Sir ROBERT (1900), *Food and the Principles of Dietetics,* London: Edward Arnold.

HUXLEY, T. H. (1877), *Anatomy of Invertebrated Animals,* London.

—— (1880), *The Crayfish*, London.

HYMAN, PHILIP (1986), 'Snail Trails', in *PPC* 23, London: Prospect Books.

—— and HYMAN, MARY (1980), 'Long Pepper: A Short History', in *PPC* 6.

IDDISON, PHILIP (1994), 'Azarole, Oleaster and Jujube', in *PPC* 48.

IPCF (l'Inventaire du Patrimoine Culinaire de la France) (1992–2000), 27 vols on 'Produits du Terroir' of regions of France, including Provence-Alpes-Côte d'Azur (1995), France-Comté (1993), and Île-de-France (1993), CNAC (Conseil National des Arts Culinaires) & Albin Michel.

IRVINE, F. R. (1934), *A Text-Book of West African Agriculture*, London.

—— (1961), *Woody Plants of Ghana*, Oxford: OUP.

IRWIN, FLORENCE (1937), *Irish Country Recipes*, Belfast: Northern Whig.

—— (1949), *The Cookin' Woman, Irish Country Recipes & Others*, Edinburgh: Oliver & Boyd.

ISSACS, J. (1987), *Bush Food: Aboriginal Food and Herbal Medicine*, Sydney: Weldons.

J.K. (trans) (1702), *The Court and Country Cook* (by Massialot), London.

JACCOTTET, J. (1973), *Les Champignons dans la nature*, 9th edn, Neuchâtel, Delachaux & Niestlé.

JACKSON, IAN (1995), 'Fragments of the History of the Pear', in *PPC* 49.

JACOBS, LOUIS (1995), *The Jewish Religion: A Companion*, Oxford: OUP.

JACQUAT, CHRISTIANE (1990), *Plants from the Markets of Thailand*, Bangkok: Editions Duang Kamol.

JAFFREY, MADHUR (1985), *A Taste of India*, London: Pavilion.

—— (1995), *Madhur Jaffrey's Flavours of India*, London: BBC Books.

JAINE, TOM (1986a), *Cooking in the Country*, London: Chatto & Windus.

—— (1986b), 'Oxalic Acid: Does it Rot Fish Bones', in *Cookery: Science, Lore and Books*, Oxford Symposium on Food History 1984 and 1985, London: Prospect Books.

—— (ed) (1988), *Taste*, Oxford Symposium on Food History 1987, London: Prospect Books.

JARRIN, G. A. (1827), *The Italian Confectioner*, London: John Harding.

JEFFREYS, M. D. W. (1975), 'Pre-Columbian Maize in the Old World', in Margaret L. Arnott (ed.), *Gastronomy*, The Hague: Mouton.

JENKINSON, ELEANOR L. (1909), *The Ocklye Cookery Book*, London: Cassell.

JENSEN, ALBERT C. (1972), *The Cod*, New York: Thomas Y. Crowell.

JOHNSON, GEORGE W. (1847), *The Cucumber and the Gooseberry*, London.

JOHNSON, ROBERT (1992), 'Saffron and the Good Life', in *PPC* 41.

JOHNSTON, JAMES P. (1977), *A Hundred Years Eating*, Dublin: Gill & Macmillan.

JONES, EVAN (1981), *American Food: The Gastronomic Story*, 2nd edn, New York: Random House.

JONES, PAUL and ANDREWS, BARRY (1980), *A Taste of Mauritius*, Mauritius: Éditions de l'Océan Indien.

JORDAN, DAVID STARR and EVERMANN, B. W. (1896), *The Fishes of North and Middle America*, vols i–iv, Washington: Government Printing Office.

—— (1902), *American Food and Game Fishes*, New York: Doubleday.

JORDAN, MICHAEL (1975), *A Guide to Mushrooms*, London [?]: Millington.

—— (1995a), *Edible Mushrooms and Other Fungi*, London: Cassell.

—— (1995b), *The Encyclopaedia of Fungi of Britain and Europe*, Newton Abbot: David & Charles.

KAHN, E. J., Jr (1985), *The Staffs of Life*, Boston: Little Brown.

KALÇAS, EVELYN LYLE (1974), *Food from the Fields*, Izmir: Birlik Matbaasý.

KALM, PETER (1972), *Travels in North America*, Barre, Mass.: Imprint Society.

KANAFANI-ZAHAR, AÏDA (1994), *Mûne: La Conservation alimentaire traditionelle au Liban*, Paris: Maison des Sciences de l'Homme.

KANEVA-JOHNSON, MARIA (1979), 'In Praise of Simplicity', in *PPC* 1.

—— (1995), *The Melting Pot: Balkan Food and Cookery*, London: Prospect Books.

KAVASCH, BARRIE (1979), *Native Harvests*, New York: Random House.

KAVENA, JUANITA TIGER (1980), *Hopi Cookery*, Tucson: University of Arizona Press.

KELLOGG, ELLA EATON (1904), *Science in the Kitchen*, rev edn, Battle Creek, Mich.: Modern Medicine Publishing.

KELLY, SARAH (1985), *Festive Baking in Austria, Germany and Switzerland*, London: Penguin.

KELSEY, MARY WALLACE (1990), 'Beans of the Southwestern United States Indians', in *Staple Foods*, Oxford Symposium on Food History 1989, London: Prospect Books.

KENNEDY, DIANA (1975), *The Tortilla Book*, New York: Harper & Row.

—— (1986), *The Cuisines of Mexico*, rev edn, New York: Harper & Row.

KENNEY-HERBERT, Col. A. ('Wyvern') (1885), *Culinary Jottings for Madras*, 5th edn, Madras: Higginbotham.

—— (1894a), *Common-Sense Cookery for English Households*, London: Edward Arnold.

—— (1894b), *Fifty Breakfasts*, London: Edward Arnold.

—— (1895), *Fifty Dinners*, London: Edward Arnold.

KETTILBY, MARY (1714), *A Collection of above Three Hundred Receipts in Cookery, Physick and Surgery*, London.

KEVILL-DAVIES, SALLY (1983), *Jelly Moulds*, Guildford: Lutterworth.

KEYS, JOHN D. (1966), *Japanese Cuisine: A Culinary Tour*, Tokyo: Charles E. Tuttle.

KHAING, MI MI (1978), *Cook and Entertain the Burmese Way*, Ann Arbor: Karoma.

KING, WILLIAM (1708), *The Art of Cookery*, London.

KIRSHENBLATT-GIMBLETT, BARBARA (1987), 'Udder and Other Extremities: Recipes from the Jews of Yemen', in *PPC* 27.

KITCHINER, Dr (1818), *The Cook's Oracle*, London.

KLEIN, MAGGIE BLYTH (1994), *The Feast of the Olive*, rev edn, San Francisco: Chronicle Books.

KLEPPER, NICOLAE (1997), *Taste of Romania*, New York: Hippocrene.

KOCH, H. and LAWSON, L. (eds) (1996), *Garlic*, Baltimore: Williams & Wilkins.

KOHL, HANNELORE (ed) (1996), *A Culinary Voyage through Germany*, New York: Abbeville Press.

KOLPAS, NORMAN (1979), *Coffee*, London: John Murray.

KOSIKOWSKI, F. V. (1977), *Cheese and Fermented Milk Foods*, New York: the author.

KOUKI, MOHAMED (1967), *La Cuisine tunisienne d'Ommote Sannafa*, Tunis.

KREMEZI, AGLAIA (1993), *The Foods of Greece*, New York: Stewart Tabori & Chang.

—— (1997), 'Paximadia (Barley Biscuits)', in *Food on the Move*, Oxford Symposium on Food History 1996, Totnes: Prospect Books.

KREUZER, RUDOLF (ed) (1974), *Fishery Products*, West Byfleet: Fishing News with FAO.

KRIEGER, LOUIS C. C. (1947), *The Mushroom Handbook*, New York: Macmillan.

KROCHMAL, CONNIE and KROCHMAL, ARNOLD (1974a), *A Naturalist's Guide to Cooking with Wild Plants*, New York: Quadrangle.

—— —— (1974b), *Caribbean Cooking*, New York: Quadrangle.

KUHN, C. G. (ed and trans) (1821–33), *Writings of Galen*, vols i–xx, Berlin.

KURLANSKY, MARK (1997), *Cod*, New York: Knopf.

KURTI, NICHOLAS (1996), 'Rumford and Culinary Science', in *Cooks and Other People*, Oxford Symposium on Food History 1995, Totnes: Prospect Books.

—— (1997), 'Space, Time and Food', in *Food on the Move*, Oxford Symposium on Food History 1996, Totnes: Prospect Books.

—— and KURTI, GIANA (eds) (1988), *But the Crackling is Superb*, Bristol: Adam Hilger.

LACAM, P. (1890), *Le Mémorial historique et géographique de la pâtisserie*, Paris: the author.

LA CHAPELLE, VINCENT (1733), *The Modern Cook*, London: Thomas Osborne.

Ladies of Toronto and Chief Cities and Towns in Canada (1877), *Canadian Home Cook Book*, Toronto.

LAGRIFFE, LOUIS (1968), *Le Livre des épices, condiments et aromates*, Haute Provence: Marabout Service.

LAKE, MAX (1989), *Scents and Sensuality*, London: John Murray.

LALLEMAND, ROGER (1986), *Les Omelettes*, Marseilles: Jeanne Laffitte.

—— (1990), *Petit Guide des douceurs de France*, Paris: Desvigne.

LAMB, PATRICK (1726), *Royal Cookery*, London.

LAMBERT, CAROLE (ed) (1992), *Du manuscrit à la table*, Montreal: Presses de l'Université de Montréal.

LANARÈS, JEAN-PIERRE (1982), *Le Bon Roy Camembert*, Paris: Bréa.

LANDEN, DINSDALE and DANIEL, JENNIFER (1985), *The True Story of HP Sauce*, London: Methuen.

LANDING, JAMES E. (1969), *American Essence*,

Kalamazoo, Mich.: Public Museum.

LANDRY, ROBERT (1978), *Guide Culinaire des épices, aromates et condiments*, Verviers: Nouvelles.

LANE, E. W. (1860), *Manners and Customs of the Modern Egyptians*, 5th edn, London: John Murray.

LANE, FRANK W. (1957), *Kingdom of the Octopus*, London: Jarrolds.

LANG, GEORGE (1971), *The Cuisine of Hungary*, New York: Bonanza.

LANNER, HARRIETTE (1981), *The Piñon Pine*, Reno: University of Nevada Press.

LARKCOM, JOY (1984), *The Salad Garden*, London: Windward.

—— (1991), *Oriental Vegetables*, London: John Murray.

Larousse gastronomique (1997), rev edn, Paris: Larousse-Bordas.

LAUDAN, RACHEL (1996), *The Food of Paradise*, Honolulu: University of Hawai'i Press.

LAUFER, BERTHOLD (1930), *Geophagy*, Chicago: Field Museum of Natural History.

—— (1978), *Sino Iranica*, repr of 1919 edn, Taipei: Ch'eng Wen.

LAURIOUX, BRUNO (1997), *La Règne de Taillevent*, Paris: Publications de La Sorbonne.

LA VARENNE, FRANÇOIS PIERRE DE (1651, 1654), *Le Cuisinier francois*, Paris.

—— (1667), *Le Parfait Confiturier*, Paris.

—— (1668), *L'École des ragouts*, Lyons.

LAVERTY, MAURA (1946), *Maura Laverty's Cookery Book*, London: Longmans, Green.

—— (1966), *Full and Plenty*, 2nd edn, Dublin: Irish Flour Millers' Association.

LAW, JAMES T. (*c*.1895), *Law's Grocer's Manual*, Liverpool.

LEA, ELIZABETH ELLICOT (1982), *A Quaker Woman's Cookbook* (1845), ed William Woys Weaver, Philadelphia: University of Pennsylvania.

LEACH, HELEN M. (1997), 'The Pavlova Cake', in *Food and Travel*, Oxford Symposium on Food History 1996, Totnes: Prospect Books.

LECLERC, HENRI (1925), *Les Fruits de France*, Paris.

—— (1927), *Les Légumes de France*, Paris.

LE COINTE, JOURDAIN (1790), *La Cuisine de Santé*, Paris.

LEE, Mrs N. K. M. (1972), *The Cook's Own Book*, New York: Arno.

LEIGHTON, ANN (1970), *Early English Gardens in New England: For Meate or Medicine*, London: Cassell.

LEIM, A. H. and SCOTT, W. B. (1966), *Fishes of the Atlantic Coast of Canada*, Ottawa: Fisheries Research Board of Canada.

LEIPOLDT, C. LOUIS (1976), *Leipoldt's Cape Cookery*, Cape Town: W. J. Flesch.

LEMERY, M. L. (1745), *A Treatise of All Sorts of Foods*, trans D. Hay, London: T. Osborne.

LEMOINE, CÉCILE and CLAUSTRES, GEORGES (1977), *Connaître et reconnaître les champignons*, Rennes: Ouest France.

LENNON, BIDDY WHITE (1990), *The Poolbeg Book of Traditional Irish Cooking*, Swords, Co. Dublin: Poolbeg Press.

LEONARD, JONATHAN NORTON (1970), *Latin American Cooking*, Netherlands: Time-Life Int.

LESLIE, ELIZA (1832), *Domestic French Cookery, Chiefly Translated from Sulpice Barue*, Philadelphia: Carey & Hart.

—— (1973), *Directions for Cookery in its Various Branches*, New York: Arno.

—— (1986), *Seventy-five Receipts for Pastry, Cakes and Sweetmeats*, San Francisco: American Institute of Wine and Food.

LEVAILLANT, FRANÇOIS (1790), *Travels from the Cape of Good Hope into the Interior Parts of Africa*, London: William Lane.

LEVENSTEIN, HARVEY (1988), *Revolution at the Table*, New York: OUP.

—— (1993), *Paradox of Plenty*, New York: OUP.

LEVY, PAUL (1986), *Out to Lunch*, London: Chatto & Windus.

LEWES, G. H. (1860), *Sea-Side Studies*, 2nd edn, Edinburgh.

LEYEL, Mrs (1937), *Herbal Delights*, London: Faber & Faber.

—— (ed) (1947), *Culpeper's English Physician and Complete Herbal*, London: Herbert Joseph.

—— and HARTLEY, OLGA (1925), *The Gentle Art of Cookery*, London: Chatto & Windus.

LIDDELL, CAROLINE and WEIR, ROBIN (1993), *Ices*, London: Hodder & Stoughton.

LIN, FLORENCE (1986), *Florence Lin's Complete Book of Chinese Noodles, Dumplings and Breads*, New York: Peter Morrow.

LIN, L. P. and HAR, L. S. (1986), *Hawkers Galore*, Penang: Penang Festival.

LINCOLN, Mrs. D. A. (1891), *Mrs Lincoln's Boston Cookbook*, Boston: Roberts.

LIND, JAMES (1757), *A Treatise on the Scurvy*, London: A. Millar.

LINDLEY, JOHN (1846), *The Vegetable Kingdom*, London.

LINSCHOTEN, JOHN HUIGHEN VAN (1598), *Discours of Voyages into ye Easte and Weste Indies*, London: John Wolfe.

LISSARRAGUE, F. (1987), *Un flot d'images*, Paris: Biro.

LISSNER, ERICH (1939), *Wurstologia*, Weihnachten.

LISTER, MARTIN (1698), *A Journey to Paris in the Year 1698*, facsimile edn, New York: Arno Press (1971).

LITTRÉ, ÉMILE (1881–83), *Dictionnaire de la langue française*, Paris.

LLANOVER, Lady (1867), *The First Principles of Good Cookery*, facsimile edn, Tregaron: Brefi Press (1991).

LLOYD, L. C. and LLOYD, A. J. (1931), 'Shrewsbury Cakes: The Story of a Famous Delicacy', *Shrewsbury Circular*.

LOCKHART, G. W. (1997), *The Scots and their Oats*, 2nd edn, Edinburgh: Birlinn.

LOCKWOOD, WILLAM G. and LOCKWOOD, YVONNE R. (1983), 'The Cornish Pasty in Northern Michigan', in *Food in Motion*, Oxford Symposium on Food History 1983, Leeds: Prospect Books.

LOESCH, JEANNE (1994), *De chou et de choucroute*, Mulhouse: Éditions du Rhin.

LOEWENFELD, CLAIRE (1957), *Britain's Wild Larder: Nuts*, London: Faber.

LONGONE, JAN (1985), 'Portable Soup', *Journal of Gastronomy*, 1/4.

—— (1986), *Mother Maize and King Corn*, Ann

Arbor: William L. Clements Library.

—— (1988–9), 'From the Kitchen', *American Magazine and Historical Chronicle*, 4/2.

—— (1996a), *American Cookery: The Bicentennial 1796–1996*, Ann Arbor: William L. Clements Library.

—— (1996b), 'Amelia Simmons and the First American Cookbook', in a special culinary issue of *Bookman's Weekly*.

—— and LONGONE, DANIEL T. (1984), *American Cookbooks and Wine Books 1797–1950*, Ann Arbor: William L. Clements Library.

LORD, W. B. (1867), *Crab, Shrimp and Lobster Lore*, London: Routledge.

LOVELL, M. S. (1884), *The Edible Mollusca of Great Britain and Ireland*, 2nd edn, London: L. Reeve.

LOVELOCK, YANN (1972), *The Vegetable Book: An Unnatural History*, London: Allen & Unwin.

LOVERA, JOSE RAFAEL (1988), *Historia de la alimentación en Venezuela*, Caracas: Monte Avila Editores.

—— (1991), *Gastronomia caribeña*, Caracas: CEGA.

LOW, TIM (1989), *Bush Tucker*, Auckland: Angus & Robertson.

—— (1991), *Wild Herbs of Australia and New Zealand*, rev edn, Ryde: Angus & Robertson.

LUARD, ELISABETH (1990), *European Festival Food*, London: Bantam Press.

LUCAS, A. T. (1960), 'Irish Food before the Potato', *Gwerin*, 3.

LUCIAN (1959–60), *Works*, vols vi and vii, Cambridge, Mass.: Loeb Classical Library.

LUCRAFT, FIONA (1992–3), 'The London Art of Plagiarism', in *PPC* 42 and 43.

—— (1997–8), 'A Study of the Compleat Confectioner by Hannah Glasse', in *PPC* 56, 57, and 58.

McCLANE, A. J. (1978a), *Freshwater Fishes of North America*, New York: Holt, Rinehart & Winston.

—— (1978b), *Saltwater Fishes of North America*, New York: Henry Holt.

MacCLURE, VICTOR (1935), *Scotland's Inner Man*, London: George Routledge.

McCORMICK, H. W.; ALLEN, T. B.; and YOUNG, W. E. (1963), *Shadows in the Sea*, Philadelphia: Chilton.

McDONALD, RONALD (1997), *The Complete Hamburger*, Secaucus, NJ: Carol Publishing.

MacDONOGH, GILES (1992a), *Brillat-Savarin*, London: John Murray.

—— (1992b), *The Wine and Food of Austria*, London: Mitchell Beazley.

McGEE, HAROLD (1984), *On Food and Cooking*, New York: Charles Scribner's Sons.

—— (1985), 'Heat', *Journal of Gastronomy*, 1/4.

—— (1990), *The Curious Cook*, San Francisco: North Point Press.

McGOVERN, WILLIAM (*c*.1927), *Jungle Paths and Inca Ruins*, New York: Century.

McIlvaine, CHARLES (1902), *One Thousand American Fungi*, rev edn, repr West Glover, VT: Something Else Press (1973).

MacKIE, CRISTINE (1987), *Trade Winds: A Caribbean Cookery Book*, Bath: Absolute Press.

—— (1991), *Life and Food in the Caribbean*, London: Weidenfeld & Nicolson.

MACKIE, I. M., HARDY, R., and HOBBS, G. (1971), *Fermented Fish Products*, Rome: FAO.

McKIRDY, MICHAEL (1988), 'Who Wrote Soyer's Pantropheon?', in *PPC* 29.

MACLEAN, VIRGINIA (1973), *Much Entertainment*, London: J. M. Dent & Sons.

—— (1981), *A Short-title Catalogue of Household and Cookery Books Published in the English Tongue 1701–1800*, London: Prospect Books.

McLAUGHLIN, TERENCE (1978), *A Diet of Tripe*, Newton Abbot: David & Charles.

McLINTOCK, Mrs (1736), *Receipts for Cookery and Pastry-Work*, repr, Aberdeen: Aberdeen UP (1986).

MacMIADHACHAIN, ANNA (1976), *Spanish Regional Cookery*, London: Penguin.

McNEILL, F. MARIAN (1929), *The Scots Kitchen*, Glasgow: Blackie.

MAGOMEDKHANOV, M. (1991), 'Feasting after Fasting in Archi Village, Dagestan', ed R. Chenciner, in Walker (1991).

—— (1993), '. . . Flavourings of some Dagestan Mountain Dishes', ed R. Chenciner, in Walker (1993).

—— and LUGUEV, S. (1990), 'Traditional Table Manners in Dagestan', ed R. Chenciner, in *Staple Foods*, Oxford Symposium on Food History 1989, London: Prospect Books.

MAHER, BARBARA (1982), *Cakes*, London: Jill Norman & Hobhouse.

MAHIAS, MARIE-CLAUDE (1981), 'Rhythmes culinaires indiens: Quelques Aspects des repas Jaina', in *National and Regional Styles of Cookery*, Oxford Symposium on Food History 1981, London: Prospect Books.

MAHON, BRID (1991), *Land of Milk and Honey: The story of Traditional Irish Food and Drink*, Dublin: Poolbeg.

MAJUPURIA, INDRA (1980–1), *Joys of Nepalese Cooking*, Gwalior: Smt S. Devi.

MAN, ROSAMOND and WEIR, ROBIN (1988), *The Compleat Mustard*, London: Constable.

MANDEVILLE, Sir JOHN (1568), *The voiage and trauayle of syr John Maundeuile, Knight, …*(first of numerous printed edns based on the original MS), London: Thomas East.

MANEKSHAW, BHICOO (1996), *Parsi Food and Customs*, New Delhi: Penguin Books India.

MANGELSDORF, PAUL C. (1953), 'Wheat', *Scientific American*.

MANGOR, A. M. (1837), *Kogebog for Maa Huusholdninger*, Copenhagen.

MARCH, LOURDES (1985), *El libro de la paella y de los arroces*, Madrid: Alianza.

—— and RIOS, ALICIA (1988), '*Oliva Sapiens*', in *Taste*, Oxford Symposium on Food History 1987, London: Prospect Books.

MARCHINGTON, JOHN (1984), *The Natural History of Game*, Woodbridge: Boydell Press.

MARGARET, LEN (1980) *Fish & Brewis*, Canada: Breakwater.

MARIANI, JOHN (1991), *America Eats Out*, New York: Wm Morrow.

—— (1994), *The Dictionary of American Food and Drink*, 2nd rev edn, New York: Hearst.

MARIN (1742), *Les Dons de Comus*, vols. i–iii, Paris.

MARINETTI, F. T. (1931), *The Futurist Cookbook*, London: Trefoil.

MARKHAM, GERVASE (1615), *The English Hus-wife*, 1st edn, London.

—— (1631), *The English Hus-wife*, 4th edn, London.

MARKS, COPELAND (1985), *False Tongues and Sunday Bread*, New York: M. Evans.

MARS, VALERIE (1994), 'Kitsch Culinary Icons', in *Look and Feel*, Oxford Symposium on Food History 1993, Totnes: Prospect Books.

MARSHALL, Mrs AGNES B. (1888), *Mrs A. B. Marshall's Cookery Book*, London: Marshall's School of Cookery.

—— (1891), *Mrs A. B. Marshall's Larger Cookery Book of Extra Recipes*, London: Marshall's School of Cookery.

—— (1894), *Fancy Ices*, London: Marshall's School of Cookery.

—— (For the same author's *Book of Ices*, 1885, see Wheaton, 1976.)

MARSHALL, HUMPHREY (1785), *Arbustum Americanum: The American Grove*, repr New York: Hafner (1967).

MARTEKA, VINCENT (1980), *Mushrooms Wild and Edible*, New York: W. W. Norton.

MARTIAL (1919–20), *Epigrams*, vols i and ii, trans Walter C. A. Ker, London: W. Heinemann.

MARTIN, FRANKLIN W. and RUBERTÉ, RUTH M. (1975), *Edible Leaves of the Tropics*, Mayaguez: Antillian.

—— et al. (1987), *Perennial Edible Fruits of the Tropics: An Inventory*, Washington: US Department of Agriculture.

MARTINEZ-LLOPIS, MANUEL (1981), *Historia de la gastronomia española*, Madrid: Nacional.

MARTINI, ANNA (1977), *Pasta and Pizza*, London: Angus & Robertson.

MASON, LAURA (1990), 'Dibs, Dabs, Lemons and Love Hearts: An Investigation into Sherbet Sweets', in *PPC* 35.

—— (1995), 'Written in Sugar: the Phenomenology of Rock', in *PPC* 49.

—— (1996), *Euroterroirs Catalogue of Traditional British Foods*, Paris: CNAC.

—— (1998), *Sugar Plums and Sherbet*, Totnes: Prospect Books.

—— with BROWN, CATHERINE (1999), *Traditional Foods of Britain: An Inventory*, Totnes: Prospect Books.

MASSIALOT, M. (1691), *Le Cuisinier roial et bourgeois*, Paris: Charles de Sercy.

—— (1712), *Le Nouveau Cuisinier royal et bourgeois*, vols i and ii, Paris: Prudhomme.

MATHIOT, GINETTE (1932), *Je sais cuisiner*, Paris: Albin Michel.

MATTIOLI, PIERANDREA (1544), *Commentarii in sex libros Pedacii Dioscoridis*.

MAXWELL, C. N. (1921), *Malayan Fishes*, Singapore: Methodist Pub. House.

MAY, R. J. (1984), *Kaikai Aniani*, Bathurst: Robert Brown.

MAY, ROBERT (1685), *The Accomplisht Cook*, repr, London: Prospect Books (1994).

MEDLIN, FAITH (1975), *A Gourmet's Book of Beasts*, New York: Paul S. Eriksson.

MEDSGER, OLIVER PERRY (1972), *Edible Wild Plants*, New York: Collier Macmillan.

MEILLER, DANIEL and VANNIER, PAUL (1991), *Le Grand Livre des fruits et légumes*, Besançon: La Manufacture.

MENDEL, JANET (1996), *Traditional Spanish Cooking*, Reading: Garnet Publishing.

MENDELSON, ANNE (1996), *Stand Facing the Stove*, New York: Henry Holt.

MENNELL, STEPHEN (1985), *All Manners of Food*, Oxford: Basil Blackwell.

MENNINGER, EDWIN A. (1977), *Edible Nuts of the World*, Stuart, FL.: Horticultural Books.

MENON (1742), *La Nouvelle Cuisine*, Paris: chez David.

—— (1746), *La Cuisinière bourgeoise*, Paris: Guillyn.

—— (1758), *Les Soupers de la cour* (first pub 1755), Paris: L. Cellot.

MERCADO, MONINA A. (1976), 'Banana Leaf Tablecloth', in G. Cordero-Fernando (ed), *The Culinary Culture of the Philippines*, Manila: Bancom Audiovision Corporation.

MERDOL, T. K. (1992), 'Libya Mutfağı', in *Proceedings of the Fourth International Food Congress, Turkey, 1992*, Konya: Konya Culture and Tourism.

MEREDITH, MARY ELLEN (1851), 'Gastronomy and Civilisation' (probably by Thomas Love Peacock), *Fraser's Magazine*, Dec.

MÉRIGOT, Mme (1795), *La Cuisinière républicaine*, Paris: Mérigot jeune.

MESSIANT, JACQUES (1998), *La cuisine flamande traditionnelle*, Morbecque: the author.

MICHAEL, PAMELA (1980), *All Good Things around Us*, London: Ernest Benn.

MICHELI, P. A. (1729), *Nova Plantarum Genera. . .*, Florence.

MICKLER, ERNEST MATTHEW (1986), *White Trash Cooking*, USA: The Jargon Society.

—— (1988), *Sinkin Spells, Hot Flashes, Fits and Cravins*, Berkeley: Ten Speed Press.

MILHAM, MARY ELLA (1998), *Platina: On Right Pleasure and Good Health: A Critical Edition and Translation of De Honesta Voluptate et Valetudine*, Tempe, Ariz.: Medieval and Renaissance Studies.

MILLER, J. INNES (1969), *The Spice Trade of the Roman Empire*, Oxford: Clarendon Press.

MILLER, JILL NHU HUONG (1968), *Vietnamese Cookery*, Rutland, VT.: Charles Tuttle.

MILLER, MARK (1992), *The Great Chile Book*, Berkeley: Ten Speed Press.

MILLER, ORSON K., Jr. and MILLER, HOPE H. (1980), *Mushrooms in Color*, New York: Dutton.

MILLER, WILLIAM (1905), *Greek Life in Town and Country*, London.

Ministero Agricoltura e Foreste (1992), *L'Italia de formaggi DOC*, Milan: Franco Angeli.

MINTZ, SIDNEY W. (1985), *Sweetness and Power*, London: Viking.

MIREL, ELIZABETH POST (1973), *Plum Crazy*, New York: Clarkson N. Potter.

MIRODAN, VLADIMIR (1987), *The Balkan Cookbook*, Wheathampstead: Lennard.

MITCHAM, HOWARD (1975), *Provincetown Seafood Cookbook*, Reading, MA: Addison Wesley.

—— (1978), *Creole Gumbo and All That Jazz*, Reading, MA.: Addison Wesley.

MOFFET, THOMAS (1746), *Health's Improvement*, London.

Molokhovets, Elena (1897), *A Gift to Young Housewives* (1861), 20th edn, St Petersburg.

Montagné, Prosper and Salles, Prosper (1929), *Le Grand Livre de la cuisine*, Paris: Flammarion.

Montandon, Jacques (1980), *Les Fromages de Suisse*, Lausanne: Edita.

Montgomery, John (1872), *The Wealth of Nature*, Edinburgh.

Montijn, Irene (1991), 'Dutch Treats', in Walker (1991).

Moore, Mary Hanson (1980), *A Yorkshire Cookbook*, London: David & Charles.

Morgan, Joan (1985), 'In Praise of Older Apples', in *PPC*, 20.

—— and Richards, Alison (1993), *The Book of Apples*, London: Ebury Press.

Moriarty, Christopher (1978), *Eels*, Newton Abbot: David & Charles.

Morris (1892), *Yorkshire Folk Talk*.

Morrissy, Lesley (1978), *Western Australian Crayfish Cookery*, Scarborough: Claire Dane.

Morsy, Magali (1996), *Le Monde des couscous et recettes de couscous*, 2 vols, Aix-en-Provence: Edisud.

Mortimer, W. Golden (1974), *History of Coca*, San Francisco: And/Or Press.

Morton, Julia F. (1976), *Herbs and Spices*, New York: Golden Press.

—— (1987), *Fruits of Warm Climates*, Miami: Julia F. Morton.

Moryson, Fynes (1617), *An Itinerary Containing his Ten Years Travel*, repr, Glasgow: J. MacLehose & Sons (1908)

Moulin, Léo (1975), *L'Europe à table*, Paris: Elsevier Sequoia.

Mulligan, Grace (1995), *The Women's Institute Book of Pies and Puddings*, London: Harper Collins.

Multhauf, Robert P. (1978), *Neptune's Gift: A History of Common Salt*, Baltimore: Johns Hopkins UP.

Mundy, G. C. (1862), *Our Antipodes*, London: Bentley.

Murcott, Anne (ed) (1983), *The Sociology of Food and Eating*, Aldershot: Gower.

Murie, Dr James (1903), *Thames Estuary Sea Fisheries*, London: Waterlow Bros. & Layton.

Murrell, John (1638), *Two Books of Cookerie and Carving*, facsimile edn, Ilkley: Jacksons.

Muskett, P. (1893), *The Art of Living in Australia*, London: Eyre & Spottiswoode.

Naj, Amal (1992), *Peppers*, New York: Alfred A. Knopf.

Nakamura, Izumi (1985), *Billfishes of the World*, Rome: FAO.

Napier, Mrs Alexander (ed) (1882), *A Noble Boke off Cookry*, London: Elliot Stock.

Nashe, Thomas (1557), *Lenten Stuffe, or the Praise of the Red Herring*.

Naso, Irma (1990), *Formaggi del Medioevo*, Turin: Il Segnalibro.

National Academy of Sciences (1979), *Tropical Legumes: Resources for the Future*, Washington: NAS.

National Research Council (1989), *Lost Crops of the Incas*, Washington: National Academy Press.

—— (1991), *Microlivestock*, Washington: National Academy Press.

Neal, Miss C. A. (as 'A Lady') (1841), *Total Abstinence Cookery*, Philadelphia: Eugene Commiskey.

Nearing, Helen, and Nearing, Scott (1950), *The Maple Sugar Book*, New York: John Day.

Needham, Joseph (1984), *Science and Civilisation in China*, vol vi pt 2, containing 'Agriculture' by Francesca Bray, Cambridge: Cambridge Univ. Press.

Nègre, Dr André (1970), *The French West-Indies Cookery*, Guadeloupe.

Nelson, Dawn and Nelson, Douglas (1980), 'Why Huss? Or Uss?', Notes and Queries in *PPC* 6, London: Prospect Books.

—— (1983), 'Chuno and Tunta', in *Food in Motion*, Oxford Symposium on Food History 1983, Leeds: Prospect Books.

Netboy, Anthony (1968), *The Atlantic Salmon: A Vanishing Species?*, London: Faber & Faber.

Newall, Venetia (1971), *An Egg at Easter: A Folklore Study*, Bloomington: Indiana University Press.

Nicholls, Anne and Nicholls, Gerald (1989), 'The Cooking Pot in China', in *The Cooking Pot*, Oxford Symposium on Food History 1988, London: Prospect Books.

Nicholson, J. (1890), *Folk Lore of East Yorkshire*.

Nicolaou, Nearchos (1983), *Cooking from Cyprus*, Nicosia: Nearchos Nicolaou.

Niethammer, Carolyn (1974), *American Indian Food and Lore*, New York: Collier.

Nightingale, Marie (1971), *Out of Old Nova Scotia Kitchens*, New York: Charles Scribner.

Noble, John (1992), 'Mrs Mary Cole's Disappearing Frenchmen', in *PPC* 40.

Nonnius, Ludovicus (1646), *Diaetiticon, sive De Re Cibaria*, Antwerp.

Norman, Jill (1990), *The Complete Book of Spices*, London: Dorling Kindersley.

—— (1997), *The Classic Herb Cookbook*, London: Dorling Kindersley.

Norrman, R. and Haarberg, J. (1980), *Nature and Language*, London: Routledge & Kegan Paul.

Nostradamus, Michael (1979), *Traité des confitures*, Gutenburg: Senlis.

Notaker, Henry (1990), 'Romania: Cooking, Literature and Politics. A Cookbook from Moldova, 1841', in *PPC* 35, London: Prospect Books.

—— (1993), *Ganens makt*, Oslo: n.p.

Nott, John (1726), *Cooks and Confectioners Dictionary*, facsimile edn, London: L. Rivington (1980).

Nylander, Margaretha (1822), *Handbok wid den nu brukliga finare matlagningen*, Stockholm.

Oberthur, J. (1937), *Gibiers de notre pays*, Paris: Librairie des Champs-Élysées.

Occhipinti, Paolo, and Stecchi, Guido (1987), *Funghi buoni e facili*, Milan: Rizzoli.

Ochse, J. J. (1931), *Fruits and Fruiticulture in the Dutch East Indies*, Batavia-Centrum: G. Kolff.

—— (1980), *The Vegetables of the Dutch East Indies* (first pub in both Dutch and English 1931), Amsterdam: A. Asher.

Oddy, Derek and Miller, Derek (eds)

(1976), *The Making of the Modern British Diet*, London: Croom Helm.

O'Drisceoil, Diarmuid (1993), 'An Experiment in Bronze Age Cooking', in *PPC* 45.

O'Hara-May, Jane (1977), *An Elizabethan Dyetary of Health*, Lawrence, KS.: Coronado Press.

—— (1984), 'The Moleschott Figures', in *PPC* 16.

Ojakangas, Beatrice A. (1964), *The Finnish Cookbook*, New York: Crown Publishers.

O'Kelly, M. (1989), *Early Ireland*, Cambridge: Cambridge University Press.

Olearius, A. (1669), *Voyages of the Ambassadors to the Great Duke of Muscovy, and the King of Persia*, London.

Olleboma, Antonio M. de Oliveira Bello (1936), *Culinária portuguesa*, Lisbon.

Olney, Richard (1974), *Simple French Food*, London: Jill Norman.

—— and the editors of Time-Life Books (1980), *Cakes and Pastries*, Amsterdam: Time-Life International.

Olszewski, Peter (1980), *A Salute to the Humble Yabby*, Melbourne: Angus & Robertson.

Organ, John (1963), *Gourds*, London: Faber.

Orlebar, Eleanor (1879), *Food for the People*, London: Sampson Low, Marston, etc.

Orosa, Maria Y. (1970), *Maria Y Orosa: Her Life and Work*, ed Helen Orosa del Rosario, Quezon City: R. P. Garcia.

Ortiz, Elisabeth Lambert (1973), *The Complete Book of Caribbean Cooking*, New York: M. Evans.

—— (1975), *The Best of Caribbean Cooking*, London: André Deutsch.

—— (1979), *The Book of Latin American Cooking*, New York: Knopf.

—— (1984), *The Book of Latin American Cooking*, UK edn, London: Robert Hale.

—— (1986), *Japanese Cookery*, London: Collins.

—— (1989), *The Food of Spain and Portugal*, Oxford: Lennard.

Ortiz y Pino, Yolanda (1979), *Original Native New Mexican Cooking*, Galisteo, NM: Galisteo Historical Museum.

Osa, Harald, and Ulltveit, Gudrun (1993), *Norsk mat gjennom tidene*, Oslo: n.p.

O'Suilleabhain, Sean (1963), *A Handbook of Irish Folklore*, London: H. Jenkins.

Owen, Sri (1986a), *Indonesian Food and Cookery*, rev edn, London: Prospect Books.

—— (1986b), 'Rendang', in *Cookery: Science, Lore and Books*, Oxford Symposium on Food History 1984 and 1985, London: Prospect Books.

—— (1993), *The Rice Book*, London: Transworld.

—— (1994), *Indonesian Regional Food and Cookery*, London: Doubleday.

Pagnol, Jean (1973), *La Truffe*, Avignon: Aubanel.

Paice, E. (1994), *Guide to Eritrea*, Chalfont St Peter: Bradt Publications.

Paige, Howard (1987), *Aspects of Afro-America Cookery*, Southfield, MI: Aspects.

Palmer, Arnold (1952), *Movable Feasts*, London: OUP.

PALMER, CARMEN SIMON (1977), *Bibliografía de la gastronomía española*, Madrid: Ediciones Velasquez.

PANJABI, CAMELLIA (1994), *50 Great Curries of India*, London: Kyle Cathie.

—— (1995), 'The Non-emergence of the Regional Foods of India', in *Disappearing Foods*, Oxford Symposium on Food History 1994, Totnes: Prospect Books.

PAPIN, DENYS (1681), *A New Digester or Engine for Softning Bones*, facsimile edn, St Louis: Mallinckrodt Food Classics.

PARENTI, GIOVANNI RIGHI (1972), *La cucina degli Etruschi*, Milan: Sugar.

PARKINSON, J. (1629), *Paradise in Sole*.

PARROTT, ARTHUR W. (1960), *The Queer and the Rare Fishes of New Zealand*, London: Hodder & Stoughton.

PASSMORE, JACKI (1991), *The Encyclopedia of Asian Food and Cooking*, New South Wales: Doubleday.

PAULET (1793), *Traité des champignons*, Paris.

PEAT, NEVILLE (1979), *Cascade on the Run*, Christchurch: Whitcoulls.

PEGGE, SAMUEL (ed) (1780), *The Forme of Cury*, London: J. Nichols.

PEGLER, D. N. and PIEARCE G. D. (1980), 'The Edible Mushrooms of Zambia', in *Kew Bulletin*, 35(3), Royal Botanic Gardens, Kew.

PEMBERTON, ROBERT (1995), 'Catching and Eating Dragonflies in Bali', *American Entomologist* (summer).

PENDERGRAST, MARK (1994), *For God, Country and Coca-Cola*, London: Phoenix.

PENSADO, EULALIA (1992, with Alan Davidson), 'The Earliest Portuguese Cookery Book Examined', in *PPC* 41, London: Prospect Books.

PERRIER-ROBERT, ANNIE (1986), *Les Friandises et leurs secrets*, Paris: Larousse.

PERRY, CHARLES (1981), 'The Oldest Mediterranean Noodle', in *PPC* 9.

—— (1982), 'Notes on Persian Pasta', in *PPC* 10, London: Prospect Books.

—— (1983*a*), 'Capirotada, Almodrote, Muthawwamah', in 'Three Notes', in *PPC* 15.

—— (1983*b*), 'Grain Foods of the Early Turks', in *Food in Motion*, Oxford Symposium on Food History 1983, Leeds: Prospect Books.

—— (1987*a*), 'Baklava not Proven Greek', in *PPC* 27.

—— (1987*b*), 'The Sals of the Infidels', in *PPC* 26.

—— (1989), 'The Central Asian Origins of Baklava', in *Proceedings of the Second International Food Congress*, Turkey 1988, Konya: Konya Culture and Tourism.

—— (1993), 'Moorish Sugar', in Walker (1993).

—— (1994) 'The Chekich', in *PPC* 48.

—— (1995*a*), 'Preserved Lemons', in *PPC* 50.

—— (1995*b*), 'The Fate of the Tail', in *Disappearing Foods*, Oxford Symposium on Food History 1994, Totnes: Prospect Books.

—— (1997), 'Trakahanas Revisited', in *PPC* 55, London: Prospect Books.

—— (1998), 'A Nuanced Apology to Rotted Barley', in *PPC* 58.

—— (ed) (2000), *Medieval Arab Cookery: Papers by Maxime Rodinson and Charles Perry with a reprint of 'A Baghbad Cookery Book'* [originally published in 1939] by the late Professor A. J. Arberry, and with a foreword by Claudia Roden, Totnes: Prospect Books.

PERSOON, C. H. (1801), *Synopsis Methodica Fungorum*, Göttingen: H. Dieterich.

PETTY, FLORENCE (1917), *The 'Pudding Lady's' Recipe Book*, London: G. Bell.

PHILLIPPS, EDWARD (1706), *New World of English Words*, London.

PHILLIPPS, KAREN and DAHLEN, MARTHA (1985), *A Guide to Market Fruits of Southeast Asia*, Hong Kong: South China Morning Post.

PHILLIPS, HENRY (1823), *Fruits Known in Great Britain*, London.

PHILLIPS, JOHN C. (1922–6), *A Natural History of the Ducks*, Boston: Houghton Mifflin.

PHILLIPS, ROGER (1981), *Mushrooms and Other Fungi of Great Britain and Europe*, London: Pan.

—— (1983), *Wild Food*, London: Pan.

—— and RIX, MARTYN (1993), *Vegetables*, London: Pan.

PICCINARDI, ANTONIO (1993), *Dizionario di gastronomia*, Milan: Rizzoli.

PICHON, le Baron JÉRÔME (ed) (1846), *Le Ménagier de Paris*, vols i and ii, Paris: Société des Bibliophiles Français.

PICTON, PIERRE (1966), *A Gourmet's Guide to Fish and Chips*, London: Four Square.

PIDOUX, PIERRE, et al. (1543), *La Fleur de toute cuisine*, Paris: Alain Lotrain.

PIERCE, CHARLES (1868), *The Household Manager*, London: Simpkin.

PILCHER, JEFFREY M. (1998), *Que vivan los tamales: Food and the Making of Mexican Identity*, Albuquerque: University of New Mexico Press.

PISCATOR (1843), *Fish: How to Choose and How to Dress*, London: Longman, Brown, Green, etc.

PLATINA (1475), *De Honesta Voluptate*, facsimile edn, trans, St Louis: Mallinckrodt (1967).

PLATT, HUGH (1609), *Delightes for Ladies*, repr London: Crosby Lockwood (1948).

PLINY (1938–63), *Natural History*, vols. 1–8, ed and trans H. Rackham, W. H. S. Jones, and D. E. Eichholz, Cambridge, MA.: Loeb Classical Library.

—— (1963), *Natural History*, vol 8, books 28–32, trans W. H. S. Jones, London: William Heinemann.

—— (1967), *Natural History*, vol 3, books 8–11, trans H. Rackham, London: William Heinemann.

PLOUVIER, LILIANE (*c*.1980), *Introduction de la dinde en Europe*, Brussels.

POILÂNE, LIONEL (1981), *Guide de l'amateur de pain*, Paris: Robert Lafont.

POKHLEBKIN, V. V. (1981), *National Cuisines of our People*, Moscow: Pishchevaia Promyshlennost.

—— (1984), *Russian Delight*, London: Pan.

POLLARD, HELEN (1991), 'Lancashire's Heritage', in C. Anne Wilson (ed), *Traditional Food East and West of the Pennines*, Edinburgh: Edinburgh University Press.

—— (1993), 'A Liquid Diet', in C. Anne Wilson (ed), *Liquid Nourishment*, Edinburgh: Edinburgh University Press.

POLLARD, HUGH B. C. (1926), *The Sportsman's Cookery Book*, London: Country Life.

POMÉS, LEOPOLD (1985), *Teoria i practica del pa ambtomaquet*, Barcelona: Tusquets.

POMET, Monsieur (1712), *A Compleat History of Druggs* (translated from the French), vols i, ii, London.

PONCELET (1774), *Nouvelle Chymie du goût et de l'odorat*, Paris: Pissot.

POPENOE, PAUL B. (1913), *Date Growing in the Old and New Worlds*, Altadena, CA.

POPENOE, WILSON (1924), *Economic Fruit-Bearing Plants of Ecuador*, Washington: Smithsonian.

—— (1932), *Manual of Tropical and Subtropical Fruits*, New York: Macmillan.

PORPHYRY (1965), *On Abstinence from Animal Food*, London: Centaur.

PORTER, HAL (1963), *The Watcher on the Cast Iron Balcony*, London: Faber & Faber.

PORTER, VALERIE (1991), *Cattle*, London: Helm.

POTTER, BEATRIX (1908), *The Tale of Samuel Whiskers or the Roly Poly Pudding*, London: Frederick Warne.

POURRAT, HENRI (1956), *The Roquefort Adventure*, Roquefort: Société Anonyme des Caves et des Producteurs.

POYNTER, MISS E. S. (1904), *'What' and 'How'*, London: Thacker, Spink.

PRESCOTT, JAMES (trans and ed) (1988), *Le Viandier de Taillevent: 14th Century Cookery*, Eugene, Ore.: Alfarhaugr.

PRINGLE, T. (1851), *Narrative of a Resident in S. Africa*, London.

PRUTHI, J. S. (1976), *Spices and Condiments*, rev edn, New Delhi: National Book Africa Trust, 1992.

PURSEGLOVE, J. W. (1985), *Tropical Crops: Monocotyledons*, 5th rev impression, Harlow: Longman.

—— (1987), *Tropical Crops: Dicotyledons* (first pub 1968), Harlow: Longman.

—— BROWN, E. G., GREEN, C. L. and ROBBINS, S. R. J. (1981), *Spices*, vols i and ii, London: Longman.

QUINN, VERNON (1938), *Roots: Their Place in Life and Legend*, New York.

RABISHA, WILL (1682), *The Whole Body of Cookery Dissected*, London.

RADCLIFFE, WILLIAM (1921), *Fishing from the Earliest Times*, London.

RAFFALD, ELIZABETH (1769), *The Experienced English Housekeeper*, Manchester: J. Harrop. Also repr 1997, Lewes: Southover Press.

—— (1782), *The Experienced English Housekeeper*, 8th edn, London: R. Baldwin (repr 1970).

RAMAIN, PAUL (1979), *Myco gastronomie* (first pub 1954), Marseille: Laffitte Reprints.

RAMAZANI, NESTA (1974), *Persian Cooking*, Charlottesville, VA.: Univ. Press of Virginia.

RAMSBOTTOM, J. (1932), 'The Fungus Stone, Polyporus tuberaster', *Proceedings of the Linnaean Society*, 144.

—— (1953), *Mushrooms and Toadstools*, London: Collins.

RANCE, PATRICK (1982), *The Great British Cheese Book*, London: Macmillan.

—— (1989), *The French Cheese Book*, London: Macmillan.

RANDOLPH, MARY (1984), *The Virginia House-wife*, ed Karen Hess, Columbia: University of South Carolina.

RANGARAO, SHANTI (1990), *Good Food from India* (1st edn 1968), Bombay: Jaico Publishing House

RAPHAEL, CHAIM (introd.) (1983), *The Jewish Manual* (by 'A Lady'), New York.

RAY, JOHN (1686–1704), *Historia Generalis Plantarum*, vols i–iii, London.

—— (1738), *Travels through the Low-Countries, Germany, Italy and France*, 2nd edn, vols i and ii, London.

RAYCHAUDHURI, HASHI and RAYCHAUDHURI, TAPAN (1981), 'Not by Curry Alone', in *National and Regional Styles of Cookery*, Oxford Symposium on Food History 1981, London: Prospect Books.

REA, JOHN (1676), *Flora: Seu, de Florum Cultura*, 2nd rev impression, London.

READ, JAN and MANJON, MAITE (1978), *Flavours of Spain*, London: Cassell.

—— —— (1981), *The Great British Breakfast*, London: Michael Joseph.

REBIÈRE, JEAN (1967), *La Truffe du Périgord*, Périgueux: Pierre Fanlac.

REBOUL, J.-B. (n.d.), *La Cuisinière provençale*, Marseilles: Tacussel.

REDGROVE, H. S. (1933), *Spices and Condiments*, London: Isaac Pitman.

REDON, ODILE; SABBAN, FRANÇOISE; and SERVENTI, SILVANO (1998), *The Medieval Kitchen*, trans Edward Schneider, Chicago: University Press of Chicago.

REDWOOD, JEAN (1989), *Russian Food*, Felixstowe: Oldwicks Press.

RENNER, H. D. (1944), *The Origin of Food Habits*, London: Faber.

RICHARDIN, J. EDMOND (1913), *L'Art du bien manger*, Paris: J. E. Richardin.

RICHARDSON, SIR JOHN (1852), *Arctic Searching Expedition*, New York.

RICHARDSON, LOUISE A. and ISABELL, J. R. (1984), 'Joseph Cooper, Chief Cook to Charles I', in *PPC* 18, London: Prospect Books.

RICHIE, DONALD (1985), *A Taste of Japan*, New York: Kodansha Int.

RICKETTS, EDWARD F. and CALVIN, JACK (1978), *Between Pacific Tides*, 4th edn (ed Joel W. Hedgpeth), Stanford, CA: Stanford Univ. Press.

—— and STEINBECK, JOHN (1978), *The Outer Shores*, ed Joel W. Hedgepeth, Eureka, CA: Mad River Press.

RIDDERVOLD, ASTRI (1986), '"Gravlax", the Buried Salmon', in *Cookery: Science, Lore and Books*, Oxford Symposium on Food History 1984 and 1985, London: Prospect Books.

—— (ed) (1988), with Andreas Ropeid, *Food Conservation*, London: Prospect Books.

—— (1990*a*), *Lutefisk, Rakefisk and Herring in Norwegian Tradition*, Oslo: Novus.

—— (1990*b*), 'The Importance of Herring in the Daily Life of the Coastal Population of Norway', in *Staple Foods*, Oxford Symposium on Food History 1989, London: Prospect Books.

—— (1993), *Konservering av mat*, Oslo: Technologist Forlag.

RIDLEY, HENRY N. (1912), *Spices*, London: Macmillan.

RILEY, GILLIAN (1990), 'Vilhjalmur Stefansson and the All-Meat Diet', in *Staple Foods*, Oxford Symposium on Food History 1989, London: Prospect Books.

—— (1993), 'Tainted Meat', in Walker (1993).

—— (1996), 'Platina, Martino and their Circle', in *Cooks and Other People*, Oxford Symposium on Food History 1995, Totnes: Prospect Books.

——(1997), *A Feast for the Eyes*, London: National Gallery Publications.

RILEY, LORNA WOODSUM (1987), *Reel Meals: Movie Lover's Cookbook*, Lombard, IL.: Wallace-Homestead

RIOS, ALICIA (1984), 'The Cocido Madrileno: A Case of Culinary Adhocism', in *PPC* 18.

—— (1987), 'El arte del tapeo', in *PPC* 27.

—— and MARCH, LOURDES (1993), *The Heritage of Spanish Cooking*, London: Limited Editions.

RIPE, CHERRY (1993), *Goodbye Culinary Cringe*, Sydney: Allen & Unwin.

RIVAL, NED (1983), *Grimod de la Reynière*, France: Le Préaux Clercs.

RIZZUTO, JIM (1977), *Modern Hawaiian Game-fishing*, Honolulu: University Press of Hawaii.

ROACH, F. A. (1985), *Cultivated Fruits of Britain*, Oxford: Basil Blackwell.

ROBUCHON, J. (foreword) and HODGSON, R. (consultant) (1996), *French Cheeses*, London: Dorling Kindersley.

ROBYNS, GWEN (1980), *The Potato Cookbook*, London: Pan Books.

RODEN, CLAUDIA (1968), *A Book of Middle Eastern Food*, London: Nelson.

—— (1977), *Coffee*, London: Faber.

—— (1981), *Picnic*, London: Jill Norman.

—— (1985), *A New Book of Middle Eastern Food*, London: Viking.

—— (1996), *The Book of Jewish Food*, New York: Knopf.

RODINSON, MAXIME (1949), 'Recherches sur les documents arabes relatifs à la cuisine', *Revue des études islamiques*.

—— (1950), 'Romania et autres mot arabes en italien', *Romania*, 71.

—— (1956), 'Sur l'étymologie de "losange" ', in *Studi orientalistici in onore di Giorgio Levi della Vida*, Rome: Istituto per l'Oriente.

—— (1973), *Mohammed*, London: Pelican.

RODRIGUES, DOMINGOS (1680), *Arte de cozinha*, Lisbon.

ROE, F. G. (1972), *The North American Buffalo*, Newton Abbot: David & Charles.

ROHDE, ELEANOUR SINCLAIR (1936), *Herbs and Herb Gardening*, London: Medici.

ROMBAUER, IRMA S. (1931), *The Joy of Cooking*, St Louis: A. C. Clayton Printing Co.

—— and ROMBAUER BECKER, MARION (1951), *The Joy of Cooking*, rev edn, Indianapolis: Bobbs Merrill.

ROOT, WAVERLEY (1980), *Food*, New York: Simon & Schuster.

ROPER, CLYDE F. E. and SWEENEY, MICHAEL J. (1984), *Cephalopods of the World*, Rome: FAO.

ROQUES, J. (1841), *Champignons comestibles et vénéneux*, Paris.

RORER, MRS S. T. (1886), *Mrs Rorer's Philadelphia Cook Book*, Philadelphia: Arnold.

—— (1902), *Mrs Rorer's New Cook Book*, New York repr 1970, New York: Ladies' Home Journal Cook Book Club.

ROSE, EVELYN (1985), *The New Jewish Cuisine*, London: Robson.

ROSE, GILES (1682), *A Perfect School of Instruction for the Officers of the Mouth*, London.

ROSE, PETER G. (trans and ed) (1989), *The Sensible Cook*, Syracuse, NY: Syracuse UP.

ROSENBLUM, MORT (1997), *Olives*, Bath: Absolute Press.

ROSENGARTEN, FREDERIC, Jr (1969), *The Book of Spices*, Wynnewood, PA.: Livingston.

—— (1984), *The Book of Edible Nuts*, New York: Walker.

ROUGHLEY, T. C. (1966), *Fish and Fisheries of Australia*, Sydney: Angus & Robertson.

ROUTHIER, NICOLE (1989), *The Foods of Vietnam*, New York: Stewart Tabori & Chang.

ROUX-SAGET, MICHÈLE and DELPLANQUE, LOUIS-PAUL (1985), *Nos 20 meilleurs champignons et leurs amis*, Avignon: Aubanel.

RUMFORD, Count (1968–70), *Collected Works*, vols i–v, ed Sanborn C. Brown, Cambridge, MA.: Belknap Press.

RUMOHR, KARL FREIDRICH VON (1822), *Geist der Kochkunst*.

—— (1993), *The Essence of Cookery*, trans Barbara Yeomans, Totnes: Prospect Books.

RUMPOLT, MAX (1581), *Ein neues Kochbuch*, Frankfurt.

RUNDELL, MRS ('A Lady') (1806), *A New System of Domestic Cookery*, London: John Murray.

—— and BIRCH, E. (c1862), *A New System of Domestic Cookery formed upon Principles of Economy*, London: Henry G. Bohn.

—— and ROBERTS, EMMA (1847), *A New System of Domestic Cookery Founded upon Principles of Economy*, London: John Murray.

RUSHDIE, SAMEEN (1991), *Indian Cookery*, London: Arrow Books.

RUSKIN, F. R. (ed) (1975), *Underexploited Tropical Plants with Promising Economic Value*, Washington: National Academy of Sciences.

RUSSELL, J. (1868), *Boke of Nurture in Early English Meals and Manners*, ed F. J. Furnivall, London: Early English Text Society.

RYMSDYK, JAN VAN (1791), *Museum Britannicum*, London.

SABERI, HELEN (1986), *Noshe Djan: Afghan Food and Cookery*, London: Prospect Books.

—— (1992), 'Public Eating in Afghanistan', in *Public Eating*, Oxford Symposium on Food History 1991, London: Prospect Books.

—— (1993), 'Rosewater, . . . and Asafoetida, . . .', in Walker (1993).

—— (1995*a*), 'Where are the Pouting Nibblers of Yesteryear? or What Happened to Boudoir Biscuits?', in *PPC* 49.

—— (1995*b*), 'Whims and Fancies of a Trifle Lover', in *PPC* 50.

—— HELOU, ANISSA; POMBO-VILLAR, ESTEBAN; et al. (1994), 'A Spicy Mystery', parts 1 and 2, in *PPC* 47 and 48.

SAHAGÚN, BERNARDINO DE (1529), *General History of the Things of New Spain: Florentine Codex*, repr Santa Fe, NM: School of American Research (1950–82).

SAHNI, JULIE (1980), *Classic Indian Cooking*, New York: William Morrow.

—— (1985), *Classic Indian Vegetarian and Grain Cooking*, New York: William Morrow.

SAINTSBURY, GEORGE and MACPHERSON, H. A. (1896), *The Partridge*, London: Longmans.

SALA, GEORGE AUGUSTUS (1895), *The Thorough Good Cook*, London: Cassell.

SALAMAN, REDCLIFFE N. (1949), *The History and Social Influence of the Potato*, Cambridge: CUP.

SALAMAN, RENA (1993*a*), Greek Food, rev edn, London: Harper Collins.

—— (1993*b*), 'Down Mastic Way on Chios', in Walker (1993).

SALLES, PROSPER and MONTAGNÉ, PROSPER (1902), *La Grande Cuisine illustrée*, Paris: Flammarion.

SALZMAN, CATHERINE (1983), 'Food in the Netherlands during World War II', in *PPC* 12.

SAMTANI, GEETA (1995), *A Taste of Kashmir*, London: Merehurst.

SAMUEL, ARTHUR MICHAEL (1918), *The Herring*, London: J. Murray.

SAMUEL, DELWEN (1996), 'Approaches to the Archaeology of Food', in *PPC* 54, London: Prospect Books.

SANDEL, Revd ANDREAS (c1988), *Andreas Sandels dagbok 1701–1743*, Uppsala: Erene.

SANDERS, ROSANNE (1988), *The English Apple*, Oxford: Phaidon.

SANTICH, BARBARA (1982), 'Capirattata and Capirotada', Notes and Queries, in *PPC* 12.

—— (1985), 'On Escabeche (and Ceviche)', in *PPC* 20.

—— (1995*a*), *The Original Mediterranean Cuisine*, Kent Town: Wakefield Press; Totnes: Prospect Books.

—— (1995*b*), *What the Doctors Ordered*, South Melbourne: Hyland House.

—— (1996), *Looking for Flavour*, Kent Town: Wakefield Press.

—— (1988), 'Sponges, Lamingtons and Anzacs: The Australian Ritual of Afternoon Tea', in *The Journal of Gastronomy* (4, 2), San Francisco: American Institute of Wine and Food.

SAUL, MARY (1974), *Shells*, London: Hamlyn & Country Life.

SAUNDERS, ALAN (1995), *A is for Apple*, Port Melbourne: William Heinneman.

SAUNDERS, CHARLES FRANCIS (1976), *Edible and Useful Wild Plants*, repr of 1934 edn, New York: Dover.

SAUNT, JAMES (1990), *Citrus Varieties of the World*, Norwich: Sinclair International.

SCAPPI, BARTOLOMEO (1570), *Opera, dell'arte del cucinare*, facsimile edn, Rome: Arnaldo Forni (1981).

SCHAUER, AMY (1909), *The Schauer Cookery Book*, Brisbane: Edwards Dunlop.

SCHELLHAMMER, MARIA (1692), *Die wohlunterwiesene Kochin*

SCHLOESSER, FRANK (1905), *The Cult of the Chafing Dish*, London: Gay & Bird.

SCHNEIDER, ELIZABETH (1986), *Uncommon Fruits and Vegetables*, New York: Harper & Row.

SCHOFF, WILFRED H. (1912), *The Periplus of the Erythraean Sea*, London: Longmans Green.

SCHORGER, A. W. (1966), *The Wild Turkey*, Norman: University of Oklahoma Press.

SCHUMACHER-VOELKER, UTA (1980), 'German Cookery Books, 1485–1800', in *PPC* 6, London: Prospect Books

SCHWABE, CALVIN W. (1979), *Unmentionable Cuisine*, Charlottesville, VA.: University Press of Virginia.

SCHWARTZ, HILLEL (1986), *Never Satisfied*, New York: Macmillan.

SCHWARTZ, ODED (1992), *In Search of Plenty*, London: Kyle Cathie.

SCHWEID, RICHARD (1980), *Hot Peppers*, Seattle: Madrona.

SCHWIND, Cap'n PHIL (1967), *Clam Shack Cookery*, Eastham, MA.: Malcolm Hobbes.

SCOTT, J. S. (1959), *Sea Fishes of Malaya*, Kuala Lumpur: Government Press.

SCULLY, TERENCE (trans and ed) (1986), *Chiquart's 'On Cookery': A Fifteenth Century Savoyard Culinary Treatise*, New York: Peter Lang.

—— (ed) (1988), *The Viandier of Taillevent*, Ottawa: University Press.

—— (1995), *The Art of Cookery in the Middle Ages*, Woodbridge: Boydell Press.

SEIGNEURIE, ALBERT (1898), *Dictionnaire encyclopédique de l'épicerie*, Paris.

SELINUS, R., et al. (1971), *Dietary Studies in Ethiopia*, American Journal of Clinical Nutrition.

SENECA (1970–9), *Moral Essays*, i–iii, trans J. W. Basore, Cambridge, MA: Loeb Classical Library.

SERVENTI, SILVANO (1993), *La Grande Histoire du foie gras*, Paris: Flammarion.

SERZHANINA, G. I. and ZMITROVICH, I. I. (1978) *Macromycetae*, Minsk.

SEUMERICHT, KARL (1959), *Fisch-Warenkunde*, Hamburg.

SEVILLA, MARIA JOSÉ (1989), *Life and Food in the Basque Country*, London: Weidenfeld & Nicolson.

—— (1992), *Spain on a Plate*, London, BBC Books.

SEXTON, REGINA (1998), *A Little History of Irish Food*, London: Kyle Cathie.

SHAIDA, MARGARET (1992), *The Legendary Cuisine of Persia*, Henley-on-Thames: Lieuse.

SHAND, P. MORTON (1934), *Book of Food*, London: Jonathan Cape.

SHAPIRO, LAURA (1986), *Perfection Salad*, Toronto: Collins.

SHARKEY, OLIVE (1994), *Old Days, Old Ways*, Dublin: O'Brien.

SHAW, TIMOTHY (1994), *The World of Escoffier*, London: Zwemmer.

SHERATON, MIMI and SHEFFER, NELLI (1997), *Food Markets of the World*, New York: Harry N. Abrams.

SHERIDAN, MONICA (1966), *My Irish Cook Book*, London: Frederick Muller.

SHERSON, ERROLL (1931), *The Book of Vegetable Cookery, Usual and Unusual*, London: F. Warne.

SHIPPERBOTTOM, ROY (1993), 'The Adulteration of Spices', in Walker (1993).

—— (1994), 'Precious Metals on Food', in *Look and Feel*, Oxford Symposium on Food History 1993, Totnes: Prospect Books.

—— (1998), 'Fish and Chips', in *Food from the Waters*, Oxford Symposium on Food History 1997, Totnes: Prospect Books.

SHURTLEFF, WILLIAM and AOYAGI, AKIKO (1983), *The Book of Tofu*, Berkeley: Ten Speed Press.

—— (1985), *The Book of Tempeh*, rev edn, New York: Harper & Row.

SIESBY, BIRGIT (1980), 'Blood is Food', in *PPC* 4.

—— (1988), 'The Turkish Crescent and the Danish Pastry', in *PPC* 30.

SIMMONDS, PETER LUND (1859), *The Curiosities of Food*, London: Richard Bentley.

—— (1885), *The Animal Food Resources of Different Nations*, London: E. and F. N. Spoon.

SIMMONS, AMELIA (1796), *American Cookery*, facsimile edn, Bedford, MA. (1996).

SIMON, ANDRÉ L. (1983), *A Concise Encyclopedia of Gastronomy* (1st edn as a single vol, 1952), London: Allen Lane.

SIMOONS, FREDERICK (1991), *Food in China*, Boca Raton, FL.: CRC Press.

—— (1994), *Eat Not This Flesh*, Madison: University of Wisconsin Press.

SING, PHIA (1981), *Traditional Recipes of Laos*, London: Prospect Books.

SINGH, Mrs BALBIR (1967), *Indian Cookery*, 3rd rev impression, London: Mills & Boon.

SINGH, DHARAAMJIT (1970), *Indian Cookery*, London: Penguin.

SITAS, AMARANTH (1968), *Kopiaste*, Limmasol: Atlas Printing.

SITWELL, OSBERT (1963), 'The Banquets of Tantalus', in *Poundwise*, London: Hutchinson.

SKINNER, GWEN (1983), *The Cuisine of the South Pacific*, Auckland: Hodder & Stoughton.

SKUSE, E. (c.1890), *Complete Confectionery*, 3rd edn, London: W. J. Bush.

SMITH, ALEXANDER H. (1975), *A Field Guide to Western Mushrooms*, Ann Arbor: University of Michigan Press.

—— (1977), *The Mushroom Hunter's Field Guide*, rev edn, Ann Arbor: University of Michigan Press.

SMITH, ANDREW F. (1991), 'The Rise and Fall of Home-Made Anglo-American Tomato Ketchup', in *PPC* 39.

—— (1994), *The Tomato in America*, Columbia, SC: Univ. of South Carolina Press.

—— (1996), *Pure Ketchup*, Columbia: University of South Carolina Press.

—— (1997), 'The Popcorn Polka', in *PPC* 56.

SMITH, E. (usually taken to be Eliza) (1734), *The Compleat Housewife*, Williamsburg.

—— (1983), *The Compleat Housewife*, King's Langley.

SMITH, EDWARD (1886), *Foods*, London.

SMITH, MARGARET M. and HEEMSTRA, P. C. (ed) (1986), *Smith's Sea Fishes*, Johannesburg: Macmillan South Africa.

SMITH, MARY (1772), *The Complete House-keeper*, Newcastle: the author.

SMITH, MICHAEL (1989), *The Afternoon Tea Book*, New York: Macmillan.

SMITH, MURIEL W. G. (1971), *National Apple Register of the United Kingdom*, London: Ministry of Agriculture, Fisheries & Food.

SMITH, PAGE and DANIEL, CHARLES (1982), *The Chicken Book*, San Francisco: North Point Press

SMITH, R. E. F., and CHRISTIAN, DAVID (1984), *Bread and Salt*, Cambridge: CUP.

SMITH, ROBERT (1980), 'Whence the Samovar', in *PPC* 4.

SO, YAN-KIT (1984), *Yan-Kit's Classic Chinese Cookbook*, London: Dorling Kindersley.

—— (1985), *Wok Cookbook*, London: Piatkus.

—— (1992), *Classic Food of China*, London: Macmillan.

SOKOLOV, RAYMOND (1976), *The Saucier's Apprentice*, New York: Alfred A. Knopf.

—— (1981), *Fading Feast*, New York: Farrar Straus Giroux.

—— (1989), *The Jewish-American Kitchen*, New York: Stewart, Tabori & Chang.

—— (1991), *Why We Eat What We Eat*, New York: Summit Books.

—— (1996), *With the Grain*, New York: Alfred A. Knopf.

SOLOMON, CHARMAINE (1996), *Encyclopaedia of Asian Food*, Port Melbourne: William Heinemann.

SOLOMON, JON (1995), 'The Apician Sauce', in Wilkins et al. (1995).

SOUYRI, JEAN-CLAUDE and GLORY, NORBERT (1986), *Le Pruneau gourmand*, Toulouse: Privat.

SOYER, A. (1847), *The Gastronomic Regenerator*, London: Simpkin & Marshall.

—— (1849), *The Modern Housewife or Ménagère*, London: Simpkin Marshall.

SPARRMANN, A. (1789), *Voyage to the Cape of Good Hope . . . and Round the World from 1772/76*, vols i and ii, Perth.

SPENCER, COLIN (1993), *The Heretic's Feast*, London: Fourth Estate.

SPENCER, EVELENE and COBB, JOHN N. (1922), *Fish Cookery*, Boston: Little, Brown.

SPICER, DOROTHY GLADYS (1948), *From an English Oven*, New York: The Women's Press.

SPOERRI, DANIEL (1982), *Mythology and Meatballs*, Berkeley: Aris.

STAEBLER, EDNA (1968), *Food that Really Schmecks*, Toronto: McGraw-Hill Ryerson.

STALLINGS, W. S. (1979), 'Ice Cream and Water Ices in 17th and 18th Century England', Supplement to *PPC* 3.

STAUB, PATRICIA T. ARROYO (1982), *The Science of Philippine Foods*, Quezon: Abaniko Enterprises.

STEAD, JENNIFER (1979), 'Greensauce', in *PPC* 3.

—— (1983), 'Quizzing Glasse: or Hannah Scrutinised', in *PPC* 13 and 14.

—— (1991a), 'Bowers of Bliss: The Banquet Setting', in C. Anne Wilson (ed), *Banquetting Stuffe*, Edinburgh: Edinburgh University Press.

—— (1991b), 'Yorkshire Pudding and Parkin', in C. Anne Wilson (ed), *Traditional Food East and West of the Pennines*, Edinburgh: Edinburgh UP.

—— (1995a), 'Dock Pudding: A Documentary History', in *PPC* 49.

—— (1995b), 'Viper Soup, Viper Broth, Viper Wine', in *PPC* 51.

STEARN, WILLIAM T. (1992), *Botanical Latin*, 4th edn, Newton Abbot: David & Charles.

STECHISHIN, SAVELLA (1979), *Traditional Ukrainian Cookery*, Winnipeg: Trident Press.

STEFANSSON, VILHJALMUR (1946), *Not by Bread Alone*, New York.

STELLA, ALAIN (1996), *Le Livre du café*, Paris: Flammarion.

STERBA, GÜNTHER (1962), *Freshwater Fishes of the World*, London: Studio Vista.

STERN, JANE and STERN, MICHAEL (1984), *Square Meals*, New York: Knopf.

—— —— (1986a), *Road Food and Good Food*, New York: Knopf.

—— —— (1986b), *Coast-to-Coast Cookbook*, New York: Knopf.

—— —— (1992), *Encyclopaedia of Pop Culture*, New York: Harper Perennial.

STEVEN, MAISIE (1985), *The Good Scots Diet: What Happened to it?*, Aberdeen: Aberdeen UP.

STOBART, TOM (1980), *The Cook's Encyclopaedia*, London: B. T. Batsford. Also repr 1999, London: Grub Street

STOUT, MARGARET B. (1968), *The Shetland Cookery Book*, Lerwick: T. & J. Manson.

STRABO (1960–9), *Geography*, vols i–viii, trans H. L. Jones, Cambridge, MA.: Loeb Classical Library.

STRĂTILESCU, TEREZA (1907), *From Carpathians to Pindus*, Boston: John W. Luce.

STREET, PHILLIP (1966), *The Crab and its Relatives*, London: Faber & Faber.

STURTEVANT, E. L. (1919), *Sturtevant's Notes on Edible Plants*, ed U. P. Hedrick, Albany, NY: New York Department of Agriculture.

STYLE, SUE (1992), *A Taste of Switzerland*, London: Pavilion Books.

SUETONIUS (1950–1), *Lives of the Caesars*, trans J. C. Rolfe, Cambridge, MA.: Loeb Classical Library.

SWINBURNE, LAYINKA (1997), '. . . Ship's Biscuit and Portable Soup', in *Food on the Move*, Oxford Symposium on Food History 1996, Totnes: Prospect Books.

SYKES, L. (*c*.1912), *An Olio of Proved Recipes and Domestic Wrinkles*, 7th edn, Manchester: Abel Heywood.

SYMONS, MICHAEL (1982), *One Continuous Picnic*, Adelaide: Duck Press.

SZATHMARY, LOUIS (1974), *American Gastronomy*, Chicago: Henry Regnery.

TAIK, AUNG AUNG (1993), *Under the Golden Pagoda*, San Francisco: Chronicle Books.

TANNAHILL, REAY (1975), *Flesh and Blood: A History of the Cannibal Complex*, New York: Stein & Day.

—— (1988), *Food in History*, rev edn, London: Penguin.

TANTTU, ANNA-MAIJA and TANTTU, JUHA (1988), *Food from Finland*, Helsingissä: Kustannusosakeyhtiö Otava.

TARUSCHIO, ANN and TARUSCHIO, FRANCO (1995), *Bruschetta, Crostoni and Crostini*, London: Pavilion Books.

TEE, GEORGE (1983), 'Samphire', in *PPC* 15.

TENG, UNG (1967), *Les Aliments usuels au Cambodge*, Phnom Penh: Université Royale.

THACKER, JOHN (1758), *The Art of Cookery*, Newcastle upon Tyne.

THAXTER, CELIA (1894), *An Island Garden*, Boston: Houghton Mifflin.

THEOPHRASTUS (1916–26), *Enquiry into Plants*, ed and trans Sir Arthur Hort, Cambridge, Mass.: Loeb Classical Library.

—— (1976–90), *De Causis Plantarum*, ed and trans B. Einarson and G. K. K. Link, Cambridge, Mass.: Loeb Classical Library.

THICK, MALCOLM (1992), 'Sir Hugh Plat's Promotion of Pasta as a Victual for Seamen', in *PPC* 40.

THIS, HERVÉ (1993), *Les Secrets de la casserole*, Paris: Belin.

—— (1995), *Révélations gastronomiques*, Paris: Belin.

THOMAS, IAN (1992), *How to Grow Herbs*, new edn, London: Bloomsbury Books.

THOMPSON, FLORA (1945), *Lark Rise to Candleford*, Oxford: OUP.

THOMPSON, STEVEN and THOMPSON, MARY (1972), *Wild Food Plants of the Sierra*, Berkeley: Wilderness Press.

THORLACIUS, SIGRIÐUR (1980), 'Do you know Skyr?', in *PPC* 4.

THORNE, JOHN, with THORNE, MATT LEWIS (1996), *Serious Pig*, New York: North Point Press.

THORNTON, P. (1840), *The Southern Gardener and Receipt Book*, Camden, SC: the author.

THRELKELD, CALEB (1727), *Synopsis stirpium Hibernicarum*

THUDICHUM, J. L. W. (1895), *The Spirit of Cookery*, London: Bailliere, Tindall & Cox.

THWAITES, R. G. (ed) (1904–5), *Original Journals of the Lewis and Clark Expedition, 1804–1806*, New York: Antiquarian Press.

TIBBOTT, S. MINWEL (1976), *Welsh Fare*, St Fagan's: Welsh Folk Museum.

—— (1991), *Baking in Wales*, Cardiff: National Museum of Wales.

TICKLETOOTH, TABITHA (1860), *The Dinner Question*, London: Routledge, Warne, etc.

TIDBURY, G. E. (1949), *The Clove Tree*, London: Crosby Lockwood.

TILSLEY-BENHAM, JILL (1986a), 'An Enquiry into Keshkul', in *Cookery: Science, Lore and Books*, Oxford Symposium on Food History 1984 and 1985, London: Prospect Books.

—— (1986b), 'Sardi/Garmi in Iran', in *Cookery: Science, Lore and Books*, Oxford Symposium on Food History 1984 and 1985, London: Prospect Books.

—— (1987), 'Sheep with Two Tails', in *The Cooking Medium*, Oxford Symposium on Food History 1986, London: Prospect Books.

—— (1989), 'Pots from an Emir's Palace', in *The Cooking Pot*, Oxford Symposium on Food History 1988, London: Prospect Books.

TOKLAS, ALICE B. (1954), *The Alice B. Toklas Cookbook*, New York: Harper & Brothers.

TOLBERT, FRANK X. (1972), *A Bowl of Red*, New York: Doubleday.

TOLKOWSKY, S. (1938), *Hesperides*, London: Staples & Staples.

TOOMRE, JOYCE (1992), *Classic Russian Cooking* (a translation of and commentary on Molokhovets, 1897), Bloomington: Indiana University Press.

TROUSSET, JULES (1879), *Grande Encyclopédie d'économie domestique*, vols i–ii, Paris.

TSUJI, SHIZUO (1980), *Japanese Cooking: A Simple Art*, Tokyo: Kodansha International.

TUCKER, ARTHUR and MACCIARELLO, MICHAEL J. (1994), 'Oregano: Botany, Chemistry, and Cultivation', in G. Charalambous (ed), *Spices, Herbs and Edible Fungi*, Elsevier: Science BV.

TURNER, ROBERT (1664), *The British Physician: or, the Nature and Vertues of English Plants*, London.

TURNER, T. (1984) *The Diary of Thomas Turner 1754–1765*, ed D. Vasey, Oxford: Oxford University Press.

TURNER, WILLIAM (1538), *Libellus de Re Herbaria Nova*, London.

—— (1551–68), *A New Herball* (in three parts), London.

TURNER-NEALE, MARGARET-MARY, with HENDERSON, JOHN (1996), *Bush Foods*, Alice Springs: IAD Press.

TUSSER, THOMAS (1557), *A Hundreth Good Pointes of Husbandrie*, London.

—— (1984), *Five Hundred Points of Good Husbandry*, repr, Oxford: OUP.

TWEEDIE, M. W. F. and HARRISON, J. L. (1970), *Malayan Animal Life*, Singapore: Longman Malaysia.

UCKO, P. J. and DIMBLEBY, G. W. (eds) (1969), *The Domestication and Exploitation of Plants and Animals*, London: Duckworth.

UDE, LOUIS EUSTACHE (1828), *The French Cook*, repr, New York: Arco (1978).

UKERS, WILLIAM H. (1922), *All about Coffee*, New York: Tea and Coffee Trade Journal Company.

—— (1935), *All about Tea*, vols i–ii, New York: Tea and Coffee Trade Journal Company.

Universidad International Menéndez y Pelayo (1982), *Conferencias culinarias*, Barcelona: Tusquets.

UPHOF, J. C. TH. (1968), *Dictionary of Economic Plants*, New York: Stechert-Hafner.

URQUHART, JUDY (1983), *Animals on the Farm*, London: Macdonald.

UTRECHT-FRIEDEL, Mme LOUISE (1801), *L'Art du confiseur*, Paris.

UTTLEY, ALISON (1966), *Recipes from an Old Farmhouse*, London: Faber & Faber.

UVEZIAN, SONIA (1976), *Cooking from the Caucasus*, New York: Harvest/HBJ.

VALENTE, MARÍA ODETTE CORTES (1973), *Cozinha regional portuguesa*, Coimbra: Almedina.

VALENTIN, MARIE (1982), *La Cuisine réunionnaise*,

VALÉRI, RENÉE (1977), *Le Confit*, Lund: Liber.

VAN DER POST, LAURENS (1977), *First Catch your Eland*, London: The Hogarth Press.

VAN DER STEEN, EVELINE J. (1995), 'Zukanda and Other Delicacies', in *PPC* 51.

VAN NIEL, ELOISE SMITH (1997), 'The Colonial Kitchen of the Dutch in Java', in *PPC* 55,

London: Prospect Books.

VAREY, SIMON (1995), 'Viper Soup', in *PPC* 50.

VEHLING, J. D. (1936), *Apicius*, Chicago.

VELDSMAN, PETER (1999), *Flavours of South Africa*, Cape Town: Tafelberg.

VENNER, TOBIAS (1628), *Via Recta ad Vitam Longam* (first pub 1622), London.

VERRALL, WILLIAM (1759), *A Complete System of Cookery*, London: printed for the author.

—— (1948), *The Cook's Paradise*, ed R. L. Megroz, London: Sylvan Press.

—— (1988), *A Complete System of Cookery*, ed Ann Haly, Lewes: Southover.

VIARD, A. (1806), *Le Cuisinier impériale*, Paris: Chez Barba.

VICKERY, K. F. (1936), *Food in Early Greece*, Urbana: University of Illinois.

VIEIRA, EDITE (1988), *The Taste of Portugal*, London: Robert Hale.

VIGEON, EVELYN V. (1993), 'The Celebrated Cookie Shop', *Manchester Genealogist*, 29/1 (Jan.).

VILLA, ANGELO and BARRIOS, VICKI (1978), *Adventures in Mexican Cooking*, San Francisco: Ortho Books.

VILMORIN-ANDRIEUX (1883), *Les Plantes potagères*, Paris.

—— (1885), *The Vegetable Garden*, English edn, trans W. Miller, London: John Murray.

VISSER, MARGARET (1986), *Much Depends on Dinner*, Canada: M. & S.

—— (1991), *The Rituals of Dinner*, London: Penguin.

W. M. (1655), *The Compleat Cook and Queens Delight*, facsimile edn, London: Prospect Books (1984).

WALDO, MYRA (1961), *The Art of South American Cookery*, New York: Doubleday.

WALKER, HARLAN (ed) (1991), *Feasting and Fasting*, Oxford Symposium on Food History 1990, London: Prospect Books.

—— (ed) (1992), *Public Eating*, Oxford Symposium on Food History 1991, London: Prospect Books.

—— (ed) (1993), *Spicing up the Palate*, Oxford Symposium on Food History 1992, Totnes: Prospect Books.

—— (ed) (1998), *Fish, Food from the Waters*, Oxford Symposium on Food History 1997, Totnes: Prospect Books.

WALLACE, ALFRED RUSSEL (1869), *The Malay Archipelago*, facsimile edn, New York: Dover (1982).

WANG, TERESA and ANDERSON, E. N. (1998), 'Ni Tsan and His "Cloud Forest Hall Collection of Rules for Drinking and Eating" ', in *PPC* 60.

WARD, ARTEMAS (1886), *The Grocer's Handbook and Directory*, Philadelphia: Philadelphia Grocer Publishing Co.

—— (1911), *The Grocer's Encyclopaedia*, New York: Stationers' Hall.

—— (1923), *The Encyclopedia of Food*, New York: A. Ward.

WARNER, Revd RICHARD (1791), *Antiquitates Culinariae*, facsimile edn, London: Prospect Books (n.d., 1980s).

WARNER, WILLIAM W. (1976), *Beautiful Swimmers*, Boston: Little, Brown.

—— (1977), *Distant Water*, Boston: Little, Brown.

WARREN, GEOFFREY C. (ed) (1958), *The Foods We Eat*, London: Cassell.

WASSON, R. GORDON (1969), *Soma, Divine Mushroom of Immortality*, New York: Harcourt Brace Jovanovich.

—— (1972), *The Death of Claudius*, Cambridge, Mass.: Harvard UP.

WASSON, VALENTINA, and WASSON, GORDON (1957), *Mushrooms, Russia and History*, vols i and ii, New York: Pantheon.

WATT, GEORGE (1889–96), *A Dictionary of the Economic Products of India*, vols i–vi and index, Delhi.

WEAVER, WILLIAM WOYS (1982), 'Shad Cookery in Old Philadelphia', in *PPC* 11.

—— (1983), *Sauerkraut Yankees*, Philadelphia: University Press of Pennsylvania.

—— (1993), *Pennsylvania Dutch Country Cooking*, New York: Abbeville Press.

WEBB, Mrs ARTHUR (*c*.1935), *Farmhouse Cookery*, London: George Newnes.

WEBSTER, THOMAS (1861), *Encyclopedia of Domestic Economy*, London.

WECHSBERG, JOSEPH (1969), *The Cooking of Vienna's Empire*, New York: Time Life Books.

WEEKLEY, ERNEST (1958), *Words Ancient and Modern*, London: John Murray.

WEIGLEY, EMMA SEIFRIT (1977), *Sarah Tyson Rorer*, Philadelphia: American Philosophical Society.

WEINER, PIROSKA (1981), *Carved Honeycake Moulds*, 2nd edn, Hungary: Corvina Kiadó.

WESTBURY, Lord (1983), *Handlist of Italian Cookery Books*, Saifer.

WESTERGAARD, ERIK K. (1974), *Dansk Egnsretter*, Copenhagen: Lindhardt og Ringhof.

WESTRIP, JOYCE (1997), *Moghul Cooking*, London: Serif.

WEYMOUTH, FRANK W. (1920), *The Edible Clams, Mussels and Scallops of California*, Sacramento, CA.: California Fish & Game Commission.

WHEATON, BARBARA KETCHAM (1976), *Victorian Ices and Ice Cream*, New York: Metropolitan Museum of Art/Charles Scribner's Sons.

—— (1983), *Savoring the Past*, Philadelphia: University of Pennsylvania Press.

—— 'No Hoax', in *PPC* 16, London: Prospect Books.

WHEELER, ALWYNE (1969), *The Fishes of the British Isles and North-West Europe*, London: Macmillan.

—— (1979), *Fishes of the World: An Illustrated Dictionary*, London: Ferndale.

WHITE, EILEEN (1994), 'First Things First: The Great British Breakfast', in C. Anne Wilson (ed), *Luncheon, Nuncheon and Other Meals*, Stroud: Alan Sutton Publishing.

WHITE, FLORENCE (1932), *Good Things in England*, London: Jonathan Cape.

—— (1934), *Flowers as Food*, London: Jonathan Cape.

—— (1952), *Good English Food*, London: Jonathan Cape.

WHITE, K. D. (1970), *Roman Farming*, London: Thames & Hudson.

WHITEAKER, STAFFORD (1985), *The Compleat*

Strawberry, London: Century Publishing.

WICKSON, EDWARD J. (1891), *The California Fruits and How to Grow Them*, San Francisco.

WILDER, KINAU (1978), *Wilders of Waikiki*, Hawaii.

WILEY, HARVEY W. (1911), *Foods & their Adulteration*, Philadelphia: P. Blakiston's Sons.

WILKINS, JOHN et al. (ed) (1995), *Food in Antiquity*, Exeter: University of Exeter Press.

WILLAN, ANNE (1977), *Great Cooks and their Recipes: From Taillevent to Escoffier*, London: Elm Tree.

—— (1989), *Reader's Digest Complete Guide to Cookery*, London: Dorling Kindersley.

WILLIAMS, JACKY (1993), *Wagon Wheel Kitchens*, Lawrence, KS.: University Press of Kansas.

WILLIAMS, MATHIEU (1892), *The Chemistry of Cookery*, London: Chatto & Windus.

WILLIAMS, VICKY (1996), 'Musings on Syllabub', in *PPC* 52.

WILSON, C. ANNE (1973), *Food and Drink in Britain from the Stone Age to Recent Times*, London: Cookery Book Club.

—— (1979–80), 'The French Connection', parts I and II, in *PPC* 2 and 4.

—— (1985a), *The Book of Marmalade*, London: Constable.

—— (1985b), 'I'll to thee a Simnel Bring', in *PPC* 19.

—— (ed) (1993), *Liquid Nourishment*, Edinburgh: Edinburgh UP.

—— (ed) (1994), *Luncheon, Nuncheon and Other Meals*, Stroud: Alan Sutton Publishing.

WILSON, HILARY (1988), *Egyptian Food and Drink*, Aylesbury: Shire Publications.

WILSON, MARY TOLFORD (1957), 'Amelia Simmons Fills a Need: American Cookery 1796', *William and Mary Quarterly*.

WINSNES, HANNA (1845), *Lærebog i de Forskellige Grene of Huusholdningen*, Christiania.

WITTEVEEN, JOOP (1983), 'Potato Recipes in Holland from 1600 until 1850', in *Food in Motion*, Oxford Symposium on Food History 1983, Leeds: Prospect Books.

—— (1986–7), 'On Swans, Cranes and Herons', parts 1 to 3, in *PPC* 24, 25, 26.

—— (1989), 'The Great Birds: Part 4, Peacocks in History', in *PPC* 32.

—— (1990), 'The Great Birds, Part 5: Preparation of the Peacock for the Table', in *PPC* 36.

—— (1995), 'Poffertjes (aka Bollebuisjes)', in *PPC* 49.

WOLFERT, PAULA (1973), *Couscous and Other Good Food from Morocco*, New York: Harper & Row.

WOLLEY, HANNAH (1661), *The Ladies Directory*, London.

—— (1670), *The Gentleman's Companion*, London.

—— (1671), *The Compleat Servant Maid*, London.

—— (1672), *The Ladies Delight*, London.

—— (1677), *The Accomplish'd Ladies Delight*, London.

—— (n.d.a), *The Cooks Guide*, n.p

—— (n.d.b), *The Queen-Like Closet*, n.p.

WONDRAUSCH, MARY (1996), 'Dorothy Hartley', in *PPC* 54.

WOOD, WILLIAM (1634), *New England's Prospect*, Boston (1898).

—— and CUPERUS, BART (1998), *Bibliotheca Gastronomica*, Amsterdam: Linnaeus Press.

WOODHAM-SMITH, CECIL (1962), *The Great Hunger, Ireland 1845–1849*, London: Hamish Hamilton.

WOODROOF, JASPER GUY (1979), *Tree Nuts*, Westport, CT: AVI.

WOOLEDGE-SALMON, ALICE (1981), 'Enduring Fantasies', in *PPC* 8.

WREN, JENNY (1880), *Modern Domestic Cookery*, Paisley: Alexander Gardner.

XENOPHON (1958), *Anabasis*, trans W. H. D. Rouse, Ann Arbor: University of Michigan Press.

YABUKI, ISAO (c.1950), *The Special Foods of Tokyo*, Tokyo: Foreign Affairs Association.

YARRELL, WILLIAM (1859), *A History of British Fishes*, vols i and ii, 3rd edn, London.

YASHIRODA, KAN, et al. (eds) (1968), *Handbook on Japanese Herbs and their Uses*, Brooklyn, NY: Botanic Garden.

YEE, KENNY and GORDON, CATHERINE (1993), *Thai Hawker Food*, Bangkok: Book Promotion and Service.

YOUATT, WILLIAM (1860), *The Pig*, 2nd edn, London.

—— (1877), *The Complete Grazier*, 12th edn, enlarged and rev Robert Scott Burn, London: Crosby Lockwood.

YOUNG, ARTHUR (1780), *A Tour of Ireland*, London.

YULE, Col. HENRY and BURNELL, A. C. (1979), *Hobson-Jobson*, ed William Crooke (1st edn pub John Murray, London, 1903), New Delhi: Munshiram Manoharlal.

ZACHARY, HUGH (1969), *The Beachcomber's Handbook of Seafood Cookery*, Winston-Salem, NC: John F. Blair.

ZEUNER, F. E. (1963), *A History of Domestic Animals*, London: Hutchinson.

ZOLA, ÉMILE (1986), *Le Ventre de Paris*, repr of 1873 edn, Paris: Gallimard.

ZUBAIDA, SAMI (1990), 'Rice and Wheat in Middle Eastern Cultures', in *Staple Foods*, Oxford Symposium on Food History 1989, London: Prospect Books.

—— (1991), 'Ramadhan', in Walker (1991).

—— (1994), 'National, Communal and Global Dimensions in Middle Eastern Food Cultures', in Zubaida and Tapper (1994).

—— and TAPPER, RICHARD (eds) (1994), *Culinary Cultures of the Middle East*, London: I. B. Tauris.

ZYW, Mrs LESLIE (1981), 'Tuscan Cold Pressed Extra Virgin Olive Oil', in *PPC* 7.

INDEX

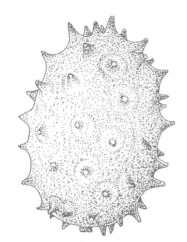

This is not a comprehensive index but a highly selective one. As explained in 'Notes On Using This Book' (p. xix), it has two main functions:
- to direct the reader from a synonym to the appropriate headword (as in 'Dublin Bay prawn > Norway lobster' and 'arugula > rocket'); and
- to show the way to something which, although not having its own entry, is mentioned or dealt with under some other headword (e.g. 'amaretti > macaroon' and 'bonnag > barley breads').

In every instance, what the reader may be looking for is to the left of the arrow and the relevant headword to the right.

PICTURE ACKNOWLEDGEMENTS

With only a few exceptions, the drawings in this book are by the Laotian artist Soun Vannithone, about whom there is a page at the website indicated on page vii. Most were specially commissioned for the present work, but a number of the drawings have been previously published in; Josephine Bacon (1988); Cost (1990); Davidson (1979, 1981, 1988a): Nathalie Hambro (1981); Sri Owen (1986a); Elizabeth Schneider (1986); and Phia Sing (1981).

The Food and Agriculture Organisation of the United Nations (FAO) have been exceptionally helpful to me over a period of nearly 30 years in allowing me to use the admirable drawings of fish and other seafood published in their various catalogues. On this occasion they are the source of the drawings of the comber on page 208 and the flounder on page 307. The Smithsonian Institution in Washington DC, source of the drawing of the tautog on page 786, have been equally helpful for more than 20 years. The drawing of mauka (page 484) was published in the valuable report on Lost Crops of the Incas (National Research Council, 1989), having been taken from a learned paper by Julio Rea and Jorge León. The drawing of fruit jellies on page 322 is by Peter Brears (1996). The drawing of a top-shell on page 802 is one of a number which Peter Stebbing was commissioned to do for Davidson (1981).